ENCYCLOPAEDIA JUDAICA

ENCYCLOPAEDIA JUDAICA

SECOND EDITION

VOLUME 20
To–Wei

Fred Skolnik, *Editor in Chief*
Michael Berenbaum, *Executive Editor*

MACMILLAN REFERENCE USA
An imprint of Thomson Gale, a part of The Thomson Corporation

IN ASSOCIATION WITH
KETER PUBLISHING HOUSE LTD., JERUSALEM

THOMSON
GALE

Detroit • New York • San Francisco • New Haven, Conn. • Waterville, Maine • London

THOMSON
GALE

ENCYCLOPAEDIA JUDAICA, Second Edition

Fred Skolnik, *Editor in Chief*
Michael Berenbaum, *Executive Editor*
Shlomo S. (Yosh) Gafni, *Editorial Project Manager*
Rachel Gilon, *Editorial Project Planning and Control*

Thomson Gale
Gordon Macomber, *President*
Frank Menchaca, *Senior Vice President and Publisher*
Jay Flynn, *Publisher*
Hélène Potter, *Publishing Director*

Keter Publishing House
Yiphtach Dekel, *Chief Executive Officer*
Peter Tomkins, *Executive Project Director*

Complete staff listings appear in Volume 1

For more information, contact
Macmillan Reference USA
An imprint of Thomson Gale
27500 Drake Rd.
Farmington Hills, MI 48331-3535
Or you can visit our internet site at
http://www.gale.com

LIBRARY OF CONGRESS CATALOGING-IN-PUBLICATION DATA

Encyclopaedia Judaica / Fred Skolnik, editor-in-chief ; Michael Berenbaum, executive editor. -- 2nd ed.
v. cm.
Includes bibliographical references and index.
Contents: v.1. Aa-Alp.
ISBN 0-02-865928-7 (set hardcover : alk. paper) -- ISBN 0-02-865929-5 (vol. 1 hardcover : alk. paper) -- ISBN 0-02-865930-9 (vol. 2 hardcover : alk. paper) -- ISBN 0-02-865931-7 (vol. 3 hardcover : alk. paper) -- ISBN 0-02-865932-5 (vol. 4 hardcover : alk. paper) -- ISBN 0-02-865933-3 (vol. 5 hardcover : alk. paper) -- ISBN 0-02-865934-1 (vol. 6 hardcover : alk. paper) -- ISBN 0-02-865935-X (vol. 7 hardcover : alk. paper) -- ISBN 0-02-865936-8 (vol. 8 hardcover : alk. paper) -- ISBN 0-02-865937-6 (vol. 9 hardcover : alk. paper) -- ISBN 0-02-865938-4 (vol. 10 hardcover : alk. paper) -- ISBN 0-02-865939-2 (vol. 11 hardcover : alk. paper) -- ISBN 0-02-865940-6 (vol. 12 hardcover : alk. paper) -- ISBN 0-02-865941-4 (vol. 13 hardcover : alk. paper) -- ISBN 0-02-865942-2 (vol. 14 hardcover : alk. paper) -- ISBN 0-02-865943-0 (vol. 15: alk. paper) -- ISBN 0-02-865944-9 (vol. 16: alk. paper) -- ISBN 0-02-865945-7 (vol. 17: alk. paper) -- ISBN 0-02-865946-5 (vol. 18: alk. paper) -- ISBN 0-02-865947-3 (vol. 19: alk. paper) -- ISBN 0-02-865948-1 (vol. 20: alk. paper) -- ISBN 0-02-865949-X (vol. 21: alk. paper) -- ISBN 0-02-865950-3 (vol. 22: alk. paper)
1. Jews -- Encyclopedias. I. Skolnik, Fred. II. Berenbaum, Michael, 1945-
DS102.8.E496 2007
909'.04924 -- dc22

2006020426

ISBN-13:

978-0-02-865928-2 (set)
978-0-02-865929-9 (vol. 1)
978-0-02-865930-5 (vol. 2)
978-0-02-865931-2 (vol. 3)
978-0-02-865932-9 (vol. 4)
978-0-02-865933-6 (vol. 5)
978-0-02-865934-3 (vol. 6)
978-0-02-865935-0 (vol. 7)
978-0-02-865936-7 (vol. 8)
978-0-02-865937-4 (vol. 9)
978-0-02-865938-1 (vol. 10)
978-0-02-865939-8 (vol. 11)
978-0-02-865940-4 (vol. 12)
978-0-02-865941-1 (vol. 13)
978-0-02-865942-8 (vol. 14)
978-0-02-865943-5 (vol. 15)
978-0-02-865944-2 (vol. 16)
978-0-02-865945-9 (vol. 17)
978-0-02-865946-6 (vol. 18)
978-0-02-865947-3 (vol. 19)
978-0-02-865948-0 (vol. 20)
978-0-02-865949-7 (vol. 21)
978-0-02-865950-3 (vol. 22)

This title is also available as an e-book
ISBN-10: 0-02-866097-8
ISBN-13: 978-0-02-866097-4
Contact your Thomson Gale representative for ordering information.
Printed in the United States of America

10 9 8 7 6 5 4 3 2

TABLE OF CONTENTS

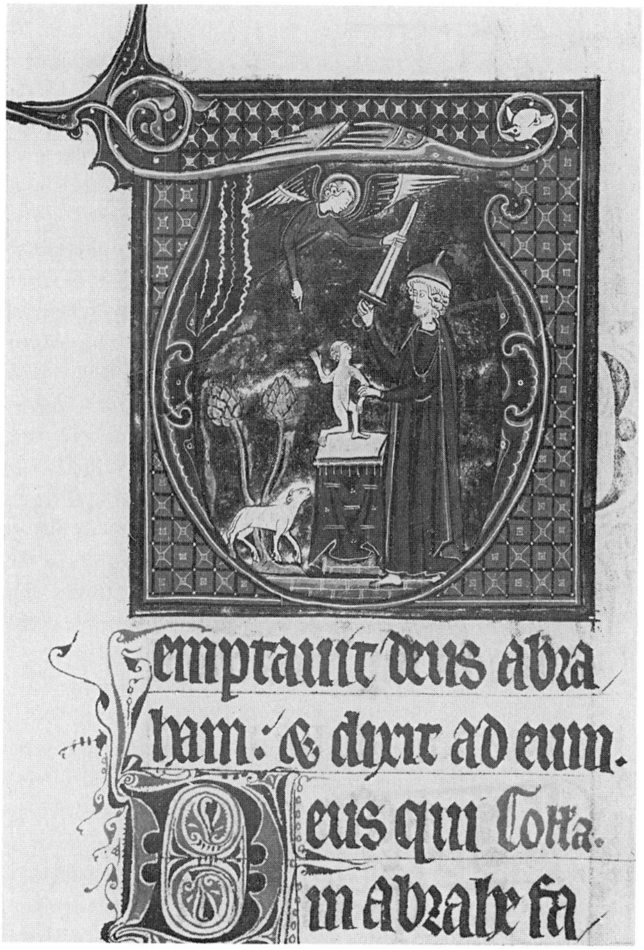

Initial letter "T" of the phrase Temptavit Deus Abraham *in a 14th-century Paris missal. The illumination shows the "sacrifice" of Isaac. Rheims, Bibliothèque Municipale, Ms. 2301, fol. 49v.*

To-Tz

TOAFF, Italian family of rabbis. ALFREDO SABATO TOAFF (1880–1963) was born in Leghorn and studied under R. Elijah *Benamozegh at the Leghorn Rabbinical College, where he was made professor, and in 1923 succeeded Samuel *Colombo as chief rabbi of Leghorn. A member of the Italian Rabbinical Council for many years (from 1931), he was several times its president. He headed the Leghorn Rabbinical College and was head of the *Collegio Rabbinico Italiano in Rome from its reopening in 1955 until his death, which occurred in his native city. He was the author of many works on, and translations into Italian of, biblical and post-biblical Hebrew literature, as well as of writings on the history and traditions of the Leghorn Jewish community (such as *Cenni storici sulla Comunità Ebraica e sulla Singagoga di Livorno*, 1955). Many of his writings show the influence of E. Benamozegh, whose *Scritti Scelti* (1955) he edited. A bibliography of the writings of Alfredo Toaff appears in: E. Toaff (ed.), *Annuario di Studi Ebraici* (1965), 215–6.

His son, ELIO TOAFF (1915–), was born in Leghorn and was the last rabbi ordained by its Rabbinical College, before its closure by the Fascist regime (reopened 1955). He was rabbi of Ancona (1941–46) and of Venice (1946–51) and was called to Rome to succeed David *Prato as chief rabbi of that community in 1951. A member of the Italian Rabbinical Council and head of the Collegio Rabbinico Italiano from 1963, he edited the *Annuario di Studi Ebraici* at the college. Elio was a member of the executive of the Conference of European Rabbis. On April 13, 1986, he welcomed Pope John Paul II on the first visit ever by a pope to a synagogue. He wrote articles and translated studies on Jewish, biblical, and historical topics from Hebrew into Italian.

BIBLIOGRAPHY: *Israel, corriere israelitico*, 49 (1963), nos. 7–13; *Ha-Tikwà, Organo della Federazione giovanile ebraica d'Italia*, 11 (1963), no. 9.

[Sergio DellaPergola]

TOB (Heb. טוֹב), biblical place name. When *Jephthah the Gileadite was expelled from his father's house, he went to the land of Tob (Judg. 11:13). "A man of Tob" (Heb. *ish Tov*) is mentioned alongside the Aramean armies which came to the aid of the Ammonites during their war with David (II Sam. 10:6, 8). The phrase "a man of Tob" apparently refers to the people of the land of Tob (cf. the usages "man of Israel," "man of God"), or to a Tobite ruler (cf. the terms for Canaanite rulers in the *El-Amarna tablets).

Documents from the second millennium B.C.E. mention a place called Ṭby or Ṭubu, along with cities in *Bashan. It has been suggested, therefore, by B. Mazar, that the land of Tob is to be located in the vicinity of the settlement of Taiyibeh, east of Edrei. It seems that the land of Tob was back country, and that it served as an asylum for outlaws.

BIBLIOGRAPHY: B. Maisler (Mazar), in: JPOS, 9 (1929), 83; M. Noth, in: ZDPV, 68 (1949), 6 (n. 6), 8 (n. 3), 27–28.

[Bustanay Oded]

TOBACCO TRADE AND INDUSTRIES. Throughout the first two centuries after the discovery of tobacco for Europe through Christopher Columbus, *Marranos took part in spreading its cultivation and in introducing it to Europe. Jews took up smoking (widespread from the 17th century) and snuff taking (widespread from the 18th), and entered the trade in tobacco, which, starting out as a luxury article, became a mass consumer commodity.

At Amsterdam, the first important tobacco importing and processing center in the 17th century, Isak Italiaander was the largest importer, and 10 of the 30 leading tobacco importers were Jews. Ashkenazi and poor Sephardi Jews were employed in processing tobacco for snuff: the profession of 14 out of 24 bridegrooms in a list of 1649–53 was tobacco dressing. In this period Jews took an active part in the tobacco trade of the *Hamburg center. The first Jews to settle in *Mecklenburg in the late 17th century were tobacco traders from Hamburg who leased the ducal tobacco monopoly; outstanding was Michael Hinrichsen nicknamed "Tabakspinner." Sephardi Jews filled an important role in the "*appalto*" system of contracting for the monopoly on the tobacco trade (or other products). The monopoly concession system was also practiced in the Austrian provinces and the southern German states. In this, Sephardi Jews were often the contractors because of their previous experience. The business carried considerable risks, including fluctuating prices, varying quality, deterioration through adulteration, and the hazards of war.

Diego d'*Aguilar managed to hold the tobacco monopoly in Austria in 1734–48, using Christian nobles as men of straw. In the second half of the 18th century the tobacco monopoly of Bohemia and Moravia was in the hands of members of the *Dobruschka, *Popper, and *Hoenig families, whereby they rose to importance and amassed wealth. Jews succeeded in holding the tobacco monopoly in only a few principalities in Germany. In the 19th century Jews entered the open tobacco market. In 1933 Jews engaged in about 5% of the German tobacco trade and industry, primarily as cigar manufacturers.

In Eastern Europe snuff processing was widespread, and tobacco was a staple ware of the Jewish *peddler. When in the mid-19th century cigars and cigarettes entered the mass market Leopold *Kronenberg, the Jewish industrialist and financier, was one of the main entrepreneurs in Poland, owning 12 factories in 1867 and producing 25% of the total. Of 110 tobacco factories in the *Pale of Settlement in 1897, 83 were owned by Jews, and over 80% of the workers were Jewish. This participation continued into the 20th century, and the Jewish tobacco workers were active in the ranks of socialism. The huge Y. Shereshevsky tobacco factory in Grodno employed, before World War I, some 1,800 workers. The nationalization in Poland of the tobacco and liquor industries in 1923–24 was a severe blow to the many Jews who gained their livelihood from them. The leading tobacco factories in Riga, Latvia, were owned by two wealthy Karaites, Asimakis and Maikapar.

On the American continent Jews traded in tobacco as early as 1658. It frequently served as legal tender and was a stock retail article of the Jewish peddler. However, Jews played a considerable part only in the snuff trade, among them the firms of Asher and Solomon, and Gomez. Judah Morris, who wrote the first Hebrew book to be printed in North America, became a snuff trader. The last quarter of the 19th century brought an influx of impoverished Jewish immigrants from Eastern Europe who entered the cigar and cigarette industry, and, after the garment industry, it had the largest concentration of Jewish workers in the United States. The first professional cigar makers were generally Jews of Dutch or German origin, who employed the immigrants in their factories or in sweatshops. The Jewish firm of Keeney Brothers, makers of "Sweet Caporals," employed approximately 2,000 Jewish workers. The Durham factory almost exclusively employed Jews. Tobacco workers, organized by Samuel *Gompers, became the spearhead of the labor union movement in the United States in the 1870s and 1880s. Subsequently Jewish participation in the cigarette industry declined through the creation of large concerns, though many cigar firms remained under Jewish ownership. In New York and the major cities the tobacco retail trade occupied a high proportion of Jews. A survey by *Fortune* magazine (*Jews in America*; 1935) stated that "Jews have practically blanketed the tobacco buying business, where Jews and buyer are synonymous words, and they control three of the four leading cigar-manufacturing concerns, including Fred Hirschhorn's General Cigar, which makes every seventh cigar smoked in America." The *Culman family of Philip Morris, involved in American tobacco from the mid-19th century, was a giant of the industry. In Canada Jews played a leading role in introducing the tobacco industry; Mortimer B. Davis was known as the "tobacco king" of Canada.

In Great Britain cigar making was traditionally associated with Dutch Jews, who formed the main body of Jewish immigrants in the mid-19th century; cigar making was the most widespread occupation in London's East End in 1860. In 1850, 44% of the meerschaum pipe makers were Jewish, and 22% of the cigar manufacturers. East European Jewish immigrants introduced cigarette making into England. In 1880 Jacob Kamusch, an Austrian Jewish cigarette entrepreneur, brought

310 workers, mainly Jewish, to his Glasgow cigarette factory. Isidore Gluckstein founded his first tobacconist shop in 1872 and became the biggest retail tobacconist in England, up to 1904. Bernhard *Baron was a large-scale cigarette manufacturer in America and England.

Sephardi Jews played an active role in the tobacco trade from its beginnings in the Ottoman Empire. The *Recanati banking family began as *Salonika tobacco merchants. Thrace and Macedonia were major tobacco-growing areas; the *Alatino (Alatini) family became sole suppliers of the Italian tobacco monopoly.

[Henry Wasserman]

In Israel

Tobacco growing was first introduced in the country in 1923/24, in order to solve problems of unemployment. New immigrants from Bulgaria and Greece took an important part in the development of the industry. All kinds of tobacco products are manufactured in Israel. In 1969 the overall production included 3,700 tons of cigarettes, 15,000 kg. of cigars, 60,600 kg. of tumbak, 40,100 kg. of snuff, and 16,600 kg. of pipe tobacco. In the same year the consumption of tobacco products amounted to nearly IL 200,000,000 (about 2% of the total private consumption in Israel), including mainly locally produced products but also about $6,000,000 worth of imported products. There were 15 manufacturing plants in Israel, employing 875 workers and processing mostly locally grown tobacco of Oriental aroma. Tobacco was grown mainly in the non-Jewish sector in northern Israel. In 1950 tobacco-growing areas amounted to 9,000 dunams, and tobacco-product manufacture reached 600 tons. By 1969 tobacco was grown in 35,000 dunams and production increased to 2,200 tons. Since that time tobacco production has dropped radically, to 150 tons on 5,000 dunams by 1990, but cigarette imports have risen dramatically, by about 2,500% between 1970 and 2000 along with a 33% increase in tobacco leaf imports. Local cigarette production rose from 3,668 million cigarettes in 1970 to 4,933 million in 1995. The industry employed around 600 workers in the late 1990s.

[Zeev Barkai]

BIBLIOGRAPHY: M. Hainisch, in: *Vierteljahrschrift fuer Sozial- und Wirtschaftsgeschichte*, 8 (1910), 394–444; W. Stieda, *Die Besteuerung des Tabaks in Ansbach-Bayreuth und Bamberg-Wuerzburg im achtzehnten Jahrhundert* (1911); M. Grunwald, *Samuel Oppenheimer* (1913), 295–300; A.D. Hart, *The Jew in Canada* (1926), 324–5, 337; S.B. Weinryb, *Neueste Wirtschaftsgeschichte der Juden in Russland und Polen* (1934), index, s.v. *Tabakindustrie*; P. Friedmann, in: *Jewish Studies in Memory of G.A. Kohut* (1935), 196, 232–3 (Ger.); H.I. Bloom, *Economic Activities of the Jews of Amsterdam* (1937); H. Rachel et al., *Berliner Grosskaufleute und Kapitalisten*, 2 (1938), 50–52; J. Starr, in: JSOS, 7 (1945), 323–6; M. Epstein, *Jewish Labor in U.S.A.* (1950), 76–78; J. Shatzky, *Geshikhte fun Yidn in Varshe*, 3 (1953), 37, 43–46; H. Schnee, *Die Hoffinanz und der moderne Staat*, 1 (1953), 89, 185; 2 (1954), 88f., 294ff.; 3 (1955), 123ff.; 4 (1963), 219–22, 239–41; S. Gompers, *Seventy Years of Life and Labour* (1957²); H. Kellenbenz, *Sephardim an der unteren Elbe* (1958), 205, 436–46; J. Frumkin et al., *Russian Jewry* (1966), 130–1; V. Kurrein, in: *Menorah*, 3 (1925), 155f.; A. Mueller, *Zur Geschichte der Judenfrage in… der Landgrafschaft Hessen-Darmstadt* (1937), 54–56; S. Simonsohn, *Toledot ha-Yehudim be-Dukkasut Mantovah*, 2 vols. (1962–64); Z. Kahana, in: *Kol Torah*, 3 (1949/50), 55–61; L.P. Gartner, *The Jewish Immigrant in England* (1960), 73–75; V.D. Lipman, *Social History of the Jews in England* (1954), index.

TOBACH, ETHEL (1921–), U.S. leader in the field of comparative psychology and the use of psychological knowledge for the public good. Tobach was born in the Ukraine to Fanya (Schecterman) and Ralph Wiener. Two weeks after her birth her parents fled with her to Palestine to escape pogroms. When Tobach's father died nine months later, her mother immigrated with her to Philadelphia and became an activist in the garment workers' union. Tobach also worked at blue-collar occupations while attending Hunter College in New York City, from which she graduated Phi Beta Kappa in 1949. Shortly after World War II she married Charles Tobach, a fellow radical who belonged to her union. He encouraged her to pursue graduate work in psychology at New York University, where she received a Ph.D. in 1957.

Tobach spent her entire career at the American Museum of Natural History, rising to the rank of curator. Although she taught at a number of universities in the New York City area, for most of her professional life she was a full time researcher in animal behavior. Her research was voluminous and broad in scope. Her empirical articles focused on the link between stress and disease in rats; she also contributed extensively to the study of emotionality in rats and mice, and explored the biopsychology of development and the evolution of social behavior. Tobach was a consistent critic of genetic determinism; one of her most important contributions to psychology was the book series, "Genes and Gender," initiated in 1978 with Betty Rosoff. These books critically examined psychology's relatively unsophisticated view of the interactions between biological and social processes.

Tobach was vice president of the New York Academy of Sciences in 1972, president of the American Psychological Association Division of Comparative and Physiological Psychology in 1984–85, president of the Eastern Psychological Association in 1987–88, and president of the APA Division on Peace in 2003–4. In 1993 she received the Kurt Lewin award from the Society for the Psychological Study of Social Issues and in 2003 she received an award for Life Time Service for Psychology in the Public Interest from the American Psychological Foundation.

BIBLIOGRAPHY: R.K. Unger, "Tobach, Ethel," in P.E. Hyman and D. Dash Moore (eds.), *Jewish Women in America*, 2 (1997), 1404–6.

[Rhoda K. Unger (2nd ed.)]

TOBACK, JAMES (1944–), U.S. writer, screenwriter-director, and producer. Born in New York City, Toback was educated at Harvard University (A.B., 1966) and Columbia University (M.A., 1967). He served as an instructor in English at the City College of the City University of New York and wrote *JIM: The Author's Self-Centered Memoir on the Great Jim Brown* (1971). He was also the author of a sports column appearing in *Lifestyle*, a film critic for *Dissent*; and contributed articles to numerous magazines, including *Esquire, Sport*, the *Village Voice, Harper's*, and *Commentary*. Toback wrote the screenplays for *The Gambler* (1974) and *Bugsy* (1991) and was the writer and director for *Fingers* (1978), *Love and Money* (1982), *Exposed* (1983), *The Pick-Up Artist* (1987), *The Big Bang* (1989); *Two Girls and a Guy* (1997), *Black & White* (1999), *Love in Paris* (1999), *Harvard Man* (2001), and *When Will I Be Loved* (2004). Subsequently he wrote the screenplay for the French remake of his film *Fingers*, translated into English as *The Beat That My Heart Skipped* (2005).

[Amy Handelsman (2nd ed.)]

TOBENKIN, ELIAS (1882–1963), U.S. journalist and author. Born in Russia and taken to the U.S. as a boy, he served as Russian expert for the U.S. Committee on Public Information. He was correspondent for the *Herald Tribune* in Eastern Europe and Germany, and in 1926 spent five months in the U.S.S.R. and wrote an uncensored account of the Communist regime. His first novel *Witte Arrives* (1916) described the Americanization of an immigrant Jewish family. *God of Might* (1925) dealt with the problems of intermarriage. Among his other books were *Stalin's Ladder* (1933) and *The Peoples Want Peace* (1938).

TOBIADS, dynastic family of political importance from the time of Nehemiah to the end of the Hasmonean revolt. The name Tobiah remained in the family on the basis of pappyonomy, handed down from grandson to son, for many generations. There is good literary evidence for at least four prominent members of the family and archaeological evidence of their country seat in Transjordan for several hundred years in the Hellenistic period. The family may have had earlier ancestors, such as Tobijah, returnee from the Exile, mentioned by Zechariah (6:9 and 14); Tubyahu, "arm" and "servant" of the king, mentioned in the Lachish letters of 588 B.C.E.; and even the "son of Tabeel," a usurper planning to replace King Ahaz (Isa. 7:6), all as claimed by Mazar (1957).

The Tobiad estate was at Tyros (Ẓur, or "rock"), some 13 mi. (20 km). west of Rabbat-Ammon (Philadelphia) and was rediscovered by Willam Bankes in 1818 (Irby and Mangles 1823), thanks to a full account of it by Josephus. He described it as a *paradeisos*, a kind of Persian country estate, consisting of a marble fortress (*birta*) with animals carved on the walls, and surrounded by a moat; a long series of defensible caves; some enclosed halls and vast parks; and located between Arabia and Judea, not far from Heshbon (Ant. 12:222–34). His account is accurate, though not in all details. The site is known today as Airaq (or 'Iraq) al-Amir ("Cliff of the Prince"), based on the cliff of caves, and the name Tyros, or Ẓur, is still preserved in that of the adjacent valley, Wadi Sir. Two of the cave entrances carry a large Aramaic inscription, TOBYAH, to the right-hand side of their doorways. The chief building, of monumental size though plainly not a fortress, sported at each corner a frieze of lions (with two eagles above) and had two unique panther fountains (Lapp 1963). It is called the Qasr al-Abd ("Castle of the Slave") and was largely restored by a French team in the years 1976 to 1986 (Will and Larché, 1991). It was built by Hyrcanus, the last of the Tobiads, and largely completed, but much of its megalithic construction was toppled by later earthquakes (Amiran 1996).

The earliest Tobiad to be described in some detail is Tobyah, "the servant, the Ammonite" (Neh. 2:10). He was one of the chief opponents of Nehemiah, when he came to rebuild the walls of Jerusalem in 445 B.C.E. As Tobyah was allied to *Sanballat of Samaria and Geshem the Arabian (2:19), all major landowners, it is likely that their opposition was mainly due to the land reforms being forced through by Nehemiah (5:11). Tobyah was well connected to other Jewish aristocratic families by oath (6:17–18) and to the priesthood by marriage. He was given rooms in the offerings chamber of the Temple by the High Priest Eliashib, but Nehemiah had him expelled and insisted that the place be ritually cleansed thereafter (13:4–11). The title given him by Nehemiah, "the servant, the Ammonite," is generally taken to be a rank implying ministerial service to the Persians in Ammon, and some have claimed that he was governor of the Persian province of Ammon. But that post is not attested to and the title could also be pejorative, as implying that Tobyah's pedigree was not faultless, seeing that, on their return from the Exile, the Benei Tobyah clan had not been able to prove "they were of Israel" (7:61–62).

The second known prominent member of the family was Toubias, who was visited by Zenon, acting on behalf of Appolonius, chief minister to Ptolemy II Philadelphos of Egypt. The papyri records of his journey through Palestine and Transjordan are dated to 259 B.C.E. He visited Surabit (Ẓur bayit), the birta of Ammonitis, where he conducted trade with its chieftain Toubias. Zenon brought grain from Egypt and several contracts record that he received slave boys and girls and exotic animals in return. The animals, consisting of horses, dogs, donkeys, and asses, were sent as gifts to Appolonius and to Ptolemy directly (Tcherikover and Fuks 1957). The contracts were witnessed by Persian and Greek soldiers and indicate that Tyros was then a military camp as well as an animal breeding center under Toubias and well known to the Egyptians.

Josephus wrote extensively on the subject of Joseph, son of Tobias, and his son Hyrcanus (Ant. 12:154–236) in a section that is generally known as the Tobiad Saga, or the "Tales of the Tobiads" (Goldstein 1975). His account had been seen as mainly fictional, as it contains many fabulous deeds of the two Tobiads, but when the evidence of the Zenon Papyri (as above) came to light in 1918, and when Josephus's description of Tyros was seen to accord with the facts on the ground, it was necessary to take him seriously. He tells us that Joseph's mother was a sister of the High Priest Onias, and that as a young man he was elected as *prostastes* (chief magistrate) of the Jews in place of Onias, who had refused to pay tribute to Ptolemy, the Egyptian Pharaoh. Joseph went to Alexandria and obtained the office of tax farmer to Ptolemy for Coele-Syria (Palestine) and, with the help of Egyptian troops, extracted tax sums that pleased his master. He also enriched himself and, according to Josephus, enhanced the status of his Jewish brethren. He carried out this work for 22 years. In his old age he sent Hyrcanus, the youngest of his seven sons, to Alexandria to attend the birthday celebrations of the new Pharaoh's son. Hyrcanus took the opportunity to supplant his father as tax farmer by offering a huge sum of his father's funds to the new Pharaoh, thus outbidding all others, and excluding his older brothers, who had not been interested in making the journey. His father and brothers naturally took umbrage and on his return Hyrcanus had to flee Jerusalem to Tyros, where he set up the family estate, as previously described. He dwelt there in conflict with his Arab neighbors for seven years and eventually committed suicide when Antiochus IV Epiphanes came to the Seleucid throne in 175 B.C.E., and made an end of the Tyros estate.

This detailed account raises as many questions as it answers. Much of the inconsistencies are due to the continuing wars between the Ptolemies and the Seleucids, who eventually gained control of Palestine from the Ptolemies in 200 B.C.E. It appears that Joseph the tax farmer was pro-Ptolemy and managed to supplant his uncle Onias, who was unwilling to pay tribute to Ptolemy when he saw the Seleucids in the ascendant. Later his sons sided with the Seleucids, while the youngest, Hyrcanus, remained loyal to the Ptolemies. Hyrcanus had to retreat to Tyros in the face of the Seleucid victory and when the Seleucids started to expand their Empire under Antiochus IV, he thought his fate was sealed. But it may not have been so.

After the discovery of the Zenon Papyri in 1918, it was assumed that Joseph, the son of Tobias was the son of the Toubias of the Zenon Papyri. However, that places him at too early a date, and it is more likely that he was the son of a grandson of that Toubias, who carried the same name. It was Onias II who had refused to pay tribute to Ptolemy III Eurgetes, and when his successor Ptolemy IV Philopater won a surprise victory against the Seleucids in 222 B.C.E., Joseph was appointed in place of his uncle, Onias II. Twenty-two years later, he sent Hyrcanus to the birth celebrations of the son of Ptolemy V and Cleopatra I, and Hyrcanus took the tax farmer post from Joseph. This may not have been such a coup, as in exactly that year, 200 B.C.E., Antiochus III finally wrested Palestine from the Ptolemies, so the taxes should now have gone to the Seleucids. However, he generously transferred those taxes to Cleopatra, his daughter (Schwartz 1998), and it seems that Hyrcanus was astute enough to see they would then go to her husband, his master, Ptolemy V. Meanwhile Ptolemy's general Scopas tried to retake Jerusalem but failed to do so in 198 B.C.E., and it is then that Hyrcanus was ousted from Jerusalem and spent the rest of his days, and his wealth, in developing the family estate at Tyros.

It is unlikely that Hyrcanus committed suicide or even died in 175 B.C.E. The Seleucids were too busy, in Jerusalem and Egypt, to take notice of him and it is more likely that he survived until at least 169 or 168 B.C.E., when Antiochus IV returned from Egypt and punished the Jews for believing him to be dead. He may then have turned his attention to the remaining pockets of Ptolemaic resistance. In any case we know that the estate stood until 163 B.C.E., when it was overrun by the Seleucid general Timotheus, who massacred about a thousand men of "our fellow Jews in the region of Tubias"(II Macc. 5:13). It also appears that Jason, the hellenizing high priest, who displaced his brother Onias III, and built the gymnasium in Jerusalem (II Macc. 4:12) had, in his turn, to flee in 171 B.C.E. from the more extreme usurper Menelaus, and came to find sanctuary in "Ammonite country" (II Macc. 4:26), probably in Tyros with his cousin Hyrcanus.

From the archeological evidence it is clear that it was Hyrcanus who built the Qasr al-Abd, it being in the Hellenistic style of the late second century B.C.E., similar to palaces at Alexandria and Ionia (Butler 1907, Nielsen 1994). For many years it was considered to be an unorthodox temple built to challenge Jerusalem, but no altar has been found and the interior, now reconstructed by the French team, is quite unsuitable for use as a shrine. The French have concluded that it is "Le Château du Tobiade Hyrcan" but that is unlikely. It was designed to stand in the center of a lake, for which there is good evidence, and was a grand monumental building whose lower floor, of small rooms surrounded by massive monoliths, could only, in their opinion, be designated as mere storerooms (Will and Larché 1991). And access via the lake would have been cumbersome. Therefore it is more likely to have been intended as a mausoleum to his distinguished family by its last scion, Hyrcanus, as surmised many years ago by W.F. Albright. The group of lion sculptures at each corner represent the guardians of a typical Ionian mausoleum, and the upper eagles represent the messengers that carry the souls of the dead to heaven. The small rooms of the monumental lower story were for burials and the columnated upper story for funereal banquets (Rosenberg 2004).

Hyrcanus turned the whole of the family estate into a Hellenistic garden city (*paradeisos*) as Josephus claims (Ant. 12:233). He renovated the ancient caves and turned two of them into *triclinia*, or feasting chambers. He built a small aedicule, as a shrine or tomb (Butler 1907), a vast dike to the lake he intended to form around the Qasr al-Abd, a *nymphaeum* (water source) on the hillside, and a monumental gateway to the estate. He converted the older buildings on the upper site – which go back to the Iron Age, and which had been the original *birta* (fortress) of the estate (Gera 1990) – into spacious halls with plastered walls (Lapp 1963). It is impossible that he could have done all this in the seven years allocated to him by Josephus, though it is clear that he did not live to finish the Qasr.

The two TOBYAH cave inscriptions are now safely dated to the fourth century B.C.E. (Naveh 1976) and show that the estate was that of the Tobiads well before the time of Hyrcanus. It was a true *paradeisos*, in that its development began in the Persian period, adjacent to the original *birta* on the upper site.

The Tobiads were clearly Hellenizers from the time of the Tobyah of the Zenon Papyri and played an important role in the events leading up to the Hasmonean revolt. Joseph, son of Tobias, in particular would have brought customs of Alexandrian life and luxury, in the wake of his increased wealth, to Jerusalem. And the Tobiads would have supported the High Priest Jason in building a gymnasium and designating Jerusalem to be a Greek *polis*. Nevertheless, when it came to the war against the Seleucids, the Tubian Jews sided with the Hasmoneans and *Judah Maccabee crossed the Jordan to avenge the death of the thousands slain by the Seleucids in the land of the Tubians (II Macc. 12:23).

BIBLIOGRAPHY: D.H.K. Amiran, "Location Index for Earthquakes in Israel since 100 B.C.E.," in: IEJ, 46:1–2 (1996), 120–30; H.C. Butler, *Ancient Architecture in Syria*, Division II, Princeton (1907); D. Gera, "On the Credibility of the History of the Tobiads," in: Kasher et al. (eds.), *Greece and Rome in Eretz Israel*, (1990) 21–38; J. Goldstein, "The Tales of the Tobiads," in: J. Neusner (ed.), *Christianity, Judaism and Other Greco-Roman Cults* (1975), pt. III, 85–123; C.L. Irby and J. Mangles, *Travels in Egypt and Nubia, Syria and Asia Minor* (1823), 473–74; P.W. Lapp, "The Second and Third Campaigns at Araq el-Emir," in: BASOR, 171 (1963), 8–39; B. Mazar, "The Tobiads," in: IEJ, 7:3 (1957), 137–45 and 229–38; J. Naveh, "The Development of the Aramaic Script," in: *Proceedings of the Israel Academy of Sciences and Humanities*, vol. 5 (1976), 62–65; E. Netzer, "Tyros, the Floating Palace" in: Wilson et al. (eds.), *Text and Artifact in the Religions of Mediterranean Antiquity* (2000), 340–53; I. Nielsen, *Hellenistic Palaces, Tradition and Renewal* (1994); S.G. Rosenberg, "Qasr al-Abd: a Mausoleum of the Tobiad Family?" in: BAIAS, 19–20 (2001–2), 157–75; D.R. Schwartz, "Josephus's Tobiads, Back to the Second Century?" in: M. Goodman (ed.), *Jews in a Greco-Roman World* (1998), 47–61; V.A. Tcherikover and A. Fuks, *Corpus Papyrorum Judaicarum*, vol. 1 (1957), 125–29.; E. Will and F. Larché, *Iraq al-Amir, le Château du Tobiade Hyrcan* (1991).

[Stephen G. Rosenberg (2nd ed.)]

TOBIAS, ABRAHAM (1793–1856), Charleston businessman and civic leader. Born in Charleston, Tobias received little formal education. He prospered as an auctioneer, vendue master, and commission merchant. He was a director of the Union Bank of South Carolina for 21 years, a member of the City Board of Health (1833–37), and a commissioner of pilotage for Charleston harbor (1838–43). He participated in the turbulent politics of the period as a States Rights Party member, supporting John C. Calhoun's position. As a trustee of Beth Elohim synagogue, of which his great-grandfather, Joseph *Tobias, was a founder (1749), he was a key figure in the 1840s when the congregation split over installing an organ and making other ritual reforms.

BIBLIOGRAPHY: B.A. Elzas, *The Jews of South Carolina* (1905), passim; A. Tarshish, in: AJHSQ, 54 (1965), 411–49.

[Thomas J. Tobias]

TOBIAS, JOSEPH (1684–1761), colonial settler of Charleston, South Carolina. Tobias, whose parentage and birthplace are unknown, was of Spanish lineage. He served as Spanish interpreter in the British navy prior to coming to Charleston in the early 1730s. During the long-standing hostilities between the English and the Spanish in the South, Tobias served the South Carolina government as a Spanish interpreter. In 1741 he became a naturalized British subject, being one of the first Jews in the colonies to apply under an act passed by Parliament in 1740. Tobias was one of the founders and first *parnas* of Charleston's congregation Beth Elohim, organized in 1749. His wife, Leah, was the daughter of Jacob De Oliviera, one of the original Savannah Jewish settlers in 1733.

BIBLIOGRAPHY: T.J. Tobias, in: AJHSP, 49 (1959), 33–38; B.A. Elzas, *The Jews of South Carolina* (1905), 24, and passim; C. Reznikoff and U.Z. Engelman, *The Jews of Charleston* (1950), passim; T.J. Tobias, in: A.J. Karp (ed.), *The Jewish Experience in America*, 1 (1969), 114–9.

[Thomas J. Tobias]

TOBIAS, MOSES (1694–1769), merchant of *Surat, India. A native of Cochin, Tobias was appointed in 1728 director of the Surat Portuguese factory by the Portuguese viceroy and undertook many important negotiations with the neighboring native rulers as accredited "agent of the Portuguese nation." The Portuguese archives in Goa have preserved many documents attesting to his diplomatic role in Surat, in which he was succeeded by his son Isaac and other members of his family throughout the 18th century. Moses Tobias conducted commercial transactions on a large scale and was a shipowner whose vessels sailed the Arabian Sea and the Indian Ocean. Dutch records of the day frequently register the movements of the "Jew's ships of Surat" under the command of presumably Jewish captains such as Jacob Moses and Moses Alexander. Tobias' tombstone inscription, in which he is styled "*nasi*," i.e., president, of the Surat Jewish community, is one of the few preserved in the old Jewish cemetery in Surat.

BIBLIOGRAPHY: W.J. Fischel, *Ha-Yehudim be-Hodu* (1960), 39–46; idem, in: JQR, 47 (1956–57), 37–57.

[Walter Joseph Fischel]

TOBIAS, PHILLIP VALLENTINE (1925–), South African anatomist and paleoanthropologist. His paternal grandfather Phillip Tobias served the Central Synagogue of London from 1854 to 1904. Professor Tobias was the great-great-grandson of Isaac Vallentine (1793–1868), founder of the *Jewish Chronicle*. Born in Durban, South Africa, Tobias taught at the Witwatersrand Medical School from 1951. From 1959 until 1990 he served as head of the department of anatomy. He was dean of the Faculty of Medicine (1980–82), member of the Witwatersrand University Council (1971–84), and the only simultaneous holder of three professorships at Witwatersrand University, Anatomy, Zoology, Palaeo-anthropology. From 1994 he was Professor Emeritus of Anatomy and Human Biology. He was founder and president of the Institute for the Study of Mankind in Africa (1961–68, 1983–84), president of the Royal Society of South Africa (1970–72) and of the South African Archaeological Society (1964–65), founder and first president of the Anatomical Society of Southern Africa (1968–72) and

South African Society for Quaternary Research (1969–73). From 1994 to 1998, he was president of the International Association of Human Biologists. Protégé and successor of Raymond Dart, who discovered the first African australopithecine, Tobias was from 1959 closely associated with Louis and Mary Leakey, who found early hominid remains in northern Tanzania. Some of these fossil hominids Leakey, Tobias, and Napier identified as a new lowly species of man, which they named *Homo habilis* (handy man) representing a more hominised lineage than the australopithecines. Tobias later adduced evidence that *Homo habilis* was the world's earliest primate with a capacity for spoken language. To a series of volumes on Olduvai Gorge, Tanzania, Tobias contributed a monograph on the biggest-toothed australopithecines, *Australopithecus boisei*, and two volumes on *Homo habilis*. His oeuvre of over 1,100 published works includes nearly 500 articles in periodicals, 125 chapters in books, and over 50 books and monographs. He is recognized internationally as a leading authority in palaeo-anthropology and has received 17 honorary doctorates, the Carmel Award of Merit of the University of Haifa, and many medals, honorary professorships, civil decorations, and memberships of academies. He has written inter alia on living Africans, genetics, race and racism, academic freedom, and the harmful effects of apartheid on South African education. Tobias was active in Jewish communal affairs, including the Board of Deputies and the Great Synagogue of Johannesburg.

[Gali Rotstein and Bracher Rager (2nd ed.)]

TOBIAS BEN MOSES HA-AVEL (or **ha-Ma'tik**, "the translator"; 11th century), *Karaite scholar. He laid the theoretical and educational foundations for establishing the Karaites in the Byzantine milieu. According to Elijah *Bashyaẓi (*Iggeret Gid ha-Nasheh*, 4a) Tobias studied under *Jeshua b. Judah, translated his works from Arabic into Hebrew, and brought them to Constantinople. He would therefore seem to have lived in the second half of the 11th century. However, two letters in Tobias' own handwriting found in the **Genizah* of Cairo indicate that he went to Jerusalem as early as the 1030s (or possibly the 1020s). At any rate he had returned by 1041, after he, like other Karaites, became involved in a bitter controversy which split the *Rabbanite community in Ereẓ Israel between the supporters of *Nathan b. Abraham and the followers of *Solomon b. Judah Gaon. Tobias could not have been a pupil of Jeshua b. Judah since both apparently studied under Joseph b. Abraham ha-Kohen "ha-Ro'eh" (al-*Baṣīr), Tobias even translating some of al-Baṣīr's letters into Hebrew. A few years later, at all events before 1048, Tobias headed the Karaite community in Byzantium. He went to Egypt, perhaps as an emissary, and there instituted regulations for the synagogues of his community. His authority was recognized by all "the communities of Edom [i.e., Byzantium] both near and far" (letter to Abraham b. Yashar *Abu Sad al-Tustarī in Egypt; see Z. Ankori, in: *Essays… S.W. Baron* (1959), 38). As the independent leader of the first Karaite center in the Byzantine Empire, he several times addressed questions on halakhic matters to the scholars in Jerusalem. Their answer to his query on intercalation was kept as a ruling for the Diaspora communities (Judah Hadassi, *Eshkol ha-Kofer*, 76a).

Epithets

The epithets by which Tobias is remembered in Karaite history are an indication of his personality and activities. His membership of the *Avelei Zion of Jerusalem while he was a student in the academy there led to his designation *ha-avel* ("the mourner") and *ha-oved* ("the worshiper"); his role as commentator and decisor on the laws of his community gained him the honorific *ha-baki* ("the erudite"), in addition to the conventional appellations *he-ḥakham* ("the sage") and *ha-maskil* ("the teacher"). Tobias attests that he was also called *ha-sofer* ("the scribe"), possibly in reference to his art (as demonstrated by his fine calligraphy in manuscripts which have survived). The title *ha-ma'tik* ("the translator") best describes Tobias, which then meant both translation and knowledge of tradition (*masoret*).

Works

With the exception of several liturgical poems (two of which were included in the Karaite prayer book), Tobias' works consist for the most part either of actual translations of works by his teacher Joseph al-Baṣīr from Arabic into Hebrew – *Sefer Ne'imot*, i.e., *Kitāb al-Muḥtawī* ("Book of Melodies"); *Sefer Maḥkimat Peti*, i.e., *Kitāb al-Tamyīz* (or *al-Manṣūrī*, "Book for the Enlightenment of Fools"); and *Sefer ha-Moladim*, one of eight chapters from *Kitāb al-Istibṣār* ("Book of Festivals") – or of compilations of Arabic material from other "Jerusalemite scholars" and its adaptation in Hebrew as the basis for Tobias' original work. This applies to his philosophical treatise *Meshivat Nefesh* (extant in manuscript), and his halakhic commentary, in many volumes, *Sefer Oẓar Neḥmad le-Va-Yikra* (only the first part, on Lev. 1–10, has survived in manuscript; passages from it have been published by Neubauer, Poznański, Mann, and Ankori). In this case Tobias himself states (at the end of the work) that his investigation is based "on Arabic works which I would have rendered into Hebrew," particularly on the Arabic commentaries of *David b. Boaz and *Japheth b. Ali ha-Levi, tenth-century Karaite scholars.

Halakhic System

In the legal field, the term *ha'takah* (Ar. *al-naql*) denotes the principle of tradition (precedence) in the determination of law. Its original (i.e., Rabbanite) meaning naturally refers to the Oral Law. But the tenth-century Karaite polemical writers, who borrowed this term from their Rabbanite opponents, attributed to it, in accordance with the classic standpoint adopted by this sect, two separate aspects and designated them as follows: on the one hand, there is acknowledgment of "*ha'takah* which all regard as authoritative," i.e., the prophetic tradition which has been preserved for posterity "in the books and prophecies transcribed with the Torah in the possession of Israel" (according to the definition of *Sahl b.

Maẓliaḥ ha-Kohen in S. Pinsker (ed.), *Likkutei Kadmoniyyot* (1860), 34); on the other, the authority of non-biblical tradition is rejected and it is laid down that "any *ha'takah* which has no support from Scripture is worthless" (Aaron b. Elijah of Nicomedia, *Gan Eden*, 8b/c, and Elijah Bashyaẓi, *Adderet Eliyahu*, 9d, 48c, 82b. All further citations are taken from the latter source). The original version of Tobias' definitive treatise on the theory of *ha'takah* has not survived and its position among his lost works is not known. However, its inherent boldness and revolutionary consequences were perceived by subsequent generations of scholars who preserved his text, with slight linguistic changes, and interpreted it repeatedly as they saw fit. In his endeavor to establish an intellectual and legal criterion for compromise solutions necessitated by time and place, Tobias recognized in both theory and practice the positive and dynamic function of the principle of *ha'takah* for his contemporaries, as it was also understood by the Rabbanites. In order to mollify conservative Karaite opinion, Tobias based this awareness on the fictitious assumption that all the activities of the Karaites, even seeming innovations, must have a foundation in and derive proof from Scripture, and "those who say that *ha'takah* exists without support from Scripture merely show that they lack the intelligence to find its legal validity in the Torah."

At the same time as the Karaite concept of tradition was in the process of being enriched, there existed in Karaism a corresponding trend whereby the concept of "community" (Heb. *edah* or *kibbutz*; Ar. *al-ijmāʿ*) was assimilated within the comprehensive context of tradition. Thus Tobias' fundamentally broader concept of *ha'takah* absorbed the ingredients of the Karaite principle of "consensus of the community," one of the earliest sectarian impediments to authoritative halakhic initiative. On the strength of this twofold development, *ha'takah* (which Tobias also called *kabbalah*, i.e., chain of tradition, while others called it *sevel ha-yerushah*, i.e., traditional custom) was harnessed in its new context to the positive process of later Karaite legislation. In the course of time *ha'takah* was to rise to the level of the two other fundaments of Karaism, the Torah (Scripture) and comprehension (*da'at* or analogy; *hekkesh*, Ar. *al-qiyās*), and even to become the leading principle. It completely changed the attitude of the Karaites toward the Talmud and its place in Jewish history, and ended by paving the way to the radical reforms effected in Byzantine-Turkish Karaism in the 15th century.

BIBLIOGRAPHY: Z. Ankori, *Karaites in Byzantium* (1959), index; idem, in: *Tarbiz*, 25 (1957), 44–65; idem, in: PAAJR, 24 (1955), 1–38; idem, in: JJS, 8 (1958), 79–81; idem, in: *Essays... S.W. Baron* (1959), 1–38; S. Poznański, in: *Oẓar Yisrael*, 5 (1911), 12–14; Mann, Texts, index; L. Nemoy, *Karaite Anthology* (1952), 124, 249, 380.

TOBIT, BOOK OF, one of the books of the *Apocrypha included in the Septuagint and Vulgate in the canon.

It is the story of Tobit, an honest, upright man of the tribe of Naphtali, who observed the precepts and was exiled to Assyria by Shalmaneser (III?). When he came to the land of his exile and the king of Assyria (Sennacherib) put many of the Jewish exiles to death, Tobit endangered his own life by defying the royal decree and arranging for the burial of the victims. His action came to the knowledge of the government and he was compelled to go into hiding until Esarhadon ascended the throne and *Ahikar, Tobit's nephew, was restored to his post as the king's scribe. Tobit then resumed his beneficent activities. It happened that on one occasion, when he had returned from burying an abandoned corpse, and lay down to sleep in his courtyard, bird's droppings fell into his eyes and he became blind. In his distress he remembered that some time before he had lent his relative in Rages of Media ten talents of silver. He therefore requested his son – called Tobias – to claim the money. The young man went in the company of a guide. On the way, as they passed the River Tigris, the guide advised him to catch a fish and preserve its heart, liver, and gall. Later as they passed Ecbatana in Media, the guide told him that his kinsman Raguel (Reuel) dwelt there, and that he had an only daughter, Sarah. She had already been married seven times, but the bridegroom had died each time on the night of the wedding, and according to the law of the Torah, since she was the young Tobias' kinswoman she was bespoken to him and not to a stranger. In order to drive away *Ashmedai, the demon who slew the grooms, the guide advised him to burn the heart and liver of the fish. Tobias did as ordered and was successful. His father-in-law, who was glad to see him alive, doubled the duration of the festivities from seven to 14 days. Meanwhile the guide, who had gone to Rages to bring the debt, came back, and they returned together to the home of Tobit the elder. When they reached Nineveh the son smeared the gall on his father's eyes, and his eyesight was restored. Tobit wanted to pay the guide his hire, but then it became known to him that the guide was none other than the angel Raphael, one of the seven angels who carry up prayers to Heaven. The aged Tobit, being aware that the end of Nineveh was near, commanded his son to leave the city and to go to Media after his father's death, which he did.

Various conjectures have been put forward with regard to the source of the tale. In the past it was usual to give the historical explanation that the story reflects the prohibition in some period against burying the dead, whether in the Persian era, or the Greek (under Antiochus IV), or the Roman (cf. Graetz; cf. Katznelson). However, the Roman era is much too late (the book is now known from the Dead Sea scrolls); there is even no reflection of the religious persecution of Antiochus IV, nor has the story any visible connection with the Persian custom of not burying the dead (moreover, its author praises Media). In recent decades the conjecture has gained acceptance that there is a connection between the story and the widespread folkloristic motif of a young man who saved a dead body from creditors who wanted to prevent its burial, and was then rescued by the deceased's spirit from mortal peril. The story of Tobit, however, does not speak even of a single creditor but of people put to death because of their devotion to burying the corpses of those executed by royal decree (as in the story of Antigone), and the bride is not a legendary king's daughter, but a kinswoman bespoken to her relative; nor is there mention of the many fabulous deeds which characterize the folklore tale. Probably, what the author really had in mind were the two popular "precepts," known from both the apocryphal and early talmudic literature: the first that one is in duty bound (even if he be a Nazirite or a high priest, who must keep away from any uncleanness) to bury a corpse found at random (*met mitzvah*, "the burial of the dead that is a precept"); and the second that there is special merit in marrying a kinswoman (cf. Tosef., Kid. 1:4; TJ, Naz. 7:1; and there are many stories of scholars who did so).

The book itself appears to be as early as the Persian era. It contains a prophecy on the building of Jerusalem, but there is no allusion to the Hasmonean wars. It appears to have been compiled in Media. To this the Iranian name "Ashmedai" (from Aeshma-Dawa) seems appropriate. There is also the very fact that the whole story turns around descendants of the ten tribes. From talmudic and other sources, it is clear that until a very late period the ten tribes were believed to thrive in Media and in the surrounding countries. Furthermore, in Babylonia (in a wide sense) more than in any other place, they were concerned about the genealogical purity of the Jews of the Exile. Moreover, and connecting of Tobit with Ahikar shows that in that place and time Ahikar was a well-known personality, which again lends support to the earlier date. The book is regarded as the most artistic story of the Apocrypha. Though dealing with various motifs, it retains a simple style and character. The original language was either Hebrew or Aramaic. Several fragments of the book were found among the Qumran scrolls both in Hebrew and in Aramaic. The Greek text is preserved in many versions, a long one (S) which is attested to in the Qumran library, a short one (A and B), and a third one, which is represented in many minuscules. Several Hebrew versions were preserved in the Middle Ages, but they all seem to be later adaptations. A very shortened version of the tale found its way into the well-known *Midrash *Tanḥuma*.

[Yehoshua M. Grintz]

In the Arts

The book's ethical message was congenial to the early Christian Reformers, notably Martin Luther (who recommended Tobit as a subject for comedy). A pioneer of the drama in Sweden was the Lutheran writer and preacher Olaus Petri (Olof Petterson), whose *Tobiae Commedia* appeared in 1550. Other works of the period were a Danish play by Hieronymus Justesen Ranch of Viborg, the German *Meistersinger* Hans Sachs' comedy, *Die gantz histori Tobie*, Joerg Wickram's German prose comedy, *Tobias* (1551), and a mystery staged at Lincoln in 1564. These were followed by several more works in the 17th century, but interest in the theme later waned, although the 19th century saw the appearance of Milovan Vidahoric's Serbian epic, *Mladi Tovija* (1825). In recent times, however, the subject has been revived in works such as James Bridie's *Tobias and the Angel* (1931) and Gonzalo Torrente Ballester's modern Spanish miracle play, *El viaje del joven Tobias* (1938). Bridie succeeded in revitalizing the Apocryphal story by injecting humor and colloquial speech into his realistic interpretation of the old theme.

In art there have been several cycles of works illustrating the story of Tobias, such as the fourth-century sarcophagus of St. Sebastian in the Appenine Way, Italy; 13th-century carvings at Chartres Cathedral; eight scenes in the Berlin Museum by Pinturiccio or Giulio Bugiardini; and paintings by Francesco Guardi for the Church of the Angel Raphael in Venice. The story of Tobias particularly appealed to *Rembrandt: the blind Tobit with his wife Anna (Tobit 2:11–14) is the subject of a meticulous early Rembrandt in the Moscow Museum and of several later works, including one in Berlin. These are studies of humble Dutch interiors, with a soft light filtering through the windows. There is also a painting by Rembrandt (Hermitage, Leningrad) of the younger Tobias taking leave of his parents as he sets out on his journey (5:17–22). Tobias and the angel (ch. 6) was a favorite subject in early Renaissance Italy. Merchants sometimes had their sons painted as Tobias accompanied by a guardian angel if they went away on business. The youth would be shown dangling his fish, followed by a little dog. The subject inspired paintings by Pollaiuolo (Pinacoteca, Turin); Filippino Lippi (Bension Collection, London); a follower of Verrochio (National Gallery, London); Botticelli (Academy, Florence); and Perugino (National Gallery, London). In "The Virgin with the Fish" by Raphael (Prado, Madrid), the kneeling Tobias holding his fish is presented by the angel to the Madonna. A painting by Rembrandt in the collection of the duke of Arenberg, Brussels, of the restoration of Tobit's sight (ch. 11) has been admired for the exactitude with which it depicts an operation for cataracts in the 17th century; and one in the Louvre shows the archangel Raphael taking leave of Tobit and his family (12:16–22).

In music Tobit's song of praise, *Magnus es Domine in aeternum*, is included among the Cantica of the Roman Catholic rite, and sung to a simple psalmodic melody. In the 16th century, a motet, *Domine deus patrum nostrorum*, is found among the works of the composer Jacobus Gallus (Handl), and there is a *Historia Tobiae* in the manuscript of Hungarian historico-biblical songs known as the Hofgreff Collection. The subject was sometimes used for oratorios by minor 17th-century composers: a work often mentioned in the history of the oratorio, Matthias Weckmann's dialogue *Tobias und Raquel*, was for long attributed to his better-known contemporary, Johann Rosenmueller (c. 1620–1684). More prominent composers turned to the subject for oratorios in the 18th century: Antonio Caldara (*Tobia*, text by Apostolo Zeno, 1720), Antonio Lotti (*Il ritorno di Tobia*, Bologna, 1723), Georg Reutter the Younger (*Il Ritorno di Tobia*, Vienna, 1733), Joseph Mysliveczek (1737–1781), and Baldassare Galuppi (1782). The outstanding work of this period was Haydn's oratorio *Il ritorno di Tobia* (text by Giovanni Gastone Boccherini, written in 1774–75). Haydn produced an augmented version in 1784 (a revised version was made by Sigismund Neukomm in 1806); and the work is still occasionally performed, as is its overture. A charming curiosity is Beethoven's jocular canon, *O Tobias, heiliger Tobias!* (1823), addressed to his publisher and friend Tobias Haslinger: according to the composer, he conceived the canon in a reverie on a coach ride during which he dreamt that he was transported to the Holy Land, felt very saintly, and through further flights of association came to think of "Saint" Tobit and his friend's good qualities. In the 19th century, the subject was taken up by several French composers in short succession, following upon Pierre-Louis Deffés' cantata (1847); Bizet (*L'ange et Tobie*, cantata, c. 1885–87, unfinished, text by Léon *Halévy); Gounod (*Tobie*, small oratorio, c. 1866, text by H. Lefèvre); and E. Ortolan (another setting of Halévy's libretto, 1867). Works of the 20th century include the opera *Tobias and the Angel* by Arthur Bliss (1959–60; text by Christopher Hassall); and Darius *Milhaud's *Invocation à l'ange Raphaël*, a cantata in four parts for women's voices and orchestra (text by Paul Claudel, published 1965).

[Bathja Bayer]

BIBLIOGRAPHY: X.L. Katzenelson, in: *Ha-Tekufah*, 25 (1929), 361–4; A. Kahana, *Ha-Sefarim ha-Ḥiẓonim*, 2 (1937), 291–311; Z. Hirsch, *Ha-Psychologyah be-Sifrutenu ha-Attikah* (1957), 70–73; H. Graetz, in: MGWJ, 28 (1879), 145–63, 385–408, 433–55, 509–20; F. Rosenthal, *Vier apokryphische Buecher aus der Zeit und Schule R. Akiba's* (1885), 104–50; F.C. Conybeare, J.R. Harris, and A.S. Lewis (eds.), *The Story of Ahikar* (1913[2]); E. Cosquin, in: RB, 8 (1899), 50–82; Charles, Apocrypha, 1 (1913), 174–201; M.M. Schumpp (tr. and ed.), *Das Buch Tobias* (1933); A. Miller (tr. and ed.), *Das Buch Tobias* (1940).

TOBY, JACKSON (1925–), U.S. criminologist and sociologist. Toby received his Ph.D. from Harvard University in 1950. He taught at Brooklyn College, N.Y., and at Harvard. He then took on the position of professor of sociology at Rutgers University, where he became chairman of the Sociology Department in 1961. He specialized in problems of adolescence and deviant behavior and was chief consultant to the Ford Foundation youth development program (1959–63). In 1966 he prepared a report on "Affluence and Adolescent Crime" for the President's Law Enforcement Commission. He served as director of the Institute for Criminological Research at Rutgers from 1969 to 1994. His subsequent research focused on undergraduate education and the causes of and remedies for school violence.

His publications include *Social Problems in America* (with Harry C. Bredemeier, 1960); *Contemporary Society: Social Process and Social Structure in Urban Industrial Societies* (1964); *The Evolution of Societies* (with T. Parsons, 1977); and *Higher Education as an Entitlement* (2005).

TOCH, ERNST (1887–1967), composer. Born in Vienna, Toch studied medicine and philosophy and was self-taught in music. After studying piano with Rehberg, he became a teacher of composition at the Mannheim Hochschule fuer Musik (1913). In 1921 he received his Ph.D. with the dissertation *Beitraege zur Stilkunde der Melodie* (published as *Melodielehre*, Berlin, 1923). In 1929 he moved to Berlin, and in 1934 he settled in the United States. From 1937 he lived in Hollywood and taught at various universities. Though his earlier compositions show a rather romantic style, he later turned to a more modern idiom and also experimented in compositions such as *Gesprochene Musik* (1930).

His music is strongly lyrical and shows a classical sense of form; in piano compositions, his style is more brilliant. Toch's works include four operas; orchestral works; chamber music; incidental music for plays, films, and radio plays; and choral works (including *Cantata of the Bitter Herbs*, a Passover oratorio, 1938). The overture to his opera *Die Prinzessin auf der Erbse* (1926) is often played.

BIBLIOGRAPHY: MGG; Grove, Dict; Riemann-Gurlitt; Baker, Biog Dict.

[Claude Abravanel]

TOCH, MAXIMILIAN (1864–1946), U.S. paint chemist. Born in New York, Toch graduated in chemistry and law before entering his father's paint business. He became an expert on the authenticity of paintings. He was professor of industrial chemistry at Cooper Union, New York (1919), and professor of the chemistry of artistic painting at the National Academy of Design, New York (1924). During World War I he invented the "Toch system" of camouflage. Among his books are *Chemistry and Technology of Mixed Paints* (1907), *How to Paint Permanent Pictures* (1922), and *Paint, Paintings and Restoration* (1931).

TOCHNER, MESHULLAM (1912–1966), Israeli literary critic. Born in the Ukraine, Tochner was taken to Bessarabia by his family during World War I. In 1925 he went to Palestine, settling in Jerusalem. He taught at the Teachers' Seminary of Beit ha-Kerem, Jerusalem.

He published literary research articles in Israel's newspapers, literary periodicals, and anthologies, and in the jubilee volumes for S.Y. *Agnon. Tochner was one of the most perceptive critics and interpreters of Agnon's works; *Pesher Agnon* (1968), a collection of his essays on Agnon, with the addition of critical remarks by D. Sadan, was published posthumously.

BIBLIOGRAPHY: S.Y. Agnon et al., *'Al Meshullam Tochner* (1967).

[Getzel Kressel]

TODD, MIKE (Avrom Hirsch Goldbogen; 1909–1958), U.S. producer and impresario. Born in Minneapolis, Minnesota, Todd was the son of a Polish-born rabbi. He produced 21 shows on Broadway, largely light musicals. These include *Call Me Ziggy* (1937); *The Hot Mikado* (1939); *Star and Garter* (1942); *Something for the Boys* (1943); *Mexican Hayride* (1944); *Up in Central Park* (1945); *As the Girls Go* (1948); *Michael Todd's Peep Show* (1950); and *The Live Wire* (1950). His production of the tragedy *Hamlet* (1945), starring Maurice Evans, set the record at the time for the longest run of any Shakespearean play on Broadway (131 performances).

Todd was a financial promoter of two motion picture filming innovations, Cinerama and Todd-AO, the latter of which he codeveloped. Cinerama was introduced to film audiences in 1952 with the stomach-churning *This Is Cinerama.* Todd-AO was introduced in 1955 with the wide-screen film *Oklahoma!* In 1956 Todd made the $6.5 million film of Jules Verne's *Around the World in 80 Days* (Academy Award winner for Best Picture) which, by the time of his death in a plane crash, had grossed $33 million.

Of his three marriages, the second and third were to the film actresses Joan Blondell (from 1947 to 1950) and Elizabeth Taylor (from 1957 until his death).

BIBLIOGRAPHY: A. Cohn, *The Nine Lives of Michael Todd* (1959); Liz Taylor, M. Todd Jr., and S. Todd McCarthy, *A Valuable Property: The Life Story of Michael Todd* (1983).

[Ruth Beloff (2nd ed.)]

TODESCO, HERMANN (1791–1844), Austrian industrialist and philanthropist. Todesco was born in Pressburg (Bratislava) to Babette, née Pick, of Breslau, and Aaron Hirschl Wellisch (Welsche) of Pressburg, a silk merchant, who acquired the surname Todesco after numerous trips to Italy (*tedesco* is Italian for "German"). In 1789 he was included in the list of Jews permitted to reside in Vienna. Hermann's business abilities soon brought him appreciable wealth and position. He was an efficient military contractor and established one of the first cotton mills in Marienthal (near Vienna), introducing modern machines and methods from abroad. In 1835 he bought an estate in Legnaro, Italy, where he planted mulberry trees for raising silk worms. Todesco was one of the founders of the Vienna temple in 1826 and was distinguished by his munificent philanthropic activities. He donated a school to the Pressburg community, made a magnificent bequest for a Jewish hospital in Baden, and gave large sums to the Vienna Jewish community to develop handicrafts. Shortly before his death he was nominated a member of the *Kollegium* of the community and opened a public kitchen for the poor. Hermann's banking firm was managed after his death by two of his seven children, Eduard (1814–1887) and Moritz (1816–1873). Eduard continued his father's philanthropic policies by establishing generous foundations to help needy army officers and impoverished Jewish students.

BIBLIOGRAPHY: B. Wachstein, *Die ersten Statuten* (1926), index; C. Von Wurzbach, *Biographisches Lexikon des Kaiserthums Oesterreich*, s.v.

[Albert Lichtblau (2nd ed.)]

TOEPLITZ, OTTO (1881–1940), German mathematician. Toeplitz was professor of mathematics at Kiel (1920) and Bonn (1928–35) until his dismissal by the Nazis. He immigrated to Palestine in 1939 and held an administrative post at the Hebrew University. He contributed to many branches of research in pure mathematics; his main interest was in matrix algebra. He wrote *Von Zahlen und Figuren* (1930) and published articles on Plato's mathematical ideas in *Quellen und Studien zur Geschichte der Mathematik, Astronomie und Physik*, a periodical which he helped found.

TOHORAH (Heb. טָהֳרָה; "cleansing," "purification"), the ceremony of washing the dead before burial, performed by *mit'assekim* ("attendants"), members of the **ḥevra kaddisha*. The body is laid on a special *tohorah* board, the feet toward the door to indicate the escape of the impurity. While the body is undressed, thoroughly rubbed and cleansed with lukewarm water, the *mit'assekim* recite biblical verses (Zech. 3:4; Ezek. 36:25; Song 5:11, etc.). Then the head and the front part of the body are rubbed with a beaten egg, a symbol of the perpetual wheel of life. (This part of the ceremony is only observed nowadays in very Orthodox circles.) Thereafter, "nine measures" (9 "*kav*," 4½ gallons) of water are poured over the body while it is held in an upright position. This process is the essential part of the *tohorah* ceremony. The body is then thoroughly dried and dressed in shrouds. The *tohorah* rite for great rabbis and scholars, called *reḥizah gedolah* ("great washing"), is more elaborate. "Nine measures" of water are used several times: the body may even be immersed in a *mikveh* ("ritual bath"). This custom, however, was strongly opposed by leading rabbis because it discouraged women from attending the *mikveh*. In addition to the washing of the body, the hair is combed and the fingernails and toenails are cut (Sh. Ar., YD 352:4). The basis for *tohorah* is in Ecclesiastes 5:15, "as he came, so shall he go" (meaning: as when man is born, he is washed, so too when he dies, he is washed; *Sefer Ḥasidim*, ed. by R. Margaliot (1957), no. 560). The ceremony of *tohorah*, as well as all other burial details, is not mentioned in the Bible. At the burial of kings, however, sweet odorous spices were used (II Chron. 16:14) and the Tombs of the Kings in Jerusalem have a bath below the entrance to the courtyard, which may have been built either for cleansing the dead or for the ritual use of priests. *Tohorah* was observed in mishnaic times, as can be derived from the statement that limited washing and anointing of the body is permitted on the Sabbath (Shab. 23:5). Talmudic literature mentions the cleansing of the body with myrtle and the cutting of the hair of the deceased (cf. Beẓah 6a; MK 8b). *Tohorah* for women is performed by the female members of the *ḥevra kaddisha*. After *tohorah*, the attendants clean their hands with salted water. Most traditional cemeteries have a special annex to the cemetery called *bet tohorah* ("cleansing house"). In recent times, however, *tohorah* is generally performed at the mortuary of hospitals (or by the undertaker). *Reform Judaism has discarded the ritual of *tohorah*.

BIBLIOGRAPHY: S. Baer, *Toẓe'ot Ḥayyim* (Heb. and Ger., 1900), 99–102 (Heb. pt.); J.M. Tukaczinsky, *Gesher ha-Ḥayyim*, 1 (1960²), 94–100; M. Lamm, *Jewish Way in Death and Mourning* (1969), 6–7, 242–5; H. Rabinowicz, *A Guide to Life* (1964), 38–39.

TOHOROT (Heb. טָהֳרוֹת; lit. "cleannesses"), the last of the six orders of the Mishnah, according to the traditional arrangement mentioned in the homily of *Simeon b. Lakish (Shab. 31a), but the fifth order according to R. *Tanḥuma (Num. R. 13:15). *Tohorot* discusses the *halakhot* of the different categories of ritual purity and impurity.

It contains 12 tractates, arranged in descending order according to the number of chapters: **Kelim*, containing 30 chapters, on vessels susceptible to impurity; **Oholot*, 18 chapters, on ritual impurity arising from the overshadowing of a dead person; **Nega'im*, 14 chapters, on uncleanness relating to leprosies; **Parah*, 12 chapters, on the *red heifer; **Tohorot*, ten chapters, mainly on conditions rendering foods unclean; **Mikva'ot*, ten chapters, on the pools for ritual immersion; **Niddah*, ten chapters, on uncleanness relating to the menstruant; **Makhshirim*, six chapters, on the fluids rendering food susceptible to becoming ritually impure; **Zavim*, five chapters, on uncleanesss from gonorrhea; **Tevul Yom*, four chapters, on uncleanness, lasting until the sunset, of one who has gone through ritual immersion during the day; **Yadayim*, four chapters, on the uncleanness of unwashed hands and their purification; and **Ukẓin*, three chapters, on the uncleanness transferred by the stalks or husks of fruits or plants – 126 chapters in all. Because of its length, some divided *Kelim* into three *bavot* ("gates"), namely *Bava Kamma, Bava Meẓia*, and *Bava Batra*, each containing ten chapters, as was done with *Nezikin (see **Bava Kamma*). In the Tosefta of *Tohorot, Kelim Bava Kamma* has seven chapters, *Kelim Bava Meẓia* 11, and *Kelim Bava Batra*, seven chapters; *Oholot* has 18, *Nega'im* nine, *Parah* 12, *Niddah* nine, *Mikva'ot* seven (or eight), *Tohorot* 11, *Makhshirim* three, *Zavim* five, *Yadayim* two, *Tevul Yom* two, and *Ukẓin* three chapters. Apart from the tractate *Niddah, Tohorot* has no *Gemara* in either the Jerusalem or Babylonian Talmud.

BIBLIOGRAPHY: Epstein, Mishnah, 980ff.; Ḥ. Albeck (ed.), *Shishah Sidrei Mishnah, Seder Tohorot* (1959), 9f.

[Abraham Arzi]

TOHOROT (Heb. טָהֳרוֹת; lit. "cleannesses"), fifth tractate in the order of the same name according to the enumeration in the standard Mishnah. According to *Hai Gaon it is the seventh. It is also the seventh in the Tosefta, if the three sections into which *Kelim* is divided there are counted as one.

The name *tohorot* ("ritual cleannesses") is actually a euphemism for *tumot* ("ritual uncleannesses") since *Tohorot* deals essentially with the rules of the lesser degrees of uncleanness, effects of which last until sunset only. It details the laws of cleanness and uncleanness regarding foodstuffs and liquids, persons engaged in their preparation or consumption, and vessels employed in the process.

Chapter 1 begins with the 13 regulations concerning the carrion of clean birds, and those relating to unclean birds and cattle. It continues with a discussion of the extent to which foodstuffs of major and minor grades of uncleanness may be combined to form the prescribed minima. Also discussed are the conditions under which the same or different grades of uncleanness may be conveyed to a number of loaves or pieces of dough that cling to one another. Chapter 2 discusses uncleanness that may be conveyed to wet or dry **terumah* by the hands of clean and unclean persons, the various grades of uncleanness a person may contract through eating, and the resultant uncleanness of foodstuff in contact with other foodstuff possessing various grades of uncleanness. Chapter 3 deals with the grades of uncleanness and minimum amounts applicable to foodstuffs capable of changing their state of fluidity to one of solidity and vice versa. Also discussed is the cleanness or uncleanness of those objects whose bulk is increased or decreased by weather conditions. The chapter concludes with an exposition of doubtful uncleanness, and this continues to the end of chapter 4 which deals with cases of doubtful uncleanness as a result of which *terumah* is to be burned, and doubtful instances that are finally regarded as clean. Chapters 5 and 6 are mainly concerned with doubtful cases of uncleanness in which a distinction is made between location in a private domain and location in a public domain. In the former, all doubtful cases are declared unclean, while in the latter, they are considered clean. Also discussed are instances in which both a private and public domain are involved. Chapter 7 discusses forms of doubtful uncleanness which result from the presence of an **am ha-areẓ* or his wife. Chapter 8 concludes the discussion regarding the *am ha-areẓ*. Rules regarding the stages when foodstuffs begin and cease to be susceptible to uncleanness are next specified. A discussion concerning the uncleanness of beverages concludes the chapter. Chapters 9 and 10 conclude the tractate with the regulations concerning the stages at which olives become susceptible to uncleanness, and the laws of cleanness and uncleanness that apply to an olive-press and a winepress. The Tosefta to this tractate is divided into 11 chapters. Since there is no *Gemara* to *Tohorot*, the Tosefta is extremely valuable for the elucidation of many difficult passages in the Mishnah. All the commentators therefore made extensive use of the Tosefta in their explanations of the Mishnah. The Tosefta does not totally correspond to the Mishnah. It does not contain any laws that correspond to Mishnah 1:1–4 or 2:1. Tosefta 4:1–4 includes material which is not contained in the Mishnah. It was translated into English by H. Danby (*The Mishnah*, 1933), and J. Neusner published a translation of both the Mishnah (1991) and the Tosefta (2002) of *Tohorot*.

ADD. BIBLIOGRAPHY: Strack-Stemberger, *Introduction to the Talmud and Midrash* (1996), 117; Epstein, *The Gaonic Commentary on the Order Toharot* (Hebrew) (1982); S. Lieberman, *Tosefet Rishonim*, vol. 3 (1939); J. Neusner, *A History of the Mishnaic Laws of Purities* (1974–77), vols. 11–12; idem, *From Mishnah to Scripture* (1984), 67–71; idem, *The Mishnah Before 70* (1987), 171–178; idem, *The Philosophical Mishnah*, 3 (1989), 207–20; idem, *Purity in Rabbinic Judaism* (1994), 74–79.

[Aaron Rothkoff]

TOHOROT HA-KODESH, an important work of ethical literature. First printed in Amsterdam in 1733, this anonymous work has been wrongly attributed to Benjamin Wolf b. Mattathias. The error arose from the fact that Benjamin's name is mentioned on the title page, not as the author but as the person who brought the work to the press, and, it seems, collected the funds necessary to finance the printing. According to his introduction, the author chose to remain anonymous in order to avoid pride of authorship, and probably also because of the harsh criticism of contemporary rabbis, institutions, and customs contained in the work. The original title of the work, the introduction indicates, was *Hanhagot Yesharot* ("Right Ways of Behavior"). Evidence in the book shows that the author was from Poland, and in the work he occasionally compares the customs of Eastern Europe with those of the Orient. It seems that the author was poor, wandered from place to place, and knew Russian. I. Halpern attempted to prove that the author lived in Poland during the *Chmielnicki persecutions (1648–49), which left a deep impression on him, and that he finished the work a decade or two later. B.Z. Dinur and D. Tamar, however, hold that the work was probably written in the first decade of the 18th century. The later date is somewhat more credible in view of the historical and biographical facts recorded in the work itself. The writer, a Lurianic kabbalist like most authors of ethical works at that time, divided the book into six parts: (1) daily behavior, including the proper way to study at night and to perform the morning rites; (2) synagogue and prayer; (3) business and ethics, and the necessity to study and pray even while attending to daily tasks; (4) evening rites; (5) behavior during Sabbath and festivals; and (6) all aspects of social conduct. Social criticism holds a central place in this work. Ethical literature's preoccupation with just social behavior as the supreme religious goal is clearly presented, especially in the criticism of contemporary rabbis. In fact, the author emphasizes that right social behavior takes precedence over study of the Torah. Dinur included *Tohorot ha-Kodesh* among those East European ethical works which anticipated modern Ḥasidism and carried some of its social and religious message.

BIBLIOGRAPHY: B. Dinur, *Be-Mifneh ha-Dorot* (1955), index; I. Halpern, in: KS, 34 (1959), 495–98 (=*Yehudim ve-Yahadut be-Mizraḥ Eiropah* (1968), 396–400); D. Tamar, in: *Aresheth*, 3 (1961), 166–72 (= *Meḥkarim be-Toledot ha-Yehudim* (1970), 131–7).

TOKAT, capital city of the province bearing the same name in northern Anatolia, situated on the banks of the Yeşil Irmak. The community was founded by Jews from *Amasya in 1530. After the Amasya blood libel in 1553, most of them returned to Amasya in 1565. During the Ottoman period there existed a small Jewish community in Tokat. Tokat then was also the scene of a blood libel, instigated by Armenians; as a result of an intervention by Moses *Hamon, Sultan *Suleiman's chief physician, the Jews were able to prove their innocence. In the 16th century Jewish silk merchants traveled via Tokat to *Aleppo and *Persia. A document from 1574/75 noted 29 Jewish households and 27 Jewish bachelors in the community. The traveler Tevernier visited the city in the 17th century, but wrote only about Muslims, Christians, and Armenians who lived there. Yet it is known that R. Zemach Narvoni lived in Tokat in 1642, and we can assume that there existed an organized Jewish community. Hebron emissaries R. Moshe Halevi Nazir and R. Yosef Hacohen visited Tokat between the years 1668 and 1671 and 1675–1677. The latter spent a short time in Tokat in 1684 when he traveled to many communities to collect money for himself. At the beginning of the 18th century the Shabbatean Ḥayyim Malach met *Shabbetai Ẓevi on his way from Bursa to Tokat. At that time Rabbi Joseph ben Mordechai from *Jerusalem lived in the city. At the beginning of the 19th century about 100 families lived in the community; by 1927 only 20 families were left. There are two Jewish cemeteries and an old synagogue, where a **genizah* was found. Jews originally handled the town's commerce, but they were gradually replaced by the Armenians who used more up-to-date methods and mastered the foreign languages required for the export-import trade. As a result of this, the Jewish community scattered.

BIBLIOGRAPHY: A. Galanté, *Histoire des Juifs d'Anatolie*, 2 (1939), 289–92; Rosanes, Togarmah, 2 (1937–38), 135–6. **ADD. BIBLIOGRAPHY:** A. Yaari, Shelohei, 373, 416, 469–70; Tevernier, *Voyages de Perse*, 1, 90; M. Benveniste, *Responsa Penei Moshe*, 1 (1971), no. 33; U. Heyd, in: *Sefunot*, 5 (1961), 135–50; M. Benayahu, in: *Sefunot*, 14 (1971–78), 92, 248; M.A. Epstein, *The Ottoman Jewish Communities and Their Role in the Fifteenth and Sixteenth Centuries* (1980), 277; H. Gerber, *Yehudei ha-Imperiyah ha-Otmanit ba-Me'ot ha-Shesh Esrei ve-ha-Sheva Esrei: Ḥevrah ve-Kalkalah* (1983), 47, 69, 159.

[Abraham Haim / Leah Bornstein-Makovetsky (2nd ed.)]

TOKER, ELIAHU (1934–), Argentinean writer, poet, translator, and researcher in Jewish literature and lore. The scope and spirit of his works are oriented both to Jewish traditions of the past, and to the building of a contemporary Jewish-Latin American identity. His eight books of poetry include *Lejaim* ("To Life," 1974); *Piedra de par en par* ("Wide Open Stone," 1974); *Padretierra* ("Fatherearth," 1977); *Homenaje a Abraxas* ("Homage to Abraxas," 1980); *Papá, mamá y otras ciudades* ("Dad, Mom and Other Cities," 1988); and *Las manos del silencio* ("The Hands of Silence," 2003). His translations include valuable anthologies such as the following: from Yiddish – *El resplandor de la palabra judía: antología de poesía ídish del siglo XX* ("The Radiance of the Jewish Word: Anthology of 20th Century Yiddish Poetry," 1981); *Poesía de Avrom Sútzkever* ("Poetry by Avrom Sutzkever," 1983); *El ídish es también Latinoamérica* ("Yiddish is also Latin America," 2003); from Hebrew – *El Cantar de los Cantares* ("The Song of Songs," 1984); *Pirké Avot* ("The Sayings of the Fathers," 1988), and anthologies of kabbalistic, talmudic, and rabbinical texts. He also published critical editions of the Argentinean Jewish writers César Tiempo, Carlos M. Grünberg, and Alberto Gerchunoff; collections of Jewish proverbs and jokes; and volumes devoted to the Holocaust and to the victims of the attack on the Buenos Aires Jewish Community building in 1994. His poems have been translated into Yiddish, Hebrew, French, German, and Portuguese. Toker received several awards in Argentina and Mexico. He was also active in Jewish cultural and community life in Argentina, and participated in national and international conferences on Jewish Latin American issues.

BIBLIOGRAPHY: D.B. Lockhart, *Jewish Writers of Latin America. A Dictionary* (1997); R. Di Antonio and N. Glickman, *Tradition and Innovation: Reflection on Latin American Jewish Writing* (1993); P. Finzi et al., *El imaginario judío en la literatura de América Latina: visión y realidad* (1992).

[Florinda F. Goldberg (2nd ed.)]

TOKHEḤAH (Heb. תּוֹכֵחָה; lit. "reproof"), the name given to the two comminatory passages in the Pentateuch (Lev. 26:14–45; Deut. 28:15–68). The Mishnah referred to them as the "chapters of curses" and they were designated as the Torah reading for fast days. These sections must not be divided, but must be read by one person (Meg. 3:6, 31b). In order to begin and end with more favorable sentences (Meg. 31b; TJ, Meg. 3:8, 74b), the reading is commenced before the curses and concluded after them (e.g., Lev. 26:10–46; Deut. 28:7–69). The Deuteronomy chapter was considered the more severe since it contains no verses of consolation and is written in the present tense. The public reading of these passages on their appropriate Sabbaths generated fear among the listeners, and it therefore became customary for the reader to recite them quickly in a low voice. People were reluctant to be called to the Torah for these portions. In some communities it became customary to give this *aliyah* to poor people who could not afford to pledge donations for the more desirable *aliyot*. The person was not called up by his name, but the sexton simply said "May anyone who wishes rise to the Torah" (Rema to Sh. Ar. 428:6). It later became the general practice for the sexton or the reader of the Torah to accept this *aliyah*. However, in some communities, the rabbis insisted on receiving these *aliyot* to demonstrate that the word of the Torah need not be feared.

[Aaron Rothkoff]

TOKYO, city in *Japan. Jewish history, culture, and religion were generally unknown to the Japanese of Tokyo before the end of World War I. Although the city had been designated the imperial capital in 1868, Jews who took up residence in Japan before World War I settled in the great port cities of *Kobe, *Yokohama, and *Nagasaki. Acquaintance with things Jewish was largely limited to Christian missionaries and their converts. This state of affairs changed somewhat after 1918 when a small number of Jews fleeing from the Bolshevik revolution in Russia made their homes in Tokyo, and many Japanese encountered Jews and witnessed antisemitism during Japan's military expedition in Siberia (1918–22). During the 1920s a handful of Japanese antisemites founded organizations and engaged in publication, mostly in Tokyo, but their work was generally ineffectual. With the spread of Nazism in Germany and the drift of Japan after 1932 toward closer relations with Hitler, professional antisemites – military and civilian – attempted with little success to spread their message of hatred among the Japanese people. When Japan surrendered to the allied powers in 1945, Tokyo soon emerged as a center of Jewish life and activity in Japan. Many of the Jews who helped to stimulate a wide variety of Jewish activities were among the thousands of American troops stationed in Tokyo during the American occupation of Japan (1945–52). The civilian Jewish community grew slowly during and after this period as hundreds of Jews, mainly from the United States and Western Europe, settled in the city for professional and commercial purposes. Jewish life gravitated toward the Tokyo Jewish Center which was established and maintained by the local community. In the late 1950s some American Jews studied briefly the feasibility of "missionary" work in Japan, especially in Tokyo, but the idea was soon abandoned. A Jewish community, supplemented by a steady stream of temporary residents from abroad, continued to exist in Japan's capital city. In 1971 there were approximately 300 Jews living in the city. In the first years of the 21st century the permanent Jewish population of Tokyo amounted to fewer than 200 people, though the transient Jewish population brought the total up to somewhat fewer than 1,000. These included representatives of businesses and financial institutions, as well as journalists and students, mostly from the U.S. and Israel. The Jewish community center houses the only synagogue in Japan as well as a school (with classes twice a week up to the eighth grade), a library, and a *mikveh*.

BIBLIOGRAPHY: S. Mason, *Our Mission to the Far East* (1918); J. Nakada, *Japan in the Bible* (1933); I. Cohen, in: *East and West*, 2 (1922), 239–40, 267–70, 652–4; H. Dicker, *Wanderers and Settlers in the Far East* (1962), incl. bibl.

[Hyman Kublin]

°**TOLAND, JOHN** (1670–1722), Irish-born deist, active in the theological and political controversies in England at the beginning of the 18th century. Toland was born in County Donegal, supposedly the illegitimate son of a Roman Catholic priest. At the age of 16 he rejected Catholicism, became a Presbyterian, and studied at Scottish universities. A friend of John Locke, he eventually became a Deist and, later, a Pantheist. Among his many publications was *Reasons for Naturalising the Jews in Great Britain and Ireland on the Same Footing with All Other Nations* (anonymously published in London in 1714, reprinted 1939). This was not as has frequently been stated a plea for the naturalization of the Jews, but for facilitating the naturalization of foreign-born Jews and thereby attracting them to England. The economic and philosophic arguments that Toland used to demonstrate the utility of the Jews to the country showed a tolerance in advance of his day. Toland also translated into English *The Agreement of the Customs of the East Indians with Those of the Jews* (London, 1705).

BIBLIOGRAPHY: Dubnow, Weltgesch, 7 (1928), 520–3; Roth, Mag Bib, 213, 380; Wiener, in: HUCA, 16 (1941), 215–42; A. Cohen, *Anglo-Jewish Scrapbook* (1943), 336–7; J. Toland, *Gruende fuer die Einbuergerung der Juden in Grossbritannien und Irland*, ed. and tr. by H. Mainusch (Eng. and Ger., 1965), incl. bibl.; Barzilay, in: JSS, 21 (1969), 75–81. **ADD. BIBLIOGRAPHY:** ODNB online; S.H. Daniel, *John Toland: His Methods, Manners, and Mind* (1984); R.E. Sullivan, *John Toland and the Deist Controversy* (1982); Katz, England, 234–36.

[Cecil Roth]

TOLANSKY, SAMUEL (1907–1973), English physicist and world authority on optics and spectroscopy. Tolansky was born in Newcastle-on-Tyne, England, to Russian parents. He received his education in Newcastle and at the Imperial College in London, where he was appointed assistant lecturer in physics in 1934. He subsequently held various appointments at Manchester University, where he conducted important research work in the field of atomic energy during World War II. He joined the Royal Holloway College of London University in 1947, becoming professor of physics. He became a fellow of the Royal Society in 1952.

Tolansky was a principal investigator for the American NASA lunar research project, and was one of the first group of scientists chosen to examine and evaluate the dust brought back by the Apollo moon astronauts. His prediction in 1969 that the moon is covered with glasslike marbles was verified a year later. Tolansky wrote a large number of works in his special field, many of which were translated into Russian, German, Japanese, and other languages. They include *Optical Illusions* (1964); *Curiosities of Light Rays and Light Waves* (1964); *Interference Microscopy for the Biologist* (1968); *The Strategic Diamond* (1968); *Microstructures of Surfaces* (1968); and *Revolution in Optics* (1968). He also published over 300 scientific papers.

Keenly interested in Jewish affairs, Tolansky was an active member of the academic advisory council of the cultural department of the World Jewish Congress, and was generally associated with Israeli scientific institutions. He was also a vice president of the British Technion society. He visited Israel on a number of occasions, delivering scientific lectures and advising on scientific affairs.

[Michael Wallach]

TOLEDANO, family of rabbis and *ḥakhamim* which originated in Toledo, *Spain. After the expulsion from Spain in 1492, the Toledanos were to be found in Safed, Salonika, and Morocco. According to a family tradition, they arrived in Fez during the 16th century from Salonika, and from there went to Meknès and became leaders of the community from the 16th century until the present day. They were prominent in the community in religious affairs, producing renowned rabbis and poets who enriched the literature of Moroccan Jewry with their works and greatly influenced the western communities, particularly those of Meknès, Salé, Tangier, and even Gibraltar; in political affairs, producing men who served as ministers and counselors to kings and were entrusted with diplomatic missions; and in economic affairs, producing outstanding merchants who developed and maintained varied commercial relations with European countries which contributed to the economic progress of Morocco.

(1) DANIEL BEN JOSEPH (c. 1570–1640) arrived in Fez from Salonika with his sons (2) ḤAYYIM and (3) JOSEPH, from whom the two principal lines of the family branched out. He is described in sources as the "head of the yeshivah of Fez" and as the "head of the Castilian scholars."

(2) Ḥayyim's sons were (4) ḤABIB (d. c. 1660) and (5) DANIEL (1600–1670?). The former was rabbi and *nagid* in Meknès and was referred to as *He-Ḥasid* ("the Pious"). He was a signatory to a *takkanah* of 1640, whose efficacy he strengthened by securing for it a royal order. The latter was a rabbi and legal authority in Meknès. (3) Joseph's sons were (6) DANIEL (d. c. 1680) and (7) BARUCH (d. 1685). The former was a rabbi and *dayyan* in Meknès and counselor of Moulay Ismāʾil together with his colleague Joseph *Maymeran. He fought Shabbateanism with R. Aaron ha-Sabʿuni and his son-in-law R. Jacob *Sasportas, and he signed legal decisions together with (9) R. Hayyim b. Habib (see below). Baruch (7) was a rabbi in Meknès, father of seven sons, including (8) MOSES, the father of four *ḥakhamim*. Among Baruch's other sons were (16) Ḥayyim and (17) Abraham, leading merchants who traded with the royal family.

(9) ḤAYYIM BEN ḤABIB HE-ḤASID (d. c. 1680), rabbi and kabbalist, copied kabbalistic and ethical works, including *Yeraḥ Yakar* of R. Abraham Galanté which was brought to him by the emissary Elisha Ashkenazi – the father of Nathan of Gaza – and *Shaʿarei Ḥokhmah* of an Ashkenazi author, thus contributing to their circulation in the West. It is almost certain that he fought the Shabbatean movement, as did his relative Daniel, with whom he shared the position of *dayyan*. He maintained contact with R. Aaron ha-Sabʿuni and copied the marginal notes of the latter's copy of the Shulḥan Arukh. One of his daughters married R. Abraham Berdugo and was the mother of R. Moses Berdugo ("ha-MaSHBIR"), and the other married R. (8) Moses b. Baruch (see above) and gave birth to R. (18) Ḥayyim ("MaHaRḤaT") and R. (21) Jacob Toledano ("MaHaRIT"). Ḥayyim (9) signed legal decisions together with his relative Daniel. His son (10) MOSES (1643–1723) was the leading rabbi of Meknès and corresponded on halakhic questions with R. Menahem *Serero, R. Vidal ha-*Sarfati, and others. Some of his responsa and legal decisions were published in the works of Moroccan *ḥakhamim*. He held rabbinical office together with his brother (11) ḤABIB (1658–1716). The latter corresponded extensively with the *ḥakhamim* of Fez. R. Judah (1660–1729), a scholar of Meknès, was known as a great talmudist.

(12) JOSEPH TOLEDANO BEN DANIEL (b) (d. c. 1700) was also a counselor of the Moroccan king Moulay Ismāʾil, who sought to develop foreign trade and exchange Christian captives for arms as well as for other goods. He sent Joseph to the Netherlands to conduct negotiations which would lead to a peace treaty and a commercial agreement between the two countries. His mission was successful and the treaty was ratified in 1683. In 1688 Joseph presented his credentials as Moroccan ambassador to the States General. The presence in Holland of his brother-in-law Jacob Sasportas obviously assisted him in the fulfillment of his mission. His brother (13) ḤAYYIM TOLEDANO (d. c. 1710), also a royal counselor, accompanied him on the mission. Once the treaty was ratified in the Netherlands, he returned to Meknès and together with the *nagid* Abraham Maymeran convinced the king to accept its conditions

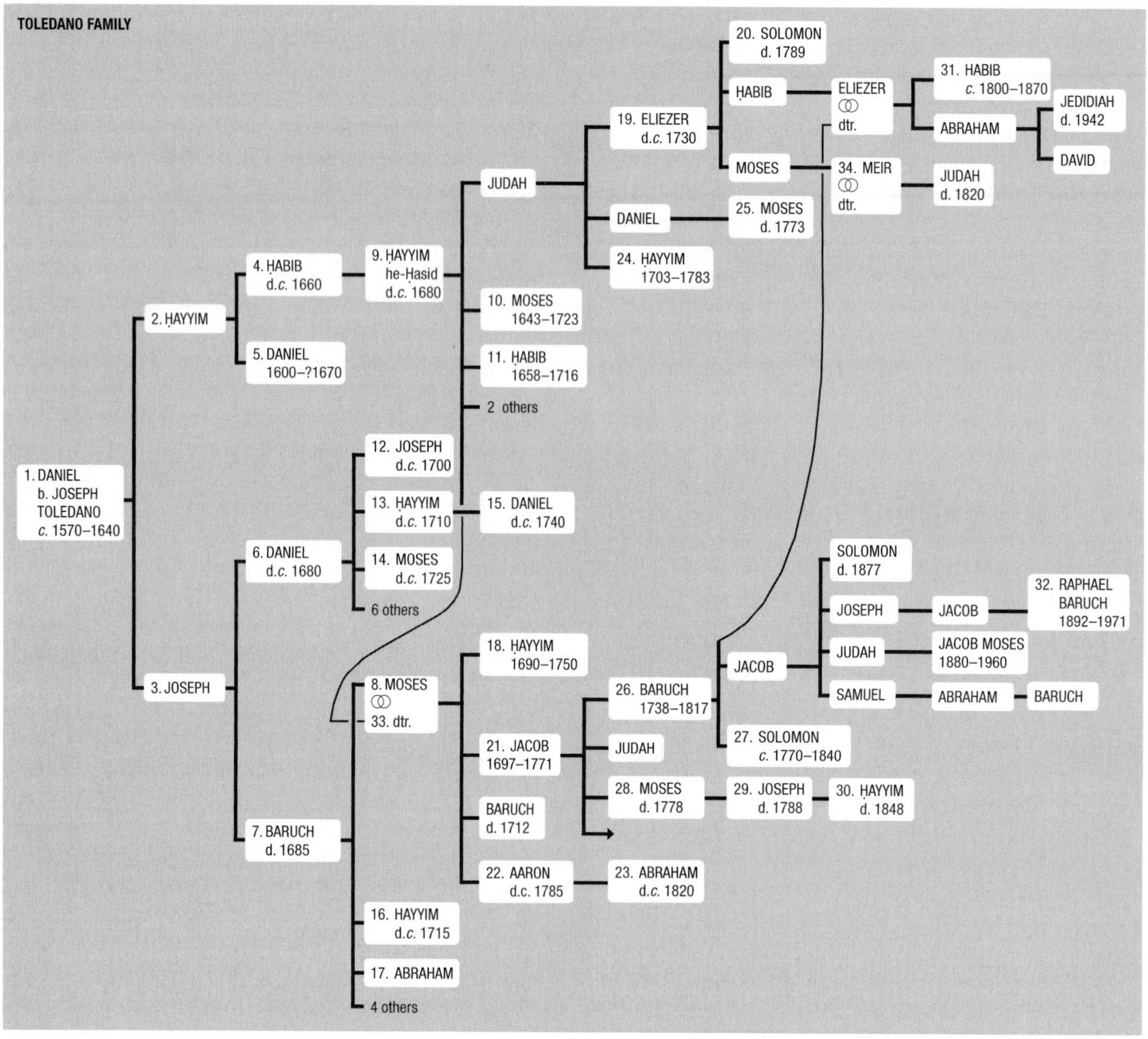

and sign. In 1690, when a crisis between the two countries appeared imminent, he traveled to the Netherlands and succeeded in renewing the treaty, afterward convincing the king to accept the conditions of the treaty. (14) MOSES TOLEDANO (d. c. 1725) was one of the favorites at the court. Together with the *nagid* Abraham Maymeran, he traded with the European countries, especially in firearms. In 1699 he traveled to the Netherlands and submitted complaints to the States General concerning his dealings with them. He won his suit and was awarded considerable compensation.

(15) DANIEL TOLEDANO (d. c. 1740), son of (13) Ḥayyim, traded, together with his father, in the Netherlands and other European countries. He dealt mainly in wax and was known as "one of the country's magnates." In about 1720, after the death of his father, he was arrested by the king. The king confiscated his family's belongings in payment for his debt, including (18) R. Ḥayyim Toledano's property, thus bankrupting him. (16) ḤAYYIM TOLEDANO BEN BARUCH (d. c. 1715), a wealthy merchant, was associated with his brother (17) ABRAHAM in various business transactions and was a favorite of the royal family. He died childless and bequeathed his estate to (18) R. Ḥayyim (MaHaRḤaT; see below), the son of his brother (8) Moses. (19) ELIEZER TOLEDANO BEN R. JUDAH (d. c. 1730) was among the wealthiest Moroccan merchants and a member of the circle of *negidim* which included Abraham Maymeran and Moses ibn Attar. Together with Maimon Toledano, he leased the meat tax of the community. He was the father of (20) R. Solomon (MaHaRshaT; see below). (18) ḤAYYIM TOLEDANO BEN MOSES BEN BARUCH (MaHaRḤaT; 1690–1750), rabbi in Meknès, became wealthy after he inherited his uncle Ḥayyim's fortune. He wrote some legal decisions which were published in Fez under the title *Ḥok u-Mishpat* ("Law and Judgment," 1931).

His brother (21) R. JACOB TOLEDANO (MaHaRIT; 1697–1771) was a prominent rabbi in Meknès and a disciple of R. Moses Berdugo, holding rabbinical office for 50 years. He was the most important halakhic authority in the Maghreb during the second half of the 18th century and played a central role in the leadership of his community. A crisis occurred in the relations between himself and his community in 1764, but the difficulties were settled and he continued to serve the community. He wrote a commentary on the Torah, a commentary to Rashi on the Torah, a work on the Shulḥan Arukh, novellae on the Talmud, legal decisions, some of which were published in the works of Moroccan *ḥakhamim*, and sermons. Another brother, (22) AARON TOLEDANO (d. c. 1785), was rabbi in Meknès. Toward the end of his life he left for Tangier, where he was appointed rabbi. His son (23) R. ABRAHAM TOLEDANO (d. c. 1820) was rabbi in Tangier after his father's death.

(24) R. ḤAYYIM BEN R. JUDAH (1703–1783), renowned for his piety, was rabbi in Salé. He was a disciple of R. Moses Berdugo and wrote legal decisions (*Teshuvot MaHaRḤat shel Salé*), *kinot*, and *piyyutim*. His nephew (20) R. SOLOMON BEN ELIEZER (MaHaRShaT; d. 1809) was a leading rabbi in Meknès and a member of the *bet din* of (21) R. Jacob b. Moses (MaHaRIT). He is said to have performed miracles, and to the present day the sick prostrate themselves and pray at his tomb. He wrote a work of legal decisions entitled *Piskei MaHaRShat*. His cousin (25) MOSES BEN DANIEL (d. 1773) was a disciple of the brothers (18) R. Ḥayyim and (21) R. Jacob Toledano (see above). From 1769 he was a member of the *bet din* of the MaHaRIT (21). He left many works on the Torah which his son-in-law (34) R. MEIR TOLEDANO edited, summarized, and published as *Melekhet ha-Kodesh* (Leghorn, 1803). His legal decisions were published as *Ha-Shamayim ha-Ḥadashim*.

(26) R. BARUCH TOLEDANO (1738–1817), son of MaHaRIT, was appointed *dayyan* after the death of his father. The opponent of R. Raphael Berdugo he wrote legal decisions and responsa. His son (?), (27) R. SOLOMON TOLEDANO (c. 1770–1840), was rabbi in Meknès. Many of his legal decisions were published in the work *Shufrei de-Ya'akov* of R. Jacob Berdugo. (28) R. MOSES TOLEDANO (d. 1778), son of MaHaRIT, was rabbi in Meknès. He wrote *Meginnei Shelomo*, on Rashi's commentary to the Torah, as well as sermons. His son (29), R. JOSEPH, collected, arranged, and copied the writings of his grandfather (MaHaRIT). (30) R. ḤAYYIM BEN R. JOSEPH (d. 1848), rabbi in Meknès, was very active in the community's administration. In Iyyar 5608 (1848) he was arrested by the sherif (ruler) – as a result of a denunciation – together with his colleague R. Joseph Berdugo and ten of the community's leaders. About two months later he died in the prison of Fez. He wrote a brief commentary on the Torah, legal decisions, responsa, a work on the *Tur* Shulḥan Arukh, a commentary on the *Haggadah*, and a collection of letters and writings.

(31) R. ḤABIB TOLEDANO BEN ELIEZER (c. 1800–1870) was brought up in Meknès. Prior to 1825 he traveled to Gibraltar, where he collected funds to save the members of his community from the famine which then ravaged Morocco. From there he went to Tunis and Italy, where he published his commentary on the *Haggadah, Peh Yesharim* (Leghorn, 1834), and *Terumat ha-Kodesh* (Leghorn, 1842). R. JACOB TOLEDANO BEN MOSES (d. c. 1928) was a rabbinical authority in Meknès and a poet. His *piyyutim* and poems were published as *Yagel Ya'akov* (in: *Yismaḥ Yisrael*, 1931). (32) R. RAPHAEL BARUCH BEN JACOB (1892–1971) was rabbi in Meknès. After his father's death he was appointed to the *bet din*, and from about 1940 he was *av bet din* of Meknès. He was very active in community affairs, and founded yeshivot. He immigrated to Israel in 1965. Toledano wrote a summarized version of the complete Shulḥan Arukh (1966), as well as a number of poems and *piyyutim*, some of which are recited by Oriental communities and Sephardim. Rabbi Jacob Moses *Toledano was also a member of the family.

BIBLIOGRAPHY: J.M. Toledano, *Ner ha-Ma'arav* (1911); J. Ben-Naim, *Malkhei Rabbanan* (1931); Hirschberg, Afrikah, index; idem, in: H.J. Zimmels et al. (eds.), *Essays Presented to Chief Rabbi Israel Brodie…* (1967), 153–82.

[Haim Bentov]

TOLEDANO, JACOB MOSES (1880–1960), rabbi and scholar. Toledano's father Judah had immigrated to Ereẓ Israel from Morocco. Jacob was born, educated, and ordained in Tiberias. During 1899–1909, his first articles appeared in the Jerusalem Hebrew paper *Ḥavaẓẓelet*, under the title *Ḥiddushei Torah*. They were written in elegant Hebrew and in a scholarly style. Toledano was also interested in ancient manuscripts preserved in the libraries and yeshivot of Oriental countries. He conceived the idea of founding a society to publish them and with this aim in mind entered into correspondence with scholars in western countries who encouraged him to implement the project. As a result of the cholera epidemic in Tiberias in 1903, he and his family left the town and settled in Peki'in. During the seven years he lived there he devoted himself to the study of the history of Oriental Jewry and its personalities, as well as to the affairs of the Peki'in community, and published his *Ner ha-Ma'arav*. At the beginning of World War I, together with 700 "French" Jews (of North African descent) from Galilee, he was exiled from Ereẓ Israel to Corsica because of his French citizenship. As the representative of the Alliance Israélite Universelle and the French government, he headed the committee of exiles and worked for their material and spiritual benefit. In 1920 he returned to Tiberias and took part in activities to revive communal life in the town; he represented it in 1921 at the rabbinical conference held in Jerusalem to establish the chief rabbinate of Ereẓ Israel. In 1926 he was appointed a member of the Tangier rabbinate, and in 1929 *av bet din* and deputy chief rabbi of Cairo. In 1933 he was appointed to the similar office in Alexandria, as well as deputy head of the rabbinical court of appeals in Cairo, and in 1937 he became chief rabbi of Alexandria. In 1942 he was elected Sephardi chief rabbi of Tel Aviv-Jaffa, succeeding Ben Zion *Ouziel. In 1958, when the religious parties had left the government coalition, he was appointed minister of religious affairs.

His *Ner ha-Ma'arav* (1911), the history of the Jews in Morocco from the commencement of their settlement and the biographies of its great rabbis, is a basic work for research into the origins of Jewry in North Africa. His other books included *Appiryon* (Jerusalem, 1905), a bibliography of the supercommentators to Rashi's commentary to the Pentateuch; *Yedei Moshe* (Safed, 1915), a commentary on the Mishnah *Pesaḥim* by Maimonides from a manuscript; *Yam ha-Gadol* (Cairo, 1931), responsa; *Sarid u-Falit* (Tel Aviv, 1945), giving passages from manuscripts on ancient works dealing with the Talmud, Jewish scholarship, the history of the settlement in Ereẓ Israel, and bibliography; and *Oẓar Genazim* (1960), a collection of letters on the history of Ereẓ Israel from ancient manuscripts, with introductions and notes.

BIBLIOGRAPHY: M.D. Gaon, *Yehudei ha-Mizraḥ be-Ereẓ Yisrael*, 2 (1938), 268–72; Tidhar, 3 (1958²), 1322–24.

[Itzhak Goldshlag]

TOLEDO, city in Castile, central *Spain; capital of Castile until 1561.

Early Jewish Settlement and Visigothic Period

There is no substantive information available on the beginnings of the Jewish settlement in Toledo, which was only a small village in the period of Roman rule over Spain. According to a Jewish tradition dating from the period of Muslim rule, the Jewish settlement in Toledo was the most ancient in the Iberian peninsula. This tradition was accepted by Isaac *Abrabanel who states (in his commentary to the Book of Kings, at the end, and to Obadiah 20) that the first settlers were exiles from the tribes of Judah and Benjamin, who had arrived there after the destruction of the First Temple, and were associated with a legend concerning Pirus and Hispan who took part in the siege of Jerusalem. Hence the name "Tuletula" (Lat. *Toletum* = Toledo) has been explained as deriving from their wanderings (Heb. *taltelah*) when they were expelled from their land.

Jews probably established themselves there when the town became the capital of the Visigoths, or during the preceding fourth to fifth centuries C.E. The Jewish settlement was, however, inconsiderable, the Jews then being mainly concentrated in the towns on the east coast. Once the Visigoths became converted to Christianity, the *Church councils held in Toledo, particularly from the reign of Sisenand onward, directed many decrees against them, which the Visigothic kings strictly applied. The legislation indicates that there were Jewish settlements in Toledo and the vicinity mainly engaged in agriculture. When the danger of a Muslim invasion seemed imminent, the 17ᵗʰ Church Council, held in Toledo in 694, accused the Jews of plotting, in collaboration with their coreligionists living across the straits, to destroy the Christian kingdom. There is, however, no foundation to the accusation that the Jews delivered the town to the Muslims at the time of its capture (c. 712). Information on the conquest and the presence of Jews in the town is extant from a later period: during the 13ᵗʰ century, Ibn al-Adhari wrote that there had been only a few Jews in the town at the time of its conquest.

[Haim Beinart]

The Jewish Quarter

The first sources referring to the Jewish quarter of Toledo are from the 12ᵗʰ century. At that time its size was much smaller and was in the district of San Martín. The Jewish population of Toledo increased considerably and with it the size of the Jewish quarter, which expanded as far as San Tomé and later reached San Román. The Jewish quarter in Toledo was situated in the western part of the town, where it remained throughout the existence of the Jewish settlement. Its location has been always known in the city. The documents related to the Jews of Toledo published by León Tello make it possible to define with a great degree of precision the boundaries of the quarter. In this area, a number of streets bear names recalling the magnificent past of the community: Samuel ha-Levi, Travesía de la Judería. The quarter spread as far as the gate known today as Cambrón, formerly named "Gate of the Jews." The principal artery of the Jewish quarter, at present known as Calle del Angel, was formerly named Calle de la Judería. This street led to a spacious square which was presumably the center of the quarter. The wall which surrounded the quarter was built as early as 820. There was also a fortress in the quarter for the protection of the Jewish population. Because of the form of its construction, the quarter constituted a kind of independent town which could provide support and assistance to the king when necessary. The Jewish quarter reached the peak of its development and size in the middle of the 14ᵗʰ century. A mistaken reading of one of the sources misled some scholars into thinking that there was a second, smaller quarter near the Cathedral.

The Jewish quarter of Toledo was not exclusively inhabited by Jews. Several well-known Christian noblemen had houses in the precincts of the Jewish quarter. The size of the Jewish population of Toledo cannot be estimated from the area of the Jewish quarter. Baer estimates that the community consisted of 350 families during the 14ᵗʰ century, including those who lived in villages in the vicinity. The historian Ayala concluded that 1,200 Jewish men, women, and children of Toledo died in the persecutions of 1355, in the Alcana quarter only, though Baer does not consider that there were so many Jews living here. In 1368, during the siege of Henry of Trastamara against the town, 8,000 Jews including adults and children died in Toledo, showing the magnitude of their numbers at that time. The community of Toledo was one of the largest in the Iberian peninsula, and at the height of its prosperity the Jews probably formed one third of the city's population, which was then over 40,000.

Jewish Edifices and Ancient Remnants

Toledo is one of the few towns of Spain where remnants of Jewish edifices have been preserved. Toward the close of the 15ᵗʰ century the sources (see Cantera, in bibliography) mention ten synagogues and a further five *battei midrash*. The synagogues included the Great Synagogue situated in the old quarter, which was destroyed by fire in 1250; the Old Synagogue, renovated in 1107, an event which Judah Halevi immortalized in a poem; the Ben-Ziza Synagogue, and many others, some of whose names have not been recorded. In addition, there was a synagogue founded by Joseph Abu 'Omar *Ibn Shoshan in 1203, converted into a church named Santa Maria la Blanca in 1411 by Vicente *Ferrer (see below). Another synagogue was built by Don Samuel Halevi in c. 1357; transferred to the Order of the Knights of Calatrava in 1494, it later belonged to the priory of San Benito and is at present named El Transito. These two synagogues, still standing, are built in pronounced Mudéjar style and are distinguished for the beauty of their arches and general appearance. They were evidently built by Moorish craftsmen, and underwent structural alterations to adapt them to church requirements. Both were declared national monuments toward the middle of the 19th century. Repairs have been carried out in the Samuel Halevi Synagogue, and the women's gallery and other parts have been restored. In 1964 it was decided to transform the synagogue into the Sephardi Museum. The museum contains very important Jewish tombstones and various articles of great historical value. The synagogue is decorated with passages from the Psalms and beautiful dedicatory inscriptions to the benefactor and builder of the synagogue and King Pedro, during whose reign it was erected. The house of Samuel Halevi, still standing, was for a while inhabited by the painter El Greco.

Toledo also has many remnants of Jewish tombstones, some of which are preserved in the archaeological museum of the town and others in the Sephardi Museum. Copying of the inscriptions on these tombstones was begun from the end of the 16th century; many of the tombstones have since been lost. During the 19th century these reproductions were seen by S.D. *Luzzatto, who published them (*Avnei Zikkaron*). A scholarly edition of these inscriptions was published by Cantera and Míllas with the addition of inscriptions and findings discovered after Luzzatto's publication. Of the tombstones whose inscriptions were published, noteworthy are those of Joseph Abu 'Omar ibn Shoshan (builder of the synagogue mentioned above) who died in 1205; several members of the *Abulafia family; *Jonah b. Abraham of Gerona (d. 1264); David b. Gedaliah ibn Yaḥya of Portugal (d. 1325); *Jacob b. Asher, author of the *Turim* (d. 1340), son of *Asher b. Jehiel (see below); his brother, *Judah b. Asher, and members of his family who died in the Black Death in 1349; the woman Sitbona (a unique tombstone preserved in the archaeological museum of Toledo); and R. Menahem b. Zerah author of *Ẓeidah la-Derekh* (d. 1385).

Other findings include a pillar with the inscription "Blessed be thy coming and blessed be thy going," with an Arabic version of a blessing, which belonged to one of the synagogues of the town; its architectural form indicates that it dates from the late 12th or early 13th century. The bath house of the Jews of the town was handed over to the San Clemente monastery in 1131 by Alfonso VII but its location is unknown. This abundance of findings is exceptional in Spain, where few Jewish remains have been preserved. All the efforts in looking for a *mikveh* or ritual bath have led to no concrete or certain results. Of special interest is a fresco in one of the exits of the Cathedral describing the blood libel leveled against the Jews, accused of murdering a child of La Guardia.

[Haim Beinart / Yom Tov Assis (2nd ed.)]

Period of Muslim Rule

During the 11th century, when Toledo was ruled by the Berber Ibn Danun dynasty, it had a large Jewish population of about 4,000, divided into separate communities generally according to place of origin (e.g., the Cordobans, Barcelonese, etc.), and a group to which was attributed *Khazar descent. Toledo was also the center of the *Karaites in Spain. Jewish occupations included textile manufacture, tanning, and dyeing, military professions, and commerce. Jews in the villages near Toledo were known for their skill in agriculture and viticulture. A wealthy class of Jewish merchants, bankers, and agents for foreign Christian rulers lived in Toledo. Toledo became a center of Jewish scholarship, translation, and science; the astronomer Zarkal (Abu Ishaq Ibrahim b. Yaḥya) lived there for a time in the mid-11th century, and the biblical commentator Judah b. Samuel *Ibn Bal'am was born and educated in Toledo in this period.

Toledo under Christian Rule

The situation of the Jews in Toledo remained unchanged after the town was conquered by Alfonso VI in 1085. During the 12th century it continued as a center of learning and Jews and apostates were among those who translated works of mathematics, astronomy, and other subjects from Arabic into the spoken vernacular and from that language into Latin. The capitulation terms of the town show that Alfonso promised the Muslims that they could retain their mosques and would only transfer to him the fortified places. There is, however, no information available on the terms affecting the Jews although the fortress situated in their quarter remained in their possession. At this time and throughout the reign of Alfonso, Don Joseph *Ferrizuel (Cidellus) held office in the royal court and was particularly active in favor of his coreligionists.

From then on, the community developed until it became the most prominent in the Kingdom of Castile and one of the most important in Spain. In 1101 Alfonso granted the Arabized Christian population a privilege establishing that the fines they might pay should amount to only one-fifth of those paid by others, excepting in the case of murder or robbery of a Jew or Moor. When Alfonso VI died in 1109, the inhabitants of the town rebelled and attacked the Jews. Alfonso VII, the crown prince, reached a compromise with the townsmen and issued a series of laws discriminating against the Jews, and laid down that lawsuits between Jews and Christians were to be brought before a Christian judge. In 1118 he actually reintroduced the Visigothic law of the fourth council of Toledo in 633, which excluded "those of Jewish origin" from all public positions.

During this period some of the most distinguished personalities of their time lived in Toledo: Isaac *Ibn Ezra who apparently left the town in 1119; Moses *Ibn Ezra who stayed there; and Joseph ibn Kamaniel, the physician, one of the wealthiest members of the community who was entrusted with an important diplomatic mission to the king of Portugal. There were also the families of Shoshan, Al-Fakhar, Halevi, Abulafia, Zadok (who were given land in a village near Toledo in 1132), and Ferrizuel. Because of their importance, the last regarded themselves as descendants of the House of David and as being of noble birth: they assumed the title of *nasi* and thus became a kind of oligarchy within the Jewish community. This family produced the leading tax lessees in the city, in the surrounding area, and in the whole kingdom, as well as other courtiers almost throughout the community's existence. During the reign of Sancho III (1157–58), the position of *almoxarife* in Toledo was held by Judah Joseph ibn Ezra (referred to as Bonjuda in documents); the king granted him lands and exempted him from the payment of tithes on these estates and taxes. R. Judah is known for his energetic activity to remove Karaism from Castile. During the reign of Alfonso VIII (1158–1214), when Toledo was again threatened by the *Almohads, the Christian soldiers maltreated the Jews, although these had actively participated in the defense of the town. Joseph Al-Fakhar and his son Abraham, originally from Granada, then acted as *almoxarifes* in Toledo, as did also members of the Ibn Ezra family and Joseph Abu Omar ibn Shoshan.

The language spoken by the Jews of Toledo and employed in their documents during the 11th to 13th centuries was partly Arabic; they customarily wrote their documents in Arabic with Hebrew characters. These sources reveal a well-developed economic life. Jews of Toledo are recorded as having sold or purchased land, as lenders and borrowers, and are also found in partnerships with Christians in real estate transactions and in commerce. The documents show that the Jews of Toledo did not turn to the non-Jewish tribunals, as was customary in other communities, in matters which involved both Christians and Jews. The Jews owned fields and vineyards and occasionally leased land and pastures in partnership with Christians; they maintained slaves, owned shops, and engaged in every kind of craft. In conjunction with Christians they even occasionally leased the revenues of churches and monasteries. The documents also indicate the status of several of their signatories within the framework of the community. Some of them bear the title of *sofer* or *ḥazzan*, as well as honorifics such as *al-ḥakim* and *al-vazir*. Apparently until the close of the 12th century, the community's style of life resembled that of a Jewish community under Muslim rule. It was only in the course of the 13th century that the prevailing Arab titles lost their luster. By the beginning of the 14th century, use of Arabic in deeds and documents was abandoned.

The administrative organization of the community does not appear to have changed throughout its existence. There is no information on the administrative organization during Muslim rule, but a responsum attributed to R. Joseph ibn Migash mentions the existence, in the early 12th century, of an organization headed by seven notables and elders and a *bet din*. During that period there were also administrative leaders in the community. Gonzalez Palencia has shown that these positions were held by members of distinguished families. From the 13th century the community was administered by ten **muqaddimūn*. Under the influence of Don Joseph ibn Wakar, changes were introduced into the procedure for the election of the community leaders: two arbitrators were elected to choose the *muqaddimūn*. After the expulsion of the Jews from Spain the regulations of Toledo became a model for the organization of the communities of Spanish refugees who settled in North Africa and throughout the territories of the Ottoman Empire.

The decisions of the Fourth *Lateran Council of 1215 influenced the relationship between the Church and the Jews of the town. Rodrigo, the archbishop of Toledo, reached an agreement with the Jews of the archdiocese according to which every Jew aged over 20 would pay one sixth of a gold coin to him as an annual tax; it was laid down that doubtful cases were to be decided by four elders, the *muqaddimūn* of the community, and two Jews chosen by the archbishop; the Jews of Toledo would be exempted from all tithe payments as decided by the Lateran Council, and any property sold by a Jew to a Christian throughout the archdiocese would be exempted from tithe payment. The archbishop undertook to protect the Jews, and the elders of the community were responsible for observance of the agreement by the Jews. Ferdinand III ratified this agreement.

In the 13th century, under the auspices of Alfonso X, the Wise, Jews were involved in translating scientific, philosophical, and medical works from Arabic into Castilian. Out of the 12 translators engaged in the program 5 were Jewish, and they translated 40 percent of all the works.

A period of crisis occurred at the time of the revolt of Crown Prince Sancho against his father (1280–81). A contemporary author relates that the community of Toledo was shaken "as Sodom and Gomorrah." Alfonso X ordered the imprisonment of the Jews in their synagogues, from which they were not to be released until the community paid him a special tax. Notables of the community remained in prison for many months. Attempts were even made there to convert them and several were executed. The distinguished poet Todros b. Judah Ha-Levi was among the prisoners, who after some self-examination decided to repent. He called on the community to amend its evil ways in transactions and commerce, and to separate from non-Jewish women, among other practices. The community accepted his appeal, and a *ḥerem* ("ban") was proclaimed in the synagogue against anyone committing these offenses. This was an act of repentance on the part of a whole community. One of the scholars of Toledo, Jacob b. Crisp, turned to Solomon b. Abraham *Adret (Rashba) and requested his opinion and sanction for the administration of "this province and the penalization of offenders." The latter advised that the same rule could not be applied to everyone: at first a gentle manner should be adopted, but if this proved of no avail, then the strict letter of the law was to be applied.

The same conditions prevailed within the community of Toledo during the reigns of Alfonso and Sancho. The main figure among the Jewish courtiers was Don Abraham El Barchillon, a native of Toledo, first mentioned in state documents as having leased the minting of coins in the kingdom. Others included Don Abraham ibn Shoshan who had already risen to importance during the reign of Alfonso x, and was the *almoxarife* of the queen. The poet Todros ha-Levi Abulafia also resumed his public activities and for a period headed a group of personalities who leased the state revenues: the port customs duties, payments to the royal office, and others.

During his own lifetime, Maimonides was challenged in Toledo by a notable adversary, Meir b. Todros ha-Levi Abulafia, whose opinions were shared by the physician Judah b. Joseph al-Fakhar, and Joseph b. Todros Ha-Levi, the brother of R. Meir. They regarded the writings of Maimonides to be dangerous in that they could undermine faith. The controversy over the study of the writings of Maimonides (see *Maimonidean controversy) received particular impetus in Toledo in 1304–05, at the time of the publication of the correspondence between Solomon b. Adret and Abba Mari *Astruc on the subject of the *ḥerem* issued against the study of the *Guide of the Perplexed*. The correspondence was published by Samson b. Meir, who went to Toledo to obtain the signatures of the community leaders to this *ḥerem* and the support of R. Asher b. Jehiel (Rosh), who from the beginning of the 14th century occupied the rabbinical seat in Toledo. During his lifetime and that of his son R. Judah, Torah learning flourished in Toledo; another of his sons, R. *Jacob b. Asher, wrote the *Turim* there. Israel b. Joseph *al-Nakawa, author of *Menorat ha-Ma'or*, was also active there.

At the beginning of the 14th century, an attempt was made by the clergy in Toledo to compel the Jews to cease from engaging in moneylending; they also compelled the Jews to return the interest which they had taken and to cancel the obligations of payment which Christians had undertaken. Ferdinand iv notified the clergy that he would bring them to account if they continued to impose a boycott on the Jews or sought to prosecute them before the Church tribunals. Nevertheless in a number of cases the king accepted the arguments of the clergy, and Jewish moneylenders of Toledo were arrested, tried before Christian judges, and condemned to lengthy terms of imprisonment. During that period there were wealthy Jews who earned their livelihood by renting houses to other Jews, a practice until then unknown. Toledo was also one of the rare places where Jews owned Muslim slaves. The reign of Alfonso xi (1312–50) was favorable to the community. Don Joseph ha-Levi b. Ephraim (identified with Don Yuçaf de Ecija) and Samuel ibn Wakar, the king's physician who in 1320 leased the minting of coins in the kingdom, were then active at court. They competed for influence there and for the leasing of the revenues of the kingdom. Don Moses *Abzardiel (or Zardiel) was a third personality of importance; as *dayyan* in Toledo and scribe of the king, his signature in Latin is found on deeds and documents concerning taxes and financial affairs, and on privileges issued to bishops, monasteries, noblemen, and towns during the 1330s.

The *Black Death (1348) took a heavy toll among the community of Toledo. During the reign of Pedro the Cruel (1350–60), Don Samuel b. Meir ha-Levi *Abulafia acted as chief agent and treasurer of the king. It was presumably he who built the synagogue in 1357 which bears his name (see above). In 1358 he left for Portugal to negotiate a political agreement, and he was signatory to several royal edicts. He was suddenly arrested in 1360 (or 1361) upon the order of King Pedro, and removed to Seville, where he died at the hands of his torturers. Other Jews after him were lessees and courtiers, more particularly members of the ha-Levi and *Benveniste families of Burgos.

In 1355, when the king entered Toledo, Christians and Muslims attacked the Jewish quarters. The Alcana quarter, near the cathedral, suffered heavily. During the civil war between Pedro and Henry (1366–69), the town changed hands several times; when Pedro once more besieged the city, in 1368–69, 8,000 Jews perished. In June 1369 he ordered that the Jews of Toledo and their belongings be sold to raise 1,000,000 gold coins. The community was ruined, and every object which could find a buyer was sold. By 1367, however, the Christian congregations had already complained that they had sunk into debts to the Jews and called for a moratorium on their debts and reduction to half of their value. Henry had remitted their debts for two years and reduced them to one third.

The Persecutions of 1391

While the Toledo community was still endeavoring to recover from the effects of the civil war, it was overtaken by the persecutions which swept Spain in 1391 and brought down upon it ruin and destruction. The riots against the Jews in Toledo broke out on 17 Tammuz (June 20) or, according to Christian sources, on August 5. Among the many who were martyred were the grandchildren of R. Asher, his disciples, and numerous distinguished members of the community. Almost all the synagogues were destroyed or set on fire, and the *battei midrash* became mounds of ruins. Many abandoned Judaism at that time, and Toledo became filled with Conversos (see below). The impoverishment of the community is also evident from the order of Henry iii, according to which certain incomes totaling 48,400 maravedis were handed over to the New Kings Church of Toledo in 1397 instead of the income provided for it by his father and grandfather from the annual tax of the Jews, which could not be collected as a result of the destruction of the community. During that year Jewish houses were also auctioned. There were, however, still Jews of Toledo who held important leases. In 1395 the archbishop of Toledo appointed his physician Pedro, who was an apostate, chief justice of the communities of his archdiocese. This was a unique case in which an apostate became a judge to dispense Jewish law. Don Abraham ibn Shoshan protested to the crown against this appointment.

The community of Toledo did not recover throughout the 15th century. In 1408 John II transferred several revenues to the chief *adelantado* of the kingdom of Castile to replace his revenues formerly derived from the communities of Toledo, Madrid, and Alcalá de Henares which had been destroyed and were so impoverished that all income from them had disappeared. Vicente Ferrer visited Toledo in 1411. He entered the Jewish quarter with an armed escort and converted the Ibn Shoshan Synagogue into a church. There is reason to believe that a number of Jews converted to Christianity as a result of the sermons he delivered. The annual taxes of Jewish Toledo amounted to only 7,000 maravedis in 1439. There were, however, still a number of Jews who held leases in the town and outside it, survivors of the old families: Don Isaac Abudraham in the archdeaconry of Alcaraz near Toledo (1439); Don Ephraim ibn Shoshan who leased taxes in Toledo in 1442 and continued to do so after the attacks on the Conversos in 1452 and 1454. When Isabella ascended the throne and the country became united with the kingdom of Aragon, Jews of Toledo again held important positions in the kingdom as lessees and courtiers. Don David Abudraham leased the tax on meat and fish in Toledo between 1481 and 1484. Don Moses ibn Shoshan leased the taxes of Molina. During that year Don Abraham *Seneor of Segovia leased the taxes of Toledo. While in Toledo in 1480, the Catholic monarchs *Ferdinand and Isabella decided on their anti-Jewish policy and the Cortes convened there adopted a series of decrees.

The Jews of Toledo were expelled with the other Jews of Spain in 1492, and the last exiles left Toledo on the seventh of Av. They left behind them the debts owed to them by Christians, and the government determined the procedure for their collection. Luis de Alcalá and Fernando Nuñez (Abraham Seneor) Coronel were entrusted with this task. At that time 40 houses in their ancient quarter were owned by Jews, who apparently were not sufficiently numerous to occupy all of them so that some were inhabited by Christians. No information is available about the destinations of the exiles, but as the regulations of the Toledo community are found in Fez and other places in North Africa they obviously settled there. Jews from Toledo settled in Turkey and also reestablished communities in Ereẓ Israel. In Toledo in 1494 Rodrigo de Marcado, the king's representative, proclaimed that the property of the community would be transferred to the crown. This included communal property, the debts owed to Jews, real estate, butchers' shops, and the lands and consecrated properties which the Jews of the town had entrusted to the municipal council or handed over to several of its citizens.

The Conversos of Toledo

Jews were living in Toledo as forced converts (see also **Anusim*) during two periods. The first was under the Visigoths, and the second period of religious persecution and forced apostasy was from the end of the 14th century. The Conversos of Toledo continued to live in the quarters they had formerly occupied as Jews, until the 1480s, when the residential area of the Jewish quarter was greatly reduced, while the Conversos were dispersed among the Christian parishes of the town.

The revolt of Pedro *Sarmiento against John II in 1449, and the attempt by the crown to have taxes collected from the inhabitants of the town by Conversos, resulted in attacks on the latter. These were followed by a trial of 12 Conversos which gave impetus to the publication in Castile of a widespread literature on the subject, as part of a public campaign both for and against the Conversos, concerning their place within Christian society. Many pamphlets of satire which ridiculed the Conversos were composed, while forged letters were circulated of a supposed correspondence between Chamorro, the "head" of the community of Toledo, with Yusuf, the "head" of the Jews of Constantinople, concerning a project to destroy Christianity.

Attempts to conduct inquiries in Toledo against suspected heresy, in *Inquisition style, were inspired by the monk *Alfonso de Espina during the 1460s. *Alfonso de Oropesa, head of the Order of St. Jerome, was appointed by the archbishop to investigate heresy in Toledo. During a whole year he interrogated Conversos and penalized them, but the overwhelming majority evidently returned to the fold of the Church. On July 19, 1467 riots again broke out against the Conversos in the Magdalena quarter, and there was again an open conflict between Conversos and Christians in various quarters of the town. When the Christians gained the upper hand, many Conversos hid in the houses of the Jews. Several of the Converso leaders were arrested and executed.

In 1485 the rabbis of Toledo were ordered to proclaim a *ḥerem* against Jews who refused to testify before the Inquisition if they knew of Conversos who observed the Jewish precepts. In 1486 and the beginning of 1487, 4,000 of the inhabitants of the town and the vicinity were involved in five autos-da-fé; some of them returned to the fold of the Church and others were burned at the stake on the site known as Sucodovar. However, the files of only 85 executions are extant for the period between 1485 and the 1660s. The Conversos sentenced in Toledo belonged to two categories: the cultured persons, holders of public office, and the ordinary craftsmen. Among the intellectuals sentenced were Alvaro de Montalbán, father-in-law of the poet Fernando de Rojas, author of the *Celestina*; and Martín de Lucena, to whom R. Solomon ibn Verga refers as a scholar. His son Juan de Lucena was one of the first in Spain to print Hebrew works and diffuse them outside the country. Juan de Pineda, a commander of the Order of Santiago and the delegate of the Order at the papal court, was also among those tried. Craftsmen tried by the Inquisition included cobblers, shoemakers, tailors, and blacksmiths. Many merchants and women were also executed. Attempts were also made to implicate the Conversos of Toledo in the *La Guardia blood libel.

[Haim Beinart]

BIBLIOGRAPHY: GENERAL: Baer, Spain, index; A.M. Gamero, *Historia de la Ciudad de Toledo* (1862); J. Amador de los Ríos, *Historia... de los Judíos de España y Portugal*, 3 vols. (1876), passim; Neuman, Spain, index. **ADD. BIBLIOGRAPHY:** A.M. López Álvarez, *Catálogo del Museo Sefardí, Toledo* (1986); J. Blázquez Miguel, *Toledot: Historia del Toledo judío* (1989). EARLY JEWISH COMMUNITY AND THE VISIGOTHIC PERIOD: S. Katz, *Jews in the Visigothic and Frankish Kingdoms of Spain and Gaul* (1937), passim; C.G. Goldaraz, *El códice Lucense* (1954); H. Beinart, in: *Estudios*, 3 (1961), 1–32 (includes bibliography). JEWISH QUARTER: Ashtor, Korot, 1 (1960), 211ff.; A. González Palencia, *Los mozárabes de Toledo en los siglos XII y XII, estudio preliminar* (1930), 72f.; L. Torres Balbas, in: *Al-Andalus*, 12 (1947), 164–98; F. Cantera, in: *Sefarad*, 7 (1947), 442–3; M. Reisz, *Europe's Jewish Quarters* (1991), 24–37. JEWISH LANDMARKS: C. Roth, in: JQR, 39 (1948), 123ff.; idem, in: *Sefarad*, 8 (1948), 3–22; F. Cantera, *ibid.*, 26 (1966), 305–14; idem, *Sinagogas españolas* (1955), 33–150; F. Cantera and J.M. Míllas, *Inscripciones hebraicas de España* (1956), 36–180, 332–9, 367–8 (incl. bibl.). **ADD. BIBLIOGRAPHY:** S. Palomera Plaza, A.M. López Alvarez, and Y. Alvarez Delgado, in: *Jewish Art*, 18 (1992), 48–57; E.W. Goldman, in: *ibid.*, 58–70. MUSLIM PERIOD: Y. Baer, in: *Tarbiz*, 5 (1934), 186ff.; S.D. Goitein, *ibid.*, 24 (1955), 21ff., 134ff.; 25 (1956), 393ff.; E. Ashtor, in: *Zion*, 28 (1963), 39–40; Ashtor, Korot; A. González Palencia, *Los mozárabes de Toledo en los siglos XII y XII, estudio preliminar* (1930), 149–51; Baer, Urkunden, index. CHRISTIAN PERIOD: N. Round, in: *Archivum*, 16 (1966), 385–446; B. Netanyahu, in: PAAJR, 44 (1977), 93–125; P. León Tello, *Judíos de Toledo* (1979), 2 vols.; J.M. Nieto Soria, in: *Sefarad*, 41 (1981), 301–19; 42 (1982), 79–102; J. Porres Martín-Cleto, in: *Anales toledanos*, 16 (1983), 37–61; N. Roth, in: AJSR, 11 (1986), 189–220; J. Aguado Villalba, in: *Arqueología medieval española, II Congreso* (1987), 247–57; L. Cardaillac (ed.), *Tolède, XIIe-XIIIe: musulmans, chrétiens et juifs; le savoir et la tolérance* (1991). CONVERSOS: A.Z. Aescoly, in: *Zion*, 10 (1945), 136ff.; H. Beinart, *ibid.*, 20 (1955), 1ff.; idem, in: *Tarbiz*, 26 (1957), 86–71; idem, *Anusim be-Din ha-Inkvizizyah* (1965), index; H.C. Lea, *A History of the Inquisition of Spain*, 4 vols. (1906), index; A. de Cartagena, *Defensonium unitatis christianae*, ed. by M. Alonso (1943); A.A. Sicroff, *Les controverses de statuts de "pureté de sang" en Espagne...* (1960); E. Benito Ruano, *Toledo en el siglo XV* (1961); Suárez Fernández, Documentos, index; F. Cantera, *Judaizantes del arzobispado de Toledo* (1969); idem, *El poeta Rodrigo Cota y su familia de judíos Conversos* (1970). **ADD. BIBLIOGRAPHY:** L. Martz, in: *Sefarad*, 48 (1988), 117–96; J-P. Dedieu, *L'administration de la foi: l'Inquisition de Tolède, XVIe–XVIIIe siècle* (1989).

TOLEDO, city in Ohio, U.S. The estimated population (2005) was 315,000, with the Jewish population somewhat less than 4,000 (5,900 in the metropolitan area), approximately 6,000 fewer than cited in the 1972 *Encyclopaedia Judaica*. Local legend has it that the name of the city, borrowed from the Spanish city, was suggested by the Jewish citizens as it derives from the Hebrew *toledot* which connotes history and continuity.

The history of the development of the Toledo Jewish community began with a handful of German and Dutch Jews who arrived via Cincinnati. They were joined by several Hungarian Jews. In 1837 when the city was chartered there were several Jewish families. Toledo and Cincinnati were connected by a series of canals and the local Jews were largely in commerce with goods that were ferried from Cincinnati. Happily, there was no need for a Jewish cemetery until 1867 when the Hebrew Benevolent and Cemetery Association was founded. The first cemetery was interdenominational. Since then, the three congregations have created separate burial grounds for their members. There is a *ḥevra kaddisha* that serves all the Jews of the community.

Among the first Jewish families were the Marx brothers. Emil, Guido, and Joseph published the *Ohio Staatszeitung* intended for the largely German-speaking population of the area. Emil was an early volunteer at the beginning of the Civil War. Joseph was appointed U.S. consul to Amsterdam by President Abraham Lincoln in 1864.

The first settlers were staunchly individualistic free thinking or atheistic Jews who were bound to the community through a network of family business and shared capital. Attempts to form synagogues were spasmodic and short lived.

The first mention of the observance of High Holidays was in 1865 but it wasn't until 1867 that Congregation B'nai Israel, now affiliated with the Conservative movement, was founded. It has been served by Rabbis Halper, Glazer, Herowitz, Epstein, Lichtenstein, Goldberg, Perlmutter, Bienstock, Ungar, Kaiman, and Leff.

Eight years later Reform Congregation Shomer Emunim ("keeper of faithfulness"; Isaiah 26:2) was founded. The name was suggested by Isaac Mayer Wise, the initiator and organizer of the then incipient Reform movement in the United States. It was assumed that a Jewish community in such a remote section of the mid-west United States deserved a name affirming its faithfulness. It appears to be the only synagogal congregation in the world with that name. The rabbis of the congregation have been Schanfarber, Meier, Freund, Alexander, Coffee, Harris, Kornfeld, Feuer, Sokobin, and Weinstein.

Congregation Etz Chaim was founded by the merger of smaller Orthodox congregations. Its rabbis have been Katz and Garsek.

Several of the rabbis of Toledo have had contributory positions in Toledo to the nation and national Jewish organizations. Following World War II when Israel was struggling to create its independence Rabbi Leon *Feuer was the chief lobbyist in Washington seeking American political support for the establishment of a Jewish State. He later became president of the Central Conference of American Rabbis. Rabbi Morton Goldberg served as both president of the Toledo Public School System and the Toledo Library system. Rabbi J.S. *Kornfeld was ambassador to Persia and Rabbi Alan Sokobin was chair of studies of the educational system as well as the court and justice systems of the City of Toledo. Both Rabbi Feuer and Rabbi Sokobin taught at the University of Toledo.

In response to the large number of Jews arriving in Toledo the need to organize led to the establishment of the Toledo Federation of Jewish Charities in 1907. The Jewish Banner Boys Club had previously been organized to assist 12 and 13 year olds integrate into the community. A Banner Club for girls was formed and the boys and girls met together on a weekly basis for a discussion group. The many social and cultural activities thrived and the need for a building was becoming apparent. In 1911 the Council of Jewish Women was given permission to solicit funds for a building. In 1912 a building was erected by the Jewish Educational League for the programs directed at children and newcomers to the area. The purpose of the league had the lofty goal "to develop and maintain a high standard of American citizenship among the Jewish Residents of Toledo."

In 1936 the Jewish Educational League, the Jewish Family Service, and the Transient Service became a part of the Jewish Community Center. Since that time the Jewish community of Toledo has been exceedingly well represented in national Jewish organizations. There are active chapters of Hadassah, ORT, and B'nai B'rith as well as chapters of Young Judea and Synagogue Youth. The United Jewish Council is the governance body for the Toledo Board of Jewish Education that maintains a Jewish day school as well as an afternoon Hebrew program serving the Orthodox and Conservative congregations. In 2004 the athletic programs of the Jewish Community Center were combined with those of the Toledo YMCA.

Jews have become an integral part of the general Toledo community. There are Jews who have been elected to important judicial as well as legislative posts. While the community began largely with merchants, today the majority of Toledo Jewry is engaged in the professions. Like many Ohio communities, elderly Jews have migrated toward the sunbelt and younger Jews have left for college and not returned home.

[Alan Sokobin (2nd ed.)]

TOLEDO, MOSES DE (fl. first part of 17th century), Jerusalem *ḥakham* and emissary. In 1628 Toledo traveled through the Greek islands, reaching the island of Corfu at the beginning of winter. He was one of the numerous emissaries who were sent out from Jerusalem after the brutalities of the governor, Muhammad ibn Farukh, in 1625. The latter impoverished the Jews, who lost all of their possessions, and as a result of his extortions he even enslaved them to the Muslims for many years. The community of Corfu was generous with all the emissaries, but since Toledo was the third emissary from Jerusalem within a brief period, the community in a special letter to Jerusalem requested that no more emissaries be sent. Furthermore, it stated that the Corfu community would send its contributions directly to Jerusalem by the safest method available, in order to save the commissioning of an emissary and his expenses.

BIBLIOGRAPHY: S. Baron, in: *Sefer ha-Shanah li-Yhudei Amerikah*, 6 (1942), 167–8; Yaari, Sheluḥei, 266.

[Avraham Yaari]

TOLEDOT HA-ARI (Heb. תּוֹלְדוֹת הָאֲרִ"י), a legendary biography of Isaac *Luria of *Safed. It is one of the most detailed and richest hagiographies written in Hebrew.

Found in many manuscripts, it seems to have been a popular work, was translated into Ladino (printed 1766), and even adapted into the story genre having a single plot (e.g., a Yemenite story based on it). It first appeared in print under the title *Kavvanot u-Ma'aseh Nissim* (Istanbul, 1720). The relationship between this work and the *Shivḥei ha-Ari*, another collection of stories about Luria (first printed in Joseph *Delmedigo's *Ta'alumot Ḥokhmah*, Basle, 1629–31, and again in a different version in *Emek ha-Melekh* by Naphtali *Bacharach, Amsterdam, 1648) is a point of discussion in modern scholarship. Benayahu maintains that the letters constituting *Shivḥei ha-Ari* (the letters of Solomon Shlumil of Dresnitz) were written in Safed in the first decade of the 17th century, and were taken from *Toledot ha-Ari* which, according to him, already existed then as a collection of stories. However, the first manuscripts of *Toledot ha-Ari* were written in the second half of the 17th century, decades after R. Shlumil's letters.

Toledot ha-Ari is a more fantastical, romantic, and imaginative work than *Shivḥei ha-Ari*. It includes, for example, a version of "The Story of the Jerusalemite," a 13th-century tale about the marriage between a man and a demon, adapted to serve as a vehicle to demonstrate Luria's greatness. The famous story of the **dibbuk* (a spirit which entered a girl's body) which appears in *Shivḥei ha-Ari* as an addendum, and is not among Shlumil's original letters, is an integral part of *Toledot ha-Ari*. The supernatural tales found in *Toledot ha-Ari* are also not in *Shivḥei ha-Ari*. In *Toledot ha-Ari*, Luria is sometimes portrayed as a famous rabbi and judge, respected in Safed and all over the Jewish East. This is not a historical fact, and nothing of the sort is mentioned in Shlumil's letters. It may therefore be inferred that *Shivḥei ha-Ari* is a compilation of intimate accounts told by Luria's pupils, whereas *Toledot ha-Ari* is a collection of fantastical and imaginary hagiographies which were associated with Luria by later admirers, after his fame had spread all over the Jewish world. At the same time, there is little doubt that *Toledot ha-Ari* also includes some true stories about Luria which Shlumil either did not know, or did not include in his extant letters. It must therefore be considered also as a source on Luria's life and works. It served as an example for later Jewish compilers of hagiographies, and, undoubtedly, influenced *Shivḥei ha-Besht* (Berdichev, 1815), the hagiographies of the founder of Ḥasidism, and other similar works.

BIBLIOGRAPHY: M. Benayahu (ed.), *Sefer Toledot ha-Ari* (1967), incl. bibl.; idem, in: *Sefunot*, 10 (1966), 213–98.

[Joseph Dan]

TOLEDOT YESHU (Heb. "The Life of Jesus"), medieval pseudo-history of the life of *Jesus. The inherent nature of the Christian version of the birth, life, and death of Jesus called forth a "Jewish" view. Beginnings to an approach can be found in the talmudic tractates *Sotah* (47a) and *Sanhedrin* (43a; 67a; 107b). When confronted by Christian critics and censors, however, Jewish scholars explained that these references were to another Jesus who had lived 200 years before the Christian era. From the geonic period at the latest, and throughout the Middle Ages, many versions on the life of Jesus were written and compiled by Jews. The authors used as sources talmudic sayings and Christian stories. The different writings merged into a single narrative of which nearly a dozen versions are extant. Most of these were printed by Samuel *Krauss, whose *Das Leben Jesu nach juedischen Quellen* (1902) includes a detailed study of nine versions of the story, and has remained the main scholarly work in the field.

The complete narrative, which could not have been written before the tenth century, used earlier sources, some of which have been preserved in the Cairo **Genizah* documents. A chronological examination of the various fragments and versions reveals the development of the narrative. The complete medieval story has versions which are so different from each other in attitude and in detail that it is impossible that one author could have written it. Undoubtedly, several storytellers wove their separate tales out of the same early material; these were then compiled. In all the versions, Miriam (Mary), Jesus' mother, is described in a favorable light. She is of a good family and marries a nobleman whose ancestry goes back to the House of David. According to the narrative, Jesus' father, a neighbor of the household, was a bad man. Some versions state that he raped Miriam, others relate that he succeeded in pretending to be Miriam's husband. The names of the husband and the villain vary in the different versions. If the husband is Joseph, the villain is Johanan, and in those which name Johanan as the husband, Joseph is the villain. All versions concur that when it became known that Mary was raped, the husband ran away, and the infant was born to his lonely mother.

The narrative in all its versions treats Jesus as an exceptional person who from his youth demonstrated unusual wit and wisdom, but disrespect toward his elders and the sages of the age. This part of the story bears some similarities to Ben Sira's youth described in *Alphabet of *Ben Sira*, leading some scholars to believe that the latter was also an anti-Christian satirical medieval work. The narrative does not deny that Jesus had supernatural powers; these, however, he obtained when he stole a holy name from the Temple. After a long struggle, in which conflicting magical powers contested for preeminence, Jesus' magic was rendered powerless by one of the sages. Naturally, the narrative intends to divest Christian tradition of any spiritual meaning. Some of the miracles, therefore, like the disappearance of Jesus' body after death, are explained either as acts of deception or as natural phenomena. In the more developed versions of the narrative, the hatred toward Jesus and his followers is not the only motif in the story. Many unnecessary details were added, secondary characters were developed, and the story became a romance about the tragic fate of a young man mistaken in his ways.

BIBLIOGRAPHY: S. Krauss, *Das Leben Jesu nach juedischen Quellen* (1902); J. Jacobs, *Jesus as Others Saw Him* (1925^2), contains *How the Jews will Reclaim Jesus* (introductory essay by H.A. Wolfson); H.G. Enelow, *A Jewish View of Jesus* (1931^2); G. Brandes, *Jesus a Myth* (1926); W. Fischel, *Eine juedisch-persische "Toledoth Jeschu"-Handschrift* (offprint from MGWJ, vol. 78, 1934).

[Joseph Dan]

TOLERANZPATENT, edict of tolerance issued by Emperor Joseph II on Jan. 2, 1782 for Vienna and Lower Austria (and subsequently for other provinces of the empire). It was one of a series of patents granted to the major, non-Catholic denominations of Austria, guaranteeing existing rights and obligations and laying down additional ones. The final version was less liberal than Joseph II's original drafts. The *Toleranzpatent* confirmed existing restrictions against any increase in the number of tolerated Jews; however, they were encouraged to engage in large-scale business, to set up factories, and to learn trades (although becoming master craftsmen remained prohibited); to establish schools and attend universities. Upper-class Jews were encouraged to integrate socially. The concluding article exhorted the Jews to be thankful and not to misuse their privileges, particularly not to offend Christianity in public, an offense which would result in expulsion. At the same time insult or violence done to a Jew would be punished.

With its leitmotif of making the Jews useful to society and the state through education and the abolishment of economic restrictions, the *Toleranzpatent* influenced much contemporary legislation in Germany. Although welcomed by N.H. *Wessely and other luminaries of the *Haskalah, it was viewed with misgiving in conservative Jewish circles, in particular by Ezekiel *Landau, who characterized it as a *gezerah* ("a disaster"); he was especially troubled by the order that within two years no document in Hebrew would be legally valid. Even Moses *Mendelssohn expressed misgivings over the new type of Christian enticement. Nonetheless, the edict was a significant milestone on the road to full emancipation.

BIBLIOGRAPHY: P.P. Bernard, in: *Austrian History Yearbook*, 4–5 (1968–69), 101–19; see also bibliography *Joseph II.

TOLKOWSKY, SHEMUEL (1886–1965), agronomist and Israel diplomat. Born in Antwerp, Belgium, Tolkowsky settled in Ereẓ Israel in 1911. In 1916–18 he served under Chaim *Weizmann in London as member of the Zionist Political Committee, which negotiated the *Balfour Declaration, and was an advisor on political matters. In 1918–19 he was the secretary of the Zionist delegation in the Versailles Peace Conference. Tolkowsky was active in various economic and public fields in Tel Aviv. In 1949–56 he was consul general and later minister of Israel in Berne, Switzerland. His books include *The Gateway to Palestine – History of Jaffa* (1924); *Hesperides, A History of the Culture and Use of Citrus Fruits* (1938); and *They Look to the Sea* (1964). His son DAN (1921–), born in Tel Aviv, was a mechanical engineer, and served in the British Royal Air Force as a flight lieutenant during World War II. From 1948 he served in the Israel air force and from 1953 until 1958 was its commander, attaining the rank of *alluf*.

[Benjamin Jaffe]

TOLLER, ERNST (1893–1939), German playwright and revolutionary. Born in Samotschin, Prussia, Toller was raised in an assimilated Jewish family which prided itself on being representative of German culture in a region heavily populated by

Poles. He volunteered for the army at the outbreak of World War I and after 13 months in the trenches at Verdun, was released as unfit for service. Toller's war experiences converted him from ultranationalism to pacifistic socialism. In Berlin he met Kurt *Eisner, and joined him in Munich as a member of the Independent Socialist Party (USPD), participating in strikes and anti-war agitation, as a result of which he was briefly imprisoned. Toller was a leader of the short-lived Bavarian Soviet Republic of 1919 and he succeeded Eisner after the latter's murder. Later he headed the Red Guard, but opposed needless violence. In June 1919, when the revolution collapsed, he was hounded by the authorities and spent five years in prison. It was while he was in jail that Toller wrote his celebrated expressionistic dramas: *Masse-Mensch* (1921; *Masses and Man*, 1923), *Die Maschinenstuermer* (1922; *The Machine-Wreckers*, 1923), *Hinkemann* (1924; *Brokenbrow*, 1926), and *Der entfesselte Wotan* (1923), which called for a new and more humane society and for man's liberation from the tyranny of the machine. The verse collection, *Das Schwalbenbuch* (1923; *The Swallow-Book*, 1924), contains some of the best poetry written during his imprisonment. After his release, Toller visited the U.S.S.R. (1926) and the U.S. (1929), shedding some of his utopian ideas. His later plays, such as *Hoppla wir leben*! (1927; *Hoppla*, 1928), and *Feuer aus den Kesseln* (1930; *Draw the Fires*, 1935), were less successful. Another drama, *Wunder in Amerika* (1931), was written in collaboration with Hermann *Kesten. Hitler's rise to power drove Toller into exile. His autobiography, *Eine Jugend in Deutschland* (1933; *I Was a German*, 1934), vividly depicted the hopes and frustrations of his generation. Toller continued the struggle against the Nazis, who regarded him with special hatred, throughout his years of exile, first in Switzerland, then in France, England, and finally, from 1936, in the U.S. He was engaged in unremitting efforts to help the cause of Spanish democracy but the fall of Republican Madrid to Franco's troops brought him a feeling of increased isolation and despair which led him to commit suicide in New York. Toller's last works include *No More Peace* (1937) and *Pastor Hall* (in English only, 1939).

BIBLIOGRAPHY: W.A. Willibrand, *Ernst Toller and his Ideology* (1945); S. Liptzin, *Germany's Stepchildren* (1961), 195–201; *Exil Literatur 1933–1945* (1967^3), 248–50.

[Sol Liptzin]

TOLSTOYE (Pol. **Tłuste**), town in Tarnopol district, W. Ukraine. Jews first settled in Tolstoye in the late 17th century. In the mid-1720s *Israel b. Eliezer, Ba'al Shem Tov, came to settle with his family and from there he started to preach his doctrine (1736). The gravestone of his mother was in the old local cemetery until World War II. From the first partition of Poland in 1772 until 1918, Tolstoye was under Austrian rule. In the 19th century the Jews traded in agricultural produce, timber, cloth, and beverages. They numbered 2,157 (67% of the total population) in 1880; 2,172 (59%) in 1900; and 1,196 (46%) in 1921. Ḥasidism was preponderant in Tolstoye; the wealthy members of the community (estate owners, contractors, and merchants of forest produce and hides) were followers of the *ẓaddik* of Chortkov, whereas shopkeepers, grain merchants, brokers, and scholars adhered to Viznitsa Ḥasidism, and the artisans were followers of the *ẓaddik* of Kopychintsy. In 1914 and 1916 the Jews suffered at the hands of the Russian army. Between the two world wars, in independent Poland, all the Zionist parties were active in the town and there was a *Tarbut Hebrew school.

[Shimshon Leib Kirshboim]

Holocaust Period

With the outbreak of war between Germany and the U.S.S.R. (June 22, 1941), groups of Jewish youth attempted to escape to the Soviet Union with the retreating Soviet army, but only a few succeeded. The city was captured by the Hungarian army, which was an ally of Germany. The Ukrainians attacked the Jews and looted their property, and Jews were drafted into work camps and agricultural farms in the area. In March 1942 the remnants of the Jewish communities of the entire area were concentrated in Tolstoye. In July 1942, 200 people were arrested and sent off in an "unknown direction." On Oct. 5, 1942, about 1,000 people were transported to the *Belzec death camp and about 150 were killed on the spot. On May 27, 1943, about 3,000 people were concentrated in the market square and were taken from there to the Jewish cemetery, where they were killed. About 1,000 people remained in the city, and they were murdered in an *Aktion* on June 6, 1943. The last 80 Jews were transported to Czortkow and found their deaths there. Many of the Jews who had fled to the forests fell into the hands of the fanatic Ukrainian Bandera gangs, but some of them joined partisan units. The remnants of the Tolstoye community were liberated from the camps in the area in March 1944. They soon immigrated to Palestine and the West. Jewish life was not reconstituted in Tolstoye after the war.

[Aharon Weiss]

BIBLIOGRAPHY: B. Wasiutyński, *Ludność żydowska w Polsce w wiekach XIX i XX* (1930), 141; G. Lindberg (ed.), *Sefer Tluste* (1965); I. Alfasi, *Sefer ha-Admorim* (1961), 9, 10; Dubnow, Ḥasidut, 44, 48, 51.

TOLUSH (pseudonym of **Iser Muselevitsh**; 1887–1962), Yiddish writer, born in Dvinsk, Latvia. Orphaned at an early age, he was virtually self-educated. Upon arriving in the U.S. in 1920, he shifted from writing in Russian to Yiddish. He worked at numerous occupations and wandered across much of Europe, Palestine, and the U.S. The designation Tolush (Heb. "detached" / "displaced") was given him by Z. *Shneour to characterize his itinerant life. His writing, influenced by Gorky and reflecting his wandering, introduced into Yiddish literature bohemian and unusual characters and settings. His works include *Der Yam Roysht* ("The Sea Roars," 1921), *A Zump* ("A Swamp," 1922), *Voglenish* ("Wandering," 1938), *Yidishe Shrayber* ("Yiddish Authors," 1953), and *Mayn Tatns Nign* ("My Father's Melody," 1957).

BIBLIOGRAPHY: M. Ḥalamish (ed.), *Mi-Kan u-mi-Karov* (1966), 27–32; Rejzen, Leksikon, 4 (1929), 891–6. **ADD. BIBLIOGRAPHY:** LNYL, 8 (1981), 804–5.

[Leonard Prager / Jerold C. Frakes (2nd ed.)]

TOMA, A. (originally **Moscovici**; 1875–1954), Romanian poet. Toma contributed to Romania's socialist and Jewish press and one of his poems, "Sion" ("Zion"), was often recited at Zionist gatherings. His verse collections include *Poezii* (1926, 1930^2) and *Cîntul vietii* (1950); a volume of children's poems, *Piuici si fratii lui mici* ("Piuici and his Little Brothers"), also appeared in English (1956). A member of the Romanian Academy after World War II, he was a prolific translator and gained many awards.

TOMAR (formerly **Thomar**), city in central Portugal. The earliest record of Tomar Jews, a tombstone of a rabbi, Joseph of Thomar, dated 1315, is found in *Faro's Jewish cemetery. A magnificent 15th-century synagogue on Rua de Joaquin Jacinto, referred to in an old document as "Rua Nova que foi judaria," reveals that there was a dynamic Jewish community in Tomar prior to the forced baptisms of 1497. The residents of the *judaria*, called *gente da naçao* or "people of the nation," were generally upper-class citizens. An *Inquisition tribunal was established at Tomar in 1540, and the first *auto-da-fé was held on May 6, 1543. After a second *auto-da-fé*, on June 20, 1544, the tribunal was suspended, owing perhaps to the discovery of administrative abuses. It was closed altogether with the publication on July 10, 1548 of a bull of pardon directing the release of all persons then held by the Inquisition.

On July 29, 1921, Tomar's historic synagogue building – which had been confiscated and used by a Christian order throughout the Inquisition period – was declared a national monument by the Portuguese government. In 1922 the antiquarian Samuel *Schwarz took title to the building, establishing there a museum for Judeo-Portuguese artifacts and inscriptions. Named Museu Luso-Hebraico Abraham Zacuto, it contains a good collection of inscriptions from early synagogues, including the notable stone from *Belmonte's 13th-century synagogue inscribed "And the Lord is in His holy Temple, be still before Him all the land," where the Divine Name is represented by three dots, in a manner also found in the *Dead Sea Scrolls.

BIBLIOGRAPHY: M. Kayserling, *Geschichte der Juden in Portugal* (1867), index; Roth, Marranos, 73; F.A. Garcez Teixeira, *A Antiga Sinagoga de Tomar* (1925); idem, *A Familia Camoes em Tomar* (1922); S. Schwarz, *Inscricões Hebraicas em Portugal* (1923); idem, *Museo Luso-Hebraico em Tomar* (1939); *American Sephardi* (Autumn 1970).

[Aaron Lichtenstein]

TOMASHPOL, town in Vinnitsa district, Ukraine; before the 1917 Revolution in the administrative province of Podolia. In 1847 there were 1,875 Jews living in Tomashpol. The town developed extensively as a result of the sugar industry and trade there. Between 1883 and 1918 Judah Leib *Levin (Yahalal) lived there, employed as an accountant in the factory owned by the *Brodski family. There were 4,518 Jews (over 90% of the total population) in the town in 1897. During the civil war many Jews in Tomashpol fell victims of the pogroms perpetrated by the armies of *Denikin in February 1920. By 1926 the number of Jews in the town had decreased to 3,252 (54.3%).

After the German occupation of Tomashpol in 1941, the Jews who remained there were murdered.

In the late 1960s the Jewish population was estimated at 1,000. There was no synagogue, the last remaining synagogue having been confiscated in 1956 and converted into a tailoring workshop.

BIBLIOGRAPHY: A.D. Rosenthal, *Megillat ha-Tevaḥ*, 3 (1931), 60–63.

[Yehuda Slutsky]

TOMASZOW LUBELSKI, town in Lublin province, E. Poland; from 1772 to 1809 under Austria, and from 1815 within Congress Poland. An organized Jewish community existed in Tomaszow Lubelski from the 1630s, but it was almost entirely annihilated in the *Chmielnicki massacres of 1648. The community was reorganized in the late 1650s. Its members earned their livelihood from trade in agricultural produce, the fur trade, tailoring, and inn keeping. The *parnas* of the community, Jacob Levi Safra, was its delegate at the Council of Four Lands (see *Councils of Lands) in 1667. In the 1670s the rabbi of the town was Isaac Shapira; he was succeeded by Judah b. Nisan. R. Phinehas bar Meir of Tomaszow was martyred in Lublin in 1677. There were 806 Jews in the town and its surroundings who paid the poll-tax in 1765. From the beginning of the 19th century the community was increasingly influenced by Ḥasidism. The Jewish population numbered 1,156 (43% of the total) in 1827; 2,090 (57%) in 1857; and 3,646 (59%) in 1897. At the close of the 19th century the Jews of Tomaszow Lubelski, among whom were many laborers, engaged in the operation of flour-mills, processing wood, weaving, tailoring, baking, and tanning. Between the two world wars, the Jewish population increased from 4,643 (65%) in 1921 to 5,669 in 1931. A library and Jewish sports club were established; branches of all the Jewish parties were active.

[Arthur Cygielman]

Holocaust Period

On the outbreak of World War II there were about 6,000 Jews in Tomaszow. On Sept. 6, 1939, the Jewish quarter suffered heavy German bombardment. The local synagogue was burned down, and about 500 houses inhabited by Jews were destroyed. The German army entered Tomaszow on Sept. 13, 1939, but withdrew within two weeks, and the Soviet army entered, only to return the town to the Germans after a few days. Many Jews (over 75%) seized the opportunity of leaving the town with the withdrawing Soviet army, and only 1,500 remained when the Germans returned. On Feb. 25, 1942, most of them were deported to the forced-labor camp in Cieszanow, where almost all died. Many Jews fled into the surrounding forests and attempted to hide there. A group of young Jews under Mendel Heler and Meir Kalichmacher organized a Jewish partisan unit, which fought the Germans for some time, but was betrayed by local Poles and annihilated.

The Jewish community was not reconstituted in Tomaszow Lubelski after the war.

[Stefan Krakowski]

BIBLIOGRAPHY: Halpern, Pinkas, index; B. Wasiutyński, *Ludność żydowska w Polsce w wiekach XIX i XX* (1930), 11, 16, 33, 60, 71; S. Bronsztejn, *Ludność żydowska w Polsce w okresie miedzywojennym* (1963), 278; M. Weinreich, *Shturmvint* (1927), 176–80: *Tomashover Yisker Bukh* (1965).

TOMASZOW MAZOWIECKI (also called **Tomaszow Rawski**), city in Lodz province, central Poland. The owner of Tomaszow Mazowiecki, Count Antoni Adam Ostrowski, invited Jewish weavers and entrepreneurs to settle there in the 1820s. Jacob Steinman from Ujazd acted as the count's agent in charge of the area. Jewish merchants who came to settle received building plots. They soon organized trade in local textile products. On the initiative of the manufacturer Leib Zilber a Jewish community was officially founded in 1831, and was granted sites for a synagogue, *mikveh*, hospital, and cemetery. The first dozen Jewish families in the city earned their livelihood as hired workers in the local weaving mills; later several became managers and owners of various textile plants. After the defeat of the Polish uprising of 1831, the Russian government of Nicholas I confiscated the Ostrowski estates, including Tomaszow Mazowiecki. Antoni Ostrowski went into exile in France, where he published *Pomysfy o potrzebie reformy towarzyskiej* ("Thoughts on the Necessity of Social Change," 1834), in which he formulated a plan for improving the conditions of the Jews in Poland.

The town grew from the early 1850s. The 1,879 Jews who lived there in 1857 comprised 37% of the population. By 1897 the number of Jews had grown to 9,320 (47% of the population); it increased to 10,070 in 1921 and 11,310 in 1931. The great synagogue was built between 1864 and 1878. In 1889 a *kasher* kitchen was built to cater for 120 Jewish soldiers serving in the Russian army who were stationed in the area. The manufacturer and community leader A. Landsberg paid for the building of a community center and donated another building to house the city's first Jewish high school. The community's first rabbi was Abraham Altschuler; Jacob Wieliczkier served there from 1857 to 1888 and Hersh Aaron Israelewicz from 1890 to 1916. In the 1880s David Bornstein founded a textile mill to employ Jewish workers, thus assuring their Sabbath observance. Besides weaving and spinning, the Jews engaged in carpentry, dyeing, and construction; many were employed as bookkeepers and foremen. In the early 20th century a Jewish workers' movement was organized. Between the world wars all the Jewish political parties were active in the city, especially the *Bund, *Po'alei Zion, and *Agudat Israel. Ludwik Frucht served as deputy mayor from 1926. In 1921 two schools merged to form the Hebrew high school. A Yiddish weekly, *Tomashover Vokhenblat*, appeared between 1925 and 1939. Samuel ha-Levi Brot, a Mizrachi leader in Poland, officiated as rabbi between 1928 and 1936. In the 1930s the Jews were damaged economically by the growing antisemitism. Natives of Tomaszow Mazowiecki include Leon *Pinsker, whose father taught in the city, the writer Moshe Dolzenovsky, and the chess champion Samuel *Reshevsky. The mathematician Ḥayyim Selig *Slonimski lived there between 1846 and 1858.

[Arthur Cygielman]

Holocaust Period

On the outbreak of World War II there were 13,000 Jews in the town. In December 1940 a closed ghetto composed of three isolated parts was established there. On March 11, 1941 the Jews from Plock were forced to settle there, so that the town's Jewish population grew to over 15,000. On April 27, 1942 about 100 people, including many members of the local underground, were arrested and shot. About 7,000 Jews were deported to the *Treblinka death camp and murdered on Oct. 31, 1942. Three days later another 7,000 Tomaszow Jews met their death in Treblinka. Only about 1,000 were left in the ghetto, which became a forced-labor camp. In May 1943 the ghetto was liquidated and its inmates transferred to the forced-labor camps in Blizyna and Starachowice, where almost all of them perished. No Jewish community was reconstituted in Tomaszow Mazowiecki.

[Stefan Krakowski]

BIBLIOGRAPHY: B. Wasiutyński, *Ludność żydowska w Polsce w wiekach XIX i XX* (1930), 28; S. Bronsztejn, *Ludność żydowska w Polsce w okresie międzywojennym* (1963), 278; M. Wejsberg (ed.), *Tomashov-Mazovyetsk Yisker Bukh* (1969); A. Rutkowski, in: BŻIH, 15–16 (1955).

TOMBS AND TOMBSTONES. Regular burial of the dead in tombs was customary even in prehistoric times as a manifestation of the beginnings of religious ritual, both among nomads and among settled peoples. In the Neolithic period, deceased tribal heads were regarded as family or tribal totems as attested by clay skulls, with human features, found at Jericho (Kenyon, in bibl.). In the Chalcolithic period it was customary to bury the bones in dry ossuaries after the flesh had disintegrated. There were various forms of ossuaries. Sometimes human features were engraved on the front of the ossuary. *Cemeteries of ossuaries were found mainly on the coastal strip of Ereẓ Israel. Death was viewed as a transition to a different world, where life was continued. The dead and their departed spirits were thought of as powerful, incomprehensible forces threatening the living with a limitless capacity for harm or for good. It was thus customary to place offerings of food and drink in special vessels, which were then buried in the tomb together with the corpse. For example, a platter with a lamb's head upon it has been found in a tomb at Afulah. Gifts given to the dead, either for their use or to propitiate them, were the items most highly prized by the person during his lifetime. Thus, during the Middle Canaanite period it was customary to "kill" the sword of the deceased after its owner's death by bending it and making it useless. During the Late Canaanite period, a man's war horse and chariot were symbolic of his noble status. It was therefore customary to bury a nobleman's weapons and horse with him. In a number of graves at Beth-Eglaim (Tell-ʿAjūl) horses are buried with their rid-ers (Petrie, in bibl.). Burial customs were the most important aspect of the early Egyptian cultic practices. These customs accompanied the death of the king-gods, nobles, and upper classes. The monumental architecture of the Egyptian burial cities, the mummification of the kings, and the embalming of sacred animals, all developed around the Egyptian burial cult (Dawson, in bibl.). Such practices were employed in the great, powerful, and stable kingdoms and in Mesopotamia, though they were not found among the tribes who arrived in Palestine with the wave of ethnic wanderings, during the patriarchal period of the second millennium B.C.E. These wandering tribes did, however, continue the practice of burying various offerings together with their dead, as was customary from the Early Canaanite period on.

During the time of the Patriarchs, when there was a change from tribal wanderings to permanent settlement, a new element was added to the burial customs. A permanent grave site was purchased in the vicinity of the settlement which was a significant indication of permanent settlement. Herein lies the importance of Abraham's purchase of a family tomb (Gen. 23:4). Jacob's request that he be buried at this place rather than in Egypt may be understood against this background (Gen. 47:29). Joseph's burial in Shechem in the land of his ancestors (Josh. 24:32) must be seen as part of the process of Exodus from Egypt and the conquest and settlement of Palestine. This identification of the patriarchal tomb with the Promised Land may be discerned in Nehemiah's remark to the Persian king from whom he requested permission to go to Palestine to rebuild its ruins: "... the place of my father's sepulchers lies waste..." (Neh. 2:3). For a long period of time, from the Patriarchs until the establishment of the monarchy, it was customary to bury the dead in a family plot (Heb. *bet ʾavotam*) in an effort to maintain contact with the place (e.g., Judg. 2:9; I Sam. 25:1).

During the period of the kingdoms of Judah and Israel, sepulchers for kings and nobles were established: "and they buried him [Uzziah] with his fathers in the burial field which belonged to the kings" (II Chron. 26:23). Special mention should be made of the discovery of an engraved tablet bearing the name of Uzziah king of Judah. The tablet cannot be the original one which marked the grave, since its script and its general form are of the Second Temple period. It appears that for various reasons the king's bones were transferred during this period. Noblemen and officers also merited lavish burial. The prophet, fighting the corrupt nobility, denigrates the elegant tombs, hewn out of the rocks (Isa. 22:16). The carving of tombs in elevated places is reminiscent of the grave sites above the Kidron Brook in Jerusalem (Avigad, in bibl.). A number of hewn graves dating to the period of the kings have been found at this location. The most striking of them is a hewn tomb, upon whose lintel appears a dedication to some person who held an administrative position: "...who was over the household." The name of this person ends with the syllable *yhw*. Conceivably, it may be the same Shebna (Shebaniahu) mentioned in Isaiah 22:16 [15]. Another tomb from the same period is the one called "the grave of Pharaoh's daughter." This tomb is cut from rock into the shape of a cube. It has a small entrance and contains the remains of a striking structure, perhaps pyramidal, on its roof. During certain periods grave markers or tombstones were part of the grave itself (Gen. 35:20). The most luxurious graves from this period found, for example, at Achzib, are hewn according to Phoenician design. The burial cave has a vaulted ceiling, cut as much as 10 m. (33 ft.) deep into the rock. At its end is a catafalque hewn out of rock, upon which the corpse was placed. In order to elevate the head of the corpse, a stone was placed beneath it, or a projection shaped like a raised pillow was left on the catafalque. As a result of the custom of burying items of value from the deceased's lifetime along with him, there arose a class of grave robbers in the Ancient East. To prevent such incursions, complicated grave sealing techniques were developed, along with difficult entrance and exit passages from the interior of the tombs. In many instances it was customary to warn grave robbers against entering. The tomb of "...*yhw* who was over the household" (mentioned above) contains the inscription: "Cursed be he who opens this." This is similar to the inscriptions common in the Second Temple Period, which contained the name of the deceased and a warning not to open the grave.

Thousands of tombs have been unearthed and investigated during the years of archaeological activities in Israel. Several characteristic grave types have been found:

(1) A communal grave within a cave from the Middle Canaanite period, like one found at Jericho. Dozens of skeletons were found in the cave as well as the offerings buried there (Garstang, in bibl.). In this case, a household or family used a natural cave, which served it for several generations. This type of mausoleum, consisting of some land and a cave, was no doubt the kind acquired by Abraham from Ephron the Hittite near Hebron, when he came to settle permanently in Palestine. The patriarchal sepulcher remained traditional among the people even as late as Herod's time. Among his massive building projects throughout the land, he constructed a Roman-style monument over the patriarchal tomb in Hebron. This monument was intended as an architectural marker of the site and its sanctity.

(2) During the same Middle Canaanite period pit burials were common. For this purpose either natural caves were used or circular or rectangular pits were dug out of the earth to a depth of one to 2 m. (3–6 ft.). The walls of the pit contained the burial niches into which were placed the bodies and the offerings. Each niche would be sealed with a single large stone, and the central pit would be filled in up to ground level, thus preventing any approach to the graves themselves.

(3) In addition to family graves, individual tombs have been found. These too contain gifts to accompany the deceased to his new life. Generally, these gifts were eating and drinking utensils, jewelry, personal seals, etc. The finds from tombs are many and variegated, and by their nature are better preserved than finds from the usual, exposed ancient sites.

(4) Among the graves unearthed from the Late Canaanite period are pit tombs, of the style of the prior period, both of family as well as of individual types and simple inhumations. Graves from this period have been found at Tell Abu Hawām (Hamilton, in bibl.), Achzib, and elsewhere. Special attention was given to the manner in which the body was placed in the grave. Generally, the hands were folded and the legs stretched out. The custom of burying gifts with the dead continued into the Late Canaanite period. Offerings in these graves are either local or imported implements.

(5) At the end of this period another form of burial appears. The corpse is placed into two large ossuaries, or jugs, whose necks have been removed, so that the bodies of the jugs enclose the corpse from the feet up and from the head down. These graves, too, contain offerings and weapons that served the deceased during his lifetime.

(6) At the end of the second millennium B.C.E., with the advent of the Philistines in the land, sites with Philistine population, such as Beth-Shean, exhibit different burial methods. The corpse was provided with a clay coffin, longer than the body. The coffin had a cover near the head, decorated with human features. Such decoration was intended to symbolize the personality of the deceased. The engraved hats and diadems resemble the headdress of the Philistines portrayed on ancient Egyptian monuments (Dothan, in bibl.).

(7) A large quantity of graves, including pit tombs, burial caves, rock-hewn tombs, and individual grave sites, from the Israelite period, have been found at Megiddo, Hazor, Beth-Shean, and other sites. The offerings placed in these graves are usually pottery vessels, such as jars and flasks, some of them imported, as well as jewelry and seals.

(8) The Israelite II and the Persian periods reveal tombs hewn into caves with ledges provided for the corpses, known mainly from the Shephelah and the coastal strip. Tombs of Phoenician style are especially to be found in the Athlit area (Hamilton, in bibl.). These are in the shape of a four-sided pit hewn into the hard rock, with ladderlike sockets for hands and feet, to be used in climbing down the pit. At the bottom of the pit there are one or more hewn openings to the burial niches themselves. These are sealed with large stones. The entrance pit itself is filled with earth and stones to block off the entrance to the graves.

(9) With the close of the Persian period and the beginning of the Hellenistic, the most common form of grave consisted of rock tombs, with raised shelves or ledges, or troughs resembling coffins, near the walls. The typical cave ceiling of this period is in the form of a large camel hump, as in the case of a grave found at Marissah. The walls and ceiling of this grave are decorated with drawings. A tomb of similar design has been found at Nazareth.

See also *Death, *Mourning.

[Ze'ev Yeivin]

Tombstones

The first tombstone mentioned in the Bible is the *mazzevah* ("monument") which Jacob set up over the grave of Rachel (Gen. 35:20; see Tomb of *Rachel). The custom continued during the First Temple period as is clear from II Kings 23:17, where King Josiah saw the *ẓiyyun* over the grave of the prophet who had prophesied that Josiah would undertake the religious reformation (cf. I Kings 13). Ezekiel (39:15) also uses *ẓiyyun* for a sign placed over the grave. The custom continued during the period of the Second Temple and the Talmud. I Maccabees 13:27–29 describes the ornate tombstone and monument which Simeon the Hasmonean erected over the grave of his father and brothers at Modi'in, of which Josephus (Ant. 13:211) also gives a detailed description. However, apart from a vague reference in the Talmud stating that one of the things which adversely affects one's study is "the reading of an inscription on a grave" (Hor. 13b), there is no evidence that these tombstones bore inscriptions either in the biblical or early Second Temple periods (but see below). In the later period their main purpose seems to have been to indicate the position of a grave in order to obviate the fear of a kohen becoming ritually unclean by being in its vicinity (cf. Tosef. Oholot 17:4). The custom of erecting these tombstones was widespread. R. Nathan ha-Bavli ruled that a surplus of the money provided for the burial of the dead was to be applied to erecting a memorial over the grave (Shek. 2:5), and the 15th of Adar was selected as the day of the year when graves were marked (Shek. 1:1) by daubing them with lime (Ma'as. Sh. 5:1). In addition to those *ẓiyyunim* which were apparently simple markers there were two kinds of more ornate tombstones (called *nefesh*, literally, "a soul"). One was a solid structure over the grave without any entrance (Er. 55b); the other had an entrance to which a dwelling chamber, probably for the watchman, was attached (Er. 5:1).

During the later Hasmonean period, under Greek and Roman influence, there developed the custom of erecting ornate monumental tombstones for the nobility, notable examples being the Yad Avshalom (Monument of Absalom), the sepulcher of Zechariah, and that of the Sons of Hezir in the Kidron Valley. The last bears the inscription "this is the grave and the *nefesh* ["soul"] of," giving the names of the members of the family buried there. For many years this was the only known inscription on a tombstone of the Second Temple period, but recent excavations have revealed a large number, including the Tomb of Jason in Reḥavyah in Jerusalem and that of Simeon the builder of the Sanctuary, among others (see *Epitaphs, and the reproductions in *Sefer Yerushalayim*, 1957, pp. 220–321 and 352–3). It has been suggested that it was this ostentation, so foreign to the spirit of Judaism, and the desire to abolish it which caused Rabbah Simeon b. Gamaliel to declare that "one does not erect *nefashot* to the righteous, for their words are their memorial" (Gen. R. 82:10; TJ, Shek. 2:7, 47a).

In view of the extensive discovery of such inscriptions, the suggestion can no longer be upheld that it was only outside Ereẓ Israel that the Jews adopted the custom from the Greeks and Romans of adding inscriptions to tombstones in addition to Jewish symbols (see below on tombstone art), and the custom is to be regarded as common from at least the second century B.C.E. Jacob Moellin (the Maharil) states that in Mainz he discovered a fragment of a tombstone over a thousand years old (i.e., of the fourth century) bearing the Hebrew inscription "a designated bondmaid" (cf. Lev. 19:20; *Likkutei Maharil* at the end of his book of that name). The earliest known tombstones bearing the inscription *shalom al Yisrael* ("Peace upon Israel"), dated 668, was found at Narbonne, one at Brindisi dates from 832, and one at Lyons from 1101. Maimonides (Yad, Avel 4:4) adopts the abovementioned view of Simeon b. Gamaliel that tombstones are not erected over the graves of the righteous. Solomon b. Abraham Adret, however (Resp. 375), regards the tombstone as a mark of honor for the dead, while Isaac Luria (*Sha'ar ha-Mitzvot, Va-Yeḥi*) even regards it as contributing to the *tikkun ha-nefesh* ("the perfecting of the soul") of the deceased. It is forbidden to derive material benefit from a tombstone (Sh. Ar. YD 364:1). At the present day it is the universal custom to erect tombstones, and a special order of service for the consecration of the tombstone has been drawn up. In Israel its main content is the reading of those portions of the alphabetical 119th Psalm which constitute the name of the deceased and the letters of the word *neshamah* ("soul"); in Western countries it consists of a selection of appropriate Psalms and biblical passages; and in both cases it concludes with a memorial prayer and **Kaddish* by the mourners. In the Diaspora it is the custom to erect and consecrate the tombstone during the 12th month after death; in Israel on the 30th day. Ashkenazi tombstones are usually vertical; among the Sephardim they lie flat (for inscriptions on tombstones see *Epitaphs; see also *Burial; *Catacombs; *Cemetery).

The tombstones of many ancient communities have been published.

Art

A desire for originality allied to an emphasis on tradition is characteristic of the tombstones in Jewish cemeteries. Here the anonymous Jewish craftsman succeeded perhaps better than in most other fields of art in establishing an individual style. There are few branches of Jewish art which are distinguished by such richness of decoration, and by such a variety of symbolism, as tombstone art. Thus a study of Jewish tombstones is a rich source of material for the study of Jewish art from ancient times to the present. The artistic and traditional development of the tombstone and of its individual style is based on two factors: (a) the desire for perpetuation; (b) artistic expression and the participation of the various branches of the plastic arts in its creation. Hence the great value of the tombstone not only lies in the study of epitaphs, but also in its ornamentation.

TOMBSTONE ART IN THE ANCIENT WORLD. The oldest graveyards are found in Ereẓ Israel. Here the original form of the cemetery, consisting of rock vaults intended for a group of graves, has been preserved. The so-called Tombs of the Sanhedrin in Jerusalem, dating from the first and second centuries C.E., are outstanding for the ornamentation at the lintel to the graves. Similar ornamentation exists at the entry to the burial chamber of the royal line of Adiabene in Jerusalem, traditionally known as the "Tomb of the Kings." At the same period, under the influence of Egyptian and Greek art, individual monuments were erected to mark graves. Examples are the monuments known as "Absalom's Tomb," "The Tomb of Zechariah," and others, all in the Valley of Kidron in Jerusalem. In Galilee, the *Bet She'arim necropolis has a wealth of ornamentation, both Jewish and mythological. In the Roman catacombs of the classical period the Jewish tomb was recognizable by symbols such as the **shofar* or the *menorah*. A very few Roman sarcophagi have been preserved which combine this Jewish symbolism with classical motifs – e.g., the *menorah* supported by putti in pure pagan style, found in the Catacomb of Vigna Randanini. The early tombstones erected over graves in the western world after the classical period were on the whole severely plain, sometimes merely embodying (in Spain and Italy) a crudely engraved *menorah* whether as a symbol of Jewish allegiance or of eternal light. In the Middle Ages, even this slight ornamentation disappeared, and the decorative element was entirely provided by the engraved Hebrew characters. In most cases, however, the inscriptions were crudely carved by inexpert hands. There now developed a tendency for the tombstones in Germany and the lands of Ashkenazi civilization to be upright, those in Spain and the Sephardi world to be sometimes horizontal, sometimes built up in the form of altar-tombs.

LATER SEPHARDI TOMBSTONES. A more elaborate form of tombstone began to emerge in the Renaissance period. While in North Africa and the Orient the utmost simplicity continued to prevail, in some of the Sephardi communities of Northern Europe (especially Amsterdam, though not London) and of the West Indies (especially Curaçao) an elaborate Jewish funerary art developed. In these places the recumbent tombstones were often decorated with scenes in relief depicting events connected with the biblical character whose name was borne by the deceased (the sacrifice of Isaac or the call of Samuel), and in Curaçao sometimes even with the actual deathbed scene. In Italy, the vertical tombstone was often surmounted by the family badge, and in the case of families of Marrano descent with the knightly helm or with armorial bearings.

ASHKENAZI TOMBSTONES. The Ashkenazim, on the other hand, used symbols which illustrated the deceased's religious status, his virtues or his trade. These then were special symbols to denote a rabbi, a kohen, a levite; an alms-box would be shown on the tombstone of a philanthropist; and a pair of scissors on that of a tailor. The depiction of the human figure is unknown on Ashkenazi tombstones, and allegorical figures are very rarely found. As in medieval Spain, Ashkenazi Jewry in Bohemia and in parts of Poland sometimes used vertical and horizontal stones together to form a sarcophagus. This sarcophagus monument was usually intended for important personages. Another type of tombstone intended for an important person, a *zaddik or an *admor, is to be found in Polish cemeteries, and in neighboring Ashkenazi countries. This was in the form of an *ohel* ("tent" or "tabernacle"). These tabernacles generally had no artistic or architectural distinction; they were built in the form of a small stone or wooden house, or of a simple hut standing on four posts, inside which the tombstone itself was placed. Sometimes the tabernacle was encircled by a wrought iron fence. But the most common form of tombstone among Ashkenazi Jewry is the vertical, rectangular stone. A few cast-iron tombstones are known, and in small, poor communities, particularly in Eastern Europe, there are wooden tombstones. The tombstones in Prague, Worms (Germany) and Lublin (Poland), dating from the mid-15th and early 16th centuries, have no special ornamentation. Most of them are in the form of square stone tablets, and were seldom topped with a semicircular or triangular decoration. From the mid-16th century onward, tombstones have more elaborate decoration, particularly in the ornamentation of the frame for the epitaph. The most common designs resemble those of the ark curtains in the synagogue, with two columns flanking the tombstone and enclosing the text. It is in this period that flora and fauna make their first appearance, mostly around the frame, while the epitaph is engraved on the main part of the stone, below the two-columned portico. Nevertheless, with its beautiful lettering the epitaph constitutes the main decoration of the tombstone. From the early 17th century, the tombstone of Eastern European Jewry developed a definite style of ornamentation. There is a clear post-Renaissance influence in the form of the tombstone and the ornamentation. In the design of this ornamentation, and the manner in which it is placed on the tombstone, there are the beginnings of the rich Jewish decoration, baroque in essence, which is characteristic of the century in Eastern Europe, and particularly in Poland. This decoration is reminiscent in both subject matter and execution of the wall-paintings of the wooden synagogues, which in fact were first built during this same period. This similarity is particularly apparent after the 1648–49 massacres in Poland. The number of Jewish motifs on tombstones was increased and more honorific descriptions of the deceased taken from the Holy Scriptures or the Talmud were added to the epitaph. Other new decorations included anagrams at the beginning and end of the text The late 17th and early 18th century tombstones, though still outstanding for their floral decoration – full-blown roses, and baskets or bowls filled with ripe fruit – have lost their Jewishness and are lacking in originality. Some of the common symbols used on the Jewish tombstone continued to appear in most Jewish communities. These were the hands of the priest in an attitude of blessing. This marked the grave of a kohen, while an ewer and basin or a musical instrument marked the grave of a levite. In Bohemia and Poland they still used occupational symbols such as chains on the grave of a goldsmith, a parchment with a goosefeather on the grave of a Torah scribe, an open book or a row of books with engraved titles on the grave of a learned rabbi or author. Apart from this, there were also animal, bird or fish motifs representing the name of the deceased, such as a lion on the grave of a man named Leib, a deer on the grave of a man named Hirsch, a bird in memory of Jonah (dove), and a fish on the tombstone of Fischel. The engraver occasionally emphasized the decorative and sculptural aspect by the addition of colors. The anonymous tombstone artists who worked in Jewish communities were excellent craftsmen, sometimes inheriting their craft from their fathers. Their work has a primitive charm and occasionally even a certain degree of professionalism. Some were gifted sculptors, whose work showed sensitivity and a poetic quality. All the religious and philosophical ideas connected with death, the phenomenon of death itself, man's mortality, his ways on earth and his relationship with God and eternity, were given artistic expression in stone. Sometimes death was depicted as a flickering flame, as a shipwrecked vessel, an overturned and extinguished lamp, or a flock without a shepherd. The fear of death was sometimes symbolized by fledglings nestling under their mother's wing. Heraldic designs were also used on tombstones, particularly in Eastern Europe. They took the form of a pair of lions, deer or even sea-horses holding the crowns of the Torah. Other animals also appeared occasionally, such as bears, hares, squirrels and ravens – the raven being the harbinger of disaster. One particular tombstone is of such exceptional beauty that it merits special mention. It is that of Dov Baer Shmulovicz, the son of Samuel Zbitkower, the founder of the Bergsohn family in Warsaw. The tombstone was made by the Jewish artist, David Friedlaender. The main decoration is two bas-reliefs, one on each side of the stone. One depicts a landscape with a river and cargo boats signifying the trade of the deceased and a walled city with towers, houses, including a synagogue, *bet midrash* and windmill, while on the horizon is a palace, which the ancestors of the deceased received as a gift from the last king of Poland, Stanislaus Augustus. The other bas-relief shows the tower (of Babylon) and a grove of trees, on whose branches are hung musical instruments, recalling the passage from Psalm 137, "By the waters of Babylon…"

In recent years there has been a tendency, at least among the orthodox, for tombstones to be increasingly simple, notwithstanding an occasional exuberance of architectural forms. In Eastern Europe they are without exception severely plain.

[David Davidovitch]

BIBLIOGRAPHY: W.R. Dawson, in: JEA, 13 (1927), pl. 18, 40–49; W.M.F. Petrie, *Beth Pelet I* (1930), passim; A. Rowe, *The Topography and History of Beth Shan* (1930), pl. 37, 39; R.W. Hamilton, *Excavation at Tell Abu Hawām* (1935); M. Werbrouck, *Les pleureuses dans l'Egypte ancienne* (1938); J. Finegan, *Light from the Ancient Past* (1946), 353–98; J. Garstang, *The Story of Jericho* (1948); A.G. Barrois, *Manuel d'archéologie biblique*, 2 (1953), 274–323; N. Avigad, *Mazzevot Kedumot be-Naḥal Kidron* (1954), 9ff.; K. Kenyon, *Digging up Jericho* (1957), 95–102, 194–209, 233–55, 665; T. Dothan, *The Philistines and their Material Culture* (1967); D. Ussishkin, in: *Qadmoniot*, 2 (1970), 25–27. SECOND TEMPLE AND TALMUD PERIODS: N. Avigad, in: *Sefer*

Yerushalayim, 1 (1956), 320–48. IN ART: N. Avigad, *Maẓẓevot Kedumot be-Naḥal Kidron* (1954); I. Pinkerfeld, *Bi-Shevilei Ommanut Yehudit* (1957); M. Gruenwald, *Portugiesengraeber auf deutscher Erde* (1902); D. Henrique de Castro, *Keur van Grafsteenen… Ouderkerk aan den Amstel* (Dutch and Ger. 1883); A. Grotte, *Alte schlesische Judenfriedhoefe* (1927); M. Balaban, *Die Judenstadt von Lublin* (1919); A. Levy, *Juedische Grabmalkunst in Osteuropa* (n.d.); O. Muneles and M. Vitimkôvá, *Starý židovský hřbitov v Praze* (1955); M. Levy, *Der alte israelitische Friedhof zu Worms am Rhein* (1913); M. Diamant, *Juedische Volkskunst* (1937); L.A. Mayer, *Bibliography of Jewish Art* (1967), index; I.S. Emmanuel, *Precious Stones of the Jews of Curaçao* (1957); Cantera y Burgos et al., *Las Inscripciones Hebraicas de España* (1955); E.R. Goodenough, *Jewish Symbols…* (13 vols, 1953–68); Roth, Art, index.

TOMSK, main city of Tomsk district (Siberia), Russia. Before the October Revolution the district of Tomsk was beyond the *Pale of Settlement and no Jewish settlement was allowed there until the cancellation of the Pale enactment. A Jewish community was nevertheless established in Tomsk in the first half of the 19th century by exiled prisoners and Jewish soldiers who served there (among them several Jewish *Cantonists who were brought to a Cantonist institute there). A number of these soldiers settled in Tomsk after their release from the army. In the second half of the 19th century, Jews of all professions who were allowed now to reside beyond the Pale began to settle in Tomsk. In 1897 the number of Jews in the entire district of Tomsk was 7,900, of whom 3,214 (6.4% of the total population) lived in the town of Tomsk proper. In October 1905 there were in Tomsk organized attacks on Jews and members of the Russian intelligentsia, fomented by the local administration. At the end of 1969 the Jewish population was estimated at about 5,000. The last synagogue was closed down by the authorities in 1959. After the mass exodus of the 1990s fewer than 1,000 Jews remained in the entire Tomsk district. However, Jewish life was revived, including an active community center and officiating rabbi.

BIBLIOGRAPHY: *Die Judenpogrome in Russland*, 2 (1909), 524–30; G. Tsam, *Istoriya vozniknoveniya v Tomske voyennoy soldatskoy shkoly* (1909).

[Yehuda Slutsky]

°**TONNA, CHARLOTTE ELIZABETH** (1790–1846), British philosemitic writer and editor. Born Charlotte Browne in Norwich, England, the daughter of an Anglican vicar, she became an extreme Protestant Evangelical writer and edited *The Christian Lady's Magazine* from 1834 until 1846 as well as other religious journals. Tonna was an outspoken philosemite who, most unusually, discarded the normal aim among Evangelicals of converting the Jews, instead adopting the position that Jews remain a Covenant people and that Judaism represented a valid alternative means of attaining salvation. Her magazine reproduced articles on Judaism by Jacob *Franklin, the editor of the Jewish newspaper *The Voice of Jacob*, and she supported the efforts of British Jews to assist persecuted Jews overseas. Tonna also believed that Protestants should themselves practice the Jewish rites, including circumcision. In contrast, she was an outspoken opponent of Roman Catholicism. Well known in her day – a collection of her works was published in 1845 with an introduction by Harriet Beecher Stowe – she was largely forgotten until recently, when her remarkable views attracted renewed interest.

BIBLIOGRAPHY: ODNB online; H.L. Rubinstein, "A Pioneering Philosemite: Charlotte Elizabeth Tonna (1790–1846) and the Jews," in: JHSET, 35 (1996–98), 103–18; W.D. Rubinstein and H.L. Rubinstein, *Philosemitism: Admiration and Support in the English-Speaking World for Jews, 1840–1939* (1999), index.

[William D. Rubinstein (2nd ed.)]

TOPARCHY (τοπαρχία), the basic administrative district in Palestine during the major part of the Second Temple period. Under the Ptolemies the division of Palestine was fashioned after that of Egypt, although the names given to each administrative district were not always identical. Thus, whereas in Egypt the largest unit was the *nomos* (νομός) which was divided into smaller districts called *topos* (τόπος), the major unit in Palestine under the Ptolemies was the *hyparchia*, subdivided into smaller units called toparchies (cf., however, I Macc. 10:30; 11:57, where the larger units of Palestine are also called *nomos*). At times the toparchy was in effect the combined territory of a number of neighboring villages, and each toparchy had a capital city or town which was probably the seat of the local governor, known as *strategos toparchos* or simply *strategos*. Under Herod Jewish Palestine was divided into approximately 21 toparchies. As for Judea, two lists are given. Pliny (Natural History 5:70) lists ten toparchies, whereas Josephus enumerates 13 (Wars, 3:54–5), including two toparchies of Idumea. Perea was probably divided into three toparchies and Lower Galilee into four, while Upper Galilee was considered a separate unit.

BIBLIOGRAPHY: Schuerer, Gesch, 2 (1907), 229–36; A. Schalit, *Ha-Mishtar ha-Roma'i be-Ereẓ Yisrael* (1937), 16 ff.

[Isaiah Gafni]

TOPLPUNKT: FERTLYOR-SHRIFT FAR LITERATUR, KUNST UN GEZELSCHAFTLEKHE FRAGES (Yid. "Colon: Quarterly of Literature, Art and Social Questions"), Yiddish literary journal published since 2000 in Tel Aviv by Der Natsyonaler Instants far Yidisher Kultur ("The National Instance for Yiddish Culture"). Nos. 1–5 were edited by Yankev Beser and co-edited by Yisroel Rudnitski, the latter becoming editor with no. 6 (Winter 2003). The closing down of the journal **Di Goldene Keyt* in 1995 created a vacuum in international Yiddish literary culture. Many of the participants in *Toplpunkt* would have been – or would have aspired to become – contributors to *Di Goldene Keyt*. *Toplpunkt* partly fills a void left by that prestigious journal's surcease and can also lay claim to a character of its own – a greater emphasis on graphic design and on a fruitful exchange between older and younger Yiddish writers. *Toplpunkt* is a serious magazine that radiates a certain vitality: two-thirds of its material is original Yiddish work, while the other third comprises translations from

Hebrew and major European languages. Of the 60–70 Yiddish-writing participants, almost a third are relatively young (mainly late-wave immigrants from former Soviet lands). The folio-size journal is visually attractive, each number featuring work by a particular artist. Those represented in issues 1–9 are among Israel's major artists: Yosl Bergner, Menashe Kadishman, Yossef Zaritsky, Arye Arokh, Tsiona Tagger, Mula Ben-Khayim, Mordecai Ardon, Reuven Rubin, Moshe Rozentalis (in that order). Each issue contains more than 100 pages of a lively variety of genres. Some readers may sense a "last Mohican" strain in this 21st-century subsidized international Yiddish literary periodical.

[Leonard Prager (2nd ed.)]

TOPOL, CHAIM (1935–), Israeli actor, who won international fame as the Shalom Aleichem character, Tevye in the musical *Fiddler on the Roof.* Born in Tel Aviv, Topol began to appear on the stage during his period of army service. He first gained a reputation at the Haifa Municipal Theater, which he co-founded and where he appeared in the Hebrew versions of Ionesco's *Rhinoceros*, Shakespeare's *Taming of the Shrew*, Brecht's *Caucasian Chalk Circle*, and the Japanese *Rashomon*. In Tel Aviv he appeared in the Hebrew production of *Fiddler on the Roof.* This led to his starring in the London West End production in English (1967), which brought him wide acclaim and the lead in the movie (1971). His films made in Israel include *Sallah Shabbati* (1964) and *Ervinka* (1967). He also appeared in *Galileo* (1975), *The House on Garibaldi Street* (1979), *Flash Gordon* (1980), and *For Your Eyes Only* (1981). He also appeared in the TV versions of Herman Wouk's *Winds of War* (1983) and *War and Remembrance* (1988). His autobiography, *Topol by Topol*, was published in London. He has illustrated 20 books.

[Dora Leah Sowden]

TOPOLCANY (Slovak **Topolčany**; Hung. **Nagytapolcsány**), town in Slovakia. The first documentary evidence of the Jewish appearance in Topolcany is from the 14th century. In the following centuries Topolcany was not a pleasant place to live because of the many wars and battles in the area.

The first Jews arrived in Topolcany from Moravia and Uhersky Brod in 1649 and established families. The anti-Jewish legislation of Emperor Charles VI (1711–1780) and of his daughter Maria Theresa (1740–1780) encouraged further settlement of Moravian Jews in upper Hungary. Jews in the city engaged in trade, including international trade. Attempts to expel Jews in 1727 and in 1755 failed. Jewish community life expanded and by 1755 there were a cemetery, a synagogue, and a *ḥevra kaddisha*. In the census of 1735, there were 50 Jews in Topolcany. The "*Toleranzpatent*" (1782) of Emperor Joseph II (1780–90) permitted further settlement of Jews and commerce. By the end of the 18th century a yeshivah was established, under the supervision and instruction of Rabbis Asher Anshel Roth (Ruta) and Abraham Ullmann.

The community grew quickly. In 1830 there were 561 Jews in Topolcany; in 1840 there were 618; and in 1850 there were 760. In 1880 there were 1,119 Jews and in 1910 there were 1,934. The 1930 census records 2,991. On the eve of World War II the number was 2,700. Toward 1942, the number reached 3,000, which included Jews from surrounding villages who moved there, concerned for their safety.

Jews lived a quiet life in Topolcany in the 19th century; but in 1848 during the Spring of Nations, Jews were attacked and robbed. In 1918–19 pogroms took place and Jewish property was looted and destroyed.

After the 1868 Congress of Hungarian Jewry, the Topolcany congregation chose the Orthodox stream. Zionist activity centered on the youth movements, and the Maccabi sports movement organized the young people. A Jewish school, a *talmud torah*, an old-age home, and women's associations extended the social life of the congregation. The Communist Party was also active, particularly among the youth. The Jewish political party clashed with parties representing the Orthodox (mainly the Agrarian Party).

About 80% of the retail trade was in Jewish hands, largely in the horse and cattle trade, wood, food and beverages, and construction material.

In 1938 Hlinka's nationalistic fascist Slovak People's Party gained supreme power in the country. On March 14, 1939, it proclaimed the Slovak state with Nazi support. Jews were the primary target. The Hlinka Guard, with a storm trooper unit, cast a dark shadow on social and political life. Under the guise of "Aryanization," the Jews lost their property and livelihoods. In 1942 the Slovak authorities began to deport the Jews to the extermination camps in Poland. The local population took the opportunity to pillage and divide up Jewish property left in the apartments and stores and grabbed Jewish real estate.

When the deportations stopped in fall 1942 about 2,500 Jews had been deported. Only several hundred Jews were left in the town. They were joined in the spring of 1944 by several dozen Jewish families transferred from eastern Slovakia when the Soviet army closed in. By August 1944 an anti-Nazi uprising spread in parts of Slovakia. Jews from Topolcany in labor camps were liberated and returned home. Thus before German troops arrived to quell the uprising, 1,000 Jews gathered in the city. A few days later, the Germans sent all the Jews to Auschwitz. Fifty who hid were found by the Slovak inhabitants and were shot by the Nazis in a field in nearby Nemcice.

In 1947, there were 320 survivors living in Topolcany. A memorial to the Holocaust victims was erected in the Jewish cemetery. One of the synagogues was restored. Antisemitism continued to plague the Jews. The gentiles who had stolen Jewish property were resentful of the Jews' demands to return their belongings. In September 1945 rumors spread that a Jewish doctor was poisoning children and that Jewish teachers were replacing nuns. A pogrom swept the town. Jewish property was pillaged and destroyed, and 47 people were injured. An army unit sent to disperse the rioters joined the mob. In 1945–49 most of the surviving Jews emigrated. The Great Synagogue was turned into a warehouse.

BIBLIOGRAPHY: L. Venetianer, *A magyar zsidóság tötének* (1922); M. Lányi and H. Propper, *A szlovenszkói zsidó hitközségek története* (1933); Y.R. Buechler, *The Story and Origin of the Jewish Community of Topoltchany* (1976); E. Bàrkàny and L. Dojč, *Židovské náboženské obce na Slovensku* (1991), 206–9.

[Yeshayahu Jelinek (2nd ed.)]

TOPOLEVSKY, GREGORIO (1907–1986), Argentine politician and physician. Born in Grodno, Russia, Topolevsky immigrated to Argentina as a child and became a physician specializing in otorhinolaryngology. Between 1933 and 1945, he was frequently arrested for political agitation against the dictatorial governments in Argentina and was again imprisoned in 1951. In 1937 he fought on the republican side in the Spanish Civil War. After World War II he was a member of the Unión Civica Radical del Pueblo party and was appointed Argentine ambassador to Israel (1955–58). Later, during the presidency of Arturo Illia, Topolevsky was appointed director general of social welfare in the Ministry of Communications. Active in Jewish communal affairs, he was chairman of a number of local Jewish organizations, among them the Instituto de Intercambio Cultural Argentino Israelí.

[Israel Drapkin-Senderey]

TOPOLSKI, FELIKS (1907–1989), pictorial chronicler and muralist. Topolski, the son of Edward Topolski, a well-known actor, was born in Warsaw and studied art at the Warsaw Academy, and also studied at the Officers' School of Artillery. He later traveled in Italy and France, studying the old masters, before he settled in England in 1935. He developed an outstanding reputation as a draughtsman, writer, muralist, and portrait painter, and also worked in the theater. Appointed an official war artist during World War II, he recorded the British and Allied forces in Russia, the Middle East, the Far East, and Europe. His drawings were used widely in the press and have appeared in a series of books he published on these wartime experiences. Topolski also excelled as a mural painter, for which he received commissions all over the world. His most famous murals are *Cavalcade of Commonwealth*, 60 × 20 feet, painted in 1951 for the Festival of Britain, and *Coronation of Elizabeth II*, 100 × 4 feet, painted between 1958 and 1960 at the request of Prince Philip, which is now in Buckingham Palace, London. Another important commission was for 20 portraits of English writers in 1961, from the University of Texas. Topolski illustrated numerous books, notably the plays of George Bernard Shaw, as well as his own 20 works, including *Was Paris Lost* (1973). From 1953 he published *Topolski's Chronicle*, a hand-printed, pictorial broadsheet on current events. In 1969 he made a television film *Topolski's Moscow* and his environmental painting, *Memoir of the Century*, in London's South Bank Arts Centre was begun in 1977. He was elected to the Royal Academy in the year of his death. Topolski wrote an autobiography, *Fourteen Letters* (1988).

[Charles Samuel Spencer]

TORAH (Heb. תּוֹרָה).

The Term

Torah is derived from the root ירה which in the *hifil* conjugation means "to teach" (cf. Lev. 10:11). The meaning of the word is therefore "teaching," "doctrine," or "instruction"; the commonly accepted "law" gives a wrong impression. The word is used in different ways but the underlying idea of "teaching" is common to all.

In the Pentateuch it is used for all the body of laws referring to a specific subject, e.g., "the *torah* of the meal offering" (Lev. 6:7), of the guilt offering (7:1), and of the Nazirite (Num. 6:21), and especially as a summation of all the separate *torot* (cf. Lev. 7:37–38; 14:54–56). In verses, however, such as Deuteronomy 4:44, "and this is the Torah which Moses set before the children of Israel" and *ibid.* 33:4, "Moses commanded us a Torah, an inheritance of the congregation of Jacob" and the references in the Bible to "the Torah of Moses" (cf. Josh. 1:7; Ezra 3:2; 7:6; 8:1, 8; Mal. 3:22), it refers particularly to the Pentateuch as distinct from the rest of the Bible. In later literature the whole Bible was referred to as *Tanakh*, the initial letters of Torah (Pentateuch), *Nevi'im* (Prophets), and *Ketuvim* (Hagiographia), a meaning it retained in halakhic literature to differentiate between the laws which are of biblical origin (in its Aramaic form, *de-Oraita*, "from the Torah") and those of rabbinic provenance *(de-rabbanan)*. The term is, however, also used loosely to designate the Bible as a whole.

A further extension of the term came with the distinction made between the Written Torah (Torah *she-bi-khetav*) and the Oral Torah (Torah *she-be-al peh*). The use of the plural *Torot* (e.g., Gen. 26:5) was taken to refer to those two branches of divine revelation which were traditionally regarded as having been given to Moses on Mount Sinai (Yoma 28b, and see *Oral Law). Justification was found in the verse of Exodus 34:27, which can be translated literally as "Write thou these words for by the mouth of these words I have made a covenant." The word "write" (*ketav*) was regarded as the authority for the Written Law (hence Torah *she-bi-khetav*, i.e., the Torah included in the word *ketav*) while "by the mouth" (*al pi*) was taken to refer to the Torah *she-be-al peh* (i.e., the Torah referred to in the phrase *al pi*; cf. Git. 60b). Lastly, the word is used for the whole corpus of Jewish traditional law from the Bible to the latest development of the *halakhah*. In modern Hebrew the word is used to designate the system of a thinker or scholar, e.g., "the *torah* of Spinoza."

See also *Judaism.

[Louis Isaac Rabinowitz]

Origin and Preexistence

"Moses received the Torah from Sinai" (Avot 1:1). Yet there is an ancient tradition that the Torah existed in heaven not only before God revealed it to Moses, but even before the world was created. The apocryphal book The Wisdom of Ben Sira identified the Torah with preexistent personified wisdom (1:1–5, 26; 15:1; 24:1ff.; 34:8; cf. Prov. 8:22–31). In rabbinic literature, it was taught that the Torah was one of the six or seven things created prior to the creation of the world (Gen. R. 1:4; Pes. 54a, et al.). Of these preexistent things, it was said that only the Torah and the throne of glory were actually created, while the others were only conceived, and that the Torah preceded the throne of glory (Gen. R. 1:4). According to Eliezer ben Yose the Galilean, for 974 generations before the creation of the world, the Torah lay in God's bosom and joined the ministering angels in song (ARN[1] 31, p. 91; cf. Gen. R. 28:4, et al.). Simeon ben Lakish taught that the Torah preceded the world by 2,000 years (Lev. R. 19:1, et al.) and was written in black fire upon white fire (TJ, Shek. 6:1, 49d, et al.). Akiva called the Torah "the precious instrument by which the world was created" (Avot 3:14). Rav *Hoshaiah, explicitly identifying the Torah with the preexistent wisdom of Proverbs, said that God created the world by looking into the Torah as an architect builds a palace by looking into blueprints. He also took the first word of Genesis not in the sense of "In the beginning," but in that of "By means of the beginning," and he taught that "beginning" (probably in the philosophic sense of the Greek *archē*) designates Torah, since it is written of wisdom (= Torah), "The Lord made me the beginning of His way" (Prov. 8:22; Gen. R. 1:1). It was also taught that God took council with the Torah before He created the world (Tanḥ. B. 2, et al.). The concept of the preexistence of the Torah is perhaps implicit in the philosophy of Philo, who wrote of the preexistence and role in creation of the Word of God (*logos*; e.g., Op. 20, 25, 36; Cher. 127) and identified the Word of God with the Torah (Mig. 130; cf. Op. and II Mos.).

*Saadiah Gaon rejected the literal belief in preexistent things on the grounds that it contradicts the principle of creation ex nihilo. In his view, Proverbs 8:22, the verse cited by Rav Hoshaiah, means no more than that God created the world in a wise manner (*Beliefs and Opinions* 1:3; cf. Saadiah's commentary on Proverbs, ad loc.).

*Judah b. Barzillai of Barcelona raised the problem of place. Where could God have kept a preexistent Torah? While allowing that God could conceivably have provided an antemundane place for a corporeal Torah, he preferred the interpretation that the Torah preexisted only as a thought in the divine mind. Ultimately, however, he expressed the opinion that the Torah's preexistence is a rabbinic metaphor, spoken out of love for the Torah and those who study it, and teaching that the Torah is worthy to have been created before the world (commentary on *Sefer Yeẓirah*, pp. 88–89; cf. Solomon b. Abraham Adret, *Perushei Aggadot*).

Abraham *Ibn Ezra raised the problem of time. He wrote that it is impossible for the Torah to have preceded the world by 2,000 years or even by one moment, since time is an accident of motion, and there was no motion before God created the celestial spheres; rather, he concluded, the teaching about the Torah's preexistence must be a metaphoric riddle (cf. Commentary on the Torah, introd., "the fourth method" (both versions); cf. also Judah Hadassi, *Eshkol ha-Kofer*, 25b–26a; and cf. Abraham Shalom, *Neveh Shalom*, 10:8).

*Judah Halevi explained that the Torah precedes the world in terms of teleology; God created the world for the purpose of revealing the Torah; therefore, since, as the philosophers say, "the first of thought is the end of the work," the Torah is said to have existed before the world (*Kuzari* 3:73).

*Maimonides discussed the origin of the Torah from the standpoint of the epistemology of the unique prophecy of Moses (*Guide of the Perplexed* 2:35; 3:51; et al.; cf. Yad, introd.). The tradition of the preexistence of the Torah was not discussed in the *Guide of the Perplexed*; however, the closely related tradition of the preexistence of the throne of glory was (2:26, 30, et al.). The discussions of Moses' prophecy and of the throne of glory are esoteric and controversial, and each reader will interpret them according to his own views, perhaps inferring Maimonides' position concerning the origin of the Torah.

Within the framework of his Neoplatonic ontology, Isaac ibn Latif suggested that the Torah precedes the world not in time, but in rank. He cited the aggadic statements that the Torah and the throne of glory preceded the world, and that the Torah preceded the throne of glory, and he intimated that the Torah is the upper world (wisdom or intellect) which ontologically precedes the middle world (the celestial spheres, the throne of glory) which, in turn, ontologically precedes the lower world (our world of changing elements; *Sha'ar ha-Shamayim*).

While the tradition of the preexistence of the Torah was being ignored or explained away by most philosophers, it became fundamental in the Kabbalah. Like Ibn Latif, the kabbalists of Spain held that the Torah precedes the world ontologically. Some kabbalists identified the primordial Torah with *Ḥokhmah* (God's wisdom), the second of the ten *Sefirot* in emanation. Others identified the Written Torah with the sixth *Sefirah, Tiferet* (God's beauty), and the Oral Torah with the tenth *Sefirah, Malkhut* (God's kingdom). Emanational precedence signifies creative power; and it was with the Torah that God created the angels and the worlds, and with the Torah He sustains all (Zohar 3, 152a; Num. 9:1).

Ḥasdai *Crescas, who in the course of his revolutionary critique of Aristotelian physics had rejected the dependence of time on motion, was able to take preexistence literally as chronological. He interpreted the proposition about the preexistence of the Torah as a metonymy, referring actually to the purpose of the Torah. Since, according to him, the purpose of the Torah and the purpose of the world are the same, namely, love, and since the purpose or final cause of an object chronologically precedes it, it follows that the purpose of the Torah (i.e., love) chronologically preceded the world. As its final cause, love (= the purpose of the Torah) is a necessary condition of the world; and this is the meaning of the talmudic statement, "Were it not for the Torah [i.e., the purpose of the Torah, or love], heaven and earth would not have come into existence" (Pes. 68b; *Or Adonai* 2:6, 4; cf. Nissim b. Reuben Gerondi, Commentary on Ned. 39b).

Joseph *Albo also interpreted the preexistence of the Torah in terms of final causality, but his position was essentially that of Judah Halevi, and not that of his teacher, Crescas. He reasoned that man exists for the sake of the Torah; everything in the world of generation and corruption exists for the sake of man; therefore, the Torah preceded the world in the Aristotelian sense that the final cause in (the mind of) the agent necessarily precedes the other three causes (*Sefer ha-Ikkarim* 3:12; cf. Jacob b. Solomon ibn Ḥabib, *Ein Ya'akov*, introd.; Joseph Solomon Delmedigo, *Novelot Ḥokhmah*, 1).

The theory, based on the statement of Rav Hoshaiah, that the Torah was the preexistent blueprint of creation, was elaborated by Isaac Arama, Isaac Abrabanel, Moses Alshekh, Judah Loew b. Bezalel, and others.

In modern Jewish philosophical literature, Nachman *Krochmal analyzed the interpretation of the Torah's preexistence by the author of *Sha'ar ha-Shamayim* (Ibn Latif and not, as Krochmal supposed, Ibn Ezra), and his analysis bears implications for his own idealistic concept of the metaphysical and epistemological precedence of the spiritual (*Moreh Nevukhei ha-Zeman*, 17; cf. 12, 16).

Franz Rosenzweig, in his existentalist reaction to the intellectualist interpretation of the Torah by German rabbis, appealed to the *aggadah* of the preexistence of the Torah in an attempt to show the absurdity of trying to base the claim of the Torah merely on a juridical or historical reason: "No doubt the Torah, both Written and Oral, was given to Moses on Sinai, but was it not created before the creation of the world? Written against a background of shining fire in letters of somber flame? And was not the world created for its sake?" ("The Builders," in: N. Glatzer (ed.), *On Jewish Learning* (1955), 78).

Nature and Purpose

In the Bible, the Torah is referred to as the Torah of the Lord (Ex. 13:9, et al.) and of Moses (Josh. 8:31, et al.), and is said to be given as an inheritance to the congregation of Jacob (Deut. 33:4). Its purpose seems to be to make Israel "a kingdom of priests and a holy nation" (Ex. 19:6). It was said that "the commandment is a lamp and the Torah is light" (Prov. 6:23). The Torah was called "perfect," its ordinances "sweeter than honey and the flow of honeycombs" (Ps. 19:8, 11; cf. 119:103; Prov. 16:24). Psalm 119, containing 176 verses, is a song of love for the Torah whose precepts give peace and understanding.

In the apocryphal book The Wisdom of Ben Sira, the Torah is identified with wisdom (see above). In another apocryphal work, the laws of the Torah are said to be drawn up "with a view to truth and the indication of right reason" (Arist. 161). The Septuagint rendered the Hebrew *torah* by the Greek *nomos* ("law"), probably in the sense of a living network of traditions and customs of a people. The designation of the Torah by *nomos*, and by its Latin successor *lex* (whence, "the Law"), has historically given rise to the sad misunderstanding that Torah means legalism.

It was one of the very few real dogmas of rabbinic theology that the Torah is from heaven (Heb. *Torah min ha-shamayim*; Sanh. 10:1, et al.; cf. Ex. 20:22 [19]; Deut. 4:36); i.e., the Torah in its entirety was revealed by God. According to the *aggadah*, Moses ascended into heaven to capture the Torah from the angels (Shab. 89a, et al.). In one of the oldest mishnaic statements, Simeon the Just taught that (the study of the) Torah is one of the three things by which the world is sustained (Avot 1:2). Eleazar ben Shammua said: "Were it not for the Torah, heaven and earth would not continue to exist" (Pes. 68b; Ned. 32a; cf. Crescas' interpretation above). It was calculated that "the whole world in its entirety is only 1/3,200 of the Torah" (Er. 21a; cf. TJ, Pe'ah 1:1, 15d). God Himself was said to study the Torah daily (Av. Zar. 3b, et al.).

The Torah was often compared to fire, water, wine, oil, milk, honey, drugs, manna, the tree of life, and many other things; it was considered the source of freedom, goodness, and life (e.g., Avot 6:2, 3, 7); it was identified both with wisdom and with love (e.g., Mid. Ps. to 1:18). Hillel summarized the entire Torah in one sentence: "What is hateful to you, do not to your fellow" (Shab. 31a). Akiva said: "The fundamental principle of the Torah is the commandment, 'Love thy neighbor as thyself'" (Lev. 19:18). His disciple Simeon ben Azzai said that its fundamental principle is the verse (Gen. 5:1) which teaches that all human beings are descended from the same man, and created by God in His image (Sifra, Kedoshim 4:12; TJ, Ned. 9:3, 41c; Gen. R. 24:7).

Often the Torah was personified. Not only did God take council with the Torah before He created the world (see above), but according to one interpretation, the plural in "Let us make man" (Gen. 1:26) refers to God and the Torah (Tanḥ. Pekudei, 3). The Torah appears as the daughter of God and the bride of Israel (PR 20; 95a, et al.). On occasion, the Torah is obliged to plead the case of Israel before God (e.g., Ex. R. 29:4).

The message of the Torah is for all mankind. Before giving the Torah to Israel, God offered it to the other nations, but they refused it; and when He did give the Torah to Israel, He revealed it in the extraterritorial desert and simultaneously in all the 70 languages, so that men of all nations would have a right to it (Mekh., Yitro, 5; Sif. Deut. 343; Shab. 88b; Ex. R. 5:9; 27:9; cf. Av. Zar. 3a: "a pagan who studies the Torah is like a high priest"). Alongside this universalism, the rabbis taught the inseparability of Israel and the Torah. One rabbi held that the concept of Israel existed in God's mind even before He created the Torah (Gen. R. 1:4). Yet, were it not for its accepting the Torah, Israel would not be "chosen," nor would it be different from all the idolatrous nations (Num. 14:10; Ex. R. 47:3, et al.).

In the Hellenistic literature contemporaneous with the early rabbinic teachings, Philo considered the Torah the ideal law of the philosophers, and Moses the perfect lawgiver and prophet and the philosopher-ruler of Plato's *Republic* (II Mos. 2). His concept of the relationship of the Torah to nature and man was Stoic: "The world is in harmony with the Torah and the Torah with the world, and the man who observes the Torah is constituted thereby a loyal citizen of the world" (Op. 3). He wrote that the laws of the Torah are "stamped with the seals of nature," and are "the most perfect picture of the cosmic polity" (II Mos. 14, 51). Josephus, in his *Against Apion*, discoursed on the moral and universalistic nature of the Torah, emphasizing that it promotes piety, friendship, humanity toward the world at large, justice, charity, and endurance under persecution. Both Philo and Josephus wrote that principles of the Torah, e.g., the Sabbath, have been imitated by all nations.

Saadiah Gaon expounded a rationalist theory according to which the ethical and religious-intellectual beliefs imparted by the Torah are all attainable by human reason. He held that the Torah is divisible into

(1) commandments which, in addition to being revealed, are demanded by reason (e.g., prohibitions of murder, fornication, theft, lying); and

(2) commandments whose authority is revelation alone (e.g., Sabbath and dietary laws), but which generally are understandable in terms of some personal or social benefit attained by their performance. Revelation of the Torah was needed because while reason makes general demands, it does not dictate particular laws; and while the matters of religious belief revealed in the Torah are attainable by philosophy, they are only attained by it after some time or, in the case of many, not at all. He taught that the purpose of the Torah is the bestowal of eternal bliss (*Beliefs and Opinions*, introd. 6, ch. 3). He held that Israel is a nation only by virtue of the Torah (see below).

In the period between Saadiah and Maimonides, most Jewish writers who speculated on the nature of the Torah continued in the rationalist tradition established by Saadiah. These included Baḥya ibn Paquda, Joseph ibn Ẓaddik, Abraham Ibn Ezra, and Abraham ibn Daud. Judah Halevi, however, opposed the rationalist interpretation. He allowed that the Torah contains rational and political laws, but considered them preliminary to the specifically divine laws and teachings which cannot be comprehended by reason, e.g., the laws of the Sabbath which teach the omnipotence of God and the creation of the world (*Kuzari* 2:48, 50). The Torah makes it possible to approach God by awe, love, and joy (2:50). It is the essence of wisdom, and the outcome of the will of God to reveal His kingdom on earth as it is in heaven (3:17). While Judah Halevi held that Israel was created to fulfill the Torah, he wrote that there would be no Torah were there no Israel (2:56; 3:73).

Maimonides emphasized that the Torah is the product of the unique prophecy of Moses. He maintained that the Torah has two purposes; first, the welfare of the body and, ultimately, the welfare of the soul (intellect). The first purpose, which is a prerequisite of the ultimate purpose, is political, and "consists in the governance of the city and the well-being of the state of all its people according to their capacity." The ultimate purpose consists in the true perfection of man, his acquisition of immortality through intellection of the highest things. The Torah is similar to other laws in its concern with the welfare of the body; but its divine nature is reflected in its concern for the welfare of the soul (*Guide of the Perplexed*, 3:27). Maimonides saw the Torah as a rationalizing force, warring against superstition, imagination, appetite, and idolatry. He cited the rabbinic dictum, "Everyone who disbelieves in idolatry professes the Torah in its entirety" (Sif. Num. 110; Guide 3:29; Yad, Ovedei Kokhavim 2:4), and taught that the foundation of the Torah and the pivot around which it turns consists in the effacement of idolatry. He held that the Torah must be interpreted in the light of reason.

Of the Jewish philosophers who flourished in the 13th and early 14th centuries, most endorsed Maimonides' position that the Torah has as its purpose both political and spiritual welfare. Some, like Samuel ibn Tibbon and Isaac *Albalag, argued that its purpose consists only or chiefly in political welfare. Others emphasized its spiritual purpose, like Levi b. Gershom, who taught that the purpose of the Torah is to guide man – the masses as well as the intellectual elite – toward human perfection, that is, the acquisition of true knowledge and, thereby, an immortal intellect.

While Maimonides and the Maimonideans generally restricted their analyses of the nature of the Torah to questions of its educational, moral, or political value, the Spanish kabbalists engaged in bold metaphysical speculation concerning its essence. The kabbalists taught that the Torah is a living organism. Some said the entire Torah consists of the names of God set in succession (cf. Naḥmanides, *Perushei ha-Torah*, Preface) or interwoven into a fabric (cf. Joseph Gikatilla, *Sha'arei Orah*). Others said that the Torah is itself the name of God. The Torah was identified with various *Sefirot* in the divine body (see above). Ultimately, it was said that the Torah is God (Menahem Recanati, *Ta'amei ha-Mitzvot*, 3a; Zohar 2, 60a [Ex. 15:22]). This identification of the Torah and God was understood to refer to the Torah in its true primordial essence, and not to its manifestation in the world of creation.

The first Jewish philosopher to construct a metaphysics in which the Torah plays an integral role was Ḥasdai Crescas, who, notwithstanding his distinguished work in natural science, was more sympathetic to the Kabbalah than to Aristotle. He taught that the purpose of the Torah is to effect the purpose of the universe. By guiding man toward corporeal happiness, moral and intellectual excellence, and felicity of soul, the Torah leads him to the love of neighbor and, finally, the eternal love of God [*devekut*], which is the purpose of all creation (*Or Adonai*, 2:6). Like Judah Halevi, he took an ultimately anti-intellectualist position, and maintained, in opposition to the Maimonideans, that the very definition of the Torah as the communication of God to man implies beliefs about the nature of God and His relation to man which cannot, and need not, be proved by philosophy.

Joseph Albo, developing some Maimonidean ideas, taught that the Torah, as divine law, is superior to natural law and conventional-positive law in that it not only promotes political security and good behavior, but also guides man toward eternal spiritual happiness (*Sefer ha-Ikkarim*, 1:7).

In the writings of Isaac Arama, Isaac Abrabanel, Moses Alshekh, Judah Loew b. Beẓalel, and other late medievals, the conflicting approaches to the Torah of Maimonideanism and the Kabbalah converged to give expression to the theme, already adumbrated in Philo, that the Torah exists in the mind of God as the plan and order of the universe (Arama, *Akedat Yiẓḥak*, 1; Abrabanel, *Mifalot Elohim*, 1:2; Alshekh, *Torat Moshe* to Genesis 1:1; Judah Loew, *Netivot Olam*, 1:1; *Tiferet Yisrael*, 25; cf. above). In Italy, *Judah b. Jehiel (Messer Leon), influenced by the Renaissance emphasis on the art of rhetoric, composed the *Nofet Ẓufim*, in which he analyzed the language of the Bible and, in effect, presented the first aesthetic interpretation of the Torah (cf. Judah Abrabanel, *Dialoghi di Amore*).

Influenced by Maimonides, Baruch *Spinoza took the position taken by some early Maimonideans that the Torah is an exclusively political law. However, he broke radically with those Maimonideans and with all rabbinic tradition by denying its divine nature, by making it an object of historical-critical investigation, and by maintaining that it was not written by Moses alone but by various authors living at different times. Moreover, he considered the Torah primitive, unscientific, and particularistic, and thus subversive to progress, reason, and universal morality. By portraying the Torah as a product of the Jewish people, he reversed the traditional opinion (but cf. Judah Halevi) according to which the Jewish people are a product of the Torah.

Like Spinoza, Moses *Mendelssohn considered the Torah a political law, but he affirmed its divine nature. Taking a position similar to Saadiah's, he explained that the Torah does not intend to reveal new ideas about deism and morality, but rather, through its laws and institutions, to arouse men to be mindful of the true ideas attainable by all men through reason. By identifying the beliefs of the Torah with the truths of reason, Mendelssohn affirmed both its scientific respectability and its universalistic nature. By defining the Torah as a political law given to Israel by God, he preserved the traditional view that Israel is a product of the Torah, and not, as Spinoza claimed, vice versa.

With the rise of the science of Judaism (*Wissenschaft des Judentums*) in the 19th century, and the advance of the historical-critical approach to the Torah, many Jewish intellectuals, including ideologists of Reform like Abraham *Geiger, followed Spinoza in seeing the Torah, at least in part, as a product of the primitive history of the Jewish nation. Nachman Krochmal, in his rationalist-idealist philosophy, attempted to synthesize the historical-critical thesis that the Torah is a product of Jewish history, with the traditional thesis that the entire Torah is divinely revealed. He maintained that, from the days of Abraham and Isaac, the Hebrew nation has contained the Absolute Spiritual, and this Absolute Spiritual was the source of the laws given to Moses on Mt. Sinai, whose purpose is to perfect the individual and the group, and to prevent the nation's extinction. The Oral Torah, which is, in effect, the history of the evolution of the Jewish spirit, is inseparable from the Written Torah, and is its clarification and conceptual refinement; which is to say, the true science of the Torah, which is the vocation of the Jewish spirit, is the conceptualization of the Absolute Spiritual (*Moreh Nevukhei ha-Zeman*, esp. 6–8, 13).

The increasing intellectualization of the Torah was opposed by Samuel David *Luzzatto and Salomon Ludwig *Steinheim, two men who had little in common but their fideism. They contended – as Crescas had against the Maimonideans – that the belief that God revealed the Torah is the starting point of Judaism, and that this belief, with its momentous implications concerning the nature of God and His relation to man, cannot be attained by philosophy. Luzzatto held that the foundation of the whole Torah is compassion. Steinheim, profoundly opposing Mendelssohn, held that the Torah comes to reveal truths about God and His work.

While Spinoza and Mendelssohn had emphasized the political nature of the Torah, many rationalists of the late 19th and early 20th centuries emphasized its moral nature. Moritz *Lazarus identified the Torah with the moral law, and interpreted the rabbinical statement, "Were it not for the Torah, heaven and earth would not continue to exist" (see above), as corresponding to the Kantian teaching that it is the moral law that gives value to existence. Hermann *Cohen condemned Spinoza as a willful falsifier and a traitor to the Jewish people for his claim that the Torah is subversive to universalistic morality. He held that the Torah, with its monotheistic ethics, far from being subversive to universalism, prepares a Jew to participate fully and excellently in general culture (in this connection, he opposed Zionism and developed his controversial theory of "Germanism and Judaism"). He maintained that in its promulgation of commandments affecting all realms of human action, the Torah moves toward overcoming the distinction between holy and profane through teaching all men to become holy by always performing holy actions, i.e., by always acting in accordance with the moral law.

In their German translation of the Bible, Martin *Buber and Franz Rosenzweig translated *torah* as *Weisung* or *Unterweisung* ("Instruction") and not as *Gesetz* ("Law"). In general, they agreed on the purpose of the Torah: to convert the universe and God from It to Thou. Yet they differed on several points concerning its nature. Buber saw the Torah as the past dialogue between Israel and God, and the present dialogue between the individual reader, the I, and God, the Thou. He concluded that while one must open himself to the entire teaching of the Torah, he need only accept a particular law of the Torah if he feels that it is being spoken now to him. Rosenzweig objected to this personalist and antinomian position of Buber's. Taking an existentialist position, he maintained that the laws of the Torah are commandments to do, and as such become comprehensible only in the experience of doing, and, therefore, a Jew must not, as Buber did, reject a law of the Torah that "does not speak to me," but must always open himself to the new experience which may make it comprehensible. Like Cohen – and also like the Ḥasidim – he marveled that the law of the Torah is universal in range. He contended that it erases the barrier between this world and the world to come by encompassing, vitalizing, and thereby redeeming everything in this world.

The secular Zionism of the late 19th and early 20th centuries gave religious thinkers new cause to define the relationship between the Torah and the Jewish nation. Some defined the Torah in terms of the nation. Thus, Mordecai *Kaplan translated *Aḥad Ha-Am's sociological theory of the evolution of Jewish civilization into a religious, though naturalistic, theory of the Torah as the "religious civilization of the Jews." Others, like Buber and Rosenzweig, considering secular nationalism dangerous, tried to "interdefine" the Torah and the nation. Whereas Buber saw the Torah as the product of a dialogue between the nation and God, he held that the spirit of the nation was transfigured by that dialogue. Rosenzweig, whose position here resembles Judah Halevi's, stated both that the nation's chosenness is prior to the Torah, and that the acceptance of the Torah is an experiential precondition of its chosenness. Other thinkers defined the nation in terms of the Torah. Thus, Abraham Isaac *Kook, whose thought was influenced by the Kabbalah, taught that the purpose of the Torah is to reveal the living light of the universe, the suprarational spiritual, to Israel and, through Israel, to all mankind. While the Written Torah, which reveals the light in the highest channel of our soul, is the product of God alone, the Oral Torah, which is inseparable from the Written Torah, and which reveals the light in a second channel of our soul, proximate to the life of deeds, derives its personality from the spirit of the nation. The Oral Torah can live in its fullness only when Israel lives in its fullness – in peace and independence in the Land of Israel. Thus, according to Kook, modern Zionism, whatever the intent of its secular ideologists, has universal religious significance, for it is acting in service of the Torah (see esp. *Orot ha-Torah*).

In the State of Israel, most writers and educators have maintained the secularist position of the early Zionists, namely, that the Torah was not revealed by God, in the traditional sense, but is the product of the national life of ancient Israel. Those who have discussed the Torah and its relation to the state from a religious point of view have mostly followed Kook or Buber and Rosenzweig. However, a radically rationalist approach to the nature of the Torah has been taught by Yeshayahu Leibowitz who, in the Maimonidean tradition, emphasizes that the Torah is a law for the worship of God and for the consequent obliteration of the worship of men and things; in this connection, he condemns the subordination of the Torah to nationalism or to religious sentimentalism or to any ideology or institution. Outside the State of Israel, a similarly iconoclastic position has been taken by the French phenomenologist Emmanuel *Levinas, who has gone further and written that the love for the Torah should take precedence even over the love for God Himself, for only through the Torah – that knowledge of the Other which is the condition of all ethics – can man relate to a personal God against Whom he can rebel and for Whom he can die.

ETERNITY (OR NONABROGABILITY). In the Bible there is no text unanimously understood to affirm explicitly the eternity or nonabrogability of the Torah; however, many laws of the Torah are accompanied by phrases such as, "an everlasting injunction through your generations" (Lev. 3:17, et al.).

The doctrine that the Torah is eternal appears several times in the pre-tannaitic apocryphal literature; e.g., Ben Sira 24:9 ("the memorial of me shall never cease") and Jubilees 33:16 ("an everlasting law for everlasting generations").

Whereas the rabbis understood the preexistence of the Torah in terms of its prerevelation existence in heaven, they understood the eternity or nonabrogability of the Torah in terms of its postrevelation existence, not in heaven; i.e., the whole Torah was given to Moses and no part of it remained in heaven (Deut. 8:6, et al.). When Eliezer ben Hyrcanus and Joshua ben Hananiah were debating a point of Torah and a voice from heaven dramatically announced that Eliezer's position was correct, Joshua refused to recognize its testimony, for the Torah "is not in heaven" (Deut. 30:12), and must be interpreted by men, unaided by the supernatural (BM 59b). It was a principle that "a prophet is henceforth not permitted to innovate a thing" (Sifra, Be-Ḥukkotai 13:7; Tem. 16a; but he was permitted to suspend a law temporarily (Sif. Deut. 175)). The rabbis taught that the Torah would continue to exist in the world to come (e.g., Eccles. R. 2:1), although some of them were of the opinion that innovations would be made in the messianic era (e.g., Gen. R. 98:9; Lev. R. 9:7).

Philo saw the eternity of the Torah as a metaphysical principle, following from the Torah's accord with nature. He believed that the laws and enactments of the Torah "will remain for all future ages as though immortal, so long as the sun and the moon and the whole heaven and universe exist" (II Mos. 14; cf. Jer. 31:32–35). The belief in the eternity of the Torah appears also in the later apocryphal works (e.g., I Bar. 4:1; Ps. of Sol. 10:5) and in Josephus (Apion, 2:277).

With the rise to political power of Christianity and Islam, two religions which sought to convert Jews and which argued that particular injunctions of the Torah had been abrogated, the question of the eternity or "nonabrogability" of the Torah became urgent.

Saadiah Gaon stated that the children of Israel have a clear tradition from the prophets that the laws of the Torah are not subject to abrogation. Presenting scriptural corroboration for this tradition, he appealed to phrases appended to certain commandments, e.g., "throughout their generations, for a perpetual covenant" (Ex. 31:16). According to one novel argument of his, the Jewish nation is a nation only by virtue of its laws, namely, the Torah; God has stated that the Jewish nation will endure as long as the heaven and earth (Jer. 31:35–36); therefore, the Torah will last as long as heaven and earth (cf. Philo, above). He interpreted the verses, "Remember ye the Torah of Moses… Behold, I will send you Elijah…" (Mal. 3:22–23), as teaching that the Torah will hold valid until the prophet Elijah returns to herald the resurrection (*Beliefs and Opinions* 3:7).

Maimonides listed the belief in the eternity of the Torah as the ninth of his 13 principles of Judaism, and connected it with the belief that no prophet will surpass Moses, the only man to give people laws through prophecy. He contended that the eternity of the Torah is stated clearly in the Bible, particularly in Deuteronomy 13:1 ("thou shalt not add thereto, nor diminish from it") and Deuteronomy 29:28 ("the things that are revealed belong unto us and to our children for ever, that we may do all the words of this Torah"). He also cited the rabbinic principle: "A prophet is henceforth not permitted to innovate a thing" (see above). He offered the following explanation of the Torah's eternity, based on its perfection and on the theory of the mean: "The Torah of the Lord is perfect" (Ps. 19:8) in that its statutes are just, i.e., that they are equibalanced between the burdensome and the indulgent; and "when a thing is perfect as it is possible to be within its species, it is impossible that within that species there should be found another thing that does not fall short of the perfection either because of excess or deficiency." Also, he mentioned the argument that the prophesied eternity of the name of Israel ("For as the new heavens and the new earth, which I will make, shall remain before Me… so shall your seed and your name"; Isa. 66:22) entails the eternity of the Torah (cf. Saadiah above). He held that there will be no change in the Torah after the coming of the Messiah (commentary on Mishnah, Sanh. 10; Yad, Yesodei ha-Torah 9; cf. *Sefer ha-Mitzvot; Guide of the Perplexed* 2:29, 39; Abraham ibn Daud, *Emunah Ramah*).

Ḥasdai Crescas listed the eternity of the Torah as a nonfundamental true belief, i.e., required by Judaism, but not essential to the concept of Torah. Unlike Saadiah and Maimonides, he did not try to found this belief directly on a biblical text (but cf. his *Bittul Ikkarei ha-Noẓerim*, 9), but solely on the rabbinic dictum: "A prophet is henceforth not permitted to innovate a thing" (see above). To elucidate the belief from the point of view of speculation, he presented an argument from the perfection of the Torah, which differed markedly from its Maimonidean precursor. The argument proceeds as follows: The Torah is perfect, for it perfectly guides men toward the ultimate human happiness, love. If God were to abrogate the Torah, He would surely replace it, for it is impossible that He would forsake His purpose to maximize love. Since the Torah is perfect, it could be replaced only by an equal or an inferior; but if inferior, God would not be achieving His purpose of maximizing love; and if equal, He would be acting futilely. Therefore, He will not abrogate the Torah. Against the argument that replacement of the Torah by an equal but different law would make sense if there were an appreciable change – for better or worse – in the people who received it, he retorted characteristically that the Torah is the excellent guide for all, including both the intellectuals and the backward (*Or Adonai*, 3, pt. 1, 5:1–2).

Joseph Albo criticized Maimonides for listing the belief in the eternity of the Torah as an independent fundamental belief of Judaism. In a long discussion, which in many places constitutes an elaboration of arguments found in Crescas, he contended that nonabrogation is not a fundamental principle of the Torah, and that moreover, no text can be found in the Bible to establish it. Ironically, his ultimate position turned out to be closer to Maimonides' than to Crescas'; for he concluded that the belief in the nonabrogation of the Torah is a branch of the doctrine that no prophet will surpass the excellence of Moses (*Sefer ha-Ikkarim*, 3:13–23).

After Albo, the question of the eternity of the Torah became routine in Jewish philosophical literature (e.g., Abraham Shalom, *Neveh Shalom* 10:3–4; Isaac Abrabanel, *Rosh Amanah*, 13). However, in the Kabbalah it was never routine. In the 13th-century *Sefer ha-Temunah* a doctrine of cosmic cycles (or *shemittot*; cf. Deut. 15) was expounded, according to which creation is renewed every 7,000 years, at which times the letters of the Torah reassemble, and the Torah enters the new cycle bearing different words and meanings. Thus, while eternal in its unrevealed state, the Torah, in its manifestation in creation, is destined to be abrogated. This doctrine became popular in later kabbalistic and ḥasidic literature, and was exploited by the heretic Shabbetai Ẓevi and his followers, who claimed that a new cycle had begun, and in consequence he was able to teach that "the abrogation of the Torah is its fulfillment!"

Like his contemporary Shabbetai Ẓevi, but for much different reasons (see above), Spinoza committed the heresy of advocating the abrogation of the Torah. Subsequently, in the 19th century, Reform ideologists held that the abrogation of parts of the traditional Torah was not a heresy at all but was necessary for the progress of the Jewish religion. Similarly, many intellectuals and nationalists held that it was necessary for the progress of the Jewish nation. Aḥad Ha-Am called for the Torah in the Heart to replace the Torah of Moses and of the rabbis, which having been written down, had, in his opinion, become rigid and ossified in the process of time.

Jewish philosophers of modern times have not concentrated on the question of the eternity or nonabrogability of the Torah. Nevertheless, it is not entirely untenable that the main distinction between Orthodox Judaism and non-Orthodox Judaism is that the latter rejects the literal interpretation of the ninth principle of Maimonides' Creed that there will be no change in the Torah.

[Warren Harvey]

BIBLIOGRAPHY: S. Schechter, *Aspects of Rabbinic Theology* (1960^2); C.G. Montefiore and H. Loewe, *A Rabbinic Anthology* (1960^2), index; G.G. Scholem, *On the Kabbalah and its Symbolism* (1965), index; S.Y. Agnon, *Attem Re'item* (1959); A.J. Heschel, *Torah min ha-Shamayim ba-Aspaklaryah shel ha-Dorot*, 2 (1965); F.E. Urbach, *Ḥazal Pirkei Emunot ve-De'ot* (1969), index.

TORAH, READING OF.

History

The practice of reading the Pentateuch (Torah) in public is undoubtedly ancient. The sources, however, do not permit the definite tracing of the historical development of the custom. The command to assemble the people at the end of every seven years to read the law "in their hearing" (Deut. 31:10–13) is the earliest reference to a public Torah reading. A second mention is made in the time of *Ezra when he read the Torah to all the people, both men and women, from early morning until midday, on the first day of the seventh month (Neh. 8:1–8). These two occasions are isolated instances, and do not help to establish when the custom of regular Torah readings arose.

Moses' command that the Israelites should read the Torah on the Sabbath, on festivals, and on new moons, and Ezra's that it should be read on Mondays, on Thursdays, and on Sabbath afternoons (TJ, Meg. 4:1, 75a; BK 82a) are not historical statements in themselves; they point, however, to an early date for the introduction of regular readings. It may be assumed that the custom dates from about the first half of the third century B.C.E., since the Septuagint was apparently compiled for the purpose of public reading in the synagogue. Josephus (Apion, 2:175) and Philo (II Som. 127) refer to public Torah readings as an ancient practice. This contention is supported by evidence in the New Testament: "For Moses of old time hath in every city them that preach him, being read in the synagogue every Sabbath day" (Acts 15:21). Elbogen is of the opinion that originally the Torah was read only on the festivals and on certain Sabbath days before the festivals; the reading was to instruct the people as to the significance of these days. If this is correct, the original Torah reading was didactic rather than liturgical.

The Mishnah shows that by the end of the second century C.E. there were regular Torah readings on Mondays, on Thursdays, and on Sabbaths; special readings for the Sabbaths during the period from before the month of Adar to before Passover; and special readings for the festivals, including those of Ḥanukkah and Purim, and for fast days (Meg. 3, 4–6). The length of the reading, however, seems not to have been fixed by that time. R. *Meir states, for instance, that the practice was to read a short portion on Sabbath mornings, the portion that followed on Sabbath afternoon, and further portions on Monday and Thursday, beginning on the following Sabbath morning from the end of the Thursday portion. According to R. Judah, the procedure was to begin the reading each Sabbath morning service where it had ended on the morning of the previous Sabbath (Meg. 31b).

The passage in the Babylonian Talmud (Meg. 29b) is the earliest reference to a fixed cycle of consecutive readings. It states that "in the West" (Palestine), they completed the reading of the Torah in three years. The old division of the Pentateuch into 153, 155, or 167 *sedarim* ("divisions") is based on this triennial cycle. Buechler, with great ingenuity, attempted to reconstruct the weekly portions of the *triennial cycle, assuming the cycle to have begun on the first day of Nisan. On the basis of his reconstruction, he proceeds to explain various traditions regarding events of the past (e.g., that Moses died on the seventh day of Adar and that Sarah was "remembered" on the first day of Tishri). Buechler contends that since the portions describing these events were read once every three years at these times, the tradition grew that the events themselves had taken place then.

In Babylon and other communities outside Palestine, an annual cycle was followed according to which the Pentateuch was divided into 54 *sedarim* (sing. *sidrah*, i.e., *parashah*). This became the universal Jewish practice, except for certain isolated instances. In Palestine, the triennial cycle was also superseded by the annual, possibly under the influence of Babylonian immigrants. However, the eminent traveler *Benjamin of Tudela writes about the community of Cairo (c. 1170): "Two large synagogues are there, one belonging to the land of Israel and one belonging to the men of the land of Babylon… Their usage with regard to the portions and sections of the law is not alike; for the men of Babylon are accustomed to read a portion every week, as is done in Spain, and is our custom, and to finish the law each year; while the men of Palestine do not do so but divide each portion into three sections and finish the law at the end of three years. The two communities, however, have an established custom to unite and pray together on the day of the Rejoicing of the Law, and on the day of the Giving of the Law" (M.N. Adler (ed.), *The Itinerary of Benjamin of Tudela* (1907), 70). Similarly, in the 12th century Maimonides (Yad, Tefillah 13:1) writes that the universal custom was to follow the annual cycle; he states, however, that the triennial cycle was nevertheless followed in some places.

The Mishnah rules that three persons read the Torah on Sabbath afternoons, on Mondays, and on Thursdays; four on *ḥol ha-mo'ed* of the festivals and on the new moon; five on a festival; six on the Day of Atonement; and seven on a Sabbath morning (Meg. 4:1–2). The privilege of reading the first portion of the day was given to a priest, the second to a levite, and the others to Israelites (Git. 5:8). Originally, each person read his own portion. In time, with the deterioration of Torah learning among the lay people, a special official of the synagogue read the portion while the person called to the reading recited the benedictions. At an early period, it was customary to translate the Hebrew text into the vernacular at the time of the reading (e.g., in Palestine and Babylon the translation was into Aramaic). The **targum* ("translation") was done by a special synagogue official, called the *meturgeman* (Meg. 4:4–10). Eventually, the practice of translating into the vernacular was discontinued.

Table of Scriptural Readings on Sabbaths

PENTATEUCH		PROPHETS
GENESIS		
Bereshit	1:1–6:8	Isa. 42:5–43:11 (42:5–21)[1]
No'aḥ	6:9–11:32	Isa. 54:1–55:5 (54:1–10)
Lekh Lekha	12:1–17:27	Isa. 40:27–41:16
Va-Yera	18:1–22:24	II Kings 4:1–37 (4:1–23)
Ḥayyei Sarah	23:1–25:18	I Kings 1:1–31
Toledot	25:19–28:9	Mal. 1:1–2:7
Va-Yeẓe	28:10–32:3	Hos. 12:13–14:10 (11:7–12:12)
Va-Yishlaḥ	32:4–36:43	Hos. 11:7–12:12 (Obad. 1:1–21)
Va-Yeshev	37:1–40:23	Amos 2:6–3:8
Mi-Keẓ	41:1–44:17	I Kings 3:15–4:1
Va-Yiggash	44:18–47:27	Ezek. 37:15–28
Va-Yeḥi	47:28–50:26	I Kings 2:1–12
EXODUS		
Shemot	1:1–6:1	Isa. 27:6–28:13; 29:22, 23 (Jer. 1:1–2:3)
Va-Era	6:2–9:35	Ezek. 28:25–29:21
Bo	10:1–13:16	Jer. 46:13–28
Be-Shallaḥ	13:17–17:16	Judg. 4:4–5:31 (5:1–31)
Yitro	18:1–20:23	Isa. 6:1–7:6 ; 9:5 (6:1–13)
Mishpatim	21:1–24:18	Jer. 34:8–22; 33:25, 26
[2] { Terumah	25:1–27:19	I Kings 5:26–6:13
Teẓavveh	27:20–30:10	Ezek. 43:10–27
Ki Tissa	30:11–34:35	I Kings 18:1–39 (18:20–39)
{ Va-Yakhel	35:1–38:20	I Kings 7:40–50 (7:13–26)
Pekudei	38:21–40:38	I Kings 7:51–8:21 (7:40–50)
LEVITICUS		
Va-Yikra	1:1–5:26	Isa. 43:21–44:23
Ẓav	6:1–8:36	Jer. 7:21–8:3; 9:22, 23
Shemini	9:1–11:47	II Sam. 6:1–7:17 (6:1–19)
[2] { Tazri'a	12:1–13:59	II Kings 4:42–5:19
Meẓora	14:1–15:33	II Kings 7:3–20
{ Aḥarei Mot	16:1–18:30	Ezek. 22:1–19 (22:1–16)
Kedoshim	19:1–20:27	Amos 9:7–15 (Ezek. 20:2–20)
Emor	21:1–24:23	Ezek. 44:15–31
{ Be-Har	25:1–26:2	Jer. 32:6–27
Be-Ḥukkotai	26:3–27:34	Jer. 16:19–17:14
NUMBERS		
Be-Midbar	1:1–4:20	Hos. 2:1–22
Naso	4:21–7:89	Judg. 13:2–25
Be-Ha'alotkha	8:1–12:16	Zech. 2:14–4:7
Shelaḥ Lekha	13:1–15:41	Josh. 2:1–24
Koraḥ	16:1–18:32	I Sam. 11:14–12:22
Ḥukkat	19:1–22:1	Judg. 11:1–33
Balak	22:2–25:9	Micah 5:6–6:8
Pinḥas	25:10–30:1	I Kings 18:46–19:21
{ Mattot	30:2–32:42	Jer. 1:1–2:3
Masei	33:1–36:13	Jer. 2:4–28; 3:4 (2:4–28; 4:1, 2)
DEUTERONOMY		
Devarim	1:1–3:22	Isa. 1:1–27
Va-Ethannan	3:23–7:11	Isa. 40:1–26
Ekev	7:12–11:25	Isa. 49:14–51:3
Re'eh	11:26–16:17	Isa. 54:11–55:5
Shofetim	16:18–21:9	Isa. 51:12–52:12
Ki Teẓe	21:10–25:19	Isa. 54:1–10
Ki Tavo	26:1–29:8	Isa. 60:1–22
{ Niẓẓavim	29:9–30:20	Isa. 61:10–63:9
Va-Yelekh	31:1–30	Isa. 55:6–56:8
Ha'azinu	32:1–52	II Sam. 22:1–51
Ve-Zot ha-Berakhah[3]	33:1–34:12	Josh. 1:1–18 (1:1–9)

[1] Parentheses indicate Sephardi ritual. [2] Brackets indicate portions that are sometimes combined. [3] This portion is not read on Sabbath but on Simḥat Torah.

Table of Holiday Scriptural Readings for the Diaspora and for Ereẓ Israel

	PENTATEUCH	PROPHETS
Rosh Ha-Shanah		
1st Day	Gen. 21:1–34; Num. 29:1–6	I Sam. 1:1–2:10
2nd Day	Gen. 22:1–24; Num. 29–1–6	Jer. 31:2–20
Shabbat Shuvah	Weekly portion	Hos. 14:2–10; Micah 7:18–20 or Hos. 14:2–10; Joel 2:15–17 (Hos. 14:2–10; Micah 7:18–20[1])
Day of Atonement		
Morning	Lev. 16:1–34; num. 29:7–11	Isa. 57:14–58:14
Afternoon	Lev. 18:1–30	The Book of Jonah; Micah 7:18–20
Sukkot		
1st Day	Lev. 22:26–23:44; Num. 29:12–16	Zech. 14:1–21
2nd Day	Lev. 22:26–23:44; Num. 29:12–16 [Num. 29:17–19][2,4]	I Kings 8:2–21 [none]
3rd Day	Num. 29:17–22 [29:20–22][2,4]	
4th Day	Num. 29:20–28 [29:23–25][2,4]	
5th Day	Num. 29:23–31 [29:26–28][2,4]	
6th Day	Num. 29:26–34 [29:29–31][2,4]	
7th Day	Num. 29:26–34 [29:32–34][2,4]	
Shabbat during the Intermediate Days	Ex. 33:12–34:26; Daily portion from Num. 29	Ezek. 38:18–39:16
Shemini Aẓeret 8th Day	Deut. 14:22–16:17; Num. 29:35–30:1 [as for Simḥat Torah]	I Kings 8:54–66 [as for Simḥat Torah]
Simḥat Torah 9th day	Deut. 33:1–34:12; Gen. 1:1–2:3; Num. 29:35–30:1 [none]	Josh. 1:1–18 (1:1–9) [none]
Ḥanukkah		
1st Day	Num. 7:1–17	
2nd Day	Num. 7:18–29 [7:18–23][5]	
3rd Day	Num. 7:24–35 [7:24–29][5]	
4th Day	Num. 7:30–41 [7:30–35][5]	
5th Day	Num. 7:36–47 [7:36–41][5]	
6th Day	Num. 7:42–53 [7:42–47][5]	
7th Day	Num. 7:48–59 [7:48–53][5]	
8th Day	Num. 7:54–8:4	
First Shabbat Ḥanukkah	Weekly Ḥanukkah portions as for Ereẓ Israel	Zech. 2:14–4:4:7
Second Shabbat Ḥanukkah	Weekly Ḥanukkah portions as for Ereẓ Israel	I Kings 7:40–50
Rosh Ḥodesh during Ḥanukkah	Weekly Ḥanukkah portions as for Ereẓ Israel and Num. 28:1–15	
Rosh Ḥodesh and Shabbat Ḥanukkah	Weekly Rosh Ḥodesh, and Ḥanukkah portions as for Ereẓ Israel	Isa. 66:1–24
Shekalim	Weekly portion; Ex. 30:11–16	II Kings 12:1–17
Zakhor	Weekly portion; Deut. 25:17–19	I Sam. 15:2–34 (15:1–34)
Purim	Ex. 17:8–16	
Parah	Weekly portion; Num. 19:1–22	Ezek. 36:16–38 (36:16–36)
Ha-Ḥodesh	Weekly portion; Ex. 12:1–20	Ezek. 45:16–46:18 (45:18–46:5)
Shabbat Ha-Gadol	Weekly portion	Mal. 3:4–24
Passover		
1st Day	Ex. 12:21–51; Num. 28:19–25	Josh. 5:2–6:1
2nd Day	Lev. 22:26–23:44; Num. 28–19:25	II Kings 23:1–9; 21–25 [none]
3rd Day	Ex. 13:1–16; Num. 28:19–25	
4th Day	Ex. 22:24–23:19; Num. 28:19–25	
5th Day	Ex. 33:12–34:26; Num. 28:19–25	
6th Day	Num. 9:1–14; 28:19–25	
Intermediate Shabbat	The order to allow for the reading as on the 5th day above	Ezek. 36:37–37:14 (37:1–14)
7th Day	Ex. 13:17–15:26; Num. 28:19–25	II Sam. 22:1–51
8th Day	Deut. 15:19–16:17[3]; Num. 28:19–25 [none]	Isa. 10:32–12:6 [none]
Shavuot		
1st Day	Ex. 19:1–20:23; Num. 28:26–31	Ezek. 1:1–28; 3:12
2nd Day	Deut. 15:19–16:17[3]; Num. 28:26–31 [none]	Num. 3:1–19 (2:20–3:19)

[1] Parenthesis indicate Sephardi custom. [2] Square brackets indicate Ereẓ Israel custom. [3] On Shabbat, 14:22–16:17.
[4] Ereẓ Israel portion read four times. [5] Ereẓ Israel portion read three times.

Table of Holiday Scriptural Readings for the Diaspora and for Ereẓ Israel (cont.)

	PENTATEUCH	PROPHETS
Ninth of Av		
Morning	Deut. 4:25–40	Jer. 8:13–9:23
Afternoon	Ex. 32:11–14; 34:1–10	Isa. 55:6–56:8 (Hos. 14:2–10; Micah [7:18–20]
Other Fasts		
Morning and afternoon	Ex. 32:11–14; 34:1–10	Isa. 55:6–56:8
Rosh Ḥodesh	Num. 28:1–15	
Shabbat and Rosh Ḥodesh	Weekly portion; Num. 28:9–15	Isa. 66:1–24
Shabbat immediately preceding Rosh Ḥodesh	Weekly portion	I Sam. 20:18–12

The practice of "completing" the Torah reading with a passage from one of the prophetic books, the **haftarah* ("completion"), is mentioned in the Mishnah (Meg. 4:1–2); the origins of the custom, however, are obscure. The custom is referred to as early as the New Testament period (Luke 4:17; Acts 13:15). The particular chosen prophetic passage accorded in theme with the day's Torah reading (see Meg. 29b). There is evidence that in some communities, selections from the Hagiographa were also read. This explains the frequent quotations from this part of the Bible found in the various midrashic passages which comment on Pentateuchal themes. The saying of R. *Akiva (Sanh. 10:1) that one who reads the external books has no share in the world to come refers, in all probability, to the public readings of such books as those of the Apocrypha.

The Reading of the Torah Today

The Pentateuch is divided into 54 portions; one is to be read each Sabbath. Two such portions are sometimes read on a single Sabbath; otherwise the cycle could not be completed in one year. (See Table: Scriptural Readings on Sabbaths.) On festivals, a special portion dealing with the theme of that festival is read from one scroll and the relevant portion of Numbers 28:16–29:39 from the second scroll. (See Table: Holiday Scriptural Readings.) The regular portion is not read on a Sabbath coinciding with a festival. Each weekly portion is divided into seven smaller ones; the actual point of division, however, varies in the different rites. The Ashkenazi and Sephardi Jews do not read the same *haftarot* on certain Sabbaths. There are also occasions when different portions are read in Israel and the Diaspora (as a consequence of the observance of second days of festivals outside Israel). The cycle of readings begins on the Sabbath after *Sukkot and is completed on the last day of this festival (Simḥat Torah). Since the early part of the 19th century, various attempts have been made to reintroduce the triennial cycle; Buechler, in reply to a query by an Anglo-Jewish congregation, observed: "If you ask me about the *din* ("law"), I have to answer that it is against our codified law from the 12th century onward, and even much earlier in Babylon whence our law proceeded. If you introduce the triennial cycle, you separate yourself from the main body of Judaism" (London, New West End Synagogue, *Report on the Sabbath Reading of the Scriptures in a Triennial Cycle* (1913), 9). Many contemporary Reform and Conservative congregations follow the practice of reading about a third of the portion for the week from the portions of the annual cycle. In some of these congregations, women are called to the reading of the Torah; the practice is substantiated by some traditional sources (see A.B. Blumenthal in *Rabbinical Assembly America, Proceedings*, 19 (1956), 168–81). In a few synagogues, it is customary to read the *haftarah* from a handwritten scroll of the prophets but in most communities, the *haftarah* is read from a printed book. The *haftarah* reading, therefore, requires less expertise and it is customary that it is read by a member of the congregation, and not a special official. In modern communities, the old practice of selling the *aliyyot* (from a root meaning "to ascend" i.e., the platform from which the Torah is read) has been discontinued.

The Laws and Customs of Reading the Torah

The Torah scroll is taken from the ark and carried in procession around the synagogue before and after the reading; the congregation stands during the procession. According to rabbinic authorities, Leviticus 19:32 "Thou shalt rise up before the hoary head and honor the face of the old man, and thou shalt fear thy God: I am the Lord," means that one must rise when a Torah scholar, as well as an old man, passes by. The argument is developed that if one must rise before those who study the Torah, how much more before the Torah itself (Kid. 33b). It has become customary for the congregation to gather around the scroll and kiss it as it passes.

The reader must prepare himself well by rehearsing the portion he is to read. He must stand erect while reading and must enunciate the words clearly but not excessively. If he reads a word incorrectly, so that its meaning is changed, he must repeat it. The Torah can only be read if at least a *minyan* ("ten adult males") are present. Although it is permitted to add to the number of persons called to the reading on the Sabbath, no less than three verses are to be read for each person. The portions are frequently subdivided for this purpose, but care must be taken not to end a passage with an unfavorable topic. A person is called to the reading by his Hebrew name and that of his father. If he is a rabbi, he is called by this title (*morenu ha-rav*). He ascends the *bimah* (raised platform from which the Torah is read) by the shortest route and descends by the longest, thus demonstrating his eagerness to be called and his reluctance to leave. If he is seated in the middle of the synagogue, so that both routes are equidistant, he should ascend to the right and descend to the left. Both before and after the reading, he recites special benedictions (see **Birkat ha-Torah*).

The kabbalists consider the reading of the Torah a dramatic re-enactment of the theophany at Sinai; the reader is in place of the Almighty, the person called to the reading represents the people to whom the Torah was given, and the *segan* ("the congregational leader who apportions the *aliyyot* and stands at the side of the reader") has the role of Moses. Others, for whom the Torah reading is also this dramatic re-enactment, consider the *segan* in place of the Almighty and the reader in place of Moses. R. Simeon said: "When the scroll of the Torah is taken out in public to be read therefrom the heavenly gates of mercy are opened and the love from above is awakened. A man should then say: 'Blessed be the name…'" (Zohar Ex. 206a). This mystical prayer, *Berikh Shemei*, is found in most prayer books and is recited in many congregations.

There are seven *aliyyot* on a Sabbath, of which the first goes to a kohen, the second to a levite, and five to Israelites. If no levite is present, the kohen is called again to the regular levite portion. If no kohen is present, either a levite or an Israelite is called to the kohen portion and a levite is not then called to the second portion, but an Israelite. A kohen or levite may not be called to any of the five Israelite portions. However, since it is permitted to add to these he may be called to the last additional portion. A father and son, or two brothers, may not be called consecutively to the Torah reading, for fear of the "evil eye" or to prevent near relatives from testifying together which is forbidden by Jewish law. (The calling up to the Torah is to attest its truth.) The following persons take precedence in being called to the Torah:

(1) a bridegroom who is to be married during the following week or was married that week;

(2) a boy who has reached his religious majority (bar mitzvah);

(3) a man whose wife has borne him a child;

(4) a man commemorating the death of a parent (*yahrzeit*);

(5) a man rising from mourning (*shivah*).

On the Sabbath it is considered an honor to receive the highly valued third and sixth *aliyyot*. It is customary to allot them to men of special learning or piety. The same applies to the last *aliyah*, particularly when the reading is from one of the concluding portions of the five books. Other valued portions are the Song of Moses (Ex. 15:1–21) and the Ten Commandments (Ex. 20:1–14 and Deut. 5:6–18). The congregation stands while these portions are being read. The portions Exodus 32:1–33:6; Leviticus 26:14–43; Numbers 11; and Deuteronomy 28:15–68 are read softly because they deal with Israel's backsliding. The last few verses of the *maftir* ("final portion") of the *sidrah* are repeated for the person called to read the *haftarah*. This can be given to a kohen or a levite and, unlike the others, also to a minor.

The Torah reading is cantillated in a specific way which is distinct from that of the *haftarah*. The Ashkenazi and the Sephardi rites have different cantillations for the reading. There are also special cantillations for the Book of Esther, the Book of Lamentations, and for the Books of Ruth, Ecclesiastes, and Song of Songs. It is considered wrong to substitute one cantillation for another. The verse: "You shall not move your neighbor's landmarks, set up by previous generations" (Deut. 19:14) is cited when such a change is attempted. The reader does not have to repeat words read with an incorrect cantillation (for the musical aspects see *Masoretic Accents, Musical Rendition). In Sephardi congregations, the open scroll is lifted (*hagbahah*) and shown to the congregation before the reading; in Ashkenazi congregations this ceremony is performed after the reading. When the scroll is raised, the congregation chants: "This is the law which Moses set before the children of Israel" (Deut. 4:44). After the reading, the scroll is rolled together again (*gelilah*) and its ornaments are replaced.

The Torah may only be read from a scroll that is *kasher* ("fit for use"), and not from one rendered *pasul* ("unfit") because it had been incorrectly written or its words or letters have been obliterated. A scroll is unfit for use, even if only one letter has been omitted. The scroll must be unpointed; it should have no other signs than the consonants. If the vowel signs or the notes for cantillation have been written in the scroll, it is unfit for use. If during the reading it is discovered that the scroll is unfit, it should be returned to the ark and another scroll taken out. The reading from the second scroll is continued from the place where the mistake was discovered. Should this occur on a Sabbath, the required number of seven persons must be called up to the reading of the second scroll, even if some have already been called up to the reading of the first.

Most Reform temples in the United States have shortened or abandoned the traditional Torah readings and a number of Conservative temples have substituted the old triennial cycle of readings. In non-Orthodox congregations where women are counted as part of the *minyan*, they may also receive an *aliyah* and girls may celebrate their bat mitzvah like boys with a reading from their portion.

BIBLIOGRAPHY: Sh. Ar., OḤ 135–49; D.B.D. Reifmann, *Shulḥan ha-Keri'ah* (1882); Zunz-Albeck, Derashot, index, s.v. *Keri'at ha-Torah*; Buechler, in: JQR, 5 (1892/93), 420–68; 6 (1893/94), 1–73; Elbogen, Gottesdienst, index, s.v. *Tora Vorlesung*; J. Mann, *The Bible as Read and Preached in the Old Synagogue*, 1 (1940); idem and I. Sonne, *ibid.*, 2 (1966).

[Louis Jacobs]

TORAH ORNAMENTS. The sacred and ceremonial objects in the synagogue revolve around the Torah scroll. These objects differ from one place to another and not every object exists in every community.

Storage of the Torah Scroll

The length of cloth known in Hebrew as the *mitpaḥat* (plural *mitpaḥot*) is the earliest known means for storage of the Torah scroll. The *mitpahḥat*, also known in the sources as *mappah*, is mentioned in the Mishnah and in the Tosefta and later in the Jerusalem and Babylonian Talmuds (Mishnah, Kel. 28:4, Meg. 4:1, Kil. 9:3; Tosef. BM 9:5; TJ, Ber. 6:4; TB, Meg. 26b, etc.). It is known from these sources that in ancient times woolen or linen *mitpaḥot* were used, sometimes with colorful stripes woven in; some were provided with bells. It is also known from Greek and Latin literature that in the ancient Middle East important scrolls were regularly wrapped in cloth. In time, the Jewish communities of the East Mediterranean Basin, as well as the Eastern communities, began to keep their Torah scrolls in special cases. Such cases were common in the classical world; they are referred to as *theca* in Greek or *capsa* in Latin. Archaeological finds from all parts of the Roman Empire attest to the shape of the case: a cylindrical or prism-shaped container used to carry various objects, including scrolls. Used in the Jewish world to carry Torah scrolls, such cases eventually became the main permanent receptacle for Torah scrolls in the communities of the East and the East Mediterranean Basin.

Torah Case and Mitpaḥat

The case is a small wooden cabinet, either cylindrical or prism-shaped with eight, ten, or twelve faces in two parts that open lengthwise. There are three main types of case: the flat-topped case used in Yemen, Cochin, Eastern Iran, and Afghanistan; the case with a circular or onion-shaped crown used in the Babylonian communities, i.e., Iraq and Western Iran; and the case with a coronet used in Libya, Tunisia, and the Greek Romaniot communities. The ornamentation of the case differs from one community to another. Cases may be adorned with colorful drawings or covered with leather, fabric, or beaten silver plates. In some communities, such as Yemen, Tunisia, and Libya, the case is usually wrapped in a rich fabric. The Torah cases generally have inscriptions around the edges, on the front, or inside. Two types of inscription are characteristic: biblical verses extolling the Torah, mainly from the books of Proverbs and Psalms, and personal information about the donor.

Our knowledge of Torah cases and *mitpaḥot* in pre-modern times is meager; the process whereby the case evolved from a mere receptacle for carrying the Torah into a sacred artifact can at most be conjectured. It may be assumed that in the first stage, when the case was used only for storage, the scroll was wrapped in a *mitpaḥat* when placed in the case. However, it was difficult to handle the Torah scroll wrapped in the *mitpaḥat* in its case, and most communities therefore removed it from the case. Only the Jews of Yemen continued to wrap the Torah in two or three *mitpaḥot*, and until they came to Israel they used colorful, geometrically patterned, cotton-print *mitpaḥot* of Indian manufacture. There, the *mitpaḥat* is used to cover the text adjacent to the text being read, thus preventing its unnecessary exposure. In other communities, the *mitpaḥat* is used only to cover the scroll during pauses in the reading, when it is placed on the case and not on the Torah scroll itself.

Wrapper, Binder, and Mantle

Two textile objects developed from the *mitpaḥat* in European communities. One, found only in Italy and in communities of the Sephardi Diaspora, is a wrapper (Hebrew *yeriʿah*), of height equal to that of the parchment sheets from which the Torah scroll is made and rolled up together with the scroll, a custom which is gradually disappearing. Another textile object wound around the Torah scroll in Ashkenazi communities, in Italy, and in the Sephardi Diaspora is the binder. The binder is a long narrow strip of cloth with which the Torah is bound, either on top of the wrapper or directly on the parchment. Its purpose is to keep the scroll securely bound when not in use.

In Italy and in the Sephardi communities, the binder is known as a *fascia*; it is made of a costly material or of linen embroidered in silk thread. From the 16th century it became customary in Northern Italy for girls and young women to embroider binders with biblical verses or original personal dedicatory inscriptions. In Germany it became customary in the second half of the 16th century to prepare a binder for the Torah scroll on the occasion of the birth of a son. This binder, called a *mappah* or *wimpel*, was fashioned from a piece of square linen cloth which was placed near the infant during the circumcision ceremony. The infant's name, his father's, name and his date of birth were embroidered or written on the cloth, as well as the blessing recited during the ceremony: "May he enter into the Torah, the nuptial canopy, and into good deeds." By the 17th century, binders often had pictures illustrating the three elements of "Torah, the nuptial canopy and good deeds."

The Torah mantle is as it were the clothing of the Torah scroll. In Sephardi communities, Italy, and Germany, and in halakhic literature, it was indeed occasionally known as *beged*, "garment," or *mappah*, but later the term *meʿil* became standard in most communities. The earliest attestation to the shape of the mantle appears in the 14th-century *Sarajevo Haggadah*, created in Spain. The mantles shown there are made of a costly material, probably not embroidered. This tradition is still common today in Sephardi communities, with the exception of Morocco and Algeria, where Torah mantles are made of velvet with elaborately embroidered patterns and dedicatory inscriptions. Common motifs on these mantles are the Tree of Life (in Morocco) and a gate (in Algeria). The shapes of the mantle differ from community to community – some are wide and open in the front (Italy and the Spanish Diaspora), others have a small cape atop the robe, still others are of simple rectangular length with material gathered at the upper borders (Algeria).

The earliest German mantles are depicted in 15th-century manuscripts. This Torah mantle is generally narrower and smaller than the Sephardi mantle, while the robe-like part is made of two rectangular lengths of material sewn together. Two openings at the upper end of the mantle enable the staves to protrude. The designs on Torah mantles in Germany and Central Europe are influenced by the ornamentation of the Torah Ark curtain, with such motifs as a pair of columns, lions, and the Torah crown most frequent.

Torah Crown

The earliest Torah ornaments are the Torah crown and the finials mounted on the Torah case or on the staves of the Torah scroll. We first hear of a Torah crown in the 11th century, in a responsum of *Hai Gaon concerning the use of a crown for a Torah scroll on *Simḥat Torah. The use of the Torah crown is linked in this responsum to the custom of crowning the so-called "*Bridegrooms of the Law," i.e., the persons called up on Simḥat Torah to complete the annual cycle of the Torah reading and to initiate the new cycle. At the time, the Torah crown was an *ad hoc* object made from various decorative items, such as plants and jewelry. About a hundred years later, fixed crowns, made of silver and used regularly to decorate Torah scrolls in the synagogue, are mentioned in a document from the Cairo *Genizah*. Their earliest depiction is in the 14th-century Spanish *Sarajevo Haggadah*.

Torah crowns are used in almost all communities (the exceptions are Morocco and Yemen), their design being influenced in each locality by local tradition. The onion-shaped or conical crown of the Iraqi-Persian Torah case follows the tradition of the crowns of the Sassanid kings, the last Persian dynasty prior to the Muslim conquest. In Cochin, India, and in Aden, the independent port of Yemen, a tapering dome-like crown developed through which protrude finials mounted on the staves on which the Torah scroll is wound; the crown is not fixed to the case. By the 20th century, the Torah crown in Cochin showed distinct European features. In Eastern Iran, where the Torah had a small crown, the outer sides of the crown lost their spherical shape and became flat dedicatory plaques. Today this crown looks like a pair of flat finials, and only their designation as "crowns" hints at their origin in the Torah crown. The circlet or coronet on the Mediterranean case, which became an integral part of the case, was based on a local medieval crown tradition typified by floral patterns. The European crown is shaped like a floral coronet with arms closing over it. In Eastern Europe a two- or three-tiered crown developed, inspired by the crown motif on the Torah Ark in this region. In Italy, on the other hand, the Torah crown was a coronet, known in Hebrew as the *atarah*.

Torah Finials

The finials evolved from knobs at the upper end of the staves (*ezei ḥayyim*) on which the Torah scroll is wound. Since the shape of the spherical finial recalled that of a fruit, it was called a *tappu'aḥ*, "apple," among the Jews of Spain and in the Sephardi Diaspora, and a *rimmon*, "pomegranate," in all other communities.

The earliest known reference to Torah finials occurs in a document from 1159, found in the Cairo *Genizah*, from which we learn that by the 12th century finials were already being made of silver and had bells. Around the same time, *Maimonides mentions finials in the *Mishneh Torah* (Hilkhot Sefer Torah 10:4). Despite the variations on the spherical shape which developed over the centuries and the addition of small bells around the main body of the finial, the spherical, fruit-like form was the basic model for the design of finials in Oriental and European communities.

A most significant variation appeared in 15th-century Spain, Italy, and Germany, where the shape of finials was influenced by that of various objects of church ritual, whose design often incorporated architectural motifs, The resulting tower-like structure, which seems to have appeared around the same time in different parts of Europe, became the main type of finial in 18th-century Germany and Italy, as well as Morocco, brought there by Jews expelled from Spain.

Breastplates and Metal Shields Hung in Front of the Torah Scroll

Breastplates – ornamental metal plates or shields hung in front of the Torah scroll – are found in all Ashkenazi communities, as well as Italy and Turkey, but designed differently in each community. In most cases the breastplate is made of silver or silver-plated metal. In Italy the breastplate is shaped like a half-coronet and known as the *keter*, "crown." In Turkey, the breastplate is called a *tass*, and assumes a variety of shapes – circular, triangular, oval, or even the Star of David. In Western, Central, and Eastern Europe the breastplate is called either *tass* or *ẓiẓ*; its function there is not merely ornamental: it designates which Torah scroll is to be used for the Torah reading on any particular occasion, with interchangeable plaques. The most notable early breastplates, from 17th-century Germany and Holland, were either square or rectangular, but over time they became rounded and decorative, and bells or small dedicatory plaques were suspended from its lower edge. During this period, the design of breastplates was influenced by that of the Torah Ark and the *parokhet* (curtain) concealing it, featuring various architectural motifs, the *menorah* (the seven-branched candelabrum), Moses and Aaron, lions, or Torah crowns.

Objects Used in the Torah Reading

TORAH POINTER. The pointer used by the Torah reader to keep the place is known in European communities as the *yad*, "hand," or the *ezba*, "finger," and in Sephardi and Eastern communities as the *moreh*, "pointer," or *kulmus*, "quill," the former because of its function and the latter because of its shape. Halakhic sources also use the terms *moreh* or *kulmus*. The pointer was originally a narrow rod, tapered at the pointing end, usually with a hole at the other end through which a ring or chain could be passed to hang the pointer on the Torah scroll.

The original form of the pointer was preserved in Eastern communities, the differences from one community to another being mainly in length and ornamentation. In certain communities a hand with a pointing finger was added, and accordingly the pointer came to be known as a *yad*, "hand," or *ezba*, "finger." Pointers are made for the most part of silver or silver-plated brass, but in a few European communities they used to be made of wood. In such cases the pointers were carved in the local folk-art style.

BIBLIOGRAPHY: P.J. Abbink van der Zwan, "Ornamentation on Eighteenth-Century Torah Binders," in: *The Israel Museum News* (1978), 64–73; G. Boll, "The Jewish Community of Mackenheim," in: A. Weber, E. Friedlander & F. Armbruster (eds.), *Mappo ... blessed be who comes, The Band of Jewish Tradition* (1997), 22–27; Y. Cohen, "Torah Breastplates from Augsburg in the Israel Museum," in: *Israel Museum News*, 14 (1978), 75–85; D. Davidovitch, "Die Tora Wimpel im Braunschweigischen Landesmuseum," in: R. Hagen (ed.), *Tora Wimpel, Zeugniss jüdischer Volkskunst aus dem Braunschweigisches Landesmuseum* (1978), 12–27; J. Doleželová, "Torah Binders in the Czech Republic," in: A. Weber, E. Friedlander & F. Armbruster (eds.), *Mappot... blessed be who comes, The Band of Jewish Tradition* (1997), 99–103; idem, "Torah Binders from Four Centuries at the State Jewish Museum in Prague," in: *Judaica Bohemiae*, 9:2 (1973), 55–71; idem, "Binders and Festive Covers from the Collections of the State Jewish Museum in Prague," in: *Judaica Bohemiae*, 10:2 (1974), 91–104; idem, "Die Sammlung der Thorawickel," in: *Judaica Bohemiae*, 16:1 (1980), 60–63; R. Eis, *Torah Binders of the Judah L. Magnes Museum* (1979); N. Feuchtwanger-Sarig, "Torah Binders from Denmark," in: M. Gelfer-Jørgensen (ed.), *Danish Jewish Art – Jews in Danish Art* (Danish,1999), 382–435; R. Grafman, *Crowning Glory, Silver Torah Ornaments* (1996); idem, *50 Rimmonim, A Selection of Torah Finials from a European Family Collection* (1998); C. Grossman, "Italian Torah Binders," in: *Jewish Art*, 7 (1980), 35–43; F. Guggenheim-Grünberg, *Die Torawickelbänder von Lengnau Zeugnisse jüdischer Volkskunst* (1967); J. Gutmann, "Die Mappe Schuletragen," in: A. Weber, E. Friedlander & F. Armbruster (eds.), *Mappot ...blessed be who comes, The Band of Jewish Tradition* (1997), 65–69; R. Jacoby, "'*Etzba*' and '*Kulmos*,' The Torah Pointer in the Persian World" (Ph.D. diss., Hebrew University of Jerusalem, 2005); B. Kirshenblatt-Gimblett, "The Cut that Binds: The Western Ashkenazic Torah Binder as Nexus between Circumcision and Torah," in: V. Turner (ed.), *Celebration: Studies in Festivity and Ritual* (1982), 136–46; F. Raphaël, "On Saturday My Grandson Will Bring the Mappah to the Synagogue," in: A. Weber, E. Friedlander & F. Armbruster (eds.), *Mappot... blessed be who comes, The Band of Jewish Tradition* (1997), 73–79; C. Roth, "Ritual Art," in: *Encyclopedia Judaica* (1973), 3:524–535; S. Sabar "'May He Grow Up to the Huppah': Representations of the Wedding on Ashkenazi Torah Binders," in: G. Cohen Grossman (ed.), *Romance & Ritual: Celebrating The Jewish Wedding* (2001), 31–45; J. Stown, "Silver English Rimmonim and Their Makers," in: *Quest* (Sept. 1965), 23–30; D. Tahon, "*Rapduni be-Tapuḥim*," in: *Rimmonim*, 4 (1994), 20–27 (Heb.); A. Weber, "The Culture of Rural Jewry in Swabia and Franconia," in: A. Weber, E. Friedlander & F. Armbruster (eds.), *Mappot... blessed be who comes, The Band of Jewish Tradition* (1997), 82–91; idem, "From Leo to Virgo – The Binders of the Synagogue at Ichenhausen," in: A. Weber, E. Friedlander & F. Armbruster (eds.), *Mappot... blessed be who comes, The Band of Jewish Tradition* (1997), 92–99; B.Yaniv, "An Attempt to Reconstruct the Design of Tower-Shaped Rimonim in Morocco according to Models from Spain," in: *Pe'amim*, 50 (Winter 1992), 69–98 (Heb.); idem, "The Mystery of the Flat Torah Finials from East Persia," in: A. Netzer (ed.), *Padyavand, Judeo-Iranian and Jewish Studies Series*, 1 (1996), 63–74; idem, "The Samaritan Torah Case," in: V. Morabito, Alen D. Crown & L. Davey (eds.), *Samaritan Researches*, 5 (2000), 4.04–4.13; idem, "Regional Variations of Torah Cases from the Islamic World," in: *For Every Thing a Season – Jewish Ritual Art* (2002), 39–76; idem, *The Torah Case; Its History and Design* (1997) (Heb.); M. Gelfer-Jørgensen (ed.), *Danish Jewish Art – Jews in Danish Art* (tr. from the Danish; 1999).

[Bracha Yaniv (2nd ed.)]

TORAH UMESORAH (National Society for Hebrew Day Schools). The largest national body serving 700 Orthodox day schools in North America, the Torah Umesorah was founded in 1944 by Rabbi Shraga Feivel Mendlowitz. From 1946 its national director was Joseph Kaminetsky, who was succeeded by Rabbi Joshua Fishman in 1982. Policy is officially dictated by a rabbinical board. Among its other activities, Torah Umesorah sponsors a teacher training institute called AishDos and represents its membership schools to the U.S. Department of Education. In the past, Torah Umesorah published the children's magazine *Olomeinu* as well as *The Jewish Parent*; and *Hamenahel*, a periodical for school principals. In 2004 they began publishing an educational magazine called *Rayanos*. Torah Umesorah organizes two yearly conferences, the National Conference of Yeshiva Principals and the National Leadership Convention, the latter of which is geared toward anyone involved in Torah education.

BIBLIOGRAPHY: D. Zvi Kramer, *The Day Schools and Torah Umesorah: The Seeding of Traditional Judaism in America* (1984); C.S. Liebman, in: AJYP, 66 (1965); A.I. Schiff, *The Jewish Day School in America* (1966).

[Asher Oser (2nd ed.)]

TORAH VA-AVODAH (Heb. "Torah and Labor"), description of the ideology of the Zionist religious pioneering movement, as well as the name of the world confederation of pioneer and youth groups of the *Mizrachi movement established in Vienna in 1925 at a conference of delegates from various countries (representing Mizrachi youth, religious *He-Ḥalutz groups, and *Ha-Po'el ha-Mizrachi). The ideology was based on the unity of the Torah, the people, and the land of Israel, as well as on the postulate that only a man who lives by his own labor can be certain that he does not exploit and abuse his neighbor. This concept, coupled with the demand for social justice, induced the movement into establishing cooperative collective pioneering settlements in Ereẓ Israel.

See also *Mizrachi, *Ha-Po'el ha-Mizrachi, *Bnei Akiva, *Ha-Kibbutz ha-Dati.

BIBLIOGRAPHY: J. Walk, in: YLBI, 6 (1961), 236–56.

TORBERG (Kantorberg), FRIEDRICH (1908–1979), Austrian novelist, journalist, and editor. Torberg, who was born in Vienna, won acclaim with his first novel, *Der Schueler Gerber hat absolviert* (1930). He worked for the *Prager Tagblatt* and the *Selbstwehr* during the 1930s. In 1938 he fled from Prague to Switzerland and fought in a Czech brigade with the French army until the collapse of France. With the help of the "Emergency Rescue Committee," he escaped to the U.S. in 1940 as a persecuted writer. There he lived first as a scriptwriter in Los Angeles and later in New York. Torberg returned to Vienna in 1951, where he was for many years the editor of *Forum*, a literary and cultural monthly.

His novella *Mein ist die Rache* (1943) and his novel *Hier bin ich, mein Vater* (1948) dealt with the fate of Jews under Nazi rule. His other novels include *Abschied* (1937) and *Die zweite Begegnung* (1950). He published two collections of verse, *Der ewige Refrain* (1929) and *Lebenslied* (1958). Among his further works are *Das fuenfte Rad am Thespiskarren* (1967), *Golems Wiederkehr* (1968), *Suesskind von Trimberg* (1972), and two collection of anecdotes on Jewish life in the Habsburg monarchy, *Die Tante Jolesch* (1977) and *Die Erben der Tante Jolesch* (1978). Torberg's collected works, including his extensive correspondence, appeared in 19 volumes (1962–91). In addition to his extensive literary output, Torberg also worked as a German translator of Ephraim *Kishon's novels.

BIBLIOGRAPHY: F. Lennartz, *Deutsche Dichter und Schriftsteller unserer Zeit* (1959⁸), 756–8; H. Zohn, *Wiener Juden in der deutschen Literatur* (1964), 101–5. **ADD. BIBLIOGRAPHY:** J. Strelka (ed.), *Festschrift* (1970); A. Tobias, in: BLB, 19 (1980), 56/57:169–73; R. Hilbrand, in: D. Axmann (ed.), *Und Lächeln ist das Erbteil meines Stammes* (1988), 89–106; D. Axmann, in: *ibid.*, 149–58; H. Zogbaum, in: *Australian Journal of Jewish Studies*, 7 (1993), 1, 71–92; J. Thunecke, in: *Modern Austrian Literature*, 27 (1994), 3–4, 19–36; E. Adunka, in: *ibid.*, 213–37; F. Tichy, *Friedrich Torberg* (1995); C. Sajak, in: J. Thunecke (ed.), *Deutschsprachige Exillyrik von 1933 bis zur Nachkriegszeit* (1998), 157–69; H. Abret, in: M. Braun et al. (ed.), *"Hinauf und Zurueck in die herzhelle Zukunft"* (2000), 521–41; S. Hart, "History through Humor … Friedrich Torberg's 'Tante Jolesch' Books, with particular Reference to the Problems of Assimilation and Anti-Semitism" (Ph.D. diss., King's College, London; 2001).

[Sol Liptzin / Mirjam Triendl (2nd ed.)]

TORCHIN (Pol. **Torczyn**), town in S. Volyn district, Ukraine; passed to Russia in 1795. In 1648–49 the Jews suffered at the hands of the Cossacks under *Chmielnicki. Because of their economic plight, the Council of the Four Lands (see *Councils of the Lands) granted the community a reduction in tax in 1726. The Jewish population numbered about 640 in 1765. During the 19th century various branches of crafts were developed whose products were sold on the Russian markets. In 1890 there were 21 tanneries and 66 shops in the town, most of them owned by Jews. The Jewish population numbered 1,748 in 1847, 2,629 (58% of total population) in 1897, and 1,480 (46%) in 1921. Between the two world wars, in independent Poland, all the Jewish parties were active in the town, as well as a branch of He-Ḥalutz, a sport association, and a library.

Holocaust Period

Before the outbreak of World War II there were about 1,600 Jews in Torczyn. In September 1939 the Red Army entered the town and a Soviet administration was established there until the outbreak of the German-Soviet war in June 1941. The Germans occupied the town on June 24, 1941. In January 1942 the Jews from Torczyn and its vicinity were concentrated in a closed ghetto in the town. The ghetto was liquidated at the end of August 1942 and most of the Jews were shot in the Jewish cemetery. During this *Aktion* some Jews succeeded in hiding and another group in escaping and joining a partisan unit that operated in the vicinity. After the war, the Jewish community of Torczyn was not reconstituted.

BIBLIOGRAPHY: Halpern, Pinkas, index; B. Wasiutyński, *Ludność żydowska w Polsce w wiekach XIX i XX* (1930), 84.

[Shimon Leib Kirshenboim]

TORCZYNER, JACQUES (1914–), U.S. Zionist leader. Torczyner was born in Antwerp, Belgium, where his father had been president of the Belgian Zionist Federation. He identified himself with Zionist activity in Belgium and was editor of the official publications of the Zionist Federation from 1937 until the outbreak of World War II. In 1940 he immigrated to the United States and became one of the leaders of the Zionist Organization of America and was closely associated with Abba Hillel *Silver. Torczyner served as president of the Zionist Organization of America for five consecutive terms and was appointed chairman of the Administrative Board of the ZOA. He is also president of the World Union of General Zionists. He has written extensively on problems connected with Zionist ideology and the future of American Jewry.

TORGOV, MORLEY (1927–), Canadian author. Morley Torgov was born and raised in Sault Ste. Marie, Ontario, where his family was part of the city's small Jewish community. A full-time lawyer with a practice in Toronto, he wrote in his leisure time.

Torgov published a memoir and five novels, each of which explores Jewish themes with humor and irony that are gentler than in either Mordecai *Richler or Philip *Roth, with whom he is often compared. *A Good Place to Come From* (1974) won the Leacock Medal for Humour and was adapted as a mini-series for television and for the stage in Canada and the United States. A series of vignettes, it describes Torgov's experience of growing up Jewish in the predominantly gentile world of Sault Ste. Marie. *The Abramsky Variations* (1977), written in three parts and set in Toronto and France, concerns three generations of the Abramsky (later Brahms) family: father Louis, son Hershel, and grandson Bart (né Kevin). Each character struggles to reconcile Jewish tradition with secular ambition, and all are more strongly attracted to fantasizing about people they want to emulate than to facing reality. Torgov's second novel, *The Outside Chance of Maximilian Glick* (1982), which also won the Leacock Medal, was first written as a children's story. It takes a comic look at 12-year-old Maximilian, so named because his parents thought it would look impressive on the door of a law office. It is the story of a boy raised in a tiny Jewish community in Steelton, northern Ontario. Maximilian seeks to escape the suffocating love of his parents and grandparents, who envision him making a career as a surgeon, judge, or scientist. With the help of Rabbi Kalman Teitelman, who replaces Steelton's former rabbi and with whom Maximilian forms a relationship, he eventually releases himself from the stifling expectations of others. *St. Farb's Day* (1990) concerns Isadore Farb, an honest, respectable lawyer on Toronto's Bay Street. As Farb struggles with an ethical dilemma – he finds himself involved in a conflict of interest with several clients – he confronts larger moral issues linked to his Jewish identity. *The War to End All Wars* (1998) brings together two former soldiers who had fought opposite one another in World War I. In the mid-1920s, Ellio Pines and Karl Sternberg are living in the small town of Oreville, Michigan, where they compete as businessmen and as suitors. *Stickler and Me* (2002) is a novel for young adults.

[Ruth Panofsky (2nd ed.)]

TORME, MEL (**Melvin Howard**; 1925–1999) U.S. singer, drummer, pianist, composer, arranger, actor, author. Although he was known as "the Velvet Fog," a nickname he loathed, and most people thought of him in terms of his creamy vocal tones, Mel Torme was a protean figure whose range of talents encompassed not only jazz and pop music but writing and acting as well. The son of Russian Jewish immigrants (the family name, Torma, was changed by an immigration official at Ellis Island), Torme was a child performer of note, singing with the Coon-Sanders Nighthawks Orchestra at four and appearing on numerous national radio programs including *Jack Armstrong, the All-American Boy* when he was nine. Trained as a pianist and drummer, he also began his songwriting career very early, with the Harry James band performing his "Lament of Love" when Torme was 15. By 1943, the teenager was touring with the Chico Marx band as a singer, drummer, and arranger. That was the year in which he also made his film debut in *Higher and Higher* alongside another newcomer, Frank Sinatra.

Sinatra's success with the Pied Pipers vocal group inspired Torme to form his own backup aggregation, the Mel-Tones, and it was his recordings with them in the mid-1940s that inspired New York disk jockey Fred Robbins to gift Torme with his famous sobriquet. (Torme eventually came to accept the nickname, sporting license plates that read LE FOG and EL PHOG.) His career continued in the ascendant with a commercial peak in the 1947 MGM musical *Good News*, which triggered a very brief enthusiasm for Torme among the bobbysoxers. But he was outgrowing this music and by the early 1950s hooked up with nascent Bethlehem Records where he became a jazz artist in earnest. The timing was probably unfortunate, as Torme's musical maturing coincided with the rise of rock 'n' roll and the ebbing of jazz as a commercial vehicle.

Torme, however, was a man of many interests and talents, and survived by broadening his horizons to include writing for television, several books of non-fiction including an autobiography (*It Wasn't All Velvet*, 1988) and a biography of his close friend and fellow Jewish child prodigy, Buddy Rich (*Traps: The Drum Wonder*, 1991). His most famous composition, "The Christmas Song," was not only a huge hit for Nat Cole but is among the most frequently recorded holiday songs in the modern repertoire. Torme continued performing and recording until a serious stroke felled him in 1996; the lingering effects of that stroke would kill him three years later.

BIBLIOGRAPHY: "Mel Torme," Biography Resource Center, Thompson-Gale Publishing, at: www.gale.com/BiographyRC; "Mel Torme," MusicWeb Encyclopaedia of Popular Music, at: www.musicweb.uk.net; J. Rosen, "Mel Torme," in *Salon Magazine* (June 12, 1999), at: www.salon.com.

[George Robinson (2nd ed.)]

TORONTO, city in Canada, with a population of approximately 2.5 million people; located on the north shore of Lake Ontario. The city is the capital of the province of Ontario and at the heart of a larger urban expanse officially known as the Greater Toronto Area (GTA), home to an additional 2.7 million people. Toronto is also one of the largest Jewish Diaspora centers. In 2001 there were approximately 114,000 Jews in the city of Toronto and another 65,000 in the surrounding GTA municipalities. That population continues to grow.

History

Many of Toronto's Jews remain clustered along what is likely the longest Jewish neighborhood in the Diaspora. It begins downtown and extends up either side of one street, Bathurst Street, for about 15 miles (24 km.). While there are no fixed boundaries along this lengthy north/south artery, it is possible to divide the Toronto Jewish community into a landscape of three connected neighborhoods.

The downtown and most southerly neighborhood is the oldest. Toronto, originally named York, was founded as a British garrison town on Lake Ontario in the late 18th century. As surrounding agricultural settlement gradually expanded, so did the town, which served as a local market and commercial center. By the late 1840s and early 1850s Toronto was home to a small number of Jews, mostly merchants active in the jewelry, clothing, and dry goods business. Many of these Jews were originally from England or Germany and retained close economic and kinship ties to Jewish merchant families in Montreal, New York, or London. As Toronto continued to grow, Jewish-owned enterprises successfully expanded to include financial services, land speculation, and manufacturing.

While few in number and generally well integrated into the larger community, the tiny Toronto Jewish community came together to found a burial society and organize High Holiday services. Confident that their numbers would gradually grow, in 1856 a group of 18 men founded Toronto's Holy Blossom Congregation. For the next decade and a half, there was slow but steady growth in the community. In the early 1880s the Toronto Jewish community stood just short of 600 members. They were not ready for the explosion in Jewish population numbers that came with the great westward migration of Jews out of Russian Poland, Lithuania, and the Ukraine that began in the early 1880s. As this migration reached Toronto the city's Jewish population expanded by more than 200 percent to almost 1,400 Jews in 1891. During the next 20 years it grew by more than one thousand percent to exceed 18,000 in 1911. In the next ten years the size of the Jewish community of Toronto doubled yet again.

The small and generally well-integrated older Jewish community offered the new immigrants what assistance it could, but it was soon overwhelmed by so many new arrivals who were so different from themselves. In turn, the new arrivals, Yiddish-speaking and largely working-class, often felt at a distance from the prosperous and largely English-speaking Jews they found in Toronto. Many of the recent immigrants first clustered in poorer inner-city neighborhoods where they found employment in the growing garment industry or struggled to make a living as peddlers and petty merchants. They built an institutional infrastructure that echoed the East European world from which they had recently arrived. Synagogues and *Landsmannschaften* were established, often tied to country or region of origin. Secular organizations of many different political stripes, left and right, Zionist and non-Zionist, also took root.

Even as Jewish immigrants to Toronto and their children struggled to secure an economic foothold for themselves in this new urban world while tenaciously holding onto their identities as Jews, they were subject to assimilationist pressures from Toronto's urban gatekeepers – school teachers, Protestant missionaries, social workers, and politicians – all preaching a vision of Toronto as an orderly outpost of British values in North America and believing it their duty to remake these "foreigners" in their own image. Some, tinged with antisemitism and fearing that Jews could not or would not assimilate, began to pressure the government for severe restrictions on immigration. As the anti-immigrant movement grew through the mid-1920s, the government responded with tough immigration barriers. Even though these regulations cut off the flow of East European immigration into Canada, antisemitism in housing, in the workplace, and in areas of social contact continued. Tensions exploded in the 1933 Christie Pits riot, where Jewish and Italian youths fought anti-immigrant gangs who had been harassing Jews.

World War II was a watershed in Toronto Jewish life. The outbreak of war in 1939 brought not only distress to the heavily Polish-Jewish population of Toronto fearful for the fate of family still in Poland, it also brought a return of economic growth, full employment, and a sense of shared contribution to the national cause. With many Canadian Jews serving with the military and contributing on the home front, Jews were increasingly unwilling to tolerate further anti-Jewish discrimination. Even as the organized Toronto Jewish community, led by the Canadian Jewish Congress, organized in support of the war effort it also began a campaign to combat antisemitism and to lobby for legally enforced human rights protections. In part as a result of this effort, in 1944 Ontario passed the first human rights legislation in Canada, barring discrimination on the basis of race or religion. In 1962 the Ontario Human Rights Code was proclaimed and the Ontario Human Rights Commission established to ensure the Code was followed. Changing attitudes can be seen in the election, back-to-back, of two Jewish mayors, Nathan *Phillips (1955–62) and Philip *Givens (1962–66). Givens, at the time he was mayor, was also president of the Canadian Zionist Federation.

In addition to a growing spirit of openness, Toronto also emerged from the war a prosperous center of commerce and industry. Continuing demand for labor in and around Toronto drew migrants from within Canada and quickly forced a reopening of immigration. Toronto continued to thrive through the rest of the 20th century. Manufacturing declined, but the government and service sectors expanded. The city grew through large-scale suburban expansion. Like most North American Jews, Toronto Jews left crowded, aging housing downtown for the second of Toronto's Jewish neighborhoods, the near suburbs – now considered the central region of Jewish Toronto – above the core along Bathurst St. The near suburbs developed as an uptown version of the dense Jewish community that had been downtown. Continued immigration as well as suburbanization brought Jews to this area. Tens of thousands of Displaced Persons, including many Holocaust survivors, settled in Toronto in the 1950s as Canada became second only to Israel in the proportion of survivors in its Jewish population. North African Jews and Hungarian Jews arrived in Toronto in the 1960s. In addition, small-town Ontario Jews seeking a more Jewish environment for themselves and their children also moved to Toronto as did many young people from Montreal who moved out of fear of separatism in Quebec during the 1970s and 1980s. Toronto also attracted immigrants from the United States, including Vietnam draft resistors, and many from the former Soviet Union, South Africa, and Israel. Each group brought its own Jewish traditions, creating a unique Jewish community pluralism that found expression in new congregations, schools, bookstores, newspapers, bakeries, restaurants, clubs, and cultural associations. By 1991, the Jewish population of greater Toronto had risen to 163,000, up from 67,000 in 1951.

Education

The near suburbs developed as population expanded from the 1950s through the 1980s. Dozens of congregations of all branches are found in the near suburbs. Forest Hill, which was the subject of an early study of suburbia, *Crestwood Heights*, is the home of Holy Blossom Temple, Canada's largest Reform congregation, and of Beth Tzedec, Canada's – and North America's – largest Conservative congregation. Toronto's extensive network of Jewish schools, which began downtown in the first wave of migration, flourished in the near suburbs. The Toronto Jewish Federation decided in the early 1970s to place considerable community resources into day school education. But instead of funding schools directly, the Federation started subsidizing tuition according to need. Day school enrollment steadily increased, reaching parity with Jewish supplementary school enrollment in the 1970s. Congregationally based supplementary schools remain the setting in which many Toronto Jews have their Jewish education, but the enrollments at Jewish day schools are now larger. And as day school enrollment grew, so did the range of day school options. Orthodox day schools were joined by secular Zionist, Conservative, and Reform day schools and others with distinctive pedagogical approaches. Orthodox schools on the yeshivah model are also late 20th century additions to the Toronto Jewish school system.

As the day schools grew at the elementary level, Federation leaders planned for a high school which would be an alternative to the public high schools that prepare students to do well at university. The Community Hebrew Academy of Toronto, which opened in the 1960s, has had continually increasing enrollment, to over 1,400 students in 2004–5. In contrast to the expansion of the day school system, there are still many school-age Jewish children who do not receive any formal Jewish education. As in other North American Jewish communities, there is support for a model of lifelong learning in summer camps, campus programs, and adult education. Both the University of Toronto downtown and suburban York University have well-staffed and well-enrolled programs in Jewish Studies and many congregations have active adult education programs.

Community Organization

The Toronto UJA Federation, which was created by the merger of the Ontario branch of the *Canadian Jewish Congress with the Toronto Jewish Welfare Fund in the 1970s, acts as the central agency of the community. By the end of the 20th century the Federation's UJA campaign in Toronto was annually raising about $50 million. It allocates funds to a wide diversity of needs. About one-third of the annual UJA income goes overseas and almost 10 percent to Canada-wide Jewish organizations. Of the part that remains in Toronto about 40 percent is allocated to Jewish education and identity. Of that amount, two-thirds is used for subsidy of Jewish day school tuition. Significant Federation allocations support a range of social services often in conjunction with funding from different levels of government. The Jewish Family and Child Service is the leading agency in this area. The Federation acquired responsibility for the two Jewish community centers in the 1990s. The Toronto Jewish community has also developed a wide range of services for the elderly. The Baycrest Centre for Geriatric Care is one of the world's outstanding facilities. In addition to the support from Federation, Jewish schools, social services, and other organizations do their own fundraising. The Orthodox community is also organized for its particular needs, sponsoring a *bet din* and maintaining a well-organized Va'ad Hakashrut, which uses the COR label.

York Region and Downtown Toronto

Jewish population expanded along Bathurst Street beyond the near suburbs into York Region, north of the city of Toronto. This area is today the third distinctive Toronto Jewish neighborhood. The first step was the intentional creation of a Jewish neighborhood in the 1980s and this set the stage for a later transformation of this previous farming landscape into dense automobile-dependent suburbs. The developer of a large tract along Bathurst Street set aside a plot for a large Orthodox synagogue and encouraged Jewish day schools to build. The area soon became an affluent, largely Orthodox neighborhood from its inception. In addition to the synagogues and schools, the local shopping center contains a large grocery chain extensively stocked with kosher items, a Jewish bookstore, and kosher restaurants. Jews, not all Orthodox, have continued to move northward in York Region, attracted by large modern housing developments, Jewish schools, and the perception of the region as the "new neighborhood." By 2001, York Region accounted for 33 percent of the Jewish population of the GTA, and with so many younger Jewish families it was home to 40 percent of Jewish children and tightly packed with hockey clubs, music lessons, and carpooling.

UJA Federation has begun building a York Region campus that will include Federation offices, a Jewish community center, and several different day schools. Synagogues, while present, are less visible parts of the area landscape than they are in the near suburbs, since a number of existing day school buildings have space in which congregations can meet. Socially, the neighborhood is also distinctive. It has a large percentage of recent immigrants from Israel and the former Soviet Union. Street life, characteristic of Toronto Jewry two generations ago and still common downtown and in parts of the near suburbs, is much reduced, shifting to the malls that dot Bathurst Street in York Region which provide the setting for the leisure-time spending on entertainment, snacks, and consumer goods.

In counterpoint to the development in York Region, downtown Toronto has also seen a rapid revival in Jewish population growth. Much of downtown Toronto was gentrified in the latter 20th century. This urban transformation brought thousands of Jewish professionals and business people into renovated homes. With its combination of safe streets, public transportation, pedestrian street culture, and access to jobs and the arts, central Toronto is considered a very desirable place to live. Some areas with competitive house prices remain, but much of the increase in the Jewish population is occurring due to extensive recent condominium construction, which is adding hundreds of thousands of residential units to the central city. Recently formed Jewish congregations have joined several historic ones. New schools were founded in the 1970s and have grown since. The downtown Jewish Community Centre was renovated in the early 2000s and the Hillel at the University of Toronto's downtown campus constructed a new center at the same time. The Ashkenaz Festival of "new Jewish culture," which grew out of the *klezmer* revival, is held over Labor Day weekend every second year at Harbourfront, an urban park on the Lake Ontario waterfront.

Multiculturalism

Toronto is today a city where immigrants from all over the world and the children of immigrants constitute a large majority of the population. This multicultural reality is celebrated by city boosters and Toronto Jews as a vital part of that urban context. The ability of people from a pluralism of origins to live together in Toronto without overt racial tensions and the widely held view that new immigrants enrich the local culture and economy are seen as measures of the city's tolerance. Multiculturalism also continues Canada's older tradition of seeing itself as a mosaic society. The separate tiles of a mosaic touch and form a richer larger whole, but they do remain separate. While there are social settings where persons of different backgrounds meet, and a growing segment of Toronto society where friendships and families are drawn from more than one group, social segmentation continues. This is aided by new technologies which allow extensive and low-cost contact with the old country. Modern transportation also encourages more travel back and forth than was possible for previous waves of migration. This applies to Toronto Jews as well as the general population. Toronto Jews, for example, maintain a strong attachment with Israel. Many Toronto Jews have family in Israel, whom they visit and stay in contact with. Others who do not have family have visited and many have friends and professional contacts there. As well, many Israelis have moved to Toronto, some temporarily and others permanently.

Multiculturalism is also associated with the clustering of Toronto Jews in their own neighborhoods. Many older downtown neighborhoods still have ethnic labels, although the residents of these neighborhoods are now quite mixed. Clustering in ethnic neighborhoods is also common in the new suburbs. A large concentration of Italian Canadians is found west of the Jewish neighborhood in York Region, and the largest Chinese urban diaspora in the world, a product of recent and continuing immigration, is to its east. Other immigrant groups, including growing Muslim and Arab populations, are residentially concentrated elsewhere in the central city and suburbs of the GTA. Multiculturalism is also associated with the willingness to respect the public show of distinctive lifestyles. Accordingly, not only is Toronto a good place to be a secular, Reform, Reconstructionist, or Conservative Jew, but it is also a good place to be an Orthodox Jew. The value placed on diversity can sometimes engender unlikely alliances. In the 1990s, supporters of Toronto Jewish day schools, and the Ontario Region of the Canadian Jewish Congress acting on their behalf, joined Conservative Christian and Muslim private school supporters in a multifaith coalition. The coalition unsuccessfully urged the Ontario government to follow a policy similar to that of other provinces, which allocate public funds to private religious schools.

Toronto, which is now by far Canada's largest city, has developed into a major world center, a node in a global network of communications, commercial, and population flows. Greater Toronto's Jewish population topped 179,000 Jews in 2001 and now accounts for approximately half of all Jews in Canada. And that population is projected to grow. Jews play important roles in sustaining and developing Toronto's social and economic network, not unlike the role Jews play in other world cities. The Jews of Toronto, as in other world cities, are also continually challenged to creatively and productively blend the separate identities fostered by multiculturalism with the cosmopolitanism of an interconnected global society.

BIBLIOGRAPHY: C.H. Levitt, and W. Shaffir, *Riot at Christie Pits* (1987); C. Shahar and T. Rosenbaum, *Jewish Life in Greater Toronto: A Comprehensive Survey of the Attitudes & Behaviors of Members of the Greater Toronto Jewish Community* (2005); S.A. Speisman, *The Jews of Toronto: A History to 1937* (1979).

[Stuart Schoenfeld and Harold Troper (2nd ed.)]

°**TORQUEMADA, TOMÁS DE** (1420?–1498), first head of the Spanish *Inquisition. Probably born in Valladolid, he entered the *Dominican Order at the age of 14, and soon took his place among the strictest members of the monastery. At the age of 32 he became prior of the monastery of Segovia. Torquemada first came in contact with Queen Isabella around 1469; he became her confessor and some time later also her husband King Ferdinand's. His influence on the royal couple, especially on the queen, made him a powerful factor in Spanish politics. In conjunction with Cardinal Mendoza he drafted a petition to the Pope requesting authorization of the establishment of a unified national Spanish Inquisition. This was given in 1478. Torquemada was among the 12 clerics whose names were submitted to the pope in 1482 for inquisitorial appointments. At that time he was already known for his extreme views on the eradication of Judaism among the *Conversos and the question of the Jews in the united Spanish kingdom. After confirmation of his appointment he started to prepare the organization of the Inquisition, and founded its general supreme council, which became one of the councils of state and a key power in the internal affairs of the united kingdom. As head of the council, Torquemada was accorded the title inquisitor general (1483).

Torquemada established a system of regional inquisitional tribunals, at first in smaller towns near centers of Converso influence where opposition from the local population to the inquisitorial methods was manifest. Later, tribunals were also set up in larger towns. Torquemada initiated conventions of inquisitors (the first was held in Seville in 1484) to discuss the activities of the tribunals. He also drew up permanent instructions for the tribunals on working methods, as well as judicial procedures. In addition to the trials held by the Inquisition, the first results of Torquemada's activities concerning Conversos and Jews were the orders of expulsion from Andalusia (1483) and Albarracín (1486). In particular, there was the libel of *Host desecration and alleged crucifixion of a Christian child involving a group of Conversos at *La Guardia (1490–91).

In the sphere of general politics Torquemada pressed for resumption of the war of Reconquest against the kingdom of *Granada. After Granada's conquest he was instrumental in obtaining the general decree of expulsion of the Jews from Spain (1492). A widely related legend – probably without historical foundation – tells of negotiations between a Jewish delegation headed by Don Isaac *Abrabanel and the king: the king was offered the sum of 30,000 dinars for abolition of the expulsion decree, but Torquemada, who was listening to the talks from an adjacent room, broke into the king's room, put a crucifix on the table, and reminded him of Judah Iscariot who had betrayed Jesus for 30 pieces of silver. Influenced by Torquemada's appearance, the king rejected the Jewish offer.

In 1494 additional inquisitors were appointed, who were allocated many of Torquemada's former competencies. The appointments were evidently made because of Torquemada's failing health, not because of a decline in his influence. In the early 1490s he proceeded severely against bishops and clerics suspected of requesting the pope's support against his methods and policy, the essence of which were to turn Spain into a country of "one flock with one shepherd."

Torquemada had already become a legend in his lifetime, and various assessments – often contradictory – have been made of his personality by writers and scholars. He became a symbol of religious and ideological fanaticism, of persecution, investigation and interrogation, and probing into the souls of men.

BIBLIOGRAPHY: Baer, Spain, index; E. de Molènes, *Torquemada et l'Inquisition* (1897); H.C. Lea, *A History of the Inquisition of Spain* (3 vols., 1906, repr. 1958), index; T. Hope, *Torquemada, Scourge of the Jews* (1939); B. Llorca, in: *Sefarad*, 8 (1948), 360–3, 374–81.

[Haim Beinart]

TORRE, ALFONSO DE LA (1421–1461), Spanish Converso author. Torre, a humanist, is known principally for his *Vysyon Delectable de la Philosophia y artes liberales*, a kind of universal encyclopedia presented in the form of a series of dialogues which he wrote c. 1450. It quoted *Maimonides extensively and was in its turn frequently cited by Solomon ibn Verga in his *Shevet Yehudah*. The sixth chapter of the work, dealing with arithmetic, includes a detailed discussion of the numerological aspects of the Kabbalah.

The *Vysyon* has been termed a link between the Judeo-Arabic thinkers of the Middle Ages and *Spinoza, and it enjoyed great influence in its own day and for the subsequent two centuries. First published in Burgos in 1485, it was one of the few non-Hebrew books printed by Abraham *Usque, who produced an Italian version in Ferrara in 1554. The Italian text was ultimately retranslated into Spanish by the Marrano Francisco (Joseph) de *Caceres (Frankfurt, 1623^1, 1663^2), who was probably unaware that its original author was himself a Spaniard and a Converso.

[Kenneth R. Scholberg]

TORRÈS, HENRY (1891–1966), French lawyer and politician. Born in Les Andelys, Torrès practiced law in Bordeaux and in 1919 moved to Paris. A communist in his youth, he published *Histoire d'un complot* (1921) protesting against the arrest of militant communists after World War I but later joined the Socialist Party and was a radical socialist deputy from 1932 to 1936. He became famous for the fiery eloquence of his advocacy as a defense counsel. His reputation reached its peak in 1926 with his successful defense of Shalom *Schwarzbard, who assassinated the Ukrainian leader Simon *Petlyura. By using the evidence of the pogroms initiated by Petlyura against the Ukrainian Jews, Torrès obtained Schwarzbard's acquittal. After the Nazi invasion of France, Torrès fled to the United States. In America he campaigned against the Pétain regime in France, publishing *La France trahie: Pierre Laval* (1941; Eng. tr., 1941) and *La Machine infernale* (1942; *Campaign of Treachery*, 1942) and edited *La Voix de France* from 1942 to 1943, a political journal for French refugees in New York. After World War II, Torrès returned to France and from 1948 to 1958 was a Gaullist senator for the Seine department. Vice president of the High Court of Justice from 1956 to 1958, he was also president of the French broadcasting authority (RTF).

Torrès was the author of several political and historical works, among them *Le Procès des Pogromes* (1927) describing his defense of Schwarzbard, and *France, terre de liberté* (1940). He also wrote plays with a legal background including French versions of the *Trial of Mary Dugan* by Bayard Veiller (1928), and *Witness for the Prosecution* by Agatha Christie (1956).

[Shulamith Catane]

TORRES, LUIS DE (15th–16th cent.), Spanish interpreter to Christopher *Columbus on his first voyage of discovery in 1492. Contrary to what was formerly believed, he was the only person of Jewish birth who was among the companions of Christopher Columbus on his first voyage, having been baptized shortly before the expedition sailed. He knew Hebrew, Aramaic, and some Arabic. When Columbus landed in Cuba, convinced it was the mainland, he took possession of it for Spain and dispatched Torres with a party into the interior to see if they could find gold. Torres reported back that the natives were friendly, that he had found no gold but that he had seen men putting thin rolls of dried leaves called tobacco into their mouths, lighting them and blowing out clouds of smoke. Torres settled in Cuba and won the friendship of the Indian ruler who gave him land and slaves. He soon set up his own small empire. As an independent ruler of Spanish territory, he received an annual allowance from the Spanish royal family.

BIBLIOGRAPHY: Roth, Marranos; M. Kayserling, *Christopher Columbus…* (1907^2).

°**TORREY, CHARLES CUTLER** (1863–1956), U.S. Bible scholar and Semitist. Born in East Hardwick, Vermont, Torrey taught Latin at Bowdoin College (1885–86), and Semitics, Bible, and Hebraica at Andover Theological Seminary (1892–1900) and at Yale University (1900–34). He was one of the founders of the American School of Archaeology in Jerusalem. Subsequent archaeological finds and advances in Semitic linguistics and in lower and higher biblical criticism have been damaging to many of Torrey's contributions in the estimation of present-day scholarship. He developed an independent exegesis of the period of Ezra and Nehemiah in *The Composition and Historical Value of Ezra-Nehemiah* (1896), *Ezra Studies* (1910; 1970), and *Chronicler's History of Israel* (1954). Following E.

Koenig's commentary on Isaiah, he argued in *Second Isaiah* (1928) for the unity of Isaiah 40–66, and assigned Isaiah 34–35 as the introduction to this corpus. In his articles on Ezekiel in the *Journal of Biblical Literature* and in *Pseudo-Ezekiel and the Original Prophecy* (1930; 1970[4]), he expounded his theory regarding the nature and composition of the Book of Ezekiel. His thesis was that the bulk of the prophecy contained in the canonical Book of Ezekiel was pseudepigraphic, composed around 230 B.C.E. but purporting to date from the period of Manasseh (692–639 B.C.E.), and later in 200 B.C.E. edited so as to appear to be an exilic work. It provoked, however, a bitter attack by S. Spiegel, who advocated caution in the critical analyses and wanton emendations of Ezekiel.

His often cited theory that the Synoptic Gospels, John, and Revelations, as they have been handed down are for the most part straightforward translations of Aramaic originals, was developed in a number of publications including *Translations Made from the Original Aramaic Gospels* (1912), *Four Gospels: A New Translation* (1934), *Our Translated Gospels* (1936), *Documents of the Primitive Church* (1941), and the posthumous *Apocalypse of John* (1958). How deeply the koranic tradition is steeped in the Hebraic culture is documented in *Jewish Foundation of Islam* (1933; 1967). His other Islamic studies are *Mohammedan Conquest of Egypt and North Africa* (1901) by Ibn Abd al-Ḥakām, edited with notes and selections of the writings of Al-Buḥāa (1948; 1969). In the area of numismatics he investigated the Aramaic graffiti on coins buried in 318 B.C.E. and belonging to Jews of Egypt (1937), and he wrote on the rare coinage of the Khans of Khokand and Bukhārā *Gold Coins of Kokhand and Bukhārā* (1950). His other publications include a treatise on the composition of Acts *The Composition and Date of Acts* (1926); and an introduction to the apocryphal literature (*Apocryphal Literature; A Brief Introduction*, 1945).

BIBLIOGRAPHY: M. Greenberg, in: C.C. Torrey, *Pseudo-Ezekiel and the Original Prophecy* (1970), xi–xxxv (prolegomenon); W.F. Stinespring, in: idem, *Ezra Studies* (1970), xi–xxviii (prolegomenon); F. Rosenthal, in: idem, *Jewish Foundation of Islam* (1967), v–xxiii (introd.).

[Zev Garber]

TORTOISE (Mod. Heb. צָב), a reptile. In Israel there are several species of both land and water tortoises; the latter lives in both sweet and salt water. Some commentators identify the צָב (*ẓav*), enumerated among the unclean reptiles (Lev. 11:29), with the tortoise, and on this basis it is so called in modern Hebrew. According to rabbinical sources, however, the *ẓav* is a species of *lizard. Thus the expression "the *ẓav* after its kind" is explained as including the salamander and other reptiles which bear no resemblance to the tortoise (see Sifra 6:5). Similarly a resemblance between the *ẓav* and the snake is mentioned (Ḥul. 127a), and the *ḥardon*, a species of lizard of the family of *Agamidae* (TJ, Ber. 8:6, 12b). From this last source it is apparent that "the *ẓav* after its kind" includes the *Agamidae* family, of which six species are found in Israel, the largest of which is the *Uromastix aegyptius* called in Arabic *dabb*. It is found in the Negev and the Arabah and is herbivorous. The Bedouin hunt it and regard its flesh as a great delicacy.

BIBLIOGRAPHY: Lewysohn, Zool, 230f.; F.S. Bodenheimer, *Animal and Man in Bible Lands* (1960), 10, 99; J. Feliks, *Animal World of the Bible* (1962), 10.

[Jehuda Feliks]

TORTOSA, city in Tarragona provinces, N.E. Spain; it had one of the oldest Jewish communities in the Iberian Peninsula. A tombstone inscribed in three languages (Hebrew, Latin, and Greek) belonging to the first centuries of the Christian era (opinions conflict as to its exact date) attests the early existence of Jews in the city. The Jewish quarter was situated in the northern part of the town, now slightly north of the district known as Remolinos; the Jewish cemetery (from which only a few tombstones have survived) was situated to the east of the city wall. The existence of the quarter is commemorated by the names of such streets as Jerusalem Alley and Jerusalem Street.

Muslim Period

During the Muslim period many Tortosa Jews engaged in agriculture and in the flourishing maritime trade, maintaining commercial ties with Jews of Barcelona and southern France. The city was also a center of Jewish learning as is shown by 10th- and 11th-century responsa which indicate a high level of talmudic knowledge and devout religious observance. The poet, grammarian, and lexicographer *Menahem b. Jacob ibn Saruq (mid-10th century) was a native of Tortosa and returned to his birthplace after losing the patronage of *Ḥisdai Ibn Shaprut of Córdoba. Another native of Tortosa, the physician and geographer *Ibrahim b. Yaqub, Menahem's contemporary, was sent by Caliph al-Ḥakam II to travel and survey Western and Central Europe. The Hebrew liturgical poet Levi b. Isaac ibn Mar Saul lived in Tortosa in the early 11th century. Ashtor (see bibliography) estimates Tortosa's Jewish population in the 11th century at about 30 families.

Under Christian Rule

Ramon Berenguer IV, count of Barcelona, captured Tortosa from the Muslims in 1148. The treaty of capitulation was similar to that of *Tudela, but the article which prohibited the appointment of Jewish officials with rights of jurisdiction over Muslims was omitted. It appears that the Jewish community was destroyed during this war of conquest and Ramon Berenguer attempted to restore it. He set aside a plot of land between the coast and the R. Ebro, which was then fortified and surrounded with towers, on which 60 residential houses were built. Berenguer also granted the Jews vineyards and gardens which had formerly belonged to Muslims, so that the cultivation of these became the principal occupation of the Jews, in addition to crafts and maritime trade. He also promised land to any Jew who would settle in Tortosa, and Jews were exempted from the payment of taxes for four years. Even after this period, they were not required to do any "work, customary tasks or duties for the count or the other lords of the land, unless of their own free will." The ruler decreed that no Muslim should exercise authority over Jews; lawsuits between Jews and Christians were to be adjudicated under the privileges enjoyed by the community of Barcelona. These conditions were an exceptional opportunity for the development of the Jewish community.

However, the hopes which Berenguer had placed in the Jews did not materialize because of the division between the various lords of the town who challenged his authority over it and severely oppressed the Jewish population. In February 1181, Alfonso II of Aragon granted the Jews of Tortosa a privilege, with the consent of Raimundo de Moncada (who held the right of jurisdiction over the Jews of the town) according to which they were authorized to present one of the town's lords with a gift without incurring the obligation of giving gifts to the others. Pledges were not to be taken from them for their debts, they were not to be confined to their houses, and if they were condemned to imprisonment, they were to be detained in the fortress (see Rashba (Solomon b. Abraham *Adret), Responsa, IV, 260). The sum which was paid in taxes in 1271 – 6,000 sólidos – testifies to the strength and wealth of the community. Tortosa and Alcañez then formed a single entity, for tax purposes.

Pedro III granted the Jews of Tortosa the right of sitting as judges in the local tribunals, though with a lower rank than the Christian judges. During the 13th century Jews were employed as bailiffs by the Moncada family and by the Templars.

At the beginning of the 14th century, the community of Tortosa addressed a complaint to James II against the moratorium on debts which he had granted to the Christian inhabitants of the town, claiming that oral promises that the debts owed to them would be repaid could not be relied upon.

Result of the Persecutions of 1391

The community of Tortosa suffered during the persecutions of the Jews in Spain in 1391. On July 24, John I wrote to the municipal council, requiring them not only to protect the Jews but also to rehabilitate the community. At the end of the month the Jews were still concealed in the fortress, but from the beginning of August they were taken away individually to the houses of the townsmen in order to be baptized, by force if necessary. Christian townsmen and Jewish apostates collaborated in these acts, the latter compelling the conversion of their wives, parents, and children. On August 14 disorders broke out against both the Jews and the municipal authorities who were accused of giving the Jews assistance and support. By arresting the instigator of the disorders, the municipal leaders succeeded in suppressing the riots; many Jews, however, abandoned their religion during these events. After more than a month (on Sept. 2), the king wrote to the municipal leaders of Tortosa requesting information concerning the heirless property of the Jews who had died as martyrs. In April 1392 he authorized the impoverished Jews who were then living in the fortress to remain there and ordered the bailiff to protect them. Turning his attention to the relations between Jews and *Conversos, the king issued a decree (Aug. 18, 1393) in which he prohibited Jews and Conversos to live in the same quarter, to eat or to pray together. Upon the instructions of the bishop, the Conversos were obliged to attend church, listen to missionary sermons, adhere to Christian observances, and immediately separate themselves from the Jews. The Jews were compelled to wear a distinctive *badge and garb, and sexual relations between Jews and Christians (obviously referring to Conversos) were punishable by burning at the stake. It nevertheless appears that toward the close of the century (1397) a number of laws favorable to both the Jews and the Moors of Tortosa were issued.

Disputation of Tortosa

In 1412 Tortosa became the focus of events which the Jews of Aragon regarded with trepidation, and that proved a turning point in their history, namely, the Disputation of Tortosa (see *Tortosa, Disputation of). The community of Tortosa itself was represented by the poet Solomon b. Reuben *Bonafed who gives a description of the tense atmosphere which pervaded throughout the kingdom in general, and in Tortosa in particular, during the disputation.

The disputation began on Feb. 7, 1413, and was continued, with interruptions until Nov. 1414.

In 1417 the community of Tortosa began to recover. Alfonso V exempted Jews who came to live there from payment of taxes for five years. There is also some information on the community from the reign of Ferdinand II, who in 1480 issued a decree in which he instructed the community of Tortosa on the procedure for electing community leaders, trustees, and **muqaddimūn*. In October 1481 he issued further instructions concerning the swearing-in of officials, and also authorized the election of relatives (e.g., father, son, brothers, father-in-law and son-in-law) to serve in the community – a practice forbidden by the regulations of the Spanish communities. Ferdinand II ordered the election of Benveniste Barzilai as the leader of the community.

An indication of the atmosphere in Tortosa on the eve of the expulsion of the Jews from Spain in 1492 can be deduced from the fine imposed on Abraham Toledano of Tortosa, who made a wager, with a number of Christians that the Catholic Monarchs would not capture Loja and Málaga from the Muslims. Tortosa, like neighboring Barcelona and Tarragona, was also a port of departure for Jewish refugees from Spain.

BIBLIOGRAPHY: MUSLIM PERIOD: Ashtor, Korot, 1 (1960), 226–9; idem, in: *Zion*, 28 (1963), 48–49. CHRISTIAN PERIOD: Baer, Spain, index; Baer, Urkunden, 1 (1929), index; H.C. Lea, *A History of the Inquisition of Spain*, 1 (1906), 544; F. Carreras i Candi, *Laljama de jueus de Tortosa* (1928); Neuman, Spain, index; F. Vendrell, in: *Sefarad*, 10 (1950), 353ff., 362f.; D. Romano, *ibid.*, 13 (1953), 79ff.; A. López de Meneses, in: *Estudios de Edad Media de la Corona de Aragón*, 6 (1952), 748–9; J.M. Font Rius, in: *Cuadernos de Historia de España*, 10 (1953), 124ff.; E. Bayerri y Bartomeu, *Historia de Tortosa y su comarca*, 4 (1954), 90ff.; F. Cantera, *Sinagogas españolas* (1955), 319f.; Cantera-Millás, Inscripciones, 267–77.

[Haim Beinart]

TORTOSA, DISPUTATION OF, disputation held in Tortosa, in 1413–14, the most important and longest of the Christian-Jewish *disputations which were forced upon the Jews during the Middle Ages. It was apparently prompted by Gerónimo de Santa Fé (the apostate Joshua *Lorki) in which he claimed to prove the authenticity of the messianism of Jesus from Jewish sources. In 1412 the anti-pope *Benedict XIII, who was recognized as pope in Spain, ordered the communities of Aragon and Catalonia to send delegates for a discussion in his presence on the claims of Gerónimo. The disputation was drawn out over some 20 months, and 69 sessions were held; it was presided over by the pope, who also actively participated in it. From the outset, the disputation did not assume the form of a free discussion between two parties but that of a propagandist missionary attack accompanied by psychological pressure – to the point of intimidation and threats – by the Christian side against Jews, in order to compel them to accept the arguments of their adversaries. The principal Hebrew source for the history of the disputation is *Shevet Yehudah* by Solomon *Ibn Verga. The Jewish sources mention about 20 participants on the Jewish side; some of these actively participated, while others were advisers and observers. A neutral Christian account of the debate is also extant. In the disputation, the most prominent personalities were rabbis *Zerahiah ha-Levi, Astruc ha-Levi, Joseph *Albo, and Mattathias ha-Yiẓhari.

Immediately upon the first encounter, the pope announced – contrary to the promises which he had previously given to the Jews – that it was not intended to hold a discussion between two equal parties, but to prove the truth of Christianity and its principles, as it emerges from the Talmud. Gerónimo opened the disputation with a veiled threat against the obstinate Jews, and during the disputation he passed to open threats. To the arguments presented by the Jews, he retorted by accusing them of heresy against their own religion, for which they would be tried by the Inquisition. In this heavy atmosphere, the Jewish delegates were overtaken by fear and confusion and occasionally did not dare – or did not succeed – in answering correctly, especially because those replies which did not please the pope aroused vulgar rebukes on his part which only intensified their fears and anxieties. During the disputation new participants appeared on the Jewish side, and their arguments were not always coordinated with the former; besides, the last word was always granted to Gerónimo, so that the impression could be formed that he had the upper hand.

During the first part of the disputation (until March 1414), the discussion revolved around the Messiah and his nature (as in the Disputation of *Barcelona). Its second part concerned the "errors, the heresy, the villainy, and the abuse against the Christian religion in the Talmud," according to the definition of the initiators of the disputation, and resembled the disputation of Paris, initiated by Nicholas *Donin. The Jews were requested to answer the claims of Gerónimo which appeared in his work that was being used as the basis of the disputation, and to explain various Midrashim which had been collected by Raymond *Martini. After a while, 12 questions were presented to the Jews on the subjects of Jesus, Original Sin, and the causes of the Exile. The discussions on these subjects were prolonged over several months. It was at this stage that some of the most brilliant answers ever given to questions of this type in similar disputations of the Middle Ages were offered.

At the beginning of 1414 Pope Benedict entered the disputation himself and demanded that the procedure be shortened and practical conclusions arrived at. Most of the Jews sought to withdraw from the disputation because during their prolonged absence from home and as a result of the mental strain prevailing among their communities, faith was being undermined and there was rising despair, while the missionary preachings of the monks had succeeded in bringing many Jews to baptism. Zerahiah ha-Levi, Mattathias ha-Yiẓhari, and Astruc ha-Levi, however, presented memoranda in which they refuted all the arguments drawn from *aggadot* and Midrashim. R. Astruc even dared to point out the injustice inhering in the actual conditions of the disputation. The delegates of the communities were away from their homes for about a year; they became impoverished and tremendous harm was caused to their communities; this may also be regarded as a reason for the failure of the Jews to reply successfully. Gerónimo reacted with words of contempt against the Talmud and the Jews who denied the validity of the *aggadah*, he argued that they ought to be tried according to their own laws as unbelievers of the principles of their faith.

The second part of the disputation opened in April 1414. Its details are not entirely known, but it is clearly evident that at first the Jews chose to remain silent. When Gerónimo brought a list of sayings which were to be effaced from the Talmud as impugning the honor of Christianity, the Jews replied that they themselves were unable to answer, although it was certain that the sages of the Talmud in their time would have been able to reply, and that consequently the value of the Talmud could not be deduced from their own weakness; they once more requested to be freed from the disputation. Gerónimo summarized his arguments and demanded of the pope that the delegates be brought to justice. The latter, with the exception of Zerahiah ha-Levi and Joseph Albo, claimed that they failed to understand the meaning of Gerónimo's citations. On November 12, the memorandum of R. Astruc was presented as the last Jewish memorandum, and on the following day the disputation was concluded with the issue of a bull on the subject by the pope, and the Jews returned to their homes.

Consequences of the Disputation

Throughout the period of the disputation, Jews continually arrived in Tortosa, where they converted to Christianity. The authorities, on their part, intensified their persecutions, and ordered that everything which had been disqualified by Gerónimo should be obliterated from the Talmud. The disputation in itself acted as an incentive for anti-Jewish incitement, and in several towns the inhabitants adopted severe measures in order to force the Jews to convert. Many broke down and accepted baptism. Three works were written after the Disputation of Tortosa in an attempt at soul-searching: *Sefer ha-Ikkarim* ("Book of Principles") of R. Joseph Albo, in which the author clarified the religious fundamentals discussed at the disputation; *Sefer ha-Emunot* ("Book of Beliefs") by R. *Shem Tov, who regarded the cultivation of philosophy as the cause of conversion; and *Iggeret Musar* ("Letter of Ethics") by R. Solomon *Alami, who considered that disrespect toward religion and ethics was the cause of the destruction of Spanish Jewry.

BIBLIOGRAPHY: S.Z.H. Halberstam, in: *Jeschurun*, 6 (1868), 45ff. (Heb.); J.D. Eisenstein, *Oẓar Vikkuḥim* (1928), 104–11; Baer, Spain, index; Y. Boer, *Die Disputation von Tortosa, 1413–1414* (1931); idem, in: *Sefer Zikkaron le-Asher Gulak u-li-Shemu'el Klein* (1942), 28–49; S. Lieberman, *Sheki'in* (1939), index; idem, in: HJ, 5 (1943), 87–102; A. Posnanski, in: REJ, 74 (1922), 17–39, 160–8; 75 (1923), 74–88, 187–204, 76 (1923), 37–46; A. Pacios López, *La Disputa de Tortosa*, 2 vols. (1957).

[Haim Beinart]

TORTS.

The Principal Categories of Torts

The liability of various tortfeasors is discussed in relative detail in the Torah. Four principal cases are considered:

(1) where someone opens a pit into which an animal falls and dies (Ex. 21:33–4);

(2) where cattle trespass into the fields of others and do damage (Ex. 22:4);

(3) where someone lights a fire which spreads to neighboring fields (Ex. 22:5);

(4) where an ox gores man or beast (Ex. 21:28–32, 35–6). To those has to be added the case where a man injures his fellow or damages his property (Ex. 21:18–19, 22–5; Lev. 24:18–20). The Talmud calls the cases contained in the Torah primary categories of damage (*Avot Nezikin*) and these serve as archetypes for similar groups of torts. The principal categories of animal torts are *shen* (tooth) – where the animal causes damage by consuming; *regel* (foot) – where the animal causes damage by walking in its normal manner; and *keren* (horn) – where the animal causes damage by goring with the intention of doing harm or does any other kind of unusual damage. The other principal categories of damage are *bor* (pit) – any nuisance which ipso facto causes damage; *esh* (fire) – anything which causes damage when spread by the wind; and direct damage by man to another's person or property. These principal categories and their derivative rules were expanded to form a complete and homogeneous legal system embracing many other factual situations. As a result they were capable of dealing with any case of tortious liability which might arise.

The Basis of Liability – Negligence

The Talmud states that a man could be held liable only for damage caused by his negligence (*peshi'ah*), and not for damage through an accident (*ones*). Negligence is defined as conduct which the tortfeasor should have foreseen would cause damage (BK 21b; 52a/b; 99b), since this would be the normal result of such conduct. Thus liability would be incurred for a fire which spread in an ordinary wind (BK 56a) or for fencing a courtyard with thorns in a place frequented by the public who habitually lean against this fence (BK 29b).

The rabbis ruled that negligence was to be determined objectively. A man is liable for conduct which people would normally foresee as likely to cause damage (see R. Ulla's statement, BK 27b; Tosef. BK 10:29). On the other hand, if his conduct was such that most people would not normally foresee it as likely to cause damage, the damage is considered a mishap and not a consequence of his act and he is not liable (see Rif, *Halakhot* on BK 61b). Even if the defendant was of above-average intelligence and foresaw that damage would occur, he could not be held liable for conduct causing damage if most people would not have foreseen damage as resulting from such conduct. In such circumstances no liability would be incurred under human law for even willful damage (see Ra'ah and Meiri in *Shitah Mekubbeẓet*, BK 56a, beginning *U-le-Rav Ashi*) unless the damage claimed was depredation (BK 27a). However, rabbinical enactments created liability for deliberate acts in certain cases in the interests of public policy (Git. 53a; Tosef. Git. 4 (3):6). The objective criterion of negligence was also applied where the tortfeasor was of below-average intelligence and incapable of foreseeing the possibility of damage. However, the deaf-mute, idiot, and minor are not liable for the damage they cause, since they have no understanding and cannot be expected to foresee the consequences of their actions. Indeed, since they frequently do cause damage, those encountering them should take suitable precautions, and if they fail to do so would themselves be liable for the resulting damage. In this respect damage caused by the deaf-mute, idiot, and minor can be compared to damage by cattle on public ground for which the owners are not liable since the injured party himself is bound to take precautions.

This test of negligence was applied to all the principal categories of damage mentioned in the Torah (see BK 55b and *Rashi* beginning *ke-ein*). Thus, if an animal was injured by falling into an inadequately covered pit, the owner of the pit was liable. On the other hand, if the pit were properly covered but the cover became decayed, he would not be liable (BK 52a). Similarly, the owner of the pit would be liable if a young ox, incapable of looking after itself, fell into an open pit, but not if the ox were fully grown and fell into the pit during the daytime (*Milḥamot ha-Shem* 52b ad finem). Likewise, liability would be incurred for a fire which spread in a normal wind but not where it spread in an unusual wind (BK 56a); and the owner of cattle which consumed and trampled on crops in another's field would be liable for the damage only if the control he exercised over his cattle was insufficient to prevent this kind of damage (BK 55b, 56a).

As to damage done by man directly, the Mishnah states: he is always *Mu'ad* (forewarned, and therefore liable for the consequences), whether he acted intentionally or inadvertently, "whether he was awake or asleep" (BK 26a). Nevertheless, many cases are mentioned where the man who did the damage was not liable and Tosafot (BK 27b) tried to solve the contradiction by distinguishing between cases of absolute "*ones*," and qualified "*ones*." Only in the latter case would liability be incurred. There is no hint of this distinction in the sources and the better view seems to be that a tortfeasor is liable only if he caused damage by *ones* (compulsion) which could have been foreseen by him, as putting himself in the hands of robbers who forced him to do damage, or lying down to sleep next to objects which he should have foreseen he might break in his sleep, aliter, if the vessels were placed next to him after he went to sleep. Likewise a person who caused damage through his lack of expertise could only be held liable where he should have foreseen that expertise was required. However, a person who caused proprietary damage to his neighbor in order to save himself is not exempt because of *ones*, as he chose to act in a way which would damage his neighbor's property and did foresee the damage.

No Liability Where No Negligence Exists

Cases where the defendant is entirely exempt from liability because he was in no way negligent are of two kinds:

(1) the plaintiff himself was negligent because he should have foreseen the possibility of damage i.e., where the defendant acted in the usual way and the plaintiff acted in an unusual way and the damage was therefore unforeseeable;

(2) neither party could have foreseen the possibility of damage and therefore neither was negligent. An instance of the second kind is where an animal, kept under sufficient control, escaped in an unusual manner and did damage, and no liability would be incurred (BK 55b). Similarly, where an animal managed to start a fire or dig a pit which caused damage, no liability would be incurred since such an unusual eventuality could not have been foreseen (see the Ravad in the *Shitah Mekubbeẓet*, BK 48a beginning "*Mat*"; BK 22a). The Talmud cites examples where no liability would be incurred, such as where an animal fell into a pit whose covering was originally adequate but which later became decayed (BK 52a); where a wall or tree unexpectedly fell onto the highway (BK 6b); where a fire spread further than could have been anticipated (BK 61b); where a burning coal was given to a deaf-mute, idiot, or minor who set fire to something (BK 59b); or experts such as physicians who acted in the usual professional manner and caused damage (Tosef. BK 9:11). As instances of the first kind the Talmud cites the case where a person running along the street collided with and was injured by another walking along the street; here the former alone would be liable since his conduct was unusual (BK 32a). Similarly, if a man broke his vessel against a beam carried by the man walking in front of him, the owner of the beam would not be liable. Aliter, however, if the owner of the beam stopped unexpectedly, thereby causing the vessel to strike the beam and break (loc. cit.). Likewise, a person who places his objects on public ground where they are damaged by animals walking or grazing in a normal manner has no claim against the owner of the animals, since animals are to be expected on public ground (BK 19b, 20a). However, the presence of a pit, fire, or a goring ox on public ground would cause liability for damage since they are not normally present and people do not expect them and take no precautions (BK 27b). It would also be unusual behavior and therefore negligence to enter another's premises or bring chattels or livestock therein, without permission. Since his presence was unexpected the owner of the premises would not be liable for damage caused to the trespasser or his property, but the trespasser would be liable for damage caused to the owner or his property (BK 47a–b, 48a).

Sometimes a person is injured even though both parties behaved in the usual manner, e.g., when both walk in the street or if one enters the premises of another with permission. In these cases the tortfeasor is not liable because the other party should have taken precautions as he ought to have foreseen the normal behavior of the tortfeasor. Likewise, damage may occur when both parties behave in an unusual manner as where both were running along the street or where both entered the premises of a third party without permission (*ibid.*, 32a; 48a/b); in these cases too, the tortfeasor is exempt, since the fact that he was behaving abnormally should have made him foresee that others may behave abnormally too (Tos. BK 48b, s.v. "*Sheneihem*").

If without negligence a man creates a situation which is likely to cause damage, he will not be liable for damage caused before he had a reasonable opportunity to know about the situation and remove it. An objective test was laid down as to when a man should have known of the existence of the nuisance and acted to remove it. If he adequately covered his pit and through no fault of his own the pit was uncovered he would not be liable for damage during the period that most people would not have known that the pit had become open and required covering (BK 52a). Similarly, if his animal escaped from his courtyard through no fault of his own, and caused damage during the period in which he could not have been expected to realize that the animal had escaped and to recapture it, he would not be liable (see BK 58a and Meiri in the *Shitah Mekubbeẓet* on 55b beginning "*nifreẓah*"). Similarly if a man's vessels broke non-negligently on the highway and, without intending to abandon them, he left them there, he is liable, except for damage caused by them before they could have been removed (BK 29a). Similarly, the owner of a wall or a tree which fell onto the highway and caused damage would be liable only if he knew that they were in a bad condition or was warned that they might fall (BK 6b).

The foreseeability test as the basis of liability for damage led the rabbis to conclude that even where negligent the tortfeasor would only be liable for damage that he could foresee. He is not liable for additional or other damage, or damage greater than that foreseeable. Thus where a fire spread in an ordinary wind the tortfeasor would be liable for whatever could be seen to be within the path of the fire but not for what was hidden, unless, according to R. Judah, he should have contemplated the existence of hidden objects (BK 61b). Similarly, if a man dug a pit and did not cover it he would be liable for injury to a young animal or to an animal who fell into it at night but would not be liable for injury to a grown animal who fell into it in daylight (BK 54b), or for a human being who fell into the pit (BK 28b). If the pit was less than ten handbreadths deep, he would be liable for injury only, since animals do not normally die when falling into such a small pit (BK 3a). Likewise, liability for injury is restricted to the extent of its original gravity. If the injury becomes worse than was originally estimated the tortfeasor is not liable for additional damage (BK 91a). However, where the degree of damage was foreseen but the way in which the damage occurred was unexpected the rabbis disagreed as to whether the defendant should be held liable, some arguing that the defendant was liable in negligence while others holding that the defendant could not be liable for what he could not foresee. This situation is known in the Talmud as *Teḥilato bi-Feshi'ah ve-Sofo be-Ones* (negligent conduct leading to accidental damage). Thus, if a man put his dog on a roof and the dog fell off and broke nearby objects (BK 21b), he would be liable in negligence for putting his dog on the roof (since a dog could be expected to jump off a roof) but not for the mode of damage, since he could not have foreseen that the dog would fall.

Indirect Damage

The foreseeability test would appear to determine liability for indirect damage (**gerama*) where the damage is the ultimate consequence of the defendant's act. Only if the defendant should have foreseen the damage occurring would he be held liable for indirect damage.

Unusual Damage by Cattle

Unusual animal torts, such as goring, lie between liability in negligence for foreseeable damage and exemption for accidental damage. In such cases the animal's owners are liable for half-damages (BK 14a). But if the animal was a habitual gorer, having gored three times, the owner would be liable for full damage, since the damage was neither unusual nor unforeseeable. On the other hand, the owner would be completely exempt if he was not negligent at all. Thus, if the defendant's animal gored the plaintiff on the defendant's premises, no liability would normally be incurred since the defendant could not have foreseen that the plaintiff would enter his premises.

Defenses to Negligence

A person who negligently causes damage is not liable for damages in three situations:

(1) where he received permission from the plaintiff to cause damage (BK 92a, 93a), e.g., was allowed to feed his cattle in the plaintiff's field;

(2) where the defendant, in his capacity as a court official was given permission by a court to harm the plaintiff, e.g., by administering punishment (Tosef. BK 9:11);

(3) where the damage inflicted was nonphysical, e.g., distress and sorrow (where there is no physical pain), or economic or commercial damage (BK 98a); for liability for damage is restricted to physical damage.

Damage Committed by the Person and by His Property

A distinction is found in several places in the Talmud between damage by a person and damage by his property (BK 4a; 4b). The difference is that liability for damage by the person is confined to negligent acts of commission whereas liability for damage by his property can also be incurred by negligent acts of omission. Thus, a man who spilt another's wine must pay for the damage, whereas if he saw the other's wine spill and did nothing to help him recover it, he would not be liable. On the other hand, the defendant whose ox grazed in the plaintiff's field would be liable for damage caused by the animal either because he put the ox there or because he did not adequately prevent its escape. Similarly, a man who did nothing to prevent a stray fire from spreading onto the highway would not be liable even though he was able to prevent the fire's spreading. He would be liable, however, if he caused the fire negligently or if he did not prevent the spread of a fire from his own premises, even though he did not start it.

Joint Tortfeasors

Where damage was caused by the negligence of two or more persons, the parties are liable in equal proportions. If the plaintiff and the defendant were equally negligent, the plaintiff recovers half damages from the defendant and loses the remainder (see Tos. BK 23a, s.v. "*U-Leḥayyev*"). The negligence of each tortfeasor is one of two types:

(1) where he should have foreseen that his negligence alone would cause damage;

(2) where he should have foreseen that damage would result from his conduct, coupled with that of the other tortfeasor, even though his conduct alone would not be expected to lead to damage.

Thus if two men dug a pit together, they would both be held liable in negligence for damage caused by the pit (BK 51a). However, if only one of them was negligent, he alone is liable. Thus, a man who concealed sharp pieces of glass in his neighbor's dilapidated wall which the latter was about to pull down onto public ground would be liable in negligence to anyone injured by the glass pieces, whereas the neighbor would incur no liability since he could not have anticipated the presence of glass pieces in his wall (BK 30a). Similarly, someone who put objects by the side of a man sleeping would be solely liable if the latter broke the objects in his sleep (TJ. BK 2:8, 3a).

Where damage was caused by two tortfeasors, the first leading the second to perform the act, the rabbis were divided as to the liability of the party performing the damage. Examples of such cases, which are known as *Garme* (see **Gerama* and **Garme*), include informing about another's property which leads to its seizure (BK 117a) and the hiring of false witnesses (BK 55b). In each case the party performing the damage had a choice as to whether to act tortiously or not. If he had no choice in the matter because of lack of intelligence or the required expertise, he is no more than a tool in the hand of the first tortfeasor and the latter is liable for all the damages. Thus a man who puts an idiot or minor in charge of fire and thorns is liable for all the damage if his neighbor's house is burnt down (BK 59b); and the defendant who tells his neighbor to bring him his animal from the premises of a third party is solely liable if it transpires that the animal does not belong to the defendant at all and that the latter attempted to steal it (Tos. *ibid.*, 79a).

Israel Law

The Israel law of torts is covered by the Civil Wrongs Ordinance (1944, new version 1968), originally enacted by the British Mandatory authorities, which came into force in 1947, and several amendments enacted by the Knesset. The ordinance is modeled on English law and section 2 explicitly refers to English law for explanations of, and supplements to, the ordinance.

See also **Avot Nezikin*; **Gerama* and **Garme*; *Damages.

[Shalom Albeck]

NEGLIGENT MISREPRESENTATION AS GROUNDS FOR ACTION IN TORTS. In the *Amidar* case (CA 86/76 *Amidar National Company for Immigrant Housing in Israel Ltd. v. Avraham Aharon*, 32 (2) PD 337, 348) Israeli Supreme Court, Justice, Menachem Elon implemented the talmudic principle regarding damage caused by negligence in providing information. He noted that in Jewish law a person is liable for damages caused as a result of negligently conveying incorrect information, through which damage is caused (*ibid.*, 350). A person who negligently conveys incorrect information to another, even in good faith, is responsible for the damage caused to the other person as a result of his acting upon that information. It makes no difference if the information was conveyed in writing or orally; in business negotiations or otherwise; by a professional or by someone with no special qualifications in the field. On the contrary, in certain cases a layman's responsibility may be even greater than that of a professional because, in addition to conveying incorrect information, the very fact that he agreed to advise and provide information in a field in which he has no professional expertise, is an act of negligence. The essential and central condition for liability is that the provider of the information knew, or should have known, under the circumstances, that the person receiving the information intended to rely on his words and to act accordingly. Liability for damages exists when the provider of the information acted negligently and without the reasonable measure of caution with which a reasonable person ought to have acted.

PAYMENT OF COMPENSATION FOR DAMAGE BEYOND THE REQUIREMENTS OF THE LAW (LI-FENIM MI-SHURAT HA-DIN). Justice Elon stressed in his decisions that under certain circumstances the tortfeasor, may be exempt from liability for damages due to various reasons, such as the absence of a causal connection between the negligence and the damage that was caused. However, he may be obliged to compensate the victim by force of his duty to act in a manner which is *li-fenim mi-shurat ha-din* – beyond the requirements of the law. The duty of behaving more generously toward others, in a manner that is beyond the requirements of the law is an established principle and binding legal norm in Jewish law, and was the basis of his ruling in the *Kitan* case (CA 350/77 *Kitan Ltd. v. Sarah Weiss*, 33 (2) 809–811). In that case Justice Elon ruled that even where a person is exempt from liability for damages according to the laws of torts, he is liable, under certain circumstances, to pay compensation for damage incurred in order to "fulfill his duty in the sight of heaven" (*laẓeit yedei shamayim*) (see, e.g., BK 55b). It is therefore appropriate that the Court inform the litigants of the obligation incumbent upon them in this sphere (see CA 842/79 *Ness v. Golda*, PD 36 (1) 220–221; and see at length: *Damages).

THE LIABILITY OF A RECALCITRANT SPOUSE. The wife or husband of a recalcitrant spouse, who refuses to give or receive a Jewish bill of divorce (*get*) is entitled to sue the spouse in the Family Matters Court for his or her losses and agony as a result of being forced to wait for a valid divorce bill (*get*), when the refusal is unjustified. Subject to conditions stipulated by Jewish divorce law, the wife or husband of the recalcitrant spouse may be entitled to damages under two grounds of action recognized in Israeli law: negligence, and breach of statutory duty.

Coercive measures, including an obligation to pay money, intended to pressure the husband or wife to give or receive a get, are occasionally considered by Jewish Law as unlawful duress that invalidates the writ of divorce. However, in other circumstances such coercive measures do not invalidate the *get*. As a result, the principles of Jewish law concerning coerced divorce (*get me'useh*) are important regarding the scope of civil liability of the recalcitrant spouse. The wife's attempts to secure her *get* by way of a damages action against the recalcitrant husband may have negative ramifications in future divorce proceedings in the rabbinical court. For example, a rabbinical court may refuse to hear an action for divorce until the woman abandons her tort action, or waives her right of action in torts, or signs over to her husband any sum obtained through a tort action. It may even refuse to arrange a *get*, on the grounds that a *get* granted by the husband or received by the wife after being obligated to pay compensation for the damage that was caused the recalcitrant spouse may be deemed unlawfully coerced (*me'useh*), and therefore invalid. Accordingly, it has been suggested that the Israeli legislator should intervene in an attempt to avoid these undesirable consequences.

Scholars have suggested a model of legislation that may, to a certain extent, alleviate the suffering of a woman or man awaiting a *get* and which would induce the recalcitrant spouse to give or receive the desired *get*. And of equal importance – such legislation would similarly ensure the validity of the *get* when actually given, so that the woman's or man's fundamental will is realized. This legislation will enable the Family Matters Courts to grant the aforementioned compensation in torts only when the rabbinical court has ruled that the husband or wife: (1) may be compelled (*kofin*) to give or receive a *get*, or (2) is obligated (*ḥiyyuv*) to render or receive a *get*. Other relevant limitations, stemming from principles of Jewish law, are also taken into consideration (see Kaplan & Perry, Bibliography).

[Yehiel Kaplan (2nd ed.)]

BIBLIOGRAPHY: Ch. Tchernowitz, *Shi'urim ba-Talmud*, 1 (1913); Gulak, Yesodei, 2 (1922), 201–37; idem, in: *Tarbiz*, 6 (1935), 383–95; B.B. Lieberman, in: *Journal of Comparative Legislation*, 9 (1927), 231–40, I.S. Zuri, *Torat ha-Mishpat ha-Ezraḥi ha-Ivri*, 3, pt. 1 (1937); J.J. Weinberg, *Meḥkarim ba-Talmud*, 1 (1937/38), 180ff.; J.S. Ben-Meir, in: *Sinai*, 7 (1940), 295–308; G. Horowitz, *The Spirit of Jewish Law* (1953), 569–623; B. Cohen, in: *Studi in onore di Pietro de Francisci*, 1 (1954), 305–36; reprinted in his: *Jewish and Roman Law* (1966), 578–609, addenda; *ibid.* 788–92; S.J. Zevin, in: *Sinai*, 50 (1961/62), 88–95; idem, in: *Torah she-be-Al-Peh*, 4 (1962), 9–17; Sh. Albeck, *Pesher Dinei ha-Nezikin ba-Talmud* (1965); Elon, Mafte'aḥ, 181–8. **ADD. BIBLIOGRAPHY:** M. Elon, *Ha-Mishpat ha-Ivri* (1988), 1:128, 138, 185, 341f., 495f., 498, 648, 750f., 823f.; 2:868; 3:1370, 1381; ibid, *Jewish Law* (1994), 1:144, 156, 207, 410f; 2:602f., 607, 802, 925f., 1008f.; 3:1060; 4:1635, 1645; idem, *Jewish Law (Cases and Materials)* (1999), 50ff., 145ff.; M. Elon and B. Lifshitz, *Mafte'aḥ ha-She'elot ve-ha-Teshuvot shel Ḥakhmei Sefarad u-Ẓefon Afrikah* (legal digest) (1986), 2:293–99; B. Lifshitz and E. Shochetman, *Mafte'aḥ ha-She'elot ve-ha-Teshuvot shel Ḥakhmei Ashkenaz, Ẓarefat ve-Italyah* (legal digest) (1997), 204–07; A. Sheinfeld, *Nezikin*, (1992); Y.S. Kaplan, "Elements of Tort in the Jewish Law of Surety," in: *Shenaton ha-Mishpat ha-Ivri*, 9–10 (1982–83), 359–96; Y.S. Kaplan and R. Perry, "Tort Liability of Recalcitrant Husbands," in: *Tel Aviv University Law Review*, 28 (2005), 773–869.

TORUN (Ger. **Thorn**), port on the R. Vistula, N. central Poland; founded by the Teutonic Order in the 13th century, and incorporated into Poland in 1454. Jews first visited Torun on *market days only; in 1766 six Jewish families were permitted to settle there, as in the 18th century there was a great demand for Jewish merchants who traded in cloth manufactured in Torun. In the second half of the 18th century some were attacked by members of the guilds because, in conjunction with the guildmasters, they lent money for interest to the craftsmen.

Torun passed to Prussia in 1793–1806. When included in the principality of Warsaw in 1806–14 it had a larger number of Jewish inhabitants. It reverted to Prussia from 1814 to 1920, when the Jewish population increased. It numbered 248 in 1828; 1,371 (5% of the total population) in 1890; 1,100 (2.3%) in 1905. Culturally, the Jews were closest to German Jewry. A Jewish primary school was founded in 1862. In 1891 a literary and cultural association was founded (Litteratur und Culturverein zu Thorn) with the objective of broadening knowledge of Jewish history and literature, without political or religious implications. A Jewish Women's Association (Israelitischer Frauenverein) to aid sick and needy women was founded in 1868. The increase of antisemitism in Pomerania and the regression in the economy of Torun at the end of the 19th century led to a decrease in the number of Jews living there. After Torun reverted to Poland in 1920, the local Jewish population became one of the smallest in Polish towns of that size, numbering 354 (0.9% of the total) in 1925.

Holocaust Period

On the outbreak of World War II there were about 1,000 Jews in Torun. The community was liquidated in the autumn of 1939, when the Jews were expelled to the territory of the General Government. After the war the community was not reconstituted.

[Jacob Goldberg]

BIBLIOGRAPHY: *Mitteilungen des Gesamtarchivs der deutschen Juden* (1910); *Dzieje Torunia* (1934); J. Wojtowicz, *Studia nad kształtowaniem sie układu kapitalistycznego w Toruniu* (1960).

TOSAFOT (Heb. תּוֹסָפוֹת; lit. "additions"), collections of comments on the Talmud arranged according to the order of the talmudic tractates. In general the point of departure of the *tosafot* is not the Talmud itself but the comments on it by the earlier authorities, principally *Rashi. Where and when the *tosafot* were compiled, their types, and their historical and literary development are among the most fundamental and difficult problems in the study of rabbinic literature. The concept of the *tosafot* was originally bound up with the method of study characteristic of the schools of Germany and France in the 12th–14th centuries. Their beginnings go back to the generation of Rashi's pupils and descendants, who undertook to expand, elaborate, and develop their teacher's commentary on the Talmud (**Kunteres*) by making it the foundation of talmudic studies in the schools which they headed. In fact Rashi's commentary is a concise summary, arrived at through precise sifting and literary adaptation, of the tradition of studying the Oral Law prevalent in the principal French and German schools where he had studied for many years. By a careful perusal of his commentary those who followed him were able to acquire for the first time a profound and harmonious comprehension of the Talmud. Through questioning Rashi's statements – on the basis of the talmudic theme under discussion, or of one found elsewhere, or of Rashi's own comments on some other passage, the tosafists sought to answer their questions by pointing to differences and distinctions between one case and another or between one source and another. In this way they produced new halakhic deductions and conclusions, which in turn became themselves subjects for discussion, to be refuted or substantiated in the later *tosafot*.

The terms *ve-im tomar* ("and if you were to say") and *ve-yesh lomar* ("and then one may answer") – almost exclusively characteristic of this literary genre – are the most commonly used in the *tosafot* and more than anything else typify their essential character. This vast work was produced entirely within the yeshivot in the form of oral, animated discussions between the heads of the yeshivot and their pupils. In these discussions, views were often put forward which, either in principle or in detail, differed from Rashi's. Such views abound in the *tosafot*, both in the names of their authors and anonymously. After Rashi's death, the teaching and study methods of Isaac *Alfasi, *Hananel b. Ḥushi'el, and *Nathan b. Jehiel of Rome, which represented a tradition of learning basically different from the local one, began to penetrate into France and Germany. The tosafists took every occasion to quote these novel views and compare them with their own traditions. Simultaneously, a large number of new versions of the Talmud also reached the tosafists, giving them almost unlimited opportunities for argumentation and for advancing new interpretations by incorporating the Babylonian-North African tradition into their own. Another novel feature was the extensive use by the *tosafot* of the Jerusalem Talmud. While this resulted from the tosafists' critical comparative method of learning itself, a contributing factor was undoubtedly their acquaintance with the teachings of Hananel b. Ḥushi'el, who had a particular predilection for the Jerusalem Talmud.

Originally and formally the *tosafot* were written as "additions" to Rashi's comments. From these modest beginnings almost nothing of which has been preserved and whose most notable representative is apparently Isaac b. Nathan, Rashi's son-in-law, a movement developed – and it was undoubtedly a movement with all the spiritual implications of the word. Within a few years this movement became the dominant force that for centuries shaped the method of learning the Torah, first in Germany and France (including Provence), and, from the days of *Naḥmanides, also in Spain. The spirit of the tosafists is already apparent in *Samuel b. Meir, Rashi's grandson. He and his brothers Jacob *Tam and *Isaac b. Meir were not only the first but the most important tosafists in France. The chief architect of the *tosafot*, and the driving force behind them for many generations, was Jacob Tam. It was he who laid down their pattern and final form. He was followed by his nephew *Isaac b. Samuel of Dampierre. These two overshadow not only the scores of tosafists, their pupils, who are known by name from collections of *tosafot*, but also the hundreds of others whose names have not been preserved. Samuel b. Meir's older contemporary, *Isaac b. Asher ha-Levi, who had studied under Rashi at Troyes and then later returned to Germany, was the first tosafist in Germany in his new yeshivah at Speyer. In the history of Torah study there was no essential difference in the 12th–13th centuries between France and Germany, for it was a common occurrence for pupils to move from one territory to the other, the subdivision of the Carolingian Empire having no relevance in the cultural life of the Jews. Nevertheless, for the sake of convenience, a distinction is made between the two when describing the successive generations of the tosafists in these centuries.

The *tosafot* were written down as "*shitot*," interpretations which the pupils of the yeshivot committed to writing under the auspices of their teachers. In these notes the pupils recorded the substance of the halakhic discussions which had taken place in the yeshivah, incorporating their teacher's views as well as the arguments for and against them, and adding their own opinions. The teachers reviewed their pupils' notes, correcting and improving them, thus giving them their personal stamp. Very little remains of the original language of Tam's statements, which are quoted everywhere in the *tosafot*, and the text of his *Sefer ha-Yashar*, too, went through many hands. The same is true of the original notes of Isaac b. Samuel ha-Zaken of Dampierre; he is cited on almost every page of the *tosafot*, but only isolated phrases of his actual wording have been preserved. These notes by the foremost pupils, which had received the approbation of their teachers, passed from one yeshivah to another between France and Germany, and in the process various additions were made to them. However, several substantial works are extant which were written by the leading tosafists themselves, such as *Sefer Yere'im* by *Eliezer b. Samuel of Metz, *Sefer Mitzvot Gadol* by *Moses of Coucy, *Sefer Mitzvot Katan* by *Isaac of Corbeil, *Sefer ha-Terumah* by *Baruch b. Isaac of Worms, *Sefer ha-Roke'aḥ* by *Eleazer b. Judah of Worms, and others. Later editions abstracted from these works statements which they incorporated in the *tosafot*.

Although the *tosafot* are characterized by keen thought and great originality, it is impossible to distinguish any individual style or approach among the many tosafists, about a hundred of whom are known by name. It was the special method of learning that determined the approach and set the intellectual standard which all the tosafists had to meet. Some of them surpassed others by reason of their eminent halakhic authority and the many pupils who spread their teachings; some produced more novellae and interpretations than others; but these are quantitative differences, and any qualitative distinctions there may have been are not reflected in their teachings. Moreover, theirs was teamwork in the full sense of the word, and a novel view quoted in the name of an individual scholar was frequently the result of an involved discussion among many, each one of whom contributed something to the final outcome.

A general account of the historical development of the tosafists movement is reliably and accurately given in E.E. Urbach's voluminous and monumental *Ba'alei ha-Tosafot* (1955), which deals in chronological order with all the important tosafists and their literary work. They lived in scores of clustered cities in France and Germany. Many are known by their own and their fathers' names, although their identification is not always certain. Sometimes the same scholar is mentioned with considerable differences in various sources. Yet a minute knowledge of this history contributes little to a better understanding of the *tosafot* themselves. For although there was undoubtedly a certain continuity and a clear link between teacher and pupil, the functional structure of the *tosafot* was based on freedom in learning and teaching, which permitted a pupil to disagree with his teacher in the theoretical apprehension and frequently even in the practical significance of the talmudic themes.

In the vast ocean of the *tosafot* a distinction is made between several "types" or rather "collections" of *tosafot*, which are the outcome of different editings, and are distinguished from one another by the contents of their argumentation but not in their methodology. This systemization is important for a historical account of the various *tosafot* and for an understanding of what is known as "our *tosafot*" – i.e., those included in the present-day printed editions of the Talmud – and also for a comprehension of the way in which the *tosafot* penetrated into Jewish cultural spheres beyond the confines of France and Germany. Generally, there are many passages among these various types of *tosafot*, which are parallel materially (in the preference for one answer to a problem over another, etc.), although not in their actual phraseology. The first important collection of *tosafot* is the *tosafot* of Sens of *Samson of Sens, whose literary heritage is greater than that of most tosafists. Portions of them are extant in the author's own words. When contemporary German scholars quoted from "French *tosafot*" they generally referred to him. Written on the whole Talmud and modeled on the French tradition which Samson had learned from Isaac b. Samuel of Dampierre, the *tosafot* of Sens served as the basis of most subsequent collections, their influence being clearly discernible in "our *tosafot*" to many tractates. Though the *tosafot* of Evreux of the brothers Samuel, Moses, and Isaac of Evreux have not yet been fully investigated with reference to their literary identity, character, and influence, it is evident that they too were influenced by the *tosafot* of Sens. Although the *tosafot* of *Meir of Rothenburg and *Perez b. Elijah, who were almost contemporaries, enjoyed great renown in earlier times, they are no longer extant, except for remnants of varying length. Some *tosafot* of theirs, and especially of Meir of Rothenburg, exist in manuscript. Particularly well known are the *tosafot* of Touques composed by *Eliezer of Touques and based on those of Sens, which he adapted, abbreviated, and expanded by including new interpretations of later dates. These new interpretations were written as marginal notes to the *tosafot* themselves, and the quotations from the *gilyonot* ("marginal notes") found largely in *Shitah Mekubbeẓet* are generally his. The *tosafot* of Touques were included by the earliest printers in their editions of the Talmud (from 1484 onward), thereby establishing a tradition generally followed up to the present, so that the printed *tosafot* in more than ten large tractates are those of Touques. Quantitatively they comprise the largest part of "our *tosafot*" so called in contrast to collections of *tosafot* in manuscript and to those later printed in the margin of the Talmud or in separate works, which are referred to as *tosafot yeshanim* ("old *tosafot*"). There are two further types, the "*tosafot* Rosh" of *Asher b. Jehiel, which were widely studied chiefly in Spain and the *tosafot* Rid of *Isaiah b. Mali di Trani of Italy, which present a difficult literary problem. Asher b. Jehiel's *tosafot* contain few original interpretations, some of which are mainly based on the *tosafot* of Sens, with "Spanish" additions. Most of them are in print. The *tosafot* of the scholars in England before the expulsion (1290) are in the process of being published from a recently identified manuscript.

The techniques and style of *tosafot* literature were not limited specifically to the Talmud, there being an extensive literature of *tosafot* on the Pentateuch. These have Rashi as their starting point also, but they go far beyond him by propounding questions and answers to them, by curtailing and expanding, in the exact manner of the *tosafot* to the Talmud. Like the latter, they are divided into German and French *tosafot*, the German "style" being generally recognizable by its numerous *gematriot*, which were used as a significant exegetical principle. Usually the same scholars are mentioned in the *tosafot* both to the Talmud and to the Pentateuch. Some scholars, however, devoted themselves exclusively to biblical exegesis, such as Joseph *Bekhor Shor, Joseph *Kara, and others of whom almost nothing except their names is known, and who were apparently mainly aggadists. The chief characteristic of the tosafists to the Pentateuch is their halakhic approach. On the basis of the talmudic *halakhah*, the actions of each biblical figure, whether righteous or evil, are weighed and explained. Thus this literature created a unique fusion between the argumentation characteristic of the talmudic *halakhah* and biblical exegesis that, in its own way, aimed at arriving at the literal interpretation.

Samuel b. Meir wrote "*tosafot*" to Alfasi's *halakhot* – although they are not *tosafot* in the usual sense of the word and are more in the nature of glosses; only a few extracts from them have been preserved. *Moses b. Yom Tov, an English tosafist, also wrote *tosafot* on Alfasi. However there is no evidence that *tosafot* were regularly written on Alfasi, although the earlier authorities studied him extensively. The same happened once again in Germany in the 15th century when following on persecutions and the resultant lowering in the status of learning there, there was a move away from the study of the Talmud to that of Alfasi.

From France and Germany the *tosafot* penetrated first to Spain, where the earliest scholar to quote the tosafist literature, although in a very limited form, was Meir ha-Levi *Abulafia. But it is evident that this literature was still a novelty for him and it is clear from his works that he preferred the Spanish tradition of learning, which differed completely from the tosafists' method of study. The latter was introduced into Spain by two scholars related to one another, Jonah *Gerondi and Naḥmanides, who had either studied in France or with teachers from there. Naḥmanides' novellae on the Talmud incorporate the best of the *tosafot*, adopting their views and comparing them with those of the earlier Spanish scholars. While assigning almost the same value to both, he preferred the superior Spanish talmudic texts and its links with the teachings of the Babylonian *geonim*. Naḥmanides was undoubtedly the first to introduce the study of the *tosafot* into Spain, and his pupils and their pupils after them, Solomon b. Abraham *Adret and *Yom Tov b. Abraham Ishbili, established the study of the *tosafot* there. Among these scholars and their contemporaries, who were the heads of large yeshivot and wrote many works on the entire Talmud, the tosafistic element increasingly predominated over that of the early "Spanish" element, so that from their time on the method of the *tosafot* was adopted in Spain both in theory and in practice. A contemporary of these two scholars, *Asher b. Jehiel, who had come from Germany to Spain with his sons, was the second scholar to bring the study of the *tosafot* to Spain, thereby encouraging and advancing the process already flourishing there. His chief contribution was to reinforce and consolidate this process by writing *tosafot* on most of the tractates of the Talmud. These were based on those of Sens in many places and incorporated the local Spanish teachings. In Spain Asher b. Jehiel's version of the *tosafot* was regarded as the more accurate, in contrast to the French *tosafot*, which had been current until then among the scholars there. Thus while Naḥmanides and his *bet midrash* introduced the tosafists' method of study and most of their teachings into Spain, the text of the *tosafot* was laid down by Asher b. Jehiel, whose *tosafot* subsequently became the only ones officially studied in all the Spanish yeshivot.

The influence which the *tosafot* have had on the entire history of learning among the Jewish people up to present times is inestimable. A "page of *Gemara*" invariably refers to the text itself, Rashi's commentary (called *perush*), and the *tosafot*, and is called Ga-Pa-T, the initial letters of *Gemara, perush* and *tosafot*. That the early printers included the *tosafot* as the companion commentary to Rashi's in their editions was not fortuitous, but because this was the customary combination. Wishing to enhance the value of their product, they accordingly printed the *tosafot* at the side of the page. In later times, from the expulsion from Spain (1492) onward, an extensive literature was produced whose object was to answer the questions raised in the *tosafot* which conflicted with Rashi, and in any event to attain a deeper comprehension of the principles underlying both. Among the most notable of these works are *Sefer ha-Maharsha* of Samuel Edels, *Ḥiddushei ha-Maharam* of Meir b. Gedaliah of Lublin, *Meginnei Shelomo* of Joshua Falk I, *Ḥiddushei Maharam Schiff* of Meir Schiff of Fulda, *Hora'at Sha'ah* of Solomon and Isaac Heilprin, and others. For greater convenience some of these works, which were highly esteemed by scholars, have been printed at the end of the editions of the Talmud. This type of literature also appeared among Jews in the East, later Spain, Egypt, etc., where an accurate and systematic methodology was produced of the principles of Rashi and the *tosafot* so that their divergent views could be better understood. The most outstanding of these works is *Darkhei ha-Gemara* by Isaac Canpanton.

On the other hand, some leading scholars considered the combined study of the Talmud and the *tosafot* at an early age as pedagogically wrong, in that it did not permit young students to arrive at an independent, straightforward, and correct comprehension of the Talmud and its themes. Instead it imposed on them from the outset the methods of **pilpul* and of *ḥillukim* (forms of talmudic casuistry), which from the beginning of the 15th century were associated with the study of the *tosafot* in Poland and Germany. In the early days of their appearance the *tosafot* were already criticized, and there were scholars in the 14th century who considered studying them a waste of time. But the criticism began to gather force only with the development of the casuistic method of *ḥillukim* which was intrinsically associated with the *tosafot*.

BIBLIOGRAPHY: Urbach, Tosafot; idem, in: *Essays Presented to... I. Brodie* (1967), 1–56 (Heb. pt.); A.F. Kleinberger, *Ha-Maḥashavah ha-Pedagogit shel ha-Maharal mi-Prag* (1962); J. Lifschitz (ed.), *Tosafot Evreux... le-Sotah* (1969), introd.; I. Ta-Shema, in: Sinai, 65 (1969), 200–5; Gross, Gal Jud; R.N.N. Rabbinovicz, *Ma'amar al Hadpasat ha-Talmud*, ed. by A.M. Habermann (1952); *Perush al Yeḥezkel u-Terei Asar le-R. Eliezer mi-Belganẓi* (1913), preface by S. Poznański; Germ Jud; Assaf, Mekorot; V. Aptowitzer, *Mavo le-Sefer Ravyah* (1938); P. Tarshish, *Ishim u-Sefarim ba-Tosafot* (1942).

[Israel Moses Ta-Shma]

TOSEFTA (Aram. תּוֹסֶפְתָּא, Heb. תּוֹסֶפֶת), literally an "additional" or "supplementary" halakhic or aggadic tradition, i.e., one not included in the *Mishnah of R. *Judah ha-Nasi. Originally the term was used to designate any individual additional or supplementary tannaitic tradition, and so was virtually synonymous with the later Babylonian term **baraita*. In the later Babylonian tradition the term "tosefta" was used to designate a particular body of such *baraitot* (Kid. 49b; Meg. 28b; Shav. 41b), and eventually it came to denote a particular literary work, "the Tosefta" – a collection of halakhic and aggadic *baraitot*, organized according to the order of the Mishnah, and serving as a companion volume to it. Though there may once have been other such collections of tannaitic *halakhot* and *aggadot*, the Tosefta is the only such collection to have come down to us, and together with the extant **Midrashei Halakhah*, it provides the student with direct access to a large body of ancient tannaitic sources, without the mediation of later amoraic and post-amoraic talmudic tradition.

In most respects, the Tosefta is identical to the Mishnah. Its Hebrew language is similar in all essential points to the language of the Mishnah, and seems unaffected by later dialects of amoraic Hebrew. The content, terminology, and formal structures of the *halakhah* in the Tosefta are the same as those in the Mishnah. The *tannaim* mentioned in the Tosefta are the same as those mentioned in the Mishnah, with the exception that the Tosefta also mentions scholars from the two following generations – almost all either direct descendents of the *tannaim* mentioned in the Mishnah, or otherwise associated closely with the circle or the family of R. Judah Ha-Nasi. From all of this it would seem clear that the Tosefta which we possess today was redacted in the same circles in which the Mishnah was redacted – the school of R. Judah ha-Nasi – some 40 or 50 years later, and by his own disciples. Since the last prominent scholar to be mentioned in the Tosefta (twice only) is none other than R. Ḥiyya – a close relative and prime disciple of R. Judah ha-Nasi – it is not surprising that tradition has ascribed to R. Ḥiyya the redaction of the Tosefta, though there is no solid historical evidence which can confirm this suggestion.

In addition to containing two additional layers of tannaitic traditions, there are two primary differences between the Mishnah and the Tosefta. First, the Tosefta is some three to four times larger than the Mishnah. Second, the overall order of the units of tradition found in the Tosefta is largely dictated, not by internal criteria, but rather by the external standard of the order of the Mishnah. It would therefore be fair to say that the Tosefta as a whole represents a kind of proto-talmud to the Mishnah – a large collection of tannaitic traditions whose purpose is to supplement, to complement, and in various other ways to expand upon the Mishnah of R. Judah Ha-Nasi (see: *Talmud, Babylonian – The Four Stages of Talmudic Tradition).

Both the critical examination of the Tosefta itself and the comparison of the Tosefta to parallel tannaitic collections (Mishnah and *Midrashei Halakhah*) point toward one simple conclusion – the Tosefta which we possess today was collected and redacted in Ereẓ Israel shortly after the redaction of the Mishnah and in the same scholarly circles. Nevertheless one of the greatest talmudic scholars, Ḥ. Albeck, rejected this conclusion. His rejection of this conclusion was not, however, based either on an examination of the internal evidence of the Tosefta itself, or on a comparison of the Tosefta to other tannaitic collections. Rather it was founded primarily on a comparison of the Tosefta to the *baraitot* found in the Babylonian Talmud and the Jerusalem Talmud. The talmudic *baraitot* are in many ways very similar to the parallel traditions found in our extent tannaitic collections. On the other hand there are also significant differences between them. Assuming that the *amoraim* would not have dared to add, omit, or in any other way intentionally change the ancient tannaitic traditions which they had received (see *Mishnah, The Redaction of the Mishnah), Albeck concluded that the *baraitot* in the *talmudim* could not have derived from the tannaitic collections which we today possess – the Tosefta and the extant *Midrashei Halakhah* – but rather must have been drawn from other collections of *baraitot* which have not survived in independent form. Consistent with this view, he also ascribed the redaction of our Tosefta to the end of the fourth century (at the very earliest), i.e., after the main body of amoraic talmudic literature had already largely taken shape. Since Albeck's assumptions concerning the nature of the talmudic *baraitot* are highly speculative at best, his views concerning the redaction of the Tosefta cannot be maintained in the face of all the internal evidence of the tannaitic sources to the contrary.

Broadly speaking the relationship between the traditions found in the Tosefta to the parallel traditions found in the Mishnah are of three kinds, the two relatively familiar and well known, the third less so. First, a tradition in the Tosefta can presuppose the exact text of our Mishnah, and comment directly upon it. Alternatively the Tosefta can transmit a different version of the same *halakhah*, either reporting the same opinion in different language, or reporting other opinions concerning the same issue. There is however, a third possibility: the Tosefta can transmit the *halakhah* of the Mishnah in an earlier and more original version. In this third case, the Tosefta may have preserved the "raw" material out of which R. Judah ha-Nasi composed the version of the *halakhah* which is included in his Mishnah. This third possibility has provided the focal point for some of the most fruitful and creative recent scholarship on the Tosefta (Friedman, *Tosefta Atiqta*). In addition to this parallel material, the Tosefta also includes additional independent tannaitic traditions which are either related topically to the halakhic or aggadic content of the Mishnah, or associatively – attaching themselves to some hint or reference which may have been mentioned in passing in the Mishnah.

With the exception of *Avot, Tamid, Middot*, and *Kinnim*, every tractate in the Mishnah has a parallel tractate in the Tosefta, though the precise character of the content of the Tosefta tractate and its relationship to the material found in the Mishnah can vary radically. Some have claimed that **Avot de-Rabbi Nathan*, once considered a late tannaitic work, serves as a kind of "Tosefta" to Mishnah *Avot*. Recent research, however, has shown that ARN is actually a rather late aggadic work with no substantial connection to the Tosefta.

The Tosefta and R. Nehemiah

The Babylonian Talmud (Sanh. 86a) ascribes to R. Johanan the statement that "*Setam Tosefta Rabbi Neḥemiah*" – "Anonymous statements in the Tosefta are to be attributed to R. Nehemiah." Both the precise sense of this statement and its historical authenticity require clarification. The full text of this statement in the Babylonian Talmud runs as follows: "R. Johanan said: Anonymous statements in the Mishnah are to be attributed to R. Meir; anonymous statements in the Tosefta are to be attributed to R. Nehemiah; anonymous statements in the *Sifra* are to be attributed to R. Judah; anonymous statements in the *Sifre* are to be attributed to R. Simeon – and all of them represent the views of R. Akiva." The first element in this statement is almost certainly the literary and historical kernel of this tradition, since it is the topic of a controversy between R. Johanan and R. Simeon ben Lakish in the Jerusalem Talmud (Yev. 4:11, 6b): "R. Johanan said: Any place where [Rabbi] taught an anonymous Mishnah, that [anonymous Mishnah] is [presumed to represent] the majority position, until one receives explicit information from one's teacher [to the contrary]; R. Simeon ben Lakish said: Any anonymous Mishnah is [presumed to represent the position] of R. Meir, until one receives explicit information from one's teacher [to the contrary]." On the one hand, the Jerusalem Talmud ascribes the view that anonymous statements in the Mishnah are R. Meir to R. Simeon ben Lakish, and not to R. Johanan. On the other hand the Jerusalem Talmud goes on to state that "R. Simeon ben Lakish does not actually disagree with R. Johanan; he just observed that most anonymous *mishnayot* happen to reflect the view of R. Meir." It seems fairly clear that the primary intent of R. Johanan's statement in the Jerusalem Talmud was not historical, but rather legal. It asserts that one may presume that an anonymous Mishnah reflects the position of the majority of sages, and hence is to be assumed to reflect the normative *halakhah*. On the basis of this understanding R. Johanan's words were summarized and transmitted in the Babylonian Talmud (cf. the list in the margin of Shab. 46a) in the following form: "R. Johanan said: The *halakhah* is in accordance with an anonymous Mishnah." Given this interpretation we may presume that the final comment of the Jerusalem Talmud represents a (perhaps somewhat artificial) conflation of the positions of these two sages: R. Simeon ben Lakish is understood to have made an empirical observation concerning the provenance of most anonymous *mishnayot*, while R. Johanan has asserted a most significant halakhic determination – that anonymous *mishnayot* are to be accepted as normative *halakhah*, unless evidence is brought to the contrary. In the Babylonian Talmud this complex tradition was summarized and transmitted in the name of R. Johanan as follows: "Anonymous statements in the Mishnah are to be attributed to R. Meir – [but they do not reflect the individual opinions of R. Meir, but rather] represent the views of R. Akiva." The tradition in the Babylonian Talmud has been further expanded to include the other canonical tannaitic works familiar to and accepted by the Babylonian Talmud: *Sifra*, *Sifre*, and Tosefta (for the relation of these works to the extant tannaitic collections known by these names, see above). It is likely that the primary intention of this expanded tradition is to extend R. Johanan's halakhic judgment concerning the presumed authority of anonymous traditions found in the Mishnah, to anonymous traditions found in these other works, by ascribing them to other well-known disciples of R. Akiva, who are all presumed to have transmitted their master's views. On the other hand, the historical reliability and significance of the ascription of anonymous passages in the Tosefta to R. Nehemiah remain highly questionable.

Nevertheless, on the basis of this relatively late Babylonian tradition, some scholars have posited the existence of a proto-Tosefta already in the days of R. Akiva and his students. There is, however, no direct evidence for the existence of such a work in this early period. Moreover, the terms *tosefet*, *tosefta*, *baraita* appear only in the amoraic literary stratum of talmudic literature, after the acceptance and dissemination of the Mishnah of R. Judah ha-Nasi. Neither these terms nor any other comparable terms are mentioned anywhere in tannaitic literature. The phenomenon of multiple literary levels within the Mishnah, and the habit of later *tannaim* to "add" comments to the traditions which they received from their teachers, should not be confused with the distinction between an accepted and official canon of select and authoritative traditions (e.g., the Mishnah of R. Judah ha-Nasi) and an extra-canonical "supplementary" tradition (*tosefet*, *baraita*), or collection of traditions (Tosefta).

Editions and Commentaries

The Tosefta was first published together with the *halakhot* of Isaac Alfasi in Venice in 1521, and it can still be found at the end of most standard editions of the Babylonian Talmud after the *halakhot* of Alfasi. There are no commentaries to the Tosefta which derive from the early period of the **rishonim*, though many passages from the Tosefta are cited and explained in their other commentaries, e.g., Maimonides' commentary to the Mishnah, and especially the commentary of R. Samson ben Abraham to Mishnah *Tohorot*. During the period of the **aḥaronim* a number of commentaries were written, the most important of which is the comprehensive commentary covering all of the Tosefta, *Ḥasdei David*, composed by R. David Pardo in the 18th century. Two volumes (covering four orders of the Tosefta) were published in his lifetime – *Zera'im-Nashim* (Leghorn, 1777) and *Nezikin* (Leghorn, 1790). A third volume, containing his commentary to *Kodashim*, was published in Jerusalem in 1890, and the final volumes, containing his most important commentary to *Tohorot*, were only rediscovered and published in Jerusalem in 1970. The commentaries and emendations of Elijah Gaon of Vilna to Tosefta *Tohorot* are also very important. Toward the end of the 19th century, M.S. Zuckermandel published an edition (1881) of the Tosefta, based mainly on the Erfurt manuscript (which ends in *Zevaḥim*, the rest being based on the Vienna manuscript), and including variant readings. While this work constituted a great step forward at the time, it suffers from two problems. First, the transcription of the Erfurt manuscript is not always accurate. More significantly, however, is the choice of the Erfurt manuscript as the basis of his edition. The Erfurt manuscript of the Tosefta does not always transmit the text of the Tosefta in its original form; rather it often reflects medieval emendations of the Tosefta, in order to bring its text in line with parallel versions of a tradition found in the Babylonian Talmud, the Jerusalem Talmud, or even the *Midrashei Halakhah*. A new critical edition of the Tosefta based on the superior Vienna manuscript, including variae lectiones, notes, and a detailed commentary (*Tosefta ki-Feshuta*) – the pinnacle of modern Tosefta studies – covering over half the Tosefta was published by S. Lieberman (*Zera'im*, 1955; *Mo'ed*, 1961–2; *Nashim*, 1967, 1973; the first half of *Nezikin*, 1988). The complete texts of all known manuscripts and *Genizah* fragments of the Tosefta are available on the website of Bar-Ilan University (http://www.biu.ac.il/JS/tosefta/).

BIBLIOGRAPHY: Annotated bibliography, up to 1953, by M.I. Abramski, in: KS, 29 (1953/54), 149–61; Ḥ. Albeck, *Meḥkarim bi-Veraita ve-Tosefta* (1944); idem, *Mavo la-Talmudim*, 1 (1969), 51–78; Epstein, Tanna'im, 241–69; B. de Vries, in: *Tarbiz*, 27 (1958), 148ff.; Strack-Stemberger, *Introduction to the Talmud and Midrash* (1996), 149–63; A. Goldberg, in: *The Literature of the Sages*, ed. S. Safrai (1987), 283–302; idem, *Tosefta Bava Kamma, A Structural and Analytical Commentary* (2001); S. Friedman, *Tosefta Atiqta* (2002); idem, in: S. Friedman (ed.), *Saul Lieberman Memorial Volume* (1993), 119–64; idem, "*Baraitot*," in: D. Boyarin et al. (eds.), *Ateret le-Ḥaim* (2000); H. Fox and T. Meacham (eds.), *Introducing the Tosefta* (1999); Y. Elman, *Authority and Tradition – Toseftan Baraitot in Talmudic Babylonian* (1994); J. Hauptman, in: S.J.D. Cohen (ed.), *The Synoptic Problem in Rabbinic Literature* (2000), 13–34; N. Braverman, in: *Meḥkarim be-Lashon*, 5–6 (1992), 153–70; idem, in: *Proceedings of the Ninth World Congress of Jewish Studies*, 4:1 (1986), 31–38.

[Stephen G. Wald (2nd ed.)]

TOUATI, CHARLES (1925–2003), French rabbi, teacher. The scion of a rabbinical family, he studied at the University of Algiers, then in Paris at the Sorbonne, the École pratique des hautes études, the École Rabbinique, and later at Dropsie College, Philadelphia, under Solomon Zeitlin. He was for a few months the rabbi of the Ohel Avraham Community in Paris; later professor at the École Rabbinique until the beginning of the 1980s and at the École pratique des hautes études, section des sciences religieuses (1967–71), as a "chargé de conferences," 1972–93, and as a "directeur d'études"; director of the *Revue des études juives* with Gérard Nahon (1981–1996). He was honored with the title of chief rabbi ("grand rabbin") but was hindered by poor health from succeeding Jacob *Kaplan as chief rabbi of France. A specialist on medieval Jewish theology and philosophy as well as talmudic literature, he is mainly known for his annotated translation of Gersonides, *Les Guerres du Seigneur. Livres III et IV* (1968); for the first thorough and momentous synthesis on *La pensée théologique et philosophique de Gersonide* (1973, repr. 1992); and for his French translation of the *Kuzari* of Judah ha-Levi (1994). Some of his articles were collected in *Prophètes, talmudistes, philosophes* (1990).

BIBLIOGRAPHY: G. Freudenthal, J.P. Rothschild, G. Dahan (eds.), *Torah et science… Études offertes à Charles Touati* (2001); "Hommage à Charles Touati (1925–2003)," in: REJ, 162 (2003), 343–56; G. Nahon, "Hommage au grand rabbin Charles Touati (1925–2003), REJ, 164 (2005), 539–46.

[Jean-Pierre Rothschild (2nd ed.)]

TOUL, city in the department Meurthe-et-Moselle in N.E. France. The earliest reference to the existence of Jews there is *The Life of St. Mansuy*, written in 974, in which the author mentions a Jewish physician in Toul. The tosafists *Eliezer of Toul, who died before 1234, and his brother Abraham, disciple of Isaac the Elder of Dampierre, lived in the town. From the Middle Ages until the French Revolution there is no evidence of Jews living there legally, although some Jews were in the region during various periods, and in 1711 a few even settled in the town temporarily. In 1791 an important community was formed and in 1808 one of its members was a delegate to the Napoleonic *Sanhedrin. The synagogue was built in 1819, and for a time after 1850, Toul was the seat of a rabbinate. In 1905 there were not more than 40–50 Jews in the community. In 1970 there were 15 Jews residing in the city.

BIBLIOGRAPHY: Gross, Gal Jud, 211–2; B. Blumenkranz, *Juifs et Chrétiens…* (1960), 54ff.

[Gilbert Cahen]

TOULON, port in the Var department, S.E. France. In the second half of the 13th century the Jews made up an appreciable proportion of the population of Toulon: at a general municipal assembly held in 1285, 11 of the 155 participants were Jews. They shared the same rights and duties as the other citizens. The community came to a brutal end on the night of April 12/13, 1348 (Palm Sunday), when the Jewish street, "Carriera de la Juteria," was attacked, the houses pillaged, and 40 Jews slain; this attack was probably related to the *Black Death persecutions. Faced with an enquiry set up by a judge from Hyères, the assailants fled; however, they were soon pardoned. After this date, in addition to a few converted Jews, there were in Toulon only individual Jews who stayed for short periods; one such man was Vitalis of Marseilles, who was engaged as a town physician in 1440. The medieval Jewish street corresponded largely to the present Rue des Tombades. In 1760 the merchants' guild of Toulon successfully prevented the arrival of Jewish merchants. On being granted rights of citizenship, a Jew from *Avignon requested permission to settle in Toulon. The community formed in the 19th century remained small. At the beginning of World War II around 50 Jewish families lived in the town, two-thirds of them refugees from *Alsace. In 1971 there were some 2,000 Jews in Toulon, the majority being from North Africa. An estimated 2,000 Jewish families lived there at the outset of the 21st century. In 2004 the community center with its synagogue was firebombed in an antisemitic incident.

BIBLIOGRAPHY: Gross, Gal Jud, 212f.; A. Crémieux, in: REJ, 89 (1930), 33–72; 90 (1931), 43–64; L. Mangin, *Toulon*, 1 (1901), index; G. Le Bellegou-Beguin, *L'Evolution des Institutions Municipales Toulonnaises* (1959), 123.

[Bernhard Blumenkranz]

TOULOUSE (Heb. טולושה), capital of the department of Haute-Garonne, in southern France. According to a legendary tradition, there were Jews in Toulouse as early as the eighth century, when as a result of their disloyalty to the ruling Franks, they were ordered to choose a member of the community every year to be publicly slapped in the face on Good Friday. This tradition also mentions a council held in Toulouse in 883 in the presence of the Jews to discuss their complaint against this custom. There is definite evidence of this practice, however, from 1020 onward. During the late 11th and early 12th centuries, the custom was waived on payment of a high fee. The Jews were also compelled to provide the cathedral with 44 pounds of wax and the bishop with incense. The Jewish quarter, whose center was the Rue Juzaygas or Joutx-Aigues, lay around the square of the Carmelites. The Jewish cemetery was at first situated near the Château Narbonnais. When the king took possession of it in 1281, the Jews acquired a field near the Porte de Montoulieu, on the site of the present Grand Rond, for a new cemetery. Communal institutions in this period included a hospital, which was destroyed in the war of the *Albigenses. The importance of the Jewish population can be deduced from the number of houses owned by the Jews. Commerce and moneylending are mentioned as the principal occupations of the Jews in Toulouse in this period. In 1209 they were excluded from holding public office, though they remained free to dispose of their real estate and often possessed the rights of ownership over land held by individuals or religious institutions, particularly the Templars. *Alphonse of Poitiers imposed a large tax on the Jews of Toulouse, as well as on the other Jews under his authority, its payment being enforced by coercive measures. Toward the end of the 13th century, there was debate between the royal officers and the count over the judicial and fiscal jurisdiction of many Jews.

At the time of the expulsion of the Jews from the kingdom of France in 1306, the community of Toulouse was still numerous and economically important, as shown by the number and value of the confiscated properties mentioned in the extant auction documents. They included several "operatoria," perhaps workshops or commercial premises. The new community formed after the readmission of the Jews in 1315 also appears to have been of considerable size, and even attracted Jews from other localities who had not been among the exiles of 1306. There is mention of Baruch "the Teuton," for example, who came from Germany. In 1320, the Jews in Toulouse became victims of the *Pastoureaux persecutions, despite efforts by government authorities to protect them; the houses in the Jewish quarter were looted, and their inhabitants were massacred if they refused immediate baptism. The *Inquisition took precautions that these forced converts should not return to Judaism. As a result, the community practically ceased to exist well before the next expulsion of the Jews of the kingdom in 1322.

A new community was organized in Toulouse after the readmission of Jews in 1359. Only about 15 families settled in the city. Although they established themselves in the former Jewish quarter of Joutx-Aigues, their situation and economic activity had radically changed. They no longer owned land, rented the houses which they occupied, and generally limited themselves to moneylending. They were taken by surprise by the publication of the "final" expulsion order of 1394. A short time earlier, butchers' regulations had laid down the procedure for ritual slaughter with the assumption that the community would remain in Toulouse for a long time. There is no definite information available on medieval Jewish scholars in Toulouse.

During the 17th century a group of *Marranos attempted to establish themselves in Toulouse. They were tried by an Inquisition tribunal in 1685 and received severe penalties. From the end of the century, Jewish merchants, mainly from *Comtat Venaissin, were authorized to trade in Toulouse four times a year. Beginning in the second half of the 18th century, several of them endeavored to settle permanently in the city. There were about 80 Marranos in 1790. After the Reign of Terror, the municipality allowed them to use a former church (the Church of the Penitents) as a synagogue. They do not appear to have taken possession of it, however, because in 1806, they were still without a synagogue. At about that time, they obtained a concession for exclusive use of the cemetery, which until the Revolution had been used for the burial of both Protestants and Jews. There were then 105 Jews in Toulouse, and their numbers increased very slowly. However, from the beginning of the 20th century, many Jewish students from Poland and the Balkans were attracted by the opportunity to study at the University of Toulouse.

[Bernhard Blumenkranz / David Weinberg (2nd ed.)]

Holocaust Period

With the flight of population from the northern zone in June 1940 after the Nazi defeat of France, many Jews settled in Toulouse. As a result, it rapidly became one of the principal centers for Jewish life and resistance in the unoccupied zone. Toulouse was in effect the capital of the southwest of France. Here a considerable number of Jews found refuge and a range of important organizations was set up, including children's homes and agricultural schools. Toulouse was also an important stopover for Jews seeking to escape to Spain. The Organisation Juive de Combat was created at Toulouse and its leaders would often meet there. In August 1942, when 1,525 foreign-born Jews from the region were "regrouped" for deportation, the archbishop of Toulouse, Msgr. Saliège, issued a vigorous protest, which was read publicly in all the churches of the diocese. Following the German occupation of all of France (November 1942), the area around Toulouse saw increased Jewish resistance, including acts of sabotage, the formation of fighting groups, the hiding of children and their transportation to safe havens, and stepped-up efforts to ferry Jews across the border to Spain en route to Palestine or England. Many men, women, and children fell victim to the Nazis and their French collaborators, however, and were tortured to death or deported to Auschwitz.

Contemporary Jewry

Many Holocaust survivors chose to remain in the city after the liberation. As a result, the postwar community gained greater importance than it had enjoyed prior to the war. In 1960 there were over 3,000 members of the community. Thanks largely to the arrival of Jews from North Africa, the Toulouse community became one of the most important Jewish centers in France. In 1987, it had a Jewish population of 12,000. The Jews of Toulouse maintain a full range of communal institutions, including three synagogues, kosher butchers and restaurants, and a community center. Toulouse is also the center for the regional consistory.

[Georges Levitte / David Weinberg (2nd ed.)]

BIBLIOGRAPHY: Gross, Gal Jud, 213f.; B. Blumenkranz, *Juifs et chrétiens…* (1960), index; G. Saige, *Juifs du Languedoc* (1881), index; Y. Dossat, in: *Archives Juives*, 6 (1969/70), 4f., 32f.; E. Szapiro, in: REJ, 125 (1966), 395–9; J.H. Mundy, *Liberty and Political Power in Toulouse* (1954), index; J. Coppolani, *Toulouse* (Fr., 1954), 44–50; A. Thomas, in: *Annales du Midi*, 7 (1895), 439–42; C. Douais, in: *Bulletin de la société archéologique du Midi*, 2 (1888), 118f.; P. Wolff, *Commerce et marchands à Toulouse* (1954), index; Z. Szajkowski, *Franco-Judaica* (1962), index; idem, *Analytical Franco-Jewish Gazetteer* (1966), 195f.; idem, in: JQR, 41 (1958/59), 278–81. **ADD. BIBLIOGRAPHY:** *Guide pratique de judaïsme* (1987), 39.

TOURAINE, former province of W. central France whose territory corresponded to the present department of Indre-et-Loire. The earliest information on the presence of Jews in Touraine is from about 570. Gregory of Tours mentions their presence in Civray and in Tours itself. Jews were subsequently to be found in several places in Touraine, more specifically in Loches, Amboise, and Chinon. During the second half of the 11th century, Philip I, king of France, held several rights in Touraine, including the right to one half of the tenure paid by the Jews of Tours. An agreement of 1215 between the Abbey of St. Martin of Tours and the squire of Loches stipulated that not a single Jew would be authorized to reside in the locality of Longueil. The common law of Touraine of

1246 declared that upon his request a Jew of the feudal lord or the king would be judged by that lord or the king because they were the actual owners of his belongings. In an entry for the year 1306 on the subject of the expulsion of the Jews from France, the "Abridged Chronicle of Touraine" relates that the Jews left Touraine on August 26. They returned in 1315, and in 1321 were among the first victims of the accusation that the Jews had poisoned the wells in collaboration with the lepers. It appears that with the next return of the Jews to France in 1359, none settled in Touraine.

BIBLIOGRAPHY: L. Lazard, in: REJ, 17 (1888), 210–34; A. Salmon (ed.), *Recueil des Chroniques de Touraine* (1854), 198.

[Bernhard Blumenkranz]

TOUREL, JENNIE (1910–1973), mezzo-soprano. Born in Montreal, Canada, Jennie Tourel was educated in Russia, Switzerland, and France, where she studied with Anna El-Tour, whose name she transposed to form her own stage name. In 1933 she began her career in the Opéra Comique, Paris, and in 1940 settled in the United States. She made her U.S. debut with the New York Philharmonic under Toscanini. In 1944 she joined the Metropolitan Opera. Her best-known non-operatic performance was the rendition of the vocal solo in Leonard *Bernstein's *Jeremiah* symphony at its premiere performance (1944); she also became known through appearances in concerts and for recording. She gave annual courses at the Rubin Academy of Music, Jerusalem.

TOURO, JUDAH (1775–1854), U.S. philanthropist. Born in Newport, Rhode Island, to Isaac Touro (d. 1873), the *ḥazzan* of the Yeshuat Israel synagogue, and his wife Reyna, sister of the merchant Moses Michael Hays, Touro had a troubled childhood. The Revolutionary War shattered the prosperity and unity of the Jewish community of Newport. Isaac Touro, a Tory, went with the British to New York City where he lived on a military dole and, in 1782, to Jamaica, British West Indies, where he officiated for a brief time until his death the following year. Touro's widowed mother returned to New England with her four children and took up residence with her wealthy brother. Judah was trained in his uncle's mercantile business, and undertook a number of voyages in his uncle's interest.

In 1801 Touro left Boston for New Orleans. Legend attributes this departure to his uncle's refusal to permit him to marry a cousin, but there is no sure evidence of this. Touro's choice of New Orleans as a center of commercial operations was a fortunate one. Still in Spanish hands at the time of his arrival, the port was soon transferred to France and then sold by Napoleon to the United States as part of the Louisiana Purchase. The population and trade of the city grew in geometric proportions, and Touro and other early merchants prospered greatly. Touro served as a civilian volunteer in the American army at the Battle of New Orleans in 1815 and was severely wounded. His life was saved by his close friend, the Virginia merchant Rezin Shepherd, who was ultimately an executor and residual legatee of Touro's estate. After his recovery Touro took no part in the civic or social life of New Orleans, in contradistinction to an active interest during prior years; some reports indicate that the wound, which left him with a limp and damaged his sexual organs, was the reason for his withdrawal from social relations with any but a few close friends. His business activities continued unabated, however, and his holdings increased. He was a commission merchant who accepted shipments on consignment from firms in the North, which were then sold for the benefit of the owners. He also invested in steamships and other vessels. At no time, however, was he a major mercantile power in New Orleans. He accumulated his fortune through prudent investments in real estate and through his modest standard of living. He said to Rabbi Isaac *Leeser that he had "saved a fortune by strict economy, while others had spent one by their liberal expenditures." He was not a speculator like many of his New Orleans colleagues, and, as a result, easily weathered the periodic panics and depressions which drove many other New Orleans business houses into bankruptcy.

Touro, a reticent, shy, and even peculiar man, took no interest in Jewish matters until late in life; he made only a modest contribution to the first New Orleans congregation, which was founded in 1827, but did not join as a member. The first person with a sense of Jewish responsibility to penetrate his shell of indifference and reserve was Gershom Kursheedt, who arrived in New Orleans in 1839 or 1840, and ultimately succeeded in arousing Touro's feelings of Jewish loyalty. He, and possibly Rezin Shepherd, persuaded Touro to purchase an old Episcopal church for the benefit of a new congregation which Kursheedt organized, Nefutzoth Yehudah, and to pay for its conversion into a synagogue. Kursheedt was also responsible for Touro's bequests, in his famous will, to a host of Jewish institutions. Among these were $108,000 to congregations and societies in New Orleans, and to the Jewish hospital which Touro had founded and which has ever since carried his name; $10,000 for the upkeep of the synagogue and cemetery in Newport, his old home; $60,000 for the relief of the poor in Ereẓ Israel to be used at the discretion of Sir Moses Montefiore; a total of $143,000 to congregations, schools, and other Jewish institutions in 17 cities throughout the land. Gifts to non-Jewish institutions in New Orleans, Boston, and Newport totaled $153,000. No American Jew had ever given so much to so many agencies and causes; nor had any non-Jew done so much in such varied ways.

BIBLIOGRAPHY: L. Huhner, *The Life of Judah Touro* (1946); M.A. Gutstein, *A. Lopez and Judah Touro* (1939); idem, *The Touro Family in Newport* (1935), 23–38; idem, *The Story of the Jews of Newport* (1936), index; J.B. Feibelman, *New Orleans Jewish Community* (1941), 77–78; M.J. Kohler, in: A.J. Karp (ed.), *The Jewish Experience in America*, 2 (1969), 158–76.

[Bertram Wallace Korn]

TOURO COLLEGE, one of the largest institutions of higher and professional education under Jewish sponsorship. Touro has grown from a small liberal arts college consisting of 35 freshmen in 1971, situated in midtown Manhattan, to an international university of over 23,000 students.

It was founded and was under the leadership of Dr. Bernard Lander. The guiding mission of the school can be noted from its being named for Judah and Isaac Touro, who both exemplified in colonial and early America a love for the democratic ethos and their Jewish heritage.

Touro's vision is to serve the larger community in keeping with the Judaic commitment to social justice, intellectual pursuit, and service to humanity.

Under Dr. Lander's guidance Touro's programs had a two-pronged thrust. One is to serve the Jewish community by developing a cadre of committed and concerned Jewish youth in the United States by giving them a higher and professional education with a curriculum based on Jewish values. Secondly, Touro's programs also serve the educational needs of the total society, non-sectarian as well as Jewish. One of Touro's mottos has been "where there is a need, Touro reaches out to help." Touro does not wait for the student to come to the school but brings the school to the student.

Touro College has satellites on three continents. In the United States Touro has several campuses in three states (New York, California, and Nevada), with another planned for Florida in 2006.

Based in New York are separate programs for men and women that meet on alternate days. The Lander College of Arts and Sciences offers a traditional yeshivah program combined with a full secular college curriculum, which is offered at the Men's Division in Kew Garden Hills, Queens. A Men's Division enabling yeshivah students from other institutions desiring to study for a college degree in secular studies was opened in the Flatbush section of Brooklyn in 1977. A Women's Division was initiated in Manhattan in 1974 with a dual Judaic and secular studies curriculum. A parallel Women's Division was opened in Flatbush in 1979. These programs offer broad appeal to Orthodox Jews and allow them to attend their respective religious institutions and earn a higher or professional degree simultaneously.

The Touro School of Lifelong Education (a mentoring program opened in 1988) provides an opportunity for ḥasidic and yeshivah students to be the first in their families to earn a higher and/or professional degree. An affiliate Machon LaParnassa allows students to earn an associates degree. A similar undergraduate program opened in Los Angeles in 2005 and one in Miami is scheduled for 2006.

Touro also has an affiliate full time yeshivah program, Ohr Hachaim (1984), and a yeshivah high school for boys, Yesodai Yeshurun in Queens (1994).

The Graduate School of Jewish Studies was opened in 1979 offering a master's degree.

Touro has opened several professional divisions. A division of Health Sciences was opened in 1972 offering a physicians assistant (PA) program, and added a medical records administration program in 1980. The Touro Center for Bio-Medical Education in Long Island offers a MS-MD degree in conjunction with the Technion Medical School in Israel (1983). A physical therapy (PT) program was added in 1984 and an occupational therapy (OT) program in 1996. A graduate program in speech language pathology began in 2000.

In 1997 Touro opened a Touro University College of Osteopathic Medicine, currently located in Vallejo, California, with a branch campus in Las Vegas in 2004. A similar school is planned for 2006 in New York State.

A school of nursing opened in 2005 in the Boro Park section of Brooklyn creating the opportunity for ḥasidic women to attain a career.

The Jacob D. Fuchsberg Law School was founded as a division of Touro in 1980 and is situated in Huntington, Long Island. In addition to the general law curriculum it has an Institute of Jewish Law.

Touro has also been a leader in innovative pedagogy establishing Touro University International based in Las Alamitos, California in 1999, offering graduate degrees in business over the Internet. The Graduate School of Education and Technology also offers many online courses as do the undergraduate departments in the Lander colleges.

Touro's international programs teach Jewish studies and business courses. Campus sites include Moscow, Berlin, and Jerusalem. Programs are planned for other sites, such as Rome and Budapest.

The Touro campus in Givat Shaul Jerusalem offers a program for Americans in Israel and an affiliate Machon Lander for Israelis. There is also a division of the Touro Graduate School for Jewish Studies in Israel.

The School for General Studies (1974) and the Division of New Americans (1985) began particularly to aid many refugees coming from the former Soviet Union. The latter division was renamed the School of Career and Applied Studies and was eventually merged with the School of General Studies. These divisions, which are community based and have several campuses in New York, have over 6,000 students from all ethnic backgrounds matriculating for the associate and bachelor's degrees.

[Ted Lauer (2nd ed.)]

TOUROFF, NISSAN (1877–1953), educator and author. Born in Nesvizh near Minsk, Touroff became principal of the Girls School in Jaffa in 1907 and later principal of the Levinsky Teachers Seminary for Girls. During World War I he headed the important Education Committee (Va'ad ha-Ḥinnukh) which was responsible for Jewish education in Palestine. He also edited, briefly, the pedagogical journal *Ha-Ḥinnukh* and the daily *Haaretz*. He immigrated to the United States in 1919 and worked in an editorial capacity for the Stybel Publishing Company. He was one of the founders of the Hebrew Teachers College (now Hebrew College) of Boston in 1921 and its first dean. He also founded the educational magazine *Shevilei ha-Ḥinnukh* in 1925. In 1926 he left Boston and became professor of education and Hebrew literature at the Jewish Institute of Religion in New York (1926–32). Touroff's major themes in education were nationalism and Zionism, Hebrew language and literature, the utilization of modern psychological insights in teaching, and the attention to aesthetics in the life of the school. His main Hebrew works in the fields of education and psychology include *Ha-Psychologyah be-Yameinu* (2 vols., 1939–41), *Be-Yode'im u-ve-Lo Yode'im* (1946), a collection of essays on problems of culture and education under the title *Ha'arakhot* (1947), and *Be'ayot ha-Hitabbedut* (1953).

BIBLIOGRAPHY: E. Silberschlag and Y. Twersky (eds.), *Sefer Touroff* (1938), 7–114 (incl. bibl.); M. Ribalow, *Ketavim u-Megillot* (1942), 246–61; A. Epstein, *Soferim Ivriyyim ba-Amerikah* (1952), 403–12; Z. Scharfstein, *Gedolei Ḥinnukh be-Ammenu* (1964), 208–25.

[Eisig Silberschlag]

TOURS, city in the Indre-et-Loire department, central France. Jewish settlement in Tours dates from at least 570, one of the earliest recorded indications of Jewish life in France. In 1171 a notable of the community of Tours intervened in favor of the Jews of *Blois, who were persecuted following an accusation of ritual murder. A council held in Tours in 1236 forbade the Crusaders – as well as every other Christian – to conspire against the lives, health, and property of the Jews. Those found guilty of such a crime would be expelled from the ranks of the Crusaders. A subsequent Council of Tours (1239), however, excluded the Jews from testifying in lawsuits. During this period, Jews lived in a quarter known as the "Juiverie," which was situated between the old bridge and the Rue de la Caserne and consisted of at least 20 houses. They owned a synagogue and leased from the archbishop a plot of land in the Saint-Vincent parish (near the present Rue du Cygne and de Lucé) to use as a cemetery. The Jews of Tours were authorized to bury the Jewish dead, not only of their community, but of any other locality. In addition, a plot of agricultural land and a vineyard were worked by Jews. Expelled from France along with other Jews in 1306, individual Jews from Tours returned in 1315. They also suffered in the persecutions of 1321, which were later justified as punishment for their supposed collusion with the lepers. The community seems to have declined precipitously afterwards, for in 1359 the municipality ordered the final destruction of the Jewish cemetery. A number of scholars are known to have lived in Tours during the Middle Ages: an individual named Solomon corresponded with *Rashi; someone named David lived there toward the middle of the 13th century, as did a Joseph b. Elijah toward the close of the 13th century. Their works, however, have not survived. Before World War II there were fewer than 100 Jews in Tours. There is little information on the community during the Holocaust and in the immediate postwar period. In the early 1970s, as a result of the arrival of North African Jews, there were about 550 Jews. In the early 21st century, the community maintained a synagogue, a community center, and a *talmud torah*.

BIBLIOGRAPHY: Gross, Gal Jud, 216ff.; L. Lazard, in: REJ, 17 (1888), 210–34; L. de Grandmaison, *ibid.*, 18 (1889), 262–75; idem (ed.), *Cartulaire de l'Archevêché de Tours*, 2 (1904), 84–87; S. Grayzel, *Church and the Jews…* (1966²), index; Z. Szajkowski, *Analytical Franco-Jewish Gazetteer* (1966), 204; B. Blumenkranz, in: *Archives Juives*, 6 (1969–70), 36–38. **ADD. BIBLIOGRAPHY:** *Jewish Travel Guide* (2002), 91.

[Bernhard Blumenkranz / David Weinberg (2nd ed.)]

°TOUSSENEL, ALPHONSE (1803–1885), French antisemitic publicist and disciple of *Fourier. From 1839 to 1843 Toussenel coedited *Phalange* and later participated in the foundation of the *Démocratie pacifique*, both Fourierist publications. His two-volume work, *Les Juifs, rois de l'époque; histoire de la féodalité financière*, was one of the most resounding attacks on the Jews published in France (1845) before the appearance of *Drumont's *La France Juive*. An even more virulent second edition of *Les Juifs…* was published in 1847 and reprinted in 1886 and 1888. To some degree Toussenel influenced Drumont. He also helped to inspire a conservative, rural antisemitism, which later found its political expression in *L'*Action Française*. Toussenel did not make a formal attack on the Jewish people as such, but tried rather to show what he believed was commonly meant by "Jew". He wrote, "I wish to point out to the reader that this word will generally be used here in the popular sense of Jew: banker, usurer."

Toussenel's antisemitism was not limited to his conception of a Jew-dominated 19th century. Reaching back into history, he affirmed his sympathy for the persecutions inflicted upon the Jews by the Romans, Christians, and Muslims. Adding another dimension to his antisemitism, Toussenel also declared, "Who says Jew says Protestant." Accordingly, the Protestant nations of Europe – the English, the Dutch, and the Swiss, in particular – were, like the Jews, "merchants and birds of prey." Toussenel's embittered antisemitic, anti-foreign, and anti-Protestant tirades later provided ample inspiration for the anti-Dreyfusards.

BIBLIOGRAPHY: R.F. Byrnes, *Anti-semitism in Modern France*, 1 (1950), index; E. Silberner, *Sozialisten zur Judenfrage* (1962), index; L. Thomas, *Alphonse-Toussenel, socialistenational, antisémite* (1941); Z. Szajkowski, in: JSS, 9 (1947), 33–47.

°TOVEY, D'BLOISSIERS (1692–1745), English clergyman. He wrote the first comprehensive history of the Jews of England, *Anglia Judaica or the History and Antiquities of the Jews in England, collected from all our historians, both printed and manuscript, as also from the records in the Tower, and other publick repositories* (1738). Though concentrating on the medieval period, the work contains a section on the resettlement and on the English Jews of his own day. It shows appreciation of the magnitude of royal exploitation of the Jews in the Middle Ages and a healthy skepticism of ritual murder charges. It is largely based on the *Short Demurrer…* (1656) of William *Prynne. Tovey estimated that in 1738 there were about 6,000 Jews in England and noted that, at the time, no settled Jewish communities existed outside of London.

BIBLIOGRAPHY: S. Levy, in: JHSET, 6 (1912), 9. **ADD. BIBLIOGRAPHY:** ODNB online; Endelman, *Jews in Georgian England*, index; Katz, England, index.

[Vivian David Lipman]

TOWNE, CHARLES (1781–1854), English painter of animals and landscapes. Born in London, Towne's work such as *The Boat Builders* (1811) and *Cattle Fair* (1826) resemble the productions of the Norwich School and show a strong feeling for English country life of the period. From the year 1806 Towne exhibited at the Royal Academy. Another English painter of animals, who was not Jewish, was also named Charles Towne (or Town). He lived from 1763 to 1840, and is known as "Charles Towner the Elder" to distinguish him from this artist.

TOZ (abbr. from the initials of **Towarzystwo Ochrony Zdrowia Ludnośći Żydowskiej**, "Society for the Safeguarding of the Health of the Jewish Population"), Jewish welfare organization officially founded in Poland in 1921. It was connected with the *OZE society, established in St. Petersburg in 1912, which engaged in medical activities in the former territories of Russia and was later integrated into a common framework in Poland. TOZ began activities in a few regions only, but from 1923 it encompassed all areas in the state. World War I and its consequences, especially in the eastern regions, where the Jews had also suffered from pogroms, brought the society up against a number of urgent problems. It had to combat the contagious diseases which developed into epidemics and were responsible for a high death rate among the Jewish population in general and children in particular. On the other hand, the hostilities along the borders until the Peace of Riga (1921) brought chaos to the state and municipal medical services and prevented the impoverished Jewish masses from benefiting from the sick funds for organized workers.

Although TOZ considered its principal role in the sphere of preventive medicine, current needs compelled it to concentrate its main efforts in preventing the spread of skin and eye diseases (ringworm and trachoma) and tuberculosis by establishing clinics, X-ray departments, pharmacies, convalescent homes, etc. TOZ published three periodicals: *Folksgezund* (for the masses), *Gezund* (for schoolchildren), and *Sotsiale Meditisin* (a scientific journal). Among its many services the psycho-hygienic assistance which TOZ offered in treating the mentally retarded or those with physical afflictions was of great importance.

In addition to its institutions, TOZ also supported numbers of Jewish hospitals with its advisory services and assistance funds. In 1939 it was responsible for over 400 medical and sanitary institutions in 50 towns. Annual membership fees were paid by 15,000 supporters, and about 1,000 people, including doctors, nurses, dentists, teachers, and medical assistants, were on its employment roll. Additional incomes were derived from support by the *American Jewish Joint Distribution Committee and the funds raised by the OZE abroad. Throughout the existence of TOZ, its central committee was presided over by the physician and public worker Gershon *Lewin, formerly director of the Jewish hospital in Warsaw. Leon Wulman also played an outstanding role in the activities of the organization in his capacity of general secretary. During World War II the institutions of TOZ attempted to assist victims of famine and epidemics until 1942, when all its branches were closed down on the order of the German occupation authorities in Poland.

BIBLIOGRAPHY: Y. Gruenbaum (ed.), EG, 1 (1953), 582–5: A. Lewinson, *Toledot Yehudei Varshah* (1953), 353–5; H.M. Rabinowicz, *The Legacy of Polish Jewry* (1965), 175–6.

[Moshe Landau]

TRABOT (Trabotto), Italian family of French origin which flourished from the 14th to the 17th centuries. The name is most probably derived from Trévoux, once Trévou, a town located in Burgundy, from where the Jews were definitely expelled in 1488. The most important members of the family are PEREZ TRABOT (14th–15th centuries), also known as Zarfati or Catalani which seems to indicate that he went from France to Catalonia in 1395, then to Italy. He composed *Makrei Dardekei*, a Hebrew–French and Hebrew–Catalan dictionary (Naples, 1488). JEHIEL TRABOT, rabbi at Pesaro in the early 16th century, was a grandson of R. Joseph *Colon, whose own father was known as Solomon Trabot. Jehiel is mentioned in *Naḥalat Ya'akov*, Jacob Alpron's collection of responsa. His son AZRIEL (d. 1569), rabbi in Florence and Ascoli in the second half of the 16th century, was noted for his responsa. Following the bull of February 1569 of Pope *Pius V, decreeing that all Jews in the Papal States except Rome and Ancona should be driven out, the congregation of Ascoli, with Azriel at its head, found refuge at Pesaro. There Azriel was entrusted with the valuable Ark. He died in Pesaro in July of the same year. His son JEHIEL was rabbi at Pesaro and Ferrara. AZRIEL, son of Jehiel, was rabbi of Ascoli at the beginning of the 17th century. He composed a list of rabbis (cf. REJ, 4 (1882), 208–25) and several responsa. NETHANEL BEN BENJAMIN BEN AZRIEL (1576–1653), was rabbi of Modena. Several of his rulings are extant. Especially important is his responsum on reform of music in the synagogue. In 1711, RAFAEL TRABOTTO was given permission by the Austrian authorities to engage in moneylending in Mantua.

BIBLIOGRAPHY: Gross, Gal Jud, 219–21; Mortara, Indice, 65–66; Ghirondi-Neppi, 179, 271, 296; S. Simonsohn, *Toledot ha-Yehudim ba-Dukkasut Mantovah* (1962), index; D. Kaufmann, in: JQR, 9 (1896/97), 255ff.

TRACHONITIS, a province of the area of *Bashan E. of the River Jordan and N. of the River Yarmuk. It was one of the three provinces into which the area was divided by the Ptolemies, the other two being Gaulonitis and Batanaea. As a result the Targum renders the name Argob as a region of Bashan and as "the province of Trachonitis" (*pelakh Terakhona*, cf. Deut. 3:4). The emperor Augustus awarded it to Herod, and it remained with his heirs until Agrippa (II; c. 100). In 106 C.E., together with all Bashan, it was annexed to the province of Arabia, the capital of which was Boẓrah and it is therefore called "Trachonitis of Boẓrah" in the Tosefta (see below). During Herod's stay in Rome, the inhabitants of Trachonitis rebelled against him, and his commander *Zamaris cleared it of marauders; it is therefore also referred to as "Trachonitis of Zamaris" (*Terakhona de-Zimra*). For halakhic purposes Trachonitis was regarded as part of the territory of Ereẓ Israel, and therefore, the laws appertaining to the Sabbatical Year applied to it (Tosef., Shev. 4:11).

TRACHTENBERG, JOSHUA (1904–1959), U.S. Reform rabbi and scholar. Trachtenberg, born in London, was taken to the U.S. in 1907. He received rabbinic ordination at Hebrew Union College (1936) and served Congregation Covenant of Peace, Easton, Pennsylvania (1930–51), and Bergen County Reform Temple, Teaneck, New Jersey (1953–59). During 1951–52 he worked on a survey of religious conditions in Israel, sponsored by the Central Conference of American Rabbis and the Union of American Hebrew Congregations. His report, displaying great depth of feeling, appeared in the *Year Book* (1952) of the Central Conference of American Rabbis. Trachtenberg was active both in the fields of scholarship and community work. In Easton he was president of the Jewish Community Council (1939–46); an ardent Zionist, he was identified with the Labor Zionist movement. His scholarly work was conducted despite the handicap of a serious eye defect. *Jewish Magic and Superstition* (1939, repr. 1961) was his Ph.D. dissertation at Columbia University. An outgrowth of this study was *The Devil and the Jews* (1943, repr. 1966), which examines the relationship of the medieval conception of antisemitism to the modern variety. *Consider the Years* (1944) is a history of the Easton Jewish community.

BIBLIOGRAPHY: A.J. Zuckerman, in: CCARY, 70 (1961), 180–1.

[Sefton D. Temkin]

TRADE AND COMMERCE.

In the Bible

The geopolitical location of Palestine, set as it is in the heart of the Fertile Crescent, made it a pivotal link in the commercial activities carried on by land and sea between, on the one hand, Egypt and the Arabian Peninsula in the south and, on the other, Phoenicia, Syria, Anatolia, and Mesopotamia in the north. Palestine also played a part in the maritime trade with the Mediterranean islands, as it did, too, in trade with the commercial centers on the Mediterranean littoral.

The special position enjoyed by Palestine among the ancient lands was due to the existence and activities of cities – harbor cities and others – which, being situated along the main arteries of communication, became important centers in the international and internal trade. The written sources in archaeological finds clearly show that trading was a favorite occupation by which a considerable proportion of the local population directly or indirectly earned a livelihood. A notable contribution to the development of economic relations in Palestine was made by the nomads who, roaming the border areas of the permanently populated regions and along the main highways, engaged in the transit trade (Gen. 37:25, 28).

Since it was poor in natural resources and raw materials, Palestine's own share in the export trade comprised agricultural products and other items, the production of which was associated with agriculture. Foreign sources (in particular those of Egypt, which imported the products of Palestine) and to some extent, too, the Bible, emphasize that Palestine sustained itself by exporting cereals and flour, oil and wine, as well as cosmetic and medicinal products extracted from plants (Gen. 43:11; Ezek. 27:17; Hos. 12:2) and, at a relatively later period, also ore and finished metal goods. In contrast to its limited exports the population of Palestine needed an unceasing stream of products, various luxury goods, and raw materials, such as timber, metal, and so on.

The destinations and composition of the commodities and the identity of the traders did not change with the conquest of Palestine by the Israelites. They did not actively participate in trade either because of the tribal structure of their autarchic society and economy or because access to the main arteries of commerce was obstructed by the autochthonous population. Thus the Bible contains no evidence of the pursuit of trade or finance (allied areas also in ancient times). Nor do the laws of the Torah make much reference to commerce, the exceptions being the laws enjoining just weights, measures, and balances (Lev. 19:36; Deut. 25:13ff.), and stringent warnings against exacting interest from Israelites, but these admonitions may reflect other spheres of economic activity and a later period when the land was being divided among the tribes. It is also probable that the sparse mention of trade is due in part to the negative attitude of the writers and redactors of the Bible and of prophetic circles to commerce and to the foreigners who engaged in it: "As the merchant [lit. Canaan] keeps balances of deceit, he loves to oppress" (Hos. 12:8). The expression "Canaanite" became a synonym for "a merchant" ("Who has devised this against Tyre, the crowning city, whose tradesmen are princes, whose merchants [Canaanites] are the honorable of the earth?" – Isa. 23:8; and see Prov. 31:24, et al.). Throughout the First Temple period (Isa. 23; Ezek. 27) and also in the early days of the Restoration (Neh. 13:16) their activities were considerable.

Israelite participation in international economic activities and commerce began with the inception of the United Kingdom. This participation was made possible by the establishment of a large kingdom whose needs were considerable and whose political ties were extensive. The control of lengthy sections of the important trade routes in Transjordan and in the coastal plain, along which commerce flowed, intensified the urge to profit from it. In the days of *David and particularly in those of *Solomon economic relations were developed with the kingdom of *Tyre, one of the most important economic powers at the time. To carry out its extensive construction projects both within and outside the confines of Jerusalem, Israel needed building materials, metal, and other commodities, which were supplied and transported to Jaffa by the Tyrians in exchange for agricultural products: "And we will cut whatever timber you need from Lebanon, and bring it to you in rafts by sea to Jaffa, so that you may take it up to Jerusalem" (II Chron. 2:15 [16]; cf. I Kings 5:21ff.).

The chronicler of Solomon's activities lays great stress on the place occupied by the royal trade. Indeed, it seems that the monarchy in Israel exercised a monopoly in this economic sphere. Solomon's Tyrian allies undoubtedly benefited from the Israelite control of the arteries of communication along which flowed the trade with southern Arabia and Egypt, for Solomon could direct the caravans to such destinations in his own kingdom and in friendly countries as he wished. Thus he profited not only from barter with Tyre but also from the international transit trade. Moreover, the royal commercial apparatus in Israel was able to initiate independent trading activities. According to the sources, this independent trade was apparently maritime commerce in which Solomon's ships, built with Tyrian help in the port of *Ezion-Geber, took part. Yet these very sources make it possible for the opposite conclusion to be drawn, for it is probable that the Tyrians insisted on being made partners in such ventures in exchange for their technical assistance and for the participation of their men in these expeditions: "King Solomon built a fleet of ships at Ezion-Geber, which is near Eloth on the shore of the Red Sea, in the land of Edom. And Hiram sent with the fleet his servants, seamen who were familiar with the sea, together with the servants of Solomon" (I Kings 9:26–27; II Chron. 8:17–18). The ships sailed to, and traded with, the African and Arabian coasts (see *Ophir). On these voyages they brought with them precious metals and precious stones, as well as rare kinds of timber: "And they went to Ophir, and brought from there gold, to the amount of four hundred and twenty talents; and they brought it to King Solomon" (I Kings 9:28; II Chron. 8:18). "The fleet of Hiram, which brought gold from Ophir, brought from Ophir a very great amount of almug wood and precious stones" (I Kings 10:11; II Chron. 9:10). According to one theory, Israelite-Tyrian ships also voyaged in the Mediterranean Sea as far as Spain (if *Tarshish is explained as a place name). Another view however maintains that "the fleet of ships of Tarshish" was a type of ship suitable for transporting metal, and hence alludes to the nature of the Israelite exports and the goods received in exchange: "For the king had a fleet of ships of Tarshish at sea with the fleet of Hiram. Once every three years the fleet of ships of Tarshish used to come bringing gold, silver, ivory, apes, and peacocks" (I Kings 10:22; II Chron. 9:21).

Barter also occupied a place in Solomon's economic activities: the royal merchants purchased horses from *Que and chariots from Egypt, and marketed them as "a finished product" to the kings of Syria: "And Solomon's import of horses was from Egypt and Keveh [Que], and the king's traders received them from Keveh at a price. A chariot could be imported from Egypt for six hundred shekels of silver, and a horse for a hundred and fifty; and so through the king's traders they were exported to all the kings of the Hittites, and for the kings of Aram" (I Kings 10:28–29; II Chron. 9:28). The enigmatic reference to "the kings of the mingled people" (מַלְכֵי הָעֶרֶב, the reading in II Chron. is "the kings of Arabia" – מַלְכֵי עֲרָב) alongside "the governors of the land" as persons with whom Solomon had commercial relations either indicates that the United Kingdom traded directly with the Arabian Peninsula, or may refer to contacts with nomads who engaged extensively in transporting goods from the south to the north (I Kings 10:15; II Chron. 9:14). The well-known story of the Queen of *Sheba's visit to Jerusalem may reasonably be explained on the assumption that the queen of this South Arabian kingdom came to Jerusalem at the head of a trade delegation to establish closer relations with Israel (I Kings 10:1ff.; II Chron. 9:1–12).

The extensive space which the Bible devotes to Solomon is not accorded to the kings who reigned after him. This, however, does not warrant the conclusion that the commercial activities ceased after Solomon's time. The continuation of these activities is attested by the products of foreign lands dating from the days of the kingdoms of Israel and Judah which have been uncovered at various archaeological sites in the country. Under King *Jehoshaphat of Judah there was a renewed attempt to sail ships from Ezion-Geber which failed owing to the destructive forces of nature: "Jehoshaphat made ships of Tarshish to go to Ophir for gold; but they did not go, for the ships were wrecked at Ezion-Geber" (I Kings 22:49 [48]). This attempt is undoubtedly to be understood against the background of the relations which Jehoshaphat established with the dynasty of Omri in Israel and with the Kingdom of Tyre. He may have been assisted in the building of his navy by the Tyrians. The close ties maintained by *Omri and Ahab with the Tyrians are similarly to be regarded as indubitably commercial relations. Jehoshaphat apparently brought the kings of Israel into association with the activities of his navy in the Red Sea: "After this Jehoshaphat king of Judah joined [אֶתְחַבַּר] with Ahaziah king of Israel, who did wickedly. He joined him [וַיְחַבְּרֵהוּ] in building ships to go to Tarshish, and they built the ships in Ezion-Geber. Then Eliezer son of Dodavahu of Mareshah prophesied against Jehoshaphat, saying: 'Because you have joined [בְּהִתְחַבֶּרְךָ] with Ahaziah, the Lord will destroy what you have made.' And the ships were wrecked and were not able to go to Tarshish" (II Chron. 20:35–37). The use of the root *ḥbr*, "to join," is intended to indicate the significance of the relations between Jehoshaphat and Ahaziah. In several Semitic languages the use of *ḥbr* denotes a commercial partnership, particularly in a maritime connection. According to I Kings 22:50, Jehoshaphat rejected Ahaziah's offer to cooperate with him in maritime commerce.

Additional evidence of trade that was conditioned by political circumstances is the presence not only of Aramean commercial agencies in Samaria in the days of Omri and in part of those of Ahab, but also, after the latter's victory over Aram, of Israelite agencies in Damascus (I Kings 20:34). Furthermore the economic tendencies to develop trade in Israel and Judah, though not explicitly mentioned in the Bible, are evident in the expansionist ambitions of these kingdoms toward Transjordan and the west, the purpose of which was to gain control both of the trade routes in these areas and of the centrally located ports that promoted trade with Phoenicia, Egypt, and other countries on the Mediterranean littoral.

The biblical references to internal trade are sparse. This trade was carried on in open places, in streets, squares, and marketplaces (Neh. 13:17–22), as also in open areas near gates (II Kings 7:1). It apparently took the form mainly of barter, in which farmers, artisans, and others who offered the products of their labors participated. Merchants and peddlers also displayed their wares. There is no information on the quality of the goods or on the organization of the internal retail trade. The Bible mentions trade in oil (II Kings 4:7), wine, grapes, and figs (Neh. 13:15–16), fish (13:16) and animals (II Sam. 12:3, et al.), in addition to products such as pottery (Jer. 19:1) and items of clothing (13:1–2). These individual mentions undoubtedly represent only a few of the potential articles of trade. The likely range of the retail trade may be inferred from the cultural and material standard of the population at various periods, and in particular from the fact that the economy of the Israelites ceased to be autarchic already at a late stage of the division of the land among the tribes, for as the standard of life rose among the inhabitants of the country, so undoubtedly did the articles of trade increase in quantity and diversity.

[Hanoch Reviv]

Post-Biblical

During the Babylonian Exile Jews became acquainted with old commercial traditions. The post-biblical, talmudic epoch shows Palestine again as an agrarian country, as is clear from the Talmud and Josephus. The growing Diaspora intensified the contacts with Phoenicians, Syrians, and Greeks, and especially Greek influence as is to be seen in the use of technical terms.

The consequence of those influences is especially notable where Jews met in an atmosphere of strong commercial activity, as in Alexandria and later in Delos and Ostia. In the late Roman Empire there were colonies of Jewish and Syrian merchants all over its realm who preserved their ethical and religious traditions. Such colonies were to be found from Britanny and Ireland as far as India and Turkestan. Hennig stressed the commerce of Jews with China which had already come into being. The superiority of the Jewish over the Syrian merchants must, according to Heichelheim, be seen in the fund of common traditions going back to Babylonia. The Talmud knows the "pragmateutes" and the "emporos" as specializations in trade in far distant lands, terms which point to their Hellenistic origins. In addition, the word "taggar" – known from Palmyra – is found, and is related to the Babylonian "tamkar." The taggar was the merchant who was occupied in local commerce. Many of these traditions passed, as pointed out by R.S. Lopez, from the late Roman Empire to the Byzantine Empire and from Sassanid Persia to the empire of the Caliphs. On the base of a widely autonomous economy, trade in the distant lands was limited to luxury goods.

Middle Ages to 18th Century

From the fifth to seventh centuries, Jews traded as far as Gaul where the ports of Provence, especially *Narbonne and *Marseilles, served them as transit places. They dealt in perfumes, glassware, textiles, and other luxury articles of the Orient. Procopius, Cassiodorus, and Pope Gregory I (the Great) mention Jewish merchants in Genoa, Naples, and Palermo. The system of trade in the *Byzantine Empire probably favored the expansion of these merchants toward the west where the vacuum created by the invasions of the Germans opened new routes for selling Oriental luxury goods. Clients of all ranks were to be found. Jewish merchants supplied kings as well as monasteries and high church dignitaries with *spices and all types of precious Oriental goods. The extent to which they obtained these wares directly from the Orient is not certain. Documentation on direct trading relations with the Orient exists only from the end of the eighth century. In 797 when *Charlemagne sent two ambassadors to the caliph Hārūn-al-Rashid from Aix-la-Chapelle the merchant *Isaac acted as a guide and interpreter, returning to Aix-la-Chapelle in 802.

At least from the seventh century, after the ports of Syria had been conquered by the Arabs, Jews were able to develop a far-flung trading network. According to Ibn Chordadbeh, the postmaster of the caliph of Baghdad (between 854 and 874), the *Radaniya traded between France and China along four routes, some of them touching at Byzantium on their return. It is not clear from where the Radaniya came, either from France or from a region east of the Tigris. These merchants brought swords, eunuchs, slaves, furs, and silks from the West, and musk, aloes, camphor, cinnamon, and other articles from the East. One of the most important spheres of trade seems to have been the *slave trade, especially in slaves from the countries of the Slavs, since the Council of Meaux in 845 (see *Church Councils) prohibited trade in Christian slaves. The chief market was the area in the Iberian Peninsula under Muslim rule. Commercial centers of the northern route were *Kiev, the valley of the Danube, where they had to pass the customs of Raffelstetten near *Passau, then *Regensburg and *Mainz.

From the tenth century, this northern route became the more important because of the rise of the Mediterranean rivalry of the Italian cities. Mainz and Regensburg then apparently became the most important starting points for trade expeditions to the East. Jews from the western regions traveled as far as Bulgar of Itil (see *Atil), the capital of the Jewish *Khazars on the Volga. Around 955 *Isaac b. Eleazar brought a letter from *Ḥisdai ibn Shaprut, when a minister in Córdoba, to the Khazar king *Joseph. The route passed through Prague and Cracow. In 965 Prague was visited by the Spanish geographer *Ibrahim ibn Yaqūb, who stressed the importance of this town for the trade with the East and mentions the role of the Jews. There he saw Jewish and Islamic merchants from the empire of the Khazars and *Crimea. At that time Italian Jews still had trading connections with Jerusalem. In particular Jews of Gaeta traded with Jaffa, and Jews of Capua with Egypt, until the rising cities of Amalfi, Bari, Venice, Genoa, and Pisa drove them from the Levantine trade. Venetian captains were forbidden to transport Jews and Jewish merchandise. The activity of the Jews of Mainz in the East European trade led to a diplomatic correspondence by the doge Pietro of Venice and the patriarch of Grado with Emperor Henry I and the archbishop of Mainz concerning the duty to compel the Mainz Jews to become Christians or else prohibit them from trading in Oriental goods.

In this period, additional Jewish settlements grew in the Rhine region, the main part of the East Franconian Empire, the most important being Metz, Trier, Cologne, Worms, and Speyer. There they were allowed to trade freely, especially in wines, hides, and drugs, as well as in meat and secondhand goods, which was often combined with lending on pawn, while slaves and Oriental products were also important. From the tenth century a new route was opened through the Danube Valley to Hungary which became accessible after the inhabitants became converted to Christianity, *Esztergom (Gran) or Ofen-Pest serving as points of transit. From there the merchants often crossed the passes of the Carpathians, continuing to *Przemysl and Kiev, where there was an important Jewish settlement. Toward the end of the 11th century *Isaac b. Asher ha-Levi at Speyer was well informed on the role and importance of this East European trade. He relates that the merchants traveled in caravans, and that each caravan formed an association, buying the merchandise jointly and distributing it by lot. During the 12th century Regensburg Jews became the main entrepreneurs of this trade. *Pethahiah of Regensburg shows that Jews from there traveled as far as Crimea, the *Caucasus, *Baghdad, and *Mosul. Later, from the beginning of the 13th century, Prague and Vienna seem to have outrivaled Regensburg. In 1221 transit through Vienna was forbidden. After the Tatar invasions Kiev's importance waned and this eastern trade declined.

Regensburg especially was a center for the silver trade and the mint business. Meanwhile, for the slave trade another route from Magdeburg and Merseburg to the Rhine came into use. The customs regulations of Coblenz from 1104 record the passage of slaves on the Rhine for the last time, since after the adoption of Christianity by the Slav countries the slave trade there was prohibited.

Along the trade routes of the Indian Ocean, as well as the Mediterranean, in the 11th to 13th centuries, Jewish merchants combined in manifold far-distance trading activities as well as more limited coastal trading in most of this period. *Yemen served as a transit station for the trade between Egypt and the Far East. Scores of categories of articles, some of them in huge quantities, were transported by this Jewish trade mainly through Muslim ports. Jewish trading activity was based on a well-established organization of Jewish merchants at the ports.

Meanwhile, the interior market in Western Europe grew, the fairs of Cologne especially attracting Jews. They met there three times a year in order to sell and buy wool, hides, furs, jewels, and pearls. With the First Crusade an epoch of persecutions began in Western Europe (see *Crusades). Local restrictions and canon law compelled Jews to concentrate on *moneylending. However, as late as the 14th century *Alexander Sueslein ha-Kohen of Frankfurt states that Jews did business at the fairs of the Christians, and that on Sabbath non-Jewish debtors came with wagons of corn. The responsa of *Meir b. Baruch of Rothenburg show that Jewish merchants used the Rhine shipping route, trading in, among other items, salted fish, wool, skins, wines, grain, silver, and gold. After the decline of the Cologne fairs Jewish merchants were attracted by the fairs of Frankfurt and Friedberg. At the same time the courts of the princes offered a market for luxury goods. In this period Jews generally seem to have bought from far-distance traders in order to sell as retailers and *peddlers. How far there were trading relations for instance with southern France and Spain is hard to ascertain. By then the distant trade had mainly passed to Christian merchants. Generally members of a family joined in partnership and women took an active part.

In the persecutions, plunder, and massacre of the Jews occasioned by the *Black Death, the patricians were not the main adversaries of the Jews – many of whom being active in far-distance trade had commercial relations with them – but the artisans, who viewed the Jewish retailers and peddlers as bringing unfavorable competition. After the persecutions Jews were again active in trade and apparently had trade connections from the Rhineland not only with the Netherlands and France but also with parts of Spain, Switzerland, and probably Italy.

Meanwhile, a new series of anti-Jewish measures began. From the end of the 14th until the beginning of the 16th centuries Jews had to leave most of the German towns. They withdrew into the small domains of local lords or went to Eastern Europe where there were possibilities open in the service of the crown of Poland and the nobles. The wealthy Jews were attracted by privileges in connection with the colonization policies of Duke *Boleslav and King *Casimir III. Witold, grand duke of Lithuania, continued this policy. In an agrarian society Jews became important representatives of commercial activity. Not only the princes, but the nobles also had good relations with them. From Poland Jews, in the same way as Armenians, participated in the trade with the Black Sea regions, especially with Caffa (*Feodosiya), Khadzhibei, Cetatea-Alba (*Belgorod-Dnestrovski), and *Kiliya. *Vladimir-Volynski, *Lutsk, Lvov, Cracow, and later Lublin and Bratislava became the main trading links in Poland and Silesia. Meanwhile a Jewish colony grew up at Caffa, and later, after its decline, Jewish merchants in *Constantinople established direct commercial relations with Poland.

In *Apulia and *Sicily Jews were active in the silk trade, Emperor Frederick II granting them the monopoly for trade in raw silk. They also organized the commerce in dyed textiles. In southern France Jews played a main part in the trade of kermes. From the ports of Provence they took part in the Levantine trade and had connections with the Spanish littoral, Sicily, and southern Italy. This trade was organized, like that of the Italian merchants in Venice or Genoa, by the practice of *commenda*. Mardoché Joseph, whose register from 1374 has been preserved, owned woods where the resin was extracted from the trees. In *Franche-Comté from 1300 to 1318 a Jewish company developed extensive trading activity in goods and money.

IBERIAN PENINSULA. On the Iberian Peninsula Jews could maintain far-reaching trading relations from the areas under Arab rule with Central Europe and the slave markets in Eastern Europe, as well as with North Africa and the Levant, their main centers being Córdoba and *Lucena. Following persecutions in the Moorish part of the peninsula, Jews settled in the areas with a Christian population, where they participated, among other commercial activities, in provisioning the soldiers who fought in the Christian Reconquest. Apart from the prohibition on the slave trade, their economic activity was unrestricted. Generally, more is known of their activity as lessees of revenues such as customs or rents than of their trading activities, but in *Toledo, the Jewish center in Castile, as well as in *Barcelona and *Saragossa, the centers in Catalonia and Aragon, some Jews must have been merchants, dealing for instance in cloth or bullion. Don Samuel ha-Levi, the richest Jew in Toledo in the 14th century, was a merchant, and the building of the synagogue of Toledo as well as that of Córdoba must have been made possible by wealth acquired by trade.

In Portugal the Abrabanel family and other Jewish cloth merchants had far-reaching trade connections. The persecutions of the Jews in Spain of 1391 resulted in major damage to Jewish workshops, to the cloth production in Aragon and Catalonia, the tanneries of Oscaña and Córdoba, the silks of Valencia, Seville, *Talavera de la Reina, and *Murcia, the carpets of Borja and Salamanca, the goldsmiths' wares of Toledo and Córdoba, and other precious articles of artisan production organized by Jewish manufacturers and merchants. At the same time there were fairs to which Jews imported silk from Persia and Damascus, leather from Tafilalet, and Arabian filigree. Records exist especially from Seville showing that even after the persecutions the production of Jewish swordsmiths, tailors, and manufacturers of embossed leather, and the activities of merchants continued. Meanwhile, the wave of conversions to Christianity among the Jews in Spain especially affected members of the upper class, including merchants. One group of them is expressly known to have continued its activity as merchants – the Villanova of Calatayud, the Maluenda, de Ribas, de Jassa from Tauste and Hijar, the Ortigas, Esprés, Vidal, and Esplugas from Saragossa. Don Alfonso of Aragon, a bastard of King John of Navarre, had three sons by Estenza, daughter of the rich cloth merchant Aviasa ha-Cohen or Coneso, and took the name of Aragon.

A last important role was played by Jewish merchants in Spain in the final phase of the Christian Reconquest. There were also trading relations with the Moorish regions, and one of the reasons for the restrictions ordered against them by the Cortes of Toledo in 1480 was that Jews were selling arms there. On the other side Abraham *Senior and Isaac Abravanel with a staff of Jewish merchants organized the supply of the troops that conquered Malaga, Baza, and finally Granada.

The edict of March 31, 1492, ordering the expulsion of the Jews from Spain was made even more severe since they had to sell their properties but were forbidden to take gold and silver away with them. In Aragon Jews sold textile workshops at Hijar, Barbastro, Huesca, Saragossa, Lerida, Manresa, Valencia, and Barcelona. One of the best-known textile manufacturers at Huesca was Solomon Abenaqua, and at Hijar, Samuel Auping.

MARRANO ACTIVITY. The exiles included many craftsmen, manufacturers, and merchants. The majority emigrated to Portugal, the nearest place of refuge. Those who preferred to stay in Spain had to accept baptism, though secretly most of them maintained their Jewish religious traditions and were regarded as a special group of New Christians (Marranos). The Spanish overseas expansion opened up new fields of activity for them, especially in the spice trade. Rui Mendes (de Brito), and subsequently Francisco and Diogo *Mendes, organized trading activities which spanned an area from the East Indies through Lisbon to Antwerp, and included not only spices, but precious stones, pearls, and other Oriental luxury goods. Additional Marrano families entered this trade. Later, toward the end of the 16th century, notably the Ximenes, the Rodrigues d'évora, Heitor Mendes, Duarte Furtado de Mendoza, Luis Gomes d'Elvas, and the Rodrigues Solis families participated in the East Indies trade.

Other fields of Marrano trading activity were the trade with Africa and Brazil which began with Fernão de Noronha, who organized the trade in Brazilian dyewood. Marrano merchants participated in the development of sugar production in Madeira, São Tomé, and Brazil. Diogo Fernandes and a group were owners of one of the five sugar plantations which existed in Brazil about 1550. Toward the end of the 16th century, as can be seen from the records of the Inquisition, among the outstanding businessmen accused of Judaizing were Bento Dias Santiago, João Nunes, and Heitor Antunes, who from localities in the northeast, especially Paraiba, Olinda, and Bahia, organized the export of sugar and other Brazilian goods as correspondents of the Marrano merchants at Lisbon and other places in Portugal, as well as of their relatives, who meanwhile had begun emigrating to Northern Europe. By maintaining commercial relations from Brazil to Buenos Aires, and from there through Córdoba to Lima and Potosi, they organized an important contraband trade for a market which, because of the monopolistic policy of the Spanish center, was underprovided. They exported textiles and other manufactured goods or slaves, and received bullion which they sent to Europe. "La complicidad grande," the large-scale investigation organized by the Inquisition, which alarmed Lima from 1635 to 1639, resulted in economic disaster; among 81 persons apprehended, 64 were "Judaizers," most of them merchants.

When the Dutch West India Company occupied part of Brazil, the Marranos and those who now openly confessed their Jewish tradition took a remarkable part in the trade both in retail business, in financing, and in the export-import trade. When the Dutch were expelled from the northeast (the last from *Recife in 1654) some of the sugar traders settled in the West Indies, where, through their European market connections they contributed, at first in Barbados and Guyana, in developing sugar export to Europe. Later Curacao and São Tomé became the main centers of Jewish trade in the Antilles.

This was a factor that exercised great influence in the expansion of Jewish trade toward Africa after the expulsion from the Iberian Peninsula. At first Morocco, Salé, and *Safed afforded them trading possibilities, and with the rise of the slave trade to America they found chances to extend their influence to the main African slave markets on the coast of Guinea, the Cape Verde Islands, São Tomé, and Angola, since these regions belonged to the sphere of Portuguese dominance. The same circumstances operated in the infiltration by Marrano merchants into Spain, especially to Seville, in order to participate from there in the American trade. Among the early families engaged in this activity was the Jorge family whose participation in the slave trade is recorded from 1540. After their bankruptcy in 1567, other representatives were Francisco Nunes de Bejar and his son Antonio Nunes Caldeira. These Seville merchants had correspondents in the important centers in the Indies and West Africa as well as in Lisbon, and especially with the slave contractors of Africa, some of whom were Marranos. From 1587 the king of Spain as monarch of Portugal signed slavetrading agreements with Lisbon merchants for the provision of slaves in Angola and Cape Verde. This system lasted until the Portuguese restoration in 1640. Meanwhile Moroccan trading connections were intensified with the Netherlands, especially through the intervention of the important family of Palache.

Jewish trading connections also intensified with the Sephardi migration to the Mediterranean.

Under Muslim Rule

In the Arab world Jewish trade in the Middle Ages followed the same trends as in the Occident. At first Arab expansion contributed to the urbanization of the Jews and favored their trading activity, especially in the era under the *Fatimids. Yaʿqūb ibn Killis (c. 991), who later adopted *Islam and became a vizier, was a merchant in the wide area between North Africa and *Iraq, where *Baghdad with its important Jewish settlement remained the principal trading center. Under al-Mustanṣir (c. 1094) the brothers *Abu Saʿd al-Tustari and Abu Harun traded as merchants between *Egypt, *Syria, and Iraq, and were influential in the finances of Egypt. In the 12th century a decline began, connected with the rise of the Christian city states in the Mediterranean, the decline of the Fatimids, and the Crusades. The Karimi merchants then obtained a leading position.

With the emigration of Jews from the Occident to the Ottoman possessions they were able to integrate into the widespread network of international trade reaching as far as Cochin and Goa, where spices and jewels attracted them. The Danube principalities were also connected with this network. From the 17th century *Isfahan Jews organized silk export to *Aleppo.

REESTABLISHMENT IN THE WEST. From the end of the 16th century Leghorn, through the granting of important privileges to its inhabitants, became the most important trading link in the West, besides Venice. Jews compelled to emigrate from Milan in the 16th century were partially reintegrated into the network of Marrano trade, as in Naples, whereas in Rome and other central and northern Italian towns, some commerce remained a Jewish occupation, though generally not on a large scale.

In Provence, Jews lost their part in the Levantine trade after their expulsion at the end of the 15th century. Meanwhile émigré settlements of Marranos grew up at Antwerp, and also along the French Atlantic coast from St. Jean de Luz, *Bayonne, and Bordeaux to Nantes and Rouen and the Lower Elbe in Hamburg and Glueckstadt, as well as in the Netherlands, especially Amsterdam, and in London. Some of the Marranos remained Catholics, mainly in Antwerp, but along the Lower Elbe and at Amsterdam they openly returned to Judaism and established Sephardi communities. All the settlements played an important role in the trade between the Iberian Peninsula and Northwestern Europe.

Leading Marrano families throughout the 16th century were among the main contractors of the Portuguese spice trade. The jewel trade was an additional branch of the Antwerp colony, establishing connections with important trade centers in the interior such as Cologne (to which during the crisis in Antwerp they partly transferred their offices), with the Leipzig and the Frankfurt fairs, with Paris, with the fairs of Lyons, and with the trading centers of Italy. Meanwhile, they participated in the export-import trade between the Netherlands, England, Germany, and Italy. This included textiles, English cloth, Netherlands fabric, Italian fustian, and silk and grain, the latter being sent by sea. The main representatives of this trade were the Ximenes, the Rodrigues d'Evora, the Álvares Caldeira, and the Jorge families. The Hamburg colony, for some time, predominated in the import of sugar and spices and contributed to the modernization of trade usages.

Álvaro Dinis and Antônio Faleiro were merchants in Hamburg from the end of the 16th century. At Amsterdam Manuel Rodrigues Vega and others participated in the financing of *voorkompagnien* which opened up direct trade by the Dutch to the East Indies. The direct participation of the Amsterdam Portuguese in the Dutch East India Company was modest. But their international trading connections with the Mediterranean, as well as with the African and the Brazilian ports and the East Indies, contributed to the rise of the Dutch international trade, as well as to that of Hamburg, Scandinavia, and the Baltic.

The last act of the Dutch struggle with Spanish domination was helped by the contribution their merchants made to the forces of the Portuguese restoration after 1640. Jeronimo Nunes da Costa at Amsterdam and his father Duarte Nunes da Costa at Hamburg were the main suppliers or agents to the Portuguese of military and naval stores. However, it was typical of the complicated situation within the communities that Lopo Ramires at Amsterdam, a brother of Duarte Nunes da Costa, and Manuel Bocarro (Jacob Rosales) at Hamburg assisted the Spaniards.

In the second half of the 17th century the Hamburg as well as the Amsterdam Portuguese increasingly retired from the trade with the Iberian Peninsula and its colonial settlements in consequence of the continuing hostility against suspected Marranos and Jews. Meanwhile new fields of commercial activity opened with the Baltic, Scandinavia, and various courts. Diogo (Diego) *Teixeira and his son Manuel, the outstanding representatives at Hamburg, traded in jewels and, with their relatives, the Nunes Henriques, at Amsterdam entered the Norwegian copper exploitation. With the emigration of the Teixeira group to the Netherlands, the Hamburg settlement soon lost its earlier importance. Closely connected with Hamburg were small colonies at Altona and Glueckstadt. The latter especially was designed by Christian IV of Denmark and his successors to be a rival of Hamburg, in particular in the overseas trade, but never fulfilled their hopes. Nevertheless, for a time some Iberian trade in the 1620s, and again some African and West Indian trade in the second half of the 17th century, was organized from Glueckstadt.

In the Netherlands Amsterdam had the largest community of Portuguese Jews. At the beginning of the 18th century these still took considerable part in the colonial trade but were more active in speculative trade in commodities and company shares. Meanwhile the Sephardi community of London also took a share in the overseas trade, especially with West Africa and the West Indies. In its eastern extremities, from the 16th century this trade system linked with the extensive trade system of the Jews in *Poland-Lithuania based on *arenda and a large and growing share in exports and imports, as well as in the transit trade of the kingdom. The memoirs of *Glueckel von Hameln, and the even more extensive activities of the *Court Jews and factors show the influence of both these systems in Central European Jewish economic activity.

ASHKENAZI TRADING ACTIVITY. For Ashkenazi Jews the 16th and 17th centuries were an epoch of repression in consequence of the Reformation and Counter-Reformation. In Germany they mostly lived in smaller settlements where they obtained licences (*Geleit*; equivalent to the Italian *condotta*) and traded in cattle, horses, *agricultural produce, or secondhand articles obtained from loans on pawn, were peddlers, or provided the mints with bullion. The brothers Oppenheim at Frankfurt and their companies dealt in silk goods and other textiles, and there already existed connections with some courts that afforded the possibility of providing them with luxury goods, and their armies with victuals and weapons. When the possibility of forming mints, especially in the Hamburg region where overseas trading connections guaranteed a steady silver market, opened, Jacob *Bassevi at Prague was an outstanding entrepreneur of mints. During the Thirty Years' War several Jews took the opportunity to organize provisions for the armies. With the rise of the absolutist state and the sumptuous baroque culture displayed at a large number of courts the presence of the Court Jew opened new paths for wide-ranging Jewish commercial activity. Partly as a consequence of the protection afforded by the princes, the Ashkenazi settlements at Frankfurt, Hamburg, Altona, Berlin, and then Vienna also became centers of Jewish trade. From Hamburg and Altona as well as from Copenhagen and Amsterdam Jews entered the overseas trade.

From the second half of the 17th and especially in the 18th century Jews of Hamburg and Amsterdam actively participated in the trade of the fairs of Frankfurt, Zurzach, Braunschweig, Naumburg, and Frankfurt on the Oder, and especially of Leipzig and Breslau. In Eastern Europe, since there was as yet no large stratum of long-distance traders, this favored the role of small traders who were mostly of Jewish origin and often traveled in caravans. Jews from Prague, Mikulov (Nikolsburg), Leczno (Lissa), Teplice, Cracow, Brody, and Lvov in particular were among those visitors, but they had rivals in the Armenians, Greeks, Wallachians, "Raitzen" (Russians), and Courlanders. In Poland many of these Jews administered the trade of the nobility. Lithuanian Jews preferred Koenigsberg, Memel, and Riga, and traveled as far as Moscow. Galician Jews traveled to the Danubian principalities and imported wines from Hungary. Jewish trade was mostly concentrated in the fairs of Lublin, Yaroslaw, Torun, Gniezno, Kopyl, Stolin, and Mir. During the 18th century Berdichev and Brody, a free city from 1779, became important. The growing Jewish population in Bohemia, Moravia, Poland, and White Russia, and their widespread artisan activity, opened up an interior market of growing importance.

19th and 20th Centuries

From the period of the Middle Ages Jewish commercial activity had undergone many changes. At first the trade in Oriental luxury goods predominated; then, with the overseas expansion and the rise of shipping, colonial and staple goods were added. The *emancipation of the Jews in consequence of the epoch of the Enlightenment, combined with the consequences of the French Revolution and the Napoleonic Wars, put the Jewish communities on a new basis. Most spectacular was the rise of Jewish banking and the activity of Jews in industrialization, whereas the part of Jews in commerce is more difficult to discern. The organization of trade, then the sector of large stores (Tietz, Wertheim, Karstadt), and the commodity trade, especially in metal, wood, grain, furs, textiles, shoes, and diamonds, remained the branches preferred by Jews. In Germany, their part in the trading sector from 1895 to 1933 declined from 5.7 to 2.5%. In 1925 in Prussia over 34% of those active in the sector of banking and stock exchange, 13.2% in brokerage, 10.8% in the real estate business, and 10.7% in the commerce of merchandise and products, were Jews. On the whole, about 50% of the Jewish population were occupied in commerce. With the growing degree of social assimilation, however, this proportion declined as did the general participation of the Jews in economic life.

In general, it may be stated that the proportion of Jewish participation in commerce diminished in Germany and rose in the East European countries. In Hungary (1920) 44.1%, in Czechoslovakia (1921) 39.1%, in Poland (1913) 35.1%, and in Russia one-fifth (1926) of the total Jewish population were active in commerce. As Simon *Kuznets stressed, in the pre-World War II epoch in all countries excepting Poland and the Soviet Union the largest sector in the industrial structure of the gainfully occupied Jewish population remained trade and finance. They accounted for such a large proportion of the nonagricultural Jewish population because small-scale entrepreneurship was more readily accessible: it did not require heavy capital investment, and personal training was not necessary. Moreover, the conditions under which Jewish minorities had lived for centuries favored the acquisition of skills and the formation of connections useful for the pursuit of trade and finance.

[Hermann Kellenbenz]

In the U.S.

COLONIAL PERIOD TO 1820. Virtually from the mid-17th-century beginnings of their settlement in North America, the Jews tended to support themselves as small businessmen – general merchants and shopkeepers – in tidewater commercial and shipping centers like New York, Newport, Philadelphia, Charleston (South Carolina), Savannah, and Montreal. Their function, like that of the non-Jewish businessmen with whom they frequently formed partnerships of more or less limited duration, was to supply the local market with hardware, textiles, and other European produced consumer goods as well as commodities like rum, wines, spices, tea, and sugar. They attempted to balance their European and West Indian imports with exports of North American products like lumber, grain, fish, furs, and whale oil. Though specialization was not unknown, these tradesmen for the most part offered a wide range of wares.

Jews were represented in nearly every branch of early American enterprise apart from the export of tobacco and iron. Seldom, however, did they play a leading role: great coastal, Caribbean, and trans-Atlantic merchant-shippers like Aaron *Lopez of Newport, Nathan Simson and Jacob *Franks of New York, and Nathan *Levy of Philadelphia, substantial inland merchants, land speculators, and fur traders like Joseph Simon of Lancaster (Pennsylvania) and Samuel Jacobs of Canada, and important army purveyors like David Franks of Philadelphia were atypical – if not always for the character, certainly for the scale, of their dealings. Not infrequently 18th-century American Jewish businessmen acted as agents for European firms. The Levy-Franks clan of New York and Philadelphia, for example, constituted a branch of the family's commercial empire headquartered in London. Though rudimentary banking often fell within a merchant's sphere of activity – since without extending credit to his customer he could not have survived – Jewish financiers on the contemporary European scale were absent from the early American scene.

The colonial American economy was precarious, offering formidable hazards as well as attractive opportunities. Even well-established merchants not uncommonly owed their European suppliers huge sums, while bankruptcies and even imprisonment for debt occurred with considerable regularity.

Post-Revolutionary and Early National America gave rise to fledgling Jewish communities in Midwestern river ports like Cincinnati and Pittsburgh, while Jewish economic activity presented in many respects a more varied scene. Though shopkeeping and merchantry continued to be characteristic, the country's westward expansion and interest in developing its own resources generated many new enterprises involving Jews: land speculation, planting, shipping, banking, insurance, garment manufacturing, mining, and distilling. Jewish railroad directors prospered in South Carolina, and Jewish bank directors were active in South Carolina, New York, and Rhode Island. The Richmond (Virginia) firm of Cohen and Isaacs employed a frontiersman like Daniel Boone to survey land in Kentucky, and the Philadelphia *Gratzes became more important in the trans-Allegheny trade. The New York Hendrickses became prominent in the copper industry. Moses Seixas was among the Bank of Rhode Island's organizers in the 1790s, and Judah *Touro established an impressive mercantile reputation in New Orleans. Peddling, though usually no more than a transitional occupation, was far more common among Jews in early 19th-century America than it had ever been during the pre-Revolutionary period.

As the American economy burgeoned in the half-century following the Revolution, people skilled in trade, moneylending, the distribution of commodities, and the establishment of wholesale and retail outlets were needed with increasing frequency everywhere in the country. Jews found a wide gamut of opportunities in a developing America and took advantage of them to become well integrated into the country's business life.

[Stanley F. Chyet]

SINCE 1820. German Jewish immigrants to the U.S. who began arriving in large numbers about 1820 devoted themselves mainly to trade. The "Jew peddler" succeeded the "Yankee peddler" in the countryside as young Jews, securing their goods on credit mostly from Jewish wholesale houses in cities, peddled household and dry goods and small luxuries among isolated farmers throughout the Northeast, Middle West, and the South. With the opening of California in 1849 Jews became purveyors to its mining camps, a function they later performed in towns of the Rocky Mountains and the Southwest from the 1870s until the towns declined in the 1890s. The Jewish peddler's foreign accent, dauntlessness, and business skill won him a distinct, rather complimentary image in American folklore. Those who usually started by carrying their stock in a pack on the back came to own a horse and wagon;

later, when their success permitted, they quit itinerant trade to open a store. Partners and employees were usually drawn from members of the family. Jewish merchants during the middle and later 19th century established themselves not only in all large cities, but in many crossroads villages and in river towns the length of the Mississippi and Ohio rivers. During this period they played a major role in establishing a continentwide commercial network. In addition they were wheat and cotton brokers, and conspicuous in U.S. international trade. The migration of Jewish merchants from small places to booming metropolitan centers is noticeable after the 1880s. Their most conspicuous activity was the establishment of *department stores, among them some of the world's largest. A retail enterprise of particular importance was Sears Roebuck, under the ownership of Julius Rosenwald, which published huge catalogs for mail order service, thereby nearly eliminating the itinerant country peddler's market. Other merchants, notably clothiers, began to manufacture the goods they sold. A small but highly important group branched into banking from their mercantile operations (see *Banking).

East European Jews who settled mainly in large cities had few opportunities for rural peddling. Their commercial efforts were mainly urban. In the Middle West they were scrap metal merchants for the steel mills; throughout the United States they were petty shopkeepers when they did not follow proletarian occupations. The great majority of New York City's 25,000 pushcart peddlers in 1900 were Jews, as were half of its 4,000 meat retailers in 1888. The city's commercial life has been largely in Jewish hands to the present day. About 1920, only 3% of Los Angeles Jews were peddlers, but manufacturers, proprietors, and shopkeepers amounted to 20%. Jews were numerous in U.S. commerce, especially in such branches as import and export, department stores, general merchants in small cities, and after 1945 in inter-city chain and discount stores. The slow decline of small retail trade in the U.S. and the movement of Jews into white-collar occupations and the professions decreased the place of Jews in U.S. commerce, but roughly one-third of gainfully employed U.S. Jews still made their living in wholesale and retail trade.

[Lloyd P. Gartner]

BIBLIOGRAPHY: ANCIENT AND BIBLICAL TIMES: F. Delitzsch, *Handel und Wandel in Altbabylonien* (1910); R. Hartmann, in: ZDPV, 41 (1918), 53–56; B. Meissner, *Babylonien und Assyrien*, 1 (1920), 336–70; G. Dalman, *Orte und Wege Jesu* (1924); idem, in: PJB, 12 (1916), 15–54; 21 (1925), 58ff.; A. Koester, *Schiffahrt und Handelsverkehr des oestlichen Mittelmeers im 3. und 2. Jahrtausend v. Chr.* (1924); W.G. Barnes, *Business in the Bible* (1926); B. Maisler (Mazar), in: JPOS, 9 (1929), 80–81; idem, in: ZDPV, 58 (1935), 73–83; M. Rostovtsev, *Caravan Cities* (1932); S. Yeiven (ed.), *Ha-Mishar, ha-Ta'asiyyah ve-ha-Melakhah be-Ereẓ-Yisrael bi-Ymei Kedem* (1937); Abel, Geog, 2 (1938), 207–22; M. North, in: ZDPV, 60 (1937), 183ff.; 61 (1938), 20ff., 277ff.; S. Smith, in: *Antiquaries Journal*, 22 (1942), 87ff.; J.J. Garstang, in: *American Journal of Archaeology*, 47 (1943), 35–62; B. Maisler (Mazar), in: RHJE, 1 (1947), 34ff.; W.F. Leemans, *The Old Babylonian Merchant* (1950); idem, in: *Journal of Economic and Social History of the Orient*, 2 (1959), 111–2; 3 (1960), 21–37; 4 (1961), 106–12; idem, *Foreign Trade in the Old Babylonian Period* (1960); M. Avi-Yonah, in: IEJ, 1 (1950/51), 56–60; G. Cardascia, *Les Archives des Murāshû* (1951); J. Lewy, in: *Orientalia*, 21 (1952), 265–92; A. Barrois, *Manuel d'archéologie biblique*, 2 (1953), s.v. *Commerce*; A.F. Oppenheim, in: JAOS, 74 (1954), 6–17; K. Polanyi et al., *Trade and Market in the Early Empires* (1957); C.H. Gordon, in: JNES, 17 (1958), 28–31; G.W. van Beck and A. Jamme, in: BASOR, 151 (1958), 9–16; F.M. Heichelheim, *An Ancient Economic History*, 1–2 (1958^2); M. Stekelis, in: *Eretz Israel*, 5 (1959), 35–37; J.B. Curtis and W.H. Hallo, in: HUCA, 30 (1959), 103–39; A. Malamat, in: JBL, 79 (1960), 12ff.; D.O. Edzard, in: *Journal of Economic and Social History of the Orient*, 3 (1960), 38–55; M. Birot, *ibid.*, 5 (1962), 91–109; W. Ward, *ibid.*, 6 (1963), 1–57; J.B. Pritchard, in: BA, 23 (1960), 23–29; E.A. Speiser, in: BASOR, 164 (1961), 23–28; W.F. Albright, *ibid.*, 163 (1961), 31–64; 164 (1961), 28; E. Anati, *ibid.*, 167 (1962), 23–31; A. Malamat, in: *Sefer Baer* (1961), 1–7; A. Millard, in: JSS, 7 (1962), 201–13; A.F. Rainey, in: *Christian News From Israel*, 14 (1963), 17–26. POST-BIBLICAL PERIOD: L. Herzfeld, *Handelsgeschichte der Juden des Altertums* (1879); L. Heybod, *Handelsgeschichte der Juden des Altertums* (1894); L. Fuchs, *Die Juden Aegyptens in ptolemaeischer und roemischer Zeit* (1924); F.M. Heichelheim, *Die auswaertige Bevoelkerung im Ptolemaeer-Reich* (1925); idem, *Roman Syria*, in: *An Economic Survey of Ancient Rome*, 1 (1938); J. Obermeyer, *Die Landschaft Babyloniens im Zeitalter des Talmuds und des Gaonats* (1929); M. Rostovtsev, *Gesellschaft und Wirtschaft im roemischen Kaiserreich*, 1–2 (1931); idem, *The Near East in the Hellenistic and Roman Times* (1941); idem, *Social and Economic History of the Hellenistic World*, 3 vols. (1941); idem, *Gesellschaft der alten Welt*, 1–2 (1942); Baron, Social², index; F.M. Heichelheim, *The Ancient Economic History from the Palaeolithic Age to the Migrations of the Germanic, Slavic and Arabic Nations*, 1–2 (1958); V. Tcherikover, *Hellenistic Civilization and the Jews* (1959). UP TO 18th CENTURY: Baer, Spain; W. Heyd, *Geschichte des Levanthandels im Mittelalter* (1879); P. Masson, *Histoire du commerce français dans le Levant au* XVIIIe *siècle* (1896); J.T. Medina, *El tribunal… de la Inquisición en… la Plata, Santiago de Chile* (1899); M. Grunwald, *Juden als Reeder und Seefahrer* (1902); I. Schiper, *Die Anfaenge des Kapitalismus bei den abendlaendischen Juden* (1907); idem, *Dzieje handlu Żdowskiego na ziemiach polskich* (1937); W. Sombart, *Die Juden und das Wirtschaftsleben* (1907); H. Waetjen, *Das Judentum und die Anfaenge der modernen Kolonisation* (1914); idem, *Die Niederlaender im Mittelmeergebiet zur Zeit ihrer hoechsten Machtstellung* (1909); idem, *Das hollaendische Kolonialreich in Brasilien* (1921); G. Caro, *Sozial-und Wirtschaftsgeschichte der Juden im Mittelalter und der Neuzeit*, 2 vols. (1908–20); B. Hahn, *Die wirtschaftliche Taetigkeit der Juden im fraenkischen und deutschen Reich bis zum 2. Kreuzzug* (1911); M. Freudenthal, *Leipziger Messegaeste… 1675 bis 1764* (1918); idem *Leipziger Messegaeste* (1928); Mann, Egypt; L. Brentano, in: *Der wirtschaftende Mensch in der Geschichte* (1923); G. Le Strange, *Baghdad during the Abbasid Caliphate* (1924); J.A. Goris, *Etude sur les colonies marchandes méridionales a Anvers de 1488 B 1567* (1925); S. Stern, *Der preussische Staat und die Juden* (1925); idem, *Jud Suess, ein Beitrag zur deutschen und juedischen Geschichte* (1929); idem, *Court Jews* (1950); J. Brutzkus, in: ZGJD, 3 (1931); M. Wischnitzer, in: *Festschrift S. Dubnow* (1930); A.S. Tritton, *The Caliphs and their Non-Muslim Subjects* (1930); J. Starr, *The Jews in the Byzantine Empire, 641–1204* (1930); W.J. Fischel, *Jews in the Economic and Political Life of Mediaeval Islam* (1931); H.I. Bloom, *The Economic Activity of the Amsterdam Jews* (1937); B. Lewin, *El judío en la epoca colonial, un aspecto de la historia rioplatense* (1939); idem, *El Santo Oficio en América y el más grande proceso inquisitorial en Perú* (1950); Brugmans-Frank; Duarte Gomes, *Discursas sobre los comercios de las Indias*, ed. by M.B. Amzalak (1943); A. Canabrava, *O comercio portugues do Rio da Prata* (1944); Roth, Italy; Roth, England; Roth, Marranos; J.L. de Azevedo, *Epocas de Portugal económico*

(1947[2]); D.S. Sassoon, *A History of the Jews in Baghdad* (1949); H. Schnee, *Die Hoffinanz und der moderne Staat* (1953–67); S.D. Goitein, *Documents on the India Trade*, vol. 1; R.S. Lopez, in: M. Postan and E.E. Rich (eds.), *The Cambridge Economic History of Europe*, 2 (1952); idem, in: *Relazioni del X Congresso Internazionale di Scienze Storiche*, 3 (Eng., 1955); H. Kellenbenz, *Sephardim an der unteren Elbe* (1958); idem, in: *Annales*, 11 (1956), 1ff.; idem, in: *Jahrbuch fuer Geschichte von Staat, Wirtschaft und Gesellschaft Lateinamerikas*, 1 (1964); idem, in: *Jahrbuch fuer Geschichte Osteuropas*, 12 (1964); idem, in: *Miscellanea Mediaevalia*, 4 (1966); idem, in: *Monumenta Judaica* (Exhibition, Cologne, 1963); W. Treue, *ibid.*; F. Guggenheim, in: Gruenberg, *Die Juden auf der Zurzacher Messe im 18. Jahrhundert* (1957); A. Wiznitzer, *Jews in Colonial Brazil* (1960); L. Hanke, in: *Revista de Historia de América*, 51 (Eng., 1961); J.A. Gonsalves de Mello (ed.), *Dialogos dos Grandezas do Brasil* (1962); Subhi y Lahib, *Handelsgeschichte Aegyptens im Spaetmittelalter, 1157–1517* (1965); L. Poliakov, *Les Banquiers juifs et la Saint-Siège du XIIIe au XVIIe siècle* (1965). 19th–20th CENTURIES: P. Silbergleit, *Die Bevoelkerungs-und Berufsverhaeltnisse der Juden im deutschen Reich*, 1 (1930); M. Wischnitzer, in: EJ, 7 (1931), 910–34; S. Kuznets, in: L. Finkelstein (ed.), *The Jews, their History, Culture and Religion*, 2 (1960[3]), 1597–666. IN THE U.S. – COLONIAL PERIOD TO 1820: S.F. Chyet, *Lopez of Newport* (1970); J.R. Marcus, *The Colonial American Jew*, 3 vols. (1970); E. Wolf and M. Whiteman, *Jews of Philadelphia* (1957); J.L. Blau and S.W. Baron, *The Jews of the United States 1790–1840: A Documentary History*, 1 (1963), 95–158; I.J. Benjamin, *Three Years in America 1859–1862*, 2 vols. (1956); H.L. Golden, *Forgotten Pioneer* (1963). SINCE 1820: R. Glanz, *The Jews of California* (1960), 19–91; idem, *The Jew in the Old American Folklore* (1961), 96–177; idem, in: JSOS, 6 (1944), 3–30; 7 (1945), 119–36; B.E. Supple, in: *Business History Review*, 31 (1957), 143–78; A. Tarshish, in: *Essays in American Jewish History* (1958); B.B. Seligman, S.J. Fauman, and N. Glazer, in: M. Sklare (ed.), *The Jews: Social Patterns of an American Group* (1958), 69–82, 101–6, 119–46; M. Whiteman, in: *Studies and Essays in Honor of Abraham A. Neuman* (1962), 503–16; idem, in: JQR, 53 (1962/63), 306–21; M. Rischin, *The Promised City: New York's Jews 1870–1914* (1962); L.J. Swichkow and L.P. Gartner, *The History of the Jews of Milwaukee* (1963), 94–109, 160–6, 296; M. Vorspan and L.P. Gartner, *History of the Jews of Los Angeles* (1970), 5–14, 25–28, 32–45, 75–78, 91–106, 120–34, 193–200, 230–7; E. Tcherikower (ed.), *Geshikhte fun der Yidisher Arbeter-Bavregung in di Fareynikte Shtatn*, 1 (1943), 224–53, 338–55; F.S. Fierman, in: AJHSQ, 56 (1966/67), 371–456; 57 (1967/68), 353–435; W.J. Parish, *The Charles Ilfeld Company* (1961); idem, in: *New Mexico Historical Review*, 35 (1960), 1–29, 129–50; R.M. Hower, *History of Macy's of New York, 1858–1919* (1943).

TRADITION (Heb. מָסֹרֶת). The term tradition derives from the Latin *tradere*, which means "to transmit" or "to give over." Generally, it refers to beliefs, doctrines, customs, ethical and moral standards, and cultural values and attitudes which are transmitted orally or by personal example. Under this designation, the process of transmission itself is also included. Theologically, in Judaism, tradition is the name applied to the unwritten code of law given by God to Moses on Mount Sinai.

Terms

Masoret is the general name for tradition. It is found in Ezekiel 20:37 and means originally "bond" or "fetter." Tradition is the discipline which establishes the correct practice and interpretation of the *Torah and was therefore regarded as a hedge or fetter about the Law (Avot 3:14). Since this knowledge was handed down by successive generations, it was also associated with the Hebrew word *masor*, denoting "to give over." In the talmudic literature, the term *masoret* is used to include all forms of tradition, both those which relate to the Bible and those which concern custom, law, historical events, folkways, and other subjects. Different kinds of traditions were given special names. Traditions which specified the vocalization, punctuation, spelling, and correct form of the biblical text were called **masorah*. Those legal traditions which were revealed to Moses at Mount Sinai and were later preserved in writing, were known as **Halakhah le-Moshe mi-Sinai* ("law given to Moses on Sinai"). A legal tradition which was handed down by word of mouth, but did not necessarily emanate from Sinai, was called *shemu'ah* ("a report"). Religious and general traditions which became binding as result of long observance by successive generations were termed **minhag* ("custom"). Prophetic traditions described in the books of the prophets and Hagiographa were known as *Divrei Kabbalah* ("words of tradition"). Esoteric and mystical traditions concerning God and the world transmitted to the elect and then passed down through the ages were called *Kabbalah, from *kibbel* ("to receive").

Origin

Many statutes were committed to writing by Moses. However, the vast majority of laws were handed down orally by him (see Written and Oral *Law). The Written Law did not always detail the manner and form of practice, giving rise of necessity to tradition. An instance of this kind is the law relating to fish which meet the biblical dietary requirements. Leviticus 11:9 states that a fish that has a fin and a scale in the water can be eaten. However, the minimum number of fins and scales that a fish must have to be ritually edible is not specified. The traditions relating to the Bible and Mishnah taught that a fish needs at least one fin and two scales to satisfy the biblical dietary requirements (see Arukh, s.v. *Akunos*). Similarly, the Bible commands that a paschal lamb be slaughtered on the 14th day of Nisan. There is no mention in the Bible as to whether it is permissible to perform this act if the 14th day of Nisan occurs on the Sabbath when the slaughtering of animals is forbidden. In the year 31 B.C.E., the 14th of Nisan fell on the Sabbath. The Sons of Bathyra, the heads of the high court, forgot the precedent previously established. Hillel, a then unknown Babylonian, volunteered the information that he had heard from Shemaiah and Avtalyon, the foremost teachers of the age, that it was permissible to slaughter the paschal lamb on the Sabbath. This reported tradition of Hillel's mentors was readily accepted (TJ, Pes. 6:1, 33a), and it is mentioned that because of this display of erudition with regard to tradition, Hillel was appointed *nasi*. Tradition was also the vehicle of transmission for the rules of interpretation, of the Written Law, such as the laws of *hermeneutics. Since it was impossible within the confines of writing to record all the laws and their applications in all situations, a medium was needed to preserve this information. Even today, with the availability of writing media, much of our culture is handed down orally. Tradition was the means whereby extant law was maintained and applied to life. Thus R. Joshua b. Levi declared that all teachings both of the Bible, Mishnah, Talmud, and *aggadah* and those that were initiated by veteran scholars were already given to Moses on Mount Sinai (see TJ, Pe'ah 2:6, 17a). Some traditions arose as a result of the common practice of the community. These practices were considered to emanate from eminent religious authorities and owed their binding character to having been handed down by previous generations, from father to son, a principle upheld by R. Johanan in the Talmud. The citizens of Beth-Shean complained to him that the custom of not going from Tyre to Sidon on the eve of the Sabbath was impossible for them to observe. R. Johanan replied, "Your fathers have already taken it (this custom) upon themselves" (Pes. 50b). As a result, this tradition could not be abrogated.

History

In rabbinic Judaism, tradition was binding and had the force of law. The divine revelation to Moses consisted of the Written Law and Oral Law with its implied exposition by the sages of Israel. *Berakhot* 5a tells that R. Levi b. Ḥama said in the name of R. Simeon b. Lakish: "What is the meaning of the verse, 'and I will give thee the tables of stone, and the law and the commandments, which I have written to teach them' [Ex. 24:12]. It means as follows: 'the tables of stone' are the Ten Commandments, 'the law' is the Pentateuch, 'the commandments' is the Mishnah, 'which I have written' are the prophets and the Hagiographa, 'to teach them' is the *Gemara*. This teaches us that all these things were given at Sinai." Originally, the Oral Law was handed down by word of mouth. When its transmission became difficult, it was set down in writing in the Mishnah and Talmud. The validity of the Oral Law was attacked by the *Sadducees, one of the early sects in Judaism. Josephus records that the Sadducees held that "only those observances are obligatory which are in the written word but that those which derived from the tradition of the forefathers need not be kept" (Ant. 13:297).

Talmudic Times

After the destruction of the Temple, the Sadducees disappeared. The body of tradition continued to grow as rites were introduced to replace the Temple ritual. *Megillah* 31b pictures the patriarch Abraham as concerned with how Israel could obtain forgiveness, once the Temple ceased to exist. God assures Abraham, "I have already ordained for them the order of the sacrifices. Every time that they read them, it is considered as if they offer up a sacrifice and I forgive them all their sins." After the destruction of the Temple, the system of public prayer was instituted to substitute for the Temple service. The liturgical traditions were handed down verbally, through the centuries, until they were compiled in the prayer book of Amram Gaon.

Medieval Times

At the end of the eighth century, rabbinic Judaism was again challenged by a new sect, the Karaites. They accepted the authority of the Bible but denied rabbinical tradition and law, which had developed further as the Mishnah and Talmud were elucidated and applied to life. Through its great exponents, Saadiah and Maimonides, rabbinic Judaism triumphed over the Karaites. The latter wrote his code of law, *Mishneh Torah* ("The Second Torah"), and showed the direct connection between the Written Law and its explanation in the Oral Law (Introd. Maim. Yad). As new situations arose, the talmudic, geonic, and post-geonic traditions were further amplified. They in turn were set down in writing in the responsa and codes. In the 16th century R. Joseph Caro produced his definitive code, the Shulḥan Arukh. With the addition of the glosses of R. Moses Isserles and later commentaries, it became the most comprehensive compendium of Jewish law and tradition to this day.

Modern Times

At the end of the 18th century rabbinic Judaism, which had maintained an unbroken chain of tradition from the days of Moses was again challenged. A *Reform movement began in Germany which sought to assimilate the Jews into the general culture by modifying Jewish traditions. Among the reforms instituted were sermons in the German vernacular, hymns and chorals in German, the use of the organ, and the confirmation of boys on the Feast of Pentecost instead of the traditional bar mitzvah. In the course of time, this movement established itself in America. Here it continued to propound its doctrine that Judaism was primarily a universalistic and moral religion. Only the moral law was binding. Ceremonial laws which could be adapted to the views of the modern environment were to be maintained. Other Mosaic and rabbinic laws which regulated diet, priestly purity, and dress could be discarded.

In reaction to the reformers' break with tradition, the *Conservative movement was formed in America. At the founding meeting of its congregational organization in 1913, it declared itself "a union of congregations for the promotion of traditional Judaism." Other aims were the furtherance of Sabbath observance and dietary laws, and the maintenance of the traditional liturgy with Hebrew as the language of prayer. As the complexion of American Jewry changed, the Conservative movement incorporated some Reform externals of worship such as family pews and the use of the organ in many congregations. However, it accepted the authority of rabbinic tradition, instituting changes advocated by its scholars, with regard for the attitude of the people and the place of the observance in Jewish tradition.

Transmitters of the Tradition

In rabbinic literature the chain of tradition is given as follows: Moses received the Torah on Sinai and delivered it to Joshua, who in turn delivered it to the elders, the elders to the prophets, and the prophets to the Men of the Great Synagogue

(Avot 1:1). According to rabbinic Judaism, the teaching of the great sages in every generation in keeping with the *halakhah* is binding (Deut. 17:88). Thus, the transmitters of tradition included the successors to the Men of the Great Synagogue down to modern times, namely: the scribes (*soferim*), the pairs (*zugot), the *tannaim*, the *amoraim*, the *savoraim*, the *geonim*, the codifiers, the world famous Torah authorities of every era, and the *rashei ha-yeshivah* ("heads of the academies").

Significance

Tradition has given Judaism a continuity with its past and preserved its character as a unique faith with a distinct way of life. As the successor of rabbinic Judaism, Orthodoxy representing tradition harks back to the Sinaitic divine revelation and can only be changed within the framework of rabbinic law. In Conservative Judaism, tradition is a vital force capable of modification according to the historical evolution of Jewish law. Reform Judaism has recently displayed a greater appreciation of traditional practices but tradition remains voluntary in character (see *Masorah*).

BIBLIOGRAPHY: S. Belkin, *In His Image* (1960), 290ff.; B. Cohen, *Law and Tradition in Judaism* (1959), 243ff.; I. Epstein, *Judaism* (1959), 49ff.; S. Freehof, *Reform Jewish Practices* (1944), 193ff.; S.R. Hirsch, *Judaism Eternal*, 2 (1956), 612ff.; L. Jacobs, *Principles of Faith* (1964), 473ff.; D. Rudavsky, *Emancipation and Adjustment* (1967), 460ff.

[Leon J. Yagod]

TRAGACANTH (Heb. נְכֹאת, *nekhot*). The identification of tragacanth with *nekhot* is attested by its Arabic name *Rathirāʾ*. It was included in spices carried by the caravan of Ishmaelites from Gilead on their journey to Egypt (Gen. 37:25), as well as in the gift sent by Jacob to the ruler of Egypt (43:11). It is the aromatic sap of a species of *Astragalus* which is called τραγακανδα in Greek. These are plants of the family Papilionaceae, short prickly shrubs which exude a sap when the roots or stalks are split open. Tens of species of *Astragalus* grow in Israel but these do not exude the *nekhot*. This is obtained from the species that grow in east Asia and the mountains of Syria and Lebanon. In former times it was used as incense but today it is used for medicinal purposes.

BIBLIOGRAPHY: Loew, Flora, 2 (1924), 419ff.; J. Feliks, *Olam ha-Ẓomeʿaḥ ha-Mikraʾi* (1968²), 274–5.

[Jehuda Feliks]

°**TRAJAN (Traianus), MARCUS ULPIUS** (52/3–117), Roman emperor, ruled 98–117 C.E. In 114 C.E. Chosroes, king of Parthia, violated the arrangement between his country and Rome regarding Armenia. Trajan went to war immediately, conquered Armenia, and annexed it to his empire together with northern Mesopotamia, also including Adiabene. In 116 he captured Ctesiphon, the capital of the Parthians, and penetrated into Babylon. However, a violent uprising among the population of Mesopotamia in which the Jews of the country even earlier played an active role and the previous uprisings in Cyrenaica and Egypt (see below) compelled him to interrupt his campaign of conquest. Nothing definite is known about Trajan's attitude to the Jews. According to the papyrus *Alilot Kedoshei Alexandria* ("Deeds of the Martyrs of Alexandria"), Trajan and his wife Plotina preferred the Jews of Alexandria to its Greeks (see *Egypt). In 115, however, at the height of Trajan's war with the Parthians, a great revolt of Jews broke out in Cyrenaica that spread to Egypt and Cyprus the following year. Trajan ordered the disturbances put down with a strong hand. In the same year the revolt spread to Mesopotamia where it also involved the Jewish inhabitants of the country particularly. Trajan ordered Lusius *Quietus to subdue the Jews of Mesopotamia, and the order was carried out with savage cruelty. An allusion to this has been preserved in rabbinic literature which refers to the "war of Quietus" (Sot. 9:14 – according to the correct reading; *Seder Olam*), and also mentions the great destruction of Egyptian Jewry generally, and that of Alexandria in particular, with the crushing of the revolt (the destruction of its magnificent synagogue is ascribed to Trajan himself – TJ, Suk. 5:1, 55b).

There is an *aggadah* that Trajan attacked the Jews because, when his son was born on the Ninth of Av, the Jews were mourning, while on the death of another child which occurred on Ḥanukkah, they kindled lamps in joy (TJ, *ibid*.; Taʿan. 18b; Lam. R. 1:16 no. 45; et al.). Another *aggadah* states that before his death he decreed the death of *Pappus and Julianus in Laodicea. In rabbinic literature the name Trajan usually appears in a corrupt form: Trogianus, Tarkinus, etc.

BIBLIOGRAPHY: Juster, Juifs, 2 (1914), 185–94; Tcherikover, Corpus, 2 (1960), introd., index; K. Friedmann, in: *Giornale della Società Asiatica Italiana*, 2 (1930), 108–24; A. Schalit, in: *Tarbiz*, 7 (1935/36), 159–80; J. Guttmann, in: *Sefer Assaf* (1953), 149–84; S. Apfelbaum, in: *Zion*, 19 (1954), 23–56; A. Fuks, *ibid*., 22 (1957), 1–9; Alon, Toledot, 1 (1958³), index; R.P. Longden, *The Wars of Trajan*, in: *Cambridge Ancient History*, 11 (1936), R. Syme, *Tacitus*, 1 (1958), 86–99, 217–35; A. Fuks, in: *Journal of Roman Studies*, 51 (1961); V. Tcherikover, *Ha-Yehudim be-Miẓrayim…* (1963²), 116–30, 160–79.

[Moshe David Herr]

TRAMER, MORITZ (1882–1963), pioneer of child psychiatry. Born in Czechoslovakia, Tramer began his career as an engineer and mathematician and is the coauthor of a textbook of higher mathematics for engineers, *Differential- und Integralrechnung* (1913). He then studied medicine and specialized in psychiatry. From 1924 to 1946 he was medical director of the Psychiatric Hospital in the Canton of Solothurn, Switzerland, and initiated the establishment in 1924 of the Observation Center "Gotthelf Haus" for emotionally disturbed children. He lectured on child and adolescent psychiatry at Berne University and in 1951 founded the Swiss Institute of Research and Information on Child Psychiatry. The designation of the specialty as "child psychiatry" owes its existence to Tramer. He was also the advocate of its recognition as a medical specialty in Switzerland in 1953.

Tramer was a prominent figure in national and international professional organizations and published numerous articles. His books include the monumental textbook *Lehrbuch der allgemeinen Kinderpsychiatrie* (1942, 1964⁴) and the well-known monograph *Allgemeine Psychohygiene* (1960s). He was the founder and editor of the first journal of child psychiatry in 1934 later known as *Acta Paedopsychiatrica* which is the official organ of the International Association for Child Psychiatry and Allied Professions.

BIBLIOGRAPHY: *Acta Paedopsychiatrica*, 30 (1963).

[Alexander Meijer]

TRANI, seaport in Apulia, S. Italy. In the 12th century, when the town had become a port of embarkation for Crusaders and an important center of Eastern trade, it contained a flourishing Jewish community. When *Benjamin of Tudela visited Trani around 1159 he found 200 Jewish families there. Recognizing their economic usefulness the Norman kings in the 12th century and Emperor Frederick II in the first half of the 13th century granted the Jews a measure of protection. Thanks to this royal patronage they were given the right to control and distribute all the raw silk in Apulia and Calabria. Under Angevin rule toward the end of the 13th century, the position of the Jews deteriorated and they were subjected to severe persecution, fomented by Dominican friars. The houses in the Jewish quarter were repeatedly sacked; *blood libels were frequently raised against the heavily taxed Jews and a growing number was forced into baptism, causing heavy losses to the community. In 1290 four synagogues were converted into churches; two of them still stand. The position did not improve in the next century and many Jewish families left the town. In 1382 other synagogues were turned into churches and the Jewish cemetery was confiscated by the friars. In 1413, when King Ladislas of Naples issued certain dispositions regarding the communal administration of the city of Trani, he decreed that the community (universitas) would have the right to elect a governing body of 16 representatives consisting of 8 nobles, 6 commoners, and *Neofiti (baptized Jews). In all probability the need for this provision arose from the continuing existence of a convert population that retained a separate identity. In 1443 Trani still had 870 families of *Neofiti, and all the commercial activities of the town were said to be concentrated in their hands. After the 1492 expulsions from the Spanish kingdoms and Sicily, many exiles settled in Trani. Jews and Neofiti were expelled from Trani in 1510–11, along with the rest of the Jews in southern Italy. Sporadic persecutions of Neofiti continued for some time. The medieval Jewish settlement is still commemorated by street names such as Vicolo Giudecca, Via Scolanova, and Via la Giudea (renamed Via Mose (di Isaiah) di Trani).

BIBLIOGRAPHY: Milano, Bibliotheca, index; Milano, Italia, index; Roth, Italy, index; U. Cassuto, in: *Rivista degli studi orientali*, 13 (1932), 172–80; idem, in: *Alexander Marx Jubilee Volume…* (1950), 387–9; Luzzatto, in: RMI, 10 (1935/36), 285–9; N. Ferorelli, *Ebrei nell'Italia Meridionale…* (1915), passim; E. Munkácsi, *Der Jude von Neapel* (1939), 47–80. **ADD. BIBLIOGRAPHY:** C. Colafemmina, "Documenti per la storia degli ebrei a Trani nei secoli XV–XVI," in: *Sefer Yuhasin*, 3 (1987), 17–24; idem, *Documenti per la storia degli ebrei in Puglia nell'archivio di stato di Napoli* (1990); D. Abulafia, "Il mezzogiorno peninsulare dai bizantini all'espulsione," in: *Storia d'Italia. Annali 11, Gli ebrei in Italia. Dall'alto Medioevo all'età dei ghetti*, ed. Corrao Vivant (1996), 5–44; C. Colafemmina, "Di alcune iscrizioni ebraiche a Trani," in: RMI, 67 (2001), 305–12.

[Arial Toaff / Nadia Zeldes (2nd ed.)]

TRANI, JOSEPH BEN MOSES (1568–1639), rabbi and halakhist. Trani, known as the "**Maharit**" (**M**orenu **ha**-**R**av Joseph **T**rani), was born in Safed, the youngest son of Moses b. Joseph *Trani. Joseph, 12 years old when his father died, was taken into the home of Solomon *Sagis, a Safed scholar, and became his pupil. In 1587, when Sagis died, Trani went to Egypt, where he attracted many pupils. After a short time he returned to Safed where he founded and taught in a yeshivah. Following the outbreak of a plague in Safed (1594), he went to Jerusalem, where he did research on the design and plan of the Temple. The resulting work, *Ẓurat ha-Bayit*, was lost, but many fragments and quotations from it have been preserved in *Derekh ha-Kodesh* by Ḥayyim *Alfandari (published in *Maggid mi-Reshit*, Constantinople, 1710). After some time Trani returned to Safed, where – as his father before him – he headed the Sephardi community. In 1599 he was sent by the Safed community to Constantinople, and in 1604 took up permanent residence there. Trani headed a large yeshivah in Constantinople which became a center of Torah for all Turkish Jewry and produced many of the great Turkish rabbis of the 17th century, including Ḥayyim b. Israel *Benveniste. Trani was eventually elected chief rabbi of Turkey, in which office he introduced *takkanot*, established societies, and became renowned for his many charitable acts. However, he took a severe attitude toward the *Karaites, who came under his authority according to the law.

In addition to *Ẓurat ha-Bayit*, the following works by Joseph have been published: Talmud novellae on the tractates of *Shabbat, Ketubbot*, and *Kiddushin* (Venice, 1645); *Ẓafenat Pane'aḥ* (*ibid.*, 1648), sermons; and responsa (Constantine, 1641; Venice, 1645). Most of his works, which encompassed all branches of Torah, have been lost, among them a supercommentary on Elijah *Mizraḥi's commentary on the Pentateuch and an abridgment of the *Arukh* of *Nathan b. Jehiel of Rome.

BIBLIOGRAPHY: Frumkin-Rivlin, 1 (1928), 119–20; Rosanes, Togarmah, 3 (1938), 96–100; Yaari, Sheluḥei, 243–4; Bloch, in: *Hadorom*, 5–6 (1958), 95–108; 7 (1958), 78–100; I. Schepansky, *Ereẓ Yisrael be-Sifrut ha-Teshuvot*, 1 (1966), 314–22; 2 (1968), index, s.v. *She'elot u-Teshuvot Maharit.*

[Ephraim Kupfer]

TRANI, MOSES BEN JOSEPH (Heb. acronym **Ha-Ma-bit**; 1500–1580), rabbi. His father emigrated from Italy to Salonika, where Moses was born, but the family was of Spanish origin. Orphaned at an early age, Moses went to Adrianople to live with his uncle Aaron, studying with him as well as at the yeshivah of R. Joseph Fasi. He later proceeded to Safed where he studied under Jacob *Berab, and was one of the four scholars ordained by him in his attempt to reintroduce ordination (**semikhah*). In 1525 Moses was appointed *marbiẓ Torah* of the

Bet Ya'akov congregation. In 1535 he visited Jerusalem. Moses devoted himself to a considerable extent to the agricultural laws which obtained in Ereẓ Israel, and in a *Sabbatical Year exempted from tithes produce that had grown in land belonging to a gentile, even though it had been stored by a Jew. This decision was disputed by Joseph *Caro and other Safed scholars. There were also spirited controversies between him and Caro on other matters. For some time he stayed in Damascus (1565). Moses was active as rabbi and *dayyan* for 54 years, but it was only after the death of Joseph Caro that he was appointed spiritual head of the whole community of Safed. Moses had two sons: Solomon, who was rabbi in Egypt, and Joseph *Trani (from his second marriage), who was rabbi in Safed and in Constantinople.

Moses' works are *Kiryat Sefer* on Maimonides (Venice, 1551); *Beit Elohim*, a moral and philosophical work with a commentary to **Perek Shirah* (Venice, 1576; Warsaw, 1872); *Iggeret Derekh ha-Shem*, a moral work (Venice, 1553); responsa (2 pts., Venice, 1629–30; Lvov, 1861).

BIBLIOGRAPHY: Conforte, Kore, 35b–36b; Fishman, in: *Sinai*, 14 (1944), 12–16; Dimitrovsky, in: *Sefunot*, 6 (1962), 71–117; 7 (1963), 41–100; Frumkin-Rivlin, 1 (1929), 88; Rosanes, Togarmah, 2 (1938), 168f., 190ff.; A. Elmaleh (ed.), *Ḥemdat Yisrael* (1946), 147–56; Joffeh, in: *Sinai*, 24 (1948/49), 290–304; S. Schechter, *Studies in Judaism*, 2 (1908), index.

[Hirsch Jacob Zimmels]

TRANSJORDAN (Heb. עֵבֶר הַיַּרְדֵּן). Geographically, Transjordan includes the area east of the Jordan River, extending from the sources of the Jordan near the *Hermon to the *Dead Sea. However, the area north of the Yarmuk River (the Golan and Bashan) are regarded as a separate entity, while the area east of the Dead Sea and the *Arabah, down to the Red Sea, is included in the region of Transjordan.

In its geographical configuration, Transjordan is composed of a series of three regions running from north to south: the eastern *Jordan Valley; the slopes descending to the valley, which face westward and are well provided with rainfall; and the mountains which slope gently eastward and merge with the desert steppe. The settled part of this area covers 6,840 sq. mi. (17,500 sq. km.), of which the Jordan-Dead Sea depression comprises 215 sq. mi. (550 sq. km.), the mountain and hill region 2,617 sq. mi. (6,700 sq. km.), the high plateau 2,051 sq. mi. (5,250 sq. km.), and the sandy southern regions approximately 1,953 sq. mi. (c. 5,000 sq. km.). Politically, in the Hashemite Kingdom of *Jordan, the region of Transjordan is considered to include 28,320 sq. mi. (72,500 sq. km.) of steppe and desert in a broad strip joining Iraq and dividing *Syria from *Saudi-Arabia.

The settled area is cut by confluents of the Jordan flowing from east to west, and by rivers emptying into the Dead Sea: the Yarmuk, forming the northern boundary of the region; the Jabbok, separating Gilead from Ammon and the Peraea; the Nimrīn, usually the northern boundary of Moab; the Arnon, at certain times the boundary of Moab; the Zered, separating Moab from Edom and the mountains of Seir. The mountain range parallel to the Jordan on the east varies in height: in the ʿAjlūn (Gilead), Tell ʿIbbīn is 3,940 ft. (1,182 m.) high, Umm al-Daraj is 4,203 ft. (1,261 m.) high, and Qalʿat Ilyās is 3,640 ft. (1,092 m.) high. South of the Jabbok, Nabī Yūshaʿ reaches to 3,710 ft. (1,113 m.) and Mount Nebo to 2,650 ft. (795 m.); south of the Arnon, Jebel Sīhān is 3,550 ft. (1,065 m.) high and Jebel al-Ḥasāʾ is 113 ft. (1,234 m.) high; the mountains of Seir reach to 5,776 ft. (1,733 m.). The greatest rainfall is in the ʿAjlūn (c. 27½ in.; 700 mm.) and in the mountains of Seir (c. 15¾ in.; 400 mm.). Most of the cultivable area receives about 8 in. (200 mm.) annually, with a rainfall of about 3 in. (80 mm.) in the desert. The mountains of Gilead are still wooded; in antiquity the area was much more thickly afforested, as is borne out by the story of Absalom. There is evidence that a large area under cultivation extended eastward. Iron was mined near Jerash and copper in the Arabah (see *Punon).

History

Paleolithic and Mesolithic remains, the earliest traces of occupation in Transjordan, have been found in the mountains of Seir and in Wadi Nimrīn. A pre-ceramic Neolithic settlement was discovered at al-Bayḍāʾ, southeast of the Dead Sea. Megalithic constructions were found at Alfa Safat and al-ʿUdayma in the Jordan Valley. Near the latter site is Tulaylāt al-Ghassūl, a Chalcolithic site of great importance, which gave its name to the Ghassulian culture. From the Early Bronze Age onward, a certain pattern of occupation can be noticed, mainly in the southern part of Transjordan, as a result of the archaeological survey undertaken by N. Glueck: periods of settlement varied with periods in which the area was abandoned to nomads.

The first period of settlement lasted from approximately the 23rd to the 19th century B.C.E. According to biblical tradition, the early populations included the Zuzims at Ham in northern Gilead, the Emims in Moab, and the Horites in Mount Seir (Gen. 14:5–6). Possibly as a result of the invasion described in this chapter, there was a decline in the settlement of Transjordan from the 19th to approximately the 14th century B.C.E. Egyptian texts do not mention any cities in Transjordan within this span of time, except for those in the Jordan Valley proper: Pehel (Pella; Execration Texts, Thutmosis III and Seti I), and perhaps Zaphon (Tell el-Amarna letters), Zarethan (Execration Texts), and Kiriath Anab (Tell al-Shihāb on the Yarmuk; Seti I, Papyrus Anastasi I). Only in the 13th century, in inscriptions of Ramses II, are cities in Moab, including Dibon, mentioned for the first time. The biblical definition of the Egyptian province of *Canaan (Num. 34) definitely excludes Transjordan, which was left to the Shasu nomads.

About a century before the Exodus, Transjordan was settled again by the Ammonites, Moabites, and Edomites, who formed a strong chain of kingdoms, with extensive areas under cultivation and a system of efficient border fortresses. Probably in the early 13th century, Moab was attacked from the north by Sihon, the Amorite king of Heshbon, who wrested the area north of the Arnon from it. The Israelites, coming from the wilderness, found it extremely difficult to cross Transjordan;

finally they passed east of the settled area of Moab and Edom; their victory over Sihon gave them the entire Jordan Valley, the Gilead, and part of Moab. This area was allotted to the tribes of Reuben (from the Arnon to the Nimrīn Valley), Gad (from southern Gilead to the Jabbok and the Jordan Valley), and half of Manasseh (from the Jabbok northward).

In the period of the Judges these tribes were subjected to the kings of Ammon and Moab, until David eventually conquered all of Transjordan down to the Red Sea. In the time of Solomon, Israelite-controlled Transjordan was organized into the three districts of Ramoth-Gilead, Mahanaim, and southern Gilead (Gad?; I Kings 4:13–14, 19). After the division of the kingdom, Ammon and Moab fell to Israel and Edom to Judah, but all three soon regained their independence. As is known from the *Mesha stele, Moab was reconquered by Omri; it revolted against Israel in the time of Ahab, finally gaining its independence in the days of Joram, the last of the Omrid kings (851–842 B.C.E.; cf. II Kings 3). In later times Israel never succeeded in subduing Moab, which under Mesha had enlarged its boundaries to the edge of the Jordan Valley. However, the kings of Judah succeeded in ruling large parts of Edom in the ninth century during the days of Jehoshaphat and Jehoram, and again in the eighth century in the days of Amaziah and Uzziah.

With the eighth century B.C.E., the settled area of Transjordan began once more to shrink, a process which lasted until the Hellenistic period. The Assyrian king Tiglath-Pileser III deported part of the Israelite population from Gilead in 732 B.C.E. The Ammonites maintained their independence, and the Edomites threw off Judean rule in the time of Ahaz (743–727 B.C.E.). After the fall of Jerusalem and the deportation of its population by Nebuchadnezzar in 586 B.C.E., the Edomites moved into southern Judea and their place was gradually taken over by the Nabateans, a people known for outstanding achievements in agriculture, architecture, and art. Their kingdom was composed of sections of Transjordan, Palestine, and Syria, and Petra was their capital (fourth century B.C.E.). In the Persian period, Ammon was ruled by the Jewish family of *Tobiads, whose roots in Gilead dated back to the time of the Israelite monarchy.

In Hellenistic times, a new period of prosperity began for Transjordan, lasting until the Arab conquest. The Ptolemies or Seleucids founded a number of cities in the northern part: Gadara and Abila to the north, followed by Pella and Gerasa. Rabbath-Ammon became the city of Philadelphia and was separated from the area of the Tobiads, who ruled the region populated by Jews between Philadelphia and the Jordan (the Peraea). Transjordan passed temporarily from Ptolemaic to Seleucid rule in 218 B.C.E. and permanently in 198 B.C.E. In the course of Hasmonean expansion, large areas of Transjordan were conquered by Jonathan (the Peraea), John Hyrcanus (Madaba and Heshbon), and Alexander Yannai (Moab to the Zered, Gerasa, Pella, and Gadara). In 63 B.C.E. Pompey restored the autonomy of the Greek cities, leaving only Peraea to the Jews. In order to strengthen the Greek element under Roman rule, he formed the Decapolis league, which included Philadelphia. For a time, Herod ruled Gadara, which was restored to Syria after his death. In the First Jewish War, the Peraea was conquered by the Romans (68 C.E.), but its Jewish population remained. In 97 the city of Capitolias was founded at Belt al-Rās near Pella. In 106 Trajan annexed the Nabatean kingdom; the cities of Madaba, Esbus (Heshbon), Areopolis (Rabbath-Moab), Charachmoba, and Petra became part of the new province of Arabia, into which Philadelphia and Gerasa were incorporated. The cities of the area reached a height of prosperity in the second century C.E. under the Antonines, due to a new paved road (the Via Nova) running from Elath (Aila) to Bostra throughout the length of Transjordan.

Christianity gained an early foothold in Transjordan, when the Jerusalem community moved to Pella in 70 C.E. In the Byzantine period southern Transjordan was attached to Palaestina III, the rest to Arabia. Churches and monasteries were built in all the large cities and the bishops took part in church councils. In the last centuries of Byzantine rule, Arab influences in the area were marked. The first battle between the Arabs and the Byzantines took place in 629, still in the lifetime of the prophet *Muhammad, in Transjordan (in Mu'ta, near Karak). The final Arab conquest was effected in several stages: southern Transjordan was taken in 630, the mountains of Seir and Moab in 634, and the rest of the region in 635. With the battle on the Yarmuk in 636, Arab rule in the area was established. In the early Arab period, the area up to Jerash was attached to the Jund al-Urdunn; central Transjordan, including Amman, to the Jund Filasṭīn; and the northern part to the Jund Dimashq (*Damascus). Under Arab rule the northern part of Transjordan together with northern Palestine constituted an administrative unit called Jund al-Urdun, with Tiberias as its capital. Central and southern Transjordan, with the equivalent parts west of the river Jordan, became Jund Filasṭīn, administered from Ramleh. The Arab period marked the beginning of a new decline in the population, which became pronounced for centuries after the Crusades (13th to 19th centuries). In the Crusades period, the Jordan Valley, part of the ʿAjlūn, and the mountains of Karak and Shawbak down to the Red Sea were combined into a principality known as Terre D'Outre Jourdain. As the Crusaders, and especially the rulers of the fortress of Montreal (Shawbak), threatened the pilgrims' route to Mecca and even the holy cities themselves, Saladin attacked and reduced the Crusader fortresses before the battle of Ḥiṭṭin. Under *Mamluk rule Transjordan was divided between Mamlakat Dimashq (the districts (*aʿmāl*) of ʿAjlūn and al-Balqāʾ) and Mamlakat al-Karak, which included Maʿān, Shawbak, Zughar (Zoar), and Karak. In the time of Baybars it was ruled by the last descendant of the *Ayyubid dynasty. In Ottoman times the population of Transjordan reached its lowest level and most of Transjordan was left to the Bedouin, although the sultans kept up a semblance of administration in the western areas. Most of the region was part of the *vilayet* of Damascus, divided into the Sanjak of Ḥawrān (to the Jabbok), the Sanjak of Nablus, which occasionally included the Balqāʾ,

and the Sanjak of al-Karak. The southern sections, Ma'an and Aqaba, were part of the *vilayet* of Hijaz. However, Ottoman rule was nominal most of the time. Transjordan was regarded as the backyard of Syria and Palestine and concerned the Ottomans only during the annual pilgrimage, as the main Hajj caravan from Damascus had to cross it en route to *Medina. Only in the second half of the 19th century, after the short-lived Egyptian occupation (1831–40) and during the reform period (Tanzimat), under *Abdul-Ḥamid II, was resettlement begun. The Ottomans had extended their direct rule over Transjordan. Karak, the capital of its namesake sanjak, was the major city in the area and the jurisdiction of its governor stretched over most of sedentary Transjordan. Local population increased when Circassian refugees from Russian-occupied Caucasus were encouraged by the Ottomans (in 1861–64, and later after the Turkish-Russian war of 1877–78) to migrate to Palestine and Transjordan. In the latter they settled in and around Amman, Zarqa, and Jarash. The 19th century also witnessed growing European interest in Transjordan, mainly for archeological and historical reasons – in 1812 Burckhardt discovered Petra and in 1806 Seetzen discovered Jarash. In the second half of the 19th century the interest of the Palestine Exploration Fund as well as of Christian churches and missions in Transjordan yielded, inter alia, the discovery of the *Mesha stele and the *Madaba mosaic map. In 1900–08 the Ottomans built the Hijazi railroad from Damascus to Medina. About one third of the 1,200 km. line passed through Transjordan, bringing it closer to the administrative centers of Damascus and *Istanbul, yet also triggering several rebellions in Karak.

For modern period after 1914, see also *Israel; *Jordan.

BIBLIOGRAPHY: G. Schumacher, *Across the Jordan* (1886); idem, *Karte des Ostjordanlandes* (1908); A. Musil, *Arabia Petraea* (1907); R.E. Bruennow and A. Domaszewski, *Provincia Arabia*, 3 vols. (1904–09); C. Sternagel, *Der Adschlun* (1927); H. Rhotert, *Transjordanien* (1938); N. Glueck, *The Other Side of the Jordan* (1940); idem, *Explorations in Eastern Palestine*, 4 vols. (1934–51); A. Konikoff, *Transjordan* (1946); L. Harding, *The Antiquities of Jordan* (1959). **ADD. BIBLIOGRAPHY:** N. Lewis, *Nomads and Settlers in Syria and Jordan* (1987); R.S. AbuJaber, *Pioneers over Jordan: The Frontier Settlement in Transjordan 1850–1914* (1989); E. Rogan, *Frontiers of State in the Late Ottoman Empire: Transjordan 1850–1921* (1999).

[Michael Avi-Yonah / Joseph Nevo (2nd ed.)]

TRANSLATION AND TRANSLATORS (Medieval). The earliest Jewish translations, apart from possible examples in the Bible, are the Greek version of the Pentateuch and, later, other books of the Bible, which were made to fill a need in the Greek-speaking Jewish community of Alexandria and other places that no longer understood the original Hebrew. Similarly, the Aramaic vernacular of Jewish settlements in Palestine and other parts of southwestern Asia explain the development of Aramaic versions of the Bible.

In the 10th century *Ḥisdai ibn Shaprut was one of the main translators of Dioscorides' work from Greek to Arabic in the court of Cordoba. During the 12th and 13th century Toledo was a very notable center of translations and the Jews played an important role in this enterprise. In the middle of the 12th century the archbishop of Toledo, Don Raimundo de la Sauvetat (1124–52), promoted the translation of Arabic philosophical works from Arabic through the Romance versions into Latin. The Jew Avendauth worked together with the Christian Gundisalvus, translating, for instance, the *De Anima* of Avicenna and Ibn Gabirol's *Fons Vitae*. One century later, King Alfonso the Sage relied on Jewish translators to get Romance versions of many scientific works. Among them, Judah ben Moses ha-Kohen, Isaac ibn Sa'id, the Alfaquim Don Abraham (Ibn Shoshan?), Samuel ha-Levi Abulafiah, and Don Moses Alfaquí, translated important astronomic and astrologic treatises.

The many translations into Hebrew which began to appear in Western Europe early in the 12th century can be attributed to several factors, among which the spread of Judeo-Islamic culture was of central importance. Cultured and scholarly men from Islamic Spain began to travel to Christian lands. Abraham Ibn Ezra, for example, traveled to Italy, France, and England, and supported himself by writing Hebrew grammars, translations, and biblical commentaries commissioned by Jewish communities. These works undoubtedly stimulated interest in the new approaches to language and learning and reflected the cultural richness of Spain. In consequence of religious persecutions and other disturbances in the Iberian Peninsula during the 12th century, some Jewish families emigrated to southern France or northern Italy, and spread something of the learning and achievements of their native land in their new homes. Works written in Hebrew, moreover, stimulated a desire for additional works in that language. In addition, the general cultural awakening in Western Europe during the 12th century affected the Jews, encouraging them to the further acquisition of knowledge. Without question, at the end of the 12th century, Maimonides' Hebrew code of Jewish law *Mishneh Torah* excited scholars in France and Italy, so that they avidly sought everything the master produced, translating it from Arabic into Hebrew.

No discernible pattern governed the books that were translated into Hebrew. Apparently, books were often translated on the request of a patron, or a scholar would select a book to translate for his own reasons. However, besides the large number of such unclassifiable translations, activity was concentrated in the fields of philosophy, mathematics, medicine, and other sciences. Generally, translators explained their undertakings as being in response to a special request. Judah ibn *Tibbon relates in the introduction to his Hebrew version of Baḥya ibn Paquda's *Ḥovot ha-Levavot* (*Duties of the Heart*) that Meshullam b. Jacob, whom he praises as an adept in both religious and secular studies, urged him to prepare a translation of the Arabic work. Similarly, Judah *Al-Ḥarizi states that he translated Maimonides' *Moreh Nevukhim* (*Guide of the Perplexed*) at the invitation of some Provençal scholars. There are many other examples of requests urging the translation of a work, yet there is no information about remuneration, although the translators presumably received some payment from those who requested the work. Perhaps a community assumed some obligation for payment, especially if the persons interested in the translation were influential members in it. While it is reasonable to assume this of professional translators, like the Tibbonids or al-Ḥarizi, it is probable that other translators were impelled by a personal interest in the work and a desire to bring it to the attention of their fellow Jews.

There was considerable complaint about the neglect of Hebrew and the employment of Arabic. Writers occasionally pointed out the difference between Jews who lived under Islamic domination and Jews who resided in Christian lands. It was not the use of the vernacular Arabic which vexed them, because it was taken for granted that for social intercourse the language of the land was the proper vehicle. But in view of the fact that Jews in Christian countries utilized Hebrew in their literary productions, Jewish writers in Islamic countries justified their use of Arabic by claiming that the subjects they dealt with – subjects not cultivated by Italian and French Jews – required a vocabulary which Hebrew did not possess and which Arabic possessed in abundance. Moses ha-Kohen *Gikatilla, who supplied a Hebrew translation of the grammatical studies of Ḥayyūj, explains that grammarians were compelled to write in Arabic "because it is the current speech of a victorious people, and it is explicit while Hebrew is vague; clear and plain whereas Hebrew is ambiguous; and it is proper to elucidate the unknown by the known and the vague by the explicit." Judah ibn Tibbon presents a brief historical survey of the course of development: "Afterward most of the *geonim* lived in the Diaspora of the Muslim Empire, Iraq, Ereẓ Israel and Iran, and spoke Arabic, and all the Jewish communities in those areas spoke that tongue. Most of their interpretations of biblical and mishnaic and talmudic books were in Arabic, as also most of their compilations and responsa in answer to inquiries made of them. All the people understood it. Moreover it is a rich language, fully adequate for every theme and every need of orator or author; straight and clear rhetoric, to express the essence of every subject more than is possible in Hebrew." Notwithstanding the conceded advantages of Arabic over Hebrew, Jews adhered to the tradition that Hebrew was the divine tongue, the first to serve mankind. But the exile and the tribulations which Jews suffered had caused the loss of a significant portion of Hebrew vocabulary, since the Bible was the only record preserved.

In view of the difference in the richness of the two languages, the role of translator imposed certain duties, the main being the coinage of words and phrases in Hebrew according to need. For translating philosophical, scientific, or medical works new technical words had to be created in Hebrew. It was also necessary to decide what method to pursue in this process. Ordinarily translation is in large measure interpretation, and the function of the translator is to transmit in the new medium the sense of the original. Before Samuel ibn Tibbon translated the *Guide of the Perplexed* into Hebrew, he asked Maimonides for suggestions. The latter offered the following instructions: a translator must first understand the content, and narrate and explain that content in the language in which he is working. He will not escape changing the order of words, or transmitting phrases in single words, or eliminating vocables, or adding them, so that the work is well ordered and expounded, and the language of the translator will follow the principles governing that language. Despite this very sensible advice, Samuel ibn Tibbon's translation of the *Guide*, and his father's version of other works, give the impression of excessive faithfulness to the original. Yet this did not prove contrary to Maimonides' demands, inasmuch as he expressed his gratitude for the accomplishment of his translator. In fact, the style developed by father and son, with strong Arabic influence in its morphology, syntax, and vocabulary, became the standard for subsequent efforts in this field (Goshen-Gottstein). Other ways of translating, searching for a pure, more literary biblical language and avoiding the numerous neologisms, was undertaken also by other Jewish scholars like Judah Al-Ḥarizi, who translated Maimonides' *Guide* in a completely different way not long after the Tibbonid translation. But the method of the ibn Tibbon family was taken as a model for the future, while Al-Ḥarizi's translation was quickly forgotten.

When the full mastery of Arabic was lacking, books were translated from Arabic to Latin by way of the Hebrew version, and occasionally Hebrew translations were made from the Latin rather than from the original Arabic. Although thorough knowledge of both tongues was theoretically necessary – to appreciate the nuances and fathom the true meaning of the original, and to render it authentically and idiomatically – in practice this was unfortunately rarely the case. Translators, even if they were qualified to produce the ideal version, were so concerned about remaining faithful to the original Arabic that they frequently violated Hebrew syntax or sentence structure, and disregarded simple rules of gender and number. Nevertheless, translators contributed greatly to the enrichment of Hebrew, adding a large scientific and philosophic vocabulary. The means utilized to expand the vocabulary were forming new words from existing roots, creating additional noun patterns, making derivations from verbal stems, or forming verbs from nouns. Occasionally a new meaning was attached to an existing term, parallel to the course followed in the coinage of the Arabic terminology. In addition, a number of words were borrowed from Arabic, and they were generally adjusted to the morphological requirements of Hebrew. It should also be kept in mind that the philosophic and scientific style introduced by the translators became the standard, so that men who composed in Hebrew followed the patterns adopted from Arabic.

Translators were not always familiar with the subject of the work they were rendering. Occasionally criticism would be voiced about translators who offered to work without adequate knowledge of the field involved. However, on the whole, translators were usually conscious of their obligations, and succeeded in transmitting authentic versions of the originals. Even in more popular literature, where greater freedom could be taken since in popular works eloquence was frequently a major quality, the Hebrew version, although it may read like an original, will still be a correct rendering. Abraham ibn Ḥasdai's **Ben ha-Melekh ve-ha-Nazir*, a beautiful Jewish book in Hebrew, is unmistakably a rendering of *Barlaam and Josaphat*. Other popular works translated into Hebrew were **Kalila and Dimna* and *Sinbad the Sailor*. In this genre, and, for that matter, in some of the more serious compositions, like Ibn Gabirol's *Improvement of the Qualities of the Soul*, translators often substituted Jewish personalities and references for foreign ones, and even replaced Arabic verses with Jewish equivalents.

Translators generally approached their task with deep humility. Statements of inadequacy and confessions of ignorance, which should have kept them from the undertaking, are often found in translators' introductions to their works. Although some of these expressions were undoubtedly *pro forma*, many others represent expressions of genuine trepidation with which translators assumed the charge. Samuel b. Judah of Marseilles, who translated Aristotle's *Ethics*, admits openly and sincerely his insufficient acquaintance with the subject and expresses the hope of studying it in depth to improve his rendering. Judah b. Nathan, who prepared a Hebrew version of Ghazali's *The Intentions of the Philosopher*, frankly describes his inadequate command of the language and the subject. Yet the results are by and large highly commendable.

Our main source of information about Hebrew translations is still the monumental work of M. Steinschneider, *Die hebraeischen Uebersetzungen des Mittelalters und die Juden als Dolmetscher* (1893, repr. 1956). The following is a survey of medieval Hebrew translations of Arabic and Latin works. It begins with philosophy, and in this field *Aristotle was far and away the outstanding representative of Greek thought among Muslim and Jewish thinkers. The latter, who were mostly unfamiliar with Greek, knew him only through the Arabic. Two Muslim philosophers are extremely important for their influence on their Jewish counterparts: Abu al-Naṣr Muhammad al-*Fārābi (c. 870–950), known as "the second teacher" (Aristotle was the first), and Abu al-Walīd Muhammad ibn Rushd (*Averroes; 1126–1198). The Jewish philosophers knew the views of the Greek master through the commentaries of these two.

The Muslim thinkers, and Maimonides among the Jews, knew of a compendium of the entire Organon; but in Hebrew translation, only some parts are to be found: (1) Porphyry's *Isagoge* was called *Kiẓẓur mi-Kol Melekhet ha-Higgayon* by its translator Moses b. Samuel ibn Tibbon. A fragment of another version of their Introduction to logic is also extant; (2) *Categoriae Sifrei Ma'amarot*, in two renderings; (3) *Hermeneutica*, in two Hebrew translations, both known to Abraham Avigdor in his commentary on Averroes; (4) *Syllogisms*, also in two translations, and an abridgment by Jacob Anatoli; (5) *Analytica Posteriora – Ma'amar bi-Tena'ei ha-Hekkesh ha-Mofet*, anonymous; (6) *Topica – Ommanut ha-Nissu'aḥ*, in two translations, both anonymous. All of these works in logic are in al-Fārābi's version.

Averroes studied Aristotle's works in three ways: (1) Summaries of the latter's teachings which he himself called Al-Jawāmi ʿal-Sighār (the brief compendia; in Heb. *Kiẓẓur*). (2) The *Middle Commentaries*, which Averroes named Talkhiṣ – *Be'ur* or *Perush*; the Hebrew renderings do not indicate in each work whether it is from this body, or from the next one. (3) The *Great Commentaries*. In these Aristotle's text is offered in sections, followed in every case by a detailed commentary. In the ensuing list 1 = *The Compendium*, 2 = *The Middle Commentary*, 3 = *The Great Commentary*. I. Logic. (1a) *Kol Melekhet ha-Higgayon le-Aristoteles mi-Kiẓẓurei ibn Rushd* by Jacob b. Inaktur, Nov. 10, 1189. (1b) *Kiẓẓur Higgayon* by Samuel b. Judah of Marseilles, December 1329. He explains in his introduction that he undertook it only because the previous one was a poor performance. (2a) by Jacob b. Abba Mari Anatoli, March 1232. (2b) *Nissu'aḥ ve-Hata'ah* by Kalonymus b. Kalonymus, Arles, 1313. (2c) *Halaẓah ve-Shir* by Todros Todrosi, Arles, 1337. (3) *Ha-Mofet* by Kalonymus b. Kalonymus, December 1314.

II. A. Physics. (1) *Ha-Shema ha-Tivi* by Moses ibn Tibbon. (2a) *Ha-Shema* by Zerahiah Ḥen of Barcelona, in Rome, 1284. It is in eight sections (*ma'amarim*), divided into principles (*kelalim*), and these into chapters (*perakim*). (2b) *Ha-Shema* by Kalonymus b. Kalonymus, Arles, 1316. (3) *Ha-Shema* by Kalonymus b. Kalonymus. It seems that another version was prepared by Moses b. Solomon.

B. *Sefer ha-Shamayim* (1) Themistius' paraphrase, by Zerahiah Ḥen, Rome, 1284. Averroes' *Kelalei ha-Shamayim veha-Olam* was done by Moses ibn Tibbon. (2) by Solomon b. Joseph ibn Ayyūb of Granada, in Béziers, 1259.

C. (1) *Ha-Havayah ve-ha-Hefsed*, by Moses ibn Tibbon, 1250. (2) by Zerahiah Ḥen, Rome, 1284. Also by Kalonymus b. Kalonymus, October 1316.

D. *Al-Āthār al-ʿAlawiyya* on meteorology. (1) *Otot ha-Shamayim* by Samuel ibn Tibbon, 1210. A work by Averroes: *Otot Elyonot* was translated into Hebrew by Moses ibn Tibbon. (2) *Be'ur Sefer ha-Otot ha-Elyonot* by Kalonymus b. Kalonymus, Arles, 1316.

E. *Ha-Ẓemaḥim* 1–2 by Shem Tov ibn Falaquera, and Kalonymus b. Kalonymus, who did Averroes' commentary, April 1314.

F. *Sefer Ba'alei-Ḥayyim*, consisting of *de Natura Animalium, de Partibus* and *de Generatione*. The last two were translated by Jacob b. Machir ibn Tibbon, December 1302.

G. *On the Soul*, translated by Zerahiah Ḥen in Rome, 1284. Averroes' treatment (1) *Kelalei Sefer ha-Nefesh*, by Moses ibn Tibbon, 1244. (2a) by Shem Tov b. Isaac of Tortosa. (2b) *Be'ur Sefer ha-Nefesh* by Moses ibn Tibbon, April 1261. (3) Of the *Great Commentary* no Hebrew translation is known, but it was used by Shem Tov Falaquera and was commented on by Joseph b. Shem Tov. It is also pertinent to mention the treatise of Alexander of Aphrodisias, which in Hebrew is *Ma'amar Nefesh*, translated by Samuel b. Judah of Marseilles in Murcia, November 1323.

H. Of the *Parva Naturalia*, consisting of *de Sensu et Sensato, de Memoria, de Somno*, and *de Berevitate Vitae*, only the first was translated as *Ha-Ḥush ve-ha Muḥash* by Moses ibn Tibbon, July 1314, in Montpellier.

Metaphysics. Al-Fārābī's introduction *Kitāb fī Aghrāḍ Aristo fī Kitāb mā ba'd al-Tabī'a* was rendered anonymously in Hebrew under the title: *Be-Khavvanot Aristo be-Sifro Mah she-Akhar ha-Teva*. Books alpha–lambda were done from the Latin by Baruch b. Ya'ish for Samuel Sarfati about 1485. Of Averroes' treatment, one was presented in Hebrew by Moses ibn Tibbon in May 1258, a second by Zerahiah Ḥen, 1284, in Rome and also by Kalonymus b. Kalonymus in May 1317. The third is by Moses b. Solomon of Salon in Beaucaire, 1310–20, of which only Hebrew fragments survive. Themistius' paraphrase of Book Lambda (12) was translated by Moses ibn Tibbon. *De Anima* plus Averroes' commentary was explained, and possibly translated by Moses Narboni under the title *Efsharut ha-Devekut ba-Sekhel ha-Po'el*. Three treatises on the same theme were translated into Hebrew by Samuel ibn Tibbon. Aristotle's *Nicomachean Ethics* were rendered in Hebrew from the Latin by Don Meir b. Solomon Alguadez, Averroes' middle commentary in Hebrew by Samuel b. Judah of Marseilles, February 1321.

His *Politics* were never translated into Arabic, although its existence was known as the practical application of the principle in the *Ethics* to the conduct of the state, but it is Plato's *Republic* which was available in Arabic under the title *Kitāb al-Siyāsa* and was translated into Hebrew by Samuel b. Judah of Marseilles in 1320–22.

Of Aristotle's *Economica*, a Hebrew version from the Arabic was prepared by David b. Solomon of Seville (1373?), and probably from the Latin by Leon Aretino. The latter carries an *Introduction* by an otherwise unknown Abraham ibn Tibbon. Several pseudo-Aristotelian works circulated in Hebrew, generally via Arabic. Of these, *Problemata* by Moses ibn Tibbon (1264); on stones – *Sefer ha-Avanim* or *De Lapidario; Theology* by Moses b. Joseph Arovas, from the Arabic, and also in Italian by him; *Secretum secretorum*, in Arabic *Sirr al-Asrār*, and in Hebrew, anonymously, *Sod ha-Sodot*, in the 13th century; *de Causis*, on the absolute good, by Zerahiah Ḥen called *Ha-Be'ur be-Tov ha-Gamur*, and also by Hillel b. Samuel of Verona, both from the Arabic, which is not known (Produs' *de Causis* was rendered in Hebrew by Judah Romano, and called *Sefer ha-Sibbot); Kitāb-al-Tufāḥa* ("On the Apple"; on immorality, and seen as an imitation of Plato's *Phaedo*) in Hebrew by Abraham ibn Ḥisdai; these are also letters which he sent to Alexander the Great, and works on auguring.

Muslim thinkers who wrote in Arabic, and whose works were translated into Hebrew, include al-Fārābi: *Fi al-Tanbīhʿ alā Sabīl al-Saʿāda* is rendered in Hebrew, *Ha-He'arah al-Derekh ha-Hazlaḥah*, by an anonymous translator; *Kitab al-Mabādiʾ* or *al-Siyāsa* was translated by Moses ibn Tibbon, and named *Sefer ha-Hatḥalah; Iḥṣāʾ al-Ulūm* (an enumeration of the sciences), in Hebrew, by Kalonymus b. Kalonymus, *Be-Mispar ha-Ḥokhmot; ʿUyūn al-Masāʾil* (answers to philosophical problems), in Hebrew *Ayin Mishpat ha-Derushim* by Todros Todrosi; Kalonymus b. Kalonymus did *Iggeret be-Siddur Kri'at ha-Ḥokhmot* from the Arabic *fi mā Yanbaghiʿan Yaqdum qabla Taʿallum al-Falsafa; Ba-Sekhel u-va-Muskal from fi al-ʿAql wa al-Mʿaqūl*; the last was also translated anonymously as *Ha Sekhel ve-ha-muskalot. Risāla fī Hayāt al-Nafs* was done in Hebrew by Zerahiah Ḥen, in 1284, Ibn Sīnā (Avicenna, d. 1037), accepted by orthodox Islam, wrote *al-Samāʾ wa al-ʿĀlam*, translated into Hebrew as *Ha-Shamayim ve-ha-Olam*, by Solomon b. Moses of Melgueil (second half of 13th century), probably from Latin; *Sefer ha-Shenah ve-ha-Yekẓah* by the same, again from Latin; *al-Najāt*, translated as *Hazzalat ha-Nefesh* by Todros Todrosi (1330–40); Ḥai ibn Yaqzān, in Hebrew *Iggeret Ḥai ben Mekiẓ* by Abraham ibn Ezra.

Al-*Ghazālī (d. 1111), the famous critic of philosophy, wrote *Maqāṣid al-Falāsifa* ("The Objectives of the Philosopher"; it was cribbed by Saádiah b. Daud al-ʿAdeni under the title *Zakāt al-Nafs*) which was adopted by Isaac al-Balagh (only the first two parts) and called *De'ot ha-Pilosofim*. A translation, *Kavvanot ha-Pilosofim*, was prepared (1352–58) by Judah b. Nathan, a Provençal physician. A third anonymous version also exists. His *Tahāfut al-Falāsifa* ("The Collapse of the Philosophers") was translated into Hebrew, by Zerahiah b. Isaac ha-Levi, called Saladin, and possibly the Rabbi Ferrer of the Tortosa disputation (1412–14). *Miʿyar al-ʿIlm* is *Moznei ha-Iyyunim* by Jacob b. Machir ibn Tibbon; *Mīzān al-ʿAmal*, an ethical work, done by Abraham b. Samuel ibn Ḥasdai and called *Moznei Ẓedek. Mishkatt al-Anwar* ("The Niche of the Lights") is *Maskit ha-Orot* by Isaac b. Joseph al-Fāsī, of the 13th century. Another, but anonymous, rendering is called *Ha-Orot ha-Elohiyyot*.

Abdallah ibn Muhammad of Badajoz (d. 1127) wrote *al-Dāʾira al-Wahmiyya* ("The Imaginary Circle") a work which was quite influential among Jewish thinkers. Moses ibn Tibbon rendered it into Hebrew, calling it *Ha-Agullot ha-Ra'yoniyyot*. It was also done by Samuel Motot, as part of his commentary on *Sefer Yeẓirah*. Ibn Baja (d. 1138 in Fez) wrote *Kitāb al-Wadāʿ* ("The Farewell" [to the world]) which was converted into Hebrew by Ḥayyim ibn Vivas, and *fī Tadbīr al-Mutawaḥḥid* (on the conduct of the recluse) which is *Be-Hanhagat ha-Mitboded*, by Moses of Narbonne who wrote a commentary on it. Ibn Ṭufayl (d. 1185 in Murcia) composed a celebrated *Risālat Ḥayy ben Yaqzān*, in Hebrew *Iggeret Ḥayawan ben Yakson*, it was also incorporated by Moses of Narbonne in his commentary. Ibn Rushd (Averroes, d. 1198) wrote an exposition of the harmony of religion and philosophy called *Faṣl al-Maqāl* etc., which was translated into Hebrew, anonymously, under the name *Ha-Hevdel ha-Ne'emar she-Bein ha-Torah ve-ha Ḥokhmah min ha-Devekut*. He refuted Ghazāli's critique of philosophy in his *Tahāfut al-Tahāfut* ("The Collapse of the Collapse"); its Hebrew version, *Happalat ha-Happalah*, was prepared by Kalonymus b. David b. Todros. A second rendering, anonymous, is also extant.

Since a number of Jewish thinkers wrote their works in Arabic, they also required conversion into Hebrew. The earliest is Isaac Israeli. Among his philosophic writings are *Kitāb al-Ḥudūd wa al-Rusūm* ("Book of Definitions"), in Hebrew, *Sefer ha-Gevulim ve-ha-Reshamim* by Nissim b. Solomon; *Kitāb al-Ustuqṣāt* as *Sefer ha-Yesodot* by Abraham ibn Ḥisdai; *Maqāla fi-Yishersku ha-Mayim*, in an anonymous Hebrew version; *Sefer ha-Ru'ah ve-ha-Nefesh*, only a small fragment of the Arabic original is extant. Saadiah b. Joseph al-Fayyumi (d. 942) composed *Kitāb al-Amānāt wa al-Iʿtiqādāt*, called in Hebrew *Sefer ha-Emunot ve-ha De'ot* by Judah ibn Tibbon. An anonymous version titled *Pitron Sefer ha-Emunot* is also extant. His commentary on *Sefer Yeẓirah* is likewise found in Hebrew, but the translator is not known with certainty.

Baḥya ibn Paquda composed the ethical-philosophical, *Farāʾid al-Qulūb*; in Hebrew it is *Ḥovot ha-Levavot* translated by Judah ibn Tibbon, who also appended an interesting introduction to his translation.

Solomon ibn Gabirol wrote a philosophic rather than a theological study, whose Arabic original has not been discovered. No medieval Hebrew translation exists (one is extant in Latin), but an epitome, *Likkutim*, prepared by Shem Tov ibn Falaquera, is extant. A modern Hebrew version is now available. Other works Ibn Gabirol rendered into Hebrew included *Iṣlāḥ al-Akhlāq* ("The Improvement of the Character") translated by Judah ibn Tibbon as *Tikkun Middot ha-Nefesh*, and a collection of aphorisms, probably by the same translator, under the title *Mivḥar ha-Peninnim*. Another version, in the rhyme, *Shekel ha-Kodesh*, was the work of Joseph Kimḥi. Joseph ibn Ẓaddik, a judge in Cordoba (d. 1149), wrote *al-ʿĀlam al-Ṣaqhīr* ("Microcosm"), which is *Ha-Olam ha-Katan* in Hebrew, but the translator is unknown.

Judah Halevi (d. 1141) is the author of *Kitāb al-Hujja wa al-Dalil* ("The Argument and Proof"), known as *Ha-Kuzari* in Judah ibn Tibbon's Hebrew rendering. A fragment is also extant of a translation by Judah b. Kardena. Abraham ibn Daud, the earliest Aristotelian among Jewish thinkers, wrote *al-ʿAqida al-Rafiʿa*, on free will and other matters. It was translated as *Ha-Emunah ha-Nissa'ah* by Samuel ibn Motot in 1312, and as *Ha-Emunah ha-Ramah* by Solomon b. Levi. Moses Ibn Ezra wrote a work of literary criticism, *Kitāb al-Muḥaḍara wa al-Mudhākara* (which is called *Shirat Yisrael* in a modern Hebrew version by B. Halper, or *Sefer ha-Iyyunim ve-ha-Diyyunim* by A.S. Halkin), and *Fī Maʿna al-Majāz wa al-Haqīqa* ("On Literalisms and Figurative Expressions"), part of which was rendered into Hebrew as *Arugat ha-Bosem*.

Many of the works of Maimonides were rendered in Hebrew translation. Of his commentary on the Mishnah, Judah al-Ḥarizi translated the general introduction and most of *Zera'im*; Joseph ibn al-Fawwāl and a certain Simḥah did *Mo'ed* and *Nashim* in Huesca; the remaining three were done in Saragossa by Solomon ibn Ya'qūb (*Nezikin*) and Nethanel ibn Almali (*Kodashim* and *Tohorot*). There are also fragments of other translations. *Avot* was done by Samuel ibn Tibbon. Maimonides' *Sefer ha-Mitzvot*, listing the 613 biblical precepts, was rendered into Hebrew by Abraham ibn Ḥisdai, of which only fragments exist, and by Moses ibn Tibbon. A third version exists by Solomon ibn Ayyūb. His epistle on forced conversion was titled *Iggeret ha-Shemad* in Hebrew; the translator is unknown; his *Iggeret Teiman* exists in three Hebrew versions: (a) by Samuel ibn Tibbon; (b) by Abraham ibn Ḥisdai; (c) by Nahum ha-Ma'aravi; his treatise on resurrection, *Ma'amar Teḥiyyat ha-Metim*, by Samuel ibn Tibbon. His major philosophic composition, *Dalālat al-Ḥāʾirīn*, was translated by Samuel ibn Tibbon and also by Judah al-Ḥarizi. His treatise on logic, *Maqāla fī Sināʿat al-Manṭiq*, is available in Hebrew, probably from Moses ibn Tibbon's hand, as *Millot ha-Higgayon*.

Joseph b. Judah ibn Aknin wrote a philosophic commentary on the Songs of Songs, which he called *Inkishāf al-Asrār wa Ṭuhūr al-Anwār*. It was recently translated into Hebrew. Of Karaite thinkers, Joseph al-Basir's two works were provided with a Hebrew translation: *Al-Muḥtawī* was translated under the title *Sefer ha-Ne'imot*, and *Kitāb al-Tamyīz*, received by the Hebrew name *Maḥkimot Peti*.

Books by Christians which are available in Hebrew translation include *Quaestiones naturale* by Adelard of Bath (c. 1120), which is *Dodi ve-Nekhdi*, by Berechiah ha-Nakdan; *Philosophia* of Albertus Magnus (1193–1286) is in a Hebrew version titled *Kiẓẓur ha-Pilosofyah ha-Tivit* by Abraham Shalom, and Aegidius de Columnas' (d. 1306) *De Regimine Principum*, in Hebrew *Hanhagat ha-Melakhim*. The *De Consolationes Philosophiae* of Boethius (d. 524) was translated into Hebrew by Samuel b, Benveniste and called *Menaḥem Meshiv Nafshi*, and again by Azariah b. Abba Mari under the name *Neḥamot ha-Pilosofyah*. Other scholastics whose works were translated are Occam (d. 1343/7) whose *Summa totius*, in Hebrew *Perakim ba-Kolel*, was translated by Eli Habillo, who called himself Don Manuel. Petrus Hispanus (d. 1276) wrote *Parva Logicalia*, a work quite popular among Jews, as can be judged from the several renderings: (a) *Higgayon Kaẓar* by Abraham Avigdor; (b) *Higgayon* by Judah b. Samuel Shalom; (c) *Trattat*, anonymous; *Be'ur ha-Mavo* by Jehezekiah b. Ḥalafta. Raimund Lull (d. 1215) created an *Ars Parva* from his *Ars Magna*, the former was rendered into Hebrew by several translators as *Melakhah Keẓarah*. Many of Thomas Aquinas' works, particularly the philosophic treatises and commentaries, were made available in Hebrew.

The Jews in the Islamic world were deeply interested in mathematics, first, because of its intrinsic challenge, and secondly, because of its use in astronomy and astrology, which had important practical and religious implications. As in philosophy, so in science, the pursuits of the Greek scientists were eagerly studied. Archimedes' work on cylinders was translated by Kalonymus b. Kalonymus under the title *Ba-Kaddur u-va Iẓtevanah* from Costa ibn Lucca's Arabic version. Kalonymus also provided a Hebrew version of the measurement of circles, *Bi-Meshiḥat ha-Agullah*; from Thābit b. Karras' Arabic. Euclid was the representative of the Greeks. His *Kitāb al-Uṣūl* or *al-Ustuqṣāt*, in 12 books, augmented by two more of Hypsicles, was rendered by Moses ibn Tibbon in 1270. Another version called *Yesodot ve-Shorashim* was made by Jacob b. Machir about 1270. Other Hebrew texts also exist, possibly from the Latin, for example, his *Data* in *Sefer ha-Mattanot* by Jacob b. Machir. The *Optics, bi-Khtilāf al-Manāthir,* and *Ḥilluf ha-Mabbatim* in Hebrew, was also the work of Jacob b. Machir. In the Hebrew manuscript *Sefer ha-Marim* of Euclid follows the preceding work. But the Arabs know only a *Kitāb al-Mir'a* by Aristotle. A book of Menelaus of Alexandria (first century; Ar. *Kitāb al-Ashkāl al-Kurriyya*) was translated into Hebrew by Jacob b. Machir and called *Sefer Mileus ba-Temunot ha-Kadduriyyot.*

Ptolemy of Alexandria (d. 150), known to Jews and Arabs as Betolomaus, is the author of *Elmegiste*, which was translated into Hebrew as *Ḥibbur ha-Gadol* by Jacob Anatoli. The introduction to *Elmegiste* was turned into Hebrew as *Ḥokhmat ha-Kokhavim*, or *Ḥokhmat Tekhunah ha-Keẓarah* by Moses ibn Tibbon. His *Hypotheses* was rendered by Kalonymus b. Kalonymus in 1317 under the title *Be-Sippur Inyenei ha-Kokhavim ha-Nevukhim.* Several works ascribed to Ptolemy also circulated, among them the *Astrolabe*, called *Ma'aseh ha-Aẓterolav* by Solomon Sharvit ha-Zahav (14th century), and *Planispherium*, called *Mofetei Kelei ha-Habbatah*, probably from the Latin.

Muslim mathematician and astronomer Jābir ibn Aflaḥ's *Kitāb al-Hay'a*, which was translated into Hebrew by Moses ibn Tibbon, is identical with the alleged *Elmegiste* in nine books, completed in 1274. His *Sector of Menelaus is Ha-Ḥibbur ba-Temunah ha-Ḥitukhit le-Mileus*; the translator is not known with certainty. Abu Batir's *De Nativitatibus* was rendered into Hebrew as *Sefer ha-Moladot* by Isḥāq abu al-Khayr from the Latin in 1498. Averroes' *Compendium* is *Kiẓẓur Elmegiste* by Jacob Anatoli in 1231. Abu Isḥāq al-Bitrinji of Seville composed *Kitāb fi al-Hay'a, Ma'amar ba-Tekhunah* in Hebrew by Moses ibn Tibbon. Costa ibn Lucca's *Al-ʿAmal bial-kurra al-Nujūmiyya* was translated by Jacob b. Machir as *Sefer ha-Ma'aseh be-Khaddur ha-Galgol.* Aḥmed al-Ferghani (d. 833/844) wrote *Jawāmiʿ al-Nujūm* which is *Yesodot ha-Tekhunah* by Jacob Anatoli (the title is not his). Muhammad al-Ḥaṣṣār composed an arithmetic which he named *Al-Bayān wa al-Tidhkār*, and it is available in the Hebrew translation of Moses ibn Tibbon as *Ḥeshbon.* Ibn Haitham's *Qawl fi Hay'at-ʿAlam* was translated as *Sefer ha-Tekhunah* by Jacob b. Machir in 1271, and by Solomon ibn Fatir ha-Kohen in 1322. Abu Yūsuf al-Kindī's astrological work on the new moon was prepared in Hebrew by Kalonymus b. Kalonymus as *Iggeret be-Kiẓẓur ha-Ma'amar ba-Moladot.* His *Iggeret ha-Maspeket ba-la-Ḥiyyut u-va-Matar* exists in an anonymous translation. Jaʿfar Abu Maʿshar (d. 885/6 at the age of 100) wrote *Al-Madkhal al-Kabīr*, which was translated into Hebrew from the Latin under the name *Mavo ha-Gadol me-Ḥokhmat ha-Tekhunah* by Jacob b. Elijah. Another work of his is *Sefer Kaẓar be-Mivḥar Liabi Maʿshar* by an anonymous translator from the Arabic *al-Ikhtiyārāt.* The astronomical *Tables*, by an unknown Muslim, were translated into Hebrew by Abraham ibn Ezra and called *Ta'amei Luḥot al-Khwarizmi.* Ibn Muʿadh's discussion of the solar eclipse of 1079, was converted into Hebrew by Samuel b. Judah of Marseilles (1320–40), who also translated Ibn Mu'adh's treatise on the Dawn, as *Iggeret be-Ammud ha-Shaḥar. Kitāb al-ʿAmal bi al-Asturlab* by Aḥmad ibn al-Saffār was rendered into Hebrew as *Perush ha-Aẓterolab* by Jacob b. Machir. Kalonymus b. Kalonymus translated Abu l-Qāsim ibn Samḥ's work under the title *Ma'amar ba-Iẓtevanot u-va-Meḥudadim.* Abu al-Kāmil Shujāʿ of Egypt (900–950) composed *Ṭharā'if al-Ḥisāb*, and it was translated from the Latin into Hebrew by Mordecai Finzi of Manta (1344–1375). Thābit b. Qurra (d.901) composed *Kitāb al-Shakl al-Qaṭāʿ.* Its Hebrew version, *Sefer ha-Temunah ha-Ḥittukhit*, is by Kalonymus b. Kalonymus. Ibrāhīm al-Nakkūsh ibn al-Zarkala (1061–80) composed *al-Ṣafīḥa al-Zarkaliya*, which was done in Hebrew by an unknown translator under the title *Iggeret ha Ma'aseh ba-Lu'aḥ ha-Nikra Ṣafīha.* Another work by this author, on the fixed stars, was translated by Samuel b. Judah of Marseilles and called *Ma'amar bi-Tenu'at ha-Kokhavim ha-Kayyamim.*

A few Jewish astronomers wrote in Arabic, and their works required translation. Mashalla (d. 820) wrote an astrological study, which Abraham ibn Ezra translated under the title *She'elot.* He also translated Mashalla's work on eclipses which in Hebrew is called *Be-Kadrut ha-Levanah ve-ha-Shemesh ve-Ḥibbur ha-Kokhavim u-Tekufat ha-Shanim.* Sahl ibn Bishr (d. c. 820) compiled a book of principles of astrology, *Kitāb al-Aḥkām.* Rendered into Hebrew by an unknown translator, it is called *Kelalim.* Maimonides' treatise on the calendar is translated by an unknown scholar as *Ḥibbur be-Ḥokhmat ha-Ibbur.* Joseph ibn Naḥmias' astronomical study, *Nūr al-ʿAlam*, was rendered into Hebrew by an unknown translator as *Ha-Shamayim ha-Ḥadashim.* The astronomical tables of Joseph ibn Wakkār were also done in Hebrew.

The *Alphonsine Tables*, prepared by the Jew Yisḥak ibn Cid in 1265, for the Christian astronomer Alphonse, have been rendered into Hebrew, as have other tables, with adjusted dates. Gerard of Sabionetta wrote a *Thearica Planetarum* which, in the Hebrew of Judah b. Samuel Shalom, is *Iyyun Shivah Kokhevei Lekhet.* Hermanus Contractus (d. 1054) produced *de Mensura Astrolabu*, which in Hebrew is called *Sefer ha-Aẓteroblin*, and, in another version, *Sefer Astrolog.* Both translators are unknown. John of Gmund (d. 1417) is the author of a treatise on the stars which David b. Meir Kalonymus translated into Hebrew and called *Marot ha-Kokhavim.* Alessandro Piccolomini (d. 1578) composed *La Spera del Mondo* and *Speculazione dei Pianete.* In Hebrew they are respectively *Sefer ha-Kidor* and *Iyyunei Kokhevei ha-Nevokhah* in the translations of an unknown author. Dioscorides (first cent. C.E.) compiled a work on *Simplicia* in which Ḥisdai ibn Shaprut participated in translating into Arabic; no Hebrew version is known, except for passages in the medical work of the so-called Asaf. His *Succeda Nea* was translated from the Latin by Azariah Bonafoux under the title *Temurat ha-Sammim.* Numerous writings of Galen were available in Hebrew. *Ars Parva (Techne)* was rendered from the Arabic as *Ha-Me'assef le-khol ha-Maḥanot* by an unknown scholar. Four of his smaller works on illnesses, their cause and symptoms, were combined in the Hebrew of Zerahiah Ḥen (1277) under the heading *Sefer ha-Ḥola'im ve-ha-Mikrim.* Zerahiah Ḥen also translated the *Kata-*

genos, which deals with compound medicines. Galen's work on crises, *al-Buḥrān* in Arabic, was made available in Hebrew under the Arabic name by Bonirac (perhaps Boniac) Solomon (c. 1300–1350). *On Blood Letting* was rendered by Kalonymus b. Kalonymus (1308) as *Sefer ha-Hakazah*. Kalonymus also translated *Ba-Ḥuknah u-va Kulang* ("on enema and colic"). The author's treatise on epilepsy was rendered in Hebrew by an unknown translator under the title *Be-Hanhagat ha-Na'ar Nikhpeh*, and his *De Malitia Complexionis Diversae* was rendered in Hebrew from the Latin by David b. Abraham Caslari (1280–1337) and called *Sefer Ro'a Mezeg Mitḥallef. The Compendia* (Ar. *al-Jawāmiʿ*) was converted into Hebrew by Samson b. Solomon (1332). Many smaller tracts of his were also made available in Hebrew, all, of course, from the Arabic or the Latin. Some writings ascribed to Galen are *Sefer ha-Em* ("Gynaecaeas") and *Sefer Issur ha-Kevurah* (on prohibition of burial before 72 hours after death) *fī Taḥrīm al-dafn*.

Hippocrates, the father of Greek medicine, was known to the medieval Jews, through the Arabs, by his aphorisms, *Kitāb al-Fusūl*, translated by Moses ibn Tibbon as *Perakim*. This work was also translated by an unknown scholar and by Nathan ha-Me'ati, in 1283. Hillel b. Samuel of Verona prepared a Hebrew version of it from the Latin with the title *Ma'amar ha-Rofe'im*, and another version under the name *Agur*, again from the Latin, was made by an unknown translator. Hippocrates' *Prognostica* with Galen's comments and titled *Hakdamat ha-Yedi'ah*, was probably translated by Nathan ha-Me'ati. It also exists as *Ḥidot ve-Hashgaḥot*, evidently rendered from Greek and Latin by an unknown translator. His work on acute illnesses, *Hanhagat ha-Ḥola'im ha-Ḥaddim*, was translated by Nathan ha-Me'ati, and by his grandson Samuel b. Solomon. Hippocrates' study of air, water, and places, *Sefer ha-Avirim u-va-Zemannim ve-ha-Memot ve-ha-Araẓot* – was rendered by Nathan ha-Me'ati, and Galen's commentary on it, in Hebrew, is the work of Solomon b. Nathan in 1299. A book, *Marot ha-Sheten* ("on the color of urine"), ascribed to the Greek physician, is extant in Hebrew in the translation of Joseph b. Isaac Yisre'eli.

In Arabic a good deal was produced on medicine, and much of it was rendered into Hebrew. The celebrated translator of Galen, Ḥunayn ibn Isḥāq, himself a physician, compiled an introduction, *Madkhal fī-al-Ṭibb*, which exists in Hebrew as *Mavo* or *She'elot* translated from the Latin by Moses ibn *Tibbon and two anonymous scholars called *Mavo*. Māsawayh (d. 857) wrote medical curiosities, *al-Nawādir al-Ṭibbiyya*, translated into Hebrew as *He'arot min ha-Refu'ah* by an unknown scholar, and *Iṣlāh al-Adwiya al-Mushila* ("on laxatives") rendered into Hebrew as *Me-ha-Eẓah ve-ha-Teva'im ve-ha-Tena'im* by Samuel b. Jacob (end of 13th century), and also by an unknown scholar. There is an antidotary by Māsawayh, *Aqrābadhīn*, of which three or four anonymous versions are in existence. Muhammad al-Rāzī (d. 932/3), one of the famous Muslim writers on medicine, wrote *al-Manṣūrī*, a general work in ten tracts, which was translated by Shem Tov b. Isaac Tartasi (d. 1264), and was later abridged. His *Aegritudine junctuarum* (*Me-Ḥolyei ha-Ḥibburim*), *de Aegritudinibus puerorum* (*Me-Hanhagat ha-Ne'arim ha-Ketannim*) are both by unknown translators from the Latin, the latter being a more literal translation than *Me-Ḥoli ha-Ne'arim ke-fi Rāzi*. *Pirkei Razi*, 119 short aphorisms, is an anonymous translation from Arabic, as is also *Sefer ha-Pesakot*. A compendium, *Liber Divisionum*, was translated by Moses ibn Tibbon as *Ha-Ḥilluk ve-ha-Ḥilluf*; he also translated Al-Rāzī's antidotary in 1257; of the latter an anonymous version also exists. Al-Rāzī's explanation of why people go to charlatans, *Ba-Meh she-Yikreh bi-Melekhet ha-Refu'ah*, is perhaps the work of Nathan ha-Me'ati. There is an anonymous *Ma'amar be-Hakkazah*, and, from the Latin, *Mi-Segullat Evrei Ba'alei Ḥayyim ve-Te'aliyyotam ve-Hezzekam* ("on limbs and organs of living beings"). Ibn Sīnā (Avicenna) is the author of the standard medical textbook of the late Middle Ages. His *Canon, al-Qānūn*, was translated by Nathan ha-Me'ati, although the manuscripts do not include the rendering of the whole. Zerahiah Ḥen also worked on a translation of the *Canon*, but only the first two books are known. Of Joseph ha-Lorki's rendering (before 1402) only book one and part of book two are extant. Avicenna's *al-Qānūm al-Ṣaghīr* was translated by Moses ibn Tibbon in Montpellier in 1272. *Canticum*, a medical book in verse (*arjūza* in Arabic), was rendered into prose by Moses ibn Tibbon, and, in verse, by Solomon b. Joseph ibn Ayyūb (*Sefer ha-Ḥaruzim ha-Nikra arjūza*), and by Ḥayyim Israel, and by an unknown scholar of whose work only a fragment exists. His *al-Adwiya al-Qalbiyya* on cures for heart disorders, is found in two anonymous Hebrew versions: *Ha-Sammim ha-Libbiyyim*, and *Ha-Refu'ot ha-Levaviyyot*, the latter from Latin.

ʿAmmār ibn Ali (d. 1020), an ophthalmologist, wrote *al-Muntakhab fī ʿIlāj al-ʿayn*, translated by Nathan ha-Me'ati under the title (not by him) *Shetalim ha-Nifradim ha-Mo'ilim la-Ayin*. Ali ibn Riḍwān (d. 1068) wrote *al-Uṣūl fī-al-Ṭibb* which Kalonymus b. Kalonymus translated into Hebrew in Arles in 1307 under the title *Ha-ʿAmmud be-Shorshei ha-Refu'ah*. His *Sharḥ Kitāb al-Ṣināʿa al-Saghīra*, on a work by Galen, is translated as *Perush Melakhah Ketannah* by Samuel ibn Tibbon, done in Béziers in 1199. Another rendering from the Latin, by Hillel b. Samuel, is called *Sefer ha-Tenge*. ʿAmmār's *al-Ustuqṣāt*, was translated into Hebrew as *Perush ba-yesodot* by an unknown scholar. Aḥmed al-Jazzār (11th century) is the author of *al-Iʿtimād*, on simple cures, which in Hebrew is the anonymous *Sefer ha-Ma'alot*. His *Zād al-Musāfir* (viaticum) is *Ẓeidat ha-Derakhim* by Moses ibn Tibbon in 1259, *Ẓeidah la-Oreḥim* by Abraham b. Isaac, and *Ya'ir Nativ* by an unknown translator. He also wrote on forgetfulness, in Hebrew *Iggeret ha-Shikhḥah* by Nathan ha-Me'ati.

Abu al-Qāsim Zahrawī of Spain (11th century) compiled *al-Taṣrīf*, on medical practice, which was rendered into Hebrew by Shem Tov b. Isaac Tartasi (1261–64) and called *Sefer ha-Shimmush*. *He-Ḥafeẓ ha-Shalem*, a medical compendium, is the version by Meshullam b. Jonah (1287) of a no longer extant Arabic original, a compendious work in two tractates and 14 sections. Ibn Ṣoar (d. 1162) wrote *al-Taysir fī-al-Mudāwāt* *wa al-Tadbīr* (which in the Hebrew of an unknown translator is *Ha-Ḥelek ha-Kolel*) and *Kitāb al-Aghdhiya*, on foods, which was converted into Hebrew by Nathan ha-Me'ati in about 1275 under the title *Sefer ha-Mezonot*. His work on the difference between sugar and honey became in the Hebrew version of Bon Senior ibn Ḥisdai *Ma'amar ba-Hevdel bein ha-Devash ve-ha-Sukkar*. Ibn Rushd (Averroes) was both philosopher and physician. In the latter capacity his work *Kitāb Kulliyyāt fī-al-Ṭibb*, a compendium, was titled *Klal* by Solomon b. Abraham in his translation, as well as in that of an anonymous translator. It is also unknown who translated *Maqāla fī-al-Teriak, Simplicia*, which is called *Peshatim be-Rippui Ḥola'ei ha-Guf*, and the work on purgatives, titled *Shorashim Kolelim*. His tract on diarrhea was translated into Hebrew by Jacob ha-Katan under the title *Ma'amar ha-Shilshul*. Among Jewish writers on medical subjects, Isaac Yisre'eli composed *Kitāb al-Adwiya al-Mufrada wa-al-Aghdhiya*, on cures and foods, and it was rendered into Hebrew by an unknown translator under the name *Sefer ha-Misadim*. Likewise anonymous are the three Hebrew versions of *Kitāb al-Bawl* ("on urine"); *Bi-Ydi'at ha-Sheten, Marot ha-Sheten*, and *Sefer ha-Shetanim*. So are also the book on fevers, *Kitāb al-Ḥummayāt*, in Hebrew *Sefer ha-Kaddaḥot*, and 50 aphorisms, not known in Arabic, called *Musar ha-Rofe'im*. *Maimonides' writings include *fī-al-Bawāsīr* ("on hemorrhoids") called, in an anonymous Hebrew version, *Bi-Refu'at ha-Teḥorim*, a work on intercourse *fī-al-Jim'a*, translated by Zerahiah Ḥen and called *Ma'amar ha-Mishgal*, and *Fuṣūl Mūsā*, aphorisms, also rendered by Zerahiah and by Nathan ha-Me'ati under the title *Pirkei Moshe*. Moses ibn Tibbon is the translator of *fī al-Sumūm* ("on poisons") which, in Hebrew, is called *Ha-Ma'amar ha-Nikhbad*. Solomon b. Yaish (d. 1343) wrote a commentary on ibn Sīnā's *Qānūn*, of which an extract in Hebrew was made by Jacob Kaphanton. As the Christian West learned the medical knowledge transmitted and composed in Arabic, its physicians also began to write, generally in Latin. Nicolaus of the Salerno school of medicine (1150–1200) prepared an *Antidotarium* which is known by the same name in the Hebrew rendering of Jacob. Petrus Hispanus (d. 1276) produced a medical compendium, *Thesaurus pauperum*, translated as *Oẓar ha-Aniyyim* in an anonymous version, and *Oẓar ha-Dallim* in the rendering of Todros Moses Bondoa, 1394. Lamprandi's (d. 1296) *Chirurgia Parva* is abridged in an anonymous Hebrew version titled *Alanfranchina*, and *ha-Yad* in Hebrew. Bernard de Gardon is the author of *Lilium Practica*, which is called *Ḥokhmah Nishlemet bi-Melekhet Medicinae* (c. 1305). In the version of Moses b. Samuel it is titled *Peraḥ ha-Refu'ot ha-Sali*, and in that of Jekuthiel b. Solomon of Narbonne, *Shoshan ha-Refu'ah* (1387). He also wrote *Regimen Acutarum Aegritudinum de Phlebotomia*, and *de Medicinarum gradibus*, all three of which were translated anonymously and titled respectively *Ḥibbur be-Hanhagot ha-Ḥaddot, Ha-Ma'amar be-Hakkazah*, and *Sefer ha-Madregot*. Arnaldus of Villanova (d. 1317/18) is the author of *Regimen sanitatis*, which in Hebrew is called *Ma'amar be-Hanhagat ha-Beri'ut* by the translator Israel Kaslari (1327), and *Hanhagot ha-Beri'ut* in the anonymous version. His *Arnavdina* is called *Practica* in Israel Kaslari's version.

Gentile da Foligna (d. 1348) composed a book on practice, *Prattiche, Nisyonot* in its anonymous Hebrew version, and *Consilium*, which is called *Eẓah* by its Hebrew translator, probably Joshua of Bologna. Guy de Gauliac, a surgeon in Avignon (d. 1363), prepared a *Chirurgia magna*, translated by an unknown scholar; the beginning and end are unfortunately missing. He also produced a *Chirurgia Parva*, translated into Hebrew by Asher b. Moses (1468), and titled *Giddu'a Kaẓar*. John Jacobi (1366), wrote *Secretarius practicus*. It is available in two anonymous Hebrew renderings: *Sod ha-Melakhah* and *Sod ha-Pratikah*. Gerard de Salo composed a commentary on the ninth book of Al-Rāzī's *al-Manṣūrī* titled in *Nomum mansoris*; Abraham Avigdor made an abridged translation, and Leon Joseph a full one in 1394. His *introductarium juvenum*, on the care of the body, was likewise done in Hebrew by Leon Joseph and called *Meishir ha-Matḥilim*, and his treatise on fever, *de Febribus*, was translated by Abraham Avigdor. Bernard Alberti (1339–58) compiled an *Introductarium in practicam*, a collection of prescriptions, done in Hebrew by Abraham Avigdor under the title *Mavo ba-Melakhah*. Albertus Magnus is the author of discussions on six needs of the body, which Moses Ḥabib called *She'elot u-Teshuvot* in his Hebrew version of it.

Jews were interested not only in philosophy and the sciences, but also in what can be called the humanities. They translated and wrote a good deal of popular literature, and they also cultivated eloquence, linguistics, and poetry. Mention should be made of the great popularity among them of all sorts of divinations, called *Goralot*, including astrology, mantic, and facial features. Among the foreign creations which made their way into Hebrew are the fables of Aesop, known as *Ḥidot Esopito*, and *Kalila and Dimna* by the Indian Bidpai. Its anonymous Hebrew translation is the source of all European versions made from its Latin rendering by the convert John of Capua (1262–78). Another Hebrew text prepared by Jacob b. Eleazar (d. 1223) is less literal than the other. The story of a demon who entered a woman and was expelled by a man, which is found in an Indian source and in the *1001 Nights*, is told in *Ma'amar Midyenei Ishaḥ*. *Mishlei *Sindabar*, the Hebrew counterpart of the very popular *Seven Sages*, although originally of Indian origin, is important as the link which connects the eastern type of individual and the western type.

The history of Alexander the Great, originating in Callisthenes' Greek story, was popular in Jewish literature from talmudic times. The medieval Hebrew book, *Sefer Alexander Mokedon ve-Korotov*, said to be the work of Samuel ibn Tibbon or Judah al-Ḥarizi, is a translation of an Arabic original. Immanuel b. Jacob did another *Toledot Alexander* from the Latin. It should also be noted that sayings gleaned by various authors were also attractive to Jews, so that books like *Sefer ha-Musar, Mishlei Arav*, or *Mishlei Anashim ha-Ḥakhamim*, not to speak of works in which they are introduced *en passant*, are all translations from the Arabic, whether from one work or from many. A good example is presented by Ibn Gabirol's *Mivḥar ha-Peninnim*, discussed above. A work of consolation, allegedly sent to a friend who sustained a loss, is the *Ḥibbur Yafeh me-ha-Yeshu'ah* by Nissim b. Jacob ibn Shahin of Kairouan, a Hebrew translation of his Arabic original. The *Maqāmāt* of al-Ḥarīrī (1054–1121), a literary genre characterized by rhymed prose and metrical verse, in which beauty of language was the major objective, were translated by Judah al-Ḥarizi under the title *Maḥbarot Iti'el*. Abraham ibn Ḥisdai produced a Hebrew version, called *Ben ha-Melekh ve-ha-Nazir*, of an Arabic translation of the original Indian tale of *Barlaam and Josaphat*, and Kalonymus b. Kalonymus composed *Iggeret Ba'alei Ḥayyim*, which is a discussion between men and beasts and is a free rendering of Epistle No. 21 of the *Epistles of the Ikwān al-Ṣafā'*.

Hebrew grammar and lexicography attracted the attention of a number of Jewish writers who were stimulated by the parallel studies of Arabic, and many of their works were originally written in Arabic, and only later translated into Hebrew. The comparative lexicographic study of Judah ibn Quraish (tenth century) was not translated until modern times. Judah Ḥayyuj (early 11th century) wrote on verbs with quiescent letters, and geminative verbs. These tracts were first translated by Moses ha-Kohen Gikatilla as *Otiyyot ha-Sefer ve-ha Meshekh*, and later, by Abraham ibn Ezra as *Otiyyot ha-Naḥ*, *Ba'alei ha-Kefel*, and *ha-Nikkud*. The master work of Hebrew grammar by Jonah ibn Janāḥ, *Kitāb al-Luma'*, was translated into Hebrew by Judah ibn Tibbon, and the lexicon, *Kitāb al-Uṣūl*, was translated by Isaac b. Judah, and by Isaac ha-Levi, both translations going only to the letter *lamed*. A complete translation was made by Judah ibn Tibbon in 1171. Ibn Jarah's shorter work, *al-mustalḥiq*, is called *Sefer ha-Hassagah* by its Hebrew translator Obadiah (c. 1300). Judah ibn Bal'am compiled a work on Hebrew particles *Ḥurūf al-Ma'āni*, rendered as *Otiyyot ha-Inyamim* in an anonymous Hebrew version; and *al-Af'āl Mushtaqqa min al-Asmā'*, a work on verbs derived from nouns, which in its anonymous Hebrew rendering is *Ha-Pe'alim she-Hem mi-Gizrat ha-Shemot*. He also is the author of a short tract on the proper reading of the Bible, *Hadāyat al-Qāri'*, which was rendered into Hebrew either by Nethanel b. Meshullam or by Menahem b. Nethanel under the title *Horayat ha-Kore*.

Some miscellaneous compositions include halakhic writings of Hai Gaon (d. 1038) such as *al-Buyū'āt*, which was translated into Hebrew by Isaac b. Reuben and was called *Sefer ha-Mikkaḥ ve-ha-Mimkar*, and, in an anonymous Hebrew version *Mishpetei ha-Tena'im ve-Halva'ot*, and the book on oaths which in its anonymous Hebrew translation is titled *Mishpetei Shevu'ot* or *Sefer ha-Shevu'ot*. A metrical version also exists, *Sha'arei Dinei Mamonot ve-Sha'arei Shevu'ot*. Joseph ibn 'Aknīn, who wrote an introduction to the Talmud and a book on biblical and talmudic weights and measures, is represented in Hebrew translation by *Mevo ha-Talmud*, perhaps by an Abraham Yerushalmi, and by an anonymous version *Ma'amar al ha-Middot*. Of Abraham Maimonides' moralistic and pietistic work *Kifāyat al-'Abidin*, only a short section was rendered into Hebrew. A work on liturgy, *Mitzvot Zemanniyyot*, by Israel Yisre'eli, was translated into Hebrew by Don Shem Tov b. Ardutiel. Of Joseph ibn 'Aknīn's *Ṭibb al-Nufūs*, only the first chapter was translated under the name *Marpeh ha-Nefashot*.

BIBLIOGRAPHY: Steinschneider, Uebersetzungen (1893, repr. 1956); E. Bevan and C.J. Singer (eds.), *Legacy of Israel* (1927), 173–314. **ADD. BIBLIOGRAPHY:** M. Goshen-Gottstein, *Medieval Hebrew Syntax and Vocabulary as Influenced by Arabic* (Heb., 1951); B.R. Goldstein, in: *Isis*, 72:2 (1981), 237–51; A. Ivry, in: *Rencontres de cultures dans la philosophie médiévale* (1990), 167–86; J. Lomba, in: *Mediaevalia, Textos e Estudios*, 7–8 (1995), 199–220; S. Harvey, in: *The Cambridge Companion to Medieval Jewish Philosophy* (2003), 258–80; S. Harvey (ed.), *The Medieval Hebrew Encyclopedias of Science and Philosophy* (2000); M. McVaugh and L. Ferre, *The Tabula Antidotarii of Armengaud Blasi and Its Hebrew Translation* (2000); G. Freudenthal, in: JQR, 93:1–2 (2002), 29–115.

[Abraham Solomon Halkin / Angel Sáenz-Badillos (2nd ed.)]

TRANSNISTRIA, geographical designation, referring to the area in the Ukraine situated between the Bug and Dniester rivers. The term is derived from the Romanian name for the Dniester (Nistru) and was coined after the occupation of the area by German and Romanian troops, in World War II. Before the war the area had a population of 3,400,000, but in the course of the occupation it was reduced to 2,250,000, as a result of the mobilization of men and of mass flights.

Jewish Population

Before 1939 the Jewish population was 300,000 according to the statistical data of 1926. According to reports of the Nazi Einsatzkommandos ("action groups") which entered the area in July 1941 in the wake of the occupying troops, two-thirds of the local Jewish population had fled the area. However, there remained local Jews and Jewish refugees, primarily from neighboring *Bessarabia; these refugees had fled previously from the advancing German troops. It must also be assumed that many local Jews were apprehended while escaping and were murdered by German troops or by Einsatzkommandos. In general, Einsatzgruppe "D" under the command of Otto Ohlendorf, was most active in Transnistria. In the north Einsatzkommando "10B," and in the south "11B" were also active. Their reports contain some information on the murder actions committed by the units (e.g., in Yampol, Kokina, Mogilev), but the figures given on the local population are far too low and unrealistic. To illustrate the magnitude of the murder actions perpetrated by the Nazis: in one town alone, *Dubossary, on the east bank of the Dniester, two common graves contained the bodies of 3,500 Jews from Dubossary itself and 7,000 from the vicinity, killed in the town after being rounded up by the Nazis.

Deportations to Transnistria

After its occupation Transnistria became the destination for deported Romanian Jews. At the end of July 1941, 25,000 Jewish survivors from towns in northern Bessarabia were expelled

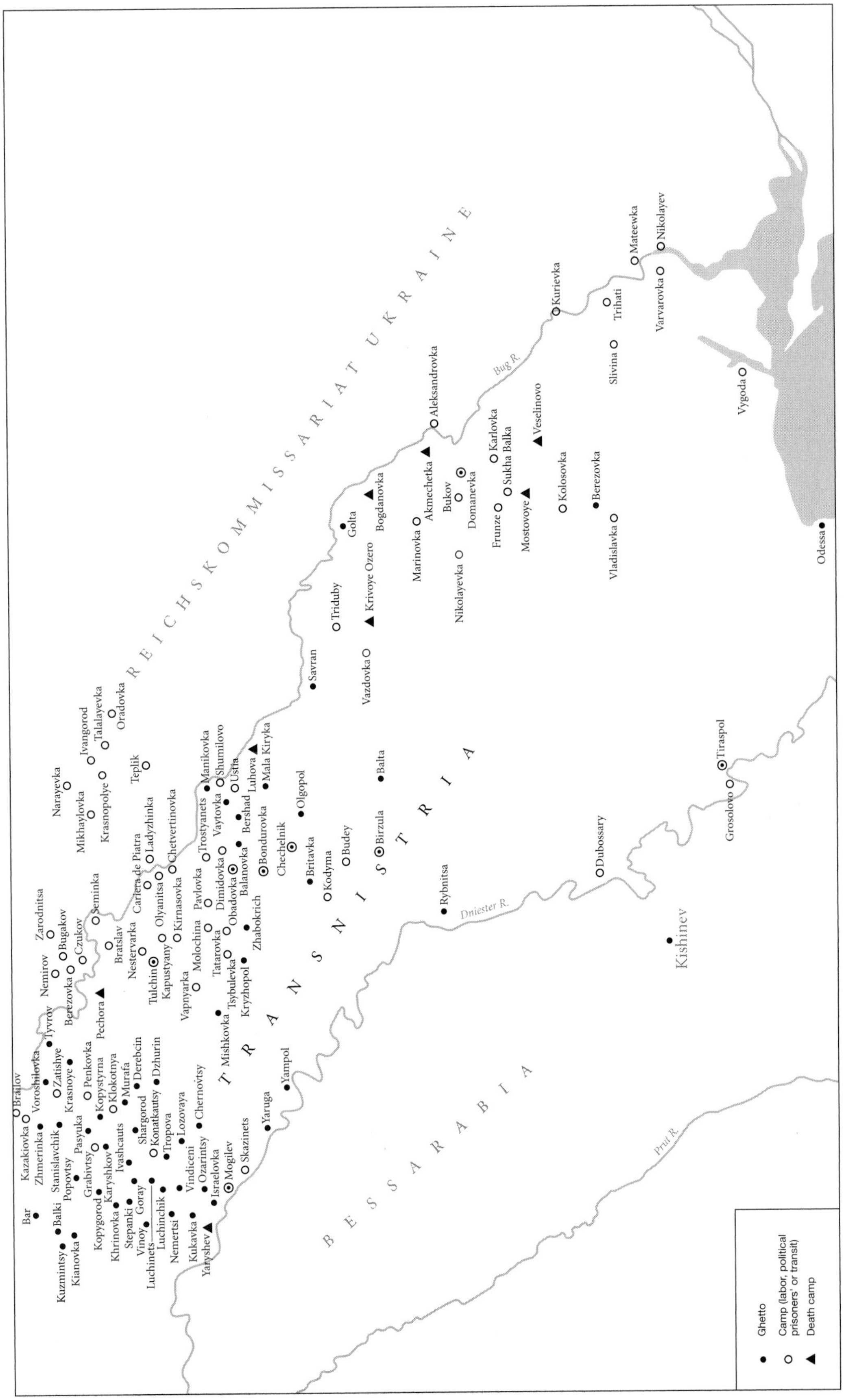

Camps and ghettos in Transnistria. Based on T. Lavi (ed.), Pinkas ha-Kehillot: Romanyah, *vol 1, Jerusalem, 1969.*

to Transnistria by the Romanians, but they were sent back to Bessarabia by the Germans, after 4,000 refugees were murdered. Other groups sent to Transnistria wandered about the area of Mogilev, Skazinets, and Yampol for about two weeks, before the Romanians agreed to their return. Finally, on August 17–18, another 20,500 were readmitted to Bessarabia; many were shot or thrown into the river, by both German and Romanian troops.

Systematic deportations began in the middle of September. In the course of the next two months, all the surviving Jews of Bessarabia and *Bukovina (except for some 20,000 Jews of *Chernovtsy) and a part of the Jewish population of the *Dorohoi district of Old Romania, were dispatched across the Dniester. This first wave of deportations reached 118,847 by mid-November 1941.

Deportations resumed at the beginning of the summer of 1942, affecting 4,200 Jews from Chernovtsy and 450 from Dorohoi. A third series of deportations from Old Romania came in July 1942 affecting Jews who had evaded the forced labor decrees, as well as their families, Communist sympathizers, and Bessarabian Jews who had been in Old Romania and Transylvania during the Soviet occupation of Bessarabia in June 1940, and had asked to be repatriated to their homes. Of the latter group, 350 Jews were shot to death by *SS troops on their arrival at Berezovka (in Transnistria).

The Communist sympathizers, among them many socialists, were taken to a special concentration camp in Vapnyarka Transnistria. Some individual deportation orders were directed against Jewish merchants and industrialists accused of economic sabotage, bribery, and similar "economic crimes."

The Romanian general staff submitted an additional list of 12,000 Jews who had violated the forced labor laws. In the meantime, however, the Romanian government policy changed and the deportation of this group was not implemented; neither did the Romanian government give its consent to Germany's insistence on the deportation of all Romania's Jews. According to a German source, a total of Romanian archival sources 146,000 Jews were deported to Transnistria. In December 1943 the Romanian Ministry of Interior informed its government that 50,741 deportees had survived.

Ghettos and Expulsions

The status of the Jews in Transnistria was determined by a decree (Nov. 11, 1941) serving to follow up the Tighina Agreement, which expressly referred to the imprisonment of Jews in ghettos. At the end of the month large numbers of Jews were dispatched to the northern part of Transnistria. In the southern part they were put into several large ghettos in the Golta district: 54,000 in Bogdanovka, 12,000 in Domanevka, and 18,000 in Akmechetka. All 48,000 Jews in the Bogdanovka concentration camp were murdered by Ukrainian police and local German members of the SS and Sonderkommando R, on the initiative of Fleischer, the German adviser to the district commander. At first, 5,000 sick and maimed Jews were locked into sheds and burned alive, and in the course of the following two months the remaining inmates of the camps were shot to death and their bodies cremated. In January and February 1942, 18,000 Jews were murdered in the Domanevka 18,000 and Akmechetka. Another 28,000 Jews were murdered by SS troops and local German police in German villages in the Berezovka area. By March 1943, only 485 Jews were still alive in the southern area, between *Odessa and Mogilev; of these 60 were in Odessa itself. When Odessa was taken, by Romanian troops in October 1941, 25,000 Jews were killed on the personal orders of Antonescu after a Russian-made time bomb exploded in a building housing high-ranking Romanian officers. The rest of the Jews of the city were driven out. Members of the local Ukrainian militia participated in the murder though in many cases Ukrainians provided Jews with food and hideouts. The deportees from Bessarabia, Bukovina, and Dorohoi were sent to the northern part of Transnistria. At first they wandered from place to place, as some of the towns refused to accept them. Some groups from southern Bukovina had money and bribed the local authorities for the right to stay (e.g., in Mogilev). In some cases entire communities were expelled as a group together with the community leaders, e.g., the communities of *Radauti and *Suceava; the latter also saved the community's funds with which they managed to obtain better living conditions. In some instances the deportees took it upon themselves to repair local factories in ruins – as in the case of the sugar factory in Vindiceni. In Mogilev, where the local Romanian authorities at first refused a residential permit to the deportees, a group of 500 Jewish deportees successfully undertook repairs of the local electric power station and a local foundry; they established a repair workshop for automobiles, and were generally useful in the rehabilitation of the city. In some of the towns – *Shargorod, Dzhurin, and Mogilev – Jewish committees were set up comprising community leaders from Romania and representatives of the local Jewish population. In other places the Romanians themselves appointed local Jewish committees and forced them to collaborate with the regime. After the war some of the latter committees were brought to trial by both the Russians and the Romanians on charges of harshly dealing with the deportees. On the other hand, others, especially former leaders of their communities, sacrificed themselves for the welfare of the refugees.

In places where the local Jews still survived, the deportees received shelter in homes or in those synagogues which had not been destroyed. Jewish refugees from the Ukraine (who had crossed the Bug River) were hidden by local Jews or by the deportees from Romania. In some cases the local committees provided them with forged identification documents. The first winter (1941–42) was extremely harsh, with temperatures dropping to 40° C below zero. Many died of cold or starved to death. The bodies of the dead accumulated in the cemeteries until the spring, when graves could be dug for them. Various epidemics, such as typhus and dysentery, also claimed tens of thousands of victims. In Dzhurin, Shargorod, and Mogilev the local committees succeeded in organizing the internal life of the refugee communities. In some ghettos the committees established public kitchens, hospitals, orphanages, bakeries, and soap factories, and organized sales cooperatives. All this helped make life more bearable. Post offices were organized by a number of Jewish committees, and a register of deaths and births was kept. Jewish police detachments were formed, but these not infrequently became a tool in the hands of the occupation power, who used them for drafting men and women for forced labor. Improved internal organization controlled epidemics. In the second winter (1942–43) only four out of 25 patients died in an epidemic in the town of Shargorod, as compared to 1,400 the year before. The doctors among the deportees vigorously combated the epidemics, and many died in the execution of their task. In those camps where no internal organization was created, the mortality rate reached almost 100%.

The Jews were completely at the mercy of the local authorities. Their situation was especially grave in the area adjoining the Bug River, as from time to time the Germans crossed the west bank to use Jews for forced labor on the other side of the river. At Pechora, a sign at the camp entrance identified it as a "death camp." There were several German raids from across the Bug, and in the fall of 1942, 1,000 Jews were dragged across the river. In the camp at *Bar, which was over the Bug River and in German occupied territory 12,000 Jews were put to death on Oct. 20, 1942. The people who had been taken to eastern Ukraine for forced labor were put to death as soon as their job was done, while those who were unable to work were instantly murdered. The head of the *Tulchin district was particularly efficient in handing Jews over to the Germans, especially to the Todt Organisation. Tens of thousands were murdered in the second deportation to the German-administered territories beyond the Bug, in such places as *Gaisin, Krasnopolye, and Trihati. In the spring of 1942 the Romanians initiated the deportation of several thousand Jews to the other side of the Bug, in order to dispose of them; this however, did not fit in with *Eichmann's overall plans for the "Final Solution" and he protested to the German Foreign Office; as a result, the Jews were returned to Transnistria where some of them were murdered. The special camp at Vapnyarka for Communist sympathizers fed the prisoners poisoned beans which caused paralysis and death.

Aid Operations

From the very beginning, Jewish leaders and institutions in Bucharest made efforts to provide help to the deportees. In December 1941 the Council of Romanian Jewish Communities received permission from Antonescu to extend aid to the refugees. The special central committee established for this purpose collected money and contributions in kind, and dispatched financial aid, clothing, and medicines to the refugees. Other sources of help were provided by the Joint and the Zionist Organization and by special committees established by natives of the deported communities who were residents of Old Romania.

The central aid committee was finally granted permission in 1943 to send a delegation to visit the area. The papal nuncio, Monsignor Andrea Cassulo, visited Transnistria from April 27 to May 5, 1943, and an International Red Cross mission arrived there in December of that year. Jewish leaders in Bucharest established contact with Jewish organizations abroad, and obtained financial aid for the deportees from the American Jewish *Joint Distribution Committee, the Rescue Committee of the Zionist Organization, the World Jewish Congress, and OSE. In the first two years, 500,000,000 lei were spent in aid to the Jews in Transnistria, of which about 160,000,000 was spent in cash and the rest provided salt, coal, glasspanes, wood, medicines, and equipment for artisans.

In February 1944, as a result of Cassulo's visit, the pope donated 1,300,000 lei to alleviate the conditions of the Jews of Transnistria.

Rescue and Assistance

At the first reports of deportations to Transnistria, W. Fildermann made efforts to stop the deportations and, failing in this, tried to alleviate the refugees' plight. A secret committee was formed in Bucharest, with both Fildermann and Zionist leaders participating. The committee's major purpose was to put a stop to the deportations. In November 1941 it persuaded Antonescu not to deport 20,000 Jews considered essential for the smooth functioning of the city. In the spring of 1942, as a result of German pressure, 4,000 of the remaining Jews of Chernovtsy were also deported. The deportation of the Jews of Southern Transylvania was canceled during the fall of 1942 for reasons yet to be understood; this deportation was intended to be the first stage in the deportation of all the Jews of Romania to the death camps in Poland. One factor was the protests of foreign diplomats, such as the ambassadors of neutral countries and the papal nuncio, and of the representatives of the International Red Cross, leaders of the Romanian Church, the queen mother Helena, and leaders of Romanian political parties. This intervention, along with the turning tide of the war, prompted the Romanian government in November 1942 to enter into negotiations with Jewish leaders in Bucharest on the return of the deportees and the emigration to Palestine of 75,000 survivors.

In March 1943 a selection commission was sent to Transnistria by the Romanian government. In April Antonescu approved the repatriation of 5,000 orphaned children, and of persons who had been "innocently" deported. As early as December 1942 the German Foreign Ministry, the German minister in Bucharest, Manfred von Killinger, and Eichmann's representative, Gustav Richter, protested against any decisions to repatriate Romanian Jews from Transnistria. In March 1943 Eichmann informed *Himmler of the planned emigration of Jewish orphans from Transnistria to Palestine and asked the German Foreign Ministry to prevent it.

In the spring of 1943 Fildermann, who in the meantime had himself been deported to Transnistria, called upon the Romanian government to permit the return of all the deportees. By mid-December 1943 the first group, consisting of 1,500 Jews from Dorohoi were allowed to go back to their homes. Repatriation was stopped at the end of January 1944, but the secret committee persevered and in March a group of 1,846 orphans, out of a total of 4,500, arrived in Jassy. Earlier, in February 1944, the chief rabbi of Palestine, Isaac *Herzog, appealed to the papal nuncio in Istanbul, Monsignor Roncalli (later Pope *John XXIII), to ensure the safety of the Transnistria deportees, now threatened by the withdrawing German armies. Roncalli transmitted this request to Monsignor Cassulo, the nuncio in Bucharest. On March 15, 1944, the Soviet armies crossed the Bug. Within five days they advanced northward up to the Dniester. A Jewish commission from Bucharest had in the meantime arrived in the south and arranged for the repatriation of 2,518 Jews in the towns of *Tiraspol and *Balta to Romania. On their arrival in Romania, 563 deportees from the Vapnyarka camp were seized by the Romanians and sent to the Targu-Jiu concentration camp in the western part of the country. The Transnistria deportations resulted in 88,294 deaths, out of a total of 146,555 persons deported. At least another 175,000 persons among the local Jewish inhabitants of Transnistria also fell victim to the Holocaust.

See also *Romania.

BIBLIOGRAPHY: A. Dallin, *Odessa 1941–1944; a Case Study of Soviet Territory under Foreign Rule* (1957), 45–110; M. Carp, *Cartea Neagră*, 3 (1947); PK Romanyah, 349–86, bibl. 386–8; J.S. Fisher, *The Forgotten Cemetery* (1970). **ADD. BIBLIOGRAPHY:** J. Ancel, *Transnistria, 1941–1943: The Romanian Mass Murder Campaigns* (2003); R. Ioanid, *Holocaust in Romania: The Destruction of Jews and Gypsies under the Antonescu Regime, 1940–1944* (2000).

[Theodor Lavi]

TRANSOXIANA, ancient region of central Asia, between the Oxus and Jaxartes rivers, known to the Arabs as Ma-Waran-Nahr ("beyond the river"). In the medieval period it was divided into several provinces, one being Khwarizm, with its two capitals Khiva and Urgench, and another Soghd, with the two capitals *Samarkand and *Bukhara. These four cities have been connected in various periods with Jewish settlements, mostly consisting of Persian Jews who had penetrated into these remote regions from the central provinces of Persia and *Khursan. According to an ancient Pahlavi tradition, Khwarizm was built by Narses (fifth century), the son of Yezdegerd I and his Jewish wife Shushan Dokt, daughter of the exilarch. That Jews lived in this region in early Islamic times can be inferred from the work of the ninth-century Arab historian, al-Ṭabarī (II, 1238); recounting that the shah of Khwarizm assembled the leaders of the various communities of his domain, he mentions the "Habar," a term usually applied to Jews. The 13th-century Muslim historian al-Umari mentions expressly in his *Masālik al-Absār* that there were in Khwarizm 100 Jewish families and the same number of Christian and that they were not permitted to exceed this total.

Khiva (see *Khorezm), a large city on the bank of the Oxus which was a central meeting place for merchants, had, according to one manuscript version of the travels of *Benjamin of Tudela (ed. A. Asher, 1 (1840), 128; 2 (1840), 168–9), a community of 8,000 Jews. *Solomon b. Samuel, the author of a Hebrew-Persian dictionary of the Bible, known as *Sefer ha-Meliẓah* (c. 1339), lived in Urgench in the 14th century.

BIBLIOGRAPHY: E.N. Adler, *Jews in Many Lands* (1905), 196ff.; A. Yaari, *Sifrei Yehudei Bukharah* (1942); idem, in: *Moznayim*, 6 (1937/38), 496–503; W.J. Fischel, in: HJ, 7 (1945), 42ff.; I. Ben-Zvi, *The Exiled and the Redeemed* (1961²), 56–58, 205–13.

[Walter Joseph Fischel]

TRANSPLANTS. Advances in medical knowledge and technology have made possible the transplantation of organs from a deceased (or, in the case of some organs such as a kidney, from a living) person into another individual stricken with disease, and this technological advance reached an acme with the transplantation of a human heart. Such operations raised many moral, theological, legal, social, and philosophical problems.

With regard to the general permissibility, Rabbi I. *Jakobovits is of the opinion that a donor may endanger his life or health to supply a "spare" organ to a recipient whose life would thereby be saved, only if the probability of saving the recipient's life is substantially greater than the risk to the donor's life or health. This principle is applicable to all organ transplantation where live donors are used as a source of the organ in question. Rabbi Y. Waldenberg (Responsa *Ẓiẓ Eliezer*, 9 (1967), no. 45) discusses at length the question of whether a healthy person may or must donate one of his organs to save the life of another. The majority opinion seems to be that a small risk may be undertaken by the donor if the chances for success in the recipient are substantial.

Most of the rabbinic responsa literature concerning organ transplantation deals with eye (cornea) transplants. The basic halakhic principles governing eye transplants, however, are applicable to nearly all other organ transplants. Kidney and heart transplants involve several additional unique questions. The classic responsum is that of Rabbi I.Y. *Unterman (*Shevet mi-Yhudah* (1955), 313ff.) who states that the prohibitions on deriving benefit from the dead, desecrating the dead, and delaying the burial of the dead are all set aside because of *pikku'aḥ nefesh* – the consideration of saving life. These prohibitions would remain if there is no threat to life involved in the condition for the treatment of which the transplant is being done. For example, there is no *pikku'aḥ nefesh* involved in a nose transplant. Rabbi Unterman considers eye transplants to involve *pikku'aḥ nefesh* because blindness is a situation in which a person so afflicted may fall down a flight of stairs or into a ditch and be killed. What of a person blind in one eye? The concept of *pikku'aḥ nefesh* does not apply. However, argues Rabbi Unterman, once the donor eye is implanted into the recipient, it is not considered dead but a living organ. Thus, the prohibitions on deriving benefit from the dead and delaying burial of the dead are not applicable since no dead organ is involved. For the same reason, the problem of ritual defilement or *tumah* is nonexistent, in regard to the transplanted eye. Rabbi J.J. Greenwald (*Kol Bo al Avelut*, 1 (1947), 45ff.) presents reasoning from which the conclusion can be drawn that one may not remove the entire eye from a deceased donor for transplantation; only the cornea may be used since a whole eye represents flesh whereas the cornea alone is considered skin. Furthermore, one cannot overcome the problems of desecrating and delaying burial of the dead without invoking the concept of *pikku'aḥ nefesh*. Thus, Rabbi Greenwald, as most authorities, would only permit eye grafts for a person blind in both eyes. Rabbi I. Glickman (*No'am*, 4 (1961), 206–17) added to Rabbi Unterman's theses described above that one may perform a transplant only if the donor gave permission prior to his death. Most rabbinic responsa agree with this requirement.

The problem of eye banks is raised by Rabbi M. Steinberg (*No'am*, 3 (1960), 87ff.). Since the permissibility of organ transplants rests primarily on the overriding consideration of *pikku'aḥ nefesh*, then it would seem that the recipient would have to be at hand (*lefaneinu*). Rabbi Steinberg states that since the number of blind persons is so large, a recipient is considered to be always at hand. Rabbi Jakobovits also permits organs or blood to be donated for deposit in banks provided there is a reasonable certainty that they will eventually be used in life-saving operations including the restoration or preservation of eyesight. Rabbi Unterman, at the end of his remarks on eye transplants, also states that donations to blood banks are permissible.

The question of whether the eye of a non-Jewish donor may be used for an eye transplant is raised by Rabbi M. Feinstein (*Iggerot Moshe*, pt. *Yoreh De'ah* (1959), no. 229). He draws the conclusion that it is permissible for a Jew to use the eye of a gentile donor.

Kidney transplants are governed by the same principles as those discussed above for eye transplants. In fact, many of the responsa deal with both eye and kidney transplants. In addition to cadaver kidneys, kidneys from live donors are used for transplantation. Here, new halakhic questions arise. Is the donor allowed to subject himself to the danger, however small, of the operation to remove one of his kidneys in order to save the life of another? Does the donor transgress the commandments to "take heed to thyself" (Deut. 4:9 and 4:15)? The Shulḥan Arukh and Maimonides in the *Yad* answer this question by stating as follows: "The Jerusalem Talmud concludes that one is obligated to put oneself even into a possibly dangerous situation [to save another's life]." The reason seems to be that the death of the sick person (i.e., the kidney recipient) without intervention is a certainty, whereas his (the donor's) death is only a possibility.

With regard to heart transplantations, medical and ethical guidelines have been established. Recommendations include the requirements that the surgical team shall have had extensive laboratory experience in cardiac transplantation, that death of the donor shall be certified by an independent group of physicians, and that the information and knowledge gained should be rapidly disseminated to the medical world.

From the halakhic point of view, the prohibitions dealing with desecrating the dead, delaying burial of the dead, and ritual defilement, are all set aside in the case of human heart transplantation, for the overriding consideration of *pikku'aḥ nefesh*, saving a life. The major halakhic problem remaining is the establishment of the death of the donor. Prior to death, the donor is in the category of a *gosses* (hopelessly ill patient) and one is prohibited from touching him or moving him or doing anything that might hasten his death. There are many types of death: mental death when a person's intellect ceases to function; social death when a person can no longer function in society; spiritual death when the soul leaves the body; and physiological or medical death. The Jewish legal or halakhic definition of death is that a person who has stopped breathing and whose heart is not beating is considered dead. This classic definition of death in the Talmud (Yoma 8:6–7; Yoma 85a; TJ, Yoma 8:5, 45a and Maimonides, Yad, Shabbat 2:19; Sh. Ar., OḤ 329:4) would be set aside if prospects for resuscitation of the patient, however remote, are deemed feasible.

On the assumption that the donor is absolutely and positively dead, most rabbinic authorities permit heart transplants. Rabbi Jakobovits has stated that "...in principle, I can see no objection in Jewish law to the heart operations recently carried out, provided the donors were definitely deceased at the time the organ was removed from them." Rabbi I. Arieli is also quoted as having said that heart transplants are permissible if the donor is definitely dead, but only with the family's consent. A similar pronouncement was made by Rabbi D. Lifshutz. Rabbi Unterman's published responsum (*No'am*, 13 (1970), 1–9) dealing specifically with heart transplants begins by stating that consent from the family of the donor must be obtained for several reasons. Touching briefly on the problem of organ banks, he states that freezing organs for later use is allowed provided there is a good chance that they will be used to save a life. Then the situation would be comparable to having the recipient at hand (*lefaneinu*). Rabbi Unterman concludes with the novel pronouncement that in the case of a human heart transplant recipient, removing the patient's old heart takes from him his hold on life (*ḥezkat ḥayyim*). Therefore, the removal of the recipient's heart can be sanctioned only if the risk of death resulting from the surgery is estimated to be smaller than the prospect for lasting success.

Dissenting from Rabbi Unterman's permissiveness toward heart transplants under the conditions described above is Rabbi J. Weiss who strongly condemns cardiac transplants as double murder (*Ha-Ma'or*, 20 (1968), no. 7, 1–9). Rabbi Feinstein also added his voice to those condemning heart transplants (*Ha-Pardes*, 43 (1969), no. 5). Careful reading of his lengthy responsum on this subject discloses the following clarification of his position: if the donor is definitely dead by all medical and Jewish legal criteria, then no murder of the donor would be involved and the removal of his heart or other organ to save another human life would be permitted. Concerning the recipient, he wrote at the time, when medical science will have progressed to the point where cardiac transplantation becomes an accepted therapeutic procedure with reasonably good chances for success, then the recipient shall no longer be considered murdered. Major obstacles such as organ rejection, tissue compatibility testing, and immunosuppressive therapy must be first overcome. Other responsa on cardiac transplantation are those of Rabbi S. *Goren (*Maḥanayim*, 122 (1969), 7–15), Rabbi Y. Gershuni (*Or Ha-Mizraḥ*, April 1969), Rabbi D.C. Gulewski (*Ha-Maor*, 21 (1969), no. 1, 1–16), Rabbi M. *Kasher (*No'am*, 13 (1970), 10–20), and Dr. J. Levi (*No'am*, 12 (1969), 289–313). The major concern of most, if not all, rabbis attempting to render legal rulings in heart transplant cases is the establishment of the death of the donor.

For a full legal discussion with later rulings, see *Medicine and the Law.

BIBLIOGRAPHY: I. Jakobovits, *Jewish Medical Ethics* (1959), 96ff.; idem, in: *Essays Presented to… I. Brodie* (1967), 188f.; F. Rosner, in: *Jewish Life*, 37 (1969), 38–51; idem, in: *Tradition*, 10 (1969), no. 4, 33–39.

[Fred Rosner]

TRANSYLVANIA (Rom. **Transilvania** or **Ardeal**; Ger. **Siebenbuergen**; Hung. **Erdély**), historic province now forming western *Romania. Each territorial component of this region has its own history, which has influenced the history of the Jews living among the Hungarians, Romanians, Germans, and other peoples inhabiting it. In 1940, as a result of the second arbitration decision of Vienna, the territory was divided between Hungary and Romania – northern Transylvania going to Hungary and southern Transylvania to Romania – where the Jews suffered different fates. In 1945 the whole of Transylvania reverted to Romania.

Transylvania has always been a center of routes connecting the Orient with the West, and southern Europe with northern Europe. Its location influenced the general development of the region, and in particular Jewish settlement from its beginnings. The first Jews arrived from the south – the Balkans and Turkey – by the trade routes to the north of Transylvania. It has, however, been surmised that a small Jewish settlement existed there, as one had also in neighboring Pannonia, during the first and second centuries C.E. when the territory was under Roman rule and constituted Roman Dacia, though there is no definite evidence for this assumption. Between 1571 and 1687, historic Transylvania and a number of the bordering territories formed an independent principality ruled by the Hungarian-Transylvanian princes. It was in this principality, which was adjacent to the Ottoman Empire and maintained close relations with it, that the first recorded Jewish settlement developed. The overwhelming majority of its members were Turkish Sephardi Jews. Their first organized Jewish community was in *Alba Iulia, the seat of the prince. A letter of protection of 1623 guaranteed the Jews extensive rights, but restricted their residence to this town only. However, despite the restrictions, Jews began to settle in other localities close to the mother community. The relations of the local Jews with the Jews in the north and the west attracted a small number of Ashkenazi settlers from distant places.

This first settlement also affected the development of the Transylvanian Christian sect of *Somrei Sabat, whose customs and prayer books were influenced by the Sephardi ritual. Although the princes, particularly Gabriel Bethlen, had promised the Jews certain rights, there were also schemings against them, and at the general assemblies of the classes it was suggested that the number of Jews be restricted. The first decision to this effect was passed as early as 1578.

With the close of the period of the independent principality and the beginning of Austrian rule, Jews also began to settle on the estates of noblemen who were not bound by the residence prohibitions already issued against Jews. (The aristocrats needed the Jews for the economic exploitation of their land, but provoked antisemitic feelings among their dependents in order to make the Jews afraid of them.) Most of the towns nevertheless remained closed to Jewish settlement. The revolutionary year of 1848 theoretically marked the end of the residence restrictions. There were then about 15,000 Jews in historic Transylvania. The number of Sephardim was declining and Ashkenazi settlers from the north – i.e., Poland – began to play an important role in community life. The number of Jews in historic Transylvania has been estimated at 2,000 in 1766; 5,175 in 1825; and 15,600 in 1850. Organizationally, between 1754 and 1879, the Jews were under the jurisdiction of a chief rabbi whose seat was in Alba Iulia. In 1866, when Transylvania was still ruled by the central government in Vienna, representatives of the Jewish communities gathered for the first time in *Cluj for a national conference to create a unified communal organization with regular organizational patterns.

The objectives of this congress did not materialize because in 1867 the whole of Transylvania was incorporated within Hungary, and Jewish communal organization followed that of Hungarian Jewry until the end of World War I. The religious schism which occurred within Hungarian Jewry after 1868–69 (see *Hungary) also left its imprint on Transylvania and, after struggles within the communities, separate Orthodox, *Neologist, and *Status Quo Ante communities were formed. The influence of *Ḥasidism, which penetrated Transylvania from the north, was powerful. During the period of the struggles and separations, the Jews of historic Transylvania numbered 25,142. By 1880, upon the completion of the new organization, they numbered 30,000. The majority of the communities, especially those with large memberships, joined the Orthodox trend. There were sharp controversies between the Ḥasidim and the rabbinist-Ashkenazi Jews, who in spiritual-religious matters turned to Pressburg (*Bratislava) as a center of authority. The Neologist communities, in which the Magyar assimilationist trend became strong, regarded Budapest as their center.

The densest Jewish population developed in northeastern Transylvania, whose territories bordered upon Poland and Moldavia, the urban centers of this region being *Sighet and *Satu Mare. Until its liquidation, the majority of Jews there remained loyal to traditional Jewish culture, and the predominant language was Yiddish. During the 19th century, Yiddish newspapers were published there, and several poets and authors published works in this language. In the western part of Transylvania, where the large urban centers were *Oradea and *Arad, the predominant language was Hungarian, while in the southwestern part of the region, whose center was *Timisoara, it was Hungarian and German. In the southeastern part, whose center was *Brasov, the Jews lived among a German population which influenced them culturally, but their social ties with it were not extensive. Although there was a large Romanian population in the whole of Transylvania, the Jews were not influenced culturally by the Romanian element until the end of World War I. On the contrary, in most places Jews were pioneers in spreading among the Romanian population the Magyar national trend of the central government in Budapest. The natural center of Transylvania, the town of Cluj – which also occasionally served as its official capital – was also a Jewish center during most of the 19th and 20th centuries. Cluj University, where Jews were also appointed professors, was an important intellectual center for Jews in historic Transylvania, while those in the western districts attended the University of Budapest.

From the beginning of the 20th century, the Jewish population in historic Transylvania only increased from 53,065 (2.2 percent of the total population) in 1900 to 64,674 (2.4 percent) in 1910. In the whole area currently known as Transylvania the Jews numbered 181,340 (3.57 percent) at the beginning of Romanian rule in 1920. The growth of the Jewish population and its dispersion throughout the region was linked to economic development, the establishment of industry, and the construction of the railway system. Jews played an important role in this development, at first in small trade and later in large-scale industrialization; they were also prominent in railroad construction. In general cultural life Jewish participation was considerable, and from 1860 Jews took an active part in political life. Jewish journalists were prominent and in particular assisted in raising the standard of the theater. Jewish producers active in Cluj before World War I were pioneers in the film industry in Hungary, among them Alexander *Korda. In the field of Jewish culture before the end of World War I there were Hebrew printing presses, and attempts were made to publish newspapers and weeklies in Hebrew, Yiddish, and Hungarian. Most communities had elementary schools.

In 1918–19 historic Transylvania and the other territories which constitute present-day Transylvania were transferred from Hungary to Romania. Links were established with Romanian Jewry and its center in Bucharest, but they remained very weak, with neither of the two sides willing to compromise; very few of the Hungarian-speaking Transylvanian Jews were prepared to change their cultural affiliations. Even after World War II and the Holocaust, many Transylvanian Jews continued to see themselves as "Hungarians of the Mosaic faith." Important secondary schools were established in Cluj (where the language of instruction was also Hebrew), Timisoara, and Oradea. A Hungarian-Jewish daily, **Uj Kelet* (first appearing as a weekly), was published in Cluj from 1918 until 1940; its publication was resumed in Israel in 1948. Jewish works were published under its aegis, and its supporters and members of the editorial board were active in Jewish cultural life and even in the general political sphere, among them the editor-in-chief, E. *Marton. In the interwar period there were 110 organized Jewish communities in Transylvania, of which 23 belonged to the Neologist organization, 80 were Orthodox, and the remainder belonged to the Status Quo Ante organization. The headquarters of the Neologist communities were in Cluj, while those of the Orthodox communities were at first in *Bistrita and later in *Turda.

Zionist activity, which had already commenced at the time of the first Zionist congress, developed to large proportions. Every trend of the Zionist movement reached the major towns and even the smallest localities of the region. Until 1927, the Zionist national headquarters were situated in Cluj, after which its organizational section was transferred to Timisoara. In association with the Zionist movement, a national Jewish party, active mainly after 1930, campaigned on a large scale in parliamentary and municipal elections. The party delegates in the Romanian Parliament fought against anti-Jewish discrimination by the government, and for promulgation of the *minority rights expressly granted the Jews by the Trianon peace treaty. A number of Jews, especially in the western districts, who had remained politically attached to the Hungarians, organized a separate political party in Transylvania. Jews rose to the leadership and were elected to municipal councils and as delegates to the Parliament in Bucharest. A limited number of Jews were also active in the national Romanian parties, and slightly more in the Social Democratic Party. Jews also belonged to the underground Communist movement, some serving among its leaders between the two world wars.

Romanian antisemitism, strong throughout this period, also made its appearance in Transylvania. In 1927 pogroms were organized by Romanian students who had convened in Oradea for their national conference. These disorders spread to the areas in the vicinity of Oradea, to localities situated near the Oradea-Cluj railway line, and to Cluj itself. In 1936–37, when the Romanian Fascist movement, the Iron Guard, formed branches throughout Romania, centers were also established in most Transylvanian towns, particularly in Arad. After 1933, the overwhelming majority of the German population – the Swabians in Banat and the Saxons in southern Transylvania – proclaimed themselves supporters of the Third Reich. Most of the German population was associated with the Transylvanian Fascist organizations. These, however, did not take active measures against the Jews and contented themselves with an economic *boycott and social ostracism. Between the end of 1937 and the beginning of 1938, when the outspokenly antisemitic O. Goga-A.C. Cuza government came to power, Jews, under the direction of the Zionists, formed clandestine *self-defense organizations which succeeded in preventing acts of brutality. A Jewish economic organization was established to assist Jews threatened with dismissal from employment. The succeeding Romanian governments continued to discriminate against Jews; severe economic problems arose, and there was growing poverty. The Jewish organizations combined in efforts to provide relief and assistance. *Aliyah* to Palestine increased, though few immigration certificates were allocated to Transylvanian Jews. The number of Jews in this period remained approximately 200,000, forming 1.8 percent of the general population of historic Transylvania, 20.9 percent of that of Maramures, 5 percent of that of Crisana, and 1.2 percent of that of Banat.

Holocaust and Contemporary Periods

In August 1940, in the second arbitration decision of Vienna, it was decided by Germany and Italy – upon the basis of political considerations of the German Nazis – to incorporate one part of Transylvania into Hungary, while the other remained within Romania, the parts being known respectively as northern Transylvania and southern Transylvania.

SOUTHERN TRANSYLVANIA. The minority of about 40,000 Jews remained in the southern, Romanian sector, where the government began severe persecution of the Jewish population. The land owned by the community bodies was confiscated, Jews were deprived of factories and shops, and many Jews of military age were forced into labor battalions. Whole Jewish populations of villages and provincial towns were expelled and concentrated in the district capitals. The communities were nevertheless able to continue their religious activities and provided assistance for the needy. The Zionist movement continued activities, and its leaders and members of the youth movement organized rescue and defense from their center in Timisoara.

NORTHERN TRANSYLVANIA. The fate of the Jews in northern Transylvania, who numbered approximately 150,000, was very different. The Fascist Hungarian government which occupied this territory during the first half of September 1940 immediately introduced economic, social, and cultural restrictions against the Jews. The newspaper *Uj Kelet* was compelled to cease publication on the first day of Hungarian rule in Cluj. Zionist activity was prohibited in most places. Jews were immediately dismissed from law offices and public positions, and the number of Jewish pupils in the general secondary schools was restricted to 4 percent of the student rolls. The Jewish organizations took steps to relieve this situation. In the fall of 1940 a Jewish secondary school was established in Cluj with eight classes for boys and eight for girls, and later absorbed pupils who had been dismissed from the general secondary schools, as well as from outlying districts. Central relief organizations were set up in which both the Orthodox and the Neologist communities cooperated. In 1942, the Hungarian military command began to conscript Jews of military age into forced labor battalions, most of which were sent to the eastern front and reached the advance lines of the German-Hungarian invasion of the Soviet Union. Most of the conscripts perished under the harsh conditions. The Jews in northern Transylvania began to resume participation in the organizational life of Hungarian Jewry, whose center was in Budapest. The Transylvanian Zionist movement functioned clandestinely, and even succeeded in sending youths and adults to Palestine through Romania and the Black Sea.

A further turning point occurred on March 19, 1944, when the Germans occupied Hungary. After a few weeks, preparations were made to establish ghettos and for deportations to the death camp at *Auschwitz. The area was declared to be a danger zone from the security aspect, and both the Hungarian and German authorities sped up the deportations to the death camps. From the end of the summer of 1944 nearly all the Jews in northern Transylvania were deported; few succeeded in hiding themselves. The Jewish institutions were liquidated and a number of synagogues were destroyed.

After the capitulation of Romania on Aug. 23, 1944, northern Transylvania became a battle zone: the Soviet and Romanian armies entered the region and defeated the German and Hungarian forces. Toward the end of this period, a few Jews left southern Transylvania for northern Transylvania. In 1945 survivors began to return to the region.

By 1947 a Jewish population had been formed from survivors of the camps, the arrivals from southern Transylvania, and others who had come to the region from Romania and northern Bukovina, occupied by the Soviet Union. According to an estimate for that year, they numbered about 44,000 in northern Transylvania, 13,000 in Crisana, and 15,000 in Banat. The traditional community institutions were revived, and Zionist organizations were also active until 1949 in finding opportunities for *aliyah*. In addition, a new Jewish Democratic Committee (Comitetul Democratic Evreesc – CDE) was established by Jewish activists of the Communist Party. However, as soon became evident, the committee was an instrument of the new Communist regime, with the principal objective of disbanding the Zionist movement so that organized Jewish activities could be placed under close government and party supervision. After the war, and especially after the establishment of the State of Israel, many thousands of Jews made their way to Israel. The Jewish population in the region in 1971 was estimated at between 6,000 and 7,000. In towns with traditional communities – Cluj, Oradea, Arad, and Timisoara – and in several other smaller towns, the community organizations continued to be active, and prayers were held in the synagogues at least on Friday evenings and festivals. The communities were affiliated to the central organization of Romanian Jews with headquarters in Bucharest. The dwindling of the Transylvanian Jewish communities continued into the 21st century, with most of the remaining Jews now being entirely assimilated.

BIBLIOGRAPHY: M. Carmilly-Weinberger (ed.), *Memorial Volume for the Jews of Cluj-Kolozsvar* (Eng., Heb., and Hung., 1970); N. Sylvain, in: P. Meyer et al., *The Jews in the Soviet Satellites* (1953); B. Vágó, in: R.L. Braham (ed.), *Hungarian Jewish Studies*, 1 (1966); idem, in: PK Romanyah, 1 (1970), 261–71 (incl. bibl.); Z.Y. Avraham, *Le-Korot* *ha-Yehudim bi-Transilvanyah* (1951); I.J. Cohen, in: KS, 33 (1957/58), 386–403; 34 (1958–59), 499–512; 35 (1959–60), 98–108; 37 (1961–62), 249–66; S. Yitzḥaki, *Battei-Sefer Yehudiyyim bi-Transilvanyah Bein Shetei Milḥamot ha-Olam* (1970); M. Eisler, *Az erdélyi zsidók multjából* (1901); D. Schoen, *Istenkeresők a Kárpátok alatt* (1964).

[Yehouda Marton / Paul Schveiger (2nd ed.)]

TRAPANI, city in Sicily. Documents suggest that 200 Jews, constituting one-tenth of the town's inhabitants, lived in Trapani in 1439. Their share of the taxes, however, was one-sixth, and from 1426 they had to provide one-third of the guard for the town walls. The affairs of the community were directed by the *prothi* ("notables"), assisted by 12 elders. In 1484 the community adopted the unusual system of having the outgoing *prothi* appoint their own successors. Like all the Jews in Sicily, the Jews of Trapani were under continuous pressure to pay special levies to the sovereigns. In 1404 King Martin urged the *prothi* to proceed energetically against Jewish tax defaulters through excommunication, denial of circumcision for their sons, and exclusion from burial in the Jewish cemetery. Two years later he reconfirmed the privileges of the Jews, in consequence of the exceptional contributions they had paid. The brothers Samuel and Elia Sala, who in 1402 had been granted special privileges for services rendered to the royal house, were commissioned in 1405 and 1409 to negotiate the peace between the rulers of Sicily and Tripoli. In the meantime they ransomed the bishop of Syracuse from the Saracens. The Jews of Trapani made their living from trade, including shipping merchandise to Tunisia, and many worked in the manufacture of coral jewelry. The number of Jews obliged to leave Trapani at the expulsion in 1492 (see *Sicily) is estimated at about 300. In 1492, at the time of the expulsion many wealthy Jewish families left Trapani, but they returned a few years later as *Neofiti (baptized Jews). In 1499 the city negotiated the taxation of Jewish property that remained after the expulsion specifying that it concerned the newly converted Jews, and referring to the "assets, debts, silver, gold, jewels, and other things of the said former Jews, at present baptized." Shortly after its establishment in 1500, the Spanish Inquisition in Sicily concentrated its efforts against the converted Jews of Trapani and many were prosecuted. Inquisitorial registers list 80 converts living in Trapani after the expulsion.

BIBLIOGRAPHY: Milano, Bibliotheca, index; Milano, Italia, index; Roth, Italy, index; Lagumina, in: *Archivio Storico Siciliano*, 11 (1887), 446–7; G. Di Giovanni, *Ebraismo della Sicilia…* (Palermo, 1748). **ADD. BIBLIOGRAPHY:** A. Precopi Lombardi, "Le comunità ebraiche del Trapanse," in: *Italia Judaica*, 5 (1995), 463–500; C. Trasselli, *Siciliani fra quattrocento e cinquecento* (1981); E. Ashtor, "The Jews of Trapani in the Later Middle Ages," in: *Studi Medievali*, 25 (1984), 1–30; A. Sparti, *Fonti per la storia del corallo nel medioevo mediterraneo* (1986); F. Renda, *La fine del giudaismo siciliano* (1993); A. Scandaliato, "Momenti di vita a Trapani nel Quattrocento," in: N. Bucaria (ed.), *Gli ebrei in Sicilia dal tardoantico al medioevo, Studi in onore di Monsignor Benedetto Rocco* (1998), 167–219; S. Simonsohn, *The Jews in Sicily*, 1–6, index; H. Bresc, *Arabes de langue, juifs de religion. L'evolution du judaïsme sicilien dans l'environment latin, XIIe–XVe siècles* (2001); N. Zeldes, *The Former Jews of this Kingdom. Sicilian Converts after the Expulsion (1492–1516)* (2003).

[Sergio Joseph Sierra / Nadia Zeldes (2nd ed.)]

°TRASKE, JOHN (c. 1585–1636), English sectarian leader and Judaizer. Born in Somerset, Traske became an Anglican minister in 1611. He then became a peripatetic preacher and, by the mid-1610s, influenced by a tailor named Hamlet Jackson, he and his followers regulated their lives by the Hebrew Scriptures, strictly observing the Sabbath and dietary laws. After being condemned to savage punishment by the Star Chamber (1618), he recanted and published *A Treatise of Libertie from Judaisme … by John Traske, of late stumbling, now happily running again in the Race of Christianitie* (London, 1620). Some of his associates, including Hamlet Jackson, immigrated to Amsterdam where the latter, at least, formally joined the Jewish community.

BIBLIOGRAPHY: Philips, in: JHSET, 15 (1939–45), 63–72; Roth, *ibid.*, 19 (1955–59), 9f. **ADD. BIBLIOGRAPHY:** ODNB online; D. Katz, *Sabbath and Sectarianism in Seventeenth-Century England* (1988).

[Cecil Roth]

TRAUB, MARVIN S. (1925–), U.S. retail executive. Traub, a native New Yorker, became synonymous with one of the city's best-known attractions, Bloomingdale's department store. Under his leadership, it evolved from dowdy to dazzling and turned shopping into show business. It was also on his watch that Bloomingdale's had its darkest days, being forced into a brief period of bankruptcy. Traub was raised in a retailing environment. His mother was a fashion director at Bonwit Teller on Fifth Avenue and his father had a licensing agreement with Christian Dior. After serving in France with the U.S. infantry in World War II and receiving a Purple Heart for a leg wound, Traub graduated from Harvard College in 1947 and Harvard Business School in 1949. He worked briefly at Macy's and Alexander's, then joined Bloomingdale's in 1950. It would be his employer for the next 41 years. When Traub arrived, the store's wares were modestly priced, "a notch below Gimbel's," he once recalled. His first assignment was to manage the 49-cent bargain hosiery table. By 1959, Traub had risen to vice president of home products and he made history by sending his buyers to Italy to look for everything from flatware to furniture. The Casa Bella promotion became the first of Bloomingdale's import events, presaging the transformation of the store into one of the most dynamic retailing operations in the U.S. The import promotions spread to other departments and eventually were storewide. Traub also advanced the concept of in-store boutiques, a key retail development. He was named president of Bloomingdale's in 1960 and chairman in 1978, retaining that post until he retired in 1991. That year, he was awarded the National Retail Federation's Gold Medal. From 1988 to 1992, Traub was also a vice chairman of Federated Department Stores, Bloomingdale's owner. In 1992, he formed Marvin Traub Associates, a marketing and consulting business. He was a senior advisor to Financo, an investment banking firm. In 1993, Traub co-authored *Like No Other Store in the World*, a chronicle of his triumphs at Bloomingdale's and an unsparing critique of Robert Campeau, a Canadian real estate tycoon who borrowed billions to complete a hostile takeover of the store in 1988. Pressed by debt, Campeau put Bloomingdale's up for sale. Traub tried and failed to buy the store, which was driven into bankruptcy in 1990 and emerged from it in 1992.

BIBLIOGRAPHY: M. Traub and T. Teicholz, *Like No Other Store in the World* (1993).

[Mort Sheinman (2nd ed.)]

TRAUBE, ISIDOR (1860–1943), German physical chemist. Traube, who was born in Hildesheim, worked at the universities of Heidelberg and Bonn. From 1901 he was professor at the Technische Hochschule of Berlin, but left Germany in 1934 and settled in Edinburgh.

Traube related the laws governing the behavior of dilute solutions to the gas laws, actually anticipating Van't Hoff and Arrhenius, the Dutch and Swedish physical chemists. Traube also propounded that absorbed films on liquid surfaces obeyed two-dimensional analogies of the gas laws, a proposition that was substantiated 30 years later. He published numerous papers on surface phenomena. His theory of the action of drugs had a positive effect on pharmacological research for years. The effect of organic compounds on the surface tension of water is governed by "Traube's Rule."

[Samuel Aaron Miller]

TRAUBE, LUDWIG (1818–1876), German pathologist; a pioneer in the field of experimental pathology. Traube was born in Silesia and graduated from the University of Berlin. In 1849 he was appointed lecturer and research worker at the Charité Hospital in Berlin and his clinic soon achieved a high reputation for exactness and thoroughness in diagnoses and therapy. His book *Gesammelte Beitraege zur Pathologie und Physiologie* (3 vols., 1871–78) earned him a worldwide reputation. He was one of the first Jewish physicians to attain the title of professor in Germany.

Traube investigated pulmonary resection of the vagus nerve and carried out studies on suffocation, effects of digitalis and other drugs, the pathology of fever, the relationship between heart and kidney diseases, and many other subjects. He was the first to introduce the thermometer in his clinic for regular checking of temperature of all patients. He described an area of the chest wall over which stomach resonance is obtained ("Traube's Space"). "Traube's Sign" is a double sound over the peripheral arteries in aortic insufficiency or mitral stenosis. He also described blood curves ("Traube's Curves") and an artificial chemical membrane ("Traube's Membrane").

BIBLIOGRAPHY: H. Morrison, *Ludwig Traube* (Eng., 1927); S.R. Kagan, *Jewish Medicine* (1952), 222–3.

[Suessmann Muntner]

TRAUBE, LUDWIG (1861–1907), master paleographer and critic of Latin texts. Born in Berlin, the son of Ludwig *Traube, the great pathologist, he became professor of the Latin philology of the Middle Ages at the University of Munich in 1904 after a long struggle in which his Jewishness played a key role. His importance lies in the fact that through his independent research he raised paleography to the status of a historical science and made a basic contribution to the intellectual history of the Latin Middle Ages. Possessed of independent means, he was able to visit all the important libraries of Europe and study the Latin manuscripts at length. His studies of contractions of Latin words and *nomina sacra* (his major work, a study of various ways of writing divine names in manuscripts) proved crucial in tracing the history of schools of copyists, tracing manuscripts to particular monks, and indicating which medieval scholars had used them. He unraveled the complicated textual histories of the Rule of St. Benedict and of the Latin historian Livy. Of his projected comprehensive work on Latin paleography, the study of the half-uncial script appeared posthumously. Despite his premature death, Traube, because of his ability to attract and influence students, continued to exercise a profound influence on the field through his students – P. Lehmann, P. Maas, C.U. Clark, C.H. Beeson, E.A. *Lowe, and E.K. Rand – not only in Germany but also in England and especially in the United States.

BIBLIOGRAPHY: F. Boll and P. Lehmann (ed.), *Vorlesungen und Abhandlungen von Ludwig Traube*, 1 (1909), 11–73 [biography and list of his writings, including a large number in manuscript, some of which were edited posthumously by Boll and Lehmann]; J.E. Sandys, *A History of Classical Scholarship*, 3 (1958), 195.

[Louis Harry Feldman]

TRAUBE, MORITZ (1826–1894), German chemist and biologist. Traube was born in Ratibor, Upper Silesia, the brother of Ludwig *Traube. For most of his life he had to combine scientific research in his private laboratory with running the family wine business. With his discovery of semipermeable membranes he pioneered the field of osmosis. He also did research into autoxidation of hydrogen peroxide, plant respiration, biological oxidation and reduction, and nutrition. Traube was a member of the Berlin Academy of Sciences.

TRAUBE, WILHELM (1866–1942), German organic chemist. Traube was born in Ratibor, Upper Silesia, the son of Moritz *Traube, and the brother of Hermann Traube, professor of mineralogy at Breslau. He studied at Heidelberg, and in Berlin. He spent his career at the University of Berlin, where he became professor in 1929, retiring in 1934. He published on aromatic and heterocylic compounds and pharmaceutical activity.

TRAVEL, PRAYER FOR (Heb. תְּפִלַּת הַדֶּרֶךְ, *Tefillat ha-Derekh*), prayer recited upon setting out on a journey to protect the traveler from the dangers associated with travel. The Talmud attributes the institution of this practice to the prophet

Elijah, who cautioned a scholar that "when thou goest forth on a journey, seek counsel of thy Maker and go forth." The talmudic text of this prayer is:

> May it be Thy will, O Lord my God, to lead me forth in peace, and direct my steps in peace and uphold me in peace, and deliver me from the hand of every enemy and ambush by the way, and send a blessing on the works of my hands, and cause me to find grace, kindness, and mercy in Thy eyes and in the eyes of all who see me. Blessed art Thou, O Lord, who hearkenest unto prayer (Ber. 29b).

With only slight alterations, this text has since been used as the traveler's prayer among both Ashkenazim and Sephardim (Hertz, Prayer, 1044). It is, however, recited in the first person plural in accordance with the dictum of Abbaye that "a man should always associate himself with the congregation" (Ber. 29b–30a). It is recited once daily at the start of each day's travels, as long as a distance of 1 Persian mile (about 3 miles) is to be covered. It is preferable to recite this prayer while standing, although it may be said while sitting in places where it is difficult to stand (Ber. 30a; Sh. Ar., OḤ 110:4–7), as in an automobile or airplane. It has also become customary to recite appropriate biblical selections (e.g., Gen. 32:2–3; Ex. 23:20; Ps. 91) at the conclusion of the prayer. Additions have also been made for sea and air travel. Alternative versions of this prayer for paratroopers, pilots, sailors, and soldiers were composed by S. Goren, the former chief rabbi of the Israel Defense Forces.

BIBLIOGRAPHY: Idelsohn, Liturgy, 172.

TRAVELERS AND EXPLORERS. In the ninth century Jewish traders known as "*Radaniya" traded between Western Europe and China, by land and sea. They were fluent in several languages and dealt in female and boy slaves, eunuchs, brocades, furs such as beaver and marten, and swords from the West. They brought back musk, aloes, camphor, cinnamon, and other products from China and India. After the Arab conquest of North Africa in the seventh century, Jewish traders had followed the Berber and Arab armies and reached the Niger Basin. As late as the 18th and 19th centuries, Jewish caravan travelers were sending geographical information about southern Morocco and the western Sahara back to Europe.

*Isaac the Jew, who accompanied Charlemagne's embassy to Hārūn al-Rashīd as an interpreter in 797, returned four years later with an elephant, Abulaboz, which was a gift from the sultan. *Eldad ha-Dani (c. 880) claimed to have made two voyages. The range of his travels seems to have extended from Baghdad and Kairouan to Spain. Jacob ibn Ṭāriq (ninth century) is supposed to have traveled from Baghdad to Ceylon to obtain books on astronomy, while an Arabian or Turkish ruler sent a Jacob Aben Sheara to India (c. 925), for the same purpose.

According to the *ʿAjaʾib al-Hind* ("The Wonders of India," c. 953), by Buzurg ibn Shahriyar of Ramhurmuz, Isḥāq (Isaac) the Jew traveled from Oman (Sohar, southeastern Arabia) to India. From there, he went to China, where he lived for 30 years and amassed a fortune. He returned to Oman in 912/13. Isḥāq was subsequently killed at Serboza in Sumatra on orders of Oman's governor Ahmad ibn Hilāl. He is also supposed to have visited Lhó or Bhutan in the Himalayas. *Ibrāhīm ibn Yaʿqūb of Tortosa (tenth century) visited France (including the area around the English Channel), Mainz, Fulda, Schleswig, apparently Bohemia, and the court of the German emperor, Otto I, in 966. According to Abraham *Ibn Ezra (12th century), a Jewish traveler brought the "Arabic" numerals from India. Ibn Ezra himself visited Rome, a number of other Italian towns, Provence, France, England, Africa, Rhodes, and perhaps Ereẓ Israel and even India. His *Reshit Ḥokhmah* contains important information on Egypt, Arabia, Ereẓ Israel, Persia, and India. *Genizah* documents attest to considerable travel by Jewish merchants from the Middle East to India and other Asian countries.

The most famous Jewish medieval traveler was *Benjamin b. Jonah of Tudela who journeyed in the second half of the 12th century. He wrote a book on his travels, which vividly depicts the many Jewish communities he visited and also gives a picture of general political and economic conditions. His contemporary, the German traveler *Pethahiah of Regensburg, journeyed throughout the Middle East and his account, although incorporating certain legendary elements, gives much valuable information on the Jewish communities he encountered. An adventurous traveler was the Hebrew poet and translator Judah *al-Ḥarizi. In his youth he traveled from his native Spain to Provence. In about 1216 he set out on his journey to the East. Some chapters of his classical work *Taḥkemoni* contain his observations, at times very critical, of the Jewish communities he visited between 1216 and 1230, which included those in Southern France, Egypt, Ereẓ Israel, Syria, and Mesopotamia. A document of King James IV of Majorca (1334) states that Yuceff Faquin, a Barcelona Jew, had circumnavigated the entire known world on the king's orders. Much Jewish travel concentrated on journeys to and from Ereẓ Israel, for which see *Travelers and Travel to Ereẓ Israel.

The Age of Discovery

Luis de *Torres, Columbus' interpreter, was a Jew who was baptized the day before the expedition's departure. De Torres, who reported the discovery of the phenomenon of tobacco, was the first person of Jewish origin to settle in Cuba.

The Portuguese, who attempted to find both a sea and an overland route to the Indies, sent João Perez of Covilhá and Alfonso de Paiva to search for such a route. When the pair had not been heard from for some time, *Abraham of Beja, known for his fluency in several languages, and Joseph Copateiro, an experienced eastern traveler, were sent to find them. They met Perez returning from India, in Cairo. De Paiva had died meanwhile. Abraham and Perez returned to Portugal via Ormuz, Damascus, and Aleppo, while Copateiro returned directly to Portugal with the information which indicated the existence of a sea route to the Far East; this information was then used by Vasco da Gama. One of the pilots and navigators who helped Da Gama in his later journey was a Jew, variously described as from Posen and Alexandria, whom he picked up on an island 60 miles from Goa. Da Gama had the Jew baptized as Gaspar da *Gama, and made him a pilot of the Portuguese fleet.

Hernando Alonso (1460–1528) had a particularly adventurous career. He was born in Niebla, Spain, immigrated to Cuba where he met Hernando Cortez (1516), and became a member of Cortez' army that sailed for Mexico (1520). A blacksmith and carpenter by trade, he helped build the ships that Cortez needed for the conquest of Tenochtitlán. He led the group that subdued the Indians of Pánuco and took part in the conquest of Guanajuato. Cortez awarded him the estate of Actopan, 40 miles outside of Mexico City, and he engaged in the lucrative business of supplying the town with meat. In 1528 he was denounced as a Judaizer and burned at the stake.

One of the most interesting and enigmatic figures of Jewish history is David *Reuveni, who appeared in Italy in 1524 claiming that his brother Joseph ruled over the tribes of Gad and Reuben and half the tribe of Manasseh in the wilderness of Habor and that he was the commander of his army. He claimed to have traveled, disguised as a Muslim, through Ethiopia, Egypt, and Ereẓ Israel, and came to Europe to elicit the military assistance of the Christian powers for the liberation of the Holy Land from the Turks. His "project" failed and he is reported to have died in prison in Spain. His Hebrew diary, which reflects his claims, describes, among other things, his talks with the pope and the king of Portugal, his visits to Italian Jewish communities, and his meetings in Portugal with Marranos, who saw in him the bearer of their hope.

Joseph *Delmedigo, who was born in Crete and studied in Padua, traveled through Egypt, Turkey, Poland, Russia, and Lithuania in the course of his career. A Jewish interpreter accompanied Captain James Lancaster (1601) on the East India Company's first expedition. He helped to negotiate the treaty between the English and the sultan of Achin in Sumatra, which served as the basis for British expansion in the Far East.

The 16th-century Yemenite poet *Zechariah al-Dāhiri traveled widely. He journeyed to Yemen, India, Persia, Babylonia, Turkey, Syria, Ereẓ Israel, Egypt, and Ethiopia. His travel impressions form the literary background of his magnum opus *Sefer ha-Musar.*

Pedro *Teixeira (c. 1570–1650), a Marrano from Lisbon, may have been the first Jew to go around the world, and is believed to have been the first white man to make a continuous journey up the River Amazon.

In 1644 Antonio de Montezinos, who had returned from a trip to the Americas, told the worthies of the Amsterdam community about Indians he had met near Quito, Ecuador, who knew the *Shema* and claimed that they were descended from the tribes of Reuben and Levi. His report encouraged *Manasseh Ben Israel to write "Hope of Israel" and later to negotiate with Oliver Cromwell to readmit the Jews to England in order to complete their dispersion to the "end of the earth," which was a prerequisite for the coming of the Messiah.

In 1687 there appeared in Amsterdam *Notisias dos Judeos de Cochin*, a report on the condition of the Jews of *Cochin, by Moses *Pereira de Paiva, an Amsterdam Jew of Portuguese descent, who visited India.

18th–20th Centuries

Sason Hai of the House of Castiel was a native of Istanbul, who from his youth evinced a great desire to travel. From his travel account, in Hebrew, published by Izhak Ben-Zvi (*Sefunot*, 1 (1956), 141–84), it is difficult to determine the route of his travels. He mentions his return to Istanbul in 1703 and that in 1709 he was in Basra. Among the countries he visited were Holland, Italy, Ethiopia, Tunisia and Morocco, Persia, and Afghanistan. Although his account abounds in legends, folk tales and hearsay, it nevertheless contains many accurate facts which he reports as an eyewitness.

The best-known Jewish travel record of the 18th century is the *Ma'gal Tov* of Ḥayyim Joseph David *Azulai, the famous rabbinical scholar and bibliographer. He twice toured European Jewish communities as an emissary of the Jewish community of Hebron. On his first journey (1753–58), he sailed from Alexandria to Leghorn, where he returned after traveling through Italy, Tyrol, Germany, Holland, England, and France, and sailed from there to Smyrna. He subsequently visited Istanbul, returning from there by boat to Ereẓ Israel. On his second journey (1772–78), he sailed from Alexandria to Tunis and from there to Leghorn. He traveled through Italy, France, Belgium, and Holland, finally settling in Leghorn. His diaries are replete with acute observations on life in the cities he visited.

A contemporary of Azulai was Simon von *Geldern. A native of Vienna, he grew up in Germany and studied at yeshivot there. He led an adventurous life, traveling through Europe and the Near East, visiting Ereẓ Israel several times. He was equally at home in the Jewish community and in high society and gentile scholarly circles in various European countries. Von Geldern, who was a great-uncle of Heine, kept a diary. His life was described by Fritz Heymann (*Der Chevalier von Geldern*, 1937). Earlier David Kaufmann had published extracts from his diary in his *Aus Heinrich Heines Ahnensaal* (1896).

A Jewish traveler whose travel record was very popular was Israel Joseph Benjamin (*Benjamin II). From his early youth he formed the desire to make a pilgrimage to Ereẓ Israel and to travel in search of traces of the lost ten tribes. After he failed in business in his home town Fălticeni, in the then Turkish province of Moldavia, he set out to realize his dream. He traveled through Turkey, Egypt, Ereẓ Israel, Syria, Kurdistan, Mesopotamia, India, Afghanistan, and Persia, and also visited Singapore and Canton. Shortly after his return to Europe, he set out on another voyage, traveling through North Africa. He published *Cinque années de voyage en Orient 1846–1851* (Paris, 1856) about his travels in Asia. The book appeared later in German with additional chapters on his travels in Africa (*Acht Jahre in Asien und Afrika*, 1858) and was translated into English, Hebrew, and Ladino. From 1859 to 1862, Benjamin was in America, and he recorded his experiences there in *Drei Jahre in Amerika* (1862; Eng. edition: *Three Years in America*, 1956).

Jacob *Saphir was the first Jewish traveler to report on the life of the Jews of Yemen. Born in Lithuania in 1812, he settled with his parents in Ereẓ Israel when he was ten years old. In 1858–63 he visited Egypt, Aden, Yemen, Bombay, Cochin, Colombo in Ceylon, Calcutta, Rangoon, Singapore, Batavia, Australia, and New Zealand, as an emissary of the Jerusalem community. He spent longer periods in Yemen and India and in his travel book *Even Sappir* (2 vols., 1866–74) gives detailed descriptions of the life and customs of the Jews of Yemen, the Bene Israel of India, and the black and white Jews of Cochin.

Jehiel Fishl Kestelmann visited the Jewish communities of Syria, Kurdistan, Mesopotamia, and Persia as an emissary of the Jewish community of Safed in 1859–61. His description of his travels was published by A. Yaari under the title *Massa'ot Shali'aḥ Ẓefat be-Arẓot ha-Mizraḥ* (1942).

Asher ha-Levi was born in Galicia. After an unhappy childhood, in 1866, at the age of 17, he left Jassy, where he had lived for several years, and traveled through the Balkans, Asia Minor, Mesopotamia, and India. Eventually he settled in a city in the Himalayan Mountains. He wrote several books in Hebrew, including an autobiography. His account of his travels in the Balkans in 1866–68 was published in 1938 by A. Yaari under the title *Harpatka'otav shel Asher ha-Levi*.

Salomon Rinman was born in Galicia. After spending many years in Cochin he returned to Europe and at the urging of the Hebrew writer Wolf Schur he wrote a description of his travels in India, Burma, and China, *Massa'ot Shelomo be-Ereẓ Hodu, Birman ve-Sinim* (1884).

In 1883–86, Ephraim *Neumark visited the Jewish communities in Syria, Kurdistan, Mesopotamia, Persia, Afghanistan, and Central Persia. His travel impressions *Massa be-Ereẓ ha-Kedem* were first printed in *Ha-Asif* (5, 1887). He was the first to report on the crypto-Jews of *Meshed in Persia.

In 1868, the Orientalist Joseph *Halévy was sent by the Alliance Israélite Universelle to study the conditions of the Falashas, describing his journey there in "Travels in Abyssinia" (*Miscellany of Hebrew Literature*, 2 (1877), 177–256). Not long after his return he went to Yemen to inquire into the state of the Jews there and to examine the Sabean inscriptions. Halévy did not write a book about his travels to Yemen, but years after the expedition Ḥayyim *Ḥabshush, a Yemenite Jew who had served as Halévy's guide, wrote an account of their travels there. Written partly in Hebrew and partly in Arabic, it was published in Hebrew in 1939 by S.D. Goitein under the title *Massa'ot Ḥabshush*.

Ephraim *Deinard wrote several travel books. His *Massa Krim* (1878) includes chapters on the life of the Karaites and the Krimchaks (original Jews of the Crimea). *Sefer ha-Massa'ot be-Ereẓ Kavkaz u-vi-Medinot asher me-Ever le-Kavkaz* (1884) by Joseph Judah *Chorny, printed after the death of the author, gives an account of his travels among the Jewish communities in the Caucasus and in Transcaucasia.

Arctic explorers and travelers of the 18th and 19th centuries include Israel Lyons (1739–1775) who served as chief astronomer with Captain Phipps' expedition to the Polar regions in 1773; Isaac Israel *Hayes (1832–1881), surgeon to the "Advance" expedition searching for Sir John Franklin, discoverer and explorer of Grinnel Land, and leader of an 1860 expedition to Greenland which encountered another expedition led by August Sonntag; Emil *Bessels (1847–1888), surgeon and naturalist of the ill-fated "Polaris" expedition to the North Pole; Edward *Israel (1859–1884), astronomer with the Greely expedition to Greenland, where he died of malnutrition; Aldo Pontremoli (1896–1928), physics professor at the University of Milan and an aviation pioneer during the interwar period, who died on Nobile's 1928 Arctic dirigible expedition; Rudolph *Samoilovich (1881–1939), who led the Russian relief expedition to the Nobile party's aid (1928), discovered the Spitzbergen coal deposit, and explored the Franz Josef Archipelago; and Angelo Heilperin (1853–1907), who made geological expeditions to Florida (1886), Bermuda (1888), and Mexico (1890), led a relief expedition to Peary's aid in Greenland (1892), took part in expeditions to North Africa (1896) and to the Klondike (1898–99), and scaled and explored Mt. Pelee (1902–03).

Explorers of Africa in the 19th century include Nathaniel *Isaacs, a member of the King expedition sent to search for Farwell, wrecked off Natal in 1825, who explored Natal for seven years; *Emin Pasha (Eduard Schnitzer), General Gordon's aide, then his successor as governor of the Equatorial Province, who made important explorations and investigations in Central Africa; Edouard *Foa, who traveled through Morocco, southern and central Africa, French Congo and Dahomey; and Louis Arthur Lucas, who traveled through the U.S. (1872), Egypt (1873), and navigated the northern part of Lake Albert Nyanza in 1876.

Other travelers, adventurers, or explorers of the 18th, 19th, and 20th centuries who were Jewish or of Jewish origin include Mantua-born Samuel *Romanelli, whose *Massa ba-Arav* (Berlin, 1792) is a vivid account of his four-year journey from Gibraltar to Algiers and Morocco; Captain Moses Ximenes (c. 1762–c. 1830), who led an expedition from England to the island of Bulama, West Africa, and made an unsuccessful attempt to establish a colony there; a U.S. Army colonel from Boston named Cohen, who traveled from Adana via Smyrna to Constantinople with a group of Egyptian soldiers; *David D'Beth Hillel, author of *The Travels From Jerusalem through Arabia, Koordistan, Part of Persia, and India, to Madras* (1832), who searched for the remnants of the Ten Tribes, and described in detail the holy places and historical sites of Christianity, Judaism, and Islam from India to Ereẓ Israel, the Yazidis in Sinjār, the Sabeans, Wahhabis, Druze, the Dāwūdiyya sect in western Persia, and the differences between the Sunnite and Shi'ite Muslims; Alexander *Salmon, an English sailor who married a Tahitian clan chieftaineess and served as adviser to the rulers of Tahiti; Heinrich Bernstein (1828–1865), who explored the Moluccas, the Malay Peninsula, and New Guinea for Holland; William Gifford Palgrave (1826–1888), who worked as a Catholic missionary in India, Syria, and Arabia and wrote *Narrative of a Year's Journey Through Central and Eastern Arabia* (2 vols., 1865); Arminius *Vambery who, disguised as a Muslim dervish, was the first European to travel from Trebizond to Teheran, Persia, and Samarkand in Central Asia (1861–63); Gottfried *Merzbacher, who climbed mountains in the Caucasus and the Tien Shan range and studied the ecology of the latter for more than five years; Ney *Elias, who traveled across the Gobi Desert, through the Pamir Mountains, and Chinese and Afghan Turkestan, and traced the Oxus River's upper course; Elio Modigliani, who explored the Malay Peninsula; Samuel *Fenichel, who explored New Guinea for bird and butterfly specimens; Nathaniel Wallich, who explored Assam, Hindustan, and Burma; Lamberto Loria, who traveled in Australia and New Guinea; Eduard *Glaser, the Austrian explorer who made four expeditions to the Yemen, located San'a, and discovered numerous old manuscripts and inscriptions; Hermann *Burchardt, German explorer and ethnographer, who traveled in the Near East, North Africa, Australia, America, India, and Iceland, and was murdered in Yemen; Julius Popper, who explored and reigned briefly over Tierra del Fuego; Sir Mark Aurel *Stein, who headed expeditions in India, Chinese Turkestan, China, Persia, and the Middle East; Raimondo *Franchetti, the "Italian Lawrence," who traveled in Indochina, Malaya, the Sudan, East Africa, and Ethiopia; the ethnologist Vladmir *Jochelson, who, in the course of a ten-year exile in Siberia (1884–94), studied the nomad Yokaghir tribe and latter accompanied expeditions to Kamchatka, Eastern Asia, and Alaska; Lev Yakovlevich Sternberg, who was also exiled to Siberia (1910–20) and studied the nomad Giyake tribe in northeastern Siberia; and Charles *Bernheimer, who explored the northern Arizona and Utah badlands for the American Museum of Natural History and undertook expeditions to Guatemala and Yucatan.

Of the many travel books which appeared in the 20th century only a few can be mentioned: E.N. *Adler's *Jews in Many Lands* (1905). Jacques *Faitlovitch, who devoted his life to the Falashas, wrote *Quer durch Abessinien* (1910; Hebrew: *Massa el ha-Falashim*, 1959). Zvi Kasdoi described his journeys in Caucasus, Central Asia, Siberia, and the Far East in *Mamlekhet Ararat* (1912) and *Mi-Yarketei Tevel* (2 vols., 1914). Among Nahum *Slouschz's many studies on North African Jewry was *Travels in North Africa* (1927). Ezriel *Carlebach's *Exotische Juden* (1932) included, among other travel reports, chapters on the descendants of the Marranos of Portugal, the Chuetas of Majorca, the Doenmeh of Turkey, and the Karaites of Lithuania. *A World Passed By* (1933) by Marvin *Lowenthal does not describe existing communities but landmarks and memories of the Jewish past in Europe and North Africa. Abraham Jacob *Brawer gave an account of his travels in the Middle East in *Avak Derakhim* (2 vols., 1944–46). Shmuel *Yavne'eli's *Massa le-Teiman* ("Journey to Yemen," 1952), Israel *Cohen's *Travels in Jewry* (1953), David S. *Sassoon's *Massa Bavel* ("Voyage to Babylonia," 1955), L. *Rabinowitz's *Far East Mission* (1952), and Joseph Carmel's *Massa el Aḥim Nidaḥim* (1957) are about the Far East. H.Z. Hirschberg's *Me-Ereẓ Mevo ha-Shemesh* (1957) is on travels in North Africa. Jacob Beller's travel books on South America included *Jews in Latin America* (1969). Henry Shoshkes circled the globe many times. His travel accounts were published in the Yiddish press, and he was the author of several books, among them *Your World and Mine* (1952). In 1972 *Jews in Remote Corners of the World* by Ida Cowen appeared. It described visits to Jewish communities in the Pacific and in the Far and Near East.

BIBLIOGRAPHY: M. Kayserling, *Christopher Columbus and the Participation of the Jews in the Spanish and Portuguese Discoveries* (1907); E.N. Adler (ed.), *Jewish Travellers* (1930); L. Zunz, in: A. Asher (ed.), *Itinerary of Rabbi Benjamin of Tudela*, 2 (1927?), 230–317, includes bibliography; C. Roth, *Jewish Contribution to Civilisation* (1938), 63–86, incl. bibl.; J.D. Eisenstein, *Oẓar Massa'ot* (1926); S.D. Goitein, *A Mediterranean Society* (1967), 42–70, 209–15, 273–352; L.I. Rabinowitz, *Jewish Merchant Adventurers* (1948); J.D. Eisenstein, *Oẓar Massa'ot* (1926); E.N. Adler, *Jewish Travellers* (1930); Yaari, Sheluḥei; A. Epstein, *Eldad ha-Dani* (1950); A.Z. Aescoly, *Sippur David ha-Reuveni* (1940); Zechariah al-Dahiri', *Sefer ha-Musar*, ed. by Y. Ratzaby (1965).

[Tovia Preschel]

TRAVELERS AND TRAVELS TO EREẒ ISRAEL.

Jewish Travelers

Jews have traveled to see the Holy Land ever since they first settled in the lands of the Diaspora, i.e., travel by Jews to Ereẓ Israel began from the time of the Babylonian Exile and in effect never ceased entirely from then to the present.

During the Second Temple period the focus of attraction for *pilgrims was the Temple. However, even after the destruction of the Temple, and after most of the people were exiled from its land, the attraction of Ereẓ Israel did not abate. Actual descriptions of the travels by the travelers themselves exist only from the middle of the 12th century. The first known Jewish traveler who left literary evidence about his travels was *Judah Halevi. He left Spain in 1140 but apparently did not reach Ereẓ Israel. The literary evidence which he left expresses the poet's feelings about the adventures which befell him on his travels, rather than the adventures themselves. Its usefulness lies in that it reveals the profound emotional motives operating within the traveler to the Holy Land. The first historical document offering a mostly factually accurate travel description is the itinerary of *Benjamin of Tudela from Spain. He arrived in Ereẓ Israel about 1170. He describes various geographic sites there, as well as the number of Jewish inhabitants he found in each place, the conditions under which they lived, the history of the places, historical identifications, etc. Benjamin arrived before the collapse of crusader rule, and his accounts are an important source of information about the situation of the Jews there during that period.

About ten years after the visit of Benjamin of Tudela, *Pethahiah of Regensburg toured the country. He completes the picture of the impoverished situation of the Jewish community at the end of the crusader period, in contrast to the comfortable situation of contemporary Babylonian Jewry under Muslim rule. His main interest was the *holy places, and he did not devote much attention to the material conditions of the Jews. Jacob b. Nethanel, who visited the country and Jerusalem, apparently before its conquest by Saladin (1187), was also mainly interested in the holy places and the tombs of the *tannaim* and *amoraim*.

The situation was different during the travels of Judah *Al-Ḥarizi. He arrived in 1218, after the country had been conquered from the crusaders, and after the immigration of 300 rabbis from France and England, some of whom he met in Jerusalem. The Muslim conquest and the immigration eased the conditions of the Jewish community there. Al-Ḥarizi himself attests: "From the day it was conquered by Ishmaelites, it was settled by Israelites." In 1238 a journey was made by R. Jacob, the emissary of R. *Jehiel of Paris, but in contrast to Al-Ḥarizi he gives almost no description of the situation of the Jewish community, and concentrates primarily on describing the holy places and the tombs. A special place among the settlers of Ereẓ Israel is held by *Naḥmanides (1267), who gives a very somber description of the conditions of the Jews during his stay. He also describes the destruction and desolation which abounded in the country. Naḥmanides' action in renewing the settlement of Jerusalem was an outstanding enterprise.

An interesting figure among travelers was *Estori ha-Parḥi, who arrived in 1322. Far from being a mere transitory tourist, he delved deep into the study of Ereẓ Israel. He investigated the problem of identifying several places in the country, displaying an outstanding expertise in Jewish literature and foreign languages, and approached his subject scientifically.

Nevertheless, love of Ereẓ Israel was not the legacy of Jewish scholars or men of letters alone. Simple people, too, greatly desired to settle there. This is evidenced by the tale about two Spanish Jews who vowed to immigrate in 1317. When their attempts proved unsuccessful, one of them asked R. *Asher b. Jehiel if he could break his vow (Resp. Rosh, 8:11). In the course of time common people (usually merchants) came, e.g., Isaac ibn al-Fara of Malaga, Spain, who visited Ereẓ Israel in 1411 and wrote a letter to Simeon b. Zemaḥ *Duran in Algiers, describing what he saw there. He also visited the important cities of Syria. In 1443 he sent a list of the locations of the holy graves in Ereẓ Israel, which he took from an ancient book in his possession, to Solomon b. Simeon *Duran. The two letters are lost but they were summarized in Abraham *Zacuto's *Sefer Yuḥasin*. In 1473 an anonymous traveler went there from Candia, and numerous others went there from Italy in the second half of the 15th century. The most famous among these were R. Meshullam of Volterra (1481), a wealthy merchant, whose book of travels is very important from a historical point of view, and Obadiah of *Bertinoro (1488–90), who became one of the greatest rabbis of Ereẓ Israel of his time; three of his letters from there are among the most beautiful in travel literature.

In the 16th century a considerable number of Italian Jews traveled to the Holy Land. The book of travels of Moses *Basola (1521–23) is a gem among travel literature. In 1563 the wealthy merchant Elijah of Pesaro settled there, and his book contains a detailed description of the means of travel from Italy to Ereẓ Israel. The description of the economic conditions prevailing there in the 16th century is also detailed and enlightening. This is reflected in a letter from David di Rossi, a merchant who was a fellow-countryman of Elijah, and who journeyed there in 1535. Solomon Shlomil Meinstril from Resnitz, Moravia, arrived in Safed at the end of 1602, and his letters are filled with realistic descriptions of the Safed community, its spiritual life, its economic situation, relations with non-Jews, climate, etc. Isaiah *Horowitz tells about his travels in his letters and describes Safed, where he arrived in 1620, and his visits to the tombs of the *ẓaddikim*, as well as his journey to Jerusalem.

During the 17th and 18th centuries Karaite pilgrims went to Ereẓ Israel from the Crimean Peninsula, after having vowed to undertake the journey. The descriptions of the travels of *Samuel b. David (1641–42), Moses b. Elijah (1654–55), and *Benjamin b. Elijah (1785–86) are filled with religious fervor and love of the Holy Land. The Karaites used to bestow the title *Yerushalmi* ("Jerusalemite") on every immigrant, and such an event was a great celebration for the entire community.

One of the travelers in the famous group of *Judah Ḥasid was Gedaliah of Siemiatycze, from Poland. In his book, *Sha'alu Shelom Yerushalayim*, he describes the adventures of the travelers, as well as life in Jerusalem. The adventures undergone by Abraham Roiyo and his group (1702) during their travels to Ereẓ Israel, as well as the yeshivah built by him, are described in a letter written by one of the travelers. There is a series of letters and stories about travels to and in Ereẓ Israel in connection with the immigration (1741) of Ḥayyim *Attar, author of *Or ha-Ḥayyim*.

In 1746 Abraham Gershom of Kutow, brother-in-law of *Israel b. Eliezer Ba'al Shem Tov, immigrated there. He served as the first bridge for the great ḥasidic immigration. As a result, there are numerous travel descriptions written by settlers and travelers who went from eastern Galicia and Volhynia, the provinces where Ḥasidism originated. In 1760 Joseph Sofer journeyed there from Berestzka in Volhynia province. He related in his letter that there was a gradual but regular immigration from Poland. In 1764 two ḥasidic leaders from eastern Galicia, *Naḥman of Horodenka and *Menahem Mendel of Peremyshlyany, arrived with the groups of ḥasidic immigrants. Information about their journey is given by a Galician Jew, who recounts the stories of his travel to Ereẓ Israel in a book entitled *Ahavat Ẓiyyon*.

In the framework of the ḥasidic immigration, an especially great role was played by the Ḥasidim of Lithuania and

Rydzyna, whose leaders describe, among other things, their travels and immigration in their letters (1777), as well as the situation of the Jews of Ereẓ Israel at the time. The most famous traveler was R. *Naḥman of Bratslav, who traveled in 1798–99, and who regarded the Holy Land as the center of his ḥasidic teaching. About 30 years after the move by Ḥasidim to settle in Ereẓ Israel, their opponents, the *Mitnaggedim*, also felt the spiritual need to settle there. The first group of the disciples of R. Elijah, the Gaon of Vilna, traveled there in 1808, and settled in Safed. Two additional groups of R. Elijah's disciples went in 1809. Their letters give expression to the religious yearning of the immigrants, and the great call on Diaspora Jewry to take part in the settlement of the land. Supplementary information about this immigration is given in the book of travels of R. *David D'Beth Hillel, who joined the disciples of the Gaon in Safed, in 1815, but did not remain with them long, and left to wander around the country. In 1824 R. David D'Beth Hillel left to tour the world. The description of his travels in Ereẓ Israel is the only one of its kind by a Jew during the first quarter of the 19th century. His diary is also of historical significance, because he is generally precise in the facts which he presents. In 1833 Menahem Mendel of Kamieniec arrived in Ereẓ Israel. He published a small work entitled *Korot ha-Ittim* in 1840, describing the terrible sufferings of the Jews of Safed as a result of the fellahin's rebellion against Ibrahim Pasha. He devotes a special chapter to describing daily life in Ereẓ Israel.

In 1833 R. Yehoseph *Schwarz from Bavaria settled in Ereẓ Israel. He was not an ordinary traveler. Like Estori ha-Parḥi in the 14th century, R. Yehoseph Schwarz devoted all his strength and energy to the study of the country. He covered its length and breadth, dealing with its borders, antiquities, flora, climate, etc. His book, *Tevu'ot ha-Areẓ* (1845), is the major product of his investigations, and was translated into German and English. In a letter written in 1837, he describes the quality of life in Jerusalem, its holy places, and the climate and productivity of the country.

Travel literature and the history of travels in the 19th century accompany the first manifestations of national revival and the renewal of Jewish settlement. Moses *Montefiore and his wife, Judith, made seven trips. She kept a detailed travel diary about her second trip with her husband (1839). Eliezer Halevi, Montefiore's secretary and right-hand man, described in four letters what he had seen in his tour throughout the country, in which he spent two months (1838).

The beginning of Zionism may be associated with the activity of Jehiel Michael *Pines, who traveled throughout the country in 1878 examining the quality of land suitable for settlement. He tells about these travels in his letter. The historian Ze'ev *Jawitz, who immigrated in 1887, tells in his letter about his arrival and his visits to various places. There is also the description by Mordecai b. Hillel, among the first of the Ḥovevei Zion, who visited the new *yishuv* in 1889. In his book of travels, he describes the situation of the moshavot, as well as the way of life of the old *yishuv* in Jerusalem.

The travels of Zionist leaders *Aḥad Ha-Am (1891) and Theodor *Herzl (1898) to Ereẓ Israel exemplify the new trend in travel (see *Zionism).

[Menahem Schmelzer]

Christian Travelers

Numerous travel descriptions were written from the 12th century to modern times by Christian pilgrims who went to Ereẓ Israel to visit the holy places of their faith, and other travelers who wandered through the countries of the East and visited the Holy Land. Among them were some who were not adept at literary expression, whose travels were described by companions or by someone to whom they told their story. Their writings are often nothing more than a list of the Christian holy places visited by pilgrims, the pilgrimage "stations," and the prayers which were to be said at these places. Many of the pilgrim-travelers, however, were priests and intellectuals, who could describe their travels in works which bore a literary character. All such works were called in Latin *itineraria*. Since many of the pilgrims visited Syria and Egypt as well, their travel books include interesting information about these countries also. These works are important sources not only for the history of Ereẓ Israel, and especially for the study of its topography, but also for the history of Oriental civilization in general, including data about the social and economic conditions. On the other hand, all the itineraries show the authors to be aliens unfamiliar with the way of life of the country, especially with the languages spoken by its inhabitants; they required the mediation of guides and translators, who often misled them. The tendency to believe legends was almost general in the Middle Ages. However, in the course of the generations in which travel descriptions were written by the Christians who went to Ereẓ Israel, the nature of these writings underwent changes according to the national and social origin of their authors, as well as according to their approach to matters relating to the country.

A few itineraries from the period preceding the Crusades have been preserved. Most of them were written in Latin by West European priests, and some of them were written in Greek by Byzantine priests. Their character was determined by that of the authors: they concentrate mainly on descriptions of the holy places, the monasteries, etc. The earliest extant itinerary is by an anonymous author called the "Bordeaux Pilgrim," who gives an account of his journey from France, through Italy and the Balkans, to Ereẓ Israel, where he describes, naturally first and foremost, the Christian holy places in Jerusalem. This journey was apparently made in the 330s (333?). About 50 years later an itinerary was written which is attributed to Saint Silvia of Aquitania. The authoress spent three years in the countries of the Orient and, after a lengthy stay in Ereẓ Israel, also visited Syria and Mesopotamia. Her description of her travels is so detailed that it is an invaluable aid for the study of topography. One of the most popular works from that time was the description of the journey undertaken by the French bishop Arculfus, around 670. Arculfus spent nine months in Jerusalem, visiting the shore of the Dead Sea, the northern part of the country, Damascus, and Tyre, and later traveling to Constantinople. He finally arrived in Scotland, where he told the head of an Irish monastery about his travels, and the latter wrote down his story. This work is important in that it is the first (known) work from the period of Muslim rule in Ereẓ Israel and the neighboring countries. A detailed travel book, which gives a lengthy description of the adventures and tribulations of a western pilgrim in the Oriental countries, is the travel description by St. Willibald, who went to Ereẓ Israel in 723. Willibald was an Englishman, but he became bishop of Eichstadt, Germany.

Beginning with the First Crusade there was an increasing number of pilgrims who wrote descriptions of their travels. The types of traveler-authors became more variegated, and the establishment of Frankish rule in Ereẓ Israel and a few Syrian provinces resulted in the broadening of the travelers' scope of interests, and they included in their books topics other than just the holy places. Of greatest interest among the works written in the second half of the 12th century are the travel descriptions of Saewulf, who went to Ereẓ Israel while making a sea voyage and visiting Greece and Constantinople (1102–03), and those by the Russian ascetic, Daniel (1106–08), whose work is one of the first written in Russian. From the second half of the 12th century, mention should be made of the travel descriptions of Nicolaeus Saemundarson, the head of a monastery in northern Ireland (1151–54), of Johannes of Wurtzburg (1165), and the description of Ereẓ Israel by Johannes Phocas (1177). The most important among the itineraries of the 13th century are the works by the Germans Wilbrand of Oldenburg (1212) and Thietmar (1217), the book by Sabbas, archbishop of Serbia (1225–27), written in ancient Slavic, and the work by Perdiccas, protonotary of Ephesus (c. 1250). From the end of the century there is a description of the "Holy Land" by Burchardus of Mount Zion (de Monte Sion; 1283), which is not actually an itinerary but rather a work by a monk who lived in Ereẓ Israel for a long time.

After the elimination of the last remnant of crusader rule in Jerusalem, i.e., the conquest of Acre in 1291, the pilgrimage movement increased. Many of the visitors and travelers wrote about their travels, and hence a greater number of itineraries is preserved from the 14th century than from earlier periods, and they are more varied. During this period the pilgrims began to write their works in their national languages as well. Of these, special mention should be made of the travel descriptions by the Irish monk Simeon Simeonis (1332); the German priest Ludolf of Suchem, who spent the years 1336–41 in the countries of the Orient and described them in a Latin and German work; the Italian monk Niccolo da Poggibonsi (1345) who wrote in Italian "A Book about the Land Across the Sea"; and the Russian priest Ignatius of Smolensk, who went to Ereẓ Israel at the end of the century and described the Christian holy places in his mother tongue. Of the emissary-spy type was a German nobleman, Wilhelm of Boldensele, who was a member of the Dominican Order and visited Ereẓ Israel (1333) as an emissary of a French cardinal connected with plans for a new Crusade. The detailed itinerary by the monk Giacomo of Verona (1335), written in Latin, is a combined guide for pilgrims and exploration of possibilities of a new Crusade. Itineraries of a completely different type were written by three Florentines, Lionardo Frescobaldi, Simone Sigoli, and Giorgio Gucci, who went to Ereẓ Israel in 1384 by way of Egypt and returned by way of Syria. The three pilgrims were secular and their travel books reflect the secular-commercial approach of the townsmen. They abound in descriptions of the economic and social life and they also contain exact data about expenditures. With the increase in pilgrimages high-ranking noblemen also went to Ereẓ Israel in that generation and their travels were described by their companions. Among these was the future King Henry IV of England (1392/93). Mention should also be made of the travelers during that century who visited in all the Oriental countries and did not go especially to Ereẓ Israel, but in whose travel books the description of Ereẓ Israel plays a major role. Among these were the Italian Odorico de Pordenone (1320), the Englishman John of Mandeville (c. 1336), and the Italian Giovanni de Marignola (1350).

The 15th century was the classic period of Christian pilgrimage to Ereẓ Israel in the sense that the pilgrimage movement was more intense, its forms were more crystallized, and the composition of the pilgrims in terms of their origins was more variegated than in any preceding period. The proportion of priests was smaller than formerly while the proportion of the bourgeois was larger. The variety of pilgrims is reflected by the variety of itineraries preserved from that century. Some travelers did not take the short sea-route from Italy to the shores of Ereẓ Israel, but wandered in many countries on the way to and from Ereẓ Israel, since their entire purpose was to gather information about the strength of the armies and fortifications in the Holy Land itself and its neighboring countries. There are many itineraries of noblemen from various countries who went to Ereẓ Israel during the 15th century and whose travels are described by their companions. Especially characteristic of the pilgrimages of that time was the broad participation of the urban laymen. These bourgeois came from various countries. However, the most important itineraries in terms of their comprehensiveness and the value of their information about the contemporary social scene in Ereẓ Israel were still those written by priests. Among the itineraries of churchmen of the 15th century, especially significant are the works of the Italians Santo Brasca (1480) and Pietro Casola (1494), and of the Germans Bernhard of Breidenbach and Felix Fabri, who went to Ereẓ Israel in 1483. Both Bernhard of Breidenbach, who was a priest in Mainz, and Felix Fabri, who was a Dominican monk in Ulm, wrote travel books. Their works, especially that by Fabri, are, on the one hand, travel descriptions, and, on the other, studies in the history of Ereẓ Israel, its settlement, and the holy places. Naturally, in many of the descriptions of travels, which were written in the course of hundreds of years, there is also information about the meetings between the pilgrims and Jews in various places and especially about the places of origin of these Jews. Although most of the authors display a marked orthodoxy and even extreme religious zealousness, with regard to this matter they were simply reporting.

Of greater historical significance are the Christian itineraries from the 16th century on, which mainly describe the population in general and the Christians in particular. However, the Jewish population was increasing in Safed and later in Jerusalem, Tiberias, and Hebron, and the Christian travelers, now mostly coming from the various German countries, from Spain, and later from France and England as well, did not miss the opportunity to describe their meetings with the Jews. They also tell about religious discussions conducted between themselves and the Jews, with whom they found a common tongue (German, Spanish) and whose houses often provided clean and secure inns, and polite hospitality (in places where there were no monasteries or inns for pilgrims). These travel books, especially because they were numerous and sometimes contained contradictory views, serve as a primary source for the history of the Jews of Ereẓ Israel during the Ottoman period, since most of them perhaps quite unintentionally gave expression to a completely objective picture. The many travel books, amounting to about 120 in all, which were written by Christian travelers in the course of 400 years (16th–19th centuries) add up to a considerable historical treasure.

It is impossible to review here all the Christian travel books published during this period, particularly since many of them merely parrot the words of their predecessors. However, some of them should be mentioned: the travel book of the Franciscan monk from Portugal, Pantaleao de Aveiro, *Itinerario da Terra Sancta* (c. 1565, publ. 1927); of the French Franciscan monk Jaques Goujon, *Histoire et Voyage de la Terre Sainte* (Lyons, 1571); of John Sanderson, who was in Ereẓ Israel in 1601, *The Travels of John Sanderson, 1584–1602* (publ. 1931); of George Sandys, *A Relation of a Journey, A Description of the Holy Land of the Jewes* (London[5], 1652); and especially the description by the monk-missionary Eugéne Roger (c. 1630), *La Terre Sainte* (1664). The learned Dutchman Olaf Dapper collected much information which he found in works by preceding scholars, added his own eyewitness accounts, and wrote a complete description of Ereẓ Israel, first published in Amsterdam in 1681, and later in German translation in Nuremberg, 1688–89, *Asia, oder genaue und gruendliche Beschreibung des gantzen Syrien und Palestins*. This is not an original work but it includes considerable geographic-historical material. The broad travel memoirs of L. de Arvieux, who served as French consul and ambassador in Algeria and Tunisia (1664–65) and later as special ambassador to the sultan in Constantinople (1672–73), and finally as consul with broad authority in Aleppo (1682–88), adapted De la Roque, *Voyage dans la Palestine* (Amsterdam, 1718). The Dutchman Cornellius le Bruya undertook a comprehensive tour of Asia Minor, the Aegean Isles, Egypt, Syria, and Ereẓ Israel at the end of the century. His work, which includes numerous illustrations (about 200 copper engravings), was published in Dutch, translated into French and from French into English: *A Voyage to the Levant, etc.* (London, 1702). Of lasting scholarly worth is the work by Thomas Shaw, *Travels or Observations relating to several parts of Barbary and the Levant* (Oxford, 1738).

Among the numerous travelers of the 18th century special mention should also be made of Richard Pococke (1738), *A Description of the East II/1* (London, 1745); Frederick Hasselquirst (1751), *Voyages and Travels in the Levant* (London, 1766); and especially the Frenchman C.-J. Volney, *Travels etc.* (1783–85; London, 1788), who visited the countries of the Orient at a young age and who in his travel description offers a brilliant analysis of the political situation and of the strategic plans already formulated at that time, ten years before Napoleon prepared to conquer Egypt.

After Napoleon's campaign of conquest in the area, and despite his failure, there was an increasing number of Christian travelers who went to Ereẓ Israel not necessarily from purely religious motives. There were among them important scholars such as Edward Robinson, E. Picrotti, C.R. Conder, and many others who opened up Ereẓ Israel for Muslim scholarship and who cannot be regarded as traveler-tourists in the accepted sense. The travel works devoted to describing the Ottoman Empire, Egypt, and North Africa, often contain descriptions dealing with Ereẓ Israel which mention Jews as well.

Muslim Travelers

Throughout the Middle Ages and in modern times numerous Muslims have gone to *Jerusalem to pray at the mosque on the Temple Mount, which is considered one of the holy places of *Islam. These pilgrims also came from many countries. However, despite the richness of Arabic literature, almost no books are devoted solely to descriptions of these travels. It should be pointed out that also in relation to travels to Mecca no literary branch developed similar to the descriptions of Christian travels to Ereẓ Israel.

A book describing travels to Ereẓ Israel and Mecca was written by the Spanish judge Abū al-Baqā' Khālid b. ʿIsā al-Balawī, who set out in 1336. This work, however, is in part a copy of itineraries by earlier writer-travelers. The mystic ʿAbd al-Ghanī b. Ismāʿil al-Nābulusī, who lived in *Damascus, wrote a description of a journey to Jerusalem at the end of the 17th century. However, these works did not become well known in Arabic literature, and if one were interested in a description of Ereẓ Israel one would have to resort to works describing long journeys and general works on geography. Especially interesting among these itineraries are the Persian work *Sefer Nāmeh* ("The Book of Travel") by Nasir-i Khosrau, who visited Ereẓ Israel in 1047; the Arabic work *Riḥla* ("The Journey"), by Abu al-Ḥusayn Muhammad ibn Jubayr, who visited Ereẓ Israel in 1184; and the work by the world traveler Ibn Baṭṭūṭa, who visited Ereẓ Israel in 1326–30, on his long journey in Eastern Asia from which he returned in 1348. The descriptions of Ereẓ Israel included in the works of Arabic geographers of the classical school were also the product of personal observations and investigations. These geographers, the most important of whom lived in the tenth century, based their works on firsthand research in various countries to which they traveled. The three outstanding representatives of this school were al-Iṣṭakhrī (c. 950), Ibn Ḥawqal al-Nasībī (977), and Muhammad b. Aḥmad, called al-Maqdisī (the Jerusalemite, who wrote in 985).

The Muslims also composed itineraries for pilgrims, similar to the itineraries written by Christian clerics for the pilgrims who came to worship at the holy places. The most famous, *Kitāb al-Ishārāt ilā maʿrifat al-Ziyārāt* ("Guide for the Places of Pilgrimage"), written by Ali b. Abī Bakr Al-Harawī (d. 1214), includes the vast material he collected on long journeys. The work is not limited to a description of the Muslim holy places in Ereẓ Israel, but lists holy places in other countries as well. Such itineraries generally contained sayings attributed to *Muhammad about the holiness of Jerusalem and especially about the mosque of the Dome of the Rock, as well as reviews of the history of Jerusalem.

More numerous were the works containing only sayings about the holiness of Jerusalem and especially of the mosques on the Temple Mount. Such works on the "praises of Jerusalem" became characteristic of the Muslim literature of Ereẓ Israel. In the second half of the 11th century Abu 'l-Ma ʿalī al-Musharraf b. al-Murajja (d. 1099), a Jerusalemite, composed such a work, entitled *Faḍā'il Bayt al-Maqdis wa al-Shām* ("The Qualities of Jerusalem and Damascus"). Al-Qāsim ibn ʿAsākir (d. 1203) wrote a work about the al-Aqṣa Mosque, and his relative, Niẓām al-Dīn (d. 1274), wrote *Faḍā'il al-Quds* ("The Qualities of Jerusalem"). While the manuscripts of these writings have not been found, there are extant manuscripts of a book praising Jerusalem which was written by the Baghdad historian, Abu al-Faraj ibn al-Jawzī (d. 1200). In the 14th century Burhān al-dīn Ibrāhīm ibn al-Firkāh, a teacher in Damascus (d. 1329), wrote *Bāʿith al-Nufūs ilā Ziyārāt al-Quds al-Maḥrūs* ("He who Stirs his Soul to Visit Preserved Jerusalem"). In 1351 in Jerusalem itself, Shihāb al-dīn Aḥmad b. Muhammad b. Ibrāhīm ibn Hilāl wrote a similar book entitled *Muthīr al-Gharām ilā Ziyārāt al-Quds wa al-Shām* ("The Arouser of Desire to Visit Jerusalem and Damascus"). In the mid-14th century the Hebronite preacher Isḥāq b. Ibrāhīm al-Tadmurī wrote about the cave of *Machpelah as a place of pilgrimage. In 1470 the Egyptian Shams al-Dīn al-Suyūtī wrote in Jerusalem about the "Outer Mosque." These works were preserved and published, and some of them were even translated into English. The most important of these books is the comprehensive work about Jerusalem and Hebron written in 1494/95 by the Jerusalemite judge Mujīr al-Dīn al-ʿUlaymī entitled *al-Uns al-Jalīl bi-Taʿrīkh al-Quds wa al-Khalīl* ("A Weighty Discussion of the History of Jerusalem and the City of the Friend [Abraham] – Hebron"). This work contains all the sayings about the holiness of Jerusalem attributed to the prophet of Islam, as well as a detailed description of the holy city and the other towns of Ereẓ Israel (the book was printed in Cairo in 1293 A.H.). Works about Jerusalem continued to be written during the period of Ottomon rule. In the mid-17th century a judge from Medina, Nāṣir al-dīn Muhammad b. Khiḍr al-Rūmī al-Jalālī, wrote a book entitled *Al-Mustaqṣā fī Faḍl al-Ziyārāt bi al-Masjid al-Aqṣā* ("The Book Concerning the Right to Visit the Outer Mosque"). This work differs from the traditional type of the Muslim "praises of Jerusalem" in that it contains a detailed guide for pilgrims.

In summation, the Arabic writings about Ereẓ Israel, most of which contain "praises of Jerusalem," generally lack factual-documentary content. In contrast, the descriptions of the Turkish traveler Evliya Çelebi, who visited Ereẓ Israel twice (first in 1649 and then in 1660–61), are of great significance. He was an experienced statesman-scholar, whose sharp eyes observed the situation of the population, the administrative division of the country, the changes which had occurred during the time between his two visits, and the amount of taxes collected. He paid attention to the Jewish populations of all the countries he visited. Of special importance in connection with the situation of Ereẓ Israel is his recounting of the mass exodus of the Jews of *Safed, which took place in his time, and the mention of the custom of pilgrimage to Meron, which in his time was not yet celebrated on Lag ba-Omer. Evliya Çelebi, however, was the last Muslim traveler to devote part of his work to Ereẓ Israel.

[Eliyahu Ashtor]

BIBLIOGRAPHY: R. Roehricht, *Bibliotheca Geographica Palaestinae* (1890); idem and H. Meisner, *Deutsche Pilgerreisen nach dem heiligen Lande* (1880); H. Michelant and G. Raynava, *Itinéraires à Jerusalem et Descriptions de la Terre Sainte* (1882); *Reysbuch des heyligen Lands* (Frankfurt on the Main, 1584); Th. Wright, *Early Travels in Palestine* (1848); *Palestine Pilgrims' Text Society Library*, 1–13 (1890–97); S.P. Khitrowo, *Itinéraires Russes en Orient* (1889); I. Ben-Zvi, *Ereẓ Yisrael vi-Yshuvah bi-Ymei ha-Shilton ha-Ottomani* (1967²); M. Ish-Shalom, *Masei Noẓerim le-Ereẓ Yisrael* (1965); E.L. Sukenik, in: KS, 7 (1930/31), 99–101; M. Narkiss, in: *Ommanut*, 2 (1941), 7–10; Z. Vilnay, *Maẓẓevot Kodesh be-Ereẓ Yisra'el* (1963²); P. Thomsen, *Die Palaestina-Literatur*, 7 vols. (1908–60), passim; T. Tobler, *Bibliographia geographica Palaestinae* (Ger., 1867, 1875); T. Kollek and M. Perlman, *Pilgrims to the Holy Land* (1970).

TRAVNIK, town in Bosnia. Under Ottoman rule until Austrian annexation in 1878; within Yugoslavia from 1918. After *Sarajevo, it had the second most important settlement of Sephardi Jews in the region; some of them originally lived in Sarajevo and transferred their residence to Travnik in the 18th century. A community was organized by the mid-18th century and a *kal santo* (synagogue) existed from 1768. The Jews themselves constructed it, working daily between the *Minḥah* and *Ma'ariv* prayers.

Trouble assailed the community when an apostate, Moses Habillo, who took the name of Derwish Aḥmed, incited a massacre of the Jews. Many Muslims rioted but disaster was prevented when Rabbi Raphael Pinto achieved a compromise. Ten Jewish hostages were taken into custody for inquiry. They were freed after a ransom was paid on the second day of Marḥeshvan (in 1807), which was celebrated for many years by the community as a feast of deliverance. In 1818 the local *qāimaqam*, the vizier's representative, accused the Jews of ritual murder. Some Jews were arrested, but were released when Muslim notables intervened on their behalf. Apart from such isolated incidents, and cases of extortions, Jewish communal life remained undisturbed and relations with the majority of the city's residents were good. The best known rabbi of Travnik was Abram Abinun. Jews were occupied as blacksmiths, joiners, saddlers, tailors, and shoemakers, dealers in medicinal plants and folk healers. Some of them were distillers and wheat merchants. In 1878, shortly after Travnik passed to Austria, a small Ashkenazi community was founded. A synagogue was erected in 1769. The community had a philanthropic association, Ezrat Dalim, and in the 20th century a "Jewish Club" existed there. Until the Holocaust, 375 Jews lived there peacefully.

In World War II the German-Croatian occupation violently and cruelly clamped down on the community. A concentration camp was established at nearby Kruščica (Krooshchitza); survivors were deported and murdered elsewhere in Croatia or Poland. The community was not renewed. The synagogue was used as a workshop.

BIBLIOGRAPHY: V. Vinaver, in: *Jevrejski Almanah* (1955/56), 28–34. **ADD. BIBLIOGRAPHY:** J. Konforti, *Travnički Jevreji* (1979).

[Zvi Loker]

TREASURE, TREASURY (Treasure: Heb. אוֹצָר, בֶּצֶר, חַיִל, חֹסֶן, מַטְמוֹן, מִסְתָּר, מַצְפּוּן, נֶעְלָם, סְגֻלָּה; Akk. *niṣirtu*; Treasury: Heb. בֵּית הָאוֹצָר(וֹת), גִּנְזֵי הַמֶּלֶךְ, גִּנְזַךְ, בֵּית נְכוֹת; Akk. *bīt niṣirti, bāt nakkamīti*). The concepts of treasure and treasury in the Bible are denoted by many different terms.

Semantic Range of Words Meaning Treasure

Most of the Hebrew words for treasure listed above may be divided into two semantic groups:

a) Words which mean both treasure and something hidden or secret (*maṭmon, mistar, maẓpun, neʿlam*).

b) Words which mean both treasure and strength (*beẓer, ḥayil, ḥosen*).

The most common Akkadian term for treasure, *niṣirtu*, belongs to the first group as may be seen from the following passage:

> *Utnapištim ana šâšuma izzakkara ana Gilgameš luptēka Gilgameš amat niṣirti u pirišta ša ilāni kâša luqbīka.* "Utnapishtim said to him, to Gilgamesh: 'Let me divulge a hidden matter to you, O Gilgamesh, And let me tell you a secret of the gods'" (Gilgamesh, 11:8–10).

Types of Treasures

While the most common type of treasure referred to is "silver and gold" (*kesef, zahav*, e.g., Isa. 2:7; Ezek. 28:4; Eccles. 2:8; I Chron. 29:3; cf. Ps. 68:31 where perhaps the reading should be *beẓer kesef*, so Tur-Sinai), treasures of clothes (e.g., Jer. 38:11; Zech. 14:14), wine (I Chron. 27:27), oil (I Chron. 27:28), food in general (Joel 1:17; II Chron. 11:11), precious stones (I Chron. 29:8), and dedicated gifts (I Chron. 26:26) are all represented. Elsewhere, temple treasures are listed in Ezra 1:9–11 (cf. Ezra 2:68–69; Neh. 7:69 ff.) and include gold and silver dishes and bowls, and gold drachmas and priestly vestments, while royal treasures are mentioned in II Chronicles 32:27–29 (period of Hezekiah) comprising silver, gold, precious stones, spices, shields, and miscellaneous items. Babylonia in particular is singled out for her opulence and is called "the one rich in treasures" (Jer. 51:13). The treasures of Israel's enemies (*ḥeil goyim*) will all come to her when God executes His punishment upon them (Isa. 60:5, 11; 61:6; Zech. 14:14). Treasures are sometimes described as being transported on the backs of beasts of burden (Isa. 30:6; I Kings 10:2 = II Chron. 9:1; cf. Isa. 66:20). The gold of Ophir is described as "the treasure of the rivers" (Job 22:24; cf. N.H. Tur-Sinai, in bibl.). Finally, treasures are used as bribes in the Bible. In Jeremiah 41:8 the ten men who remained after Ishmael son of Nethaniah's massacre of the rest of their group bribed Ishmael to let them live in return for treasures of wheat, barley, olive oil, and honey, hidden in the fields. In I Samuel 12:3 and Amos 2:6; 8:6, there are additional instances of bribes involving treasure. In all three cases the word *nʿelam*, "hidden treasure" (the vocalization of which is still uncertain) must be restored to the text (in place of *naʿalayim*, "shoes" in Amos 2:6; 8:6, and *ʾaʿalim*, "I shall hide" in I Sam. 12:3, cf. Septuagint which also reads *naʿalayim*, "shoes"). This meaning is demonstrated both by Ben Sira 46:19 which paraphrases I Samuel 12:3, by juxtaposing the Hebrew word *kofer*, "gift," with the word *naʿalayim*, and by Targum Jonathan which translates *naʿalayim* in Amos 2:6 and 8:6 by a form of the word *ḥosen*, "treasure" (see above).

In extra-biblical sources, mention must be made of the Copper Scroll discovered in 1952 in Cave 3 of Qumran. This Copper Scroll consists of three sheets of very thin copper on which is engraved a Hebrew text. The Hebrew text is a register of 64 deposits of buried treasure supposed to be hidden in and around Qumran (in an area extending from Hebron to Mt. Gerizim). The objects listed include a silver chest, ingots of gold and silver, jars of all shapes and sizes, bowls, perfumes, and perhaps, vestments. It should be noted that the purpose of the scroll is still a mystery. Among the theories advanced by scholars are that it is a list of the treasures of the First Temple, the Second Temple, or the Qumran community. A fourth theory, posited by T.H. Gaster (see bibl.), is that the scroll represents "an unconscionable fraud [or even a cruel practical joke] perpetrated by some cynical outsider upon the naive and innocent minds of the ascetics of Qumran."

Treasures in War

The defeated nation often was obliged to give up all of her treasures to the victor (Isa. 39:6 ff.). For example, Shishak of Egypt took from Jerusalem the royal treasures, the Temple treasures, and everything else (I Kings 14:26 = II Chron. 12:9). While no part of the *ḥerem* of Jericho after Joshua's conquest could be taken by any Israelite, all the silver and gold, and the copper and iron vessels were to be added to the Temple treasury (Josh. 6:19, 24). As part of Israel's punishment, Babylon would carry off all of her treasures as spoil (Jer. 15:13; 17:3; 20:5); but the day would also come when Babylon would be punished in kind (Jer. 50:37). Likewise, Moab (Jer. 48:7) and the Ammonites (Jer. 49:4), who trusted in their treasures, and Edom (Jer. 49:10; cf. Obad. 6) would suffer the same consequences. In extra-biblical sources, the same situation prevailed in times of war. Sennacherib of Assyria in describing his defeat of Merodach-Baladan of Babylon claims:

> *Ann ekallišu ša qereb Bāb-ili ērumma aptēma bīt niṣirtišu ḫurāṣa kaspa unūt hurāṣi kaspi abnu aqartu bušê makkūr ēkallišu ašlula.* "I entered his palace in Babylon and I opened his treasury. I took as spoil – gold, silver, gold and silver vessels, precious stones, valuables, and property of his palace" (D.D. Luckenbill, *The Annals of Sennacherib* (1924), p. 67, lines 5–6).

Symbolic Treasures

Both Israel and God are spoken of as each other's treasure. Israel is spoken of as God's *segullah*, "treasured/private possession" (Ex. 19:5; Deut. 7:6; 14:2; 26:18; cf. Mal. 3:17; Ps. 135:4; for this meaning compare likewise Akk. *sikiltu*). Eliphaz instructs Job to return to God and consider the Lord his treasure (Job 22:23–25). There are many references to the heavens as God's treasure (Deut. 28:12; Jer. 10:13; 51:16; Ps. 135:7), while various forces of God are described as His treasure (Jer. 50:25; Ps. 33:6–7; Job 38:22). Finally, wisdom and devotion to God are described as the treasure of faith (Isa. 33:6).

Concept of Treasure in Wisdom Literature

The connection between wisdom and treasure may best be seen from those passages where wisdom is personified. Wisdom fills the treasuries of those who seek her (Prov. 8:21), and, in turn, should be sought after like buried treasure (Prov. 2:4). Elsewhere, there are many references to the treasures of the wise man, but the fool has none (Prov. 15:6; 21:20). Treasures gained through wickedness are of no avail (Prov. 10:2), while a little in the way of material goods plus a good deal of faith are better than the most precious treasures (Prov. 15:16). Finally, the acquisition of treasures through deceitful means will cause their owner's downfall (Prov. 21:6ff.), a theme which has several extra-biblical parallels. In an Akkadian composition entitled "Counsels of Wisdom," the following advice is given:

> My son, if it be the desire of the prince that you be his, if you are entrusted with his closely guarded seal, open his treasure house [*niṣirtašu*], enter into [it]; apart from you there is not another man [who may enter into it]. You will find therein untold wealth. Do not covet anything. Do not take it into your head to conceal something. For afterwards, the matter will be investigated, and what you have concealed will come to light … (W.G. Lambert, *Babylonian Wisdom Literature* (1960), p. 102, lines 81ff.).

Treasury

Of the three words for treasury listed above, only one, *bet nekhot*, was not understood until fairly recently. The context of the single biblical verse in which this term occurs (II Kings 20:13 = Isa. 39:2) showed that it must mean treasury, but the origin of the term was still a mystery. It is now known that *bet nekhot* is a loanword from the Akkadian *bīt nakkamāti*, "treasury." Both the Hebrew and Akkadian nouns have corresponding verbs, *ʾẓr* and *nakāmu*, meaning "to amass, store up." For example, Ashurbanipal boasts in his annals about his conquest of Susa:

> *Aptēma bīt nakkamātišu (nu) sa kaspu ḫurāṣu bušû makkūru nukkumū qrebšun.* "I opened his treasure house wherein silver, gold, valuables and property were stored …" (M. Streck, *Aššurbanipal…* (1916), p. 50, lines 132–4).

Elsewhere, *ʾoẓrot bet* YHWH, "Temple treasury" (e.g., I Kings 7:51 = II Chron. 5:1), and *oʾẓrot bet ha-melekh*, "palace treasury" (e.g., I Kings 14:26), are often mentioned together. For example, Asa gave all he had in both treasuries to Ben-Hadad (I Kings 15:18 = II Chron. 16:2), Joash gave up both his treasuries to Hazael (II Kings 12:19), and Nebuchadnezzar took everything from the treasuries in Jerusalem (e.g., II Kings 24:13; II Chron. 36:10, 18). Another instance is the discussion between Isaiah and Hezekiah concerning the delegation sent by the Babylonian king to see Hezekiah (II Kings 20:12ff. = Isa. 39:1ff.). Finally, the term *genazim* is used three times in the latest biblical books to refer to the treasury of Persia (Esth. 3:9; 4:7) and the treasuries of multicolored garments of many nations (Ezek. 27:24).

BIBLIOGRAPHY: H. Zimmern, *Akkadische Fremdwoerter* (1917), 8; M. Greenberg, in: JAOS, 71 (1951), 172–4; T.H. Gaster, *The Dead Sea Scriptures* (1956), 382–5; M.Z. Segal, *Sifrei Shemuʾel* (1964), 86–87; N.H. Tur-Sinai, *The Book of Job* (1967), 347–8.

[Chayim Cohen]

TREBIC (Czech **Třebič**; Ger. **Trebitsch**), town in W. Moravia, Czech Republic. The Trebic community was considered one of the oldest in Moravia; it is alleged that a synagogue was built in 938. During the wave of massacres of Jews in 1338, which commenced in *Pulkau, some Trebic Jews were killed. The first documentary mention of the community concerns an attack on Jews and robbery in 1410. In 1464 it was destroyed along with the rest of the town. Jewish matters were included in the *Stadtordnung* ("municipal regulations") of 1583. In 1604 the majority of Trebic's merchants were Jews. The old synagogue was allegedly built in 1639–42; in 1757 its roof had to be lowered so that its lights could not be seen from the castle. It was damaged three times by fire and was redesigned several times, the last time in neo-Gothic style in 1880. Services were held until World War I. Since 1954 it has been used by the Hussite Church. The new synagogue was built in the early 17th century and renovated in 1845. After World War I, it fell into disuse. After World War II, it was converted into a Jewish museum.

In 1727 Jews were compelled to live segregated from Christians. In 1848 the Jews were prevented from organizing a Jewish unit in the National Guard. Becoming one of the Politischen Gemeinden ("political communities," see *Politische Gemeinde) in 1849, Trebic retained this status until the dissolution of the Hapsburg monarchy. After freedom of movement and settlement had been granted to Jews, the community began to decline, many moving to *Vienna, *Brno, *Jihlava, and other larger cities. Whereas in 1799 there were 1,770 Jews in the Jewish quarter of Trebic, and in 1850 the community numbered 1,605, in 1890 their number declined to 987; in 1900 to 756; in 1921 to 362; and in 1930 to 300. During the German occupation, in May 1942, 1,370 Jews from *Jihlava province were assembled in Trebic and deported to *Theresienstadt; only 35 of them survived the war. A small congregation was reestablished in 1945. In 1957 a memorial tablet for the victims of the Holocaust was dedicated.

Born in Trebic were Wolfgang *Wessely, the first Jewish university teacher in Austria; Adolf Kurrein (1846–1919), one of the first Zionist rabbis in Austria; and Sigmund Taussig (1840–1910), a pioneer in the field of hydro-engineering.

BIBLIOGRAPHY: Kořatek, in: H. Gold (ed.), *Die Juden und Judengemeinden Maehrens* (1929), 523–37; A. Engel, in: JGJJČ, 2 (1930); Kahana, in: *Kobez al Jad*, 4 (1946/47), 183–92; *Věstnik židovské obce náboženské v Praze*, 20:1 (1958), 4; *Der Orient*, 5 (1844), 308. **ADD. BIBLIOGRAPHY:** J. Fiedler, *Jewish Sights of Bohemia and Moravia* (1991), 184–85.

[Meir Lamed / Yeshayahu Jelinek (2nd ed.)]

TREBITSCH, ABRAHAM (**Reuven Hayyat**; b. 1760), Moravian historical author. Born in Trebic, he attended a Prague yeshivah c. 1775, and later in *Mikulov was secretary of the Moravian *Landesrabbiner. His history, *Korot ha-Ittim* (Bruenn, 1801), contains "tales of all the wars from 1741 to 1801 which were waged in the countries of Austria, Prussia, France, and England and all that Jews went through in those days." Intended as a continuation of Menahem *Amelander's *She'erit Yisrael* (Amsterdam, 1743), it differs from it by covering non-Jewish as well as Jewish history. It was published simultaneously in Yiddish as *Tsaytgeshikhte*. The work is important mainly for its traditionalist evaluation of the reforms of *Joseph II. In 1851 Jacob *Bodek published a revised edition entitled *Korot Nosafot*, and there also exists an edition apparently plagiarized by Bodek's brother-in-law. Along with Hirsch Menaker, Trebitsch wrote *Ru'aḥ Ḥayyim*, an account of the exorcism of a **dibbuk* in Mikulov (Vienna, 1785; Yid. (same title), Bruenn, 1785; repr. in several editions of Moshe Graf's *Zera Kodesh*).

BIBLIOGRAPHY: R. Kestenberg-Gladstein, *Die neuere Geschichte der Juden in den boehmischen Laendern*, 1 (1969), index; I. Halpern, in: KS, 29 (1953/54), 174–5.

[Meir Lamed]

TREBITSCH, MOSES LOEB BEN WOLF (18th century), Central European Hebrew scribe-illuminator, from Trebic in Moravia. He was one of the pioneer figures in the renaissance of Jewish manuscript art at the beginning of the 18th century. At least a dozen works from his gifted pen are known – most of them Passover *Haggadot*. His pen drawings, usually set off by wash, are well-composed, small genre paintings. The family scene which he prefixed to the *Van Geldern Haggadah* (1723) and a companion work now in the Hebrew Union College, Cincinnati (1716–17), are among the outstanding specimens of the new Jewish miniature art of the period.

BIBLIOGRAPHY: Landsberger, in: HUCA, 23 (1950–51), 503–21; Naményi, in: REJ, 16 (1957), 59–60.

[Cecil Roth]

TREBITSCH, NEHEMIAH (**Menahem Nahum**; 1779–1842), Moravian rabbi. Trebitsch taught at the Prague yeshivot of Jacob Guensburg and Simon Kuh before becoming rabbi in Prossnitz (1826–32). He was subsequently appointed Landesrabbiner of Moravia with his seat in Nikolsburg. The right bestowed upon him by the provincial government (1833) to appoint candidates for vacant rabbinates was canceled in 1838 because of his persistent refusal to nominate rabbis with liberal leanings. This cancellation was also influenced by his opposition to the use of German in sermons for which he had been officially censured. However, he consented to, and participated in, the establishment of a Hebrew-German industrial school. He wrote glosses to the Jerusalem Talmud, and *Kovez al Yad ha-Ḥazakah* (8 vols., 1835–42), notes on Maimonides' *Yad*.

BIBLIOGRAPHY: A. Schlesinger, *Kol Nehi* (Heb. and Ger., 1842), eulogy and biography; L. Loew, *Gesammelte Schriften*, 2 (1900), 195–212; H. Gold (ed.), *Juden und Judengemeinden Maehrens* (1929), 500 and index; I. Kahn, in: A. Engel (ed.), *Gedenkbuch im Auftrag des Kuratoriums Nikolsburg* (1936), 71–74; A.H. Weiss, *Zikhronotai* (1895), 41–45.

[Oskar K. Rabinowicz]

TREBITSCH, SIEGFRIED (1869–1956), Austrian novelist, playwright, and translator. The son of a Viennese silk merchant, Trebitsch was a great traveler. His first volume of poetry, *Gedichte* (1889), was followed after prolonged intervals by *Wellen und Wege* (1913) and *Aus verschuetteten Tiefen* (1947). He was, however, better known as a prose writer and wrote many psychological novels, including *Genesung* (1902), *Spaetes Licht* (1918), and *Renate Aldringen* (1929). *Die Rache ist mein* (1934) was a volume of novellas. Trebitsch's plays include *Ein Muttersohn* (1911), *Frau Gittas Suehne* (1920), and *Das Land der Treue* (1926). His German translations of George Bernard Shaw's plays (in various editions from the turn of the century on) paved the way for Shaw's European vogue. Following the *Anschluss* in 1938, Trebitsch, a convert to Christianity, settled in Switzerland. His autobiography, *Chronik eines Lebens* (1951; *Chronicle of a Life*, 1953), is an informative and entertaining firsthand account of the European literary scene.

[Harry Zohn]

His stepbrother, ARTHUR TREBITSCH (1880–1927), was also a writer in Vienna. Like Siegfried he abandoned Judaism and, as a disciple of Otto *Weininger, was a notorious antisemite. His book *Geist und Judentum* (1919) blamed the defeat of the Central Powers during World War I and the subsequent collapse of the Hohenzollern and Hapsburg dynasties on Jewish machinations. His *Deutscher Geist – oder Judentum* (1921) utilized the forged *Protocols of the Elders of Zion* to prove the existence of a Jewish conspiracy to dominate and debauch the world. An admirer of Houston Stewart *Chamberlain, whose racial theories he developed to a pathological extreme,

Trebitsch vilified his fellow Jews until his death and even offered his services to the Austrian Nazis.

BIBLIOGRAPHY: G. Schuberth, *Arthur Trebitsch, sein Leben und sein Werk* (1927); R. Mueller-Guttenbrunn, *Der brennende Mensch: Das geistige Vermaechtnis von Arthur Trebitsch* (1930); T. Lessing, *Juedischer Selbsthass* (1930), 101–31; F. Heer, *Der Glaube des Adolf Hitler* (1968), index; S. Liptzin, *Germany's Stepchildren* (1944), 189–94.

TREBLINKA, one of the three Aktion Reinhard death camps during World War II, second only to *Auschwitz in the number of Jews killed. Known until then as a small railroad station between Siedlce and Malkinia, located approximately 62 miles (100 km.) northeast of Warsaw. The Germans built a railway spur that led from the labor camp to the death camp and to the railway station in the village of Treblinka. Heavily wooded, it could be hidden from view. Treblinka became the final destination for transports that brought Jews from the ghettos of the General Government and about ten European countries to their death. The Jews were brought to Treblinka under the pretext of resettlement in former Soviet territories that had been occupied. The actual site of mass slaughter was located approximately 2.5 miles (4 km.) from the station, camouflaged inside a pine forest. On the border of this area was a platform for the train that carried the Jews from the station in consignments of 15–20 cars, which reached the camp on a side track especially built for this purpose.

However, the name Treblinka refers to two camps: the first one (later called Treblinka I), which began operating in 1941, was openly and officially designated as a forced-labor camp for offenses against the occupation authorities; the second camp, located approximately 1 mile (1.5 km.) from the first, and designed for mass extermination, was treated by the German authorities as a state secret, and its name was coded even in confidential letters as T.II.

Treblinka I: For Jews and Poles (December 1941–July 1944)

Unlike Treblinka II, this camp was intended not only for Jews, but also for Poles deported for economic or political offenses. The Poles would remain in the camp for the duration of their punishment, and only part of those charged with political crimes were killed or transferred to concentration camps. Jews were transferred there after roundups or from forced-labor contingents required from the Judenrate, and only in a very few cases would they leave the place alive. Devastated by hunger, overwork in the nearby gravel pit, brutal beatings, and cruel harassment, they died in large numbers. Others perished in occasional executions or were transferred to Treblinka II to be murdered after they lost all their strength. The last execution at Treblinka I took place on July 24, 1944, just prior to the entrance of the Soviet army.

According to the statistical estimates of Judge Z. Lukaszkiewicz, who conducted an investigation of both camps in 1945 on behalf of the Main State Commission for the Investigation of Nazi Crimes in Poland, approximately 10,000 individuals had passed through Treblinka I, 70% of whom were either shot or murdered in other ways. In light of the practices for mixed camps, according to which the Aryans benefited from larger food rations and were allowed to receive provisions from their families, it can be assumed that at least 90% of those who perished were Jews. After the war more than 40 mass graves were dug up in the nearby forest and as many as 6,500 bodies were counted. Deeper in the forest were more graves that were not dug up.

The commanding officer of Treblinka I was SS Hauptsturmfuehrer von Eupen. His favorite sport was horseback riding, which gave him the opportunity to trample and kill prisoners. The statements of surviving witnesses from Treblinka I include a particularly gruesome description of how 30 children brought there during the *Warsaw ghetto uprising were killed with an ax by a Ukrainian from the auxiliary service under the supervision of Hans Heinbuch, an SS man, who was a university graduate and worked as a teacher after the war.

Treblinka II: The Culmination of "Efficiency" in the Extermination of Jews (July 23, 1942–Oct. 14, 1943)

After the beginning of mass slaughter in the *Belzec and *Sobibor camps in March and May 1942, Treblinka II became the third and, in terms of capacity, the largest camp for the death camps of Jews in the General Government. It measured 1,312 feet by 1,968 feet, trees camouflaged the camp, and watchtowers were placed along the fence. The camp was divided into three sections: the reception area, the killing area, and the living area. The living area was used by camp personnel, Germans and Ukrainians. It had storerooms and workshops. There were also barracks for Jews. Construction on the killing center began in May and was completed on July 22. A day later massive deportations began arriving from Warsaw.

The stationary gas chambers installed in the above-mentioned camps used a uniform organizational and technical system based on a common operational center located in Lublin. The creator and head of this center, the SS and Polizeifuehrer of the district, Odilo *Globocnik, was appointed by *Himmler as a high official in charge of the "Final Solution" of the Jewish question on a European scale. He acted in close collaboration with Reichsamtsleiter Victor Brack, the former chief of the euthanasia program in Germany.

Mobile gas chambers constructed on the model of the lethal sanitary vans tested in Germany were put into operation in the parts of Poland annexed by the Reich (Wartheland) and in some former Soviet territories. The main obstacle to the mass application of these vans was their limited capacity, their frequent breakdowns and the disposal of bodies; in short, they lacked efficiency. Mass shooting of the Jewish inhabitants in the U.S.S.R. by the *Einsatzgruppen* was no less problematic from the Nazi point of view. These massacres caused misgivings in commanding military circles; they caused too much noise and were carried out in broad daylight, and also left too many wounded or unhurt witnesses who could flee the graves. To employ this method on territories near European centers and even to Germany itself was out of the question.

The death camp reversed the process: instead of sending mobile killers to stationary victims, the victims were made mobile – by being placed on a train – and were sent to stationary execution centers, death camps that operated on an assembly line basis. Arriving prisoners had their values confiscated, they were stripped naked, hair was shaven, and then they were murdered in gas chambers, gold was removed from their teeth, and their bodies were burned in crematoria or open pits. The solution was achieved by the division of labor and the coordination of individual sections. The functions of rounding up the victims at their places of residence and their extermination at the place of execution were separated. One of the *Einsatzgruppen* (the notorious *Einsatz Reinhardt*) was to continue to act, but in the framework of Globocnik's camps its activities were connected mainly with deportation. As a result, the transports directed to the camps had fixed quotas. After a fixed number of "heads" and transports had been dispatched from a given place, the *Einsatz* team was free to perform its *Aktion* in another place. This ensured the death factories a regular and plentiful supply of human material.

The services of the railway network of the Reich and the occupied countries comprised a link in this chain. Transport was a difficult matter at a time when all the railways were swamped with military personnel and supplies. In addition, the trains for transporting Jews from Western and Central Europe had to be ordinary long-distance passenger trains in order to prevent the suspicions of the victims and soothe the conscience of some satellite circles. Jews from the Polish ghettos were being "resettled" without such ceremonies. Freight trains and cattle cars escorted by murderers were filled beyond capacity with people designated for death. They were cold in winter, hot in the summer and a bucket was used for sanitation. Jews had to sit in their own excrement prior to arrival. For hours, and sometimes days, these trains would stand on the side tracks allowing other transports to pass, and thus a large proportion of the deportees (mainly babies, the aged, and the sick), lacking water, air, and sanitary arrangements, frequently died before reaching their destination.

Those who arrived alive were awaited by the third link in the chain – a team of executioners. It was their duty to get the largest possible number of victims through the respective stages of the procedure at lightning speed: to strip them of the last remnants of their possessions including their hair, gold teeth and dentures; to supervise the removal of the corpses; and to sort out the remaining belongings for shipment to Germany.

The large area of Treblinka (32 acres; 13 hectares) was divided into two sectors. In the first, the larger one, the victims were received and classified and their remaining possessions were sorted out and dispatched. In the second were two buildings containing gas chambers and a field of mass graves dug up by mechanical excavators. Three gas chambers (measuring 25 sq. m. each) were located in the building erected earlier, and ten more chambers, twice as large, were in the building erected at a later date. The staff of both sectors consisted of about 30 SS men, 120 so-called Ukrainians (that is, members of the auxiliary services), and about 1,000–1,500 Jewish prisoners who were recruited for the work from among the younger men and, after having been brought to a state of emaciation, were often replaced by men from new transports.

Both buildings had annexes outside. Inside were passages containing narrow, hermetically shut doors to the gas chambers fitted out with small peepholes. On the opposite wall of each chamber there was a hermetically adherent trapdoor that could be opened from the outside. The walls of the chambers were set with tiles and on the ceiling there were openings fitted out with shower heads, to give the obviously false impression that the chambers were showers. The openings in the ceilings were connected to pipes leading to diesel engines located in the annexes. After the engines were started, fumes containing carbon monoxide (CO_1) emanated from the pipes and consumed all the oxygen in the hermetically closed room, causing the suffocation of the people crowded inside. Death in the chambers was calculated to occur within 15–20 minutes, however it sometimes lasted much longer, especially in the larger chambers of the building constructed later on and also when the engines were out of order.

In Treblinka there were also camouflage buildings such as "*Lazarette*" and "train change stations" intended to prevent any self-defending from the victims. The entire procedure was set in motion the moment the vans arrived at the loading platform. After the doors of the vans were pulled aside, a horde of Germans and Ukrainians rushed at the victims, shouting, and beating them. They would throw the victims out of the vans, wounding and injuring them straightaway and causing the miserable people unbelievable shock. Shortly thereafter the *Hoellenspektakel* ("inferno show") would begin. Men and women were separated and families were broken up without being allowed the opportunity for farewells. Men were ordered to undress at the square. While their heads and faces were being whipped, they had to snatch armfuls of clothing and bring them to a large pile to be sorted. A prisoner from the Jewish staff dealt bits of string to men to tie their shoes into pairs. In a nearby barrack another Jewish prisoner would distribute bits of string to women for the same purpose. From the "changing room," women would go over to the "hairdressers," where their hair would be cut off. It would then be used in some industries of the Third Reich.

No pain and no humiliation were spared to those sentenced to death.

Jews arrived on transports from Theresienstadt, Greece, and Slovakia as well as Poland. Jews from Bulgarian-occupied zones of Thrace and Macedonia were sent to Treblinka – but no Jews from Bulgaria itself. There were also Jews from Austria, Belgium, France, Germany, and the occupied Soviet Union. Some 2,000 Roma and Sinti (gypsies) were also deported to Treblinka.

The victims would be stood in a row – ready for the "chase" – naked and barefoot, even in the worst winter days. Before them stretched a 150-yard path connecting both sectors of the camp, called by the Germans *Schlauch* (tube) or, more "wittily," *Himmelstrasse* ("Way to Heaven"). The condemned ran between the rows of torturers, who shouted, battered them with their whips, pricked them with bayonets. Among the shouts, the barking of an enormous hound (the famed dog Bari who belonged to the principal sadist of the camp, nicknamed "Doll") would be heard. Excited by the cries, the hound would tear chunks of flesh from the victims' bodies. The victims screamed as well, and cursed; some of them calling *Shema Yisrael* or "down with Hitler." All inhibitions abandoned, even the men howled with pain; children cried, women were frantic with fear. This route to the gas chambers also had its name, *Himmelfahrt* ("Ascension"), in the camp slang.

Perhaps Brack's experts instructed the executioners that if victims arrived at the chambers out of breath, the effect of the gas would be hastened and the time of agony shortened. The condemned were probably oblivious of this aspect, but they would already be hurriedly running and pushing in order to get to their only refuge left in the world after what had happened to them.

After it was ascertained, by looking through the peepholes, that all movement had ceased, the trapdoor was lifted from the outside and a sight unparalleled in its ghastly nightmarishness would be revealed. The corpses "stood" pressed one against the other ("like basalt pillars") and appeared to be staring with the horror of suffocation. The first corpses had to be pulled out with hoops, and after that they fell out in heaps on the concrete platforms. They were pale and damp and bathed in perspiration and the secretions of the last defecation. The buttocks and faces were blue, mouths open, teeth bared, and bloody effusions oozed out from the mouths and noses.

In the corridors, the staff began cleaning and washing the chambers for the next shift, sprinkling the *Himmelstrasse* with fresh sand, while on the side of the graves, men began the run with the corpses, under a storm of blows and threat of pistols, toward the enormous graves. The gravediggers placed corpses in the gigantic cavities head to feet, and feet to head, in order to put in the maximum number. On the way to the graves stood a squad of "dentists" whose duty it was to pull out gold teeth and dentures from the mouths of the corpses. Another group of specialists was to check quickly whether there were any diamonds hidden in the corpse's rectums or in the women's vaginas. From time to time single shots were fired by the guards to increase the zeal of the gravediggers standing in the grave full of blood, pus, and dreadful stench. Whoever was beaten up, had a trace of blood, or a bruise left on his face, was finished off with a bullet after the roll call. And there was also musical accompaniment to the shows of Treblinka; at first *klezmerim* from the surrounding villages and later an excellent chamber orchestra played under the direction of Artur Gold known for his jazz ensemble from Warsaw. In addition there was a choir which every evening sang the idyllic song *Gute Nacht, Gute Nacht, schlaft gut bis der Morgen erwacht* and a marching song composed by one of the prisoners. None of those musicians survived Treblinka. During roll call and on their way to work prisoners were forced to sing the Anthem of Treblinka written by Artur Gold at the insistence of Kurt Franz.

> We look straight out at the world,
> The columns are marching off to their work.
> All we have left is Treblinka,
> It is our destiny.
> We heed the commandant's voice,
> Obeying his every nod and sign.
> We march along altogether,
> To do what duty demands.
> Work, obedience and duty
> Must be our existence.
> Until we too, will catch a glimpse at last
> Of a modest bit of luck.

Yechiel Reichman, one of the very few to survive the camp, described the lives of those who worked there:

> We tried to encourage and calm each other. "Leibel," I said to him. "Yesterday at this time my little sister was still alive." And he answered: "And my whole family, my relatives, and 12,000 poor Jews from our city." And we were alive, spectators to this great calamity and we became like stone, so that we could eat and carry with us this great pain.

Acts of Resistance

The greatest number of transports occurred in the late summer and autumn of 1942; in the summer of 1942 beginning on July 23 and continuing through September 12, at least 265,000 Jews were transported from the Warsaw Ghetto alone. During the winter the frequency and number of transports abated. After the German defeat at Stalingrad and foreseeing the need to retreat from the Eastern front, the Nazi authorities decided to cremate the corpses in order to eliminate the traces of their crimes.

A special corps of Jewish prisoners, coded by the number 1005, was set up on the grounds where the mass graves were placed. After Himmler's visit to Treblinka in February 1943, the monstrous action of pulling the corpses out of the mass graves and burning them on iron grates began. In most of the 1005 squads, the commandants of this difficult task were forced to stop killing the already trained prisoners and their replacement by new ones. This, however, did not lessen the prisoners' belief that they would also be shot and burned the moment their task was finished. That is when plans for rebellion and escape were born and ripened in almost all such groups in the second half of 1943 and in the first half of 1944. Sometimes these plans even partially succeeded, despite losses. The same happened in Treblinka.

Isolated escapes from the camp began as early as the first weeks of its existence. The runaways would escape under the piles of clothing taken from the dead, that is, in the dispatch vans that had been cleared of the victims. There were also acts of resistance, although only a few have been reported because of the limited number of witnesses who survived to tell the story. On Aug. 26, 1942, a young man from the Kielce transport armed with a penknife threw himself at a Ukrainian who had prevented him from bidding farewell to his mother. As a punishment, all the men who had arrived on the same transport were shot. On Sept. 10, 1942, while the selection was being carried out, Meir Berliner, a citizen of Argentina who was caught by the occupation while visiting his parents in Warsaw, lethally wounded an SS man, Max Biel, with a knife.

Among the better known cases was the resistance of a group of men from Grodno who had refused to undress. They had thrown themselves in unison at the guard but only achieved being shot by automatic fire instead of being gassed in the chambers. Statements by a number of witnesses claim that the news of the armed resistance in January and of the April uprising in Warsaw reached the prisoners and influenced the activities of the conspirators. Their aim now was not only to escape and save their lives, but also to take revenge on the murderers.

Such a group had come into existence in Treblinka II toward the end of 1942. Members of the committee were the physician, Dr. Julian Chorażycki; the head of the Jewish squad, engineer Galewski; Shmuel Rajzman (d. 1979); Kurland; a former captain of the Czech army, Zielo Bloch; and others. They began to make efforts to obtain arms, which they had hoped to smuggle in from the outside with the help of bribed Ukrainian guards. However, they paid for these activities with the loss of Chorażycki, who managed to commit suicide when caught with a packet of bank notes. After various failures the conspirators succeeded, with the help of a copied key, in obtaining arms from the camp arsenal and hiding them in a workshop. Contact was established with the second sector in Treblinka II, where the conspirators had only shovels and spades. They set a date and a signal: a shot and the explosion of a hand grenade. The revolt was to begin on August 2 at 4:30.

At the beginning everything went well. On the appointed day, benzine had been substituted for a solution of lysol during the disinfecting of the wooden buildings. Each active member had a task assigned to him and waited for the signal. At 3:40 a shot suddenly resounded in the first sector, followed soon by the explosion of a hand grenade. Only those in the front barrack knew what had happened. Two young boys there had unearthed some hidden money from a hiding place and a Kapo had caught them. Soon the commanders at their observation points caught sight of Germans leading the youngsters at gunpoint for interrogation to the guardhouse. They realized that they had to begin immediately. The first shot heard in the camp killed the Kapo.

Immediately thereafter one of the leaders dashed through the square with a hand grenade that he was supposed to hurl at the SS men's canteen. He realized that there would not be enough time, and, in order not to confuse the signal, he threw it before he reached his target. The prematurity of the outbreak of the revolt had disastrous consequences. They had not managed to remove the Ukrainian staff guarding the machine guns on the turrets (the conspirators had planned to lure them away with gold); nor had the telephone connections with the outside world been cut.

The leaders of the revolt did not lose their heads. All the barracks were set on fire immediately. They managed to kill one of the main hangmen, Kuetner, cut through the barbed-wire entanglements, and open the way to escape. They tried to kill the Ukrainians operating the machine guns on the guard turret, but did not succeed. Although a few gunners were killed and some wounded, it was impossible for the rebels, with only a few hand grenades and pistols, to lead a systematic struggle under the torrent of machine gun fire from above. Almost all those in command fell. They tried to cover the escape of those who rushed at the wires, but could do little more than die with honor. Apart from the heavily armed Germans and the Ukrainians of the staff, "relief" troops had arrived from Treblinka I. The whole district was alerted by telephone.

Most of the rebels fell while forcing their way through the barbed-wire entanglements. Most of those who escaped (between 300 and 500) from the range of fire were caught in the first weeks of the manhunt and killed or betrayed by the local peasants, who were on the lookout for the riches carried out of Treblinka. There were, however, Poles who gave shelter to the fugitives, either in their houses or in haystacks, dressed the wounded, fed them, and helped them to survive. However, almost a year was to pass before the area was liberated and there were casualties day after day and week after week. Only a total of about 50 survivors, including those who had escaped from Treblinka at an earlier time, could be counted after the liberation. And yet the rebellion and the escape from Treblinka were a great phenomenon in those times: as an act of resistance and revenge and as a bridge to the future struggles of the Jewish nation.

The Aftermath

As a result of interviews and investigations conducted after the liberation, it appeared that although the wooden barracks were burned down, Aug. 2, 1943 was not the last day of activities in Treblinka II. Most of the German and Ukrainian staff remained alive. They completed the burning of the corpses and dealt with some transports, in the main from the General Government, up to September. In October 1943 all buildings were blown up and the entire area was plowed and sown with fodder, in order to obliterate all traces of the crime. According to the data collected by the Polish authorities, apart from Jews from the General Government and Reichskommissariat Ost (Bialystok and Grodno), Jews from several Central and West European countries (Germany, Austria, Bohemia-Moravia, Slovakia, Holland, Belgium, Luxembourg) and from Balkan countries (Greece, Yugoslavia, and Bulgaria) were murdered there. Coins and identity cards of the citizens of more than 30 countries were found among other exhibits unearthed in the camp grounds. In addition to Jews, a certain number of Poles and gypsies were also murdered there. According to the calculations of Judge Z. Lukaszkiewicz, the number of victims murdered in Treblinka amounted to at least 731,600. The basis of this calculation was the railway documentation and an estimation of the average number of vans and people. This number, which was published in 1946, must be enlarged and rounded out to about 750,000 on the basis of German documents discovered later on by Jewish researchers.

After the liberation of Poland, a Central Jewish Historical Committee came into existence almost simultaneously with the Main State Commission for the Investigation of Nazi Crimes. It established itself in Lodz and later transferred to Warsaw as the Jewish Historical Institute. The committee pursued the contacts established with a group of 35 survivors of Treblinka. In November 1945 representatives of the Polish Main Commission and of the Central Jewish Historical Committee visited the scene of the crimes; they were assisted by five former prisoners and accompanied by a unit of militia men and representatives of the local Polish authorities. The most explicit evidence of the monstrous crimes that had taken place there were the human skulls and bones scattered all over; they had been unearthed when the local inhabitants and scavengers of a nearby station of the Soviet army, out for gold teeth and other treasures of the murdered Jews, tore up the grounds.

The document that remained after this visit was a memorandum of the Jewish participants to the Central Committee of Jews in Poland appealing for action to prevent further profanation of the place of martyrdom and disaster of close to three-quarters of a million Jews. This appeal remained unanswered, and only in 1961 was the building of a monument begun on behalf of the Jewish division for the preservation of places of commemoration in Poland, presided over by S. Fischgrund. A pamphlet was published in several languages urging Jews from all over the world to contribute toward this goal.

In 1963 a delegation from Israel arrived in Poland for the commemoration of the 20th anniversary of the Warsaw ghetto uprising. It also went on a pilgrimage to Treblinka, where a monument and a mausoleum in the form of a symbolic railway and cemetery, designed by A. Haupt and F. Duszenko, had in the meantime been erected. The delegation returned to Israel with a case of remains, and a profoundly moving funeral was held at the Naḥalat Yiẓḥak cemetery near Tel Aviv. Since then, the former prisoners of Treblinka have held an annual memorial service there.

In kibbutz *Loḥamei ha-Getta'ot, a model of Treblinka planned and executed by the senior of the former prisoners of Treblinka II was erected. The number of former prisoners of Treblinka in Israel amounted to 20 and they remained in contact with the surviving fellow prisoners scattered all over the world.

Three trials directly concerning the crimes at Treblinka were conducted in Germany. The first was of Joseph (Sepp) Hirtreiter (Frankfurt, 1951) who was sentenced for life. The second was of ten defendants from Treblinka II (Dusseldorf, 1965), in which the chief defendant from this camp, Kurt Franz (called "Doll") was sentenced to life imprisonment, while his companions received various sentences up to a maximum of 12 years, one of them being acquitted. The third was of Franz Stangl, the commandant of Treblinka, who was arrested in Brazil and delivered to the German authorities. After a six-month trial he was sentenced to life imprisonment in January 1971. Under extradition agreement this punishment was reduced to 20 years, but in June of the same year he died in prison.

BIBLIOGRAPHY: G. Reitlinger, *Final Solution* (1968^2) index; R. Hilberg, *Destruction of the European Jews* (1961, 1984, 2003), index; Y. Virnick, *A Year in Treblinka* (1945); *German Crimes in Poland*, 1 (1946), 95–106; V. Grossman, *Ha-Gehinnom bi-Treblinkah* (1945); R. Auerbach, *Oyf di Felder fun Treblinka* (1947); A. Krzepicki, in: *Bleter far Geshikhte*, 9 no. 1–2 (1956), 71–141; Israel, Attorney General against A. Eichmann, *Eduyyot*, 2 (1963), 1084–113; Rajzman, in: Y. Suhl (ed.), *They Fought Back* (1967), 128–35; See also the indictments of the Treblinka trials 12:870 10 904/19, and the decision of the court 3.9. 1965 A. 2 8IKS. **ADD. BIBLIOGRAPHY:** Y. Arad, *Belzec, Sobibor, Treblinka: The Operation Reinhard Death Camps* (1987); W. Chrostowski, *Extermination Camp Treblinka* (2004); G. Sereny, *Into that Darkness: An Examination of Conscience* (1983).

[Rachel Auerbach / Michael Berenbaum (2nd ed.)]

TREFOUSSE, HANS LOUIS (1921–), U.S. historian. Born in Frankfurt, Germany, Trefousse became professor of history at Brooklyn College, New York. After he retired from teaching, he was named professor emeritus of history. He published books on American diplomacy and on the role of Republicans in the American Civil War and Reconstruction. His biographies *Ben Butler, the South Called Him Beast* (1957) and *Benjamin Franklin Wade, Radical Republican from Ohio* (1963) were significant preludes to his *Radical Republicans* (1969).

Some of his other published works include *Germany and American Neutrality, 1939–41* (1951), *Reconstruction* (1971), *Lincoln's Decision for Emancipation* (1975), *Andrew Johnson: A Biography* (1989), *Pearl Harbor: The Continuing Controversy* (1982), *Carl Schurz: A Biography* (1998), *Thaddeus Stevens: 19th-Century Egalitarian* (2001), and *Rutherford B. Hayes* (2002).

°**TREITSCHKE, HEINRICH VON** (1834–1896), German historian and politician. Treitschke was a member of the National Liberal Party and author of a popular German history of the 19th century (*Deutsche Geschichte im 19. Jahrhundert*, 5 vols., 1879–94). He became well known as a staunch advocate of German nationalism increasingly critical of liberalism. The Berlin historian was very vocal in various campaigns for a cultural unification and homogenization of the young German nation-state. In this context, he published an anti-liberal article in 1879 entitled "Unsere Aussichten" in the *Preussische Jahrbuecher* in which he justified the antisemitic movement which had emerged in Germany since 1873. Behind this, Treitschke saw "a brutal but natural reaction of German national feeling against a foreign element," and he praised the "instinct of the masses, which has perceived a grave danger," that of Jewish domination of Germany. He launched the famous slogan: "The Jews are our misfortune!"

As a result, the antisemitic agitation, which until then had been considered vulgar, especially in intellectual circles, now received the approval of one of the most illustrious thinkers in Germany at the time and acquired a warrant of respectability. Over the course of the following year, controversies about his attacks broke out among the educated bourgeoisie; participants included the historian Heinrich *Graetz, who had been personally attacked in Treitschke's article, and the historian of Rome, Theodor *Mommsen, who accused Treitschke of disturbing the public peace in Germany. Treitschke was not a "racist" in the radical sense of the word. He limited himself to demanding the rapid and complete assimilation of the Jews in the Germanic culture, yet he became more and more skeptical about the likelihood of accomplishing this objective. In the years after 1879 his political and historical writings, therefore, remained persistently antisemitic.

BIBLIOGRAPHY: A. Dorpalen, *Heinrich Von Treitschke* (Eng., 1957); H. Liebeschütz, *Das Judentum im deutschen Geschichtsbild* (1967). **ADD. BIBLIOGRAPHY:** U. Langer, *Heinrich von Treitschke...* (1998); K. Krieger (ed.), *Der "Berliner Antisemitismusstreit" 1879–1881...* (2003); U. Jensen, *Gebildete Doppelgänger...* (2005), 197–324.

[Leon Poliakov / Uffa Jensen (2nd ed.)]

TREMELLIUS, JOHN IMMANUEL (1510–1580), Italian Hebraist and apostate Jew. Born in Ferrara and educated at the University of Padua, Tremellius became a Catholic in about 1540, his godfather being Cardinal Reginald Pole, archbishop of Canterbury. A year later, he abandoned Catholicism for Protestantism, and in 1542 was appointed professor of Hebrew at the University of Strasbourg. The European wars of religion drove Tremellius to England, where Archbishop Thomas Cranmer, a leading Protestant, gave him lodgings for a time in Lambeth Palace. Following the death of Paulus *Fagius, Tremellius served as king's reader in Hebrew at the University of Cambridge, where he remained from 1549 until the Catholic reaction under Queen Mary (1553), when he left for Germany. He was professor of Old Testament at the University of Heidelberg between 1561 and 1576, but paid a second visit to England in 1565. As a Calvinist, he incurred Lutheran displeasure at Heidelberg and was expelled in 1576, concluding his teaching career at Sedan.

Tremellius' main work was his Latin translation of the Bible from Hebrew and Syriac (Old Testament with F. Junius, Frankfurt on the Main, 1575–59; New Testament, Geneva, 1569), of which many editions were published. He also issued an Aramaic and Syriac grammar (Geneva, 1569). His Latin Bible had a profound impact on Hebrew studies in England during the 17th century.

BIBLIOGRAPHY: DNB, s.v.; W. Becker, *Immanuel Tremellius* (Ger., 1890^2); H.P. Stokes, *Studies in Anglo-Jewish History* (1913), 207–9; F. Secret, *Les Kabbalistes Chrétiens de la Renaissance* (1964), 201, 229; Baron, $Social^2$, 13 (1969), 167, 396; Roth, England, 146f.

[Godfrey Edmond Silverman]

TRENCIN (Slovak **Trenčín**; Hung. **Trencsén**; Ger. **Trentschin**), town in western Slovakia.

In the 14th century there were several Jews in Trencin. In the 16th century Jews reappeared. After the Kuruc invasion of Ubersky Brod in 1683, some Jews took refuge in Trencin. For the next 100 years, the community was under Ubersky Brod's jurisdiction. In 1734 the Jews took a secret oath to use only Ubersky Brod's court in disputes and to avoid the Hungarian court system.

The Trencin Jews tried to develop community life. They established a *ḥevra kaddisha* and held services on the Sabbath and holidays in private homes. They also had a *mikveh*. In 1736 there was a Jewish school, and in 1760 the community hired its first rabbi, David Kahn Casid (d. 1783). The municipal authorities were not well disposed toward the Jewish community. It charged the Jews municipal and state taxes and prohibited several religious rituals, such as marriage and circumcision. To perform these rituals, the Jews were charged heavy taxes. They were forbidden to employ Christian servants. The authorities tried to curtail the expansion of the community.

In 1703 Jews opened a factory that produced a scarce oil for tanning hides. During the first quarter of the 18th century, Jews were engaged in trade in hides and bones, and in producing spirits. In 1787 a fire destroyed the community's archives. In 1834 the congregation owned a small wooden synagogue. During the first half of the 19th century, the school system was expanded. Most of the schools had been privately owned but slowly became public and then government-owned. The major government-run Jewish elementary school was established in 1857. It had an excellent reputation, and many gentile children were enrolled.

After the Congress of Hungarian Jewry in 1868, the Trencin congregation joined the Reform (Neolog) stream of Jewry. In 1911 a new synagogue was constructed, often described as one of the most beautiful in Hungary. The congregation had a *ḥevra kaddisha*, a cemetery, and a kosher butcher. There were several social, women's, religious, and charitable societies. During World War I, 150 men enlisted in the army.

From 1785 the community underwent rapid expansion. In that year there were 388 Jews in Trencin. In 1848 there were 688, while 50 years later the community numbered 1,113. An increase was seen in 1922 when the community reached its peak of 2,115. In 1930 the number decreased to 1,539.

At the end of World War I, mobs looted Jewish property and homes and injured and even murdered Jews. When the disturbances subsided, the Jewish community recovered and contributed significantly to economic life. Several local factories were owned by Jewish entrepreneurs. Outstanding among them was one that produced natural oil. It supported local agriculture and provided employment. Jews were well represented in the educated strata and comprised much of Trencin's intelligentsia. There was active political and social life in the community. In 1932 five Jews were elected to the municipal council, four of them from the Jewish party. A number of Zionist groups influenced the community. The congregation belonged to the Slovakia-wide Jeshurun association, which unified the Neolog and Status Quo congregations. There was also a small Orthodox group.

On the eve of the deportations in 1942, there were 2,500 Jews in Trencin and environs; in Trencin itself there were 1,619. Most of them perished in the extermination camps in Poland. In 1947 there were 228 Jews in Trencin. In the small synagogue, the names of the victims were inscribed on the walls. Most of the survivors emigrated or settled in other parts of Czechoslovakia. The rest attempted to preserve Jewish life.

In 1968, during the Prague Spring, another wave of emigration took place. In 1978 a memorial was unveiled in the cemetery for Jewish anti-Fascist fighters and victims of the Holocaust. The Reform synagogue served as the city's cultural center.

BIBLIOGRAPHY: M. Lányi and H. Propper, *A szlovenszkói zsidó hitközségek története* (1933); R. Iltis (ed.), *Die aussaeen unter Traenen mit Jubel werden sie ernten* (1959), 195–8; *Magyar Zsidó Lexikon* (1929), 913; E. Bárkány-L. Dojc, *Zidovské nábozenské obce na Slovensku* (1991), 221–24.

[Yeshayahu Jelinek (2nd ed.)]

TRENT, city in northern Italy. The presence of some Jews in Trent, most of them emigrants from Germany, is mentioned from the first half of the 14th century. The usury regulations of the Jews of Trent served as a model elsewhere in the Tyrol. In the 15th century Jews in Trent possessed a synagogue, a house for study, and three other houses. The Jewish physician Tobiah practiced among the Christian as well as the Jewish population. In 1475, the fanatical Franciscan, Bernardino da *Feltre, preached there against the Jews in his Lenten sermons, and foretold that their sins would soon be manifested to all.

A few days after this, on Maundy Thursday, a Christian infant named Simon disappeared. Shortly afterward his body was discovered near the house of the head of the Jewish community, and the whole community, men, women, and children were arrested. After 17 of them had been tortured for 15 consecutive days they "confessed" to the crimes of which they had been accused. One of the tortured died in prison, six were burnt at the stake, and two (who had converted to Christianity) were strangled. At this stage Pope *Sixtus IV intervened in the affair and the judicial proceedings were temporarily halted. A papal commissary was sent to Trent to investigate the circumstances of the incident, but was forced to leave when the results of his inquiries led him to contradict the findings of the local "trial." Proceedings were reopened in Trent in face of violent opposition from the commissary, and at the end of the year five more Jews were executed (two of them were converted to Christianity before their deaths). A papal court of inquiry in 1476 justified the libel, and in 1478, as a result of its proceedings, Sixtus published the *Bull *Facit nos pietas* endorsing the "legality" of the trial. In the meantime four Jewish women of Trent had accepted the Christian faith and the property of the murdered Jews had been confiscated. Jews were henceforth excluded from Trent, and in the 18th century were still not allowed to pass through the town (see Ḥ.J.D. Azulai, *Ma'gal Tov*, 10–11).

Simon was beatified. The libel had widespread repercussions and served for intense antisemitic propaganda both inside and outside Italy. According to legend, the rabbis of Italy imposed a ban on Jewish settlement in Trent after 1475: this was formally raised when Simon was de-beatified in 1965.

BIBLIOGRAPHY: J.E. Scherer, *Die Rechtsverhaeltnisse der Juden in den deutsch-oesterreichischen Laendern* (1901), 579–611; G. Divina, *Storia del Beato-Simone da Trento*, 2 vols. (1902); G. Menestrina, *Gli ebrei a Trento* (1903); V. Manzini, *La superstizione omicida e i sacrifici umani con particolare riguardo alle accuse contro gli ebrei* (1930), 106, 218; M. Shulvass, *Bi-Ẓevat ha-Dorot* (1960), 67–75; W.P. Eckert, in: P. Wilpert (ed.), *Judentum im Mittelalter* (1966), 283–336; Milano, Biblioteca, index.

[Shlomo Simonsohn]

TRENTON, capital of the state of New Jersey, U.S., situated between Philadelphia and New York City. Greater Trenton has a population of about 341,000 (2003); the Jewish population of Greater Trenton numbered about 10,000 in 1970, but by the mid-1990s, the Jewish population numbered approximately 6,000 as Jews from the city migrated to surrounding suburban areas. Greater Trenton in 2005 included most of Mercer County and its Jewish population remained at some 6,000 in 2005.

Trenton was founded in 1679. The first Jew connected with Trenton was Simon *Gratz, of Philadelphia, who bought shares in the Trenton Banking Company when it was established in 1805. In 1839, Daniel Levy Maduro *Peixotto, of New York City, became editor, for a few months, of the *Emporium* and *True American*, a daily and weekly newspaper. Judge David *Naar, who bought the *True American* in 1853 and was its editor until 1869, played a prominent role in the political life of New Jersey as well as in local civic and educational affairs. German Jews began to settle in the late 1840s. The first prominent Jew was Simon Kahnweiler, a merchant and manufacturer. The Mt. Sinai Cemetery Association was incorporated in 1857 and the Har Sinai Hebrew Congregation held its first service in 1858 in rented quarters, and held its first formal services in 1860 when the congregation formalized its organization. In 1866 it bought a small Lutheran Church. Chevra Bikkur Cholim, "for the mutual relief of the sick and the burial of the dead," was incorporated in 1877.

The East European immigration, started in the late 1870s, was composed mainly of Lithuanian, Polish, and Hungarian Jews. They organized the synagogues Achenu Bnai Yisroel (1883); Anshey Emes (1891); Ahavath Israel (1909); and Poaley Emes (1920). Until 1903 Jewish education was conducted by private teachers, after which the Brothers of Israel Synagogue founded a Hebrew school. Later, in 1945, it became partly a day school, under the leadership of Rabbi Issachar Levin, who served the community from 1927 to 1969. In 1969 it became a full-fledged day school, the Trenton Hebrew Academy. Renamed in 1981 as the Abrams Hebrew Academy (named for a local foundation that made a significant endowment to the school), it moved from Trenton, New Jersey, to Yardley, Pennsylvania. In 2006, the school had 30 faculty teaching 300 students from nursery school through eighth grade in a secular/religious day school curriculum.

An influx of Jews into Trenton after World War I resulted in a proliferation of social, literary, and recreational societies as well as political groups. Har Sinai joined the Reform movement in 1922. Adath Israel was organized in 1923 as a Conservative congregation. The Workmen's Circle began its activities in 1924. The YMHA was organized in 1910, reorganized in 1916, and acquired its first building in 1917 – the forerunner of the Jewish Community Center (1962). Zionist societies started in the early 1900s. The Jewish Federation of Trenton was organized in 1929. The Jewish Family Service (1937) dates back to its predecessor the Hebrew Ladies Aid Society (1900). The Home for the Aged Sons and Daughters of Israel, now called the Greenwood House, was organized in 1939 and had 132 beds in 2006. An assisted living center, Abrams Residence, was added in 2003 using money provided by a local Jewish foundation called the Abrams Foundation. It was created from the fortunes of the last surviving members of the Abrams family, brothers Samuel and David and sister Susan. The family's fortune came from diversified holdings financed originally by a retail furniture operation; they began their diversification by purchasing single shares of General Motors Corporation stock during the Great Depression. The Abrams Foundation also helped finance the activities of the Abrams Day Camp, a Jewish day camp operated by the Jewish Community Center since 1963. An eight-week program, it offers activities for about 400 Jewish children each summer. In 1937 a Jewish census study showed that there were 7,191 Jews, or about 6 percent of the population; 32 organizations including 6 synagogues; and that 59 percent of the Jewish population was in trade, 13.3 percent in mechanical and manufacturing enterprises, and 12.3 percent in professions. The 1949 and the 1961 census showed increases in the professions which in 1970 probably amounted to nearly 30 percent. In 1970 there were 40 organizations, including three Conservative congregations as well as two Orthodox and one Reform. By the beginning of the new millennium, the community within the city limits had diminished to two congregations, one Conservative and the second a Reform congregation.

It was the culmination of a general migration of Jewish families out of the city and into surrounding suburban communities in Pennsylvania and New Jersey. In 2006, the last two congregations within the city limits, Congregation Brothers of Israel (200 families) and Har Sinai Temple (500 families), were each in various stages of relocating. In 2006, Brothers of Israel was in the process of purchasing land for a new synagogue in Yardley, Pennsylvania, and Har Sinai was building a new facility approximately 15 miles north of Trenton, in Pennington, New Jersey. At that time, Har Sinai announced its intention to remain vested in the city of Trenton by continuing its charitable programs there.

The Jews have been well-integrated in the communal life of the city, participating actively in the United Fund and other charitable and educational institutions. Outstanding leaders in the general and Jewish community include Judge Phillip Forman, United States Circuit Court; Judge Sidney Goldmann, presiding judge of the Appellate Division of the Supreme Court of New Jersey; Bernard Alexander; Leon Levy; comedian Jon Stewart; and Expressionist painter Max *Weber.

BIBLIOGRAPHY: Trenton Historical Society, *History of Trenton, 1679–1929*, 2 (1929); J.S. Merzbacher, *Trenton's Foreign Colonies* (1908); Kohn, in: AJHSQ, 53 (1964), 373–95; S. Robinson, *Jewish Population of Trenton*, N.J. (1949).

[S. Joshua Kohn / David Weinstock (2nd ed.)]

TREPMAN, PAUL (1916–1987), journalist, author, community leader. Born in Warsaw, Trepman was an only child. His father's family were followers of the Gur Rebbe, and one of Trepman's earliest memories was going with his father to meet the him. Trepman attended both traditional and modern cheders, as well as the Takhkemoni Yeshivah in Warsaw. In his youth, he joined the Betar Zionist movement, and was a strong supporter of Ze'ev *Jabotinksy and his Revisionist Zionism. He began to publish in Polish, and his works appeared in a journal edited by Janusz *Korczak and in the Revisionist press. He also began university at the Stefan Batory University in Vilna, but the war halted his studies.

During the war, Trepman had the opportunity to escape east to Russia but refused to abandon his mother in Warsaw. He returned to Warsaw to find his mother in the ghetto, weak and stricken with typhus. He narrowly escaped his mother's fate – deportation to Treblinka – and lived in the Warsaw area with Aryan papers. His Jewish identity hidden, he was arrested in June 1943 and accused of being a Soviet spy. He was sent to *Majdanek and subsequently saw the inside of various camps. He was in *Bergen-Belsen when it was liberated by the British in April 1945, and only after liberation did Trepman resume his Jewish identity. He was soon involved in the cultural and political life of the Bergen-Belsen Displaced Persons Camp. In July 1945 he was the founding co-editor (with Rafael Olewsky and David Rosenthal) of *Undzer Shtimme*, the first Jewish newspaper in the British Zone. In December 1947 *Undzer Shtimme* was replaced with the more substantial *Vochnbalatt*. Trepman was also an editor of Zamy Feder's *Anthology of Songs and Poems from the Ghettos and Concentration Camps*, and was co-editor, again with Olewsky and Rosental, of an early photo album of the Holocaust, the multilingual *Undzer Churbn in Bild*, (*Our Destruction in Pictures*, Bergen-Belsen, 1946).

With the support of Hirsch *Wolofsky, the editor of Montreal's Yiddish daily, *Keneder Adler*, Trepman and his wife immigrated to Montreal in 1948. He was hired to teach at the Jewish People's Schools, where he remained for 23 years. In the summers he directed the Labor Zionist Camp Undzer – Camp-Kindervelt. Between 1971 and 1981 he was the executive director of the Jewish Public Library of Montreal. Trepman became a central figure in the Montreal survivor community. In 1961 he established the Montreal chapter of Bergen-Belsen survivors, and served as its president for a number of years.

In Montreal, Trepman was a frequent contributor to the *Adler*, often writing under pen-names, including the tongue-in-cheek pen-name Pinchas Batlan (Pinchas the Loafer). He also wrote several books focusing on his life before the war and his wartime experiences. These include *A Gesl in Varshe* (1949; *Among Men and Beasts*, 1978), based on newspaper articles he had written between 1946 and 1953; and his description of going back to visit Poland, *A Traumatic Return to Poland* (1980), a translation of six articles he had written for the *Keneder Adler* about a return trip he took to Poland in 1979.

BIBLIOGRAPHY: B. Widutchinsky Trepman and E. Trepman, *Paul Trepman: Bikher, Pulikazyes, Arkhivn* (1999); C.L. Fuks (ed.), *Hundert Yor Yidishe un Hebreyishe Literatur in Kanade* (1982), 137–38.

[Richard Menkis (2nd ed.)]

TREPPER, LEOPOLD (Leiba Domb; 1904–1982), former Soviet intelligence agent, head of the anti-German spy network known as "The Red Orchestra." Trepper was born in Nowy Targ near Zakopane, Poland. He was active in the Polish Communist youth movement and was imprisoned for several months. Afterwards he joined Ha-Shomer ha-Ẓa'ir and in 1926 went to Ereẓ Israel, where he soon became affiliated with the illegal Communist party and was detained several times by the police for his clandestine activities. In the Histadrut he became known as the leader of the Eḥud (Unity) faction which advocated workers' unity, intending to include Communists and Arabs. After the first conference of Eḥud (1927), Trepper was expelled from Ereẓ Israel and went to France. There he became active in the Jewish section of the French Communist party as well as in the Soviet secret service. In 1932, in consequence of the discovery of a Soviet spy network, referred to in the French press as the "Fantomas" affair, Trepper had to leave France and proceeded to the Soviet Union. In Moscow he studied at the Communist University for Western Workers (KUNZ) and was probably also trained for intelligence work. In 1938 he was sent to France and Belgium, where, under various covers, he played a central role in Soviet military intelligence. He organized and headed a widespread clandestine radio service which had agents in high echelons of the German military machine in Berlin. German counter-intelligence called the network "The Red Orchestra."

In 1941 Trepper warned Moscow of Germany's imminent attack on the U.S.S.R., predicting even its exact date, but Stalin disregarded these warnings as originating in "British provocation." During the German-Soviet war "The Red Orchestra," under Trepper's direction, contributed greatly, and sometimes decisively, to Soviet strategy and tactics. In November 1942 Trepper was captured in Paris by a combined team of German counter-intelligence and the Gestapo. They attempted to enlist his services for a sophisticated anti-Soviet operation in which he would continue his radio transmissions under secret German control (the so-called *Funkspiel*). According to previous orders from his superiors for such a contingency, Trepper pretended to respond to these overtures, thus saving his life and even succeeding in escaping less than a year later. During his imprisonment, he managed to smuggle out a detailed report, written in a mixture of Hebrew, Yiddish, and Polish, which was transmitted to Moscow by underground Communist party channels and which contained exact information about his arrest as well as about the German control already established over parts of "The Red Orchestra." After his escape he resumed his intelligence activity.

In 1945 he was recalled to Moscow and on arrival immediately arrested. He spent ten years in prison and was constantly interrogated by the highest Soviet security officials. At a certain stage, during Stalin's antisemitic Black Year, one of the main charges leveled against him was the fact that in "The Red Orchestra" he had "surrounded himself with Jews" (some of them, like Hillel Katz, were old comrades from Ereẓ Israel), to which he replied that at that time Jewish Communists were the most reliable people he could find. In 1955 he was released and completely "rehabilitated." From then on Trepper devoted himself exclusively to Jewish interests. He submitted to the post-Stalin leadership a detailed plan to revive Jewish cultural life and institutions in the Soviet Union, but in 1956, after the Twentieth Congress of the Soviet Communist party, he was officially informed that his plan had been rejected. He then went to Warsaw, where, under the name Leiba Domb, he headed the government-sponsored Jewish Cultural-Social Society (Yidisher Kultur-Gezelshaftlekher Farband) and its publishing house Yiddish Bukh.

In 1968, during the violently anti-Jewish period in Polish policy, Trepper decided to return to Israel, where members of his family had already settled, but was constantly denied an exit permit. This attitude of the Polish government, possibly a result of Soviet pressure, aroused in 1971–72 worldwide publicity and many protests, including hunger strikes by Trepper's sons in Jerusalem, in Canada, and at the United Nations building in New York.

Toward the end of 1972 a French court heard a libel action by Trepper against the former French secret agent Jean Rochet, who had accused Trepper, in a letter to *Le Monde*, of having collaborated with the Nazis and betrayed his comrades in the underground. Despite Trepper's inability to appear because he was not allowed to leave Poland, he won the case and Rochet was fined and ordered to publish the court's verdict.

Trepper was finally granted permission by the Polish authorities to leave Poland for England in order to undergo a serious operation. He stated that his plans included the writing of "the full and true account of the 'Red Orchestra,'" not merely as an intelligence network, but as an organization of anti-Nazi resistance in which Jews played such a prominent part. His memoirs, *Le Grand Jeu*, were published in 1975 and in English translation by the author in 1977 as *The Great Game: The Story of the Red Orchestra.*

Trepper settled in Israel in 1974. He died early in 1982 and was buried in Jerusalem.

BIBLIOGRAPHY: D.J. Dallin, *Soviet Espionage* (1964³), 139–40, 156–68, passim; G. Perrault, *L'Orchestre Rouge* (1967), passim.

[Joseph Berger-Barzilai]

TREST (Czech **Třešt**; Ger. **Triesch**), town in Moravia, Czech Republic. R. Jacob of Triesch is mentioned in a query addressed to Solomon b. Abraham *Adret. The community developed after the expulsion from nearby *Jihlava (1426) but it may be assumed that it existed earlier. In 1678 Jews owned fields and in 1693 they were permitted to distill spirits and to fatten cattle. Trest Jews were connected with the textile industry as sellers of wool, and in 1723 a distillery, tannery, and butchery were rented to a Jew. In 1789 there were 102 Jewish families permitted by the *Familiants Laws; 20 others also lived in the town. One hundred years later the community numbered 316. Trest was the seat of an important yeshivah and among its rabbis was Eleazar *Loew. In 1930 the community numbered 64 (1.3% of the total population). It came to an end in the Holocaust period, some immigrating to England and Palestine and the rest deported to the death camps of Poland via Theresienstadt. Its sacred objects are now in the Jewish State Museum in Prague.

BIBLIOGRAPHY: H. Gold and B. Wachstein, in: H. Gold (ed.), *Juden und Judengemeinden Maehrens in Vergangenheit und Gegenwart* (1929), 539–48; Germ Jud, 2 (1968) 833.

[Meir Lamed]

TRETS (Heb. טְרִייץ), town in the department of Bouches-du-Rhone, S. France. Jewish sources indicate that a Jewish community, which included some scholars, existed there at least from 1269. The non-Jewish sources mention the protection given by the lords of Trets to local Jews in the 14th and 15th centuries, granting them equality with Christian inhabitants. However, in 1413, the Jewish community was obliged to request an order, which they obtained, placing them under the protection of the lord and imposing a heavy fine of 50 silver marks "for any injury or offense to them." The community continued to exist until the expulsion of the Jews from Provence in 1501.

BIBLIOGRAPHY: Gross, Gal Jud, 244ff.; H. de Gerin-Ricard, in: *Répertoire des travaux de la Société de statistique de Marseille*, 48 (1911–20), 41–45; B. Blumenkranz, in: *Bulletin philologique et historique* (1965), 611.

[Bernhard Blumenkranz]

TREVES, a ramified family which produced scores of scholars, rabbis, and communal workers. It is usually assumed that the family's origins were in Troyes, France, *Rashi's birthplace, from where it spread throughout Italy and Germany. Others hold that it came from Treviso near Venice, Italy, in the 14th century, while a third opinion is that it originated in Trier (Germany), called Trèves in French. In France members of the family were called Triverzans and in Germany, Drifzan. Branches of the family spread through the different countries of Europe from the 14th to the 20th centuries. From the original family there afterward branched off the Trefouse, Dreyfuss, and Tribas families. JOHANAN, the founder of the family, lived in Germany in the second half of the 13th century. The first to be called Treves was JOSEPH B. JOHANAN (the Great), rabbi of Paris or Marseilles in the first half of the 14th century. His son MATTATHIAS (c. 1325–died c. 1385) of Provence lived in Spain, studied under his father, and was a pupil of Nissim b. Reuben *Gerondi and Perez b. Isaac ha-Kohen. He returned to France when the edict of expulsion was repealed in 1361. In Paris he founded a yeshivah which had a large number of students. He was given the title of honor *Morenu*, and in 1363 was appointed rabbi of Paris by Charles v. Mattathias and the members of his family were among those exempted from wearing the Jewish badge decreed upon the Jews of France by Charles v. He is mentioned in the responsa of *Isaac b. Sheshet Perfet (No. 271) and in the fragments of the *Kiryat Sefer* of Isaac *Lattes published by Neubauer (*Seder ha-Ḥakhamim ve-Korot ha-Yamim*, pt. 2 (1893), 241). Mattathias had three sons, Johanan *Treves, ABRAHAM, and JOSEPH, the last apparently being ordained rabbi in Italy, where he died in 1429. Joseph's great-grandson NAPHTALI HERTZ (Drifzan) was the author of the kabbalistic commentary *Dikduk Tefillah*, on the prayer book *Malah ha-Areẓ De'ah* (Thuengen, 1560), and *Naftulei Elohim*, a supercommentary on the commentary of *Baḥya b. Asher (Heddernheim, 1546). He was cantor in Frankfurt on the Main and was renowned as "the great kabbalist." Naphtali Herz's son JOSEPH together with his brother ELIEZER (1495–1566) published their father's commentary on the prayer book. Eliezer served as rabbi of Frankfurt for 22 years. A third son SAMUEL settled in Russia (see below). He wrote *Yesod Shirim* (Thuengen, 1559) on the Book of Ruth, giving both literal and kabbalistic explanations. Many members of the Treves family settled in Italy. The first known is Johanan b. Joseph *Treves, author of the commentary *Kimḥa de-Avishuna* (Bologna, 1540). His son RAPHAEL JOSEPH (16th century) was rabbi in Ferrara, engaged in the publication of books, and in 1559 worked as a proofreader in the Hebrew press in Sabbioneta. JOSEPH B. MATTATHIAS in Svigliano was involved in the notorious Tamari-Venturozzo case (1566) in which the rabbis of Venice and Mantua took part (see Moses b. Abraham *Provençal).

From the 16th century onward the Treves family is found in Russia. The Russian branch of the family traces its descent to Samuel, the son of Naphtali Herz of Frankfurt, who crossed into Russia and adopted the family name of Ẓevi. He had two sons, one of whom, ELIEZER, called Ashkenazi or Ish Ẓevi, served as rabbi in Opatow, and wrote commentaries on the Talmud, and glosses to tractate *Ḥullin*, which were published under the title *Dammesek Eliezer* (Lublin, 1646). He was also the author of a collection of prayers, *Si'ah ha-Sadeh* (*ibid.*, 1645).

Still another branch of the Treves family is found in Turkey from the end of the 15th century. From there a number of them also went to Ereẓ Israel. Of these the following may be mentioned: ABRAHAM B. SOLOMON ẒAREFATI (1470–1552) was born in Mantua, but in 1495 went to Salonika. In 1505 he was appointed rabbi of Ferrara, and in 1522 went to Constantinople. He subsequently lived for several years in Adrianople with Joseph *Caro, where he became friendly with Solomon *Molcho. Immediately after Molcho's death he moved to Ereẓ Israel, settling in Jerusalem. He was the author of the *Birkat Avraham* (Venice, 1552), on the ritual washing of the hands. His copy of the *Halakhot* of Isaac *Alfasi contained his own glosses and those of his ancestors. Another member of this branch was ISAAC B. MORDECAI GERSHON, one of the scholars of Safed and a pupil of Moses *Alshekh. He became rabbi in Constantinople (1583), but from there went to Venice. He became renowned as a proofreader and publisher of the works of the scholars of Safed. RAPHAEL TREVES was born in Smyrna and from 1710 lived in Jerusalem, where he died around 1745. His works are *Ẓaḥ ve-Adom* (Constantinople, 1740), giving the order of prayers for those settling in Ereẓ Israel, and *Dagul me-Revavah* (*ibid*., 1743), a commentary on the Song of Songs.

BIBLIOGRAPHY: Michael, Or, nos. 245, 426; Bruell, *Jahrbuecher…*, 1 (1874), 87–122; Gross, Gal Jud, 242, 532f.; A. Epstein, in: MGWJ, 46 (1902), 159f.; Frumkin-Rivlin, 1 (1929), 91–93; 3 (1929), 84; H. Chone, in: *Sinai*, 11 (1942), 183–213; D. Tamar, in: KS, 33 (1958), 377; M. Benayahu, *Rabbi Ḥayyim Yosef David Azulai* (Heb., 1959), 344.

[Yehoshua Horowitz]

TREVES, EMILIO (1834–1916), Italian publisher. Born in Trieste, Treves began to work as a proofreader in a local office and wrote anonymously for magazines prohibited by the Austrian censor. He was forced to leave for Paris when his association with the prohibited journals was discovered, and after working as a journalist and translator he became a publisher in Fiume. He joined Garibaldi's legion in 1859 in the war against the Bourbon regime in Naples, and after peace was declared he founded the Treves publishing company with his brother Giuseppe. The Treves brothers published the highly successful *Illustrazione Italiana*, and later the works of many famous Italian writers including De Amicis, D'Annunzio, and Verga, as well as translations from foreign languages. By the end of the 19th century the Treves publishing company was the most important in Italy.

[Giorgio Romano]

TREVES, JOHANAN BEN JOSEPH (1490?–1557?), Italian rabbi and scholar. His place of birth is unknown. In his youth he studied together with Joseph of Arles in the yeshivah of Moses *Navarro in Ferrara, where he later became a member of the *bet din*. For about 20 years he wandered in different towns of northern and central Italy, serving as religious instructor and rabbi, and as a result he was termed one of "the peripatetic rabbis." For a number of years during this period, he lived in the house of Ishmael Rieti in Siena as his private tutor, a practice common in Italy. He then lived in Sabbioneta and Bologna (1540). It was assumed that he worked in the Hebrew press in Bologna from 1537 to 1541; and it is possible that in the years 1545–46 he worked as a proofreader in the printing press of Daniel *Bomberg in Venice.

Johanan was an author, publisher, and writer of responsa. Widely known is his commentary, *Kimḥa de-Avishuna* (Bologna, 1540), on the festival prayer book according to the Roman rite, published anonymously. He endeavored to establish the correct readings "and did not invent anything; well nigh everything was gathered from existing authors … as the gleaner follows the harvester." The work was designed for the untutored, and its title is explained in the statement that "he was not concerned to produce fine flour but flour made from roasted ears [*Kimḥa de-Avishuna*; see Pes. 39b] … that had already been ground and roasted." His commentary is based almost entirely upon Midrashim, some of which are otherwise unknown, and upon commentaries on early *piyyutim*, his purpose being simply to explain the words and subject matter. He was extremely active as a proofreader of midrashic works and in the establishment of accurate readings of the tractates he studied with his pupils. His glosses to the *Halakhot* of Isaac *Alfasi, his approbations to the works of his contemporaries, and his responsa (one of which, no. 58, was included in the responsa of Moses *Isserles), are extant. He also compiled a commentary on the laws of **shehitah u-vedikah* and the *halakhot* of **issur ve-hetter* of the *Mordekhai* of *Mordecai b. Hillel (Venice, 1550). His *piyyutim* and poems are also known. Of his three sons the best known is Raphael Joseph who was a *posek*, as well as a book publisher. In 1559 he was working in the Sabbioneta press.

BIBLIOGRAPHY: Ghirondi-Neppi, 167, 178–80; Bruell, Jahrbuecher, 1 (1874), 108; D.W. Amram, *The Makers of Hebrew Books in Italy* (1909), 205; Davidson, Oẓar, 4 (1933), 398; A. Marx, in: *Tarbiz*, 8 (1936/37), 173, 176; idem, *Koveẓ Madda'i le-Zekher M. Schorr* (1944), 189–219; I. Sonne, in: HUCA, 16 (1941), Heb. pt. 42, no. 11; H.D. Friedberg, *Toledot ha-Defus ha-Ivri be-Italyah…* (1956^2), 30, 65, 79.

[Yehoshua Horowitz]

TREVES, JOHANAN BEN MATTATHIAS (d. 1429), French rabbi. Treves was ordained by his father Mattathias b. Joseph. He was a son-in-law of the procurator-general, *Manessier de Vesoul. Treves first served as rabbi to a single French community but on the death of his father in 1385 was appointed chief rabbi of Paris with the consent of Charles VI and served in this office from 1385 to 1394. After some years of tranquility, a distinguished pupil of his father, Isaiah Astruc b. Abba Mari, became his enemy and claimed for himself the sole right of appointing rabbis in France and of conducting a yeshivah. With the help of Meir b. Baruch ha-Levi of Vienna, Isaiah Astruc tried to remove Johanan from his post by proclaiming that all arrangements of the rabbinate not confirmed by him were null and void. Johanan turned for help to the greatest rabbis of Catalonia, Ḥasdai *Crescas and *Isaac b. Sheshet Perfet (the Ribash). These two supported the persecuted rabbi and in their responsa opposed both Isaiah Astruc and Meir b. Baruch. They claimed that Johanan, "besides inheriting his rabbinate from his father with the approval of the monarch in accordance with the wishes of the communities, was also worthy of it on account of his learning and activities" (Resp. Ribash, 270–72). Some justify the intervention of Isaiah Astruc on the grounds of his constructive criticism of the affairs of the French communities and Johanan's inability to halt the religious decline which had taken place. It was Johanan who characterized the attitude of Isaiah Astruc as prompted by a desire to oust him from office. The expulsion of the Jews from France in 1394 ended the quarrel. Johanan went to Italy, where he lived until his death. He achieved great renown among his contemporaries who referred to him as "the greatest in our times," and "the paragon of the generation." His rulings were much referred to by contemporary scholars. From Italy he corresponded with Jacob b. Moses *Moellin (the Maharil). His responsa on the prayers to be said by orphans and a responsum to the Padua community are extant.

BIBLIOGRAPHY: Graetz, Gesch, 8 (n.d.), 4, 35f., 70 n.2; Bruell, Jahrbuecher, 1 (1874), 95–99; Guedemann, Gesch Erz, 1 (1880), 247–9; Gross, Gal Jud, 508, 534; Weiss, Dor, 5 (1904^4), 147, 164–7, 239 n. 1; I. Lévi, in: REJ, 39 (1899), 85–94; G. Lauer, in: JJLG, 16 (1924), 1–42; A.M. Hershman, *Rabbi Isaac b. Sheshet Perfet and his Time* (1943), 203–13; S. Schwarzfuchs, *Etudes sur l'Origine et le Développement du Rabbinat au Moyen Age* (1957), 38–75.

[Yehoshua Horowitz]

TREVIÑO DE SOBREMONTE, TOMÁS (1592–1649), Marrano martyr in Mexico. His father came from an old aristocratic Christian family and his mother, Leonor Martínez de Villagómez, was a Judaizing New Christian. Born in Medina de Riosoco, Spain, he studied Latin in two Jesuit schools and canon law at Salamanca, and became a page for a nobleman in his home town. When a fellow page called him a Jew, he killed him and went into hiding. In 1612 Tomás fled to New Spain, where he prospered as a merchant, with connections at the commercial centers of Zacatecas, Guadalajara, Acapulco, and Vera Cruz. His brother, Gerónimo, was arrested with their mother by the Inquisition in Spain, and revealed under torture that Tomás was a Judaizer. Consequently, the Mexican Inquisition arrested Tomás in November 1624 and reconciled him to the Church the following year after he expressed repentance. The repentance was feigned, however, for Tomás had no intention of relinquishing his Judaism. He even had himself circumcised in jail by a cell mate. In 1629 he married the Judaizer, Maria Gómez, and despite the interdict of the Inquisition he dressed in finery, wore arms, and rode on horseback. When his wife and her family were arrested by the Inquisition, he found various ways of communicating with them, but refused to take his wife back after her reconciliation with the Church until he was ordered to do so by the Inquisition. He was planning to flee New Spain, most probably to Holland, when he was rearrested as a relapsed heretic on Oct. 11, 1644, and after a lengthy trial condemned to the stake. He was the only one of over a hundred prisoners to be burned alive at the great **auto-da-fé* of Apr. 11, 1649. To his last moment, learned theologians tried to convert him, but could not budge him from his devotion to Judaism. The poet Miguel de Barrios dedicated a eulogy to Tomás Treviño de Sobremonte, but it is apparent that he confused him with another Marrano victim, Francisco Maldonado de *Silva, who died at the stake a decade earlier.

BIBLIOGRAPHY: J.T. Medina, *Historia... de la Inquisición en México* (1905), 148, 199, 206; A. Wiznitzer, in: AJHSQ, 51 (1962), 229–39; B. Lewin, *Mártires y conquistadores judíos en la América Hispana* (n.d.), 116–76.

[Martin A. Cohen]

TREVISO, city in N. Italy. The presence of Jews in Treviso and its vicinity is first mentioned in 905. A document from May 28, 972, records that the Emperor Otto I donated to the Monastery of San Candido D'Indica a farm situated near a property owned by a certain Isaac the Jew. In 1235 a certain Vascono Judeo is mentioned in a document. In 1294, Solomon, presumably an Ashkenazi Jew, founded loan banks in the town.

After the annexation of Treviso by the Venetian Republic in 1339 the position of the Jews there was similar to that of the other Jews of the Veneto region. A decree from 1390 orders the local authorities to supervise the activity of the moneylenders. In 1398 the Doge Antonio Venier authorized a tax of 3,000 ducats to be paid by the Jews living in Treviso and Ceneda. By the end of the 14th century five loan banks in Treviso were owned by Jews, among whom were Jacob di Alemagna and Elhanan de Candida, who signed the renewal of their license in 1401. At this time also, the Sicilian scholar *Abulrabi was a student at a yeshivah in the town. At the end of the 15th century R. Benedict Alexander Axelrod was head of a yeshivah in Treviso. A halakhic question addressed by the Jews of Treviso to Judah *Mintz at the end of the 15th century (responsum no. 7) contains references to the construction of a new synagogue and a *mikveh* as well as to a method for treating eye complaints used by Treviso Jews. In 1443 the obligation to wear the yellow badge was reintroduced. In 1480, five Jews were arrested in Treviso and accused of killing a Christian child, Sebastian Novello, in the wake of similar cases following the affair of Simon of *Trent (1475); they were burned at the stake in Venice. It seems that the Jews of Treviso were banned from moneylending from 1483 until 1487. A Christian loan bank (**Monti di Pietà*) was established in Treviso in 1496, and the citizens asked the Venetian government to banish the Jews from the town. After the Jews had agreed to give up moneylending, they were permitted to remain.

In 1509, when Treviso was captured by the armies of the League of Cambrai, the populace rioted against the Jews under the pretext that they had collaborated with the Germans. All Jewish homes were destroyed, except the house of "Calman the Jew, friend of the people of Treviso," or Calimano de Treviso, head of the Venetian family of the same name. That year the doge issued a decree of expulsion, prohibiting Jews from living in Treviso: the ordinance was engraved on a marble pillar in the town square. The Jews moved to nearby Asolo. In 1547 rioting broke out there also when, without apparent motive, a gang of peasants killed eight and wounded ten out of the 37 Jews living there at the time. The rest fled from the area. In the latter half of the 16th century a few individual Jews were to be found in Treviso. In 1880, 27 Jewish gravestones were found during excavations. In 1909–10 fragments of Jewish tombstones dating from the 15th century were found in the Borgo Cavour (then the Borgo Santi Quaranta). In the second half of the 19th century a small Jewish community was again founded in Treviso, but has since ceased to exist.

BIBLIOGRAPHY: *Leket Yosher*, pt. 1 (1903), 44; pt. 2 (1904), 29, 76, 80; E. Morpurgo, in: *Corriere Israelitico*, 48 (1909–10), 141–4, 170–2; A. Marx, *Studies in Jewish History* (1944), 128, 130; M.A. Shulvass, in: HUCA, 22 (1949), 6–8 (Heb.); I. Sonne, *ibid.*, 26–27 (Heb.); N., Pavoncello, "Le epigrafi dell'antico cimitero ebraico di Treviso," in: RMI, 34 (1968), 221–32. **ADD. BIBLIOGRAPHY:** F. Brandes, *Veneto Jewish Itineraries* (1996), 100–3; I.M. Peles, "Rabbi Moshe Vinek," in: RMI, 67 (2001), 27–31 (Heb.).

[Shlomo Simonsohn / Samuele Rocca (2nd ed.)]

TRÉVOUX (Heb. טרבוט), town in the department of Ain, E. France. Article 49 of the charter of freedom of Trévoux of 1300, which prohibited the residence of Jews in the town, was not respected; however, in exchange for an annual payment of 15 pounds, many Jews were authorized to live there. The Jewish population increased considerably in 1420 with the arrival of the Jews who had been expelled from *Lyons, who introduced the gold- and silver-thread industry. In 1429 an investigation was carried out against the books of the Jews. This act closely resembled the trial of Paris of 1240; the books were seized, and several Jews were subjected to an interrogation concerning their contents. The sentence was a double one: the books were burned and the Jews were expelled. This expulsion did not remain in force for long, however; three years later, Jews were again found in Trévoux. In 1433 there were several Jews among the prisoners taken in Trévoux by the Duke of Savoy. In 1467 the inhabitants of Trévoux obtained the expulsion of the Jews by taking upon themselves the payment of their taxes. The few Jews who were spared from this expulsion were driven out in 1488. The Rue des Juifs, subsequently known as Rue Japperie, was situated in the eastern part of the town. Near this quarter was a stone building known as the "Tower of the Jews." The synagogue was situated in the Grande Rue. The only scholars who bore the name of "Trévoux" or Trabot lived in Italy.

BIBLIOGRAPHY: Gross, Gal Jud, 219–23; J.F. Jolibois, *Histoire de la Ville et du Canton de Trévoux* (1853), 9–16; C. Jarrin, *La Bresse et le Bugey*, 1 (1883), 477ff.; I. Loeb, in: REJ, 10 (1885), 33ff.; E. Dreyfus and L. Marx, *Autour des Juifs de Lyon et Alentour* (1958), 93–102; H. Merḥavya, in: KS, 45 (1969–70), 592f.

[Bernhard Blumenkranz]

TRIBE, LAURENCE H. (1941–), U.S. lawyer, legal scholar. Born in Shanghai, China, Tribe and his family moved to San Francisco when he was five. He graduated from Harvard summa cum laude in mathematics in 1962 and Harvard Law School in 1966, magna cum laude. After serving as a clerk on the Supreme Court, Tribe joined the Harvard Law faculty in 1968 and became recognized as one of the foremost constitutional law experts in the country. He was the author of *American Constitutional Law* (1978), the most frequently cited textbook in that field. He served as a consultant to several government committees, including the Senate Committee on Public Works (1970–72). In 1978 he helped write a new constitution for the Marshall Islands. He was also noted for his frequent testimony before congressional committees and his extensive support of liberal legal causes. His book, *God Save This Honorable Court* (1985), in which he warned against "presidential court-packing," was considered the main influence in the failure of Robert H. Bork to win confirmation to a seat on the United States Supreme Court in 1987. Tribe's expertise was in legal, constitutional, and jurisprudential theory, the role of law in shaping technological development, and the uses and abuses of mathematical methods in policy and systems analysis. He argued many high-profile cases before the Supreme Court, including those for Al Gore during the disputed presidential election of 2000. The court had also ruled against Tribe in *Bowers v. Hardwick* in 1986, holding that a Georgia state law criminalizing sodomy, as applied to consensual acts between persons of the same sex, did not violate fundamental liberties under the principle of substantive due process. However, Tribe was vindicated in 2003 when the court overruled Bowers in *Lawrence v. Texas*. Although Tribe did not argue that case, he wrote the amicus, or friend of the court, brief on behalf of the American Civil Liberties Union urging that Bowers be overruled. Tribe was widely respected by the justices, as indicated by the fact that many of them referred to him as Professor Tribe during oral arguments, a sign of respect not generally shown toward law professors arguing before the court. In 2004, it was revealed that several passages in *God Save This Honorable Court* were copied without proper attribution from the 1974 book *Justices and Presidents*, written by Henry J. Abraham, a University of Virginia political scientist. In 2005, Harvard's president and dean released a statement saying that Tribe's admitted failure to provide appropriate attribution was a "significant lapse in proper academic practice," but that they regarded the error as "the product of inadvertence rather than intentionality." Tribe was the J. Alfred Prufrock University Professor at Harvard, one of 19 holding the title university professor.

[Stewart Kampel (2nd ed.)]

TRIBES, THE TWELVE, the traditional division of Israel into 12 tribes: Reuben, Simeon (Levi), Judah, Issachar, Zebulun, Benjamin, Dan, Naphtali, Gad, Asher, Ephraim, and Manasseh. Biblical tradition holds that the 12 tribes of Israel are descended from the sons and grandsons of Jacob (Gen. 29–30; 35:16–18; 48:5–6). The tribes are collectively called Israel because of their origin in the patriarch Jacob-Israel. Jacob and his family went into Egypt as "70 souls" (Ex. 1:1–5). In Egypt "the Israelites were fertile and prolific; they multiplied and increased very greatly" (1:7), and there they became the "Israelite people" (1:9). A pharaoh, "who did not know Joseph" (1:8), oppressed them by burdensome labor. God "remembered His covenant with Abraham, with Isaac, and with Jacob" (2:24), made Himself known to Moses (Ex. 3), and rescued the Israelites from Egypt. By this time the nation numbered "600,000 men on foot, aside from *taf*" which apparently means women as well as children (12:37). At Sinai, the nation received its laws and regulations, covenanting itself to God (Ex. 19–24). After wandering for 40 years in the desert under the leadership of Moses, the 12 Israelite tribes penetrated the land of Canaan with Joshua in command. The united force of the 12 tribes was sufficient to conquer the land, which was then distributed among them. During this period of settlement, and the subsequent period of the Judges, there was no predetermined pattern of leadership among the tribes, except for deliverer-judges sent to them by God in time of need (see also *Judges, Book of). Such crises forced the tribes into cooperative action against enemies under the leadership of the "deliverer." *Shiloh served as a sacral center for all the tribes, housing the Ark of the Covenant under the priestly family of Eli (I Sam. 1:3, 12; 2:27). Under the impact of military pressures, the Israelites felt compelled to turn to *Samuel with the request that he establish a monarchy, and *Saul was crowned to rule over all the tribes of Israel (I Sam. 11:15). Upon his death, *Ish-Bosheth, Saul's son, was accepted by all the tribes save Judah and Simeon who preferred David. David's struggle with the house of Saul ended in victory for him, and all the elders turned to David for royal leadership. He ruled from Jerusalem over all the tribes of Israel (II Sam. 5:3), and was succeeded by his son. After the death of *Solomon, the tribes once again split along territorial and political lines, with Judah and Benjamin in the south loyal to the Davidic house, and the rest of the tribes in the north ruled by a succession of dynasties.

Modern scholarship does not generally accept the biblical notion that the 12 tribes are simply divisions of a larger unit which developed naturally from patriarchal roots. This simplistic scheme, it is felt, actually stems from later genealogical speculations which attempted to explain the history of the tribes in terms of familial relationships. The alliance of the 12 tribes is believed to have grown from the organization of independent tribes, or groups of tribes, forced together for historical reasons. Scholars differ as to when this union of 12 took place, and when the tribes of Israel became one nation. One school of thought holds that the confederation took place inside the country toward the end of the period of the Judges and the beginnings of the Monarchy. All of the traditions which see the 12 tribes as one nation as early as the enslavement in Egypt or the wanderings in the desert are regarded as having no basis in fact. This school recognizes in the names of some of the tribes the names of ancient sites in Canaan, such as the mountains of Naphtali, Ephraim, and Judah, the desert of Judah, and Gilead. With the passage of time, those who dwelt in these areas assumed the names of the localities. M. Noth feels that the Leah tribes, Reuben, Simeon, Levi, Judah, Zebulun, and Issachar, existed at an earlier stage as a confederation of six tribes whose boundaries in Canaan were contiguous. Only at a later stage did other tribes penetrate the area, eventually expanding the confederation to 12. A second school grants that the union of 12 existed during the period of wanderings in the desert, but that Canaan was not conquered by an alliance of these at any one time. Rather, there were individual incursions into the land at widely separated periods. However, the covenant among the 12 tribes and their awareness of national unity flowing from ethnic kinship and common history, faith, and sacral practices had their source in the period prior to the conquest of the land.

The number 12 is neither fictitious nor the result of an actual genealogical development in patriarchal history. It is an institutionalized and conventionalized figure which is found among other tribes as well, such as the sons of Ishmael (Gen. 25:13–16), the sons of Nahor (Gen. 22:20–24), of Joktan (Gen. 10:26–30 – so LXX), and Esau (Gen. 36:10–13). Similar organizational patterns built about groups of 12, or even six, tribes, are known from Asia Minor, Greece, and Italy. In Greece, such groupings were called amphictyony (Ἀμφικτυονία), from ἀμφικτίζω, meaning "to dwell about," that is, about a central sanctuary. Each tribe was assigned a prearranged turn in the provision and maintenance of the shrine. The amphictyonic members would make pilgrimages to the common religious center on festive occasions. The exact measure of correspondence between the amphictyony of the Hellenic world and the duodecimal structure of the tribes of Israel may be the subject of scholarly controversy, but there can be little doubt that this pattern of 12 attributed to the Hebrew tribes is very real and historically rooted. Thus, if one tribe were to withdraw from the union or to be absorbed into another, the number 12 would be preserved, either by splitting one of the remaining tribes into two or by accepting a new tribe into the union. When, for example, the tribe of Levi is considered among the 12 tribes, the Joseph tribes are counted as one (Gen. 35:22–26; 46:8–25; 49:1–27). However, when Levi is not mentioned, the Joseph tribes are counted separately as Manasseh and Ephraim (Num. 26:4–51). For the same duodecimal considerations, Simeon is counted as a tribe even after having been absorbed into Judah (Josh. 19:1), and Manasseh, even after having split in two, is considered one. Among the six Leah tribes, Gad, although the son of Zilpah, is counted as one of them when Levi is missing (Num. 1:20–42; 26:5–50).

The confederation of the 12 tribes was primarily religious, based upon belief in the one "God of Israel" with whom the tribes had made a covenant and whom they worshiped at a common sacral center as the "people of the Lord" (Judg. 5:11; 20:2). The Tent of Meeting and the Ark of the Covenant were the most sacred cultic objects of the tribal union. Biblical tradition shows that many places served as religious centers in various periods. During the desert wanderings, "the mountain of God," that is, Sinai, known as Horeb, served as such a place (Ex. 3:1; 18:5; cf. 5:1–3; 8:23–24), as did the great oasis at Kadesh-Barnea where the tribes remained for some time

(Deut. 1:46). From there the Israelite tribes attempted a conquest of the land (Num. 13:3, 26). Many sites in Canaan are mentioned as having sacred associations or as being centers of pilgrimage. Some of these, such as Penuel, where Jacob, the nominal progenitor of the tribes, received the name Israel (Gen. 32:24–32), Beth-El (28:10–22; 35:1–15), where the Ark of the Lord rested (Judg. 20:26–28), and Beer-Sheba (Gen. 21:33; 46:1–4; Amos 5:5; 8:14) go back to patriarchal times. Jacob built an altar at Shechem (Gen. 33:18–20) and the tribes gathered there "before the Lord" and made a covenant with Him in Joshua's time (Josh. 24). Shiloh enjoyed special importance as a central cultic site for the tribes. There they gathered under Joshua to divide up the land by lot, and it was there that they placed the Tent of Meeting and the Ark of the Covenant (Josh. 18:1–8). Eli's family, which traced its descent from Aaron, the high priest, served at Shiloh (I Sam. 2:27), and it was to Shiloh that the Israelites turned for festivals and sacrifices (Judg. 21:19; I Sam. 1:3; cf. Jer. 7:14; 26:9). The multiplicity of cultic places raises the question of whether all 12 tribes were, indeed, centered about one amphictyonic site. It may be that as a tribe's connections with the amphictyony were weakened for various reasons, the tribe began to worship at one or another of the sites. Possibly, different sites served the several subgroups among the tribes. Beer-Sheba and Hebron, for example, served the southern groups of tribes (Gen. 13:18; Josh. 21:10–11; II Sam. 2:1–4; 5:1–3; 15:7–10); Shechem, Shiloh, and Gilgal (Josh. 5:9–10; I Sam. 11:14–15; 13:4–15; Amos 5:5) were revered by the tribes in the center of the country; and the shrine at Dan served the northern tribes (Judg. 18:30–31). The likelihood of a multiplicity of shrines is strengthened by the fact that clusters of Canaanite settlements separated the southern and central tribes (of the mountains of Ephraim), and divided the central tribes from those in Galilee. It is possible that various shrines served different tribes simultaneously, while the sanctuary which held the Ark of the Lord was revered as central to all 12.

The changes which occurred in the structure of the 12 tribes and in their relative strengths, find expression in the biblical genealogies. The tribes are descended from four matriarchs, eight of them from the wives Leah and Rachel, and four from the handmaids Bilhah and Zilpah (Gen. 29–30). It is a widely held view that attribution to the two wives is indicative of an early stage of tribal organization, the "tribes of Leah" and the "tribes of Rachel." The attribution of four tribes to handmaids may indicate either a lowered status or late entry into the confederation. In the list of the 12 tribes, Reuben is prominent as the firstborn (Gen. 46:8), followed by Simeon, Levi, and Judah, the sons of Leah, who occupy primary positions. Reuben stood at the head of a tribal league and had a position of central importance among his confederates prior to the conquest of the land (Gen. 30:14; 35:22; 37:21; 42:22, 37; Num. 16:1ff.). On the other hand, the same tribe is inactive during the period of the Judges. It did not provide any of the judges, and during Deborah's war against Sisera, Reuben "sat among the sheepfolds" and did not render any aid (Judg. 5:16). Possibly, because this tribe dwelt on the fringes of the land (I Chron. 5:9–10), its links with the others were weakened, and its continued existence as one of the tribes of Israel was in jeopardy (cf. Deut. 33:6). Simeon was absorbed by Judah. Levi spread throughout Israel as a result of its sacral duties. Judah was cut off from the rest of the tribes by a Canaanite land strip that separated the mountains of Judah and Ephraim. Reuben's place as head of the 12 tribes was taken by the house of Joseph which played a decisive and historic role during the periods of the settlement and the Judges. Joshua came from the tribe of Ephraim (Num. 13:8). Shechem and Shiloh were within the borders of the house of Joseph (cf. Ps. 78:59, 67–68). Samuel came from the hill country of Ephraim (I Sam. 1:1). Ephraim led the tribes in the war against Benjamin over the incident of the concubine in Gibeah (Judg. 19–21). At the beginning of the Monarchy, the leadership passed to Judah (cf. Gen. 49:8ff.). The passage in I Chronicles 5:1–2 illustrates well how the dominant position among the tribes passed from Reuben to Ephraim and from Ephraim to Judah.

Each of the 12 tribes enjoyed a good deal of autonomy, ordering its own affairs after the patriarchal-tribal pattern. No doubt there were administrative institutions common to all the tribes, situated beside the central shrines, though information about them is exceedingly scanty. During the desert wanderings, leadership of the people was vested in the princes of each of the tribes and the elders who assisted Moses. They met and legislated for the entire people (Ex. 19:7; 24:1, 9; Num. 1–2; 11:16–24; 32:2; 34:16–29; Deut. 27:1; 31:28). There are references to meetings of tribal leaders and elders during the periods of the settlement and the Judges. "The princes of the congregation, the heads of the thousands of Israel" along with Phinehas the priest, conducted negotiations with the Transjordanian tribes, in the name of the entire nation (Josh. 22:30). Joshua summoned "the elders, the heads, the judges, and the officers of Israel" to make a covenant in Shechem (Josh. 24). The elders of Israel, speaking for the entire nation, requested Samuel to appoint a king (I Sam. 8:4). The incidents of the concubine in Gibeah (Judg. 19–21) and Saul's battle with Nahash the Ammonite (I Sam. 11) are classic examples of joint action taken by the league of 12 tribes acting "as one man, from Dan even to Beer-Sheba, with the land of Gilead" (Judg. 20:1; I Sam. 11:7). In the one case, unified action was taken by the tribes against one of their members, Benjamin, for a breach of the terms of the covenant (Judg. 20:7). The war against Nahash the Ammonite proves that the tribes were required to come to the aid of any one of the league that found itself in difficulty. Because of the sacral nature of the league, the wars of the tribes were considered "wars of the Lord" (Ex. 17:16; Num. 21:14). Nevertheless, the narratives in the Book of Judges regarding the battles which Israel waged against its enemies make it clear that the league must have been rather weak in those days. The consciousness of national and religious unity had not yet led to a solid politico-military confederation. The Song of Deborah gives clear expression to the lack of solidarity among the tribes, for some of them did not come to the aid of the Galilean tribes. It is impossible to designate even one war against external enemies during the period of the Judges in which all the tribes acted in concert. Indeed, there are indications of intertribal quarrels and disputes (Judg. 7–8; 12). In this connection, there are scholars who hold that the judge-deliverers were not pantribal national leaders, but headed only individual tribes, or groups of them (see *Judges). It was only toward the end of the period of the Judges when the Philistine pressure on the Israelite tribes increased in the west and that of the Transjordanian peoples in the east, that the religio-national tribal confederation assumed political and military dimensions. The Israelite tribes then consolidated as a crystallized national-territorial entity within the framework of a monarchical regime. David, Solomon, and afterward the kings of Israel and Judah tended to weaken tribal consciousness in favor of the territorial and monarchical organization. It is apparent, however, from Ezekiel's eschatological vision (Ezek. 47–48) that the awareness of Israel as a people composed of 12 tribes had not, even then, become effaced.

See also *Ten Lost Tribes.

[Bustanay Oded]

In the *Aggadah*

In aggadic literature the word *shevatim* ("tribes," sing., *shevet*) applies to both the 12 sons of Jacob and to the 12 tribes descended from them. When Jacob left home and had his dream, he took 12 stones as a headrest and declared: "God has decreed that there are to be 12 tribes; yet they did not issue from Abraham or Isaac; if these 12 stones will join into one I will know that I am destined to beget them" (Gen. R. 68:11), and in fact the 12 stones coalesced into one (Gen. 28:11 being contrasted with v. 18). Whereas Abraham and Isaac both begat wicked sons, Ishmael and Esau, all of Jacob's 12 sons were loyal to God (Shab. 146a; cf. Ex. R. 1:1). They were all named in reference to Israel's redemption (Tanḥ. Shemot 5), and God declared, "Their names are more precious to me than the anointing oil with which priests and kings were anointed" (Eccles. R. 7:1, 2).

All the tribal ancestors were born outside the Land of Israel, save Benjamin, and all, with the exception of Benjamin, participated in the sale of Joseph. Therefore the tribe of Benjamin was privileged to have the *Shekhinah*, i.e., the Temple, in its portion (Sif. Deut. 3:5, 352). None of the tribes maintained its family purity in Egypt, and all except for Reuben, Simeon, and Levi, engaged in idolatry there (Num. R. 13:8). Just as the heavens cannot endure without the 12 constellations (Ex. R. 15:6), so the world cannot endure without the 12 tribes, for the world was created only by their merit (PR 3:10). The names of the tribes are not always enumerated in the same order, so that it should not be said that those descended from the mistresses (Rachel and Leah) took priority over the descendants of their handmaids (Bilhah and Zilpah; Ex. R. 1:6).

The tribe of Zebulun engaged in trade and supported the tribe of Issachar, to enable it to devote itself to the study of the Torah; therefore in his blessings, Moses gave priority to the tribe of Zebulun (Yal. Gen. 129). All the tribes produced judges and kings, except Simeon, on account of the sin perpetrated by Zimri (Mid. Tadshe 8; see Num. 25:1–2, 14). Every tribe produced prophets; Judah and Benjamin produced kings by prophetic direction (Suk. 27b).

Whereas the tribes of Benjamin and Judah were exiled to Babylon, the Ten Tribes were exiled beyond the river *Sambatyon (Gen. R. 73:6). The Ten Tribes shall neither be resurrected nor judged; R. *Simeon b. Yoḥai said, "They shall never return from exile," but R. Akiva maintained that they would return (ARN 36:4). But see *Ten Lost Tribes. The Davidic Messiah will be descended from two tribes, his father from Judah and his mother from Dan (Yal. Gen. 160).

[Harry Freedman]

BIBLIOGRAPHY: B. Luther, in: ZAW, 21 (1901), 37ff.; E. Meyer, *Die Israeliten und ihre Nachbarstaemme* (1906), 498ff.; W.F. Albright, in: JPOS, 5 (1925), 2–54; A. Alt, *Die Landnahme der Israeliten in Palaestina* (1925); idem, in: PJB, 21 (1925), 100ff.; idem, in: *E. Sellin Festschrift* (1927), 13–24; Alt, Kl Schr, 2 (1953), 1–65; M. Noth, *Das System der Zwoelf Staemme Israels* (1930), 85–108; W. Duffy, *The Tribal History Theory on the Origin of the Hebrews* (1944); Albright, Arch Rel, 102–9; C.V. Wolf, in: JBL, 65 (1946), 45–49; idem, in: JQR, 36 (1945–46), 287–95; Noth, Hist Isr, 53–137; Bright, Hist, 142–60; R. Smend, *Yahweh War and Confederation* (1970). IN THE AGGADAH: Ginzberg, Legends, 7 (1938), 481 (index), s.v. *Tribes, the twelve.*

TRIENNIAL CYCLE, term denoting the custom according to which the weekly Pentateuchal readings on Sabbaths are completed in a three-year cycle. The triennial cycle was practiced in Palestine and in Egypt as late as 1170 C.E., whereas in Babylonia the reading of the Pentateuch was completed in one year, from Tishri to Tishri. The latter became the accepted traditional custom the world over (Meg. 29b; Maim., Yad, Tefillah 13:1).

The masoretic text of the Pentateuch has 154 divisions, known as *sedarim*. According to other traditions, however, the Pentateuch consists of 161 and even 175 portions (Sof. 16:10); the Yemenites divide the Pentateuch into 167. It has been suggested that the 154 division corresponds to the minimum number of Sabbaths in the triennial cycle and 161 to the maximum. The difference is due to the occurrence of festivals on Sabbaths when the regular Pentateuch portions were superseded by special Pentateuch readings appropriate to the festivals. The 175 division stems from the practice of completing the reading of the whole Pentateuch within a cycle of three and a half years (twice within seven years). In general, the different Jewish communities arbitrarily divided the Pentateuch, either by joining portions or dividing them. In the triennial cycle, the Pentateuch reading started on Nisan the first, which was regarded as the Jewish *New Year (see: Ex. 12:2); while the reading of each of the five books of the Pentateuch started on one of the New Years mentioned in the Mishnah (RH 1:1), as can be seen in the following list (p. 142):

Triennial cycle

	FIRST YEAR		SECOND YEAR		THIRD YEAR	
	PENTATEUCH	HAFTARAH	PENTATEUCH	HAFTARAH	PENTATEUCH	HAFTARAH
	GENESIS					
NISAN	1:1	Isa. 42:5	12:29	Isa. 21:11	6:22	(not extant)
	2:4	(not extant)	13:1	Isa. 46:3	8:1	Zech. 4:14
	3:24	(not extant)	13:21	Isa. 45:24	9:22	(not extant)
	5:1	Isa. 30:8–15	15:21	Isa. 49:10	11:1	(not extant)
IYYAR	6:9	Isa. 54:9–10	16:25	Isa. 58:23	12:1	–
	8:1	Hab. 3:1–5	18:1	Isa. 6; 61:6–10	13:1	Josh. 2:1; Judg. 18:7
	8:15	Isa. 42:7–21	21:1	Jer. 34:1	14:1	–
	9:18	Isa. 49:9–13	22:26	Isa. 49:3	15:1	–
	11:1	(not extant)			16:1	I Sam. 11
SIVAN	12:1	Josh. 24:3–8	24:1	Isa. 60:17–61:9	17:16	Ezek. 44:15
	14:1	Isa. 41:2–14; I Kings 10:9	25:1	Isa. 66	18:25	Ezek. 44:29
	15:1	Zeph. 3:9–19; Isa. 1:1–17	26:31	Ezek. 16:10–19	20:14	Judg. 11
	16:1	Isa. 64:1	27:20	Hos. 14:7; Ezek. 43:10	22:2	Micah 5:6
			29:1	Isa. 61:6		
TAMMUZ	17:1	Isa. 63:10–11	30:1	Mal. 1:11–2:7	23:2	(not extant)
	18:1	Isa. 33:17–34:12; II Kings 4	30:12	II Kings 12:5	25:10	Mal. 2:5
	19:1	Isa. 17:14–18:7	31:1	Isa. 43:7–21	26:52	Josh. 17:4
	20:1	Isa. 61:9–10	32:14	II Sam. 22:10–51	28:1	Ezek. 45:12
	21:1	I Sam. 2:21–28				
AV	22:1	Isa. 33:7–22	34:27	Jer. 31:33–40; I Kings 18:27–39	30:1	Jer. 4:2
	23:1	I Kings 1:1	37:1	I Kings 8:8–22	32:1	Jer. 2
	24:1	Judg. 19:20	38:21	Jer. 30:18	33:1	(not extant)
	24:42	Isa. 12:3–14:2	39:1	Isa. 33:20–34:8; I Kings 7:13	34:1	Ezek. 45:1; Josh. 21:41
	25:1	II Sam. 5:17–6:1				Josh. 20:1
ELUL	26:11	Isa. 65:23–66:8	**LEVITICUS**		**DEUTERONOMY**	
	27:1	Isa. 46:3–6	1:1	Isa. 43:21; Jer. 21:19; Micah 6:9–7:8	1:1	Jer. 30:4; Amos 2:9
	27:28	Micah 1:1; 5:7–13	3:1	Ezek. 44:11; 20:41	2:1	(not extant)
	28:10	Hos. 12:13	4:1	Ezek. 18:4–17	3:23	Jer. 32:16
	29:31	Isa. 60:15	5:1	Zech. 5:3–6:19	4:1	(not extant)
			6:1	Jer. 7:21		
TISHRI	30:21	I Sam. 1:11	6:12	Mal. 3:9	5:1	(not extant)
	31:3	Jer. 30:10–16; Micah 6:3–7:20	8:1	Ezek. 43:27	6:4	I Kings 10:39
	32:4	Obad. 1:1	9:1	I Kings 8:56–58	8:1	Jer. 9:22–24
	33:18	Nah. 1:12–2:5	12:1	Isa. 66:7	9:1	Jer. 2:1; II Kings 8:30
ḤESHVAN	35:9	Isa. 43:1–7	13:29	II Kings 5	10:1	II Kings 13:23
	37:1	Jer. 38:8	14:1	II Kings 7:8	11:26	Isa. 54:11–55:6
	38:1	Isa. 37:31–37	15:1	(not extant)	12:20	Jer. 23:9
	39:1	Isa. 52:3–9	16:1	Ezek. 44:1	15:7	Isa. 61:1–2
KISLEV	40:23	Amos 1:3–15; 2:6	17:1	(not extant)	17:14	I Sam. 8:1
	41:1	Isa. 29:8	18:1	Ezek. 22:1	17:24	I Sam. 10:24
	41:38	Isa. 11:2–9	19:1	Amos 9:7	18:1	Jer. 29:8
	42:18	Isa. 50:10–52:11	21:1	Ezek. 44:25	20:10	Josh. 24:1
TEVET	43:24	Jer. 42:12–17; 43:12–14; I Kings 3:15	22:1	(not extant)	21:10	Isa. 54:1–10
	44:18	Josh. 14:6; Ezek. 37:10	24:1	(not extant)	(not extant)	(not extant)
	{47:28	{I Kings 13:14	25:1	Jer. 36:6; Ezek. 34	(not extant)	(not extant)
	48:1	I Kings 2:1	25:39	Isa. 24:2	26:1	Isa. 60:1–22
	49:1	Isa. 43:2				

Triennial cycle (cont.)

	FIRST YEAR		SECOND YEAR		THIRD YEAR	
	PENTATEUCH	HAFTARAH	PENTATEUCH	HAFTARAH	PENTATEUCH	HAFTARAH
SHEVAT	49:27	Zech. 14:1; Micah 2:12	26:3	Jer. 16:19; Ezek. 12:20	29:9	Isa. 55:6–58:8; Micah 7:18–20
	EXODUS		NUMBERS		31:1	Jer. 12:15
	1:1	Isa. 27:6; Ezek. 16:1; 20	1:1	Hos. 2:1	31:14	Judg. 2:7
	3:1	Isa. 40:11; II Kings 20:8	2:14	(not extant)	32:1	Ezek. 17:22
	4:14	Isa. 55:12	3:14	Isa. 43:9		
	6:2	Ezek. 28:25–29:21				
ADAR	7:18	Joel 3:3	4:17	I Sam. 6:10	33:1	Josh. 1:1–18
	8:16	Isa. 34:11	4:21	Judg. 13:2–25	34:1	(not extant)
	10:1	Isa. 19; Jer. 4:6; I Sam. 6:6	5:11	Hos. 4:14	Shekalim	
	12:13	Jer. 46:13–28	6:1	Judg. 13:2	Zakhor	
					Parah	
					Ha-Ḥodesh	

The reading of the book of

Genesis started on Nisan the 1st	1st
Exodus started on Shevat the 15th	1st
Leviticus started on Tishri the 1st	2nd
Numbers started on Shevat the 15th	2nd
Deuteronomy started on Elul the 1s	3rd

The above division corresponds with biblical events narrated in aggadic legends:

(1) The creation story was read in the month of Nisan (in the first year of the cycle) as it was held that the world was created in this month (R. Joshua's view, in RH 11a).

(2) The sin of Cain (Gen. 4) was always read on the third Sabbath in Nisan (on Passover) which tallies with the legend that Cain offered his sacrifice on Passover (PdRE, sect. 21).

(3) The story of Rachel giving birth to Joseph after having been barren for years (Gen. 30:22ff.), was always read at the beginning of Tishri (in the first year) which corresponds to the legend that Rachel, Sarah, Hannah, etc., were remembered by God on Rosh Ha-Shanah (RH 10b).

(4) Exodus 12, whose subject is the exodus from Egypt and was read in Nisan (second year), coincides with the Passover festival.

(5) The reading of the Ten Commandments (Ex. 20:1–14) on the 6th of Sivan (second year) tallies with the *Shavuot festival.

(6) Exodus 34, read on the last Sabbath of Av, records Moses receiving the two tablets of the law for the second time (80 days after the 6th of Sivan). This is in accordance with the tradition that Moses spent twice 40 days on Mount Sinai. With the first two tablets he descended on the 17th of Tammuz but broke them because of the sin of the Golden Calf (Ex. 32); he then ascended for another 40 days and returned with the second two tablets on the 29th of Av.

(7) The reading of Leviticus always started (second year) at the end of Elul. Leviticus 8:1; 10:7, whose subject is the sacrificial cult of the priests in the Temple, was read on the *Day of Atonement on which the high priest performed the most sacred ritual in the Holy of Holies.

(8) Numbers (6:22ff.), always read at the beginning of Nisan (in the third year), corresponds to the biblical date of Moses' inauguration of the tabernacle.

(9) Deuteronomy 34, on the death of Moses, always read at the beginning of Adar (third year), tallies with the tradition that Moses died on the 7th of Adar.

The intention behind the triennial cycle was that the weekly portions correspond to the character of the festivals on which these are read (as may be seen from the above examples). This thematic coincidence was not always possible and did not always occur. There is, for example, no thematic correspondence between the portions to be read in Tishri (the first year) with the festivals in this month. The Mishnah (Meg. 3:5), therefore, ordered for all festivals special readings from the Pentateuch dealing with the commandments, etc., of each particular festival. Since the reading of the whole Pentateuch ended in Adar of the third year of the cycle and a few Sabbaths were left until Nisan (when the cycle started anew), the particular portions for the Four Sabbaths (*Arba Parashiyyot; Shekalim, Zakhor, Parah,* and *Ha-Ḥodesh*) were read as is customary nowadays (see *Torah, Reading of and *Sabbaths, Special).

In traditional synagogues, the Pentateuch is read in one year. *Reform Judaism (and some *Conservative synagogues) has, however, reverted to the ancient Palestinian custom of a triennial cycle. It was done in response to the spiritual need of the congregants most of whom do not understand Hebrew, and consequently, cannot follow – with proper attention – the lengthy reading in Hebrew of the entire weekly **sidrah*. The weekly reading was shortened to approximately one third. In order that the portion should not be different from that read in traditional synagogues, the first part of each weekly *sidrah* is read in the first year, the second in the next, and the third in the last year of this triennial cycle. Consequently, three different *haftarot* were provided for every standard Pentateuch portion to correspond to the central theme of the particular part of the portion read. (See *Union Prayer Book*, 1 (1924), 399–406.)

The accompanying Table: Triennial Cycle is based on a number of hypotheses, first developed by Buechler and later taken up, with significant modification, by Mann (see bibl.). According to Buechler, the triennial cycle began in Nisan. According to Mann, it began in Tishri. Both of them worked with references in the Midrash and with *genizah* fragments. There is, however, no lectionary extant which, with any certainty, can be ascribed to either the tannaitic or the amoraic period. On the contrary, all available evidence seems to point in the direction of a complete absence of a definite triennial cycle in the talmudic period – although a number of such "cycles" were definitely in existence in the post-talmudic period. During the talmudic period – whence comes the ruling that each one of the seven people, "called" to read from the Torah, must not read "less than three verses" – various congregations seem to have begun and completed the reading of the Pentateuch at different times of the year.

BIBLIOGRAPHY: A. Buechler, in: JQR, 5 (1892/93), 420–68; 6 (1893/94), 1–73; Jacobs, in: JE, 12 (1905), 254–7 (with tables); J. Mann, *The Bible as Read and Preached in the Old Synagogue*, 1 (1940); 2 (1966; completed by I. Sonne); Ḥ. Albeck, in: *L. Ginzberg Jubilee Volume* (1946), 25–43 (Heb. pt.); L. Morris, *The New Testament and the Jewish Lectionaries* (1964); L. Crockett, in: JJS, 17 (1966), 13–46; J. Heinemann, in: *Tarbiz*, 33 (1963/64), 362–8; idem, in: JJS, 19 (1968), 41–48; J.J. Petuchowski, *Contributions to the Scientific Study of Jewish Liturgy* (1970), xvii–xxiii.

TRIER (Treves), city in Germany and formerly also a bishopric. Archaeological evidence seems to point to the presence of Jews in Trier as early as the end of the third century C.E., although the existence of a Jewish community there at the time is uncertain. Traces of Jewish commercial activity in the sixth century suggest the possibility of Jewish settlement. The first definitive evidence for the presence of a Jewish community dates from 1066, when the Jews were saved from an attempted expulsion on the part of Archbishop Eberhard through his sudden death at the altar. The Jewish community was accused of the use of black magic in order to bring about his death. On April 10, 1096, the first day of Passover, Peter the Hermit appeared before the gates of Trier armed with a letter from the Jewish communities of France to their coreligionists in Germany, requesting that they provide provisions for Peter and his crusaders for their expedition to the Holy Land. The Jewish community responded to the letter, and Peter and his followers went on their way. Sometime later the burghers of the city rose against the Jews; they discovered the community's Torah scrolls, which had been placed in a building for safekeeping, and desecrated them. In panic the Jews fled to the palace of Archbishop Egelbert; somehow they rescued their desecrated scrolls and took them along. The archbishop did his best to protect them, and the Jews hoped to remain under his protection until the imminent return of Emperor *Henry IV to Germany. A number of Jews were murdered and others committed suicide; the archbishop and his retinue were themselves attacked for shielding the Jews. Under increasing pressure from a mob outside the palace, the archbishop prevailed upon the remaining Jews to convert, including their leader, Rabbi Micah, who was converted by the archbishop himself. One year later, however, with the return of Emperor Henry IV to Germany, all of them were permitted to return to Judaism.

Other Jewish communities in the bishopric were also severely affected by the First Crusade; soon, however, the Jews of Trier returned to their homes and rebuilt their community life. The *Gesta Trevarorum* tells of a Jew named Joshua who served as a physician in the retinue of Archbishop Bruno of Trier (d. 1124). Joshua, who later converted to Christianity, was also a mathematician and astronomer. During the Second Crusade (1146), R. Simon of Trier fell as a martyr in the vicinity of Cologne; the community as a whole, however, remained undisturbed. During the course of the 12th-century, its economic position was strengthened considerably. The communal organization, known as *universitas Judeorum Treverensium*, had as its leader a so-called "Jewish bishop" (**Episcopus Judaeorum*) with considerable authority. The community possessed a cemetery, and in 1235 a synagogue and community building (*domus communitatis*). A *Judenstrasse* is mentioned at the beginning of the 13th century. The Jews occupied themselves mostly in trading and moneylending, although other occupations were known. They reached, in fact, such a level of economic well-being as to arouse the cupidity of Archbishop Henry (1260–86), who extorted a considerable amount of money from the Jews in 1285. There was some measure of cultural contact between Jews and gentiles. Lambert of Luettich, a monk at the monastery of St. Matthew in Trier, was taught Hebrew by a Jew and with the aid of his teacher succeeded in deciphering a rare Hebrew manuscript. Sources dating from the 14th century indicate that Jews continued to own houses and vineyards outside the Jewish quarter and that Christians were living on the *Judenstrasse*. The community profited from the liberal and energetic administration of Archbishop Baldwin (1307–54), who entrusted a considerable portion of his financial administration to Jewish hands. Although Jews suffered during the *Armleder uprising of 1336, its effects were limited by the prompt action of the archbishop. In 1338 he was forced to guarantee to the burghers that the number of Jewish families in the city would not rise above 56. During the *Black Death persecutions of 1349, the burghers attacked the Jews, murdering some, stealing their property, and desecrating their cemetery. The community fled in panic, although Baldwin and his successor Boehmund sought to compensate them for the expropriation of their property. It was only in 1356 that King *Charles IV gave permission for the Jews to return, although in 1354 Bishop Boehmund made Simeon b. Jacob of Trier his court physician.

By 1418, however, the Jews were expelled once more from the entire bishopric of Trier; among the properties of the Jewish community in the city that were disposed of in 1422 was a hospital. Jews did not reappear again in the bishopric until the beginning of the 16th century; in 1555 they were permitted the services of a rabbi to care for the needs of all who were resident in the bishopric. Elector Johann von Schoeneberg expelled them in 1589, only to readmit them in 1593. In a regulation put into force in that year, a yellow *badge was prescribed for Jews to distinguish them from Christians. In 1597 a consortium of Jewish merchants headed by Magino Gabrieli were granted special trading privileges that were to last 25 years. However, in 1657, among other restrictive provisions, legislation was approved which severely limited the interest rate of Jewish moneylenders.

In 1675 Jews were accused of giving aid to French troops quartered in the city; after the French surrendered, Jewish homes were plundered and the Jewish community sustained overwhelming losses. A fast day was declared in perpetuity for the 15th of Elul to mark the event; a **Memorbuch* also dates from the period. At the head of the community at the time was David Tevele b. Isaac Wallich (d. 1691), a physician. In 1723 Elector Franz Ludwig limited the number of Jews in the bishopric to 160; in addition to some highly restrictive provisions, legislation of that year reaffirmed the authority of the rabbinate in the bishopric. A synagogue was constructed in 1762, formerly a house occupied by R. Mordecai Marx, grandfather of Karl *Marx. The French conquered the city in 1794, bringing with them civic equality for the Jews, a measure acknowledged fully by the Prussian administration only in 1850. Among the rabbis who served the community in the 19th century were Moses b. Eliezer Treves (d. 1840) and Joseph Kahn, who was rabbi at the time of the dedication of a new synagogue in September 1859. The modern community also developed a number of philanthropic organizations and an elementary school. There were 568 Jews in the city in 1871; 823 in 1893; 802 in 1925; 796 in 1933; 400 in 1938; 210 in 1939; and 450 in 1941.

The onset of Nazism brought with it accelerated emigration, aided by the efforts of Adolf Altmann, rabbi in Trier, who helped to develop a program of adult Jewish education that involved many other communities in the area as well. On *Kristallnacht*, Nov. 9–10, 1938, the synagogue was destroyed. Almost all the Jews remaining in the city in 1941 were deported to Poland and *Theresienstadt, never to return.

[Alexander Shapiro / B. Mordechai Ansbacher]

Post Word-War II

A new community of displaced persons was established after the war, and a new synagogue was erected in 1957. In 1971 there were 75 Jews living in Trier. The Jewish community numbered 61 in 1984; 54 in 1989; and 457 in 2004. The increase is explained by the immigration of Jews from the former Soviet Union after 1990. The house where Karl Marx was born has housed a museum of his life and work since 1947. In 1996–97 the Arye Maimon Institute for Jewish History was founded at Trier University. The institute's work is focused on the research of Jewish history in central and Western Europe.

[Alexander Shapiro and B. Mordechai Ansbacher / Larissa Daemmig (2nd ed.)]

BIBLIOGRAPHY: Aronius, Regesten, 160, 22, 439, 773; *Germania Judaica*, 1 (1963), 376–83; 2 (1968), 826–33; 3 (1987), 1470–81; Salfeld, Martyrol, index; F. Haubrich, *Die Juden in Trier* (1907); A. Altmann, *Das frueheste Vorkommen der Juden in Deutschland – Juden im roemischen Trier* (1932); A.M. Habermann, *Gezerot Ashkenaz ve-Ẓarefat* (1946); K. Duewell, *Die Rheingebiete in der Judenpolitik des Nazionalsozialismus vor* 1942 (1968), index; *Die Feier der Einweihung der neuen Synagoge zu Trier* (1859); K. Baas, in: MGWJ, 55 (1911), 745–6; 57 (1913), 458; S. Schifress, in: ZGJD, 3 (1931), 243–7; *ibid.*, 7 (1937), 156–79. **ADD. BIBLIOGRAPHY:** R. Laufner and A. Rauch, *Die Familie Marx und die Trierer Judenschaft* (Schriften aus dem Karl-Marx-Haus in Trier, vol. 14) (1975); J. Jacobs, *Existenz und Untergang der alten Judengemeinde der Stadt Trier* (1984); R. Nolden (ed.), *Juden in Trier* (Ausstellungskataloge Trierer Bibliotheken, vol. 15) (1988); idem (ed.), *Vorlaeufiges Gedenkbuch fuer die Juden von Trier 1938–1943* (1994); A. Haller, *Der juedische Friedhof an der Weidegasse in Trier und die mittelalterlichen juedischen Grabsteine im Rheinischen Landesmuseum Trier* (2003).

TRIER, WALTER (1890–1951), cartoonist and illustrator. Trier, who came from a Prague German family, settled in Berlin. He is best known for his witty and ironic drawings and for his illustrations of books by famous German authors, especially those of Erich Kaestner. Trier was one of the leading contributors to the German humorous weeklies *Simplicissimus* and *Lustige Blaetter* and published several collections of his drawings in volume form. He was one of the first to infuse contemporary content into "imitations" of the old masters. After escaping from Germany before World War II, he contributed to publications in England and America. His own collections included *1000 Bauernwitze* (1917), *Fridolins Siebenmeilenpferd, Fridolins Harlekinder,* and *Fridolins Zauberland,* all of which appeared in 1926.

BIBLIOGRAPHY: *Allgemeines Lexikon der bildenden Kuenstler* (1939); Roth, Art, 837. **ADD. BIBLIOGRAPHY:** L. Lang, *Walter Trier. Klassiker der Karikatur,* vol. 4 (1984).

[Avigdor Dagan]

TRIESTE, port in Friuli, N. Italy. Although Jews may have lived in Trieste before the end of the 14th century, there is no authoritative information. After the city's annexation to Austria in 1382 Jews from Germany settled there; some were subject to the dukes of Austria and some to the local rulers. Jews soon took the place of Tuscan moneylenders in the economic life of the city. The Jewish banker Moses and his brother Cazino, who lived in the Rione del Mercato, are mentioned in 1359. The Jews tended to live in the Riborgo neighborhood, then the civic and commercial center. The 15th century was a period of development for the small Jewish community. Two Jewish bankers dominated the period, Salomone D'Oro and Isacco da Trieste. In 1509 the Emperor Maximilian I granted to Isacco the position of *Schutzjude*, or protected Jew. It is important to stress the position of Jewish women, who sometimes directed the family's banking establishment. As in the other Imperial possessions, Jews were obliged to wear the yellow badge. In 1583 there was an abortive attempt to expel the Jews.

In 1620 Ventura Parente and the Grassin brothers received from the City of Trieste the concession of the title of public banker and moneylender. In 1624 Ventura Parente obtained from the Emperor Ferdinand II the title of Hoffaktor. During the 17th century Trieste's Patriciate took an unfavorable stand toward the Jews, asking the imperial authorities for their expulsion. The imperial authorities resisted the pressure and Jews were not expelled. However, in 1695 the 11 Jewish families in the city, around 70 people, were enclosed in the so-called Old Ghetto, or Trauner Ghetto. The Jews petitioned the authorities successfully for a healthier site, and in 1696 the Jewish ghetto was erected in the Riborgo neighborhood, near the harbor.

From the beginning of the 18th century the Hapsburgs adopted a mercantilist policy, which led to the development of the port of Trieste. In 1746 the Università degli ebrei, or Jewish community, was constituted. In this period there were 120 Jews living in Trieste. The most important families were the Morpurgo, Parente, Levi, and Luzzatto. In the same year the first synagogue was erected, the so-called Scuola Piccola. Maria Theresa permitted the richest Jewish families to live outside the ghetto. Moreover, Marco Levi, head of the community, received the title of Hoffaktor in 1765. In 1771 Maria Theresa granted a series of privileges to the Nazione Ebrea of Trieste. In the 18th century Jews were traders and craftsmen and some of them were factors to the Austrian court (see above). One of the most distinguished scholars of the mid-18th century was Rabbi Isacco Formiggini. Emperor *Joseph II's *Toleranzpatent* of 1782 gave legal sanction to the gradually improving condition of the Jews in Trieste, and in 1785 the gates of the ghetto were destroyed. There were around 670 Jews in 1788. In 1775 the Scuola Grande or Great Synagogue was erected on the plan of the architect Francesco Balzano. The building included also a Sephardi synagogue.

In 1796 the community inaugurated a Jewish school under the Chief Rabbi Raffael Nathan Tedesco. This school was in part inspired by the proposals of N.H. *Wessely. The first Hebrew work printed in Trieste was Samuel Romanelli's Italian-Hebrew grammar, published in 1799.

In 1796 the French under Napoleon arrived in Trieste. In 1800, 1,200 Jews lived in Trieste. From 1809 to 1813 Trieste was part of the Kingdom of Italy. Some Jews were supporters of the French Revolution and Napoleon, although Napoleon's economic blockade ruined the city's trade. Thus, when the Austrians returned in 1814, the Jewish community was relieved. Tedesco was followed by Abramo Eliezer Levi, who was the chief rabbi of Trieste between 1802 and 1825.

The 19th century was the golden age of Trieste Jewry. In 1831 Giuseppe Lazzaro Morpurgo established the Assicurazioni Generali, which dominated the economic life of the city for more than a hundred years. During the 19th century some members of the community played an active part in the Risorgimento and the Irredentist struggle which culminated in Trieste's becoming part of Italy in 1919. Trieste Jews, such as the writer Italo *Svevo and the poet Umberto *Saba, were central in the creation of the Italian intellectual world. *Il Corriere Israelitico*, a Jewish newspaper in Italian, was published in Trieste from 1862 to 1915. In 1862 S.D. *Luzzatto issued there his dirge on Abraham Eliezer Levi. In the 1850s some Hebrew books were printed at the Marinigha press, including Ghirondi-Neppi's *Toledot Gedolei Yisrael* (1853). The Jewish printer Jonah Cohen was active in the 1860s. His illustrated Passover *Haggadah* (by A.V. Morpurgo) with and without Italian translation (1864) was a memorable production.

The number of Jews increased gradually in the 19th century. In 1848 there were around 3,000 Jews, in 1869 there were 4,421, and in 1910, 5,160 Jews lived in Trieste. Most of the chief rabbis of Trieste were Italian Jews, such as Marco Tedeschi, elected in 1858, and Sabato Raffaele Melli from 1870 to 1907. The monumental new synagogue in Via Donizzetti opened in 1912 and it was inaugurated by Chief Rabbi Zvi Perez Chajes. It followed the Ashkenazi rite. After World War I Trieste was the main port for Jews from Central and Eastern Europe who immigrated to Ereẓ Israel.

[Shlomo Simonsohn / Samuele Rocca (2nd ed.)]

Holocaust Period

According to the census of 1931, the Jewish community of Trieste had 4,671 members, including 3,234 Italians and 1,437 foreigners. Census data for 1938 recorded 5,381 Jews in Trieste, belonging for the most part to the lower and middle sectors of the middle class. The racial laws at the end of 1938 caused an initial period of disorientation, including many conversions, the withdrawal of membership of many Community leaders and members, and the emigration of most foreign Jews. By 1939, however, the elected council had been replaced by one appointed by the Italian government. In October 1941, the first visible acts of real intimidation occurred. The facade of the central temple of the German rite and the headquarters of the community in Via del Monte were defaced with antisemitic slogans and red ink. Vandalism and violence recurred in July 1942, when several Fascist squads devastated the temple and assaulted defenseless passers-by. Similar incidents occurred in May 1943, when Jewish and Slavic businesses and shops were sacked. By then, the Jewish community of Trieste had no more than 2,500 members.

After the Italian armistice with the Allies on September 8, 1943, and the German occupation of Italy, Trieste and the surrounding area were incorporated into the Adriatisches Kustenland and formally annexed as an integral part of the Reich, with dire consequences for the Jews. Not all Jews were able to go into hiding before a German *Einsatzkommando* initiated the first roundup of Jews on October 9. A second roundup occurred on October 29, and a third on January 20, 1944. During the latter event, Dr. Carlo Morpurgo, secretary of the community, remained at work in order not to abandon the elderly patients at the Jewish Pia Casa Gentilomo hospice. He was arrested and deported with them to Auschwitz, where he was murdered on November 4, 1944.

In March 1944, other Jews recovering in various hospitals throughout the city, including the Regina Elena, the psychiatric hospital, and the hospital for the chronically ill, were seized. After being arrested, the Jews were taken to the Coroneo prison and, after February or March 1944, also to the Risiera di San Sabba, the only concentration camp with a crematorium in Italy. Some Jews arrested in Fiume, Venice, Padua, and Arbe were also sent to the Risiera. From October 1943 to February 1945, about 60 convoys left Trieste, all headed for the concentration camps of Central and Eastern Europe. According to estimates, Jews deported from the Adriatisches Kustenland numbered 1,235, of whom 708 were from Trieste. Of the latter, only 23 returned.

Some Jews from Trieste joined the partisans and died in combat. Sergio Forti was killed in battle near Perugia on June 16, 1944; Rita Rosana died near Verona on September 17, 1944, at the age of 22; and Eugenio Curiel, a university teacher, was killed by Fascists in Milan on February 24, 1945, just a few weeks before the liberation.

[Adonella Cedarmas (2nd ed.)]

After the war about 1,500 Jews remained in Trieste; by 1965 their number had fallen to 1,052, out of a total of 280,000 inhabitants, partly because of the excess of deaths over births. In 1969 the community, numbering about 1,000, operated a synagogue and a prayer house of the Ashkenazi rite, a school, and a home for the aged. In the early 21st century the Jewish population of Trieste was around 600.

[Shlomo Simonsohn / Samuele Rocca (2nd ed.)]

BIBLIOGRAPHY: Roth, Italy, index; Milano, Italia, index; Milano, Bibliotheca, index; Bachi, in: *Israel* (Aug. 11–18, 1927); Colbi, *ibid.* (March 22, 1928); idem, in: RMI 17 (1951), 122–9; Curiel, *ibid.*, 6 (1931/32), 446–72; Volli, *ibid.*, 24 (1958), 206–14; Botteri and Carmiel, in: *Trieste…*, 6 (1959), May-June issue, 6–16; L. Buda, *Vicende e notizie della comunità ebraica triestina nel Settecento* (1969); H.D. Friedberg, *Ha-Defus ha-Ivri be Italyah* (1956²), 90. **ADD. BIBLIOGRAPHY:** T. Catalan, *La comunità ebraica di Trieste (1781–1914), Politica, società e cultura, Quaderni del dipartimento di storia, Università degli studi di Trieste* (2000); S.G. Cusin, and P.C. Ioly Zorattini, *Friuli Venezia Giulia, Itinerari ebraici, I luoghi, la storia, l'arte* (1998), 108–71; L.C., Dubin, *The Port Jews of Habsburg Trieste, Absolutist Politics and Enlightenment Culture* (1999); M., Stock, *Nel segno di Geremia, Storia della comunità israelitica di Trieste dal 1200* (1979); S. Bon, *Gli Ebrei a Trieste 1930–1945. Identità, persecuzione, risposte* (2000); S.G. Cusin and P.C.I. Zorattini, *Friuli Venezia Giulia, Itinerari ebraici* (1998).

TRIETSCH, DAVIS (1870–1935), Zionist leader and author. Born in Dresden, Germany, Trietsch was educated in Berlin and subsequently studied migration problems in New York (1893–99). There he conceived (1895) the idea of settling Jews in *Cyprus, but he pursued this notion only after attending the First Zionist Congress (1897). He opposed Theodor *Herzl's political Zionism, insisting on immediate practical settlement wherever possible in the vicinity of Palestine. He tried in vain to persuade the Zionist Movement to adopt his conception of a "Greater Palestine," which was to comprise Palestine proper, Cyprus, and *El-Arish. After negotiations with the High Commissioner of Cyprus in 1899, Trietsch brought a group of 11 Boryslaw miners to the island (March 1900). This attempt ended in failure, however, because of inadequate preparation of both the settlers and of the land. He regarded Herzl's negotiations with the British authorities for a settlement in El-Arish (1902–03) as "an acceptance by Herzl of his program without him." This led to a permanent rupture between the two men (Sixth Zionist Congress, 1903). He subsequently organized the Juedische Orient-Kolonisations-Gesellschaft in Berlin, in whose name he negotiated with the London Colonial Office (1903) concerning a settlement in Cyprus, but was turned down.

Trietsch was a delegate to the First Zionist Congress and at many subsequent ones. In 1905 Trietsch opened an Information Office for Immigration in Jaffa, with branches in other cities in Ereẓ Israel, but was unable to maintain it. In 1906 he organized and participated in an expedition to El-Arish to investigate the area for Jewish settlement with a view to reopening negotiations with the British government, but this effort, too, ended in failure. He was a member of the Zionist General Council in 1907–11 and 1920–21. Some of his suggestions regarding practical settlement in Ereẓ Israel were adopted by Zionist Congresses. At first he supported the new leadership consisting of practical Zionists (from 1911 onward), but soon fell out with them and opposed Arthur *Ruppin's "slow settlement methods." During World War I he served in the statistical department of the German army, and after 1915 he published a number of officially sponsored pamphlets in which he pleaded for collaboration between Zionism and Germany after the war. At the request of the British government, Arnold J. Toynbee opposed these ideas and pleaded (in *Turkey: A Past and A Future*, 1917) for cooperation between Zionism and the Allies. After World War I Trietsch fought for his "Zionist maximalism" with still more fervor, believing that a chance for large-scale immigration to Ereẓ Israel was at hand and that the agricultural methods of the Zionist Organization were inadequate to handle it. He suggested planned industrial development of the country in conjunction with numerous small "garden cities" and propagated these ideas at Zionist Congresses and in his periodical *Volk und Land* (Berlin, 1919).

Trietsch was coeditor and cofounder (with Leo Wintz) of *Ost und West* (Berlin, 1901–02) and with Alfred *Nossig of *Palaestina* (Berlin, 1902). He propagated his ideas in a great many books, pamphlets, and articles, including *Palaestina-Handbuch* (1907 and nine subsequent editions), *Juedische Emigration und Kolonisation* (1917), *Palaestina Wirtschaftsatlas* (1922), *Der Widereintritt der Juden in die Weltgeschichte* (1926).

BIBLIOGRAPHY: O.K. Rabinowicz, in: *Herzl Year Book*, 4 (1962), 119–206; *Juedische Rundschau* (Jan. 9, 1930); A. Boehm, *Geschichte der zionistischen Bewegung*, 1 (1935), 247ff.; 2 (1937), 20–21.

[Oskar K. Rabinowicz]

TRIGANO, SHMUEL (1948–), French sociologist and intellectual, born in Blida, Algeria. A professor of sociology of religion and politics at the Nanterre University Paris x, Trigano's main purpose was to investigate the enigma of modernity and the nature of Jewish politics. By studying the Jews as agents and subjects of history, he tried to understand why Jews disappeared from the public space in the modern world in the aftermath of the Emancipation and how Jewish politics have been restored in the historical arena with the creation of the State of Israel. He developed his reflections in two directions: an analysis of modernity and an attempt to understand the essence of Jewishness, with regard to the political dimension of the world. Following an hermeneutical method, Trigano developed, from his initial *Le Récit de la disparue* (1977) to *La demeure oubliée, genèse religieuse du politique* (1982), *Philosophie de la Loi, l'origine de la politique dans la Tora* (1992), and *La séparation d'amour, une éthique d'alliance* (1998), an anthropological approach to Judaism.

He published numerous books, which are not only concerned with the Jewish sphere but also with the essence of politics and democracy as such. Assuming that the attitude of democracy towards the Jews is a key to the understanding of its very nature, he postulates that the Jewish question could illustrate the failure of the human rights theory to account for collective identity and to face the question of transcendence, which modernity can not paradoxically avoid despite the phenomenon of secularization and civil religion. Trying to pinpoint the origins of the presence and topicality of Jewishness in the modern world through Jewish history, Trigano conceives the idea of the Jewish State not as a regression to the past but as an invention of a new age. A special part of his work is devoted to French Judaism, considered as an exemplary case of the civil political status of the emancipated Jew. More recently Trigano focused on the new European antisemitism. In *Les frontières d'Auschwitz, les ravages du devoir de mémoire* (2005), he intended to demonstrate the way Europe expects the Jews to remain in the role of victims, the only recognition allowed to them. He assumes that as soon as they depart from this role, as is the case when they live in a sovereign political state, they are subjected to reprobation.

Being one of the main figures in contemporary French Judaism, Trigano was the founding director of the College of Jewish Studies at the *Alliance Israélite Universelle (1986–) and initiated the periodical *Pardès*, an European Journal for Jewish Studies and Culture (1985). In 2001, he created a research center devoted to the analysis of contemporary antisemitism. He was a president of the Observatory of the Jewish World. He also was the editor of the 4-volume series *La Société juive à travers l'histoire* (1992) intended to illustrate the permanence, unity, and continuity of the Jewish people over 30 centuries.

[Perrine Simon-Nahum (2nd ed.)]

TRIGERE, PAULINE (1908–2002), U.S. fashion designer. Trigere was born in Paris to parents who had emigrated there from Russia. As a child, she thought about becoming a doctor, but her father, Alexandre, a tailor, and mother, Cecile, a seamstress, persuaded her to learn dressmaking. She studied at Victor Hugo College, designed her own party dresses, and at 19 married Lazar Radley, a Russian-born tailor. Trigere and her brother, Robert, opened a store in Paris that became known for its smart suits and dresses, but in 1937, the looming Nazi threat forced Trigere and her family to head for New York City. In 1941, she and her husband separated, eventually to divorce. To support her two sons, she took a job as an assistant designer at Hattie *Carnegie for $65 a week. In 1942, with her brother, she opened her own business with an 11-piece collection. Her strength was being able to make dresses in the French style: instead of sketching a garment, she would actually cut the fabric to shape while it was draped on the model, wielding her scissors like a sword. It was a skill she was able to demonstrate for the rest of her life. Trigere was among the first to use common fabrics like cotton and wool in evening wear. She developed a thin wool called Trigeen that she used for 50 years. Her clothes, which combined elegance with practicality, were sold in the finest stores and became popular with such style icons as the Duchess of Windsor and Bette Davis. Trigere became known for her reversible capes and coats, and her jumpsuits, which became a fashion staple in the 1960s. In 1949 she won the first of three Coty Awards and in 1959 was inducted into the Coty Hall of Fame. In 1961 she was among the first major U.S. designers to hire an African-American model for an important runway show. She was honored by the Fashion Institute of Technology in 1992 on the 50th anniversary of her company. A year later, she closed the business, citing increasing retail consolidation as a reason. Its volume had peaked about a decade earlier at some $5 million. More honors followed: a Lifetime Achievement Award from the Council of Fashion Designers of America, induction into the Fashion Industry Walk of Fame and the French Legion of Honor. In 2001, Trigere – then 92 – went into a new business with an online retailer, designing accessories for older people: canes, pill boxes, cases for eyeglasses, and hearing aids. Although her clothes had become collectibles, she had never licensed out her name, something she said she regretted. She was a fiercely independent woman whose individual sense of style was evident not only in the clothes she designed, but in the life she lived. She learned English by sitting through multiple showings of Hollywood movies, collected turtles, practiced yoga, and never hesitated to speak her mind.

[Mort Sheinman (2nd ed.)]

TRIKKALA (Trikala), city in W. Thessaly, Greece. In the third and fourth centuries, Trikkala was an important Hellenistic city that probably had a Jewish population, but little is known about it. From 1421 to 1451, there were an estimated 387 Jewish families in the area, most of whom were Judeo-Greek–speaking *Romaniote Jews. After the Ottomans conquered Constantinople, they began sending Jewish sorgunim (those forcibly exiled) from Trikkala to the capital. In Istanbul, the Trikkala Jews formed their own community and in 1540, it had ten family heads who paid the *jizya* (head tax). In 1545, there were only six family heads listed, and by the 17th century, no more traces of the community.

The Kahal Kadosh Yevanim ("Greek Community") synagogue in Trikkala confirmed the ancientness of the Jewish community, which grew during the 16th century with the arrival of refugees from Hungary, after the Ottoman conquest of Buda, Spain, Portugal, and Sicily. There were also Kahal Kadosh Sephardim and Kahal Kadosh Sicilyanim (Sicilians) synagogues in the town. While the Romaniot Jews absorbed the Iberian Sephardi exiles, eventually the Sephardim achieved communal hegemony. The refugees from Spain introduced the weaving of wool. In 1520–35, there were 1,000 Jews in the city and in the region. The Jews of the city worked in wool production, and in trading wool and hides. The Trikkala Jewish merchants had commercial relations with Larissa and Arta as well as with Venice and Ragusa (Dubrovnik).

Though **dhimmis*, they enjoyed communal autonomy and toleration from the authorities. In 1497 the community requested from the authorities exemption from the Ispenja tax, claiming that the Jews did not work in agriculture, but commerce and the crafts. Thus, they also were exempt from serving in the Janissary military units.

The Jews of Trikala were in contact with the rabbinic authorities of Salonika and Arta. Among the rabbis active in Trikkala in the 16th century were Romaniot rabbi Benjamin b. Rav Shmariya (Papo) of Arta (R. Samuel *Kalai was his student), *Benjamin b. Shmariya (rabbi of the Romaniot *kahal*), Solomon ben Maior, Menachem b. Moses *Bavli; Menachem b. Shabbetai ha-Rofeh (*av bet din*), and Eleazar Belgid.

In the failed Greek rebellion of 1770, Jews in Trikkala were robbed of their money and property. In the 18th century, the community was served by Rabbi Abraham Amarilio, author of *Sefer Berit Avraham* (1802). In 1873, the community number 150 families or 600–700 people, with Jews working as tinsmiths, moneychangers, and mainly small fabric merchants.

In 1881, Trikkala became part of the Greek sovereign state. In October King George I visited the city, stayed in the home of a local Jewish family, and was well received in a ceremony in the synagogue.

In the 1880s, the community was led by Jacob Joseph Sidis, who came in the 1870s from Ioannina and made improvements, including a boys' choir, hiring of new teachers for the *talmud torah*, renovation of two of the cities' three synagogues, and the building of a *mikveh*. At the end of the 19th century the community rabbi was Simeon Pessah, later of Larissa.

Ḥevrat Yetomot was a philanthropic society that helped poor girls, assisted in education, contributed to the *talmud torah*, assisted the Bikkur Holim society, and aided, in the religious sphere, *Tikkun Hatzot* and *Amirat Tehilim* (recitation of psalms). There were *blood libel accusations in 1893, in 1898 (followed by anti-Jewish riots), and in 1911. At the end of the 19th century there were about 800 Jews in Trikkala. In 1906, 17-year-old Yomtov Yakoel, who became a prominent Jewish community leader and lawyer in Salonika, founded the Zionist Eretz-Zion movement. Caught in hiding in Athens in 1944, he was deported to Birkenau and died as a crematorium *Sonderkommando* worker. Thirty-five local Jews fought in the Greek army in the Balkan Wars, two dying and some wounded.

In 1912, the wealthy landowner Elias Cohen housed the royal family on a visit to Trikkala. During World War II, as a result of this connection, Princess Alice (Aliki), mother to English Prince Philip, provided shelter for the widow and four sons of Haimaki (Elias's son), and was recognized as Righteous Among the Nations by Yad Vashem in Israel in the early 1990s.

In 1917–19, Judah Matitiya, edited the Greek publication *Israel*, organ of the Zionist Federation of Trikkala, Larissa, and Volos. Asher *Moissis assisted in its publication. Two large department stores in Trikkala were owned by Jews, and Lazarus Muchtar and Meir Solomon were known as wealthy local Jewish bankers. The Ohavei Tzion Zionist organization's club had an important function for the youth of the community.

In 1925, the community numbered 120 families. The Jews worked in commerce and banking. In the mid-1920s, there was a Jewish theatrical group in Trikkal.

In the Assembly of Representatives of the Jewish Communities of Greece in Salonika in 1929, the Jewish community of Trikkala was represented by the young lawyers Asher Moissis and Yomtov Yakoel (both of whom moved to Salonika in the 1930s).

On the eve of World War II the number of Jews had decreased to 500. Many local Jews fought in the Greek army against the invading Italians in Albania from October 28, 1940, until April 1940. During Italian military rule from April 1941 to September 1943, the Jews fared relatively well. After the Germans replaced the Italian military occupation in September 1943, Rabbi Kastel led more than 300 community members to the mountains under the protection of the ELAS-EAM leftist-leaning resistance movement. The Greek Orthodox clergy also assisted Jews to hide. A few days after the Nazis arrived, the communal leaders, including Abraham Baruch, were invited to the mayor's office, where the commander said they would not be deported to Poland like Salonikan Jewry and requested that they persuade the Jews who had fled to return, promising *matzot* for Passover, sugar, and travel permits to other cities, but the Jews did not agree. During the Nazi persecutions the majority of the Jews escaped to the region controlled by the Greek partisans. On March 23, 1944, the Germans spread false rumors that the partisans had killed a German commander and called a general curfew for the city. A Greek-Orthodox townsman, Alexander Tchatjigakis, warned the Jewish community that they would be deported to Poland the next day, so many Jews fled. The next day, early in the morning, remaining Jews were arrested; mostly the elderly, women, children, and a few people who returned to the city from hiding. Some 50 Jews were deported to extermination camps. In October the city was liberated from the Nazis. The Sephardi and Sicilian synagogues were destroyed and the Romaniot synagogue was burned, but renovated after the war.

In 1946, the Jewish community numbered 73 families (267 people – of whom 65 were children (32 orphans) and 12 widows) as opposed to 492 people before the war. Twenty stores and 23 houses were returned to the Jews as well as the school and the damaged synagogue; which was in need of repair. The cemetery was in ruins and it took three years to refurbish it. Jews began to leave for Athens, Israel, and the United States. Trikkalan Jewish youth were among the founders of moshav Neveh Yemin in Israel in 1949. In 1954 the synagogue was damaged and repaired two years later with the financial help of Judah Perahia of Xanthi. In 1958 there were 123 Jews in the city and by 1967 they numbered 101.

In the 1970s and 1980s, Ovadiah Sabbas was community president and local WIZO leader Betty Haleva was community vice president. The Jews worked in the textile and clothing trade, and two prominent local Jewish families were Yesulas and Kabellis. The religious leader of the community was Moses Ganis and later Rabbi Eli Shabbetai. In the synagogue, there is a memorial tablet for the local Jewish Holocaust victims and the Jewish cemetery is situated on both sides of the interurban highway, which crosses the city. The cemetery was desecrated in neo-Nazi activities in the early 2000s. The city also has a Holocaust memorial statue.

BIBLIOGRAPHY: *Mosè*, 7 (1884), 196; M. Molho and J. Nehama, *In Memoriam, Hommage aux victimes juives des Nazis en Grèce*, 2 (1949), 61, 156, 164; B. Rivlin, and L. Bornstein-Makovetski, "Trikkala," in: *Pinkas ha-Kehillot Yavan* (1999), 125–31; Y. Kerem, *The History of the Jews in Greece, 1821–1940*, Pt. 1 (1985), 197–214; D. Benveniste, *Jewish Communities of Greece, Notes and Impressions* (Heb., 1979), 66–69.

[Simon Marcus / Yitzchak Kerem (2nd ed.)]

TRILLIN, CALVIN (1935–), U.S. journalist, humorist, and novelist. Trillin, who was born in Kansas City, Mo., went to Yale University, where he was chairman of the *Yale Daily News*. After a stint in the U.S. Army, he worked as a reporter for *Time* magazine before joining the staff of the *New Yorker* in 1963, and from 1967 to 1982 he produced a series of articles called "U.S. Journal," 3,000-word articles every three weeks from somewhere in the United States on subjects that ranged from the murder of a farmer's wife in Iowa to the author's effort to write the definitive history of a Louisiana restaurant. Trillin's reporting for the *New Yorker* on the racial integration of the University of Georgia was published in his first book, *An Education in Georgia* (1964). From 1978 through 1985, Trillin wrote a humor column for *The Nation* called "Uncivil Liberties." From 1986 he produced a nationally syndicated column under the same name. He won acclaim in remarkably diverse fields of writing, writing about his family; about his adventures in eating (*American Fried: Adventures of a Happy Eater*, 1974); *Barnett Frummer is an Unbloomed Flower* (1969), short stories about trendiness in the 1960s; *Runestruck* (1977), a novel about a small town after the discovery of what could be a Viking artifact; *Killings* (1984), *New Yorker* articles on sudden death; *Travels with Alice* (1989), a book about traveling with his wife, mostly in Europe and the Caribbean; and *Deadline Poet: My Life as a Doggerelist* (1994). He also wrote and performed two one-man shows, *Calvin Trillin's Uncle Sam* (1988) and *Words, No Music* (1990). The most autobiographical of his books is *Messages from My Father* (1996), a memoir in which he discusses his father's fluency in Yiddish and the experience of growing up Jewish in the Protestant Midwest.

[Stewart Kampel (2nd ed.)]

TRILLING, DIANA (1905–1996), U.S. literary critic. Born in New York to Polish immigrants, Diana Rubin graduated from Radcliffe College. In 1927 she met Lionel *Trilling, a graduate student in literature at Columbia who was to become one of the foremost literary critics and teachers in the United States. They married in 1929. "With marriage I had entered Lionel's world," she wrote. "It was with his friends that I chiefly associated. They were not easy companions, these intellectuals. They were overbearing and arrogant, excessively competitive; they lacked magnanimity and often they lacked common courtesy. Ours was a cruelly judgmental society, often malicious and riddled with envy." These intellectuals included Alfred *Kazin, Irving *Howe, Philip *Rahv, Sidney *Hook, Delmore *Schwartz, Dwight McDonald, Hannah *Arendt, Saul *Bellow, Mary McCarthy, Clement *Greenberg, Irving Kristol, and others who helped set the intellectual agenda of the United States in the 1940s and 1950s. Diana Trilling began writing in 1941 and continued into her 90th year, despite failing eyesight, composing a 75-page article on a Welsh literary figure for *The New Yorker*. At one point, as a critic for *The Nation*, she read a novel a day for six and a half years, delivering challenging reviews on some of the most important works of the modern era: Evelyn Waugh's *Brideshead Revisited*, Robert Penn Warren's *All the King's Men*, Jean-Paul Sartre's *Age of Reason*, and George Orwell's *1984*. No novels, volumes of poetry, or short fiction bore her name, but among her writing credits were five books: three collections of essays and reviews, an impressionistic piece of journalism, *Mrs. Harris: The Death of the Scarsdale Diet Doctor* (1981), and *The Beginning of the Journey* (1984), a memoir. Her work appeared in leading magazines, including *The Atlantic, Harper's, The Saturday Review*, and *The Partisan Review*, to which she contributed essays. In 1975 Lionel Trilling died, and in the years that followed she worked to assure his legacy, editing a 12-volume uniform edition of his work. She also published two collections of her criticism, *Reviewing the Forties* and *We Must My Darlings* (1977).

[Stewart Kampel (2nd ed.)]

TRILLING, LIONEL (1905–1975), U.S. author, critic, and public intellectual. Born in New York City, Trilling attended Columbia University and then began teaching there. He eventually was appointed as the first Jewish assistant professor of English at Columbia University in 1939, receiving full professorship in 1948. Trilling was part of a group of largely Jewish New York intellectuals who dominated American culture and letters in the 1940s and 1950s. He brought a nearly religious devotion to his study of literature and thought, and through his writings revived interest in many neglected authors and works. He was praised for his erudition, the elegance, clarity, and care of his prose, and his high moral thoughtfulness. He was particularly interested in the Victorian poet Matthew Arnold, whose works he examined using the methods of modern psychology. His first published book, *Matthew Arnold* (1939), gave new insight into Arnold's character. The same critical methods were evident in *E.M. Forster* (1943), *The Liberal Imagination* (1950), *The Opposing Self* (1955), *A Gathering of Fugitives* (1956), *Beyond Culture: Essays on Learning and Literature* (1965), and *Sincerity and Authenticity* (1972). Trilling's books and his essays in various journals and reviews were highly influential in intellectual circles, with his most influential book being *The Liberal Imagination*, an attempt to complicate and redeem liberalism with the addition of the imagination, ethical stoicism, and new-found ironies. His work also includes several short stories and a novel, *The Middle of the Journey* (1947), which introduced themes found in his criticism. He edited *The Portable Matthew Arnold* (1949) and *The Selected Letters of John Keats* (1951), and wrote *Freud and the Crisis of Our Culture* (1955). He often returned to studies involving Freud, and later co-edited with Steven Marcus *The Life and Work of Sigmund Freud* (1961).

Trilling did not often deal with Jewish subjects in an overt manner, and many other Jewish American scholars of the period, including Irving Howe and Alfred Kazin, believed that he was uncomfortable with his Jewish origins. However, early in his career, in the 1920s, Trilling wrote short stories focused on Jewish American identity for the humanist *Menorah Journal*, and he continued to write on Jewish writers and Jewish themes throughout his career. In "Wordsworth and the Rabbis" (1955), he explored what he saw as a common quality in Wordsworth's thought and Rabbinic Judaism: namely, devotion to a divine object – Nature for Wordsworth and Torah for the rabbis. In an essay on the Russian-Jewish writer Isaac *Babel (in the introduction to Babel's *Collected Stories*, 1961), he observed that Babel, the Jew who wrote about a Jew among the Cossacks, was painfully aware of the dialectic of Cossack and Jew, body and mind, society and self. Trilling was also interested in the problems of antisemitism facing American Jews, but only as far as these problems worked to exclude Jews from public life. He also served at Columbia as a supportive mentor to numerous important Jewish writers, including Allen *Ginsberg, John *Hollander, Steven Marcus, and Norman *Podhoretz. Trilling's wife, the literary critic Diana (Rubin) *Trilling (1905–1996), wrote *Claremont Essays* (1964) and edited works by D.H. Lawrence. She headed the American Committee for Cultural Freedom (1955–57).

BIBLIOGRAPHY: H.R. Warfel, *American Novelists of Today* (1951), 430; D. Daiches, in: *Commentary*, 24 (1957), 66–69; S.J. Kunitz (ed.), *Twentieth Century Authors*, first supplement (1955). **ADD. BIBLIOGRAPHY:** J. Rodden (ed.), *Lionel Trilling and the Critics* (1999).

[Irving Malin / Craig Svonkin (2nd ed.)]

TRIOLET (Blick), ELSA (1903–1970), French novelist. Born in Moscow, and a student of Maxim Gorki, Elsa Triolet first wrote in Russian. She settled in France, where she married the French poet Louis Aragon whose poems, *Les yeux d'Elsa* (1943) and *Elsa* (1959), she inspired. Her first book in French, *Bonsoir Therésè* (1938), revealed her narrative and stylistic gifts. Her novels *Mille regrets* (1942), *Le cheval blanc* (1943; *The White Charger*, 1946), and *Le premier accroc coûte deux cents francs* (1945; *A Fine of 200 Francs*, 1947, a winner of the Prix Goncourt), combined social and political concern with inventiveness, wit, and charm. Elsa Triolet's chronicle of the Resistance, *Les Amants d'Avignon* (1943), deals with serious, even somber, subjects with an unusual lightness. Her communist ideology is felt more strongly in *L'Inspecteur des Ruines* (1948; *The Inspector of Ruins*, 1953), *Le Cheval Roux* (1953), and *Le Rendez-vous des étrangers* (1956). However, in *Le Monument* (1957), the balance between social ideology and aesthetic approach was restored. In the trilogy, *L'Age de nylon* (*Roses à crédit*, 1959; *Luna-Park*, 1959; and *L'Ame*, 1963), Elsa Triolet revealed new breadth and power. *Le Grand Jamais* (1965), a meditation on death, displays considerable depth and richness of technique. She never lost touch with Russian literature, translated many of Chekhov's plays, and in 1939 published a study of the poet Vladimir Mayakovski, who was her brother-in-law.

BIBLIOGRAPHY: J.P. Madaule, *Ce que dit Elsa* (1960).

[Denise R. Goitein]

TRIPOLI, port in N. *Lebanon (Ar. **Tarabulus al-Sham**; called in Hebrew sources *Sinim*, on the basis of Gen. 10:17). From the seventh century there was a Jewish community in the town, although it never was large. At the beginning of the Arab conquest, Muʿāwiya, the *Umayyad governor of *Syria, established a garrison of Jewish troops in the harbor fortress to guard it against Byzantine attacks. At the beginning of the 11th century – after Syria came under *Fatimid rule – the caliph al-Ḥākim imposed severe restrictions on non-Muslim communities; as a result the Tripoli synagogue was turned into a mosque and several Jewish houses were destroyed. When the decrees were abolished, the Jews asked for the return of the synagogue; the Tripoli Muslims, unlike those in other towns, refused their demand, claiming that the place had already become a Muslim sanctuary. The Jews in turn asked for a royal permit to build a new synagogue. A document from the community, dated 1079, and which is signed and witnessed by the local *bet din*, has been preserved. There were Jews from Tripoli who immigrated to *Egypt in the Arab period. During the First Crusade, R. *Abiathar b. Elijah Ha-Kohen, the Ereẓ Israel *rosh yeshivah*, took refuge in Tripoli and sent a letter from there.

After its conquest by the crusaders in 1109, Tripoli became the capital of an independent principality, but remained a busy port and industrial center. The Jewish community continued its existence throughout the period of crusader rule. *Benjamin of Tudela, the 12th-century traveler, reported that there were many Tripoli Jews among the victims of the earthquakes that struck Syria in the middle of the 12th century. In 1289 the town was captured by the *Mamluks, who razed it and built a new town on a nearby hill and at its base. The Jewish community reestablished itself on the new site. During Mamluk rule there were *Karaites and Samaritans in the town, in addition to the Rabbanite Jews. In a letter written in 1489 R. Obadiah of Bertinoro reports that there were 100 Jewish families living in Tripoli at the time, but this figure seems exaggerated. At the end of the 15th century the Spanish scribe Abraham ha-Sefaradi lived in the city. In the 16th century Sephardi Jews came to settle in Tripoli and some became wealthy merchants. According to R. Moses Basola there were 100 Jewish households (400 people) in Tripoli in 1521, some of which were Musta'arabs and the others immigrants from *Spain and Sicily. The Jews owned shops and many of them were merchants and workmen. They had one synagogue. Tripoli rabbis are mentioned in the responsa dating from this period. In mid-16th century Isaac Mishan was the rabbi of the town and was followed by R. Samuel ha-Kohen and by the latter's son, R. Joseph ha-Kohen, who officiated until 1590. At the beginning of the 17th century Tripoli Jews suffered from the oppressive rule of Yūsufoglu Seyf Pasha and many left. A small community remained and is mentioned in the diary of a Hebron emissary who visited the town in 1675. The community went into a further decline during the 19th century due to the economic decline of the city and the emigration from Tripoli of many local Jews heading for *Beirut, *Aleppo, and other cities. In 1824 the traveler David D'Beth Hillel visited the city and found there 15 Jewish families who had a little synagogue. Yehoseph Schwarz noted 112 Jewish families in Tripoli. In 1843 there were only 11 Jewish families in the city, numbering 50 people. The head of the community at that time was Isaac, an oil merchant. The majority of the Jews were poor. Eliezer L. Frenkel visited the city in 1856 and found 17 families (80 people) there. The older graves survived 400 years. The Jews of Tripoli spoke Arabic. The community had no *talmud torah*. There were a few merchants who participated in international trade. On the eve of World War II only four Jewish families were left.

ADD. BIBLIOGRAPHY: E.L. Frenkel, *Yerushalayma* (1860), 142–146; Rosanes, Togarmah, 2 (1937–38²), 145f.; Ashtor, Toledot, 1 (1944), 274–5; 2 (1951), 121, 427, 445. **ADD. BIBLIOGRAPHY:** A. Yaari, *Masot Ereẓ Israel*, 527; B. Dinur, *Israel ba-Golah*, 1:104, 199, 274, 298, 331; 2:337, 427, 428, 441, 448, 463, 525; S.D. Goitein, *Ha-Yishuv be-Ereẓ Israel be-Reshit ha-Islam u-va-Tekufah ha-Ẓalbanit* (1980), 278–284, 302; M. Rozen, in: *Pe'amim*, 14 (1982), 32–44; M. Gil, *Ereẓ Israel ba-Tekufah ha-Muslemit ha-Rishonah (634–1097)*, 1–3 (1983), index; N. Shor, in: *Pe'amim*, 24 (1985), 117, 136–38; I. Abramsky-Blei, in: *Pe'amim*, 28 (1987), 131–57; H. Gerber, *Yehudei ha-Imperiyah ha-Otmanit ba-Me'ot ha-Shesh-Esrie ve-ha-Sheva-Esrei: Ḥevrah ve-Kalkalah*, 172; E. Bareket, *Shafrir Miẓrayim* (1995), 17, 154.

[Eliyahu Astor / Leah Bornstein-Makovetsky (2nd ed.)]

TRIPOLI, port city of *Libya. Tripoli was built by the Phoenicians in the seventh century B.C.E. They called the town Wiat (Latin Oea). Together with its two neighbors, Sabratha and Leptis (Homs), the town was included in the Greek designation Tripolis (i.e., three towns); they all paid tribute to Carthage. There is little information available on the Jews of Tripoli during the Roman and Byzantine periods. A Roman road map from the fourth century indicates a Jewish locality named Scina (or Iscina) *Locus Judaeorum Augusti* ("Scina, locality of Jews belonging to the emperor") in the vicinity of Oea. They were probably captives. Converts from Libya are mentioned at the end of the fourth century (TJ, Kil. 8:3). There was also a Jewish community in Oea during the fifth century.

The sources for the Arab period are also very scarce. During the second half of the 11th century, there was a *bet din* in Tripoli which was independent of the Palestinian one. The Jewish community suffered greatly under the rules of *Spain and the Knights of Malta (1510–51), but prospered again with the Ottoman conquest (1551) when many Jews from the small rural communities settled in Tripoli. It seems that at the end of the 16th century descendants of the Spanish Jews expelled from Christian Europe settled in Tripoli; during the 17th century they were joined by Jews from *Leghorn (Livorno, referred to as Gornim) most of whom were merchants of Sephardi origin. During the reign of the Turkish Qaramanlī dynasty (1711–1835), Tripoli became a haven for Jewish refugees from *Tunis (1756) and *Algiers (1805). Jews played an important role in the Trans-Saharan trade with Europe and the African continent, while others held diplomatic and consular positions. In 1705 and 1793 the Jews of Tripoli were saved from the danger of extermination by foreign invaders and two local Purim days were fixed to commemorate these events: Purim ash-Sharif on 23 Tevet and Purim Burgul on 29 Tevet, respectively.

In 1835, when Tripoli once more came under the direct rule of the *Ottoman Empire, there was a further improvement in the social and legal status of the community. The kingdom of *Italy – from its establishment in 1861 – attempted to wield its influence in Tripoli, especially among the Jews, many of whose big traders had strong economic and social ties with Italy. The community was divided between the traditionalist conservatives, who generally supported the Muslim authorities, and those who favored European culture and consequently Italy. The Italian influence increased during the period of Italian rule (1911–43), when the Jews enjoyed complete emancipation except for the World War II period. They engaged in the crafts and commerce as builders, carpenters, blacksmiths, tailors, cobblers, and wholesale and retail merchants. The gold- and silversmith crafts, as well as the textile trade, were entirely controlled by the Jews. In 1943 the Jews of Tripoli numbered about 15,000 (for the World War II period, see *Libya). In November 4, 1945, riots broke out with the Arabs attacking their Jewish neighbors while the British authorities were slow to intervene. During these riots 120 Jews were murdered in Tripoli and its vicinity, hundreds were injured, and a great deal of property was looted. As a result of these events, a secret Jewish defense organization was formed with covert help from Palestine and small arms were acquired. When riots again occurred in June 1948, there were some Jewish victims, but the Jews were ready, fought back, and killed many of their attackers.

Religious and Communal Life

The community of Tripoli held the exclusive leadership over the Jews of the country. From the middle of the 18th century the presidents of the community represented Libyan Jewry before the government and were empowered to inflict corporal punishment and imprisonment. During the second period of direct Ottoman rule (1835–1911), these presidents attended the council meetings of the governor.

The revival of Jewish learning and the establishment of community *takkanot* (regulations) are attributed to R. Simeon *Labi (mid-16th century). In 1663 Abraham Miguel *Cardozo, who was later one of the leaders of the Shabbatean movement, settled in Tripoli. From the middle of the 18th century several *dayyanim* and prominent *ḥakhamim* of Tripoli came from *Turkey and *Palestine, returning home after a period of office in Tripoli. In 1749 R. Mas'ūd Hai Rakah, an emissary from Jerusalem, arrived in Tripoli. He was joined by his son-in-law R. Nathan Adadi, who was born in Palestine and returned there in his old age. His grandson, Abraham Ḥayyim Adadi, settled in Tripoli after the earthquake in *Safed in 1837 and accomplished a great deal as *dayyan* and *ḥakham* of the community. He also retired to Safed in his old age. After his death, the Ottoman government in Istanbul appointed Elijah Ḥazzan as *ḥakham bashi* (chief rabbi) (1874–88) by royal *firman* (order). The latter was also the representative of Tripolitanian Jewry before the government. The Italian government at first continued this tradition and appointed R. Elia Samuele *Artom to this position (1920–23).

Jews lived in two exclusively Jewish neighborhoods within the walled old city of Tripoli, though many carried out their business in trade in specific streets in the Muslim parts of town. With the establishment of new neighborhoods outside the walled city, wealthier Jews moved there and lived in mixed neighborhoods with Italians and Muslim Arabs.

[Haïm Z'ew Hirschberg / Rachel Simon (2nd ed.)]

Contemporary Period

Approximately 20,000 Jews lived in Tripoli in 1948. Following mass immigration to Israel in 1949–52, only 6,228 Jews remained, comprising 3% of the town's population of 198,000, according to the 1962 census. The majority of the Jews who remained after 1962 were wealthy merchants who were closely connected with Italy and spent part of the year there. After the riots that occurred in Tripoli during the Six-Day War in 1967 (see *Libya), most of the Jews immigrated to Italy and some to Israel. In 1970 there were only several dozen Jews living in the town and none by the end of the century.

The Tripoli community was headed by a committee, whose subcommittees provided services such as aid for paupers and dowries for brides (to help poor girls marry). The committee's incomes derived from the gabelle (Qābilah), a tax on kosher meat, the sale of unleavened bread, and from community dues. In 1916 the Zionist organization gained 11 out of 31 seats in the committee. Due to internal conflicts, the Italian authorities dispersed the committee in 1929 and appointed an Italian non-Jewish official to administer the affairs of the community. Only 700 paid dues in 1948, their number having fallen from 2,300 in 1944. Spiritual affairs were conducted by the chief rabbi, who also headed the rabbinical court of three members. The first European school in Tripoli was established in 1876 by Italian Jews in response to the local initiative of Jews with economic contacts with Italy. This was followed by a school run by the Paris-based *Alliance Israélite Universelle in 1890. The latter was attended by 70 pupils in 1949 with the number of pupils rising to 601 in 1951, but after the mass immigration to Israel, enrollment fell to 129 in 1953 and to 38 in 1960 when the Alliance school closed down. In addition, in 1950 the town possessed a *talmud torah*, with 371 pupils, a Youth Aliyah school with 68 pupils, and a school with 300 children of Jews who had moved from villages to Tripoli. A total of 1,800 Jewish children attended Italian schools. Emigration reduced the number of synagogues from 30 in 1948 to seven in 1951. The branch of the Maccabi Zionist sports and culture organization, which functioned in Tripoli from 1920, was closed in December 1953, as was the bureau of the Jewish Agency for Israel in January 1953, after having functioned there for four years.

For further information, see *Libya.

[Haim J. Cohen / Rachel Simon (2nd ed.)]

BIBLIOGRAPHY: Scholem, in: *Zion*, 19 (1954), 1–22; *Yahadut Luv* (1960); Hirschberg, Afrikah, index; Attal, in: *Sefunot*, 9 (1964), 398 (index); H. Goldberg, in: JJSO, 9 (1967), 209–25. For additional bibliography, see *Libya.

°**TRISTRAM, HENRY BAKER** (1822–1906), Anglican theologian, archaeologist, and naturalist whose work dealt with Palestine. Born in Eglingham, Northumberland, England, and educated at Oxford, Tristram became an Anglican vicar. He served as secretary and army and navy chaplain to the governor of Bermuda (1847–49), rector of Castle Eden near Durham (1849–60), vicar in Greatham (1860–74), and resident canon at Durham Cathedral. Delicate health forced him to spend winters in warmer climates such as North Africa, the Sahara, and the Far East. He visited Palestine several times from 1861 onward. In 1879 Tristram was offered by Disraeli the Anglican Bishopric of Jerusalem but declined. During his visits to Palestine he inspected missionary establishments and at the same time carried on geological, botanical, and zoological research, which earned him the title of "father of the nature study of Palestine."

Apart from numerous articles in periodicals, Tristram's published work concerned with Palestine included *The Land of Israel, a Journal of Travels with Reference to Its Physical History* (1865, and many editions), *Natural History of the Bible* (1867), *Land of Moab* (1874), *Pathways of Palestine* (1882),

Fauna and Flora of Palestine (1884), and *Eastern Customs in Bible Lands* (1894).

ADD. BIBLIOGRAPHY: ODNB online; Y. Ben-Arieh, *The Rediscovery of the Holy Land in the Nineteenth Century* (1979).

[Aviva Rabinovich]

°**TRITHEMIUS, JOHANNES (Johann Heidenberg of Tritheim**; 1462–1516), German churchman, scholar, and alchemist. Born in Trittenheim, he entered the Benedictine order in 1482 and became abbot of Sponheim three years later. Trithemius, who endeavored to reform the monastic system and to promote the "new learning," established a famous library at Sponheim containing manuscripts in five languages, mainly Hebrew and Greek. It was visited by many of the leading scholars of the age, notably Johann *Reuchlin (1496). Trithemius published several works, such as a *Catalogus scriptorum ecclesiasticorum* (1494) and *De viris illustribus Germaniae* (1495), but is best remembered for two celebrated works on magic, *Polygraphia* (1507) and *Chronologica mystica* (1508). Though no Hebraist, the abbot dealt in these books with subjects such as numerology, planetary influences, and the Kabbalah. He immersed himself in alchemy and occult sciences and was eventually condemned and deposed from office.

An opponent of the Inquisition, in 1510 he defended the Jews against charges of profaning the Host and of ritual murder (see *Blood Libel). Trithemius greatly influenced the astrologer and alchemist Henry Cornelius Agrippa (1486–1535), who wrote a controversial defense of magic, *De Occulta Philosophia* (Cologne, 1531; *Three Books of Occult Philosophy*, London, 1651), the last part of which drew on Reuchlin and the Kabbalah. Both Trithemius and Agrippa further influenced the celebrated philosopher and alchemist Paracelsus (Theophrastus Bombastus ab Hohenheim, 1493–1541). The careers of Trithemius and his two disciples became fused in popular imagination to produce the tragic figure of the legendary magician Faust.

BIBLIOGRAPHY: R.W. Seton-Watson (ed.), *Tudor Studies Presented to A.F. Pollard* (1924), 79; M. Pachter, *Paracelsus: Magic into Science* (1951), index; F. Secret, *Les kabbalistes chrétiens de la Renaissance* (1964), 157ff.; J. Silbernagel, *Johannes Trithemius* (1967). **ADD. BIBLIOGRAPHY:** N.L. Brann, *The Abbot Trithemius* (1981); W. Vogt, in: *Ebernburghefte*, 20 (1986), 7–20; E. Hellgardt: in: *Sprache, Literatur, Kultur* (1989), 355–75; R. Auenheimer (ed.), *Johannes Trithemius: Humanismus und Magie…* (1991); N.L. Brann, *Trithemius and Magical Theology…* (1999).

[Godfrey Edmond Silverman]

TRIVALE, ION (originally **Iosef Netzler**; 1889–1917), Romanian literary critic. His *Cronici literare* (1915) and *Vina Războiului de Azi* ("War Guilt of Our Days," 1915) were outstanding works of criticism hailed by the leading pundits. Trivale also published a volume of translations from Mark Twain. His death in action during World War I robbed Romania of one of its most promising critical essayists.

°**TRIVETH (Trevet), NICHOLAS (Trivetus**; 1257/65–1334 or after), English theologian and historian. A Dominican preacher, Triveth taught at Oxford University and is best known for his English chronicle work, *Annales sex Regum Angliae*, covering the years 1136–1307 (published in Oxford, 1719). He also wrote a commentary on St. Augustine's *De Civitate Dei* (c. 1468–73). Many of his theological writings, manuscripts of which are in various Oxford and Cambridge libraries, reveal Triveth's extensive knowledge of Hebrew and rabbinic literature.

Outstanding among these is his commentary on Jerome's translation of the Psalms (*In Psalterium*, written 1317–20; Bodleian, Oxford). Triveth, a pioneer English Hebraist and the first recorded student of *Maimonides in England, often quotes the *Guide of the Perplexed*. His commentary was used by another medieval English Hebraist, Henry of Cossey, who was Triveth's contemporary at Cambridge. Other works by Triveth include *De Computo Hebraeorum*, and commentaries on Genesis, Exodus, Leviticus, and other books of the Old Testament. He lived on the Continent from about 1300 until 1314.

BIBLIOGRAPHY: R. Loewe, in: V.D. Lipman (ed.), *Three Centuries of Anglo-Jewish History* (1961), 136ff.; idem, in: J.M. Shaftesley (ed.), *Remember the Days. Essays… Presented to Cecil Roth* (1966), 28ff.; B. Smalley, *The Study of the Bible in the Middle Ages* (1952^2), 400. **ADD. BIBLIOGRAPHY:** ODNB online.

TRIWOSCH, JOSEPH ELIJAH (1855–1940), Hebrew writer and biblical commentator. Born in Vilna, Triwosch grew up in its Haskalah atmosphere. He first published poems and short stories – which were among the earliest Hebrew modern fiction – in *Ha-Levanon* (1873). His story "*Ha-Lita'i*" (in: *Ha-Shaḥar*, 10 (1880)) and especially his book *Dor Tahpukhot* (1881) made a great impression. His stories "*Din ve-Ḥeshbon*" (1895) and "*Pesi'ot Ketannot*" (1904) appeared separately. In addition to his stories he also published over the years articles and feuilletons, mainly in *Ha-Zeman*. After World War I, Triwosch taught at the Hebrew secondary school of Vilna. In his last years, he also engaged in biblical and philological research.

His translations into Hebrew include many works of world literature, among them Tolstoy's *War and Peace* (1921–24) and *Anna Karenina* (1918–22). He wrote the major part of the commentary, as well as the introductions, to the individual books of *Mikra Meforash* (1909, and after), a project of biblical exegesis, which he edited together with N. Lewin, D. Lewin, and D. Nottick. Triwosch also published an anthology of medieval Hebrew literature (1925) together with M.Y. Nadel.

BIBLIOGRAPHY: Kressel, Leksikon, 2 (1967), 34–35; Zeitlin, Bibliotheca, 398.

[Getzel Kressel]

TRNAVA (Hung. **Nagyszombat**; Ger. **Tyrnau**), city in Slovakia. There were Jews in Trnava from the 14th, perhaps even the 12th century, making it one of the oldest Jewish communities in ancient Hungary. Economic life was organized in guilds, which would not accept Jews. Fierce competition developed between the guild members and the Jews. Adverse relations prevailed in wine production and trade as well. The local vineyard owners wanted a monopoly to dictate prices; but the Jews imported wine, reduced the price, and thus evoked hostility (1471–86).

In the second half of the 14th century, Rabbi Eisig (Isac) Tyrnau officiated. He wrote the *Sidur ha-Minhagim*, a manual of Sabbath prayers used for centuries by Slovak, Czech, Hungarian, and Austrian Jews.

In the late 15th century, the burghers established a ghetto, locking the Jews in and depriving them of free movement. In 1539 a *blood libel was invented, and several Jews were executed. Hapsburg King Ferdinand ordered all Jews expelled. Jews were prohibited from staying in or even passing through Trnava. Only the few Jewish students of the local university could stay in the town.

In 1717, under royal insistence, Jews were allowed to pass through the city. Emperor Joseph II permitted the family of Joseph Loeb Wolf to live in the city; they were later joined by three other families. Encountering great hostility, they sometimes had to be protected by the military. In 1801 Wolf appealed to the court in Vienna to be allotted land for a cemetery. From that date, the *ḥevra kaddisha* was established in Trnava. In 1790 there were 78 Jews in the town. Until 1855, the community was under the jurisdiction of the nearby congregation Cifer, where Rabbi Simeon Sidon (1815–1891) resided. In 1855 he moved to Trnava. In 1814 a synagogue was erected. In 1855 the first Jewish school was installed. In 1848 a wave of plundering of Jewish property swept the city. Several neighboring communities joined the Trnava congregation. The Jewish school expanded in 1864. The next year, the community numbered 524. It was recognized by local and state authorities, which supervised its administration. After the 1868 Congress of Hungarian Jewry, the congregation chose the *status quo ante trend, refusing to join either the Orthodox or the Reform. In 1891 it erected an impressive synagogue and owned a *mikveh*. That year, Rabbi Sidon died. Five years later, Rabbi Mayer Maximilian Stein assumed the position, holding it until 1934. Among his achievements, he compiled a book about Hungarian rabbis.

In 1881, part of the congregation split and established an Orthodox congregation. It established its own school, *mikveh*, and synagogue (1914). It founded a renowned yeshivah, under the leadership or Rabbi David Unger (1885–1944). In 1930 it moved to Nitra.

In 1918 the Czechoslovak Republic was founded. In its first month, the new state saw a wave of violence. The population looted the property of the wealthy and the followers of the previous regime. But the main target was Jewish property of both the rich and poor.

In the 19th century, Jews were deeply engaged in the economic life of the city, and Jewish entrepreneurs established or advanced several branches of industry, such as breweries, sugar refineries, and confectionaries, providing employment for hundreds; their products were sold at home and abroad. Textile mills and ironworks also provided jobs. Jewish physicians and lawyers were part of the expanding middle class, which turned Trnava into a modern town.

The Zionist movement had deep roots in the community. Samuel Diamant participated in the First Zionist Congress in Basel in 1897; the following year he and friends founded Beit Yaakov. The Jewish party, supported by the Zionists, played an important role in public and municipal life. Both congregations developed social and philanthropic organizations; cultural activity was promoted by many clubs and organizations.

In 1830 there were 84 Jews in the city. In 1850 the Jewish population grew to 200; in 1880 there were 1,325 Jews. In 1904 they numbered 1,715; in 1910 there were 2,126. In 1930 there were 2,728.

Trnava was one of the Slovak centers of antisemitism. The first antisemitic party in Slovakia, the White Brotherhood (*Biel Bratstvo*), was founded there; it published "*Streicher-type" literature. The vicious antisemitism of this small organization influenced the Slovak storm troopers, the Rodobrana, and the Hlinka Guard. In December 1938, the status quo synagogue was torched by the mob.

Trnava was one of the first Slovak cities to deport Jews to extermination camps in Poland in 1942. In 1941 the Jewish population was augmented by hundreds of Jews expelled from Bratislava. The first transport to leave Slovakia departed from Trnava on April 12, 1942. Altogether, some 2,500 Jews were deported from Trnava.

In 1947 there were 336 Jews in Trnava. After the war, the status quo synagogue was made into a memorial for the murdered Trnava Jews. During the Communist regime, the memorial was destroyed. The synagogue was reconstructed and is used by the local art museum for exhibits. Most of the surviving Jews emigrated after returning to Slovakia. After 1989, some 15 Jews lived in Trnava.

BIBLIOGRAPHY: *Der Israelit*, 5 (1864), 228f., 244, 310, 339; S. Kohn, *A zsidók története Magyarországon* (1884), index, s.v. *Nagyszombat*; J. Bergel (Bergl), *Geschichte der ungarischen Juden* (1879), 52; MHJ, passim; *Magyar Zsidó Lexikon* (1929), s.v. *Nagyszombat*; R. Iltis (ed.), *Die aussaeen unter Traenen…* (1959), 199–205; E. Bárkány-L. Dojc, *Zidovské nábozenské obce na Slovensku* (1991); *Dejiny Trnavy* (1989).

[Yeshayahu Jelinek (2nd ed.)]

TROKI (Lith. **Trakai**; Ger. **Traken**), city in S.E. Lithuania; annexed to Russia after the third partition of Poland (1795), under Polish rule from 1922 to 1939. Troki is known as the site of an extended struggle between *Karaites and *Rabbanite Jews. It was the most ancient and important of the Karaite communities in the kingdom of *Poland-Lithuania, having apparently been founded by Karaites brought from the Crimea by the Grand Duke of Lithuania, Witold (Vitovt). In 1388 Witold gave the Troki Karaites a charter of rights (in which they were called Jews) which assured them the status of freemen, commercial and professional freedom, religious liberty, and the right to their own jurisdiction. These privileges were confirmed and even extended by the Lithuanian dukes and Polish kings of the 15th to 17th centuries. In 1441 Casimir IV (see *Poland) granted the status of a city with *Magdeburg rights to that half of Troki occupied by the Karaites, under a special judge who was to deal with their internecine quarrels. After 1625 some Rabbanite families settled in Troki and engaged in trade, but in 1646 the Karaites obtained from Ladislaus IV an order banning those Jews from living in Troki and competing with the Karaites in commerce.

The Karaites of Troki, who up to recent times spoke a peculiar Tatar dialect, were comfortably situated, some of them becoming very wealthy. Although they were expelled along with the Jews of Lithuania in 1495, they resettled after the decree was canceled in 1503. They cooperated on many occasions with the Rabbanite communities in matters of taxes and confirmation of privileges, and lent Troki charters of rights to those communities for purposes of intercession with the authorities. The representatives of Troki were the acknowledged leaders at the councils of all the Lithuanian Karaites. The regulations of the all-Lithuanian Karaite Council, which met in Troki in 1553, were handed over to the heads of the Rabbanite communities for their approval in 1568, when the latter assembled at *Grodno. In 1579 the Karaite community of Troki was called on to join the discussions of the organization of Lithuanian Jewish communities concerning taxation; during the activity of the Council of Lithuania (see *Councils of the Lands), Troki paid the royal taxes through the Council. Up to the *Chmielnicki massacres of 1648 good relations obtained between the Karaites of Troki and the communities of Lithuania. Among the learned Karaites of Troki in the 15th and 16th centuries were Isaac b. Abraham *Troki, author of *Ḥizzuk Emunah* (against Christianity); his pupil Joseph b. Mordecai *Malinovski; *Zerah b. Nathan; Ezra b. Nisan (d. 1666); and Josiah b. Judah (d. after 1658). The last three were influenced by Joseph Solomon *Delmedigo.

Troki was so severely affected by the Russian-Polish struggle over the Ukraine in 1654–67 that by about 1680 there were no more than about 30 families in the declining Karaite community, divided by disputes with the other Karaite communities and with the Council of Lithuania regarding taxation demands. With the encouragement of King John III Sobieski, in 1688 a number of householders moved from Troki to Kukizov (Krasny Ostrov) near Lvov, to establish a Karaite community there. At the beginning of the 18th century Troki was again hit by war, famine, and plague, so that only three Karaite families remained. About that time another conflict broke out over the Rabbanites' right of domicile (permission was granted in the end). But in 1765 there were about 150 Rabbanites and 300 Karaites in Troki and its environs.

After Troki passed to Russia, many Jews who had been expelled from the villages settled there in 1804. In the same year the Karaites began to fight for the expulsion of those refugees, and in 1835, after protracted legal debates, the Rabbanites were ordered to leave the city within five years. In 1862 this order was rescinded and the Rabbanites returned to Troki. In 1879 there were about 600 Karaites there and in 1897, 377 Karaites and 1,112 Rabbanites (out of a total population of 3,240). Some of the Troki Karaites left the town and established a new community in Vilna. In the 19th and 20th centuries relations between Karaites and Jews were strained and hostile.

[Mordekhai Nadav]

Before the outbreak of World War II, there were about 300 Jews in Troki. The Jewish community was liquidated on Sept. 30, 1941. Only the Karaite community remained, and according to the 1959 Soviet census there were 5,700 Karaites in Troki. After the war the Jewish community was not reconstituted.

BIBLIOGRAPHY: Y. Luria, in: *He-Avar*, 1 (1918): M. Balaban, in: *Ha-Tekufah*, 25 (1929); J. Brutzkus, in: *YIVO Bleter*, 13 (1938; repr. in *Lite*, vol. 1, 1951); S. Shomroni-Shtraz (ed.), *Troki-Sefer Zikkaron* (Heb. and some Yid., 1954); M. Nadav, in: KS, 33 (1957/58), 260–8; Mann, Texts, 2 (1935); S. Bershadski, *Litovskiye yevrei* (1883), 178–82; Yu. Hessen, in: *Yevreyskaya Starina*, 3 (1910); I.A. Klienman, *ibid.*, 13 (1930); I. Schiper, *Dzieje handlu żydowskiego na ziemiach polskich* (1937), index.

TROKI, ISAAC BEN ABRAHAM (c. 1533–c. 1594), *Karaite scholar, born in Troki (according to Mann's hypothesis, he was born and died eight years earlier than the above dates). Troki's learning earned him the respect and deference of his fellow Karaites, and his knowledge of Latin and Polish enabled him to hold conversations on theological subjects with Roman Catholic, Protestant, and Eastern Orthodox clergymen, as well as with Socinian and other sectarian adherents. The result of these discussions was his famous apology for Judaism entitled *Ḥizzuk Emunah*. Troki himself did not live to complete the work and his pupil Joseph b. Mordecai *Malinovski (Troki) supplied it with preface and index.

Troki's reasoned defense of Judaism and his penetrating examination of the vulnerable points of Christian tradition and dogma caused his work to achieve immediate popularity. It was circulated in manuscript by interested Jewish readers, and each copyist felt free to modify the text according to his own views, so that at present, pending the discovery of more authentic manuscripts, it would probably be impossible to restore Isaac's original text in its entirety. In about 1629 *Zeraḥ b. Nathan of Troki offered the work to *Manasseh Ben Israel for publication at the latter's press in Amsterdam, but it was not printed there (presumably Manasseh declined the offer). Several decades later, another manuscript copy, apparently amended by a *Rabbanite copyist, fell into the hands of Johann Christoph *Wagenseil, who published it with a Latin translation and an extensive refutation in his *Tela ignea Satanae* ("The Fiery Darts of Satan"; Altdorf, 1681). The Latin version made Troki's work accessible to wider Christian circles, and some of his arguments were later taken over by the 18th-century anticlerical writers; Voltaire mentions the *Ḥizzuk Emunah* as a masterpiece of its kind. Troki would probably have been dismayed at this notoriety; he no doubt intended to have his work circulate among Jewish scholars only.

Wagenseil's text of the *Ḥizzuk Emunah* was reprinted for Jewish use at Amsterdam in 1705, and a Yiddish translation was printed there in 1717. An English translation by Moses Mocatta, uncle of Sir Moses Montefiore, was issued at London in 1851, with the statement on the title page "Printed but not published" (republ. 1970 with introd. by T. Weiss-Rosmarin). A German translation was published by David Deutsch (with the Hebrew text; 2nd edition, Sohrau, 1873). Among other editions, one appeared in Calcutta in 1846, and another in New York in 1932.

Some of Troki's hymns are included in the official Karaite prayer book. He is also said to have composed some works on Karaite ritual law.

BIBLIOGRAPHY: Mann, Texts, 2 (1935), passim; Waxman, Literature, 2 (1966), 449–51.

[Leon Nemoy]

TROTSKY (Bronstein), LEV DAVIDOVICH (Leon; 1879–1940), Russian revolutionary, Soviet and Communist leader. Trotsky was the son of a Jewish farmer of Ivanovka, Ukraine. He studied mathematics at Odessa University, but gave up his studies to devote himself to revolutionary activities and joined the illegal Social Democratic Party in 1896. Arrested by the czarist authorities in 1898 and sent to Siberia, he escaped to England in October 1902, arriving on a forged passport issued in the name of "Trotsky." In London he cooperated with *Lenin, *Martov, and *Axelrod in editing the Social Democratic organ *Iskra*. At the second congress of the Russian Social Democratic Party in 1903, Trotsky attacked Lenin and supported the Mensheviks. In 1904 he left *Iskra* and published a pamphlet *Nashi Politicheskiye zadachi* ("Our Political Tasks"), in which he again attacked Lenin, exposing the dictatorial tendencies of the Bolsheviks. He became an independent socialist and worked for reconciliation between the various factions. At that time, under the influence of Helphand (Parvus), he formulated the theory of permanent revolution, according to which a bourgeois revolution in Russia would, by its inner momentum, lead quickly to the socialist stage, even before the socialist revolution in the West.

Trotsky returned to Russia at the outbreak of the 1905 Revolution and became a leader of the revolutionary workers' council (soviet) in Petersburg. He was arrested while chairing a meeting of the council and deported to Siberia a second time. Again he escaped and arrived in London in 1907 to take part in the congress of the Social Democratic Party. Later he moved to Vienna where he lived for several years as a correspondent for the popular liberal newspaper *Kiyevskaya Mysi* and wrote numerous articles devoted mainly to revolutionary theory.

At the outbreak of World War I Trotsky left for neutral Switzerland and wrote a detailed exposition of his anti-war policy entitled *Der Krieg und die Internationale*. He went to Paris in November 1914 to propagate his ideas in the émigré newspaper *Nashe Slovo*. Expelled two years later, he went to New York.

Trotsky returned to Russia shortly after the outbreak of the Revolution of February 1917, and was given a tremendous welcome by the Petrograd workers. He now cooperated with Lenin. Kerensky's provisional government arrested him, but he was soon released. While in prison he was elected to the Central Committee of the Bolsheviks. He also became head of the Petrograd Soviet and of its Military Revolutionary Committee. Trotsky voted for the armed insurrection at the decisive meeting of the Bolshevik Central Committee. He directed the operation of the armed uprising on November 7, when the members of the provisional government were arrested and Soviet rule established. From then on Trotsky was one of the main organizers and leaders of the October Revolution and the Soviet regime, and played a part second only to that of Lenin. He became people's commissar for foreign affairs and head of the Russian delegation at the Brest-Litovsk peace talks. It was during this period that Trotsky and Lenin clashed over the question of peace with Germany. Trotsky, believing the German revolution to be imminent, was against signing a peace treaty which would give imperial Germany large parts of Russian territory; he proposed to stop the war unilaterally, but not to make peace under these conditions, coining the formula, "neither war nor peace." But the more skeptical Lenin insisted upon signing the peace treaty in order to save the revolution from a renewed Russo-German war.

In March 1918, Trotsky became people's commissar for military affairs, organizing the Red Army and directing military operations on the various civil war fronts from his famous armored train. After the bloody suppression of the Kronstadt fleet mutiny, aimed against the Bolshevik dictatorship, he took the salute at the victory parade in April 1921. He also served as people's commissar for transport and was responsible for preventing the complete collapse of the railway system.

In internal party debates during Lenin's lifetime, he expounded a harsh "left-wing" approach to the problems of the legitimacy of revolutionary terror against the regime's opponents, how to induce the peasants to supply the cities with food, and labor discipline in the nationalized industry.

After Lenin's death in 1924, however, Trotsky's position in the Communist hierarchy weakened quickly as a result of a campaign by party veterans aimed at discrediting him. He fought back with great determination. He headed the semilegal left-wing opposition in the party and even enjoyed, from time to time, demonstrative support, mainly from younger party members and students. Stalin, however, played the various leaders and factions against each other until he assumed sole control of the party machine, and within two years succeeded in ousting Trotsky from the political life of both the Soviet Union and the Communist International. In January 1925, Trotsky was forced to resign from the Ministry of War and subsequently held only lesser posts in the Supreme Economic Council. Removed from the Politburo and the Central

Committee in 1926, he was eventually expelled from the Communist Party on November 14, 1927, on the grounds that he was an "instigator of counterrevolutionary demonstrations."

In January 1928, Trotsky was convicted of counterrevolutionary activities and sent to Alma-Ata in Turkestan. Even there he fearlessly continued to lead the left-wing opposition in the Communist Party and a year later was expelled to Turkey with his wife and son. In Turkey he maintained contact with the opposition to Stalin in an attempt to organize a new Communist International, independent of Moscow. He went to Norway in 1936, but was forced to leave after several defendants at the Moscow trials accused him of joining *Zinoviev and *Kamenev in "an imperialist plot" to murder Stalin. He later settled in Mexico. During his years in exile he produced his vast literary output, including *My Life* (1930), *The History of the Russian Revolution* (3 vols., 1932–33), and *The Permanent Revolution* (1931), and edited *The Living Thoughts of Karl Marx*, published in 1939. On August 21, 1940, he was assassinated in Mexico City by a "friend" who is generally assumed to have acted on Stalin's orders. Remarkably gifted, a brilliant writer and orator, Trotsky fought all his life to bring about the socialist world revolution. He was opposed to Stalin's policy of building up "Socialism in one country," arguing that Socialism could only be achieved through revolution on a world scale. In 1938, his followers assembled in Switzerland to found the Fourth International which would be independent of the Moscow-centered Third (Communist) International, but they failed to create a mass movement in support of Trotsky. In the Soviet Union his name and the term Trotskyism officially became synonymous with treason and perfidy and served as the main object of hatred and slander during the famous purge-trials of veteran Bolsheviks in the middle and late 1930s. Trotsky's role in the revolution and the early Soviet regime was expunged from all official historical records in the Soviet Union and in the "orthodox" Communist movement everywhere, but he has had supporters and admirers in many countries including, silently, in the Soviet Union as well.

Trotsky and the "Jewish Question"

Convinced that there was no future for the Jews as a separate people, Trotsky favored their assimilation. At the second congress of the Russian Social Democratic Party (1903), he attacked the *Bund, claiming that despite its opposition to Zionism, it had adopted the nationalist character of Zionism. After the Sixth Zionist Congress he wrote an article in *Iskra* prophesying the disappearance of the movement (Jan. 1, 1904).

Trotsky visualized the solution of the Jewish problem only through the socialist reshaping of society within an international framework. But he was quite aware of the fact that his Jewish origin was a political handicap. When Lenin, after the victory of Nov. 7, 1917, proposed to put him at the head of the first Soviet government, Trotsky refused, and – in his own words (*Moya Zhizn*, II, 62–63) – mentioned "among other arguments the national aspect: would it be wise to give into the hands of the enemies such an additional weapon as my being Jewish?" Later he was shocked at the antisemitic innuendos of the campaign conducted against him in the late 1920s in the Soviet Union and he later emphasized the antisemitic undertones of the Moscow trials against Zinoviev, Kamenev, and others. In an interview with the New York *Jewish Daily Forward*, he admitted, in 1937, that the reemergence of antisemitism in Germany and the U.S.S.R. had brought him to the conclusion that the Jewish problem required a territorial solution, but he did not believe that Palestine was the answer; and the final solution would come only through the emancipation of all humanity by international socialism. "The longer the rotten bourgeois society lives, the more and more barbaric will antisemitism become everywhere," he said in the same interview.

In *Trotsky and the Jews* (1972), J. Nedava has made a special study of this question, throwing new light on the subject and revealing, inter alia, that Trotsky sat as an adviser at the Sixth Zionist Congress in Basle (1903), and later became increasingly interested in the Jewish Labor Movement in Ereẓ Israel.

BIBLIOGRAPHY: I. Deutscher, *The Prophet Armed, Trotsky 1879–1921* (1965); idem, *The Prophet Unarmed, Trotsky 1921–1929* (1965); idem, *The Prophet Outcast, Trotsky 1929–1940* (1963); B.D. Wolfe, *Three Who Made a Revolution* (1948, paperback 1966); L. Shapiro, *The Communist Party of the Soviet Union* (1960).

TROYES, chief town of the department of Aube, in northeast central France. Evidence of the earliest period of Jewish settlement in Troyes is derived from rabbinic sources. From the first half of the 11th century, an organized Jewish community collected taxes from its members, and Jews owned real estate, more particularly vineyards. The *synods which were reputedly held in the town may have been little more than assemblies convened by the local community and expanded to include the representatives of a number of dependent communities. It may be assumed that in *Rashi's time the community numbered no more than 100 people. Only from the beginning of the 13th century is there evidence of the Jews of Troyes engaging in *moneylending; their clients included the Saint-Loup Abbey. On the other hand, a number of Jews owed this abbey a regular quitrent, which was calculated in measures of wheat and wine, presumably for plots of land or vineyards leased from it.

In 1288 the community was persecuted, with accompanying bloodshed, as a result of an accusation of ritual murder (see *Blood Libel). On Good Friday, March 26, during the Jewish Passover, a body was surreptitiously placed in the house of one of the Jewish notables, Isaac Châtelain. The inquiry was carried out by the Franciscan and Dominican Orders, and 13 Jews (most of them members of Châtelain's family) sacrificed themselves in order to spare the remainder of the community. They were handed over to the "secular arm" and burned on April 24. The shock which was aroused in the Jewish world by this auto-da-fé can be measured by the fact that six elegies, in Hebrew or in Judeo-French, relate the details of it. The most moving account is the famous *Complainte de Troyes*, a Judeo-French elegy, the author of which Arsène *Darmesteter identified as Jacob b. Judah de Lotra (Lorraine), who also wrote a Hebrew elegy on the subject (manuscript in Vatican Library). Although King *Philip IV the Fair prohibited the religious orders from prosecuting any Jew in France without informing the civil authorities – even if it be for a religious crime (1288) – he did not disregard the material benefit accruing from this auto-da-fé when he ordered the confiscation of the victims' property for the treasury.

Following the banishment of the Jews of France in 1306, Jews returned to Troyes after 1315. In 1320 King *Philip V the Tall addressed a series of criticisms to the bailiff of Troyes because he tolerated Jews not wearing their distinctive sign and permitted them to make so much noise in their synagogues (indicating that at least two were still in existence) that even the predicant friars and the minor canons were disturbed in the execution of their duties. The Jews do not appear to have returned to Troyes after the expulsion of 1322, although several Jews in the duchy and county of Burgundy between 1332 and 1388 originated in Troyes. During the 14th and 15th centuries, however, Christians bearing the surname "le Juif" are mentioned in Troyes and were possibly descendants of converted Jews. The Jewish quarter, also known as "La Broce-aux-Juifs," was situated in the St. Frobert parish, and the St. Frobert Church is thought to be a former synagogue. The cemetery was situated at the entrance of the Faubourg de Preize. Troyes was the native city of Rashi, the great commentator on the Bible and Talmud. Rashi served as the rabbi of Troyes, where he founded (c. 1070) a school which became famous. The present-day streets rue de la Synagogue and rue Salomon Rachi perpetuate the memory of the flourishing medieval community, although their topographical relationship to the ancient location has not been determined. After Rashi, the scholars who taught or were born in Troyes included R. Jacob b. Meir *Tam, R. *Joseph b. Moses, the tosafist R. Samson, R. Joseph Ḥazzan b. Judah, his son Menahem, and the disciple of the latter, Judah b. Eliezer.

In 1808, there was not a single Jew in Troyes or in the whole of the department of Aube. The community was reorganized only during the second half of the 19th century (the synagogue was erected in 1877). On the eve of World War II there were some 200 Jews in Troyes. During the war, however, a large number of non-French Jews, as well as those who came from "prohibited" departments, were interned in the town by the Germans. The community, which was reconstituted after World War II, numbered 400 in the early 1970s and has since 1966 maintained the Rashi Community Center.

BIBLIOGRAPHY: Gross, Gal Jud, 223–43; A. Darmesteter, in: REJ, 2 (1881), 199–247; idem, in: *Romania*, 3 (1874), 443–86; P. Pietresson De Saint-Aubin, in: *Le Moyen Age*, 22 (1920), 84–87; A. Lane, *Quelques aspects de la vie économique et sociale à Troyes* (thesis, Paris Univ., 1956), passim; J. Roserot De Melin, *Le Diocèse de Troyes* (1957), passim; C. Lehrmann, *L'Elément juif dans la littérature française*, 1 (1960), 39–41; Z. Szajkowski, *Analytical Franco-Jewish Gazetteer* (1966), 163.

[Bernhard Blumenkranz]

TRUJILLO, town in Estremadura, W. Spain, on an important junction near the Portuguese border. Trujillo was taken by Alfonso VIII in 1184, then reconquered by the Moors; it definitely became part of the kingdom of Castile only in 1233. It may be assumed that there was a Jewish settlement there in the Muslim period, but the available data mainly concerns the Christian period. Toward the end of the 13th century, the community of Trujillo was the second largest in Estremadura, after Badajoz. In the 14th century Jews in Trujillo owned land, vineyards, and houses, which apparently had belonged to them before. There also were merchants and craftsmen among them. No data has survived about the fate of this community during the 1391 persecutions, but there were Jews who forsook their faith under duress in Trujillo as elsewhere. Yet the community was able to pay 6,000 maravedis in 1439 and 7,500 in 1474. A year before the edict of expulsion, in 1491, it spiraled to 11,400 maravedis, owing to an influx of refugees from other Jewish communities and to a special tax imposed as a contribution toward the war against Granada. In 1480 the segregation of Jews and Conversos into different quarters was carried out in Trujillo. The Jews were ordered to leave their quarter within two years and resettle in another part allotted to them. Exchange of houses was arranged, and the Jews were allowed to build a synagogue in their own area. Abraham *Seneor collected taxes and imposts in the town and its surroundings in the 1480s. The community existed until the edict of expulsion, when the exiles from elsewhere in Spain passed through Trujillo and Badajoz on their way to Portugal.

BIBLIOGRAPHY: Baer, Urkunden, 2 (1936), index; J. González, *El Reino de Castilla en la época de Alonso VIII*, 3 vols. (1960), index; Suárez Fernández, Documentos, index.

[Haim Beinart]

°**TRUMAN, HARRY S.** (1884–1972), 33rd president of the United States. From 1922 to 1924 his partner in an unsuccessful haberdashery business in Kansas City was Eddie Jacobson, a Jewish businessman. Truman was elected to the U.S. Senate in 1935, in 1945 became vice president, and a few months later (April 12, 1945) – on Roosevelt's death – president.

Among the vast problems faced by Truman following the defeat of Germany and Japan in 1945 were Jewish refugees and the disposition of Palestine. In 1945 and 1946 they were only remotely related to the major crisis of the Cold War, but it nevertheless proved uncommonly difficult to find a solution. In the short run, Truman desired to bring 100,000 displaced Jews to Palestine. This was supplemented by a request to Congress, repeated in his address of Oct. 4, 1946 (which fell on the Day of Atonement), to liberalize the immigration laws so that more displaced persons, "including Jews," might enter. The U.S. Legislation permitting 200,000 displaced persons to enter above the quota was passed in 1948. Truman's desire to send Jewish DPs to Palestine was subsequently supported by the recommendation of the Anglo-American Committee of Inquiry (April 1946) and also by the United Nations Special Committee on Palestine (UNSCOP; August 1947). But Truman was less certain regarding the establishment of a Jewish state, maintaining that the UN was the proper agency for handling the long-range solution of the Middle East problem. Even such steps as Truman was willing to advocate – the entrance of more Jewish refugees into Palestine and tentative support of the concept of partition – faced the stubborn opposition of his closest advisers in the State Department and the Joint Chiefs of Staff, and resentment by the British government. When the State of Israel was proclaimed on May 14, 1948, Truman personally made certain that within its first half hour of existence de facto U.S. recognition was extended to it. Nevertheless, he continued to advocate a temporary UN Trusteeship for the area. He subsequently opposed severing the Negev from the new state, a key element of the Bernadotte partition plan.

There was some speculation concerning Truman's motives in precipitously reversing U.S. policy for Palestine. The critical situation of the Democratic Party preceding the election of 1948 fueled suspicion that Truman acted purely for political reasons. It had become clear in the years after Roosevelt's death that the coalition of southern conservatives and urban-based liberal elements which formed the core of the Democratic Party, was no longer viable. The former components broke away from the party to form the Dixiecrats. At the same time a strong pull from the left developed when Henry Wallace formed the Progressive Party. Its platform of "progressive capitalism" and sincere negotiations with the Soviet Union to nip the developing Cold War in the bud exercised a strong attraction for the traditional left-wing elements in the Jewish voting bloc. At the same time the imposition of an arms embargo for the Middle East in December 1947 and the fact that the Republican Party candidate, Thomas Dewey, had given strong pledges of support to the U.S. Zionists, threatened to capture the Jewish vote or at least deny it to the Democrats, who needed it desperately to keep their chances alive. In February 1948 the worst fears of Democratic leaders regarding the loss of the Jewish vote were confirmed when Leo Isaacson ran on the Wallace platform in a largely Jewish congressional district in the East Bronx, New York, and won by a two to one margin. It was at this juncture that Truman supposedly decided to make an all-out bid to win back the Jewish vote. He did so by recognizing the State of Israel in May 1948.

Undoubtedly some political capital did accrue to Truman as a result of this step and his strong support for the new state between May and the election in November. The election results show that the Republican ticket was able to attract only two to three percent more of the Jewish vote in the election of 1948 as compared to 1944. But like the theory that Truman chose to recognize Israel because of the influence of his longtime friend and former business partner Eddie Jacobson, such theorizing is too simplistic to fit the facts. The considerable vote for Henry Wallace, especially in the poorer Jewish districts of the urban northeast, indicates that the great majority of Jewish voters were still drawn to the party of liberalism and Franklin Roosevelt which both Truman and Wallace were heir to. Truman himself adamantly denied that his recognition was based on domestic political imperatives: "The fate of the Jewish victims of Hitlerism," he explains in his memoirs, "was a matter of deep personal concern to me…" It may well be that in Truman the Jewish voter finally found the powerful Christian leader who personified that sense of civilized world conscience which they had hopefully assigned to his predecessor, Franklin Roosevelt.

On the whole, it can be said that the liberal, "Fair-Deal" administration over which Truman presided from 1948 to 1952 remained popular with Jewish voters even when the tide of general public opinion began to run against it as a result of the Korean War. The Jews were the one constituent of the original New Deal coalition put together by Roosevelt to show practically no defection to the Republican camp during the Eisenhower-Stevenson campaign of 1952, a fact which reflected on Truman's ability to satisfy Jewish sentiments both in his policy toward Israel and his stand on domestic issues.

BIBLIOGRAPHY: Harry S Truman, *Memoirs: Year of Decision*, 1 (1955); *Years of Trial and Hope*, 2 (1956); C. Phillips, *Truman Presidency: History of a Triumphant Succession* (1966); F.E. Manuel, *Realities of American Palestine Relations* (1949); N. Safran, *United States and Israel* (1967); E. Jacobson, in: AJA, 20 (April 1968), 3–15.

[Henry L. Feingold]

TRUMPELDOR, JOSEPH (1880–1920), soldier, symbol of pioneering and armed defense in Ereẓ Israel. Joseph's father, Ze'ev (Vladimir; 1830–1915), was a soldier in the army of Nicholas I. His son Joseph, born in Pyatigorsk (northern Caucasus), was sent to a religious school in Rostov-on-Don before he attended a Russian municipal school. Since, as a Jew, he could not attend high school, he studied dentistry. He was influenced by the idea of the collective commune as described by Tolstoy and practiced by the Tolstoyan settlers near his hometown. In Trumpeldor's mind, this ideal became intertwined with his concept of Zionism through the establishment of agricultural communes in Ereẓ Israel, which, if necessary, would be defended by armed force. In 1902 Trumpeldor was drafted into the army, volunteered for the 27th East Siberian Regiment, and was sent with it to Port Arthur. By volunteering for dangerous missions, Trumpeldor distinguished himself in the Russo-Japanese War (1904), in which he was severely wounded, and his left arm had to be amputated. Upon recovery, Trumpeldor asked his commanding officer to send him back to the front although he had the right to be demobilized. His request was granted and received mention in a special order for the day, in which he was promoted to the rank of a noncommissioned officer. When Port Arthur surrendered (late 1904), Trumpeldor was transferred to a prisoner-of-war camp in Japan, where he worked for the welfare of his fellow prisoners and devoted special attention to the Jews among them, organizing a Zionist group and a group of Jewish soldiers, whose aim was to go to

Ereẓ Israel and establish an agricultural commune there. In 1906 he was returned to Russia. Although a Jew, he received the rank of officer and was awarded several major decorations for distinguished service.

Trumpeldor entered the law faculty of the University of St. Petersburg, simultaneously working to form a group that would implement his idea of collective settlement in Ereẓ Israel. In 1911 Trumpeldor and his comrades, whose declared aim was the liberation of the Jewish people from national oppression through an independent existence in Ereẓ Israel, held their first meeting in Romny (Ukraine). In 1912, together with a group of his comrades, Trumpeldor went to Ereẓ Israel and worked for a time at the Migdal farm and the kevuẓah *Deganyah. He participated in the defense of the Jewish settlements in Lower Galilee. When World War I broke out, he refused to take Ottoman citizenship and was deported to Egypt. In Alexandria he advocated the establishment of a legion of volunteers from among the Ereẓ Israel deportees that would put itself at the disposal of the British to help liberate the country from the Turks. He accepted the British army's proposal to form the Zion Mule Corps (see *Jewish Legion), which he regarded as a first step toward the formation of a Jewish military force to liberate Ereẓ Israel. With the corps, of which he was deputy commander, Trumpeldor left for Gallipoli and between May and December 1915 took part in the major British offensive against the Turks. He set an example by his bravery and his willingness to undertake the most difficult tasks. After the Gallipoli campaign, Trumpeldor returned to Alexandria, and, after the corps' disbandment, proceeded to London, where he joined Vladimir *Jabotinsky in efforts to form a Jewish Legion from among the Russian Jews living in England, using a group of soldiers of the Zion Mule Corps as a nucleus.

In June 1917, Trumpeldor left for Russia to persuade the Provisional Russian Government to form Jewish regiments in the Russian army that could be sent to the Caucasian front and from there could break through to Ereẓ Israel. Trumpeldor was active in the Jewish Soldiers' movement in Russia and at its conference in Kiev, at which it was decided to form the General Federation of Jewish Soldiers in Russia and the General Federation for Self-Defense. He was elected commissar for Jewish Soldiers' Affairs. After the October Revolution Trumpeldor received permission to form the first Jewish regiment, whose chief objective was to combat the massacre of Jews; but the plan was canceled when Soviet Russia signed the peace treaty with Germany (January 1918). The regiment was disbanded and the Jewish defense organization outlawed; Trumpeldor was arrested at Petrograd but was soon released. He then devoted himself to the establishment of the *He-Ḥalutz movement in Russia, whose aim was to organize and prepare young Jews for settlement in Ereẓ Israel. He was elected chairman of He-Ḥalutz at its first conference in 1919, at which he demanded the introduction of military training for He-Ḥalutz members. He tried to gather groups of pioneers from various parts of Russia and to form centers for training and migration to Ereẓ Israel in Minsk and in the Crimea.

In 1919, Trumpeldor went back to Ereẓ Israel, stopping at Constantinople, where he founded an information office and a transit farm for immigrants and pioneers going to Palestine to the Jewish settlement Mesillah Ḥadashah. Upon arrival in Palestine, he proposed to the British military authorities to bring 10,000 Jewish soldiers from Russia as part of the Jewish Legion, and regarded the plan as a question of life or death for national existence in Ereẓ Israel. He also urged labor leaders in Palestine to unite into a single labor federation, which could efficiently absorb the new pioneering immigration. His proposal to form Jewish regiments was rejected. When news arrived of the danger facing the Jewish settlements in Upper Galilee, the scene of armed skirmishes between the French authorities and Arab rebels, Trumpeldor was asked to organize the defense of the settlements, and on Jan. 1, 1920, he reached *Tel Ḥai, which, together with the settlers and volunteers from the south, he began to fortify along with *Kefar Giladi and Metullah. On March 1, 1920, large numbers of armed Arabs attacked Tel Ḥai. During negotiations with their leaders, an exchange of fire took place in which Trumpeldor received a stomach wound. The battle continued all day. Toward evening, Trumpeldor was taken with other casualties to Kefar Giladi, but died on the way. His last words were, "*Ein davar, tov lamut be'ad arẓenu*" ("Never mind; it is good to die for our country"). Trumpeldor and five of his comrades were buried in the courtyard of Kefar Giladi; their remains were later removed to a new cemetery between Tel Ḥai and Kefar Giladi, where, in 1934, a memorial by the sculptor A. Melnikov was erected. The pioneers who arrived from Crimea shortly after Trumpeldor's death founded the Joseph Trumpeldor Labor Legion (*Gedud ha-Avodah), and named their settlement at the foot of Mount Gilboa *Tel Yosef in his memory.

The life and death of Trumpeldor became a symbol to pioneer youth from all parts of the Diaspora. Songs, poems, and stories were written about him. A collection of his correspondence, his diary, and memoirs, edited by M. Poznansky in 1922, became a standard text of the youth and pioneer movement. Trumpeldor inspired both the pioneering socialist movements and the right-wing youth groups. The movement Berit Trumpeldor (*Betar) concentrated on the military and nationalist aspects of his ideology and activity. A Trumpeldor House was established at Tel Yosef, and collects material connected with Trumpeldor's life and death and with the history of the Gedud ha-Avodah.

BIBLIOGRAPHY: *Me-Ḥayyei Yosef Trumpeldor* (1945^2), includes his diary; P. Lipovetzky, *Joseph Trumpeldor* (Eng., 1953); N. Benari and A. Kena'ani, *Yosef Trumpeldor, Po'olo u-Tekufato* (1960); S. Laskov, *Trumpeldor* (1972); Dinur, Haganah, 2 pt. 1 (1959), 24–28, 50–51 and index; Syrkin, in: *Mi-Bifnim* (Feb. 1947), 360–70; R. Freulich and J. Abramson, *The Hill of Life* (1969).

[Yehuda Slutsky]

TRUNK, ISAIAH (**Yesha'ah**; 1905–1981), historian in Poland and U.S. Trunk was the last major representative of the Eastern European Jewish historians who were trained before the Holocaust and worked primarily in Yiddish.

Born in Kutno, Poland, he was a descendant of the Trunk rabbinical family of that city. He received his master's degree in history from the University of Warsaw in 1929, and joined the Warsaw "Circle of Young Historians" (later a branch of YIVO) led by Emanuel Ringelblum and Rafael Mahler. He taught history and Latin for the Central Yiddish School Organization in Bialystok and Warsaw until the German invasion of 1939. During World War II, he took refuge in the Soviet Union, and returned to Poland in 1946, serving as a leader of the Jewish Historical Institute in Warsaw from 1948 to 1950. Trunk lived in Israel from 1951 to 1953 and helped to found the research archives at Ghetto Fighters House. In 1953, he became director of the Peretz-Shul in Calgary, Canada. In 1954, he settled permanently in New York City, where he became a research associate and, later, chief archivist at YIVO.

Trunk's works reflect three areas of interest. In accordance with the research program of Ringelblum and Mahler, his earliest works are histories of Jewish communities in Poland, based on archival sources, including *A yidishe kehile in Poyln baym sof 18ᵗⁿ yorhundert*: Kutno (1934), *Geshikhte fun di yidn in Plotsk*, 1237–1567 (1939), and monographs on Polish-Jewish history published in the leading Yiddish journals of pre-war Poland. A common feature is his emphasis on the "internal" aspects of Jewish life, including the economic, legal, cultural, religious, and social organization of Jewish communities.

After World War II, Trunk focused on Jewish life during the Holocaust. His research concerned daily life in the ghettos of German-occupied Europe and problems of health, education, social life, self-government, and resistance. These are exemplified by his "Shtudye tsu der geshikhte fun yidn in 'varteland' in der t'kufe fun umkum, 1939–1944" (1948) and *Lodzsher geto: a historishe un sotsyologishe shtudye* (1962).

Trunk is best known for his comprehensive study of imposed Jewish governing bodies, *Judenrat: The Jewish Councils in Eastern Europe Under Nazi Occupation* (1972), which won the 1973 National Book Award for history. Here, Trunk extended his research to continue a project commenced by his colleague Philip Friedman, who died in 1960. Trunk based his work on archival records of Jewish councils, Nazi government documents, and questionnaires of ghetto survivors. He dealt with the contentious moral issue of whether the Councils were complicit, from the time of their initial planning of ghetto life, in aiding in the destruction of Jews within their realms. Trunk found the actions of most Council leaders to rest on sound, but inapplicable, historical experience. He concluded that Jewish survival would not have been greater if Jews had refused to participate in the Councils. He wrote this work at a time when Hannah Arendt's *Eichmann in Jerusalem: A Report on the Banality of Evil* had charged that Jewish leadership enabled the Germans to annihilate the Jews.

This book was the subject of a symposium in 1975 in which the leading Holocaust historians of the time debated the role of the Councils (see bibl.: Bauer). Trunk also compiled and edited a collection of survivors' accounts in *Jewish Responses to Nazi Persecution* (1979). Additional Holocaust studies appeared in Yiddish and Hebrew journals and encyclopedias.

Trunk's third area of interest was Jewish historiography. He published studies of Russian-Jewish historiography and the role of YIVO in Jewish historiography as well as critical appreciations of many Eastern European Jewish historians of his and the preceding generation, including Simon Dubnov, Meir Balaban, Ringelblum, Mahler, and Friedman.

Trunk compiled three collections of his Yiddish historical essays: *Geshtaltn un gesheenishn* (1962), *Shtudyes in yidisher geshikhte in poyln* (1963), and *Geshtaltn un gesheenishn [naye serye]* (1983). His personal papers may be found in the YIVO special collections.

BIBLIOGRAPHY: LNYL, 4 (1961) 128–30; Y. Kermish (preface), in: Y. Trunk, *Geshtaltn un Gesheenishn [naye serye]* (1983), 7–16; *Imposed Governing Bodies Under Nazi Rule: YIVO Colloquium* (1972); Y. Bauer and N. Rotenstreich (eds.), *The Holocaust as Historical Experience* (1981).

[Mark L. Smith (2nd ed.)]

TRUNK, ISRAEL JOSHUA (1820–1893), Polish rabbi and one of the early supporters of *Ḥibbat Zion. Born in Plock, Poland, Trunk soon developed a reputation as a prodigy and great scholar. He served as the rabbi of Szrensk (from 1840), Gabin (from 1847), Warka (from 1850), Poltusk (from 1853), and from 1861 to the end of his life he was rabbi of Kutno and was known throughout the Jewish world as Israel Joshua Trunk of Kutno. He was close to Ḥasidism, especially to the *rebbe* of *Gur, Isaac Meir. He joined the Ḥibbat Zion movement with the initial activity of Ẓevi Hirsch *Kalischer, whom he encouraged in his letters. In 1886 Trunk visited Ereẓ Israel and encouraged the pioneers who were then experiencing the initial difficulties of settlement. He was among the rabbis who permitted agricultural work during the sabbatical year in Ereẓ Israel. A halakhic authority, only one of his books on *halakhah, Yeshu'ot Yisrael* (1870), on Shulḥan Arukh *Ḥoshen Mishpat*, was published during his lifetime. The remainder were published posthumously by his grandson as *Yeshu'ot Malko* (1927–39), novellae, and *Yavin Da'at* (1932), on Shulḥan Arukh, *Yoreh De'ah* with responsa. His grandson, ISAAC JUDAH (1879–1939), was one of the leaders of the *Mizrachi movement in Poland. The best known of his books is the Bible commentary *Mikra Meforash* (1936). At the end of his life he drew close to Po'alei Agudat Israel.

BIBLIOGRAPHY: I. Judah Trunk, in: *I.J. Trunk, Yeshu'ot Malko*, 1 (1927), 154–6; D. Weissbrod (Halaḥmi), *Arzei Levanon* (1955), 126–31; Bath Yehudah, in: EẒD, 2 (1960), 433–9.

[Getzel Kressel]

TRUNK, YEHIEL YESHAIA (1887–1961), Yiddish essayist and writer. Born near Warsaw to a landowning family with rabbinic ancestry, his most popular work was his memoirs, *Poyln* ("Poland," 7 vols., 1944–53), a rich source of Jewish folk-culture in Poland. He depicts his ḥasidic background grotesquely, satirically, but mostly lovingly. A member of the *Bund from 1923, he wrote many essays on socialism and Diaspora culture. His work reflects its classical, biblical, talmudic, kabbalistic, and European literary influences. As had many others, he shifted from Hebrew to Yiddish under the influence of I.L. *Peretz. He set a high level of literary criticism in *Idealizm un Naturalizm in der Yidisher Literatur* ("Idealism and Naturalism in Yiddish Literature," 1927) and in his analyses of the work of *Sholem Aleichem: *Sholem Aleykhem* (1937), *Tevye der Milkhiker* ("Tevye the Dairyman," 1939), and *Tevye un Menakhem Mendl in Yidishn Velt Goyrl* ("Tevye, Menakhem Mendl and Jewish Fate," 1944). He wrote in a light parodic vein in his works on Hershele *Ostropolyer, *Der Freylekhster Yid in der Velt* ("The Happiest Jew in the World," 1953), *Khelmer Khakhomim* ("The Wise Men of *Chelm," 1951), and *Simkhe Plakhte fun Narkove oder der Yidisher Don-Kikhot* ("Simkhe Plakhte of Narkove or the Jewish Don Quixote," 1951).

BIBLIOGRAPHY: LNYL, 4 (1961), 121–8. **ADD. BIBLIOGRAPHY:** D. Roskies, *A Bridge of Longing: The Lost Art of Yiddish Storytelling* (1995), 312–18; B. Davis, in: J Sherman (ed.), *Biographical Dictionary of Yiddish Writers* (2005).

[Barry Davis (2nd ed.)]

TRUTH (Heb. אֱמֶת, *ʾemet*). The Bible often speaks of God as "the God of truth" (e.g., Jer. 10:10; Ps. 31:6), as does the Talmud where this synonymity climaxes in the famous dictum: "The Seal of God is truth" (Shab. 55a; TJ, Sanh. 1:5). The same idea is also found in medieval Jewish philosophy (Maim., Yad, Yesodei ha-Torah 1:4; Joseph Albo, *Sefer ha-Ikkarim*, 2:27). In rabbinic theology "Truth" is one of the 13 attributes of God (cf. Ex. 34:6).

In Judaism truth is primarily an ethical notion: it describes not what is but what ought to be. Thus, in the Bible, truth is connected with peace (Zech. 8:16), righteousness (Mal. 2:6ff.), grace (Gen. 24:27, 49), justice (Zech. 7:9), and even with salvation (Ps. 25:4ff.; cf. Avot 1:18, "The world rests on three things – truth, justice, and peace"). In *Maimonides' and Hermann *Cohen's concept of God as the absolute paradigm of morality, from "the God of truth" follows the human virtue of "truthfulness" (H. Cohen, *Religion der Vernunft* (1929), index, s.v. *Wahrhaftigkeit*). Since God keeps truth (Ps. 146:6), only the man who speaks truth can come near Him (Ps. 145:18; Yoma 69b). Thus, also, Moritz *Lazarus (*Ethik des Judentums*, 2 (1911), 123ff.) and E. Berkovits (*God and Man* (1969), ch. 2) translate *emet* as "faithfulness" (*emunah*), identifying it ultimately with Jewish faith.

God acts truthfully in that He keeps His word. Human truthfulness is to be faithful to God and man. This is specified in many ways: to speak truth even in one's heart (Ps. 15:2ff.); always to quote correctly (Meg. 16a); to engage in commerce honestly (Mak. 24a); and to abstain from all deceit and hypocrisy (BM 49a; Yoma 72b; Maim., Yad, De'ot 2:6). In sum, as God is truth so Judaism as a whole is the practice of truth (BB 74a).

Jewish philosophers generally accepted the Greek notion of truth as "correspondence with reality" (*Saadiah Gaon, *Book of Beliefs and Opinions*, preface and 3:5; Abraham *Ibn Daud, *Emunah Ramah*, 2:3). Even such intellectualism, however, is ultimately superseded by biblical ethicism (e.g., Maimonides, *Guide of the Perplexed*, 3:53, end).

In modern Jewish philosophy, Hermann Cohen designates the normative unity of cognition and ethics as "the fundamental law of truth" (*Ethik des reinen Willens* (1904), ch. 1). Martin *Buber also identifies Jewish faith (*emunah*) with truth as interpersonal trust. Thus, truth as a human, ethical criterion is commonplace throughout the mainstream of Jewish thinking.

[Steven S. Schwarzschild]

TRZCIANKA (Ger. **Schoenlanke**), town in Poznan province, Poland. Jews were present in Schoenlanke from the first quarter of the 18th century; documentary evidence for the presence of a Jewish community dates from 1739 when the Jews of Schoenlanke were granted a privilege that secured for them certain trading and commercial rights. The privilege remained in force until 1756 when the town passed into the hands of Anton von Lasocki. It was then renewed, but at great cost and with highly restrictive conditions. After Poznan passed to Prussia (1772) the community (286 persons) successfully appealed the restrictions and their rights were reaffirmed. The synagogue burned down in 1779; a permanent one was built only in 1883. A *bet midrash* was functioning in 1772; in 1869 a new one was built but closed down in 1897 for lack of students. In 1790 there were 75 families in 31 Jewish-owned houses. The community was served by Rabbi Joel Meyer Asch (d. 1811) as well as his son Judah (d. 1831). The Jews, mainly large-scale wool merchants, were economically dominant and constituted a high but decreasing percentage of the total population: 863 in 1830 (23%); 584 in 1880 (14%); 590 in 1905 (8.1%); and 380 in 1932 (4.3%). Before the war the community maintained a school, library, *mikveh*, cemetery, and synagogue; its last rabbi was Curt Peritz (1932–36).

BIBLIOGRAPHY: A. Heppner and J. Herzberg, *Aus Vergangenheit und Gegenwart der Juden… in den Posener Landen* (1909), 926–45; M.L. Bamberger, *Geschichte der Juden in Schoenlanke* (1912); FJW, 85; PK, Germanyah.

TSABAN, YA'IR (1930–), Israeli socialist politician and publicist, member of the Tenth to Thirteenth Knessets. Tsaban was born in Jerusalem to parents who had emigrated from Poland in the 1920s. After completing high school, in 1948 he joined the Palmaḥ. He participated in the burial of the Arab victims of the Dir-Yassin massacre committed by the IẒL in April 1948. In December 1948 he was one of the founders of kibbutz Ẓor'a, near Beit-Shemesh, which he left four years later.

In the War of Independence Tsaban fought in the Sixth Palmaḥ Brigade, participating in the unsuccessful attempt to conquer the Latrun area on the way to Jerusalem. During a course for company commanders he first met Moshe *Sneh, who became his mentor. In 1952–54 he trained as a teacher at a kibbutz seminary, and started working as a teacher and youth instructor. In this period he became active in *Mapam. In January 1953 he left Mapam with Sneh, and for the next 27 years was active in various radical left-wing groups. He was a member of the Israel Communist Party (Maki) from 1954 to 1973, participating in various Communist youth delegations abroad. He also initiated opposition by the young guards of various political parties in Israel to the Statute of Limitations for Nazi Crimes, and to the establishment of relations with the Federal Republic of Germany. In 1969–72 Tsaban studied philosophy at Bar-Ilan and Tel Aviv universities. After Sneh's death in 1972, he served briefly as chairman of Maki's Political Bureau. He was later a member of Moked, and Maḥaneh Sheli. Over the years he represented Maki, Moked, and Maḥaneh Sheli in the Israel Executive of the World Jewish Congress, and in the Histadrut Executive Committee. In 1980 he returned to Mapam and was elected as its political secretary.

Tsaban was elected to the Tenth Knesset in 1981 within the framework of the Alignment between the *Israel Labor Party and Mapam. In 1984–92 he was a member of the Mapam parliamentary group in the Knesset, heading the list in the elections to the Twelfth Knesset. In 1992–96 he was a member of the Meretz parliamentary group, which Mapam had joined. In the governments formed by Yitzhak *Rabin and Shimon *Peres in the course of the Thirteenth Knesset, he served as minister of immigration absorption, and was a member of the Ministerial Committees on Absorption, and Political and Security Issues. In the Knesset he concentrated on social and humanitarian issues, initiating and supporting legislation affecting workers' rights and social welfare. He consistently supported peace initiatives with the Palestinians, and fought against religious coercion, and for the recognition of the non-Orthodox streams in Judaism. On several occasions in this period he appealed to the High Court of Justice on issues relating to the religious parties and personalities, and won.

In the Knesset he was noted for his diligence and graciousness.

After leaving the Knesset he was active in the meetings that led to the signing of the Geneva Initiative on December 1, 2003, and continued to campaign, together with others, for a variety of ideological and humanitarian causes. Since 1996 he has served as chairman of the College for Judaism as a Culture, and as chairman of the academic council of the Lavon Institute for Research on the Labor Movement, and has taught courses in public policy at Tel Aviv University. In 2000 he initiated the Encyclopedia of Jewish Culture in the Era of Modernization and Secularization and is a member of its editorial board.

Since 2002 he has served as a member of the Board of Trustees of the Jewish Agency.

[Susan Hattis Rolef (2nd ed.)]

TSALKA, DAN (1936–2005), Hebrew writer. Born in Warsaw, Poland, Tsalka spent the war years in the Soviet Union and lived up to the age of ten in Siberia and in Kazakhstan; in 1946 he returned to Poland. He studied philosophy and literature and immigrated in 1957 to Israel, where he continued his studies. Later on, he spent some time in Grenoble, France. His first book, *Doktor Barkel*, a collection of stories, appeared in 1967. This was followed by stories and novels, including *Si'aḥ ha-Beru'im* ("The Dialogue of Creatures," 1967), *Philip Arbes* (1977), *Yaldei ha-Shemesh* ("Children of the Sun," 1979), *Misḥak ha-Malakhim* ("The Angels' Game," 1986), and others. The novel *Ananim* ("Clouds," 1994; German, 1997), tells the story of a 13-year-old Jewish boy, the only survivor of a pogrom in a German town, who shares his fate with a German hangman. Set against the backdrop of medieval Germany, the relationship between the survivor and the executioner becomes a metaphor for Jewish-Christian history. Steeped in European culture, Tsalka developed an ambivalent attitude to the Hebrew language, which was not his mother tongue, and often focused on figures who opposed the Israeli mainstream and the Zionist narrative. His magnum opus is the novel *Elef Levavot* ("A Thousand Hearts," 1991; German, 2002), a sweeping epic about Jewish life in the 20th century. Oscillating between pre-state Tel Aviv, the Oriental Samarkand, and Poland, the saga presents a wide range of characters, following an intricate baroque-like structure. Tsalka published his autobiography under the title *Sefer ha-Alef Bet* in 2003. He taught at the Art Department of Tel Aviv University, and was writer-in-residence at the Hebrew University. He also published essays, poetry, books for children, and drama. Among the prizes he received are the Brenner Prize and the Sapir Prize (2004). A collection of stories in English, *On the Road to Aleppo*, appeared in 1999. Further information concerning translation is available at the ITHL website at www.ithl.org.il.

BIBLIOGRAPHY: D. Miron, "*Immut she-Huḥmaẓ*," in: *Hadoar*, 58:24 (1978); N. Mirsky, in: *Yedioth Aharonoth* (September 14, 1979); G. Moked, in: *Haaretz* (August 3, 1979); Y. Schwartz, "*Kemo Ẓippor ba-Keluv*," in: *Siman Keriah*, 10 (1980), 480–81; G. Shaked, *Ha-Sipporet ha-Ivrit*, 5 (1998), 445–80; Y. Peuys, "*Go'alei Olam al Saf Teruf*," in: *Devarim*, 1 (1999), 44–55; Y. Sharon, in: *Maariv* (July 15, 2005); Sh. Lev-Ari, in: *Haaretz* (June 16, 2005).

[Anat Feinberg (2nd ed.)]

TSANIN, (Yeshaye) MORDKHE (1906–), Yiddish writer. Born in Sokołow-Podlaski (Poland), he settled in Warsaw (1920), where he had a traditional and secular education and became a writer and cultural organizer (publications in *Oyfgang*, which he also edited, and *Naye Folksysaytung*) until the Nazi invasion, when he fled to Vilna (1939), Japan (1940), and Palestine (1941). After several years of manual labor, he worked full-time as a journalist and writer. His consistent and adamant advocacy of Yiddish in Israel was of signal importance. His *Iber Shteyn un Shtok: a Rayze iber Hundert Khorev-Gevorene Kehiles in Poyln* ("Through Thick and Thin: A Journey through 100 Destroyed Jewish Communities in Poland," 1952) collected his columns from the *Forverts* (for which he was also the Israeli correspondent, 1947–56), based on his postwar travels through Poland, posing as a gentile (1945–6). He contributed to Yiddish newspapers and periodicals throughout the world, including *Tsukunft*, *Di Goldene Keyt*, *Davar*, and edited *Ilustrirte Veltvokh* (1956–) and founded and edited *Letste Nayes* (1949–), Israel's first Yiddish daily, where the first part of his *magnum opus*, *Artopanus Kumt Tsurik Aheym* ("Artopanus Comes Home") began to appear serially; it was published in six volumes: *Yerusholayim un Roym* ("Jerusalem and Rome," 1966), *Fremde Himlen* ("Foreign Skies," 1968), *Libshaft in Geviter* ("Love during a Storm," 1972), *Di Meride fun Mezhibozh* ("The Revolt of Mezhibozh," 1976), *Der Yardn Falt Arayn in Yam Hamelekh* ("The Jordan Flows into the Dead Sea," 1981), and *Der Gzar-Din* ("The Verdict," 1985). The epic series of historical novels traces the history of Jews and Jewish culture from the Roman conquest of Judea up to the present as a series of cycles of persecution, survival, exile, and personal memory that comes to function as cultural memory and cultural tradition, projecting a moral and intellectual code that transcends individuals and even historical periods. It is one of the great achievements of Yiddish narrative, especially in postwar literature. Among his other books are *Vivat Lebn!* ("Live!," 1933; stories), *Oyf Zumpiker Erd* ("On Swampy Ground," 1935; novel), *Vuhin Geyt Yapan* ("Whither Japan," 1942; journalism), *Shabesdike Shmuesn* ("Sabbath Chats," 1957; feuilletons), *Megiles Ruth / Shir Hashirim* ("Ruth / Song of Songs," 1962; Yid. tr.); *Oyf di Vegn fun Yidishn Goyrl* ("The Paths of Jewish Fate," 1966; also Heb., 1967; essays), *Der Dekadents fun a Meshiekh* ("Decadence of a Messiah," 1967; essays), *Grenetsn biz tsum Himl* ("Borders up to Heaven," 1969/70; autobiography), *Der Shlisl tsum Himl* ("The Key to Heaven," 1979; stories), *Fuler Yidish-Hebreisher Verterbukh* ("Complete Yiddish-Hebrew Dictionary," 1982), *Fuler Hebreish-Yidisher Verterbukh* ("Complete Hebrew-Yiddish Dictionary," 1983), *Fun Yener Zayt Tsayt* ("Behind the Times," 1988), *Zumershney* ("Summer Snow," 1992; stories, essays), *Herts Grosbard* (1995; biography), *Shluf Nit Mameshi* ("Do Not Sleep, Mama," 1996; stories), and *Dos Vort Mayn Shverd* ("Word My Sword," 1997; essays). For several decades Tsanin served as president of the Association of Yiddish Writers and Journalists in Israel.

BIBLIOGRAPHY: M. Ravitsh, *Mayn Leksikon*, 3 (1958), 350–5; LNYL, 7 (1968), 532–4; S. Liptzin, in: *Yiddish*, 2:4 (1977), 91–5; D. Sfard, in: *Yidishe Kultur*, 42:5 (1980), 33–7; Y. Shargel, in: *Bay Zikh*, 18 (1981), 66–72; Y. Yanasovitch, in: *Bay Zikh*, 19 (1981), 68–74; A. Lis, in: *Yerusholaymer Almanakh*, 25 (1996), 280–7.

[Jerold C. Frakes (2nd ed.)]

TSCHLENOW, JEHIEL (Yefim Vladimirovich; 1863–1918), Zionist leader. Born in Kremenchug, Ukraine, into a well-to-do ḥasidic family, Tschlenow studied medicine in Moscow where his family had settled in 1876. He graduated as a physician in 1888 and became a well-known practitioner. The pogroms of 1881 turned Tschlenow from a sympathizer with the revolutionary populists (Narodniki) into a Jewish nationalist. In 1883 he became active in the Moscow *Ḥibbat Zion group, Benei Zion (to which Menaḥem *Ussishkin, Jacob *Mazeh, and Abraham *Idelson belonged). After some hesitation, he joined *Herzl's Zionist Organization and attended Zionist Congresses. Tschlenow presided at the all-Russian Zionist Conference in Minsk in 1902. During the *Uganda controversy at the Sixth Zionist Congress (1903), Tschlenow left the hall after the vote in favor of Herzl's proposal and 128 other opposition delegates followed him. He published a series of articles in the Zionist press against the Uganda scheme entitled "Zion and Africa." At the *Helsingfors Conference (1906), he was an articulate promoter of the idea that the political goal of Zionism must be closely associated with immediate settlement work in Ereẓ Israel and particularly with large-scale purchases of land.

A visit to Ereẓ Israel in 1907 and the revolution of the Young Turks in 1908 strengthened his conviction. From 1908 he was head of the Zionist Movement in the Moscow district and developed extensive activities, including the arrangement of meetings and conferences, opening of information offices on questions of Jewish education, publication of programs for the study of Jewish history, and preparation of catalogues for Jewish libraries. In 1909 he organized a group of Russian Jewish investors that established the farm *Migdal on the shores of Lake Kinneret. He also actively supported the settlement work of the *Odessa Committee. Since the general trend in the Zionist Movement was in this direction, Tschlenow's role steadily increased. He was a member of the board of the *Jewish Colonial Trust. At the Tenth Zionist Congress he was elected to the Zionist Executive, and at the 11th Congress (1911) he was elected vice president of the Executive (under Otto *Warburg). He moved to Berlin and directed Zionist activities from there. In 1912 he again visited Ereẓ Israel. During this visit he laid the cornerstone of the Haifa *Technion, as a member of its governing board, and purchased the plot of land on which the Hadassah Hospital in Tel Aviv was later located.

Forced to leave Berlin at the outbreak of hostilities in 1914, Tschlenow returned to Russia (1915). By the end of that year he was in London for consultations with Naḥum *Sokolow and Chaim *Weizmann on the political situation and the program of the movement. During the war he was active in aiding Jewish refugees expelled from the front area by the Russian army command. After the February Revolution in Russia (1917) Tschlenow headed the all-Russian Zionist Convention in *Petrograd. In July 1917 he left for London, where he participated in the negotiations that led to the *Balfour Declaration. He died in London. In 1961 his remains were reinterred in the old cemetery in Tel Aviv. His Zionist writings included *The Second Zionist Congress, Zion and Africa* (in J. Tschlenow, *Pirkei Hayyav…* (1937), 101–302; on the Uganda project); *Five Years of Work in Palestine* (1913); *The World and Our Prospects* (1917). Tschlenow was known for his emotional warmth and sincerity, his deep devotion and gentle sagacity, and his ability to handle people and situations.

BIBLIOGRAPHY: N. Sokolow, *History of Zionism*, 1 (1919), index; A. Boehm, *Die zionistische Bewegung* (1935), index; S. Eisenstadt (ed.), *Yehi'el Tschlenow* (Heb., 1937); Y. Gruenbaum, *Penei ha-Dor*, 1 (1958), 137–48; S. Kling, in: *Herzl Year Book*, 6 (1965), 83–108.

[Mark Perlman]

TSFASSMAN, ALEXANDER NAUMOVICH (1906–1971), Soviet jazz pianist and composer. Born in Zaporozhe (formerly Alexandrovsk), Ukraine, Tsfassman began to study piano at an early age, and in 1930 he graduated from the piano class of Feliks Blumenfeld at the Moscow Conservatory. While still a student he formed an ensemble of jazz orchestra and piano soloist, a novelty at that time in Soviet Russia, and it was attacked by the Association of Proletarian Musicians for introducing "decadent" Western music. From 1939 to 1946 he headed the large jazz orchestra of Radio Moscow. In later years he appeared mostly as a piano soloist with stage orchestras in performances of his own works or his piano arrangements of popular Soviet songs. In 1957 he was named "Meritorious Artist." His best known works are instrumental jazz music (including a piano concerto with jazz orchestra, 1941) and music written for choir, the theater, and films.

BIBLIOGRAPHY: Baker, Biog Dict, s.v.; A.N. Tsfassman, in: *Sovyetskaya Musika*, 5 (1971), 159.

[Michael Goldstein]

TSHEMERISKI (Chemeriski), ALEXANDER (Solomon; 1880–193?), leading member of the Russian *Bund and later of the *Yevsektsiya in the Soviet Union. Born in Bar, Podolia, in the late 1890s Tshemeriski worked as a photographer in Minsk, and ranked among the activists of the Bund. In 1901 he was among the founders of the *Independent Jewish Workers Party. When the party was liquidated, he once more became a revolutionary and conducted illegal propaganda among the peasants. After he addressed a letter of "confession" to the central committee of the Bund, however, he was again accepted within its ranks. As a committee member of the Bund in Lodz, he played an important role in the 1905 Revolution. During the years 1908–10 he was exiled to Siberia. Upon his return, he was the delegate for Lodz at the eighth (Lemberg, 1910) and ninth (Vienna, 1912) conferences of the Bund. He also represented Jewish workers of Lodz at the all-Russian convention of craftsmen (St. Petersburg, 1911), after which he was again arrested. During World War I he lived in Vienna and Geneva. Upon his return to Russia, he was arrested, but set free after the February revolution (1917). Tshemeriski was co-opted as a member of the central committee of the Bund, active in Yekaterinoslav (Dnepropetrovsk) and Kiev, and became a member of the central executive of the trade unions of Ukraine. At the 11th conference of the Bund (March 1919), having been nominated as a candidate for the central committee, he rapidly turned to the Bolsheviks and participated in the foundation of the "Komfarbund," which was the result of merging the "Kombund" with the United Jewish Communist Party (May 1919). At first a member of the head office of the Yevsektsiya in the Ukraine, he was subsequently appointed member of the central bureau of the Yevsektsiya and its secretary (1920). He wrote for *Emes* and was active in social and economic reconstruction and education among the Jews. In the mid-1930s he was arrested and tried on charges which included his previous affiliation to the "Independents." He apparently died in prison. Tshemeriski published memoirs in *Krasny Arkhiv*, no. 1 (1922), on the "Independents," and in *Royte Bleter* (1929), on his activities in Lodz in 1905. His publications of the Soviet period are listed in Ch. Shmeruk (ed.), *Pirsumim Yehudiyyim be-Verit ha-Mo'aẓot* (1961), index.

BIBLIOGRAPHY: M. Altshuler (ed.), *Russian Publications on Jews and Judaism in the Soviet Union 1917–1967* (1970), index; J.S. Hertz et al. (eds.), *Geshikhte fun Bund*, 3 vols. (1960–66), index; LNYL, 4 (1961), 153–4; *Avram der Tate [= Leib Blekhman], Bleter fun Mayn Yugnt* (1959), 179–85.

[Moshe Mishkinsky]

TSOMET (Tzomet), right-wing Israeli political party, founded in 1984, prior to the elections to the Eleventh Knesset, by Raphael *Eitan. In keeping with Eitan's views, Tsomet supported the concept of Greater Israel, compulsory military service for yeshivah students, and reduction of state financing for the yeshivot. Tsomet ran in a single list with Teḥiyyah, but only Eitan was elected to the Knesset from the party. In 1987 Tsomet broke away from the joint parliamentary group owing to differences of opinion between Eitan and Ge'ulah *Cohen. Tsomet ran independently in the 1988 election to the Twelfth Knesset, and gained two seats. After the *Israel Labor Party left the National Unity Government, Tsomet joined the narrow government formed by Yitzhak *Shamir in June 1990, and Eitan was appointed minister of agriculture. However, due to opposition to the Madrid Conference of October/November 1991, Tsomet left the government at the end of the year. Toward the end of the Twelfth Knesset Yo'ash Zidon of Tsomet was one of the four MKs who were responsible for the passing of the Law for the Direct Election of the Prime Minister. In the 1992 elections to the Thirteenth Knesset Tsomet ran under the slogan of "clean politics," and won eight seats, gaining many former *Likud votes. Tsomet opposed the Oslo Accords and the possibility of territorial concessions on the Golan Heights to Syria. In the field of economics it supported privatization. However, in 1995, in view of growing discontent in the Tsomet parliamentary group over Eitan's domineering leadership, Labor successfully wooed away three Tsomet members, two of whom were offered ministerial positions. In the 1996 elections to the Fourteenth Knesset, Tsomet ran in a joint list with the Likud and Gesher, and as part of the joint parliamentary group became a member of the government formed by Binyamin *Netanyahu. However, in March 1999 Tsomet broke away from the Likud. At the same time several of its members left to join other parties, either further to the Right or further to the Left. Tsomet was not elected to the Fifteenth Knesset, and of its eight members in the Fourteenth only one – Eli'ezer (Mudi) Sandberg – remained in the Knesset, as a member of Shinui. Eitan was killed in an accident during a storm in 2004.

[Susan Hattis Rolef (2nd ed.)]

TSUKUNFT (Zukunft), U.S. Yiddish monthly. Founded in New York in 1892 as an organ of the Socialist Labor Party,

Tsukunft was one of the first serious Yiddish periodicals to be published anywhere and the oldest still appearing at the turn of the 21st century. Despite a dwindling readership and an ever-declining group of potential writers, *Tsukunft* continues to appear, albeit approximately twice a year, publishing poetry, literary reviews, and essays in Yiddish under the editorship of Itzik Gottesman. Edited from the first by some of the most distinguished Yiddish literary figures in the U.S., including Philip *Krantz, Abe *Cahan, and Morris *Vinchevsky, *Tsukunft* quickly outgrew its original dogmatic base and opened its pages wide to all sectors of opinion in American Yiddish life, while itself remaining secularist and socialist. In 1912 it was acquired by the Forward Association, publishers of the **Forverts*. Under the editorship of Abraham *Liessin (1913–38) the magazine published the work of practically every Yiddish writer and thinker of note in the U.S. and of many others from all over the world. After Liessin's death, *Tsukunft* was edited by many prominent figures in the Yiddish world, including Hillel *Rogoff, David *Pinski, Nochum Boruch *Minkoff, Shmuel *Niger, Jacob *Glatstein, and Eliezer *Greenberg. From 1940 it was published by the Central Yiddish Cultural Organization.

BIBLIOGRAPHY: Y. Yeshurin, in: *Zukunft, 70th Anniversary Issue* (Nov.–Dec. 1962), 503–20; H. Bez, E.R. Malachi, and M. Shtarkman, *ibid., 75th Anniversary Issue* (April 1968), 100–15.

[Hillel Halkin / Samuel Spinner (2nd ed.)]

TSUR (Tchernowitz), JACOB (1906–1990), Israel diplomat and Zionist leader. Born in Vilna, the son of Samuel *Tchernowitz, Tsur settled in Ereẓ Israel in 1921. He was educated in Jerusalem and the universities of Paris and Florence. In 1929–48 he was public relations officer and later director of the Information Department of the *Jewish National Fund in Jerusalem. He served as the liaison officer of the Jewish Agency headquarters with the British army in Cairo from 1943 to 1945, and in 1945 became head of the UNRRA, Israel relief mission to Greece. From 1949 to 1953 Tsur was the first Israel minister to Argentina, Uruguay, Paraguay, and Chile, and in 1953–59 he was Israel ambassador to France. During his term of office there, Israel-French relations achieved a degree of cordiality which became virtually an alliance. He served on the Jewish Agency Executive as head of its Information Department in 1960–61. From 1960 he was chairman of the board of directors of the Jewish National Fund and held the presidency until 1977. In the years 1960–68 he was chairman of the Zionist General Council. Tsur was the president of the Central Institute of Cultural Relations with Ibero America, Spain, and Portugal and active in a number of national institutions. His books include his memoirs *Shaḥarit shel Etmol* (1965; *Sunrise in Zion*, 1968), and *Yoman Paris (Ambassador's Diary in Paris*, 1968). His *Epopée de Zionisme*, published in 1975 in French, has been translated into English (*The Saga of Zionism*), German, Italian, and Portuguese. His sister is the Hebrew writer, Yemimah *Tchernovitz-Avidar.

[Benjamin Jaffe]

TUAT, with the Gurara, an oasis complex stretching over 360 mi. (600 km.) in the Algerian Sahara. Tuat's center was Tamentit, "the Jewish town." Traditions reported by Arab historians fix the arrival of the first Jews as early as 5 C.E., and in large numbers in the "year of the elephant" (570), which coincided with the foundation of settlements in the oasis. Hebrew inscriptions, dating from 1329, were discovered there. The artesian wells there are attributed to the Jews who planted palm groves and built fortified villages. A responsum of R. *Isaac b. Sheshet (end of 14th century) was sent to Tuat via Honain, the important port of the Beni Zayan. The Jews were largely landowners, farmers, and warriors and lived in peace until 1437 when they were besieged for four months. They were rescued by friendly Muslims. The nomads envied their wealth. The Jewish traders from Tuat controlled the gold traffic. The preacher al-Maghili who had been expelled from Fez (end of the 15th century) incited the people to revolt against the Jews, and a new synagogue was destroyed. The high *qadi* ("judge") of Tuat came out in defense of the Jews. When al-Maghili ordered war against the Jews, the tribes united and there was a general massacre in 1492. The tombs of the victims are still a place of pilgrimage for the inhabitants of Tuat-Gurara. The family name Tuati (Touati, Toaty) derives from Tuat.

BIBLIOGRAPHY: *Archives Marocaines*, 12 (1908), 244–65; G. Vajda, in: *Etudes... Levi-Provençal*, 2 (1962), 805–13; Corcos, in: JQR, 54 (1963/64), 275–7; 55 (1964/65), 73; Hirschberg, Afrikah, 1 (1965), 282, 296f.; 2 (1965), 18–19.

[David Corcos]

TUBAL-CAIN (Heb. תּוּבַל־קַיִן), son of *Lamech. Genesis 4:22 states that "Zillah bore Tubal-Cain, who forged implements of copper and iron; Tubal-Cain had a sister Naamah." Various attempts have been made to identify Tubal-Cain as the name of an ancient tribe somewhere in the Near East. S. Mowinckel, however, followed by W.F. Albright, understands Tubal as a generic name for smith, derived from *ybl*, "to bring, produce." The second element of the name is universally connected with the Arabic *qāyin*, Aramaic *qaināyā* (*qainā'ah*), "smith, metalworker." In later times, Tubal-Cain was confused with the Tubal of Genesis 10:2, for example, and mistakenly identified with the Tuscans, well-known smiths of the ancient world. A. Dillmann pointed to the parallel between Tubal-Cain and his beautiful sister Naamah and the Greek smith-god, Hephaestus, and his sister Aphrodite.

[Daniel Boyarin]

In the *Aggadah*

The aggadic interpretation of the meaning of Tubal-Cain's name, is based upon the biblical record that he was "the forger of every cutting instrument" (Gen. 4:22). The *aggadah* teaches that by thus furnishing mankind with the means to repeat Cain's act of killing, with even more ease, he perfected (*tibbel*, תִּבֵּל) Cain's sin (Gen. R. 23:3).

BIBLIOGRAPHY: S. Mowinckel, *The Two Sources of Pre-deuteronomic Primeval History in Genesis*, 1–11 (1937), 81–82; W.F. Albright, in: JBL, 58 (1939), 95–96. IN THE AGGADAH: Ginzberg, Legends, index; I. Ḥasida, *Ishei ha-Tanakh* (1964), 430.

TU BI-SHEVAT (Heb. ט״ו בִּשְׁבָט; Fifteenth of Shevat), name for the festival of the New Year of Trees. According to *Bet Hillel, the 15th of Shevat marked the beginning of the separation of the *tithes of fruit (RH 1:1). This date was chosen because most of the annual rain in Ereẓ Israel falls before the 15th of Shevat (RH 14a; TJ, RH 1:2, 57a); consequently the fruits of those trees which blossom after the 15th of Shevat are considered to belong to another year for the levying of tithes and for the prohibitions of **orlah* (see: Lev. 19:23–25; Maim., Yad, Terumot 5:11; *ibid.*, Ma'aser Sheni 19:9–10). The New Year of Trees is regarded as a minor or semi-holiday for liturgical purposes; no penitential prayers are said and fasting is not permitted. In the Ashkenazi communities in Europe it was customary to eat 15 different kinds of fruits on the 15th of Shevat; special preference was given to the kinds of fruit grown in Ereẓ Israel. The eating of fruits was accompanied by the recital of Psalm 104 and of the 15 "ascending" psalms (nos. 120–34). In many communities the children had no school on this day. The Sephardi Jews gave the New Year of Trees a greater significance. Under the influence of the kabbalists of Safed in the 16th century the Sephardi liturgy and customs for this festival were expanded. From Safed the liturgy spread to Sephardi communities in Europe (Turkey, Italy, Greece) and, finally, to Sephardi centers in other parts of Europe, Asia, and North Africa. Among Sephardi Jews this day was called the Feast of Fruits and the special poems sung were called "complas." A special order of service for the 15th of Shevat, *Ḥemdat ha-Yamim*, was believed to have been compiled by *Nathan of Gaza. It was modeled on the Passover *seder* and included drinking four cups of wine. This liturgy, expanded by additional poems, *piyyutim* for the *Amidah* on the 15th of Shevat, and readings from the Scriptures and midrashic literature, was collected and published under the name *Peri Eẓ Hadar* ("Citrus Fruit," 1753).

Since the establishment of the agricultural settlements in Palestine in the last decades of the 19th century, the New Year of Trees has acquired great significance symbolizing the revival and redemption of the land by the conquest of the desert. In Israel Tu bi-Shevat is celebrated with children's songs in honor of the feast of the trees and with tree-planting ceremonies by kindergarten schoolchildren and others under the auspices of the afforestation department of the Jewish National Fund.

BIBLIOGRAPHY: C. Pearl, *Guide to the Minor Festivals and Feasts* (1961^3), 23–33; Y.T. Levinsky, *Sefer ha-Mo'adim*, 5 (1954), 317–492; H. Palagi, *Mo'ed le-Khol Ḥai* (1861), 252b–253a.

[Meir Ydit]

TUCACAS, a town on the northern coast of Venezuela, surrounded by two rivers making access from the interior of Venezuela difficult. In 1693 a large group of Jews originally from Leghorn left Curaçao for Tucacas. With the settlement of Jews there, the place became a lively commercial center. The Jews built houses, grew cattle, erected a fortress, and built a synagogue. They began to purchase cocoa beans from the interior of Venezuela, and mule trains carrying cocoa from Colombia and Ecuador would arrive in Tucacas, sell their produce to the Jews, and purchase textiles and other European goods in return. The attempts by Spanish forces to attack the settlement failed, owing to the protection of Dutch naval units, the local Venezuelan population, and the defense by the Jews themselves. This Dutch enclave was under the command of Jorge Christian, Marquis of Tucacas, and Samuel Hebreo (Samuel Gradis Gabai), under the title Señor de las Tucacas. Samuel Hebreo was also president of the Hebrew congregation called "Santa Irmandad" (the Holy Brotherhood).

The Spanish provincial authorities collaborated with the Jews, since they saw them as an outlet for export and the suppliers of much-needed European goods, since the overextended Spanish fleet could not meet the demands of all its American colonies.

At the end of 1717, the province of Venezuela became part of the viceroyalty of "Nueva Granada," which also included Colombia and Ecuador. The Viceroy Jorge de Vilalonga, because of complaints from the Catholic clergy and from Spain, decided to eliminate Tucacas. Pedro Jose de Olivarriaga was nominated commissioner against the so-called Jewish "contraband trade." With special army units and 40 ships he attacked and captured the town in 1720. According to eyewitnesses the synagogue was destroyed, the Jews burned their own houses, and left for Curaçao on 30–40 ships.

BIBLIOGRAPHY: C.A. Arauz Monfante, *El Contrabando Holandes en el Caribe, Durante la primera mitad de Siglo XVII* (1984); M. Arbell, "Rediscovering Tucacas," in: American Jewish Archives, 48: 1 (1996), 35–43; C.F. Cardot, *Algunas acciones de los Holandeses en la region del oriente del Venezuela (primera mitad del siglo XVII)* (1962).

[Mordechai Arbell (2nd ed.)]

TUCHIN (Pol. **Tuczyn**), village in Rovno oblast, Ukraine, within Poland before 1772 and between the two world wars. Jews began to settle there at the beginning of the 18th century. There were 514 Jews paying the poll-tax in Tuchin in 1765. Jews of Tuchin in the 19th century were occupied in small-scale trade in agricultural products, the raising of livestock, and crafts. The establishment of an army garrison in the vicinity at the beginning of the 20th century brought improvements in the economic sphere. The Jewish population numbered 1,180 in 1847; 2,535 (67% of the total) in 1897; and 2,159 (73%) in 1921. During the civil war in 1918–20, the Jews in Tuchin suffered from the frequent changes of the forces in control of the area (Ukrainians, Soviets, and Poles). Within Poland, in the interwar period, Zionist parties were active in the community. The livelihood of the Jews in Tuchin was severely affected from 1925 by the support given by the Polish authorities to Poles who settled there.

[Shimon Leib Kirshenboim]

Holocaust and Contemporary Periods

The number of Jews in Tuchin increased to some 3,000 in 1941 when refugees from western Poland found temporary shelter there. Under the Soviet occupation (1939–41), the Jewish organizations were not permitted to function. Tuchin was captured by the Germans on July 4, 1941, and the signal given to the Ukrainians to carry out pogroms in which 70 Jews were killed. That month 20 Jewish leaders were arrested and shot. In the following years various forms of persecution including restriction of movement, the seizure of able-bodied people for slave labor, and the wearing of the yellow *badge were introduced. Some of the intelligentsia were murdered. A ghetto was established in August 1942. At this time, news reached the community about the wholesale murder of the Jewish population in the neighboring cities. On Sept. 23, 1942, an order was given for all Jews to assemble at the ghetto gate. The leaders of the community were aware of the impending disaster and a decision to revolt was then taken by the head of the Judenrat, Gecel Schwarzman, supported by his two deputies, Meir Himmelfarb and Tuwia Czuwak. The Jews themselves set fire to many houses in the ghetto for defense purposes when the Germans began to break into it. Some young Jews had managed to acquire firearms, and the Jews in the ghetto offered strong resistance. Many fell in the fighting that ensued. Subsequently some 2,000 Jews escaped to the forests, but many of them were delivered up by Ukrainian peasants to the Germans. The Nazi authorities issued a proclamation that those who returned to the ghetto voluntarily would be allowed to live on there. Approximately 300 Jews returned, and were immediately taken to the local cemetery and shot. Those who remained in the forests suffered from hunger and exposure and were harassed by the Ukrainian gangs of Stefan Bandera. A few Tuchin Jews managed to reach the Soviet partisans and joined them in their struggle against the Germans. The revolt of the Tuchin Jewish community was exceptional in that an entire and united community challenged the German forces.

After the war, the community was not revived. The survivors settled in Israel, the United States, and Canada. A memorial book, *Sefer Zikkaron li-Kehillot Tuchin-Krippe* (Heb. and Yid.), was published in 1967.

[Aharon Weiss]

BIBLIOGRAPHY: B. Wasiutyński, *Ludność żydowska w Polsce w wiekach XIX i XX* (1930), 85; Cholavski, in: *Yalkut Moreshet*, 2 (1964), no. 2, 81–95, English summary.

TUCHMAN, BARBARA WERTHEIM (1912–1989), U.S. author, journalist, and historian. Born in New York City, she was a daughter of Maurice *Wertheim and a granddaughter of Henry *Morgenthau, Sr. She engaged in journalistic and editorial work, including coverage of the Spanish Civil War and service as editor of the Far Eastern Desk of the U.S. Office of War Information (1943–45). One of her principal achievements was making scholarly history readable to the general public. Her best-known book, *The Guns of August* (1962), which won the Pulitzer Prize, is a dramatic portrayal of the diplomatic prelude to, and early days of, World War I.

Bible and Sword: England and Palestine from the Bronze Age to Balfour (1956) expressed strong sympathy for the Zionist cause and an appreciation of Palestine's role in world history. Her other works include *The Lost British Policy* (1938); *The Zimmerman Telegram* (1958), on German intrigues in Mexico during World War I; and *The Proud Tower* (1966), a study of the years 1890–1914, which includes a chapter on the *Dreyfus Affair.

[Catherine Silverman]

In 1972 Tuchman was the recipient of the Pulitzer Prize for the second time for her book *Stilwell and the American Experience in China, 1911–1945*, and her book *A Distant Mirror: The Calamitous 14th Century* (1978) was an outstanding bestseller. These were followed by *The March of Folly: From Troy to Vietnam* (1984) and *The First Salute: A View of the American Revolution* (1988).

In May 1978 she was awarded a gold medal for history by the American Academy and Institute of Arts and Letters and in February 1979 was elected its president, the first woman to hold this position. In April 1980 she delivered the Thomas Jefferson lecture, the highest award of the American government for intellectual achievement outside of science; her subject was "Mankind's Better Moments."

BIBLIOGRAPHY: *Current Biography Yearbook 1963* (1964), 426–8; J.M. Ethridge and B. Kopala (eds.), *Contemporary Authors*, 1–4 (1967), first revision, s.v.

TUCHOLSKY, KURT (1890–1935), German satirist and journalist. Born in Berlin, Tucholsky was conscripted immediately after his graduation from law school in 1915. He spent most of World War I at the front and his experiences made him an ardent pacifist and socialist. In 1912 he had published *Rheinsberg*, a remarkably mature novella (which had its 100th edition in 1932). From 1913 he was encouraged by Siegfried *Jacobsohn to write for his periodical *Die Schaubuehne* (later called the *Weltbuehne*), one of the most aggressive and effective magazines of its time. His articles appeared under various pseudonyms (e.g., Peter Panter and Theobald Tiger), often side by side. He also wrote for many other newspapers and periodicals, publishing essays, stories, poems, and cabaret songs. Disillusioned with the Weimar Republic, Tucholsky moved to Paris in 1924, and worked as a foreign correspondent for the *Weltbuehne* and other publications. For six months after the death of Siegfried Jacobsohn he was the interim editor of *Weltbuehne* (1926–27). Tucholsky traveled throughout Europe and in 1929 settled in Sweden. Although he was drawn toward Communism, its excesses repelled him and the triumph of Nazism made him despair of Germany's future. He finally committed suicide in Hindas, Sweden. Tucholsky is considered one of the greatest German-Jewish satirists after *Heine, with whom in his apostasy and his ability to be witty and subtle in the German language he has often been compared. He was a man of the left, an ardent European, and an antinationalist. Tucholsky's satire was aimed at militarism, injustice, entrenched privilege, deep-rooted flaws in the German national character, stupidity, and greed.

His prose satire was collected in *Mit 5 PS* (1928), *Das Laecheln der Mona Lisa* (1929), and *Lerne lachen, ohne zu weinen* (1931). An early volume of cheeky poems, *Fromme Gesaenge* (1920), was followed by light satirical verse, often using the Berlin dialect in which Tucholsky excelled. Other works include *Ein Pyrenaeenbuch* (1927); the controversial *Deutschland, Deutschland ueber alles* (1929), a volume of photos and photomontages containing his prose and poetry, which mercilessly pilloried the Germany of the Weimar Republic; and *Schloss Gripsholm* (1931). Having abandoned Judaism in 1911, Tucholsky presented in the figure of Herr Wendriner an assimilated, opportunistic, spiritually empty German Jew. After World War II his works were frequently reprinted in both East and West Germany. Two which appeared posthumously were *Politische Briefe* (1969) and *Briefe an eine Katholikin* (1970).

BIBLIOGRAPHY: H. Zohn (ed.), *The World is a Comedy; A Tucholsky Anthology* (1957); H. Prescher, *Kurt Tucholsky* (Ger., 1959); F.J. Raddatz, *Tucholsky. Eine Bildbiographie* (1961); E. Pawel, in: *Commentary*, 46 (1968), 100–6; H.L. Poor, *Kurt Tucholsky and the Ordeal of Germany*, 1914–1935 (1968; incl. bibl.); H. Zohn and K. Ross (eds.), *Kurt Tucholsky: What if…?* (1968); I. Deak, *Weimar Germany's Left-Wing Intellectuals: A Political History of the Weltbuehne and Its Circle* (1969); F. Gotfurt, in: AJR *Information*, 25:2 (Feb. 1970), 6.

[Harry Zohn]

TUCK, RAPHAEL (1821–1900), British art and greeting card publisher. Born to a Jewish family in Germany, Tuck probably came to England at the time of the 1848 revolution, settling in London. He became a noted art publisher and, ironically in view of his religion, one of the earliest and most successful publishers of Christmas cards (which date from 1843). In 1880 he held a competition to design the best-looking card and did much to make them popular. Tuck employed a variety of famous artists to design his cards, including Sir Edward Poynter, and once paid Alfred Tennyson £1000 to write some verse for a card. His son SIR ADOLPH TUCK, FIRST BARONET (1854–1926) is often credited with introducing the picture postcard into England with a card showing Mount Snowdon in Wales and designed to be sold to tourists visiting the spot. He also introduced the first full-color postcards of fine art works, a set of Turner paintings, in 1898–99. Tuck, who received a baronetcy in 1910, served as treasurer of Jews' College, London, and was a member of the committee, founded in December 1917 and headed by Lord Rothschild, to further the policies of the *Balfour Declaration.

BIBLIOGRAPHY: ODNB online.

[William D. Rubinstein (2nd ed.)]

TUCKER, RICHARD (1914–1975), singer and **ḥazzan*. Born in New York, Tucker sang in a synagogue choir and studied singing under Paul Althouse. From 1939 to 1944 he was *ḥazzan* at Temple Adath Israel, Brooklyn, and also appeared in concerts and on radio. In 1944 he was engaged by the Metropolitan Opera, but continued officiating as *ḥazzan* at the Brooklyn Jewish Center until 1947. At the Metropolitan he became one of the leading lyric tenors, specializing in French and Italian operas. Tucker was distinguished for the volume and quality of his voice, and sang in the world's leading opera houses. Throughout his career Tucker continued to perform occasionally as *ḥazzan* or in cantorial recitals, and also made several cantorial recordings.

TUCKER, SOPHIE (née **Kalish**; 1884–1966), vaudeville artiste. Tucker was taken as a baby from Russia to the United States. As a child in Hartford, Connecticut, she worked in her parents' kosher restaurant and rooming house, which catered to many show business professionals and stars of the Yiddish theater. She got her start in the profession by singing her heart out to the celebrated customers. Going to New York in 1906, she played the lesser vaudeville circuits, but by 1915 she was topping the bill at the Palace Theater. She toured frequently and presented her act in English and in Yiddish. Known as the "Last of the Red-Hot Mamas," she was described as "big, brassy, flamboyant, laughing and crying, if need be, so that audiences were swept up in an irresistible torrent of lush sentiment." Among her best-known songs were "A Good Man Is Hard to Find," "M-O-T-H-E-R," and "I'm the Last of the Red-Hot Mamas." The audience favorite in the U.S. and Europe was "My Yiddishe Momma," written in 1925 by Jack Yellen. After Hitler came to power in Germany, it was decreed that her recordings of that song were to be destroyed, and it was forbidden to sell them. Tucker's signature song was "Some of These Days," written in 1910 by Shelton Brooks, to which she purchased the excusive rights to sing.

Tucker appeared on Broadway in *Lulu's Husbands* (1910); *Earl Carroll's Vanities* (1924); *Leave It to Me* (1938); and *High Kickers* (1941). She also appeared in several films, among them *Honky Tonk* (1929); *Broadway Melody of 1938* (1937); *Thoroughbreds Don't Cry* (1937); *The Heart of Show Business* (1937); and *Follow the Boys* (1944). In the 1950s and 1960s she was a frequent guest singer on Ed Sullivan's TV variety show *Toast of the Town*.

The Sophie Tucker Foundation, which she established in 1945, distributed millions of dollars to various charities. In 1955 she endowed a theater arts chair at Brandeis University. She also set up two youth centers in Israel bearing her name – the Sophie Tucker Youth Center in Bet Shemesh and a youth center in kibbutz Be'eri in the Negev. In 1962 she sponsored the Sophie Tucker Forest near the Bet Shemesh amphitheater as well as funding many hospitals and homes for the aged.

Her autobiography, *Some of These Days*, appeared in 1945. The 1963 Broadway musical *Sophie*, written by Phillip Pruneau with music by Steve Allen, was based on the early years of Tucker's career.

BIBLIOGRAPHY: M. Freedland, *Sophie: The Sophie Tucker Story* (1978); A. Fields, *Sophie Tucker: First Lady of Show Business* (2003).

[Lee Healey / Ruth Beloff (2nd ed.)]

TUCSON, city located in the S.E. part of Arizona. The 2005 Jewish population is estimated at somewhere around 25,000 (exclusive of about 3,000 university students and untold numbers of winter visitors). Although the general population, numbering about 750,000 in Pima County (Tucson is the county seat), keeps growing, the Jewish population fluctuates too much to make any kind of definitive statement. Of the Jews present in the city in 1994, 38% no longer reside there, while 24% of the Jews living in Tucson in 2005 did not reside there in 1994. In this sense, Tucson is a typical southwestern town where roots do not go back more than a generation or two because so much growth has occurred since the end of World War II.

Tucson was part of the Gadsden Purchase when a small area of land in southern Arizona and New Mexico was acquired from Mexico in 1854. At first there were relatively few people, Jews and gentiles, in the community, but some Jews came because of merchandising opportunities. Some opened general stores, others acquired Indian trading licenses, and some also served as contractors for the U.S. Army. The settlement in the 19th century consisted mostly of young men out to seek their fortunes. Marriages were made with Mexicans and/or Indians, or else with German or eastern Jewish women who some of the men went back to marry. The total Jewish population of Arizona in the 1880s was estimated at about 50 people, so the numbers in Tucson must have been fewer. A number of men from the city's pioneer Jewish families, the Drachmans, Franklins, Jacobs, Ferrins, Zeckendorfs, Steinfelds, and Mansfields, could be found in elected political positions: on the school board, on the county Board of Supervisors, and even as mayor. One Jew who represented Tucson in the territorial legislature, Selim Franklin, won the University of Arizona for his community in 1885 although at the time it was considered the "booby" prize. Prescott kept the state capitol, Phoenix was awarded the state insane asylum, and Yuma remained home to the state prison.

Almost none of the descendants of the pioneer families are counted among the Jews of Tucson today. Many of the original Jewish settlers fled to other parts of the West or the nation in the late 1880s and 1890s when an economic depression hit the Arizona territory. Moreover, those Jews who had already made money left the community because of the unbearable heat, often over 100 degrees Fahrenheit, which could last sometimes from May through October.

In the early 20th century a number of Jews remained in Tucson as is evidenced by the presence of a Hebrew Ladies' Benevolent Society and the building in 1910 of the first Jewish temple in Arizona: Temple Emanu-el (Reform).

Until World War II, and even among some of the pioneers, the Jews who arrived in Tucson came because someone in the family needed the dry air for his/her health. The whole Jewish population of Arizona, for example, increased from 1,150 people in 1920, to 1,847 in 1937. How many of these Jews lived in Tucson is difficult to judge but in 1940 census takers estimated their number at 480. The one new establishment in Tucson in the 1930s occurred with the founding of a second Jewish synagogue, Conservative, at the beginning of the decade. In 1939 this congregation, Anshei Israel, acquired its first small building.

During World War II the population grew because the United States government established an air force base in Tucson. After the war many of those whose first experience of the southwest occurred during the conflagration returned as settlers because during most of the year the daytime climate ranged from 50 to 80 degrees F. with cool nights except during the summer monsoon season in July and August. The impact of the influx on the city's Jewish community was enormous. In 1948 Tucson counted about 4,000 Jews. Within the next few years Jews in Tucson had established an Orthodox synagogue, a Jewish Community Council, and a wealth of organizations to provide a variety of social services to Jews in the city.

Growth spurts in Tucson occurred in the 1950s and thereafter. Air conditioning came into vogue in that decade which made the city a more tolerable place to live. The 1960s witnessed a depression in the city. At the end of the decade, however, the continued growth of the University of Arizona and the establishment of its medical college spawned a huge mushrooming of the population, Jewish as well as gentile. Whereas in 1970 the city had about 250,000 people and 6,000 or so Jews, today, as mentioned, there are 750,000 people, about 3–4% of whom are Jewish.

In the early 21st century Tucson and the Jews within the community were thriving. Most Jews who work were in professional occupations while a sizeable number were involved with real estate development. There was a host of cultural activities, both Jewish and in the greater community, a strong Jewish Federation with social welfare and social service groups that provide for the needs of every age group, and some indication that young Jewish adults, who in previous decades had to seek employment opportunities elsewhere, were remaining in the city and working in the community.

A community survey taken in 2002 revealed that fewer than half of all Tucson Jews participate in Jewish activities. The community was the second from the bottom among comparably sized Jewish communities whose Jewish respondents have attended synagogues only on special occasions; it had the highest percentage of Jewish single-family households under the age of 65; Tucson was fourth from the bottom in making donations to Jewish charities and fourth from the top (46%) in young adults marrying non-Jews. Forty-two percent of Jewish children under the age of 17 were being raised in households where one of the parents is not Jewish.

On the other hand, Tucson also had the lowest perception of antisemitism in its midst of any Jewish community in the United States. Jews did not find any kind of discrimination in the areas that were of concern in previous decades: housing, employment, areas of recreation. In the 1980s four of the seven members of the State Board of Regents were Jewish (these are gubernatorial appointees), and in the 1990s the chief justice of the Arizona Supreme Court was also Jewish. The year's major societal charity event in Tucson, the Angel Ball, is totally non-discriminatory.

BIBLIOGRAPHY: L. Dinnerstein, "From Desert Oasis to the Desert Caucus: The Jews of Tucson," in: M. Rischin and J. Livingston (eds.), *Jews of the American West* (1991), 136–63; Jewish Federation of Southern Arizona, *A Roadmap for the Future: The 2002 Population Study & Tucson's Jewish Community Planning.*

[Leonard Dinnerstein (2nd ed.)]

TUDELA, city on R. Ebro, in Navarre, N. *Spain. Tudela was the most important Jewish community in the medieval kingdom of Navarre that remained independent until 1512. No information is available on the beginnings of the Jewish settlement in Tudela, which however appears to have been the most ancient of the communities of Navarre. In the period of Muslim rule Jews engaged in agriculture and international commerce, and owned and rented land in the area. Tudela was the birthplace of *Judah Halevi (at the latest in 1075), Abraham *Ibn Ezra (1092), and Shem Tov ibn *Falaquera. In this period there were around 1,000 Jews in Tudela. The Jews of Tudela dominated the life of Navarrese Jewry, both under Muslims and Christians.

With the end of Muslim rule (1115), Tudela passed to *Alfonso I (*el Batallador*), king of Aragon. Two treaties of the conquest period concluded by the king with the local Muslims and Jews have been preserved. With the Muslims, it was agreed that all those who desired to remain in Tudela once it passed under Christian dominion would leave their quarter, including their mosques, within one year and settle in the suburbs of the town. They were promised religious and national autonomy and were prohibited from bringing Muslim captives into the town in order to sell them to Jews; in the same treaty, Jews were forbidden to purchase Muslim prisoners of war. Jews who molested Muslims by word or deed would be prosecuted, and no Jewish officials were to be appointed with rights of jurisdiction over the Muslims or their property. However, the local Jews were granted several rights: Jews who had fled from the town during the siege or at the time of the conquest were authorized to return (there appears to have been some tension between them and the Muslims), their rights over their houses and property were guaranteed, and the Jews were required to pay to the Christian governor the taxes which they had formerly paid under Muslim rule. In the judicial sphere, the charters which had been granted to the Jews of *Nájera were also applied to those in Tudela, undoubtedly at their request. Comparison of the two treaties indicates that the Jews were more favored than the Muslims, especially as they were not required to leave their quarter within a year. According to F. Cantera, this quarter was situated within proximity of the cathedral, while in the opinion of L. Torres-Balbás, it lay in the southeastern part of the town (see bibliography). Jews owned a large number of estates, gardens, and vineyards in the district known as Mosquera, near Tudela. Occupations of the Jews in Tudela included *slave trading (already practiced under Muslim rule) in addition to spinning, trade in wool, the production of textiles, and various crafts, including gold- and silversmithing.

It was at the height of this period of prosperity, in the 1160s, that the traveler *Benjamin of Tudela left his city for the countries of the Orient and the Mediterranean basin. His account of the towns he visited included mostly information about the local Jewish community and the economy of the towns. He was most probably a merchant with a great interest in the Jewish world. His book, written in Hebrew, often provides the only information available on the Jews of the time. In 1170 Sancho VI "the Wise" granted the Jews of Tudela a privilege which did much to regularize community life. It permitted Jewish houses in the Jewish quarter, which was now established in the fortress, to be sold and transferred to any buyer, ratified the charters of Nájera, and granted a tax exemption on condition that the Jews of Tudela assumed responsibility for maintaining the fortress of Tudela (with the exception of the tower). A site was allocated to them for a cemetery. A year later Sancho granted the Jews of Tudela the charters applying in Funes and alleviated the severity of the Jewish *oath. The privilege of 1170 secured a place of residence for the Jews in the fortress of Tudela where they could protect themselves against rioters and attackers. Thus there were two Jewish quarters in Tudela. The first, the Vieja (the Old), existed during the Muslim period and continued to exist during the first 50 years of the Christian conquest. This quarter was in the southeastern part of the city, within the walls, in the area stretching from the Cathedral as far as the Queiles River, today El Muro street. The second quarter was established in the fortress in 1170. This new quarter, the Nueva, occupied part of Paseo del Castillo and San Miguel street. In the new quarter there were the following synagogues: the Sinagoga Mayor, the Sinagoga Menor, and the Bet Midrash of Bene Orabuena. We have no information about the locality of these synagogues or of other communal institutions of whose existence we know.

When Navarre passed to the house of Champagne in 1234, French rulers introduced their modes of behavior into the new possessions, while economic and religious rivalry between the Jews and the Christian townsmen also increased. The tax registers show the heavy burden of taxation imposed on the Tudela community. It was affected by the revolt of the townsmen against King Theobald I in 1235. R. Shem Tov *Falaquera, of a distinguished family of Tudela, still complained in 1264 of the situation in his *Ha-Mevakkesh*. Many Jews lost their fortunes, while the debts which were owed to Jews by the peasants could not be collected. The community administration was concentrated in the hands of several prominent families.

14th and 15th Centuries

The community regulations of 1305 show that the administration was modeled on the institutions of the municipal administration. The "Institution of the Twenty" was comparable to the institution of the 20 town notables found in the towns of Aragon by the beginning of the 12th century, and the 20 *jurados* who administered the town at the beginning of the 13th century; there were also the "Institution of the Eleven," by which several of the community's regulations were established, and the *muqaddimūn. Every regulation required the signatures of eight of the community's notables. Three of the community's leaders, Joseph b. Shem Tov Falaquera, Samuel b. Joseph Abbasi, and Ḥayyim b. Shem Tov Menir, were to be the decisive authority in matters connected with denunciations by *informers.

Like many of the communities of Aragon and Navarre, Tudela became a haven for the refugees from French territory after the expulsion of 1306. However, difficult times followed. In 1319 several *Conversos who had returned to Judaism were burned at the stake in Tudela. A year later the community was only spared a massacre by the *Pastoureaux (Shepherds) through the latter's defeat near the capital of *Pamplona. The community again suffered from the riots of 1328, and was not spared in the economic decline of the 14th century. Like the other communities of Spain, the Tudela community also appears to have suffered in the 1360s at the hands of the foreign armies which invaded Spain and Castile during the civil war between the brothers Pedro the Cruel and Henry of Trastamara.

During the 14th century Tudela had several outstanding personalities. In 1322 the infante Alfonso of Aragon conducted negotiations with Ishmael b. Joseph ibn Abbas (the same as Ishmael de Abelitas) concerning his settlement in Aragon. The members of this family were prominent merchants who controlled a large part of the trade of that period. R. Joseph *Orabuena, who acted as physician and confidant to Charles III of Navarre, and accompanied him on several journeys to France, presided over the community of Tudela after 1391. R. Shem Tov b. Isaac *Shaprut, a philosopher and a rabbinic authority, who was involved in a disputation with Cardinal Pedro de Luna (later Pope Benedict XIII) in Pamplona in 1375, was also a native of Tudela. There were also some Converso artists in Tudela, including Juan de Levi, whose paintings are to be found in the local church.

Hebrew sources found in the archives in Pamplona and Tudela show the extensive economic activities of the Jews of Tudela. These sources were mostly written in Hebrew, sometimes in Judeo-Navarrese, that is, in Navarrese dialect but in Hebrew characters. Some of these sources also provide information about the organization of the community.

In 1391 there were 90 houseowners in Tudela who paid taxes, but these represented only a remnant of the community's former population at the height of its prosperity, although Tudela was not itself affected by the 1391 persecutions. Subsequently the community continued to decline.

The phenomena characterizing the communities of Spain in the 15th century were also evident in the Tudela community, and a number of its members abandoned Judaism. The community was also depleted by a plague which struck the town during the 1430s. A Cortes convened in Tafalla in 1482 prohibited the Jews of Navarre from going out of their quarters on Christian festivals; they were forbidden to walk in the streets among the Christians who were celebrating until the conclusion of the prayer service. Only physicians and surgeons were authorized to visit the sick. After the assassination of the inquisitor Pedro de *Arbués in Saragossa the town of Tudela refused to deliver several Converso fugitives to the *Inquisition.

At the time of the expulsion of the Jews from Spain in 1492, about 2,000 refugees crossed the border of the kingdom of Navarre. Like the other communities in Navarre, the Tudela community ceased to exist after the expulsion of the Jews from this kingdom in 1498. Although the Spanish border was closed, a number of Jews moved to Provence. Tudela was included within the jurisdiction of the Inquisition tribunal of the kingdom of Navarre which was set up in 1512, whose seat was at first in Pamplona and subsequently in Estella. The tribunal established itself in Tudela in 1515 and was later incorporated within the tribunal which had its seat in Logroño. In 1521 the Conversos in Navarre rose in support of the French armies then invading the kingdom. When the invasion had been repelled, the Inquisition turned its attention to the Conversos, many of whom fled from Tudela and the other towns in Navarre. A list of those condemned in Tudela by the Inquisition, known as La Manta, still hung in the cathedral at the close of the 18th century.

BIBLIOGRAPHY: Baer, Spain, index; Baer, Urkunden, 1 (1929), index; J. Yanguas y Miranda, *Historia de Navarra* (1832); M. Kayserling, *Juden in Navarra...* (1861), 3–110; H.C. Lea, *A History of the Inquisition of Spain*, 1 (1906), 551; H. Malter, in: JQR, 1 (1910/11), 151–81, 451–501; Neuman, Spain, index; J.M. Sanz Artibucilla, in: *Sefarad*, 5 (1945), 337–66; J.M. Lacarra, in: *Estudios de Edad Media de la Corona de Aragón, Seccion de Zaragoza*, 3 (1949), index; F. Idoate, in: *El Pensamiento Navarro* (Oct. 12, 1954); F. Cantera, *Sinagogas españolas* (1955), 320–4; L. Torres Balbás, in: *Al-Andalus*, 19 (1954), 193ff. **ADD. BIBLIOGRAPHY:** B. Leroy, in: REJ, 136 (1977), 277–95; idem, in: *Miscelánea de estudios árabes y hebraicos*, 32:2 (1983), 81–93; idem, *The Jews of Navarre* (1985), index; idem, *Une famille sépharade à travers les siècles: les Menir* (1985); J. Carrasco Pérez, in: *Miscelánea de estudios árabes y hebraicos*, 29:2 (1980), 87–141; idem, in: *Príncipe de Viana*, 166–67 (1982), 909–48; J.L. Lacave, in: *Sefarad*, 43 (1983), 169–79; idem, in: *ibid.*, 44 (1984), 3–32; J.E. Avila Palet, in: *Sefarad*, 45 (1985), 281–314; idem, *ibid.*, 47 (1987), 9–57; B.R. Gampel, *The Last Jews on Iberian Soil* (1989), index; Y. Assis and R. Magdalena, *The Jews of Navarre in the Late Middle Ages* (Heb., 1990), index; Y. Assis, R. Magdalena and C. Lleal, *Aljamía romance de los documentos hebraiconavarros (siglo XIV)* (1992).

[Haim Beinart / Yom Tov Assis (2nd ed.)]

TUEBINGEN, city in S. Germany. The first mention of Jews in Tuebingen concerns a short-term guarantee in 1335 by the counts of Tuebingen, who sold the city to *Wuerttemberg in 1342, to their "burghers: clerics, laymen, Jews or Christians." The Judengasse was south of the town's bridge and is fortuitously mentioned only in 1398, but it dates probably from a much earlier period. A 1458 source, of which only a résumé is extant, speaks of the privileges of the Tuebingen Jews. In 1459 they were accused of charging higher interest than specified therein. The two major creditors, Kaufman and his wife Bela, were imprisoned by 14-year-old Count Eberhard V of Wuerttemberg, but they were released by his guardian Count Ulrich v of Wuerttemberg, who ordered a three-year debt moratorium and interest annulment. In 1460 he helped them to move, under favorable terms, to the Black Forest town of Wildberg, and two other Jewish families followed them to this town. By 1471 five Jewish families remained in Tuebingen. The founding of the university at Tuebingen in 1477 occasioned the expulsion of the Jews from the city and a ban against doing any business there.

In 1815 the first Jewish student, Samuel Harum Mayer, was admitted to the university by special permission of the Wuerttemberg king; Jewish students were admitted generally from 1821. In the nearby village of Wankenheim, a Jewish community of peddlers and *livestock merchants started in 1775; a synagogue was built there in 1833, and a cemetery was acquired in 1845. By 1852 the Wankenheim Jews began moving to Tuebingen, a process nearly completed in 1882 when a synagogue was consecrated in the city; like the cemetery, it was used by Jews of Reutlingen and several other towns and villages. Seventy-five Jews lived in Tuebingen in 1875; 139 in 1910 (0.73 percent of the total population); and 90 in June 1933. The attorney Simon Hayum had a municipal position prior to 1933. With the rising of Nazism, a general boycott of Jewish establishments was initiated, and Jewish students had to leave the university. (The law office of Simon Hayum was maintained until November 1938.) Twenty Jews moved elsewhere after 1933, and 50 emigrated between 1933 and 1940. The synagogue was burned in November 1938, and the community was dissolved in 1939. Fourteen Jews were deported to the east in 1941–43.

[Toni Oelsner]

Contemporary Period

In 1968, eight Jews lived in Tuebingen. They were affiliated with the community in *Stuttgart. The university's theological faculty had an *Institutum Judaicum that conducted seminars and lectures, and published Judaistic works. The philosopher Ernst *Bloch taught from 1956 at Tuebingen University. In 1978/79 a memorial was inaugurated to commemorate the destroyed synagogue and the former Jewish community. In 2000 a new memorial was consecrated. About 1% of the members of the Jewish community of Wuerttemberg (2,881 members in 2004) live in Tuebingen.

[Toni Oelsner / Larissa Daemmig (2nd ed.)]

BIBLIOGRAPHY: M. Crusius, *Schwaebische Chronick*, tr. from Latin by J.J. Moser (1733), 72f.; R. Roth, *Urkunden zur Geschichte der Universitaet Tuebingen 1476–1550* (1877), 72f.; Wuerttembergisches Staatsarchiv, Wuerttembergische Regesten (1916–40), nos. 159, 1466, 1499; *Feiertagsschrift israelitische Kultusvereinigung Wuertemberg* (Sept. 1964), 34; A. Marx, *ibid.* (Oct. 1967), 23f.; P. Sauer (ed.), *Dokumente ueber die Verfolgung der juedischen Buerger in Baden-Wuerttemberg* (1966), index; idem, *Die juedischen Gemeinden in Wuerttemberg* (1967); *Germania Judaica*, 2 (1968), 835–7; 3 (1987), 1489–90. **ADD. BIBLIOGRAPHY:** L. Zapf, *Die Tuebinger Juden* (1981^3); *Zerstoerte Hoffnungen. Wege der Tuebinger Juden* (Beitraege zur Tuebinger Geschichte, vol. 8) (1995); B. Schoenhagen and W. Setzler, *Juedisches Tuebingen. Schauplaetze und Spuren* (Orte juedischer Kultur) (1999). **WEBSITE:** www.alemannia-judaica.de.

TUGAL, PIERRE (1895–1964), French writer, born in Russia. In 1931 he was co-founder (with Rolf de Maré) and curator of the Paris Archives Internationales de la Danse until its dissolution in 1952. In 1935 Tugal was a founder of L'Association de la Presse Chorégraphique. Delegate to UNESCO, doctor of law, with a diploma in social and political sciences, Tugal devoted himself to literary and art research, specializing in the theater and dance. He engaged in research on the use of dance in rehabilitation of the handicapped and the mentally ill. He was the author of many articles and several books on dance, including *Initiation à la Danse* (1947), *Petite histoire de l'art et des artistes* (1952), *La Danse Classique sans Maître* (with Lucien Legrand, 1956); and a work on Noverre, an 18th-century French ballet master (1959).

BIBLIOGRAPHY: *The Dance Encyclopedia* (1967); *The Concise Oxford Dictionary of Ballet* (1977, 1982).

[Naama Ramot (2nd ed.)]

TUGENDHOLD, JACOB (1794–1871), author and an early adherent of the Galician *Haskalah. He was born near Cracow, Poland and graduated from the University of Breslau. In 1819 he founded a model school in Warsaw, which aroused the antagonism of the Orthodox teachers, and a year later was appointed governmental vice censor of Hebrew books. He served as head of the governmental rabbinical seminary in Warsaw during its last years (1856–63). An author of many Polish books and pamphlets aimed at improving the lives of the Polish Jews, he also defended Judaism from hostile attacks.

Among his books are *Jerobaał* (Pol. 1831), and the leaflet *Koshet Imrei Emet ve-Shalom* (1844), on the attitude of Judaism toward people of other faiths. Tugendhold also wrote a Polish-Hebrew catechism titled *Ben-Yakkir* (1834) and translated into Polish *Beḥinat Olam* (1846) by *Jedaiah ha-Penini, *Vindiciae Judaeorum* (1831) by *Manasseh Ben Israel, in defense of the Jews against the blood libel, M. *Mendelssohn's *Phaedon* (1842), and other books.

[Yehuda Slutsky]

His younger brother WOLF TUGENDHOLD (1796–1864), born in Vilna, was an educator and author. In 1827 he was appointed government censor of Hebrew books at Vilna, using his office with particular severity against ḥasidic writings. His relations with the Vilna circle of *maskilim* were tenuous, as he advocated a germanizing Haskalah and had little interest in Hebrew culture. He also taught history at the rabbinical seminary in Vilna. His published works include *Der Denunziant* (1833; Heb. tr. by M.M. Bendetsohn, *Hamoser…*, 1847), a story of Jewish life in Poland; and *Der Mensch im Ebenbild Gottes* (1830).

BIBLIOGRAPHY: J. Nirnstein (ed.), *Proverbia Salomonis: Przysłowia Salomona* (1895), 1–7 (list of his works); J.L. Landau, *Short Lectures on Hebrew Literature* (1938^2), 125, 133; J. Shatzky, *Geshikhte fun Yidn in Varshe* (1947–53), index to each volume; A. Levinson, *Toledot Yehudei Varshah* (1953), 117–8; Kressel, Leksikon, 2 (1967), 10; B. Weinryb, in: MSWJ, 77 (1933), 280ff.

°**TUKA, VOJTECH** (1880–1946), prime minister of Slovakia during World War II and one of those responsible for the deportations of Slovak Jewry. A professor of law at Pecs and later at Bratislava University, Tuka became secretary of the separatist Slovak People's Party and editor of its publication *Slovak* after World War I. He adopted a strong anti-Czech line, collaborated with the Hungarian Irredenta movement, and in 1923 established the fascist Rodobrana ("Homeguard"). In 1929 he was found guilty of high treason by a Czechoslovak court. In the pre-Munich days Tuka renewed his activity in the pro-German radical wing of the People's Party led by Hlinka. He became the ideologist of "independent" Slovakia, its prime minister (1939–44) and foreign minister (from 1940). Tuka acted as the moving spirit behind the persecution of the Jews, negotiating with the Germans for the deportations of Slovak Jewry and collaborating fully with Hitler and his officials in the "Final Solution." He opposed intervening against the expulsion of the Slovak Jews. He was condemned to death by the National Tribunal of Bratislava but died before the sentence could be carried out.

BIBLIOGRAPHY: J. Lettrich, *History of Modern Slovakia* (1956), index; L. Rothkirchen, *Ḥurban Yahadut Slovakia* (1961), index, (incl. Eng. summary); O.J. Neumann, *Be-Ẓel ha-Mavet* (1958), passim.

[Livia Rothkirchen]

TUKUMS (Ger. **Tuckum**), city in Zemgale province, Latvia. In 1800 Tukums had a Jewish population of 272, of whom 17 were merchants. Records from the following year show that the Jewish community had a rabbi, a *ḥevra kaddisha*, a community council, and a minute-book (**pinkas*). In the late 1897 census Tukums showed a Jewish population of 2,561 (34% of the total population). After World War I there were 597 Jews in Tukums (13.4%) in 1920; 968 (12.6%) in 1930; and 953 (11.7%) in 1935. Most of the Jews were shopkeepers and artisans. Members of the Lichtenstein family served for several generations as rabbis in Tukums. In the summer of 1941 Tukums was occupied by the Germans. The Jews of the town, with those of surrounding smaller communities, were then all driven into the local synagogue and burned. Early in 1961 the synagogue of Tukums was closed by the authorities after pressure to resign had been brought to bear on its board. The Torah scrolls, religious articles, and hundreds of books were removed to the Riga synagogue.

In the late 1960s the Jewish population of Tukums was estimated at about 750, but it dwindled as a result of emigration and Soviet repression.

[Joseph Gar]

TULCHIN, city in Vinnitsa district, Ukraine. A Jewish community is first mentioned in 1648 when Tulchin was conquered by the Cossack forces of *Chmielnicki, who massacred the Jews of the town and those of the surroundings who had sought refuge in the fortress of Tulchin, as well as the Poles who were there at the time. According to two varying, widely circulated accounts the Poles betrayed the Jews to the Cossacks after fighting them together, but were in turn massacred by their common enemy in Tulchin. The massacre of Tulchin was the subject of a play written by the Jewish-Russian author N. *Minski under the title *Osada Tulchina* ("The Siege of Tulchin," in the monthly *Voskhod*, 1889). Shalom *Asch in his tale *Kiddush ha-Shem* (Eng., 1926) and A.S. *Friedberg in part III of his *Zikhronot le-Veit David* also wrote on the massacre of Tulchin. After the rebellion the Jewish settlement of Tulchin was renewed, but in 1743 and 1768 the community was again attacked by the *Haidamacks. In 1765 there were 452 Jews in Tulchin. At the end of the 18th century the *ẓaddik* R. Baruch, the grandson of *Israel b. Eliezer Ba'al Shem Tov, lived in Tulchin. The number of Jews in Tulchin increased during the 19th century, and with 10,055 Jews in 1897 formed 62% of the total population. During the civil war in the Ukraine at the end of World War I the Jews of Tulchin were attacked several times; the most severe pogroms took place on July 1, 1919, when about 170 Jews were massacred. In 1926 there were 7,708 Jews in Tulchin (44.3% of the total population). After the German occupation of the Ukraine in World War II, Tulchin was incorporated into the region of *Transnistria, which had been handed over to Romania. During the autumn of 1941 the 3,000 Jews who remained in Tulchin were transferred to the camp of Peczara. In 1959 there were about 2,500 Jews in Tulchin (21% of the total population). The last synagogue was closed by the authorities in 1959.

BIBLIOGRAPHY: J. Gurland, *Le-Korot ha-Gezerot al Yisrael* (1887–89); M. Litinski, *Tsu der Geshikhte fun Yudn in Podolien* (1888), 420–1; A.D. Rosenthal, in: *Reshummot*, 3 (1923), 399–401; idem, *Megillat ha-Tevaḥ*, pt. 3 (1931), 57–60; N.N. Hannover, *Yeven Meẓulah* (1945), 40–43; M. Osherowitch, *Shtet un Shtetlekh in Ukraine*, 1 (1948), 9–21; Y. Heilperin, in: *Zion*, 25 (1960), 22–27; PK Romanyah, 1 (1969), 443–4.

[Yehuda Slutsky]

ṬŪL KARM, Arab town in Ereẓ Israel 9 mi. (15 km.) E. of Netanyah. According to archaeological evidence, the place was inhabited in the Roman period. The Arabic name is derived from the Aramaic Tur Karma (טוּר כַּרְמָא) so-called by its *Samaritan inhabitants who constituted the majority of its population in the Middle Ages. Over the last few centuries, Ṭūl Karm was a small place, but expanded in the 20th century when through traffic increased, particularly with the building of a highway along the eastern rim of the Sharon and the construction of the Haifa-Lydda railway line. The planting of citrus groves and progress in other local farm branches also favorably affected its growth. Ṭūl Karm's development slackened somewhat in the 1930s when a main highway was completed further west, between Petaḥ Tikvah and Ḥaderah. In the armistice agreement with Jordan (1949), Ṭūl Karm was in Jordanian territory and the border was so drawn that it was separated from the railway and from certain landholdings. Nevertheless, the town resumed its growth as farming and administrative services provided new employment opportunities. A farm school was established in the 1920s through a contribution by Sir Elly *Kadoorie. Ṭūl Karm was taken by

Israeli forces in the *Six-Day War (June 7, 1967). According to the census of the fall of 1967, the town had 10,157 inhabitants, all of whom were Muslim Arabs, except for 103 Christians. Of the total, 5,020 lived in a refugee camp. The town's economy continued to be based mainly on intensive farming. In the wake of the Oslo II Agreement of September 1995, Ṭūl Karm was transferred to the jurisdiction of the *Palestinian Authority. In 1997 its population was 33,921, of whom 31.4% were refugees.

[Efraim Orni]

TUMARKIN, IGAEL (1933–), sculptor and painter. Tumarkin was born in Dresden, Germany, the son of Berta Gurevitch and Martin Hellberg, a German theater actor and director. His mother and his stepfather, Herzl Tumarkin, raised Tumarkin in Israel from the age of two. In 1955–57, after his service in the navy, Tumarkin traveled to Europe. In East Berlin he met his father and worked as a set designer for Bertolt Brecht's Berliner Ensemble. The sculptors Rudy Lehman and Itzhak *Danziger influenced his turn to the medium of sculpture, and his first iron sculptures appeared in the summer of 1956.

The landscape of the desert also inspired him. Tumarkin created reliefs made from sand using a unique spraying method. Through the 1960s Tumarkin turned to assemblage techniques and his sculptures were created from the junk of Israeli ships, weapons, and machines. Over time the weapons became integrated into figurative sculptures of males and females made from casts taken from show window mannequins (*He Walked in the Fields*, 1967, Tel Aviv Museum of Art).

Tumarkin's visits to New York in the mid-1970s influenced the composition of his sculptures. They became horizontal as counterpoints to the skyward orientation of modern architecture. The use of glass reflecting the environment was also based on the urban landscape. In 1974–75 he completed his monument dedicated to the Holocaust and renewal in Tel Aviv. With his interest in earth architecture he traveled to Egypt, Tunisia, Morocco, Senegal, and elsewhere. The works created under the inspiration of these trips were made of iron, earth, and fabric. The subject matter dealt with nature, religion, sacrifices, and the connection among them (*Bedouin Crucifixion*, 1982, Israel Museum, Jerusalem).

Iron became Tumarkin's main material, and from the 1990s he improved his technique, shaping the iron by himself at a temperature of 1200 degrees using heavy tools in a process that required the utmost concentration.

Tumarkin's sculptures were placed all over the world and he gained international recognition. In Israel he was one of the dominant figures in modern Israeli art. A feature of his art is its connection to the history of the country. Israeli ideals, wars, and the social situation were all part of his artistic content. The fact that his art involved controversial political statements created enormous objection to his being awarded the Israel Prize in 2004.

BIBLIOGRAPHY: Jerusalem, Israel Museum, *To Paint a Mustache on the Zamir – Igael Tumarkin New Works* (1999); Tel Aviv, Tel Aviv Museum of Art, *Tumarkin Sculptures 1957–1992* (1992); Tel Aviv, Tel Aviv Museum of Art, *Tumarkin Prints 1962–1991* (1992).

[Ronit Steinberg (2nd ed.)]

TUMIN, MELVIN MARVIN (1919–1994), U.S. sociologist. Born in Newark, New Jersey, Tumin first taught at Wayne State University, Detroit, and from 1947 was professor of sociology and anthropology at Princeton. Tumin specialized in race and intercultural relations. His book *Desegregation: Resistance and Readiness* (1958), based on survey data from Guilford County, North Carolina, is a careful account of a white population's attitude toward the American black.

Among his other works are *Social Class and Social Change in Puerto Rico* (1961), *Education, Social Class and Intergroup Attitudes in England, France and Germany* (1964), *Social Stratification: The Forms and Functions of Inequity* (1967), *Patterns of Society* (1973), and *Caste in a Peasant Society* (1975). In all these investigations, Tumin emphasized the correlation between social structure and intergroup attitudes. He was a consultant on race and intergroup relations to the Anti-Defamation League of B'nai B'rith, for which he wrote *An Inventory and an Appraisal of Research on American Anti-Semitism* (1961) and edited *Race and Intelligence: An Evaluation* (1963). Tumin also edited *The Research Annual on Intergroup Relations* of the A.D.L.

[Werner J. Cahnman]

TUNIS, TUNISIA, country in N. Africa between *Libya and *Algeria. After their conquest of the country, the Romans named it Provincia Africa, Africa Propria, or, more generally, Africa. Roman Africa included, in addition to the territories of present-day Tunisia, a large stretch of Algeria's territory to the west, which was called Numidia, and Libya's coast to the east.

Second Temple Period

As many scholars have often assumed, it is probable that Jews lived in Punic *Carthage; a Judeo-African legend has it that the Jews came to the island in the southeast (e.g., in the island of *Djerba (Jerba)) in King Solomon's time. Another legend relates that the kohanim, escaping from Jerusalem in the year 70 C.E., carried one of the Temple's doors to the island, and it is believed to be walled in the synagogue called *Ghriba* (the wondrous). However, there is no factual evidence positively stating that Jews lived in Punic Carthage or its territories. The "*Tarshish" of the Bible has nevertheless been identified with Carthage by the Septuagint and the Aramaic Targum of the prophets. On the other hand, for the Arab authors of the Middle Ages, Carthage – later confused with Tunis – has always been synonymous with "Tarshish." The Talmud echoes ancient traditions regarding the connection between, on the one hand, Punic Africa and Canaan's country and the Jewish world of Ereẓ Israel, on the other.

Under Roman rule the province of Africa included many Jewish communities whose existence has been proven by numerous texts and archaeological findings. From Cyrenaica to *Morocco a series of Jewish communities have left their landmarks in these countries. Their center was Africa Propria, whose living conditions were well known in ancient rabbinic literature. The most important of these communities was Latin Carthage which from the second to the fourth centuries C.E. was the home of such sages as R. Ḥinna, R. Ḥanan, R. Isaac, and R. Abba, who are mentioned in the Talmud. A great number of Jewish lamps and many epitaphs, mostly written in Latin and accompanied by the seven-branched *menorah*, which were discovered in the cemeteries of Carthage, Marsa, Byrsa, or Gamarth, bear witness to the existence of a large population of the Jewish faith in Carthage. The extension of the Jewish necropolis at Gamarth indicates the importance of the community against which, Tertullian, who knew it intimately, wrote a special treatise (c. 200–06). Later, St. Cyprian, St. Augustine, and many other Christian authors of Africa Propria wrote against their Jewish fellow countrymen and the numerous Judaizing sects of ancient Tunisia.

Jews and Judaizers were widely scattered throughout the entire country, especially at Naro on the Hammam-Lif beach where a magnificent synagogue stood, the ruins of which are well known; at Hippo-Diarrhytus (present-day Bizerta), whose governor at the time of the Arab conquest was, according to the historian al-Qayrawānī, a Jew; at Utica; at Simittu (present-day Chemtou); at Hadrumetum (present-day Sousse); and at Henchir-Gouana, west of the site where the present-day Kairouan was to be built. On the Libyan littoral, included in Africa Propria, there was a Jewish community at Oea (present-day Tripoli); at Leptis Magna (present-day Lebda); and at Locus Judeorum Augusti, also called Scina (Iscina), whose Jews were among those sent by the Romans as slaves from Ereẓ Israel to Africa after the war of 70. After they were set free, they settled in areas granted to them by the Romans. Inland, according to Ibn Khaldūn, the tribe of Nefusa practiced the Jewish faith before the Arab conquest. It is known that there were Jewish communities in Numidia – which also belonged to Carthage – at Hippo Regius (present-day Bone), at Cirta (Constantine), and at Henchir-Fouara, not far from Souk-Ahras, the center of nomadic Jews called Baḥusim under Arab rule. Concentrations of Jews were also found at Thusurus (the present-day Tozeur), as well as Jewish tribes who lived before the Arab rule in the mountains of Aurès.

Living and economic conditions of Jews in Africa seem to have been satisfactory during the Roman era and before Christianity's triumph. In Carthage especially, the luxury of the decorations of most of the hypogea in the Jewish cemeteries of Gamarth bear witness to the prosperity of the community and to the wealth of certain families. It seems that most of the island Jews were engaged in agriculture. In the harbors many Jews were involved in maritime trade: trade relations between Rome and North Africa were of exceptional importance owing to the transport of foodstuffs to Rome, and later on also to Constantinople. This trade – as much evidence indicates – was almost completely in the hands of African Jews

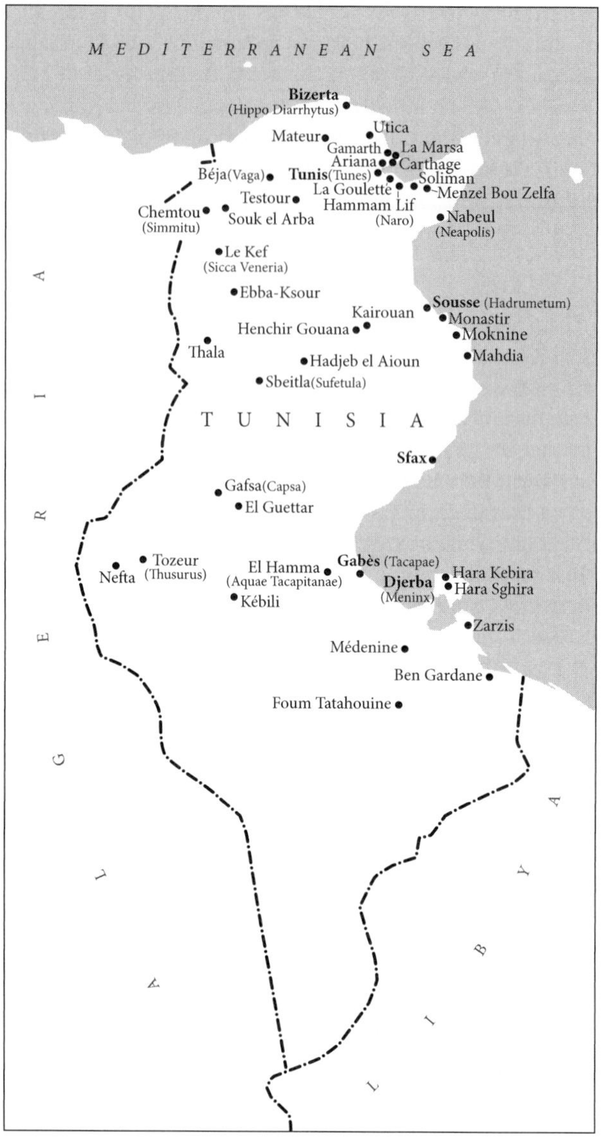

Jewish communities in Tunisia. Names in boldface indicate those still in existence in 1971.

who lived in Rome on Mount Colius, in a special district between the Coliseum and the Appian Way. Jews were entrusted with the transport of foodstuffs destined for Rome (*annona urbis*), which consisted mainly of cereals and olive oil; at that time Africa was the main producer in the Mediterranean; they were then called *navicularii*. One of the main tasks of these Jewish owners of big vessels was to engage in transport for state requirements, for which they received official honors in Africa Propria, as elsewhere. Jewish *navicularii* formed a separate corporate body. When the Roman Empire became Christian, the state took advantage of the Jewish ship owners and misused them so that their task became an overwhelming burden. Mass arrivals of Jews to Africa were mainly the aftermath of the disasters they were subject to in Ereẓ Israel, Egypt, and Cyrenaica from 70 to 118 C.E.

Their number increased as a consequence of the intense proselytic propaganda to which they dedicated themselves, first among the descendants of the Punics, then among the Berbers. The situation of the Jews facing Christians changed considerably after the time of Constantine, when triumphant Christianity became persecutor in Africa as elsewhere. When the Vandals dominated Africa Propria, the Jews were better treated but little is known about their true condition during that era. There is more information about their condition during the Byzantine period. In pursuance of the edicts of 535, applied by *Justinian at the same time to the Christian heretics, Jews were excluded from all public office, their worship outlawed, all meetings prohibited, and their synagogues transformed into churches. By the emperor's order the Jews of Borion, on Cyrenaica's frontiers, were forcibly converted, but toward the end of the sixth century the Byzantine administration slowly let the strictness of its rules lapse.

The persecutions by Justinian contributed to the expansion of African Judaism. Tracked down and sometimes even expelled, many Jews took refuge with the Berbers of the mountains and of the desert where they doubtlessly met coreligionists who had already settled there. In those regions the newcomers again took up their propaganda. This is probably how the great Judaized Berber tribes of Africa Propria were established, especially the Jarrāwas of the Aurès Mountains and the Nafūsas of Libya. According to some scholars other Jews left Africa for *Sicily and southern Italy. After the Arab conquest this latent immigration – started under Justinian – took the form of mass flight for the Jews of the African coast.

Tunisia under Arab Rule (to the Advent of the Hafsid)

The Arab conquest of this part of the world began in 643 when they took *Tripoli, but it did not take on a permanent aspect until the foundation of *Kairouan in 670. The resistance of the Byzantines rapidly decreased as the Berbers withstood the conquerors stubbornly. The *Berber leader Kusayla was a Christian. After having gained control of Kairouan in 688, he was defeated and killed. *Kāhina, who according to certain sources was a Jewess and whose life is surrounded in legends, then reigned over the powerful Jarrāwa tribe in the Aurès. Ibn Khaldun asserts that the Jarrāwas were Jewish. After the death of Kusayla, Kāhina – followed by all the Berbers – directed the military operations. A new Arab chief, Ḥassān ibn Nuʿmān, received a mighty army from the caliph *Abd al-Malik. Ḥassān seized Carthage and its inhabitants, doubtless including a number of Jews, and sailed for the islands of the Mediterranean. Kāhina advanced with her Jarrāwas on the Arab army, which she overwhelmed near Tebessa and drove out of Ifrīqiya. The Berbers then lived in security for a few years; once Ḥassān ibn Nuʿmān had received reinforcements, he launched another offensive in 702. Moreover, the Arabs found allies among the Greek inhabitants of the towns as well as the Berber farmers, who were opposed to Kāhina because she had destroyed their crops in order to prevent them from falling into the hands of the invaders. The old queen fought a desperate battle against Ḥassān ibn Nuʿmān but her army was beaten and pursued into the Aurès Mountains. In the wake of a second battle Kāhina was killed and her head was sent to the caliph ʿAbd al-Malik as a trophy. With the death of this woman, who was called the "Berber Deborah," the period of heroic defense was brought to a close.

The Arabs then subordinated the whole of North Africa. The "people of the Book" (see *Ahl al-Kitāb) and the Christians were authorized to live under their domination upon the condition that they paid the **jizya* (an annual poll tax, sometimes called also in the Maghreb (as elsewhere) *jawāli*, the tax of the expellees; see **Galut*). Although the Berbers converted to *Islam, they were also compelled to pay these levies. The demands of the Arabs soon incited large-scale revolt. In Ifrīqiya an Arab governor, Ibrāhīm ibn al-Aghlab, established the dynasty of the *Aghlabids, which reigned from 800 to 909. There is evidence that from this period important groups of Jews were found particularly in the towns, where the revenue of their poll tax constituted an appreciable income for the state. They coexisted peacefully with the Muslim masses. Muslim scholars maintained friendly relations with Jewish scholars and important Muslim merchants and ship owners were content to trade with their Jewish colleagues. Under the Aghlabids, their successors the *Fatimids (Fātimids), and the Zīrids, until the invasions of Ifrīqiya by the Bedouin in the mid-11th century, an exceptional prosperity was enjoyed, which was followed by a period in which remarkable intellectual activity prevailed. The Jews played an important role in this progress. In Kairouan, the leading city of an immense empire, there were famous yeshivot which were headed by eminent scholars who for a long time maintained relations with the **geonim* of the academies of *Sura, *Pumbedita, and Palestine. Shortly after the city's foundation the *Umayyad caliph of Damascus had 1,000 families – which are thought to have been Jewish – transferred from *Egypt to Kairouan. It was there that Isaac Israeli, the most famous physician of his day, studied in about 900. He became the private physician of the last of the Aghlabids, Ziyādat-Allah III, and held the same position under the first of the Fatimid caliphs, the mahdī ʿUbaydallah. The most famous of Israeli's disciples was *Dunash ibn Tamīm, who, like his teacher, left a number of valuable works including a treatise on astronomy which refuted the principles of astrology, a commentary on the *Sefer Yeẓirah*, and a textbook on Hebrew grammar. Jewish scholars who possessed a wide, profound, and diversified knowledge – as was customary in the Middle Ages – flourished in Ifrīqiya. In addition to Kairouan they were to be found in such important communities as al-Mahdiya and Gabès. Outstanding among the talmudists in Tunisia were the scholars of the Ibn Shahūn family: R. Nissim, his son Jacob to whom R. Sherira and R. Hai addressed their famous *Iggeret* (responsum concerning the history of the Oral Tradition), and his grandson *Nissim, author of many talmudic treatises. Not less important was R. Ḥushi'el (one of the *Four Captives), and especially his son R. *Hananel. The leading family of scholars in Mahdiya was the

Ibn Sīghmār (or Zūghmār), four generations of which served as *dayyanim*. But according to Abraham ibn Daud (*Sefer ha-Kabbalah*, 77–8) after the demise of R. Hananel and R. Nissim, the talmudic learning came to an end in Ifriqīya. Ibn Daud did not hold in high esteem later scholars in Mahdiya and in Galʿat Hammad.

From the thousands of documents preserved in the Cairo **Genizah* and recently studied it is particularly evident that the class of Jewish-Tunisian businessmen (which was also – as was almost always the case in North Africa – the intellectual class) was a factor of considerable importance at this time not only in Tunisia but also throughout the Mediterranean countries. The importance of these other merchants, whether indigenous or from places in the Maghreb – but who often established themselves in Tunisia – lay in the decisive role they played in the trade with *India and their dominant position in the trade of the western Mediterranean. A large number of the leading and most active merchants in Egypt – in Fostat, *Alexandria, the large textile centers of Bushir and Tinnis, and the smaller localities where flax and indigo were grown – were Tunisian Jews who stayed in the country or had recently established themselves there; their families generally remained in Tunisia. Others lived in *Aden or even further away, as in India.

Jewish *Jerusalem of the 11th century was also inhabited by many Jews from the Maghreb. The majority of the Jews of *Sicily, which had been conquered by the Muslim natives of Tunisia from the ninth century, were Tunisians. Their extensive activity on the island – in *Palermo, *Messina, and later *Syracuse – was felt as far as in northern *Italy and *Spain to the west. The principal goods which the Jews exported from Tunisia were linen and cotton textiles of every category, which they themselves occasionally manufactured, especially in the large industrial center of Sousse. Silk cloth and valuable brocades were also exported. Their carpets, manufactured in Tunis, Sfax, or Gafsa, and the canopies of Gabès, well-known in the Middle Ages, were much sought after. They exported many metals: copper from *Morocco, Spanish tin, lead, and mercury. The reexport of Spanish and Sicilian silks was practiced on a large scale. The agricultural products exported by the Jews included primarily olive oil and its by-product soap, beeswax, almonds, saffron, and occasionally wheat. They sent salted tunny (fish) to Egypt. One of their main exports was raw or tanned hides; they also exported coral, which was found abundantly along the African coasts, and all kinds of ornaments which were made from them. Finally, books, written in Hebrew in Kairouan, were a very important item in the export trade to the west.

The Jews of Ifrīqiya imported spices of every kind, Oriental perfumes, indigo, walnut peel for its dyes and varnishes, sugar, medicinal drugs and plants, jewelry, precious stones, and pearls. The most important import, however, was Egyptian linen. All these goods were mainly transported by sea. The Jews of Tunisia were occasionally ship owners or partners in this trade. The ships, however, were generally owned by the government or members of the royal family, who maintained excellent relations with the Jews and entrusted them with the administration of their wealth. This enormous traffic was largely controlled by powerful Jewish families. These families, only about 20 in number, were large, wealthy, and influential. They organized into clans, contracted marriages among themselves, and were also related to the distinguished families of other countries. Rivalry existed to a degree among these clans; thus, members of the family Majjāni (originally from Majzāna) were the antagonists of the powerful Tāhertis (from Tāherē), who were related by marriage to the Berakhias – all leading clans of merchants who also produced eminent scholars and community leaders especially known from the responsa of the *geonim* of Iraq. On their part, the Majjānis considered the Ben Allans their implacable adversaries. Whether they were related by blood or by marriage, or were enemies, other important families dominated the Tunisian trade. These included the Ibn Sighmārs (Zūghmār) of Mahdiya, the Nahrāys, among whom there were also prominent scholars and others who lived in the same centers.

It can be said that in general the Jews of Tunisia enjoyed a life of ease. Yet, among the masses as well as among the aristocracy – even among a number of scholars – there was such an exaggerated passion for music that the *gaon* *Hai addressed his famous responsa against instrumental music to the communities of Gabès and Kairouan. The Tunisian Jews also manifested a misguided enthusiasm for perfumes and some extravagance in their dress. Great prosperity obviously prevailed, and in spite of their status of **dhimmī*, their condition was excellent. They did not suffer from persecutions until about 1057, when Kairouan was destroyed by hordes of Arabs, and about 1087, when they were among the victims of the Christians who came from Italy and attacked Mahdiya and other coastal towns. On these occasions the Jews suffered the same fate as their Muslim compatriots. The Arab invasion of the 11th century marked the end of the golden era of the Jews of Ifrīqiya.

In 698 Ḥassān ibn Nuʿmān chose Tunis, a small and ancient townlet, to replace the fallen capital of Carthage, but it never attained the importance of Kairouan. In time, after the invasion of the Bedouins, it succeeded together with Mahdiya in overshadowing Kairouan. On the other hand, the closed towns of the coast escaped the Arab peril only to fall into the hands of the Christians. Roger II the Norman, who had conquered Sicily, attacked the coast of Ifrīqiya (1118–27) and seized the island of *Djerba (1134), Gabès, Sfax, and Sousse (1148), as well as Mahdiya (1156), in all of which there were important Jewish communities. It does not, however, appear that the Jews of all these ports suffered extensively under Norman rule. Those of Tunis, who were governed by the small and tolerant Banu-Khorassan dynasty, continued to control the large maritime trade of Tunisia. In 1159 the *Almohads invaded Tunisia. When they conquered Tunis, they confronted both Jews and Christians with the alternative of conversion to Islam or death. Other communities, also, suffered heavily as a result of this conquest. Thus, according to ancient additions to the famous elegy of Abraham *Ibn Ezra, the communities of Mahdiya, Sousse, Gafsa, al-Hamma, Gabès, Djerba, and the town of Tripolitania shared the same fate. Many Jews converted, while others fled and dispersed throughout the country or chose to die as martyrs. In the wake of this catastrophe, the strength of Ifrīqiya Jewry was impaired for a long period, and its social organization, economic situation, and intellectual and religious conditions greatly declined. In a letter attributed to *Maimonides, who left North Africa in 1165, it is said that between Tunis and Egypt, including Djerba, the standard of the Jews was very low. If this letter is authentic, it at least proves the presence of Jews in Tunisia who were able to remain there from 1165 onward.

Hafsid (Ḥafṣid) Rule (1228–1534)

In 1228 the governor of Ifrīqiya, Abu Zakariya, severed relations with the Almohad caliph of *Marrakesh, and in 1236 proclaimed himself emir and chose Tunis as his capital. It appears that from then onward many Jews who had been forced to convert were able to return to Judaism; from that date they lived under relatively normal conditions together with those who had fled from the towns. At least the constant threat to their lives and property was lifted. The synagogues, which were closed under the Almohads, were reopened. Although the Jewish communities of Ifrīqiya did not in general enjoy their former prosperity, a class of important merchants, which appears to have survived the Almohad conquest, succeeded in reassuming its earlier position. They resumed their maritime trade immediately after the consolidation of Almohad rule – well before the advent of the Hafsids. There is a mention in Maimonides' responsa of a Jew from Egypt who traveled to Tunis in the course of his affairs. The reign of Abu Zakariya and his successors was propitious, and the Jews of Tunisia once more developed their trade. In 1227 a detainer was lodged against them in a commercial lawsuit by the podesta of Pisa. In 1239 the Jews of Djerba established a colony in Sicily. Frederick II granted them a concession to cultivate indigo, which had until then been imported from the Orient, as well as henna, which only Tunisia supplied to Italy. The royal palm plantation near Palermo was also given to them as a concession. In 1257 the Jews of *Barcelona, who maintained permanent relations with their coreligionists on the Barbary Coast, demanded diplomatic intervention in Tunis so as to render their trade with Ifrīqiya more profitable. The expenses of the mission were included in the taxes which were paid by the Jewish community. From that time excellent relations existed between the king of Aragon and the Hafsid sultan, who recommended to Pedro III a considerable number of his Jewish subjects wishing to settle in Majorca and Catalonia (see *Spain). The king then granted them privileges and favors. Other Jews of Ifrīqiya established themselves in the Aragon states, having been encouraged to do so by Pedro III, who granted safe conduct to Ḥayon b. ʿAmar, Isaac b. Bul-Faraj, Ismael Ḥazzān, and the astronomer Isaac *Nifoci (Nafusi) among others.

There was constant movement of Jews between the Barbary Coast and the Aragon states (see *Spain), and they became useful and even indispensable intermediaries. The monarchy of Aragon maintained excellent relations with the Jews of southeastern Ifrīqiya; moreover, the king of Aragon showed special concern for the Jews of the Barbary Coast and accorded them particularly advantageous facilities to establish themselves in the Aragon states. In 1285 the Hafsid sovereign sent a delegation to Pedro III requesting that he grant the concession of all the *funduqs* (marts) which belonged to him in Tunis to one of his Jewish subjects, Solomon b. Zahit – probably one of his favorites. For a period of two years Solomon b. Zahit was able to appropriate for himself one half of the income of these *funduqs*, through which the majority of the goods imported from Europe passed in transit. A Jew of Djerba was entrusted with the proposal and the payment of a ransom of 14,000 dinars for the liberation of the Muslim ruler of the island, which was occupied by the Catalonians from 1286 until about 1335. Djerba then became the center of the trade between Catalonia and Ifrīqiya and Jews played the leading role in it. In 1308, when James II of Majorca decided to wage war against Tunisia, the goods of his Jewish subjects in Tunisia were seized by the Hafsid *makhzan*. All trade with Tunisia was prohibited, but the Jews, who had tremendous interests in Ifrīqiya, disapproved of this measure. As a result the Jewish community of Majorca did not contribute to the equipping of the fleet which was sent against Tunisia. A short while later, when negotiations were opened in order to resume cordial relations with the Hafsid state, a prominent Jewish merchant, Maimon b. Nono, assisted James III of Majorca's ambassador in the negotiations which led to the peace treaty of July 1329. In Tunis the collector of custom duties, an important official, was often a Jew. In 1330 Joseph Assusi, who held this position and was zealous in upholding the interests of his sovereign, sought to impose additional taxes on the Catalonian Christians and his Jewish coreligionists.

Alongside of these influential businessmen the Jewish masses engaged in peddling. These petty tradesmen carried textiles, leather, spices, and other goods from one village or hamlet to another; others joined caravans which went deep into the desert. A number were exceedingly wealthy and a very important factor in the trans-Sahara trade of Tunisia. Though its volume and importance could not be compared to the scope of that of the kingdoms of Tlemcen and *Morocco, they nevertheless greatly enriched the Hafsid sovereigns and their subjects. The Jews of Ifrīqiya thus earned their livelihood almost exclusively from their economic activity, a situation which prevailed throughout the Hafsid period and also later. However, there were probably also a number of physicians, and aside from their religious officials the Jews also had a few representatives in other liberal professions. They hardly engaged in manual occupations, with the exception of those connected with precious metals, an ancient Jewish craft in North Africa.

The great anti-Jewish persecution which broke out in Spain in 1391 deeply affected North African Jewry. The Jewish emigration from Spain which followed this persecution was largely directed to the Barbary Coast. The eastern towns of Ifrīqiya, which form part of present-day Tunisia, received only a limited number of these emigrants. Their influx was felt to the greatest extent, in quality and quantity, in the territory of the kingdom of *Tlemcen. Many of the emigrants originated in the countries to which they now turned. In Tunisia, hostility which prevailed against the newcomers and their coreligionists who had left the country, was unknown. The influence of Jews of Catalonia and Majorca does not seem to have been as appreciable in Tunisia as in Algeria where more backward communities had benefited from their contact with the newcomers. Even so, Tunis, Sousse, and Bizerta, as well as the communities of the central Maghreb, often turned for orientation and leadership to Algiers, the center of such outstanding rabbis as R. *Isaac b. Sheshet Perfet and the *Duran family.

There were a number of rabbis and *dayyanim* in the communities of eastern Ifrīqiya. Although they were not as numerous, and especially not as influential, as those of the western part of the country – in Miliana, Bougie, Bône, or *Constantine – there were nevertheless some outstanding scholars among them, such as the *dayyan* of Tenes, Samuel Ḥakim, who was native born and had studied astronomy under the Spanish immigrant Abraham b. Nathan; the learned Isaac of Tunis; and the financier Ḥayyim Méllili, who was also from Tunis and corresponded with R. Simeon b. Ẓemaḥ *Duran. Occasionally however, such important towns as Tunis found themselves without a rabbi-*dayyan* and were compelled to seek them elsewhere. Although the Hafsids decreed that newcomers would not be taxed to the same extent as the native Jews, the number of immigrants does not appear to have increased. The local Jews always constituted a majority in Ifrīqiya. It seems that the interpreters and translators who maintained the contacts between the native Arab dynasty and the European authorities in the cities and ports were recruited from among Jewish immigrants. Such one seems to be Moses, who in 1267 was interpreter into Arabic for the Genoese merchants who had settled in Tunis. In 1421 a Jew, Abraham, was entrusted with the translation from Arabic into Italian of the peace treaty which had been concluded between *Florence and Tunis. In 1485 Abraham Fava drew up the Latin version of the Tunis-Genoa treaty.

European Jews were also raised to the rank of ambassador in the foreign relations of the Hafsids. In 1400 the physician *Bondavin was entrusted with a diplomatic mission to the king of Aragon; in 1409 Samuel and Eli Sala negotiated the peace treaty between Sicily and Tunis, which they signed themselves. The above examples of Jews who played an important role in the political life of Ifrīqiya were rare under the Hafsids. Even though Tunisia did not have eminent Jewish statesmen like those who flourished in Morocco during the same period, the community was at least spared bloody pogroms such as were perpetrated in *Fez at the beginning and the end of the Merenid dynasty (1269–1465).

The legal status of the Jews in the Hafsid State conformed to the legislation pertaining to the **dhimmi*, which tolerated and protected the "people of the Book" but at the same time looked upon them as inferior to Muslims. As in all Islamic countries, the Hafsids subjected the *dhimmi* to a number of restrictions: they imposed the payment of special taxes and, at the whim of the sovereign or his representatives, the obligation to wear distinctive garments or signs. As elsewhere, the *jizya* was the characteristic levy which was imposed on the *dhimmi*. Only rabbis who had achieved a degree of fame were exempted by the Hafsid government from its payment. The government also extorted arbitrary payments from the Jewish communities on fixed dates, or as exceptional measures. This category of imposition was known as *qānūn*. The community, in the person of its leaders, was responsible for its payment. The Jews of the Hafsid State were compelled as a matter of principle to distinguish themselves from the Muslims by the color of their clothes or the donning of a distinctive sign. The severity of the application of these laws varied widely. The decree of the Almohad al-Manṣūr which stipulated that the Jews were to wear a special costume and a distinctive sign called a *shikla* fell into disuse with time. In 1250 the Hafsid al-Mustanṣir reimposed this discriminatory measure. As late as 1470 the Jews of Tunis still wore special dress and displayed a piece of yellow cloth on their head or neck. At the same time, the Jews of the Hafsid State were not affected by any official impediment to their rights of ownership. They freely acquired and sold real estate everywhere, including houses which they erected, and thus were occasionally important landowners. They could also own non-Muslim slaves. The government authorities strictly protected the Jewish communities of Ifrīqiya, where anti-Jewish outbreaks of violence were unknown. In spite of the difference of religion and the feeling of contempt which was often expressed by the Muslim masses toward Jews, commercial relations were maintained on a permanent basis and both parties reaped benefits from them. Conflicts which arose were brought sometimes before the qadis. Occasionally, the qadi himself referred complicated cases to the *dayyanim* of Algiers. In fact, the rabbis of Algiers often campaigned against the exaggerated tendency of the Jews of Tunisia to resort to the tribunal of the qadi.

According to legend the Jews lived in the center of Tunis from the tenth century onward, when the Muslim mystic Sidi Mahrez founded the *Ḥāra* (*Ḥārat al-Yahūd*, i.e., the Jewish quarter of the town). In the Middle Ages the Jews concentrated themselves in a quarter of the town around one or several synagogues. On other occasions, they preferred to live in groups among the Muslim population. Foreign Jewish merchants used to live in a special *funduq* in Tunis.

The Jewish communities were granted official recognition and enjoyed a wide measure of administrative and cultural autonomy. They were headed by "notables" (*gedolei ha-kahal, ziknei ha-kahal*) who were – as in Morocco – a plutocratic oligarchy. This was in contrast to the leaders (*ne'emanim*) of the communities of Spanish or *Leghorn (Italy) origin – to be later established in the country – who were elected by all the members of the community. The *gedolei ha-kahal* were entrusted with the management of charitable funds, while others known as *parnasim* or *gizbarim* were responsible for the administration of the synagogues and religious funds. They held these functions – which were often financially burdensome – on an honorary basis and were referred to with confidence. The notables were headed by the *zekan ha-Yehudim* (elder of the Jews), who under Ottoman rule assumed the title of *qa'id*. This eminent personality was always feared when he was nominated by the sovereign and loved and respected when he was chosen by his coreligionists. He was always a native of the country, because, in the first place, he exercised his control over the destinies of the communities of the native Jews; his authority, however, also included the communities of foreign born Jews. Moreover, in Tunisia the native Jews were far more numerous than their coreligionists of European origin. As a general rule the rabbis, and particularly the *dayyanim*, played a role in the administration of the community.

In the wake of the expulsions from Spain and Sicily in 1492 and from Portugal in 1497, a number of Jewish refugees took refuge in Tunisia. They do not appear to have been very numerous; furthermore, many of them were only transients. There were several scholars among these refugees, including such highly eminent personalities as the commentator on Rashi, Abraham *Levy-Bacrat, the talmudist Moses *Alashkar, and the astronomer and historian Abraham *Zacuto, who completed his *Sefer Yuḥasin* ("Book of Genealogy") while in Tunis in 1504.

Tunisia under Ottoman Rule

The anarchy which prevailed in North Africa during the late 15th and early 16th centuries facilitated the Portuguese invasions of Morocco and the Spanish invasion of Algeria and Tunisia. Only the unexpected intervention of the Ottoman Turks in the latter two countries finally spared them from Spanish occupation. In the meantime the menace of anti-Jewish Spain overshadowed the Tunisian communities. In 1515 the Spanish fleet raided Djerba and the Jews suffered extensively. In 1535 Charles v occupied Bizerta and La Goulette, their small communities being expelled or massacred. When the emperor occupied Tunis, he immediately turned the town over to his soldiers who ransacked it and massacred 70,000 persons, including a large numbers of Jews, while others were sold as slaves. Several Tunisian ports were taken, liberated, and retaken by the Spaniards until 1574, when Turkish military victories finally brought these attacks to an end. As a result of this climate of insecurity and constant danger, the Jewish communities of the coast were almost completely depleted of their members; many of them, natives and Spanish expellees, left for the Orient or Italy.

When the grand duke of Tuscany called upon the Jews to establish themselves in his ports of Pisa and Leghorn in 1593, the many Conversos and Jews from various Mediterranean countries who immediately settled there were joined by African Jews who had already taken refuge in Italy and sought a permanent home there. Leghorn thus became a large Jewish center and its trade underwent considerable expansion. The Jewish community soon sent representatives to Africa, and from the early 17th century there was a sizable number of Leghorn Jews in Tunis, where they were known as "Grana" from the Arab name for Leghorn – "Gorna." All the foreign Jews, former Marranos, or Tunisians who returned to their native country after spending one or two generations in Italy were gradually integrated among the Jews of Spanish or Sicilian origin remaining in Tunisia, as well as those who had recently arrived from Algeria or Morocco. In fact, those people who possessed a common language – Spanish or Italian – customs, and ways of life which were more or less similar were called "Granas" or "Gornim." From 1685 they designated themselves as "la nation livornese [from Leghorn] ebrea en Tunes," although many of them had never set foot in Leghorn.

From the beginning, the Jews known as "Touansa" (natives of Tunisia), who formed the overwhelming majority of the community, looked upon the "Grana" with suspicion. Although both groups lived together in the *Ḥāra* for a long time, their relations continually deteriorated until they bordered upon hatred. Indeed, in the middle of the 17th century Hamūda Pasha prohibited all the Jews, whether "Grana" or "Touansa," to own real estate; they were confined to residential quarters where they could only be tenants. As a result of overcrowding, rents soared. The rabbis then decided that anyone who was the first tenant of a house thus acquired the right of *ḥazakah* (possession). No other Jew could have the first tenant evicted by offering a higher rent. The right of *ḥazakah* remained in force for a long time among Tunisian Jews, only falling into disuse when the government of Muhammad Pasha authorized the Jews to acquire real estate in the wake of the Pacte Fondamental of 1857. The decrees which prohibited Jewish ownership of real estate or confined them to a special quarter were by no means generally observed in Tunis. In fact, after having coexisted for several generations the "Touansa" realized that they were despised by the "Grana," whose religious practices differed from their own; they subsequently assigned them special places in their synagogues, as a result of which life in common became unbearable. The "Grana" finally separated from their native-born coreligionists completely and established an independent community which possessed its own administration, cemetery, slaughterhouses, rabbinical tribunal, *dayyanim*, and chief rabbi. This secession, in 1710, prevailed until 1899 when the authorities issued a decree calling for an official merger of the two communities. From that time there was a single chief rabbi for the whole of Tunisia, one rabbinical tribunal and one slaughterhouse in each town, and a single delegation within the council of the community and the cabinet of the Tunisian government. In practice, however, the schism persisted and the authorities were compelled to issue a further decree of amalgamation in 1944.

After 1710 the "Touansa" waged a veritable holy war against the "Grana," going so far as to treat them as false Jews in light of their pride. They finally succeeded in having them expelled from the *Ḥāra*. The "Grana" then founded the *sūq al-Grana*, the commercial artery of the old part of Tunis, and opened three new synagogues and two houses of prayer, one of which was situated in the heart of the Christian quarter of that period. The struggle between the groups continued and the "Grana" of Tunis attracted every newcomer in the town to their community, whether he was of European, African, or Asian origin. Moreover, their slaughterhouses, which were more popular, also sold meat to the "Touansa," thus depriving this ancient community of a part of its meat taxes, raised for the benefit of its poor. An arrangement became imperative, and in July 1741 a *takkanah* was signed by the rabbis of the two communities under the supervision of R. Abraham Tayyib, their leader. The following agreements were reached: (1) that all Jews who had originated in Christian countries would form part of the community of the "Grana," while all those who had originated in Muslim countries would belong to the community of the "Touansa"; (2) that two-thirds of the general expenses of the community would be covered by the "Touansa" and one-third by the "Grana"; and (3) that the "Touansa" could not buy meat in the "Grana" slaughterhouses. This prohibition was not observed and had to be renewed in 1784.

The community organization of the Tunisian Jews remained unchanged for several centuries, with only a single leader, the *qa'id* of the Jews. This leader wielded extensive powers and was responsible for the collection of taxes – an honorary position of considerable importance with material advantages. He was generally a member of the ancient community. Thus, for the most part the "Touansa" dominated the "Grana." Moreover, the bey regarded both as his own subjects. This state of affairs was even maintained during the first half of the 19th century – when there was an intensified immigration of Leghorn Jews – by the inclusion of a number of clauses in the treaty signed in 1822 between Tuscany and the regency of Tunis. In fact, it was anticipated therein that Leghorn Jews who settled in the regency would always be considered and treated as subjects of the country and would enjoy the same rights as the native-born Jews. Occasionally, the authorities even adopted policies toward the ancient community differing from those for the new one, which was thus discriminated against. In 1686 the latter – through the intercession of their leaders Jacob and Raphael Lombroso, Moses Mendès Ossuna, and Jacob Luzada – requested a loan from the consul of France in order to pay a huge tax imposed on them by the Muslim authorities. They then informed the consul of the extreme poverty to which the "Leghorn nation" had been reduced. They claimed that the extortions and assassinations, both past and present, had impoverished them and that it was their intention to seek the assistance of their coreligionists of Leghorn in order to repay the loan which "with tears in their eyes, they now solicited for the love of God so as to redeem a nation and a community." Under these circumstances, as others, the "Touansa" supported the "Grana." Moreover, it was a rule among the Jews of Tunis to redeem their coreligionists who had been captured by pirates.

There were instances when a single spiritual leader headed both communities at the same time. In such a case the chief rabbi was always a native of the country or a personality whose ancestors were of African origin. There was, however, one exception: the renowned talmudist R. Isaac Lombroso, who was born in Tunis but was of Leghorn parentage. His teachers, however, were Tunisians: R. Ẓemaḥ Serfati and R. Abraham Tayeb (d. 1714), the famous "Baba Sidi" who exerted a great influence on the whole of Tunisian Jewry. The grandson of the latter, also named R. Abraham, wrote *Ḥayyei Avraham* (1826), a voluminous commentary on the Talmud accompanied by important notes on *Alfasi, *Rashi, and *Maimonides. His son R. Ḥayyim Tayeb wrote *Derekh Ḥayyim* (1826) and R. Isaac Tayeb (1830) was also the author of several valuable works. The Bordjel family were Leghorn Jews of Tunisian origin. Their ancestor, R. Abraham *Bordjel (d. 1795), was a well-known author and *dayyan* in Tunis. Members of this family ranked among the leaders of Tunisian Jewry for two centuries. The most famous, R. Elijah *Bordjel, simultaneously held the positions of chief rabbi and *qa'id* of the Jews. From 1750–1850 the Bonan family, Leghorn Jews of African origin, presided over the destinies of the "Grana" of Tunis, who were also headed by other Africans, such as members of the Darmon family. In the sphere of learning and Jewish studies all enmity between the two factions disappeared.

The authority of the rabbis of Tunis was very broad: they supervised the strict observance of religious precepts and the moral conduct of the individual, also issuing regulations pertaining to clothing and condemning the fancy of young women for elegance, jewelry, and fineries. These rabbis were widely known and were consulted from Ereẓ Israel and other countries. They were the first to abolish flogging in Tunis, substituting a heavy fine on behalf of the poor for it; they also compelled the members of all the communities to donate one tenth of their annual profits to charitable and religious institutions. Furthermore, they encouraged marriage between the "Grana" and the "Touansa." From the 17th century Tunis became an important center of Jewish learning: there was a particularly brilliant revival of the study of *Talmud and *Kabbalah. Ḥ.J.D. *Azulai, who visited Tunis in 1773, was impressed by the extensive learning and piety of Tunisian scholars, such as that of his hosts the Cohen-Tanoudjis family, among whom there were scholars and *qa'īds*. He also became acquainted with the chief rabbi of Tunis, R. Masʿud Raphael al-*Alfasi (d. 1776), author of the novellae *Mishnah de-Revuta* (1805), and his two sons, Solomon (d. 1801) and Ḥayyim (d. 1783), author of *Kerub Mimeshaḥ* (1859). In Tunis there were other eminent scholars, such as R. Uzziel Al'-Haik (*Alhayk), the author of *Mishkenot ha-Ro'im* (1760), a rabbinic code in the form of an encyclopedia which deals with every category of problem encountered in the internal and public life of the Jews of Tunisia during the 17th–18th centuries and thus constitutes a valuable source of information that is indispensable to the writing of the history of the Jews of Tunisia. R. Mordecai *Carvalho (d. 1785) was a wealthy merchant in

Tunis who devoted a large part of his life to rabbinical studies. In 1752 he was appointed rabbi of the Leghorn community and as such was widely known as a rabbinical authority. Of his works, the *To'afot Re'em* (1761), a commentary on the works of R. Elijah *Mizraḥi, is the best known. R. Abraham Boccara (d. 1879), author of *Ben Avraham* (1882), was also a leader of the "Grana."

The Jews of Tunisia occasionally played important roles in diplomatic capacities: in 1699 Judah *Cohen was sent to Holland as ambassador in order to negotiate a peace and commercial treaty; in 1702 he was the intermediary between Tunisia and the States General of the United Provinces, which ratified the secret decisions pertaining to their relations with the Barbary states. Moreover, Tunisian Jews were often appointed by the Christian powers to official positions in the capacity of interpreters or vice consuls. In 1814 Mordecai Manuel *Noah arrived in Tunis to fulfill the function of consul of the United States; upon his return he wrote a work on his travels which includes information on Tunisian Jews – yet, he never maintained relations with them as he sought to conceal his Jewish identity. It was, however, precisely because he was a Jew that the president of the United States, James Madison, relieved him of his functions. In a letter which he addressed to the president, Noah declared that his Jewish identity – when it became known in Washington – had left an unfavorable impression and he was therefore asked to leave the U.S. consulate in Tunis.

Their capacity as merchant magnates enabled the Jews of Tunisia, who were particularly well placed, to redeem Christian captives. In their trade with France, Italy, and the Orient these merchants employed bills of exchange and controlled the maritime trade in spite of the fact that the bey imposed higher export and import duties on them than on the Christians. For the latter the duty was 3% of the value of the goods, while for Jews it was 10% – reduced to 8% in the 18th century. Many Tunisian Jews were treasurers or bankers; they were employed at the mint; and it was to them that the authorities assigned the monopolies on fishing of tunny and corals and the trade in ostrich feathers, tobacco, wool, and the collection of customs duties. In 1740 the customs duties of Tunis were leased to the "Grana" for an annual payment of 80,000 piasters. In 1713 the bey sent a Jew from Bizerta to Sicily to sign a treaty on coral fishing. By this treaty the Sicilians committed themselves to bring in their haul of coral to Bizerta, where it would be sold to the Jews who had signed the treaty. From the 17th century to 1810 the Jews manufactured over 20,000 shawls of wool or silk in Tunis. More than one half of these were *tallitot*, which were sent to the Jews of *Trieste and Leghorn, from where they were exported to Poland for the religious requirements of the Jews of that country. The bey defended the interests of the Jewish merchants. In 1784 he declared war on the Republic of *Venice as it had not indemnified them for the loss of several cargoes in which the Venetian fleet was involved. Yet, during the same century the Jews of Tunis were the victims of pillaging on two occasions: in 1752 by the troops of the bey himself, when he was deposed from the throne for a time by a marabout; and in 1756 by Algerian troops who took the lives of thousands of Muslims and committed the worst outrages on Jewish women and children.

In contrast to the information on the Hafsid period, the Jews of Tunisia from the 16th century onward engaged in a variety of crafts. They were clock makers, artistic ironworkers, smelters, and joiners; others were glaziers, tailors, lace makers, shoemakers, and the only ones who worked with precious metals. They also manufactured musical instruments. Moreover, many of them were musicians, particularly on festive occasions. The members of every craft, as well as the petty tradesmen, were organized in guilds, presided over by a Muslim *amīn* (chief of the corporation) appointed by the authorities. All controversies between Jewish businessmen, industrialists, craftsmen, or workers, and all disputes over salaries, the price charged for the execution of a piece of work, and the like, were settled by three competent Jewish colleagues who were designated by their coreligionists. Occasionally the parties concerned challenged these persons and demanded the intervention of the *amīn*. The rabbis and the leaders of the community were then compelled to accept his judgment and enforce it under the threat that a ban would be issued against the parties involved if they bribed the *amīn*.

The native adult Jews of Tunisia wore a kind of small violet turban which was wound around a black skullcap, while the remainder of their dress was patterned after the Turkish fashion. During the 18th century the Leghorn Jews wore hats and wigs like the Europeans of the West. Until the beginning of the 19th century the "Grana" and a large number of "Touansa" merchants had the habit of wearing European clothes and round hats as a result of their trade, which required them to stay in Europe for various periods of time. The authorities shut their eyes to this departure from the Covenant of Omar. In the end this tolerance gave rise to abuses when a number of Jews, under the cover of their European dress, sought to evade certain obligations to which they had been subjected. The bey then decided to compel all Jews, whether "Touansa," "Grana," or foreigners, to wear a cap or a three-cornered hat. This decree was at the source of the so-called "affair of the hats" which took place in 1823 and almost caused the breaking off of diplomatic relations between Tunisia and the European states. The execution of the bey's orders was accompanied by many acts of cruelty and extortion perpetuated by the officers responsible for their application.

From the beginning of the century the Jews of Tunis manifested their approval of the French Revolution, whose armies emancipated the Jews of Europe in the name of human rights. They all wore the cockade. One of them, who appeared before the bey with this badge, received the bastinado. The Jews subsequently became ardent supporters of Napoleon and the "Grana" returned to wearing the French cockade. In order to restrain them the bey wanted to have one of them burned alive; he was only saved through the intervention of the consuls. The bey Aḥmad (1830–55) treated the Jews favorably on every occasion. When he visited the king of France, many Jews formed part of his retinue. He bestowed many honors on his Jewish private physicians, the baron Abraham Lombrozo, Dr. Nunez Wais, and the baron Castel Nuevo, all of whom endeavored to improve the status of their coreligionists. The Muslims referred to the bey Aḥmad as the "bey of the Jews." During his reign and those of his successors, a large number of Jews held important positions in his government. The bey Muhammad (1855–59) abolished the collective responsibility of the Jews in the sphere of taxation, exempted them from all degrading tasks, declared that they would pay the same duties on goods as Muslims and Christians, and attempted to include them in the common law. In 1857, however, a Jew, Batto Sfez, who had quarreled with a Muslim, was accused of having blasphemed Islam. The mob dragged him before the qadi, who condemned him to death. In spite of a vigorous protest by the consul of France, the bey Muhammad ratified the sentence and Batto Sfez was executed; the promises which were given to the consular authorities and the Jewish population that his life would be spared were disregarded. A squadron of Napoleon III's then took up positions in front of La Goulette so as to coerce the bey to apply the principles of equality and tolerance toward all the inhabitants of the regency. The equality of all Tunisian subjects of every religion was then proclaimed in a kind of declaration of human rights known as the Pacte Fondamental (September 1857). All the laws which discriminated against the Jews were repealed.

In 1861 Muhammad al-Ṣadiq-Bey (1857–82) promulgated edicts for drawing up civil and penal codes to be applied by the newly constituted tribunals. There was widespread discontent among the Muslim masses as a result of these laws. The government was reproached for favoring the infidels and raising the taxes paid by the Muslims, while the ministers were accused of having ruined the state. This was during a period in which the minister of finance, the *qa'id* Nissim Samama, contracted onerous loans in Europe. An insurrection of the tribes broke out. In the north of the country the ill-treated Jews were convinced that their salvation only lay in the intervention of European warships, whose presence indeed restrained the rebels. In the south, pillaging against the Jews of Djerba and Sfax took place. In 1864 the bey was compelled to abolish the new constitution, but the abuses which it had suppressed did not reappear. The bey ordered that the Jewish victims of the insurrection be indemnified. The International Financial Commission, imposed on Tunisia in the wake of these financial upheavals, received the collaboration of the Jews and succeeded in its mission. From then on the French found in the Jewish population a very useful instrument for support of its policy, while the "Grana" remained the champions of the Italian presence in the country.

In 1878 the *Alliance Israélite Universelle founded its first school in Tunis. The French Protectorate, which was established in 1881, brought considerable changes in the material life of the Jewish masses of Tunisia. During the 19th century the Jewish population of the country was mainly concentrated in the towns: there were 60,000 Jews in Tunis in 1786, 30,000 Jews in 1815, but only 15–16,000 in the following years; Jews also lived in Matra, Le Kef, Nefta, Gafsa, Gabès, Sfax, Sousse, Naloeul, Mahdiya, and Testour. There were also many Jews in the villages and on the island of Djerba. The total Jewish population of Tunisia at the end of the 19th century was estimated by some scholars as 50,000 persons, by others as 60,000, and still others as 100,000, but all estimates were tentative only.

[David Corcos]

Changes on the Eve of the French Protectorate

The interference of France and Great Britain in Tunisia's internal affairs and the relations between the Grana and Italy were not the only examples of the involvement of external elements in Tunisian and Tunisian Jewish affairs. The opening of the Alliance Israélite Universelle school in 1878, 12 years after the foundation of the first such school in Morocco, was an important factor that influenced Jewish life. The Bey did his best to prevent the foundation of the first school but he could not resist French pressure. Those schools were not only a framework for learning, but also a challenge to the Jewish community because they offered new opportunities for social and economic improvement. An agreement, which insured that Jewish and religious materials would be part of the school curriculum was signed between the representatives of the Jewish community and of the Alliance Israélite Universelle in Tunisia.

Another change at the end of the 19th century was the activity of Jewish scholars ("*maskilim*"). This activity was mainly intellectual: they wrote letters and reports to the international Jewish newspapers of that time such as *Ha-Maggid, Ha-Ẓefirah, Ha-Levanon*, and others. Despite the fact that these reports constitute important historical material due to the descriptions of the Jewish community of that time, the main objective of the *maskilim* was to arouse the awareness of the Jewish leaders in Europe and encourage them to became involved in Tunisian affairs and to improve Jewish life there. One of the famous scholars was Shalom Flach who wrote Hebrew text books and history books such as *Ẓedek ve-Shalom* ("Peace and Justice") about the relations between the Grana and Touansa. The *maskilim* published newspapers and also books of Jewish enlightenment from East Europe in Judeo-Arabic. Until World War II this would be one of the main sources of conflict between them and the Alliance Israélite Universelle school director. At that time, the Alliance school was a cornerstone of French influence and an opportunity for youth to bring about social and cultural changes.

The Tunisian Jews in the French Protectorate (1881–1956)

Tunisia was conquered by the French in 1881. From that year on, it was the French – both in theory and in practice – who molded the development of modern Tunisia. Freedom from the restrictions of traditional society, new opportunities for the improvement of their economic situation, new modes of expression and activity that became possible for Jews through French acculturation, all of these were part of the modernization process. Three basic factors characterized modernization under colonial rule. First, the patterns of modernization were set by colonial rule. The modes were political, economic, or social or a combination of the three. French colonialism was assimilatory: it sought to instill French values and mold the ruled society by the standards of the ruling society according to its perceptions. Second, the pace of modernization was set by the considerations and needs of the French colonial powers. Third, the relationship between the colonial government and the local population lacked equality and was based on the exploitation of the ruled. The major basic problem of the Jews in this colonial society was the fact that they lived within a Muslim majority with very set patterns for Jewish existence. In the past a Jew had been obliged to be part of an autonomous Jewish community, living side by side yet in the shadow of Islam. The new colonial society gave the Jew the freedom, within certain limitations, to choose how he desired to identify himself. French culture presented a challenge which was irresistible. French rule was both the source of the Jews' security and their means of release from the degradation of Islam. Consciously – but not necessarily by choice – the Jews tied their fate with that of French colonial rule. Naturally, this process distanced them from the Muslim majority in Tunisian society.

Demographic Aspects

Before the mass emigration of Tunisian Jews the Jewish population was estimated at around 105,000 people, which means that in less than 100 years the Jewish population had increased more than fourfold. Most lived in Tunis, the capital. As a result of the modernization process the Jews left the small villages and immigrated to larger centers; the capital was the most attractive as it offered the Jews new employment opportunities. Changes were also felt in the Jews' occupations, since the opportunities or options for employment had grown. Jews, who were no longer restricted in their choice of occupation, entered the liberal professions and the French administration, playing a significant role in clerical work. Salaried work, which was the basis of union organizations and syndicates, where Jews played an important role, spread. The working Jewish population increased with the years, women workers were more common than in the past, and children rarely worked. In the peripheral towns and villages those changes were not as intense as in the capital.

Naturalization and Emancipation

One of the issues concerning the Jewish community was the question of French citizenship, since, at least in the case of Algerian Jewry, French citizenship was forced upon them. In the case of Tunisia, there was a small group of Jews which tried to force the French authorities to duplicate the Algerian experience with Tunisian Jewry. Mardochee Smadja was born in Tunis in 1864 and educated at the Alliance schools. His grandfather was one of the rabbis who had signed the agreement with the Alliance Israélite Universelle in 1874. Smadja was the leader of the campaign to encourage the French to grant Tunisian Jews the same rights as those awarded to Algerian Jews. He published the first manifesto of that group ("L'extension de la jurisdiction et de la nationalité françaises en Tunisie") in 1905 and was the publisher of the important newspaper *La Justice*. Smadja also represented the group at the Colonial congress held in Madrid and organized the mass demonstration in Tunis in 1910. All these efforts were not in vain. The demands presented the French general resident with a dilemma. The case of Tunisia was not similar to that of Algeria. First, Tunisia was only a protectorate while Algeria was annexed to France. Second, the existence of a considerable colony of Italian Jews who had Italian citizenship and no desire to renounce it posed a particular problem. Third, the French general resident was afraid of Muslim reactions as had occurred in Algeria following the law of 1870. After taking everything into consideration, the French authorities in Tunisia decided to naturalize the Tunisian Jews on an individual and selective basis. Thus, every Jew who wanted to acquire French citizenship was asked to demand it personally and to prove that he answered all the French conditions such as special service to France, knowledge of the French language, and French education. In the beginning of the French Protectorate, only a few Jews could be naturalized, but as a result of Jewish pressure the French general resident agreed to facilitate the conditions of naturalization. This was the background to the laws of 1910 and 1923. In the 1920s and 1930s, Jews acquired French citizenship in large numbers. For example, 1,222 became French citizens in 1926, 747 in 1928. However, in the 1930s there was a decrease in the naturalization of Tunisian Jews owing to French antisemitism and influences from Germany. The consequence of this naturalization policy was that the Jewish population was divided into three main categories: French citizens, Tunisian subjects, and Italian ones. Moreover, the second group, which constituted the majority of the Jewish population, was subdivided according to its acculturation to French culture. In Djerba, the most religious town of Tunisia, Jews did not want to have any connection with French culture, while in the capital most of the Jews were assimilated into French culture even if they were not French citizens. The second consequence was that the struggle for French naturalization proved that the French general resident would agree to change his policy under concrete pressure and defined goals. Tunisian Jews became more active and politically involved in order to achieve social change.

Communal Organization

The function of the Jews' *qa'id* was gradually abolished and its seems that Michael Uzan was the last one. At the beginning of the French protectorate, the French created a new institution, L'Assemblée des Notables. Furthermore, there was also a president and a chief rabbi for both the Touansa and the Grana. The chief rabbi of Tunis represented all the Jews, including the Grana, and received his salary from the French treasury. More important and durable was the creation of the Caisse de Secours et de Bienfaissance, which consisted of nine people who were nominated by the French, and which replaced all the traditional functions of the Jewish community. In order to adequately solve all the needs of Jewish society, a solution was devised: more than ten voluntary organizations, such as Société de l'Asile de Nuit (1909), Caisse de Secours et d'Habillement des Ecoles de l'Alliance (1904), were created under the patronage of Jewish notables. The most important change occurred in 1921 when the French decided to create the Conseil de la Communauté Israélite. It is not clear what the exact reasons were for that change. Perhaps the contribution of the Jewish volunteers in World War I or the desire of the French to conciliate the Jews after their refusal to legislate in their favor regarding naturalization contributed to this. The Conseil de la Communauté Israélite was elected quite democratically: a secret ballot was held every four years, but only the men who had paid their taxes to the community were eligible to vote. There were separate elections in each part of the community. The electoral campaign was the stage for debates which reflected struggles between political parties. Zionists tried to insure the Zionization of the council's activities, while the La Justice party hoped to use the power of that institution to persuade the French authorities to exert French influence over the Jewish community. The fighting over the character of the Jewish council was further proof of the political and social awareness of the Jewish community.

Intellectual and Spiritual Activity

Other expressions of political and social awareness may be found in the enormous number and variety of newspapers and periodicals that were published in Tunisia. From R. Attal's works it can be noted that about 160 periodicals, newspapers, and year books were published in Tunisia between 1878 and 1962. Seventy-eight were written in Judeo-Arabic, 65 in French, and 16 in Hebrew, most of the latter in Djerba. The majority of the newspapers in Judeo-Arabic were issued during the first generation of the French occupation. During the second generation, the domination of the French language was absolute and was also an expression of the community's assimilation to French culture. Forty-six of them could be defined as informative in character, 30 of them were Zionist-oriented newspapers, 15 were political, 12 rabbinical, and about 27 were literary. Some of the newspapers appeared for more than ten consecutive years; the most famous and important papers were *La Justice* (1907–14, 1923–33), *L'Egalité* (1912–32, 1940), *Le Réveil Juif* (1924–35), *La Gazette d'Israël* (1938–39, 1945–51), and *El-Najma* (1920–61). These newspapers, like the elections for the community, were the stage for the political, social, and intellectual struggle within Jewish society and of the Jews with the Muslims and the French in Tunisia. Jews were also employed by French newspapers as journalists, editors, and publishers. In 1921 out of a total workforce of 13,303, some 1,079 Jews declared that they were journalists, while in 1936, 3,114 Jews out of 15,928 made the same declaration, i.e., about 20% of the Jewish working population. As regards Jewish intellectual and spiritual life, it should be added that hundreds of Jewish books, mainly from East Europe, were translated into Judeo-Arabic by Jewish scholars, and the rabbinical literature in Djerba and the capital ran into hundreds of volumes of religious commentaries and interpretations.

Jewish-Muslim Relations

French domination in Tunisia slowly changed the pattern of Muslim-Jewish coexistence. The Jews' process of assimilation to French culture gradually detached them from the Muslim society with which they had lived for hundreds of years. From the beginning of the French protectorate, a new ethnic element – the French settlers – was added to Muslim-Jewish relations. Those three ethnic elements had different, and occasionally opposing, interests. Owing to the increasing Tunisian national struggle, tension between the French and the Muslims was more obvious and understandable than between French and Jews, and even Muslims and Jews. As far as is known in the collective memory of Tunisian Jews, Muslim-Jewish coexistence was convenient and tranquil. This is not an idyllic, nostalgic point of view. Most Tunisian Jews do not remember any of the violent outbreaks that occurred in Tunisia. Apart from the three days in August 1917 and fragments of information in the Jewish newspapers about violent incidents or outbreaks in the early 1920s, one does not know of any significant outbreaks of violence. At the end of the 19th century, a short wave of French antisemitism influenced French-Jewish relations. This wave reappeared in the 1930s, but by then it was more aggressive. From this relatively favorable atmosphere, the Palestinian issue emerged as a new factor in the relations among the three ethnic groups. The Palestinian issue concerned all the aspects of the relations and connections between the Palestinian national movement and the Arab world, and in the Jewish case, with the Tunisian national movement.

In society at large, an interesting struggle developed during the 1930s between the Tunisian national movement, the Destour, and the Zionists. The Destour took advantage of French sensitivity to public order and thereby prevented the Zionists from parading their strength and their victories publicly. For example, the Destour prevented *Jabotinsky's appearance in Tunisia in 1932 and the screening of the film *The Promised Land*. They sabotaged the visit of Betar's study ship, *Sarah A*, in 1937, and condemned the Zionists at every opportunity. A close examination of the relations between the Zionists and the Destour shows that, in spite of the attitude of the Destour towards Zionism, the Zionists were not significantly harmed. The reason for this is simple. The Tunisian national movement's struggle was primarily directed against French rule, and it used Zionism only as a means by which to attack the French. For example, the denunciation of British colonialism in Palestine could be taken as a condemnation of French colonialism, if only indirectly. The damage done to Zionism was an indirect indication of the level of relations between the French administration and the leaders of the Tunisian nationalists. In this manner the Muslims learned how far they could strain relations with the French without significantly harming themselves. Moreover, such activity allowed them to test their ability to organize the Muslim crowds, to consolidate movement cells, and to prepare movement leadership. In spite of attacks of the Destour on Zionism, the fact that both were nationalist movements prevented the Destour from condemning the right of free speech and the self-determination of the Zionists. A negation of such rights would have been self-defeating. As far as is known, the relationship between Jews and Muslims did not deteriorate in the following years. During the period of Vichy and the German occupation of Tunisia the relations did not change, and the Muslims did not turn the situation to their advantage. While in most of the Arab world violent eruptions between Jews and Muslims occurred, Tunisia experienced no more than attacks in the newspapers or public demonstrations.

Zionism and Political Activity

Zionism was one response of Tunisian Jews to French colonialism and the modernization processes which affected them. Zionism was not only a reaction to modernity, but also an expression of modernity. The influence of Zionism increased over the years. The internal dynamics of the colonial situation on the one hand, and the possibilities for achieving the aims of Zionism, on the other, were principal factors in the development of Zionism in Tunisia. Tunisian Zionists saw in their movement a means to achieve political and social expressions, adapted to the spirit of the times.

Expressions of Zionism appeared at the end of the 19th century. Organized Zionism began only in 1910 with the foundation of the first Zionist society, Agudat Zion ("Society of Zion"). The French authorities legalized Zionism, but restricted it to cultural activities. Zionist political activity was forbidden. French authorization of Zionism was part of the colonial policy towards a plurality of cultural activities. During this period there was almost no opposition from other social groups in Tunisian Jewry. Zionism had been established, but was not yet an important factor in the social and political fabric of Tunisian Jewry. By World War I, other organizations had been founded in all the major cities of Tunisia. Agudat Zion published a Zionist newspaper, *Kol Zion*, collected the Zionist tax (the shekel), sent a representative to the Tenth Zionist Congress, contributed to Keren Kayemet (the Jewish National Fund), and held Zionist propaganda meetings. World War I interrupted Zionist activity, which virtually ceased until the end of the war.

Zionists participated fully in all major activities of the Jewish community of this period. During 1898–1918, Zionism reinforced individual interest in the general political movement, and defined itself on the social and political landscape of the Jewish community. This process of consolidation emerged from a stage of individual interest in Zionism to prominence in the public sphere and finally to a basis for activity. Zionism in this period established itself throughout Tunisia, and relationships were formed between activity in the periphery and in Tunis, the center. Zionists understood that without their own newspaper, they could not maintain themselves in the struggle against other political camps. The years 1918–26 were the formative years of Zionism in Tunisia. During this period the Tunisian Zionist Federation was established (October 1920) as an organizational framework for all Zionist activities. The founding of additional Zionist organizations, their geographic dispersion, and the policy of the World Zionist Organization made the establishment of the Federation compulsory. The Federation dealt with all necessary organizational matters – the collecting of money, propaganda, Zionist newspapers, elections to the Zionist congresses, and the struggle against other ideologies. However, the Federation did not succeed in rising above internal problems and leading Tunisian Zionism. Its weakness stemmed from its inability to impose its authority upon its constituent components, its lack of a fixed budget and, therefore, a good, regularly published newspaper, and the disregard and neglect on the part of the World Zionist Organization. In addition, opposition to Zionist activities by various sections of the Jewish community increased the difficulties.

Opposition to Zionism stemmed from two sources. Foremost was that of the Alliance Israélite Universelle. Its opposition was ideological. Zionism was nationalistic, whereas the Alliance presented an emancipatory ideology, seeking to integrate Jews into the general society in which they lived. In the Tunisian framework this meant integration into the French colonial society. The Zionists demanded that more Jewish history and Hebrew, as a living modern language, be taught in the Alliance schools, whereas the Alliance emphasized a deep attachment to French culture, based on the emancipatory model of French Jewry. The forces behind the struggle were not equal. The Alliance had a strong organization, considerable financial backing, and the support of the French authorities. Zionism, on the other hand, was in its initial stages of establishment. In spite of this, the Zionists succeeded in their struggle against the Alliance, at least in respect to the social legitimization of Zionism as a viable Jewish cultural, social, and communal alternative.

By actively participating in all aspects of Jewish communal life, the Zionists compelled the various communal groups to publicly recognize their presence. In addition to their struggles within the Jewish community, Zionists strove to make a place for themselves among the other social movements of the time, particularly vis-à-vis the socialist movement and the communist party, which were strongly attractive to Jewish youth. These struggles, however, were general and ideological in character and, because of this, their impact on Zionism was minimal. During 1926–39 Zionism was at the forefront of the struggle to define the character of Jewish life and its position in society. Two major changes occurred during this period. One was the creation of Zionist youth movements, the Eclaireurs Israélites de France (EIF), the Union Universelle de Jeunesse Juive (UUJJ), Ha-Shomer ha-Ẓa'ir, and Betar. The youth movements brought an element of vitality to the full range of Zionist activity. Education, an important and central element of the youth movements, was accompanied by Zionist indoctrination. A child educated in one of these youth movements had a deep Zionist consciousness and commitment. The youth movements lowered the age level of Zionist activists. The frameworks for activity were more rigid in the youth movement than in the former Zionist organizations. In addition, youth movements made it possible for girls to participate in Zionist activity, which had formerly been impossible.

Another change in Tunisian Zionism during this period was the penetration of world Zionist political parties: the Revisionists accompanied by the Betar youth movement, and Ha-Shomer ha-Ẓa'ir. Bitter struggles took place between the two ideological approaches to Zionism: the integral Zionist program of the Revisionists versus the Marxist Zionism of Ha-Shomer ha-Ẓa'ir. The struggle culminated when the Revisionists accused their rivals of atheism, destroying family life, a bias towards communism, and aspirations to be fulfilled only in a kibbutz. Ha-Shomer ha-Ẓa'ir was forced to defend itself against harsh attacks and retaliated by accusing the Revisionists of fascism and Hitlerism. This contest could be seen in public demonstrations as well as in newspapers and was also reflected in information passed on to the police by informers. Ha-Shomer ha-Ẓa'ir was forced to disband in 1935. The Revisionists' victory was a result of having a strong newspaper, a simple ideological ethic, being well-suited to a society in transition, and effective meshing between the party and its youth movement.

The greatest importance of Tunisian Zionism during this period was its primary position in the struggle against all antisemitic manifestations in the country, both that of the French colonists and of the Italian ones. Tunisia did not escape the world-wide wave of antisemitism in the 1930s. The Zionists initiated and encouraged the Jewish community to boycott German, Italian, and Japanese goods. The Zionists called for public demonstrations against German antisemitic outbreaks. In this way, they both paved the way for themselves within the Jewish society and took a stand on behalf of the Jewish community among the various social elements.

The war years in Tunisia, 1939–43, totally changed the character of local Zionism. Until World War II, the importance of Zionism was within Jewish society. Zionism made possible a modern mode of expression and activity for Jews who had not received French citizenship, yet wished to express their aspirations without violating the Jewish character of their society. After World War II, Zionists understood that without *aliyah* to Ereẓ Israel, without severing themselves from life in Tunisia, there was no meaning to Zionism. Therefore the period between the end of World War II and the creation of the State of Israel is characterized as "A Time of Achieving Zionism."

Ideologically, all the various Zionist streams believed in the fulfillment of Zionism as an obligation of the individual to the movement. There were arguments between the various streams of Zionism about the character of fulfillment, for example whether to live in a kibbutz or a city, but none about the need for its realization. Preparation was now required prior to embarking on a new life in Israel. Hebrew became significant and a Zionist was required to invest time learning the language as part of his preparation for *aliyah*. No less important for the Zionists were the attempts to establish preparatory camps in Tunisia and elsewhere. However, the number of Zionists who succeeded in completing this preparation was small. One particular aspect of this ideology was the mission of Tunisian Zionism in North Africa. Almost all the Zionist parties saw Tunisia as the base for overall activity in North Africa. The strength and importance of Zionism in Tunisia led to its primary position in all Zionist activity in North Africa. The significance of achieving Zionism was practical. During this period the immigration of Tunisian Jews to Israel began. At first immigration was legal, but it was small in numbers, encompassing not more than several dozens. The gap created between the desire to immigrate and the possibilities for legal *aliyah* in 1947–48 forced the Zionists to turn to illegal immigration. Tunisian Zionists were among the planners and implementers of the Ha'palah (*"illegal" immigration movement). Only some 300 Jews left Tunisia illegally during this period, but in terms of responsibility, the role of Tunisian Zionism was more significant.

The war years were characterized by an increase in the number of ideological parties, particularly those connected to world movements. The Revisionists still enjoyed Zionist hegemony as exemplified in the results of the elections to the Zionist Congress in 1946 and in its strong Zionist and Revisionist newspaper. Among the other movements, which combined socialism and Zionism, were Ẓe'irei Zion, which was aligned with the Kibbutz ha-Meuḥad, and Ha-Shomer ha-Ẓa'ir, which renewed its activities in 1946. Among the religious movement, two trends were established. One was aligned with Torah va-Avodah and the Mizrachi party, and the other, religious Zionists, such as the Ateret Zion in Djerba, were without any affiliation. Other groups remained politically neutral. In this period, it is significant that the Zionists were the first to understand that the Jewish community under French rule was at its end. Restricted modernization under colonial rule had brought about the end of Jewish existence in Tunisia. Such was the Zionists' advantage in the colonial drama.

World War II

Tunisian Jewry was influenced during World War II by developments which had taken place mainly in France. French territories, including Tunisia, were under Vichy government rule and all its anti-Jewish legislation was applied there. The laws and decrees published by the Vichy government concerned three main areas: the legal status of the Jews, the *numerus clausus* in education, and the measures that were taken against the Jews' economic influence. The Jewish Statute was published in Tunisia on November 30, 1940, but its implementation was only partial because of the small number of French Jews and their importance in the economy, the positive attitude of the French résident général towards Tunisian

Jews, and the involvement of the Italian government representative in Tunisia who looked after Italian interests. In Tunisia, the Italian representative strongly opposed all French attempts to aryanize Jewish property as part of Italy's policy to protect the Italian colony in Tunisia.

During a period of six months, between November 1942 and May 1943, the situation of Tunisian Jewry steadily deteriorated as a result of the German occupation which was a counter-attack against the American Operation Torch and also the British military campaign from Libya. The Jews suffered from the aerial bombardment of the Allied Forces as well as that of the German ones. As far as is known, most of the Jews who died during the German occupation were killed by these bombings. The Germans created a new Jewish communal committee most of whose functions were similar to the *Judenrat. The most important task of the community was to supply forced labor for military purposes. It is estimated that approximately 5,000 young Jews were sent to forced labor. The recruiting of the Jews was carried out by a special Comité de Recrutement de la Main d'Oeuvre which was headed by Paul Ghez, a famous lawyer. The Jewish workers were interned at about 30 military camps along the battle fields. The dissatisfaction of the Jews with the work of this committee was natural and understandable, because they had to take care of all the workers' necessities, such as food, clothes, transportation, links with families, etc. The Germans confiscated Jewish property, houses, cars, blankets, radios, public buildings such as the Alliance school, etc., for their own purposes. They imposed a 53 million franc fine on the community. The French résident général, did not, and probably could not, help the Jewish leaders to argue with, or at least to minimize the Germans' demands. Thus, Jewish feelings of isolation, abandonment, and disappointment with France as a Protectorate, were quite understandable. As far as is known, the Tunisian Muslims did not harm the Jews during this tragic period and no incidents occurred between Jews and Arabs. On the contrary, Arabs offered shelter to Jews in their villages until the German threat passed. On July 7, 1943, Tunisia was liberated from Nazi occupation by the Allied Forces. A new era began, while in Europe the destruction of the Jewish communities was still going on.

The period of Vichy and the German occupation was a turning point in the history of the Tunisian Jews and proved that the attempts to assimilate to French culture were an illusion. Not only did France fail to protect the Jews against harsh attacks, but it also initiated antisemitic activity itself. The process of decolonization, disappointment in France, and the rise of Tunisian national aspirations for independence were among the major factors in the change in the view of France. French military and economic power was reduced to such levels that the Jews lost their confidence that France would help them when necessary. The alternatives to a French protectorate were Zionism and immigration to Israel, communism, or waiting for other developments. In addition to the disappointment with France there was also disappointment with the leaders of the Jewish community who were accused of nepotism as well as cooperation with the Germans. They had to submit their resignation and a provisional committee was established. The economic situation deteriorated due to the war and the German oppression. Moreover, France could not give any economic assistance to Tunisia because of its economic situation after the war.

From World War II to Independent Tunisia

The main development after World War II was the emigration from Tunisia which was due partly to the disappointment with France and the decline of colonialism, partly to the fear of an independent Tunisia, and above all to the creation of the State of Israel. As mentioned before, the first stage of *aliyah* was the illegal immigration of 1947–48. The second stage began with the creation of the State of Israel with more than 4,000 immigrants in 1951, and 2,500 in 1952. But the two following years were marked by a strong decrease in immigrants: about 600 in 1953 and 2,600 in 1954. The political autonomy given to them by the French and the forthcoming independence influenced the Jews' decision to leave the country. More than 6,000 Jews immigrated to Israel in 1955 and 6,500 in 1956. The *aliyah* was organized by the Jewish Agency which sent emissaries to Tunisia. This was the period when the Tunisian Jewish leaders lost their standing in the community to the Israeli emissaries and Israeli political party representatives. One such expression of this was the decrease in the number of Jewish newspapers published in Tunisia.

Jews in Independent Tunisia until the Six-Day War

The character and attributes of independent Tunisia were influenced by several basic factors: the nature of the party in power (Neo-Destour), the almost bloodless struggle for independence, Tunisia's role in the Maghreb states and in the Arab world, its pro-Western inclinations, and the domestic problems it faced during the first years of independence. These factors had a consequential influence on the character of Tunisian Jewry and on the manner in which Israel handled the issue of immigration from Tunisia.

Independent Tunisia's policy vis-à-vis its Jews favored their full integration into the new Tunisian society. Thus, for example, all Tunisians were given the franchise in elections to the Constituent Assembly, ten Jewish judges were appointed to the country's courts to decide cases dealing with Jewish litigants, and though the rabbinical courts were abolished, special courts dealing with matters of personal status were established within the Tunisian legal system that were open to Jews just as they were to all other Tunisians. The Jewish community council was disbanded and replaced by an "Interim Committee for the Management of the Affairs of the Jewish Community" until "associations for religious matters" would be established.

Two of the steps taken by the authorities for the development of the capital city of Tunis proved detrimental to the Jewish community: the transfer of the old Jewish cemetery to another site and the razing of *Ḥārat al-Yahūd*, the Jewish quarter. These were carried out as part of an urban renewal plan in which the Muslim cemetery was also removed to a new location. Aware of the Jews' sensitivity, Habib Bourguiba personally supervised all work related to the transfer of the Jewish cemetery, during which the Tunisians displayed a reasonable degree of consideration for Jewish feelings.

The years from Tunisian independence until the events in Bizerta in 1961 were marked by a decrease in tension between those Jews who remained in the country and the authorities. Jews were appointed to some of the positions vacated by the French, and Yom Kippur was proclaimed an official holiday, enabling Jews to absent themselves from work. The Jews' sense of security and the degree of their identification with Tunisia are exemplified in the role they played in the "Campaign for the Dinar" (in which all Tunisians were called upon to shore up the declining value of the Tunisian dinar). The extent of *aliyah* to Israel in these years also reflects the general climate of opinion in Tunisia. In 1955, over 6,000 Jews immigrated to Israel, while in 1956 – the year of Tunisian independence – another 6,500 arrived. In the year following independence, however, the figure dropped to about 2,600 and was even lower in the succeeding years until the fighting in Bizerta in 1961 between the French and the Arabs. The events in Bizerta increased the Jews' doubts as to their future in Tunisia. French military presence, limited as it was, was a sort of lifebelt for them and made them feel more secure. The best proof of their sense of insecurity lies in the figures for Jewish emigration during these years. Of the 65,000 Jews in the country in 1960, 60,000 remained in 1962, while in 1965 the Jewish population of Tunisia amounted to no more than half of that of 1962. In less than five years, over 30,000 had left the country, most of them professionals or businessmen. The extent and character of emigration during these years are quite similar to that of the period which immediately preceded Tunisian independence. Those who remained were primarily the elderly.

In the interim period between the Bizerta affair and Bourguiba's proposals in 1965 for a peaceful solution of the Arab-Israeli conflict, the condition of Tunisia's Jewish community deteriorated. After a plot to assassinate Bourguiba was uncovered in 1962, many Jewish families closed down their businesses and immigrated to France. Gradually, it was forbidden to send letters and parcels to Israel, and direct telephone communications between the two countries were cut off. Only Jews bearing French citizenship were allowed to leave with their belongings, and this only if they were able to present proof of their citizenship and an affidavit certifying their destination as France. Jews holding Tunisian citizenship could leave the country without their property, except for 30 dinars and some clothes. Thirty-five Jews from Djerba were arrested on suspicion of trying to smuggle gold from Tunisia to Libya. They were imprisoned, tortured, and tried in court, where they were very heavily fined. Only intervention by the community leadership managed to alleviate their condition somewhat. Eyewitness accounts from the time of the Six-Day War in Tunisia talked of anti-Jewish demonstrations in Tunis, heavy damage done to Jewish retail establishments throughout the city, where more than 100 shops were looted and smoke poured out of scores of Jewish establishments. Only intervention by President Bourguiba brought the demonstrations to an end. In a speech broadcast over the radio and the television, he called on the mobs to stop the riots and denounced them severely. His action prevented even more severe attacks on the Jews, especially in the smaller towns.

Since the Six-Day War

The character of this period was influenced by the Arabization of the new state including its relations with the Arab world and the effect of the Israeli-Arab conflict, the economic situation, and the size of the Jewish population. These years can be divided into three main periods: from the Six-Day War to the Lebanese War (June 1982, known as Peace in Galilee); from the Lebanese War to the beginning of the Zin Ben-Ali regime in 1987; and from the beginning of the Zin Ben-Ali regime until the early 21st century.

In 1966 only 23,000 Jews lived in Tunisia. Two years afterwards, the Jewish population was estimated at about 10,000, which means that more than 13,000 Jews had left Tunisia, most of whom emigrated in the six months after the end of the Six-Day War. From 1965 to 1971, 7,753 Tunisian Jews immigrated to Israel, in 1972–79 only 2,148 did so, and 1,232 left for Israel in 1980–84. Most of the Jews who left Tunisia after the Six-Day War immigrated to France and created a Tunisian colony there which exerted considerable influence on French Jewish life. Under the Bourguiba government the situation of the Jewish community did not deteriorate; it was a time of relative calm for those Jews who preferred to stay in Tunisia.

During the Lebanese War, June 1982, and especially after the events in Sabra and Shatilla, some incidents occurred in the south of Tunisia. On September 23, 1982, the daily journal *al-Sabach* denounced the chief rabbi of Tunisia for his unclear position on the events in Sabra and Shatilla. Some days afterwards, and in accordance with Bourguiba's position, which called for an Israeli-Palestinian dialogue, the chief rabbi dedicated a place in his prayers for the innocent victims of Sabra and Shatilla. This declaration, however, did not prevent riots against Jews in the small towns of Zarzis and Ben-Garden which caused much damage to Jewish property. The authorities arrested those responsible for the incidents and put them on trial. The Lebanese War changed the Tunisian Jews' situation as a result of the transfer of the Palestinian Liberation Organization's headquarters and the Arab League bureau after the Camp David agreements. Consequently, Tunisia became a center for anti-Jewish and anti-Israel propaganda. Other elements that influenced the Jews' situation were the fundamentalist activities which were encouraged by the Khomeini Islamic revolution and its impact on Muslims in Libya and Algeria. On October 1, 1985, an Israeli aircraft bombed the Palestine Liberation Organization's headquarters. Fifty-six Palestinian were killed and about 100 injured. The steps which were taken by the Tunisian authorities failed to protect the Jews.

Some Jews were killed in the synagogue of Djerba. The Israeli bombings caused a wave of Jewish emigration from Tunisia. More than 700 Jews left Tunisia during the years 1985–89; thus only 2,500 Jews continued to live in Tunisia, most of them in Djerba and Tunis.

Zin Al-Abidin Ibn-Ali took power in Tunisia on November 6, 1987, after the dismissal of Bourguiba. His internal policy improved the economic situation and opened the country to a democratic process. During 1987–91 the Jews expressed their fear and increasing doubts regarding their future in Tunisia. The assassination of Abu Jihad, one of the most important commanders of the PLO, in April 1988, in his house in Tunisia, and the Gulf War in February-March 1991 contributed to those fears and doubts. However, since the Oslo agreements there has been a gradual improvement in the Jews' situation due to the significant part played by Tunisia in those agreements. Tunisia opened its borders to Israeli tourists and most Palestinians were evacuated from Tunisia, as was the Arab League bureau, and diplomatic relations were established with Israel.

As of 2005 the Jewish community consisted of about 1,500 Jews, most of them living in Tunis and Djerba, which is a religious center and very attractive to tourists. Jews have all the requisites for leading a religious life. Relations with Israel are still at a very low level and are influenced by the progress (or its absence) in the peace process and also by Tunisia's position in the Arab world.

[Haim Saadoun (2nd ed.)]

BIBLIOGRAPHY: GENERAL: D. Cazès, *Essai sur l'Histoire des Israélites de Tunisie* (1888); E. Vassel, *La littérature populaire des Israélites tunisiens avec un essai ethnographique et archéologique sur leur superstitions* (1904–07); Baron, Social², index; A. Chouraqui, *Between East and West* (1968), index; R. Attal, *Les Juifs d'Afrique du Nord – Bibliographie* (1994); H.Y. Cohen, *Asian and African Jews in the Middle East – 1860–1971; Annotated Bibliography* (1976); Hirschberg, Afrikah, index; R. Attal, in: *Sefunot* (1961), 480–9. ANTIQUITY: D. Kaufmann, in: REJ, 12–13 (1886), 45–61; P. Delattre, *Gamart ou la Nécropole juive de Carthage* (1895); Ch. Diehl, *L'Afrique Byzantine* (1896), passim; P. Monceaux, in: REJ, 44–45 (1902), 1–28; H. Leclercq, *L'Afrique Chrétienne*, 2 vols. (1904), passim; M. Mieses, in: REJ, 92–93 (1932), no. 184, 133–5, no. 185, 53–72, no. 186, 135–56, no. 187, 94–96 (1933), 73–89; M. Simon, in: RHPR (1946), 1–31, 105–45; idem, *Verus Israel* (1948), passim; idem, *Recherches d'Histoire judéo-chrétienne* (1962), 30–87; J. Ferron, in: *Cahiers de Byrsa* (1951), 176–224; (1956), 99–102, 105–52. UNDER ARAB RULE TO THE ADVENT OF THE HAFSIDS, 665–1236: I. Goldziher, in: REJ, 46–47 (1903), 179–86; S.D. Goitein, in: *Etudes d'Orientalisme dediées à la mémoire de Levi-Provençal* (1962); idem, in: *Speculum* (1954), 181–97; idem, *A Mediterranean Society* (1967), passim; H.Z. Hirschberg, in: *Eretz Israel, Mazar Jubilee Volume* (1958), 213–9; D. Corcos, in: *Zion* (1967), 146ff. HAFSID RULE: R. Brunschvig, *La Berbèrie Orientale sous les Hafsides*, 1 (1940), 396–430; J. Pinkerfeld, in: *Cahiers de Byrsa* (1957), 127–88; A.M. Hershman, *Rabbi Isaac ben Sheshet Perfet and his Time* (1943), index. UNDER OTTOMAN RULE: M.R. Elfasi, *Mishna Direbuta* (1805); J.H. Dunant, *Notice sur la Régence de Tunis* (1858), 229–46; U. Elhaik, *Mishkhenot Haro'im* (1860); P. Faynault, *Tunis et Kairouan* (1889), 138–71; D. Cazès, *Notes bibliographiques sur la littérature juive tunisienne* (1893); R. Darmon, *La Situation des Cultes en Tunisie* (1930); P. Grandchamp, *La France en Tunisie de la fin du XVIe siècle á l'avènement de la dynastie hassanide*, 10 vols. (1920–33), index; C. Masi, in: *Revue Tunisienne* (1938), 155–7, 323–42; J. Bercher, *ibid.* (1939), 67–86; (1940), 59–69; M. Uzan, *Fêtes et Solennités d'Israël* (1950); M. Eisenbeth, in: *Revue Africaine* (1952), 115–87, 344–84; J. Ganiage, *ibid.* (1955), 153–73. **ADD. BIBLIOGRAPHY:** M. Abitbol, *The Jews of North Africa during World War II* (1986), 37–40; A. Attal, "Jews in Independent Tunisia," in: *Bi-Tefuzot ha-Golah*, 8, nos. 2–3 (37–38) (1967), 87–96; A. Attal and C. Sitbon, *Regards sur les Juifs de Tunisie* (1979); idem, *Le Caïd Nessim Samama de Tunis, mécène du livre hébraïque* (1995); idem, *Mémoires d'un adolescent à Tunis sous l'occupation nazie* (1996); A. Arrouas, *Livre d'Or* (1942); A. Itzak, *Pinkas ha-Kehillah ha-Yehudit ha-Portugezit be-Tunis 1710–1944* (1996); I. Avramski-Blai, *Pinkas ha-Kehillot, Enziklopediyah shel ha-Yeshuvim ha-Yehudim, Tunisia* (1997); M. Ben-Sasson, *Ẓemiḥat ha-Kehillah ha-Yehudit be-Arẓot ha-Islam, Qayrawan, 800–1057* (1997); R. Borgel, *Etoile Jaune et Croix Gammée* (1944); B. Cohen, *Malkhei Tarshish, Toledot Rabbanei Tunis ve-Ḥibburehem* (1986); M. Gil, *Be-Malkhut Ishmael bi-Tekufat ha-Geonim* (1997), 611–721; Ch. Haddad De Paz, *Juifs et Arabes au pays de Bourguiba* (1977); Sh. Deshen, "Southern Tunisian Jewry in the Early Twentieth Century," in: S. Deshen and W.P. Zenner (eds.), *Jews among Muslims…* (1996), 133–43; Sh. Deshen and M. Shoked, *Dor ha-Temurah* (1999); M. Hamdane, *Guide des périodiques parus en Tunisie de 1838 au 20 mars 1956*, fasc. 1 (in Arabic); *Guide des périodiques en arabe et en judéo-arabe* [= pp. 267–308]; fasc. 2 (in French); *Guide des périodiques en langues européennes* (1989); A. Larguèche, "La communauté juive de Tunis à l'époque Husseinite," in: *Histoire communautaire, histoire plurielle; la communauté juive de Tunisie, Actes du colloque de Tunis…* (1999), 165–80; *ibid.*, "Les ombres de la ville; pauvres, marginaux et minoritaires à Tunis (XVIIIe et XIXe siècle)," in: *La Communauté juive* (1999), 339–92; L. Lévy, *La communauté juive de Livourne; le dernier des Livournais. Essai* (1996); S. Haim, "The Effect of the Palestinian Issue on Muslim-Jewish Relations in the Arab World; the Case of Tunisia (1920–1939)," in: T. Parfitt (ed.), *Israel and Ishmael* (2000), 105–23; idem, "L'influence du sionisme sur les relations judéo-musulmanes en Tunisie," in: S. Fellous (ed.), *Juifs et musulmans en Tunisie; fraternité et déchirements (Actes du Colloque… Paris, 1999)* (2003), 219–29; idem (ed.), *Kehillot Israel ba-Mizraḥ ba-Me'ot ha-Tesha-Esre ve-ha-Esrim, Tunisia* (2005); P. Sebag, *Histoire des Juifs de Tunisie* (1991); idem, *Les noms des Juifs de Tunisie; origines et significations* (2002); L. Valensi, "Espaces publiques, espaces communautaires aux XIXe et XXe siècles," in: *Confluences Méditerranée*, 10 (1994), 97–109; E. Schely-Newman, *Self and Community in Historical Narratives; Tunisian Immigrants in an Israeli Moshav* (1991); A. Shiloah, "Témoignages sur le rôle des musiciens juifs dans le musique tunisienne," in: S. Fellous (ed.), *Juifs et musulmans en Tunisie; fraternité et déchirements (Actes du Colloque…1999)* (2003), 309–16; Y. Tobi and Z. Tobi, *Ha-Sifrut ha-Aravit-ha-Yehudit be-Tunisia (1850–1950)* (2000); Y. Zur, *Sippur Tarbut, Yehudei Tunisia ve-Arẓot Muslemiyyot Aḥerot* (2003).

TUNKEL, JOSEPH (**Yoysef Tunkl**; pseudonym **Der Tunkeler**; 1881–1949), Yiddish humorist, satirist, and cartoonist. Born in Bobruisk, Belorussia, he immigrated to New York in 1906, where he founded and edited the satirical weeklies *Der Kibitser* (1909–10) and *Der Groyser Kundes* (1910), but in 1910 returned to Warsaw, where he edited *Der Krumer Shpigl* ("The Crooked Mirror"), the weekly humor supplement of the Yiddish daily *Der *Moment*. In 1939 he succeeded in escaping to France and, in 1941, to the U.S., where he wrote for the Yiddish daily *Forverts. Der Tunkeler* was popular in the Yiddish press. His humorous pamphlets and books were widely read, his one-act plays often performed, and his comic sketches recited by many artists. His humor was good-natured and his satire was mild. A sharp social and cultural critic, he was a master of the spoken idiom of his day and can be read with profit for his literary parodies in particular.

BIBLIOGRAPHY: Rejzen, Leksikon (1926), 1168–70; LNYL, 4 (1961), 48–52; M. Ravitch, *Mayn Leksikon*, 1 (1945), 101–3. **ADD. BIBLIOGRAPHY:** Y. Szeintuch, *Sefer ha-Humoreskot ve-ha-Parodiyot ha-Sifrutiot be-Yiddish* (1990).

TUR BROTHERS, pseudonym of **Leonid Davydovich Tubelski** (1905–1961) and **Peter Lvovich Ryzhey** (1908–), Soviet Russian playwrights. Both were originally newspapermen, and some of their plays were written in collaboration with Lev Romanovich Sheinin (1906–1967), a lawyer by training. Most have swiftly moving plots, and many deal with political intrigue and the struggle against criminal elements. A number of their plays have Jewish protagonists. Noteworthy among these is *Komu psodchinyayetsya vremya* ("To Whom Time Bows," 1946), written by all three authors, which portrays a Jewish watchmaker in Nazi-occupied Russia. This central character, an anti-Nazi resistance fighter, is deeply attached to Jewish tradition and is shown observing the Passover festival. An earlier play by the same authors (*Neravny brak*, "The Misalliance," 1940), was set in what had been a Jewish **shtetl* in the Pale of Settlement. A visiting American millionaire does not recognize the town which his father has described to him: gone are the traditional Jewish occupations, even the matchmaker has become a bookkeeper in a collective farm, and no Soviet Jewish girl is interested in marrying an American Jewish capitalist.

[Maurice Friedberg]

TURDA (Ger. **Thorenburg**; Hung. **Torda**), town in Transylvania, N.W. Romania; until the end of World War I within Hungary. Jews began to settle there at the close of the 18th century although individual Jews had visited the locality earlier. A document of 1669 mentions a Jew of *Alba Iulia who had stayed in Turda in order to sign an agreement with the local inhabitants. A community was organized between 1830 and 1840. There were already houses of prayer during that period. The community remained Orthodox throughout its existence, but there were also many *maskilim* in Turda who had an affinity for the Western trends promoted by the Neolog communities in Hungarian-speaking Transylvania. The Jewish population numbered 48 families (175 persons) in 1866; 203 (2.1 percent of the total) in 1870; 326 (3.5 percent) in 1900; 482 (3.5 percent) in 1910; and 852 (4.2 percent) in 1930.

The community, which was wealthy and well organized, employed some distinguished rabbis, among them Ben-Zion Albert Wesel (1900–38) and Joseph Adler (1938–44). For most of the period between the two world wars these two rabbis also held the position of president of the central office of the organization of Orthodox communities of Transylvania, and the community thus played a leading role among Orthodox Jewry in Transylvania. An Orthodox Hungarian-language weekly, *Hoemesz*, was published in Turda from 1933 to 1940. A large synagogue was erected in 1932. Zionist activities were also organized, and there was a group of Jews which supported the Hungarian minority movement in Romania; a Jewish club, established in 1936, played an important part in Jewish life.

Holocaust and Contemporary Periods

There were 726 Jews in Turda (2.2 percent of the total population) in 1940. Their numbers increased to 1,805 in 1942 after Jews from the surrounding areas were concentrated in Turda by the Romanian Fascist authorities. From 1940 to 1944, because of the location of Turda near the Romanian-Hungarian border and within 18 mi. (approx. 30 km.) of *Cluj, the capital of northern Transylvania, Jews of Turda played an important role in underground rescue activities among the Jewish population. Members of the community collaborated with the representatives of the Zionist youth movements in contact with the rescue centers in Bucharest and Budapest and rescue workers in Palestine through their center in Istanbul. They organized secret routes for the transfer of refugees from neighboring Hungary to Romania, where the situation of the Jews was less dangerous, subsequently directing the refugees toward Bucharest, from where most of them reached Palestine. Hundreds of refugees passed along this escape route, most of them from Hungary, some from Slovakia, and even a number from Poland. In the fall of 1944, the town was taken by Hungarian forces. However, they were defeated by the Russians about five weeks later before they had succeeded in organizing the deportation of the local Jews.

After World War II the community continued activities but its institutions lost their importance with the decline of the Jewish population as a result of emigration to Israel and elsewhere. There were about 150 Jews living in Turda in 1971, and their numbers continue to dwindle into the 21st century. Prayers were still held in the Great Synagogue on Jewish festivals.

BIBLIOGRAPHY: MHJ, 5 (1959), 380–1; A.D. Finkelstein, *Fénysugár a borzalmak éjszákajában* (Tel Aviv, 1958); PK Romanyah, 304–7.

[Yehouda Marton]

TURECK, ROSALYN (1914–2003), U.S. pianist. Born in Chicago, Rosalyn Tureck played with the Chicago Symphony Orchestra at the age of 11, studied at the Juilliard School of Music, and specialized in the performance of Bach's keyboard works. In 1937 she gave the first of her Bach concerts in New York, and in 1947 set out on the first of her extensive European tours. She was a faculty member of the Juilliard School of Music (1943–53), lecturer at Columbia (1953–55), and Regent's Professor at the University of California (1966). She founded the Society for the Performance of International Contemporary Music (1951–55), the Tureck Bach Players (1959), and the International Bach Society (1966). She published many Bach works in pedagogical editions.

TURIN (It. **Torino**), city on the Po River, N.W. Italy. Turin was the capital of the duchy of Savoy and later of the kingdom of Sardinia; it is now the capital of Piedmont province. The presence of Jews in Turin was recorded by Bishop Maximus of Turin in the fourth century, but thereafter there is no evidence of Jews until 1424 when the French Jewish physicians and bankers Elias Alamanni and Amedeo Foa moved there with their families. They received a ducal privilege and a pontifical patent. The Turin Communal Council gave them the final authorization to settle there. Two documents dated to 1424 confirm it. The first document is a permission to live in the city and open a bank. The second mentions that the Jews could not be injured or insulted. Also a plot was purchased for a burial ground. Other Jewish bankers followed and a small group was formed. In 1425 the Jews were compelled to live in a restricted area where they could be watched more easily and prevented from lending money at excessive rates of interest. In 1430 Duke Amadeus VIII of Savoy issued statutes regulating Jewish residence, synagogues, civil and criminal jurisdiction, and relations with Christians. In addition, the statutes required Jewish men to wear a *badge in the shape of a disk, four fingers in width and red and white in color. For the following four centuries the interpretation of these regulations by the various rulers of Savoy ranged from literal to lenient. When in 1436 Ludovico of Savoy had the *Studium*, or university, erected, he decreed that the mansions of the Jews would be used by the students. At the same time the Jewish scholar and banker Bonafé de Chalon was invited to make low-interest loans to the university's students. During the pestilence of 1450–51 the care of the sick was given over to a Jewish doctor, Bono.

Jewish moneylending was permitted in Turin for a longer time than anywhere else in Italy. The taxes paid by the Jews were particularly high and the imposition of new taxes threatened the Jews with ruin or expulsion. In 1560 and 1566 Duke Emmanuel Philibert decreed that the Jews be expelled, but the decrees were canceled because of the intervention of influential people and the annual payment by the Jews of 20,000 florins.

From 1561 a guardian (*conservatore*) was given jurisdiction over the Jews and in some cases also represented them. The duke chose the guardian from among the senators from 1603 to 1626: thereafter he chose him from the names of three senators submitted by the Jews. Charles Emmanuel I (1580–1630) allowed the monopoly granted to Jewish moneylenders to remain in force, and he rejected Cardinal Carlo *Borromeo's demands for the expulsion of the Jews and the establishment of a ghetto in Turin. The most outstanding rabbi in the 16th century was Nethanel b. Shabbetai ha-Dani.

The majority of the Jews engaged in moneylending and were in close economic cooperation with the dukes of Savoy, extending to them large loans. In 1624 there were nine Jewish banks in Turin. The Talmud Torah Fraternity was founded in 1662. In 1679, after the death of Charles Emmanuel II, the reigning duchess, Maria Giovanna of Nemours, guardian of Duke Victor Amadeus II, decreed the establishment of the ghetto. Thus in 1680 the approximately 750 Jews of Turin were collected in one building which had been used as a hospital for beggars. The most important rabbis of 17th century Turin were Joseph Calvo, Daniel b. Joseph Calvo, and Joseph b. Michael Ravenna.

In 1702 there were 800 Jewish residents in Turin. In 1720 Victor Amadeus II transferred the Jewish codices that had been collected by his ancestors to the library of the University of Turin. These codices were described by Pasini Regi in the 18th century, B. Peyron in the 19th, and E.S. Artom in the 20th (*Soncino Blaetter* (1925), 43–70). However, at the beginning of the 20th century, they were almost entirely destroyed by fire. In the 17th and 18th centuries the Jews were urged to engage in the production and sale of fabrics.

Victor Amadeus II issued new statutes in 1723 and 1729 that substantially renewed those of 1430. The Jews were forbidden to own real estate and it was stipulated that they should live in the ghetto. Despite the trade in woolen and silk fabrics, the economic position of the Jews deteriorated. There are, however, no records of complaints; in fact, the Jewish population increased to about 1,300 by 1794. This implies that the Jews were better off in Turin than in other parts of Italy, both because of the comparative prosperity and the greater liberality of King Charles Emmanuel III. Turin continued to produce outstanding scholars. Eighteenth-century rabbis from Turin were Joshua Colon, Isaac Formiggini, Abraham Sanson b. Jacob ha-Levi Fubini, Michael Solomon Jonah, Gabriel Pontremoli, Jacob b. Joshua Benzion Segre, Abraham b. Jehuda Segre, and Daniel Valabrega.

The first real breath of liberty came with the French Revolution. Following the annexation to France in 1798, the Jews of Turin enjoyed greater liberty and were no longer compelled to live in the ghetto. Thus in 1797 a group of Jews, Ghidiglia, Guastalla, Treves, Nizza, Todros, and Malvano, bought a palace in front of the ghetto. In 1799 the Austro-Russian allies reconquered Piedmont from the French Republic, and the ancient statutes were reestablished. However, after Napoleon's victory at Marengo in 1800, Piedmont was annexed to France, and Turin became the capital of the new department. Turin's Jews were well established in the Napoleonic period and continued to purchase real estate outside the ghetto. Moreover, some of the Jews from the most prominent families were selected as guards of honor for Napoleon's visit.

With the fall of Napoleon in 1814, Victor Emmanuel I reenacted all the previous regulations. In theory the Jews had to go back to the ghetto and wear the badge. However, the reality was different. The Jews were soon exempted, in 1816, from wearing the yellow badge. Moreover the Sardinian government found it impossible to force the Jews to sell their land outside the ghetto and reside inside the ghetto only. A series of extensions and respites continued under the rule of Carlo Felice, until the Emancipation in 1848 under Carlo Alberto. Some of Turin's Jews took part in the 1821 *carbonari* insurrection, such as the banker Davide Levi. In 1848 there were 3,200 Jews living in Turin. By this time, however, the spirit of liberty was asserting itself as the voices of Gioberti, Franchi, Maffoni, Romagnosi, *Cattaneo, and Roberto and Massimo D'*Azeglio were raised in favor of the emancipation of the Jews everywhere in Italy. In 1848 M. D'Azeglio published his booklet *Dell'emancipazione degli Israeliti*. In the same year King Carlo Alberto, on March 29, granted the Jews full emancipation, and hence liberation from the ghetto. The wealthier families left the ghetto immediately. Encouraged by the rabbi of Turin Lelio *Cantoni and the poet David Levi, the Jews of Turin participated in the First Italian War of Independence, and 65 Jews volunteered for the Sardinian Army. After the defeat in 1849, under the strong hand of Vittorio Emanuele II, the legal situation of the Jews living in the Kingdom of Sardinia became a model for the Jews living in the other states of Italy, which still lacked full emancipation. Jews had access to the administration and the diplomatic corps as well as the army. In 1852 Cavour, a friend of the Jews who had at one time asked for their emancipation became the prime minister under King Victor Emmanuel II. Cavour was aided by the Jews Isaac Artom, his secretary, and Giacomo Dina, director of *L'opinione*, a newspaper backing Cavour's policy.

Piedmont having become the center of Italian unification and the symbol of Jewish emancipation attracted some Jews to Turin. In 1871 4,500 Jews lived in Turin. In 1859 the Jewish community commissioned the architect Antonelli to plan a monumental synagogue, the tangible symbol of the emancipation. However the building, the so-called Mole Antonelliana, was so expensive that the Jewish community donated it to the Turin Municipality. The main synagogue of Turin was erected in 1884 in Moorish style on St. Pius V Street. Various Jewish scholars lived or worked in 19th century Turin, such as Abraham de *Cologna, a member of Napoleon's Sanhedrin, Felice Bachi, Elijah Aaron Lattes, Samuel Solomon Olper, Isaiah Foà, Lellio *Della Torre, director of the Rabbinical College of Padua, Sabbato Graziadio Treves, Giuseppe Lattes, and Samuel Ghiron. Rabbi Olper's decision in 1865 to shorten the period of mourning aroused controversy among Italian rabbis. The decision was accepted only within Turin, where it was carried out until the beginning of the 20th century.

Although the capital of Italy moved to Florence in 1861 and to Rome in 1870, Turin Jewry still played a disproportionate role in Italy's cultural history. Among Turin's outstanding Jewish personalities during the following period were E.S. *Artom; R. *Bachi; S. *Foa; and B. *Terracini, who studied the history and dialect of the Jews of Piedmont. Other notables included G. Bolaffi, the jurist M. *Falco, the writers *Carlo and Primo *Levi, the historian A. *Momigliano, E. *Artom, and Senator U. *Terracini.

A Hebrew printing establishment existed in Turin in the 18th century (E.S. Lattes, in *Mosè* (Corfu, 1879), 263–5). In the 20th century the Marietti graphics company published, under the guidance of Rabbi Disegni, the Bible and some *maḥzorim* with Italian translation; and, under the supervision of R. Bonfil, a Passover *Haggadah*.

[Alfredo Mordechai Rabello / Samuele Rocca (2nd ed.)]

Holocaust and Contemporary Periods

In 1931 4,040 Jews lived in Turin. In 1938 the Racial Law particularly affected the Jewish community of Turin, much assimilated to Italian life. In 1942 a bomb destroyed the interior of the synagogue. In November and December 1943, the Germans began to deport the Jews of Turin. A total of 246 Jews were deported to Auschwitz. Only 21 came back. One of them was the writer Primo Levi. Various gentiles helped the Jews in ingenious ways. Thus Dr. Coggiola of Mauriziano Hospital organized a "quarantine section" housing Jews, and the judge Germano subpoenaed Jews as witnesses in various legal processes. Jews joined the local partisan movements, such as E. Artom, political commissar of the 5th Regiment of the Giustizia and Libertà brigades, and G. Bolaffio, who was the commander of the 4th Regiment of Giustizia and Libertà. At the end of World War II 2,885 Jews were left in Turin, apart from numerous refugees who were temporarily housed in the surrounding districts. The Jewish Brigade helped restore the confidence of the community. In 1949 the synagogue was repaired.

Various rabbis dominated Jewish life in Turin in the 20th century, such as Giacomo Bolaffio; Dario *Disegni, chief rabbi of Turin from 1924 to 1960, founder of the Margulies Rabbinical School, and editor of a translation of the Pentateuch and of the Bible; and Sergio Joseph *Sierra.

Due to a high mortality rate (as compared with their birthrate) the Jewish population of Turin in 1970 was around 2,000 (only 0.16% of the total inhabitants). Educational institutions included a school for higher Hebrew studies, the Margulies Sierra Rabbinic School, a kindergarten, an elementary school, and a Jewish high school. The other institutions included a rest home for elderly people and an orphanage. The Jewish community of Turin continued to publish a monthly newspaper, *Notiziario della Comunita' ebraica di Torino*. In 2005, 924 Jews lived in Turin. The chief-rabbi was Alberto Somech.

[Sergio DellaPergola / Samuele Rocca (2nd ed.)]

BIBLIOGRAPHY: Mortara, Indice, passim; Milano, Bibliotheca and *supplemento 1954–1963* (1964), index s.v. *Torino*; Milano, Italia, index; idem, in: RMI, 34 (1968), 295–7; G. Bachi, *ibid.*, 12 (1938), 197ff.; B. Terracini, *ibid.*, 164ff.; 7 (1932), 93ff.; 15 (1949), 62–77; R. Bachi, *ibid.*, 28 (1962), 37; Roth, Italy, index; G. Volino, *Condizione giuridica degli Ebrei in Piemonte prima dell'emancipazione* (1904); G. Valabrega (ed.), *Gli ebrei in Italia durante il fascismo* (1963), 29–33; M. Benayahu, in: *Miscellanea Disegni* (1969), 5ff.; S. Foa, in: RMI, 16 (1950), 188ff.; 19 (1953), 542ff.; *Scritti S. Mayer* (1956), 89ff.; *Vicende del ghetto di Torino* (1963). **ADD. BIBLIOGRAPHY:** AA.VV., *Ebrei a Torino, Ricerche per il centenario della sinagoga (1884–1984)* (1984); G. Arian Levi and G. Disegni, *Fuori dal ghetto, Il 1848 degli ebrei* (1998); D. Colombo, "Il ghetto di Torino ed il suo antico cimitero," in: RMI, 5–6 (1975); R., Segre, *The Jews in Piedmont*, 1–3 (1986–90); A.M. Tedeschi Falco, *Piemonte, Itinerari ebraici, I luoghi, la storia, l'arte* (1994), 151.

TURKA, city in Lvov district, W. Ukraine. Jews first settled in Turka in the early 19th century when the city was under Austrian rule. They engaged in trading in forest products, the manufacture of building materials, shopkeeping, and crafts – tailoring, shoemaking, carpentry, and transportation. In the second half of the 19th century the ḥasidic groups of *Belz and Sadgora had great influence within the community. On the eve of World War I, M. Landes, the Jewish representative on the city council, was mayor. Between the two world wars, when Turka was incorporated into Poland, Zionist parties were active, including Agudat Israel, Ha-Shomer ha-Ẓa'ir, and Agudat Akiva. Among Jewish educational institutions were the Degel Torah yeshivah, and *Tarbut and *Beth Jacob schools. The community founded a new orphanage in 1927. The Jewish population numbered 2,368 (51% of the total) in 1890, 2,892 (48%) in 1900, 4,887 (45%) in 1910, 4,201 (42%) in 1921, and 4,117 in 1931. The mayor of Haifa, Abba *Khoushi, was born in Turka.

[Shimon Leib Kirshenboim]

Holocaust Period

Before the outbreak of World War II, there were about 6,000 Jews in Turka. On Sept. 17, 1939, the Red Army entered the town and a Soviet administration was established there until the outbreak of the German-Soviet war in June 1941. The Germans occupied the town at the beginning of July 1941. The first *Aktion* took place in January 1942, when about 500 Jews were killed. In August 1942 about 4,000 Jews were deported to the *Belzec death camp. The Jewish community was liquidated in December 1942, when the Jews were transported to the *Sambor ghetto, where they were killed together with the local Jews. After the war, the Jewish community was not reconstituted. An organization of former residents of Turka is active in Israel.

BIBLIOGRAPHY: B. Wasiutyński, *Ludność żydowska w Polsce w wiekach XIX i XX* (1930), 124, 128, 155, 157; *Almanach gmin żydowska w Polsce* (1938), index; S. Bronsztejn, *Ludność żydowska w Polsce w okresie międzywojennym* (1963), 279; I. Zigelman (ed.), *Turka: Sefer Zikkaron* (Heb. and Yid., 1966).

TURKEY, modern republic in Asia Minor and S.E. Europe (see *Ottoman Empire for previous period). In the peace treaty of Lausanne (July 24, 1923), Turkey established complete sovereignty in Anatolia, the southeastern part of Thrace, and some islands in its territorial waters. The international status of the Turkish republic established in 1923 was secured, and in the following year the caliphate was abolished. The Treaty of Lausanne secured the rights of the religious and ethnic minorities (par. 39), who were permitted to have their own social institutions, funds, and schools (par. 40). In paragraph 41 the Turkish government assured the minorities their personal status as provided by their religious canons. The Jews showed their Turkish patriotism in the new republic: they relinquished the claims connected with their rights as a minority, and many renounced their foreign nationality and became Turkish citizens. Turkish Jewry was represented in parliament by Solomon Adato (from 1946 until his death in 1953) and by Henry Suriano (from 1954). The Turkish republic was declared a secular state, and Mustafa *Kemal Atatürk, its founder, attempted to erase all signs of the religious-institutional influence of Islam and also to maintain equality of Christianity and Judaism in public life. Even the wearing of "clerical" garb was prohibited and permitted only to the heads of the autonomous churches. For the Jews the prohibition on teaching Hebrew in schools was a hard blow. After Atatürk's death in 1938 many of the prohibitions he introduced were eased (e.g., the use of Arabic during the call for prayer in the mosques), but the general attitude toward religious minorities remained unchanged.

Economic Activities

In 1926 G. Bie Raondal, the U.S. consul general in Istanbul, wrote: "In the former Ottoman Empire they [the Jews] occupied important government positions, but the tendency of the new nationalism, ushered in by the republic, has been to put them in the same relative position as other non-Muslims, although they have never been persecuted in Turkey. [Now they] have carved out for themselves a place in every branch of the national life and are found as traders, bankers, professional men, office workers, and even laborers" (*Turkey*, 1926). Since 1926 many changes have occurred in modern Turkey, and the Jewish community has dwindled to an almost insignificant minority from the economic aspect. Although the severe blow of the capital tax (see below) was only temporary, it had a psychological effect on the Jewish community and was one of the causes of Jewish emigration from the country.

Jewish national life did not develop in *Istanbul and the towns which remained within the boundaries of Turkey; the Zionist idea had only few followers in the capital. The negative attitude of the Turkish government to Zionism was a heritage from Young Turk and Ottoman times, and influenced Turkish Jews. However, the idea of full integration in the Turkish state appeared to be unrealistic. The Jews, like the Greeks and the Armenians, unofficially remained second-class citizens. This was both demonstrated and felt in particular during World War II, so long as Hitler's antisemitic propaganda gained ground and it seemed that the Axis powers were moving toward victory. To meet wartime needs in the neutral Turkish republic a capital tax (*varlik vergisi*) was approved (1942) which was to be levied on owners of large farms (Muslims) and other taxpayers. However, it soon became apparent that the really important determinants of a taxpayer's assessment were his religion and nationality. The taxpayers' lists were prepared according to denominational indications. M (for Muslims) had to pay 5% of their capital or income (the same grade was accorded to foreign citizens); the tax rate for D (*Doenmeh) was about twice as much as for Muslims; for G (Gayri Muslims, non-Muslims) assessments would be made by special commissions, in accordance with their opinions. In fact the poorest among the non-Muslims, especially Jewish artisans, wage earners, and others, were taxed at figures wildly beyond their ability to pay. Members of the minorities who had retained or obtained foreign protection at the time of the armistice and Allied occupation (1919–23) were able to have their assessments reduced to the Muslim level. The Jews who had trusted

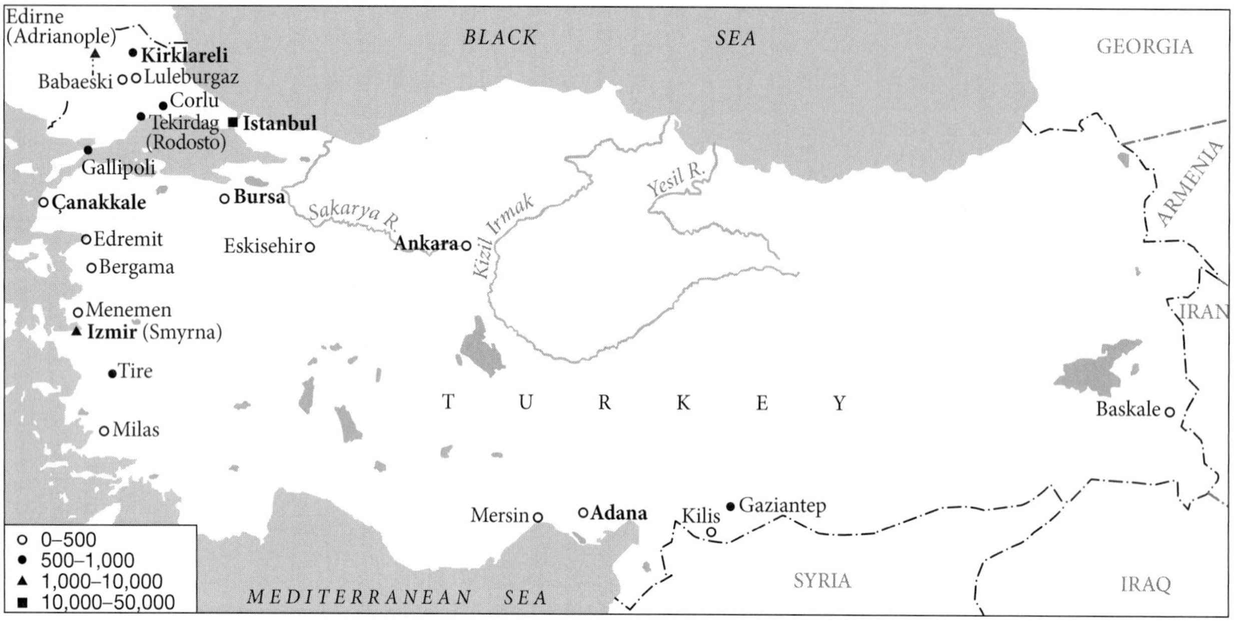

Jewish communities in Turkey in 1930. Names in boldface indicate those still in existence in 2005.

in the new republic and thrown their lot in with it were subject to victimization and punishment. Through the spring and summer of 1943 the continuing arrests, seizures, and deportations to labor camps were almost all of non-Muslims, the majority of whom were Jews. Many businessmen were ruined by assessments higher than their total possessions; others, though wealthy enough to pay, went bankrupt because no time was allowed them to find sufficient liquid money. The pro-Axis press expressed cordial approval of these developments, and denounced people of "alien blood," "Turks by name only," who should be punished for their disloyalty and ingratitude. With the decline of German power, as the downfall of the Axis became evident, a law was passed (1944) releasing all defaulters still detained and canceling all amounts still unpaid. The Democratic Party even promised compensation for damages caused to health and wealth.

After the end of the war the general economic situation and its structure changed for the better. Primarily, the reforms introduced after the establishment of the republic began to be felt. In addition, the aid given by the United States, aimed to strengthen the social structure of the population and hence the strategic value of the country, showed its efficacy. The Jewish population also took part in this recovery. In 1968 the economic situation of Turkish Jewry was good and the community contained some wealthy men. Most Jews were merchants, employees (very few of them in government service), or artisans. There were few underprivileged since most of the needy had settled in Israel soon after the establishment of the state.

Minor discrimination against Jews in Istanbul occurred, however, influenced by the tension between Turkey and Greece over Cyprus. During the anti-Greek riots in 1955 and 1964 the Jews were among the victims. The *Six-Day War (1967) also aroused anti-Jewish feelings and led to some small-scale incidents. The Turkish government, which had established diplomatic relations with Israel in 1949, always attempted to quell mob turbulence, but not with full effect. As the government's attitude toward Muslim religious activities became more tolerant, the rightist parties used it as a cover for anti-Jewish propaganda. Antisemitism being prohibited by law, anti-leftist and anti-Communist slogans were employed demagogically. By use of these tactics a small daily, *Bugün*, raised its circulation from 10,000 copies to 60,000. Some Turkish newspapers published articles in 1948 and later condemning emigration to Israel, and a few attacked the government for allowing it. They argued that the exodus of Jews would undermine the economy, and that communists were helping to organize emigration. Later, the amount of anti-Jewish material published in Turkey was reduced. Among those continuing to publish such material was Cevat Rifat Atilhan, who wrote *Le Sionisme, Danger pour l'Islamisme* (1951; almost all copies were seized by the authorities) and "Turks, Here is Your Enemy" (Turkish, 1959). Atilhan also wrote anti-Jewish articles in the newspaper *Yeni Istiklal*. Between 1951 and 1961 the newspaper *Büyük Doğu* ("Great East"), whose editor was Necip Fazil Kisakürek, printed many anti-Jewish articles.

Demography

The first census of the Turkish republic, held in 1927, showed some 79,454 Jews in a total population of over 13.5 million (see Table: Distribution of Jewish Population in Turkey), of whom half were in Istanbul. By 1945, the total Jewish population had decreased to 76,965, and in 1955 to 40,345. Immediately after the establishment of the State of Israel there was large-scale emigration of Turkish Jews. However, in November 1948, as the result of pressure exerted by the Arab states, emigration was forbidden until early 1949. Later in that year Turkey recognized the State of Israel *de jure*, and Jews were again permitted to emigrate. The government even put ships of its merchant shipping line at the disposal of the emigrants, but forbade Israel representatives to organize emigration (until 1950). A total of 4,362 Turkish Jews went to Israel in 1948, and 26,295 in 1949–50. After 1950 the number of emigrants fell, although the Turkish government made no difficulties for those wishing to leave, except for the prohibition of taking out money. Between 1952 and 1955 only 2,182 Jews went to Israel. It is presumed that about 37,000 Jews left Turkey for Israel between 1948 and 1970; however about ten percent of these, principally from Istanbul and Izmir (peddlers, bootblacks, small wage earners, etc.), returned to Turkey, as conditions had improved in the country. Since 1960 the official Turkish census commission has not compiled statistics by religion, hence it is impossible to know precise figures for Turkey's Jews. Estimates are 38,000 for 1965, and about 20,000 in 2005: some 17,000 in Istanbul, 2,000 in Izmir, and smaller groups in Ankara, Adana, Çanakkale, Bursa, and Kirklareli.

Distribution of Jewish Population in Turkey

	Year 1927 official census	Year 1965 chief rabbinate estimates[1]	Year 1965–70 Jewish institutions estimates[2]
1. Adana	159	60	70
2. Ankara	663	800	3,200
3. Antakya (Antioch)	–	100	6
4. Bursa (Brusa)	1,915	350	400
5. Çanakkale	–	420	300
6. Çoclu	592	40	20
7. Dardanelles	1,109	–	–
8. Edirne (Adrianople)	6,098	400	120–400
9. Gallipoli	736	200	200
10. Gaziantep	742	160	–
11. Iskenderun	–	60	60
12. Istanbul	47,035	35,000	30,000
13. Izmir (Smyrna)	17,094	5,000	4,800–4,000
14. Kirklareli	978	90	67–35
15. Mersin	122	90	50
16. Milas	259	–	79
17. Tekirdag (Rodosto)	889	170	120
18. Tire	1063	–	100
Total	79,454	42,940	40,000

1 According to letter Aug. 3, 1965
2 World Jewish Congress; Jewish Agency

Cultural, Religious, and Social Life

There was a dramatic decline of interest in Judaism and Jewish culture among Turkish Jewry in the period between the two world wars and for a few years after it. The last Hebrew press closed in 1944, when its proprietor emigrated to Ereẓ Israel. After the death in 1931 of the *ḥakham bashi* R. Bekhor Ḥayyim *Bejarano, the official representative of Turkish Jewry, the community did not even feel an immediate necessity to appoint a successor. This absence of a spiritual leader not only led to religious indifference but also to apathy. As the *ḥakham bashi* was responsible for leading all activities of all Jewish communities in the Turkish republic, his absence was felt in every field of Jewish life. After a long interval Turkish Jewry decided to elect another *ḥakham bashi*, and R. Raphael David Saban was appointed to head the chief rabbinate (1953–60). He was succeeded by R. David *Asseo in 1960 and R. Isak *Haleva. The *ḥakham bashi* is assisted by a religious council consisting of a *rosh bet din* (also bearing the title *mara de-atra*) and four *ḥakhamim*. The lay council of the *ḥakham bashi* deals with secular-social matters concerning the Jewish community; it consists of 19 members (Sephardim and Ashkenazim). Together they support communal institutions such as synagogues, hospitals, cemeteries, old age homes, and schools.

Jewish Communal Schools

Turkish Jewry maintained its own educational institutions. However, the syllabus in all of them was the same as in government schools. When state opposition to religion was reduced (1948), Jews were permitted to teach Hebrew and religion in their schools (for following the prayers). The Turkish government forbade all Zionist activity as well as the existence of organizations with centers abroad which propagated non-Turkish nationalism. Since most Jewish children attended school, illiteracy fell, and almost all of them spoke and read Turkish, although most of them also spoke Ladino.

In the 1920s and 1930s Istanbul had eight Jewish communal schools for boys and girls together and one high school (founded in 1922 as Lycée Juif by the *B'nai B'rith Lodge); their number has decreased since. The Turkish language was the compulsory medium of instruction in all state schools, and in private schools at the primary level. The Jewish schools obtained permission to give one course in elementary Hebrew, needed for reciting the prayers, but not to give instruction in Jewish history and literature. Hebrew studies were de-emphasized as a result of a 1932 law which forbade religious instruction in all Turkish schools.

Abraham *Galanté was one of the enthusiastic supporters of the spread of Turkish and one of the sponsors of replacing the Arabic script by the Latin alphabet (1928). Ladino periodicals, which had previously appeared in Hebrew script, began to be printed in Latin characters; one, in Istanbul, was *La Vera Luz* (edited by Eliezer Menda), later closed down. *Shalom*, first edited by Avram Leyon, continues, but only some of its articles were in Ladino, the rest in Turkish. A third, *Etoile du Lévant*, published in French, ceased in 1948. The monthly periodical (later a quarterly) *Hamenorah*, published by the B'nai B'rith (1923–38) and edited by David Marcus in three languages (Hebrew, Ladino, and French), carried many important articles concerning the history of Ottoman Jewry. Present-day Jewish writers publish their works in Turkish or French. The Jewish poet Joseph Habib *Gerez wrote in Turkish and described the glories of Istanbul. The library of the chief rabbinate was little used, and Italian Jews made efforts to promote interest in religion and culture. The Turkish authorities did not hinder Jews from religious observance. Nevertheless, most of the younger generation by the 1960s was not observant, and some young people were entirely ignorant of Judaism. The number of marriages to non-Jews increased too.

The Maḥazikei Torah institutions provided religious instruction (and elementary Hebrew language courses) in the evenings and Sunday mornings (Sunday being the official rest day in the Turkish republic) for Jewish boys and girls who attended the Turkish state schools where no Hebrew was taught. There were about 2,000 pupils in these institutions. The Maḥazikei Torah also trained religious functionaries: *ḥazzanim, shoḥatim, mohalim*. Turkish Jewry also had a rabbinical seminary. It was established in Istanbul in 1955, and about 50 students were registered in the mid-1960s, some of whom were awarded rabbinic ordination. After years of general decline in Jewish life this indicated noticeable progress and a reaction to the general apathy in Jewish education. Izmir is the second largest Jewish community in modern Turkey, with approximately 2,000 Jewish inhabitants (2005). It had two Jewish elementary schools and a secondary one. Other communities were too small to have their own schools.

The usual Jewish philanthropic and social institutions also existed in Istanbul and Izmir: orphanages, hospitals, assistance for poor, etc., all supervised by the Türkiye Hahambashiliği, the chief rabbinate of Turkey (letter from the *ḥakham bashi* dated Aug. 3, 1965).

Ashkenazim and Sephardim

Of Turkey's Jews in 1969, about 95 percent were Sephardim, the rest Ashkenazim, called *lehli*, the Turkish name for Poles, because during the 17th and 18th centuries the Ashkenazi immigrants had come from Poland. Later, however, there was Ashkenazi immigration from Austria; the German-speaking Austrian Jews formed the elite of the community, and the Great Synagogue built by them became known as the "Oesterreichischer Tempel." Their last officiating rabbi, David Marcus, was born in Russia, studied in Germany, and then settled in Istanbul (1900–44). After his death the congregation remained without a rabbi and went into a decline, being in danger of complete disintegration, although their percentage in the Jewish population increased somewhat. The older generation of Sephardi Jews continued to speak *Ladino, in which language they produced sacred literature, and since the 19th century published many periodicals. In the 1955 census 64 percent among the Jews declared that their mother tongue was Yahudice (Ladino) compared with 84 percent in 1927, but knowledge of Ladino decreased. Neither the Jews nor the Greeks mastered the Turkish language until, under the new regime, it was introduced into the schools and the younger generation learned to speak, read, and write it fluently.

Karaites

Since all the *Karaite Jews of Egypt left for Israel during the 1950s, as did the remnants of the Karaite community in Hith (Iraq), the Karaite community in Istanbul remained the last in non-Communist Europe. There were about 200 Karaite families (1,000 persons) in Hasköy, a suburb of Istanbul, whose forefathers settled in the city in Byzantine times. They established their own synagogue and cemetery and were completely separated from the Jewish Rabbanite community. They did not intermarry with Rabbanites, with whom the only link was a Rabbanite *mohel* whom they too employed for circumcisions. Their rabbi, Isaac Kerimi, came from the Crimea. Many Karaites spoke Greek. Their attitude toward Israel was neutral, or even unfriendly.

[Haïm Z'ew Hirschberg and Hayyim J. Cohen]

Later Developments

In general, the 1980s were a period of well-being for the Jewish community in Turkey. In spite of increasing Islamic fundamentalist trends and economic difficulties due to high inflation, the Jews of Turkey witnessed a demographic growth, an improvement of the relations between the authorities and the community, and a visible awakening of Jewish identity among the members of the community.

The traumatic event of the decade to hit the community, which is usually out of the spotlight, occurred on September 6, 1986, when Arab gunmen attacked worshipers in Istanbul's Neveh Shalom synagogue during Sabbath morning services. Nineteen of the congregation, two of them Israelis, were killed in the massacre, as were the two gunmen who apparently blew themselves up. A wave of horror ran through the world and condemnations were heard on all sides, while the subsequent funeral became a protest demonstration. The Turkish prime minister, Turgut Özal, immediately called an emergency cabinet meeting and sent a message of condemnation and sympathy to the chief rabbi of Turkey, David Asseo. A subsequent government statement linked the murderers to *Iran and pro-Iranian terror organizations. The synagogue was restored and reinaugurated the following year. A monument in memory of the victims was dedicated at the Ulus/Istanbul cemetery in 1989. In another bomb outrage in 1992, an Israeli diplomat was killed.

In spite of pressures created by the gradual revival of the Islamic spirit in the country, the Turkish government has shown a close interest in the problems of the Jewish community and encouraged direct personal contacts to develop between it and the leaders of the community. Unprecedented permission was granted to Jews by allowing members of the community to take part in the meetings of the World Jewish Congress (WJC). However, this permission marks the only instance, with the exception of *Morocco, of a Muslim government allowing its Jews to participate in a worldwide Jewish activity; it is valid solely for the WJC but applies to no other international Jewish organization, and has been granted on condition of the Turkish community's not becoming a full member but being present only as an "observer."

Synagogues, as well as property owned by the community, are considered as *vakif* ("foundations") by Turkish law, and all foundations in Turkey, non-Muslim and Muslim alike, are subject to the control and regulations of the *vakif.* Jewish communities have felt the effect of these regulations in their efforts to obtain firm and autonomous possession of their patrimony. By the existing regulations, communities are regarded merely as administrators and not as absolute owners of their immovable property. In the event of Jewish population movement, either within the cities or to the suburbs, if Jewish community real estate remains in the area where Jews no longer live, it is forfeited by the community to the *vakif* administration.

Two main events marked Jewish communal life during the latter part of this period: the reorganization in March 1989 of the Lay Council of the Chief Rabbinate and the positive approach of the Turkish authorities to Jewish communal problems.

Through the reorganization of the Lay Council, communal affairs have been taken over by a younger and more dynamic group which adopted a bolder attitude in solving problems. Both the 80-member General Assembly of the Council and its 15-member Executive Committee include representatives from even the smallest Jewish congregations all over the country. The Chief Rabbinate has thus gained authority and jurisdiction over all the Jews of Turkey; previously its authority was practically limited to Istanbul and was often subject to the whims and goodwill of the communities in other cities.

The new Lay Council also succeeded in establishing closer relations with the authorities which, parallel to the changing international political developments, have been inclined to view the problems of the Jewish community from a more positive angle. As a result of this approach a number of developments beneficial to the community have been achieved: the permission to transfer the Jewish lycée and primary school in Istanbul to an area where Jews had moved during the last 20 years, for which permission had been requested ten years ago and been left pending, was granted; a law passed six years earlier rendering the teaching of Islamic religion an obligatory part of the curriculum in all primary and secondary schools was abolished; *talmud torah* education in synagogues was officially allowed; a special foundation to commemorate and celebrate the 500th anniversary of the arrival on Turkish-Ottoman soil of Jews fleeing the Inquisition was created jointly by Muslim and Jewish citizens with the support of the government; and a disused synagogue, the Zülfaris, is being turned into a Jewish museum, the only one of its kind in a Muslim country, where Jews constitute less than 5 per 10,000 of the general population; and for the first time ever, Jewish sportsmen were officially authorized to take part in the 1991 Maccabi games in Marseilles under the Turkish flag.

Immigration to Israel has almost ceased while the number of Jews who had moved to Israel but decided to return to Istanbul in particular has increased considerably. Further, the improved political and social conditions in Turkey have resulted in a sense of security for Jews, and the number of births has risen. The Jewish population grew from 22,000 to 27,000, of whom 2,000 live in Izmir; a few hundred are scattered over western Turkey; and the rest reside in Istanbul. (Censuses do not state the religion of citizens so it is difficult to determine exact figures.) Roughly 1,000 Turkish Jews are Ashkenazim; the rest Sephardim. The two groups live in complete harmony and all communal welfare institutions are administered jointly by members of both rites. There is only one Ashkenazi synagogue in all Turkey. The religious activities of the two rites are run by the Sephardi chief rabbinate and *bet din* which satisfactorily fulfill Ashkenazi needs.

Economically most of the Turkish Jews continued to be rather well off, except for some 300 families who were partly or totally supported by the community. However, Jews in general suffered due to the rampant inflation in the 1990s (a limited number of prominent businessmen constituting an exception).

Members of the community have displayed a marked return to religion and traditions and a keener Jewish consciousness. The number of people who have voluntarily offered to take an active part in communal work and assume their obligations toward the community has grown. The weekly paper *Shalom*, the publication of which had been stopped as a result of its former owner's illness and death, has been taken over by a group of young people who have succeeded in increasing its circulation to 5,000 (thus turning it into a paper read in almost every Jewish household) and giving special emphasis to the revival of Ladino. About one third of the contents of the paper is in *Ladino and the younger generation has begun to show a greater interest in the language.

A new club was founded to serve the Jewish residents of fashionable quarters on the Asian coast of Istanbul, where almost a fourth of the Jewish population lives, and its new building with sports, recreation, and cultural facilities was inaugurated in 1987. A trend of more intense searching for a Jewish identity has emerged among the younger generation and a greater number of people of all ages are volunteering for communal work. However, in spite of the sociocultural revival, the number of intermarriages has increased and has been put at ten percent.

The chief rabbi (*ḥakham bashi*) is the official leader and representative of Turkish Jewry. He is assisted by a Religious Council (*bet din*) and the Lay Council. In contrast to its glorious past of world-famous rabbis and religious scholars, the community is beginning to feel the shortage of qualified rabbis and other religious functionaries. The only *kasher* restaurant closed when its owner retired.

Jews continue to be politically inactive in the country. As in the past, this is due both to their insignificant numbers as well as to their reluctance to take part in politics. While the majority of Jews voted for the middle-right Motherland Party in power during the 1986 elections, a religious party advocating antipathy and even hostility towards Israel and the Jews grew much stronger. Occasional incitements by this party have caused the Jewish community anxiety.

The approval by the authorities and their encouragement of the decision to celebrate the 500th anniversary of the settling of the Sephardi Jews on Turkish-Ottoman soil in 1492 was a high point in Jewish communal life. To celebrate the anniversary a series of national and international symposiums, publications, the creation of a Jewish museum and concerts of local Jewish music were prepared for 1990, with the climax in 1992. (See also *Sephardim.)

[Hanri Yasova]

Relations with Israel

In the 1947 UN General Assembly, Turkey voted against the partition of Palestine and the creation of a Jewish state out of Muslim solidarity and also because of its interest in the continued existence of British positions in the Middle East in the event of a Soviet attack. When the State of Israel became a reality, however, Turkey extended to Israel *de jure* recognition in November 1949, and agreed to the establishment of diplomatic relations. Legations were established and relations between the two countries developed satisfactorily. A commercial agreement in July 1950 facilitated trade relations based on the complementary character of the two countries' economies. An air-transport agreement was signed in February 1951 inaugurating regular Lydda-Istanbul flights by El Al and Turkish Airlines. The Turkish maritime company also initiated passenger and cargo lines to Israel. Israeli contracting firms started working in Turkey, and cultural relations also developed.

The Democratic Party, which came to power in May 1950, slowed down (especially from 1952) the pace of strengthening relations with Israel. It initiated a policy of rapprochement with the Arab countries in order to form a regional defense treaty and to please religious elements within Turkey. The level and scope of relations with Israel were reduced mainly after the signing of the Baghdad Pact with Iraq in February 1955. In December 1956, a few weeks after the *Sinai Campaign, Turkey recalled its minister from Israel, leaving its legation under a chargé d'affaires, and asked Israel to reciprocate. This step was a compromise, as Turkey resisted Arab pressure to sever diplomatic relations with Israel. When Iraq withdrew from the Baghdad Pact in 1959 after the revolutionary coup of 1958, Turkey again changed its attitude vis-à-vis Israel. The ousting of the Democratic Party from power in May 1960 also contributed to the improvement of relations between the two countries. Official visits, some of them at the level of cabinet ministers, were exchanged, and close cooperation began in technical assistance. This stage came to an end following the intercommunal riots in Cyprus in 1963–64. Turkey needed Arab support at the UN and decided to reduce its relations with Israel to a minimum, limiting them mainly to the economic sphere. (In 1969, for example, Israel exported $2,000,000 worth of chemicals, medicaments, and paint to Turkey and imported $4,700,000 worth of sugar, dried fruits, and lentils.) After the Six-Day War (1967), Turkey called for "the establishment of a just and lasting peace" in the Middle East, declaring its opposition to the acquisition of territories by force. It demanded that Israel withdraw from the occupied territories and that there be no change in the status of *Jerusalem. In 1971, the Israel consul in Istanbul, Ephraim Elrom, was kidnapped and after a few days was found murdered. The Turkish government ascribed the crime to extreme left-wing circles whose action was directed not only against Israel but also against the Turkish regime.

[Baruch Gilead]

The years from 1967 to the present may be divided into two: the period which ended in the late 1980s and the second one that continued into the early 21st century. The first period was characterized by official alienation towards Israel by Turkey, culminating in November 1980 in the downgrading of diplomatic relations to the level of junior chargés d'affaires. This happened as a result of the Israeli Knesset's decision to apply Israeli law to the eastern parts of Jerusalem (held by Israel since the 1967 Six-Day War). The pressure of Arab countries, loans and credits from *Saudi Arabia, and large quantities of cheap oil from Iran, *Libya, and *Iraq persuaded Turkey to adopt this position. Turkey supported the Arab position that the occupation of lands in the June 1967 war, including East Jerusalem and the Muslim holy places, amounted to aggression. In October 1973 Ankara refused to grant the right of passage through its airspace, and landing facilities, to American cargo planes that carried urgent supplies to Israel during the October 1973 war; Turkey did, however, allow Russian weapon convoys to cross its territory on their way to *Syria.

This pattern of relations continued until the late 1980s. However, three processes helped change the relations and the atmosphere of alienation. A sharp decrease in energy prices resulted in the Arab countries' losing their ability to exert pressure on Turkey's foreign policy. The second process was the collapse of communism and the disintegration of the Soviet Union. Thus, relations with Israel were no longer a component of the Cold War, to be used as an asset for communism or the Arab states against anybody who had decided to improve relations with Israel, or as a threat of punishment against anyone upgrading relations with Israel. The third process that encouraged Turkey to improve relations with Israel was the withdrawal of Israel from much of southern Lebanon (1985), the Madrid Conference (1991), and the ensuing thaw in Arab-Israeli relations, culminating in the Oslo accords (1993) between Israel and the Palestinians and the peace agreement between Israel and Jordan (1994). Another component that brought about greater cooperation between Israel and Turkey was the growing influence of Muslim radicalism and threats to the Middle Eastern status quo emanating, respectively, from Iran and Iraq. As a result the 1990s were marked by dramatic changes in Turkish-Israeli relations. Cooperation and contacts were conducted openly, a sharp contrast to the previous period, which was marked mostly by secret and clandestine relations. Diplomatic relations were elevated to ambassadorial level (December 2001). A military agreement (February 1996) resulted in intensive cooperation between the armies, navies, air forces, and weapons industries of the two countries. Growing numbers of Israeli tourists visit Turkey (more than 300,000 annually since the mid-1990s, about five percent of Israel's population). Cultural contacts have also increased resulting, among other things, in the teaching of the Turkish and the Hebrew languages in Israeli and Turkish universities, respectively. Thus, mutual civilian trade of all kinds, tourism not included, has amounted to more than $2 billion a year since the early 21st century. Roughly speaking, the entire volume of trade can be divided into one-quarter military contracts and three-quarters civilian. The two countries signed an agreement (March 2004) according to which Israel would purchase annually, for a period of 20 years, the amount of 50 million cubic meters of Turkish fresh water. The upshot of all the above is that Turkey and Israel have a greater volume of civilian trade than between any two states in the Middle East.

The coming to power in Turkey of the Muslim Justice and Development Party (AKP) in November 2002, the war in Iraq which erupted in March 2003, and the December 2004 decision of the EU to conduct membership negotiations with Turkey (to begin in October 2005) provided new inputs to Turkish-Israeli relations. The worsening of relations (as from the year 2000) between Israel and the Palestinians also detrimentally affected Turkish-Israeli relations. Unlike Israel, which supported the American war in Iraq, Turkey opposed it and looked with great concern at the Iraqi mayhem and the possible disintegration of that country into its ethnic components. Turkey repeatedly voiced concern lest a Kurdish entity be established in northern Iraq. Even more, the growing interaction between Ankara and the EU resulted, inter alia, in Turkish policies and statements vis-à-vis Israel and the Palestinians which resemble those of the EU. And while the basic pattern of the bilateral cooperation has not changed – economic, cultural, and military contacts continue to improve, even to thrive; Ankara supported the Israeli disengagement from the *Gaza Strip; high-level contacts are routinely conducted (in August 2005 Turkey used its good offices to mediate between Israel and Pakistan and arranged the first public meeting between the foreign secretaries of the two states) – still, occasionally, Turkey openly criticizes certain Israeli measures in the Israeli-Palestinian conflict.

[Amikam Nachmani (2nd ed.)]

Jewish Musical Tradition

The arrival of the waves of Jews expelled from Spain in the newly established Ottoman Empire marks a turning point in the history of this country's Jewish musical life. The newcomers brought with them a rich musical tradition, which they continued to preserve and cultivate jealously in the new environment. Their contact with the highly developed Turkish art music as well as with the vestiges of the Romaniot-Byzantine musical style gave rise to an interesting situation in which the Turkish and Sephardi styles became subsequently the two dominant strains of the diverse musical activities in the major cities of the Ottoman Empire. The Byzantine style that characterized the music of old Romaniot communities of Constantinople, Bursa, Adrianople and others continued to be preserved among the Karaites of the Hasköy district of Constantinople and much more overtly in the area where Greek is still the spoken language: at Ioanina, Chalkis, Arta, and Patras. One may even assume that even after the great changes the Byzantine style did not disappear without leaving some traces.

THE COEXISTENCE OF TWO DIFFERENT STYLES. The Spanish Jews continued to maintain a distinctive Judeo-Spanish idiom for secular purposes and Hebrew and Ladino for liturgical functions, and maintained the musical repertory of the Spanish tradition with a remarkable persistence. The latter has been prominent mainly in secular life, and to a lesser extent in liturgical and paraliturgical instances, and essentially became the province of women in the new environment. Jewish women were not involved in the performance of Turkish classical music, and as a rule they did not take part in the liturgical practice. Nevertheless, some daughters of rabbis and cantors involved in the religious activities of their fathers were proficient in the singing of synagogal pieces in the men's ornamented and nasalizing Turkish style.

THE TURKISH STYLE IN SYNAGOGAL MUSIC. The fervent identification of the Jews with the Turkish art music style as a vehicle leading the worshipers to religious elevation and compassion, known as *ḥizzun* (a derivative from the Arabic *ḥuzn*, meaning sadness and introspection), appears in a statement made by the religious scholar, kabbalist, and talented poet-musician rabbi Menahem di *Lonzano (1550–before 1624). In the preface to his collection of *piyyutim* set to Turkish tunes (published about 1575 in Constantinople, probably his birthplace) he claims that he found the Turkish tunes "to be the expression of a broken and contrite heart." In the 19th century, Rabbi Moses Hazzan, who served in Jerusalem's High Religious Court, reports in his book *Kerekh shel Romi* (Livorno, 1886, fol. 72) the following astonishing testimony, which may imply the influence of Turkish-Byzantine style:

> And I testify by heaven and earth that when I was in Izmir, the great city of scholars and mystics, I saw some of the most outstanding religious authorities who were also great creators of the science of music, headed by the wonderful Rabbi Abraham ha-Cohen Ariash of blessed memory, who secretly used to go (behind a screen) in the Christian church on their holy days to learn the special melodies from them and to adapt them to the High Holidays prayers which require great humility. And from those same melodies they would arrange the most remarkable blessings and holy prayers.

Interestingly, the aforementioned Rabbi Abraham Ariash made a name as a composer of 80 Turkish musical pieces in different modes and was known as *hadje-i beskusar* ("a consummate master").

The singing of *piyyutim* in the framework of the normative liturgy music as well as all other types of religious rituals, such as that of the *maftirim* (see below), is only one aspect of synagogal music; the other concerns the recitation of the prayer and the cantillation of Holy Scriptures. While the latter realizes only partially and in a floating manner the melodic content of the *Maqam principles, such as the use of *Maqam Sika* for the reading of the Torah and various other *maqamat* for the Sabbath prayers' recitation, the singing of the *piyyutim* fully adheres to the Turkish *maqam* system. The Jews also adhere to the related doctrine of ethos and its psychological influence; cantors and readers of the sacred texts frequently relate the tune to an emotive term, and to the typical intonations characterizing the voice inflections and timbres of the Turkish performing style.

Solomon Mazal Tov published the earliest Hebrew collection of sung *piyyutim*: *Shirim u-Zemirot ve-Tishbaḥot* (Constantinople, 1545).

The Maftirim. At Edirne (Adrianople), a choral society of *Maftirim* was founded in the 17th century; it developed an extensive repertoire paralleling the **Bakkashot* tradition of the mystic circles in Aleppo, Morocco, and elsewhere. They used in their celebrations of the Sabbath a book of *piyyutim* called *jonk,* the term being derived from Turkish/Persian *conk,* which is similar to the Arabic *diwan*, meaning a collection of poetry. The activity and the reputation of the *Maftirim* society helped Adrianople become a center for hymn writers and composers. Among the best known were composer Aaron ben Isaac Hamon (18th c.); Joseph Danon (d. 1901), who collected and published in 1896 a large repertoire of Ladino folksongs from Adrianople; and Isaac Eliahu Navon (b. 1859). Navon was a prominent personality in the community and a member of the choir society of the *Maftirim*. He moved with his parents at the age of 18 to Istanbul where he composed poems and hymns; he gathered and edited a collection of old *piyyutim* of Jewish poets, *Shirat Ẓiyyon be-Ereẓ ha-Kedem* (Istanbul, 1921), which reflects the choral repertory of the *Maftirim* from Edirne. At the age of 70, Eliahu Navon immigrated to Ereẓ Israel where he published his collection *Yinnon* (Jerusalem, 1937), including both religious and secular compositions; some of his songs became part of Israeli folk song.

The repertory of the *Maftirim* is modeled after the Turkish classical multisectional *fasil* (lit. "section"). This prestigious form seems to have grown from the eastern *nawba*. It was customary to perform a fixed sequence of pieces of different genres, allowing a certain amount of freedom to introduce new combinations.

THE MUSICAL ACTIVITY IN IZMIR. Izmir was an important center of a rich Jewish musical life from the 17th through the 20th century. In his book *Histoire des Juifs d'Anatolie* (vol. 1, 163–67) Abraham Galanté mentioned several Jewish musicians who made a name as proficient composers and performers in the Turkish society. They include Hakham Yomtov Danon (17th century) known among the Turks as "the little *Hakham*"; the aforementioned Rabbi Abraham Ariash; the composer and *santur* (trapezoidal cithara) player Elia Levy; the violinist Isaac Barki; composer Shemtov Shikiar, known among the Turks as Hodja Santo; and Salomon Algazi, a noted *ḥazzan* and composer known among the Turks as Salomon the Nightingale, thanks to his most beautiful voice. He is the father of the famous *ḥazzan* and composer Isaac *Algazi (1882–1964). At an early age Isaac joined the *Maftirim* Choir led by his father and served as *ḥazzan* in his native town. His performing style as a *ḥazzan* and singer of secular pieces was highly expressive, enhanced by a moving and pleasant voice. He also became proficient in Turkish art music and a noted performer of classical Turkish music; Ataturk invited him to sing at his palace. Among his pupils was another native of Izmir, composer and musicologist Alberto *Hemsi who published in 1924–5 five notated groups of *piyyutim* organized in the form of *Fasil* (a Turkish suite). Isaac Algazi ended his life in Uruguay. A selection of Isaac Algazi's poetry has been published in *Shirei Yisrael be-Ereẓ ha-Kedem* (1921).

In dealing with the various Jewish societies in Izmir, Galanté refers to the activity during the 18th and 19th centuries of a unique society, largely supported by charity, called *La Dansa*. It involved a group of singers and dancers whose function was to gladden poor newly married couples in their house on Sabbath afternoon. To avoid the interdiction of playing instruments on the day of Sabbath, they used to accompany their singing and dancing with a copper plate on which they beat the rhythm. Some religious authorities expressed dissatisfaction with this practice, while others justified it by virtue of the *mitzvah* "To gladden the bridegroom and bride" (*ibid.*, p. 93).

[Amnon Shiloah (2nd ed.)]

BIBLIOGRAPHY: Galanté, *Histoire des Juifs d'Anatolie*, 1–2 (1937–39); D.J. Elazar (ed.) et al., *Balkan Jewish Communities: Yugoslavia, Bulgaria, Greece, and Turkey* (1984); N. Nathan, in: JJSO, 6 (1964), 172–89; B. Lewis, *Emergence of Modern Turkey* (1961); *Revue encyclopédique juive*, 4:18 (1970); N. Robinson, in: J. Freid (ed.), *Jews in Modern World*, 1 (1962), 50–90; A. Tartakower, *Shivtei Yisrael* 3 (1969), 253–8. **ADD BIBLIOGRAPHY:** The best bibliography on Jews in the Republic of Turkey is R.N. Bali, *Türkiye'de Yayinlanmiş Yahudilikle ilgili kitab, tez ve makaleler bibliyografyasi 1923–2003* (2004). See also: B. Lewis, *The Emergence of Modern Turkey* (1960); J.M. Landau, *Tekinalp: Turkish Patriot* (1984); idem, "Comments on the Jewish Press in Istanbul," in: *Etudes Balkaniques*, 2 (1990), 78–82; idem, "Turkish-Israeli Cultural and Scientific Relations," in: Ali Ihsan Bagiş (ed.), *Actual Situation and Prospects of Turkey's Bilateral Relations with Israel* (1992), 85–96; S.J. Shaw, *The Jews of the Ottoman Empire and the Turkish Republic* (1991); A. Levi, *Toledot ha-Yehudim ba-Republikah ha-Turkit* (1992); N. Güleryüz, *Türk Yahudileri tarihi* (1993); E.J. Zürcher, *Turkey: A Modern History* (1997); R.N. Bali, *Cummhuriyet yillarinda Türkiye Yahudileri* (1999); idem, *Les Relations entre Turcs et Tuifs dans la Turquie moderne* (2001); M. Tütüneü (ed.), *Turkish-Jewish Encounters* (2001); G.E. Gruen, "Turkey," in: R.S. Simon et al. (eds.), *The Jews of the Middle East and North Africa in Modern Times* (2003), 303–15; Sh. Tuval, *Ha-Kehillah ha-Yehudit be-Istanbul 1948–1992* (2004); A. Nachmani, *Turkey Facing A New Millennium* (2003); O. Bengio, *The Turkish-Israeli Relationship* (2004). JEWISH MUSICAL TRADITION: A. Galanté, *Histoire des Juifs d'Anatolie*, 2 vols.

(Istanbul, 1937); E. Seroussi, *Mizimrat Qedem: The Life and Music of Isaac Algazi from Turkey* (1989); idem, "From the Court and *Tarikat* to the Synagogue: Ottoman Art Music and Hebrew Sacred Song," in: *Sufism, Music and Society in Turkey and the Middle East*, papers edited by A. Hammarlund, T. Olsson, E. Özdalga, Swedish Research Institute in Istanbul, Transactions, vol. 10 (2001), 81–93; P. Dorn, *Change and Ideology: The Ethnomusicology of Turkish Jewry*, UMI Dissertation Services (2001).

TURKOW, Polish family originating in Warsaw. ITZḤAK TURKOW (pen name Grudberg; 1906–1970), Yiddish actor and writer. From 1925 to 1957, Itzhak Turkow worked with the Yiddish Art Theater in Warsaw, the Vilna Troupe, and the Jewish State Theater. From 1946 to 1950 he also edited a weekly "Lower Silesia." He settled in Israel in 1957, edited the weekly *Folksblat* (1958–68), and was the author of *Yidish Teater in Poyln* (1951), *Mame Esther Rachel*, a biography of Esther Rachel *Kaminska (1953), *Varshever Purim-Shpiler* (1957), memoirs *Oyf Mayn Veg* (1964), *Geven a Yidish Teater* (1968), and monographs on Peretz, Asch, Goldfaden, and Gordin. He was director of Bet Shalom Ash in Bat-Yam from 1959.

ZYGMUNT TURKOW (1896–1970), Yiddish actor and director. Turkow toured with Rachel Kaminska, and with her founded the Jewish Art Theater, Warsaw, 1929. He toured widely playing in Molière, Shalom Aleichem, Gogol, Goldfaden, and the early Yiddish play *Serkele* by *Ettinger. He went to Brazil after World War II and was co-founder of the Brazilian National Theater. He also directed and acted in Yiddish films. He settled in Israel in 1952, founded Zuta, a traveling theater, in 1956, and directed it until it disbanded in 1967. He also wrote plays and four volumes of memoirs.

JONAS TURKOW (1898–1988), actor, in charge of theatrical entertainment in the Warsaw ghetto during World War II. He started his career with the Kaminska Theater in Warsaw, and managed theaters in Vilna, Warsaw, and Cracow. He took part in several Yiddish films, playing the title role in *Lamed-Vovnik* and directing J. Opatoshu's *In Poylishe Velder* (1929). He and his wife, Diana Blumenfeld, were in the Warsaw ghetto until 1943 and were the only two actors to come out of it alive. In his book *Azoy Is Es Geven* ("That's How it Was," 1948), Turkow describes ghetto life in much detail and explains how the theater he organized functioned amid want and peril. After the war he toured the Displaced Persons camps and continued writing of his wartime experiences: *In Kamf farn Lebn* ("Fighting for Life," 1949), *Farloshene Shtern* ("Stars Extinguished," 1953), and *Nokh der Bafrayung* ("After the Liberation," 1959). Settling in New York in 1947, he became archivist for the theater department of *YIVO in 1958. He settled in Israel in 1966.

Marc *Turkow (1904–1983) was a Yiddish journalist and writer in Warsaw and Buenos Aires.

BIBLIOGRAPHY: LNYL, 2 (1958), 369–70; 4 (1961), 56–62.

TURKOW, MARC (1904–1983), journalist and writer in Yiddish and Spanish. He was born in Warsaw, Poland, where he was a journalist and started his public career. Turkow settled in Buenos Aires, Argentina, in 1930. From 1946 he headed the bureau of HIAS. From 1954 he was the representative of the World Jewish Congress for Latin America. One of his contributions to Jewish culture in Spanish in Argentina was the publication of dozens of booklets on distinguished Jewish intellectuals and spiritual leaders under the name Biblioteca Popular Judía (Jewish Popular Library). The Centro de Documentación e Información sobre Judaísmo Argentino (Documentation and Information Center on Argentinean Jewry), established in 1983 under the auspices of AMIA – the Ashkenazi Jewish Community of Buenos Aires, was named after him.

[Efraim Zadoff (2nd ed.)]

TURNER, YA'AKOV (1935–), 10th inspector general of the Israeli police and mayor of Beersheba. Turner joined the IDF in 1953 and served for 32 years in the Israel Air Force, flying over 300 combat missions and serving as a squadron commander in the Six-Day War and afterward as commander of the IAF flight school. In 1977 Turner was named commander of one of the major bases of the Israel Air Force, a position he held until 1981, when he became head of the human resource department of the force. During his military service he graduated in human behavioral sciences from Ben-Gurion University. He was one of the founders of the Air Force Museum, becoming its head. In 1985 he joined the Israeli police as head of the human resource section. In 1989 he was promoted to head the Central District and in 1990 he became inspector general, a position he filled until 1993. Under his leadership, the police faced the first Intifada. He also created a number of important units: the traffic police to deal with traffic problems and felonies; the helicopter unit aimed to assist forces on the ground; and the Southern District with headquarters in Beersheba. Six years after his retirement from the police, in 1999, he was elected mayor of Beersheba.

[Shaked Gilboa (2nd ed.)]

TURNOV (Ger. **Turnau**), town in N. Bohemia, Czech Republic. Jews are first mentioned in Turnov in 1526. The town manual of 1568 lays down regulations on Jewish-gentile relations. When the community increased during the 17th century, a cemetery (still in existence in 1969) was consecrated. After the wooden synagogue burned down in 1707, the authorities ordered the community to rebuild it in stone. In 1717 there were 23 Jewish houses in the town. The Jewish population numbered 280 in 1880 and 478 (2.9% of the total population) in 1910, but by 1930 had fallen to 110 (1.4%). In 1942 all Jews were deported to the Nazi extermination camps. The synagogue equipment was transferred to the Central Jewish Museum in Prague. Most of the members of the small congregation organized in 1945 were from *Subcarpathian Ruthenia; it was administered by the *Liberec community. In 1952 a memorial tablet to Nazi victims, with 93 names from Turnov and 25 from the surrounding area, was unveiled in the cemetery. Author Ivan Olbracht (1882–1952), known for his stories about Jews in Carpatho-Rus, was born in the neighboring town of Sedlice.

BIBLIOGRAPHY: Geger, in: H. Gold (ed.), *Die Juden und Judengemeinden Boehmens…* (1934), 679–83. **ADD. BIBLIOGRAPHY:** J. Fiedler, *Jewish Sights of Bohemia and Moravia* (1991).

[Jan Herman / Yeshayahu Jelinek (2nd ed.)]

TURÓCZI-TROSTLER, JÓZSEF (1888–1962), Hungarian literary scholar, critic, and translator. Born in Moskóc, then Hungary, Turóczi-Trostler became a high school teacher. Between 1917 and 1943, he was literary critic of the German-language newspaper, *Pester Lloyd.* During the revolution of October 1918, he became a senior official in the Hungarian Ministry of Education, and, following Béla *Kun's Communist revolution, was professor of world literature at Budapest University. Removed from his post by the counterrevolution, he became a teacher at the Jewish *Neolog community's girls' high school in Budapest. From 1945, Turóczi-Trostler was a member of the Hungarian Academy, a member of the Hungarian parliament, and professor of world literature at Budapest University. In 1947, he was made professor of German literature. He edited an anthology of German literature in Hungarian translation and translated works by German authors. His Jewish sympathies and associations declined over the years.

As a young man he contributed poems to József *Patai's periodical, **Mult és Jövő*; following his expulsion from Budapest University he wrote several works on Jewish themes; but, when he returned to academic life after World War II, he severed all connection with Judaism. Turóczi-Trostler's major studies include *Magyar Simplicissimus* (1915), *Stefan George* (1920), *Wassermann* (1927), *A magyar nyelv felfedezése* ("The Discovery of the Hungarian Language," 1933), *Thomas Manns Weg zum Mythos* (1936), *Stefan Zweig* (1942), *A magyar irodalom európaizálódása* ("The Europeanization of Hungarian Literature," 1946), and "Wassermann Literature," (2 vols., 1961), selected research.

BIBLIOGRAPHY: *Magyar Zsidó Lexikon* (1929), 915; *Magyar Irodalmi Lexikon*, 3 (1965), 430.

[Baruch Yaron]

TUROW, SCOTT (1949–), U.S. novelist. Turow, who was born in Chicago, graduated from Amherst College. On a fellowship he attended Stanford University's Creative Writing Center for two years and then taught there for three years. In 1975 Turow entered Harvard Law School and graduated with honors in 1978, but not before publishing *One L*, a book about his first year there. From 1978 to 1986 Turow was an assistant United States Attorney in Chicago, where he prosecuted several high-profile corruption cases, including the tax-fraud case of the state attorney general. Turow was also lead counsel in the federal prosecution of Illinois judicial corruption cases. After leaving the U.S. Attorney's office, Turow became a novelist, achieving his greatest success with legal thrillers like *Presumed Innocent* (1987), *The Burden of Proof* (1990), *Pleading Guilty* (1993), *The Laws of Our Fathers* (1996), *Personal Injuries* (1999), and *Reversible Errors* (2002). His books were translated into 20 languages, sold more than 25 million copies worldwide, and won many literary awards. The film based on *Presumed Innocent* (1990), starring Harrison Ford and directed by Alan J. Pakula, was also a major box-office success. Turow sought to make a break from the courtroom fiction genre with *Ordinary Heroes* (2005), a story set in World War II in which the major characters are Jewish. In addition to his writing, Turow continued to practice law. He was a partner in the Chicago office of Sonnenschein, Nath & Rosenthal, a national law firm. His practice centered on white collar criminal litigation, but he devoted a substantial part of his practice to pro bono work, including representing defendants facing the death penalty. In one of those cases, a prisoner was exonerated after 11 years in prison. In 2003, Turow published *Ultimate Punishment: A Lawyer's Reflections on Dealing With the Death Penalty.* He served as president of the Authors Guild, the national organization for professional writers, and was active in a number of public bodies and charitable causes, including Literacy Chicago and Illinois's Executive Ethics Commission.

[Stewart Kampel (2nd ed.)]

TUR-SINAI, NAPHTALI HERZ (Harry Torczyner; 1886–1973), Hebrew philologist and Bible scholar. Born in Lemberg, Tur-Sinai was raised in Vienna. He studied at the University of Vienna, 1905–09, and the Rabbinical Seminary, where his teachers included Meir Friedmann and Heinrich Mueller. His first teacher, however, was his father, an important patron of Jews in science, literature, and art and among the first active Zionists. In 1910 Tur-Sinai was appointed lecturer at the University of Vienna on the basis of his work on accents and vowels in Semitic languages. That same year he went to Jerusalem where he was elected a member of the *Va'ad ha-Lashon and taught Bible and Hebrew at a high school. From 1913 to 1919 he lectured in Semitic languages at the University of Vienna, and from 1919 to 1933 taught Bible and Semitic philology at the Hochschule fuer die Wissenschaft des Judentums in Berlin. In 1933 he settled in Jerusalem and was professor of Hebrew language at the Hebrew University. He was one of the presidents of the Va'ad ha-Lashon and president of the *Academy of the Hebrew Language from its founding in 1953. The following are among his publications: *Deutsch-Hebraeisches Woerterbuch* (together with S.M. Laser; 1927); substantial contributions to the new Jewish translation of the Bible into German (1935–37; see *Bible: Translations); commentary on the Book of Job (1941; 1954²); and *The Lachish Letters* (1938), a deciphering of the Lachish letters. In addition to editing the periodical *Leshonenu* from 1934 to 1954, he edited and completed E. *Ben-Yehuda's dictionary from vol. 10 (1944), and translated essays by *Aḥad Ha-Am into German (1916; 1923). Among his works in German are *Das Buch Hiob* (1920); *Die Bundeslade und die Anfaenge der Religion Israels* (1922; 1930²); and *Die Entstehung des semitischen Sprachtypus* (1916), where he sought to establish new origins of the Hebrew language, and which met with the opposition of most scholars.

In his writings, Tur-Sinai did not shrink from daring conjectures, but at the same time he continually criticized his own views and publicly repudiated assumptions of whose invalidity he had become convinced. A summary of his studies is given in the three volumes of *Ha-Lashon ve-ha-Sefer* (1951–56), and a collection of his expositions on the Bible are published in *Peshuto shel Mikra* (1962–68). Tur-Sinai's approach to the problems of the Bible was formed against the background of the documentary theory in its classical form, which, however, he explicitly rejected. In his view the Bible in our possession is merely a collection of remnants of ancient works that spoke of early times. Within the framework of these ancient stories the laws, parables, poems, and prophecies were interwoven. Accordingly, the life of David was intertwined with the Psalms, and the life of Solomon with apothegms from the Books of Proverbs and Ecclesiastes and with poetry from the Song of Songs. Our Book of Job is an adaptation of ancient stories about Job and his friends (who lived in Edom). The skeleton of the story was fleshed out by many poetic sections in the form of polemics placed in the mouth of Job and his comforters. Tur-Sinai maintained that the original language of the book was Aramaic and that our Hebrew translation was made by one who did not sufficiently understand Aramaic. He believed, moreover, that anonymous texts, fragmentary and corrupt, formed the bases for fixing the biblical texts and assembling the canon during the Babylonian exile and later. Hence, in an effort to reconstruct the original version, his many bold suggestions for textual emendation derived from linguistic novellae – the majority of which did not gain acceptance. From his research in the Ugaritic writings, Tur-Sinai concluded that the content of the Bible is very ancient.

BIBLIOGRAPHY: S.I. Feigin, in: *Haolam*, 26 (1938), 56f., 75f., 96–98; idem, *Anshei Sefer* (1950), 78–130, 417–23; J. Klausher, in: *Leshonenu*, 15 (1947), 3–9, bibl. of his writings; *ibid.*, 10–26, 21 (1957), 149–54; *Pirsumei ha-Ḥevrah la-Ḥakirat ha-Mikra be-Yisrael*, 81 (*Sefer Tur-Sinai*; 1960), 7–10 (first pagination).

TURTLE DOVE (Heb. תּוֹר, an onomatopoeic word), the *Streptopelia turtur*. Large flights arrive in Israel in spring, and their cooing, which fills the wood, heralds the advent of spring (Song 2:12). It nests in trees and lays two clutches of eggs. In October it migrates to southern countries, returning in the spring, and Jeremiah states that the exact times of its migrations were known (8:7). Like the dove, the turtle dove was used for various sacrifices (Lev. 5:7; 12:6; Num. 6:10). It was included among the birds Abraham offered at the covenant between the pieces (Gen. 15:9). It symbolizes the innocent Israelite nation against whom its enemies plot (Ps. 74:19). In a passage which advocates that "one should be ever of the persecuted, but not of the persecutors," the Talmud states that no birds are more persecuted than turtle doves and young pigeons – yet the Bible regarded only them as worthy of being offered upon the altar (BK 93a). The turtle dove, a beautiful bird with colorful feathers, is recognizable by the bright stripes at the side of its neck. A closely related species, *Streptopelia senegalensis*, the palm dove, is found in Israel throughout the year, and lays its eggs on roofs and eaves.

BIBLIOGRAPHY: I. Aharoni, *Torat ha-Ḥai* (1923), 192–3; J. Feliks, *Animal World of the Bible* (1962), 55. **ADD. BIBLIOGRAPHY:** Feliks, Ha-Tzome'aḥ, 286.

[Jehuda Feliks]

TUSCANY, region in central Italy. No information on Jews in Tuscany during the Roman era is available but it is likely that a Jewish community existed then at least in *Florence. The first reliable data comes from Benjamin of *Tudela who found Jews in *Pisa and in *Lucca (c. 1159). There were Jews in *Siena by 1229. Jews presumably engaged in moneylending in Tuscany in the 13th century. In 1309 three Jewish loan bankers were invited to San Gimignano; the negotiations with them and others did not succeed, but in 1392 the first agreement regulating Jewish loan banking activities (*condotta*) there was concluded. Until 1437 Jewish moneylenders were excluded from Florence itself, but not from the provincial cities under its sovereignty. In 1393 a *condotta* was concluded at San Miniato with a group of Jewish bankers headed by members of the Min ha-Keneset or Min Bet-El (Della Sinagoga) family of Rome. A concession to maintain a loan bank in San Gimignano was granted in 1410, and in 1423 a similar license was extended to the city of Pisa, again to this family. At the beginning of the 15th century the family also engaged in moneylending in Pescia, Prato, Colle Val d'Elsa, and perhaps in Pistoia; authorization to permit Jews to engage in moneylending was also extended to the cities of *Arezzo, Montepulciano, Castiglion Fiorentino, Volterra, Castrocaro, and Empoli. In exchange, the central authorities demanded a tax which varied between 50 and 250 florins yearly, according to the importance of the locality.

In 1416 representatives of the communities of Tuscany took part in the Council of *Bologna. The establishment of Christian loan banks (**Monti di Pieta*) in the 16th century caused some difficulty to Jewish moneylenders in Tuscany, but there was no conspicuous change in their situation, though there was an unsuccessful attempt to excommunicate the Jews of Empoli. The reign of Duke Cosimo de' Medici was originally beneficial for the Jews. In 1553 however he yielded to papal pressure and ordered the burning of the *Talmud. In 1551 he had issued an invitation to merchants from the Levant, including Jews, to settle in Tuscany and do business there; previously, Marranos also had been permitted to settle in Tuscany. In 1557 and before, he gave asylum to Jewish refugees from the Papal States. The same year he refused to implement the anti-Jewish restrictions issued by Pope *Paul IV or to hand over the Jews to the jurisdiction of the Inquisition. But when Cosimo wished to gain the support of Pope *Pius V for his aspirations to the title of grand duke, his attitude toward the Jews changed. In 1567 he rigorously applied the obligation to wear the Jewish *badge. Refugees from the Papal States who wished to settle in Volterra were not accepted. In 1570 information was collected on the Jews in Pisa, Cortona, Foiano, Pieve-Santo-Stefano, Arezzo, Prato, Anghiari, Castrocaro, Modigliana, Bibbiena, and Montepulciano, apparently as a preliminary to concentrating them in Florence. On the pretext that Jews had violated some of the articles of their moneylending concessions, all their agreements in Florence were abrogated in 1570, and in the district of Siena in 1571. Subsequently the expulsion of the Jews from all cities excepting Florence and Siena was ordered. In these cities the Jewish inhabitants were segregated in a ghetto along with refugees from other localities. At the end of the century, however, the Grand Duke Ferdinand I (1587–1609) invited Jews, including Marranos, to settle in Pisa and the free port of *Leghorn, which before long became one of the great Jewish centers of the Mediterranean area. The Lucca community, however, had ceased to exist.

At the end of the 16th century a new community was established in Pitigliano, which served as a haven for the Jews from the Papal States. This community prospered mainly in the 18th century, when the Jewish population reached 300. In the 17th century Jews settled again in Arezzo, Monte San Savino, Borgo San Sepolcro, and Lippano, although in 1680 Cosimo III intensified the papal anti-Jewish restrictions which were now strictly enforced. At the end of the 17th century the preaching of the apostate Paolo Medici led to anti-Jewish riots, and serious disturbances occurred in Borgo San Sepolcro. A marked improvement in the conditions of the Jews in Tuscany began in the 18th century under the Lorraine dynasty. Leopold I (later Emperor Leopold II of Austria), who reigned in Tuscany from 1765 to 1790, granted all the Jews there the same rights as the Jews of Leghorn. In 1779 he permitted Jews to sit on the municipal councils, and in 1789 to hold official positions.

In 1798 the French occupied Tuscany and granted the Jews full rights of citizenship. These were abrogated in 1799 after the retreat of the French forces. In the wake of the reaction, there were serious anti-Jewish disturbances, especially in Siena and in Monte San Savino and the community ceased to exist. In 1801, on the establishment of the kingdom of Etruria by Napoleon, the Jews in Tuscany were again granted full rights. Between 1810 and 1814, when Tuscany was incorporated in the French Empire, the communities were organized on the lines of the French *Consistory. Jews began to acquire land and to enter middle-class society.

After the Restoration, however, the situation reverted to much the same as before, but Jews were no longer required to live in the ghettos, although most continued to reside there. The House of Lorraine continued its liberal policy, and consequently Tuscany attracted many Jews in poor economic circumstances from Rome. Jews were permitted to attend public schools and universities in Tuscany. They took part in all branches of the economy in business and industry. Only government positions, military service, and the legal profession remained closed to them. On April 30, 1859, Tuscany was incorporated in the kingdom of Sardinia (later the kingdom of Italy) and the principle of equal rights without discrimination on religious grounds was introduced there also. Henceforth the history of the Jews of Tuscany does not differ from the general history of Italian Jewry. Concerning the organization of the communities, legislation of the House of Lorraine remained in force. This obliged every Jew to belong to the community and pay dues to it. However, between 1865 and 1905 the communities successively dispensed with levying compulsory dues. The Italian law of 1931 regulating the organization of the Jewish communities applied to Tuscany, and the principle of compulsory taxation was again introduced. The provincial Tuscan communities dwindled in the 19th century like most of the small communities of Italy. In 1969 there were only a few fully organized communities in Florence, Pisa (including Viareggio and Lucca), and Leghorn (Livorno), and partially in Siena.

BIBLIOGRAPHY: U. Cassuto, *Ebrei a Firenze nell'età del Rinascimento* (1918); Roth, Italy, index; Milano, Italia, index; De Rubertis, in: RMI, 18 (1952), 10–20; J.E. Rignano, *Sulla attuale posizione giuridica degl'israeliti in Toscana…* (1847).

[Menachem E. Arom]

TUSKA, SIMON (1835–1871), U.S. rabbi. The son of the Reverend Mordecai Tuska, Tuska was born in Veszprém, Hungary. He went to the U.S. with his parents in 1849 and his father then became "rabbi, Reader … *shoḥet* … *mohel*" in Rochester, New York. After two years of U.S. schooling Tuska was awarded one of the first scholarships to the University of Rochester, founded in 1850. Although he specialized in Greek and Latin, his chief interest was Judaism. While still a student, he wrote and published "The Stranger in the Synagogue" to explain Jewish rites and ceremonies to both his Christian colleagues and the Jewish public. He was warmly praised by Isaac Mayer *Wise, but his critique of talmudic law drew the censure of Isaac *Leeser. Tuska wrote letters and articles for both *The Israelite* and *The Occident*, and Wise encouraged him to pursue the rabbinate. Upon graduation in 1856 Tuska attended courses at the Rochester Theological Seminary. He did not seek a pulpit because of his youth and the fact that most Reform congregations of the day required a German-speaking rabbi. However, as a result of Wise's constant urging, he decided in 1858 to go to the Breslau seminary to prepare himself for the rabbinate. In 1860 Tuska tried unsuccessfully to become English lecturer at Temple Emanuel in New York. He subsequently was also rejected by Congregation Berith Kodesh in his hometown, Rochester, because of his radical religious views. Shortly thereafter he was elected to the Reform pulpit in Memphis, Tennessee, where he served until his death. Tuska's importance lay in the pattern he set for the training of U.S. rabbis – English-speaking, with university degree plus theological training.

BIBLIOGRAPHY: A.J. Karp, in: AJHSQ, 50:2 (1960), 79–97.

[Gladys Rosen]

TUSSMAN, MALKA HEIFETZ (1893–1987), U.S. Yiddish poet and teacher. Born in Ukraine, the second of eight children, Tussman, who came to the United States in 1912 to join family members in Chicago, married cantor Shloyme Tussman soon after her arrival. She and her husband, who had two sons, lived in Milwaukee and later in Los Angeles. Tussman studied at the University of Wisconsin and briefly at the University of California at Berkeley. She taught for many years in Yiddish secular schools and in 1949 became an instructor in Yiddish language and literature at the University of Judaism in Los Angeles. After spending 1971–72 in Israel, following her husband's death, she lived for the rest of her life in Berkeley, Calif.

Tussman began publishing poems, short stories, and essays in Yiddish newspapers and journals in 1918. She published six volumes of poetry in Yiddish between 1949 and 1977; her poems appear in many anthologies. She also translated poems by a wide range of writers into Yiddish. Tussman was a mentor for a number of younger poets, some of whom translated her works into English. She thus "served as a bridge between the generations of Yiddish poets who emigrated from Eastern Europe and of those American-born Jewish poets who have taken up the task of making Yiddish poetry known to a readership that knows little Yiddish" (Hellerstein). Her works include *Bleter Faln Not* (1972); *Haynt Iz Eybik: Lider* (1977); *Lider* (1949); *Mild Mayn Vild* (1958); *Shotns fun Gedenkn* (1965); and *Unter Dayn Tseykhn: Lider* (1974). *With Teeth in the Earth: Selected Poems* (1992) is an English translation of some of her poetry, edited and with an introduction by Marcia *Falk.

BIBLIOGRAPHY: K. Hellerstein. "Tussman, Malka Heifetz," in: P.E. Hyman and D.D. Moore (eds.), *Jewish Women in America*, vol. 2 (1997), 1422–23.

[Judith R. Baskin (2nd ed.)]

TUTSI. Since the late 1990s, a group of Tutsi, who have their origin in the Great Lakes area of Africa (Burundi and Rwanda), claim that this region was the home of a Hebraic community in ancient times, and claim a Jewish identity. Their homeland, supposedly extending far beyond the regions where the Tutsi now reside, is called *Havila* by them, according to the name applied in Genesis 2:11 to the legendary territory watered by the Pishon River. The Tutsi claim to perpetuate either the pharaonic monotheism of the 18th dynasty of Egypt or Moses' faith as transcribed in the Hebraic Torah. The Hamitic-Semitic myth of the origins of these Tutsi, which was largely inspired by missionaries and colonists of the 19th century, now appears to be strongly reinforced by the symbolic uses they make of Judaism. Following their terrible suffering during the genocide of 1994, these Tutsi have increasingly claimed a Jewish identity and describe their history as a microcosm of World Jewish history, evoking the common experience of persecution to give more weight to their Jewish identity claim. The group is based in Belgium, where its president, Professor Yochanan Bwejeri, and the Havila Institute call upon Israel and the international community to condemn and take measures against the "antisemitic" violence in Africa towards the Tutsi ethnic group.

BIBLIOGRAPHY: L. Ndayongeje, "Mythe des origines, idéologie hamitique et violence en Afrique des Grands Lacs: comprendre et agir," in: *Grands Lacs Confidentiel* (Aug. 16, 2004); E. Kennes, "Judaïsation des Tutsi: identité ou stratégie de conquête," in: *Grands Lacs Confidentiel* (March 18, 2000).

[Tudor Parfitt (2nd ed.)]

TUWIM, JULIAN (1894–1953), Polish poet. Tuwim, who was born in Lodz, was one of the outstanding Polish poets of the first half of the 20th century. His family background on his father's side was strongly Jewish; and, in fact, his father's relatives included several Zionists prominent in Russia and later in Ereẓ Israel. His mother, an assimilationist, educated him in a staunchly Polish spirit. Tuwim studied in Warsaw and was one of the founders of the literary group associated with the *Skamander* monthly. His early verse collections – *Czyhanie na Boga* ("Lying in wait for God," 1918), *Sokrates tańczący* ("Socrates the Dancer," 1920), and *Siódma jesień* ("The Seventh Autumn," 1922) – were full of youthful enthusiasm and vigor, expressing the poet's faith in the newly liberated Poland. Harsh realities soon disillusioned him, provoking his angry criticism of the rich and the "profiteers" in the epics *Słowa we krwi* ("Words in Blood," 1926) and *Rzecz czarnoleska* ("The Czarnolesie Affair," 1929). Here his hero was the ordinary man suffering from poverty and oppression. Tuwim eventually turned to socio-political themes, vehemently attacking Poland's militarist and capitalist regime in *Biblia cygańska* ("The Vagabonds' Bible," 1933), *Treść gorejąca* ("Burning Contents," 1936; Heb. tr., *Tokhen Lohet*, 1954), and *Bal w operze* ("The Opera Party," published in part in 1936). The last work appeared in full ten years later in 1946. Despite his clearly expressed sympathy for the poor, Tuwim was remote from the proletarian revolutionary movement at this period, his poems merely voicing an isolated intellectual's protest against the grim effects of the capitalist system.

Tuwim never attempted to conceal his Jewish identity and upbringing, and was subjected to vicious attacks by extreme Polish nationalists during the years preceding World War II. As an exile in France, South America, and the United States during the Nazi era, he was an active anti-Fascist and his outspoken declarations about the fate of European Jewry were heard throughout the free world. During the war years he wrote the epic *Kwiaty polskie* ("Flowers of Poland," 1940–44), one section of which, "Modlitwa" ("A Prayer"), became the anthem of the Polish resistance movement. In April 1944, Tuwim published a manifesto entitled *My, Żydzi polscy* ("We Polish Jews"), the sheer fury, power, and irony of which it would be hard to match in any nation's literature. After his return to Poland in 1946, he mainly devoted himself to literature, journalism, and the training of young poets. A literary craftsman and acknowledged master of the Polish language, Tuwim was one of the great revolutionary innovators in the history of Polish verse. He was also a prolific translator, particularly from Russian (e.g., Pushkin), and he published many delightful children's books (e.g., *Lokomotywa*, 1938), as well as satires, philological research papers, and various anthologies. A selection of his works was published in English (1942).

During the last years of his life, Tuwim supported the State of Israel and the Hebrew University of Jerusalem. His family relationships and his Jewish loyalties find reflection in the correspondence with his cousin, Immanuel Tuwim, a Haifa engineer, and with the Zionist leader and poet Leib *Jaffe, a close friend of his, which was published in the Israeli press by Moshe Altbauer. His sister, the poet and translator IRENA TUWIM (1900–1987), described her brother and family in *Lódzkie pory roku* ("Lodz Years," 1958[2]).

BIBLIOGRAPHY: R. Matuszewski, *Literatura po wojnie* (1950[2]); idem, *Literatura polska w latach 1918–1955* (1958); P. Dembowski, in: *Canadian Slavonic Papers*, 1 (1958); J. Stradecki, *Julian Tuwim: Bibliografia* (1959), 609; W. Jedlicka and M. Toporowski (eds.), *Wspomnienia o Julianie Tuwimie* (1963), 467.

[Shlomo Dykman]

TWERSKI, JACOB ISRAEL (1899–1973), U.S. ḥasidic rabbi. Twerski, a descendant of a long line of famous ḥasidic rabbis, was born in Hornistopoli, near Kiev, Russia. In accordance with time-honored ḥasidic tradition, he was pledged in marriage at the age of 11 to his future wife, who was then aged 10, the actual marriage taking place in 1922. He immigrated to the United States in 1927, and after serving congregations in various parts of New York, settled in Milwaukee, where in 1939 he founded Congregation Beth Yehudah, whose spiritual leader he remained until his death. For Jews in Milwaukee and throughout Wisconsin, Twerski was a counselor and friend to whom people turned for guidance and arbitration. Following the family tradition, all his five sons were ordained as rabbis, but only one of them, Michael, officiated as such, succeeding his father on his death. Of the other sons, Shlomo became a research scholar in Talmud at Denver; Abraham was clinical director at St. Francis Psychiatric Hospital, Pittsburgh; Aaron served as a law professor at Hofstra University in Hempsted, N.Y.; while Motel (Mordecai) became a certified public accountant in Brooklyn, N.Y.

[Manfred Eric Swarsensky (2nd ed.)]

TWERSKY, ḥasidic dynasty in the Ukraine. The founder of the dynasty, MENAHEM NAHUM BEN ẒEVI of Chernobyl (1730–1787), was educated in Lithuanian yeshivot. After his marriage he eked out a living as a teacher. Influenced by the kabbalistic teachings of Isaac *Luria, he practiced self-mortification, and with the spread of *Ḥasidism he journeyed to Medzhibozh to visit *Israel b. Eliezer Ba'al Shem Tov. After the latter's death Menahem became one of the prominent disciples of *Dov Baer of Mezhirech, and was one of the first to propagate Ḥasidism; he was then accepted as *maggid* (preacher) at Chernobyl, where he lived in penury. The *Mitnaggedim* were extremely hostile toward him and sometimes insulted him while he was preaching. It is doubtful whether Menahem became a ḥasidic *ẓaddik*; as an itinerant preacher he wandered among the towns of the Ukraine, engaging also in pious deeds and the "redemption of captives" (in this case, Jewish tax farmers who had been imprisoned for failing to pay rents to the landowners). He wrote *Me'or Einayim* (Slavuta, 1798), on the Torah and *aggadah*, and *Yismaḥ Lev (ibid.*, 1798), both of which were frequently reprinted. Menahem added no innovations to his teachers' expositions of Ḥasidism, but among the principles he stressed in particular was the purification of man's moral attributes: "so long as his moral attributes are not purified [a man] will not be worthy of the Torah" (*Me'or Einayim, Lekh Lekha*); "every day of the week should be devoted to the purification of one particular attribute; the first day to love; the second to fear of God; etc." (*ibid., Be-Shallaḥ*).

Menahem's son, MORDECAI OF CHERNOBYL (1770–1837), replaced him as *maggid* in Chernobyl, where he was born. He was the real founder of the Chernobyl dynasty of *ẓaddikim*. Unlike his father, who had spread the teachings of Ḥasidism while wandering and living in poverty, Mordecai lived in a splendid house and exercised his functions as leader in opulence and power. While maintaining a high standard of living he introduced the payment of *ma'amadot*, a financial contribution which every ḥasid paid for the benefit of the *ẓaddik's* "court," collected by emissaries sent from Chernobyl. He was revered by Ḥasidim who traveled to visit him in their thousands. Mordecai wrote *Likkutei Torah* (1860) on the Bible, and sermons. He added nothing new to the teachings of Ḥasidism. His outstanding pupil was Israel Dov Baer, the *maggid* of Weledniki, whose *She'erit Yisrael* was an important ḥasidic treatise of his time.

After Mordecai's death his place was taken by his eight sons, who settled in different cities in the Ukraine. His eldest son (1) AARON (1787–1872) lived in Chernobyl itself. He was educated by his grandfather, Menahem Nahum, and already during his father's lifetime was considered to have a saintly inclination. He based his sermons on his grandfather's teachings and the commentary *Or ha-Ḥayyim* by Ḥayyim b. Moses *Attar. Thousands of admiring Ḥasidim flocked to him. Aaron was confident of his spiritual abilities and holiness; he once wrote in a letter: "Even if they [his Ḥasidim] live as long as Methusaleh they will never realize even a thousandth part of the good I – with God's help – have bestowed on them." He was convinced that the Messiah would come in his lifetime. He headed the Volhynia *kolel* in support of settlement in Ereẓ Israel. A dispute concerning the presidency of the *kolel* between himself and one of his brothers ended in Aaron's favor. Two of his sons, ZUSIA and BARUCH, continued the dynasty of Chernobyl. (2) MOSES (1789–1866) lived at Korostyshev. (3) JACOB ISRAEL (1794–1876), author of *Shoshannat ha-Amakim* (1884), lived at Cherkassy; he had begun to lead a congregation while his father was still alive, and after the latter's death did not recognize his eldest brother's authority, but after a fierce controversy was forced to yield. His grandson MORDECAI DOV of Hornistopol (1840–1904), son-in-law of Ḥayyim *Halberstamm of Sandz, was a noted scholar and wrote several works, including *Emek She'elah* (1906), responsa, and *Emek ha-Ḥokhmah* (1928). (4) NAHUM (1805–1852) lived at Makarov. (5) ABRAHAM (1806–1889) was also known as the *maggid* of Trisk (Turiysk), where he lived. He exercised his leadership with a high hand although he tried to act in keeping with the simplicity of the Polish ḥasidic leaders. His Ḥasidim were mainly learned men, wealthy and distinguished persons, and rabbis, including several famous *ẓaddikim*. He treated his Ḥasidim, who flocked to him in their thousands, as his personal guests and maintained them at his expense. His sermons are a mixture of ḥasidic teachings and Kabbalah, spiced with numerology and *gematria* in the manner of Samson b. Pesaḥ *Ostropoler. Two years before his death he published *Magen Avraham* (1887) on the Pentateuch and the festivals. In his *Shalosh Hadrakhot Yesharot li-Zemannim Shonim* he strives to teach "a method of divine service and ways to repentance." He wielded great influence. During the reign of Nicholas I he was imprisoned on the slanderous charge that his sayings questioned obedience to the government. He was quickly released once the charges were proven false. His three sons, NAHUM, MORDECAI, and JACOB LEIB, continued the dynasty of Trisk. (6) DAVID (1808–1882), the most celebrated of the brothers, first lived at Vasilkov and later at Talnoye, where he held his luxurious court in great splendor. It is said that he sat on a silver throne with the words "David King of Israel lives for ever" inscribed in gold. For this the Russian authorities kept him under arrest for a long time. David loved singing and music, being visited sometimes by popular Jewish musicians. His teaching was spiced with secular references and parables, which increased his popularity. He wrote *Magen David* (1852), *Birkat David* (1862), and *Kehillat David* (1882). (7) ISAAC (1812–1895) lived at Skvira. (8) JOHANAN (1802–1885) lived at Rotmistrovka. The courts of these *ẓaddikim* dominated Ukrainian-Russian Jewry throughout the 19th century. The influence of the Twersky family increased particularly after Israel of Ruzhin left Volhynia to settle in Galicia. After the Russian Revolution of 1917 descendants of the Twersky *ẓaddikim* left for Poland, the United States, and Ereẓ Israel.

BIBLIOGRAPHY: Horodezky, Ḥasidut, 2 (1951³), 59–69; 3 (1951³), 85–96; idem, *R. Naḥum mi-Tshernobil ve-Ẓe'eẓa'av* (1902); Dubnow, Ḥasidut, 2 (1931), 199–203, 315–6; M.J. Guttmann, *Rabbi Naḥman mi-Tshernobil* (1932 = *Mi-Gibborei ha-Ḥasidut*, no. 5); A.D. Twersky, *Sefer ha-Yaḥas mi-Tshernobil ve-Ruzhin* (1938²); Y. Alfasi, *Sefer ha-Admorim* (1961), 24–27.

[Zvi Meir Rabinowitz / Avraham Rubinstein]

TWERSKY, ISADORE (1930–1997), scholar and teacher. Born in Boston, Massachusetts, the son of R. Meshullam Zalman Twersky (Tolnaer Rebbe), a member of the well-known ḥasidic dynasty, Twersky was ordained as a rabbi by the Isaac Elchanan Yeshiva (University). At Harvard University he earned a bachelor's degree in 1952, a master's in 1953, and a doctorate in 1956. He became a faculty member at Harvard in 1956 as professor of Hebrew literature and philosophy, and chairman of the Department of Near Eastern Languages from 1965. He served as director of Harvard's Center for Jewish Studies from 1978 to 1993.

Twersky's formidable expertise in Jewish literature encompassed such areas as the rabbinic texts, Bible commentaries, and legal writing of the Middle Ages. He was a fellow of the American Academy for Jewish Research and the American Academy of Arts and Sciences. In 1989 he won a Guggenheim Fellowship.

His published works include *Rabad of Posquières, a 12th-Century Talmudist* (1962); *Judaism and World History* (1969); and *A Maimonides Reader* (1969). He edited *Studies in Medieval Jewish History and Literature* (vol. 1, 1979; vol. 2, 1985; vol. 3, 2000); *Danzig: Between East and West* (1985); *Jewish Thought in the 17th Century* (1987); and *Studies in Maimonides* (1991).

Twersky was the son-in-law of the eminent rabbinic thinker and scholar Rabbi Joseph *Soloveitchik.

[Ruth Beloff (2nd ed.)]

TWERSKY, YOḤANAN (1900–1967), Hebrew novelist. Born in Shpikov (Ukraine), of the famous ḥasidic family, Twersky immigrated to the United States in 1926 and taught for 20 years (1927–47) at the Hebrew College in Boston. He settled in Israel in 1947, and served on the editorial staff of the Dvir Publishing House in Tel Aviv. From 1924 he steadily produced historical novels which centered around Jewish and non-Jewish heroes, both in the remote past and in the present. These novels include *Uriel Acosta* (3 vols., 1935–38); *Aḥad Ha-Am* (1941); *Alfred Dreyfus* (1946); *Rashi* (1946); and *Rom u-Tehom* (1951), a novel with the Second Commonwealth as background. He also authored *Lappidim ba-Laylah* (1954), a series of historical stories on Saadiah, Descartes, Leibnitz, Spinoza, Moses Ḥayyim Luzzatto, Leone Modena, Mordecai Emanuel Noah, and Herzl. Both his stories and novels have a lively, staccato style.

Of special interest is Twersky's work on Ḥasidism. From his knowledge and his observation, he was able to reconstruct the exciting innovations of the founders of the movement and its latter-day epigones in a number of narrative works: *He-"Ḥaẓer" ha-Penimit* (1954), a partly fictionalized autobiography; *Ha-Lev ve-ha-Ḥerev* (1955), a novel on R. Naḥman of Bratslav; and *Ha-Betulah mi-Ludmir* (1950), a fictional biography of the Ḥasidic Maid of *Ludomir.

Twersky also edited a memorial volume *Sefer Maximon* (1935) and, together with E. Silberschlag, a Festschrift, *Sefer Touroff* (1938). In addition, he published many essays on education and educational psychology. Before his death, he was engaged in a multi-volume work on the story of human thought from its inception to the present time, of which only one volume appeared, *Toledot ha-Filosofyah ve-ha-Filosofim* (1967). His four-volume encyclopedia of world literature, *Sifrut ha-Olam* (1953–54), is a useful reference work.

BIBLIOGRAPHY: M. Ribalow, *Im ha-Kad el ha-Mabbu'a* (1950), 230–7; A. Epstein, *Soferim Ivrim ba-Amerikah*, 2 (1952), 352–69.

[Eisig Silberschlag]

TWILIGHT, the transition period between day and night, called in the Bible *bein ha-arbayim* (Heb. בֵּין הָעַרְבַּיִם, Ex. 12:6), and in rabbinic literature *bein ha-shemashot* (Heb. בֵּין הַשְּׁמָשׁוֹת, Ber. 2b; Avot 5:9). Whether twilight forms part of day or the night is a moot question in the Talmud (Shab. 34b). Its exact duration was also a matter of dispute. According to R. *Yose, the transition from day to night is instantaneous, whereas R. *Nehemiah said twilight lasted for nine minutes after sunset (i.e., the length of a walk of half a mile = 1000 ells, approx. 560 meters). The *amora* Samuel said it lasts for 13½ minutes and according to another opinion 12 minutes (Shab. 34b). The codifiers established the duration of twilight at 18 minutes, i.e., when the sun is about 3½ degrees below the horizon (Tur, OḤ 293). Actual night begins only with the appearance of three stars in the sky (called *ẓet ha-kokhavim*, Ber. 2b; see also Neh. 4:15). This traditional calculation of the duration of twilight deviates only slightly from the exact astronomical twilight.

Twilight on Friday is reckoned as Sabbath eve and consequently no work may be performed then. The Sabbath candles must be lit before twilight (Shab. 2:7). The twilight at the end of the Sabbath is calculated as still belonging to the Sabbath day which concludes with the appearance of three stars in the sky. This rule applies also to the beginning and conclusion of the holidays. Before the beginning of the Day of Atonement, twilight is reckoned from approximately one hour before the stars would become visible. All religious ceremonies which ought to be performed only at night, e.g., the recital of the evening service, the kindling of *Ḥanukkah lights, the reading of the **Megillah*, should be observed only after twilight; but if they are performed during twilight they are valid and do not have to be repeated.

BIBLIOGRAPHY: Sh. Ar., OḤ 261:1–3; Eisenstein, Dinim, 39; JE, 3 (1903), 501; 11 (1905), 591–7; ET, 3 (1951), 121–9, s.v. *Bein ha-Shemashot*.

TWORKOV, JACK (1900–1982), U.S. educator, printmaker, painter. Tworkov was born in Biala, Poland and immigrated to the U.S. in 1913. He studied at Columbia University, the National Academy of Design, and the Art Students League. Tworkov worked as an artist for the Works Project Administration's Federal Art Project in 1935, where he met Willem de Kooning. Both men emerged as forces in the Abstract Expressionist movement. Tworkov was also one of the founders of The Club, a loose New York association of Abstract Expressionists which met to discuss matters relating to art making. Like many other Abstract Expressionists, Tworkov's early work consisted of figures and still-lifes. He also rendered images in a cubist style before adopting the visual aspects of Abstract Expressionism. As to be expected, his early work shared many stylistic characteristics with that of de Kooning. As Tworkov gained eminence along with his colleagues in the New York School representational subject matter became subsumed in abundantly textured long, dashing, diagonal brush strokes, as in his painting *Blue Note* from 1959. Among other influences, Tworkov also turned to the art of the marginalized Expressionist painter Chaim Soutine as a source of inspiration; in fact, Tworkov wrote an article on Soutine during the latter's 1950 show at MOMA. Tworkov achieved the illusion of vibrating and multiple fields or screens of color from a cool, restricted palette and subtle nuances of tone. Likely influenced by the Minimalists, Tworkov integrated grids and other ordering systems into his images from the 1960s onward, such as *Shield* (1961) and *Variables II* (1964–65). One of his major series of paintings, *House of the Sun,* refers to Ulysses, whose epic adventures suggested a variety of themes to the artist. Tworkov taught at numerous institutions: the American University, Black Mountain College (other luminaries of this period such as John Cage, Franz Kline, and Lyonel Feininger also taught here during the 1940s), Queens College, the Pratt Institute, and Yale University, where he functioned as chairman of the art department. He was a recipient of a Corcoran Gold Medal in 1963. Tworkov's art has been exhibited at numerous major museums, including the Art Institute of Chicago, the Guggenheim Museum, the Museum of Modern Art, New York, the Pennsylvania Academy, and the Whitney Museum, among other venues. His work is in the collections of the Hirschhorn Museum and Sculpture Garden, the National Gallery of Art, Washington, D.C., and the Smithsonian Museum of American Art.

BIBLIOGRAPHY: D. Ashton, *The New York School: A Cultural Reckoning* (1972); *Jack Tworkov: Paintings, 1950–1978* (Glasgow: Third Eye Center, 1979); I. Sandler, *The Triumph of American Painting: A History of Abstract Expressionism* (1970).

[Nancy Buchwald (2nd ed.)]

°TYCHSEN, OLAUS GERHARD (**Oluf Gerard**; 1734–1815), Danish Orientalist. Born in Tönder, Schleswig, Tychsen is said to have learned Hebrew in Altona as a pupil of Jonathan *Eybeschuetz, and later to have studied rabbinics and Oriental languages at the University of Halle. After conducting unsuccessful missionary activities among Jews in Denmark and northern Germany (1759–60), he taught at the University of Buetzow in Mecklenburg (which subsequently became Rostock University), serving as professor of Oriental languages from 1763 until 1789.

Tychsen wrote on a variety of subjects, including the Bible, Hebrew coinage, and cuneiform inscriptions. He was a violent controversialist, and his views foreshadowed the German school of biblical criticism. His six-volume *Buetzowische Nebenstunden* (1766–69) reflects his Hebrew and rabbinic scholarship. He reputedly mastered Yiddish and also became an expert on Arabic and Syriac philology. His publications include *Dialecti rabbinicae elementa* (1763); *De delectu veterum Ebraeorum* (1763); *De Pentateucho Ebraeo-Samaritano* (1765); *Abbreviaturarum Hebraicarum supplementum secundum* (1769); an introduction to the *Sefer Tikkunei Shetarot*, on Jewish deeds of contract (1773); and *De numis Hebraicis* (1791).

BIBLIOGRAPHY: F. Perez Bayer, *Legitimidad de las monedas hebreo-samaritanas…* (1793); A.T. Hartmann, *Biblisch-asiatischer Wegweiser zu Oluf Gerhard Tychsen* (1823); Steinschneider, Cat Bod 2687, no. 7321; Ḥ. Heller, *Untersuchungen zur Septuaginta*. vol. 1: *Die Tychsen-Wutzsche Transkriptionstheorie* (1932); *Soncino-Blaetter*, 2 (1927), 155.

TYKOCIN (in Jewish sources, **Tiktin**; Rus. **Tykotsin**), village in Bialystok province, N.E. Poland. Tykocin was formerly a town on the border between the kingdom of Poland and the principality of Lithuania. In 1522 the noble family of Gashtold, who owned Tykocin, invited ten Jewish families from *Grodno to settle there. They were given sites for homes and were later allowed to establish shops, a synagogue, a cemetery, and an autonomous community. A charter (1536) provided that the rabbi and the head of the town council should jointly judge cases between a Jew and a gentile. By 1576 there were 54 houses owned by Jews, who engaged in wholesale trading of salt, spices, and cloth. Their rights were confirmed by special royal privileges in 1576 and 1639. In 1642 a baroque synagogue was erected, which until 1740 was the finest building in the town (it still stood in 1970, preserved as a historical site, although the Nazis ruined the interior and the women's section).

With the growth of the community Tykocin achieved independence from the *kahal* of Grodno. Between 1621 and 1654 Tykocin conducted a successful struggle with Grodno involving the hegemony over the communities of Choroszcz, *Zabludow, *Gorodok, and Wasilkow. In 1623 Tykocin severed its ties with the Council of Lithuania and instead declared allegiance to the *Council of Four Lands. It became one of the most important communities in the region in the 17th and 18th centuries. The communities of Podlasie (*Siemiatycze, Wysokie Mazowieckie, *Miedzyrzec Podlaski, Bransk) and eastern Masovia (*Ciechanow) were under the jurisdiction of the Tykocin *kahal*, which was the chief community in the *galil* (province) of Tykocin. In 1660 the Jews of Tykocin suffered at the hands of the Swedish army and the troops of the Polish general, S. Czarniecki. In the 18th century the Tykocin community weakened and its influence in the area diminished.

Tykocin's rabbis until the end of the 18th century included some important halakhic authorities: Mordecai (1568); Menahem David b. Isaac, a student of Moses *Isserles; Samuel Eliezer *Edels (in the 1620s); Joshua b. Joseph, author of the talmudic commentary *Penei Yehoshu'a* (early 1630s); Isaac Aizik b. Eliezer Lipman Heilperin (1667–81); Elijah *Shapira, head of the rabbinical court of Prague, who became nonresident rabbi of Tykocin in 1703; and Shalom ben Eliezer Rokeaḥ (1756–66). In 1765 there were 2,694 Jews in Tykocin and nearby villages who paid the poll tax, and in 1808 there were 1,652 (56% of the total population). In 1815 the town was annexed to Congress Poland and the Russian administration allowed free Jewish settlement of the area. There were 2,701 Jews (64%) in 1827; 3,456 (70%) in 1857; and 2,484 (59%) in 1897. The Jews earned their livelihoods in small trade and crafts. Between 1919 and 1920 the community suffered at the hands of Russian and Polish armies which passed through the town. Between the two world wars the Jews manufactured brushes and prayer shawls (*Talitot Tiktin*). In 1921 there were 1,401 Jews (49%) in Tykocin. Various Zionist parties, mainly *He-Ḥalutz, were active and there was a *Tarbut school.

[Shimshon Leib Kirshenboim]

Holocaust Period and After

At the end of June 1941 after the outbreak of the German-Soviet war, Tykocin was captured by the Germans. During the first days of the occupation, a pogrom was conducted by the Poles (with the encouragement of the Germans), and Jewish property was looted. The Jews were drafted for forced labor and freedom of movement was limited. On Aug. 25, 1941, the Jews of the town were called to assemble in the market square. After a *Selektion* about 1,400 people were transported to large pits that had been prepared near the city and were murdered. Some of the Jews succeeded in hiding, but the next day they were caught and executed by the Polish police. About 150 people found temporary shelter in the *Bialystok ghetto and in the surrounding townlets, later perishing together with the members of those communities. After the war a few of the survivors returned to Tykocin, but they were subject to attacks by gangs of Polish nationalists that were active in the area; as a result they left the city. A memorial book, *Sefer Tykocin*, was published in Tel Aviv in 1949.

[Aharon Weiss]

BIBLIOGRAPHY: Halpern, Pinkas, index; idem, *Yehudim ve-Yahadut be Mizraḥ-Eiropah* (1959), 139–51; E. Schreiber, *Abraham Geiger* (Eng., 1892), 20, passim; S. Dubnow (ed.), *Pinkas ha-Medinah* (1925); idem, in: *Sefer ha-Yovel li-Khevod Naḥum Sokolow* (1904); M. Tolczyn (ed.), *Pinkes Tiktin* (1949); M. Bar-Juda and Z. Ben-Nahum (eds.), *Sefer Tiktin* (1959); H.H. Ben-Sasson, *Hagut ve-Hanhagah* (1959), index; M. Baliński and T. Lipiński, *Starożytna Polska*, 2 (1845), 533; B. Wasiutyński, *Ludność żydowska w Polsce w wiekach XIX i XX* (1930), 36; S. Zajczyk, in: Zakład architektury polskiej… Politechniki warszawskiej, *Biuletyn naukowy*, 1:4 (1933); I. Schiper, *Dzieje handlu żydowskiego na ziemiach polskich* (1937), index; A. Kubiak, in: BŻIH, 8 (1953), 81–84; Przyboś (ed.), *Polska w okresie drugiej wojny północnej, 1655–1660*, 2 (1957), index.

TYKOCINSKI, ḤAYYIM (1862–1942?), Jewish historian. Tykocinski, born in Poland, was one of the editors and main contributors of the important work in German-Jewish history *Germania Judaica* (1917–34), continuing with this work until he was killed by the Nazis and the material was lost. He also wrote *Die gaonaeischen Verordnungen* (1929).

His scholarly articles appeared in the *Monatsschrift fuer Geschichte und Wissenschaft des Judentums*, *Devir*, and *Tarbiz*, as well as in the *Festschriften* for M. Philippson (1916) and S. *Dubnow (1930). They dealt with such subjects as Moses b. Ḥisdai and Moses Taku (MGWJ, 54 (1910), 70ff.); Isaac *Or Zaru'a* and his pupils (MGWJ, 55 (1911), 478ff.; 63 (1919), 333ff.); and the history of the Jews in Halle (MGWJ, 47 (1913), 32ff.).

BIBLIOGRAPHY: T. Preshel, in: S. Federbush (ed.), *Ḥokhmat Yisrael be-Ma'arav Eiropah*, 2 (1963), 115ff.

[Siegbert Neufeld]

TYKOCINSKI, JEHIEL MICHEL (1872–1955), rabbi and author. Tykocinski was born in Lyakhovichi, Belorussia. Orphaned of his father while still young, he was taken to Ereẓ Israel in 1882. He studied under Samuel *Salant, whose granddaughter he married in 1890. In 1900 he began to take part in the administration of Ez̧ Ḥayyim in Jerusalem, at first as head of the junior department and then as chief administrator. He contributed greatly to the development of the institution – both when it was in the Old City of Jerusalem, and later when it moved outside. He was also active in the foundation of new suburbs in Jerusalem, and favored the unification of all sections of the Jewish population, new and old. Tykocinski specialized in the laws and customs pertaining to Erez̧ Israel, and from 1904 onward published an annual *Lu'aḥ* ("calendar") detailing liturgical and other customs for the whole year. This calendar was accepted as the authoritative guide for the liturgical and synagogal customs of the Ashkenazim in Israel; it continued to appear under the editorship of his son even after his death.

Tykocinski devoted himself especially to halakhic problems connected with astronomy, in which field he published *Tekufat ha-Ḥamah u-Virkatah* (1924); *Bein ha-Shemashot* (1929); and *Sefer ha-Yomam* (1943), on the international date line (see *Calendar). His other works are *Tohorat Yisrael* (c. 1910); *Ha-Ishah al pi Ḥukkat Yisrael* (1920); *Hilkhot Shevi'it* (1910) and *Sefer ha-Shemittah* on the laws of the Sabbatical Year; *Gesher ha-Ḥayyim* (1947, 1960^2) on the laws of mourning; and *Sefer Erez̧ Yisrael* (1955) on the laws and customs appertaining to Erez̧ Israel. He also published many articles in various journals and left behind in manuscript novellae on the Talmud and responsa.

BIBLIOGRAPHY: J.M. Tykocinski, *Gesher ha-Ḥayyim*, 1 (1960^2), introd. by Nissan A. Tykocinski.

°TYNDALE, WILLIAM (c. 1490–1536), English Bible translator and religious reformer. An Erasmian humanist, Tyndale began work on a new, vernacular Bible in 1520, but met so much opposition from his fellow-churchmen that he had to seek refuge on the Continent, where his New Testament, based directly on the Greek, appeared in various editions (Cologne/Worms, 1525; Antwerp, 1526^3, etc.). Having visited Martin *Luther at Wittenberg and declared himself a Protestant, Tyndale proceeded to smuggle his publications into England, where they were condemned as heretical: Cardinal Wolsey ordered his arrest, but failed to capture him. Of all the English scholars of his time, Tyndale was the only competent Hebraist. His translation of the Old Testament, which referred to the original Hebrew text, appeared only in part (Pentateuch, 1530; Jonah, 1531), although the section from Joshua to Chronicles – which remained in manuscript at the author's death – is thought to have inspired Miles Coverdale's Bible (1535) and to have been included in Matthews' Bible (by J. Rogers, 1537). Tyndale's Old Testament was Protestant more in its prefaces and marginal glosses than in its actual English text, which maintained a great measure of independence. Anglo-Saxon outweighs Latin in the translator's vigorous English style, since he believed, that "… the properties of the hebrue tonge agreth a thousande tymes moare with the english then with the latyne…" (*The Obedience of a Christian Man*, 1528). In fact, the English language's saturation in Hebrew idiom may largely be credited to the popular appeal of Tyndale's Bible which, after Henry VIII's quarrel with Rome, was allowed to circulate in England. Tyndale was finally arrested, condemned, and burnt at the stake for heresy.

BIBLIOGRAPHY: J.F. Mozley, *William Tyndale* (1937); W.E. Campbell, *Erasmus, Tyndale, and More* (1950).

[Godfrey Edmund Silverman]

TYNYANOV, YURI NIKOLAYEVICH (1894–1943), Soviet Russian novelist and literary theoretician. Born in Rezhitsa (Rezekne), Latvia, a small Jewish town in the old Pale of Settlement, Tynyanov moved at an early age to St. Petersburg, where he spent the rest of his life. His assimilation into the milieu of the Russian literary intelligentsia was almost complete. None of his works display any interest in Jewish subjects, and even in his posthumously published memoirs there is no hint of any Jewish identification. A brilliant literary scholar, Tynyanov was one of the foremost exponents of Formalism, a school of literary criticism fashionable in the early 1920s. This, like New Criticism in the U.S., emphasized the study of structure and artistic devices rather than of literature's social and ideological content. He was equally well known as a creative writer, particularly as the author of polished, whimsical works of historical fiction.

His best-known books included *Kyukhlya* (1925), a novel about Wilhelm Kuechelbecker, a Russian poet, eccentric, and friend of Pushkin; *Smert Vazir-Mukhtara* (1927–28; *Death and Diplomacy in Persia*, 1938), on the 19th-century Russian poet and diplomat Alexander Griboyedov; and *Pushkin* (3 vols., 1936–43). The suite *Lieutenant Kijé* by Sergei Prokofiev is based on Tynyanov's satirical novella *Podporuchik Kizhe* (1928) set in the reign of the oppressive Czar Paul I.

BIBLIOGRAPHY: A.V. Belinkov, *Yuri Tynyanov* (Rus., 1960); V.A. Kaverin, *Yuri Tynyanov pisatel i uchony* (1966); V.V. Vinogradov, in: Y.N. Tynyanov, *Pushkin i yego sovremenniki* (1969), 5–22.

[Maurice Friedberg]

TYPOGRAPHERS. Within the past century and a half the concept of typography as a special art distinct from the ordinary mechanics of printing has gained ground. Originally typography was another term for printing, but the meaning has changed. Typography now covers choice of paper, ink, design of layout, type forms, and illustrations.

Impetus was given to this modern attitude, after nearly four centuries of fairly static practice, by the technical improvements of the 19th century: the inventions of lithography and the halftone screen process of making blocks for pictures; rotary and power-driven presses in place of flatbed; and machine in place of hand typesetting, ensuring fresh type for every job instead of worn pieces. Probably most significant of all in this last respect was the solid-line setting machine, the Linotype – line o' type – invented by a man of German-Jewish origin, Ottmar Mergenthaler (1854–1899), and first used in New York in 1886.

The Private Presses

Typesetting by hand has, however, never lost its votaries. This can be seen in the rise during the last hundred years, especially in the U.S. and England, of the private presses, whose aim was not commercial profit so much as beautiful books. An authoritative survey, *The Private Presses*, written by Collin Ellis Franklin, a Jewish publisher in London, appeared in 1969. At the same time, after centuries of dependence on relatively few styles of type, there has been a widespread renaissance in type and book designing, not to mention the opportunities afforded by the tremendous growth of advertising. Jews have been prominent in these modern movements. As early as the 1870s, for example, a National Typographical Society was founded in Milan, Italy, among whose activities was the holding of exhibitions of printed matter. One of its chief supporters, elected president in 1881, was Emilio *Treves, son of the rabbi of Trieste, who was director and editor of 15 journals. Eminent among the founders of the finest private presses was Lucien Pissarro (1863–1944), the artist son of the French impressionist, Camille *Pissarro. His Eragny Press (1894–1914) is among the two or three credited with bringing wood engraving back into the hands of artists. He also designed a new type known as the Brook type. One of the services to printing performed by the private presses, and the commercial presses in their wake, has been the encouragement of illustrators and type designers, and in both these fields – sometimes combined – there have been a great many Jews. The revolutionary halftone screen process, which enables any sort of picture or photograph to be faithfully reproduced for printing in black and white or color, was perfected in the late 19th century by Georg Meisenbach (1841–1912) and Max Levy.

In Britain

One of the presses to introduce distinctive typography was the Hogarth Press, established in 1917 by Leonard *Woolf and his wife Virginia, and now part of a large commercial group. One of Francis Meynell's two partners in the fine Nonesuch Press which he founded in 1923 was Vera Mendel. In 1917 a firm originally founded in 1863 to print music, the Curwen Press, began to achieve fame by turning to general printing. Associated with it was a Jewish artist who played a great part in its art work and patterned papers, Albert Rutherston, brother of the artist Sir William *Rothenstein. In 1920 their nephew Oliver Simon joined Curwen, later to become its head. He was one of the greatest experts on typography, on which he wrote some standard works. His brother Herbert and other members of the family were also associated with the firm. Oliver Simon greatly influenced the revival of good printing by founding, and editing from 1923 to 1927, *The Fleuron*, a fine typographical annual, and the journal *Signature* (1935–54), as well as by founding, in 1924, an international association of distinguished typophiles called the Double Crown Club. Other Jews who have figured prominently in typography in England are Dennis David Myer Cohen (1891–1969), who founded the Cresset Press in 1927; John Gustave Dreyfus (1918–2002) of the Cambridge University Press; Barnett *Freedman, artist, letterer, and lithographer of genius; René Ben-Sussan, Salonika-born French artist; and two men of German birth: Hans P. Schmoller (1916–1985) of Penguin Books, and Berthold Wolpe (1905–1989), designer of books, symbols, and numerous typefaces. One of the last typefaces, Albertus, which he created for the U.S. Monotype Corporation in 1932, was described nearly 40 years later as "perhaps the most successful modern display face that has yet been designed."

In Other European Countries

Jewish typographers include Imre Reiner (1900–1987), who was born in Hungary but became known for his work in Switzerland, where he designed Corvinus and other types; and two Dutchmen: Sem L. Hartz, engraver and art director for the famous printers Enschedé, and S.H. de Roos (b. 1877), who as chief designer to the Amsterdam Type Foundry had several typefaces to his credit. Russia was very late in producing its own type; until the latter half of the 19th century, type was generally imported. The first native type foundry and printing machine factory was established, probably some time in the 1870s, by a St. Petersburg Jew, Isidore Goldberg. In 1886 he founded the first typolithographic establishment in Askabad, Transcaspian Territory, and the following year, remarkably in that antisemitic period, was decorated with the Order of St. Stanislas for his services to printing.

In the U.S.

Simon's counterpart in the U.S. was Elmer *Adler, who established Pynson Printers in 1922 to do fine printing. Modern typographers of eminence in the U.S., where Jewish names in the craft form a high proportion, are J.B. Abrahams (b. 1884), calligrapher; Peter Beilenson and his wife Edna (Peter Pauper Press); Lucian Bernhard (1883–1972), designer of Fraktur and nearly 40 other types; Joseph *Blumenthal (1897–1990) of the Spiral Press, designer of Monotype Emerson; Henry Dreyfuss (1904–1972), designer of complete magazines, especially for the McCall Company; William Henry Friedman, printing educationist; Reuben Leaf, specialist in Hebrew lettering; Robert *Leslie, Alvin Lustig, Sol Marks, and Sidney Solomon of Macmillan, New York. An American Jewish expert, N.I. Korman, dealt with the development of electronic typesetting and gave an authoritative precast of its future in an article entitled "The Editorial Revolution" in the 1968 edition of the printers' handbook, the *Penrose Annual*.

[John M. Shaftesley]

TYPOGRAPHY. Hebrew *printing began about 1475, the date of publication of two books, one at *Reggio di Calabria and the other at *Piove di Sacco, near Venice. It is sometimes claimed that a group of undated and unlocated early Hebrew books by different printers were issued earlier, and by conjecture, are believed to have originated in Rome. The year 1476 appears in the imprint of a book printed at *Guadalajara, Spain, the first of about 15 books to be printed there during the following six years. In the short span of the following few

1
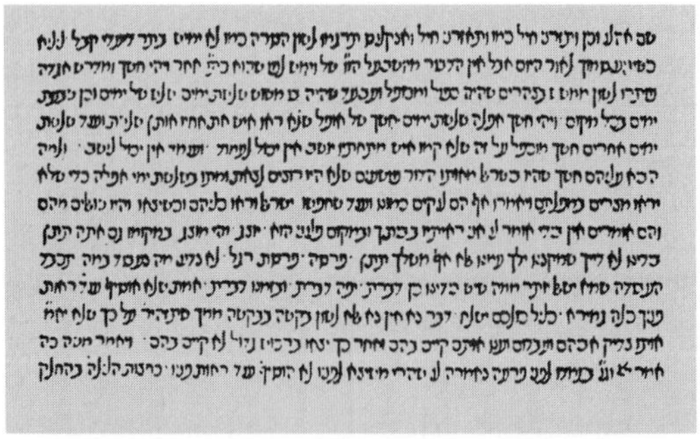

2
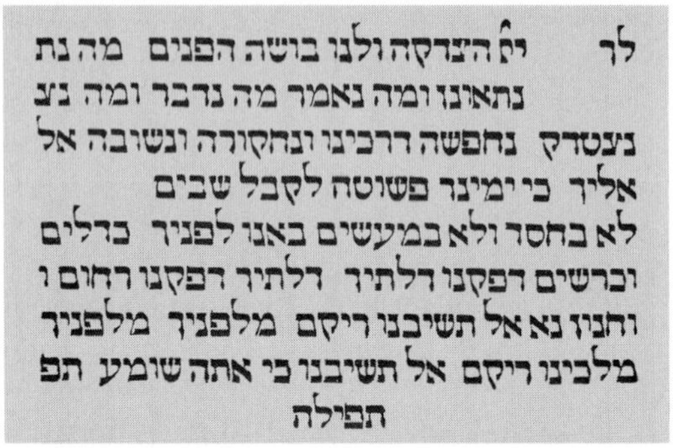

3
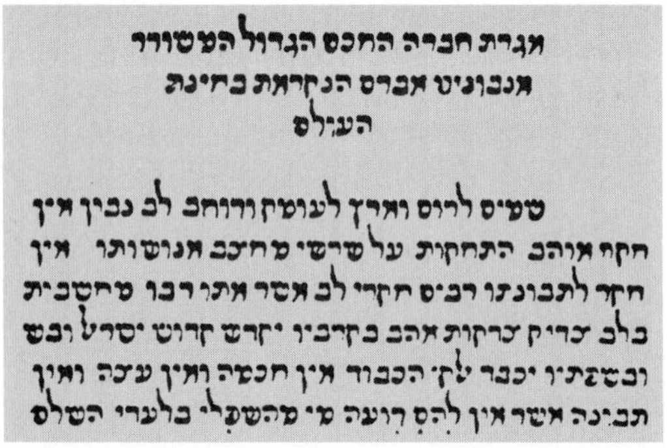

4

5
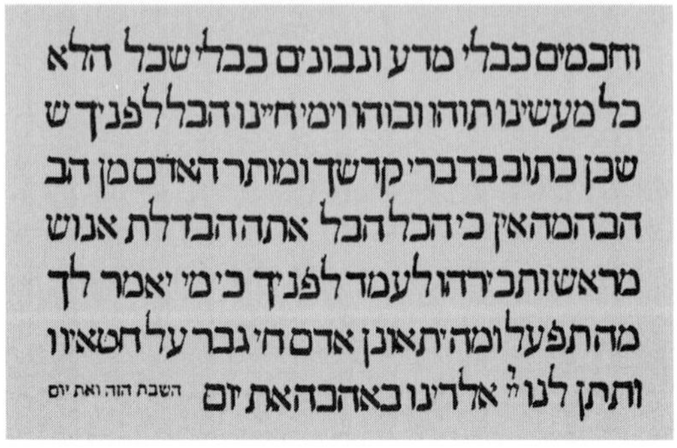

6

Figure 1. The cursive Sephardi letter used in an incunabulum of Rashi's commentary on the Pentateuch printed by Abraham b. Garton in Reggio di Calabria 1475. Incunabula list, no 171. From A. Freimann (ed.), Thesaurus Typographiae Hebraicae, *1924.*

Figure 2. Example of quill-shaped Ashkenazi manuscript letter from an edition of Seliḥot *printed by Meshullam Cusis's sons in Piove de Sacco, Italy, 1475. Incunabula list, no 98. From A. Freimann, ibid.*

Figure 3. A square, Ashkenazi-style cursive letter used by Abraham ben Solomon Conat of Mantua. Detail of a page from Beḥinat ha-Olam, *printed by Conat's wife, Estillina, assisted by Jacob Levi, from Tarascon, between 1476 and 1480. Incunabula list, no 138. From A. Freimann. ibid.*

Figure 4. A large, light, square letter of Sephardi style used for the Pentateuch, with the commentary in a smaller, Italian-type, cursive letter, in an edition of the Pentateuch with Targum Onkelos and Rashi's commentary printed by Abraham b. Ḥayyim the Dyer in Bologna, 1482. Incunabula list, no 13. From A. Freimann, ibid.

Figure 5. Alphabet based on the Sephardi style and adapted to the mechanical demands of printing. From the Maḥzor Minhag Roma *printed and published by the sons of Soncino at Soncino and Casalmaggiore, 1485–86. Incunabula list, no 102. From A. Freimann, ibid.*

Figure 6. Beginning of the famous Bible printed and published by Joseph Athias in Amsterdam, 1661. Jerusalem J.N.U.L.

Figure 7. Passage from Ezekiel in a small Bible printed by Stephanus' printing house, Paris, 1544–46.

7
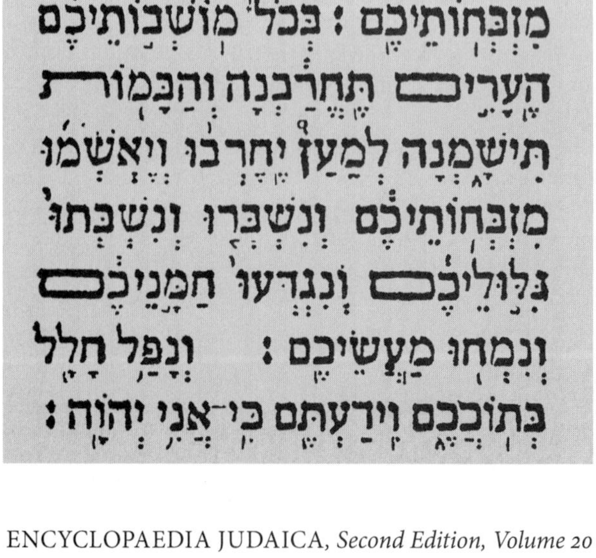

1 שׁוֹמֵעַ תְּפִלָּה עָדֶיךָ כָּל־בָּשָׂר יָבֹאוּ:
יָבוֹא כָּל־בָּשָׂר לְהִשְׁתַּחֲוֺת לְפָנֶיךָ יְיָ:
לְפָנֶיךָ

2 שׁוֹמֵעַ תְּפִלָּה וכו׳. הַפְּסוּקִים הָאֵלֶּה כֻּלָּם מְלֻקָּטִים הֵנָּה וְהֵנָּה מִסְּפָרֵי קֹדֶשׁ
כָּל חָבֵר לְיִרְאֶיךָ עָלֶיהֶם, וְהָרוֹצֶה לַעֲמֹד עַל טַעֲנוֹת וְקוּשְׁיוֹת, יְעַיֵּן בְּמִסְפְּרֵי תּוֹלְדוֹתָם,
נִסְתַּכְּמוֹת לִמְבוּכוֹת. שׁוֹמֵעַ, תְּהִלִּים ס״ה ג׳. יְבוֹא, עֶז״ס שֶׁעָ״ה ק״ז כ״ג.

3 וואַלְטֶע חוּנְזֶער פֿלֶהֶן פֿאַם זֶבֶּער, בֵּין בִּיר כָּאמַפֿרְשְׁטַייגֶען,
רָמָה חֵן וֵרְאַגֶּען פֶֿערְגֶעבְּנָעס עֶרְפֿאָלְגַּע
אוּנְזֶער חוּנְזֶער מִינְבָּרִיזְסְטַייגֶּען! בִּיטְּטֶט אִיר גֶעפֶֿעהלַאָ בִּין לֹאָם מֶעבֶען!

9

וְתוֹלְדוֹת הַנְּבִיאִים שֶׁיִּשְׂרָאֵל נִמְשְׁלוּ בַגֶּפֶן וְדַלִּיּוֹתֵיהֶ הֵם הַנְּבִיאִים
וְשָׁרָשֶׁיהָ הֵם הָאָבוֹת וַיּוֹנַקְתָּהּ הֵם הַחֲכָמִים מַצְדִּיקֵי הָרַבִּים״.

אַתָּה נָטַעְתָּ גֶּפֶן שׂוֹרֵקָה
מֻשְׁבַּחַת הָיְתָה מִכָּל הַגְּפָנִים
בְּמִגְדַּל דָּוִד הָיְתָה שְׁתוּלָה

10

1 אבגדהוזחטיכלמנסעפצקרשת דמזףץ ל 321
§—*‛«»’„[]()!?׃;‚.־ 0987654
בַּתְּחִלָּה נִתְּנָה תּוֹרָה לְיִשְׂרָאֵל בִּכְתָב עִבְרִי וּלְשׁוֹן הַקֹּדֶשׁ.
חָזְרָה וְנִתְּנָה לָהֶם בִּימֵי עֶזְרָא בִּכְתָב אַשּׁוּרִית וּלְשׁוֹן אֲרַמִּי.

2 אבגדהוזחטיכלמנסעפצקרשת דמזףץ 7654321
098 .,־׃:!?»«‛’„()—§
בַּתְּחִלָּה נִתְּנָה תּוֹרָה לְיִשְׂרָאֵל בִּכְתָב עִבְרִי וּלְשׁוֹן הַקֹּדֶשׁ. חָזְרָה
וְנִתְּנָה לָהֶם בִּימֵי עֶזְרָא בִּכְתָב אַשּׁוּרִית וּלְשׁוֹן אֲרַמִּי. בֵּרְרוּ לָהֶם

3 אבגדהוזחטיכלמנסעפצקרשת
דמזףץ 0987654321 .,:׃?!()[]□’”„—-§

4 אבגדהוזחטיכלמנסעפצקרשת דמזףץ 7654321
§—*‛«»’()!?׃;‚.־ 098
בַּתְּחִלָּה נִתְּנָה תּוֹרָה לְיִשְׂרָאֵל בִּכְתָב עִבְרִי וּלְשׁוֹן הַקֹּדֶשׁ.
חָזְרָה וְנִתְּנָה לָהֶם בִּימֵי עֶזְרָא בִּכְתָב אַשּׁוּרִית וּלְשׁוֹן אֲרַמִּי.

5 אבגדהוזחטיכלמנסעפצקרשת דמזףץ 4321
098765 .,־׃:»«’()—*
בַּתְּחִלָּה נִתְּנָה תּוֹרָה לְיִשְׂרָאֵל בִּכְתָב עִבְרִי וּלְשׁוֹן הַקֹּ
דֶשׁ. חָזְרָה וְנִתְּנָה לָהֶם בִּימֵי עֶזְרָא בִּכְתָב אַשּׁוּרִית וּלְשׁוֹן
אֲרַמִּי. בֵּרְרוּ לָהֶם לְיִשְׂרָאֵל כְּתָב אַשּׁוּרִית וּלְשׁוֹן הַקֹּדֶשׁ

6 אבגדהוזחטיכלמנסעפצקרשת דמזףץ 654321
0987 .,־׃:»«’()—
בַּתְּחִלָּה נִתְּנָה תּוֹרָה לְיִשְׂרָאֵל בִּכְתָב עִבְרִי וּלְשׁוֹן הַקֹּדֶשׁ.
חָזְרָה וְנִתְּנָה לָהֶם בִּימֵי עֶזְרָא בִּכְתָב אַשּׁוּרִית וּלְשׁוֹן אֲרַמִּי.
בֵּרְרוּ לָהֶם לְיִשְׂרָאֵל כְּתָב אַשּׁוּרִית וּלְשׁוֹן הַקֹּדֶשׁ

7 אבגדהוזחטיכלמנסעפצקרשת דמזףץ
*—־.;:?׃!()[] 0987654321
בַּתְּחִלָּה נִתְּנָה תּוֹרָה לְיִשְׂרָאֵל בִּכְתָב עִבְרִי
וּלְשׁוֹן הַקֹּדֶשׁ. חָזְרָה וְנִתְּנָה לָהֶם בִּימֵי עֶזְרָא

11

״...בְּיוֹם עֶשְׂרִים וְאַרְבָּעָה לְנוֹבֶמְבֶּר אֶלֶף שֵׁשׁ מֵאוֹת שִׁשִּׁים וְשָׁלֹשׁ

הֻפְקַד בְּלִינְדָה אוֹטוֹ לְבֵית רִילְקֶה / אֲשֶׁר עַל לַנְגְנָאוּ / גְּרִינִיצִי וְצִיגְרָה עַל אֲחֻזַּת

לִינְדָה נַחֲלַת אָחִיו כְּרִיסְטוֹף שֶׁנָּפַל חָלָל בְּאוּנְגָּארְן / אוּלָם הוֹטֶל עָלָיו לַעֲרֹךְ כְּתָב

פְּרוֹבּוּל / אֲשֶׁר לְפִיו תְּהֵא חֲזָקָה זוֹ בְּטֵלָה וּמְבֻטֶּלֶת / בְּמִקְרֶה שֶׁאָחִיו כְּרִיסְטוֹף

(אֲשֶׁר לְפִי תְּעוּדַת הַמִּיתָה נִפְטַר וְהוּא קוֹרְנֶט בִּפְלֻגָּתוֹ שֶׁל הָאָדוֹן לְבֵית פִֿירוֹבָֿאנוֹ,

בִּגְדוּד הָאוֹסְטְרִי הַקֵּיסָרִי שֶׁל פָּרָשֵׁי הַהַייסְטֶר) יָבוֹא חֲזָרָה...״

12

אֶחָד:

א וַיֹּאמֶר אֱלֹהִים יְהִי רָקִיעַ בְּתוֹךְ הַמָּיִם וִיהִי מַבְדִּיל בֵּין מַיִם
לָמָיִם: ב וַיַּעַשׂ אֱלֹהִים אֶת־הָרָקִיעַ וַיַּבְדֵּל בֵּין הַמַּיִם אֲשֶׁר
מִתַּחַת לָרָקִיעַ וּבֵין הַמַּיִם אֲשֶׁר מֵעַל לָרָקִיעַ וַיְהִי־כֵן: ח וַיִּקְרָא
אֱלֹהִים לָרָקִיעַ שָׁמָיִם וַיְהִי־עֶרֶב וַיְהִי־בֹקֶר יוֹם שֵׁנִי:
ט וַיֹּאמֶר אֱלֹהִים יִקָּווּ הַמַּיִם מִתַּחַת הַשָּׁמַיִם אֶל־מָקוֹם אֶחָד
וְתֵרָאֶה הַיַּבָּשָׁה וַיְהִי־כֵן: וַיִּקְרָא אֱלֹהִים לַיַּבָּשָׁה אֶרֶץ וּלְמִקְוֵה
הַמַּיִם קָרָא יַמִּים וַיַּרְא אֱלֹהִים כִּי־טוֹב: יא וַיֹּאמֶר אֱלֹהִים תַּדְשֵׁא
הָאָרֶץ דֶּשֶׁא עֵשֶׂב מַזְרִיעַ זֶרַע עֵץ פְּרִי עֹשֶׂה פְּרִי לְמִינוֹ אֲשֶׁר

13

שָׂרָה וְרִבְקָה טִפְּלוּ בְּיִצְחָק וְלֹא הֵסִיחוּ דַּעְתָּן מֵר׳ פַייש. בְּאוֹתָם הַיָּמִים
נִדְמֶה הָיָה שֶׁר׳ פַייש נִשְׁתַּנָּה קְצָת לְטוֹבָה, וּכְבָר הָיָה זוֹקֵף אֶת רֹאשׁוֹ עַל
כְּרוֹ וְהָיָה פּוֹלֵט חֲצָאֵי מִלִּים. כָּל אֵימַת שֶׁרִבְקָה אוֹ שָׂרָה הָיוּ שׁוֹמְעוֹת
אֶת קוֹלוֹ שֶׁל ר׳ פַייש הָיוּ מְמַהֲרוֹת וְרָצוֹת אֶצְלוֹ. כֵּיוָן שֶׁבָּאוּ אֶצְלוֹ הָיָה
שׁוֹתֵק. אֵין סָפֵק שֶׁהָיָה ר׳ פַייש מִשְׁתַּדֵּל לְהַחֲזִיר לְעַצְמָם אֶת לְשׁוֹנוֹ, אֲבָל
לֹא הָיָה מִתְכַּוֵּן שֶׁיָּבִינוּ מַה הוּא אוֹמֵר. בֵּין כָּךְ וּבֵין כָּךְ טוֹרְחוֹת הָיוּ
עָלָיו הַרְבֵּה, שֶׁמָּא יִשְׁמְעוּ דָּבָר מִפִּיו. הָיוּ רָצוֹת מֵר׳ פַייש לְיִצְחָק וּמִיִּצְחָק
לְר׳ פַייש, עַד שֶׁתָּשַׁשׁ כֹּחָן וְלֹא הָיוּ יְכוֹלוֹת לַעֲמֹד עַל רַגְלֵיהֶן. וְאִלְמָלֵא
גִּטְשִׁי אִשְׁתּוֹ שֶׁל מַנְדִּיל הָרַפָּד שֶׁהָיְתָה עוֹזַרְתָן לֹא הָיְתָה לָהֶן תְּקוּמָה.

14

גֹּדֶל הַמְּגִלָּה וְאָרְכָּהּ אֵינוֹ מוּגְבָּל. קַיָּמוֹת מְגִלּוֹת בְּאֹרֶךְ עֲשָׂרוֹת
מֶטְרִים. בְּמִצְרַיִם הָעַתִּיקָה הָיָה זֶה דָּבָר רָגִיל. בְּסִין קַיָּמוֹת מְגִלּוֹת
עַד לְאֹרֶךְ כְּשִׁבְעִים מֶטֶר, בִּמְיֻחָד מְגִלּוֹת צִיּוּרִים כְּמוֹ לְמָשָׁל שֶׁל נוֹף
הַנָּהָר יָאנְג-טְסִי-קִיאַנְג; פּוֹרְשִׂים אֶת הַמְּגִלָּה וְרוֹאִים אֶת הַנּוֹף, כְּפִי
שֶׁרוֹאֶה נוֹסֵעַ בְּסִירָה עַל הַנָּהָר. בְּסִין קַיֶּמֶת גַּם צוּרָה אַחֶרֶת לַמְּגִלָּה,
מְגִלָּה הַנִּפְתַּחַת בְּכִוּוּן לְגֹבַהּ (2). בְּקָצֶה הָעֶלְיוֹן יֶשְׁנָם מַקֵּל וְחוּטִים
לִתְלִיַּת הַמְּגִלָּה. וּבְקָצֶה הַתַּחְתּוֹן פַּס לְגָלִילָה. הַטֶּקְסְט כָּתוּב מִלְמַעְלָה
לְמַטָּה, וְהוּא פָּתוּחַ בְּבַת אַחַת. מוּבָן מֵאֵלָיו. שְׁמַגִלָּה כָּזֹאת אֵינָהּ
נִתֶּנֶת לְשִׁמּוּשׁ כְּסֵפֶר, אַךְ מְשַׁמֶּשֶׁת כְּעֵין תְּמוּנָה: שִׁיר אוֹ פִתְגָּם

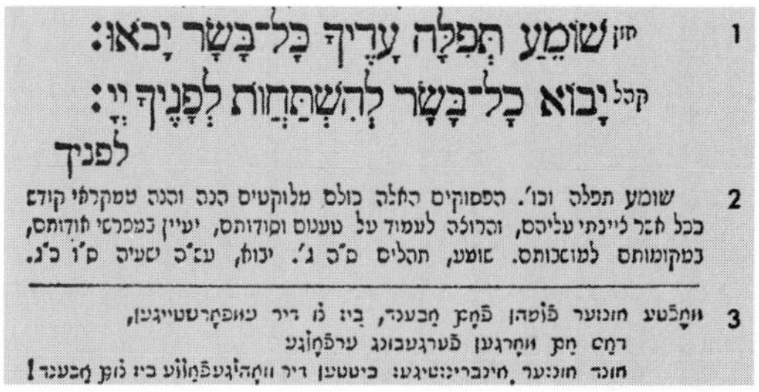

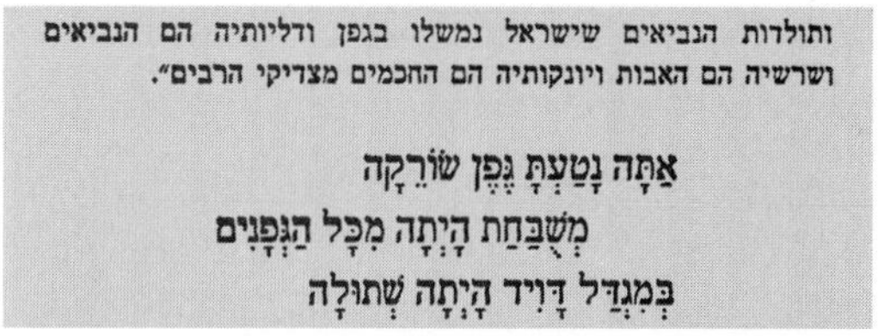

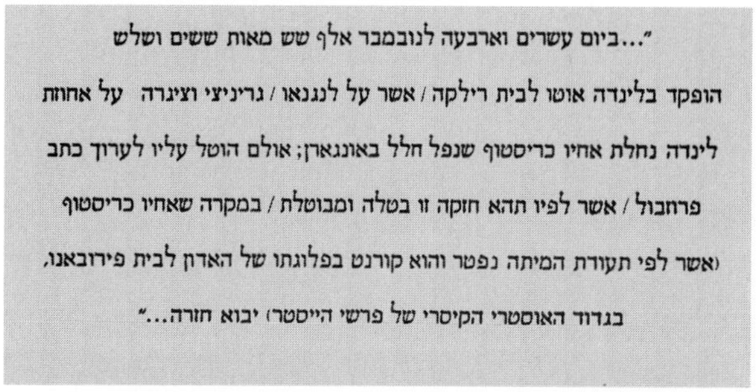

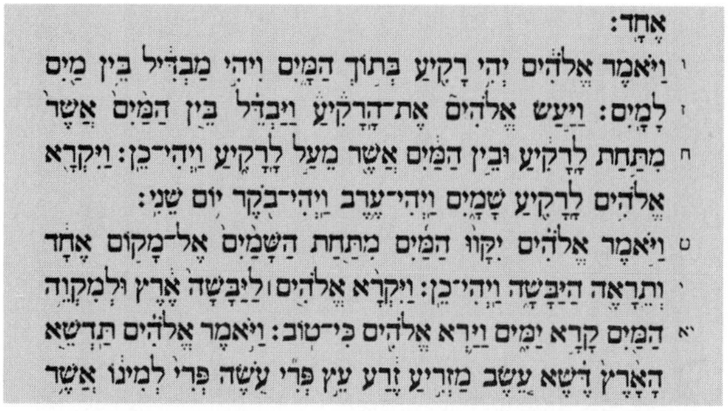

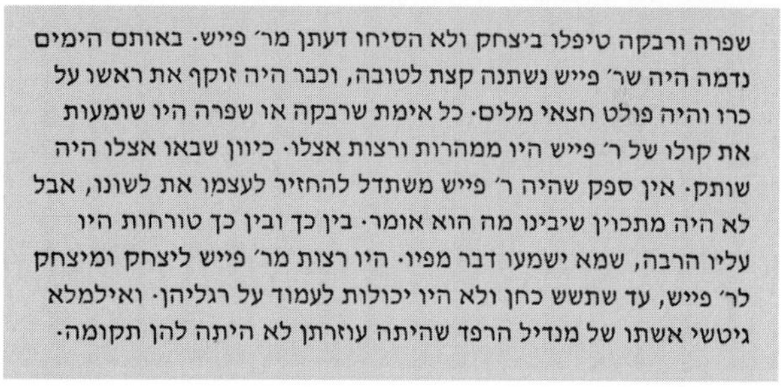

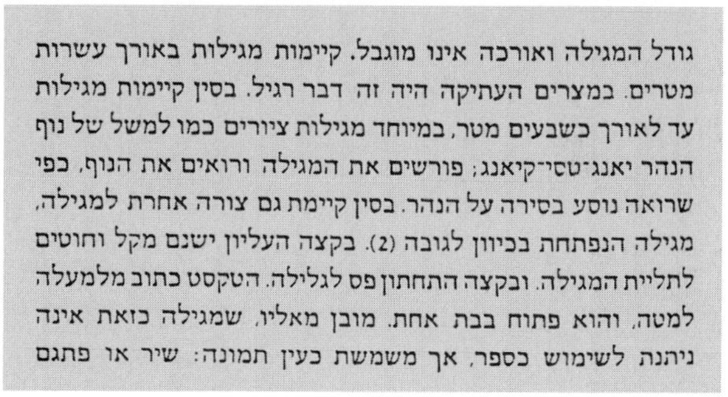

Figure 8. Sephardi square letters for the text (1), cursive for the commentary (2), and cursive Ashkenazi for the German translation (3) in Maḥzor Minhag Ashkenazi *published by W. Heidenheim and B. Baschwitz, Roedelheim, 1800–97, Jerusalem, J.N.U.L.*

Figure 9. Example of Frank-Ruehl, from Mivḥar ha-Shirim, *a collection of poems' printed at Haaretz Press, Tel Aviv, 1948.*

Figure 10. Twentieth-century Hebrew type faces (1) Frank-Ruehl, (2) Haim, (3) Aharoni, (4) Stam, (5) Gill, (6) Mayer-Baruch, (7) Ha-Ẓevi.

Figure 11. The "Schocken" typeface designed by Franziska Baruch used for Yizḥak Shenhar's translation of Die Weise von Liebe und Tod des Cornets Christoph Rilke *by Rainer Maria Rilke, Jerusalem, 1952.*

Figure 12. From the Koren Bible, set in the "Koren" typeface, Jerusalem, 1958.

Figure 13. From S.Y. Agnon's Kelev Ḥuẓot *set in "David" typeface, Jerusalem, 1960.*

Figure 14. From Henri Friedlaender's textbook on printing, Melekhet ha-Sefer, *using the author's typeface. "Hadassah," and produced by the Hadassah Apprentice School of Printing, Jerusalem, 1962.*

years new Hebrew presses were established in *Mantua, *Bologna, *Ferrara (Italy), and *Hijar (Spain). Thus, within a short time Hebrew printing spread to relatively distant places. Since printers at that time had to provide their own letter founts, a remarkable variety of alphabets and styles appeared at the inception of Hebrew typography.

The books printed in Spain and in Reggio di Calabria display the reed-born alphabets (square and cursive, a sort of italics) customary in the manuscripts of the Jews centered in Spain (Sephardi). These alphabets are distinguished by a great elegance in their curves and in the modeling of their strokes; the artist who cut the ones used in Guadalajara was mentioned by name, Piedro de Guadalajara, and was ostensibly a gentile. It is remarkable that the cursive Sephardi letter is already used as text letter in the first book printed in Reggio di Calabria, Rashi's commentary on the Pentateuch (hence its later name "Rashi-letter"), 26 years before a (non-Hebrew) cursive letter was used for the first time by the Venetian printer Aldus Manutius in 1501. In Piove di Sacco, where the printer was of German origin – as were most of the early Hebrew printers in Italy – the alphabets used were developments of the quill-shaped Ashkenazi (German) manuscript letter, angular and based on heavy contrast between bold and fine strokes. The edition of *seliḥot*, undated and probably the first book by that printer, displays a distinguished page set in quite large letters and long lines with wide margins in quarto size.

The founder of the press in Mantua, Abraham *Conat, who was a physician and scribe by profession, had an alphabet cut for himself, for which his own Italian-German cursive hand served as a model. His square letter was of the Ashkenazi type and similar to that used in Piove di Sacco. In 1477 Psalms, with the commentary of David Kimḥi, appeared in Bologna, the letters being of a similar type to those used in Mantua. In the same year Abraham b. *Ḥayyim, "The Dyer," of Pesaro started a short-lived press in Ferrara, buying the equipment from Abraham Conat. In 1482 he printed in Bologna an edition of the Pentateuch with Rashi's commentary; the text is set in a pleasantly large and elegantly light Sephardi new square letter and the commentary in a much smaller cursive letter of the Italian type. This edition fixed the layout for biblical texts with commentaries for all following editions.

The decisive turn in Hebrew typography after these initial trials was instituted with the activity of the *Soncino family. This family, hailing from Germany, printed Hebrew books through five generations, starting in 1484 in Soncino and later publishing works in Casalmaggiore, Pesaro, Brescia, Naples, Rimini, Salonika, Istanbul, and Cairo until 1557. The Soncinos, the most prolific and most creative Jewish Hebrew printer-publishers of all time, stabilized the style of letters used in Hebrew printing, employing an alphabet based on the Sephardi type and well adapted to the mechanical exigencies of printing, and which served as a base for later printers. They put out works of basic Hebrew literature in editions which became classic, as well as non-Hebrew books. The non-Hebrew books printed by Gershom Soncino typographically take a place of honor among the book productions of this time. He employed as a letter cutter the most accomplished letter artist of his time, and possibly of all time, Francesco Griffo, a friar of Bologna who had also worked for the famous Venetian printer Aldus Manutius, the first to print books in cursive letters (*cancellaresca*), which were cut by Griffo, in pocket size.

In the meantime *Venice became a new center of Hebrew printing. A rich gentile humanist from Antwerp, Daniel *Bomberg, assembled an impressive team of scholars – Jewish and baptized – as editors and proofreaders, as well as competent craftsmen, had excellent letters cut, and erected a Hebrew press in Venice which was to excel in quantity and quality all those that had preceded him in this field. All of the products of Bomberg's press were distinguished by faultless composition and layout, improved typefaces, and high-quality paper. His products constituted the high mark of achievement of the first decades of Hebrew typography. Based on the shapes pioneered by the Soncinos, Bomberg's typefaces became dominant and greatly influenced the further development of Hebrew typography.

While the Spanish-Italian branch of Hebrew printing developed – after some initial wavering – a square and cursive typeface based on the Sephardi tradition of lettering, another Hebrew printing center came into being in the second decade of the 16th century in *Prague (and somewhat later in *Basle) whose lettering was based decidedly on the Ashkenazi letter shapes. From the start the Prague printers achieved high typographical excellence and their influence spread to various parts of Germany and to Poland. Hebrew printing in Prague started in 1512; in 1514 the printers' company was joined by new partners, among them Gershom *Kohen, and from then on he was the central figure in the enterprise. His family continued his work well into the 17th century. In 1526 the Kohen press published a typographically outstanding work, a Passover *Haggadah* in large quarto with many woodcuts, the text being set in a superb large-size Ashkenazi typeface, which was probably cut in wood and displays to the best advantage all the beauty in this late Gothic style of Hebrew lettering. The many initial words are of exceptional beauty and are set in a still larger size, or, more probably, cut as whole words in wood. Four of the woodcut illustrations have the letter *Shin* (ש) unobtrusively incorporated, probably the signature of one of the partners, Ḥayyim *Shaḥor (he had already left the partnership when the *Haggadah* was published but seems to have been responsible for the woodcuts, or some of them). The *Haggadah* was reprinted in the same year with slight alterations by the original printers and was closely copied in 1560 in Mantua, with altered woodcuts and initial words; parts of the text were printed in smaller type.

Shaḥor set up a press in Oels (*Olesnica), near Breslau, moving from there to Augsburg, Ichenhausen, Heddernheim (all in Germany), and finally to Lublin, Poland. He took typefaces from Prague and continued to use the skill he gained there. The *Halicz brothers set up a press in Cracow about 1530, using mostly Prague type and style. The Hebrew Bible

(c. 1551–52), with Rashi's commentary, printed by Samuel Halicz in Istanbul – of which only the Pentateuch with the Five Scrolls and *Haftarot* is known (in a unique copy) – is in good typographical tradition; the letters which were used show a strange mixture of Ashkenazi and Sephardi style.

In the 16th century the interest of Christian humanists in Hebrew printing became of the utmost importance. Apart from Daniel Bomberg in Venice, there was Johannes Froben of Basle, who used the Ashkenazi type of letters to great advantage, including the Ashkenazi cursive (chiefly for texts in Judeo-German). Froben printed quite a number of Hebrew and Judeo-German books in cooperation with the Christian Hebraists Sebastian *Muenster and the two Buxtorfs, among them the biblical cantillation rendered in musical notes for the first time (in a Hebrew grammar written in Latin by Sebastian Muenster, 1534). Paulus *Fagius in Isny and Paulus Aemilius in Augsburg carefully produced books in Ashkenazi Hebrew type. At the same time in France Robertus Stephanus (Etienne), who was responsible for editions of many Latin and almost all Greek texts, printed the Hebrew Bible twice, once in a small format and once in octavo in beautiful letters of the Sephardi type, cut specially for these editions. Guillaume Le *Bé, the man who influenced the further development of the Hebrew printed alphabet possibly more than any other single figure, emerged from Stephanus' printing house. A native of Troyes, France, he was a letter designer and punch cutter who in 1545 was employed on Stephanus' recommendation by the Venetian humanist M.A. *Giustiniani, the founder in that year of a Hebrew press in Venice. Le Bé, 21 years old when he came to Venice, mainly specialized from then onward in designing and cutting Hebrew letters (until 1550 in Venice and later again in Paris). He carefully studied the Hebrew letter shapes, collected what he considered the best samples from everywhere, and continued cutting Hebrew founts to the end of his long life. Almost 20 Hebrew founts are credited to him. Not only did Giustiniani and the Italian-Jewish printer Meir *Parenzo depend on his typefaces but they were also later copied in Italy until the 19th century. The press of *Belforte in Leghorn (closed in 1939) used a derivative of his letters, and the Nebiolo type foundry in Turin still produced them in 1970 in a later rendering.

More important still, Le Bé provided Christopher *Plantin, the great printer of Antwerp, with Hebrew letters which the latter used in his Polyglot Bible (Antwerp, 1569–72), a superb piece of printing. Le Bé's letter style (and probably even some of the original letters) was passed on from Plantin to Christian printers in Germany, on one hand, and on the other to Holland, which took the lead in Hebrew printing in the 17th and 18th centuries, and by which Hebrew printing in Germany, England, Eastern Europe, and even the Near East was decisively influenced. The first Hebrew printer in Holland was *Manasseh Ben Israel, who had his letters cut from models prepared by the chief Hebrew scribe of Amsterdam, Michael Judah. His first publication, a prayer book of the Sephardi rite, appeared in 1627. Further Hebrew presses were set up soon after in *Amsterdam. The Jewish printers there, who were learned and cultured men, ordered their letters from the most accomplished punch cutters of their time, among them Christopher van Dyck and Johann Michael Fleischmann of Nuremberg. Since Hebrew books became an important export item in the economy of Amsterdam, all the important type foundries there produced Hebrew fonts. These were used everywhere, and printers mentioned the use of "Amsterdam type" on their title pages rather than the places and names of the printers. Typographically outstanding among the Amsterdam Hebrew presses was that of the *Athias family, which produced, among others, the famous Hebrew Bible (1661) and the beautiful edition of Maimonides' *Mishneh Torah* (1702–03). Another Hebrew press in Amsterdam of high standing was that of the *Proops family, which published a very large quantity of Hebrew books and continued its work into the late 19th century.

In the 17th and 18th centuries Hebrew printing spread widely to Germany, Poland, and some Oriental countries, and continued at some presses in Italy. The centers all derived from Amsterdam, Prague, and Venice and continued their respective typographical traditions, mostly with loss of quality. Some Hebrew type is also used in the first book printed on the North American continent, the *Bay Psalm Book* (Cambridge, Massachusetts, 1640). The 19th century brought further innovations. In *Roedelheim (near Frankfurt) W. *Heidenheim and B. Baschwitz published a new *maḥzor* in 1800 in nine volumes, using newly cut letters – square and cursive Sephardi for the commentary, and cursive Ashkenazi for the German translations – with a great deal of skill. This press continued printing in the same style and with the same letters throughout the 19th century, and its products were reprinted from stereotypes until the Holocaust, being reproduced in Basle even after World War II. In Eastern Europe the most important typographical production was the superb edition of the Babylonian Talmud by the house of *Romm in Vilna (1880–86). In England Z.H. *Filipowski printed Hebrew text editions in a pleasant small type.

The 19th century, with its deep changes in Jewish life, made new claims on Hebrew typography. A secular literature arose, with newspapers and periodicals not only in Hebrew but also in Yiddish and Ladino. By the end of the century changes in typographical techniques had taken place. The large European type foundries produced new Hebrew letters on traditional lines which were used in the printing of Bibles by the British and Foreign Bible Society and the Wuerttemberg Bible Institute, as well as in other scholarly editions. The most successful Hebrew type innovation was created through the cooperation of the Leipzig cantor and scribe Raphael Frank and the graphic artist Ruehl who worked for the Berthold type foundry. The Frank-Ruehl letter spread quickly, and after it was incorporated in the program of all the chief typesetting machines (Linotype, Monotype – under the name of Peninim – and Intertype) it held a near monopoly for quite a long period, in spite of its being an expression of the Art Nouveau style.

The rapid expansion of the press and of art and literature publications in Hebrew and Yiddish after World War I and the growing influence, first of the German expressionism and then of the New Typography promoted by the Bauhaus, were a new challenge to Hebrew typography. The existing letters were of little use in shaping the new typographical images. New Hebrew letters of the sans serif type were therefore created, at least for display, the first a letter called "Haim" by Jacob Levit (in Warsaw) and the second by the Tel Aviv graphic artist Aharoni which was published under his name in Germany. Both these typefaces were widely used for display and gave Hebrew printing an entirely new look. At the same time the cursive (Rashi) alphabet was totally abandoned in secular literature – a fact which resulted in a deplorable impoverishment of typographical possibilities.

The renascence of Hebrew literature, its concentration in Israel, and the tremendous growth of the production of books and periodicals, as well as of commercial printing, necessitated swift developments in Hebrew typography. They took shape chiefly from the end of World War II onward, and from the foundation of the State of Israel with accelerated energy. Between the two world wars new Hebrew types were still intended chiefly for what could be called ceremonial printing: this is true of the Ashkenazi square letter called "Stam," which was cut by the Berthold foundry and was dependent on a design by Franziska Baruch, and of the type designed by Marcus Behmer and ordered by the *Soncino Society for its monumental Bible, of which only the Pentateuch was printed before the Nazis put an end to the project. From this time a different sort of typeface was needed. Serious attempts began in the period between the two world wars, such as those of Eric Gill and L.A. Meyer, together with Franziska Baruch, but were not successful in providing new letters for general use; others, such as those of the German letter designer E.R. Weiss (whose drawings were lost), the American F.W. Goudy, and the Englishman H.G. Carter, were abortive. A radical step forward was made in the Ha-Ẓevi family of typefaces (Jerusalem Type Foundry), which were designed by Ẓevi Hausmann in collaboration with M. Spitzer. Based on a quasi-sans serif style, it went back to old letter shapes and reduced the overdecoration which had crept into Hebrew letter design in the course of centuries. In this way it achieved a modern appearance, but (being in its light rendering a book face) available for hand composition only, it could not be used for book work. The David Hebrew, a letter built on somewhat similar principles but more cursive, was designed by Ismar David with some help from M. Spitzer, and is available on Intertype; it is used in book work and allows for a very light look of the page in contrast to the heavy look traditional in Hebrew printing. Other new types are a modern renewal of the Ashkenazi letter by Henry Friedlaender, Hadassah (Amsterdam Type Foundry), also available on Intertype; Franziska Baruch's Schocken-Hebrew (Monotype); Z. Korngold's Koren (Deberny et Peignot, Paris), a traditional letter useful for traditional literature; and Ẓvi Narkis' Narkis Hebrew on Linotype. As a result of the progress of photo setting new faces were created. The general appearance of Hebrew typographical work – which in the present day covers the whole range of printing from belles-lettres through scholarly and technical literature to art books, periodicals of all sorts, and a very wide range of commercial printing – will go on changing. Some substantial advances in bibliophile book production have also taken place.

BIBLIOGRAPHY: A.M. Habermann, *Ha-Sefer ha-Ivri be-Hitpattehuto* (1968), includes a comprehensive bibliography; M. Spitzer, in: *Alei Ayin; Minḥat Devarim le S.Z. Schocken* (1952), 481–501; D.W. Amram, *The Makers of Hebrew Books in Italy* (1909); A. Freimann, *Thesausus Typographiae Hebraicae Saeculi XV* (1924–31, 1968); M. Marx, in: HUCA, 11 (1936), 427–501; J. Prijs, *Die Basler hebraeischen Drucke* (1964); H. Omont, *Spécimens de Caractères Hebreux Gravés à Venise et à Paris par Guillaume Le Bé* (1887); M. Steinschneider and D. Cassel, *Juedische Typographie und juedischer Buchhandel* (1938); C. Enschedé, *Fonderies de Caractéres et leur Matériel dans les Pays Bas du XVe au XIXe Siècle* (1908); *Soncino Blaetter* (1925–30).

[Maurice Moshe Spitzer]

TYRE (Heb. צוֹר), port in Lebanon, S.S.W. of Beirut. An ancient competitor of *Sidon, Tyre by 1200 B.C.E. became the leading port of Phoenicia and is mentioned in the *El-Amarna Letters. By the 10th century Tyre had founded the colonies of Uttica, Godes, and perhaps Carthage. Tyre was famous for its temple and craftsmen, and *Hiram of Tyre supplied Solomon with wood for the Temple (I Kings 5). A later Hiram built a huge breakwater in front of the port, then situated on an impregnable island, making Tyre one of the most important ports in the Mediterranean.

In 332 B.C.E. Alexander marched on Tyre for refusing to submit to him as the other Phoenician towns had done. After a siege of seven months Alexander took Tyre by building a mole, which joined the island to the mainland for the rest of its history. Tyre was destroyed and its inhabitants killed or enslaved (Arrian, Anabasis 2:5–21). The town rapidly recovered and was ruled by a native dynasty under Ptolemid suzerainity until 274 B.C.E. (Era of Tyre), when power was passed to the suffetes. Conquered by the Seleucids in 200 B.C.E. (Justinian 18:3:18), Tyre gained independence in 126 B.C.E. It expanded its silk, glass, and purple dye industry for which it was famous in the ancient world. During the Maccabean wars Tyre joined Sidon and Ptolemais (Acre) in attacking the Jews of Galilee, only to be repulsed by Simeon (Jos. Ant. 12:331; I Macc. 5:16).

In 63 B.C.E. Tyre came under Roman rule and Mark Antony demanded the restoration of Jewish property taken by the Tyrians during the wars of Hyrcanus and forbade damage to it (*ibid.* 14:313–22). Cleopatra begged him to grant her Tyre as a gift with the other territories south of R. Eleutherus that she received. Antony refused as Tyre was a free city (*ibid.* 15:95). There was a Jewish community at Tyre but the Tyrians were bitter enemies of the Jews (Jos., Apion 1:70). Like Sidon, Tyre under Augustus lost her rights because of some disturbances, but she administered territories up to the Jordan until Byzantine times. Tyre established centers for commerce at Puteoli and Rome, but when Ostia was rebuilt by Trajan they began to fail (CIG, 5853; CIL 10: 1601). By this time Tyre was the richest town of the eastern provinces. In the second century *Simeon b. Yoḥai lived there.

Excavations by P. Bikai in 1973–1974, on behalf of the Lebanese Department of Antiquities, produced a sequence of architecture and pottery from the site dating from between 2700 and 1600 B.C.E. The visible archaeological remains from the city are essentially from the Roman and Byzantine periods, notably a colonnaded street, a monumental archway, a large Roman bath, and a hippodrome that could seat some 60,000 spectators. A fourth-century basilica and a large Crusader cathedral represent some of the later remains in the city.

In the Middle Ages

In the Middle Ages Tyre was a rich and well-fortified city with a large Jewish community, whose high economic and cultural standard made it one of the most important communities in the Near East. The *Genizah and other sources contain a wealth of material on the community in the 11th and 12th centuries. It transpires from these records that the Jews of Tyre derived their income mainly from the manufacture of glass and the export of glass products. They also traded in spices and flax with Jews from Egypt and the Maghreb, who came there on business. According to the testimony of an Italian Jew who settled in Ereẓ Israel in the 11th century, many Jews came to settle in Tyre during that period. During the great Bedouin revolt against *Fatimid rulers in the 1030s the Jewish community in Tyre was spared the sufferings that afflicted most of the other communities in Ereẓ Israel and southern Syria. It was the center of religious scholars who engaged in literary works and maintained close contacts with the Ereẓ Israel academy; in 1071, when Jerusalem was conquered by the *Seljuqs, the academy moved to Tyre. In 1081 the *rosh yeshivah* *Elijah ha-Kohen traveled to Haifa to ordain his son Abiathar as his successor, honoring the principle that ordination is not to be carried out beyond the confines of Ereẓ Israel. Ten years later a violent controversy broke out between the *ḥakhamim* of the academy and *David b. Daniel, when the latter demanded recognition as *nasi* by the Jews of Ereẓ Israel and Syria. As a result, Abiathar, the *gaon* of the academy, was forced to leave Tyre, and was followed by the *av* of the academy, *Solomon ha-Kohen. The controversy was finally settled in 1094, when the *nagid* *Mevorakh succeeded in gaining the upper hand over David b. Daniel; the academy was reestablished and Abiathar returned to resume his office. After the Crusader conquest of Tyre in 1124, Italian merchants, led by Venetians, established trade colonies in the city. The Jews lived in the Venetian quarter, which was under the direct control of the Venetian republic, and attempts by the last of the Frankish kings of Jerusalem to wrest jurisdiction over the Jews from their Venetian overlords were of no avail. *Benjamin of Tudela, who visited Tyre in the second half of the 12th century, reports on having found about 400 Jews in the city; they were engaged mainly in glass manufacture, but also included shipowners, i.e., international traders. The rabbis of Tyre in this period addressed numerous inquiries to *Maimonides. In the 13th century the community seems to have declined since there is an absence of reports dating from that period. After the *Mamluk conquest in 1291, the Tyre Jewish community ceased to exist.

BIBLIOGRAPHY: IN THE MIDDLE AGES: S. Schechter, *Saadyana* (1903), 88ff.; S.A. Wertheimer, *Ginzei Yerushalayim* 3 (1902), 15–16; Mann, Egypt, 1–2 (1920–22), index; S. Assaf, in: *Tarbiz*, 9 (1938), 196–9; idem, *Mekorot u-Meḥkarim* (1946), 134–7; idem, in: *Ereẓ-Israel* 1 (1951), 140–4; *Teshuvot ha-Rambam* ed. by J. Blau, 3 (1961), index; I. Ben-Zvi, *She'ar Yashuv* (1965), index; S.D. Goitein, in: JQR, 49 (1958–59), 40ff. **ADD. BIBLIOGRAPHY:** H. Katzenstein, *The History of Tyre: From the Beginning of the Second Millennium* B.C.E. *until the Fall of the Neo-Babylonian Empire in 538* B.C.E. (1973, 1997²); M.S. Joukowsky (ed.), *The Heritage of Tyre: Essays on the History, Archaeology and Preservation of Tyre* (1992); W.A. Ward, "Tyre," in: *The Oxford Encyclopedia of Archaeology in the Near East*, vol. 5 (1997), 247–50.

[Eliyahu Ashtor]

TYRE, LADDER OF (Heb. סֻלָּם צוֹר; Sullam Ẓur), a steep road cut in steps which connected the territory of Acre with that of Tyre and formed part of the coastal road passing the twin capes of Rosh ha-Nikrah (Ras en-Naqura) and Rosh ha-Lavan (Ras el-Abyad) partly in Israel and partly in Lebanon. It is first mentioned in I Maccabees 11:59 as the northern boundary of the coastal province of Paralia, entrusted by the Seleucid king to Simeon the Hasmonean. Josephus describes it as the northern boundary of Ptolemais (Acre), 100 stadia (c. 11½ mi.; 18½ km.) from that city. In talmudic sources, the Ladder of Tyre (Aramaic: *Sulma de Sor*) is frequently mentioned as the northern limit of the Holy Land, beyond which certain ordinances referring to that region no longer applied (Tosef., Pes. 1:28; et al.). The area from which the snails yielding purple dye were collected extended from Haifa to the Ladder of Tyre (Sab. 26a). The name has been revived as the appellation of a regional council in northwestern Galilee.

[Michael Avi-Yonah]

TYRE OF THE TOBIADS, fortress in Transjordan, built by Hyrcanus, the last of the Tobiad rulers of Peraea (Jos., Ant., 12:228–34). It is identified with the ruins of ʿIrāq al-Amir, approximately 10½ mi. (17 km.) W. of Amman (see full description of the site under entry *Tobiads). Another suggested identification is with Birtha of the Ammanitis, the Tobiad capital in the third century, which is mentioned in the *Zeno Papyri* (ed. by Edgar, no. 59003).

BIBLIOGRAPHY: Conder-Kitchener, 1 (1881), 72ff.; H.C. Butler, *Syria…, Architecture*, 2a (1919), 1ff.; Abel, Geog, 2 (1938), 131; Lapp, in: BASOR, 165 (1962), 16–34; 171 (1963), 8ff.

[Michael Avi-Yonah]

TYRNAU, ISAAC (end of 14th century), Austrian rabbi and compiler of a book of *minhagim*. Tyrnau's teachers were Abraham *Klausner, Sar Shalom of Neustadt, and *Aaron Neustadt. Until recently it was assumed that his name derived from Trnava (Tyrnau) in Hungary (now Slovakia), but modern scholars incline more to the view that he came from

Austria. He was born in Vienna and apparently subsequently moved to Tyrnau in Austria, from where it is possible that he went to minister as rabbi of Pressburg although some scholars deny that he was ever in Pressburg. Little is known about his life except that in 1420 he contacted Jacob *Moellin regarding a divorce.

Tyrnau's fame rests upon his book of *minhagim*. Basing himself largely on his teacher, Klausner, he set down customs and codes of conduct for the whole year, and they were subsequently adopted in most communities in Austria, Hungary, and Styria. As Tyrnau wrote in the preface, his aim was to create a common *minhag*. As a result of the *Black Death (1348–50), which had uprooted most of the communities of Germany, "scholars became so few.... I saw localities where there were no more than two or three persons with a real knowledge of local custom." His description is concise and his style easy. The book enjoyed great popularity among German and Polish Jewry. Glosses by a Hungarian scholar, whose identity is not certain, apparently were added to the book and published together with it. The first edition was printed in Venice (1566) and has been frequently republished often as an appendix to the prayer book. Similarly a German translation by Simon Guenzburg (Mantua, 1590) has often been reprinted. A legend has been preserved to the effect that the Hungarian crown prince fell in love with the beautiful daughter of Tyrnau, and out of love for her renounced the throne, became converted to Judaism, and went to study Torah from Sephardi rabbis. On his return to Hungary he entered into a clandestine marriage with her and continued to study under his father-in-law. His identity was accidentally discovered by Catholic priests who demanded that he revert to his original faith. When he refused, he was burned at the stake and the Jews expelled from Tyrnau (*Eẓba Elohim, o Ma'aseh Ray she-Eira le-ha-Rav Yiẓḥak Tyrnau*; "The Finger of God, or What Happened to R. Isaac Tyrnau," the author of *Sefer ha-Minhagim*, 1857).

BIBLIOGRAPHY: Michael, Or, no. 328; J.J. Cohen in: *Ha-Ma'yan*, 8 (1968), no. 4, 4–12; Weingarten, *ibid.*, 10 (1970), no. 2, 48–56.

[Shmuel Ashkenazi]

TYROL, autonomous province in W. Austria. Jews are first recorded in the Tyrol in the late 13th century: Isaac of Lienz was a large-scale moneylender and leased the income from the customs. A "Mayr the *Monetarius*" (*mintmaster) is mentioned in 1310 in *Merano. The few Jews living in *Innsbruck were massacred during the *Black Death persecutions in 1348–49, and in the following decades few are recorded in the province. In Bozen (*Bolzano) and Trient (*Trent), scene of the notorious blood libel in 1475, Jews are first mentioned in 1403. In 1442 a blood libel also occurred in Lienz. The alleged murder of Andreas of Rinn on the local "*Judenstein*" was an early 17th-century fabrication on the lines of the Trent blood libel. Although Andreas was never beatified, his cult was tolerated by the Church in 1755; an attempt to revive the "Anderl" play in 1954 was not permitted.

Expulsion orders of Jews from the Tyrol issued in 1520 and 1569 were not enforced, and a few Jews were found living there soon afterward, mainly in Innsbruck. After the expulsion from nearby *Hohenems in 1676, a few families settled in Innsbruck and elsewhere. Though Tyrol produced few scholars of distinction, two of the 17th century should be mentioned: Solomon b. Isaac and Shemaiah b. Meir Halevi Horowitz. During the anti-French uprising of Andreas *Hofer the Jewish settlement in Innsbruck was pillaged. Legal and economic restrictions on the Jews were not abolished under Bavarian rule and were ratified by the estates in 1817. In 1850 about 90 Jews were living in the province, mainly in Innsbruck. In Merano, where the first Jew settled in 1832, a Jewish settlement developed following the growth of the resort town. The Koenigswarter burial foundation was established in 1872, a hospital was opened in 1893, and a synagogue in 1901. In 1914 there were 130 Jews living in the province; that year Joseph Link, formerly of Hohenems, became provincial rabbi of the Tyrol and *Vorarlberg at Innsbruck, officiating until 1932. He was succeeded by E.S. Rimalt, under whom Zionism gained ground. After World War I *sheḥitah* was prohibited in Tyrol. The early 1930s saw a rise in the support of Nazism by the local population. Isolated Jews living in the province were not molested during **Kristallnacht* in November 1938, but the Jews of Innsbruck suffered extensively from Nazi attacks. Soon afterward all the Jews of Tyrol moved to Vienna. After World War II about 11 families established a new community in Innsbruck.

BIBLIOGRAPHY: E.S. Rimalt, in: J. Fraenkel (ed.), *Jews of Austria* (1967), 375–85; *Germania Judaica*, 2 (1968), 537, 823; K. Kruby in: W.P. Eckert and E.L. Ehrlich (eds.), *Judenhass – Schuld der Christen?* (1964), 301ff.; B. Muenz, in: AZJ, 70 (1906), 116f., 141f.

TYSMENITSA (Pol. **Tyśmienica**), town in Ivano-Frankovsk oblast, Ukraine; within Poland until 1772 when it passed to Austria, reverting to Poland between the two world wars. An organized Jewish community existed in Tysmenitsa from the early 18th century, under the jurisdiction of the council of the "province of Russia" (see *Councils of the Lands). In the mid-18th century Jews from Tysmenitsa attended the *Breslau fairs. In the 1760s, during the rabbinate of Meshullam b. Samson *Igra, a new stone synagogue was erected to replace the old wooden one which had burned down in 1754. In 1765 there were 856 Jews paying the poll tax in the town. The Ḥasidim in Tysmenitsa were persecuted in the early 19th century. The Jewish population numbered 2,529 (36% of the total) in 1880, 2,049 (26%) in 1900, and 2,305 (23%) in 1910. They mainly engaged in trade of agricultural products and timber, shopkeeping, furriery, and carpentry. In the 1850s Menahem Mendel of Tysmenitsa, author of *Elef Alfin* (1876), was rabbi of the community. He was followed by Saul b. Meshullam Issachar ha-Levi Horovitz, author of responsa (*Besamim Rosh he-Ḥadash*). Before World War I there was a Jewish school financed by the *Baron de Hirsch Fund. Between 1914 and 1920 many Jews moved to *Stanislav, *Lvov, and *Stry. Between 1919 and 1939 when Tysmenitsa was within Poland, the Zionist movement was active. The community had a library. The Jewish population numbered 1,090 (16%) in 1921. The community was destroyed in the Holocaust. There were 56 survivors, some 30 of whom immigrated to Israel.

BIBLIOGRAPHY: R. Mahler, *Yidn in Amolikn Poyln in Likht fun Tsifern* (1958), index; Dov of Bolehov, *Zikhronot*, ed. by M. Wischnitzer (1922), 62; B. Wasiutyński, *Ludność źdowska w Polsce w wiekach XIX i XX* (1930), 124; I. Schiper, *Dzieje handlu hydowskiego na ziemiach polskich* (1937), index; I. Lewin, *Przeczynki do dziejł i historji literatury żydow Polsce* (1935), 9, 15.

[Shimshon Leib Kirshenboim]

TYSZOWCE (in Jewish sources **Tishvits**), a village in Lublin province, near the city of *Tomaszow Lubelski, E. Poland. Tyszowce was granted municipal rights in 1453. Jewish merchants settled there in the early 16th century, and by the 1630s they actively participated in the fairs at Lublin and *Lvov. In 1565 King Sigismund II Augustus granted the Jews equal rights and forbade market days to be held on the Sabbath. The *Council of the Lands sometimes met in Tyszowce and discussed such important matters as autonomous governance of communities, independent choice of rabbis, guardianship of orphans, marriage arrangements (Takkanot Tishvits, 1583), intercession with the government (1624), and financial support for Jews in Ereẓ Israel (1742). In 1649 and 1655/57, the Jews suffered from the armies of S. *Czarniecki and *Chmielnicki. In the 18th century they engaged in shoemaking and pottery, in addition to commerce. In 1765, 925 Jews living there paid the poll tax. In 1815 the town was included in Congress Poland, and from 1823 to 1862 the Russian authorities limited Jewish settlement in the area because of its proximity to the Austrian border. The 732 Jews living there in 1827 comprised 34% of the population. In 1857 there were 956 Jews (36%); in 1897/98, 851 Jews (85%); in 1921, 2,454 Jews (55%). Between the world wars all the Jewish parties were represented in the town and there was an active community life.

Holocaust Period

On the outbreak of World War II, there were about 3,800 Jews in Tyszowce. In September 1939 the Red Army entered the town but withdrew after a short time, according to a new Soviet-German agreement on the partition line. About 1,000 Jews left the town for the East with the withdrawing Red Army. The German army occupied the town at the beginning of October 1939. In May 1942 about 1,000 Jews were deported to the *Belzec death camp. The Jewish community was liquidated in November 1942, when the remaining Jews were sent to the same camp. After the war the Jewish community of Tyszowce was not reconstituted.

BIBLIOGRAPHY: Halpern, Pinkas, index; B. Wasiutyński, *Ludność żydowska w Polsce w wiekach XIX i XX* (1930), 60; M. Balaban, *Historja Żydów w Krakowie i na Kazimierzu*, 1 (1931) 330, 433; idem, in: *Istoriya yevreyskogo naroda*, 11 (1914), 166; M. Schorr, *Organizacja wewnętrzna Żydów w Polsce* (1899), 11, 17, 18, 82.

TZARA, TRISTAN (originally **Sami Rosenstein**; 1896–1963), Romanian and French poet. Born in Moinesti, Romania, Tzara was one of several Jews who enjoyed literary repute both in their native country and in their adopted land, France. His earliest poems in Romanian appeared in 1912 (under the pen name S. Samiro) in *Simbolul*, a short-lived review which he founded together with the poet Ion Vinea (1895–1964). Tzara's symbolist verse was thereafter published in other leading Romanian periodicals and its unusual imagery already heralded "the great Faun of poetry" – a title which the French writer Louis Aragon was later to bestow on him. In 1916 Tzara left Romania, settling first in Zurich and, three years later, in Paris. He continued to write Romanian poetry, however, publishing his work in avant-garde reviews, mainly in *Unu*. His collected Romanian verse, edited by *Unu's* chief editor, Sasa *Pana, appeared as *Primele poeme* ("First Poems," 1934). In Romania Tzara exerted a powerful influence on the younger generation of poets.

In Zurich, Tzara was co-founder of the *Dada* movement and editor of its official organ. Until the rise of surrealism in 1924, *Dada* was a literary and artistic sensation, making a "clean slate" of traditional forms, dislocating the rules of language and logic, and transforming poetry into an ideological weapon. Some of Tzara's collections of this period are *Vingt-cinq poèmes* (1918) and *Cinéma, calendrier du coeur abstrait* (1920). In the course of time, his poetic tone became more sober and restrained, revealing genuine poetic gifts. In 1931 Tzara turned to surrealism with *L'Homme approximatif* and published an important theoretical essay, *Sur la situation de la poésie*. He became a Communist in 1935 and was active in the French underground during World War II. There is little trace of Jewish sentiment or expression in his verse, but Tzara became increasingly preoccupied with an imminent universal catastrophe. His later works include *O – boivent les loups* (1932); *L'Antitête* (1933), essays; *Le coeur à gaz* (1946); *La Fuite* (1947), a drama; *La Face intérieure* (1953); and *Parler seul* (1950). In 1970 La Monnaie de Paris stamped a medal with the effigy of Tristan Tzara "the father of dadaism" engraved by Andre-Henri Torcheux.

BIBLIOGRAPHY: E. Lovinescu, *Istoria literaturii române contemporane*, 3 (1927), 441; G. Călinescu, *Istoria literaturii române...* (1941), 803; R. Lacôte and G. Haldas (eds.), *Tristan Tzara* (1960[2]).

[Wladimir Rabi / Dora Litani-Littman]

TZELNIKER, MEIR (1896–1980), Yiddish actor. Tzelniker began his career at 12 in Bessarabia, Russia, and attended the Odessa School of Drama. He played for three years on the Russian stage and joined a Yiddish company in 1922. Immigrating to London in 1927, he played in Yiddish at the Pavilion Theater, Whitechapel, and then headed the Yiddish National Theater Company. In 1939 he took over the Yiddish Theater in the Grand Palais, Whitechapel, which played throughout World War II in modern repertoire and in Shakespeare. He made a hit in *The King of Lampedusa* based on an amusing war episode. He subsequently appeared in films and television. His daughter, ANNA TZELNIKER (1922–), who was born in Romania, was also a well-known Yiddish actress in London.

ADD. BIBLIOGRAPHY: D. Mazower, *The Yiddish Theatre in London* (1987).

Historiated initial "U" depicting Joseph being pulled from the well by his brothers, Tuscan School, 15th century. Vellum, 16 x 16.5 cm. Musée Marmottan, Paris, France. © Visual Arts Library (London)/Alamy.

Uc-Uz

UCEDA, SAMUEL BEN ISAAC (1540–?), talmudist, preacher, and kabbalist. Uceda, who was born in Safed, studied Kabbalah under Isaac *Luria. After the latter's death, he studied under Luria's disciple Ḥayyim *Vital and Elisha *Gallico. At the age of 40, he established a great yeshivah in Safed where Talmud and Kabbalah were taught. The yeshivah was supported by the *Nasi family of Constantinople. Uceda also spent some time as a merchant in Aleppo. In 1597, when the financial resources of the yeshivah were depleted, he went to Constantinople in an attempt to raise funds. There he was helped by the philanthropist and scholar Abraham Algazi.

Uceda was apparently the owner of a large library which contained many manuscripts. In his *Midrash Shemu'el* (Venice, 1579), a commentary on the tractate *Avot*, he quotes some of the early Spanish scholars and his contemporaries from books which were in his possession. He also wrote a commentary on the Five Scrolls. The commentary on Ruth was published as *Iggeret Shemu'el* (Kuru-Chesme, near Constantinople, 1597). It includes sayings of early Spanish scholars and of Uceda's contemporaries. His commentary on Lamentations was published as *Leḥem Dimah* (Venice, 1606). His books had wide circulation and his commentary on *Avot* was printed three times during his life. His sermons are to be found in manuscript (Moscow, Guenzburg Ms. 1054).

BIBLIOGRAPHY: Rosanes, Togarmah, 3 (1938), 282; G. Scholem, in; *Zion*, 5 (1940), 134, 145; D. Tamar, in; *Sefunot*, 7 (1963), 173–4; M. Benayahu, *Sefer Toledot ha-Ari* (1967), index.

UCKO, SIEGFRIED (**Sinai**; 1905–1976), rabbi and educator. Born in Gleiwitz (Gliwice), Upper Silesia, Ucko studied at the Juedisch-Theologisches Seminar, Breslau, and at the Hochschule (Lehranstalt) fuer die Wissenschaft des Judentums, Berlin. After serving as rabbi in Mannheim and Offenburg, he settled in Palestine in 1935, teaching at Kiryat Bialik and at a teachers' training college in Tel Aviv (from 1946). In 1951 he was appointed head of the teacher's seminary at Givat ha-Sheloshah and was instructor in education at the Hebrew University, Jerusalem. In 1955 Ucko became head (later professor) of the education department of Tel Aviv University, also serving as inspector of teachers' training at the Israel Ministry of Education. His published works include *Der Gottesbegriff in der Philosophie Herrmann Cohens* (1927) and *Al ha-Osher re-ha-Tov* ("On Happiness and Goodness," 1951).

UDIM (Heb. אוּדִים), moshav in central Israel, 5 mi. (8 km.) S. of Netanyah, affiliated with Ha-Mo'aẓah ha-Ḥakla'it. Founded in 1948, Udim had 369 inhabitants in 1970 and 661 in 2002. The first settlers, from Poland and Hungary, were later joined by Israelis and immigrants mainly from Yemen and Iraq. Farming was based on irrigated citrus groves, vegetable gardens, and livestock. Other source of livelihood were from various retail outlets. The "Roman Breach" in a nearby sandstone ridge was once assumed to have been opened in the Roman period to provide an outlet for the waters in the Poleg swamp, but later archaeological investigation identified the breach as belonging to the fortification installations of a settlement dating from the Israelite period. The name, "Embers [i.e., Drawn from the Fire]," refers to the founders, who were survivors of the Holocaust.

[Efram Orni / Shaked Gilboa (2nd ed.)]

UDIN, SOPHIE A. (1896–1960), founder of the Women's Organization for the Pioneer Women of Palestine (*Pioneer Women, subsequently Na'amat U.S.A.). Udin was born in Zhinkov, Ukraine, and emigrated as a child to Pittsburgh, Penn., with her socialist parents. Trained at Columbia University School of Library Science (M.L.S., 1929), she married Pinchas Ginguld, head of the network of secular Yiddish Folk Schools and Teachers Seminary and Po'alei Zion officer in New York (1922). Udin, who served on the staff of New York Public Library (1914–29), specializing in foreign collections, helped organize the American Mogen David Adom (March 13, 1918) and served as its first national secretary (1918–19). In 1921 and 1925–27, she went to Palestine to help organize and build the Jewish National and Hebrew University Library, introducing the Dewey decimal system and Anglo-American cataloguing and American-style library education for the staff. Living in Jerusalem, she became involved in clandestine Haganah work. In 1924 she raised American funds to produce the first Kiryat Sefer, the bibliography of Jewish and Hebrew publications of the National Library. According to the "legend of the well," Udin, with the assistance of six wives of Po'alei Zion members, responded to the plea of Raḥel Yanait *Ben-Zvi to raise money for a well to water trees at a tree nursery near Jerusalem. In 1925 they founded the Women's Organization for the Pioneer Women of Palestine to achieve this immediate goal as well as to support working women in Palestine and to campaign for auto-emancipation for all women. Udin established and directed the Zionist Archives and Library in New York, collecting documentation of the Zionist movement and editing *The Palestine Year Book* annual (1945–49) and three-volume *Palestine and Zionism* (1947–48); she published "A List of References Leading to the Establishment of the Jewish State of Israel" in *The Journal of Educational Sociology*. Leaving her husband to continue his work in New York, Udin made *aliyah* with her children in 1949 when David Ben-Gurion appointed her to set up and direct the Israel State Archives (now the National Archives) in the government complex in Tel Aviv. When the government moved to Jerusalem, she also moved the archives. She helped organize the Association of Americans and Canadians (AACI) in Israel in 1951 to ease the absorption of American immigrants to Israel; she died in Jerusalem.

BIBLIOGRAPHY: T. Keren. *Sophie Udin: Portrait of a Pioneer* (1984); J.F. Rosen, "Sophie A. Udin," in: P.E. Hyman and D. Dash Moore (eds.), *Jewish Women in America: An Historical Encyclopedia*, vol. 2 (1997), 1425–26.

[Judith Friedman Rosen (2nd ed.)]

UDLICE (Czech **Údlice**; Ger. **Eidlitz**), village in N.W. Bohemia, Czech Republic. It is assumed that the Jewish community of Udlice was founded by refugees who fled from the nearby community of *Chomutov (Komotau) when the *Hussites attacked it in 1421. Eleven families were recorded in 1570 and the oldest gravestone (still extant until the Holocaust) dated from 1572. The *ḥevra kaddisha* was founded in 1680. The synagogue was rebuilt in 1694 and again in 1782. Judah Loew b. Isaac Lipschitz, the author of *Hanhagot Adam* (Fuerth, 1691) was rabbi in the 17th century. In 1724 the community numbered 76 families; 15 houses owned by the local lord were given to 24 heads of families in 1727; in 1815 they were destroyed by fire. The community numbered 597 in 1809, and in 1824, 111 families (481 persons) lived in 40 houses. In 1840 the synagogue was rebuilt in Reform style. (It was demolished in the 1920s and services were held in the school.) After 1848 the community diminished rapidly, most of its members moving to Chomutov and until 1869 returning to Udlice only for services. Only 150 Jews (9.2% of the total population) were left in Udlice in 1880 and these had declined to 21 (1.02%) in 1910; by 1926 only two families remained. Under Nazi occupation, both cemeteries and the school were destroyed. The memory of the community is perpetuated in the family name "Eidlitz."

BIBLIOGRAPHY: Krakauer, in; H. Gold (ed.), *Die Juden und Judengemeinden Boehmens in Vergangenheit und Gegenwart* (1934), 130–3.

[Jan Herman]

UEBERLINGEN, town in Baden, Germany. Although the oldest gravestones discovered in Ueberlingen date from 1275–76, a Jewish community with a synagogue and cemetery was in existence in 1226. In 1240 the bishop of Constance forbade the setting up of a private mint in Ueberlingen either by a Jew or a Christian. A Jewish witness to an agreement appears in a source dated 1253. Most Jews made their living through *moneylending: in 1289 a Jewess, Guta of Ueberlingen, lent a considerable sum of money to Bishop Frederick of Montfort to permit him to participate in a Church Council in Wuerzburg. The Jew Samuel lent money in 1290 to a minister of high position and to the bishop of Constance; even King Louis IV, the Bavarian, was a debtor of Ueberlingen Jews. A tax list of 1241 indicates that the Jewish population was one of the smallest in Germany at the time, but by the beginning of the 14th century the Jewish population had grown considerably. A *Judenstrasse* is also noted during this period. A Rabbi Menlin of Ueberlingen is mentioned by Jacob b. Moses *Moellin (MaHaRil, 1365–1427). In 1332 an accusation was made that Jews had murdered a Christian child. A threatening mob surrounded the Jews who had gathered in the synagogue and set the structure afire, about 300 Jews perished as a result. The remaining Jews continued to live in the city, and two years later when King Louis IV, the Bavarian, visited the city he imposed a fine on those who had perpetrated the massacre. More Jewish lives were claimed by the *Black Death persecutions of 1349, after which the city confiscated the synagogue, cemetery, and houses of the victims. Jewish gravestones were used to build a cathedral. Jewish settlement was renewed, however, in 1378. In 1429 a *blood libel in Ravensburg brought about the arrest of all the Jews in Ueberlingen: 12 Jews were burned in 1430, and 11 saved themselves by accepting baptism. Jewish settlement came to an end in 1431 and was not renewed until 1862. The modern community remained extremely small; in 1895 there were only five Jewish families in the town and the community combined with that of Constance. All five families recorded as living in Ueberlingen in 1938 emigrated to England and the U.S.

BIBLIOGRAPHY: *Germania Judaica*, 1 (1962), 389–90; 2 (1968), 838–42; F. Hundsnurscher and G. Taddey, *Die juedischen Gemeinden in-Baden* (1968), 167–8; L. Loewenstein, *Geschichte der Juden am Bodensee und Umgebung* (1879), 1–56; B. Rosenthal, *Heimatsgeschichte der badischen Juden* (1927), index; M. Stern, in; ZGJD, 1 (1887), 216–29.

[Alexander Shapiro]

UFA, capital of Bashkortostan, Russia. Under the czars, Ufa was beyond the *Pale of Settlement. Its Jewish community was established by veteran Jewish soldiers. In 1855 a synagogue was built. In 1897 the Jews in Ufa numbered 376 (0.8% of the total population). In World War I about 1,000 Jewish refugees came to Ufa from areas near the front. The Jewish community suffered from the battles between the Red Army and the White Army in 1918. In 1923 there were 1,588 Jews (1.8% of the total population). In the entire Bashkir Republic there were 7,167 Jews in 1959. In 1971 some thousands of Jews were thought to be still living in Ufa, but there was no information available about Jewish communal or religious life in the town. When the community re-emerged in the post-Communist period, a full range of communal services developed, a chief rabbi was installed, and the Jewish population was estimated at as much as 10,000.

BIBLIOGRAPHY: E. Tcherikower (ed.), *In der Tkufe fun Revolutsie* (1924), 101–16, 126–9.

[Yehuda Slutsky]

UGANDA SCHEME. In the spring of 1903 Joseph Chamberlain, the British colonial secretary, offered Herzl the Guas Ngishu plateau near Nairobi in East Africa – not Uganda, as Chamberlain and others later erroneously called it – for a Jewish settlement under the British flag. Herzl thought it politically imprudent to reject it, since the very fact that a Great Power was negotiating with him amounted to a de facto recognition of his movement. He considered the offer primarily in political terms. Rather than being an impediment, it might bring the realization of his ultimate goal nearer. For him it was merely a ploy to obtain British recognition of the Zionist movement, recognition of Jews as a people, and to bring Britain gradually to the conclusion that only in Palestine would the Jewish Problem be solved. In these tactics he was eminently successful. At no time did Herzl abandon Palestine.

The storm that erupted during the Sixth Zionist Congress in August 1903 was unforeseen. The acrimonious controversy was largely due to a misunderstanding. It was not the choice between "Zion or Uganda" that had been put on the agenda. What had been proposed was the dispatch of a Commission of Inquiry to East Africa, and Herzl anticipated that the report would be negative, as it was crystal clear to him that the Jews would not go to Africa in any case.

Moreover, all the controversy was irrelevant, because the subject matter became unreal. In view of the protests raised by the white settlers in Kenya against the very idea of a Jewish settlement, the Foreign Office changed its mind. Herzl did not shed any tears. In a circular letter to the members of the Zionist Executive, he declared that the East Africa project was dead. In mid-April 1904, during a meeting of the Executive, the leading opponents, the Neinsagers, admitted that they were mistaken and expressed their unswerving confidence in Herzl.

For a fuller treatment see *Herzl, Theodor.

BIBLIOGRAPHY: R.G. Weisbord, *African Zion: The Attempt to Establish a Jewish Colony in the East African Protectorate, 1903–1905* (1968); *The Complete Diaries of Theodor Herzl*, ed. R. Patai, tr. M. Zohn (1960); O.K. Rabinowicz, *Herzl and England* (1951); A. Bein, *Theodor Herzl: A Biography* (1962); M. Heymann, *The Uganda Controversy*, 2 vols. (1970); I. Friedman, "Herzl and the Uganda Controversy," in: R. Robbertson and E. Timms (eds.), *Theodor Herzl and the Origins of Zionism* (Austrian Studies 8) (1997), 39–53; also in Heb. in: *Iyyunim*, 4 (Annual 1994), 175–203.

[Isaiah Friedman (2nd ed.)]

UGARIT, ancient city located about 7 mi. (11 km.) north of Latakia. Though it is not mentioned in the Bible, its discovery has had a profound effect on biblical studies, especially in the fields of religion, literature, and language.

Excavation

The ancient mound of this city, known as Ras Shamra ("Hill of Fennel"), first came to the attention of modern scholars after a Syrian farmer accidentally uncovered a stone from the roof of a well-built tomb chamber containing Cypriot and Mycenean pottery. C. Virolleaud, then director of archaeological works for the (French mandatory) government of Syria, first excavated the tomb in 1928. In the following year the Mission de Ras Shamra under the direction of Claude F.A. *Schaeffer began systematic excavations that continued into the 1970s except for several years during World War II.

Nine seasons from 1929 to 1937 were devoted to the seaport at Mînet el-Beiḍa (classical Leucos limen, "White Harbor") and to the acropolis on the western half of the tell, where two temples, one to Dagon and the other to Baal, were found; between them was the high priest's house, containing a rich collection of literary texts. The site of the town rises c. 65 ft. (20 m.) above the surrounding plain and stands about 3,980 ft. (1,200 m.) from the bay. Its total surface area is 22 hectares. From 1937 to 1939 and from 1948 to 1955 work was concentrated on the northwestern corner of the mound, where stables, various important residences, and above all the royal palace, were uncovered. The palace archives have furnished invaluable historical and social data. From 1953 to 1958 a large residential quarter came to light, and during the years 1959–66 the craftsmen's quarter on the south side of the tell was investigated. Some private archives have provided both legal and literary texts. An abundance of artifacts including statuettes, bowls, and other objects of bronze and gold have been found in various points on the mound.

Early Stratigraphy

The basic chronology for prehistoric Ras Shamra has been established by a series of deep soundings and can be briefly summarized thus: Level V, Neolithic, five meters of deposit beginning from the pre-pottery to the later ceramic Neolithic Age (seventh–fifth millennia B.C.E.); Level IV, early phase represented by wares of Hassuna and Tell Halaf (early fifth millennium B.C.E.), later phase with influence from el-Ubaid (c. 4500–4000); Level III C and B, Chalcolithic (4000–3000 B.C.E.); Level III A1 and A2, Early Bronze Age (3000–2350), probably destroyed during one of the campaigns of the rulers of the Akkad Dynasty – throughout this long period the settlement developed into a formidable city with ample storage space for surplus grains, etc.; Level III A3 reflects the nomadic invasion by foreign elements that settled on the ruins of the previous civilization – they were the "torque wearers," whose only traces at this site are their tombs (c. 2250 to 2050 B.C.E.).

History – Middle Bronze (2050–1500 B.C.E.)

After the disappearance of the "torque wearers" a new ethnic element, the Amorites, became the dominant people of the Levant. The new urban center which they built at Ras Shamra must have arisen shortly before approximately 2000 B.C.E. (Level II). The pharaohs of the 12th dynasty (1990–1780) strove to maintain strong diplomatic and commercial ties with Ugarit, as evidenced by the presence of numerous statuettes and other objects. The earliest known thus far is a bead inscribed with the cartouche of Senusret I (1971–1928); this is followed by the statuette of a queen of Senusret II (1897–1877) and two sphinxes of Amenhemet III (1842–1797). Other statues include that of an Egyptian vizier and his family and those of other priests and important women. Since Ugarit is not mentioned in the Egyptian Execration Texts, there is no reason to suppose that the city was under the direct suzerainty of Egypt.

In the later Middle Bronze Age, Ugarit is mentioned a few times in texts on the Euphrates. Hammurapi, king of Yamhad (Aleppo), wrote to Zimri-Lim (c. 1779–1761), king of *Mari, informing him that the ruler of Ugarit wanted to see the famous palace at Mari. Another letter, by an official who was evidently writing to Zimri-Lim, suggests that the latter planned a trip to Ugarit. Five other references to Ugarit appear in unpublished economic texts. The city was obviously one of the flourishing "Amorite" city-states of the Old Babylonian Age. The "Amorite" origin of the dynasty at Ugarit is also reflected in the rulers' names, which are also attested as Amorite in a later age. The "dynastic seal" used by kings of Ugarit in the Late Bronze Age was of Old Babylonian style and bears the name of Yaqarum son of Niqmaddu; one of these two, either the father or the son, was probably the founder of the dynasty. These two names also appear at the end of an unpublished list of deified rulers. A man from Ugarit is recorded on an administrative list from neighboring *Alalakh (Level VII) just slightly later than the Mari texts. During the 1969 excavations, Schaeffer began to uncover the palace from this period.

History – Late Bronze (1500–1100)

There are two allusions to Ugarit in the later Alalakh tablets (Level IV) from the 15th century B.C.E. One is an epistle or agreement having to do with thieves and the other is a fragment. A letter found at Ugarit from Niqmepa (of Alalakh?) to a certain Ibira, probably ruler of Ugarit, can be dated to about the same period; the subject was a fugitive groom. The dynastic roster alluded to above included three kings named Ibrn (for Ibiranu); one of them may have been this 15th-century Ibira(nu).

Though Thutmose III (1490–1436) does not claim the conquest of Ugarit in his northern campaigns, he did overrun the neighboring states of Alalakh, Nughasse, and Niyi. A vase found at Ugarit is inscribed with the name of Thutmose III. In addition, Amenhotep II (1436–1416) apparently made a thoroughgoing foray into Ugarit's territory on his first campaign as sole ruler. The name of Ugarit is preserved only imperfectly in his annals; the initial error must have occurred in the first "historical" digest prepared as a preliminary to making the inscriptions. It would appear that the local ruler was loyal to the pharaoh and had an Egyptian garrison in his city. Another faction was plotting against the pro-Egyptian king. Amenhotep II quelled the rebellion in the countryside and pacified the city.

The next information about Ugarit pertains to Ammistamru I, a contemporary of Amenhotep III (1405–1367). He appealed to the pharaoh for help, evidently when the Hittite Suppiluliumas (1375–1335) was making his first foray into northern Syria. He seems to have had a dispute with a certain Niqmepa of Amurru. Other Tell *el-Amarna letters lacking the name of the sender must have come from Ugarit about this time or during the reign of Ammistamru's successor, Niqmaddu II. They indicate that the ruler of Ugarit was a loyal "servant" of the pharaoh. A scarab and some vase fragments found at Ugarit bear the name of Amenhotep III. The commercial relations between Ugarit and Egypt under this pharaoh are further illustrated by an epistle, apparently from the overseer of Ugarit's main port, *Ma'h-adu* (Mînet el-Beiḍa), addressed to Nimmuria (praenomen of Amenhotep III). It is no surprise, therefore, that Ugarit is mentioned in a topographical list of Amenhotep III.

The next ruler of Ugarit, Niqmaddu II, seems to have continued his allegiance to Egypt. His portrait appears on the side of an alabaster vase; before him stands a lovely Egyptian maiden. She is evidently of noble birth and represents a marriage tie between Ugarit and Egypt. Niqmaddu sent a letter to Egypt asking for two Cushite page boys and a physician. His loyalty to the next pharaoh, Amenhotep IV (1367–1350), is proven by the name of the latter and of his wife, Nefertiti, on other alabaster vases discovered at Ugarit.

During the First Syrian War of Suppiluliumas in which he defeated the Mitannians and subdued the pro-Mitannian states of northern Syria, the Hittite ruler recognized that Ugarit was more closely allied to Egypt than to Mitanni and thus made the very clever offer to Niqmaddu of an alliance against the neighboring states of Mugish and Nughasse. These latter had also sought Niqmaddu's support against Suppiluliumas and had attacked Ugarit when he refused. Hittite troops were sent to rescue Ugarit. The ensuing conflict resulted in a conclusive Hittite victory throughout the area. Niqmaddu was rewarded with large portions of territory taken from Mugish on the north and Nughasse on the east. A report from Tyre to the pharaoh to the effect that Ugarit's palace had been burned may pertain to this affair.

Niqmaddu thus became a loyal vassal of the Hittites. Just as his father had clashed with the expansionist rulers of Amurru, so he and his own vassal, Abdi-khebat of Siyannu, ran foul of Baʿluya, brother of the infamous Aziru (probably while the latter was called to Egypt to give an accounting).

After Aziru's return, he continued the feud until he too was compelled to submit to Hittite rule. Since both states were now vassals of the same overlord, a treaty was arranged between them. Henceforth, the entire coastline from Ugarit to Byblos was subject to the Hittites.

Later, in the seventh year of Mursilis (c. 1334–1306), Niqmaddu was asked to furnish troops against his neighbors who were staging an Egyptian-inspired revolt. He evidently did so, and the revolt was suppressed; but just at this time he was followed on the throne by his son Arkhalbu, the only ruler of Ugarit to bear a Hurrian name. It would appear that pro-Egyptian elements at Ugarit had staged a coup at the instigation of Pharaoh Horemheb (c. 1335–1309; whose inscribed vases were also found in the Ugaritic palace); this would explain Ugarit's inclusion in a topographical list by that pharaoh. A second revolt by Nughasse, to which Ugarit may have been partner, was smashed by Mursilis who then removed Arkhalbu and placed his brother, Niqmepa, on the throne of Ugarit. The size of the kingdom was much reduced and even Siyannu was taken out of Ugarit's jurisdiction.

Niqmepa was the ruler of Ugarit who joined the Hittite allied forces in their confrontation with Pharaoh Ramses II (1290–1224) at the battle of Kadesh (1285). He continued to reign for a considerable time after Mutawallis' death (1282). Under Hattusilis (1275–1250), his kingdom enjoyed a renewed era of wealth and prosperity, doubtless facilitated by the peace treaty between Hatti and Egypt. Ugarit's position as a key center in the Hittite imperial economy is illustrated by the fact that the Hittite king agreed to restrain the activity of even his own merchants from Ura (in Cilicia) vis-à-vis Niqmepa. Another decree by Hattusilis prevented Ugaritic citizens from deserting their own sovereign and fleeing to the *ʿapiru* territory, i.e., they could not escape the jurisdiction of Niqmepa by joining the freebooters.

At the demise of Niqmepa, there seems to have been some dispute over the succession. Two sons of Niqmepa's widow Ahatmilku (formerly a princess from Amurru), Hishmi-sharruma and Abdi-sharruma, committed an act of treason (lit. a "sin") against the new incumbent, Ammistamru II. The queen mother was held responsible for seeing that the rebels took their shares of personal property and went into exile to Alashi (on Cyprus).

Ammistamru's domestic troubles were just beginning. He decided to divorce his own Amorite wife and apparently discovered, after she had gone back to her home country, that she had not only been a troublemaker but had also committed a "great sin" against him – probably adultery. Various attempts were made to adjudicate the affair, first before the Hittite viceroy in Carchemish and later before the emperor in Hattusas, now Tudkhaliyas. After certain acts of hostility between Ugarit and Amurru, the emperor imposed a settlement. The erring lady was returned to Ammistamru and promptly executed; in return an indemnity payment was made to her brother, the king of Amurru. Certain difficulties arise from the documents pertaining to this case; in fact, two separate women may be involved though it seems most unlikely that Ammistamru would have taken a second wife from Amurru after divorcing the first.

When the Assyrians (probably under Shalmaneser I; 1274–1245) began to put pressure on the eastern Hittite frontier, Ammistamru was not required to furnish support troops, but a payment of 50 minas of gold was imposed upon him as financial backing for the war. Neighboring Amurru did have to send troops.

The next ruler of Ugarit was Ibiranu, another son of Ammistamru (rather than the son of the deposed Amorite wife). A certain indifference toward the Hittites can be discerned in his failure to present himself at the capital and in his not sending the customary gifts upon his accession to the throne. His recalcitrant attitude may have been the result of the new Assyrian threat under Tukulti-Ninurta I (1244–1208). This time the Hittites were not content to accept money in lieu of soldiers. Ibiranu tried to stall, but they sent an officer to muster the troops of Ugarit.

Ibiranu was followed by his son Niqmaddu III, whose reign must have been short. The last known king at Ugarit bore the name Hammurapi. Under the leadership of the last Hittite monarch, Suppiluliumas II, he was more cooperative than his predecessors. The reason is clear; a new threat was looming, this time on the western horizon. The Ugaritic fleet was the backbone of Hittite resistance by sea. Tablets still baking in the kiln when the palace was finally destroyed tell the sad tale of failure and retreat in the face of an advancing foe. Some Ugaritic ships were lost near Cyprus; there was apparently an advance raid on the coast of Ugarit while the rest of the fleet was away. Land forces from Ugarit, led by the king, had joined the Hittites in an attempt to stem the tide of enemy troops advancing from the west and north.

Ugarit was sacked and burned in a mighty conflagration. Its civilization remained buried until the excavator's spade revived it in modern times. The small colony of Hellenic tradespeople that lived for a time at Ras Shamra during the Iron Age had no idea of the rich cultural treasures buried beneath their feet.

Social Structure

The Late Bronze Age archives from Ugarit provide a unique source for the study of social structure and institutions in the Levant on the eve of the Israelite conquest. Geographically and politically Ugarit was never a part of *Canaan; in fact, a Canaanite at Ugarit was listed like any other foreigner. The most prominent element in the Ugaritic population was West Semitic; but there were also many Hurrians there who seem to have been considered an integral element in the society. Unlike neighboring Alalakh, Ugarit has furnished administrative records in both the standard lingua franca, Akkadian, and the West Semitic dialect of the indigenous population, *Ugaritic. Thus many West Semitic equivalents for Akkadian social and political terms are available.

Ugarit was a monarchical despotism ruled by a dynasty that apparently had its roots in the previous "Amorite" culture of the Levant (cf. above). The kings, though themselves vassals of the Hittite emperor (and of the pharaoh before that), were recognized by international law as the absolute lords of all persons and real estate in their realm. At least for a time, the neighboring state(s) of Siyannu-Ushnatu stood in a vassal relationship to Ugarit.

By virtue of his ownership of all the lands in the kingdom, the king of Ugarit was able to provide estates for all his loyal supporters, especially the aristocracy of officials, soldiers, and other noble classes (including the priesthoods). In return, the landholders were obligated to serve the crown. A person who committed treason against the state or who fell hopelessly into debt to a foreign creditor would lose his patrimony. If an estate were left temporarily without an adult male to fulfill the incumbent duties to the crown, the king would protect the widow as well as his own interests.

The upper class included the principal palace officials such as the high commissioners (*rābiṣū*) and the overseers (*sākinu*), whose offices were either identical or parallel (the former term is Akkadian, the latter West Semitic). Scribes (*tupšarrū/‡sāpirūma*) had the great responsibilities of keeping official records and composing correspondence; many of them rose to higher government positions. There was also an elite band of "royal acquaintances," who shared special privileges in the palace.

Yeoman classes included various craftsmen, such as carpenters, shipwrights, metalsmiths, cooks, fowlers, etc. Many of these lived in a special quarter of the city (cf. above). Farmers and herdsmen were doubtlessly located in the many village precincts throughout the realm. Little is known about the administration of the local town or village. Sometimes a whole town would be given to a high-ranking officer as his patrimony. Overseers and village headmen governed most of the others. Each township was responsible for furnishing a certain number of man-days, evidently for corvée labor, each year. The peasantry was doubtless employed in the cultivation of the nobles' estates.

Ugarit's role as a major metropolitan focus of international trade is underlined by the presence of numerous foreign elements in the personnel rosters. Assyrians, Hittites, Egyptians, and Canaanites all made their way to Ugarit on diplomatic and commercial missions. The Ugaritic merchant fleet sailed the entire eastern Mediterranean from Egypt to Caphtor. The evidence from written records has been abundantly confirmed by the material finds produced in excavation. Vessels of gold and ivory reflect artistic styles of Semitic and other cultural traditions. Alabaster vessels testify to frequent and close contacts with Egypt (whenever political factors permitted).

BIBLIOGRAPHY: C.F.A. Schaeffer (ed.), *Ugaritica*, vols. 1–6 (*Mission de Ras Shamra*, vols. 3, 5, 8, 9, 16, 17 (1939–69)); J. Nougayrol, *Le palais royal d'Ugarit*, vols. 3, 4 (*Mission de Ras Shamra*, vols. 6, 9, 11 (1955–70)); Ch. Virolleaud, *Le palais royal d'Ugarit* vols. 2, 5 (*Mission de Ras Shamra*, vol. 7, 11 (1957, 1965)); K.A. Kitchen, *Suppiluliuma and the Amarna Pharaohs* (1962); M. Liverani, *Storia di Ugarit nell' età degli archivi politici* [= *Studi Semitici*, 6] (1962); J.M. Sasson, in: JAOS, 86 (1966), 126–38; M.C. Astour, in: *American Journal of Archaeology*, 69 (1965), 253–58; idem, in: *Orientalia*, 38 (1969), 381–414; idem, in: *Journal of the Economic and Social History of the Orient*, 13 (1970), 113–27; M.S. Drower, in: CAH², 2 (1968), ch. 21. **ADD. BIBLIOGRAPHY:** M.S. Smith, *Untold Stories: The Bible and Ugaritic Studies in the Twentieth Century* (2001); D. Psrdee, "Ugaritic Studies at the End of the 20th Century," in BASOR, 320 (2000), 49–86; W.G.E. Watson and N. Wyatt (eds.), *Handbook of Ugaritic Studies* [Handbuch der Orientalistik, Abteilung 1: Der Nahe und Mittlere Osten, Band 39] (1999).

[Anson Rainey]

UGARITIC, a Northwest Semitic language spoken and written in northern Syria during the second millennium B.C.E. Documents written in this tongue have been discovered at Ras Shamra, site of the ancient *Ugarit, and at nearby Ras ibn Hani.

The texts were written on clay tablets in a unique cuneiform alphabetic script. This represented a revolutionary adaptation of the Mesopotamian writing method, which was in its original form syllabic and logographic and required hundreds of symbols; thus there were separate symbols for *ba* and *ab*, *ik* and *ki*, etc. The Ugaritic repertoire consisted, in contrast, of 27 basic consonants. An additional sign for *samekh* and two supplementary *alefs* served to distinguish the three fundamental Semitic vowels in combination with that consonant, i.e., *a*ʾ, *i*ʾ, *u*ʾ. Rare instances have been noted in which these consonant-plus-vowel signs were utilized as pure vowel indicators and in two texts the *yod* seems to stand for a final vowel; otherwise the Ugaritic method of writing was entirely consonantal. Five small inscriptions show certain unusual features such as minor divergences in the shapes of letters and especially a preference for only 22 consonants as in the traditional Canaanite *alphabet. Three of these texts with the shorter alphabet were found not at Ugarit but in Ereẓ Israel.

The corpus of Ugaritic inscriptions so far published represents a wide range of literary and nonliterary types. The former have attracted the widest attention because of their parallels to biblical poetry and epic prose. Of special interest are the tablets pertaining to the adventures of Baal and his consort Anath which outnumber the other literary works discovered. In many instances, the language and poetic style are – as shown especially by U. Cassuto and H.L. Ginsberg – very close to passages in the Hebrew poetry, e.g., the god of death, Mot, warns Baal not to boast "because you have smitten Lotan [Leviathan] the evil serpent, you have destroyed the crooked serpent, the mighty one of seven heads." The analogy with Isaiah 27:1 is indeed striking.

Other mythical works include an ode on the marriage of the Moon god (masculine) with the goddess Nikkal (a deity of Mesopotamian origin), and a drama about the birth of the good and lovely gods which even contains stage directions for the cast and parenthetical remarks by the narrator. Two legendary stories are worthy of special notice, viz. that of a certain renowned king named Keret (Kirta) and a judge known as Danʾil. The latter is probably to be equated with the Daniel of Ezekiel 14:14, 20; 28:3; he was famous for his fairness as a judge, revealed especially in his care for the widow and the orphan. A major theme of both the Keret and the Danʾil epics is the desire for an heir to maintain the family line.

As the archaeological researches at Ras Shamra continue, the variety of religious and literary texts increases. Ritual inscriptions include dedicatory formulae on stelae and votive objects, lists of sacrifices to the various deities of the Ugaritic pantheon, and descriptions of ceremonial acts of worship. Extispicy, the "science" of omens, is also represented. One unpublished tablet deals with ominous predictions founded on unusual births; another is a clay model of a sheep's liver with textual allusions to certain marks and other features which the examining priest had to learn to recognize and interpret. All of these have their counterparts or prototypes in Mesopotamian and Hittite sources; it is quite clear now that all these facets of cuneiform science and culture had made their mark on the life of Ugarit. For the first time scholars can compare the linguistic expressions in these ancient literary genres in both the East Semitic Akkadian and the West Semitic Ugaritic (with many Hittite and Hurrian parallels as well).

The classification of Ugaritic within the Northwest Semitic family is a disputed issue. Many scholars hold that it is Canaanite or north Canaanite. It certainly is not identical with the dialect(s) spoken further south in the original land of Canaan as reflected in Egyptian transcriptions and glosses in the *El-Amarna letters.

The Ugaritic language bears many resemblances to other members of the Northwest Semitic family, and to Hebrew and *Phoenician in particular. There are, however, also a number of significant differences: Ugaritic used a *shin*-causative stem instead of *h(ifil)*, *a(fel)* or *y(ifil)*; its long [*a*] vowels had not shifted to long [*o*]; the old Semitic case system was still in full force and short final vowels had generally not been elided from various verb forms. Barth's law of thematic and preformative vowels in imperfect verb tenses is shared by both Ugaritic and Hebrew but, unlike the latter, these forms still distinguished four modes, indicative, volitive, jussive, and energic, in correspondence with classical Arabic (except that the jussive had already begun to assume the function of a past or completed-action tense).

To date the Ugaritic lexicon consists of over 2,000 words. Many personal names are similar in form and construction to those in the Bible. The Ugaritic script was even utilized to write texts in the Hurrian language and Hurrian names appear alongside those of local Semites. Although the royal scribes of Ugarit carried on their international correspondence and drew up most of their local documents in Akkadian, they also used Ugaritic for various administrative purposes.

The decipherment of Ugaritic was achieved almost simultaneously by H. Bauer, E. Dhorme, and C. Virolleaud, each working independently. Various scholars have contributed to the analysis and elucidation of the inflection, syntax and lexicography of the language. A major pioneer was H.L. *Ginsberg, whose fundamental researches put the grammar on a solid, scientific basis. C.H. *Gordon made a systematic presentation of the various aspects of the grammar, to which a comprehensive glossary was added, along with transcriptions of all texts published to date. Interest in the linguistic, literary, religious, and cultural information in this newly discovered body of inscribed material has been international. Relationships with the Bible and biblical Hebrew have received most of the attention. As more examples of major compositions from the Mesopotamian sphere have come to light at Ugarit, the influence of Babylonian literature on that of Ugarit has attracted further research. Attention has also been paid to Ugarit against the larger world of ancient Syria including Emar and *Mari. Since the 1970s Ugaritology has emerged as a discipline in its own right rather than a handmaiden of biblical studies. *Ugarit Forschungen* ("Ugaritic Researches"), 1969 ff., which has been publishing articles in several languages, is in the main devoted to Ugaritic studies. A scholarly series is published by Ugarit Verlag in Muenster, Germany.

BIBLIOGRAPHY: A. Herdner, *Corpus des tablettes en cunéiformes alphabétiques*, 1 (1963), includes a comprehensive bibliography, 293–339; C. Virolleaud, *Le palais royal d'Ugarit*, 2 (1957) and 5 (1965); C.H. Gordon, *Ugaritic Textbook* (1965), with glossary; H. L Ginsberg, *The Legend of King Keret* (1946); idem, in: Pritchard, Texts, 1929–55 (Eng. tr. of texts); C.H. Gordon, *Ugarit and Minoan Crete* (1966), ch. 4 (Eng. tr. of texts); F. Gröndahl, *Die Personennamen der Texte aus Ugarit* (1967); C. Virolleaud, in: *Ugaritica*, 5 (1968), 545–606. TEXTS IN THE "SHORTER" ALPHABETIC CUNEIFORM SCRIPT – FROM UGARIT: C.H. Gordon, *Ugaritic Textbook* (1965), 176 (no. 57), 180f. (no. 74), 185 (no. 94); A. Herdner, *Corpus des tablettes en cunéiformes alphabétiques*, 1 (1963), 285 (no. 207), 274 (no. 187), 284f. (no. 206); (parallel texts to the preceding source, see above); Virolleaud, in: *Comptes rendus de l'Académie des Inscriptions et Belles-Lettres* (1960), 85–90. FROM EREẒ ISRAEL: Yeivin, in: *Kedem*, 2 (1945), 32–41; Albright, in: BASOR, no. 173 (1964), 51–53; Hillers, *ibid.*, 45–50; S.E. Loewenstamm, in: *World History of Jewish People*, ed. by Mazar, 2 (1970), 9–23. **ADD. BIBLIOGRAPHY:** GENERAL: M. Yon, in: ABD, 6:695–706; D. Pardee and M. Bordreuil, in: *ibid.*, 706–21; W. Watson and N. Wyatt, *Handbook of Ugaritic Studies* (HdO; 1999; extensive bibl.). GRAMMARS: S. Segert, *A Basic Grammar of the Ugaritic Language* (1984); J. Tropper, *Ugaritische Grammatik* (2000); D. Sivan, *A Grammar of the Ugaritic Language* (HdO; 2001); P. Bourdreuil and D. Pardee, *Manuel d'Ougaritique*, 2 vols. (2004). TEXT COLLECTIONS: M. Dietrich, O. Loretz, and J. Sanmartin, *The Cuneiform Alphabetic Texts from Ugarit, Ras ibn Hani and Other Places* (1995). TRANSLATIONS: G. del Olmo Lete, *Mitos y leyendas de Canaan segun la tradicion de Ugarit* (1981); B. Margalit, *The Ugaritic Poem of* AQHT (1989); M. Smith, *The Ugaritic Baal Cycle* (1994); D. Pardee, in: COS, I, 241–45; 287–98; 302–9; idem, *Les texts rituels*, 2 vols. (2000); DICTIONARY: G. del Olmo Lete and J. Sanmartin, *A Dictionary of the Ugaritic Language* (HdO; 2004).

[Anson Rainey / S. David Sperling (2nd ed.)]

UGODA (Pol. "Compromise"), a type of arrangement between the Polish administration and the Jewish Parliamentary Club of the *Sejm known as the Koło Zydowskie. According to this agreement, certain indispensable requirements were granted to the Jews in return for a declaration of loyalty to several demands by the Polish government. The compromise came as the conclusion to prolonged talks involving a limited circle of notables including Foreign Minister Skrzynski and Minister of Religion and Education Stanislaw *Grabski on the Polish side, and the leaders of the Koło, Leon *Reich and Osias *Thon. The negotiations resulted in an official meeting on July 4, 1925, in the chambers of Premier Wladyslaw *Grabski. Among the matters discussed, which were later announced publicly, were economic questions, political rights of citizens, organization of Jewish communities, and problems of culture, religion, and education.

The agreement aroused hopes that many painful matters would be rectified, such as compulsory stoppage of work on Sundays, the *numerus clausus at the universities, and discriminatory practices in taxation and credit, and that aid would be rendered to foster a national Jewish culture and autonomous institutions. Nonetheless, of the 42 original paragraphs, only 12 were officially publicized in July 1925 with the stamp of approval of the Polish government; they were limited to reforms concerning the organization of Jewish communities, educational aid to schools, the right to use a Jewish national language, and religious considerations for soldiers and students in government schools. The more serious problems that the Ugoda was expected to alleviate were solved on paper only, a fact which led Yiẓhak *Gruenbaum, as spokesman of the Jewish populace, to criticize the leadership of the Koło. On the other hand, the antisemitic camp criticized the government for its leniency in granting concessions to the Jews. While the Ugoda negotiations were in progress, Poland had been undergoing a financial crisis due to a tariff war with Germany. The situation caused political repercussions which resulted in the ousting of the Grabski administration in November 1925. The Ugoda was thenceforth regarded with disappointment by the Jews.

BIBLIOGRAPHY: H.M. Rabinowicz, *The Legacy of Polish Jewry* (1965), 49–50; I. Schwarzbart, *Tsvishn Beyde Milkhomes* (1958), 201–6.

[Moshe Landau]

UHDE, MILAN (1936–), Czech playwright, publicist, essayist, and prose writer. Born in Brno, Moravia, into a Czech-Jewish assimilated family, Uhde completed his studies of Czech and Russian at the Faculty of Philosophy in Brno in 1958. He worked at the literary monthly *Host do domu* ("Guest in the House"). After the Soviet occupation of Czechoslovakia, the journal was banned in 1970. Uhde lost his job and was forced to publish either in *samizdat* or under assumed names. In 1977 he signed Charter 77. In 1989–90 he became editor-in-chief of the Atlantis Publishing House. Entering political life, he served as minister of culture (1990) and chairman of the House of Deputies of the Czech Parliament (1992–96). Uhde started his literary career with three collections of stories and a satirical anti-regime play *Král-Vávra* ("King Vávra," 1964), followed by a work in verse, *Děvka z města Théby* ("The Bitch of Thebes," 1967). In the 1970s he adapted three novels – by V. Páral, I. *Olbracht, and V. Mrštík – for the stage (under a pen name). The play *Zvěstování aneb Bedřichu, jsi anděl* ("The Annunciation, or Bedřich, You Are an Angel," 1990), written in 1986, is a parody of Karl Marx's biography. Jewish themes are reflected in some characters, names, and stories in Uhde's radio and TV plays, such as *Velice tiché ave* (1981, 1987; German, "A Very Quiet Ave") in which a Jewish woman who wants to save herself from being sent to a concentration camp uses fake evidence to show that she had non-Jewish parents; *Pán plamínků* ("The Master of Small Flames," 1977, 1990); *Hodina obrany* ("An Hour of Defense," 1978, 1991); and *Zázrak v černém domě* ("Miracle in the Black House," 2004). After 1989 Uhde wrote essays against racism in *Česká republiko, dobrý den* ("Czech Republic, Good Day!" 1995); on tolerance and freedom in a collection of articles entitled *Čeští spisovatelé o toleranci* ("Czech Writers on Tolerance," 1994); and on Czech-German relations. In 2000 he was awarded the State Medal of Merit in the Cultural Sphere by President V. Havel. Uhde lived in Brno.

BIBLIOGRAPHY: J. Čulík, *Knihy za ohradou. Česká literatura v exilových nakladatelstvích* 1971–1989 (s.d.); J. Lehár et al., *Česká literatura od počátků k dnešku* (1998); V. Menclová a kol., *Slovník českých spisovatelů* (2000); A. Mikulášek et al., *Literatura s hvězdou Davidovou*, vol. 1 (1998), vol. 2 (2002); *Slovník českých spisovatelů* (1982).

[Milos Pojar (2nd ed.)]

UHERSKE HRADISTE (Czech **Uherské Hradiště**; Ger. **Ungarisch-Hradisch**), town in S.E. Moravia, Czech Republic; in the Middle Ages one of the six royal cities in Moravia. The first documentary evidence about Jews residing in the town dates from 1342. In 1453, when Jews were expelled from all the other Moravian royal cities, Uherske Hradiste refused to follow suit; but in 1514, under King Ladislaus II, they were expelled from there too. They settled in small rural communities and smaller towns and were not permitted to return to Uherske Hradiste until 1848. In 1857 there were 67 Jews in the town, rising to 342 in 1869 and 488 in 1880. A new synagogue was constructed in 1875; it was redesigned in the Art Noveau style in 1904. In the early 21st century it was used as the municipal library. A prosperous community developed, the majority of Jews joining Zionist organizations. By 1930 the number of Jews had fallen to 353. The few who returned after World War II were incorporated into the community of *Uhersky Brod and later into that of *Brno.

On the site of the former cemetery, devastated by the Nazis, a memorial to the Holocaust victims was erected.

BIBLIOGRAPHY: H. Gold (ed.), *Juden und Judengemeinden Maehrens* (1929), 561–2. **ADD. BIBLIOGRAPHY:** J. Fiedler, *Jewish Sights of Bohemia and Moravia,* (1991).

[Chaim Yahil / Yeshayahu Jelinek (2nd ed.)]

UHERSKY BROD (Czech **Uherský Brod**; Ger. **Ungarisch Brod**; in rabbinical literature, **Broda**), town in S.E. Moravia, Czech Republic. It was an important Jewish community, probably from the 13th century, first mentioned in a municipal document in 1470. Four Jewish families lived there in 1558; 18 in 1615; 59 in 1753; 160 in 1745; and 110 families by the late 18th century. In 1843 there were 827 Jews; 1,068 in 1857; and 825 in 1900.

Uhersky Brod Jews suffered severely during the Thirty Years' War (1618–48). After the expulsion of the Jews from Vienna in 1670, many settled in Uhersky Brod. In 1683 a plague killed 438 Jews, and another 100 were massacred by Kuruc soldiers defending Vienna. The massacre forced many inhabitants to take refuge in upper Hungary. There they established new Jewish communities, such as Nove Mesto, *Vahom *Trencin, Cachtiace, Beckov, and Vrbove, which after the rehabilitation of Uhersky Brod remained under its religious jurisdiction for more than 50 years. Among those killed by the Kuruc was Nathan Nata *Hannover, author of *Yeven MeẒulah* and *Sha'arei Ẓiyyon*, who had escaped the *Chmielnicki massacres and settled in Uhersky Brod. An elegy in memory of the Kuruc catastrophe (composed in Judeo-German) was customarily recited in the Uhersky Brod community on the 20th of Tammuz. The community was reconstituted a short time after the disaster and developed rapidly. Since the first half of the 17th century, some 20 noted rabbis served there, including *David ben Samuel ha-Levi (the "Taz") and, in the 19th century, Moses Nascher (1844–54), Moses David Hoffmann (1864–89), and Moritz Jung (1890–1912), who established the first high school that combined Jewish studies with general education. The rabbis, who came from such cities as Vienna, Frankfurt a. M., and Cracow, wrote significant theological and historical works.

The community was one of the largest in Moravia. In the 18th and 19th centuries, many left the overcrowded ghetto and moved to Slovakia.

During the 1848 Revolution, Jewish members of the National Guard prevented the outbreak of anti-Jewish riots in Uhersky Brod; they were subsequently forced out of the militia. Uhersky Brod was one of the most Orthodox communities in Moravia. In 1872 the ultra-Orthodox group in the community seceded, in protest against the moving of the *bimah* and the introduction of a choir; bitter strife divided the community for more than a generation. Both factions adhered to the Orthodox tradition.

In the nearby village of Drskovice, the well-known Jelinek family originated and from there spread throughout the Jewish world. The rabbi of Vienna, Abraham Adolf *Jellinek, was a member of this family.

[Isaac Ze'ev Kahane / Yeshayahu Jelinek (2nd ed.)]

Holocaust Period

In March 1939 the community of Uhersky Brod numbered 489. Religious services were held in two synagogues. In 1941 the head of the community, Felix Brunn, and seven members of the communal council were arrested by the Gestapo and executed for alleged "underground anti-German activity." At the end of that year, local Fascists set fire to the great synagogue. In early 1942, 350 Jews from Uherske Hradiste were taken to Uhersky Brod, to be quartered with and supported by the local Jewish families. Subsequently Uhersky Brod became a center of concentration for Jews from the whole of southeast Moravia before deportation. In January 1943, three transports totaling 2,837 Jews were sent first to the Theresienstadt ghetto, and later to the Auschwitz death camp; only 81 survived.

In 1945, 30 Jews returned; the community was supported by the American Jewish Joint Distribution Committee. It became a center of religious and social life for the smaller neighboring communities. In 1948 the Uhersky Brod community donated 500,000 crowns to purchase arms for Israel and financed the training of two of its members for the Israeli Air Force. After the rise of Communism in 1948, antisemitic riots occurred and many Jews were deprived of their livelihood. In 1948, 20 Jews immigrated to Israel, and the independent community ceased to exist; the few remaining Jews were served by the Kyjov community. In 1948 a monument was erected in the local cemetery, bearing the names of the Holocaust victims.

[Erich Kulka / Yeshayahu Jelinek (2nd ed.)]

BIBLIOGRAPHY: D. Kaufmann, *Die Verheerung um Ungarisch Brod durch den Kuruzzen Ueberfall* (1894); A. Frankl-Gruen, *Jahresbericht der Privat Gymnasial-Lehranstalt zu Ungarisch Brod* (1905); idem, *Geschichte der Juden in Ungarisch Brod* (1905); M. Jung, in: *Jahresberichte der Ungarisch Broder Schule*; H. Gold (ed.), *Juden und Judengemeinden Maehrens* (1929), index; *Památnik vydaný při 250 letém výročí vypleněni Židovské obce Uherského Brodu…* (1936); B. Bretholz, in: JGGJČ, 4 (1932), 107–81. HOLOCAUST PERIOD: Z. Lederer, *Ghetto Theresienstadt* (Eng., 1953), 254; R. Iltis (ed.), *Die aussaeen unter Traenen…* (1959), 58; E. Kulka and O. Kraus, *Továrna na smrt* (1946), 298; *Terezin* (Eng., 1965), 55–56. **ADD. BIBLIOGRAPHY:** J. Fiedler, *Jewish Sights of Bohemia and Moravia* (1991); *Archive der Familie aron Dauf Jellinek und deren Verzeigung* (1929).

UHLMAN, FRED (**Manfred**; 1901–1985), English painter and writer. Born in Stuttgart, Germany, and trained as a lawyer, Uhlman began to paint when he fled to Paris after the Nazis came to power. In Germany, he was at risk both as a Jew and as a prominent lawyer for the outlawed Social Democratic Party. His first works, studies of French life, resembled the productions of "Sunday" painters. His first exhibitions were held in Paris by the mid-1930s. In 1936 Uhlman moved to England and married Diana Page Croft, the daughter of an extreme right-wing Member of Parliament, Sir Henry Page Croft. Uhlman was briefly interned as an "enemy alien" in 1940. When Uhlman moved to England, his work developed more sophistication. He became an interpreter of the English provincial scene in a linear style, as in his paintings of cathedral cities. After the war he held many exhibitions. He was the author of an interesting autobiography, *The Making of an Englishman* (1960), and also became a novelist of some note, whose *Reunion* (1971) was translated into many languages.

ADD. BIBLIOGRAPHY: ODNB online.

UJ KELET (Hung. "New East"), Zionist newspaper in the Hungarian language which first appeared in Kolozsvár (Cluj), Transylvania, and was later revived in Tel Aviv. On the initiative of Chajjim Weiszburg, a leader of the Zionist Movement, *Uj Kelet* was launched as a weekly on Dec. 19, 1918. It became a daily in 1920. The first editor was Béla Székely, who was succeeded in 1919 by E. *Marton. From 1927 until the end of its Transylvanian period, the responsible editor was Ferenc Jámbor. After the Hungarian annexation of Cluj in 1940, the Fascist regime banned the paper because of its strong Zionist line. Marton emigrated to Ereẓ Israel after World War II, and in 1948 the paper reappeared under his editorship in Tel Aviv. David Dezső Schőn, who had been a contributor, participated in its reestablishment and was appointed responsible editor. In Transylvania the paper had always reacted strongly to events affecting world Jewry and fought for the rights of the Jewish communities. Reestablished in Tel Aviv, *Uj Kelet* encouraged the integration of Hungarian immigrants into Israel's cultural life. Its contributors were mostly survivors of the Holocaust who had been contributors in Transylvania. E. Marton, who died in 1960, was succeeded by his widow, Gisela Marton, while the running of the paper was entrusted to his son Michael Marton.

BIBLIOGRAPHY: L. Marton, in: *Uj Kelet* (Jan. 15, 1954); A. Barzilai, in: *Sefer ha-Shanah shel ha-Ittonai'im*, 28 (1968), 322–4.

[Yehouda Marton]

UJVÁRI, PÉTER (1869–1931), Hungarian author and journalist. Ujvári, the son of Wolf Groszmann, rabbi of Érsekújvár (Nové-Zámky), Slovakia, was born in Tolcsva. He was educated at various yeshivot until the age of 20, when he became a journalist in Szeged. By the time he moved to Budapest, in 1907, he was already well known. In Budapest he joined the editorial boards of a number of liberal newspapers, as well as the Jewish newspaper *Egyenlőség*. It was in this paper that his first and most important novel, *Az új keresztény* ("The New Christian," 1907), was serialized. This is the tragicomic story of the conversion to Christianity of the head of a small Jewish community, so that his son may be elected to parliament. The book gives a realistic picture of Jewish life in the late 19th century, of the people who strove to preserve it, and of those who helped to destroy it. He never gained a wide readership and lived most of his life at starvation level. After World War I, he wandered from one Central European country to another and, when he returned to Budapest, every one of his attempts to establish a Jewish newspaper met with disaster. His only successful enterprise was the Hungarian-Jewish encyclopedia, *Magyar Zsidó Lexikon* (1929), a carefully written and responsible work which, after the extermination of Hungarian Jewry, became an important source of information.

Ujvári's other works include *Legendák és krónikák* ("Legends and Stories," 1905), *A túlsó parton* ("Across the River," 1920), and *A mécs mellett* ("By Candlelight," 1908), memories of his yeshivah days. Ujvári's play, *Leviathán* (1929), on life during the Ukrainian pogroms, was banned in Hungary.

BIBLIOGRAPHY: *Magyar Zsidó Lexikon* (1929), 922–3; *Magyar Irodalmi Lexikon*, (1965), 444–5.

[Baruch Yaron]

UKBA (**Ukva**), **MAR,** Babylonian *amora* of the early third century C.E. Ukba's name is usually prefixed by the title *mar*, which was customarily adopted by members of the exilarch's family. According to the letter of Sherira Gaon (ed. Lewin, 77), Ukba succeeded Huna as exilarch; Bacher (JE, 5 (1903), 289) dates his accession to a period shortly before the rise of the Sassanids. His principal teacher was *Samuel (Er. 81a; Shab. 108b), who praised his qualities as a judge. A dispute between Samuel and Karna was referred to Ukba's court at Kafri (Kid. 44b). To his court were applied the words of Jeremiah (21:12): "O house of David [the exilarch was traditionally descended from David] execute judgment in the morning, and deliver him that is spoiled out of the hand of the oppressor" (Shab. 55a). Moreover, although Samuel's knowledge exceeded that of Ukba, the latter passed judgment in his teacher's presence (MK 16b). He nevertheless continued to show his respect for Samuel by accompanying him home every day. When he once neglected to do so, he acknowledged his fault (*ibid.*). Ukba and his court had close ties with Palestinian scholars, who consulted him and by whom he was highly respected (Sanh. 31b). He corresponded with the *nesi'im* on matters relating to the calendar, such as the incidence of leap years (TJ, Meg. 1:7, 71a), and the timing of festivals (RH 19b). Among his Babylonian colleagues was Matna (MK 26b). His closest pupil was *Ḥisda, who also lived in Kafri, and who transmitted many of his sayings (Ber. 10b, etc.)

Ukba was renowned for his charity, of which the Talmud gives three particular examples (Ket. 67b). On one occasion, he and his wife, in order to avoid being seen and thanked by a poor man to whom they were accustomed to give four zuz every day, took refuge in a furnace from which the fire had barely been swept. On another, his son reported that a man to whom Ukba had sent him to give 400 zuz on the eve of the Day of Atonement was not, in fact, a pauper. Ukba nevertheless immediately doubled the amount. Finally, even when he discovered, on his deathbed, that he had already donated 7,000 golden denarii to charity, he gave half of his remaining wealth to charity (Ket. 67b). Ukba had two sons: Meri (Ḥul. 43b) and Nathan (Ber. 13b).

BIBLIOGRAPHY: Hyman, Toledot, 975–8; Margalioth, Ḥakhmei, 649–51.

UKBA (Ukva), MAR, *exilarch in the late ninth-early tenth centuries. Ukba was appointed exilarch in succession to his uncle Zakkai b. Aḥunai (d. c. 890), as Zakkai's son *David, who later became known for his dispute with R. *Saadiah Gaon, was then very young. A violent controversy broke out between Ukba and the *rosh yeshivah* of *Pumbedita, R. Judah b. Samuel, who acted as *Gaon* from 905 to 917, over the question of the income of the academy from the region of *Khorasan. As a result of the interventions of the wealthy communal leaders *Netira and his father-in-law *Joseph b. Phinehas, Mar Ukba was banished from 909 to 916. According to *Nathan ha-Bavli, he was banished to *Kermanshah, in the east of the Abbasid Empire. After a time Ukba returned to *Baghdad, but the interventions of Netira and his father-in-law caused him to be banished for a second time. According to *Abraham b. Nathan ha-Yarḥi (*Sefer ha-Manhig*, ch. 58), it is known that he settled in *Kairouan, where he received all the honors due an exilarch. The position of exilarch was left vacant until the appointment of David b. Zakkai.

BIBLIOGRAPHY: Neubauer, Chronicles, 2 (1895), 78–79; Mann, Texts, 1 (1931), 209, 229; idem, in: *Tarbiz*, 5 (1934), 148–54; Goode, in: JQR, 31 (1940/41), 159. **ADD. BIBLIOGRAPHY:** H.Z.(J.W.) Hirschberg, *A History of the Jews in North Africa*, 1:207–8; M. Gil, *Be-Malkhut Ishmael*, 1:208–16; M. Ben-Sasson, in: *Tarbut ve-Ḥevrah be-Toledot Yisrael bi-Ymei ha-Beinayim* (1989), 143–44, 150, 155, 181–88.

[Abraham David]

ʿUKBARĀ (Okbarā), Babylonian town. The three towns of ʿUkbarā, Avana (Awana), and Busra, which were all situated near each other on the left bank of the Tigris, were regarded as the northern extremity of Babylonia during the talmudic period. The largest of these was ʿUkbarā; the geographer al-Muqaddasī said at the close of the tenth century that it was a big town with a large population. It fell into decline and was destroyed as a result of a change in the course of the Tigris, whose chief river bed moved eastward during the 12th century; this explains the fact that the town's ruins are now located to the west of the river. During the town's period of prosperity there was also a large Jewish settlement (see allusions to it in A.E. Harkavy, *Zikkaron la-Rishonim ve-gam la-Aḥaronim*, 4 (1887), no. 285). During the ninth century *Meshvi of ʿUkbarā achieved fame; he founded a sect which deviated from both traditional Judaism and *Karaism. According to the testimony of *Benjamin of Tudela, the 12th-century traveler, there were about 10,000 Jews in ʿUkbarā during the second half of the 12th century. After the decline and destruction of the town, the Jewish settlement also disappeared. However, when the Jewish researcher Jacob *Obermeyer visited the site in 1877, he found many potsherds bearing Hebrew inscriptions in square script.

BIBLIOGRAPHY: J. Obermeyer, *Die Landschaft Babylonien* (1929), 81ff.; A. Ben-Jacob, *Yehudei Bavel* (1965), 53.

[Eliyahu Ashtor]

UKHMANI, AZRIEL (1907–1978), Israel writer and literary critic. Born in Sanok, Poland, Ukhmani studied in Sanok at the *yeshivah* of Rabbi Meir Shapiro and was ordained by the Taḥkemoni Rabbinical Seminary in Warsaw, later graduating in agronomy from the University of Toulouse, France. In 1932 he joined kibbutz Ein Shemer and was secretary of the labor council of Karkur. He served as editor of the literary supplement of Ha-Shomer ha-Ẓa'ir.

Ukhmani was one of the founders and editor of the daily newspaper *Al ha-Mishmar.* Together with Lea *Goldberg, R. Eliaz and Ezra *Sussman, he was a member of the editorial board of the literary weekly *Ittim*, which was edited by *Shlonsky. He was a founder of the progressive culture (*Tarbut Mitkademet*) and Ẓavta movements. He was editor of the *belles lettres* section (now the poetry section) of the Sifriat ha-Poalim publishing company and a member, for 20 years, of the Central Committee of the Hebrew Writers' Association in Israel, and for a number of years edited its publication *Moznayim*. He was a member of the PEN committee in Israel and was co-editor with Israel *Cohen of the annual for literature, criticism, and thought – *Me'assef.* Ukhmani published works on literary criticism: *Le-Ever ha-Adam* (1935); *Tekhanim ve-Ẓurot* (1957, enlarged and expanded edition, 2 vols. 1977); and *Kolot Adam* (1967). His poetical works, written under the pseudonym of Ron Adi, are *Aval Laylah Laylah Ani* (1968), *Mi-Sha'ah le-Sha'ah, mi-Nes le-Nes* (1970), *Emor Pelaim* (1973) and *Atar Kadum* (1976, awarded the Talpir Prize). Yehudit Kafri edited a volume in his memory, entitled *Bi-Ẓeva'im mi-Makor Rishon* (1983).

BIBLIOGRAPHY: Y. Rabi, *"Mah Yitaron la-Sofer be-Khol Amalo?"* in: *Moznayim*, 50:2 (1980), 135–37; R. Kritz, '"*Azriel*

Ukhmani ve-Ran Adi: Bibliografiyyah," in: *Erev Rav* (1990), 334–39; A. Holtzman, "*Le-Ever ha-Adam o me-Ever la-Sifrut*," in: *Alei Siaḥ*, 36 (1995), 127–40.

[Getzel Kressel]

UKMERGE (Pol. **Wilkomierz**; Rus. **Vilkomir**), city in Lithuania. The Jewish community of Ukmerge is first mentioned in a document of 1685. In the census of 1766, 716 Jews were counted there, and by 1847 their number had risen to 3,758, the majority of whom were engaged in commerce and crafts, including tanning. The community of Ukmerge was renowned for its conservatism. M.L. *Lilienblum lived there during the 1860s and it was there that he began his public career and literary activity. The community continued to develop and by the 1880s the number of Jews reached 10,000. A period of decline followed, however, when the town was bypassed by the railroads which were built at that time. In 1897 there were 7,287 Jews (54% of the total population) and 6,390 (49%) in 1910. At the beginning of May 1915 the Jews were expelled from Ukmerge, together with those of the province of Kovno. Some returned after the war and in 1923 there were 3,885 Jews (37% of the population). During the period of independent Lithuania (1918–40), Jewish life in Ukmerge prospered. A *yeshivah ketannah* (preparatory yeshivah) which prepared pupils for the larger Lithuanian yeshivot was established and there were also two secondary schools, Hebrew and Yiddish. The last rabbi of Ukmerge, R. Joseph Zussmanowitz (of Palestinian birth), ranked among the most prominent Lithuanian rabbis. With the annexation of Lithuania to the Soviet Union in June 1940, religious and nationalist Jewish life was systematically destroyed. A year later, Ukmerge fell into the hands of the Germans. On Sept. 18, 1941, the Jews remaining in Ukmerge, together with those of the neighboring towns, were assembled in the nearby forest and massacred.

BIBLIOGRAPHY: *Słownik geograficzny królestwa polskiege*, 13 (1893), 535–41; *Yahadut Lita*, 3 (1967), 303–6.

[Yehuda Slutsky]

UKRAINE (Rus. **Ukraina**), East European republic, formerly the Ukrainian S.S.R. At the close of the 16th century there were about 45,000 Jews (out of the 100,000 Jews who were then presumably in the whole of Poland) living in the eastern regions of Poland which were inhabited by Ukrainians. Before the *Chmielnicki massacres of 1648–49 their numbers had increased to at least 150,000; in the census of 1764, 258,000 Jews were enumerated, though in fact their number was over 300,000. In 1847, according to official sources, there were almost 600,000 Jews in the Ukrainian regions belonging to Russia (the provinces of southwestern Russia – *Volhynia, *Podolia, and *Kiev; of "Little Russia" – *Chernigov and *Poltava; and of "New Russia" – Yekaterinoslav (*Dnepropetrovsk), *Kherson, and Taurida), though they actually numbered up to 900,000. According to the population census of 1897 (the first general census in Russia), there were 1,927,268 Jews in these regions, 9.2% of the total population of the Ukraine. The census of 1926 enumerated 1,574,391 Jews in the Ukraine, subsequent to the detachment of half of the province of Volhynia (the second half was then within the borders of Poland), half of the province of Taurida, and a small section of the province of Chernigov, while several districts of the Don region had been incorporated into it. The Jews then constituted 5.43% of the total population of the Ukraine. The census of 1939 enumerated 1,532,827 Jews in the Ukraine (4.9% of the total). According to the census of 1959, which also included the Jews of the regions which had passed to Russia after World War II (eastern *Galicia, northern *Bukovina, *Subcarpathian Ruthenia), there were 840,319 Jews in the Ukraine (2% of the total). According to this census, which was generally regarded as underestimating their numbers, Jews were concentrated in the towns of Kiev (153,500), *Odessa (106,700), *Kharkov (84,000), Dnepropetrovsk (52,800), *Chernovtsy (Czernowitz; 36,500), *Lvov (24,700), and *Donetsk (21,000). About 80% of the Jews of the Ukraine declared their mother tongue as Russian, about 17% (142,240) as Yiddish, and only about 3% as Ukrainian.

Development and Distribution of the Jewish Settlement

The Jewish settlement in the Ukraine preceded the unification of the area and the formation of the Ukrainian nation. Jewish settlements already existed on the banks of the River Dnieper and in the east and south of the Ukraine and the *Crimea in the periods of the *Khazar kingdom, while ancient Jewish communities were only established in the west, in Volhynia and "Red Russia" (eastern Galicia), in the 12th century. Of these the most ancient was apparently *Vladimir-Volynski. It seems that the "Russia" mentioned in 13th-century rabbinical literature refers to "Red Russia." These communities absorbed the Jewish migration from Germany and Bohemia caused by the persecutions and massacres of the 14th (the *Black Death) and 15th centuries; later, Jews were drawn to the Ukraine by the colonizing activities of the Polish nobility that intensified in the 16th to 17th centuries with the consolidation of the rule of *Poland-Lithuania over the region. The important role taken by the Jews in the economic sphere in this colonization made the Ukraine one of the Jewish centers in Poland-Lithuania. The number of the communities there increased from 25 during the 14th century to 80 in 1764. Even the Chmielnicki massacres in 1648–49 did not halt Jewish migration to the Ukraine and they played a prominent role in its economic recovery during the second half of the 17th and the 18th centuries. After the Ukraine was annexed by Russia, according to the census of 1764, about 15% of the Jewish population lived in provinces having communities over 1,000 Jews, while in other provinces – Volhynia, Podolia, Kiev, and *Bratslav – their proportion was only 11%. The census of 1897, however, shows that 72% of the Jewish population there were living in 262 communities of more than 1,000 persons, which, taken together with the communities having more than 500 Jews, meant that 37% of the Jewish population there lived in towns and townlets in which the Jews formed an absolute majority and 22% in localities where they formed 40–50% of the total population. In contrast, in the part of the Ukraine which lay beyond the Dnieper, in the provinces of Poltava and Chernigov (where about 225,000 Jews lived and constituted a majority in about two places only and 40% of the total population in three others), 65% of the Jewish population lived in 39 communities of more than 1,000. The same situation obtained in "New Russia" (the provinces of Kherson, Yekaterinoslav, and Taurida) where over 500,000 Jews lived: 76% of the Jewish population was concentrated in 58 communities of over 1,000, and Jews formed a majority only in their agricultural settlements. In 1897 Jews constituted 30% of the urban population of the Ukraine, 26% of them living in 20 towns, in each of which there were over 10,000 Jews.

After the abolition of the *Pale of Settlement, with the October 1917 Revolution, the civil war, and the disorders which accompanied it, more than 300,000 Jews left the Ukraine for other parts of the Soviet Union. Hence they formed only 5.4% of the total population and 22% of the urban population of the Ukraine in 1926, and 4.1% and 11.7% respectively in 1939. In 1926, 44% of them lived in 20 towns, each having over 10,000 Jews; while in 1939, 39% lived in the four cities of Odessa, Kiev, Kharkov, and Dnepropetrovsk. This intensified urbanization did not, however, give them predominance in the cities, since there also was a stream of Ukrainian peasants from the villages into the towns, which assumed a pronounced Ukrainian character.

For the history of Ukrainian Jewry after World War I and in the Holocaust see *Russia.

Economic Situation

The migration of Jews from the western provinces of Poland to the Ukraine in the 16th century was mainly due to their economic role in the **arenda* business on a large or small scale. Hence, the Ukraine became a region where Jews managed a considerable proportion of the agricultural economy, administering complexes consisting of a number of estates, single estates, or a sector of their economy. Jews also engaged in *arenda* there in the collection of customs duties and taxes, and played an important role in the export and import trade in the region. The Cossack authorities of the part of the Ukraine annexed by Russia beyond the Dnieper opposed the frequent expulsions of the Jews from there (1717, 1731, 1740, 1742, 1744), and argued in favor of their free admission to the Ukraine (1728, 1734, 1764) stating that the Jews promoted the region's trade. When the Ukraine (with the exception of eastern Galicia) became part of the Pale of Settlement after the partition of Poland-Lithuania, the Jews continued to play a considerable and dynamic role in the economy of the region. In 1817, 30% of the factories in Ukraine were owned by Jews. They were particularly active in the production of alcoholic beverages. In 1872, before the anti-Jewish restriction in this sphere, 90% of those occupied in distilling were Jews; 56.6% in sawmills, 48.8% in the *tobacco industry, and 32.5% in the *sugar industry. Only a limited number of Jews were occupied in heavy industry, where they were generally employed as white-collar workers. In 1897 the occupational structure of the Jewish population of Ukraine was 43.3% in commerce; 32.2% in crafts and industry; 2.9% in agriculture; 3.7% in communications; 7.3% in private services (including porterage and the like); 5.8% in public services (including the liberal professions); and 4.8% of no permanent occupation. Under the Soviet regime, by 1926, it had become 20.6% in arts and crafts; 20.6% in public services (administrative work); 15.3% workers (including 6.6% industrial workers); 13.3% in commerce; 9.2% in agriculture; 1.6% in liberal professions; 8.9% unemployed; 7.3% without profession; and 3.2% miscellaneous (pensioners, invalids, etc.). The proportion of Jews in various administrative branches was 40.6% in the economic administration and 31.9% in the medical sanitary administration. After large numbers of Jews had been absorbed under the Five-Year Plan in heavy industry (especially the metal and automobile industries), in the artisan cooperatives (in which there were over 70,000 Jewish members – 12.9% of the membership), and in agriculture (16,500 families in the cooperative farms), the proportion of Jews living in villages rose to 14% of the Jewish population.

Hatred of the Jews

When the Jews settled in the Ukraine during the period of Polish rule, they found themselves between hammer and anvil: under the *arenda* system the Jewish lessee administered the estate in the name of the Polish landowner, and, if living in the town, he found his customers among the nobility, officials, the Catholic clergy, and the local army garrison. To the enslaved peasants and rebellious Cossacks, Ukrainians, and Greek-Orthodox the Jewish lessee appeared both as an infidel and an alien – an emissary of the Polish Catholic noblemen who sought to dominate them. The Ukrainian townsman was jealous of his urban rival, the unbelieving Jew, whose success was due to the assistance of the foreign and hated Polish regime. In times of rebellion and war, this hatred and jealousy was vented in severe persecutions and horrifying massacres, such as the Chmielnicki massacres of 1648–49, when over 100,000 Jews were brutally killed and almost all the communities of the Ukraine were destroyed, and the persecutions of the *Haidamaks in the 18th century, which were more limited in scope but even more terrible in their cruelty. These massacres, whose perpetrators were admired as national heroes, gave rise to a popular tradition of hatred toward the Jews in the Ukraine; it was nurtured by the increase of the Jewish population in the country, by its economic position, and later by the propagation of the Russian language and culture by Jews – an act which the nationalist Ukrainian intellectuals (the "Ukrainophiles") regarded as collaboration with the "Muscovite" Russian government in its campaign against their awakening as a separate nation. This tradition of hatred toward the Jews found its expression in both folk songs and literature (T. Shevchenko; N. Gogol), in historiography (N. Kostomarov), and in political thought (M. Dragomanov). The Nationalist and Socialist Party of the Ukraine was also imbued with anti-Jewish feelings. The *pogroms of 1881–82 broke out and spread through the provinces of the Ukraine; after 1917, in the Civil War and under the regime of S. *Petlyura (the "Socialist" government), about 100,000 Jews were murdered in the Ukraine (1919–20), as in the days of Chmielnicki and with the same cruelty. Two decades of Soviet regime did little to eradicate the hostility against the Jews: during World War II great parts of the Ukrainian population wholeheartedly collaborated with the Nazis in exterminating the Jews in the occupied Ukraine.

The Period of the Independent Ukraine and Jewish National Autonomy

The period from March 1917 to August 1920 constitutes a special chapter in the history of the Jews of the Ukraine. The Ukrainians established a National Council (the Rada), which in January 1918 proclaimed the separation of the Ukraine from Russia; this episode came to an end in August 1920, when the Red Army completed the conquest of the Ukraine. During this time the leaders of the Ukrainian nationalist movement attempted to reach an agreement with the Jews. They established relations with the leaders of Zionism in eastern Galicia, and jointly waged a struggle against Polish aims in the Ukraine. During this period the Jews were represented in the Rada (with 50 delegates), a secretariat for Jewish affairs was established (July 1917), and a law passed on "personal national autonomy" for the national minorities, among which, the Jews were included. The Jewish ministry (M. *Silberfarb was the first minister; he was succeeded by J.W. *Latzki-Bertholdi) passed a law providing for democratic elections to the administrative bodies of the communities (December 1918), a Jewish National Council was formed, and the Provisional National Council of the Jews of the Ukraine was convened (November 1918). These institutions were short-lived. In July 1918 the autonomy was abolished, the Jewish ministry was dissolved and the pogroms which then took place – without the Ukrainian government taking any effective measures to assure the security of the Jewish population – proved that the whole of this project had been directed more at securing the assistance of the Jewish parties in order to achieve complete separation from Russia than at really developing a new positive attitude toward the Jews.

Religious and Social Movements in Ukrainian Jewry

Ukrainian Jewry became a focus of religious and social ferment within Judaism from the late 17th century. The massacres and sufferings endured by the Jews in the Ukraine also introduced spiritual and social trends. The messianic agitation which followed the massacres of 1648–49 paved the way for the penetration of *Shabbateanism, while at the time of the Haidamak persecutions and the revival of *blood libels, the *Frankist movement made its appearance, and *Ḥasidim as inaugurated by *Israel b. Eliezer Ba'al Shem Tov developed and spread rapidly through the country. After the pogroms of the 1880s, the Ukraine was not only the birthplace of the *Ḥibbat Zion, the *Bilu, and the *Am Olam movements but also of the Dukhovno-bibleyskoye bratstvo ("Spiritual Biblical Brotherhood," founded by Jacob *Gordin and his circle) which sought to "bring back" the Jews to the religious purity of the Bible and thus draw them closer to Christianity. Activist and revolutionary trends were also prominent in the Hebrew and Yiddish literature which emerged in the Ukraine during the 19th and 20th centuries.

During the 1920s and the early 1930s three Jewish districts were created in the areas of Jewish settlement in southeastern Ukraine (*Kalininskoye, Stalinskoye, and *Zlatopol; see also *Yevsektsiya).

[Benzion Dinur (Dinaburg)]

After World War II

During the last stages of World War II and in the period after it, when Nikita Khrushchev was the ruling party man of the Ukraine, Ukrainian Jews who, during the occupation, fled or were evacuated to Soviet Asia, began to stream back and claim their previous housing, possessions, and positions. They were met with outspoken hostility by most of the Ukrainians who had taken their place. The administration refused to interfere in favor of the Jews and generally showed "understanding" for the anti-Jewish reaction, even hushing up violent clashes (as, e.g., in Kiev). When Khrushchev became the ruling figure in the U.S.S.R. after Stalin's death, and particularly in the 1960s, the traditional hatred of Jews in the Ukraine was again allowed to find free expression in pseudo-scientific literature (e.g., the book by the professional antisemite Trofim Kichko, *Judaism without Embellishment*, which appeared in 1963 under the auspices of the Ukrainian Academy of Sciences) and in various popular brochures and periodicals. This official anti-Jewish atmosphere prevailed in the Ukraine during the whole postwar period. The only synagogue in Kharkov was closed down in 1948 and its aged rabbi sent to a labor camp. In Kiev the only remaining synagogue was put under severe surveillance of the secret police, more than in other Soviet cities. Yiddish folklore concerts and shows were almost completely banned from the Ukrainian capital, Kiev, though they were allowed to take place occasionally in Ukrainian provincial towns.

An interesting reaction to this trend "from above" became noticeable in the late 1960s among Ukrainian intellectuals who openly strove to achieve more freedom in civil and national rights. Though engaged in defending the Ukrainian character of their republic against "russification," some of them went out of their way to emphasize their solidarity with Jewish demands for the revival of Jewish culture and education. They also identified with the Jewish attempt to keep alive the remembrance of the Holocaust against the official policy of obliterating it. Young Ukrainian writers, most of them Communist Party members, expressed this new trend in Ukrainian national thought in various ways, and even in labor camps after their arrest for "bourgeois nationalism." A particular impression was made in 1966 by the speech of the writer Ivan Dzyuba in *Babi Yar on the anniversary of the massacre (October 29). It was published only in the West, but it became widely known among Jews and educated non-Jews in the Ukraine.

From 1969 some Jewish families in Kharkov, Kiev, and Odessa were allowed to leave the U.S.S.R. for Israel. In the following two decades Jewish life continued to be repressed as in the U.S.S.R. as a whole. Religious life was centered in the synagogues. In the mid-1970s there were an estimated dozen functioning in the Ukraine. Many Jews were able to leave during the large wave of emigration in the 1970s, arriving largely in the United States and Israel. During the 1970s and 1980s Kiev became a major center of underground Jewish culture and pro-*aliyah* agitation. (For general developments, see *Russia.)

In Independent Ukraine

According to the Soviet census there were 487,300 Jews living in Ukraine in 1989. This figure included 100,600 in Kiev, 69,100 in Odessa province (city and surrounding oblast), 50,100 in Dnepropetrosk province, and 48,900 in Kharkov province. By late 1991 the number of Jews in the Ukraine was estimated at 325,000. The number of Ukrainian Jews emigrating from the late 1980s was the following: 1988 – 8,770; 1989 (to Israel) – 32,547; 1990 – 60,074, and 1991 (to Israel) – 41,264. The geographical breakdown of emigration for 1989–1991 (from 1990 only to Israel) was: from Kiev – 33,818; Odessa province – 19,741; Kharkov province – 11,945; Dnepropetrosk province – 7,501; and Zhitomir province – 5,005. Large-scale emigration continued through the 1990s. At the end of the process over 80% had left, leaving an estimated 84,000 in 2005.

Ukraine declared its independence on August 24, 1991, with the majority of the republic's Jews also voting for independence. On a number of occasions the leaders of the Ukrainian national movement "Rukh" expressed a positive attitude toward the Jews of the Ukraine and the desire to cooperate with them. To further that goal, an international conference was held in Kiev in June 1991 on Ukrainian-Jewish relations, with the participation of leading Ukrainian public figures. Ukrainian president Kravchuk spoke at the public meeting commemorating the 50th anniversary of the mass murder of Kiev's Jews at Babi Yar. In his speech the president acknowledged the Ukrainian people's share of guilt for the destruction of the Jews and asked for the Jewish people's forgiveness. He also called for the UN to support the initiative of U.S. president George Bush and rescind the UN resolution equating Zionism with racism. In 1990, before the splitting up of the U.S.S.R., four Jewish deputies were elected to the Supreme Soviet of the Ukrainian republic.

Under Soviet rule, Bogdan *Chmielnicki, the leader responsible for the unprecedented Cossack slaughter of Jews in the mid-17th century, had been considered a Ukrainian national hero. With the growth, however, of Ukrainian separatist feeling, Chmielnicki became less of a hero due to the fact that he had concluded a pact with Moscow which transformed Ukraine into a Russian colony. Today Simon *Petlyura (1879–1926) is considered the pre-eminent national hero since he headed the country during the brief years of its independence after World War I. Petlyura's responsibility for pogroms during the Civil War is denied by Ukrainian nationalists. In Ukraine the Jewish hero Shalom *Schwarzbard, who assassinated Petlyura in Paris for supporting the perpetrators of pogroms, is today viewed as having been a Soviet secret police agent.

Grass roots antisemitism has not disappeared in Ukraine. According to the results of a sociological survey conducted in November 1990, 7 percent of the population firmly believe in the existence of an international "Zionist" conspiracy, while 68 percent believe that such a conspiracy may exist; 10 percent believe that the Jews bear considerable responsibility for the suffering of other peoples (e.g., the Ukrainians) in the Soviet Union in the 20th century; and 20 percent believe that Jews have an unpleasant appearance.

A law on ethnic minorities grants Ukrainian Jews the right of national-cultural autonomy. In 1992 several Jewish publications appeared, including three (*Vozrozhdenie-91, Evreiskie vesti*, and *Khadashot*) in Kiev. Study (often by amateurs) of local Jewish history is being developed in the republics. The Jewish Culture Association of Ukraine was headed by Ilya Levitas; the rival Association of Jewish Public Organizations of Ukraine was headed by the co-chairman of VAAD of the CIS, Iosif Zisels.

In late 1991, 120 Jewish organizations were operating in Ukraine. The Ukrainian Jewish Congress was established in Oct. 1991. The American rabbi Yankel Blau was named chief rabbi of Ukraine. Several synagogues confiscated in the 1920s and 1930s were returned by Ukrainian authorities, among them those of the Jewish communities of Kharkov, Donets, Vinnitsa, Odessa, Lvov, Shepetovka, Kirovograd, and Drahobych.

[Michael Beizer]

In 1993 Leonid Kuchma was elected president of the Ukraine, which put an end to the moderate nationalist government in the country; Kuchma was regarded as a more pro-Russian leader, who favored closer ties with Moscow. The Black Sea fleet and the Crimean question continued to be, however, burning issues in the relations with Russia.

In April 1994, the Academies of Sciences in the Ukraine and in Israel signed an agreement on cooperation. In September 1995 Prime Minister Yitzḥak Rabin paid an official visit to the Ukraine.

JEWISH LIFE. The main umbrella organization of Ukrainian Jewry in the 1990s was the Association of Jewish Communities and Organizations of Ukraine (VAAD). The Jewish Council of the Ukraine (JCU) was registered in the Ministry of Justice of the Ukraine in January 1993 as the second umbrella organization of Ukrainian Jewry. In the words of the Jewish activist Arkadii Monastyrsky, the JCU united all the Jews of the Ukraine, whereas the VAAD was merely a council of chairpersons of Jewish organizations. Despite the obvious rivalry between both federations, there was no lack of cooperation between them. In 1993 both rival umbrella organizations agreed on cooperation in such matters as Holocaust commemoration and the program "Righteous Gentiles" (in June), and also on common endeavors for the establishment of the Methodological Center for Jewish Education under the aegis of the Ukrainian Ministry of Education (in September 1993).

The Solomon's University in Kiev, one of the four Jewish universities operating in the former Soviet Union, was formerly established in 1993. The International Memorial Foundation Ianovsky Camp was established in Lvov in the beginning of 1993. The newly established foundation issued a declaration in which it explained its goals: to liquidate a penitentiary colony at the site of the former Nazi camp in the outskirts of Lvov; to set up a memorial complex, which would include a Holocaust museum and the international center of documentation on the Jews of Galicia.

In March 1994, the training center for teachers in Jewish day and Sunday schools in the Ukraine, Belarus and Moldova opened in Kiev. It was supported by the JCU, VAAD, the Ukrainian Ministry of Education, and the Foundation for Culture and Education in the Diaspora.

There were 19 Jewish periodical publications in the Ukraine in 1993, among them 10 were issued only in Kiev, 2 in Kharkov, 2 in Dnepropetrovsk, 2 in Chernovtsy, others in Donetsk, Simferopol and Bershad. The papers were issued in Russian, Ukrainian, and, to a lesser extent – in Yiddish. The oldest and the most important Jewish newspapers were the monthly *Vozrozhdenie-91* ("Revival-91"), the continuation of *Vozrozhenie* (see JDB, 1993, p. 364), *Khadashot-Novosti* ("The News"), and *Evreiskie vesti* ("Jewish Reports"), all published in Kiev.

A number of academic conferences on Jewish issues were held in the Ukraine. In October 1993 alone there were three such events: two international scientific conferences, "The Holocaust of Galician Jewry – Problems of History, Politics and Morality," held in Lvov, and "The Beilis Trial: Current Perspectives," held in Kiev; and the conference "Overcoming Chauvinism and Extremism – the Prerequisite for Inter-Ethnic Harmony and Civil Peace in the Ukraine," held in Kiev. At the end of 1994, the conference "Jewish Culture, History and Tradition" was held in Odessa.

Jewish communal life continued to flourish in the following years. By 2005 over 250 Jewish organizations were active and education had expanded into a network that included 14 Jewish day schools, 10 yeshivot, and 70 Hebrew and Sunday schools. Large and active Jewish communities thrived in Kiev, Kharkov, Odessa, and Dnepropetrovsk. In late 2004, a new Jewish community complex opened in Zaparozhye with a theater, gym, kosher kitchen, library, Jewish school, kindergarten, orphanage, and welfare center.

The All-Ukrainian Jewish Congress (AUJC), founded in 1997, united the country's disjointed Jewish organizations in order to promote the Jewish national renascence. It is a volunteer, independent action organization whose membership includes over 120 different public associations, cultural associations, and funds. Also in 1997 the Jewish Foundation of Ukraine was founded as a Jewish charitable organization collecting funds for needs of Jewish organizations and communities in Ukraine.

In 1998, a new umbrella organization, the Jewish Confederation of Ukraine (JCU), was founded, uniting the Association of Jewish Communities and Organizations of Ukraine (VAAD), the Jewish Council of Ukraine, the Union of Jewish Religious Organizations of Ukraine, and the Kiev Municipal Jewish Community.

Another group, the Congress of Jewish Religious Organizations, under Chabad Lubavitch, has also been active in recent years. The World Union for Progressive Judaism has a rabbi based in Kiev and additional Reform congregations operate in Lvov and Kerch; the World Union also runs leadership seminars as well as holiday and summer programs. The Masorti (Conservative) movement runs a Sunday school and youth group in Kiev, and operates day schools, youth activities, and summer camps in several smaller cities.

Antisemitism

There were a number of right-wing nationalist and antisemitic groups in the Ukraine in 1993–94. Among the most conspicuous were the Organization of the Ukrainian Idealists, based in Lvov, the State Independence of the Ukraine party, and the Ukrainian National Assembly with its strong para-military wing "Ukrainian National Self-Defense" (IMA-UNSO). The OUI managed to organize several mass rallies in Lvov, which attracted more than 2,000 participants each; at the rallies antisemitic placards were displayed, and anti-Jewish speeches delivered.

Riots broke out in September 1993 in Vinnitsa, where UNA-UNSO members picketed the offices of the city's Jewish mayor Dmitrii Dvorkis, whom they accused of being a mafia boss. Following the arrest of the leaders of the organization, approximately 10,000 people reportedly blockaded roads and demanded their release. In 1993–94 Dvorkis, as well as other Jewish mayors – Odessa's Eduard Hurvich and Donetsk's Efim Zviahilsky – became victims of antisemitic campaigns.

There were a number of antisemitic periodicals in the Ukraine in recent years: *Nova Ukraina, Za vilnu Ukrainu* ("For Free Ukraine"), *Nezalezhna natsiia* ("Independent Nation"), *Holos natsii* ("The Voice of the Nation"), *Neskorena natsiia* ("Unconquered Nation"), which in 1994 serialized the "Protocols of the Learned Elders of Zion." The main accusation of the Ukrainian nationalist press against the Jews has been their alleged organizing of the mass famine in the Ukraine in 1932–33. A columnist wrote in *Neskorena natsiia* in November 1994: "It is difficult to find a people who have done Ukraine more harm than the kikes. Compared to their crimes, all the misdemeanors of Moscow, Warsaw, and Berlin combined pale into insignificance." Antisemitism in the Ukraine, based on a long tradition, continued to raise its head into the early years of the 21st century.

[Daniel Romanowski (2nd ed.)]

BIBLIOGRAPHY: I.I. Malyshevski, *Yevrei v yuzhnoy Rusi i Kiyeve v X–XII vekakh* (1878); *Arkhiv yugo-zapadnoy Rossii*, 5 pt. 2 (1890); M. Zilberfarb, *Dos Yidishe Avtonomye in Ukraine* (1919); L. Khazanovich, *Der Yidisher Ministerium un di Yidishe Khurbn in Ukraine* (1920); E. Heifetz, *The Slaughter of the Jews in the Ukraine in 1919* (1921); J. Lestschinsky, *Dos Yidishe Folk in Tsifern* (1922); idem, *Ha-Yehudim be-Rusyah ha-Sovyetit* (1943); A. Druyanow (ed.), *Reshummot*, 3 (1923); E. Tcherikower, *Anti-semitizm un Pogromen in Ukraine 1917–1918* (1923); Committee of Jewish Delegations, *The Pogroms in the Ukraine under the Ukrainian Governments, 1917–1920* (1927); E.D. Rosenthal, *Megillat ha-Tevah*, 3 pts. (192731); H. Landau, in: YIVO *Shriftn Jar Ekonomik un Statistik*, 1 (1928), 98–104; *Eshkol, Enẓiklopedyah Yisre'elit*, 1 (1929), 1054–83; J, Kantor, *Di Yidishe Bafelkerung in Ukraine* (1929); J. Shatzky, in: YIVO Historishe Sektsye, *Gzeyres Takh* (1938); L. Zinger, *Dos Banayte Folk* (1941); B. Dinaburg, in: *Zion*, 8–10 (1943–45); S. Ettinger, *ibid.*, 20 (1955), 128–52; 21 (1956), 107–42; R. Mahler, *Toledot ha-Yehudim be-Polin* (1946); I. Halpern, *Beit Yisrael be-Polin*, 1 (1948), 80–91; Dubnow, Divrei, 7 (repr. 1958); O.S. Brik, *Ukrayinsko-yevreysky vzayemovidnosyny* (1961); S.I. Goldelman, *Jewish National Autonomy in Ukraine, 1917–1920* (1968); V. Chornovil, The *Chornovil Papers* (1968), 222–6 (speech of Ivan Dzyuba). CONTEMPORARY PERIOD: U. Schmelz and S. DellaPergola in JYB, 1995, 478; *Supplement to the Monthly Bulletin of Statistics*, 2, 1995, Jerusalem; Y. Florsheim in *Jews in Eastern Europe*, 1 (26) 1995, 25–33; M. Beizer and I. Klimenko, in *Jews in Eastern Europe*, 1 (24) 1995, 25–33; *Antisemitism World Report 1994*, London: Institute of Jewish Affairs, 153–155; *Antisemitism World Report 1995*, London: Institute of Jewish Affairs, 232–234; *Mezhdunarodnaia Evreiskaia Gazeta* (MEG), 1993–1994. **WEBSITES:** www.fjc.ru; www.ukraineinfo.us.

UKẒIN (Heb. עֻקְצִין; "Stalks"), 12th and last tractate in the order *Tohorot* in the Mishnah and the Tosefta. There is no *Gemara*, either in the Babylonian or the Jerusalem Talmud. *Ukẓin* deals, in three chapters, with the problems of ritual impurity affecting roots, stalks, husks, shells, kernels, etc., and the imparting of the uncleanness to the fruits to which they are attached. This tractate was considered one of the most difficult even in talmudic times (Ber. 20a; Hor. 13b).

Chapter 1 distinguishes first between *yad* ("handle") and *shomer* ("protection"), the former referring to that part of the fruit which one holds when eating the fruit, and the latter to such parts as protect the fruit; both are relevant to the question of ritual purity. It then goes on to consider the roots and stalks of a great variety of vegetables and fruits, determining whether or not (or to what extent) they fall under the terms of *yad* and *shomer*. Chapter 2 continues this subject, in particular whether kernels, shells, husks, and encasing leaves are to be regarded as part of the fruit. Toward the end of the chapter, the problem of *hekhsher is touched upon, i.e., the susceptibility of food to ritual impurity, a subject dealt with in detail in tractate *Makhshirin*. Chapter 3 continues with the subject of *hekhsher*, introducing also the associated notion of *maḤashavah*, i.e., the intent to use the respective foods (vegetable or meat) for human consumption. Then there is a detailed discussion of various cases where one of the elements, *hekhsher* or *maḥashavah*, or neither of them, or both, are required in order to make the food susceptible to impurity.

Most of the laws in this tractate are found scattered among the other tractates, e.g., *Tohorot* 1:1–4; 8:9; *Tevul Yom* 3:1–3; and *Makhshirin*. R. Samson of Sens (in his commentary at the beginning of *Tohorot*) suggests that *Ukẓin* logically precedes *Tohorot*, which continues with the subject matter of *Ukẓin*'s final chapter. The laws of *Ukẓin* were known to be very difficult to understand, and when Rav Judah studied it he would say, "we see here questions of Rav and Samuel." In *Horayot* 13b it is related that several rabbis strove to embarrass the *nasi* Simeon b. Gamaliel by challenging him to teach them *Ukẓin*. If the reference is to the tractate and not to the individual laws, it proves that at least parts of the Mishnah were edited before Judah ha-Nasi. According to Epstein, Mishnah 3:2 represents the revised opinion of Akiva (cf. Tosefta 3:2) and Mishnah 3:10 represents the view of Meir.

The Tosefta also consists of three chapters, but many paragraphs in it, such as 2:1–10 and 3:6–14, are not directly related to any Mishnah; and even when there is a correlation, the order of the Tosefta does not correspond to that of the Mishnah. It may be noted that the view of Resh (Simeon b.) Lakish, placing *Tohorot* as the sixth and last order of the Mishnah, having been accepted (Shab. 31a), *Ukẓin* appears as the last tractate of the whole Mishnah (as well as of the Talmud and Tosefta). It is an unusual subject with which to round off the Oral Law. According to Maimonides, its position does not express any particular appreciation for this tractate; on the contrary "it has been left to the end", he says, "because it is based on rabbinical speculation, without any foundation in the Bible" (Introduction to *Zera'im*). To give the Mishnah a fitting close, later editors of the Mishnah added an aggadic passage to the original text of *Ukẓin*, speaking of great reward for the pious and the divine blessing of peace, and quoting in conclusion Psalm 29:11: "The Lord will give strength unto His people, the Lord will bless His people with peace." It was translated into English by H. Danby in *The Mishnah* (1934). For bibliography see main articles *Mishnah; *Talmud; *Tosefta.

[Arnost Zvi Ehrman]

ULAM, STANISLAW MARCIN (1909–1984), mathematician. Ulam was born in Lvov, Poland (then Austro-Hungary), and educated at the Lvov Polytechnic Institute, receiving his doctorate in mathematics in 1933. In 1935 he was invited to work at the Institute for Advanced Study in Princeton. After a brief period in Poland, he returned to the U.S. in 1938, first to Harvard and then in 1940 to the University of Wisconsin as assistant professor. He became a U.S. citizen in 1943, the same year that he joined the Manhattan Project group at Los Alamos working on the development of nuclear weapons. With Von Neumann, he developed the "Monte Carlo" approach to computational problems, paving the way for the "simulation" methods of physics research. His major contribution to the development of thermonuclear weapons was to suggest that compression was essential to inducing a sustained fusion reaction. With Edward *Teller, he devised the system by which this was achieved with radiation implosion from a fission explosion rather than mechanical shock. In 1965 he left Los Alamos for the chair in mathematics at the University of Colorado in Boulder, a post he retained until his death in Santa Fe. With

K.C. Everett, he proposed a scheme for nuclear propulsion of space vehicles. He was essentially a theorist and his intellectual creativity survived the effects of encephalitis contracted in 1946. He was elected a member of the U.S. National Academy of Sciences, the President's Science Advisory Committee, and the Board of Governors of the Weizmann Institute (1975). His publications mainly feature books on mathematical theory.

[Joseph Gillis / Michael Denman (2nd ed.)]

ULIANOVER, MIRIAM (1890–1944), Yiddish poet. Born in Lodz, Poland, Ulianover published poems in journals such as the *Lodzher Folksblat* and *Lodzher Togblat*, until deported to *Auschwitz where she perished. A single volume, *Der Bobes Oytser* ("Grandmother's Treasure," 1922), with an introduction by David *Frischmann, led to her being acclaimed as one of the outstanding women poets in Yiddish. Only extracts of a second volume, *Shabes* ("Sabbath"), appeared in E. Korman's anthology *Yidishe Dikhterins*. Her poems combined the simplicity of folk songs with tender romantic mysticism and nostalgia for the lost traditional world of her grandmother and great-grandmother in Polish villages.

BIBLIOGRAPHY: LNYL, 1 (1956), 34; E. Korman (ed.), *Yidishe Dikhterins* (1928), 134–46, 339.

[Sol Liptzin / Sarah Ponichtera (2nd ed.)]

ULLA I (**Ulla b. Ishmael** in the Jerusalem Talmud; second half of third century), Palestinian *amora*. Ulla studied in Ereẓ Israel under *Johanan b. Nappaḥa (Ḥag. 19a), Resh Lakish (Git. 50b), and *Eleazar b. Pedat (Er. 21b), and transmitted halakhic decisions in their names. He also recorded some of the teachings of Oshaiah and Joshua b. Levi. He was known to be extremely strict in his interpretation of religious laws (Shab. 147a; 157b). Among his halakhic decisions were those concerning the benedictions to be made on different occasions (Ber. 38b; Pes. 53b; 104b). He censured decisions he disliked and on one occasion commented, "As vinegar to the teeth and as smoke to the eyes are the words of *Huna" (Kid. 45b). Some of his other colleagues were *Abba (BM 11 b), *Judah (Ḥul. 76a), and particularly, *Rabbah b. Bar Ḥana (Ḥul. 34a).

Ulla was greatly respected both in Ereẓ Israel and in Babylon, which he visited frequently, and he was one of the first *nehutei* (TJ, Kil. 9:3). In Babylon he reported on current Palestinian customs and decisions and was often invited by the exilarch to deliver halakhic discourses (Ket. 65b; Kid. 31a; Shab. 157b). It is related that once, when returning to Ereẓ Israel from Babylon, Ulla was in danger of being murdered by one of his fellow travelers. In order to save himself he had to condone the murder of another, and Johanan excused his conduct as having been done in self-defense (Ned. 22a). Ulla's maxims reveal how intensely he felt the tragedy of the destruction of the Temple; for instance: "Since the destruction of the Temple, God has nothing in this world save the four cubits of *halakhah*" (Ber. 8a); and "Jerusalem will be redeemed through the performance of charity" (Sanh. 98a). He died in Babylon on one of his visits (before c. 279 C.E.). On hearing the news, Eleazar, adapting Amos 7: 17, exclaimed, "That you, Ulla, should have died in an unclean land" (Ket. 111a), and had his remains taken to Ereẓ Israel for burial. He was survived by his only son, Rabba (Shab. 83b). Among those who transmitted his sayings were Aḥa b. Adda, Ḥisda, and Joshua b. Abba.

BIBLIOGRAPHY: Hyman, Toledot, 970–4; Bacher, Pal Amor; Frankel, Mevo, 119b–120b; Ḥ. Albeck, *Mavo la-Talmudim* (1969), 302–4.

ULLENDORF, EDWARD (1920–), British linguist. Ullendorf, who received his schooling in Germany and his university education in Jerusalem, served with the British in Eritrea and Ethiopia during and after World War II (1942–46) and was an assistant secretary in the Palestine government in 1947–48. He then took up a research post at Oxford; in 1950 he became reader in Semitic languages at St. Andrews University, Scotland. In 1959 he was appointed professor of Semitic languages and literatures at Manchester University and in 1964 professor of Ethiopian studies at the School of Oriental and African Studies of the University of London, retiring in 1982. Ullendorf's service in Eritrea and Ethiopia led him to concentrate his research on studies of the Semitic languages of those areas.

Among his published works are *The Definite Article in the Semitic Languages* (1941), *Exploration and Study in Abyssinia* (1945), *The Semitic Languages of Ethiopia* (1955), *The Ethiopians* (1959), and *The Challenge of Amharic* (1965). He was chairman of the Anglo-Ethiopian Society.

ULLMAN, MICHA (1939–), sculptor and painter. Ullman was born in Tel Aviv, the son of Yitzhak Ullman and Lily Hirsh, who emigrated from Germany in 1933. Ullman spent his childhood in Tel Aviv where he lived with his extended family. After his army service, he studied art in the Bezalel Academy of Art and Design (1960–64). In 1965 he studied in London at the Central School of Arts and Crafts. From 1970 until 1978 Ullman taught at Bezalel, but after an ideological rebellion by the teachers and the students there, Ullman was fired. He began to teach at Haifa University and from 1991 was also a lecturer at the Academy of Art in Stuttgart, Germany.

Ullman participated in the Venice Biennale (1980) and in the Sao Paulo Biennale (1989). He was awarded many art prizes in Israel as well as in Germany and became a well-known artist in both countries.

Ullman used graphic techniques and sculpture in his art. In most cases the drawings of the sculptures were printed and exhibited beside them or in a separate exhibition. For a better understanding of Ullman's abstracts it is recommended to observe all those components.

From 1982 Ullman began to create public sculptures. He created site specific works, some of which were so minimal in size that they became almost unseen. Some of his public sculptures were placed at ground level or even beneath it, so most of the time the audiences stood on them without being aware of it. This subversive style is a characteristic of Ullman's art. One of his first digging works was created in 1972. Ullman excavated two potholes one in kibbutz Mezer and the other one was situated in the nearest Arabic village Meser. In a symbolic act Ullman took the earth of each hole and filled the other one with it. This conceptual action was connected to the art style of the 1970s as well as to the political meaning of Ullman's art.

One of his noted works is the monument *Library* (1995, Bebelplatz, Berlin), which commemorates the book burning of May 10, 1933. The sculpture was a closed hall, below the ground, covered with a glass square. All the walls were covered with shelves and in general was reminiscent of a library which could contain around 20,000 books, similar to the amount of books burned that night. The white hall is lit with constant artificial light so the surroundings, the sky and the viewer, are reflected in the glass. This modest monument was very heartrending and it attracted a great public.

The shape of Ullman's works was abstract, but their content was very symbolic. Ullman used linguistic double meanings in his works, referring to literary, philosophical, religious as well as historical meanings. Being an Israeli who was working outside of his country was expressed in the meaning of the works, for example, by creating a linkage between the works and Jerusalem (*Molad – New Moon*, 1994, Schloss Solitude, Stuttgart).

BIBLIOGRAPHY: Tel Aviv, Tel Aviv Museum of Art, *Library – Drawings* (1996); Tel Aviv, Tel Aviv Museum of Art, *Month – 29 Drawings* (1996); Wiesbaden, Museum Wiesbaden, *Micha Ullman* (2003).

[Ronit Steinberg (2nd ed.)]

ULLMAN, TRACEY (1959–), British comedienne, actress, and singer. Ullman was born in Berkshire, England, to Dorin and attorney Antony Ullman, a Polish immigrant who died when Tracey was six. Her mother enrolled her in the Italia Conti Academy of Theatre Arts at 12. Ullman dropped out at 16 and spent six months performing in a Berlin production of *Gigi* before returning to England, where she was cast in West End productions of *Grease* and *The Rocky Horror Show.* At 21, Ullman won the London Theatre Critics Award for her part in the improvisational play *Four in a Million* (1981). This led to roles on British television, including the BBC sketch comedy shows *Three of a Kind* (1981–83) and *A Kick Up the Eighties* (1981–84), as well as the ITV Jennifer Saunders-Dawn French sitcom *Girls on Top* (1985). Ullman recorded a comically romantic album under punk label Stiff Records, *You Broke My Heart in Seventeen Places* (1983), which featured the hit single "They Don't Know About Us." The song's video featured a cameo from Paul McCartney, who at the time was shooting *Give My Regards to Broad Street* (1984) with Ullman. After Ullman finished the Meryl Streep film *Plenty* (1985), she moved to Los Angeles with her husband and took time off to have her first child. Soon after, producer James L. Brooks helped her create the highly popular Sunday night variety show *The Tracey Ullman Show* (1987–90). The series received five Emmy nominations; earned Ullman a Golden Globe Award for best actress in 1988; and spun off one of America's longest-running animated series, *The Simpsons.* Ullman starred in *I Love You to Death* (1990) and appeared opposite Morgan Freeman in *The Taming of the Shrew* (1990) in Central Park. She made her Broadway debut in the one-woman show *The Big Love* (1991), which earned her a Drama Desk nomination. Ullman gave birth to a son in 1991. In 1993, she won an Emmy for her guest spot on the CBS sitcom *Love & War,* while 1994 saw her take another Emmy for her HBO special *Tracey Ullman Takes On New York* (1993). Ullman continued to star in films, including Mel Brooks' *Robin Hood: Men in Tights* (1993), *Bullets over Broadway* (1994), and James L. Brooks' *I'll Do Anything* (1994). HBO turned Ullman's award-winning special into a series, *Tracey Takes On…* (1996–99), which earned her a sixth Emmy in 1997. Her turn as Dr. Tracy Clark on *Ally McBeal* earned a second guest actress Emmy for Ullman in 1999. After starring in Woody Allen's *Small Time Crooks* (2000), Ullman received two more Emmy nods for her HBO specials *Tracey Ullman in The Trailer Tales* (2003) and *Tracey Ullman: Live & Exposed* (2005). Ullman became a naturalized American citizen in 2003.

[Adam Wills (2nd ed.)]

ULLMAN, VIKTOR (d. 1944), theater conductor and composer. Ullman studied under *Schoenberg in Vienna. Among his compositions were two operas, a piano concerto and much chamber music.

Ullman was arrested by the Nazis, imprisoned in Theresienstadt and murdered at Auschwitz in about 1944. While in Theresienstadt, he wrote an opera entitled *The Emperor of Atlantis,* but it was never performed since the Nazis realized its anti-Hitler implications and banned its performance. It was thought that the work had perished with the author, but a mutilated copy turned up in London. It had been written on scraps of paper, including the backs of Theresinstadt entrance forms. A young British composer, Kerry Woodward, succeeded in piecing it together, except for six bars which had disappeared; he therefore composed new ones. The text was written by a Czechoslovakian Jew, Peter Kien, who perished in Theresienstadt. The opera, written in German, had its world premiere in Amsterdam in 1975. The American premiere was performed in San Francisco by the Spring Opera on Apr. 21, 1977, in an English version translated by Aaron Kramer.

ULLMANN, ADOLPH (1857–1925), Hungarian baron, economist, and member of the Hungarian Upper House. He entered the service of the General Hungarian Credit Bank. In 1885 he was appointed director of the petroleum refinery, a subsidiary of the bank, and in 1909 (after the death of N. Kornfeld) he became the bank's chief executive. Ullmann played a decisive role in the financial activities of the Hungarian government and in establishing factories and industrial enterprises. He was also the president of the national industrial union. His articles on economic problems were published (in German) in the daily Hungarian government newspaper, *Pester Lloyd*.

BIBLIOGRAPHY: K. Tolnay, *Báró Ullman Adolph emlékezete* (1931); J. Radnóti, *Kornfeld Móric* (Hung., 1931), 50–51; N. Katzburg, *Antishemiyyut be-Hungaryah* (1969), 45.

[Jeno Zsoldos]

ULLMANN, ERNEST (1900–1975), South African artist. Born in Munich, he worked as illustrator for *Auslandspost* and later in Berlin for *Mitropa-Zeitung*. In 1935 he settled in Johannesburg and the following year won the Empire Exhibition poster competition.

He was art editor of the weekly, *The Forum*, 1938–46, worked independently in various media, and took up sculpture. In 1950 he toured Israel and painted ten murals for the "Israel Cavalcade" exhibition in Johannesburg. His designs for wood panels and glass engravings for "Yad Vashem," the Etz Chaim Memorial Hall, Johannesburg, were unveiled in 1969. Ullmann's other works include book illustrations, designs for tapestries, and monumental sculptures in various South African cities, notably a large bronze group, *Playmakers*, for the Civic Theatre, Johannesburg, 1964. A park and recreation center in Johannesburg is named in his honor. He wrote an autobiography, *Designs on Life* (Cape Town, 1970).

[Lewis Sowden]

ULLMANN, SALOMON (1806–1865), French rabbi. Ullmann, who was born in Zabern (Saverne; Lower Alsace), first studied in Strasbourg, and then at the Ecole Centrale Rabbinique in Metz, where he was the first to receive the diploma of *grand rabbin* (1832). He officiated as rabbi in Lauterbourg (Lower Alsace) from 1834, and in Nancy (Lorraine) from 1844. In 1853 he succeeded Marchand Ennery as *grand rabbin* of France. One of his major achievements was the organization of the Central Conference of the *Grands Rabbins* of France, the first of its kind, over which he presided in Paris in May 1856. The conference resolved on a number of practical measures, including the introduction of the organ in synagogues.

BIBLIOGRAPHY: *L'Univers Israélite*, 20 (1865), 457–70; AI, 26 (1865), 417.

ULLSTEIN, family of German publishers whose newspaper and magazine empire was at one time one of the largest in the world. The Ullstein company was founded in 1877 by LEOPOLD ULLSTEIN (1826–1899), the son of a wholesale paper merchant of Fuerth, Bavaria. Ullstein left his father's paper business in 1848 and went to Berlin, where he founded his own wholesale paper firm and became a progressive member of the Berlin City Council (1871–1877). In 1877 he bought up the failing *Neues Berliner Tageblatt* and brought it out as an evening paper with the name *Deutsche Union*. A year later Ullstein bought the *Berliner Zeitung*. In 1904 this paper, which reflected Ullstein's liberal political views, was merged by his sons with the *Berliner Zeitung am Mittag*. The new paper's circulation reached the unprecedented figure of 40,000 and made the Ullstein company one of the biggest publishers in Germany. All five of Ullstein's sons entered the family firm. HANS (1859–1935) was legal advisor for many years; LOUIS (1863–1933) was business head after his father's death, and FRANZ (1868–1945), who was editorial director, was the guiding force behind the company for many years. The younger sons, RUDOLF (1873–1964) and HERMANN (1875–1943) joined the firm after their father's death, Rudolf becoming technical director and Hermann managing the magazine and book departments. In 1887 Louis Ullstein founded the *Berliner Abendpost;* in 1898 the three eldest sons founded the *Berliner Morgenpost* and raised its circulation to 600,000, the largest of any German daily. They made the *Berliner Zeitung am Mittag* the first German newspaper to be sold by street vendors instead of by subscription. They also produced a series of other newspapers, including the *Berliner Allgemeine Zeitung*, the *Montagspost*, the *Vossische Zeitung*, and *Tempo*. In addition, the Ullsteins had their own picture and news services, radio equipment, music division, dress pattern division, movie studios, and even a zoo to serve one of their children's papers. The other major ventures of the Ullstein company were its book publishing house (Ullstein, renamed Propylaeen in 1919) and magazine empire. They published the *Berliner Illustrierte Zeitung*, a new type of paper with many illustrations, photographs and drawings, from 1894 with a circulation of two million. In 1919 the Ullsteins began publishing on a large scale, producing many other magazines on the sciences, the arts and literature, broadcasting, automobiles, and aviation. The advent of Hitler, however, spelled the end of the Ullstein enterprise. In 1934 the family was forced to sell the colossal empire to a Nazi-backed consortium for one-fifth of its value and the company became known as the *Deutscher Verlag*. In 1938 Franz and Hermann immigrated to the U.S.; Rudolf went to England in 1939 and to the U.S. in 1943. After World War II, the American authorities in West Berlin rebuilt the Ullstein plant and appointed Rudolf Ullstein as chairman. By 1957 the *Berliner Zeitung* and *Morgenpost*, owned by the Ullstein group, had the largest circulation in West Berlin. In 1960, however, the controlling interest in the group was sold to Axel Springer and the Ullstein family interest in the concern came to an end.

BIBLIOGRAPHY: H. Ullstein, *Rise and Fall of the House of Ullstein* (1943). **ADD. BIBLIOGRAPHY:** P. de Mendelssohn, *Zeitungsstadt Berlin* (1959; revised edition 1982); H. Ullstein, *Spielplatz meines Lebens* (1961); W.J. Freyburg and H. Wallenberg (eds.), *100 Jahre Ullstein 1877–1977* (1977); E. Linder (ed.), *Presse- und Verlagsgeschichte im Zeichen der Eule: 125 Jahre Ullstein* (2002); S. Nadolny, *Ullsteinroman* (2003).

[Stewart Kampel / Archiv Bibliographia Judaica (2nd ed.)]

ULM, city in Wuerttemberg, Germany. The first documentary evidence of a community in Ulm dates from 1241, when a sum of six silver marks in taxes was paid by Jews. The first settlers undoubtedly arrived much earlier. An unbroken series of gravestones (dated from 1243 to 1491) from the cemetery, first mentioned in 1281, indicates the continued existence of the community. As it grew during the 13th and early 14th centuries, its members were engaged primarily in moneylending. Jews were allowed to own houses, and although a *Judengasse* is mentioned in 1331, Jews were not restricted to one quarter. In 1348 the emperor *Charles IV allowed the imperial taxes paid by the Jewish community to be kept by the city for the purpose of its fortification. Despite measures taken by the municipal council to protect the Jews, on Jan. 30, 1349, during the *Black Death persecutions, the Jewish quarter was stormed by a mob and the community was all but destroyed. Nevertheless, it rapidly revived. The synagogue, cemetery and dance hall that had been appropriated by the city were relinquished to the Jewish community in 1354 and 1357. In 1366 a number of Jews were granted partial citizenship. Jud Jacklin, a local Jewish moneylender, monopolized the southern German money market, lent the city funds, and aided it in its struggle against the emperor. The municipality gradually replaced the emperor as protector of the Jews and recipient of their taxes.

In the 15th century, Ulm grew in economic and political importance, while the Jewish community, oppressed by heavy taxation and regulations restricting their financial activities, declined. In 1457 Jewish noncitizens were expelled; in 1499 all Jews were given five months to leave the city. These acts were carried out under a policy known as *Judenfreiheit* ("freedom from Jewish settlement"), which was vigorously observed for two centuries. Only in 1712 were Jews even allowed to trade at the cattle market. In 1786 a single Jew possessing the right of residence was known to have resided in Ulm. During the wars of the 18th century, *Court Jews lived in the city.

From 13 in 1824 the community grew to a peak of 667 in 1886, and thereafter gradually declined. A synagogue was consecrated in 1873 and a cemetery in 1885. The community consisted mostly of prosperous merchants and manufacturers. Albert Mayer, a lawyer, was the first Jew elected to the Wuerttemberg parliament, serving from 1906 to 1909. Julius Baum, the museum director, and the artist L. Moos were two well-known residents of the community. The most famous Jew born in Ulm was Albert *Einstein. During the Nazi era, the population of the community declined from 530 in 1933 to 162 in August 1939, in part due to the boycott of Jewish business establishments and antisemitic harassment; the old cemetery was desecrated in 1936; the same year, Jewish children were no longer able to attend the public schools and a Jewish school was established in its place. On Nov. 10, 1938, the synagogue was burned down and many Jews were viciously beaten. Of 116 Jews deported from Ulm during World War II (45 were sent to *Theresienstadt on Aug. 22, 1942), only four returned. Approximately 25 Jews were living in Ulm in 1968. In 1958 a plaque was mounted to commemorate the former synagogue. In 1988 an additional memorial was erected. In 2002 a Jewish community was founded as a branch of the Jewish community of Wuerttemberg in Stuttgart. A new community center was consecrated in the same year. The community had 450 members in 2004, mostly immigrants from the former Soviet Union who went to Germany after 1990.

BIBLIOGRAPHY: M. Brann, in: *Festschrift... Kroner* (1917), 162–88; M. Stern, in: ZGJD, 7 (1937), 243–8; H. Dicker, *Die Geschichte der Juden in Ulm* (1937); H. Keil (ed.), *Dokumentation ueber die Verfolgungen der juedischen Buerger von Ulm/Donau* (1961); P. Sauer (ed.), *Die juedischen Gemeinden in Wuerttemberg und Hohenzollern* (1966); *Germania Judaica*, 1 (1963), index; 2 (1968), 843–6; 3 (1987), 1498–1522. **ADD. BIBLIOGRAPHY:** P. Lang, "Die Reichsstadt Ulm und die Juden 1500–1803," in: *Rottenburger Jahrbuch fuer Kirchengeschichte*, 8 (1989), 39–48; *Zeugnisse zur Geschichte der Juden in Ulm. Erinnerungen und Dokumente* (1991); M. Adams and C. Maihoefer, *Juedisches Ulm. Schauplaetze und Spuren* (1998). **WEBSITE:** www.alemannia-judaica.de.

[Henry Wasserman / Larissa Daemmig (2nd ed.)]

ULMAN, ABRAHAM (1791–1849), Hungarian rabbi. Ulman served as rabbi in Szabadka (Subotica) and from 1824 to his death in Lackenbach. Moses *Sofer had a high opinion of him and said that "his teaching is sacred" (ḤM no. 197).

Ulman published *Divrei Rash* (1826), the work of his father, Shalom Ulman. His own son, David, published Ulman's writings posthumously under the title *Beit Avraham* (1909), pilpulistic and halakhic responsa and talmudic novellae. David succeeded his father as rabbi in Lackenbach, serving until his death in 1906.

BIBLIOGRAPHY: P.J. Schwartz, *Shem ha-Gedolim me-Ereẓ Hagar*, 1 (1913), 5a no. 16, 24a no. 15; A. Krauss, *Lackenbach* (Ger., 1963).

[Naphtali Ben-Menahem]

ULMAN, JOSEPH N. (1878–1943), U.S. lawyer and jurist. Ulman, who was born in Baltimore, Maryland, taught at the University of Maryland Law School during 1908–28 and served as judge of the Supreme Bench of Baltimore from 1924. As a judge, he advocated modernization of the state's divorce laws (1932), and a year later he wrote *A Judge Takes the Stand*, in which he discussed justice in Maryland, based on specific cases he had tried. About the same time, he told a convention of lawyers that the country's penal system "would be ludicrous if it were not so tragic." President Franklin D. Roosevelt appointed him head of a committee to study prison labor, then appointed him chairman of the newly-created Prison Industries Reorganization Board (1934–36), where he acted as a mediator in disputes concerning privately- and prison-made goods. Ulman was also active in civic affairs, serving as president of the Hebrew Benevolent Society (1925–28), president of the Baltimore Urban League (1931–34), and vice president of the Baltimore branch of the American Jewish Congress (1937–41).

ULPAN (Heb. אֻלְפָּן), center for intensive study by adults, especially of Hebrew by newcomers to Israel. The term comes from an Aramaic word meaning custom, training, instruction, law. It is also used to mean a broadcasting studio or artist's atelier. The term was coined in 1949 when the first center for intensive adult Hebrew study by immigrants was opened at the Eẓion immigrants' camp in Jerusalem and was called an ulpan in distinction to *bet sefer*, the usual term for a school.

The term has since spread to the Diaspora, where it is applied to all kinds of educational activity.

Mass immigration in the early years of the state brought a babel of tongues, and it became imperative to provide centers where the new arrivals could acquire Hebrew and a knowledge of Jewish culture. The Ministry of Education and Culture and the Absorption Department of the *Jewish Agency set up the Eẓion ulpan as a pilot project. Others were soon set up, primarily for professional men who could not find suitable work because of their ignorance of the Hebrew language and Israeli culture. The ulpan network became one of Israel's most significant features, essential in aiding immigrant settlement.

The major ulpanim are residential and intensive, offering four to five months' study with 30 hours of classwork per week. At a kibbutz ulpan younger people work half a day and pay no fees. Other ulpanim are nonresidential, and there are also morning and evening courses; the term *ulpanit* is also used for the less intensive courses. In 1969 there were 89 ulpanim in Israel (including those run by local authorities but supervised by the Ministry of Education). Between 1949 and the end of 1969, over 120,000 adults studied in them, some 11,000 in 1969 alone. The major residential ulpanim are in Jerusalem, Tel Aviv, Haifa, Netanyah, Beersheba, and Nazareth. In the 1990s, with the renewal of mass immigration, the ulpanim hosted Russian and Ethiopian newcomers. At the turn of the century there were 220 ulpanim nationwide teaching 27,000 students at 350 sites in cities, kibbutzim, factories, hospitals, army bases, universities, community centers, and government offices.

Ulpan teaching is intensive, eclectic, and functional. The curriculum combines study of the past (Bible, *aggadah*, Jewish history and traditions, folklore, and literature) with the needs of everyday communication. It includes civics, information on professional life, and the different aspects of modern Israel in its various aspects – geography, economy, security, and so forth.

BIBLIOGRAPHY: *Orḥot: Dappei Hadrakhah le-Morim li-Mevugarim*, vol. 3: *Hora'at Ivrit li-Mevugarim – Takẓirim u-Bibliografyah* (1963); UNESCO, *Teaching of Modern Languages* (1955), index; M. Kamrat, *Hanḥalat ha-Lashon ha-Ivrit* (1962); D. Marani, *Ha-Metodikah shel Hora'at ha-Lashon ha-Ivrit li-Mevugarim* (1956); *Enẓiklopedyah Ḥinnukhit*, 3 (1967), 586ff.; Israel, Misrad ha-Ḥinnukh ve-ha-Tarbut, Ha-Maḥalakah le-Hanḥalat ha-Lashon, *Ba-Ulpanim* (1955–57), 8 nos.; idem, *Yalkut* (1956); idem, *Haẓa'at Tokhnit Limmudim* (1959); idem, *Derakhim u-Fe'ullot* (1960).

[Mordechai Kamrat]

ULPIAN (Ulpianus Domitius of Tyre; d. 228 C.E.), Roman jurist. Some scholars in the early part of the 16th century, believing that the Latin of Ulpian had been corrupted by an Oriental influence, sought for traces of "Hebraisms" in the fragments of his works, many passages of which are included in the *Digest* of Justinian. One, Otto, even went so far as to affirm, in his *Thesaurus of Roman Law*, that Ulpian, together with two other great Roman jurists, Papinian and Modestinus was half-Jewish. In the 18th century, this hypothesis was completely refuted by Heineccius, who not only pointed out the lack of reliable evidence for the supposed Eastern origins of Ulpian, since many Roman families lived in Tyre, but also showed that the alleged "Hebraisms" in Ulpian's Latin were also used by Livy, Cicero, and Quintillian, authors whose Roman origin is beyond question. Although in the 19th century, Orientalists such as Revillout and Lapauge revived this theory in an attempt to prove the Eastern origin of Roman law, it has been again discredited and abandoned by serious modern scholarship.

BIBLIOGRAPHY: J.G. Heineccius, *De Ulpiani Jurisconsulti Hebraismis* (1730), reprinted in his: *Opera Omnia*, 2 (1746), 707ff.; Ch. Wolle (Wollius), *Epistola Critica de Hebraismis Ulpiani Jurisconsulti* (1739); E. Volterra, *Diritto romano e diritti orietali* (1937); idem, in: *Studie et Documenta Historiae Juris*, 3 (It., 1937), 158–63.

[Alfredo Mordechai Rabello]

°**ULRICH, JOHANN CASPAR** (1705–1768), Swiss Protestant theologian and historian. After his ordination in 1727, he studied Hebrew and the Talmud in Bremen under the Jewish apostate Gottlieb Fromann, and in Lengnau with Jacob Guggenheim. His missionary activities in Surbtal brought him into contact with the Jews of *Endingen and Lengnau. In his *Sammlung juedischer Geschichten…* (Basle, 1768; repr. 1922), the first comprehensive history of the Jews of Switzerland, he exonerates the Jews from complicity in causing the *Black Death and from similar allegations. For his work, Ulrich used Jewish sources as well as cantonal records, and it remains a valuable work of reference, especially the section on the Jews of Zurich.

BIBLIOGRAPHY: L. Rothschild, *Johann Caspar Ulrich von Zuerich…* (1933); F. Guggenheim-Gruenberg, *Pfarrer Ulrich als Missionar im Surbtal* (1953); A. Weldler-Steinberg, *Geschichte der Juden in der Schweiz* (1966), index; *Historisch-biographisches Lexikon der Schweiz*, s.v.

UMAN (Pol. **Human**), city in Kiev district, Ukraine; in Poland-Lithuania until the 1793 partition. In 1749 the *Haidamacks massacred many Jews of Uman and burned part of the town. Count Potocki, the landlord of the city, rebuilt it in 1761, held fairs there, and otherwise stimulated its development. In 1768 Haidamacks annihilated the Jews of Uman, together with the Jews from other places who had sought refuge there. On June 19, 1788, the peasant revolutionary, Maxim Zheleznyak, marched on Uman after he had butchered the Jews of Tetiyev. When the Cossack garrison and its commander, Ivan Gonta, went over to Zheleznyak (despite the sums of money he received from the Uman community and the promises he had made in return), the city fell to Zheleznyak, in spite of a courageous defense in which the Jews played an active role. The Jews then gathered in the synagogues, where they were led by Leib Shargorodski and Moses Menaker in an attempt to defend themselves, but they were destroyed by cannon fire. The remaining Jews in the city were subsequently killed. The massacre lasted three days and did not spare old men, women, or children. Gonta threatened death to all Christians who dared to shelter Jews. The number of Poles and Jews who were killed in the "massacre of Uman" is estimated to be 20,000. The anniversary of the commencement of the massacre, Tammuz 5, hereforth known as the "Evil Decree of Uman," was observed as a fast and by a special prayer. Naḥman of Bratslav settled in Uman and before his death there he said, "the souls of the martyrs (slaughtered by Gonta) await me." After his death in 1811, the Ḥasidim of Bratslav used to come to Uman in large numbers to prostrate themselves on his grave.

Uman had the reputation of being a city of *klezmerim* ("Jewish musicians"). The grandfather of the violinist Mischa *Elman was a popular *klezmer* in the city, and the tunes of Uman were widely known. It was also known as one of the first centers of the *Haskalah movement in the Ukraine. The leader of the movement was Chaim (Ḥaikl) *Hurwitz. In 1822 "a school based on Mendelssohnian principles" was established in Uman several years before the schools in *Odessa and *Kishinev. The founder was Ẓevi Dov (Hirsch Beer), the son of Chaim Hurwitz and a friend of the poet Jacob *Eichenbaum; the school closed after a few years.

In 1842 there were 4,933 Jews in Uman; in 1897, 17,945 (59% of the total population), and in 1910, 28,267. During the Bolshevik Revolution, the Jews of Uman endured great suffering. In the spring and summer of 1919, a number of troops passed through the city and perpetrated pogroms; there were 170 victims in the first pogrom and more than 90 in the subsequent one. This time the Christian inhabitants helped to hide the Jews. The Council for Public Peace, most of whose members were prominent Christians, with a minority of prominent Jews, saved the city from danger several times; in 1920, for example, it stopped the pogrom initiated by the troops of General A. Denikin. In 1926 there were 22,179 Jews (49.5% of the total population).

During World War II, the Nazis exterminated the Jews of Uman. In 1959 there were 2,200 Jews (5% of the total population). In the late 1960s the Jewish population was estimated at about 1,000. The last synagogue was closed by the authorities in the late 1950s, and the Jewish cemetery was badly neglected. A monument to the memory of 17,000 Jewish martyrs of the Nazis bears a Yiddish inscription. Jews still visit the tomb of Naḥman of Bratslav.

After the breakup of the Soviet Union, pilgrimages to Rebbe Naḥman's grave were renewed, with thousands arriving from all around the world on Rosh ha-Shanah.

BIBLIOGRAPHY: Ḥ.J. Gurland, *Le-Korot ha-Gezerot al Yisrael*, 1–3 (1887–89); YIVO, *Historishe Shriftn*, 1 (1929), 27–54; S. Bernfeld, *Sefer ha-Dema'ot*, 3 (1926), 290–302; A. Druyanow (ed.), in: *Reshumot*, 3 (1923), 132–40; M. Osherovich, *Shtet un Shtetlakh in Ukraine*, 1 (1948), 165–73; M.N. Litinsky, *Sefer Korot Podolya ve-Kadmoniyyot ha-Yehudim Sham* (1895); E. Bingel, in: *Yad Vashem Studies*, 3 (1959), 303–20.

[Baruch Shohetman]

UMAYYADS, dynasty (660–750) under which the Arabs established their empire, extending from Central Asia and the Indian border to the Atlantic Ocean. The religious ties which had unified Muslims under the first four Orthodox caliphs ("al-Rāshidūn") were weakened under ʿUthmān. Muʿāwiya, the first Umayyad caliph (661–680), transformed the community of the faithful into a secular Arab state in which religion took second place. For the first time, leadership was in the hands of a person who had not been one of the Prophet's eminent associates. Muʿāwiya was proclaimed caliph in *Jerusalem in 660, but was not finally recognized as such until 661 – after ʿAlī had been assassinated and his son Ḥasan had abdicated. Muʿāwiya organized the empire on the Persian and Byzantine model, introduced the *barīd* (postal horse) service, the official service of Post and Intelligence, and was the first to create an Arab fleet.

The capital of the Umayyad caliphate was *Damascus, and *Syria and Ereẓ Israel were the center of the Muslim world. Muʿāwiya built a wooden mosque on the Temple Mount (mentioned in an apocalyptic Midrash; Wertheimer, *Battei Midrashot* (1894), 30 and by the Christian pilgrim Arculfus: J. Wilkinson, *Jerusalem Pilgrims before the Crusades* (1977), 9–10). He and his successors confiscated land from the Jews of Ereẓ Israel and distributed it among the new Arab settlers, causing great disappointment to the Jews among whom the Arab conquest of Ereẓ Israel had caused messianic stirrings (see: PdRE, ch. 30 and *Nistarot de-Rabbi Shimon bar Yoḥai*), and it seems that they settled some of those Jews in *Tripoli, Lebanon. Muʿāwiya established the principle of heredity for the caliphate and four years before his death appointed his son Yazīd as his successor. The majority of the tribal chiefs supported the appointment. After his death, opposition to Umayyad rule resulted in civil war, the main centers of the unrest being in *Persia, *Iraq, and the *Ḥejāz. Abdullah ibn Zubayr proclaimed himself caliph in Mecca, having gained the support of the Muslim aristocracy; the Umayyad caliphs Yazīd I (680–3), his son Muʿāwiya II (683–4), and ʿAbd al-Malik ibn Marwān (685–705) warred against him. Ḥusayn, the grandson of Muhammad, revolted and was killed in Karbalāʾ, Irak (680). ʿAbd al-Malik built the Dome of the Rock (691–2), the costs being covered by the tax revenue which he received from *Egypt for a period of seven years. *Goldziher assumes that the purpose of the grandiose structure was to divert the pilgrims from Mecca to Jerusalem, but *Goitein is of the opinion that the aim was to compete with the Holy Sepulcher. A. Elʿad, according to older traditions than those used by both researchers, thinks that Goldziher was right ("Al-Ḥaram al-sharīf: ʿAbd al-Malik's Jerusalem," in: *Oxford Studies in Islamic Arts*, 9:33–58) and that ʿAbd al-Malik or his son al-Walīd (705–715) built the Al-Aqṣā Mosque.

Al-Wasiṭī (Jerusalem, 1019), the author of the oldest remaining book of *Faḍā'il al-Bayt al-Muqaddas* ("The Praises of Jerusalem"; I. Hasson ed. 1979, 43–44) reports that a group of Jewish attendants were in charge of cleanliness in the mosque and on the Temple Mount and responsible for the maintenance of the lighting, for which service they were reimbursed by exemption from the poll tax. This monopoly was inherited by their descendants until it was abolished by Omar II. The

Umayyad caliphs employed both Jews and Christians, some of whom attained high posts in the government hierarchy. Under ʿAbd al-Malik a Jew was in charge of the mint. In spite of the existing prohibition on the building of new churches, some were in fact built. In general Umayyad caliphs exercised tolerance in religious matters, the exception being Omar ibn ʿAbd al-ʿAzīz (the Second; 717–20), a religious fanatic who was the first to apply the restrictions of the Covenant of *Omar to the religious minorities. It was presumably Omar II who excluded the Jews from the Temple Mount and restricted them to prayers at only one gate (*Salmon b. Jeroham in his commentary on Psalms 30:10; see Dinur in bibl.).

During the rule of the Umayyads, Ereẓ Israel was the scene of construction and development projects. Sulaiman ibn ʿAbd al-Malik (715–7) built *Ramleh, which became a district capital in Jund Falastin. Walīd II (743), the son of Yazīd II, embarked on a project of diverting the Jordan for irrigation purposes, but the project came to an abrupt end when a landslide caused the death of some of the workers; Walīd was then assassinated by his opponents. This event is described in *Midrash Nistarot de-Rabbi Shimon bar Yoḥai*: "Another king will arise and will seek to separate the waters of the Jordan, and he will bring laborers from distant lands to dig a canal to raise the water level and irrigate the land; and the land they dig up will collapse upon them and kill them, and when their princes learn of this event they will rise against the king and assassinate him" (J. Even Shemuel, *Midreshei Ge'ullah* (1954²), 193). This report was confirmed by the Arab chronicler al-Ṭabarī.

Toward its end, the Umayyad regime was plagued by natural catastrophes and internal strife. Between 746 and 749 a number of earthquakes occurred in Ereẓ Israel. The most severe took place in 748 and caused a heavy loss of life and the collapse of a part of the Dome of the Rock. Against a background of inter-Muslim sectarian strife, Shiʿite opposition to the ruling house, and wars against the Byzantine Empire, which raised messianic hopes among the Jews of a Muslim victory over the Christians, Jewish sects came into being in the East in the beginning of the eighth century. Some of these sects advocated revolt against the established order, hoping to bring about redemption by force. One of these sects was headed by Serenus (or *Severus) of Syria, who was active at the time of Yazīd (720–4); reports of his appearance even reached Spain. The climax of anti-Umayyad stirrings in Persia came in the 740s, when an insurrection headed by Abdullah ibn Muʿāwiya was successful in establishing a short-lived independent kingdom. This was the background for the rise of the Jewish pseudo-messiah Abū ʿIssa (or Obadiah) from *Isfahan, who lived during the rule of Marwān II (744–50), the last Umayyad caliph. The internal strife in various parts of the empire was among the major causes for the collapse of the Umayyad dynasty and paved the way for the rise of the *Abbasids.

[Eliezer Bashan]

Umayyad Caliphs in Syria

Muʿāwiyah ibn Abī Sufyān, 661–680
Yazīd ibn Muʿāwiyah, 680–683
Muʿāwiya II ibn Yazīd, 683–684
Marwān ibn al-Ḥakam, 684–685
ʿAbd al-Malik ibn Marwān, 685–705
al-Walīd ibn ʿAbd al-Malik, 705–715
Sulaymān ibn ʿAbd al-Malik, 715–717
ʿUmar ibn ʿAbd al-ʿAzīz, 717–720
Yazīd II ibn ʿAbd al-Malik, 720–724
Hishām ibn ʿAbd al-Malik, 724–743
al-Walīd II ibn Yazīd II, 743–744
Yazīd III ibn al-Walīd, 744
Ibrāhīm ibn al-Walīd, 744
Marwān II ibn Muḥammad, 744–750

In Spain

The Umayyad dynasty began its rule in Spain in 756. ʿAbd al-Raḥmān I (reigned 756–88), a survivor of the slaughter of the Umayyad dynasty in Damascus by the newly proclaimed Abbasid caliphate, and grandson of the 10th Umayyad caliph Hishām, made *Cordoba the capital of his emirate. The Jews under his jurisdiction enjoyed the same rights and status as they had previously under the former Muslim rulers. Both they and the Christians had to pay the special poll tax (*jizyah*) of 12, 24, or 48 *dirhems* each year, according to income. The activity of the Umayyad dynasty at first was the consolidation of the conquest of Spain and the conciliation of a hostile Christian population, a task which continued well into the mid-9th century. The Jewish minority, which had welcomed the Muslim takeover, did not suffer from the Muslim attacks on rebellious Christians, particularly prevalent in Cordoba. The first cultural flowering came under ʿAbd al-Raḥmān II (822–852) through the patronage of literature and science and the refinement of customs and traditions: Al-Andalus became the center of western Islam. There is little information on the Jews under early Umayyad rulers in the 8th and 9th centuries, except that the population increased rapidly as Umayyad tolerance encouraged Jewish immigration to Spain. Under Umayyad rule, the Jews attained wealth, developed their culture, and even acquired influential positions at the center of power. *Ḥisdai ibn Shaprut was physician and adviser to ʿAbd al-Raḥmān III (912–61), who proclaimed himself caliph in 929. The latter's reign marks the height of Umayyad military, economic, and cultural supremacy, and the caliph was considered the most tolerant toward minorities of all the Umayyads. Ḥisdai, head of the Jewish community, was in charge of trade and commerce and foreign affairs, traveling to the generally hostile northern Christian provinces of Spain on diplomatic missions. Cordoba was then the center of Muslim civilization in the West and an important seat of Jewish culture. Other prominent Jewish communities included *Tarragona, *Granada, and *Lucena. Under ʿAbd al-Raḥmān's successors, al-Ḥakam II (961–76), Hishām II (976–1013), and al-*Manṣūr (Hishām's chamberlain who in effect managed affairs of state from 996 to 1002), the Jewish community in the caliphate rose to great wealth and cultural prominence. Just as the western caliphate had declared its independence of Abbasid Baghdad,

Spanish Jewry began to assert its independence of the Babylonian academies and the *geonim. The 12th-century historian Abraham *Ibn Daud describes the relations between the Jewish community of Cordoba and the caliph (Ibn Daud, Tradition, 63–71). Apparently the Umayyad ruler intervened in the appointment of the head of the Jewish community (*nasi) and the head of the academy, as exemplified in the case of the conflict between R. *Ḥanokh b. Moses and R. Joseph *Ibn Abitur in the late tenth century. At first, al-Ḥakam acknowledged the leadership of R. Ḥanokh. During Hishām's reign, al-Manṣūr appointed a supporter of Ibn Abitur, Jacob *Ibn Jau, a wealthy silk merchant who supplied the royal house with his costly wares, *nasi* of all Jewish communities in his domain. Ibn Jau, however, did not collect enough tribute from his people to suit al-Manṣūr, and was imprisoned. He was released by Hishām. The wealth of the Cordoba community and especially of Ibn Jau is attested to by Ibn Daud. The intellectual exchange and high cultural level of the Umayyad house may be ascertained from the statement that Ibn Abitur "interpreted the whole of the Talmud in Arabic for the Muslim king al-Ḥakam." The *Berber invasion and sack of Cordoba (1010–13) resulted in the decline of the Umayyad dynasty in Spain. Cordoba never regained its supremacy as a Muslim and Jewish cultural center; many Jews fled to Granada, Malaga, Lucena, and other cities. The constant internecine strife between the Muslim principalities contributed to a longing for the stability and peace of the Umayyad reign which had endured for nearly 250 years. The dynasty ended with the demise of the weak Hishām III in 1031.

Umayyad Emirs of Spain

ʿAbd ar-Raḥmān ibn Muʿāwiya, 756–788
Hishām ibn ʿAbd ar-Raḥmān, 788–796
al-Ḥakam ibn Hishām, 796–822
ʿAbd ar-Raḥmān II ibn al-Ḥakam, 822–852
Muḥammad ibn ʿAbd al-Raḥmān, 852–886
al-Mundhir ibn Muḥammad, 886–888
ʿAbdallāh ibn Muḥammad, 888–912
ʿAbd ar-Raḥmān III ibn Muḥammad ibn ʿAbdallāh, 912–929

Umayyad Caliphs of Spain

ʿAbd ar-Raḥmān III al-Naṣir, as caliph, 929–961
Al-Ḥakam II ibn ʿAbd ar-Raḥmān, 961–976
Hishām II ibn al-Ḥakam, 976–1009
Muḥammad II ibn Hishām, 1009–1009
Sulaymān ibn al-Ḥakam, 1009–1010
Hishām II, restored, 1010–1012
Sulaymān, restored, 1012–1017
ʿAbd al-Raḥmān IV ibn Muḥammad, al-Murtaḍā 1018–1023
ʿAbd al-Raḥmān V ibn Hishām, 1023–1024
Muḥammad III ibn ʿAbd al-Raḥmān, al-Mustakfī, 1024–1025
Hishām III ibn Muḥammad, 1027–1031

[Isaac Hasson (2nd ed.)]

BIBLIOGRAPHY: I. Goldziher, *Muslim Studies*, 2 (1971), 35–37; A.F. von Kremer, *The Orient under the Caliphs* (1920), 133–218; T.W. Arnold, *The Caliphate* (1924), 7–22, 57–58; J. Wellhausen, *The Arab Kingdom and its Fall* (1927); G.E. Von Grunebaum, *Classical Islam. A History 600–1258* (1970), 64–79; M. Zulay, in: YMḤSI, 3 (1936), 153–83; M. Margaliot, in: BJPES, 8 (1941), 97–104; idem, in: *Tarbiz*, 29 (1960), 339–44; H.Z. Hirschberg, in: BJPES, 13 (1947), 156–64; idem, in: *Yerushalayim le-Dorotehah* (1968), 109–19; B. Lewis, in BSOAS (1950); S.D. Goitein, in: JAOS, 70 (1950), 104–8; idem, in: *Yerushalayim*, 4 (1953), 82–103; J. Braslavsky, *Le-Ḥeker Arẓenu* (1954), 53–61; Dinur, Golah, 1 (1960²), 41–53; D. Iron, in: *Perakim be-Toledot ha-Aravim ve-ha-Islam*, ed. by Ḥ. Lazarus Yafeh (1968²), 128–55; P.M. Holt et al. (eds.), *The Cambridge History of Islam*, 1 (1970), 57–103; A.A. Dixon, *The Umayyad Caliphate* (1970); P. Crone, *Slaves on Horses. The Evolution of the Islamic Polity* (1980), 29–57; P. Crone and M. Hinds, *God's Caliph* (1986); G.R. Hawting, *The First Dynasty of Islam* (1986); Kh.Y. Blankinship, *The end of the Jihad State: The reign of Hisham b. ʿAbd al-Malik*, (1994); Ch. Robinson, *ʿAbd al-Malik* (2005); IN SPAIN: Ashtor, Korot, 1 (1966²); E. Levi-Provençal, *Histoire de l'Espagne Musulmane*, 1–2 (1950); P. Hitti, *History of the Arabs* (1960), 493–536; Baron, Social, index. **ADD. BIBLIOGRAPHY:** W. Montgomery Watt, *A History of Islamic* Spain (1965), 5–94; J.Y. O'Callaghan, *A History of Medieval Spain* (1075), 89–162; R. Fletcher, *Moorish Spain* (1993); M. Fierro, *ʿAbd al-Raḥmān* (2005)

UMAYYA IBN ABĪ AL-SALT, one of the "true seekers of God" (*Ḥanīf*, pl. *Ḥunafāʾ*) who are mentioned several times in the *Koran. Umayya was an older contemporary of *Muhammad. According to Muslim tradition, he desired to be the apostle, the prophet to the Arabs. Muhammad, however, regarded him as a deviationist who led others astray and did not accomplish his mission. There is an allusion to him in Sura 7:174–5, which, according to most commentators, refers to *Balaam. Many long and short extant fragments of ancient Arabic poetry deal with the same biblical subjects that are found in the Koran. Scholars differ as to the originality of these poems and their independence from the narratives of the Koran. Undoubtedly, many came from the Jewish and Christian legends used by Muhammad and therefore there is neither plagiarism nor borrowing from the Koran.

BIBLIOGRAPHY: *Umajja b. Abi ṣ-ṣalt: die unter seinem Namen ueberlieferten Gedichte*, tr. by F. Schulthess (1911); J.W. [= H.Z.] Hirschberg, *Juedische und christliche Lehren im vor-und fruehislamischen Arabien* (1939), 34ff., and passim; idem, *Yisrael be-Arav* (1946), index.

[Haïm Z'ew Hirschberg]

U-NETANNEH TOKEF (Heb. וּנְתַנֶּה תֹּקֶף; lit. "Let us declare the mighty importance [of the holiness of the day]"), a *piyyut* (*silluk*) recited before the *Kedushah* of the *Musaf* of Rosh Ha-Shanah and the Day of Atonement. The prayer epitomizes the significance of the High Holy Days as "the day of judgment" on which all creatures pass, one by one, before God, like a flock before the Shepherd Who decrees their fate. It emphasizes man's precarious and painful lot and his futile strivings. Following an enumeration of the manifold fates which may be decreed for a man during the year to come, the prayer, however, goes on to stress the belief that "repentance, prayer and charity avert the severe decree": God is full of forgiveness toward man who "came from dust and who shall return to dust" and whose days are "as a fleeting shadow, as a passing cloud … and as a dream that vanishes." Because this prayer, in simple yet very expressive words, voices the basic idea of the Day of Judgment, it came to be one of the most solemn parts of the High Holy Day liturgy and is recited with awe and in a soul-stirring mood.

Written by Kalonymus b. Meshullam *Kalonymus, the *paytan* of Mayence (11th century), a well-known legend ascribed its composition to a R. Amnon of Mainz (for details see *Amnon of Mainz). The prayer became part of the traditional Ashkenazi, Polish, and Italian liturgies.

BIBLIOGRAPHY: Davidson, Oẓar, 2 (1929), 199, no. 451; Landshuth, Ammudei, 45f.; Idelsohn, Liturgy, 220; P. Birnbaum, *High Holiday Prayer Book* (1951), 359–64.

UNGAR, BENJAMIN (1907–1983), **ḥazzan*. Born in Jaslo, Galicia, Poland, Ungar studied with several notable cantors and composers before taking his first position as *ḥazzan* in Magdeburg, Germany. From there he moved to Stendal and in 1938 went to Israel. He officiated in several Tel Aviv synagogues and in 1959 became chief *ḥazzan* of the Tel Aviv Great Synagogue. The possessor of a powerful and rich tenor voice, Ungar gained a reputation through his many concert, radio, and television appearances, and became known internationally through his records and concert tours. In 1966 he became chairman of the Association of Cantors of Israel. In May 1983 Ungar was made a Distinguished Citizen of Tel Aviv.

[Akiva Zimmerman (2nd ed.)]

UNGAR, JOEL OF RECHNITZ (1800–1885), Hungarian rabbi. Ungar was born in Rechnitz, where his father Eliezer was a merchant. At about the age of 15, he went to the yeshivah of Mordecai *Banet in *Mikulov (Nikolsburg) and finally to the yeshivah of Moses *Sofer in Pressburg. In addition to his talmudic studies, he studied German, French, and mathematics. In 1824 he married the daughter of the wealthy Joseph Yust of Csejte, who wished him to devote himself to commerce. Once, however, when traveling to the Vienna fair on behalf of his father-in-law, he called upon his teacher and became so engrossed in halakhic discussion that he arrived too late for the fair, bringing about the impoverishment of his father-in-law. As a result, Ungar was compelled to accept the rabbinate of Csejte and became known as an outstanding Torah scholar. He was later appointed rabbi of *Paks, where he remained until his death. He maintained and administered a large yeshivah and several of the great Hungarian talmudists were his pupils. His protest against the resolutions of the Brunswick conference in 1844 was printed in the *Torat ha-Kena'ot* (1845). He was nevertheless opposed to the schism of Hungarian Jewry, and when it took place, he withdrew from national Jewish affairs, devoting himself wholly to his own community and to teaching.

He was very strict in his personal life. On the morrow of the Day of Atonement, he would eat only such minute quantities of food as did not constitute eating according to the *halakhah* because of his doubt as to whether one was obliged to fast for two days, so that he would technically be fasting. After his death, his son-in-law Susman Sofer published several of his responsa on the four parts of the Shulḥan Arukh under the title *Teshuvat Riba* (Riba = Heb. acronym **R**abbi **J**oel **B**en **E**liezer).

BIBLIOGRAPHY: *Magyar Żsidó Szemle* (1886), 134–9; Sofer, in: J. Ungar, *Teshuvot Riba* (EH, ḤM; 1924); S.B.D. Sofer, *Mazkeret Paks* (1962), 116–26.

[Samuel Weingarten-Hakohen]

UNGER, IRWIN (1927–), U.S. historian. Born in New York, Unger received both his M.A. (1949) and Ph.D. (1958) in American history from Columbia University. He taught at the universities of Columbia and California and was appointed professor of history at New York University, where he taught U.S. economic and 19th-century history. His main areas of interest were radicalism and reform; the 1960s; the Gilded Age; and economic history.

Unger's book *The Greenback Era: A Political and Social History of American Finance, 1865–1879* (1964) won the Pulitzer Prize in history. Meticulously researched, it recognized the variety of economic interests on either side of the paper money issue and emphasized the impact of intellectual, religious, and political leaders on that controversy. In a different vein, Unger perceptively analyzed "New Left" historians in "The 'New Left' and American History…" in *The American Historical Review* (72, no. 4 (July 1967), 1237–63).

Other books by Unger include *The Movement* (1974); *These United States* (1978; 2002^2); *Turning Point, 1968* (with his wife, Debi, 1988); *20th-Century America* (with D. Unger, 1990); *Postwar America* (with D. Unger, 1991); *America in the 1960s* (with D. Unger, 1993); *Instant American History* (1994); *The Best of Intentions* (1996); *LBJ: A Life* (with D. Unger, 2000); *Recent America: The United States since 1945* (2001); and *The Guggenheims: A Family History* (with D. Unger, 2005). The Ungers also compiled *The Times Were a Changin'* (1998), an anthology of the 1960s.

[Ari Hoogenboom / Ruth Beloff (2nd ed.)]

UNGER, JOSEF (1828–1913), Austrian statesman and jurist. Unger converted to Christianity at a young age. He was appointed professor of jurisprudence at the University of Vienna in 1857. He entered parliament in 1867, was minister without portfolio 1871–79, and president of the Supreme Court in 1881. His principal work, *System des Oesterreichischen Allgemeinen Privatrechts* (6 vols., 1856–64) gained him a European reputation.

UNGER, MAX (1883–1959), musicologist. Born in Germany, Unger worked as a conductor and critic, and in 1919–20 edited the *Neue Zeitschrift fuer Musik*. In 1933 he went to Switzerland and Italy and returned to Germany after World War II. An authority on Beethoven, he published *Auf Spuren von Beethovens unsterblicher Geliebten* (1911), *Beethovens Handschrift* (1926), *Ein Faustopernplan Beethovens und Goethes* (1952), and the catalogs of two important Beethoven collections. Unger gathered material for a revised edition of Beethoven's letters and established many of their datings for the first time.

UNGERFELD, MOSHE (1898–1983), Hebrew literary critic. Born in Galicia, Ungerfeld was active in the Zionist and Hebrew movement in Vienna, where he was also a teacher and journalist. He emigrated to Palestine in 1938 and from the following year served as director of the Bialik House in Tel Aviv.

He contributed articles and book reviews to many Hebrew and Yiddish periodicals. Ungerfeld wrote literary essays for the Hebrew press, concentrating on material from the Bialik archives. He published *Vinah* (1946), *Ḥ.N. Bialik vi-Yeẓirotav* (1960), a bibliography of Bialik's works, and *Ketavim Genuzim shel Bialik* (1971), as well as a collection of essays *Orot u-Ẓelalim* (1977) and *Hogim and Meshorerim* (1974).

[Getzel Kressel]

UNGERMAN, IRVING (1922–) sports promoter, manager, and member of Canadian Boxing Hall of Fame and the International Sports Hall of Fame. Ungerman was born in Toronto and grew up in the downtown heavily Jewish Kensington Market area. During World War II, he enlisted in the Royal Canadian Air Force and served as a bombardier.

Ungerman was one of Canada's most prolific promoters of amateur and professional sports. He managed and represented many Canadian boxers during his career, notably the champions George Chuvalo and Clyde Gray. Ungerman's contribution includes television broadcasting. He initiated the broadcast of boxing on Canadian closed-circuit television in the early 1950s and he was also responsible for establishing Canada's Friday Night at the Fights on commercial TV. Ungerman was also involved in sports other than boxing. He served on the organizing committee that developed the inaugural hockey series between Team Canada and the Soviet National Team in 1972. He was a prominent figure on the organizing committee that brought the Blue Jays and major league baseball to Toronto.

Outside the realm of sports, Ungerman was a longtime supporter of many Toronto-based charitable organizations, including the Salvation Army, Variety Village, the Reena Foundation serving special needs children within a framework of Jewish culture and values, the Hospital for Sick Children, and Mount Sinai Hospital. In 2000 Ungerman was honored by the Government of Ontario with the Order of Ontario.

[Avi Hyman and Brenda Cappe (2nd ed.)]

UNION, OESTERREICHISCH-ISRAELITISCHE (Union of Austrian Jews, later **Union oesterreichischer Juden**), association representing the interests of the Jews of the Austrian Empire and standing for implementation of their equal rights. It was founded in 1882 in part as an outgrowth of J.S. Bloch's battle against a rising tide of antisemitism. The union operated a legal office which kept a watchful eye on every violation of equality in all the provinces, supporting legal action up to the highest courts, exposing and prosecuting calumnies against Jews, and intervening against any administrative discrimination. It believed that the only legally relevant criterion of a Jew was his religion, following the same line as the Central-Verein Deutscher Staatsbuerger Juedischen *Glaubens in Germany. This tenet brought it into conflict with Jewish aspirations for national autonomy. The union rejected the creation of any special category for the Jews, pointing to the fact that this was the aspiration of the antisemitic parties in order to deprive the Jews of equality in the professions and the economy. After the partition of old Austria, the union limited its activity to the Austrian Republic. It welcomed the Balfour *Declaration and supported colonization in Palestine but remained unalterably opposed to nationalist domestic policy. It lost its majority in the Vienna religious community in 1932, but in general elections the Jewish electorate did not support the Jewish national candidates. The union published an annual, *Kalender fuer Israeliten* (1892ff.), a weekly, *Die Wahrheit* (1899ff.), and a monthly, *Mitteilungen* (1888f.). After the 1938 *Anschluss*, the union and its publications ceased to exist.

BIBLIOGRAPHY: J. Kreppel, *Juden und Judentum von heute* (1925); *Festschrift zur Feier des 50 jaehrigen Bestandes der Union oesterreichischer Jude* (1937); H. Gold, *Geschichte der Juden in Wien* (1966).

[Hugo Knoepfmacher]

UNION COUNTY, county in N.E. New Jersey. Of Union County's 532,000 residents (2004 census), about 35,000 were Jews. Major Jewish communities are in Elizabeth-Hillside, Westfield, Scotch Plains, Springfield, Union, Cranford, and Linden.

Although German Jews came to Elizabeth in the middle of the 19th century, by 1880 only 25 families had settled there. At the turn of the century, immigrants came from Eastern Europe; there were 550 Jewish families in 1905 and the large influx continued until a limit was placed on immigration in 1920. In the mid-1930s, 10,000 Jews lived in Elizabeth, a number of them American-born. A parallel settlement occurred in Plainfield where four congregations and two charitable associations were already active in 1904. The Plainfield community grew to 6,000 Jews in 1960.

YM-YWHA's were founded in Elizabeth in 1883 and in Plainfield in 1929, and a Jewish community council for eastern Union County based in Elizabeth in 1940, and one in Plainfield in 1937. In 2006 one synagogue struggled to continue its existence in Plainfield, where most of the Jewish population had moved to Somerset County, while Elizabeth continued to attract young families.

The major difference was the strength of the Jewish Educational Center (JEC), founded by Rav Mordechai Pinchas Teitz. The JEC grew from a *mikveh* and an elementary school, founded in 1940, to high schools, five synagogues (with a Sephardi as well as an Ashkenazi minyan in one synagogue), a second *mikveh*, an institute for Talmud study for college-age students, and an adult education system. Rabbi Teitz initiated the move from the downtown Elizabethport neighborhood to the more affluent Elmora and Westminster areas. Elmora Avenue has several kosher restaurants, a kosher bakery and a kosher supermarket.

Three distinctive features of Elizabeth are that it is a united *kehillah*; it is a center for Holocaust survivors who were integrated into the community and joined in all facets of Jewish life; *aliyah* is encouraged, with more than 100 families, especially those of scientists who worked in research in nearby pharmaceutical, communications, and other companies, settling in Israel.

The YM-YWHA is now on Green Lane in Union, near Kean University, at the edge of Elizabeth's Elmora section. The Wilf Jewish Community Campus of Central New Jersey, located in Scotch Plains, is a major Jewish Community Center. The Jewish Family Service (www.jfscentralnj.com) is in Elizabeth with branches in Fanwood and Warren (Somerset County).

Temple Emanu-El in Westfield had over 1,100 members (2005) (www.tewnj.org); Beth Israel in Scotch Plains had 463 members (2005); the JEC in Elizabeth had over 1,000 members (2005) (www.thejec.org). B'nai Israel, a Conservative synagogue in Elizabeth, merged with a congregation of the same name in Millburn in 1992, a few years after its centennial, while Beth El, a Reform synagogue founded in 1950, also closed.

BIBLIOGRAPHY: P. Wolgin, "Visions of America, Visions of Judaism: Jewish Immigrant Community Development, Elizabeth, N.J., 1900–1950," paper presented for the Elizabeth Historical Society (May 5, 2005).

[Rivkah Blau (2nd ed.)]

UNION GÉNÉRALE DES ISRAÉLITES DE FRANCE

(UGIF), official body created by the Vichy government under German pressure, to represent French Jewry during the German occupation. Soon after the occupation of France (June 1940) the Germans unsuccessfully tried to organize a representative body in Paris, to be directed by consistorial leaders who remained in the city. In connection with relief work, a Comité de Coordination des Oeuvres de Bienfaisance du Grand Paris was organized on Jan. 30, 1941, and officially declared in April 1941 as a French association. French officials had long resisted the German pressure, mainly led by Theodor Dannecker, Eichmann's representative in Paris, to organize a centralized Jewish organization that could serve as a German tool to implement antisemitic measures. The French government finally accepted the setting up of such a body, under the threat of a purely German organization. By a law of Nov. 29, 1941, the Vichy government created the UGIF, which became an official French body representing both French and foreign-born Jews, with two divisions, one in the occupied and one in the Southern zone. The UGIF was officially to be controlled by the Commissariat Général aux Questions Juives, then headed by Xavier Vallat. Like the Germans in Paris, the Vichy authorities also tried to choose veteran Jewish leaders to direct the affairs of the new body. Vallat frequently discussed the UGIF with Jewish leaders, since its creation separated French Jewry into two sharply divided groups: those willing to participate in the UGIF in order to retain some form of independence for Jewish relief activities and to be able to pursue them, as they became ever-more necessary, and to prevent the takeover of the new body by less responsible Jews; and those willing to stick to the traditional Jewish organizational scheme, set up by the Republic, mainly the Consistory. The fight against the UGIF was conducted in the free zone mainly by the Consistoire Central (Central Consistory) which protested against the creation of such a quasi-political organization with its own juridical and fiscal structure. The Consistoire Central stated that such a body would be called upon to give indirect or even direct approval to anti-Jewish measures; traditional voluntary Jewish relief would have to give way to forced relief controlled by the government and financed by funds from confiscated Jewish properties. Jacques Helbronner, president of the Consistoire Central, stated in a protest to Vichy that the creation of the UGIF was based on legislation of a racial character and of foreign inspiration, and the basic idea of which stood in contradiction to the spirit of French legislation. Albert Lévy, a member of the Consistoire Central, became the UGIF's first president, with André Baur, vice president for the occupied zone, and Marcel Stora as administrators, respectively, of the free and occupied zones. Among the members of the board, the majority were former members of the Comité de Coordination. They were all French Jews, coming from a professional or upper-class background, who had been active in relief organizations. The first task of the UGIF, almost immediately after it was set up, was to collect the levy of 1 billion francs imposed by the German Military Command in Paris (Majestic) on the Jews of France as "reprisals" for the first attacks by the French Resistance. This levy was imposed on December 12, 1941. As the money available was not sufficient, and as the threats of deportation and the shooting of hostages became stronger, the UGIF had to organize a loan from the main French banks, of 250 millions francs, to pay the first installment. Then, it could use money raised by the selling of Jewish-owned stocks on the Paris stock exchanges to pay the rest of the levy. All pre-war Jewish organizations, according to the law, would be disbanded and merged into the UGIF, the only authorized Jewish body in France. The UGIF took over the properties of these defunct organizations, and also all their relief tasks. In the spring of 1942, the UGIF was helping half of the Jews in France, mostly through payments, as the aryanization policy had struck severely and impoverished the Jewish population. In the occupied zone the UGIF had no fewer than 24 offices (for services in the free zone there were seven directorates, each of which was a former association that had been absorbed by UGIF). In the French Jewish circles which were opposed to involvement in the UGIF, the old enmity to foreign-born Jews played an important role. Many French Jews did not favor a plan which forced all Jews, foreign as well as French, to belong to the UGIF. Participation in the UGIF indicated not only acknowledgment of the anti-Jewish legislation, but also a recognition of separate Jewish identity, which repudiated the established tenet that Jews were to be regarded solely as a religious group. The UGIF never became strictly an organization of collaboration with the Germans, although the UGIF leaders were forced to negotiate constantly with the Gestapo, the Sipo-SD. Leaders of the UGIF had to acquiesce to some of the logic of the perpetrators, for example in giving more attention to French Jews in comparison to foreign Jews. Raymond-Raoul Lambert proved, however, more sympathetic to foreign Jews, people he had tried to help in the late 1930s who had entered prior to the beginning of the German Occupation, in contrast to the French Consistory. When negotiating with the Germans, the UGIF tried to use its margin of maneuverability, always very small, to have French Jews released or not deported. The Union hired many Jews as employees, to serve the needs of a growing despairing population. Officially, employees of the UGIF were exempt from deportation though the protection proved unstable. For example, a roundup in the office of Lyons, organized by Klaus Barbie, led to the arrest of the employees, later deported to Auschwitz. On July 21, 1943, André Baur, then the president of the Union in the northern zone, was arrested. He was deported, together with his family, to Auschwitz. In the days before his arrest he had protested, once again, directly to Marshall Pétain, on the poor conditions of Jews in the Drancy camp. In September 1943, Raymond-Raoul Lambert was also arrested, then deported with his wife and children. The question, raised as early as February 1943, became then whether or not to maintain the activities of the UGIF or to dismantle it. Such a decision was never made, and the UGIF continued officially to work till the very end of Occupation. The support it provided for Jews, whether in freedom or imprisoned in camps in France, proved to be necessary. Underground activities developed then rapidly, not organized by the leaders of the UGIF but under the cover and with the financial help of the Union. The most notable was the underground fight of the Eclaireurs Israélites, officially absorbed into the 6th department of the UGIF, which led to the purchase of weapons and the organization in the Southeast of France of a maquis, a group of youth that fought for the liberation of the city of Tarbes. The policy of the UGIF was always to negotiate in order to keep as many Jews as possible on French territory, whatever the German conditions might be. This led to the creation of agricultural colonies in the northern part of France, and to three camps in the heart of Paris, annexes of Drancy for "privileged Jews," mostly spouses of Aryans. These persons were entirely fed and taken care of with the finances of the Union. The leaders were not able to make the necessary steps to go underground nor to disperse children's homes that sheltered youngsters whose parents had already been deported. Numerous such houses were raided by the Gestapo, such the one in La Verdière or Izieu. On July 21, 1944, the houses in the suburbs of Paris were raided; 242 children and 33 UGIF employees were arrested and immediately deported to Auschwitz. Soon after the Allied invasion (June 1944) in Normandy, members of the Comité Général de Défense, an underground Jewish body consisting of representatives of all Jewish groups, discussed the possibility of closing the UGIF offices. At a secret meeting held on July 13, 1944, in Paris, the UGIF leaders of the former occupied zone adopted a resolution against the voluntary dissolution of the UGIF because it would induce immediate reprisals against the Jews in both zones. Raymond Geissmann, who was then director general of the UGIF in the former free zone, strongly defended the record of the UGIF. As early as July 1944, the newly (clandestinely) created body representing all Jews in France, the CRIF, considered the fate of the UGIF and possible trial for its leaders. In October 1944, a commission set up by the CRIF started to investigate the activities of the Union. This led only to a reprimand that was even not made public. The debate continued within the CRIF until 1947 but its president, Léon Meiss, avoided any further determinations. The debate about the UGIF started anew in 1980, with the publication of a book by Maurice Rajsfus, *Des Juifs dans la collaboration*. It lasted more than 10 years, with the judgment on the UGIF remaining equivocal: the Union was seen as either a body whose leaders, French bourgeois Jews, were ready to deliver foreign Jews to the Germans to save the French Jews, or as a Resistance body. Further research, and comparison with other countries, could clarify both versions of history and give a more accurate, balanced description of this tragic episode.

BIBLIOGRAPHY: Z. Szajkowski, *Analytical Franco-Jewish Gazetteer 1939–1945* (1965), 39–65, 125–46; idem, in: JSOS, 9 (1947), 239–56; R. Billig, *Le Commissariat Général aux Questions Juives (1941–1944)*, 1 (1955), passim; J. Adler, *Face à la persécution: les organisations juives à Paris de 1940 à 1944* (1985; Eng. edition, *The Jews of Paris and the Final Solution: Communal Response and Internal Conflicts, 1940–1944* (1987)); V. Caron, *Uneasy Asylum. France and the Jewish Refugee Crisis, 1933–1942* (1999); R. Cohen, *The Burden of Conscience* (1987); D. Epelbaum, *Aloïs Brunner* (1990); G. Kohn, *Journal de Drancy* (1999); M. Laffitte, *Un engrenage fatal. L'UGIF face aux réalités de la Shoah 1941–1944* (2003); R.R. Lambert, *Carnets d'un témoin*, preface by R. Cohen (1985); M. Rajsfus, *Des Juifs dans la collaboration* (1980); idem, *Des Juifs dans la collaboration*, vol. 2: *Une Terre promise? (1941–1944)* (1989); S. Schwarzfuchs, *Aux prises avec Vichy. Histoire politique des Juifs de France (1940–1944)* (1998); C. Steur, *Theodor Dannecker ein Funktionnär der Endlösung* (1987); the archives of the UGIF are deposited with YIVO in New York.

[Jean-Marc Dreyfus (2nd ed.)]

UNION OF COUNCILS FOR JEWS IN THE FORMER SOVIET UNION (UCSJ; formerly **Union of Councils for Soviet Jews**).

Voice of the Refuseniks (1970–1999)

In the mid-1960s, with the sense that American Jews had not done enough to rescue Europe's Jews during the Holocaust still fresh in their minds, a small number of American Jewish activists concluded "Never Again": that the needs for rescue from persecution and quarantine of the Soviet Union's 4-plus million Jews was receiving inadequate attention.

Following the inspiration of Student Struggle for Soviet Jewry, activists in half a dozen cities organized local "action" committees and, in 1970, they established the umbrella organization, Union of Councils for Soviet Jews (UCSJ). In the 1970s, UCSJ established itself as the principal grassroots and activist component of the Soviet Jewry Movement. Prior to the internet, it pioneered a number of innovations to assure an integrated campaign. It purchased fax machines for each local council to receive their information and to compile and distribute to them a weekly packet of information about new developments in the former Soviet Union and provide up-to-date UCSJ policies and projects.

Virtually every Refusenik and Prisoner of Conscience was "adopted" by at least one council which, in turn, developed and shared official biographies and coordinated their respective cases. The councils provided regular information to local media and officials and to their Congressional delegations. UCSJ organized a Congressional Vigil, headed by Congressmen John Porter (R-Ill) and Tom Lantos (D-Cal); assisted by UCSJ, congressmen placed profiles of Refuseniks and Prisoners into the Congressional Record every Friday for nearly two decades.

UCSJ's greatest political triumph came in the early 1970s with its successful advocacy in the Congress of the interventionist Jackson-Vanik Amendment, sponsored by Senator Henry Jackson and Congressman Charles Vanik, to U.S. Trade legislation, which made "most favored nation" trade concessions contingent on the free emigration of the Jews – this over the vehement opposition of the Nixon-Kissinger administration and the Israeli and American Jewish leadership.

By the late 1980s, the organization had swelled to nearly 40 local councils with a combined membership of 50,000, matching the approximately 50,000 unaffiliated members and supporters of the national organization. In its campaigning, throughout the 1970s and 1980s, UCSJ briefed thousands of visitors not only about who to visit among the Refuseniks but on how to collect vital, strategic information from their leaders. They supplemented these reports with weekly telephone calls to activists across the Soviet Union. Refuseniks especially valued the leadership of UCSJ's 10-year president, Pamela B. Cohen of Chicago Action for Soviet Jewry. When she made an unannounced two-week visit in 1987, word of her arrival spread across the 11 time zones and hundreds of Refusenik leaders traveled to Moscow and Leningrad to brief her on conditions in their communities.

Although it was largely unknown to the million-plus American Jews who responded to the rallying cry, "Let My People Go," there existed a serious, principled political and operational divide between the Israel-dominated "Establishment" wing of the Soviet Jewry movement and the grassroots activists. The difference often produced a measure of vitriol during the Refusenik era but, since the fall of the Iron Curtain, it is seen by UCSJ as affecting far more dangerous stakes. Among the questions that divided the "establishment" from the activists were "Who spoke for Soviet Jews? How to position the struggle? Was the ultimate goal of the movement "*aliyah*" or "freedom," including the freedom not to choose to live in Israel, and to what extent was the movement devoted to human rights as well as *aliyah*.

The Jewish Establishment conceded to the State of Israel the international voice of Soviet Jewry. They argued that only Israel was prepared to accept all Soviet Jews, and the demographics of a proportionately rising Arab population in greater Israel was a time bomb that massive immigration from the U.S.S.R. could help defuse. What's more, the Soviets were prepared at least to consider granting Jewish emigration if it were seen as repatriation to homeland rather than a human rights category – freedom of movement. Hence, it was seen as the duty of every departing Soviet Jew to make *aliyah*.

Further, as the movement began, in the post-1967 era, Moscow had severed its diplomatic relations with Israel, and Israel's vital interests were at stake in promoting a modus vivendi with the then powerful Soviet Union. Israel had a long agenda with the Soviet Union; Soviet Jews were only one part of that agenda, which also included trade, military security, and Soviet diplomatic support of its hostile neighbors. Accordingly, Israel was convinced that the only effective approach to the Soviets was what they termed "quiet diplomacy." It therefore rejected grassroots activism aimed at "making noise" and opposing antisemitism and the broad violations of human rights – concerns that the 35-nation Helsinki Process, and UCSJ, routinely addressed.

But to the activists in the U.S.S.R. and UCSJ alike, "quiet diplomacy" and the *aliyah*-only campaign smacked of paternalism and violated the Russian Jews' internationally guaranteed "freedom of choice and movement." It also unacceptably isolated the targeted Jews from their equally oppressed majority, their non-Jewish neighbors, and especially from the politically courageous dissident Helsinki monitors led by such international luminaries as Andrei Sakharov, Yuri Orlov, and Anatoly (Nathan) Sharansky. In contrast, UCSJ and the activist Refuseniks, including Sharansky and Leonid Stonov, viewed the activists as full, non-paternalistic partners – with UCSJ as the Western "voice of the Refuseniks."

Antisemitism and Human Rights Monitor

In the late 1990s, with grassroots antisemitism rising dangerously in Russia (Ukraine and Belarus as well), UCSJ established a nationwide antisemitism and xenophobia monitoring network – the only one of its kind. And it forged a full working coalition with the prestigious Moscow Helsinki Group, a human rights coalition still opposed by the Jewish Establishment. Although Russian President Vladimir Putin has made many excellent speeches inveighing against antisemitism and xenophobia in Russia, as well as terrorism, antisemitism remains the principal language of extremist violence and propaganda, from the 50,000 neo-Nazi skinheads, to the exclusionary Russian Orthodox Church, to the nationalistic and fascist political factions. By 2005 these factions constituted one-third of the deputies in the Duma (parliament); strongly antisemitic attitudes garnered upward of 50% approval in public opinion sampling. Putin has tolerated a fully corrupt and dysfunctional rule of law infrastructure incapable of providing protection to citizens let alone economic stability, has systematically outlawed political opposition parties, and has imposed virtual control of the major media.

In sum, with the collapse of the Iron Curtain, half a million Soviet Jews "dropped out" in Vienna and came to America; and more than a million made *aliyah*. In the early 21st century, with the Russian Jewish leadership dependent upon President Putin's good intentions, Russia still remained an authoritarian country that hand picked its presidents. With the pool of future contenders so contaminated, Jews and democracy itself are in jeopardy. With Jews also challenged and targeted in Ukraine and Belarus, advocacy and the monitoring of antisemitism and xenophobia in the FSU remained UCSJ's unique mandate as 2005 drew to a close.

[Micah H. Naftalin (2nd ed.)]

UNION OF ORTHODOX JEWISH CONGREGATIONS OF AMERICA (UOJCA), commonly referred to as the OU, largest organization of Orthodox synagogues in the U.S. Founded in 1898, the UOJCA was originally oriented toward the few English-speaking, rather than Yiddish-speaking, congregations. The call for establishing the organization was sent from the address of the Jewish Theological Seminary, and a few early UOJCA leaders, such as Henry Pereira *Mendes, were also identified with that institution. The UOJCA remained a small group until about 1950, and its status rested more on the reputation of its presidents, men such as Rabbi Herbert S. *Goldstein, than on the activities or the number of its affiliates. Since then it has experienced tremendous growth and in 2005 claimed nearly 1,000 affiliated synagogues.

The UOJCA is best known for its *kashrut* supervision; founded in 1923, today it is a multinational operation that certifies 400,000 industrial and consumer products manufactured in 73 countries. The *kashrut* division employs 300 full-time supervisors and produces its own rabbinic journal about *kashrut* called *Mesorah,* as well as a quarterly called *Behind the Union Symbol.* Under the leadership of Rabbi Menachem Genack, the *kashrut* division also seeks to educate the Jewish community about various aspects of *kashrut.*

Aside from programming geared towards its constituent synagogues, the UOJCA seeks to promote its perspective and values through its Institute for Public affairs in Washington, headed by the UOJCA director for public policy, Nathan J. Diament. The National Council of Synagogue Youth (NCSY), a division of the UOJCA, has a cadre of 850 volunteers and reaches unaffiliated youth who do not attend Jewish day schools. Yachad, the National Council for Jewish Disabilities, also a division of the UOJCA provides mainstream programming for children and adults with developmental disabilities.

In addition to their offices in New York and Los Angeles, which employ over 200 people, the UOJCA also maintains an office in Jerusalem, which aims to bring secular Israelis closer to Orthodox Jewish observance through adult education programs and summer camps across 25 Israeli cities and towns. The UOJCA also services Orthodox college students through their Jewish Learning Initiative on Campus, which deploys rabbinic couples to serve as Torah leaders and mentors on college campuses. Additionally, the UOJCA sponsors the Sha'alavim High School in Kharakov, Ukraine, and produces a quarterly magazine called *Jewish Action*. In 2005 the executive vice president of the UOJCA was Rabbi Dr. Tzvi Hersh Weinreb and its president was Stephen J. Savitsky.

BIBLIOGRAPHY: Jeffrey S. Gurock *American Jewish Orthodoxy in Historical Perspective* (1996); C.S. Liebman, in: AJYB, 66 (1965), 21–97; E. Markovitz, in: AJHSQ, 55 (1966), 364–84.

[Asher Oser (2nd ed.)]

UNION OF ORTHODOX RABBIS OF THE UNITED STATES AND CANADA (Agudath Harabbonim), the oldest organization of Orthodox rabbis in the U.S. in 2005 it had 450 members. The Agudath Harabonnim was founded on July 29, 1902, in New York City with a goal of strengthening "the weakened hands of the rabbinate and to remove stumbling blocks from the path of our nation." In 1914 the organization set up the Central Relief Committee, which was later absorbed into the American Jewish Joint Distribution Committee, and in 1915 a charity called Ezras Torah, which still operates today. During World War II, Agudath Harabbonim founded the *Vaad ha-Hatzalah, which rescued leading Orthodox Torah scholars. Occasionally the Agudath Harabbonim clashed with the Rabbinical Council of America over a variety of issues, this was exacerbated by the fact that the former represented the older European-trained generation of rabbis and the latter American-trained rabbis, most of whom were ordained by the Rabbi Isaac Elchanan Theological Seminary at Yeshiva University. Originally, membership in the Agudath Harabbonim was limited, almost exclusively, to rabbis ordained in Europe, and it still insists on the more comprehensive *yadin yadin* ordination. The monthly Torah journal *Ha-Pardes* had close ties with the Aggudath Harabbonim and carried a lot of information relevant to it, until it stopped appearing in 2004. The Agudath Harabonnim maintains its own *bet din* (ecclesiastical court) that was headed in 2005 by Rabbi Hersh Ginsberg. Rabbi Yehuda Levin of Brooklyn, New York, although not a member of the Agudath Harabonnim, lobbied on its behalf since 1979.

For many years Rabbi Eliezer *Silver was the president and central figure in the Agudath Harabbonim. The organization has not had a president since the passing of Rabbi Moses Feinstein in 1986. In the early 21st century, it was led by a Va'ad ha-Meẓumẓam that included Rabbi David Feinstein, son of the late Rabbi Moses Feinstein.

BIBLIOGRAPHY: Charles S. Liebman, in: AJYB, 66 (1965), 21–97; A. Rakeffet-Rothkoff, *The Silver Era in American Jewish Orthodoxy: Rabbi Eliezer Silver and His Generation* (1981); J.S. Gurock, *American Jewish Orthodoxy in Historical Perspective* (1996).

[Asher Oser (2nd ed.)]

UNION OF REFORM JUDAISM (formerly the **Union of American Hebrew Congregations** (UAHC)), association of the more than 900 Reform and Liberal congregations of the U.S. and Canada, representing some 1.5 million Jews, with headquarters in New York. Founded in 1873 as the first nationwide cooperative organization of Jewish congregations – after 32 years of unsuccessful efforts to establish a semblance of unity among U.S. Jewish communities – the UAHC's first goal was to coordinate support for the establishment of a seminary for the training of rabbis. Two years after the first meeting of the UAHC, its leaders announced the founding of the *Hebrew Union College, with Isaac Mayer *Wise, the prime mover in the creation of the UAHC, as its president. Wise had hoped that the UAHC would be an "umbrella" organization which would include traditional as well as progressive congregations. This hope was doomed to defeat, however, and a number of Conservative rabbis, who at first cooperated in the program of the Hebrew Union College, withdrew and established the *Jewish Theological Seminary in New York City. In 1876 the UAHC succeeded in reconciling the disparate aims of the eastern and Midwestern Reform leaders, and absorbed the *Board of Delegates of American Israelites, which had been founded in 1859 under the impact of the *Mortara case in Italy. The UAHC gradually developed an extensive program of administrative activity, including such fields as religious education (1886), congregational organization (1903), sisterhoods (1913), brotherhoods (1923), youth work (1939), synagogue administration (1941), and social action (1949). For many years its greatest contribution was a broad range of religious school textbooks which were utilized in Orthodox and Conservative as well as Reform congregations. For much of the period prior to World War II the UAHC was the weakest partner in the trio of agencies of the Reform movement; its lay leaders regarded it simply as a service organization, rather than one which would stimulate and lead its congregations and their members. The Reform Movement was the first to establish the tri-partite system of organization – a seminary, a rabbinic body, and a union of congregations.

The direction of the UAHC's activity was changed beginning in 1941, however, with the appointment first of Rabbi Edward *Israel and then of Rabbi Maurice N. *Eisendrath as executive secretary. In 1951 the UAHC moved its offices from its former Midwestern stronghold in Cincinnati to New York City, thereby dramatizing the adoption of an active, dynamic program of leadership within the Reform Movement and in U.S. Jewish life generally and moving out of the shadow of Hebrew Union College. The change of location to the center of U.S. Jewish affairs and the assumption of prerogatives of national leadership were both preceded and followed by conflicts between those who favored emphasis on the local autonomy of the individual congregation and those who supported the concept of national action. Generally, the proponents of national assertiveness won out, and the UAHC took strong stands on such issues as civil rights for blacks and the Vietnam War. And the leader of the Union became not only the titular head of Reform Judaism but its actual leader. In Conservative Judaism by contrast, the chancellor of the Seminary was the titular head of the movement. The leadership of the UAHC attempted in such matters to present a Jewish view that would match that of newly vocal forces within the Catholic and Protestant churches. From an ideological and theological point of view, however, this trend was part of the search by the entire U.S. Jewish community, during the post-World War II period, for a definition of Jewish distinctiveness and identity.

The governance of the Union is different than its counterparts. The Union's policy-making body is the General Assembly, which meets every other year at the Biennial, in accordance with the Union of Reform Judaism's Constitution and Bylaws. The General Assembly is composed of delegates who are members of and selected by Union congregations in proportion to the size of their synagogue.

The Union's Board of Trustees meets twice each year and is responsible to the General Assembly. Its more than 242 board members come from all parts of the United States and Canada. Fifty percent of the board is elected directly by the Union's regions, while the remaining membership is made up of at-large members elected by the General Assembly and ex officio members.

The 90-member Union for Reform Judaism's Executive Committee also meets twice each year.

The UAHC has had two strong and dynamic leaders since 1973, Rabbi Alexander M. Schindler, who became president of the UAHC in 1973, and his successor Rabbi Eric Yoffie, who assumed office in 1976. Schindler gained renown for his assertive support of the social action agenda of the Reform Movement of the 1970s and 1980s, including civil rights, world peace, nuclear disarmament, a "Marshall Plan" for the poor, feminism, and gay rights, as well as his opposition to the death penalty. He was the head of the Conference of Presidents of Major American Jewish Organization and as such the titular leader of American Jewry when Menachem Begin became prime minister of Israel, and although they disagreed, strongly and directly with each other, they got along famously and Schindler paved the way for Begin's acceptance by American Jewry shocked by the transition from Labor leadership. He strengthened the ties of the Reform Movement to Israel and also got along quite well with the leaders of Orthodox Jewry, including Moshe Sherer of the Agudah, who also were his intense ideological opponents. Within the Reform Movement, Schindler is associated with a period of growth, which overtook Conservative Judaism as the largest denomination of American Jews. During his presidency, the UAHC grew from 400 congregations in 1973 to about 875 in 1995. He was an advocate of outreach to intermarried couples and of patrilineal descent. His efforts at outreach broke the taboo against dealing with the subject of intermarriage except to condemn it. He called upon the Reform Movement to reach out to the non-Jewish spouses in interfaith marriages and also to unchurched Americans. His second initiative was even more controversial. During his tenure the Reform Movement adopted the patrilineal descent resolution, which stated that the child of one Jewish partner is "under the presumption of Jewish descent." Traditionally, only the child of a Jewish mother was considered Jewish. As Schindler advocated, the UAHC approved a resolution that said that the child of a Jewish father (and a non-Jewish mother) would be regarded as Jewish, *provided that the child was raised as a Jew.* The Conservative and Orthodox movements and the statutes of the State of Israel did not agree with this position, so that there are now two operative standards for being considered Jewish. During Schindler's presidency, the Reform Movement allowed women to assume a more central role in the synagogue, a direct consequence of the feminist movement that influenced every aspect of American life. He also was associated with the move to welcome gays and lesbians – and their congregations into the movement as well as into the rabbinate. And rare in Jewish life, he was the mentor to his successor and retired gracefully to make way for Eric Yoffie.

Under Yoffie's leadership the name of the organization was changed to better reflect its task. Since 2003 it has been called the Union for Reform Judaism (URJ). He moved the organization from its Fifth Avenue headquarters and used the bully pulpit to change the direction of the Union, including congregational worship, adult and religious school education, and Jewish camping. The Religious Action Center of Reform Judaism in Washington, D.C. – headed by David Saperstein – which has long been a feature of the movement, sought to translate its prophetic mandate into practical political action; lobbying and working with other coalition groups generally on liberal issues and for the state of Israel.

Yoffie himself, and by extension the URJ, has been a strong critic of President George W. Bush on the domestic agenda and an equally strong critic of the war in Iraq. He has been critical of the Israeli government, but supportive of the disengagement from Gaza and the peace process and within the President's Conference, a strong advocate of the peace camp much to the chagrin of right-wing and some Orthodox religious forces. Like the Union – and like Schindler before him – he is a force to be reckoned with.

Yoffie has expanded the Union's work to strengthen Progressive Judaism in Israel, and has been a strong advocate of Jewish religious pluralism in the Jewish state. Reflecting on the work of the URJ, Yoffie has stated: "We are a union of Jews committed to a particular vision of Jewish life: to spirituality, Torah, and social justice – the highest ideals of Reform Judaism."

Yoffie is leading the restructuring and revitalization of the Reform Movement with new approaches to study, worship, and ritual practice. He proposed a plan to reform Reform. "I propose, therefore, that at this biennial assembly we proclaim a new Reform revolution. Like the original Reform revolution, it will be rooted in the conviction that Judaism is a tradition of rebellion, revival, and redefinition; and like the original too, this new initiative will make synagogue worship our Movement's foremost concern." Yoffie urged that this "worship revolution" be built on a partnership among rabbis, cantors, and lay people. He stressed music as a central element of worship, a reintensification of the commitment to study Torah, a return to *mitzvot.* He has moved to strengthen Reform youth programs and to expand its camps and its trips to Israel. During the height of the Intifada, he was roundly criticized for canceling a series of trips to Israel, but with the diminution of tension and the increase in safety, Reform Judaism has redoubled its efforts to get its youth involved.

In the past years, Reform Judaism has at once been more traditional and less so; more willing to return to the practices that classical Reform left behind such as the *kippah*, the *tallit*, forms of *kashrut*; more engaged in Torah study, but also more confident in its own unique synthesis of a Judaism at home in tradition and at home in the liberal wing of American life.

BIBLIOGRAPHY: J.G. Heller, *Isaac M. Wise* (1965), index; W.G. Plaut, *The Growth of Reform Judaism* (1965).

[Bertram Wallace Korn]

UNION OF THE RUSSIAN PEOPLE (**"Soyuz russkogo naroda"**), a right wing political movement, fanatically antisemitic, in czarist Russia; founded in November 1905. It demanded the exclusion of Jews from military service and their payment of a special tax instead; annulment of all the privileges enjoyed by the more prosperous Jewish merchants, artisans, and academic intelligentsia; negation of the Jews' right to vote, either actively or passively, for the Duma (the Russian parliament); a prohibition against Jews trading in books, maintaining printing presses, or editing newspapers. In December 1905, Czar Nicholas II consented to take the Union under his auspices. Among its leaders were A. Dubrovin and V.M. Purishkevich, who was a member of all the national Dumas except the First. The official paper was *Russkoye znamya* ("The Russian Flag"). The union was active among the city and rural roughs and the lower middle class, whence it recruited the "Black Hundreds" (*chernosotentsy*), armed gangs who initiated *pogroms against Jews and members of the radical intelligentsia. In 1907 Purishkevich and a group of his followers broke away from the union to create the "Chamber of the Archangel Michael." There was little difference between the two groups in their attitude toward the Jews.

A few members of the union were elected to the Second Duma, and many more entered the Third. The union conducted a virulent propaganda campaign, and published a large number of pamphlets and papers. In many towns, the union's "tea houses" were the headquarters of anti-Jewish propaganda and assaults on Jews. The union organized the murder of two progressive members of the Duma, Professor M.Y. *Herzenstein (of Jewish origin) and G.B. Yollos (a Jew). The union was especially successful in its election propaganda within the *Pale of Settlement, and its members were influential behind the scenes in the highest government circles. They also had an important role in the *Beilis trial. After the Revolution of February 1917, the Provisional Government established a committee to investigate the activities of the union. In many aspects the Union of the Russian People was the precursor of

*Nazism. It bequeathed to Nazism the use of the Protocols of the *Elders of Zion, and probably directly influenced the Nazis via the Baltic Germans, among whom were Scheubner-Richter and Alfred *Rosenberg.

BIBLIOGRAPHY: N.D. Spector, *The Doctrine and Program of the Union of the Russian People in 1906* (dissertation, Columbia University, 1952); W. Laqueur, in: *Survey: a Journal of Soviet and East European Studies* (Oct. 1962); H. Rogger, in: *Journal of Modern History*, 36 (1964), 398–415; L. Greenberg, *The Jews in Russia*, 2 (1946), index; A. Chernovski, *Soyuz russkogo naroda* (1929); V. Levitski, in: Yu. O. Martov et al. (eds.), *Obshchestvennoye dvizheniye v Rossii v nachale XX-go veka*, 3 (1914).

[*Encyclopaedia Hebraica*]

UNION OF SEPHARDIC CONGREGATIONS, THE. The Union of Sephardic Congregations was established in 1929 by leaders of Sephardi communities in America to promote the religious interests of Sephardi Jews. Its primary aim was to give cohesion and the strength of union to the scattered and comparatively weak congregational units of the Sephardim. It also assisted Sephardi communities outside of the United States.

The main activity of the union was the preparation and publication of Sephardi prayer books with English translations by the union's first president, Dr. David de Sola Pool. These books were distributed to Sephardi communities throughout the world, including South America, Europe, Africa, India, Canada, Rhodesia, and Iraq. The union also assisted American Sephardi communities in finding and bringing to the United States trained Sephardi rabbis, cantors, and scholars, and it provided scholarships for religious training for promising Sephardim in yeshivot in the United States. During the 1930s and 1940s it assisted in the rescue of Sephardi scholars and religious leaders from Europe, was involved with the Sephardi refugees interred at Fort Ontario in Oswego, New York, and collected financial support for the Marranos in Portugal. Additionally, the union supported the adoption of Sephardi Hebrew for use in Israel.

[Mark Angel (2nd ed.)]

UNITED JEWISH COMMUNITIES, organization incorporated in 1999 as a result of merger discussions held between representatives of the *Council of Jewish Federations, (CJF), United Israel Appeal (UIA), and United Jewish Appeal (UJA).

Prior merger discussions began in 1948, both privately and publicly, by various representatives of sometimes two and three organizations. The new organization subsumed the functions formerly performed separately by CJF, UIA, and UJA. The structure established five pillars (the word used to describe various departments or divisions of UJC), one of which was closed a year or so after the United Jewish Communities began. The pillars still functioning are:

1. Financial Resource Development
2. Human Resources and Social Policy
3. Israel and Overseas Needs, now called ONAD
4. The Trust for Jewish Philanthropy Development

Financial Resource Development monitors trends in Jewish and general fundraising, provides consultation, various publications, and fund raising tools to local Jewish Federations in improving their fund raising.

Human Resource and Social Policy is devoted to addressing human and social needs of the Jewish community. Staff training and consultation is provided for local federations regarding planning and allocation of resources, staff development and staff placement. Through this pillar, UJC plays a significant role in Washington regarding government allocations for health and human services under local Jewish auspices.

ONAD assesses the needs of Jewish communities worldwide and aids in the educational process on the local level in enhancing the awareness of Jewish needs. The allocation of local federation funds, dedicated to overseas use is done through this pillar. Representatives work closely with the *Jewish Agency for Israel (JAFI) and the *American Jewish Joint Distribution Committee (JDC), who are the major recipients of these funds.

The now closed Philanthropic pillar was originally intended to evaluate the field of Jewish philanthropy by conducting Jewish outreach, provide consulting services to Jewish philanthropists and non-profits, and catalyze new ventures in American Jewish life.

Before being closed it developed two initiatives; one devoted to Jewish women and their career advancement in the Jewish community and the other to developing a coalition for service in the larger Jewish community.

UJC continues to evolve in response to suggestions and evolving needs and interests within the American Jewish community and is a work in progress.

UIA continues with its name as a department within UJC and continues as an agent for friends to JAFI (UJC, 2003).

Historical Context

What follows is a brief historical summary of the major national and international institutions which served the Jewish community from 1914 to 1999 until the formation of UJC. Included are two organizations that were not partners in the merger but are integral elements of the Jewish philanthropic and communal system – American Jewish Joint Distribution Committee and the Jewish Agency for Israel.

AMERICAN JEWISH JOINT DISTRIBUTION COMMITTEE (JDC). In 1914, as the shadow of World War I began to spread over Europe, JDC was established. Its mission is "to serve the needs of Jews throughout the world, particularly where their lives are threatened or made more difficult." JDC's focus is on rescue, relief, and renewal of Jewish communities around the world to rebuild Jewish culture and religion while advancing Jewish continuity. In addition, JDC is committed to assisting Israel in providing social services to her vulnerable communities. JDC estimates that it has assisted millions of Jews in 85 countries through its efforts, starting with the distribution of $50,000 raised in 1914 to help Jews in Palestine and Europe from starving to death through to the respose to the current economic crisis faced by the Jewish community in Argentina.

At its inception, JDC focused on maintaining the vibrancy of worldwide Jewish communities and assisting them with rescue and relocation to Palestine when they were at risk of destruction. That stance changed with the formation of the State of Israel. The majority of JDC's annual budget came from UJA. Additional resources included grants from the United States Government for specific programs such as the resettlement of Jewish emigrants from the Soviet Union, individual private donations, donations from foundations, international organizations, and Jewish communities around the world.

COUNCIL FOR JEWISH FEDERATIONS (CJF). Nearly two decades before the founding of JDC, the first federation was established in Boston. This model was believed to be a more efficient way to raise funds and address the needs in local Jewish communities. Almost 40 years later, a national organization was created to service the more than 200 local federations in the United States. It was originally named "National Council of Jewish Federations and Welfare Funds." In 1932, it became known as CJF. Organizers aimed to develop standards, principles, and programming in social and communal welfare work for federations, welfare funds, and other Jewish communal service organizations in North America. The Council was primarily concerned with organizing resources to best serve the Jewish communities on local and national levels, without concentrating on issues abroad.

UNITED ISRAEL APPEAL (UIA). Created in 1925, to unify fundraising efforts of organizations including Jewish National Fund, Hadassah and Hebrew University, "United Palestine Appeal" was dissolved in 1930. But in 1936, it was revived. In 1939, it became one of the founders of United Jewish Appeal, and was its principal beneficiary. UIA was the main source of tax-deductible contributions from American Jewry to the people of Israel and was the primary source of funding for the Jewish Agency for Israel. By 1952 it became known as United Israel Appeal (UIA). In 1971, the Jewish Agency was reconstituted, and UIA's role in the Agency as representative of the U.S. fundraising community was enhanced to encompass the monitoring as well as the transfer of funds. From its inception, UIA served as the sole fundraising agency for the *Jewish Agency for Palestine (Israel), and provided a link between the American Jewish community and Palestine (Israel). Though UIA had the smallest operating budget of the three organizations involved in the merger, its power and land holdings in Israel surpassed both CJF and UJA's influence on Israel.

The formation of UIA created the need for an agency abroad to allocate funds collected in North America, and the Jewish Agency for Israel (JAFI) was established. UIA distributed these funds raised by UJA/federation campaigns to JAFI for allocation. These funds accounted for three-fourths of JAFI's annual operating budget. Due to the funding UIA provided, its board had influence on JAFI's policies, including representation on JAFI's Board of Governors and Assembly. The composition of UIA's board changed over the years as various American Jewish organizations vied for seats in order to influence JAFI. From 1973, UIA annually secured and monitored grant money from the United States Government for the resettlement of Jewish refugees to Israel.

JEWISH AGENCY FOR ISRAEL (JAFI). In 1929, World Zionist Organization (WZO) created the Jewish Agency for Palestine, which today is known as JAFI. Before the birth of Israel, JAFI was recognized by the League of Nations as the official representative of World Jewry in forming a Jewish National Home in Palestine. It was the de facto government for the territory before the State of Israel was created. After the State of Israel was recognized, JAFI remained in place to finance and organize mass immigrations and to welcome and initiate settlement of those moving to Israel. Its Board of Governors is equally composed of members of WZO and Diaspora Jews. JAFI's mission is dedicated to rescuing Jewish communities at risk, resettling new immigrants' to Israel, encouraging and assisting those who make *aliyah*, building new settlements, bolstering Israel's economic development, providing local and worldwide Jewish Zionist education, promoting Israeli culture, enhancing Jewish unity and identity, supporting health services in Israel, and strengthening Israel as a home for all Jews. JAFI is as concerned about the well being of American Jews as it is about Israelis since so much of its own and Israel's funding comes from the United States. JAFI remains influential in both effecting Israeli politics and maintaining American-Israeli relationships. Before 1999, JAFI was the major recipient of CJF, UIA, and UJA funds raised or transmitted for Israel. Any exceptions were locally selected programs and organizations in Israel to which a number of local federations had begun to provide direct funding.

UNITED JEWISH APPEAL (UJA). UJA was formed in 1939 in order to unite fundraising efforts with the American Jewish Joint Distribution Committee and the United Palestine Appeal as principal partners and with the National Refugee Service as a beneficiary for efficient fundraising to help European Jews in response to *Kristallnacht*. It was preceded by United Jewish Appeal campaigns in 1934 and 1935 for the American Jewish Joint Distribution Committee and for the Keren Hayesod, and by a similar joint effort in 1930 by the Allied Jewish Campaign. Over the following decades, UJA grew to become the "largest voluntary philanthropy in Jewish history." Part of the impetus for the merger came from CJF, pressuring the organizations to unify their fundraising efforts to reduce the strain on the American Jewish community in deciding which overseas efforts to support.

From the beginning, UJA decided it would implement its campaigns through the local federations. It had a profound impact on how federations raised money. Under the leadership of Rabbi Henry *Montor, American Jews were challenged as never before to give and to increase their contributions in support of the Jewish State. This drive forever changed how federations raised funds. Their combined efforts in overseas and domestic campaigns helped to bring Zionism to the American Jewish community, while at the same time strengthen Jewish communities in America. After World War II, UJA's fundraising assisted in the resettlement of Holocaust survivors – some 370,000 Jews to the United States, Canada, and France – and aided Israel and Jewish communities, worldwide. It grew to provide leadership development, educational programs, twinning of American and Israeli communities, and various missions to Israel (Davis, 1994).

From 1939 through 1966, the United Jewish Appeal distributed $924 million to the United Israel Appeal and to its predecessor United Palestine Appeal, $582 million to the American Jewish Joint Distribution Committee, $55 million to the United Service for New Americans and its predecessor the National Refugee Service, $29 million to the New York Association for New Americans, and $4 million to United HIAS Service. Over 200 Jewish Federations and Welfare Funds, including the New York United Jewish Appeal, provided about 95% of United Jewish Appeal income. The remainder was secured directly by United Jewish Appeal in hundreds of small communities where federated appeals did not exist The chairmen of the United Jewish Appeal included Rabbi Abba Hillel Silver, Rabbi Jonah B. Wise, William Rosenwald, Rabbi James G. Heller, Charles J. Rosenbloom, Henry Morgenthau, Jr., Edward M. Warburg, Morris Berinstein, Philip M. Klutznick, Joseph Meyerhoff, Max Fisher, and Edward Ginsberg. The executive vice chairmen of the United Jewish Appeal included Isidor Coons, Henry Montor, Joseph J. Schwartz, and Rabbi Herbert A. Friedman.

The UJA receives its fund through 229 federation and welfare funds and 665 independent and combined campaigns. It supports the UIA; the JDC; United HIAS Service, which helps Jews settling in countries other than Israel; and the New York Association for New Americans (NYANA), which aids Jewish immigrants settling in the Greater New York area.

BIBLIOGRAPHY: P. Bernstein, *To Dwell in Unity: The Jewish Federation Movement in America Since 1960* (1983); M. Davis (ed.), *UJA Memoirs: Irving Bernstein: An Oral History Anthology* (1994); D.J. Elazar, *Community & Polity: The Organizational Dynamics of American Jewry* (1976, rev. 1995); M. Golensky and G.L. DeRuiter, "The Urge to Merge: A Multiple-Case Study," in: *Nonprofit Management & Leadership*, 13:2 (2002), 169–186; A.J. Karp, *To Give Life: The UJA in the Shaping of the American Jewish Community* (1981); M.L. Raphael, *A History of the United Jewish Appeal 1939–1982* (1982); J.R. Solomon and S.H. Wachsstock, "Reflections on the UJC Merger: Issues Faced and Lessons Learned," in: *Journal of Jewish Communal Service*, 79:1 (2002), 23–27; E. Stock, *Partners and Pursestrings: A History of the United Israel Appeal* (1987).

[Gerald Bubis (2nd ed.)]

UNITED JEWISH SOCIALIST WORKERS' PARTY (SS and JS; abbr.: Fareynigte, i.e., "United"), short-lived group in revolutionary Russia and interwar Poland. It was formed in June 1917 through the union of the *Zionist Socialist Workers' Party (SS, who were *territorialists), and the *Jewish Socialist Workers' Party (JS, who were *autonomists), which revived after the February revolution. The program of the Fareynigte was based on the "unity of the Jewish working class as an organic part of the 'ex-territorial' Jewish nation and the international proletariat." The former divergences of opinion on the realization of territorialism were declared to be lacking in actual significance, and the central element of the party program became "national personal autonomy."

Several leaders of the two parties did not join the Fareynigte: J.W. *Latzky-Bertholdy, N. *Shtif, I. *Yefroykin, and J. Tschernikhov. They became *Folkists. For a brief period, the party became influential, particularly in the Ukraine, where it played an important role in the experiment of national autonomy. Its spokesmen included M. Rashkes, Moses *Katz, the brothers Joseph and Jacob *Lestschinsky, Y. Churgin, M. Gutman, M. *Litvakov, M. *Schatz-Anin, and *Ben-Adir. In September 1917, the party called on the Provisional Government of Russia to declare the equality of languages and to set up a council for national affairs which would represent all nationalities and cover the financial requirements of Jewish schools and social institutions. At the third All-Russian Conference of the Trade Unions (June), the Fareynigte proposed the establishment of "national sections," but only the eventual formation of national "committees" was decided upon. In the *Ukraine, the party joined the Central *Rada* (national council) and the party leader, M. *Silberfarb, held the position of vice secretary (minister) for Jewish affairs in the government (called General Secretariat) from July 1917 to January 1918. After the manifesto ("third *universal*") of the *Rada*, which proclaimed a free Ukraine federally allied to Russia, Silberfarb drafted the law on "national personal autonomy" for the minorities in the Ukraine – the Jews, the Poles, and the Russians – and simultaneously pursued his activities in organizing a system of Jewish institutions. The Fareynigte abstained from voting on the "fourth *universal*" (January 1918), which proclaimed the complete separation of the Ukraine from Russia, but, in practice, the party complied with it. Silberfarb resigned from the government for general reasons as well as because of the anti-Jewish pogroms in the Ukraine. In the elections to the Jewish community councils in the Ukraine, the Fareynigte obtained 8.2% of the votes, as compared with the *Bund (14.4%) and Po'alei Zion (6.3%). In the elections to the Jewish National Assembly of the Ukraine, they obtained 19,689 out of the 209,128 votes. In 1918 the Fareynigte also supported Belorussian statehood federally allied with Russia. The party, on the whole, opposed the seizure of power by the Bolsheviks, and its delegates left the second All-Russian Congress of the Soviets. One of the leaders of the Fareynigte, D. *Lvovich, was elected to the Constituent Assembly on the list of the Socialist Revolutionaries with which the Fareynigte had allied themselves in their political activity.

In independent Ukraine, the Fareynigte at first enthusiastically supported the government (called Directory, in 1918–19) but its tolerant attitude toward the pogroms changed their stand. At the second conference of the party in the Ukraine, a pro-Soviet program was adopted, although it opposed joining the Communists. The pogroms and the stimulus of the revolution in Germany prompted the majority of the party, headed by the leaders (Novakovsky, Levkovsky, and M. Levitan) to establish the United Jewish Communist Party in March 1919. In May 1919, together with the Ukrainian Kombund, it established the Yidisher Komunistisher Farband. In August the Komfarband was included within the Ukrainian Communist Party which began to form branches of the *Yevsektsiya. At the third conference of the branches of the Yevsektsiya (July 1920), the former Fareynigte led the faction which sought a greater measure of autonomy for these "Jewish sections." The first national conference of the Fareynigte decided to adopt a stance of loyalty to the Soviet regime (July 1919). The second national conference of the Fareynigte (Gomel, April–May 1920) adopted a Communist program and, together with the Communist faction of the Bund, they formed the Kombund (June 1920), which in turn decided to join the Communist Party of Russia (March 1921).

In Poland there was no JS movement, but the SS, at their conference in November 1918, changed their name to "United Jewish Socialist Workers' Party (Fareynigte)." The party was short-lived. Some of its members joined the Bund and others the Communists. In summer 1922, the party, led by J. Kruk (d. 1972), joined the Independent Socialist Party (from 1924, "Independent Socialist Labor Party") as a Jewish section. Its program called for "national personal autonomy" for the Jews. Among its proposed activities, the "section" also included "regulation of the emigration of the Jewish working masses." Kruk represented the party on the executive council of the Socialist International. In 1937 it was dissolved by the government. To a limited extent the Fareynigte subsisted within the territorialist movement Freyland (Freeland League). The organs of the Fareynigte included the weekly, *Der Yidisher Proletaryer* (Kiev, 1917); a daily, *Naye Tsayt* (Kiev, 1917–19); the collections *Der Yidisher Proletaryer*, 1–2 (Warsaw, 1918); and *Unzer Vort* (Warsaw, 1920).

BIBLIOGRAPHY: S. Agurski, *Der Yidisher Arbeter in der Kommunistisher Bavegung 1917–1921* (1925); Ch. Shmeruk (ed.), *Pirsumim Yehudiyyim bi-Verit ha-Mo'aẓot 1917–1960* (1961), index; I. Shayn, *Bibliografye fun Oysgabes Aroysgegeben durkh di Arbeter Parteyen in Poylen in di Yorn 1918–1939* (1963), 133–43; I. Gordin, *Yorn Fargangene, Yorn Umfargeslekhe* (1960), 206–35; I. Rubin, *Fundanen Ahin* (1952), 187–208; E. Rosental-Schneiderman, *Naftulei Derakhim* (1970), 124–242; O. Janowsky, *The Jews and Minority Rights* (1933), index; E. Tcherikower, *Yehudim be-Ittot Mahpekhah* (1957), 459–546; M.Astor, *Geshikhte fun der Frayland-Lige un funem teritorialistishn Gedank*, 1–2 (1967).

[Moshe Mishkinsky]

UNITED NATIONS (UN), a worldwide organization of states established in 1945, in the wake of World War II, with a view, primarily, to maintain international peace and security and also bring about cooperation among nations in the economic, social, cultural, and humanitarian spheres.

Most, though not all, countries are members of the UN, which has become the most important international forum for states to exchange views, conduct diplomatic negotiations, and adopt resolutions calling for concerted action by the world community. As a medium of discussion and resolution, the UN has been instrumental in the process leading to the creation of the State of Israel, as well as in the course of Israel's ongoing struggle for survival. It has also been utilized as a forum for debates on a number of issues pertaining to the plight of distressed Jewish communities in the Diaspora, particularly Arab countries and the Soviet Union.

The Partition Resolution (1947)

At the inception of the UN, Palestine was still a *Mandate territory under the administration of the United Kingdom. In Chapter XII of the UN Charter, adopted on June 26, 1945, an international trusteeship system was established applying, inter alia, to territories subject to mandate. The founding conference of the UN, convened in San Francisco in April 1945, had before it a memorandum submitted by the *Jewish Agency for Palestine requesting that the special rights of the Jewish people under the Mandate be secured. It proposed that the Charter include a general stipulation safeguarding rights acquired under existing mandates. Despite Arab objections, a "conservatory clause" was indeed incorporated in Article 80 of the Charter, but it was circumscribed in terms of temporal applicability to the period pending the conclusion of trusteeship agreements. Article 79 made the transformation of a mandate into a trusteeship dependent on the agreement of the mandatory power. With regard to Palestine, the United Kingdom did not choose to follow the procedure envisaged in the Charter. Initially, it insisted on awaiting the report of the Joint Anglo-American Committee of Inquiry appointed to examine the question of Palestine and of European Jewry after the war. On April 2, 1947, when the United Kingdom finally transmitted the Palestine issue to the UN, it went beyond the purview of Chapter XII. Asserting that the Mandate had proved unworkable, the United Kingdom requested that the UN recommend a solution for the settlement of the problem.

A special session of the UN General Assembly, the first of its kind, was summoned in April 1947 and decided, in Resolution 106 (S-l) of May 15, to establish the UN Special Committee on Palestine (UNSCOP), consisting of representatives of 11 states. UNSCOP members visited Palestine, neighboring countries, and camps of *displaced persons in Europe. They heard oral testimonies, received written communications from individuals and organizations, and finally submitted a report to the General Assembly. The UNSCOP report (A/364) unanimously recommended that the Mandate over Palestine be terminated and that Palestine be granted independence as soon as possible, after a brief transition period. The majority of the UNSCOP members proposed the political partition (subject to an economic union) of Palestine into a Jewish state, an Arab state, and a separate City of Jerusalem. A minority of the members urged the formation of a Federal State of Palestine. (See *Palestine, Inquiry Commission). The report was discussed by the General Assembly, at its second regular session, in the Ad Hoc Committee on the Palestine Question, which, after a prolonged debate, endorsed, with modifications, the UNSCOP majority plan. Strong Arab opposition was countered by a unique alliance between the United States and the Soviet Union, supported by many smaller countries. On Nov. 29, 1947, a plenary meeting of the General Assembly adopted the Ad Hoc Committee's report (A/516) containing the scheme of the partition of Palestine, by a vote of 33 in favor, 13 against, and 10 abstentions. This is the famous Partition Resolution N. 181 (II).

The Israel War of Independence

The State of Israel, however, was not "created" by the UN partition resolution. The resolution was only an important link in a chain of events that brought the state into being. Under international law, Israel emerged as an independent state from the throes of its War of Independence, when it proved its viability as a legal unit by meeting the four cumulative conditions: nation, territory, government, and independence. The partition resolution was hardly a matter of record when the Arab leadership in Palestine resolved to oppose it by force. Confronted with a challenge to its moral authority, the UN convened a second special session of the General Assembly early in 1948. Some delegates felt that the partition plan could no longer be implemented and that a new approach to the Palestine problem should be sought. The United States put forward a proposal (A/C. 1/277) for the establishment of a "temporary" trusteeship for Palestine, thereby discarding, in effect, the partition scheme. Initially, the new idea gained ground – against Jewish protests – and a special subcommittee (No. 9) was designated to formulate the necessary details. Still, when the establishment of the State of Israel was proclaimed in Tel Aviv on May 14, 1948, the United States granted it immediate de facto recognition, and the trusteeship project was abandoned.

The partition resolution constituted a Palestine Commission to supervise its implementation under the guidance of the Security Council. The commission indeed submitted several reports to the Security Council, but on May 14, 1948, it was relieved of its responsibilities by the General Assembly in Resolution 186 (S-2). Instead, the General Assembly created the post of a UN mediator on Palestine, to which Count Folke *Bernadotte of Sweden was appointed on May 20.

The Partition Resolution requested the Security Council to take required action for its implementation, including enforcement measures within the scope of Chapter VII of the Charter. It was the consideration of the Palestine Commission's reports, however, that generated the constantly increasing involvement of the Security Council with the Palestine question. At the outset, the council proceeded cautiously and on March 5, 1948, merely made a general appeal to all concerned to prevent or reduce disorders in Palestine (S/691). By April 17, however, it had already adopted a detailed truce resolution (S/723), and on April 23 it established a Truce Commission for Palestine (S/727). Following the armed attack by a number of Arab states against Israel on May 15, the Security Council resumed debate. A call for a cease-fire, within 36 hours, was issued only on May 22 (S/773). After the 36 hours had passed and the Arab governments still refused to stop fighting, the council continued the discussion for several more days. It was not until May 29 that it finally adopted a strong resolution (S/801) calling for a four-week cease-fire by June 1, instructing the mediator on Palestine and the Truce Commission to supervise its observance, and, for the first time, referring to Chapter VII of the Charter, implicitly threatening sanctions.

The June 1 deadline was also ignored by the Arab states, which insisted that Jewish immigration to Israel halt during the course of the cease-fire. After lengthy negotiations through the mediator, however, cessation of hostilities, commonly known as the "first truce," was accepted as of June 11. When the four-week duration of the truce drew to a close, on July 7, the Security Council addressed an appeal to the parties to accept its prolongation (S/867). As in previous cases, Israel agreed but the Arabs did not, and hostilities were renewed. On July 15 the council passed its most vigorous resolution on the war (S/902), wherein it took into account Arab rejection of appeals for the continuation of the truce; determined that the situation constituted a threat to the peace within the meaning of Chapter VII; declared that failure to comply with the resolution would demonstrate the existence of a breach of the peace entailing action under that chapter and ordered a cease-fire "until a peaceful adjustment of the future situation of Palestine is reached." The renewed cease-fire, commonly known as the "second truce," took effect on July 18.

The second truce was frequently violated, and the poignant phrasing of the resolution of July 16 had only an initial impact on the antagonists. On August 19, the Security Council passed another resolution (S/983), which is of particular interest as a precursor of things to come. It was stated that each party "is responsible for the actions of both regular and irregular forces operating under its authority or in territory under its control" and that violations of the truce on the ground of "reprisals or retaliation" were impermissible. The observance of the cease-fire was supervised by the mediator, who simultaneously attempted to propose a solution of his own to the Palestine question. On September 16 Bernadotte presented a progress report (A/648), in which he recommended a number of crucial changes in the partition plan, e.g., that the Israel Negev "should be defined as Arab territory." The following day Bernadotte was assassinated by unknown terrorists in the Israel sector of Jerusalem. (Israel paid reparations to the UN, according to a ruling of the International Court of Justice in 1949 that the UN had the "capacity to maintain its rights by bringing international claims.") Ralph Bunche, a member of the UN Secretariat, was appointed acting mediator.

In October, when heavy fighting again broke out between Israel and Egypt, the Security Council adopted a resolution (S/1044; October 19) calling for restoration of the cease-fire and suggesting withdrawal of forces, as well as negotiations between the parties either directly or through the UN. The unheeded call was reiterated by the council on November 4 (S/1070), November 16 (S/1080), and December 29 (S/1169). Negotiations between Israel and Egypt, under the chairmanship of the acting mediator, opened at Rhodes in January 1949. An *Armistice Agreement was signed on February 24, followed by a series of similar agreements between Israel and Lebanon (signed March 22), Jordan (signed April 3), and Syria (signed July 20). All the Armistice Agreements were concluded without prejudice to territorial rights, and it was specifically stated that the armistice demarcation lines were not to be construed as political boundaries. The agreements established certain demilitarized zones and set up Mixed Armistice Commissions (MACS) to supervise the implementation of the truce. The chairman of each MAC was the chief of staff of the UN Truce Supervision Organization (UNTSO).

In its role in the course of the Israel War of Independence the UN, for the first time, faced a clear-cut case of a concerted armed attack, in flagrant contravention of the Charter, but ultimately failed to discharge its peace-keeping responsibility. The collective security system structured in San Francisco remained practically a dead letter, and it was left to the State of Israel to defend itself as best it could. In the Security Council, protracted discussions replaced action, and as the number of resolutions increased, the specific weight of each decreased. When agreement was finally reached between Israel and the Arab states, it was almost entirely due to Arab defeat on the battlefield and to negotiations between the parties.

Israel Membership

Israel applied for admission to membership in the UN in November 1948 (S/1093). Under Article 4 of the Charter, such admission is effected by a decision of the General Assembly upon the recommendation of the Security Council, but the latter did not initially endorse Israel's application. In February 1949, however, when Israel requested renewed consideration of the matter (S/1267), recommendation was granted by the council (A/818). The General Assembly considered the issue at great length and finally accepted Israel to the fold, in Resolution 273 (III), on May 11, 1949.

Israel soon perceived that as a result of the bloc system permeating every facet of life in the UN, it could scarcely take a major part in the institution's affairs. Being beyond the pale of all blocs, in its decades of membership Israel failed to get elected even once to any of the UN councils: the Security Council, the Trusteeship Council, or the Economic and Social Council. The most important elective office that Israel ever held in the UN framework was the vice presidency of the General Assembly during the eighth session in 1953 (the position was held by Abba *Eban). Resolutions sponsored by Israel were practically doomed to failure, and even cosponsorship was not sought by other states, since Arab opposition would ensue almost automatically. Israel did extend aid to developing countries through the UN and did receive technical assistance from the organization, although regional cooperation with the Arabs proved impossible.

In the beginning, Israel enjoyed at least a relative degree of support on the part of both the United States and the U.S.S.R. In a short while, however, the U.S.S.R., trying to gain a foothold in the Middle East, began to support the Arab cause, putting its veto power in the Security Council and its significant bargaining position in every UN organ at the Arabs' disposal. According to Soviet policy, as of the mid-1950s, the Arabs could do no wrong against Israel and Israel could almost never do right. Not one single pro-Israel resolution was passed by the Security Council subsequent to 1951. Although Israel made impressive efforts to win friends and influence new states and was consequently able to thwart many pro-Arab resolutions aimed at undermining its political independence and stifling its economic development, the atmosphere in the UN became increasingly hostile to her, and, particularly after the *Six-Day War (1967), Israel found itself frequently isolated and even ostracized.

Israel's political insulation in the UN had its psychological impact on many of the organization's officials (especially within UNTSO), some of whom flaunted their partiality to the Arab cause in a variety of ways. As a result, Jewish public opinion, which in 1947 deeply believed the UN to be an objective moral arbiter in international affairs, became disenchanted in the 1950s and defiant by the late 1960s.

Jerusalem

The partition resolution prescribed a special international regime for the city of Jerusalem as a *corpus separatum*, to be administered by the UN through the Trusteeship Council. Thus in December 1947, the Trusteeship Council appointed a working committee on Jerusalem to elaborate a statute for the city. The committee formulated a draft, which the council discussed and modified, but had not completed by the end of April 1948. During the War of Independence, many UN debates revolved around the fate of Jerusalem and the need to protect the holy places. At the second special session of the General Assembly (April and May 1948), a special subcommittee (No. 10) was established to consider the question of Jerusalem. A resolution dealing with the temporary administration of the city was adopted by the subcommittee, but failed to be carried by the General Assembly. Specific clauses relating to the protection of Jerusalem were incorporated in the Security Council's cease-fire resolutions of May 29 (S/801) and July 15 (S/902) 1948. General Assembly Resolution 194 (III) of Dec. 11, 1948, declared that "in view of its association with three world religions," Jerusalem should be placed under an international regime. Israel and Jordan, however, were equally opposed to the *corpus separatum* concept. Since the city was in effect divided between them by the War of Independence, the Armistice Agreement stabilized the situation along the lines of the status quo.

In 1949 the fourth session of the General Assembly adopted Resolution 303 (IV), which restated the case for an international regime in Jerusalem, and in 1950 the Trusteeship Council resumed its work on the statute for the city and approved a new text (A/1286). Nonetheless, Jordan and Israel's united opposition to the internationalization scheme was so strenuous, and the actual state of affairs so removed from the atmosphere prevailing in the UN, that the efforts toward internationalization began to flag. A proposal to initiate further study on the subject by the Trusteeship Council was introduced at the fifth session of the General Assembly, and approved by the Ad Hoc Political Committee (A/1724), but did not obtain the required two-thirds majority in plenary. A Philippine amendment endorsing "the principle of the internationalization of Jerusalem" (A/L. 134) was submitted in plenary at the seventh session of the General Assembly in 1952, but once more fell short of the necessary majority. During the next 15 years, the issue of Jerusalem remained dormant in the General Assembly.

In the Security Council questions pertaining to violations of the Armistice Agreement in Jerusalem engendered several debates over the years. As early as 1950 Israel complained about Jordan's noncompliance with Article VIII of the agreement, which had accorded to Israel rights of access to holy places, normal functioning of the institutions on Mount Scopus (the Hebrew University and the Hadassah Hospital), and free movement of traffic on vital roads. The Security Council, however, adopted only a noncommittal resolution (S/1899), and the article was never implemented by Jordan. Israel renewed the complaint in 1957 (S/3883), but to no avail. The UN did help in supervising the observance of a special agreement for the demilitarization of Mount Scopus, concluded between Israel and Jordan on July 7, 1948. The agreement provided for supplies to be brought to Mount Scopus by special convoys, and occasionally Jordan suspended the line of communication. Late in 1957 Secretary-General Dag Hammerskjöld paid a special visit to the Middle East and in 1958 appointed a number of personal representatives to conduct negotiations between the parties with a view to the full implementation of the 1948 agreement.

In 1957 Jordan brought the issue of Israeli activities in the zone between the demarcation lines in Jerusalem before the Security Council, which called for their suspension (S/3942). In 1961 Jordan complained that Israel planned to hold a military parade in Jerusalem on Independence Day despite the prohibition against heavy armaments in the city under the Armistice Agreement. Israel pointed out that the equipment was brought into Jerusalem for ceremonial purposes only and that military parades had been conducted in the city earlier by both sides. The Security Council refused to accept Israel's explanation and urged it to comply with a MAC decision upholding Jordan's position (S/4788). The question of an Independence Day military parade was again raised in the Security Council in April 1968 (after the reunification of the city). In Resolution 250 (1968) the council called upon Israel to refrain from proceeding with the parade. When Israel ignored the call, and held the event, the Security Council adopted another resolution (No. 251; 1968) deeply deploring that action.

The reunification of Jerusalem after the Six-Day War revived UN interest in establishing an international regime in the city. The idea was espoused in a Latin American draft resolution submitted in June 1967 to the fifth emergency special session of the General Assembly (A/L. 523), but it was not adopted, having failed to gain the necessary two-thirds majority. On July 4, the General Assembly nevertheless, approved a Muslim-sponsored resolution, No. 2253 (ES-V), calling upon Israel to rescind and desist from any measures to alter the status of Jerusalem and considering such steps invalid. Israel did not participate in the vote and ignored the call. On July 14, the General Assembly voted in favor of a second resolution, No. 2254 (ES-V), deploring Israel's noncompliance and reiterating the demand. In May 1968 the Security Council adopted a resolution of its own (No. 252; 1968) in the same vein and in July 1969 it approved resolution 267 (1969), which censured "in the strongest terms" the measures taken by Israel. In September of that year, after the arson committed at the Al Aqṣā Mosque, the Security Council adopted resolution 271 (1969), condemning Israel for its failure to carry out any of the previous pronouncements. In the midst of the spate of resolutions, the secretary-general sent Ernesto A. Thalman of Switzerland to Jerusalem in August 1967 as his personal representative. Thalman's report (S/8146) tried to reflect impartially the conflicting viewpoints about a complicated matter, but it was swept aside by the descent of one-sided attacks against Israel. Israel's stand was that Christianity and Islam, like Judaism, have legitimate claims to their holy places in Jerusalem, and the concern of the UN, representing the world community, with the fate of the city is understandable. Yet the UN kept silent for 15 years, when Jordan totally disregarded the rights guaranteed Israel by the Armistice Agreements, and the general desecration of Jewish holy places by Jordan's army and population occurred. It can, therefore, hardly expect Israel automatically to submit to its sudden concern for law and order in Jerusalem when the city became reunited under Israel jurisdiction, particularly in view of the fact that since the reunification, Muslim and Christian religious rights have been scrupulously observed, and Israel has often voiced its readiness to guarantee these rights by special legal arrangements.

The Arab Refugees

The problem of the Arab refugees (see State of *Israel, Arab Refugees) was spawned by the War of Independence and augmented by a myopic and self-deluding approach to the subject by Arab governments. The General Assembly, in the pace-setting paragraph 11 of Resolution 194 (III), dated December 11, 1948, proclaimed that "the refugees wishing to return to their homes and live at peace with their neighbors should be permitted to do so at the earliest practicable date, and that compensation should be paid for the property of those choosing not to return." The Palestine Conciliation Commission (PCC), established by the same resolution, was instructed to facilitate repatriation, resettlement, rehabilitation, and compensation.

Israel, having admitted back tens of thousands of Arab refugees on the basis of a reunion of families project and having agreed in principle to the admission of others (sometimes the figure of 100,000 was used), always emphasized that, on the whole, the solution to the problem lay in resettlement rather than repatriation. Israel pointed out that the Arab refugees, far from willing "to live at peace with their [Jewish] neighbors," have been subjected to a continuous propaganda campaign, beginning in primary schools, based on hatred for Israel, and have always been regarded by the Arab states as a means to bring about the disintegration of Israel from within. In addition, it raised the issue of Jewish refugees, from Palestine as well as from Arab countries, which also emanated from the War of Independence. Israel always expressed its readiness to contribute to the payment of compensation for Arab property abandoned in Israel, though it has also drawn attention to the seizure of Jewish property in Iraq and elsewhere in the Arab world and indicated that a balancing off is in order. As a gesture of good will, it agreed to release frozen accounts of Arab refugees. At times Israel insisted on dealing with the problem of the Arab refugees only as part and parcel of a comprehensive settlement with the Arab states, but on other occasions it agreed that solution was not contingent on an overall reconciliation. The Arab states, on the other hand, consistently repeated that repatriation of the refugees, as distinct from resettlement, is their only goal, and, as of 1948, they turned this essentially humanitarian issue into their main political weapon against Israel. Since then not a single year passed without an acrimonious debate on the subject in the UN.

In the beginning, hectic negotiations relating to the Arab refugees were held between Israel and the Arab states under the auspices of the PCC. In 1949 the latter set in motion an Economic Survey Mission for the Middle East, headed by Gordon R. Clapp of the United States, which suggested that the immediate constructive step was to give the refugees an opportunity to work in their new locations (A/AC. 25/6). The Arabs rejected the idea, and for a long time the PCC was inactive. Then, at its 15th session in 1961, the General Assembly requested the PCC (in resolution 1604 (XV)) to renew efforts to secure the implementation of paragraph 11 of resolution 194 (III). Accordingly, the PCC appointed Joseph E. Johnson of the U.S. its special representative and sent him to the Middle East. The mission, however, did not bear fruit, and Johnson resigned in 1963. For many years the PCC, through its Technical Office, conducted a program of identification and assessment of individual parcels of immovable refugee property left in Israel. It was hoped that, once concluded, the project could serve as a basis for the initiation of a compensation scheme; however, inasmuch as the Arabs were interested in repatriation only, the endeavor faded out.

In resolution 212 (III) of 1948 the third session of the General Assembly decided to appoint a director of UN relief for Palestine refugees. In 1949 the assembly's fourth session established the UN Relief and Works Agency for Palestine Refugees in the Near East (UNRWA) in Resolution 302 (IV). The term "Palestine refugees," used in the definition of UNRWA's mandate, covered not only Arabs but also Jews displaced as a result of the War of Independence, and originally UNRWA dealt also with thousands of cases of Palestine Jewish refugees. These, however, were quickly absorbed in the economic life of Israel and needed no further assistance from the UN. The problem of the Palestine Arab refugees, on the other hand, kept inflating, with children and grandchildren of 1948 refugees, born and reared outside Israel, automatically joining the lists.

The Arab refugee problem did not expand as a result of the Sinai Campaign of 1956, but the Six-Day War of 1967 caused many Arabs – some of them already refugees, others displaced for the first time – to leave the territories coming under Israel control. Israel permitted many thousands of them to return, and some of them, but not all, availed themselves of the opportunity. At its 23rd session (in 1968), the General Assembly adopted resolution 2452 A (XXIII), which called upon Israel to take effective steps for the immediate return of those inhabitants who had fled the occupied areas since the outbreak of hostilities. This call was renewed at the 25th session in 1970 in resolution 2672 (XXV).

Perhaps the greatest impact of the Six-Day War on the Arab refugee problem is reflected in the fact that most of the refugees (in the Gaza Strip and the West Bank) found themselves under Israeli administration for an indefinite period of time. Instead of returning to their old homes in Israel, Israeli control reached their new ones. At long last Israel was given a chance to prove in practice that resettlement, rehabilitation, and compensation were a valid alternative to repatriation. Due to the more urgent requisites of the "war after the war," however, Israel has not of yet found its way to exploit the unique opportunity.

In the 1960s the Arabs endeavored to have the General Assembly pass a resolution safeguarding the property rights of the Arab refugees, as well as appointing a custodian to administer and protect them. Draft resolutions along these lines were submitted to the Special Political Committee but were not pressed to a vote (A/SPC/L.90 at the 17th session in 1962; A/SPC/L.99 at the 18th session in 1963) or were rejected by the committee (A/SPC/L.116 at the 20th session in 1965; A/SPC/L.128 at the 21st session in 1966; A/SPC/L.168 at the 23rd session in 1968). On other occasions the drafts were approved by the committee but not put to a vote in plenary (A/SPC/L.157 at the 22nd session in 1967) or failed to receive the necessary two-thirds majority in the final vote (A/SPC/L.61 at the 15th session in 1961; A/SPC/L.81 at the 16th session in the same year).

All these drafts, designed implicitly to undermine the sovereignty of Israel, proved abortive. At the 24th session of the General Assembly in 1969, however, an explicit resolution (No. 2535 (XXIV)) reaffirming "the inalienable rights of the people of Palestine" and requesting the Security Council to take effective measures against Israel, was accepted. At the

25th session, in 1970, two resolutions (2672 (XXV) and 2628 (XXV)) were adopted, declaring that respect for the rights of the people of Palestine was indispensable for the establishment of a just and lasting peace in the Middle East. Still another resolution carried in the same session (2649 (XXV)) condemned unnamed governments for denying the rights of self-determination of peoples, including, *expressis verbis*, the people of Palestine. Resolution 2535 (XXIV) thus created a new trend, which probably reflects Israel's greatest defeat at the UN in more than two decades. The problem of the Arab refugees was transformed into the problem of the so-called people of (the no longer existent) Palestine. Resolution 2535 (XXIV) and its sequels are the antithesis of Resolution 181 (II).

Direct Negotiations

Israel always insisted on direct negotiations with the Arab governments as the only way of arriving at a peaceful settlement of the conflict. The Armistice Agreements were in effect an outcome of such negotiations, albeit under UN auspices. In 1950 Israel submitted to the Ad Hoc Political Committee of the General Assembly, at its fifth session, a draft resolution (A/AC.38/L.60) urging direct negotiations upon the parties concerned. The draft was withdrawn prior to a vote, but the resolution finally adopted (No. 394 (V)) did call upon the parties to seek agreement by negotiations conducted either through the PCC "or directly." At the seventh session of the General Assembly, in 1952, the Ad Hoc Political Committee endorsed a resolution (A/AC.61/L.23/Rev.4) urging the parties "to enter at an early date, without prejudice to their respective rights and claims, into direct negotiations," but the required two-thirds majority was not obtained in plenary. At the 16th session of the General Assembly, in 1961, Israel canvassed sponsors for a draft resolution appealing for direct negotiations and managed to get 16 states, most of them from Africa and Latin America, to submit the resolution to the Special Political Committee (A/SPC/L.80). Although the resolution failed in the vote, the initiative was renewed with 21 sponsors at the 17th session, in 1962 (A/SPC/L.89), 19 sponsors at the 18th session, in 1963 (A/SPC/L.100), and the sole sponsorship of Israel at the 20th session, in 1965 (A/SPC/L.115), but another confrontation on the floor of the committee was avoided. Following the Six-Day War, Israel revived the demand for direct negotiations, but in 1967, when the secretary-general appointed (in keeping with the instructions of Security Council Resolution 242 (1967)) Gunnar V. Jarring of Sweden as his special representative to the Middle East, Israel was willing to cooperate. Jarring traveled extensively on several missions to the capitals of Israel and her neighbors, and submitted a number of reports, but at first he could not bring the Arabs to accept anything remotely like negotiations on a peace settlement with Israel, while Israel, in spite of its adherence to the principle of direct negotiations was ready to agree to an initial stage of indirect talks under Jarring's auspices. However, in March 1971, after Nasser's death and the secession of the right-wing Gaḥal from the Israeli government, a certain change seemed to occur in the attitude of both Cairo and Jerusalem. To a questionnaire of Jarring Cairo in principle agreed to sign a peace settlement with Israel, but demanded complete withdrawal of Israel forces from all territories occupied in the Six-Day War, according to the Arab-Soviet interpretation of the Security Council resolution of Nov. 22, 1967. Israel for its part responded to Jarring's questionnaire by reiterating its readiness to negotiate with Egypt on all outstanding issues "without any preliminary conditions," but refused to answer in the affirmative Jarring's question, whether, in exchange for a signed peace settlement and agreed security arrangements in Sharm el-Sheikh, Israel would evacuate all Egyptian territory and withdraw its forces to the previous international boundary between Egypt and Palestine (which excludes the Gaza strip from Egyptian territory). Israel stressed that the withdrawal should be effected to "secure and recognized" frontiers, not identical with any previous line of demarcation, to be agreed upon between the parties in unconditional negotiations. Egypt regarded this response as a "total rejection" of its "peace offer."

Armistice: The First Phase

The PCC entered upon its task of looking for ways and means of reconciling Israel and the Arab states with a great deal of zeal. Its essay culminated in a conference convoked at Lausanne on May 12, 1949, when a rather ambiguous protocol (A/927) was signed separately by the parties. In 1951, at another conference convened in Paris, the PCC suggested that a declaration of pacific intentions be accepted. Israel agreed in principle, but the Arabs refused, and when further attempts to bring the adversaries together failed, the PCC reached the conclusion that it was unable to discharge its duties (A/1985). Nevertheless, the sixth session of the General Assembly 1952 decided (in Resolution 512 (VI)) to keep the PCC alive. Similar resolutions were passed in later years, but to all intents and purposes the PCC ceased to be a factor in the political picture of the Middle East.

Once the armistice agreements were signed, in 1949, the Security Council relieved the acting mediator of his assignment, and the supervision of the truce was entrusted to UNTSO (1/1376). UNTSO and the MACs, however, could not maintain the armistice, mainly because their senior officers often tried to appear scrupulously "neutral" by "balancing" the number of infringements from the both sides against each other or, in some cases, showed pro-Arab bias and declared Israel's retaliatory self-defense measures as aggressive acts, while ignoring infiltrations of saboteurs and terrorists which provoked them. Thus, many meetings of the Security Council were monopolized by the Middle East question. In 1950 Israel complained to the council about Egypt's interference with passage of goods destined for Israel through the Suez Canal. On Sept. 1, 1951, the Security Council resolved that such practice was illegal and called upon Egypt to terminate the restrictions imposed on Israel-bound shipping (S/2322). This is perhaps the only unequivocally pro-Israel resolution to have emerged from that body. When Egypt refused to conform and even extended its interference beyond the canal to the Gulf of Akaba, Israel renewed its complaint to the Security Council in January 1954. A New Zealand draft resolution (S/3188), noting "with grave concern" Egypt's noncompliance and calling for the implementation of the 1951 resolution, foundered on a Soviet veto in March. In September 1954, when the Israel vessel *Bat Gallim* was seized by Egypt at the entrance to the Suez Canal, Israel again complained to the Security Council, which was still unable to surmount the obstacle of the veto. On Oct. 13, 1956, after Egypt nationalized the Suez Canal Company, the Security Council adopted a resolution (S/3675) stating that any settlement of the Suez question should meet six "requirements," including "free and open transit through the Canal without discrimination, overt or covert." These requirements were accepted by Egypt, but access to the Suez Canal nonetheless continued to be denied to Israel and Israel-bound shipping until the canal's closure during and after the Six-Day War.

In the early 1950s a pattern began to be formed in the Security Council. Backed by the U.S.S.R., the Arabs seized the initiative and started to submit a spate of complaints about violations and alleged violations of the armistice by Israel. Israel also turned to the council occasionally, but was generally rebuffed. Many of the disputes before the Security Council related to the demilitarized zones, which thus became a source of friction, instead of fulfilling their intended role as a buffer. In 1951 fighting erupted between Syria and Israel concomitant to the drainage of the Ḥuleh marshes. The matter was brought before the Security Council, which first issued a directive of cease-fire (S/2130) and then, in effect, called upon Israel to desist from all operations in the demilitarized zone (S/2157). In 1953, when Israel began to construct a Jordan River canal as part of a hydroelectric project, the Security Council quickly called for the temporary suspension of operations in the demilitarized zone (S/3128). The suspension became indefinite as a Western draft resolution (S/3151/Rev.2), containing a compromise formula, encountered a Soviet veto in 1954.

In 1953, after an Israel retaliatory raid on the Arab village of Qibya, as a reprisal for terrorist attacks on Israel territory emanating from there, the Security Council expressed "the strongest censure" of Israel's action (S/3139/Rev. 2). This was the first among many resolutions in which the council tried to curb Israel reprisals without dealing explicitly with the terrorist Arab attacks that had motivated them. Israel reprisals were again condemned by the council in 1955, subsequent to the Gaza raid (S/3378), and in January 1956, following reprisal on terrorist bases east of Lake Kinneret (S/3538). By 1956 it became clear that the armistice structure was crumbling. In March of that year, at the request of the United States, the Security Council took up the general issue of compliance with the Armistice Agreements and its own resolutions. In April it requested the secretary-general to arrange with the parties for the adoption of certain measures designed to reduce the tension (S/3562). Dag Hammarskjöld visited the Middle East and submitted a progress report (S/3594). In June the council called for reestablishment of full compliance with the Armistice Agreements, and requested the secretary-general to continue his good offices (S/3605). Hammarskjöld returned to the region in July and transmitted to the council two more reports (S/3632 and S/3659). Conditions continued to deteriorate, however, and murderous fedayeen raids into Israeli territory increased, mainly from the Gaza Strip and Sinai, which in turn provoked Israeli retaliation. On Oct. 29, 1956, the *Sinai Campaign began, and Israel announced that the Armistice Agreement with Egypt was no longer valid.

The early 1950s thus represented a constant deterioration of the conditions on the Israel-Arab armistice lines and proved the inadequacy of the UN as a peace and law-enforcing agency. Not once did a Security Council resolution refer specifically to the operations of the fedayeen. Hardly any distinction was made between aggressor and victim. In fact, judging by the peculiar attitude of the UN members, who treated measures which Israel regarded as self-defense as more criminal than the aggression which provoked them, it would appear that it was Israel who continuously motivated trouble in the Middle East and endangered world peace.

The Sinai Campaign

The UN, which was slow to react in 1948 to the War of Independence, showed remarkable alacrity when the Sinai Campaign and the Anglo-French Suez War began. This time the two superpowers, the United States and the U.S.S.R., acted initially in full harmony. By Oct. 30, 1956, the Security Council was already in session. The same evening a vote was taken on a U.S.-sponsored draft resolution (S/3710) calling for immediate withdrawal of Israeli troops and urging other states not to assist Israel. The resolution was vetoed by France and the United Kingdom, but an emergency special session of the General Assembly was convened forthwith. On November 1 the General Assembly met and the following day in Resolution 997 (ES-I) it appealed for an immediate cease-fire and prompt withdrawal of forces. Another resolution (No. 998 (ES-I)), restating the case more strongly, was approved on November 4. Still another resolution (1002 ES-I), again urging immediate withdrawal of Israel troops, was taken on November 7.

New ground was broken at the emergency special session with the adoption of Resolution 998 (ES-I), originally introduced by Canada, on November 4. It requested the secretary-general to present a plan for the creation of a UN emergency force, and he quickly responded to the idea. The UN Emergency Force (UNEF) was established on November 5 by Resolution 1000 (ES-I). Its purpose was "to secure and supervise the cessation of hostilities." Resolution 1001 (ES-I), dated November 7, approved guidelines proposed by the secretary-general for the functioning of UNEF. The formation of UNEF was carried out against strong protests from the U.S.S.R., which adhered to the view that only the Security Council, as distinct from the General Assembly, was empowered to take such action. The U.S.S.R., as well as several other countries, refused to participate in covering UNEF's expenses, and in time this refusal precipitated a financial and political crisis for the UN. (The question was eventually brought before the International Court of Justice, which, in 1962, in the matter of *Certain Expenses of the United Nations* (Article 17, paragraph 2 of the Charter), gave an advisory opinion to the effect that these were "expenses of the organization" within the meaning of Article 17 of the Charter.)

The 11th regular session of the General Assembly continued the deliberations begun in the first emergency special session. On November 24, in Resolution 1120 (XI), it noted "with regret" that no withdrawal of Israeli, French, or British troops had been effected and reiterated its call to comply with former resolution on the subject. In Resolution 1121 (XI), adopted the same day, it noted the "basis for the presence and functioning" of UNEF in Egypt, in line with points made by the secretary-general in an *aide-mémoire* (A/3375). The *aide-mémoire*, based on the secretary-general's conversations in Cairo, contained a clear Egyptian undertaking to be guided by Resolution 1000 (ES-I) and enable UNEF to operate until its task had been completed. The first UNEF contingents arrived in the Middle East within a matter of days.

Throughout this period Israel was subjected to intense pressure by the United States and the secretary-general (in person) to commence withdrawal. Dag Hammarskjöld was a strong and active secretary-general who interpreted his authority in a way that permitted him to play a direct and major role in the affairs of the Middle East. Gradual withdrawal of Israeli troops started late in November, but Israel and the secretary-general were in constant disagreement over the schedule of the evacuation of Sinai and the Gaza Strip. On Jan. 19, 1957, pursuant to a report by the secretary-general, the General Assembly in Resolution 1123 (XI), noted "with regret and concern" that withdrawal had not yet been completed, and lent its support to the secretary-general's uncompromising stand. Israel then put forward an *aide-mémoire* (A/3511) indicating that withdrawal from *Sharm el-Sheikh must be accompanied by related measures ensuring free navigation in the Straits of Tiran and the Gulf of Akaba. Furthermore, Israel propounded that certain steps be taken to ascertain that the Gaza Strip would not again be used as a springboard for attack and raised practical questions pertaining to the conditions for the termination of UNEF's functions.

The secretary-general continued to insist on total and immediate withdrawal (A/3512). Debate in the General Assembly resumed, and on February 2, in Resolution 1124 (XI), the assembly deplored Israel's noncompliance with former resolutions and urged the completion of withdrawal without delay. In a complementary resolution (No. 1125 (XI)), adopted on the same day, the General Assembly also called for the scrupulous observance of the Armistice Agreement. Israel then had a new round of exchanges with the secretary-general (A/3527 and A/3563), and on March 1 Israel announced that it was prepared to proceed with full withdrawal on the basis of certain "assumptions," founded in part on statements made by the U.S. government. Withdrawal followed suit. During the Sinai Campaign and immediately thereafter, the UN suddenly reawakened as a peace-keeping organization. Its energetic pursuit of the goal of cease-fire and withdrawal had no precedent in the Middle East conflict. The same UN members, who remained aloof during weeks of bloodshed in 1948 and who totally ignored the activities of the fedayeen in subsequent years became agitated when the pace of Israel's withdrawal from Sinai was not rapid enough, and, under pressure from the UN and the United States, Israel complied.

Armistice: The Second Phase

The presence of UNEF contributed to the relative stability that characterized the southern border of Israel in the decade following the Sinai Campaign, but the attention of the Security Council was frequently drawn in the same period to clashes between Israel and Syria (which, for a while, formed part of the United Arab Republic). Most of the disputes again involved the demilitarized zones.

In 1958 and 1959 the Security Council convened to discuss complaints by Israel against Syrian violations of the armistice (S/4123 and S/4151), but no resolution could be reached because of Soviet intransigence. Conversely, in 1962, when Israel again retaliated against Syria in the Lake Kinneret area, the council adopted a resolution (S/5111) reaffirming the January 1956 condemnation of Israel (S/3538) and determining that the recent reprisal constituted a "flagrant violation" of that decision. In 1963, after terrorist bloodshed at Almagor, a Western draft resolution condemning the "wanton murder" of Israeli citizens (S/5407) was once again vetoed by the U.S.S.R. In 1964, when fighting erupted around Tel Dan, the Security Council rejected an Arab-sponsored draft resolution condemning Israel (S/6085), whereupon the Soviets cast their veto on a Western text which deplored the renewal of military action on both sides (S/6113). In July 1966, following a flare-up of fighting as a result of Syrian support of terrorist activities and attempts to divert the source of the Jordan River, another Arab-sponsored draft resolution condemning Israel (S/7437) was rejected by the Security Council. In October of that year Israel complained about the Syrian-backed terrorist attacks. A Western resolution calling upon Syria to prevent the use of its territory by the terrorists (S/7568) was not even put to a vote. A weaker and broader draft (S/7575) was vetoed by the U.S.S.R. In November 1966, subsequent to the Israeli reprisal action in the village al-Samʿu, in Jordan territory, the Security Council approved resolution No. 228 (1966), which, for the first time, "censured" Israel for its action and emphasized that such retaliation "cannot be tolerated" and may entail "further and more effective steps."

The decade of relative quiet between Israel and Egypt came to an abrupt end in May 1967. On May 16 Egypt demanded the withdrawal of UNEF from observation posts along the border. By May 18 Egypt insisted on the total evacuation of UNEF from Sinai and the Gaza Strip. Secretary-General U Thant immediately conceded that UNEF could remain in Egypt only as long as that country consented to its presence. On the same day he issued instructions to UNEF to withdraw and merely reported his decision to the General Assembly (A/6669), without requesting permission from the General Assembly or the Security Council; without consideration for Israel's views; and without serious study of the legal rights of Egypt unilaterally to terminate the presence of UNEF (in the light of the agreement reached in 1956 in Cairo with Secretary-General Hammarskjöld (A/3375) and endorsed by General Assembly Resolution 1121 (XI)). UNEF was ousted at the moment when its presence was most needed. On May 19, after issuing the withdrawal instructions, the secretary-general submitted a further report to the Security Council (S/7896) and left for consultations in Cairo. On May 23, while U Thant was in Egypt, Canada and Denmark requested an urgent meeting of the Security Council to examine the deteriorating situation. In the ensuing debates, held on May 24, the council proved its complete ineffectiveness as a peace-keeping organ, particularly when the U.S.S.R. and other pro-Arab states regarded the situation as favorable to Arab aggression against Israel. The representatives of the U.S.S.R. and Bulgaria claimed that events in the Middle East were over-dramatized and that there was no reason for an urgent meeting of the council in the first place. Other representatives, from Asia and Africa, also contended that the discussion was untimely. A draft resolution, submitted by Canada and Denmark (S/7905), merely requesting all member states to refrain from steps which might worsen the situation, was not even put to a vote. On May 26 the secretary-general returned from Cairo and issued a new report (S/7906). On May 29 the Security Council reconvened, and ineffective discussions continued, until the canons began thundering in the Middle East.

The Six-Day War and After

The Security Council met in emergency session on June 5, nearly as soon as the news of the outbreak of fighting reached New York. The United States was immediately willing to adopt a resolution calling for the cessation of hostilities, but, inasmuch as it was not yet clear which side had the upper hand in battle, the U.S.S.R. preferred to await developments. Only on June 6, when the Egyptian military debacle became obvious, was the Security Council in a position to adopt resolution 233 (1967), calling for an immediate cease-fire. On June 7 a second resolution, No. 234 (1967), urging the cessation of all military activities (particularly between Israel and Jordan) was approved. On June 9 resolution 235 (1967) demanded that hostilities between Israel and Syria come to an end immediately. On June 11 the Security Council (in resolution 236 (1967)) condemned all violations of the cease-fire. On June 14 (in resolution 237 (1967)) it called upon Israel to ensure the security of the inhabitants of the areas where military operations had taken place and urged the governments concerned to respect the humanitarian principles governing the treatment of prisoners of war and protection of civilians. However, a Soviet-sponsored draft resolution (S/795 Rev.2) condemning Israel as the aggressor and demanding immediate withdrawal was rejected by the Security Council the same day.

Having failed to achieve the denunciation of Israel in the Security Council, the U.S.S.R. took the initiative to convene the fifth emergency special session of the General Assembly. The session opened on June 17, and two days later the chairman of the council of ministers of the U.S.S.R., Aleksei Kosygin, personally presented a draft resolution to the effect that the General Assembly vigorously condemn Israel; demand immediate withdrawal of Israel troops as well as compensation for damages inflicted on Arab countries; and appeal to the Security Council to take effective measures to eliminate all the consequences of Israel's aggression (A/L.519). This proposal was rejected by the General Assembly on July 4. A similar draft submitted by Albania, which also condemned the United States and United Kingdom for their complicity in the aggression (A/L.521), was voted down on the same day. Yugoslavia introduced another text, ultimately sponsored by 17 (mostly African and Asian) states, which generally restricted itself to a call for immediate withdrawal (A/L.522/Rev.3). An alternative Latin American draft resolution, sponsored by 20 states, also made a request for withdrawal, but coupled it with a call for an end to the belligerency, a request that the Security Council look into the question of navigation and Arab refugees, and reference to the issue of Jerusalem (A/L.523/Rev.1). The Yugoslav and the Latin American proposals met the same fate on July 4, having failed to obtain the required two-thirds majority. The only resolution adopted by the General Assembly on that day (No. 2252 (ES-V)), like Security Council Resolution 237 (1967), related to the need for respecting humanitarian principles.

By July 1967 it was already necessary for the Security Council to convene to examine complaints about breaches of the cease-fire along the Suez Canal, but no formal resolution was voted upon. The discussion resumed in October, after the sinking by the Egyptians of the Israel destroyer *Eilat*. On October 25 the council approved Resolution 240 (1967), generally condemning all violations of the cease-fire. On November 22 the reconvened Security Council adopted the famous Resolution 242 (1967), initially proposed by the United Kingdom, which affirmed that the establishment of "a just and lasting peace in the Middle East" was based on both withdrawal of Israeli forces and termination of belligerency, as well as respect for the right of every state in the area "to live in peace within secure and recognized boundaries." The resolution further affirmed the necessity for (1) guaranteeing freedom of navigation; (2) achieving a just settlement of the refugee problem; and (3) guaranteeing the territorial inviolability and political independence of every state in the region. Finally, the resolution requested the secretary-general to designate a special representative to proceed to the Middle East in order to promote a settlement between the parties. This resolution became a milestone in the period following the Six-Day War. Its precise meaning, however, was controversial, and its validity in later years, in view of the disintegration of the cease-fire on which it was based, was often subject to doubt. It also reflected the low-water mark of Arab postwar efforts to bring about the adoption of unequivocally one-sided, anti-Israel resolutions at the UN. From that point on, the tide of resolutions, which practically challenged Israel's right to self-defense and self-preservation, became an almost routine performance, losing much of its political and moral impact. In March 1968, after the Karameh battle (in which Israel attacked the main Arab terrorist base in Jordan), the Security Council adopted Resolution 248 (1968), condemning the military action launched by Israel "in flagrant violation" of the Charter and the cease-fire and declaring that it would have to consider more effective steps to prevent the repetition of such acts. The Security Council was reconvened almost immediately for further debate on new violations of the cease-fire along the Israel-Jordan line, but no formal resolution was taken. The discussion resumed in August, when the council approved Resolution 256 (1968), again condemning Israel and reaffirming the warning that more effective measures might be taken. Once more, the deliberations continued in March and April 1969, and the council accepted Resolution 265 (1969), adding still another condemnation of Israel to the record, while repeating the same warning.

In September 1968 the situation along the Suez Canal was brought up before the Security Council, which insisted, in Resolution 258 (1968), that the cease-fire "must be rigorously respected." In November 1968 the discussion recommenced, but no vote was taken.

In December 1968, after the attacks of Arab terrorists based in Beirut on El Al planes in Europe, the pendulum swung to Lebanon, and the Security Council met to examine Israel's reprisal action against the international airport in Beirut. The Security Council (in Resolution 262 (1968)) condemned Israel, adding "a solemn warning" about further steps that might be taken. The question of Lebanon was also raised in August 1969, when Israel attacked terrorists operating from Lebanese territory and the council (in Resolution 270 (1969)) condemned Israel again. In May 1970 the same problem produced a similar resolution (S/9807), including condemnation of Israel and reiteration of the "solemn warning." It is notable that the (actual) cease-fire within a (technical) cease-fire, agreed upon for a period of three months in August 1970 – and extended for an equal length of time in November of that year – was brought about as a result of a U.S. rather than UN initiative. In November 1970 the General Assembly adopted Resolution 2628 (XXV), recommending the extension of the cease-fire. This resolution, however, was totally unbalanced against Israel in its thrust and formulation. The advent of the second series of talks with the parties, conducted by the secretary-general's special representative, Gunnar Jarring, early in 1971, was again due to U.S. diplomatic efforts.

Antisemitism

At its first session in 1946 the UN General Assembly confirmed the principles of international law introduced by the legislation of the International Arbitrary Tribunal in Nuremberg and later embodied in the *Genocide Convention (resolutions 95 (I), 96 (I)), thus outlawing the worst antisemitic crimes ever committed in the history of mankind. After that the UN for years ignored the issue of antisemitism. In 1959–60 a "swastika epidemic" swept through large parts of the world. Consequently, several members submitted to the UN subcommission on Prevention of Discrimination and Protection of Minorities at its 12th session (in January 1960) a draft resolution condemning manifestations of antisemitism and other religious and racial prejudices (E/CN.4/Sub.2/L.159). There was a consensus in the subcommission that it was necessary to take action against antisemitism, but some members had qualms about the explicit use of that term in the resolution. Finally a decision was taken to condemn antisemitism without resorting to euphemisms, and the subcommission recommended that its parent body, the UN Commission on Human Rights do the same (Resolution 3 (XIII)). The Commission on Human Rights, followed the recommendation, in a somewhat altered form, in Resolution 6 (XVI), adopted at its 16th session (in March 1960). The matter was discussed later in the year in the Third Committee of the General Assembly. The General Assembly in Resolution 1510 (XV) condemned all manifestations of racial, religious, and national hatred, but deleted a specific reference to antisemitism. The item of "manifestations of antisemitism and other forms of racial prejudice and religious intolerance of a similar nature" was placed on the agenda of the subcommission at its 13th session (in 1961). The subcommission studied material on the subject obtained from governments (E/CN.4/Sub.2/208) and nongovernmental organizations (E/CN.4/Sub.2/L.216), and discussed the nature of the manifestations of antisemitism, as well as the causes of the swastika epidemic. It also examined public reaction to the incidents and measures taken by governments. Objections were again raised to the specific reference to antisemitism in the emerging resolution. Finally the term was relegated to the preamble of Resolution 5 (XIII); the operative paragraphs were of general character and dealt with the need to combat racial, religious, and national hatred. At the 17th session of the Commission on Human Rights (in 1961) manifestations of antisemitism were further studied, but Resolution 5 (XVII) almost entirely ignored antisemitism as such. The Economic and Social Council of the UN (ECOSOC) continued the trend in Resolution 826B (XXXII) of that year, calling for the eradication of racial prejudice and religious intolerance wherever they exist. The General Assembly debated the subject at its 17th session, in 1962, when another resolution, No. 1779 (XVII), was adopted along the same lines.

As an outcome of the deliberations on the subject in the Third Committee, in 1962 the General Assembly also resolved to initiate the drafting of a series of declarations and conventions on the elimination of all forms of racial discrimination (Resolution 1780 (XVII)) and religious intolerance (Resolution 1781 (XVIII)). The Declaration on the Elimination of All Forms of Racial Discrimination (Resolution 1904 (XVIII)) was adopted by the General Assembly at its 18th session, in 1963. In the course of drafting the accompanying convention, at the

20th session of the Commission on Human Rights, a representative of a Jewish nongovernmental organization (see below), the Agudat Israel World Organization, suggested that a specific condemnation of antisemitism be incorporated in the document. The United States embraced the idea and officially proposed that Article 3 of the draft prepared by the subcommission, condemning "racial segregation and apartheid," be amended to include a condemnation of antisemitism as well. Objection to the proposal was voiced on the ground that Article 3 dealt exclusively with segregation and apartheid, and that antisemitism was out of place in this context. The United States therefore withdrew the amendment and offered the addition of a new article instead: "States parties condemn antisemitism and shall take action as appropriate for its speedy eradication in the territories subject to their jurisdiction" (E/CN.4L.701, later revised). The U.S.S.R., for its part, proposed to expand the new article to cover Nazism also (including Neo-Nazism) and genocide (E/CN.4/L.710).

Most members of the Commission on Human Rights endorsed, in principle, the concept of the condemnation of antisemitism, but since the United States and the U.S.S.R. could not reach a mutually accepted formula, it was decided to transmit both versions to the General Assembly. The Third Committee debated the issue only at the 20th session, in 1965. By that time, opposition to the express mention of antisemitism had grown and congealed, particularly among Arab and Soviet bloc delegations. The U.S.S.R. was no longer satisfied merely with the joint listing of antisemitism and Nazism and now insisted on adding Zionism to the same category (A/C.3/L.1231). Many other delegations wanted to avoid a confrontation on the subject, inasmuch as they had reservations even about the direct reference to antisemitism. Therefore, at the suggestion of Greece and Hungary (A/C.3/L.1244), the Third Committee decided, by an overwhelming majority, not to insert in the convention "any reference to specific forms of racial discrimination," i.e., to delete from the text all the "isms" (the condemnation of apartheid in Article 3 was left intact). Thus, the International Convention on the Elimination of All Forms of Racial Discrimination, adopted by the General Assembly in Resolution 2106 (XX), does not condemn antisemitism in so many words. However, the interpretation that antisemitism is covered by the general injunctions of the convention, is based on good authority (see Schwelb, "The International Convention on the Elimination of All Forms of Racial Discrimination," in: *International and Comparative Law Quarterly*, 15 (1966), 996, 1011–5).

Whereas progress in the UN codification on racial discrimination was very quick, many obstacles have impeded the drafting of the instruments regarding religious intolerance. The declaration was in effect abandoned in the Commission on Human Rights in favor of a convention, and the prospects that the latter will be quickly adopted by the General Assembly do not appear to be good. In the process of drafting, however, at the 22nd session of the Commission on Human Rights in 1966, Israel proposed to add in Article 5 (later enumerated as No. 6) of the text prepared by the subcommission a specific reference to antisemitism (E/EN.4/L. 791). This amendment was subsequently withdrawn in favor of a similar draft submitted by Chile (E/CN.4/L.797). The Chilean formulation was accepted by the Commission on Human Rights, which, once more, was not sufficiently sensitive to the atmosphere prevailing in the General Assembly. In the 22nd session of the General Assembly (in 1967) Libya proposed (in the Third Committee) adding the words "Nazism, Fascism and Zionism" after antisemitism (A/C.3/L.1461). Before discussion of Article 6 as a whole was about to begin, however, the General Assembly adopted Resolution 2295 (XXII), which decided not to mention "any specific examples of religious intolerance" in the convention. Thus specific mention of antisemitism, past or present, has become a taboo in UN resolutions. The closest that the UN ever came to denouncing the Nazi Holocaust was in a 1960 Security Council resolution in the case of Adolf Eichmann (S/4349). In response to an Argentinean complaint against Israel's abduction of Eichmann, the council noted, with Soviet support, "the universal condemnation of the persecution of the Jews under the Nazis" and concern that Eichmann should be brought to appropriate justice for his crimes. However, it nonetheless requested Israel "to make appropriate reparation."

Jewish Communities in Arab Countries and the U.S.S.R. Israel, as the only Jewish member state of the UN, has always felt itself duty-bound to raise the issue of oppressed, sometimes silent, Jewish minorities in Diaspora countries. The same sense of responsibility has been shared by some Jewish nongovernmental organizations in consultative status with the Economic and Social Council. The greatest efforts to appeal to the conscience of the world were made on behalf of Jews in Arab lands and in the U.S.S.R. The plight of Jews in Arab lands, directly affected by the Middle East conflict, was first brought to the attention of the UN early in 1948 by the World Jewish Congress, which initiated the adoption of two rather bland formal resolutions on the subject by the Economic and Social Council (Resolutions 133 (VI) H of March 1948 and 214 (VIII) B of February 1949). The Jewish nongovernmental organizations and the State of Israel later found it impossible to have formal resolutions placed before the United Nations. The campaign was therefore confined to the debating ground.

Israel used the opportunity of the annual General Assembly discussion on the subject of the Arab refugees to air in public the grievances against the Arab governments' maltreatment of Jews. Occasionally more dramatic action was taken, and at the sixth session of the General Assembly (in January 1952), Israel publicly withdrew from meetings of the Ad Hoc Political Committee (47th meeting) and the Third Committee (398th meeting) as a protest against the hangings of Jews in Iraq following useless appeals for UN intercession on their behalf. When other incidents of hanging Jews in Iraq occurred early in 1969, Israel proposed to the Commission on Human Rights (at its 25th session) that it dispatch a special communication to the Baghdad government in an effort to prevent further summary executions. The commission was unresponsive, even though the year before, when Arab houses connected with terrorist actions were blown up in Israel-administered territories, a telegram appealing to Israel "to desist forthwith from indulging in such practices" had been promptly adopted at its 24th session.

The Sinai Campaign compounded the plight of the Jewish community in Egypt, and Israel brought the matter up in detail before the 11th session of the General Assembly. The Six-Day War ignited an anti-Jewish campaign of unprecedented dimensions throughout the Arab world, and Israel strove to mobilize world public opinion on behalf of the persecuted Jews. A special representative of the secretary-general, Nils G. Gussing, was nominated in July 1967, pursuant to Security Council Resolution 237 (1967), relating to respect for humanitarian principles by "the Government concerned," and sought to obtain information with regard, inter alia, to the treatment of Jewish minorities in Egypt and Syria (A/6797). Israel requested that the condition of Jewish communities in the whole area of the conflict, including Iraq and Lebanon, be investigated by a projected second mission, but the Security Council (in Resolution 259 of September 1968) called upon Israel alone to receive a special representative of the secretary-general to examine the situation in the territories under its control. Israel insisted that the assignment of the special representative include the issue of Jews in Arab countries, and when this demand was denied, it refused to cooperate with any new mission. For the same reason, Israel also expressed its unwillingness to cooperate with a Special Committee to Investigate Israel Practices Affecting the Human Rights of the Population of the Occupied Territories, established by General Assembly Resolution 2443 (XXIII) in 1968 (renewed in Resolution 2546 (XXIV) in 1969 and in Resolution 2727 (XXV) in 1970), as well as a special Working Group of Experts set up by Commission on Human Rights Resolution 6 (XXV) in 1969 (and renewed in Resolution 10 (XXVI) in 1970).

The plight of about 3,000,000 Jews in the U.S.S.R. was generally not raised in the UN during the Stalin period. An exception was made in 1953, just before Stalin's death, when Israel castigated in the First Committee of the General Assembly, at its seventh session, "the libel of an alleged world Jewish conspiracy" underlying the notorious *"Doctors' Plot." With the advent of the 1960s, however, the UN gradually became an important arena for exposing the suffering of Soviet Jewry. First Jewish nongovernmental organizations, then Israel, and eventually many other states from all continents raised their voices denouncing the denial of human rights and fundamental freedoms to the Jews of the U.S.S.R. Initially, the accusations leveled at the U.S.S.R. were muted and circumspect, scarcely mentioning that country by name; but in time, a systematic and sustained offensive developed. It covered, under a variety of agenda items, almost every possible session of the subcommission, the Commission on Human Rights, the Economic and Social Council, and the General Assembly. Since 1967 even debates in the Security Council served as a forum for the topic.

The campaign for Soviet Jewry in the UN served to enlist world opinion in exerting moral pressure upon a government defaulting the human rights of an oppressed minority group to persuade it to mend its ways. Most of the critical statements at the UN have hinged on the U.S.S.R.'s violations of fundamental freedoms proclaimed by the Universal Declaration of Human Rights and related instruments: communal Jewish activities that were not permitted; synagogues that were closed down; Jewish schools, religious facilities, publishing houses and cultural institutions that were practically nonexistent; reunion of families torn asunder by World War II that was not made possible. After the Six-Day War (1967) the focus shifted from charges of discriminatory practices to protests against the virulent antisemitic propaganda, thinly disguised as attacks against Israel and "world Zionism," which spread over the U.S.S.R. and practically revived the paranoiac concept of The Protocols of the *Elders of Zion. On a number of occasions, special emphasis was placed on the poisonous writings of the Ukrainian antisemite Trofim Kichko. His first book, *Judaism Without Embellishment*, was strongly reprehended by Israel and other delegates at the 20th session of the Commission on Human Rights in 1964. His later book, *Judaism and Zionism*, and, for that matter, the whole phenomenon of "Kichkoism" was rebuked by Israel at the 25th session of the commission in Israel in 1969. As of November 1969 Israel has publicly raised the demand that Soviet Jews be permitted to go and settle in Israel, and circulated in the UN official communications on the subject – the first one containing a letter addressed to the Israel government and various UN bodies by a group of 18 families in Soviet Georgia who expressed the wish to settle in the Jewish homeland (A/7762).

Soviet response to the statements made at the UN on behalf of Jews in the U.S.S.R. was uneven. Soviet representatives tried to muzzle such statements, contending that they were irrelevant to the agenda under discussion. They took strong exception to Israel's circulation of official documents on Soviet Jewry and claimed that the procedure constituted "a gross violation" of the Charter, inasmuch as it intervened in the domestic jurisdiction of the U.S.S.R. (A/7787). The U.S.S.R. accused those who spoke out on behalf of Soviet Jews of slander and distortions, of creating a smokescreen to conceal their own violations of human rights, and even of an attempt to undermine the Soviet system. At times the U.S.S.R. also responded with elaborate statements, replete with statistics and quotes, designed to disprove any discriminatory practices against Soviet Jews. However, the fact that the Soviets, who consistently denied the existence of antisemitism in their country, became the standard-bearers of the fight against the condemnation of antisemitism at the UN, voided their statements of any moral content. Often, the debate on antisemitism at the UN became synonymous with a debate on Soviet policies.

See also *Antisemitism, In the Soviet Bloc; *Russia, The Struggle for Soviet Jewry.

[Yoram Dinstein]

UN Bodies and Specialized Agencies

Israel's participation and activities in the framework of the various UN bodies and specialized agencies has been relatively fruitful and in some cases even outstanding, mainly in view of her role as a source of aid to other developing countries.

ECONOMIC AND SOCIAL COUNCIL. At the sessions of the Economic and Social Council, which consists of 27 members elected by the General Assembly, Israelis participated as observers and frequently raised the issue of discrimination against the Jews in the U.S.S.R.

Regional Commissions. Due to Arab refusal to cooperate with Israel in regional bodies, no Regional Commission for the Middle East, similar to those for Europe (ECE), Asia and the Far East (ECAFE), Latin America (ECLA), and Africa (ECA), was established. Israel, however, sent observers to the ECA, ECAFE, and ECLA, some of whose sessions had to be transferred from cities closed to Israel (e.g., Karachi, Algiers, or Kabul) to those open to her (Bangkok or Addis Ababa). In the framework of these commissions, Israel experts took part in development schemes, as, e.g., in the Mekong Delta Development Project in the Far East, regional development in Upper Volta, and various projects in Latin America.

Functional Commissions. Israel was an active member in the functional commissions elected by the Economic and Social Council. As a member of the Commission for Human Rights (from 1957 until 1959 and from 1965 until 1970), Israel, together with other delegations, incessantly raised the issue of Soviet Jewry and was active in drafting the Convention on the Right of Asylum. The problem of Soviet Jewry was also raised by Israeli members, as well as by members from other countries, in the Subcommission on the Prevention of Discrimination and the Protection of Minorities, where Israel's membership lasted from 1966 until 1968. Israel was also a member of the Social Commission; the UN Refugee Fund Executive Committee (UNREF), the Technical Assistance Committee; the Population Commission; the commissions for Social Development, on the Status of Women, on Housing, Building and Planning; the Advisory Committee on the Application of Science and Technology to Development; and the International Law Commission. Israel was a member on the Executive Committee of the UN High Commissioners' Program (1970).

Other Bodies. Israel played an outstanding part in the International Children's Emergency Fund (UNICEF), not only as a member of the Executive Board from 1957 but also as its vice chairman (in 1957–58) and member, and several times as chairman, of its Program Committee. Israel's representative, Zena *Harman, received on UNICEF's behalf the Nobel Prize for Peace in 1965. Israel was active in extending aid through UNICEF by participating in the establishment of the plant for sterilized milk, of centers for mothers, and care for prematurely born children. Israel became a member of the High Commissioners' Advisory Committee on Refugees in 1951, the rapporteur in 1952, and chairman of the session in 1954.

AD HOC COMMITTEES. Israel was also a member of a number of ad hoc committees, appointed by the General Assembly, such as the Ad Hoc Committee on Refugees and Stateless Persons; the Special Committee on the Methods and Procedures of the General Assembly for Dealing with Legal and Drafting Questions; the Committee on International Criminal Jurisdiction; the Special Committee on Review of Administrative Tribunal Judgments; the Peace Observation Committee; the Panel for Inquiry and Conciliation; several committees of the UN Trade and Development Board, e.g., the Committee on Manufactures, the Group on Preferences, etc.

SPECIALIZED AGENCIES. *International Labor Organization (ILO).* ILO's director general from 1948 to 1970 was an American Jew, David *Morse. Israel joined the ILO in 1949 and signed 36 of the 130 conventions drafted by it, including the convention against forced labor. Arab and Soviet representatives failed in their attempt to establish that the *Naḥal (in the Israel army) is a form of forced labor. The Israeli government is represented in the ILO by its Ministry of Labor; Israeli workers by the *Histadrut; and employers by the Manufacturers' Association. The Histadrut delegate was elected in 1954 as workers' deputy member, and the Israeli government delegate was elected in 1960–61 as government group deputy member. ILO assisted Israel, from her early days, in establishing a vocational school network and workers' training courses for developing countries in cooperation with the Histadrut. Israeli experts were sent by the ILO to developing countries (e.g., Cyprus) to assist in trade union organization.

Food and Agricultural Organization (FAO). Israel joined the FAO in 1949 and until 1953 belonged to its Near Eastern Region. In view of the Arabs' refusal to attend regional conferences of FAO with Israel, the latter moved to its European Region in 1954. In 1967–68 Israel was a member of the FAO's Council. FAO assisted Israel in matters of irrigation and the drainage of underground water, e.g., in Naḥal Shikmah. Israel cooperated with the FAO in establishing courses in poultry raising, irrigation, multi-seasonal crops, food production, etc. for developing countries. Israel contributes to the World Food Program of the FAO.

World Health Organization (WHO). Israel joined WHO in 1949 and at first belonged to its Eastern Mediterranean Region, together with Cyprus, the Arab states, Pakistan, Iran, and Ethiopia. Arab refusal to participate together with Israel in regional activities prevented the convocation of its meetings until 1953. In 1954 WHO decided to split the regional organization into two subcommittees, and Israel belonged to subcommittee B, together with Iran, Cyprus and Ethiopia; these, however, gradually seceded from it, and the subcommittee ceased to exist. Despite Arab opposition, Israel continues its participation in the region and in 1961–64 was represented by the director general of its Ministry of Health on WHO's Executive Board. On WHO's initiative, Israel and Arab states cooperated in combating rabies and venereal diseases. WHO assisted Israel in establishing medical courses and nursing courses as well as postgraduate medical courses in various fields for students from developing countries. WHO also assisted Israel in sending experts and equipment to other countries for combating malaria and producing vaccine against tuberculosis.

International Civil Aviation Organization (ICAO). Israel joined ICAO in 1949, and on her initiative the organization adopted a resolution in 1970 against plane hijacking.

Universal Postal Union (UPU). Israel joined UPU in 1949, but Arab states refused to maintain mutual postal services with Israel.

International Telecommunication Union (ITO). Israel joined ITO in 1949, but Arab states refused to maintain telegraphic contacts with Israel.

World Meteorological Organization (WMO). Israel joined WMO in 1949, and Israeli experts were sent by WMO to African states. WMO experts and equipment assisted Israel in establishing a meteorological station at Beit Dagon.

Israel also participates in the following specialized agencies of the UN: the Inter-Governmental Maritime Consultative Organization (IMCO), from 1958; the International Bank for Reconstruction and Development (IBRD), from 1954; the International Monetary Fund (IMF), from 1954; the International Financial Corporation (IFC), from 1965; the General Agreement on Tariffs and Trade (GATT), from 1962. The International Atomic Energy Agency (IAEA) was joined by Israel in 1957, and Israel's Atomic Energy Commission maintained close contact with it.

UNESCO. A particularly fruitful cooperation developed between the UN Educational, Scientific and Cultural Organization (UNESCO) and Israel. Léon *Blum played a prominent role in UNESCO's foundation in 1946, and the opening sentence of its constitution ("since wars begin in the minds of men, it is in the minds of men that the defense of peace must be constructed") is attributed to him. Israel joined UNESCO in 1949 and was a member of its Executive Board, represented by Moshe Avidor, from 1962 until 1970. Until 1967 Israel belonged, in most fields of UNESCO activity, to the organization's Asian region. Later UNESCO's regional organization became more specified, and Israel's participation in the Asian region greatly diminished; Israel is now the only developing country that does not belong to any regional sector of UNESCO. UNESCO experts, equipment, and scholarships assisted Israel in many fields of education, science, and cultural activities. UNESCO international conferences on adult education, the social sciences, and science instruction in elementary schools took place in Israel. Israeli professionals and scientists are often invited by UNESCO to participate in expert meetings, panels, and study groups on specific issues, such as hydrology, racialism, sociology, communal integration, adult education, etc. Israel raised the issue of discrimination against Jewish education in the U.S.S.R. at UNESCO's general conferences from 1964. In 1964 the UNESCO conference adopted an Israel-proposed resolution demanding education toward tolerance and against racialism in kindergartens and elementary schools. In 1960 Israel was active in drafting the Convention against Discrimination in Education.

In November 1967, after the Six-Day War, Israel raised the issue of using textbooks containing material of anti-Jewish and anti-Israel hate and incitement in UNWRA-UNESCO schools. In 1968, in accordance with a decision by its Executive Board, the director general of UNESCO appointed a committee of outside experts to examine the textbooks in Jordan, Lebanon, and Egypt, and it confirmed Israel's complaint. After prolonged negotiations, these states undertook to expunge the objectionable passages from the textbooks. Syria refused to abide by UNESCO's Executive Committee's decisions, declaring that "the hatred we instill in our children from birth is a sacred emotion." In 1969–70, under UNESCO auspices, matriculation examinations, according to the Egyptian curriculum, were held in the Israel-administered Gaza Strip. In 1967, in accordance with the Convention on Protection of Cultural Property in the Event of Armed Conflict, applied for the first time, UNESCO sent general commissioners to Israel and her neighbors. The Arabs accused Israel of destroying historical sites, but the reports of UNESCO's general commissioners denied this charge. The Arabs also failed in their attempt to have UNESCO denounce Israel for the fire in the Al-Aqṣā mosque in Jerusalem. On the other hand, the Arabs succeeded in having UNESCO adopt a resolution which called on Israel to refrain from archaeological excavations and town planning in East Jerusalem in order to preserve its specific character. Israel did not vote and declared that the status of Jerusalem is not within UNESCO's sphere of responsibility.

UNESCO published books and pamphlets on Jewish topics in several languages, as well as anti-racialist literature, such as *Israel Ancient Mosaics* (prefaced by Meyer Shapiro with an introduction by M. Avi-Yonah, 1960); *Social Life and Social Values of the Jewish People*, in: *Journal of World History*, 11 (1968/69); Leon Roth, *Jewish Thought as a Factor in Civilization* (1961); Claude Levi-Strauss, *Race and History* (1961–4); Cyril Bibby, *Race, Prejudice and Education* (ed. by Z. Adar, Jerusalem, 1962); Arnold M. Rose, *L'Origine des Préjugés* (Jerusalem, 1963); Harry L. Shapiro, *The Jewish People: A Biological History* (1963[2]). UNESCO's monthly *Courier* began to appear in Israel in 1968 in a Hebrew edition called *Eshnav la-Olam* ("Window to the World").

NONGOVERNMENTAL ORGANIZATIONS (NGO). By 1970 there were some 620 nongovernmental organizations a consultative status on the Economic and Social Council and other UN bodies, as well as on regional bodies outside the UN framework.

NGOS delegate observers to the meeting of the bodies with which they have a consultative status and distribute written material on the topics under discussion. The Jewish NGOS were active in various fields, such as denouncing racialism, discrimination of all kinds, antisemitism, oppression of minorities, as well as demanding freedom of religion, and particularly persisting in defending the rights of the Jewish communities in the Soviet Union and the Arab countries.

In 1968 the Arab and Soviet delegations opened an intensive campaign to oust the Jewish NGOs that have consultative status on the Economic and Social Council, arguing that their "Zionist" character deprives them de facto of their nongovernmental character, since they are closely linked with the State of Israel. Their main target was the Coordinating Board of Jewish Organizations. At its spring session in 1970, the ECOSOC decided not to change the status of the Jewish NGOs.

[Anne Marie Lambert]

For Israel, the collapse of the Soviet Union and the end of the Cold War, as well as significant weakening in the Arab position following the Gulf War and the opening of peace talks after the Madrid Conference, led to a significant change in its standing in the United Nations. This manifested itself in the unprecedented repeal on December 15, 1991, of General Assembly Resolution 3379 passed in 1975 that had equated Zionism with racism. The resolution, which had been passed by a vote of 72 in favor, 35 against and 32 abstentions, was repealed in 1991 by a vote of 111 in favor, 25 against (including almost all the Arab and Muslim states), and 13 abstentions.

Even following the resolution's repeal, critics pointed to an anti-Israel bias at the UN, in the General Assembly and other UN forums, such as UNESCO. Israel's position within the UN was nevertheless considered to have improved since 1991, as it was elected to several UN bodies that were previously closed to it. At the end of 1992 Israel was approached for the first time by the secretary general of the UN, Dr. Butrus-Ghali, about sending professional personnel to participate in UN peacekeeping forces, and agreed.

Resolution 3379 (November 10, 1975), which declared that "Zionism is a form of racism and racial discrimination," had marked the climax of what critics denounced as an ongoing anti-Israel and antisemitic campaign in the United Nations, especially since the 1970s. The U.S. ambassador to the UN, Daniel Patrick Moynihan called it a "terrible lie... an infamous act." Israel's then ambassador to the UN, Chaim Herzog, told the General Assembly: "For us, the Jewish people, this resolution based on hatred, falsehood, and arrogance is devoid of any moral or legal value," and then he tore the text of the resolution in two.

For most Israelis, the UN resolution equating Zionism with racism was an Orwellian inversion of language, deemed common practice at the Soviet-Arab-Third World-dominated General Assembly of the mid-1970s. But unlike other regular generalized attacks on capitalism, democracy, or freedom of the press, here the Israeli delegation felt the target was clear and specific: to delegitimize a member state – Israel – and to legitimize antisemitism. The adverse ramifications for Jews and Israelis went far beyond the narrow confines of the United Nations, as would become explicit in an alarming increase of antisemitic incidents in Western Europe.

Subsequently, critics point out, the attacks on Israel and Zionism, replete with antisemitic nuances, spread to all the UN institutions and special agencies, bearing the nature of a campaign to delegitimize the right of the Jewish people to its own independent state. More than 30 anti-Israel resolutions were adopted on various aspects of the Arab-Israel conflict. Israel was singled out in General Assembly resolutions for policies of "hegemony" and "racism" and was accused of being a "non-peace-loving country" (a characterization, which, according to the UN Charter, could be grounds for expulsion from the organization), "an affront to humanity" and a perpatrator of "war crimes."

The resolutions and papers accepted and distributed within the various organizations of the United Nations were mostly collections of condemnations, abuses, and retouched histories that disregarded and even challenged the right of Israel to exist as a state. At the General Assembly, resolutions called for economic, diplomatic, and military sanctions against Israel which, had they not been vetoed in the Security Council, would have left Israel helpless against military attacks as well as political and economic ones. UN records contain many antisemitic outbursts, delegitimization attacks, obscene accusations, and diatribes against Israel. Critical reviews of the UN General Assembly records, of diplomatic efforts as well as the media coverage involved in passing these resolutions pointed to the annual and special UN conferences as forums for anti-Israel attacks. The UN played a major role in enhancing the prestige and international standing of the Palestine Liberation Organization (PLO) when its leader, Yasser Arafat, addressed the General Assembly in November 1974.

In the early 1980s the anti-Israeli campaign shifted to an effort to have the credentials of the Israeli delegation to the General Assembly disqualified, with the goal of having Israel suspended from the deliberations. As a result of the determined American position, accompanied by U.S. threats that it would withdraw if Israel were to be suspended, no deliberation on the disqualification of Israel's credentials took place. The revelations in 1986–7 on the Nazi past of Dr. Kurt Waldheim, the former Secretary General of the UN, dealt another blow to the prestige of the UN. Waldheim's file in the UN War Crimes Commission was not known to the public when he was elected, serving 10 years in this post.

In the field of UN peacekeeping forces, the Middle East and the Arab-Israeli conflict continued to be an active laboratory for various operations. In addition to the UN Disengagement Observer Force (UNDOF) in the Golan Heights since 1974, the UN Interim Force in Lebanon (UNIFIL) has been stationed in southern Lebanon since 1978. Criticism within the UN General Assembly of the Camp David Accords and the peace agreements between Israel and Egypt as well as the opposition of the Soviet Union in the Security Council prompted the creation of a new framework outside the UN, the Multinational Force, led by the United States, which was stationed in Sinai after Israel's final withdrawal to the international border in April 1982. This Multinational Force replaced the UN forces in Sinai.

There are still about 300 UN personnel in the UN Truce Supervision Organization (UNTSO) that was established in 1948 to supervise the cease-fires and later the armistice agreements between Israel and its neighbors. The UN Relief and Work Agency (UNRWA) has been operating in the Palestinian refugee camps in the territories.

[Avi Beker]

After the short honeymoon in the wake of the Oslo Accords, hostility to Israel again reared its head as the Arab-Israel peace process became stalled and the second Intifada got under way in 2000. The Israeli perception of being labeled the primary aggressor in the Arab-Israel conflict was reinforced by events at the UN World Conference Against Racism, held in Durban, South Africa, in the summer of 2001, which steadfastly refused to concern itself with antisemitism and instead held up the Palestinians as victims of Israeli racism, as well as in the 2004 condemnation of Israel's security fence by the UN's International Court of Justice. In 2002 the UN was quick to call Israel's incursion in Jenin against Palestinian terrorists a "massacre" though it later had to admit that most of the 52 dead were armed combatants. In 2003 the General Assembly passed 18 resolutions critical of Israel, but only four mentioning any other country, with such gross violators of human rights as Syria and China not mentioned at all. International sentiment, as expressed by the United Nations' General Assembly, remained critical of Israel in the Middle East equation, implying that it could not play a meaningful role in the peace process.

On a more positive note, in 2005 the UN General Assembly proclaimed January 27 as International Holocaust Day, marking the first time that a resolution introduced by Israel was adopted by the General Assembly.

BIBLIOGRAPHY: R. Higgins, *United Nations Peacekeeping 1946–1967: The Middle East* (1969); A. Lall, *The UN and the Middle East Crisis* (1967); Hebrew University of Jerusalem, *Israel and the United Nations* (1956); A.G. Mezerik, *The Arab-Israeli Conflict and the UN; The 1967 Round: Prelude, June War, Jarring Mission* (1969); J. Robinson, *Palestine and the United Nations* (1947); P. de Azcarate, *Mission in Palestine 1948–52* (1966); D. Brook, *Preface to Peace…* (1964); N. Safran, *The United Nations and Israel* (1963); E. Lauterpacht, *Jerusalem and the Holy Places* (1968); M. Sharett, *Be-Sha'ar ha-Ummot 1946–1949* (1958); Y. Dinstein, in: *St. John's Law Review*, 44 (1970), 466, 476–82; Y. Lador-Lederer, *International Non-Governmental Organizations and Economic Entities* (1963); B. Akzin, in: N. Feinberg and J. Stoyanovsky (eds.), *Jewish Yearbook of International Law* (1948), 87ff., E. Elath, *Yoman San Francisco* (1971). **ADD. BIBLIOGRAPHY:** A. Bayefsky, "The UN and the Jews," in: *Commentary* (Feb. 26, 2004); D. Tell, "The UN's Israel Obsession," in: *The Weekly Standard* (May 6, 2002).

UNITED RESTITUTION ORGANIZATION (URO), legal aid society for claimants outside Germany for restitution and compensation. During World War II the Allies declared they would obtain restitution of the property of Nazi victims which had been confiscated, taken, or sold under duress; and financial compensation for their suffering – loss of liberty, health, profession, and employment, and loss of parents and family. Failing to agree on a uniform law, separate Ordinances on Restitution in each of the occupied zones were enacted, initially by the Americans (1948), and followed two years later by the English and French. A decree governing the Western Sectors of Berlin was promulgated about the same time. When the Western Allies agreed to recognize the sovereignty of the German Federal Republic in 1952, they stipulated that the Bonn government must pass a federal law on compensation at least as favorable to the refugees as any provincial law in force.

The United Restitution Organization was founded in 1948 as a legal aid society, to help claimants of limited means, living outside Germany, to recover both in restitution and compensation what was due to them. Legal offices were set up for this purpose, staffed by expert Jewish and European lawyers in the countries of refuge and in Germany itself and later in Austria. The URO was sponsored by the British Foreign Office as a qualified and responsible public service to undertake the preparation and pleading of claims in return for a modest fee in case of success. The administrative center, established in London, was headed from 1949 until his death in 1964 by Secretary-General Hans Reichmann, a German-Jewish civil servant. The number of clients soon reached 100,000, and rose in the peak period of activity to 250,000. For the first five years the URO was financed by Jewish voluntary bodies concerned with refugees: the *Jewish Agency for Palestine, the *American Jewish Joint Distribution Committee, and the *Central British Fund for relief and rehabilitation.

When the Government of Israel and the *Conference on Jewish Material Claims against Germany (formed in 1952), together demanded reparations, restitution, and compensation, the latter, as the representative of the Jews in the Diaspora, advanced sums from funds which it received from the German government and took over financial responsibility for the URO. A central office was opened in Frankfurt, and Benjamin Ferencz, an American lawyer and former head of the Jewish Restitution Successor Organization, became the first director general, succeeded in 1955 by Kurt May, a German lawyer. In 1958 the URO maintained 29 branch offices in 15 countries including South America and Australia; and had a staff of 1,000, of whom 200 were legal officers. The original estimate of the liability of the German government for compensation claims, i.e., excluding restitution, was DM 7,000,000,000 ($1,750,000,000). After the final legislation in 1966, it rose to DM 45,000,000,000 ($11,250,000,000). Ten percent of the claimants are clients of the URO. By 1967 the URO recovered for its clients over DM 2,000,000,000 ($500,000,000) and with the fees from claims which were successful, it has repaid the sums advanced by the Claims Conference and other philanthropic bodies. Later, the amount recovered for the clients and the fees paid declined considerably.

The total sum recovered includes compensation for Jews who resided in the Eastern Zone or Eastern Sector of Berlin, as the federal German government took over the liability which was rejected by the Soviet authorities and the East German government. It also includes compensation for the confiscation of movable property, furniture, jewelry, securities, and bank accounts of Jews living in countries occupied by the Nazi armies, provided the claimant could prove that the property had been transferred to Germany. Since the Nazi bureaucratic system kept careful record of the Nazi spoliation, the research staff of the URO was able to trace it. The URO is a legal British nonprofit organization limited by guarantee since 1954. The organization did not take up the claims of Jewish and other victims of the Nazi Holocaust living in any part of Germany. It had offices in Frankfurt, Berlin, Munich, Cologne, and Hanover. At the peak of its operations the URO maintained 29 branch offices in 15 countries. Over the years it assisted more than 200,000 claimants.

By the end of 1965 the filing deadlines under the principal restitution and compensation laws expired. The scope of the URO's activities began to gradually diminish. Currently (2006) the URO maintains six offices located in Israel, the United States, Canada, and Germany.

BIBLIOGRAPHY: N. Bentwich, *The United Restitution Organization* (1969); URO, *Zusammenstellung der Gesetze, Verordnungen, Verfuegungen, Erlasse, Rundschreiben, und Schnellbriefe* (n.d.); idem, *Dokumente ueber Methoden der Judenverfolgung im Ausland* (1959); Bentwich, in: YLBI, 10 (1965), 204–24.

[Norman Bentwich]

UNITED STATES HOLOCAUST MEMORIAL MUSEUM. The United States Holocaust Memorial Museum adjacent to the National Mall in Washington, D.C., is America's national memorial to the Holocaust, whose mission is to advance and disseminate knowledge about that unprecedented tragedy, preserve the memory of those who suffered, and encourage reflection upon the moral and spiritual questions raised by those events. Most of the museums and monuments on the National Mall in Washington, D.C., celebrate the fruits of democratic freedoms. Standing as a sobering counterpoint, the United States Holocaust Memorial Museum reflects the opposite – the disintegration of civilized values and the perversion of technological achievements. The museum is housed in an award-winning building designed by architect James Ingo *Freed of Pei, Cobb, Freed and Partners. Freed's family fled Nazi Germany when he was a child. The Memorial Museum won the American Institute of Architects' Honor Award in 1994. The museum is a unique public-private partnership, built on public land with funds donated by the American people. The museum remains a joint effort of the United States government and private contributors from across the nation.

Background

The initiative for the creation of the museum began when President Jimmy Carter appointed the President's Commission on the Holocaust on November 1, 1978, to study the idea of an American national memorial to the Holocaust. Chaired by Elie *Wiesel, the commission issued its *Report to the President*, on September 27, 1979, calling for a permanent "living memorial" in Washington, D.C. The commission felt that such a memorial would fulfill the obligation to learn from the past and to teach future generations, in its words, "A memorial unresponsive to the future would also violate the memory of the past." The president accepted the Commission's recommendations and appointed a United States Holocaust Memorial Council.

By a unanimous vote on October 7, 1980, Congress established the United States Holocaust Memorial Council and charged it with raising funds for and building the memorial museum, conducting an annual national Days of Remembrance observance for the victims of the Holocaust, and establishing a Committee on Conscience to serve as an influential voice on issues of contemporary genocide and related crimes against humanity. Elie Wiesel and Mark Talisman were named the first chairman and vice chairman of the Council, respectively.

The Building of the Museum

An official groundbreaking ceremony on the site of the future museum took place on October 16, 1985, just south of Independence Avenue, bordering 14th and 15th Streets, Southwest. On October 8, 1986, the section of 15th Street, Southwest, in front of the site was officially renamed Raoul Wallenberg Place, in honor of the Swedish diplomat responsible for rescuing thousands of Hungarian Jews during the Holocaust.

In February 1987, President Ronald Reagan appointed Harvey M. Meyerhoff as chairman of the Council, succeeding Elie Wiesel, who had resigned the Council chairmanship in December 1986 after being given the Nobel Peace Prize.

President Reagan appointed William J. Lowenberg to serve as Meyerhoff's vice chairman. Albert Abramson chaired the Museum Development committee that oversaw the creation of the museum. Miles Lerman chaired the International Relations Committee and the Campaign to Remember, the fundraising arm of the Museum, and Benjamin Meed chaired the Content and Days of Remembrance Committees.

To spearhead the creation of the museum, in 1989, the council appointed Jeshajahu (Shaike) Weinberg to serve as museum director. Weinberg, whose background was in theater and museums, had pioneered the idea of a storytelling museum when he led the development of Beth Hatefutsoth, the Nahum Goldmann Museum of the Jewish Diaspora, in Tel Aviv, Israel.

The Museum Opening

The United States Holocaust Memorial Museum opened to the public on April 26, 1993, with a dedication ceremony attended by President Clinton, Vice President Gore, and many national and international dignitaries.

The museum opened at a time of dramatically increased attention to the Holocaust in the United States. The Museum of Tolerance had opened some two months before; *Schindler's List* premiered that fall; and in Bosnia ethnic cleansing was taking place in Europe for the first time since 1945. The museum drew large crowds, predominantly non-Jewish, from the day it opened. Almost 20 million visitors saw the museum during its first decade, including about six million schoolchildren. Visitation is 90 percent non-Jewish. The museum has been an important destination for international visitors. Eighty heads of state have visited, as have almost 3,000 foreign officials from more than 130 countries.

Though the Holocaust did not take place on American soil, the museum's core messages are very much intended for American audiences as it reflects on American history and American values.

The museum, of course, has special meaning to Holocaust survivors and to the American Jewish community. Its creators felt free to create this memorial in the heart of America's civic landscape. The choice of Washington and not New York was a decision to take what could have been kept as the parochial memoirs of a bereaved community to the American people as a lesson for humanity, while preserving the Judeocentricity of the event.

Remembrance is at the heart of the museum and it resonates throughout the building. The hexagonal Hall of Remembrance and the Wall of Remembrance, which memorializes the murdered children, are the two specific memorial spaces.

Another memorial component is the Benjamin and Vladka Meed Registry of Jewish Holocaust Survivors, which contains information on more than 190,000 survivors and their family members, including names, cities of birth, places of transit and incarceration, wartime locations, and communities of resettlement. Remembrance is also central to the museum's programming, both onsite and around the country, ranging from the oral testimony in exhibitions to talks by survivors at the Museum and around the country. Perhaps most important, the enduring commitment to remembrance is affirmed annually when the Museum leads the nation in observing the Days of Remembrance with ceremonies in the United States Capitol Rotunda and at the Museum, and in commemorations in cities and states throughout the country. Every president since 1979 has spoken at the Days of Remembrance commemoration as well as many cabinet officials and Supreme Court justices.

Directed by Jeshajahu Weinberg, designed by Ralph Appelbaum, who worked in collaboration first with Martin Smith 1989–91 and later with Raye Farr as director of the Permanent Exhibition, to implement the storyline developed by a team of scholars, curators and museum conceptual developers headed by Holocaust scholar and Museum Project Director Michael *Berenbaum, the Permanent Exhibition presents a chronological account in a self-guided format that is designed for visitors 11 years of age and above. Traversing three floors, it is divided into three sections, "Nazi Assault – 1933 to 1939," "The 'Final Solution' – 1940 to 1945," and "Last Chapter."

The story is told through photographs, film, documents and artifacts – such as a barracks from Birkenau, a railcar of the type used to transport Jews from Warsaw to Treblinka, a milk can hidden by Jews under the Warsaw ghetto, and a Danish boat that transported Jews to freedom. Four themes underlie the permanent exhibition: personalizing the story of the Holocaust, making it accessible to American visitors intellectually and conceptually, including all victims of Nazi tyranny without diluting from the Judeocentricity of the event, and understanding the unique perspective of those who were there. The exhibition personalizes the history, encourages visitors to understand the Holocaust as an event that people did to other people, and encourages identification with the victims and the understanding that the victims were very much like us. Another permanent installation is *Remember the Children: Daniel's Story*, which recounts the history of the Holocaust from the perspective of a young boy growing up in Nazi Germany. This interactive exhibition with recreated environments was designed for younger audiences, eight years and above, accompanied by their families and teachers. Although intended for younger audiences, it is also very moving for adult visitors.

The museum also offers special exhibitions in the Sidney Kimmel and Rena Rowan Exhibition Gallery and the Gonda Education Center, as well as topical displays in the Museum's Wexner Learning Center. Designed as a destination for visitors to explore and discuss Holocaust history and its meaning today, the Wexner Learning Center examines various themes and features an array of digital media, group-discussion areas, artifact displays, and videos of eyewitness testimonies. It has explored such topics as liberation, war crimes trials, and contemporary genocide in Darfur, Sudan.

The National Institute for Holocaust Education

The museum has become a worldwide leader in Holocaust education in the broadest sense. Its stature has enabled it to work nationally, internationally, and with an array of U.S. and regional governmental entities.

The Teacher Fellowship Program provides advanced professional development training to highly experienced secondary level teachers in all 50 states. The Law Enforcement and Society Program serves police and federal law enforcement officers, as well as FBI agents and judges, encouraging participants to explore the implications of Holocaust history for their own professions. The Holocaust, the Military, and the Defense of Freedom Program reaches cadets from the U.S. Naval Academy, officers in training at West Point, foreign liaison officers at the Pentagon, and soldiers, sailors, pilots and marines from military bases, aircraft carriers, and active duty locations nationwide. Finally, the museum's Leadership and Diplomacy Programs reach out to senior civil servants within the Federal Executive Institute and foreign service officers in training with the State Department so they might approach their public service with a sophisticated level of moral discourse rooted in awareness of Holocaust history and a commitment to vigorous response when faced with contemporary threats of genocide.

Rescue the Evidence

The Museum's educational work depends on its collections and ensuring the vitality of Holocaust scholarship. Already housing the most comprehensive collection of Holocaust-related resources in a single location, the museum was fortunate to have negotiated with East European governments at transitional moments, before, during and after the revolutionary regime changes that swept across Eastern Europe in the years just prior to the museum's opening. It is also fortunate to receive donations of artifacts and material from Americans of all walks of life, survivors, rescuers, and liberators as well as their descendants. The museum is continuing its efforts to acquire materials through its Rescue the Evidence Initiative, seeking donations of objects and documents from Holocaust survivors, liberators, eyewitnesses, and their family members, as well as institutions and governments. The museum makes a concerted effort to offer access to highly relevant archival materials, otherwise widely dispersed internationally, via a centralized collection of microfilm copies. Many of these microfilms are also available in Jerusalem at *Yad Vashem and the museum has a policy of sharing microfilmed material to maximize its accessibility to scholars.

The Photographic Reference Collection is one of the museum's most widely used resources, containing copies of images from collections worldwide. It is an indispensable source of information for educators, filmmakers, curators, researchers, journalists, and publishers throughout the world.

In addition, the museum's Library comprehensively collects books, dissertations, music scores, sound recordings, periodicals, audiovisual materials, and other electronic media on the historiography and documentation of the Holocaust and the Third Reich, personal accounts of Holocaust survivors and victims, and materials relating to war crimes and war crimes trials. In order to support background research on the Holocaust and related topics, the Library also collects materials on World War II, genocide studies, antisemitism, and Jewish genealogical and cultural history as affected by the Holocaust.

Center for Advanced Holocaust Studies

From its inception the Museum was conceived of as an educational and scholarly institution, a center for both research and teacher training. Within months of its opening the Research Institute was opened with a scholarly conference. In 1998 the Center for Advanced Holocaust Studies was established to foster the continued growth and vitality of the academic study of the Holocaust. The center has taken the lead in training and supporting new scholars in the field through rigorous academic programs and is working to ensure that students at colleges and universities are taught at the highest levels of excellence by conducting programs for faculty members who specialize in this field. The center offers conferences, fellowships, awards, and stipends. It also publishes in the field of Holocaust studies, including the *Journal of Holocaust and Genocide Studies*, published in association with Oxford University Press.

As part of its effort to encourage a balanced and comprehensive approach to the field of Holocaust scholarship, the center launched its Jewish Source Study Initiative to encourage research on how Jews – as individuals and communities – responded during the Holocaust. This research program is an effort to balance the established research focus on the perpetrators with a commensurate level of attention to documenting the perspectives of those targeted.

Committee on Conscience

As the museum is a living memorial to the victims, its Committee on Conscience works to raise public awareness and alert the national conscience to contemporary acts or threats of genocide and related crimes against humanity. The committee has addressed areas such as Rwanda, Kosovo, Chechnya, and Sudan (both southern and Darfur regions). Working with the U.S. State Department and other federal entities, the committee recently launched an Academy for Genocide Prevention.

Museum Governance

The museum is overseen by the United States Holocaust Memorial Council, which includes 55 private citizens appointed by the U.S. president, five members of the Senate and five members of the House of Representatives, and three ex-officio members from the Departments of State, Education, and Interior.

Since the museum opened, the council has been led by Chairman Miles Lerman and Vice Chairman Ruth B. Mandel, appointed by President Clinton in 1993; Chairman Rabbi Irving Greenberg, appointed by President Clinton in 2000; Chairman Fred S. Zeidman, appointed by President Bush in 2002; and Vice Chairman Joel M. Geiderman, appointed by President Bush in 2005.

The council has appointed these individuals to serve as directors of the museum: Jeshajahu Weinberg, 1987–94; Walter Reich, 1995–98; Sara J. Bloomfield, from 1999.

BIBLIOGRAPHY: M. Berenbaum, *After Tragedy and Triumph: Modern Jewish Thought and the American Experience* (1990); idem, *The World Must Know: The History of the Holocaust as Told in the United States Holocaust Memorial Museum* (2005^2); T. Cole, *Selling the Holocaust: From Auschwitz to Schindler; How History Is Bought, Packaged, and Sold* (1999); E.T. Linenthal, *Preserving Memory: The Struggle to Create America's Holocaust Museum* (1995); T.W. Luke, "Memorializing Mass Murder: The United States Holocaust Memorial Museum," in: *Museum Politics: Power Plays at the Exhibition* (2002), 37–64; P. Novick, *The Holocaust in American Life* (1999); President's Commission on the Holocaust, *Report to the President* (1979); J. Weinberg and R. Elieli, *The Holocaust Museum in Washington* (1995). **WEBSITE:** www.ushmm.org.

[Dara Goldberg (2nd ed.)]

UNITED STATES LITERATURE.

The Influence of the Bible and Hebrew Culture

The Jewish influence on American literary expression predated the actual arrival of Jews in the United States in 1654, for the Puritan culture of New England was marked from the outset by a deep association with Jewish themes. No Christian community in history identified more with the Israelites of the Bible than did the first generations of settlers of the

Massachusetts Bay Colony, who believed their own lives to be a literal reenactment of the biblical drama of the chosen people: they were the children of Israel; the American continent was the promised land; the kings of England were the pharaohs of Egypt; the Indians were the natives of Canaan or, alternatively, the *Ten Lost Tribes; the pact of Plymouth Rock was God's holy covenant; and the ordinances by which they lived were His divine law. Since they viewed themselves as the persecuted victims of the sinful Christian establishment of the Old World, the Puritans also had a natural sympathy for the Jews of their own time, at least in the abstract. The Puritan leader Cotton Mather repeatedly referred to the Jews in his prayer for their conversion as God's "Beloved People," and the lasting influence of this attitude no doubt accounts in large measure for the striking philo-Semitism that prevailed in American life and letters long after Puritanism as such had ceased to be a vital force.

A striking feature of the Puritan identification with the Old Testament was the high place accorded to the study of Hebrew in New England's intellectual life. Until late in the 18th century, Hebrew was a required subject at Harvard and Yale, and was also taught at Princeton, Dartmouth, Brown, and King's (Columbia) College. Commencement addresses were given in Hebrew and scholars such as Yale President Ezra *Stiles even conversed in the language. The very fact that the Puritans produced next to nothing of a literary nature apart from sermons and theological tracts bears witness in itself to their affinity to Judaic modes of thought, which were on the whole traditionally hostile to secular writing and to literary expression for its own sake.

[Milton Henry Hindus]

The Image of the Jew

It was only in the 19th century that Jews themselves first came upon the American literary scene, as both authors and fictional characters. Curiously enough, during this period it is only in the writings of non-Jews that Jewish characters appear. The works of the early 19th-century Jewish playwrights Mordecai Manuel *Noah, Isaac *Harby, and Jonas B. Phillips are conventional melodramas, conspicuously devoid of Jewish subject matter, despite the active involvement of Noah and Harby in Jewish community life. Perhaps they felt that Jewish life was too insubstantial to provide the working basis for a dramatic theme; or perhaps they wished to vie with their contemporaries on more universal ground. On the other hand, as drama critic of the New York *Evening Post*, Harby attacked the antisemitic stereotype of Shylock in Shakespeare's *Merchant of Venice*. A fourth Jewish dramatist of the period, Samuel Judah, was hostile to his background, and his unperformed biblical play, *The Maid of Midian*, was an attack on Old Testament religion. In contrast to the playwrights, two 19th-century Jewish poets, both women and southerners, wrote verse of a specifically Jewish character. The legendary Adah Isaacs Menken deservedly gained fame more for her romantic personality than for her poetry, but her volume *Infelicia* received considerable attention when it appeared shortly before her death in 1868. Her first poems, largely on Jewish national themes, were published by Isaac M. Wise in his *Israelite.

In contrast to the generally sympathetic treatment of Jews as a collective entity in American journalism and political writing of the age, the few portraits of Jewish characters in fiction and drama tended to draw heavily on the negative stereotypes of Jews that predominated in British literary tradition, on which American authors were greatly dependent until well into the 19th century. Perhaps the first such Jewish character to appear in American literature was in Susanna Haswell Rowson's *Slaves in Algeria* (1794), a drama about piracy along the Barbary Coast in which a central role was played by a rapacious Jewish miser and swindler. A similar character appeared in James Ellison's *The American Captive* (1812). In fiction, George Lippard's Gothic novel *The Quaker City* presents a minor Jewish character named Gabriel von Gelt as a misshapen incarnation of greed.

In the middle of the 19th century, Jewish characters began to make their appearance in serious works of American fiction. Significantly, their entry occurred at the time of the first large increase of the American Jewish population, which was created by the arrival of German Jews in the wake of the European upheavals of 1848. The critic John J. Appel has observed that in Hawthorne's well-known story *Ethan Brand* (1851) "the German-Jewish peddler reflected American awareness of the growing numbers of German-Jewish immigrants who traveled the backwoods with their moveable stocks of goods." These peddlers also appear in the correspondence of Emily Dickinson and may be the source of some odd images in her poems, such as one in which she describes her orchard "sparkling like a Jew!"

In contrast, Longfellow's moving poem "The Jewish Cemetery at Newport," which was written in 1852, delineates Jewish martyrdom and antisemitic persecutions throughout the ages with the profoundest sympathy for the victims. Yet its concluding stanza is hardly calculated to inspire any hope or nurse illusions in the heart of its Jewish readers:

> But ah! What once has been shall be no more!
> The groaning earth in travail and in pain
> Brings forth its races, but does not restore,
> And the dead nations never rise again.

This dispiriting ending prompted a protest by Emma *Lazarus – the author of the sonnet "The New Colossus," which is inscribed on the base of the Statue of Liberty – who pointed out that it was hardly consonant with the facts.

Walt Whitman's voracious curiosity about the inhabitants of the city of New York led him to consider the Jews. Long before the appearance of *Leaves of Grass*, he had published two sizable articles, in a newspaper he was editing at the time, recording his impressions of the customs of the Sabbath service that he had witnessed at the Crosby Street Synagogue. The philo-Semitic temper of the time is nowhere more evident than in the writings of William Cullen Bryant, who was not only a distinguished American poet but also, for almost 50 years, the influential editor of New York's *Evening Post*, a newspaper that enjoyed the greatest prestige in mid-19th-century America. Commenting on a performance by the Shakespearean actor Edwin Booth in the role of Shylock, Bryant took the opportunity to find fault with Shakespeare for his repulsive caricature of the Jew and paid eloquent tribute to –

> That superiority of intellect which has survived all persecutions, and which, soaring above the prejudice of the hour, has filled us with reluctant admiration on finding how many of the great events which work the progress of the age or minister to its improvement or elevate its past may be traced to the wonderful workings of the soul of the Hebrew and the supremacy of that spiritual nature which gave to mankind its noblest religion, its noblest laws, and some of its noblest poetry and music.

The mass immigration to the United States of East European Jews that began in the 1880s and lasted until after World War I totally transformed both the character and the size of the American Jewish community and, concomitantly, the attitudes of American intellectuals toward it. On the whole, the first reactions still echoed the generous sentiments of an earlier age. William Dean Howells wrote with great insight and compassion about the Jewish immigrants on New York's Lower East Side in his *Impressions and Experiences* (1896), and in the same year he wrote an article hailing the advent of Abraham *Cahan's novel of immigrant life, *Yekl*, for which he himself had helped to find a publisher. Howells' friend Mark Twain expressed himself equally strongly on the subject of Jewish immigration. The Jews' "contributions to the world's list of great names in literature, science, art, music, finance, medicine, and abstruse learning," he wrote in an article in *Harper's* in 1899, "are… out of proportion to the weakness of his numbers … [the Jew] is now what he always was, exhibiting no decadence, no infirmities of age, no weakening of his parts, no slowing of his energies, no dulling of his alert and aggressive mind…"

It is impossible to pinpoint with any precision the exact moment when far-reaching historical changes first began to challenge this hitherto predominant image of the Jew in American literature. If anything, it tended somewhat to predate the time when the tide of popular tolerance toward Jews began to recede in America, which the historian Oscar Handlin has dated to "the portentous period between 1913 and 1920." During this time, as Handlin puts it, "great numbers of Americans became obsessed with fear of the Jew." The new attitudes of the 20th century are already anticipated by Henry James in his novel *The American Scene* (1907), in which he speaks of his impressions on New York's Lower East Side of "a Jewry that had burst all bounds.… The children swarmed above all – here was multiplication with a vengeance.… There is no swarming like that of Israel when once Israel has got a start." In a similar vein, some years later in his novel *The Beautiful and Damned* (1922), F. Scott Fitzgerald described a trip down the length of the island of Manhattan:

> Down in a tall busy street he read a dozen Jewish names on a line of stores; in the door of each stood a dark little man watching the passers from intent eyes – eyes gleaming with suspicion, with pride, with clarity, with cupidity, with comprehension. New York – he could not dissociate it now from the slow, upward creep of this people – the little stores, growing, expanding, consolidating, moving, watched over with hawk's eyes and a bee's attention to detail – they slathered out on all sides. It was impressive – in perspective, it was tremendous.

Even the normally sympathetic Mark Twain commented wryly on the enormous increase of Jewish numbers in America:

> When I read [in the *Encyclopaedia Britannica*] that the Jewish population of the United States was 250,000, I wrote the editor and explained to him that I was personally acquainted with more Jews than that in my country, and that his figures were without a doubt a misprint for 25,000,000.

The same impression is communicated humorlessly in the correspondence of Theodore Dreiser, who was inclined to assume the existence of a sinister conspiracy on the part of official agencies to minimize Jewish population statistics in the United States. Dreiser's antisemitism, which was unusual at the time for one who held radical left-wing opinions, surfaced so unmistakably during the Depression following the financial crash of 1929, and especially after the accession of the Nazis to power in Germany, that he was publicly taken to task for it by his Communist comrade Michael *Gold, the author of *Jews Without Money* (1930).

During the first four decades of the 20th century, it became almost fashionable for many American writers of distinction – especially among the expatriates – to express antisemitism. It is sometimes present in the writings of Edith Wharton (who once described Fitzgerald's gangster-villain Wolfsheim in *The Great Gatsby* (1925) as the "perfect Jew"), Henry James, T.S. Eliot, Ezra Pound, Ernest Hemingway, e.e. cummings, and others. It is strong in those of German ancestry like Dreiser, H.L. Mencken, and Thomas Wolfe, and it even touches a writer like Gertrude *Stein, who was herself, as Wyndham Lewis described her, "a brilliant Jewish lady." In 1920, the year which saw the publication of the spurious Protocols of the *Elders of Zion in Henry Ford's *Dearborn Independent*, Mencken wrote: "The case against the Jews is long and damning; it would justify ten thousand times as many pogroms as now go on in the world." Yet such sentiments did not seem incompatible with Mencken's having Jewish friends and even Jewish publishers! Among those who wrote about urban Jewry was Damon Runyon, whose *Guys and Dolls* (1932) and other short story collections teem with amiable Jewish gangsters and Broadway characters.

In the late 1930s, the pendulum began to swing back again, as the emerging barbarism of the Nazis developed an inhibiting effect upon intellectual antisemitism in America. A number of American writers, including Thomas Wolfe, T.S. Eliot, and F. Scott Fitzgerald, whose sentiments concerning the Jews had hitherto been less than friendly, now gave signs of regretting that their own position might be confused with or lend comfort to that of the Hitler regime. After being lionized by the Nazis on his visit to Germany in the mid-1930s,

Wolfe returned to the United States to write a report on what he had seen, which promptly resulted in the suppression of all his books in the Third Reich. The outbreak of World War II and its aftermath once again generated a new wave of philo-Semitic sympathies in American intellectual life.

[Milton Henry Hindus / Hillel Halkin]

Works on Palestine and Israel

American writers who visited Palestine in the 19th century found the land both inviting and forbidding. The climactic experience of Herman Melville's trip to Europe and the Near East (1857) appears to have been the 18 days he spent in Ereẓ Israel, mainly in the area of Jerusalem. His *Journal* (published in 1955) contains a vivid metaphor summing up the writer's impression of the desolation there: "In the emptiness of the lifeless antiquity of Jerusalem, the emigrant Jews are like flies that have taken up their abode in a skull." All Judea, in fact, seemed to him an accumulation of stones, rubbish, and the "mere refuse of creation." Yet the experience haunted Melville's imagination, and almost 20 years later he published his two-volume *Clarel; A Poem and Pilgrimage in the Holy Land* (1876), which was inspired by this visit to Jerusalem. Ten years after Melville's journey, Mark Twain embarked on the steamship *Quaker City* for a tour of the Mediterranean, which he describes in *The Innocents Abroad* (1869). His impressions of Palestine were similar to those of Melville, but though anxious to debunk the guidebooks, he recognized that "Palestine is no more of this work-day world. It is sacred to poetry and tradition – it is dreamland …" Twain's testimony to the true fascination of the ancient land did more to promote foreign travel among Americans than all the tourist brochures of his day.

One of the earliest novels by a U.S. writer dealing with Ereẓ Israel was Henry Gillman's *Hassan: A Fellah; A Romance of Palestine* (1898). This account of romance and adventure in the Holy Land was in general very hostile toward the Jews, although as U.S. consul in Jerusalem (1886–91) Gillman had succeeded in preventing the Turks from expelling the Jews from the country.

Among the early American-Jewish poets inspired by the Holy Land was Jessie *Sampter. In *The Emek* (1927), she portrayed the first pioneers in the Valley of Jezreel through a series of vivid prose poems; and in the verse collection *Brand Plucked from the Fire* (1937), she expressed her attitude to Judaism and Zionism. Judah Stampfer (1923–), a poet deeply conscious of his Jewish roots, published several poems about Israel, which he knew as both soldier and teacher, in the collection *Jerusalem Has Many Faces* (1950). *Israel* (1925) by Ludwig *Lewisohn, was both a Zionist-oriented study of the Jewish question in the 1920s and an evocative and reflective travel book covering the development of the country. Meyer *Levin wrote two novels on the subject: *Yehuda* (1931), a first-hand description of the life on a kibbutz in the late 1920s; and *My Father's House* (1947), the story of a Polish boy's escape to Palestine during World War II. Michael Blankfort's novel *Behold the Fire* (1965) tells the story of the Palestinian Jews who assisted British intelligence during World War I, and another of his novels, *The Juggler* (1952), is also set in Israel. A defiant Zionist work of the post-World War II era was Ben *Hecht's drama, *A Flag is Born* (1946). Probably the most famous of all the novels about Israel's establishment and the idea of independence is Leon *Uris' *Exodus* (1958). Daniel Spicehandler's *Burnt Offering* (1961) also deals with the war, as does his autobiographical *Let My Right Hand Wither* (1950). Robert *Nathan's novel, *A Star in the Wind* (1962), tells how a young American gradually discovers his identity as a Jew while witnessing the events in Palestine in May 1948. The scene in Jerusalem at the same period is described in Zelda Popkin's (d. 1983) *Quiet Street* (1951). In the 1960s the most popular novel about Israel was James Michener's *The Source* (1963). Weaving his tale around a fictional archaeological site ("Makor"), Michener made his readers realize afresh the historical significance of Ereẓ Israel and its continuing relevance to the present and future.

The Jewish Contribution (to 1970)

Curiously enough, one of the first writers to realize that the growth of a Jewish audience provided the conditions for the evolution of a distinctive American-Jewish literary school was the non-Jew Henry Harland (well known in England during the 1890s as editor of *The Yellow Book*), who, under the pseudonym of Sidney Luska, wrote a number of popular novels during the 1880s on subjects of Jewish concern. One of them, *The Yoke of the Thora* (1887), dealt with the tragic difficulties of intermarriage more than 40 years before Ludwig Lewisohn's eloquent treatment of the same subject in *The Island Within* (1928). Although there were representatives of American Jewry in the field of belles lettres before 1880, the most significant Jewish writing had been in the form of biographical documents (rather than of works that aspired to art), such as those collected by Jacob Marcus in the three volumes of his *Memoirs of American Jews, 1755–1865* (1955–56). Few literary productions by American Jews concerning Jewish life at the turn of the century in the immigrant ghettoes or elsewhere are as interesting and significant as such memoir-type works as Mary *Antin's *The Promised Land* (1912), Ludwig Lewisohn's *Up Stream* (1922) and *Mid-Channel* (1929), Charles *Reznikoff's *Early History of a Sewing-Machine Operator* (1936) and *Family Chronicle* (1963), Anzia *Yezierska's *Red Ribbon on a White Horse* (1950), Morris Raphael Cohen's *Dreamer's Journey* (1949), Jacob *Epstein's autobiography *Let There Be Sculpture* (1940), S.N. *Behrman's *The Worcester Account* (1954), and Myer Levin's *In Search* (1950).

Abraham Cahan was the first American Jewish writer of considerable power to attempt the ascent from memoir and journalism, where he was initially at home (for the better part of his career he led the dual life of English novelist and editor in chief of the Yiddish Jewish Daily *Forward), and he undoubtedly met with exemplary success. In many ways, he succeeded in writing the great American-Jewish novel as well as any of the writers who later followed him and reaped richer awards in popularity and critical acclaim. While Cahan wrote a number of novels, his magnum opus was indisputably *The Rise of David Levinsky* (1917), the value of which has been continually rediscovered by American-Jewish literary critics to their own surprise. Although *David Levinsky* is, among other things, a scathing indictment of the American "success story," the dream of so many millions of immigrants, it is also representative of the first generation of Jewish immigrants to America after 1880 in its refusal to make any sweeping rejection of American life as such. Although nearly all Jewish immigrant writers were critical in one degree or another of the American realities that confronted them, such as poverty (Mary Antin, Anzia Yezierska) or social discrimination (Ludwig Lewisohn), they were nevertheless grateful to America and could never forget the contrast between the freedom and opportunity they found there and the repressiveness and narrowness of the old world. None of them could ever have written, as did native-born Michael Gold in his "proletarian" novel about Jewish immigrant life in New York, *Jews Without Money* (1930), "America has grown so rich and fat because she has eaten the tragedies of millions of immigrants." Such an attitude arose from a depth of alienation, hostility, and resentment that they simply never experienced.

In this respect alone, a book like *David Levinsky* is superior to such second-generation "proletarian" successors of the 1920s and 1930s as *Jews Without Money*, Samuel *Ornitz's *Haunch, Paunch, and Jowl* (1923), and Isidor Schneider's (d. 1977) *From the Kingdom of Necessity* (1935). For all the genuine indignation over the social injustices of American life, out of which such novels were written, the schematic Communist theory to which they were molded turned out to be a Procrustean bed for the imagination to lie in. One feels that the predatory capitalists, venal and reactionary schoolteachers, corrupt rabbis, and sentimentalized workers who populate the pages of this Jewish-American school sprang more from some economic or political textbook than from their authors' actual observations of the life around them. The lessons of moderation, patience, and fortitude that were learned by the first generation of immigrants through hard experience seem to have been lost upon their rebellious offspring, whose psychological experience of American reality may have been even harsher because of the higher level of expectation with which they, as native sons, were raised. It was precisely the paradoxical contradiction so often evident in American life between limitless promise and limited performance that turned so many of them to social and political extremes.

The best literary work of this second, native generation of Jewish Americans was done by writers who, while they were by no means oblivious to social ills and may even have been for a time sympathetic to their more "activist" fellow authors, were more aesthetically oriented, more inclined to take professional pride in their literary workmanship, and more apt to look upon the art that they created as an end in itself. For the propagandist school of Ornitz, Schneider, Gold, and even Joseph *Freeman and Howard *Fast, art was an adjective. What was important to them was the substantive matter or views which it modified. But for writers like Henry *Roth and Charles Reznikoff, art was not only a noun, but a noun with a capital letter. Their great idol, as Reznikoff's *By the Waters of Manhattan* (1930) and Roth's *Call It Sleep* (1934) reveal, was James Joyce. Indeed, sharp-eyed observers of the American literary scene, like Scott Fitzgerald, had seen the shape of things to come before they actually materialized. In an article in *The Bookman* in 1926, Fitzgerald predicted the coming of a "novel off the Jewish tenement-block, festooned with wreaths out of *Ulysses* and the later Gertrude Stein." *Call It Sleep* appeared eight years later. Like *David Levinsky*, it has since enjoyed periodic rediscoveries by prominent Jewish critics. A powerful evocation of a Jewish childhood in a New York immigrant slum, it is a book worth reading and remembering, though to call it one of the great novels of the 20th century, as has been done on occasion, seems to be an unfortunate type of cultural inflation. Such enthusiastic overestimation by critics may originate in sheer delight at discovering that American-Jewish authors more than 30 year ago were capable of ascending into an atmosphere of pure aestheticism from the common ground of documentary social realism and political propaganda in which so many fellow authors of their generation were mired.

An anomaly among Jewish novelists of the 1930s was Nathanael *West, who in the course of his short life wrote only a few thin works, the best-known of which, *Miss Lonelyhearts*, is today generally considered a minor American classic. Though West avoided writing about Jews (characteristically, he changed his own name from Weinstein), in a sense he was, more than any other figure of his age, a precursor of the great flowering of American-Jewish writing that took place in the years after World War II. Whereas nearly all of his contemporaries wrote naturalistic fiction, West was inclined to imaginative fantasy; where his contemporaries cultivated a tone of dramatic seriousness, West's preference was for comedy; and whereas his contemporaries were for the most part concerned with the problems of immigrant life and/or the great depression, his own interest lay in that psychological alienation of the individual in modern, atomized, American industrial society that, in the final analysis, had little to do with either poverty or wealth. In all of these respects, West foreshadowed tendencies that were to be fully and exuberantly developed in the American-Jewish literature of the late 1940s, 1950s, and 1960s, which was undoubtedly one reason for the revival of interest in him in those decades.

Among Jewish playwrights in the 19th century was Mordecai M. *Noah whose historical plays, notably *The Fortress of Sorrento* (1808), *Paul and Alexis* (1812), and *She Would Be a Soldier* (1819), were well received. Another important figure was David *Belasco, whose *The Return of Peter Grimm* (1911) was considered an important play. The most prominent of Jewish playwrights in the first half of the 20th century were

George S. *Kaufman, S.N. *Behrman, Clifford *Odets, Elmer *Rice, and Lillian *Hellman.

[Milton Henry Hindus]

The quarter of a century of American literary life that followed the end of World War II witnessed a conspicuous emergence of Jewish talent and activity that reached its peak in the late 1950s and early 1960s, which were on occasion even referred to by critics as American literature's "Jewish decade" and as a period of "Jewish renaissance." I. Malin and I. Stark wrote in their anthology *Breakthrough: A Treasury of Contemporary American-Jewish Literature* (1964): "For the first time in history a large and impressively gifted group of serious American-Jewish writers has broken through the psychic barriers of the past to become an important, possibly a major reformative influence in American life and letters." While there is perhaps an element of hyperbole in such phrases, it is well worth considering why the phenomenon described here came into existence and what its defining characteristics were.

The period after World War II roughly marked the coming of age of a third generation in American-Jewish life dating back to the great East European immigration of the turn of the century. Three main features distinguished this generation from its predecessor: American-born itself, it was for the most part raised by parents who were either native-born or who had broken away physically and culturally from the immigrant ghetto; unlike these parents, most of whom grew up in relative poverty, it was largely the product of middle- or lower-middle-class homes, where physical want was unknown; and unlike its parents again, it was overwhelmingly college-educated. Forming a more thoroughly acculturated, economically secure, and better educated group than its parents, it was only natural that third-generation American Jewry should have included a higher percentage of academicians, artists, intellectuals, and writers.

At the same time, the salient fact about this third-generation intelligentsia, at least to judge by the literature that it produced, was an unmistakable sense of estrangement not only from the generation that raised it but in a subtler sense from American culture as a whole. The former reaction is perhaps the easier to understand. In a sense, the conflict between the generation of American Jews that reached intellectual maturity after World War II and the preceding generation was more intense and exacerbated than the conflict between the latter and the original immigrant generation. Whereas the earlier struggle was a clear-cut one between the desire to preserve certain old-world values and the urge to "Americanize" at any cost, the later one was between two conflicting versions of "Americanism" itself. If anything, it was precisely what the second generation looked upon as its successful adaptation to American life that was repeatedly excoriated and satirized in "third generation literature" as a vulgar materialism.

More difficult to explain is the definite sense of not being entirely at home in the general American landscape. Possibly this may be regarded as the surfacing of a residual Jewish unease, an atavistic sense of exile that continued to exist beneath the accomplishments of Americanization. In part, it may also be a reaction to the overall complacency and thinly veiled anti-intellectualism of a great deal of American life in the 1940s and 1950s, which made adjustment difficult for many non-Jewish artists and intellectuals as well. In any case, whatever its roots, what is significant about this feeling of estrangement is that time after time it is deliberately expressed in openly Jewish terms, as in Delmore *Schwartz's poem "Abraham":

> It has never been otherwise: /Exiled, wandering, dumbfounded by riches, /Estranged among strangers, dismayed by the infinite sky, /An alien to myself until at the last caste of the last alienation, /The angel of death comes to make the alienated and indestructible one a part of his famous and democratic society.

And in a remark which might be applied to the work of numerous Jewish writers of these years, Schwartz commented how "… the fact of being a Jew became available to me as a central symbol of alienation … and certain other characteristics which are the peculiar marks of modern life, and as I think now, the essential ones."

These words help to explain why Jewish writing played the crucial role that it did in America during this period, for if the theme of social and spiritual alienation seemed immemorially Jewish to the Jewish author, in an age when the individual was increasingly being viewed as a helpless pawn of the manipulations of big business, big government, mass communications, and modern technology, it was fast becoming basic to American intellectual life in general. The result of this overlap was, paradoxically, that at the very historical moment that American-Jewish writers were feeling sufficiently confident of their position in American life to express their sense of estrangement from it, non-Jewish readers and intellectuals were prepared for the first time to see in the figure of the "alien Jew" a genuine American culture hero of the times – or, more precisely, an anti-hero, since the treatment of alienation in the American-Jewish writing of these years was a self-directed irony by means of which the predicament of the alienated character was simultaneously intensified and mocked. This attitude owed much, it would appear, to traditional East European Jewish humor and is an excellent example of how fragments of immigrant folk culture survived among American Jews to be eventually transmuted into serious art.

If one takes for example the three postwar Jewish novelists whose work has aroused the greatest interest among the serious reading public in America, one finds that the most representative characters of all three share much with the traditional Jewish folk-humor figure of the *shlemiel*. For all the differences between these characters and the authors who created them, Saul *Bellow's Herzog (*Herzog*, 1964), Bernard *Malamud's Levin (*A New Life*, 1962) and Fidelman (*Pictures of Fidelman*, 1969), and Philip *Roth's Portnoy (*Portnoy's Complaint*, 1969) share a common private war against a society to which they cannot adjust and against which their only retaliation is to play the comic buffoon. The harder each tries, the more miserably each fails, yet none is ultimately defeated, for in terms of a highly Jewish paradox, to win such battles is to lose, to lose is to win. If success corrupts within the moral universe set down by these books, absolute success corrupts absolutely; or, in the words of Ivan Gold, another Jewish novelist who made his debut in the 1950s, with a long comic story (*Taub East*) about Jewish servicemen in Japan: "There must be an outgroup. This is the divine order of things. If lucky enough to be one, rejoice!"

This association of the Jew with the eternal outsider – less by virtue of any sustained social prejudice directed against him than of his own ingrained sensitivities, which make it impossible for him to integrate successfully into the aggressive, competitive fabric of American life – occurs as a unifying theme in much Jewish fiction of the 1950s and 1960s, despite the wide variety of backgrounds and environments invoked. One finds it in the Kafkaesque stories of Isaac Rosenfeld; in Wallace Markfeld's recollections of boyhood in Jewish Brooklyn; in Herbert *Gold's short stories about life in Jewish suburbia; in Leslie *Fiedler's fiction about Jewish intellectuals on the campus; Edward Wallant's urban novels; in the Glass family stories of J.D. *Salinger; and in the writings of many other Jewish novelists and short-story writers of the period. Hardly any of the central characters created by such authors have any active sense of identification with the Jewish community or Jewish tradition as such. In fact, nearly all are more alienated from the organized Jewish life of the communities in which they lived than from their surroundings in general, yet few are not obsessed with the moral implications of being Jewish and the sometimes bewildering problems of dealing with them.

It is debatable to what extent the emergence in the 1960s of the so-called "novel of the absurd," with a wide range of grotesquely comic situations reflecting the meaninglessness of contemporary existence, was again indebted in part to the surfacing in American life of a traditional mode of Jewish humor. It is a matter of record, however, that among the earliest practitioners of "black humor" as a tool of social criticism were such stand-up Jewish comedians as Lennie Bruce and Mort Sahl (the former, in particular, acquired a devoted avant-garde audience before his early death). This same sensibility appears as a defining stylistic element in the works of a number of prominent Jewish novelists of the 1960s, such as Bruce Jay *Friedman and Joseph Heller. Heller's morbidly comic novel of army life during World War II, *Catch-22* (1961), became practically a Bible for a generation of young Americans who came to political consciousness at the time of the Vietnam War and for whom it epitomized the struggle of the individual to survive in a mindlessly bureaucratic world.

By far the most radical in his indictment of American society among major American Jewish novelists has been Norman *Mailer, whose prose virtuosity and intellectual boldness made him for many readers the most exciting American novelist and essayist of his time. On the whole, Mailer studiously avoided Jewish characters and concerns in his work, a fact that is itself of some critical interest and that constitutes the exception rather than the rule among his Jewish contemporaries.

American Jewish poets of this period have also, for the most part, drawn freely on their experience as Jews. Many would no doubt agree with Muriel Rukeyser (d. 1980) when she writes that

> To be a Jew in the twentieth century
> Is to be offered a gift. If you refuse,
> Wishing to be invisible, you choose
> Death of the spirit, the stone insanity

or with Hyam Plutzik's lines in "The Priest Eskranath," in which the Jew is portrayed as the eternal outsider, the compulsive intellectual critic who can never be at rest:

> Listen, you nations:/They will lure you from your spontaneous ecstasies,/And positive possessions, and with themselves,/Carry you forth on arduous pilgrimages,/Whose only triumph can be a bitter knowledge."

If one were to compile a list of leading American Jewish poets of these years – Charles Reznikoff, Louis Zukofsky (d. 1978), Karl *Shapiro, Howard Nemerov (d. 1991), Delmore Schwartz, David Ignatow, Irving Feldman, Babette *Deutsch, Denise Levertov, John Hollander, Kenneth Koch – one would find that few have not availed themselves at times of the wealth of symbolic and allusive material that the Jewish heritage provides, though few have actually made this heritage the theme of an entire volume, as did Karl Shapiro in his *Poems of a Jew* (1958). Unique among American Jewish poets in his impact upon both the American and the international world of poetry has been Allen *Ginsberg, whose long free-verse poem *Howl* (1955) was a landmark in the development of contemporary American prosody and one of the first poetic trumpet blasts of the "beat generation" and of the profound cultural transformation that began to affect American life in these years. Ginsberg has Jewish motifs, as in his poem *Kaddish* (1960), and his mystical inclinations have led him to take an interest in the symbolism of Ḥasidism and the Kabbalah.

In drama, Arthur *Miller was widely regarded throughout the 1950s as the leading American playwright of his age. His reputation faded somewhat in the 1960s with the decline of realistic theater in general, but his *Death of a Salesman*, at least, was certain to remain a classic of the American repertoire. Among the leading experimental playwrights of the 1960s were Jack Gelber, Arthur Koppitt, and Israel Horovitz. An avant-garde company that pioneered in the creation of what came to be known in the late 1960s as "total" or "action" theater, with its emphasis on improvisation, audience involvement, and radical social and political content, was Julian Beck's and Judith Malina's Living Theater, which spent much of the decade in political exile in Europe. One of the most accomplished troupes to arise under its influence was Joseph Chaikin's Open Theater, located in New York. In the commercial theater, Paddy *Chayefsky wrote a number of highly successful Broadway dramas and Neil Simon was the author of numerous popular comedy hits.

Particularly prominent among American literary critics in the postwar period were Philip Rahv, Alfred *Kazin, Irving *Howe, Lionel Trilling, and Leslie Fiedler. Common to all was a rejection of "new" or "form" criticism, with its insistence on regarding the literary work as an isolated artifice to be analyzed only in its own internal terms, and an interest in the study of literature for the sake of its wider cultural, political, and psychological ramifications. Among the leading exponents of this "neo-new" criticism of the 1960s, on the other hand, was Susan *Sontag. Also noteworthy in the 1950s and 1960s was the key role played in American literary life by cultural and critical publications presided over by Jews, among them the *Partisan Review*, edited by Philip Rahv; the *New American Review*, edited by Theodore Solotaroff; *Commentary, edited by Norman *Podhoretz; and the *New York Review of Books*, edited by Robert Silvers and Barbara Epstein.

No discussion of the Jews and American literature in this era would be complete without mention of the unique phenomenon of the Jewish "best-seller" – the popular book or novel on a Jewish subject whose sales ran into the hundreds of thousands or millions, frequently leading all other contenders on national "best-seller" lists. Since one can assume that such books – among the most popular of which were Herman *Wouk's *Marjorie Morningstar*, Leon Uris' *Exodus*, Harry *Golden's *Only in America*, Harry Kemelman's *Friday the Rabbi Slept Late*, Chaim Potok's *The Chosen*, John Hersey's *The Wall*, and James Michener's *The Source* (the last two by non-Jewish authors) – were in large measure purchased, or at least promoted, by Jewish readers, the dimensions of their success reveal the extraordinary impact of Jewish readership on the American book market in general. Characteristic of the Jewish "best-seller" was the fact that unlike most of the more serious American-Jewish novels mentioned previously (some of which also, however, were highly successful commercially), it tended to portray Jewish life in America and elsewhere in highly flattering and often sentimental terms. Of generally slight literary value, such books will nonetheless interest future historians for the picture they give of how the majority of American-Jewish readers during these years preferred to view themselves and their tradition.

[Hillel Halkin]

1970–2005

I

Modern American-Jewish literature is a colloquy between an America in process and a Judaism in change. This literature expresses the interplay amongst self, community, and *heritages*. This body of letters is also a dialogue with theology in large, and theologies in small, whether found in text, or in a determined seeking for engagement with God. Often, American-Jewish literature presents these complex relationships as the comportment of a Jewish ethic with the American present: the belief that justice and compassion transcend the *mores* and self-interest of the historical moment. The strong relay between Jewish existence, culture, and God is self-reflective, and communally defining. Significant readings of this are found in Max Schulz's *Radical Sophistication: Studies in Contemporary Jewish-American Novelists* (1969), which studies the Jewish writer's search for a balance between existential despair and the Jewish tradition of affirming a meaningful life; Allen Guttmann's *The Jewish Writer in America: Assimilation and the Crisis of Identity* (1971), exploring the claims made upon the idea and act of being Jewish; Alan Berger's *Crisis and Covenant: The Holocaust in American Jewish Fiction* (1985), emphasizing the secular and religious value systems of Judaism; L.S. Dembo's *The Monological Jew: A Literary Study* (1988), dealing, for example, with the impact of Buber and Sartre on modern American-Jewish writing, and Norman Finkelstein's *The Ritual of New Creation: Jewish Tradition and Contemporary Literature* (1992), covering such figures as Gershom *Scholem, Walter *Benjamin, Harold *Bloom, and Cynthia *Ozick.

By now, American-Jewish literature is also a sustained meditation on Jewish life as a civic identity, one authorized by American pluralism and democracy. The republication of Paul *Goodman's *The Empire City* (2001) once again reminds the reader that America's representative citizens could be portrayed by a Jewish writer. The always suggestive, if not polemical author names his protagonist Horatio Alger. As social critic and therapist, Goodman insists that his characters utilize the entitlements of American democracy, as well as their "natural" strengths, to overcome political obstruction and psychological impasse.

More often than not, this America for the contemporary Jewish writer is *not* an America of outward passage, attended by the themes of breaking away from the European past, learning English, earning a living, and creating or suffering one's future. Instead, American-Jewish literature charts the refashioning of a difficult, contemporary identity. It takes into account the assertions that Zionism is the end of Diaspora; that the Holocaust demands a new understanding of surety, theology, and politics; and that America is not simply a new chapter of Diaspora, but a new beginning in which Jewish text in a borrowed tongue redefines the Jewish past and opens up a unique future.

Contemporary American-Jewish literature often takes Judaism and Jewishness as the inescapable context of life. Whether set in a Europe lost to the imagination, or modern America, such a framework embraces both continuity and an imagined unity. To cite several examples: Chaim *Potok's *My Name Is Asher Lev* (1972); Francine *Prose's *Judah the Pious* (1973); Isaac Bashevis *Singer's *The Penitent* (1983); Anne *Roiphe's *Lovingkindness* (1987); Elie *Wiesel's *Twilight* (1988); Wendy *Wasserstein's drama *The Sisters Rosenzweig* (1993); Steve Stern's *The Wedding Jester* (1999); Joshua Hammer's *Chosen by God* (1999); Nathan Englander's *For the Relief of Unbearable Urges* (1999); Allegra *Goodman's *Paradise Park* (2001); and Jonathan Rosen's *Joy Comes in the Morning* (2004). There are also examples of women rebelling against the constraining religious life of the Orthodox: Naomi *Ragen's *Jephte's Daughter* (1989); Pearl Abraham's *The Romance Reader* (1995); Boaz Yakin's film *A Price above Rubies* (1998), and Hortense *Calisher's *Sunday Jews* (2002).

There is a marked return to biblical and rabbinic text. In the contemporary period, writers allude to the Hebrew Scripture and Talmud, as well as explore the possibilities of interpretation and retelling. Salient examples are Neil *Simon's play *God's Favorite* (published 1975), based on *Job*; David Rosenberg and Harold Bloom's *The Book of J* (1990) with its theory of authorship; Joseph Heller's *God Knows* (1984), which casts David's voice into modern idiom; Alicia Ostriker's *The Nakedness of the Fathers: Biblical Visions and Revisions* (1994), which is a writer's meditation on biblical themes, speaking across "boundaries" as well as addressing the character of women in the text; Norma Rosen's *Biblical Women Unbound* (1996), which seeks to recover the power of biblical matriarchs and their voices; Anita Diamant's *The Red Tent* (1997) which recreates Dinah's story; and Robert *Pinsky's *The Life of David* (2005). (Over these works looms, of course, Thomas Mann's Joseph novels which are probably the most compelling engagement of writer and Hebrew Scripture in the 20th century).

There are also studies of rabbinic exegesis and secular writing, as well as the relationship between Hebrew Scripture and contemporary literature: selected examples are, respectively, *Midrash and Literature* (ed. Geoffrey Hartman and Sanford Budick, 1986) and Robert *Alter's *Canon and Creativity: Modern Writing and the Authority of Scripture* (2000). During this contemporary period, Jewish writers seem to be eager to write about their grappling with text and how they came to do so. Among recent works are *Congregation: Contemporary Writers Read the Jewish Bible*, edited by David Rosenberg (1987), and *People of the Book: Thirty Scholars Reflect on Their Jewish Identity* (1996), edited by Jeffrey Rubin-Dorsky and Shelley Fisher Fishkin.

The modern American-Jewish writer and reader are doubly fortunate: foundational texts and traditions of interpretation are democratized and decentralized. Computer software for the Bible offers commentary, word searching, parsing, and multiple translations stacked across the screen (as for example with Bibleworks, which is Christian-centered), as well as the sea of Jewish text and commentary (as with Davka, which is in Hebrew). There are new hard-copy editions of the Talmud with English-language translation and gloss (for example the Steinsaltz and Schottenstein, complementing the classic Soncino). And, of course, new translations of, and commentary on, Hebrew Scripture, including W. Gunther Plaut and Bernard Bamberger's *The Torah: A Modern Commentary* (1967/1981); The *JPS Torah Commentary* (General Editor, Nahum Sarna; its five volumes were published between 1989 and 1996); The *Stone Edition* of *Tanach* (1996); Michael Fishbane's *The JPS Bible Commentary: Haftarot: The Traditional Hebrew Text with the New JPS Translation* (2002); Adele Berlin's and Marc Zvi Brettler's *The Jewish Study Bible* (2004); Richard Elliott Friedman's *Commentary on the Torah: With a New Translation and the Hebrew Text* (2001); *Etz Hayim: Torah and Commentary* (Senior Editor, David Lieber, 2001); and Robert Alter's *The Five Books of Moses: A Translation with Commentary* (2004). As a result, rabbinic and secular commentary jostle each other, supplementing, if not challenging, each other's authority. These works make contemporary interpretive communities abound by crossing intellectual, class, gender, and theological lines.

Given the ease of Jewish life in America, the authority of estrangement that the American-Jewish writer once possessed has diminished. Yet the modern canon is still deeply – and rightly – informed by an earlier generation of critics who made a moral use of alienation and its insights. Men of letters such as Leslie Fiedler, Irving *Howe, Alfred *Kazin, Philip *Rahv, Isaac *Rosenfeld, and Lionel *Trilling helped establish both the American as well as the American-Jewish literary imaginations, exemplifying the democratic tradition in which proverbial outsiders create national and world traditions. Modern representative examples of their work are Rahv's *Essays on Literature & Politics, 1932–1972* (1978); *Preserving the Hunger: An Isaac Rosenfeld Reader* (ed. Mark Shechner, 1988); Howe's *Selected Writings, 1950–1990* (1990); Fiedler's *Fiedler on the Roof: Essays on Literature and Jewish Identity* (1991); Leon Wieseltier's anthology of Trilling's writings, *The Moral Obligation To Be Intelligent: Selected Essays* (2000); and *Alfred Kazin's America: Critical and Personal Writings* (ed. Ted Solotaroff, 2003). The arc of their times, traversing ideologies and interpretations of a literature relevant to both American and American-Jewish culture is described by such critics as Bernard Rosenberg and Ernest Goldstein in *Creators and Disturbers: Reminiscences by Jewish Intellectuals of New York* (1982); Alexander Bloom in *Prodigal Sons: The New York Intellectuals & Their World* (1986); Alan Wald in *The New York Intellectuals: The Rise and Decline of the Anti-Stalinist Left from the 1930s to the 1980s* (1987); Mark Shechner in *After the Revolution: Studies in the Contemporary Jewish-American Imagination* (1987); and Carole Kessner in her edition of *The "Other" New York Jewish Intellectuals* (1994).

As an immigrant *Yidishkayt* passed from being a seemingly cohesive culture of the East European Diaspora, to being a creative minority presence in the United States, it also became an adjunct of an American civic faith. Its language became English; its rhetoric became increasingly receptive to a democratic, pluralistic, and diversifying society. *Yidishkayt* became an American "Jewishness." It defined the issues of American-Jewish life in terms of American political and social history. *Yidishkayt* retained its charms as an almost otherworldliness, indicating a putatively richer, thick life that was lost: Although this is a rightly disputed claim, its imaginative recall indicates that the past is not yet over: witness Rebecca *Goldstein's *Mazel* (1995). Readers ought to consult as well Karen Brodkin's *How Jews Became White Folks and What That Says about Race in America* (1998). The two-volume anthology edited by Ellen Schiff, *Awake and Singing: 7 Classic Plays from the American Jewish Repertoire* (1995) and *Fruitful and Multiplying: 9 Contemporary Plays from the American Jewish Repertoire* (1996) contain notable examples of the past suffusing the present.

For the contemporary American-Jewish writer, nostalgia is also a rite of recalled passage. Such homesickness wards off an uncertain future by creating a haven of memory, measuring the passage of the Jew from one bitter exile to a modernity that is sweet, but precarious. As David Roskies' and Diane Roshkies' *The Shtetl Book* (1975) indicates, the shtetl is now textualized. Important examples are *The Shtetl* (ed., Joachim Neugroschel, 1979); and the republication of A.J. *Heschel's poignant *The Earth Is the Lord's: The Inner World of the Jew in Eastern Europe* (1950/1987/1995). The shtetl's cultural assignment as a world more charmed because of its known extinction animates, for instance, the groundbreaking, somewhat rosy *Life Is With People: The Jewish Little-Town of Eastern Europe* by Mark Zborowski and Elizabeth Herzog (1952; ten years later, perhaps prompted by a growing American desire to "authenticate" a lost world, the book was subtitled *The Culture of the Shtetl*); the perennial revivals of *Fiddler on the Roof*; Melvin *Bukiet's *Stories of an Imaginary Childhood* (1992); and also the New American Library's two-volume collection of I.B. Singer's *Collected Stories* (2004). Although the shtetl's charm is denied by immigrant autobiographies, and early American-Jewish novels written by those fleeing Eastern Europe, there are few novels that have done so: perhaps the most significant are Peter Martin's *The Landsmen* (1952); and Bernard *Malamud's *The Fixer* (1966). Jonathan Safran Foer's *Everything Is Illuminated* (2002) depicts the betrayal of Jews within a shtetl. An important study about immigrant memories, often entailing the shtetl, and the Pale of Settlement is Jan Schwartz's *Imagining Lives: Autobiographical Fiction of Yiddish Writers* (2005).

Nonetheless, there is a return of sorts open to the American-Jewish writer: the homecoming to a definable locality, binding together the immediacy and *mores* of the past, and usually the past of one's childhood. For the American-Jewish literary protagonist, the other side of acculturation is the longing for the particularity of belonging, of enjoying the perceived solidarity of the Jewish community. Jay *Neugeboren's *The Stolen Jew* (1981) deals with his protagonist's return to Brooklyn. Steven Stern discovered the American "ghetto" life of "the Pinch" in Memphis, setting much of his fiction there (see, for example, his *A Plague of Dreamers: Three Novellas* (1994). In *American Pastoral* (1997), Philip *Roth's Nathan Zuckerman judges both the "Swede" and contemporary America in the light of childhood and adolescent values rich with irony and naiveté. Paradoxically, many acculturated American Jews now have come back to a community of Jews, but this time to a supportive community of the often elderly, remembering (or keeping at bay) all that is now past: Leslie Epstein's *Goldkorn Tales* (1985); Alan Isler's *The Prince of West End Avenue* (1994); Stanley *Elkin's *Mrs. Ted Bliss* (1995); and Andrew Furman's rendition of a young man among the Florida elderly, in *Alligators May Be Present* (2005).

Diasporas, both physical and intellectual, give American-Jewish literature possibilities for futures not solely determined by one national narrative but by many. So often defined in the late 19th and early 20th centuries as the migration away from the Eastern seaboard, whether that of the moving frontier, the mid-Western settlements, a commonizing America is now conscious of its histories. Nonetheless, an industrialized, urbanizing America, World War II, the Korean War, Viet Nam, and the Civil Rights movement give Jewish life in America the certainty of shared national, and international experience. As American-Jewish literature has moved away from the lamentation over the loss of a past rooted in places other than America, editors have preserved its diverse intellectual and cultural genealogies. Impressive examples are found in Jerome Rothenberg's *A Big Jewish Book: Poems & Other Visions of the Jews from Tribal Times to the Present* (with Harris Lenowitz, and Charles Doria, 1978); Howard Schwartz and Anthony Rudolf's *Voices Within the Ark: The Modern Jewish Poets* (1980); Ilan Stavans' *The Oxford Book of Jewish Stories* (1998); and Derek Rubin's anthology, *Who We Are: On Being (and Not Being) A Jewish American Writer* (2005). A companion work is Murray Baumgarten's *City Scriptures: Modern Jewish Writing* (1982).

Jewish thinkers and writers, who were not far from their immigrant pasts or its comportment with American promises of success, called into being a new understanding of American culture as well as American-Jewish literature. Their *Yidishkayt* and their Jewishness domesticated as well as made insurgent the values of a pluralizing American civilization. Louis Harap's indispensable *The Image of the Jew in American Literature: From Early Republic to Mass Immigration* (1974) analyzes how the figure of the Jew and the Jewish public appeared to American people-of-letters. His three volumes entitled *Creative Awakening: The Jewish Presence in Twentieth-Century American Literature, 1900–1940s*, (1987); *In the Mainstream: The Jewish Presence in Twentieth-Century American Literature, 1950s–1980s* (1987); *Dramatic Encounters: The Jewish Presence in Twentieth-Century American Drama, Poetry, and Humor and the Black-Jewish Literary Relationship* (1987); Susanne Klingenstein's *Jews in the American Academy, 1900–1940: The Dynamics of Intellectual Assimilation* (1991); and her *Enlarging America: The Cultural Work of Jewish Literary Scholars, 1930–1990* (1998); Andrew Furman's study, *Contemporary Jewish American Writers and the Multicultural Dilemma* (2000); and David Biale, Michael Galchinsky, and Susannah Heschel's anthology *Insider/Outsider: American Jews and Multiculturalism* (1998) address how American Jews are viewed on a cultural spectrum from the oppositional to appositional.

Diasporas, belongings, and returns involve the poetics of remembrance. The shaping of the American-Jewish canon calls attention to traditions of memory, rhetoric, and languages: the classic work is Henry *Roth's *Call It Sleep* (1934); a contemporary example is Myla Goldberg's *Bee Season* (2000). Critical discussion of this complexity is explored variously in Rael Meyerowitz's *Transferring to America: Jewish Interpretations of American Dreams* (1995); Sidra DeKoven Ezrahi's *Booking Passage: Exile and Homecoming in the Modern Jewish Imagination* (2000); and Ranen Omer-Sherman's *Diaspora* *and Zionism in Jewish American Literature: Lazarus, Syrkin, Reznikoff and Roth* (2002).

Speaking in "American," a "trans-national" American rhetoric as Randolph Bourne might have called it, the American-Jewish novelists' characters invariably engage the past rather than dismiss it. Individuality is affirmed though at the expense of the sustaining community. American-Jewish novelists usually portray the ironic ease and anxiety of the American self as it moves between and within communities. Cases-in-point are Francine Prose's *A Changed Man* (2005) in which a former member of the Aryan Resistance Movement comes to support a Jewish reconciliation organization; and again in Prose's *Guided Tours of Hell* (1997), in which the protagonist, a minor American playwright, questions the authenticity of his life when measured against a Holocaust survivor's; Philip Roth's *The Human Stain* (2000) in which an African American poses as a Jewish professor of the classics; Emily Prager's *Eve's Tattoo* (1991), in which a character usurps what is thought to be a Holocaust victim's tattoo; and Michael *Chabon's *The Amazing Adventures of Kavalier and Clay* (2000), in which two young Jewish men, one gay and the other a refugee fleeing the Nazis, invent a comic book hero who becomes an American icon.

Yet America is not so liberally conceived as a humorous theater of invented selves. A good instance is Norma Rosen's novel, *John and Anzia: An American Romance* (1989), depicting the affair between John Dewey and Anzia *Yezierska. Both find each other exotic and iconic: Yezierska represents – to Dewey – the unbridled spirit of a colorful people, attuned to their instincts; Dewey remains the thinker whose New England background of order and obligation – as understood by Anzia – cannot accommodate a pragmatism that takes into account emotional directives.

Equally important, during this period the cultural relationships between Jews and African Americans began to unravel. On the one hand, African Americans wanted to shape their politics and culture without interference or control by others. On the other hand, Jews often felt that there was a shared heritage, best expressed by Hebrew Scripture: God authorizes freedom. The literary relationship between African Americans and Jews in this modern period reaches back, for a convenient origin, to Norman *Mailer's *The White Negro: Superficial Reflections on the Hipster* (published freestanding in 1957, and later, in the accessible *Advertisements for Myself*, 1959). Mailer reads the plight of the African American as an existential triumph: the living of felt needs. The "Negro" could stay alive by following "obligatory" pleasures. The hipster could model freedom upon the African American's "instantaneous existential states." The hipster's desire for the consecrated present would be shaped, in the future, by the African American's achievement of equality. The "potential superiority" of the African American, one that was feared, is "the underground drama of domestic politics." Hatred could be lived; violence is romanticized.

Whereas the African American could be viewed as part of the existential quest for the creation of self, other American-Jewish writers often spoke in terms of moral endowment. In Malamud's "Angel Levine" (1955), a feckless black angel inspires a small, defeated man to assent to the nature of the "other." The act is one of mutual confidence; both are transformed. *Bellow's eponymous protagonist of *Henderson the Rain King* (1959) encounters Africa not as Conrad's metaphor of darkness but as land that offers him a mentor in, and for, freedom. Jay Neugeboren's *Sam's Legacy* (1974) plays out the drama of freedom against *the* American sport, baseball. Mason Tidewater, an African American, gives to Sam his moving autobiography, "My Life and Death in the Negro Baseball League: A Slave Narrative," which weighs the issues of socially imposed identities against the moral strength of our devotion to others. *Doctorow's *Ragtime* (1975) portrays an African American as someone whose dignity demands that he challenge the injustices done to him. Lore Segal's *Her First American* (1985) explores the shock of surprise and comfort between a refugee and an African American.

As African American politics came to veer into antisemitism, so did American-Jewish writers portray the potential (and sometimes real) flashpoints of contact. Malamud's *The Tenants* (1971) presents the author's impasse reconciling an African American and a Jewish character. Bellow's *Mr. Sammler's Planet* (1970; discussed below), portrays an African American as a thief who displays his aggressive, flamboyant sexuality. In Bellow's *The Dean's December* (1982) the African American is yet more sinister. Philip Roth's *The Human Stain* (2000; discussed below) further complicates this difficult relationship; an African American assumes (or usurps) the identity of an American Jew, becoming a professor of the classics. Selected critical works on this topic are Louis Harap's *Dramatic Encounters: The Jewish Presence in Twentieth-Century American Drama, Poetry, and Humor and the Black-Jewish Literary Relationship* (1987); *Bridges and Boundaries: African Americans and American Jews* (ed. Jack Salzman with Adina Back and Gretchen Sorin, 1992); Emily Budick's *Blacks and Jews in Literary Conversation* (1998); and *Strangers & Neighbors: Relations between Blacks and Jews in the United States* (eds. Maurianne Adams and John Bracey, 1999).

Whereas the heritage of 19th-century realism remains strong, innovative narrative strategies question its adequacy. Although this experimentation is neither unique nor particular to Jewish letters, formal creativity challenges both our understanding of tradition and our reading of it. Cases are – and these are just a few – Norman Fruchter's *Single File* (1970); Norman Mailer's *The Executioner's Song* (1979); Art *Spiegelman's *Maus: A Survivor's Tale, I: My Father Bleeds History* (1986); and *Maus: A Survivor's Tale, II: And Here My Troubles Began* (1991); Doctorow's *City of God* (2000); Benjamin Zucker's *Blue* (2001); and Steve Stern's *The Angel of Forgetfulness* (2005). These works formally reconcile the heritages (and claims) of Diaspora cultures and gentile nations: a mingling of diaries, welfare reports, and characters' reflections for Fruchter; for Mailer, the new journalism which combines fact with novelistic rendition; the Talmud page for

Zucker; the comic book format for Spiegelman; narrative vying with narrative, and fiction becoming counter-fiction for Stern; and the novel of multiple voices, and narrative montage for Doctorow.

For a contemporary generation, the Holocaust is a memory challenging notions of a safe American haven. A God who vouchsafes the existence of the Jewish people has been splintered into a God who has committed Himself to accept historical choice, or has turned His face, or who demands a reconstruction of moral nature and engagement, or a delusion. Each of these possibilities challenges the hope of life without peril. Each choice creates an identity based on the conditioned and contingent. The literature is so vast that a few contemporary examples indicate the reach of the Holocaust into the present: Isaac Bashevis Singer's *Enemies, A Love Story* (1972) and his *Shosha* (1978); Susan Fromberg Schaeffer's *Anya* (1974); Philip Roth's *The Ghost Writer* (1979); Jerome Badanes' *The Final Opus of Leon Solomon* (1985); Ozick's "The Shawl" (1981) and "Rosa" (1984), published as one volume in the accessible *The Shawl: A Story and a Novella* (1989); Elie Wiesel's *The Fifth Son* (1985) and his *The Forgotten* (1992); Jon Baitz's drama, *The Substance of Fire* (published 1993); Melvin Bukiet's *Stories of an Imaginary Childhood* (1992), and his anthology, *Nothing Makes You Free: Writings by Descendants of Jewish Holocaust Survivors* (2002); Thane Rosenbaum's *Second Hand Smoke* (1999); Aryeh Lev Stollman's *The Illuminated Soul* (2002); Leslie Epstein's *King of the Jews* (1979); and Arthur *Miller's drama, *Broken Glass* (1994). Well worth viewing is the 1991 film, *The Quarrel,* based on Chaim *Grade's "My Quarrel with Hersh Rasseyner."

Questions of authority and sincerity dog a younger generation. Is the factual nature of the Holocaust open to the task of fiction *as* fiction? Can fiction formalize an experience that goes beyond the limits of representation? Is a speculative, if not interim rhetoric needed? Fire, ashes, smoke, railroad tracks, tattoos, the literal and metaphorical uncovering of human nature – the jigsaw pieces of life and death under Nazism are close to the surface but part of a new politics and rhetoric.

As with Holocaust fiction, there is a large body of critical commentary dealing with the roles of language, memory and representation. Part of such discussion are Terence Des Pres' *The Survivor: An Anatomy of Life in the Death Camps* (1976); James Young's *Writing and Rewriting the Holocaust: Narrative and the Consequences of Interpretation* (1988); *Probing the Limits of Representation: Nazism and the "Final Solution"* (edited by Saul Friedlander, 1992); Lawrence Langer's *Admitting the Holocaust: Collected Essays* (1995); and Edith Wyschogrod's *An Ethics of Remembering: History, Heterology, and the Nameless Others* (1998).

Zionism brings with it celebration and critique. A new Zion carved out of the wilderness, and an America affirming its history as redemptive make American-Jewish literature's depiction of Zionism rife with sincerity as well as irony. Portraits of Israelis and Americans wandering in Zion implicate the authenticity of American-Jewish existence and the authority of Jewish life in Israel. Examples are Philip Roth's *The Counterlife* (1986) and *Operation Shylock: A Confession* (1993); Anne Roiphe's *The Pursuit of Happiness* (1991); and the personal reflections found in Hugh *Nissenson's *Notes from the Frontier* (1968) and Bellow's *To Jerusalem and Back* (1976). Sabras and pioneers have long been replaced by characters – Americans in Israel and Israelis themselves – ranging from the manipulative to the naïve, as in Tova Reich's *Master of the Return* (1988) and *The Jewish War* (1995). Andrew Furman's *Israel Through the Jewish-American Imagination: A Survey of Jewish-American Literature on Israel, 1928–1995* (1997) and Ranen Omer-Sherman's *Diaspora and Zionism in Jewish American Literature: Lazarus, Syrkin, Reznikoff and Roth* (2002) explicate the American literary dialogue with Israel.

II

The generation of writers that came to maturity from the 1930s to the 1960s could draw upon the inheritance of being Jewish as inseparable from being ill at ease in the American Diaspora. The contemporary stylistic deployment of Yiddish words and diction by those whose native tongue is English; the reliance on the Jew as neurotic, or as schlemiel, or as divested of the strengths of Judaism are tics rendering the Jew harmless but provocative. The unease of writer and writing made estrangement the appropriate moral and political response to modern American culture. (It should be noted that V.L. Parrington, Van Wyck Brooks, and Lewis Mumford made the same case.) Dreams of socialism, the promise of psychoanalytic theory – all of these gave an edge to earlier American-Jewish writers' depiction of a specific America, one at variance with their families' understanding of America itself. At their most minatory, American-Jewish letters is overly suspicious of the literature of affirmation that argues that Jewish life not only endured in America, but also flourished. Norman *Podhoretz's *Making It* (1967) seemed – to its critics – less the tracing of choice and success than a surrender to cynicism and irony.

For contemporary readers and writers, American-Jewish literature seems blunted, incapable of bringing the cutting edge of politics and a shrewd cynicism to America's failures. And equally important, to the failures of Judaism to keep constant the Prophetic vision of the just society. The contemporary authorial task, so it seems, is witnessing. This, too, is a moral act, akin to the Prophets enumerating the refusal of those who confuse Hellenism with Hebraism.

Irving Howe, in his magisterial *World of Our Fathers: The Journey of the East European Jews to America and the Life They Found and Made* (with the assistance of Kenneth Libo, 1976); and in *Jewish American Stories* (1977), writes about the American-Jewish literary imagination as both regional and centralizing. American-Jewish literary culture draws upon the great tide of Jewish immigration (usually to the lower East Side), as well as Jewish tradition. Howe's work is part of a larger body of literature studying what he called this "regional" style. Selected works, dedicated to exploring the ferment of the lower

East Side and its influence are Ronald Sanders' pioneering *The Downtown Jews: Portraits of an Immigrant Generation* (1969); Mario Maffi's *Gateway to the Promised Land: Ethnic Cultures in New York's Lower East Side* (1995); and Hasia Diner's *Lower East Side Memories: A Jewish Place in America* (2000).

By now, the Jewish writer in America has moved beyond the culture of a thick *Yidishkayt*, and its immigrant traditions. American-Jewish writers have appropriated the geography of America as *the* sustenance of memory. Examples are Saul Bellow's Chicago (*Ravelstein*, 2000); Adam Berlin's Las Vegas (*Headlock*, 2000); Leslie *Epstein's West Coast (*San Remo Drive: A Novel from Memory*, 2003); Michael Chabon's Pittsburgh (*The Mysteries of Pittsburgh*, 1988); Rebecca Goldstein's Princeton (*The Mind-Body Problem*, 1983); the American South of Steve Stern (*A Plague of Dreamers*, 1994) and Tova Mirvis (*The Ladies Auxiliary*, 1999); Philip Roth's rural community in the Berkshires (*The Human Stain*, 2000); Malamud's "Wild West" (in his unfinished novel, *The People, and Uncollected Stories*, 1989) and his New England (*Dubin's Lives*, 1979); and Allegra Goodman's upstate New York (*Kaaterskill Falls*, 1998). Unsurprisingly, New York City remains a center for the imagination: the metropolis of Paul *Auster (*The New York Trilogy*, 1990); Jonathan Safran Foer (*Extremely Loud & Incredibly Close*, 2005); Hugh Nissenson (*Days of Awe*, 2005); and Cynthia Ozick (*The Puttermesser Papers*, 1997; and *Heir to the Glimmering World*, 2004).

Modern American-Jewish writers and anthologists have enlarged the American-Jewish present by expanding the canon, rescuing often-neglected works written by women, Sephardim, as well as gay and lesbian Jews. The following selected works are significant additions to the literature of and about American-Jewish women: Melanie Kaye/Kantrowitz and Irena Klepfisz's *The Tribe of Dina: A Jewish Women's Anthology* (1989); Joyce Antler's anthology, *America and I: Short Stories by American Jewish Women Writers* (1990); Sharon Niederman's *Shaking Eve's Tree: Short Stories of Jewish Women* (1990); Sylvia Barack Fishman's reader, *Follow My Footprints: Changing Images of Women in American Jewish Fiction* (1992); Ellen Uffen's *Strands of the Cable: The Place of the Past in Jewish American Women's Writing* (1992); Marlene Marks' *Nice Jewish Girls: Growing Up in America* (1996); Janet Burstein's *Writing Mothers, Writing Daughters: Tracing the Maternal in Stories by American Jewish Women* (1996); Paula Hyman and Deborah Dash Moore's *Jewish Women in America: An Historical Encyclopedia* (1997, 2 vols.); Ann Shapiro, Sarah Horowitz, Ellen Schiff and Miriyam Glazer's *Jewish American Women Writers: A Bio-Bibliographical and Critical Sourcebook* (1994); and Lois Rubin's *Connections and Collisions: Identities in Contemporary Jewish-American Women's Writing* (2005).

The experiences of gay and lesbian American Jews are found notably in works by Harvey Fierstein (*Torch-Song Trilogy*, consisting of *The International Stud, Fugue in a Nursery*, and *Widows and Children First!*, published in one volume in 1979); Tony *Kushner (*Angels in America: A Gay Fantasia on National Themes*, consisting of *Part 1: Millennium Approaches* and *Part 2: Perestroika*, and published in one volume, 1995); and Larry Kramer (*The Normal Heart* and *The Destiny of Me*, published in one volume, 2000). In addition, gay or lesbian characters are found, for example, in Alice Bloch's *The Law of Return* (1983); Leslea Newman's *A Letter to Harvey Milk* (1988); Lev Raphael's *Dancing on Tisha B'Av* (1990); and Adam Berlin's *Belmondo Style* (2004). Significant readers on this topic are *Nice Jewish Girls: A Lesbian Anthology* (ed. Evelyn Torton Beck, 1982) and Christie Balka and Andy Rose's anthology *Twice Blessed: On Being Lesbian, Gay and Jewish* (1989).

Diane Matza's anthology, *Sephardic-American Voices: Two Hundred Years of a Literary Legacy* (1996), spans categories from "The Descendants of the Colonial Sephardim" (for example, Penina Moise, Mordecai Noah, and Emma Lazarus) to "Issues of Identity" (including Rosaly Roffman, Herbert Hadad, and Jordan Elgrably, among others).

There is also a Jewish literature of imagined futures and mythographies. Envisaged futures and fantasias are found notably in the works of Isaac Asimov and Harlan Ellison; in Jack Dann's anthologies *Wandering Stars: An Anthology of Jewish Fantasy and Science Fiction* (1974); his *More Wandering Stars* (1981); as well as in Marge Piercy's *He, She and It* (1991). Examples of mythographies are Cynthia Ozick's title story of *The Pagan Rabbi and Other Stories* (1971); Arthur Cohen's *In The Days of Simon Stern* (1973); and Steve Stern's *Lazar Malkin Enters Heaven* (1986).

The image of the American Jew as timid, neurotic, and small, found for example in Woody *Allen's films (such as *Take the Money and Run*, 1969, and *Bananas*, 1971) has yielded to what might earlier have been considered as a Hellenizing of the American-Jewish man. Among these are Michael Chabon's *The Mysteries of Pittsburgh* (1988) with a protagonist choosing to plunge into chaos leading to self-revelation; Philip Roth's unbridled *Sabbath's Theater* (1995); and Adam Berlin's *Headlock* (2000), with its epigraph from Homer, offering a narrator exulting in his strength. That American-Jewish writers could be attracted to violence, and depict it with panache is an unsettling note but certainly offered in the works of dramatist and screenwriter David *Mamet, especially in his portrait of marginal people in *American Buffalo* (published 1977) and *Glengarry Glen Ross* (published 1984).

Modern American-Jewish humor, both defensive and aggressive, can be read in a slightly different way than its immigrant counterparts. American life was strange. The American-Jewish immigrants' humor was usually based on the shock of transplantation and surprise. The immigrant was unsure of American freedom, and dismayed by the insecurity of employment. In contrast, modern American-Jewish humor appears to have two movements. The first is its characteristic, sharp irony that hedges uncertainty: a major theme found in Diaspora Jewish humor. For the Jewish immigrant in the United States, though, this irony marked a refusal to accept fully American promises of surety. The second movement is the adoption of the attitude of American surety in order to retroject present insecurities into an earlier generation. Often, this historical irony is found in the durable themes of the Jewish overbearing mother, the feckless husband, the "Jewish-American Princess," the psychologically damaged child, and the appeal of the *shiksa*. (A convenient point of origin for the jagged edge of modern American-Jewish literary humor is Nathanael *West's fiction. Though his works rarely deal with Judaism, the alienation his fiction presents is that of the outsider who is too urbane to be shocked and yet the insider who is too shocked to accept American myths. The acceptance of his fiction's enormous savagery can be measured by the publication of his *Complete Works* in 1957; its re-issue in 1978, and his *Collected Works* in 1975). The double nature of modern American-Jewish humor is found in various degrees in Bruce Jay *Friedman's "black-humor" novels *Stern* (1962) and *A Mother's Kisses* (1963); Philip Roth's parody of the dominating Jewish-mother and neurotic Jewish son in *Portnoy's Complaint* (1969); Woody Allen's protean Jew, the eponymous protagonist of the film *Zelig* (1983); and Neil Simon's play *Lost in Yonkers* (1991). Notable works are *The Big Book of Jewish Humor* (eds. William Novak and Moshe Waldoks, 1981); Robert Menchin's *Jewish Humor from Groucho Marx to Jerry Seinfeld* (1997); *Encyclopedia of Jewish Humor: From Biblical Times to the Modern Age* (ed., Henry Spalding, 2001); and *Classic Jewish Humor in America* (ed. Henry Spalding, 1995). Important critical studies are *Jewish Wry: Essays on Jewish Humor* (ed. Sarah Blacher Cohen, 1990); and James Bloom's *Gravity Fails: The Comic Jewish Shaping of Modern America* (2003). Lawrence Epstein's *The Haunted Smile: The Story of Jewish Comedians in America* (2001) supplements these works.

All of the above-mentioned works indicate the possession of America's open imagination and opportunity. Philip Roth's Nathan Zuckerman sums up this appropriation by the America Jew. Recalling his adolescence in the late 1940s, he writes that he "wanted to become part of the national character." With her novel *O My America!* (1980), Johanna Kaplan captures the excitement as well as the anxiety of what we have come to call the "American experience." She prefaces it with two epigraphs. The first is Donne's, and provides the novel with its title. The body of a woman, for Donne, is as richly enticing as is America's conquest. The novel's second epigraph is from De Tocqueville, addressing the paradoxical nature of a country that does not seem to be historical so much as ahistorical. Democracy, De Tocqueville opines, produces an historical amnesia, making one forget genealogies. Democracy shears the self of the comfort and support of lineage, and could confine the individual "*entirely within the solitude of his own heart.*"

The sequesterment of the American, and especially that of the American-Jewish literary character, speaks to the ironic solitude of the Jew in an inviting pluralistic society. On the one hand, Jewish culture is now often experienced away from ritual and rite. On the other hand, American-Jewish literature has both civic and Prophetic signatures: its ethical spirit is invariably a preachment for a renewed community within and for a nation. The judgment pronounced maintains its force because it is spoken with the fervor of an other-worldliness, one not indebted to historical variability but paradoxically addressing the immediate moment. As a result, the American-Jewish novel forces the reader to examine anew the implications of a timeless ethic within an historical present; and a mandated, ahistorical way of being described within the immediacy of the day.

From 1970 to the present, as numerous critics have pointed out, a generation of American-Jewish writers did not have as points of cultural and political reference the immediacy of the Holocaust, the founding of the State of Israel, and the feeling of a marginal American existence. Nonetheless, the enormous trepidation that marked an older generation's coming to maturity in the 1930s and 1940s, in which the Jewish future was far from assured, has left its mark.

For all the comfort America offers, there is a premonitory insecurity, a sense that American-Jewish life may be precarious. There are looming examples. In Philip Roth's "Eli, the Fanatic" (1959), Eli Peck, an acculturated young lawyer, reflects upon the America that he accepts as indisputable. Thinking about the safety America offers Jewish families, Eli muses, "What incredible peace." The irony is thick, but it is shared only by narrator and reader, not by Eli. In her 1970 essay, "Toward a New Yiddish," Cynthia Ozick reminded her readers that American-Jewish life, with its flowering of creativity in America, was not similar to Germany but analogous to Spain. Both led, she writes, to "abbatoir." Paul Auster endows a future that is just as ominous for Jews. *In The Country of Last Things* (1987), the simplicity of realism is cautionary fable. Anna Blume, a Jewish woman in search of her brother, wanders across a nameless, anarchic city. During a hard winter, she pushes her way into the National Library and comes upon a room in which she discovers Jewish men, talking urgently and animatedly. "I thought all Jews were dead," she whispers, yet hears the reply that only a small number remain. "It's not so easy to get rid of us...." Years later, there is an equally assertive wariness, again, from Philip Roth: *The Plot Against America* (2004). The novel begins in the present, with the narrator remembering with trepidation his boyhood. In this alternative history, a companion piece to Sinclair Lewis's *It Can't Happen Here*, a family named Roth finds itself living in a pre-World War II semi-totalitarian American state. Led by Lindbergh, America initiates state-sponsored antisemitism. Only by authorial intervention, history is righted; Roosevelt assumes the presidency.

III

American-Jewish literature produced its own histories, arguing for a conserved and preserving identity: a sign that American Jews are intent upon preserving a shared life through creating and assessing a common tradition. These re-evaluations may well be interim canons, suggesting how the strengths of the past can be used to shape the present. Among others, there are valuable histories and critical bio-bibliographies of American-Jewish literature by Louis Harap (mentioned above); *Twentieth-Century American-Jewish Fiction Writers* (ed. Daniel Walden 1984); *Handbook of American-Jewish Literature* (eds. Lewis Fried, Gene Brown, Jules Chametzky and Louis Harap, 1988); Sanford Pinsker's *Jewish American Fiction, 1917–1987* (1992); *Contemporary Jewish-American Novelists* (1997) and *Contemporary Jewish-American Dramatists and Poets* (both works edited by Joel Shatzky and Michael Taub, 1999); Stephen Wade's *Jewish American Literature Since 1945: An Introduction* (1999); *The Cambridge Companion to Jewish American Literature* (eds. Michael Kramer and Hana Wirth-Nesher, 2003); and Rosalind Reisner's *Jewish American Literature: A Guide to Reading Interests* (2004).

A point and counterpoint in these histories is the claim of the universal against the particular. A modern beginning for these pressures is Cynthia Ozick's "Toward a New Yiddish" (1970, and published again in 1983, in Ozick's *Art & Ardor*). Ozick later pointed out that she was "no longer greatly attached to its conclusions." (Well worth looking at is the strongly differing George Steiner's "Our Homeland, the Text" in *Salmagundi*, Winter-Spring, 1985.) The essay draws upon a large literary history: Aḥad Ha-Am's notion of Diaspora culture; Matthew Arnold's discussions of Hebraism and Hellenism; Isaac Rosenfeld's notion of creative estrangement; and the autonomous text of the New Critics. The points Ozick makes are hard, and not without irony. Ozick imaginatively summons for the reader a new Yavneh, a "Displaced Jerusalem." (The reader, of course, should recall that the original Yavneh had as its foreboding background the siege of Jerusalem. Yavneh rebelled against the might of empire by turning powerlessness into transmission of decree and commentary.) America, this new, metaphorical Yavneh, Ozick points out, is a temporary haven.

"Toward a New Yiddish" insists upon de-idolization: a rejection, by the Jew, of ideologies and acts effacing the divinely mandated and rabbinically authorized particularism of the Jewish people. Sinai condemns any desire obstructing the just community. The essay paints an alluring Hellenism, a metonym for universalism: from the declaration that all religions are the same, to the abandonment of an ethically demanding imperative, to ecstasy, to the individual as "mediator of the sacral." And, when Jewish novelists efface their particularity, they become lost to history. In effect, Hebrew Scripture funds the grand moral imagination. The commanding 19th-century novels were Judaized, represented by writers such as George Eliot, Dickens, and Tolstoy, who dramatized conduct and its consequences.

A "centrally Jewish" literature impinges on the liturgical. It is bound to the "reciprocal moral imagination" and resounds within and for the community. It echoes God's voice, "the Lord of History." Ozick's concession is one to the form of the liturgical voice itself. Our houses of Jewish worship may well be empty, she argues, because we have done with the idea and form of the "cathedral." Whether in text or talk, our conversations reveal the possibilities of our future. And these may be large.

The new Yiddish, a language commensurate with the upbuilding of Yavneh in America, will be the language of Jewish discourse, spoken as well as written "by Jews for Jews." It will renew the American Jew for it will nourish new talmudic forms of creative literature. Although the new Yiddish will not be explicitly religious, it will feel the touch of the Covenant. We can try to be a holy people in America, developing our own *Aggadah*.

Ozick's essay gave later critics the chance to explore the association of the Covenant, with a covenanted literature. Two works, among several, deal with this relationship. *In The New Covenant: Jewish Writers and the American Idea* (1984), Sam Girgus points out how Jewish writers, transforming the rhetoric and myths of America, reshape and modernize these communalizing forces. Their work make significant "the American ideal," pitting it against "authoritarian and totalitarian ideologies." In terms drawn from their own background, these writers formulate anew a narrative of American redemption.

In *What Happened to Abraham?: Reinventing the Covenant in American Jewish Fiction* (2005), Victoria Aarons argues that the contemporary American-Jewish writer takes the "laws of the covenant" and transforms them into "metaphors and allegories of invention, promise, and design." The law may reappear in a number of forms and modes: for example, as assessment, and as framework. The writer's recognition of the Covenant involves a revitalization, a re-telling of a heritage leading to a dialogue with the large assumptions and concerns of "the Hebrew Bible." Aarons points out that this retelling involves an understanding of America, often presented as a radical metonym for "displacement and loss."

Anthologies of American-Jewish writing offer a reading of a canon in process, enhancing the terms of analysis. The anthologies' principles of selection provide a characteristic tension – that of being Jewish and being American. Strikingly, many of these anthologies do not emphasize a conversation with theology but rather focus on the living of Jewishness (which may well be such a conversation itself). Equally intriguing, some do not strongly accentuate a potentially unsettling conversation with Israel. Such choices indicate a confidence in America as a home for Jews. American-Jewish anthologies – and they are groundbreakers – have a large subject: the making of an American Judaism, the comportment of faith with a democracy that is experimental and unique. Important supplementary texts are Arnold Eisen's *The Chosen People in America: A Study in Jewish Religious Ideology* (1983), and Jonathan Sarna's *American Judaism: A History* (2004).

In 1974, Daniel Walden put together one of the first anthologies of contemporary American-Jewish writing. *On Being Jewish: American Jewish Writers from Cahan to Bellow* illuminates Walden's discussion of American-Jewish writing as obligated to narratives of immigration and acculturation. The anthology reflects a period in which the term "American-Jewish" writing was a triumphal designation, a narration of largely unchallenged success which was the significant literature of the American present. Roth, Malamud, and Bellow, major voices then and now, bespeak an American-Jewish identity. (Walden includes them in the book's last section, entitled "The American Jews, The Jewish Americans"). Confidently, Walden's "Introduction" asserts the congruence of Jews and Judaism. The Jewish writer's work often conveys a Jewish ethic. Following biblical imperative, even in the face of American secular culture, American-Jewish writers "still choose life."

In the same year, 1974, Abraham Chapman's *Jewish-American Literature, An Anthology* was published. His collection takes note of the tension between an American culture and the legacy of Hebrew Scripture. Within a secular American culture, the modern Jewish-American writer usually expresses the dignity of humanity, a central theme of the Prophets. American-Jewish literature resists an easy conformity with American culture; its unease marks its heritage and chance for creativity.

In his anthology *Jewish American Stories* (1977), Irving Howe finds regional literature a useful category in understanding Jewish-American literature. Arguing that "regional" can be used in a metaphorical way, Jewish American writers (who are indisputably American writers) derive the subjects of their work from the early neighborhoods of Jewish settlement, or the more affluent areas of upward and outward migration. In an almost Hegelian moment, Howe compares American-Jewish writing with that of Southern literature, both "subcultures" finding their "voice" when they approach "disintegration." The immigrant milieu offers both a usable past as well as characteristic problems: the search for an adequate way to preserve and order the past. Moreover, the American Jewish writer has access to those traditions and implications designated as "Jewishness." Calling this the "persuasion of distinctiveness," Howe finds it to be a "rich moral perspective." Yet, such distinctiveness is protean, felt as "urgency and need."

For Howe, the culture of Yiddish is threnody and theory: narratives of immigration are exhausted. Nonetheless, Howe wonders about the cultivation of a new sensibility, the "post-immigrant Jewish experience" which may inform younger writers. His *World of Our Fathers* funds this claim, exploring the cultural variousness and political convictions of the lower East Side's Jews. Clearly a secular rendition of *Yidishkayt*, the book presents the Jew entering modernity through the harshness of the laboring day, the promise of socialism, and the reality of rough and tumble American politics.

In his *American Jewish Fiction: A Century of Stories* (1998), Gerald Shapiro disputes Irving Howe's claim that the major narrative line of the American-Jewish experience has thinned. Rather, he finds that the perennial topics Jews have engaged with are still being posed: Jewish identity and its implications, notably the tension "between skepticism and belief…"

Ted Solotaroff and Nessa Rapoport's introductory essays to *Writing Our Way Home* (Schocken, 1992; republished as *The Shocken Book of Contemporary Jewish Fiction* in 1996) also contest Howe's lament. *Writing Our Way Home* identifies the acts that kept afloat Jewish life. The *Yidishkayt* of the immigrant became a presence in American literature by finding its place in "the dynamic of acculturation." This took place decades after the great East European migration to America. But equally important, Solotaroff and Rapoport's work illuminates a tradition coming into being: post-acculturation alternatives for Jewish life. Could not the modern Jewish imagination be nourished "as much by imagination as by memory?" The victory of the Six-Day War, the emergence of spoken Hebrew, the fervent identification of American Jews with Israel, the rise of exciting learning communities – all of these suggest a new, assertive American-Jewish life.

For Michael Lerner, the guiding figure of *Tikkun*, Jewish writing can be seen as healing, a redemption from injustice and the will to power of politics. In his *Best Contemporary Jewish Writing* (2001), Lerner writes that his selections emphasize works that suggest the healing "that our planet and our community so badly need." Lerner sees Jewish text affirming that we make our freedom, and *can* make this freedom for the betterment of our society. He appeals to Jewish mystical tradition, recounting the contraction of God and the effulgence of sacred light that shattered their vessels: holy fragments that "need repair." Our labor is to liberate these sparks, returning the *Shekinah* to our world As Lerner suggests, this can be translated into political, social, and personal terms.

The most comprehensive and spacious anthology to date is Jules Chametzky, John Felstiner, Hilene Flanzbaum, and Kathryn Hellerstein's *Jewish American Literature: A Norton Anthology* (2001). Situating itself in a multicultural American literary history, the anthology addresses the widening term "Jewish American literature" so that it "signifies an American literature that is Jewish." Setting Jewish literature within the development of American civilization makes much sense. Chronology reflects the phases of immigration, estrangement, acculturation, and critique. The Norton's last section, "Jews Translating Jews," though a small part of the book, shines light on how an American language – its style, its pace, what Whitman might term its voice *en masse* – absorbs the Jewish polylingual heritage. This section also reminds us of the Jewish dialogue with its own imagination, making its past enter the present.

IV

The period from 1970 to the present had its major themes articulated by Malamud, Bellow, Ozick, and Philip Roth. Their literature has a broad descriptive trait which is best expressed as the claim of the ethical within and upon ordinary life. The oft-described quest for an American-Jewish identity becomes a search for the adequate, purposive community. This community can be made possible by text, tradition, or neighborhood. The works of these writers insist that dignity, justice, and compassion are ordinal virtues at the core of a desirable existence. For these authors, moral decision illuminates the contemporary situation but is not of it. It is akin to the Prophetic declamations about the just society. Moreover, the wellsprings of the ethical life, to paraphrase Mosaic exhortation, are not hidden. Given the autonomy America offers the self, moral dereliction is an act of will. As Artur Sammler wearily puts it, "we know."

This ethical temperament is often described in earlier terms as a contest between what cultural historians, *pace* Arnold, have called Hellenism and Hebraism. In theme, these poles represent the civic culture of nations and the culture of the Covenant. Bellow describes the recoil from the sensual Byzantine city and its chaos. Ozick writes forthrightly about the Judaic strain of the novel, its ethical import, and a liturgical voice. Much of her fiction examines the boundaries enclosing the Jewish self. Malamud dramatizes the demand that one yield to a higher notion of selfhood than egoism. Roth envisions a community intent upon preserving a tradition of comportment, so much so, that an individual's turn against the *mores* and boundaries of American-Jewish culture undoes the self.

Several of their works form a "communalizing text," a representation of dominant themes that have been relevant to, and are still vibrant in American-Jewish literature. This large text is a colloquy exploring the social contract we make with civil society (its laws, its customs, its culture), and the covenant that we uphold with the Jewish ethic bespeaking the dignity of self. These multiple, rich, and often contradictory relationships take the form of explanation: an attempt to separate what is forbidden by *the* Covenant and what is permitted by modern society. Separation is presented in these exemplary works as the anxiety entailed by our making our selves discover a relationship to secular and sacred history. These encounters are not without awe. Such trepidation involves not simply the making of a self, but the willingness to live within a particular people and a pluralizing culture.

From 1970 onward, *Mr. Sammler's Planet* is the towering presence in American-Jewish writing and modern American literature as well. Bellow's later works, notably *Humboldt's Gift* (1975), *The Dean's December* (1982), and *Ravelstein* (2000), are deprived of a character whose history separates him from normalizing experience. *Mr. Sammler's Planet*'s cultural background is the *idea* of the city itself. American and European regionalist thinkers, from Patrick Geddes to Lewis Mumford, defend the city as concentrating human symbols and resources, allowing for creativity and the possibility of a balanced life. Cultural, social, and environmental assets can be cultivated and shared. The democratic city expresses the equanimity of the good life, countering the dangers posed by poverty, density, and injustice. This city is the aureate dream of civilization, and embraces Athens as well as Jerusalem.

Mr. Sammler's Planet (1970) addresses what the city has become. The Holocaust, the rise of a technics shorn of moral evaluation, and a democracy deprived of thoughtfulness give the novel its chance for judgment. Sammler's New York ingathers these. Bellow turns away from the eponymous adventurers of *The Adventures of Augie March* (1953), and *Henderson the Rain King* (1959), presenting Sammler, a man whose experience has been refined so that his action *is* judgment. Sammler is a collector of selves and of identities. No stranger to mass murder as well as intellectual society, his character easily moves amongst urban communities: the would-be students, speculators, the criminal, the deranged, urbane intellectuals, and his own family. A well-born Polish Jew; a journalist who knew H.G. Wells; a thinker drawn to a utopian project to regulate social life; and a Holocaust survivor, Sammler is blind in one eye. When the novel begins, he is living in Manhattan on the pension provided by a distant relative, Dr. Elya Gruner.

The novel's characters are people whose lives are truncated, either by history or dereliction. They celebrate their personal liabilities. As Sammler understands them, they are oblivious to the implicit moral "contract" that makes society just. The obligations to the "contract," as Sammler poses it, are obligations to ethical order and satisfaction, making the attainable – if not the good – life possible. Conduct is not justified by sentiment, but by consciousness of what is good for both self and others. His claim takes us back to rabbinic dictum: "the rest is commentary. Go and learn it."

A novel confronting the romantics of violence, and the imperatives of the ethical self, *Mr. Sammler's Planet* does not propose how we know the good: we simply know it. In Sammler's case, this world-weary knowledge is the recoil from untrammeled individuality, from mass movements that are based on rationales, not rationality, and from the fables of modern autonomy. A survivor who literally lived in a tomb, Sammler is resurrected in a world uncomprehending of the traditions of language, and of "high ceiling" thought. New York has become a society without an intellectual framework that makes room for moral judgment. Sammler possesses the authority of survival almost extinguished by barbarism. He is enabled to ask how we *should* live, not *how* we live. Sammler's task is to assess, to demand, and to pronounce. The company Sammler keeps has to be disenchanted of its banality. Easy explanations, the novel's massive collecting of nonchalant behavior, have to be traced to the myths for keeping them.

The novel's plot is architectural; layers imbricating layers. Images of the sea, of pipes bursting, of an aneurism, and of a reservoir punctuate the novel. They are offset by images of height: the moon, an airplane scraping a house and long-distance flight. They suggest the human desire to live in other places, to escape the limiting conditions of location, history, and mortality. As a result, the novel presents us with human boundaries and their crossings.

Sammler recoils from a city of crime and theatrical selves. As he traverses Manhattan by bus, the city becomes a modern theater. Individuals adopt historical costumes and roles: the bohemian, the hippie, the prince, the sexually provocative, and the deranged. His bus route to the library is also that of an African American pickpocket, elegantly dressed. Later, he confronts Sammler, pushing him against a wall, and exposing himself.

Beginning his meditations upon the contained as well as limitless self, Sammler reads the Bible and Meister Eckhart. Eckhart's writing on the purification of individuality as well as biblical ethical injunction are clues to Sammler's recoil from the contemporary city. His conversation with Professor V. Govinda Lal, a biophysicist, is a plea for a renewed humanism. Lal's manuscript, "The Future of the Moon," has come into Sammler's possession. Their talk is built upon Sammler's defense of the necessary, ordered society, and Lal's vision of a lunar colony, an escape from the density of an ever-growing population and human limits. For Sammler, philosophy is grounded, literally and metaphorically. There can be no flight from the human condition or human betterment. On the one hand, H.G. Wells (whom Sammler knew from his days in London, and about whom Sammler is rumored to be writing a book) provides a point of critical departure. An explainer, a believer in mass education, Wells refused to abandon the high role of education in a mass society. On the other hand, modern culture witnesses a call to "noble actions" on the part of those who can least understand what this demands. Sammler's fear of disorder is his trembling before murder.

Lal's version of the planned society takes place on the moon. It is a metonym for the unbinding of man from humanistic tradition: a flight from the bounded. Philosophically interesting, it is a technological fugue that is captivating as well as implicative. For an American reader, Lal's proposals summon up Henry Adams' speculations about the age of ether, Lewis Mumford's discussions of unbridled technics, and Paul Goodman's understanding of the depersonalizing society. For Sammler, Lal's advocacy of the order of technics leads to the demolition of the species.

By the novel's end, the imagery Bellow has drawn becomes a tight knot: Elya's aneurism in the brain bursts. His feckless son has pulled the pipes apart of Elya's house, looking for hidden money. Sammler's former son-in-law, another survivor, Eisen, comes to America to interest people in his grotesque, pyrite "medallions," bearing the word "*Hazak*." As New Yorkers merely watch, Eisen slams the pickpocket in the head with his medallions. Though called a lunatic, Eisen acts and justly so. In the last scene. as Sammler sees Elya's body, he understands that Elya has met the terms of his contract. And, as Sammler concludes, we know those terms.

During this period, Malamud's works reveal the Jewish self as metaphorically all selves and as hapless as all humanity. For Malamud, Jewish history preserves if not *the*, at least *a* moral imagination. In an interview with Shlomo Kidrin in 1968 ("Malamud Explains Jewish Contribution to U.S. Writing," reprinted in *Conversations with Bernard Malamud*, ed. Lawrence Lasher, 1991), Malamud pointed out that he envisioned the Jew as a metaphor for "'universal man.'" For "'every man is a Jew'" even if he is unaware of this.

In Malamud's fiction, empathy and compassion are shown by the powerless because the powerful have lost this humanly defining response. They refuse or are unable to accept a common life. While hardly mandated by Jewish law, concern for others at the expense of self becomes authorized as a recognition that we are bound to others as we are bound to our notion of our best selves. "But if I am for myself only," Hillel asks in *Pirkei Avot*, "what am I?" An encounter with God becomes the daily encounter with an unfinished self and society.

Arguably his best work, *Dubin's Lives* (1979) deals with the quarrel between art and the ordered life: the opposition rendered as the struggle between Hellenism and Hebraism. The knowing of terms is Sammler's pathos. For Malamud's Dubin, action itself is unsettling, destabilizing his notion of himself. In terms of the novel, Dubin's character remains a theory read in the light of experience. Malamud depicts Dubin's limited abilities to live within the poetics of Hellenism, to nurture the instincts that D.H. Lawrence praised as authoritative and liberating.

Dubin is a middle-aged man, an eminent biographer, living in a now loveless marriage. While working on his *Passion of D.H. Lawrence*, he is swept by desire for the young Fanny Bick, whom he thinks of as "Venus revived." Of course, passion's ambiguity – need as well as desire – serves the book well. Dubin is helpless before his procreant urge. His pathos is his struggle to hold his idea of himself to account, and yet, to know that he will be tormented by its constraints: fidelity, honesty, and clarity. Dubin's life is Hebraic pain, as Emma Lazarus so aptly termed it: the Jew's abject bow before the culture of Hellas.

As Dubin hopefully enters this liaison, replete with humiliation and deception, he is reminded that he is now living Lawrence's myth of the natural self. Lying with Fanny in her New York apartment, he thinks he comprehends what Lawrence has meant by his celebration of paganism. Nevertheless, Malamud will not grant Dubin an easeful sensuality. Looking out the bedroom window, he sees a Jew praying in a synagogue. Dismissing the idea of a God ever listening to humanity, Dubin wonders, wistfully, whom should he pray for?

The image of a people apart claims him. Whereas Malamud ignores the Hebraic celebration of sexuality, he does not diminish the antisemitic notion of the Jew as an intruder within nature. Jogging along a road near his rural home, a farmer on horseback comes alongside him. Pointing to tractors bulldozing trees, the farmer shrilly raises the notion of deicide. The Jews, the farmer declaims, are "crucifyin'" the land. The spectral Lawrence confronts Dubin, hectoring him that his Jewish mind opposes "the active Male Principle." The Jew fears "primal impulses."

Malamud's struggle for the novel's ending is his labor for equipoise between Hebraism and Hellenism. On the crest of a renewed youthfulness, Dubin had declaimed that he wanted all of life. This Faustian wish is granted. Comforting his daughter who believes that Zen will bring her serenity, he argues that Jews do not withdraw from the world. In the last scene, Dubin, who now all too chaotically lives in the world, rushes from mistress to wife, holding his "half-stiffened phallus … for his wife with love." Even given the clumsiness of this ending, there is a victory over irresoluteness. The triumph is not Dubin's, though it is of his making. Fanny has been encouraged by him to fashion a purposeful life.

In her "Innovation and Redemption: What Literature Means" (found in *Art & Ardor*), Cynthia Ozick accentuates the claim that literature "*is* the moral life." Repelled by the notion that one could abandon moral judgment in art, that one could wrest art away from its all-too-real address of the human situation, she argues that those who assert that the moral sense in art is irrelevant are part of the Hellenic legacy. Writers under the influence of Hellas invariably lead to Hellas. Ozick's "Preface" to *Bloodshed and Three Novellas* (1976) enhances these claims. "Usurpation (Other People's Stories)" invokes what Ozick calls the "dread of imagination." As Ozick puts it, "Usurpation" militates against Apollo. The story counters "magic and mystification" because the drive to create stories can lead to the worshipping of idols, to adoring the "magical event." (A good companion piece is Heine's "The Greek Gods.") However, Ozick wonders if the urge to write stories is another form of idolization.

From "The Pagan Rabbi" (found in the accessible *The Pagan Rabbi and Other Stories*, 1971) through "Usurpation (Other People's Stories)" to *The Cannibal Galaxy* (1983) through *The Messiah of Stockholm* (1987) and to her *Heir to the Glimmering World* (2004), Ozick embroiders this theme, She poses the American-Jewish writer's dilemma: what can be heard both within and outside what Ozick has called the liturgical voice of Jewish writing? Saul *Tchernichowsky, and his poem about obeisance to Hellas, "Before the Statue of Apollo," haunt Ozick's work. Her fiction suggests that if Jewish writers accept the heritage of abomination, reading their own lives within gentile myth, they worship the forbidden on its own terms. As she puts it in *Bloodshed and Three Novellas*, the Canaanite idols will speak of such a writer "in the language of the spheres, kike."

Her *Heir to the Glimmering World* (2004) strongly defends the tradition of Jewish commentary that is an unfolding address to creation and Covenant. Such meditation is also a renewal of the human. The novel encloses fables of identity within each other, asking what acts of interpretation and enhancement sustain self and community. Told through the eyes of a young woman, Rose, the book takes two figures – the Bear Boy and Professor Mitwisser – as examples of Karaitism. Ozick's deployment of *Karaites in both historical and literary usages suggests its boundaries. In her "Toward a New Yiddish," she contends that the New Critics are "Christian Karaites," extracting the text from the richness of human circumstance, and hence making it an idol. In "Innovation and Redemption," she marks the Karaites as those who would obey the strict letter without accepting its halo of meaning.

At the novel's center are James A'Bair (known as Bear Boy, called so after being the model for his father's illustrated children's books) and Prof. Mitwisser, a scholar of Karaitism. Both seek a return (the latter in text; the former, in self) to an original state of being, free of elaboration by others. Called a Karaite by Mrs. Mitwisser, James (who is Mitwisser's patron) wants to throw off his identity as Bear Boy. He wants to fashion anew his own individuality by acts of self-will. He ends as a suicide, the classic argument for self-determination. Pursuing the meaning of a fragment by al-*Kirkisani, a Karaite writer, Mitwisser, discovers this figure is a unique theological rebel. As Mitwisser argues, al-Kirkisani "receives, in order to refuse." Mitwisser understands that he has comprehended al-Kirkisani's grand renunciation, a descent into a depth in which, finally there is only *the* authentic divinity, a God "who disbelieves in man." This God is God "the heretic." Mitwisser's claim, though, may well be untenable. His work and conclusions, returning to an unelaborated tradition, an ever-present moment of the new, have been too hasty.

More so than any other American-Jewish writer, Philip Roth's work encompasses the history of contemporary America. His last novels, those narrated by Nathan Zuckerman, depict an America that remains, in spite of its contradictory promises of freedom, a nation in which Jews can determine their identities. Set against this freedom is the stabilizing norm of American myth: the pastoral as possessed by the *American* consciousness. This pastoral is offered through images and dreams that ennoble, even in tragic defeat, Roth's characters. An "arcadian mountain," a farmhouse, a lake, a life of abundance and achieved repose – these constitute an American myth of imagined completeness. As Roth well makes clear, this cluster of images and ideas, delusory or not, holds chaos at bay.

Roth's America (of *American Pastoral*, 1997; *I Married a Communist*, 1998; and *The Human Stain*, 2000) reveals the broken self, one bereft of the adequate, morally informing community. His works offer a reading of the fables of American culture lauding autonomy, eradication of the past, and the planned life. Even so, these novels catalogue private and public injustices that the spirit cannot heal: murder, betrayal, malevolence, slander, and gossip.

Roth's gift for discerning the large drift of American *mores*, its claims for an invented self, describes both the comic and tragic art of these works. The endings of these novels are caustic, setting the tragic undoing of individuals by their own wishes, within an indifferent nature. Foreground and background no longer comport. The self's putative grandeur has long been diminished. The pastoral images suffusing his novels belittle the passions animating his characters. His self-confident American Jews survive only by a creative deception: assurance. Neither good intentions nor communal traditions stay their pathos. In fact, their Judaism is civic and thin. It is a fidelity to the lessons of democracy learned from hard-working parents, from neighborhoods, and schools – all of which evoke the poignancy of youthful beliefs still informing the present.

In these three novels, an older Nathan Zuckerman bears witness. He records the fates of those whose acculturation is ironic and bitter. His sensibilities and frailties (variously, cancer, a by-pass operation, and deliberate seclusion near Athena College) shape his narrations. In turn, these traits fund his ideas of the self and history. The reader is never far from Nathan's New Jersey childhood and the work-ethic of the Jewish families he knew. His own limitations are strengths. He admits that writing is revealing and concealing. As a result, he discovers himself while he is compelled to write about lives that have been unimaginable to him. (The most salient analogue in American letters is Faulkner's *Absalom, Absalom!*, in which Quentin and Shreve invent Southern history, shredding its empirical nature to lay bare its fables of race and identity.)

Nathan reminds the reader that the novelist always gets it wrong. As he puts it, he is given to dream a realistic chronicle. His narrations, though, are far from this. They question his own sense of self, so much so that he is forced to change his life. He, and those whose lives he imagines he has reconstructed, discover that the past can neither be betrayed nor buried. As *I Married A Communist's* Murray Ringold puts it, quoting Shakespeare, "'And thus the whirligig of time brings in his revenges.'"

Nathan invokes Greek tragedy and Shakespearean drama; he echoes Fitzgerald and Faulkner; he is never far from Turgenev and Tolstoy, pushing his work into the great narrative of human failing, attendant upon success and arrogance. Nathan strains to find the majesty of failure within the seeming normalcy of lives: lives which cannot bear the gravity of such tragedy until they represent a summa and summation of what we recognize as an American character. The endings of his novels are less resolutions than they are commentaries about a civilization opposing the soft pastoral to its intent: the present cannot sustain myth. The pastoral now judges human incompleteness. In Nathan's understanding, it is the human stain that we must accept.

Roth's *American Pastoral* has as companion pieces both the novels of Russian moral realism and those classics of literature that speak directly to the ironies of naiveté: Tolstoy and Fitzgerald come easily to mind. For Nathan, the pull of his Jewish past unprepares him for the astonishing present. Nathan's idea of his childhood separates obligation from indulgence. The place of his boyish years was marked by industriousness, he remembers. "The goal was to *have* goals…."

The novel's protagonist, Seymour "Swede" Levov, a man without wit or irony as Nathan points out, enacts his understanding of America. A high school hero (Nathan calls Swede "the household Apollo" of the community's Jews), and a former Marine, he is raised on the virtues of responsibility and rationality. His self-imposed civic obligations and his concern for his family's glove manufacturing business make him stay in Newark, a city ruined by crime and riots.

The Swede has moved away, literally and communally, from the Jewish past of his father, and the Jews of his neighborhood. He marries a gentile, former Miss New Jersey and buys a farmhouse in the countryside, Old Rimrock, where his wife breeds cattle. American culture is both his charmed pastoral, and his destruction. His, and America's, dreams of insulation from violence by means of affluence, distance, and cultural myth are porous. His daughter, Merry, is responsible for the bombing of a local general store and post-office, killing one person. Fleeing her home, she is passed along a radical underground railway, aided in her flight, at first, by friends of the Swede. She becomes the nightmare of America's choice. She matures. She becomes expert at bomb-making, and later kills other people. Finally, starving herself and incapable of recognizing the horror of her crimes, she meets with her father, telling him she has become a Jain.

The last blow that the Swede takes is at a dinner party in his house. He realizes his wife is having an affair; that his daughter can no longer be defined as a sweet, gentle child manipulated by radicals, and that Merry's therapist and the therapist's husband have sheltered the child after the first bombing, leaving him in anguished ignorance of his daughter's whereabouts. At the same time, his father leaves the table, trying to coax a drunk, mentally ill woman to eat. She stabs him close to the eye. At the end of this chaos, a dinner guest sarcastically laughs at the fragility of seemingly "robust things." Roth's last lines – how sarcastically Olympian – ask what *could* be wrong with them? "What on earth is less reprehensible than the life of the Levovs?"

The novel takes unredeemable action as its center. Its Job-like litany of disease and death, success and affliction are built upon Nathan's recollection of one of the Swede's childhood books, *The Kid from Tomkinsville*. This book is a counter-narrative of American promise. The book is spun around baseball, yet in the book every success is met with disappointment and "accident." At one point, Nathan considers entitling his own account of the Swede as *The Kid from Keer Avenue*.

American Pastoral explores the stabilizing myths of the older generation of its Jews. It also depicts unforeseen consequences: the fables of revolution that children such as Merry use to define American history and social justice. An illuminating, elementary morality is destroyed within civic life. Yet the Swede is also morally sightless. At the dinner party, the Swede believes that Merry has opened his eyes; she has made him see. He is, however, no blind seer. He is only someone who understands his own self-deceptions as well as those of others. *American Pastoral* becomes an elegy for Nathan's and the Swede's youth. Nathan's grasp of his own mortality, and the Swede's death from cancer address the mortal heritage: the self's fate is particular. It cannot be determined.

I Married a Communist carries on the grand theme of social realism: a protagonist who is undone by willed self-ignorance. The novel depicts the career of Ira Ringold who has tried to prevent his past from engulfing man. His education is crisis, as well as a dogmatic Communist Party reading of crisis. The theme of what sort of education can America provide is a durable one, and finds its great examples in Dreiser's *An American Tragedy*, Farrell's *Studs Lonigan*, and Wright's *Native Son*. With Roth's novel, the American Jew enters again this pedagogy of insincerity.

Ira's life is a series of duplicities. A Communist who is exposed by a conniving gossip columnist and politician; a youthful murderer on the run; a radio actor married to Eve Frame, a Jewish antisemite; a husband beset by Eve's tyrannical daughter, Sylphid – these are the shards of Ira's life. His marriage and desire for a family are shields. They protect him from his childhood, his violent anger and HUAC.

Ira, and his well-intentioned brother, Murray, a high-school English teacher, represent American-Jewish types. For Murray, education is an education in the culture of democracy. He succeeds because he thinks America nourishes a liberalizing culture of reason and opportunity. Ira also succeeds; his path away from the past is the Party. Yet both fail: Murray's wife is killed, in part, because of his liberal good will. Ira's understanding of others and himself is destroyed by ideology. Murray Ringold's pronouncement about his brother is final and decisive: "He never discovered his life." His judgment upon himself is just as bitter: the myth of his own goodness was his "final delusion." Nathan, who has listened to Murray's story for six nights, later looks at the heavens. They are part of a universe without conflict, fixed by no human machination. "The stars," he reflects, "are indispensable."

Nathan appears again in *The Human Stain*. The title's allusion is multiple, referring to the infamous stain on Lewinsky's dress, the imperfection of being human, and the stain of skin color. Its protagonist is Coleman Silk, an African American, who decides as a young man that he could pass the color line. And he does. His journey from his East Orange, New Jersey past to his professorship in the classics at Athena college, is a bargain made to protect what Nathan calls "the elaborate clockwork" of his life. Coleman has broken with his mother, and siblings, invented himself as a Russian Jew, and has married Iris Gittelman.

His life is undone because of political incorrectness. "Do they exist or are they spooks?" he asks his class about two missing students. "Spooks" is the word that undoes him. The two students are black. Silk is accused of racism. He is undefended and shunned by his colleagues. He is also victimized by a parody of the academic woman, Delphine Roux, who presents herself as a French "depaysee" professor, stranded at Athena College, and persecuted by Coleman. Sending a letter that is meant to intimidate Coleman, revealing his affair with Faunia, a seemingly illiterate woman, who works as a janitor, Delphine begins by writing "Everyone knows…."

This phrase resounds in Nathan's narrative: it is banal, reducing the complexity of life to malicious gossip. For what "everyone knows" opposes the revelation of the novel. Nathan opens up what had been seen as the simple arrogance and stubbornness of Coleman's life. Nathan enfolds the time-worn American fable of self-invention within the pattern of tragedy. Yet, as Nathan has mentioned elsewhere, literature depends upon particularity, upon the authenticity and uniqueness of character. His strategy, as always, recreates the painful moments when the self is recalled to its past, when its vaunting sense of individuality is caught by the furies that are the haunting of the past. Coleman's pedagogy speaks to his life – and to Nathan's art: the rage of Achilles, the Greek gods' quarrels, the cruelty exposing the human stain. Coleman's grandeur is his refusal to abandon his calibrated life. His refusal is also his fate.

Nathan's meditation on Coleman's life becomes Roth's dialogue with classical literature. Hellenism and Hebraism confront one another: can Hebraism be usurped or even adopted in order to judge as well as present Hellenism? The book's epigraph about blood expiation is taken from *Oedipus Rex*, bespeaking both an identity and a destiny that are interwoven. Roth easily leads the reader to one of Coleman's lectures, as Nathan reconstructs it. In a course dealing with heroes, gods, and myths, Coleman ironically encapsulates the crisis of his life and the recurrent despair of the epic hero. There is no repose for the Greek warrior, for *The Iliad*'s opening lines, Coleman declaims, provide European literature with its origin. The rage of Achilles, Coleman points out, is like "a barroom brawl." Faunia's ex-husband is Nathan's Americanization of the Greek warrior. Les Farley is a Viet Nam veteran, at the mercy of trauma and rage. He is cunning, stalking Faunia and Coleman, and, Nathan believes, later forces their car off a road so that they are killed.

To borrow Arendt's now classic phrase, Nathan confronts the banality of evil. For Nathan, it is a leave-taking. His romantic indulgence of the solitudinous life is over. The novel ends with Nathan looking at Les Farley who is ice fishing. Nathan calls the scene "pure and peaceful," a man fishing alone on an "arcadian mountain." It is a vision particularly fitting. It calls for, as Nathan himself has called for, an end to a deception so enormous and with such entitlement that America can no longer be looked upon as a civilization commensurate with unconstrained dreams.

[Lewis Fried (2nd ed.)]

POETRY. Jewish-American poetry since 1970 has come into its own. A relative late-bloomer compared to Jewish-American drama and prose fiction, this genre has virtually exploded in the past 35 years, producing a rich and diverse body of work representing nearly all aspects of Jewish life and thought in the United States. The earlier 20th century witnessed the publication of a number of important Jewish poems, such as Louis *Zukofsky's *Poem Beginning "The"* (1928) and *"A"*-12 (1950–51), and Allen *Ginsberg's *Kaddish* (1961). It was also the period during which Charles *Reznikoff (1894–1976), the one major American poet who wrote consistently about Jewish experience, produced nearly all his work. By contrast, the post-1970 period encompasses much of the careers of a number of important poets for whom Jewish experience is fundamental to their writing in terms of both form and content. We also see an increasingly serious engagement not only with Jewish-American daily life, but, perhaps even more importantly, with traditional Jewish texts and textuality, and with Jewish philosophy, religious practice, ritual and belief.

As is true of other literary genres and the arts in general, a widening and deepening of what it means to be Jewish in America marks the poetry of recent times. Never an "immigrant" or "ethnic" literature to the same extent as Jewish-American fiction, Jewish-American poetry at its most profound addresses longstanding concerns of the Jewish worldview that are, in effect, reconceived through American history and culture. Then again, this recent work cannot be truly understood and appreciated without taking important trends and schools in modern American poetry into account; thus Jewish-American poetry must be recognized as a peculiar fold in a set of American literary and cultural concerns that have roots extending at least as far back as early-20th century modernism. This is especially true in regard to matters of style and form: the traditional English versification of a "Jewish" poem by Anthony Hecht or John Hollander is a far cry from the avant-garde practices shaping an equally "Jewish" poem by Jerome Rothenberg or Charles Bernstein. Because American poetry of the last 30 years has been marked by vigorous debate – if not outright conflict – in regard to issues of style, voice, personal and group identity, canon formation, and cultural institutionalization, we must acknowledge at the outset that recent Jewish-American poets have both shaped and been shaped by concerns that extend well beyond Jewishness per se.

This is clearly the case for those figures who have also made significant contributions to the *poetics* of Jewish-American poetry. The first of these poet-critics whom we will consider is Allen *Grossman (1932–). Grossman's engagement with Judaism dates from his first collection of poems, *A Harlot's Hire* (1961) and remains constant throughout his career. Deeply influenced by the Anglo-American Romantic tradition (his first critical study was on Yeats, and he has written distinguished essays on Whitman and Crane), Grossman acknowledges himself to be "a high-style writer," since "The high style is the style of high hope." Using elevated rhetoric, cunning irony, and phantasmagoric imagery, Grossman synthesizes the Romantic sublime with Jewish psalmic utterance and a weirdly deadpan, midwestern American humor; the result is one of the most unique voices in American poetry of the last 50 years. Thus in "The Song of the Lord," the poet announces that "The voice of the Lord opens the gates of day," while in "How to do things with tears," he affirms that "In thy springs, O Zion, are the water wheels / of my mind!" At the same time, however, Grossman raises doubts about the relationship of Jewish belief to the poetic imagination. As he declares in "Out of the Blue," "The meaning of the world / Is being made in defiance of the Jew."

What Grossman means by this enigmatic statement – along with many others in his passionately propaedeutic and dialogical poems – can only be understood in relation to the "long schoolroom" (the phrase comes from Yeats' "Among School Children") that constitutes the body of his writings on poetics, gathered in *The Sighted Singer* (1992) and *The Long Schoolroom: Lesson in the Bitter Logic of the Poetic Principle* (1997). The latter is particularly important for Jewish poetry, for it contains his early, penetrating review of Ginsberg's *Kaddish*, his article on "Holiness," originally written for the collection *Contemporary Jewish Religious Thought*, and above all, "Jewish Poetry Considered as a Theophoric Project," arguably one of the most profound essays ever written on poetry and the Jewish literary imagination. The argument of this essay is too complex to be rehearsed here, but Grossman's self-consciously problematic idea of Jewish poetry as "theophoric," i.e. "God-bearing," and dedicated to a "culture of holiness," actually stands in partial opposition to poetic creation as it is conventionally understood. For Grossman, "the Jew's one word (the Jew's poem of which I write) does not 'create', for that would be redundant, but repeats the one word [God's Word, the Word of Holiness and Presence] that is." Be that as it may, Grossman still concludes that the Jewish poet, dedicated to God's Presence, the Shechinah, "has an obligation to construct the place where 'Light and Law are manifest', to which the nations may come because it is where they are."

The Jewish invocation of the *Shekhinah* and its concomitant call to the nations lead us to a second highly influential figure in recent Jewish-American poetry, Jerome Rothenberg (1931–). A leading figure in the ethnopoetics movement, Rothenberg is a prolific poet, translator and anthologist whose influential work synthesizes the anthropological study of "primitive" cultures with the experimental practices of American and European modernism. Rothenberg sees in the Jews a "primal people," and understands Jewish culture, back to its most archaic origins, as sharing with other tribal cultures a power of *poesis* or imaginative making: "magic, myth, & dream; earth, nature, orgy, love; the female presence the Jewish poets named Shekinah." This quote comes from the "Pre-Face" to Rothenberg's *A Big Jewish Book* (1978; republished in a shorter version as *Exiled in the Word*, 1989), co-edited with the translator Harris Lenowitz. Constructed along the lines of his other ethnographically-inspired literary anthologies, *A Big Jewish Book* juxtaposes modern and traditional texts, orthodox and heretical, religious and secular, to present an immense collage of Jewish *poesis,* understood as "an inherently impure activity of individuals creating reality from all conditions & influences at hand." For Grossman, the *Shekhinah* represents the unique, monological nature of a Jewish poetry of presence, whereas for Rothenberg, the Shekhinah as Jewish muse links the Jews to all other peoples through the universality of poetic activity.

The "inherently impure activity" of Jewish *poesis* is nowhere more in evidence than in Rothenberg's *Poland/1931* (1974). Described by the poet as "an experimental attempt to explore, and recover, ancestral sources in the world of Jewish mystics, thieves, and madmen," this "supreme Yiddish surrealist vaudeville" is both an exercise in deep parody of Jewish ritual and textual practices and an altogether serious enactment of a "timeless" ancestral world. Beginning in a mythic Jewish Poland (which owes a great deal to the fiction of I.B. Singer), the book progresses through the immigration to America of the primal Jewish couples, Esther K. and Leo Levi, to culminate in the outrageous sexual conquest of the American west in the final poem, "Cokboy." Yet Rothenberg's vision of Jewish life is not altogether comic: *Khurbn & Other Poems* (1989) presents a wrenchingly bleak but equally uncanny vision of the Holocaust in Poland, based on the poet's visit to the town from which his parents emigrated in 1920, just twenty miles from Treblinka. *Gematria* (1994), perhaps Rothenberg's boldest experiment in Jewish poetry, reworks into English the traditional interpretive system based on the numerological equivalents of the Hebrew alphabet, producing brief, exquisite poems that read like dictated portents inscribed by one of the ancient Jewish kabbalists that this postmodern poet continually invokes.

Kabbalah is also at the heart of *Spectral Emanations* (1978), John *Hollander's greatest achievement in Jewish poetry, though this elegant craftsman has written many other lyrics and sequences drawing on Jewish tradition and history. Hollander (1929–) has also distinguished himself as a critic of English poetry, and his own work bears the mark of a poet who has immersed himself in the formal values of that tradition. Measured, witty, and full of elegant word play, it nonetheless rises often to the level of the sublime, and nowhere more frequently than in *Spectral Emanations*. Structured according to the colors of the spectrum, with a text for each color, the poem also purports to be a quest for the lost Menorah of the Temple in Jerusalem, carried off by the Romans when they destroyed the city in 70 C.E. Yet it is also an unfolding vision of God's Presence through the figure of the *Shekinah*, who appears in various guises throughout, and an attempt at *tikkun*, or mystical restoration of the vessels that contain the supernal lights of the godhead in kabbalistic myth.

Like all of Hollander's Jewish poems, *Spectral Emanations* reflects the poet's observation, in his essay "The Question of American Jewish Poetry" (1988), "that the American Jewish poet can be either blessed or cursed by whatever knowledge he or she has of Jewish history and tradition." Though his knowledge proves a blessing, Hollander also warns that "Literalness is the death of the poetic imagination, and all groups in the cultural community that speak for Jewishness will always be very literal about 'Jewish experience' is, as will all groups that want to speak for 'American experience.'" Thus Hollander, like nearly all Jewish American poets, refuses to recognize any religious or cultural authority when it comes to the use of Jewish materials by the literary imagination.

Nowhere is this more apparent than in the work of the feminist poet and critic Alicia Ostriker (1937–). Vigorous, forthright, passionate and engaged, Ostriker's poetry casts a wide net in regard to Jewish matters: she writes about Jewish-American family life, about the Holocaust, about religious ritual, and most especially, about the Hebrew scriptures. One of the most ambitious midrashists among Jewish-American poets, Ostriker returns again and again to biblical tales and figures, probing, revising, turning and transforming the tradition in the light of her sharply critical but deeply humane social and political commitments. Perhaps her boldest venture into midrash is *The Nakedness of the Fathers: Biblical Visions and Revisions* (1994), in which poetry and prose, narrative and hermeneutic, personal reflection and scholarly exegesis are combined in a remarkably comprehensive reconsideration of nearly all the major tales and figures in the Torah. Concentrating on the nature of fatherhood and the tensions of gender relations in these familiar texts, Ostriker deconstructs patriarchal power, opening a space for "the return of the mothers." But in no sense does she dismiss or seek to dispense with the unpredictable God of the Fathers and his all too human patriarchs. An enlightened, modern rationalist, Ostriker, for all her passionate revisionism, insists on the notion of *progress* in Jewish history. For her, the original weight of Sinai dropped and upon Moses and the Israelites gradually lessens over the course of time: ironically, Jewish accomplishment, from those of King David to those of Maimonides to those of Kafka, Chagall, and Heifetz, lead her to "suppose that the mass of Sinai has decreased by the weight of a sparrow. Let it be pronounced we are making excellent progress. We are making history."

Such persistent tribal connections continue to reshape recent Jewish American poetry and poetics – or as Michael Heller puts it in his crucial poem "For Uncle Nat," "Not to make / Too much of it, but I know history / Stamps and restamps the Jew; our ways / Are rife with only momentary deliverance." In addition to a significant body of poems, many of them engaged not only with his own sense of identity but with the historical and philosophical dimensions of modern Jewish life, Heller (1937–) is also the author of *Living Root* (2000), a brilliant memoir which braids together Heller's family history, his early poetic development, midrashic commentary on his own poems, and more abstract, virtually kabbalistic considerations of language and being. Heller becomes, in effect, one of his own best critics, maintaining a striking sense of rigor and objectivity while at the same time gracefully illuminating his poems from within. Ranging from "Bialystock Stanzas," a meditation on photographs of his ancestral hometown in Poland destroyed in the Holocaust, to "The American Jewish Clock," a mordant consideration of the passage of generations in Jewish American life, to "Constellations of Waking," a stirring elegy on the suicide of Walter Benjamin, the German Jewish writer who has profoundly influenced Heller's work, the poems upon which Heller comments in *Living Root* constitute a remarkable tapestry of some of the most important moments of Jewish history and culture in the 20th century.

Heller is also a wide-ranging, exceptionally nuanced critic of modern and postmodern poetry. *Conviction's Net of Branches* (1985), the first full length study of the Objectivists, brings to light many of the ethical and linguistic concerns which make this largely Jewish group of poets one of the most important in 20th-century American literature. More recently, Heller's critical acumen has been confirmed with *Uncertain Poetries* (2005), a generous gathering of his essays, including pieces on George Oppen, Armand Schwerner, David Ignatow, and poetry of the Holocaust. The collection also includes "Diasporic Poetics," a definitive consideration on the Jewish dimension of Objectivist poetry which contains some of the most far-reaching remarks on the Jewish-American poetic sensibility. As Heller revisits his lifelong connection to this poetry, he concludes that "there is no such stable category as Jewishness.... What is religious, after all, are the very things that question the boundaries of our being, which enable a traverse of psychic chasms, of difference and otherness." Nevertheless, "From so much utilitarian secularity, one might derive a nontheological theology of language, as if to say: thank Whomever (ironically of course) or whatever has designed this world. For I find new languages daily; I find that not all is written out, and that therefore I too am allowed to speak and write."

What Heller identifies as the "utilitarian secularity" of modern, urban America, dialectically generating "a nontheological theology of language," may well serve as a paradigm for many recent Jewish-American poets, however different from each other they may be in terms of poetic style, as well as the particularities of their Jewish experience. Keeping in mind the extraordinary stylistic diversity of modern American poetry in general, it must also be stressed that many Jewish American poets address Jewish matters (be they cultural, historical, political, religious, or, as is most often the case, biographical) only intermittently, and in relation to their other themes and interests. One may cite a major figure such as Adrienne *Rich (1929–), for instance, who for much of her career hardly addresses Jewish matters at all. An icon of modern feminism, Rich's reputation is built on a complex, highly politicized body of poetry and prose in which issues of identity and shifting subject positions are continuously filtered through a resolute, passionate sense of self. Yet the ethical imperative that drives Rich's work forward is decidedly Jewish, and her search for justice, as in the earlier instance of Muriel Rukeyser, one of Rich's most important precursors, does indeed find expression in Jewish matters. A poem such "Yom Kippur 1984" (from *Your Native Land, Your Life*, 1986) begins with the resonant line "What is a Jew in solitude?" and explores the political and dilemmas of various marginalized social groups, rising to a prophetic intensity in its last lines, "when leviathan is endangered and Jonah becomes revenger."

The same ethical imperative and concern for the enlivening diversity of modern American culture can also be found in the work of Charles Bernstein (1950–), one of the leading figures of the Language poets, who has become one of the most widely-recognized and influential avant-garde literary groups of the last thirty years. Unlike Rich, whose political commitment is often expressed through a rhetoric of righteous biblical wrath, Bernstein's vision of community, related to what he calls "the civic practice of Jewishness," often manifests itself more obliquely. His poetry is typically marked by a sly, mockingly self-conscious verbal play, owing as much to Borscht Belt comedy and the monologues of Lenny Bruce as to his more firmly "poetic" precursors like Gertrude Stein and Louis Zukofsky. As Bernstein puts it in "Poetry and/or the Sacred" (1999), "Against the priestly function of the poet or of poetry I propose the comic and bathetic, the awkward and railing: to be grounded horizontally in the social and not vertically in the ethers." Again, much of Bernstein's work is not explicitly engaged with Jewish matters; especially in the earlier part of his career, he adopts and furthers the defamiliarizing techniques of high modernism while developing a comic version of the "politics of the signifier" associated with postmodern literary theory. Yet Jewish cultural concerns are never remote from him. One of his best essays, "Reznikoff's Nearness," carefully relates the earlier poet's Jewishness not only to his subject matter, but to the seriality and discontinuities of his poetic forms. As for an instance of Jewishness in Bernstein's own poetry, consider the poem "Solidarity Is the Name We Give to What We Cannot Hold" (1996), consisting entirely of a long list of possible poetic identities carried to absurd lengths ("I am a serial poet, a paratactic poet, a / disjunctive poet, a discombobulating poet / … I am a capitalist poet in Leningrad / and a socialist poet in St. Petersburg; / a bourgeois poet at Zabar's [the famous Manhattan deli]"). When the poem was reprinted in *Jewish American Poetry: Poems, Commentary, and Reflections* (see below), Bernstein offered the following commentary: "But is it Jewish? / – I think, probably, maybe so / But it could also be not Jewish / – Exactly." For Bernstein then, as for so many other recent Jewish writers, the indeterminate and decentered nature of modern Jewish identity becomes, paradoxically, the ground on which a new sense of the self can be established.

The potential for comedy in the dilemmas of modern Jewish identity is nowhere more in evidence than in *Chelmaxioms* (1977), a booklength poem by Allen Mandelbaum (1926–). Mandelbaum, a translator noted for his magisterial versions of the *Divine Comedy*, the *Aeneid*, the *Odyssey* and the *Metamorphoses*, brings all his linguistic talents and breathtaking erudition (both classical and Jewish) to bear on this unique work, consisting of the "Maxims, Axioms, Maxioms of Chelm." For Mandelbaum, "Chelm is the Diaspora writ small, but nurtured in the narrow compass of its walls by the scoriae, residues, sediments of all the encounters of the Jew in exile." But this Chelm is not the well known "counterfeit, usurping Chelm of Yiddish folklore…so derivative of – so indebted for its humor to – early German lumpen humor." Rather, Mandelbaum claims to write of "the *echt* Chelm, the meandering Chelm of the maxioms, which follow the non sequiturs – yet arabesque – of talk of talk and talk of text, which mime the riverlike careers of the Oral Law and the Written Law but carry a cargo of alegalities." Inhabited by wandering tribes of scholars (legalists, spinozists, kabbalists, etc.), Mandelbaum's Chelm is a free-floating textual paradise forever remaining to be uncovered, layer after layer, like Schliemann's Troy. The poem is thus structured as a sequence of "Findings," and its maxioms, Mandelbaum suggests, constitute a virtual third redaction of the Talmud, following those of Jerusalem and Babylon. Inspired by "the Perfect Woman" (a.k.a. the Sabbath Queen or *Shekhinah*), the scholars of Chelm pass through the various gates of their city engaged in endless disputation, conveyed to us through Mandelbaum's elaborately rhymed lyrics and absurd but always elegant digressions, footnotes, and scoriae.

Mandelbaum's voice in *Chelmaxioms* is mediated by that of "the Hoarse Savant," an inspired pedant, a kabbalistic schlemiel who gathers the fragments of word and act and binds them into the semblance of a unified poem. He is a close relation to the "Scholar/Translator" through whom we receive the text of Armand Schwerner's long poem *The Tablets* (1999). This boldly experimental work, written over the course of thirty years, has been compared to such works as Charles Olson's *Maximus Poems* and Zukofsky's *"A,"* but in its fascination with archaeology, ethnography, and the textually restorative powers of philology, it resembles the more overtly Jewish *Chelmaxioms* as well. A colleague of Rothenberg's in the ethnopoetics group, Schwerner (1927–1999) was also a translator, musician and performance artist, and like Rothenberg, Schwerner's interest in primitive and archaic cultures and their links to contemporary poetic practices is fundamental to *The Tablets* and his other poetry. Genealogically, *The Tablets* goes back further than any other exercise in ethnopoetics: it consists of a sequence of texts (mixing prose and poetry of various genres) that purports to be translations of Sumerian/Akkadian clay tablets more than four thousand years old. The "translations" and their commentaries come to us via Schwerner's "Scholar/Translator," an eccentric, perhaps even mad figure in constant dialogue with the voices of the archaic past, and much of the weird humor of the work arises from the discrepancies between the Scholar/Translator's observations and the materials he has managed to decipher with varying degrees of certainty. Appended to the poem is Schwerner's own "Tablets Journals / Divagations." These fragmentary observations, aphorisms, reflections and self-criticisms, many of them brilliantly insightful, further complicate the issues of commentary and of the transmission of scriptural traditions so fundamental to a Jewish understanding of textuality.

Thus, *The Tablets*, although neither ethnically nor historically "Jewish" in any overt fashion, is paradoxically one of the most important religious poems written by a Jew in recent years (though in all fairness, it should be noted that Schwerner, like a number of other prominent Jewish-American poets of his generation, such as Allen Ginsberg, was also a practicing Buddhist). For Schwerner, the poem in the process of uncovering – and making – reality, is simultaneously an act of sanctification and an interrogation of the sacred. The archaeological, linguistic, and paleographical methods of *The Tablets* lead us to reconsider some of our most reified assumptions about religious texts, scriptural canons, prophetic and priestly authority, and most importantly, the relation of the sacred to the profane. Positioned precisely in the space between ritual and scholarship, poetry and religion, Schwerner's masterpiece effectively deconstructs these polarities and reinstates the primacy of the linguistic imagination.

Given the radical degree to which *The Tablets* challenges what we have seen Michael Heller call any "stable category of Jewishness," Schwerner's work represents a limit case for Jewish-American poetry. Be that as it may, within these limits or categories, Jewish Americans of a number of generations continue to produce a richly varied body of work. The imminent publication of Harvey Shapiro's *The Sights Along the Harbor: New and Collected Poems*, for instance, marks the triumphant culmination of a career of over fifty years, which blends a Jewish search for "the Way" (*halakah*) with a sense of American openness and freedom that is also fully aware of the nation's political failures and historical disasters. Shapiro (1924–), who served as an Air Force gunner in World War II and went on to a distinguished career in journalism (including an eight-year editorship of the *New York Times Book Review*), represents the richness of recent Jewish-American poetry as fully as any of his contemporaries. Shapiro starts out, like so many poets of his generation, as a formalist, though his style changes dramatically under the influence of the Objectivists, whom he met in New York City in the 1960s (he became particularly close to George Oppen). By then, he had already published *Mountain, Fire, Thornbush* (1961), one of the most vivid instances of (to use Allen Grossman's term) a "theophoric" poetry, a poetry that participates in Jewish thought and history without being limited to a particular vision of Jewish ethnicity, but rather returns to biblical and rabbinic origins in order to understand the power of the Law and the overriding demands of the Holy. The elaborate rhetoric of this book will gradually modulate, in Shapiro's later work, into a looser, more conversational free verse, a greater sense of Objectivist economy, and the edgy, streetwise sound. With an eye that rivals Reznikoff's for urban detail, and a voice inflected with the rhythms of both the synagogue and the jazz club, Shapiro's poetry since the 1970s has become one of the best representatives of a New York Jewish style: wry, wise, restless and suffused with a sense of the blessedness of what he calls, to borrow the title of one of his books, "a day's portion."

In 2000, at the start of a new millennium, a book appeared that suggests, perhaps better than any other collection or anthology, the continuities and future of Jewish-American poetry. Edited by Jonathan N. Barron and Eric Murphy Selinger, *Jewish American Poetry: Poems, Commentary, and Reflections* offers a broad but also in-depth introduction to the field. In addition to a number of important historical and cultural analyses, it includes individual poems by twenty-six poets, along with their commentaries on the poems. This unique feature provides, as it were, a snapshot of contemporary Jewish-American poetry. The poems deal with virtually every aspect of Jewish life and thought, from religious meditations to ethnic memories, from ancient visions to modern American scenes. They represent well known poets with established reputations (Gerald Stern, Anthony Hecht, C.K. Williams, Philip Levine, and a number of the poets already mentioned here) as well as poets in mid-career (Ammiel Alcalay, Jacqueline Osherow, Bob Perelman, Norman Finkelstein). The commentaries are scholarly, playful, anecdotal, ironic, sentimental, intimate, hermeneutical, devout, profane. They convince the reader that Jewish-American poetry will continue to thrive, reflecting the remarkable heterogeneity and braided traditions of the culture from which it comes.

[Norman Finkelstein (2nd ed.)]

UNITED STATES OF AMERICA, country in N. America.

This article is arranged according to the following outline:

Introduction

American Jewish history is the product of a unique New World environment. It is also the outcome of centuries of social, religious, cultural, and political developments that reflect the myriad complexity and cross-currents of the history of East and West in the modern era, including the distinctive role played by the Jews in a variety of Christian and Islamic host societies and settings. This article traces the evolution and shaping of American Jewish life over time, from the colonization of North America in the early 17th century to the present age. It highlights broad themes and major topics in the American Jewish experience, examines divergent attitudes and perspectives on American Judaism, and investigates critical historical junctures in the relationship between the Jews and American society.

To understand the nature of American Jewish society and how American Jewry has organized itself for local, national, and international purposes, several factors specific to this continental community must be borne in mind. First, it is important to note the relative youth of American Jewry, a post-emancipationist community virtually devoid of persecution and expulsion, themes of special significance in the history of Jewish civilization. The overwhelming majority of today's American Jews date their arrival or that of their ancestors in America to the turn of the 19th century, the era in which czarist Russia's severe legal restrictions and widespread pogroms in Eastern Europe triggered the relocation of millions of Jews to Western Europe, Ottoman Palestine, and North and South America. To be sure, the first 23 Jews to settle in North America arrived in New Amsterdam (later New York) in 1654, but until the middle of the 19th century the total number of Jews in the United States was relatively sparse, especially in comparison to the vast numbers that arrived between 1881 and 1924.

A distinctive historical paradox of American Jewish life is that it tends toward being both chaotically over-organized *and* lacking in any central organizational structure. In fact, American Jewish life is typified by decentralization and competition in the marketplace of ideas over the direction of its communal agenda, and there has never been a figure (such as a chief rabbi) or group (such as the French General Assembly of Jews in the Napoleonic era) that can speak authoritatively for the entire Jewish community on social, religious, political, and philanthropic issues. The Council of Jewish Federations, an umbrella framework of Jewish Federations from across the country, wields considerable authority in regional affairs and often seeks to influence matters of domestic and international policy. Meanwhile, a host of formidable countrywide membership organizations have grown over time to exercise a profound impact on American, Israeli, and global Jewish affairs. This is true of the secular arena – consider, for example, the variety of non-religious American Jewish activity represented by the *American Israel Public Affairs Committee (AIPAC), the *Anti-Defamation League, *Hadassah, the *Jewish Labor Committee, the *National Jewish Democratic Council, the *Republican Jewish Coalition, and the *World Jewish Congress – *and* the religious spectrum demarcated by the Reform, Conservative, and Orthodox synagogue movements. Competition among and between these and other branches of institutional American Jewish life can be vigorous, especially in matters of theology, community relations, and philanthropy.

There have been frequent attempts in the United States to establish a central representative authoritative body of American Jews as well as strong counter pressure to preserve fragmentation, local autonomy, with large segments of the community refusing to become a part of any central organization. The impulse towards unification of the wider American Jewish community in the 20th century manifested itself in the *American Jewish Congress of 1917 and the *American Jewish Conference of 1943–45 and later in frameworks such as the *Conference of Presidents of Major American Jewish Organizations, the National Jewish Community Relations Advisory Council, and the General Assembly of the Council of Jewish Federations. More recently, the *United Jewish Communities was created in 1999 out of a merger of the Council of Jewish Federations, the United Jewish Appeal, and the United Israel Appeal to mobilize the energies of the American Jewish community. At the dawn of the 21st century, the United Jewish Communities constituted the fifth largest charity in the country, with a combined income of over $2.2 billion.

That no centralized authority exists in American Jewish life is, in large measure, a reflection of the anti-hierarchical model of American society as a whole. To borrow a phrase coined by the historian Ben Halpern, "America is different" in numerous ways, not only in size and age but, most importantly, in the absence of any established church or governmental recognition or support of religion. This is markedly unlike other host societies in Europe and the Middle East where there are long histories of officially recognized Jewish *Kultusgemeindes*, chief rabbis, and other spokespeople. The American constitutional system has hallowed the separation of powers and the ban on any support of religious activities, which is strictly monitored by the courts and other organizations, including many Jewish organizations, for any incursion of government involvement in religious concerns. The American tradition does not recognize the perpetuation of separate ethnic or linguistic communities such as exist in Canada. This is one of the reasons for the lack of a religious census taken as part of the decennial census as well as the absence of definitive data about the size of the Jewish population in the United States. The estimate over the past 40 years has usually hovered around six million American Jews.

Many factors have contributed to the remarkable progress of the American Jewish community in almost every area of Jewish concern from the decline of antisemitism, the explosion of Jewish affluence, the emergence of higher institutions of Jewish learning and educational institutions, from elementary to post-graduate, to the growing influence and support of the community for Israel both politically and materially. It is hard to determine the extent to which the impact of the Holocaust and the creation of the State of Israel have contributed to the makeup of contemporary American Jewish life. Undoubtedly, both events were significant in reinforcing American Jews in their determination not to allow the repetition of what happened in the 1930s and 1940s when the United States stood by as European Jewry (one-third of the modern Jewish world) was destroyed by the Nazi regime.

In the three centuries since Jews first set foot on American soil – and roughly a century after the United States was but a distant, numerically insignificant outpost of the Jewish people – American Jewry has attained robust proportions, prosperity, cultural eminence, and political prestige. Humanitarianism, skill at organization, liking for innovation, and confidence in unlimited social and material improvement profoundly influenced the American Jewish experience. Such growth and achievements found no precedent in the history of the Jews, just as those of the United States itself were unparalleled. In post-emancipationist America – essentially devoid of feudal, aristocratic, and clerical roots – most of the legal and social problems that preoccupied European Jewry during and long after its era of emancipation were pointless. Discussions of Jewish status in the United States have sometimes had an apprehensive tone and antisemitism palpably existed. But American Jews, shaped in part by a continent-wide society composed of many religions and ethnic groups, has largely lacked the sense of the historical problematics that for centuries permeated Jewish life in Europe and the Islamic world. In American life, the Jewish role has been far in excess of the small Jewish percentage of the population. Only the State of Israel has played a greater role than its American counterpart in the transformation of the Jewish people in the modern period.

The Colonial Era, 1654–1776

THE PURITAN SETTING. The Hebrew Bible influenced the Pilgrims' journey from their native England to the new "Promised Land." The *élan vital* of the Pilgrim voyage was the profoundly biblical perception of a supernatural orientation to human history. After fleeing England, the "Separatists" (as the Pilgrims were known to their contemporaries) sojourned in Leyden, Holland. Before long, however, they began to fear that their children might be assimilated into the alien environment, and the group decided to resume its voyage to America without further delay. When this assemblage, The Scrooby Congregation, was ready to depart for the new land, the members fasted in a manner reminiscent of the ancient Israelites. Once settled in America, the custom was retained and frequently renewed. Early in 1620, the very year of the Pilgrims' landing in the new Plymouth, a solemn day of prayer was observed. This custom, combining prayer and fasting with biblical readings on important occasions, persisted at least until 1774, when Massachusetts declared a solemn day of prayer and fasting after the passage of the Intolerance Acts by the British Parliament. As late as 1800, President John Quincy Adams likewise called for a national day of prayer and fasting during the Napoleonic Wars. English colonists possessed of a similar sensibility soon followed in the footsteps of the pioneering Pilgrims. They, too, were impelled to forsake their native land owing to the political and religious persecution they endured under the prevailing ecclesiastical and civil authorities in England.

Of equal significance is the fact that the Puritan voyages to America were also part of a commercial phenomenon. The Endicott group, for instance, among the first to be sent to New England in 1628, was organized and financed entirely by a commercial concern established by English Puritans with the practical aim of turning a profit. Although it is difficult to disentangle the diverse strands woven into the Puritan effort to establish a new society, the two different elements – the search for religious liberty and the rise of capitalist enterprise – should be kept in mind when the colonization of North America is assessed.

In 1630 John Winthrop led the next major group of Puritan settlers to arrive in New England. He brought with him an organized form of government that attempted to fuse diverse political, social, and religious elements. The Massachusetts Bay Colony founded by Winthrop was ruled initially by an oligarchy of leading Puritan families, whose natural instrument of rule – since the colony itself was based on biblical principles and was moved by the Puritan spirit of the Scriptures – was the Holy Bible. The Puritans wholeheartedly believed it was their special mission to establish in America a society modeled on the precepts of Sacred Scripture. While there is considerable debate over whether the society established in the new colony was in effect a theocracy, the Massachusetts Bay Colony was at the very least a state inspired by and thoroughly devoted to the Bible.

The Puritans in coming to America believed they were entering a wilderness ruled by Satan and his attendant forces of idolatry, and they felt it their sacred duty to secure the rule of God in this latter-day Canaan. The Puritans' conviction that they were the Lord's chosen people *redivivus*, and, as such, partners in a new covenant with Him, pervaded every aspect of colonial life, political as well as religious. This had a twofold effect. First, it distinguished them from other Christian sects in the New World; the well-known intolerance of the Massachusetts colony stemmed directly from this fervent belief in their divine election. Secondly, it reinforced their sense of autonomy from England; the Puritans were certain they had been led to America at God's express command, and that their successes were the direct result and special sign of divine favor, protection, and guidance. This prevailing belief found expression and confirmation in the Synod of 1679, which declared "the ways of God towards this His people are in many respects like unto His dealings with Israel of old. It was a great and high undertaking of our fathers when they ventured themselves and their little ones upon the rude waves of the vast ocean, that so they might follow the Lord into this land."

The Scriptures were not simply left to the clergy but also read and studied by the laity who related the Bible to their New World experience. Such active lay participation and control in matters that were not the ordinary concern of lay members of a church in Europe was due to the dominant role the laity generally played within the larger Puritan religious establishment. The New England "meeting house" was consciously modeled on the synagogue, serving as the central place of learning as well as the social center of the community. The emergent spiritual sensibility in the colonies had political implications as well. The Puritan practice of restricting political rights to Church members was justified by reference to the Hebrew Bible. If worldly men were electors, wrote John Cotton, they "would as readily set over us magistrates like themselves, such as might hate us according to the curse" (Lev. 26:17). A curious but illuminating sidelight of the conception of the Bible as a living document was the Puritan proclivity to view the indigenous Native American population as remnants of the "ten lost tribes of Israel."

Such conscious analogy with the Hebrew Bible was a regular feature of Puritan thinking in New England. If Israel had its Pharaoh, the Puritans had their King James I. The Atlantic Ocean was their Red Sea, America their Promised Land, and the "founding fathers" their Moses and Joshua. Such analogies came naturally to a people who so thoroughly incorporated the Bible into their lives. Accordingly, the first settlers in New England called themselves "Christian Israel."

The names of early cities, towns and settlements likewise derived from Hebraic sources. The names Salem (peace), Bethlehem (house of bread), and countless others bear witness to this phenomenon. For example, the name Nahumkeik, conferred upon the later Salem plantation original settlement in 1628, was clearly of Hebraic origin. It derived, according to Cotton Mather, from the combination of two Hebrew words, *naum* (comfort or consolation) and *keik* (haven): "And our English not only found in it an Haven of Comfort, but happened also to put an Hebrew name upon it; for they called it Salem for the peace which they had and hoped in it; and so it was called unto this day."

The practice of investing the strange New World environment with the more familiar nomenclature of the Bible was widespread in colonial America and continued for many generations. Very often, names were chosen because the implications they carried or the impression they conveyed seemed appropriate to the chosen site. Thus one minister chose the name "Rehoboth," meaning "the Lord hath made room." Names such as Goshen, Canaan, and Sharon were probably selected because they suggested rich valleys or lush plains. Many early American towns – Bethesda, Bethany, Zion, to mention but a few – received their biblical names in this way, and the custom continued throughout the country's history. The rugged terrain of the New World filled the early settlers with awe, and the names of many biblical heights were eventually bestowed upon the great mountains of America, e.g., Mount Carmel, Mount Horeb, Mount Nebo, etc.

That the early settlers showed an active interest in Hebrew language and nomenclature should not be surprising. Cotton Mather, to cite only one example, was extremely preoccupied with Hebrew. He reportedly began studying Hebrew grammar at the age of twelve and likewise taught his eldest daughter, Katherine, to read Hebrew. Hebrew words and phrases are found throughout his writings. In general, the Puritans drew inspiration from the Hebrew Bible and interpreted it to serve their own peculiar needs, often in an arbitrary fashion. Biblical Judaism thus served as a touchstone for America's early settlers, and it was this spirit that infused the colonization of the New World with intense religious devotion.

ARRIVAL OF JEWS IN NORTH AMERICA. After the medieval Crusades, European Jewish immigration moved eastward to Poland, but with anti-Jewish hostilities in the east, culminating in the *Chmielnicki uprising of 1648, the pendulum swung westward. Meanwhile, the Spanish *Inquisition and the expulsion of the Jews from Spain in 1492 and Portugal in 1497 prompted a transcontinental Jewish migration from the Iberian peninsula to Holland and England. Thus as the modern age dawned, Jews began rejuvenating their communities in Central and Western Europe.

Induced by the commercial and industrial revolutions and the exploitation of the Americas in this period, a relatively small number of Jews sought the opportunities of the Western Hemisphere. For those who did, the prime motivation was economic. One result was the establishment of a Jewish community in the Dutch colony of Pernambuco (*Recifé) in northeastern Brazil. With the recapture by the Portuguese of Dutch colonies in Brazil, the local Sephardi Jewish community disbanded. Not only did the Jews wish to flee from the Inquisition, but they also feared Portuguese retribution for having aided the Dutch in the development of the colonies. Those with means escaped to Amsterdam and London, but a small boatload of 23 Jewish refugees eventually landed in Dutch-controlled New Amsterdam aboard the St. Charles. The New Holland colony was small, with a population of approximately 750 persons, but it was also highly cosmopolitan. There the Jewish refugees expected to find a haven. However, though technically Dutch subjects, Peter Stuyvesant, former director of the Dutch West India Company's colony in Curaçao in 1643–1644 and now governor of New Amsterdam, denied the Jews entry to the colony. In a letter dated September 22, 1654, Stuyvesant wrote a letter of protest to the Amsterdam Chamber, the most significant of the Dutch West India Company's five chambers of directors. He argued that the Jews would defile the colony.

> The Jews who have arrived would nearly all like to remain here, but learning that they (with their customary usury and deceitful trading with the Christians) were very repugnant to the inferior magistrates, as also to the people having the most affection for you; the Deaconry also fearing that owing to their present indigence they might become a charge in the coming winter, we have, for the benefit of this weak and newly developing place and the land in general, deemed it useful to require them in a friendly way to depart; praying also most seriously in this connection, for ourselves as also for the general community of your worships, that the deceitful race – such hateful enemies and blasphemers of the name of Christ – be not allowed further to infect and trouble this new colony, to the detraction of your worships and the dissatisfaction of your worships' most affectionate subjects.

Meanwhile, Amsterdam Jewry interceded vigorously on behalf of the St. Charles refugees. In January 1655 the Jewish community submitted a petition to the company's Amsterdam Chamber. They explained that the Jewish colonists had shed their blood to defend the Dutch possessions in Brazil, that the French and English allowed Jews in their colonies, and that there were several Jews among the company's "principal shareholders." They argued, correctly, that Holland's Jews enjoyed greater freedoms than Jews anywhere else. Their concerns were no doubt informed by a reflexive effort to protect their own liberties. In the event, the vigorous intercession of Amsterdam Jewry, Dutch fear of English competition, and the imperatives of mercantilism impelled the Dutch West India Company's board of directors to reject Stuyvesant's request. In a reply to Stuyvesant dated April 26, 1655 permission for the Jews to remain in New Amsterdam was grudgingly given.

> Honorable, Prudent, Pious, Dear, Faithful [Stuyvesant]... We would have liked to effectuate and fulfill your wishes and request that the new territories should no more be allowed to be infected by people of the Jewish nation, for we foresee therefrom the same difficulties which you fear. But after having further weighed and considered the matter, we observe this would be somewhat unreasonable and unfair, especially because of the considerable loss sustained by this nation, with others, in the [Portuguese re-]taking of Brazil, as also because of the large amount of capital they still have invested in the shares of this company. Therefore after many deliberations we have finally decided and resolved to apostille upon a certain petition presented by said Portuguese Jews that these people may travel and trade to and in New Netherland and live and remain there, provided the poor among them shall not become a burden to the company or to the community, but be supported by their own nation. You will now govern yourself accordingly.

The utilitarian rationale of the bigoted Dutch West India Company stemmed from the directors' overriding concern with the manufacture of raw goods, their consumption, and the quest for Dutch mercantile supremacy over their Western competitors. True to the mercantilist spirit of the age, they placed a premium on turning a profit rather than the character of the emerging North American colony. Stuyvesant, however, whose life was impacted by events thousands of miles from the mother country, viewed matters differently. "To give liberty to the Jews will be very detrimental there," he argued on October 30, 1655, "because the Christians there will not be able at the same time to do business. Giving them liberty, we cannot refuse the Lutherans and Papists." In time, he reluctantly acquiesced and the Jews gained a foothold in New Amsterdam. Although Stuyvesant subjected the Jewish newcomers to numerous and severe disabilities, by 1657 their lot had improved considerably and they were able to carry on as traders with little hindrance. Yet in a very few years the new Jewish community began to fade because of larger opportunities in other parts of the Atlantic Basin, especially in the West Indies. By the early 1660s the New Amsterdam Jewish community was moribund.

JEWISH LIFE IN THE ENGLISH COLONIES. In 1664 the English eliminated the Dutch wedge between Long Island and Maryland by conquering the province of New Netherland. Henceforth New Amsterdam was known as New York. Under the English, synagogue communities were established in six towns: *Montreal, *Newport, *New York, *Philadelphia, *Charleston, South Carolina, and *Savannah. Except for Montreal, all were in the tidewater, where most Jews lived. By 1700 there were at most 200 to 300 Jews in the country; by 1776, about 2,500. Up to 1720 the majority of the Jews were of Spanish-Portuguese provenance; after that year Central and East European Jews predominated, although they accepted the Sephardi *minhag* (custom). Many of the Ashkenazim who landed in North America came by way of England, where they had learned some English and had even Anglicized their names. When the Dutch left in 1664, the few Jews in New Amsterdam were not allowed, officially at least, to practice a craft or to sell at retail. They could hold no public religious services and, of course, no honorific offices. Conditions under the English changed for the better. By 1700 Jews were permitted to sell at retail, to practice crafts, and to worship openly. In New York City and in other places they were compelled to support the established churches. In a few colonies they were granted the franchise, certainly in town elections; nowhere however could they hold office, except onerous positions, such as that of constable. Shortly thereafter, however, the British authorities, more liberal than the colonists themselves and eager to further intercolonial trade, passed the British Naturalization Act of 1740.

> An act for naturalizing such foreign Protestants, and others therein mentioned, as are settled or shall settle, in any of His Majesty's colonies in America....
>
> Whereas the increase of people is a means of advancing the wealth and strength of any nation or country;

> And whereas many foreigners and strangers, from the lenity of our government, the purity of our religion, the benefit of our laws, the advantages of our trade, and the security of our property, might be induced to come and settle in some of His Majesty's colonies in America, if they were made partakers of the advantages and privileges which the natural born subjects of this realm do enjoy; Be it therefore enacted by the King's Most Excellent majesty... all persons... who have inhabited and resided, or shall inhabit or reside for the space of seven years or more, in any of His Majesty's colonies in America... and shall take and subscribe the oaths... shall be deemed, adjudged, and taken to be His majesty's Natural born subjects of this kingdom....
>
> Be it further enacted by the authority aforesaid, that whenever any person professing the Jewish religion shall present himself to take the said oath of abjuration in pursuance of this act, the said words – "upon the true faith of a Christian" – shall be omitted out of the said oath... shall be deemed a sufficient taking of the said oaths, in order to intitle such a person to the benefit of being naturalized by virtue of this act....

The naturalization law did not confer any political rights on colonial Jews. Indeed, Jews would not gain equality until the American Revolution. However, the British act did permit Jews to carry on trade anywhere in the empire. This was an important gain and it opened the door to the Jewish community's economic advancement.

Rare individuals like Francis Salvador were planters; a few were farmers, and some in Georgia ran cattle in the pine barrens. A considerable number were artisans, tailors, soapmakers, distillers, tobacconists, saddlers, bakers, and silversmiths. The economic aristocrats were the army purveyors who provisioned the British armies on the North American continent. During the frequent wars Jews also engaged in privateering. These economic activities were exceptional, however, since the typical Jew in the coastal plains was a small shopkeeper selling hardware, dry goods, and liquors. If successful, the Jew became a merchant or merchant shipper, engaged in retailing, wholesaling, commission sales, importing, and exporting. Moses Franks is an outstanding example in this regard. A talented and successful entrepreneur, Franks' fortune stemmed from speculation in the western region of the Illinois territory. His considerable business dealings with the British crown eventually impelled him to relocate to London, where he became a prominent merchant, shipowner, and financial investor. Like Franks, most Jews were exporters, limited primarily to the British Empire by the Trade and Navigation Acts, and they exchanged raw materials for English consumer wares. Jews also played a significant role in the sale of American provisions to the West Indies in exchange for molasses and rum. A merchant shipper like Aaron *Lopez of Rhode Island, who was denied naturalization in 1762, was also an industrialist contracting for anything from a work apron, to a prefabricated house, to a ship. A number of Jews were members of the United Company of Spermaceti Candlers, the first American syndicate to attempt control of the production and price of candles. Some of the candle manufacturers sent out their own whalers that penetrated as far south as the Falkland Islands. A few entrepreneurs, notably a handful of Newport merchant families engaged in the slave trade, including Lopez and his father-in-law Jacob Rodrigues Rivera, who invested in the international Guinea trade to Africa. Jewish participation in the slave trade, however, was relatively minor in comparison to the dominant role played by Christian merchants of the period. In the main, Jewish mercantile activity was governed by economic rather than moral considerations. A 1762 directive illustrates the matter-of-fact attitude of two Newport Jewish merchants toward the slave trade:

> [October 29, 1762]
> Captain John Peck,
>
> As you are at present master of the sloop Prince George with her Cargo on board and ready to sale you are to observe the following orders:
>
> That you Imbrace the first fair wind and proceed to sea and make the best of your way to the windward part of the Coast of Africa and at your arrival there dispose of your Cargo for the most possible can be gotten, and Invest the neat proceeds into as many good merchantable slaves as you can, and make all the Dispatch you possibly can. As soon as your Business there is Completed make the best of your way from thence to the Island of New Providence and there dispose of your Slaves for Cash, if the markets are not too dull; but if they should [be], make the best of your way home to this port... You are further to observe that all Rum on board your Sloop shall come upon an average in case of any Misfortune, and also all the slaves in general shall come upon an Average in case any Casualty or Misfortune happens, and that no Slaves shall be brought upon freight for any person...
>
> And also we allow you for your Commission four Slaves upon the purchase of one hundred and four, and the privilege of bringing home three slaves and your mate one.
>
> Observe not neglect writing us by all opportunitys of every Transaction of your Voyage. Lastly be particular Carefull of your Vessell and Slaves, and be as frugal as possible in every expense relating to the voyage....
>
> Isaac Elizer
> Samuel Moses

Jews of the 14th colony, Canada, were almost all in the fur trade. Others active in the buying and selling of this commodity were the New Yorkers and Pennsylvanians. These fur entrepreneurs rarely traded directly with the Native American tribes. They were the wholesalers supplying goods to traders who went directly to the army posts and Indian villages. It was an easy shift from Indian trading to land speculation, and Jewish businessmen soon helped launch huge enterprises in the trans-Allegheny West involving millions of acres. None of the proposed colonies in which they were concerned proved successful, but they did help in opening the West to American settlers.

The typical Jewish shopkeeper was an immigrant devoted to Judaism. The *kehillah* (communal framework) established by Jews in this period was a voluntaristic one, with a certain measure of compulsion built in. Recalcitrant Jews with nowhere else to turn could theoretically be excluded by the collective. However, communal discipline, especially in matters of *kashrut* (dietary law), was constantly ameliorated by the need not to offend. There were simply too few Jews and the fact of voluntary association acted as a break on the authority of the Jewish community's leadership. Permanent cemeteries were established in 1678 at *Newport, and in 1682 at New York. Religious services that had begun in New Amsterdam in 1654 or 1655 were revived in New York not later than the 1680s. The typical colonial congregation had a *parnas* (sexton) and a board (*mahamad* or junta). Sometimes there was a treasurer (*gabbai*), but no secretary. New York had first-class (*yehidim*) and second-class members. No congregation in North America had a rabbi until 1840, but each employed a *ḥazzan* (cantor), *shoḥet* (ritual slaughterer), and *shamash* (sexton). On occasion the first two offices, and that of *mohel* (ritual circumciser) too, were combined in one individual.

A sizable portion of the budget, in New York, at least, went for "pious works," charities. Itinerants were constantly arriving from the Caribbean islands, Europe, and Palestine, and were usually received courteously and treated generously. Once in a while a Palestinian emissary would arrive seeking aid for oppressed Jews in the Holy Land. Impoverished members of the congregation were granted loans to tide them over, the sick and dying were provided with medicine, nursing, and physicians, respectable elders who had come upon hard times were pensioned, and the community itself saw to all burials. There is no conclusive evidence that a separate burial society functioned anywhere in British North America. Education was not a communal responsibility except for the children of the poor. *Rebbes*, private teachers, were generally available. By 1731 a school building had been erected in New York by a London philanthropist. At first the curriculum consisted only of Hebraic studies to train the boys for *bar mizvah*, but by 1755 the school had become a communally subsidized all-day institution also teaching secular subjects. The instruction was by no means inadequate. Gershom Mendes *Seixas, the first native-born American *ḥazzan*, received his education in this school.

There were surprisingly few anti-Jewish incidents in the North American colonies. A cemetery was desecrated now and then, "Jew" was a dirty word, and the press nearly always presented a distorted image of Jewish life both in the colonies and abroad. Despite the fact that Jews were second-class citizens, physical anti-Jewish violence was very rare. Rich Jews like the Lopezes and the army-purveying Frankses were highly respected. They were influential even in political circles. Jews were accepted in the English North American settlements because they were needed. Men, money, and talent were at a premium in the mercantilistic age. It was not their Christian interest in the Hebrew Bible that led Protestants to tolerate Jews. Christian Hebraists were enamored of Hebrew, but not of actual Jews or their descendants. Hebraism was an integral part of Christian culture. Nonetheless, Jews were often welcomed as business partners. At one time or another most Jewish merchants had worked closely with Christian businessmen. Many of these Jews had intimate Christian friends. Children of the wealthy went to college where they were made welcome, but on the whole the Jews showed little interest in formal higher education. Careers in law were closed, while medicine, apparently, had little appeal.

As illustrated by the well known Franks-Levy portraits, one of the most significant collections of extant colonial portraiture, Jews in this period typically dressed, looked, and acted like gentiles. Like the Franks-Levy clan, a prominent New York City Jewish family of merchants and arms purveyors, they were completely acculturated. Moreover, away from the community and its rigid controls many of the younger generation abandoned traditional observances and dietary laws. Social intimacies led to mixed marriage. Practically every Jew who permanently settled in Connecticut married out of the faith and most of them assimilated completely. Intermarriages even in the larger towns of the country were not unusual. The latter was a source of great concern for Abigail Franks, who in 1743 wrote to her son Naphtali, imploring him to remain faithful to Jewish customs and expressing her distress over the elopement of her daughter Phila to Oliver DeLancey, a gentile aristocrat.

> Flatt bush, June 7th, 1743
> Dear Heartsey:
>
> My wishes for your felicity are as great as the joy I have to hear you are happily married. May the smiles of Providence waite always on y'r inclinations and your dear [wife] Phila's whome I salute with tender affections, pray'g kind Heaven to be propitious to your wishes in making her a happy mother....
>
> I am now retired from town and would from my self (if it where possible to have some peace of mind) from the sever affliction I am under on the conduct of that unhappy girle [your sister Phila]. Good God, wath a shock it was when they acquaintyed me she had left the house and had bin married six months. I can hardly hold my pen whilst I am writing it. Itt's wath I never could have imagined, especially after wath I heard her soe often say, that noe consideration in life should ever induce her to disoblige such good parents.
>
> I had heard the report of her goeing to be married to Oliver Delancey, but as such reports had often bin off either of your sisters, I gave no heed to it further than a general l caution of her conduct wich has always bin unblemish'd, and is soe still in the eye of the Christians whoe allow she had disobliged us but has in noe way bin dishonorable, being married to a man of worth and character.
>
> ...My house has bin my prison ever since. I had not heart enough to goe near the street door. It's a pain to me to think off goeing again to town [lower Manhattan] and if your father's buissness would permit to live out of it I never would goe near it again. I wish it was in my power to leave this part of the world; I would come away in the first man of war that went to London.
>
> Oliver has sent many times to beg leave to see me... tho' I never will give him leave to come to my house in town, and as for his wife, I am determined I never will see nor lett none of the family goe near her.

He intends to write to you and my brother Isaac [Levy] to endeavour a reconciliation. I would have you answer his letter, if you don't hers, for I must be soe ingenious to confess nature is very strong and it would give me great concern if she should live un happy tho' it's a concern she does not merit…

Your affectionate mother,
Abigaill Franks

Although some Jews retained a strong sense of their identity, many identified easily with the larger community into which they were integrated. The desire for low visibility induced even the Sephardi *ḥazzan*, Saul *Pardo, to change his name to its English equivalent, Brown. In 1711 the most prominent Jewish businessmen of New York City, including the *ḥazzan*, made contributions to help build Trinity Church. In the days before the American Revolution the Union Society, a charity composed of Jews, Catholics, and Protestants, made provision for the poor of Savannah, Georgia.

The typical American Jew of the mid-18th century was of German origin, a shopkeeper, hardworking, enterprising, religiously observant, frequently uncouth and untutored, but with sufficient learning to keep accounts and write a simple business letter in English. This is well illustrated by a communication from Isaac Delyon of Savannah to Barnard Gratz of the respected Philadelphia mercantile firm B. and M. Gratz.

Savannah, 24 Sept., 1760
To Mr. Barnard Gratz,
Marchant in Philadelphia.
Mr. Gratz,
Sir:

By Capt. Joseph Howard I have inclosed you an invoice of sundry [goods] shipped you on my one [own] account; four barrels rice; four bundles of drear [deer] skins, one hundread dressed ones, fifteen onery [ordinary] six in the heir [undressed], which [you] will be good enuph to seal [sell] them to the best advantage. Please to seal them so that I may git the remittence by this schooner, because I don't know when the[re] will be a nother opertunity. Even if you should oblige to seal them something cheepor than the common rate, I should be glad if you would send me an account of the seals [sales] of which I have shipped you in all.

I should be glad if you have received the money of what you sould for me. If you have, you will be good enuph to remit it by this.

You rote me by Capt. Nezbet to let you know if starch seals heir [here]. It is now from 30s. to 40s. [shillings].

Pleas to send me the following artcles. You will mutch oblige me if you do send theme this time, because it will be mutch to my advantage. Pleas to inshure what you send. From

Your most humble servant,
Isaac Delyon

25 lb. chokolet
1 barrel linced [linseed]oil
1 doz best black grane [grain] calf skins
9 barrels makarels
1 ditto herrings
150 lb. gingerbread
2 barrels cranberys
10 barrels of apples

If there is any thing remaing, plead to send it in milk and butter bread if the wether is not low. Could send me 15 barrels ables [apples], but do let them be the last you put on board, for fear of the frost.

The American Jews of the pre-Revolutionary era brought with them from Europe to the New World a sense of Jewish communalism. Despite their absorption in business as they struggled for economic self-sufficiency, they kept their congregation alive. In general, Jews in British North America tended to be careless in matters of ritual, governed less by traditional prescriptions than by the unconscious principle of salutary neglect and a readiness to make concessions in order to keep more negligent fellow-Jews within the ambit of the *minyan* (religious quorum). There were exceptions to this rule, however, and fear of assimilation sometimes prompted bitter recriminations by communal leaders. In 1757, for example, having received disturbing reports that Jews were ignoring basic religious customs and laws, Shearith Israel, the flagship synagogue of New England and the mid-Atlantic provinces, issued a stern public warning. On the eve of Yom Kippur (Day of Atonement), the leaders of the New York congregation denounced those community members who flouted Jewish practices.

The *parnasim* [presidents] and elders having received undouted testimony that severall of our brethren that reside in the country have and dayly violate the principles [of] our holy religion, such as trading on the sabath, eating forbidden meats, and other heinous crimes, and as our Holy Law injoins us to reprove one another agreeable to the commandments in Liviticus … that is no one is to be punished unless first admonished:

Therefore whosoever for the future continues to act contrary to our Holy Law by breacking any of the principles command will not be deem'd a member of our congregation, have none of the mitzote [honors] of the sinagoge conferred on him, and when dead will not be buried according to the manner of our brethren … the Gates of our Community will be shut intirely against such offenders, but thos that repent and obey the precepts of the Almighty, we beseech the divine goodness to open to them the gates of mercy, and all their enterprises will be attended with the blessing of haven.… All who obey will be blessed [Hebrew].

In reality, however, the leaders of Shearith Israel and other early synagogues commanded few if any social controls. For although most colonial Jews were synagogue-goers, so too were they strongly influenced by the New World's relaxed social and economic rhythms. In time, a variety of synagogue communities emerged and the competition among them made it possible for Jews of varying attitudes and behaviors to find suitable religious and communal frameworks. Lack of a centralized authority in Jewish life, along with the considerable influence of synagogue lay leaders whose mercantile lifestyles predisposed them to benign acceptance of non-traditional behaviors and attitudes, undermined the fixity of *halakhah* in Jewish affairs. In sum, the Jewish newcomers of this period seem not to have felt that they were in *galut* (exile). Rather, America for them was home.

Early National Period, 1776–1820

THE REVOLUTIONARY ERA. When the American Revolution broke out in 1775, the Jewish population of the New World numbered approximately 2,500, or less than one-tenth of one percent of the entire population. In accord with centuries of social conditioning some Jews, including Isaac Touro of Newport, were Tory loyalists and clung to the status quo. Others such as Aaron Lopez, a merchant of considerable importance who owned more than 30 ships and was heavily invested in inter-colonial and international trade, were not Tories and only quietly supported the revolution. When 8,000 British and Hessian troops occupied and sacked Newport, Lopez, his father-in-law Jacob Rodriguez Rivera, and his son-in-law, Abraham Pereira Mendez, relocated their families to Leicester, Massachusetts until the war's end. Still other families divided into opposing camps (like the Gomezes, Frankses, Hayses, and Harts), and a fair number were Jewish Hessians (that is, German mercenaries hired by King George III to help put down the American insurrection). However, the majority of Jews – once they were forced to make a choice and vacillation no longer remained an option – were Whigs. Indeed, by this time most Jews had few ties to England and were determined to become first-class citizens. They accepted the revolutionary propaganda that had already been aired for half a generation, and they were fascinated by the "Great Promise" of July 4, 1776, the Declaration of Independence. Quite a number were in the militia, which was compulsory, and some served in the Continental line as soldiers and officers. Three officers attained relatively high rank. Jewish merchants ventured into privateering and blockade-running, but the Jew was in general still a shopkeeper somehow or other finding the consumer goods so desperately needed in a nonindustrial country whose ports were often blockaded by the British fleet.

Among the most notable Jewish rebels was the Polish immigrant, Haym Salomon, an ardent patriot who served as an underground agent for the American forces while working for the British. When discovered, he fled to Philadelphia to avoid being arrested, leaving his family and considerable resources behind. The following memorial addressed to the Continental Congress, in which a penniless Salomon requested public employment, provides a detailed account of his services during the first three years of the war.

> Philad^a Augt 25th 1778.
>
> To the Honorable the Continental Congress
> The Memorial of Hyam Solomon of the City of New York, Merchant.
> Humbly sheweth,
>
> That Your Memorialist was some time before the Entry of the British Troops at the said City of New York, and soon after taken up as a Spy and by General Robertson committed to the Provost – That by the Interposition of Lieut. General Heister (who wanted him on account of his Knowledge in the French, polish, Russian Italian &ca Languages) he was given over to the Hessian Commander who appointed him the Commissary War as purveyor chiefly for the Officers – That being at New York he has been of great Service to the French & American prisoners and has assisted them with Money and helped them off to make their Escape – That this and his close Connexions with such of the Hessian Officers as were inclined to resign and with Monsieur Samuel Demezes has rendered him at last so obnoxious to the British Head Quarters that he was already pursued by the Guards and on Tuesday the 11th inst. He made his happy Escape from Thence – This Monsieur Demezes is now most barbarously treated at the Provost's and is seemingly in danger of his Life And the Memorialist begs leave to cause him to be remembered to Congress for an Exchange
>
> Your Memorialist has upon this Event most irrevocably lost all his Effects and Credits to the Amount of Five or six thousand Pounds sterling and left his distressed Wife and Child of a Month old at New York waiting that they may soon have an Opportunity to come out from thence with empty hands –
>
> In these Circumstances he most humbly prayeth to grant him any Employ in the Way of his Business whereby he may be enabled to support himself and family – And Your Memorialist as in duty bound &c^a.
>
> Haym Salomon

The Congress seems to have ignored Salomon's request and he subsequently opened his own brokerage business. He eventually became the best known war broker in the country. Indeed, it was in his capacity as a chief bill broker to Robert Morris, the superintendent of finance, that Salomon helped make funds available for the successful expedition against General Charles Cornwallis, which brought the war to an end.

Independence from England did not at once materially improve the political status of the American Jew. But in 1787 the Northwest Ordinance guaranteed that the Jew would be on the same footing as his fellow citizens in all new states. The Constitution adopted a year later gave the equality on the federal level. At the time this was not a great victory, for most rights were still resident in the states. This meant that while a Jew could be elected president of the American republic, he might be barred from becoming a local or state official. As late as 1820 only seven of the 13 original states had recognized the Jew in a political sense. Ultimately men of talent were appointed or elected town councilors, judges of the lower courts, and members of the state legislatures. The national authorities appointed them marshals and consuls; outstanding individuals made careers for themselves in the army and the navy, though the latter branch of the service was particularly inhospitable to Jewish aspirants.

In spite of these advances, in an era when the American form of government was still raw and new, the Jewish community as a whole was susceptible to the ambivalence of the dominant Christian majority and wary of the possibility of social discrimination in the New World. A telling illustration in this regard is the entreaty of the Jews of Newport, Rhode Island, presented to President George *Washington in 1790 as he campaigned along the eastern seaboard to win support for ratification of the federal constitution. The letter reveals an early American Jewish sensibility that was conditioned, on the one hand, by life under the *ancien regime* and shaped, on the other, by the recent history of Jews in the new American society-in-the-making.

> Sir,
>
> Permit the Children of the Stock of Abraham to approach you with the most cordial affection and esteem for your person and merits – and to join with our fellow citizens in welcoming you to New Port.
>
> With pleasure we reflect on those days – those days of difficulty and danger, when the God of Israel, who delivered David from the peril of the sword – shielded your head in the day of battle: – and we rejoice to think the same Spirit, who rested in the bosom of the greatly beloved Daniel, enabling him to preside over the provinces of the Babylonish Empire, rests, and ever will rest upon you, enabling you to discharge the arduous duties of Chief Magistrate in the States.
>
> Deprived as we have been hitherto of the invaluable rights of free citizens, we now (with a deep sense of gratitude to the Almighty Disposer of all events) behold a government (erected by the majesty of the People) a Government which gives to bigotry no sanction and to persecution no assistance – but generously affording to all liberty of conscience, and immunities of citizenship – deeming every one, of whatever nation, tongue, or language equal parts of the great governmental machine. This so ample and extensive federal union whose basis is Philanthropy, mutual confidence, and public virtue, we cannot but acknowledge to be the work of the Great God, who ruleth in the armies of Heaven, and among the inhabitants of the Earth, doing whatsoever seemeth him good.
>
> For all the blessings of civil and religious liberty which we enjoy under an equal and benign administration we desire to send up our thanks to the Antient of days, the great Preserver of Men – beseeching him that the Angel who conducted our forefathers through the wilderness into the promised land, may graciously conduct you through all the dangers and difficulties of this mortal life – and when like Joshua full of days, and full of honor, you are gathered to your fathers, may you be admitted into the heavenly Paradise to partake of the water of life and the tree of immortality.
>
> Done and signed by order of the Hebrew Congregation in New Port, Rhode Island, August 17th, 1790.
>
> Moses Sexias [sic] Warden

Washington's judicious and cogent reply addressed the Jewish community's concerns in a respectful and dignified manner. Nonetheless, he also gently reproached them, offering a brilliant object lesson in civic rights. In the gracious and brief formulation that follows, he incorporated some of Jewish petitioners' felicitous language, while elevating the dialogue to the level of an ultimate test of America's hallowed principle of inalienable rights.

> Gentlemen:
>
> While I receive with much satisfaction your address replete with expressions of affection and esteem, I rejoice in the opportunity of assuring you that I shall always retain a grateful remembrance of the cordial welcome I experienced in my visit to New Port from all classes of Citizens.
>
> The reflection on the days of difficulty and danger which are past is rendered the more sweet from a consciousness that they are succeeded by days of uncommon prosperity.
>
> If we have the wisdom to make the best use of the advantages with which we are now favored, we cannot fail, under the just administration of a good government to become a great and happy people.
>
> The Citizens of the United States have a right to applaud themselves for having given to mankind examples of an enlarged and liberal policy, a policy worthy of imitation. All possess alike liberty of conscience and immunities of citizenship.
>
> It is now no more that toleration is spoken of, as if it was by the indulgence of one class of people, that another enjoyed the exercise of their inherent natural rights. For happily the government of the United States, which gives to bigotry no sanction, to persecution no assistance, requires only that they who live under its protection should demean themselves as good citizens, in giving it on all occasions their effectual support.
>
> It would be inconsistent with the frankness of my character not to avow that I am pleased with your favorable opinion of my administration, and fervent wishes for my felicity.
>
> May the children of the stock of Abraham, who dwell in this land, continue to merit and enjoy the good will of other inhabitants, while every one shall sit in safety under his own vine and fig-tree and there shall be none to make him afraid.
>
> May the Father of all mercies scatter light and not darkness in our paths, and make us all in our several vocations useful here, and in his own time and way everlastingly happy.
>
> G. Washington

The exchange of letters between the Hebrew Congregation of Newport and George Washington underscores the centrality of liberty of conscience and religious toleration in the struggle to create a free and open American society. The eloquent phraseology articulated by the Jewish petitioners and Washington – that the government of the United States "gives to bigotry no sanction, to persecution no assistance" – would in time become a classic formulation of the American attitude to minority rights.

From a global perspective, the ratification of the U.S. Constitution and subsequent amendments between 1788 and 1791 portended a significant and unprecedented departure from the general trajectory of Jewish history. In a mere 45 words, Article 1 (known today as the "establishment clause") erased the scourge of legalized social and religious discrimination which hitherto prevented Jews from participating fully in modern society: "Congress shall make no law respecting an establishment of religion, or prohibiting the free exercise thereof; or abridging the freedom of speech, or of the press, or the right of the people peaceably to assemble and to petition the government for a redress of grievances."

The Newport Jewish community disappeared after 1800, but the other Sephardi congregations continued to prosper, reinforced by the growth of communities in Philadelphia, New York, Charleston, and Richmond. The apparatus of all these synagogues was modified and enlarged: the status of the *ḥazzan* was raised to that of the Christian minister; secretaries and committees were common, and eleemosynary societies

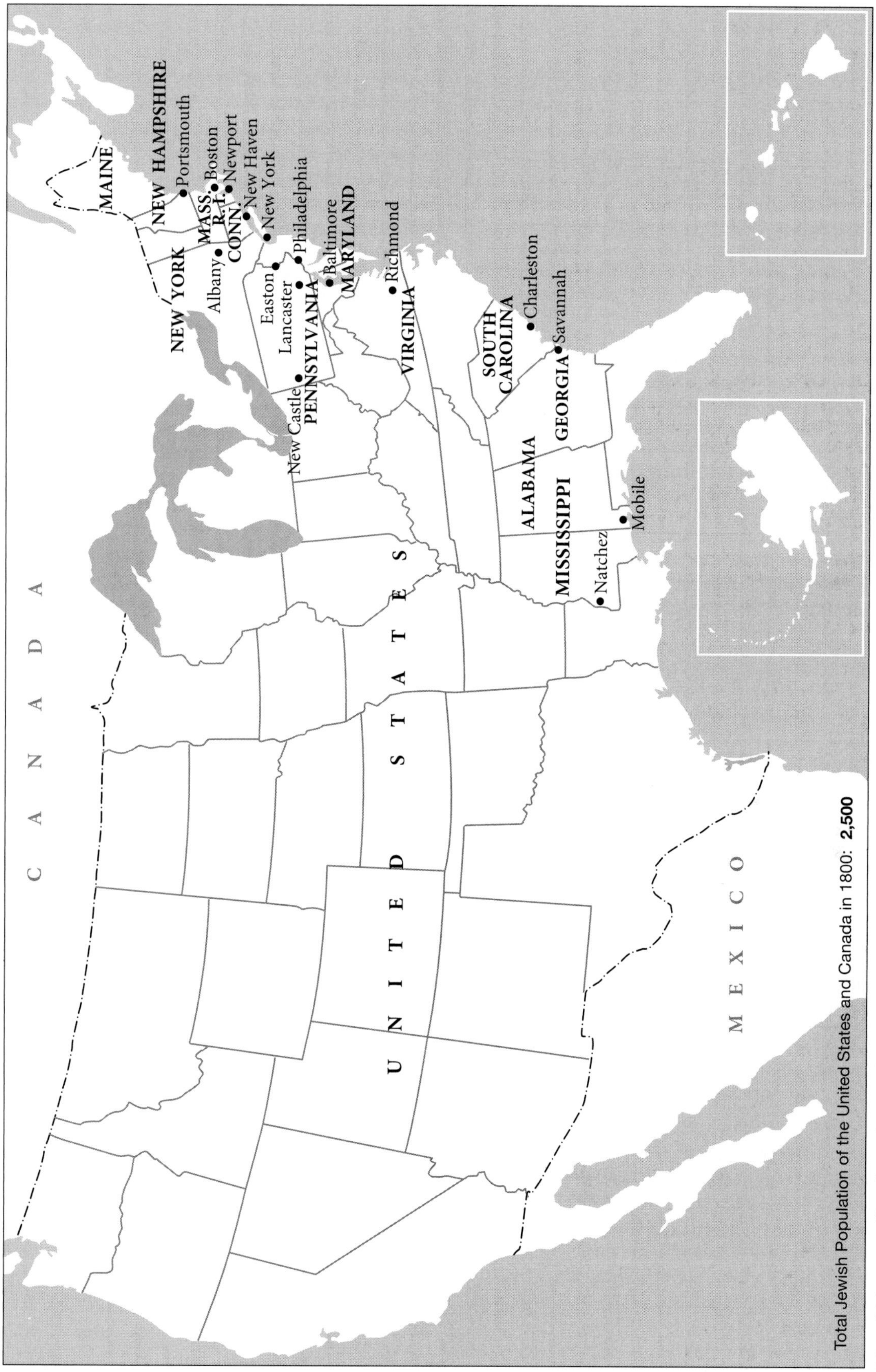

Map 1. Main centers of Jewish population in the U.S., 1800, within state borders of today.

and confraternities (*ḥevrot*) rose in every congregation during this post-Revolutionary period. From then on special organizations took care of the poor, the sick, and the dead. Some of these societies, primarily concerned with mutual aid, offered sick and death benefits. Originally these new groups – whether composed of men or women – were closely affiliated with congregations, but from the very beginning they enjoyed a degree of autonomy. Given the voluntaristic nature of emergent American Jewish life, the charities would ultimately emancipate themselves from congregational control.

Changes also occurred in the economic activities of the Jews. As cotton became "king," Jewish planters increased. Merchant shippers, though still rich and powerful, lost their relative importance as the retail and wholesale urban merchants turned away from the sea and became specialists. With good titles possible, land speculation within the ambit of states and territories assumed increasing importance; Cohen & Isaacs of Richmond employed Daniel Boone to survey their holdings in Kentucky. Independence and affluence brought new economic fields into prominence in the United States. Jews began turning to banking and moneylending, insurance, industry, and the stock exchange. By 1820 they had entered the professions of law, medicine, engineering, education, and journalism.

Many Jews in the post-Revolutionary period, especially in South Carolina, were men of education and culture, at home in the classics, in modern languages and literatures, devotees of music and poetry. A number of *literati* both in the North and in the South were playwrights of some distinction; all were ardent cultural nationalists. Patriotism, however, was no guarantee against Judeophobia, which increased as the Jew rose in wealth, prominence, and visibility. For example, an antisemitic letter published in 1800 in the *Gazette of the United States*, a Federalist newspaper, publicly ridiculed and defamed Benjamin Nones in mocking tones for not having contributed to a collection of the Democratic Society of Philadelphia: "*Citizen N – the Jew*. I hopsh you will consider dat de monish ish very scarch, and besides you know I'sh just come out by de Insholvent Law. – *Several*. Oh yes let N – pass." When the *Gazette* refused to print Nones' reply, he turned to the *Philadelphia Aurora*, a leading Republican organ, with the following eloquent and damning refutation:

> Philadelphia Aug 11, 1800
> To the Printer of the Gazette of the United States.
>
> Sir,
>
> I hope, if you take the liberty of inserting calumnies against individuals, for the amusement of your readers, you will at least have so much regard to justice, as to permit the injured through the same channel as conveyed the slander, to appeal to the public in self defence… I can shew, that the want of prudence of this Mr. Marplot [the anonymous writer], in his slander upon me is equally glaring with his want of wit, his want of veracity, his want of decency, and his want of humanity.
>
> I am accused of being a *Jew*; of being a *Republican*; and of being *Poor*.
>
> I *am* a *Jew*. I glory in belonging to that persuasion, which even its opponents, whether Christian, or Mahomedan, allow to be of divine origin – of that persuasion on which Christianity itself was originally founded, and must ultimately rest – which has preserved its faith secure and undefiled, for near three thousand years – whose votaries have never murdered each other in religious wars, or cherished theological hatred so general, so unextinguishable among those who revile them…
>
> To be of such persuasion, is to me no disgrace; though I well understand the inhuman language of bigoted contempt, in which your reporter by attempting to make me ridiculous, as a Jew, has made himself detestable, whatever religious persuasion may be dishonored by his adherence…
>
> I am a *Republican*! Thank God, I have not been so heedless, and so ignorant of what has passed, and is now passing in the political world. I have not been so proud or so prejudiced as to renounce the cause for which I have *fought*, as an American throughout the whole of the revolutionary war, in the militia of Charleston, and in Polafskey's legion, I fought in almost every action which took place in Carolina, and in the disastrous affair of Savannah, shared the hardships of that sanguinary day, and for three and twenty years I felt no disposition to change my political, any more than my religious principles. – Your correspondent… cannot have known what it is to serve his country in time of danger and difficulties, at the expence of his health and his peace, of his pocket and of his person, as I have done; or he would not be as he is, a pert reviler of those who have done so… On religious grounds I am a republican…
>
> In the history of the Jews are contained the earliest warnings against kingly government…
>
> How then can a Jew but be a Republican? in America particularly. Unfeeling & ungrateful would he be, if he were callous to the glorious and benevolent cause of the difference between his situation in this land of freedom, and among the proud and priviledged law givers of Europe.
>
> But I am *poor*, I am so, my family also is large, but soberly and decently brought up. They have not been taught to revile a Christian, because his religion is not so old as their. They have not been taught to mock even as the errors of good intention, and conscientious belief. I hope they will always leave this to men as unlike themselves, as I hope I am to your scurrilous correspondent.
>
> I know that to purse proud aristocracy poverty is a crime, but it may sometimes be accompanied with honesty even in a Jew. I was bankrupt some years ago. I obtained my certificate and was discharged from my debts. Having been more successful afterwards, I called my creditors together, and eight years afterwards unsolicited I discharged all my old debts, I offered interest which was refused by my creditors, and they gave me under their hands without any solicitations of mine, as a testimonial of the fact (to use their own language) as a tribute to my honor and honesty…
>
> This is a long defence… but you have called it forth, and therefore, I hope you at least will not object to it. The Public will now judge who is the proper object of ridicule and contempt, your facetious reporter, or
>
> Your Humble Servant,
> Benjamin Nones

Not unlike Nones' predicament vis-à-vis anti-Republican sentiment, Jews who entered politics and joined the Jeffersonians were vilified in the Federalist press as "democrats," which was at the time used in public debate as a derogatory epithet. In this manner, Jews seeking public office, even Christians of Jewish ancestry, were frequently and viciously attacked. Aside from a few plays, miscellaneous orations, addresses, and literary anthologies, however, Jews wrote relatively little of note in this period. Meanwhile, Jewish publishers in New York City did begin to make themselves known by reprinting significant European books. In the area of Jewish culture, American Jewry was equally uncreative. In the 1760s two English translations of Hebrew prayer books had appeared. After the Revolution, Jews brought out a few sermons and eulogies, a Hebrew grammar, and by 1820 a rather interesting polemic entitled *Israel Vindicated*, though there is no absolute proof that this was written by a Jew. More important was the reprinting of a number of apologetic works directed against deists and Christian missionaries. Some of these books had originally appeared in England.

The typical American Jew of the post-Revolutionary period was native born and completely acculturated. Intermarriage was not uncommon. Though nominally a follower of Jewish customs, most Jews of this era were in reality largely indifferent to the tenets and practices of traditional Judaism. Despite such an attenuated profile, they were nonetheless strongly and even belligerently attached to American and world Jewry by a strong sense of kinship. Altogether there were about 4,000 Jews in the United States by 1820, most of them in the Allegheny regions, but there was no town in the United States, even distant St. Louis, which did not shelter some Jews. Many of them were recent German immigrants who had drifted in after the Napoleonic wars. By the turn of the 18th century Central Europeans had already started a little Ashkenazi synagogue in Philadelphia. Within a generation Ashkenazi culture dominated the American Jewish scene.

German Jewish Period, 1820–1880

POPULATION, IMMIGRATION, AND SETTLEMENT. The salient development in American Jewry during the four decades before the Civil War was its growth from a small group, estimated at 6,000 in 1826, to a major world Jewish community. The number of Jews, which stood at about 15,000 in 1840, was authoritatively estimated at 150,000 in 1860, and probably reached 280,000 in 1880. This vast increase was largely due to foreign immigration, especially from German lands. In general, the Metternichian age in Central Europe was one of conservatism. Jews feared conscription, their right to move about freely and settle in the German lands was often limited, they were not always free to marry, the new industrialism was a threat to their traditional economy, the German guild system hemmed them in, and anti-Jewish prejudice was constant. This was the push that impelled them to emigrate; American liberties and opportunities attracted them.

In Bavaria, dozens of small largely Jewish villages saw most of their inhabitants leave for the United States, while in Posen (Prussian Poland) there was a steady outward movement. Germanized Jews from Bohemia and Hungary also emigrated. Immigration attained a peak during the early 1850s, when economic depression and the repressive aftermath following the abortive Continental revolutions of 1830 and 1848 impelled the greatest movement to the prospering American republic. Consequently, the Jewish community in the United States long spoke English with a German accent when it was not speaking its native German. The German Jews also proved to be hard working and highly adaptive to their New World environment. The swift Americanization and cultural elasticity that characterized German Jews in the antebellum period is evident in the following letter (translated from German) in which Jacob Felsenthal, originally of Cologne, invites his brother to join him in San Francisco.

> San Francisco, Calif., Jan, 13, 1854
> Dear Brother,
>
> It was a wonderful surprise to learn from a fellow named Liwey [Levy?] that you are in America! And also that you are living in Baltimore with a family named Herzog. I could not remember who the Herzogs are but it finally dawned on me that must be Jacob Herz and his wife from Limburg!
>
> How are you getting along and how's business? It's not great here since as you can imagine things don't just fall in your lap. Here I have learned what business means, and I have put up with a lot, especially in Panama. I was sick for several months and had no money, not even enough to eat. As I got a little better I got various jobs to pay for board and room, which cost a dollar-and-a-half a day. I was too weak even to play my guitar.
>
> But with God's help I got well, and after 4–5 months in Panama in that awful heat I was able to put away 120 dollars in gold which I earned in just five weeks. Then I was able to go to California! Luckily, through a doctor I know, I got a place on a steamer as a cook so I didn't have to pay any fare. Also, I made a deal with Carl Reis and made some money in potatoes, which cost 1 schilling a pound. I don't have to tell you how expensive everything is.
>
> I have now been in California seven months, in San Francisco, and am married! I have a fine wife and thank God things are going quite well. I have already taken in several hundred dollars. If you would want to come here then you and I and my wife would start up a nice café with music and singing every evening. Here a cigar costs 1 or 2 schillings each, and drinks the same, so there is money to be made. Also I am as well known in San Francisco as I was in Cologne …
>
> Write immediately of you are coming or not. If you don't have 50 dollars then let me know and I will send you the money. It would be better if you have the money and then I can put more into the business. In any case, answer by return mail so I can start arranging things. Don't buy a through ticket because it will cost 25 dollars more from Panama to San Francisco by steamer. Take a sailing vessel. As I said, write me by return mail. I won't leave you in the lurch. The sooner you come the better for you and me. An ordinary worker gets 4–5 dollars a day, so you can see how you'll do.
>
> I imagine you already speak good English. So do I since my wife is American and doesn't speak a word of German. She was born in Boston and speaks a little Spanish. But here every language in the world is spoken. If you get to Panama, then go to the pharmacist – take your right, then left – he is also German. They both know me; tell them you are my brother and ask their help to get you a job on the steamer so you won't have

to pay passage. Don't stay in Panama long; it is very unhealthy. And don't eat too much meat. The sooner you leave the better. Do what is best for you.

Regards from my wife who is looking forward to meeting you.

Your brother,
J. Felsenthal

In the decades prior to the Civil War, Jewish settlement traversed the North American continent. Old seacoast Jewish communities like those in Charleston, South Carolina, Newport, Rhode Island, and Norfolk, Virginia, failed to grow and declined in importance. The most important expansion took place along the route of the Erie Canal, which crossed upstate New York after 1825, and on the shores of the Great Lakes. The Jewish population of such cities as *Albany, *Syracuse, *Rochester, and *Buffalo in New York State, and *Cleveland, *Chicago, *Detroit, and *Milwaukee in the Middle West quickly rose to the thousands. On the banks of the Ohio and Mississippi rivers scores of smaller towns had Jewish settlements. *Cincinnati on the Ohio River stood second only to New York during the mid-nineteenth century, while *Louisville, *Minneapolis, *St. Louis, and *New Orleans on the Mississippi drew upon vast developing hinterlands for the commercial and industrial growth in which Jews took a prominent role. Dozens of towns in the southern Cotton Kingdom sheltered little groups of German Jews, who traded in the freshly picked cotton and kept general stores. A striking growth occurred in northern California during and after the Gold Rush of 1849–52; perhaps 10,000 Jews lived in the boom city of *San Francisco and scattered among the mining camps by 1860. New York City's numerical predominance in American Jewish life was well established by that date with 40,000 Jews, and Philadelphia and Baltimore were also important communities. Jews in New England, on the other hand, were very few.

The last significant traces of legal inequality disappeared early in this period. The most significant episode was the public agitation and debate in the State of Maryland over the disqualification of Jews for public office, which was finally removed by the "Jew Bill" of 1826. Like the debates during the period of the American Revolution, these deliberations concerned the alleged Christian basis of the state, rather than a contest between pro-Jewish and anti-Jewish feeling. The states of North Carolina and New Hampshire retained legal obstacles to Jewish tenure of public office but very few Jews resided there and prescribed Christian oaths appear to have been a dead letter issue.

The middle of the 19th century was the day of the German Jewish peddler. At a time when retail trade outlets outside large cities were few, the peddler was an important functionary of emergent American commerce. Thousands of men, mostly recent young immigrants, trudged the countryside east of the Mississippi River with packs on their back, successors of the Yankee peddler. Peddling proved to be a hard-scrabble existence and was susceptible to the attacks of those, like the anonymous author of *Men and Manners in America* (1833), who believed "the whole race of Yankee peddlers are proverbial for their dishonesty. These go forth annually in thousands to lie, cog, cheat, swindle… In this respect they resemble the Jews…" To the profile of the Jewish peddler must therefore be added the occasional encounter with petty antisemitism which, as the following text demonstrates, illustrated the darker side of America's European legacy.

I continued my peddling until January 1835, when one evening, in deep snow and quite frozen I came to Easton, a pretty little town in Delaware, and entered an inn. A number of guests sat around the glowing stoves; and as they saw me enter, a pale and snow-covered merchant, a feeling of compassion must have come over them, for nearly every one bought something of me, and thus even in the evening, I did some good business, after I had run about the whole day in terrible winter weather, earning scarcely enough for a drink.

While preoccupied with my business, I was watched by an oldish-looking, occasionally smiling, but apparently unconcerned man behind the stove. He allowed me to finish the business in peace but then he got up, tapped me on the shoulder and bade me follow him. Out of doors his first question was whether I had a trade-license for peddling? I still felt so strange in America, and he spoke in so low a voice that I did not understand him and, therefore, looked at him in astonishment. My long, ten-days-old beard struck him, and he asked me further whether I was a Jew. He did not want to believe me when I denied it. Fortunately, I had with me the passport of my homeland, which I presented to him. Now he grew somewhat better disposed, looked at me sympathetically and said: "Since I see that you are an honest Protestant Christian I shall let you go, although I am losing 25 dollars through it. I have no kind feelings for the Jews, and were you one of them, I would not treat you so gently. If I wanted to arrest you, you would have to pay 50 dollars fine or, until you were able to raise it, you would have to go to jail, and half the fine would be mine. Still I shall forge that; but you better give up your trade and look for another one. Sooner or later you will be caught and then you'll be out of luck."

Jews also became the purveyors of nearly all the necessities of gold prospectors in California. Although many had been trained in crafts and trades in Europe, few held to them in the United States and were instead drawn into grueling but lucrative peddling. Isaac Mayer *Wise, who served as a rabbi in Albany, New York, from 1846 to 1854, described his community as composed mostly of men who departed on Sunday morning for their peddling routes through the countryside, returning only for the following Sabbath. The progress of many of these men followed a classic pattern: from peddler on foot, to peddler on a wagon, to crossroads shopkeeper, to large merchant. Jews who practiced trades were mostly tailors and cigarmakers. The overwhelming majority of American Jews, native and immigrant, were occupied in commerce at its various levels and in skilled crafts. Very few tilled the soil. The proportion of Jews in the professions of the day – medicine, law, teaching, and journalism – was low. Here and there a man of significance stood forth in his profession, such as the physicians Daniel Peixotto *Hays, Jonathan P. *Horwitz,

Daniel L.M. *Peixotto, and Abraham *Jacobi. However, during the period of mass immigration into a very small original settlement, commerce remained the Jewish livelihood par excellence.

CULTURAL, RELIGIOUS, AND COMMUNAL ACTIVITY. The first countrywide stirrings of cultural activity, religious diversity, and communal organization beyond the synagogue appeared in the middle of the 19th century. German Jewish immigrants included a considerable number of persons versed or learned in Judaism. Thus while ordained rabbis were extremely few, many teachers from Europe assumed the rabbinic title and became spiritual heads of congregations. (This is best exemplified by the case of Isaac Mayer Wise, arguably the most important American Reform leader of the 19th century, whose own rabbinic qualifications were uncertain and never verified.) German-speaking culture was also widespread. As part of the vast German migration to the United States, many were active in German American cultural life. Jews were prominent in German theatrical societies, as writers and subscribers to German newspapers, members of German musical societies, leaders of German immigrant aid and charitable societies, and political personalities within the German ethnic group. For a large but indeterminate group of Jews in the United States German culture was a full substitute for their ancestral Judaism.

The decades between 1820 and 1860 were a period of broad freedom and social acceptance for American Jews. The small native bourgeois group readily entered United States life and politics in such centers as Charleston, South Carolina, New York City, and Philadelphia. Of actual antisemitism there was very little. Indeed, the antagonisms and tensions within American society found expression in anti-Catholicism, which was directed especially at recent Irish immigrants. By contrast, instances of antisemitism were infrequent – e.g., an attack on Jewish businessmen in the California legislature during a debate on a Sabbath closing law, explicitly phrased insistence that the United States was "a Christian country," or a biased courtroom address by a lawyer against a Jewish adversary. Branches of American Protestantism continued to produce extensive missionary literature, including newspapers, books, and pamphlets, but Jewish conversions to Christianity by such means were negligible. Linked to such proselytizing endeavors were expressions of faith that the Jews would ultimately be restored to their homeland, and sympathy for Jewish efforts, real or rumored, toward that end. If the biblical people of Israel still lay deep in the American mind, the contemporary Jews were on the whole not a preoccupation.

The most characteristic form of German Jewry's religious expression in the United States in this period was Reform Judaism. After an early episode in Charleston between 1824 and 1828, where the demand was mainly for more aesthetic ritual, Reform took root during the 1840s with the beginning of the Emanu-El Reformverein in New York and the founding of Reform congregations. Few synagogues, however, were founded on professed Reform principles. Usually an Orthodox congregation of German immigrants changed at first in a relatively superficial manner: it might omit the prayer for the long defunct Babylonian academies (*yekum purkan*), the incense formula (*pittum ha-ketoret*), and the complimentary benedictions during the reading of the Torah (*mi she-berakh*). More far-reaching alterations followed thereafter, such as the shift to a mainly English liturgy, the elimination of the second day of festivals, and the doffing of hats. It was less the initiative of the members of these early congregations than that of their rabbis which produced these changes. By the time of the Civil War several dozen congregations had taken their first steps toward Reform under the major rabbinic figures of the day: Isaac Mayer Wise, who settled in Cincinnati from 1854 after a stormy term in Albany to become the spokesman and organizer of American Reform; David *Einhorn, a theological radical of deeply Germanic and classical Reform thought; Bernard *Felsenthal, a moderate reformer; and Samuel *Hirsch and Samuel *Adler, similar to Einhorn in their Germanism and religious radicalism. The theological approach of these rabbis satisfied the widespread desire for Americanized forms of Judaism that harmonized with contemporary liberalism, rationalism, and optimism. Thus a version of Judaism was formulated in the United States that sought to bridge the chasm between Jews and Christians and refute the millennial view that Jews were living in exile.

To the difficulties of communication and transportation in this period may be added some apprehensiveness on the part of recently arrived German Jews over Jewish separatism and isolation. The synagogue was frequently the basic institution in the communal structure, although the founding of the fraternal order *B'nai B'rith in 1843 and its rapid growth outside the synagogue framework as a representative social and benevolent organization provided an alternate and rival form of Jewish affiliation and identification. Most cities also had their Jewish "literary" and charitable group. During the agitation over the *Damascus blood libel in 1840, protest meetings were purely local, but with some overall coordination. Repeated calls by Isaac *Leeser and Samuel M. *Isaacs of New York brought about the formation of the Board of Delegates of American Israelites in 1859, intentionally resembling in name and structure the Board of Deputies of British Jews. Like many central representative bodies thereafter, the Board of Delegates was founded on account of crises – on this occasion a not insignificant one in 1854 over the United States government's ratification of a treaty with Switzerland that enabled the latter country to bar foreign Jews from entry, and the more serious *Mortara Affair of 1858–59 in which a Jewish boy, Edgar Mortara, was secretly baptized by his Christian nurse and taken from his parents. The Board of Delegates was initially controlled by traditionalists and opposed by the Reformers. It claimed no more than 30 congregations – perhaps one-fifth of the number in existence.

The main ideas of American Reform Judaism were already articulated before 1860, but large-scale expansion of the movement took place in the 1860s and 1870s. In 1873, Isaac Mayer Wise, author of *Minhag Amerikah* ("The American Custom," 1857), a prayer book intended to be the unifying text of American Judaism, led the movement in cohering around a relatively small organization calling itself the *Union of American Hebrew Congregations. The constitution of the new Union scrupulously avoided theological and ideological references. In the wake of the Civil War, the notion of "union" became a hallowed principle in itself and Wise and his followers sincerely hoped all American Jews would join them.

> [July 9, 1873]
>
> PREAMBLE, CONSTITUTION, AND BY-LAWS OF THE UNION OF AMERICAN HEBREW CONGREGATIONS PREAMBLE
>
> The congregations represented in this convention, in faithful attachment to the sublime principles of Judaism, and in consciousness of Israel's sacred duties, feel impressed with the conviction, that in order to discharge these obligations beneficially, a closer union of the congregations is necessary. To this end, under the protection of the benign Providence and the laws of our country, we hereby establish this sacred covenant of the American Israelites, as set forth in the following:
>
> CONSTITUTION
>
> *Name*
>
> *Article I.* The body hereby constituted and established shall be known as "The Union of American Hebrew Congregations."
>
> *Object*
>
> *Article II.* It is the primary object of the Union of American Hebrew Congregations to establish a Hebrew Theological Institute – to preserve Judaism intact; to bequesth it in its purity and sublimity to posterity – to Israel united and fraternized; to establish, sustain, and govern a seat of learning for Jewish religion and literature; to provide for and advance the standard of Sabbath-schools for the instruction of the young in Israel's religion and history, and the Hebrew language; to aid an encourage young congregations by such material and spiritual support as may be at the command of the Union; and to provide, sustain, and manage such other institutions which the common welfare and progress of Judaism shall require – *without, however, interfering in any manner whatsoever with the affairs and management of any congregation.*

Opposition to the Reform movement came from a few Orthodox and proto-Conservative figures, most notably Isaac Leeser, lecturer, editor, author of *Olat Tamid* ("Eternal Offering," 1858) – a traditionalist prayer book – and *ḥazzan* of the Sephardi congregation in Philadelphia. Leeser stressed the immutable character of Judaism as a revealed religion, and insisted that under American freedom the Jewish religion had to be observed in full, rather than truncated. In the final analysis, however, the times were not with Leeser and his companions.

In the 1840s and 1850s Jewish schools teaching both Hebrew and general subjects (usually under the auspices of a synagogue) opened around the country. They existed during the absence of adequate public schooling or because of a Christian sectarian tinge to the public schools. During the same decades the movement for free, universal, religiously neutral public schools spread throughout the United States. As they were established in city after city, the recently founded Jewish schools closed and their children were sent to the new public institutions. By 1860 a new pattern was set for Jewish children of the public school combined with the afternoon or Sunday supplementary Jewish school.

For much of the 19th century Jewish communal organization seldom reached above the local level. However, several notable instances of intensive regional activity did set the stage for later countrywide innovations. An excellent example in this regard is the case of Rebecca *Gratz, daughter of a family of successful German Jewish merchants, who used her considerable talents to help create and lead five benevolent associations: the Female Association for the Relief of Women and Children in Reduced Circumstances (1801), the Philadelphia Orphan Asylum (1815), the Female Hebrew Benevolent Society (1819), the Hebrew Sunday School (1838), and the Jewish Foster Home (1855). Gratz herself was religiously observant. But her participation in Philadelphia's elite social circles, her commitment to nondenominational civic causes, and her appreciation of successful Gentile communal agencies underscore the capacity and rapidity of Jewish integration into wider American culture. Her pioneering mindset led to experiments in communitywide Jewish organization and philanthropy that would ultimately transform the American Jewish scene.

THE CIVIL WAR. Moses Judah, a New York merchant, was apparently the first American Jew to play a leadership role in the emergent abolitionist movement. In 1799 he joined New York City's Society for Promoting the Manumission of Slaves and in 1806 he was elected to the group's executive committee. Judah was an exception, however, and before the American Civil War (1861–65) few Jews took part in the mounting debate over slavery. The 150,000 or so American Jews generally sided with their respective regions before and during the conflict. As tensions escalated, some American Jewish leaders and activists engaged in fierce public debates. In 1860 Rabbi Morris J. *Raphall of Congregation Bnai Jeshurun, the first Jew to open a session of the U.S. House of Representatives with prayer, and Michael *Heilprin of New York City engaged in a printed debate over the alleged biblical legitimization of slavery. The exchange garnered nationwide attention. Asserting that "the slave is a person in whom the dignity of human nature is to be respected," Raphall nonetheless sought to justify the institution of slavery on theological grounds. "If our Northern fellow-citizens, content with following the word of God," he stated in a widely disseminated sermon, "would not insist on being 'righteous overmuch,' or denouncing 'sin'… they would entertain more equity and less ill feeling towards their Southern brethren." In response, Heilprin offered a cogent exegetical and scholarly retort, printed on January 15, 1861 by the *New York Daily Tribune*, which reached a substantial newspaper audience.

> If [Raphall's pro-slavery] assertion needs a refutation you can find it in the concluding passages of the Book of Job, in which

> you will find how the martyr was rewarded for his constancy, all his former possessions being restored double, his sheep, his camels, his oxen, and his she asses – but is there a word of slaves? So much for your proofs from passages of the Scriptures.
>
> Another ample and general refutation of our Rabbi's view can be found in the history of the Hebrews as a nation, a history of fifteen centuries, full of wars, revolutions, civil strifes and catastrophies, but without a mention of a single slave rising, or a single similar event. And how often do the Helots figure in Spartan history! How often slaves in the history of Rome! The history of this country, alas, has scarcely a page on which is not written the black word "Slavery." Shall its history be so continued? Answer, statesmen and people of America!
>
> And you, Rev. Rabbi Raphall, make your Bible, by some process of reasoning, to be pure, just, and humane, if you want to have it regarded as divine; or reject it as full of human frailty, if you dare! *Shalom!*

In addition to the secular abolitionist worldview of Heilprin, the American Jewish landscape was dotted with rabbis who took different positions on the question of abolition. An especially courageous communal leader was Rabbi David *Einhorn, the Baltimore reformer, who called slavery "the cancer of the Union" in the German-language monthly *Sinai*. He also staunchly upheld abolitionism in the slaveholding state of Maryland, in the heart of a city where one-tenth of the population consisted of slaves, and despite the opposition of his congregation *and* threats to his personal safety. He fled to New York City from a mob in 1861. On the other hand, Rabbi Isaac M. Wise probably reflected the mixed sympathies in his border city of Cincinnati by remaining silent about the Civil War and its issues; the reverends Isaac Leeser and Samuel M. Isaacs did likewise. Meanwhile, Judah P. *Benjamin, a distinguished Southern Jewish jurist, slave owner, and plantation farmer, who rose to become a United States senator representing Louisiana, played a key role in the secessionist movement. Benjamin, a close personal advisor to Jefferson Davis, would later serve as attorney general, secretary of war, and secretary of state of the Confederacy. Although Benjamin's attachments to Jewish life were minimal, he swiftly became an object of ridicule for antisemites in the North and the South, who feverishly accused him of treason, profiteering, and the like.

Perhaps 10,000 Jews served, about 7,000 in the Northern armies and 3,000 in those of the South, and over 500 lost their lives. Many of these soldiers, recent immigrants from Germany, served in the numerous units of German-born soldiers. The Union army began to appoint Jewish military chaplains in 1862, after the restriction under the law of 1861 on the appointment of military chaplains to Christian clergy was abolished.

Among the extant documents that illustrate the wartime experience of American Jews is an anonymous letter by a Union soldier, in which the writer discloses the self-consciousness of Jews in the military.

> As a general rule, the Jews do not care to make their religion a matter of notoriety, as it would at once involve them in an intricate controversial disquisition with the Christian chaplains, for which they do not always feel themselves qualified, and which, of course can, under no circumstance, afford them anything but annoyance. Some of our brethren fear that, were they known as Hebrews, it would expose them to taunts and sneers of those among their comrades who have been in the habit of associating with the name of the Jew, everything that is mean and contemptible; but I must say, and it redounds much to the credit of the army, that in the course of my experience in the camps, which has been considerable, I have heard but of a single instance in which a Jew was wantonly insulted on account of his religion, and that was by a drunken Scotchman, who commenced damning in every variety of language and motion, when he learned that he was addressing an Israelite, declaring them all to be cheats and thieves....
>
> Most people take it for granted, that every soldier is an infidel, and that no sooner does he enter on active duty, than he banishes all the idea of religion from his mind. This is a great mistake, at least as far as the Jews are concerned. My own observation has convinced me that military life does not injuriously affect their ideas of duty and devotion.... It is quite common for Jewish soldiers belonging to the same company, to meet together for worship on Sabbath, in some secluded spot, and I know a young soldier, who was on Kippore [sic] morning, ordered to take part in a skirmish, near Harper's Ferry, which he had to go through, without having tasted food, and as soon as the enemy retreated, he retired to the woods, where he remained until sunset, reading his prayers....
>
> Some Jewish soldiers suggested the idea of organizing all the Jewish soldiers in the army, into distinct regiments, with Hebrew banners, etc., so that both our food and religious services may be more consonant with our habits and ideas, and we may have the pleasure of associating with our own brethren. I was further informed that such was actually the custom among the Dutch Jews.... The suggestion of my friends to form themselves into separate regiments was, however, disapproved of by wiser heads, which was altogether unnecessary, as it is at present impracticable, and we are quite satisfied to fight with our Christian comrades for one cause, one country, and THE UNION.

Another useful example of American Jewish life during the Civil War is the memoir of German-born Marcus Spiegel, who served as a second lieutenant in the 67th Ohio Infantry and then as a colonel in the 120th Ohio Infantry. Marcus' extensive correspondence with his wife Caroline, a convert to Judaism, underscores the conflict's tragic impact on family life in this period. Addressing his "good, lovely and abused Wife," Marcus noted:

> I speak truly when I say "abused Wife": a Woman as good and lovely, as saving and industrious, as kind a wife and good mother as you are should [not] be left alone hundreds of miles from her husband who loves her more and more with fervor, zeal, and devotion... with three small children and one coming, or that he should leave her at all.

Somewhat later, Marcus lay dying in 1864 from a mortal wound and wept to an attending surgeon, "This is the last of the husband and father, what will become of my poor family?"

As the tragedy of the war deepened, casualties mounted, and hardships intensified, the beleaguered Confederacy became subject to serious antisemitic agitation, most of which focused on Judah P. Benjamin. The agitation was mainly felt in the smaller towns, however, no instance appeared of antisemitic physical assaults. By contrast, in the North, General Ulysses S. *Grant's General Order No. 11 was a serious albeit short-lived instance of official antisemitism. Predicated on the claim that "the Jews as a class" were engaged in illegal trade with the Confederate army, specifically that they were profiting from illicit traffic in cotton, Grant unilaterally expelled all Jews from the Department of Tennessee, the region along the lower Mississippi occupied by the Union army.

> Head Quarters 13th Army Corps
> Department of the Tennessee.
> Oxford, Miss. Dec. 17th 1862
> General Orders No. 11 (12)
>
> I. The Jews, as a class, violating every regulation of trade established by the Treasury Department, and also Department orders, are hereby expelled from the Department.
>
> II. Within twenty-four hours from the receipt of this order by Post Commanders, they will see that all of this class of people are furnished passes and are required to leave, and any one returning after such notification, will be arrested and held in confinement until an opportunity occurs of sending them out as prisoners unless furnished with permits from these Head Quarters.
>
> III. No permits will be given these people to visit Head Quarters for the purpose of making personal application for trade permits.
>
> By order of Maj. Genl. U.S. Grant
> Jno. A. Rawlins
> Ass't Adj't Genl.

The Jews of Paducah, Kentucky, led by Caesar Kaskel, immediately petitioned President Abraham *Lincoln for removal of "this inhuman order, the carrying out of which," they argued, "would be the grossest violation of the Constitution and our rights as good citizens under it, and would place us, besides a large number of other Jewish families of this town, as outlaws before the world." President Abraham Lincoln promptly nullified and rescinded the order.

> War Department
> Washington, January 4, 1863
> Major General Grant,
> Holly Springs, Miss.
>
> A paper purporting to be General Orders, No. 11, issued by you December 17, has been presented here. By its terms it expels all Jews from your department.
>
> If such an order has been issued, it will be immediately revoked.
>
> H.W. Halleck
> General-in-Chief

Like the wider Christian society of the North, Jews also shared in the prosperity that was a byproduct of the Civil War. The demands of military supply provided unusual opportunities to entrepreneurial businessmen and provisioners, who developed and expanded the ready-made clothing industry from large-scale orders for army uniforms. For example, the Jewish communities of Buffalo and Rochester experienced a wartime boost as result of their significant participation in the local garment making and tailoring industries. Similarly, American banking in general was vastly stimulated by the needs of government finance. The success of the *Seligman brothers in marketing Union bonds on the European market was a critically important contribution to the war effort. Numerous Jewish bankers of the 1870s and 1880s started with capital they amassed during the Civil War years as clothing manufacturers and merchants.

POST-CIVIL WAR STABILITY. The years between the end of the Civil War in 1865 and the onset of mass immigration from Eastern Europe during the 1880s marked the maturity of German Jewry in the United States. Jewish community leaders and heads of households in this period were predominantly merchants, manufacturers of clothing and other consumer goods, and bankers in large cities and also in the small towns of the West and South. "Germandom" reached its peak in this time and Reform Judaism became the dominant institutional religious form in American Jewish society.

Meanwhile, Jews also played a visible role in the economic and political development of the South following the emancipation of the slaves and the breakup of the plantation system. Jewish peddlers and storekeepers played an important part in the economic development of the region. One contemporary attributed part of their success to the habit they had of addressing black customers as "Mister" rather than by given name. This cultural openness signaled the Jews' lack of attachment to the region's racial system. In this period, several Jews became prominent politicians, notably Raphael J. *Moses in South Carolina.

Jewish immigration to the United States resumed after its near cessation during the Civil War period. The Jewish population rose from about 150,000 in 1860 to perhaps 280,000 in 1880, much of it due to a substantial excess of births over deaths within a young immigrant population, but even more to continued immigration. For the first time there were serious discussions in the Jewish community over the possibility of organizing Jewish immigration from Europe. In 1870 about 500 East Prussians and Lithuanians were brought from their famine-stricken region. Oppressed Romanian Jews also figured as potential immigrants in 1872. Despite these discussions, Jewish migration to the United States remained a matter of individual initiative. Of profound significance was the shift in its geographic sources from Germanic to Slavic areas of Europe. To be sure, some small immigration arrived from Alsace following the German annexation of the province in 1871, and scattered immigration continued from many other lands.

The German Jewish merchant class climbed rapidly in the post-Civil War age of industrial and financial expansion and the private banker also reached his zenith during the last decades of the century. Joseph Seligman and his brothers in New York and San Francisco were among the foremost bankers of their day. He declined President Ulysses S. Grant's offer

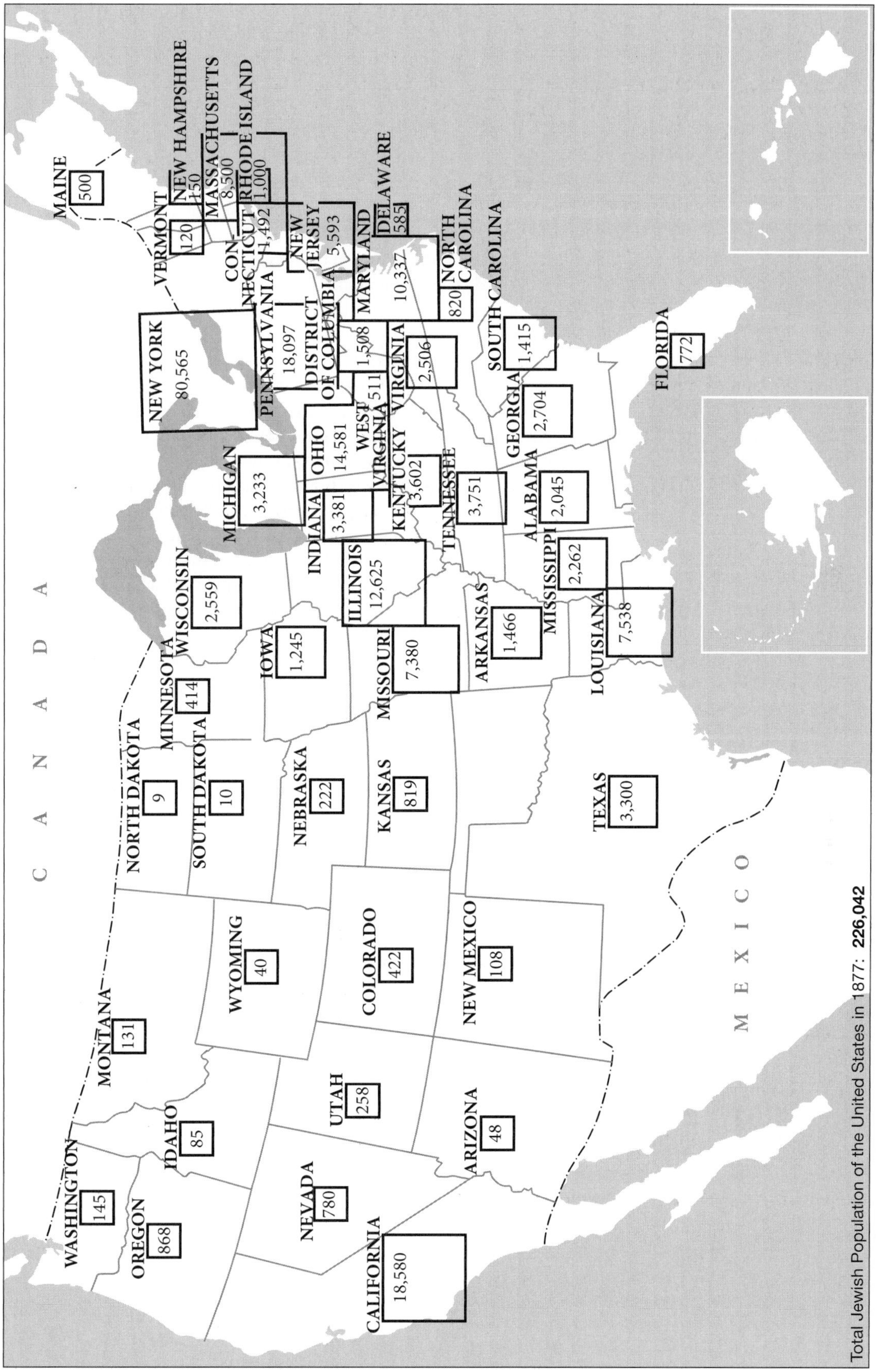

Map 2. Jewish population of the U.S., 1877, within state borders of today.

to appoint him secretary of the treasury in 1869. Entrepreneurs like Max A. Meyer of New York City, a leading domestic and foreign dry goods dealer, Philip Heidelbach of Cincinnati, a significant clothing manufacturer, the banker and city alderman Henry *Greenebaum of Chicago, and I.W. *Hellman in Los Angeles, then still a village, were important personages. In particular, Jacob H. *Schiff swiftly rose in this period to become one his generation's and the country's most influential investment bankers.

The decades after the Civil War witnessed the greatest period of synagogue construction up to that time. Dozens of congregations founded ten and twenty years earlier had achieved size, stability, and prosperity, and the numerous edifices they erected during this period, many with elaborate decoration in Romanesque Moorish style, attest to the confidence and optimism of their builders. (Three outstanding surviving specimens are the Plum Street Temple, at Plum and Sixth Streets, Cincinnati, built in 1869, the Central Synagogue, New York City, built in 1870, and the former home of Congregation Beth Emeth, at Swan and Jay Streets, Albany, built in 1891.) Reform Judaism reached the peak of its influence during the 1870s and 1880s, when it came close to being synonymous with American Judaism, the growth of which its organizer and leader Isaac Mayer Wise anticipated in the 1850s. The ritual in Reform congregations made the rabbi its moving force, and his sermon the focus. The use of English (or in some congregations, German) greatly outweighed that of Hebrew. A shortened public worship was held on Sabbaths and the first day only of festivals. Theological changes were even more profound, probably the most basic of them being the transformation of the conception of Jewish exile and ultimate messianic redemption into a Jewish mission to spread the enlightenment of ethical monotheism to the world, and to hasten the millennium of human perfection and true faith. The Reform theological position was epitomized in the *Pittsburgh Platform of 1885, drawn up by Rabbi Kaufmann *Kohler, which remained the standard Reform creed for 50 years. The organizational strength of Reform Judaism was solidified by the founding of the *Union of American Hebrew Congregations in 1873, the *Hebrew Union College in 1875, and the *Central Conference of American Rabbis in 1889.

While Reform attained structural maturity and theological stability, traditionalists, both Orthodox and proto-Conservative, were confined to a few synagogues and were linked by personal and family ties. Their strength grew out of the mass immigration of East European Jews that reached the United States from the 1880s to the 1920s in unprecedented numbers.

Jewish participation in mainstream American culture grew considerably in the late 19th century as ever increasing numbers of Jews interacted socially, economically, and politically with their gentile peers. For many, the fraternal order B'nai B'rith, established in 1843 by German Jews, provided a pluralistic non-religious framework for meaningful association. By 1876 B'nai B'rith's reach grew to include lodges all across the country. All in all, however, Jewish participation in the arts remained marginal, with the exception of music, which was extensively cultivated by German Jews. Nor did any novelist, poet, essayist, artist, or scholar hold major rank. The emergence of Emma *Lazarus in this period was a notable exception and her sonnet "Ode to Colossus" would later adorn the base of the Statue of Liberty. Nevertheless, Lazarus' early work showed little concern with Jewish themes and issues. Her attitude would change dramatically in the 1880s following the outbreak of anti-Jewish violence in czarist Russia that impelled the mass waves of East European Jewish immigration to the United States. Of scientists there were few, but physicians became comparatively numerous and some were distinguished. Among them were the father of American pediatrics Abraham *Jacobi and Ernst Krakowitzer, who first used the laryngoscope, and others.

The phenomenon of Jewish exclusion from upper-level social circles was especially notable in the 1870s. It erupted notoriously in 1877, with the refusal to admit prominent Jewish financier Joseph Seligman to the fashionable Grand Union Hotel in Saratoga Springs, New York. In the event, the hotel's manager Henry Hilton gave explicit "instructions that no Israelites shall be permitted in the future to stop at this hotel." This act aroused widespread anger and indignation, not only among Jews but in the general press and among such liberal Protestants as Henry Ward Beecher. The social clubs for the wealthy that were being established in the 1870s and later mostly kept Jews out and the German gymnastic and social *Turnvereine* were also inhospitable. In 1879 the *New York Herald* published an interview with Austin Corbin, president of the Long Island Railroad and the Manhattan Beach Company, in which Corbin candidly explained his rationale for barring Jews from Coney Island, which he planned to develop as a fashionable resort. The interview with Corbin captured the genteel antisemitism of America's elite in the *fin de siècle*.

> The war against the Jews, which was carried on at Saratoga two years ago, is apparently to be revived at Coney Island. This time it is in a quarter where Jewish residents of New York City are particularly aimed at. Several days ago a rumor was circulated to the effect that Austin Corbin, the President of the Manhattan Beach Company, had taken an open stand against admitting Jews to the beach or hotel. The report was on Sunday strengthened by a statement by Mr. P.S. Gilmore, the leader of the Manhattan Beach band, who said that Mr. Corbin told him he was going to oppose the Jews, and that he would rather "sink" the two millions invested in the railway and hotel than have a single Israelite take advantage of its attractions. A representative of the *Herald* called upon Mr. Corbin at his banking establishment in the new Trinity building, No. 115 Broadway, yesterday, to ascertain what foundation there was for these most extraordinary rumors. Mr. Corbin at first exhibited some timidity about talking on the subject, but finally invited the reporter into his private office, where he was joined by his brother and partner, Daniel C. Corbin.
>
> "You see," he began, "I don't want to speak too strongly, as it might be mistaken for something entirely different from its intended sense. Personally I am opposed to Jews. They are

a pretentious class, who expect three times as much for their money as other people. They give us more trouble on our road and in our hotel than we can stand. Another thing is, that they are driving away the class of people who are beginning to make Coney Island the most fashionable and magnificent watering place in the world."

"Of course, this must affect business?"

"Why, they are hurting us in every way, and we do not want them. We cannot bring the highest social element to Manhattan Beach if the Jews persist in coming. They won't associate with Jews, and that's all there is about it."

"Do you intend to make an open stand against them?"

"Yes, I do. They are contemptible as a class, and I never knew but one 'white' Jew in my life. The rest I found were not safe people to deal with in business. Now, I feel pretty warm over this matter, and I will write a statement which you can publish."

Mr. Corbin sat down at his desk and wrote a few sentences on a slip of paper, as follows:

"We do not like the Jews as a class. There are some well behaved people among them, but as a rule they make themselves offensive to the kind of people who principally patronize our road and hotel, and I am satisfied we should be better off without than with their custom."

"There," said he, handing the statement to the reporter, "that is my opinion and I am prepared to follow up the matter. It is a question that has to be handled without gloves. It stands this way: We must have a good place for society to patronize. I say we cannot do so and have Jews. They are a detestable and vulgar people. What do you say, eh, Dan?"

This last sentence was addressed to his brother, Mr. Daniel Corbin, who had taken an active part in the conversation. Dan said, with great emphasis, "Vulgar? I can only find one term for them, and that is nasty. It describes the Jews perfectly."

Mr. Austin Corbin then spoke warmly of the loss sustained by the Manhattan Beach Company in consequence of Israelitish patronage.

"Do you mean, Mr. Corbin, that the presence of Jews attracts the element of ruffianism?" asked the reporter.

"Not always. But the thing is this. The Jews drive off the people whose places are filled by a less particular class. The latter are not rich enough to have any preference in the matter. Even they, in my opinion, bear with them only because they can't help it. It is not the Jews' religion I object to; it is the offensiveness which they possess as a sect or nationality. I would not oppose any man because of his creed."

"Will the other members of the Manhattan Beach Company support you in your position?"

"I expect them to. They know just as much about it as I do, and no reasonable man can deny that the Jews will creep in a place just as it is about to become a grand success and spoil everything. They are not wanted at the beach and that settles it."

"Have you spoken to any other members about it?"

"No, but I guess they know my opinions."

Mr. Corbin rose from the chair he had been sitting in and paced the floor. "I'll tell you," he said, running his fingers through his hair, "if I had my way and there was no one to consult with in the matter but myself, I would have stopped the Jews from coming long ago. You just publish my statement. It covers the whole ground, and I mean every word of it."

Mr. Corbin concluded the conversation by telling the reporter to be sure not to give the impression that he was warning against the Jewish religion, but he stigmatized the Jews as having no place in first-class society.

In contrast to the major urban centers of the eastern seaboard, it generally appears that during the early development of many midwestern cities Jews had the freest opportunities for social mingling and political advancement. Indeed, it was quite usual for a Jew, as one of the few literate, stable settlers, to become mayor or a leading official of a so-called frontier town. However, once these pioneer years ended and more fixed social groupings came into being, a tendency to exclude Jews from elite social and business circles became evident.

WOMEN. Over the course of the 19th century, the profile of American Jewish women changed dramatically. In the antebellum period, German Jewish immigrant women participated actively in the family economy as their male counterparts made the transition from itinerant peddling to stationary businesses such as small stores and boardinghouses. Within a short period, German Jewish immigrant families achieved a measure of economic stability. The liberal climate and dynamic social setting of America provided the scope and inducement for American Jewish women to opt out of a traditional Jewish lifestyle marked by domesticity and religious piety. Moreover, the Reform movement's concomitant emphasis on Americanizing Judaism and eliminating aspects of Jewish practice that set Jews apart from the dominant middle-class Protestant culture of the period, including the labor intensive activity of maintaining a Jewish household in accordance with traditional dietary laws, paved the way for new models of female behavior.

As early as the 1820s and 1830s, upper-middle-class German Jewish women in urban centers transformed the activity of *ḥevrot nashim*, women's groups that sought to fulfill the commandment of performing *mitzvot* (charitable acts) such as preparing the dead for ritual burial, visiting and caring for the sick, and assisting the poor, into an emerging network of self-governing female benevolent societies devoted to a wide array of communal and philanthropic work. In 1819 Rebecca Gratz established the prototype of the Ladies' Hebrew Benevolent Society in Philadelphia. In ensuing decades, this innovative framework became a countrywide phenomenon characterized by voluntary membership, democratic procedures, and fundraising. Following an initial phase during which such female societies were attached to synagogues and run by male officers, they evolved into truly independent non-synagogal frameworks managed and directed by women. Meanwhile, the steady acculturation and secularization of German Jewry, the swift upward mobility of the German Jewish family and its embourgeoisment, and the development of an intricate web of new sociocultural institutions in wider middle-class American society – including in 1843 the creation of the B'nai B'rith fraternal order – provided a context in which Jewish women's groups became normative.

In the decades following the Civil War, a variety of Jewish female social agencies and charitable institutions emerged. Among the most notable examples from this period are the

Henry Street Settlement house, created in 1893 by social activist Lillian *Wald, and the Clara De Hirsch Home for Working Girls, a trade school established in 1897 that quickly became a model for similar enterprises across the country. The year 1893 also witnessed the founding of the *National Council of Jewish Women, organized during a Jewish Women's Congress held as part of the World's Parliament of Religions at the Chicago World's Fair. Thereafter, with the support of Lillian Wald and Jane Addams, the National Council of Jewish Women established more than a dozen settlement houses in immigrant neighborhoods across the country. In the decades that spanned the 19th and 20th centuries, American Jewish women of German ancestry opened the door to new social patterns and political roles that would ultimately transform the place of women in Judaism and American Jewish life.

East European Jewish Period, 1880–1930s

MASS WAVES OF IMMIGRATION. The "East European Era" in American Jewish history started in 1881–82 with widespread pogroms in tsarist Russia and reached a climax with the implementation of the Johnson-Reed Act in 1924 when the United States Congress effectively closed the doors to the "Golden Land." During these years, the number of Jews in the United States grew from about 280,000 in a U.S. population of 50,155,000 in 1880, to approximately 4,500,000 of 115,000,000 in 1925. Some 2,378,000 Jews arrived in the United States between 1880 and the end of free immigration in 1925. The peak was reached during the five consecutive years 1904 to 1908, when 642,000 reached American shores. This movement, which formed part of the mass waves of migration from Europe to the United States in general, was indeed epoch-making. Vast numbers of Jews who moved from Eastern Europe into the world's fastest growing economy were automatically emancipated from all legal discrimination and rapidly entered Western culture.

Events stimulating European emigration, such as the pogroms of 1881–83, the expulsion from Moscow in 1890, and Russia's years of war, revolution, and pogroms between 1903 and 1907 were notorious episodes. Other causes of the mass migration lay deeper, however, and were more influential. Probably the most important cause was the growth of East European (Russian Empire, Austrian Poland, Hungary, Romania) Jewry from perhaps 1,500,000 in 1800 to some 6,800,000 persons in 1900, generating nearly insoluble questions of sheer physical survival. The economic development of Eastern Europe failed to provide sufficient livelihood for its Jews, and Russian governmental policies excluded Jews from the new industrial cities, kept them off the land, and burdened them with drastically restrictive decrees. The feeling among Russian Jews grew stronger that their lot would never improve by normal political and economic processes but required emigration abroad or revolution at home. The Jews of Romania, mostly 19th-century immigrants from Russia who attained a better economic position by their move, suffered greatly from arbitrary and occasionally violent treatment as aliens without rights. In Galicia, under Habsburg rule, the Jews enjoyed emancipation from 1867, but the economic backwardness of that area fostered the highest emigration rate in Eastern Europe. By then emigrants could travel by fully developed railroad and steamship lines, so that the journey from a town in Eastern Europe to the port of New York City might be consummated in two weeks. Entry into the United States was virtually free, with barely one percent of arrivals turned away, mainly because of contagious diseases.

The pace of immigration increased with each decade. The annual average between 1881 and 1892 stood at approximately 19,000; between 1892 and 1903, at 37,000; and for the decade between 1903 and the outbreak of war in 1914, at 76,000 for each year. The mass waves of immigration triggered alarm bells in nativist circles, particularly among the established segments of white Protestant America who feared the mongrelization of the Christian West by so-called "new immigrants." This theme gained widespread credence as a result of the work of the Immigration Commission of the 61st U.S. Congress, chaired by the xenophobe Senator William P. Dillingham of Vermont. In 1910, the Dillingham Commission resolved "within a half hour of the time when, under the law," its report must have been filed – and with nary a reference to the findings of a 42-volume report concerning recent immigrant groups in the United States – to recommend that the American government henceforth place a premium on immigrants of "Aryan stock" from northern and western Europe and severely restrict the flow of immigration from southern and eastern European lands. Even before its formal recommendation to the U.S. Congress, news of the Dillingham Commission's nativist predisposition sent shock waves through the organized American Jewish community. The officers of the American Jewish Committee and the lay leadership of the Union of American Hebrew Congregation assumed an active role in trying to defend the interests of the American Jewish community as a whole, while protecting the burgeoning Yiddish-speaking immigrant communities now heavily concentrated along the eastern seaboard and in the Middle West. Testifying before the commission in 1909, Simon *Wolf, a prominent Washington, D.C., lawyer and Jewish leader of German ancestry active in both groups, attempted to disabuse Senators William P. Dillingham, Henry Cabot Lodge, and other commission members of their hostile attitude toward the Jews. Much of the commission's antipathetic attitude to the Jews derived from antisemitic assumptions and pseudo-scientific assumptions about race and genetics. "The point we make is this," Wolf asserted, "a Jew coming from Russia is a Russian; from Roumania, a Roumanian; from France, a Frenchman; from England, an Englishman; and from Germany, a German; that 'Hebrew' or 'Jewish' is simply a religion."

> Senator [Henry Cabot] Lodge: How would you classify those coming from the seventeen provinces of Austria – men of utterly different races, historically speaking? We classify the Croatians, the Bohemians, according to the race they represent in Austria …

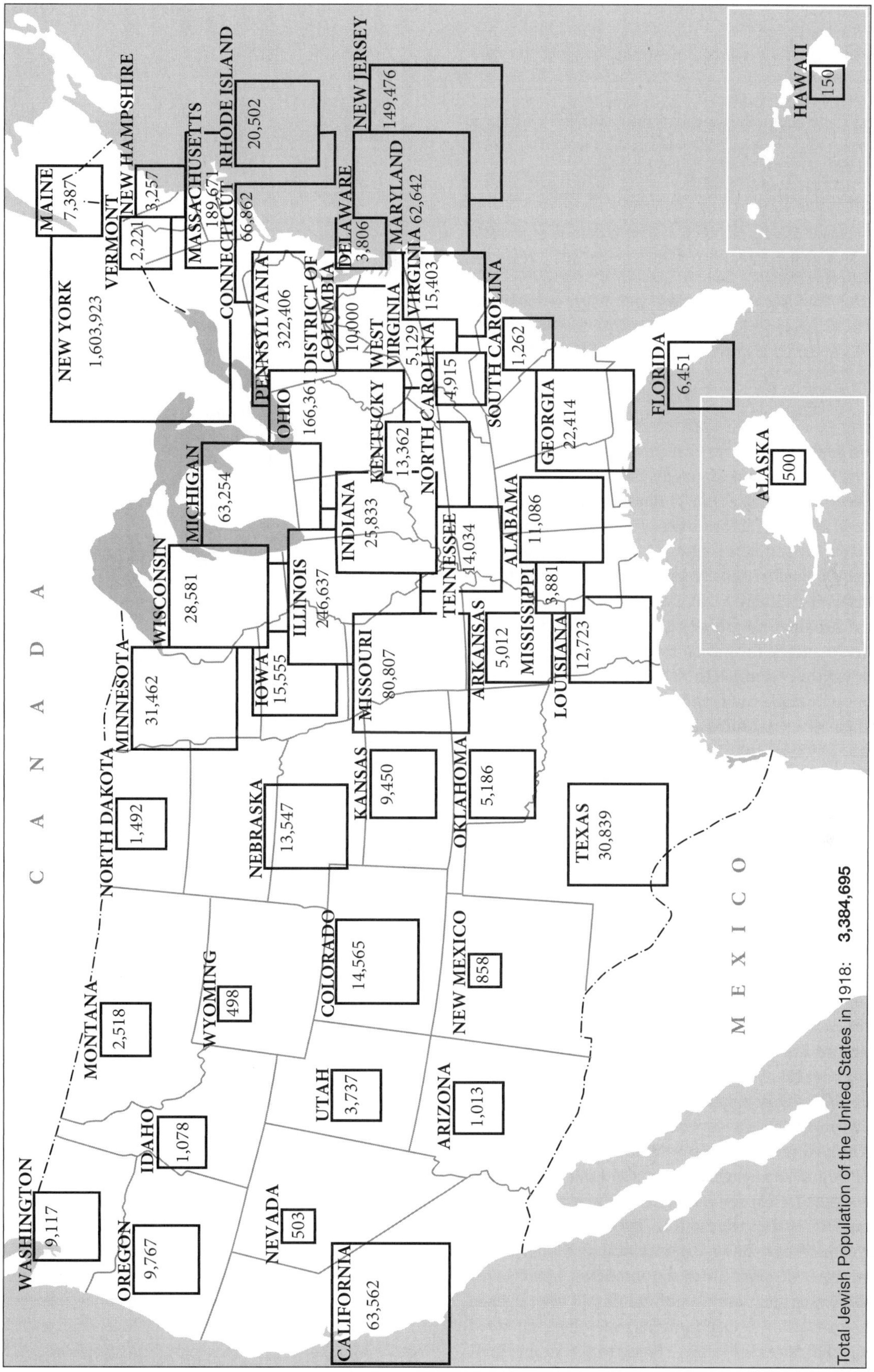
CANADA
MEXICO
WASHINGTON 9,117
OREGON 9,767
CALIFORNIA 63,562
IDAHO 1,078
NEVADA 503
MONTANA 2,518
WYOMING 498
UTAH 3,737
ARIZONA 1,013
COLORADO 14,565
NEW MEXICO 858
NORTH DAKOTA 1,492
NEBRASKA 13,547
KANSAS 9,450
OKLAHOMA 5,186
TEXAS 30,839
MINNESOTA 31,462
IOWA 15,555
MISSOURI 80,807
ARKANSAS 5,012
LOUISIANA 12,723
WISCONSIN 28,581
ILLINOIS 246,637
MISSISSIPPI 3,881
TENNESSEE 14,034
ALABAMA 11,086
MICHIGAN 63,254
INDIANA 25,833
KENTUCKY 13,362
GEORGIA 22,414
FLORIDA 6,451
OHIO 166,361
NORTH CAROLINA 4,915
SOUTH CAROLINA 1,262
WEST VIRGINIA 5,129
VIRGINIA 15,403
DISTRICT OF COLUMBIA 10,000
PENNSYLVANIA 322,406
MARYLAND 62,642
DELAWARE 3,806
NEW JERSEY 149,476
NEW YORK 1,603,923
CONNECTICUT 66,862
RHODE ISLAND 20,502
MASSACHUSETTS 189,671
VERMONT 2,221
NEW HAMPSHIRE 3,257
MAINE 7,387
ALASKA 500
HAWAII 150
Total Jewish Population of the United States in 1918: 3,384,695

Map 3. Jewish population of the U.S., 1918, within state borders of today.

> Mr. Wolf: I am aware of that.
>
> Senator Lodge: The Irish are a perfect illustration of that. They are not classified according to their religion. They are British subjects –
>
> Mr. Wolf: Certainly.
>
> Senator Lodge: But we classify them as Irish because they are Irish, and undoubtedly there is a great deal of mixed blood in Ireland – English, Scotch, and Welsh blood.
>
> Mr. Wolf: That is altogether geographical, and so with respect to the seventeen Austrian provinces.
>
> Senator Lodge: The Irish are not classified geographically. An Irishman is classified as an Irish immigrant wherever he may come from.
>
> Mr. Wolf: You seem to forget – and you are certainly sufficiently versed in the history of all people and especially the people I represent to know – that when a Jew is spoken of, a Jew in faith is meant.
>
> Senator Lodge: Not at all... There is where we start off with a vast difference....

As manifest by the Dillingham Commission's monumental report and the Lodge-Simon exchange, the American political establishment had ample access to objective data and information about Jews and Jewish immigrants. But Dillingham, Lodge, and other key political figures were hardly predisposed to view such evidence rationally. Instead, they set in motion a chain of legislative initiatives that ultimately succeeded in closing the doors to the United States between 1921 and 1924.

Notwithstanding the wave of xenophobia and isolationism that swept the country in these years, the vast majority of East European Jewish immigrants proved successful in transplanting themselves to American soil. Indeed, the 42-volume report of the Dillingham Commission's report included considerable documentation in this regard. Meanwhile, the proportion of immigrants that returned to Europe from among the immigration of the 1880s has been estimated at 25 percent. From that point it steadily declined; in 1908 and after, when statistics began to be taken, the rate of return was about eight percent; after 1919 it sank below one percent. Clearly, the Jewish immigrant came to stay, to a greater extent than all his immigrant contemporaries except the Irish. A negligible number followed the advice of the Palestinian sage *Israel Meir ha-Kohen, known as the "Ḥafez Ḥayyim," in his emigrant guide *Niddeḥei Yisrael* ("The Dispersed of Israel") to return as early as possible and live in prosperous piety. Indeed, the Jewish immigrants who came to the United States became a permanent addition to the population. They raised the number of Jews in the United States to approximately 1,000,000 in 1900, 3,250,000 in 1915, and 4,500,000 in 1925, establishing the Jews as a major ethnic and religious group, and made American Jewry the largest Jewish community in the world after 1918.

Almost 80 percent of the East European newcomers were 15 to 45 years old, the age range typical of immigrants to the United States generally. Men outnumbered women only slightly, indicating the permanence and family character of this emigration, even though families were often separated for considerable periods of time. Owing to the sizable quotient of female Jewish immigrants of child-bearing age, the Yiddish-speaking immigrant community was a very fecund group; very high birthrates are recorded for urban districts where they preponderated.

Meanwhile, the earlier German Jewish stock, joined by later middle-class German Jewish immigrants and a few from England and France, shifted from predominantly mercantile occupations to a more varied spectrum. Law and politics, banking and finance, department store ownership, publishing, medicine, and literary, academic, and scientific pursuits all became widespread. A comparatively noticeable group functioned as collectors and patrons of the arts, and as philanthropists. During the 1870s German Jewish settlement had spread wide, with hundreds of small towns in California, along the Mississippi River, and throughout the South and Middle West where there were small Jewish communities. A stream of East European Jewish immigrants followed in their wake, including would-be farmers who established Jewish agricultural communities along the eastern seaboard with the support of the Baron De Hirsch Fund and the Jewish Agricultural and Industrial Aid Society. Additionally, small groups of Am Olam (Eternal People) pioneers created quasi-socialist Jewish pioneering colonies that dotted the American landscape from New Jersey to Oregon. Within the space of a generation, however, most Jews quit these towns and colonies. The great expansion of America's industrial cities, the depression of the agricultural economy upon which many small towns and rural communities were reliant, and the antisemitic undertones and religious fundamentalism to be found in remote areas of the country helped to make Jews of the 20th century a largely metropolitan group.

SOCIAL AND CULTURAL LIFE. The Jewish labor movement helped to foster a secular Yiddish-speaking environment that flourished from the 1910s into the 1930s and offered a modern, social democratic alternative to Jewish tradition. About 80,000 families, mainly members of Jewish unions and small businessmen, belonged to the Arbeter Ring (*Workmen's Circle) at its peak in the mid-1920s. Like the socialist Zionist Farband, it provided sick and death benefits as well as a diverse Yiddish cultural program. In this period, there was a lively and robust Yiddish daily press with a combined circulation of about 700,000 at its peak in 1916. Through a variety of weeklies, monthlies, literary journals, and periodicals, a rich diet of news as well as Yiddish literature was supplied by prominent writers, poets, and literary critics including Sholem *Asch, M. *Boraisha, David *Einhorn, R. Eisland, Mendel Elkin, Jacob *Glatstein, Moshe Leib *Halpern, Peretz *Hirschbein, Zishe *Landau, Mani Leib, A. Leiles, N. *Minkoff, Samuel *Niger, David *Pinski, Abraham *Reisin, J. *Rolnick, Morris *Rosenfeld, H. *Rosenblatt, I.J. *Schwartz, L. *Shapiro, Isaac Bashevis *Singer, Israel Joshua *Singer, J. Slonim, and *Yehoash.

Among the most significant Yiddish newspapers in this period were the traditionalist *Yidisher Tageblatt* ("Jewish Daily News"), the Labor Zionist weekly **Yidisher Kemfer* ("Jewish

Fighter"), which attracted significant public intellectuals including Nachman *Syrkin, Chaim *Zhitlowsky, and Ḥayyim *Greenberg, *Zukunft* ("Future"), which became the leading Yiddish monthly under the editorship Abraham Liessen, the conservative-leaning *Morgen Zhurnal* (**Morning Journal*), and the liberal pro-Zionist *Tog* (**Jewish Day*). In the final analysis, however, the *Forverts* (**Jewish Daily Forward*), edited by Abraham *Cahan, was unquestionably the most influential newspaper of the day. The most popular feature of the *Forverts* was "*Bintel Brief*" (Bundle of Letters), a forum edited by Cahan himself in which he dispensed advice to thousands of Yiddish-speaking immigrants who wrote seeking advice about their everyday concerns, struggles, hopes, fears, and needs. The column was wildly popular, and it also proved to be important to the *Forvert's* general commercial success. Viewed in historical perspective, *Bintel Brief* throws considerable light on the daily experiences and hardscrabble lives of East European Jewish immigrants in this period. For example, a debate over secularism and tradition in 1908 prompted the following exchange:

> Worthy Mr. Editor,
>
> Please help us decide who is right in the debate between friends, whether a Socialist and freethinker should observe *yohrzeit* (the traditional anniversary of mourning one's relatives)?
>
> Among the disputants there is a Socialist, a freethinker, who observes his mother's *yohrzeit* in the following manner: He pays a pious man to say the *kaddish* prayer for the dead, and burns a *yohrzeit* candle in his home. He himself doesn't say *kaddish*, because he doesn't believe in religion. But his desire to respect the memory of his mother is so strong that it does not prevent him from performing this religious ceremony.
>
> Among the debaters there are those who do not want to know of such an emotion as honoring the dead. But if one does desire to do so, one should say *kaddish* himself, even if he does not believe in it.
>
> Therefore, our first question is: Can we recognize the beautiful human emotion of honoring the dead, especially when it concerns one so near as a mother? The second question: If so, should the expression of honor be in keeping with the desires of the honored? Third: Would it be more conscientious and righteous if the freethinker said *kaddish* himself, or if he hired a pious man to do it for him?
>
> Being convinced that this matter interests a great number of people, we hope you, Mr. Editor, will answer us soon.
>
> With regards,
> The Debating Group

To which Cahan responded:

> Honoring a departed one who was cherished and loved is a gracious sentiment and a requisite for the living. And everyone wants to be remembered after his death. Socialists and freethinkers observe the anniversaries of their great leaders – just recently they commemorated the twenty-fifth anniversary of the death of Karl Marx.
>
> Saying *kaddish* is certainly a religious rite, and to pay someone to say *kaddish* is not the act of a freethinker. But we can understand the psychology of a freethinker who feels that hiring someone else is not as much against his own convictions as to say *kaddish* himself.

Women, too, wrote to Cahan about their travails in the New World. Many female writers discussed their struggles as workers, wives, and mothers. The following exchange from 1908 provides a glimpse of a dilemma that faced many Jewish immigrant women: abandonment by their husbands. Known in Jewish tradition as *agunot* (abandoned wives), such women often suffered deep personal and intense social and economic trauma. Indeed, the *Forverts* frequently published lists of husbands who deserted their wives in an effort to reunite broken families.

> Worthy Editor,
>
> Have pity on me and my two small children and print my letter in the *Forverts*.
>
> Max! The children and I now say farewell to you. You left us in such a terrible state. You have no compassion for us. For six years I loved you faithfully, took care of you like a loyal servant, never had a happy day with you. Yet I forgive you for everything.
>
> You ever asked yourself why you left us? Max, where is your conscience: you used to have sympathy for the forsaken women and used to say their terrible plight was due to the men who left them in dire need. And how did you act? I was a young, educated, decent girl when you took me. You lived with me for six years, during which time I bore you four children. And then you left me.
>
> Of the four children, only two remain, but you have made them living orphans. Who will bring them up? Who will support us? Have you no pity for your own flesh and blood? Consider what you are doing. My tears choke me and I cannot write anymore.
>
> Be advised that in several days I am leaving with my two living orphans for Russia. We say farewell to you and beg you to take pity on us and send us enough to live on…
>
> Your Deserted Wife and Children

As the foregoing illustrates, many Jewish immigrants to the United States experienced downward mobility and consequently thousands did return to Europe despite the dangers and uncertainty they might face, particularly in tsarist Russia. That the Old World continued to exert a strong pull for many immigrants, even after they had been living in America for several years, is evident in the following exchange from 1912.

> Dear Editor,
>
> Twenty-two years ago I came to America with my wife and four little children. We lived in Chicago nineteen years, and we have been in New York for three. I am not skilled in a trade, but I am a businessman, and all these years I've struggled because I never made a living. I know English, I am not lazy, I've tried everything and never succeeded.
>
> When the children were young I had to appeal for aid to my wealthy family in Warsaw, and they helped me many times. Later, as the children grew up and began to earn money, it was easier, but I, with all my ability as a businessman, couldn't get myself settled in this country. In the city of Warsaw, where I lived before immigrating to America, there were times when

things weren't too bad. In America, however, it always went badly and I haven't been able to adjust to the country.

Now, when my children are all married and in good positions, I got an idea that it might be good for me and my wife to go back to Warsaw. It is very hard to part with the children, but to live in poverty is also bad. It seems strange to me that I must go away from the free America in order to better my condition. But the chances for me are still better there. I ask your advice and I thank you in advance.

Respectfully,
The Unlucky One

Cahan's responded to the unfortunate man with a mixture of sympathy and hard-headed realism as follows:

> The advice to this letter writer is not to go back to Warsaw, because after so many years in this country he would feel like a stranger there. He must understand he is no longer the same man he was twenty-two years ago and the city of Warsaw is also not the same as it was in the past.

Over the course of the next half a century, the *Forverts* emerged as the central publication of the Yiddish-speaking milieu. Following World War I, it gradually warmed to the cause of Zionism and became disenchanted with Soviet-style Communism. In time, although it never completely abandoned its socialist ethos and concern for the Jewish workers movement, the paper was gradually transformed into a vehicle of Jewish liberal opinion. In 1922 the prominent American publicist Oswald Garrison Villard, owner of *The Nation*, offered the following description of a typical issue of the *Forverts* at the height of its influence and prosperity:

> Its eight pages of eight columns each (28 or 32 pages on Sundays) offers a variegated bill of fare. Pictures, of course, occasional cartoons; little of crime (about two columns a day); often sensational matter… extraordinarily valuable letters from abroad, together with a great deal of Jewish and labor news, all with Hearst-like headlines. In one week in July 1922 it carried 24 columns of letters and cablegrams from its own correspondents (in eastern Europe)… In that same week it carried 154 columns of serious reading matter and 137 columns which can be termed "light matter," though this does not adequately describe it, for while the *Forward* writes down to its readers it is also printing today by far the best fiction and *belles lettres* of any newspaper in America.

Beyond the world of print, vast audiences also responded enthusiastically to the musical artistry and liturgical compositions of cantorial singers, some of whom recorded the earliest gramaphone records. One of the most celebrated figures in this regard was Yossele *Rosenblatt, who immigrated to the United States from Germany to conduct services at the First Hungarian Congregation in Harlem, New York. He quickly attracted a following of Jewish and non-Jewish music lovers who flocked to his services and concerts. There was also a flourishing of scholarly public Yiddish lectures, Yiddish afternoon schools sponsored by a variety of organizations, and a burgeoning Yiddish theater scene, of which there were numerous troupes. The case of Abraham *Goldfaden, a pioneer of the Yiddish theater, exemplifies the complexity of the East European Jewish scene in this period. Goldfaden himself fled to the United States in 1903 after his plays were banned by the tsarist regime which feared their incendiary and revolutionary nature. He went on to write some 60 plays, including many popularly acclaimed comedies and melodramas. In the process, as historian Martin Gilbert writes, "Goldfaden became a strong critic of Jewish assimilation and participation in the life of other nationalities."

In his play *Ben Ami* (*Son of My People*) he called for Jewish national redemption in Palestine as an answer to the Russian pogroms. The play's aristocratic hero, on discovering his Jewish origins and witnessing a pogrom in Odessa, leaves the bloodstained soil of Russia for a new life, not in America, but in Palestine. Once there, the hero sets as his task the training of Jewish youth to till the soil and to work for the national regeneration of the Jewish people. As assimilation gained ground in the United States, and Zionism saw emigration to Palestine as the countermeasure to it, Goldfaden's play – it was the last that he wrote – held a particular resonance.

Somewhat later there were Yiddish films and part-time as well as full-time radio stations. It was here that many Jewish performers and actors got their start. For example, the Hollywood film star Theda *Bara (born Theodosia Goodman in Cincinnati, Ohio) appeared in more than 40 films between 1914 and 1919 including *A Fool was There* (1915), in which she was cast as a vamp and acquired her signature role as an object of intense sexual desire. Another significant Jewish celebrity in this period was Fanny *Brice, who immigrated to the United States from Hungary with her family at the turn of the century, and made her debut in 1916 performing in the Ziegfield Follies. She launched her career dressed as an American Indian speaking English with a heavy Yiddish accent, a routine she would later develop and make famous in her role as Mrs. Cohen, a gossip who ordered her husband around. Years later, reflecting on her career in show business, Brice explained her comic strategy in the following terms: "In anything Jewish I ever did, I wasn't standing apart, making fun of the race. What happened to me on stage is what could happen to them. They identified with me, and then it was all right to get a laugh, because they were laughing at themselves as well as at me."

Most Yiddish-speaking Jews were secular and abandoned religious practice, but they retained strong ethnic attachments and folk loyalties. Except for the small socialist Zionist groups, they were generally indifferent or opposed to Zionism, although such attitudes waned after the 1920s as Palestine Jewry grew and concretized many socialist ideals. They were divided bitterly and irreconcilably in their attitude to Soviet Russia.

Very few Jewish immigrants, especially before 1900, were highly educated; they were mainly from the poorer working classes. Virtually all knew the rudiments of Jewish law and ritual, Hebrew Bible, and frequently some talmudic and rabbinic literature. Very few women, however, possessed any formal education. Only a minority maintained a brand of East European orthodox Judaism unswervingly against the overpowering force of the urban, industrial, and secular life into which they were cast. Another minority, mostly of younger intelligentsia, embraced socialism in one of its numerous contemporary forms, and in smaller numbers Zionism, Hebraism, or literary modernism. The mass of immigrants, it appears, retained a measure of outward signs of religious observance while, for example, neglecting the Sabbath rules and other daily stringencies. Only a tiny minority had time or inclination for pious study before or after work. Characteristically, they flocked to the synagogues on Rosh Hashanah (the Jewish New Year) and Yom Kippur (the Day of Atonement), and were diligent in matters of filial piety like the recitation of *yizkor* (the traditional memorial service) and the mourner's *kaddish* (memorial prayer). The *bar mizvah* of the sons of East European immigrants, symbolizing generational and ethnic continuity, was all but universally desired.

The most widespread immigrant organization was the *ḥevrah* (society), usually founded on a **landsmanshaft* (hometown) basis. In New York City alone at least 1,200 *landsmanshaften* (pl.) existed in 1915. In addition to providing a fraternal social atmosphere for their members who knew each other still from Europe, the *landsmanshaften* invariably provided funeral arrangements and burial rights. Sick benefits and occasionally unemployment help were also granted. The societies probably reached their peak during the World War I era, when assistance to the war-smitten Jews of the native town became another major activity. A large proportion of such *landsmanshaften* affiliated with the Arbeter Ring, the Federation of Galician Jews, and other central organizations. Many maintained synagogues, all of which were Orthodox and Yiddish-speaking and preserved East European habits of worship. The little houses of worship known as *shtieblakh* (pl.) – New York City alone numbered over 500 in 1916 – were generally transitory venues and few of them survived the immigrant founders and the shift to areas of second settlement.

The entire immigrant milieu thus described was largely a generational experience. Sons and daughters generally did not follow their parents into the Jewish trade unions, so that the proportion of Jews in their ranks fell below half by the 1920s. The Yiddish press, theater, and literature steadily declined, for the next generation's language was English. They could care little for the ancestral town and its *landsmanshaft* and preferred other voluntaristic forms of Jewish life in the New World including Americanized synagogues, fraternal orders, membership societies, and institutions that offered benefits for death and illness. Indeed, the entire immigrant environment – problem-ridden, colorful, and dynamic – existed by grace of the stream of arrivals that continued until the restrictive legislation of the 1920s took full effect. Lacking replenishment from overseas, the Yiddish-speaking immigrant milieu contracted and shriveled; by the 1940s it was a relic.

NEIGHBORHOODS, OCCUPATIONS, AND THE JEWISH LABOR MOVEMENT. The East European Jewish immigrants clustered in distinct urban neighborhoods, which were generally older or slum districts close to downtown. The streets where they lived became all but exclusively Jewish in population, and the stores, the Yiddish heard on the streets, and the festive atmosphere on the Jewish Sabbath and holidays reflected the character of the inhabitants. Every American metropolitan center had such an area between the 1890s and 1920. The largest of them, the Lower East Side of New York City, sheltered an estimated 350,000 Jews in 1915 in less than two square miles. These neighborhoods were very seriously congested with dangerous problems of health and sanitation. Yet their prevailing atmosphere was one of hope and confidence, with a rich and varied cultural life. As material circumstances improved families quit the immigrant district for more attractive neighborhoods – resettlement locales referred to by historians as "areas of second settlement."

The immigrants' prime motive in coming to the United States was to improve their material and economic conditions. European fables about the "*goldene medine*" (golden land) notwithstanding, their lot was a hard one. They made their living among a vast variety of trades, although hardly any Jews worked on railroads, docks, or in mines and large factories. As was true of American occupations generally, habits of ethnic concentration could be found among the Jews. Petty trade proliferated as Jewish immigrants opened small stores throughout booming metropolises and in smaller cities as well. The venerable peddling trade, however, lost its luster. As a nationwide network of retail trade and mail order companies spread – the greatest of which, Sears Roebuck, was built by the Jewish entrepreneur Julius Rosenwald – the peddlers' status declined from an important agent of commerce to a marginal tradesman.

The Yiddish-speaking Jewish immigrant generally joined the working class, working mainly in the ready-made clothing industry that was growing with remarkable rapidity. The number of Jews employed in it as workers, entrepreneurs, salesmen, and so forth may have reached 300,000 around 1915. The ready-made garment industry was composed mainly of shops where workers labored on one or two parts of the total product. In such important centers as Rochester, Cleveland, and Chicago, clothing was produced in substantial factories, owned mostly by Jews. On the other hand, in 1910, in the Borough of Manhattan within New York City, there were 11,172 clothing firms employing 214,428 persons; 78 percent of them, in 1913, averaged five employees each. These were the notorious sweatshops – tiny, crowded, dirty, unventilated, often the petty employer's dwelling – where the employee often worked for 16 hours a day during the busy period of this highly seasonal industry. Despite all their evils, the workshops did enable thousands of immigrant wage workers to enter the garment business on their own. Failure only meant that the unsuccessful entrepreneur returned to wage work, while success in the ferociously competitive industry might lead to independence and wealth. New York City was the great center of the clothing industry; its East Side and then lower West Side, and finally midtown Seventh Avenue were the foci of manufacturing. Chicago was a second major center, especially for men's clothing. Philadelphia, Baltimore, Rochester, Boston, and Cleveland were also important in this regard. After 1900 successful East European immigrant entrepreneurs moved into the leadership of the industry as the earlier German Jewish capitalists tended to quit it. In Cleveland, by contrast, the earlier families held sway.

Highly decentralized, low-cost ready-made clothing production was as nearly Jewish an industry as ever seen in the United States, although large numbers of Italian, German, and Irish workers, especially women, also held jobs. It inspired the Jewish trade union movement, beginning in the 1880s. The Jewish labor movement spoke in revolutionary tones during early years, but made little headway before 1900. The seasonal fluctuations of the industry, the virtually unorganizable mass of puny workshops, the relation of employer and employee who might be relatives and *landsmen* (fellow townsmen from Eastern Europe) and could readily exchange places under the conditions of the industry, the failure of the early unions to organize solidly, the legal obstacles and public hostility to trade unionism, especially when it was professedly socialist and revolutionary – were all factors which hindered the development of the Jewish labor movement before 1900. However, larger clothing factories became more common after 1900, and their size and overhead tended to reduce seasonality and sever personal relations between worker and employer. The downfall of the revolutionary movement in Russia in 1906, moreover, caused a considerable number of able labor organizers to flee to the United States. In this period, American public opinion also began to sympathize with trade unionism.

The period of the successful organization of Jewish labor, from 1909 to 1916, coincided with the great drive by American trade unionism at large. In New York City the surge of trade unionism began with the tragic Triangle Shirtwaist fire of 1911, in which 146 Italian and Jewish workers, almost all girls and young women, perished. It was followed by the bitter "revolt of the shirtwaist [blouse] makers," an unsuccessful six-week strike which drew widespread public sympathy but failed nevertheless.

The most important labor event of the period was the three-month strike of 60,000 cloakmakers in 1910 under the direction of the previously ineffectual *International Ladies Garment Workers Union, founded in 1900. In this largest sustained strike in the city's history up to that time, the main demand was for recognition of the union as the exclusive bargaining agent for the workers, and it was on this point, rather than those which concerned wages, hours, and subcontracting, that employers' resistance was bitterest. Such acculturated American Jews as Judah L. *Magnes, Louis *Marshall, and Jacob H. *Schiff intervened in the struggle, but the settlement was worked out by Louis D. *Brandeis, making his first appearance in the Jewish public arena. The "Protocol of Permanent Peace" provided for a system of joint employer-employee-public boards to deal with grievances, sanitation, and other issues, while the contest over union recognition was settled by "the preferential shop," i.e., preference in employment given to union members. The success of the protocol attracted countrywide attention in labor and governmental circles. As well, both the American and Jewish press helped to spread the word of Brandeis' skill and authority as an arbitrator. In a carefully crafted letter written in 1912 to Lincoln Steffens, the era's leading muckraking American journalist – copies of which were forwarded to several major newspapers and their editors – Brandeis spelled out his Progressive vision of employee-employer relations.

> In my opinion the time is ripe for a great advance in the scope and influence and the quality of trade unionism.
>
> On the one hand, the disclosures incident to the labor policies of the strong trusts and particularly the hours of labor, wages, and conditions in the steel industry are making many Americans recognize that unions and collective bargaining are essential to industrial liberty and social justice.
>
> On the other hand, the abuses of trade unionism as we have known them during the last twenty years with their violence, restriction of output, and their lack of constructive policy, are in large part the result of the fact that they have been engaged in a bitter struggle for existence. When public opinion is brought actively to the support of labor unions these abuses will, I believe, tend rapidly to disappear. But the American people should not and will not accept unionism if it involves the closed shop. They will not consent to the exchange of the tyranny of the employer for the tyranny of the employee. Unionism therefore cannot make a great advance until it abandons the closed shop; and it cannot accept the open shop as an alternative. The open shop means the destruction of the union.
>
> The advance of unionism demands therefore some relation between the employer and the employee other than the closed or open shop, and I feel confident that we have found a solution in the preferential union shop.
>
> ...This seems the time to commence the campaign of education. Much hammering will be necessary; for the employers will be loath to enter into so comprehensive an agreement with unions; and unions will be loath to give up the closed shop. But the preferential shop seems to be a way out of our present serious difficulty; and we must pursue it unless a better can be found.

Though Brandeis' letter to Steffens ostensibly deals exclusively with the question of the preferential union shop, it also provides a glimpse of the amalgam of political liberalism and sensitivity to the rights of disenfranchised groups that would become a hallmark of the American Jewish community in the 20th century. Meanwhile, the size, duration, and the unprecedented settlement of the cloakmakers' strike made it a milestone in the history of American labor and a pivotal event which turned the Jewish labor movement into a powerful force. The episode also elevated the visibility and underscored the political capital of other Jewish participants, most notably the union lawyers Morris *Hillquit and Meyer *London. In fact, London subsequently won election in 1914 to the U.S. House of Representatives as the standard bearer Socialist Party for the Lower East Side; he was reelected in 1916.

The cloakmakers' strike was followed by several other successful ones, including in 1912–13 the strike of the furriers, men's tailors, and ladies' waist- and dressmakers. Surveying this turbulent period, the historian Jonathan Frankel has observed that "at one point in 1912, an estimated 175,000 workers in the 'Jewish trades' were out on strike." Another important strike that followed was the Chicago men's clothing strike in 1914 and 1915. Here leaders of the United Garment Workers, whose preponderant ethnic elements were not Jewish and did not work at ready-made clothing, made an unauthorized deal with the employers which brought about the secession of the Jewish and other ready-made tailors and the founding of the Amalgamated Clothing Workers of America, led by Sidney *Hillman. The new union conducted a series of victorious strikes in Chicago and then in other major centers of the trade. However, neither they nor the International Ladies Garment Workers Union (ILGWU) were uniformly successful. Thus in Cleveland the factory employers defeated strikers and union organizers until 1917. By 1920 at least 250,000 Jews belonged to the Jewish unions.

WOMEN. American Jewish women lived under a set of unique circumstances at the turn of the 19th and 20th centuries. In stark contrast to their counterparts in much of Europe, Jewish women in the United States enjoyed increasing freedom of individual movement and expression, and some even possessed funds for philanthropic activities. Such liberties and assets were almost totally lacking in Eastern Europe, where traditional gender-differentiated Jewish values and systems prevailed and where the possibility for Jewish participation in the host society was marginal. In many situations, Jewish women experienced double oppression – as Jews in an antisemitic milieu and as women in a patriarchal society. The lack of birth control, opportunities for education, and a secure income severely restricted the lives of Jewish women in Eastern and Central Europe. In the United States, these forces were muted.

In late 19th century America, Jewish women expanded and deepened their participation in American Jewish life. The mass waves of East European Jewish immigrants, including many thousand radicalized young Yiddish-speaking women, helped create the American Jewish labor movement and some of the most important American labor entities including the International Ladies Garment Worker's Union. They also became involved in the anti-prostitution movement, the Settlement House movement, the suffrage movement, and in the birth control movement.

Women leaders of the early American Jewish labor movement included Clara Lemlich (*Shavelson), Pauline *Newman, and Rose *Schneiderman, who served as president of the New York Women's Trade Union League. These women proved especially adept at negotiating the delicate relationship of women workers, the male-dominated labor establishment, and various progressive and middle-class allies of the labor movement. The significance in this regard became evident in the wake of the notorious Triangle Shirtwaist Fire of 1911, in which more than 140 women workers perished as result of inhumane sweatshop conditions on the Lower East Side of New York City. Following the tragedy, these and other women campaigned for the regulation of safety standards, sanitary conditions, wages, and working hours. Meanwhile, the establishment of the Amalgamated Clothing Workers of America was due, in large measure, to the organizational talents of political activist Bessie Abramowitz (*Hillman), who shortly thereafter married American labor leader Sidney Hillman. At its peak between World Wars I and II, approximately 40 percent of all Jewish laborers could be found in the American garment industry, including a sizable quotient of women, the majority of whom belonged to International Ladies Garment Workers Union and the Amalgamated Clothing Workers of America. In this period, Dorothy Jacobs Bellanca, Fannia *Cohen, and Rose *Pesotta assumed national prominence as influential American labor leaders. The importance of Jewish rank-and-file participation in the American labor movement and the impact of Jewish workers' activity on American Jewish life is indicated by the ringing editorial endorsement of the International Ladies Garment Workers' Union by the Yiddish-language daily *Forverts*, which at the time had a circulation of well over a quarter million.

> In Chicago a convention of the International Ladies Garment Workers' Union opens today [May 3, 1920] at which there will be present about three thousand delegates from the entire length and breadth of the country.
>
> For the first time in the history of this powerful labor organization, the most important trade in the general women's clothing industry comes to the convention one hundred percent organized. The cloak makers have, during the past two years, captured the last stronghold of the employers, who have always been considered invincible. Cleveland fell; the last factories in Canada were captured; cities in the far West were organized; and the cloak trade comes to the convention entirely under the flag of the union.
>
> Of great significance is the recommendation of the executive committee that the union should organize cooperative shops. This plan reflects the spirit of the new tendencies in the union movement of the world, the spirit which leads workers to control industries themselves.
>
> The ILGWU stands now in the foremost ranks of the American labor movement, both materially and spiritually. It is one of the most important unions in the country. It has won for its members such conditions that very few of the real Americans may compare with it. Spiritually it is in every respect one of the most progressive. It responds to every movement for justice, for light. It is always prepared to help the workers in other trades in their struggles to help the oppressed and the suffering.
>
> The International Ladies Garment Workers' Union is a blessing to its members, a pride to the general labor movement, and a hope for the progress of humanity at large.

The twin themes of female and Jewish liberation also impelled many thousands – and later hundreds of thousands – of American Jewish women to view the new Jewish community in the Land of Israel as a model. This Jewish country could embody, they believed, a reflection of what modern society ought to be: pluralistic, healthy, welcoming, egalitarian, and accessible to all Jews. The fact that very few American Zionist women expected to actually set foot in Palestine did not represent a contradiction for them. It simply meant that their ideology would remain romantic and insulated from the harsh reality of Jewish life in Ottoman and then British Palestine. Zionism for these women became a way of fighting their own assimilationist tendencies, rather than a way of addressing the ideological imperative of emigration.

The groundswell of popular interest in Zionism in the United States, especially among East European Jewish immigrants, led to the creation of a diverse array of Zionist women's organizations and groups by the 1920s and 1930s. In fact, women's Zionist organizations in the United States were frequently stronger and more effective than their male counterparts. For example, since its inception in 1897, the *Zionist Organization of America (ZOA) purported to be *the* representative body of the American movement. Though the rank and file was comprised of men and women, the organization's leadership was entirely male. Relegated to conventional and secondary roles, female ZOA members performed social functions rather than substantive ones, and were shunted to the margins of political activity. In 1912, a few Jewish women had created their own Zionist organization, named Hadassah. As Hadassah grew and flourished, the ZOA leadership demanded that it fold into the male-dominated ZOA. In a remarkable instance of resistance, American Zionist women decided to take matters into their own hands and establish a separate independent organization, rather than allow Hadassah to become the ZOA's female auxiliary. The new American *women's* Zionist organization determined to assume a full range of social, financial and political roles.

Not only did the ZOA stand to lose a significant portion of its membership and the women's services, it was also threatened with stiff competition. In the event, the ZOA leadership sought to compel Henrietta *Szold to merge Hadassah into the organization's ranks. Szold refused. She was interested in mobilizing American Jewish women and foresaw the potential and power of a distinct Zionist women's organization. Indeed, American women's colleges, medical schools and other institutions had already successfully employed a similar strategy. A crisis ensued, but Szold held firm. Since that time, Hadassah has grown to become the largest Jewish women's organization in the world. It remains a powerful and, arguably, the most significant Zionist group in the United States. By contrast, the ZOA has enjoyed only sporadic organizational and political success.

With some variation, the scenario described above was repeated in other Zionist quarters. For example, *Poalei Zion (Workers of Zion), the American wing of the Russian socialist-Zionist party, opposed the establishment of a separate women's organization. Similarly, when *Pioneer Women was created in 1925, it too became more successful than its male counterpart. But Pioneer Women is instructive in an additional way: it demonstrates the impact of Jewish women *from* Palestine on the mobilization of American Jewish woman. In this case, American women's Zionist activity and ideology were not exclusively a product of conditions in America, of Jews generally, or of women. Rather, these spheres were strongly influenced by female emissaries from Palestine, charismatic leaders such as Raḥel Yanait *Ben-Zvi and Manya Wilbushewitz Shohat.

Last, American Zionist women leaders like Irma *Lindheim and Henrietta Szold traveled back and forth between Palestine and the United States, bringing with them compelling descriptions and instructive reports of life in the Yishuv and forging a bond between the two communities. In general, Hadassah appealed to a new generation of middle-class English-speaking American Jewish women, while Pioneer Women attracted working-class first- and second-generation Jewish women from the Yiddish-speaking immigrant milieu. There were also American female Zionist organizations within the Orthodox community. In all cases, ranging among the varied classes and religious spheres, American Jewish women understood their Zionist activities both in terms of aiding the Jewish community in Palestine, and in retaining their own Jewish identity through self-education. The focus of the women's organizations was on fundraising and social projects, particularly projects that would aid women and families. In short, American Zionist women's groups – whether left-leaning, middle-class, or religious – emerged as a loosely constructed coalition that emphasized a residual national consciousness in American Jewish life and worked alongside other women's groups who sought to participate in and shape the larger public conversation about the Americanization of Jewish identity and culture.

CLASH BETWEEN "GREENHORNS" AND "NATIVES". Unlike the many other immigrant groups that reached the United States at the same time as the East European Jews, the latter had the important patronage and protection of their established German Jewish predecessors. By this time, settled Jews had largely fallen away from Germanism and were beginning to feel the impact of systematic social and political exclusion from mainstream American culture – a phenomenon that reached an abrupt climax during World War I with the swift rise of nationwide anti-German sentiment. Feelings between New York City's uptown "native" Jews and downtown "greenhorns" – and those in Jewish communities elsewhere where German and East European Jews also derisively referred to each other, respectively, as *yahudim* and *yidn* – were none too fond. Meanwhile, strong anti-immigrant sentiment was to be found especially among working-class native Jews, such as cigar makers and skilled tailors. Notwithstanding irritation over the allegedly "clannish" and "backward" character of the Yiddish-speaking immigrants, their political radicalism, and their presumed ingratitude for the philanthropy they received, the native Jews regarded the East European newcomers as their wards, to be helped, chided, and guided. Writing in 1915, Israel *Friedlaender, a Polish-born, German- and French-educated

Jewish public intellectual and professor of Semitics and Bible at the Jewish Theological Seminary, described the American setting and the cultural clash between German and East European Jews in the following terms:

> America has, in less than one generation, become the second largest center of the Jewish Diaspora, and bids fair to become the first, instead of the second, within another generation. No other country in the world offers, even approximately, such a favorable combination of opportunities for the development of Diaspora Judaism, as does America: economic possibilities, vast sparsely populated territories, freedom of action, liberty of conscience, equality of citizenship, appreciation of the fundamentals of Judaism, variety of population, excluding a rigidly nationalistic state policy, and other similar factors. It is no wonder, therefore, that in no other country did Reform Judaism [brought from Germany], as the incarnation of Diaspora Judaism, attain such luxurious growth as it did in America. It discarded more radically than in Europe, the national elements still clinging to Judaism, and it solemnly proclaimed that Judaism was wholly and exclusively a religious faith, and that America was the Zion and Washington the Jerusalem of American Israel.
>
> On the other hand, the emigrants from Russia brought the antithesis on the scene. They quickly perceived the decomposing effect of American life upon Jewish doctrine and practice, and they became convinced more firmly than ever that Diaspora Judaism was a failure, and that the only antidote was Palestine and nothing but Palestine. The nationalists among them beheld in the very same factors in which the German Jews saw the possibilities of Diaspora Judaism the chances for organizing Jewry on purely nationalistic lines. Nowhere else, except perhaps in Russia, can be found a greater amount of Palestinian sentiment, as well as a larger manifestation of a one-sided nationalism, than is to be met with in this country.
>
> This conflict of ideas became extraordinarily aggravated by numerous influences of a personal character. The division between the so-called German Jews and the so-called Russian Jews was not limited to a difference in theory. It was equally nourished by far-reaching differences in economic and social position and in the entire range of mental development. The German Jews were the natives; the Russian Jews were the newcomers. The German Jews were the rich; the Russian Jews were the poor. The German Jews were the dispensers of charity; the Russian Jews were the receivers of it. The German Jews were the employers; the Russian Jews were the employees. The German Jews were deliberate, reserved, practical, sticklers for formalities, with a marked ability for organization; the Russian Jews were quick-tempered, emotional, theorizing, haters of formalities, with a decided bent toward individualism. An enormous amount of explosives had been accumulating between the two sections which if lit by a spark might have wrecked the edifice of American Israel while yet in the process of construction.

The ubiquitous Hebrew Relief Societies that arose in different parts of the country in this period rapidly transformed into social agencies dedicated to the relief of economic distress and family aid. Most changed their names between 1910 and 1925 to reflect the American sensibility of self-help and became known as Jewish Social Service Associations. Such institutions as the Educational Alliance in New York, the Council Educational Alliance in Cleveland, the Jewish People's Institute in Chicago, and the Abraham Lincoln House in Milwaukee all demonstrated the interest of native Jews in bringing social and cultural amenities to immigrant Jews, particularly the youth, hastening their "Americanization." The founders' and directors' frequent indifference or antagonism to the cultural heritage and aspirations of their clientele generated an undertone of tension that occasionally broke into open conflict. However, the art, music, sports, health education, mothers' classes, lectures, and other activities of these institutions proved of enduring value. The Jewish immigrant districts also developed numerous social services, including hospitals and medical clinics, as well as non-Jewish institutions such as (in New York City) Cooper Union, the Rand School, and the Labor Temple.

A subtler issue between natives and immigrants was religious life. The Reform temples of native American Jewry were uninviting, while the *ḥevrot* and *landsmanshaft* synagogues could only attract their own devotees. Several prominent communal leaders and religious figures worried about the young generation who rejected the religion of their forebears in favor of secularism and radical social doctrines. In the eyes of some, a modernized form of traditional Judaism was required for the rising generation of Jews of East European ancestry who were raised or born on American soil. Against this background, the moribund *Jewish Theological Seminary of America was revived in 1902 for the training of modern rabbis (and from 1909, teachers for Jewish schools). It was substantially endowed by a group of German Jewish patrician leaders and under the direction of Solomon *Schechter, a distinguished scholar-theologian, an outstanding library and faculty were quickly assembled. The growth of the seminary was slow, but its professors deeply influenced many of the younger religiously oriented intelligentsia.

For their part the immigrants had unflattering perceptions of the native "uptown" Jews, whom they regarded as snobbish and patronizing, excessively assimilated, and lacking Jewish kindness and sympathy. Yet the natives did provide the immigrants with a model for being American and Jewish. Immigrants and their problems were the main content of Jewish communal life and concerns from the 1880s until the 1930s. The intellectuality and Jewish fervor common among the newcomers, and such achievements as their labor movement and the New York City Kehillah, showed some natives – of whom Louis D. Brandeis might be cited as the outstanding example – a more authentic, passionate way to be a Jew. Quite a few native Jews were thus drawn into the cultural life and social movements of the Yiddish-speaking immigrant milieu, including Zionism.

East European Jewish immigration brought about the establishment of Orthodoxy in the United States, although only a minority of immigrants and few of their children actually remained Orthodox Jews. Several hundred East European rabbis settled throughout the country, but their influence was far more limited than it had been in their native lands. Before the 1930s most Orthodox synagogues were immigrant *ḥevrot*. At the other end of the spectrum Reform Judaism reached its greatest distance from Jewish tradition at the turn of the 19th and 20th centuries. Proposals were considered at length for a Reform synod to settle matters of belief and practice, but they were not accepted. Extensive discussion took place over shifting the Sabbath from Saturday to Sunday, and several large congregations did so. The Reform rabbinate began to take an active interest in contemporary social problems and its strong anti-Zionism slowly softened so that it was able to countenance the *Balfour Declaration of 1917. There was also considerable preoccupation with the inroads made by Christian Science, *Ethical Culture, and New Thought. If Orthodox Judaism was hampered by its intimate identification with Old World life and customs, and Conservative Judaism lacked a strong congregational constituency and depended for recruits upon acculturated immigrants, Reform after the 1890s tended to lose contact with the mainstream of American Jewish life and affairs. Its layleaders, who included many significant leaders of American Jewry, participated in Jewish life mostly outside the framework of Reform Judaism. During the 1920s Reform interest in tradition and Jewish peoplehood revived largely as a result of the developments in Palestine and the widening influence of East European forms of secular Jewish life.

COMMUNAL STRUCTURE AND EDUCATION. Before the fin-de-siècle, American Jewry as a body consisted essentially of dozens of local communities. The de facto communal leaders were lawyers, substantial merchants, bankers, and some political activists in the large metropolitan centers. Such elites were often the pillars of the Reform temples, the B'nai B'rith lodges, the Hebrew Relief Societies, the Jewish social clubs, and the emerging Jewish labor movement. The most significant countrywide organizations were B'nai B'rith (and several other internally oriented fraternal bodies), the Union of American Hebrew Congregations, and the National Council of Jewish Women. Mass immigration and increasing manifestations of antisemitism, however, brought charity and the defense of Jewish rights to the foreground of American Jewish concerns, while the development of nationwide transportation and communications provided the means of making Jewry an organic, nationwide body. Beginning in 1895 with the creation of Boston's Combined Jewish Philanthropies, local Jewish charities set up federations for unified fundraising and allocation purposes. This federation method was soon taken up by every larger community, and essentially covered the United States with the founding in 1917 of the Federation for the Support of Jewish Philanthropic Societies (see *Philanthropy) in New York City. These bodies tended to assume local Jewish leadership, developing a quasi-ideology that philanthropy was the one tie uniting Jews of all kinds. The most influential national Jewish spokesman from its founding in 1906 was the American Jewish Committee, which drew its membership by invitation from the leading Jews of every city but was centered in New York City. The elitist viewpoint of the American Jewish Committee frequently conflicted with such movements as Zionism and Jewish trade unionism, which drew their strength from East European Jewish immigrant mass followings. However, the wealthy, well-connected, and extremely able leadership of the American Jewish Committee, notably Jacob H. Schiff, Mayer *Sulzberger, and above all Louis Marshall, exhibited a talent for compromise and enjoyed prestige which gave the committee's membership of bankers, merchants, lawyers, and politicians its leadership.

Well before massive East European immigration began, American Jews were committed to the public school for the education of their children. With the firm establishment of free, state, compulsory, universal elementary and then secondary schools, Christian, i.e., Protestant influence, was largely removed. Catholics rejected religiously neutral public schools and erected a parochial school system, but Jews gladly saw their children educated in the public schools. Jewish education in the specific sense became the responsibility of synagogues, most of which maintained Sunday schools attended by their own children and some others. In these schools the course of study lasted three years, and the teaching usually involved a moralistic interpretation of Bible stories and an inculcation by catechism of the principles of Judaism.

When East European immigrants first undertook to educate their sons in Judaism – virtually nothing was done initially for daughters – they merely copied traditional *ḥeder* instruction with its shortcomings. After about 1905 a new direction became prominent in Jewish education as a synthesis of religion, modern Hebraism, and Zionism, came to prevail in the afternoon Hebrew schools, known as Talmud Torahs. A new curriculum emphasized the study of the Hebrew language by the "natural method," Hebrew Bible, music, and Jewish customs and ceremonies. The new Hebrew pedagogues were often learned and devoted men, but they had to struggle against financial adversity even in prosperous times, and to overcome widespread parental indifference to Jewish education beyond sketchy *bar mitzvah* lessons. A variety of secular Yiddish-speaking supplementary schools also flourished in this period. Supported by the Arbeter Ring, the Labor Zionist movement, and other socialist groups, these schools – known as *folkshuln* (pl.) (people's schools) – emphasized a mix of classes on Yiddish and Hebrew language, Jewish history, culture, and literature, and contemporary Jewish society. They also sought to educate Jewish youth in the ideologies of Jewish socialism, Yiddishism, and Zionism. The swift adaptation of the East European Jews to American society is evident in the plethora of aforementioned institutions and the fact that the children of Yiddish-speaking immigrants frequently moved seamlessly between them. Thus, for example, in addition to the modernizing influence of American public schools, it would not have been at all unusual for a child to receive traditional instruction in an Orthodox *shul* (synagogue), regularly attend a Talmud Torah or *folkshul* which emphasized a variety of contemporary educational methods and concerns, and even belong to a Zionist or socialist group.

WORLD WAR I AND ZIONISM. World War I (1914–18), which the United States entered in 1917, proved decisive in welding together the various segments of American Jewry and affirming their place in American society. When the war started there was considerable Jewish sympathy with Germany as the enemy of Russian tsarism, a bastion of socialist strength, and the ancestral land of a large proportion of American Jewry. In November 1914 early efforts for overseas relief were unified by the establishment of the *American Jewish Joint Distribution Committee, led by Jacob H. Schiff, his son-in-law and partner Felix M. *Warburg, Nathan *Straus, Herbert H. *Lehman, and prominent personages from immigrant circles. As the war raged, Jewish opinion moved with American opinion generally toward a pro-Allied policy. Another by-product of this complex era was the waning of the decades old American Jewish attachment to German culture. But there were also dissident and pacifist voices heard amidst the din of battle and growing anti-Hun sentiment, including that of the socialist Zionist ideologue Nachman Syrkin, who resigned from the Poalei Zion party's central committee when the latter adopted a pro-war stance, and the radical anarchist Emma *Goldman, a brilliant orator who inspired audiences in Yiddish, English, Russian, and German. Sounding the clarion call of labor militancy, Goldman frequently exhorted striking workers to "demonstrate before the palaces of the rich; demand work. If they do not give you work, demand bread. If they deny you both, take bread. It is your sacred right." As a result of her anarcho-syndicalist and anti-war activity, she spent two years in prison in the United States before being deported in 1919 to the recently established Soviet Union.

The critical year during World War I was 1917. The overthrow of Russian tsarism, the idealistic motivation of the United States' entry into the war, and the British conquest of Palestine, soon followed by the Balfour Declaration which recognized Palestine as the "national home" of the Jewish people, stirred a fever of enthusiasm. Approximately 250,000 Jews served in the United States Armed Forces in 1917 and 1918, a majority of them young immigrants. As a consequence, Zionism acquired influence in American Jewish circles that it had not previously enjoyed. The organized movement dated from 1897, but there had been proto-Zionist groups as early as 1882. The leadership was composed of several acculturated businessmen and Hebraic intelligentsia, centering on such persons as Richard J.H. *Gottheil, Harry *Friedenwald, Judah L. Magnes, Stephen S. Wise, Jacob *De Haas, Philip *Cowen, Henrietta Szold, and Israel Friedlander. Funds and outlets for activity were extremely limited, however, and membership was mostly young people of immigrant parentage, with modest means and connections. The coming of war and the neutrality of the United States, with the probability of the breakup of the Ottoman Empire, stirred considerable interest in Palestine's Jewish society-in-the-making. In addition, Louis D. Brandeis entered the movement and in 1914 assumed active leadership of the Federation of American Zionists (later renamed the Zionist Organization of America). Brandeis' participation in Zionism brought the movement instant recognition and credibility. The Zionist idea began to elicit excitement among American Jews as it appeared to be a Jewish counterpart of the "self-determination of nations" propounded by President Woodrow *Wilson. It was adapted to the American Jewish outlook by stressing Palestine as a refuge for oppressed Jews and a place where an ideal society would be built. American Zionist ideology avoided interpreting all lands except Palestine as exile (*galut*). At one and the same time, Brandeis proved to be an especially eloquent spokesman for American Zionism as well as an exemplar of the rise of a new American Jewish consciousness. In a public address given to the Eastern Council of Reform Rabbis in 1915, he addressed the question of divided loyalties.

> Let no American imagine that Zionism is inconsistent with patriotism. Multiple loyalties are objectionable only if they are inconsistent. A man is a better citizen of the United States for being also a loyal citizen of his state, and of his city; for being loyal to his family, and to his profession or trade; for being loyal to his college or lodge. Every Irish American who contributed towards advancing home rule [in the Irish Free State] was a better man and a better American for the sacrifice he made. Every American Jew who aids in advancing the Jewish settlement in Palestine, though he feels that neither he nor his descendants will ever live there, will likewise be a better man and a better American for doing so.

With the escalation of the war, American Jewish sentiment increasingly favored Russian Zionist leader Ze'ev *Jabotinsky's call to establish the Jewish Legion. In the United States, David *Ben-Gurion, Yitzhak *Ben-Zvi, and Pinḥas *Rutenberg, all three of whom were expelled from Palestine by the Turkish authorities and spent much of the war in exile, threw their support behind the idea of a Jewish military force and assumed the leadership of the American campaign. Marshaling the support of the fledgling Zionist group *He-Ḥalutz (The Pioneer), they organized the 39th and 40th Battalions of Royal Fusiliers, the American regiments of the British-sponsored *Jewish Legion. The He-Ḥalutz members formed the idealistic core of the legion's American recruits who, according to one member, were motivated by "the strong desire to participate in the liberation of the land of our forefathers and, if spared, to remain among its builders." One observer offered the following description of a Jewish immigrant recruit:

> A Jewish driver entered the recruiting office and asked in uncouth Yiddish, "Do you take soldiers here for Palestine? I want to go myself." "Your age?" "Thirty-one." "Are you an American citizen?" "No." "Are you out of work?" "I make thirty to thirty-five dollars a week." "Why do you want to go?" He burst out in a rage and came near hitting the recruiting officer. "Are you a Jew? When they are fighting for Palestine will I stay here? I can kill twenty Turks for one breakfast."

In fact, a majority of the 5,000 legionnaires were not members of the Zionist movement. As a report to the American Poalei Zion convention of 1918 indicated, most were workers, clerks, students and individuals from white collar professions. Yet the groundswell of interest in the Jewish Legion illustrates the allure the notion of liberating the Jewish National Home held for a broad cross-section of American Jews. Public displays of support for the legionnaires were common. For example, as hundreds of young recruits traveled along the eastern seaboard en route to the legion's British military training camp in Windsor, Ontario, they evoked an enthusiastic response from the region's Jewish communities. One sympathetic witness observed:

> At every town in New England where the train stops on the way to Canada crowds come out to wish God-speed to the men who are going to fight for the Jewish people, for them… *Hatikvah* [The Hope] takes on a new sound and a new meaning in gatherings such as [these]. It is not the wail of a people which protests that its hope is not yet dead. It is the triumphant battle-cry of a people whose hope is to be realized.

Of the American recruits, only 2,500 legionnaires actually fought during World War I. The 39th Battalion, together with the British 38th "Judean" Battalion, played notable roles in this regard. Both the 38th and 39th Battalions were stationed in Palestine near Jericho. On September 22, 1918, the Jewish Legion routed the Turks from a strategic ford of the Jordan River, north of the lake of Galilee, and opened the way to Damascus for the Australian and New Zealand cavalry. After the war's conclusion, a group of 280 American legionnaires provided the nucleus for the establishment of Aviḥayil, a moshav ovedim (workers cooperative) near the oceanside town of Natanyah. Although relatively few in number, the former legionnaires comprised a significant segment of the 600 American Jews who settled in Palestine during the 1919–23 postwar wave of Zionist immigration.

The Jewish Legion's task was defined in Wilsonian terms as making the world safe for democracy and in Zionist terms as establishing a Jewish foothold in Ereẓ Israel. Although the Jewish Legion's contribution to the total Allied war effort was minimal, the unit had great symbolic value for American Jews. American Jews relished the image of a Jewish military force that would combat the stereotype of immigrant Jews as rootless, cowardly, and defenseless. The Jewish Legion thus assumed an importance in the public sphere disproportionate to its actual wartime role. The legionnaires themselves sustained this myth; they were credited with and took credit for successes in which they played only a part. Military experience was an intensive acculturation to the larger American scene for a sizable number of Jews who came from urban immigrant districts.

Under Brandeis, Zionist membership and influence in this period grew rapidly. Significant headway in this regard was made when the American Jewish Committee's dominance in American Jewish affairs was challenged by the Zionist-inspired movement for an American Jewish Congress which, it was rightly supposed, would include the realization of the Zionist goal among postwar Jewish demands. The congress movement succeeded in calling a countrywide Jewish election on June 4, 1917, at which pro-Zionist delegates were chosen. By this time the American Jewish Committee compromised, and soon thereafter the Balfour Declaration, endorsed by the United States, appeared to settle the Palestine question. After the war, the delegation sent to the Paris Peace Conference by the American Jewish Congress was headed by the Zionist leader Julian W. *Mack and non-Zionist leader Louis Marshall, both distinguished jurists, who collaborated with other European Jewish representatives in acquiring national minority rights for Jews in the newly created states of Central and Eastern Europe. Another important American Jewish figure to attend the conference was Bernard *Baruch, a senior advisor to President Woodrow Wilson and outspoken opponent of Zionism. In the event, Baruch helped design the Versailles Treaty's economic sanctions, which ultimately imposed heavy reparations payments on Germany and contributed to the instability of the Weimar Republic. American Jewry thus made its debut at the center of world Jewish affairs, like the United States itself – at the very moment when postwar withdrawal from European involvements was reflected in decreased American Jewish interest in foreign matters and a drastic drop in the funds raised for overseas purposes, with the notable exception of Palestine.

THE TURBULENT TWENTIES. Flanked by the swift rise of new ethnic and immigrant groups, on the one hand, to which entrenched American elements responded with a mixture of xenophobia and racism, and the collapse of America's economy, on the other, historian John Higham has dubbed the interlude between World Wars I and II as "The Turbulent Twenties." In this period, the American Zionist movement entered into prolonged decline after Brandeis, who Wilson in the meanwhile elevated to the United States Supreme Court, and his well-connected leadership group withdrew from Zionist activities following their defeat in 1921 by the *Weizmann wing of the Zionist Organization. The conflict at hand arose from whether Palestine was to be developed by large-scale public corporate enterprise or by mass contributions to the new *Keren Hayesod (Palestine Foundation Fund) general development scheme. It also derived from a lack of personal chemistry between Brandeis and Weizmann. Thereafter deprived of access to large givers, the principal Zionist funds could raise no more than $15,000,000 during the 1920s. Meanwhile, Hadassah, founded by Henrietta Szold in 1912, continued to raise increasingly substantial sums for health services projects in Palestine, as did the Labor Zionist movement – the Po'alei Zion (Workers of Zion), Zei'rei Zion (Youth of Zion), Pioneer Women's Organization, and Farband (Labor Zionist fraternal order) – in the name of the Geverkshaften campaign for Palestine labor institutions.

The United States' turn toward isolationism, the "Red Scare" of 1919–21, and the surge of nativism and anti-urbanism during the 1920s bore serious consequences for American Jewry. A great wave of anti-foreignism and fervor for "Americanization," as propagated in the press, books, and the public schools, bore down hard on Jewish cultural distinctiveness.

Jews were prominent among political radicals of all shades, few of whom felt anything but indifference or hostility to their Jewish origins, but antisemitism in the United States in lurid tones tied Jews as a body to Bolshevism and political radicalism. The canard of an international Jewish plot to overthrow Western civilization spread countrywide. At the same time doctrines of the inferiority of specific racial types became widely accepted in academic as well as popular thinking. This philosophy had a vigorous proponent of unlimited financial means in the automobile magnate Henry Ford, who published the *Dearborn Independent* and *The International Jew* in millions of copies until forced by a lawsuit in 1927 to cease and to retract his statements. Louis Marshall spearheaded the latter effort and succeeded in extracting a public apology from Ford. The hooded southern society of the Ku Klux Klan, refounded about 1915, spread far beyond its original locale in the South to the Middle West and even the East, propagating antisemitism alongside its racism and anti-Catholicism. It gained short-lived political power in some states. Public revulsion at the Klan's corruption and weariness with its antics caused the organization virtually to disappear by 1927.

By far the most important result of these movements was the Johnson-Reed Act of 1924 restricting immigration, which took effect in several stages beginning in 1925. An earlier immigration act of 1921 established the principle of the national origins quota, by providing that the number of immigrants to be admitted in any year was not to exceed three percent of their respective native lands' stock (i.e., immigrants and their children) residing in the United States in 1910. Following vigorous agitation by racist intellectuals like Prescott F. Hall and Madison Grant, and their ally Senator Henry Cabot Lodge of Massachusetts, and by Southern and Western nativist opponents of foreign immigration, the Johnson-Reed Act was passed in 1924. Its provisions were founded on a belief in "Nordic" (Northern and Western European: English, Irish, German Scandinavian) superiority over Mediterraneans, Slavs, Orientals, and Jews, for it not only limited yearly immigration to 154,000 but also gave overwhelming preference to immigrants from Northern and Western Europe. This was accomplished by setting the quota at two percent of the foreign stock living in the United States in 1890, a census year before "undesirable" Slavic and Mediterranean elements were heavily represented in the population. Thus, only 5,982 immigrants could be admitted yearly from Poland, 2,148 from Russia, and 749 from Romania. A prospective immigrant was categorized for quota purposes by his/her land of birth so that, for example, a Jew born in Poland who spent his/her life in England was a Pole under the Johnson-Reed Act. The only means of reaching American shores outside the quota was by affidavits guaranteeing support submitted by relatives in the United States. The quota system, worked out in detail during the late 1920s, closed off the great stream by which almost 2,500,000 Jews came to the United States between 1880 and 1925. The effect of the Johnson-Reed Act, therefore, was to hasten the day when the majority of American Jews were native born, which was around 1940.

Racist and nativist movements became rife during a period of massive movement of Jews out of the immigrant quarters into newer, more attractive urban districts, and out of immigrant trades into commercial, clerical, and professional occupations. During the prosperity of the 1920s large numbers of young Jews, children of immigrant parents reaching maturity, tended to enter the professions of law, medicine, dentistry, teaching, and to some extent social work. As far as can be reckoned, the largest trend was toward small, independent business and clerical, managerial ("white collar") employment. It was in this connection that antisemitism in the United States assumed the most directly injurious forms. Large insurance companies, banks, retail chains, law firms, and large companies generally did not employ Jews, with the exception of a few who had no chance of advancement in the positions they held. Private colleges and universities habitually imposed quotas on Jewish student admissions, usually between five and ten percent. Most rigorous were antisemitic restrictions in almost all medical schools that forced many intelligent and capable young Jews to study abroad. Antisemitism in the medical profession also applied to opportunities for specialty training and appointment to hospital staffs, even in public institutions. The Jewish hospitals founded late in the 19th century for the needs of Jewish patients became devoted from the 1920s to alleviating the plight of the Jewish physicians. College and university faculties were with few exceptions closed to Jews, and Jewish teachers could usually secure employment in public schools only in the largest cities.

These occupational trends into clerical, managerial, entrepreneurial, and professional employment coincided with the gradual departure of Jews from the heretofore Jewish trades, mainly in the garment industry. By the 1930s Jews constituted only two-fifths of the membership of the International Ladies Garment Workers Union and the number in the Amalgamated Clothing Workers dropped, although the leadership continued to be Jewish. A similar Jewish union arose during the 1920s, the Fur and Leather Workers Union. These unions were torn by factional disputes between Communist and anti-Communist groups.

The 1920s were the ripest years of Yiddish culture. There were eleven Yiddish theaters in New York City and seventeen elsewhere in the United States which, during a one-month period in the fall of 1927, presented 645 performances of 85 plays, many of high artistic quality. The Yiddish school system also reached its peak during these years, enrolling approximately 12,000 children, while such a Yiddish organization as the Workmen's Circle (Arbeter Ring) attained its maximum membership of about 80,000. Symptomatic of future decline, however, was the lowered circulation of the Yiddish press from its 1915 peak. Hebrew culture attracted a devoted but much smaller following, organized in the Histadruth Ivrith of America and publishing the weekly *Hadoar* ("The Mail"). Hebraists were particularly prominent in the rabbinate and Jewish education.

During the 1920s Jews began to appear in American literature. Several semi-autobiographical novels about Jewish immigrant life appeared in English – two noteworthy examples are Ludwig *Lewisohn's *Up Stream* (1922) and Anzia *Yezierska's *Bread Givers* (1925) – while persons like Gertrude *Stein and Maxwell *Bodenheim were literary modernists. Other gifted American Jewish writers, whose work reached a broad Yiddish and English readership in this period, were Sholem Asch, Moshe Leib Halpern, Anna Margolin, Joseph *Opatoshu, I.J. Schwartz, and Yehoash (Yehoash-Solomon Bloomgarden). Such publishers as Alfred A. *Knopf and Horace *Liveright specialized in issuing the best of contemporary literature. The first American Jewish literary magazine, the *Menorah Journal*, began publication in 1915 and enjoyed its most distinguished years of "fostering the Jewish 'humanities'" during the 1920s. The door was thus opened for the rise of other Anglo-Jewish journals of high quality, many of which focused on questions of literature, art, religion, and contemporary politics. Consequently, the emergence of **Commentary*, the *Contemporary Jewish Record*, *Jewish Frontier*, the *Jewish Spectator*, *New Palestine*, the *Reconstructionist*, and others in the 1930s and 1940s – and their success as a platform for vigorous Jewish public debate – can be traced to the pioneering efforts of the *Menorah Journal*.

At a different cultural level, the advent of mass film entertainment in the United States was largely the work of Jewish producers and entrepreneurs who made Hollywood the world's film capital after 1920. Poor immigrants like Adolph *Zukor, Carl *Laemmle, Louis B. *Mayer, Lewis J. *Selznick, Jesse L. *Lasky, and the *Warner brothers eventually developed motion pictures into a worldwide entertainment industry in the 1920s and 1930s. They virtually dominated the new industry for several decades and in the meantime made themselves and others multimillionaires. In turn, these "moguls" attracted a rich cadre of Jewish immigrant talent that helped shape Hollywood's golden age and set 20th-century American culture on a new path.

In fact, the first "talkie," *The Jazz Singer* (1927) – the story of a Jewish boy struggling to escape his Yiddish-speaking immigrant background and make it as a show business entertainer – was produced by Warner Brothers and featured the vaudeville singing and dancing star Al *Jolson. The film ushered in the new mixed technology of celluloid photography and synchronized sound and quickly became a countrywide sensation. It also promoted a positive and liberal view of the Americanization process and introduced a variety of theater audiences to East European Jewish culture and life, including traditional Jewish rituals, liturgical music, and the Yiddish language. In the story, the protagonist Jakie Rabinowitz (played by Jolson), runs away from home, adopts the non-Jewish stage name Jack Robin, and works hard to achieve success and acclaim. He is eventually reconciled with his dying traditionalist father, honors his parents' wishes by chanting the **Kol Nidrei* service on Yom Kippur eve, and then resumes his Broadway career. The film ends with Jolson singing "Mammy" in blackface, while his adoring widowed mother looks on. "If God wanted him in His house," she reasons, "He would have kept him there."

Notwithstanding *The Jazz Singer*'s unapologetic use of Jewish subject matter and its commercial and artistic success, the story line serves to illustrate the trajectory of many Jews in the growing American film industry. From the producers and movie makers behind the scenes to the box office celebrities who became iconic figures of the silver screen, Hollywood offered many Jews the opportunity to jettison their East European ancestry and remake themselves fully as Americans. They distanced themselves from the organized Jewish scene and played nary a visible role in the wider community. "When I arrived at Paramount [movie studio] as a contract writer," Abraham Polansky later reported, "another Jewish writer told me to change my name. He told me it sounded Jewish and that movies were seen all over America. I didn't change my name… but many actors did." Thus, following in the tradition of many German Jewish immigrants, including Erich Weiss, the celebrated escape artist of the early 20th century who became Harry *Houdini, Israel Iskowitz became Eddie *Cantor, Julius Garfinkle became John *Garfield, Emanuel Goldberg became Edward G. *Robinson, Melvyn Hesselberg became Melvyn *Douglas, and Marion Levy became Paulette *Goddard. Among other especially popular Jewish performers in this period were the radio comic Jack *Benny (born Benjamin Kubelsky in Chicago, Illinois), who later became a pioneer of television comedy, and Julius Henry (Groucho) *Marx and his brothers Chico (Leonard), Harpo (Adolph), Gummo (Milton), and Zeppo (Herbert) whose wild antics in films like *Animal Crackers* (1930) and *Duck Soup* (1933) quickly made these sons of German Jewish immigrants a household name. Younger Jewish aspirants, including Jerry *Lewis who in the 1940s would get his start doing vaudeville sketches in the Catskills and go on to become a major comic celebrity in the 1950s and 1960s, followed in their wake. Meanwhile, George *Gershwin's American operetta *Porgy and Bess* (1935) appeared in the same year as the virtuoso clarinetist Benny *Goodman (born Benjamin David Gordon), the son of poor East European Jewish immigrants in Chicago's Maxwell Street neighborhood, established himself as the "King of Swing." The stage was now set for the future participation of Jews in American culture on a major scale.

THE GREAT DEPRESSION. The Great Depression which began in 1929 and did not fully end until World War II struck Jews and other Americans very hard. Mass unemployment severely affected the Jews with their distinct economic stratification, although precise statistics are not available. Thousands of small Jewish businesses, many established a few years earlier by ambitious immigrants, were ruined, and established businessmen and Jewish communal leaders often fared no better. One result of these economic disasters was the abandonment by Jewish philanthropies of the claim that "Jews take care of their own," for the numbers requiring relief were far too great for any but governmental support. Against this background of unemployment and business crisis, the Jewish community suffered severely as the income of its institutions drastically declined. Saadia Gelb, a Labor Zionist youth leader, later recalled the impact of these uncertain times on left-leaning Jewish youth like himself:

> It is difficult to conceive what a sense of helplessness engulfed the country after the crash. Not only the headlines of tycoons turned paupers, news of millionaire suicides, confusing government statements, but gnawing doubts about the very foundation of our society upset every American. Those of us who were then in the Young Poalei Zion had the answers. We knew that Zionism would solve the Jewish problem; socialism the problem of society as a whole.

During the Depression, the income of charitable institutions dropped by more than half, campaigns for overseas aid were virtually given up from 1930 to 1935, and synagogues and schools fell far in arrears of pay to their employees. The occupational distribution of the Jews at this time was summarized by Benjamin M. Selikman:

> Jews are not widely represented on the farms or in manual jobs. The needle trades have employed large numbers, although even here other nationalities have been supporting them in recent decades. The heavy industries engage few Jews either among employers or workers. Banking, stock brokering, moving pictures and other forms of amusement, real estate and the distributive trades account for most of our Jewish wealth. The professions, small business, and white-collar occupations yield our large Jewish middle class.

Earlier discrimination against Jews in employment became much sharper as jobs became fewer. Many Jews entered expanding governmental service, which offered extensive employment to professional and technically trained Jews on terms of equal opportunity. Widespread Jewish communal concern that under conditions of depression and antisemitism American Jewry would presently consist of a few large businessmen, many independent salesmen, a large proletariat drifting unwillingly into factory labor, and an element of restless, bitter intellectuals prompted much talk and a few efforts to "balance" Jewish occupational distribution, none of which came to anything. Jewish youth, aided by their often impoverished families, continued to go to free colleges, especially in New York City, and to somewhat more costly state universities, while the prosperous went to private institutions. Proportions in this regard continued to be far higher among Jews than the general population. For example, in the mid-1930s approximately 49 percent of all college students in New York City were Jewish, while the 105,000 Jewish college students in the entire country were just over nine percent of total college enrollment. Student ambitions were toward business and the professions, and this foretold the Jewish economic future in the 1950s more accurately than the predictions of the sociologists and economists of the 1930s.

From the New Deal to the Rise of the State of Israel, 1932–1948

POLITICAL ACTIVITY. As the Democrats became the party of urban-oriented reform, exemplified in 1928 by the presidential candidacy of Alfred E. Smith, Jews moved into its ranks en masse and away from their earlier Socialist or Republican affiliation. The New Deal and its leader, President Franklin D. *Roosevelt, attracted enthusiastic Jewish loyalty. Roosevelt, who had strong ties with New York City reformers, many of them Jews, was greatly admired. Throughout his presidency (1933–45) 85 to 90 percent of Jewish votes were cast for him and candidates who supported him. In this period, Jews appeared in politics with unprecedented prominence: one cabinet member (Henry *Morgenthau, Jr. who served as secretary of the treasury), three United States Supreme Court justices (Louis D. Brandeis, Benjamin *Cardozo, and Felix *Frankfurter as Brandeis' successor), five governors (Ernest *Gruening of the Alaskan territory, Herbert H. *Lehman of New York, Arthur Seligman of New Mexico, Julius L. *Meier of Oregon, and Henry *Horner of Illinois), and several hundred assistant secretaries, mayors, judges of lower courts, and high appointive officials. Such New Deal legislation as bank deposit insurance, the protection of trade unionism, work relief, establishing wage and hour standards, and social security, directly benefited the mass of working-class and lower-middle-class Jews. In the final analysis, however, vigorous Jewish support for Roosevelt and the unprecedented number of elite Jewish officials – antisemites spoke of the "Jew Deal" – yielded very little governmental aid for Jews imperiled abroad beyond sympathetic presidential statements.

In addition to the overwhelming support among Jews for the New Deal, the vogue of "popular front" Communism during this period attracted many Jews. Troubled by seemingly insoluble economic crisis and menaced by antisemitism, the security of employment in Soviet Russia and its "prohibition" of antisemitism made that country appear a utopia to thousands. Communism appealed especially to some segments among garment workers and to professionals, like teachers and social workers, who were sensitive to social ills and encountered great difficulty in establishing themselves. Outside the Communist Yiddish enclave, the movement was indifferent to Jewish needs and problems. In fact, it was favorable to the Arab cause in Palestine. Communists claimed that their triumph would solve all Jewish problems. A rapid deflation of their popularity occurred with the Hitler-Stalin pact of 1939.

If the liberal American Jewish *Weltanschauung* of the 1930s and 1940s was buoyed by the twin visions of the Roosevelt administration in the United States and the Zionist movement in Jewish public affairs, it is also true that the social realities in both instances tested American Jewry's political resolve and the durability of its attachments. Like Roosevelt's New Deal coalition (in which American Jews played an important role), the Zionist Organization's prevailing Labor-led coalition (in which American Zionist groups played a crucial part) consolidated its power and authority around grand strategies and the global *Realpolitik* of the 1930s. Roosevelt persuaded the country to accept the proposition that the national government is responsible for the welfare of its citizens and that the New Deal would provide social and economic security for all Americans. Meanwhile, David Ben-Gurion, who emerged as Labor Zionism's undisputed leader in 1935, articulated a similar set of priorities: "Zionism means the growth of a state, and a state does not build itself, nor is it built by those who seek their own interests and survival. Only through mobilization of mass strength and movement, with pioneer training and a readiness for self-sacrifice can this be made a reality." In sum, the Labor-Centrist coalition that dominated Zionist politics in Palestine and world affairs from the mid-1930s onward – and which came to power as a result of the achievements in Palestine of the Histadrut, a countrywide socio-economic infrastructure organized along cooperative and nationalist lines – also captured the hearts and minds of broad array of American Jewish socialists, progressives, and liberals. This remained true even after the outbreak of World War II, when both Roosevelt and Ben-Gurion led their respective nations into the international arena as part of the Allied fight against the Nazi Germany.

IMPACT OF NAZI GERMANY AND ANTISEMITISM. American Jews were profoundly shocked and frightened by Germany's turn to Nazism in 1933 and its unprecedented treatment of the Jews, and to a lesser degree by official antisemitism in lands such as Poland and Romania. Against this backdrop, antisemitism in the United States was therefore particularly disturbing, although its major sources were Catholic and populist rather than Nazi in origin and focused in the person of the notorious "radio priest," Father Charles E. Coughlin. Probably more significant, however, was that every political leader and virtually every intellectual and cultural figure opposed antisemitism, led by President Franklin D. Roosevelt who earned strong Jewish support in part for his unconcealed detestation of Nazism and antisemitism.

The Nazi regime drove increasing numbers of its Jewish victims to the United States. However, owing to severe economic conditions, a rise in xenophobia, the hostility of the State Department, and the intransigence of United States consuls empowered to grant visas, total Jewish immigration to the United States, most of it from Germany, did not exceed 33,000 from 1933 through 1937. With the extreme worsening of the situation, 124,000 refugees arrived from 1938 through 1941, mostly from Germany and the lands conquered by the Nazi regime. Refugee immigrants encountered great difficulty in adjustment owing not only to the trauma of their readjustment but also to Depression conditions. Indeed, most Jewish refugees experienced significant downward mobility and had to start and long remain at a socio-economic level beneath that which they enjoyed in Europe. They concentrated in New York City, focusing on particular neighborhoods, and tended to establish their own congregations, welfare organizations, and social clubs. A coordinating body, the National Coordinating Committee for Aid to Refugees and Emigrants Coming from Germany, was established 1934, and in 1939 it became the National Refugee Service, a functional agency.

Several thousand of these refugees were scientists and academic intellectuals. Their symbolic leader was Albert *Einstein, who received the Nobel Prize in physics in 1921 for his work on the photoelectric effect of quantum mechanics and who now assumed a post at Princeton University. A few hundred of these refugee scholars wielded tremendous intellectual influence on research and teaching in the United States in such fields as music, art history, psychiatry and psychoanalysis, history, sociology, and incomparably in nuclear physics. This intellectual migration, nearly all Jewish, ensured the transfer of much of the world's intellectual leadership from Europe to the United States, including many well known figures such as the composers Arnold *Schoenberg and Kurt *Weill, the conductors Otto *Klemperer and Bruno *Walter, the writer Stefan *Zweig, the piano virtuoso Artur *Rubinstein, the theatrical producer Max *Reinhardt, and the architect Erich *Mendelsohn.

RELIGION AND EDUCATION. Few of the 3,728 known congregations flourished financially or spiritually. Synagogue membership and contributions sharply declined, and many congregations were burdened by mortgages on buildings erected during the 1920s. Reform Judaism became quite vigorous in its espousal of liberal political program, emphasizing trade unionism and international peace, and the Conservatives spoke likewise. The Orthodox were disorganized and inarticulate, losing strength as their immigrant constituents passed on without leaving replacements. Jewish education was hit hardest, as enrolled students failed to pay tuition and communal sources of funds dwindled and disappeared. Large arrears were owed to teachers, especially in traditional Hebraic and Orthodox schools. About 1940 communal interest began to rise as the Jewish Education Committee of New York was founded to improve schooling in that metropolis and the American Association for Jewish Education was established in 1939.

COMMUNAL ORGANIZATION. The Jewish communal structure was profoundly shaken by the Great Depression as the mood of Jewish life changed. The old leaders, many of them of German Jewish origin, were dying out and their children were for the most part disinterested in the Jewish community. Many leaders' personal wealth and status declined sharply. The Depression, the New Deal, and the Jewish crisis in Germany and Europe shook established Jewish values and practices and opened the way for communal restructuring and a newer leadership, drawn from East European immigrant origins, which was strongly pro-Zionist. Jewish labor and socialist groups decisively joined the community after decades of abstention on account of class differences.

The Jewish Labor Committee, established in 1934 to combat totalitarianism and aid labor refugees, collaborated with other Jewish bodies. Many of them gave up their anti-Zionism on account of the socialist character of Jewish Palestine and disillusion with international socialist brotherhood. The Zionist movement was weak during the 1930s. The combined income of its two fundraising arms, the Keren Hayesod

(Palestine Foundation Fund) and the *Jewish National Fund (Keren Kayemet), dropped as low as $339,000 in 1933. The raising and allocation of philanthropic funds was in fact the key issue in American Jewish communal life. Zionists waged a prolonged campaign to increase the proportion given to Palestine from the welfare fund drives conducted in most cities. In their attempt to increase the allocations to Palestine, Zionists encountered consistent opposition from the controlling oligarchy of large givers who generally favored European relief and distrusted Zionist projects. In 1939 the United Palestine Appeal (UPA) began independent national campaigns with Rabbi Abba Hillel Silver as its principal tactician and orator. In 1939 it reached an agreement with the Joint Distribution Committee and its allied National Refugee Service, which led to the creation of the United Jewish Appeal (UJA). The UJA raised $7,000,000 in 1939 and $14,500,000 in 1940, but the diminishing allocation to Palestine caused a rupture in 1941 which was healed by a 63:37 division of funds. During the 1940s, the UJA raised $638,000,000, and ultimately as much as 75 percent of its income went to Palestine. These sums established the UJA as one of the greatest voluntary fundraising organizations ever known.

These developments at the national level were made possible in many cities by the newly founded Jewish community councils. (There was a General Jewish Council of Jewish defense organizations from 1938 to 1941 which subsequently became the National Community Relations Advisory Council.) Synagogues, B'nai B'rith lodges, and Zionist societies were heavily represented and the tone was decidedly pro-Zionist. The Jewish community councils were heavily involved in the overseas philanthropic campaigns, or Jewish welfare funds as they were known locally, in addition to their functions of promoting Jewish education, settling internal disputes, and watching over Jewish rights in their cities. They thus became the representative local Jewish organizations during the 1940s and strongly influenced philanthropic allocations toward Palestine.

WORLD WAR II AND ZIONISM. Well before the outbreak of World War II, American Jewish public support crystallized around the anti-Nazi movement, which was organized in 1935 and among whose earliest and most outspoken leaders was Stephen S. Wise. The anti-Nazi boycott served as an organizational hub for American Jewry in the years leading up to the war and America's fateful decision to enter the fray. On the eve of the Japanese bombing of Pearl Harbor on December 7, 1941, for example, Wise gave one of his many anti-Nazi addresses to the Inter-American Jewish Conference meeting in Baltimore, Maryland. The conference included delegates from Diaspora Jewish communities in North, Central, and South America. Anticipating the sea change in the postwar composition of world Jewry, Wise called for unified action by the free Diaspora Jewish communities of the Americas.

> We are gathered in part in order to bethink ourselves touching the infinitely mournful fate of our fellow Jews, who have dwelt in European lands. Addresses other than my own will deal with the oceanic tragedy which has befallen the peaceable and loyal populations of many European lands, who were the first and will be the last victims of Nazism until the day of liberation from the monstrous calamity of Nazism. And that day is not far off…
>
> But even though, not if, Hitlerism or Nazism is to be banished from the earth… there will still remain a number of the most difficult and taxing Jewish problems. The economic basis of Jewish living has been willfully destroyed by Nazism. Jews who, like you and like us, are free must give to the succor of Jews who for nearly a decade have been enslaved and dispossessed. Even though after the war, inter-governmental programs must have special reference to a people in many lands deprived of the basic possibilities of self-support, the fate of our brother Jews in European lands cries out to us for immediate succor. When peace shall have come, as it will, demands will be made for ultimate and permanent redress from the nations which will have it in their power to bring about the organization of a new world.
>
> Woe betide us, if amidst the comparative plenty and prosperity of American life, we forget our brother Jews, whose agonies and suffering have come about largely, if not solely, because they are Jews…

Another outstanding expression of American Jewish idealism as well as fidelity to the United States was Irving *Berlin's "God Bless America." Written and composed by Berlin (born Israel Baline in Russian Siberia) – a gifted secular Jewish musical artist who also wrote the wildly popular "White Christmas" – and first broadcast on Armistice Day in November 1938, "God Bless America" swiftly attained the elevated status of a secular national prayer.

> While the storm clouds gather far across the sea,
> Let us swear allegiance to a land that's free,
> Let us all be grateful for a land so fair,
> As we raise our voices in solemn prayer.
> God bless America, land that I love.
> Stand beside her and guide her,
> Thru the night with a light from above.
> From the mountains to the prairies,
> To the oceans white with foam,
> God bless America, my home sweet home.

In the public debates that raged over American foreign policy between September 1939, when Nazi Germany invaded and conquered Poland, and December 7, 1941, when the Japanese bombed the American naval base located at Pearl Harbor, Hawaii, American Jews were generally found on the side favoring maximum foreign and military aid to England and France, and later Russia. American Jewish sympathies were less with Great Britain per se, whose imperialism and White Paper of 1939 essentially brought to a halt European Jewish immigration to Palestine and whose anti-refugee policies were deeply resented. But as American Jewry's fear and loathing of Nazi Germany increased, so too did its growing sympathy (along with mainstream American society) for the Allied cause in general, including the besieged British Isles. Quite apart from this consensus stood the America First Committee, which attracted a large following of antisemites and even some Jews. As late as 1941, the America First Committee sponsored a speech by Charles A. Lindbergh charging that Jews were attempting to draw the United States into war. The coming of World War II ended the debate over isolation and also proved a blow against such antisemitism, which was now identified with the Nazi enemy. Jews served in all branches of the United States armed forces, their numbers reaching approximately 550,000. About 10,500 lost their lives, 24,000 were wounded, and 36,000 were decorated for gallantry. Jewish refugees from Germany furnished many American soldiers, while refugee scientists played an indispensable role in the development of atomic and other advanced weapons. Jewish soldiers in the American armed forces were served by 310 Jewish chaplains holding military rank, and the National Jewish Welfare Board provided for some social and religious needs.

While battles raged throughout the world, European Jewry was being systematically murdered by Nazi Germany. Information about the destruction of European Jewish life became public during the fall of 1942, and subsequent stages in the Nazi "final solution" were widely known. Notwithstanding private and public efforts by various Jewish leaders and groups, including the vigorous public criticism of the right-wing Zionist Bergson group, American Jewry as a whole, uncertain of its own situation and fearful of appearing to ask for "special treatment" or of encouraging propaganda that the country was engaged in a "Jewish war," shied away from demanding direct United States intervention to save Jews under Nazi rule. In general, the prevailing view was that early victory was the sole means to rescue European Jewry. Nevertheless, public controversy abounded and many American Jewish leaders expressed despair of the powerlessness of American Jews to alter the Allies wartime priorities. Among the most poignant statements in this regard was a speech delivered by the Labor Zionist leader Ḥayyim Greenberg in February 1943. His summation, reprinted at length below, illustrates the profound anguish, self-recrimination, and anger of the American Jewish leadership in this cataclysmic period.

> The time has come, perhaps, when the few Jewish communities remaining in the world which are still free to make their voices heard and to pray in public should proclaim a day of fasting and prayer for American Jews. No – this is not a misprint. I mean specifically that a day of prayer and of fasting should be proclaimed for the five million Jews now living in the United States. They live under the protection of a mighty republic governed by democratic laws. They move about freely through the length and breadth of the land. The vast majority of them have enough food to eat, clothes to wear and roofs over their heads. And if any wrong is committed against them, they are free to protest and to demand their rights. Nevertheless, they deserve to be prayed for. They are not even aware what a misfortune has befallen them, and if they were to look at themselves with seeing eyes they would realize with shock how intolerable this misfortune is. This misfortune consists of the vacuity, the hardness and the dullness that has come over them; it consists in a kind of epidemic inability to suffer or to feel compassion that has seized upon the vast majority of American Jews and of their institutions; in pathological fear of pain; in terrifying lack of imagination – a horny shell seems to have formed over the soul of American Jewry to protect and defend it against pain and pity.
>
> At a time when the American Jewish community is the largest and most influential in the world, at a time when the eyes of millions of Jews in Europe who are daily threatened with the most terrible and degrading forms of physical extermination are primarily turned to American Jewry, this American Jewish community has fallen lower than perhaps any other in recent times, and displays an unbelievable amount of highly suspect clinical "health" and "evenness of temper." If moral bankruptcy deserves pity, and if this pity is seven-fold for one who is not even aware how shocking his bankruptcy is, then no Jewish community in the world today (not even the Jews who are now in the claws of the Nazi devourer) deserves more compassion from Heaven than does American Jewry…
>
> The basic fact is evident to any Jew who has the courage to look at the situation as it is: American Jewry has not done – and has made no effort to do – its elementary duty toward the millions of Jews who are captive and doomed to die in Europe!…
>
> Quite some months have passed since representatives of Jewish organizations have even met to engage in earnest discussion whether and what can still be done for European Jewry. The President made his statement, and then came the declarations of some governments of the United Nations regarding the punishment to be meted out to the guilty *after the victory*, and most, or is it all, the Jewish organizations were satisfied and appeared to be calmed by it… Everyone knew that this declaration had little effect on the situation. And now we are informed that both Warsaw and Vienna are completely *Judenrein*….
>
> The murder of two million Jews with the most inhuman methods of torture and degradation which sadistic fantasy has ever devised, still has not sufficiently impressed those among us who have donned the *shtreimels* of Jewish guardianship, those who have assumed responsibility for Jewish interests so that they could sit down around one table and look into each other's eyes and together try to do something to rescue at least one percent of the doomed millions. There have even appeared some Zionists in our midst who have become reconciled to the thought that it is impossible to stay the hand of the murderer, and therefore, they say, it is necessary "to utilize this opportunity" to emphasize to the world the tragedy of Jewish homelessness and to strengthen the demand for a Jewish National Home in Palestine. (A Home for whom? For the millions of dead in their temporary cemeteries in Europe?) And there have arisen *sages* in our midst who have reached the profound conclusion that the sole response to the mass extermination of our people should be the earliest possible opening of a second front. The delegation of the Bund in America has satisfied the demands of its conscience both as Jews and as human beings, by organizing a protest conference of European socialist leaders, and is now boastfully claiming "sole credit" for its own little clique for this great achievement. And only some days ago the Revisionist-controlled Committee for a Jewish Army, succumbing to its own ambitions and hunger for prestige, has put other Jewish organizations in an uncomfortable position by publishing huge ads in the newspapers – ads which also seek "to utilize the opportunity" – calling for the establishment of

> a Jewish armed force of 200,000, knowing very well that this is a mythical figure concocted for purposes of cheap and irresponsible propaganda…
>
> Every "Committee" cherishes its own committee-interests, its sectarian ambitions, its exclusively wise strategy and its "power position" in the teapot of Jewish communal competition…
>
> No less characteristic is the fact that such a highly reputable organization as the American Jewish Committee could hold its annual conference one week ago, at the end of which there was issued a declaration dealing with all the bakers' dozen areas in which they differ from the Zionists or from other Jews, but not mentioning with even a single word the extermination of the Jews in Europe and what the American Jewish Committee proposes to do now, today, without delay, so that after the victory there should remain someone across the ocean whom the Committee could defend in accordance with its own program and ideology, someone whose rights and human dignity they could protect.
>
> The only Jewish organization which, formally at least, remained on guard and tries to create the impression that it does something, is the American Jewish Congress. But it would be criminal negligence to conceal from the public the fact that at a time when the Angel of Death uses airplanes, the American Jewish Congress employs an oxcart-express…
>
> I confess that I am unable to draw concrete, practical conclusions from the above. If it is still objectively possible to do anything, then I do not know who should do it and how it should be done. I only know this, that we are all – all five million of us, with all our organizations and committees and leaders – politically and morally bankrupt. And I refuse to understand how and why all of us here have fallen to such a state of shameful degradation.

In all, roughly a year and a half elapsed until in 1944, following a direct approach by Treasury Secretary Henry *Morgenthau, Jr., who was profoundly disturbed by State Department's ongoing indifference and hostility to all rescue proposals, President Roosevelt established the *War Refugee Board. The board energetically attempted, with some success, to work through neutral countries and third parties to prevent further Nazi murder of Jews and others. The efforts in this regard were ultimately realized in the rescue of some 100,000 Jews. Within the American Jewish community, the American Zionist Emergency Council, the Va'ad ha-Hazzalah (Rescue Committee) under Orthodox leadership, and other Jewish and Zionist groups also worked to rescue as many Jews as possible, mainly by ransom. By this point, the sole remaining community of any significant size was that of Hungarian Jewry.

In the spring 1942 Zionist leaders, headed by David Ben-Gurion and Chaim Weizmann, set their postwar program as Jewish control over immigration to Palestine, leading to the founding of a Jewish commonwealth. This vision was embodied in the *Biltmore Program of May 1942 (named after the New York City hotel where the conference was held) and it gradually won over American Jewry by vigorous Zionist public relations efforts, and above all by the widening realization of the full fate of European Jewry. Under Rabbis Stephen S. Wise and Abba Hillel Silver, the American Zionist Emergency Council, which conducted Zionist political affairs in the United States, continued the traditional method of winning sympathy and good will from American political, religious, and intellectual leaders. Wise was supplanted in 1944 by Silver and more aggressive tactics of converting American public opinion to the Zionist program and applying continuous pressure to the makers of American foreign policy were adopted.

The representative *American Jewish Conference in 1943, swayed by Silver's oratory, rejected a compromise demanding only free Jewish immigration to Palestine and adopted the Biltmore Program. The scales were tipped when Silver gave an unexpected address during the general debate on Palestine. By all accounts, his forceful argument reversed the moderate trend of the Conference. His speech laid the groundwork for the final resolution on Palestine. "There is but one solution for national homelessness," Silver declared. "That is a national home!"

> Not new immigration opportunities to other countries for fleeing refugees, for new colonization schemes in other parts of the world… The only solution is to normalize the political status of the Jewish people in the world by giving it a national basis in its national and historic home…
>
> …The reconstitution of the Jewish people as a nation in its homeland is not a playful political conceit of ours, a sort of intellectual thing of ours calculated to satisfy some national vanity of ours. It is the cry of despair of a people driven to the wall, fighting for its very life…
>
> I am for unity in Israel, for the realization of the total program of Jewish life: relief, rescue, reconstruction and the national restoration in Palestine. I am not for unity on a fragment of the program, for a fragment of the program is a betrayal of the rest of the program and a tragic futility besides. We cannot truly rescue the Jews of Europe unless we have free immigration into Palestine. We cannot have free immigration into Palestine unless our political rights are recognized there. Our political rights cannot be recognized unless our historic connection with the country is acknowledged and our right to rebuild our national home is affirmed. The whole chain breaks if one of our links is missing…

Silver's eloquent case for an immediate political solution based on wartime realities and his assertion of the critical role to be played by the Zionist enterprise in any plans for postwar reconstruction cut across ideological and philosophical lines. The Palestine vote was carried with only four dissenting votes. The delegates resoundingly called for "the fulfillment of the Balfour Declaration" and the reconstitution of Palestine as the Jewish Commonwealth. Next, the assemblage spontaneously "rose, applauded, and sang Hatikvah [The Hope]."

By contrast, on three other occasions – early in 1944 and late that year as well as early in 1945 – the U.S. House of Representatives Foreign Affairs Committee stood poised to pass resolutions endorsing the Jewish commonwealth. Nonetheless, despite every prospect for early passage in both houses of Congress, the War Department, at the request of the State

Department, succeeded in having the legislative proposals tabled as "prejudicial" to the war effort.

As American Jewish support for Zionism and the Yishuv intensified, anti-Zionist views became more isolated and aggressive. The American Council for Judaism was founded late in 1942 upon an ideology of classical Reform opposition to Jewish nationalism. It conducted an assiduous anti-Zionist propaganda campaign that was vigorously countered by Zionists. The American Jewish Committee turned in a similar direction and advocated free Jewish immigration to Palestine under a rather vague international trusteeship. However, much of its once great influence and public stature was lost over this issue.

The American Jewish community's domestic affairs remained in relative suspense during the war. Jews shared in American prosperity as unemployment almost vanished, charitable aid became superfluous, and business flourished. However, antisemitism continued in sectors of public opinion and manifested itself in petty street molestations of Jews, especially in Boston and somewhat in New York. President Roosevelt's alleged remark to "clear it with Sidney [Hillman]" was used with special malice by antisemites against him during the 1944 election. A strong wave of postwar antisemitism was expected, especially if there were an economic depression, during the difficulties of conversion from wartime to peace.

During the five years following the war's end in 1945, American Jewish communal life was dominated by developments among Jewish refugees in Europe and by the Jewish struggle in Palestine. Mass public meetings were frequently convened, while gentile political and religious leaders were won over by persuasion or pressure, and funds raised for overseas needs reached levels previously unknown. Thus, the Zionist Organization of America (ZOA) raised its membership from 49,000 in 1940 to 225,000 in 1948, while Hadassah numbering 81,000 in 1940, multiplied more than threefold. As the United States exercised a dominant position in international affairs, American Zionist leaders became important in framing world Zionist policy and played an increasingly important role vis-à-vis the Palestinian leadership on the international scene. Several thousand American Jewish volunteers participated in Aliyah Bet efforts, the Jewish Agency's clandestine immigration scheme, some helping to navigate *illegal immigrant ships across the Mediterranean, and eventually many joined the *Haganah and fought in Palestine in 1948–49. With the founding of the State of Israel in 1948 and its War of Independence until 1949, American Zionism reached an organizational peak that quickly declined. Membership in Zionist organizations dropped drastically, in the case of the ZOA to less than 25,000 in the mid-1950s, and monies raised, as well as the proportion of them actually allocated to Israel, slid slowly downward. Paradoxically, the development and security of Israel now became a pervasive philanthropic, political, and cultural concern of American Jewry as a whole.

In common with American citizens generally, Jews enjoyed an era of prolonged prosperity during the post-World War II years. Homecoming soldiers found jobs or attended college en masse under the liberal terms of the "GI Bill of Rights." Antisemitism in the United States all but disappeared from public view. Father Charles Coughlin had been silenced by his church, and a few agitators, notably G.L.K. Smith, were practically ignored. Active and largely successful efforts were made by American Jewish defense organizations to root out antisemitic and every other form of religious and racial discrimination in employment, housing, and higher education. Legislation to these ends in many states was spearheaded by the Jewish community, often in alliance with African American bodies such as the National Association for the Advancement of Colored People (NAACP), the Urban League, and a variety of church organizations. On the other hand, efforts to eliminate the exclusion of Jews from upper-level social clubs and from the management of major banks and corporations proved less successful. The basic trend for two decades following the end of World War II was the decline of antisemitism to the point where its disappearance was widely predicted. Even the feverish atmosphere of the anti-Communist fright from about 1947 to 1954 and the hunt for alleged Communists in government and strategic positions, during which a high proportion of the accused were Jews, did not significantly stir antisemitic sentiment.

The Cold War Era, 1950s–1980s

THE POSTWAR SETTING. For American Jews, the Cold War era centered around a paradox: The astonishing success and rapid upward mobility of the American Jewish community in the post-World War II era was accompanied by America's growing fear of the Soviet Union and potentially subversive anti-American elements, including instances in which Jews played a highly visible role. On the one hand, the postwar decades, as historian Lucy Dawidowicz has noted, were something of a "golden age" in which Jews became thoroughly acculturated, Americanized, economically prosperous, and professionally successful in virtually all quarters of American society. The self-confidence of organized American Jewry was perhaps nowhere more apparent than in the 1954 commemoration of the 300th anniversary of Jewish settlement in North America. The tercentenary committee deployed the inoffensive and patriotic branding message of "Man's Opportunities and Responsibilities under Freedom." Indeed, there was nothing particularly Jewish about this theme which (after months of deliberation and counsel with a variety of Jewish communal leaders and scholars) was noteworthy for its scrupulous neutrality. Rather, as the tercentenary committee explained, the anniversary was intended to celebrate the presumed congruence of American ideals and Jewish values:

> The theme should express the outstanding fact of the past 300 years of our participation in America; that it should describe the significance of the present day for American Jews, and that it should express the hopes and aspirations and objectives of the future for ourselves and for all Americans – indeed, for all human beings throughout the world.

Despite the note of triumphalism sounded by the committee – a recurring feature of the American Jewish experience termed the "cult of synthesis" by historian Jonathan D. Sarna – American Jewish society was in fact also shaped by the discordant social, cultural, and political realities of the Cold War era, including the Red Scare. Joseph McCarthy's persecutorial anti-Communist witch hunt, FBI director J. Edgar Hoover's ruthless subversion of numerous left-leaning American individuals and groups, and the widespread fear of Communist insurgency in American society leavened the American Jewish experience. Thus was Jewish communal success tempered by collective anxiety about the group's social status, lingering doubts about the promise of acculturation, and fear for the fragility of the liberal political enterprise.

Some outstanding examples help to illustrate this paradox. The case of communal leader Philip M. *Klutznik, for instance, is in many ways emblematic of American Jewish success in this period. Rising through the ranks of B'nai B'rith to become the fraternal organization's national president, Klutznik's professional career in public service led him from commissioner of Federal Public Housing under Presidents Franklin D. Roosevelt and Harry S. *Truman, to United States representative to the United Nations in the *Eisenhower, *Kennedy, and *Johnson administrations, and finally to the position of secretary of commerce under President Jimmy *Carter. Likewise, Henry *Kissinger, a refugee from Nazi Germany and Harvard-trained scholar, rose to become President Richard M. *Nixon's national security advisor in 1969 and was appointed secretary of state in 1975. The ending of the war in Vietnam, the normalization of relations with China, the conclusion of the Yom Kippur War, and the attempt to find a Middle East settlement were among the activities that made him the most iconic holder of this office in recent times. Speaking at a farewell luncheon given in his honor in 1977 by the Conference of Presidents of Major American Jewish Organizations, Kissinger declared, "I have never forgotten that thirteen members of my family died in a concentration camp." His authority in the realm of foreign affairs was enhanced not only by his negotiating skill but also by the fact that for many months Nixon was entangled in the Watergate Affair. His authority was reaffirmed when Gerald Ford, on succeeding Nixon, retained him in office. The meteoric trajectory of Klutznik, Kissinger, and other Jewish figures – for which there are precious few equivalents among other ethnic minorities in mid-20th century American society – was truly astonishing.

Meanwhile, a darker side of American society is reflected in the spectacle of three widely publicized episodes of anti-Communist activity in the United States in the 1950s, all of which centered on Jewish protagonists. First, the arrest in 1950 of Julius and Ethel Rosenberg, Jewish Communists alleged to have passed on atomic secrets to the Soviets, their highly controversial trial, and subsequent execution for treason in 1953 sent shock waves through the American Jewish community. Second, the vigorous campaign conducted by the Atomic Energy Commission to strip the credentials of German Jewish physicist J. Robert *Oppenheimer, the "father of the atomic bomb" and first director of the Los Alamos National Laboratory, garnered considerable public notoriety. In the event, Oppenheimer aroused the ire of scientists and politicians alike with his outspoken concern about the bomb's potential for mass destruction. Lewis L. Strauss, who served as chairman of the Atomic Energy Commission and was himself a prominent Republican and national leader of the American Jewish Committee, spearheaded the effort to discredit Oppenheimer as a Communist sympathizer and opponent of plans to develop the hydrogen bomb. The Oppenheimer affair proved to be a high water mark of the Red Scare; Oppenheimer's reputation was tarnished and Strauss resigned under fire. Subsequently, when President Dwight D. Eisenhower nominated Strauss to be secretary of commerce, his appointment was narrowly rejected in a Congressional showdown between U.S. Senate Democrats and Republicans. Finally, an excellent example of the complexity of this period is the case of *The Goldbergs*, a comedy about an American Jewish family that aired over radio from 1929 to 1947 and became a nationally popular television program from 1949 to 1956. Starring the actor Philip Loeb as Goldberg, the show became a target of the McCarthy witch hunt when Loeb was blacklisted after the right-wing anti-Communist magazine *Red Channels* accused him of being a Communist. Loeb denied the accusation, but the climate of fear induced by the McCarthy era and the hearings conducted by the House Committee on Un-American Activities caused him to lose his job and the CBS network soon dropped the show. Although Loeb continued to eke out a living as an actor thereafter, he succumbed to depression in 1955 and committed suicide.

Suspended between the antipodes of success and marginalization, American Jews faced the Cold War with a mixture of self-congratulatory confidence and well-founded anxiety. The ensuing decades would be marked by these themes, even as American Jews continued to develop and strengthen the infrastructure of their communal life.

POPULATION, DEMOGRAPHY, AND ECONOMIC ACTIVITY. The size of the American Jewish population increased rather slightly in the decades immediately following World War II. However, Jewish population estimates, while comparatively accurate for many cities, were unreliable for the country as a whole. The Jewish population, probably overestimated at 5,000,000 in 1950, stood at close to 5,500,000 in 1960, and then peaked at approximately 6,000,000 in the 1970s and 1980s. In comparison, the general American population numbered 140,000,000 in 1950 and rose to over 250,000,000 by the 1990s. In other words, Jews comprised slightly more than 3.5 percent of the American population at mid-century, but barely more than 2 percent by the close of the century. The reasons underlying the small Jewish population increase are strongly suggested by the median Jewish household size and the mean number of children born per 1,000 women, both lower than that of other religious or ethnic groups. With no more than about 12 percent of Jewish families having four or more children, Jewish natural increase was well below that of the U.S. as a whole.

Prior to the collapse of the Soviet Union in the late 1980s, immigration provided little of the Jewish increase in this period. From the end of World War II through the 1950s, for example, over 191,000 Jews settled in the United States, of whom nearly 120,000 arrived between 1947 and 1951. The large majority were Holocaust survivors, over 63,000 of whom entered under the provisions of the Displaced Persons Act of 1949. Otherwise, the quota system of the Johnson-Reed Act and its successor McCarran-Walter Act of 1952 remained intact until practically abolished by new legislation in 1965. In the late 1950s and 1960s about 73,000 Jewish immigrants arrived, most of whom tended to be Israelis (frequently of European birth), Cubans leaving the Castro regime, and Jews from Islamic lands. The United Service for New Americans, a descendant of the previous National Refugee Service together with the *Hebrew Immigrant Aid Society (HIAS), and local community organizations aided the immigrants. Some "new Americans" were professionally trained, but most tended to enter traditional Jewish occupations, such as garment cutters, salesmen, or shopkeepers.

Until the close of the 1960s, American Jewry retained a largely metropolitan character. Approximately 40 percent of American Jews dwelled in the New York City area, as had been the case since 1900. Meanwhile, the sum total of Jews living in the greater New York City region, northeastern New Jersey, and the nine next largest communities (Los Angeles, Chicago, Philadelphia, Boston, Miami, Washington, Cleveland, Baltimore, and Detroit) comprised 75 percent of American Jewry. The most notable demographic phenomenon in these and other urban centers was movement to the suburbs. As income and aspirations rose, large numbers of Jews quit the ever more congested and aging cities seeking greater space, more relaxed living, and a more affluent social environment. By the 1960s, 85 percent of Cleveland Jews lived beyond the city boundaries, and the same happened to virtually the entire Jewish population in Detroit, Newark, and Washington, D.C., within the decade. Every large city saw a considerable proportion of its middle class, including the Jewish community, relocate to the suburbs, while African American migration to many formerly Jewish neighborhoods precipitated formidable social tensions and problems between Jews and blacks.

Coincidental with the suburban movement, was the migration of large numbers of Jews within the United States. The increase of the Los Angeles Jewish population from 150,000 at the end of World War II to over 500,000 in the 1970s, and of Miami from 40,000 in the late 1940s to roughly 150,000 in 1970, was almost wholly the result of internal migration. Much of it came from the Middle West whose Jewish population failed to increase after the 1920s. Thus, Chicago, with 333,000 in the city at the end of World War II, actually declined to 285,000 for its metropolitan area by the 1970s. Milwaukee also lost – 30,000 to 24,500 – and centers such as Cleveland and Detroit did not increase. Boston's Jewish population increased from 137,000 in 1948 to over 176,000 in the 1970s, apparently owing to heavy Jewish participation in that area's scientific and technological growth.

In the decades following World War II a new occupational pattern of American Jewry also became evident. No systematic nationwide surveys were conducted until the 1970s, but until then many studies of individual communities made clear that employment in the professions was rising greatly, and proprietorship and management somewhat less so; skilled, semiskilled, and unskilled labor was sharply decreasing, and clerical and sales employment somewhat declining. Forestry, mining, and transportation in all forms hardly employed any Jews, as in the past, and the small contingent of Jewish farmers slowly decreased in size. The ascent of Jewish professionals in these decades was also a general phenomenon. In addition to the continuing prominence of Jews as physicians, lawyers, accountants, and teachers, they were prominent as scientific professionals in such new industries as electronics. Earlier occupational patterns lasted longer in New York City where a concentration of skilled and unskilled workers comprised about 28 percent of the Jewish labor force until the early 1960s.

In such professions as law, medicine, dentistry, and teaching Jews formed a clear majority of those employed. Industries in which they had once been the labor force, especially the garment industry, remained Jewish only at the higher levels of skill and in entrepreneurship. As entrepreneurs, Jews were extensively represented in urban retail trade, the building of homes and shopping centers, and in metropolitan real estate. The same could be said of such mass media areas as television, films, and advertising, and of cultural enterprises like book publishing, art dealing, and impresarioship in music and theater. Stock brokerage and other spheres of finance continued to involve Jewish firms and brokers, setting the stage for the return to prominence in subsequent decades of Jewish financiers, as was previously the case in the late 19th and early 20th centuries.

In sum, for the country as a whole the "baby boom" of the post-World War II era was followed by a steep decline in the birthrate. The American Jewish community shared generally in this trend. Ḥasidic Jewish communities were an exception in this regard; traditional values and attitudes prevailed and large families with an average of 6.5 children were the norm. Nonetheless, reinforcement of American Jewish life in this period came from unexpected sources. Estimates of the number of Israelis who settled in the United States in the 1970s and early 1980s vary between 300,000 and 500,000. Meanwhile, 70 percent of the Jews allowed to leave the Soviet Union between 1972 and 1981 chose to immigrate to the United States – more than 75,000 – and an additional 100,000 Jewish immigrants arrived from other countries in these years. By the end of the Cold War era, American Jews comprised 43 percent of world Jewry and 60 percent of diaspora Jewry.

COMMUNAL STRUCTURE. Economic prosperity, the gradual neutralization of once sharp internal ideological differences, the diminution of antisemitism, the waning of the cultural rift that once separated native-born and immigrant Jews, and growing social homogeneity resulted in a lengthy period of Jewish communal consensus that extended from the post-World War II years to the 1970s. In this period, the State of Israel became a unifying rather than divisive force. Funds were ample for generally agreed communal purposes in the United States and overseas. Communal interests focused primarily on local matters as Jewish suburbia built its institutions, while in older urban areas they had to struggle to survive or relocate. Nearly every city, except New York and Chicago, conducted a combined campaign for overseas and domestic needs and had some form of central Jewish community organization. The Jewish community councils, founded during the 1930s, generally merged with the older federations of Jewish philanthropies and were governed by an executive board and a none too potent community assembly of representatives from organizations. In some cities, however, contributors to the combined campaign above a minimal level (usually $10) were enfranchised to vote for a fixed proportion of the delegates to these assemblies. These central Jewish communal bodies promoted equal rights through their community relations committees, which coordinated the local efforts of the leading American Jewish membership organizations – e.g., American Jewish Committee, American Jewish Congress, B'nai B'rith, Hadassah, Jewish Labor Committee, Jewish War Veterans, and the National Council for Jewish Women. They also sponsored the local bureaus of Jewish education, settled intra-communal disputes, in some communities supervised *kashrut* (Jewish dietary law), and generally functioned as the recognized Jewish spokespersons in the general community. The social service agencies affiliated with the antecedent federations enjoyed far-reaching autonomy. The most important activity by far was the annual campaigns, whose proceeds were allocated, after negotiations, by carefully devised formulas.

At the national level, ideological groupings and specialization of activities evolved, but no stable central body developed. The aforementioned organizations coordinated some of their activities in the National Community Relations Advisory Council. The American Zionist Council did likewise for Zionist groups, especially on political issues related to Israel and the Middle East, and the Synagogue Council, with little power or religious authority, obtained occasional consensus among the denominational federations of synagogues. The military functions of the National Jewish Welfare Board were largely replaced by its peacetime activity of providing coordination and program assistance to approximately 300 Jewish community centers, and their 645,000 members, affiliated with it by 1960. The Council of Jewish Federations and Welfare Funds guided and counseled its constituents by means of nationwide meetings, through intensive studies of Jewish philanthropic policy, of the role of government in education and social service, and through the activities of various beneficiaries. In 1954 the Conference of Presidents of Major American Jewish Organizations (the "Presidents' Club") was established to consult informally in matters concerning Israel and overseas Jewish problems. By virtue of its age, size, prestige, and non-partisan Jewish character, B'nai B'rith tended to play a central role in such efforts. In 1963, in response to grass roots activity and pressure, the *National Conference of Soviet Jewry was established. With some variation, these groups and agencies defined the infrastructure of American Jewish life for the remainder of the 20th century.

SOCIAL AND CULTURAL LIFE. By mid-century the Jews as an overwhelmingly native-born group, extensively college-educated, and heavily concentrated in the mercantile and professional classes, with widespread social and cultural interests, began to assume a remarkable degree of prominence in American society. Their previously notable position as physicians, scientists, lawyers, psychoanalysts, and musicians not only continued but increased exponentially. As well, Jews began to excel in fields once closed or inaccessible to them. General estrangement from the American academy's longstanding preoccupation with British literature and the relative inattention of American Jews to the thematic content of American literature had tended to make Jewish writers in English very few. But beginning in the 1950s and 1960s a considerable number of American Jewish writers attained importance and true distinction. In this period, significant works were produced by the writers Saul *Bellow, Meyer *Levin, Norman *Mailer, Bernard *Malamud, Tillie *Olsen, Cynthia *Ozick, Grace *Paley, Chaim *Potok, Philip *Roth, Isaac Bashevis *Singer, Leon *Uris, and Elie *Wiesel, the playwright Arthur *Miller, the poets Delmore *Schwartz, Allen *Ginsberg, and Karl *Shapiro, and the critics Lionel *Trilling, Leslie *Fiedler, Alfred *Kazin, and Irving *Howe. (Interestingly, Kazin, originally an East European Jewish immigrant, helped to define the field of American literature with *On Native Grounds* (1942), one of the first systematic and comprehensive studies of literature by native-born American writers.) The wave of postwar literary creativity opened the door to many other successful American Jewish writers in the 1970s and 1980s including the poets Allen *Grossman, Joseph *Heller, Robert *Pinsky, and Adrienne *Rich, the novelists E.M. *Broner, Melvin Jules *Bukiet, E.L. *Doctorow, Howard *Fast, Allegra Goodman, Marge Piercy, Kate *Simon, and Art *Spiegelman, the playwrights Tony *Kushner and Wendy *Wasserstein, and the critic Harold *Bloom.

As Jewish subjects surged to the forefront of literary interest, novels and short stories of extremely varied quality on themes including the Holocaust, Israel, and middle-class American Jewish life, sold in the millions to gentiles as well as Jews. Plays and television programs on Jewish themes attracted vast audiences and were eventually produced on nationwide television. Many of the writers mentioned above contributed to this movement, and "Jewish" became a literary genre that now competed commercially with the "Southern" and "Middle Western" genres in popularity. Occasional voices, questioning its integration into American literature and even alleged domination by a New York Jewish circle, surfaced in *Commentary*, *Partisan Review*, and the *New York Review of Books*. Whether literary politics or legitimate criticism, there was no doubt that Jews were among the principal purveyors of American culture – as impresarios of music, theatrical producers, editors, book publishers, and film and television producers.

Another major trend was that of Jews into the arts and sciences on university faculties. During the 1930s and earlier only a few hundred Jews held academic positions, mainly in the municipal colleges of New York City, but at the close of the 1960s an estimated 30,000 Jews composed about one-tenth of all college faculty members. They were distributed in all fields, although physics, sociology, and psychology particularly attracted a high proportion of Jews. No field of study, however, lacked notable Jewish contributors. Jewish professors could be found in almost all colleges, but especially in public research universities and in the "Ivy League."

By and large, Jewish contributors to American cultural life, at least until the middle 1960s, continued to be the liberal left, with echoes of earlier radicalism. To the wider Jewish community its Jewish public intellectuals were somehow a source of concern. Could they be made to demonstrate positive interest in established American Jewish life and American Judaism, and why did most of them shy away from participation in the communal infrastructure of American Jews? A symposium on "Jewishness and the Younger Intellectuals," published in *Commentary* in 1961, strongly suggested that under the cultural consensus and religiosity of the 1950s lay the alienated restlessness of many of the highly acculturated, talented younger generation.

Especially visible in the postwar decades was the rise of an elite cohort of Jewish artists around whom the world of American musical theater grew and flourished. It is difficult to overstress the profound impact in this period on American culture of musical figures Leonard *Bernstein, Marvin *Hamlisch, Oscar *Hammerstein II, Sheldon *Harnick, Larry *Hart, Jerome *Kern, Alan Jay *Lerner, Frank *Loesser, Jerome *Robbins, Richard *Rodgers, Stephen *Sondheim, and other lesser known figures. Like Irving *Berlin, Aaron *Copland, George *Gershwin, and Ira *Gershwin before them, whose impact on the decades prior to mid-century was profound, the second-generation of American Jewish composers, conductors, lyricists, and choreographers left an indelible imprint on the Broadway musical tradition with such classics as *South Pacific* (1949), *Guys and Dolls* (1950), *The King and I* (1951), *My Fair Lady* (1956), *Gypsy* (1959), *The Sound of Music* (1959), *Camelot* (1960), *West Side Story* (1961), *A Funny Thing Happened on the Way to the Forum* (1962); *Fiddler on the Roof* (1964), *Company* (1970), *A Chorus Line* (1975); *Sweeney Todd* (1979), and *Into the Woods* (1987).

Parallel to the Broadway musical tradition was the arena of American popular music, whose ranks swelled throughout these decades to include a variety of influential Jewish musical artists and record producers. Even a cursory review in this regard illustrates the diverse wealth of American Jewish talent that helped shape this dynamic aspect of American culture. Some singers and entertainers openly identified with American Jewish life while others, like the diva Beverly *Sills (born Belle Miriam Silverman), one of America's greatest opera sopranos, did not and remained virtually indistinguishable from the larger canvas of American popular music. Any list in this regard must include artists as diverse as band leader Herb *Alpert, the singer-entertainers Sammy *Davis, Jr. (a convert to Judaism), Eydie *Gorme, Bette *Midler, Allan *Sherman, Dinah *Shore, and Barbra *Streisand, the singer-songwriters Neil *Diamond, Art *Garfunkel, Billy *Joel, Carole *King, Barry *Manilow, Linda *Ronstadt, Neil *Sedaka, Carly *Simon, and Paul *Simon, and the folk singers Theodore *Bikel, Bob *Dylan, Arlo *Guthrie, Janis *Ian, and Phil *Ochs.

Likewise, the world of modern American art was enriched and shaped by an array of Jewish artists including the painter-sculptors Boris *Aronson, Leonard *Baskin, Judy *Chicago, Helen *Frankenthaler, Marc *Rothko, George *Segal, Richard *Serra, Ben *Shahn, Raphael *Soyer, and Max *Weber as well as the influential art critic Clement *Greenberg and even the comic book creators Jack *Kirby and Stan *Lee.

As noted previously, Hollywood, too, played an increasingly central role in the complex relationship between Jews and American culture. Among the most visible and important Jewish actors, television stars, and film makers from mid-century forward were Woody *Allen, Alan *Arkin, Milton *Berle, Mathew *Broderick, Adrien Brody, Mel *Brooks, George *Burns, Sid *Caesar, Billy *Crystal, Tony *Curtis, Kirk *Douglas, Michael *Douglas, Richard *Dreyfuss, Peter *Falk, Marty *Feldman, Tova *Feldshuh, Harvey *Fierstein, Fyvush Finkel, Harrison *Ford, Jeff *Goldblum, Elliot *Gould, Harold Gould, Joel *Grey, Charles Grodin, Goldie *Hawn, Judd Hirsch, Dustin *Hoffman, Madeline *Kahn, Danny *Kaye, Alan *King, Jack *Klugman, Harvey Korman, Lisa *Kudrow, Hal Linden, Jackie *Mason, Walter *Matthau, Zero *Mostel, Jerry Orbach, Sarah Jessica *Parker, Mandy *Patinkin, Gilda *Radner, Tony *Randall, Carl *Reiner, Rob *Reiner, Adam *Sandler, Roy *Scheider, Jerry *Seinfeld, Peter *Sellers, Joan Micklin *Silver, Ron *Silver, Steven *Spielberg, Ben *Stiller, Barbra *Streisand, Chaim *Topol, Gene *Wilder, and Henry *Winkler.

The broad range of Jewish participation in American culture and, likewise, the integration of American themes, rhythms, and modalities into the work of Jewish artists in the 20th century, defies easy explanation. Reflecting on the complexity of this phenomenon, the historian Stephen J. Whitfield has observed that "like religion, culture should not be regarded as the stable expression of a people with an immutable set of attributes. The features that are more evident are borrowing, adaptation, and inventiveness as well as continuity." In the process of negotiating the dynamic and creative tensions that link their Jewish and American identities, Jewish artists from all walks of the contemporary scene – music, sculpture, painting, theater, and literature – have imbued American society with important and unparalleled cultural achievements.

WOMEN. In the 1960s and 1970s, against the backdrop of the counter-culture movement that spread across the country, there emerged a wave of feminism that sought to refashion the place of women and introduce new ways of considering gender in American society. Among the outstanding early leaders of the feminist movement were two Jewish activists, the theorist Betty *Friedan (born Bettye Naomi Goldstein in Peoria, Illinois) and political maverick Bella *Abzug. Friedan's book *The Feminine Mystique* (1963), which depicted the repressed domestic lives of middle-class American women in the decades following World War II, became a national best-seller and is often credited with energizing the women's movement in this period. Abzug, a daughter of poor Russian Jewish immigrants, who grew up in the Bronx where she joined the socialist Zionist youth group Ha-Shomer ha-Ẓa'ir as a teenager, went on to become active in New York State and national Democratic politics. In 1970 Abzug garnered countrywide attention while campaigning for election to the U.S. House of Representatives with the statement, "This woman's place is in the House – the House of Representatives." Friedan, a co-founder of the National Organization for Women in 1966, and Abzug were both outspoken advocates for the passage of the Equal Rights Amendment and public opponents of the Vietnam War. In 1979 they were among the founders of the National Women's Political Caucus.

A figure of equal importance to the emergence of American feminism in this period was Carol (Friedman) *Gilligan, who single-handedly transformed the field of psychology with the publication in 1982 of her pathbreaking study *In a Different Voice: Psychological Theory and Women's Development*. Gilligan, who as a child participated actively in the Reconstructionist movement's flagship Society for the Advancement of Judaism in New York City, has described herself "a Jewish child of the Holocaust era." Her strong moral and political convictions, which soon found expression through her participation in the civil rights movements, were ultimately manifest in her scholarship. In 1964 she completed a Ph.D. in psychology at Harvard University. After teaching at the University of Chicago, she returned to Harvard, where she worked closely with Erik Erikson and Lawrence Kohlberg, two eminent psychological theorists. At this juncture, Gilligan began to closely examine the ways female identity and experience were virtually ignored by mainstream psychology. *In a Different Voice*, which stemmed from research conducted at the Emma Willard girls school in Troy, New York, provoked a national debate and catapulted Gilligan to the forefront of the American feminist movement and utterly revolutionized the fields of education, psychology, and women's studies. Subsequently, Gilligan was named "Woman of the Year" in 1984 by *Ms.* magazine and in 1996 *Time* magazine named her one of the 25 most influential figures in American society.

While Jewish female activists such as Friedan, Abzug, and Gilligan swiftly became household names in wider American society, an equally explicit albeit more subtle Jewish brand of feminism emerged in this period, too – with profound implications for the future of American Jewry. The burgeoning of American Jewish publications in these years throws light on this trend as well as a pervasive desire to reorient perceptions of women in modern Jewish life generally. Consider, for example, a few disparate works that illustrate significant shifts on the American Jewish scene. First, *The Jewish Catalog* (1973), an enormously popular do-it-yourself guide to Judaism and Jewish life in American society, contained a chapter on Jewish women emphasizing "consciousness-raising" and suggesting new "areas of priorities for interested Jewish women." Second, *Women in the Kibbutz* (1975), a controversial multi-generational study by the sociologists Lionel Tiger and Joseph Shepher, focused attention on the unique experiment of Israeli communal living and, in the words of the publisher, raised "new questions about the goals of the Women's Liberation Movement." Third, Anne Lapidus Lerner's "'Who Hast Not Made Me a Man': The Movement for Equal Rights for Women in American Jewry," published in the *American Jewish Year Book* of 1977, accurately pointed to the vitality and durability of feminism in contemporary American Jewish life. The sentiment of the period was summed up in Lerner's bold assertion that "Queen Esther no longer reigns supreme in the hearts of young Jewish women. More and more of them are admiring Vashti's spunk instead." In the final analysis, she optimistically intoned, as "the image of Queen Esther is becoming less persuasive … the new Jewish feminism must be confronted and accommodated to ensure the survival of American Jewry."

As participants and observers alike created a new literature and public arena about Jewish women and for feminist discourse – e.g., Trude *Weiss-Rosmarin's "The Unfreedom of Jewish Women" (1970); **Lillith* magazine, established in 1976 by Susan Weidman Schneider and Aviva Cantor; Blu Greenberg's *On Women and Judaism* (1979); etc. – some female scholars turned to history in order to discern "models from [the] past." "From them we learn," explained Elizabeth Koltun in *The Jewish Woman: New Perspectives* (1976), "that we are not the first Jewish women discontent with 'women's place' and that, concomitantly, Jewish feminism does not, in fact, represent the total break with our past which our critics would have us believe."

It was not by chance that of the four role models featured in Koltun's anthology, two were Zionists: Henrietta Szold, the American founder of Hadassah and head of Youth Aliyah, and Raḥel Yanait Ben-Zvi, a Labor Zionist leader and founder of the *Ha-Shomer self-defense organization in the Yishuv (pre-state Israeli society). Likewise, a bibliographic "Guide to Jewish Women's Activities" in *The Jewish Catalog* begins with five autobiographical works written and edited by Zionist women activists: Raḥel Yanait Ben-Zvi, Geula *Cohen, Irma L. Lindheim, Raḥel *Katznelson-Shazar, and Ada *Maimon. It also contains numerous references to women in the Zionist movement, the Yishuv, and contemporary Israel. In another instance, a slim volume titled *Sisters of Exile* (1974), published by the American Zionist youth movement *Habonim, focused on the lives of significant women in Jewish history and elevated Zionist activists to the pantheon of modern Jewish heroes. It also found its way into many Jewish studies classes on American college campuses in an era when such information was still largely ignored and inaccessible. Finally, it is worth noting Golda *Meir's bestselling autobiography, *My Life* (1975), which enjoyed a mass distribution in the United States.

Viewed historically, the developments described above are not surprising. As sociologist Sylvia Barack Fishman has observed, the close identification of Jewish women with Zionism and Israel in the 1970s and 1980s – despite the checkered track records of both vis-à-vis the equality and empowerment of women – was a self-defining characteristic of American Jewish feminism in this period. In fact, despite external pressures many Jewish feminists refused to sever their links to Zionism. The scholar Paula *Hyman explains the strong similarities between Jewish feminism and Zionism from a historical perspective:

> Like Zionism, Jewish feminism emerged from an encounter of Jews who were deeply concerned with the fate of their group with secular Western culture… Jewish feminism, too, did not spring in an unmediated way from Jewish tradition… It took secularized Jews, influenced by the rise of feminism in America in the 1960s, to establish a Jewish feminist movement that provided a radically modern form to strivings for gender equality.

The profile of American Jewish feminism in this period reveals a *mélange* of secular, spiritual, modern, radical, and feminist impulses as well as a broad range of perspectives on women, Judaism, Zionism, and Israel. In the words of historian Judith R. *Baskin, "expanding our knowledge of Jewish women not only enlarges what we know about Jewish history and the Jewish experience but redefines our very conceptions of what Jews and Judaism were and continue to be about."

RELIGION. American Jewish religious life broadened considerably in the decades following World War II as Judaism was all but officially recognized as the third religion of American society. Will Herberg's celebrated polemic *Protestant, Catholic, Jew* (1960) and the widespread use of the term "Judeo-Christian" illustrate this trend. Public commissions habitually included a Jewish member alongside Protestants and Catholics, and official ceremonies, including presidential inaugurations, arranged for Jewish as well as Christian clerical participation. The 1950s was a period of unprecedented interest in Jewish religious life and thought, as part of the "revival of religion" in American culture during those years. The writings of such figures as philosopher Martin *Buber and theologian Abraham J. *Heschel received widespread attention. Numerous interfaith institutes and assemblies were held. It is no accident that among the ideologues who had the most impact on the various denominations of American Judaism – Abraham J. Heschel, Joseph *Soloveitchik, Menachem *Schneersohn, and Emil *Fackenheim – all, with the exception of Fackenheim, were scholars with deep roots in Eastern Europe who spent some of their most formative years pursuing higher education in Western Europe, primarily, Berlin, and then emigrated to the United States where they quickly emerged as the most creative authorities for their disciples on how to relate to the Jewish religious tradition in a pluralistic, technological, and open society.

Although it is customary to divide American Judaism in this period according to the tripartite model of Reform, Conservative, and Orthodox synagogue movements, each with central institutions and recognized leaders, the reality resembled more a spectrum in which the membership, beliefs, and practices, and even the rabbinate of one group shaded into the next. The number of denominationally identified congregations grew rapidly. In the early 1950s there were nearly 500 Reform congregations, 100 more than in the previous decade, while the Conservative movement added more than 150 synagogues in the same period and rose beyond 500 congregations. (Many had been Orthodox and evolved into Conservatism.) There were more than 700 affiliated Orthodox congregations, but many were inactive leftovers from immigrant days. The increase continued, so that in the 1960s the congregations numbered more than 550 Reform, 600 Conservative, and 700 Orthodox. The organized American rabbinate in 1955 counted 1,127 men in the two large Orthodox professional bodies, 677 Reform, and 598 Conservative. In 1960 the U.S. Bureau of Labor Statistics reached similar conclusions when it identified 2,517 congregational rabbis, 944 in "specialized Jewish community service," and 148 at temporary work or unemployed. To these 3,609 rabbis the Bureau of Labor Statistics added some 650 retired or out of the profession, and there were probably others privately ordained not functioning as rabbis. A 1950 estimate placed total synagogue membership at a maximum of 450,000 families, besides about 250,000 persons who occupied seats in the synagogue on the High Holy Days. Perhaps 1,485,000 Jews were thus synagogally affiliated, and this figure apparently increased during the 1950s. Thus around 1960 there were over 450,000 families in Conservative and Reform congregations. The number of Orthodox Jews could not be properly determined, but a 1965 study suggested 300,000 committed Orthodox individuals. Altogether, the largest institutional and membership growth was found in the Conservative movement, which counted over 800 congregations affiliated with the United Synagogue of America in 1970 as compared with some 700 in the Union of American Hebrew Congregations in that year.

A wave of synagogue construction illustrated this increase of affiliation, as did the burgeoning of Jewish communities in new suburban districts. In the decade following World War II an estimated $50–60 million was spent on synagogue building, and the ten-year period that followed may have seen twice that amount expended. Many synagogues, especially in the suburbs, accommodated not only worship and study but also quite elaborate social functions and even sports and social recreation. The tendency of synagogues to act as Jewish community centers sometimes brought them into rivalry with non-synagogal Jewish centers and Young Men's Hebrew Associations and Young Women's Hebrew Associations, which were professionally equipped for such work. The latter were engaged in reorienting their outlook and activities toward a more explicit Jewish program, as recommended in the influential Jewish Welfare Board survey (1948) directed by Oscar I. *Janowsky. The synagogue-Jewish center rivalry had some ideological basis: synagogal claims to primacy as the embodiment of Jewish religion and tradition, versus the centers' emphasis on their broadly Jewish character accommodating secular as well as religious members.

Notwithstanding great material growth, Jewish religious life hardly became more intensive. Although American Jews in surveys tended to describe themselves as "conservative," this no doubt indicated a general preference for traditional religious rituals rather than actual Conservative religious belief or synagogue affiliation. There was widespread well-documented interest in Judaism on college campuses, and numerous instances occurred of young people adopting traditional religious life and beliefs. Altogether, however, only small minorities, estimated variously between 10 and 20 percent, observed the Sabbath scrupulously, maintained the dietary laws in full, and observed daily prayer. Reform, Conservative, and Orthodox religious groupings were found in every Jewish community of any size, but some were strong in particular cities. Thus, the centers of Orthodoxy in the 1950s and 1960s were in Boston, Baltimore, and above all New York City. Philadelphia and Detroit were strongholds of Conservative Judaism, while Cincinnati, Cleveland, San Francisco, and Milwaukee were especially favorable environments for the Reform movement.

The denominations had their struggles over internal issues. The Reform majority, now pro-Zionist, moved toward increased ritual and traditionalism, over the opposition of a vigorous "classical Reform" minority, and congregations leaned in either direction. The majority of Reform rabbis attempted to utilize the classic sources of Jewish law in religious problems. Among the Conservatives differences tended to be muffled in loyalty to the central institution, the Jewish Theological Seminary of America and its profoundly traditionalist faculty. The main issue was Jewish law and the extent to which it could be modified and by whom. Yet while Conservative rabbis and scholars debated the *halakhic* problems of change, the lay membership proceeded in its own un-*halakhic* way of life.

Orthodoxy meanwhile shed its status as the Judaism of Yiddish-speaking East European immigrants after the number of acculturated, middle-class congregations with modernist American-trained rabbinic leadership sharply increased. There was also a large accretion to Orthodoxy from post-1945 immigration, among whom ḥasidic and yeshivah leaders were prominent. Tensions arose between these two segments for the latter tended to be non-Zionist or anti-Zionist and considered the secular world and non-Orthodox forms of American Jewishness to have improperly influenced American Orthodoxy. As well, Orthodoxy became intellectually active and vibrant in this period as religious and philosophic writing was produced, including American reprintings of the Talmud and nearly the entire corpus of rabbinic classics.

Nonetheless, the *National Jewish Population Survey* of 1970 revealed that American Jewish life was marked by substantial acculturation among young people and the break up of family cohesion. These findings aroused considerable concern among American Jewish leaders from across the social, religious, and political spectrum and reinvigorated the long-standing public debate over the maintenance of a separate Jewish identity and the wholehearted acceptance of the Jews by a society that stands for the elimination of barriers based on race or creed.

The prospective decline of American Jewish religious life prompted some rabbis and congregational lay leaders to call on the synagogue movements to review their traditional reluctance to accept proselytes. Small groups encouraging converts had been at work for some time but the idea took on a new dimension in 1978 when Alexander *Schindler, president of the Union of American Hebrew Congregations (UAHC), proposed that American Judaism (or at any rate its Reform wing) actively seek converts from among the religiously unaffiliated: "I believe that it is time for our movement to launch a carefully conceived Outreach Program aimed at all Americans who are unchurched and who are seeking roots in religion." The UAHC board of trustees responded positively to Schindler's proposal.

Renewal efforts were manifest in other areas of the Reform movement as well. The most dramatic illustration in this regard was the ordination in 1972 by the Hebrew Union College – Jewish Institute of Religion of America's first woman rabbi, Sally *Priesand.

> As I sat in the historic Plum Street Temple [in Cincinnati, Ohio], waiting to accept the ancient rite of *smikhah* [ordination], I couldn't help but reflect on the implications of what was about to happen. For thousands of years women in Judaism had been second-class citizens. They were not permitted to own property. They could not serve as witnesses. They did not have the right to initiate divorce proceedings. They were not counted in the *minyan* [quorum]. Even in Reform Judaism they were not permitted to participate fully in the life of the synagogue. With my ordination all that was going to change; one more barrier was about to be broken.

Priesand's ordination represented not only a major departure from Reform's institutional culture but also portended a sea change in the American rabbinate and, in time, American Judaism as a whole. Meanwhile, Reform liturgical innovations resulted in a triad of new prayer books: *Gates of Prayer* (1973), the *Union Haggadah* (1974), and *Gates of Repentance* (1978). In direct line of succession to the *Union Prayer Book*

(1892), the volumes retained traces of Reform's earlier radicalism, but exhibited in style and content important theological changes and an emphasis on ceremonial tradition. Likewise, *Shaare Mitzvah* (Gates of Observance) (1979) encouraged Reform Jews to "return" to personal observances. Moreover, as a consequence of the rise of intermarriage, the CCAR called upon its members not to participate in such ceremonies. The New York Board of Rabbis subsequently resolved to bar those who did so from membership. In 1975 the Rabbinical Council of America passed a similar resolution.

Conservative Judaism underwent a significant paradigm shift in this period. In 1972 the Rabbinical Assembly published a new High Holiday *maḥzor* (prayer book). It departed from earlier versions in its modern translation and the incorporation of new material, including an alternative to the silent *amidah* (personal recitation). The martyrology for Yom Kippur was revised considerably to include non-liturgical texts and commemorative material related to the Holocaust. The question of women's rights, which for opposite reasons excited no significant discussion in either Orthodoxy or Reform, was a matter of vigorous debate in the Conservative movement. In 1972 the Rabbinical Assembly of America determined it should be left to individual congregations whether or not to include women in the *minyan* (religious quorum). The ordination of women to the Conservative rabbinate also came under discussion at the Assembly's 1974 convention, where it was rejected. The issue caused deep division within the seminary faculty and the Conservative rabbinate. In the meantime, however, one Conservative congregation appointed Sandy Eisenberg *Sasso, who was ordained by the Reconstructionist Rabbinical Seminary.

A survey of Conservative movement members presented to the 1979 biennial convention of the United Synagogue of America generated pessimistic conclusions as to the future of that body. The findings were based on age composition, the low proportion of members among third-generation American Jews, and the failure to bring about a commitment to Conservative Judaism among the majority of the children of Conservative synagogue members. Moreover, despite the enthusiastic efforts of a group of young Israel-oriented activists, the United Synagogue of America refused to endorse the establishment in 1977 of Mercaz (Hebrew for "Center"), a Conservative Zionist group that claimed an enrollment of 10,000 members. Ironically, the American Zionist Federation accepted Mercaz as an affiliate. In 1979 Mercaz announced plans for the creation of a moshav (collective settlement) in Israel. On the eve of Rosh Hashanah 5740 (September 1979) the chief rabbis of Jerusalem issued a statement vigorously denouncing Conservative Judaism. In connection with this it was revealed that there were 29 Conservative congregations in Israel.

The twinning of the Reform and Conservative movement's positions vis-à-vis Israel became apparent in this period. In 1977 Reform and Conservative representatives together met Israeli Prime Minister Menahem *Begin and sent a deputation to the Jewish state in an effort to prevent an alteration in the *Law of Return called for by the Orthodox. In addition they worked together in 1978 to secure from the Twenty-Ninth World Zionist Congress a resolution calling for equal rights for all quarters of Jewish life. The determination of the Orthodox to resist any encroachment on their special status in Israel generated a strong counterforce among American Jewish leaders, and the ambiguities of Reform in the matter of *halakhah*, particularly as related to marriage and conversion, made cooperation with the Conservative movement problematic.

Orthodoxy, too, increased its assertiveness in this period within and beyond the organized American Jewish community. The growth of Orthodoxy conformed to the climate of the times. Throughout the 1970s liberal churches in the United States lost support while fundamentalist Christianity (which developed a distinct political thrust) gained in strength. Of the several strata of Orthodox Judaism, the ḥasidic sector became the most conspicuous. Among the Ḥasidim those adhering to the Lubavitcher *rebbe* became the most widely known because of the missionary work they conducted among the non-Orthodox.

Ḥasidic strength was centered in Brooklyn, where identifiable groups settled in specific sections of the borough – the Satmar (see *Teitelbaum) in Williamsburg, the Lubavitcher (see *Chabad) in Crown Heights, and the *Bobover in Borough Park. In 1977 the serious differences between the Lubavitcher and Satmar sects deteriorated to the extent of an inter-ḥasidic riot in Brooklyn. In 1979 differences between the *Belzer and Satmar Ḥasidim in Jerusalem spilled over in violence between them in New York. Though they maintained complete independence of the organized American Jewish community, the ḥasidic leaders developed an important web of contacts in the world of politics. An expanding group of followers (owing to a high birthrate and proselytism), well-defined communal goals, and high voter turnout gave them considerable political leverage, resulting in increased government aid for their projects.

EDUCATION AND CULTURE. The relation between church and state, especially in the field of education, was a sensitive issue in this period. The Jewish community maintained its historic opposition to religious observances in governmental functions and particularly in the public school system. This stand was put to the test, especially over Catholic demands for government aid to their parochial school system. A series of United States Supreme Court decisions that permitted private schools to receive school buses, lunches, and textbooks from the government was generally regretted, while decisions that barred school prayers and any active role for schools in sponsoring outside sectarian religious instruction were widely applauded by Jews. The passage of the Education Act of 1964 and subsequent legislation, providing limited federal aid for private schools, tended to quiet the issue.

American Jews also opposed school programs that aimed to inculcate "moral and spiritual values" in children. Local disputes frequently erupted, typically in predominantly Christian suburbs to which a substantial number of Jews had moved, due to Jewish opposition to Christmas observances in the public schools; combined Christmas-Hanukah observances were a syncretistic "compromise." Thus, the American Jewish community continued its historic affinity for the public schools provided they were religiously neutral. Among Jewish organizations the American Jewish Congress took the most rigorous separationist position, while the American Jewish Committee leaned toward a more pragmatic acceptance of the prevailing public policy. Orthodox Jewry, which had few children in the public schools, opposed rigorous church-state separation in education, partly in hopes of securing public funds for their hard-pressed day schools.

After 1950 Hebrew literary creativity in the United States nearly vanished as Israel increasingly monopolized talent and provided a mass audience for writers. Yiddish letters also continued their decline, largely on account of linguistic assimilation. Significant Yiddish writers continued to publish, however, including Chaim *Grade and Isaac Bashevis Singer, who in English translation became an American literary celebrity during the 1960s. Yiddish was no longer the language of the Jewish masses. In 1971 the *Tag-Morgen Zhurnal* (Day-Morning Journal) one of the two remaining Yiddish dailies in New York City ceased publication while the *Forverts* (The Forward) remained afloat only through philanthropic support. Only the *Allgemeine Journal*, a Yiddish weekly newspaper close to the Lubavitcher movement, enjoyed a measure of success. The remaining publications of note were the monthly *Zukunft*, scientific literature produced by the *YIVO Institute for Jewish Research, and various organizational periodicals. Ironically, as the prestige of Yiddish seemed to peak in the 1970s, Irving Howe's celebrated *World of Our Fathers* (1976), an epic history of East European Jewish immigration to the United States, became a national bestseller, and in 1978 Isaac Bashevis Singer was awarded the Nobel Prize for literature. In short, Yiddish as a living language – except among ḥasidic Jews – all but disappeared.

By contrast, American Jewish cultural activity in English surged throughout this period. The mainstay of the weekly Anglo-Jewish press, whose news came from the *Jewish Telegraphic Agency, were Jewish monthlies and quarterlies like *American Jewish Congress Monthly*, *Commentary*, *Hadassah Magazine*, *Jewish Frontier*, *Judaism*, *Midstream*, *Moment Magazine*, the *Reconstructionist*, *Shma*, and *Tikkun* – some of which were of the highest standard. Nor was it longer unusual to read of Jewish affairs in the general press, and television and general magazines also frequently presented Jewish material from which unpleasant stereotypes had long been eliminated.

University presses and commercial publishers issued serious works on Jewish subjects, in addition to the best-selling novels. Jewish scholarship, while still concentrated in seminaries and yeshivot, slowly began to find a place in universities with the establishment of academic chairs in Jewish studies and the rise to national prominence under its founding president Abram *Sachar of *Brandeis University, a Jewish-sponsored non-sectarian university which was established in 1948. To the generation of mature, European-trained scholars was added a new one educated in the United States and frequently in Israel. Learned studies of outstanding merit in Bible, theology, and homiletics, medieval and modern Jewish languages and literature, and Jewish philosophy, history, political science, sociology, anthropology, and folklore were produced by elder scholars and their younger American-born colleagues. Notwithstanding a new, respectful attitude toward Jewish scholarship, the relatively low Jewish educational level of much of American Jewry often made such works inaccessible.

Meanwhile, participation in Jewish educational institutions surged as school enrollment increased, owing particularly to the post-1945 "baby boom" from some 268,000 in 1950 to over 589,000 in the 1960s. In this period, an estimated 80 percent of American Jewish children received Jewish education at some time during their school years. Over half went to Sunday schools, which were generally attached to Reform congregations, and perhaps one-third to weekday congregational schools, usually branches of Conservative synagogues. A striking and somewhat controversial increase was that of day schools, most of them under Orthodox auspices, which enrolled approximately 80,000 children in 1970. The lesser expansion of yeshivah high schools and of yeshivot for full-time talmudic study was also conspicuous. As these schools grew the communally supported Talmud Torahs of earlier decades sharply declined owing to changing religious trends within the Jewish community and the change of urban neighborhoods. In this climate, secular Yiddish education barely survived. Local Jewish welfare funds began to appropriate more for Jewish education, mainly toward central bureaus and specialized services. Notwithstanding financial improvement and the desire of most parents to send their child to some Jewish school, Jewish education remained brief and superficial for most pupils, and was severely handicapped by a seemingly insoluble shortage of qualified teachers.

At the beginning of the 1970s, the *National Jewish Population Survey* reported that more than 80 percent of Jewish males received some Jewish education at some time in their lives, and about the same percentage of Jewish boys celebrated their bar *mitzvah*. For females the proportion receiving some Jewish education was less. Within this general framework, the picture of Jewish education exhibited some marked contrasts. A survey undertaken in 1979 by the American Association for Jewish Education estimated total student enrollment in Jewish educational institutions to be 357,107. Furthermore, the study noted the growth of the Jewish day school movement. Whereas in 1946 there were 69 Jewish day schools with 10,000 pupils, in 1979 there were 378 with 90,675 pupils. Total enrollment figures showed that 35.6 percent of all pupils attended Reform schools, 29.5 percent Conservative, 24.1 percent Orthodox, 7.1 percent communal, 3.6 percent independent, and 0.1 percent Yiddish. The proportion of Orthodox schools in greater New York was greater, amounting to 53.6 percent.

THE CONVULSIONS OF THE 1960S. Toward the end of the 1960s, the American Jewish position seemed stable. Population held to predictable rates, immigration was minimal and readily absorbed, and demographic and occupational trends continued as they had from approximately 1950. Meanwhile, Israel attracted considerable political and financial support and tourism, and the institutions of the Jewish community were generally well financed and seemed capable of dealing with most of the problems coming up on their agendas. Late in the 1960s, however, quite unanticipated matters and issues arose which stirred unusual interest and anxiety.

The accession of Pope *John XXIII in 1958 and the Vatican II Ecumenical Council, which he convened, inaugurated sweeping changes in the Roman Catholic Church. These included a major attempt to rectify the ancient anti-Jewish record of the Church and to meet belated worldwide criticism of the generally passive and indifferent attitude of Pope *Pius XII during the Holocaust. The movement within the Church to "exonerate" the Jews collectively of the charge of "deicide" and to formally recognize the theological legitimacy of Judaism was highly active in the United States, and stirred considerable American Jewish participation and enthusiasm. A period of Catholic-Jewish theological conversation and inter-faith dialogue commenced, in which Cardinal Augustine Bea and American prelates were leaders. The most prominent American Jewish spokesman in this regard was the theologian Rabbi Abraham J. Heschel. The final document issued by Vatican II in 1965 disappointed high hopes. While Catholic silence (as well as that of Protestants) during the Arab preparations to annihilate Israel in May 1967 was very disillusioning, Catholic-Jewish dialogue continued, but in a subdued key.

The acquisition of equal rights by African Americans had long been a goal of legal and political action, as well as philanthropic endeavor, by Jews. Not only did such Jewish organizations as the American Jewish Committee and the American Jewish Congress possess considerable track records as supporters of legislation and litigants in court in order to secure black rights, but individual Jews since the days of Louis Marshall, Julius Rosenwald, and others had long been a source of activists and funds in these struggles, dating back to significant charitable gifts to historically black colleges in the South. During the Civil Rights era of the mid-1960s young Jews constituted, by some reports, as high as 50 percent of all the white student youth who participated in grassroots political activity aimed at the enfranchisement and improvement of the African American community's socio-economic conditions, particularly in the southern United States. A particularly cogent expression of the American Jewish perspective was voiced in 1963 by Rabbi Joachim Prinz, president of the American Jewish Congress, at the March on Washington, where he stood together with the Rev. Martin Luther King and Rabbi Abraham Joshua Heschel before the Lincoln Memorial:

> I speak to you as an American Jew.
>
> As Americans we share the profound concern of millions of people about the shame and disgrace of inequality and injustice which make a mockery of the great American idea.
>
> As Jews we bring to this great demonstration, in which thousands of us proudly participate, a twofold experience – one of the spirit and one of our history.
>
> In the realm of the spirit, our fathers taught us thousands of years ago that when God created man, He created him as everybody's neighbor. Neighbor is not a geographic term. It is a moral concept. It means our collective responsibility for the preservation of man's dignity and integrity.
>
> From our Jewish historic experience of three and a half thousand years we say: Our ancient history began with slavery and the yearning for freedom. During the Middle Ages my people lived for a thousand years in the ghettos of Europe. Our modern history begins with a proclamation of emancipation.
>
> It is for these reasons that it is not merely sympathy and compassion for the black people of America that motivates us. It is above all and beyond all such sympathies and emotions a sense of complete identification and solidarity born of our own painful historic experience.
>
> When I was the rabbi of a Jewish community in Berlin under the Hitler regime, I learned many things. The most important thing that I learned under those tragic circumstances was that bigotry and hatred are not the most urgent problem. The most urgent, the most disgraceful, the most shameful and the most tragic problem is silence.
>
> A great people which had created a great civilization had become a nation of silent onlookers. They remained silent in the face of hate, in the face of brutality, and in the face of mass murder.
>
> America must not become a nation of onlookers. America must not remain silent. Not merely black America, but all of America. It must speak up and act, from the President down to the humblest of us, and not for the sake of the Negro, not for the sake of the black community but for the sake of the image, the idea, and the aspiration of America itself.
>
> Our children, yours and mine in every school across the land, each morning pledge allegiance to the flag of the United States and to the republic for which it stands. They, the children, speak fervently and innocently of this land as the land of "liberty and justice for all."
>
> The time, I believe, has come to work together – for it is not enough to hope together, and it is not enough to pray together – to work together that this children's oath, pronounced every morning from Maine to California, from North to South, may become a glorious, unshakable reality in a morally renewed and united America.

An especially tragic illustration of the youthful Jewish commitment to this idealistic vision was the murder in 1964 of Andrew Goodman and Michael Schwerner (along with other voting rights activists) in Mississippi by members of the Ku Klux Klan. Against this backdrop, the passage of the Civil Rights Acts of 1964 and 1965, and the legal and judicial prohibition of racial segregation in all forms, were viewed by American Jews with deep satisfaction.

After these victories, the black-Jewish alliance was gravely strained and broken at many points, largely owing to dynamic social, economic, and political trends. The presence within African American areas of numerous Jewish merchants and slum landlords – many of who were holdovers from earlier years when such districts were heavily Jewish – was a source of major friction. The whites with whom the masses of southern black migrants to northern cities came in contact were also disproportionately Jewish, including social case workers, communal service professionals, and, especially in New York City, public school teachers. The wave of riots that swept African American communities in northern cities between 1964 and 1968 compelled the departure of most of their white businessmen, including Jews, and violently shook the fragile urban setting. Militant groups espousing "black power," separatism, and nationalism denounced whites and repudiated their assistance in terms that were sometimes antisemitic. Proposals for social policy from some black and establishment white sources stirred deep Jewish fears that the economic and social gains of African Americans were to be at the expense of American Jews, with Jewish opportunities in higher education and broad areas of professional employment reduced to make room for African Americans. Other American ethnic groups shared similar fears.

A strike by New York City teachers in 1968, most of them Jews, arose from the intention of "school decentralization" to ease Jews out or reduce their opportunities for advancement in order to advance African Americans (and Puerto Ricans, in that city's situation) in the school system. Serious eruptions of antisemitism accompanied the strike, and the Jewish community was disturbed at white intellectual and upper-class indifference to them. Deep cleavages appeared within the American Jewish community as feelings emerged, especially among urban-working and lower-middle-class Jews, that the established Jewish organizations with their prosperous, suburban supporters were unconcerned with their plight and heedless of rising antisemitism. The rapid growth of the militant Jewish Defense League in New York and other cities, with its tactics of physical defense, public demonstrations, and retaliation, was, in part, an expression of this fear.

The Middle East crisis of May 1967 brought American Jewish concern for Israel to a peak. Some volunteers were able to leave for Israel before June 5, 1967, but the escalating political anxiety and subsequent astonishing military triumph by Israel in the Six-Day War found its main outlet in unparalleled charitable contributions – $232 million to the United Jewish Appeal and $75 million in State of Israel bonds. Hardly had the euphoria of victory dissipated when the New Left in shaky combination with militant black elements vigorously espoused the Arab cause. Like Soviet Russia and Poland, they used the term "Zionist" as an epithet and synonym for "Jew" in attempting to obscure the antisemitic character of their propaganda. Together with numerous Arab students on American campuses, they propagandized vigorously for their cause. The American Zionist movement – largely quiescent for almost 20 years as the vast majority of American Jews expressed their pro-Israel convictions outside its framework – somewhat revived after 1967. This was particularly noticeable at many colleges and universities, especially those swept by campus disturbances and the militant tone of leftist and black demands. Jewish students spontaneously founded Zionist organizations, which they named (in contemporary parlance) as "radical" and "liberation" groups, e.g., the Jewish Activist League (Boston), the Jewish Liberation Project (New York City), the Jewish Radical Community (Los Angeles), Jews for Urban Justice (Washington, D.C.), the Radical Zionist Alliance (New York City), etc. At a more sedate level, American business investment in Israel as well as tourism, both overwhelmingly Jewish, greatly increased despite the danger to Israel's security. *Aliyah* (Jewish immigration to Israel), long debated in American Zionist and Jewish circles, enjoyed a relative surge as approximately 17,000 American Jews settled in Israel between July 1967 and the end of 1970.

Antisemitic discrimination and the near-suppression of Jewish life in the Soviet Union, together with the Soviet regime's refusal to permit Jewish emigration, furnished the main cause for agitation and protest by American Jews at the end of the 1960s. The American Conference on Soviet Jewry, the Academic Council on Soviet Jewry, and especially the Student Struggle for Soviet Jewry were the major organizers in this regard. The continued threat to the existence of Israel, urban problems weighing heavily on an overwhelmingly urban community, and the surge of antisemitism, anti-Zionism, and anti-Israel sentiment, together with the well-publicized glorification of violence by some militant black demagogues and white followers, angered American Jews and tended to stimulate a siege mentality. Assertions were common that Jewish communal life and institutions were "useless" and "irrelevant," and the supposed revolt of American youth stirred concern. Nevertheless, American Jews continued to support liberal political programs and candidates and played a prominent role in American cultural and economic life.

THE INSECURE 1970S. The 1970s brought many changes as well as insecurity and anxiety to the fore of American society. The Vietnam War's conclusion was as humiliating as its pursuit and the scars took time to heal. The Arab oil embargo of the period and subsequent price increases exposed the vulnerability of the world's most advanced technological society to Middle Eastern oil supplies. The Watergate scandal revealed a corruption of power that had eaten into the political structure and weakened public respect for government. Scarcely had this receded when the overthrow of the Shah of Iran again threatened oil supplies, and the humiliation of the prolonged detention of the occupants of the Teheran embassy underscored the extent to which the giant economies of the West did not control their own destinies. The manner in which their appetite for oil continued, despite the warning of the earlier crisis, made the West dependent on the whim of a handful of Arab countries, whose control over substantial portion of the world's oil reserves portended dramatic changes in the balance of Cold War geo-political power – in the Middle East and worldwide. All this was driven home by a background of seemingly unbeatable inflation, accompanied, as the decade drew to a close, by a depressed American economy – the effects of which provided the context for the work of Simon *Kuznets, a leading American economist of Ukrainian Jewish origins who won the Nobel Prize in 1971 for his empirical studies of economic growth and the socio-economic structure of society.

The impact of the economic and political climate on American Jews was complicated by the shock of the Yom Kippur War, and the ensuing concern that – quite apart from its decisive 1967 victory – Israel's long-term survival was far from certain. American Jews responded to the crisis of the Yom Kippur War almost reflexively and immediately undertook a dizzying campaign to lobby American policy-makers, coordinate a massive fundraising campaign on Israel's behalf, and activate local American Jewish communities to support Israel's war effort. Within hours of the outbreak of hostilities, American Jewish leaders mobilized to secure political support for Nixon's request for a $2.2 billion Congressional appropriation that allowed Israel to purchase American military supplies. Meanwhile, the United Jewish Appeal pledged to raise $900 million, while the Israel Bond's organization and a plethora of Jewish and Zionist groups initiated emergency fund raising initiatives. The Conservative movement alone raised a total of $82 million. Finally, some 35,000 prospective American Jewish volunteers barraged the offices of the Jewish Agency including a disproportionate number of doctors whose prior experience in Vietnam made them ideal candidates for service. Of the tens of thousands who offered their services, only a couple thousand were actually sent to Israel in the first weeks following the outbreak of the war. Most of the volunteers paid for their own passage to Israel.

The flurry of negotiations that followed the Yom Kippur War provided exhilaration and depression, satisfaction and resentment in quick succession, as did the involved discussions that followed Anwar Sadat's historic visit to Jerusalem. For in spite of Israel's hard won victory and Egypt's momentous policy change, the majority of the Arab world remained implacably determined to crush Israel. Meanwhile, the 1975 United Nations resolution condemning Zionism as racism resounded like a thunderclap. The United States condemned the vote, but its impact on the American Jewish community and militant left-wing anti-Israel elements was significant.

Against this backdrop, two major ideological debates underscored a significant shift in the trajectory of American Jewish life. One centered on the role of pluralism in the American Jewish community. The other was, in effect, a political conflict waged in print, at the ballot box, and through various forms of activism, between Jewish liberals and conservatives who took sides over a variety of social, economic, and foreign policy issues. The net result proved to be a widespread trend toward communal decentralization, the increasing demand by constituents and donors for accountability on the part of local Jewish Federations and the agencies they supported, and the creation of new educational, cultural, political, and philanthropic institutions that arose alongside the American Jewish Joint Distribution Committee, B'nai B'rith, the Council of Jewish Federations, Hadassah, and other venerable institutions of American Jewish life.

POLITICS. The visibility of Jews in the American political process grew in the 1970s not merely by virtue of being openly courted in presidential elections but through their appointment to high office. Under the Nixon administration Herbert *Stein became chairman of the president's Council of Economic Advisors, Arthur *Burns chairman of the Federal Reserve Board, and Walter *Annenberg ambassador to Great Britain. Edward H. *Levi, president of the University of Chicago and descendant of a well-known rabbinical family, was appointed attorney general in 1975. The most noteworthy Jewish figure in the Nixon administration was Henry Kissinger. A refugee from Nazi Germany, he became the president's national security advisor in 1969 and was appointed secretary of state in 1975. Kissinger's authority was apparent not only in the critical diplomatic and foreign affairs role he played vis-à-vis the Soviet Union, Vietnam, the Middle East, and China but also by virtue of the fact that he was for many months the administration's most effective senior official as Nixon himself became deeply entangled in the Watergate Affair. Kissinger's authority was sustained and reaffirmed when Gerald Ford, on succeeding Nixon, retained him in office.

Although the Republican Party labored under the handicap of the Watergate scandal in the presidential election of 1976, it was clearly no longer the case that a liberal viewpoint crystallizing into support for the Democrats could be predicted of Jews. For example, despite a heavy concentration of Jewish voters in New York's Democratic primary, Jimmy Carter captured only 4 percent of the Jewish vote and succeeded in winning only 33 delegates as compared to 90 for Senator Henry M. Jackson, a conservative Democrat who was an ardent supporter of aid to Israel and the right of Soviet Jews to emigrate. Indeed, one report published after the presidential election estimated 54 percent of the Jewish vote going to Carter, as against 45 percent to Ford; another gave the proportion as two to one. Even this figure falls far short of the 83 percent preference for the Democrats reported in 1968.

In the Carter administration Stuart *Eisenstadt and Mark *Siegal were appointed to responsible positions on the White House staff, and Marvin Warner became ambassador to Switzerland. Two converts from Judaism became members of the cabinet – W. Michael *Blumenthal, as secretary of the treasury, and James Schlesinger, as secretary of the Department of Energy. Both retired in 1979 when Carter reorganized his administration. Subsequently, Neil *Goldschmidt, mayor of Portland, Oregon, and a practicing Jew, was appointed secretary of transportation, and Philip M. Klutznick, long an active figure in Jewish affairs, was appointed secretary of commerce.

Despite the historic Israel-Egypt peace treaty of 1978 brokered by President Jimmy Carter, the administration's open criticism of Israeli policy, which reached a climax in 1980 with support for a United Nations resolution calling on Israel to dismantle Jewish settlements in the West Bank and Gaza Strip, alienated many American Jewish voters. In the end, the presumed Jewish disposition to support Carter's bid for reelection in 1980 did not materialize. It was estimated that Carter won approximately 40 percent of the Jewish vote and Ronald Reagan about 35 percent, with the balance going to independent candidate John Anderson. Because of the concentration of Jewish voters in large urban areas, the effect of the Jewish vote in the election remained disproportionate to its size in the body politic. This explained the attention drawn by even minor political shifts within the American Jewish community. A Gallup poll taken after Reagan's landslide reelection to a second presidential term revealed that while the number of Jewish Republicans had doubled to 16 percent, the number of Jewish Democrats was 50 percent.

Some observers viewed the American Jewish community's steadfast support for Israel as evidence of its parochial and increasingly conservative interests. This support was repeatedly demonstrated in public opinion polls. Meanwhile, an active, articulate, well funded, and growing conservative minority proved to be a force to be reckoned with in American Jewish life. The most popular forum for Jewish neo-conservative ideas was *Commentary* edited by Norman *Podhoretz and originally founded in the 1930s by Elliot *Cohen. It swiftly proved to be the most significant Jewish-sponsored intellectual journal of the period and featured many of the country's leading Jewish and non-Jewish neo-conservatives in its pages – a group dubbed the "New York intellectuals" that over the course of a few decades included political journalists Midge *Decter, *Irving Kristol, and Gertrude *Himmelfarb, literary critics Diana *Trilling, Lionel *Trilling, Leslie *Fiedler, Philip *Rahv, and William *Phillips, social scientists Daniel *Bell, Sidney *Hook, Seymour Martin *Lipset, and Nathan *Glazer, art critics and historians Hannah *Arendt, Clement *Greenberg, Harold *Rosenberg, and Meyer *Schapiro, and the novelist Saul *Bellow. This group also had a major impact on the quality and vitality of other influential political and literary journals including *Dissent*, *Partisan Review*, and *The New York Review of Books*. But it was *Commentary* in particular that emerged as an intellectual laboratory for neo-conservatism. It served as a training ground for many of the American right's most important thinkers and policymakers in the 1970s and eventually blossomed with the "Reagan revolution" in the 1980s. In the final analysis, however, as the voting behavior of American Jews demonstrated, neo-conservativism within the Jewish community, no matter how articulately formed, remained a minority view. The liberalism associated with the Roosevelt-Kennedy-Humphrey branch of the Democratic party was simply too much a part of the American Jewish ethos.

DISCRIMINATION IN REVERSE. The decline of antisemitism since World War II and the lowering of the residential, occupational, educational, and social barriers that previously cast a shadow over Jewish life in the United States helped to sustain American Jewry's liberal orientation in the second half of the 20th century. Used to regarding themselves as "outsiders," Jews were surprised and dismayed to find that other minority groups regarded them as "insiders" whose entrenched position was standing in the way of their own legitimate aspirations. This turn in inter-group relations took place against a background of urban decay in areas in which important Jewish communities had lived for decades. In addition to crime and violence in the streets, Jews found themselves plagued by the wider problems of school integration, quotas, low-income housing, ethnic rights, and inter-group relations, as well as by antisemitism.

This situation faced the Jews with contradictions that made them highly uncomfortable. Their traditional liberalism had made them accustomed to the posture of strong supporters of the underdog; they were now suddenly forced to defend their own status, their neighborhoods, their safety and the adequate education of their children. Having fought for a society from which discrimination would be eliminated, they now found that society proposed to discriminate in favor of other less privileged groups. Now the priority given to the African American and Latino populations (along with other minority groups), forced them to reconsider their status as a minority, albeit, a neglected one. There were strong feelings of anger, of being at a disadvantage, of frustration, of a new insecurity.

These feelings were much more intense among the lower middle and working class than among the more affluent Jews, among those whose homes or whose occupations remained in the decaying cities than among those who lived in the suburbs under entirely different conditions. Whatever kind of pressure had been built up was felt much more directly by the poor shopkeeper, the schoolteacher, the Orthodox Jew whose life centered on his synagogue. They suffered from the changed composition of their neighborhoods. In many instances, they had to face the violence brought into formerly quiet, homogeneous areas by ethnic groups who had moved into what used to be Jewish territory. While the sheltered suburbanites, not exposed to these pressures to the same degree as the poorer Jews, tended to maintain their traditional liberalism, those in violence-prone neighborhoods began to feel less sympathy for those minorities who, while struggling to better themselves, were bringing a good deal of hardship into the lives of lower-middle-class Jews. The continuing migration from the city to the suburb by the more affluent contributed to the creation of a vicious circle: Jewish neighborhoods became poorer, and more space became available to minorities and low-income whites, exacerbating the already existing problems.

In addition to crime, the priority treatment of minorities and the quota system, both in education and employment, was a cause of concern. The necessity to provide blacks and members of other minorities with jobs, and giving them preference apart from their qualifications affected the rights of Jews as part of the white population. Still more important were the consequences of this preferential treatment in the field of education, especially higher education. Even where no discrimination against Jews was intended, any quota system prescribing an increased number of minority students without increasing the overall number of students meant that qualified white students, particularly high achieving Jewish students, were not admitted. In the event, many of those admitted under quotas did not meet the regular qualifications and the standards of higher education had to be lowered.

In 1978 the United States Supreme Court considered the issue of "discrimination in reverse" in the case of Allan P. Bakke, a white engineer who claimed the minority admissions of the University of California Medical School denied him his equal rights. The court ruled that the school's special admission program was illegal, though the university could consider race as one factor in choosing among applicants for admission. Jewish groups favored the ruling, while black and Hispanic groups were against it.

ZIONISM AND ISRAEL. Throughout the 1970s and 1980s Israel-related matters held a critical place in American Jewish life. In 1977 the national conference of the United Jewish Appeal was held in Israel for the first time, with the participation of some 3,000 American Jewish leaders. Tourism to Israel continued at a high level and contact with a new generation of young people was fostered through participation in kibbutz volunteer programs and study at Israeli universities. Notwithstanding Arthur Hertzberg's statement that Zionism and Israel had become the "religion" of American Jewry, immigration to Israel actually declined during this decade. When Pinḥas *Sapir, chairman of the Jewish Agency, toured the United States in 1974 in order to draw attention to the need for American immigrants, he received a lukewarm reception. The figure for 1970 was 7,658 American Jewish immigrants; by 1975 it had fallen to 2,964.

Occasionally voices were heard suggesting a desire to tone down the popular emphasis on the primacy of Israel. In 1973, for example, Jewish Theological Seminary chancellor Gerson D. *Cohen called for an equal partnership between the Jews of Israel and the diaspora. "The legitimate place of the Jewish people, of Jewish culture and Jewish religion," he asserted, "is not limited to a single geographic location." Meanwhile, however, so active politically and economically had American Jewry become in its support of Israel that it registered from afar every disturbance and challenge to Israel's situation. Scarcely a day passed but that the *New York Times* and other major American newspapers, by way of articles, news items, editorials or correspondence, did not contain information and discussions concerning Israel. At every level the engagement of the American Jewish community was demonstrated – from meetings of organizational delegations with the president, the secretary of state, senators and members of Congress to contacts with local politicians and news outlets. Financial aid to Israel, the supply of arms, economic aid given to neighboring Arab countries, recognition of the Palestine Liberation Organization, diplomatic support for Israel's position on the occupied territories and Jerusalem, possible overtures to the Arab states, the involvement of American business in the Arab boycott of Israel – all drew vigorous responses from the American Jewish community.

Some viewed the flurry of American Jewish Israel-oriented activity as political maneuvering devoid of substantial impact, others as involving unusual danger and genuine opportunity to advance Israel's interests. The Yom Kippur War of 1973, which demonstrated the singularity of United States as Israel's chief ally, was recognized in the community as belonging to the latter category. Unremitting preoccupation with Israeli concerns brought into prominence the Conference of Presidents of Major American Jewish Organizations. Thus, in 1974 Secretary of State Henry Kissinger met the leaders Conference no less than six times within a period of seven months. Another instance in this regard was the United Nations resolution of 1975, condemning Zionism as a form of racism, which raised the ire of Jewish groups across the country and provoked a storm of organized lobbying activity. The American Jewish community responded similarly a year earlier when PLO chairman Yasser *Arafat was invited to address the United Nations General Assembly.

The general standpoint of the organized American Jewish community in this period was one of unqualified support for Israel's foreign policy. This was exemplified in an emphatic way by Hadassah president Charlotte Jacobson who in 1977 condemned Jewish personalities who criticized Israeli policies publicly because such criticism was used by anti-Israel factions to weaken support for Israel. Indeed, notwithstanding the criticism of groups like the American Council for Judaism on the one side and the Satmar Ḥasidim on the other, which stood far beyond the American Jewish mainstream, unqualified acceptance of the Israeli point of view was difficult to controvert in the atmosphere of deliverance that followed Israel's hard won victories in the Six-Day War of 1967 and Yom Kippur War of 1973. The policy of standing firm, based on the bargaining power of Israel's territorial gains, received general acceptance among American Jews. But even under the shock of the Yom Kippur War, questions began to be raised as to the validity of Israel's policies – particularly with respect to the treatment of the Palestinian Arabs and the continued occupation of the West Bank, Gaza Strip, Golan Heights, and Sinai peninsula – that American Jews were being called upon automatically to support. The procedures of the organized American Jewish scene, which aimed at maximum publicity for lobbying purposes, but provided minimum access for arriving at community decisions – and the absence of an open Jewish press – meant there was no channel for the ventilation of these misgivings.

Against the backdrop of growing leftist Jewish political activity on college campuses across the country, including open questioning by student leaders of the American Jewish establishment and Israeli policy makers, this conflict surfaced in 1977 when the venerable Anti-Defamation League attacked a small organization known as Breira (Alternative). Established in 1973, the left-leaning Breira obtained considerable press coverage for its views and it was rumored that Nahum *Goldmann was helping to finance it. It advocated the creation of an independent Palestinian State in the West Bank and the Gaza Strip and negotiations with any Palestinian who would renounce terrorism and recognize Israel's right to exist. The attacks on Breira not only criticized this policy, but impugned the motives of its advocates. The Anti-Defamation League sought to prevent B'nai B'rith staff members from associating with Breira, especially rabbis associated with the *Hillel Foundation who were among its supporters on American college campuses. Shortly thereafter, Breira disappeared from the scene almost as quickly as it had attracted attention, due, it was said, to difficulty in raising funds. However, the countercurrent of disquietude it represented did not disappear.

In 1977 the electoral victory in Israel of the *Likud party, led by Menahem Begin, was received by leaders of the American Jewish community with surprise tinged with consternation. The rule of the Labor-led coalition, dominated by the elite founders of the Jewish state, had come to be regarded as one of the fixities of the Israeli scene, and their Likud opponents had been dismissed as extremists in whose hands such possibilities of peace as existed between Israel and her neighbors would be cast away. In short order, most American Jewish organizations publicly adjusted themselves to Israel's new right-wing political order. Begin's personality contributed to the smoothness of the transition. He related well to the rank-and-file members of the American Jewish community; his stubbornness and pertinacity quickly established his image as a fighter for whom no power was too formidable where the curtailment of Jewish rights was involved; and within six months of his accession to power Anwar *Sadat's visit to Jerusalem demonstrated his capacity for political leadership and compromise.

The news of Sadat's intention to visit Jerusalem was received by American Jews with elation, and they watched closely the diplomatic moves which led to the historic signing in 1979 of the Israel-Egypt peace treaty on the White House lawn and the three-way handshake of President Jimmy Carter, Sadat, and Begin. Meanwhile, one policy move foreshadowed by the Begin government created grave discomfort within the American Jewish community. To win the support of Israel's Agudat Israel party for support of the peace treaty, Begin promised an important extension to the privileges enjoyed by Orthodox Jews under Israeli law – namely, that for the purposes of the Law of Return only conversions to Judaism conforming to the requirements of Orthodoxy would be recognized. This proposal aroused concern on the part of the Reform and Conservative organizations in the United States, who promptly met with Begin and dispatched rabbinic delegations to Israel to interview the chief rabbis. No accommodation to the non-Orthodox viewpoint was announced, and more urgent matters supervened to delay the taking of decisive steps.

Many elements within the American Jewish community felt misgivings over the Begin government's announced policy to expand Jewish settlements in the occupied territories. Since 1967 successive Labor-led governments had implemented the unofficial "Allon Plan," which called for limited Jewish settlement in the Jordan Rift Valley, Golan Heights, and along the borders of the Gaza Strip. The settlements – deemed strategic expedients in the absence of a comprehensive peace agreement with Israel's Arab neighbors – were intended to secure Israel's border and ensure its safety. The Begin government's explicit policy of creating a durable Jewish presence throughout "Greater Israel" resulted in the establishment of scores of new Jewish outposts and communities in the West Bank and Gaza Strip. Even as prominent leaders sought privately to persuade Begin to adopt a more moderate policy, others publicly voiced their support of Israel's growing "*Peace Now" movement, which called for an end to Israeli occupation of the territories and recognition of Palestinian Arab rights.

In the interim, a highly publicized struggle occurred in 1979 when the organized American Jewish community vigorously opposed the Carter administration's plan to sell $4.8 billion worth of jet warplanes to Egypt, Saudi Arabia, and Israel. In the event, much to the dismay of American Jewish leaders and the community's pro-Israel lobbyists, the United States Senate approved the sale. The importance attached to the Jewish vote is illustrated by the application of emolients in the aftermath of the struggle. Carter and several members of his administration telephoned and met American Jewish leaders to inform them of Washington's continued support for Israel. At the same time expressions of satisfaction were heard in Washington that the pro-Israel lobby had sustained a defeat.

HOLOCAUST-RELATED MATTERS. As early as 1949, the Jewish community had been aware of the presence of Nazi war criminals in the United States. However, interest in the subject remained generally low until the mid-1970s and the beginning of the 1980s. As a result of document research and field investigations performed by the *Office of Special Investigations, established in 1979 as a special unit within the Criminal Division of the United States Justice Department, it was revealed that in the years following World War II over 1,000 Nazi war criminals or collaborators had found refuge in the United States. Many were actually brought to the United States through the efforts of the State Department, the intelligence branches of the Army, Navy, and Air Force, the FBI, and the CIA, having been recruited to serve as agents and consultants in anti-Communist operations during the late 1940s and the 1950s.

By the beginning of 1980, the Office of Special Investigations had collected documentation on 413 war criminals residing in the United States. Among the high profile cases prosecuted during this period were Valerian Trifa, a Romanian, who was expelled by the United States in 1983 and made his way to Portugal where he died; Feodor Fedorenko, a Pole, who was deported to the Soviet Union in 1984 and executed in 1987; Andrija Artukovic, a Croatian, who was extradited to Yugoslavia in 1986 and sentenced to death; Karl Linnas, an

Estonian, deported to the Soviet Union in April 1987 where he died three months later in a hospital; and Ukrainian-born John *Demjanjuk, alleged to have been "Ivan the Terrible" of Treblinka, who in 1986 was stripped of his naturalized American citizenship and extradited to Israel to stand trial.

A major controversy erupted over President Ronald Reagan's 1985 visit to the military cemetery in *Bitburg, West Germany. The visit was planned to commemorate the 40th anniversary of Nazi Germany's surrender and to symbolize the spirit of reconciliation between the United States and Germany. The controversy, which provoked an international response, lay in the fact that among the 2,000 dead soldiers interred were 47 members of the Nazi Waffen SS. Furthermore, at the time the president's itinerary was first announced, it included no visit to Bergen-Belsen, a nearby concentration camp. In spite of growing criticism and pressure, Reagan proceeded with his planned visit to the cemetery where he laid a wreath. He, however, also visited the site of Bergen-Belsen where in his speech he addressed the feelings of Holocaust survivors.

Holocaust Revisionism succeeded in drawing increased attention during the 1980s. The most active revisionist organization in the United States during this period was the California-based Institute for Historical Review (IHR), founded in 1978 by Willis Carto, a known antisemite. Other known Holocaust revisionists operating in the United States included Arthur Butz of Northwestern University, author of *The Hoax of the Twentieth Century: The Case Against the Presumed Extermination of European Jewry* (1976); David McCalden, a co-founder of the IHR; Bradley Smith, publisher of *Prima Facie*, a racist and antisemitic monthly newsletter; and Charles E. Weber of the University of Tulsa and author of *The Holocaust: 120 Questions and Answers* (1983).

One significant response to the pressing need for Holocaust education in the United States was the creation in 1988 of the bi-annual March of the Living program. The program was organized to bring together thousands of American and Israeli high school students in a week of workshops and lectures about the Holocaust, culminating in a procession beginning at the Auschwitz concentration camp in Poland and ending nearly two miles away at the Birkenau crematoria. From Poland, participants flew to Israel in time to celebrate Israel Independence Day. The march recreated the first steps of the infamous Forced March of January 1945 toward Germany of 60,000 Jews who were still alive near the end of the war, of whom only some 6,000 survived. The results of social scientific surveys of Jewish teenagers who participated in the March of the Living indicated that by the 1990s the program was having a strong positive effect on all markers related to Jewish identity and identification with Judaism and Israel.

SOVIET AND ETHIOPIAN JEWRY. An historic demonstration on behalf of Soviet Jewry was held in Washington, D.C., during the first week of December 1987. This mass rally, co-sponsored by some 50 national Jewish organizations and 300 local Jewish federations from throughout North America, brought over 200,000 demonstrators together on the eve of the Reagan-Gorbachev summit. It also marked a rare display in organizational unity. The Soviet Jewry movement in the United States had been split for years between the more moderate National Conference on Soviet Jewry, on the one hand, and the more confrontational Union of Councils for Soviet Jews and the Student Struggle for Soviet Jewry on the other.

With the advent of *glasnost* in the late 1980s, Soviet Jewish emigration figures soon began to climb. The American Jewish community now found itself confronted by two major issues, one ideological, but with very pragmatic implications, the other material. As the emigration of Soviet Jews continued, the American Jewish community found itself in a confrontation with the State of Israel over the émigrés' destination. The United States was willing to accept a fixed number of Soviet Jewish immigrants as refugees and was by far the émigrés' most popular destination. But Israel argued that its willingness to accept unconditionally all emigrating Soviet Jews belied their refugee status. Israel wanted cooperating authorities to direct virtually all emigrating Soviet Jews to its shores. During the first year of the Soviet Union's more liberal emigration policy, the monthly dropout rate, a figure that referred to those Soviet Jewish emigrants who changed their destination from Israel to another country (usually the United States) while in transit, often reached over 90 percent.

Most American Jews supported the policy of "freedom of choice." The Union of Councils for Soviet Jews and the Student Struggle for Soviet Jewry criticized Israeli pressure on American Jewish organizations and the United States. The National Conference on Soviet Jewry and other major Jewish organizations, while upholding the principle of "freedom of choice," accepted a dual track compromise whereby the large backlog of Jews already holding Israeli visas would emigrate to Israel through Romania, while those as yet without visas and seeking to emigrate to the United States would have to apply for an American visa in Moscow.

The number of Soviet Jews who applied for and received exit visas grew significantly. In September 1988, as a result of the new dimensions of Soviet Jewish emigration, the United States became more selective in awarding refugee status to applicants. This status was now meted out on a more selective basis, so that by August 1989, nearly one quarter of all applicants for U.S. immigrant visas were being refused. In July 1989 the United States announced that its immigration budget for Eastern European refugees was exhausted and temporarily stopped processing visa applications for the thousands of Soviet Jews who were by now languishing in transit centers in Ladispoli, near Rome, and in Vienna.

In the fall, following negotiations with American Jewish groups, the administration of President George H.W. Bush announced that it was fixing a new annual immigration quota for Soviet Jews at 43,000 with priority extended to those with immediate, or first degree, family members already residing in the United States. It was also allocating $75 million to resettlement programs. As a result of this new policy, which also involved closing down the transit centers and requiring applicants to apply for immigrant visas in Moscow, the majority of Soviet émigrés gave up trying to seek entry to the United States. Even with the new, more stringent quota on Soviet Jewish immigration, the American Jewish community was faced with the huge task of resettling tens of thousands of new arrivals. In the last quarter of 1989, some 18,000 Soviet Jews arrived in the United States. The funds set aside by the American government for total Soviet resettlement were insufficient. In order to insure that the Soviet Jews coming to the United States were provided with all the means and opportunities for successful resettlement, defined to mean their material resettlement as well as their religious, cultural, and educational integration into the Jewish community, the Council of Jewish Federations (CJF) and the United Jewish Appeal (UJA) launched a $75 million voluntary campaign called "Passage to Freedom," but its national goal was never reached. By the end of the year, only about two-fifths of the money had been collected.

The combination of stricter American immigration laws and the difficulties involved in resettling Soviet Jews locally gradually influenced American Jewish leadership to heed the government of Israel's calls for receiving the bulk of émigrés. In 1990 the UJA and CJF announced "Operation Exodus," a $420 million campaign, whose goal was to bring directly to Israel and resettle the overwhelming majority of Soviet Jews seeking to emigrate. Operation Exodus was a financial success and 95 percent of the goal was reached within ten months, the majority pledged by the biggest givers in the largest Jewish communities. "Exodus II," the worldwide campaign in 1991 to raise an additional $1.3 billion, was launched when the number of Soviet Jews coming to Israel turned out to be more than double the original estimate. From the results of the Exodus II campaign, it became clear that the desire of American Jewry lay in assisting the emigrating Soviet Jews to resettle in Israel.

By the end of 1990 it was reported that over 181,000 Jews had left the Soviet Union. In response to this new situation, President George H.W. Bush, in December 1990, waived key agricultural restrictions of the Jackson-Vanik Amendment, which since 1974 stood as a symbol of American Jewish opposition to the Soviet Union's disregard for human rights.

American Jews played an active role in bringing Ethiopian Jewry to Israel. The major airlifts in 1984–85 and 1991 were largely made possible by behind-the-scenes diplomacy by the United States government and through funds raised by the American Jewish community. The American Association for Ethiopian Jews was established in 1969 and the North American Conference on Ethiopian Jewry in 1982. The objectives of these activist groups included raising the awareness of Jews and the world to the condition of the Jews of Ethiopia and visiting Jewish communities in Ethiopia to demonstrate solidarity and to provide material assistance. The subsequent cost of resettling the Ethiopian Jews in Israel was absorbed into the United Jewish Appeal's Operation Exodus campaign.

These humanitarian activities on behalf of Soviet and Ethiopian Jews were representative of the efforts by American Jews on behalf of distressed Jewish communities worldwide. The International Coalition for the Revival of the Jews of Yemen, based in New York, was established in 1989 to offer assistance to Yemen's remaining Jews. The Syrian Jewish community of Brooklyn continued its own efforts to secure the emigration of kinsmen remaining in the Jewish centers of Damascus, Aleppo, and Qamishli. Other organizations, such as the American Jewish Joint Distribution Committee, continued their contacts with these communities or remained otherwise involved on their behalf throughout the 1990s.

The Contemporary Period, 1980s to 2000s

THE FUTURE OF AMERICAN JEWRY. American Jewish life in the decades spanning the 20th and 21st centuries has been marked by a high degree of self-awareness, economic success, political engagement, institutional innovation, and globalization. Responding to a variety of social, cultural, and political changes and challenges, both internally and externally, the organized American Jewish community continues to display a remarkable capacity for adaptability and elasticity within an ever-changing and dynamic American setting. Even so, American Jewry's belief in pluralism and the promise of a free and open Western society has over time become intertwined with deep concern about the community's ultimate survival, its cultural vitality, and its ability to sustain itself into the future. All of the statistical data gathered since the start of the 1980s points to the Jewish community's heightened Americanization *and* a general weakening and diminution of its tribal identity. The astonishing success of Jewish life in the American setting, an experience without precedent in modern history, is in many ways a mixed blessing. Absent the binding forces of history that have sustained Jewish life in a variety of settings – namely, religious faith, antisemitism, ethnic cohesion derived from a shared immigrant past, or the social and political activism characteristic of American Jews in the 20th century – what will be the glue that holds American Jewish life together in the 21st century? Arthur *Hertzberg, a rabbi, scholar, and veteran observer of American Jewish scene, has argued "the essential crisis of the American Jewish community" stems from the fact that "it has essentially defined its Jewish experience without classic texts." Given the community's general affluence, he proposes:

> The American Jewish community is capable of deciding to create a network of elite boarding schools and day schools which would educate many more, perhaps even most, of the American Jewish young. It is at least conceivable that American Jews might decide that activism and togetherness are running down as forces of cohesion and as sources of meaning. It is conceivable that American Jews might decide that they cannot be the only Jewish community in all of history in which Jewish learning is not a prerequisite for Jewish belonging and Jewish leadership.

Many analysts, scholars, and communal leaders share Hertzberg's perspective and concur with his diagnosis of the crisis facing contemporary American Jewish society. To this end, the organized Jewish community has in recent decades generated billions of dollars to support Jewish community centers, educational and communal training programs, highly subsidized Israel trips for high school and college students, and various academic and experiential models aimed at infusing future generations of American Jews with meaningful and substantive content. A handful of Jewish philanthropists led by Edgar M. *Bronfman, Sr., Charles and Andrea Bronfman, Harold Grinspoon, Ronald *Lauder, Felix Posen, Lynn and Charles *Schusterman, and Michael and Judy *Steinhardt have been especially influential in this dynamic and evolving project.

An alternate assessment, one decidedly more optimistic about the trajectory of the American Jewish experience in toto, has been offered by Jacob Rader *Marcus, the dean of American Jewish historians. "Most frequently the future is but an extension of the past," Marcus wrote in 1996. "Throughout the 19th century amateur prophets suggested that the Jew [in the United States] had no future. They were wrong…" Taking a long view of history, Marcus further argued:

> Jewry in the twenty-first century will not experience substantial growth. Intermarriages eventuate in loss for the Jewish body politic, but then numbers are not really important: in the first quarter of the 20th century German Jewry counted but some 600,000 souls, yet it exercised spiritual hegemony over world Jewry, some 15,000,000 strong. From all indications – statistical surveys made in the 1990s – American Jewry is surviving and prospering in an open society. Jews are Jewish because they prefer to remain Jewish; they are blending Americanism and Jewishness. Because of the fusion of these two cultures they are content, if not happy; they strive to become enlightened human beings. For them, patently, the United States is still "the land of unlimited opportunity."

As the positions staked out by Hertzberg and Marcus illustrate, observers of American Jewish life in the contemporary period have engaged in an escalating debate over whether the proverbial glass is half full or half empty. This highly complex and sensitive issue, which in the 1990s quickly assumed the catchphrase "Jewish continuity," continues to dominate the board rooms, meetings, and conferences of a wide variety of American Jewish organizations, groups, and academics. Critics point to an unprecedented rise in the rate of intermarriage, an ominously low Jewish birth rate, the migration of younger professionals away from Jewish population centers, increasing Jewish cultural illiteracy, and the rise of anti-Zionism and militant Palestinian nationalism. Viewed from this perspective, it indeed appears that American Jewish communal life is fractured and its future is in jeopardy. On the other hand, optimists see a Jewish community that is the most materially secure in history, fully integrated into the surrounding society, and well represented in all branches of American science, art, academia, government, and commerce.

DEMOGRAPHY AND POPULATION. The study of the contemporary American Jewish scene has benefited enormously in the last quarter of the 20th century from a veritable cottage industry of demographic analysis based at leading universities in the United States and Israel. In general, this effort is sponsored by the major Jewish communal agencies and philanthropies. Though not without controversy, the studies have nonetheless become central to the work of a wide variety of professionals, communal leaders, policy analysts, and scholars. Demographic, social, and attitudinal data gathered throughout 1980s and 1990s in several national surveys have had a profound impact on organized American Jewry's countrywide agenda and the implications of such studies for future of the community as a whole are considerable.

The generally accepted figure for the number of Jews in the United States in the present era varies between an estimated 5.5 million "core" Jewish population and approximately 6 million, making it the largest Jewish community in the world. (The global Jewish population is estimated to be approximately 13 million.) A 1993 report issued by Israel's Ministry of Education determined that while the largest concentration of Jews continues to reside in the Northeast (43.5 percent), the trend in population movement during the 1980s and 1990s continued to be away from the Northeast and Midwest (11.3 percent) to the South (21.8 percent) and West (23.4 percent). By comparison, in 1970 the *National Jewish Population Survey* had found 64 percent of the Jewish population living in the Northeast, 17 percent in the Midwest, and only 19 percent, combined, in the South and West. Other demographic studies produced in this period also noted the greater distribution of American Jews among smaller urban areas than in the past. The migration was characterized by Jews who had moved from the largest Northeastern and Midwestern cities, such as New York, Philadelphia and Boston, to smaller urban areas in the South and West such as Atlanta and Phoenix. As a result, the Jewish population in the New York metropolitan area had decreased since mid-century from about 2.6 million to 2.2 million. Likewise, Chicago's Jewish population decreased from 378,000 to about 250,000. By the mid-1980s the Jewish communities of Philadelphia, Pittsburgh, Cleveland, Detroit, and St. Louis had all declined. By the 1980s there were six Jewish communities west of the Rocky Mountains whose populations had grown to over 100,000. Consequently, Los Angeles, with an estimated 604,000 Jews became the second largest Jewish community in the United States, followed by Miami/Ft. Lauderdale metropolitan region, with an estimated 367,000 Jews. The historian Deborah Dash Moore has examined this phenomenon and concludes:

> In many ways, the Jewish worlds of Los Angeles and Miami and other Sunbelt cities can be seen as the offspring of the large urban Jewish settlements of New York, Chicago, Philadelphia, and Boston, and of the more modest communities of such cities as Omaha, Milwaukee, Cleveland, and Detroit. As Jewish New York, Chicago, and Philadelphia represent continuity with a European past because they were created by immigrants from cities and towns of Eastern Europe, so Jewish Miami and Los Angeles are the creations of the Midwestern and northeastern

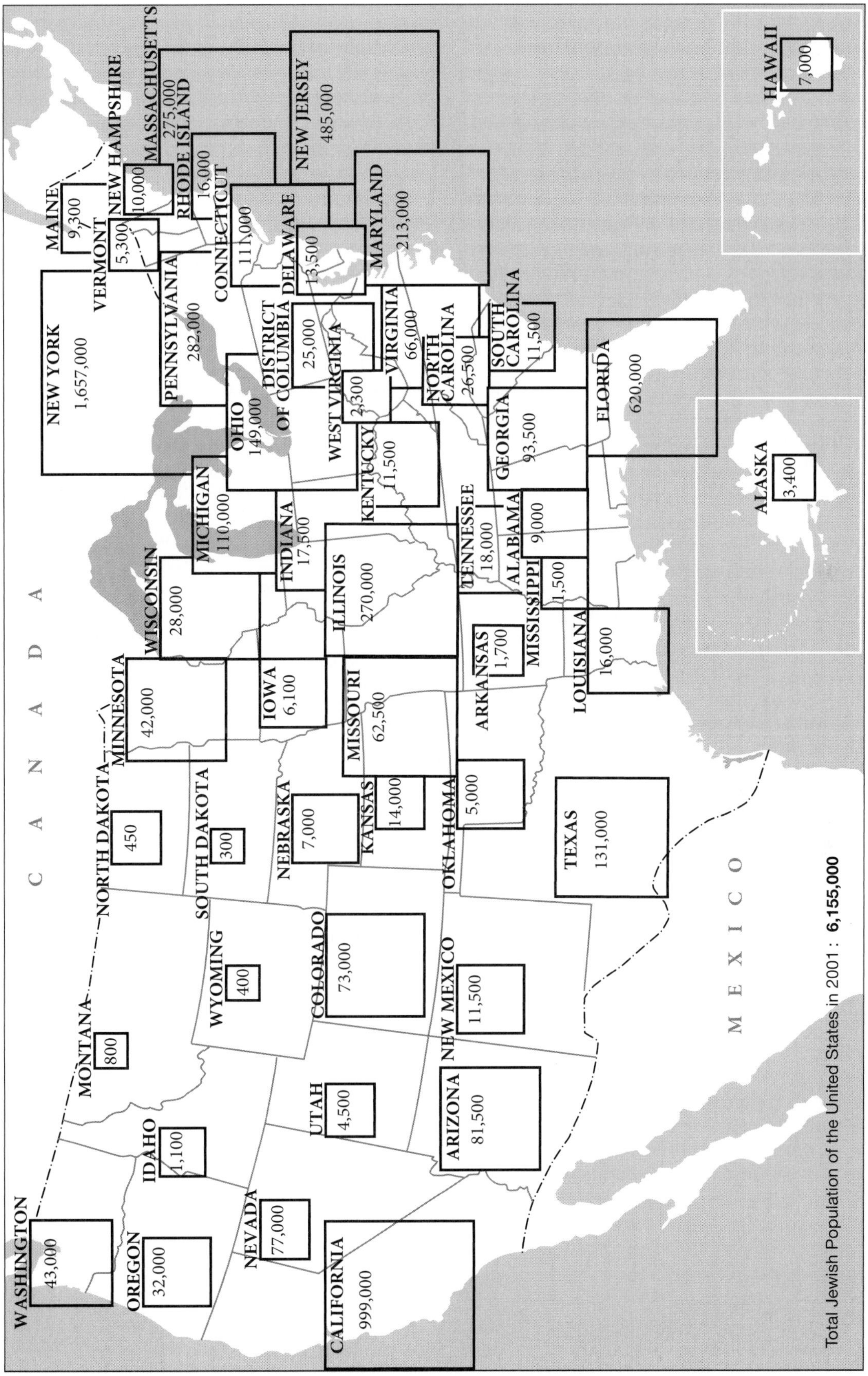

Map 4. Jewish population of the U.S., 2001. Based on American Jewish Year Book.

> cities, representing continuity with an American past. American Jews produced in the postwar era a second generation of cities, offspring of the first generation.

The findings of the *National Jewish Population Survey* in 1990 bear out Moore's assessment. The survey demonstrates that between 1985 and 1990, some 700,000 respondents, or 23.5 percent of the American Jewish population had migrated to at least one new out of state residence. Many of the migrants sought a residential area that included or was in proximity to a synagogue, Jewish school, or a Jewish community center. However, nothing comparable to the highly concentrated Jewish neighborhoods or post-World War II suburbs were being recreated.

With respect to income, the aforementioned 1993 Israeli Ministry of Education study indicated that some 35 percent of American Jews were reported to have earned more than $40,000 a year, compared to only 17 percent of the general American population. About 40 percent of the United States' 400 richest families were reported to be Jewish. The study also revealed that more than half of the American Jewish population under the age of 65 had graduated college, while some 85 percent of young Jews were active in higher education programs, either as students, teacher or researchers. At the other end of the economic spectrum were American Jews living below the poverty line. In the 1980s it was estimated that approximately 250,000 Jews in New York City were living on annual incomes of less than $3,500. In Chicago, where the estimated number of poor Jews was thought to be around 35,000, the Jewish Federation during the mid-1980s created Project Ezra, an umbrella project that coordinated the skills and resources of its various agencies. The majority of the Jewish poor were elderly.

"The High Cost of Jewish Living," a report commissioned by the American Jewish Committee, examined the costs of an active Jewish lifestyle in the 1990s. It estimated that a family of four would have to spend between $18,000 and $25,000 in order to pay for enrollment in a Jewish day school, retain synagogue and Jewish community center membership, cover the cost of a Jewish summer camp or travel to Israel, and make respectable charitable donations to various Jewish philanthropic causes. Other expenses, such as kosher food, regular Sabbath and holiday observance, dues to one or more additional organizations, the purchase of Jewish books and a subscription to one or more Jewish magazines, necessitate "an annual income of $80,000 to $125,000, depending on the region of the country."

A 2001 *Census of United States Synagogues* sponsored by the United Jewish Communities (the umbrella organization formed in 1999 by the Council of Jewish Federations, the United Jewish Appeal, and the United Israel Appeal) revealed that at the close of the century American Jews remained a primarily urban population. "A remarkably high 50 percent of American Jews live in the top three metropolitan areas," it concluded, "and 94 percent in the top 50. Their synagogues are almost as concentrated, with 43 percent in the top three metro areas and 82 percent in the top 50." The study also suggested "Orthodox synagogues are highly overrepresented relative to the Orthodox population."

The 2001 study pointed to 11 regions which sustained communities with Jewish populations of over a hundred thousand: New York-Northern New Jersey-Long Island (2,051,000); Los Angeles-Riverside-Orange County (668,000); Miami-Ft. Lauderdale (331,00); Philadelphia-Wilmington-Atlantic City (285,000); Chicago-Gary-Kenosha (265,000); Boston-Worcester-Lawrence (254,000); San Francisco-Oakland-San Jose (218,000); West Palm Beach-Boca Raton (167,000); Baltimore (106,000); and Detroit-Ann Arbor (103,000). The study also identified eight regions with Jewish communities of over 50,000 inhabitants: Cleveland-Akron (86,000); Atlanta (86,000); Las Vegas (75,000); San Diego (70,000); Denver-Boulder-Greeley (67,000); Phoenix-Mesa (60,000); St. Louis (54,500); and Dallas-Ft. Worth (50,000). There are currently (2001) five regions with Jewish communities of over 40,000 inhabitants (Houston-Galveston-Brazoria; Tampa-St. Petersburg-Clearwater, Minneapolis-St. Paul, Pittsburgh, and Seattle-Tacoma-Bremerton); nine with Jewish communities of over 20,000 inhabitants (Hartford, Portland-Salem, Cincinnati, Rochester, Columbus, Sacramento-Yolo, Milwaukee-Racine, Orlando, and Tucson); 12 regions with Jewish communities ranging from 10,000 to 19,000 inhabitants; and five regions with greater than 8,000 Jewish inhabitants. In all, some 5,806,500 Jews (82.5 percent of the total American Jewish population) resides in the top 50 metropolitan areas in the country. Meanwhile, approximately 348,500 Jews (or roughly 17.5 percent) reside elsewhere in the United States.

CHANGES IN AMERICAN JEWISH IDENTITY. Notwithstanding the wealth of data collected in the past 30 years, the results of various surveys offered analysts, at best, an imperfect picture of the American Jewish scene. The difficulty associated with measuring ethnic identification reflects, at least in part, the ambiguity of the surveys themselves. For example, synagogue affiliation or membership, a standard survey item, did not necessarily accurately reflect a respondent's attitude toward matters of religious observance. Nor was it at all certain that useful assessments could be made on the basis of tabulating behaviors such as attendance at Sabbath services, participation in a Passover *seder*, or the observance of dietary laws, since such practices meant different things to different respondents. The complexity in this regard is illustrated by the following figures, which compare responses to five religious observance survey items that appeared in national surveys undertaken in 1981 and 1990: (1) attend a Passover *seder* – 1981, 77%; 1990, 86%; (2) light Ḥanukkah candles – 1981, 67%, 1990, 77%; (3) belong to a synagogue – 1981, 51%, 1990, 41%; (4) light Sabbath candles – 1981, 22%, 1990, 44%; (5) maintain dietary laws – 1981, 15%, 1990, 17%. At best, the data show that, in general, infrequently practiced activities were more likely to be adhered to than those involving more regular participation.

Global measures of Jewish identification, a concept even more abstract than religious observance, were also evaluated in such surveys. The following comparison of three standard survey items suggests certain trends, namely: (1) most/all friends are Jewish – 1981, 61%; 1990, 45%; (2) contribute to UJA/Federation – 1981, 49%, 1990, 45%; (3) have visited Israel – 1981, 37%, 1990, 31%. Although these items do not define the parameters of Jewish identity, it is significant that responses to all of these items in the 1990 survey had fallen to below 50 percent. Results such as these, combined with additional information from the *National Jewish Population Survey* of 1990, which indicated that only 28 percent of all intermarried couples were raising their children as Jews and over 70 percent were raising their children with no religion or as Christians, intensified expressions of pessimism. Another important trend that came into view by the beginning of the 1980s was that the postponement of marriage, high geographic mobility, a preference for small families, and a growing divorce rate, traits that typified the American middleclass, were now all becoming characteristic of American Jewish life. Indeed, a major finding of the *National Jewish Population Survey* of 1990 was that only 17 percent of all households containing a "core Jew" (a born Jew or a convert) reflected the stereotyped nuclear family consisting of two Jewish parents and children. Thus, the "alternative household," referring variously to a single parent household, a non-married, including same sex couple raising children, a couple that has chosen to remain childless, or a remarried couple raising the offspring of previous marriages together as siblings, was becoming more normative as American Jews continued marrying later, divorcing more frequently, and having fewer children.

The *National Jewish Population Survey* of 1990, the most comprehensive study of American Jewry undertaken since 1970, revealed not only that one-third of all American Jews were married to non-Jews, but among those who had married since 1985, the intermarriage rate had reached an unprecedented 52 percent. The *National Jewish Population Survey* study also reported that the American Jewish community had lost more members (210,000) through conversion than it had gained (185,000). Additional findings of the study, including an increasing divorce rate, greater geographic dispersion, decreasing ritual observance, minimal Jewish education, infrequent synagogue attendance, decreasing formal affiliation among college students and adults, and a decline in Jewish charitable giving, pointed to the further erosion of Jewish communal life. However, for most people it was the revelation regarding high intermarriage rates and low fertility rates that raised the fear of group extinction.

As speculation abounded about the future size of the Jewish community, "assimilationists" argued that the American Jewish community could soon lose the ability to biologically replace itself. To counter these fears "transformationalists" asserted that American Jewish women were openly following the trend of American women in general, who were registering a sharp increase in marriage and fertility between the ages 30–39. This, they argued, combined with an appreciable number of converts to Judaism, would contribute to the stabilization and subsequent growth of the Jewish population, assuming the American Jewish community maintained the minimum replacement average of 2.1 children per couple.

Such concerns about the future of American Jewish life did not dissipate in any appreciable way in the ensuing decade. Furthermore, studies like Charles E. Silberman's *A Certain People: American Jews and Their Lives Today* (1985), Jack Wertheimer's *A People Divided: Judaism in Contemporary America* (1993) and Samuel G. Freedman's *Jew vs. Jew: The Struggle for the Soul of American Jewry* (2000) garnered considerable public and scholarly attention and helped to define and sharpen the parameters of the discussion about the future of American Jewry. After nearly three decades of systematic study and examination by social scientists, communal leaders, and policy makers, the chances for Jewish survival in the shape of ongoing acculturation resulted in a vigorous debate between two camps. The "transformationalists," as the first group became known, posited that American Jews were not abandoning Judaism, Jewish identity, and Jewish communal life, but were instead transforming the concepts associated with Jewish practice and affiliation. They tended to view American Judaism and the American Jewish community as being inclusive rather than exclusive in responding to the challenges of modernity. By contrast, the "assimilationists" interpreted contemporary trends as signifying an ongoing process of assimilation, i.e., the eventual integration beyond recognition of Jews into the general society, a process which, assuming similar ongoing social and economic conditions, they felt was likely to continue.

Among the most cited indicators of this process by analysts and scholars was the rate of intermarriage. By the start of the 1980s the national rate of intermarriage, estimated at roughly 30 percent, was becoming a serious concern within the organized American Jewish community. Studies showed that intermarriage was more common both among younger Jews marrying for the first time and among divorcees who had married for a second or third time. A Council of Jewish Federations/North American Jewish Data Bank report indicated that for the years 1982–87 the percentage of intermarriage among American Jews was 14 percent for first marriages and 40 percent for second marriages. In all studies on the subject, a significant difference was found between men and women in every age group with Jewish men constantly demonstrating a higher rate of intermarriage.

Concern over the high rate of intermarriage was compounded by evidence of the growing number of Jews who had either never married or had not begun a family by the time they had reached their mid-thirties. A 1983 survey of American Jews by the *American Jewish Year Book* estimated that 38 percent of the adult Jewish population of the United States was single. Twenty-one percent reported never having been married. The growing phenomenon of single Jews served as an impetus for the proliferation of Jewish dating services throughout the country. The venerable tradition of Jewish matchmaking was transformed during the 1980s and 1990s into a nationwide industry. Some services, established mainly in large urban areas, were operated on a private commercial basis. Others were run under the non-profit auspices of community agencies such as B'nai B'rith, the Jewish Community Centers, or a local synagogue. With the boom in internet usage, several Jewish dating services went on-line, where they became highly popular and accessible to Jewish singles across the country.

Coupled with gender, denomination was also found to play a role among Jews who had intermarried. While studies showed the intermarriage rate among Orthodox Jews to be negligible, the estimated intermarriage rate among Conservative Jews is about 10 percent and among Reform Jews it is roughly 30 percent. As pointed out by the *American Jewish Identity Survey* of 2001, those calling themselves secular Jews, humanist Jews, or "just Jews," had the highest rate of all groups, with an intermarriage rate of over 50 percent. The findings also indicated that the longer a Jewish family had been in America, the greater the chance that the youngest generation of that family would intermarry.

Another manifestation of such trends was the diminution in strength of several venerable American Jewish organizations. With the notable exception of traditionalist Orthodoxy, the synagogue movements and most of the national Jewish organizations suffered a considerable decline in membership. Zionist organizations that 50 years earlier boasted tens of thousands and even hundreds of thousands of members saw their memberships virtually erode and vanish. This did not necessarily mean that American Jews had become less concerned about Zionism and Israel, but rather that fewer American Jews found it necessary to join a Zionist organizations when they could just as easily express their loyalty to the Zionist cause through contributions to their local Jewish Federations, Israel Bonds, voting for political candidates who support Israel, Israeli tourism, alternative charitable groups like the New Israel Fund, and, in some instances, even urging their children and grandchildren to settle in Israel.

Another indication of increasing acculturation was the growth in the number of reported cases of Jews involved in gambling, alcoholism, drug abuse, and domestic violence, such as incest and rape. The rise in public awareness to these problems could be attributed either to a true increase in the number of incidents or more assiduous documentation by professionals and community officials. Estimates were that between five and ten percent of American Jews could be classified as alcoholics. A smaller percent suffered from drug addiction. The origins of these problems appeared to be unrelated to background, profession, or position in the community. As the seriousness of alcohol and drug addiction within the Jewish community became better appreciated, Jewish support groups were established as an alternative to the Christian-oriented Alcoholics Anonymous.

Cases of domestic violence in the Jewish community, although relatively atypical, became reported more frequently. In 1988 B'nai B'rith women began sponsoring events in chapters across the country geared toward heightening awareness of domestic violence within the Jewish community. The chapters also sponsored the establishment of kosher safe-houses for women in different parts of the country. Meanwhile, social workers reported the tendency of some rabbis to dismiss reports of domestic violence in their congregations because of the difficulty they had conceptualizing this phenomenon within a Jewish household. Nationally, the problem was estimated to affect from one-quarter to one-third of the community. Reported incidents involved physical, emotional, and sexual abuse as well as neglect of spouses, children, and older parents. Until the 1980s little was written about the occurrence of incest among Jewish families. As a result of greater openness and support for victims, the reporting of incidents became more frequent. Instances involving Jewish families were found to be without any relationship to socio-economic or denominational background.

A critical point in social and demographic analysis was reached with the publication of the results of the *National Jewish Population Survey* of 2000–01, which emphasized that "a continuing low Jewish fertility rate, the consequent aging in population composition, and continuing erosion in the willingness to identify with Judaism among the younger age groups [was] apparently [leading] to a significantly lower total core population size" of American Jews. Such findings were generally corroborated by the independent *American Jewish Identity Survey*, sponsored by the Posen Foundation and published in 2001 by the Center for Cultural Judaism. But the latter also went further than any previous study in its assessment of non-religious forms of American Jewish life. In fact, it determined that roughly half of the American Jewish population self-identified as "secular" in its orientation. "America's Jews are divided, perhaps as never before," the report explained, "over a question that would surprise most other Americans who are not familiar with the Jewish heritage or the Jewish community in any way. That question is, quite simply: 'Who is Jewish?' At a more subtle level, the questions asked are, 'What does 'Jewish' mean?' and 'Who gets to decide?' or 'How are those who call themselves 'Jewish' or are labeled as such by others signify that identity or social status to themselves and others?'" Deploying the "dispassionate tools of modern social science," the *American Jewish Identity Survey* analyzed these questions on the basis of a data set comprising a broad spectrum of individuals "who describe[d] themselves as Jewish when asked about their religious adherence or who might be reasonably labeled as Jewish by virtue of their family origins." In the final analysis, the survey produced the following profile of American Jewry:

- Nearly 4% of America's 105 million residential households have at least one member who is Jewish by religion or is of Jewish parentage or upbringing or considers himself/herself Jewish.

- The number of such households has increased since 1990 from about 3.2 million to about 3.9 million.
- The number of persons living in a household that has at least one member who is Jewish by religion or parentage or upbringing or considers himself/herself Jewish has increased since 1990 from about 8 million to nearly 10 million.
- About 5.5 million American adults are Jewish by religion or of Jewish parentage or upbringing or consider themselves Jewish.
- About 3.6 million American adults (or just 65% of the 5.5 million total) have a Jewish mother.
- More than 1.5 million American adults have only one Jewish parent.
- The number of persons who regard themselves as Jewish by religion or say they are of Jewish parentage or upbringing but have no religion (the "core Jewish" population) has declined from about 5.5 million in 1990 to about 5.3 million in 2001.
- The number of persons who are either currently Jewish or of Jewish origins has increased from about 6.8 million in 1990 to nearly 7.7 million in 2001.
- The majority (73%) of America's adults who are Jewish by religion or of Jewish parentage or upbringing but say they have no religion believe that God exists. But nearly half of this population regards itself as secular or somewhat secular in outlook.
- About one million American households report affiliation with a Jewish congregation (synagogue, temple, or an independent havurah). That number represents an increase of some 15% over the 880,000 households reporting congregational affiliation in 1990.
- About 44% of America's adults who are Jewish by religion or say they are of Jewish parentage or upbringing report membership in a Jewish congregation (synagogue, temple, or an independent havurah).
- The Reform branch of Judaism is the largest in terms of the number of adult adherents: about 1.1 million or 30% of America's Jewish-by-religion adults or adults of Jewish parentage or upbringing identify with it.
- The other branches of Judaism in size order are Conservative Judaism with about 940,000 adult adherents (24% of the total), Orthodox Judaism with about 300,000 adult adherents (8% of the total), Secular Humanist Judaism with about 40,000 adherents, and Reconstructionist Judaism with about 35,000 adherents (about 1% each).
- Nearly one million American adults who are Jewish by religion or are of Jewish parentage or upbringing but say they have no religion are affiliated with some noncongregational Jewish community organization such as a Jewish community center or a Jewish fraternal organization.
- Nearly a third of America's adults who are Jewish by religion or say they are of Jewish parentage or upbringing but have no religion have visited Israel. That figure represents a modest increase from the roughly 28% reporting visiting Israel in 1990.
- Nearly 60% of adults who are Jewish by religion are married; of those who report being of Jewish parentage or upbringing but of no religion, just 45% are married. More of the latter group is likely to be separated or divorced or living in a non-marital couple relationship (cohabiting).
- Of all adults married since 1990, who say they are Jewish by religion or of Jewish parentage or upbringing, just 40% are married to a spouse who is also of Jewish origins; 51% are married to a spouse who is not of Jewish origins and an additional 9% are married to a spouse who is a convert to Judaism.
- Of all cohabiting adults who say they are Jewish by religion or of Jewish parentage or upbringing, 81% are living with a partner who is not of Jewish origins.

While observers and scholars of American Jewish society widely agree on the veracity of the *American Jewish Identity Survey*, there is considerable debate about the implications of its findings. It remains for different quarters of the organized American Jewish scene to come to terms with the trends underscored by the survey and develop policies that address the American Jewish community's short- and long-range needs. In the final analysis, although it is impossible to predict the future, a general observation drawn from an overview of American Jewry's past makes clear at least the general contours of future American Jewish policy: Rooted in a historical context shaped by a unique and open liberal environment, the American Jewish community's future very much depends upon its ongoing capacity for innovation, inclusion, and pluralism even as it faces new challenges and seeks new ways for strengthening the bonds of Jewish communal life.

RELIGION. The polarization of American Judaism's denominational groups became a major communal issue at the turn of the 20th and 21st centuries. A chief reason was that by the 1980s Orthodoxy in America had undergone a process of completely unanticipated revitalization. Its growth resulted in greater resources, new and bigger institutions, and subsequently more influence and greater assertiveness within the wider Jewish community. American Orthodoxy's new confidence was bolstered by its ties to the Orthodox establishment in the State of Israel. Traditional American Orthodoxy, in contrast to the modern, or moderate, Orthodoxy associated with New York's *Yeshiva University, was openly committed to reinstituting the type of religious Jewish community life that had flourished in Europe until the eve of World War II. Its leaders reviled American society's emphasis on individualism and pluralism. They recognized as legitimate only their own interpretation of Judaism, which was based on the strict rigid interpretation of *halakhah*.

The historic 1983 decision by the Reform movement's Central Conference of American Rabbis to accept the child of a Jewish father and non-Jewish mother as Jewish without need of conversion; its religious outreach program to families of mixed religions or the unchurched; the decision by the Jewish Theological Seminary in 1983 to ordain Conservative women rabbis; and the announcement in 1987 to graduate women as Conservative cantors all served to exacerbate existing tensions within American Judaism. Although united with Reform Judaism over the legitimacy of religious pluralism, the Conservative movement's understanding of *halakhah* forced it to reject the Reform position on patrilineal descent. The decision by the Reform movement to recognize patrilineal descent was so controversial as to prompt the appearance in 1985 of Alexander Shapiro, president of the Conservative Rabbinical Assembly, before the Central Conference of American Rabbis. Addressing his Reform colleagues, Shapiro cautioned that "if patrilinealism remains in place, then Conservative rabbis might have to question the Jewish status of someone from a sister movement," resulting in "a cleavage in Jewish life which would threaten the survival of the Jewish people."

Orthodox leaders were also outspoken on this issue. Haskel *Lookstein, a moderate Orthodox spokesman and president of the New York Board of Rabbis, characterized Reform's adoption of patrilineal descent as "a wedge… that fosters polarization, anger, resentment, bitterness, and divisiveness." Traditional Orthodox leaders went further and denounced what they viewed as the continuing erosion of Jewish life in America. In 1986 America's Agudat Israel and its Council of Torah Sages attacked Reform and Conservative Judaism, refusing to sanction any form of dialogue with any of its representatives.

The ongoing ferment within Conservative Judaism over the flexibility of Jewish law, especially controversy over the status of women, led to a major ideological fracture. In 1984 a breakaway organization calling itself the Union for Traditional Judaism (UTJ) succeeded in drawing rabbis and lay people who were disgruntled over the Rabbinical Assembly's 1983 decision to ordain women rabbis. In 1992 the UTJ incorporated the approximately 100 rabbis belonging to the Fellowship of Traditional Orthodox Rabbis. The latter group constituted the more liberal wing of the Orthodox rabbinate concerned about the growing strength and influence of its more right-wing elements. By the mid-1990s the UTJ had grown to include some 8,000 families and approximately 350 rabbis.

The increasing polarization between Orthodoxy's modern and sectarian streams beset communities throughout the United States and was both ideological and pragmatic. Modern Orthodoxy defended the legitimacy of combining the ethos of contemporary society and traditional Judaism. The more conservative, sectarian Orthodox, generally referred to as the "ultra-Orthodox," rejected this approach, preferring to minimize communication and social interaction with those outside their own groups. By the early 1990s, traditional Orthodox circles came to dominate Orthodox community life. Among younger Jews in particular, the religious stringencies associated with traditional Orthodoxy became more normative.

In the early 1990s the Chabad-Lubavitch Ḥasidim, based in the Crown Heights neighborhood of Brooklyn, received considerable media attention following the physical incapacitation of their leader Menachem Mendel Schneersohn. Lubavitch openly split between those who believed Schneersohn had the potential to be the messiah and those who were certain he had already been anointed. As Schneersohn's physical condition continued to deteriorate, a power struggle ensued over the control of the worldwide Lubavitch empire. Schneersohn's death in 1994 left Chabad-Lubavitch Ḥasidim all over the world stunned and uncertain. His New York funeral was attended by tens of thousands of Ḥasidim and other admirers, including dignitaries from the United States and abroad.

Although the majority of American Jews shunned formal synagogue affiliation in the 1980s and 1990s, some sought religious expression in alternative settings. In 1992 the Reconstructionist movement, a branch of Conservative Judaism established in 1934 by Mordecai M. *Kaplan, claimed about 2 percent of American Jews and some 70 congregations. In 1994 the *American Jewish Year Book* called *Seek My Face, Speak My Name* by Arthur *Green, president of the Reconstructionist Rabbinical College, "the first serious attempt to arrive at a contemporary understanding of Judaism based not on rationalism, ethics, or *halakhah*, but on the Jewish mystical tradition." Green's personal interest in mysticism permeated the Reconstructionist movement. This paralleled the interest in mysticism and New Age philosophies expressed by many young Jewish adults. Though inconsistent with Kaplan's rational philosophical approach, Green's orientation reflected the movement's incorporation of current social and cultural trends.

While many "New Age" Jews turned to Reconstructionism for spiritual fulfillment, others opted for community-based havurot (Jewish fellowships). These groups, which spread throughout the country in the 1980s and 1990s, functioned either independently of or in association with a synagogue. Though not always spiritual or even prayer-focused (some centered on text study, politics, culture, or Jewish cuisine), havurot represented the informal and intimate Jewish community experience thought to be lacking in most established synagogues. Still other Jewish seekers after spirituality cultivated an interest in Jewish meditation. In 1993 the Jewish Telegraphic Agency reported that "for many meditators who were estranged from the Jewish community and traditional practices, and who have little Jewish education, contemplation has provided a port of re-entry." Among centers of practice were the Jewish Meditation Circle of Manhattan, the School of Traditional Jewish Meditation in Los Angeles, and a mountaintop retreat center located some 40 miles northwest of Boulder, Colorado.

In some cases, Jewish meditation served as a bridge back to Jewish practice for many Jews who had been involved with cults. Although the actual number of Jews in cults was not known, it was estimated that as many as 70 percent of participants in Buddhist and Hindu groups in North America were Jews. Among the cults in which Jews were believed to be disproportionately represented were Sun Myung Moon's Unification Church (Moonies), Hare Krishna, the Oregon-based followers of Bhagwan Shree Rajneesh, Synanon, and Scientology. Contemporary observers attributed the latter phenomenon to (1) the openness of liberal minded Jews to alternative political and theological ideas; (2) the strong presence of Jews on college and university campuses where cults invested heavily in recruitment; and (3) the difficulty many young Jews had in forming independent adult identities as a result of coming from nurturing and secure families.

WOMEN. Surveying the dynamic role of women in American Jewish life and the impact of Jewish feminism on the American scene, the scholar Sylvia Barack Fishman offered the following perspective on the period under investigation:

> Remembering that women comprise, after all, at least one-half of the Jewish people, it seems appropriate for Jewish survivalists of all denominations to reconsider the validity of feminist goals case by case and to search for constructive ways in which to reconcile Jewish feminism with the goals of Jewish survival. It is hard to imagine what communal good could be served by adhering to an automatic anti-feminist stance. On the other hand, it seems appropriate for Jewish feminists, to the extent that they are serious about Jewish survival, to weigh carefully the repercussions of proposed changes and to consider their responsibility to the community as a whole. Indeed, it is one of the achievements of American Jewish feminism that women are now in a position to examine these issues – and to make choices.

Of particular note in this period was the greater role of women in almost every area of communal leadership. In 1986 Peggy *Tishman became head of New York City's United Jewish Appeal-Federation, the largest in the country, while Shoshana *Cardin became chair of the Council of Jewish Federations and Welfare Funds. In general, however, Jewish women professionals working for the Jewish community found themselves victims of the "glass ceiling" phenomenon. At a Women's Economic Summit convened in 1993 by the National Jewish Community Relations Advisory Council and the American Jewish Congress, a number of speakers suggested that Jewish communal agencies should begin addressing women's economic inequity by evaluating their own hiring, promotion, pay and benefits patterns and policies.

In a survey of 42 national Jewish agencies, including the American Jewish Congress, the Council of Jewish Federations, the Hebrew Immigrant Aid Society, and the Jewish Telegraphic Agency, it was discovered that 37 were run by men. Similarly, out of the 157 Jewish federations with paid professional leadership, the 30 run by women executive directors were almost all small or mid-size. Only the Jewish Federation of Hartford, Connecticut, one of 23 federations categorized as larger intermediate-size, was directed by a woman. In spite of the fact the 60 percent of employees at federations were female, none of the 18 largest federations employed a woman as executive director. A separate Council of Jewish Federations survey revealed that about one-third of the campaign directors in large and intermediate-size federations were women. While entry-level positions in Jewish federations offered equal remuneration to men and women, senior-level female staff earned between 67 and 92 percent of what men in comparable positions were earning; 80 percent of the respondents to an internal survey of senior professional women at federations cited the "old boys" network as the primary factor behind hiring and advancement discrimination.

In a parallel vein, although the Reconstructionist, Reform, and Conservative synagogue movements opened the doors of their respective seminaries to growing numbers of women, this did not mean that women in these streams of Judaism were free of harassment and sexism. The results of a survey conducted in 1992 by the American Jewish Congress revealed that 73 percent of the 142 women rabbis who responded claimed to have been sexually harassed by congregants and other rabbis; 54 percent claimed to have experienced sexual discrimination consisting of denial of equal pay, benefits, or differential treatment in hiring, firing or job responsibilities. The women reported that only one in five of the synagogues, organizations or institutions at which they worked maintained a sexual discrimination policy.

Even as traditional and mainstream Orthodoxy remained firmly opposed to the notion of women rabbis, a few voices from within the movement called for dialogue on the issue. The most vociferous advocate in this regard was author and community leader Blu Greenberg, who pointed out the extensive learning and erudition among American Jewish women, which, if they were men, would qualify them for Orthodox rabbinical ordination. "I believe the ordination of Orthodox women is close at hand," she wrote in 1993. "The cumulative impact – of a critical mass of students of Talmud and *halakhah*, a plethora of rising-star teachers, the support of educational institutions and the presence of respected women rabbis in the liberal denominations – will be to transform the expectations of Orthodox women. This will be a powerful agent for change." To this end, womens' *tefillah* (prayer) groups were organized in a number of Jewish communities in the United States. The groups followed an Orthodox prayer service, without men, that included a full Torah reading. In 1993 over a hundred women from around the country met in New York for the third Women's Tefillah Conference.

Additionally, Jewish women continued to play significant and visible roles in wider American society. A striking example in this regard is the case of the scientist Gertrude B. *Elion, who in 1988 won the Nobel Prize in medicine. The daughter of Polish and Lithuanian immigrants and descended from a line of distinguished rabbis, Elion's family immigrated to the United States before World War I. She graduated in 1937 from Hunter College in New York City, but was rejected by fifteen graduate school programs and research institutes owing to discrimination against women in the sciences in the 1940s and 1950s. After working as an unpaid lab assistant in order to acquire further research experience, she was hired by a pharmaceuticals company to work with nucleic acids. Her pathbreaking medical research led to the discovery of the drug, azathioprine, used to facilitate kidney transplants and treat rheumatoid arthritis, and the development of thioguanine and mercaptopurine, which is used in chemotherapy to treat children with leukemia. Her name is attached to some 23 honorary degrees and 45 patents, including a drug that can be used to treat chicken pox, genital herpes, encephalitis, and shingles. By the time of her death in 1999, she was regarded as one of America's most eminent scientist.

HOMOSEXUALITY. Homosexuality drew increased communal attention during this period as the different denominations either proclaimed or debated their official position on the subject. The position of Orthodoxy remained that such activity under any circumstances constituted, as stated in the Torah, a moral abomination. Abstinence in combination with therapy or medication was the only prescribed treatment. Nonetheless, by the end of the 1980s approximately 20 gay and lesbian congregations existed around the country.

In 1990 the Reform movement's Central Conference of American Rabbis endorsed a resolution accepting the view that "all rabbis, regardless of sexual orientation, be accorded the opportunity to fulfill the sacred vocation which they have chosen..." and that "all Jews are religiously equal regardless of their sexual orientation." Although the Reform rabbinate officially accepted homosexuality, including homosexual rabbis, it continued to affirm heterosexual relations as the ideal. This sent something of a mixed message, not only to Reform congregants, but also to the movement's clergy. As a consequence, some gay rabbinical students chose not to reveal their sexual orientation. Likewise, homosexual pulpit rabbis were confronted with the dilemma of "coming out" with the support of their colleagues while possibly offending their congregations.

It was the Reconstructionist movement that went the farthest in embracing homosexuality. In 1992 the Federation of Reconstructionist Congregations and Havurot issued a formal statement calling for an end to all distinctions between heterosexuals and homosexuals in Jewish life. Homosexual Jews, of both genders, were welcomed into the Reconstructionist rabbinate. The Reconstructionist position was that since homosexuality is a fundamental component of an individual's psychological makeup and not subject to change, it was natural and acceptable in the eyes of God. Same-sex relationships were considered as holy as those between a man and a woman and could, in the same manner, comprise a legitimate and stable Jewish family. To solemnize these relationships, Reconstructionist clergy performed "commitment" ceremonies. The Reconstructionists encouraged gay and lesbian Jews to develop their own rituals, to celebrate their own special lifecycle events, and to introduce the stories of gay and lesbian Jews into Jewish history.

Participants at the 1992 annual meeting of the Conservative movement's Rabbinical Assembly voted to allow their colleagues to be employed by gay and lesbian congregations. In addition, a commission was created to study human sexuality and to develop a Conservative perspective on the issue. That same year, the Jewish National Fund (JNF) and the World Congress of Gay and Lesbian Jewish Organizations resolved a dispute that had been ongoing for 13 years. The JNF agreed to affixing a plaque bearing the words "Fourth International Congress of Gay and Lesbian Jews" at Lahav in southern Israel. Members of this organization had planted a 3,000 tree forest at the site in 1979.

The May 1993 New York City Israel Day Parade was clouded by the controversy over the request for formal participation by Manhattan's Beth Simchat Torah, the nation's largest gay and lesbian synagogue. The main opponents were the heads of Orthodox primary and high school yeshivot whose pupils traditionally comprised at least half of the parade's marchers. The schools' principals would not allow their students to participate if the gay synagogue marched as an identifiable unit, reasoning this would sanction its legitimacy. In spite of protracted negotiations over a compromise formula, none was found and the parade's sponsor, the American Zionist Youth Foundation, excluded the gay synagogue from the event.

PHILANTHROPY AND COMMUNAL ORGANIZATION. During the 1980s and 1990s, there developed a complex web of regional agencies and institutions. The swift expansion of local bureaus of Jewish education, Jewish day schools and yeshivot, and the growing number of departments and programs of Jewish studies in colleges and universities across the country underscored a deepening commitment to matters of Jewish education and scholarship. In addition, the Jewish Welfare Board became the national umbrella group for the Jewish community center movement, providing guidance, personnel and other resources to the growing number of community centers, many of which expanded to include adult education programs, summer camps, Israel trips, and elaborate health clubs as well as other services of a recreational nature. In short, regional Jewish communities became, in many respects, autonomous. They no longer necessarily looked to New York or Chicago for leadership, but now set their own agendas and turned to local Jewish agencies, philanthropists, and scholars for support and guidance. A parallel phenomenon was the diminished role of volunteers and increased importance of permanent professionals in most organizations and philanthropic agencies.

The remarkable successes of American Jewish philanthropy in this period underscore the extent to which community affairs revolved around campaigns for charitable funds. By far, the Council of Jewish Federations, the United Jewish Appeal, and the United Israel Appeal – brought together in 1999 under the banner of the "United Jewish Communities" – was the single most effective vehicle for collecting funds for a variety of institutions, local, national, and overseas. In 1980 the United Jewish Appeal reported pledges amounting to $528 million; cash collected amounted to $301 million. Of this sum $245 million went to the United Israel Appeal. The United Jewish Appeal's Israel Emergency Fund, originally launched in 1967 in response to the Six-Day War, in 1970 received pledges amounting to $124 million, in addition to cash receipts of $180 million for its regular campaign. Again a crisis in the Middle East had its effect on the level of American Jewish giving. Following the outbreak in 1973 of the Yom Kippur War, the United Jewish Appeal results for 1974 (including the Israel Emergency Fund) rose to $481 million. In the 1980s and 1990s, the national trend was toward a decrease in the proportion sent to Israel. Thus, in 1983 national United Jewish Appeal received approximately 48 percent of the combined federation campaign, domestic needs received 29 percent, and the remaining 23 percent went to other overseas causes. By comparison, in 1991 the national United Jewish Appeal received 40 percent, 36 percent was retained for local agencies, and 24 percent was allocated overseas.

The Chronicle of Philanthropy ranked the United Jewish Appeal first in fundraising contributions in 1992, "more than any other non-profit organization." The $668.1 million reported was not based on total income because government grants and other earning (such as income from endowments and investments) were not included. The death of billionaire Baltimorian Harry *Weinberg in 1991 resulted in the largest Jewish-oriented foundation in the world. With assets of $762.8 million, it ranked as the 22nd largest foundation in the United States. A quarter of its annual grants were reserved for Jewish groups, another 25 percent for non-Jewish causes, and the remaining 50 percent was not earmarked for any particular group.

Fund raising efforts for Israel outside the United Jewish Appeal or the Federation structure are also noteworthy. Sales of State of Israel Bonds in the United States which, when inaugurated in 1951 amounted to $52 million, reached $175 million in 1970, $295 million in 1978, and in excess of $350 million in 1981. By 2000 the leadership of Israel Bonds reported that over $20 billion in investment capital for the development of every aspect of Israel's economic infrastructure had been raised in the previous 50 years.

Further solidifying its role as the "central address of the Jewish community" during these years, the United Jewish Communities proved its ability to respond to various emergencies and natural disasters. At the turn of the 20th century, the organization developed a close working relationship with the Federal Emergency Management Agency (FEMA), the American Red Cross, the Salvation Army, and other aid groups. Together with these agencies, it provided hundreds of millions of dollars in emergency relief to communities in the Miami area devastated by Hurricane Andrew in 1992, to the victims of the earthquake that shook Los Angeles in 1994, to the families of victims killed in the Al Qaeda terrorist attack of September 11, 2001, and to the communities of Louisiana, Mississippi, Texas, Alabama, and Florida devastated in 2005 by Hurricanes Katrina, Rita, and Wilma. While a sizable quotient of these monies specifically targeted Jewish communal needs, substantial sums were also raised for general rescue and relief purposes. Nonetheless, critics charged the United Jewish Communities – which by this period had a combined income of $2.2 billion – with exploiting crises affecting American society and the Jewish people in order to meet the organization's predetermined fundraising goals and solidify its centralized control of community resources. Allegations of impropriety were also raised concerning the United Jewish Communities' dependency upon political consensus as well as the generous salaries and benefits enjoyed by high-ranking Jewish Federation executives, especially some who earned six-figure salaries akin to America's leading corporate executives.

Parallel to the framework of the organized Jewish community, American Jews generally continued to be active on behalf of a wide variety of social, political, and philanthropic causes that exceeded the orbit of the community's specifically Jewish interests, including considerable grassroots support for the civil rights of homosexuals, assistance for the victims of the AIDS virus and support for medical research to find a cure for the disease, abortion rights, the struggle against apartheid in South Africa and militant regimes around the globe, the nuclear freeze movement, protecting the environment, the feminist movement, support for the homeless, and putting an end to worldwide poverty and hunger. While many Jews comfortably opted for membership in social and humanitarian organizations at large, others felt the need to establish alternative organizations comprised solely of Jewish membership since they viewed their commitment to these causes as an expression of their Jewish identity. Specific examples of the latter included the Jewish Fund for Justice, which provided grants to fight poverty in America; the American Jewish World Service, which funded environmental development programs in the Third World; Mazon: A Jewish Response to Hunger, which supported anti-hunger programs among Jews and non-Jews in the United States and abroad; the National Jewish AIDS Project, an educational body created to raise the consciousness of Jewish communal leaders and organizations about the AIDS virus; the Jewish Fund for Justice, which disbursed money to both Jewish and non-Jewish housing and community revitalization projects; the Shefa Fund, which supported projects related to social and economic justice, the impact of gender and the arts; and the New Israel Fund, which disbursed money to a wide range of programs in Israel dedicated to social change, including civil rights, women's rights, and Israeli-Palestinian coexistence. Together these groups raised hundreds of millions of dollars.

American Jewish commitment to the commonweal was also exemplified by the Jewish Volunteer Corps (JVC), which sent Jewish professionals to assist in developing countries. The JVC, established in 1993, grew out of the American Jewish World Service, another worldwide relief organization operating under private Jewish auspices. Like the more established American Jewish World Service, the JVC dedicated itself exclusively to providing grass-roots level assistance to non-Jews in Third World countries. Participants were trained and dispatched for up to six months to remote areas of Nepal, Mexico, Zimbabwe, Tanzania, Senegal, Bangladesh and Honduras, as well as other countries. Modeled on the American Peace

Corps, JVC volunteers were assigned to agricultural projects, rural medical clinics, nutritional programs, small business development schemes, environmental preservation and soil conservation efforts, and basic literacy programs.

By contrast, mainstream Jewish organizations suffered a serious decline in membership during this period. B'nai B'rith, the oldest national Jewish membership organization in the United States, saw its membership drop from a post-World War II era high of some 200,000 in the 1960s to about 136,000 in the 1980s and then to under 100,000 in the 1990s. With an accumulated deficit of over $4 million, a largely middle-class and working-class membership whose average age was in the mid-60s, and a membership shrinking at an average rate of 9 percent a year, B'nai B'rith president Kent E. Schiner acknowledged in 1995 that the fraternal order had become "irrelevant to a new generation of successful, more assimilated Jews with no need or desire for their own private club." Likewise, the growing involvement of professional Jewish women in the workplace during this period made it more difficult for organizations like Amit, Hadassah, the National Council for Jewish Women, ORT, and Naamat USA (formerly Pioneer Women), to recruit new members. As noted previously, the synagogue movements were also threatened by steadily declining membership and all studies pointed to the inescapable conclusion that in this period the majority of third- and fourth-generation American Jews were even less likely to join a congregation than their parents or grandparents.

A handful of national Jewish organizations experienced significant growth and development in the 1990s. The most successful was the Los Angeles-based *Simon Wiesenthal Center. By the end of 1992, it reported approximately 385,000 contributors, an annual budget of about $12 million, and a professional staff of 100. Another organization which grew in popularity toward the end of this era was American Friends of Peace Now (renamed Americans for Peace Now in 1989). Throughout most of the 1980s, American Friends of Peace Now was on the margins of American Jewish life, but its credibility was firmly established with the ascendancy of the Labor-led coalition government in Israel after the 1992 election. It reported 10,000 members divided among 21 chapters throughout the United States, and was accepted for membership in the Conference of Presidents of Major American Jewish Organizations.

Both as individuals and through the auspices of various organizations, American Jews continued to play a role in causes beyond the borders of the Jewish community. Some national Jewish organizations increased their Middle East activities. In 1992, for example, American Jewish Congress leaders made an unprecedented trip to Saudi Arabia for talks with King Fahd and senior Saudi officials. That same year, the American Jewish Joint Distribution Committee (JDC) was asked by the United States government to assist in the distribution of aid in the new republics of the Commonwealth of Independent States. This included an agreement that the JDC signed with the U.S. Department of Agriculture to distribute $7 million worth of food. The escalating inter-communal turmoil in Bosnia-Herzegovina took on special significance for many American Jews who reacted with alarm to reports of "ethnic cleansing" by Serbian troops. Television news coverage of skeletal figures languishing in Serbian prisoner-of-war and concentration camps evoked painful memories of the Holocaust. Against this backdrop, all the major American Jewish organizations adopted the cause of the former Yugoslavia. The JDC organized the rescue in 1993 of some 350 Jewish, Muslim, Serbian, and Croatian refugees under siege in Sarajevo. Such philanthropic and humanitarian activity continued unabated over the course of the decade. In 1999–2000 the JDC spearheaded a concerted effort by several leading American Jewish groups, including the American Jewish Committee, the American Jewish World Service, the Hebrew Immigrant Aid Society, ORT, and the Simon Wiesenthal Center in Los Angeles, to provide assistance to hundreds of thousands of Kosovar refugees who fled to Albania and Macedonia following the NATO air strikes. In this period, the JDC also raised over $500,000 for the victims of the calamitous earthquake that struck Turkey.

EDUCATION AND CULTURE. At the midpoint of the period under review, the 1990 *National Jewish Population Survey* reported that 3,350,000 of those surveyed were estimated to have received some form of Jewish education at some point in their lives. Even so, fewer women than men were the recipients of formal Jewish education. The survey also reported the median years of Jewish education for this age group to have been 6.2 for males and 4.6 for females.

Jewish education was not restricted to formal classroom education. Particular effort was devoted to developing and marketing "the Israel experience." Research confirmed that "the short-term summer-time Israel experience very often profoundly influences how youngsters relate to Israel and to their Jewishness." At the General Assembly in 1993, the CRB (Charles R. Bronfman) Foundation of Montreal announced an "Israel experience" incentive program. The foundation would commit one dollar towards sponsoring the participation of a Jewish youth in one of many Israel experience programs for every three dollars contributed by a local Jewish federation and other community resources. Its objective was to make a trip to Israel affordable to every Jewish North American high school student so that by the turn of the century 50,000 Jewish teenagers would visit Israel each year. (In fact, in 2006 the program reported a total of over 100,000 participants.) As conceived, the Israel Experience was intended to complement, if not replace, the more conventional American Jewish summer camp experience. Over the years the latter had a demonstrable positive effect on the Jewish identity of youth.

In spite of the availability of adult or continuing Jewish education classes in synagogues, community centers, and Jewish community colleges around the country, outside of the Orthodox community Jewish education remained primarily a part-time activity associated with Jewish childhood.

The quality of American Jewish education varied greatly from one communal context to the next. An attempt to improve the quality of Jewish education nationally came in 1981 when the Federation movement established the Jewish Education Service of North America (JESNA). JESNA was founded "to improve the quality and strengthen the impact of Jewish education by providing leadership and a broad range of services and informational resources locally, throughout North America, and in relationships with Israeli and world educational institutions." Despite such efforts, there was a clear impression by the end of the decade that Jewish education as a nationwide communal enterprise was not succeeding.

In an attempt to remedy this situation, a private, interdenominational and non-partisan body consisting of noted Jewish educators and top philanthropists calling itself the Commission of Jewish Education in North America was created in 1988. Unofficially it was known as the Mandel Commission, having been spearheaded by Jewish community leader and philanthropist Morton L. Mandel of Cleveland. In 1990 the commission produced a major report, "A Time to Act," which analyzed the condition of Jewish education in North America and offered a concrete plan of action whose goal was to "significantly improve the effectiveness of Jewish education (within) a coalition of community institutions, supplemented with continental institutions and resources."

The question of state aid to parochial schools continued to divide the American Jewish community. It was long axiomatic for the major Jewish organizations to uphold the strict separation of church and state, thus precluding anything in the nature of state support, but in the 1976 American presidential election the Orthodox community made it clear that it would welcome government subsidies to its Jewish day schools. As the debate intensified in the 1990s over the place of Jewish day schools in the American setting, an increasing number of organizations, agencies, and communal leaders acceded to the agenda set out by the Mandel commission. In 1999, the Jewish Educational Service of North America (JESNA), a branch of the United Jewish Communities whose stated goal is "to make engaging, inspiring, high quality Jewish education available to every Jew in North America," announced that "No Jewish family that desires to send its children to a Jewish day school should be prevented from doing so due to financial reasons." As part of this ideological trend and in response to growth of the Jewish day school movement countrywide, many major metropolitan Jewish Federations increased the size of their allocations to local Jewish day schools. Notwithstanding mixed assessments over the effectiveness of many of these schools, the day school movement continued to spread while supplementary afternoon and Sunday schools declined in importance everywhere. In 2000, a study released by the Avi Chai Foundation revealed that the number of students enrolled in Jewish day schools had in fact risen by 25,000 since 1990, reaching a nationwide total of approximately 185,000. This figure cut across all denominational categories and included student enrollments in hundreds of Orthodox schools, more than 70 Conservative movement-sponsored schools (e.g., Solomon Schechter schools), 22 Reform movement-sponsored schools, and a growing number of pluralistic nondenominational community day schools. The success of the Jewish day school movement alarmed some critics, who worried openly that it might result in a weakening of Jewish support for the American public education system. In the context of this debate, it was observed that the proportion of Jewish children in public schools had declined from roughly 90 percent in 1962 to 65 percent in 2000. Some voiced concern about non-Jewish perceptions of the Jewish day school movement and the continued integration of Jews in American life. Others called for a reassessment of American Jewry's time honored liberal tradition of support for public education and proposed the community as whole embrace the concept of government vouchers for private education.

In this period, studies also revealed that an estimated 80 to 85 percent of American Jews received some college or university education, with more than 50 percent earning at least a bachelor's degree. It was also during these years that about 350 colleges and universities, excluding seminaries and divinity schools, undertook the teaching of Judaica in one form or another. The Association for Jewish Studies, composed of scholars and academicians in the field, grew to over 900 members. Courses in Hebrew and Yiddish language and literature, the Holocaust, and Zionism and Israel were among those garnering the most substantial student interest. By the end of the 20th century, more than half of all American Jews under the age of 65 were college graduates. A disproportionate number of Jewish college graduates went on to graduate studies in pursuit of a professional career. It was further estimated that some 85 percent of young Jews were active at colleges and universities either as students, teachers, or researchers.

Among areas of educational and cultural life that experienced a swift revival in this period was Yiddish. The establishment of the *National Yiddish Book Center, located at Hampshire College in Amherst, Massachusetts, signaled the dramatic growth of interest in Yiddish among college students. By 1994, according to center founder and director Aaron Lansky, the center had managed to collect 1.2 million Yiddish books and managed an annual operating budget of $1.2 million.

Meanwhile, the 70-year-old national Jewish student organization *Hillel generally attracted no more than 15 percent of the local Jewish student body. With few exceptions, Hillel's ostensibly parochial agenda proved unattractive to a majority of Jewish students otherwise engaged in the open and liberal American campus environment. To complicate matters, Hillel's parent organization, B'nai B'rith, experienced severe financial difficulties and was forced to cut its support to less than 1 percent of Hillel's annual budget. In 1992 Hillel determined to expand and offer a more sophisticated array of Jewish cultural and social programs. To accompany its new image, the organization's name was officially changed to "Hillel: The Foundation for Jewish Campus Life." Under the leadership of

Hillel's new international director, Richard Joel, the organization set out to secure private endowments in order to pay for new outreach, leadership, and professional development programs. A major source of support was Edgar M. Bronfman, Sr.'s Fund for Jewish Campus Life. Additional funding came from the Council of Jewish Federations (the predecessor of the United Jewish Communities). In previous years, Jewish student leaders and activists had vigorously criticized the Council of Jewish Federations for neglecting to allocate sufficient support to campus programs. Now, in response to an organized student lobbying effort, the Council of Jewish Federations agreed to double its previous annual contribution of $8.5 million to the Hillel organization. The reinvigoration of Hillel as a national organization was only partly successful. Meanwhile, another strategy for strengthening the identity of young American Jews was designed and led by a small group of philanthropists. In 1998 Michael Steinhardt and Charles Bronfman launched Birthright Israel, a program created to ensure that every American Jew between the ages of 15 and 26 would have – as his/her "birthright" – the opportunity for a free ten-day visit to Israel. Despite the program's success, the concept as a whole yielded mixed results. It was hampered in part due to the complex interplay between, on the hand, the American Jewish philanthropists who created it and, on the other, the regional Jewish Federations and Israeli government which pledged to support it but who were reluctant to assume responsibility for its long-range support.

The area of the arts in American Jewish life advanced in this period, too, as evidenced by the productions of Jewish theater groups across the country including San Francisco's "Traveling Jewish Theater," the establishment of annual Jewish art and film festivals in major cities, and the success of the American Jewish Theatre in New York City, Theatre J in Washington, DC, and the Martin Steinberg Center for the Arts, an American Jewish Congress affiliate. Three forms of Jewish music, choral, klezmer, and contemporary liturgical, contributed to the cultural revival of the period. The former was especially well represented by the highly accomplished Boston-based Zamir Chorale. Originally founded in New York in 1960 under the direction of Stanley Sperber, by the 1980s there were similar choral organizations in Boston, Washington, D.C., Connecticut, Chicago, and Los Angeles. The proliferation of Jewish choirs was sufficient for the creation of the American Hebrew Choral Festival whose annual performances drew capacity audiences. Klezmer music, a form of popular Jewish music based largely on the wedding melodies used in Eastern Europe and songs from the golden age of Yiddish theater, experienced a remarkable revival in the United States after having become virtually extinct. The rise of klezmer bands began in the 1970s but experienced the greatest growth during the 1980s and 1990s. Virtually every major American city became home to at least one klezmer ensemble – with colorful and playful names such as Brave Old World, Beyond the Pale, the Chicago Klezmer Ensemble, the Klezmatics, the Klezmer Conservatory Band, the Maxwell Street Klezmer Band, and the Sabras Klezmer Band – and as a result klezmer music garnered considerable recognition and popularity among young audiences. Finally, contemporary Jewish liturgical and folk music, especially the recordings and performances of singer-songwriter Debbie *Friedman, but also the work of other artists including Rachel Cole, the Zmiros Project (Frank London, Lorin Sklamberg, and Rob Schwimmer), and Paul Zim, became widely popular.

Handcrafted Judaica developed into a major form of Jewish artistic expression in the latter decades of 20th century. Jewish ritual objects and symbols such as the *ḥanukkiyyah* (Ḥanukkah *menorah*), the wine goblet, the *mezuzah*, the spice box, and the prayer shawl, found new forms of expression in various media, including wood, metal, precious metals, fabrics, plastic, and glass. The *ketubbah* (marriage contract) was developed into a sophisticated form of artwork. The legal text was hand-written calligraphy, often on genuine parchment and embellished with Jewish and Israeli motifs and themes.

The largest single event for Jewish youth in North America was the Maccabi Youth Games, organized every two years under the auspices of the Jewish Community Centers of North America (JCCA), in association with the United States Sports Committee for Israel, Maccabi Canada, and Maccabi World Union. The games attracted some 2,500 participants between the ages of 13–16. Represented at the games were some 70 American Jewish communities, as well as Canada, Mexico, Australia, Great Britain, and Israel. An Olympic-style event featuring athletic competition in more than 12 different sports, regional games are held every other year.

Unprecedented growth also took place in the area of Jewish children's literature. It has long been the case that American children's literature has been enriched and shaped by the infusion of well-produced creative fiction and non-fiction by American Jewish authors, including early popular works such as Sydney Taylor's *All-of-a-Kind Family* (1951), Joanne Greenberg's (pseud. Hannah Green) *I Never Promised You a Rose Garden* (1964), Maurice Sendak's *Where the Wild Things Are* (1964), Elaine L. Konigsburg's *From the Mixed-Up Files of Mrs. Basil E. Frankfurter* (1967), Judy Blume's *Are You There God? It's Me, Margaret* (1970), Barbara Cohen's *The Carp in the Bathtub* (1972), Judith Viorst's *Alexander and the Terrible, Horrible, No Good, Very Bad Day* (1972), and Bette Greene's *Summer of My German Soldier* (1973). The 1980s and 1990s witnessed a veritable surge in children's literature produced by American Jewish authors as well as a plethora of works of specifically Jewish content including, for example, the following wide array of books: Sandy Asher's *Summer Begins* (1980), Anita and Arnold Lobel's *On Market Street* (1981), Fran Arrick's *Chernowitz* (1981), Hazel Kranz's *Henrietta Szold* (1987), Chaya Burstein's *A Kid's Catalog of Israel* (1988), Patricia Polacco's *The Keeping Quilt* (1988), Jane Breskin Zalben's *Beni's First Chanukah* (1988), Ann Morris and Lily Rivlin's *When Will the Fighting Stop? A Child's View of Jerusalem* (1990), Laurie and Ben Dolphin's *Neve Shalom-Wahat Al Salaam: Oasis of Peace* (1993), Susan Goldman Rubin's *Emily Good as Gold*

(1993), Lois Ruby's *Miriam's Well* (1993), and Sylvia Rouss' popular children's series of Sammy Spider Jewish holiday stories (1993–2006).

Jewish educational software for computers, which entered the commercial market a decade earlier, reached the stage where many classic Jewish texts, from the Bible and Prophets to the Talmud, including the Soncino English translation as well as later works from Maimonides, Rashi and the Zohar, as well as self-teaching courses in modern Hebrew language, were now available on CD-ROM. In the 1990s both the medium of electronic mail (e-mail) and the Internet, the world-wide network of computer communication, experienced a sudden large rise in use by the Jewish community. The immediacy of communication provided by e-mail and the myriad Internet "sites" was a boon to the organized Jewish community, particularly for organizational activities and Jewish education. Internet enthusiasts pointed to the benefits of this technology to Jews living alone or at a distance from established Jewish community life. Through the use of e-mail, mailing lists, newsgroups, or message boards, Jewish individuals and groups readily and regularly communicated with one another. The developing "communications superhighway" was used to facilitate discussion around issues of common Jewish interest, pose and respond to questions, exchange information, and even for teaching and study. While some expressed concern that over-reliance upon this medium would result in the loss of a "sense of shared cultural experience" and other attributes of traditional community life, most American Jews viewed such activities with enthusiasm.

POLITICS. On virtually all the key social issues at the turn of the 20th and 21st centuries, which included protection of the environment, guaranteeing the rights of homosexuals, support for the Equal Rights Amendment, nuclear freeze, handgun control, federal spending for social programs, abortion rights, and opposition to prayer in public schools, American Jews as a whole, in public opinion surveys and at the ballot box, overwhelmingly and consistently supported the liberal position. A series of surveys demonstrated the positive relationship between youth and education and liberalism, i.e., the younger and better educated the respondent, the higher was his/her score on the survey's liberal public opinion index. Contrary to popular assumptions, young Jewish leaders in the 1980s and 1990s did not turn to the right in large numbers. The majority remained both Democrats and liberals on a broad range of social and economic issues.

On church-state matters involving court cases or proposed legislation, the Jewish community frequently split between Orthodox and more liberal non-Orthodox groups. As they had since the late 1940s, most American Jews continued to support the strict separation between state and religious matters as guaranteed by the United States Constitution. This guarantee, referred to as the "establishment clause" of the First Amendment, provides that "Congress shall make no law respecting an establishment of religion, or prohibiting the free exercise thereof." However, throughout the 1980s and 1990s right-wing Christian and Jewish groups, notably Chabad-Lubavitch and Agudath Israel of America, mounted a series of legal challenges to the establishment clause centered on the issues of religious activity in public schools and government assistance to parochial schools. These and other attempts to blur church-state separation through legislation favoring sectarian interests, or by facilitating sectarian activities on government-owned property, were vigorously opposed by liberal organizations such as the American Jewish Committee, the American Jewish Congress, the Anti-Defamation League, the National Jewish Community Relations Advisory Council, and the Union of American Hebrew Congregations. The latter postulated the denial of government assistance, in any form, to any religious group to be the most fair and effective way to preclude religious discrimination and avoid religious favoritism within American society.

A distinctive feature of this period was the open concern shown by the Democratic and Republican parties to win the favor of American Jews. As Jews constituted slightly less than 2.5 percent of the total United States population and 5 percent of American voters, this concern was not due solely to the size of the Jewish vote. Rather, given the Jewish community's concentration in six important states – New York, Florida, California, Ohio, Pennsylvania, and Illinois – where historically they voted in large numbers and earned a reputation of being generous to liberal causes, it was believed that a swing on the part of the Jewish electorate might have important results. On the Jewish side, a consciousness of their own common political interests heightened the disposition to be wooed. Concern for the State of Israel, the plight of Soviet Jewry, fear of "discrimination in reverse" and urban violence, and the example of political assertiveness set by other minorities, provided the scope and inducement for American Jews to scrutinize candidates and their parties in the light of their record on matters of cardinal importance to the organized Jewish community.

Meanwhile, certain ideologues of the left, Jewish and non-Jewish, argued that there was an intrinsic conflict between being liberal and supporting Israel. These critics declared that Israel was guilty, inter alia, of a series of human rights violations in the West Bank and Gaza Strip, had engaged in secret nuclear testing and weapons sales to the apartheid government of South Africa, and had played a key role in the Iran-Contra (Irangate) affair. While most American Jews rejected such views, some Jewish leftists found an outlet in 1986 with the birth of *Tikkun*. Founded by 1960s activist Michael Lerner, *Tikkun* was a reaction to the "over-materialism and lack of spirituality in Jewish life." Pragmatically, it challenged the conservative interests of *Commentary* and defended Jewish liberalism against allegations by those on the far left. Like Breira in the 1970s and, to a certain extent, the New Jewish Agenda in the 1980s, *Tikkun* adopted the mandate of formulating a progressive political agenda for the American Jewish community. It gained immediate prominence because of the noted intellectuals, Jewish and non-Jewish, whose articles and interviews it published and because of the outspoken dovish opinions of its editor, especially with regard to Israel's treatment of the Palestinians in the West Bank and Gaza Strip.

The image of the Reagan White House as a bastion of Republican, white, Christian values encouraged political assertiveness among fundamentalist church groups. This resulted in an unprecedented effort on the part of national Christian fundamentalist organizations such as the Moral Majority to align themselves with the conservative New Right political movement in attempting to influence both the electoral and legislative processes. The difficulty the Jewish community had with these groups went beyond their opposition to its own positions on most social issues. By 1990 discontent with the Republican administration of George H.W. Bush, Reagan's successor and former vice president, helped return the number of Jewish Democrats to just under 60 percent, although the number of Jewish Republican voters remained at 15 percent. According to a 1992 University of Michigan study, American Jews remained an active political force, since about 90 percent of the Jewish population was spread among only 12 states, namely, New York, New Jersey, Massachusetts, Pennsylvania, Illinois, California, Florida, Maryland, Connecticut, Ohio, Texas, and Michigan. But the voter apathy which came to characterize the general American population had its effect on the number of American Jewish voters which declined from 92 percent in 1952 to 67 percent at the time of the study. As a result, the Jewish community stood at risk of losing the high-voter-turnout edge that had been the source of its national political influence.

As the country prepared for the 1992 presidential election, the Jewish community took stock of its relationship with the Republican Administration. During Bush's tenure, hundreds of thousands of Jews from the former Soviet Union, as well over fifteen thousand Jews from Ethiopia, arrived in Israel with the active support of the United States government. Bush also ended Saddam Hussein's aggression in the Middle East by enlisting and leading a military coalition in the 1991 Gulf War's Operation Desert Storm. American military personnel and equipment were stationed in Israel for the first time to assist in its defense against Iraq's SCUD missiles. At the same time, Bush stayed Israel's hand during the height of the war and prevented the Israel Defense Force from carrying out retaliatory air strikes against Western Iraq. This policy engendered much resentment among American Jews. After intensive and sensitive negotiations, the Bush Administration succeeded in establishing the first face-to-face peace talks between Israel and most Middle East Arab states. Still, Bush maintained his policy of linking Israel's request for $10 billion in loan guarantees, intended for the resettlement and absorption of immigrants from the former Soviet Union, to a freeze by the Israeli government of Yitzhak *Shamir on all construction in the West Bank. In response, the Jewish community mounted a concerted campaign in Washington to reverse Bush's opposition, or if need be, to persuade the Congress to grant the loan guarantees in spite of it. Bush revealed his ire at these efforts in 1991, when he said in a press interview, "…I'm up against some powerful political forces, but I owe it to the American people to tell them how strongly I feel about deferral [of the loan guarantees]… I heard today that there were something like a thousand lobbyists on the Hill working the other side of the question. We've got one lonely guy down here doing it." His remark, implying the exercise of undue political influence by American Jews, engendered great consternation throughout the Jewish community. After being made aware of the effect of his words, he offered clarification and an apology.

Bush's attitude toward Israel and appeal to the Christian Right troubled American Jews deeply. In contrast to Bush's public endorsement of the importance of religion and Christian values within American society, Democratic presidential candidate Bill Clinton and his party represented the more liberal domestic tradition that American Jews had supported since the New Deal Administration of Franklin D. Roosevelt. Clinton, who was personally known to be a friend of the Jewish state, made it clear to the Jewish community that he would be a much more unequivocal ally of Israel in its search for peace than had the Bush Administration. At the party's national convention in 1992, the Democrats drafted the strongest pro-Israel platform in recent decades. Its Israel plank affirmed the "special" U.S.-Israel relationship, criticized the Bush administration for not being an "honest broker" in the peace process, recognized Jerusalem as the capital of Israel, condemned antisemitism, and called upon the United States to further assist in the absorption of immigrants in Israel. When the election was held, Jewish voters overwhelmingly supported Bill Clinton and the Democratic Party. A combination of exit polls indicated that Clinton received approximately 80 percent of all Jewish votes. Incumbent George Bush received between only 10–15 percent and independent candidate H. Ross Perot between 5–10 percent. Analysts attributed American Jews' disproportionate support for Clinton to a tradition of voting Democratic, dissatisfaction with the Bush Administration's treatment of Israel, and a feeling of alienation from Bush's patrician background. These factors appeared to outweigh speculation that more Jews, feeling confident and secure in their socio-economic position, might abandon the Democratic Party in 1992 and vote Republican.

In 1993 President Clinton announced his nomination to the U.S. Supreme Court of Federal Appeals Court Judge Ruth Bader *Ginsburg, 60, to replace retiring Justice Byron White, considered a moderate. For 25 years, the so-called "Jewish seat" on the Supreme Court remained unoccupied. Beginning in 1916 with the appointment of Louis Brandeis, this seat was held consecutively for over a half-century by justices Benjamin Cardozo, Felix Frankfurter, Arthur *Goldberg, and finally Abe *Fortas, who resigned in 1969. The matter of filling the "Jewish seat" on the Supreme Court was dealt with cautiously among Jewish groups. No Jewish organization ever actively lobbied for this cause. While there was little doubt that most

American Jews looked forward to the appointment of another Jewish justice and were personally pleased over Ginsburg's nomination, the community's traditional and ardent public opposition to filling any position on the basis of religion, race, or ethnicity resulted in constrained enthusiasm. Steven Freeman of the Anti-Defamation League summarized the Jewish position by saying: "The criteria (sic) should be merit, the best qualified person for the job. We would not recommend that the person be chosen by ethnicity. By the same token, we would be pleased if the best qualified person happened to be Jewish." Most public commentary on Ginsburg's nomination emphasized her feminist, not her Jewish, interests. Ginsburg had won five out of six womens' rights cases which she had argued before the Supreme Court. In announcing her nomination, Clinton noted: "Many admirers of her work say that she is to the Women's moment what former Supreme Court Justice Thurgood Marshall was to the movement for the rights of African Americans." Ginsburg had served as a law professor at Columbia and Rutgers universities.

In 1984, as a presiding justice, Ginsburg indicated support for the right of a Jewish Air Force Captain, Dr. Simcha Goldman, to continue wearing a yarmulke while in uniform in spite of this constituting a technical violation of the military dress code. A Federal District Court ruled in favor of Goldman, but this ruling was later reversed by the Circuit Court of Appeals. Ginsburg was also one of the judges who rejected convicted spy Jonathan *Pollard's 1992 appeal against his life sentence. Pollard's attorneys argued that his 1987 life sentence constituted a miscarriage of justice since the government had violated its plea bargain agreement and implied to the court a preference for a maximum sentence. Ginsburg and Laurence Silberman, also Jewish, rejected Pollard's argument, while the only non-Jew on the three-judge panel, Judge Stephen Williams, dissented.

Ginsburg's appointment was confirmed 96–3 by the U.S. Senate. The only senators to oppose Ginsburg were conservative Republicans Jesse Helms of North Carolina, Robert Smith of New Hampshire, and Don Nickles of Oklahoma. They expressed concern over Ginsburg's support for abortion rights as well as her opposition to any form of discrimination against gay men and lesbians. Earlier, however, the Senate Judiciary Committee had unanimously approved her nomination. In her testimony before the committee, Ginsburg spoke of her strong distaste for discrimination which she related to her grandparents fleeing of pogroms in Eastern Europe as well as her personal experience with antisemitism in the United States. On August 10, Ginsburg, standing alongside President Clinton and her husband, and using a Hebrew Bible, was sworn in by Chief Justice William Rehnquist, thereby becoming the first female Jewish U.S. Supreme Court Justice in history.

After a quarter of a century without a Jewish justice, one year later there were two. Initially passed over by President Clinton in 1993, Gerald Stephen *Breyer was appointed by the president to the Court in 1994. His appointment came following the resignation of Justice Harry A. Blackmun.

Other significant American Jewish appointees who rose to national prominence during the Clinton administration were Secretary of Labor Robert *Reich, Secretary of the Treasury Robert *Rubin, Secretary of State Madeline Albright (who was raised Episcopalian by converted parents), Secretary of Defense William *Cohen, and National Security Advisor Sandy *Berger. Under Clinton, Alan *Greenspan continued his term as chairman of the Federal Reserve. (Greenspan's successor, Ben Bernanke, who was appointed by President George W. Bush, is also Jewish and active in Jewish communal life.)

Jewish mayors, at least in large cities, remained a rare commodity for much of the 1970s and 1980s. An important exception in the earlier phase of this period was the election in 1975 of Abraham D. *Beame as mayor of New York City. This was the first time New York, which long boasted the largest Jewish community in the world, elected a Jewish chief magistrate. Beame's term of office coincided with a fiscal crisis that threatened New York with bankruptcy and he consequently failed to secure the Democratic nomination for reelection. In 1978 Democrat Edward Koch, an especially colorful and outspoken figure, became the city's second Jewish mayor; he was elected to three consecutive terms. In 2001 the influential investment advisor Michael *Bloomberg, a Jewish Democrat-turned-Republican, prevailed over a field of opponents, including another popular Jewish Democrat, and was elected mayor. Bloomberg handily won reelection in 2005, garnering considerable of support from a plurality of the city's ethnic constituencies.

By contrast, American Jews succeeded in being elected and reelected to Congress in numbers disproportionate to their percentage of the general population, even in districts with an insignificant number of Jewish voters. Some of the most prominent figures in this regard were Senators Barbara *Boxer (California), Russell *Feingold (Wisconsin), Diane *Feinstein (California), Herb *Kohl (Wisconsin), Frank *Lautenberg (New Jersey), Joseph *Lieberman (Connecticut), Charles *Schumer (New York), Arlen *Specter (Pennsylvania), and Paul *Wellstone (Minnesota), and Ron *Wyden (Oregon). Noteworthy Jews elected to the U.S. House of Representatives included Bella *Abzug (New York), Barney Frank (Massachusetts), Holocaust survivor Tom *Lantos (California), the socialist Bernie *Sanders (Vermont), and Henry Waxman (California).

The presidential election of George W. Bush in 2000 marked a turning point for the country and was greeted cautiously by the American Jewish community. Memories of the previous Bush administration's anti-Jewish sentiment – former Secretary of State James Baker was reported to have once said, "F—k the Jews, they don't vote for us anyway" – and the younger Bush's evangelical Christian orientation prompted widespread suspicion in American Jewish circles. On the other hand, the excitement that accompanied the unprecedented selection by former Vice President Al Gore of Senator Joseph Lieberman, a modern Orthodox Jew, to be his running mate was palpable in American Jewish circles. For a majority of American Jews, the Gore-Lieberman ticket was an ideal combination – moderate on economic policy, liberal on social policy, and activist with respect to foreign policy. A Gore administration also virtually guaranteed a continuation of Clinton's Middle East diplomacy. In the event, fewer than 20 percent of American Jews cast their ballots for the Republican standard bearer. Furthermore, many American Jewish voters were deeply disappointed when, owing to voting irregularities, the U.S. Supreme Court decided the presidential election in favor of Bush.

Despite the wide gap between the Bush administration's conservative views – its opposition to abortion and church-state separation – and American Jewry's moderate liberalism, the president himself reached out to the American Jewish leadership. He was aided in this regard by Ari Fleischer, the White House press secretary. In addition to modest efforts like hosting the first Ḥanukkah celebration at the White House, Bush displayed unequivocal, open, and even warm support for Israel and its leaders, while pointedly denying Yasser Arafat and the Palestinians similar treatment. This was markedly different from the support Clinton had shown to the Arab parties.

In the wake of the terrorist attacks of September 11, 2001, American Jews, like other American constituencies, closed ranks behind the president. But the American Jewish community soon found itself at odds with the Bush administration's views on the necessity of invading Afghanistan to hunt the Al-Qaeda terrorist group and its leader Osama bin Laden as well as its concomitant determination to curtail civil liberties in order to fight the "War on Terrorism." What emerged in 2001 as concern over the broadly construed USA-Patriot Act, which critics feared could lead to egregious violations of the constitutional rights of law-abiding citizens, reached a pivotal juncture with the imprisonment of noncitizens at Guantanamo. Captured by American forces in Afghanistan and deemed "unlawful combatants" by the American government, they were denied the procedural safeguards customarily afforded prisoners of war and held indefinitely. Meanwhile, U.S. Attorney General John Ashcroft issued a series of directives aimed at elevating surveillance activities among the prisoners and across the country generally.

The American Jewish community was divided over what, if any, public response might be warranted under the circumstances. For example, the annual conference of the Jewish Council for Public Affairs (JCPA), meeting in 2002, passed a resolution criticizing the administration for undermining civil liberties in the name of national security. But to satisfy a split between the groups opposed to the Bush policies – led by the Reform movement's Religious Action Center and the National Council for Jewish Women – and the moderates who believed such a resolution to be "premature" – the American Jewish Committee, the Anti-Defamation League, B'nai B'rith, and Hadassah – a supplementary statement was issued that the JCPA supported "strengthening domestic antiterrorism measures that enhance law enforcement capabilities" without infringing upon "basic constitutional rights." Next, the passage of the Homeland Security Act, which created a new cabinet-level department, gave the U.S. government unprecedented surveillance powers over "federal government, state and local government agencies (including law enforcement agencies), and private sector entities." The widespread unease displayed by American Jewish groups over such an open-ended mandate was tempered, at least temporarily, by the assurances of Congressional leaders like Senator Arlen Specter who, in a speech to the American Jewish Committee in 2002, announced his intention "to craft a new bill that maintained the law's core provisions while ameliorating the problematic civil liberties issues." Two notable exceptions in this regard were Senators Russell Feingold and Paul Wellstone, who vigorously opposed the war from the beginning.

Over the course of several months, the Bush administration continued to make the case for isolating and invading Iraq. It alleged the totalitarian regime of Saddam Hussein possessed "weapons of mass destruction" and that Iraq was linked to the 9/11 terrorist attacks on the U.S. Though the charges remained unproven, approximately 65 percent of Americans supported the president's position when in March 2003 the U.S. launched a massive offensive against Iraq. Within weeks, an American-led military coalition succeeded in toppling the Hussein regime and occupying the country. While it was widely presumed the American Jewish community supported the war, owing especially to Iraq's profile as one of Israel's most dangerous foes, polls revealed that 54 percent of American Jews disapproved of Bush's handling of the conflict. Still, antisemitic and anti-Israel groups as well as some antiwar activists accused the Jews of fomenting the war to further Zionist aims. In reality, however, although a poll sponsored by the American Jewish Committee on the eve of the 2004 presidential election discerned strong American Jewish backing for the Bush administration's Israel policy, including the president's tacit endorsement of Israel's unilateral withdrawal from the Gaza Strip and the establishment of the West Bank security barrier, antiwar sentiment among American Jews persisted at high levels. The poll also found that American Jews backed the Democratic candidate Senator John F. Kerry (Massachusetts) by a nearly 3-to-1 margin and that disapproval of the Iraq war among Jews had risen to 66 percent. David Harris, executive director of the American Jewish Committee, suggested the poll gave a "bird's eye view of where American Jews are on the important issues of the day." The data painted a picture, he explained, of a community that was "very supportive of Israel, very multilateralist, skeptical of the Bush administration's policy in Iraq, and domestically very liberal." Following Bush's reelection to office in 2004, it was determined that Kerry won 77 percent of the Jewish vote and Bush received 22 percent. While this pattern was consistent with past Jewish support for Democratic candidate, Bush actually made modest gains among younger American Jewish voters since he was first elected in 2000.

In the ensuing months, as the Iraq war continued and revelations emerged of abuses by American military personnel at the Abu Ghraib prison, American Jewish opposition to the war increased to 70 percent. This figure was no doubt influenced by the growing death toll of American soldiers and Iraqi civilians which rose, respectively, to over 2000 and approximately 35,000 in 2005. Meanwhile, according to Pentagon estimates, the cost of the war grew to more than $5.8 billion per month.

BLACK-JEWISH RELATIONS. Relations at the community level between blacks and Jews were troubled and strained in the period under review. American Jewish Committee leader Murray Friedman's assertion that "the black-Jewish alliance of the civil rights days is simply gone" was borne out in various surveys that reflected a growing resentment of Jews by blacks, especially among younger blacks on college campuses. A handful of black leaders gained notoriety for their anti-Jewish sentiments, which were accompanied by anti-Israel and pro-Palestinian statements. Less frequently reported were examples of cooperation taking place among black and Jewish leaders in Congress, in city halls, and in inter-communal dialogues around the country.

Undoubtedly, some of the outstanding issues between the two communities were rooted in the past. But the issues themselves were current. For example, prominent black leader the Rev. Jesse Jackson had made himself anathema to many American Jews in 1979, the year he embraced PLO Chairman Yasser Arafat in front of the press, called for the establishment of an independent Palestinian state, and criticized the Jewish community for the dismissal by President Jimmy Carter of Andrew Young, American ambassador to the United Nations, after his unauthorized contact with Yasser Arafat.

During the 1980s Jackson continued to be critical of Israel for its relationship with South Africa, and called Zionism a "kind of poisonous weed that is choking Judaism," while he continued to support Palestinian demands for an independent state. However, the nadir of Jackson's relationship with American Jews came in 1984 when in a private conversation with a black *Washington Post* reporter, Jackson referred to Jews as "Hymies" and to New York as "Hymietown." The Jewish community, aghast at the candidate's remark, subsequently received an apology by Jackson during a speech made at a synagogue. By the beginning of the 1990s, Jackson had made attempts to improve his relationship with the Jewish community, initially by condemning antisemitism at the 1992 World Jewish Congress on antisemitism in Brussels and later by spearheading efforts of black-Jewish cooperation.

By far the nation's most controversial black personality, known for his direct attacks upon the Jewish community, was Chicago-based Louis Farrakhan, head of the black Muslim sect Nation of Islam. Farrakhan frequently made derogatory and insulting statements about Jews, Judaism, and the State of Israel. In his sermons he referred to the "lying and deceit" of Jews, and the "tyranny of Jewish shopkeepers and landlords who swarmed the ghetto communities to prey upon our people." In a 1984 radio broadcasts he declared Hitler a "great man" and referred to Judaism as a "gutter religion." He also accused Jewish doctors of injecting the AIDS virus into black babies. Furthermore, the Nation of Islam published and sold two antisemitic tracts, *The Protocols of the Elders of Zion* and *The Secret Relationship between Blacks and Jews*. While Farrakhan's vituperative statements strained black-Jewish relations, within the black community he was criticized by the NAACP, the Urban League, and many church groups.

A third black personality to have stirred controversy with his statements about Jews was Leonard Jeffries, founding chairman of the black studies department at the City College of New York. In a 1991 speech at a black culture festival in Albany, New York, he defended New York State's multi-cultural education reform plan and attacked Jews in particular for opposing the plan. Among his most controversial statements, Jeffries accused Jews of dominating the slave trade and "conspiring for the destruction of black people" through control of Hollywood. After being removed as department head for making statements, Jeffries brought suit against CCNY, claiming his First Amendment rights had been violated. In May 1993, a U.S. district court, agreeing with Jeffries, awarded him $400,000 in damages, an amount reduced by the judge to $40,000. The judge noted Jeffries' behavior to be "repugnant, hateful, poisonous, and reprehensible," but instructed City College to return him to the chair of the Afro-American Studies Department.

An eruption broke out in the Crown Heights section of Brooklyn in 1991 when a station wagon driven by a ḥasidic Jew careened out of control and crashed into a sidewalk, killing a seven-year-old black boy and badly injuring a black girl. When the driver stepped out of the car, he was attacked and robbed by angry black bystanders. Before police and medical personnel reached the scene, the crowd broke up into smaller groups and turned in different directions throwing rocks and bottles at people, cars, and homes. One of these frenzied groups came upon 29-year-old Yankel Rosenbaum, an ultra-Orthodox Jew from Australia who was visiting New York City. Rosenbaum was severely beaten and stabbed to death. Though 17-year-old Lemrick Nelson, Jr. was arrested for Rosenbaum's murder, he was acquitted by a mostly black and Latino jury.

The episode was followed by three days and four nights of rioting by blacks in Crown Heights, a community variously estimated to include 12,000 to 25,000 mostly ḥasidic Jews and 100,000 to 180,000 blacks. The New York Police Department and the city's first black mayor David Dinkins were criticized for not being able to control the riots. The Crown Heights affair acted as a catalyst for additional rioting by blacks in other large cities around the country over the next few days. Although well-intentioned community leaders initiated attempts at inter-community dialogue, the development of the case and the coverage it received in the press exacerbated tensions between blacks and Jews.

Following federal and state investigations, which criticized the mayor, the police, and even the courts for mishandling of the Crown Heights affair, Dinkins lost the 1993 mayoral election to Republican candidate Rudolph Giuliani. Giuliani became the first Republican elected mayor of New York since 1965. Exit polls conducted determined that only 4 percent of all those questioned were influenced by Dinkins' handling of the Crown Heights riots. Jewish – especially ḥasidic – neighborhoods, however, voted overwhelmingly for Giuliani. Meanwhile, a Roper Organization poll demonstrated the persistence of ethnic rivalry, with almost half of New York City residents, 47 percent, answering that Jews had "too much influence" in city life and politics. Among African Americans, the figure was 63 percent and among Hispanics 66 percent. A hopeful but provocative response to this rivalry was a *New Yorker* cover drawn by Art Spiegelman, author/artist of *Maus: A Survivor's Tale*, a popular comic book-style rendering of the history of the Holocaust and its impact on American Jews. Spiegelman's wish for reconciliation took the metaphoric form of an ḥasidic man kissing a black woman. Both the Jewish and black communities expressed ire over this illustration.

In the 1990s Jesse Jackson took determined steps towards rapprochement with the Jewish community. Speaking at a conference on antisemitism convened by the World Jewish Congress in Brussels in July 1992, he condemned "racism and antisemitism (as) scientifically and morally wrong." In marked contrast to his previous public position on the subject, he also praised Zionism as a "liberation movement." In 1993, he met with Israel's foreign minister Shimon *Peres and pledged to help seek freedom of emigration for Syria's Jews. Jackson also played a constructive mitigating role in the controversy that erupted that year over the nomination by President Bill Clinton of Lani Guinier, a black legal studies scholar, to the position of assistant attorney general for civil rights in the U.S. Department of Justice. The Jewish community reacted critically to her nomination and expressed concern over Guinier's support for an interpretation of the Voting Rights Act favoring blacks and other minorities. In the event, President Clinton withdrew his nomination and the black community was angered by what it viewed as the successful torpedoing of its candidate by Jewish interest groups. Meanwhile, Jewish groups sought to downplay their influence over the president's decision.

These tensions dissipated over time – at least among the leaders of both communities – and within the space of a few years black-Jewish relations exhibited noticeable improvement. A turning point was signaled in 2000 when the New York-based Foundation for Ethnic Understanding, originally established in 1989 by Rabbi Marc Schneier and Joseph Papp, launched a Web site devoted to supporting the improvement of dialogue between African Americans and American Jews. The Web site, which promoted the collaborative efforts of Jewish and black leaders and organizations, announced: "We are committed to the belief that direct, face-to-face, dialogue between leaders of ethnic communities is the most effective path toward the reduction of bigotry and the promotion of reconciliation and understanding." That same year, Jesse Jackson gave a keynote address to a World Jewish Congress-sponsored meeting focused on the question of black-Jewish relations. Jackson called the relationship "better than ever," but also emphasized that "we still have unfinished business." Jackson's rehabilitation in the eyes of American Jews was completed later that year when he publicly and actively devoted himself to securing the release of thirteen Iranian Jews detained by the Iranian regime on charges of spying for Israel.

CHRISTIAN-JEWISH RELATIONS. On the whole, relations between the Jewish community and most Christian denominations were positive in this period. However, one serious area of contention between American Jewish leaders and mainline Christian churches was the Middle East. In 1992, these groups continued to express their objection to Israel's presence in the Occupied Territories, by publicly opposing Israel's request to the United States for $10 billion in loan guarantees. "An Open Statement of Religious Leaders to President George Bush," proffered by the National Council of Churches (NCC), called upon the president to "oppose housing loan guarantees to Israel until it halts construction and expansion of settlements in the West Bank, Gaza, and East Jerusalem." It was signed by representatives of the Presbyterian Church (U.S.A.), the Lutheran Council, the Episcopal Church, the Mennonites, the American Baptist Church, the United Church of Christ, the Reformed Church of America, and the Unitarian-Universalist Association. An even stronger tone was used in a resolution debated by the United Methodist Church; it failed to pass for technical reasons. In general, criticism of Israel by these bodies continued until the 1993 signing of the Israel-PLO Declaration of Principles in Washington, D.C.

In the areas of social and economic justice, Protestant and Jewish groups shared concern over the growth of the Christian Right. *The Religious Right: The Assault on Tolerance and Pluralism* (1994), published by the Anti-Defamation League, analyzed the ongoing and well-funded effort by evangelical Christian groups to blur the traditional separation between religion and politics in America and initiate new legislation, both at the local and national level, reflecting their anti-pluralistic, fundamentalist religious values. It pointed to efforts led by Pat Robertson and the Christian Coalition, preacher Jerry Falwell, and activist Time LaHaye as well as those of organizations with innocuous-sounding names like CARE (Citizens Advocating Responsible Education) and CEE (Citizens for Excellence in Education) who promoted candidates for school board seats, local Republican party committees, water commissions, and real estate zoning boards. These forces, it was argued, sought control of the Republican party by the year 2000 and constituted a threat to American democracy. They were thus to be regarded as a special threat by American Jews and other non-Protestant and non-white groups. Nonetheless, because of many issues on which the Religious Right coincided with Jewish concerns, including active and loyal Evangelical support of Israel, the relationship between the groups remained complicated.

There were also important developments in Catholic-Jewish relations in this era. The most significant breakthrough occurred in 1993 when Israel and the Vatican signed an agreement establishing full diplomatic relations between the Holy See and the Jewish state. Against this backdrop, a joint American Jewish-Catholic delegation visited Poland in order to address a number of issues in Polish-Jewish relations. Foremost was the progress on the construction of a new Carmelite convent and education-prayer center in the town of Oswiecim, not far from the Auschwitz/Birkenau death camp site. The new facility was an alternative to the existing convent situated nearer the entrance to the camp, over whose presence Jewish organizations long objected. In 1993, the office within the Church that oversees Catholic orders, with the support of the Pope, directed the nuns to relocate. On the other hand, Jewish groups expressed ambivalence about the Catholic Church's Catechism for the Universal Church (1992), which noted Christianity's Jewish roots and rejected the charge of deicide, but stopped short of an explicit condemnation of antisemitism. The catechism "gives final authority to what we have worked on for thirty years," stated James Rudin of the American Jewish Committee, "but [it] doesn't break any new ground." Next, in 1994 the Synagogue Council of America and the National Conference of Catholic Bishops issued a joint statement condemning pornography and asking communities and parents to exercise greater vigilance to prevent its exposure to young people.

Toward the end of the decade, a highly sensitive aspect of Catholic-Jewish relations emerged into a full-blown controversy. The matter concerned a panel of historians appointed in the late 1990s to investigate the role of Pope Pius XII during World War II and the Holocaust era. The panel had been assembled, in part, to address questions and assuage tensions resulting from Pope John Paul II's plans for the beatification and sainthood of Pius XII, who was alleged by many historians and Jewish community leaders to have been indifferent to the fate of European Jewry and even culpable within the wider context of the Nazi regime's plans to exterminate the Jews. When the panel was denied access to the Holy See's archives for "technical reasons," it disbanded and protested to the Vatican's Commission for Religious Relations with the Jews that "we cannot see a way forward at present to the final report you request, and believe we must suspend our work." The matter heated up further when Cardinal Walter Kasper, the senior figure charged with responsibility for the Vatican's relationship with the Jewish community, accused the Jewish members of the panel of "indiscretion" and making "polemical remarks to the press." The Jewish scholars responded that they had been "singled out for blame" and should be allowed unfettered access to the Vatican's historical documentation. The imbroglio prompted some Jewish historians to resign from the panel and historian Robert S. Wistrich of the Hebrew University called the episode "the lowest ebb in Catholic-Jewish relations since the 1960s." The matter remained an open source of contention, but the strained relations were eased somewhat in the spring of 2001 when the pontiff, together with the chief rabbi of Ukraine, paid a visit to Babi Yar, where thousands of Jews had been killed in 1941 by the Nazis.

HOLOCAUST-RELATED MATTERS. In the 1980s and 1990s, Holocaust memorialization efforts on the part of American Jewry developed into a major activity and social psychological phenomenon. Faced with the reality of Holocaust survivors succumbing to natural attrition and aided by the retrospective vision of two generations, American Jews focused considerable resources, including time, money and skills, on producing an unprecedented number of Holocaust projects to serve as testaments and memorials for posterity. This was expressed in everything from the creation of artwork, books, films, school curricula, events and conferences for survivors and their children to organized tours to Eastern Europe to visit the sites of former Jewish communities and Nazi death camps. A number of Jewish communities, among them Baltimore, Boston, Chicago, Miami, New York, Pittsburgh, San Francisco, and St. Louis, established regional Holocaust monuments, museums, and educational centers. Furthermore, many states adopted new statutes and mandated the teaching of the Holocaust in middle and senior high school across the country. Most American Jews supported these efforts and responded favorably to the commemoration and normalization of the Holocaust in American Jewish life. Support was also manifest in the countrywide growth of Holocaust studies as an academic field and the convening of scholarly meetings such as the annual conference of the Holocaust Education Foundation.

Two major efforts in this period were the opening in 1993 of the Beit Hashoah-Museum of Tolerance in Los Angeles and the *United States Holocaust Memorial Museum in Washington, D.C. Although funding for the institutions was raised mainly through private donations, both were surrounded by controversy even before they opened their doors to the public. Five million dollars for the Wiesenthal project came from the State of California and the land upon which the U.S. Holocaust Memorial Museum in Washington stands was donated by the federal government. In both cases, questions arose over whether these donations violated the constitutional principle of separation between religion and state. The Wiesenthal museum's many state of the art high-tech educational exhibits also aroused controversy because, as critics charged, they detracted from the solemnity of the subject. Repeated changes in its design and plans resulted in it taking six years to complete at a cost of $55 million instead of two years and $15 million.

The U.S. Memorial Holocaust Museum, built at a cost of $168 million, faced a controversy of a different nature. Since its founding in the 1970s under the Carter administration, the U.S. Holocaust Memorial Council, the body charged with the planning and development of the project, was split over the issue of which message the museum was to communicate. The Council was divided into two camps, one which wished to emphasize the specifically Jewish aspect of the Holocaust, the other which sought to convey a more universal theme it thought would increase its relevance to non-Jewish visitors. Less than a month before its opening, Harvey Meyerhoff and William Lowenberg, chairman and vice chairman of the council respectively (and both aligned with the universal camp), were forced to resign under pressure from the new Clinton administration. Meyerhoff and Lowenberg, appointed by former President Ronald Reagan, had opposed extending an invitation to speak at the opening ceremony to President of Israel Chaim Herzog. President Bill Clinton wanted the participation of Herzog, and saw the disagreement as an opportunity to relieve the two Republicans. They were replaced by Miles Lerman and Ruth Mandel. The two new heads sought to place more a Jewish emphasis on the institution that included its closing on Yom Kippur, in addition to Christmas.

The dedication ceremony for the museum in 1993, attended by President Clinton, was marred by controversy over the presence of Croatian President Franjo Tudjman. Tudjman, author of *Wastelands – Historical Truth* (1988), in which he attributed the accounting of six million Jews murdered by the Nazis to "too much on both emotional, biased testimonies and on exaggerated data in the postwar reckonings of war crimes," was also known to have made antisemitic remarks in public, including the statement that Jews are "selfish, crafty, unreliable, miserly and underhanded." The author and Nobel laureate Elie Wiesel publicly criticized Tudjman's participation in the event. The controversy was partially tempered by the visit to the museum of His Holiness the Dalai Lama, who was, in fact, the institution's first official visitor.

A third major American Holocaust center, New York City's A Living Memorial to the Holocaust – *Museum of Jewish Heritage, opened in 1994 on a plot of land situated on the waterfront in Battery Park City, directly opposite the Statue of Liberty and Ellis Island. Construction of the museum had been postponed for many years, partly due to complicated lease negotiations with the municipality. This long-term project was initiated in 1981 when then Mayor Edward I. *Koch appointed a Holocaust Memorial Task Force (later a commission) to begin work to create such an institution.

Next, five years after a Jerusalem court sentenced John Demjanjuk (alleged to be "Ivan the Terrible" of Treblinka) to death and placed him in solitary confinement, the Israeli Supreme Court ruled in 1993 there was not enough evidence to convict him. Demjanjuk subsequently returned to the United States, where a lengthy judicial process produced "clear, unequivocal, and convincing evidence" of his service in Nazi death camps and in 2005 the 6th U.S. Circuit Court of Appeals ruled he could be stripped of his American citizenship. Demjanjuk's lawyers appealed the court's decision, arguing that "having marked Mr. Demjanjuk with blood scent, the [United States] government wants to drop him into a shark tank." Chief U.S. Immigration Judge Michael J. Creppy asserted there was no evidence, however, to substantiate Demjanjuk's claim he would be mistreated if deported to his native Ukraine. Assistant Attorney General Alice S. Fischer stated: "The chief immigration judge's decision reaffirms the important principle that the United States will continue to track down and remove individuals who assisted the Nazis in their brutal campaign of terror, and secure a measure of justice on behalf of the Nazis' victims."

In 1994 *Schindler's List*, a feature film about German industrialist Oskar *Schindler, who was personally responsible for saving the lives of over a thousand Jews by employing them in his factory, opened to American audiences. The $23 million film production, conceived of and directed by Steven *Spielberg, was based on a book by Thomas Keneally. The worldwide critical and financial success of *Schindler's List* was unprecedented. The film won seven Oscar awards and generated revenues estimated at $300 million. Spielberg used some $50 million from the film's profits to establish The Righteous Persons Foundation. A second project was the creation of the *Survivors of the Shoah Visual History Foundation, with assets of over $30 million, which developed a state-of-the-art multi-media archive comprising in-depth interviews with Holocaust survivors as well as educational materials such as books, documentary films, and CD-ROMS.

In stark contrast to the widespread success of *Schindler's List* and the highly visible projects sponsored by Spielberg, throughout the 1990s Holocaust denial, the propagation of the argument and the dissemination of information minimizing the degree to which the Nazis persecuted the Jews during World War II, including the denial of the Nazis' systematic mass murder of European Jewry, continued unabated in a variety of public arenas. For example, Holocaust denial activists made a special effort to target college campuses throughout the United States. The Committee for Open Debate on the Holocaust (CODOH), led by Bradley R. Smith, succeeded in placing full-page advertisements and op-ed pieces in dozens of college newspapers. One ad was entitled "The Holocaust: How Much is False? The Case for Open Debate." A second, published in the spring of 1992 was called "Falsus in Uno, Falsus in Omnibus… the 'Human Soap' Holocaust Myth." A widely reprinted essay that first appeared in 1993 was "A Revisionist's View on the U.S. Holocaust Memorial Museum in Washington, D.C.," which argued that the homicidal Nazi gas chambers never existed. The appearance of these materials engendered great media attention followed by an immediate backlash of criticism from students, faculty, the local Jewish community and national Jewish organizations. The scholar Deborah E. Lipstadt documented the extent of this campaign in *Denying the Holocaust: The Growing Assault on Truth and Memory* (1993). Meanwhile, as part of its "Confronting Antisemitism Project," the Anti-Defamation League launched a Web site titled "Holocaust Denial: An Online Guide to Exposing and Combating Anti-Semitic Propaganda," which aimed to make available information to counter Holocaust denial claims and expose the activities of "career antisemites" including Willis Allison Carto, David *Irving, Ingrid Rimland, Bradley R. Smith, Mark Weber, and Ernst Zundel.

The explosion of interest in Holocaust history reached something of a fever pitch with the publication in 1996 of

Daniel Goldhagen's *Hitler's Willing Executioners*. In this highly provocative work, Goldhagen advanced the argument that ordinary Germans not only knew about the Hitler regime's efforts to exterminate the Jews but were predisposed to accept the Nazi worldview owing to a unique and virulent "eliminationist" strain of antisemitism endemic to German culture. The book generated a firestorm of controversy in academic circles and, at the same time, became an international best-seller. Virtually overnight, Goldhagen became a familiar figure on national television and on the lecture circuit throughout the United States and Europe. He was also attacked by many established Holocaust scholars who challenged his findings and questioned his research, including Yehuda *Bauer, Christopher *Browning, Saul Friedman, and Fritz Stern.

Critics of American Jewry's seemingly inexhaustible fascination with the Holocaust charged that the success of phenomena like the film *Schindler's List*, the Goldhagen volume, and even the opening of Holocaust museums and memorials in different parts of the country illustrated American Jewry's base impulses and lack of a substantive grasp of world and Jewish history. They further argued the Holocaust itself was being exploited by many American Jews for contemporary political and social purposes, including shielding Israel from public criticism and offering a temporary salve to those who feared the weakening of American Jewish identity. The historian Peter Novick articulated this view in a controversial book titled *The Holocaust in American Life* (1999). Novick's detractors, however, averred that although *The Holocaust in American Life* was painstakingly researched, its scholarly value was undermined by the author's "evident distaste for the idea of Jewish distinctiveness and his commitment to a universalistic political agenda."

Parallel to the public debates described above were the highly visible Holocaust restitution efforts which began in the early 1990s and assumed special intensity between 1995 and the turn of the centuries. Concerted efforts were made during these years to address the restitution and compensation claims of Holocaust survivors worldwide, a group estimated to be as high as 935,000 individuals. The main actors in the drama surrounding compensation for survivors of the Holocaust were the Claims Conference, the World Jewish Restitution Organization, and the World Jewish Congress. As a result of varied legal efforts that emanated from different corners of the globe, this triad was quickly enlarged to include a broad range of American and European officials as well as class action lawyers. Stuart *Eizenstat represented the U.S. government for much of the period in question. Working closely with Israel Singer and Edgar M. Bronfman, Sr., of the World Jewish Congress as well as other American Jewish leaders, Eizenstat sought to navigate a complex array of legal, diplomatic, economic, and political issues while negotiating competing claims made by European governments, insurance companies, and banks – particularly Swiss banks – and even Bank Leumi, the Israeli successor to the Anglo-Palestine Bank, and the Jewish National Fund. Between 1998 and 2001, more than $6.5 billion in restitution settlements were concluded for Jewish and non-Jewish victims of the Nazi regime. Even so, there remained considerable debate about the status of formerly Jewish-owned individual and communal properties in central and eastern Europe as well as works of art plundered by the Nazis. The relative success of the aforementioned compensation and restitution efforts could not, of course, erase or dim the impact of the catastrophic destruction of European Jewry by the Nazis during World War II. Speaking before the third international conference on the Holocaust in Stockholm in 2000, which focused on the theme of Holocaust education and remembrance, Eizenstat emphasized the enduring importance of efforts to come to terms with the Holocaust:

> We have been dealing heavily with the restitution of assets, trying to bring some measure of justice to surviving victims in everything from communal property to art to Swiss bank accounts to German slave and forced labor and insurance. These are all important and we are making progress in each of those areas. The significance of this historically important conference is that it begins, as we enter a new century, to move us away from what is important and immediate – money and assets – to what is enduring and lasting – memory and education. Financial restitution, while critical, cannot be the last word on the Holocaust. This conference assures [that] education, remembrance, and research will be.

Fifty years after World War II and the Holocaust, the issues and controversies outlined above surfaced with dramatic intensity and had a profound impact on American Jewry. In part, the flurry of American Jewish commemorative, artistic, scholarly, and restitution activity, which followed in the wake of the Soviet Union's collapse and the end of the Cold War, signaled the end of an era. Hitherto inaccessible archives in eastern and central Europe poured forth information about the assets of hundred of thousands of Holocaust victims, including survivors and their heirs who now lived in the United States. The turn of the centuries also proved to be a juncture for widespread communal and national introspection – in Europe and America. As the generation of war-era survivors began to fade, American Jews vigorously pursued avenues for preserving the memory and legacy of European Jewry and securing material compensation for Holocaust survivors worldwide.

Many of the controversies highlighted here have yet to dissipate; some of the disputes will probably never be resolved. Meanwhile, popular and scholarly interest in Holocaust studies, literature, films, documentaries, museums, memorials, and financial restitution continues unabated. According to the directory of the Association of Holocaust Organizations, by the year 2005 dozens of institutions in the United States were officially classified as Holocaust museums and the organization itself had a combined membership of over a hundred affiliated agencies, institutes, and educational operations. In addition, numerous resource centers, libraries, and archives, from Maine to Hawaii, offer seminars and workshops, operate speakers bureaus, collect and categorize historical documents, record and classify oral histories, organize commemoration ceremonies, and sponsor academic research and essay contests on the subject of the Holocaust. Many of the latter were established under Jewish communal auspices, with support from local and state government agencies. Some are also the beneficiaries of funding recovered as a result of Holocaust restitution efforts.

SOVIET JEWRY. Immigrants from the former Soviet Union constituted a distinct sub-population within the American Jewish community. According to the 1994 *American Jewish Year Book*, over 280,000 Jews from the former Soviet Union had immigrated to the United States since the mid-1960s. The waves of Russian Jewish migration generally fell into two periods: 1976–79 and 1989–92. A high point was reached in the years 1992 and 1993, for which the Hebrew Immigrant Aid Society (HIAS) reported the number of Russian Jewish immigrants to be 45,888 and 35,581, respectively. This movement was the immediate result of the breakdown of the Soviet regime, which also saw the emigration over half a million Jews to the State of Israel. The 1989 Lautenberg Amendment, named after Democratic Senator Frank Lautenberg of Pennsylvania, had eased the evidentiary requirements for refugees applying from certain countries. It permitted entry to the United States to individuals based on "persecution or a well-founded fear of persecution based on race, religion, nationality, membership in a particular social group, or political opinion." The Refugee Act of 1980, reauthorized in 1991, facilitated employment training and job placement, as well as English-language training, "in order to achieve economic self-sufficiency among refugees as quickly as possible." This law, combined with other legislation, made possible a variety of resettlement services to be offered to new Soviet Jewish immigrants. These services were primarily administered through the national network of Jewish organizations, including HIAS, local federations, and other local agencies.

The New York Association for New Americans (NYANA), for example, was responsible for resettling over 30 percent of the Soviet Jewish immigrants to have arrived in the United States since 1990. The second largest community of former Soviet Jewish immigrants resided in Los Angeles, with other large new immigrant groups settling in Chicago, San Francisco, Boston, and Miami. While short-term resettlement programs for former Soviet Jews won recognition both inside and outside the Jewish community, the immigrants' social and cultural integration into American Jewish life proved to be more of a challenge. After officially completing the resettlement process, relatively few sought affiliation with the Jewish community at large.

Unlike Russian Jewish immigrants from the former Soviet Union, Israelis residing permanently in the United States had, as a group, never been eligible for the package of resettlement services made available by the local Jewish community. Although seeking the bounty of America, Israelis were not recognized as refugees. Residing mainly in New York and Los Angeles, they succeeded in developing their own vibrant, Hebrew-speaking community life, separate from American Jews. While a number continued working for the organized Jewish community as supplementary, Sunday school, and day school teachers, in Jewish community centers, and summer camps, the majority found employment throughout all sectors of the economy. Many did not live in Jewish areas, and their children attended local American public schools.

A controversy with implications for Jewish philanthropy that arose within the social service field in this period concerned the large and increasing proportion of the Jewish émigrés from the Soviet Union who chose to settle in the United States rather than in Israel. The Hebrew Immigrant Aid Society (HIAS) extended to them the usual assistance it gives to Jewish immigrants. To this the Jewish Agency took exception on the ground that it was discouraging settlement in Israel. The two bodies reached an agreement as to procedure to be followed in Vienna, the principal staging point, whereby HIAS would deal with the émigrés only after they had declined the Agency's persuasions to proceed to Israel. Still the majority opted to settle in the United States, and the Jewish Agency continued its pressure on HIAS to withhold assistance. Meanwhile, the controversy reached back to the local Federations, and in a few cases they were reported to have declined to assist Russian Jews settled in their midst. Ultimately, Israeli Prime Minister Menahem Begin in 1980 presented a compromise plan to the directors of the Council of Jewish Federations (CJF). The CJF accepted the greater part of the plan but rejected a directive to HIAS that it assist only those émigrés with close relatives in the United States. Twelve months later HIAS acceded to further requests from the Jewish Agency to curtail its assistance to Russian émigrés, but by this time the flow from Russia had diminished to a trickle.

ZIONISM AND ISRAEL. The 1980s was a period in which the relationship between American Jews and Israel underwent measurable change, characterized by the disenchantment on the part of many American Jews with Israel's image and a willingness to publicly criticize Israel for adopting policies and actions perceived to be detrimental to itself or the Jewish people. Many identify the ascendancy of Begin and the rightwing Likud-led coalition government in 1977 as the beginning of this change. Begin's ideology and rhetoric, especially his desire to secure the borders of "Greater Israel," were viewed by many American Jews as jingoistic and provocative. His successor, Yitzhak Shamir, bore the same political ideology.

After nearly a decade of unflagging admiration and support, the aura surrounding the State of Israel began to dim. Research findings from this period indicate a steady decline in interest in Israel among American Jews, particularly among individuals under the age of 40. Nevertheless, it was also apparent that despite external circumstances, which could and did alter the American Jewish landscape in important ways, American Jewry's fundamental attitude to Israel was one of unconditional support. Put another way, the erosion of Arab intransigence over making peace with Israel, which exac-

Members of the Jewish community known as Abayudaya in Mbale, Uganda, 224 km east of Kampala, leave their synagogue after morning prayers, 2005. © *Patrick Olum/Reuters/Corbis.*

In 2005, the worldwide Jewish population was estimated to be close to 14 million persons, with its largest numbers in North America and Israel. Despite the large concentrations in these two geographical areas, there are Jews all over the world who come from a variety of racial and ethnic backgrounds. Here are a few faces that illustrate the diversity and vibrancy of Jewish life in its many world-scattered communities.

COMMUNITIES

*ABOVE: **Sukkah*** in the Jewish Quarter (Mellah) of Marrakesh, Morocco, 1994. Moroccan Jews often build their ***sukkot*** with palm-tree branches or reeds, so that they look completely green from the outside. ***Sukkot*** are decorated with pictures of venerated rabbis, mainly of R. Simeon bar Yohai, traditional author of the Zohar. Every night during Sukkot selected portions from the Zohar are recited.
Photo: Alex Levac, Israel. By courtesy of Beth Hatefutsoth Photo Archive, Tel Aviv.

(opposite page): A teenage Ethiopian boy prepares to pray at the Beta Israel School in Addis Ababa, Ethiopia, 2003. Although many members of the Jewish community in Addis Ababa were airlifted by the Israeli government in the 1980s and 1990s, in 2003 17,000 Ethiopian Jews were still awaiting ***aliyah***, or emigration to Israel. *Photo by Natalie Behring-Chisholm/Getty Images.*

(opposite page) TOP: An Israeli dressed as a clown performs for a group during Purim celebrations in Hebron, West Bank, 2006. *GALI TIBBON/AFP/ Getty Images.*

(opposite page) BOTTOM: Matisyahu, a Lubavitch Hasidic Jew who raps over reggae music about traditional Jewish beliefs, performs the night before the beginning of Passover in Northampton, Massachusetts, 2006. *Photo by Mario Tama/Getty Images.*

(this page) TOP: *Sukkah* posed on a boat in the canals of the Ghetto in Venice, Italy, 2004. The idea was initiated by Chabad House, the Lubavitch institution in the city. *Photo: Ya'akov Brill, Israel. By courtesy of Beth Hatefutsoth Photo Archive, Tel Aviv*

(this page) BOTTOM: Members of Congregation Beth Simchat Torah celebrate Hanukkah, 2004. The synagogue serves the gay, lesbian, bisexual, and transgender communities in New York City. *Courtesy of Congregation Beth Simchat Torah. Photo by Donna Aceto.*

ABOVE: Students at Heschel High School, a private Jewish school in New York City, listen to a lecture from behind their laptop computers. © *Richard Levine/Alamy.*

(opposite page): A rabbi arrives to run the mechanical grape sorter to begin the winemaking process at a Kosher winery in Saint-Émilion, France, 2003. © *Lucille Bass/Corbis.*

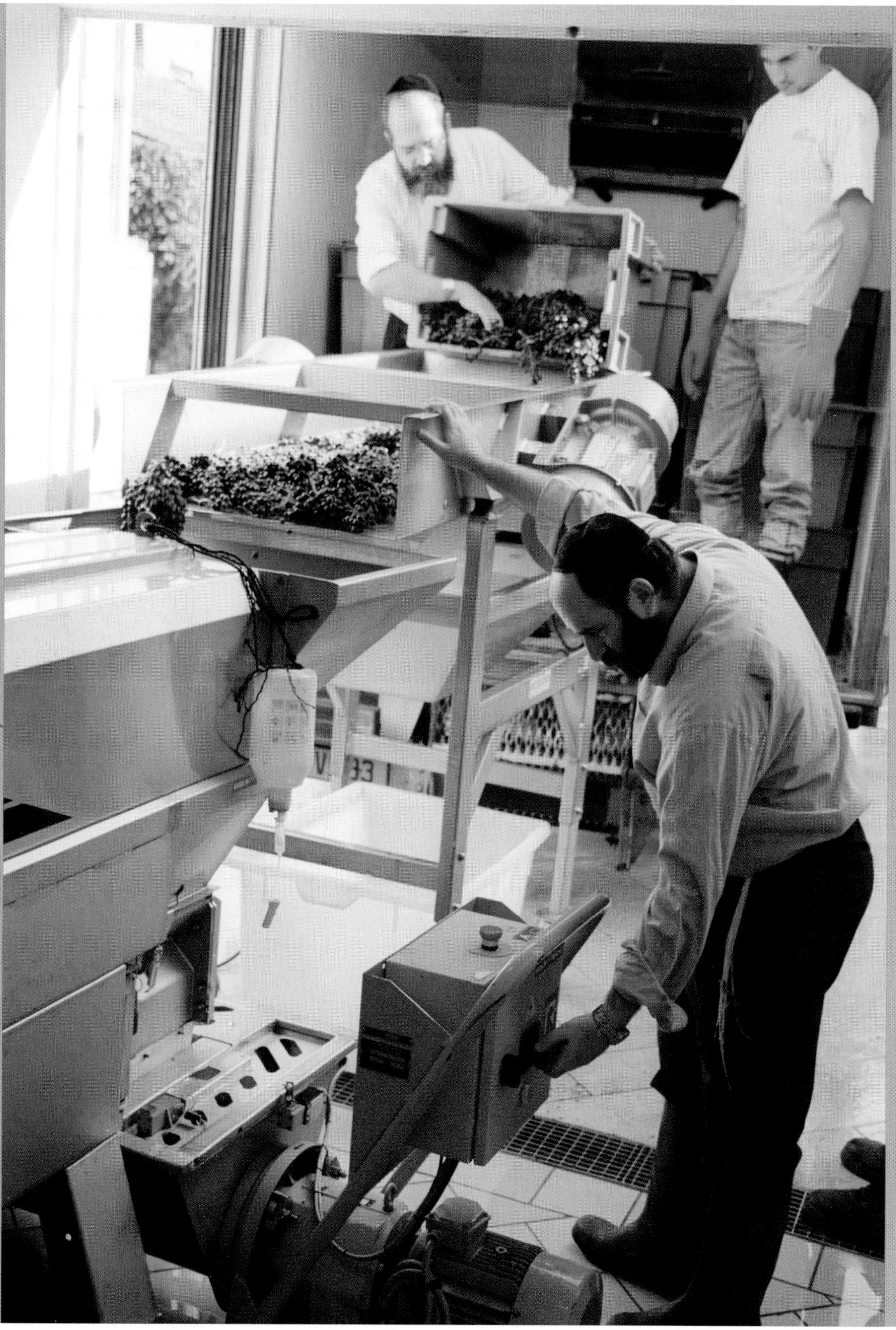

月 日

SHANGHAI MUNICIPAL COUNCIL
上海工部局衛生處
PUBLIC HEALTH DEPARTMENT

誕生報告書

第六一四號

嬰孩題名尹利亞
性　　別男
產生日期一九四二年一月十三日
產生地點宏恩醫院
父親姓名巴尔德
父親職位或業務巴尔德眼鏡公司
籍　　貫俄國
母親姓名卡氏
雙親住址靜安寺路一一七三號

上海公共租界工部局衛生處
註冊員冼嘉士簽印
註冊日期 中華民國卅一 西曆一九四二年一月廿九日

ABOVE: **A group of Israeli women pray at the Western Wall, 2000.** *© Ricki Rosen/Corbis.*

LEFT: **Birth certificate of Ilia Bard issued by the health department of the municipal council of Shanghai, China, December 1942.** *Photo: Eliahu Bard, Israel. By courtesy of Beth Hatefutsoth Photo Archive, Tel Aviv.*

erbated rifts in Israeli society, weakened the disposition of American Jews to sublimate or mask criticisms of Israeli policy. As the scholar Melvin I. Urofsky observed in this period, despite "deep divisions... over the wisdom of [the Begin government's] diplomatic and settlement policies" relations between American Jews and Israel were "strained yet still intact." Such an assessment could hardly have been made in the 1970s when it appeared the divisions referred to obtained mainly in intellectual circles but were not reflected in the alignment of organizations. With the passage of Israel's Golan Heights law, however, a new juncture was reached. Now, as Rabbi Alexander M. Schindler, chairman of the Conference of the Presidents of Major American Jewish Organizations reported, there was "no unanimity... among American Jewish leaders" on matters of Israeli policy.

In addition to the Likud government's extensive settlement program in the West Bank and Gaza Strip, other issues and events that led to this change included Israel's bombing of Iraq's atomic reactor in June 1981, the extension of Israeli law to the Golan Heights in December 1981, the bombing of Beirut and Israel's indirect role in the Sabra and Shatilla refugee camp massacres during the 1982 Lebanon War, the sale of arms to Iran prior to the Irangate scandal, Israel's military and commercial ties to South Africa's apartheid government, the emergence of the still unresolved and highly charged "Who is a Jew?" issue, and Israel's role as portrayed in the media during the Palestinian Intifada. Certain American Jewish intellectuals were among the most critical of Israel's policies and actions.

Especially upsetting from the point of view of American Jews, and the only issue to have brought about a direct confrontation between the American Jewish community and the government of Israel, was the revival of the "Who is a Jew?" controversy. Although the roots of the argument lay in internal Israeli political developments going back to the beginning of the state, a string of events reignited the crisis at the end of 1988 and brought about the direct involvement of American Jewish leaders. The two contenders for the Israel premiership, Yitzhak Shamir and Shimon Peres, after the general elections were angling for the support of ultra-religious parties who stipulated the condition that Israeli law would be changed to recognize as Jews only those who underwent conversion under the auspices of an Orthodox rabbi in accordance with *halakhah* (traditional Jewish law).

Employing a Washington, D.C.–style lobbying effort, American Jews flew to Israel and met personally with government ministers, members of the Knesset, academicians, heads of industry, and the arts. The professional and lay heads of federations and other major American Jewish organizations came to state emphatically that any change in Israeli law would bring about the spiritual and possibly the physical alienation of American Jews from the State of Israel. In exchange for other concessions, the religious parties demanding this amendment agreed not to insist on their demand. A new government led by the Likud party was formed and the "Who is a Jew?" law was not amended.

In a controversial March 1987 op-ed article that appeared in the *Washington Post* the Judaica scholar Jacob *Neusner wrote: "It's time to say that America is a better place to be a Jew than Jerusalem." In addition to concern over the general instability of the region and Israel's external and internal political dilemmas, Neusner was disappointed that the Jewish State had not proven to be the world center of Jewish spirituality, scholarship, art, or literature. The Jewish community in the United States, he felt, had equal claim to that title.

The psychological gap between American and Israeli Jews was experienced in both directions, particularly during the 1991 Gulf War. While American Jews identified with the threat posed to Israel to the point of experiencing personal anguish, Israelis reported feeling abandoned by American Jews. As noted in the *Jerusalem Report* in 1992: "From August 1990, when Iraq invaded Kuwait... through March 1991, Israel lost a full 500,000 tourists, as compared to the year before... most of the drop was among American Jewish visitors; tourism from Europe and Christian America remained more or less stable."

The start of large-scale immigration from the U.S.S.R. in 1989 and its continuation after the breakup of the Soviet Union in 1991 increased Israel's population by some 400,000 by 1992 and gave a significant boost to Israel-Diaspora relations. Many of the new Russian immigrants were academicians and scientists with backgrounds in applied research, as well as a number of other professionals and entrepreneurs. As a result of initiatives taken by Israel, attempts at economic partnership between both private and communal American Jewish sources and the Jewish state began to develop alongside traditional philanthropic projects. Sensitive to the negative effects on Israel-diaspora relations which would inevitably result from a string of business failures, American Jewish investors developed a broad range of carefully researched investment opportunities, from startup incubator schemes, to the privatization of government-run concerns, to creating new partnerships within large, established corporations. One example was the "strategic alliance model" developed by the Jewish community of Boston. This program was based on the principle of allocating about 20 percent of funds raised for Israel to help create partnerships between Israeli hi-tech firms and their Massachusetts counterparts.

At the outset of 1992, pro-Israel activists were torn over how to respond to the President George H.W. Bush's insistence on linking approval of Israel's request for $10 billion in loan guarantees from the United States to a complete freeze on the construction and expansion of Jewish settlements in the West Bank. Israel was requesting the guarantees in order to secure $10 billion of credit on the international loan market needed for the absorption of the recent large wave of immigrants from the former Soviet Union. Meanwhile, Israel's Prime Minister Yitzhak Shamir declared that none of the money secured through the loan guarantees would be used to support settlement expansion. However, as Shamir's detractors pointed out, including those within the American Jewish community, the money would most likely be used to free funds from Israel's own treasury for support of West Bank settlement.

Liberal organizations, such as the American Jewish Congress, the Union of American Hebrew Congregations, and the Jewish community relations councils of Milwaukee and Detroit, supported the idea of a total freeze. Conservative groups, such as Americans for a Safe Israel and the Union of Orthodox Jewish Congregations of America, felt that to back the U.S. administration's demands would jeopardize Israel's future security. While Americans for Peace Now and the Jewish Peace Lobby condemned "the settlements" and publicly advocated a two-state solution to the Israeli-Palestinian controversy, other Jewish organizations such as the National Council of Jewish Women and the Zionist Organization of America, stood behind Israeli government policies and its application for the loan guarantees. AIPAC implemented a particularly vigorous public relations campaign over the issue. It was not until mid-August 1992, after Labor leader Yitzhak Rabin had succeeded Shamir as prime minister and announced a gradual halt to the construction of new West Bank settlements, that Israel and the United States announced an agreement on the basic principles that would allow the loan guarantees to proceed. Next, in a speech before B'nai B'rith, Bush announced he would recommend to Congress that it approve Israel's $10 billion loan guarantee request.

Jewish opinion of the Bush administration's overall record on Israel was mixed. On the one hand, the United States played a vital role in the May 1991 airlift operation of nearly 14,200 Ethiopian Jews to Israel in Operation Solomon. On the other hand, some American Jews resented the constraints placed on Israel by the United States during the Gulf War, which prevented Israel's air force from retaliating against Iraq for bombarding Israel with SCUD missiles. The relationship between the American Jewish community and the Bush administration ended rather poorly, mainly because of the loan guarantees struggle.

The return to power in 1992 of Israel's Labor party under the leadership of Yitzhak Rabin and the election that November of Democratic presidential candidate Bill Clinton ushered in a new era in Israel-American relations. As a result of these twin victories, American Jews were faced with a new situation. The government of Israel was now dovish instead of hawkish. Israel's new leaders were willing to negotiate for a settlement in far reaching terms, something their predecessors would never consider. Second, Israel's position towards the PLO confused many American Jews, who for decades knew the organization to be a ruthless terrorist group. One American Orthodox rabbi described the dilemma as a "psychological issue." "People have been told for twenty years the PLO is out of bounds," he explained. "You can't expect them to turn on a dime." Meanwhile, Clinton, who lacked George H.W. Bush's patrician background, was closer to the Jews generally and warmer to the Jewish state. The Clinton administration immediately embraced the peace process undertaken by the Rabin government, and it was felt that the tensions and strains that characterized recent American-Israel relations would now cease. Even so, a small but influential group of American Jewish public intellectuals spoke out against the policies of the new Rabin government and Clinton administration. These included, among others, *Commentary* editor Norman Podhoretz and former *New York Times* editor A.M. *Rosenthal. Podhoretz saw the peace process as a trap that, sooner or later, would lead Israel into a war in a diminished capacity.

Although the number of active pro-Israel American Jews was but a small percentage of the total Jewish population, both the Likud and Labor parties maintained supporters in the United States. The Labor party established a new organization, the Israel Policy Forum, to promote its policies. Its American-based Friends of Labor Israel, was set up outside the umbrella American Zionist Federation to raise funds for the party. Likud also had an American Friends organization and but continued to rely especially on the support of the mainstream Zionist Organization of America. Polls showed that over 60 percent of American Jews were more optimistic about the chances for peace in the Middle East as a result of Rabin's election.

Like most of the world, American Jews were surprised to hear in 1993 that secret talks taking place in Oslo between representatives of his government and the PLO had resulted in an historic agreement. According to its terms, Israel would hand over Gaza and Jericho where the Palestinians would create the first two autonomous self-rule areas. According to the *New York Times*, most American Jews reacted to the news with "a kind of hard-headed optimism, a feeling that recognition of the PLO and establishing relations with its leader, Yasser Arafat, [was] risky but promising." A minority felt that recognizing the PLO and its leader in spite of its record of terror was wrong.

On September 13, 1993, Rabin and Arafat were brought together on the White House lawn by President Bill Clinton to sign an accord of mutual recognition between Israel and the Palestinian Liberation Organization (PLO). A community survey conducted by the American Jewish Committee found that in the weeks following, some 90 percent of American Jews felt the Israel-PLO agreement to be a "positive development from Israel's point of view," with 57 percent favoring the establishment of a Palestinian state and 30 percent opposed. That summer, Rabin urged American Jewish leaders to complete the $1.2 billion Operation Exodus campaign intended to underwrite the resettlement costs of Jews from the former Soviet Union. No longer perceived as vulnerable or besieged, American Jews deployed the "Israel's Risks for Peace" campaign.

One of the most shocking news items of 1994, while ostensibly an internal Israeli affair, had a distinctively American Jewish angle. Early in the morning on the holiday of Purim, which fell on February 25, a Jewish physician and resident of the community of Kiryat Arba, entered the Cave of the Patriarchs in the adjacent city of Hebron and opened fire with an automatic rifle on a large group of Moslem worshipers. Twenty-nine Muslims died from their wounds and the physician, Dr. Baruch Goldstein, was killed on the spot by the enraged crowd. The fact that Goldstein was an American Jew was strongly emphasized in all media coverage of the event. American Jewish organizations, who swiftly and unconditionally condemned the massacre, took pains to distance Goldstein from the mainstream Jewish community. Nevertheless, Goldstein's deed raised the issue, both in Israel and the United States, of the seemingly disproportionate number of American-Jewish immigrants in Israel involved in extremist political groups such as Kach and Kahane Chai.

Israel's Deputy Foreign Minister Yossi *Beilin surprised Jews around the world, but particularly American Jews, with remarks he made before a WIZO convention held in Jerusalem in January 1994. Beilin claimed that the State of Israel was financially self-sufficient and no longer dependent on charity from Diaspora communities. Diaspora fundraising efforts, he argued, would be better directed towards local Jewish education. In reacting to Beilin's remarks, Rabin characterized them as "brainless," noting: "If Israel could not ask diaspora Jews for money, how could it ask the [non-Jewish] American taxpayer?"

In 1994, after more than four years, the absorption of 500,000 new immigrants, and nearly $900 million in aid, the United Jewish Appeal's Operation Exodus officially came to a close. Funds from Operation Exodus were used to help Jews immigrate to Israel from the former Soviet Union and Ethiopia. The campaign was launched in 1990, with an original three-year goal of $420 million needed for an estimated 200,000 immigrants. When 185,000 new immigrants arrived in 1990, the goal of the campaign was doubled. The $910 million actually raised, fell just short of the campaign's declared goal of $1 billion.

American Jews were shocked in 1995 by the assassination of Prime Minister Yitzhak *Rabin, who was murdered by Yigal Amir, a right-wing zealot, at a peace rally in Tel Aviv. Rabin's murder led to a series of major political shifts, including the election in 1996 of a Likud coalition under Binyamin *Netanyahu, an opponent of the Oslo process. The Netanyahu government agreed in principle to fulfill Israel's negotiated commitments, starting with the redeployment of Israeli troops from Hebron, but meanwhile insisted on the Palestinian Authority's full compliance with the terms of the Oslo agreement. As a result, the peace process now entered a period of protracted stagnation. Accusations of non-compliance were compounded by sporadic Palestinian violence and ultimately led in 2000 to a second Intifada (Palestinian uprising). The rapid deterioration in Israel-Palestinian relations resulted in widespread despair among the Israeli public and dampened the spirits of the American Jewish community. The crisis resulted in yet another dramatic shift on the Israeli political scene and the consequent victory in 2000 of Labor leader Ehud *Barak, a highly decorated war hero and former chief of staff. Despite the country's overwhelming support for Barak and his commitment to advancing the peace process, he lacked the political experience and steady hand of Rabin, his predecessor and role model. Moreover, the Palestine Authority under Yasser Arafat proved powerless if not unwilling to stem the tide of Palestinian terrorist violence directed at Israel, including the seemingly endless cycle of suicide bombings aimed at border checkpoints and Israel's major urban centers – much of which was clandestinely financed and supported by hostile Arab regimes in the region and the militant Hamas organization. Following a series of delicate and unsuccessful negotiations brokered by the Clinton administration between Israel and Syria, Barak turned his full attention to reaching a swift and final agreement with the Palestinians. Owing to numerous obstacles, Barak's efforts were, in practice, stillborn and he quickly lost his public support and his hold on power.

At the turn of the 20th century, the context for the Israel-Palestinian conflict underwent a shift to the right and a major sea change. Against the backdrop of the election of President George W. Bush in the United States, the landslide victory of Likud leader Ariel *Sharon in Israel, and the 9/11 attacks, Israel publicly adopted a new three-pronged strategy vis-à-vis the Palestinians. First, the new Sharon government sought to increase pressure on the Palestine Authority and drive forward its signed commitments to peace and security by exerting economic and political pressure on the Palestinian leadership, including the isolation of Yasser Arafat. Second, the Likud coalition, with the support of the Labor party, unilaterally initiated the redeployment of Israeli troops from the West Bank and Gaza Strip and, where necessary, forcibly removed Jewish settlers from settlements in the occupied territories. Finally, the government built a separation wall between Israel and the Palestinian lands – some of which was reconfigured after the Israeli Supreme Court determined certain sections of the barrier to be in violation of Palestinian rights – and in this way sought to ensure Israel's territorial integrity while safeguarding the country from further terrorist attacks and strengthening its hold on borders established since the June 1967 war, including its sovereignty over Jerusalem and the surrounding metropolitan region.

A striking result of this process was the transformation of American Jewry's attitude toward Sharon himself, once vilified by those on the American Jewish left and even many centrists as a dangerous right-wing fanatic, and now rehabilitated as a warrior-turned-elder statesman – much like Rabin before him. Indeed, American Jews proved largely supportive of Sharon's policies and diplomatic maneuvers, a combination that was, in essence, a continuation and extension of the semi-transparent strategy first implemented under Rabin a decade earlier. Having closely followed the waxing and waning of Israel-Arab relations in the recent past, a majority of American Jews responded favorably to Sharon's pragmatic and bold leadership which seemed to vouchsafe Israel's interests while neither ignoring the reality of the Palestinian situation nor extending the reach of the Jewish state in a way that exceeded its grasp. As noted in the memoir of Middle East envoy Dennis *Ross, chief peace negotiator in the presidential administrations of

George H.W. Bush and Bill Clinton and arguably the most significant American Jewish figure in U.S. diplomacy since Henry Kissinger, Sharon's approach was a pro-active and rational response to an ineluctable and historic dilemma faced by Israel which had evolved since the very establishment of the Jewish state in 1948.

> Partition was bound to happen at some point. For Yitzhak Rabin, who understood both the demographic and security arrangements for partition, his preference was to produce it through agreement with the Palestinians. But he was prepared to "separate" from the Palestinians if agreement was not possible. Prime Minister Sharon, though a pronounced opponent of building a separation fence when Yitzhak Rabin first proposed it in 1995 and Ehud Barak reintroduced it after the outbreak of the Intifada, has now become a proponent of both the fence and the concept of disengagement. Partly, he has been driven by the security reality: The fence around Gaza has proven effective in preventing suicide attacks into Israel from Gaza… Small wonder, therefore, that 83 percent of the Israeli public favors the building of a comparable fence or barrier on the West Bank… For Sharon and other leaders [on the Israeli right], the issue is no longer whether to build the fence, but where to do so… That is why Ehud Olmert has spoken about withdrawing from 80–85 percent of the West Bank unilaterally…

The congruence of the Rabin and Sharon pragmatic policies helps to explain why the Anti-Defamation League's *2005 Survey of American Attitudes toward Israel and the Middle East* found that 67 percent of Americans generally supported the Sharon government's policy of disengagement. As well, the American Labor Zionist group Ameinu conducted a separate poll in the same year which demonstrated that 62 percent of American Jews supported Sharon's plan for disengagement. "In the context of a peace agreement," the Ameinu report explained, "42 percent thought Israel should be willing to withdraw from most Jewish settlements in the West Bank – even though only 24 percent believe most Palestinians are willing to live in peace next to the Jewish state, and 70 percent believe the Palestinians will continue terrorist attacks even if a peace agreement is reached."

Since the Persian Gulf War of 1991, American Jews watched anxiously as Israel, the Palestinians, and the neighboring Arab countries entered new and uncharted territory. What was once unthinkable in the Middle East barely a few decades ago has become a matter of established precedent and each hopeful episode in the troubled Arab-Israeli peace process has in general been accompanied by an upswing in American Jewish support for Israel's bold diplomatic and political moves. Starting with the Madrid Peace Conference in 1991, where Prime Minister Yitzhak Shamir participated in unprecedented direct negotiations with Jordan, Lebanon, Syria, and the Palestinians and continuing with the Declaration of Principles in 1993, the Israel-Jordan peace treaty in 1994, and Interim Agreement with the Palestinians in 1995, and the Wye River Memorandum of 1998, American Jews have consistently supported the emergent Rabin-Sharon strategy-in-the-making. Following Sharon's sudden illness and departure from the political scene, it appears that Ehud *Olmert and a new generation of Israeli political leaders will continue on this path. To be sure, Israeli policies and methods frequently provoke considerable controversy among diverse American Jewish circles and American Zionist groups. Nonetheless, since the 1990s the majority of American Jews have consistently responded favorably to Israel's notion of "land for peace" and the ensuing prospects for a comprehensive solution to the Arab-Israel conflict. Today, it is widely believed that the issue of Israel's survival, which dominated much of the American Jewish agenda from 1967 to 1991, will soon be consigned to the past, like the Cold War itself.

Conclusion

> "American Jewish history weds together two great historical traditions: one Jewish, dating back to the Patriarchs, the prophets, and the rabbis of the Talmud, the other American, dating back to the Indians, Columbus, and the heroes of the Revolution. Bearing the imprint of both, it nevertheless forms a distinctive historical tradition of its own, now more than three centuries old. It is a tradition rooted in ambivalence, for American Jews are sometimes pulled in two different directions at once. Yet it is also unified by a common vision, the quest to be fully a Jew and fully an American, both at the same time. It is closely tied to Jews worldwide, and just as closely tied to Americans of other faiths. It is perpetuated generation after generation by creative men and women, who grapple with the tensions and paradoxes inherent in American Jewish life, and fashion from them what we know as the American Jewish experience – a kaleidoscope of social, religious, cultural, economic, and political elements that makes up the variegated, dynamic world of the American Jew."
>
> Jonathan D. Sarna, *The American Jewish Experience* (1986).

It is, perhaps, a commonplace observation that almost any statement made about the Jewish condition in North America and its opposite are both true. On the one hand, much of the data collected on American Jews in the past quarter century reveals high levels of apathy, assimilation, and indifference to Jewish values and observance. At best, no more than 50 percent of the American Jewish population in this period has been directly involved in any form of organized communal or religious life. At the same time, the general opening up of American society since the mid-20th century for all minorities contributed significantly to the opening up of American Jewish life. Merit and achievement have generally taken precedence over other factors and enabled Jews to rise quickly in a variety of professions, especially those requiring advanced academic training. In fact, never before in the history of Jewish civilization has there been a Jewish community with more affluence, influence, and access to the highest levels of government, business, and the professions. Virtually, no barriers exist at the present time to the most elite levels of American business, law, or government. Nor have there ever been so many American Jews involved in such a variety of well funded Jewish-sponsored communal frameworks, including hospitals, social welfare agencies, retirement homes, day schools, summer camps, Israel programs, college-level studies in Judaica, and so on. In a word, American Jewish life is arguably one of the most robust voluntary and self-sustaining ethnic-communal frameworks in contemporary American society.

Today, the American Jewish community covers a continent with numerous major communities of substantial numbers as well as hundreds of smaller-sized communities consisting of from a handful to several hundreds of families. The last one hundred years have witnessed the wide scale migration of the American Jewish population from inner city ghettos to vast sprawling suburban areas and back again to many center-city now-gentrified neighborhoods. From the Northeast, where almost half the total Jewish population once resided in New York City, there has been a massive relocation to the sun belt, where communities such as southern Florida and southern California now boast populations of more than half a million Jews each, most of whom have settled there in the past 50 years.

With tap roots in centuries of Jewish history and top roots in the American experience, contemporary American Jewry presently stands at a crossroads. Free to participate in the social, religious, and political fabric of American life as no other western Jewry before it, American Jews – individually and collectively – can decide to strengthen their communal bonds or loosen them, to shore up the larger community's sense of cohesion or allow it to dissipate. As the historical record suggests, the antipodes of engagement and disengagement have long demarcated much of the American Jewish experience. But it is also evident that American Jewry has emerged from its history in the New World largely intact and enriched. In each phase of its development, American Jewry has discerned possibilities and created opportunities for negotiating the delicate balance of modern life in an open society – that is, calibrating oneself and one's community to the requirements of living as a Jew *and* as an American. This tension is arguably a fundamental component of life in a pluralistic democratic society.

It is not the task of this study to predict "Wither American Jewish life?" or determine whether it is "good for the Jews or bad for the Jews" to sustain their tribal identity in America of the 21st century. These are, to be sure, vitally important questions and they have been raised here owing to their centrality in the American Jewish public arena. But the "answers" to such questions, which surely warrant serious and thoughtful deliberation, go well beyond the scope of an historical analysis such as this. It is clear, however, that American Jewry is a dynamic and multidimensional creature with considerable intrinsic talents and material resources. Possessed of the capacity to enrich Jewish life even as it enlarges America's bounty, American Jewry boasts a remarkable history of success and legacy of achievement. How present and future generations of American Jews will be informed and shaped by this inheritance and will, in turn, seek to determine their destiny remains to be seen.

American Antisemitism in Historical Perspective

In 1811 Rabbi Gershon Mendes Seixas of New York wrote that "The United States is, perhaps, the only place where the Jews have not suffered persecution, but have, on the contrary, been encouraged and indulged in every right of citizens." While it is true that American antisemitism never attained the virulence and baneful consequences of European antisemitism, it is equally clear that an undercurrent of anti-Jewish prejudice, sometimes open, more often subtle, has existed throughout the history of the United States.

The early colonial settlers in America brought with them the old stereotype of the Jew as the mysterious outsider, heretic, and despoiler. These prejudices, however, were rarely translated into direct anti-Jewish actions. The very first Jewish settlers in New Amsterdam in 1654 did face an immediate threat when Peter Stuyvesant, the Dutch governor, attempted to expel them. Overruled by the Dutch West India Company, Stuyvesant was forced to grant them the right of residency, and by 1657 they were granted the status of burghers. Nevertheless, the Jews remained in effect second-class burghers even after the British took control of New York. Although economic rights were secured by the end of the seventeenth century, political rights were not fully granted throughout the colonial period.

The need for immigrants, particularly those with economic skills, and the growing ethnic and religious diversity of the American colonies were powerful factors counteracting traditional prejudices. Still, each colony had an established church and, consequently, Jews, Catholics, and Protestant dissenters were all subject to discrimination. In 1658 Jacob Lumbrozo, a physician, the first Jewish settler in Maryland, was charged with blasphemy in that colony, but the prosecution was never completed. In no colony, however, were Jews physically harmed for religious motives, as were Quakers and Baptists, and no 18th-century law was enacted for the sole purpose of disabling Jews. Colonial American Jewry achieved a considerable degree of economic success and social integration, and intermarriage was frequent by the mid-18th century.

Anti-Jewish prejudice during the period from independence until the Civil War, while present in the form of the persistent Shylock image and related stereotypes, did not seriously impinge on the rights of the relatively small Jewish community. The 1840s and 1850s saw a fairly large immigration of German Jews, but by 1860 there were still fewer than 200,000 Jews in a population of 30,000,000. The invisibility of the Jews, the availability of other targets of discrimination, the all-absorbing slavery issue, and the rapid economic growth of the country combined to reduce the possible development of any real group antagonism based on latent prejudice. The Know-Nothing movement of the 1850s and other nativist phenomena of the pre-Civil War era concentrated their ire on Catholics, not Jews.

Still, there were occasional outbursts of antisemitism. The political strife between Federalists and Republicans at the turn of the 18th century produced a noticeable outpouring of slurs upon Jews who were Jeffersonian partisans. A Federalist in New York condemned the local Democratic-Republican Society by saying that they all seemed to be "of the tribe of Shylock." In 1809 Jacob Henry was at first refused a seat in the North Carolina House of Commons to which he had been elected, but was eventually seated by a legal subterfuge. Mordecai M. Noah, one of the outstanding Jewish figures of this period, was recalled in 1815 by Secretary of State James Monroe from his post as U.S. consul in Tunis because his faith allegedly interfered with the performance of his duties. In 1820, the editor of a prominent magazine, the *Niles Weekly Register*, wrote that the Jews "create nothing" and act "as if they had a home no where." Uriah P. Levy, an officer in the United States Navy, was subjected to several courts-martial, partly due to anti-Jewish prejudice. Jews were concerned also with questions of church-state relations, including the vexing problem of public school education. Yet these incidents and remarks cannot be construed as evidence of significant antisemitism; Henry was seated, Levy was acquitted and restored to rank, and the editor of the *Niles Weekly Register*, while critical, urged equal rights for Jews.

The first substantial and open antisemitic agitation in the United States was evidenced during the Civil War (1861–65). The economic dislocations and frayed tempers of this critical period released prejudices that had slumbered below the surface. Both in the North and in the South, Jews were accused by some newspapers and political leaders of aiding the enemy, smuggling, profiteering, draft dodging, and speculating. Almost every political opponent of Judah P. Benjamin, the Confederate secretary of state, made unflattering references to his Jewishness. Among the prominent figures who displayed antisemitic tendencies were Generals William T. Sherman and Benjamin F. Butler, Parson William Brownlow, Congressman Henry S. Foote, and Senator Henry Wilson. The major antisemitic incident of the war originated with General Ulysses S. Grant. In what has been called the most sweeping anti-Jewish regulation in all American history, Grant, in his General Order No. 11, December 17, 1862, ordered the expulsion of all Jews "as a class" within 24 hours from the Department of the Tennessee, comprising parts of Kentucky, Tennessee, and Mississippi. However, President Abraham Lincoln directed the revocation of Grant's order.

The unpleasant episodes of the Civil War years should not obscure the fact that the Jews of the United States were perhaps freer than Jews had ever been since their dispersion from Palestine. No price had been exacted from them in return for complete political emancipation, and the community flourished economically and religiously. Official or governmental discrimination on the European model was absent and systematic antisemitism did not exist. Beginning with the 1870s, however, antisemitism in the form of social discrimination was increasingly evident, and was accompanied by the development of ideological antisemitism. The refusal of accommodations to Joseph Seligman, a prominent New York Jewish banker, at the Grand Union Hotel in Saratoga Springs in the summer of 1877 drew widespread adverse comment in the public press, but it symbolized a growing tendency toward the exclusion of Jews from areas involving leisure-time facilities. Summer resort advertisements including statements such as "We prefer not to entertain Hebrews" were common after the 1880s. From the resorts, social discrimination worked back into the cities. Important social clubs, such as the Union League Club, barred Jewish members. Private schools were closed to Jewish children, and, in general, Jews were not welcome at any institution or association that conferred prestige and status. Behind the groundswell of social discrimination lay the profound social changes of the "Gilded Age" of the late 19th century. The older, elite white Protestant groups faced a growing struggle for their social status and power as their security was threatened by rapid industrialization and the rise of new middle- and upper-class elements, whom they regarded as crass nouveaux riches. Social discrimination thus served the dual purpose of keeping Jews "in their place" while enhancing and defining the social status of the older elite and the newer non-Jewish wealthy class.

During the turbulent and xenophobic decades that spanned the 19th and 20th centuries, an ideological antisemitism began to appear as a by-product of American nativism and in response to the perceptible cultural gap between the older population and the massive numbers of Jewish immigrants from Eastern Europe. Men like Henry Adams, representing Eastern patrician intellectuals, and Ignatius Donnelly, representing Western agrarian radicals, while far apart in basic orientation, both viewed the Jew as conniving and grasping, and as the cause and symbol of their discontent. The anti-Jewish stereotype which emerged clearly during this period contained elements of the earlier Christian antisemitism, the Shylock image, the wielding of undue power through manipulation of gold, and an identification of Jews with the hated, feared city.

From 1881 to 1910, over 1,500,000 East European Jews arrived in the United States, and by 1925 there were close to 4,000,000 Jews in the country. Their very presence, the competition engendered by their rapid rise in economic status, and their pressure to achieve social integration lent credence to the anti-Jewish stereotype, sharpened antisemitic feelings, and confirmed a widespread system of social discrimination. For their part, Jews did not accept antisemitism without protest, especially when it appeared to involve public matters. Led by the older German Jewish community, American Jewry formed self-defense organizations, including the American Jewish Committee in 1906, the Anti-Defamation League of B'nai B'rith in 1913, and the American Jewish Congress in 1920.

One of the most serious issues faced by the Jewish community during the first quarter of the 20th century was the movement for restriction of immigration to the United States. Although there was no direct antisemitism reflected in the legislation resulting from restrictionism, it was clear that the intellectual fathers of the movement, such as Henry Cabot Lodge, Prescott Hall, John R. Commons, Henry Pratt Fairchild, and Edward A. Ross, considered Jewish immigration deleterious to the welfare of the nation. Ross, for example, predicted "riots and anti-Jewish legislation" if unrestricted immigration continued. Madison Grant, a thoroughgoing racist, condemned the Jews in his book *The Passing of the Great Race* (1916) for mongrelizing the nation. The campaign for immigration restriction reached its height after World War I when the nation reacted with horror at the prospect of unlimited immigration. Burton J. Hendrick, a well-known journalist, while disclaiming antisemitism, wrote a widely publicized attack on Jewish immigration in 1923, as did Kenneth Roberts, a popular novelist. The ultimate result of the restrictionist movement – the U.S. Immigration Act of 1924 – established a national origins quota system that discriminated heavily against South and East European immigration. Although antisemitism was not the primary motivation for restrictionism, it was a useful propaganda weapon and, subtly, became enshrined in American legislation for over 40 years.

The first-class citizenship of American Jews was indirectly challenged during the late 19th and early 20th centuries by the general refusal of Tsarist Russia to issue visas to American Jews and its mistreatment of those who did receive them. American Jewry, led by Jacob H. Schiff and Louis Marshall of the American Jewish Committee, argued that tacit acceptance of this situation by the U.S. government constituted a slur on its full citizenship. Diplomatic pressure having failed, a determined and successful campaign was instituted in 1911 for the unilateral abrogation of the Russo-American Treaty of 1832. To Louis Marshall the victory symbolized "the removal of the last civil disabilities to which the Jews of this country have been subjected."

In 1913, however, American Jews were shocked when Leo Frank, a New York Jew who had relocated in Atlanta, Georgia to become manager of a pencil factory, was convicted of the slaying of one of his female employees. The evidence against Frank was flimsy and the trial, which unleashed fantasies of Jewish ritual murder and garnered widespread public attention, showcased the darkest racist and antisemitic tendencies of white southern Christian society. In the event, the circumstances surrounding Frank's trial and conviction reflected came to be viewed as a transparent example of mob antisemitism. In 1915, after the governor of Georgia stayed Frank's death sentence, a lynching party abducted Frank from jail and hanged him.

The emergence of overt antisemitism in the Frank case was a harbinger of an upsurge of anti-Jewish feeling, expression, and actions during the 1920s. The hatred of Jews was rooted both in older stereotypes and renewed economic antisemitism which was an element in the outlook of some of the Populists, the movement of protest against capitalism and monopoly that prevailed in southern and western states at the turn of the century. Jewish capital was identified with Wall Street financiers and oppression by the financial system of farmers and small businessmen. Some of the then young Populists, such as the later Senator Burton K. Wheeler from Montana, were to remain anti-Jewish on such economic grounds into the 1930s. Antisemitism did not involve all of Populism, but what there was of such prejudice represented its only appearance in American history within an important left-wing movement.

The artificially stimulated unity of World War I cracked under the impact of postwar disillusionment, and a sense of imminent danger from internal and external subversive forces seized the nation. The old way of life appeared to be disappearing under the onslaught of the foreign born, the city, the new moral relativism, and liberal religion. Many Americans adopted ideologies stressing coercive political and religious fundamentalism and sought scapegoats for the ills, real and imaginary, that beset them. Antisemitism was part of this reaction. Although incidents of antisemitism during America's participation in World War I were sporadic, a new wave of nativist nationalism gripped the land. Many German Jews, including America's elite Jewish patricians of Austrian and Bavarian extraction, outwardly disassociated from their central European past. Meanwhile, foreign radicalism, often associated with East European Jews, became the chief target in the postwar Red Scare of 1919–20. This alleged Jewish-Bolshevik nexus remained a permanent part of antisemitic propaganda.

The concern of Jews over these charges was heightened considerably by the appearance of an American edition of the spurious *Protocols of the Elders of Zion* in 1920, followed by a work based on it, *The Cause of World Unrest*. The basic message of these volumes was that the Bolshevik Revolution was Jewish in origin and part of an international Jewish conspiracy to destroy Christendom and dominate the world. Discredited by serious investigators, these libels nevertheless remained alive. In May 1920 The *Dearborn Independent*, a magazine owned and published by Henry Ford, the automobile magnate, launched an antisemitic propaganda campaign without precedent in the United States which lasted, with varying intensity, for almost seven years. Charging American Jews with a plot to subvert traditional American ways, Ford's propaganda found acceptance in rural areas and small towns, but met a negative reaction in the large urban areas and among leading American policy and opinion makers. Notwithstanding such condemnations as that of January 16, 1921, when a declaration, signed by 119 leading Americans, headed by President Woodrow Wilson and former president William Howard Taft, denounced the anti-Jewish calumnies, Ford's campaign continued unchecked until in 1927, under pressure of an unofficial consumer boycott and several lawsuits, Ford issued a public apology through Louis Marshall, head of the American Jewish Committee. However, the *Protocols* and *The International Jew* persisted as staple items in the arsenal of American antisemitism in succeeding decades. The stereotype of the international Jewish banker-Bolshevik had been superimposed on the earlier stereotype of anti-Christ, Shylock, and Rothschild.

The most significant expression of American nativism during the 1920s was the spectacular revival of the Ku Klux

Klan which, at its height in 1924, counted over 4,000,000 members in all parts of the country. Although its primary targets in the defense of "one hundred percent Americanism" were Catholics and blacks, Klan leaders in their propaganda also included Jews as one of the chief obstacles to the preservation of the "real America." Thus, the Klan of the 1920s was the first substantial, organized mass movement in the U.S. that utilized antisemitism. Politically ineffective except as an adjunct to the immigration restriction movement, the Klan never proposed a specific anti-Jewish program, but sporadic boycotts of Jewish merchants and similar harassments did occur before the collapse of Klan power in the late 1920s.

Social discrimination reached new heights in the 1920s as Jews continued to be the most swiftly rising ethnic group in American society. Although Jewish leaders had obtained passage of a civil rights statute applying to places of public accommodation in New York in 1913, and subsequently in other states, exclusion of Jews from summer resorts and hotels continued unabated. Particularly galling to upper-class Jews was their exclusion from social clubs, both of the city and country types. As Jews began to leave the crowded immigrant quarters of the large cities, they tended to settle in concentrated areas, partly in response to residential discrimination. Jews with high incomes found themselves unwelcome in the fashionable sections of the cities and in many suburban developments.

The form of social discrimination that concerned Jews most directly occurred in higher education, which they sought in larger numbers and earlier than any other immigrant group as the key to economic and cultural advancement. Eastern colleges in particular were faced with increasing waves of Jewish students and reacted by establishing quota systems under a variety of guises. Once admitted, Jewish students often faced social aloofness and resistance, and responded by the formation of Jewish fraternities. Educational discrimination became a national issue in June 1922 when A. Lawrence Lowell, president of Harvard College, announced that Harvard was considering a quota system for Jewish students. Jewish leaders reacted strongly to this open evidence of prejudice, and Lowell's proposal was rejected by a Harvard faculty committee in April 1923. Defeated in its most blatant form, the quota system survived at Harvard and at most other leading colleges indirectly through various underhanded techniques. In the meantime, Harvard itself would nonetheless come to boast a distinguish cohort of Jewish alumni who later assumed national prominence as jurists, physicians, scholars, and business leaders including Louis D. Brandeis, Felix Frankfurter, Horace M. Kallen, Walter Lippman, Julian W. Mack, and Harry Wolfsohn.

Jews encountered considerable resistance as they attempted to move into white-collar and professional positions. Employers increasingly specified that Christians were preferred for office, sales, and executive positions. Banking, insurance, and public utilities firms were in the forefront of anti-Jewish prejudice. In medicine, the most ardently desired profession for Jews, there was a steady decline in the proportion of Jewish applicants accepted to medical schools during the 1920s and 1930s. In addition, Jewish doctors faced considerable difficulties in securing internships and staff positions in hospitals. Law schools did not discriminate against Jewish applicants, but Jewish lawyers were generally not accepted into large, well-established firms. Jews increasingly entered the teaching profession, especially where open, competitive examinations were required, but they were virtually excluded from faculty positions in American universities until after World War II.

Antisemitism in the form of social discrimination continued during the 1930s, but the chief distinction of this decade was an upsurge of ideological and politically motivated antisemitism. The combined impact of the Great Depression, the hysterical hatred of opponents for President Franklin D. Roosevelt, and the triumph of Nazism in Germany produced an outpouring of antisemitic propaganda and scores of antisemitic organizations in the United States. The major themes of this agitation were drawn from reprints of *The Protocols* and Henry Ford's *The International Jew: The World's Foremost Problem*, repeating the old charges of a Jewish international conspiracy, to which was added alleged Jewish responsibility for the depression and Jewish control of the Roosevelt administration. Nazi-inspired antisemitism was disseminated by such groups as the Friends of New Germany and the German-American Bund. The latter never achieved wide membership and was discredited when its leader, Fritz Kuhn, was convicted of embezzlement. More serious was the revival of native American antisemitism of the fundamentalist, pseudo-agrarian type. Among the major figures were William Dudley Pelley, organizer of the Silver Shirts, Gerald Winrod, Gerald L.K. Smith, Gerald Deatherage and the Knights of the White Camelia, and Major General George van Horn Moseley.

The most potentially dangerous antisemitic leader of the 1930s was Charles E. Coughlin, a Roman Catholic priest and an opponent of the New Deal. Coughlin, whose weekly radio broadcasts reached millions of listeners, launched an open antisemitic campaign in 1938. His magazine, *Social Justice*, reprinted *The Protocols* with Coughlin's commentary placing responsibility for the world's plight on the Jews. Street riots and disturbances occurred when vendors sold his publication in the large cities. Coughlin was supported in his efforts by some official Catholic publications, including the *Boston Pilot* and the *Brooklyn Tablet*. The organizational expression of this predominantly Irish Catholic version of antisemitism was the Christian Front, led by Joe McWilliams, which held street-corner meetings and sponsored boycotts of Jewish merchants.

The approach of World War II in the late 1930s saw the formation of a powerful isolationist movement in the United States. The America First Committee, organized in 1940, attracted antisemites to its banner. At an America First rally, on September 11, 1941, Charles A. Lindbergh, hero of American aviation, called the Jews the most dangerous force pushing the United States into war. Although his speech was followed by the protest resignation of the more liberal members of the committee, Lindbergh and the conservative faction persisted in their propaganda. Similar remarks were heard on the floor of Congress from such isolationist senators as Burton K. Wheeler and Gerald Nye. After the attack on Pearl Harbor and the entrance of the United States into the war, open antisemitic agitation declined. The tensions of the war years, however, stimulated a considerable amount of antisemitic sentiment. In 1944, for example, a public opinion poll showed that 24 percent of the respondents still regarded Jews as a "menace" to America and one-third to one-half would have supported a hypothetical countrywide antisemitic campaign. The fate of European Jewry appeared to have little impact on the prejudices of the American public.

The noisy antisemitism of the 1930s did not seriously endanger the American Jewish community, although it created much anguish and discomfort. The prevailing political traditions, the participation of the Jews in the New Deal alliance of ethnic groups, the inability of the antisemites to unite, self-defense and interfaith activities, and the intellectual discrediting of racism were all factors in preventing a potentially dangerous situation from materializing.

After 1945 antisemitism in the United States did not assume the ideological strength it had achieved in the preceding decades. Direct anti-Jewish agitation after World War II was limited, for the most part, to isolated fringe groups that were declining in number. Among the active exponents of antisemitism were such individuals and groups as the Columbians, the miniscule but vociferous American Nazi Party, the National Renaissance Party, and such publications as Gerald L.K. Smith's *The Cross and the Flag* and Conde McGinley's *Common Sense*. Much more threatening from the Jewish viewpoint was the persistence and growth of ultraconservative groups that officially denied antisemitic proclivities but provided a rallying point for many who were inclined to antisemitism. Significantly, however, the anti-Communist crusade initiated by Senator Joseph McCarthy in the early 1950s, while receiving widespread popular support, never attacked Jews as such.

Political antisemitism has shown few signs of strength in the post-World War II period and there have been only sporadic antisemitic episodes. There has been a noticeable decline in the system of social discrimination that prevailed in the United States between the 1880s and the 1950s. Notwithstanding a series of bombings of synagogues in the American south in the early 1950s, American Jewry in the 1950s and 1960s attained a high degree of behavioral acculturation, economic affluence, and educational achievement. The declining hostility to the Jews, their absorption into the dominant middle-class suburban society, the disreputability of openly avowed prejudice, continued economic prosperity, and the role of government in fostering major civil rights legislation have combined to produce a diminution in social antisemitism. In 1945 the president of Dartmouth College openly admitted and defended a quota system against Jewish students; 20 years later Jewish students comprised 25 percent of the student body at the prestigious Ivy League universities. Discrimination in admission of Jews to medical schools ended in the 1950s. In the same decade, Jewish students increasingly choose careers in such fields as engineering, architecture, science, which in the 1930s were highly discriminatory. By the late 1960s Jewish professors constituted over 10 percent of the faculties in the nation's senior colleges. At this juncture, surveys of discrimination by city and country clubs and by resorts showed a marked decline in the proportion excluding Jews. Nevertheless, subtle forms of social antisemitism persisted, especially in what came to be known as "executive suite" discrimination. Thus, in the 1970s, while Jews constituted 8 percent of the college-trained population in the United States, they comprised less than ½ percent of the executives of America's major companies or presidents of American colleges.

The American Jewish community was deeply concerned with problems of church-state relationships at mid-century. Occasionally, as in the strong public reaction to the Supreme Court's decision in the Regents prayer case of 1962 in which public school prayers were declared unconstitutional, antisemitic overtones were apparent.

Jewish participation in the civil rights movement of the 1950s and early 1960s brought charges from Southern extremists of attempts to "mongrelize" and "Communize" America. In the late 1960s the shift in the black community to greater militancy, the growth of black nationalism, and the emphasis on "black power" generated considerable friction in black-Jewish relations. Although surveys indicated that antisemitism among the mass of black Americans was no greater, and perhaps less, than that existing among white Americans, and although moderate black American leaders condemned antisemitism, continued inter-group conflict seriously disturbed American Jewry and influenced black-Jewish relations in the late 1960s.

Despite conflicting evidence, public opinion surveys conducted in the United States during the decades after World War II generally documented a substantial decline in antisemitic attitudes. Whereas 63 percent of the American public attributed "objectionable traits" to the Jews as a group in 1940, only 22 percent felt this way in 1962. A continuation of this trajectory was ascertained in surveys conducted by the Anti-Defamation League in the mid-1980s, including a 1986 study in which 82 percent of respondents characterized their attitude toward Jews as "favorable and warm." Meanwhile, four Roper polls in the 1980s demonstrated that only 7 or 8 percent of Americans believed Jews possessed "too much power." Further evidence of antisemitism's decline – apparently a reflection of a larger generational and societal pattern – was discerned in a 1992 Anti-Defamation League study that found a correlation between the intensity of antisemitism and access to formal education. Thus in comparison to one-fifth of survey respondents under the age of 39, two-fifths of those over 65 scored high on the survey's antisemitic index. This contrast was amplified by the finding that among those possessed of such attitudes 17 percent were college graduates compared with 33 percent who had only a high school education or less.

For most of the 1970s antisemitism in the more restricted sense was a matter of apprehension as much as of actuality; but by 1981 the feeling was general among those active in community relations that antisemitic incidents were on the increase. Fears that the oil embargo imposed by the Arab states after the Yom Kippur War would lead to anti-Jewish feeling did not materialize. Propaganda directed against Jews as such has continued all along, but it has been the work of a lunatic fringe. The lifting of barriers that at one time prevented the advancement of Jews was exemplified in the public sector by the appointment in 1973 of Henry Kissinger as secretary of state and in the private sector by the appointment in 1974 of Irving Shapiro as chairman of Du Pont.

On the other hand, American Jews viewed attacks on Zionism in the 1970s by the New Left and militant blacks as a new manifestation of antisemitism. Added to the turbulence and demoralization of the inner cities in this period, which frequently pitted Jews and blacks against each other on the local scene, anti-Zionism on college campuses exacerbated inter-communal tensions. The situation reached a climax in 1979 when Andrew Young was forced to resign his office as U.S. Ambassador to the United Nations because of contacts with the Palestine Liberation Organization and leaders of important black organizations made a pilgrimage to the Middle East, during the course of which they met with the leaders of the PLO.

One incident from this period may be singled out as an illustration of the tenacity of antisemitism. Speaking to the Duke University Law School in 1974, General George S. Brown, chairman of the Joint Chiefs of Staff, spoke about an alleged Jewish influence in the U.S. and said: "It's so strong you wouldn't believe it … We have the Israelis coming to us for equipment. We say we can't possibly get the Congress to support a program like that. They say 'Don't worry about Congress. We'll take care of the Congress.' Now this is somebody from another country, but they can do it. They own, you know, large banks in this country, the newspapers, you just look at where the Jewish money is in this country." The reaction was strong and President Gerald Ford personally reprimanded the general. Brown himself apologized, but there were continued calls for his removal. The Senate Armed Services Committee rejected a proposed enquiry into General Brown's fitness for office and he was retained.

Events during the 1980s seemed to indicate that antisemitism in America was operating at two levels. In 1981 a public debate arose over the sale of AWACS planes to Saudi Arabia, to which Israel strongly objected. A public opinion survey at the time reported a substantial increase in negative feeling towards the Jews on two issues: 23 percent of Americans (as opposed to 13 percent in 1964) thought that Jews had "too much power in the U.S."; 48 percent (as opposed to 39 percent in 1964) believed that "Jews are much more loyal to Israel than to America." Nonetheless, it also found a general decrease in discriminatory antisemitism in comparison to previous decades. This type of antisemitism was based on discriminatory practices in the workplace, in schools, especially colleges and universities, at country clubs and in upper-class communities. In July 1981, a survey conducted on behalf of the American Jewish Committee reported that antisemitism of this nature had in fact declined significantly over a 17-year period.

The success of Jews within American academia, at one time a domain known for restrictions against Jews and other ethnic minorities, was equally impressive. In the 1980s, Jews became increasingly visible as the presidents of Ivy League and other elite American universities and colleges. By the decade of the 1990s Richard Levin, Harold T. Shapiro, and Neil Rudenstine had become the presidents of the American academic pantheon, Yale, Princeton and Harvard, respectively. Interestingly, the latter had at one time in the 20th century maintained a strict quota on Jewish student enrollment. For many, all of this was indisputable proof that previously unbreachable social barriers in America had finally been torn down.

Such achievements notwithstanding, antisemitism in America had not disappeared. In 1987, after a five-year downward trend, the Anti-Defamation League's annual "Audit of Antisemitic Incidents" reported an increase in isolated incidents of antisemitic vandalism. The latter threat was realized in the 1984 machine-gun slaying of Denver radio talk show host Alan Berg by a white supremacist organization calling itself "The Order." However, most antisemitic acts in this category were expressed through vandalism and damage to property, including swastika daubings on synagogues, Jewish homes, storefronts, and Jewish cemetery headstones, the slashing of automobile tires, the breaking of windows, threatening telephone calls, arson, and bombings. Not until 1992 did the Anti-Defamation League report an 8 percent drop in antisemitic incidents, the first decline in six years. A report issued by the Anti-Defamation League stated that 20 percent of American adults are "hard-core" antisemites and an additional 39 percent "mildly" antisemitic, a group equaling approximately 100 million Americans.

From approximately the middle of the 1990s additional attention was paid by the media to groups whose statements and activities threatened the sense of well-being and security of American Jews, blacks, and other minorities. These included certain Christian fundamentalist groups, racist organizations such as neo-Nazis groups, skinhead gangs, the Aryan Nation, and The Order. Anti-Jewish statements or activities disguised as politically legitimate anti-Israel expressions originated in either politically far left circles, the Arab American community, or black Muslim groups.

Election campaigns focused the country's attention on two formerly relatively unknown personalities, Lyndon La Rouche and David Duke. La Rouche was a local left-wing politician in the 1970s and 1980s who changed his world outlook and ran three times as a marginal right-wing presidential candidate, a purveyor of Communist and antisemitic conspiracy theories. In 1989, La Rouche was sentenced to 15 years in federal prison for fraud and tax evasion. David Duke was a former grand wizard of the Knights of the Ku Klux Klan and the leader of the National Association for the Advancement of White People. In 1988, Duke ran as a presidential candidate on the slate of the neo-Nazi Populist Party. At the beginning of the following year he narrowly won a seat in the Louisiana state legislature. In December he announced his intention to run as a Republican for the U.S. Senate. He was strongly denounced by both the Republican Party and President George Bush. Although Duke lost the election, his relative popularity among Southern white voters and others raised considerable concern among Jews and non-Jews alike.

To the surprise of many observers, the well-publicized Wall St. "insider" scandals of 1986, among whose key figures were extremely wealthy Jewish businessmen, did not result in an appreciable rise in antisemitic or anti-Israel feelings among the American public. The principle figures included Ivan Boesky and Michael Milken, both of whom received prison sentences.

Nor was there any general rise in antisemitism attributable to the Jonathan Pollard affair. This dramatic real-life spy episode, which stunned the American Jewish community, and had direct, albeit short-term, implications for U.S.-Israel diplomatic relations, went almost unnoticed by most Americans. It served as the most dramatic and poignant example to date of the dual loyalty issue to which the organized American Jewish community is sensitive. Pollard, who served as a civilian intelligence analyst for the U.S. Navy, was arrested by the FBI in 1985 and charged with providing Israel with classified security information involving "scientific, technical and military" data, specifically intelligence information on Arab and Soviet weapons development. Pollard's spying and the punishment he received, a life sentence in a U.S. federal prison, aroused widespread and heated debate, but the controversy was mainly limited to Jewish circles.

Nor did the 1986 Irangate, or Iran-Contra, Affair result in any perceptible increase in antisemitism. The possibility arose from the role Israel played in this U.S. government scandal. In response to a secret request from the Reagan administration, Israel's government under then Prime Minister Shimon Peres supplied American-made arms to Iran. The profit from the sale was diverted through a Swiss bank account belonging to Contra rebels fighting the leftist Nicaraguan government. Israel officially denied handling the funds for this covert operation that was illegal according to U.S. federal law.

American Jews remained relatively sheltered throughout the 1980s from acts of international terror related to the conflicts in the Middle East, but there were two dramatic exceptions. The first was the hijacking in 1985 by members of the Palestine Liberation Front of the Italian pleasure ship *Achille Lauro* traveling between the ports of Alexandria and Ashdod. During the episode the terrorists, who were led by Palestine Liberation Organization faction head Mohammed Abu al-Abbas, killed a 69-year-old disabled American Jewish tourist, Leon Klinghoffer, who was shot and thrown overboard along with his wheelchair. The second exception was the assassination of Rabbi Meir Kahane on American soil. Kahane, founder of the American Jewish vigilante group the Jewish Defense League (JDL), immigrated in 1975 to Israel where he established the extreme right-wing anti-Arab political party Kach. He was elected to Israel's Knesset, serving from 1984 to 1988, and in 1990 was shot dead at close range inside a Manhattan hotel minutes after addressing an audience.

According to survey findings, antisemitism during the first years of the 1990s appeared to be declining. One Anti-Defamation League survey reported antisemitism among Americans having reached a low 20 percent in 1992. At the same time, a Roper survey conducted on behalf of the American Jewish Committee indicated that 47 percent of New York City residents felt Jews had "too much influence in New York City life and politics." Among blacks this figure rose to 63 percent. The poll also revealed that Jews were admired for intelligence and for not being prone to violence. In 1993 an Anti-Defamation League report noted that neo-Nazi "skinheads" posed an increasing threat in the United States. The report noted the seven states with the greatest number of skinheads to be New Jersey, Texas, Oregon, and Colorado, Florida, Michigan and Virginia, each with approximately 200–400 members. A 1994 Anti-Defamation League report titled "Armed and Dangerous: Militias Take Aim at the Federal Government" summarized the activities of right-wing paramilitary organizations in thirteen states. The report noted the informal but close ties, including overlap in membership, between many of these militias and local neo-Nazi groups or the Ku Klux Klan.

Polls conducted by the Anti-Defamation League in the mid-1990s showed that roughly 35 percent of blacks, in contrast to about 15 percent of whites, fell into the "most antisemitic" category, i.e., those who answered "Yes" to six out of 11 possible Jewish stereotypes. Similar polls over the years showed that blacks, in fact, share mixed positive and negative attitudes towards Jews.

Two separate incidents involving antisemitic comments by public figures received significant media coverage toward the end of 1992. First, at a press conference in Yugoslavia held prior to a major championship match, American chess master Bobby Fischer, a controversial recluse, blamed the Jews and Israel for many of the world's present problems, including persecution of Palestinians. Second, Marge Schott, owner of the Cincinnati Reds major league baseball team, caused a stir with her racist remarks including the word "nigger" and the phrase "money-grubbing Jews." Major league baseball suspended Schott for eight months from the day-to-day operation of the team and fined her $25,000.

Among the many acts of antisemitism reported in this period was the defacing of some 100 grave markers at a New Jersey Jewish cemetery, and the spray-painting of swastikas and hate slogans on the side of the home of Sandra Klebanoff, the Jewish mayor of West Hartford, Connecticut, and her husband Howard Klebanoff, a former state legislator.

According to the Anti-Defamation League, incidents of antisemitism also rose on college campuses in the 1990s. Antisemitic activities, often couched in anti-Israel terms, typically took place surrounding the appearance on campus of well-known controversial speakers, such as City College of New York professor Lionel Jeffries or Nation of Islam speaker Khalid Abdul Muhammad, or in conjunction with the celebration of Israel Independence Day or Palestinian student-sponsored events. *The Jewish Onslaught: Despatches from the Wellesley Battlefield*, was a virulently antisemitic tract published in 1994 by Anthony "Tony" C. Martin, a tenured professor of Africana studies at Wellesley College in Massachusetts. In his book, Martin accused the Jewish people of masterminding the black slave trade in the 17th century, blocking the economic advancement of African Americans, and controlling American banking, media, and politics. The book engendered a storm of protest from students, faculty, and a number of Jewish organizations.

In a similar vein, the Russian ultranationalist Vladimir Zhirinovsky visited the United States in 1994 and angered American Jews by blaming the Jewish people for the Bolshevik Revolution and the breakup of the former Soviet Union.

Holocaust denial, which became a virtual cottage industry in the late 20th century owing to the unprecedented reach of the World Wide Web, gave renewed energy to such antisemitic canards. A loose coalition of Arab American groups, for example, exploited the complexity of the Middle Eastern political arena and promoted overt and hostile antisemitic agendas on many internet sites. Nor were such polemics limited to the flickering screen. In 1998, the American Muslim Council, the American Muslim Alliance, and the Council on American-Islamic Relations held a rally at Brooklyn College in New York City where militant speakers described the Jews as "pigs and monkeys" and urged listeners to adopt the path of *jihad*. Together with the Muslim Public Affairs Council, these groups sponsored a rally the following year in Santa Clara, California, at which one speaker explicitly called for the murder of Jews. These groups and others were emboldened by the invective of militant Arab groups abroad. Such was the case in 2000, for example, when, following the third international conference on the Holocaust, held in Stockholm, Hamas spokesmen in Palestine issued a statement denouncing Zionist efforts "aimed at forging history by hiding the truth about the so-called Holocaust, which is an alleged and invented story with no basis…" This statement resonated and was picked up by anti-Israel activists in the United States, including opportunistic supporters of the anti-globalization movement on the far right and far left of the American political spectrum.

Against this backdrop, many American colleges, including the mainstream institutions Columbia University, Florida Atlantic University, the University of Michigan, the University of Pennsylvania, and the University of South Florida, became flashpoints for hosting and, in some instances, even serving as the home institutions of scholars who openly professed vigorous anti-Israel and antisemitic views. Such trends prompted Harvard University's president Lawrence Summers, a former secretary of the treasury under President Bill Clinton, to publicly decry calls for economic divestment from Israel as "antisemitic in result if not intent" and denounce the "profoundly anti-Israel views [which] are increasingly finding support in progressive intellectual communities" in American higher education. He was joined in this stance by Columbia president Lee Bollinger and Barnard president Judith Shapiro. Bollinger called the comparison of Israel to South Africa at the time of apartheid a "grotesque and offensive" analogy.

In the final analysis, a nationwide *Survey of American Attitudes Towards Jews in America* released by the Anti-Defamation League in 2005 showed a slight overall decline since 2002 in the number of Americans holding antisemitic views. Based on a national poll of 1,600 American adults, the survey noted the persistence of antisemitic attitudes, especially with regard to issues of "Jewish power," and determined the number of Americans with "hardcore antisemitic beliefs" fluctuated from 20 percent in 1992 to 12 percent in 1998 to 17 percent in 2002 and finally to 14 percent in 2005. These findings support the assessment of scholars Seymour Martin Lipset and Earl Raab who contend that although "the cultural reservoir of antisemitism [in the United States] is variable," a long view of the historical record indicates that American antisemitic attitudes "soared in the 1930s, then declined sharply in the 1950s, and have slowly fallen further since."

Antisemitism in the United States, while far from extinct, is usually no longer expressed openly. In fact, over time the American political system has acted as a brake on antisemitism and the civil position of Jews in the United States has never been fundamentally endangered. Nevertheless, latent anti-Jewish stereotypes are persistent and their history has demonstrated that prejudice is translated into open discrimination when social conflict and tensions are severe.

United States-Israel Relations

The interest of the American people in the return of the Jews to the Land of Israel long precedes the establishment of the Jewish state. It was influenced partly by faith in biblical prophecy and partly by revulsion at the persecution of the Jews in tsarist Russia and other lands. A high point was the Blackstone Memorial to President Benjamin Harrison, signed by more than 400 leading Americans in 1891 – six years before the First Zionist Congress. However, America did not become involved with Palestine until World War I, when the British government consulted and gained the approval of President Woodrow Wilson before issuing the Balfour Declaration of 1917. Wilson's endorsement encouraged American Zionist groups to engage in a large-scale lobbying effort. This campaign concluded successfully with the U.S. Congress' unanimous adoption of the 1922 Lodge-Fish Resolution, an official call for a Jewish national home, signed by President Warren G. Harding. Next, in 1925 a treaty on Palestine was signed by the U.S. and British governments. Subsequently, however, America remained aloof from Middle East problems. The region was regarded as a British and French sphere of influence, although many Americans were actively engaged in the search for oil and in educational and missionary activities.

In the 1930s, the United States was disinclined to intervene when the British Mandatory regime yielded to Arab pressure and restricted Jewish immigration and settlement. Like their British colleagues, American diplomats feared that support for Zionism might facilitate fascist and Nazi propaganda among the Arabs. Meanwhile, the disunity of American Jews on the Palestine question was exploited by Washington diplomats, who tried unsuccessfully to dissuade the American Jewish Conference of 1943 from demanding the establishment of a Jewish commonwealth in Palestine after World War II. (The conference nevertheless voted overwhelmingly in favor of it.) With that resolution as their platform, American Jews undertook a campaign to win the support of the American people, the U.S. Congress, the national political parties, and the media. Rabbis Stephen S. Wise and Abba Hillel Silver spearheaded Zionist efforts in the United States as mass meetings, protest rallies, letter writing and telegram campaigns, publications and the press were utilized countrywide in the struggle for Jewish statehood. The American Palestine Committee, chaired by Senator Robert F. Wagner, played a key role in winning substantial public support for a Jewish state in Palestine.

When World War II ended, there was a power vacuum in the Middle East. Britain and France, weakened in the great struggle, were in retreat and under pressure to surrender their mandates and bases in the Mediterranean area in Syria, Lebanon, North Africa, Iraq, Egypt, and Palestine. The Soviet Union, for its part, was pushing into Iran, and Communist guerrillas were attempting to subvert Greece and Turkey. Washington promulgated the Truman Doctrine to block the Soviet thrust. Disregarding the opinion of State Department advisers, President Harry S. Truman sent Earl G. Harrison into the Displaced Persons camps in Europe to investigate the plight of the Jewish survivors of the Holocaust. After he urgently recommended that they be allowed to go to Palestine, the British proposed that the United States join in a new Anglo-American Committee of Inquiry. This committee unanimously voted to recommend the immediate admission of 100,000 displaced Jews into Palestine and the deferment of a political settlement. President Truman enthusiastically supported the committee's recommendations and declared that the U.S. would be ready to finance the settlement of the refugees. He rejected the proposal to establish autonomous Arab and Jewish regions in Palestine under British rule. The British then turned to the United Nations to end the impasse.

The 11-nation United Nations Special Committee on Palestine (UNSCOP) recommended the termination of the British Mandate in Palestine and the partition of the country into a Jewish and an Arab state and a *corpus separatum* consisting of Jerusalem and its environs as an international enclave. The United States delegation supported the proposal in accordance with Truman's instructions who overruled the position of his State Department. Veteran American diplomats were unreconciled, however. Soon after the partition resolution was adopted, supporters of the Arab cause – missionaries, oil lobbyists, and Arabists – organized a powerful committee to demand its nullification, assisted by key State and Defense Department officials. Their campaign seemed to succeed, and the United Nations Security Council proved impotent to cope with Arab pressure and belligerence. The United States then proposed that the General Assembly be convened in special session to recommend the establishment of a United Nations trusteeship in Palestine. But this attempt to block the establishment of the Jewish state failed. Events in Palestine moved faster than diplomacy. The British withdrew their forces in anticipation of the termination of the mandate, and the Haganah forces in combat with Arab armies and irregulars secured well-organized Jewish political authority over a substantial part of the country.

On May 14, 1948, at 6:00 P.M. eastern standard time, Israel was established as a state and, 11 minutes later, Truman granted de facto recognition by the United States, much to the dismay of the State Department. By quickly recognizing Israel, Truman overcame internal opposition from the State Department, maintaining that Congress' passage of the Lodge-Fish Resolution in 1922 affirmed the principles of the Balfour Declaration. Two days later the Soviet Union granted it *de jure* recognition. In the ensuing United Nations debates, the Soviet Union and the United States both supported Israel, while the British delegation remained aligned with the Arab states.

After a grueling year of war in which Israel suffered more than 6,000 fatalities (roughly 1 percent of Israel's Jewish population at the time), the Jewish state finally initiated efforts toward building secure territorial borders. The task would first involve the absorption of two large-scale waves of immigration. The first group comprised Holocaust survivors from Europe as well as returnees from British detention camps, primarily in Cyprus. The second wave comprised refugees from Arab countries in the Middle East and North Africa, who had been persecuted in revenge for the creation of the Jewish state. In all, Israel's Jewish population doubled in less than three years with the arrival of some 700,000 new immigrants.

In this period, the United States also provided Israel with significant economic support. In 1949 the U.S. Export-Import Bank extended a $100,000,000 loan to help Israel develop her agricultural economy. Two years later, Congress urged the administration to provide Israel with economic aid and amended the administration's Mutual Security Act to include a grant of $65,000,000. This was the first of many economic grants and loans, most of it in loans or the sale of surplus commodities. All loans were repaid on time. During most of the 1950s, however, the United States declined to make arms available to Israel.

U.S. policy toward Israel and the Arab-Israel conflict was deeply affected by other major conflicts in the area: the traditional, centuries-old conflict between East and West, with the Soviet Union and the United States emerging as the contemporary principals; enmity in the Arab world between the conservative, western-oriented states some of them oil-rich and the nominally socialist-oriented, which gradually turned to the Soviet Union. As a consequence, the United States, though explicitly committed to support Israel's existence and security, tended to be restrained in its day-to-day attitude. In part, this was due to the influence of American diplomats, missionaries, and businessmen who had cultural, religious, and economic interests in the Arab world. Above all, the United States was sensitive to the dynamic Soviet policy in the area.

After 1948, and particularly from 1955, the Soviets steadily increased their influence throughout the area, putting the West very much on the defensive. By adopting a policy of absolute hostility to Israel as a major card in winning Arab friendship, the Soviet Union left Israel no option but to become increasingly dependent on the West and particularly on the U.S. In this way it also endeavored to establish Israel's reputation as a "satellite" of the U.S., whereas Israel and the U.S. understood the relationship as one of overlapping interest in limiting hostile Soviet influence in the area. American diplomacy feared the region would become polarized, with all Arab states eventually oriented toward Moscow and the United States isolated as a kind of protecting power of Israel. Moreover, American diplomats were concerned that oil concessions might be nationalized by radical Arab governments, adversely affecting the strategically important flow of oil to Europe, as well as oil dividends and bank deposits to the West. The gradual growth of Soviet power in the area during the 1950s and 1960s posed grave problems, as the U.S.S.R. sought substantial control of the Mediterranean communication lines and sources of intelligence, thus furthering its basic aims of disorganizing NATO and weakening U.S. voting strength in the United Nations.

The American reaction to the Soviet expansionist trend in the Middle East was inconsistent, sometimes swinging from one extreme to the other. As early as 1945 the United States insisted that the Soviets quit Iran. Two years later, the Truman Doctrine helped to bolster Greece and Turkey. In 1950 the United States joined Great Britain and France in a Tripartite Declaration that included a vague commitment to maintain a balance of armaments between Israel and her Arab neighbors and prevent the change of the armistice lines by violent means. Shortly afterward the United States and Great Britain attempted to rally the Arab states in defense arrangements to "contain" the Soviet Union, which would have permitted the West to retain the bases in Egypt and in Iraq that were being politically vacated by the British. This eventually led to the Baghdad Pact, which the United States cemented with arms shipments to Iraq. Israel, as well as Nasser's Egypt, opposed the pact, and Nasser even accepted the Soviet offer of arms and large-scale economic aid, thus upsetting the balance of power with Israel precariously maintained by the Tripartite Declaration. Soviet expansion into the Middle East now gained a firm foothold, while the Baghdad Pact itself exploded in the antimonarchist coup in Iraq in 1958, which left Turkey, Iran, and Pakistan in it, in addition to British and American backing.

The United States then swerved to another extreme. It sought to win Nasser's Egypt and the other radical Arab states by an attempt to persuade them to adopt a pro-Western attitude. As a result of East-West competition, they were able, in accordance with Nasser's positive neutralism, to secure aid from both the United States and the Soviet Union, to the increasing military disadvantage of Israel. Washington was still maneuvering to freeze the Soviets out of the Middle East long after they had penetrated the area but was slow and indecisive in its actions. Preoccupation with the cold war competition was reflected in the U.S. attitude to many aspects of the Arab-Israel conflict. On such issues as military aid, boundaries, utilization of water resources, the resettlement of refugees, navigation through international waterways, the Arab boycott, terrorism, and retaliation, U.S. diplomacy was often vacillating and undecided so as not to offend Arab sensitivities.

On the question of Jerusalem there were also considerable divergences of opinion between the United States and Israel. While in 1950, the United States supported the Swedish proposal at the United Nations for a functional internationalization of the holy places, thereby abrogating the former decision for territorial internationalization as a *corpus separatum*, after the defeat of the proposal the United States steadfastly refused to recognize Jerusalem as Israel's capital and even used its influence on other states to desist from establishing or transferring their diplomatic missions to Jerusalem. This attitude was suspended by many nations only in the early 1960s, after strong Israeli protests.

Meanwhile, the United States strongly supported Israel on the question of international navigation. Since the 1949 Armistice Agreement, Egypt insisted that it was in a state of war with Israel and closed the Suez Canal to Israel and Israel-bound shipping. In 1951 the United Nations Security Council upheld Israel's complaint and ordered Egypt to keep the canal open, but Egypt ignored the decision and later in 1954, when Israel renewed its complaint to the Security Council, the Soviet Union, already closely linked to Egypt, used its veto to block enforcement of the council's order. The council was thenceforward powerless to force an end to Arab belligerence against Israel.

In 1953 the American administration and Israel clashed over Israel's irrigation program, and President Dwight D. Eisenhower dispatched Eric Johnston as special envoy to the Middle East to devise a plan for the sharing of the water resources in the Jordan Valley. Agreement was reached with U.S. mediation between Israel and Arab experts on the technical level, but the Arab states refused to approve the plan for political reasons, and water development had to proceed unilaterally. Israel completed its national water carrier in 1964, with the discrete but efficient backing of the United States.

There was a sharp controversy between Israel and the United States over the U.S. proposal to send arms to Iraq in 1954 in the framework of the Baghdad Pact. Later, when the Soviet Union began to arm Egypt, Israel appealed to Washington for arms, but Secretary of State John Foster Dulles referred

Israel to the French. Growing Soviet support emboldened the Egyptians, who barred Israel from the Straits of Tiran as well as from the Suez Canal. The crisis deepened as Arab *fedayeen*, based mainly in the Egyptian-held Gaza Strip, increasingly attacked Israeli settlements and population centers. Late in 1956, Jordan and Egypt entered into a military alliance against Israel, which now became virtually surrounded by aggressive enemies. This was one of the main causes of the Sinai Campaign in which Israel won a swift victory. The United States and the Soviet Union then joined diplomatic forces to press Israel to withdraw from the occupied areas. During this period, relations between Israel and the U.S. were greatly strained and many American Jewish bodies and individuals made representations in Washington in support of Israel's position. A United Nations Emergency Force (UNEF) was stationed in the Gaza Strip and at Sharm el-Sheikh to prevent the recurrence of terrorist attacks, and the United States and most other maritime powers gave Israel assurances about the maintenance of free passage through the Straits of Tiran.

In 1957 Israel acceded to the Eisenhower Doctrine, aimed at guaranteeing the independence of states and governments in the Middle East against Communist oppression or subversion. The doctrine was effectively implemented during the Lebanon crisis of 1958, but later disintegrated. In 1958, the American administration launched a new initiative to win the friendship of Egypt through economic aid, and this policy continued when President John F. Kennedy took office in 1961. During this period, the United States tried to work out an elaborate proposal for the solution of the Arab refugee problem, which would have obliged Israel to absorb a substantial number of refugees. This attempt came to naught due to the Arabs' refusal to enter into any substantial negotiations. Another diplomatic issue that divided Israel and the Kennedy administration was U.S. opposition to Israel's insistence that a solution to the Arab-Israel conflict could be achieved only by direct Arab-Israel peace talks. When the Soviet Union provided Egypt with long-range bombers, MIG planes, and other modern arms, Israel renewed its appeal for U.S. arms. In 1962 Kennedy lifted the American arms embargo and approved the sale of U.S. Hawk anti-aircraft missiles to Israel. This was the first important arms deal between the U.S. and Israel, which incidentally, was the first country outside NATO to receive this weapon. In the words of historian Warren Bass, Kennedy's was thus the "pivotal presidency" – it laid the groundwork for a new close U.S.-Israeli relationship in the latter decades of the 20th century. In 1965 President Lyndon B. Johnson and his administration deepened the U.S.-Israel relationship by assisting Israel in maintaining its military strength through the sale of American warplanes to Israel for the first time.

A new crisis erupted in the Middle East in 1966–67 when the Soviet Union encouraged Syria and Egypt to take a more belligerent attitude toward Israel and the West. Anti-Israel terrorism mounted and the United Nations was unable to curb or even censure attacks against Israel, which came largely from Syria by the newly established al-Fatah organization and Syrian artillery. In addition, Soviet and Arab confidence was bolstered by the belief that the United States would not intervene in an explosive Middle East conflict because of heavy commitments in Southeast Asia and growing unrest and isolationist sentiment at home. This led in May 1967 to the dispatch of heavy Egyptian forces into Gaza and the Sinai Peninsula, the blockade of the Straits of Tiran, and the sudden withdrawal of the United Nations forces from the area.

At the end of the Six-Day War (June 1967), the United States did not repeat its 1956–57 attitude. It was largely instrumental in blocking in the United Nations various Soviet-Arab initiatives to brand Israel as an aggressor and demand the unconditional withdrawal of its forces from the occupied territories (i.e., the West Bank, Gaza Strip, Golan Heights, and Sinai peninsula). The United States insisted that Israel should not be required to withdraw from occupied territories until there was agreement between the parties on "recognized and secure boundaries," according to the Security Council resolution of Nov. 22, 1967. Nonetheless, there were substantial differences between the United States and Israel. In 1969 President Richard M. Nixon's administration agreed to Four Power talks to draw up guidelines for a settlement, and Secretary of State William Rogers publicly outlined a plan that entailed Israel's withdrawal to the lines of June 4, 1967, with little emendation, in exchange for a peace agreement with Egypt and Jordan. Israel feared that the United States was again joining with the Soviet Union in an attempt to impose a settlement. A difference also arose because of protracted delays on responding to Israel's urgent request for arms.

Until 1970 any military equipment Israel obtained from the United States represented hard currency dollar purchases. In the Military Assistance Act of 1970, the U.S. government provided credits up to $500 million for military aid to Israel. This represented a major change in U.S.-Israel relations. Over the years, Israel obtained a variety of loans from the U.S. government-owned Export-Import Bank. This bank's principal function was to provide financing for U.S. exports. However, assistance from the private sector, including public institutions, was of greater importance to Israel's growth than U.S. government programs. Transfers through the United Jewish Appeal and similar public institutions and sales of Israel Bonds totaled over $2 billion from 1948. Philanthropic transfers were used predominantly for social welfare and development purposes, while the proceeds of bond sales, which were initiated in 1951, were used for economic development as well as current account purchases. In addition, loans to Israeli companies and the government by private American banking institutions were substantial. Even more important was the development of U.S.-Israel trade. From 1949 to 1959, imports from the United States averaged $100 million per year. During the next ten years, this amount doubled. Imports from the United States in 1969 were $310 million, 24 percent of Israel's total imports. Exports from Israel to the United States averaged $13 million from 1949 to 1959 and $60 million during the next ten years. In 1969, exports to the U.S. were $136 million, 19 percent of Israel's total exports. There was thus an annual balance of payments of approximately $175 million in favor of the United States.

In 1970 it became clear that the Soviet Union and Egypt were determined to increase their military power in the area and weaken Israel by a "war of attrition" in the canal zone in contravention of the cease-fire order of the Security Council of June 1967. Israel's counteraction against Egyptian military targets proved highly effective, and the United States continued to slow down delivery of arms to Israel in the hope that the Soviet Union would join in a program of arms limitations in the conflict area. It made repeated efforts to bring about a cease-fire and peace negotiations, and in August 1970, American initiative brought about a new cease-fire agreement between Egypt and Israel, which entailed a complete "standstill" of military installations on both sides of the canal as well as the renewal of indirect Israel-Arab peace talks through United Nations representative Gunnar Jarring. In an effort to make Egypt's skies impenetrable and shift the balance of power, the Soviet Union and Egypt violated the "standstill agreement," introducing new missiles in the canal area. This was not only a threat to Israel but a challenge to U.S. prestige and power. Washington then moved to sell weapons to Israel, including modern and sophisticated equipment, and Congress voted large-scale credits to enable Israel to buy them. This decision was a major development in U.S.-Israel relations, as it constituted the decisive element in strengthening Israel's capacity to withstand Soviet-Arab pressure. On the other hand, the United States also induced Israel to agree to a resumption of the Jarring talks in January 1971. It soon emerged, however, that there was still a wide divergence between Israel and U.S. views on the contents and aims of the talks. Israel emphasized the principle of new, secure, defensible, agreed, and recognized borders, substantially different from the pre-June 4, 1967 lines, while the U.S. attitude still seemed to be guided by the Rogers plan of 1969.

In determining its policy throughout the 1960s and 1970s, the U.S. sought to balance its efforts to retain a maximum role within Arab states and the desirability of maintaining a militarily and economically strong Israel as a counter to Soviet penetration into the Arab neighboring countries. Israel's military successes, although performed by Israel for the sake of its own security, had the effect of checking the extension of Soviet influence. Certain Washington circles consequently favored (especially after the Six-Day War) the maintenance of a strong Israel in order to maintain the balance of power that had been achieved in the area, uneasy as it was.

However, these Washington circles were countered by elements in the State Department that emphasized maintaining the friendship of pro-Western Arab regimes and thus winning a measure of influence in those states where the Soviet Union was largely dominant. The latter argued that a too blatantly pro-Israel policy could endanger other U.S. footholds in the Middle East, especially Saudi Arabia, Jordan, and Lebanon, and that by appearing as Israel's backer, the U.S. could drive these countries into the Soviet orbit. Strongly advocated by certain State Department officials, this line of thinking was massively backed by the powerful oil lobby which represented a major group of U.S. capital that had heavily invested in the Arab lands. The oil lobby was active not only in Washington but in financing pro-Arab activities and pressure groups throughout the U.S.

A further factor that U.S. policy makers had to take into consideration was the Jewish reaction in the U.S. Although the strategic issues frequently might have led to differences of opinion in the American administration, resulting from differing assessments of the global consequences of policies, the ultimate decisions of the politicians had also to take into consideration the demands of the oil companies, on the one hand, and the Jewish vote on the other. The last factor became of particular significance as major election periods approached.

On March 26, 1979, the Camp David accords were formalized in the Egypt-Israel peace treaty signed by Prime Minister Menahem Begin and President Anwar Sadat and witnessed by President Jimmy Carter. The peace treaty marked a turning point in the history of Arab-Israel relations. It held out the hope for peaceful coexistence between Israel and other Arab countries as well as a resolution of the Palestinian Arab problem. "The critical importance of the agreement with Egypt," Prime Minister Begin declared, "lies in the fact that this time we undertook to sign a peace treaty..."

> No more interim agreements... It means complete normalization of relations [between Israel and Egypt]... The basis for the framework agreement concerning Judea, Samaria and Gaza is our autonomy plan... The military government and its civilian administration will be withdrawn.

The peace treaty with Egypt did indeed lead to a complete Israeli withdrawal from Sinai in 1982. In the meantime, however, the Likud-led government annexed the Golan Heights in 1981. The Golan legislation demonstrated the Begin government's commitment to the concept of territorial maximalism and defused right-wing and religious criticism that crystallized around the Gush Emunim settlers and the "Stop the Withdrawal" movement.

In 1981 controversy erupted when the sale of five AWACS aircraft to Saudi Arabia was announced. As in the recent past, the arms sale was opposed by the State of Israel and American Jewish organizations lobbied intensively against it. Although the U.S. House of Representatives voted overwhelmingly against the sale, the Senate voted to permit it. On this occasion emolients were less in evidence. Apparently alluding to the efforts by Israel and its supporters, President Ronald Reagan observed: "It is not the business of other nations to make American foreign policy." An additional critical statement by ex-President Richard M. Nixon brought an angry response from leaders of the American Jewish community.

The public relations damage caused by the AWACS sale receded in 1981 when Israel and the United States entered into a strategic pact directed against Russian intervention in the Middle East. However, the sudden adoption by the Knesset in December 1981 of a bill extending Israeli law to the Golan Heights drew a sharp rebuke from Washington and aroused considerable misgiving in American Jewish circles. In response to the new Golan Heights law, the American government suspended the strategic pact. In due course, Begin replied by addressing to the U.S. ambassador to Israel a series of complaints, including the charge that the Reagan administration's effort to ratify the AWACS sale was "accompanied by an ugly antisemitic campaign."

The political horizon was also clouded in this period by the Palestine Liberation Organization, which over the years established itself as a virtual state-within-a-state in southern Lebanon and amassed a considerable arsenal. It now possessed the capability of shelling much of the Upper Galilee. Syria, too, escalated tensions by installing sophisticated long-range missiles in the Beqaa Valley that threatened Israeli aircraft and violated the longstanding cease-fire agreements reached after the Yom Kippur War.

In June 1982, on the heels of an attack by Palestinian Arab extremists against Shlomo Argov, Israel's ambassador to Great Britain, Israel launched major air strikes against PLO bases in southern Lebanon and in Beirut. The PLO responded by shelling Israeli settlements in the Galilee. These events prompted the Israeli invasion of Lebanon known as "Operation Peace for Galilee." The operation, intended to be a limited initiative with precise military objectives, brought a rapid Israeli victory. It successfully pushed PLO artillery outside the range of settlements and towns in northern Israel. At the same time, however, the Israel Defense Forces failed to destroy or capture most of the PLO forces in southern Lebanon. Moreover, the Israeli public was shocked by the Sabra and Shatilla massacres of September 1982.

Following the Lebanon War, Reagan announced his administration's intention to advance the peace process within the framework of the Camp David accords. Reagan acknowledged the rights of the Palestinian Arab people but emphasized that "America's commitment to the security of Israel is ironclad." American diplomatic initiatives notwithstanding, tensions between Israel and the Palestinian Arabs continued to escalate. In 1983 the United States and Israel signed a Memorandum of Understanding for strategic cooperation, and in 1988 Israel became a major non-NATO ally of the United States. The two countries next became involved in joint research and development efforts on high technology projects such as the Arrow and anti-ballistic missile system. A generous program of American economic and financial aid eased Israel's defense burden and allowed Israel to invest in its economic and social infrastructure and focus on the absorption of Jewish refugees. Moreover, the United States was an instrumental player in the struggle to ensure the emigration of 750,000 Jews from the former Soviet Union, Ethiopia, and other countries to Israel. Through loan guarantees granted in 1992, Israel was able to finance the mammoth task of absorbing, since 1990, approximately one-fifth of its total population. Additional cooperation between Israel and the United States took the form of a Free Trade Agreement (1985) and the establishment of the U.S.-Israel Science and Technology Commission (1993).

October 1991 marked a significant milestone on the road to Mideast peace when following the Persian Gulf War, the United States cosponsored, with the Soviet Union, the Arab-Israeli Peace Conference in Madrid. As a result of the negotiations that followed, Israel signed a peace treaty with Jordan (1994) as well as a Declaration of Principles (1993) and an Interim Agreement (1995) with the Palestinians. In these years, Israel also expanded its relations with many other Arab countries. Like Egyptian President Anwar Sadat before him, Israeli Prime Minister Yitzhak Rabin made the ultimate sacrifice for Mideast reconciliation. On November 4, 1995, Yigal Amir, a right-wing zealot assassinated Rabin at the end of a peace rally in Tel Aviv. Following Rabin's murder the peace process continued fitfully under his successor Shimon Peres and then stalled under the Likud government of Benjamin Netanyahu, despite the potential breakthrough represented by the Wye River Memorandum (1998). Diplomatic momentum was renewed in 1999 when Ehud Barak handily won Israel's general election and brought a new Labor-led government to power. Vowing to continue Rabin's approach to securing Israel's borders and a negotiated settlement for Palestinian self-government, Barak embarked on an ambitious plan to "conclude all Middle East peace negotiations within 15 months." At this juncture, President Bill Clinton invested considerable energy and political capital in an effort reinvigorate the peace process, pressing for both a Syria-Israel peace treaty and a final resolution to the Israel-Palestinian negotiations. Despite high hopes and great expectations, the process was ultimately stymied by a recalcitrant Assad, a reluctant Arafat, a brash Barak, and a lame-duck Clinton administration. Before leaving office, Clinton brought the Israeli and Palestinian negotiators together in 2000 and outlined the parameters of possible agreement that addressed the issues of Israeli and Palestinian territorial sovereignty and security, the status of Jerusalem, the question of the Palestinian refugees, and an end of claims to be implemented through the United Nations. He concluded his presentation with the following statement:

> I believe this is the outline of a fair and lasting agreement. It gives the Palestinian people the ability to determine their future on their own land, a sovereign and viable state recognized by the international community, al-Quds as its capital, sovereignty over the Haram, and new lives for the refugees.
>
> It gives the people of Israel a genuine end to the conflict, real security, the preservation of sacred religious ties, the incorporation of 80 percent of the settlers into Israel, and the largest Jewish Jerusalem in history, recognized by all as your capital.
>
> This is the best I can do. I would ask you to brief your leaders and let me know if they are prepared to come for discussions based on these ideas. I want to be very clear on one thing. These are my ideas. If they are not accepted they are not just off the table. They go with me when I leave office.

Clinton's proposal came to naught, but it did anticipate the subsequent approach adopted by the Israeli government under Likud leader and veteran military strategist Ariel Sharon. Sharon, who was elected in 2001 following the Labor party's humiliating defeat after only a brief period in power, implemented a strategy that was in practice an extension of the hard-headed and pragmatic policy first introduced by Yitzhak Rabin a decade earlier. Meanwhile, the election of George W. Bush as president – who defeated Democratic standard bearer Al Gore and his running mate Senator Joseph Lieberman of Connecticut (the first Jewish candidate for vice president of a major political party) – brought about a dramatic shift in American policy vis-à-vis the Middle East peace process. In stark contrast to Clinton, whose close personal engagement with Israeli and Arab leaders was well known, the Bush administration remained relatively remote from week-to-week and month-to-month affairs of Israeli and Palestinian diplomatic activity. Moreover, with the tacit support of Bush himself, Sharon moved swiftly to isolate Yasser Arafat, unilaterally redeploy Israeli troops from areas of the occupied territories, build a separation fence around the Gaza Strip and the West Bank, and remove Jewish settlers from the former area, if necessary, by force. Notwithstanding some minor criticisms, particularly with respect to the impact of the separation barrier on the Palestinian economy, the Bush administration staunchly supported the Sharon government. The U.S. government signaled its continued support of Sharon's policies even after a sudden stroke in 2006 resulted in the latter's abrupt departure from the political arena. Ehud Olmert, Sharon's heir apparent and immediate successor, now appeared determined to stay the course. Thus the torch was passed from the generation of Rabin and Sharon – warriors-turned-peace makers who succeeded the founding generation of Zionist leaders – to a younger generation, Olmert and others who had come of age in the era of the Six-Day War of 1967 and the Yom Kippur War of 1973.

As the historical record demonstrates, American foreign policy in the Middle East over the decades did not steer a consistent course because of the conflicting and even contradictory interests involved. Developments must be viewed against the background of both global strategy and internal pressures. In large measure, certainly until the late 1980s, American decisions were made within the framework of the ongoing rivalry between the U.S. and the U.S.S.R. (with the rise of Communist China a constant background consideration). The Middle East as a whole served as a flashpoint for the American and Soviet governments, each of which exerted considerable efforts to control the region while avoiding a direct confrontation. It continues to be a key area culturally and geographically – as one of the world's critical geo-political arenas, a gateway to Africa, and because of the immense oil deposits possessed by the Arab world.

Apart from all this, United States policy makers had to take into consideration a widespread sympathy for Israel among the general American public – despite the extensive efforts made by hostile elements to blacken this image – based among other things on a Christian appreciation for the Jews' attachment to the Holy Land, a sense of horror at Jewish suffering in the 20th century, Israel's support of American efforts to check Soviet expansionism during the Cold War, and an affinity for the democratic nature of the State of Israel. In the wake of the 9/11 attacks and the Iraq War, the United States and Israel have stepped up joint efforts to combat international terrorism. Although the special relationship between the two countries has deepened over time and Israel is today one of the United States' closest allies, support for the Jewish state is not unconditional. Indeed, the United States has exerted considerable pressure on Israel at the turn of the 20th and 21st centuries in the quest for a comprehensive solution to the Israel-Arab conflict. For its part, since the breakthrough of the Oslo peace talks, Israel has gradually implemented a phased withdrawal from the territories it captured in the Six-Day War of 1967, with the exception of Jerusalem, and cautiously supported plans for the creation of an independent Palestinian state in the West Bank and Gaza Strip. It is against the background of this canvas that the ongoing development of U.S.-Israel relations must be assessed. The factors and considerations outlined here are also critical to the historic decisions that will determine the future of the Jewish state.

BIBLIOGRAPHY: There is a voluminous body of scholarly literature on the history of the Jews of the United States. What follows here is a selected bibliography of significant and representative works. For references on various cities, organizations, and individuals, see their respective articles in the *Encyclopaedia Judaica*. A number of scholarly journals publish material specifically related to the history of American Jews. See *American Jewish Archives*; *American Jewish History* (formerly *Publications of the American Jewish Historical Society* and *American Jewish Historical Quarterly*); *American Jewish Year Book*; *Chicago Jewish History*; *Commentary*; *Jewish History*; *Jewish Quarterly Review*; *Jewish Socials Studies*; *Judaism*; *Journal of Israeli History; Modern Judaism*; *Proceedings of the American Academy of Jewish Research*; *Studies in Contemporary Jewry*; *Western States Jewish History*; *YIVO Annual*. Some general history journals that publish articles related to American Jewish history are *American Historical Review, Journal of American Ethnic History, Journal of American History, Journal of Modern History; Religion and American Culture*. DOCUMENTARY AND REFERENCE MATERIALS: J. Blau and S. Baron, *The Jews of the United States: A Documentary History, 1790–1840* (1963); J. Cohen and D. Soyer (eds.), *My Future is in America: Autobiographies of East European Jewish Immigrants* (2005); D. Elazar, J. Sarna, and R. Monson, *A Double Bond: The Constitutional Documents of American Jewry* (1992); J. Fischel and S. Pinsker, *Jewish-American History and Culture: An Encyclopedia* (1992); A. Goren (ed.), *Dissenter in Zion: From the Writings of Judah L. Magnes* (1982); S. Greenberg (ed.), *The Ordination of Women as Rabbis: Studies and Responsa* (1988); H. Hapgood, *The Spirit of the Ghetto* (1967); B. Harshav and B. Harshav (eds.), *American Yiddish Poetry* (1986); L. Hershkowitz, *Wills of Early New York Jews, 1704–1799* (1967); L. Hershkowitz and I. Meyers (eds.), *The Lee Max Friedman Collection of American Jewish Colonial Correspondence: Letters of the Franks Family, 1733–1748* (1968); A. Hertzberg, *A Jew in America: My Life and a People's Struggle for Identity* (2002); P. Hyman and D. Moore (eds.), *Jewish Women in America: An Historical Encyclopedia* (1997); W. Jacobs (ed.), *Amer-*

ican Reform Responsa (1983); *Jewish Communal Register of New York City, 1917–1918* (1918); E. Kaplan and S. Dresner (eds.), *Abraham Joshua Heschel: Prophetic Witness* (1998); M. Kaplan, *Judaism as a Civilization* (1994); A. Kohanski (ed.), *The American Jewish Conference: Its Organization and Proceedings of the First Session* (1944); R. Kohut, *My Portion: An Autobiography* (1925); E. Lazarus, *An Epistle to the Hebrews* (1987); I. Leeser, *Discourses on the Jewish Religion* (1867); L. Levi, *Memorial Volume* (1905); J. Liebman, *Peace of Mind* (1946); S. Litman, *Ray Frank Litman: A Memoir* (1957); J. Marcus (ed.), *The American Jewish Woman: A Documentary History* (1981); idem (ed.), *American Jewry – Documents-Eighteenth Century* (1959); idem, *The Colonial American Jew, 1492–1776* (1970); idem, *The Handsome Young Priest in the Black Gown: The Personal World of Gershom Seixas* (1970); idem (ed.), *The Jew in the American World: A Sourcebook* (1996); idem (ed.), *Memoirs of American Jews, 1775–1865* (1955); idem (ed.), *This I Believe: Documents of American Jewish Life* (1990); P. Mendes-Flohr and J. Reinharz (eds.), *The Jew in the Modern World: A Documentary History* (1995); I. Metzker (ed.), *A Bintel Brief: Sixty Years of Letters From the Lower East Side to the Jewish Daily Forward* (1971); R. Moses, *Last Order of the Lost Cause: The Civil War Memoirs of a Jewish Family from the "Old South"* (1995); D. Philipson (ed.), *Letters of Rebecca Gratz* (1929); D. Philipson and L. Grossman (eds.), *Selected Writings of Isaac M. Wise* (1900); *Prayer Book Abridged for Jews in the Armed Forces of the United States* (1945); *Proceedings of the National Federation of Temple Sisterhoods* (1941); M. Raider and M. Raider-Roth (eds.), *The Plough Woman: Records of the Pioneer Women of Palestine. A Critical Edition* (2002); *Reports of the U.S. Immigration Commission, 1910* (reprint 1970); C. Reznikoff (ed.), *Louis Marshall, Champion of Liberty: Selected Papers and Addresses*, 2 vols. (1957); H. Ribalow, *Autobiographies of American Jews* (1968); M. Rischin (ed.), *Grandma Never Lived in America* (1985); J. Rikoon (ed.), *Rachel Calof's Story: Jewish Homesteader on the Northern Plains* (1995); D. Ross, *The Missing Peace: The Inside Story of the Fight for Middle East Peace* (2004); C. Rubenstein, *A History of the Har Sinai Congregation of the City of Baltimore* (1918); J. Sarna (ed.), *People Walk on Their Heads: Moses Weinberger's Jews and Judaism in New York* (1982); M. Schappes (ed.), *A Documentary History of the Jews of the United States, 1654–1875* (1971); S. Schechter, *Seminary Addresses and Other Papers* (1915); M. Scult (ed.), *Communings of the Spirit: The Journals of Mordecai M. Kaplan* (2001); R. Siegel et al. (eds.), *The Jewish Catalog* (1973); M. Spiegel, *A Jewish Colonel in the Civil War: Marcus M. Spiegel of the Ohio Volunteers* (1995); J. Staub and R. Alpert, *Exploring Judaism: A Reconstructionist Approach* (1995); M. Staub, *The Jewish 1960s: An American Sourcebook* (2004); M. Stern, *The Rise and Progress of Reform Judaism* (1895); E. Umansky and D. Ashton (ed.), *Four Centuries of Jewish Women's Spirituality: A Sourcebook* (1992); I. Wise, *Reminiscences* (1973); S. Wise, *As I See It* (1944). SECONDARY WORKS: S. Ahlstrom, *A Religious History of the American People* (1972); M. Alexander, *Jazz Age Jews* (2001); S. Almog et al. (eds.), *Zionism and Religion* (1998); J. Antler, *The Journey Home: Jewish Women and the American Century* (1997); A. Antonovsky and E. Tcherikower (eds.), *The Early Jewish Labor Movement in the United States* (1961); G. Arad, *America, Its Jews, and the Rise of Nazism* (2000); E. Ashkenazi, *Business of Jews in Louisiana, 1840–1875* (1998); D. Ashton, *Unsubdued Spirits: Rebecca Gratz and Women's Judaism in America* (1997); A. Aufuses and B. Niss, *The House of Noble Deeds: The Mount Sinai Hospital, 1852–2000* (2002); K. Avruch, *American Immigrants in Israel: Social Identities and Change* (1981); N. Baldwin, *Henry Ford and the Jews: The Mass Production of Hate* (2001); L. Barash (ed.), *Rabbis in Uniform: The Story of the American Jewish Military Chaplain* (1962); A. Barkai, *Branching Out: German Jewish Immigration to the United States, 1820–1914* (1994); S. Baron, *Steeled by Adversity: Essays and Addresses on American Jewish Life* (1971); W. Bass, *Support Any Friend: Kennedy's Middle East and the Making of the U.S.-Israel Alliance* (2003); Y. Bauer, *My Brother's Keeper: A History of the American Jewish Joint Distribution Committee, 1929–1939* (1974); M. Bauman and B. Kalin (eds.), *The Quiet Voices: Southern Rabbis and Black Civil Rights, 1880s to 1990s* (1997); M. Bazyler and R. Alford (eds.), *Holocaust Restitution: Perspectives on the Litigation and Its Aftermath* (2005); J. Bendersky, *The "Jewish Threat": Antisemitic Policies of the U.S. Army* (2000); M. Berman, *Richmond's Jewry, 1769–1976* (1979); P. Bernardini and N. Fiering (eds.), *The Jews and the Expansion of Europe to the West, 1450–1800* (2001); E. Bingham, *Mordecai: An Early American Family* (2003); S. Birmingham, *Our Crowd: The Great Jewish Families of New York* (1967); idem, *The Rest of Us: The Rise of America's East European Jews* (1984); A. Bloom, *Prodigal Sons: The New York Intellectuals and Their World* (1986); J. Blumberg, *One Voice: Rabbi Jacob M. Rothschild and the Troubled South* (1985); P. Bonomi, *Under the Cope of Heaven: Religion, Society and Politics in Colonial New York* (1986); R. Breitman and A. Kraut, *American Refugee Policy and European Jewry, 1933–1945* (1987); R. Brilliant, *Facing the New World: Jewish Portraits in Colonial and Federal America* (1997); M. Brown, *The Israeli-American Connection: Its Roots in the Yishuv, 1914–1945* (1996); K. Caplan, *Orthodoxy in the New World: Immigrant Rabbis and Preaching in America, 1881–1924* (Heb., 2002); J. Chametzky, J. Felsteiner, H. Flanzbaum, and K. Hellerstein (eds.), *Jewish American Literature: A Norton Anthology* (2001); S. Chyet, *Lopez of Newport* (1980); M. Cohen and A. Peck (eds.), *Sephardim in the Americas: Studies in Culture and History* (1993); N.W. Cohen, *The Americanization of Zionism, 1897–1948* (2003); idem, *Encounter With Emancipation: The German Jews in the United States, 1830–1914* (1984); idem, *Jews in Christian America: The Pursuit of Religious Equality* (1992); idem, *Not Free to Desist: The American Jewish Committee, 1906–1966* (1972); S. Cohen and A. Eisen, *The Jew Within: Self, Family, and Community in America* (2001); M. Cone, H. Droker, and J. Williams, *Family of Strangers: Building a Jewish Community in Washington State* (2003); D. Dalin and J. Rosenbaum, *Making a Life, Building a Community: A History of the Jews of Hartford* (1997); H. Danziger, *Returning to Tradition: The Contemporary Revival of Orthodox Judaism* (1989); J. Dash, *The Life of Henrietta Szold* (1979); L. Davidman, *Tradition in a Rootless World: Women Turn to Orthodox Judaism* (1991); M. Davis, *The Emergence of Conservative Judaism: The Historical School in Nineteenth-Century America* (1965); L. Dawidowicz, *On Equal Terms: Jews in America, 1881–1981* (1984); E. Diamond, *"And I Will Dwell in Their Midst": Orthodox Jews in Suburbia* (2000); H. Diner, *In the Almost Promised Land: American Blacks and Jews, 1915–1935* (1995); idem, *A Time for Gathering: The Second Migration, 1820–1880* (1992); idem, *Lower East Side Memories: A Jewish Place in America* (2000); H. Diner and B. Benderly, *Her Works Praise Her: A History of Jewish Women in America From Colonial Times to the Present* (2002); L. Dinnerstein, *Antisemitism in America* (1994); idem, *The Leo Frank Case* (1968); M. Dobkowski, *Jewish American Voluntary Organizations* (1986); M. Dollinger, *Quest for Inclusion: Jews and Liberalism in Modern America* (2000); A. Dushkin and U. Engelman, *Jewish Education in the United States* (1959); W. Ehrlich, *Zion in the Valley: The Jewish Community of St. Louis* (1997); D. Elazar and R. Gefen, *The Conservative Movement in Judaism: Dilemmas and Opportunities* (2000); P. Erens, *The Jew in American Cinema* (1984); E. Faber, *A Time for Planting: The First Migration* (1992); E. Evans, *The Provincials: A Personal History of Jews in the South* (1997); E. Faber, *Jews, Slaves, and the Slave Trade: Setting the Record Straight* (1998); I. Fein, *The Making of an American Jewish Community: The History of Baltimore Jewry from 1773 to 1920* (1971); H. Feingold, *A Time for Searching: Entering the Mainstream, 1920–1945* (1992); idem, *Bearing Witness: How America and Its Jews Responded to the Holocaust* (1995); idem, *Lest Memory Cease: Finding Meaning in the American Jewish Past* (1996); idem, *The Politics of Rescue: The Roosevelt Administration and the Holocaust, 1938–1945* (1970); R. Fierstein, *A Different Spirit: The Jewish Theological Seminary of America, 1886–1902* (1990); S. Fishman, *A Breath of Life: Feminism in the American Jewish Community* (1993); idem, *Changing Minds: Feminism in Contemporary Orthodox Jewish Life* (2000); idem, *Jewish Life and American Culture* (2000); C. Ford, *The Girls: Jewish Women of Brownsville, Brooklyn, 1940–1995* (2000); J. Frankel, *Prophecy and Politics: Socialism, Nationalism, and the Russian Jews, 1862–1917* (1984); S. Freedman, *Jew vs. Jew: The Struggle for the Soul of American Jewry* (2000); M. Friedman (ed.), *Jewish Life in Philadelphia* (1983); idem (ed.), *When Philadelphia Was the Capital of Jewish America* (1993); M. Friedman and A. Chernin (eds.), *A Second Exodus, The American Movement to Free Soviet Jews* (1999); E. Friesel, *The Zionist Movement in the United States, 1897–1914* (Heb., 1970); A. Gal (ed.), *Envisioning Israel: The Changing Ideals and Images of North American Jews* (1996); Z. Ganin, *An Uneasy Relationship: American Jewish Leadership and Israel, 1948–1957* (2005); L. Gartner, *History of the Jews of Cleveland* (1978); D. Gerber (ed.), *Anti-Semitism in American History* (1986); M. Gilbert, *The Jews in the Twentieth Century* (2001); N. Glazer, *American Judaism* (1989²); S. Godfrey and J. Godfrey, *Search Out the Land: The Jews and the Growth of Equality in British Colonial America, 1740–1867* (1995); J. Goldberg, *Jewish Power* (1996); K. Goldman, *Beyond the Synagogue Gallery: Finding a Place for Women in American Judaism* (2000); S. Goldman, *God's Sacred Tongue: Hebrew and the American Imagination* (2004); E. Goldstein, *The Price of Whiteness: Jews, Race, and American Identity* (2005); J. Goldstein, *The Politics of Ethnic Pressure: The American Jewish Committee Fight Against Immigration Restriction, 1906–1917* (1990); S. Goldstein and C. Goldscheider, *Jewish Americans: Three Generations in a Jewish Community* (1968); S. Goldstein and A. Goldstein, *Jews on the Move* (1996); R. Goldy, *The Emergence of Jewish Theology in America* (1990); S. Goodman (ed.), *The Faith of Secular Jews* (1976); A. Gordon, *Jews in Suburbia* (1959); A. Goren, *New York Jews and the Quest for Community: The Kehillah Experiment, 1908–1922* (1970); M. Greene, *The Temple Bombing* (1996); H. Greenstein, *Turning Point: Zionism and Reform Judaism* (1981); A. Grobman, *Battling for Souls: The Vaad Hatzala Rescue Committee in Post-War Europe* (2004); J. Gurock, *American Jewish Orthodoxy in Historical Perspective* (1996); idem, *The Men and Women of Yeshiva University: Higher Education, Orthodoxy, and American Judaism* (1997); J. Gurock and J. Schacter, *A Modern Heretic and a Traditional Community: Mordecai M. Kaplan, Orthodoxy, and American Judaism* (1997); M. Gutstein, *A Priceless Heritage: The Epic Growth of Nineteenth-Century Chicago Jewry* (1953); idem, *The Story of the Jews of Newport* (1936); W. Hagy, *This Happy Land: The Jews of Colonial and Antebellum Charleston* (1993); B. Halpern, *The American Jew: A Zionist Analysis* (1983); S. Halperin, *The Political World of American Zionism* (1985); L. Harap, *Creative Awakening: The Jewish Presence in Twentieth-Century American Literature, 1900–1940s* (1987); idem, *In the Mainstream: The Jewish Presence in Twentieth-Century American Literature, 1950–1980s* (1987); A. Heilbut, *Exiled in Paradise: German Refugee Artists and Intellectuals in America from the 1930s to the Present* (1983); A. Heinze, *Adapting to Abundance: Jewish Immigrants, Mass Consumption, and the Search for American Identity* (1990); W. Helmreich, *The World of Yeshiva: An Intimate Portrait of Orthodox Jewry* (1982); W. Herberg, *Protestant-Catholic-Jew: An Essay in American Religious Sociology* (1960); A. Hertzberg, *The Jews in America: Four Centuries of an Uneasy Encounter* (1989); S. Hertzberg, *Strangers Within the Gate City: The Jews of Atlanta, 1845–1915* (1978); J. Higham, *Send These to Me: Immigrants in Urban America* (1984); idem, *Strangers in the Land: Patterns of American Nativism, 1860–1925* (1963); J. Hoberman and J. Shandler, *Entertaining America: Jews, Movies, and Broadcasting* (2003); E. Hoffman, *Despite All Odds: The Story of the Lubavitch* (1991); S. Hornstein, L. Levitt, and L. Silberstein, *Impossible Images: Contemporary Art after the Holocaust* (2003); B. Horowitz, *Connections and Journeys: Assessing Critical Opportunities for Enhancing Jewish Identity* (2000); I. Howe, *World of Our Fathers: The Journey of East European Jews to America and the Life They Found and Made* (1976); P. Hyman, *Gender and Assimilation in Modern Jewish History: The Roles and Representations of Women* (1995); W. Jacob (ed.), *The Changing World of Reform Judaism: The Pittsburgh Platform in Retrospect* (1985); O. Janowsky, *The JWB Survey* (1948); J. Kugelmass (ed.), *Key Texts in American Jewish Culture* (2003); L. Jick, *The Americanization of the Synagogue, 1820–1870* (1976); J. Joselit, *New York's Jewish Jews: The Orthodox Community in the Interwar Years* (1990); idem, *The Wonders of America: Reinventing Jewish Culture, 1880–1950* (1994); A. Kahan, *Essays in Jewish Social and Economic History* (1986); D. Kaplan, *American Reform Judaism: An Introduction* (2003); S. Karff (ed.), *Hebrew Union College-Jewish Institute of Religion at One Hundred Years* (1976); A. Karp, *Haven and Home: A History of the Jews in America* (1985); idem, *A History of the United Synagogue of America, 1913–1963* (1964); idem, *Jewish Continuity in America: Creative Survival in a Free Society* (1998); D. Kaufman, *Shul with a Pool: The "Synagogue Center" in American Jewish History* (1999); idem, *Rachel's Daughters: Newly Orthodox Women* (1991); I. Kaufman, *American Jews in World War II* (1947); G. Klaperman, *The Story of Yeshiva University: The First Jewish University in America* (1969); S. Klingenstein, *Enlarging America: The Cultural Work of Jewish Literary Scholars, 1930–1990* (1998); idem, *Jews in the American Academy, 1900–1940: The Dynamics of Intellectual Assimilation* (1998); B. Korn, *American Jewry and the Civil War* (1970); idem, *The American Reaction to the Mortara Case, 1858–1859* (1957); idem (ed.), *A Bicentennial Festschrift for Jacob Rader Marcus* (1976); J. Kramer and S. Leventman, *Children of the Gilded Ghetto: Conflict Resolutions of Three Generations of American Jews* (1961); P. Levine, *Ellis Island to Ebbets Field: Sport and the American Jewish Experience* (1992); M. Kramer and H. Wirth-Nesher, *The Cambridge Companion to Jewish American Literature* (2003); G. Kranzler, *Hasidic Williamsburg* (1995); B. Kraut, *From Reform Judaism to Ethical Culture: The Religious Evolution of Felix Adler* (1979); J. Kugelmass (ed.), *Key Texts in American Jewish Culture* (2003); S. Kuznets, "Immigration of Russian Jews to the United States," *Perspectives in American History* 9 (1975), 35–124; E. Lederhendler, in: *The Six-Day War and World Jewry* (2000); idem, *New York Jews and the Decline of Urban Ethnicity, 1950–1970* (2001); A. Levin, *The Szolds of Lombard Street* (1960); T. Levitan, *Islands of Compassion: A History of the Jewish Hospitals of New York* (1964); R. Libowitz, *Mordecai M. Kaplan and the Development of Reconstructionism* (1983); C. Liebman, *Pressure Without Sanctions* (1977); D. Lifson, *The Yiddish Theater in America* (1965); S. Lipset and E. Raab, *Jews and the New American Scene* (1995); D. Lipstadt, *The American Press and the Coming of the Holocaust, 1933–1945* (1986); S. Lowenstein, *Frankfurt on the Hudson: The German Jewish Community of Washington Heights, 1933–1983. Its Structure and Culture* (1989); J. Marcus, *The American Jewish Woman, 1654–1980*, 2 vols. (1981); idem, *Studies in American Jewish History* (1969); A. Mason, *Brandeis: A Free Man's Life* (1946); L. Mayo, *The Ambivalent Image: Nineteenth-Century America's Perception of the Jew* (1988); C. Mauch and J. Salmons (eds.), *German-Jewish Identities in America* (2003); E. Mayer, *From Suburb to Shtetl: The Jews of Boro Park* (1979); M. McCune, *"The Whole Wide World, Without Limits": International Relief, Gender, Politics, and American Jewish Women, 1893–1930* (2005); J. Melnick, *A Right to Sing the Blues: African Americans, Jews, and American Popular Song* (1999); R. Melnick, *The Life and Work of Ludwig Lewisohn*, 2 vols. (1998); M. Meyer (ed.), *German Jewish History in Modern Times*, 4 vols. (1996); M. Meyer, *Judaism Within Modernity: Essays on Jewish History and Religion* (2001); idem, *Response to Modernity: A History of the Reform Movement in Judaism* (1988); T. Michels, *A Fire in Their Hearts: Yiddish Socialists in New York* (2005); J. Mintz, *Hasidic People: A Place in the New World* (1992); D. Moore, *At Home in America: Second Generation New York Jews* (1981); idem, *B'nai B'rith and the Challenge of Ethnic Leadership* (1981); idem, *To the Golden Cities: Pursuing the American Dream in Miami and L.A.* (1994); D. Moore and S. Troen, *Divergent Jewish Cultures: Israel and America* (2001); E. Morawska, *Insecure Prosperity: Small Town Jews in Industrial America, 1890–1940* (1996); A. Most, *Making Americans: Jews and the Broadway Musical* (2004); P. Nadell, *Conservative Judaism in America: A Biographical Dictionary and Sourcebook* (1988); idem, *Women Who Would Be Rabbis: A History of Women's Ordination, 1899–1985* (1998); P. Nadell and J. Sarna (eds.), *Women and American Judaism: Historical Perspectives* (2001); P. Novick, *The Holocaust in American Life* (1999); W. Orbach, *The American Movement to Aid Soviet Jews* (1979); A. Orleck, *The Soviet Jewish Americans* (1999); S. Ortner, *New Jersey Dreaming: Capital, Culture, and the Class of '58* (2003); N. Pasachoff, *Links in the Chain: Shapers of the Jewish Tradition* (1997); J. Pilch (ed.), *A History of Jewish Education in America* (1969); W. Plaut, *The Jews of Minnesota: The First Seventy-Five Years* (1959); idem, *The Magen David* (1991); J. Podair, *The Strike That Changed New York: Blacks, Whites, and the Ocean Hill-Brownsville Crisis* (2002); D. Polish, *Renew Our Days: The Zionist Issue in Reform Judaism* (1976); M. Polner, *American Jewish Biographies* (1982); D. Pool and T. Pool, *An Old Faith in a New World: Portrait of Shearith Israel, 1654–1954* (1955); R. Prell, *Fighting to Become Americans: American Jews, Gender, and the Anxiety of Assimilation* (1999); idem, *Prayer and Community: The Havurah in American Judaism* (1989); W. Pritchett, *Brownsville, Brooklyn: Blacks, Jews, and the Changing Face of the Ghetto* (2002); M. Raider, *The Emergence of American Zionism* (1998); M. Raider, J. Sarna and R. Zweig (eds.), *Abba Hillel Silver and American Zionism* (1996); M. Raphael, *A History of the United Jewish Appeal, 1939–1982* (1982); idem, *Judaism in America* (2003); idem, *Abba Hillel Silver: A Profile in American Judaism* (1989); S. Reinharz and M. Raider (eds.), *American Jewish Women and the Zionist Enterprise* (2004), S. Rezneck, *Unrecognized Patriots: The Jews in the American Revolution* (1975); I. Richman, *Borscht Belt Bungalows: Memories of Catskill Summers* (1998); M. Rischin, *The Promised City: New York's Jews, 1870–1914* (1970); F. Rogow, *"Gone to Another Meeting": The National Council of Jewish Women, 1893–1993* (1993); R. Rosen, *The Jewish Confederates* (2000); T. Rosengarten and D. Rosengarten (eds.), *A Portion of the People: Three Hundred Years of Southern Jewish Life* (2002); I. Rosenwaike, *On the Edge of Greatness: A Portrait of American Jewry in the Early National Period* (1985); A. Rothkoff, *Bernard Revel: Builder of American Jewish Orthodoxy* (1972); I. Rubin, *Satmar: Two Generations of an Urban Island* (1997); S. Rubin, *Third to None: The Saga of Savannah Jewry* (1983); J. Rubin-Dorsky and S. Fishkin (eds.), *Thirty Scholars Reflect on Their Jewish Identity* (1996); H. Sachar, *A History of the Jews in America* (1993); J. Salzman and C. West (eds.), *Struggles in the Promised Land: Toward a History of Black-Jewish Relations in the United States* (1997); M. Sanua, *Going Greek: Jewish College Fraternities in the United States, 1895–1945* (2003); J. Sarna, *American Judaism: A History* (2004); idem, *Jacksonian Jew: The Two Worlds of Mordecai Noah* (1980); idem, *JPS: The Americanization of Jewish Culture* (1989); J. Sarna and D. Dalin (eds.), *Religion and State in the American Jewish Experience* (1997); J. Sarna and N. Klein, *The Jews of Cincinnati* (1989); J. Sarna, E. Smith, and S. Martin-Kossofsky (eds.), *The Jews of Boston* (2005); A. Scoener, *Portal to America: The Lower East Side, 1870–1925* (1967); A. Schulman, *Like a Raging Fire: A Biography of Maurice N. Eisendrath* (1993); L. Schwartz, *Jews and the American Revolution: Haym Salomon and Others* (1987); S. Schwartz, *The Rabbi's Wife: The Rebbetzin in American Jewish Life* (2005); M. Scult, *Judaism Faces the Twentieth Century: A Biography of Mordecai M. Kaplan* (1993); R. Seltzer and N. Cohen (eds.), *The Americanization of the Jews* (1995); J. Shandler, *While America Watches: Televising the Holocaust* (1999); E. Shapiro, *A Time for Healing: American Jewry Since World War II* (1992); H. Sharfman, *The First Rabbi: Origins of Conflict Between Orthodox and Reform: Jewish Polemic Warfare in Pre-Civil War America: A Biographical History* (1988); R. Shermay, "Defining Lessons: The Holocaust in American Jewish Education" (Ph.D. diss., Brandeis University, 2001); C. Sherman, *The Jew Within American Society* (1961); C. Silberman, *A Certain People: American Jews and Their Lives Today* (1985); A. Silverstein, *Alternatives to Assimilation: The Response of Reform Judaism to American Culture, 1840–1930* (1994); M. Sklare, *Conservative Judaism, An American Religious Movement* (1972); M. Sklare and J. Greenblum, *Jewish Identity on the Suburban Frontier: A Study of Group Survival in an Open Society* (1979); M. Slobin, *Chosen Voices: The Story of the American Cantorate* (1989); G. Sorin, *Tradition Transformed: The Jewish Experience in America* (1997); D. Soyer, *Jewish Immigrant Associations and American Identity in New York, 1880–1939* (1997); M. Staub, *Torn at the Roots: The Crisis of Jewish Liberalism in Postwar America* (2002); C. Stember, *Jews in the Mind of America* (1966); M. Stern and M. Angel, *New York's Early Jews: Some Myths and Misconceptions* (1976); H. Strauss (ed.), *Jewish Immigrants of the Nazi Period in the U.S.A.*, 6 vols. (1978–86); L. Sussman, *Isaac Leeser and the Making of American Jewry* (1995); S. Svonkin, *Jews Against Prejudice: American Jews and the Fight for Civil Liberties* (1997); D. Swetschinski, *Reluctant Cosmopolitans: The Portuguese Jews of Seventeenth-Century Amsterdam* (2000); L. Swichkow and L. Gartner, *History of the Jews of Milwaukee* (1963); Z. Szajkowski, *Jews, Wars and Communism*, 2 vols. (1972–74); E. Tcherikover and A. Antonovsky, *The Early Jewish Labor Movement in the United States* (1961); J. Teller, *Strangers and Natives: The Evolution of the American Jew from 1921 to the Present* (1968); S. Temkin, *Isaac Mayer Wise, Shaping American Judaism* (1992); S. Tenenbaum, *A Credit to Their Community: Jewish Loan Societies in the United States, 1880–1945* (1993); J. Trachtenberg, *Consider the Years: The Story of the Jewish Community of Easton, 1752–1942* (1944); M. Urofsky, *American Zionism from Herzl to the Holocaust* (1975); idem, *A Voice That Spoke for Justice: The Life and Times of Stephen S. Wise* (1982); idem, *We Are One! American Jewry and Israel* (1978); M. Waxman (ed.), *Tradition and Change: The Development of Conservative Judaism* (1958); C. Webb, *Fight Against Fear: Southern Jews and Black Civil Rights* (2001); S. Weinberg, *The World of Our Mothers: The Lives of Jewish Immigrant Women* (1988); B. Wenger, *New York Jews and the Great Depression: Uncertain Promise* (1996); J. Wertheimer (ed.), *The American Synagogue: A Sanctuary Transformed* (1987); idem (ed.), *Jews in the Center: Conservative Synagogues and Their Members* (2000); idem, *A People Divided: Judaism in Contemporary America* (1997); idem (ed.), *Tradition Renewed: A History of the Jewish Theological Seminary* (1997); S. Whitfield, *In Search of American Jewish Culture* (1999); G. Wigoder, *Jewish-Christian Relations Since the Second World War* (1988); R. Wischnitzer, *Synagogue Architecture in the United States* (1955); A. Wiznitzer, *Jews in Colonial Brazil* (1960); idem, *The Records of the Earliest Jewish Community in the New World* (1954); E. Wolf, *The History of the Jews of Philadelphia from Colonial Times to the Age of Jackson* (1975); G. Wolfe, *The Synagogues of New York's Lower East Side* (1978); J. Woocher, *Sacred Survival: The Civil Religion of American Jews* (1986); D. Wyman, *The Abandonment of the Jews: America and the Holocaust, 1941–1945* (1984); idem, *Paper Walls: America and the Refugee Crisis, 1938–1941*

(1985); C. Wyszkowski, *A Community in Conflict: American Jewry During the Great European Immigration* (1991); J. Young, *The Texture of Memory: Holocaust Memorials and Meaning* (1993); G. Zola, *Isaac Harby of Charleston, 1788–1828* (1994); idem (ed.), *Women Rabbis: Exploration and Celebration* (1996); E. Zuroff, *The Response of Orthodox Jewry in the United States to the Holocaust* (2000).

[Maurice Atkin, Lloyd P. Gartner, Arden J. Geldman, Isaiah Kenen, Jacob Rader Marcus, and Sefton D. Temkin / Mark A. Raider (2nd ed.)]

UNITED SYNAGOGUE (Heb. ק״ק כְּנֶסֶת יִשְׂרָאֵל), association of Ashkenazi congregations in London – originally formed by the Great Synagogue, Duke's Place (c. 1690), and four other constituent synagogues – which was established by Act of Parliament on July 14, 1870. The project, apparently inspired by Michael *Sachs' model federation in Berlin, was initiated by Chief Rabbi Nathan Marcus *Adler in 1866 and the organizational work developed under his son and successor, Hermann *Adler. The United Synagogue (popularly known as the "U.S.") rapidly became one of the most powerful centralized bodies of its type in the Jewish world, and its name was later borrowed by Solomon *Schechter for the Conservative synagogue body in the U.S. The United Synagogue was arguably at its peak in the half-century from about 1920 until 1970, when it was, generally, the synagogue of choice of England's second generation immigrants as they moved into the middle class. During this time it opened many new venues in north and northeast London and elsewhere. Its ambiance emphasizes decorum, conservatism in behavior, and British patriotism. Before 1948, while not anti-Zionist, it was seldom associated as a rule with the extreme supporters of a Jewish state. Since the establishment of the State of Israel, it has become a loyal supporter of the Jewish state, although recent chief rabbis have occasionally been critical of some Israeli actions. It is the bastion of the British chief rabbinate and of the London *bet din* and all its synagogues accept the religious authority of the Chief Rabbi. By 1971 there were 23 constituent synagogues (with some 20,000 members), a further 23 district synagogues, and 35 affiliated congregations; about 40,000 families, representing half the Jewish population of Greater London, were United Synagogue members. After World War II, these activities were expanded to include new congregations in a few provincial centers such as Peterborough and Worcester. Income is paid into a common pool so that poorer synagogues can be supported by wealthier ones and a number of general communal services can be supported.

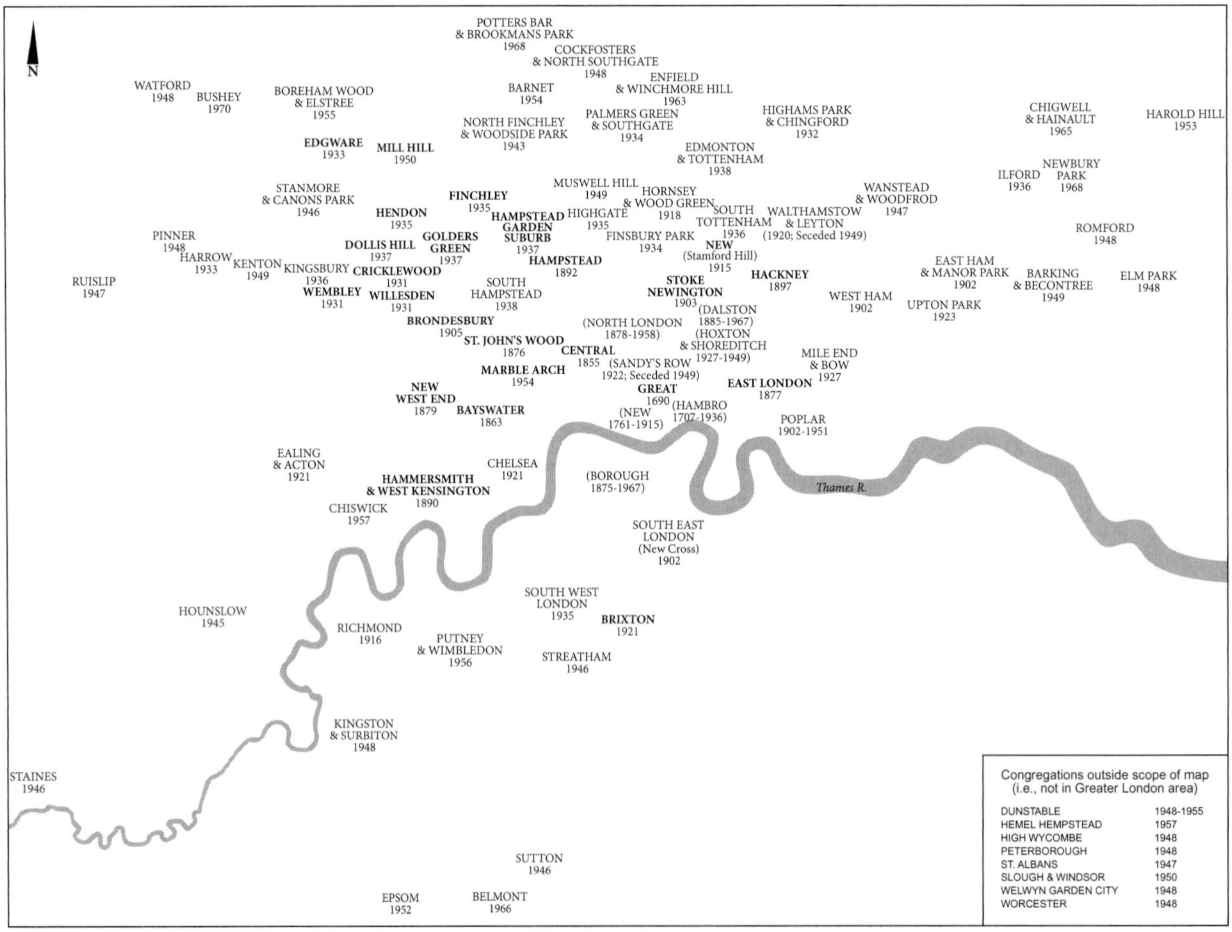

United Synagogue congregations in Greater London. Constituent synagogues in boldface. Prepared by G.E. Silverman.

Although the United Synagogue has long claimed to preserve and represent traditional Judaism in Great Britain, its Orthodoxy had been so diluted by the early 20th century that it came near to emulating the French Central *Consistory. There were also religious and organizational conflicts and rivalries with the more right-wing Federation of Synagogues (1887) founded by Lord Swaythling and the Union of Orthodox Hebrew Congregations (Adath Yisroel) established by Victor (Avigdor) *Schoenfeld in 1926. Its dominating figure in the mid-20th century was its president, Sir Robert Waley *Cohen. With the emergence of a more staunchly Orthodox lay leadership after World War II, and especially following Sir Isaac *Wolfson's election as president in 1962, the United Synagogue swung to the right. The United Synagogue's centenary celebrations in 1970 were attended by Queen Elizabeth. In recent years it has been repeatedly challenged from both the theological right and left and has diminished somewhat in popularity – as measured, for instance, by the marriages it performs – compared with either Strict Orthodoxy or non-Orthodox strands. In the mid-1960s, the rise of the Masorti movement, led by Rabbi Louis Jacobs and linked with the American Conservative movement, represented a significant challenge to the "U.S." Both recent chief rabbis, Immanuel *Jakobovits and Jonathan *Sacks, have engaged in high-profile disputes with other strands in Anglo-Jewry, especially with the Progressive movement. In 2004 there were 46 member synagogues of the "U.S." in London, together with another 20 London synagogues affiliated to it and several dozen outside of London. Aubrey Newman's *The United Synagogue, 1870–1970* (1977) is a history of the group's first century.

BIBLIOGRAPHY: C. Roth, *Archives of the United Synagogue. Report and Catalogue* (1930); idem, *The Great Synagogue, London, 1690–1940* (1950); B. Homa, *A Fortress in Anglo-Jewry: the Story of the Machzike Hadath* (1953), index; V.D. Lipman (ed.), *Three Centuries of Anglo-Jewish History* (1961), index; idem, in: JHSET, 21 (1968), 78–103; A. Barnett, *Western Synagogue through Two Centuries (1761–1961)* (1961), index. **ADD. BIBLIOGRAPHY:** G. Alderman, *Modern British Jewry* (1992); W.D. Rubinstein, *Jews in England.*

UNITED SYNAGOGUE OF CONSERVATIVE JUDAISM (formerly **United Synagogue of America**), association of Conservative synagogues in the United States and Canada. The United Synagogue of America was founded by Solomon *Schechter, president of the Jewish Theological Seminary, on February 23, 1913. The 22 synagogues that constituted the original membership of the organization had reached well over 700 congregations by 2006.

In creating the United Synagogue, Schechter hoped to tie together those congregations that supported the seminary's goal, to strengthen "historical Judaism" in North America. Although his dream of unifying the entire Jewish community did not materialize, Schechter's labors created a major instrumentality for preserving and fostering traditional Jewish religious life across the continent.

The United Synagogue has sought to provide its affiliated congregations with help in fulfilling their religious and educational responsibilities. The United Synagogue Commission on Jewish Education has conducted many studies on the operation of congregational religious schools, which led eventually to the formulation of standards and curricula for Conservative schools. The commission has also produced hundreds of textbooks in Hebrew and English, school administration materials, and audio-visual aids. Since the late 1950s, it has spurred a system of Conservative day schools. Today, the Solomon Schechter Day School Association represents a network of more than 80 elementary and high schools.

Through the National Academy for Adult Jewish Studies, the United Synagogue has stimulated the development of adult education programs. To make prayer responsive to contemporary needs, the United Synagogue has published from time to time revised versions of the prayer book both for adults and children; its most recent is the revised *Siddur Sim Shalom*, which uses updated language and deals sensitively with issues of language and gender.

In 1952 the United Synagogue took an important step to raise standards of conduct for synagogues by adopting its "Guide to Standards for Congregational Life," and in 1959 the organization adopted the "Statement of Standards for Synagogue Practice," which became binding upon its affiliated congregations. In cooperation with the Rabbinical Assembly and the National Women's League, it also established the Commission on Social Action. The commission's purpose was to bring the wisdom of Judaism to bear on the burning social issues of the day.

Into the 21st century, United Synagogue's Social Action and Public Policy Committee still takes on that mandate; it also responds to emergencies with financial and other forms of help, and lobbies Congress to support issues of concern to the Jewish community.

In 2006 United Synagogue supported offices in 14 regions, which spanned the United States and Canada. Each region had an executive director and a network of regional officers, who met in regional councils and who were represented by their presidents on the national level. Presidents and past presidents share ideas and information with each other over the Presidents' List, a listserv run out of the national office. New leaders, on the congregational, regional, and international levels, are provided through retreat programs Sulam and Imun.

United Synagogue is particularly strong in informal education for teenagers and young adults, both in North America and in Israel. In North America, its network of United Synagogue Youth groups, for high-school students, covers the country, and often is the entry point to an independent Conservative Jewish life for teenagers. Kadimah, for middle-schoolers, is an active group that successfully feeds into USY; Koach, for college-students, operates on many campuses and holds regional gatherings for the Sabbath. On the other end of the life cycle, Hazak, provides classes, trips, discussion groups, and a range of other services for people 55 and older.

The United Synagogue of America has been committed to the cause of Israel and world Jewry generally since it was founded. As far back as 1926, it was instrumental in creating the Yeshurun Synagogue in Jerusalem as a gift to the Jews of what was then Palestine.

United Synagogue now has a six-building campus in Israel, the Fuchsberg Jerusalem Center of the United Synagogue of Conservative Judaism. The change of name is an indication of the reality that the organization stands for a movement and not for the entirety of the synagogues of America. The center houses the Conservative Yeshivah, an institution dedicated to high-level study for Jews who wish to take weeks, months, or even a year out of their lives to study for its own sake. It also provides headquarters for Nativ, the United Synagogue program for young adults who spend a year in Israel between high school and college, and often houses high-school students in Israel for USY's extremely successful Israel Pilgrimage trips.

[Alvin Kass / Joanne Palmer (2nd ed.)]

UNIVERS ISRAÉLITE, French-language periodical which was published in Paris from 1844 to 1940. In its first issue it was described as a "monthly religious, moral, and literary journal," but from January 1846, it adopted as a subtitle "journal of the conservative interests of Judaism." Then a bimonthly publication, it proposed to consider all political or social events that might have some direct or indirect bearing on the Jewish community. From 1896 it appeared as a weekly until the fall of France in May–June 1940. For decades it had been the organ which published the principal statements of the chief rabbis of France. The chief editors were S. Bloch (1844–78), Lazare *Wogue (1879–93), Israel *Lévi (1894–95), Maurice *Liber (1919–34), and Raymond *Lambert (from September 1934).

BIBLIOGRAPHY: G. Wormser, *Journal de la communauté* (1950).

[Roger Berg]

UNIVERSITIES. Jewish interest in education, including its advanced forms, goes back to the early history of the people. Specialists in the history of education, both Jewish and non-Jewish, have long recognized that the *academy of ancient Judea and Babylonia was an institution of advanced instruction and research in theology and in other subjects as well. According to Lewis J. Sherrill, the academy was "a university," in which "learned scholars" pursued "the most advanced studies" and instructed those who were capable of learning.

In the Middle Ages

The advent of Christianity, with its opposition to Judaism, made impossible any Jewish identification with the learning represented by such institutions as the University of Constantinople. However, Jewish scholars were welcome in the University of Jundishapur during the reign of Nurshirwan the Just, the renowned sixth-century monarch of Sassanid Persia. In this, "the greatest intellectual center of the time" (George Sarton), Jews, Christians, Hindus, Greeks, and others furthered study and research in philosophy, science, and *medicine. Jews also played an educational role in the House of Wisdom (Bayt al-Ḥikma), the research and translation center founded in Baghdad by Caliph Abdallah al-Mamun (813–833). At this institution, alchemy, astronomy, mathematics, law, philosophy, philology, and other learned subjects were promoted by the combined efforts of Jews and Christians under the aegis of al-Mamun.

The study of medicine drew many Jews to medieval and Renaissance universities. During the latter half of the 14th century Abraham Avigdor studied medicine at the University of Montpellier. He was apparently one of the earliest Jewish students of note at a Christian institution of higher learning. In later times Jewish names were not rare in the medical faculties of European universities, especially at those in Italy.

During the 15th and 16th centuries there were several recorded instances of Jews' affiliation with universities, as a rule in connection with science, medicine, and Hebrew. Elijah Levita, the Hebrew grammarian, invited by Francis I to accept the professorship of Hebrew at the University of Paris, refused because other Jews were not permitted to live in Paris at that time. Elijah b. Shabbetai (Sabot) taught at Paris in the 15th century.

At most, the contacts between the Jews and the European universities were sporadic and tenuous. The desire for higher education could not be satisfied through such arrangements. Hence it is not surprising that the desire for advanced learning led to the formation of plans for the establishment of an institution under Jewish auspices. In 1466 King John of Sicily gave formal permission to the Jews to organize a university of their own with faculties of medicine and law, and possibly also philosophy. It appears likely that the aim of this university was to prepare young Jews for the medical and legal professions. In any event, nothing came of this proposal, especially since the Jews were expelled from Sicily in 1492 by order of the Spanish crown.

An echo of the drive for university education came a century after the Sicilian plan. In a publication in 1604, R. David *Provençal of Mantua and his son Abraham called for the establishment of a Jewish college to teach Jewish religious and secular subjects. This plan evidently anticipated a bull by Pope Pius IV prohibiting the admission of Jews to examination for doctoral degrees. With the aid of his son, a doctor of philosophy and medicine, R. David presented a suitable program of study, "so that anyone who wishes to become a physician need not waste his days and years in a university among Christians in sinful neglect of Jewish studies." Owing to the intolerance of the times, the Provençals were not able to open this yeshivah-university, but only a talmudical institute instead.

If there was discouragement from without, there can be little doubt of opposition from within regarding secular education for Jews. Opposition to secular learning arose repeatedly, on the grounds of safeguarding the integrity of Judaism against alien ideology. However, despite such disapproval, there were always traditional Jews who made an effort to combine the sacred with the secular.

Whatever the case, some Jews in the 16th century managed to obtain doctoral degrees from several Italian universities – Bologna, Ferrara, Pavia, Perugia, Pisa, Rome, and Siena. The University of Padua conferred 228 doctorates upon Jews from 1517 to 1721. Aiding the Jews in their quest for higher learning in Italy was the Senate of Venice, which bypassed the papal ban on degrees by empowering an official to grant degrees without regard to religion, thus safeguarding academic freedom at the University of Padua.

The attitude of the Catholic Church toward study by Jews changed with the times. According to the 24th canon of the Council of Basle, Sept. 7, 1434, a ban was placed upon conferring any university degree upon Jews. However, even churchmen found it advisable to ignore this decree. Thus, Pope Julius III ordered the University of Padua (on Jan. 9, 1555) to examine a Jewish student, Simon Vitale, for the doctorate. The pope's motivation was neither religious tolerance nor academic freedom, but rather the hope that conversion of the candidate and, consequently, of other Jews would be facilitated.

Even when admitted to a university, Jewish students were faced by special problems and difficulties, some originating from their religious principles and others from discriminatory treatment. An example of the former was when students had to resort to various devices to avoid desecration of the Sabbath and holidays in connection with examinations. Jews had to pay larger graduation fees than did the Christian students, and in the 15th century they were required to invite all the students to dinner. If the Jewish students were excused from wearing the Jewish cap, they were also prohibited from practicing medicine on Christians. Jewish physicians of the 16th century had few, if any, opportunities for medical research and teaching or for admission to the leading hospitals.

17th and 18th Centuries

During the 17th and 18th centuries, the barriers to Jewish study were still very firm. No doubt taking their cue from traditional Catholic practice (as well as from Luther), European universities, hospitals, and official bodies carried on a boycott of Jewish physicians (generally identified as "Italian doctors," since it was impossible for a practicing Jew to get a doctoral degree outside of Italy). Johann Jakob *Schudt, the Lutheran theologian and Orientalist from Frankfurt and author of *Juedische Merckwuerdigkeiten* (1714–1717), was distressed at the Catholic Italians' disregard for the canon law of the Council of Basle. He accused the Italian universities, particularly the University of Padua, of permitting "every ignoramus and even the despised Jews" to take their degrees because of their pecuniary greed. Johann Heinrich Schuette provided proof in 1745 that conferring a medical doctorate upon a Jew was "contrary to the Christian religion." Under these circumstances, it is clear that Jews were separated at this time from the universities of virtually all of Europe by a formidable iron curtain.

However, here and there were chinks in this curtain. The philosopher Baruch *Spinoza, who had been excommunicated in 1656 by the Amsterdam Jewish community, but who was still identified as a Jew, was offered a professorship at the University of Heidelberg in 1673. Spinoza turned this invitation down because he feared losing his independence of thought and expression.

The usual association between medicine and higher education is also evident in the early history of the Jews of Poland. In their society talmudic and rabbinic studies were predominant, the physicians alone obtaining secular learning at universities. The earliest Jewish physicians in Poland were Spanish exiles and alumni of the University of Padua. They were seeking a place of refuge and hoped to practice the arts forbidden to them elsewhere. It was probably their example that influenced some Polish Jews (e.g., R. Moses Fishel of Cracow) to study medicine at the University of Padua in the early 16th century. From the second half of the century to the 18th, an increasing number of Polish Jews enrolled as students of medicine at Padua.

Interesting case studies are provided by R. Tobias *Cohn and Gabriel Selig or Felix of Galicia, who succeeded in getting their doctorates in medicine and philosophy at Padua in 1683. Both had succeeded in 1678, with the intervention of the great elector Frederick William of Brandenburg, in gaining admission to the University of Frankfurt on the Oder in the face of strong opposition on the part of the faculty. Only when the Lutheran faculty, citing the Catholic Council of Basle in 1434, refused to admit Jewish students to doctoral examinations, did Jewish students go to study in the south.

Once the barrier was broken, it became less difficult for Jewish students to enter German universities. Those whom the University of Cracow refused in the 18th century ventured to study medicine (and sometimes other disciplines) not only at Frankfurt on the Oder, but also at the University of Heidelberg. Only Padua exceeded the number of Jewish students at Frankfurt. It was most difficult for a Jew in the 18th century to obtain an appointment as a university lecturer in Europe, even on a temporary basis and in a subject such as the Hebrew language. The experience of Isaac Abraham *Euchel at the University of Koenigsberg in 1786 illustrates this. Euchel, who was an observant Jew, applied to the rector, Immanuel Kant, but was rejected by the university senate (minus Kant's signature) on the ground that he lacked the master's degree and that he was not a Christian.

During the 18th century, Jews studied at Harvard, Yale, the University of Pennsylvania, Columbia, and Brown University (where they were excused from attendance on Saturday). Moses Levy, who graduated from Pennsylvania in 1772, became a lawyer and judge; Isaac Abrahams (A.B., Columbia, 1774) practiced medicine; and Sampson Simson (B.A., Columbia, 1800) was the first Jewish lawyer in New York. A Jew in higher education was Rabbi Gershom Mendes *Seixas of the Spanish-Portuguese Congregation of New York, who became a regent of the University of the State of New York when it was founded in 1784, and who served as a trustee of Columbia College (1785–1815).

Enlightenment

The change in the European attitude toward opening higher education to the Jew, originating in the Enlightenment, was evident in the "Patent of Tolerance" (1782) issued by Emperor Joseph II of Austria. By this Jews could enroll their children at public schools and their young men at universities. In general, however, the change was more apparent than real, in actual practice. Nonetheless, during the course of the 19th century, young Jews began to attend European universities, at first slowly and then increasingly.

The reforms in 1812 of Karl von Hardenburg, Prussian minister of state, and of Wilhelm von Humboldt, minister of education, opened the universities to Jews. The closed door policy of the universities of Oxford, Cambridge, and Durham, which restricted entrance to Anglicans only, led to a movement for a secular university in England. The opening in 1827 of University College, the foundation school of the University of London, resulted in the admission of dissenters (Catholics and Jews). Finally, a parliamentary law in 1871 abolished the religious tests for Cambridge, Oxford, and Durham. The admission of Jewish faculty members followed that of Jewish students.

In the United States slow but perceptible change was made during the 19th century. Early in the century Joel Hart, possessor of a medical degree from the Royal College of Surgery in London, became a founder of the New York Medical Society and of the College of Physicians and Surgeons in New York. David Levi Maduro *Peixotto received an M.D. from the College of Physicians and Surgeons in 1819 and became professor of medicine at Willoughby College. Lorenzo *da Ponte (Emanuele, son of Geremia and Rachele Conegliano), a convert to Christianity, was appointed in 1830 to the professorship of Italian language and literature at Columbia College. As a poet and famous librettist of Mozart's opera he became one of the early contributors to the development of the teaching of foreign culture at American universities.

The 19th-century Russian policy of repression of minorities, especially the Jews, as well as that of reactionary political philosophy, was instrumental in the exodus of young Jews to universities in Germany and other countries. A Jewish scholar could become a faculty member at a Russian university only at the cost of conversion to the Russian Orthodox Church. The outstanding example of this was Daniel *Chwolson, professor of Hebrew and Syriac at the University of St. Petersburg.

The professional rosters of the German universities indicate the presence of a significant number of Jewish scholars in the 19th century. Jews also made their mark as scholars in Oriental studies in Germany.

The establishment of the first real university in the U.S., the Johns Hopkins University, in 1876, led to the appointment of several Jewish scholars, James J. *Sylvester and Fabian Franklin in mathematics, and Maurice *Bloomfield in Sanskrit and comparative philology. The Hopkins atmosphere was one of learning and research, rather than one of Christian piety. By the end of the 19th century, with the gradual growth of secularism, the spread of science, and the impact of industrialization and business, Jews attended Columbia and other universities in various parts of the United States.

The situation in imperial Russia regarding university attendance by Jews changed somewhat for the better under Czar Alexander II. However, the liberal privileges were severely curtailed under his successor, Alexander III, with the result that only a small percentage of Jews could receive a higher education in Russia during the late 19th century. The Jewish drive for higher education, stimulated by the Haskalah movement, but somewhat inhibited by the anti-secularist influence of the yeshivot, found an outlet in the universities of Germany, Switzerland, and other countries.

Modern Period

The forces which operated during the last decades of the 19th century to liberalize opportunities for Jews as professors and students in higher education were even stronger during the advancing decades of the 20th. The interest by young Jews in new fields of knowledge, such as psychology, sociology, experimental physics, and linguistics, brought about calls for their services when universities expanded their areas of teaching and research. The multiplication of the media of publication brought Jewish research scholars to the attention of academic audiences everywhere.

The growth of democratic sentiment in some countries opened the doors wider to Jewish students. On the other hand, Poland, Hungary, and Romania introduced the *numerus clausus* to limit Jewish enrollment. In Poland, particularly, Jews were relegated to the "ghetto benches" in university lecture halls, while periodic riots were organized by antisemitic students. During the later years of the Weimar Republic, German university students began to harass Jewish students and put pressure on Jewish professors, thus preparing for the academic repression characteristic of the Nazi regime. The opening of the Hebrew University (Jerusalem, 1925) and of the Yeshiva College (now Yeshiva University; New York City, 1928) served notice that Jews were now determined and prepared to undertake an active, leading role in the world of higher education. They would not now merely wait for Christian benevolence and for the vicissitudes of scientific and intellectual development. As time went on during the 20th century, it became evident that in universities in various parts of the world Jewish professors and students were common in virtually all fields of study. Although one cannot say that antisemitic restrictions had been abolished universally, it is clear that in the 1960s it was not at all difficult for capable Jews to make progress as students, professors, and even as administrators in higher education.

A special factor of significance during the 20th century was the impact of the policies of Nazism in Germany and elsewhere in Europe. With the application of the Nazi racial doctrines to the universities, there took place a migration of professors, research workers, and students to other countries, especially to the United States, Canada, England, and Palestine. As a result, higher education all over the world became enriched, even as the university systems of Germany and Austria became impoverished.

Of special interest is the situation in the U.S.S.R., where large numbers of Jews have been enrolled in institutions of higher education, and where professors and research workers have won signal recognition in the universities, institutes, and academies. During Stalin's "black years" (1948–53), however, a drastic reduction of their number took place, when Jewish scholars were dismissed in great numbers from their posts and many of them arrested or exiled. After Stalin's death the situation improved, but the complete absence of discrimination prevalent in the early post-revolutionary period was not restored.

In addition to teaching and scholarship, Jews have made growing contributions, in recent decades, to the administration of higher education (see below). Apart from heading institutions such as Yeshiva University (Bernard Revel, Samuel Belkin) and Brandeis (Abram L. Sachar and Charles Schottland), Jews have served as deans, vice presidents, and presidents of various institutions of higher learning. Among the rectors and presidents are Samuel Steinberg (Prague), Vittorio Polacco (Padua), Paul Klapper (Queens College), Martin Meyerson (University of Pennsylvania), Edward H. Levi (Chicago), Edward J. Bloustein (Rutgers State University of New Jersey), Maitland Steinkopf (Brandon University, Canada), Marvin Wachman (formerly at Lincoln), David N. Denker (New York Medical College), Maurice B. Mitchell (Denver), Jacob I. Hartstein (formerly at Kingsborough Community College, Brooklyn, N.Y.), and Jerome B. Wiesner (MIT). Samuel B. Gould, a convert to Christianity, was president of the State University of New York. David H. Kurtzman, formerly a professor of political science, served as acting chancellor of the University of Pittsburgh. Also to be mentioned are Abraham Flexner, director of the Institute for Advanced Study (Princeton), and Simon Flexner, former professor at Johns Hopkins and Pennsylvania, and director of the Rockefeller Institute for Medical Research (now Rockefeller University).

[William W. Brickman]

In the U.S.

STUDENTS: DATA AND TRENDS. Since the end of the 19th century, the number and proportion of Jewish students in American colleges and universities has increased rapidly, parallel to the growth of the Jewish community and of the American university population in general. In 1890 general enrollment in American colleges and universities was 157,000; it passed a million in 1934–35, reached 2,100,000 in 1946, increased to 3,570,000 in 1960, and virtually doubled once again by 1968, when it reached 7,571,636. The number of institutions of higher learning grew from 998 in 1890 to 2,008 in 1960.

The growth in Jewish enrollment has been equally rapid. By the beginning of the 20th century Jewish university students were numerous enough to permit the founding of Jewish fraternities and Zionist societies and especially of Menorah chapters at several universities. A survey by the Menorah Association between 1911 and 1913 reported 21 Jewish students at Colorado, 400 at Cornell, 160 at Harvard, 100 at Minnesota, 75 at Missouri, 62 at Ohio State, 325 at Pennsylvania, 50–60 at Penn State, 50 at Rutgers, and 70 at Wisconsin.

Prior to World War I, only scattered data about Jewish campus life are available. The first statistical survey of Jewish student enrollment, in 1915, found 7,300 Jewish students, or 3.1 percent of the total student population, at 534 institutions. Subsequent studies showed 14,837 Jewish students (9.7 percent) at 108 institutions in 1919, 104,906 (9.3 percent) in 1,319 institutions in 1953, 200,000 (7.5 percent of the total college population) at 1,610 institutions in 1955, 275,000 (6.5 percent) at 850 institutions in 1963, and 375,000 Jewish students (5 percent) at 840 institutions in 1968. A survey of 59,707 college seniors of the class of 1961 by the National Opinion Research Center found that 8.4 percent were Jews; of these 62 percent were male and 38 percent female, as compared with 67 percent and 33 percent respectively in the non-Jewish student population.

Although the number of Jewish students has increased continually since 1900, the Jewish percentage of the total American college population dropped from 9.3 percent in 1935 to about 5 percent in 1968 as the overall growth of college enrollment moved at a faster pace than the Jewish enrollment. Less than 40 percent of the U.S. college-age population was in college in 1968; the Jewish percentage attending college was nearly 80 percent. More than half of all Jewish students (51.3 percent) attended public institutions, 41 percent were at privately supported colleges, and denominational institutions accounted for 7.7 percent.

New York City continued to have the largest number and proportion of Jewish college students in the world, reflecting its large Jewish population and the city's unique system of tuition-free city colleges. Nevertheless, New York City declined as a center of higher education for Jewish students after 1935, when 53 percent of all Jewish collegians in the United States studied in New York City institutions, to 50 percent in 1946, 38 percent in 1955, and 27.6 percent in 1963. The decrease was due to several factors: growing affluence enabled more parents to give their children a college education away from home; the growth of the State University of New York opened additional opportunities for study at colleges outside the metropolitan area. The liberalization of admissions policy by private colleges, mainly but not exclusively in the east, and the steady movement of the Jewish population from the inner city to the suburbs contributed further to these tendencies.

The distribution of Jewish students by professional fields of study showed 23.6 percent (as compared with 16.5 percent of all students in business administration), 18.9 percent (compared with 28 percent) in education, 17.6 percent (19.8

percent) in engineering, 8.2 percent (3.3 percent) in law, 7.6 percent (3.4 percent) in medicine, and 5.2 percent (1.7 percent) in pharmacology. Other professional fields in which Jewish students were highly represented were dentistry, optometry, psychology, and philosophy; they were proportionately underrepresented in agriculture, nursing, home economics, physical education, and physical therapy (data for 1964).

RESTRICTIVE ADMISSIONS PRACTICES. Jewish students, however, did not always gain admission to the colleges and professional schools of their choice. While admission to institutions of higher learning was, in theory, open to all students who had the necessary scholastic and financial qualifications, many institutions restricted the admission of members of minority groups, including Jews. The use of quotas was rarely admitted, but they were a persistent feature in numerous private institutions, usually reflecting the social prejudices and desire for social homogeneity of the university community, its alumni, and its supporters. In 1922, Harvard president A. Lawrence Lowell defended the existence of a 10 percent quota for Jews at Harvard by expressing concern about "the large and increasing proportion of Jewish students in Harvard College," and his policy was supported by Harvard undergraduates who claimed that "Jews do not mix [and] they destroy the unity of the college" (in: *Harvard Graduates' Magazine*, Sept. 1922). In 1945, Dartmouth president E.M. Hopkins justified a quota for Jewish students by emphasizing that "Dartmouth is a Christian college founded for the christianization of its students." In 1947, President Truman's Commission on Higher Education charged that quota systems and policies of exclusion had prevented young people of many religious and racial groups, but particularly Jews and blacks, from obtaining a higher education and professional training. A study by the American Council on Education (1949) showed that the average Jewish applicant for college admission had considerably less chance of acceptance than a Catholic or Protestant of comparable scholastic ability. In the same year, application forms of 518 colleges and universities and of 88 schools of medicine and dentistry were still found to contain at least one and usually several potentially discriminatory questions.

Restrictive admissions and social practices at universities began to yield to concentrated public criticism after World War II. Many veterans returning to the campus under the GI bill vigorously objected to discriminatory practices in civilian life as incompatible with the mandates of democracy for which the war had been fought. Reports and studies by federal agencies and educational associations criticized restrictive policies. Several states outlawed discriminatory practices in education and employment. As a result, scholastic merit gradually became the major criterion for admission to private institutions, although other factors – geography, preferential treatment of children of alumni, the extracurricular activities of the applicant, the desire for a balanced student body – remained operative. As a result, Jewish enrollment at private institutions rose substantially between 1940 and 1968 (at Princeton from 2 percent to 12 percent, at Harvard to 21 percent, in the Ivy League colleges as a whole to 20 percent).

At the same time, however, many state universities began to restrict their enrollment of out-of-state students. In 1969, 73 (more than one-half) restricted the admission of nonresidents. Inasmuch as New York and New Jersey constituted a major Jewish population center of the United States and both states consistently "exported" large numbers of students because their own college systems could not accommodate all applicants, this restriction grew as an obstacle to the admission of Jewish students in the rest of the country. The demands for the admission of more black students to American universities, especially to tax-supported institutions, also caused increasing concern that such redistribution would cut down Jewish admissions.

FACULTY MEMBERS AND ADMINISTRATORS. While Jewish student enrollment, despite restrictions, rose steadily after the turn of the century, the number of Jewish faculty members remained proportionately small. Before World War I, the supply of qualified American-trained Jewish college teachers was small; but even after the supply increased, restrictive policies continued to bar many Jews from academic appointments until the late 1930s, when burgeoning student enrollment and the demands of enlarged or new institutions created a growing need for additional academic staff. The way was smoothed further by federal and state legislation, especially after World War II, prohibiting discriminatory employment practices. Virtually no ethnic restrictions in faculty appointments have remained. According to a 1968–69 survey, 10 percent of more than 60,000 faculty members of all ranks and from all types of institutions (94.4 percent white) indicated they had been reared as Jews, though only 6.7 percent still gave their present religion as Jewish at the time of the survey. (A similar drop in religious identification was found among non-Jews; the percentages for Protestant faculty members were 64 percent and 45.3 percent; for Catholics, 15.4 percent and 11.8 percent.) At the same time, some leading universities, such as California, Chicago, Columbia, Harvard, Michigan, Pennsylvania, Princeton, the City University of New York, were estimated to have 15–20 percent Jewish faculty. Few Jews could, however, be found among college presidents and other top-echelon university administrators. A 1966 survey found that, although Jews constituted 10–12 percent of the student body at the 775 nonsectarian senior colleges and universities in the United States at that time, only 5 of 397 private and one of 378 publicly supported institutions had Jewish presidents (less than 1 percent). Of the 1,720 deanships at the same institutions, 45 (2.6 percent) were held by Jews; two-thirds of them were, however, concentrated in half a dozen institutions. Eleven (42.3 percent) of the 26 deans of the City University of New York were Jewish in 1966. Jewish deans could be found mainly at graduate schools of social work and schools of government and international affairs. While anti-Jewish restrictions had largely disappeared on the professional level, they seemingly continued to exist on the top level of academic administration. See also *Students' Movements.

By the early 2000s 85 percent of American Jews received some college or university education, and more than 50% received at least a bachelor's degree. In all, it was estimated that more than half the Jews in America under the age of 65 were college graduates.

Jewish Studies

Jewish studies, defined as the systematic study of Judaism and Jewish life and experience through the ages, began to emerge in the American university curriculum to a significant degree only in the late 1930s. The Old Testament and Hebrew had long been taught, but only insofar as a knowledge of the Hebrew Bible was considered necessary for an understanding of Christianity and the training of Christian clergymen.

The first courses in post-biblical Judaism were introduced into the curriculum of American universities only toward the end of the 19th century. The development led to the appointment of the first Jewish scholars to American university posts in Judaica or related subjects. Despite persistent efforts by interested individuals and groups in the Jewish community, the number of institutions offering Judaic studies remained small; in 1945, full-time teaching staff in Judaica could be found only at Berkeley, Chicago, Columbia, Harvard, Iowa, Johns Hopkins, Missouri, New York University, Pennsylvania, and several New York City colleges. The number began to increase rapidly in the 1950s; by 1969, nearly 80 Jewish scholars were teaching full-time in American universities, and courses in Judaica were taught part-time at nearly 200 additional institutions in the country. By 2005 the number of Jewish scholars in the *Association for Jewish Studies (AJS), founded in 1969, was more than 1,500, most of whom were faculty teaching some area of Jewish studies in an institution of higher education, while 20% of the membership consisted of graduate students.

A variety of factors contributed to the growth of Judaic studies, among them the articulation of a growing demand for such studies arising from increased Jewish self-awareness generated by the impact of the Holocaust and the creation of the State of Israel; the democratization of academic policies and admission practices which, together with the increased social mobility and affluence of the Jewish population, led to substantial increases in Jewish enrollment and greater Jewish visibility throughout the United States; the climate of greater acceptance of Jews and Judaism by the general and academic communities, especially after World War II; the growing recognition and acknowledgment of Hebrew as a living language and of Judaism as an essential component in the fabric of Western civilization deserving of serious academic interest and study; and the postwar growth of specialized area studies and of courses and departments of religious studies.

The efforts aiming at the introduction of new or the enlargement of existing programs of Judaic studies were usually spearheaded by Jewish students, faculty members, and Hillel directors, frequently joined by other groups or agencies. Although some of there efforts may also have been stimulated by pressure for the introduction of black studies, university responses were generally based on recognition of the significance of Judaism as a major matrix of Western civilization and of its rightful claim as an authentic field of study. Some Jewish studies programs offered a major for undergraduates either in departments of religion or in departments of Near Eastern studies; others were interdepartmental.

The funds required for the support of Judaic studies came from a variety of sources. About two-thirds of the support for full-time staff was provided by university budgets; 10 chairs of Judaic studies were fully endowed; others were supported by various Jewish communal or private sources. Numerous individual courses were taught by Hillel directors (at 40 institutions) and by visiting staff provided by the Jewish Chautauqua Society, the National Foundation for Jewish Culture, and similar groups.

The number of undergraduates majoring in Judaica was estimated to be about 600 in 1969. A 1972 survey (by the Hillel Foundation) listed more than 350 institutions, not including seminaries and divinity schools, which offered at least one and usually several courses in some area of Jewish studies. Graduate studies leading to an advanced degree could be undertaken at 25 institutions as well as the major rabbinical seminaries and some Hebrew Teachers Colleges. The expansion of programs of Judaic studies in American universities was, at that time, slowed by a shortage of competent academic personnel. By 2005, more than 70 institutions had degree-granting programs of one kind or another in Jewish studies.

[Alfred Jospe]

BIBLIOGRAPHY: H. Hurwitz and L. Scharfman, *The Menorah Movement* (1914); L.J. Levinger, *The Jewish Student in America* (1937); E. Roper, *Factors Affecting the Admission of High School Seniors to College* (1949); R. Shosteck, *The Jewish College Student* (1955); S. Kaznelson (ed.), *Juden im deutschen Kulturbereich* (1959²); A. Jospe, *Judaism on the Campus* (1963); American Jewish Committee, *Jews in College and University Administration* (1966); L. Fermi, *Illustrious Immigrants: The Intellectual Migration from Europe 1930–41* (1968); L.A. Jick, *The Teaching of Judaism in American Universities* (1970); A. Band, in: AJYB (1966), 3–30; A. Jospe, *ibid.* (1964), 131–45; Elbogen, *ibid.* (1943), 47–65; Bloomgarden, in: *Commentary* (Feb. 1960), 112–9; Neusner, in: *Journal of the American Academy of Religion* (June 1969), 131–40.

UNIVERSITY OF JUDAISM, THE (UJ). The University of Judaism was founded in 1947 in Los Angeles, California, based on the vision of Dr. Mordecai *Kaplan who called for an institution that would further Jewish education by advancing the thought and culture of "Jewish Civilization." In his article, "A University of Judaism – A Compelling Need," he outlined the basic elements of his proposed university. He called for a rabbinical school, a school of education, a school of the arts, a research institute, a school of democracy, and a junior college. His paper also called for a school of social service to train Jews, already committed to social work, to view their occupation through the lens of Jewish culture.

In writing his article, Kaplan did not intend to create a west coast institution. Rather, he hoped to convince his *alma mater*, the Jewish Theological Seminary (JTS) to refashion itself in the image he proposed. However, JTS used his blueprint to create a west coast outpost for itself in cooperation with the Los Angeles Bureau of Jewish Education. Initially, an attempt was made to include the leadership of the Orthodox and Reform communities in this effort, but this effort was unsuccessful. Shortly afterward, the Hebrew Union College opened its own branch school, and some years later, Yeshivah University followed suit.

From the very beginning, the University of Judaism had a dual constituency. As the west coast branch of the Jewish Theological Seminary, it had links to the various arms of the Conservative movement, and much of its professional leadership was drawn from the ranks of JTS graduates. At the same time, Kaplan's vision impelled the university to offer broad-based programs geared toward the entire Jewish community. So although the professional leadership was decidedly Conservative, the programs themselves were nondenominational in character and often emphasized the cultural aspects of Jewish life.

The community leadership for the UJ was initially drawn from the entertainment community. The first two chairmen of the UJ's board of directors were writer-producer, Dore Schary, followed by Milton Sperling. The UJ's first president was Dr. Simon Greenberg who also served as vice chancellor of the Jewish Theological Seminary.

Although the university did not implement all aspects of Kaplan's vision, many of its programs reflected the realization of his plan. In the 1950s and 1960s the University of Judaism served primarily as a Hebrew teachers college that also provided adult education courses for the community. David Lieber followed Greenberg as UJ's president in 1963 and began a 29-year tenure. During these early years the university relied almost entirely on part-time faculty and full-time administrators who also taught. Nevertheless, the UJ was able to attract prominent guest faculty including Martin *Buber, Abraham Joshua *Heschel, Leo *Strauss, and Mordecai Kaplan.

Much of Lieber's presidency was marked by a partnership forged with his vice president, Dr. Max Vorspan. While Lieber occupied himself with the academic side of the institution, Vorspan, a devoted Kaplanite, emphasized the growing adult education and cultural programs. Under Vorspan's direction, the UJ launched the first Jewish Elderhostel program in the United States. And although Vorspan retired in 1993, by 2005 the UJ had the largest and most comprehensive Jewish adult education program outside of Israel. In 1956, the UJ also established Camp Ramah in Ojai, California, which still serves both as a summer camp for children and as a retreat center for the UJ.

In the first few years of its existence, the UJ held classes at the site of Sinai Temple in downtown Los Angeles. Later the UJ moved to the former site of the Hollywood Athletic Club where it remained until moving in 1977 to its present 27-acre campus in the suburb of Bel Air.

In 1973 the University of Judaism took its first steps toward independence from JTS when its board of directors, under Jack M. Ostrow, assumed full responsibility for the financial welfare of the institution. The UJ board of directors undertook to finance and build the new Bel Air campus, which was finally completed in the mid-1980s.

During David Lieber's administration, the first full-time faculty members were hired including Bible scholar Ziony Zevit, philosopher Elliot Dorff, educator Ron Wolfson, and historian Steven Lowenstein. Lieber also established a two-year pre-rabbinic program, the Fingerhut School of Education, a graduate school of nonprofit management, and an undergraduate college. At the same time, Vorspan continued to focus on community education and culture by creating programs in the plastic arts, dance, music and theater. His part-time faculty included dancer Bella Lewitsky, actor Benjamin Zemach, and sculptor Max Finkelstein.

With the establishment of its undergraduate College of Arts and Sciences in 1982, the UJ made the transition from Hebrew college to a small university. Since the undergraduate program included majors in areas such as political science, psychology, bio-ethics (pre-medical), and literature, the institution began to hire its first faculty members in scholarly areas outside of Jewish studies. The UJ underwent an academic reclassification, such that it became recognized as an independent liberal arts institution rather than as a type of religious seminary.

In 1991, David Lieber announced his intention to retire from the presidency. Although the University of Judaism had already been functionally independent from the Jewish Theological Seminary for almost 20 years, it was felt that the time had come to transform a *de facto* relationship into a *de jure* one. Lieber negotiated an official separation agreement before stepping down as president in fall 1992.

Lieber was succeeded by Robert Wexler. Wexler had been a member of the UJ faculty and staff since 1978 and was himself a graduate of the University of Judaism having attended there from 1969 to 1973. Although Wexler received his rabbinical ordination at JTS, he also had personal connections to the Reform and Orthodox movements and was an ardent Zionist. These facts shaped his approach to the future growth of the university.

Almost immediately, Wexler began to guide the UJ toward a nondenominational status that he believed to be consistent with the initial vision of Mordecai Kaplan. This realignment meant that the UJ would no longer be formally identified as an institution of the Conservative movement.

The new chairman of the UJ board, Francis Maas encouraged Wexler's efforts.

During the 1990s and early 2000s, the University greater improved its financial position. After many years of deficits, the operating budget was brought into balance. Additionally, the UJ's endowment, which stood at $5 million in 1992, grew to more than $50 million by the end of 2005. The university also undertook to expand its facility by adding a student union and conference center; in 2006, it began construction on its new Ostrow Library.

In 1995, the UJ opened the first American rabbinical school in the western United States, the Ziegler School of Rabbinic Studies. Despite the UJ's nondenominational status within the Jewish community, it was felt that an American rabbinical school should be affiliated with a specific religious movement, and it was determined that the Ziegler School would become an official constituent of the Conservative Movement.

The university continued to expand with the establishment of the Ziering Institute which examines the ethical and religious implications of the Holocaust. A Center for Israel Studies was also created with the purpose of increasing the knowledge of Israeli history, politics, culture, and society among American Jews.

[Iris Waskow (2nd ed.)]

UNJUST ENRICHMENT.

The Concept

The law of *obligations deals with obligations arising from both contract and tort, i.e., those undertaken by the party or parties concerned of their own free will and those imposed by law on a person – against his will – in consequence of damage resulting from an act or omission on his part. There is a further group of cases which fall under a branch of the law known as unjust enrichment and relate to a person's liability which arises neither from his undertaking nor delictual act, but from the fact that he has derived a benefit to which he is not entitled, at the expense of another.

A general exemplification of this class of obligations in Jewish law is the discussion in the Mishnah of the matter of a person who hires from his neighbor a cow, which dies of natural causes after the hirer has lent it to a third party (BM 3:2). One opinion is that the hirer is not liable to the owner for the value of the cow – since the death of the cow is attributable to **ones* and the hirer has no liability for loss resulting therefrom – but the borrower must compensate the hirer (i.e., the person from whom he received the animal) – since the borrower is liable for loss resulting from *ones* (see **Shomerim*). However, R. Yose differs, questioning the hirer's right to "traffic with his neighbor's cow," i.e., it is inconceivable that the hirer shall enrich himself at the expense of the owner of the cow, who is the real loser, without any color of right thereto, and the hirer must therefore restore to the owner the value of the cow received from the borrower. R. Yose's opinion was accepted as *halakhah* (BM 36b; Yad, Sekhirut 1:6; Sh. Ar., ḤM 307:5). The same principle is enunciated by R. Johanan: "it is forbidden for a person to benefit [without authority] from another's property" (BM 117b), and the *halakhah* was decided as follows: "similarly, whenever a person performs an act or benefit in favor of another, the latter may not say, 'you have acted for me gratis since I did not authorize you' but he must give such person his reward" (Rema, ḤM 264:4; see also Ran on Rif, Ket. 107b). The problems of unjust enrichment are treated in Jewish law under the following five headings: (1) rescue of another's life; (2) rescue of another's property; (3) payment of another's debt; (4) improvement of another's property; (5) deriving benefit from another's property.

Rescue of Another's Life

The duty to rescue the life of another when endangered is enjoined in the Pentateuch: "Thou shalt not stand idly by the blood of thy neighbor" (Lev. 19:16). This duty includes the obligation to hire other persons against payment in order to rescue the person in danger (Sanh. 73a), who must refund to his rescuer all the expenses thus incurred by the latter: "For it is not a person's duty to save the life of his fellow with his own money when the person saved has money" (*Piskei ha-Rosh* 8:2; Sanh. 73a; Sh. Ar., ḤM 426:1, Sma and Siftei Kohen ad loc.). It was likewise decided that the heirs of the deceased must refund the expenses incurred by a third person in connection with the medical treatment of the deceased, even if not expended at the latter's request, since a person who of his own accord seeks a cure for the sick must not lose inasmuch as it is a matter of *pikku'aḥ nefesh* ("saving life") and whoever hurries to do so is praised (Resp. Rosh no. 85:2). This too is the law as regards the rescue and ransom of a Jewish prisoner in the hands of a gentile, and the latter – if he has the means thereto – must refund the ransom money to his rescuer (Rema, YD 252:12), since it is inconceivable that such a person "shall enrich his children while being a burden on the community" (Resp. Maharam of Rothenburg, ed. Cremona, no. 32; *Mordekhai* BM sec. 59).

Rescue of Another's Property

Under this heading are included cases in which a person knowingly, and without being requested to do so, acts to the benefit of another in a manner whereby the rescuer does not add to the other anything he did not have before but prevents the latter from suffering pecuniary loss. The basic laws concerning the duty to rescue another's property are expressed in two pentateuchal enjoinders, relating respectively to the duty of restoring lost property (Ex. 23:4; Deut. 22:1–3) and that of releasing an animal lying under its burden (Ex. 23:5; Deut. 22:4). In both cases the duty carries no return consideration (as regards restoring lost property, see Sh. Ar., ḤM 265:1; as regards releasing an animal, see BM 32a; Yad, Roẓe'aḥ 13:7; Sh. Ar., ḤM 272:6). However, the duty to provide aid gratuitously exists only as long as the rescue activities cause no loss to the rescuing party, but when he is likely to suffer loss therefrom he will not be obliged to act gratuitously (BM 2:9; Yad, Gezelah 12:4; Sh. Ar., ḤM 265:1; Tur. ḤM 272:2). The result is that even in cases where the very act of beneficence toward another is imposed as a duty of the Torah, the beneficiary will be obliged, whenever the benefactor has suffered pecuniary loss, to compensate the latter on account of the benefit derived by himself. It was similarly laid down (BM 93b) that a paid herdsman must take precautions against possible circumstances of *ones*, for instance by hiring others to guard against beasts of prey, and that the owner of the herd must pay the herdsman for such expenses. This too is the law as regards any person, who hires people to protect another's herd from the threat of harm, and even though he has acted without being requested to do so by the owner of the herd, is entitled to receive from the latter his expenses and remuneration (Tos. BK 58a).

As regards the duty to compensate the rescuer for a loss he has suffered, a distinction is drawn as illustrated in the following two examples. The Mishnah mentions the case where one person has a jar of wine and another a jar of honey; because of a crack in the honey jar, the owner of the other jar spills his wine and rescues the honey by pouring it into his own jar (the honey being the more expensive) and the Mishnah holds the latter is entitled "to his remuneration [*sekharo*] alone" (BK 10:4, and the further example there cited). According to this Mishnah the beneficiary has to remunerate the rescuer for his efforts alone and is not obliged to refund the latter the cost of his wine. On the other hand, in the Talmud in like circumstances it is stated in the name of R. Ishmael, the son of R. Johanan b. Beroka, that the person pouring out the wine "receives his wine out of the honey of his fellow" (BK 81b; 114b), i.e., that the owner of the wine is entitled to payment of the value of the wine spilled in order to rescue his fellow's honey. The contradiction between the two cases was reconciled on the basis that in the former case the owner of the rescued property was present at the place and time of the rescue but the rescuer, not having sought express consent for his action, is not entitled to a full refund of his expenses or the value of his wine, but only to his remuneration; in the latter case, however, the owner of the rescued property was not present as aforementioned and therefore the rescuer is entitled to a full refund of his expenses (for an explanation of this distinction, see Tos. BM 31b; *Piskei ha-Rosh* BM no. 28; *Mordekhai* BK no. 57).

In contrast to the above cases, the Talmud quotes the case of rescue of another's property (*mavri'aḥ ari* – one who chases away a lion from another's property) without the knowledge of the beneficiary, in which the latter is exempt from making any payment whatever to the rescuer (Ned. 33a; BK 58a; BB 53a). The Talmud mentions two elements which characterize the category of *mavri'aḥ ari* cases in which the rescuer is not entitled to remuneration. First, that the rescuer acted as he did of his own initiative; secondly, that he suffered no loss whatever as a result of such action. Some of the *rishonim* were of the opinion that this category of *mavri'aḥ ari* includes only those cases in which both the above elements operate and that the absence of one of them renders the beneficiary liable to payment for the benefit derived by himself (Tos. Ket. 107b; *Mordekhai* BK no. 57). Others held that this category includes also cases in which only one of the two elements is present and that there is no need for both to operate together (Tos. BK 58a; Rosh, loc. cit.). The *rishonim* added a further requisite for the beneficiary's exemption from payment in *mavri'aḥ ari* cases, namely, that the loss which the rescuer sought to avoid was of doubtful contingency. That is, when it may reasonably be accepted that even without the rescuer's intervention no loss would have occurred, as for instance in the case where the lion was far from the beneficiary's herd. Hence the rescuer will be entitled to payment of his remuneration if the beneficiary, but for the intervention of the former, was certain to have suffered loss (Tos. BK 58a; Rosh and *Mordekhai*, loc. cit.). Yet another material requirement (for the beneficiary's exemption from liability) is that the rescuer's action was not calculated to enrich the beneficiary in any way but merely to have prevented him loss (Tos. Ket. 107b; Tos. BK 58a).

Payment of Another's Debt

This question is discussed in the Mishnah (Ket. 13:2) in relation to the obligation of maintenance, in the case of a person who supports a wife whose husband has gone abroad – without being requested to do so by either the wife or her husband. Some of the *tannaim* hold the benefactor to have "put his money on the horn of a deer" and to have no claim, neither against the wife nor her husband, since he acted as he did of his own accord. Other *tannaim* take the view that the benefactor may deliver an oath as to the exact amount expended on the wife and recover this amount from her husband. The *halakhah* was decided according to the former opinion (Yad, Ishut 12:19; Sh. Ar., EH 70:8).

As regards debts arising from other causes, there is a difference of opinion among the scholars. In the Jerusalem Talmud (Ket. 13:2; 35d) two opinions are quoted. One is that the dispute concerning a debt for maintenance extends also to the case of any other regular debt paid on behalf of another and without the latter's knowledge; the other opinion is that the dispute relates solely to payment of a debt owed by the husband for the maintenance of his wife, but with regard to a regular debt paid on behalf of the debtor, the opinion of all is that it may not be reclaimed from the debtor since it cannot be said that the latter received an absolute benefit because of the possibility that his creditor may have granted a waiver of the debt, and therefore the person who has paid it is in the position of a *mavri'aḥ ari* (see above). From the Babylonian Talmud (Ned. 33a–b; Ket. 108a) it may be concluded, according to most of the commentators, that the dispute relating to a maintenance debt extends also to regular debts. Some of the commentators (R. Hananel and R. Tam) interpreted the statements in the Babylonian Talmud to mean that a debt not arising from maintenance and paid by another may, in the opinion of all, be reclaimed from the debtor because of the certainty of the benefit caused the latter (Tos. Ket. 108a). The majority opinion of the *posekim* is that a person who has paid another's debt of any kind whatever may not recover payment from the debtor (Yad, Malveh 26:6; Sh. Ar., ḤM 128:1; some scholars also explain the debtor's exemption on the grounds that it is a matter of *gerama* – Tos. Ket. 108a).

Improvement of Another's Property

This category includes cases in which a person knowingly, and without being requested thereto, acts so as to confer an actual benefit on another by affording him a gain or increment which he did not previously have. The classic example is the case of a person who "goes down" to another's property to plant it or erect a building thereon, without any request from the owner to do the work or undertaking on his part to pay for it (analagous to the Roman law *negotiorum gestio*). Thus, for instance, if a hired worker should work in the field of a third party, whether in error or because he was directed thereto by his employer, the owner of the field will have to pay for the benefit derived, even though he did not request the work, for otherwise he will be in the position of having been enriched without right at another's expense (Tosef. BM 7:7; BM 76a).

In the case where a person plants another's land without permission, Rav's opinion is that "an assessment is made and he is at a disadvantage," whereas Samuel holds, "an estimate is made of what a person would pay to plant such a field." In the Talmud it is stated that there is no dispute between Rav and Samuel but that Rav refers to a field which is unsuitable for that which has been planted thereon, while Samuel refers to a field which is suitable for such planting (BM 101a). The scholars disputed the meaning of the expression "an assessment is made and he is at a disadvantage." R. Hai Gaon (*Sefer ha-Mikkaḥ ve-ha-Mimkar*, 7:33) and R. Zerahiah ha-Levi (*Ha-Ma'or ha-Gadol* to Rif BM 101a) held it to mean that the planter is only entitled to payment on the basis of the lowest price at which cheap workers can be hired to execute the same work; according to Rashi (BM 101a), Rosh (ad loc.), and others, the expression means that if the planter's expenses exceed the gain derived by the owner of the field then the former is only entitled to the value of such gain, but if the other way round then the planter is only entitled to the sum of his expenses. The *halakhah* was decided that a person who plants another's field without permission is at a disadvantage when the field is unsuitable for such planting, but if it is so suitable an estimate is made of how much one would be prepared to pay for planning that field (Yad, Gezelah 10:4).

Another example is the case where a person whose property surrounds the property of another on all sides fences the interior borders of his property, thereby enclosing at the same time also the surrounded property – without the authority of its owner. In the Mishnah (BB 1:3) there is a difference of opinion as regards the measure of liability of the owner of the surrounded property to pay toward the cost of the fence by which he too is served, and in the Talmud these divided opinions are interpreted in various ways (BB 4b and Codes; Rashi BK 20b; *Ha-Ma'or ha-Gadol* (see above) to Rif BB 4b; cf. Tos. BK 20b; Maim., Comm. to BB 1; *Yad Ramah* BB 4b; Ramban, Nov. BB 4b; *Milḥamot ha-Shem* thereto, etc.). All opinions agree that the owner of the surrounded property has liability for payment toward the costs of the fence from which he benefits, even though he has neither requested its erection nor undertaken to bear the costs thereof; the dispute – even among the *posekim* – centers on the varying measure of his liability, according to the factual circumstances. Liability for payment derives from the consideration that the "enclosing owner" (the *makkif*) is caused special expenses by the surrounded property since it causes a lengthening of the boundaries of the surrounding property and because the owner of the surrounded property benefits without right on account of the special expenses caused to the other (see BK 20b; for a further example, see BK 9:4; BK 101a; Yad, Sekhirut 10:4; Sh. Ar., ḤM 306:3, 6).

The *posekim* did not fail to observe that the consequence of the above law was to submit everyone to the constant danger of being placed in the position where he might be caused a benefit from and become obligated to pay for expenses incurred by his fellow in which he is not at all interested. Hence it was decided that such a beneficiary was to be exempted from liability if he had declared in advance that he had no interest in the proposed benefit and was not prepared to make any payment whatever in connection therewith (*Maggid Mishneh* Shekhenim 3:3; *Beit Yosef* ḤM 155:13).

Deriving Benefit from Another's Property

This category includes the cases in which a person benefits without authority from another's property, the benefit taking the form of a saving of expenses or the prevention of harm. The classical case discussed in the Talmud is the matter of a person who lives on another's property without the latter's knowledge or consent (BK 20a). Four possibilities are discussed: (a) If the premises are anyhow not available for letting and, in addition thereto, it is clear that even without such premises the occupier, for whatever reason, would not have hired some other residence for himself, then the latter is absolved from payment; the explanation for this is that he has neither caused a loss to the owner of the premises nor enjoyed any benefit himself since a benefit is expressed in some measure of monetary gain – nonexistent in this case. (b) If the premises are for hire and the occupier, but for his occupation thereof, would have hired some other residence, he will be liable for payment since he has derived a benefit at the cost of the owner's loss. (c) If the premises are not for hire and the occupier, but for his occupation thereof, would have hired some other residence, he will be absolved from payment since the benefit he has derived is not at another's expense, the owner having lost nothing; however, if enjoyment of the benefit should involve any measure of loss to the owner, the benefit will be at another's expense and the occupier liable for the full value of his benefit (BK 20a–b; Yad, Gezelah 3:9; Sh. Ar., ḤM 363:6–7). (d) Opinions are divided as regards the case where the premises are for hire but the occupier, even without his occupation thereof, would not hire other premises. Some of the *rishonim* held that the occupier, because he derives no benefit, need make no payment at all on account of enrichment at another's expense and that the loss suffered by the owner is in the nature of *gerama* only, for which there is exemption (Tos. BK 20a, R. Perez, quoted in *Mordekhai* BK 16). The majority of the other *posekim* took the view that there is room for holding the occupier liable on account of causing a loss to the owner (Rif, *Halakhot* BK 21a; Yad, Gezelah 3:9; Sh. Ar., ḤM 363:6); that even if it be true that the occupier enjoys no benefit – since he might find some other residence free of charge – he is nevertheless the one who eats up that which is the loss of his fellow (*Piskei ha-Rosh*, BK 2:6).

A person who benefits unawares must pay for the benefit. The laws of *tort prescribe that the owner of an animal is absolved from paying for the produce of another which the animal has eaten up while grazing in a public domain; however, "if you have benefited, you must pay for the benefit" (BK 2:2), i.e., if the owner should derive benefit from the fact that his animal has fed in the aforementioned manner (by saving himself the cost of the animal's feed for that day), he will be liable to the owner of the devoured produce for the value of the benefit, lest he enjoy an undue gain at another's expense (BK 20a and Codes, *Nimmukei Yosef* thereto, TJ, BK 2:4, 3a; see also the difference of opinion there quoted concerning the manner of assessing the value of the benefit; for a further illustration of this class of case, see BK 6:2).

[Yechezkel Rottenberg]

Services Benefiting Another Person Without His Knowledge

As stated, a person who "goes down" to another person's field and plants it is the prototype for cases in which one person benefits another by improving his property in a manner for which a fee is normally charged. However, dicta of halakhic authorities indicate that the service does not necessarily relate to unsolicited improvement of property in the simple sense, and may relate to any service performed for the benefit of others. One of Rashba's responsum (Resp. Rashba vol. 4, no. 125) discusses the case of a person who brought clients to his neighbor's shop. Rashba awarded him a fee, for "What is the difference between a person who goes down… and someone who enters his shop and improves his business, in a place where it is customary to pay a fee for such things."

Another example that engaged the halakhic authorities is that of brokerage or matchmaking without the other person's advance knowledge. A person notified his fellow about a suitable woman whom he then married, or about an appropriate apartment which the latter bought, without any advance contract between them. Some of the *posekim* awarded him a fee on basis of the precedent of "one who goes down to another person's field" (see *Bi'ur ha-Gra*, ḤM 87:7 & 185:3). In another case the *posekim* were divided: Thus, Rema writes (Sh. Ar., ḤM 331:5): "A person who teaches his friend's son without the father being aware, some rule that he is obliged to pay him, by analogy to the law of a person who goes down to another person's field without his knowledge, …while others disagree." There are a two possible rationales for the view of those who disagree: it might be argued that the service rendered is not regarded as a real benefit, similar to the case of improvement of property, either in general or in those particular circumstances; or, that teaching is deemed as a *mitzvah* that ought to be performed *gratis* (see *Taz*, ad loc.). There is also a discussion of whether a judge who has adjudicated between two adversaries without a prior contract is entitled to a fee on the basis of the law of "goes down to another person's field" (see Sh. Ar., ḤM 9:5, *Sema* and *Taz*, ad loc.). It was suggested that this law applies to a service that enhances the financial situation of another person. However, with respect to a service that simply saves the other from incurring a loss, the relevant analogy is to that of a person who saves another's property by chasing away a lion, who is not entitled to remuneration; hence, a bailiff (*shomer*) who protects another person's property without his knowledge is generally not entitled to reimbursement (see *Shenaton ha-Mishpat ha-Ivri*, 13, p. 95).

Indeed, if the insured property was damaged and the insurance company paid its value, there is extensive discussion on the question of who should receive the money: the insurer who paid the premium, or perhaps it could be claimed that "a person should not do business with his neighbor's cow" (BM 35b), and the owner of the property is entitled to the money after he pays the premium to the insurer (see N. Rakover, *Osher ve-Lo be-Mishpat*; M. Slae, *Ha-Bitu'aḥ ba-Halakhah*, ch. 6–7; E. Bazri, *Teḥumin*, 2, p. 449).

[Itamar Warhaftig (2nd ed.)]

BIBLIOGRAPHY: Gulak, Yesodei, 2 (1922), 176f., 199f.; A. Karlin, in: *Ha-Mishpat*, 1 (1927), 214–21; Herzog, Instit, 2 (1939), 49–59; A. Goldberg, in: *Ha-Peraklit*, 8 (1951/52), 314–25; ET, 12 (1967), 1–16; S. Warhaftig, *Dinei Avodah ha-Mishpat ha-Ivri* (1969), 212–28, 279–86, 802ff. **ADD. BIBLIOGRAPHY:** M. Elon, *Ha-Mishpat ha-Ivri* (1988), 2:1279; 3:1424; idem, *Jewish Law* (1994), 3:1526; 4:1697; E. Bazri, *"Shomer she-Bite'aḥ Rekhusho shel Aḥer,"* in: *Teḥumin*, 2 (1981), 449–58; H. Dagan, *"Dinei Asiyyat Osher: Bein Yahadut le-Liberalizm,"* in: *Mishpat ve-Historyah* (1989), 165; B. Jackson, "Introduction to Symposium: Unjust Enrichment," in: *Jewish Law Annual*, 3 (1980), 6; A. Kirschenbaum, *Equity in Jewish Law* (1991); B. Lifschitz, *"Zeh Neheneh ve-Zeh Lo Ḥaser,"* in: *Ha-Peraklit*, 37 (1987), 203; N. Rakover, *Osher ve-Lo be-Mishpat*, pt. 2 (1987); M. Slae, *Ha-Bitu'aḥ ba-Halakhah* (1980); I. Warhaftig: "Unjust Enrichment in Jewish Law," in: *Shenaton ha-Mishpat ha-Ivri*, 9–10, (1982–1983), 187 (Heb.); idem, "Unsolicited Improving of Another's Property," in: *Shenaton ha-Mishpat ha-Ivri*, 13 (1987), 65 (Heb.).

UNNA, PAUL GERSON (1850–1929), German dermatologist. Born in Hamburg, Unna served in the German army during the Franco-Prussian war. He was discharged after being severely wounded, continued his studies and later moved to Vienna where he worked under two famous dermatologists, Moriz *Kaposi and Ferdinand von Hebra. He returned to his native city where he started a private clinic and later a hospital for skin diseases. In 1919 he was appointed professor of dermatology at the University of Hamburg.

Unna is considered a pioneer in applying biological and physical sciences to dermatology. He made studies of the chemical aspects of the skin and by using staining methods he demonstrated changes in the structure of the epidermal cells. He was the first to describe various skin diseases such as sebarrhoic eczema, erythema acneformis, etc. He discovered the Ducrey-Unna bacillus.

[Suessmann Muntner]

UNRRA (abbreviation of **United Nations Relief and Rehabilitation Administration**), international organization (1943–47) founded to give economic and social aid to countries that were under German occupation during World War II. UNRRA, a division of the *United Nations, was actually founded before the establishment of the United Nations, by an agreement signed by the delegates of 44 countries at a White House ceremony on Nov. 9, 1943. The UNRRA Council, its governing body, was convened for the first time in Atlantic City, New Jersey the next day, and elected Herbert *Lehman as its director general; he was succeeded by Fiorello *La Guardia in 1946. The United States contributed the bulk of its budget and the organization received significant support from Britain, the Soviet Union, and China, which provided 75% of its budget and formed its central committee. It was later expanded to include other countries, including France, Canada, Australia, Brazil, and Yugoslavia. The relief activities of UNRRA encompassed the liberated countries of Europe, with extensive aid provided for the Soviet Union, Poland, and the Balkan countries. Relief was also given to Far Eastern and Middle Eastern countries. The services supplied amounted to almost $3 billion and included food supplies amounting to over $1.2 billion, medicines and medical services, clothing, and machines and materials for agricultural and industrial rehabilitation.

Another prominent function of UNRRA was care for *Displaced Persons, for which it assumed responsibility in October 1945. It was overwhelmed by the task at first – no one had prepared for the scope of the problem – but later it geared up to perform the task. At its peak, in the summer of 1946, UNRRA cared for some 850,000 persons. During this period, it operated with a staff of about 25,000 people and was also assisted by many voluntary agencies. About one-quarter of the Displaced Persons under the care of UNRRA in the summer of 1946 were Jews. Voluntary Jewish organizations active within UNRRA and attached to it included the American Jewish *Joint Distribution Committee, the *Jewish Agency, the Jewish Committee for Relief Abroad, *Ort, and the Va'ad Hazzalah. UNRRA activities ended in the summer of 1947, when its role in the care of DPs was transferred to the new International Refugee Organization (IRO).

BIBLIOGRAPHY: G. Woodbridge, *UNRRA*, 3 vols. (Eng., 1950). **ADD. BIBLIOGRAPHY:** M.R. Marrus, *The Unwanted European Refugees in the Twentieth Century* (1985); M.J. Proudfoot, *European Refugees: 1939–1945* (1956).

[Chaim Yahil / Michael Berenbaum (2nd ed.)]

UNSCOP, abbreviation of the United Nations Special Committee on Palestine, appointed by the General Assembly of the United Nations at a special meeting convened in April 1947 at the request of the British government. The committee consisted of 11 members, representing the governments of Australia, Canada, Czechoslovakia, Guatemala, India, Iran, The Netherlands, Peru, Sweden, Uruguay, and Yugoslavia. In their report, published in August 1947, the majority recommended the partitioning of Palestine into an independent Jewish state, an independent Arab state, and an internationalized "*corpus separatum*" for the city of Jerusalem. This recommendation was approved by the General Assembly of the United Nations on November 29, 1947.

UNTERMAN, ISSER YEHUDA (1886–1976), Ashkenazi chief rabbi of Israel. Born in Brest-Litovsk, Belorussia, he studied at the Maltash, *Mir, and *Volozhin yeshivot and was ordained by R. Raphael Shapiro. At the age of 24 he was appointed *rosh yeshivah* in Vishova, Lithuania, and served subsequently as rabbi of various Lithuanian communities. His last position there was as rabbi of *Grodno during 1921–24. Possessing oratorical and expository talents of a high order, he attained a distinguished record during World War I as a communal leader after representing the community before the authorities, and in the postwar period he displayed outstanding organizational gifts in the reconstruction of the Lithuanian yeshivot. In 1924 he was appointed rabbi of *Liverpool, England, and, rapidly mastering English, soon made his influence felt. A fervent Zionist, he became president of the British Mizrachi Organization and appeared before the Anglo-American Committee of Inquiry on Palestine in 1946. He championed the rights of aliens and was a member of the Council of Christians and Jews.

In 1946 Rabbi Unterman was elected Ashkenazi chief rabbi of Tel Aviv-Jaffa in succession to Rabbi M.A. *Amiel, and in 1964, Ashkenazi chief rabbi of Israel, succeeding Rabbi I. *Herzog. During his period of office in Tel Aviv he organized the rabbinic courts, making them a model of efficiency. He founded two *kolelim* (graduate talmudical academies) – Shevet mi-Yhudah in Tel Aviv and Shevet u-Meḥokekim in Jerusalem – where he introduced a systematic method of Talmud study, based on the practical *halakhah*, for select students preparing for the rabbinate and for service as religious functionaries and teachers in advanced yeshivot. While he insisted on unflinching loyalty to the minutiae of the *halakhah*, he approached public issues with moderation and understanding. In 1952 he toured the U.S. on behalf of the United Jewish Appeal and helped to strengthen the relationship between the American and Israel rabbinates. Rabbi Unterman wrote *Shevet mi-Yhudah* (1952), on problems of *halakhah*. He contributed to many rabbinical periodicals and made valuable additions to the *Ozar ha-Posekim*, the digest of responsa literature. Many of his responsa appear in the works of others and are a model of lucidity.

BIBLIOGRAPHY: Tidhar, 3 (1958²), 1510f.

[Jacob Goldman]

UNTERMEYER, LOUIS (1885–1977), U.S. poet, author, anthologist, editor, and translator. The son of a New York jewelry manufacturer, Untermeyer entered his father's firm as a designer and rose to be its vice president. Largely self-educated, he was chiefly interested in literature and in 1923 retired from business to devote himself to poetry. A prolific writer and skilled editor, Untermeyer published more than 70 volumes of prose and verse, short stories, travel books, parodies, essays, and critical anthologies. His earliest collection of lyrics, *First Love* (1911), was composed under the influence of *Heine and Laurence Housman; his second, *Challenge* (1914), showed greater maturity. His other collections were *These Times* (1917), *The New Adam* (1920), *Roast Leviathan* (1923), *Burning Bush* (1928), *Food and Drink* (1932), and *Long Feud: Selected Poems* (1962). His humorous verse includes *Collected Parodies* (1926).

Untermeyer's lifelong interest in Heine found expression in a volume of translations, *The Poems of Heinrich Heine* (1917), and in the two-volume biography, *Heinrich Heine: Paradox and Poet* (1937). He reproduced the spirit of the dying Heine with much pathos in the poem "Monolog From a Mattress." *The Firebringer and Other Great Stories: Fifty-Five Legends That Live Forever, Newly Written by Louis Untermeyer* appeared in 1968. His fictional works include the biblical novel *Moses* (1928). It was, however, with his interpretations and anthologies of English and American poetry that Untermeyer was most influential. Outstanding among these were his *Lives of the Poets* (1961) and the *Britannica Library of Great American Writing* (1960). Another of his anthologies was *The World's Great Stories* (1964). Two volumes of autobiography, *From Another World* (1939) and *Bygones* (1965), portrayed not only his own development but also the period in which he lived. *The Letters of Robert Frost to Louis Untermeyer* appeared in 1963.

JEAN STARR UNTERMEYER (1886–1970), also a poet, was Louis Untermeyer's wife from 1907 until 1923. Born in Zanesville, Ohio, she became a singer in Vienna and London, taught literature in various schools and colleges, and wrote several books of verse, including *Growing Pains* (1918), *Steep Ascent* (1927), *Love and Need* (1940), and *Later Poems* (1958). She published her autobiography, *Private Collection*, in 1965.

BIBLIOGRAPHY: LOUIS: E.L. Pound, *EP to LU: Nine Letters Written to Louis Untermeyer by Ezra Pound* (1963), incl. bibl.; S. Liptzin, *The Jew in American Literature* (1966), 141–9; *Current Biography Yearbook 1967* (1968), 423–6. JEAN STARR: L. Untermeyer, *American Poetry since 1900* (1923), 227–33; *Twentieth Century Authors*, first suppl. (1955), s.v.

[Sol Liptzin]

UNTERMYER, SAMUEL (1858–1940), U.S. lawyer and civic and communal leader. Untermyer, born in Virginia and raised in New York City, graduated from Columbia Law School in 1878. A member of the prestigious firm of Guggenheimer, Untermyer and Marshall, he engaged in a varied legal practice, including corporate, civil, criminal, labor, family, and international law. He achieved national prominence as counsel for the Congressional Committee known as the Pujo Committee which in 1912 investigated the "money trust." Untermyer's contribution to the drafting and passage of such legislation as the Federal Reserve Act, Federal Trade Commission Act, and Clayton Anti-Trust Act was substantial. A political liberal, he exerted considerable influence on Democratic political affairs, especially in New York City. His participation in Jewish affairs included service as attorney for Herman Bernstein who sued Henry Ford in 1923 following antisemitic attacks in Ford's *The Dearborn Independent*; vice president of the American Jewish Congress; president of the Palestine Foundation Fund; and, during the 1930s, president of the Non-Sectarian Anti-Nazi League and leader in the boycott of German goods.

BIBLIOGRAPHY: M. Gottlieb, in: AJHSQ, 57 (1967/68), 516–56.

[Morton Rosenstock]

UR, one of the largest towns in Sumer and later in Babylonia. Today it is a wide expanse of ruins in which stands a high tell, the ruins of the Ziggurat of Ur, known as al-Muqayyar. Ur developed on the bank of a large canal, which carried water from the Euphrates to the area and served as an important trade route, through which trade boats passed to Ur's two ports. In present times the canal is silted up and the entire region is desolate.

The origin of the name Ur is not clear. Some maintain that it is the Sumerian word *uru*, meaning "town." Some point to the group of cuneiform symbols in which the Sumerian name is written, and translate the name as: "the place of the dwelling of light." In the Bible, the city is referred to as Ur of the Chaldeans (Heb. אוּר כַּשְׂדִּים), since in the biblical period it was included in the area occupied by the Chaldeans.

According to the legendary tradition of Sumer, Ur was settled even before the flood and was the center of a dynasty of rulers, each of whom reigned for thousands of years. In later periods too the rule of Sumer and Akkad was in the hands of a dynasty of kings, whose capital was Ur. The English scholar Taylor was the first to undertake excavations on the site (1854), and it was he who identified the tell of Ur, on the basis of an inscription from the time of Nabonidus king of Babylonia. At the end of the 19th century, an expedition on behalf of the University of Pennsylvania excavated at Ur, but the results of this excavation were not published. In 1918, the English scholar Campbell Thompson conducted an experimental excavation on behalf of the British Museum, and a short while later (1918–19), the English scholar Hall excavated, on behalf of the same institution, at Ur, Eridu, and el-Ubaid, near Ur. A joint expedition on behalf of the University of Pennsylvania and the British Museum led by Sir Leonard *Woolley excavated at Ur for 12 consecutive seasons (from 1922 to 1934). Although only a small section of the area of ruins was excavated, the reports of the last expedition make it possible to know the history of the town and its cultural development from its beginnings to its final destruction. It began in the Chalcolithic Era (beginning of the fourth millennium B.C.E.).

At the end of the fourth millennium B.C.E. there are sudden signs of a new culture. After a long period there was a great flood that (according to Woolley) wiped out most of the settlements in an area of 100,000 sq. km, in the region of the lower reaches of the Euphrates and the Tigris. Only the towns located on high places, including Ur, were saved. Outside the wall of Ur, in its lower environs, Woolley found a layer of red soil without any archaeological remains, about 2.5 m. deep, which separated the early remains (below) from the later ones (above). According to Woolley it is possible that a reference to this terrible tragedy is reflected in the Sumerian-Babylonian flood mythology. However, his theory is not accepted by other scholars.

Above this "barren" layer from the time of the flood is a large cemetery from the time of the first dynasty of Ur (26th–25th centuries B.C.E.) with which the historical period of Sumer and Akkad begins. Here were found the tombs of several kings and queens. Later, Ur was transferred from one conqueror to another. Among these, mention should be made of Eannatum king of Lagash, Lugal-zagge-si king of Umma and Erech (Uruk), and Sargon of Akkad, all of whom left sacred vessels in the temple at Ur. In the 22nd century, Ur was apparently again ruled by a dynasty of local independent rulers. However, Ur reached its peak of power and development during the "Third Dynasty of Ur" (c. 22nd–21st centuries B.C.E.). Ur-Nammu, founder of this dynasty, was at first the governor of Ur on behalf of Utu-hegal of Uruk. After freeing himself from the domination of Uruk, he apparently succeeded in extending his rule to all the towns of Sumer. He also called himself "king of Sumer and Akkad," though the extension of Ur's domination outside the boundaries of Sumer occurred primarily in the time of his son and heir Shulgi, who called himself, like the kings of Akkad, "king of the four corners of the earth." During his reign, which lasted 47 years, Shulgi extended the borders of his kingdom and conquered Assyria. However, at the end of Shulgi's time the danger of the Amorites was already threatening Ur from the northwest. In the time of his successors there was an additional danger from the northeast: the consolidation and expansion of Elam. In the time of Ibbi-Sin, the last king of the third dynasty of Ur, the Sumerian and Akkadian monarchy of Ur was defeated in its battles against the invading Western Semites (Amorites) and Elam (in the northeast). Ur never recovered from this blow, although it did enjoy some additional periods of religious or economic flourishing, such as in the middle of the second millennium B.C.E. (in the time of Kurigalzu I, of the Kassite dynasty of Ur) and the beginning of the seventh century B.C.E. (in the time of Essarhaddon's active governorship). From the 11th century B.C.E., the area was occupied by the nomadic tribes of the Chaldeans; hence the biblical combination Ur of the Chaldeans. The numerous architectural changes made in the time of Nebuchadnezzar II (beginning of the sixth century B.C.E.) in the religious sphere of Ur attest to this king's attempt to infuse a new spirit into the cult of Sin in Ur. This too, however, did not help Ur. Similarly unhelpful were the attempts of Nabonidus (in the middle of the sixth century) to encourage this cult. From that time on there is no mention of Ur in the historical sources. The latest commercial document discovered in Ur is from 400 B.C.E., i.e., from the time of Persian rule. It may be assumed that not long afterward the town was destroyed and abandoned, although a Hellenistic tradition from the second century B.C.E. can be interpreted to mean that during that period the place still served as a kind of center for nomadic Arab tribes.

According to biblical tradition, Ur was the place of origin of the Patriarchs (Gen. 11:28, 31). Indeed, the first quarter of the second millennium B.C.E., with the economic decline of Ur after the downfall of the third dynasty and the emergence of the Amorites from the west, was a fitting time for the migration from Ur of various families who were not tied to Ur as were farmers who were enslaved to the soil. From there the Patriarchs wandered to Haran; this wandering too is explained by the special ties between these two centers of the moon-cult.

BIBLIOGRAPHY: L. Woolley, *Ur of the Chaldees* (1929); idem, *Ur, The First Phases* (1946); idem, *Excavations at Ur* (1954); W.F. Albright, in: BASOR, 140 (1955), 31–32; 163 (1961), 44; C.H. Gordon, in: JNES, 17 (1958), 28–31; H.W.F. Saggs, in: *Iraq*, 22 (1960), 200–9; A. Parrot, *Abraham et son Temps* (1962), 14–52; A.F. Rainey, in: IEJ. 13 (1963), 319; P. Artzi, in: *Oz le-David* (1964), 71–85; I. Ben-Shen, *ibid.*, 86–91.

[*Encyclopaedia Hebraica*]

URBACH, EPHRAIM ELIMELECH (1912–1991), Israeli researcher in talmudic and rabbinic literature. Urbach, who studied in the Breslau Rabbinical Seminary and at the universities of Breslau and Rome, served as lecturer at the Breslau Rabbinical Seminary from 1935 to 1938. After immigrating to Ereẓ Israel in 1938, he subsequently served as a teacher and headmaster of grammar schools in Jerusalem. During the years 1950–53, he was an inspector and head of a department in the Ministry of Education and Culture. From 1953 he taught *aggadah* and subsequently rabbinical literature at the Hebrew University and in 1958 became professor of Talmud. During the years 1956–60, he served as head of the Institute for Jewish Studies and in 1960/61 he was prorector. In 1962 he was elected chairman of the section of Jewish affairs of the Israel Academy of Sciences and Humanities and from 1980 to 1986 was president of the Academy.

Urbach's studies cover practically every branch of research in the Talmud and in rabbinic literature. His most important work is the *Ba'alei ha-Tosafot* (1956 and later editions), for which he was awarded the Israel Prize. This deals with the history of the *tosafists and their creations and, at the same time, illuminates both their Jewish and gentile historical, social, and ideological background, and analyzes their methods of study, their methodological theories, and their contribution to the development of the *halakhah*. In this large work that touches on all the problems connected with its field, Urbach shed light on one of the most neglected sections of Jewish history in general and rabbinical literature in particular. He also published the *Arugat ha-Bosem* (vols. 1–4, 1939–63) of *Abraham b. Azriel, with notes and a comprehensive introduction. Urbach's interest also turned to the religious and theological principles of rabbinic Judaism. He contributed several important articles in this field to various *festschriften* and periodicals. He has incorporated his researches in this field in an important book, *Ḥazal: Pirkei Emunot ve-De'ot* ("The Rabbis: Doctrines and Beliefs"; 1969) in which he outlines the views of the rabbis on the important theological issues such as creation, providence, and the nature of man. In this work Urbach synthesizes the voluminous literature on these subjects and presents the views of the talmudic authorities. In addition he published numerous articles (in Hebrew, English, French, and German) discussing, among other topics, the history of the *halakhah*, the ideological world of the rabbis, the aggadic Midrashim, and medieval polemical literature. Great importance is attached to those studies in which he proved the close connection between the *aggadah* and Christian-Jewish polemic. From 1970 Urbach was the editor of *Tarbiz*, and president of *Mekiẓe Nirdamim. In 1966 Urbach was a founder of the *Tenu'ah le-Yahadut shel Torah* ("Movement for Torah Judaism"), one of whose aims was to bring about basic and progressive changes in the politics and values of religious Jewry in Israel.

[Moshe David Herr]

URBINO, town in central Italy, formerly capital of an independent duchy. The earliest record of Jews dates from the beginning of the 14th century, when Daniel of Viterbo was authorized to trade and open a loan bank. His family long continued to head the community. Other loan bankers, ultimately eight in number, received authorization to operate later. However, in 1468 a monte di *pieta was established in Urbino in order to restrict Jewish activities. In the 15th century the dukes of the house of Montefeltro favored Jewish scholars and were interested in Jewish scholarship; Federico II collected Hebrew manuscripts. When the duchy passed to the Della Rovere family in 1508, they enacted a more severe policy, not rigidly enforced. Hebrew books were burned in Urbino in 1553 and in 1570 the ghetto was introduced, with all the accompanying indignities. The degraded status of the Jews was confirmed when the duchy of Urbino passed under papal rule in 1631. At this time there were 369 Jews (64 families) in the town, a number that steadily decreased thereafter. In 1717 they were mostly poverty-stricken; many houses in the ghetto were empty, and the synagogue itself was partly owned by non-Jews. There was a temporary improvement with the invasion of the French revolutionary armies, but during the reaction of 1798 anti-Jewish excesses took place. Papal rule, with the accompanying degradation, was reestablished with intervals from 1814 to 1860, when Urbino was annexed to the kingdom of Italy and full emancipation automatically followed. Nevertheless the community continued to decline in number and now is virtually extinct.

BIBLIOGRAPHY: Milano, Bibliotheca, index; Milano, Italia, index; C. Roth, *Personalities and Events in Jewish History* (1953), 275–82; Vitaletti, in: *Giornale storico della letteratura italiana*, 85 (1925), 98–105; G. Luzzatto, *Banchieri ebrei in Urbino*… (1902).

[Cecil Roth]

URI, PIERRE EMMANUEL (1911–1992), French economist. Uri was born in Paris. From 1936 to 1940, he taught in the U.S. In 1944 he entered public service, with the Institut de Science Economique Appliquée. From 1947 to 1951, he taught at the École Nationale d'Administration concurrently serving with the United Nations Experts Committee on Employment. In 1952 he became chief economist with the European Coal and Steel Community and left in 1959 to join *Lehman Brothers as their adviser on European affairs (1959–61).

Among his numerous publications were the following: *La Réforme de l'enseignement* (1937); *Le Fonds monétaire international* (1945); *La Crise de la zone de libre échange* (1959), published under the pseudonym "Europeus"; *Dialogue des continents* (1963, 1964²); *Partnership for Progress*, 1963); and *Une politique monétaire pour L'Amérique latine* (1965).

[Joachim O. Ronall]

URIAH (Heb. אוּרִיָּה), the name of four biblical figures (in one case in the variant form Uriahu). The most important of these is Uriah the Hittite, listed as one of David's "heroes" in II Samuel 23:39. While Uriah was away on one of David's campaigns (II Sam. 11), the king noticed his young wife *Bath-Sheba bathing on the roof of her house. He had the young woman brought to him and lay with her. When Bath-Sheba informed him that she was pregnant, David had Uriah recalled from the front in an attempt to cover his sin, but the attempt failed because Uriah felt bound by a vow or a general taboo to shun conjugal relations for the duration of the war. David then sent Uriah back to the very thick of the battle in the hope that he would be killed, which is what occurred. David then married Bath-Sheba and incurred the rebuke of the prophet *Nathan for his behavior.

There have been many attempts by scholars to explain the origin and name of Uriah. H. Gunkel dismissed the whole story as a legend having no historical basis. However, the story may have been well based and Uriah could have been one of the original Jebusite inhabitants of Jerusalem. This people, from whom David conquered the city, were probably of Hittite origin. A. Gustavs identified the name as a Hebrew folk etymology of the Hurrian name Ariya. The name would then mean something like king or ruler. B. Maisler (Mazar) suggested that the name could originally have been a compound of the Hurrian element *ur* plus the name of a pagan god, which then received an Israelite form. S. Yeivin compared the name Uriah with the other Jebusite name mentioned in the Bible, *Araunah (perhaps from the same root), and suggests that Uriah may have been a high official or perhaps the intended successor of that last Jebusite ruler of Jerusalem.

[Daniel Boyarin]

In the Aggadah

Uriah was not a Hittite; the name merely indicates that he dwelt among them (Kid. 76b). It was Uriah who revealed to David how the various suits of armor of Goliath were joined together so that David could remove them and cut off the head of the giant. Uriah did this on condition that David secure him a Jewish wife. David kept his promise and thus it was that Uriah married Bath-Sheba (unknown Midrash quoted by Moses Alshekh on II Sam. 13). Uriah had incurred the death penalty by his refusal to take his ease in his own house in accordance with the king's command (Shab. 56a); this amounted to an act of rebellion. However, the sin of David was that he did not put him to death, but let him be killed by the sword of the Ammonites (II Sam. 12:9) which was an abomination (Zohar Ex. 107a).

The other bearers of the name Uriah in the Bible include a priest in the reign of Ahaz (Isa. 8:2; II Kings 16:10f.), a priest in the time of Nehemiah (Ezra 8:33; Neh. 3:4, 21; 8:4), and with the slightly variant form of the name, Uriahu (אוּרִיָּהוּ no doubt understood as "YHWH is fire [or light]"), a prophet killed by Jehoiakim (Jer. 26:20–23) for prophesying doom like Jeremiah

BIBLIOGRAPHY: A. Gustavs, in: ZAW, 33 (1913), 201ff.; Noth, Personennamen, 168; H.L. Ginsberg and B. Maisler, in: JPOS, 14 (1934), 250–61; S. Yeivin, in: *Zion*, 9 (1944), 49–69; B. Maisler, in: *Yedi'ot*, 13 (1947), 105ff; URIAH THE HITTITE IN THE AGGADAH: Ginzberg, Legends, 4 (1913), 88, 103, 126; 6 (1928), 252, 256, 264–5.

URI (Phoebus) BEN AARON HA-LEVI (also called **Uri Witzenhausen** or **Witmund**; 1625–1715), Hebrew printer. Uri's father was *ḥazzan* of the Neveh Shalom congregation, Amsterdam, and his grandfather Moses Uri ha-Levi, rabbi of Emden and one of the founders of the Portuguese Jewish community in Amsterdam. Uri established his first press in Amsterdam in 1658 and was active there until 1689. He published numerous rabbinical and religious works, some of them in Yiddish, including the first Yiddish translation of the Bible by Jekuthiel Blitz (1679); the *Josippon* (1661); and the *Bava Bukh* (1661) by Elijah Baḥur *Levita. Uri also published the first Yiddish newspaper, which appeared every Tuesday and Friday (*Dienstagishe un Freytagishe Kurant* 1680–87). The greater part of the works he printed were for distribution among the Jews of Poland. In 1692 he moved to *Zholkva where he was reportedly invited by the Polish king John Sobieski to print Hebrew books, which previously were imported from abroad. At the sessions of the Council of the Four *Lands in Jaroslaw in 1697 and 1699, Uri obtained rabbinical backing against business competitors in Lublin and Cracow. His press was continued by his children and their descendants for some time after his death. His descendants include the author and poet Meir ha-Levi *Letteris whose father Gershon was still printing in Zolkiev in 1828, including those works written by his son.

BIBLIOGRAPHY: M. Letteris, *Zikkaron ba-Sefer* (1848), 12–13; idem, in: *Bikkurim*, 1 (1844), 52f.; Steinschneider, Cat Bod, 3061–63; M. Erik, *Di Geshikhte fun der Yidisher Literatur* (1928), 232–9; Ḥ.D. Friedberg, *Toledot ha-Defus ha-Ivri be-Polanyah* (1950), 62–64.

URI BEN SIMEON OF BIALA (second half of the 16th century), emissary of Safed to Europe. Uri was born in Biala, Poland, and immigrated to Ereẓ Israel, settling in Safed. From there he was sent as an emissary of the Ashkenazi congregation of the city to Italy, Germany, and Poland. In 1575 he was in Verona, as well as Venice, where he published, one year on each page, a 40-year calendar, and *Yiḥus Avot*, a description of the holy places and the graves of the righteous in Ereẓ Israel. He took these pages, which served to publicize his mission, with him to Germany, where they were reprinted many years later by Christian theologians.

The calendar was reprinted in 1594 in Frankfurt by Jacob Christmann, and *Yiḥus Avot* was reprinted twice in a Latin translation by Johann Heinrich Nottinger, under the title *Cippi Hebraici*, with drawings (Heidelberg, 1659 and 1662). This list of holy places and graves of the righteous in Ereẓ Israel served emissaries of succeeding generations as a pattern for similar lists called *Iggeret Mesapperet Yeḥusta de-Ẓaddikei de-Ara de-Yisrael* ("A genealogical tree of the righteous of the Holy Land," Venice, 1626, 1640, 1646, 1649; Verona, 1646, 1647; Mantua, 1676; Frankfurt, c. 1700).

BIBLIOGRAPHY: Yaari, Sheluḥei, 80f., 248.

[Avraham Yaari]

URIEL, one of the four angels of the Presence first mentioned in I Enoch 9:1. Together with Michael, *Gabriel, and *Raphael he addressed a prayer to God requesting Him to bring to an end the rule of violence and bloodshed which the *Nephilim had brought to the earth. In His reply God charged Uriel with announcing to Noah the "end of all flesh" which would be brought about by the flood. Along with the other angels of the Presence, Uriel served as a guide to Enoch in the upper heavens (I En. ch. 19ff.), but his particular function was to govern the army of angels and the *Netherworld, Sheol (20:1). It would appear that this same function is mentioned in I Enoch 75:3ff.: "[Uriel], whom the Lord of glory hath set for ever over all the luminaries of the heaven, in the heaven and in the world, that they should rule on the face of the heaven and be seen in the earth, and be leaders for the day and the night." A special function is assigned to Uriel in IV Ezra (II Esdras), where he replies to Ezra's questions on the state of the world and the divine plan for the world and the people of Israel. By means of visions, he reveals to Ezra the course and duration of the present age and the conditions of life and the place of the people of Israel in the new world to come (II Esd. 4ff.).

According to *Midrash Rabbah* (Num. 2:10), Uriel is one of the four angels whom God placed around His throne. In the Kabbalah (including the Zohar), these angels of the Presence are identified with the four holy beasts which *Ezekiel saw in the *Merkabah and the figure of Uriel with that of the eagle, and sometimes with that of the lion. These four angels shed their light on the four winds of heaven, and the light which is shed over the west, the most perfect light, is that of Uriel. The Zohar (I, 6b; III, 32b, 211a) ascribes to Uriel a special function in connection with the sacrifices at the time of the First Temple. The altar, which is called *Ariel (Isa. 29:1–2), is thus named because of Uriel, who descended in the likeness of a lion to crouch on the altar and devour the sacrifices. At his descent, the hearts of the priests and the children of Israel were gladdened for they recognized thereby that the sacrifices had been accepted with favor. The appearance of Uriel in the altar fire caused all those who could see the flames to suffer a change of heart and repent. Yet for Israel's sins Uriel's primary strength was taken from him, and instead of the fire containing divine inspiration a strange fire descended on the altar, which took the form of a [demonic] dog. In several passages of the Zohar, Uriel and Nuriel are the same angel, seen under different aspects. He is called Uriel under the aspect of mercy, but Nuriel under the aspect of rigor and severity.

BIBLIOGRAPHY: S.A. Horodetzky, in: *Sefer Klausner* (1937), 277–82; R. Margaliot, *Malakhei Elyon* (1964²), 5–10; Zunz, Poesie, 470; P. Bloch, in: MGWJ, 37 (1893), 18ff.

[Joshua Gutmann]

URIM (Heb. אוּרִים; "Lights"), kibbutz in Israel's western Negev 7½ mi. (12 km.) W. of Ofakim, affiliated with Iḥud ha-Kevuẓot ve-ha-Kibbutzim. Urim was founded as one of the 11 settlements established on the same night in the South and Negev (Oct. 6, 1946). Its members included Israeli-born settlers and immigrants from Bulgaria and the United States. Its farming was irrigated in part by water from the National Water Carrier and was based on field crops, citrus groves, poultry and dairy cattle. Noam Urim Enterprises Ltd. was the largest nonwoven needle punch processing plant in the Middle East. Its products included finished wipes and rolled fabrics and waddings for different industries. In 1970 the kibbutz had 384 inhabitants; in the mid-1990s the population rose to 545, but then dropped to 413 in 2002.

[Efraim Orni / Shaked Gilboa (2nd ed.)]

URIM AND THUMMIM (Heb. אוּרִים וְתֻמִּים), a priestly device for obtaining oracles. On the high priest's *ephod (an apronlike garment) lay a breastpiece (חֹשֶׁן) – a pouch inlaid with 12 precious stones engraved with the names of the 12 tribes of Israel – that held the Urim and Thummim (Ex. 28:15–30; Lev. 8:8). By means of the Urim, the priest inquired of YHWH on behalf of the ruler (Num. 27:21; cf. Yoma 7:5, "only for the king, the high court, or someone serving a need of the community"); they were one of the three legitimate means of obtaining oracles in early Israel (Urim, dreams, prophets; I Sam. 28:6). Owing to the oracular character of the Urim, the breastpiece is called "the breastpiece of decision" (חֹשֶׁן הַמִּשְׁפָּט). (The concept evokes "the Tablets of Destiny" in Babylonian mythology – the symbol of supreme authority that lay on the breast of the chief god; Pritchard, Texts, 63, 67, 111.) The right to work this oracle was reserved for the levitical priests (Deut. 33:8).

Occasionally the term ephod is used with reference to the Urim-oracle associated with it (I Sam. 14:3, 18 [according to LXX]; 23:6, 9; 30:7). The latest period for which there is evidence of use of the ephod-Urim is that of David (but cf. Hos. 3:4); subsequently, oracles are conveyed exclusively by prophets. In postexilic times, when the Urim oracle was extinct, difficult questions were reserved "until a priest would appear with Urim and Thummim" (Ezra 2:63; Neh. 7:65; cf. Sot. 9:12: "After the former (i.e., pre-exilic) prophets died, the Urim and Thummim became extinct"; and Josephus (Ant. 3:218), who avers that the oracle ceased 200 years before his time).

There is no biblical information on the appearance of the Urim, the material out of which they were made (the Samaritan text of Ex. 28:30; 39:21 adds a command to manufacture the Urim and tells of its execution), or the technique of their use. The most illuminating passage is the Greek of I Samuel 14:41, whose underlying Hebrew is mutilated in the received texts: הָבָה תָמִים, conventionally rendered "Give a perfect answer":

> Saul said: "O YHWH God of Israel, why have you not answered your servant this day? If the guilt be in me or in my son Jonathan. O YHWH God of Israel, give Urim (הָבָה אוּרִים). But if this guilt is in your people Israel, give Thummim (הָבָה תֻמִּים)."

(For a defense of the received Hebrew, however, see M. Tsevat. in *Sefer Segal* (1955), 78–84.)

From the use of the verbs *hippil* and *nilkad* in connection with the Urim (verses 41–42), it appears that they were a kind of lot ((marked) stones or sticks?), since these verbs occur in connection with the casting of lots (Isa. 34:17; I Sam. 10:20). They were suitable for indicating which of two alternatives was right; hence inquiries to be decided by them were designed to elicit "yes" or "no" answers (I Sam. 23:10–12;30:8).

The etymology of the terms is obscure. From the Greek passage adduced above, it seems that the two terms are the names of two objects. Hence the conjecture that Urim derives from *ʾarar*, "curse," and Thummim from *tammam*, "be whole," indicating negation and affirmation respectively. Tradition has connected the first term with light (*ʾor*) or instruction (Aram. *ʾoraita*). Thus both Greek δήλωσις καὶ ἀλήθεια, "declaration/revelation and truth," and Vulgate *doctrina et veritas*, "teaching and truth," treat the pair as a hendiadys meaning true instruction – with reference to the oracle. (An apparent derivative with this meaning is the novel coinage אורתום, found in the Qumran Thanksgiving Psalms Scroll with reference to divine illumination (4:6, 23; 18:29; see J. Licht's commentary to 4:6)). A talmudic interpretation finds an allusion to the unequivocalness of the oracle in two words: "They cause their message to be lucid [מאירין]… and carried out [משלימין]" (Yoma 73b).

The earliest speculation on the technique of the oracle is reflected in Josephus (Ant. 3:217), who states that victory was forecast by the shining of the stones in the breastpiece. The talmudists fancied that the oracle was spelled out by the miraculous protruding of letters out of the tribal names engraved on the stones (Yoma 73b; Maim. Yad, Kele ha-Mikdash, 10:11). Rashi takes account of the separate existence of the Urim by making them a document bearing the tetragrammaton, whose presence inside the breastpiece insured the clarity and perfection of the oracle (comment to Ex. 28:30 and Yoma 73a; cf. Samuel b. Meir, who calls the Urim a kind of conjuration by divine names). Naḥmanides (at Ex. 28:30) combines the various strands of interpretation: the Urim was a text bearing divine names placed inside the breastpiece, by virtue of which various letters out of the tribes' names lit up; the Thummim were other divine names by whose virtue the priest was able to combine the letters perfectly into the divine message.

[Moshe Greenberg]

In the Aggadah

To the names of the 12 tribes engraved on the breastpiece were added those of the three Patriarchs, together with the word *shevet* ("tribe") so as to encompass the whole alphabet (Yoma 73b). Interpreting Urim to mean "those whose words give light" and Thummim as "those whose words are fulfilled," the rabbis explain that the oracle was effected by rays of light shining on the letters, or protruding from them and forming themselves into groups (Yoma 73b), so that the high priest could read them. Only priests speaking by means of the holy spirit and upon whom the *Shekhinah* rested could invoke them. The inquirer had his face directed toward the high priest, who directed himself to the *Shekhinah*. One did not inquire either in a loud voice or silently in his heart, but like Hannah, who muttered her prayer (I Sam 1:13). Only one question was to be put at a time, and if two were asked, only the first was answered. However, if the occasion required two questions, both were answered. Unlike the decrees of a prophet, those of the Urim and Thummim could not be revoked. Only a king or a head of the Sanhedrin could inquire from the Urim and Thummim (Yoma 73a–b). The division of the land was effected by means of the Urim and Thummim (BB 122a). Saul and David consulted them (Mid. Ps. 27:2). The Urim and Thummim ceased to give oracular answers immediately after the death of the first prophets (Sot. 9:12), i.e., the destruction of the First Temple (Sot. 48b). However according to the Jerusalem Talmud (Sot. 9:14, 24b), the "first prophets" refers to Samuel and David and according to this view the Urim and Thummim did not function in the First Temple period either.

BIBLIOGRAPHY: N.H. Tur-Sinai, *Ha-Lashon ve-ha-Sefer*, 3 (1956), 103–13; De Vaux, Anc Isr, 349–53; A. Cody, *A History of the Old Testament Priesthood* (1969); E. Robertson, in: VT, 14 (1964), 1–6. IN THE AGGADAH: Ginzberg, Legends, 3 (1911), 172–3; 4 (1913), 75–76; 6 (1928), 69–70; Guttmann, Mafteʿaḥ, s.v.

URIS, family of U.S. builders and philanthropists. Percy Uris (1899–1971), who was born in New York City, entered the investment building business in 1920 with his father Harris Uris (1870–1945), a Lithuanian immigrant and previously an ornamental iron manufacturer. Uris Brothers eventually became one of the largest building companies in the United States, and when its various real estate and building holdings were merged into the Uris Buildings Corporation in 1960, Percy Uris became president. His brother Harold Uris (1905–1982), who was born in New York, entered the building business with his father and brother in 1925, and he became chairman of the board upon the firm's amalgamation in 1960. A patron of the arts, he served on the board of the New York City Center for Music and Drama. He also served as a trustee of the New York Federation of Jewish Philanthropies for many years.

In 1957 Percy and Harold founded the Uris Brothers Foundation as a means to "give something back" to the city that had been so accommodating to their father and to their own entrepreneurial endeavors. The foundation has donated millions of dollars to New York City charities, especially those that deal with education and housing.

URIS, LEON (1924–2003), U.S. novelist. Born in Baltimore, Uris joined the U.S. Marines at the age of 17 and participated in the campaigns on Guadalcanal and Tarawa Islands in the Pacific. On his return to the U.S., he worked for a San Francisco newspaper and then used his war experience in writing his first work, *Battle Cry* (1953), which was acclaimed as a major war novel. For another book, *The Angry Hills* (1955), Uris drew on the war diary of an uncle who was a member of the Palestine Brigade that fought in Greece. Two of his novels, *Exodus* (1958) and *Mila 18* (1961), dealt exclusively with the momentous events of recent Jewish history. Uris' other works include *Armageddon* (1964), on the Berlin airlift; *Topaz* (1967), a novel about Soviet anti-NATO espionage in France, with some savage satire against General De Gaulle; and *QB VII* (1970; made into a drama for television, 1974), about a libel suit brought by a doctor against an author who had written that the former had conducted medical experiments in a concentration camp during World War II.

Exodus, one of the greatest fiction sellers in American history, depicts the establishment of the State of Israel. Before writing it, Uris read 300 books on Israel and the Middle East, traveled throughout Israel, and interviewed 1,200 people there. *Mila 18* deals with the Jewish community in the Warsaw Ghetto and describes how the Jews finally revolted against the Nazis. Like *Exodus*, it was read by millions and enhanced Uris' reputation as a novelist, although both books were criticized for their awkward prose. Several of Uris' novels were made into motion pictures, the film version of *Exodus* by Otto Preminger being released in 1960. Uris also wrote a photo essay, *Exodus Revisited* (1960). Uris was also a screenwriter for *Battle Cry* (1955) and *Gunfight at the O.K. Corral* (1957).

He collaborated with his wife Jill, a photographer, in *Ireland: A Terrible Beauty: The Story of Ireland Today* (1975) and *Jerusalem, Song of Songs* (1981). His later works include *Trinity* (1976), *Redemption* (1995), and *O'Hara's Choice* (2003).

BIBLIOGRAPHY: M.M. Hill and L.N. Williams, *Auschwitz in England* (1965). **ADD. BIBLIOGRAPHY:** K. Cain, *Leon Uris: A Critical Companion* (1998); Gale Literary Databases/Contemporary Authors Online, "Leon Uris" (2004).

[Harold U. Ribalow]

URMAN, DAN (1945–2004), Israeli archaeologist and historian. Born in Haifa, Urman completed his military service (1963–65), and began studying archaeology and history at the Hebrew University in Jerusalem. Between 1965 and 1968, Urman made a countrywide investigation of the archaeological remains within abandoned Arab villages. Following the 1967 war, Urman was appointed the staff officer for the antiquities of the Golan Heights, and in the following years he studied many ancient sites there, notably at Rafid, including salvage excavations at some of them. On completing his M.A., Urman undertook his doctoral studies at New York University. His Ph.D. dissertation was completed in 1979 with distinction and published in 1985 as *The Golan: A Profile of a Region During the Roman and Byzantine Periods* (BAR Int. Series, Oxford). In 1979 Urman joined the faculty of the Ben-Gurion University of the Negev at Beersheba. Urman conducted numerous excavations, but he is best remembered for his excavations at the Byzantine site of Nessana in the Negev between 1987 and 1995. Among his numerous publications, one should note his books *Ancient Synagogues: Historical Analysis and Archaeological Discovery* (1995, co-edited with P.V.M. Flesher) and *Jews, Pagans and Christians in the Golan Heights* (1996, co-authored with R.C. Gregg), and, just before his death, the first volume of his excavation report *Nessana* (2004).

BIBLIOGRAPHY: V. Avigdor Hurowitz and S. Dar, "Obituary: Dan Urman (1945–2004)," in: *Bulletin of the Anglo-Israel Archaeological Society*, 22 (2004), 83–85.

[Shimon Gibson (2nd ed.)]

URUGUAY, South American republic, general population: 3,080,000; Jewish population: 24,200.

The Beginning

There are few documents relating to Jewish history during the colonial period in Uruguay. In 1726 the governor of *Montevideo, Bruno Mauricio de Zabala, still adhered to the accepted Spanish formula when he stipulated that the first settlers be "persons of worth, of good habits, repute and family, so that they be not of inferior nor of Moorish or Jewish race," and in 1760 Pedro Lago, a clergyman from Colonia del Sacramento, expressed to the Inquisition his suspicions regarding the existence of Jewish life in his city. More reliable sources, however, are lacking. With the demise of the Inquisition in 1813, the political and legal system prevailing in Uruguay, together with its tolerant population, provided the viable foundation for Jewish residence during the modern period.

The Modern Period

BASIC DATA. Geographically Uruguay is the smallest country in South America. The last official estimate of Uruguay's area is 186,925 km^2 (instead of the former estimation of 187,500 km^2). Of its 3,080,000 inhabitants, 1,200,000 (40%) live in the capital Montevideo.

Prof. Sergio DellaPergola of the Hebrew University of Jerusalem concluded that the number of 50,000 Jews in Uruguay often mentioned in different publications is unfounded and exaggerated. Instead he concluded that the number of Jews between 1936 and 1992 was as follows:

1936–1940: 25,000
1945–1946: 37,000
1990–1992: 24,200

Some 13,000 former Uruguayan Jews live in Israel. This is the highest proportion of *aliyah* from the Free World.

MODERNIZATION. The independent Uruguayan Republic was definitively established in 1830. In more recent times, the Constitution of 1918, championed by José Batlle y Ordóñez, established the principle of separation of church and state and defined the legal status of aliens, as well as their role in the political life of the country. The generally liberal-minded public, as well as the constitution, which accords social and economic equality to native and alien alike, provided the conditions for a successful Jewish community from the 1920s. The constitutions of 1934 and 1952, which altered the composition of the government, did not affect the prevailing legislation. The earliest available information about Jewish immigration to Uruguay dates from 1898; a 1909 report indicates that there were 1,700 Jews in the country, 75% of whom were Sephardim, the rest of them Russian, Romanian, Polish, and of Alsatian origin. Other reliable sources based on first-hand documentation from the first communal institutions, consistently report about a 50–50 parity between Sephardim and Ashkenazim from the beginning until the 1920s.

Immigration increased notably between 1925 and 1928, when Uruguay also served as a transit point – in some cases for illegal transit – to Argentina, which at that time had stringent immigration regulations. In 1933 there was again an increase in immigration, although just prior to World War II new limitations were imposed. In 1939 2,200 Jews entered the country, while in 1940, only 373.

KEHILLOT, ZIONISTS, AND ANTI-ZIONISTS. The Zionist movement began in 1911, when Dorshei Zion was founded, initially as an extension of the Argentinean Zionist Federation. The events affecting world Jewry and the activities of the Zionist movement evoked sympathy and support from the Jewish populace. During World War I, mass demonstrations acclaimed the Balfour Declaration, members of the community joined the Jewish Legion, protests were registered against the pogroms in Central Europe during the 1920s, and campaigns were staged to protest the Arab riots in Palestine in 1928–29. The Zionist movement was divided into the separate organizations of General Zionists, Po'alei Zion, Mizrachi, Revisionists as well as to WIZO and later on smaller women's organizations. For many years there was a "key" for the distribution of functions in the Consejo Central Sionista (later Organizacion Sionista del Uruguay), in the KKL, and in the KH: president – General Zionists; vice president – WIZO; secretary general – Po'alei Zion (Mapai); treasurer – Mizrachi, and so on. In 1945 the Zionist movement began to gain great momentum. The Consejo Central Sionista, comprising representatives of all the institutions, including the Federación Juvenil Sionista, was formed, and in 1960 the Federación Sionista Territorial Unificada, renamed in 1963 Organizacion Sionista del Uruguay (OSU), was founded as a central body of all Zionist parties and organizations as well as the Jewish Agency in charge of *aliyah* and other Zionist endeavors, including youth, pioneer, women's institutions, etc.

In 1970 the Montevideo Jewish community comprised four *kehillot*: Comunidad Israelita de Montevideo (Ashkenazi, founded in 1932), with 4,000 members; Comunidad Israelita Sefaradí (founded in 1932), with 1,500 members; Nueva Congregación Israelita (German-speaking, founded in 1936), with 1,500 members; and the Sociedad Israelita Hungara – SIHDU – (founded in 1942), with 200 members. The cemeteries of Ashkenazim and Sephardim, both on the outskirts of Montevideo, together with the respective *ḥevra kaddisha* funeral associations, were established a short time after World War I. As a matter of fact, the *kehillot* in Uruguay (and also in Argentina) evolved from a *ḥevra kaddisha* to a more diversified communal structure. Later on, the Yiddish-speaking communist sector established its own secular cemetery. The four *kehillot* noted are united under the umbrella organization Comité Central Israelita (CCI), which is affiliated with the *World Jewish Congress. The presidency of the CCI alternates between representatives of the four communities. Established in 1940 as the overall representative of the Jewish community vis-à-vis the government, the CCI played a pivotal role in combating antisemitism, especially during World War II, during subsequent sporadic resurgences of neo-Nazism, and at the time of Adolf *Eichmann's capture and trial. The vast majority of the leadership of the communities was Zionist. Consequently, the CCI usually maintained pro-Zionist positions and policies.

One of the former presidents of the CCI, professor of criminal law Nahum Bergstein, was later a senator, deputy minister of education and culture, and a member of the House. He introduced in the Uruguayan Parliament important resolutions concerning human rights, antisemitism, and solidarity with Israel in its struggle against terrorism.

Parallel to growing identification with Zionism among most Jewish inhabitants of Uruguay, there were also during the second and third decades of the 20th century isolated expressions of syndicalism; militant anti-Zionist Yiddishism; a small but very active Bund, especially in the cultural field through the I.L. Peretz Association; and a large, well organized Yiddish-speaking communist sector, self-defined as "progressive Jewry" as opposed to "national (Zionist) Jewry." The most important organization for the latter was the Asociación Cultural Jaim Zhitlowsky (founded around 1935), which also had a youth organization consisting of 300 members. Members of the Asociación received medical benefits provided by the Mutualista Israelita del Uruguay (founded 1940), and the Asociación maintained the above-mentioned separate, secular (non-religious) cemetery. Partisan discord characterized relations between the Zionist and "progressive" blocs, particularly during the 1930s. In the face of steadily increasing antisemitism, in 1938 an attempt was made to forge a united front through the short-lived Comité Contra el Nazismo y el Antisemitismo in order to defend the community and represent it vis-à-vis the government. Nevertheless, the confrontation between both sectors continued and deepened particularly after the Hitler-Stalin agreement of August 1939, openly backed by the Jewish "progressive" local daily *Unzer Fraint*, and the bankruptcy of the "progressive"-dominated "Banco Israelita," which badly affected the savings of recently arrived refugees from Germany and annexed Austria. After the establishment of the State of Israel and during the Stalinist persecutions of 1948–52, some "progressives" joined the ranks of the Zionist-oriented community; the majority, however, maintained their pro-Communist affiliations. The situation was not the same among their younger generation: part of them assimilated and another part went over to the Zionist youth movements and their presence in Israel, especially in kibbutzim and academic life, is visible and successful.

ECONOMY. At first the Jews in Uruguay engaged primarily in minor commerce (food, clothing, used articles), peddling, light industries (needles, leather, furs, textiles), independent or salaried crafts (tailors, hairdressers, watchmakers, printers), and salaried jobs (construction, factories). During the 1929–33 economic crisis, the Jewish community suffered severely, but it regained prosperity with the economic revival. At the same time, the German immigration of the 1930s gave impetus to commerce and minor crafts, and the economic upswing continued during World War II. In 1970 industry, commerce in textiles, furs, furniture, pharmaceutical products, plastics, metallurgy, and electronics were well established. Members of the professions occupied intermediate positions on the economic ladder, and a small number of Jews were partners in agricultural corporations that dealt in rural land and its products.

Attempts at Jewish agricultural settlement in Uruguay proved abortive. The first was the "19 de Abril" settlement, founded in Paysandú by 38 families that had previously tried to settle in the ICA settlements in Brazil. They received 9,880 acres of land from the Institute de Colonización of the Uruguayan Republic. Overcoming a difficult beginning, the settlers met with success after a ten-year period, but the settlement gradually lost its Jewish members; during the 1930s, five Jewish families remained, and in 1950 there was only one. Another Jewish colony founded in 1924 in Mercedes failed shortly afterward. The third, the "Tres Árboles" settlement (1938–39), was a Communist-inspired Jewish venture, but it failed primarily because of the bankruptcy of the Banco Israelita del Uruguay, on which it depended. Its collapse in 1939 precipitated a chain of bankruptcies among small merchants and industrialists and brought about the failure of the agricultural settlement "Tres Árboles." The bank managed to reopen and resume operations, however. The Centre Commercial e Industrial Israelita del Uruguay (1933), known from 1950 as the Banco Palestino-Uruguayo, was a well-established institution with branches even outside the country. In Israel it worked in particular with Bank Leumi. Later on, it was acquired by other general, non-Jewish financial enterprises. Two well-established commercial cooperatives, originally peddlers cooperatives, were the Corporación Comercial SA (pro-Zionist, founded in 1930) and the Cooperative Comercial del Uruguay (progressive, founded in 1936), which closed with the collapse of the Banco Israelita and recommenced activities in 1945 under the name La Amistad. There are still, here and there, some Jewish peddlers, but with large shopping centers and the extensive use of credit cards, this is undoubtedly an outmoded and old-fashioned source of "parnose" (livelihood), classical among Jewish immigrants in the whole American continent. The predominantly labor, artisan, and small business class of the 1920s gradually gave way to a social group of middle class merchants, industrialists, salaried employees, and professionals, with few laborers and few wealthy individuals.

In the early 21st century, the younger generation of Uruguayan Jews includes a very high proportion of professionals. People tried to reach upper class or upper middle class standards of living even when their wealth was in many cases more apparent than real, at least by international Western criteria. At the same time the remaining lower middle class Jews (such as small merchants or employees in small businesses or factories) were in a very unsure and weak economic situation. Even when they arrive in Israel when making *aliyah* or immigrate to other countries, their adaptation to different languages and present-day technological requirements is far from easy.

ANTISEMITISM. In January 1919, under the pretext of repressing revolutionaries and Bolsheviks and as a result of the events during Argentina's "Tragic Week," punitive measures were taken against workers and certain elements of the lower class. Eighty percent of the Jewish population was investigated by the police and there were many instances of imprisonment and expulsion.

During the 1930s "anti-alien" campaigns were organized, posing a serious threat to the Jewish community. Their instigators were radical nationalists and local and foreign Fascists (Vanguardia de la Patria), but large numbers of traditionally liberal elements also participated. Familiar forms of racial discrimination were invoked in sidewalk demonstrations, in the press, and on the radio. The alien character of the Jews was underscored, and demands were voiced for a ban on Jewish immigration and for the exclusion of Jews from commercial activities and other sources of income. The community organized itself in self-defense. Measures against the rise of Fascism were adopted by the administration of General Alfredo Baldomir (inaugurated 1938), and during World War II the community enjoyed the protection of the government. During the Eichmann trial (1961) serious antisemitic disturbances were provoked by local neo-Nazi associations linked to foreign cells. The Jewish community, supported by certain branches of the government and liberal political and intellectual groups, organized its defense once again. In the 1960s there were sporadic antisemitic outbursts associated with nationalist-radical and neo-Nazi-affiliated groups, some of them originating in Argentina.

EDUCATION, YOUTH, RELIGIOUS LIFE, AND JEWISH MEDIA. Since their inception, both the Ashkenazi and the Sephardi communities have maintained religious studies. In 1929 the Ashkenazi *ḥevra kaddisha* established an educational network in collaboration with ICA. The most prominent educational institutions were the Zionist Herzl School founded in 1928; the Talmud Torah Eliezer ben Yehuda, founded in 1928 by the Sephardi *ḥevra kaddisha;* the Scholem Aleichem School founded in 1941 by the left Po'alei Zion; the Mizrachi school and Yeshivah ha-Rav Kook, founded in 1945, which added the Ma'aleh secondary school in 1956; and the ultra-Orthodox *talmud torah* and *ḥeder* Adat Yere'im, founded in 1948. In the early 21st century Jewish education was concentrated in three big integral schools (day schools): the Integral School, the Ariel School (which includes the former schools Scholem Aleichem and Ivriah), and the Yavne School (religious Zionist). All of them include kindergarten, elementary school, and secondary school, and all are Zionist – their Jewish program is handled by Israeli teachers and local teachers who complete one year of pedagogical studies in Jerusalem. The curriculum includes in general subjects, in addition to Spanish and Hebrew, and also English. The so-called "workers' schools," active from 1925 to the 1950s, followed the Yiddishist, leftist, non-Zionist ideology. The only remaining school of this trend is the Jaim Zhitlowsky school (founded in 1930). The Jewish ORT School, specializing in hi-tech, is recognized as a university. Even though a large proportion of its students are not Jews, the curriculum also includes a program of Jewish studies. The educational network is coordinated by the Vaad-Hachinuch, the "Education Ministry" of Uruguayan Jews.

Informal education is given by the Zionist and pioneer youth groups, including Bnei Akiva, Dror, Ha-Shomer ha-Ẓa'ir, Ha-No'ar ha-Ẓiyyoni, Israel ha-Ẓe'ira, and Betar. Local youth organizations include the Hebraica-Macabi (social and sports activities); Juventud Sefaradí; and the youth section of the Nueva Congregación Israelita. A pivotal function was filled in the past by the student organization Union Universitaria Kadimah (founded in 1940), later continued by the Association of Professionals "Jaim Weizman." The activities of all Zionist-oriented youth-organizations are coordinated by the Federación Juvenil Sionista (founded 1941). The "progressive" youth is organized in the Federación Juvenil Jaim Zhitlowsky, which has two centers. Its membership declined in the post-Stalin period.

In view of the predominantly secular trends in the community, there is little religious extremism. Basic tradition is observed, and the communities assume responsibility for the fulfillment of ritual. There are small groups of extreme Orthodox Jews who came from Hungary and Transylvania in the 1950s and formed the Kehillah Adat Yere'im. But they are members of the Ashkenazi community and submit to its decisions. An interfaith organization made up of Catholics, Evangelists, and Jews is active in promoting inter-religious harmony and engages in social work.

Cultural life is predominant and is integrated into the program of the majority of the communal social, political, and educational institutions, such as B'nai B'rith. For the most part, the cultural activities are of an informative character on subjects of both Jewish and general interest and are usually carried on in Spanish. Among members of the older Ashkenazi generation, Yiddish continues to be spoken. A small number of Hebraists tried on different occasions to establish a Moadon Ivri. A few authors among the first generation wrote original literary works on Jewish philosophical, religious, and historical themes in Yiddish and Hebrew. Authors of the second generation wrote essays and literature of a general nature in Spanish. *YIVO has a branch in Uruguay with an archive and a library, and the Jewish writers and journalists had, in the recent past, their own association.

The Jewish press in Uruguay was at first closely linked with the Argentinean press. Starting in 1920 with the Spanish *Voz Hebrea* through the dailies *Der Tog* and *Morgentsaytung* of the 1930s, the Uruguayan Jewish community still had three dailies in the 1960s: *Folksblat* (founded in 1934), *Haynt* (founded in 1957), and the Communist *Unzer Fraynt* (founded in 1935). All of them closed. The only surviving publication in the early 21st century was the Spanish weekly *Semanario Hebreo* (founded in 1954). In the past a Zionist religious weekly *Der Moment* (founded in 1940) also appeared. There were several other periodicals, the most prominent being the *Gemeindeblatt* (founded in 1938), a weekly of the German-speaking community.

There are 14 Orthodox and one Conservative synagogues, with two Orthodox and two Conservative rabbis. The Chabad Center, with its own rabbi, has no communal affiliation. The Jewish schools are attended by 40% of the Jewish children. Nearly all of Uruguay's 24,200 Jews live in the capital, Montevideo. About one hundred families live in Paysandu. Many Jews – particularly Argentineans – come to the Punta del Este summer resort for the summer and even for weekends during the rest of the year. As a result, there are four synagogues functioning in the summer and one year-round.

In the past an important function was performed by the Jewish radio broadcasts. The most important were "Hora Cultural Israelita" continued later by "Voz de Sion en el Uruguay." Both of them transmitted daily except Yom Kippur from 12 to 14:30. They began in the 1930s and the last broadcast of "Voz de Sion" was in 2000. Another daily program, called "Hora Israelita Polaca," was transmitted two hours daily until the 1960s. All of them were Zionist-oriented and used Spanish and Yiddish alternatively. The German-speaking Jews have two daily broadcasts in German, one at lunchtime and one in the evening, even though both of them try to define themselves as "international and interconfessional." There were also weekly broadcasts.

The official government TV station included a once-a-week, one-hour transmission (on Sunday morning) dedicated to Jewish matters and to the relationship with Israel. The program was halted, but there is a similar program today (2005). Jewish institutions intensively use the Internet. For example, the German-speaking community, instead of its former German weekly *Gemeindeblatt*, now disseminates information and comments in Spanish through the Internet.

[Rosa Perla Reicher / Nahum Schutz (2nd ed.)]

Relations with Israel

Immediately after the Balfour Declaration of Nov. 2, 1917, promising British backing for the establishment of a Jewish National Home in Palestine, the Uruguayan government initiated a clear-cut policy in favor of the Zionist aspirations. The main champion of that policy, Dr. Alberto Guani, was Uruguay's delegate at the 1920 *San Remo Conference of the League of Nations establishing the British Mandate on Palestine, specifically destined to foster the realization of the Balfour Declaration.

The same Dr. Guani was President Alfredo Baldomir's foreign minister in 1940, valiantly facing very direct and crude threats from Adolf Hitler during the *Graf Spee* affair: the giant battleship *Graf Spee*, described by Churchill as "the terror of the South Atlantic," was badly mauled by three small British destroyers near the Uruguayan summer resort of Punta del Este. The ship reached the neutral port of Montevideo and Dr. Guani decided that by international law the ship would be permitted to bury the dead, leave the wounded in hospitals, and repair its engines but not its guns. Berlin pressed strongly but Dr. Guani did not yield. The *Graff Spee* left Montevideo and sank itself. At that time Uruguay was an honorable exception, since the rest of the Latin American countries oscillated between a pro-Nazi or pro-fascist position or – at least – a kind of neutrality. Instead, Uruguay was openly anti-Nazi.

In April 1947, Uruguay was among the nations that voted for the establishment of the United Nations Special Committee on Palestine (UNSCOP), one of whose members was Prof. Enrique Rodriguez Fabregat of Uruguay. Rodriguez Fabregat, together with the delegate of Guatemala, Dr. Jorge Garcia Granados, was the architect of the partition plan approved by the UN General Assembly on Nov. 11, 1947, including the establishment of a Jewish state in Palestine.

Friendly relations between the two countries began with the enthusiastic support of Uruguay for the new state. Two successive Uruguayan presidents, Tomas Berreta and Luis Batlle Berres, strongly favored the policy advocated by Rodriguez Fabregat who was advised by the historian of the Near East, Prof. Oscar Secco-Ellauri, future Uruguayan foreign minister and president of the Uruguay-Israel Institute of Cultural Relations.

Uruguay was also the first Latin American country, and the fourth country in the world, to recognize the State of Israel (May 19, 1948). Montevideo was the first Latin American capital and the fourth city in the world in which an Israeli diplomatic representation was set up (Nov. 1, 1948). On May 11, 1949, Uruguay stood out in its negative vote on the question of international administration over Jerusalem. The Uruguayan legation established in Tel Aviv in 1951 was transferred to Jerusalem in 1956. After the Six-Day War (1967), Uruguay was among the states that abstained in the UN vote against the union of Jerusalem. Later on, under strong international pressure the diplomatic representation was transferred from Jerusalem to Herzliyyah.

Streets in the capital of each country have been named in honor of the other, and parliamentary delegations have exchanged visits. The two countries have signed a trade and maritime agreement, and a forest has been planted in the Judean Mountains honoring the Uruguayan national hero, Artigas (1958). A forest named "Uruguay" was also planted in the hills of Western Galilee. Also in 1958, the diplomatic representations in Montevideo and Jerusalem were raised to the status of embassies, and the foreign ministers of each state exchanged visits at different opportunities. A visit by the president of the State of Israel to Uruguay and the reciprocal visit of Uruguayan ministers, members of parliament, scientists, authors, and artists have been dear expressions of the friendly relations between the two states. When the then foreign minister of Israel, Moshe Sharett, visited Uruguay in 1953, he signed a cultural agreement with the government. The Uruguay-Israel Institute for Cultural Relations has been set up there. In 1968 the export from Israel to Uruguay was $214,000 and in 1969 it was $212,000. Israel imported $3,360,000 worth of goods from Uruguay in 1968 and $4,433,000 worth in 1969. Israel exports mostly minerals and chemicals to Uruguay and imports meat and wool. A trade agreement was signed between the two countries on June 13, 1968, and an agreement for scientific and technical cooperation was signed at the same time. Uruguay is one of the most important exporters of meat to Israel and during various periods Israel was the number one client for Uruguayan meat. An agreement for cooperation in the field of atomic development was signed on June 23, 1966. Israel had provided Uruguay with scholarships in such fields as agriculture, cooperative living, social work, and education. Years ago, a post-graduate scholarship in medicine was awarded to the present-day (2005) Uruguayan president, Dr. Tabare Vazquez.

The state of the relations between Uruguay and Israel as of 2005 can be summed up as follows:

1) Excellent bilateral relations.

2) As far as the Middle East conflict is concerned, Uruguay is no longer the idealistic "Don Quixote" backing Zionism for idealistic reasons. Uruguay has continued to be more friendly to Israeli positions and more responsive to issues such as terror and open antisemitism than other countries, but under pressure from various international parties, its voting record vis-à-vis anti-Israel proposals is not positive – at best its representatives abstain.

Cordial relations between the two peoples, on the non-governmental level, were fostered from the mid-1980s on by the Asociacion de Amistad Israel-Uruguay. The Uruguayan embassy cooperates intensively with the association and, in addition, some cultural initiatives are undertaken by the embassy through the framework of a foundation specifically dedicated to that type of activity.

[Nissim Itzhak / Nahum Schutz (2nd ed.)]

BIBLIOGRAPHY: J. Beller, *Jews in Latin America* (1963), 218–30; J. Shatzky, *Yidishe Yishuvim in Latayn-Amerike* (1952), 15–25; World Jewish Congress, *Judíos en el Uruguay* (Sp., 1957); I. Ganon, in: *Commentario*, 14:54 (1967), 52–56; J. Jerosolimsky, *ibid.*, 76–83; B. Lewin, *Los Judíos bajo la Inquisición en Hispanoamérica* (1960); A. Monk and J. Isaacson (eds.); *Comunidades Judías de Latinoamérica* (1968), 115–21. **ADD. BIBLIOGRAPHY:** R.H. Fitzgibbon, *Uruguay, Portrait of a Democracy* (1966); H. Avni, R.P. Raicher, David Bankier (eds.), *Memorias del Uruguay e Israel, Proyecto Seroussi* (1989); R.P. Raicher, *El Uruguay, la Comunidad Israelita y el Pueblo Judio* (2003); W. Eytan, *Los Primeros Diez Anios* (1959); J. Veinshenker, *Builders and Co-Builders of the Jewish Community in Uruguay* (Yid., 1957); I. Nemirovsky, *Albores del Judaismo en el Uruguay* (1987); "The Jewish Immigrants in Uruguay," in: *Haaretz* (Heb., Oct. 10, 1931); T. Porzecansky, *Historias de Vidas de Inmigrantes Judios al Uruguay* (1988); N. Schutz, *The K.K.L. in Uruguay 1930–1960* (Heb., 1996); idem, *The KKL in Uruguay 1930–1960* (Sp., 1998); M.A. Tov, *El Murmullo de Israel, historial diplomatico* (1983); C. Aldrighi, M.M. Apou, M. Feldman, G. Abend, T. Porzecansky, *Antisemitismo en el Uruguay* (Sp., 2000); N. Bergstein, *Jew: An Uruguayan Experience* (1993).

URY, ELSE (1877–1943), bestselling German author. Born in Berlin into a upper-middle-class Jewish family, Ury first received recognition for her story "Studierte Maedel" ("Academic Girls," 1906), which touched on a controversial topic, as women gained access to universities in Prussia only in 1908. Later she became famous for her children's book series *Nesthaekchen* (1918–1925) in ten volumes; she wrote a total of 39 books.

Else Ury was murdered in Auschwitz-Birkenau in January 1943.

BIBLIOGRAPHY: M. Brentzel, *Nesthaekchen kommt ins KZ: eine Annaeherung an Else Ury* (1992); M. Berger, in: *Beiträge Jugendliteratur und Medien* (1993), 123–24; G. Stern, in: *Gegenbilder und Vorurteil* (1995), 217–28; G. Wilkending, in: *Hinauf und Zurueck in die herzhelle Zukunft* (2000), 177–88.

[Elisabeth Dessauer (2nd ed.)]

URY, LESSER (1861–1931), German painter. Ury, who was born in Birnbaum, Prussia, went to Berlin at the age of 12 and two years later was apprenticed to a clothing merchant. When he had saved enough money, he began to study art, first in Duesseldorf and then in Brussels and Paris. A prize from the Berlin Academy enabled him to train further in Italy. Although he was something of a vagrant, Ury made his headquarters in Berlin from 1886 and there led a poverty-stricken, asocial life until he was over 60. It was only then that his melancholy paintings of city streets in stormy weather began to sell for high prices. He was a versatile artist and some of his earlier works, particularly his landscapes and his flower studies, achieved a glow of color that anticipated the goal of the expressionists. He produced drawings, lithographs, and etchings, but his finest works were his pastels. Ury repeatedly attempted ambitious subjects on a monumental scale, some of them suggested by events in contemporary Jewish life. His *Jerusalem* is a study of refugees from czarist Russia at the turn of the century sitting aimlessly on a bench, staring into nothing. The most famous of his somewhat theatrical biblical paintings, *Jeremiah* – the brooding prophet reclining under a vast, star-studded sky – is in the Tel Aviv Museum. Ury's fame had spread far beyond Germany. The retrospective exhibition arranged by the Berlin National Gallery to celebrate his 70th birthday turned into a memorial exhibition. After World War II, West Germany tried to repair the damage done to his reputation in the Nazi era with several comprehensive shows.

BIBLIOGRAPHY: A. Donath, *Lesser Ury* (1921). **ADD. BIBLIOGRAPHY:** D. Rosenbach (2002); H.A. Schlögl, *Lesser Ury – Zauber des Lichts* (1995); C.C. Schuetz (ed.), *Lesser Ury. Bilder der Bibel – Der Malerradierer.* Brochure for the exhibition at the Käthe-Kollwitz-Museum Berlin and in the "Neue Synagoge Berlin – Centrum Judaicum" Foundation (2002); J. Seyppel, *Joachim: Lesser Ury. Der Maler der alten City. Leben – Kunst – Wirkung* (1987; with catalogue raisonné).

[Alfred Werner]

U.S. ARMY AND THE HOLOCAUST. On April 5, 1945, units from the American Fourth Armored Division of the Third Army were the first Americans to discover a camp with prisoners and corpses. Ohrdruf was a Buchenwald sub-camp, and of the 10,000 male slave inmates, many had been sent on death marches, shot in pits, or their corpses were stacked in the woods and burned. The Americans found the camp by accident – they did not set out to liberate camps, they happened upon them – and found starved, frail bodies of hundreds of prisoners who had managed to survive, as well as the corpses. In Nordhausen, on the 11th, the American Timberwolf Division found 3,000 corpses and 700 starving, ill, and war-wounded survivors who were slaves in the V-2 rocket factories.

An Austrian-born Jewish U.S. soldier, Fred Bohm, helped liberate Nordhausen. He described fellow GIs as having "no particular feeling for fighting the Germans. They also thought that any stories they had read in the paper, or that I had told them out of first-hand experience, were either not true or at least exaggerated. And it did not sink in, what this was all about, until we got into Nordhausen."

When the American Combat Team 9 of the 9th Armored Infantry Battalion, Sixth Armored Division were led to Buchenwald by Russians, the camp contained 30,000 prisoners in a pyramid of power, with German Communists at the top, in the main barracks, and Jews and gypsies at the bottom, living in Little Camp, in an assortment of barns.

Buchenwald barrack prisoners were reasonably healthy looking. The Little Camp had 1,000 to 1,200 prisoners in a space meant for 450. Witnesses described prisoners as "emaciated beyond all imagination or description. Their legs and arms were sticks with huge bulging joints, and their loins were fouled by their own excrement. Their eyes were sunk so deep that they looked blind. If they moved at all, it was with a crawling slowness that made them look like huge, lethargic spiders. Many just lay in their bunks as if dead." After liberation, hundreds of prisoners died daily.

Generals George Patton, Omar Bradley, and Dwight Eisenhower arrived in Ohrdruf on April 12, the day of President Franklin D. Roosevelt's death. They found 3,200 naked, emaciated bodies in shallow graves. Eisenhower found a shed piled to the ceiling with bodies, various torture devices, and a butcher's block for smashing gold fillings from the mouths of the dead. Patton became physically ill. Eisenhower turned white at the scene inside the gates, but insisted on seeing the entire camp. "We are told that the American soldier does not know what he was fighting for," he said. "Now, at least he will know what he is fighting against."

After leaving Ohrdruf, Eisenhower wrote to Chief of Staff General George Marshall, attempting to describe things that "beggar description." The evidence of starvation and bestiality "were so overpowering as to leave me a bit sick," Bradley later wrote about the day: "The smell of death overwhelmed us." Patton, whose reputation for toughness was legendary, was overcome. He refused to enter a room where the bodies of naked men who had starved to death were piled, saying "he would get sick if he did so," Eisenhower reported. "I visited every nook and cranny." It was his duty, he felt, "to be in a position from then on to testify about these things in case there ever grew up at home the belief … that the stories of Nazi brutality were just propaganda." (Seemingly, he intuited then that these crimes might be denied.)

Eisenhower issued an order that American units in the area were to visit the camp. He also issued a call to the press back home. A group of prominent journalists, led by the dean of American publishers, Joseph Pulitzer, came to see the concentration camps. Pulitzer initially had "a suspicious frame of mind," he wrote. He expected to find that many of "the terrible reports" printed in the United States were "exaggerations and largely propaganda." But they were understatements, he reported.

Within days, Congressional delegations came to visit the concentration camps, accompanied by journalists and photographers. General Patton was so angry at what he found at Buchenwald that he ordered the Military Police to go to Weimar, four miles away, and bring back 1,000 civilians to see what their leaders had done, to witness what some human beings could do to others. The MPs were so outraged they brought back 2,000. Some turned away. Some fainted. Even veteran, battle-scarred correspondents were struck dumb. In a legendary broadcast on April 15, Edward R. Murrow gave the American radio audience a stunning matter-of-fact description of Buchenwald, of the piles of dead bodies so emaciated that those shot through the head had barely bled, and of those children who still lived, tattooed with numbers, whose ribs showed through their thin shirts. "I pray you to believe what I have said about Buchenwald," Murrow asked listeners. "I have reported what I saw and heard, but only part of it; for most of it I have no words." He added, "If I have offended you by this rather mild account of Buchenwald, I am not in the least sorry."

It was these reports, the newsreel pictures that were shot and played in theaters, and the visits of important delegations that proved to be influential in the public consciousness of the still unnamed German atrocities and the perception that something awful had been done to the Jews.

Then the American forces liberated Dachau, the first concentration camp built by the Germans in 1933. There were 67,665 registered prisoners in Dachau and its subcamps; 43,350 were political prisoners; 22,100 were Jews, and a percentage of "others." As Allied forces advanced, the Germans moved prisoners from concentration camps near the front to prevent their liberation. Transports arrived at Dachau continuously, resulting in severe deterioration of conditions. Typhus epidemics, poor sanitary conditions, and the weakened state of the prisoners worsened conditions further and spread disease even faster.

On April 26, 1945, as the Americans approached Dachau about 7,000 prisoners, most of them Jews, were sent on a death march to Tegernsee. Three days later, American troops liberated the main camp and found 28 wagons of decomposing bodies in addition to thousands of starving and dying prisoners. Then in early May 1945, American forces liberated the prisoners who had been sent on the death march.

After World War II, the Allies were faced with repatriating 7,000,000 *displaced persons in Germany and Austria, of whom 1,000,000 refused or were unable to return to their homes. These included nationals from the Baltic countries, Poles, Ukrainians, and Yugoslavs who were anti-communists and/or fascists afraid of prosecution for collaborating with the Nazis and Jews. The Allies were forced to service citizens of 52 nationalities in 900 DP camps, under the aegis of the United Nations Relief and Rehabilitation Administration (UNRRA). Lack of trained personnel, absence of a clear policy, and poor planning and management prevented the agency from fulfilling its role properly. Private relief organizations were gradually permitted to operate in the camps, but at best could provide only partial aid. Consequently, the United States Army, with a shrinking budget and inexperienced personnel, assumed major responsibility for the DPs. It was not a responsibility they anticipated or they welcomed but they had no other choice.

Each national group and religious denomination demanded recognition of its own problems. In order to avoid charges of discrimination, the American army adopted a policy of evenhandedness toward all the DPs, a policy that adversely affected Jewish DPs housed in the same camps with Poles, Baltic nationals, and Ukrainians. In those camps, the Jews who survived the Holocaust remained exposed to antisemitic discrimination. They were living among antisemites who had hostility toward them. Furthermore, only after liberation could survivors begin to feel, to sense what had been lost. Others could return home, Jewish survivors had no homes to which to return.

The American army was beleaguered. Trained for war, they had to juggle multiple assignments: the occupation, the Cold War, and the problems of survivors who were naturally distrustful of all authority and in need of medical and psychological attention.

Short-term problems, such as housing, medical treatment, food, and family reunification, were acute. The army had no long-term strategy. The survivors had nowhere to go. Britain was unwilling to permit Jewish immigration to Palestine and the United States was not ready to receive refugees.

Homosexuals continued to suffer, even with the end of the war. Paragraph 175 of the German legal code stated that male homosexuality, but not female lesbianism, was punishable by imprisonment. After 1943, male homosexuals had been forced to wear a pink triangle and were sent to the death camps. After the liberation, the Americans did not repeal Paragraph 175 and sent homosexual inmates liberated from the camps to other prisons.

Preferential treatment to Jews was denied on the ground that this would be a confirmation of the Nazi racial doctrine, which differentiated between Jews and others. The Jews were therefore dealt with according to their country of origin; Jews from Germany, for example, were classified as "enemy aliens," just like the Nazis.

American troops who liberated the concentration camps felt sympathy for the Jewish DPs, and many Jewish GIs and officers went out of their way to assist the survivors. But that sympathy did not extend to men who arrived on following troop rotations. Unfamiliar with history and facts, they had little or no sympathy for the Jews. It did not help that concentration camp survivors mistrusted people, were hypersensitive, and had acquired habits that did not compare favorably with the local German and Austrian population. Some objected to the fact that they took care of their biological needs in hallways and outside; one officer provided a simple solution of latrines and the problem ceased.

Americans' contacts with antisemitic Germans stirred up innate personal prejudices held by troops. Some American commanders suspected that the DPs from Eastern Europe included Soviet agents, and that Jews had a predisposition to communist beliefs. The Army also treated the DPs as if they stood in the way of the pre-Cold-War rush to rehabilitate Germany. By June 1945, conflicts were heated enough for President Truman to send Earl G. Harrison to the American Zone on a fact-finding mission. His visit was complete with political overtones and his report was a bombshell.

His conclusions were harsh, even overstated:

> We appear to be treating the Jews as the Nazis treated them except that we do not exterminate them. They are in concentration camps in large numbers under our military guard instead of SS troops. One is led to wonder whether the German people seeing this are not supposing that we are following or at least condoning Nazi policy.

His recommendations were equally dramatic:

> Jews must be recognized as Jews. They should be evacuated from Germany quickly. One hundred thousand Jews should be admitted to Palestine. President Truman endorsed the Report, rebuked the army, and intensified pressure on Britain. He opened up the United States for limited immigration.

After the pogrom by Polish fascists that killed 60–70 Jews in *Kielce, Poland, on July 4, 1946, more than 100,000 Jews fled to the American Zone aided by *Beriḥah, overcrowding the camps and straining the Army's budget, but when the administration tried to close the borders, the American Jews pressured them to reopen them. Twice the American government kept the borders open.

From April 1945 to the summer of 1947, the Jewish DP population in the American Zone exploded from 30,000 to 250,000 as the Jews fled the Soviet Bloc. The Jews had no place else to go, since no one would take them in. As their needs grew, and U.S. Army charged with caring for them was being restricted by budget cuts, the U.S. tried to transfer control of the Jews to the local German governments, which the Jews refused to accept under any circumstances.

On April 19, 1947, General Lucius Clay, commander of the American forces in Germany closed the borders to the American Zone and denied UN aid to newcomers, but 12,000 Jews from Romania and Hungary managed to enter. The American Army usually closed their eyes to illegal immigration, especially when the immigrants were Jews. But as time went by, and troops were replaced, the communication, tolerance, and relationships deteriorated between the Americans and the Jews, especially in matters concerning the black market, which led to raids and even violence.

When Israel was established in May 1948 and Congress passed the Wiley-Revercomb Displaced Persons bill allowing 100,000 DPs to come to America, the situation changed again. The camps were essentially empty and changed the Army's attitude to those who remained behind.

At the end of the day, the Army has been praised by some historians and scholars, and reviled by others. Typical are Abraham Hyman who calls the postwar period and the Army's treatment of the Jewish DPs the Army's finest hours. Leonard Dinnerstein, a historian, criticized the Army for being insensitive and unduly harsh.

BIBLIOGRAPHY: I. Gutman (ed.), *Macmillan Encyclopedia of the Holocaust* (1990); A. Grobman, *Battling for Souls, The Vaad Hatzalah Rescue Committee in Post-War Europe* (2004).

[Jeanette Friedman (2nd ed.)]

USHA (Heb. אוּשָׁה).

(1) Town in Lower Galilee mentioned in the annals of Sennacherib (a, 40). An ancient Hebrew seal found there attests to the existence of an Israelite settlement on the site in biblical times; one side reads Elzakar b. Yehoḥil and the other side Shobai b. Elzakar.

The place was of importance in mishnaic and talmudic times. In about 140 C.E., at the end of the period of persecution following the suppression of Bar Kokhba's revolt, the surviving scholars gathered there, reestablished the Sanhedrin (see next entry), and instituted the regulations known as the "Enactments of Usha" (Song R. 2:5, no. 3). For some time, it was the seat of R. Simeon b. Gamaliel; R. Judah ha-Nasi studied there under R. Judah b. Ilai, an inhabitant of the town (Tosef., Meg. 2:8). R. Isaac Nappaḥa owned five courtyards there (Tosef., Er. 7:7). It is the present-day Hūsha, a small ruin. Remains of a splendid building, perhaps a synagogue, were uncovered on the site.

[Michael Avi-Yonah]

(2) Kibbutz in Lower Galilee in the Haifa Bay area, near Kiryat Ata, founded in 1937 by a group of Ha-No'ar ha-Ẓiyyoni originating from Galicia. The kibbutz was based on irrigated field and fodder crops, avocado plantations, citrus groves, and dairy cattle. It operated a factory producing lenses for eyeglasses. In 2002 the population was 354.

[Efraim Orni]

BIBLIOGRAPHY: S. Klein (ed.), *Sefer ha-Yishuv*, 1 (1939), s.v.

USHA, SYNOD OF, convention of sages reviving the Sanhedrin held at *Usha at the close of the period of persecution following the Bar Kokhba revolt, i.e., about the middle of the second century C.E.

During the rule of *Antoninus Pius (137–161), the restrictive decrees of Hadrian were abrogated, and in consequence a renewal of Jewish spiritual and communal life became possible. This renewal found its main expression in the convention of sages at Usha, described as follows: "When the persecution ended, our teachers convened at Usha, these being R. Judah, R. Nehemiah, R. Meir, R. Yose, R. Simeon b. Yoḥai, R. Eliezer son of R. Yose ha-Galili, and R. Eliezer b. Jacob. They sent the following message to the elders of Galilee: Let everyone who has learned come and teach and everyone who has not learned let him come and learn – they convened and learned and took all necessary steps" (Song R. 2:5, no. 3). Thus the synod inaugurated all the activities of the Sanhedrin: the teaching and study of Torah as well as legislative and judicial functions referred to by the phrase that there they took "all necessary steps." The scholars who convened at Usha included men like *Meir who had fled abroad, and others who had concealed themselves in the country during the persecutions, like Simeon b. Yoḥai. The designated *nasi*, Rabban *Simeon b. Gamaliel, who was apparently still in hiding because of a pending death sentence against him, is not mentioned. The parallel tradition in the Babylonian Talmud (Ber. 63b) states that the convention took place in *Jabneh and not in Usha, but this does not seem to be correct, either in the light of historical circumstances and the conditions in Judea at that time, or from the context in the Babylonian Talmud itself, according to which R. Judah, who lived in Usha, was the host of the convention.

Together with the Sanhedrin the office of nasi was also revived and Rabban Simeon b. Gamaliel was appointed to this post with R. *Nathan ha-Bavli as *av bet din* and R. Meir as *ḥakham*. It is difficult to determine how the functions of leadership were divided between these three, but clearly the division indicates the growth of the importance of the Sanhedrin against that of the nasi in comparison with the situation existing in the period of Rabban *Gamaliel of Jabneh. It is possible that the limitation of the power of Rabban Simeon

b. Gamaliel resulted from his not having participated at the initial convention of the scholars in Usha. In the course of time, Simeon b. Gamaliel strengthened the status of the nasi once more, penalizing Nathan and Meir for their unsuccessful attempt to unseat him.

The tradition in tractate *Rosh Ha-Shanah* of the ten migrations of the Sanhedrin includes the following stages: "And from Jerusalem to Jabneh, and from Jabneh to Usha, and from Usha [back] to Jabneh, and from Jabneh [back] to Usha, and from Usha to Shefaram" (RH 31b). The problem of the repeated moves between Jabneh and Usha has been the object of considerable study: some scholars believe that the Sanhedrin came to Usha for the first time in the era preceding the Bar Kokhba revolt, partly basing their opinions on the tradition "who are meant by the travelers to Usha? R. Ishmael" (BB 28b); others consider that this source proves that following the convention of Usha in the middle of the second century, an attempt was made to renew the Sanhedrin at Jabneh, which came to grief because Judea lacked a sufficient basis of population, and the Sanhedrin returned to Usha; still others hold that the tradition itself is corrupt or that the wanderings of the Sanhedrin were artificially rounded out to the number ten, particularly as the addition "and from Usha to Jabneh, and from Jabneh to Usha" does not occur in the versions and manuscripts of the Babylonian Talmud (see Dik. Sof.), nor does this addition appear in the parallel tradition in *Genesis Rabbah* (97; Theodor-Albeck, p. 1220). Whatever the truth, however, it is clear that the Sanhedrin of Usha which is of historical significance is the convention of scholars that took place there after the end of the persecutions following the Bar Kokhba revolt.

The *tannaim* of Usha occupied themselves to a great extent with *halakhah*, and the "Usha period" constitutes an important stage in the compilation and codification of the Mishnah. The scholars of Usha applied themselves particularly to the laws of ritual purity and it may be assumed that some of them adopted the principles of the *Ḥasidim, which included eating ordinary food in a state of ritual purity. Despite this, Buechler's view that the concepts of **am ha-areẓ* and **ḥaver* – which were much discussed by the scholars of Usha – came into historical existence in the period of Usha and were confined solely to Galilee cannot be accepted.

There exist several *takkanot* which are called "*takkanot* of Usha" in talmudic literature. A substantial number of them are connected with the laws of the home and family life, one being "that a man must maintain his young children" (TJ, Ket. 4:8, 28d). The urgent need for this *takkanah* becomes evident when it is viewed against the background of the great poverty that prevailed after the Bar Kokhba revolt. Another such *takkanah* states: "It was enacted at Usha that a man must support his son until he is 12 years old: from then onward "יורד עמו לחייו", which apparently means "helps him in his trade." Another historically important *takkanah* was "not to excommunicate an elder" (TJ, MK 3:1, 81d), which may be regarded as extending the rights of scholars, enlarging their independent status, and preventing the possibility of a repetition of such incidents as the excommunication of Eliezer b. Hyrcanus in the time of Rabban Gamaliel of Jabneh.

Some scholars believe that a number of these *takkanot* are of a later date than the synod of Usha. Thus G. Alon thinks there was another meeting of scholars presided over by the *nasi* (apparently Gamaliel b. Judah ha-Nasi), which met only once toward the end of the rule of the Severi dynasty (c. 230 C.E.), and a section of "the *takkanot* of Usha" should be attributed to this synod. Mantel considers that some of them are local *takkanot* of the *bet din* of Usha headed by Judah b. Ḥanina, some of which became generally accepted in the course of time.

BIBLIOGRAPHY: Weiss, Dor, 2 (1904[4]), 129ff.; A. Buechler, *Studies in Jewish History* (1956), 160–78: idem, *Der galilaeische Amha'Arez des zweiten Jahrhunderis* (1906); idem, in: *Abhandlungen… H.P. Chajes* (1933), 137–67 (Heb. pt.); S. Klein, *Ereẓ haGalil* (1946), index s.v.; M. Avi-Yonah, *Bi-Ymei Roma u-Bizantiyyon* (1952[2]), index s.v.; Alon, Toledot, 2 (1961[2]), 69ff.; H. Mantel, *Studies in the History of the Sanhedrin* (1961), passim. esp. 140–74; idem, in: *Tarbiz*, 34 (1964/65), 281–83.

[A'hron Oppenheimer]

USHPIZIN (Aram. אֻשְׁפִּיזִין; from the Lat. *hospes*, "guest"), according to kabbalistic tradition, the mystical seven "guests" – Abraham, Isaac, Jacob, Moses, Aaron, Joseph, and David – who visit the *sukkah* during the seven days of Tabernacles (cf. Zohar, 5:103b). According to the Zohar, Joseph comes after Moses and Aaron, but in most Ashkenazi *maḥzorim* and prayer books the order is chronological. The spiritual guest of each day is invited before the meal and the text of this invitation, "Enter, exalted holy guests…," is found in several Ashkenazi and Sephardi prayer books. The custom was adopted by the Ḥasidim and many pamphlets entitled *Seder-Ushpiz*, including liturgy based upon the practices of certain *ẓaddikim* (e.g., the rabbis of Belz, Zanz, etc.), began to be published in the 19th century. Decorating the *sukkah* wall with a plaque which bears an inscription including the names of the seven guests has also become an accepted practice. Moroccan Jews have a special compilation of prayers in honor of the *ushpizin*, called *Ḥamad Elohim*, from which special sections are recited each day of the festival.

BIBLIOGRAPHY: Eisenstein, Dinim, 12ff.

ʿUSIFIYYĀ (Isfiya), Druze and Arab village, with municipal council status, on Mount Carmel, 5.5 mi. (9 km.) S.E. of Haifa. The village is spread over an area of about 20 sq. mi. (50 sq. km.). Remnants of a fifth- or sixth-century synagogue with a mosaic floor depicting a seven-branched *menorah, etrogim, lulav, shofar,* grapevines, a peacock, and other birds and bearing the inscription *Shalom al Yisrael* have been found in the village. The antiquities give substance to ʿUsifiyyā's identification with Ḥusifah, mentioned in an ancient *kinah* lamenting the destruction of its Jewish community. Although S. Klein (see bibl.) dates this event to the fourth century C.E., Y. Press assumes that it may be connected with the Byzantine reconquest of the country from the Persians under Heraclius at the beginning of the seventh century. Due to its proximity to Haifa, ʿUsifiyyā, which had about 1,100 inhabitants in 1947, progressed well under Israeli statehood, attaining a population or 4,000 in 1969 and 9,530 in 2002, of whom 75.5% were Druze, 16% Christians and 7.5% Muslims. The village's economy was based on hill farming (vegetables, field crops, fruit orchards, cattle, sheep, etc.) with a tourist industry bolstered by the beautiful surroundings. Together with neighboring *Daliyat al-Karmil, it constituted one of Israel's major Druze centers. In 2003 it was united with the latter as the city of Karmil. In the 1950s a Greek Catholic church was built there.

BIBLIOGRAPHY: M. Avi-Yonah, in: QDAP, 3 (1933), 118–31; Press, Ereẓ, 4 (1955²), 745; S. Klein, in: *Yediʿot ha-Ḥevrah la-Ḥakirat Ereẓ Yisrael ve-Attikoteha*, 7 (1943), 60ff., 107ff.

[Shlomo Hasson]

USOV (Ger. **Maehrisch-Aussee**; in Jewish sources אויסא) town in N. Moravia, Czech Republic. The first mention of a Jew in Usov was in 1564, and by 1600 Jews were living in nine houses. The community suffered during the Thirty Years' War but recuperated to build a synagogue in 1690. It was one of the 15 communities of the "supreme [northern] district" in Moravia. On the Day of Atonement 1721, a Catholic priest who had profaned the prayers and ceremony was ejected from the synagogue: After complicated legal proceedings, the supreme court in Vienna overruled the lower instances of Brno and Prague and in 1722 ordered the synagogue to be destroyed and prohibited the holding of any public services. The *dayyan* of the community, Abraham Broda Leipniker (1690–1774), a respected merchant, succeeded in obtaining permission to build two prayer houses in 1753 and recorded the proceedings in his *Megillat Sedarim*, to be read yearly on *Simḥat Torah (published in 1895 by Emanuel M. *Baumgarten). At that time, there were 59 heads of families, 35 of them engaged in peddling and five sailors. The community numbered 10 Jewish families in 1657 and 59 in 1753. By the end of the 18th century, 110 Jewish families were permitted to reside there.

In 1830 there were 110 families (656 persons) in Usov, out of 5,200 permitted Jewish families in the whole of Moravia. The community continued to grow until 1848 but declined thereafter, both as a consequence of the right of free movement and of the general decline of the town. In 1890 the Jewish population had declined to about 150, and the community was unified with the growing community of Sumperk (Maehrisch Schoenberg). In 1900 there were 101 Jews. In 1929, there was only one Jewish family left. In 1930 there were 30 Jews. Today there are no Jews in the town, which numbered 1,114 inhabitants in 1961.

One Usov Jew survived the Holocaust. While there was no Jewish community in Usov after World War II, a well-preserved Jewish quarter recalls the Jewish existence in Usov. The synagogue built in 1784, the third one in a row, was renovated after the war and is used as a house of prayer by the Czech Brethren Protestant Church.

BIBLIOGRAPHY: H. Gold, *Die Juden und Judengemeinden Maehrens in Vergangenheit und Gegenwart* (1929), 331–42; E. Baumgarten, in: *Gedenkbuch… D. Kaufmann* (1900), 506–37; M. Haendel, *Temunot min he-Avar* (1955) 201–13. **ADD. BIBLIOGRAPHY:** J. Fiedler, *Jewish Sights of Bohemia and Moravia* (1991).

[Oskar K. Rabinowicz / Yeshayahu Jelinek (2nd ed.)]

USQUE, ABRAHAM, Marrano printer. Born in Portugal and known there as Duarte Pinel (Pinhel), Usque fled from the Inquisition shortly after 1543, established himself at Ferrara, and became associated with the press established by the Spanish ex-Marrano, Yom-Tov ben Levi Athias (Jerónimo de Vargas). He followed Athias' plan of publishing Jewish liturgies in the vernacular, as well as other texts intended to facilitate the Marranos' return to Judaism. Usque's name first appears in connection with the famous Bible translation of 1553, the so-called Ferrara Bible. This Bible was published in two forms: one intended for a Jewish audience, bearing a Hebrew date (14 Adar 5313) and a dedication to Doña Gracia *Nasi, and listing the Hebrew names of the printer and publisher (Usque and Athias); the other for the Christian world, dated March 1, 1553, with a dedication to Duke Ercole d'Este of Ferrara and the names of Duarte Pinel and Jerónimo de Vargas. Books published by Usque also include the enigmatic *Menina e Moça*, by Bernardim *Ribeiro, Samuel *Usque's *Consolaçam as tribulaçoens de Israel* (1553), and various works in Hebrew. The fury of the Counter-Reformation gradually halted Usque's printing activities. He published no books in Spanish or Portuguese after 1555 and continued the publication of Hebrew books only to 1558.

Solomon *Usque may be identical with Usque's son and assistant Solomon, but his relationship to Samuel Usque is impossible to determine.

BIBLIOGRAPHY: C. Roth, in: *Modern Language Review*, 38 (1943), 307–17; M.A. Cohen (ed. and tr.), S. Usque, *Consolation for the Tribulations of Israel* (1965).

[Martin A. Cohen]

USQUE, SAMUEL (16th century), Portuguese Marrano. All that is known about Usque comes from his *Consolaçam as tribulaçoens de Israel* ("Consolation for the Tribulations of Israel", Ferrara. 1553; second ed., Amsterdam, 1599). This unusual work reveals that the author was a man of unusually broad culture and of Spanish descent – his family having emigrated from Spain in 1492. He knew many languages, including Hebrew; he was versed in classical literature, in the Bible, and in Jewish and Christian postbiblical literature. There is no evidence that he is to be identified with Solomon *Usque, the poet-playwright, or with Abraham *Usque, who printed the first edition of the *Consolaçam*, or with the Portuguese belletrist, Bernardim *Ribeiro.

Written in limpid Portuguese prose, the *Consolaçam* was dedicated to the great patroness of Jewish art and culture, Doña Gracia *Nasi. Its avowed purpose was to persuade Marrano refugees from Spain and Portugal, and perhaps also those Marranos who were still in those two countries, to return wholeheartedly to Judaism. To this end the author, in a sweeping review of Jewish history, based upon traditional Jewish apologetics, demonstrated that the Jews, despite their centuries of hardship and persecution, had not been abandoned by God; they were rather, he declared, standing on the threshold of the golden messianic age.

The *Consolaçam* takes the form of a typically Renaissance pastoral dialogue between three shepherds, Zicareo, Numeo, and Ycabo – the names being thin disguises for those of the prophets Zechariah (the "Recaller"), Nahum (the "Comforter"), and Jacob, the eponymous hero of the Jewish people, who narrates the history of the Jews in the first person. The three sections of the book, dealing respectively with the eras of the First Temple, the Second Temple and subsequent Jewish history up until Usque's own day, form an integrated work which yields numerous insights into the mind of Usque's generation. Furthermore, the third dialogue contains invaluable accounts and impressions of events which the author experienced personally.

The first edition of the *Consolaçam* was, for the most part, destroyed by the Inquisition shortly after its publication. The second edition, also rare, marks the beginning of Sephardi literature in the Netherlands. The work is regarded as a major contribution to Jewish historiography, and as a classic of Portuguese prose. An English translation by M.A. Cohen appeared in 1965.

BIBLIOGRAPHY: J. Mendes dos Remedios (ed.), *Consolaçam as tribulaçoens de Israel* (1906–08); M.A. Cohen (tr. and ed.), *Consolation for the Tribulations of Israel* (1965), 3–5; E. Lipiner (tr.), *Bay di Taykhen fun Portugal* (1949).

[Martin A. Cohen]

USQUE, SOLOMON (c. 1530–c. 1596), Portuguese poet of Marrano descent; probably born in Portugal, he spent most of his life in Italy and later in Turkey. It is believed that he was the son of Abraham *Usque, who printed the Ferrara Bible. In collaboration with Lazzaro di Graziano Levi, Solomon Usque wrote the earliest known Jewish drama written in the vernacular – a Purim play in Spanish entitled *Esther*, first staged in the Venice ghetto in 1558. Leone *Modena, a nephew of Lazzaro Levi, was responsible for an Italian version of the play early in the 17th century. Usque published a much-admired Spanish translation of the final part of Petrarch's sonnets (Venice, 1567); many copies appearing under the contracted pseudonym of Salusque Lusitano (i.e., Solomon Usque the Portuguese). This edition, which did much to spread Petrarch's fame abroad, was dedicated to Alexander Farnese, duke of Parma. Usque also wrote some Italian verse, including a poem on the Creation entitled *Canzone sull' opera de' sei giorni*; this was included in an anthology compiled by Cristoforo Zabata (Genoa, 1572). Usque was also active in Constantinople, where he is known to have engaged in Hebrew printing in collaboration with Abraham Ashkenazi in 1560–61. In 1595 at the request of the English ambassador, Usque wrote a report on events in Turkey after the death of Sultan Muted III which was closely studied by Queen Elizabeth's ministers in London.

BIBLIOGRAPHY: C. Roth, *Gleanings* (1967), 179–99; Piattelli, in: RMI, 34 (1968), 163–72.

USSISHKIN, ABRAHAM MENAḤEM MENDEL (1863–1941), Zionist leader, member of Ḥovevei Zion, and the president of the *Jewish National Fund (JNF). Born in Dubrovno in the district of Mogilev, Russia, Ussishkin moved to Moscow with his family in 1871. From 1878 he became an enthusiastic reader of the works of contemporary Hebrew writers, and from then the revival of the Hebrew language became one of his guiding principles. The 1881 pogroms shocked Russian Jewry and led to the emergence of the *Bilu movement. At a meeting of Jewish students at Moscow University, Ussishkin and his friend Jehiel *Tschlenow founded a Society of Pioneers to Ereẓ Israel. In 1882 he entered the Technological Institute in Moscow, where he immediately founded a Jewish students' society. In August 1884 the Benei Zion society, which nurtured many Zionist leaders, was founded in Moscow. Ussishkin was elected to the society's committee and in 1885 was chosen secretary of all the Ḥovevei Zion groups in Moscow. From 1887 on he published reports and articles in *Ha-Meliẓ*. Together with M.L. *Lilienblum, he was elected secretary of the Druzkieniki Conference (1887). A clash took place at the conference between the Orthodox faction of Samuel *Mohilewer and Leon *Pinsker's liberal Ḥovevei Zion faction, but Ussishkin managed to bring about a reconciliation. The practical proposals made by him at the conference were early signs of his Zionist pragmatism. He viewed agricultural settlement in Ereẓ Israel as the essence of the whole.

When *Aḥad Ha-Am founded the *Benei Moshe society in 1889, Ussishkin became one of its active members. In the same year he qualified as a technical engineer at the Technological Institute. In 1890 he participated in the founding meeting of the *Odessa Committee. Ussishkin visited Ereẓ Israel for the first time in 1891 and described his journey in a booklet (written in Russian and later translated into Hebrew) that made a considerable impression. Upon his return from Ereẓ Israel, he settled in Yekaterinoslav, where he remained for 15 years (1891–1906). At first he was active in Hebrew educational work as well as in Zionist propaganda and fund raising; he was instrumental in founding the modernized Hebrew-speaking *ḥeder* (*ḥeder metukkan*) and a Hebrew library, became a member of the board of the publishing house Aḥi'asaf, etc. The publication of Theodor *Herzl's *Der Judenstaat* in 1896 and his meetings with Herzl and Max *Nordau in Paris and in Vienna on the eve of the First Zionist Congress made a deep impression on Ussishkin, despite his reservations regarding a concept of Zionism based exclusively on political activity, to the neglect of settlement and cultural work. He was elected Hebrew secretary of the First Zionist Congress (1897) and took an active part in the debate centered on the formulation of the first, political article of the *Basle Program. He expressed his fear that too explicit a formulation of Zionist aims might rouse the Turkish government against the existing *yishuv*. His opposition to pure political Zionism at the First Congress precluded his election as the leader of Russian Zionism, but at the Second Congress (1898) he was elected to the Zionist General Council and served on it for the rest of his life. When Russia was divided into districts for the purpose of Zionist activities at the Third Congress (1899), he was chosen to head the Yekaterinoslav district, which included all of southern Russia and the Caucasus. Under his direction, this district became one of the most active in Russian Zionism, both in its cultural and in its practical activities.

At the Fifth Congress (1901) Ussishkin delivered the address on the "United Organization," in which there was no room for separate "groups" and "societies," and proposed the establishment of the Anglo-Palestine Company in Ereẓ Israel as a branch of the *Jewish Colonial Trust. On his return from the Congress, he convened a conference of Zionists in the Caucasus, thus introducing Zionist activities into the non-Ashkenazi communities there. In the same year he was a member of a delegation that approached Baron Edmond de *Rothschild protesting the "paternalistic" methods of his officials in Ereẓ Israel. Rothschild rejected the delegation's demands, and when Aḥad Ha-Am insisted that the demands be accepted – even if it meant withdrawal of Rothschild's support of the settlements – Ussishkin's opposition to Aḥad Ha-Am's intransigence saved the situation. In 1902 at the *Minsk Conference of the Russian Zionists, he delivered an address that exerted a great influence on the future development of the Zionist movement. The call to recruit youth for pioneer work in Ereẓ Israel was then heard in the movement for the first time.

After the Kishinev pogrom in April 1903, Ussishkin went to Kishinev and was profoundly shocked. He was moved to call for action, which for him meant primarily the organization of the Jewish population of Ereẓ Israel – the embryo from which the future Jewish state would develop. After he traveled to Vienna and received Herzl's approval for his plan, Ussishkin set out for Ereẓ Israel for the second time and remained there for four months (July–September 1903). Immediately upon his arrival in Jaffa, he published a leaflet on the need to "organize the *Yishuv*," and in August 1903 the Great Assembly (Ha-Keneset ha-Gedolah) of the Jews of Ereẓ Israel was held in Zikhron Ya'akov under his direction. It lasted for three days and aroused great enthusiasm and hopes, but this atmosphere was shattered by the subsequent controversy in the Zionist Movement over the *Uganda Scheme. The only practical outcome of the convention was the founding of the Teachers' Association at a meeting in Zikhron Ya'akov immediately following the Great Assembly (Sept. 28, 1903). Upon his return from these two meetings, Ussishkin was confronted with the news that Herzl had received a proposal from the British government to establish an autonomous Jewish colony in Uganda, East Africa. He bitterly opposed the Uganda Scheme and became one of the leaders of the opposition to Herzl. He was the initiator and the moving spirit behind the *Kharkov Conference (1903), which demanded that Herzl abandon the scheme. At the beginning of 1905, Ussishkin convened a conference of the anti-Uganda Zionists, called Ẓiyyonei Zion, in Vilna. The second conference of this faction, also organized by him, took place in Freiburg three days before the Seventh Congress (July 1905) and was instrumental in influencing the congress to abandon the Uganda Scheme and concentrate wholeheartedly on settlement activities in Ereẓ Israel. During the conflict over the Uganda Scheme, Ussishkin published *Our Program* (at first in Russian and later in Hebrew, German, and English translations), which laid the five-point foundation for "synthetic Zionism": political action, acquisition of land, *aliyah*, settlement, and educational and organizational work among the people. This approach thereafter dominated the Zionist Movement. In this pamphlet, he spoke for the first time of farms and of settlements in which Jewish workers would cultivate the land acquired by the JNF "with their own hands, without help from hired laborers." This was the earliest form of the idea of the moshav ovedim. *Our Program* became the platform of practical Zionism, which gave rise to the Second Aliyah.

While engaged in the great debate over the Uganda Scheme, Ussishkin was fighting the tide of assimilation prompted by the first Russian Revolution (1904–05). He struggled to promote the Zionist Movement in general and the Hebrew language in particular. In 1906 he was elected head of the Odessa Committee and retained this post until the committee itself was abolished by the Soviet regime (1919). Under his leadership, the committee supported the establishment of the settlements Ein Gannim, Be'er Ya'akov, and Naḥalat Yehudah. Ussishkin also proposed support for the training farm at *Kinneret and for all the existing educational and cultural institutions in the young *yishuv*.

During the revolution of the Young Turks in 1908, Ussishkin went to Constantinople in an attempt to promote the Zionist cause with the help of influential Sephardi Jews. In 1913, after his third visit to Ereẓ Israel, he published in a pamphlet his "general survey" (translated into Hebrew under the title *Massa Shelishi le-Ereẓ Yisrael*), which discussed the various problems of the *yishuv*. In the winter of 1912, at the eighth conference of Ḥovevei Zion, he spoke of the need for a Hebrew university and put through a resolution in the committee to allocate the sum of 50,000 gold francs for the purpose of acquiring land on Mount Scopus. At the 11th Zionist Congress in Vienna (1913), he reported together with Chaim *Weizmann on the idea of the Hebrew University. During World War I, in February 1915, the Copenhagen office of the Zionist Organization was established, and a secret Zionist conference, attended by delegates from all the warring countries, was held in that city. Despite the danger involved (for the Czarist government regarded every contact with enemy subjects as an act of treason), Ussishkin attended the conference. Upon his return to Odessa, he was informed that there was a deportation order against him and was obliged to flee to Moscow, where he remained until the situation in Russia had changed. During the days of the February Revolution (1917), he waged a bitter struggle against the Yiddishists, who wished to eliminate Hebrew as the recognized national language of the Jewish people, and against all those who thought that the granting of equal rights to Russian Jews had made Zionism obsolete.

Ussishkin organized a mass demonstration in Odessa to celebrate the *Balfour Declaration that was attended by 200,000 people, Jews and non-Jews alike. At the invitation of Weizmann and Nahum *Sokolow, he attended the Paris Peace Conference, and on Feb. 27, 1919, he stood before the assembled representatives of the nations of the world as the representative of the Jewish people and addressed them in Hebrew.

In November 1919 Ussishkin settled in Palestine and was the head of the *Zionist Commission. For more than three years (1919–23) he guided the *yishuv* in its first and difficult steps toward the materialization of the national home. He was instrumental in organizing the Hebrew school network in Palestine and in establishing the settlement Kiryat Anavim near Jerusalem. In the spring of 1921 he left for the United States with Albert *Einstein to promote the fund-raising campaign for *Keren Hayesod. At the 13th Congress in Karlsbad (August 1923), Ussishkin's election as chairman of the Zionist General Council was prevented by his disagreement with Weizmann's moderate policy toward the Mandatory regime in Palestine. However, he was chosen to head the JNF and retained this position for nearly 20 years (1923–41). He devoted himself completely to the idea of acquiring land as the property of the nation, making trips to Europe (1924) and Canada (1927) to raise funds. Due to his tireless efforts, large tracts of land in the Jezreel Valley (1921), Ḥefer Plain (1927), Haifa Bay area (1928), Beth-Shean (1930), and other parts of the country were purchased. He increased the landed property of the JNF from 22,000 to 561,000 dunam and its income from £70,000 to £600,000.

Ussishkin played an important role in the establishment of the Hebrew University and was among those who officially inaugurated it on April 1, 1925. He was elected to both the Board of Trustees and the Executive Committee of the university and took an active interest in its affairs until he died. He was elected chairman of the Zionist General Council at the 19th Congress in 1935. When the Arab riots broke out in Palestine in 1936 and the Royal Commission (the Peel Commission) proposed the partition of the country, he fought against the proposal at the 20th Congress in Zurich (August 1937) and participated in the Round Table Conference in London in 1939. He fought against the British White Paper of May 1939 that forbade Jews to purchase land in most areas of the country.

Ussishkin's activities were widely admired. In 1939, when the JNF purchased land in Upper Galilee, north of the Ḥuleh Valley, it was decided to found a series of settlements there called Meẓudot Ussishkin ("Ussishkin Forts") – moshavei ovedim and kevuẓot in which all sections of the nation and members of all Zionist parties would participate. For 60 years no Zionist or Jewish national activity took place in which he had not participated and on which he had not left his own unique stamp. Ussishkin's writings have been collected in two volumes (which also include appreciations): *Sefer Ussishkin* (1933) and *Devarim Aḥaronim* (1946).

BIBLIOGRAPHY: S. Kling, *The Mighty Warrior, the Life Story of Menaḥem Ussishkin* (1965), incl. bibl.; H. Sacher, *Zionist Portraits and Other Essays* (1959), 52–56; L. Lipsky, *A Gallery of Zionist Profiles* (1956), 72–78; N. Sokolow, *Ḥibbath Zion* (Eng., 1935), index; Kressel, Leksikon, 1 (1965), 43–44; J. Klausner, *Menaḥem Ussishkin; his Life and Work* (1942); A. Druyanow, *Ketavim le-Toledot Ḥibbat Ẓiyyon*, 2, 3 (1925–32), indexes; S. Schwartz, *Ussishkin be-Iggerotav* (1950).

[Joseph Gedaliah Klausner]

USSISHKIN, DAVID (1935–), Israeli archaeologist, expert on the Iron Age of the Land of Israel. Born in Jerusalem, Ussishkin studied archaeology at the Hebrew University of Jerusalem (1955–66) after completing his army service. In 1961 he obtained his M.A. with distinction, writing a thesis on Macalister's excavations at Gezer. Ussishkin received his Ph.D. in 1966 and his thesis "The Neo-Hittite Monuments, Their Dating and Style," was written under the supervision of Y. Yadin. From 1966 Ussishkin taught archaeology at Tel Aviv University, and from 1996 was the incumbent of the Austria Chair in Archaeology of the Land of Israel in the Biblical Period at the Institute of Archaeology. Ussishkin's excavation experience spans close to 50 years, with his first experience in the field as a staff member on the Chalcolithic Beersheba digs (1956–65); Hazor (1958); Azor (1958); Kültepe, Turkey (1959); Megiddo (1960, 1965); Judean Desert, Cave of Letters (1960–61); En Gedi (1961–62); Masada (1964–65). His own directorial experience began with the work at Tel Eton and Beth Yerah (1967–68) and the Silwan Village survey (1968–71) and continued with the major project conducted at Tel Lachish between 1973 and 1994, which has been fully published. Following smaller excavations conducted at Bethar (1984) and at Tel Jezreel (1990–1996), Ussishkin was a co-director of the renewed excavations at Tel Megiddo from 1992. Ussishkin took on many different administrative duties over the years, including the directorship of the Institute of Archaeology at Tel Aviv (1980–84), serving also as a member of various councils (the Israel Exploration Society, the Israel Archaeological Council) and as editor of the journal *Tel Aviv* (1975–2004). Ussishkin was a prolific writer of scientific papers and research articles (more than 100). His books include *The Conquest of Lachish by Sennacherib* (1983) and *The Village of Silwan – The Necropolis from the Period of the Judean Kingdom* (1993), and he is the main author and editor of the five-volume final report on the Lachish excavations (2004).

[Shimon Gibson (2nd ed.)]

USTEK (Czech **Úštěk**; Ger. **Auscha**), small town in N. Bohemia, Czech Republic. The local lord received permission in 1327 to allow Jews to settle on his domains, but documentary evidence for the presence of Jews dates only from the 16th century, when the Serymas were lords of the town. There were ten Jewish families in 1570. After the Thirty Years' War, Ustek became a possession of the Jesuit order. The number of Jewish families was limited to eight. In 1794 a synagogue was built (rebuilt in Reform style in 1851). There were 42 Jews (eight families) in the town in 1745, 60 in 1830, 172 in 1880, 108 in 1910, and only 54 in 1930. At the turn of the century, 12 Jewish firms dealt in the export of hops. At the time of the Sudeten crisis (September 1938) the Jews left Ustek; the synagogue was destroyed on Nov. 10, 1938. After World War II the community was not reestablished.

BIBLIOGRAPHY: Germ Jud, 2 (1968), 42; Jarschel, in: H. Gold (ed.), *Juden und Judengemeinden Boehmens...* (1934), 13–18; Klambert, in: *Zeitschrift fuer die Geschichte der Juden*, 3 (1966), 203–10; Hráský, in: JGGJČ, 9 (1938), 252, 257–8.

[Jan Herman]

USTI NAD LABEM (Czech **Ústí nad Labem**; Ger. **Aussig**), town in N. Bohemia, Czech Republic. Isolated Jewish families may have settled in the town in the 16th century, but later the German burghers did not permit Jews to live there. Jews returned to the town after 1848. In 1880 there were 30 Jewish families in Usti; 95 families in 1863; and 985 persons in 1930. The first prayer room was established in 1863 and *Kultusgemeinde* in 1866. A formal congregation was established in 1869 which, in 1888, hired its first rabbi.

In the years before World War II, Usti was one of the centers of the Nazi Party (Sudetendeutsche Partei), and Jews were subjected to violence. In the summer and fall of 1938, most Jews left Usti for Prague and other localities. In November 1938, after the Munich agreement, the few Jews that remained in Usti were sent to extermination camps. In 1945–48, most of the German inhabitants were expelled to Germany. After the Soviet annexation of Carpatho-Rus, local Jews opted for Czechoslovakia; many of them settled in the depopulated Suden region. A new Jewish congregation was established in Usti. In 1948 it totaled 800. The congregation continued to exist in the early 21st century.

Usti is the native town of artist Ernst Neuschul-Norland (1895–1968), who painted the portrait of the first Czechoslovak president. Another Usti native, Ignatz Petschek, owned the north Bohemian lignite mines.

BIBLIOGRAPHY: J. Stoessler, in: H. Gold, (1934), 19–22; *Beitraege zur Heimatkunde des Aussig-Karbitzer Bezirkes* (1926); J. Fiedler, *Jewish Sights of Bohemia and Moravia* (1991).

[Yeshayahu Jelinek (2nd ed.)]

USURY.

Biblical Law

SOURCES. "If thou lend money to any of My people, even to the poor with thee, thou shalt not be to him as a creditor (*nosheh*), neither shall ye lay upon him interest" (Ex. 22:24). "And if thy brother be waxen poor and his means fail with thee... Take no interest of him or increase; but fear thy God; that thy brother may live with thee. Thou shalt not give him thy money upon interest, nor give him thy victuals for increase" (Lev. 25:35–37). "Thou shalt not lend upon interest to thy brother: interest of money, interest of victuals, interest of anything that is lent upon interest. Unto a foreigner thou mayest lend upon interest; but unto thy brother thou shalt not lend upon interest; that the Lord thy God may bless thee in all that thou puttest thy hand unto..." (Deut. 23:20–21). The prohibition on taking interest in Exodus and Leviticus seems to be confined to the poor in straits and not to extend to moneylending in the normal course of business, but the deuteronomic prohibition clearly applies to all moneylending, excluding only business dealings with foreigners.

DEFINITION. The biblical term for interest is *neshekh* (Ex. 22:24; Deut. 23:20), but in the levitical text it occurs alongside *tarbit* or *marbit* (25:36–37). In the Jewish Publication Society translation (1962) *neshekh* is rendered as "advance interest" and *tarbit* or *marbit* as "accrued interest" – the one being deducted in advance, the other being added at the time of repayment. This is only one of many interpretations that were made of the terms *neshekh* and *tarbit* from the time of the Mishnah (BM 5:1) onward and by no means the best one. One commentator regards *neshekh* as accumulating interest and *tarbit* as a fixed sum of interest that never increases (Ramban to Lev. 25:36). The most authoritative view is that of Rava, that there is no difference in meaning between *neshekh* and *tarbit* (BM 60b); but while Rava maintains that the Torah used two synonyms in order to make the prohibition of interest a twofold one (*ibid.*), the better explanation etymologically would be that *neshekh*, meaning bite, was the term used for the exaction of interest from the point of view of the debtor, and *tarbit* or *marbit*, meaning increase, was the term used for the recovery of interest by the creditor (Solomon Luntschitz, *Keli Yakar*, Be-Ḥukkotai, Lev. 25:36).

The prohibition on interest is not a prohibition on usury in the modern sense of the term, that is, excessive interest, but of all, even minimal, interest. There is no difference in law between various rates of interest, as all interest is prohibited.

LEGAL CHARACTER OF PROHIBITION. It has been said that the prohibition on interest rests on two grounds: firstly, that the prosperous ought to help the indigent, if not by gifts, then at least by free loans; and secondly, that interest (or excessive interest) was seen to lie at the root of social ruin and was therefore to be outlawed in toto. Both these considerations would apply only internally: there could be no obligation to help foreigners, nor was public policy concerned with their well-being. Moreover, moneylending transactions with foreigners were motivated solely by the legitimate desire to make profits, while the internal economy was eminently agrarian and had no money markets of any importance. It follows from the charitable nature of the prohibition on interest that its violation was not regarded as a criminal offense to which any penal sanctions attached, but rather as a moral transgression; in other words, while taking interest would not entail any punishment, granting free loans and refraining from taking interest would lead to God's rewards and blessings (Deut. 23:21 and Ramban thereto). It was only in the prophecies of Ezekiel that usury came to be identified with the gravest of crimes: it is mentioned in the context of larceny, adultery, homicide, and other such "abominations" that are worthy of death (18:11–13). The threat of death for usury was later interpreted as the divine sanction against irrecoverable and illegitimate self-enrichment (BM 61b). "He that augmenteth his substance by interest and increase" is listed among the "evil men" (Prov. 28:8); while "He that putteth not out his money on interest" is among the upright and righteous (Ps. 15:5).

IMPLEMENTATION. The prohibition on taking interest does not appear to have been generally observed in biblical times. The creditor (*nosheh*), far from giving free loans, is often described as exacting and implacable (cf. I Sam. 22:2; II Kings 4:1; Isa. 50:1; et al.); and the prophet decries those who have "taken interest and increase" and forgotten God (Ezek. 22:12). Nehemiah had to rebuke the noble and the rich for exacting interest, "every one to his brother" (Neh. 5:7); and he had formally and solemnly to adjure them to abstain from levying execution (12–13). From the *Elephantine papyri it appears that among the Jews in Egypt in the fifth century B.C.E. it was a matter of course that interest would be charged on loans: not only did they disregard the biblical injunctions as far as the taking of interest was concerned, but they made no recourse to any legal fictions in order to evade the prohibition (R. Yaron, *Mishpat shel Mismekhei Yev* (1961), 136).

Talmudic Law

EXTENSION OF PROHIBITION. It is not only the creditor who takes interest who is violating the biblical prohibition, but also the debtor who agrees to pay interest, the guarantor who guarantees the debt that bears interest, the witnesses who attest the creation of an interest-bearing debt, and even the scribe who writes out the deed (BM 5:11; BM 75b; Yad, Malveh 4:2). This is one of the very rare cases in which accessories to the offense are held responsible (see *Penal Law). "Although the creditor and debtor transgress these biblical prohibitions, there is no flogging for it, as the interest must be repaid" (Yad, Malveh 4:3). The *Ḥinnukh* (no. 74) says further that none of the accessories is flogged "for since even the creditor is not flogged… it would not be right that those who are mere accessories should be liable for flogging."

The most far-reaching extensions of the prohibition relate, however, to the nature of the "interest" prohibited. Interest is no longer only the lending of four dinars for five, or of one bushel of wheat for two (BM 5:1), but is extended to all benefits that smack of interest or might look like it. Thus, the borrower may not let the lender live on his premises without payment of rent or at a reduced rent (BM 5:2), and if he had resided there without paying rent before borrowing the money, he must now be charged rent (BM 64b). The prohibition of lending one bushel of wheat for two was also extended to the lending of one bushel of wheat for one, since it was possible that the value of the wheat might increase between the date of the loan and the date of the return, and such increase in value would amount to prohibited interest (BM 5:9; TJ, BM 5:7); but the rule does not apply where seeds are lent for sowing and not for consumption (BM 5:8), and where the borrower possesses even the smallest quantity of the same species, he may borrow any quantity (BM 75a; Yad, Malveh 10:1–5). Where two men agree to do work for each other in turn, they may agree only on the same kind of work for each, as otherwise the work of one might be more valuable than that of the other and thus amount to prohibited interest (BM 5:10; Yad, Malveh 7:11). Gifts that one man may send to another in view of a forthcoming request for a loan, or in gratitude for a loan granted and returned, fall within the prohibition on interest – as are also "words," conveying to the lender, for instance, any valuable information (BM 5:10), or even greetings, where they would not otherwise have been exchanged (BM 75b; Tosef., BM 6:17). A mortgagee, even if he is in possession of the mortgaged property, is not allowed to take its produce; if he has taken it, he must either return it or set it off against the capital debt (BM 67a–b; Yad, Malveh 6:1–8; see also *Lien; *Pledge).

Interest in the guise of *sale was also prohibited. Fruit and other agricultural produce may not be sold unless and until its market price is established (BM 5:7), for otherwise the purchaser might, by paying in advance a price below the eventual market value, receive interest on his money; such advance purchases amounted in effect to financing the farmers, and were thus in the nature of loans rather than sales. But there is nothing to prevent the farmer from selling below the market value, once that value has been established: this would no longer be a disguised loan but a genuine if ill-advised sale (BM 63b; Yad, Malveh 9:1), subject always to the seller's remedies for **onaʾah* (BM 4:4). Sales of products without current market values would be recognized as such, and not be invalidated as disguised loans, only where the goods sold were actually in the hands of the seller at the time of the sale (Tosef., BM 6:2–5), or, where they had to be processed or manufactured, were almost completed at the time of the sale (BM 74a; Yad, Malveh 9:2).

Any payment is prohibited interest that compensates a party to any transaction for money being left, for any length of time, in the hands of the other party, although it should, according to law or custom, have already been paid over (BM 63b). Thus, as rent is legally due only at the end of the period of lease, a discount may be given for rent paid in advance (see *Lease and Hire); but as the purchase price for goods or land sold is payable at the time of the sale, any price increase for later payment would amount to prohibited interest (BM 5:2; BM 65a; Yad, Malveh 8:1).

A further notable extension of the prohibition on interest relates to contracts of *partnership. An arrangement by which one partner finances a business and the other manages it, and losses are borne by the managing partner only while the profits are shared between them is illegal, for it comes within the prohibition on interest (BM 70a; BM 5:6; Yad, Malveh 8:12). Where the financing partner bears or shares the losses, such an arrangement is valid only if the managing partner is being paid a salary for his work instead of, or in addition to, a share in the profits (BM 5:4; Yad, Malveh 5:9).

All these talmudic extensions of the prohibitions on interest are known as *avak ribbit*, i.e., the dust of interest, as distinguished from *ribbit kezuzah*, i.e., interest proper in an amount or at a rate agreed upon between lender and borrower (BM 61b, 67a, et al.). The difference in law between *avak ribbit* and *ribbit kezuzah* is that the latter, if it has been paid by the borrower to the lender, is recoverable from the lender, while the former, once paid, is not recoverable, though a contract tainted with the dust of interest will not be enforced (BM 61b; Yad, Malveh 4:6; Sh. Ar., YD 161:1–2; see also *Contract).

EVASION OF PROHIBITION. It has been said that the evasion of the prohibitions on interest reflects the conflict between law and life (Globus, see bibl., p. 39). It is remarkable how the talmudic jurists extended the prohibition on interest so as to cover, and invalidate, transactions far removed from the loans to which the biblical prohibition had attached, and at the same time sought ways and means to validate transactions clearly or conceivably falling within that prohibition. This phenomenon can only be explained by the change of economic conditions: it was in the amoraic period in Babylonia that the prohibitory laws against interest proved to be no longer compatible with the economic needs of the community; and ever since the necessity of finding legal subterfuges to evade those laws has persisted. The prohibition of price increase for payment that is made after a time lapse was practically abolished by the provision that any price may be agreed upon and recovered so long as the increase involved is not expressly but only tacitly stipulated (BM 65a; YD 173:1). The mishnaic rule that a managing partner must be paid a salary in order to validate the partnership agreement was set at nought in practice by the provision that such a salary need be nominal only (BM 68b). Profit-sharing partnerships were validated by regarding the investment of the financing partner as half loan and half deposit. While the borrower is responsible for the loan, the bailee is not responsible for the loss of the deposit; thus, the financing partner (as bailor) will also bear his share in the losses, and the partnership is legal (BM 104b). Even where the financing partner's share in the profits is redeemed in advance by a down payment, the agreement is upheld, provided that the business could reasonably be expected to be profitable (TJ, BM 5:8); and, later, deeds were formulated in which a pre-estimate of the expected profits was stipulated in advance as a fixed sum (BM 68a).

A farmer who had received a loan was allowed to make a formal conveyance of his lands (or part of them) to his creditor and still remain on his lands as his creditor's tenant; the creditor would be entitled to the produce of the land, not as interest on the loan but as income from his property (BM 68a). One jurist even held that it was permissible to let money on hire, like chattels, against payment of rent, as distinguished from giving a loan against payment of interest (BM 69b). A vendor may sell goods on credit at a price of 100 units payable at a future date, and immediately repurchase the goods at the price of 90 units payable cash down: each of the two contracts of sale would be valid (BM 62b).

Another form of evasion was to lend money on interest to a non-Jew, in order that the non-Jew might relend the money to the intended Jewish debtor; both lending transactions are valid (BM 61b).

Some of these forms of evasion, though practiced in talmudic times, have not become the **halakhah* (BM 68a per Rava; Yad, Malveh 5:8; 5:16; 6:4–5); others, though recognized as legally valid and feasible, were deprecated as reprehensible and forbidden (BM 61b–62b; Yad, Malveh 5:15) because of the stratagem involved in the device (*ha'aramah*).

SANCTIONS. Originally, courts appear to have been empowered to fine the creditor for taking interest by refraining from enforcing even his claim for the repayment of the capital (Tosef., BM 5:22), but the rule evolved that taking interest did not affect the creditor's enforceable right to have his capital debt repaid (BM 72a; Yad, Malveh 4:6). Where a bill, however, includes both capital and interest without differentiating between them, the bill is not enforceable (YD 161:11; Sh. Ar., ḤM 52:1), and "whoever finds a bill which includes interest, shall tear it up" (Tosef., BM 5:23; see also *Contract). Moneylenders who take interest are disqualified as *witnesses and are not administered oaths (Sanh. 3:3), and even the borrower who pays interest is disqualified (Sanh. 25a). In their moral turpitude, moneylenders who take interest are likened to apostates who deny God (Tosef., BM 6:17) and to shedders of blood (BM 61b); and they have no share in the world to come (Mekh. Sb-Y 22:24). They are doomed to lose all their property and go bankrupt (BM 71a; Sh. Ar., YD 160:2).

LEGALITY OF INTEREST. While biblical law allowed the taking of interest from foreigners, excluding alien residents (Lev. 25:35), talmudic law extended the exemption: "One may borrow from them [foreigners] and lend them on interest; similarly in the case of an alien resident" (BM 5:6, 70b–71a). However lawful interest transactions with foreigners were, they were looked upon with disapproval: some jurists held that they were permissible only when no other means of subsistence was available (BM 70b); others would allow them only to persons learned in the law, as the uneducated might fall into the error of believing that interest is permissible in general (BM 71a). The psalmist's praise of the man who would not lend his money on interest (Ps. 15:5) was interpreted to apply to the man who would not take interest from a foreigner (Mak. 24a).

Post-Talmudic Law

TRANSACTIONS AMONG JEWS. The talmudic evasions of the prohibition against interest served as precedents for the legalization of transactions involving interest. Thus it was deduced from the evasions reported in the Talmud that it would be permissible for a lender to lend 100 units to a businessman for him to use in his business; when it had increased to 200, the lender would be entitled to the 200, provided that he had paid the borrower some salary in consideration of his work (*Piskei ha-Rosh* BM 5:23; *Mordekhai* BM 319). Rashi is reported to have ruled that you may send your friend to take a loan on interest from another for you, or you may send your friend to give your money on interest to another; for interest is prohibited only as between lender and borrower, but not as between their respective agents. The general rule that a man's agent is like himself (see *Agency) would not apply here, as the taking of interest is a criminal offense, and in criminal matters no man can be made responsible for the deed of another (see *Penal Law; *Mordekhai* BM 338).

In time, a standard form of legalization of interest was established, known as *hetter iskah*, meaning the permission to form a partnership. A deed, known as *shetar iskah*, was drawn up and attested by two witnesses, stipulating that the lender would supply a certain sum of money to the borrower for a joint venture; the borrower alone would manage the business and he would guarantee the lender's investment against all loss; he would also guarantee to the lender a fixed amount of minimum profit. The deed would also contain a stipulation that the borrower would be paid a nominal sum as a salary, as well as an agreement on the part of the lender to share the losses. In order to render this loss-sharing agreement nugatory, provision would normally be made for such loss to be proved by particular, mostly unobtainable, evidence (*Naḥalat Shivah*, no. 40; cf. *Terumat ha-Deshen*, Resp. no. 302). The amount of the capital loan plus the guaranteed minimum profit would be recoverable on the deed at the stipulated time it matured.

In the course of the centuries this form of legalizing interest has become so well established that today all interest transactions are freely carried out, even in compliance with Jewish law, by simply adding to the note or contract concerned the words *al-pi hetter iskah*. The prohibition on interest has lost all practical significance in business transactions, and is now relegated to the realm of friendly and charitable loans where, indeed, it had originated.

TRANSACTIONS WITH NON-JEWS. In 1179 the Church decreed that the taking of interest was forbidden by Scripture as well as by the laws of nature, and that all Christian usurers would be liable to excommunication. As canon law did not apply to Jews, this decree did not prevent them from lending money on interest, and moneylending soon became a typically Jewish business. The Jews were practically forced into it by the severe restrictions placed upon them in the pursuit of any other trade or profession in most countries of Europe. From the point of view of Jewish law, the taking of interest from non-Jews was permitted; and the talmudic restriction that it should not be done unless there were no other means of subsistence was duly held to be complied with: "If we nowadays allow interest to be taken from non-Jews, it is because there is no end to the yoke and the burden king and ministers impose on us, and everything we take is the minimum for our subsistence, and anyhow we are condemned to live in the midst of the nations and cannot earn our living in any other manner except by money dealings with them; therefore the taking of interest is not to be prohibited" (Tos. to BM 70b s.v. *tashikh*). With the renewed change in circumstances, the prohibition on taking interest would apply to Jews and non-Jews alike (YD 159:1).

For nonlegal aspects see also *Moneylending.

[Haim Hermann Cohn]

The Rabbinical Period

The history of the prohibition of usury, in the sense of taking interest on loans, during the rabbinical period is the history of an ideal succumbing to the dictates of reality. The talmudic prohibition on taking interest, to which there was a plethora of lenient exceptions, fell into almost total desuetude as a result of socioeconomic circumstances. The trend toward erosion of this prohibition was identical in all of the Jewish Diasporas, although the means used to limit or evade it varied.

Many halakhic decisors permitted the charging of interest pursuant to judicial decision, insofar as it did not involve a credit transaction (Resp. *Sho'el u-Meishiv Tanina*, vol. 4 no. 123). The charging of interest as an arrears fine was also permitted by many authorities, even though they were aware that this was a means of circumventing the prohibition (Resp. Ribash 335; *Haggahot Mordechai* BM, no. 454). The authorities were also lenient regarding the prohibition of interest with regard to charitable and educational institutions, both as borrowers and as lenders (Resp. *Ha-Maharit*, YD, 45).

The halakhic sages also needed to deal with new kinds of financing arrangements resulting from economic developments. Thus, for example, the first maritime insurance contracts, which were a mixture of financing the shipment and insuring it, in consideration for a certain percentage of the value of the merchandise, was legitimized (Resp. Radbaz, Pt. 6, 2290). The granting of credit through the sale of promissory notes at a discount even before the time of repayment was permitted, notwithstanding the clear element of interest in such transactions (Sh. Ar., YD, 173:4).

The transition from consumer-oriented credit to business credit, that produced income for the borrower, and the finding of ways to permit interest-bearing loans led to the creation of general financial doctrines intended to protect the lender from a borrower who attempted to evade repayment of the loan under the pretext that he does not wish to transgress the proscription against interest. Rabbinical law provided that, in any transaction that may be interpreted as legal, even if the claim is far-fetched, there is an irrefutable presumption that the transaction was indeed carried out legally. This is consistent with the talmudic expression that "a person does not eat forbidden food and leave permitted food untouched" (Responsa Maharam 2: 80; Tosafot at Gittin 37b, s.v. *la shavik heteira*).

Moreover, it frequently occurs that merchants and businessmen may take interest-bearing loan from others on the basis of a factual presentation that enabled such a loan. After trading with the money, when the time comes for repayment of the loan, the borrower may become overly righteous and deny the original presentation of facts by claiming that he does not want to transgress the prohibition of interest.

The halakhic sages were morally outraged by such an argument and recognized that accepting such an argument would close the door upon potential borrowers in the future. The solution they found was that, at the time of the litigation between borrower and the lender, the borrower was not allowed to claim that at the time of the transaction he was a "transgressor." The borrower would be barred from raising a factual claim, even if it might be correct, if it conflicted with the facts presented at the time the transaction was entered into and of its result would be the invalidation of the transaction and his exemption from paying interest. This doctrine is similar in its mechanisms and results to the English equitable doctrine of estoppel that developed several hundred years later.

This doctrine was given a halakhic basis through the "civil" application of the well-known talmudic rule that "no man may call himself a wrongdoer." This rule was originally used in criminal law and precluded conviction of a person on the basis of self-incrimination. The transference of this rule to the area of civil law leads to obligating the defendant to repay on the basis of the irrefutable presumption that the borrower, who was a party to the transaction, did so with permission and not as a transgressor (Resp. Rosh, Rule 108,12:32; Sh. Ar., YD 177, and *Taz* and *Shakh* ad loc.; Resp. *Iggerot Moshe*, YD 66; ibid., ḤM 22).

Linked Loans

The steep inflation that has become a relatively common economic phenomenon has given rise to a new financial instrument: loans whose values are linked to the inflation index. This financial instrument is intended to protect the lender from a decrease in the value of his loan in terms of its buying power. In a linked loan, the borrower undertakes to repay the amount of the loan linked to the value of a foreign currency, to the cost of living index, or to the building price index, as agreed between the parties. The issue of linked loans is problematic vis-à-vis the prohibition on interest and remains complicated and convoluted.

The central problem regarding this context is the tension existing in defining the meaning of money: should it be defined in nominal terms, or should it be defined in real terms (i.e., its real value)? During a period of inflation, the borrower will insist on repaying the loan according to the specified, nominal amount of the loan, while the lender will argue that what is of importance is not the nominal value of the loan, but rather its actual value, that is, the purchasing power of the money in the marketplace of goods and services. It is clear that, if the nominal value is the criterion, any nominal addition will be considered as prohibited interest.

The governing principle in the talmudic *halakhah* was that of nominalism. An extreme expression of this principle is the prohibition of loaning (*seah be-seah*) "a bushel for a bushel [of grain]" (Mishnah, BM 5:9).The Mishnah prohibits loaning a bushel of grain in return for the future payment of the same amount, even if the lender received no additional payment. The rationale of this rule is that the criterion for defining "addition" is exclusively monetary. In as much as the value of the *se'ah* to be returned on the date of payment may exceed its value at the date of the loan, the result is that the lender receives a prohibited addition, which is defined as interest, even though in real terms, the lender did not receive more than the same *se'ah*. The basis of this prohibition is the sharp distinction drawn between "*tebea*" (currency) and "*pera*" (products and services) in which the latter is defined as the entirety of goods, merchandise, and services that are assessed in monetary terms. Currency, on the other hand, is regarded as an absolute and stable entity of unchanged value, while only the "fruits" become more or less costly. In practice, the prohibition became eroded and emptied of all content. The *amora* R. Isaac ruled that if a borrower had a *se'ah* "he may borrow against an unlimited amount of bushels" (BM 75a), while at a later time a legal fiction was created stating that there is no person who does not own at least one bushel (Tur, *Beit Yosef*, YD 162). Paradoxically, Jewish law in the Middle Ages relied on the fiction of "bushel for bushel (*se'ah be-se'ah*)" as a central instrument for permitting linked loans. It was done in a manner that circumvented the prohibition of *se'ah be-se'ah*: The nominal subject of the loan was bushels or gold, and this form of loan was permitted on the basis of a legal fiction that any borrower owned at least a minimal amount of grain or gold, and on this basis he could borrow a large amount of the same product, when, and despite that fact that the loan was actually a monetarily linked loan (*Bet Yosef*, Tur, YD 172; Resp. Ribash no.19). At the same time, loans that were formally referred to as linked loans continued to be prohibited.

Talmudic *halakhah* based on the formal, nominalistic doctrine based on the "bushel for bushel" prohibition was confronted by the realistic approach to monetary changes initiated by the government, as opposed to market based currency fluctuations. Jewish law distinguished between price rises as a result of market forces and price rises as a result of government-initiated reduction of the value of currency. Regarding the devaluation or revaluation of the currency itself, which had an immediate effect on the price of goods and services, Rav Ashi ruled that the question of whether or not the lender received an additional sum would be answered not on the basis of the nominal test, but rather through a comparative examination of the purchasing power at the time of the loan and at the time of repayment (BM 94b; *Sefer ha-Terumot*, [1586], Pt. 8:3). This conservative trend, of distinguishing between currency fluctuations resulting from governmental initiatives as distinct from changes in the actual buying power of money due to *existing market forces*, persists even today. While the *posekim* require valuation of the debt in the event of changes in the value of the currency initiated by the government, they forbid such valuation as usurious if the change is the product of market factors. One of the leading *posekim* of the 20th century, Rabbi Karelitz, was well aware that the value of money – like that of any other merchandise – rises and falls in relation to the quantity available, but nevertheless adhered to the original talmudic law according to which money is an absolute value to which the concepts of expensive and cheap do not apply (*Hazon Ish*, YD 104b). Rabbi Moshe Feinstein, who uses a realistic criterion when it comes to the obligation to tithe money from inflationary profits, also prohibits linked loans (Resp. *Iggerot Moshe*, YD, Pt. 2:104). This doctrine reflects the accepted approach taken by contemporary rabbinical authorities and of rabbinical court rulings in Israel (Responsa *Yaskil Avdi*, Pt. 5, YD, sec. 18; *Berit Yehudah* 20:20). Nevertheless, the high rate of steep inflation in Israel in the 1970s led to movement in a more realistic direction (thus Rabbi Goren in PDR 11:235).

Hetter Iskah

Global economic development has changed the general function of credit, from being a means of assisting the poor to serving primarily as a business tool. This change in the nature of credit has led halakhic scholars to seek moral justifications for circumventing the prohibition of interest. From the beginning of the period of the *aḥaronim* (ca. 15th century) until today, the accepted means for legitimizing the free flow of interest bearing credit has been the *hetter iskah*. The basic idea underlying this financial tool is the distinction drawn by the *halakhah* between a loan and a deposit.

A loan is defined in *halakhah* as a transfer of ownership from the lender to the borrower against the borrower's commitment to return assets similar to those borrowed upon a particular date. A deposit, by contrast, is defined in *halakhah* as transfer of possession without transfer of ownership.

The promulgation of the *hetter iskah* by the Sages during the talmudic period was not necessarily to avoid the prohibition of interest. The Sages intended to create a uniform model for partnership of capital and labor (whether for manufacture, trade, or enterprise). The legal structure of the *iskah* is that half of the money invested is considered as a deposit, over which the one "giving" continues to be the owner, while the other half of the sum is treated as a loan, over which the one "engaged" in business (i.e., the borrower) is considered the owner. He is the sole party to absorb losses from that half and he is the only one entitled to any revenue from it. The practical result is a division of both opportunities for profit and of risk between the owner of the capital, on the one hand, and the entrepreneur, manufacturer or merchant, on the other hand. In order to avoid transgressing the prohibition of interest, talmudic *halakhah* provided that the owner of the capital should pay wages, even if only a symbolic sum, to the one receiving the capital for his handling of that part of the capital that is considered as a pledge.

The first *hetter iskah* document is attributed to Rabbi Menachem Mendel of Cracow, known as the Maharam (*Naḥalat Shiva*, 40), at the end of the 16th century. The *hetter* received the halakhic approval of the sages of Ashkenaz and even attained legislative status (*Kuntres ha-Ribbit* by the author of *Me'irat Einayim*, and the decision of the Council of the Four Lands at the Kremnitz fair in 1607). This *hetter* became popular and many of the loan agreements incorporated this classic formulation, which was accepted by all of the halakhic decisors of Ashkenaz, by way of reference – that is, that a provision was made that all transactions between parties be in accordance with the *hetter iskah* as promulgated by the Maharam (Rabbi Jacob Blau, *Brit Yehudah*, chap. 41.8). During this time similar *hetteirim* were fashioned by the Sephardi authorities (*Ginat Veradim*, YD, *klal* 6, no. 4), which have long been accepted by all Jewish communities.

The legal structure upon which the *hetter iskah* rests involves three basic components: (1) *iskah* (the transaction); (2) the investor (the lender); and (3) the one intended to use the money (the borrower).

Every loan or credit transaction is considered as a partnership between the investor (i.e., the lender) and the one intended to use the money (the borrower). On the basis of the Talmudic model of *iskah*, the investor is entitled to a portion of the revenue because of that portion of the loan that is considered as a "deposit." There are also *hetterim* based upon the classical talmudic model, i.e., a partnership between the "deposit" portion of the capital and that portion which is a "loan" throughout the period of the credit. There are other *hetterim*, such as that of the Maharam, based upon a deposit which, once it realizes an agreed-upon level of profit, is turned into a loan.

Given that the parties are free to make conditions, the lender can protect his investment by including in the agreement a condition that the loan may only be used for solid, profitable businesses – a condition making it difficult for the borrower to claim that he suffered a loss, one that even obligates him to pay profits.

Essentially, the *hetter iskah* is based upon the freedom to make conditions in laws of evidence. The lender/"investor" is entitled to receive a detailed report of the objectives of the investment, profits, losses, etc. He is entitled to set forth stringent means of proof regarding all these subjects in the loan/"partnership" agreement. Along with these stringent means of proof, there is also a clause exempting the borrower/"business user" from the requirements of reporting, in exchange for payment of a predetermined percentage of the value of the loan.

In practice, the borrower "acquires" from his partner the potential profit and the need to provide proofs in exchange for payment of a fixed amount or percentage agreed-upon in advance. Thus, the "interest" is paid as a waiver fee for the loaner's right to accounting and proof ("compromise fee"), and not as an addition to the principal of the loan. In this way, the prohibition of interest is circumvented.

These *hetterei iskah* were accepted by all of the later decisors and there is no one who questions their validity. This is the accepted manner of entering into credit agreements where the parties observe *mitzvot*. The use of *hetter iskah* for banking transactions is mentioned in the responsa literature at the end of the 19th century (Responsa Maharsham, Pt. I, no. 20). The banking industry in Israel has also adopted this device, and in many bank branches the accepted version of the *hetter iskah* is displayed in public. The classic *hetter iskah* has been expanded to include investments that do not realize profits, on the basis of the assumption that even consumer credit allows the borrower to invest time or money in other pursuits (Resp. *Sho'el u-Meishiv*, Pt. I, no. 137; Resp. Maharsham, Pt. II, no. 216). Decisions of Israeli civil courts have likewise recognized the *hetter iskah* as part of the contractual framework obligating the parties and has analyzed its provisions as part of the agreement between them (Motion 5317/86 *Bank Mizrahi v. Tishler et al.*, PSM 48(2) 353).

The *hetter iskah* as a valid contractual provision was also recognized in a decision of a New York State court (290 NYS 2D 997, *Leibovici v. Rawicki*). The positive attitude to the *hetter iskah* and its perception as a vital instrument for the capital market, which prevents doors being closed to borrowers, has also been recognized in contemporary rabbinical court decisions (File 17046/44, 16 PDR 74).

[Ben-Zion Eliash (2nd ed.)]

BIBLIOGRAPHY: J. Marcuse, *Das biblisch-talmudische Zinsenrecht* (1895); E. Cohn, in: *Zeitschrift fuer vergleichende Rechtswissenschaft*, 18 (1905), 37–72; J. Hejcl, *Das alttestamentliche Zinsverbot im Lichte der ethnologischen Jurisprudenz sowie des altorientalischen Zinswesens* (1907); H.L. Strack, in: *Realencyklopaedie fuer protestantische Theologie und Kirche*, 21 (19083), 518–21; I.S. Zuri, *Mishpat ha-Talmud*, 5 (1921), 63f., 134–9; Gulak, Yesodei, 2 (1922), 72, 107, 172–6; I. Bernfeld, *Das Zinsverbot bei den Juden nach talmudisch-rabbinischen Recht* (1924); S. Rosenbaum, in: *Ha-Mishpat ha-Ivri*, 2 (1926), 27, 191–4; E.L. Globus, in: *Ha-Mishpat*, 2 (1927), 23–43; E.S. Rappaport, in: *Zeitschrift fuer vergleichende Rechtswissenschaft*, 47 (1932/33), 256–378; A. Gulak, *Toledot ha-Mishpat be-Yisrael bi-Tekufat ha-Talmud*, 1 (*Ha-Ḥiyyuv ve-Shi'budav*, 1939), 45, 117f., 145; Herzog, Instit, 2 (1939), 135; S.J. Rabinowitz, in: *Yavneh*, 3 (1949), 165–74; R. Katzenelboigen, *ibid.*, 175–9; B.N. Nelson, *The Idea of Usury, from Tribal Brotherhood to Universal Otherhood* (1949); ET, 1 (1951^{3}), 46f.; 2 (1949), 51; 4 (1952), 111; 7 (1956), 394; 9 (1959), 714–22; 10 (1961), 102f., 108; J. Rosenthal, in: *Talpioth*, 5 (1951/52), 475–92; 6 (1952/53), 130–52; T. Be'eri, in: *Ha-Torah ve-ha-Medinah*, 5–6 (1952/54), 296–301; J. Segal, *ibid.*, 9–10 (1957/59), 451–90; E. Neufeld, in: JQR, 44 (1953/54), 194–204; idem, in: HUCA, 26 (1955), 355–412; M. Elon, in: *Ḥok u-Mishpat*, 1 (1955), issue 22, pp. 6–8; S. Stein, in: JSS, 1 (1956), 141–64; B. Rabinowitz-Te'omim, in: *Ha-Torah ve-ha-Medinah*, 11–13 (1959–62), 16–45; J.T. Noonan, *The Scholastic Analysis of Usury* (1957); N.N. Lemberger, in: *No'am*, 2 (1958/59), 33–37; J. Wassermann, *ibid.*, 3 (1959/60), 195–203; M.N. Lemberger, *ibid.*, 4 (1960/61), 251–7; Z. Domb, *ibid.*, 258–65; Elon, Mafte'aḥ, 302–7; B. Cohen, *Jewish and Roman Law*, 2 (1966), 433–56, 784f.; S.E. Loewenstamm, in: EM, 5 (1968), 929f. **ADD. BIBLIOGRAPHY:** M. Elon, *Ha-Mishpat ha-Ivri* (1988), 1:94, 97, 114, 197, 489, 575, 577, 642, 654, 660, 730, 738, 764, 787–89; 2:993, 1031, 1051, 1053, 1069, 1073, 1231, 1247; 3:1443; idem, *Jewish Law* (1994), 1:105, 109, 128, 222; 2:596, 708, 711, 795, 809, 816, 901, 910, 941, 966–68; 3:1201, 1246, 1269, 1272, 1294, 1475; 4:1716; M. Elon and B. Lifshitz, *Mafte'aḥ ha-She'elot ve-ha-Teshuvot shel Ḥakhmei Sefarad u-Ẓefon Afrikah* (legal digest) (1986), 2:448–59; B. Lifshitz and E. Shochetman, *Mafte'aḥ ha-She'elot ve-ha-Teshuvot shel Ḥakhmei Ashkenaz, Ẓarefat ve-Italyah* (legal digest) (1997); B-Z. Eliash: "Ideological Roots of the Halakhah: A Chapter in the Laws of Interest," in: *Shenaton ha-Mishpat ha-Ivri*, 5 (1977), 7; A. Hacohen, *"Banka'ut lelo Ribit ve-Hetter Iskah bi-Medinah Yehudit ve-Demokratit, Halakhah ve-Eein Morin Ken?"* in: *Sha'arei Mishpat*, 2 (1999) 77; N. Dreyfus, *"Dinei Ribbit ve-Hetter Iskah be-Re'i ha-Kalkalah ha-Modernit,"* in: *Teḥumin*, 14 (1992), 207; Z.Y. Ben-Yaakov, *"Hetter Iskah – Setimat Kol ha-Perazot,"* in: *Teḥumin*, 23 (2003), 373.

UTAH, Rocky Mountain state between Nevada and Colorado. The proposed State of Deseret, founded by members of the Church of Jesus Christ of Latter-day Saints, LDS, (Mormons), in 1847 and acknowledged as Utah Territory in 1850, became a state in 1896. Utah is the rare place on earth where the Jews are considered "Gentiles," in this case non-Mormons.

While the Mormon flight to the West was one of religious liberty, western Jewish migration was spurred by a sense of adventure, romance, economics, risk, and personal and religious freedom away from the stigma of antisemitism encountered in Europe.

As early as 1826, Jewish trappers traversed the territory. In 1854, Jewish daguerreotypist and writer Solomon Nunes *Carvalho traveling with Colonel John C. Fremont's mapmaking expedition yielded unparalleled images of the young Mormon community. That same year, Julius and Fannie Brooks became Utah's first Jewish family. Many Jewish entrepreneurs followed, establishing commercial shops and business ventures both large and small.

Believing themselves members of a lost tribe, Mormon theology maintains a special affiliation with Judaism, and at the same time identifies Jews as "Gentiles," non-Mormons. By the 1860s, increasing numbers of Gentiles in the Territory posed a threat to Mormon autonomy. LDS Church leaders adopted a resolution pledging its members to be self-sustaining and to boycott Gentile-owned businesses.

Bitterness between Gentiles and Mormons reached such heights that non-Mormons feared for their livelihood and

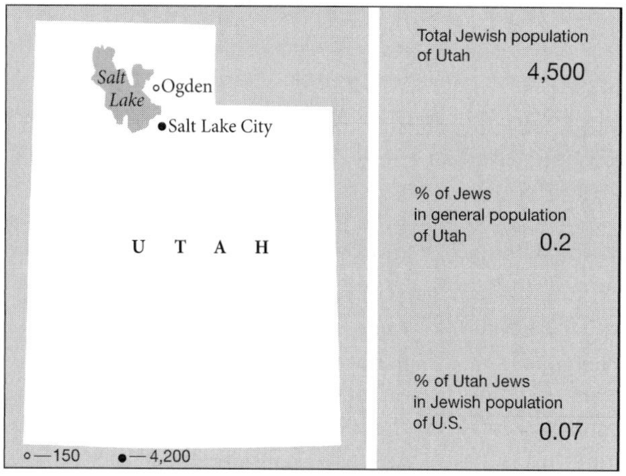

Jewish communities in Utah. Population figures for 2001.

safety. Rental property stood vacant, merchants forced into bankruptcy fled the Territory; others relocated to the railroad town of Ogden and the all-Gentile tent city of Corrine. When the transcontinental railroad (1869) and subsequent mining enterprises precluded all possibilities of Mormon seclusion, sanctions were lifted. (By 1930, 100 Jewish-owned businesses lined the downtown streets of Salt Lake City.)

Utah's early Jewish population was comprised of mostly middle-class and educated German émigrés (1857–1874) and pious Eastern European Jews (1890–1920).

Early on, people worshipped in their homes. In 1866 on property loaned by Brigham Young, the newly-formed Hebrew Benevolent Society dedicated the first cemetery in the Intermountain West. In Salt Lake City, 1881, Reform German members incorporated Congregation B'nai Israel. In 1889, Russian and Polish Jews held Conservative services in the home of Nathan Rosenblatt and in 1904 built Congregation Montefiore. The short-lived (1915–1930) but lively Shaarey Tzedek offered Orthodox services. In Ogden, Congregation Brith Sholem (formed in 1890 and built 1916), remains the state's oldest, continuously operating synagogue. In 1972, the two Salt Lake synagogues merged into Congregation Kol Ami. In 1990, the Chabad Lubavitch synagogue, Bais Menachem, opened its doors; earlier the Chavurah B'Yachad offered Reconstructionist programs; and in 1995, Reform Temple Har Sholem was founded in Park City.

In Clarion, 300 immigrant Jewish farmers (1911–1916) created a new chapter in western history with the last major attempt of Jewish colonization on land in the United States. Jews have contributed much to Utah history, including Senator Simon Bamberger (1903–1907), who became the first Democrat, first non-Mormon, and only Jewish Utah governor in 1916; Salt Lake City mayor Louis Marcus (1932–1935); Tooele mayor Sol Selvin (1942–1946); Toquerville mayor, Dr. David Dolowitz (1980); and in 2005, Patrice Arent, the highest-ranking woman in the Utah legislature, and Representative David Litvack. Jews have also been involved in higher education representing major Utah universities, medical schools, and colleges.

In a state of 2,400,000 people, an estimated 4,500 Jews reside in Utah (2001), primarily in Salt Lake City, but also in Park City and Ogden.

BIBLIOGRAPHY: Eileen Hallet Stone, *A Homeland in the West: Utah Jews Remember* (2002).

[Eileen Hallet Stone (2nd ed.)]

UTENA (or **Utyana**; Rus. **Utsyany**; Heb. and Yid. אוטיאן), town in E. Lithuania. One of the earliest Jewish communities in Lithuania, Utena had a Jewish cemetery with tombstones from the 16th century. In 1765 there were 565 Jews in Utena and the communities under its jurisdiction; in 1847 they numbered 1,416, increasing to 2,405 (75% of the total population) in 1897. During the period of Lithuanian independence (1918–39) the town developed considerably and its Jewish population increased; in 1935 their number was estimated at 5,000 (about 33% of the population). The major source of livelihood was trade in flax, skins, and boar bristles. The community supported both a *Tarbut and a Yiddish school. The Germans arrived on June 25, 1941. On July 14 they removed the Jews from the town and during the month of August murdered most of them in the Rzhech forest. After the war the community was not reconstituted. There were about 50 Jews in the late 1960s, and no synagogue. In 1963 the Jewish cemetery was completely destroyed and its land earmarked for a building project. A monument has been erected for the Jews murdered by the Nazis.

BIBLIOGRAPHY: *Yahadut Lita*, 3 (1967), 284–5.

[Yehuda Slutsky]

UTICA, commercial and industrial center in the Mohawk Valley in central New York State; population (2002) 59,684, estimated Jewish population 1,100. Both the city and its Jewish population have declined from the 1970s; the decline of Jews has been proportionately greater. Utica was first settled in 1786. The first Jew to make it his home was probably Abraham Cohen, who brought his family there in 1847 from Poland, the homeland of nearly all of Utica's early Jewish settlers. In 1848 the first synagogue, Beth Israel, was established with 20 families and by 1871 there were at least 225 Jewish family heads. Waves of Russian and Polish immigrants in the years after 1870 increased the number of Jews to 2,517 by 1920. Most of the early Jewish settlers were peddlers, while many of the post-1870 immigrants started out as manual workers. The peddlers generally went into wholesaling or branched out into new enterprises, and after 1915 Jews began to enter the professions. Not many Utican Jews became wealthy, but among those who did, several attained national prominence, such as Miles Rosenberg, president of the Miles Shoe Store chain, and David Bernstein, vice president of the Loew's theater concern. From the 1930s on, Jews began to take an increasingly active interest in local civic organizations. Between 1904 and 1958, 22 Jews held political office, including state judge H. Myron Lewis.

Utica's Jews have generally followed traditional Judaism. Congregation House of Jacob, founded in 1870, brought to Utica its first ordained rabbi, Moses Reichler, in 1897. An attempt to establish a Reform temple in 1903 ended in failure but in 1919 Temple Beth El, a Conservative synagogue, was founded with Rabbi Reuben Kaufman as its head. During the first quarter of the 20th century Jews served their social needs through fraternal lodges, a YMHA and YWHA and a Workmen's Circle (1892). Local chapters of several organizations such as Hadassah (1917) and the Zionist Organization of America (1938) were formed and Jews contributed to World War I relief funds, the United Jewish Appeal and other charities. Through the initiative of Rabbi S. Joshua Kohn of Temple Beth El a Jewish Community Council was organized in 1933 to supervise and unify the many functions of the Jewish community. A Jewish Community Center was founded in 1955 and after 1949 the community's affairs were recorded in the *Jewish Community News*. In the early 21st century the community still supported three synagogues Temple Beth El, Temple Emanu-El (Reform), and Congregation Zvi Jacob which is Orthodox.

BIBLIOGRAPHY: S.J. Kohn, *Jewish Community, of Utica, 1847–1948* (1959).

UTITZ, EMIL (1883–1956), philosopher. Born in Prague, Utitz was professor at Halle and Prague. From 1942 to 1945 he was interned in the German concentration camp at Theresienstadt. His principal fields of interest were (1) aesthetics, in which he used a phenomenological analysis to assert the autonomy of art: art and aesthetics are related but not identical, the latter being a branch of the philosophy of culture; (2) characterology, i.e., the scientific study of the drives of the human personality in its manifold manifestations. Utitz edited the *Jahrbuch fuer Charakterologie* (6 vols.); and (3) the philosophy of man and the philosophy of culture: culture is explained as man's attempt to overcome his finite limitations, hence its universality.

Utitz sought to expound the problem of time; he also wrote on the psychology of the concentration camp at Theresienstadt and on "Germany between yesterday and tomorrow." As a young man Utitz dissociated himself from the Jewish community, but the influence of Nazism brought about his return.

His principal works are *Grundlegung der allgemeinen Kunstwissenschaft* (2 vols., 1914–20); *Der Kuenstler* (1925); *Geschichte der Aesthetik* (1932); *Psychologie der Simulation* (1918); *Charakterologie* (1925); *Kultur der Gegenwart* (1922); *Ueberwindung des Expressionismus* (1927); *Mensch und Kultur* (1933); *Sendung der Philosophie in unserer Zeit* (1935); "Erinnerungen an F. Brentano", in: *Wissenschaftliche Zeitschrift der Universitaet Halle* (4 no. 1, 1954); and *Egon Erwin Kisch, der klassische Journalist* (1956). As a young man Utitz published (c. 1904) a book of poems under the pseudonym Ernst Limé.

BIBLIOGRAPHY: S. Ẓemaḥ, *Al ha-Yafeh* (1939), 242–64; Bergman, in: *Hogim u-Ma'aminim* (1959), 211–23.

[Samuel Hugo Bergman]

UTKIN, JOSEPH PAVLOVICH (1903–1944), Soviet Russian poet. Born in Manchuria, Utkin was the son of an employee of the Russian-owned Chinese Eastern Railroad and was raised in Irkutsk, far from the main centers of Jewish life. Nevertheless, he succeeded in learning enough about Jewish customs and traditions, and acquired a sufficient knowledge of Yiddish, to produce the most important long Russian poem on a Jewish theme yet to appear in Soviet literature. His adolescence was far from idyllic. In a poem sarcastically titled "My Beloved Childhood" (*Miloye detstvo*, 1933), he recalled his bossy aunt who wanted him to devote himself "to God and commerce." Utkin's rebellion led him to the fringes of the underworld and eventually prompted him to join Siberia's Bolshevik guerrillas. His first poems were militant exhortations to greater efforts for a Communist victory. Utkin's most famous poem, highly praised by such writers as Maxim *Gorki and Vladimir Mayakovski, was written in his early twenties. It was *Povest o ryzhem Motele* ("The Tale of Motele the Redhead," 1925). This was unique in its use of a mixture of Russian and Yiddish. The poem's hero, a humble tailor from Kishinev, is a typical *shtetl*-dweller. The proletarian Motele shaves off his side curls and sheds his kaftan to become a commissar, but the reactionary Rabbi Isaiah pines after the good old days. Most of Kishinev's Jews, however, are simply confused, and complain in the synagogue about food shortages. They forget that the fleshpots of Egypt were paid for with suffering and humiliation, and that the bread of affliction is also the symbol of freedom and of future happiness. "The Tale of Motele the Redhead," an original and striking poem. is now also a wistful monument to the great expectations awakened among pauperized Russian Jews by the Bolshevik Revolution.

Despite Utkin's unquestionable allegiance to the Soviet cause, orthodox Soviet critics began in the late 1920s to attack him for what they considered the dangerously individualistic lyrical and sentimental character of his verse. He was urged to mend his ways and to write about themes such as industrialization and the collectivization of agriculture. After resisting these pressures for some years, he finally gave in and promised to reform. He was never, however, entirely accepted as a Stalinist poet in good standing and continued to be hounded by the critics until the outbreak of the Nazi-Soviet war in the summer of 1941. His book *Ya videl sam* ("I Saw," 1942) described the German invasion of the U.S.S.R. Utkin's first war poem was written the day after hostilities began, and he continued to write patriotic verse for army newspapers until the end of his life. Severely wounded in action, he dictated his poems in an army hospital, and though an invalid, returned to active duty. He died in a plane crash a few months before the end of the war.

There is reason to believe that Utkin wrote poems inspired by the Holocaust that were never published.

BIBLIOGRAPHY: A.A. Saakyants, *Iosif Utkin, ocherk zhizni i tvorchestva* (1969), incl. bibl.: A.Z. Lezhnev, *Sovremenniki. literaturno-kriticheskiye ocherki* (1927), 95–118; V.G. Veshnev, *Vzvolnovannaya poeziya* (1928), 27–43.

[Maurice Friedberg]

°**UVAROV, SERGEY SEMYONOVICH** (1786–1855), minister of education in Russia (1833–49), and president of the Academy of Sciences. In 1846 he was granted the title of count. Uvarov originated the political slogan *Pravoslaviye, Samoderzhaviye, Narodnost* ("Orthodoxy [i.e., of the Eastern Church], Autocracy, Nationhood"), a slogan which was accepted by the Russian "Slavophiles," who adopted it as the catchword of their program. As the minister of education, along with his other duties, Uvarov concerned himself with Jewish education, considering it part of the Jewish problem in general. In a memorandum to Czar *Nicholas I, he noted that many governments who had tried for generations to solve the Jewish problem through persecution and coercion had finally abandoned these methods for an approach based on wielding influence by reason. He concluded that it was incumbent upon the Russian government to adopt the latter method, and stated that nations could not be exterminated, especially a nation which during its modern history "stood at Mount Golgotha." The Jews were to be "reformed" and through education brought closer to the general population. In order to achieve this, Uvarov proposed the establishment of a network of Jewish government schools at various levels, in the *Pale of Settlement, to be maintained by the special taxes paid by the Jews. In 1841 he invited Max *Lilienthal to act as adviser and director of the program. Uvarov and Lilienthal planned to invite 200 teachers from abroad to assist them in their endeavors and also called upon Jewish scholars and intellectuals abroad (including I.M. *Jost, L. *Philippson, A. *Geiger, I.N. *Mannheimer, S.D. *Luzzatto, and others) to come to Russia to participate in the fulfillment of the program. In 1842 a "Committee of Rabbis" (or "Committee for the Education of the Jews") was convened in order to give an official cachet to the project; its members were R. Mendel *Schneersohn of Lubavich, R. Isaac b. Ḥayyim *Volozhiner, Y.Y. Halperin, a banker of Berdichev, and Bezalel *Stern, the director of the Jewish school in Odessa.

In 1844 the bill providing for the establishment of Jewish government schools was ratified. With certain amendments which were made during the 1870s, it remained in force until the end of the czarist regime. Uvarov considered that the Talmud was the source of all evil, and a corrupting influence on the Jews, and he attempted to minimize this by reducing the hours given to its instruction. He did not entirely prohibit the study of the Talmud so as not to turn the Jews against his educational endeavors. Uvarov sought to gain the sympathy of Moses *Montefiore and I.A. *Cremieux, and although he invited them to attend the above conference they did not do so. In 1846 Montefiore visited Russia and met Uvarov. Uvarov was anxious to prove to Montefiore that he intended only to promote the welfare of the Jews and he complained to Montefiore about the religious fanaticism and ignorance of the Jews of Russia. Uvarov's attitude toward contemporary Hebrew literature was, however, favorable, and the *maskilim* in Russia welcomed his program.

BIBLIOGRAPHY: Dubnow, Hist Russ, index; Klausner, Sifrut, 2–4 (1952–53[2]), Russian index in each volume; M.G. Morgulis, *Voprosy yevreyskoy zhizni* (1889); P.S. Marek, *Ocherki po istorii prosveshcheniya yevreyev v Rosii* (1909).

[Baruch Shohetman]

UVILLER, HARRY (1897–1973), U.S. trade union leader. Born in Brooklyn, Uviller joined the women's garment industry in 1915 as part-time bookkeeper and salesman in the coat trade, at the same time attending the evening division of the New York University School of Law, but after graduation he chose to remain in the garment industry. He organized the coat contractors and became general manager of the American Coat and Suit Manufacturers Association. In 1936, with the support of Mayor Fiorello H. La *Guardia and the International Ladies Garment Workers Union, Uviller became impartial chairman of the industry; concurrently, he held the post of chairman of the New York State Mediation Board from 1955 to 1958. Under his leadership, there was no market-wide strike in the industry from 1936 to 1958. In the garment strike in the latter year, Uviller and Senator Herbert H. *Lehman acted as mediators. As chairman of the New York State Mediation Board, Uviller mediated hundreds of labor disputes, earning a reputation for integrity and fairness with both labor and management. In 1961 the Harry Uviller Chair in Economics was established in his honor at Brandeis University, and in the same year he served as chairman of the Greater New York Histadrut Council.

UZ (Heb. עוּץ). The identification of the land of Uz, Job's home, is rendered difficult by the fact that two distinct locations are called Uz in the Bible. In Genesis 10:23; 22:21; and I Chronicles 1:17 Uz is clearly associated with Aram. However, in Genesis 36:28 and I Chronicles 1:42 it is, though less clearly, associated with Edom, and in Lamentations 4:21, "the land of Uz" seems to be a designation for an extensive region of which Edom is a part, or else a generic designation of Edom. S.R. Driver and G.B. Gray solve this contradiction by suggesting that Uz is the name of widely scattered Arab tribes, but in Job it refers to Aram. N.H. Tur-Sinai suggests that Job (and perhaps a tribe called Uz) once lived in Edom and then moved to Aram, and all other occurrences in the Bible placing Uz in Edom derive from this tradition. P. Dhorme, on the basis of clear association between the names of Job's friends and southern localities, placed Uz in Edom. M.H. Pope concludes that, "It seems impossible to reconcile the conflicting evidences and opinions as to the exact location of Uz."

BIBLIOGRAPHY: S.R. Driver and G.B. Gray, *A Critical and Exegetical Commentary on the Book of Job* (ICC 1921), 2ff.; P. Dhorme, *Le Livre De Job* (1926); N.H. Tur-Sinai, *The Book of Job* (1957); M.H. Pope, *Job* (1965), 3ff.

[Daniel Boyarin]

UZAL (Heb. אוּזָל), a geographic designation in the Bible, appearing in two different and seemingly unrelated contexts.

(1) In the Table of Nations, Uzal is a descendant of Shem and son of Joktan (Gen. 10:27; I Chron. 1:21), and probably refers to Sanʿa, the capital of Yemen, since the family of Joktan represents the inhabitants of Southern Arabia and Azal is the pre-Islamic name of Sanʿa.

(2) The Uzal mentioned in Ezekiel 27:19 was, apparently, one of the places which traded with Tyre, Although the meaning of the text is uncertain, in the light of the Septuagint reading of *yayin* (יַיִן, "wine") instead of *Javan (יָוָן), it seems to be dealing with a wine-producing region comparable to that of Helbon (near Damascus), mentioned in the preceding verse. Now, wine from Izalla is compared to wine from Helbon in a lexical text from Nineveh. Accordingly, the Uzal of Ezekiel 27:19 is probably to be identified with the Izalla of cuneiform sources, which was located near the Upper Tigris (Izalla Mountain of Byzantine historians).

BIBLIOGRAPHY: R. Strothmann, in: EL, 4 (1934²), 154; J. Lewy, in: *Orientalia*, 21 (1952), 1–12; A. Millard, in: JSS, 7 (1962), 201–3.

[Irene Grumach]

UZAN, family of North African origin. SOLOMON (d. 1812) was *dayyan* in the town of Sousse, *Tunisia. His family settled in Tunis, where many of its members became distinguished lawyers and physicians. In 1886 MICHAEL (d. 1889) was appointed head of Tunisian Jewry and given the title of caʿid. His grandson, also named MICHAEL (1881–?), was a chemist and agronomist as well as a diplomat and a philanthropist. VICTOR (1863–?), scholar and linguist, translated the poetry of several French poets into Hebrew. In 1885, together with M. Castro, he established a press in Tunis which published literary works in Judeo-Arabic. His recommendations on the personal status and the matrimonial law of the Jews were accepted by the courts of appeal of France and Tunisia.

BIBLIOGRAPHY: P. Lambert, *Choses et gens de Tunisie* (1912), 417; *Livre d'Or de Tunisie* (1932), 182–3.

[David Corcos]

UZAN, AHARON (1924–), Israeli politician. Uzan was born in *Tunisia and immigrated to Israel in 1948. Although a goldsmith by profession, he became a farmer and building worker in moshav Gilat in the Negev, where he remained. He was manager of the Negev Purchasing Organization (1957–65), secretary of Tenu'at ha-Moshavim (the moshav movement), and president of the Negev Economic Club. He became recognized as Israel's expert on the future of the Negev.

He was elected a member of the Sixth Knesset in 1965 as a representative of the Labor Alignment and served as deputy minister of agriculture from 1965 to 1969. He was appointed minister of communications in the government of Golda Meir in March 1974 and minister of agriculture in June of the same year, remaining in that office until the elections of May 1977. He was the first cabinet minister to be appointed from the members of the mass immigration from North Africa after the establishment of the State.

In the 1981 Knesset elections he joined with Aharon Abuhazeira in forming Tami and served in the Knesset as one of its representatives. He also served as deputy minister of absorption and subsequently as welfare minister and absorption minister.

UZBEKISTAN, one of the independent CIS republics from 1990, formerly a U.S.S.R. republic in Soviet Central Asia.

The Jews in Uzbekistan were affiliated with two communities: (1) the ancient one, the Jews of *Bukhara, who speak a Tajik-Jewish dialect; (2) the new one, of Eastern European origin.

According to their tradition, the Bukharan Jews emigrated from *Persia at the time of the persecutions of King Peroz (458–485), while some consider themselves descendants of the exiles of Samaria, on the assumption that "Habor" (II Kings 17:6) is Bukhara. Anthropological examinations undertaken by L.V. Usbanin in 1926–29 proved that they originated in the Middle East, although there is no information on their exact non-Jewish origin. Precise information on the spiritual works of the Jews of Uzbekistan is, however, available only from the 14th century onward.

Jews of Uzbekistan emigrated to Khazaria and *China because of their location at the crossroads of the caravans that traveled there. The principal traffic between the Muslim world and Itil (*Atil), the capital of Khazaria, passed through northern Uzbekistan, and the information on "many Jews who came to the king of the Khazars from the towns of the Muslims" (the author al-Masʿūdī, of the tenth century) and the Jews who came "from Khurasan and strengthened the hands of the inhabitants of the country" (the anonymous "Cambridge Document") refers essentially to the Jews of Uzbekistan, which was considered an annexed territory of Iranian Eastern Khurasan.

There is a tradition concerning another wave of Jewish emigration from *Iran to Uzbekistan as a result of the Mongolian conquests of the 13th century, and the surnames of the Jews of Uzbekistan show that even during subsequent periods emigrants from Iranian-speaking communities of the west and the south were integrated among them. In modern times, however, the fanatical Muslim domination severely prejudiced the growth and economic development of the community. The Russian conquest of the 19th century came as a blessing, especially in those regions subjected to direct Russian rule, where the local Jews were granted complete judicial equality with the native Muslims and enjoyed rights which the Russian government withheld from the Jews of Eastern Europe (such as the freedom to acquire real estate). A migration from Bukhara to *Tashkent continued through several generations. The economic progress of these Jews was also reflected in their considerable contribution to the Jewish settlement of Ereẓ Israel. The Soviet regime, which liquidated private commerce, brought about the transfer of the more than 200,000 local Jews into administrative positions, industry and agriculture.

The Soviet regime did not bring about any considerable emigration of East European Jews to Uzbekistan because of linguistic difficulties and the warring gangs of Muslim insurgents (Basmachi) of the 1920s and 1930s. World War II, however, suddenly converted Uzbekistan into an important Jewish center. The Jews of the western and central European U.S.S.R. found refuge there, and Tashkent accommodated some of the Jewish institutions of Moscow. Many Jews who had been deported by the Soviet regime between 1939 and 1941 from the annexed eastern parts of Poland and the Baltic states to labor camps or exile in Siberia because of "bourgeois" class origin or political affiliations (Zionist or socialist) also migrated to Uzbekistan upon their release from the camps or places of exile. Some succeeded in continuing on to Palestine through *Persia, either as Polish soldiers in General Anders' army or as orphaned children (the so-called "Teheran children"). With the retreat of the German army from Eastern Europe, many of the refugees and evacuees returned to their places of origin, but a considerable number of East European Ashkenazi Jews settled in Uzbekistan and became integrated into administration, industry and education there. A certain rapprochement between them and the local Jews resulted from the propagation of the Russian language within both communities and the feeling of the common Jewish fate, which was emphasized by the events of the war. The census of 1959 registered 94,344 Jews (1.2 percent of the total population) in Uzbekistan; 50,445 of them lived in the capital of the republic, Tashkent. Only 19,266 of them declared Tajik to be their native language; about 27,560 Yiddish; and the remainder Russian. The 1970 Soviet census showed 103,000 Jews in Uzbekistan.

[Abraham N. Poliak]

In Independent Uzbekistan

In 1979 Uzbekistan had 99,900 Jews and in 1989 94,900, including 51,400 in Tashkent. A large proportion of Jews in the republic were Central Asian (Bukharan) Jews who mainly lived in Samarkand, Tashkent, and Bukhara and spoke the Jewish dialect of Tajik. They preserved their identity more than the local Ashkenazi Jews.

Emigration in 1989 was recorded at 4,358 Jews (with 2,379 from Tashkent, 218 from Fergana province, and 772 from Samarkand province). Emigration to Israel in 1990 totaled 20,192, with 9,786 from Tashkent. Emigration rose from Fergana province and Andizhan in the wake of the violent ethnic conflicts there. After the pogrom against Jews and Armenians in Andizhan in May 1990, emigration from that province jumped to 2,202. In 1991, 13,515 Jews went from Uzbekistan to Israel, including 7,179 from Tashkent and 1,220 from Andizhan. In 1992, 5,533 immigrants to Israel from this country constituted 9.1 percent of the entire immigration wave from the former U.S.S.R., and in 1993, Uzbekistan, with its 8,471 emigrants to Israel, contributed 14.0% to the whole "Soviet" *aliyah* of that year. At the end of the process of emigration during the 1990s around 5,500 Jews remained in Uzbekistan, mostly in Tashkent. Tashkent had a Jewish culture center. The monthly newspaper *Shofar* in Russian and Tajik began appearing in Samarkand in 1992. Two Jews were elected to the Supreme Soviet of the republic in 1990.

An air route from Tashkent to Israel via Varna was inaugurated in June 1991. The Jewish Agency has been operating openly since January 1992. Diplomatic relations were established between Uzbekistan, independent since 1991, and Israel in 1992.

[Michael Beizer]

BIBLIOGRAPHY: R. Loewenthal, *The Jews of Bukhara* (1961); Z.L. Amitin-Shapiro, *Ocherk pravovogo byta sredneaziatskikh yevreyev* (1931); idem, *Ocherki sotsialisticheskogo stroitelstva sredi sredneaziatskikh yevreyev* (1933); U. Schmelz and S. DellaPergola, in: AJYB (1995), 478; *Supplement to the Monthly Bulletin of Statistics*, 2 (1995); *Mezhdunarodnaia Evreiskaia Gazeta* (MEG), 1993–94.

UZHGOROD (Czech **Užhorod**; Hung. **Ungvár**), city in Transcarpathian district, Ukraine; part of Austro-Hungary until 1920, when it passed to Czechoslovakia; between 1938 and 1945 in Hungary; 1945–1991, in the Soviet Union. The Jewish community of Uzhgorod, probably dating from the 16th century, developed at the end of the 18th century (after the partition of Poland) and expanded further in the second half of the 19th century. Some of the outstanding rabbis of Hungary served in Uzhgorod, notably R. Meir *Eisenstadter (MaHaRaM Esh; officiated until 1852) who had great spiritual influence on Uzhgorod and Hungarian Jewry in general; and Solomon *Ganzfried, author of the *Kiẓẓur Shulḥan Arukh*, who served as *dayyan* in 1866. In 1864 Karl Jaeger established a Hebrew printing press with types bought in Vienna. The first book printed was M. Eisenstadter's responsa *Imrei Esh* (part 2). Printing continued until 1878. In 1926 another press was set up by M.S. Gelles and continued to be active until World War II. About 70 items were printed in Uzhgorod. In 1868 the community split to found a separate *Neolog community, whose first rabbi was M. *Klein, translator of Maimonides' *Guide of the Perplexed* into Hungarian. Subsequently the Neologists joined the status *quo trend, whereupon many joined the mother community.

Uzhgorod was a stronghold of the Orthodox as well as of Ḥasidism. From 1890 a Jewish elementary school, whose language of instruction was first Hungarian and later Czech, functioned there. Subsequently Hebrew schools were established. The community also maintained a *talmud torah* school and a yeshivah. In 1904 a central synagogue was established in a magnificent building. There was also a Jewish hospital and home for the aged. Between the two world wars Uzhgorod became a center of intense Jewish national and Zionist (Revisionist) activities. In 1930 the community numbered 7,357, about one-third of the total population. Following the Munich pact (1938), Uzhgorod was annexed by Hungary, which immediately implemented anti-Jewish legislation. In the winter of 1939/40, all Jews of Polish citizenship or Czech citizens originally from Poland were expelled to Poland, and many died under the severe conditions. The young were conscripted into forced labor and sent to the Russian front, never to return. On Passover (April 21–23) 1944, all the Jews of Uzhgorod and the surroundings (25,000 persons) were concentrated in a ghetto located outside the city (in a brick factory and a lumber yard), and three weeks later all were deported to *Auschwitz.

Following the war several hundred survivors returned to city, most of whom later went to Czechoslovakia.

By 2005, the Jewish community had a synagogue, a Jewish community center, a Jewish day school, and a magazine entitled *Gut Shabbos*, which covers Jewish activities in the region of the Carpathian Mountains. The Uzhgorod Jewish community oversees the nearby Jewish communities of Munkatch, Chust, Vinogradova, and Rachov.

BIBLIOGRAPHY: EG, 7 (1959); Y. Spiegel, in: *Arim ve-Immahot be-Yisrael*, 4 (1950), 5–54; A. Solel, in: *Jews of Czechoslovakia* (1968), 125–52. PRINTING: P.J. Kohn, in: KS, 24 (1947/48), 276ff.; N. Ben-Menahem, *ibid.*, 25 (1948/49), 231f.; H. Lieberman, *ibid.*, 27 (1950/51), 115f.

[*Encyclopaedia Hebraica* / Ruth Beloff (2nd ed.)]

UZIEL (**Uzziel**), family of prominent Spanish exiles whose members were to be found in Salonika, Safed, Italy, and Fez. JOSEPH UZIEL BEN ABRAHAM (d. c. 1520) arrived in Fez immediately after the Expulsion. He was a disciple of R. Samuel Valenci and had many disciples in Spain. In a dispute over ritual with the old settlers in Fez, he supported the opinion of his disciple R. Ḥayyim *Gagin. JUDAH UZIEL (d. c. 1542), a leading *ḥakham* of his time, took an active part in the aforementioned controversy, together with his colleague Naḥman ibn Sunbal. He signed decisions and *takkanot* between 1526 and 1542 and wrote commentaries on the Bible. Abraham *Gavison (in *Omer ha-Shikhḥah*) and R. Vidal ha-Sarfati (in *Ẓuf Devash*) quote some of his commentaries, sermons, prayers, and *piyyutim*. R. ABRAHAM UZIEL (d. c. 1570) was a poet and pietist. His disciples included R. Vidal ha-Sarfati. A signatory to the *takkanot* of 1545, he engaged in halakhic discussions with Algerian *ḥakhamim* and is mentioned with esteem in the responsa of R. Solomon Duran (*Tashbeẓ*, pt. 4 (1959), ch. 41). He exchanged poems with the abovementioned R. Abraham Gavison. His son was Isaac *Uziel.

R. JUDAH UZIEL BEN SAMUEL (grandson of Judah; d. c. 1600) signed decisions and *takkanot* between 1584 and 1591. He wrote *Beit ha-Uzi'eli* ("House of Uziel," Venice, 1604), commentaries on the Bible and on Rashi's commentary to the Torah. He left two sons, R. SOLOMON (c. 1550–1610) and R. JOSEPH (c. 1555–1625), both of whom were rabbis in Fez. R. ḤAYYIM UZIEL (c. 1575–1646), who was possibly his third son, was a rabbi and *dayyan* in Fez. He signed decisions in 1626 and 1645. His synagogue was destroyed during the uproar caused in Fez by the chief of the Muslim brotherhood at Dila, in 1646. He died a few days later. R. JUDAH UZIEL (1620–1689), the son of R. Joseph, was rabbi and *dayyan* in Fez. A member of R. Saadiah ibn Dannan's *bet din*, he became the chief rabbi of Fez after the former's death in 1680. He was versed in Torah and in Kabbalah, and propagated Torah learning among the masses. R. Jacob b. Ẓur was his son-in-law. A number of his decisions were published in the works of Moroccan *ḥakhamim*. R. DAVID UZIEL BEN R. ḤAYYIM (c. 1626–1700) was rabbi in Fez and scribe of the *bet din*. He served under R. Judah Uziel (his uncle?) and R. Menahem Serero. His relative, R. Jacob b. Ẓur, said of him: "the great scribe of Israel … my teachers always relied on the traditions which he handed down from the earliest *ḥakhamim* in matters concerning *takkanot* and customs."

BIBLIOGRAPHY: J.M. Toledano, *Ner ha-Ma'arav* (1911), s.v.; J. Ben-Naim, *Malkhei Rabbanan* (1931), s.v.; Hirschberg, Afrikah, index; G. Vajda, *Un recueil de textes historiques judéo-marocains* (1951), 46.

[Haim Bentov]

UZIEL, BARUCH (1900–1977), educator, lawyer, folklorist, and politician. Born and educated in Salonika, Uziel helped to found the youth organization "Maḥzikei Ivrit" whose goal was to spread the Hebrew language in the spirit of the *Haskalah. In his home, he published the first Hebrew newspaper in Salonika, *Ha-Teḥiyyah*. Sent to Palestine in 1913 to study teaching, he was caught there by World War I and as a Greek citizen was exiled in 1917 to Syria by the Turkish authorities. After the British conquered Palestine, he returned to continue his studies and remained in the country. He was among the organizers of the Sephardi faction in the *Va'ad Le'ummi. He taught in various places and also graduated in law and became involved in politics.

Uziel always maintained a close connection with Salonika and in the 1920s, helped the *aliyah* of Salonikan fishermen to Acre and later organized the immigration of Salonikan stevedores to Haifa port. He also helped to lay the foundations for research into Sephardi folklore, in particular from Salonika. He wrote stories about Judeo-Spanish life in Salonika, eventually published in *Be-sha'arei Saloniki, Novelot* (1973).

He initiated the founding of the "Haifa-Saloniki" committee, which eventually received the name Va'adat ha-Yam ("the sea committee"). This committee together with the Va'ad le-ma'an Haifa ("the committee for Haifa") organized and brought 300 Jewish Salonikan seamen and their families to Haifa. As secretary of Va'ad ha-Yam he coordinated their immigration and absorption and served as a liaison between the committee and the relevant bodies in Greece and Ereẓ Israel.

In 1931 he was elected a member of the executive of Maccabi in Palestine and was in charge of the department of culture and propaganda. He served as president of the Association of Greek Immigrants and after World War II went to Greece in order to release property confiscated by the Nazis in the Holocaust.

In 1959 he wrote *Berit ha-Periferiyyah-Haẓa'ah le-Mediniyyut Yisraelit* proposing non-Arabic people of the Middle East ally with Israel to curb Arab imperialism.

Active in the General Zionist party, he was elected to the Fifth Knesset in 1961 and was head of the Knesset Education Committee. He was re-elected to the Sixth Knesset.

Uziel was the chief editor of *Guinzaḥ Saloniki* (1961) and edited the Salonika commemorative memorial book *Saloniki Ir va-Em be-Yisrael* (1967).

[Yitzhak Kerem]

UZIEL, ISAAC BEN ABRAHAM (d. 1622), rabbi and poet. Isaac was the son of Abraham Uziel, a rabbi of Fez where Isaac was born. In consequence of the famine in Morocco during 1604–05, he left Fez and settled in Oran, Algeria, where he served as rabbi. From there he went in 1606 to Amsterdam where he became a teacher in the community's *bet ha-midrash* and also engaged in business. In 1610 when Judah Vega, the first rabbi of the Neveh Shalom congregation, retired, Isaac was invited to succeed him. He was a very strong personality, and in his sermons inveighed against those who were lax in their observance and against the Marranos who had not completely abandoned Christian views. As a result many of the Marranos left his community and in 1618 established a separate congregation. Among his pupils were *Manasseh Ben Israel and Isaac Athias.

He wrote a large number of poems which have real literary value, but only a few were published, some of them in the festival prayer books of North Africa. Uziel also studied grammar, writing *Ma'aneh Lashon* (Amsterdam, 1627) on this subject. He translated from Spanish into Hebrew legends and fables of Indian origin well known throughout the world that were called in Latin *Historia Septem Sapientium* and in Hebrew *Mishlei Erasto*. These were first published in serial form by Abraham *Elmaleh in the periodical, *Mizraḥ u-Ma'arav*. Uziel appears to have been one of the Amsterdam rabbis who excommunicated Uriel da *Costa. As a result of his conservative extremism and excessively stern persecution of his opponents, relations between him and Leone *Modena became strained.

BIBLIOGRAPHY: Brody, in: JQR, 13 (1922/23), 70–73; Davidson, Oẓar, 4 (1933), index; C. Roth, *Life of Menasseh Ben Israel* (1934), 22–24, 32–34; Hirschberg, Afrikah, 2 (1965), 102–3.

[Abraham David]

UZZA AND AZA'EL, heroes of a medieval tale based on the biblical story of the Nephilim (cf. Gen. 6:4), which was developed in the second century B.C.E. in the Book of *Enoch.

According to the medieval story, Uzza and Aza'el were two angels who set out to prove man's wickedness before God, and they sinned with mortal women. One girl, Istehar, succeeded in escaping by compelling them to reveal to her the sacred name which they invoked when they went up to heaven; and she used it and became a star. The two sons of Uzza and Aza'el, Ḥiwwa and Ḥiyya, died in the Flood; Uzza and Aza'el themselves were exiled by God but they are still alive, and are responsible for some of the evils of this world: they teach sorcery, and they show women how to make themselves beautiful to men.

The legend, which is part of the general revival of Second Temple period literature in medieval Hebrew prose, was adapted by the Kabbalah; the Zohar gives a long account of it, introducing in addition a number of special kabbalistic meanings. Some manuscripts of magic, the *Havdalah de-Rabbi Akiva* for example, use the names of the two angels in magical formulae.

BIBLIOGRAPHY: Ginzberg, Legends, 1 (1961), 147–51; A. Jellinek, *Beit ha-Midrash* (1938), 127f.; I. Tishby, *Mishnat ha-Zohar*, 1 (1949), 471–3. **ADD. BIBLIOGRAPHY:** A.Y. Reed, in: *Jewish Studies Quarterly*, 8: 2 (2001), 105–36; G. Stemberger, in: A. Lange et al. (eds.), *Die Daemonen* (2003), 636–61.

[Joseph Dan]

UZZAH (Heb. עֻזָּא, עֻזָּה), the son of Abinadab (in, II Sam. 6:3; cf. I Chron. 13:7). When David brought up the Ark of the Lord from the house of Abinadab on the hill in Baalah (II Sam. 6:2) or Kiriath-Jearim (I Sam. 7:1; I Chron. 13:5–6), Uzzah and Ahio, the two sons of Abinadab, drove the cart upon which the Ark was borne. When they reached the threshing floor of Nacon (II Chron. 13:9, Chidon), the oxen stumbled, and Uzzah put out his hand to steady the Ark, whereupon he died. Apparently, he had violated the sacrosanct nature of the Ark. Because of this incident the place was called "Perez-Uzzah," meaning, "the breach of Uzzah." David diverted the Ark to the house of *Obed-Edom the Gittite (II Sam. 6:3–10; I Chron. 13:5–13), and did not venture to bring it into Jerusalem until three months later. According to Josephus (Ant., 6:18; 7:79), Abinadab and his sons were levites.

UZZIAH (Heb. עֻזִּיָּה), also called Azariah (Heb. עֲזַרְיָה, עֲזַרְיָהוּ), king of Judah; succeeded his father *Amaziah (II Kings 14:21–22; II Chron. 26). The name Uzziah derives from the stem עזז, whose meaning in Hebrew is similar to that of עזר, "to assist." He reigned over Judah for 52 years (c. 785–734 B.C.E.). When his father Amaziah was murdered by conspirators in Lachish, "all the people of Judah" (II Kings 14:21; II Chron. 26:1) chose Uzziah, who was then only 16 years old (II Kings 14:21–22), for their king. There is very little information on the reign of Uzziah in II Kings 15. Apart from phrases which occur in connection with every other king, there is only one additional fact – the "leprosy" (probably psoriasis, rather than true leprosy, Hansen's disease) which struck Uzziah, and his residence in "a house set apart," while his son *Jotham was appointed "over the household judging the people of the land." On the other hand, there is much information on the reign of Uzziah in II Chronicles, and the subject of his "leprosy" is enlarged upon. According to II Chronicles 26:16–21, Uzziah was struck with "leprosy" after he had entered the Temple of God and tried to burn incense on the altar without heeding the words of the priests who declared that the offering of incense on the altar of God was a prerogative of the priests.

Josephus (Ant., 9:223ff.) mentions a more detailed tradition concerning this "leprosy." According to this tradition, on an important festival day, the king put on the priestly garment and in spite of the priests' opposition, he attempted to bring the offering on the golden altar. While he was preparing to do so, the earth trembled, the Temple was split, and a ray of sun shone on the face of the king who was immediately struck with "leprosy." Uzziah's "leprosy," his attempt to offer incense on the altar, and the earthquake which occurred in Jerusalem during his reign (also recorded from additional sources) may be accepted as historical facts. An Aramaic burial inscription of the Second Temple period found on the Mount of Olives reads in Albright's translation: "Hither were brought the bones of Uzziah, king of Judah – do not open." This inscription proves that the bones of Uzziah were removed from their first grave. According to halakhic tradition, it was forbidden to move the graves of the House of David. It has thus been concluded that Uzziah was not buried in the graves of the House of David but "in the field of burial which belonged to the kings; for they said he is a leper" (II Chron. 26:23). Various biblical passages also testify that the kings of Israel and Judah carried out various ritual acts (I Sam. 13:9–10; II Sam. 6:14; 8:18; I Kings 3:15; Ps. 110:4) similar to those of the priests. The attempt of the priests to prevent Uzziah from offering the incense points to the struggle between the monarchy and the priesthood for supremacy over the ritual of the Temple. It is quite probable that emboldened by his successes in his external and internal policies and his reliance on the merits of his ancestors, the king sought to demonstrate his authority in the Temple by offering the incense (II Chron. 26:16). Reports of the earthquake mentioned by Josephus (*ibid.*) are also to be found in Amos (1:1) and Zechariah (14:4–5). Thus, some believe that the data in the biblical tradition and in Josephus concerning the "leprosy" of Uzziah are historical, but that the connection between them is tendentious and folkloristic and not really historical. The story related in Chronicles and Josephus is based on a popular tradition around the rare phenomenon of the king's "leprosy."

The reign of Uzziah is described in historical sources, especially in Chronicles, as one of the golden eras of the kingdom of Judah. Uzziah appears as a firm and active king in both his interior and exterior policies. He pursued the policy of his father Amaziah for supremacy over the southern part of the land up to Elath, situated on the Red Sea coast. He returned Elath to Judah (II Kings 14:22) and built a line of fortifications and towers in the Arabah and the Negev in order to safeguard the transit routes from Jerusalem to Elath. The archaeological excavations of Tell al-Khalayfa (near Akaba) brought to light the renewed settlement of the locality (third stratum) in the days of Uzziah and his son Jotham, although opinions among archaeologists differ as to whether Tell al-Khalayfa is to be identified with Ezion-Geber and whether the findings are the installations of metallurgic works. At the same time, the fortresses and towers built by Uzziah in the Arabah and Negev served to protect the herds of cattle, the shepherds, the pasture lands, and the water sources from nomadic tribes, such as the Meunites and the Arabians (II Chron. 26:7). He also took measures for the economic development of the arid regions in the mountains, the lowlands, and the desert. In the west he fought against the towns of Philistia (Gath, Jabneh, and Ashdod) and expanded his territory at the Philistines' expense (26:6). Uzziah's objective was to break through to the west and secure a section of the "Via Maris." He also expanded eastward to the eastern bank of the Jordan and subjugated the Ammonites (26:8, but in LXX – Meunim). His successes in his foreign policies were preceded by an intensive strengthening of the economic and military power of the country. He fortified Jerusalem (26:9), reorganized the army (26:11–12), increased the number of soldiers, and prepared a great amount of weapons (26:13). The biblical author sums up the activities of Uzziah with the words: "his name spread abroad even to the entrance of Egypt; for he waxed exceedingly strong" (26:8). He may also have recovered from lsrael territory north of Jerusalem which had been lost by Amaziah.

Because of a faulty join of cuneiform tablets it was thought that "Azriyau māt Iaudaya" was mentioned in the annals of Tiglath-Pileser III (1:103–133). This led to some scholars identifying him with Uzziah, king of Judah. At present the Azriyau of the cuneiform text remains without a country. Na'aman has assigned the relevant tablets to Sennacherib. It is quite possible that Uzziah's status was equal to that of *Jeroboam son of Joash, about whom it is distinctly said that he subjugated Damascus and Hamath (II Kings 14:28). The expansion of Assyria marked the beginning of the decline of the kingdom of Judah, which reached its lowest ebb during the reign of Uzziah's grandson *Ahaz, when the armies of Damascus and Samaria invaded Judah and besieged Jerusalem, impelling Ahaz to become an Assyrian vassal. Even so, Judah was not directly harmed by Assyria during Uzziah's reign. The number of years during which Jotham reigned together with his father is one of the most difficult problems in biblical chronology. According to some opinions, the 52 years mentioned as being those of Uzziah's reign include the years during which he reigned together with his father, all the years of Jotham's reign, and even some of the years of the reign of Ahaz, son of Jotham.

BIBLIOGRAPHY: Albright, in: BASOR, 44 (1931), 8–10; Morgenstern, in: HUCA, 12–13 (1938), 1–20; 15 (1940), 267–77; Tadmor, in: *Scripta Hierosolymitana*, 8 (1961), 232–71; Glueck, in: BA, 28 (1965), 70–87; Thiele, in: VT, 16 (1966), 103–7; Ginsberg, in: *Fourth World Congress of Jewish Studies, Papers*, 1 (1967), 92b–93. **ADD. BIBLIOGRAPHY:** M. Cogan and H. Tadmor, *II Kings* (AB; 1988); N. Na'aman, in: BASOR, 214 (1974), 25–38; idem, in: *Die Welt des Orients* 9 (1978), 229–39; H. Tadmor, *The Inscriptions of Tiglath-Pileser III King of Assyria* (1996), 274–76.

[Bustanay Oded]

Initial letter "V" for the word Verbum *at the beginning of the Book of Zephaniah in a 13th-century Latin Bible from France. The letter is formed by two figures wearing medieval Jewish hats, and wielding clubs against snakes, which represent the enemies of Judah. Boulogne, Bibliothèque Municipale, Ms. 21, fol. 239v.*

VA-VY

VAAD HA-HATZALAH, a body originally established to rescue rabbis and yeshivah students during World War II. Though originally focusing exclusively on rabbis and yeshivah students, it expanded its agenda to assist all Jews in the wake of the revelation of the Final Solution and became the representative relief agency of American Orthodox Jewry.

Established in mid-November 1939 by an emergency meeting of the *Union of Orthodox Rabbis of the United States and Canada, then the largest and most important association of Orthodox rabbis in North America, the Vaad was initially founded to rescue the Polish rabbis and yeshivah students who had escaped to Lithuania following the German and Soviet invasions of September 1939, including the *rashei yeshivah* and students of leading talmudic academies such as Mir, Kletsk, Radin, Kamenets, and Baranowitz. Initially dubbed the "Emergency Committee for War-Torn Yeshivos," its leadership, headed by Rabbi Eliezer *Silver of Cincinnati, originally envisioned the relocation of the refugee yeshivot to safe havens, preferably in Palestine or the United States, as its main goal, but found itself increasingly preoccupied with maintenance as emigration from Lithuania proved extremely difficult.

As the number of refugee Polish rabbis and students in Lithuania increased and the financial burden of supporting them grew, the Vaad, which upon its foundation declared that it would seek support exclusively from Orthodox sources, sought to expand its fundraising efforts to the entire American Jewish community. This development led to serious tension between the Vaad and the *American Jewish Joint Distribution Committee (and the Council of Jewish Federations and Welfare Funds) which bore communal responsibility for administering overseas relief to Jews in distress and had joined in creating the United Jewish Appeal in January 1939 to unify American Jewish fundraising for the first time ever. While ostensibly based on practical considerations affecting fundraising, the debates between the Vaad and the JDC and CJFWF also related to two extremely serious issues: rescue priority; i.e., who should be rescued first, and the attitude toward increasingly stringent U.S. regulations, which hampered rescue and relief efforts. While the leaders of the Vaad sought absolute priority for rabbis and yeshivah students, the JDC saw things differently. While the Vaad actively sought means of circumventing the spirit, and in some cases even the letter, of American regulations, which might adversely affect rescue and relief initiatives, the JDC leadership refused to approve the slightest deviation from U.S. directives.

During the initial year and a half of its existence, the Vaad concentrated its efforts on assisting the over 2,600 Polish rabbis and yeshivah students who had escaped to Lithuania and trying to arrange their emigration overseas. (When the Soviet Union occupied Lithuania in June 1940, the Vaad also sought to facilitate the emigration of Lithuanian Torah scholars, yet in most cases they were barred from leaving by the Soviet authorities.) In the summer of 1940, for example, they sought to enlist communal support for the mass transfer of all the refugee scholars to the United States, but encountered stiff opposition from Rabbi Stephen *Wise and most of the American Jewish leaders and organizations. Ultimately, the Vaad helped obtain American visas for several leading *rashei yeshivah* and the members of their families in the framework of a special program to rescue the scientific and cultural elite of Europe.

When a possibility for large-scale emigration from Soviet Lithuania developed in the fall of 1940 based on visas to Curaçao and Japanese transit visas, the Vaad helped fund the rail and ship tickets for numerous Torah scholars, but the bulk of the funds for the project were provided by the Joint Distribution Committee. All told, of the approximately 2,300 Polish refugees who emigrated from Lithuania to the Far East from October 1940 until the German invasion in June 1941, some 650 were rabbis and yeshivah students; many of whom were assisted by the Vaad; among the refugees were such leading *rashei yeshivah* as Rabbi Aaron *Kotler of Kletsk, Reuben Grazowsky of Kamenets, and Abraham Yaphin of Bialystok and communal rabbis such as David Lifshitz of Suwalk and Moses Shatzkes of Lomza, all of whom reached the United States in 1941. Together with Rabbi Abraham Kalmanowitz of Tiktin, who had arrived in America a year earlier, several of these rabbis and especially Rabbi Kotler, were to play leading roles in the activities of the Vaad. The bulk of the refugee scholars who reached the Far East, however, were sent by the Japanese to *Shanghai, where – with the exception of 29 who immigrated to Canada in the fall of 1941 with visas obtained with the help of the Vaad – they remained for the duration of the war.

Following the American entry into World War II, the Vaad concentrated primarily on providing assistance to the refugee Torah scholars in Shanghai as well as to the group of several hundred rabbis and yeshivah students in Soviet Central Asia. Many of the latter were among the thousands of Polish citizens deported by the Soviets to Siberia or to prison camps prior to the German invasion, who were released in the wake of the Sikorski-Stalin Pact of August 1941. The Vaad provided funds for both groups and sent parcels of food and clothing to the latter, enabling them to maintain their unique life-style and continue their Torah studies despite the difficult physical conditions in both places.

Following the receipt by the Vaad of news from Switzerland concerning the scope of the mass murder of European Jewry, the rabbinic rescue organization began to play a more active role in political activities designed to facilitate the rescue of Jews from German-occupied Europe. Joining forces with the leaders of American Agudat Israel, the Orthodox activists tried to promote efforts to unite American Jewry and to make rescue the community's number one priority. Rabbi Israel Rosenberg, one of the key figures in the Vaad, was among the Jewish leaders who met with President Roosevelt on December 8, 1942, to urge him to take action to save European Jewry, and the Vaad's leadership initially participated in the attempts to establish the American Jewish Conference as a representative umbrella organization for American Jewry.

The highlight of these activities was the protest march of some 400 rabbis in Washington on October 6, 1943, the only public demonstration by Jewish leaders in the American capital during the war. The march was organized together with the "Emergency Committee for the Rescue of the Jewish People of Europe," a group headed by revisionist Zionists, which led the efforts to convince the American government to establish a special rescue agency, which ultimately led to the creation of the *War Refugee Board.

In early January 1944, the Vaad officially decided that henceforth it would attempt to rescue all Jews regardless of religiosity and/or affiliation. This decision was a product of two major developments – the dissolution of the Joint Emergency Council on European Jewish Affairs and the creation by the Vaad of practical means to transfer funds to rescue activists, headed by Rabbi Michael Dov *Weissmandl, in German-occupied Europe. The former had been the only framework which included representatives of all the major Jewish organizations and could have coordinated unified political action to promote practical rescue initiatives. The creation of the latter meant that for the first time ever, the Vaad could actively support rescue activities inside German-occupied Europe. From this point on, the Vaad channeled most of its resources to assist the Jews living under German rule, initiating several rescue projects primarily through its Swiss branch (the HIJEFS relief agency headed by Recha and Isaac Sternbuch), but also via its representatives in Turkey (Jacob Griffel), Tangiers (Renee Reichman), and Sweden (Wilhelm Wolbe). The culmination of these efforts was the release to Switzerland on the night of February 6–7, 1945, of a train with 1,210 inmates from the Theresienstadt ghetto/concentration camp, a product of negotiations conducted by Swiss politician Jean-Marie Musy on the Vaad's behalf with top Nazi leaders. During the same period, the Vaad continued to send considerable sums of money to the refugee scholars in Shanghai and Central Asia, which allowed these Torah scholars, who simultaneously received aid from other Jewish organizations, to continue their studies and maintain their life-style.

After World War II, the Vaad played an active role in the spiritual rehabilitation of the survivors, continuing its operations until the early 1950s. From its establishment in 1939 until the end of 1945, the Vaad spent more than three million dollars on relief and rescue activities and in the process helped

"Americanize" the American Orthodox leadership. While its insistence on according rescue efforts top priority and circumventing bureaucratic and legal obstacles has been favorably acknowledged by historians, its particularism and insistence on priority for Torah learning at the possible expense of rescue activities continue to be a source of debate and polemic in the Jewish community.

[Efraim Zuroff (2nd ed.)]

VA'AD HA-PEKIDIM VE-HA-AMARKALIM, an organization established in 1810 for the support of the *yishuv* in Ereẓ Israel. Until the 18th century, the majority of the Jewish community in Ereẓ Israel were Sephardim, who were supported by the *Va'ad Pekidei Ereẓ Israel be-Kushta. Toward the end of the 18th century and at the beginning of the 19th century, however, the Ashkenazi community grew in number and with it the contributions toward their upkeep from European countries. With the decline of the Turkish empire, the support coming from there diminished and the burden of the economic support of the Jewish community fell upon the communities of Europe, with Amsterdam becoming the center for the collection of the necessary funds. An additional factor was the growing interest of the European powers in Ereẓ Israel. The Va'ad was established by Western European Orthodox Jews for clearly defined ideological purposes. On the one hand there was the idea that the *yishuv* in Ereẓ Israel had to be supported by its brethren in Europe so that the former could study and pray for them, and on the other was the Va'ad's part in the struggle against *Haskalah and *Reform Judaism, which were spreading in Western Europe. It was based on the idea of the importance of the *yishuv* and the need to guard it against the spread of religious Reform.

The most prominent heads of the Va'ad were its founders, the *Lehren brothers, who headed it during the major part of the 19th century. They received authorization for their activities from the communities in Ereẓ Israel and from the Va'ad Pekidei Ereẓ Israel be-Kushta. Although their main activity was in Western and Central Europe, their influence spread to Eastern Europe. Among their activities was the incessant struggle to abolish the system of *shadarim* (emissaries) from the various communities in Ereẓ Israel and to concentrate the collection of funds in their own hands by improving the methods of collection. This concentration of funds gave them enormous influence. They intervened in the disputes between Sephardim and Ashkenazim as to the allocations of the **ḥalukkah*, establishing a key which changed every few years as a result of pressure by the various groups. Belonging as they did to the extreme Orthodox circles, they exercised their influence in this direction. They opposed every proposed innovation in the economic, social, or religious life of Ereẓ Israel, regarding it as the last stronghold of Judaism against the inroads of Haskalah and Reform, which might pose a threat to their powers. They even intervened in such matters as the appointment of the **ḥakham bashi* and came out in support of the Sephardim in their struggle to prevent the Moroccan Jews from establishing an independent communtity. Their main struggle, however, was against attempts to establish schools, hospitals, and new suburbs in Jerusalem. In their opposition to the establishment of a modern educational system, they clashed with Sir Moses *Montefiore and the enlightened Jews of Germany and Austria, and this struggle reached its peak with their campaign against the establishment of the Laemel school of Ludwig August *Frankl. Their opposition to the founding of the first hospitals was based on the fact that the initiative came from Reform circles in Germany, and they fought tenaciously against all attempts by enlightened Orthodox circles to abolish the *ḥalukkah* system.

These struggles must therefore be viewed in the perspective of what was happening in Jewish society in Europe during the 19th century. The special interest of the European powers in Ereẓ Israel, the establishment of consulates and the capitulations, the pluralism of the communities and *kolelim*, the penetration of new factors into the *yishuv* and finally the Zionist settlement all combined to bring about the weakening of the Va'ad's influence in Amsterdam, the Lehren brothers' deposition from the dominant position they maintained in Jerusalem, and the demise of the ideology of the *ḥalukkah*.

BIBLIOGRAPHY: M. Eliav, in: *Chapters in the History of the Jewish Community in Jerusalem* (1973), 48–50; B.Z. Gat, *Ha-Yishuv ha-Yehudi be-Ereẓ Yisrael ba-Shanim* 1840–1881 (1963), 72, 78, 94, 98–02, 133–5, 195, 221; B.Z. Dinaburg (Dinur), in: *Zion* (Me'asef), 1 (1926), 85 121; L.A. Frankl, *Nach Jerusalem* (1859); J. and B. Rivlin (eds.), *Iggerot ha-Pekidim ve-ha-Amarkalim me-Amsterdam*, 1–2 (1965–70).

[Jacob Barnai]

VA'AD LE'UMMI (Heb. lit.: "National Committee"), the National Council of Jews of Palestine, which functioned from Oct. 10, 1920, until the establishment of the Provisional Government of the State of Israel in May 1948 as the executive organ of the Asefat ha-Nivḥarim (the Elected Assembly) of the *yishuv*. It was preceded by a "provisional committee" (Va'ad Zemanni), established at a conference of representatives of various bodies in the *yishuv*, including soldiers of the *Jewish Legion, in 1918, at the time when only southern Palestine was occupied by the British army. Though elected in 1920 by the first Asefat ha-Nivḥarim and recognized immediately as a representative body in a letter from the *high commissioner, Sir Herbert Samuel, the Va'ad Le'ummi achieved formal legal status only on Jan. 1, 1928, when *Keneset Yisrael, the organizational framework of the *yishuv*, was legally established under the Religious Communities Organization Ordinance, 1926.

The Va'ad Le'ummi elected a smaller body to conduct its day-to-day business and was headed by a chairman, or sometimes by a president assisted by a chairman. It cooperated closely with the Zionist or *Jewish Agency Executive, which was responsible for major policy on immigration, settlement, economic development, legal defense, etc. The Va'ad Le'ummi represented the *yishuv* in its relations with the Mandatory government and the Arab leaders and dealt with internal matters (such as the school system) which were delegated to it by the

Zionist Executive. It also cooperated closely with the Chief Rabbinate and the local community councils, which were part of the official framework of Keneset Yisrael. The Va'ad Le'ummi served as the main organ of the Jews of Palestine before the *League of Nations Permanent Mandates Commission and the numerous inquiry commissions into the "Palestine problem," up to the United Nations Special Committee on Palestine (*UNSCOP), which proposed partition in 1947.

Not all sections of the Jewish population in Palestine were represented in the governing bodies of Keneset Yisrael and, consequently, in the Va'ad Le'ummi. *Agudat Israel and the ultra-Orthodox circles of the old *yishuv* boycotted it, and from 1944 the Sephardi list, the *Revisionists, the *General Zionists, and the Farmers Union were not represented, because of their boycott of the elections to the fourth Asefat ha-Nivḥarim when their demands for a reform of the electoral system were rejected.

The Va'ad Le'ummi was headed from 1920 to 1925 by a presidium consisting of I. *Ben-Zvi, J. *Thon, and D. *Yellin; from 1925 by Yellin as chairman and Ben-Zvi and Thon as deputy chairmen; between 1929 and 1940 P. *Rutenberg twice served as president and Ben-Zvi served as chairman; from 1940 to 1944 by Ben-Zvi as chairman; and from 1944 to 1948 by Ben-Zvi as president and D. *Remez as chairman.

BIBLIOGRAPHY: M. Atlas (ed.), *Sefer ha-Te'udot shel ha-Va'ad ha-Le'ummili-Keneset Yisrael, 1918–1948* (1963).

VA'AD PEKIDEI EREẒ ISRAEL BE-KUSHTA ("The Council of Representatives of the Land of Israel in Constantinople"), a body established to organize assistance for the Jewish community of Ereẓ Israel. It flourished in the 18th century, but continued to exist until the beginning of the 19th century.

The first stage in the organization of this body involved the need to assist the followers of Judah Ḥasid, the Shabbatean preacher who had died in Jerusalem in 1700 a few days after arriving there. His followers were disheartened by this tragedy, immersed in heavy debts, and suffering from the oppression of their creditors and from deaths through plague. Both the Jews of Constantinople and the communities of Europe took steps to assist them by intervening with the authorities and collecting funds. This effort was unsuccessful, however, and when the Ashkenazi synagogue in Jerusalem was set on fire by Muslim creditors in 1720, the group dispersed. The dominant Sephardi community also suffered in consequence, and many had to leave the capital and go into hiding. As a result, the Va'ad Pekidei Ereẓ Israel be-Kushta was reorganized during this decade with the aim of reconstituting the community. When they obtained a *firman* permitting the Ashkenazim to make good their debts by annual payments, the Sephardim returned, but the Ashkenazim were still fearful, and only a handful returned (their leader in the middle of the 18th century was *Abraham Gershon of Kutow, a brother-in-law of Israel Ba'al Shem Tov). The *Pekidim* reorganized the community, appointing representatives in Jerusalem and drawing up enactments with regard to taxation and expenditure. In 1727 the Va'ad Pekidei Ereẓ Israel became a permanent, well-organized body. They demanded that their representatives provide detailed reports of income and expenditure and organized regular contributions from the whole Jewish world, fixing the amounts which each community had to pay and renewing them every ten years. A special fund was also instituted called "Parah contribution" (the *parah* was a Turkish coin). Special collectors were appointed throughout the Ottoman Empire and in Europe, and the considerable proceeds were transmitted to Constantinople. Funds thus collected were applied mostly to repayment of debts and to taxes and bribery: the poor benefited only to a small extent, but the monies sent to them by relatives abroad were also administered by the *Pekidim*. The *Pekidim* reserved to themselves the sole right of appointing emissaries to the Diaspora. They established useful connections with the authorities in Constantinople, Damascus, and Jerusalem, bribing them heavily.

In a short time, sub-committees were established for each of the four "Holy Cities" of Ereẓ Israel – Jerusalem, Hebron, Safed, and Tiberias – of which the most important was Jerusalem, where there were seven *Pekidim*. As a result, during the 1730s the Jewish population of Jerusalem increased rapidly, and in the 1740s rose to some 3,000. The *Pekidim*, apprehensive of the economic and political effects of this rapid growth, enacted a *takkanah* allowing only immigrants above the age of 60 to settle in Jerusalem.

These activities made the *Pekidim* absolute rulers of the Jewish communities of Ereẓ Israel, particularly Jerusalem, which became to all intents a branch of the community of Constantinople, losing every vestige of autonomy. They appointed officials, intervened in the appointment of rabbis (sometimes even appointing the chief rabbi), and all enactments were subject to their approval. The *Pekidim* even organized pilgrimages to Ereẓ Israel by ship, imposed taxes on the pilgrims, and established yeshivot. They intervened in all the disputes between Sephardim and Ashkenazim over the question of distributing funds coming from Europe.

Their dictatorial attitude toward the communities in Ereẓ Israel could not extend to other Jewish communities, apart from Turkey and the Balkan states, and disputes arose with regard to the distribution of funds emanating from them, with the *Pekidim* more than once threatening to resign. They nevertheless maintained strong ties with leading European rabbis, such as R. Ezekiel Landau of Prague, who was the "representative of Ereẓ Israel" there.

The weakening of the Ottoman Empire and the decline of the community of Constantinople, the war between Turkey and Russia, and the growing *aliyah* of Ashkenazim brought about a decline in the importance of the institution toward the end of the 18th century. By the 19th century, it was virtually moribund, its place being taken by the "Va'ad Pekidim ve-Amarkalim" of *Amsterdam.

BIBLIOGRAPHY: *Pinkas Pekidei Kushta* (MSS), microfilm, Makhon Ben-Zvi, Cat. No. 1857; *Sefer Takkanot* (1842); M. Benayahu, *Ha-Ḥida* (1959), 379–420; I. Ben-Zvi, *Ereẓ Israel ve-Yishuvah*

(1955), 265–74. A. Yaari, in: *Sinai*, 25 (1949), 149–63; idem, Sheluḥei 373–6, 387–9.

[Jacob Barnai]

VAC (Hung. **Vác**; Ger. **Waitzen**), city in N. central Hungary. A Jewish community was organized in Vac after the publication of the law on free residence (1841). A permanent synagogue was erected in 1864. After the separation (1869), it retained its former orientation of status quo *ante. The elementary school of the community was established in 1857, and a secondary school for girls in 1922. The majority of the members of the community were merchants, contractors, and craftsmen. The first rabbi of the community was Anshel Neumann (1832–62) and its last rabbi was Sh.F. (Fülöp) Pollak (until 1944), who was deported together with the community. The Orthodox community had already been founded in 1868, and its synagogue and school were opened in 1882. Its rabbis were David Judah Leib *Silberstein (1876–84), his son Isaiah Silberstein (1884–1930), and his grandson Leib Silberstein (1935–44). In 1885 a yeshivah was established. D.Z. *Katzburg published the Torah periodical *Tel-Talpiyyot* (from 1892 to 1938) in Vac. There were five Jews in Vac in 1840; 139 in 1869; 2,131 in 1910; 2,059 in 1920; 1,854 in 1941; and 377 in 1946. After the German invasion (March 19, 1944), the Jews of Vac were deported to Auschwitz, and only a few survived.

[Baruch Yaron]

VADÁSZ, LIPÓT (1861–1924), Hungarian lawyer and politician. Born in Kisvárda, Vadász practiced law for a short time, and became a deputy in the lower house of the Hungarian parliament in 1910. In 1913 he was appointed undersecretary of state in the Ministry of Justice and was a close adviser of Count Stephan Tisza, the "strong man" of Hungary. During World War I Vadász was responsible for restrictive wartime legislation and the law on parliamentary prerogatives became known as "Lex Vadász." He also collaborated in preparing a new Hungarian civil code. Tisza's failure to obtain public support during the war led Vadász to retire from public life and return to private practice. He was active in Jewish communal affairs and president of the Hungarian Jewish Literary Society. Vadász gained a considerable reputation as an orator and his principal speeches were published under the title *Vadász Lipot Beszédei* (1925).

[Josef J. Lador-Lederer]

VAD RASHKOV, town in Bessarabia, on the Dniester, today Moldova. Under the Moldavians (up to 1812) the town was called Rashkov, the same name as the city facing it on the opposite bank of the river. In 1817 there were 88 Jewish heads of households there. As a result of Jewish emigration to Bessarabia during the 19th century, the community grew, and by 1857 it supported two synagogues and a house of prayer. In 1897 the community numbered 3,237 (69.7% of the total population), but in 1930 the number had decreased to 1,958 (49.2% of the total). Jews engaged in trade, crafts, and also in agriculture (mainly viticulture). Among 379 members registered in the local loan fund in 1925, 154 were tradesmen, 113 artisans, and 65 farmers. When the Germans and the Romanians invaded Bessarabia in July 1941, most of the Jews escaped to the Russian side of the Dniester River.

[Eliyahu Feldman]

VAEZ, ABRAHAM (d. 1694?), French Sephardi rabbi. Vaez was the earliest-known *ḥazzan* and *ḥakham* of the Nefuẓot Yehudah community formed by ex-Marranos at Bayonne and is probably to be identified with the R. Abraham "Davan" (a misreading of Da Vaez) who died there on July 29, 1694.

His works include *Arbol de Vidas* (Amsterdam, 1692), a handbook on Jewish religious law and practice in Spanish, followed by a sermon on human frailty, with a commendatory poem by Abraham Rodriguez Faro; *Discursos predicables y avisos espirituales* (Amsterdam, 1710), moral sermons, published after his death by his son, Jacob, with an introduction by Isaac (de Mattatia?) *Aboab. He also contributed a commendatory letter to the *Historia Sacra Real* by Isaac Acosta, who subsequently succeeded him at Bayonne.

BIBLIOGRAPHY: Kayserling, Bibl, 107f.; M. Schwab, *Rapport sur les Inscriptions Hébraïques de la France* (1904), 374 [232].

[Cecil Roth]

VÁGÓ, JÓZSEF (1877–1947), Hungarian architect. Vágó was born in Nagyvárad (now Oradea, Romania) and completed his studies at the Polytechnicum in Budapest. As a student, he gained a prize for the plan of a synagogue in Budapest. He later became the associate of the leading Hungarian architect, Ö. Lechner. Vágó's style was modern with the clean uncluttered lines then in vogue. Many buildings in the Hungarian capital were designed by him. In 1919 he settled in Switzerland and later in Italy. He was co-recipient of first prize in a competition for design of the League of Nations headquarters in Geneva (1926), in the realization of which he also took part. He worked in partnership with his brother *László.

BIBLIOGRAPHY: *Magyar Zsidó Lexikon* (1929), 932.

[Baruch Yaron / Eva Kondor]

VÁGÓ, LÁSZLÓ (1875–1933), Hungarian architect. He worked in partnership with his brother Jószef *Vágó. They worked in partnership until 1910. After setting up an independent firm, László specialized in the reconstruction of theater buildings. At the end of the 1920s he and his co-workers designed the Heroes' Synagogue and its arcaded courtyard adjacent to the Great Synagogue in Dohany street in Budapest.

[Eva Kondor]

VAJDA, GEORGES (1908–1981), French Arabist and Hebraist. Born in Budapest, a student of Bernard Heller, he went to Paris in 1928. From 1936 to 1960 he was a professor of Bible and theology at the Séminaire Israélite of France. He lectured at the École pratique des hautes études (EPHE) in 1937, and was appointed "directeur d'études" in 1954. In 1940 he founded the Oriental department of the Institut de Recherches et d'Histoire des Textes (CNRS). He died on its premises in 1981. He directed (and wrote himself a large part of) the *Revue des études juives* from the end of World War II to 1980. In 1970 he was appointed professor at the University of Paris (Sorbonne). There and at the EPHE he proved himself an impressive, scrupulous, and paternal scholar, though a severe teacher. He wrote numerous works, notably on Arabic and Jewish philosophy, on the *Kabbalah, and on Arab manuscripts. He specialized in the study of the beginnings of Jewish philosophy and Kabbalah and of the relationship between these two disciplines. Gifted with a vast erudition, he also produced minute and precise analyses of a number of unknown or misconstrued works. He contributed to the second edition of the *Encyclopedia of Islam* (1960–2004), with articles concerning Judaism. His most important works include *Introduction à la pensée juive du Moyen Age* (1947); *La théologie ascétique de Bahya ibn Paquda* (1947; Spanish translation with additions, 1950); *Judah ben Nissim ibn Malka, philosophe juif marocain* (1954); *L'Amour de Dieu dans la théologie juive du Moyen Age* (1957); *Isaac Albalag, averroïste juif, traducteur et annotateur d'Al-Ghazali* (1960); *Recherches sur la philosophie et la Kabbale dans la pensée juive du Moyen Age* (1962); and *Le Commentaire d'Ezra de Gérone sur le Cantique des Cantiques* (1969). Among his last main concerns was the theology of Yûsuf al-Baṣîr (REJ, 128 (1969); 131 (1972); 134 (1975); 137 (1978); 140 (1981)). The catalogue of his works embraced no fewer than 1,657 items in 1991 (among which were more than 1,200 book reviews) to which can be added unpublished material (e.g., the catalogue of the Hebrew scientific and philosophical mss. at the Bibliothèque Nationale in Paris). His later books were the critical editions of Isaac Albalag's *Tikkun ha-De'ot* (1973) and an abridgment of R. Judah Ibn Malkah on *Sefer Yeẓirah* (1974), the *Catalogue des manuscrits arabes* [de la B.N.]. *Manuscrits musulmans*, vol. 2 (1978), to which may be added the posthumous *Catalogue… Mss. musulmans*, vol. 3 (1985), *Al-Kitâb al-Muḥtawi de Yûsuf al-Baṣîr* (1985), *Le commentaire sur le Livre de la Création de Dûnash ben Tâmîm… éd. revue et augmentée* (2002), and four volumes of *scripta minora*: G.E. Weil (ed.), *Mélanges G. Vajda* (1982); N. Cottard (ed.), *La transmission du savoir en Islam, VIIe–XVIIIe siècles* (1983); D. Gimaret, M. Hayoun, J. Jolivet (eds.), *Études de théologie et de philosophie arabo-islamiques à l'époque classique* (1986); and *Sages et penseurs sépharades de Bagdad à Cordoue* (1989).

BIBLIOGRAPHY: "Hommage à Georges Vajda," in: REJ, 139 (1980), 111–27; G. Nahon, Ch. Touati (eds.), *Hommage à Georges Vajda. Études d'histoire et de pensée juives* (1980); G. Nahon, "Georges Vajda, président de la Société des études juives," in: REJ, 140 (1981), 297–302; G. Nahon and Ch. Touati, "Georges Vajda," in: *Annuaire de l'éphé, Ve section, sciences religieuses*, 90 (1981–82), 31–35; A. Caquot, "Georges Vajda," in: *Journal asiatique*, 270 (1982), 225–28; P. Fenton, *Alfei Yehudah. Bibliographie de l'œuvre de Georges Vajda* (1991).

[Charles Touati / Jean-Pierre Rothschild (2nd ed.)]

VAJS, ALBERT (1905–1964), leader of Yugoslav Jewry. Born in Zemun (Semlin), Vajs grew up in a mixed Serbo-Croat, German, and Hungarian cultural milieu, but from his youth he was a Zionist and was greatly influenced by Alexander *Licht and the Zemun rabbi H. Urbach. Until 1941 he was a barrister in Belgrade. During World War II he was a Yugoslav officer and was captured by the Germans. After the war he was a member of the State War Crimes Commission in Yugoslavia and the deputy head of the Yugoslav delegation to the International Military Tribunal in Nuremberg. From 1947 he was a professor in the faculties of law and philosophy at Belgrade and wrote numerous essays on legal matters and a book on the history of civilization.

In postwar Yugoslavia, Vajs devoted his energies to Jewish interests, mainly to the rehabilitation of the Jewish communities, becoming the president of their federation. He represented Yugoslav Jewry at world Jewish conventions, particularly of the *World Jewish Congress and its Executive. He was helpful in organizing the great *aliyah* to Israel of Yugoslav Jewry in 1948–49, which encompassed about 8,000 Jews.

BIBLIOGRAPHY: Institut za pravnu istoriju, *Zbornik radova iz pravne istorije posvećen Albertu Vajsu* (1966); *Bilten Udruženja Jevreja iz Jugoslavije u Izraelu* (May 1964).

[David Alcalay]

VALABREGA, CESARE (1898–1965), Italian pianist, critic, and musicologist. Born in Pesaro, Valabrega studied piano and composition in Bologna. He took a diploma in piano at Pesaro conservatory (1916) and an arts degree at Bologna University. He toured as a concert pianist and critic in Italy and abroad and gave lecture recitals throughout his life. He founded in 1950 the Associazione Romana dei Concerti Storici and became its artistic director in 1953. He taught the history of music at Naples Conservatory (1953) and the University of Perugia (from 1954); he was head of music for the Associazione Nazionale per l'Educatione Artistica at Rome University. He published *Schumann arte e natura* (1934, 3/1956), *Il clavicembalista Domenico Scarlatti* (1937, 2/1957), and *Johann Sebastian Bach* (1950), and he edited in 1959–63 the historical anthology of 40 long-playing records, *Storia della Musica Italiana*, with explanatory booklet, sponsored by the Italian government, the International Council for Music, and UNESCO. He was awarded a silver medal by the government for his contribution to Italian music.

BIBLIOGRAPHY: Grove Music Online.

[Amnon Shiloah (2nd ed.)]

VALABRÈGUE, MARDOCHÉE GEORGES (1852–1930), French soldier. Born in Carpentras, he was commissioned as a high artillery officer in 1873 and in 1877 was appointed instructor at the military academy. He became secretary to the French army's High Committee on Methods of Warfare in 1881 and was assistant to the minister of war, General André, from 1886 to 1902, when he was made head of the French artillery academy. Subsequently, Valabrègue commanded the 12th infantry division with the rank of major general and following the outbreak of World War I was given command of a group of two reserve divisions at the battle of the Marne. In the following year he was made a member of the French High Command and in 1917 inspector general of the Armed Forces.

[Mordechai Kaplan]

VALEA-LUI-VLAD, Jewish agricultural settlement in Bessarabia prior to World War II. It was founded on an area of some 934 acres which had been purchased in 1839 by approximately 350 Jews from Podolia. In 1899 there were 255 families (1,385 persons), including 82 landowners owning an average of 11.4 acres per family. The cultivated area amounted to 791 acres; of these 321 acres were set aside for crops and 430 for pasture. Because of a lack of agricultural implements – there was only one plow in the colony – plowing was hired out. In 1925 the 247 members of the local loan fund included 89 farmers, 56 artisans, and 79 tradesmen. In 1930 there were 1,281 Jews on the settlement (94.5% of the total population). The community was destroyed with the entry of the Germans and Romanians into Bessarabia in July 1941.

[Eliyahu Feldman]

VALENCE, chief town of the department of Dôme, S.E. France, part of the ancient province of Dauphiné. The establishment of the Jewish community in Valence does not go back earlier than 1323; however, the decision of the council held in the town in 1248 that prohibited all relations between Christians and Jews may lead to the assumption that isolated Jews were living there at the time. This decision appears to have been decreed in the wake of the accusation of ritual murder of *Valreas in 1247 as a result of which the high constable of Valence had all the Jews on his lands imprisoned and their possessions confiscated. In 1441, when the community numbered 18 families, the bishop recalled the obligation of the Jews to wear the distinctive sign so that "guests be not regarded as citizens." In 1463, 14 Jews of Valence were ordered to pay a severe fine to the dauphin "for having practiced excessive usury and having spoken evilly of His Majesty…." In 1476 the same dauphin granted the Jews of Valence a new letter of protection; however, at the close of the century this community disappeared, as did the other communities of Dauphiné. At the beginning of World War II, there were about 50 Jewish families in Valence, half of whom were refugees from *Alsace. In the early 1970s, there were about 800 Jews in Valence, mainly of North African origin.

BIBLIOGRAPHY: Gross, Gal Jud, 204; A. Prudhomme, in: REJ, 9 (1884), 235–41; S. Grayzel, *The Church and the Jews* (1960²), 234f.; P. de Torey, *Catalogue des Acres du Dauphin Louis II* (1899), passim; Z. Szajkowski, *Analytical Franco-Jewish Gazetteer* (1966), 186.

[Bernhard Blumenkranz]

VALENCIA, city in Valencia province, E. Spain; it had the largest and most important community of the medieval kingdom of Valencia. The date of the first Jewish settlement is unknown, but there was already an important community during the Muslim period. Jews then engaged in crafts such as tanning and shoemaking and often bore the name of their craft. They also engaged in the marketing of agricultural products, a major occupation in Valencia, and maintained commercial ties with other Jewish merchants in Spain. There were few scholars in the Valencia community in this period. E. Ashtor (see bibliography) estimates that there were 162 Jewish families in Valencia, forming 6.5% of the total population, at the time of the Christian Reconquest in 1238. The fragment of a rewritten Hebrew marriage contract from Valencia, dating from the middle or late 11th century, was discovered in the Cairo **Genizah*. Solomon ibn *Gabirol died in Valencia between 1055 and 1058.

After the Christian Reconquest

In 1086 the Jewish emissary of King Alfonso VI of Castile arrived in Valencia and represented him there. The capitulation treaty is connected with el Cid, who captured Valencia in 1095; the treaty stipulated that Jews were forbidden to acquire Muslim prisoners of war, Jews who molested Muslims would be prosecuted, and Jews would not be appointed to functions of authority over Muslims and their property.

During the period of Muslim rule and after the final conquest of the town by King James I of Aragon in 1238, the Jewish quarter was situated on the eastern side of the Rahbat el-qadi and in its vicinity, on the site where the Santa Catalina church stands at present. In 1244 James I granted the Jews the whole quarter. A special gate, known as the Jews' Gate, led to the Jewish cemetery. James I granted the Jews of Valencia, and those who settled there, extensive rights. The community enjoyed a very wide autonomy and its judiciary could even deal with criminal offenses. In 1273 James I ratified the boundaries of the quarter. A special wall was erected around it a short while before the persecutions of 1391 (see below). There were many synagogues in the quarter. A number of them were destroyed in 1391 and others were converted into churches. The Jewish quarter of Valencia was one of the largest in the Iberian Peninsula, but nothing of it has survived. This was due to the urban development that began in 1412, two decades after the total destruction of the Jewish community in the massacres of 1391. However, thanks to the archival documents we know where the Jewish quarter was. Following the constant growth of the Jewish population throughout the 13th and 14th centuries, the city authorities decided in 1390 to enlarge the Jewish quarter. This decision barely one year before the complete destruction of the Jewish community aroused very strong opposition on the part of the Christian inhabitants.

The register of the apportionment of properties (*Repartirmiento*) after the Christian Reconquest gives much information on the period which followed. Jewish court favorites received land and properties. Among the Jewish settlers were several of the king's interpreters, including Baḥya and Solomon *Alconstantini, and Solomon Bonafos, who acted as treasurer of Catalonia. One hundred and four Jews received houses and estates in Valencia and the vicinity; these should be regarded as new settlers. In 1239 James I granted the Jews of Valencia the same privilege as had been granted to the Jews of *Saragossa. Among other provisions, the Jews were granted the right to have lawsuits between them judged according to Jewish law; the king would adjudicate in matters of criminal law; in lawsuits between Christians and Jews, both Jewish and Christian witnesses were required; the form of the Jewish *oath was established (a version of it in Catalonian is extant); Jewish prisoners would be released to be in their homes on the Sabbath. In 1261 James I confirmed the right of the Jews to acquire farming and urban land from all the inhabitants of the country, including noblemen and clergymen – an unusual right in those days, which can perhaps be understood by the importance attached to Jewish settlement in this border region of the kingdom. One of these owners of land, cattle, and sheep was Don Judah de la *Cavalleria, who was appointed bailiff of Valencia after 1263. King Pedro III entrusted the Jews with additional functions in Valencia. When the revolt of the Muslims in the southern part of the kingdom was suppressed in 1277, Moses Alconstantini was appointed bailiff there. Among Jews appointed to administrative office were Muça de *Portella, Aaron ibn Yaḥya, and Joseph *Ravaya.

The authority of these Jews in Valencia was short-lived. Moses Alconstantini was deposed in 1283. The properties of the Ravaya family were confiscated after the death of Joseph, and Moses Ravaya was also dismissed. The anti-Jewish policy formulated at the time by James I was now enforced in Valencia: the laws on loans and interest and the regulations on oaths were reintroduced; Jews were forbidden to slaughter their animals in the abattoirs of the town, and they were ordered to wear a "cloak," as was the custom in Barcelona.

During the reign of James I, in 1271, the Jews of Valencia paid an annual tax of 3,000 solidus in the currency of the kingdom. In 1274 this amount was increased to 5,000 solidos. Pedro III imposed a special levy on the Jews of the town to cover the expenses of his wars, which amounted to 25,000 solidos in Jaca currency in 1282. The sum was collected by coercive and oppressive methods and Solomon b. Abraham *Adret (Rashba), then rabbi of the community, already pointed out (Responsa, vol. 1, no. 427) that the loans and contributions were destroying the foundations of the community's existence. The localities of *Jativa, *Murviedro (Sagunto), Alcira, and Gandia were incorporated in the tax district (*collecta*) of Valencia, and the annual tax raised generally amounted to 25,000 solidos. At the close of the 13th century, about 250 taxpaying families lived in Valencia whose names have been recorded; they spoke Arabic. After the destruction of the community of Valencia in the persecutions of 1391, however, Ḥasdai *Crescas estimated its population to have been 1,000 "houseowners." This figure may be due to his own impressions or could have referred to the whole of the kingdom of Valencia.

Toward the close of the 13th century, as a result of the activities of Jewish merchants, Valencia became an important center of maritime trade. These "seamen" traded with *Majorca, North Africa, and most of the Mediterranean ports. The merchants purchased raw materials, wool, wool products, and grain, and exported them through Valencia to other ports of the Mediterranean.

Another occupation of the Jews was brokerage, and in 1315 there were 43 Jewish brokers; evidently all those engaged in this occupation were Jews. Even after the destruction of the community of Valencia, the town remained a center of Jewish trade. Alfonso V issued letters of protection to Jewish merchants from Barbary who came to trade in Valencia.

The community administration of Valencia was similar in organization to that of the other large communities of Aragon. The community was headed by a council of 30 members, among whom five were chosen as *muqaddimūn* by lot (Solomon b. Abraham Adret (Rashba), Responsa, vol. 3, no. 417). The community was supervised by the bailiff-general, the representative of the king. A Jewish *mustaçaf* was appointed to supervise the market and its activities. In 1300, after members of the community had complained that the wealthy and prominent personalities were throwing the burden of taxation onto "the middle class and the little people," King James II ordered that all payments to the kingdom and the community, including debts of former years, were to be divided up by a system of "declaration," and that everyone should take the oath in the presence of three Jews (one each of the upper, middle, and lower strata). Many problems arose in the Valencia community as a result of disputes and informing (there was a special regulation against informing; *Isaac b. Sheshet Perfet, Responsa, no. 79). Many queries were addressed to R. Solomon Adret and R. Isaac b. Sheshet on these matters. In 1348 Pedro IV ordered the bailiff to arbitrate in community disputes concerning the methods of collecting the tax: whether it was to be imposed by assessment or by "declaration."

The Jews of Valencia suffered during the *Black Death in 1348, and the persecutions which broke out in the town in its wake. In 1354 the leaders of the Valencia community collaborated in the rehabilitation of the communities of the kingdom of Aragon. Each provincial delegate was offered a seat on the national administration. The regulations of the national organization were signed by the resolute *parnas* of the community of Valencia, Judah Eleazar, a wealthy merchant and landowner who had financial transactions with the crown but was not outstanding for his learning or piety. In 1363 Pedro IV imposed a tax of 50,000 solidos on him as a contribution toward the expenses of the war against Castile. A tax was also imposed on the community and its wealthiest members, totaling 152,000 solidos.

The adoption in 1364 of the regulations of the community of *Barcelona of 1327 may be regarded as a further attempt to reconsolidate the authority of the community. In 1369 Pedro IV authorized the burial society of the community of Valencia to collect interest from a certain income. The prohibitions issued by the community administration included one against gambling, for money or real estate, with Christians.

In 1385 Isaac b. Sheshet Perfet (Ribash) was appointed rabbi of Valencia, his native town, holding this position until the destruction of the community in 1391. He organized activities in Valencia to restore the importance of Torah study and piety. Valuable historical material on the community is contained in his responsa (nos. 253–355).

The Persecutions of 1391

On July 9, 1391, the community of Valencia was attacked and destroyed by rioters who arrived from Castile and soldiers who were stationed in the port from where they were due to sail for Sicily with the infante Martín. In this assault 250 Jews died, while the remainder agreed to convert to Christianity or found refuge in the houses of the townspeople. Isaac b. Sheshet Perfet was among those who fled. Those who converted included distinguished personalities such as Don Samuel Abravalia (who took the name Alfonso Fernández de Villanova after his apostasy), the king's physician Omar Tahuel, who ranked among the *muqaddimūn*, and his relative Isaac Tahuel. According to some documents, it seems that R. Isaac b. Sheshet was also among the forcibly converted, before he fled. On July 16 the king ordered that Jews who had hidden in the houses of Christians should not be compelled to convert, but be taken to a place of safety. He also prohibited the conversion of synagogues into churches. However, on September 22 the king instructed that a list of the property of the Jews who had perished should be drawn up, in order to have it transferred to him. In November a pardon was granted to the Christian inhabitants of Valencia for the attack because, according to the city elders, the town was being emptied of its inhabitants who were fleeing in every direction. None of the synagogues of Valencia survived the 1391 massacres. The Jewish market, the *zoco,* which was just outside the Jewish quarter, was in Gallinas Street, at the beginning of Mar Street. The Jewish cemetery was outside the Jewish quarter but within the walls of the city. At the expulsion it was given by Ferdinand to the Dominicans. In its place today stands the El Corte Inglés department store.

After this destruction, the community proved unable to recover, even though in 1393 the king and the queen entrusted Ḥasdai Crescas and the delegates of the communities of Saragossa and *Calatayud with the task of choosing 60 families who would settle in Barcelona and Valencia. A year later John I ordered that their cemetery should be restored to the Jews of Valencia. A small community may have been reconstituted, because, according to Simeon b. Ẓemaḥ *Duran, there were Jews living in Valencia at the close of the century (Responsa, *Yakhin u-Vo'az*, pt. 2, paras. 14–15).

In 1413 Vicente *Ferrer is known to have endeavored to convert Jews in Valencia, but these may have been concentrated in localities in the vicinity. Only Jewish merchants continued to visit the town. In 1483 King *Ferdinand canceled the permission given to the Jews for prolonged stays in Valencia. He also abolished the privilege exempting Jews who came there from wearing a distinctive *badge.

The Conversos in Valencia

Files of those who were sentenced by the *Inquisition of Valencia within the framework of the Papal Inquisition during the 1460s are extant. In 1464 the Inquisition discovered that many *Conversos had sailed from Valencia port to the Orient, particularly Ereẓ Israel, in order to return to Judaism. A number were apprehended, including families who had arrived there from Andalusia. Numerous testimonies to the Inquisition reported that Conversos had returned to Judaism in all the towns in the area of the eastern Mediterranean.

The Conversos in Spain were seized by an overwhelming desire to leave the country, and many made their way to Valencia for this purpose. When apprehended, however, they were only condemned to expulsion from the region or fined. In 1482, when the Spanish national Inquisition was established and Cristóbal Gualves was appointed inquisitor, the Conversos of Valencia submitted a complaint to the pope against his acts of cruelty and his acceptance of invalid testimonies. Pope *Sixtus IV removed him from his position in Valencia, but King Ferdinand strongly protested against his intervention. In 1484 investigators of heresy were appointed in Valencia to act upon instructions by *Torquemada. It is evident that they had hesitations about their duties, for up to 1492 they issued "orders of grace" three times, a rare occurrence in those days. This may also have been because many Conversos had been hidden in the houses of noblemen and Muslims throughout the kingdom of Valencia.

Up to June 1488, 983 men and women in Valencia returned to the fold of the Church, while another 100 persons were burned at the stake. In the trials the accused were interrogated as to whether they had committed acts against the Christian religion, such as having struck crucifixes, etc. The trial proceedings reveal the overwhelming yearnings of the accused for anything Jewish and their profound adherence to the Jewish religion. Prayer books in the Valencia dialect were found in their possession, and many Jewish prayers were well known to them. The messianic agitation manifested in 1500 was also apparent in Valencia, and the Inquisition took severe measures to eradicate it. The tribunal of Valencia was a regional one, and it continued to function until the general abolition of the Inquisition during the 19th century.

Valencia was the port of embarkation for Jews who left for the Orient after the expulsion from Spain in 1492. The number who left from there is not known, although there is such information on the other Spanish ports. Isaac b. Judah *Abrabanel and his family embarked from Valencia in June 1492 by special permission granted to him by King Ferdinand.

There was a small Jewish population in Valencia in the 1970s, which had recently affiliated to the organization of Spanish communities.

BIBLIOGRAPHY: The following bibliography also contains items that relate to the entire medieval Kingdom of Valencia. Baer, Spain, index; Baer, Urkunden (incl. bibl.); I. Loeb, in: REJ, 13 (1886), 239ff.; 14 (1887), 264–8; H.C. Lea, *A History of the Inquisition of Spain*, 1 (1906), index; J.E. Martínez Fernando, *Catálogo de la documentación relativa al reino de Valencia*, 2 vols. (1934); B. Llorca, *La Inquisición en Valencia, Homenaje a Antonio Rubio i Lluch*, 2 (1936), 395f.; M.

Ballesteros Gaibrois, *Valencia y los Reyes católicos* (1944); Neuman, Spain, index; L. Piles Ros, in: *Sefarad*, 6 (1946), 137–41; 7 (1947), 151–6, 354–60; 8 (1948), 89–96; 15 (1955), 89–101; L. Torres Balbas, in: *Al-Andalus*, 9 (1954), 194f.; F. Cantera, *Singogas españolas* (1955), 325–31; F.L. Schneiderman, in: *Hispania*, 7 (1958), 181–9; Suárez Fernández, Documentos, index; A. López de Meneses, in: *Estudios de Edad Media de la Corona de Aragón Sección de Zaragoza*, 6 (1952), 682–83; F.A. Roca Traver, in: *Escuela de Estudios Medievales*, 5 (1952), 120, Ashtor, Korot, index. **ADD. BIBLIOGRAPHY:** R. Burns, *Medieval Colonialism: Postcrusade Exploitation of Islamic Valencia* (1975); idem, *Jaume I els valencians del segle XIII* (1981); idem, *Muslims, Christians, and Jews in the Crusader Kingdom of Valencia* (1984); J.R. Magdalena Nom de Déu, in: *Anuario de filología* 2 (1976), 181–25; idem, in: *Sefarad,* 39 (1979), 309–31; idem, in: *Afers*, 7 (1988–9), 189–205; R. Garcia Càrcel, *Orígenes de la Inquisición española: el Tribunal de Valencia, 1478–1530* (1976); J. Ventura Subirats, *Inquisició espanyola I cultura renaixentista al País Valencià* (1978); J. Hinijosa Montalvo, in: *Saitabi*, 29 (1979), 21–42; idem, *ibid.*, 31 (1981), 47–72; idem, *ibid.*, 33 (1983), 105–24; idem, in: *Sefarad*, 45 (1985), 315–39; idem, in: *Hispania*, 175 (1990), 921–40; idem, *The Jews of the Kingdom of Valencia* (1993); L. Piles Ros, in: *Sefarad,* 44 (1984), 217–82; idem, *ibid.*, 45 (1985), 69–30; J. Guiral-Hadziiossif, in: *Anuario de estudios medievales,* 15 (1985), 415–65; D. Bramon, *Contra moros y judíos* (1986) [trans. from Catalan (1981)]; A. García, *Els Vives; una família de jueus valencians* (1987); L. García Ballester, *La medicina a la Valèncai medieval: medicina I societat en un país medieval* (1988) 23–51; S. Haliczer, *Inquisition and Society in the Kingdom of Valencia, 1478–1834* (1990).

[Haim Beinart]

VALENSI (al-Valensi, Balansi, Valença, Valencin, Valencia, Valenciano), family which originated in *Valencia (Spain). R. SAMUEL BEN ABRAHAM VALENSI (1435–1487), talmudist in Zamora, *Spain, was the disciple of R. Isaac Campanton and the teacher of several scholars, including R. Jacob *Ibn Ḥabib, the author of *Ein Ya'akov.* Of his works only a brief treatise, entitled *Kelalei Kal va-Ḥomer* (Venice, 1599), on the methodology of the Talmud, is extant. After the expulsion from Spain, his family took refuge in *Morocco. MOSES VALENSI and his son ABRAHAM VALENSI countersigned the first *takkanot* of the *megorashim* ("exiles") in Fez (1494, 1554). SAMUEL VALENSI, an inhabitant of Azemmour, distinguished himself by his military valor in the war near *Ceuta, where he led 1,400 Jewish and Muslim soldiers. He came to the assistance of the besieged *Safi with his ships and compelled the large army of attackers to abandon its campaign (1534). In *Marrakesh, JOSEPH VALENCIA was the private physician of three successive sovereigns from 1590 to 1628.

Some of the Valensis of Morocco settled in *Venice in about 1650. JOSEPH VALENSI was a rabbi there in about 1680. Several members of the family later settled in Leghorn, while others moved to *Tunis before 1690. The origin of the members of Valensi family in Tunis is France and not Leghorn. They came to Tunis at the end of the 18th century and during the 19th. In many documents, they appear as the leaders of the Grana community (the name of the community founded in Tunis by the immigrants from Leghorn) in Tunis and also as the representatives of the French nation ("Notables Français" and "Députés de la Nation française") from 1858 onward. They served the Grana community for a period of 100 years. In the minute book of the marriage contracts of the Grana community are recorded many members of this family from the end of the 18th century onward, many of them as bridegrooms and brides, and others as leaders and *dayyanim*. Many of the Valensi family members in Tunis were French citizens. The Valensis distinguished themselves especially as physicians, scholars, soldiers, and diplomats in Tunis, where the first known family member was GABRIEL DE MANUEL VALENSI (1686), a financier. JOSEPH VALENSI became involved in Franco-Tunisian political affairs between 1792 and 1812. His son SAMUEL VALENSI had a successful career in politics, and his grandson GABRIEL VALENSI, who was appointed official interpreter between the beys and the French sovereigns, was charged with diplomatic missions to Paris in 1867 and 1878. HAYYIM DAVIS VALENSI was a *dayyan* and signed many marriage contracts in the Grana community in Tunis between the years 1821 and 1824; GABRIEL BEN YA'ACOV VALENSI signed marriage contracts in the Grana community between 1806 and 1810; GABRIEL BEN REUVEN VALENSI was the treasurer of this community in 1815; MOSES VALENSI (1825–1909) was sent on a Tunisian government mission to the United States. GABRIEL VALENSI (1845–1915) was a lieutenant general in the army of the bey. He was involved in the charities of his sister Zodika, who dedicated property to the Eẓ Ḥayyim synagogue of the Grana community. He served also as the treasurer of this community and was a philanthropist. His signature appears on many regulations of his community from 1860 until 1893. In 1890 he was the opponent of the qa'id and chief rabbi Eliyahu Burgel and opposed him when Burgel wanted to diminish the autonomy and the property rights of the Grana community. The dispute broke out when the Jewish community in Tunis had severe economic difficulties, and Burgel took from the Grana community its 20 percent share in the new cemetery. Before this dispute Gabriel Valensi succeeded in achieving for his community a good new agreement with the Touansa community. In 1895 Gabriel Valensi wrote a letter to the chief rabbi of France, Rabbi Zadok Kahn, and to the *Alliance Israélite Universelle about the dispute with Burgel, and he was victorious in this struggle.

His son RODOLPHE VALENSI, linguist and engineer, wrote scientific works.

JOSEPH VALENSI (d. 1908) was the Austro-Hungarian consul and the chief administrator of the municipal services of Tunis. He was famous for his philanthropy. RAYMOND VALENSI (1847–1920) represented his country abroad, and his son JOSEPH VALENSI, professor of fine arts, was one of the architects of the Paris Exhibition (1925–31). THÉODORE VALENSI (1886–1954), philanthropist, novelist, painter, and barrister, was called to Paris, where he was a senior adviser in the ministries of Clémenceau and Briand and chief private secretary of the Cabinet du Ministre. VICTOR RAYMOND VALENSI (d. 1942) was the last member of the Valensi family who served the Grana community. He died at the age of 95. In 1881 he was appointed the head of the Alliance Israélite Universelle in Tunis and was its representative.

ALFRED VALENSI (1878–1944), philanthropist and barrister, contributed to leading European newspapers. He wrote on legislation and sociology and was an active Zionist. He founded the first Zionist organization in Tunis in 1910. He was seized by the Nazis and died during deportation. VICTOR VALENSI, a notable Tunisian architect in the 1920s and 1930s, published studies of the local architecture of northern Africa and is best known for designing the Grand Synagogue of Tunis in 1938. He died in Buchenwald. MAURICIO VALENSI was mayor of Napoli after World War II.

BIBLIOGRAPHY: Neubauer, Chronicles, 1 (1887, repr. 1965), 107, 113; J.M. Toledano, *Ner ha-Ma'arav* (1911), 72, 78–80; D. Corcos, in: *Sefunot*, 10 (1966), 68, 78; P. Lambert, *Choses et gens de Tunisie* (1912), 418–20; *Livre d'or de la Tunisie* (1932), 184–5. **ADD. BIBLIOGRAPHY:** A. Rodrigue, *Ḥinukh, Hevrah ve- Historyah, Kol Yisrael Ḥaverim vi-Yehudei ha-Yam ha-Tikhon, 1860–1929* (1991),150; P. Sebag, *Histoire des Juifs de Tunisie* (1991), 81–82; A. (R). Attal and Y. Avivi, *Pinkas u-Ketubot shel ha-Kehillah ha-Portugezit be-Tunis ba-Me'ot ha-18–19*, 1 (1993); idem, *Pinkas ha-Ketubbot, Taryag–Taryad*, 2 (2000); Y. Avrahami, *Pinkas ha-Kehillah ha-Yehudit ve-ha-Portugezit be-Tunis, 1710–1944* (1997); S. Bard, *Le-Toledot ha-Tenu'ah ha-Ẓiyyonit be-Tunisia* (1980), 135, 147.

[David Corcos / Leah Bornstein-Makovetsky (2nd ed.)]

VALENTIN, GABRIEL GUSTAV (1810–1883), German physiologist, anatomist, and embryologist. Born and educated in Breslau, Valentin practiced medicine there and later moved to Berne, Switzerland, where he became professor of physiology and zootomy. Valentin, a pioneer in the study of physiology and embryology, investigated the blood circulation in the lungs, the electrical conduction in muscles and nerves, and the physiology of the senses.

Together with Czech physiologist J.E. Purkinje and F.G.J. *Henle, he laid the foundation for the cell theory of M.J. Schleiden and Theodore Schwann. He discovered the diastatic role of the pancreatic juice in the digestion of carbohydrates, and also found a method of improving microscope observations by applying polarized light. He was the author of *Handbuch der Entwicklungsgeschichte des Menschen* (1835); *Histiogenia Comparata* (1835), for which he received the Grand Prix des Sciences Physiques; and *Lehrbuch der Physiologie des Menschen* (1844; *Textbook of Physiology*, 1853).

BIBLIOGRAPHY: S.R. Kagan, *Jewish Medicine* (1952), 160; B. Kisch, *Forgotten Leaders in Modern Medicine* (1954).

[Suessmann Muntner]

VALENTIN, HUGO MAURICE (1888–1963), Swedish historian and Zionist leader. Born in Sweden, Valentin first served as a teacher of history at a high school in Falun, but in 1930 was appointed lecturer, and in 1948 professor, at the University of Uppsala. His main topics of research were European and particularly Prussian history of the 18th century, and the history of the Jews in Sweden. In 1925 he became a Zionist, and from then on dedicated himself passionately to spreading Zionism to Swedish Jews. He became president, and later honorary president, of the Zionist Federation and was respected and beloved by all. He died suddenly in the studio of Stockholm Radio as he was preparing to defend the case of Israel in a disputation with an anti-Zionist.

Among his works on Jewish topics are *Judarnas historia i Sverige* ("History of the Jews in Sweden," 1924), the standard work on the subject; *Anti-Semitism* (1925, Eng. tr. 1926), a historical and critical examination; *Kampen om Palestina* ("The Struggle for Palestine," 1940); "Rescue Activities in Scandinavia" (in: YIVO *Annual of Jewish Social Science* (1953), 22–51); and *Judarna i Sverige* ("The Jews in Sweden," 1964). For many years until his death, he was editor of the monthly *Judisk Tidskrift* ("Jewish Review"), originally established by Marcus *Ehrenpreis.

[Chaim Yahil]

°**VALERIUS GRATUS**, Roman *procurator of Judea, 15–26 C.E., appointed by the emperor Tiberius. Little is known of his administration, but his frequent replacement of the high priest is indicative of his attitude toward the Jews. After deposing Anan b. Seth, he appointed in turn Ishmael b. Phabi I, Eleazar b. Ananius, and Joseph Caiaphas. That his motive was bribery is hinted in the Talmud: "Because money was paid for the purpose of obtaining the position of high priest, [they]were changed every 12 months," and "Since they used to hire it [the office of high priest] out for money, their days were shortened" (Sif. Num. 131).

BIBLIOGRAPHY: Schuerer, Hist. 198: Klausner, Bayit Sheni, 4 (1950^2), 203f.

[Edna Elazary]

°**VALERIUS MAXIMUS** (first century C.E.), compiler of historical anecdotes in *Tiberius' reign. He mentions that Cornelius Hispalus expelled the Jews from Rome in 139 B.C.E. for corrupting Roman customs with their worship of Jupiter Sabazius (= Sabaoth?).

[Jacob Petroff]

VALERO, Sephardi family in *Jerusalem. JACOB (d. 1880) was a banker. Born in Constantinople, he settled in Ereẓ Israel in 1835. In 1848 he founded the first modern bank in Jerusalem to have contacts with European capitals. He was a leader of the Jerusalem Sephardi community. His son ḤAYYIM AHARON (1845–1923) was born in Jerusalem and from 1875 acted as the director of the bank his father had founded. He expanded the bank which became the agent for foreign royalty who visited the Holy Land. He was also the agent for the Russian government, which purchased the Russian Compound in the center of the Holy City. He contributed to the unification of the Sephardi and Ashkenazi communities in Jerusalem. His son JOSEPH MOSHE (1882–1945) was born in Jerusalem and studied law in Switzerland, where he was active in Zionist student groups. On his return to Palestine, he practiced law in Jerusalem and became a magistrate there. From 1929 he was a district court judge in Jerusalem. He was one of the three trial judges in the *Arlosoroff murder trial (1934), and he alone vindicated the accused completely. He was also active in public institutions and the Sephardi community.

[Benjamin Jaffe]

VALLADOLID, city in N. central *Spain. As the chief city of the kingdom of Castile and the meeting place of the Cortes, Valladolid attracted many Jews to settle there; it is also connected with decrees and edicts issued there against both the local Jews and those in the kingdom as a whole. Jewish settlement in Valladolid is first mentioned in 1221. However, Jews probably already lived there during the Arab period, as well as immediately after the Christian Reconquest in the 11th century.

Information is extant from the second half of the 13th century concerning houses of the Jewish quarter bought from Christians and the butchery situated near the old synagogue. One of the landowners was Joseph b. Moses de Gerondi (perhaps the son of *Naḥmanides), who was a favorite at the court of *Alfonso x. In 1288 Sancho iv prohibited the Jews of Valladolid from acquiring land in its vicinity. The community appears to have consisted of 50 to 100 families; it was thus of average size in comparison with other Spanish communities.

In 1322 the municipal council prohibited Christians from attending Jewish and Moorish weddings and from receiving treatment from Jewish physicians. Jews were also excluded from holding public office. Nevertheless, the right to farm the *alcabala* tax of Valladolid were leased to Jews. as was the tax imposed on owning livestock. Details are known from the beginning of the 14th century about litigation brought before R. *Asher b. Jehiel (Rosh) between R. Menahem and the community administration of Valladolid, which had sold the right to farm tax collected from it to the community of Carrion. During that period the apostate *Abner of Burgos settled in the town. He was appointed sexton of the church of Valladolid, and even became known as Alfonso of Valladolid. In 1336, on the orders of *Alfonso xi, he engaged in a public *disputation with the Jews of Valladolid on the subject of the **Birkat ha-Minim*. His arguments were accepted by the king who ordered the removal of this prayer from the prayer books.

At the time of the civil war between the brothers Pedro the Cruel and Henry of Trastamara, the inhabitants of the town joined with Henry in 1367, and the local Jews were subsequently subjected to attacks in which eight synagogues were destroyed. The survivors had to receive assistance and support from the communities of the kingdom of Aragon. The community apparently recovered, however, for in 1390 John i granted the monastery of San Benito an income of 15,000 maravedis from the annual tax and service tax which the Jews of Valladolid had paid him. This income was again ratified in 1412, though granted to the monastery from other sources because the majority of the local Jews had by then converted to Christianity as a result of the anti-Jewish persecutions in Spain of 1391.

The community was then in the process of disintegration. At that time Vicente *Ferrer lived in the town. Through his influence, in conjunction with *Pablo de Santa Maria, a series of severe anti-Jewish laws was issued, known as the Laws of Valladolid. The legislation was intended to undermine the foundations of Jewish existence and bring the Jews to conversion. It abolished Jewish autonomy, the Jews' rights of independent jurisdiction, and their special tax administration, among other measures. Christian judges were appointed to administer Jewish law. A special decree prohibited the Jews and the Moors of Valladolid from leaving the town, in conformity with the prohibition forbidding the Jews to leave the kingdom. The local rulers were warned not to offer protection to the Jews.

In 1413 John ii authorized the erection of a new Jewish quarter in Valladolid. The representatives of the community leased land for the quarter from the San Pablo monastery for an annual payment. The contract stipulated that the lease would be annulled if the quarter was removed to another site, if the king ordered the expulsion of the Jews from the town, or if all the Jews converted to Christianity.

An attempt to restore community life in the kingdom, however, was made by an assembly of delegates of the communities of the kingdom of Castile; "scholars and good men" convened between April 4 and May 2, 1432, under the leadership of Don Abraham *Benveniste of Soria in the great synagogue of Valladolid in the Jewish quarter, where they discussed the organization of the communities and their rehabilitation. This meeting was significant since, in addition to the regulations issued there, it was held in the chief city, which was the seat of the "court rabbi" (**rab de la corte*), the leader of Spanish Jewry, and thus expressed the idea of a national Jewish organization. The assembly issued five unique sets of regulations aimed to restore the life of the communities to their former greatness. The Regulations of Valladolid promoted an internal revival of the communities by their own initiative and also demonstrated that it was the policy of the king to encourage their recovery.

In the tax registers of 1439, an annual tax assessment of 15,000 maravedis in old currency is still mentioned, but as few Jews by then remained in Valladolid, John ii reduced the payment to 11,400 maravedis of the same currency. In 1453 he further exempted the Jews and the Moors from various taxes, excepting the annual tax and the service tax. In 1474 the community paid a total of 5,500 maravedis in taxes.

The delegates of the communities met again in Valladolid in 1476. Apparently, a request was made by the communities to appoint R. Vidal Astori chief rabbi of the communities beyond the town of Burgos. Ferdinand agreed to the appointment, but later nominated Abraham *Seneor of Segovia chief rabbi of the whole kingdom in appreciation of his services. Ten years later in 1486, Ferdinand and Isabella took the part of the Jews of Valladolid against the decisions of the municipal council which tried to prevent Jews from settling there by prohibiting marriages of their children outside the town, with the intention of settling there after the marriage. In this period the delegates of the communities met in Valladolid under the leadership of Abraham Seneor to discuss raising funds for the expenses of the war against Granada. The atmosphere of this period, shortly before the expulsion of the Jews from Spain, is reflected in the resolutions of the Christian craftsmen's guilds demanding that the Jews should leave the town because they did not wish to live beside them.

The relations between Jews and *Conversos and between Conversos and Christians by birth in Valladolid emerge in a satirical poem directed against the Converso poet Juan Poeta de *Valladolid, a native of the town. According to the poem, Juan intended to emigrate to Ereẓ Israel but fell into the hands of the Muslims in Fez and adopted Islam; his father, it is stated, sold rags in Valladolid. In 1485, after reports had been received that Conversos had returned to Judaism in Zamora, an investigation was carried out in Valladolid by the royal tribunal, although the *Inquisition tribunals were already active and one had been established in Valladolid that year. It is possible that the court intended thereby to suppress knowledge of the affair. After the expulsion of the Jews from Spain in 1492, Fernán Núñez Coronel (Abraham Seneor) and Luis de Alcalá were appointed to collect the unpaid debts which the Jews had left in Valladolid in favor of the crown.

Apparently because few Conversos returned to Judaism in Castile, the Inquisition tribunal in Valladolid did not develop large-scale activity, though its investigations were renewed in 1499. The tribunal was abolished in 1560 when the area of its jurisdiction was included in the tribunal of Toledo.

BIBLIOGRAPHY: Baer, Spain, index; Baer, Urkunden, index; Neuman, Spain, index; H. Beinart, in: *Sefunot*, 5 (1961); J. Ortega y Rubio, *Historia de Valladolid* (1887), 92ff.; J.A. Revilla, *Los privilegios de Valladolid* (1906), 151f.; H.C. Lea, *A History of the Inquisition of Spain*, 1 (1906), 544–5; A. Ballesteros, in: *Sefarad*, 6 (1946), 255, 259n., 263ff.; Suárez Fernández, Documentos, index; P. León Tello, *Judíos de Palencia* (1967), Docs. 40, 84.

[Haim Beinart]

°VALLAT, XAVIER (1891–1972), French antisemitic politician. A member of the Chamber of Deputies from 1919, he changed his political affiliations several times, but always belonged to the extreme right and was an outspoken antisemite. He strove for de-emancipation of the Jews who were to be treated as strangers and in the Chamber (1936–40) "distinguished" himself by his fierce attacks on Leon *Blum. In July 1940 Pétain appointed him secretary general of the veterans' organization. The Nazi occupants suspected him because of his patriotism and dismissed him. However, when Darlan appointed him head of the Commissariat Général aux Questions Juives in March 1941, they did not object. Vallat enlarged the existing anti-Jewish legislation, thereby restricting the Jews' civil rights. He created the framework for the spoliation of Jewish property and founded the *Union Generale des Israelites de France (UGIF), a compulsory association over all Jews. He collaborated with the Nazi authorities but tried to safeguard French interests. Finally, in March 1942 the Nazis obtained his dismissal, but his organization served in the framework of the "Final Solution" in France (see *Holocaust, General Survey). Vallat, who afterward continued to serve Pétain in different offices, was condemned to ten years imprisonment in 1947, but released in January 1950.

BIBLIOGRAPHY: Z. Szajkowski, *Analytical Franco-Jewish Gazetteer 1939–1945* (1966), index; J. Billig, *Le Commissariat Général aux Questions Juives (1941–1944)*, 1 (1955), index; *Le Procès de Xavier Vallat* (1948).

[Yehuda Reshef]

VALLE, MOSES DAVID BEN SAMUEL (1696–1777), Italian physician and kabbalist. Valle was born in Padua. In his youth he wrote in Italian a book against Christianity entitled *I Sette Giorni della Verita*, but his major field was Kabbalah. He was considered to possess spiritual powers and receive mystical revelations. He is mentioned many times in documents relating to the circle of Moses Ḥayyim Luzzatto, of which he was one of the most important members. In this group, Valle seems to have been considered the Messiah. After Luzzatto left for Amsterdam, Valle became the leader of the Padua circle, which was not maintained for a long time. Most of his life he spent in seclusion, studying; he never occupied a rabbinic post, although he served as the cantor in the Sephardi synagogue. He wrote many disquisitions on kabbalistic subjects and other matters. From extant works found in his handwriting, it is possible to fix his date of birth and many details about his career. From all his works, only 70 kabbalistic interpretations on the last verse of the Torah were published (at the end of Luzzatto's **Megillat Setarim*, Warsaw, 1889). His rich legacy of nearly 20,000 pages is as yet unexplored.

BIBLIOGRAPHY: Ghirondi-Neppi, 247; J. Almanzi, in: *Kerem Ḥemed*, 3 (1838), 130; S.D. Luzzatto, in: HB, 6 (1863), 49–51; I. Tishby, in: *Sefer Yovel le-Y. Baer* (1960), 384; idem, *Netivei Emunah u-Minut* (1964), 193–6; M. Benayahu, in: *Sefunot*, 5 (1961), 300–16.

[Gershom Scholem]

VALMASEDA, town in Vizcaya province, N. Spain. The beginning of the Jewish settlement dates back to the 15th century, in the days of King Henry IV. The Jews were brought here and protected by the constable of Castile, the count of Haro. The Jewish quarter was then situated near the old bridge in the present San Lorenzo quarter. The settlement owed its importance to its proximity to the ports of Cantabria from which wool, skins, and other goods were exported to France, Flanders, and England. The Jews in Valmaseda consequently engaged mainly in commerce, and also owned houses and vineyards. In 1474 they paid a total of 1,100 maravedis in taxes which were imposed on them by Jacob ibn Nuñez, court physician and tax farmer. Influenced by the local craftsmen's guilds, and in opposition to crown policy, the town council from 1483 on began to adopt a decidedly anti-Jewish attitude. In 1486 the council of the Basques, which convened in Guernica, decreed the expulsion of the Jews from the area. In 1487 the town council in Valmaseda agreed to negotiate with the local community concerning their voluntary departure.

BIBLIOGRAPHY: Baer, Urkunden, 2 (1936), 368, 383; A. Rodríguez Herrero, *Valmaseda en el siglo xv y la aljama de los judíos* (1947); Suárez Fernández, Documentos, 312–3.

[Haim Beinart]

VALONA (Vlor, Vlone, אבילונה), port city in S.W. Albania. The Jewish community is considered one of the most ancient in Europe. Its beginnings are garbed in legend, relating that a Roman ship with a cargo of Jewish slaves from Palestine was blown off course and landed on the Albanian coast. Travelers' narratives mention the presence of Jews in Valona selling salt and pitch and trading with Venice. After the blood libel in Apulia, Italy, in 1290, Apulian Jews settled in Valona. The Jewish situation there improved after the Ottomans captured the city from the Byzantines. Jews from Spain (Castille and Catalonia) and Portugal arrived at the end of the 15th century. Turkish documents show that in 1520 there a total of 945 families in Valona, of which 528 were Jewish. The Jews transformed Valona into a large commercial center trading with Italy, Istanbul, Vienna, and Poland. Practically all commerce in the port was in Jewish hands, and from 1541 to 1637 all the consuls of Ragusa (Dubrovnik) in Valona were Jewish. In 1512, to unite all the Jewish congregations (Byzantine, Italian, Spanish, and Portuguese), the renowned rabbi Messer David *Leon (from Italy) was invited to the city. His strict ways, however, alienated the Spanish and Portuguese and he had to leave. The community amalgamated in the mid-17th century under the *ḥakham* Moses *Albelda.

During the Venetian siege of Valona in their war against the Turks (1688), most of the Jews left the city and escaped to Berat, and later on dispersed to Ioannina, (Greece), Monastir, Bitalya, and Kastoria (Macedonia). The old Torah scroll "Sefer Avilona" – said to be 1,500 years old – was deposited in Salonika, where it was burned by the Nazis. The old synagogue was destroyed by the great fire of 1915.

In 1938 there were 15 Jewish families in Valona. During the Nazi period, the Albanians hid and saved not only all Valona Jews but also the Jewish refugees that reached the city. In 1991 almost all of Valona's Jews settled in Israel.

BIBLIOGRAPHY: B. Hrabak, *Jevrei in Albaniji od Kraja XVII do Kraja XVIII veka* (1971); N. Tudorov, *Demografichekoto sustoianie na balkanskia Polnostrov XV–XVI vek* (1960); *Historia e Shqipertes* (1959); I. Burdelez, "Jewish Consuls in Service of the Dubrovnik Republic," in: *Diplomacy of the Republic of Dubrovnik* (1998).

[Mordechai Arbell (2nd ed.)]

VALRÉAS, town in the department of Vaucluse, S.E. France. Evidence of the medieval Jewish community in Valréas is the result of the persecution to which it was subjected in 1247 in the wake of a *blood libel. A two-year-old child disappeared on March 26 before Passover; it was found on the next day with the traces of many wounds. The statements of two brothers, both young children, brought suspicion upon the Jews of the town. Three Jews who were imprisoned confessed, after seven days of torture, that they had perpetrated a ritual murder on the child. Six other Jews were then accused and subjected to torture; with the exception of one, they admitted all that their interrogators wished to hear. The cruel sentence that ensued appears to have struck an even larger number of the Jews of Valréas: some were quartered, others burnt alive; men were castrated, and women were mutilated by the ablation of their breasts. The bishop of Saint-Paul-Trois-Châteaux and the high constable of Valence confiscated all the possessions of the Jews under their administration and then imprisoned them. On the other hand, Pope *Innocent IV ordered the archbishop of Vienne to assure the protection of the Jews in two letters (May 28, 1247), two months after the beginning of the persecution. Some regard the decision of the Council of *Valence of 1248, which prohibited all relations between Christians and Jews, and the authorization which Pope Innocent IV granted to the archbishop of Vienne to expel the Jews from his diocese in 1253, as an aftermath of the Valréas affair. The assertion that the final expulsion of the Jews from Valréas took place in about 1570, which would imply that a new community was established, lacks documentary confirmation.

BIBLIOGRAPHY: A. Molinier, in: *Cabinet Historique*, 29 (1883), 121–33; S. Grayzel, *The Church and the Jews* (1960²), index; J. Bauer, in: REJ, 29 (1894), 254.

[Bernhard Blumenkranz]

VALUES OF A JEWISH AND DEMOCRATIC STATE. In Israel, in 1992, two Basic Laws were passed: "Basic Law: Human Dignity and Freedom," and "Basic Law: Freedom of Occupation." These laws have constitutional status, and enumerate a series of rights protected by the Basic Laws (see *Human Dignity and Freedom; *Rights, Human). Section 1a of the Basic Law: Human Dignity and Freedom, declares that "The purpose of this Basic Law is to protect human dignity and liberty, in order to establish in a Basic Law the values of the State of Israel as a Jewish and democratic state." Similarly, Section 2 of the Basic Law: Freedom of Occupation, contains a similar provision regarding freedom of occupation. These sections outline the interpretive principles of the Basic Laws, according to which the court is required to interpret and apply the values entrenched in them, and interpret Israeli legislation in a manner consistent with the constitutionally protected values of the Basic Laws. However, the key phrase, "a Jewish, and democratic state," has been interpreted differently by various jurists and justices.

Justice Aharon Barak holds that:

> The expression "Jewish and democratic" does not imply two opposites, but rather their being complementary and harmonious. The contents of the term "Jewish State" is determined in accordance with the level of abstraction assigned… It should be assigned a high enough level of abstraction to unite all members of society and seek out their common ground. It should be high enough that it is consistent with the democratic nature of the state. Indeed, the state is Jewish not in the religious-halakhic sense, but in the sense that Jews have the right to migrate there, and that their national being is reflected in the being of the state (the matter finds expression, inter alia, in language and in days of rest). The fundamental values of Judaism are the fundamen-

> tal values of the state – namely, love of man, the sanctity of life, social justice, doing what is good and right, preserving human dignity, the rule of law, etc. – values bequeathed by Judaism to the entire world. These values must be approached on a universal level of abstraction, befitting the democratic character of the State. Hence, the values of the State of Israel as a Jewish State cannot be identified with Jewish Law. One must not forget that a sizeable non-Jewish population lives in Israel. Indeed, the values of the State of Israel as a Jewish State are those same universal values that are common to democratic societies, which emerged from Jewish tradition and history. These values are accompanied by the selfsame values of the State of Israel, which spring from the democratic nature of the state. The combination and synthesis between the two are what have shaped the values of the State of Israel" (see bibliography, Barak, *Mishpat u-Mimshal*, I .30).

In contrast to the above position, Justice Menachem Elon holds that Justice Barak is employing disparate criteria in interpreting the terms "Jewish" and "democratic," notwithstanding that both terms are meant to describe the nature of the State of Israel. Such interpretation, he asserts, transforms the term "Jewish" into an unimportant, secondary addendum to the term "democratic," without any exegetical rationale or justification for doing so. According to Justice Elon, in setting out to interpret the values entrenched in the aforesaid Basic Laws, the court must have recourse to sources from Jewish Law dealing with the values anchored in these basic laws, in the same way as it has recourse to democratic sources for these values. All this is mandated by the directive set out by the legislator in the law's statement of purpose, according to which the aforesaid basic laws are intended "to establish in a Basic Law the values of the State of Israel as a Jewish and democratic state." The legislator's intent was to find the common ground between the world of Judaism and that of democracy, in such a way that the two worlds will complement one another:

> In coming to interpret the basic rights in the Basic Law: Human Dignity and Freedom with the goal of anchoring the values of the State of Israel as a Jewish and democratic state, we must examine the substance of every individual right that comes before us; we must deliberate on it and come to grips with its content. In addressing the fundamental values of the Jewish heritage with regard to the fundamental rights in The Basic Law: Human Dignity and Freedom, the legislator must relate to the body and content of these values. He must deliberate and examine their philosophical underpinnings and examine the rulings and responsa in the remarkable Jewish legal and philosophical heritage throughout the ages, just as the legislator's relation to the fundamental values of democracy must consist of his examining and analyzing their body and content, sources and rulings – as we judges indeed do when we sit in judgment of the cases that come before us. Only after such examination and analysis do we arrive at our judicial conclusion regarding any of the fundamental rights found within the Basic Law: Human Dignity and Freedom. The resulting synthesis, from the standpoint of the State of Israel being a Jewish and democratic state, is reached by the judge in accordance with his approach, understanding and interpretation. (See Elon, in *Iyyunei Mishpat,* 17 p. 670). See also CA 294/91 *Ḥevra Kaddisha Gachsha Kehillat Yerushalayim v. Kastenbaum,* PD 46(2) 464, 510ff; 506/88 *Shefer v. the State of Israel,* PD 48(1) 87,102ff., 167ff.).

An important source relied upon by Justice Elon in interpreting the term "Jewish and democratic state" was the comment made by the chairman of the Knesset Constitution Committee in the Knesset plenum, during the deliberations over the Basic Law: Human Dignity and Freedom:

> This law was prepared with the understanding that we must create a broad consensus of all parties in the house. We were aware of the fact that we cannot pass a basic law which fixes the values of the State of Israel as a Jewish, democratic state unless we reach a broad consensus of all the parties in the house.... The law opens... with a declaration that it is intended to protect human dignity and freedom so as to entrench in the law the values of the State of Israel as a Jewish, democratic state. In this sense, the law already determines in its first section that we view ourselves as committed to the values of the heritage of Israel and of Judaism, for the law positively and explicitly states "the values of the State of Israel as a Jewish and democratic state." The law defines several of the fundamental freedoms of the individual, not one of which contradicts the Jewish heritage or the values system that is widespread and accepted today in the State of Israel by all parties of the house (Knesset Session 125 (1992 – 5752) (3782–3783).

Section 1 of the Basic Law: Human Dignity and Freedom, and the Basic Law: Freedom of Occupation ("Fundamental Principles") constitutes an additional focal point in the controversy between Justice Barak and Justice Elon. According to these sections, which are identical in their wording, "Basic human rights in Israel are founded on recognition of man's worth, the sanctity of life and his being free, and they shall be respected in the spirit of the principles in the Declaration of Independence of the State of Israel." This section was inserted in the Basic Laws in the 1994 amendments, and it raised the question of the relationship between the new fundamental principles and the previous statement of purpose appearing in the original versions of the two Basic Laws. According to Justice Barak, "Every one of the paragraphs assists in interpreting the others. Thus, for example, the statement of purpose of the Basic Law: Human Dignity and Freedom should be assumed to espouse the appreciation of man's worth, the sanctity of his life and his intrinsic freedom. Moreover, wherever there is an irresolvable internal contradiction between the values of the State of Israel as a Jewish State and its values as a democratic state, that contradiction can be resolved in light of the fixed fundamental principles in the clause pertaining to such principles" (see Barak, *Parshanut Ḥukatit*).

Justice Elon, who criticized the hasty way in which, in his view, the sections of the fundamental principles were legislated, holds that these sections are declarative and no more, and that they bear no practical relevance. Justice Elon concludes this from the section's declarative wording, and from the fact that it is based on "principles in the Declaration of Independence of the State of Israel." According to Justice Elon, that declaration includes many topics, making it difficult to determine which of the principles in the Declaration are meant to be the basis for respecting basic human rights in Israel (see Elon, *Meḥkerei Mishpat,* 12, pp. 289ff.).

The dispute between Justices Barak and Elon continues their earlier dispute regarding Section 1 of the Foundations of Law Act, 1980 (see: **Mishpat Ivri,* Jewish Law in the State of Israel; *Lost Property). According to that law, "Where the court, faced with a legal question requiring decision, finds no answer to it in statute law or case law or by analogy, it shall decide the issue in the light of the principles of freedom, justice, equity and peace of the Jewish heritage." According to Justice Barak's interpretation of this section, those cases in which a lacuna cannot be answered by way of statute law, case law, or analogy are very limited; hence, there are very few cases, if any, in which the court will "decide in light of the principles of freedom, justice, equity and peace of the Jewish heritage."

By contrast, according to Justice Elon, Section 1 implies *that wherever an uncertainty arises in the interpretation of a legal provision of statute in the Israeli legal system,* the Foundation of the Law directs the court to have recourse to Jewish Law, its source of inspiration and interpretation, except where the law in question explicitly contradicts Jewish Law. Justice Elon criticizes Justice Barak's interpretation of Section 1, which he sees as divesting it of all practical content since, according to Barak's approach, there is almost no chance of a lacuna being created that would direct the court to the principles of the Jewish heritage (see HC 1635/90 *Jerczewsky v. the Prime Minister,* PD 45(1) 749). Justice Elon holds that, once the aforementioned Basic Laws were passed, there was no longer a specific need for lacunae – which according to Justice Barak are almost nonexistent anyway – in order to have recourse in the values of the State of Israel as a Jewish state. Justice Elon criticizes Justice Barak's approach to interpreting "the values of the State of Israel as a Jewish and democratic state," as suffering from the same defects as does his interpretation of Section 1 of the Foundations of Law Act:

> His approach to interpreting the Foundations of Law Act… has led to… closing the door on recourse to the principles of the Jewish heritage. By those means the Foundations of Law Act was rendered essentially useless. Moreover, employing Justice Barak's approach to interpretation of the Basic Law: Human Dignity and Freedom precludes *a priori* ever having recourse to the sources of the Jewish heritage and the Jewish world. The Law and its purpose are thus stymied. (See Bibliography: M. Elon, *Iyyunei Mishpat* 17, p. 688.)

It should nevertheless be noted that in recent writings Justice Barak has attributed more weight to Jewish Law in the framework of the relevant sources for interpreting Basic Laws, and for the interpretation of legislation in general (see Barak, *Shofet be-Ḥevrah Demokratit,* pp. 156–159).

Justice Haim Cohn interprets the terms "Jewish and democratic state" differently. In his view, the interpreter must adopt, from within the principles of Jewish Tradition, only those principles befitting and appropriate to a democratic society. According to this approach, when the discussion concerns a universal, democratic value that also exists in Jewish Law, the particular notes and emphases found in Jewish Law should be applied, and these should be preferred over the interpretation given to the same value in other legal systems. In any case, according to Justice Cohen, "Jewish values will generally not have to conflict with democratic values. Yet when they do conflict, democracy must always take precedence" (see Cohn, *Ha-Praklit,* 50, 24).

Another one of the numerous interpretations offered for the term "Jewish and democratic" is that of Ariel Bendor. Bendor contends that according to the limitation clause of the Basic Laws, the constitutionality of a law that violates a right entrenched in the Basic Law is determined in accordance with its consistency (or inconsistency) with the "values of the State of Israel." The implied reference is to the State of Israel as a Jewish, democratic state, as appears previously in the law's statement of purpose. Accordingly, Bendor holds that the law in question must undergo a twofold examination: Is the law consonant with the values of the State of Israel as a Jewish state, and is it consonant with the values of the State of Israel as a democratic state? If it turns out that the law is inconsistent with one of these values, that law does not meet the conditions of the limitation clause, and the court is entitled to declare the law void.

Bendor emphasizes that, under certain circumstances, the principles of Jewish Law protect human rights more effectively than democratic principles. Thus, for example, under certain circumstances, rights afforded suspects and defendants on trial in Jewish Law, as emerged from a ruling by Justice Menachem Elon, are broader than those afforded suspects and defendants on trial according to democratic principles (see: *Detention; *Imprisonment; *Imprisonment for Debt). Where the law is inconsistent with the values of Jewish Law in these matters, the court is entitled, as noted, to declare a law void (see Bibliography: A. Bendor, *Mishpat u-Mimshal,* 2).

A striking example of the application of Justice Elon's interpretation of "Jewish and democratic state" was the Shefer case (CA 506/88 *Shefer v. the State of Israel,* 48(1) 87), in which the Supreme Court, inter alia, adjudicated the question of active euthanasia (see *Medicine and the Law: Euthanasia). Justice Elon examined the problem in accordance with the need to balance between the Jewish values of the State of Israel and its democratic values. He ruled that, according to *halakhah,* the point of departure of this question is:

> [T]he supreme value of the sanctity of human life. This supreme value has its foundation, as noted, in the supreme tenet of man's having been created in the image of God, with everything necessitated and implied by that. All this being so, there does not exist, nor can there exist, any way of measuring a man's value… This being the case, actively hastening death, actively shortening a man's life, even if it be labeled 'mercy killing,' is absolutely forbidden, even if performed at the patient's request. Our great duty under the circumstances is to ease the patient's pain and suffering in every possible way (page 144 of the ruling).

Justice Elon also discussed the position of the various democratic systems on this question, and then turned to discussing a synthesis of these systems:

> We are committed to finding a synthesis between the dual purposes of the Basic Law: Human Dignity and Freedom – namely, entrenching the values of the State of Israel as a Jewish and democratic state in its laws… One of the fundamental issues in the case before us is the possibility of actively hastening death. Jewish Law absolutely forbids this possibility, and there is no opinion or even a trace of opinion which permits this act, which in the world of *halakhah* is viewed as murder. Among democratic legal systems, American law prohibits actively hastening death. By contrast, in the Dutch legal system, active euthanasia is permitted and has even been legislatively regulated. It is clear and goes without saying that on this question synthesizing Jewish Law with that of a democratic country means accepting the common ground of Jewish Law and American law regarding the prohibition against actively hastening death, while absolutely rejecting the Dutch position that permits actively hastening death. Moreover, even if most of the democratic legal systems permitted, under certain circumstances, active euthanasia… A synthesis would be achieved through finding the common ground between Jewish Law and the legal system of any one country that still forbade it. Even more to the point, even if in actual fact not one democratic legal system forbade active euthanasia… since active euthanasia contradicts the essence of the State of Israel as a Jewish State, as we emphasized above, synthesizing the two concepts – "Jewish and democratic" – would mean preferring the conclusion necessitated by the values of a Jewish State and interpreting "democratic state" accordingly (pp. 167–68 of the ruling).

(For additional instances in which Justice Elon's approach to interpreting "Jewish and democratic state" was applied, see *Mishpat Ivri: Jewish Law in the State of Israel.)

In the topic under discussion, it would be appropriate to refer to points emphasized in the entry, "Law and Morality" regarding the instructive position of Jewish Law in terms of the role of the court, where appropriate, in compelling litigants to go "beyond the letter of the law." Toward the end of that discussion, Elon said:

> As written above, in rulings touching on these questions, and handed down before passage of the Basic Laws of the State of Israel, the court could only recommend going beyond the letter of the law. Yet in 1992, Basic Laws were enacted whose declared purpose was to establish in a Basic Law the values of the State of Israel as a Jewish and democratic state." In those laws, the term "Jewish" precedes the term "democratic," thereby according a preeminent role to Jewish Law within the values of the State of Israel as a Jewish State. In wake of these Basic Laws, it would seem appropriate for the issue of ruling beyond the letter of the law to emerge anew. The courts should adopt the approach of compelling litigants, under appropriate circumstances, to go beyond the letter of the law. A central sphere in the integration of Jewish and democratic values is the relationship between law and morality, and it is clear that Basic Laws need to have an influence on this sphere, and on the interpretation of associated legislation.

Examples of this from the realms of statute law and case law have been brought in our discussion of the topic, *Law and Morality.

BIBLIOGRAPHY: M. Elon, *Ha-Mishpat ha-Ivri* (1988), 3:1465; idem, *Jewish Law* (1994), 4:1740; idem, *Jewish Law (Cases and Materials)* (1999), 435–39; idem, "*Derekh Ḥok be-Ḥukah: Arakheha shel Medinah Yehudit ve-Demokratit le-or Ḥok Yesod: Kevod ha-Adam ve-Ḥeruto*," in: *Iyyunei Mishpat*, 17 (1992), 659; idem, "*Kevod ha-Adam ve-Ḥeruto: Mada'ei ha-Yahadut ve-Arakheha shel Medinat Yisrael ke-Medinah Yehudit ve-Demokratit*," in: *Mad'ei ha-Yahadut*, 34 (1994) 9; idem, "*Kevod ha-Adam ve-Ḥeruto be-Moreshet Yisrael*" (President of Israel Study Group for Bible and the Jewish Heritage, 1995), 15; idem, "*Ḥukei ha-Yesod: Darkhei Ḥakikatam u-Parshanutam – Me-Ayin u-Le'an?*" in: *Meḥkerei Mishpat*, 12 (1995), 253; idem, "*Ḥukei ha-Yesod Iggun Arakheha shel Medinah Yehudit ve-Demokratit: Sugyot be-Mishpat ha-Pelili*," in: *Meḥkerei Mishpat* (1996) 27; idem, "*Ha-Aḥer be-Mishpat ha-Ivri u-vi-Pesikat Bet ha-Mishpat ha-Elyon*," in: *Mada'ei ha-Yahadut*, 42 (5754), 31; idem, *Ma'amad ha-Ishah* (2005), 384–451; H. Cohn, "*Arakheha shel Medinah Yehudit ve-Demokratit – Iyyunim be-Ḥok Yesod: Kevod ha-Adam ve-Ḥeruto*," in: *Ha-Praklit* (Jubilee Volume, 1994), 9; A. Barak, "*Ha-Mahapekhah ha-Ḥukatit: Zekhuyyot Yesod Mugganot*," in: *Mishpat u-Mimshal*, 1 (1993) 9; idem, *Parshanut be-Mishpat – Parshanut Ḥukatit*, 3 (1994), 299–354; idem, *Shofet be-Ḥevrah Demokratit* (2004), 156–59; A. Bendor, "*Pegamim be-Ḥakikat Ḥukei ha-Yesod*," in: 2 (1994–95), 443, 451–54; D. Avnon, "'*Ha-Ẓibbur ha-Na'or': Yehudi ve-Demokrati o Liberali ve-Democrati'?*" in: *Mishpat u-Mimshal*, 3 (1995–96), 417; A. Rozen-Zvi, "'*Medinah Yehudit u-Demokratit': Avhut Ruḥanit, Nikkur ve-Simbioza – Ha-Efshar le-Rabbe'a et ha-Ma'agal?*" in: *Iyyunei Mishpat*, 19 (1995), 479–519; A. Levontin, "'*Yehudit ve-Demokratit' – Hirhurim Ishiyyim*," in: *Iyyunei Mishpat*, 19 (1995), 521–546; A.. Maoz, "*Arakheha shel Medinah Yehudit ve-Demokratit*," in: *Iyyunei Mishpat*, 19 (1995), 547–630; R. Gavison, "*Medinah Yehudit ve-Demokratit: Zehut Politit, Ide'ologyah u-Mishpat*," in: *Iyyunei Mishpat*, 19 (1995), 631–82; R. Margolin (ed.), *Medinat Yisrael ke-Medinah Yehudit ve-Demokratit – Rav Si'aḥ u-Mekorot Nilvim* (5759).

[Menachem Elon (2nd ed.)]

VALYI, PETER (1919–1973), Hungarian statesman. Valyi was born in Szombathely, Hungary. His father, Emanuel, the owner of a brick factory, was for some time head of the local Jewish community. There was even a suggestion that Valyi should train for the rabbinate, and for this purpose, in addition to his secular studies at the local high school, he was taught Bible and Talmud privately. During the period of Nazi rule in Hungary in 1944, the Valyi family was exempted from transportation to Auschwitz in view of the fact that the head of the family had been awarded a gold medal for bravery in World War I.

Valyi graduated as an engineer at the Technion of Budapest. As soon as the Red Army entered Hungary, he joined the ranks of the Communist Party, gradually rising to a position of importance. In 1954, he was appointed deputy director of the planning organization of the Communist Party and continued in this office until 1967, when he was appointed minister of finance in the government of Hungary. In 1970, he was appointed deputy prime minister, and put in charge of economic planning. He was regarded as the father of the new policy which produced a remarkable growth of Hungary's economy. This policy, which included the establishment of strong economic ties with the West, was not viewed favorably by the Russians and it also met with internal opposition. As a result, it was only in his last years that Valyi was elected to the Central Committee of the party, and he was never made a member of the Politburo. From the time that he rose to prominence, Valyi severed all relations with the Jewish community, and even with members of his family. He died in mysterious circumstances in 1973. According to reports, he fell into a furnace while inspecting the processes of steel manufacture at a factory.

VAMBERY, ARMINIUS (1832–1913), Hungarian traveler and Orientalist. He was born Hermann Vamberger (erroneously referred to as Bamberger) of Orthodox parents in Dunajska Streda on the island of Schütt, Hungary, Vambery, who was congenitally lame, worked to maintain himself from the age of 12 as a tailor's apprentice and later as a tutor. Possessed of an extraordinary capacity for languages and a phenomenal memory, he mastered numerous European languages and then turned to Arabic, Turkish, and Persian, achieving magisterial fluency and control in these.

In his early twenties, fired by the dream of exploring the putative homeland of the Magyars in Asia, he moved to Constantinople where he lived as a tutor of European languages and executed translations from Turkish history. He became a Muslim and entered the service of the Turkish government as secretary to Mehmet Fuad Pasha, five times foreign minister of Turkey. While in Constantinople he earned the esteem of Sultan Abdul-Hamid II.

During his six years in Constantinople, he published a Turkish-German dictionary (1858) and other linguistic works, acquired a variety of Oriental languages and dialects, and traveled extensively. In 1863–64 he undertook a long and arduous journey through Armenia, *Persia, and Turkestan, disguised as a Sunnite dervish under the assumed name Rashid Effendi. He journeyed across the Turkoman desert on the eastern shore of the Caspian to Khiva, *Teheran, Trebizond, *Bukhara, Samarkand, Herat, and back to Constantinople maintaining his disguise to the end despite many difficult tests, which might have cost him his life had the Muslim authorities known his identity. Said to have been the first European to make such a journey, the account of his exploits, *Travels and Adventures in Central Asia* (1864), aroused great interest throughout Europe. This was the case especially in England appearing as it did at a time of acute tension between Russia and England for the mastery of Central Asia. During his peregrinations in Persia he established contact with the British legation and his pro-British orientation combined with his masterful knowledge of the Near East and *India were to make him an important and useful advocate of British foreign policy.

After his return from the long trek in the spring of 1864, he visited London where he was lionized for his triumph as an intrepid adventurer and his impressive polyglot achievement. Then after a stop in Paris, Vambery, who had apparently become a Protestant, accepted an invitation from the University of Budapest to teach Oriental languages and in this capacity he served until 1905. Among his students were I. *Goldziher, B. *Munkacsi, and I. Kunos.

He produced a whole range of works on Oriental languages and ethnology and in addition, essays on political questions and popular accounts of his travels, one of which was a favorite boys' book. His books were translated into many languages but his autobiography, *Arminius Vambery, His Life and Adventures* (1883), and his memoirs, *The Story of My Struggles* (1904), were written in English. One of his scholarly contributions to Turkology was the discovery of the relation of Turkish and Magyar. He also contributed to the ethnology of Central Asia and India. A staunch protagonist of British dominance in the East he placed his vast knowledge of Central Asia at the disposal of Great Britain, serving as her adviser on Indian and Asiatic policy, executing various diplomatic missions in the Near East, and becoming a personal friend of the prince of Wales, later Edward VII. His preoccupation with the "Eastern question" is documented in various political essays, e.g., *The Coming Struggle for India* (1885).

Vambery supported *Zionism in its emergent stage by introducing Theodor *Herzl to Sultan Abdul-Hamid in 1901. After Herzl's death Vambery's counsel in respect of the Zionist cause was solicited by David *Wolfssohn. Vambery married Cornelia Aranyi (a niece of Joseph *Joachim, the violin virtuoso) and their son was the criminologist Rustem Vambery.

BIBLIOGRAPHY: T. Herzl, *Complete Diaries*, ed. by R. Patai, 5 (1960), index; N. Sokolow, *Ishim* (1958^2), 398–408; G. Hazai, *Armin Vámbéry-A Bio-Bibliography* (1963); M. Nordau, in: *Life and Adventures* (1914); N.S. Tikhonov, *Vambery* (Rus., 1957). **ADD. BIBLIOGRAPHY:** J.M. Landau, "Arminius Vambéry: Identities in Conflict," in: M. Kramer (ed.), *The Jewish Discovery of Islam* (1999), 95–102.

[Ephraim Fischoff]

°VANCE, ZEBULON BAIRD (1830–1894), North Carolina lawyer and politician who supported Jewish rights. Vance, a colonel in the Confederate army in the Civil War, served in his state legislature (1854–61) and was governor. He went on from there to the U.S. Senate (1879–94). Vance is known to the Jewish world primarily for a lecture, *The Scattered Nation* (1904, 1916), that he delivered many times. It is a tribute to the Jewish people, praising their love of learning and their having flourished despite a history of persecutions.

VANCOUVER, city in British Columbia and largest in Western Canada, with a population of nearly 2 million in 2001, including a Jewish community of 22,590.

Jewish life in Vancouver began in the early 1880s, when a small number of pioneers arrived at the town site of the future metropolis, drawn by the prospects of its deep-sea harbor on the Pacific Ocean and impending status as the terminus of the trans-Canada railway. One of the city's most prominent early builders was David Oppenheimer (1834–1897), a Jewish resident of German origins who served as Vancouver's second mayor from 1887 to 1891. During his term in office, Oppenheimer opened foreign trade and initiated the construction of Vancouver's water supply, sidewalks, bridges, transit, and lighting. He also donated large tracts of his personal property for civic facilities and the promotion of local industry. Oppenheimer was popularly known as the "father of Vancouver," and his bust still stands at the entrance of Stanley Park, the world-famous green space that he procured for the city in 1888.

Until the beginning of the 20th century, Vancouver's Jewish population remained below 200, split between a small congregation (Temple Emanuel) of acculturated West European Jews living in the west end and an increasing number of East European newcomers. Most of the latter concentrated initially in Vancouver's immigrant district in the Strathcona and Chinatown areas, many working in the clothing trade or secondhand goods. By 1911, the East Europeans had swelled the Jewish community to 1,024, becoming the dominant element. In 1907 the Orthodox congregation B'nai Yehuda (Sons of Israel) was established under the presidency of Zebulon Franks (1864–1926), a merchant in whose store and home the first Orthodox services in Vancouver had been held 20 years earlier. The congregation opened its first synagogue in 1911 and changed its name to Schara Tzedeck (Gates of Righteousness) in 1917, building a much larger synagogue in 1921, when Vancouver's Jewish population had reached 1,376. For the next three decades Schara Tzedeck was led, for the most part, by Nathan Mayer Pastinsky (1887–1948), a qualified *shoḥet* who became the religious leader for the Jewish community, universally respected for his citywide welfare work and spiritual leadership.

As the Jewish community grew to 2,440 by 1931, a vigorous organizational life became the hallmark of Vancouver Jewry. The first secular group to form was a B'nai B'rith lodge in 1910. During the 1930s to 1950s, the lodge sponsored a highly successful interfaith "Goodwill Dinner" each year, honoring leading representatives from different areas of public life. A Zionist and Social Society was founded in 1913, the official beginning of the community's long history of support of a Jewish state. The first of numerous Hadassah chapters was organized in 1920, and for many years the group ran the largest annual bazaar in the city. The National Council of Jewish Women has also been very prominent in Vancouver since 1924, initiating a number of innovative social programs for children and the elderly. A women's B'nai B'rith section was formed in 1927 and Pioneer Women in 1933. Among the community's youth groups during these years were Young Judaea and Aleph Zadik Aleph, and slightly later, Hillel and one of the most active Habonim chapters in North America.

Early mutual aid organizations included a Hebrew Immigrant Aid Society, a Hebrew Free Loan Association, and an Achduth Society (credit union) established in 1927. A Jewish Community Chest was founded in 1924 to centralize the community's fundraising, later serving as the model for the Vancouver-wide Community Chest. In 1928, a Jewish community center was opened and began publishing a weekly newssheet, the precursor to the *Jewish Western Bulletin*, which has served as the community's newspaper since 1930. To coordinate these new institutions and organizations, a Jewish Administrative Council was established in 1932, superseded by an enlarged representative body in 1950, the Jewish Community Council and Fund. Internal community welfare work was also strengthened through the 1936 creation of a Jewish Family Service Agency, run for many years by social worker Jessie Allman, and the 1946 founding of the Louis Brier Home for the Aged.

In addition to a strong tendency toward institutional affiliation, since the end of World War II rapid growth has become a dominant feature of Vancouver's Jewish community. In 1951 the population was 5,467, and by 1971 it was 10,145. Although the majority of newcomers were Jews from other parts of Canada, particularly the prairie provinces, there were also several hundred Holocaust survivors and, later, refugees from Hungary and the Soviet bloc. Vancouver's generally high level of postwar prosperity allowed for considerable upward mobility and economic diversification in the Jewish community, marked by a residential shift away from the east end to the more affluent Oak Street corridor in the south-west part of the city. In 1948, a Talmud Torah day school was built in the area, as was the Schara Tzedeck's new synagogue. The Beth Israel, a Conservative congregation that had been incorporated in 1932, also opened a new Oak Street synagogue in 1948, eventually surpassing Schara Tzedeck in membership. Further cultural and religious diversity emerged with the revival of a Reform group in the 1960s, the incorporation of a Sephardi congregation in 1973, and the arrival of Lubavitch in 1974.

In the midst of this rapid expansion, the 1962 opening of an ambitious new Vancouver Jewish Community Centre created a focal point for communal activities, housing many of the Jewish community's organizations as well as providing cultural and athletic facilities. The Pacific Region of the Canadian Jewish Congress (CJC), which had become its own branch in 1949, also assumed a leading role in community public relations, advocacy for Israel, and a number of educational initiatives. Although antisemitism in Vancouver was never a serious threat, the CJC was particularly active in calling for anti-discrimination legislation, co-founding the Vancouver Civic Unity Council for this purpose during the 1950s. Congress also sponsored a number of Christian-Jewish dialogues in the 1970s, and during the 1980s helped found an umbrella organization known as the Committee for Racial Justice. Longtime Pacific Region Executive Director Morris Saltzman (1918–1988) was especially active in inter-ethnic outreach, and in tandem with Lou Zimmerman (1911–1987), the first and longest-serving Jewish community civil servant in Vancouver, provided much of the organizational leadership throughout the postwar decades.

In addition to several programs and facilities for the religious education of youth and adults, most recently the Community Kollel and the Pacific Torah Institute, a Vancouver Peretz Centre has been providing secular, humanist Jewish education since 1945, also maintaining a small Yiddish presence. Other Jewish cultural initiatives in Vancouver have included the establishment of a Judaica library and a program of Jewish Studies at the University of British Columbia. A Vancouver-based Jewish Historical Society of B.C. has been in operation since 1971, with a museum devoted to local Jewish history scheduled to open. The very successful annual Jewish Film Festival and Jewish Festival of the Arts have also become part of the community calendar. Since the mid-1970s, Holocaust awareness has taken on increasing prominence as a vehicle for education, most notably through the 1976 inception of an annual symposium for high school students and the 1995 opening of a Vancouver Holocaust Education Centre.

Vancouver now has the third largest Jewish community in Canada, with its 2001 Jewish population of 22,590 just over 1% of the total population of the city. Although the Oak Street corridor remains home to approximately half of the city's Jews, considerable expansion has taken place into the suburbs, with new synagogues and Jewish community centers in Richmond, Burnaby/Coquitlam, North Vancouver, and Surrey. There are more than a dozen congregations across the metropolitan area, with affiliations ranging from Egalitarian to Chabad. To provide services to this increasingly dispersed community, a Jewish Federation of Greater Vancouver was established in 1987, assuming responsibility for the Combined Jewish Appeal campaign, which supports over 30 local agencies as well as Israeli and overseas Jewish causes. A Shalom B.C. welcoming center also provides newcomers with information about local Jewish life.

There have been many Vancouver Jews to have an important impact on both the Jewish and non-Jewish communities. Businessman Jack *Diamond (1910–2001) was an extremely prominent leader and benefactor, helping to found several major charities such as the local Variety Club, the B.C. Heart Foundation, and the Diamond Foundation. He also served as chancellor of Simon Fraser University (SFU), as did prominent businessman and philanthropist Joseph Segal (1925–). Morris Wosk (1917–2002) was one of SFU's greatest benefactors, particularly in the establishment of the downtown Harbour Centre campus. Judge Nathan *Nemetz (1913–1997) was the first Jewish chancellor of the University of British Columbia as well as the first Jewish chief justice of the B.C. Supreme Court and B.C. Court of Appeals. The first Jewish judge in Canada, Samuel *Schultz (1865–1917), was also a Vancouver resident. In politics, Dave *Barret (1930–) served as the provincial premier in 1972–75, while Harry Rankin (1920–2002) served on the Vancouver City Council for over 20 years and journalist Simma Holt (1922–) was the first Jewish woman to serve as a member of Parliament, representing the Vancouver-Kingsway district. Between 1969 and 1983, Muni Evers (1914–2002) was re-elected seven times as the mayor of New Westminster, part of Greater Vancouver.

[Barbara Schober (2nd ed.)]

VAN DAM, HENDRIK GEORGE (1906–1973), leader and recognized spokesman of the post-war Jewish community in Germany. Born in Berlin, Van Dam studied law, but his legal career came to an abrupt end with Hitler's rise to power. After spending several years in Holland and Switzerland, he emigrated to England, and in 1941 enlisted in the British Army, later serving in Holland and occupied Germany. After his release from the army in 1946, he volunteered for the Jewish Relief units and served as their legal adviser and later as director for the British Zone of Occupation in Germany. With the establishment of the Central Council (Zentralrat) of the Jews in Germany, he was appointed secretary general of the Council in October 1950, with residence first in Hamburg and later in Duesseldorf, continuing in that capacity until 1972. He participated in the negotiations between the *Conference on Jewish Material Claims against Germany and was a delegate of the German Government at The Hague in 1952, and became one of the foremost legal experts in the field of restitution and indemnification.

Van Dam's book, *Das Bundesentschaedigungsgesetz* ("The Federal Indemnification Law," 1953) became a classic and has been published in several revised editions. He also wrote *Die Haager Vertragswerke* ("The Hague Treaties," 1952), *KZ Verbrechen vor deutschen Gerichten* ("Concentration Camp Crimes before German Tribunals," 2 vols., 1962–66), and *Die Unverjaehrbarkeit des Voelkermordes* ("No Statute of Limitation for Genocide," 1969).

Early in 1950, Van Dam was asked by the Israel Ministry of Finance to prepare an opinion on the legal basis and prospects of a claim by the Government of Israel to inherit heirless Jewish property. In a memorandum submitted to the Ministry on July 1, 1950, Van Dam advised the Israel Government to enter into negotiations with the Government of the Federal Republic of Germany. His advice, though at that time premature from both the Israeli and German points of view, proved his foresight.

Van Dam was one of the chief protagonists of the reconstitution of a Jewish community in Germany. He believed that the reestablishment of the community was not only an inalienable right of the Jews but also in the interest of world Jewry. He maintained that the reemergence of a viable and strong German Republic was a world necessity, and that it was in the interests of the free world – and therefore also of the Jewish people – that the new Germany be integrated in the new world as a reformed and truly democratic component. Normalization of relations between the Jewish people and the new Germany, he felt, was unavoidable in the long run, and should therefore not be delayed, and in this process the Jewish community in Germany could and must play a decisive role. A large-scale German reparations program (in the sense of undoing the wrong; in German, *Wiedergutmachung*) would not only meet a justified Jewish claim, but also act as a catalyst in the process of normalization. Although Van Dam refused to advocate the return of Jews to Germany, he also refused to dissuade Jews from returning. Since the community existed and should exist, its voluntary dissolution would not serve the interests either of world Jewry or of the State of Israel. He coined the slogan: "We insist on existing" and maintained his view against the opposition of many Jewish leaders and movements.

Although he recognized the need for a Jewish State after the Holocaust and was always ready to lend his advice and active assistance to Israel, Van Dam emphasized that he was not a Zionist, believing rather in a polycentric world Jewish community. He died in Dusseldorf.

[Chaim Yahil]

VAN DER HOEDEN, JACOB (1891–1968), bacteriologist. Van der Hoeden was born in Utrecht, Holland, where he received his doctorate in 1922. From 1920 to 1930 he was senior bacteriologist in the medical department of the Dutch National Institute for Public Health and from 1930 to 1949 director of the bacteriological laboratory of the Hospital of the University of Utrecht. In 1949 he was invited by the government of Israel to advise on the organization of veterinary research and decided to settle there, heading the department of epidemiology of the Biological Research Institute in Nes Ẓiyyonah until 1955. In 1956 he was appointed clinical professor of bacteriology at the Medical School of the Hebrew University and was elected a member of the committee on zoonosis of the World Health Organization. He was awarded the Israel Prize for agriculture in 1961.

VÁNDOR, LAJOS (1913–1945), Hungarian poet. His wry and sophisticated verses were published in the 1930s and again in 1989 in a volume titled *Egy költö élt itt köztetek* ("A Poet Lived Here Amongst You"). Vándor was a victim of the Holocaust.

[Eva Kondor]

VANE, SIR JOHN R. (1927–2004), U.K. pharmacologist. Vane was born in Tardebigg, Worcestershire, the son of a father descended from Russian immigrants and an English mother. His family lived in Birmingham where he was educated at King Edward VI High School. Although he gained his B.Sc. in chemistry from the University of Birmingham University (1946), he realized that this subject of his boyhood fascination no longer interested him. He studied pharmacology at Oxford University, where he obtained his D.Phil. (1953) from the University's Nuffield Institute for Medical Research under the direction of Geoffrey Dawes. He was assistant professor in the department of pharmacology of Yale University (1953–55) before joining the Institute of Basic Medical Sciences of the University of London, eventually sited at the Royal College of Surgeons (1955–73) where he became professor of experimental pharmacology. He left to become Group Research and Development Director of the Wellcome Physiological Research Laboratories in Beckenham, Kent (1973–86). In 1986 he founded a new laboratory at St Bartholomew's Hospital Medical College, University of London which developed into the William Harvey Research Institute. Vane established a novel method for directly detecting and measuring unstable hormones and mediators in small blood samples from experimental animals. His main interest was the large and complicated group of substances called prostaglandins and the manner in which these regulate blood flow. He made major contributions to the discovery of the member of this group called prostacyclin clarifying its role in inhibiting blood clots. He showed that the therapeutic effects of aspirin and other anti-inflammatory drugs result from inhibiting the enzyme cyclo-oxygenase, also part of the prostaglandin group. For these discoveries, he was awarded the 1982 Nobel Prize in physiology or medicine, shared with Sune Bergström and Bengt Samuelsson. He also participated in and directed research that led to the introduction of drugs inhibiting angiotensin-converting enzyme (ACE), now routinely used to treat high blood pressure and some forms of heart disease. He also worked on the pharmacological regulation of the specialized cells lining blood vessels. He was deeply concerned with international scientific collaboration and especially with Polish scientists. His many honors included election to the Royal Society (1974), the Bunim Medal of the American Rheumatism Association (1979), and foreign membership in the American Academy of Arts and Sciences (1982) and the U.S. National Academy of Sciences (1983). He was also awarded the Lasker Award in Basic Medical Science (1977), a knighthood (1984), and the Polish Order of Merit (2003).

[Michael Denman (2nd ed.)]

VAN HODDIS, JAKOB (Hans Davidsohn; 1887–1942), German poet. Born into an assimilated family, Van Hoddis chose as a pseudonym an anagram of his surname, Davidsohn. He was among the founders of the "*Neue Club*" in Berlin, regarded as the heart of German expressionism. His poem "Weltende" ("End of the World"), published in 1911, made its author famous overnight, becoming "the Marseillaise of the expressionist rebellion" (J.R. Becher). Showing first symptoms of psychosis at the age of 25, van Hoddis received private foster care from 1915 on. Twelve years later, incapacitated, he was referred to psychiatric clinics in Tuebingen and Goeppingen. While the rest of his family immigrated to Palestine just after Hitler's seizure of power, van Hoddis – like all Jewish psychiatry patients – was taken to the "Israelite Convalescent Home for the Mentally Ill" in Bendorf-Sayn; from there he was deported in April 1942 and murdered in a Polish concentration camp (presumably Chełmno or Sobibor).

BIBLIOGRAPHY: I. Stratenwerth, *All meine Pfade rangen mit der Nacht. Jakob van Hoddis, Hans Davidsohn (1887–1942)* (2001); H. Hornbogen, *Jakob van Hoddis: die Odyssee eines Verschollenen* (1986); H. Schneider, *Jakob van Hoddis. Ein Beitrag zur Erforschung des Expressionismus* (1967).

[Philip Theisohn (2nd ed.)]

VAN LEER, LIA (1924–), founder of the Jerusalem Cinematheque and Jerusalem Film Center. Van Leer was born in Bessarabia, Romania, and immigrated to Israel in 1940. In 1955 she established, together with her husband, Wim van Leer (who died in 1992), the Israel Film Club in Haifa. A year later the couple established film clubs in Tel Aviv and Jerusalem. In 1960 they founded the Israel Film Archive, in 1972 the Haifa Cinematheque, and in 1973 the Jerusalem Cinematheque. The latter screens quality films seven nights a week and houses the Jerusalem Film Center as well as the archive. It has a collection of 30,000 films and 50,000 negatives, including the world's largest collection of Jewish films, and 20,000 videos and cassettes, a library, and an education department. In 1983 Van Leer was a judge at the Cannes Film Festival and in 1984 she founded the annual Jerusalem Film Festival. In 1988 she hosted a large delegation from Russia at the Festival. She has also been a judge at the Berlin, Chicago, and Venice film festivals. In 1998 she was awarded an Israeli Film Academy Award. She also received the French Chevalier des Artes et Lettres award in homage to Israeli culture and art. In 2004 she received the Israel Prize for her special contribution to Israeli society.

[Shaked Gilboa (2nd ed.)]

VAN OVEN, English family of physicians and communal workers. The founder is said to have been an Italian Jew named Samuel Bassan who settled in Oven (Hoven, Holland). ABRAHAM VAN OVEN (d. 1778) settled in London in 1759 after graduating in medicine at Leiden, and became physician to the Great Synagogue in 1767. He translated into Hebrew R. Dodsley's *Oeconomy of Human Life* (London, 1778). His son, JOSHUA VAN OVEN (1766–1838), was also surgeon to the Great Synagogue and a leading figure in London communal life. His *Letters on the Present State of the Jewish Poor in the Metropolis* (London, 1802), in answer to the strictures of the magistrate Patrick Colquhoun, initiated a systematic attempt to grapple with the social problems of London Jewry. He was foremost among the founders of the Jews' Free School and published a *Manual of Judaism* in 1835 for school use. Van Oven served as the school's president for many years. He was the father of BARNARD VAN OVEN (1796–1860), physician to the Great Synagogue from 1827, who was active in the movement for Jewish emancipation in England and published some effective pamphlets. He was a founder of the Jews' Infant Schools in 1841. Barnard's son, LIONEL VAN OVEN (1829–1905), besides being active in Jewish communal work, was a pioneer in the oral instruction of deaf-mutes.

BIBLIOGRAPHY: J. Picciotto, *Sketches of Anglo-Jewish History* (1950^2), index; C. Roth, *History of the Great Synagogue* (1959), index; P. Emden, *Jews of Britain* (1943), index; Levin, in: JHSET, 19 (1955–59), 97–114; Roth, Mag Bibl., index; JC (Jan. 13,20,27, 1905). **ADD. BIBLIOGRAPHY:** ODNB online; G. Black, *JFS: The History of the Jews' Free School since 1832* (1998).

[Cecil Roth]

°**VAN PAASSEN, PIERRE** (1895–1968), writer and journalist; among the most fervent non-Jewish Zionists. Born in Gorinchem, Holland, to a Calvinist family, Van Paassen was raised on the Bible and love for the people and the land of Israel. From 1914 he lived in Canada. He became a world-famous journalist, noted for his travel articles and interviews with leading personalities. His attachment to the Jewish people and land of Israel emerged after his first visit to Palestine in 1925, and from then on his books and articles reflected his enthusiastic attitude toward Zionism. In 1942 Van Paassen headed in the U.S. the Committee for a Jewish Army. His book *The Forgotten Ally* (1943) was a sharp indictment of British anti-Zionist policy; its Hebrew version was banned by the Mandatory government in Palestine in 1946. He also polemicized against Jewish and Zionist leaders whom he accused of a moderate, compromising stance toward anti-Zionist Britain.

Van Paassen published many books, some of them autobiographical (*Days of Our Years*, 1943; *To Number Our Days*, 1964). He was the author of *That Day Alone* (1941), *The Time is Now* (1941), and *Jerusalem Calling* (1950) and the editor (together with J.W. Wise) of *Nazism, an Assault on Civilization* (1934).

[Getzel Kressel]

VAN PRAAGH, WILLIAM (1845–1907), English educator. Born Wolf Saloman in Rotterdam, Van Praagh pioneered the lip-reading method for deaf-mutes in England. He received his training from D. Hirsch, director of the Rotterdam School for the Deaf and Dumb, who had introduced into Holland the German oral method of instructing the deaf and dumb. When Baroness Mayer de Rothschild established the Jews' Deaf and Dumb Home in London (1866), Van Praagh was appointed principal. His patience and kindness endeared him to his pupils, and his methods proved successful. In 1872 the Association for the Oral Instruction of the Deaf and Dumb, which the baroness had founded, established a college for training teachers in the oral method, and a nonsectarian school for the deaf and dumb. Van Praagh became director of the college and principal of the school. In 1894 he founded the Union of Pure Oral Teachers.

Van Praagh's publications include *Plan for the Establishment of Day-Schools for the Deaf and Dumb* (1871), *Lessons for the Instruction of Deaf and Dumb Children in Speaking, Lip-Reading, Reading, and Writing* (1884), and *Lip-Reading for the Deaf* (1900^6). Dame (Margaret) Peggy Van Praagh (1910–1990), the well-known ballerina and director of the Australian Ballet, was his granddaughter. She was knighted in 1970.

BIBLIOGRAPHY: *Cornhill Magazine* (1868), 573–7; A. Farrar, *Arnold on the Education of the Deaf* (1901), 75, 79.

[Shnayer Z. Leiman]

VAN RAALTE, EDUARD ELLIS (1841–1921), Dutch lawyer and statesman. Born in The Hague, after his academic studies he became a solicitor in Rotterdam, where in 1877 he joined the city council as a Liberal member, serving as an alderman in the period from 1892 to 1897. From 1885 to 1901 he was a member of the Liberal Union Party, of which he became chairman in 1907. Twice he served as a member of Parliament, namely, in the periods 1897 to 1905 and 1913 to 1918. In the De Meester administration (1905–08) he was minister of justice; in 1907 he initiated the Labor Contracts Act that bears his name. That same year an attempt was made against his life by a malcontent musician. Van Raalte was appointed Knight in the Order of the Dutch Lion.

BIBLIOGRAPHY: *Onze Afgevaardigden, bevattende portretten en biographieën der leden van de Eerste en Tweede Kamer der Staten Generaal* (1897; 1901; 1905; 1913).

[Peter Manasse (2nd ed.)]

VANUNU AFFAIR, case of an Israeli nuclear reactor technician who disclosed Israel's nuclear arms secrets to the London *Sunday Times*. Mordechai Vanunu (1954–) was born in Morocco to a Sephardi religious family and immigrated to Israel in 1963. In 1977 he began work as a technican at Israel's nuclear research reactor at Dimonah, attached to Machon 2, where plutonium is separated from uranium. In 1985 he was laid off, moving to Australia. Prior to leaving, he took 57 photographs inside the reactor. On October 5, 1986, the *Sunday Times* published a three-page disclosure drawing on Vanunu's information. According to the newspaper, Israel possessed 100–200 nuclear warheads, which was much higher than most earlier estimates of the country's nuclear arsenal. It was also claimed that Israel was developing neutron and thermonuclear capabilities. The newspaper arrived at its estimate of the number of warheads on the basis of Vanunu's description of the amount of plutonium produced. Given that the fact that Israel had never confirmed whether or not it possessed the Bomb, Vanunu became the first eyewitness to the nuclear program to speak without authorization. He was abducted to Israel from Europe by Mossad agents and stood trial for espionage and treason. He was sentenced to 18 years' imprisonment, 12 of which were served in solitary confinement. In 2004 he was released from prison but prevented from leaving the country. Vanunu, who studied philosophy at Ben-Gurion University while working at the reactor, and converted to Christianity in Australia, said that he leaked the information so that the Israeli public and the world community would know about the nuclear danger. Vanunu became an icon in the international anti-nuclear movement. While the disclosure lowered incrementally the ambiguity surrounding Israel's nuclear program, it generated little international pressure on Israel, most Western governments recognizing that Israel should not be pressured on the nuclear issue at the same time it was being pressured to make territorial concessions to the Palestinians. Moreover, while most foreign governments adjusted their estimates of Israel's nuclear capability upwards – strengthening Israel's nuclear deterrent posture – not all countries, including the United States, went so far as to accept the *Sunday Times*' estimates. Vanunu was awarded a number of prizes from organizations promoting anti-nuclearism.

BIBLIOGRAPHY: Y. Cohen, *Whistleblowers and the Bomb: Vanunu, Israel & Nuclear Secrecy* (2005); idem, *Nuclear Ambiguity: The Vanunu Affair* (1992).

[Yoel Cohen (2nd ed.)]

VAN VRIESLAND, SIEGFRIED ADOLF (Zadok; 1886–1939), Zionist leader. Born in Haarlem, Holland, Van Vriesland practiced law in Rotterdam and joined the Zionist movement in 1910. He became secretary of the Dutch Zionist Organization before World War I and, in 1919, settled in Palestine, where he was appointed treasurer of the Zionist Executive and was later active in the Haganah. He was Dutch consul-general in Palestine from 1929 and a member of the Zionist Executive from 1923 to 1927. Van Vriesland served as treasurer of the Executive during the difficult period for the *yishuv* and tried to balance its budget despite the economic crisis. From 1929 he was a member of the board of directors of the Dead Sea potash company. In 1936 he became manager of the port of Tel Aviv, opened during the Arab riots of that year. Three years later he decided to retire from public life and devote himself to art.

BIBLIOGRAPHY: Tidhar, 2 (1948), 602–3.

[Eliezer Livneh]

VAN VRIESLAND, VICTOR EMANUEL (1892–1974), Dutch poet, literary critic, and journalist. Born in Haarlem, Van Vriesland first worked as a journalist on the staff of *De Nieuwe Gids* and *De Vrije Bladen*, became literary editor of the daily *Nieuwe Rotterdamse Courant* (1931–38), and in 1937 edited *De Groene Amsterdammer.*

After World War II Van Vriesland published several collections of poetry, some of which was collected in *Drievoudig verweer* ("Threefold Resistance," 1949). Ten years later he published another collection, *Tegengif* ("Antidote"). His only novel, *Het afscheid van de wereld in drie dagen* ("Farewell to the World in Three Days," 1926; shortened version, 1936), had little success. He also wrote short stories, collected in *De ring met de aquamarijn en andere verhalen* ("The Ring with the Aquamarine and Other Stories," 1939), and some plays, notably *De Havenstad* ("The Seaport," 1933).

Van Vriesland was one of the few Dutch critics who dealt with Jewish literature in Western Europe. In his essay *De cultureele noodtoestand van het Joodsche volk* ("The Jewish People's Cultural State of Emergency," 1915), he adopted an extreme Zionist view in rejecting a future for Jewish art in Europe. Just before World War II he wrote a study of Dutch verse, *Spiegel van de Nederlandsche poezie door alle eeuwen* ("Mirror of Dutch Poetry throughout the Centuries," 1939). A collection of his critical essays was published as *Onderzoek en Vertoog* ("Research and Exposition," 2 vols., 1958).

[Gerda Alster-Thau]

VARAŽDIN, town in the district of Zagorje, on the Drava River, Croatia; important communications center on the Vienna-Trieste line. Jews arrived there in the mid-1750s, coming from Hungary, Burgenland, and Moravia. They traded in cattle, a fact documented in the 1761 municipal decree debarring them from this source of income. Their settlement was slow and gradual, since each individual had to procure for himself an "*inkolat*," i.e., a residence permit, which was not easily accorded. Among the first Jews on record, two are of note: Isaac the Jew and Moses Jacobsohn. In 1793 a prayer-house was built near the city's fortification. Jewish physicians and merchants suffered from robbery and plunder. Mirko Breyer, the first librarian and publisher in Croatia, originated from Varaždin.

Among rabbis who officiated, notable is Yekutiel Hirschenstein, who served the community for more than three decades; he advanced proto-Zionist ideas and during his term a Jewish school was established. A synagogue was erected in 1861.

In the 19th century the community grew to over 500 members, many of whom were active in free professions. They endured some antisemitic harassment. An expulsion was threatened but not carried out.

In the 1920s and 1930s, the leaders were Dr. Oscar Pulgram, Dr. Hinko Blau, and Hermann Herzer, along with Rabbi Rudolf Reuven Glueck. During the Holocaust almost all Jews perished soon after the Nazi and Ustashe (Croat fascists) took power. The survivors re-established the community in 1945 and the synagogue was nationalized and partially repaired in 1946. It is used as a movie theater.

BIBLIOGRAPHY: MGWJ, 81 (1937), 447–48; Y. Eventov, *Toledot Yehudei Yugoslavyah*, vol. 1 (1971), 278–87, 304–5; *Jevrejski Almanah* (Vrsac, 1928), 42–52; *Novi Omanut*, no. 11 (1995), 8.

[Zvi Loker (2nd ed.)]

VARDI, ARIE (1938–), Israeli pianist, educator, and conductor. Born in Tel Aviv, he studied with Ilona Vincze, beginning his artistic career at the age of 15. He won the Chopin Competition in Israel, appeared with the Israel Philharmonic Orchestra with *Mehta, won the George Enescu International Competition in Bucharest, and gave recitals throughout Europe. Alongside his studies at the Rubin Academy of Music, Vardi also obtained a law degree at Tel Aviv University. He continued his piano studies in Basel with Paul Baumgartner and his composition studies with Pierre Boulez and Karlheinz Stockhausen. He performed widely as soloist with major orchestras and leading conductors in Eastern and Western Europe, the United States, Latin America, the Far East, Australia, and Japan. In 1992 he had his first Russian tour, playing in Moscow, St. Petersburg, and other cities. Vardi performed regularly as soloist-conductor the complete Bach and Mozart concertos. In later years, he included in his repertoire the complete piano works of Debussy and Ravel. His extensive repertoire also includes various Israeli works, many of which were dedicated to him. His recordings for RCA won several prizes. Vardi received international acclaim as one of the country's foremost pedagogues. He was a professor of piano at the Hochschule fuer Musik in Hannover and at the Rubin Academy of Music, Tel Aviv University, having served as its director (1977–9) and chaired the Piano Faculty. He held master classes and presented lecture recitals in Israel, the Juilliard School of Music, the London Royal Academy of Music, and other leading music institutions. In 1999, he was invited to the Yale University School of Music as a visiting professor. Vardi was the artistic adviser and chairman of the jury of the Arthur *Rubinstein International Master Competition, and served as juror of other great piano competitions. Devoted to the task of simultaneously guiding students, he successfully taught a vast number of great pianists, among them Yefim *Bronfman and Li Yundi. From the 1970s Vardi was known throughout Israel for his television series *Master Classes* as well as the family series of the Israel Philharmonic Orchestra, which he conducted and presented, and for his series "Intermezzo with Arik." He received Israel's Minister of Education Award in 2004 for lifetime achievement. He supervised Open University publications on music (1978–2004, in Hebrew) and published articles in Israeli music magazines and periodicals (1988–9, 1992–3).

BIBLIOGRAPHY: R. Baldassin, "Tuning up: An Interview with Concert Artist Arie Vardi," in *Piano Technicians Journal*, 32 (Nov. 1989), 16–18.

[Naama Ramot (2nd ed.)]

VARDI, MOSHE (1938–), Israeli journalist. Vardi was born in Tel Aviv, the son of Dr. Herzl *Rosenblum, editor of **Yedioth Aharonoth*. He studied international relations in London, and in 1962 was appointed London correspondent of *Ha-Boker*. In 1965 he joined *Yedioth Aharonoth* as news editor. (In order not to be identified as his father's son, he hebraized his last name.) Vardi possessed a finely tuned sense for evaluating the news value of events, and a skilled pen in newswriting. Against the growth of television news, Vardi widened the role of the newspaper to also provide background analysis to news events. In 1986 he left the newspaper after Dov *Yudkovsky was chosen as editor instead of him, following Rosenblum's retirement, and joined *Haaretz* as deputy editor. But after Yudkovsky's dismissal in 1989, Vardi was appointed editor. His editorship was interrupted in the 1990s when he stood trial in the so-called wiretapping affair involving *Maariv* and *Yedioth Aharonoth*. Vardi, along with *Yedioth Aharonoth's* assignments editor Ruth Ben-Ari, were convicted of tapping the phones of *Maariv* publisher Ofer *Nimrodi and editor Dov *Yudkovsky, though the court determined that Vardi did not know where the tapes had come from. Vardi was given a suspended sentence. When the trial over, *Yedioth Aharonoth*'s publisher, Arnon *Mozes, reinstated Vardi as editor, a post he held until his retirement in 2004. His son, Doron Rosenblum, was also a journalist.

[Yoel Cohen (2nd ed.)]

VARGA, YEVGENI SAMOILOVICH (1879–1964), economist. Born to a poor family in Hungary, he became a shop assistant, studied in his free time, and obtained a degree. In 1906 he became associated with the Hungarian Social Democratic Party, and from 1914 was a member of its central executive. Appointed professor of economics at the University of Budapest during the 1918 revolution, he attached himself to the Communists and became finance commissar under Bela *Kun. After the regime's fall, he fled to the Soviet Union. In 1922 he was sent to Berlin as head of the Soviet Foreign Trade

Mission and from 1926 to 1932 he served as editor of *Inprekorr Internationale Presse-Korrespondenz*, where his analyses of the foreign economics attracted attention. On his return to the Soviet Union he took charge of the newly formed Institute of World Economy and World Politics, and after its merger in 1936 with the Academy of Sciences of the U.S.S.R., Varga headed the academy's department of law and economics. His main achievements were his analyses and forecasts on which the Soviet Government widely relied for their information and orientation. Despite his erudition and industry he did not make an independent contribution to economics, mainly because he frequently saw the need to adjust his theories to the political exigencies of the day. However, in 1946 he surprised the public when he warned that an imminent crisis in the Western world – similar to the slump of 1929 – was unlikely. The Stalin regime removed him from his post and virtually impounded his book, but he lived to see his views come true. The Khrushchev regime officially vindicated his opinions and used them as the basis for its policy of peaceful coexistence.

Besides his many monographs and his articles in *Inprekorr*, he published his major study in 1946 under the title of *Osnovnye voprosy ekonomiki i politiki imperializma posle Vtoroy mirovoy voyny* (1946; *Problems of the Post-war Industrial Cycle…*, 1957^2).

BIBLIOGRAPHY: *New York Times* (Oct. 9, 1964), 39.

[Joachim O. Ronall]

VARLIN (**Willy Guggenheim**; 1900–1977), Swiss expressionist painter, born in Zurich. Varlin studied under Emil Orlik in Berlin and then went to Paris, where he worked as a caricaturist. The dominant mood of his expressionist paintings is one of loneliness and alienation. His favorite subjects are nudes, portraits, and public places such as deserted restaurants and hotel interiors. In the latter he expressed the loneliness of the individual in an impersonal environment.

VARMUS, HAROLD ELIOT (1939–), U.S. microbiologist and Nobel laureate. He was born in Freeport, New York to Beatrice Barasch and Frank Varmus, and graduated with a B.A. from Amherst College, an M.A. in literary studies from Harvard University, and an M.D. from Columbia College of Physicians and Surgeons (1966). After clinical training at Presbyterian Hospital, New York (1966–68), he received his research training with Ira Pastan at the National Institutes of Health (NIH), Bethesda (1966–68) where he became interested in basic research. He then joined the department of microbiology of the University of California, San Francisco (1970–93) becoming professor (1979–83) and American Cancer Society Professor of Molecular Virology (1984–93). He returned to NIH as director (1993–99) before his appointment as president of Memorial Sloan-Kettering Cancer Center, New York, from 2000. His early interest in gene regulation started at NIH. In San Francisco he and his colleagues studied the relationships between retroviral and cellular genes. They discovered that oncogenic (cancer-causing) viruses contain altered versions of growth regulating genes found in normal cells; mutation or inappropriate activation of these normal genes, now known as proto-oncogenes, was proposed to be an important step in malignant transformation even in the absence of viral infection and as the result of other factors. These observations fundamentally influenced the subsequent direction of cancer research. For these discoveries he received the Nobel Prize for physiology or medicine (1989), jointly with his close collaborator Michael Bishop. His subsequent research interests have included retroviruses, hepatitis B viruses, and the development of drugs that inhibit enzymes on which the growth of cancer cells is dependent. His honors include election to the U.S. National Academy of Sciences (1984) and the American College of Arts and Sciences (1988), the Lasker Award for Basic Medical Research (1982) and the Gairdner Award (1984) (both with Michael Bishop), and the National Medal of Science (2001). Varmus was an influential adviser to many academic, national, biotechnology, and international organizations including WHO, concerned with health and scientific education in the developed world and Third World. His highly regarded books on science include *Genes and the Biology of Cancer* 1992 (with Robert Weinberg) written for general readers. Varmus has retained his passion for literature and the arts, and also for outdoor pursuits.

[Michael Denman (2nd ed.)]

VARNA, major seaport on the Black Sea coast of Bulgaria; ancient **Odessus**; called **Stalin** 1949–1956). During the 1880s there were 300 Jews in Varna. The organization of the community was made possible by the Tedeschi brothers. In 1919 there were 1,500 Jews; in 1938, 2,000; and in 1943, 1,254. Besides the Sephardi community, there was also a small Ashkenazi community. The Alliance Israélite Universelle opened an elementary school for boys and girls in the town in 1880 and two vocational centers, one for boys in 1885 and one for girls in 1898. A newspaper in Ladino, *Il Judio*, which had at first been published in Constantinople, was published in Varna from 1922 to 1927 under the editorship of David Elnecavé. In 2004 there were 217 Jews in Varna, affiliated with the local branch of the nationwide Shalom organization.

BIBLIOGRAPHY: S. Mézan, *Les Juifs espagnols en Bulgarie*, 1 (1925), passim; M.D. Gaon, *Ha-Ittonut be-Ladino* (1965), passim.

[Simon Marcus / Emil Kalo (2nd ed.)]

VÁRNAI, ZSENI (1890–1981), Hungarian poet. Zseni Várnai's verse expressed her Socialist and pacifist outlook. The tone of her writing changed, however, under the impact of World War II, during which she was active in the anti-Nazi underground. Two of her prose works are *Mint viharban a falevél* ("Like Leaves in the Storm," 1943) and the autobiographical *Fényben, viharban* ("In Light and Storm," 1958).

VARNHAGEN, RAHEL LEVIN (1771–1833), German intellectual and salon host. The oldest daughter of a prosperous Berlin merchant, Rahel Levin was raised in a home with only minimal elements of Jewish practice. In 1795, she welcomed the opportunity to escape from Jewishness and into aristocratic Germany through an engagement to Count Karl von Finckenstein. However, after four years she broke off the engagement. Levin was a person of culture and intellect; her home became an informal meeting place for the literary, intellectual, social, and political luminaries of the day, such as Prince Louis Ferdinand, Prince Radziwill, Alexander von Humboldt and Wilhelm von *Humboldt, Friedrich Schlegel, Ludwig Tieck, Jean Paul (Friedrich Richter), Clemens Brentano, Friedrich von Gentz, Friedrich *Schleiermacher, Adelbert von Chamisso, and F.H.K. Fouqué. Among them were Jews and former Jews, Protestants and Catholics, nobility and commoners. In 1801 Rahel became engaged to the secretary of the Spanish Legation, Don Raphael d' Urquijo, but the engagement ended in 1804. After many difficult years of financial privation during the Napoleonic wars, Rahel married her confidant and admirer, Karl August Varnhagen von Ense. Weeks before their marriage in September 1814, she became a Protestant. The ceremony took place in the home of one of her brothers, who also later converted. Varnhagen's diplomatic career ended in 1819, when his liberal views ran counter to the rising reactionary tide. In Berlin, at the couple's renowned salon, Heinrich *Heine, Ludwig *Boerne, Karl *Gutzkow, and other authors close to the Young Germany movement found a congenial, liberal, and intellectual atmosphere. Varnhagen maintained an extensive correspondence; after her death, her husband published a collection of her letters, *Rahel; Ein Buch des Andenkens fuer ihre Freunde* (1834). In recent years a reconstructed documentary archive at the Jagiellonian Library in Cracow, Poland, has illuminated aspects of her life and legacy. Although Rahel Levin never denied her Jewish origin, it was always a source of conflict for her. In 1795 she wrote: "I imagine that just as I was being thrust into this world a supernatural being plunged a dagger into my heart with these words: 'Now, have feeling, see the world as only a few see it, be great and noble; nor can I deprive you of restless, incessant thought. But with one reservation: be a Jewess.' And now my whole life is one long bleeding. By keeping calm I can prolong it; every movement to stop the bleeding is to die anew, and immobility is only possible to me in death itself."

BIBLIOGRAPHY: H. Arendt, *Rahel Varnhagen* (Eng., 1956; Ger; 1959); O. Bredow, *Rahel Varnhagen* (Ger., 1902); S. Liptzin, Germany's Stepchildren (1944). **ADD. BIBLIOGRAPHY:** B. Hahn, *"Antworten Sie mir": Rahel Levin Varnhagens Briefwechsel* (1990); idem, *The Jewess Pallas Athena* (2005); D. Hertz, *Jewish High Society in Old Regime Berlin* (1988); C. Stern, *Der Text meines Herzens: Das Leben der Rahel Varnhagen* (1994); R. Varnhagen, *Briefwechsel* (1979).

[Sol Liptzin / Deborah Hertz (2nd ed.)]

°**VARRO, MARCUS TERENTIUS** (116–27 B.C.E.), Roman scholar. Varro mentions the date palms of Judea (*De re rustica* 2:1, 27). Augustine reports that Varro identified the Jewish God with Jupiter (*De consensu Evangelistarum* 1:30, 31, 42). Elsewhere he notes that Varro, in praising a bygone era when Romans did not use images in worshiping gods, points to Judaism as proof of the greater piety in such practice (*De Civitate Dei* 4:31, 2). If the citation is accurate, it indicates a rare appreciation of Judaism, in contrast to the anti-Jewish remarks usually found in Roman literature.

[Jacob Petroff]

VARSHAVSKI, ABRAHAM (1821–1888), Russian philanthropist and *railroad builder. Varshavski was one of the builders of the Moscow Brest-Litovsk-Poltava railroad. He went to St. Petersburg from Poltava province at the beginning of the 1860s and was a member of the *Society for the Promotion of Culture among the Jews of Russia. In his last years (1883–88), he acted as expert in the High Commission for the Revision of the Jewish Legislature (The Pahlen Commission).

BIBLIOGRAPHY: E. Tcherikower, in: *Historishe Shriftn*, 3 (1939), 109.

VAS, ISTVÁN (1910–1991), Hungarian poet, playwright, and translator. Grandson of a rabbi but never an observant Jew, Vas converted to Christianity in 1938. Jewish themes are absent in his work, but Budapest, his home city, plays an important part in it. On his 70th birthday he was honored with the highest state award.

[Eva Kondor]

°**VAŠEK, ANTON** (1905–1946), lawyer and head of the department in charge of deportations in the Slovak pro-Nazi Ministry of the Interior under Sand Mach. Vašek was nicknamed "King of the Jews" (*Židovský král*). During the cessation of deportations in the autumn of 1942, he was bribed by the "Working Group" (see Gisi *Fleischmann). He wrote historical articles on the Jewish problem and a book, *Die Loesung der Judenfrage in der Slowakei* (1942), compiled with the aid of Jewish functionaries who meant to distract him from other activities. After the war he was hanged following sentence by the National Tribunal of Bratislava (1946).

BIBLIOGRAPHY: L. Rothkirchen, *Ḥurban Yahadut Slovakia* (1961), incl. comprehensive Eng. summary, index.

[Livia Rothkirchen]

VASHTI (Heb. וַשְׁתִּי; perhaps "beauty" in Persian), queen of Persia and Media, wife of *Ahasuerus (Xerxes; 485–465 B.C.E.). When King Ahasuerus, in the third year of his reign, held a banquet "for all the people that were found in *Shushan" in the king's gardens, Queen Vashti also held a banquet in the palace. On the seventh day, when the king was drunk from all the wine, he ordered Vashti brought before him "to show the peoples and the princes" her beauty. Vashti refused to appear. At the advice of his counselors the king ordered her deposed from her position and proclaimed that "every man should be lord in his house" (Esth. 1:9–22). Later she was replaced by Esther (Esth. 2). Attempts to identify Vashti with known historical figures have not been persuasive. As a proper name, Vashti has survived in inscriptions.

[Yehoshua M. Grintz]

In the Aggadah

Vashti was the granddaughter of Nebuchadnezzar (Meg. 10a). She witnessed the Persian conquest of Babylon from her father, Belshazzar. On the night that the city fell, Vashti was so alarmed by the confusion that, unaware that Belshazzar had already been killed, she ran to his private quarters. There she was confronted by Darius who, out of compassion for her, betrothed her to his son, Ahasuerus (Yalk. Est. 1049). Her action in having her banquet for women "in the royal house which belonged to Ahasuerus" (Esth. 1:9) was that her guests would be hostages if their husbands should rise and rebel against the king (Est. R. 3:10). According to R. Abun, however, the location of the banquet was dictated by the consideration that "women would sooner have well-decorated rooms and beautiful clothes, than eat fatted calves" (*ibid.*). Vashti had low moral standards: it was not for reasons of modesty that she refused to comply with Ahasuerus' command to appear before his guests (Esth. 1:11) in the nude. She was as immoral as her husband (Meg. 12a). Her refusal was occasioned either by the fact that she was suffering from leprosy (*ibid.*), or by fear for Ahasuerus' life. She remonstrated with him: "If they consider me beautiful, they will want to enjoy me themselves, and will kill you; if they consider me plain, I shall be a disgrace to you" (Est. R. 3:14). When Ahasuerus nevertheless repeated his request, Vashti insulted him by reminding him of his lowly descent as servant to her father (cf. Song R. 3:5), Belshazzar, before he was murdered. According to one version, she exclaimed: "You used to be the stable boy of my father's house, and you were used to bringing naked harlots before you. Now that you have ascended the throne you have still not changed your habits" (*ibid.*). She was put to death on the Sabbath because, when she was queen, she would force the daughters of Israel to strip and work in the nude, on the Sabbath (Meg. *ibid.*).

BIBLIOGRAPHY: Cooke, *North Semitic Inscriptions* (1903), no. 85; L.B. Paton, *Esther* (ICC, 1908), 66–67, 88–89, 142ff. IN THE AGGADAH: Ginzberg, Legends, index; I. Ḥasida, *Ishei ha-Tanakh* (1964), 142.

VASILKOV, city in Kiev district, Ukraine. In 1648 Vasilkov was conquered by *Chmielnicki's Cossacks who massacred its inhabitants, Jews and Poles alike. Since Vasilkov was annexed to Russia in 1686, no Jewish community existed there until the second partition of Poland in 1792. There were 1,478 Jews in Vasilkov in 1799, 2,407 in 1847, and 5,156 (39.2% of the total population) in 1897. Vasilkov was a ḥasidic community and for some time David b. Nahum *Twersky of Chernobyl lived there. The Jews in Vasilkov engaged in crafts, small-scale business, and worked in local tanneries. In February 1919, S. *Petlyura's armies conducted pogroms in Vasilkov, massacring 50 Jews and 60 Russians suspected of being Communists; the Jewish community was forced to pay a special contribution. When the Soviet regime was established, Jewish communal life was discontinued. In 1926 the Jews in Vasilkov numbered 3,061 (14.4% of the total population). In 1941 the Jews of Vasilkov were exterminated by the Nazis.

BIBLIOGRAPHY: A.D. Rosenthal, *Megillat ha-Tevaḥ*, 2 (1929), 81–82.

[Yehuda Slutsky]

VASLUI, district capital in Moldavia, E. Romania. The oldest tombstones in the Jewish cemetery indicate that Jews settled there in the first half of the 18th century, most of them from *Bukovina and *Galicia, and from the 1850s many Jewish *Cantonists who fled from Russia. In 1851 two Jewish inhabitants were raised to the nobility (boyarhood) for service to Vaslui. The early Jewish population was joined later on by Jews expelled from villages in the vicinity of Vaslui (in 1867, 1889, 1901, and 1908). The Jewish population numbered 892 in 1839, 1,202 (25.3% of the total) in 1859, and 2,823 (41%) in 1889; in 1899 their number increased to 3,747. Difficulties were encountered in the organization of the community because the merchants and the artisans each had their own institutions, and even their own rabbis. In 1877 a primary school was founded, but the craftsmen had their own *talmud torah*. In 1904 an attempt was made to unite the community's institutions but this lasted only two years. The community was finally unified only in 1923.

Zionist activity began in Vaslui in the 1880s. Rabbis of the town included Alexander Taubes (1841–1913) and Benjamin Rabinovici. *Ẓaddikim* of the Ruzhin-Buhus dynasty lived in the town. On the eve of World War II there were in Vaslui eight prayer rooms, a hospital and clinic, an old-age home, a *mikveh*, a primary school, and a kindergarten. After the naturalization laws were passed (in 1919), two to six Jews were active in the local council. In 1947 the Jewish population numbered 3,200, decreasing to 2,400 in 1950. In 1960 there were about 70 Jewish families with one synagogue.

BIBLIOGRAPHY: I. Brociner, *Chestiunea israeliților români…*, 1 (1910), 114–6; *Almanachul ziarului Tribuna evreească*, 1 (1937/38), 242–8; N. Leven, *Cinquante ans d'histoire*, 1 (1911), 121, 143; I. Loeb, *La situation des Israélites en Turquie, en Serbie et en Roumanie* (1877), 168; PK Romanyah, 120–3.

[Theodor Lavi]

VATICAN, residence of the *pope, who is the ruler of Vatican City in Rome.

The Vatican and Zionism

Theodor Herzl was the first Zionist leader to understand the political importance of the Catholic Church in the Middle East. He also realized the necessity for Zionists to come to terms with the Church and gain its support or at least try to neutralize its influence. The Vatican wished to safeguard Catholic rights in the holy places, and therefore Herzl was ready to propose an extraterritorial status for the holy places when he was received by the nuncio in Vienna, Msgr. Antonio Agliardi, on May 19, 1896, a short time after the publication of his book *The Jewish State*. Herzl repeated the idea of extraterritoriality to Secretary of State Cardinal Rafael Merry del Val on January 22, 1904, but Merry del Val answered that the holy places could not be regarded as entities separate from the Holy Land. On January 25 Herzl was received by the pope, *Pius x, who told him: "We cannot prevent the Jews from going to Jerusalem but we could never sanction it. The Jews have not recognized our Lord, therefore we cannot recognize the Jewish people. If you come to Palestine and settle your people there, we will have churches and priests ready to baptize all of you."

During World War i new realities were changing the political situation in the Middle East. The Vatican was aware at a very early stage of the secret *Sykes-Picot Agreement dividing the region between France and Great Britain and putting the central part of Palestine under an international regime. France had been for centuries the protecting power for Catholics in the Ottoman Empire, but the Holy See hinted that the Vatican would not be averse to British patronage of the Holy Places. This is what Sir Mark *Sykes heard on April 11, 1917, from Msgr. Eugenio Pacelli, undersecretary for extraordinary affairs at the Secretariat of State, and a few days later from Pope *Benedict xv himself.

Following the advice of Sykes, Nahum *Sokolow of the Zionist Executive in London met Msgr. Pacelli on April 29, 1917, and Secretary of State Cardinal Pietro Gasparri on May 1, and was received by the pope on May 4, 1917. Pacelli wanted clear geographical boundaries acceptable to the Vatican to be demarcated, while Gasparri wanted the Church to have a "reserved zone" that would include Jerusalem, Bethlehem, Nazareth, Tiberias, and Jericho. The pope said: "The problem of the holy places is of extraordinary importance for us. The sacred rights must be protected. We will settle this between the Church and the Great Powers. You must respect those rights to their full extent."

Sokolow could well understand that the Holy See had clear territorial claims on the central part of Palestine. Furthermore the Holy See would not accept a solution giving extraterritorial status to the holy places, and would in any case negotiate with the Great Powers, not with the Zionists.

Despite the content of these talks, the Zionists were impressed by the positive manner of the Church's representatives. On the basis of Sokolow's reports Dr. Chaim *Weizmann could announce to a Zionist conference in London on May 20, 1917: "We have assurances from the highest Catholic circles that they will favor the establishment of a Jewish National Home in Palestine and from their religious point of view they see no objections to it and no reason why we should not be good neighbors." Nothing could have been further from the truth. By "good neighbors" the pope probably meant that the Vatican would maintain a presence in the central area of Palestine that was to be internationalized, while the Zionists would remain outside of it in the bordering areas.

At the end of the year 1917 two events dramatically changed the situation of Palestine: the Balfour Declaration of November 2, and the conquest of Jerusalem by British troops on December 9.

Cardinal Gasparri clearly expressed opposition to a Jewish state in Palestine when he said on December 18, 1917, to the Belgian representative, Jules Van den Heuvel: "The transformation of Palestine into a Jewish state would not only endanger the Holy Places and injure the feelings of all Christians, it would also be very harmful for the country itself."

A few days later, on December 28, the pope expressed his fear to De Salis, the British representative, that Great Britain might hand Palestine over "to the Jews to the detriment of the Christian interests."

In January 1919 the Peace Conference met in Versailles (France) but the Holy See was not admitted to it. The reason was that Italy had included Article 15 in the secret London Treaty, excluding the Vatican from the future conference, since the question of Rome was still open between them. On March 10, 1919, the pope convened a secret consistory in the Vatican and said that "it would be a terrible grief for us and for all Christians if infidels [in Palestine] were placed in a privileged and prominent position; much more if those most holy sanctuaries of the Christian religion were given into the charge of non-Christians." As Gasparri explained some days later to the Belgian representative: "The danger that we most fear is the establishment of a Jewish state in Palestine. We would have found nothing wrong in Jews entering that country, and setting up agricultural colonies. But that they be given the rule over the Holy Places is intolerable for Christians."

Three cardinals visited Palestine in those years: the British Francis Bourne, the Italian Filippo Giustini, and the French Louis Ernest Dubois. In January 1919 Cardinal Bourne sent a letter to the British prime minister and to the foreign secretary, writing that Zionism had not received the approval of the Holy See, and if the Jews would "ever again dominate and rule the country, it would be an outrage to Christianity and its Divine founder." In October 1919 Cardinal Giustini cabled the pope from Jerusalem asking for his intervention "to prevent the reestablishment of Zionist Israel in Palestine." Cardinal Dubois was reported in March 1920 to have said that Jewish immigration to Palestine and the establishment of a Zionist state should not be permitted. On July 20, 1920, the Latin patriarch of Jerusalem, Msgr. Luigi Barlassina, also published a pastoral letter strongly protesting against the Great Powers' decision to establish a Jewish national home in Palestine. He added: "Let Palestine be internationalized rather than someday be the servant of Zionism."

On May Day 1921, the Jewish workers in Jaffa organized a celebration and parade in the streets. The Arabs attacked them and about 50 Jews and the same number of Arabs were killed and many hundreds injured. Instead of condemning the aggressors, the *Osservatore Romano* (the Vatican daily) explained a few days later that the Bolsheviks had infiltrated Palestine thanks to the Zionist Organization. The paper also raised the question of whether the Bolshevik Revolution was coordinated with Zionism or whether Zionism had raised a Bolshevik viper in its bosom.

A few days later Pope Benedict xv attacked Zionism in his allocution to the cardinals of June 13, 1921. He said that the Jews were given a "position of preponderance and privilege in Palestine"; that their activity is meant "to take away the sacred character of the Holy Places"; he admitted that no damage should "be done to the rights of the Jewish element" but "they must in no way be put above the just rights of the Christians."

Pope Benedict XV died in January 1922 and a month later, a new pope was elected, assuming the name *Pius XI. Dr. Weizmann, the leader of the Zionist Organization in London, met Secretary of State Cardinal Gasparri on April 2, 1922. Gasparri did not hide his antagonism to Zionism and gave voice to a series of objections to the draft text of the Mandate over Palestine concerning religious rights, the recognition of the Jewish Agency, and Article 14 on a commission for the holy places. Weizmann learned on this occasion that the Vatican's opposition to the Mandate would take the form of an official memorandum submitted to the League of Nations.

During Weizmann's second meeting with Cardinal Gasparri on April 20, 1922, Gasparri said that Zionist colonization work caused him no anxiety, but added: "It is your university that I fear."

On May 15, 1922, Cardinal Gasparri sent an official note to try to stop, at the very last moment, the assignment of the Mandate to Great Britain. The note sent to the League of Nations stated that the Holy See cannot agree to "the Jews being given a privileged and preponderant position in Palestine vis-à-vis the Catholics" or to "the religious rights of the Christians being inadequately safeguarded." The Holy See also opposed the recognition of the Jewish Agency, and the favoring of immigration and naturalization of Jews. Nevertheless a few weeks later, on July 22, 1922, the League of Nations approved Great Britain as the mandatory power and included the Balfour Declaration in the Preamble to the Mandate. The Vatican finally accepted the British Mandate as the lesser evil.

In the 1920s the Vatican opposed Zionism for a variety of reasons. They believed the Zionists were antireligious, that Zionist immigration would sweep the Christians out of Palestine and destroy the Christian character of the country, and that the Jews were causing radical changes in the traditional life-style of the local population and damaging moral values. During this period the Vatican was strongly opposed to Jewish statehood in the Holy Land. In August 1929 the Arabs attacked the Jewish quarters in Hebron, Safed, and other places. The daily *Osservatore Romano,* rather than blaming the Arabs for the attack, wrote that it was "the politics of Zionism, and not the religion of Israel, which lay at the root of the trouble."

In 1936 the Arabs started the Great Arab Rebellion which resulted in many acts of violence against the Jews. The British government sent the *Peel Commission, which published its proposal for partition in 1937, and on August 6 the Vatican sent a verbal note in which it expressed its objection to the principle of partition and requested that all Holy Places be included in the British zone.

In October 1938 the *Osservatore Romano* wrote that "only one of the two races which contended the hegemony in Palestine can live in the country." Along the same lines of thought, Msgr. Domenico Tardini, the Vatican undersecretary of state, told a British diplomat in 1938: "There was no real reason why [the Jews] should be back in Palestine. Why should not a nice place be found for them, for instance, in South America?"

In May 1939 the British government published the MacDonald White Paper, considered to be a betrayal by Weizmann. Land regulations prohibited or restricted land sales, Jewish immigrants were limited to 75,000 during the next five years and later would be subject to Arab consent. An independent Palestinian state would be created at the end of a transition period of 10 years.

The *Osservatore Romano* remarked with satisfaction that "the White Paper denied the historical basis of the Zionist claims."

During World War II, while the Holocaust was already raging and hundreds of thousands of Jews were being killed by the Nazis, anti-Zionist attitudes prevailed among Vatican diplomats.

Msgr. Domenico Tardini wrote in March 1943 that the Holy See "has never approved the project of making Palestine a Jewish home." Cardinal Maglione, secretary of state, wrote in May 1943 to his apostolic delegate in the United States, Cicognani, that it would not be difficult "if one wants to establish a 'Jewish Home,' to find other territories [than Palestine] which could better fulfill this aim, while Palestine, under Jewish predominance, would bring new and grave international problems."

Cardinal Maglione wrote in the same month that "Catholics would be wounded in their religious sentiments and would rightly fear for their rights if Palestine became the exclusive property of the Jews."

In August 1944 the secretariat of state of the Holy See wrote that they regarded Palestine "not as a Jewish home or a possible Arab home but also as a Catholic home and Catholic center."

On April 10, 1945, while the war was still going on in Europe, Moshe Shertok (later *Sharett) of the Jewish Agency was received by Pope *Pius XII. He hoped for the "moral support" of the Catholic Church for "our renewed existence in Palestine." But he did not receive any support; on the contrary the Holy See started a campaign for the internationalization of Jerusalem, supported by France. The Vatican considered Zionism to be an enemy, only suitable as a springboard for a new alliance between Christians and Moslems in Palestine.

In 1947 Great Britain decided to renounce the Mandate and to deliver the Palestine issue over to the United Nations. On November 29, 1947, the General Assembly approved Resolution No. 181 on the partition of Palestine and the creation of a corpus separatum for Jerusalem and its environs. The Holy See avoided interfering in the vote, probably in order not to jeopardize the internationalization of Jerusalem. The war that the Arab states opened against the State of Israel, and which made null and void the project of internationalization, started even before the state was proclaimed.

The Vatican and the State of Israel

The creation of the State of Israel in 1948 ran counter to certain theological ideas in the Catholic Church according to which the Jews were condemned to remain homeless because of the crime of deicide. Some believe that the Holy See did not oppose the partition plan of the United Nations in 1947 because it included Jerusalem in an international "corpus separatum." Pope Pius XII wrote three encyclicals on the question of the Holy Land. The first one, *Auspicia quaedam* of May 1, 1948, expressed hope "that the situation in Palestine may at long last be settled justly and thereby concord and peace be also happily established."

In the second, *In multiplicibus*, of October 24, 1948, the pope said that "it would be opportune to give Jerusalem and its outskirts, where are found so many and such precious memories of the life and death of the Savior, an international character which, in the present circumstances, seems to offer a better guarantee for the protection of the sanctuaries. It would also be necessary to assure, with international guarantees, both free access to Holy Places scattered throughout Palestine, and the freedom of worship and the respect of customs and religious traditions."

In his third encyclical, *In redemptoris nostr*, of April 15, 1949, Pope Pius XII advocated giving "to Jerusalem and its surroundings a juridical statute internationally guaranteed" and appealed that all rights of the Catholics "should be preserved inviolate."

Some Catholic states opposed the acceptance of Israel in the United Nations on May 11, 1949, because Israel had "failed to carry out the full internationalization scheme" for Jerusalem. The dispute on the war damages to churches and other properties in Israel was solved satisfactorily for the Holy See in 1955 when Msgr. Antonio Vergani received the final compensation for war damages to Catholic institutions. But even the name of the State of Israel was omitted by the *Osservatore Romano* in 1955 when a visit of the *Israel Philharmonic Orchestra to the Vatican was described as that of "Jewish musicians of fourteen different nationalities." The coronation of Pope *John XXIII in 1958 was attended by Ambassador Eliyahu *Sasson as a "special delegate of the State of Israel." This, it was later claimed by the Vatican, proved that the Holy See did recognize the State of Israel even if it did not establish normal diplomatic relations.

On January 5, 1964, *Paul VI became the first pope to visit Israel. He said in Megiddo, where he entered Israel: "We are coming as pilgrims, we come to venerate the Holy Places; we come to pray." He ended his speech with the Hebrew words "Shalom, shalom." But Paul VI never addressed President Shazar by his title; even when he sent a telegram with his thanks, it was sent to Tel Aviv, not to Jerusalem, the residence of the president of the State of Israel. Every effort was made to stress the non-recognition of Israel by the Holy See.

The Ecumenical Council Vatican II approved in 1965 an important declaration, *Nostra Aetate*, modifying the accusation of deicide and stating: "True, authorities of the Jews… pressed for the death of Christ; still what happened in His passion cannot be blamed upon all the Jews then living nor the Jews of today." The text was influenced by politics and it was watered down because of the violent protest of the Arab states.

After the liberation of Jerusalem in 1967, Pope Paul VI, on June 26, 1967, recalled that he had done his best "to avoid at least to Jerusalem the suffering and the damages of the war" and that he was very saddened by the conditions of the Palestinian refugees, and said that "the Holy City of Jerusalem should remain for ever a town of God, a free oasis of peace and prayer, with its own statute internationally guaranteed."

Thus the old formula for seeking the internationalization of Jerusalem and its environs was changed into one that spoke of an "internationally guaranteed statute."

In July 1967 Msgr. Angelo Felici, undersecretary for extraordinary affairs at the Vatican Secretariat of State arrived in Israel for talks with Prime Minister Levi *Eshkol. The pope in his allocution of December 23, 1968, had spoken of his wish to see "an internationally guaranteed agreement on the question of Jerusalem and the Holy Places."

On October 6, 1969, the pope received the Israeli foreign minister, Abba *Eban, and discussed the question of "the refugees, the holy places, and the unique and sacred character of Jerusalem."

On December 22, 1969, the traditional Christmas wishes for the Arab refugees and the special mention of the Christian communities in Palestine expressed a new preoccupation. "They have diminished and they are diminishing, the faithful of Jesus in that blessed earth," said the Pope. This was the first time that the pope had expressed publicly his concerns about the diminishing number of Catholics in the Holy Land, a preoccupation would manifest itself time and again in his subsequent speeches.

In January 1972, Deputy Secretary of State Msgr. Giovanni Benelli visited Israel and had several talks with Minister of Finance Pinḥas *Sapir, and Minister of Justice Ya'akov Shimshon *Shapiro on the question of the sale of the Notre Dame de France building to the Hebrew University. The assumptionist had sold the monastery but according to the Vatican the sale had to be considered null and void because Canon Law required authorization by the Vatican. A hearing in an Israeli court in Jerusalem was curtailed by the Israeli government's decision to cancel the sale, but no reciprocal gesture of goodwill was made by the Holy See. The Vatican transformed the building into a modern hotel and for years refused to pay municipal taxes "for services rendered." Finally, in 1987, the Vatican consented to pay the Jerusalem municipality a token sum.

On December 22, 1972, in his customary allocution to the Holy College on the eve of Christmas, the pope criticized "situations without a clear juridical basis, internationally recognized and guaranteed," referring to Jerusalem, where also the followers of Christ "must feel themselves full 'citizens.'" He spoke also of the sons of the Palestinian people waiting for years "for an equitable recognition of their aspirations, not in opposition to but in necessary harmony with the rights of other peoples."

On January 15, 1973, Israeli Prime Minister Golda *Meir was received in a private audience by Pope Paul VI. It was the first official visit of this kind, and therefore an important one. The final communiqué recalled the suffering of the Jewish people; the pope in his humanitarian mission was interested in the Arab refugee problem and the problems of the Christian communities living in the Holy Land, while in terms of his religious mission he expressed concern about the Holy Places and the universal and holy character of Jerusalem.

At the end of the same year, after the Yom Kippur War, during which Israel was attacked by Syria and Egypt, the pope dedicated most of his yearly message of December 21, 1973, to the cardinals, to the Middle East. He expressed his approval of the Peace Conference convening on that same day in Geneva, but considered it incomplete in terms of representation, referring probably to the nonparticipation of the PLO. The Holy See was ready "to offer cooperation … in agreements that would guarantee to all parties concerned a calm and secure existence and the recognition of respective rights." The pope spoke of the hundreds of thousand of Arab refugees "living in desperate conditions"; even if their cause "has been endangered by actions that are repugnant to the civil conscience of people and are in no case justified, it is a cause that demands human consideration and calls with the voice of abandoned and innocent masses for a just and generous response."

On December 9, 1974, Msgr. Hilarion Capucci, the Greek Catholic archbishop (melkite) of Jerusalem and vicar of the Patriarch Maximos, was sentenced to 12 years' imprisonment; he was found guilty of smuggling arms and explosives for the Fatah organization from Lebanon into Israel, exploiting his diplomatic immunity. Some years later, on November 6, 1977, President Ephraim *Katzir, in response to a personal letter from the pope, commuted the sentence and Archbishop Capucci was immediately released. The written promise of the pope that Msgr. Capucci would not "bring any harm to the State of Israel," i.e., would no more indulge in political activity, was not respected and the prelate participated in many propaganda meetings organized by the PLO after regaining his freedom.

The foreign minister of Israel, Moshe *Dayan, was received in private audience by the pope on January 12, 1978. The pope stressed again his concerns about the question of Jerusalem, stating that the "well-known solution proposed by the Holy See for Jerusalem could satisfy the unique and religious character of the city." The Israeli side stressed what had been done "to guarantee the protection of the Holy Places of all religions and free access to them."

Paul VI died on August 6, 1978. His successor was Pope John Paul I, who had been patriarch of Venice and as such had good relations with the Jews. He died suddenly on September 28, 1978.

The new pope, *John Paul II, was born in Poland, so that for the first time in centuries the pope was not an Italian. An Israeli delegation participated in the funeral of the previous pope and the coronation ceremony of the new pope, whom it invited to visit Israel.

The permanent observer of the Holy See to the United Nations made a declaration on Jerusalem on December 3, 1979, in which he explained the meaning of a "special statute internationally guaranteed" for Jerusalem. The content of this statute would include two orders of guarantees: parity for the three religious communities regarding freedom of worship and access to the Holy Places; and equal enjoyment of rights by the three religious communities, with guarantees for the promotion of their spiritual, cultural, civil, and social life, including adequate opportunities for economic progress, education, and employment.

Pope John Paul II spoke about the State of Israel on October 5, 1980, in Otranto, saying: "The Jewish people, after tragic experiences connected with the extermination of so many sons and daughters, driven by desire for security, has established the State of Israel. At the same time, the painful condition of the Palestinian people was created, as a large part of it were extirpated from their land."

Yitzhak *Shamir, Israeli minister for foreign affairs, was received on January 7, 1982, by the pope, who stressed the importance of the Palestinian question, which should find a solution "taking into account also the problem of security for the State of Israel." The pope also spoke about "a just and agreed solution for the question of Jerusalem," a center for the three religions. Shamir emphasized the concessions made by Israel in order to reach the peace agreement with Egypt and his concerns about the arms race in the area and the serious problem of terrorism.

On September 15, 1982, the pope received Yasser *Arafat, who had just been forced to abandon Beirut, giving him a political victory after a military defeat.

Pope John Paul II dedicated an Apostolic Letter, "*Redemptionis Anno*," on April 20, 1984, to the question of Jerusalem and the Holy Land. The pope wrote: "Jews ardently love [Jerusalem] and in every age venerate her memory, abundant as she is in many remains and monuments from the time of David who chose her as the capital, and of Solomon who built the Temple there. Therefore they turn their minds to her daily, one may say, and point to her as the symbol of their nation."

After explaining why Jerusalem is holy also to the Christians and the Moslems, he recalled the Holy See's appeals for an adequate solution. He said: "Not only the monuments or the sacred places, but the whole historical Jerusalem and the existence of religious communities, their situation and future cannot but affect everyone and interest everyone."

Shimon *Peres, then prime minister, was received by the pope on February 19, 1985, and for almost an hour discussed the peace process. It was clear that Peres would not press for the establishment of normal diplomatic relations nor extend a formal invitation to the pope to visit Israel, leaving the initiative to the Holy See. Seemingly in the conversation with Secretary of State Casaroli there was a discussion on the status of Jerusalem and the Palestinian question.

In the "Notes," a Vatican commentary to *Nostra Aetate* published in 1985, there is reference for the first time to the State of Israel. In this statement issued on the 20th anniversary of Vatican II declaration, Christians are invited to understand the religious attachment of Jews to the State of Israel, but "the existence of the State of Israel and its political options should be envisaged not in a perspective which is itself religious, but in their reference to the common principles of international law."

This was the way to overcome the theological obstacle to the recognition of Israel.

John Paul II was the first pope to visit a synagogue when on April 13, 1986, he went to Rome's Great Synagogue. In his speech he spoke of the Jews as "our elder brothers," a characterization that was changed in 2004 to "our dearest brothers."

In September 1987, when Jewish leaders were received in Castel Gandolfo, near Rome, sources close to the pope said that there was no longer any theological obstacle to full relations with Israel. This can be seen as an outgrowth of the line adopted in June 1985 denying that there was any temporal link between the Jewish people and the State of Israel. While such a view might serve to overcome theological obstacles, at the same time it denies the spiritual basis of Zionism and seeks to separate the Jews in the Diaspora from the State of Israel.

On April 10, 1989, Renato Martino, permanent observer at the UN, said: "For us the Holy Land is our homeland, our country of origin; Jerusalem is the Church hometown. The Holy See is not only interested in preserving the archaeology, artifacts and architecture of the historical Christian communities, but also those communities themselves. The lack of diplomatic relations does not imply denial of the existence of the State of Israel. That such recognition exists is clear from the constant contacts."

On January 25, 1991, during the first Gulf War, the Holy See published a long document on the issue of diplomatic relations with Israel. It stated that the lack of diplomatic relations is certainly not due to theological reasons, but to juridical ones. The three main juridical difficulties were the presence of Israel in the occupied territories, Israel's annexation of Jerusalem, and the situation of the Catholic Church in Israel and in the administered territories.

On March 6, 1991, Pope John Paul II, closing the synod of bishops from the Middle East, said: "We have spoken of the Holy Land where two peoples, the Palestinians and that of the State of Israel, have been engaged in conflict for decades; the injustice of which the Palestinian people is a victim demands engagement by all men."

After the opening of the Madrid Peace Conference in November 1991, Msgr. Michel Sabah, the Latin patriarch of Jerusalem, emphasized that the Holy See had not been invited to attend, saying: "The invitation we were waiting for did not arrive." Probably the Holy See understood that without establishing normal diplomatic relations with Israel it could not be associated with the peace process, where perhaps the status of Jerusalem could be discussed. As they themselves were engaged in a dialogue with Israel, the Arabs could not very well reproach the Holy See establishing a bilateral permanent commission with Israel in July 1992 to discuss outstanding questions and normalize relations. The status of Jerusalem, a multisided question, was not discussed there.

After the meeting between Prime Minister Yitzhak *Rabin and Chairman Yasser Arafat at the White House on September 13, 1993, the Holy See decided to sign a Fundamental Agreement with Israel. It was signed by Msgr. Claudio Maria Celli and Deputy Minister for Foreign Affairs Yossi *Beilin on December 30, 1993. Only after the Cairo Agreement between Israel and the PLO, on May 4, 1994, did the Holy See agree to an exchange of ambassadors. It also signed an accord in November 1997 on the juridical status of the Church and Catholic institutions in Israel, which grants the Church autonomy to handle its affairs while respecting Israeli laws.

In a detailed exposition in a Jerusalem lecture on October 26, 1998, Archbishop Jean-Louis Tauran, secretary for relations with states, presented the Holy See's position on Jerusalem. Tauran stated that the Holy See cannot accept any distinction between the question of the Holy Places and the question of Jerusalem. The Holy See is present "to ensure that it does not become, as is the situation today, a case of manifest international injustice. East Jerusalem is illegally occupied. It is wrong to claim that the Holy See is only interested in the religious aspect or aspects of the city and overlook the political and territorial aspect… Any unilateral solution or one brought about by force is not and cannot be a solution at all… There must be equality of rights and treatment for those belonging to the communities of the three religions found in the city… the simple 'extraterritoriality' of the Holy Places would not suffice… The Holy See believes in the importance of extending representation at the negotiating table."

On March 9, 1999, Msgr. Tauran described the main reasons of disagreement with Israel: "It must also be recognized that relations between the Holy See and the Jewish world – above all with the State of Israel – have hardly been helped by the failure to resolve the Palestinian problem, the lack of respect for certain UN Security Council Resolutions and duly concluded international agreements, without forgetting the annexation by force of a part of the City of Jerusalem."

On April 27, 1999, Foreign Minister Ariel *Sharon was received by Pope John Paul II. Sharon thanked the pope for his efforts in combating antisemitism and his relations with the Jews. "Israel will warmly welcome and ensure the security of the pilgrims who will come, including, first and foremost, the 'First pilgrim,' the Pope."

In December 1999, another item of disagreement between the Holy See and Israel was the project of building a new mosque in Nazareth just in front of the Basilica of the Annunciation.

The Catholic Church under the guidance of Msgr. Michel Sabah, the Latin patriarch of Jerusalem, reacted strongly to the government's authorization to build the mosque. Msgr. Sabah succeeded in closing down the Christian Holy Places in Jerusalem for two days in protest and managed to create a united front with other Christian communities. Sabah also accused the Israeli government of fomenting tension between Christians and Moslems, an accusation promptly re-echoed by the Holy See's spokesman, Joaquin Navarro-Valls. Some years later the Israeli government withdrew the authorization and the mosque was not built.

The official visit of Pope John Paul II to the Holy Land in March 2000 was undoubtedly an historical event. John Paul II arrived at Ben-Gurion Airport, where he was formally received by President Ezer *Weizman and Prime Minister Ehud *Barak on March 21, 2000. He visited the two chief rabbis, Israel Meir *Lau and Eliahu *Bakshi-Doron, at Hechal Shlomo in Jerusalem, and the president of the State in his official residence in Jerusalem on March 23, 2000.

The pope said to President Weizman: "Mr. President, you are known as a man of peace and a peacemaker. We all know how urgent is the need for peace and justice, not for Israel alone but for the entire region." On the same occasion the pope added: "It is my fervent hope that a genuine desire for peace will inspire your every decision."

There were two other highlights to the pope's visit to Israel: the encounter in Yad Vashem on March 23 with Holocaust survivors from his home town and the visit to the Western Wall. The Pope said at Yad Vashem: "Only a godless ideology could plan and carry out the extermination of a whole people." Thus all the responsibility fell upon a "godless ideology," unrelated to or even in opposition to the Church. Already in March 1998, the Holy See, in the document "We Remember: a Reflection on the Shoah," had stated: "The Shoah was the work of a thoroughly modern neo-pagan regime. Its antisemitism had its roots outside of Christianity."

In a crevice of the Western Wall, following the Jewish custom, the pope inserted on March 26 a note which reads: "God of our fathers, / you chose Abraham and his descendants / to bring your Name to the Nations: / we are deeply saddened / by the behavior of those / who in the course of history / have caused these children of yours to suffer, / and asking your forgiveness / we wish to commit ourselves / to genuine brotherhood / with the people of the Covenant."

This text is identical to that included in a ceremony of forgiveness in Rome on March 12, 2000, but it lacks the preamble in which the Church asked forgiveness from the Jews. Without the preamble, the Jews are not expressly mentioned.

In his meeting with Yasser Arafat in Bethlehem, the pope offered him 14 sea shells representing the 14 stations of the Way of the Cross and explained that this was a way to symbolize the Passion of the Palestinians. So again the pope made the comparison between the suffering of the Palestinians and those endured by Jesus.

In his speeches in Israel, the pope drew a parallel between antisemitism and anti-Christianity several times. Upon his arrival in Tel Aviv he said: "Christians and Jews together must make courageous efforts to remove all forms of prejudice. We must strive always and everywhere to present the true face of the Jews and Judaism as likewise of Christians and Christianity." Two days later at Hechal Shlomo, before the two chief rabbis, he said: "We must work together to build a future in which there will be no more anti-Judaism among Christians nor anti-Christian sentiment among Jews." At Yad Vashem the pope repeated: "No more anti-Jewish feeling among Christians or anti-Christian feeling among Jews."

This convenient symmetry between Jews and Christians is not supported by history.

During his visit in Israel the pope sent a letter protesting the approval given by the Israeli authorities to the building of the Nazareth mosque. This was a rather rare and strong act of censure.

On April 1, 2002, some 200 armed Palestinians entered one of the most important shrines and holy places in Christianity, the Church of the Nativity in Bethlehem – marking the place where Jesus was born – and remained inside until May 12, holding hostages. The *Osservatore Romano* wrote on April 2, 2002: "Palestinian terrorism is only a pretext," because the true objective of Israel is "to profane with fire and iron the land of the Resurrected." Msgr. Tauran, of the Secretariat of State, said that the Holy See's position included "an unequivocal condemnation of terrorism," "disapproval of the conditions of injustice and humiliation imposed on the Palestinian people, as well as reprisals and retaliations, which only make the sense of frustration and hatred grow."

Pope John Paul II in his Angelus message of August 11, 2002, said: "From 1967 till today, unspeakable sufferings have followed one upon another in a frightening manner: the suffering of the Palestinians, driven out of their land and forced, in recent times, into a state of permanent siege, becoming as it were the object of a collective punishment; the suffering of the Israeli population, who live in the daily terror of being targets of anonymous assailants. To this we must add the violation of a fundamental right, that of freedom of worship. In effect, because of a strict curfew, believers no longer have access to their places of worship on the day of weekly prayer."

Archbishop Renato Martino, permanent observer to the United Nations, wrote on November 2, 2002: "The Holy See renews its consistent call for internationally guaranteed provisions to ensure the freedom of religion and conscience of its inhabitants, in order to safeguard the special character of the City and of the sites sacred to Jews, Christians and Muslims."

On November 16, the pope said: "In this context I repeat my firm condemnation also of every terrorist action committed recently in the Holy Land. I must at the same time affirm that, unfortunately, in those places the dynamism of peace seems to have stopped. The building of a wall between the Israeli people and the Palestinians is seen by many as a new obstacle on the road toward peaceful coexistence. In effect, the Holy Land needs not walls but bridges! Without reconciliation of the souls, there cannot be peace."

In autumn 2003, Msgr. Jean-Baptiste Gourion was named auxiliary bishop of the Latin patriarch of Jerusalem for the pastoral care of the Hebrew-speaking Catholics in Israel. The Holy See named on May 15, 2004, Fr. Pierbattista Pizzaballa as the new custos of the Holy Land. He had studied modern Hebrew in Jerusalem at the Hebrew University and was general assistant to Msgr. Gourion. Some observers saw in both appointments a sign of good will toward Israel.

Minister for Foreign Affairs Silvan *Shalom was received by Pope John Paul II on December 11, 2003.

In June 2004 Cardinal Dionigi Tettamanzi, archbishop of Milan, was the first bishop ever to be received in the Knesset and delivered a speech.

Pope John Paul II died in 2005 and was replaced by Benedict XVI, the German-born Joseph Ratzinger. The new pope began his pontificate with a visit to the Roonstrasse Synagogue in Cologne, the oldest in northern Europe, and spoke out there against "new signs of antisemitism," thus following the line of his predecessor. In 2006 he visited Auschwitz.

BIBLIOGRAPHY: S.I. Minerbi, *L'Italie et la Palestine, 1914–1920* (1970); idem, *The Vatican and Zionism* (1990); A. Kreutz, *Vatican Policy on the Palestinian-Israeli Conflict, The Struggle for the Holy Land* (1990); S. Ferrari, *Vaticano e Israele dal secondo conflitto mondiale alla Guerra del Golfo* (1991); G. Rulli, *Lo Stato d'Israele* (1998); M. Mendes, *Le Vatican et Israël* (1990).

[Sergio Itzhak Minerbi (2nd ed.)]

°VATKE, WILHELM (1806–1882), German theologian and biblical scholar. Vatke taught biblical studies at the University of Berlin from 1830. His scholarly work was profoundly affected by G.W.F. *Hegel, whom Vatke considered as a "philosophical messiah." He published only a few books and of these the most important was the first, *Die biblische Theologie wissenschaftlich dargestellt* (vol. 1, pt. 1 only, 1835), a critical description of the biblical religion. This was the first attempt to approach the Bible from the viewpoint of historical evolution based on the philosophy of Hegel. Thus, he was the first to argue that the priestly sections in the Pentateuch originated in the final phase of biblical history, i.e., the Babylonian exile. The scholar E. Reuss of Strasbourg reached a similar conclusion the previous year, but did not publish his theory until 1881 (in his *Die Geschichte der heiligen Schriften des Allen Testaments*). Vatke's book was also overlooked for about 30 years, and it was not until the 1860s, with the publication of the works of K.H. *Graf and A. *Kuenen, that it was recognized. Vatke divided the history of biblical religion and cult into three main phases; the primitive phase, which is reflected in the books of Former Prophets and the earliest layers of the Pentateuch; the phase of moral consciousness, as expressed in the prophetic writings and in Deuteronomy; and the institutionalized-ritual phase, as reflected in the priestly sections of the Pentateuch. This conception became widely accepted toward the end of the 19th century, and was especially developed by J. *Wellhausen, and through his work became axiomatic in biblical studies for a long time. Wellhausen himself admitted that he was indebted to Vatke for "the most and the best" of his own work.

BIBLIOGRAPHY: H. Benecke, *W. Vatke in seinem Leben und seinen Schriften* (1883); T.K. Cheyne, *Founders of Old Testament Criticism* (1893), 131–42; R.C. Dentan, *Preface to Old Testament Theology* (1950), 16–18, 27; H.J. Kraus, *Geschichte der historisch-kritischen Erforschung des Allen Testaments* (1956), 178–82; L. Perlitt, *Vatke und Wellhausen* (1965).

[Menahem Haran]

VATRA DORNEI, town in Suceava province, N. Romania. Vatra Dornei was a way station on the trade route between Transylvania and Moldavia and was visited by Jewish merchants in the 14th and 15th centuries. Intensive Jewish settlement, however, did not begin until the late 17th century, when the city was still under Moldavian control. In 1774, under Austrian rule, census officials counted 45 Jews in the city. There were 494 Jews (12.4% of the total population) in 1880; 1,921 (12.3%) in 1910; and 1,737 (22.3%) in 1930. In 1908 the Austrian authorities expelled six Jews from the city, claiming that they did not contribute to its agricultural development. In the second half of the 19th century, Jewish hotel managers helped to develop Vatra Dornei as a therapeutic and vacation center. The Romanian annexation of Vatra Dornei in 1918 inaugurated a difficult period for the Jews. Riots were incited, one Jew was killed and Jewish homes were burned. From 1930 the city became the regional center for antisemitic activities. When the Goga-*Cuza regime assumed power in 1938, the Jewish situation became critical. In its religious life, the Jewish community was associated with that of Campulung, the previous capital of the region. In 1896 the Vatra Dornei community became independent. A large synagogue was built at the start of the 20th century. Vishnitz (*Vizhnitsa) Ḥasidim maintained a prayer house and had considerable influence in the community. Zionist organizations were founded in the city in 1900 and later organized a private elementary school associated with the government school. In 1941 the Jews of the region were concentrated in a ghetto in Vatra Dornei, and in October of that year they were deported to camps in *Transnistria. After 2,029 Jews were moved from the city, only 21 remained. About 1,500 Jews lived in the city in 1947, including refugees from areas annexed to the Soviet Union. Subsequent emigration to Israel and other countries depleted the Jewish population.

BIBLIOGRAPHY: H. Gold (ed.), *Geschichte der Juden in der Bukowina*, 2 (1962), 82–84.

[Yehouda Marton]

VAUGHAN, FRANKIE (1928–1999), English entertainer. Born Frank Fruim Abelson in Liverpool, he trained as a commercial artist before entering show business in 1952. He became one of Britain's most popular and successful entertainers and, as a singer and actor, appeared in cabaret, films (such as *These Dangerous Years*, 1957), and television programs. Vaughan supported Jewish causes, and worked mainly for boys' clubs. Known as "Mr. Moonlight," he made many hit records in the 1950s, such as *The Green Door.*

ADD. BIBLIOGRAPHY: ODNB online.

°**VAUX, ROLAND DE** (1903–1971), biblical scholar and archaeologist. Born in Paris, he became a member of the Dominican Order in 1929. From 1945 to 1965 De Vaux served as director of the Ecole Biblique et Archéologique Française in Jerusalem, where he was professor of Palestinian archaeology from 1934. From 1938 to 1953 he was the editor of the *Revue Biblique*, in which he has written most of his articles, and from 1947 on he was editor in chief of the *Bible de Jérusalem.* Having played one of the leading roles in the Qumran discoveries, he was also the editor in chief of *Discoveries in the Judaean Desert* (1955–). De Vaux began his archaeological career at Maʿin (biblical BethBaal-Meon) in 1937 and successively carried out excavations at Abu-Gosh (1944); Tell el Farʿah (1946–1960), which he identified with biblical *Tirzah; Qumran and ʿAin Feshkha (1949–58); Murabbaʿat (1952); and Jerusalem (1961–63).

In his books as well as in his articles, he always sought to combine the rigorous use of the "internal criticism" of the biblical traditions together with the criticism of the "external evidence of the Bible." Thus, for him, as a biblical scholar, archaeology is primarily a tool of biblical investigation and will, occasionally, bring an "external confirmation" to the traditions recorded in the written sources. But as an independent discipline, archaeology purports only to study the material remains of the past, and its results do not always have a direct bearing on the Bible. His major work, *Ancient Israel: Its Life and Institutions* (trans. from French, 2 vols. 1961, 1965), is a good illustration of this methodology.

His books include: *Les Fouilles à Qaryet el-ʿEnab Abu-Gosh* (with M. Stève, 1950); *L'Archéologie et les Manuscrits de la Mer Morte* (1961); *Die hebraeischen Patriarchen und die modernen Entdeckungen* (1959; first appeared in French in *Revue Biblique*, vols. 53, 55, 56); *Studies in Old Testament Sacrifice* (1964); and *Bible et Orient* (1967). The first volume of his *Histoire ancienne d'Israël* (*Des origines à l'installation en Canaan*) was published posthumously along with the first five chapters of the uncompleted second volume (*La période des juges*).

[Jean Ouellette]

VAV (**Waw;** Heb. וָו;ו), the sixth letter in the Hebrew alphabet; its numerical value is therefore 6. In the mid-second millennium B.C.E. proto-Sinaitic inscriptions the letter resembled a mace or a peg (= *vav)* ꝭ. Later the circular top opened and in the tenth century B.C.E., the letter had two variants: the Y-shaped *vav* Y and the 4-shaped one 𐤅. While the first form was accepted in the Hebrew script and was written Y → 𐤅 → 𐤅 → 𐤅 (Samaritan 𐤅), the Phoenician and the Aramaic scripts adapted the 4-shaped *vav*. In the Phoenician script it developed 𐤅 → 𐤅 → 𐤅, and in the Aramaic – 𐤅 → 𐤅 → 𐤅 → 𐤅. The Nabatean *vav* closed its top and hence the Arabic و evolved. The Jewish *vav* ו → ו basically preserved the Aramaic shape of the letter.

The old Phoenician *waw* is the ancestor of some Latin letters: the consonant "*F*", which developed from the Archaic Greek *digamma;* "*Y*" (the Greek vowel (*upsilon*), which is the first of the five letters added by the Greeks to their alphabet and which the Romans turned into "*U*" and "*V*". See *Alphabet, Hebrew.

[Joseph Naveh]

VÁZSONYI, VILMOS (1868–1926), Hungarian lawyer and politician who was the first Jew in Hungary to become minister of justice. When a law student in Budapest, Vázsonyi joined the extreme nationalist group which protested against the submerging of the Magyar nationality in the combined Austro-Hungarian army. He founded the club of Junior Democrats in Budapest of which he was lifelong chairman. This club was devoted to improving the living conditions of the petit bourgeoisie whom the socialists had previously ignored. In 1894 Vázsonyi was elected to the Budapest municipal council. He collaborated with the mayor István Bárczy in fighting municipal corruption and the result of his efforts was the transfer of transport and other public utilities from private ownership to city management. Vázsonyi was elected deputy to the lower house of the Hungarian Parliament in 1901 and continued his fight against graft in public life. During World War I, he became minister of justice and was made a privy counselor, but he retired from public life when his scheme to extend the franchise was rejected; later he went into exile. He returned to Hungary during Count Bethlen's counterrevolutionary regime of terror (1921–31) and helped to expose the counterfeiting of French banknotes which influential political circles had arranged for as part of their foreign policy. In his youth Vázsonyi fought for equal rights for the Jewish religious community in Hungary. His writings were published posthumously *Vázsonyi Vilmos beszédei és írásai*, 2 vols. (1927). His son, JÁNOS (1895–1944), continued his fight in Parliament against anti-Jewish discrimination at a time of growing Hungarian Nazism.

BIBLIOGRAPHY: V. Vázsonyi, *Az én uram* (1932).

[Josef J. Lador-Lederer]

VECINHO, JOSEPH (end of 15th century), scientist and physician to King John II of Portugal (1481–95). A pupil of Abraham *Zacuto, he translated his teacher's tables into Spanish, and his translation, *Almanach Perpetuum*, published in Leiria in 1496 by Samuel d'Ortas, a Jew, became the basis for the Hebrew version of Zacuto's work. Along with the voyager and cosmographer Martin Behaim and the then court physician Rodrigo, he participated in a commission on navigation, concerned especially with improving the techniques for establishing direction and location at sea. Through his improvements in the nautical astrolabe, Vecinho gave a boost to Portuguese maritime activity. Vecinho sat on the commission when it rejected Columbus' request for a westward journey to the Indies on the grounds that it was a chimera. However Vecinho gave Columbus a copy of his translation of Zacuto's tables, which the discoverer found useful and carried with him.

BIBLIOGRAPHY: M. Kayserling, *Geschichte der Juden in Portugal* (1867), 86, 123; idem, *Christopher Columbus and the Participation of the Jews in the Spanish and Portuguese Discoveries* (1907), index; C. Roth, in: JQR, 27 (1936), 233–6; C. Singer, in: *Legacy of Israel* (1927), 242–3.

[Martin A. Cohen]

VEGETABLES. A distinction must be made between the two kinds of vegetables which the Mishnah calls respectively "garden vegetables" and "field vegetables," i.e., that grow wild in the field. Field vegetables were gathered from earliest times as is reflected in the curse upon Adam and Eve, "And thou shalt eat the herb of the field" (Gen. 3:18). A large number of field vegetables grow in Ereẓ Israel, particularly in the winter, and some are tasty and nutritious. There is a probable reference to them in Proverbs 15:17, "Better is a dinner of herbs where love is, than a stalled ox and hatred therewith." *Mallow leaves, *orach, and species of *maror were consumed by the indigent, and in times of famine they wandered about in search of wild vegetables such as *rocket. There must also have been many other varieties. The growing of garden vegetables developed from the wild variety, and there is no doubt that their cultivation dates from ancient times, both in Israel and neighboring countries, particularly Egypt and Babylon, which are rich in water (Deut. 11:10). In Israel, too, there were many gardens which received their water from wells, springs, and rivers by means of pumps (see *Agricultural Methods and Implements in Ancient Ereẓ Israel).

Vegetables were also served at royal tables; Ahab coveted Naboth's vineyard, "that I may have it for a garden of vegetables" (I Kings 21:2). Seasonal vegetables were served at royal tables all the year round; the Midrash states of Solomon's household that it was supplied with *beet (*teradin*) in the summer and with "chate *melons" (*kishu'in*; the *Cucumis melon var chate*) in the winter (Deut. R. 1:5). Similarly, it is related of the emperor Antoninus and Judah ha-Nasi, "that *lettuce, chate melon, and *radish were not absent from their tables either summer or winter" (Av. Zar. 11a). Vegetables in season were abundant and cheap. Opinions differed on the nutritional value of vegetables. Generally speaking, cooked vegetables were valued, although people were apprehensive about eating them raw (see Ber. 44b). Five garden vegetables are mentioned in one verse among the foods eaten by the Israelites in Egypt for which they yearned in the wilderness (Num. 11:5), these being chate melon, watermelon, *leek, *onion, and *garlic. In rabbinical literature, scores of species of garden and field vegetables are mentioned, and in addition to those on which separate articles appear, the following are important.

Artichoke

Called in the Mishnah *kinras*, it is the *Cynara scolymus*; a very similar species grows wild in Israel and several *halakhot* discuss this vegetable (Kil. 5:8; Uk. 1:6). The word *dardar* in the verse, "Thorns also and *dardar* ['thistles'] shall it bring forth to thee; and thou shalt eat the herb of the field," was explained to mean "artichokes," because it consists of rows (*darim*) upon rows (Gen. R. 20:10), referring to the leaves of the edible inflorescence.

Celery and Parsley

The *karpas* of rabbinical literature has been identified with celery – *Apium graveolens* – which grows wild in Israel in damp localities. Apparently it is the wild species which is called *karpas she-ba-neharot* ("celery of the rivers"; Shev. 9:1), which the Jerusalem Talmud (Shev. 9:1, 38c) identifies with *petrosilinon* – parsley. According to another view, "the graft of fennel with celery produces *petrosilinon*" (TJ, Kil. 1:4, 27a). These three plants belong to the family Umbelliferae and are alike in appearance also and slightly similar in taste. It should be noted that Ashkenazi Jews use parsley instead of celery for the *seder* of Passover.

Colocasia

The *Colocasia antiquorum*, whose large tuber is rich in starch, in rabbinical literature is called *kolkasyah* (TJ, Shev. 2:10, 34b) or *kolkas* (*ibid.*, Pe'ah 1:5, 16c). It appears to have been recently introduced into Ereẓ Israel in the time of the Mishnah and the question of its liability to tithing is discussed (Pe'ah, *ibid.*). The Mishnah calls it *karkas* (Ma'as. 5:8). Ginger lily (Black cola) – *Arum palaestinum* – belongs to the same family. It is often mentioned in rabbinical literature where it is called *luf.* Its leaves and tuber were eaten after cooking to remove its bitter taste, and it was highly regarded. There are many references to the methods of growing and preserving it (v. Kil 2:5; Shev. 5:2 and 4). It grows wild in Israel and to the present day is eaten by Oriental Jews. Wild ginger – *Arum dioscoridis* – called *lof ha-shotah* also grows in Israel, its leaves being used for human consumption and its tubers for animal fodder (Shev. 7:1–2).

Cress

Two species of cress are mentioned in the Mishnah. *Shiḥlayim*, garden cress – *Lepidium latifolium* – grew wild by the banks of rivers. Its pungent leaves were "sweetened" with salt or vinegar (Uk. 3:4). Purslane, the *Portulaca oleracea*, is a wild vegetable common during summer in gardens and fields. Its fleshy leaves are eaten raw as a salad or cooked. It is referred to in the Mishnah under two names, *ḥalaglogot* (Shev. 9:1) and *regelah* (Shev. 7:1, 9:5), and in the Talmud is called *porpeḥinah* (Meg. 18a). The Aramaic name *porpeḥinah* was current in the second century, and an interesting fact is recorded in connection with it. The rabbis did not know to what the Hebrew name *ḥalaglogot* referred until they learned from a maidservant of Judah ha-Nasi's household, where Hebrew was spoken, that it was *porpeḥinah* – purslane (*ibid.*).

Turnip and Rape

The turnip, *Brassica rapa*, called in the Mishnah *lefet*, was a common kitchen vegetable. It was eaten raw, cooked or ground (TJ, Ter. 2:3, 41c), and "improves with long cooking" (TJ, Ber.

6:1, 10a). It was mainly the food of the poor, and hence the statement. "Woe to the house where the turnip is common." It was used to improve the flavor of meat (Ber. 44b). Rape, *Brassica napus*, in Hebrew *nafos* or *nafoẓ*, is very similar to the turnip in shape and flavor. They were therefore not regarded as mixed species (Kil. 1:3; see *Mixed Species), whereas radish and rape, alike in shape but different in flavor, were regarded as different species (TJ, Kil 1:5, 27a; but see Maim. Yad, Zera'im 3:6).

BIBLIOGRAPHY: Loew. Flora, passim; Krauss, Tal Arch, 1 (1910), 116f.; J. Feliks, *Olam ha-Ẓome'aḥ ha-Mikra'i* (1968^2), 164–203; idem, *Ha-Ḥakla'ut be- Ereẓ Yisrael bi-Tekufat ha-Mishnah ve-haTalmud* (1963), 300–12; idem, *Kilei Zera'im ve-Harkavah* (1967), 44–88. **ADD. BIBLIOGRAPHY:** Feliks, Ha-Ẓome'aḥ, 62, 90, 94, 95, 98, 103, 141, 149.

[Jehuda Feliks]

VEIGELSBERG, LEO (1846–1907), Hungarian journalist. Born in Nagyboldogasszony, Veigelsberg studied medicine in Vienna, became a teacher in Hungary and contributed essays to the Prague newspaper, *Politik*. Later he joined the *Neuer Freier Lloyd*, then the *Neues Pester Journal*, and from 1872 was editor (later editor in chief) of the *Pester Lloyd*, the semiofficial newspaper of the Hungarian government. Veigelsberg's witty and well-informed articles became popular in the new Hungarian press of which he, and other Jewish journalists, were the founders. He died by his own hand.

VEIL, covering for the face. In the Bible there are several terms usually translated as veil. However, the exact connotation for these terms is not known, and they may refer to other garments used to cover the face as well. The term צָעִיף is used of Rebecca (Gen. 24:65) and Tamar (Gen. 38:14, 19). Other terms used in the Bible for veil – though the meaning is not always certain – are צַמָּה (Isa. 47:2; Song 4:1, 3; 6:7); רְדִיד (Isa. 3:23; Song 5:7) and רְעָלָה (Isa. 3:19); cf. Shab. 6:6, where Arab women are said to go out רְעוּלוֹת (veiled), which implies that Jewish women did not. The מַסְוֶה worn by Moses after descending from Mt. Sinai to screen his radiant face (Ex. 34:29–35) was some kind of mask; the leper had to cover his upper lip (Lev. 13:45), by pulling his head-cover over his face (cf. MK 24a).

The Talmud has no Hebrew word for veil except the Aramaic בייכא or בייבא (BB 146a) and the Persian-Arabic פדאמי or פרמי (Shab. 66b). The word הינומא (Ket. 2:1, and 17b; TJ, *ibid.* 26a; cf. the Greek ὑμέαιος) describes the bridal litter (see M. Petuchowski's note in Baneth-Hoffmann etc. *Mishnayot*, 3 (1933), 100f.), but is interpreted by Rashi as "a veil over her (the bride's) head, let down over her eyes, as is customary in our region"; see also *Ḥushi'el of Kairouan, who lived before Rashi (JOR, 11 (1898–99), 649). This custom for the bride to veil her face or, as it is done now, for the groom or the rabbi to cover her face before the marriage ceremony ("*bedecken*," see *Marriage), goes back at least to the early Middle Ages. In 15th-century Rhineland bridal veils were part of the groom's presents to his bride (*sivlonot*). In the late 17th and 18th centuries communal regulations (*takkanot*) forbade women to wear veils of gold or spun gold with gold or pearls or even braided (Metz, 1692), to visit the synagogues unveiled (Metz, 1697), or betrothed girls to appear in public without their faces covered (Amsterdam, 1747). In Muslim countries Jewesses had sometimes to wear distinctive veils, but Tunisian Jewish brides wore gold-embroidered veils in the 19th century. In certain ḥasidic circles brides have their faces completely wrapped and covered.

BIBLIOGRAPHY: Krauss, Tal Arch, 1 (1910), 189, 196; idem, *Kadmoniyyot ha-Talmud*, 2 pt. 2 (1945), 265f.; I. Abrahams, *Jewish Life in the Middle Ages* (1932^2), 108, 304; A. Rubens, *History of Jewish Costume* (1967), index; L.M. Epstein, *Sex Laws and Customs in Judaism* (1948), index.

VEIL, LEWIS (Daniel) COMPIÉGNE DE (1637–?), convert and Hebraist. Veil was the son of a Metz scholar. With his brother Charles-Marie (1630–1685), he was baptized in 1665. Under Colbert, Louis XIV's minister of finance, he translated into French Maimonides' *Mishneh Torah*, part of which was published in Paris (1678), and he also translated into Latin Abraham *Jagel's Hebrew catechism (London, 1679). He became a Protestant, immigrated to England, and continued to translate Maimonides. His patron, Viscount Hyde, procured for him various payments from Charles II's secret services accounts (1679–81); the assumption that he was a spy appears unfounded, since these accounts were often used for purposes unconnected with espionage. His son was Sir Thomas de Veil (1684–1746), who became well known as a Bow Street magistrate.

BIBLIOGRAPHY: Roth, Mag Bibl, 154, 329, 330, 428; Roth, England, 178; Levy, in; JHSEM, 4 (1942), 71–74; E.B. Weill, *Weil-De Veil, a Genealogy, 1360–1956* (1957).

[Vivian David Lipman]

VEIL, SIMONE (née **Jacob**; 1927–), French politician. Veil, the daughter of architect André Jacob, was born in Nice. Deported by the Nazis to Auschwitz – where all the members of her family perished – and Bergen-Belsen from March 1944 to May 1945, she survived, and resumed her studies and married Antoine Veil in 1946 on her return to France after World War II. She graduated in law and received the diploma of the Institute of Political Studies in Paris. She was appointed a magistrate in 1956. She was attaché titulaire to the Ministry of Justice (1957–59) and substitute detaché to the ministry (1954–65). Her first political steps came in 1969 when she joined the cabinet of René Pleven. Minister of Justice Veil represented France at the International Society of Criminology in 1959 and devoted herself to the reform of the laws concerning adoption, handicapped adults, and parental authority, and in conjunction with Professor Launay and Dr. Soule published *L'Adoption, données médicales, psychologiques et sociales.* She was appointed technical counselor in the cabinet of President René Pleven and was placed in charge of press relations, problems of civil law, and the judiciary. In 1970 she was appointed secretary to the Superior Council of the Magistracy. She is a chevalier of the National Order of Merit, and a member of the

Council of the French ORT and of the Fondation de France. She served as minister of health in the cabinet of Jacques Chirac (1974–76), minister of health and social security in the cabinet of Raymond Barre (1976–79), and state minister in charge of social affairs, health and life in towns in the cabinet of Edouard Balladur (1993–95). In her capacity of minister of health, she initiated the law legalizing abortion in France. Her courage and dignity during that period gained her immense popularity in the country, far beyond the limits of her political camp. In July 1979 she resigned from the cabinet to devote herself to the European Parliament which she entered on a centrist list; she was elected its president on July 17. She served as president of the parliament for three years (1979–82) and was a regular member until 1993. In March 1980 she was awarded the Athenae Prize of $100,000 from the Aristotle Onassis Fund for her contribution to the rapprochement of peoples and the respect of human dignity. Her husband was appointed director general of Air Transport of France in 1971.

Continuously active in organizations of former deportees and Shoah survivors, Veil enjoyed widespread respect in the field of World War II memorialization. In 2000, she was appointed the first president of the newly created Fondation pour la Mémoire de la Shoah.

BIBLIOGRAPHY: M. Sarazin, *Une femme Simone Veil* (1987); M. Szafran, *Simone Veil: un destin* (1999); J.N. Jeanneney et al., *Les femmes dans l'histoire* (2005).

[Nelly Hansson (2nd ed.)]

VEINBERG (Weinberg), MOISSEY SAMUILOVICH (1919–1996) composer. Veinberg was born in Warsaw, where he studied piano at the conservatory and graduated in 1939. Soon after, he was forced to flee the oncoming German invasion to Minsk, where he studied composition at the Belorussian conservatory. In 1941, with the outbreak of the German Soviet war, he was evacuated to Tashkent. There he met the pianist Emil *Gilels, who became interested in him and performed his second piano sonata (1942) and his piano quintet with the Quartet of the Moscow Bolshoi Theater (1945). In 1943 Veinberg settled in Moscow. His marriage to the daughter of the actor *Mikhoels, a victim of Stalin's anti-Jewish purge, led to his temporary arrest; he was released through the intervention of Shostakovich. His compositions range over many media and are marked by deep emotion and dramatic expression. They include operas: *Passazhirka* ("The Passenger," 1967–68), *Madonna and the Soldier* (1970), *Lyubov' D'Artanyana* ("D'Artagnan in Love," 1972), *Congratulations* (after S. Aleichem, 1975), *Lady Magnesia* (after G.B. Shaw, *Passion, Poison and Petrification, or the Fatal Gazogene*), *The Portrait* (1980), and *The Idiot* (1986); a ballet, *The Little Golden Key* (1962); 25 symphonies written between 1942 and 1992; and many other orchestral works, including instrumental concertos; 18 piano sonatas; over 100 romances; and incidental music.

ADD. BIBLIOGRAPHY: NG²; A. Nikolayev: "*O tvorchestve M. Vaynberga*," in: *Sovetskaya muzyka*, 1 (1960), 40–47; L. Nikitina: *Simfonii M. Vaynberga* (1972); M. Weinberg: "*Chestnost', pravdivost', polnaya otdacha*," in: Sovetskaya muzyka, 9 (1988), 32–36.

[Michael Goldstein / Marina Rizarev (2nd ed.)]

VEINER, HARRY (1904–1991), Canadian farmer, rancher, mayor. Veiner was born in Dysart, Saskatchewan, into a family of Jewish immigrant farmers. In 1930 he moved to Medicine Hat, Alberta, where he opened a retail hardware business. Soon a prominent local businessman, Veiner expanded his holdings by successfully investing in a series of ranches and farms in southern Alberta. With the outbreak of World War II, Veiner enlisted in the South Alberta Regiment. He rose to the rank of lieutenant colonel and was responsible for overseeing the logistics of prisoner-of-war camps in Canada. He was repeatedly elected mayor of Medicine Hat from 1952 to 1966 and again from 1968 to 1974. With 20 years in public office, he became the second longest-serving mayor of the city.

Regarded as one of Canada's most colorful small-town mayors and a tireless municipal booster, Veiner was something of a local folk hero with articles written about him in *Time*, *Life*, and *Maclean's* magazines and appearances on radio and television. Athletic and competitive, Veiner entered and won numerous competitions at fairs and rodeos and enjoyed challenging other mayors and officials to compete against him in skating, boxing, and racing.

Veiner's wife, Fanny, served as president of the local Hadassah and was involved with Youth Aliyah. Veiner visited Israel several times and was proud to have met the prime minister and other government officials. He was prominent in the sale of Israeli bonds in Alberta and, at the request of the agriculture department of the Hebrew University, he arranged for a shipment of sheep to be sent to Israel for research. Dedicated to communal service as well as Zionist ideals, Veiner was active in both the Medicine Hat Rotary Club and B'nai B'rith and participated in many fundraising events. In memory of his mother, in 1982 he donated 26 hectares of land valued at $1.1 million to build a branch campus of Medicine Hat College in Brooks.

[Aliza Craimer (2nd ed.)]

VEINGER, MORDECAI (**Mordkhe**; 1890–1929), Yiddish linguist. Born in Poltava and educated at the University of Warsaw, Veinger's first publications appeared before World War I, during which he served in the Russian army. In 1925 he became director of Yiddish linguistic research at the Institute for Jewish Culture of the Belorussian Academy of Sciences in Minsk. Veinger published studies that spanned syntax, historical phonology, ethnographic methodology, and dialectology, notably his *Yidishe Dialektologye* ("Yiddish Dialectology," 1929). He was the first Yiddish linguist to demonstrate variation in the realization of a phonological feature for a single speaker and for a given geographic location (*Tsaytshrift*, 2–3 (1928), 619–32). He was the proponent of a radical reform of Yiddish spelling, partly implemented in the official Soviet Yiddish orthography. His main achievement was the *Yidisher*

Shprakhatlas fun Sovetn-Farband ("Yiddish Language Atlas of the Soviet Union," 1931), published after his suicide by Leyzer Vilenkin.

BIBLIOGRAPHY: Rejzen, Leksikon, 1 (1926), 945–7; LNYL, 3 (1960), 356–8; M. Weinreich, in: *YIVO Bleter* 1 (1931), 81–4; A. Zaretski, in: *Di Yidishe Shprakh* 14 (1929), 3–13, 35–8; 16 (1929), 48; 17–18 (1929), 72. **ADD. BIBLIOGRAPHY:** R. Peltz, in: I. Kreindler (ed.), *Sociolinguistic Perspectives on Soviet National Languages* (1985), 277–309; B. Kagan, *Leksikon fun Yidish Shraybers* (1986), 238.

[Menahem Schmelzer / Rakhmiel Peltz (2nd ed.)]

VEIT, family of German bankers active also in politics and arts. JUDAH VEIT (SINGER; 1710–1786), the son and grandson of rabbis, settled in Berlin in 1738. He married the daughter of Hirsch David, a Potsdam textile manufacturer, and himself went into the textile business. In 1780 three of his five sons – SOLOMON VEIT (1751–1827), DAVID VEIT (1753–1835), and SIMON VEIT (1754–1819) – established the banking partnership Gebrueder Veit. The business was a small one, specializing in money market and securities arbitrage, but it enjoyed the highest reputation both in Germany and abroad. It existed for 150 years, until the depression of 1931 forced its liquidation, but it was not until 1927 that anyone outside the family was admitted into the partnership. The eldest of the three founders of the firm, Solomon, represented the Berlin association of Bankers and Merchants of the Jewish Religion within the United Stock Exchange Corporation in 1803. He was a city councilor from 1809 to 1822, and an elder of the Jewish community. Simon married Moses *Mendelssohn 's daughter, Dorothea, but they were divorced. An older brother, JOSEPH (1745–1831), who worked as a clerk in the family enterprise, contributed German translations from the Bible to the Mendelssohn-inspired periodical, *Ha-Me'assef. Simon's sons, JOHANNES (1790–1854) and PHILIPP (1793–1877), both of whom were baptized, were artists of the Nazarene school, specializing in religious paintings and portraits. Another PHILIPP, the son of Joseph, looked after the Berlin interests of the brothers Joseph and Abraham Mendelssohn while they were residents of Hamburg between 1804 and 1811. In this same generation, one of Judah Veit's (Singer) grandsons, Moritz *Veit (1808–1864), was a publisher, liberal politician, and prominent communal leader. Three generations of Veit descendants served as board members and presidents of the Lehranstalt fuer die Wissenschaft des Judentums.

BIBLIOGRAPHY: T. Zondek, in: BLBI, 4 (1961), 171–220, index; S. Wenzel, *Juedische Buerger und kommunale Selbstverwaltung in preussischen Staedten 1808–1848* (1967), index; E. Hamburger, in: YLBI, 9 (1964), index; idem, *Juden im oeffentlichen Leben Deutschlands* (1968), index.

[Hanns G. Reisnner]

VEIT, MORITZ (1808–1864), German publisher, politician, and Jewish leader. A member of the wealthy Veit family of Berlin, Moritz studied philosophy, history, and philology at the University of Berlin (1825–32) and earned his doctorate at Jena in 1833. At the same time he wrote poetry and edited a literary journal, *Berliner Musenalmanach* (1831–31). In the publishing house he set up in 1834, his authors included L. von Ranke, J.G. Fichte, A. von Chamisso, and F.K. von Savigny. He was chairman of the German publishers' organization (Boersenverein) from 1853 to 1861. Veit also played an active part in public life. In 1847 he opposed the proposed Jewry Law which attempted to organize Prussian Jewry according to the corporatist-medieval ideas of King *Frederick William IV. He was elected to the 1848 Frankfurt Parliament, and after the revolution he was again one of the few Jewish representatives in the first chamber of the Prussian Parliament (1851); later, as a member of the Prussian House of Representatives (1858–61), he again raised his voice against attempts to infringe on Jewish rights. He was a member of the Berlin municipal council for 20 years. An elder of the Berlin Jewish community (1839–48), he was later chairman of its council. He was instrumental in the appointment of his close friend, Michael *Sachs, to the Berlin rabbinate, developed communal schools and institutions, and drafted the 1860 statutes of the community.

BIBLIOGRAPHY: L. Geiger (ed.), *Michael Sachs und Moritz Veit, Briefwechsel* (1897); idem, in: MGWJ, 52 (1908), 513–39; idem, in: JJGL, 13 (1910), 129–58; idem, in: ADB; E. Hamburger, in: YLBI, 9 (1964), 207, 208, 219, 224. **ADD. BIBLIOGRAPHY:** W. Wehrenpfennig, *Moritz Veit* (1870); L. Geiger, in: *Die Deutsche Literatur und die Juden* (1910), 182–211.

[Ed. / Archiv Bibliographia Juadaica (2nd ed.)]

VEITH, JOHANN EMANUEL (1787–1876), writer, apostate Roman Catholic priest in Vienna. A native of *Chodova Plana (Kuttenplan), Bohemia, Veith received a medical degree in Vienna (1812), was baptized (1816), and became professor at the Veterinary School and its director (1819). At the time he came under the influence of the Catholic romantic philosopher Clemens Maria Hofbauer (1751–1820). Veith was ordained to the priesthood in 1821 and later played an important role in the Catholic revival. He became a popular preacher at St. Stephen's Cathedral (1832–45), and his sermons were often published. During the 1848 March revolution he founded the *Wiener Katholikenverein*, which edited a paper called *Aufwaerts. Ein Volksblatt fuer Glauben, Freiheit und Gesittung*. At the time of the *Damascus affair (1840), he publicly took an oath on the crucifix that there was no truth whatsoever in the *blood libel. This oath was much referred to in the apologetic literature of the 19th century. In the antisemitic propaganda of the 1880s, the truth of the incident was impugned; therefore, Ludwig August *Frankl secured a sworn deposition as to its veracity from Veith's baptized brother (1882); it appeared in *Die Neuzeit* (24 (1884), 441). Another brother, Joseph, was for many years secretary of the Vienna Jewish community and a contributor to *Kokhevei Yiẓḥak*.

BIBLIOGRAPHY: H.L. Strack, *Das Blut* (1911), 173–6; Goerlich, in: *Judaica*, 9 (Ger., 1953), 47–52; M. Grunwald, *Vienna* (1936), index; H. Tietze, *Die Juden Wiens* (1935), index; L. Loew, *Aron Chorin: eine biografische Skizze* (1863), 136–7; E. Baumgarten (ed.), *Die Blutbeschuldigung gegen die Juden* (1883), 28–29; C. von Wurzbach, *Biographisches*

Lexikon des Kaiserthums Oesterreich, 50 (1884), 81–95. **ADD. BIBLIOGRAPHY:** K. Honek, *Johann Emanuel Veith (1787–1876)...* (1984); Ch. Stanek and Ch. Mache, in: *Sudetendeutsche Familienforschung*, 9:4 (2004), 125–31.

[Meir Lamed]

VEKSLER, VLADIMIR (1907–1966), Soviet physicist. Born and educated in Moscow, Veksler specialized in the physics of X-rays, cosmic rays, and in high-energy accelerator theory. For his last ten years he was head of the High Energy Laboratory at the well-known Joint Institute for Nuclear Research at Dubna. He was a member of the U.S.S.R. Academy of Sciences. Veksler improved the performance of cyclotrons (the first atom-smashing machines), by showing how the speed of the "bullets" used to smash atoms could be increased by varying the magnetic field, or the frequency of the electrical surge. This led to the development of the synchrontons. In 1963, he shared with Edwin M. Millikan, who had suggested this independently, the United States Atoms for Peace Award of $75,000. He received the Lenin Prize in 1959 and contributed to the basic research for Sputnik I, the world's first man-made satellite launched in 1957.

BIBLIOGRAPHY: *Current Biography Yearbook, 1966* (1967), 39–41.

[Maurice Goldsmith]

VELIZH, city in Smolensk district, Russia. A *blood libel which stirred up Russian Jewry during the first decade of the reign of Nicholas I (1825–55) took place there. In 1817 the czar, Alexander I, issued an edict according to which Jews were not to be accused of the murder of Christians "merely upon the basis of the ancient tradition that they required Christian blood": in each particular case an investigation of the murder was to be conducted according to those rules which applied to an accused of another religion. Six years later a blood libel occurred in the district town of Velizh (then in the province of Vitebsk). In April 1823 the stabbed body of the three-year-old child Feodor, who had disappeared three days before from the house of his parents, was found near the town. Rumors were immediately spread through the town that the child had been assassinated by the Jews for their Passover requirements. A drunken prostitute, Maria Terentyeva, testified that on the day of his disappearance she had seen the child being led away by a Jewish woman. The local tribunal decided that although the investigation had not revealed any conclusive proof against the Jews who were suspected of the murder, it was nevertheless to be assumed that they had perpetrated it "out of their hostile attitude toward the Christians." The verdict was then referred to the provincial tribunal in Vitebsk, which decreed that the accused were to be acquitted of all suspicion and that the witness Terentyeva was to receive an ecclesiastic penalty for the sin of "leading a life of prostitution." The tribunal also ordered a new investigation into the murder. but it did not produce any results.

Nevertheless, groups of antisemites in the town, who were headed by several Uniate clergymen and were supported by the chief governor of Belorussia, Count Khovanski, continued to stir up the blood libel. In the autumn of 1825, when Alexander I passed through the town, Terentyeva submitted a complaint to him against the local authorities, who had not brought the murderers of her son [sic], the child Feodor, to justice. Ignoring his edict of 1817, the czar ordered the chief governor Khovanski to reopen the investigation. One of Khovanski's officials, Strakhov, was sent to Velizh for this purpose. Terentyeva was arrested, and on this occasion she related that she herself had brought the child to the houses of the Jews, Zeitlin and Berlin, and had been present in the synagogue when he was put to death after having undergone much torture. His blood was then poured into barrels which were transported to Vitebsk and Liozno. Two Christian maids who, according to her words, had participated in these acts were arrested and also "interrogated." On the strength of their evidence over 40 of the Jews of the town were arrested. In August 1826 it was decreed (from above) that all the Velizh synagogues were to be closed because "the Jews abused the tolerance which was shown to their religion." The investigators then began to search for proof of the actual existence of a custom among the Jews to murder Christian children. They collected material and testimonies which had been deposited on the occasion of previous blood libels in Poland and Russia; they found several apostates, one of whom – Grodzinski – brought a Hebrew manuscript before the commission of inquiry which, according to his words, described the ceremony that accompanied the execution of Christian children. At the same time, Terentyeva and the Christian maids testified that they had also participated in the murders of other Christian children.

The czar himself, who received reports on the progress of the investigation, then began to doubt the truth of the charge. He ordered an inquiry to determine who the other children were who had been murdered ("It can easily be clarified whether or not a despicable lie is present"). It rapidly became obvious that there was no foundation to the new libel and that the manuscript which was "discovered" by Grodzinski dealt with the ritual slaughter of animals and poultry. Grodzinski was ordered by the court to serve in the military, and in 1830 the investigation was handed over to the Senate. In the Senate there were divergences of opinion as to the actual accusation which was brought against the Jews and the guilt of the Jews who had been arrested. The deputy minister of justice, Panin, who was responsible for the analysis of the material concerning the accusation, declared that from a legal point of view there was no reason to accuse the Jews of Velizh and he called for their immediate release.

The first decision was then placed in the hands of the State Council. The Jews were defended by the head of the department for civil and religious affairs, Admiral N. Mordvinov, who, as the owner of estates in the surroundings of Velizh, was well acquainted with the Jews of the town and their way of life. In his memorandum to the State Council, Mordvinov declared that the trial of the Jews of Velizh was a premeditated conspiracy led by Count Khovanski, and that the testimony which had been deposited by Terentyeva and her colleagues had not been given of their own free will but "as a result of a powerful influence." In January 1835 the State Council ordered the release and exoneration of the accused Jews. Terentyeva and her colleagues were sentenced to exile in Siberia on the charge of libel. Mordvinov's proposal to indemnify the Jews for their sufferings was rejected. Four of the arrested died during their nine years of imprisonment.

The trial of Velizh revived the belief in ritual murder among the Christian masses. When he ratified the final verdict, Nicholas I himself commented that he was not convinced that the Jews had not committed the murder. In his opinion, "there are religious fanatics or sectarians among the Jews who required Christian blood for their ceremonies." Accordingly, the czar refused to renew the edict of 1817, and blood libels remained one of the instruments of agitation against the Jews until the abolition of the czarist regime (see also *Blood Libel).

In the 1880s the Jewish community had a synagogue, as well as seven houses of prayer. A state Jewish school was opened in 1883, and a private Jewish boys' school in the early 1900s. During the Soviet regime, the Jewish population dropped from 3,274 in 1926 to 1,788 in 1939.

In July of 1941 the Germans captured the city and relegated the Jews to a camp under a Judenrat. In November they sent 1,000 Jews from Velizh and its environs to a ghetto, which they torched in January of 1942, killing the hundreds who were inside and shooting anyone who tried to flee. Twenty managed to escape.

BIBLIOGRAPHY: Yu. Hessen, *Velizhskaya drama* (1906); Dubnow, Divrei, 9 (1958[6]), 113–6; R. Mahler, *Divrei Am Yisrael, Dorot Aḥaronim*, 2 bk. 1 (1970), 68–74. **ADD. BIBLIOGRAPHY:** Jewish Life, 1382.

[Yehuda Slutsky / Ruth Beloff (2nd ed.)]

VELTWYCK, GERARD (d. 1555), German Hebraist and apostate. Little is known of Veltwyck's origins or early life. He was for a time the envoy of Emperor Charles V in Constantinople, and the Marrano physician Amatus *Lusitanus, in his book *In Dioscoridis... de medics materia... enarrationes* (Strasbourg, 1554), mentions that Veltwyck supplied him with medicinal herbs from Turkey.

Veltwyck is mainly remembered for his violently anti-Jewish Hebrew polemical work entitled *Shevelei Tohu – Itinera deserti, de Judaicis disciplinis et earum vanitate* (Venice, 1539), printed by Daniel *Bomberg. The text, translated into Latin by Conrad *Pellicanus in 1545, forms part of the manuscript (now in Zurich, Zentralbibliothek Ms. Car. 1102) containing Pellicanus' copy of Guillaume *Postel's kabbalistic treatise *Or Nerot ha-Menorah* (*Candelabri typici... interpretatio*), which appeared in Venice in 1548. In his *Shevilei Tohu* – a mixture of verse and prose – Veltwyck revealed his hostility toward the Kabbalah, which he declared to be both devoid of authority and riddled with lies and fancies.

BIBLIOGRAPHY: Steinschneider, Cat Bod, 2701; M.G. Rosenberg, *Gerard Veltwyck, Orientalist, Theolog und Staatsmann* (1935); F. Secret, *Les kabbalistes chrétiens de la Renaissance* (1964), 249; idem, in *Bibliothèque d'Humanisme et Renaissance*, 26 (1964), 164; Baron, Social[2], 13 (1969), 180.

[Godfrey Edmond Silverman]

VENETIANER, LAJOS (1867–1922), Hungarian rabbi and historian. Venetianer, born in Kecskemet, attended the Jewish Theological Seminary in Breslau (1888–89) and was ordained at Budapest's Landesrabbinerschule. Venetianer became rabbi in Csurgo (1893), rabbi in Lugos three years later, and from 1897 to his death chief rabbi in Ujpest and professor at the Landesrabbinerschule.

A versatile scholar, he was interested in the history of religion, in the common elements in Roman Catholic liturgy and Judaism, and in Jewish literature and history. His profound knowledge of the Christian liturgy and his scholarship were evident in his publications in this field: *Ursprung und Bedeutung der Prophetenlectionen* (in: ZDMG, vol. 73, 1909) and *Juedisches im Christentum* (1913). He edited the publications of the first Jewish medical writers in linguistic and medical-historical respects: *Asaf Judaeus* (1–3, 1915–17), a work of pioneering importance despite the sharp criticism that Immanuel Loew leveled against it. On a more popular level, Venetianer wrote about the organization of Jewish communities, *A zsidóság szervezete az európai államokban* ("The Organization of Jewry in the European States," 1901), a unique work on the subject and about the history of the Hungarian Jews, tending toward the apologetic, *A magyar zsidóság története a honfoglalástól napjainkig* ("The History of Hungarian Jewry from the Beginning of Hungarian History to Our Days," 1922).

BIBLIOGRAPHY: S. Halpert, in: *Magyar Zsidó Szemle*, 40 (1923), 3–10; N. Katzburg, in: *Sinai*, 40 (1957), 174–6; K. Ödön, *Venetianer Lajos emlékezete* (1928).

[Alexander Scheiber]

VENEZIANI, EMMANUEL FELIX (1825–1889), French philanthropist, born in Leghorn (Italy). He became a director of the relief fund of *Baron de Hirsch and in 1877 traveled to the Balkans and Bulgaria where he organized relief for Jewish and gentile victims of the Russo-Turkish war. At the Congress of Berlin in 1878, Veneziani and Charles *Netter worked for religious liberty in the former Ottoman territories, and in 1880 he was similarly active at the Congress of Madrid on behalf of Moroccan Jewry. In 1882 he and Netter were sent by the *Alliance Israélite Universelle to help organize Jewish emigration from Russia. In 1883 Veneziani toured the Jewish settlements in Palestine. In conformity with Hirsch's views, he advised limiting Russian Jewish immigration there.

BIBLIOGRAPHY: *L'Univers Israélite* (Feb. 1889); Z. Kahn, *Souvenirs et Regrets* (1898), 278–83; I. Klausner, *Ha-Tenu'ah le-Ẓiyyon be-Rusyah*, 2 (1965), 71, 145, 225–7; A. Chouraqui, *L'Alliance Israélite Universelle...* (1965), index.

VENEZUELA (Span. **República Bolivariana de Venezuela**), republic in northern South America; general population:

24,000,000; Jewish population (2005), est. 15,500 (mainly in the cities of *Caracas, Valencia, Maracay, Maracaibo, Barquisimeto, San Cristóbal, and the Margarita Island).

Colonial Period

Venezuela was discovered by Columbus on his third voyage in 1498, when Columbus, after sailing round the island of Trinidad entered the Gulf of Paria and landed on the mainland without realizing that he was setting foot for the first time on the South American continent. Having observed the huge and powerful currents of fresh water flowing into the gulf, Columbus believed he was at the mouth of one of the four rivers of paradise and, fascinated by the pearl ornaments of the native population, concluded that he was at the doorstep of the Garden of Eden described in Genesis. He was really on the eastern coast of what is now Venezuela.

EARLY JEWISH PRESENCE. Three streams flowing from the same Iberian source shaped the character of the initial Jewish presence in Venezuela: that of Portuguese, Italian, and Dutch Sephardim.

Even though many Portuguese arrived in Venezuela in the years after its discovery and at that time Portuguese was considered a synonym for *Crypto-Jew, contrary to what happened in other lands of South America most of those who came to Venezuela were not of Jewish origin. Only the names of a few of those who arrived and lived in Caracas and Maracaibo between 1642 and 1649 have remained registered. Therefore, their presence must have been very limited. It is only in 1693 that we find the first Jewish establishment in Venezuelan territory, when a group of Leghorn Jews (Italians), who had fled from *Recife (Brazil) to *Suriname, and from there moved to *Curaçao, settled in an inlet neighboring Tucacas, a village on the western coast of the country. Unfortunately, this small community, which was known under the name of Santa Irmandade (Holy Fraternity), also disappeared leaving no traces or documents, not even a cemetery or any other mark. One has to wonder if the only way to survive in the Spanish dominions was to cover one's tracks so as not to be discovered or persecuted by the Inquisition. Yet, the actions of the Inquisition in Venezuela were more sporadic and picturesque than frightening. The judges and commissioners who were sent by Spain lacked jurisdiction and, as a result, their jobs consisted only of reporting acts that had been denounced and sending the suits along to Cartagena de Indias. In 1821 the government of Venezuela definitively abolished the Inquisition, decreeing that it was extinguished and that it never would be reestablished.

18TH CENTURY. After these brief incursions of Portuguese and Italian Jews, it fell upon Sephardi Dutch to provide leadership in the years that followed. At the beginning of the 18th century the economic conditions in Venezuela and the proximity of islands belonging to the Netherlands gave rise to a commerce which would result in a significant Jewish presence in Venezuela. Due to the monopoly imposed on the colonies by the Spanish government, foreign ships bearing illegal merchandise were rife along the Venezuelan coasts. Dutch schooners were seen very frequently and smuggling flourished between Tucacas and Curaçao. Dutch Jews, attracted by the possibility of trade between the Antilles and the continent, participated extensively in the large-scale interchange which evolved under the Dutch flag. A major factor in the boom that ensued was due to the compliance of the Dutch, the very authorities appointed by the Spanish Crown, the Spanish clergy, and even the slaves. At this time, Tucacas was the most active port that sprung up along the west coast and the largest market for products from overseas. From there cocoa, tobacco, indigo and hides were shipped and food, liquors, clothing, and metals received and an active slave trade developed. This commerce between the mainland and the Netherlands Islands spurred the insistent permanence of a small colony of Jews in Tucacas from 1708. There, despite the attacks and devastation they suffered periodically by the Spanish mayors in order to suppress smuggling, they erected 17 houses and the first synagogue on Venezuelan territory and stayed until 1720 when the synagogue and the homesteads were burned and destroyed by Pedro José de Olavarriaga and the inhabitants were obliged to move away.

Jewish communities in Venezuela, 2005.

Even though the only extant reference to this first synagogue had been a single communication (now lost) sent in 1720 by this congregation to the *parnassim* of Curaçao, the existence of the synagogue was subsequently confirmed when in the files of the West India Company in The Hague was found a letter sent in 1737 by one of the *parnassim* to his colleagues in Amsterdam, where he related that "despite Governor van Collen's hostilities toward the Jews, he recognized the significance of their commercial dealings with Venezuela where, according to him, they had incensed the Spanish by erecting a synagogue on the coast near Caracas."

In spite of the intense trading activities developed by the Jews along the Venezuelan coasts, the 18th century did not favor their permanent settlement in Venezuela. The ban on foreign and Jewish establishments in the Spanish colonies was widely enforced. With the exception of a few known cases, any dealings which were not purely commercial were strictly limited.

Initial Period of Independence

A Spanish colony for more than 300 years, Venezuela became one of the first Spanish South American colonies to declare its independence in the early 19th century. Since becoming a sovereign nation, Venezuela has undergone periodic episodes of civil conflict and dictatorship. Much of Venezuela's 19th- and early 20th-century history was characterized by periods of political instability, dictatorial rule, and revolutionary turbulence, with the military exerting a strong influence over politics.

19TH CENTURY. The year 1811 is that of the Venezuelan Declaration of Independence. Nevertheless, the Spanish forces confronted the patriots inflicting upon them great losses. Simón Bolívar, forced to flee to Curaçao, received there the enthusiastic support of Mordechai Ricardo (in commemoration of this event, the government of Venezuela issued a set of stamps in 1989). The Sephardim of Curaçao saw in Bolívar a hero who, inspired by ideals of equality, with no distinction of race or religion, would fight for the separation of Venezuela from the Spanish Crown. In so doing, he would re-open the doors of the Hispanic world to them. With the onset of the War of Independence, the Dutch Jews were the first to provide aid to the young republic, participating in the war effort by means of financial support. Benjamin and Samuel Henríquez were active officials in the army, and Juan Bartolomé de Sola participated in the famous Battle of Carabobo.

Between 1819 and 1825 many Jews abandoned the island of Curaçao and relocated in various regions of Venezuela and, while some of them established themselves in Puerto Cabello, Maracaibo, Barcelona, Valencia, and Caracas, most of them chose to settle in Coro, where their coreligionists had been living since as early as 1779. There, they began to demonstrate the characteristics which would distinguish them: a unitary spirit, hard work, and an intellectual ability hardly seen in this territory in those days. Besides these skills, the Jews who arrived in Coro carried with them the baggage of religious knowledge and Sephardi traditions that had been cultivated in Curaçao and which they wanted to preserve in their new homes. With this group, a fruitful period of planting roots began. This historical period started in 1829 with Joseph Curiel, and it was the origin of the Jewish social, political, cultural, and economic integration that spread through all of Venezuela. From that time on, Coro has been considered the cradle of the Venezuelan Jewish community.

Since the arrival of Jews in Coro, many of them made important contributions to the economy, science, and culture of the region. Prominent are the names of Joseph Curiel, dedicated to the cause of public health; David Curiel, who contributed largely to pharmaceutical science; his son José David Curiel, president of the Supreme Court of the State; and the important poets Elías David Curiel and Salomón López Fonseca; other residents, such as members of the Jesurun, Senior, Maduro, Capriles, Valencia, Pereira, de Sola, Henríquez, Hoheb, Abenatar, and Salcedo families were outstanding businessmen, doctors, and politicians. But, although the newcomers celebrated religious services in some houses, had a *mohel* and practiced circumcision, celebrated marriages according to the Jewish rite and buried their dead in the Jewish cemetery, they could not be termed as Jewish practitioners. We have to remember that in Venezuela the freedom of religion was accorded in 1834. With the passage of time and although separated by only a thin strip of ocean from the center of Jewish life that was Curaçao, the adherence to the ancestral tradition diminished. These Jews, and at a later date those of the younger generations who were born in the country, soon assimilated into Venezuelan culture.

By the middle of the 1860s, new forms of political relations and business began to develop in Venezuela. The Jews and the people from Curaçao who had settled in Venezuela understood the needs of the country. Given the proportion of the population they represented, they contributed a larger than expected share to the modernization efforts. The trading company of Jacobo Abraham Jesurum & Zoom expanded the commerce between La Guaira and Curaçao. In 1865 Jesurum established a shipping line between Curaçao, La Guaira, Puerto Cabello, St. Thomas, and Europe and signed a contract to construct the eastern railroad and to issue postage stamps for the mail service he provided. Jacobo Abraham Jesurum made several loans to the government, guaranteed by the revenues of the Coro customs office. In 1879, President Antonio Guzmán Blanco, who had cultivated in France the friendship of the banker Isaac Pereire, signed a contract with a son of Isaac to develop natural resources and several enterprises in Venezuela. By the last quarter of the century, a group of industrial managers with a modern mentality and contacts in the United States and Europe arose in the commercial sector. Among them were Manasés Capriles Ricardo, Tomás Chapman, Isaac A. Senior, Salomón López Fonseca, Julio César Capriles and Jacob M. Chumaceiro.

Before the end of the 19th century, a new wave of Sephardi immigration arrived in Venezuela. They were from northern Morocco. These immigrants settled mainly in the cities of Caracas, Barcelona, Carúpano, Cumaná, La Victoria, Villa de Cura, and Caucagua, and some of them went to places as distant as the uninhabited San Fernando de Apure and Ciudad Bolívar. The life of these people was hard at the beginning. Without capital or skills, they became traveling salesmen. Because of their dedication to commerce and trade, they spread out and no longer lived together as a community. Religious life did not exist because there was neither a synagogue nor rabbis. For many of them, this situation contributed to their forgetting their Jewish roots.

Immigration and Communal Organization

20TH CENTURY. By the year 1907, 230 Jews lived in the country. Through perseverance, sacrifice, and savings, those who had arrived at the end of the 19th century started opening commercial houses in prime locations in Caracas and initiated some manufacturing facilities. Gradually they began to prosper. The adoption of local customs was not an obstacle to narrow links of solidarity among themselves; the improvement of their economic situation helped them continue to maintain their faith and the bonds with the family they had left in Morocco. To satisfy the growing needs of the group, they founded in Caracas in 1907 a charitable society named "Sociedad Benéfica Israelita" which remained active until some time after 1909; they used to meet in private houses to pray and celebrate the holidays and in 1916 they inaugurated a cemetery. By 1917 the number of Jews had increased to 475. The National Census of 1926 recorded 882 Jews.

In the 1910s, under the dictatorship of General Juan Vicente Gómez and the boom of Venezuelan oil, Sephardi Jews from Eastern Europe, Yemen, Persia, Syria, and Lebanon arrived in Caracas. At the same time, Ashkenazi Jews coming from Central Europe crossed the Atlantic Ocean to reach Venezuelan shores. These new immigrants had left Europe under the most precarious conditions. They traveled third class on miserable ships to trade their poverty for the almost universal poverty of the rural country that Venezuela then was, and to find an older community of Moroccan origin, now mostly wealthy and well established. These newcomers had to live in houses where each family had a single room with kitchen and bathroom shared. After walking through neighborhoods and climbing steep hills to sell their merchandise for monthly payments, their greatest aspiration was to create their own commercial establishments. With nostalgia for the customs and traditions of their ancestors, they soon formed groups based on places of origin, and Poles, Russians, Hungarians, and Germans came together out of affinity to share memories. These affiliations served as a mutual support in time of need. In 1931 they established the Sociedad Israelita Ashkenazit and 12 years later the Centro Social y Cultural Israel. In 1936, aware of the need to unite forces and to create a congregation, both groups merged and in 1950 they gave birth to the Unión Israelita de Caracas (UIC). Other small Ashkenazi institutions were founded in Maracaibo (1941), Maracay (1944), and San Cristóbal (1945). During all these years the Ashkenazi groups used rented houses to celebrate religious services and organize social activities. It was not until 1961 that the UIC began the construction of its synagogue in Caracas.

Greatly devoted to religious tradition, the Moroccan Sephardi group that lived in Caracas founded in 1930 the Asociación Israelita de Venezuela (AIV), whose first objective was to build a synagogue and which has become since then the representative organization of the whole Sephardi community. The Synagogue El Conde (1939–54) and the Gran Sinagoga Tiferet Israel de Caracas built in the period 1956–63, as well as the group of new synagogues that developed during the last two decades of the 20th century, are an expression of the traditional deep-rooted religious feelings of this Jewry.

The Holocaust and the Subsequent Period

By the end of the 1930s, the Venezuelan government had imposed restriction on Jewish immigration. While during the Nazi regime some Caribbean countries closed their ports to the ships carrying human cargo that tried to escape the annihilation that extended in Europe in those years, in 1939 General Eleazar López Contreras, president of the Republic, had humanitarian feelings. At the initiative of the Comité Israelita Pro-refugiados, he granted permission to land to the passengers of the only two ships under the German flag that anchored at Puerto Cabello and La Guaira, the *Koenigstein* and the *Caribia*. Most of these refugees were intellectuals and educated professionals whose influence would be decisive in the subsequent development of the community and whose contribution to the country has been notable.

The 1940s were framed by the tragic events of World War II. The nucleus that gave rise to the Unión Israelita de Caracas together with the members of the Asociación Israelita de Venezuela showed their solidarity with their coreligionists who, escaping from the Holocaust, arrived in Venezuela in search of shelter. In their desire to help the refugees fleeing events that were developing in Europe, in 1941 a Jewish group from the Middle East and North Africa set up the Centro Benéfico Israelita. Starting in 1946 and continuing well into the 1950s, a new contingent of Askenazim, survivors of the Holocaust, bolstered the Venezuelan community.

During this same decade a succession of events contributed largely to strengthen and consolidate the future of communal life: the bases of the Consejo Central de Sociedades Israelitas de Venezuela (Central Council of Jewish Societies of Venezuela) were established; *Mundo Israelita*, a weekly newspaper, began its appearance in 1943; WIZO de Venezuela was constituted and the first copies of the magazines *Prensa Judía* (1944) and *Paz* (1946) were issued. The Colegio Moral y Luces Herzl-Bialik was founded in 1946, beginning its activities with a registration of 40 students.

Zionist youth movements were established by young Venezuelan Jews who, enthusiastic over the creation of the State of Israel, took names such as Grupo Universitario Scopus (1946), Grupo Juvenil Kadimah (1946), Javerim (1954), Ken Najshón del Hashomer Hatzair y Bnei Akiva (1955), Hanoar Hatzioni, and Young Israel.

Contemporary Period

With the death of the General Juan Vicente Gómez (1935) after 27 years of a strong-arm government, Venezuela adopted the constitutional system. The decisive political changes at the end of the "gomecismo" coincided with the beginning of the modernization of the country (the presidencies of Gral. Eleazar López Contreras (1936), General Isaías Medina Angarita (1941), Rómulo Betancourt (1945), Rómulo Gallegos (1948), and General Marcos Pérez Jiménez (1950)), and with the reaping of the benefits of oil.

For Venezuela, starting on the path of modernization, two of the ingredients necessary to accomplish it were at hand: the oil wealth that sprang spontaneously from the earth and the people's desire for transformation; the only missing component was the human factor. In this circumstance, the country opened its doors to immigration. Spaniards, Italians, and Portuguese arrived in waves as did Jews who had survived the European catastrophe. By 1950, the Jewish population had grown to about 5,000–6,000 persons. In 1958 the dictatorship of General Marcos Pérez Jiménez fell. During the period 1957–59 about 1,000 Jews from Egypt, Hungary, and Israel were admitted. Others came from South American countries, escaping from their political instability.

After the withdrawal of the military from direct involvement in national politics (1958), Venezuela started to enjoy an unbroken tradition of democratic civilian rule, though not always without conflict. The 1960s were deeply convulsive in political matters, giving rise to a mainly intellectual left. The 1970s were marked by the energy crisis in consequence of the revolution in Libya, the Yom Kippur War, and the fall of the shah of Iran. Presidents Rafael Caldera (1968), Carlos Andrés Pérez (1973), and Luis Herrera Campíns (1978) had to navigate the difficulties of those years.

A highly organized and supportive Jewish community developed then. Since 1966 the Confederación de Asociaciones Israelitas de Venezuela (CAIV) is the umbrella organization that officially represents the whole community. At the beginning of the 1970s the Colegio Moral y Luces Hebraica, spanning Jewish education from kindergarten to high school, opened its door and received in its classrooms 95 percent of the Jewish student population. It was in this setting that Sephardi-Ashkenazi interrelations began to grow steadily, pointing toward the total unification of both communities. In 1970 the Jewish population was estimated at 15,000, most of them living in Caracas. This number had increased to 20,000 in the mid-1990s.

Institutions such as the Instituto Cultural Venezolano-Israelí (1956), the Federación Sionista (1959), the Instituto Superior de Estudios Judaicos (ISEJ, 1977), the Centro de Estudios Sefardíes (1980), the Colegio Sinai (1983), the Museo Raquel Kern (1983), the Beth Avot (Home for the Aged, 1984), the Museo Sefardí Morris E. Curiel (1998), the Centro de Salud Yolanda Katz (1998), the Library Leo and Anita Blum (1998), and the Centro Cultural Gonzalo Benaím (1998), are but a sample of the many educational, cultural, and welfare organizations that provide valuable communal services through intense activity. Cordial relations with churches are maintained through the Comité de Relaciones entre Iglesias y Sinagogas establecidas en Venezuela (CRISEV, 1973). A chair on Judaism opened at the Universidad Católica Andrés Bello.

Throughout these years, the Jewish contributions to the country have been significant. Outstanding individuals among them received national prizes in a variety of fields, examples being in physics (Estrella Abecasis de Laredo) and chemistry (Gabriel Chuchani); plastic arts (Harry Abend; Sofia Imber); theater (Isaac Chocrón); literature (Elisa Lerner); and cinematography (Alfredo Roffé). Jews who have presided over academic organizations were Paul Lustgarten (National Academy of Physical, Mathematics and Natural Sciences), Benjamin Sharifker (rector of the University Simón Bolívar), Rafael Reif (provost of the Massachusetts Institute of Technology), Paulina Gamus (deputy to the National Congress), Ruth de Krivoy (president, Banco Central), Rubén Merenfeld and Gonzalo Benaím (outstanding professionals and community and social activists), and many others.

In 1992 there was a military attempt under the leadership of Lieutenant Colonel Hugo Chávez to remove President Carlos Andrés Pérez from power. Though the coup ultimately failed and Chávez was jailed, his role in resisting the then unpopular president made him a prominent figure in national politics after he was released from jail in 1994. In 1998 he was elected president of the Republic.

The political turmoil of the early 2000s and the social and economic transformations the country has faced under the administration of Hugo Chávez have imposed new responsibilities upon the community. The Jewish environment did not escape the serious crisis that economically affected the less favored people. By the year 2005 the total number of registered students in the Jewish school had decreased due to the recent phenomenon of migration and *aliyah* made by a considerable number of Venezuelan Jewish families. The number of students attending the Colegio is 1,381.

In 2005 it was education and social welfare activities that required the maximum attention from the community authorities. There was an increased need for scholarships for the day school and a considerable number of families required monthly financial assistance. Apparently, the years of prosperity were reaching an end and uncertainty was what characterized the future.

Antisemitism

Leaving aside the anti-Jewish outbursts that occurred in Coro in the mid-19th century and ended in an arrangement with the government, Venezuela is a country where discrimination by origin, race, or religion had been almost nonexistent and where antisemitism was not widespread. Even during the periods of dictatorship which prevailed during part of the 20th century, the Jewish community was not singled out for oppression.

It is since the Six-Day War (1967) that anti-Israeli and anti-Zionist propaganda reared its head and was echoed by the leftist parties, although public opinion and the press remained friendly to Israel and to the Jewish people.

In Venezuela the Jewish and Arab communities had been living and trading together in harmony for years. Successive governments had maintained their neutral position in the

Middle East conflict and had tried to keep peace among these groups, although they were unable to prevent the outbreak of antisemitism that poisoned the press, the university campus, and the politic atmosphere in the 1970s.

More recently (2005), even though President Chávez had affirmed and repeated that a total and absolute climate of liberty exists, intermittent broadcasts of the official radio and TV stations attempted very often to denigrate the integrity of the Jewish people and the State of Israel; degrading concepts and prejudiced expressions are heard in some media; antisemitic watchwords appear painted on walls; posters and "cartelones" incite against the Zionism; antisemitic mottoes are daubed on the façades of Jewish institutions. As a result of a political assassination and in order to explain problematic national and political events, the police carried out an unsuccessful search in the Hebrew school and the Hebraica social club (2005). It is possible that these are isolated actions, but to the surprise of many people, the distribution of antisemitic literature has increased greatly in bookstores and newsstands.

Relations with Israel

Special mention should be made of the close relationships that have always existed between Venezuela and Israel. Diplomatic relations are on the ambassadorial level. The embassy was located in Jerusalem for many years but eventually moved to Tel Aviv. Commercial ties between the two countries are well developed. Visits of ministers and cooperation in specialized professional projects and agricultural development programs have been very frequent.

Venezuelan Jews have maintained strong ties with Israel and many have visited the country several times. The financial contributions to Jewish causes used to be large. To celebrate the 50th anniversary of Israel, a set of commemorative postal stamps was issued by the government in 1998.

The Comité Venezolano pro-Palestina was formed in 1946 and, under the Rómulo Gallegos presidency, the Venezuelan government gave its affirmative vote to the Partition Plan in the United Nations (1947) and was one of the first nations to recognize the State of Israel (1948).

Since the establishment of the Cámara Económica Venezolana-Israelí in 1976, trade between the two countries has grown considerably. In 1970 the total amount per year was $3 million ($1.5 million for each side). In 1980 the total was $21.6 million (of which Israel exported $21.3 million). This Venezuelan deficit continued in 1990 with total trade of $92.9 million (Israel exported $90.7 million). A big drop in trade was registered in 2000, down to $36.7 million, Venezuela exporting $10.4 and Israel 26.3 million. Total trade in 2003 was $29.3 million (3.8 and 25.5, respectively) and in 2004 $56.8 million (9.6 and 47.2, respectively).

With respect to *aliyah* (emigration to Israel), the first years of the 21st century showed a pattern of steady growth (52 people in 2002; 113 in 2003; 117 in 2004; and 129 in 2005).

BIBLIOGRAPHY: J. Carciente, *Presencia Sefardí en la Historia de Venezuela* (1997); "Sephardi Jews in Venezuela," in: *Synagogues in Venezuela and the Caribbean. Past and Present* (1999); M. Nassi, *La Comunidad Ashkenazí de Caracas. Breve Historia Institucional* (1981); M. Beker, "Ashkenazic Jews in Venezuela," in: *Synagogues in Venezuela and the Caribbean. Past and Present* (1999); Nuevo Mundo Israelita, *Memorias de una Diáspora* (2004); *Maguen*, Revista del Centro de Estudios Sefardíes de Caracas, 2000/2004.

[Jacob Carciente (2nd ed.)]

VENGEANCE (Heb. *nekamah, nekimah*), inflicting punishment on another in return for an offense or injury, or the withholding of benefits and kindness from another for the same reason. The Bible distinguishes between vengeance that is proper and vengeance that is sinful. Vengeance is proper for man only in the restricted sense of dispensing justice for a legally punishable crime or sin, meted out in the prescribed manner. The one who inflicts the punishment is thus acting as an instrument of the court of law, or in rare cases, of God's revealed will, but never merely to satisfy personal animosity. Examples are "When a man strikes his slave… and he dies there and then, he must be avenged" (Ex. 21:20) and "The Lord spoke to Moses, saying, 'Avenge the Israelite people on the Midianites'" (Num. 31:1–2). Similarly, vengeance is appropriate when it is directed in a legally just war against the enemies of the entire people of Israel, who are at the same time considered enemies of God: "To execute vengeance upon the nations and punishments upon the peoples" (Ps. 149:7). Vengeance is a divine prerogative, as the following verses indicate: "For He will avenge the blood of His servants, wreak vengeance on His foes" (Deut. 32:43); "I will bring a sword against you to wreak vengeance for the covenant" (Lev. 26:25); and "O Lord God of vengeance, O God of vengeance, shine forth" (Ps. 94:1). While the rabbis considered the imitation of God's ways, such as mercy, forgiveness, and so on, to be the ethical ideal for man (see, e.g., Sot. 14a; Sif. Deut. 49; Shab. 133b), they did not fail to point out that certain activities attributed by the Bible to God, such as vengeance, should not be imitated, the reason being that "with a human being wrath controls him, but the Holy One blessed He controls His wrath, as it is said, 'The Lord avengeth and is full of wrath'" [the Hebrew is *ba'al ḥemah*, literally 'master of wrath'; Nah. 1:2] (Gen. R. 49:8).

Human vengeance as the expression of personal animosity is explicitly prohibited in the Bible in the verse, "You shall not take vengeance or bear a grudge against your kinsfolk. Love your neighbor as yourself: I am the Lord" (Lev. 19:18). The rabbis offer a precise definition of this passage: "What is vengeance and what is bearing a grudge? If one said to his fellow: 'Lend me your sickle,' and he replied 'No,' and tomorrow the second comes to the first and says: 'Lend me your ax,' and he replies: 'I will not lend it to you just as you would not lend me your sickle' – that is vengeance. And what is bearing a grudge'? If one says to his fellow: 'Lend me your ax,' he replies 'No,' and on the morrow the second asks: 'Lend me your garment,' and he answers: 'Here it is, I am not like you who would not lend me what I asked for' – that is bearing a grudge" (Yoma 23a; Maim. Yad, De'ot 7:7, 9; *Sefer ha-Ḥinnukh*, nos. 247, 248). Various reasons have been offered by Jewish thinkers for the injunction against vengeance, besides the obvious one that it increases hatred and strife among men. One consideration is that a man and his neighbor are really one organic unit, so that one retaliating against the other is analogous to the situation in which one hand slicing meat with a knife slips and cuts the second hand: "would the second hand retaliate by cutting the first?" (TJ, Ned. 9:4, 41c). Or, from another aspect, one ought always to consider the harm that befalls him as ultimately deriving from God as punishment for sin, the human perpetrator of the injury being merely an unwitting instrument of divine providence, so that, actually, repentance, rather than vengeance, is called for (*Sefer ha-Ḥinnukh*, no. 247). Maimonides states that "one should rather practice forbearance in all mundane matters, for the intelligent realize that these are vain things and not worth taking vengeance for" (Maim. Yad, De'ot 7:7).

There is, according to the Talmud, one notable exception to the injunction against vengeance. "Any *talmid ḥakham* (pious Torah scholar) who does not avenge himself and retains anger like a serpent, is no real *talmid ḥakham*" (Yoma 22b–23a), the reason being that offense against him entails a slur against the Torah itself. This dispensation granted the *talmid ḥakham* is, however, highly qualified by the rabbis. It is limited to cases where the scholar has suffered personal, rather than monetary, injury; the scholar may not take overt action, but may merely withhold interference if another takes up his cause; the dispensation is terminated if the offender seeks forgiveness (Yoma, *ibid.* and Rashi *ibid.*). Furthermore, according to Maimonides (Yad, Talmud Torah 7:13), the special permission granted the scholar applies only to instances where he was publicly reviled, thus involving a gross desecration of the honor of Torah; and finally, the purpose for allowing vengeance in such a case is that it causes the offender to recant, after which he must be forgiven.

In all other instances where one has been wronged, vengeance in all its forms is forbidden. The ideal, according to the Talmud, is to be of those, "who are insulted but do not retaliate with insult, who hear themselves put to shame without replying" (Yoma, *ibid.*). Concerning such people, the rabbis declare, "he who forbears to retaliate will find forbearance [from God] for all his failings" (Yoma, *ibid.;* Shab. 88b; RH 17a.)

BIBLIOGRAPHY: A. Cohen, *Everyman's Talmud* (1949^2), 210–30; Eisenstein, Yisrael, 7 (1951), 110–1.

[Joshua H. Shmidman]

VENICE, city in N. Italy.

The Medieval Community

Although some individual Jews had passed through Venice in the Middle Ages, legislation enacted in 1382 allowing moneylending in the city for the following five years marked the start

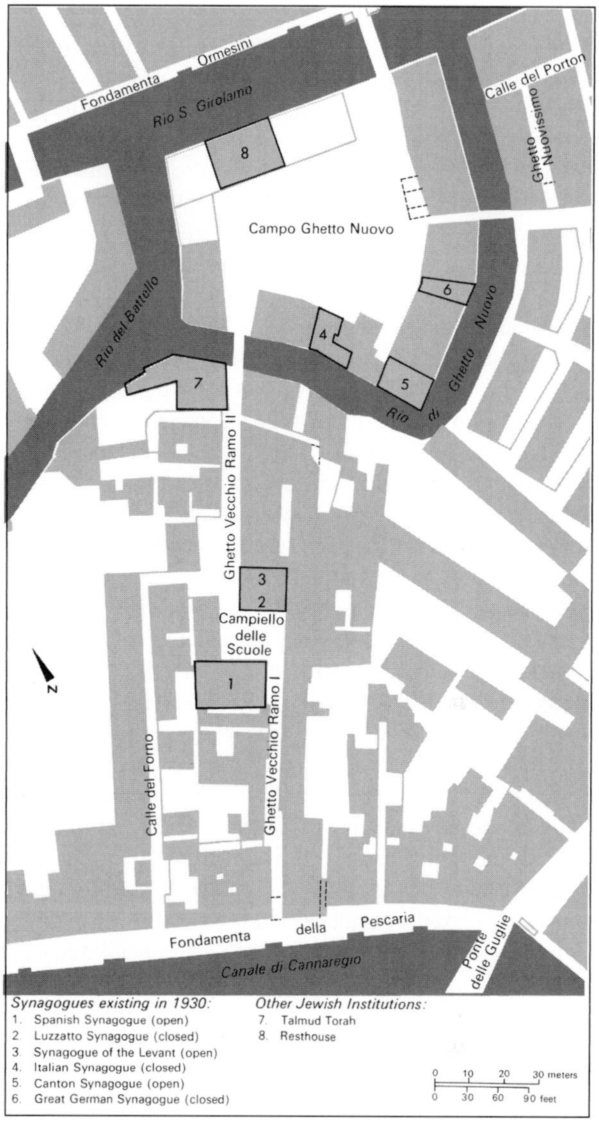

Plan of Venice ghetto, 1930.

of the authorized Jewish presence in the city, and at its expiration in 1387 a 10-year charter came into effect exclusively for Jewish moneylenders. However, at the end of the ten years, they had to leave, and officially no Jew could stay in Venice for longer than 15 days at a time, with exceptions made only for merchants arriving by sea and for doctors; also henceforth all Jews coming to the city were required to wear on their outer clothing a yellow circle, changed in 1496 to a yellow head-covering to make evasion more difficult.

The authorized continuous residence of Jews in the city of Venice and the emergence of its Jewish community was a 16th-century development not initially planned by the Venetian government. Its restrictive policy toward the residence of Jews in Venice in the 15th century was not extended either to the Venetian overseas possessions or to the Venetian territory on the Italian mainland, and the charter issued in 1503 to Jewish moneylenders in Mestre permitted them to come to Venice in case of war. Consequently, in 1509, as during the War of the League of Cambrai, the enemies of Venice overran the Venetian mainland, Jewish moneylenders and other Jews residing in Mestre, as well as in Padua and elsewhere, fled to Venice. The Venetian government soon realized that allowing them to stay was doubly beneficial, for they could provide the hard-pressed treasury with annual payments while their moneylending in the city itself was convenient for the needy urban poor. Consequently, in 1513 the government granted the Jewish moneylender Anselmo del Banco (Asher Meshullam) from Mestre and his associates a charter permitting them to lend money in Venice. Then, two years later, the Jews obtained permission to operate stores selling *strazzaria*, literally rags, but, by extension, secondhand clothing and other used items such as household goods and furnishings, which were sought by a large part of the population, especially foreign diplomats and visitors to the city and even the government itself for state occasions, prior to the Industrial Revolution when less-expensive mass-produced items first became available.

Many Venetians, especially clerics, objected to the residence of Jews all over the city, so in 1516 the Senate decided, despite the objections of the Jews, as a compromise mediating between the new freedom of residence all over the city and the previous state of exclusion, to segregate them. Accordingly, all Jews residing in the city and all who were to come in the future were required to move to the island known as the Ghetto Nuovo (the New Ghetto), which was walled up and provided with two gates that for most of the time that the ghetto existed were locked all night, from one hour after sunset in the summer and two hours after sunset in the winter, when it got dark earlier, until dawn.

Initially, the site adjacent to the island of the Ghetto Nuovo had served as the location of the Venetian municipal copper foundry, *il ghetto* from the verb *gettare,* in the sense of to pour or caste metal, while the Ghetto Nuovo to which the Jews were relegated in 1516 had been used for dumping waste material from the copper foundry. Accordingly it was referred to as "the terrain of the ghetto" (*il terreno del ghetto*) and then eventually the Ghetto Nuovo, while the area of the actual foundry became known as the Ghetto Vecchio (the Old Ghetto). But since the foundry was unable to process a sufficient quantity of metal, its activity came to be consolidated in the Arsenal, and in 1434 the government auctioned off the foundry and adjacent island, both of which became residential areas.

Although a few compulsory, segregated, and enclosed Jewish quarters had existed in Europe prior to 1516, the best-known and longest lasting of which was that of Frankfurt am Main established in 1462, they were never called ghettos because that word came to be associated with Jewish quarters only after the Venetian development of 1516. Thus, the oft-encountered statement that the first ghetto was established in Venice in 1516 is correct in a technical, linguistic sense but misleading in a wider context.

The establishment of the ghetto, however, did not assure the continued residence of the Jews in Venice, for that privilege was based on a charter granted by the Venetian government to the Jews in 1513. Upon its expiration in 1518, very extensive discussions took place in the Senate, as numerous proposals, including the expulsion of the Jews from Venice, were advanced, but eventually a new five-year charter was approved and subsequently renewed for generations.

Overall, the attitude of the Venetian government toward the Jews was highly ambivalent. While the majority of the senators allowed utilitarian socio-economic considerations to be foremost in their decision-making, thereby in retrospect making the residence of the Jews in the city continuous from 1513 on, there was a constant undercurrent of hostility that could find its expression at the time of the charter renewal. An examination of the actual terms of the charters reveals that over the years, clauses were added to further regulate the status of the Jews. Most important was the change in attitude toward moneylending. Increasingly, the Venetian government viewed Jewish moneylenders as a source of cheap credit for the urban poor rather than of revenue for the state treasury, and accordingly, it lowered the interest rates and correspondingly reduced the required annual payments of the Jews. Finally, in 1573, it eliminated the annual payment, but the Jews were required to make loans of up to three ducats each at five percent per annum interest to any borrower with a suitable pledge. Since the native Jews of Venice, whom the government referred to as Tedeschi (i.e., German) Jews because many of them were ultimately of Germanic origin even though their families might have lived on the Italian peninsula for generations, claimed that they could not support the expenses of the pawnshops (sometimes misleadingly referred to as banks) on their own, the Jewish communities of the mainland were required to contribute and that responsibility was also extended to the Jewish merchants, despite their strong objection. Thus the nature of Jewish moneylending completely changed from a voluntary profit-making activity engaged in by a few wealthy individuals to a compulsory responsibility imposed on the Jewish community which passed it on to individual Jews who had the resources to fund the pawnshops, and then subsidized them with a premium over the five percent interest that they could legally charge on their loans.

In 1541, some visiting Ottoman Jewish merchants, known as Levantine Jews, complained to the Venetian government that they did not have sufficient space in the ghetto. Legislation of that year designed to make trading in Venice more attractive to foreign merchants, primarily by lowering customs duties on certain imports, pointed out that these Jewish merchants were importing the greater part of the merchandise coming from the Ottoman Balkans and ordered that their complaint be investigated. Upon confirmation of its validity, they were assigned the area of the Ghetto Vecchio, which was ordered walled up with only one gate at each end, one of which opened up to a bridge to the Ghetto Nuovo.

Meanwhile, the establishment of the Inquisition in Portugal in 1536 increasingly induced many *New Christians to leave, either because they were secretly judaizing or were afraid that they might falsely be accused of doing so. The existence of a Jewish community in Venice and the growing presence of Levantine Jewish merchants in the city after 1541 made it more attractive for judaizing Iberian New Christians to come to Venice, where many reverted to Judaism and either stayed or went on elsewhere, primarily to the Ottoman Empire.

Although the Venetian government was always doctrinally Catholic and concerned with the religious faith of its inhabitants, it usually did not concern itself with the origin and background of those New Christians who upon arriving in Venice went directly to the ghetto and there assumed Judaism and henceforth lived unambiguously as Jews. On the other hand, officially it did not tolerate New Christians who lived outside the ghetto and passed themselves off ostensibly as Christians while nevertheless still secretly judaizing, both because their conduct was an affront to Christianity and also because it was feared that they might lead more simple Christians astray. Only once in the 16th century, in 1550, apparently under the pressure of Emperor Charles v, did the Venetian government take action against judaizing New Christians as a group as it forbade *Crypto-Jews from settling in Venice and the Venetian state.

Yet despite the legislation of 1550, the pressure of the papal nuncio, and the presence of the Venetian Inquisition – revived in 1547 in order to deal with the growth of Protestant heresy rather than with Crypto-Jews as had been the case with the Inquisition on the Iberian peninsula (although once established it concerned itself with all manifestations of heresy, including cases of Crypto-Judaism) – Venice continued to serve judaizing New Christians as both a place of settlement as well a major point of transit.

The cause of the judaizing New Christian merchants in Venice was taken up by Daniel Rodriga, a Jew of Portuguese New Christian origin, in 1573. He submitted to the Venetian government numerous proposals and projects intended primarily to restore the declining maritime commerce of Venice and augment its diminishing customs revenue while simultaneously benefiting Jewish merchants and, above all, obtaining for them privileges in Venice. Keenly aware of the far-flung merchant kinship networks of the Jewish-New Christian Iberian Diaspora in the ports of the Mediterranean, Rodriga claimed that if given suitable guarantees of security, these merchants would bring their merchandise to Venice, increasing its customs revenue and enabling it to maintain its entrepôt function. Finally, in 1589, Rodriga's persistence was rewarded, as the Venetian government, recognizing the need to take some action in view of the serious decline in Venetian maritime commerce, concluded that inviting Jewish merchants to the city constituted the least serious possible modification of its long-standing commercial protectionist policy and accordingly the least objectionable way of attempting to alleviate the situation. Consequently, it issued a charter allowing both New Christian merchants from the Iberian Peninsula (who were called Ponentine – i.e., Western – Jews in order to avoid referring to them as New Christians or Marranos) and also Levantine Jewish merchants from the Ottoman Empire to reside in Venice as Venetian subjects with the coveted privilege of engaging in maritime trade between Venice and the Levant on condition that they resided in the ghetto and wore the special yellow Jewish head-covering.

These Jewish merchants were so successful that their charter was subsequently renewed for successive 10-year periods, and when in 1633 they assured the Venetian government that additional merchants would come to Venice if granted adequate living space, it assigned the newcomers an area containing 20 dwellings across the canal from the Ghetto Nuovo, in a direction almost opposite to the Ghetto Vecchio, that almost immediately became known as the Ghetto Nuovissimo, i.e., the newest ghetto. In light of the spread of the use of the term "ghetto" to refer to compulsory and segregated Jewish quarters on the Italian peninsula in the wake of the harsh papal bull of 1555 known as *Cum Nimis Absurdum*, it is understandable that this third compulsory Jewish quarter in Venice was referred to as a ghetto. However, the Ghetto Nuovissimo differed from the Ghetto Nuovo and the Ghetto Vecchio in one important respect. While the last two designations had been in use prior to the residence of the Jews in those locations and owed their origin to the former presence of a foundry in that area, the Ghetto Nuovissimo had never been associated with a foundry. Rather, it was called the Ghetto Nuovissimo because it was the site of the newest compulsory, segregated, and enclosed Jewish quarter. Thus, the term ghetto had come full circle in the city of its origin: from an original specific usage as a foundry in Venice to a generic usage in other cities designating a compulsory, segregated, and enclosed Jewish quarter with no relation to a foundry, and then to that generic usage also in Venice.

The number of Jews residing in Venice apparently reached around 2,000 (roughly 1.5% of the total population of the city) in the last years of the 16th century, rising to a peak of almost 3,000 (roughly 2% of the population) toward the middle of the 17th century, and then dropped to a low of slightly over 1,500 in the last years of the Republic, although according to some very questionable sources at times it was substantially higher. Especially in the 16th and 17th centuries, the number of dwellings available in the ghetto was very often insufficient, so they were constantly subdivided into smaller units while stories were added to the existing buildings, thereby starting a virtually constant process of alteration and modification.

The Venetian government enforced the regulations regarding residence in the ghetto and the requirement to remain there after the hour established for the closing of its gates. Only Jewish doctors treating Christian patients and Jewish merchants who had to attend to their business enjoyed routine permission to be outside the ghetto after hours, while additionally on occasion individual Jews, including representatives of the Jewish community who had to negotiate charter renewals with the government, singers and dancers who performed in the homes of Christians, especially at carnival time, and others who had special needs and skills were granted the privilege, often only until a specified hour of the night. Only extremely rarely indeed was permission granted – usually to doctors – to reside outside the ghetto. Along with residence in the ghetto, the requirement that the Jews wear a special head-covering, initially yellow, which for some undetermined reason became red although Levantine Jews continued to wear yellow, constituted a very significant part of the Venetian socio-religious policy of segregating the Jews.

Reflecting the heterogeneous ethnic backgrounds of the Jews of Venice, several synagogues were established in the ghetto. Five were generally considered to be major synagogues. Three were located in the Ghetto Nuovo: the Scuola Grande Tedesca and the Scuola Canton, both of the Ashkenazi rite, and the Scuola Italiana. Situated in the Ghetto Vecchio were the Scuola Levantina and the Scuola Ponentina or Spagnola, officially Kahal Kadosh Talmud Torah. Additionally, at least three smaller synagogues existed in the Ghetto Nuovo: the Scuola Coanim or Sacerdote, the Scuola Luzzatto, and the Scuola Meshullam. Only the cemetery, initially established in 1386, of necessity was located outside the ghetto on the Lido. The Scuola Ponentina acquired an additional significance as its by-laws served as a model for the Sephardi community of Amsterdam, whose procedures in turn were utilized by the Sephardi Jewish communities of London and of the English colonies of New York, Philadelphia, and Montreal in the New World.

The rabbis of Venice constituted overall a distinguished cadre that provided leadership for their day and a few outstanding figures of more than local significance. The best known was the prolific Leon *Modena (1571–1648), whose numerous works include a remarkably frank Hebrew autobiography which sheds much light on his own life as well as providing unique and fascinating insight into the everyday life, practices, and values of the Jews in early-modern Venice, including their extensive relationships with their Christian neighbors on all levels, from intellectual exchanges to joint participation in alchemy experiments and gambling. Also of special prominence was Modena's contemporary, Rabbi Simone *Luzzatto (ca. 1583–1663). Today he is remembered primarily for his *Discorso sopra il stato degl'Ebrei et in particolar demoranti nel'inclita città di Venetia* ("Discourse on the Status of the Jews and in Particular Those Living in the Illustrious City of Venice," 1638), written in Italian for the Venetian nobility in order to avert a possible expulsion of the Jews as a result of a major scandal involving the bribery of Venetian judges through Jewish intermediaries. In the course of his presentation, Luzzatto displayed considerable insight into the economic and commercial situation, combined with a thorough acquaintance with classical Graeco-Roman literature and an awareness of contemporary intellectual trends, especially in philosophical and political thought, as well as new scientific discoveries in mathematics and astronomy, as he argued that the presence of Jewish merchants and moneylenders was very useful indeed for the Venetian economy and therefore the Jews should not be expelled. Additionally, Venice served as a significant center for the development, transformation, and popularization of the Lurianic Kabbalah from Safed as Rabbi Menachem Azariah mi Fano began to publicly expound it, and eventually it was transmitted from Venice to Eastern Europe.

Additionally significant in Venice was the presence of Jewish doctors, many of whom had been attracted by the educational experience offered by the nearby medical school of Padua. The attendance of Jewish students there was especially significant since it was generally regarded as the best medical school in Europe, with the humanities integrated into the scientific curriculum, and provided one of the richest opportunities for Jews to familiarize themselves with the best of European intellectual and cultural achievements. Jewish students from all over Italy as well as central and eastern Europe came to Padua, and many returned to serve in their communities and elsewhere. Especially noteworthy was the Jewish doctor David dei Pomis (1525–c. 1593) who left Rome as a result of *Cum Nimis Absurdum*, eventually settling in Venice, where he resided for the rest of his life and published, among other works, his *De Medico Hebraeo Enaratio Apologica* (1588), which refuted charges often brought against Jews and Jewish doctors in his own days in the bull of Gregory XIII.

Hebrew Printing

Understandably 16th-century Venice, with available capital, technical proficiency, good paper, a skilled labor force, and constituting a convenient location for exporting emerged as a major center of printing not only in Italian, Latin, and Greek but also Hebrew, Judeo-Italian, Ladino (Judeo-Spanish), and Yiddish (Judeo-German). Indeed, the Venetian printing press made a very extensive and lasting contribution to Jewish learning and culture through its assuming a major role in the early history of Hebrew printing and publishing. One of the outstanding publishers of Hebrew books in Renaissance Italy, and indeed of all times, was Daniel Bomberg, a Christian from Antwerp who, with the help of numerous editors, typesetters, and proofreaders, mostly either Jews or converts from Judaism to Christianity, printed around 200 Hebrew books. Of prime significance for Jewish religious life and culture is his complete edition of the Babylonian Talmud (1520–23) with the commentary of Rashi and the Tosafot, whose format and pagination has been followed in virtually all subsequent editions up to the present, and also his edition of the rabbinic Bible (*Mikra'ot Gedolot*) (1517–18; 1524–25^2), with the Aramaic translation and traditional rabbinic commentaries, which also became the standard model for most subsequent editions, as well as other major works, including the Palestinian Talmud.

After Bomberg, the more important subsequent printers of Hebrew books included the Christians Marco Antonio

Giustiniani, whose activity overlapped the last years of Bomberg, and Alvise Bragadini. Their competition in rival editions of Maimonides' *Mishneh Torah* led to a papal decree of 1553 condemning the Talmud and ordering it burned. Consequently, on October 21, 1553, Hebrew books were burned in Piazza San Marco, to the great loss of the Jewish community and the Christian printers alike. Subsequently, in the early 1560s, Hebrew printers in Venice resumed their activities, printing books by Jewish authors from all over who sought out the resources of the city on the lagoons, from which the books were exported throughout Europe and the Mediterranean world, although from 1548 on, Jews were officially not allowed to be publishers or printers. Indeed, it has been estimated that of 3,986 Hebrew books known to have been printed in Europe prior to 1650, almost a third (1,284) were printed in Venice. Eventually, during the course of the 17th century, the quantity and quality of Venetian Hebrew imprints declined and other centers of Hebrew printing gradually emerged.

The Modern Community

By the 18th century, Venice as a whole had declined economically, certainly in a relative if not absolute sense, and with it also the financial condition of the Jewish community as a corporate entity, even though an impoverished community did not mean that all of its individual members were impoverished. The Venetian government was very concerned, above all because it required that the Jewish community be solvent in order to operate the pawn shops, especially since it was unwilling to establish in Venice a charitable pawnshop known as a **monte di pietà* in order to eliminate Jewish moneylending and the presence of the Jews or at least to minimize their role as had been done in many places on the Italian peninsula, although that possibility was raised on several occasions during the course of the 18th century. Consequently, in 1722 it took the major step of creating the magistracy of the Inquisitorato sopra l'Università degli Ebrei for the purpose of restoring and maintaining the financial solvency of the community. For the rest of the century, the Inquisitorato, together with the Senate and other relevant magistracies, constantly worked out detailed regulations in attempts to promote the smooth functioning of the pawnshops, to arrange for the repayment of the substantial debts of the Jewish community owed both to Venetian Christians and to the Jewish communities of Amsterdam, The Hague, and London, and generally to restore its solvency, eventually closely supervising all aspects of its everyday financial affairs.

In 1738 the separate charters of the Tedeschi Jews and of the Levantine and Ponentine Jews ended as one unified 10-year charter was issued for all Jews residing in the Venetian state. In a sense, such a charter was long overdue, since the charters of the Tedeschi Jews, which antedated those of the Levantine and Ponentine Jewish merchants, contained general provisions which were also applied to the merchants. Yet, the once distinct economic activities and responsibilities of the two groups of Jews had merged over the years, as for well over a century the merchants had been subjected to payments to the pawnshops of the Tedeschi Jews, while since 1634 the Tedeschi Jews had been eligible to engage in maritime trade with the Levant. The charter of 1788 was slightly over a year away from its expiration when in May 1797 the Venetian government dissolved itself in favor of a municipal council as the army of *Napoleon Bonaparte stood poised across the lagoons. The ghetto gates were spontaneously torn down and the special restricted status of the Jews of Venice came to an end.

After Napoleon ceded Venice to Austria by the Treaty of Campo Formio later in 1797, some restrictions were reinstituted but not the requirement to reside within the ghetto. After Napoleon defeated Austria in 1805, Venice became a part of the Napoleonic Kingdom of Italy and the rights of the Jews were again restored, only to be partially revoked when after the fall of Napoleon, Venice was reassigned to Austria by the Congress of Vienna in 1815. They were briefly restored during the revived Republic that emerged during the revolution of 1848–49, led by Daniel Manin, of Jewish descent, and with two Jewish ministers. Only after Venice became a part of the emerging Kingdom of Italy in 1866 were the Jews granted complete emancipation. In the following decades, the Jewish community decreased in numbers as a result of emigration and intermarriage, numbering around 2,000 in 1938.

[Benjamin Ravid (2nd ed.)]

Holocaust Period

Between the issuing of the racial laws in September 1938 and the summer of 1943, the Jewish community of Venice experienced a difficult period of exclusion and racial discrimination, first under the leadership of Aldo Finzi, who had been appointed by the government, and then, after June 16, 1940, under the presidency of Professor Giuseppe Jona.

The German occupation of Mestre and Venice on September 9 and 10, 1943, however, signaled the beginning of the actual Shoah in the region. On September 17, Professor Jona committed suicide rather than deliver the membership list of the Jewish community to the Germans. The political manifesto of the Italian Social Republic (the so-called Republic of Salò) on November 14, 1943, and subsequent decrees at the end of that month declared that all Jews in Italy were enemy aliens and ordered their arrest and the confiscation of their property. Some Jews were able to escape to Switzerland or to the Allied-occupied south of Italy. Some young people joined the armed resistance, especially the Garibaldi Brigade Nannini. Most of the others were rounded up by Italian police and Fascist militia and held in special assembly points such as the prison of Santa Maria Maggiore, the women's prison on the island of Giudecca, and the Liceo M. Foscarini. From there, they were sent to Fossoli until July 1944, and after that to a camp at Bolzano or to the prison of Risiera di San Sabba in Trieste. Nearly all were deported from those camps to Auschwitz-Birkenau.

Most arrests and deportations of Jews in Venice occurred between the major roundup on December 5, 1943, and the late summer of 1944, but incidents continued at a slower pace until the end of the war. Particularly hateful was the arrest of 21 patients at the Casa di Ricovero Israelitica on August 17, 1944. Among the victims there was the elderly Rabbi Adolfo Ottolenghi, who chose to share the fate of his fellow Jews. All of these victims were deported, most of them to Auschwitz-Birkenau.

The Nazi-Fascist persecution of Jews in Venice lasted 18 months, during which time, despite the dangers, Jewish life in the former ghetto and religious services at the synagogue continued. There was also some help from non-Jews and from the Church. Some 246 Venetian Jews were captured and deported during this period. A commemorative plaque at the Campo del Ghetto Nuovo records their names forever. Near the plaque is a monument to the Shoah by the sculptor Arbit Blatas.

[Umberto Fortis (2nd ed.)]

Contemporary Period

At the time of the liberation in 1945 there were 1,050 Jews in the community. In the early 21st century Venice had an active Jewish community of around 500 members, with services still conducted in its beautiful synagogues and a Jewish museum established in the ghetto.

BIBLIOGRAPHY: B. Pullan, *Rich and Poor in Renaissance Venice* (1971); idem, *The Jews of Europe and the Inquisition of Venice* (1983); B. Ravid, *Economics and Toleration in Seventeenth Century Venice: The Background and Context of the Discorso of Simone Luzzatto* (1976); idem, *Studies on the Jews of Venice, 1382–1797* (2003); P.C.I. Zorattini, *Processi del S. Uffizio di Venezia contro ebrei e giudaizzanti*, 14 vols. (1980–99); G. Carletto, *Il Ghetto veneziano nel settecento attraverso i catastici* (1981); L. Modena, *The Autobiography of a Seventeenth-Century Venetian Rabbi: Leon Modena's Life of Judah*, ed. M.R. Cohen, with introductory essays by T.K. Rabb and M.R. Cohen, H.E. Adelman and N.Z. Davis, and historical notes by H.E. Adelman and B. Ravid (1988); D. Malkiel, *A Separate Republic: The Mechanics and Dynamics of Jewish Self-Government, 1607–1624* (1991); E. Concina, U. Camerino, and D. Calabi, *La città degli Ebrei: Il ghetto di Venezia: Architettura e urbanistica* (1991); G. Cozzi, *Giustizia Contaminata* (1996); U. Fortis, *The Ghetto on the Lagoon* (rev. ed. 2000); A. Luzzatto, *La comunità ebraica di Venezia e il suo antico cimitero* (2000); R.C. Davis and B. Ravid (eds.), *The Jews of Early Modern Venice* (2001); S. Levis Sullam, *Una comunità immaginata: gli ebrei a Venezia 1900–1938* (2001); D. Carpi, *Minutes Book of the Council of the Italian Jewish Community of Venice, 1644–1711* (Heb., 2003); R. Segre (ed.), *Gli Ebrei a Venezia 1938–1945. Una comunitá tra persecuzione e rinascita* (1995); P. Sereni, *Gli anni della persecuzione razziale a Venezia: appunti per una storia*, in *Venezia ebraica*, ed. by U. Fortis (1982), 129–51; idem, *Della comunitá ebraica a Venezia durante il fascismo*, in *La Resistenza nel Veneziano*, ed. by G. Paladini and M. Reberschak (1984); G. Luzzato and E. Perillo (eds.), *Pensare e insegnare Auschwitz. Memorie storie apprendimenti* (2004); M. Sarfatti, *Gli ebrei nell'Italia fascista* (2002); idem, *Le leggi antiebraiche spiegate agli italiani di oggi* (2004).

VENOSA, town in S. Italy. A group of Jews probably settled in this ancient and flourishing Roman colony long before the third century C.E., the date of the earliest Jewish inscriptions discovered there. Fifty-four epitaphs originating from a Jewish catacomb have been brought to light; they date from the third to the sixth centuries and are composed in Greek or Latin, with a few containing some Hebrew words. In the 1970s more inscriptions were discovered there. Another 23 epitaphs belonging to a cemetery are all in Hebrew and date from the ninth century. These two series of inscriptions constitute valuable source material. Apart from giving data on various individuals, the first series of epitaphs indicates that there was a well-organized community with religious office holders; there were also *rebbites* (or rabbis) and *apostuli* (delegates of the Palestinian patriarchate or the Babylonian exilarchate); moreover, some Jews figure as *maiores* and *partes civitatis*, i.e., as elected administrators of the town. The later series of epitaphs belongs to a period when Venosa had greatly declined as a result of frequent devastations, particularly by the Saracens. However, the prevalence of Hebrew is proof of the revival of Hebrew learning in southern Italy. The 11th-century chronicle of Ahimaaz b. *Paltiel tells of an emissary of the academy of Jerusalem who came to Venosa presumably to collect funds. He stayed there for a considerable time and used to read the Midrash and to interpret it every Sabbath while the local scholar *Silano, talmudist and liturgical poet, rendered it into the vernacular. After the conquest of the town by the Normans (1041), Venosa no longer afforded favorable ground for the cultivation of Hebrew studies.

BIBLIOGRAPHY: Milano, Bibliotheca, index; Milano, Italia, index; Roth, Italy, index; Roth, Dark Ages, 416 n. 17; Frey, Corpus, nos. 569–619; G.I. Ascoli (ed.), *Iscrizioni inedite o real note, greche, latine, ebraiche, di antichi sepoleri giudaici…* (1880); F. Lenormant, in: REJ, 6 (1883), 200–7; H.J. Leon, in: JQR, 44 (1953/54), 267–84; F. Luzzatto, in: RMI, 10 (1935/36), 203–5; D. Columbo, *ibid.*, 26 (1960), 446–7; L. Levi, *ibid.*, 31 (1965), 358–65. **ADD. BIBLIOGRAPHY:** C. Colafemmina, "Nova et Vetera nella catacomba ebraica di Venosa," in: *Studi storici* (1974), 87–95; idem, "Nuove iscrizioni ebraiche a Venosa," in: *Studi in memoria di P. Adiuto Putignani* (1975), 41–46; idem, "Nuove scoperte nella catacomba ebraica di Venosa," in: *Vetera Christianorum*, 15 (1978), 369–81; idem, "Tre iscrizioni ebraiche inedited," in: *Vetera Christianorum*, 20 (1983), 443–47; E.M. Meyers, "Report on the Excavations at the Venosa Catacombs, 1981," in: *Vetera Christianorum*, 20 (1983), 445–60; G. Lacerenza, "L'epitafio di Abigail da Venosa," in: *Henoch*, 11 (1989), 319–25; D. Noy, "The Jewish Communities of Leontopolis and Venosa," in: J.W. Van Henten and P.W. Van der Horst (ed.), *Studies in Early Jewish Epigraphy* (1994), 162–82.

[Attilio Milano / Nadia Zeldes (2nd ed.)]

°**VENTIDIUS, PUBLIUS** (**Bassus**), Roman general sent to Asia by Mark Antony (40 B.C.E.) to repel the Parthian invasion of Syria. Ventidius defeated the combined forces of Quintus Labienus (the representative of Brutus and Cassius to Parthia) and the Parthians in Syria (39 B.C.E.), thus forcing the Parthian king, Pacorus, to evacuate the country. From Syria Ventidius marched into Judea and encamped near Jerusalem. His purpose, according to Josephus, was to extort as much money as possible from *Antigonus, the Hasmonean prince restored to the throne by the Parthians. Having achieved this purpose Ventidius withdrew with the greater part of his force, leaving behind a detachment under the command of one of his officers, Silo, who continued to receive bribes from Antigonus. Ventidius remained in Palestine, however, and was occupied with the suppression of local disturbances arising out of the Parthian invasion. At the urging of Mark Antony, Ventidius sent an army under Machaeras to assist Herod, who returned to Palestine at the time and was slowly consolidating his position there. Ventidius subsequently completed the subjugation of Syria, was relieved of his command in the summer of 38 B.C.E., and celebrated his triumph in Rome in November of that year. See Jos., Wars 1:288; Jos., Ant., 14:394ff., 434.

BIBLIOGRAPHY: N. Debevoise, *Political History of Parthia* (1938), 114–20; A. Schalit, *Koenig Herodes* (1969), index.

[Isaiah Gafni]

VENTSPILS (Ger. **Windau**; Rus. **Vindava**), city in N.W. Latvia. Under czarist rule Ventspils was a town in the province of *Courland. Jewish settlement was authorized in 1795 after Courland was annexed to Russia. Some Jews from Lithuania and the German states began to settle in the town, but the majority came from neighboring Pilten. In 1835 the community numbered 513, in 1864 it grew to 920, and by 1897 the number had increased to 1,313 (18.5% of the total population). The community was a wealthy one, and during the period of Latvian independence a network of Jewish schools was established in the town. In 1925 the Jewish population amounted to 1,276 (7.8% of the total). Under German occupation a small part of the community succeeded in escaping to the interior of the Soviet Union: the remainder were executed by the Germans and their Latvian collaborators in 1941.

BIBLIOGRAPHY: S. Azaz, in: *Yahadut Latvia* (1953), 301–4.

[Yehuda Slutsky]

VENTURA, MICHON (1881–1961), lawyer. Born in Istanbul, he graduated in 1905 from the Faculty of Law of Istanbul University. Later on he went to Paris and graduated in 1912 from the Paris Faculty of Law. In 1916 he registered in the Istanbul Bar Association. He was elected as a member of the parliament in 1919 in the last elections to the Ottoman Parliament. He lectured on Roman maritime trade law and philosophy of law at the Faculty of Law of Istanbul University from 1916 to 1934. In 1934 he resigned from his position as he was charged with tax evasion, a charge he denied vehemently. He was a fervent believer in the Turkification of the Jews of Turkey. He wrote *Felsefe-i Hukuk* (1330/1914); *Hukuk-ı Ticariye-i Bahriye* (1330/1914); *Roma Hukuku. Mekteb-i Hukukun İkinci Senesinde Takrir Olunan Dersler* (1330/1916); *Mukayese-i Kavanin-i Medeniye* (1330/1914); *Roma Hukuku Dersinin İmtihan Programı* (1330/1916); *İsviçre Hukuk-ı Medenisi Vecaib Kısmı* (1926); and *Roma Hukuku* 1 (1934).

BIBLIOGRAPHY: R.N. Bali, *Devlet'in Yahudileri ve ?Öteki" Yahudi* (2004), 187–220.

[Rifat Bali (2nd ed.)]

VENTURA, MOÏSE (1893–1978), rabbi and scholar. Born in Smyrna, Ventura, studied at the rabbinical seminary at Istanbul and at Paris University. In 1938–48 he served as chief rabbi at *Alexandria, *Egypt; lectured at Yeshiva College, New York, 1951–53; and was head of Montefiore College, Ramsgate, England, 1953–55. In 1955 he settled in Israel. Apart from a number of textbooks of Hebrew and religious instruction in French, Ventura wrote *Le livre du Kuzari* (1932); *Le Kalam et le peripatétisme après le Kuzari* (1934); and *La philosophie de Saadia Gaon* (1934). He also prepared a critical edition of the Hebrew text (and part of the Arabic original) of Maimonides' *Millot ha-Higgayon* (*La terminologie logique de Maimonide*, with French translation and commentary, glossary, etc., 1935); and published a series of homiletical talks on biblical books and *Avot*.

VENTURA, RUBINO (1794–1858), Italian soldier from *Finale Emilia who became commander of an Indian army in Lahore (Punjab). Ventura enlisted in Napoleon's army in 1814 and following the defeat of Napoleon returned to Finale Emilia. His short and fiery temper caused him problems with the police and he was forced to leave Italy for Constantinople. In 1818 he sailed to Persia, where he volunteered to train the forces of the shah, Faith Ali. Ventura became a colonel in the Persian army but in 1821 after some friction between Persia and England he was dismissed like other officials from Europe. He went to India where he joined the army of Ranjit Singh, Maharaja of Lahore and became General of the Army with a yearly salary of 100,000 francs. After his departure from Italy he always kept his Jewish identity secret. Ventura organized the Lahore army and led it in battle against the Afghans and other enemies of Lahore. Under the name of Jean Baptiste Ventura, he married the Armenian Anna Moses, daughter of a French official, in 1825. From 1830 he engaged in archaeological excavations in Manikyala. In 1831, for his military services, he was appointed governor of Derajat. On the death of Ranjit Singh in 1839 he remained in the service of his successors. Under the rajhas Sher Singh he extended the boundaries of Lahore. In 1841 he left Lahore for Paris, where he lost much of his fortune in unsuccessful commercial speculations. In 1847 he returned to Lahore and tried unsuccessfully to enter the British military service against the Sikhs of Lahore. He repudiated his wife and he came back to Paris in 1853 with his daughter Victorine. He spent his last years in Lardenne. He was buried in the Christian cemetery of the town.

BIBLIOGRAPHY: F. Servi, in: *Corriere Israelitico*, 10 (1871/72), 47ff.; idem, in: *Vessillo Israelitico*, 31 (1883), 308–11; JE, 12 (1907), 417; M.P. Balboni, *Ventura. Dal Ghetto del Finale alla Corte di Latore* (1993).

[Federica Francesconi (2nd ed.)]

VEPRIK, ALEXANDER MOISEYEVITCH (1899–1958), composer. Born in Balta (Podolia), Veprik studied at the Leipzig, St. Petersburg, and Moscow conservatories. In the Moscow school he taught orchestration from 1923 to 1942.

He belongs to the Russian and Polish Postimpressionistic school.

His works of Jewish music include *Songs and Dances of the Ghetto* with orchestra; *Jewish Songs* with orchestra; and *Kaddish*, a song without text. His other works include two symphonies, choral works, and the opera *Toktughul* (1940), which was also adapted as a choral suite (1942 and 1955).

BIBLIOGRAPHY: Baker, Biog Dict.; Riemann-Gurlitt²; MGG; Grove, Dict; Sendrey, Music, index.

[Edith Gerson-Kiwi]

VERA Y ALARCON, LOPE DE (1620–1644), Spanish martyr. Vera was born at San Clemente in La Mancha, Spain, to a Christian noble family. At 14 he entered the University of Salamanca, where he excelled in ancient languages, particularly Hebrew. He competed, albeit unsuccessfully, for a university professorship in Hebrew when only 19. The continual reading of the Hebrew Bible led him to follow the Law and he came to consider himself a practitioner of Judaism. When he tried to share his new convictions with a friend – perhaps his brother – he was denounced to the Inquisition and arrested for heresy on June 24, 1639. The trial dragged on for over a year. At the hearing of May 29, 1641, Vera announced that he was intent on becoming a Jew. The Holy Office subjected him to torture, to confrontations with leading churchmen, and to the harassment of his relatives, but could not change his mind. One night in his cell, Vera fashioned a bone knife and circumcised himself, thereafter calling himself Judah the Believer. The tribunal tried to compromise him by means of theological debates, but Vera remained silent even under duress and he was finally permitted to set out his views fully in writing. Having lost all hope of reclaiming Vera's soul, the Inquisition consigned him to the stake at Valladolid on June 25, 1644. Vera's martyrdom made a profound impression on the *Marranos and Jews throughout Europe. Interest in the particulars of the episode was so intense that the document in which Vera propounded his views was smuggled out of the Inquisition palace and deposited in the library of the *talmud torah* at *Leghorn, Italy, where it remained. The inquisitor Bartholomeo Marques Mirezo noted with a tinge of admiration, "Vera was the Church's greatest heretic"; but 100 years later a Spanish writer explained away Vera's heresy as the result of his probably having had a Marrano nursemaid during infancy.

BIBLIOGRAPHY: C. Roth, *Personalities and Events in Jewish History* (1953), 182–91; L.D. Barnett, in: JQR, 15 (1924–25), 229–39.

[Aaron Lichtenstein]

VERBAND DER DEUTSCHEN JUDEN (Ger. "Alliance of German Jews"), organization of representatives of the major communities and organizations. It was formally founded on April 24, 1904, as an attempt to constitute the sole and recognized representation of German Jewry and all its factions, particularly the *Central-Verein (CV) and the Zionists. The Verband was established, after almost a decade of hesitation and planning by Jewish leaders such as Bernhard Breslauer (1851–1928) and Eugen Fuchs (1856–1923), owing to the threat of increasing antisemitism and the growing disenchantment with the progressive parties, in spite of opposition by many Jewish leaders to a separate organization. Its first chairman was Martin *Philippson. The Verband's main goal was the defense of equality and an attack on official discrimination in Germany. Brochures on discrimination in the universities and in the legal and military professions were compiled and publicized for this purpose. The Verband also published works explaining the principles of Judaism to gentiles. It was a roof organization that did not interfere with the work of other organizations. The Verband did not succeed in winning the support of the Orthodox separatists, the younger and more radical generation of Zionists, and the Eastern European Jews. After World War I, it lost much of its influence, owing partly to the fact that the Weimar Republic had largely stopped the official discrimination against the Jews and that the Verband's tactics were not fit for the fight against the new and much more radical antisemitism, and partly to the increasing significance of sectors within German Jewry that did not support it; it ceased to exist around 1922.

BIBLIOGRAPHY: W. Breslauer, in: BLBI, 7 (1964), 345–79; idem, in: YLBI, 14 (1969), 259–65; Y. Toury, *Die politischen Orientierungen der Juden in Deutschland* (1966); idem, in: YLBI, 13 (1968), 57–90; idem, in: *Ha-Ẓiyyonut*, 1 (1970), 9–56; M. Lamberti, *Central European History*, 3 (1970), 73–93. **ADD. BIBLIOGRAPHY:** P. Pulzer, *Jews and the German State* (1992), 280–82.

[Jacob Borut (2nd ed.)]

VERBAND DER VEREINE FUER JUEDISCHE GESCHICHTE UND LITERATUR (Ger. "Association of Societies for Jewish History and Literature"), association of societies founded in Berlin in 1893 under the leadership of Gustav *Karpeles. The Verband was founded following a wide-ranging process that saw the formation of such societies throughout Germany, a process that bore witness to a great rise in the interest in Judaism, its culture and history in the early 1890s. The societies aimed at increasing their members' knowledge of Jewish history and literature, especially through lectures and discussions. The society in Berlin, founded in 1892 and headed by Karpeles, was among the leaders of that process, encouraging and supporting the foundation of other societies and initiating the founding of the Verband as an umbrella organization. The Verband became the largest Jewish organization in Germany, with 12,149 members in 131 societies by 1900. Karpeles led it until 1909, and was followed by I. *Elbogen, who remained in office until 1938. The Verband tried to coordinate the activities of its constituent societies and published popular literature. From 1898 it published an annual, *Jahrbuch fuer juedische Geschichte und Literatur*, which reached a peak of 5,000 subscribers. After World War I other organizations assumed some of the functions of the Verband, leading to a decline in its membership. Nevertheless, it continued to exist until 1938.

BIBLIOGRAPHY: J. Borut, in: LBIYB 41 (1996), pp. 89–114.

[Zvi Avneri / Jacob Borut (2nd ed.)]

VERBAND NATIONALDEUTSCHER JUDEN (Ger. "Association of National German Jews"), extreme assimilationist organization founded in 1921 by Max Naumann (1875–1939), a Bavarian officer and lawyer. The organization remained numerically weak but was vociferous and supported by certain wealthy and established quarters of German Jewry. Eligible for membership were "Germans of Jewish descent, who, while openly acknowledging their descent, nevertheless felt so completely rooted in German culture and *Wesen* that they could not but think and feel as Germans." The "*Ostjudenfrage*," the problem of unwanted Jewish immigrants from Eastern Europe, served as the raison d'être of the Verband, which identified itself with the mass of right and center parties and viewed the problem from an "objective" German standpoint. The Verband accused the Zionists of hypocrisy in not carrying out their own programs, and of indulging in double loyalty. It called upon the Jews to acknowledge the truth of some antisemitic charges, and to shed themselves of all traces of Jewish nationalism. It established branches in the major cities of Germany and in Vienna, but did not succeed in gaining official recognition or encouragement from any right-wing party, whose negative attitude toward the Weimar Republic it shared.

Max Naumann acclaimed the "national awakening" of 1933 and sought, in vain, for a *modus vivendi* with the Nazi regime (mainly through Gregor Strasser). The Verband called upon the Jews to vote for the unification of the offices of president and prime minister in the plebiscite of Aug. 19, 1934, and tried to erect a counter-organization to the Reichsvertretung, which included Zionists. The Verband published a monthly *Der nationaldeutsche Jude* (1921–35) (circulation reportedly 5,000 in 1926 and 15,000 in 1935) and had its own youth movement, Schwarzes Faehnlein (formerly part of Kameraden with c. 400 members in 1932), which had approached the Hitlerjugend. Despite repeated vows of loyalty, the Verband was summarily rejected by the Nazis, who dissolved the association in 1935–36 because of attitudes "hostile to the State."

BIBLIOGRAPHY: K.J. Herrmann (ed.), *Das dritte Reich und die deutsch-juedischen Organisationen 1933–1934* (1969); M.T. Edelheim-Muehsam, in: YLBI, 1 (1956), 169–70. **ADD. BIBLIOGRAPHY:** C.J. Rheins, in: LBIYB, 25 (1980), 243–68; M. Hambrock, *Die Etablierung der Aussenseiter. Der Verband nationaldeutscher Juden, 1921–1935* (2003); J. Wright: in: LBIYB, 50 (2005) 199–211.

[Henry Wasserman]

VERBITSKY, BERNARDO (1907–1979), Argentinean author. The son of Russian immigrant parents, he was born in Buenos Aires and became a major figure in Argentine literature of the 20th century. His family was quite poor as he was growing up and he had a rather difficult childhood. In his 1977 autobiographical novel *Hermana y sombra,* Verbitsky describes his early family life, fraught with poverty, and the general immigrant milieu in which he was raised. Verbitsky's upbringing in a lower-class working family made him sensitive to the plight of the poor and working classes. Through his parents' sacrifice, he was able to attend the university where he studied journalism, medicine, and law, as well as the humanities. He worked primarily as a journalist for more than 20 years and he held a variety of editorial posts, including for the journal *Davar,* one of the leading Jewish publications in Buenos Aires, and was press officer of the Israel embassy. Verbitsky wrote a vast corpus of books including some 20 works of fiction and three volumes of literary criticism. He established himself as a central figure in Argentinean literature, and was particularly known for his works of social realism. He belonged to the Boedo group of writers, a politically motivated group of authors who cultivated the idea of literature as means of political protest. Verbitsky received numerous literary awards and prizes throughout his career.

His most well-known works include the novels *En esos años* (1947), which deals partially with the Holocaust; *Es difícil empezar a vivir* (1963), a critical look at being Jewish in Argentina; and *Villa miseria también es América* (1957), one of his most widely read novels for its denunciation of social inequities in Latin America. He was also an accomplished short-story writer, with his best known works in this genre being *Café de los angelitos* (1949), *Calles de tango* (1966), and *A pesar de todo* (1978). This last volume contains the story "La culpa," which is an eloquent allegory of the Shoah.

[Darrell B. Lockhart (2nd ed.)]

VERCELLI, city in Piedmont, N. Italy. In 1446 the commune granted Abramo della Vigneria and his son Angelo a concession to establish a loan-bank in Vercelli on condition that they be prepared to lend the commune up to 100 florins on request. A small Jewish community formed around these bankers, regulated by the severe statutes issued in 1430 by Amadeus VIII, duke of Savoy. In 1448 the Jews were compelled to live in a separate quarter. They were expelled in 1556 but readmitted on payment of 200 florins. Renewing Jewish privileges in 1572, Duke Emanuel Philibert improved conditions in some minor respects. Jews expelled from Milanese territory were absorbed by the Vercelli community in 1597. There were eight Jewish loan-banks in Vercelli in 1624. In the 18th century the condition of the Jews in Vercelli deteriorated, though it was still better than the general situation of the Jews in Italy. A ghetto was not established until 1724; in 1740 a large new synagogue was inaugurated in the ghetto. On his death Elijah E. Foa (d. 1796) bequeathed his fortune to the community; among the institutions stemming from this bequest was the Collegio Foa (established 1829) which became an important training center for rabbis and Jewish teachers in Italy. The liberating influence of the French Revolution made itself felt in Vercelli; in 1816 they were released from many disabilities including the obligation to wear the Jewish *badge; emancipation was completed when they were granted citizenship in 1848. In that year there were about 600 Jews in Vercelli, economically well-situated. In 1853 Giuseppe Levi and Esdra Pontremoli founded in Vercelli the journal *Educatore Israelita,* which became the most widespread organ of Italian Jewry (it was superseded in 1878 by the *Vessillo Israelitico*). A new synagogue, in Arabic-Moorish style, was opened in 1878. Until 1600, the Jews of Vercelli followed the Italian synagogal rite; through the influence of some bankers of German origin the Ashkenazi rite was adopted and remained in use. In the 20th century the community dwindled considerably.

In 1931 there were 275 Jews in the community of Vercelli. During the Holocaust period 26 Jews were sent to extermination camps. After the war the community, including the industrial center of Biella, had a membership of 130, which declined to 75 by 1969.

BIBLIOGRAPHY: F. Servi, in: *Educatore Israelita*, 14 (1866), 311ff.; 15 (1867), 36ff.; Milano, Bibliotheca, 183; Milano, Italia, index; Roth, Italy, index; J. Pinkerfeld, *Synagogues of Italy* (1954), 48 and illust. no 27; A. Colombo, in: RMI, 34 (1968), 527ff.; L. Mortara Ottolenghi, *Miscellane Disegni* (1969), 153ff.; Mortara, Indice, passim.

[Alfredo Mordechai Rabello]

VERCORS (pen name of **Jean Bruller**; 1902–1991), French author and engraver. Born in Paris, an engineer by training, he published albums of satirical drawings before World War II. During the Nazi occupation, Vercors founded the clandestine press, Editions de Minuit, launching it with the publication of his own novella, *Le silence de la mer* (1942; *Put out the Light*, 1944). This portrays a francophile and unusually humane German officer, who despite his dignified attitude and his profound understanding of France, ultimately proves incapable of resisting totalitarianism. Accclaimed as the first sign of French moral revival, the book was widely regarded as a minor masterpiece. *La marche à l'Etoile* (1943), which also appeared clandestinely, is based on memories of the writer's own father. A half-Jewish Hungarian settles in France, the land of freedom and justice. There, although legally exempt, he chooses to wear the yellow star. He finally comes to realize that the Vichy-French police are powerless tools of Nazi inhumanity, and his world crumbles.

A starkly humanitarian and ethical message pervades Vercors' works, which include *Plus ou moins homme* (1949); *Les yeux et la lumière* (1948); *Les animaux dénaturés* (1952); *Colères* (1956); *Sylva* (1961); and his wartime memoirs, *La bataille du silence* (1967). He also wrote for the theater and published albums of etchings. An essay of Jewish interest, "La sédition humaine et la pensée judaïque" (first published in *Cahiers du Sud*, no. 297, Dec. 1949), appeared in revised form in E.J. Finbert's *Aspects du génie d'Israël* (1950), 321–30.

BIBLIOGRAPHY: R.D. Konstantinović, *Vercors, écrivain et dessinateur* (1969); K.F. Bieber, *L'Allemagne vue par les écrivains de la Résistance française* (1954), 126–44.

[Konrad Bieber]

VERDUN, town in the department of Meuse, E. France. During the ninth and tenth centuries it was a stronghold and a station on the trading route of slaves captured in Germany or England and who were sold in Spain. According to Christian sources, merchants engaged in this trade were Jews, but from Hebrew sources this appears to be doubtful. On the other hand, the latter mention the tosafists of Verdun, Samuel b. Ḥayyim, a disciple of Jacob b. Meir Tam (Rabbenu Tam), Samuel b. Joseph the Younger (Ha-Baḥur), and his brother Jacob. Later the Jews were no longer authorized to live in Verdun and in the bishopric, and it was in vain that the town appealed to the Council of *Basle, in 1434, for the right to admit them temporarily. During the 18th century some Jews of *Metz unsuccessfully attempted to obtain this same right (in 1710, 1748) and others, who had illegally settled there, were expelled (1752, 1774). The community, which was founded at the time of the Revolution, was affiliated with the consistory of *Nancy in 1808. At first it rapidly increased in numbers, reaching 217 Jews in 1806. From then until the 20th century its size was more or less constant. In 1970 there were about 80 Jews in the town. At Douaumont there is a monument to the 10,000 French Jews who fell between 1914 and 1918. Desecrated by the Nazis, it was restored in 1959.

BIBLIOGRAPHY: B. Blumenkranz, *Juifs et chrétiens dans le Monde Occidental* (1960), 13; C. Verlinden, in: *Mélanges Félix Rousseau* (1958), 673; Gross, Gal Jud, 205–7; G. Weill, in: REJ, 125 (1966), 297–8.

[Gilbert Cahen]

VERDUN-SUR-GARONNE, village in the Tarn-et-Garonne department, in southwestern France. According to non-Jewish historians, particularly the Dominican Bernard Gui, 500 Jews took refuge in a tower which was besieged by the renegade Crusader group, the *Pastoureaux, in the 13th century and committed suicide when they realized the impossibility of escaping from their persecutors. A Jewish community existed in Verdun-sur-Garonne from before 1200 until the expulsion of 1306. When the Jews were readmitted to France in 1315, they preferred to return to the localities in which they had lived previously. A number of Jews from *Comtat Venaissin who traded in Verdun-sur-Garonne during the 18th century were accused by the local merchants of dealing in stolen property. There was little development of a community in the 19th and 20th centuries. In the early 21st century, a small community existed in Verdun and maintained its own synagogue.

BIBLIOGRAPHY: Gross, Gal Jud, 546; G. Saige, *Juifs en Languedoc* (1881), index; N. Roubin, in: REJ, 36 (1898), 78. **ADD. BIBLIOGRAPHY:** *Jewish Travel Guide* (2002), 91.

[Bernhard Blumenkranz / David Weinberg (2nd ed.)]

VEREA (Wechsler), ADRIAN (1876–1944), Romanian poet and playwright. A Bucharest physician, Verea published verse collections such as *Iasi* ("Jassy", 1917) and plays, notably *Appolonius din Tyane* (1932) and *Delfinii din Vaikiki* ("The Dolphins of Waikiki", 1933). As a sequel to *Roman-Ronetti's *Manasse*, Verea wrote *Dupa moartea lui Manasse* ("After Manasse's Death", 1915), which relates the unfortunate outcome of a mixed marriage. He was killed in an air-raid during World War II.

VEREIN FUER KULTUR UND WISSENSCHAFT DES JUDENTUMS (“**Kulturverein**”), Society for the Culture and Science of Judaism, founded in Germany in 1819. It was initiated by Eduard *Gans, Leopold *Zunz, Isaac Marcus *Jost, Moses *Moser, and others. At a later date, Heinrich *Heine also joined the society. Founded in the aftermath of the anti-Jewish riots that took place in 1819 (see *Hep! Hep!), young Jewish intellectuals, most of them university students, proposed as the object of the society the investigation of the nature of Judaism by modern scientific methods in order to bring to light the universal value of Jewish culture and controvert the stereotype of the inferior image of the Jew. The society sponsored an institute for the scientific study of Judaism, which arranged lectures on Jewish history and culture and published (1822–23) a periodical *Zeitschrift fuer die Wissenschaft des Judentums*, edited by Zunz. The first issue contained a programmatic lecture by Immanuel Wohlwill (Wolf), in which he dealt with the great idea embodied in Judaism since the revelation on Sinai, an issue that found its consummate expression in the teachings of *Spinoza. After Spinoza, the idea was eclipsed by the alleged backwardness of the Jews and their failure to keep up with the general advance of culture. It was the task of the society to restore to the idea of Judaism its ancient glory and to adapt it to the scientific spirit of the times. This led to the idea of the Jewish mission: “The Jews must once again show their mettle as doughty fellow-workers in the common task of mankind. They must raise themselves and their principle to the level of a science … and if one day a bond is to join the whole of humanity, then it is the bond of science, the bond of pure reason …” The society also established a school at which Heine lectured on Jewish history. The society failed to gain the recognition of either Jews or non-Jews and folded in May 1824. Some of its members, among them its president, Eduard Gans, chose to become baptized in order to gain the acceptance of Christian society. Despite its demise, however, the society succeeded in furthering scientific study of the Jewish heritage, especially as a result of the research into rabbinic literature carried out by Zunz.

ADD. BIBLIOGRAPHY: M.A. Meyer, *The Origins of the Modern Jew* (1968), 144–82; I. Schorsch, *From Text to Context* (1994); R. Livneh-Freudenthal, in: *Streams into the Sea* (2001), 153–77; N. Roemer, *Jewish Scholarship and Culture in Nineteenth-Century Germany* (2005), 26–34.

[Michael Graetz /Nils Roemer (2nd ed.)]

VEREINIGUNG FUER DAS LIBERALE JUDENTUM IN DEUTSCHLAND (Ger. “Union for Liberal Judaism in Germany”), organization that was founded in 1908 by Bernhard Breslauer (1851–1928), who became its first chairman. The union included the Reform communities of the major cities, rabbis of the Vereinigung der liberalen Rabbiner Deutschlands (“Union of Liberal Rabbis in Germany”), founded in 1899 by Rabbi H. *Vogelstein, as well as private persons. Vogelstein was also one of the founders of the Union for Liberal Judaism; however, the lay element was traditionally predominant in the governing bodies of the organization. Its guiding spirit was Caesar *Seligmann, editor of the Union's periodical, *Liberales Judentum* (1908–22). It had 6,000 members in its first year but the number increased to only 10,000 by 1933. It ceased to exist in the Nazi period. After the Union published its program (*Richtlinien zu einem Programm fuer das liberale Judentum*), signed by 60 rabbis, it was attacked in Orthodox circles. The Union did not champion radical reforms; its ideas had been prevalent in Germany for decades and had already found wide expression and acceptance. It emphasized the universal and humanitarian mission of Judaism in the Diaspora, and took up a strong anti-Zionist stand, particularly through its affiliated youth movement. It combated the increasing strength of the Zionists in the communal organizations after World War I by means of the *Jeudisch-liberale Zeitung*. It affiliated with the World Union for Progressive Judaism at the congress held in London in 1926.

BIBLIOGRAPHY: W. Breslauer, in: BLBI, 9 (1966) 302–29.

VEREIN ZUR ABWEHR DES ANTISEMITISMUS (**Abwehrverein**, Ger. “Association for Defense against Antisemitism”). The association was founded in December 1890 in the building of the Berlin Reichstag by 12 men, including its initiator, Edmund Friedemann, a progressive lawyer, and most likely also the philanthropist Charles Hallgarten. Among the founders were also non-Jewish participants, such as the liberal politician Heinrich Rickert and the lawyer and professor of law Rudolf von Gneist, who were both among the signers of a public denunciation of antisemitism aimed against A. *Stoecker 10 years earlier. Soon after its founding, the organization published a list of 585 supporters, “Christian gentlemen of repute” (including 56 members of the Reichstag), drawn from educated Protestant and liberal circles; among the signers were the pathologist Rudolf Virchow, Theodor *Mommsen, Max Weber, and the author Gustav Freytag. Bureaus were opened in Berlin and Frankfurt and were soon followed by smaller branches in Stuttgart, Cologne, and other cities. In 1893 the Abwehrverein boasted almost 14,000 members in Germany. The association published its own periodical, the *Mitteilungen aus dem Verein zur Abwehr des Antisemitismus* (1891–1933, from 1925 on called *Abwehrblaetter*, ed. by Ludwig *Jacobowski et. al.) as well as educational literature against antisemitism (such as the *Antisemitenspiegel* (1891), or the *Abwehr-ABC* (1920)). It observed, documented, and denounced all manifestations of antisemitism and supported political parties in their fight against antisemitism, although the prospects of success were sometimes uncertain. The association was known among antisemites as “*Judenschutztruppe*” (“Jew protectors”). The Abwehrverein regarded the fight against antisemitism as a task of non-Jews and Jews alike. Although it was represented as a Christian organization and was mainly based on non-Jewish members, Jewish participation played an essential role in it from the beginning. Later on it was made a principle to reach equal non-Jewish and Jewish participation. After the founding of the *Central-Verein as an explicit Jewish “self-defense organization” in 1893, the two associations cultivated a relationship that was respectful but not too close. After the chairmanships of Rudolf von Gneist, Heinrich Rickert, and Theodor Barth, the Abwehrverein lost its impetus under the presidency of Georg Gothein (from 1909 to 1933). Despite efforts made in the difficult period after World War I, the association lost most of its non-Jewish members and waned into insignificance after 1930. In July 1933 the Abwehrverein dissolved itself. In 1891, just eight months after the German association was founded, an Austrian Verein zur Abwehr des Antisemitismus was established in Vienna. Among its founders and prominent members were Theodor *Billroth, Arthur von Suttner, Hermann Nothnagel, and Johann Strauss. The Viennese Abwehrverein published a periodical called *Freies Blatt* from 1892 to 1897 (ed. by E.V. Zenker). Although it had around 5,000 members in 1893, it already declined in 1897. Despite the fact that both defense associations bore the same name and were liberal and inter-confessional, no cooperation was maintained between them.

ADD. BIBLIOGRAPHY: I. Schorsch, *Jewish Reactions to German Antisemitism* (1972); B. Suchy, in: LBIYB, 28 (1983), 205–39; idem, in: LBIYB, 30 (1985), 67–103; J. Borut, in: LBIYB, 36 (1991), 59–96; E. Lindner, in: LBIYB, 37(1992), 213–36; A.T. Levenson, in: *Journal of Israeli History,* 15:2 (1994), 213–22; B. Hamann, in: *Die Macht der Bilder* (1995), 253–63; J. Kornberg, in: *Central European History,* 28 (1995) 153–173; idem, in: LBIYB, 41 (1996), 161–96; J. Borut, in: *Aschkenas,* 7 (1997) 467–94; A.T. Levenson, *Between Philosemitism and Antisemitism* (2004), passim.

[Henry Wasserman / Mirjam Triendl (2nd ed.)]

VERGELIS, AARON (**Arn**; 1918–1999), Soviet Yiddish poet, novelist, and editor. Born in Lubar, Ukraine, he attended secondary school in Birobidzhan, where his family moved in 1932. From 1934 his poems began to appear in the newspaper *Birobidzhaner Shtern* and the almanac *Forpost*. He studied in the Yiddish department of the Moscow Teachers' Training Institute, graduating in 1940, the same year his first book appeared and he was called up to the army. After the war, he returned to Moscow, directed the Yiddish radio program, and was secretary of the Yiddish section of the Writers' Union and a member of the editorial board of the literary almanac *Heymland*. Following the Stalinist suppression of Yiddish culture in the late 1940s, he briefly edited a Moscow factory's (Russian) newspaper. From the late 1950s, his name was associated with the post-Stalinist period of Soviet Jewish culture. In 1961 he was appointed editor of the journal *Sovetish Heymland*. In this role he traveled to the West as a propagandist of Soviet politics. He was widely reviled for his involvement in anti-Zionist campaigns, though some readers appreciated his poetic talent. In his articles he divided the whole of Yiddish literature into "progressive" and "anti-Soviet" and often ridiculed writers of nostalgic literature which, in his view, expressed an outdated and even reactionary viewpoint. After 1991, he renamed his journal *Di Yidishe Gas* ("The Jewish Street") and published almost until the end of his life. Ironically, his former ideological opponents in the United States and Israel turned sponsors, hailing his commitment to Yiddish culture.

BIBLIOGRAPHY: LNYL, 3 (1960), 497f. **ADD. BIBLIOGRAPHY:** A. Vergelis, *On the Jewish Street* (1971); idem, in: Ch. Beider (ed.), *Native Land* (1980); G. Estraikh, in: *East European Jewish Affairs*, 2 (1997), 3–20.

[Gennady Estraikh (2nd ed.)]

VERKHNEUDINSK (today **Ulan-Ude** and part of the Russian Federation), capital city of Buryat-Mongol Autonomous S.S.R., Russian S.F.S.R. The first Jews to settle in Verkhneudinsk were exiles from European Russia. In 1879 its 65 Jewish families received authorization to erect a synagogue. In 1897, 908 Jews (11.2 percent of the total population) lived in the city and engaged mostly in commerce. At that time another 1,220 Jews were living in the surrounding district, of whom several hundred earned their livelihood in agriculture. The majority of the 2,244 urban Jews counted in Buryat-Mongol in 1959 probably lived in Ulan-Ude. In addition, 450 Jews lived in the rural regions of the Republic. About 92 percent of the Jews of Buryat-Mongol declared Russian to be their spoken language. In the early 21st century the community operated a Sunday school, library, and sports club.

[Yehuda Slutsky]

VERMES, GEZA (1924–), leading scholar in the study of the Dead Sea Scrolls, Judaism during the Second Temple Period, and Jesus. Vermes led a unique and varied career. Born in Mako in Hungary to an assimilated Jewish family, Vermes' primary and secondary studies were undertaken at Gyula, with his higher education beginning at Budapest in 1945. Vermes lost his parents in the Holocaust when they were sent to extermination camps in Poland. Studying theology at St. Albert, Louvain (Belgium) between 1947 and 1952 (receiving his D.Theol. in 1953 on the Dead Sea Scrolls), Vermes continued with his studies at the Institut Orientaliste at the Université Catholique in Louvain, between 1950 and 1952, where he obtained a License in Oriental History and the Philology with distinction. On leaving Roman Catholicism and the priesthood in 1957, Vermes went on to obtain an M.A. (1965) and a D.Litt. (1988) from Oxford University. Vermes held many different academic positions and fellowships over the years, notably serving as Senior Lecturer in Divinity at the University of Newcastle upon Tyne (1964–65) and at the University of Oxford as reader in Jewish Studies (1965–89); professor of Jewish Studies (1989–91), and professor emeritus of Jewish Studies (1991–). He was also the recipient of numerous honors and distinctions (including Fellowships of the British Academy (1985) and the European Academy (2001)) and served as chair and president on many academic boards and research societies. He was the incumbent editor of the *Journal of Jewish Studies* from 1971. Vermes was a very meticulous researcher and prolific writer with a great many research articles and books to his credit, among them: *The Dead Sea Scrolls in English* (1962, rev. ed. 1995; see now, *The Complete Dead Sea Scrolls in English*, 1997), *Jesus the Jew: A Historian's Reading of the Gospels* (1973, rev. ed. 1994), and *Jesus and the World of Judaism* (1984). He also edited and revised Emile Schürer's classic *The*

History of the Jewish People in the Age of Jesus Christ (1973–87, 3 vols., together with F. Millar, M. Black, and M. Goodman) as well as editing numerous volumes of essays. He also wrote *The Changing Faces of Jesus* (2001), *The Passion* (2005), and *Who's Who in the Age of Jesus* (2005).

BIBLIOGRAPHY: P.S. Alexander, *Blackwell's Companion to Jewish Civilization* (1988); P. Davies and R. White (eds.), *A Tribute to Geza Vermes: Essays on Jewish and Christian Literature and History* (1990); P. Alexander and M. Goodman (eds.), *Journal of Jewish Studies: Special Issue to Commemorate the Twenty-Fifth Year of Geza Vermes as Editor* (1995); G. Vermes, *Providential Accidents: An Autobiography* (1998).

[Shimon Gibson (2nd ed.)]

VERMONT, New England state, estimated population (2004), 621,394; estimated Jewish population, 5,500. Vermont was the 14th State of the Union, admitted in 1791. Although there were no known Jews living in Vermont until after George Washington's administration, there are documented instances prior to the American Revolution of Jews speculating in Vermont lands with no intention of settlement. The earliest known Jew to settle in Vermont was Joshua Vita Montefiore, a pamphleteer and author of several books on commercial law, who was an indigent uncle of Sir Moses *Montefiore. Settling in St. Albans, Vermont, in 1835, he continued to maintain some Jewish observances while raising his large family as Protestants. He died and was buried in St. Albans in 1845. After 1840 the large migration of German Jews to the United States seeped into northern Vermont to where there were few towns that did not have at least one Jew or Jewish family.

Shortly after the Civil War, a Jewish community was established in Poultney, Vermont. As a thriving center of the slate industry it had attracted Jewish merchants as well as transient peddlers seeking fellow Jews for *minyanim* (prayer quorums) and social opportunities. Poultney acquired Vermont's first Jewish cemetery in 1873 and supported a house of worship and a *shoḥet*. The Jewish community survived until circa 1906 when its Jewish population relocated to Rutland and provided the seedbed for the Rutland Jewish community.

In 1880 a concentration of Jewish families appeared in Burlington, Vermont, the largest city in the state, then a lumber center on the east shore of Lake Champlain. Weekly services were held in Burlington in rented quarters until 1885, when Congregation Ohavi Zedek was formally established and shortly thereafter a synagogue built. Burlington's rabbi was Israel *Rosenberg, who accepted the pulpit in 1909 and served as community rabbi, filling the pulpit of Burlington's three synagogues and building a Hebrew Free School. He left Burlington in 1911 to become the head of the Agudath Rabbonim in New York City. Vermont's longest tenured rabbi was Max Wall who came to Ohavi Zedek directly from military service in 1946 and served until his retirement in 1987. Under Rabbi Wall's guidance, the congregation evolved from largely Yiddish speaking to English speaking and built the synagogue building in which it is presently quartered.

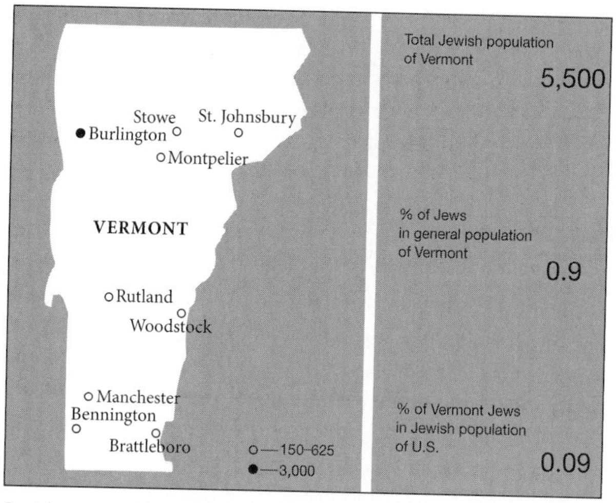

Jewish communities in Vermont. Population figures for 2001.

Burlington remains the site of Vermont's largest Jewish community (3,000) with the conservative Ohavi Zadek the largest congregation closely followed by the Reform synagogue Temple Sinai. Burlington also boasts a highly visible Chabad movement. After 1905 Jewish congregations were organized in other communities. Although congregations in St. Albans and Newport no longer exist, Bennington, Brattleboro, Manchester, Rutland, Middlebury, St. Johnsbury, Stowe, Woodstock-Waitsfield, and Montpelier now boast organized Jewish communities. Other illustrations of an increased Jewish presence in the state include establishment of Jewish Lights, a publishing firm in Woodstock; a prominent Holocaust Studies program at the University of Vermont, which was the home for a generation of the preeminent scholar Raul *Hilberg; and the Rabbi Max Wall Lecture Series at St. Michael's College in Colchester. From 1985 to 1991 Madeleine *Kunin was the governor of Vermont, the first Jewish woman in the U.S. to hold such a position, and during the Clinton administration was ambassador to Switzerland during the dispute over Holocaust victim's bank accounts, when much to her amazement she found that the list of account holders included her grandfather.

BIBLIOGRAPHY: B. Postal and L. Kappman, *Jewish Tourist's Guide to the U.S.* (1954), 615–9; L.M. Friedman, in: AJHSP, 40 (1950/51), 119–34; Myron Samuelson, *The Story of the Jewish Community of Burlington Vermont* (1976).

VEROIA (**Karaferia, Beroea, Veria**), city in Macedonia, Greece; W. of Salonika. When the apostle Paul was expelled from Salonika (49 or 50 C.E.), he fled to Veroia and preached in its synagogue (Acts 17:1–10). Inscriptions testify to the existence of a Jewish population there during the first centuries of the Christian era. Judah Ibn Moskoni visited in the 14th century and found a small Jewish library there, pointing to the existence of a small Jewish community. During the first half of the 15th century the preacher Ephraim b. Gerson of Veroia was well known. There was a Romaniot synagogue in the Balat Quarter of Constantinople named after the Jews of Veroia, who were forced to relocate to the capital after the Ottomans conquered it in 1453. In 1540 there were 54 Jewish family heads from Veroia in the capital. In 1688–89, the Karaferia (Veroia) Synagogue in Istanbul had 45 family heads (220 people).

After the 1391 riots in Spain, Jewish refugees arrived in Veroia in the first half of the 15th century. In the latter part of the 16th century, the Veroia Jewish community had 200 families or 1,000 people. Expellees from Spain and Marranos who migrated first to Salonika eventually moved to Veroia. There amassed three groups in Veroia; veteran Romaniot Jews, Spanish and Portuguese Jews, and Italian Sicilian Jews. The known Iberian families were Estruza (Strumza), Sidis, Perpinian, and the descendants of Joseph Pinto and Daniel Solomon.

The Jews lived in an area called Barbuta, a street with 50 houses. The Jewish quarter was triangular and its gates were locked at night. The current synagogue building was only built in the 18th century.

During the 16th and 17th centuries the Jews of the city of Veroia engaged in weaving, tailoring, and the making and selling of cheese. The Spanish and Portuguese Jews brought to the city the wool industry. With the arrival of more Iberian Jews, the authority of Salonika over religious life increased and the Romaniot influence waned. The Veroia Jewish community took on the *minhagim* of Salonikan Jewry, with an emphasis on leniency as opposed to strictness and adopted the Salonikan "*neficha*" system of **sheḥitah*.

The 19th century was tranquil and prosperous for the Jews of Veroia. Most of the Jewish children learned in Greek and Turkish schools and only a minority learned Hebrew in the "*Hevra*" or *talmud torah* as it was called. The synagogue was expanded and a *mikveh* was added in the back. The Jewish women dressed like Salonikan Jewish women, but outside of the Jewish ghetto they wore veils like Muslim women. The Jews of Veroia had handwritten Hebrew *piyyutim*, in a mixture of Hebrew, Turkish, Spanish, and Greek, which they chanted on the Sabbath, festivals, and special events.

In 1880 there were 149 Jews; in 1904, 500; and in 1908, 600. After the 1897 Turkish-Greek war, Jews from Thessaly left Larissa, Trikkala, and elsewhere and settled in Veroia. The Ottoman Turks of Veroia called the local Jews "*andaluzus*" in accordance with their Castillian origin. In the first decade of the 1900s at the end of Ottoman rule, Jews in Veroia had a *ḥevra kadidsha* for burials and an organization for mutual assistance. The La Hermanidad Club hosted social events. After the 1908 Young Turk Revolution, Jews began to move out of the Jewish Ghetto into the new city. The level of the Jewish school was not high, and most Jewish children learned in Turkish and Greek schools. Thus, they lacked knowledge of Jewish history and Jewish law. With help from the *Alliance Israélite Universelle, the community bought a building, and brought a principal from Salonika. Within a short time, 120 boys and 40 girls studied in the school.

Veroia was annexed to Greece after the Balkan Wars of 1912–13. After the wars several Jewish families left for Turkey and Bulgaria. On the other hand, Jews from Salonika fled to Veroia to escape the epidemics of 1911 and 1913. The Jews in Veroia lived in wooden houses in their own quarter. Their dialect, except for slight variations, was similar to that of Salonika. They owned fields and vineyards near the town, which were cultivated by tenant farmers. The Jews also engaged in agricultural trade, moneychanging, and moneylending. However, they also had small stores, were artisans (mainly shoemakers), tinsmiths, broom makers, and olive pickers. Other Jews worked as goldsmiths, as bankers, and in industry.

In 1923, 60 children studied in the Jewish community school. The Jewish girls, for lack of a Jewish girls' school, went to local Greek schools. In 1920, Zionist activists formed a mutual assistance society. In 1925 there was a blood libel against the Jews and a local Jewish leader was accused of kidnapping and hiding a Christian boy. The Jews went to the police and the matter was settled without further reverberations. In 1927, 80 children studied in five grades in the Jewish school.

In 1940 there were about 850 Jews (150 families) in Veroia. Many young Jewish men from Veroia fought against the invading Italians in Albania from October 28, 1940, until April 1941. When the Germans invaded Salonika and famine erupted due to neglect; some 170 Salonikan Jews came to Veroia. The Nazi Rosenberg Commission also came to Veroia to survey Jewish books and archival material, and to look for anti-German material and documentation on anti-German activities in the synagogue. The Germans made the Jews wear yellow stars, and warned them not to hide partisans or other Jews in their homes.

Jewish community president Menachem Strumza encouraged local Jews to flee from the city and hide. However, in Veroia many believed Salonikan Chief Rabbi *Koretz, who tried to calm the Salonikan Jewish population under Nazi occupation. Not only did Jews in Veroia hesitate to hide, but many of those who hid returned to their homes. Rabbi Shabbetai Azaria fled after he gave a talk to the Jewish community, upon German orders, that encouraged enduring the hardships and urged staying at home and remaining in the city. Menachem Strumza also hid in the mountains with the help of Greek-Orthodox friends. On the evening before the day of the deportation, 144 Jews from Veroia fled from the city to the villages in the Bulgarian occupation zone. A local Greek-Orthodox notary, Sideropoulos, collaborated with the resistance and brought Jews from Veroia to two hiding places in the mountains – to Peiria, and to Vermion. On the last day of Passover 1943, at the time of the morning Shaḥarit prayer, the Nazis arrested the Jews, and locked them for three days in the synagogue. Gathered there were also Jews who had fled from Salonika and Jewish refugees from the Bulgarian occupation zone in eastern Macedonia and western Thrace. The Jews of Veroia, together with the Jews of Phlorina and Soufli, were brought to Salonika and from there were sent to Auschwitz/Birkenau.

The Nazis deported 680 Jews from Veroia to Poland in 1943. The agronomist Lazaros Azaria joined the partisans in

1942 and set up agricultural cooperatives in the villages of the mountainous areas of the partisan strongholds to provide food for all in the area. After the war, once the civil war began, he was pursued as a Communist, and fled to Ereẓ Israel through *"illegal" immigration, eventually reaching Palestine in December 1946, after internment in Cyprus.

Thirty-four families (numbering 132 people) remained in Veroia after the war. The Metropolit Polikarpos guarded the ritual ornaments and Torahs scrolls during the German occupation and returned them to the community after the liberation. The synagogue structure and interior was neglected. David Cohen took care of the synagogues for decades.

In 1948 there were 111 Jews, but they eventually moved to Salonika or Israel. About 70 were left in 1949, 36 in 1958, and three by the 1960s. Rabbi Shabbetai Azaria moved to Salonika and served there as rabbi until his death in ca. 1982. The cemetery deteriorated, and though KIS, the Central Board of Jewish Communities of Greece, in Athens knew of the problem, it did nothing. The Greek architect Elias Messinas led a campaign for the renovation of the synagogue in the 1990s. The synagogue is preserved as a Greek national historic monument. Two Jewish families remained in the early 21st century.

BIBLIOGRAPHY: M. Molho, in: *Minḥah le-Avraham... Elmaleh* (1959), 192–96; M.L. Wagner, in: *Libro del Homenaje a Menéndez Pidal*, 2 (1924), 193–94. **ADD. BIBLIOGRAPHY:** L. Bornstein-Makovetsky and B. Rivlin, "Veria," in *Pinkas ha-Kehillot Yavan* (1999), 110–16; M. Novitch, *Le Passage des Barbares; Contribution a l'Histoire de la deportation et de la Resistance des Juifs grecs* (1982), 72–77.

[Simon Marcus / Yitzhak Kerem (2nd ed.)]

VERONA, city in N. Italy. Jews may have settled there as early as the Roman period, and certainly not later than the early Middle Ages. In the tenth century they were expelled from the city as a consequence of incitement by the bishop Ratherius. Jewish settlement was renewed in the 12th century, and in this period and the following century most of the Jews apparently engaged in trade. Several scholars lived in Verona, including the tosafists *Eliezer b. Samuel of Verona (grandfather of the philosopher and physician *Hillel b. Samuel of Verona) and Isaiah b. Mali di Trani (the Elder). The *bet din* of Verona and the teaching of its scholars are mentioned by the scholars of Germany. The poet *Immanuel of Rome was in Verona at the beginning of the 14th century. After an interval, Jewish settlement was renewed at the beginning of the 15th century, when the city passed to the Republic of Venice, and Jewish loan-bankers settled there. The Jews were again expelled from Verona after the establishment in 1490 of a Christian loan bank (*Monte di Pietà). However, at the beginning of the 16th century the community became permanent, consisting largely of immigrants who had been arriving from Germany. In the 17th century a number of Sephardim settled there, among them members of the well-known *Aboab family, and organized a separate community. The two communities eventually set up a common organization, but friction between them lasted for a long while. The Verona community numbered about 400 at the end of the 16th century, and approximately 900 at the end of the 18th century. A ghetto was set up in Verona in 1599 after a threatened expulsion. The community succeeded in securing charge of the keys, an event commemorated by the Verona Jews in the 17th and 18th centuries by an annual festivity. The community suffered numerous deaths (about 200) in the great plague which swept Italy in 1629–30. Jewish banking diminished in importance in this period and the Jews of Verona mainly earned their livelihood from trade and crafts. Another important source of subsistence for Verona Jews in the 17th and 18th centuries was lease of the tobacco monopoly. Many Jews from other centers attended the great fairs held in Verona, and in the middle of the 18th century the Verona community demanded that levies should be paid by Jews visiting the fairs from outside. In consequence a bitter dispute broke out between the Verona Jews and the communities of Mantua, Modena, and Ferrara.

The Jews in Verona were not spared the economic crisis from which the communities of Italy suffered in this period. The number of poor dependent upon the community continually increased. The structure and organization of the community were similar to those of the other communities in Italy. Apparently the Verona community was the first to establish the reform of the tax system known as the "casella", which was introduced at the end of the 17th century and in the course of time was adopted in many of the communities in Italy. Rabbis of Verona from the 16th century on included Johanan b. Saadiah, Joez b. Jacob, Samuel *Aboab, Samuel *Meldola, Menahem Navarra, and members of the *Bassani, *Hephetz (Gentile), Marini, Pincherle, and other families.

A few books in Hebrew type were printed in Verona at the press of Francesco delle Donne between 1592 and 1595, one of them in Judeo-German (*Pariz un Viena*, 1594). Most important of the Hebrew books was the *Tanḥuma* of 1595, produced by Jacob b. Gershon *Bak, of Prague, and Abraham b. Shabbetai Bath-Sheba (*Basevi). Fifty years later Hebrew printing was resumed at the press of Francesco de' Rossi (1645–52), on the initiative of the Verona rabbis Samuel Aboab (and his sons Jacob and Joseph) and Jacob *Ḥagiz, the first part of the latter's edition of the Mishnah with his commentary *Eẓ Ḥayyim* appearing in 1649 (the rest in Leghorn, 1650). Abraham Ortona was employed as typesetter. Two other printers were active in Verona late in the 18th and early in the 19th century, printing mainly liturgical items.

When the French revolutionary armies appeared in the vicinity of Verona, the local population made an assault upon the ghetto and its inhabitants. After the capture of the city by the French in 1796, however, the ghetto was abolished, its gates were symbolically torn down, and the Jews were granted civil equality. Israel Cohen from Verona took part in the deliberations of the French *Sanhedrin. When subsequently Verona came under Austrian rule, their civil rights were slightly curtailed, but the Jews of the city were not again confined to the ghetto. Full civil equality was restored to them when Verona was incorporated into the Kingdom of Italy. There were about

1,200 Jews living in Verona in the middle of the 19th century. Subsequently their numbers steadily diminished through emigration or assimilation and at the beginning of the 20th century they numbered about 600. In 1931 there were 429 Jews in the community of Verona. During the Holocaust 30 Jews were taken to the extermination camps. After the war the membership of the community was about 120, which remained constant over the next few decades.

BIBLIOGRAPHY: Milano, Bibliotheca, 183–4, supplement: 1954–63 (1964), 68; Milano, Italia, index; Roth, Italy, index; idem, *History of the Jews in Venice* (1930), index; idem, *Gleanings* (1967), 200–39; I. Sonne, in: *Kobez al-Jad*, 13 (1940), 151–83; D.W. Amram, *Makers of Hebrew Books in Italy* (1909), 388–91; B. Friedberg, *Toledot ha-Defus ha-Ivri…* (1950²), 84f.

[Shlomo Simonsohn]

VERTOV, DZIGA (originally **Denis Kaufman**; 1897–1954), Russian pioneer in newsreel-documentary movie director and founder of the "cine-eye, cine-ear" theory. He edited (early 1920s) the newsreel *kino-pravda* from film taken by cameramen he dispatched throughout the U.S.S.R. After 1924 Vertov headed his own group of movie theorists and filmmakers; his brother and chief cameramen MIKHAIL KAUFMAN went with him. Among his documentaries are *One Sixth of the World* (1927), *Three Songs of Lenin* (1932), and *Lullaby* (1937).

VESOUL, town in the Haute-Saône department, E. France. There were already a few Jews in Vesoul before the end of the 13th century, but it was at the turn of the century that an important Jewish community was formed. It owned a synagogue in the Grande-Rue, the remains of which could still be seen during the 16th century. One of the leading personalities of this community was Héliot, who, together with a number of other Jews, engaged in banking, moneylending, and commercial and agricultural transactions within a very extensive radius of the town. The names which appear in various documents indicate that there were at least 15 families living there in 1332. When the *Black Death occurred in the autumn of 1348, the duke ordered the Jews to be arrested throughout the duchy and their property seized. Eighty Jews, some of whom may have belonged to neighboring localities, were imprisoned at Toul. Although the sale of their belongings did not raise much, it should not be concluded that the Jews had been impoverished since the days of Héliot, but rather that they succeeded in hiding their precious objects in good time. Condemned to banishment on Jan. 27, 1349, they soon reappeared in Vesoul, though for a short time only. The economically powerful medieval community did not produce any scholars. On the other hand, *Manessier de Vesoul, who negotiated the return of the Jews to France in 1359 and became the syndic of those who established themselves in Languedoil, was a native of Vesoul. At the time of the French Revolution, at least two Jews lived at No. 3 Place du Palais, and a Renaissance bust in the courtyard of this building is known as "du Juif." A small community existed in Vesoul from the middle of the 19th century until the beginning of World War II.

BIBLIOGRAPHY: Gross, Gal Jud, 190; J. Morey, in: REJ, 7 (1883), 10, 16; I. Loeb, *ibid.*, 8 (1884), 161–96; M. Griveaud, *Vesoul* (1929), 39; L. Monnier, *Histoire de … Vesoul* (1909), 43–50, 73–75; Z. Szajkowski, *Analytical Franco-Jewish Gazetteer* (1966), 254; L. Gauthier, in: *Mémoires de la société d'émulation du Jura*, 3 (1914), 57–253.

[Bernhard Blumenkranz]

°**VESPASIAN, TITUS FLAVIUS** (c. 9–79 C.E.), Roman emperor 69–79 C.E. After the defeat of *Cestius Gallus in Judea, Nero appointed Vespasian commander of the army with the duty of crushing the revolt in Judea. Vespasian conquered Galilee, the coast of Judea, and Transjordan in 67–68, and began making preparations for a decisive attack on Jerusalem. On learning of Nero's death he interrupted the war. When Servius Sulpicius Galba was proclaimed emperor, Vespasian sent his son *Titus to him to pay his respects, and subsequently also swore allegiance to Otto and to Vitellius Aulus, who were appointed emperors after Galba. The idea had apparently already entered his mind to gain the throne but only under the influence of the Syrian governor, Caius Licinus *Mucianus, did he resolve to implement it. Vespasian was proclaimed emperor by the governor of Egypt, *Tiberius Julius Alexander, on July 1, 69, which was subsequently officially recognized as the day he ascended the throne (*Dies imperii*). The legions in Judea followed in the wake of the Egyptian legions and also proclaimed him emperor. Vespasian decided to remain in Egypt for some time to prevent grain from being sent to Rome. Gradually, all the army commanders and their legions went over to Vespasian; the last opposition was in Rome. However, the Praetorian guard which fought on the side of Vitellius was subdued, Vitellius was killed, and Vespasian was recognized as emperor by the Senate.

In 69 he proceeded to Rome and began to bring order into the state which had been in a chaotic condition since the death of Nero. In 71 Vespasian arranged a magnificent triumph over conquered Judea and closed the doors of the temple to the god Janus as a sign that peace had returned to the state. The building of the temple of the god of peace, Pax, served the same purpose. For Vespasian's attitude to the rebels in Ereẓ Israel and to the Jews in the Roman Empire generally, see *Josephus, *Rome.

BIBLIOGRAPHY: A. Shalit, in: *Tarbiz* (1936), 159–80; W. Weber, *Josephus und Vespasian* (1921); G.A. Stevenson, in: *Cambridge Ancient History*, 10 (1934); M.P. Charlesworth, *ibid.*, 11 (1936); L. Homo, *Vespasian* (1950).

[Abraham Schalit]

VESSILLO ISRAELITICO, Italian Jewish monthly review founded in 1875, superseding *Educatore Israelita*. It was edited until its closure in 1921 by Rabbi Flaminio Servi and then by his son Ferruccio. Imbued with an Italian national revival vision of Italian Judaism, the review – especially when the editor was Flaminio Servi – opposed the penetration of the Zionist movement's influence among the ranks of Italian Jewry. In this way, the *Vessillo Israelitico* took sharp issue with the *Corriere Israelitico* and with *Israel,* which supported Zionism.

The effects of World War I (and last but not least the Balfour Declaration) brought about the end of that specific cultural environment within Italian Judaism from which *Vessillo* drew its readers.

BIBLIOGRAPHY: A. Milano, "Un secolo di stampa periodica ebraica in Italia," in: *La Rassegna Mensile di Israel*, 12 (1937–38), 96–136.

[Massimo Longo Adorno (2nd ed.)]

VÉSZI (Weiss), ENDRE (1916–), Hungarian poet and author. Vészi, who abandoned Socialism in order to adhere to the Communist party line, wrote many poems and stories on proletarian themes. His verse collections include *Ünneprontó* ("The Desecrator of the Festival," 1936); among prose works are the novel *Felszabadultál* ("You are Liberated," 1937) and *A küldetés* ("The Mission," 1954).

VÉSZI, JOZSEF (1858–1940), Hungarian editor and journalist. A poet and translator in his youth, he became editor in chief of the daily *Pesti Napló* in 1894, founded the *Budapesti Napló* in 1896 and brought before the public, among other writers, Ferenc *Molnár and Lajos Biró (who later became his sons-in-law). He founded the *Budapester Presse* in 1911, and then was appointed editor in chief of the semiofficial *Pester Lloyd*, a position he held until 1938. During the turbulent years following the outbreak of World War I, Vészi continued to serve successive governments. He maintained his interest in Hungarian Jewry, and during the White Terror persecution of the Jews, which followed the fall of the Communist regime of Béla Kun in 1919, was a member of the delegation which went to the terrorist headquarters to seek cessation of the terror. In ensuing years, he acted as apologist of the Hungarian government even when in 1920 it introduced a *numerus clausus* law restricting the number of Jewish students to five percent. Vészi was given a seat in the Upper House of the Hungarian Parliament in 1927. He was a member of the Hungarian delegation to the League of Nations (1929–30).

BIBLIOGRAPHY: *Magyar Zsidó Lexikon* (1929); *Magyar Irodalmi Lexikon*, 3 (1965), 526.

[Stewart Kampel and Baruch Yaron]

VESZPREM (Hung. **Veszprém**), city in W. central Hungary. Between 1723 and 1725 three Jewish families settled in the city, and in 1736 there were 16 Jews there. By 1830 the community numbered 100 persons. Although Veszprem Jews leased land for a synagogue in 1799, it was not built until 1865. A school was founded in 1805 and existed until the Holocaust. After the schism of 1869 the community joined the Neologists. The first rabbi appointed was A. Fuchs (1809–33), followed by A. Hochmuth (1859–89), A. Kiss (1897–1901), A. Hoffer (1902–28), and L. Kun (1929–44). The majority of Veszprem Jews engaged in trade and crafts. The community had grown to 1,685 by 1880 but the number had fallen to 850 in 1930 and 887 in 1941. After the German conquest (March 19, 1944) about 880 Jews were deported to *Auschwitz and only a few of them returned. In 1947 there were 84 Jews in the city.

BIBLIOGRAPHY: L. Kun, *A veszprémi zsidóság multja és jelene* (1932).

[Baruch Yaron]

°**VIBERT OF NOGENT (Guibert of Nogent** (1053–1124), French Benedictine author and abbot of Nogent-sous Coucy, France. Vibert wrote a well-known history of the First Crusade – the *Gesta Dei per Francos* – and was a theoretician of preaching and the first critic of the traditional hagiography. His treatise *De incarnatione contra Judaeos* was addressed to both the count of Soissons, whom Vibert reproached for his close relations with the Jews, and to the Jews themselves. In referring to the Jews, his tone is extremely vehement.

In his autobiographical work, *De vita sua*, Vibert reports the anti-Jewish persecution of *Rouen at the time of the preaching of the First Crusade and the forced conversion of a Jewish child who, having become a monk himself, wrote an anti-Jewish treatise.

BIBLIOGRAPHY: PL, 156 (1880), 489–528, 837ff. (texts); J. de Ghellinck, *L'Essor de la littérature latine* (1946), index; P. Browe, *Die Judenmission im Mittelalter* (1942), index.

[Bernhard Blumenkranz]

VICENZA, city in N. Italy. In the second half of the 14th century the commune of Vicenza invited a group of Jews to establish a loan-bank there. They were followed by other Jewish bankers, among them the Musetto family (1425), forming a small Jewish settlement whose members engaged in commerce in addition to moneylending. In 1453 there was an unsuccessful attempt to expel the Jews. The rumor that the Jews of *Bassano had in 1485 murdered a child for ritual purposes (see Blood *libel) and the public sermons of the fanatical Bernardino da *Feltre (who also initiated the establishment of a Monte di *Pieta at Vicenza) provided the climate for a ducal decree, issued in April 1486 and implemented in June, expelling the Jews from the city and its environs.

BIBLIOGRAPHY: Milano, Bibliotheca, nos. 253 m, 1418s; Milano, Italia, 140, 209; Roth, Italy, 162, 169, 173; D. Carpi, in: *Archivio Veneto*, 68 (1961), 17ff.; idem, in: I. Klausner et al. (eds.) *Sefer ha-Yovel… N.M. Gelber* (1963), 199–203; G. Volli, in: RMI, 34 (1968), 513–26, 564–9.

[Alfredo Mordechai Rabello]

VICH, town in Catalonia. At the height of its prosperity in about the middle of the 13th century, the Vich Jewish community had 40 families. In 1277 some 15 families lived in the Jewish quarter, but there were only ten in 1318 when King James II (1291–1327) imposed an annual tax of 500 sólidos on the community; it also paid the same amount in 1329, during the reign of Alfonso IV (1327–36). The Jews of Vich engaged in activities similar to those of the other communities in Catalonia. They owned houses, vineyards, and gardens, and were moneylenders who had the local bishop and various nobles among their clients. In return for loans received, the latter pledged Moorish slaves of both sexes, and/or movable and immovable property. The community had its own cemetery, in a place called Colldasens. In 1277 land was acquired by the community for the construction of a synagogue. During the persecutions of 1391 the majority of the Jews of Vich were massacred. The six left alive owed their survival to conversion to Christianity. The intestate Jewish property in the town was seized by the crown.

BIBLIOGRAPHY: Baer, Spain, index; Baer, Urkunden, 1 (1929), index; M.R. Corbella, *La aljama de juheus de Vich* (1909); J.M. Millás Vallicrosa, in: *Sefarad*, 22 (1962), 312–20, 422–3.

[Haim Beinart]

VICOL, ADRIAN (1922–), Romanian ethnomusicologist. From his youth Adrian Vicol was inclined toward the study of music from a critical and theoretical standpoint. As a result, he became one of the most profound and disciplined minds in Romanian ethnomusicology. He collected thousands of folk music pieces and transcribed numerous items from his musical field collections. Thus, from 1949 until his retirement in 1980 he consistently enriched the largest archival funds of traditional cultures in Romania, including those in the National Archives of the C. Brăiloiu and the Institute of Ethnography and Folklore in Bucharest. Besides this type of fundamental research, he also published several academic essays of particular intellectual acumen. Vicol's research focused on the analytical dimension of the study of traditional music, such as the architectural structures of tunes, the typologies of various genres, and rhythm; these are just a few of the topics he discussed within seminal academic papers. He devoted decades to studying "the parlato recitation in Romanian epic songs." From the 1950s up to the late 1970s he studied and wrote on topics ranging from the construction of peasant flutes and the cymbalom's performing techniques to *Premise teoretice la tipologia muzicală a colindelor* ("Theoretical Premises for a Musical Typology of Carols," 1970). His anthology *Typology and Analysis of Romanian Ballads – A Pioneering Approach* was published in 2004. The event gave Vicol new energy, prompting him to publish his old collection of dance music from Muscel-Arge, as well as his old ethomusicological essays (which were scattered among the issues of the *Revista de etnografie şi folclor* (Journal for Ethnography and Folklore) of the Romanian Academy of Sciences.

[Marin Marian (2nd ed.)]

VIDAL, CRESCAS (end of 13th century), Spanish talmudic scholar. Vidal belonged to a distinguished family of Barcelona. He studied in his home town under *Aaron ha-Levi, whom he frequently quotes in his commentary on *Ketubbot*. This commentary was familiar to many later scholars, including *Isaac b. Sheshet, Bezalel *Ashkenazi, who quoted parts of it in his *Shitah Mekubbeẓet* on that tractate, Ḥayyim *Algazi, who quotes it extensively in his *Netivot Mishpat*, and Ḥ.J.D. *Azulai. There are indications that Vidal's talmudic commentary covered a number of other tractates, but, apart from his commentary to *Yevamot*, no other manuscript has been preserved. Vidal is also known for his participation at an early age in the polemic of Solomon b. Abraham *Adret against the study of philosophy and for the subsequent ban on pursuing such inquiries. After receiving the letter of *Abba Mari b. Moses on this subject, Adret first turned to Vidal, who was then (c. 1303) living in Perpignan, where he was held in very high esteem. Adret requested that he exert his authority against those "who dabbled in philosophy" in the Languedoc region. At first Vidal thought Adret had been unduly influenced by extremists who exaggerated the dangers of heresy inherent in the views of *Levi b. Abraham b. Ḥayyim, but afterward Vidal changed his mind. It was Vidal who proposed the text of the rather moderate ban on studying philosophy at an early age, which was in the end accepted by Adret (see Abba Mari b. Moses ha-Yarḥi, *Minḥat Kena'ot* (Pressburg, 1838, 44–48)).

BIBLIOGRAPHY: Baer, Spain 1 (1961), 292ff, 442.

[Israel Moses Ta-Shma]

VIDAL-NAQUET, PIERRE (1930–2006), French historian of antiquity, an emeritus professor at Ecole des Hautes Etudes en Sciences Sociales (EHESS). Vidal-Naquet was born in Paris into a typical assimilated and bourgeois French Jewish family, as the eldest of five in a family originating from Carpentras, in the Comtat Venaissin. His father, Lucien, was a lawyer and his mother, Marguerite Valabregue, a relative of the famous musician Darius *Milhaud. He attended a private school until the outbreak of World War II in 1939. As his father was enlisted in the army, he lived with his mother, brother, and sister for a while in Bretagne, and then moved to Marseille after the defeat of France in 1940, where he stayed until the deportation of his parents in 1944. Coming back to Paris after the liberation, he had to face the death of his parents. He finished high school in 1947 living with his cousins and grandmother. He joined the École Normale in Paris and Marseilles, and began a lifelong friendship with Pierre Nora, Jerome Lindon, and Charles Malamoud. While working with the French periodical *Esprit*, he met there Alex Derczanski, who trained him in some cultural aspects of Judaism. As a student at the Sorbonne in the 1950s he was challenged by the question of decolonization and was actively engaged against torture during the war in Algeria. From then on he became a widely recognized public figure in two venues: the scholar in Hellenistic studies and the active militant against torture and against Holocaust denial. Internationally renowned as one of the leading specialists in the history of Ancient Greece, he was one of the founders – with Jean-Pierre Vernant, Nicole Loraux, Marcel Détienne – of a new approach to classical Greece. His numerous books were widely translated into many languages. Among them are *Myth and Tragedy in Ancient Greece* (1994; French, 1972, 1986) published with Jean-Pierre Vernant; *The Black Hunter: Forms of Thought and Forms of Society in the Greek World* (1986; French, 1966); *Flavius Josèphe ou du bon usage de la trahison* (1987); *Politics Ancient and Modern* (1995; French, 1991). In 2005 he published *L'Atlantide, petite histoire d'un mythe platonicien*.

As a militant against French policies during the war in Algeria in the 1950s and 1960s, he wrote *L'Affaire Audin* (1958); *La torture dans la République, essai d'histoire et de politique contemporaine, 1954–1962* (1975); and *Les crimes de l'armée française en Algérie* (2001). And as a fighter against the denial of the Holocaust he published *Assassins of Memory: Essays on the Denial of the Holocaust* (1992; Hebrew, 1991; French, 1987); and with Limor Yagil, *Holocaust Denial in France: Analysis of a Unique Phenomenon* (1994).

About the Israeli-Palestinian conflict, he wrote *The Jews: History, Memory, and the Present* (1996; French, 1981), and explained his political stance in a volume written as a dialogue, *Questions au Judaisme: entretiens avec Elisabeth Weber* (1996).

Among his autobiographical works are *La brisure et l'attente* (1995); *Le trouble et la lumière* (1998); and *Le choix de l'histoire: pourquoi et comment je suis devenu historien* (2004).

[Sylvie Anne Goldberg (2nd ed.)]

VIDAL YOM TOV OF TOLOSA (second half of the 14th century), Spanish rabbi and commentator on Maimonides. Vidal came from Tolosa, Catalonia, where he compiled his commentary known as *Maggid Mishneh*, to Maimonides' *Mishneh Torah* (often called the *Yad*) of which only the commentary to Books 3; 4; 5, chapters 1–9; 11; 12, chapters 1–3; and 13 is extant. According to one opinion, the commentary covered the whole of the *Mishneh Torah*, but because of the troubles of the period in which Vidal lived, most of it was lost, only a small part remaining (Conforte, Kore (1840², 26a)). It is more probable, however, that he limited his commentary to those *halakhot* which have a practical application. Since the Constantinople (1509) edition of the *Yad*, it has invariably been published with Vidal's commentary. Its purpose was to clarify difficult passages and to indicate Maimonides' sources. Vidal deals with the *hassagot* ("criticisms") of *Abraham b. David of Posquieres, endeavoring to answer them and objecting to their sometimes disrespectful tone. He tries to explain the basis of Abraham b. David's criticism, and at times justifies the views of both men, by proving that they were the result of different versions of the text. In his introductions to the various books of the *Mishneh Torah*, he explains the order of the *halakhot* given by Maimonides, stressing his view that much of the criticism of Maimonides would not have arisen if only the final arrangement of the *Mishneh Torah* had been in accordance with its author's conception. He emphasizes that Maimonides expressed his view in a methodical manner, explaining every topic in its correct context, and that he was especially successful in dividing up the laws, statutes, and precepts of the Torah "by giving the general principles before the details, the earlier in time or in cause before the later, and the more stringent before the more lenient" (Introduction to *Zemannim*). Vidal gives the sources and explanations in clear and succinct style and he tends to be stringent in his rulings, quoting *Naḥmanides, Solomon b. Abraham *Adret, and others.

Joseph b. Ephraim *Caro, in his introduction to the *Kesef Mishneh*, states that Vidal was a colleague of Nissim b. Reuben Gerondi, but his name does not occur in Nissim's works. *Isaac b. Sheshet, however, mentions him in his responsa. Caro refers to Vidal as *kadosh* ("holy"), and as a result it has been suggested that he died a martyr's death. A commentary in Arabic to the work on logic of al-Ghazzali, translated into Hebrew by Moses b. Joshua of Narbonne (in the Vatican library) has been ascribed to Vidal, as has a commentary on Job. Vidal died during the lifetime of Nissim Gerondi (Resp. Ribash no. 388). The *Maggid Mishneh* has been accepted as the standard commentary to the *Mishneh Torah* and many scholars have spoken in praise of Vidal, relying upon his rulings and describing his soul as having a spark of the soul of Maimonides. He is respectfully designated *Ha-Rav ha-Maggid* from the title of his work, *Maggid Mishneh*. Vidal's son Nizak (Isaac) was a talmudic scholar who lived in Alcolea de Cinca and was in contact with Isaac b. Sheshet (Resp. Ribash 473), who calls him "the son of holy ones."

BIBLIOGRAPHY: Conforte, Kore (1846), 26a, 27a; Michael, Or, no. 806; Fuerst, Bibliotheca, 3 (1863), 435; Weiss, Dor, 5 (1904⁴), 129–31; Waxman, Literature, 2 (1933), 154f.; Baer, Toledot, (1945), 274, 276, 301; Baer, Spain, 1 (1966), 38, 40, 83; C. Tchernowitz, *Toledot ha-Posekim*, 1 (1946), 299–301.

[Yehoshua Horowitz]

VIDAS, ELIJAH BEN MOSES DE (16th century), kabbalist, author on morals, one of the great kabbalists of Safed. Vidas was a disciple and close friend of Moses *Cordovero, whom he always called "my teacher" without mentioning his name. In 1575 he completed his major work *Reshit Ḥokhmah*, one of the outstanding books on morals in Judaism. In contrast with previous authors in this field, Vidas included kabbalistic theories in his work, which was aimed at a popular audience; in particular, he quoted at length all that is said in the *Zohar on the question of morals and religious conduct. Quotations from the Zohar were annotated from manuscripts still found in Safed. The book is encyclopedic in character and is divided into five long chapters, "Fear," "Love," "Repentance," "Holiness," and "Humility." Vidas added five chapters from Israel *Al-Nakawa's *Menorat ha-Ma'or* which was then known only in manuscript. They include chapters on the *mitzvot*, on education, on business dealings in good faith, and on manners. At the end of these, he added *Ḥuppot Eliyahu Rabbah*, a collection of rabbinical sayings which list qualities (e.g., "three good qualities…"), and *Or Olam*, moralizing sayings which open with the word "forever" or with the word "great"; for example, "great is charity, even more than sacrifices."

Vidas' book is written in an easy and engaging style, avoiding metaphors. It was immediately accepted as one of the most important books on morals and was printed some 40 times. The first edition was printed in Venice in 1579 during the author's lifetime. The date of Vidas' death is still unknown. Because of its great length, his book was summarized several times: *Reshit Ḥokhmah Kaẓar* (Venice, 1600), completed in 1580 in Asti, Italy, by Jacob b. Mordecai Poggetti; *Tappuḥei Za-*

hav, by Jehiel Melli (Mantua, 1623); *Toze'ot Ḥayyim* (Cracow, before 1650) by Jacob Luzzatto, a preacher in Poznan. These three summaries were published many times.

BIBLIOGRAPHY: Steinschneider, Cat Bod, 950–2, no. 4973; Michael, Or. 184–5; M. Wilensky, in: HUCA, 14 (1939), 457–69; S.A. Horodezky, *Olei-Ẓiyyon* (1947), 69–82.

[Gershom Scholem]

VIDIN, port city on the right bank of the Danube in N.W. Bulgaria. The fortress of Judaeus, which was rebuilt in the vicinity of Vidin by Justinian I (527–565), confirms the presence of Jews at that time (Procopius of Caesarea (6th century) *War with the Goths*, Dewing translation, 1954, B. IV. VI. 21). After the expulsion of the Jews from Hungary in 1376, some of them settled in Vidin. When Vidin fell to the Turks in 1394, the community was led by Shalom Ashkenazi of Neustadt (Hungary), who founded a yeshivah in the town and whose pupil Dosa ha-Yevani ("the Greek") wrote in 1430 the work *Perush ve-Tosafot*. Refugees from Bavaria, who were expelled in 1470, also settled in Vidin. Refugees from Spain arrived there via Salonika. In 1778 David Shabbetai Ventura, the author of *Nehar Shalom* (Amsterdam, 1774), and Elijah Ventura, the author of *Kokheva de-Shavit* (Salonika, 1799), arrived in Vidin. To commemorate the escape of the Jews of Vidin during the rule of the Turkish leader Pazvantoglu (1794), a local Purim was fixed on the fourth of Adar. The number of Jews in Vidin at the end of the 19th century was between 1,300 and 1,500; in 1919 there were 2,000 Jews and in 1926, 1,534. The members of the community did not suffer severely during World War II. The decree of expulsion in 1943 was not carried out (see *Bulgaria). After the establishment of the State of Israel, most of the Jews of Vidin immigrated there together with most of Bulgarian Jewry. In 2004 there were 55 Jews in Vidin, affiliated to the local branch of the nationwide Shalom organization.

BIBLIOGRAPHY: M. Gruenwald, *Algo de la Istoriya de la Comunidad Israelitah di Vidin* (1894); S. Rosanes, in: *Jevrejska Tribuna* 1 (1926–27, Bulgarian) 381–95; 6 (1927), 504–14.

[Simon Marcus / Emil Kalo (2nd ed.)]

VIDVILT (**Kenig Artis Houf**), anonymous 15th–16th-century Yiddish epic. This Arthurian romance of the chivalric adventures of Sir Vidvilt (and his father Gawain), based on Wirnt von Gravenberg's 13th-century Middle High German *Wigalois*, proved to be one of the most enduringly popular secular narratives in Yiddish literary history, with numerous manuscript recensions, printings (the first in an extensively expanded version by Joseph b. Alexander Witzenhausen, Amsterdam 1671), and reprintings, in rhymed couplets, *ottava rima* (Prague 1671–79), and prose, over the course of three and a half centuries. The anonymous poet of the earliest Yiddish version composed more than 2,100 rhymed couplets (probably in northern Italy), following Wirnt's plot rather closely through the first three-quarters of the narrative (abbreviating much and generally eliminating specific Christian reference), before offering quite a different conclusion. Typical of early Yiddish epic, vocabulary from the Semitic component is avoided.

BIBLIOGRAPHY: L. Landau (ed.), *Arthurian Legends, or the Hebrew-German Rhymed Version of the Legend of King Arthur* (1912); I. Linn (ed.), "Widwilt, Son of Gawain" (Diss., New York University, 1942); R.G. Warnock, in: V.M. Lagorio (ed.), *King Arthur Through the Ages* I (1990), 189–208; J.C. Frakes (ed.), *Early Yiddish Texts: 1100–1750* (2004), 453–60, 692–713.

[Jerold C. Frakes (2nd ed.)]

°**VIEIRA, ANTONIO** (1608–1697), Portuguese priest politician, and writer. Born in Lisbon, Vieira was taken to Brazil by his parents when he was six years old. In 1641 Vieira was sent to Portugal with an embassy to the new king, John IV, who became fascinated with the dynamic priest and eventually came to look upon him as his most trusted counselor. Vieira represented Portugal diplomatically – and the king personally – in Italy, France, and the Low Countries from 1646 to 1650. When recommending the formation of a company to develop Brazil he advocated a repeal of New *Christian disabilities, proposing as a first step the abolition of confiscation of Crypto-Jewish property. Since the *Inquisition was the major beneficiary of such confiscations, Vieira made a powerful enemy. Pressure was brought on his Jesuit superiors to have him reassigned safely to Brazil. After the death of John IV in 1656 and the political realignment of 1662, Vieira was left without friends in the palace. The Inquisition seized him for preaching supposedly Judaistic ideas about the Messiah, but it was common knowledge that he was imprisoned more for proposing the removal of Jewish disabilities than for voicing heretical ideas. When another palace revolution in 1667 returned his friends to a measure of power, he was released. In 1669 he went to Rome, where he was given a papal grant of immunity from the jurisdiction of the Inquisition. From 1669 to 1675 he was a major factor in the Roman political arena, and is credited with securing a relaxation of inquisitorial activities in Portugal for the years 1676–81. This he accomplished by backing the efforts of the Marrano lobbyist Francisco *d'Azevedo to buy the freedom of accused Judaizers, and by presenting for papal review a 200-page exposé of Portuguese inquisitors that characterized them as inspired more by greed than by piety. Vieira's incisive memorandum was later included in David *Nieto's defense of Jews, *Recondite Notices of the Inquisition of Spain and Portugal* (London, 1722).

BIBLIOGRAPHY: C.R. Boxer, *A Great Luso-Brazilian Figure: Padre Antonio Vieira* (1957); R. Southey, *Letters Written During a Short Residence in Spain and Portugal* (Bristol, 1799), 452–4; Roth, Marranos, 342, 348; J.L. d'Azevedo,… *História de Antonio Vieira*, 2 vols. (1918–20).

[Aaron Lichtenstein]

VIENNA, capital of *Austria. Documentary evidence points to the first settlement of Jews in the 12th century. The first Jew known by name is *Shlom (Solomon), mintmaster and financial adviser to Duke Leopold V. The community possessed a synagogue at the time and Jews owned houses in the city. In

1196 Shlom and 15 other Jews were murdered by participants in the Third *Crusade. Under Leopold VI (1198–1230) a second synagogue was erected. Its existence is noted in 1204. In 1235 the Jew *Teka (Tecanus) is mentioned as living in Vienna; he acted as state banker for Austria, and had far-flung financial interests. A charter of privileges was granted by Emperor Frederick II in 1238 giving the Jewish community extensive autonomy. A Jewish quarter is mentioned at the end of the century, although its origins are somewhat earlier. The oldest Jewish tombstone found dates from 1298; a Jewish cemetery is noted only in 1368, but probably dates from the second half of the 13th century. A slaughterhouse is noted in 1320.

At the close of the 13th and during the 14th centuries, the community of Vienna was recognized as the leading community of German Jewry. In the second half of the 13th century there were in the community 1,000 Jews, living in 70 houses. The influence of the "Sages of Vienna" spread far beyond the limits of the town itself and continued for many generations. Of primary importance were *Isaac b. Moses "Or Zaru'a," his son *Ḥayyim "Or Zaru'a," Avigdor b. Elijah ha-Kohen, and *Meir b. Baruch ha-Levi. At the time of the *Black Death persecutions of 1348–49, the community of Vienna was spared and even served as a refuge for Jews from other places; it developed rapidly during the reign of Rudolf IV (1339–65).

Nonetheless, toward the end of the 14th century there was growing anti-Jewish feeling among the burghers; in 1406 during the course of a fire that broke out in the synagogue, in which it was destroyed, the burghers seized the opportunity to attack Jewish homes. The need of Duke Albert V for money and the effects of the uprising by the *Hussites, combined with the hatred for the Jews among the local population, led to cruel persecutions in 1421 (the *Wiener Gesera). Many of the community's members died as martyrs; others were expelled, and the children forcibly converted. The community was destroyed and its property passed to Duke Albert.

After the persecutions some Jews nevertheless remained there illegally; in 1438 Christian physicians complained about Jews practicing medicine illegally in the city. In 1512 there were 12 Jewish families in Vienna, and a small number of Jews continued to live there during the 16th century, often faced with threats of expulsion. In 1582 a Jewish cemetery is noted. They suffered during the Thirty Years' War (1618–48) as a result of the occupation of the city by Imperial soldiers. In 1624 Emperor *Ferdinand II confined the Jews to a ghetto situated on the site of the present-day Leopoldstadt quarter. In 1632 there were 106 houses in the ghetto, and in 1670 there were 136 houses accommodating 500 families. A document of privilege issued in 1635 authorized the inhabitants of the ghetto to circulate within the "inner town" during business hours and Jews also owned shops in other streets of the city. Some Jews at this time were merchants engaged in international trade; others were petty traders. The community of Vienna reassumed its respected position in the Jewish world. In addition to other communal institutions the Jews maintained two hospitals. Among rabbis of the renewed community were Yom Tov Lipman Heller, and Shabbetai Sheftel *Horowitz, one of the many refugees from Poland who fled the *Chmielnicki massacres of 1648.

Hatred by the townsmen of the Jews increased during the mid-17th century, fanned by the bigotry of Bishop Kollonitsch. Emperor Leopold I, influenced by the bishop as well as the religious fanaticism of his wife and sustained by the potential gains for his treasury, decided to expel the Jews from Vienna once again. Though Leo *Winkler, head of the Jewish community at the time, arranged for the intervention of Queen Christina of Sweden on behalf of the Jews it was of no avail, as was an offer to the emperor of 100,000 florins to limit the expulsion. The poorer Jews were expelled in 1669; the rest were exiled in the month of Av, 1670, and their properties taken from them. The Great Synagogue was converted into a Catholic church, the "Leopoldskirche." The Jews paid the municipality 4,000 florins to supervise the Jewish cemetery. Of the 3,000–4,000 Jews expelled some made their way to the great cities of Europe where a number succeeded in regaining their fortunes. Others settled in small towns and villages. According to the testimony of the Swedish ambassador at the time, some of the Jews took advantage of the offer to convert to Christianity so as not to be exiled.

By 1693 the financial losses to the city were sufficient to generate support for a proposal to readmit the Jews. This time, however, their number was to be much smaller, without provision for an organized community. Only the wealthy were authorized to reside in Vienna, as "tolerated subjects," in exchange for a payment of 300,000 florins and an annual tax of 10,000 florins. Prayer services were permitted to be held only in private homes. The founders of the community and its leaders in those years, as well as during the 18th century, were prominent *Court Jews, such as Samuel *Oppenheimer, Samson *Wertheimer, and Baron Diego *Aguilar. As a result of their activities, Vienna became a center for Jewish diplomatic efforts on behalf of Jews throughout the empire as well as an important center for Jewish philanthropy. In 1696 Oppenheimer regained possession of the Jewish cemetery and built a hospital for the poor next to it. The wealthy of Vienna supported the poor of Ereẓ Israel; in 1742 a fund of 22,000 florins was established for this purpose, and until 1918 the interest from this fund was distributed by the Austrian consul in Palestine (see *Hierosolymitanische Stiftung). A Sephardi community in Vienna traces its origins to 1737, and grew as a result of commerce with the Balkans.

During the 18th century the restrictions on the residence rights of the "tolerated subjects" had prevented the rapid growth of the Jewish population in Vienna. There were 452 Jews living in the city in 1752 and 520 in 1777. The Jews suffered under the restrictive legislation of *Maria Theresa (1740–80). In 1781 her son, Joseph II, issued his *Toleranzpatent, which though attacked in Jewish circles, paved the way in some respects for later emancipation. Religious studies and sermons were delivered illegally by the scholars of the community or by rabbis who had been called upon to visit the town. By 1793 there was a Hebrew printing press in Vienna that soon became the center for Hebrew printing in Central Europe (see below). During this period the first signs of assimilation in the social and family life of the Jews of Vienna made their appearance, and there was a decline in the observance of tradition. At the time of the Congress of *Vienna in 1815 the salons of Jewish hostesses served as entertainment and meeting places for the rulers of Europe. In 1821 nine Jews of Vienna were raised to the nobility.

From the close of the 18th century, and especially during the first decades of the 19th, Vienna became a center of the *Haskalah movement. The influence and scope of the community's activities increased particularly after the annexation of *Galicia by Austria. Despite restrictions, the number of Jews in the city rapidly increased. Several Hebrew authors, including the poet and traveler Samuel Aaron *Romanelli, the philologist Judah Leib *Ben Zeev, the poet Solomon Levisohn, Meir *Letteris, etc., wrote their works in Vienna. Some of them earned their livelihood as proofreaders in the city's Hebrew press. The character of Haskalah and the literature of the Jews of Vienna was gradually Germanized. The first Jewish journalists, such as Isidor Heller, Moritz Kuh, and Zigmund Kulischer, inaugurated an era of Jewish influence on the Viennese press.

At a later period the call for religious reform was heard in Vienna. Various *maskilim*, including Peter Peretz Ber and Naphtali Hertz *Homberg, tried to convince the government to impose Haskalah recommendations and religious reform on the Jews. This aroused strong controversy among the Vienna community. The appointment of Isaac Noah *Mannheimer as director of the religious school in 1825 was a compromise between the supporters of reform and its opponents. In 1826 a magnificent synagogue, the Stadttempel, in which the Hebrew language and the traditional prayers were retained, was built by Josef Kornhaeusel. It was the first legal synagogue to be opened since 1671, but had to be hidden from the street because the law demanded it. The activists around Mannheimer, who founded the synagogue, were Michael Lazar Biedermann, Isak Loew Hofmann von Hofmannsthal, Heinrich Sichrovsky, and Leopold von Wertheimstein. Mannheimer and the *ḥazzan* Salomon *Sulzer tried to improve the decorum of the services in the new synagogue, rejected radical Reform, created the Viennese rite, and prevented a split in the community. Sulzer's *Shir Ẓiyyon* ("Song of Zion") became a model for many Ashkenazi synagogues throughout the world.

Jewish intellectuals were in the forefront of the revolution of 1848. The physician Adolf *Fischhof pleaded for press freedom, Ludwig August *Frankl, Moritz *Hartmann, and Ignaz *Kuranda published poems and articles and founded newspapers. The burial of the Jewish and Christian dead of the revolution together, with Mannheimer and Sulzer participating, was the first ecumenical service in Austria. Among the dead was Hermann Jellinek, the brother of Mannheimer's successor, Adolf *Jellinek. With the new constitution of 1849 the Jews gained equality before the law.

Kuranda, a member of the German National Assembly in Frankfurt and of the Vienna City Council, became president of the Jewish community in 1872. The writer, poet, and journalist Ludwig August Frankl became archivist and secretary of the Jewish community. In 1856 he traveled to Jerusalem, where he founded the Laemel School, which was financed by Elise Herz. He published his experiences in the two volumes, *Nach Jerusalem*. Joseph Ritter von *Wertheimer, who became the first president of the Jewish community in 1864, founded in 1830 the first general kindergarten in Vienna and in 1843 a Jewish kindergarten. He also established an orphanage for girls and a children's home and became founder and president of the Israelitische Allianz zu Wien.

During the second half of the 19th century and the first decades of the 20th, the Jewish population of Vienna increased as a result of immigration there by Jews from other regions of the empire, particularly Hungary, Galicia, and Bukovina. There were 3,739 Jews living in Vienna in 1846, 9,731 in 1850, and about 15,000 in 1854. After 1914 about 50,000 refugees from Galicia and Bukovina established themselves there, so that by 1923 there were 201,513 Jews living in Vienna, which had become the third largest Jewish community in Europe. In 1936 there were 176,034 Jews in Vienna (8% of the total population). The occupations of the Jews in Vienna became more variegated. Many of them entered the liberal professions: out of a total of 2,163 advocates, 1,345 were Jews, and 2,440 of the 3,268 physicians were Jews.

Before the Holocaust there were 19 temples and 63 smaller houses of prayer in Vienna. Together they had 29,200 seats. The first free-standing temple in Vienna was built in 1858 by Ludwig von Foerster in Vienna's main Jewish quarter in the Leopoldstadt district. With 2,000 seats it was the biggest temple in Vienna. In 1929 the last temple – a modern Jugendstil building – was inaugurated in the Viennese district of Hietzing. The Orthodox faction of the Jewish community had two large temples, the famous Schiffschul, built in 1864, where Jesaia Fuerst was rabbi from 1897 until 1938, and the Polnische Tempel (Polish temple) in the Leopoldsgasse with Mayer Mayersohn as rabbi from 1899 until 1937.

In 1857 Adolf Jellinek became preacher of the Leopoldstaedter temple. Eight years later he became Mannheimer's successor in the Stadttempel. He avoided the term rabbi, was one of the greatest preachers of his day, and remained antagonistic to the new national movement. He published many apologetic articles in the newspaper *Neuzeit*, from 1861 edited by Leopold Kompert and Simon Szanto. He also edited many Midrashim and published several studies on the Kabbalah.

In 1866 Moritz *Guedemann, a graduate of the Jewish Theological Seminary in Breslau, became rabbi of the Leopoldstaedter temple. In 1869 he became head of the *bet din*, and in 1894 Jellinek's successor as chief rabbi of Vienna. He was more Orthodox than his predecessors and was an open enemy of the Zionist movement. As a scholar he published a multi-volume history of Jewish education. His memoirs are stored in the Leo Baeck Institute in New York and, except for short extracts, were never published.

In 1890 the Israelitengesetz was passed, which ruled that only one Jewish community was allowed in one geographical region.

The Jewish community of Vienna had many Jewish educational, cultural, and social institutions. To name only the most important, in 1864 Adolf Jellinek founded the Beth Hamidrasch, where Isak Hirsch Weiss, Meir Friedmann, Salomon Rubin, and Sigmund Gelbhaus taught Bible, Talmud, the Shulḥan Arukh and *Mishneh Torah*, and Jewish history.

The rabbinical seminary, founded in 1893, was a European center for research into Jewish literature and history. It was modeled on the Jewish Theological Seminary in Breslau, of which its first director, Adolf Schwarz, was as a graduate. The most prominent scholars were Adolf *Buechler, David *Mueller, Victor *Aptowitzer, Z.H. *Chajes, and Samuel *Krauss.

After World War I the Zionists – most prominent among them the new Viennese chief rabbi Zwi Perez Chajes – founded several new educational institutions. Among them was the Hebrew Pedagogium, opened in 1918. It offered courses for kindergarten teachers and Hebrew teachers; its language of instruction was Hebrew. Its first director was Harry Torczyner, who moved to Berlin in 1919 to teach at the *Hochschule fuer die Wissenschaft des Judentums and went in 1933 to Jerusalem, where he taught at the Hebrew University under his Hebraicized name Naphtali *Tur-Sinai. His successor was Abraham Sonne. Other instructors were Salo W. *Baron, Zwi Diesendruck, and M.A. Wiesen.

In 1920 a seminary for the training of religious teachers was founded; its director was Moritz Rosenfeld. Also in 1920 a Jewish high school was opened. It was Zionist-oriented; its director was Viktor Kellner, a former teacher of the Herzliah High School in Tel Aviv. After the death of Zwi Perez Chajes the school was named after him.

In 1924 Rabbi Armand Kaminka, who also was the secretary of the Israelitische Allianz and who had taught at the Beth Hamidrasch, founded the Maimonides Institut, where the same traditional Jewish subjects were taught. Its teachers were Moses Zickier; the Vienna community rabbi Moritz Bauer; the lawyer Nissan Goldstein; Moses Horowitz, before he became rabbi of Stanislau; and Salomon Rappaport, who later became the director of the Hebrew seminary in Johannesburg, South Africa.

In 1844 a Jewish institution for the deaf and dumb was founded. It was directed by Moritz Brunner and Salomon Krenberger, but had to be closed in 1926 because of financial difficulties. In 1876 Ludwig August Frankl founded a Jewish institution for the blind. Its directors were Simon Heller (until 1923) and Siegfried Altmann, who emigrated in 1938 to New York. Both were renowned experts in the education of the blind.

In 1869 Anselm Freiherr von Rothschild financed the new building of a Jewish hospital in memory of his father (called Rothschild hospital).

In 1896 the Jewish Museum was opened. It was the first Jewish museum in the world; it was maintained by the Society for the Collection and Conservation of Jewish Art and Historic Monuments. Its curator was Jakob Bronner, who fled to Palestine in 1938. The collection of the museum was dispersed; only parts of it could be found and reconstituted after 1945. The same happened with the famous library of the Jewish community, which had about 50,000 volumes and was directed by Bernhard Muenz, the historian Bernhard *Wachstein, and after his death in 1936 by Moses Rath, the author of the Hebrew textbook *Sefat Amenu.*

Vienna also became a Jewish sports center; the soccer team Ha-Koah and the *Maccabi organization of Vienna were well known.

Though in the social life and the administration of the community, there was mostly strong opposition to Jewish national action, Vienna was also a center of the national awakening. Peretz *Smolenskin published **Ha-Shaḥar* between 1868 and 1885 in Vienna, while Nathan *Birnbaum founded the first Jewish nationalist student association, *Kadimah, there in 1882, and preached "pre-Herzl Zionism" from 1884. It was due to Herzl that Vienna was at first the center of Zionist activities. He published the Zionist movement's organ, *Die *Welt*, and established the headquarters of the Zionist Executive there. The Zionist movement in Vienna gained in strength after World War I. In 1919 the Zionist Robert *Stricker was elected to the Austrian parliament, although he was not reelected in 1920. Three Zionists, Leopold Plaschkes, Jakob Ehrlich, and Bruno Pollack-Parnau, were elected to the Vienna City Council. The well-known Zionist social worker Anita *Mueller-Cohen, who set up a whole network of social institutions for thousands of Jewish refugees who had fled during World War I from Galicia and Bukovina to Vienna, was elected as the youngest member of the Vienna City Council on a non-Zionist list. The Zionists did not obtain a majority in the Jewish community until the elections of 1932, when the Zionist lawyer Desider *Friedmann became president.

After the establishment of the Austrian Corporate State (*Staendestaat*) in 1934 following the defeat of the Social Democrats in the Austrian Civil War, Desider Friedmann became *Staatsrat* (a member of the new governing body), Salomon Frankfurter *Bundeskulturrat* (a member of the advisory council), and Jakob Ehrlich, an appointed member of the body which replaced the democratically elected Vienna City Council.

[Yomtov Ludwig Bato / Evelyn Adunka (2nd ed.)]

The Holocaust Period

The experience and practice in dealing with the Jews, gained in Germany since 1933, were utilized by the Nazis when they occupied Vienna in March 1938 with great harshness and brutality. In less than one year they introduced all the discriminatory laws, backed by ruthless terror and by mass arrests (usually of economic leaders and intellectuals, who were detained in special camps or sent to Dachau). These measures were accompanied by unspeakable atrocities. Vienna's chief rabbi, Dr. Israel Taglicht, who was more than 75 years old, was forced to clean the Seitenstettengasse, where the Stadttempel and the community offices were, and to stand in front of a shop with an anti-Jewish poster. He was able to immigrate to England, were he died in 1943.

The president of the community, Desider Friedmann, the vice president, Robert *Stricker, and the director, Josef Loewenherz, as well as the president of the Zionist organization, Oskar Gruenbaum, were immediately arrested. The historian of the Zionist movement, Adolf Boehm became insane, dying in prison shortly afterward. During *Kristallnacht* (November 9–10, 1938), 42 synagogues were destroyed, hundreds of people perished, and thousands were arrested; shops and flats were plundered by the SA and the Hitler Youth, subsequently being confiscated.

Nonetheless, the organization of immigration and the transfer of property necessitated the release of some Jewish leaders who had to form the *Aeltestenrat*. Aryanization was practiced by the forced sale and liquidation of thousands of enterprises; apartments had to be evacuated. Moreover, for the first time, forced emigration (legal and "illegal") was systematically organized by Eichmann's Zentralstelle fuer juedische Auswanderung. Consequently, of Vienna's 166,000 Jews (approximately 10% of the city's population) about 100,000 emigrated before the war; about 18,000 of them were later caught in other European countries; an additional 18,500 succeeded in getting out before the general ban on emigration in the fall of 1941. With the outbreak of war deportation of Austrian Jews increased, whereas previously mainly those of Polish and Czech nationality had been expelled. The first transports were sent to the notorious Nisko, in the Lublin district (October 1939). The last mass transport left in September 1942; it included many prominent people and Jewish dignitaries, who were sent to Theresienstadt, from where later they were mostly deported to Auschwitz. In November 1942 the Jewish community of Vienna was officially dissolved. The "Council of Jewish Elders," with Loewenherz at its head, continued to exist. About 800 Viennese Jews succeeded in remaining underground.

For further details and bibliography, see *Austria, Holocaust.

Postwar Period

According to the historian Jonny Moser in April 1945 there were 5,512 Jews living in Austria, who had survived as employees of the *Aeltestenrat,* in hiding, or in concentration and labor camps. Their number decreased due to excess of deaths over births, and emigration; the loss was soon more than compensated for by the return of several thousands of Austrian Jews, and the addition of a number of *Displaced Persons and refugees who had settled in Vienna. The population of the community reached its postwar peak in 1950 with 12,450 registered Jews, and decreased to 8,930 in 1965. It was estimated that there were at least 2,000 Jews living in Vienna who did not register with the community.

Vienna was the main transient stopping-place and the first refuge for hundreds of thousands of Jewish refugees and emigrants from Eastern Europe after World War II. This applies to the greater part of the exodus of Polish Jews in 1946 (see *Beriḥah), and, to a lesser degree, to Jews from Romania and Hungary in 1946–47, when the Rothschild Hospital of the Viennese community became the main screening station on the way to the DP camps of Germany, Austria, and Italy. It was true also for the great stream of refugees from Hungary during and after the revolt of 1956, when at least 18,000 Jewish refugees found temporary shelter in Vienna, as well as for several thousand refugees from Czechoslovakia after the Soviet invasion of 1968. Emigration to Israel from Poland, the Soviet Union, Czechoslovakia, Hungary, and partly also from Romania passed through Vienna as well.

The Community was reconstituted shortly after the war, with a president appointed by the occupation authorities, but by April 1946, elections were held for the community council. As a result of these first elections, David Brill of the left-wing Unity party was elected president. In April 1948 the Unity party was defeated by a coalition of the Zionists and the non-Zionist Social Democrats (the Bund Werktaetiger Juden), and the Zionist, David Schapira, was elected president.

After two short and turbulent presidencies of the General Zionist Wolf Hertzberg and the Communist Kurt Heitler, both of them lawyers, the long era of the rule of the Social Democratic Party Bund werktaetiger Juden (Union of Working Jews) began in 1952. The lawyer Emil Maurer was elected president, but retired in 1963, and was replaced by Ernst Feldsberg, also a representative of the Bund. Akiba Eisenberg served as rabbi from 1948. The sole synagogue functioning was the old Stadttempel in the Seitenstettengasse, the only synagogue that was not destroyed on *Kristallnacht* on November 9–10, 1938. Though the Zionists constitute a minority, there are intensive and diversified Zionist activities. Their most important event was the transfer of the remains of Theodor Herzl, who had been buried at the Doebling cemetery in Vienna, to Jerusalem in 1949.

In the 1960s and early 1970s it was not possible for the Jewish community, for financial reasons, to rebuild its infrastructure. In 1963 an attempt to build a community center failed because of lack of funding, although the cornerstone had already been laid. A provisional room for a Jewish museum was opened in 1964 and closed after a few years; the same happened with the reading room of the library. In 1966 the Jewish community opened a youth center. In 1967 the ceremonial hall of the main Jewish cemetery was built, but the Jewish hospital was closed in 1970.

As successor to the lawyer Anton Pick, the first non-socialist president of the Vienna Jewish community – the lawyer Ivan Hacker – was elected in 1981. Two new factions of the Jewish community were founded by younger members in the 1970s and 1980s with the aim of a renewal of the Jewish community and its institutions. In 1980 the Jewish community center was opened, in 1984 the Jewish High School (the

Chajesgymnasium), in 1987 a second Jewish high school by Chabad, and in 1989 the Jewish Institute of Adult Education were founded. In 1987 the furrier Paul Grosz became successor to Ivan Hacker. In 1988 the Jewish Old Age Home was enlarged and named after Maimonides. In 1963, as in 1988, the Stadttempel was renovated. In 1994 the psychological and social services center Esra was opened.

Besides the Stadttempel 14 smaller synagogues and prayer rooms existed. In 1992 the Sephardi Center with two synagogues was built. In 1993 the Vienna Jewish Museum was opened in the Palais Eskeles in the heart of the city. The old library of the Jewish community was given on permanent loan to the Jewish Museum and could thus be reopened in 1994. From the early 1990s Jewish cultural weeks, street festivals, and film and theater weeks were regularly organized.

In 1983 Chief Rabbi Akiba Eisenberg died and was succeeded by his son Paul Chaim Eisenberg, the chief rabbi as of 2006. From 1998 the real estate tycoon Ariel Muzicant was president of the community. He was the first president who was born after the Holocaust.

In the early 21st century Vienna had a small but thriving and active Jewish community that played an active part in the public and cultural life of the city. In contrast to the Austrian state, which in early 2005 was still negotiating restitution payments, the city of Vienna strongly supported the Jewish community and its many projects from the late 1970s on. In 2004 the community had 6,894 members.

[Evelyn Adunka (2nd ed.)]

Hebrew Printing

In the 16th century a number of books were published in Vienna which had some rough Hebrew lettering (from woodblocks?): Andreas Planeus' *Institutiones Grammatices Ebreae*, printed by Egyd Adler, 1552; J.S. Pannonicis' *De bello tureis in ferendo*, printed by Hanns Singriener, 1554; and Paul Weidner's *Loca praecipuo Fidei Christianae*, printed by Raphael Hofhalter, 1559. Toward the end of the 18th century extensive Hebrew printing in Vienna began with the court printer Joseph Edler von Kurzbeck, who used the font of Joseph *Proops in Amsterdam. He employed Anton (later: von) Schmid (1775–1855), who chose printing instead of the priesthood. Their first production was the Mishnah (1793). In 1800 the government placed an embargo on Hebrew books printed abroad and thus gave him a near monopoly. His correctors were Joseph della Torre and the poet Samuel Romanelli (to 1799), who with Schmid printed his *Alot ha-Minḥah* for Charlotte Arnstein's fashionable marriage (1793). Among the works they printed were a Bible with Mendelssohn's *Biur* (1794–95) and David Franco-Mendes' *Gemul Atalyah* (1800). Schmid also issued the 24th Talmud edition (1806–11) and the *Turim* (1810–13) with J.L. Ben-Zeev's notes on *Ḥoshen Mishpat.* Besides Kurzbeck and Schmid there were other rivals and smaller firms: Joseph Hraszansky, using a Frankfurt on the Main font, opened a Hebrew department in Vienna. Among his great achievements is an edition of the Talmud (1791–97). In 1851 "J.P. Sollinger's widow" began to print Hebrew texts including a Talmud, with I.H. *Weiss as corrector (1860–73). Special mention must also be made of the Hebrew journals printed in Vienna including *Bikkurei ha-Ittim* (1820/21–31), *Kerem Ḥemed* (1833–56), *Oẓar Neḥmad* (1856–63), *Bikkurei Ittim* (1844), *Kokhevei Yiẓḥak* (1845–73), and *Ha-Shaḥar* (1868–84/5).

[Israel O. Lehman]

BIBLIOGRAPHY: Germ Jud, 1 (1963), 397–425; 2 (1968), 886–903. M. Gruenwald, *Vienna* (1936); idem, *Samuel Oppenheim und sein Kreis* (1913); S. Krauss, *Die Wiener Gesera vom Jahre 1421* (1920); J.E. Scherer, *Die Rechtsverhaeltnisse der Juden in den deutsch-oesterreichischen Laendern* (1901); H. Tietze, *Die Juden Wiens* (1935, 1987²); Aronius, Regesten, index; A.F. Pribram, *Urkunden und Akten zur Geschichte der Juden in Wien* (1918); L. Bato, *Die Juden im alten Wien* (1928); B. Wachstein, *Die Inschriften des alten Judenfriedhofes in Wien*, 2 vols. (1912/1917); A. Zehavi-Goldhammer, in: *Arim ve-Immahot be-Yisrael*, 1 (1946), 176–289; D. Kaufmann, *Die letzte Vertreibung der Juden aus Wien* (1889); J. Fraenkel, *The Jews of Austria* (1967), incl. bibl., 549–51; N.M. Gelber, in: JSOS, 10 (1948), 359–96; R. Dan, in: SBB, 9 (1970), 101–5; M. Kohler, *Jewish Rights at the Congresses of Vienna and Aix-la-Chapelle* (1918), index; G. Wolf, *Geschichte der Juden in Wien (1156–1876)* (1876); idem, *Vom ersten bis zum zweiten Tempel…* (1861); I. Schwarz, *Das Wiener Ghetto* (1909); G. Fritsch and O. Breita, *Finale und Auftakt…* (1964); H. Gold, *Geschichte der Juden in Wien* (1966); L. Goldhammer, *Die Juden Wiens* (1927); M. Letteris, in: *Bikkurim*, 2 (1865), 20–38, 244; B. Wachstein (ed.), *Die hebraeische Publizistik in Wien* (1930); Ḥ.D. Friedberg, *Toledot ha-Defus ha-Ivri be-Arim ha-Elleh she-be-Eiropah…* (1937), 94–104. **ADD. BIBLIOGRAPHY:** E. Adunka, *Die vierte Gemeinde. Die Geschichte der Wiener Juden in der Zeit von 1945 bis heute* (2000); R. Beckermann (ed.), *Die Mazzesinsel. Juden in der Wiener Leopoldstadt 1918–1938* (1984); S. Beller *Vienna and the Jews 1867–1938. A Cultural History* (1989); G. Berkley, *Vienna and its Jews. The Tragedy of Success 1880s–1980s* (1988); B. Dalinger, *Verloschene Sterne. Geschichte des juedischen Theaters in Wien* (1998); idem, *Quellenedition zur Geschichte des jüdischen Theaters in Wien* (2003); H.P. Freidenreich, *Jewish Politics in Vienna, 1918–1938* (1991); P. Genée, *Wiener Synagogen 1825–1938* (1987); D. Hecht, *Zwischen Feminismus und Zionismus. Anitta Mueller-Cohen. Die Biographie einer Juedin* (2005); M. Heindl, R. Koblizek, *125 Jahre Rothschildspital* (1998); E. Hoeflich (Moshe Ya'akov Ben-Gavriel), *Tagebücher 1915–1927*, ed. by A.A. Wallas (1999); *Juedisches Wien/Jewish Vienna* (2004); K. Kempter, *Die Jellineks 1820–1955* (1998); P. Landesmann, *Rabbiner aus Wien. Ihre Ausbildung, ihre religiösen und nationalen Konflikte* (1997); E. Malleier, *Juedische Frauen in Wien 1816–1938* (2003); J. Moser, *Demographie der juedischen Bevoelkerung Oesterreichs 1838–1945* (1999); D. Rabinovici, *Instanzen der Ohnmacht. Wien 1938–1945. Der Weg zum Judenrat* (2000); D. Rechter, *The Jews of Vienna and the First World War* (2001); M.L. Rozenblit, *The Jews of Vienna 1867–1914. Assimilation and Identity* (1983); R.S. Wistrich, *The Jews of Vienna in the Age of Franz Joseph* (1990); W. Schott, *Das Allgemeine österreichische israelitische Taubstummen-Institut in Wien 1844–1926* (1999).

VIENNA, CONGRESS OF, international congress held in Vienna, September 1814 to June 1815, to reestablish peace and order in Europe after the Napoleonic Wars. The congress met in the Apollosaal built by the English-born Jew, Sigmund Wolffsohn, and the delegates were often entertained during the course of the proceedings in the *salons of Jewish hostesses, such as Fanny von *Arnstein and Cecily *Eskeles.

The Jewish question, raised explicitly for the first time at an international conference, arose in connection with the constitution of a new federation of German states. The Jews of Frankfurt and of the Hanseatic towns of *Hamburg, *Luebeck, and *Bremen had previously attained equal civil rights under French rule. The Hanseatic cities were annexed to France in 1810, and Jewish emancipation in France was effective ipso facto there. The Frankfurt community paid the French staff of the duke a vast sum of money in 1811 in return for being granted equality. They now sent delegates to the Congress to seek confirmation of their rights, as well as emancipation for the Jews of the other German states. The delegates for Frankfurt were Gabriel Oppenheimer and Jacob Baruch (the father of Ludwig *Boerne), while the Hanseatic towns were represented among others, by the non-Jew Carl August *Buchholz. They succeeded in gaining the support of such leading personalities as Metternich (Austria), Hardenberg, and Humboldt (Prussia). In October 1814 a committee of five German states met to prepare proposals for the constitution of the new federation. Bavaria and Wuerttemberg, fearing the curtailment of their independence, opposed Austria, Prussia, and Hanover, especially on the question of Jewish rights. At the general session of the Congress in May 1815, the opposition to Jewish civic equality grew, despite favorable proposals by Austria and Prussia. On June 10, paragraph 16 of the constitution of the German Federation was resolved:

> The Assembly of the Federation will deliberate how to achieve the civic improvement of the members of the Jewish religion in Germany in as generally agreed a form as possible, in particular as to how to grant and insure for them the possibility of enjoying civic rights in return for the acceptance of all civic duties in the states of the Federation; until then, the members of this religion will have safeguarded for them the rights which have already been granted to them by the single states of the Federation.

This formulation postponed Jewish equality to the far distant future, while by changing one word in the final draft to "by," instead of "in the states," a formulation arrived at only at the meeting on June 8, a loophole had been left by which the states could disown rights granted by any but the lawful government, namely, those bestowed by the French or their temporary rulers. The Congress, therefore, did nothing to better the status of the Jews but, in effect, only worsened their position in many places.

The Jewish question arose again at the Conference of Aix-la-Chapelle (1818), when the powers met to determine the withdrawal of troops from France and consider France's indemnity to the allies. Various Jewish communities turned to the conference for relief, and Lewis *Way, an English clergyman, presented a petition for emancipation to Alexander I of Russia. Despite a sympathetic reception, however, there were no practical results.

BIBLIOGRAPHY: M.J. Kohler, in: AJHSP, 26 (1918), 33–125; L. Wolf, *Notes on the Diplomatic History of the Jewish Question* (1919), 12–15; S.W. Baron, *Die Judenfrage auf dem Wiener Kongress* (1920); M. Grunwald, *Vienna* (1936), 190–204.

[Shmuel Ettinger]

VIENNE, town in the department of Isère, S.E. France. The earliest confirmed Jewish presence in France was in Vienne. In the year 6 C.E., *Archelaus, ethnarch of Judah, was consigned there by Emperor Augustus; he died there in about 16 C.E. This fact was probably the source of the error in the *Roman provençal* of Girard de Vienne, in which it is asserted that a Jew named Joachim arrived in Vienne after the conquest of Jerusalem by Titus. At the beginning of the ninth century there was an important Jewish community in Vienne that was confronted by the coercive missionary activities organized by *Agobard, bishop of Lyons. After Agobard's failure, he induced the bishop of Vienne to call on his community to avoid all relations with the Jews. From 849 a plot of land inside the town was commonly owned by the Jews. This may have been the nucleus of the Jewish quarter, Burgus publicus Hebraeurum, which is mentioned from the last quarter of the tenth century and is commemorated by the "Saint-Pierre entre Juifs" parish and the Rue de Juiverie near the St.-Maurice church. From the tenth century the Jews of Vienne also owned and cultivated agricultural estates, including many vineyards within the proximity of Vienne. They constantly expanded these properties and the purchase of land by Jews was often camouflaged under a fictitious promissory note, for which a pledge in real estate was taken. Also, the Jews often exchanged plots of land, occasionally with the Church itself. At the close of the tenth century the Jew Astier was invested with the function of steward by the abbot of St.-André-le-Bas to deal with business (*negotia monachorum*). The tenor of the relationship with the Christian community changed radically in 1247, when the archbishop of Vienne had to be exhorted by Pope Innocent IV to guarantee the protection of the Jews of his diocese after the *Valréas blood libel. One of the last details known about the Jews of Vienne during the Middle Ages concerns the search carried out in 1389 to seize the promissory notes. Among the Jewish scholars of Vienne during the Middle Ages were the legal authority Tobiah b. Elijah (first half of the 13th century) and the *posek* Yakar (second half of the 13th century).

BIBLIOGRAPHY: Gross, Gal Jud, 191–4; L. Clair, in: *Vienne; Mélanges d' Archéologie et d'Histoire*, 1 (1923/24), 59–62; *Roman Provençal de Girard de Vienne*, ed. by G. Ranier (1829), 32; B. Blumenkranz, in: *Comptes-Rendus de l'Académie des Inscriptions et Belles-Lettres* (1969), 162; idem, *Juifs et Chrétiens dans le Monde Occidental* (1960), index; see also A. Prudhomme, in: REJ, 9 (1884), 232, 253f.

[Bernhard Blumenkranz]

VIERTEL, BERTHOLD (1885–1953), Austrian writer, stage and film director, essayist, and translator. Viertel was a cofounder and dramatic supervisor of the *Volksbuehne* in his native Vienna (1912–14) and later directed plays in Dresden as well as in Berlin and Duesseldorf. He also contributed to the satirical weekly *Simplicissimus* and to Karl *Kraus' *Die Fackel*, in which his first poems appeared. He wrote a study of the satirist, *Karl Kraus, ein Charakter und die Zeit* (1921). His comedy *Die schoene Seele* appeared in 1925, and a novel, *Das Gnadenbrot*, in 1927. Of far greater importance, however, was his lyric poetry. He produced four volumes of verse: *Die Spur* (1913), *Die Bahn* (1921), *Fuerchte dich nicht! Neue Gedichte* (1941), and *Der Lebenslauf* (1946). From 1928 to 1931, Viertel was a movie director in Hollywood and from 1933 he worked in London and broadcast anti-Nazi programs over the BBC. Christopher Isherwood's short novel, *Prater Violet*, is regarded by many as a *roman à clef* about Viertel. He settled in the United States in 1939, but in 1947 returned to Vienna, where he directed plays at the Burgtheater, including his own translations of Tennessee Williams' *The Glass Menagerie* and *A Streetcar Named Desire*. He was especially noted for his productions of expressionist dramas. After his death his collected works appeared in the volumes *Dichtung und Dokumente* (1956), *Schriften zum Theater* (1970), *Die Ueberwindung des Uebermenschen* (1989), and *Berthold Viertel: Studienausgabe in vier Baende* (1994). Among the collections of his poems are the books *Dass ich in dieser Sprache schreibe* (1981) and *Das graue Tuch* (1994). Viertel's recollections were gathered in the book *Kindheit eines Cherub* (1991).

BIBLIOGRAPHY: *Berthold Viertel... zur 80; Wiederkehr seines Geburtstages* (1965; incl. bibl.). **ADD. BIBLIOGRAPHY:** J. Mayerhoefer, *Berthold Viertel* (1975); F. Pfaefflin (ed.), *Berthold Viertel* (1969); I. Jansen, *Berthold Viertel* (1992); S. Bolbecher et al. (eds.), *Traum von der Realitaet* (1998); N. Weiss (ed.), *Berthold Viertel zum hundertzwanzigsten Geburtstag* (2005).

[Harry Zohn / Noam Zadoff (2nd ed.)]

VIGÉE (Strauss), CLAUDE (1921–), French poet and essayist. Born in the small Alsatian town of Bischwiller, Vigée was active in the French Jewish underground movement in World War II. He escaped to Spain in 1942 and reached the U.S. in 1943. After completing his studies there he taught at several American universities, including Brandeis. In 1960 he went to Israel as visiting professor of French literature at the Hebrew University of Jerusalem, assuming a permanent post there in 1963.

Vigée's poems, stories, and recollections, with their excursions into childhood and a philosophical quest for Jewishness, testify to a prolonged search for roots. This is especially evident in *La lutte avec l'ange* (1950), *L'été indien* (1957), and *Canaan d'exil* (1962). Consciousness of his own alienated condition led him, in the essays in *Les artistes de la faim* (1960) and *Révolte et louanges* (1962), to an examination of other great exiles searching for an absolute, such as Mallarmé, Camus, and *Kafka. After settling in Israel, Vigée was able to reach a harmony between his poetic urge and the surrounding everyday reality (*Le poème du retour*, 1962). The landscape of Israel inspired *Moisson de Canaan* (1967). Vigée also sought the fundamental bond between Hebrew and Western culture, and in "Civilisation française et génre hébraïque" (essay in his *Moisson de Canaan*) tried to define the role and importance of the specifically Jewish message in Western civilization. His essays on Goethe, Claudel, and Rilke also bear witness to his strong desire to reveal the imprint of the Bible on a civilization which declares itself heir to the Hellenic tradition alone. His works include various translations, such as *Cinquante poèmes de R.M. Rilke* (1953^2) and *L'Herbe du songe*, as well as the autobiographical *La lune d'hiver* (1970). His later works include *Dans le silence de l'aleph: Écriture et Révélation* (1992); *La lucarne aux étoiles: dix cahiers de Jérusalem, 1967–1997* (1998); *Vision et silence dans la poétique juive: demain la seule demeure: essais et entretiens, 1983–1996* (1999); *Danser vers l'abîme ou La spirale de l'extase: choix de poèmes et d'essais: 1995–2004* (2004); *La lutte avec l'ange: un chant de sombre joie dans l'agonie du temps: poèmes, 1939–1949* (2005).

BIBLIOGRAPHY: S. Doubrovsky, in: *Critique*, 18 (1962), 233–40; F. Tourret, in: *Preuves* (Feb. 1965), 83–84; *L'Arche*, 134 (1968), 65; G.E. Silverman, in: *Jerusalem Post*, Dec. 11, 1970. **ADD. BIBLIOGRAPHY:** M. Finck and H. Péras (ed.), *La terre et le souffle. Rencontre autour de Claude Vigée* (1998); *L'oeil témoin de la parole: rencontre autour de Claude Vigée*, essays collected by D. Mendelson and C. Leinman (2001).

[Max Bilen]

°**VIGENÈRE, BLAISE DE** (1523–1596), French diplomat, humanist, and Christian kabbalist. As French ambassador in Rome from 1566, Vigenère sought out Jewish scholars and immersed himself in Hebrew studies and the Kabbalah. He became a pupil of Gilbert *Génébrard and Nicolas Le Fèvre de la Boderie, two eminent French Christian Hebraists, and first began to publish at the age of 50. Vigenère was a well-known translator, but mainly achieved fame as the author of books on alchemy, astrology, cryptography, and Kabbalah.

His works include a *Traité des comètes avec leurs causes et effets* (Paris, 1578); and a *Traité des chiffres, ou Secrète manière d'écrire* (Paris, 1586), which was quoted at length by his cousin, Claude Duret, in his work *Thresor de l'histoire des langues de cest univers* (Paris, 1613). Kabbalistic material was more prominent in his *Prières et oraisons* (Paris, 1595), probably based on the second translation of the *Zohar undertaken by Guillaume *Postel. Vigenère himself wrote that the contents were "mainly drawn from the Zohar, the Sefer ha-*Bahir or Book of Splendor, the Midrash *Tehillim*, and other little-known works." The Christian Kabbalah is again prominent in a work which appeared posthumously, the *Traité du feu et du sel* (Paris, 1608; *Discourse of Fire and Salt*, 1649). In his *Traité des chiffres*, Vigenère paid generous tribute to Guy *Le Fèvre de la Boderie and his brother Nicolas, whose achievements had never fully been recognized.

BIBLIOGRAPHY: F. Secret, in: *Bibliothèque d'Humanisme et Renaissance*, 17 (1955), 294ff.; idem, *Le Zôhar chez les kabbalistes chrétiens de la Renaissance* (1964^2), 83–88; idem, *Les kabbalistes chrétiens de la Renaissance* (1964), 200, 203–8; *Nouvelle Biographie Générale*, 46 (1866), 140–2.

[Godfrey Edmond Silverman]

VIGODA, SAMUEL (1895–1990), *ḥazzan*. Vigoda, one of the star *ḥazzanim* of the Golden Age, was born in Dubrozin, Poland, but the family moved to Hungary, where his father was *ḥazzan*. He studied at the *yeshivot* of Galante and Pressburg and as a child lived for two and a half years with the famous *ḥazzan*, Yossele *Rosenblatt; later he also learned music at the conservatories of Klausenberg and Budapest as well as medicine at the university there. After serving as *ḥazzan* to the Arena Temple in Budapest, he immigrated to the United States in 1933, where he served as *ḥazzan* to important congregations in New York and Washington, including Rosenblatt's Oheb Zedek, the position that was given to him following Rosenblatt's untimely death. He published many articles on the history of *ḥazzanut* in Europe and the United States and produced many records. In 1980 he was given an award by the Ḥazzanim Farband of America and Canada. In 1981, Vigoda published *Legendary Voices* in English, which contains material concerning Ashkenazi *ḥazzanim.*

[Akiva Zimmerman / Raymond Goldstein (2nd ed.)]

VIHAR, BELA (1908–1978), Hungarian poet and teacher. Vihar, the son of a cantor, was born in Hajdunanas, Hungary, and received a traditional Jewish education. After completing his studies in the Jewish Teachers' Training College in Budapest he taught in various Jewish schools. During World War II he served in the Jewish Forced Labor Battalion on the Russian Front. From 1945 to 1948 he was principal of a Jewish school in Budapest and in 1949 was appointed organizer of culture for national minorities in the Hungarian Ministry of Education. From 1959 onwards, however, he devoted himself solely to journalism.

In his poems, which are of a high standard and full of profound thought, the influence of the Bible and Ḥasidism, as well as of Walt Whitman and Marc Chagall, is evident. In addition to his poetry, he occupied himself with Jewish themes and, together with Aladar *Komlos, published a collection of tales for children entitled *Kincsorzo fa* ("Treasure-Guardian Tree," 1940). He also published the first documentary work on the Holocaust, *Sarga konyv* ("Yellow Book," 1945), and the theme recurs from time to time in his works.

The following collections of his poems have been published: *Ut onmagadhoz* ("Road to Yourself," 1933); *Betuk bekessegeben* ("In Peace of Letters," 1941); *Onarckep* ("Self Portrait," 1962); *Negy felelet* ("Four Responses," 1965); *Kigyoenek* ("Serpent Song," 1970).

BIBLIOGRAPHY: *Magyar Irodalmi Lexikon*, 3 (1965).

[Baruch Yaron]

VILA REAL, town in N. central Portugal, in the province of Tras-os-Montes. Founded in the 13th century, it contains ancient architecture which exhibits Moorish influence. Vila Real became a Crypto-Jewish center after the forced conversions of 1497 (see *Portugal). The *Marranos there maintained their separate identity for four centuries, surviving the *Inquisition. Their survival was due in part to the character of the region – grapes for Porto's port wines are still grown there – which contributed to an independence of spirit and secretiveness. The Marranos narrowly won a contest of time against the Inquisition. For by 1718, when the Marranos had been effectively purged from the accessible coastal cities, the inquisitors began a systematic campaign into the hill country along the Spanish border. Concentrating on individual towns in the Tras-os-Montes, Beira and Alentejo provinces, the campaign extirpated the Crypto-Jewish center in upper Alentejo and prosperous industries collapsed as a result of the sudden decimation of the Marrano population. For 30 years the Marranos in a dozen towns throughout rural Portugal were sought out by the Inquisition, including Lamego (15 mi. south of Vila Real) and Braganza (to the north). By the 1750s, when Pombal suppressed the Inquisition, it had not yet reached Vila Real.

In 1928 the ex-Marrano Arturo Carlos de Barros *Basto visited Vila Real in an attempt to rouse the surviving Marranos to return to Judaism. Although he found that they feared to make a public declaration of their Jewish affiliation, he remained in touch with a nucleus of the Vila Real group. In 1930 he returned to found a Jewish congregation, under the presidency of Eugenio Cardoso. The Marranos in Vila Real then numbered a few hundred, out of a total population of 6,700. Its neo-Jewish community subsequently had but occasional contact with the Jewish world.

BIBLIOGRAPHY: Roth, Marranos, 273, 345, 368; Portuguese Marrano Committee, *Report for the Year 1928* (1929); idem, *Marranos in Portugal* (1938).

[Aaron Lichtenstein]

VILKAVIŠKIS (Pol. **Wylkowyski**; Rus. **Volkovyshki**), town in S.W. Lithuania. According to tradition, Jews were living in this area in the 14th century and a synagogue was built at the beginning of the 16th. By the 19th century a flourishing Jewish community had developed. Between 1823 and 1862 no new Jews were permitted to settle in Vilkaviškis, which was near the border with Germany, under the czarist legislation restricting Jewish settlement in border towns. Nevertheless, the community numbered 4,417 in 1856 (as against 834 Christians), 3,480 in 1897 (60% of the total population), 3,206 in 1923 (44%), and 3,609 in 1939 (45%). The majority were occupied in commerce and crafts. Some derived their livelihood from agriculture and garden plots close to the town. The sizable brushmaking industry in Vilkaviškis was predominantly Jewish and employed hundreds of Jewish workers. These organized a workers' union, the Jewish "Brushmakers Bund," and in 1898 published a clandestine periodical entitled *Veker*. The industry diminished in scope in the years between the two world wars. The Vilkaviškis community had an active Jewish social and cultural life. Its educational institutions included a large Hebrew primary school, a science-oriented Hebrew secondary school, and a vocational school.

The day of the outbreak of the German-Russian war, June 22, 1941, Vilkaviškis was occupied by the Germans. Most of the Jewish houses, including the synagogues, were destroyed during the fighting. On July 28, 1941, the systematic murder of the Jews in Volkaviškis began. At first about 900 men were murdered. A ghetto was established for the remaining Jews, most of them women and children, in the local barracks, close to the mass graves of the executed men. The Jews in the ghetto were killed on the day after Rosh Ha-Shanah, Sept. 24, 1941. Only a few survived until the liberation. The number of Jews in Vilkaviškis after the war remained low.

BIBLIOGRAPHY: B. London, in: *Lite*, 1 (1951), 1567–73; 2 (1965), index; *Yahadut Lita*, 1 and 3 (1959, 1967), indexes; Mats, in: *Yalkut Moreshet*, 2 no. 2 (1964); J. Gar, in: *Algemeyne Entsiklopedye:Yidn*, 6 (1963), 330–74.

[Joseph Gar]

VILLADIEGO, town in N. Spain, west of *Burgos. It is not known when Jews first settled there, but as early as 1222 Ferdinand III extended his protection to 20 Jewish families who went to stay in Burgos. He granted them the same rights as were generally enjoyed by the Jews in Castile. Important evidence, possibly the oldest of its kind in Castile, indicates that in 1240 Ferdinand ordered the community of Villadiego to pay 30 denarii yearly for the benefit of the cathedral of Burgos. In 1290 there were 20 Jewish families in Villadiego, who lived in a separate quarter close to the city walls. In the war between the brothers Pedro and Henry (1366–69), the community was destroyed by English soldiers serving under Pedro. It recovered around 1390, when it again numbered 20 Jewish families. During the 15th century some Jews of Villadiego served as tax farmers. In 1485 the community, then one of the smallest in northern Castile, contributed a special impost of 23 castellanos toward the war against Granada. In 1491 it paid an annual tax of 6,020 maravedis.

BIBLIOGRAPHY: Baer, Spain, index; Baer, Urkunden, 2 (1936), index; F. Cantera y Burgos, in: *Sefarad*, 2 (1942), 363; A.I. Laredo, *ibid.*, 5 (1945), 431; Suárez Fernández, Documentos, 25, 72, 76; P. León Tello, *Los judíos de Palencia* (1967), documents 41, 45, 110, 255.

[Haim Beinart]

VILLAFRANCA DEL PANADÉS, town near Barcelona, in Catalonia, N.E. Spain. Jews apparently first settled there at the beginning of the 12th century; the community belonged to the *collecta* (tax administrative unit) of Barcelona. The earliest extant record of its existence, dated 1207 and signed by the bailiff of Barcelona, concerns the selling of its revenues. Solomon b. Abraham Adret refers to the relationship between the Villafranca community and that of Barcelona in one of his responsa (vol. 3, no. 401).

More information on the Villafranca community is available from the mid-14th century. R. Ḥasdai Crescas, grandfather of the illustrious Ḥasdai Crescas, negotiated with the community around 1345 concerning its contribution to a loan destined for Pedro IV's campaign in Majorca. After 1346, Salomo de la Cavalleria, Vidal de Tolosa, Vidal de Beders, and Isaac b. Moses Ḥen are known as community trustees (*ne'emanei ha-kahal*). The names of two of them, Vidal de Tolosa and Vidal de Beders, show they were of French origin. When riots broke out following the Black *Death in 1348, Pedro IV ordered that measures be taken to protect the community; he repeated these instructions in 1353. During the 1391 persecutions the fate of the community of Villafranca was similar to that of *Barcelona. John I ordered that the Jews be protected, but after the rioting subsided he asked for a list of Jewish property left intestate by the victims, so that it could be handed over to the crown. Nothing further is known about the community.

BIBLIOGRAPHY: Baer, Spain, index; Baer, Urkunden, 1 (1929), index; A. Cardoner Planas, in: *Sefarad*, 1 (1941), 332ff.; A. Lopez Meneses, *ibid.*, 19 (1959), 127.

[Haim Beinart]

VILLAREAL, family name of Portuguese notables. The best known is Manoel Fernandez *Villareal (1608–1652). His son, JOSÉ DA VILLAREAL, migrated to France, where he served as a professor of Greek at Marseilles from about 1695.

Other bearers of the name include JOSÉ DA COSTA VILLAREAL (d. 1731), who was comptroller of the Portuguese royal army during the 1720s. A charge of Judaizing was brought against him, and in 1726 his arrest was ordered. Taking advantage of a conflagration then raging in Lisbon, he slipped away to London by sea with 17 members of his family and 300,000 pounds sterling of his wealth. In London the group re-entered the Jewish fold, when all the males in the family were circumcised and each marriage was recontracted "according to the law of Moses and Israel." As a token of thanksgiving they founded the Villareal girl's school. His widow was later sued for breach of promise by her profligate cousin Philip (Jacob) da Costa. The consequent publication, "*The proceedings at large in the Arches Court of Canterbury, between Mr. Jacob Mendes da Costa and Mrs. Catherine da Costa Villareal, both of the Jewish religion, and cousin Germans. Relating to a marriage contract*" (London, 1734), throws much light on social conditions in 18th-century Anglo-Jewry. Philip lost the case. When Kitty later married William Mellish, a non-Jew, she and her children by Villareal were baptized, the daughter marrying the future Viscount Galway.

The name is attested throughout the Marrano *Diaspora. MANUEL LOPEZ VILLAREAL took an important role in European business activity and established commercial ties between Hamburg and Amsterdam during the 1660s. In the New World the name Villareal appears at Hampstead, Georgia, where ISAAC VILLAREAL (VILLAROEL) was a Jewish settler around 1733. The origins of Benjamin *Disraeli have been traced back to the Villareals of Portugal. The Jewish descent of the Villareal family, and in particular of Manoel Fernandez Villareal, was indicated by the researches of Cecil Roth – a position also held by Martin A. Cohen and other scholars in the field. On the other hand, Antônio Jose Saraiva (see bibliography) concluded that Fernandez Villareal was probably neither Jewish nor a New *Christian, but that the Inquisition had used Judaism as a pretext for discrediting of Fernandez Villareal's liberal pronouncements and confiscating his property. Saraiva goes on to generalize that the majority of confessed Judaizers were not Marranos, but that they made confessions because they could escape death at the hands of the inquisitors only in this way.

BIBLIOGRAPHY: M. Kayserling, *Geschichte der Juden in Portugal* (1867), 310f.; idem, *Sephardim* (1859), index; C. Roth, *Menasseh*

Ben Israel (1934), 136–9, 324; Roth, Marranos, index; A.J. Saraiva, *Inquisição e Cristãos-Novos* (1969); Rosenbloom, Biogr Dict, 172; H. Kellenbenz, *Sephardim an der unteren Elbe* (1958), 176; *American Sephardi*, 4 nos. 1–2 (Autumn 1970), 103.

[Aaron Lichtenstein]

VILLEFRANCHE-DE-CONFLENT, village in the department of Pyrénées Orientales, S. France, which formed part of the former county of Roussillon. There was a small Jewish community there during the 13th century, most probably founded by Jews who came from *Perpignan. There is evidence of continual migratory movement between the two localities, in addition to regular commercial relations. At the end of the 14th century, the Jewish community of Villefranche ceased to exist. The theologian *Levi b. Abraham, who is known for his participation in the polemics of the early 14th century on the subject of philosophical studies, originated there. Villefranche-de-Conflent is not to be confused with two localities in Spain, called Villafranca, which were inhabited by Jews during the Middle Ages, or with Villefranche-sur-Saône, whose municipal charter of 1260 prohibited the residence of Jews.

BIBLIOGRAPHY: Gross, Gal Jud, 199f.; R.W. Emery, *The Jews of Perpignan* (1959), index; M. Meras, *Le Beaujolais au Moyen Age* (1956), 214.

[Bernhard Blumenkranz]

VILLINGEN, town in Baden, Germany. The first documentary evidence for the presence of Jews in Villingen dates from the beginning of the 14th century; in 1324 Emperor Louis IV, the Bavarian, granted to the dukes of Fuerstenberg the revenues from his Villingen Jewry in recognition of their service to him, reserving the right to repurchase them for 50 silver marks. The Jews lived in a quarter of the upper part of the town, where a synagogue was also located, mentioned for the first time in 1379. In 1342 some Jews of Villingen, together with Jews of *Freiburg and *Schaffhausen, were denounced for stealing church objects. During the *Black Death persecutions (1348–49) Jews were martyred and the community destroyed. In 1464 their moneylending activities are noted. In 1504 all the Jewish men were temporarily imprisoned in the town's tower because of the *Freiburg blood libel. In 1510 all Jews were expelled, after Emperor Maximilian I accused Jewish doctors of mistreating a sick old man, one of his veteran soldiers. Thereafter Jews could enter the town and trade only when accompanied by the town servant.

Jewish settlement in the town was not renewed until 1862; it grew from 20 in 1875 to 60 in 1933. Of that number, 42 managed to emigrate after the Nazi rise to power. The prayer hall was demolished on Nov. 10, 1938. On Oct. 20, 1940, 11 Jews were deported to Gurs; two returned at the end of the war from Theresienstadt. The building that housed the prayer hall still exists. A plaque commemorating the hall was consecrated in 1978. In 2002 the Jewish community Rottweil/Villingen-Schwenningen was founded. It numbered 179 in 2004. Most of the members are immigrants from the former Soviet Union. The community's prayer hall is in Rottweil.

BIBLIOGRAPHY: M. Ginsburger, in: REJ, 47 (1903), 125–8; F. Handsnurscher and G. Taddey (eds.), *Die juedischen Gemeinden in Baden* (1968), 242–3; *Germania Judaica*, 2 (1968), 854–5; 3 (1987), 1536–40; PK Germanyah. **ADD BIBLIOGRAPHY:** K. Engel, K. Hauser, and T. Kzimann, *Judenschicksale in Villingen* (1994) (Blaetter zur Geschichte der Stadt Villingen-Schwenningen, vol. 1, 1994); A. Faustein et al., *Juden in Villingen im 14. und 15. Jahrhundert* (1997) (Blaetter zur Geschichte der Stadt Villingen-Schwenningen, vol. 2, 1997). **WEBSITE:** www.alemannia-judaica.de.

[Larissa Daemmig (2nd ed.)]

VILNA (Pol. **Wilno**, Lithuanian **Vilnius**), from 1323 capital of the grand duchy of *Lithuania; from 1940 to 1991 capital of the Lithuanian S.S.R.; from 1991 capital of Lithuania; called by East European Jewry, especially in the modern period, the "Jerusalem of Lithuania" (*Yerushalayim de-Lita*).

The Early Settlement

In 1527 the townsmen of Vilna obtained from the Polish king, Sigismund I, the right to debar Jewish settlement there. However, a number of individual Jewish residents are found in the middle of the 16th century, including lessees of the customs, mintmasters, moneylenders, and large-scale merchants. In 1551 royal permission was granted to two Jews and their servants to lease out houses and shops, to do business in the city as visiting traders, and to engage in pawnbroking. In the same year Jews were permitted to reside in buildings owned by members of the ducal council, which lay outside the municipal jurisdiction. The first information of an organized Jewish community in Vilna dates from 1568, when it was ordered to pay the poll tax. According to tradition, a wooden synagogue was erected in Vilna in 1573. As early as 1592 the street adjoining the synagogue was called "Jew's Street." Although in that year a mob attacked the Jews of Vilna and plundered shops and houses of the Jews as well as the synagogue, in the following year Sigismund II renewed the privileges enabling them to trade and reside in the city.

In February 1633 Vilna Jewry was granted a charter of privileges permitting Jews to engage in all branches of commerce, distilling, and any crafts not subject to the guild organizations, but restricting their place of residence in the city. They were also granted permission to erect a new synagogue, which was built of stone. At the same time new regulations limited to 12 the number of shops under Jewish ownership which might be open to the street, and they might be held for a term not exceeding ten years. The Jews were exempted from payment of the municipal tax but instead were obliged to pay 300 zlotys annually in peacetime and 500 zlotys in time of war. During 1634, and in particular in 1635, the Jews in Vilna were again attacked and their property pillaged. The following year a commission of inquiry nominated by Ladislaus IV bound the municipality to protect the Jewish residents; to compensate for the damages suffered, the Jews were licensed to sell alcoholic liquors in 20 buildings. However, students of the Jesuit academy committed acts of violence (called in Yiddish *shiler-geloyf*) against Jewish residents in 1639 and 1641.

During the first half of the 17th century the Vilna community was augmented by arrivals from *Prague, *Frankfurt, and Polish towns, who included wealthy Jews and scholars. The number of petty traders and artisans also increased, and in this period about 3,000 Jewish residents are recorded out of a total population of some 15,000. Although the Vilna community, now an important Jewish entity, claimed the status of a principal community, or "community head of the courts" (*kehillah rosh bet din*), within the organizational framework of the Council of Lithuania (see *Councils of the Lands), the status was not conceded until 1652. After 1630 the Vilna community suffered from the general economic deterioration experienced by Lithuanian Jewry, as a result of which the Council of Lithuania accorded it a number of economic concessions in 1634. These subjected the conduct of trade by "residents of the Land of Lithuania visiting Vilna for the purposes of business" to detailed regulation. An additional improvement was "permission to the community of Vilna to undertake business in all the townlets, villages, boroughs, and settlements" within the jurisdiction of the other principal communities of Lithuania. A further financial burden for Vilna Jewry in 1648–49 was the aid it gave to fugitives from the *Chmielnicki massacres. Subsequently, in 1655, Vilna itself was threatened by the armies of the Muscovites and nearly all the Jewish inhabitants fled from the city. During the Russian occupation the Jewish quarter was burned down in the general conflagration that ensued. Three years later Czar Alexis endorsed the Vilna municipal charter but banished the Jews from the city precincts.

With the rehabilitation of the community in 1661, the leadership of Lithuanian Jewry passed to Vilna. The hostility between the Jews and the townsmen continued, fanned by the Jesuits and the reaction engendered by the Counter-Reformation then prevailing throughout the realm. An assault by townsmen on Jews who mustered for the census of defenders of the city in 1681 was condemned by King John Sobieski, who ordered the punishment of the guilty and freed the Jews from the obligation of the city's defense in the future. In 1687 a riot was instigated by Jesuit students, artisans, and shopkeepers, evidently in an attempt to force the distressed Jews to defray their debts. The material damage was estimated at 120,000 zlotys. The municipality was again served a stringent admonishment by the king, and students and the nobility were forbidden to distrain debts from Jews. By 1690 there were 227 Jewish families resident in the Jewish quarter of Vilna, while a similar number, perhaps more, were living outside, in areas falling within the jurisdiction of the magnates or government.

During the Northern War (1700–21) the Swedish invaders levied heavy taxes on the Vilna community, now so impoverished it was forced to place ritual objects in pawn with Christians. In addition, the famine and plague rife in the city took their toll. After the conflagration of 1737 the Vilna community turned to Jews abroad for relief, and its emissaries received a generous response from the Jews of Amsterdam. The opposition of the Christian merchants and artisans to the Jews even continued in the 18th century. In 1712 a commission recommended the promulgation of ordinances by the city council to limit the branches of trade and crafts practiced by Jews and restrict the area of Jewish residence. In 1713 the community board (*kahal*), the organ of Jewish self-government, was forced to bring actions against a number of discriminatory measures passed by the municipality. The charters of privileges conferred on Vilna Jewry were confirmed in 1738 by Augustus III, who extended the license to open shops to a term of 20 years and enabled Jews to deal in alcoholic liquors and other commodities. The townsmen, who lodged an appeal against the grant, managed to obtain a judgment in 1740 recognizing the 1527 prohibition on Jewish residence in Vilna, so that the Jews were again faced with the danger of expulsion. Exhausting negotiations ensued, in which the wealthy communal leader *Judah b. Eleazar took a prominent part. The community was forced to consent to a compromise agreement with stringent terms, including restrictions on the plying of trade and crafts and on place of residence. These the Jews were both unwilling and unable to implement. Litigation continued until a judgment was pronounced in 1783 which lifted the restriction on the occupations. The limitation on their place of residence was also abrogated, excepting two streets still barred to Jewish settlement. Jews were now made subject to the same tax regulations as other citizens and the annual poll tax was abolished. During the uprising against Russia in 1794 a number of Vilna Jews demonstrated their loyalty to Poland in the fighting and the *kahal* made contributions to the participants in the uprising. Thirty Jews were killed in one of the suburbs during the siege. After the conquest of the city by the Russians, however, the Jewish position in commerce and crafts improved. The Russian government abrogated the jurisdiction of the municipal court over Jewish citizens and rescinded the previous enactment of the Polish Sejm. The 1795 census shows 3,613 Jewish poll tax payers in Vilna and its environs.

Scholarship and Communal Affairs

Vilna had already become a preeminent center for rabbinical studies by the beginning of the 17th century. Among scholars born in Vilna were *Joshua Hoeschel ben Joseph and *Shabbetai ha-Kohen, who served as *dayyan* of the community. The rabbi of Vilna in the middle of the 17th century was Moses b. Isaac Judah *Lima. The existence of a *talmud torah* is reported in the second half of the 17th century, when a fund was also established by a philanthropist for the support of students. Among the scholars of Vilna in the second half of the 17th century and the beginning of the 18th were R. Moses, called Kremer, a forefather of Elijah Gaon; his son-in-law Joseph, author of *Rosh Yosef*, halakhic and aggadic novellae (Berlin, 1716); R. Baruch Kahana, known as Baruch Ḥarif; the grammarian Azriel and his two sons Nisan and Elijah; and Ẓevi Hirsch *Kaidanover (Kaidany). Also living in Vilna was the Gordon family of physicians, one of whom, Jekuthiel *Gordon, studied medicine in Padua and became influenced by the poet and kabbalist Moses Ḥayyim *Luzzatto. Joshua Heshel *Ẓoref of Vilna was among the crypto-Shabbateans. From the second half of the 18th century the personality and activities of *Elijah b. Solomon Zalman, the "Vilna Gaon," who attracted numerous disciples, had a lasting impact on Vilna Jewry. The circle thus formed became the most stimulating religious and spiritual center there and had a profound influence on Judaism in the sphere of both *halakhah* and Kabbalah.

The 1770s and 1780s marked a period of acute social tension for the Vilna community, expressed in a serious crisis over the rabbinate. In 1740 *Samuel b. Avigdor was chosen as rabbi of Vilna – partly because of the contributions to the community made by his father-in-law Judah b. Eleazar (see above). The fierce controversy that arose around the personality, status, and aspirations of Samuel b. Avigdor continued for 30 years and threatened the basis of communal autonomy. Diverse social and ideological forces in the community became implicated in the conflict, as well as external bodies. The Jewish artisans of Vilna, now a strong numerical force which remained without representation in community affairs or the means of exerting influence, took the side of the rabbi, as did also the Ḥasidim, who afforded him surreptitious support, while a number of powerful leaders in the community opposed him. Non-Jewish elements that entered the arena included the governor of Vilna, the bishop, and the crown tribunal. The opposition accused the rabbi of accepting bribes, of unfair decisions, and other practices. In theory the controversy terminated with the removal of Samuel b. Avigdor from office. However, the representatives of the popular faction turned to the non-Jewish authorities and complained about the way the *kahal* was levying taxes. The Gaon of Vilna also intervened. Simeon b. Wolf, the popular representative who had been imprisoned by the governor in Nieswiez (Nesvizh), applied to the Sejm with proposals for amending the community organization; he also demanded that the communities should be deprived of their secular authority, leaving Jewish jurisdiction over religious matters only.

When the Enlightenment (*Haskalah) movement spread to Vilna it did not encounter strong opposition from the leadership, and to begin with was largely conservative in character. About 14 important members of the community subscribed to the commentary on the Torah, the *Be'ur* initiated by Moses *Mendelssohn. Typical of the first adherents of the movement (*maskilim*) were the physician and author Judah ben Mordecai ha-Levi *Hurwitz and Moses *Meisel, the *shammash* of the community, who was acquainted with German literature and wrote several treatises. He had access to the Gaon of Vilna and also became an adherent of *Chabad Ḥasidism.

At the end of the 18th century, under the influence of the Gaon, Vilna became the center of the way of life and system of religious study followed by the **Mitnaggedim* and the focus of their struggle against Ḥasidism. In 1772 the *kahal* disbanded the congregation (*minyan*) formed in Vilna by the Ḥasidim and issued a ban or excommunication against them. Bitter opposition to Ḥasidism continued throughout the lifetime of the Gaon. Nevertheless, groups of Ḥasidim still assembled clandestinely in Vilna and formed their own *minyanim*, and after 1790 the movement even found support among members of the *kahal*. Persecution of the Ḥasidim was renewed when Vilna passed to Russia in 1795, and after the death of the Gaon two years later the conflict became more bitter. Members of the community were forbidden to buy liquor, a major source of livelihood, from Ḥasidim. The Ḥasidim now attempted to break the hegemony wielded by the *kahal*, and the two parties sought the intervention of the Russian authorities. In 1798 the Vilna *kahal* was prohibited from imposing fines or corporal punishment for religious offenses. When the ḥasidic leader *Shneur Zalman of Lyady was denounced to the authorities and imprisoned, 22 Ḥasidim from Vilna and its environs were also incarcerated, although afterward released. The *kahal* elders and *dayyanim* were dismissed from office in 1799, and the *kahal* accounts were examined. A new *kahal* was then chosen from among the Ḥasidim, which controlled the Vilna community for over a year. Subsequently the two parties became reconciled and a new *kahal* was elected with representatives of both parties. The Ḥasidim were permitted to maintain their own *minyanim* (congregations).

Between 1799 and 1802 an attempt was made by the Jewish residents of Vilna, according to the census of 1800, numbering 6,917 taxpayers, to obtain the right to take part in municipal affairs. A grant to this effect was twice obtained from the authorities, but the opposition of the Vilna citizens each time frustrated Jewish representation in practice. During the Napoleonic invasion of 1812 Vilna Jewry generally remained loyal to Russia in spite of the disabilities from which it suffered. (The provisional Lithuanian government established in Vilna by the French levied heavy taxes and war loans on the community, and the troops desecrated the Jewish cemetery, turning it into a cattle pen and destroying tombstones.) Nevertheless, under Czar *Nicholas I the right to take part in municipal government was rescinded, and the autonomy of the *kahal* was abolished in 1844. The directors (*gabba'im*) of the charitable fund (*ha-ẓedakah ha-gedolah*) continued to guide communal affairs unofficially. A visit was paid to Vilna by the philanthropist Moses *Montefiore in 1846.

Vilna's preeminence as the seat of Jewish learning continued in the 19th century. As an important center of Haskalah, it attracted many Hebrew writers. When the government commenced its policy of Russification of the Jews (see *Russia) it made Vilna a center of its activities. Max *Lilienthal was sent there in 1842 to encourage the establishment of modern schools, and in 1847 a government-sponsored *rabbinical seminary was established. Polish language and culture, which had influenced the *maskilim* and men of letters at the beginning of the 19th century, was now superseded by Russian. The *maskilim* of Vilna in this period included Mordecai Aaron *Guenzburg, Adam ha-Kohen *Lebensohn and his son Micah Joseph *Lebensohn (Mikhal), Isaac Meir *Dick, Kalman *Schulman, J.L. *Gordon, Joshua *Steinberg, and Eliakum *Zunser.

1860–1939

The restriction limiting Jewish residence to certain streets in Vilna was abrogated under *Alexander II in 1861. Untold harm was wreaked on the Jewish community when the apostate Jacob *Brafmann arrived in Vilna and conducted a vicious anti-Jewish propaganda campaign. He was vigorously opposed by R. Jacob *Barit, head of the yeshivah and communal leader. In 1860 S.J. *Fuenn began publication of a Hebrew weekly, *Ha-Karmel*, with Russian supplements. Among authors in Vilna who wrote in Russian was J.L. *Levanda, who occupied a government post there as an expert on Jewish matters, called "learned Jew." It was in this period that the first Jewish Socialists in Russia began to be active in the official rabbinical seminary, among them Aaron Samuel *Liebermann and his associates.

Anti-Jewish riots took place in 1881 when a band of military conscripts attacked Jewish shops. The Jewish butchers, who organized themselves to oppose the attackers, turned them over to the police. Owing to the Russian government's prohibition on Jewish settlement in the villages, many Jews in rural areas had to move to Vilna. The 1897 census shows 63,831 Jewish inhabitants, forming 41.5% of the total population. The congested conditions and increasing unemployment led to large-scale emigration. Large numbers left for the United States and South Africa, and a few went to Ereẓ Israel. Vilna became an active meeting ground for Jewish Socialists in the 1890s. A convention of Jewish Social Democrats was held in 1895, while in 1897 the *Bund labor party held its founding convention and Vilna became the center of its activities. In 1902 the shoemaker Hirsch *Lekert attempted to shoot the governor-general of Vilna, Von Wahl, after his treatment of a First of May demonstration. Lekert was condemned to death and hanged. In 1900 a wave of anti-Jewish feeling swept Vilna over the *Blondes blood libel case.

At the beginning of the 20th century Vilna became the center of the *Zionist movement in Russia, and saw the rise of a flourishing Hebrew and Yiddish literature. One of the first societies of the *Ḥovevei Zion movement was founded there; Ḥovevei Zion conventions were held in Vilna in 1889, and subsequently those of the Zionist organizations (the founding convention of the *Mizrachi party in 1902, and others). Theodor *Herzl, who visited Vilna in 1903, was given an enthusiastic popular reception. The central bureau of the Zionist Organization in Russia functioned in Vilna between 1905 and 1911, and for some time the *Po'alei Zion party made Vilna its headquarters. The well-known Zionist leader Shmaryahu *Levin was elected as deputy for Vilna to the *Duma. Orthodox circles were organized under the leadership of R. Ḥayyim Ozer *Grodzenski, and afterward amalgamated with the *Agudat Israel. Among the many Yiddish and Hebrew periodicals published in Vilna was the Hebrew daily *Ha-Zeman*. An excellent library of Judaica was established from the bequest of Mathias *Strashun.

Vilna became a transit center and asylum for Jewish refugees from the vicinity during World War I. Under German occupation lack of food and discriminatory levies on the Jewish population made conditions increasingly difficult. The situation was not improved after the war when the struggle between the Poles and Lithuanians for the possession of Vilna (1919–20) entailed frequent changes of government. In April 1919, 80 Jews were massacred by Polish troops.

The interwar period from 1922 to 1939 was a time of fruitful and manifold social and cultural activities for Vilna Jewry, although Vilna, now part of Poland, was affected economically by the severance of its former ties with Russia and Lithuania. According to the 1921 census, 46,559 Jews were living in Vilna (36.1% of the total population), and in 1931, 55,000 (28.2%). This period saw the establishment of a network of elementary and secondary schools in which Hebrew was either the language of instruction or the principal language, and of Hebrew and Yiddish teachers' seminaries and trade schools. Vilna was a world center for Yiddish culture, and a Yiddish daily and evening press, numerous weekly and other political, literary, educational, and scientific journals were published there. The Jewish historical and ethnographical society, founded by S. *An-Ski, established a museum and archives in 1919. The *YIVO research institute for Yiddish language and culture was founded in Vilna in 1924. The institute attracted Yiddish scholars and authors, among them Zalman *Rejzen, Max *Weinreich, Z. *Kalmanowicz, and Max *Erik. The Yiddish writer Moshe *Kulbak lived in Vilna. A circle of young Yiddish authors (*Yung Vilne*) included Abraham *Sutzkever, Shemariah *Kaczerginski, and Ḥayyim *Grade. Several poems of Zalman *Shneour, who stayed in Vilna for some time, express the glorious place of the city in Jewish life. Among its Hebrew scholars and writers were the linguist M.B. Shneider, S.L. *Zitron, and J.E. *Triwosch. The strong antisemitism rife in Poland in the 1930s was especially noticeable in the university, where the Jewish students often had to organize in self-defense.

[Israel Klausner]

Hebrew Printing

Hebrew printing in Vilna began in 1799 with three ethical books: a short version of Kalonymus b. Kalonymus' *Even Boḥan* by Phinehas b. Judah Polotsk; Abraham Lichtstein's *Hin Ẓedek* on Maimonides' *Shemonah Perakim* (1 and 2), by the press of Aryeh Loeb and Gershom Luria and Moses b. Menahem; and Gershon b. Benjamin's *Shemirat ha-Mitzvot*. The former two were printed by the Canonicus Joseph Mirski (d. 1812) and the third in the printing house Jan Jasienskie Luria's firm produced various small books and a Bible (1806). The firm still existed in 1823. The Drukarnia Djecezjalna (Mirski) and Vilna University had their own Hebrew press.

Hebrew printing in Vilna, however, owes its fame mainly to the house of *Romm. Baruch b. Joseph (d. 1803), after some years in Grodno, set up in Vilna in the last years of the 18th century. Baruch's son Menahem Man Romm (d. 1842) and Simḥah Zimel b. Menahem Nahum of Grodno printed some liturgical items in 1815–17. Menahem Man's three sons – David (d. 1860), assisted by his second wife Deborah, née Harkavy;

Ḥayyim Jacob; and Menahem Man Gabriel – greatly developed the firm. Due to the censorship, by 1845 the firm practically enjoyed a monopoly in Russia and Poland.

Trouble arose when the Talmud was to be printed, which eventually led to the closing of all Jewish printing presses in Lithuania and Volhynia except one in Vilna and another in *Zhitomir (until 1862). In 1835 Man Romm, in association with Simḥah Zimel, began printing the Talmud against the protest of the *Slavuta printers; as a result, Slavuta's second printing (their first dates from 1815/16–1822/23) was never finished. Romm completed their edition in 1854. It was their masterpiece; in 1846 even Sir Moses Montefiore came to visit their establishment. From 1871 it was known as the firm of "the widow and the brothers Romm" (i.e., Deborah, Ḥayyim Jacob, and Menahem Man). The 1866 edition was produced by 100 devoted workers and 14 correctors. Many standard texts, among them the Mishnah, the *Turim*, Maimonides' *Mishneh Torah*, the Jerusalem Talmud, and S. Buber's Midrash editions, made Vilna printing famous for its beauty and accuracy.

There were also a number of small firms. Abraham Ẓevi Rosenkranz and his brother Menahem Schriftsetzer, originally typesetters with the Romms, established their own press in 1863. They also took over the Samuel Joseph Fuenn press in 1893, after it had existed for 30 years. In 1920 the firm was bought up by A.L. Shalkowitz (Ben Avigdor). Among smaller presses that of Boris Kletzkin (d. 1938) employed more than 50 workers and printed some newspapers.

The Vilna presses made some very important contributions before being closed down. Romm's famous *Mishnayot* (vols. 2 and 5) were published in Vilna in 1938, one year before the Nazi invasion of Poland. Their Talmud and other rabbinic standard works continue to be reproduced photographically in a great variety of sizes and editions in Israel and the U.S.

[Israel O. Lehman]

Holocaust Period

With the outbreak of World War II, Soviet Russia invaded Vilna and in October 1939 ceded it to Lithuania. Jewish refugees from divided Poland – the German-occupied part and the Soviet-occupied one – found refuge in Vilna. Among the refugees were many rabbis (and ḥasidic rabbis), scholars, community and party leaders, as well as Zionists and members of Zionist youth movements who immediately organized into temporary "kibbutzim." By long and tortuous ways (even via the Far East), some succeeded in reaching Ereẓ Israel. In June 1940, Lithuania was annexed to the U.S.S.R. The Soviet authorities closed down Hebrew cultural institutions and Zionist organizations. All Yiddish press was replaced by the Communist Party's organ.

Many Jews – active Zionists, Bundists, and "bourgeois" – were exiled in 1941 into the Soviet interior and many were interned in camps there. Some active Yiddishists, including writers (Z. Rejzen, Joseph Chernikhov, and others), were arrested, deported to Russia, and murdered there. In June 24, 1941, the Germans entered Vilna and were welcomed by the Lithuanian population with flowers and cheers. Persecution of Vilna's Jewish population (approximately 80,000) began immediately. Prior to the establishment of the ghetto, about 35,000 Jews were murdered in *Ponary, a wooded area 10 mi. from Vilna. Among them were leaders of the Jewish community and members of the first *Judenrat.

On September 6, 1941, the remaining Jews were herded into two ghettos (the smaller was liquidated 46 days later), and a second Judenrat was established. In January 1942 the various political organizations in the ghetto created a unified fighting organization, FPO (Fareynigte Partizaner Organizatsye), commanded by Yiẓḥak *Wittenberg, Joseph Glazman, and Abba *Kovner. In the beginning, the FPO decided to fight in the ghetto rather than escape to join the partisans in the forests. They planned to blow up the German ammunition dumps and lead the Jews into the forests if they could first arm the ghetto sufficiently. A separate fighting organization, led by Yechiel Sheinboim and comprising several groups that wanted to fight in the forests, eventually joined the FPO. In addition to smuggling in ammunition, the FPO carried out acts of sabotage, issued an underground bulletin, and forged documents. In July 1942 Jacob Gens, chief of the Jewish police, was appointed "ghetto head" by the Germans. In this capacity Gens was responsible to the German authorities for law and order in the ghetto. The Judenrat established various departments through which it supervised and controlled all aspects of ghetto life: a police department; a labor department, which provided employment in German and Lithuanian public and private businesses; an industry department; a supply and distribution department, primarily for food; a health department, which provided a hospital, medical services, and children's care; a housing department, which included a sanitation and sewage disposal section; a social welfare department, which administrated the institutions for aid to the needy and provided free food, clothing, and shelter; and a cultural department, which coordinated the activities of schools, theaters, an orchestra, choirs, a library, archives, a bureau of statistics, a bookstore, a museum, and a wall bulletin, *Getto Yedies*, that contained announcements and regulations issued by the Judenrat. Writers, musicians, actors, and artists created an organization to sponsor lectures and concerts and encourage cultural expression in the ghetto. Religious life, yeshivot, and synagogues continued functioning underground.

Gens was the ghetto's most controversial figure. Some condemned him as an outright German collaborator, while others regarded him as a man who fulfilled German orders in an effort to save as many Jews as possible. Accused by the *Gestapo of aiding the underground, he was shot on September 15, 1943.

On July 5, 1943, Wittenberg, the commander of the FPO, was arrested. While he was being led out of the ghetto, the FPO attacked the guard and freed him. Realizing that a price would have to be paid for this act of defiance, the underground ordered mobilization of all its units. The Germans issued an ultimatum for Wittenberg to surrender by morning or the ghetto would be wiped out. After hours of difficult deliberation, Wittenberg surrendered himself to the Germans and was murdered by the Gestapo. The FPO then decided to evacuate to the forests. The first detail of fighters to leave for the forest was ambushed, and Glazman, its leader, was among those who died fighting. In reprisal for the flight of the fighters, the Germans killed their families and work brigadiers in the ghetto. Thereafter, no fighters left the ghetto for fear that their capture would result in the death of many Jews.

The destruction of Vilna Jewry continued with the establishment of the ghetto. Various mass murder *Aktionen* were carried out, the largest of which totaled 14,000 killed during the liquidation of the smaller ghetto, 7,000 during the two "yellow certificate actions," and 5,000 during the "*Kovno Aktion*." In August 1943, deportation of the surviving ghetto inmates to Estonia began. That marked the beginning of total liquidation. On September 1, 1943, the ghetto was sealed off, The FPO was mobilized at once, and in the morning the German soldiers entered. Fighting erupted in several areas of the ghetto. In one battle Sheinboim and other fighters lost their lives. Fearing that a continued battle would bring immediate destruction to the ghetto, Gens successfully petitioned the Germans to leave. Between September 1–4, 1943, while 8,000 more Jews were deported to labor camps in Estonia, 200 fighters left the ghetto to join the partisans. On September 15, 1943, the ghetto was again surrounded, but the Germans withdrew when they learned that the remaining FPO fighters were again mobilized for battle. On September 23 the Jews were ordered to prepare for the final deportation, which would liquidate the ghetto. The FPO at this opportunity evacuated the last of its fighters through the sewers. In the following days, the surviving men were sent to Estonia, the young women to Latvia, and the old, children, and sick to *Majdanek.

After liquidating the ghetto, the Germans left two work installations outside its walls: Keilis (a Lithuanian fur factory) and the HKP (army vehicles park), where approximately 3,000 Jews worked. On July 2–3, 1944, they were all taken to *Ponary and murdered there. There are no accurate figures on the number of Vilna Jewry killed. It is estimated that approximately 100,000 Jews from Vilna and the vicinity perished in the Vilna ghetto. Those who were not killed in Vilna died in labor concentration camps in Estonia and other places.

[Abraham H. Foxman]

Contemporary Period

After the Soviet Army liberated Lithuania (July 12, 1944) about 6,000 survivors from the forests and other places assembled in the city. Writers and Jewish communal workers (S. Kaczerginski and others) tried to organize a Jewish museum, a Jewish school, an orphanage, etc. To provide for religious needs, a *kehillah* was organized, but the Soviet authorities immediately suppressed any secular Jewish activity and prevented the existence of any Jewish organization. By provocative means, as e.g., by deceptively organizing "illegal" flights over the border to Poland, the Soviet security police captured and arrested in 1945 scores of Lithuanian Jews who wished to emigrate in order to reach Palestine. In the 1959 census 16,354 Jews (6.96%) were registered in Vilna, 11,326 of whom declared Yiddish to be their mother tongue. In 1970 the number of Jews was estimated much higher. The only synagogue left generally served a small number of elderly Jews, except on holidays, particularly on Simḥat Torah, when many hundreds congregated, including younger people. The deliberate effacement of the Jewishness of the Nazi victims during World War II as well as other measures designed to stifle Jewish cultural expression stimulated Jewish youth to counter-demonstrations, e.g., through identifying more and more with Israel, and studying Hebrew. Eventually, in the 1960s, the authorities permitted the establishment of a Yiddish amateur theater company (in the framework of the local trade unions' cultural activities, alongside Russian and Lithuanian groups), which performed plays by *Shalom Aleichem and some other Yiddish classics. The company's performances drew great crowds, and it was sometimes allowed to perform in other cities of the Baltic republics. In the early 1960s, during the campaign against "economic crimes," Vilna became the scene of one of the first anti-Jewish expressions of the campaign. A show trial against a group of Jewish "speculators" ended in death sentences and executions, accompanied by an antisemitic campaign in the local press.

After the Six-Day War in the Middle East (1967) identification with Israel became more pronounced, especially among the young, in spite of the official anti-Israel campaign, and Jews from Vilna were among those who protested against the refusal to grant them exit permits to Israel. These protests were sometimes published abroad.

See also *Russia.

UNDER LITHUANIAN INDEPENDENCE. Jewish life in Vilna revived with Lithuanian independence in 1990. Chabad was active in restoring religious life and the Shalom Aleichem State School had around 200 students, studying Hebrew, the Bible, and the history of the Jewish people in addition to general subjects. The community published *Jerusalem of Lithuania*, a periodical in Yiddish, Lithuanian, English, and Russian with special emphasis on the cultural life of the community. The community organized meetings, lectures, and exhibitions dedicated to such subjects as Israel, Jewish holidays, and the Holocaust. With the help of Jewish organizations, especially the American Joint Distribution Committee, and private donors, the community ran a wide-ranging welfare program for needy members. At the outset of the 21st century most of Lithuania's 3,500 Jews lived in the Vilna.

BIBLIOGRAPHY: I. Cohen, *History of the Jews in Vilna* (1943); S.J. Fuenn, *Kiryah Ne'emanah* (1860); H.N. Maggid-Steinschneider, *Ir Vilna* (1900); *Vilner Zamlbukh*, 2 vols. (1917–18); *Pinkas far der Geshikhte fun Vilne in di Yorn fun Milkhome un Okupatsye* (1922); E. Jeshurin (ed.), *Vilne* (1935); I. Klausner, *Toledot ha-Kehillah ha-Ivrit be-Vilna* (1937); idem, *Vilna bi-Tekufat ha-Ga'on* (1942); idem, *Korot Beit ha-Almin ha-Yashan be-Vilna* (1935); idem, in: *Zion*, 2 (1937); idem, in: *Yahadut Lita*, 1 (1959), 23–123; idem, in: *Turei Yeshurun*, 16 (1970), 26–30; I. Halpern, in: *Yehudim ve-Yahadut be-Mizraḥ*

Eiropah (1968), 159–62. HOLOCAUST: *Algemeyne Entsiklopedye*, 6 (1964), index; S. Kaczerginski, *Ḥurban Vilna* (Yid., 1947); M. Dvorjetski, *Yerushalayim de-Lita in Kamf un Umkum* (1948); R. Korchak, *Lehavot ba-Efer* (1965^3) 311–22; H. Kruk, *Togbukh fun Vilner Geto* (1961); idem, in: YIVOA, 13 (1965), 9–18; M. Balberyszski, *Shtarker fun Ayzn* (1967; includes short Eng. summary); G. Reitlinger, *Final Solution* (1968^2), index; R. Hilberg, *The Destruction of the European Jews* (1961, 1967), index.

VILNA TROUPE, Yiddish theatrical company. It began as an amateur group in Vilna in 1916, organized by the teacher Mordecai Mazo and the painter Leib Kadison, who was its first producer. It moved to Warsaw in 1917 and came to be regarded as the symbol of the "better Yiddish theater" which others had tried to achieve with limited success. The Vilna Troupe's strength lay in its ensemble and in the ideas of its producers, among them Chaim Schneir, Mark Arnstein, Michael *Weichert, who directed *Asch's *Kiddush ha-Shem*, and David *Herman, who directed *Peretz' *Bay Nakht oyfn Altn Mark* ("At Night in the Old Market"). Herman's outstanding work, however, was his production of *An-Ski's *The Dybbuk* in 1920, which brought the company international fame. The tour with *The Dybbuk* in England, France, and the U.S. in 1921 was triumphant. Success spoiled some of the players, however, and the company broke up not long afterward. One group went to the United States and toured until 1930; the other group remained in Europe and was active in Romania and Poland into the 1930s. Mordecai Mazo, the founder, and his wife, actress Miriam Orleska, perished during World War II in the Warsaw Ghetto.

BIBLIOGRAPHY: Zylbercweig, *Leksikon fun Yidishn Teater* (1934).

[Joseph Leftwich]

VILNAY (VILENSKY), ZEV (1900–1988), Israeli geographer, author, and lecturer. Born in Kishinev, Vilnay moved to Palestine with his parents as a child of six and settled in Haifa. In the middle 1920s Vilnay became one of the principal guides in the walking tours (*tiyyulim*) over the country, popular among workers and youth groups; they included areas in Lebanon, Syria, Transjordan, and Sinai. He was an instructor of military topography in the Haganah and later during the War of Independence (1948) and the Six-Day War (1967). He was awarded the Israel Prize in 1982 for *yedi'at ha-areẓ* ("knowledge of Israel").

Vilnay lectured under many auspices on Israel geography, ethnography, history and folklore. He published many books and pamphlets, including the following in English: *Legends of Palestine* (1932), *The Guide to Israel* (1955; 14 editions until 1971); *The Holy Land in Old Prints and Maps* (1965^2); *The New Israel Atlas: Bible to Present Day* (1968); and in Hebrew: *Enziklopedyah li-Ydi'at ha-Areẓ* (3 vols. (1956)); *Yerushalayim* 2 vols. (1960–62, new edition 1970); *Tel Aviv-Jaffa…* (1965); *Yehudah ve-Shomeron* (1968); *Sinai, Aver ve-Hoveh* (1969); *Golan ve-Ḥermon* (1970); *Maẓẓevot Kodesh be-Ereẓ Yisrael* (1963^2); and *Ereẓ Yisrael bi-Temunot Attikot* (1961).

BIBLIOGRAPHY: Tidhar, 3 (1958^2), 1513–14; 17 (1968), 5239.

[Benjamin Jaffe]

VINAVER, CHEMJO (1900–1973), conductor and composer. Vinaver was born in Warsaw and raised in the ḥasidic court of his grandfather, R. Isaac of Vorka, where he absorbed the Vorka and other ḥasidic musical traditions. From 1916 to 1920 he studied in Warsaw, and then in Berlin (conducting and composition with Hugo Ruedel and Siegfried Ochs). There he organized the Hanigun choir for the propagation of Jewish music, which toured in Europe and Palestine. From 1926 to 1933 Vinaver was the chief conductor at the temple of the Berlin community, with whose choir he recorded over 20 liturgical works. He also taught music at the teachers' college of the Reichsvertretung der deutschen Juden and published articles on Jewish music in the Jewish press and cantorial periodicals. In 1938 Vinaver emigrated to New York, where he organized the Vinaver Chorus and the Vinaver Symphonic Voices. From 1952 he was music consultant in the cultural department of the Zionist Organization of America. In 1967 he settled in Jerusalem, where he also established a choir.

Among his compositions may be mentioned "The Seventh Day" for cantor and chorus, for the Friday night service (1946), *Kol Nidrei*, and *Omnam Ken*. He edited several collections of ḥasidic, Yiddish, and Israeli folk songs, and in 1955 published the *Anthology of Jewish Music*, which contains traditional synagogal music, ḥasidic *niggunim*, and religious folk songs (many of them of his own collection), several synagogal compositions, including Vinaver's own, and Psalm 130, "Out of Depths," composed by Arnold *Schoenberg especially for the anthology. Vinaver's wife was the poet Masha Kaleko.

BIBLIOGRAPHY: Sendrey, Music, index.

[Haim Bar-Dayan]

VINAWER, MAXIM (1862–1926), lawyer and communal worker in Russia. Born in Warsaw, Vinawer completed his studies at the university of Warsaw (1886), and then settled in St. Petersburg, where he became a prominent lawyer in the field of civil law. In court Vinawer was outstanding for his clear and profound analyses, which influenced the shaping of judicial law. His influence was also felt through his literary activity, his presence among judicial colleagues at the university of St. Petersburg, and at conferences on civil law reforms. The fact that he was a Jew interfered with his professional standing and until 1904 he was registered only as an advocate's assistant. After the February Revolution (1917) he was allowed to sit as supreme judge for the short period preceding the liquidation of the old courts as a result of the October Revolution.

Through his literary publications he encouraged social astuteness and interest on the part of advocates in regard to public affairs. As a result of the 1905 Revolution and the introduction of a restricted parliamentary regime, he became one of the founders and leaders of the "Constitutional Democratic Party" (Cadets), or "Freedom of the Nation Party," which called for a genuine parliamentary system, based on the example of Great Britain. He was a delegate to the first parliament (*Duma) in 1906. As the vice chairman of his faction (the largest), he was the principal drafter of its policies and acted as mediator both within the group and between the group and other factions. When the Duma dispersed he joined its former members in a protest convention at Vyborg and signed the manifesto calling for civil disobedience. As a result he and all the other participants in the convention were sentenced to three months in prison and deprived of the right to vote. In 1917, after the February Revolution, he was a member of the commission that prepared the elections to the constituent assembly as well as a participant in the temporary parliament ("Council of the Republic"). The October Revolution and the banning of his party caused him to emigrate to the Crimean Peninsula, where he acted as foreign minister in the regional government formed by his party (described in his memoirs). In 1919 he emigrated to France, where he continued his activities among the Russian and Jewish emigrants.

Vinawer's Jewish communal activities began with the *Society for the Promotion of Culture among the Jews of Russia. Heading also the historio-ethnographic commission which gathered and published historical material on the Jews of Russia, he developed it into a special society. He also acted as advocate in the trials following the pogroms of *Kishinev and *Gomel. Although he was, too, among the founders and leaders of the *Society for the Attainment of Full Civil Rights for the Jewish People in Russia (1905–07), he opposed the formation of a separate Jewish faction in the Duma. Vinawer founded the newspaper *Yevreyskaya Tribuna*, one of whose objectives was to disprove the allegation of the "Jewishness" of the Russian Revolution. Vinawer's personality assumed an important place in the memoirs of his contemporaries, both Russian (i.e., *Witte, P.N. Milyukov) and Jewish (S. *Dubnow, M. *Vishniak). Vinawer himself published a collection of memoirs, *Nedavnoye* (1917; second, enlarged edition 1926).

BIBLIOGRAPHY: P.N. Milyukov et al. (eds.), *M.M. Vinawer* (collection; Rus., 1937); *Russian Jewry, 1860–1917* (1966), index.

[Abraham N. Poliak]

°**VINCENT, LOUIS HUGUES** (1872–1960), French Dominican monk and archaeologist; one of the heads of the Ecole Biblique et Archéologique Française in Jerusalem. Vincent was born in Varèze and as a youth entered the Dominican Monastery of St. Etienne in Jerusalem, where he lived until his death. His reputation as an archaeologist was established in 1907 when he published the first survey of the results of archaeological excavations in Ereẓ Israel (*Canaan d'après l'exploration récente*). In 1909 he took part in the Parker expedition, an adventurous enterprise which sought to discover the treasures of the Temple and dug in the tunnels of the Gihon. Vincent, however, turned it into a scientific excavation and published the results in *Jérusalem sous terre* (1911; *Underground Jerusalem*, 1911). In collaboration with L.F. Abel and afterward with A.M. Stève, he was the author of a series of monumental works on the remains of Jerusalem (*Jérusalem ancienne et nouvelle*, 1912–14). The concluding work on the Temple was published in 1956. Vincent and Abel also studied the antiquities of Bethlehem, Hebron and Emmaus. A visitor at almost every excavation in Ereẓ Israel and a prolific writer, Vincent was recognized as the doyen of Catholic archaeologists in Ereẓ Israel.

[Michael Avi-Yonah]

VINCHEVSKY, MORRIS (pseudonym of **Benzion Novakhovich**; 1856–1932), Yiddish and Hebrew writer and socialist leader. Born in Yonovo, Lithuania, he began his literary career in 1873 as a Hebrew poet and journalist, often writing under the pseudonyms "*Ben Nets*" ("Son of a Hawk") and "*Yigal ish ha-Ru'aḥ*" ("Yigal, the Man of Spirit"). Hailed by the Soviet Yiddish critics of the 1930s as the "grandfather" of Socialist Yiddish literature, Vinchevsky turned to writing Yiddish poetry in the 1880s. He lived in Germany (which he left when Bismarck's anti-socialist laws went into effect), France, and England (where he wrote pseudonymous articles in English for the socialist journals of H.M. Hyndman, one of the founders of British Socialism), before settling in New York in 1894. He was an active and committed socialist who expressed his sympathies in his often politically tendentious poetry. His work appealed to readers not only in the U.S. but also in pre- and post-revolutionary Russia. The basic trend of his work was humanitarian and deeply Jewish. Vinchevsky was also active in the Yiddish press, regularly contributing essays, poems, and translations to socialist publications such as the *Forverts, Der Emes,* and *Di Tsukunft*, which he also edited. He remained politically active throughout the first decades of the 20th century and was appointed to the Jewish Commission (*Comité des délégations juives), which represented Jewish interests at the Versailles Conference after World War I. In the 1920s Vinchevsky's sympathies veered sharply to the left. He broke with many of his socialist friends and in 1924–25 spent a number of months in the U.S.S.R. In 1927 he became paralyzed and remained in poor health until his death. Vinchevsky had a long and prolific career and, in 1927–28, a 10-volume edition of his works appeared under the editorship of Kalman *Marmor. Vinchevsky's library, manuscripts, and archives (YIVO), comprise a rich source for research into Yiddish literature and Jewish radical movements beginning in the 1860s.

BIBLIOGRAPHY: Reyzen, Leksikon, 1 (1928), 977–82; LNYL, 3 (1960), 432–3; Klausner, Sifrut, 5 (1955[2]), 115–20; 6 (1958[2]), 275–311; N.B. Minkoff, *Pionern fun Yidisher Poezye in Amerike*, 1 (1956), 19–85; S. Liptzin, *Flowering of Yiddish Literature* (1963), 136–9; Kressel, Leksikon, 1 (1965), 659–61; Malachi, in: *Yad la-Koré*, 4 (1956) 54–8, list of his Hebrew writings; M. Vinchevsky, *Works*, 1 (1927), biography by K. Marmor. **ADD. BIBLIOGRAPHY:** I. Howe, *World of Our Fathers* (1976), 420; S. Liptzin, *A History of Yiddish Literature* (1972), 96.

[Henry J. Tobias / Marc Miller (2nd ed.)]

VINCZE, PAUL (1907–1994), medalist. Vincze was born in Hungary, and settled in England, where he rapidly earned a reputation as having a classical gift of portraiture, which was balanced by allegorical reverses on his medals. His talent was also expressed in coins; he designed some of the new currency for Ghana, Libya, Nigeria, Malawi, and Guinea. Vincze has struck some of the finest Jewish commemoratives in modern times, including the 300th Anniversary of the Jewish Resettlement in Great Britain (1956). He executed medals for the private Israeli mint, Isnumat, and for the government of Israel. Examples of strikings he did for the former are the John F. Kennedy Memorial and the Visit of Pope Paul VI to the Holy Land. Examples of his work for the Israeli government are the 1966 Commemorative for Edmond and James de Rothschild and the 1967 Jubilee of the Balfour Declaration. Vincze executed several medals of distinguished Jews such as Ben-Gurion, Lord Samuel, and Yehudi Menuhin. Just before his death he designed the monetary coins of Malawi.

[Daniel M. Friedenberg]

VINE (Heb. גֶּפֶן). Of the various agricultural products mentioned in the Bible and talmudic literature, the vine and its products – *yayin* ("wine"), *tirosh* ("new wine"), *ḥemer* ("sweet red wine"), and *shekhar* ("strong drink") – occupy the central place. Sixteen times the Bible mentions in juxtaposition "corn, new wine, and oil," which represented the principal produce and the chief blessing of the soil (Deut. 7:13; et al.). Of the seven species with which Ereẓ Israel was blessed the vine figures first among the fruit (Deut. 8:8). "Every man [sitting] under his vine and under his fig-tree" symbolizes the ideal past and the hope of future peace (I Kings 5:5; Micah 4:4). Many biblical parables and allegories are associated with the vine, grapes, and wine. The people of Israel in its youth is compared to grapes which the traveler came upon in the wilderness (Hos. 9:10). Isaiah likens God to the owner of a vineyard and Israel to the vineyard (Isa. 5), a similar metaphor being employed by Jeremiah (2:21), and Ezekiel (17:1–10, 19:10–14) regards the vine as symbolizing the people of Israel and its fate.

Viticulture in Ereẓ Israel goes back to antiquity. An Egyptian inscription of the third millennium B.C.E. states that the Egyptian conqueror of the country ordered its vines and fig trees to be destroyed. The spies, sent ahead of the Israelites to spy out the land, brought back from the valley of Hebron a cluster of grapes of remarkable size (Num. 13:23). Situated in the inheritance of Judah, which was blessed with fruitful vines (Gen. 49:11), was the settlement Beth-Cherem ("the house of the vineyard"; Jer. 6:1), and passing through it was the valley of Sorek (Judg. 16:4), so named after the red grapes (*sorek*) grown there. Excellent wine was produced from the vines growing on Mount Ephraim and in Samaria (Isa. 28), where, Jeremiah prophesied, the vineyards of Samaria, destroyed after the desolation of the kingdom of Ephraim, would again be planted (Jer. 31:4–5). In the vineyards of Shiloh annual festivities accompanied by dances were held (Judg. 21:21), apparently connected with the vintage season, which was an occasion for great joy (cf. Isa. 16:10). According to an ancient tradition preserved in the Mishnah (Ta'an. 4:8) "the daughters of Jerusalem came out and danced in the vineyards" on the 15th of Av and the Day of Atonement. During these dances, the young girls found husbands for themselves. The Hasmoneans and Bar Kokhba struck a cluster of grapes on their victory coins as a symbol of the fertility of the country. Josephus highly praised the vineyards in the valley of Ginnosar (War, 3:519), and many places in Judea and Galilee are mentioned in talmudic literature as noted for their thriving vineyards.

The Bible refers to large vineyards in the kings' inheritance that contained "a thousand vines at a thousand pieces of silver" (Isa 7:23; cf. Song 8:11). Those mentioned in talmudic literature, however, were usually smaller, five vines in a field being considered a vineyard (Kil. 4:6). Individual vines were also planted among other trees, this being permitted by the laws of the Pentateuch, though sowing mixed seeds among the vines is prohibited (Deut. 22:9), and talmudic literature deals with many *halakhot* connected with this strict prohibition (Kil. 4–7; see *Mixed Species). Various strains of grapes were grown. Since the main product of grapes was the sweet red wine called *ḥemer*, there was a preference for the strains which produced red-black grapes known as *sorek*. Inferior white grapes were called *be'ushim* (Isa. 5:2, 4; cf. Ma'as. 1:2). Grapes were grown in two ways: either the trunk and branches trailed along the ground – the *gefen soraḥat* of the Bible (Ezek. 17:6) and the *rogeliot* of the Mishnah (Pe'ah 7:8); or the vine was trained over a pole, the *gefen adderet* of the Bible (Ezek. 17:8) and the *dalit* of the Mishnah (Pe'ah 4:2). The importance of the vine is attested by the Bible's many synonyms for its branches: *baddim, banot, daliyyot, zalzallim, zemorah, ḥoter, yonek, kannah, matteh, netishot neẓer, anaf, porah, keẓirim, sheluḥot, sarigim*, and *sorek*.

More than 40 expressions connected with viticulture are mentioned in the Bible and talmudic literature. Isaiah's song about the vineyard (Isa. 5) gives a detailed account of the different stages from its planting to the harvesting of the grapes: first the soil is dug up and the large stones are removed and used for the fence. Then the shrubs and thorns growing in the uncultivated field are cut down and used as "the hedge" of the fence; the fence protects the vineyard from being "trodden down" by cattle, and the hedge prevents goats from jumping over the fence. Next the field is cleared of small stones, which are put on top of the hedge, and all is ready for planting the sapling vines. The soil between the rows of vines is hoed, and at the end of the summer the branches are pruned. After three to four years, with the approach of the first vintage, the owner of the vineyard hews out a vat, and its stones are used to build a tower for watching over the vineyard during the vintage. Isaiah apparently describes a nonirrigated vineyard that awaits the rains of heaven (*ibid.* 5:6). The vine responds well to irrigation, flourishing particularly near fountains (Gen. 49:22; Ezek. 19:10).

The vine referred to in the Bible and in talmudic literature is the cultivated one, *Vitis vinifera*. In the region of Ereẓ Israel the wild vine does not grow, although in various places in Israel, especially near springs, such as Tel Dan and Naḥal Ammud in Galilee, seeds of the cultivated vine have sprouted and grow wild climbing trees. Various strains of vines, some local, others imported, are grown in Israel. In Samaria and on Mount Ephraim nonirrigated wine grapes, and in other regions of the country mostly irrigated and trellised eating grapes, are grown.

BIBLIOGRAPHY: Loew, Flora, 1 (1926), 49–189; J. Feliks, *Olam ha-Ẓome'aḥ ha-Mikra'i* (1968[2]), 17–24.

[Jehuda Feliks]

VINELAND, city in southern New Jersey, 30 miles (50 km) from Philadelphia. The Jewish community of Vineland dates back to the early 1880s, with the establishment of immigrant colonies outside of the city limits. Synagogues were prohibited within city limits until toward the end of the first decade of the 20th century. The first such colony was Alliance, founded in 1882 in Salem County by the Alliance Israélite Universelle (France) and the Baron de Hirsch Fund (Belgium), three miles out of Vineland, followed by others with biblical names like Carmel. In nearby Cape May County, the Baron de Hirsch Fund established Woodbine in 1891, which was incorporated by 1903 as an all-Jewish borough. Some settlers embraced the *Am Olam ideology of return to the soil as a means of salvation for the oppressed Jews of Russia. Men like Moshe Herder, H.L. Sabsovich, Sidney Bailey, and Moses Bayuk envisioned in well-balanced rural communities the basis for creative life. Subsidies were provided by philanthropic organizations in Western Europe and the United States – Alliance Israélite Universelle, Hebrew Immigrant Aid Society and the Baron de Hirsch Fund – as well as American Jewish leaders such as Jacob Schiff and Myer S. Isaacs, who hoped to create viable communities on the principles of self-help within American society. In each colony the fabric of life developed, including at least Orthodox synagogues and religious schools, as well as an array of clubs, fraternal orders, and debating and athletic groups.

An early necessity was manufacturing to supplement farm incomes. The soil was poor, the 10–15 acre lots inadequate; markets were distant, and the settlers untrained in agricultural methods. Subsistence depended on the sewing machine, especially in Carmel, Rosenhayn, Norma, and Brotmanville, as well as Woodbine, where industry was subsidized from the outset. Although the Jewish population grew slowly to about 3,500 in 1901, it dropped to 2,700 by 1919. To some extent this reflected growing American urbanization, as well as the second generation's struggle for better educational and economic opportunities. Among their sons who achieved prominence were Jacob G. Lipman, an agronomist and dean of Rutgers' College of Agriculture; Gilbert Seldes, author, critic, dean of the School of Communications, University of Pennsylvania; and Benjamin M. Golder, Philadelphia congressman. Some moved to New York or Philadelphia, but many settled in Vineland proper, operating stores or small factories. Arthur Goldhaft, a distinguished veterinarian, founded the Vineland Poultry Laboratories. During the 1960s, the Jewish community peaked at just over 10,000 people, with five synagogues in the city and another six in surrounding communities. The largest influx to the community was from several hundred survivors of the Nazi Holocaust, drawn to the area from large cities such as New York and Philadelphia with offers of assistance in the establishment of poultry farms and a quiet country life. These immigrants formed the Jewish Poultry Farmers' Association and a free loan society, as well as several diverse congregations. A Jewish day school, founded in 1953, supplemented the established congregational schools. Community life has included Zionist organizations, B'nai B'rith, Hadassah, Hebrew Women's Benevolent Society, Jewish War Veterans, and participation by Jews in all civic and political activities. The Jewish Community Council, which is today Jewish Federation of Cumberland County, was established in 1924, has been active in local, national and Israeli affairs, and has helped to maintain the community's vibrant Jewish life. Notable residents of national acclaim include Miles Lerman, founding chairman of the United States Holocaust Memorial Museum; Ben Zion Leuchter and Magda Leuchter, a local newspaper publisher and founding chairman of The National Jewish Center for Learning and Leadership (CLAL); and Esther Raab, a tireless Holocaust survivor and educator, upon whose life are based the play *Dear Esther* and the film *Escape from Sobibor*. Samuel Gassel served as borough commissioner and mayor of the City of Vineland; I. Harry Levin as municipal judge in adjoining townships; Dr. Tevis Goldhaft as chairman of the Board of Education; and Stanley S. Brotman as presiding senior judge of the U.S. District Court. The population in 2005 was 1,800.

BIBLIOGRAPHY: P.R. Goldstein, *Social Aspects of the Jewish Colonies of South Jersey* (1912); A.D. Goldhaft, *The Golden Egg* (1957) J. Brandes, *Immigrants to Freedom* (1971).

[Joseph Brandes / Kirk Wisemayer (2nd ed.)]

VINER, JACOB (1892–1970), U.S. economist. Born in Montreal, Canada, Viner began teaching at the University of Chicago in 1916 and returned there after federal government service in World War I. In 1925 he reached the rank of professor. From 1946 to 1960 he was professor of economics at Princeton, and was simultaneously a member of the Institute for Advanced Study at Princeton. Viner served the U.S. government in a number of capacities: he was representative at the League of Nations (1933), and consulting expert to the Treasury (1935–39) and to the State Department (1943–52). His research, writing, and teaching covered many aspects of international economics, including trade and commercial policy, foreign exchange, international finance, and economic development. He was particularly interested in the application and adaptation of the theory of international trade to current problems and was among the first critics of the Keynesian neoeconomics. He claimed that the use of oversimplified and otherwise unrealistic models reduced the usefulness of the theory of international trade. Viner demanded the incorporation into the classical theory of what he regarded as the valuable elements of Keynes' analysis, without abandoning the fundamentals that had been developed by the older theory.

His publications include *Canada's Balance of International Indebtedness* (1924); *Dumping: A Problem in International Trade* (1923, repr. 1966); *Studies in the Theory of International Trade* (1937, repr. 1965); *The Customs Union Issue* (1950); *International Trade and Economic Development* (1953); *The Long View and the Short* (1958); and *Problems of Monetary Control* (1964).

[Joachim O. Ronall]

VINKOVCI, town in Croatia, capital of Srijem Province. Jews are known to have lived there only from the second half of the 19th century. Ignatz Gross opened a retail store in 1866. A *kehillah* was formed in 1870 and Jacob Schlesinger installed a flour mill at that time. Jews were tanners, tailors and merchants. Leaders of the community were L. Stein, Dr. Armin Lederer, and Dr. Ignatz Lang. Zionist activists were Max Lederer, Adolf Beck, and Vilim Orenstein. The first rabbi was Solomon Neumann, followed by R. Schoenfeld and Dr. Mavro Frankfurter, who was horrendously tortured by the Ustashe and died in the Jasenovac death camp. His son, David *Frankfurter, killed the Swiss Nazi leader Wilhelm Gustloff in Davos on February 2, 1936, in an effort to call the world's attention to the dangers of Nazism.

During World War I, Jews were molested and robbed by deserters from the Austro-Hungarian army, but they organized self-defense and successfully resisted the assaults. In 1923 a national conference of Yugoslavia's rabbis took place in Vinkovci. In 1931 about 1,000 Jews lived there; their number dwindled, however, in later years due to emigration, mostly to Zagreb. On the eve of the Holocaust, only 630 Jews remained there. Nevertheless, it was a thriving community.

During the Holocaust most Jews perished and the synagogue was demolished.

BIBLIOGRAPHY: *Jevrejski Almanajh* (Vrsac, 5690 (1929/30)); PK (1988).

[Zvi Loker (2nd ed.)]

VINNIKOV, ISAAC N. (1897–), Soviet Orientalist. Born in Khotimsk, Belorussia, in 1922 Vinnikov was sent by the "People's Commissariat for Education" to study in the faculty of linguistics and ethnology at the University of Leningrad. Two of his teachers were L.Y. *Sternberg and P.K. *Kokovtsov. His first works were connected with pre-Islamic Arabic history and culture. Later he devoted himself to the study of the customs and languages of the Arab tribes living in Central Asia. In 1941 he wrote his doctoral thesis on "The Arabs in the U.S.S.R."; he also engaged in the study of Tyrean and Aramaic inscriptions and devoted many years to compiling a concordance to the Aramaic of Ereẓ Israel (in the Jerusalem Talmud and the Palestinian Midrashim). For many years he gave courses at the University of Leningrad in Semitic languages, among them Hebrew, supervising many students in the field of research.

BIBLIOGRAPHY: *Narody Azii i Afriki*, no. 6 (1967), 155–7.

[Yehuda Slutsky]

VINNITSA, town in Vinnitsa district, Ukraine. The earliest information available on the Jews of the town dates from 1532: there is a mention that year of the wealthy Jewish merchant Mekhel, who traded with Turkish Moldavia (in livestock and wool cloth). Until the end of the 18th century, the community remained rather small and suffered from the attacks of the Ukrainian rebels who fought against Polish rule (*Chmielnicki, the *Haidamacks), the oppression of the Polish governors and mayors, as well as from the wars which brought about the disruption of commerce on the nearby borders. In 1776, 381 Jews belonged to the *kahal* of Vinnitsa; of these, 190 lived in the town and the rest in the surroundings. The Russian annexation (1793) resulted in continuous growth of the Jewish population in the town and its region. The census of 1897 found 11,689 Jews (over one-third of the population) living in the town and in 1910, there were 20,257 Jews (45.5% of the total population). They earned their livelihood mainly in tailoring and from commerce in agricultural produce. The community of Vinnitsa did not suffer in 1919–20 because the town served as the regional capital of the successive governments in the region. In 1926 there were 21,812 Jews (41%). The *Yevsektsiya waged a savage campaign to destroy the religious and national life of the Jews of Vinnitsa, and the town became a center of its activities throughout Podolia. A Jewish pedagogic institute was established and during the late 1930s, a Communist Yiddish newspaper (*Proletarisher Emes*) was published in Vinnitsa. A few months after the occupation of the town by the Germans, on Rosh Ha-Shanah, Sept. 22, 1941, 28,000 Jews of the town and its surroundings were exterminated in Vinnitsa. According to the 1959 census, there were about 19,500 Jews (c. 16% of the total population) in Vinnitsa. The former Great Synagogue was closed by the authorities in 1957 and converted into a storehouse.

Though most of the Jews had left in the mass emigration of the 1990s, by 2005, Vinnitsa had a Jewish day school and a club for Hebrew-speaking youth. A new education center was being built.

BIBLIOGRAPHY: Y. Zusmer, *Be-Ikvei ha-Dor* (1957), 267–80; E. Bingel, in: *Yad Vashem Studies*, 3 (1959), 303–20.

[Yehuda Slutsky]

VIRBALIS (Ger. **Wirballen**; Pol. **Wierzbolow**; Rus. **Verzhboloro**), town in S.W. Lithuania. Due to the position of the town on an important commercial route between Russia and Germany, the Jewish community was financially prosperous. In 1897 there were 1,219 Jews (37% of the total population). Among Lithuanian Jewry, the community of Virbalis was outstanding for its nationalist cultural activity and its promotion of Hebrew both as a language for study and for daily speech. Following World War I, the Jews returned to the ruins of Virbalis, the majority of them having abandoned the town during the war. According to the census of 1923, they numbered 1,233 (30% of the population). Many of them were engaged in agriculture, either as landowners or as lessees of orchards, vegetable gardens, and tobacco plantations. Near the town was located the training farm of *He-Ḥalutz. This also included a Hebrew secondary school, a Tarbut school, and a kindergarten. There were, in addition, several Zionist organizations and welfare institutions. The mayor of the town was a Jew. The Germans invaded Virbalis on June 22, 1941. A week later they massacred the men, and a short while after that, the women and children. The poet *Yehoash was a native of Virbalis.

BIBLIOGRAPHY: M. Sudarski, in: *Lite*, 1 (1951), 1633–44.

[Dov Levin]

°**VIRGIL** (**Vergil**; **Publius Vergilius Maro**; 70–19 B.C.E.), greatest Roman poet. Though Virgil nowhere mentions the Jews directly, there are several indications in two of his greatest works, the *Eclogues* and the *Aeneid*, that he was aware of Jewish tradition.

The brief Fourth Eclogue speaks apocalyptically of the imminent return of the last and greatest age sung of by the Cumaean Sibyl and ushered in by the maiden (*virgo*) goddess Artemis and by the birth of a newborn boy, when a golden race will be sent down from heaven which will consort with the gods. All remaining traces of men's guilt will be removed; and the world, made peaceful by the virtues of the baby's father, will be a veritable utopia, with the earth producing its products without tilling, goats bringing forth udders swollen with milk, and herds cavorting fearlessly with lions. The age will be marked by the death of the snake and the replacement of poisonous herbs by Assyrian nard, though a few traces of men's ancient deceit will remain and though battles will have to be refought and rewon before the age can be ushered in. Virgil says that this Messianic-like age will begin during the consulship of *Asinius Pollio (40 B.C.E.), to whom the poem is addressed; and Pollio may well have been Virgil's major link with the Jewish tradition, since Pollio was one of the consuls who in this very year accompanied *Herod to deposit in the Capitol the decree which the Senate had passed naming Herod king (Jos., Ant. 14:388–9). Later, when Herod sent his sons *Alexander and *Aristobulus to Rome to complete their education, they lodged at his home, since, as Josephus (Ant. 15:343) adds, he was proud of Herod's friendship. Pollio was, moreover, closely associated with *Julius Caesar, who showed special consideration for the Jews (*Suetonius, 84:5); *Horace, who mentions them prominently; and *Timagenes of Alexandria, who wrote a universal history, with comments on the Jews, quoted by Josephus (Ant. 13:319, 344; Apion 2:84). The parallels with *Isaiah's vision (chapters 6, 7, 9, 11) of the birth of a wonderful child and the age of peace which he will usher in and with the snake motif (Gen. 3), suggest that Virgil may have read the Septuagint, which certainly was known to the large and Greek-speaking Jewish community of Rome, though they also resemble well-known details of the traditional Golden Age in classical literature.

*Constantine, *Jerome, *Ambrose, and *Augustine also regarded the poem as alluding to the birth of Jesus; and consequently throughout the Middle Ages, culminating in *Dante, Virgil had a special status as a prophet. The allusion to the Cumaean song may well indicate that Virgil's immediate source was the *Sibylline Oracles; for while it is true that the extant Sibylline Oracles, which are to a considerable degree of Jewish and Christian origin, have little to do with the Sibylline Books associated with the city of Cumae in Italy, they do contain a number of passages based on Isaiah which are parallel to Virgil's Eclogue. Indeed, Horace's apocalyptic Sixteenth Epode, which has similar affinities with the Sibylline Oracles, may well be his reply to this Eclogue of Virgil. The reference to Assyrian spice may be Virgil's indication of an Eastern source.

The Fourth Eclogue, especially in its utopian vision of peace, has been called a blueprint for the *Aeneid*. The fact that Virgil in the *Aeneid* consciously differs from *Homer in making his hero a devout wanderer with the mission of leading his people and their household gods by a roundabout route to a promised ancestral land, during which they are subjected to many trials, offers an obvious parallel with Moses. There are numerous apocalypses in the poem, notably in the Sixth Book, which again suggest the influence of the Sibylline Oracles. The fact that the greatest temptation of all occurs during the year which Aeneas spends at Carthage, a Semitic city, again emphasizes the contact with the Near East. Finally, though the parallels should not be strained, one may cite the similarity between Augustus standing on the shield of Aeneas (8:680) with twin beams of light darting from his temples and Moses (cf. Ex. R. 47:6), and the hitherto unnoticed Hebraic-like parallelism in both thought and language in such lines as *Aeneid* 1:9–10 (… *tot volvere casus…. tot adire labores*).

BIBLIOGRAPHY: T.F. Royds, *Virgil and Isaiah* (1918); E. Norden, *Die Geburt des Kindes* (1924); H.J. Rose, *The Eclogues of Vergil* (1942), 162–217; L.H. Feldman, in: *Transactions of the American Philological Association*, 84 (1953), 73–80; M. Hadas, *Hellenistic Culture* (1959), 238–45, 253–6; C.H. Gordon, in: C.F.A. Schaeffer (ed.), *Ugaritica*, 6 (1969), 267–88.

[Louis Harry Feldman]

VIRGIN, VIRGINITY.

Terminology

The biblical *betulah* (בתולה) usually rendered "virgin," is in fact an ambiguous term which in nonlegal contexts may denote an age of life rather than a physical state. Cognate Akkadian *batultu* (masculine, *batūlu*) and Ugaritic *btlt* refer to "an adolescent, nubile, girl." That the woman who is so called need not necessarily be a *virgo intacta* is shown by the graphic account in a Ugaritic myth of the sexual relations of Baal with the goddess Anath, who bears the honorific epithet *btlt* (see Pritchard, Texts, 142). Moreover, in an Aramaic incantation text from Nippur there is a reference to a *betulta*ʾ (בתולתא) who is "pregnant but cannot bear" (Montgomery, in bibl. 13:9, p. 178). The male counterpart to *betulah* in the Bible is often *baḥur* (בָּחוּר), "young man," e.g., Jeremiah 31:12 [13] and Amos 8:13 (cf. Joel 1:8, where a *betulah* moans for her bridegroom); and the word *betulah* interchanges with the somewhat synonymous age term *ʿalmah* (עַלְמָה), which also describes a young woman. Thus, in Genesis 24:16, 43, Rebekah is first called a *betulah* and then an *ʿalmah*. (Exactly the same interchange of the two words appears in a Ugaritic text.) *ʿAlmah*, despite a two-millennium misunderstanding of Isaiah 7:14, "Behold a young woman [LXX:παρθένοσ, "virgin"] shall conceive and bear a son," indicates nothing concerning the chastity of the woman in question. The only way that the term "virgin" can be unambiguously expressed is in the negative: thus, Sumerian and Akkadian, "undeflowered," and Akkadian, "not experienced," "unopened," and "who has not known a male." The description of Rebekah (Gen. 24:16), who is first called a *betulah*, "young woman," and then "whom no man had known" (cf. Judg. 21:12), is similar. In legal contexts, however, *betulah* denotes a virgin in the strict sense (as does *batultu* in certain Akkadian legal contexts).

In the Laws

Virginity in a woman was an asset of financial as well as moral significance: a "bride price for virgins" (*mohar betulot*, מֹהַר בְּתוּלוֹת), clearly higher than for non-virgins, was payable to her father for the privilege of marrying her. Biblical laws deal with litigation that may arise over the financial and moral stakes of virginity:

(a) Exodus 22:15–16: A man who seduces a virgin who has not been betrothed must marry her by the payment of a bride price. If the father is unwilling to permit his daughter to marry her seducer, he must still pay her father "in accordance with the bride price for virgins." In either case the father is compensated for his monetary loss. (A similar law pertaining to the seduction of an unmarried girl is found in the Middle Assyrian Laws, A, 56 (in: Pritchard, Texts, 185), where the equivalent of the Hebrew *mohar betulot*, in Akkadian, *sīm batulti*, "price for virgins," must be paid by the seducer. There, too, the father is not bound to give his daughter in marriage to the seducer. The law contains an additional clause which is absent from its biblical counterpart: "The father shall treat his daughter as he wishes," i.e., he may punish her in any way he sees fit.)

(b) Deuteronomy 22:28–29: A man who rapes a virgin who has not been betrothed must pay 50 shekels of silver (later understood as the price of a virgin), is forced to marry her, and is deprived of all future rights of divorce. (Similarly, in the Middle Assyrian Laws, A, 55 (in: Pritchard, Texts, 185), after describing the physical status of the young woman and the various places where the offense might have occurred, the law requires the culprit, if unmarried, to pay the price for virgins, marry the girl, and forfeit rights of divorce. The father in this case, having received the monetary compensation, still has the right to marry her off to whomever he pleases. If the culprit is married, the father may choose to give his daughter in marriage to him, but it is further stipulated that the father shall take the wife of the culprit to be raped in turn!)

(c) Deuteronomy 22:23–27: In the case of a man who violated a virgin who was betrothed, the place of the offense is the criterion of whether she was coerced or willingly consented (cf. Middle Assyrian Laws, A, 55 (above) and Hittite Laws, 197–8, in: Pritchard, Texts, 196). If the offense took place in town, both are stoned to death, "the girl because she did not cry for help in the town, and the man because he violated his neighbor's wife." If, however, it took place in open country, it is considered rape and the man alone is put to death. It is to be noted that as regards inviolability, a betrothed virgin is like a married woman: violation of either is a capital offense. (The Laws of Eshnunna, 26 (in: Pritchard, Texts, 162) and the Laws of Hammurapi, 130 (Pritchard, Texts, 171) may be compared; both prescribe the death penalty for the rape of virgins who are legally married.)

(d) Deuteronomy 22:13–22: If a bridegroom accuses his wife of not being a virgin at the time of marriage, the girl's parents must produce evidence of their daughter's virginity before the elders at the town gate. If he has falsely defamed his wife, he is flogged, fined 100 shekels, and is deprived of all rights of divorce. The large fine befits the gravity of his accusation, which would have resulted in the execution of his bride by stoning if his charge were proven correct, i.e., if she did transgress while yet in her father's house. (For cuneiform analogues to the accusation of adultery, cf. Laws of Hammurapi, 131, 132 (Pritchard, Texts, 171), and Middle Assyrian Laws, A, 17 (Pritchard, Texts, 181).)

Esteem of the unsullied purity of the virgin is reflected in the rule of Leviticus 21:13ff. that a high priest may marry only a virgin of his clan (cf. Rashbam). Ezekiel 44:22 obliges all priests to marry virgins (or a priest's widow), but they need only be Israelites.

In Nonlegal Literature

That virgins were particularly desired and sexually provocative comes out in several passages. Lot tries to appease the frenzy of the Sodomites by offering them his daughters, whose virginity he specially mentions (Gen. 19:8; cf. Judg. 19:24). In massacres, virgins alone might be spared, to be taken as slaves or wives (Num. 31:18; Judg. 21:12). Expanding on II Samuel 13:18, Josephus writes that "in ancient times virgins wore long-sleeved tunics reaching to the ankle in order not to be exposed" (Ant., 7:171).

As a figure of purity and moral worth, *betulah*, "maid," is used to personify countries and peoples in poetry (often construed with *bat*, "daughter," "woman"); e.g., Lamentations 2:13, *betulat bat Ẓiyyon*, "fair maiden Zion" – the genitives being explicative (as in *nehar Perat*, "River Euphrates").

[Shalom M. Paul]

In the Talmud and Halakhah

In *halakhah* a virgin is not necessarily a maiden whose hymen is intact. She can be legally regarded both as a virgin with a ruptured hymen and as a non-virgin when it is intact. The former applies when she can claim, according to Rabban Gamaliel and R. Eliezer, or prove, according to R. Joshua b. Hananiah, that the rupture was caused by an injury (*mukkat eẓ*, literally, "injured by a piece of wood"; Ket. 1:7). On the other hand, although a maiden divorced or widowed after *betrothal only has the legal status of a virgin, if she was divorced or widowed after marriage, even though no intercourse took place, she is legally classed as a non-virgin (Ket. 1:2 and 4). Nor is the statement in the Tosefta (Shev. 3:5) that a virgin is "one who has never had intercourse" exact. Intercourse with a girl child aged less than three years and a day does not invalidate her status as a virgin, as it was stated that in this case the hymen grows again, and it is regarded as merely "poking a finger in the eye" (Nid. 5:4). A woman taken captive by foreign soldiery or a manumitted bondswoman is regarded as a non-virgin, since it is assumed as a fact that in these circumstances she was raped or seduced. The legal disability of a non-virgin expresses itself in the fact that her *ketubbah* is only 100 *zuz* instead of the 200 of the virgin (Ket. 1:2; the priests during the Second Temple period instituted a *ketubbah* of 400 *zuz*, to which the rabbis did not object – Ket. 1:5) and the fact that she was forbidden to marry a high priest (Lev. 21:13).

The Mishnah states that the marriage of a virgin used to take place on Wednesdays so that, should she be found to be a non-virgin, the aggrieved bridegroom could immediately make application to the *bet din*, which sat regularly on Thursdays (Ket. 1:1). However, the custom arose to anticipate it and have it take place on Tuesdays in order to foil the custom of *jus primae noctis* exercised by the local governor (cf. Rabinowitz in bibl. for other examples).

Proof that on her wedding day she "went forth to her marriage in a *hinnuma*" (either "in a litter" or "under a veil" – (Ket. 17b)), or accompanied with ὑμέναιος ("the bridal song"), or with her hair unbound, or that "roasted corn was distributed" at her wedding, was sufficient to establish the fact that she was a virgin when she married (Ket. 2:1), since these ceremonies and customs were carried out only with regard to a virgin. Unnatural intercourse does not affect her status as a virgin (Kid. 9b; cf. Rashi, ad loc.; and Maim. Yad, Issurei Bi'ah, 3:6.

[Louis Isaac Rabinowitz]

BIBLIOGRAPHY: J.A. Montgomery, *Aramaic Incantation Texts from Nippur* (1913); E. Neufeld, *Ancient Hebrew Marriage Laws* (1944), index, s.v., *signa virginitatis*; F. Zimmerman, in: JBL, 73 (1954), 98, n. 4; J.J. Finkelstein, in: JAOS, 86 (1966), 355–72; B. Landsberger, in: *Symbolae iuridicae et historicae Mortino David dedicatae*, 2 (1968), 41–105. IN THE TALMUD AND HALAKHAH: ET, 5 (1953), 4–7; J. Preuss, *Biblisch-talmudische Medizin* (1923^{3}), 558–61; idem, in: *Allgemeine medizinische Zentral-Zeitung* (1905), no. 5ff.; L.M. Epstein, *Marriage Laws in the Bible and the Talmud* (1942), index; L. Rabinowitz, in: JQR, 58 (1967/68), 152–60.

VIRGINIA, state on the east coast of the U.S. In 2001, approximately 66,000 residents were of the Jewish faith, comprising just 0.9% of the state's total population. One of the fastest growing Jewish populations in the country, the largest Jewish community resides in Northern Virginia (35,000), followed by the Tidewater (20,000), Richmond (12,500), Roanoke (1,050), and Charlottesville (1,000). Fredericksburg, Harrisonburg, Petersburg, Staunton, and Lynchburg have small Jewish populations. Northern Virginia was once considered not a place where Jews would live, but its Jewish population has grown

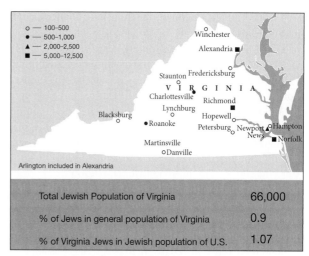

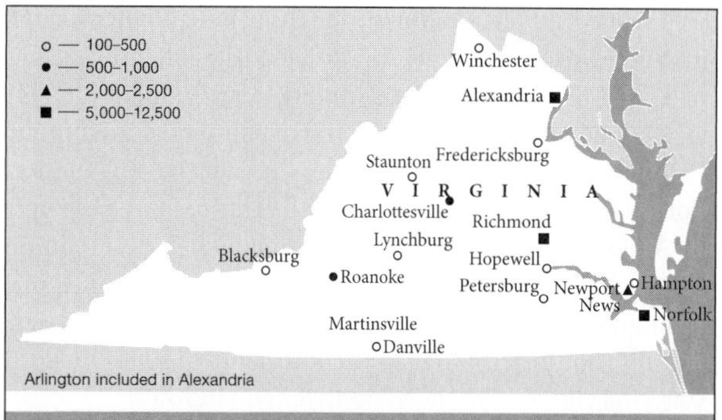

Total Jewish Population of Virginia	66,000
% of Jews in general population of Virginia	0.9
% of Virginia Jews in Jewish population of U.S.	1.07

Jewish communities in Virginia. Population figures for 2001.

both within the inner areas of suburban Washington and in the regions that have developed beyond Dulles Airport.

The Jewish experience in Virginia dates back to Sir Walter Raleigh's ill-fated Roanoke Colony, then a part of the Virginia territory. Joachim Gaunse, a Prague metallurgist, landed with Raleigh in 1585. Elias Legardo joined the colony at Jamestown in 1621; John Levy received a patent for 200 acres on Powell's Creek in James City County in 1648; and there are references to brothers Silvedo and Manuel Rodriguez, Sephardi Jews, in Lancaster County from the middle of the century. In 1658, Moses Nehemiah was discharged from debt in York County. Michael Franks and Jacob Myer accompanied George Washington in his 1754 expedition across the Allegheny Mountains and received rewards for gallant service. In 1757, Michael Israel and his wife, Sarah, bought 80 acres of land near the mountain pass between North Garden and Batesville, a pass since known as Israel's Gap. Dr. John de Sequeyra, who lived in Williamsburg, was credited by Thomas Jefferson with introducing the custom of eating tomatoes. Solomon Israel bought land in Albemarle in 1764. The Gratz brothers of Philadelphia were trading in Fredericksburg and Williamsburg in 1776. Jacob Darmstadt, who arrived in the colonies as a Hessian soldier, was an early resident of Richmond, as were Isaiah Isaacs and Jacob I. Cohen, both veterans of the Revolution, who became merchants and owners of the Bird-In-Hand tavern. Moses Meyers settled in Norfolk in 1787. Samuel Myers settled in Petersburg in 1789. Commodore Uriah P. Levy of New York purchased and began the first restoration of Thomas Jefferson's Monticello in 1836. He and his nephew Jefferson Monroe Levy preserved and restored the estate, acquired by the Thomas Jefferson Memorial Foundation in 1923. Rachel Levy, the commodore's mother, is interred on the grounds.

Although Jews enjoyed more rights in the British Colony of Virginia than almost anywhere else in the world, they were not give equal status with their Christian neighbors until well after the Revolution. Many were members of the Masonic order. William Byrd II, George Wythe, and Richard Lee II studied Hebrew, and James Waddell's school in Lancaster County instructed young gentlemen in the language. After the passage of Jefferson's Statute for Religious Freedom (1786), Jewish immigration increased in Tidewater, Fredericksburg, Richmond, Petersburg, and Albermarle County. It came through eastern ports, including New York City, Philadelphia, and Baltimore, to Alexandria, Richmond, and Norfolk along the Piedmont belt and Tidewater region. A second route taken by German immigrants ran from Pennsylvania and Maryland through the Valley of Virginia, with settlements extending south to North Carolina and west to the Ohio River and beyond.

The first Jewish congregation in Virginia, Kahol Kadosh Beth Shalome, was established in Richmond in 1789. In 1848, Jews in the Tidewater region founded the House of Jacob Congregation, later known as Ohef Sholom; Congregation Rodef Sholom was formed in Petersburg in 1858; Congregation Beth El was organized in Alexandria in 1859; the Hebrew Friendship Congregation was established in Harrisonburg in 1870; Major Alexander Hart helped to establish the House of Israel Congregation in Staunton in 1876; Danville's Beth Sholem Congregation was founded in 1881; in Newport News, organization of the synagogue was in 1887; Portsmouth's Congregation Adath Jeshurun was organized in 1893; Roanoke's Temple Emmanuel was organized in 1897; and Congregation Agudath Achim was founded in Lynchburg the same year.

In the mid-19th century, immigrant German Jews founded some of the state's major retail concerns. William Thalhimer arrived in Richmond in 1840 and established Thalhimer Bros. department store that later became the largest in Virginia with branches throughout the state. Anthony Rosenstock opened A. Rosenstock and Co. in Petersburg in 1859; the Guggenheimer family was in business in Lynchburg in 1850; the Bachrach family in Warrenton; the Leterman family opened a store in Charlottesville in 1852; Leopold Wise, Herman Heller, Samuel Loewner, and Jonas Heller settled in Harrisonburg in 1859 and started businesses there. Records show that Virginia Jews served in the Confederate Army. Many of the sons entered professions or continued in the retail businesses established by their parents. Later waves of immigration, bringing the East European Jews, repeated to a large extent this pattern of economic activity. During WWI and WWII, construction of important military bases in Virginia attracted many new Jewish settlers, especially in the Norfolk, Richmond, and Petersburg areas. The Jews continue to be prominent in the retail field as well as in the professions and in the distributing and manufacturing fields.

Since 1991, Virginia has exported over $1.5 billion of goods and services to Israel. The Virginia Israel Trade Commission, established in 1986 to investigate cultural, educational, and economic opportunities, was reformed in 1991 under Governor George Allen as the Virginia Israel Partnership. Norman Sisisky was first elected as the delegate representing Petersburg in the Virginia General Assembly in 1973; and later served nine terms as U.S. Representative for Virginia's Fourth Congressional District. Eric Cantor was elected as a delegate for Henrico County to the Virginia House of Delegates from 1992 to 2000; and in 2006 the U.S. Representative for Virginia's Seventh Congressional District served as chief deputy majority whip in the U.S. House of Representatives. Michael Schewel served as Virginia's secretary of commerce and trade under Governor Mark Warner.

BIBLIOGRAPHY: H.T. Ezekiel and G. Lichtenstein, *History of the Jews of Richmond* (1917); L. Ginsberg, *History of the Jews of Petersburg* (1954); idem, *Chapters on the Jews of Virginia (1658–1900)* (1970); J.R. Marcus, *Early American Jewry*, 2 (1953), 165–225; L. Huhner, in: A.J. Karp (ed.), *The Jewish Experience in America*, 1 (1969), 93–113. **ADD. BIBLIOGRAPHY:** M.I. Urofsky, *Commonwealth and Community: The Jewish Experience in Virginia* (1997).

[Susan Morgan (2nd ed.)]

VIRGIN ISLANDS, archipelago in the West Indies. In the late 20th century there was a total population of over 100,000 in the Virgin Islands, which included about 300 Jews. On any given Sabbath they would be joined by tourists visiting the island. There were also Jews on St. John and other islands but the synagogue was located on St. Thomas.

One of the first Jews in the Virgin Islands was Gabriel Milan, whom King Christian of Denmark sent there in 1684 to be governor. The Danes, like the Dutch, who had colonized the islands before them, were liberal toward all religions. Complete freedom of religion was granted to Catholics and Jews on St. Thomas Island in 1685. The story of the St. Thomas community is typical of West Indian Jewry. Its prosperity increased with the rise of sugar plantations and shipping lines, and at its peak the St. Thomas community numbered 400. A house of worship was built in the town of Charlotte Amalie in 1833 to replace an older one destroyed by fire. Called Sephardic Synagogue at St. Thomas, (now known as The Hebrew Congregation of St. Thomas (or *K"K Bracha v'shalom u'gimilut chasadim*) it is the only one on the island and is a landmark, being the second oldest synagogue in the United States and its territories, the oldest in continuous use. The cemetery of the St. Thomas Jewish community is filled with Spanish and Portuguese names and was the subject of a study done by the Danish Jewish community: J. Margolinski, *299 Epitaphs from the Jewish Cemetery in St. Thomas, W.I., 1837–1916* (1957).

From this congregation have come two governors of the Virgin Islands: Morris Fidangue de Castro and Ralph Paiewonsky. Two American politicians were from the Virgin Islands: David Levi, who as David *Yulee became one of Florida's first senators in 1845, and Judah P. *Benjamin, born in St. Croix. The house where Camille *Pissarro was born in 1830 can still be seen in the heart of the commercial center. The Grand Hotel located at Charlotte Amalie's main square was built by Pissarro's father in 1841.

[Benjamin Schlesinger]

Synagogue Restoration

In 1973 the Sephardi Synagogue of St. Thomas, Virgin Islands, had its original plaster on the walls removed after 140 years of service, revealing handsome walls of Danish brick. The synagogue (with the plaster) was restored in 1999 and received national recognition for its restoration. It became a National Historic Monument in 1997, the year after its bicentennial. Like certain other synagogues in the Caribbean, its marble floor is kept covered with a layer of sand to remember the conversos (secret Jews) of Spain who prayed secretly in their cellars with floors covered with sand to muffle the sound of their prayers. It employs a rabbi, Arthur Starr, who serves the community.

[Arthur F. Starr (2nd ed.)]

VISEUL-DE-SUS (Hung. **Felsöviső**; referred to by the Jews as **Oybervisha**), town in N. Romania; until the end of World War I and between 1940 and 1944 in Hungary. The Jewish community in Viseul-de-Sus was organized in 1877, although Jews had already been living there for a long time. The Jewish population developed rapidly during the 1880s. In 1885 the community was designated as the Jewish center for the three villages of Felsöviső, Alsóviso (Viseul-de-Jos), and Középvisó (Viseul de Mijloc), and later for a number of other villages. The *ḥevra kaddisha* was established in 1895. The community was Orthodox and Ḥasidism wielded a powerful influence. There were four synagogues, a number of additional prayer houses, and a yeshivah. In the main, the occupations of the Jews, including ordinary laborers, were connected with the forests and the wood industry of the town and its environs. In 1896 a Hebrew press was established; as it was the only press in the town it also printed works in other languages. The Hebrew religious periodical, *Degl ha-Torah*, was printed there from 1922 and ran to about 80 issues. In 1930 there were 3,734 Jews (33.7 percent of the total population) in Viseul-de-Sus. About the same number of Jews lived there in the spring of 1944, when the Fascist Hungarian authorities set up a ghetto, in which Jews from the surrounding villages were also concentrated. It is estimated that about 35,000 Jews passed through this ghetto on their way to *Auschwitz. After World War II about 700 Jews returned to the town. Their numbers declined through emigration and by 1971 the Jewish community had ceased to exist.

BIBLIOGRAPHY: *Magyar Zsidó Lexikon* (1929), 272; I. Benoschofsky and E. Karsai, *Vádirat a nácizmus ellen*, 2 (1960), 259, 266, 272.

[Yehouda Marton]

VISHNEVETS (Pol. **Wisniowiec**; in Jewish sources, Vishniets), village in N. Ternopol oblast, Ukraine. Jews first settled in Vishnevets in the early 17th century, and Tatars from Crimea who invaded the locality in 1653 massacred them. In the 18th century the community of Vishnevets was under the jurisdiction of the *kahal* of Kremenets (Volhynia). The village was annexed to Russia in 1795. There were 501 Jews in Vishnevets in 1765, 3,178 in 1847, 2,980 (70% of the total population) in 1897, and 2,825 (70%) in 1921. In the 19th century, Ḥasidism gained a following in the community. Between the two world wars, in independent Poland, there were branches of Agudat Israel and He-Ḥalutz. The community was annihilated in the Holocaust.

BIBLIOGRAPHY: Halpern, Pinkas, index; B. Wasiutyński, *Ludność żydowska w Polsce w wiekach XIX i XX* (1930), 85.

[Shimshon Leib Kirshenboim]

VISHNIAC, ROMAN (1897–1990), photographer. Born in St. Petersburg, Vishniac studied biology at Russian universities. When Berlin University under the Nazis refused to grant his Ph.D. in art, he left Germany and traveled throughout Poland, Austria, Holland, France, Romania, and Czechoslovakia, documenting with his camera the lives of the Jews in the cities and in the hinterlands. He was in Poland taking photographs of the Jewish community when Hitler's troops marched in. Vishniac was apprehended and sent to a concentration camp in Zbąszyń, Poland. He escaped to France but within a short time he was again incarcerated in another concentration camp, Camp du Richard in Clichy, France. Early in 1941 he managed to escape from Europe and went to the United States where he renewed his studies in medicine and began to use his camera for research in the biological sciences.

He specialized in photomicroscopy, pioneering in the field of cytoplasmic circulation in microscopic algae as connected with photosynthesis, and photographing the formation of thrombosis in blood vessels. Vishniac immediately won widespread recognition in the field of scientific cinematography. His books include *Polish Jews* (1947) and *Life of the Six Millions* (1969) illustrating European Jewish life before and during the Holocaust.

BIBLIOGRAPHY: E. Kinkead, *Spider, Egg and Microcosm* (1955), 157–244; Keppler, in: *Modern Photography*, 23 (Feb. 1959), 78–86.

[Peter Pollack]

VISIONS. The Hebrew Bible contains descriptions of many visions, especially those of God and His angel (or angels). When the appearance of God is mentioned as part of the biblical narrative, it is difficult to say if, in that specific case, the author thought that it was reality or a vision. The idea developed already at a very ancient period of Judaism that God has no shape, and, therefore, the appearance of God and His angels to the prophets was evidently understood by them as a vision (see *Prophecy). This is surely so in the case of Ezekiel's vision of God and the heavenly world. Prophets, however, have also seen visions of simple or imaginary objects and persons, which they interpreted in a symbolic way, the persons or objects themselves having already acquired a symbolic meaning. At the beginning of the Second Temple period visions were often interpreted to the prophets by an angel. This is also the manner of visions and their interpretation by angels in the later apocalyptic literature.

It may be asked if the later prophets at the beginning of the Second Temple period really believed they saw what they describe and interpret, or if visions merely became a literary form for prophecy or teaching. Sometimes, such descriptions evidently contained only a grain of actual vision (cf. the apocalyptic literature), and sometimes there was obviously no actual foundation (cf. the Vision of Seventy Shepherds in the Book of Enoch). In many cases (e.g., in the Fourth Book of Ezra), the question of an actual basis for a symbolic vision cannot be clearly answered, because this often depends on the extent to which the true author persuaded himself. The literary convention overcomes the religious or visionary experience in apocalyptic literature, because the authors did not write in their own names, but in the names of biblical persons of the past. A special type of vision in the apocalyptic literature is celestial journeys of biblical personalities, during which they visited both heaven and earth (heavenly paradise and hell). The oldest book which contains such visionary trips is the Book of Enoch; this book is thus the beginning of a chain leading to Dante. Chapter 14 in the book contains a description of God's heavenly palace, where Enoch sees the Glory of God. This is the oldest example in the tradition of visionary ascents to God's dwelling place following similar descriptions by biblical prophets, the earliest precursors of the *heikhalot* and the *Merkabah literature. A fragment describing God's dwelling place in the same spirit is also preserved in the Dead Sea Scrolls.

Jewish mystics in antiquity, as well as other persons, definitely had visionary experiences. Josephus refers to John Hyrcanus, who saw God announcing to him which of his sons would be his heir. Both Josephus and rabbinic literature relate that John Hyrcanus heard a heavenly voice in the Temple announcing the victory of his sons. This heavenly voice (*bat kol*) is often attested in rabbinical literature; the incidents referred to are both from the Second Temple period and later. Rabbinic literature often mentions the appearance of the prophet Elijah (see *Elijah in the *Aggadah*); the oldest reference comes from Ben Sira (48:11; "blessed is he who sees him"). The Second Book of Maccabees often speaks about visions of angels, especially as signs for future victory. The story of the appearance of angels to Heliodoros and punishment meted through them, narrated in this book, are also famous.

[David Flusser]

In Medieval Hebrew Literature

Following the prophetic visions in the Bible, and the frequent appearance of angels and other divine beings in talmudic and midrashic literature, medieval literature contains many descriptions of different kinds of visions. They appear chiefly in mystical works, but they are also to be found in the fiction of the period (see *Fiction) as well as in its popular literature. The fundamental Jewish tenet that God and His guardian angels are always close to man served as a basis for the belief in the objective reality of such visions. There prevailed, moreover, a profound belief in the existence of *demonic powers, which were also held to reveal themselves supernaturally.

The earliest body of Hebrew mystical works – the *heikhalot* and the Merkabah literature – is essentially devoted to visions. The mystics who make the ascent to the Divine Chariot, a practice usually attributed in these texts to R. Akiva and R. Ishmael b. Elisha and their circle, behold and then describe the glory of the heavenly world, the hierarchy of the angels and other heavenly beings, the Throne of Glory (*kisse ha-kavod*), and the songs of praise sung by the angels. The visitors are usually guided by an angel, very often *Metatron, the angelic incarnation of the mortal Enoch, who did not die but was translated to heaven and became one of the greatest angels in the divine hierarchy. This motif of a visionary "guided tour" in the divine world reappears in the literature of the Middle Ages.

Early Middle Ages

In the literature of medieval Europe, visions were most commonly seen in a dream; they might either occur spontaneously or be deliberately invoked. Whoever wished to invoke a vision would purify himself before going to sleep, and then ask *she'elat ḥalom* ("a question asked of a dream"), believing that his question would be answered by the nature of the dream that he was about to have. It was customary to make a *she'elat ḥalom* not only for matters relating to mysticism but also in connection with practical problems; and even questions of *halakhah* were answered in this way. A collection of such answers by *Jacob of Marvège is still extant, and it is known that other halakhists made similar compilations. The answer in the dream was frequently, although not always, accompanied by a vision.

Neither the mystic nor the ordinary Jew doubted the objective reality or the authenticity of angelic and demonic visions; even philosophers and Ashkenazi ḥasidic scholars (see *Ḥasidei Ashkenaz) devoted lengthy treatises to the nature of such visions, and also to those witnessed by the prophets. But most of the philosophers, and some of the Ḥasidim, believed the visions, albeit inspired by God, to be a product of the imagination of the individual. This view, however, was not widely accepted and both scholars and simple folk told and retold numerous stories of visions reported to have been seen.

One of the most common beliefs concerned the prophet Elijah, who did not die but ascended to the heavens. Following the pattern of talmudic literature, countless medieval folktales recount how he appeared to human beings in order to assist or to punish them. For scholars and mystics his most important role was that of teaching to mortal beings hidden truths which were known only to the *Academy on High. Thus, contemporaneous with the initial development of the Kabbalah in Provence in the 12th century are stories describing how Elijah appeared in the schools of the rabbis who were teaching the new ideas there.

At the same time, it was commonly believed, especially among the Jews of medieval Germany, Northern France, and Central Europe, that demons and the spirits of the dead appeared in visions to the living, either when they were awake or else in a dream. Many descriptions of such visions have been preserved in *Sefer Ḥasidim and other works written by the Ḥasidei Ashkenaz. The object of the visions was not always the same. Sometimes the dead appeared in order to request the completion of an act which they had begun in their lifetime but had not lived to finish; sometimes it was to pay a debt, or to complain of a fault in the way or the place in which they were buried. Sometimes they spoke of the other world, of the way that the righteous were rewarded and the wicked punished. Demons made their appearance either when invoked by magical means in order to perform a certain task, or else to punish those who had dealt too much in magic. One of the methods most widely used to invoke such visions was to pour oil upon a bright surface, whereupon the demons appeared and were obliged to answer any request asked of them. This practice was used even for such purposes as catching a thief or finding a lost article.

Later Middle Ages

There are manifold descriptions of visions in the kabbalistic literature written after the 13th century. The prophetic kabbalism of Abraham b. Samuel *Abulafia and his followers is merely one example; many other kabbalists had mystical experiences – sometimes when awake, sometimes when in a state of dream or trance – and in these visions they were granted revelations of hidden truths from the heavenly spheres. *Isaac b. Samuel of Acre describes in detail the frequent visitations which he received from Metatron, some in dreams and some while he was in the state between sleeping and waking; he also had revelations from even higher *Sefirot*. The 14th-century author of *Sefer ha-*Kanah* and of *Sefer ha-*Temunah* relates numerous stories describing how esoteric knowledge was revealed to members of the devout Kanah family, many of whom were mystics. The Castilian kabbalists that gathered around Jacob ha-Kohen b. Mordecai Gaon and his sons and disciples in the second half of the 13th century also give accounts of such contacts with higher beings.

The *Zohar contains numerous descriptions of visions revealed to Simeon b. Yoḥai and his followers. For example, while the mystics were sitting and studying the Kabbalah, heavenly fire surrounded them, the **Shekhinah* rested upon them, and they saw allegorical visions of hidden truths. Some of these revelations also intimate the appearance of evil powers representing Satan, the *sitra aḥra*. Later kabbalistic writings, modeling themselves upon the Zohar and the descriptions which it gave, also narrated occurrences in the higher spheres as if they were visions actually witnessed by the kabbalists.

Visions of a completely different nature appear in some literary works, and particularly in Hebrew *maqamāt* and prose narratives, for instance in Ibn Zabarra or Al-Ḥarizi, or in some polemic writings, such as the *Mostrador de Justicia* of the Converso Abner de Burgos, where "a big man" appears in dreams for explaining the "craziness and stupidity" of the Jews that do not recognize the truth. Something equivalent appears also in a rhymed prose composition written as an answer to it by Samuel ibn Sasson, a poet from Carrion and a contemporary of *Santob de Carrion.

Later Writings

The motif of visionary ascents to higher spheres, with an angel or some other divine being as a guide, appeared very frequently in Hebrew literature after the works of Dante became popular, and after *Immanuel b. Solomon of Rome followed Dante in describing a visit to heaven and hell (although even before Dante, Abraham *Ibn Ezra had dealt with a similar theme in his *Ḥai Ben Mekiẓ*). In Italy from the Renaissance on, many Hebrew writers composed works of a similar nature, one of the most notable being Abraham b. Hananiah de Galicchi *Jagel's *Sefer Gei Ḥizzayon* ("Book of the Valley of Visions"). The author, who was in prison at the time, relates how his dead father visited him and took his soul upon a visionary tour of the heavens. There many secrets were revealed to them, different spirits told them stories, and answers were given to their theological questions.

The *Shekhinah*, Metatron, and other heavenly beings appear frequently in the later Kabbalah, usually in order to reveal divine secrets. After the 16th century they were often described as **maggid* (heavenly mentor), and important kabbalistic works were written as if dictated by them, as for example Joseph *Caro's *Maggid Meisharim* and Moses Ḥayyim *Luzzatto's *Zohar Tinyana*.

Visions constituted an important element in the *Shabbatean movement founded by the prophet *Nathan of Gaza, and many of its adherents described the different messianic visions that were revealed to them. Belief in visions persisted in the ḥasidic movement as late as the 18th century, and several stories of *Israel b. Eliezer Ba'al Shem Tov describe how his soul ascended to heaven and the visions he experienced there.

[Joseph Dan]

BIBLIOGRAPHY: Scholem, Mysticism, 119–56 and passim; idem, *Jewish Gnosticism, Merkabah Mysticism and Talmudic Tradition* (1960); E. Gottlieb, in: *Fourth World Congress of Jewish Studies, Papers*, 2 (1968), 327–34; R. Margaliot, *She'elot u-Teshuvot min ha-Shamayim* (1957); R.J.Z. Werblowsky, *Joseph Karo; Lawyer and Mystic* (1962), 38–83; J. Dan, in: *Tarbiz*, 32 (1963), 359–69; A.Z. Aescoly (ed.), R. Ḥayyim Vital, *Sefer ha-Ḥezyonot* (1954).

VISSER, LODEWIJK ERNST (1871–1942), Dutch jurist and communal leader. He was born in Amersfoort into an old Dutch Jewish family. Prevented as a Jew from achieving his ambition of becoming a diplomat, Visser was appointed general prosecutor in Amsterdam and in 1903 became a district court judge in Rotterdam. In 1915 he was raised to the Supreme Court of which he eventually became president in 1939, but was dismissed by the Nazis after they entered Holland. Visser was an authority on commercial law and helped draft the Dutch Company Law of 1928. He also became vice chairman of the Dutch Royal Commission on Civil Legislation and a member of the Privy Council.

A conscious Jew, Visser was instrumental in helping Jewish refugees from Eastern Europe in 1918 and was founder of the Jewish Aid Committee for German Jews after 1933.

For many years, he was chairman of the executive of *Keren Hayesod in Holland, and as well chairman of the Permanent Committee of the Ashkenazi community in the Netherlands. During World War II, Visser opposed the German-appointed "Joodse Raad" (Jewish Council) and refused to accept the degrading identity cards. He tried to intervene for Jews arrested by Germans and participated in general resistance activities, becoming a symbol of Jewish wartime resistance in Holland. His wife and son died in concentration camps. In 1968 a square in front of the Sephardi synagogue in Amsterdam was named after him.

BIBLIOGRAPHY: J.A. Polak, *Leven en werken van mr. L.E. Visser* (1974); J. Michman, in: *Studia Rosenthaliana*, 8:1 (1974), 107–30.

[Henriette Boas / Bart Wallet (2nd ed.)]

VITAL, Italian family which produced numerous scholars of whom the most noted were:

JOSEPH VITAL (15th–16th century), a talented scribe, was especially noted for his precision in writing *tefillin*, which were widely known as *Tefillin Rav Calabrash* (*Tefillin* of the Rabbi of Calabria from where his family stemmed). His *tefillin* were highly praised by Menahem Azariah da *Fano (Resp. no. 38). He was the father of the celebrated kabbalist Ḥayyim *Vital.

MOSES BEN JOSEPH VITAL (d. middle of the 17th century), younger brother of Ḥayyim Vital, was rabbi in Safed. Like his brother, he was an enthusiastic kabbalist and many legends enveloped his life; some, in fact, actually related to his brother. Other legendary accounts assigned to him a central role for seeing to it that Rabbi Isaac Luria's legacy was saved for posterity. After his brother's death, he assumed a more important role in the kabbalistic community of Safed. Legendary material on his life is to be found in *Ma'aseh Nissim shel ha-Am* by Naphtali Herz Bachrach.

MOSES VITAL, son of Samuel b. Ḥayyim *Vital, was a rabbi in Egypt from the second half of the 17th until the beginning of the 18th century. He was a penetrating halakhist and brilliant kabbalist. All that remains of his published work is one responsum, included in *Abraham b. Mordecai ha-Levi's *Ginnat Veradim*.

BIBLIOGRAPHY: Conforte, Kore, 40b; M. Benayahu, *Sefer Toledot ha-Ari* (1967), index.

[Guiseppe Laras]

VITAL, DAVID BEN SOLOMON (first half of 16th century), rabbi, preacher and *paytan*, often called *Ha-Rofe* ("the doctor"). It is conjectured that David Vital was born before 1492 in Toledo (or southern Italy) and was among the Spanish exiles (or those leaving Calabria) who went to Turkey and Greece, eventually settling in Patras. During the Turco-Venetian war (1532), the community of Patras was severely affected and Vital's house was destroyed and his library and works lost. He moved to Arta, where he was apparently accepted as a halakhic authority, and remained there for the rest of his life. In 1534 he signed, together with the local rabbis, *takkanot* designed to preserve order and modesty in the town. He died apparently after 1536.

Vital was the son-in-law – and perhaps the pupil – of *David b. Ḥayyim of Corfu, whose responsa he collected and for which he prepared a table of contents. He corresponded on *halakhah* with many contemporary scholars, including Jacob Tam ibn Yaḥya (Responsa *Oholei Tam* in *Tummat Yesharim* (Venice, 1622), 81d–83d) and Meir *Katzenellenbogen of Padua, who writes eulogistically "that our father Abraham has in you a son of such caliber that if, God forfend, the Torah were to be forgotten in Israel, you could restore it through your dialectic" (Responsa Maharam Padua, no. 31).

Vital composed rhymed verse on halakhic and theological topics, which reveal his mastery both of Talmud and *posekim*, grammar and poetry. They include *Keter Torah* (Constantinople, 1536), a rhymed summary of the 613 commandments, in accordance with the enumeration of Maimonides, plus the seven rabbinical commandments (hence the title, the numerical value of *keter* being 620). He based himself upon the tradition that the 620 letters of the Ten Commandments hint at the 620 commandments. The work is regarded as a succinct commentary on the *Sefer ha-Mitzvot* of Maimonides, in that each commandment begins with Maimonides' formulation and concludes with an explanation of it, which sometimes even includes a reply to the critics of Maimonides. Another work is an alphabetic rhymed work on the examination of the lung of an animal after *sheḥitah* in accordance with the view of Maimonides, which appears as an appendix to the *Zivḥei Teru'ah* (Leghorn, 1872). *Mikhtam le-David* (Venice, 1546/7) is a composition intended to prove that the 13 Principles of the Faith are deduced from the *Shema* (translated into Latin by J.H. Wolf in 1726), to which are appended *piyyutim*, supplicatory prayers and poems, including a supplication consisting of 1,000 words, each word beginning with the letter "*he*." *Shirei David* (1882) is a work on grammar, the intercalation of the calendar, and some biblical expositions.

BIBLIOGRAPHY: Zunz, Gesch, 231; Zunz, Lit Poesie, 533f.; Fuerst, Bibliotheca, 3 (1863), 481f.; Michael, Or, no. 714; Ghirondi-Neppi, 83 no. 13; S.M. Chones, *Toledot ha-Posekim* (1910), 313; Rosanes, Togarmah, 2 (1937–38²), 42–44; C. Tchernowitz, *Toledot ha-Posekim*, 2 (1947), 291–3; H. Friedenwald, *Jews and Medicine*, 2 (1944), 768f.

[Yehoshua Horowitz]

VITAL, ḤAYYIM BEN JOSEPH (1542–1620), one of the greatest kabbalists. Vital was born in Ereẓ Israel, apparently in Safed. His father, Joseph Vital Calabrese, whose name indicates his origin from Calabria, South Italy, was a well-known scribe in Safed (see responsa of Menahem Azariah da *Fano, no. 38). His son is also called Ḥayyim Calabrese in several kabbalistic works. Ḥayyim Vital studied in yeshivot in Safed, especially under Moses *Alshekh, his teacher in exoteric subjects. In 1564 he began to study Kabbalah, at first according to the system of Moses *Cordovero, although Vital did not call Cordovero his teacher. He was also attracted to other esoteric studies and spent two years (1563–65) in the practice of *alchemy, which he later regretted. After Isaac *Luria's arrival in Safed, Vital became his principal disciple, studying under him for nearly two years until Luria's death in the summer of 1572. Later he began to arrange Luria's teachings in written form and to elaborate on them according to his own understanding of them. Vital tried to prevent Luria's other disciples from presenting their versions of his doctrine in writing, and he gathered around him several who accepted his spiritual authority. But he did not entirely succeed in his ambition to be the only heir to Luria's spiritual legacy and to be accepted as the sole interpreter of Lurianic Kabbalah. In 1575, 12 of Luria's disciples signed a pledge to study Luria's theory only from Vital, and promising not to induce him to reveal more than he wished and to keep the mysteries secret from others (*Zion*, 5 (1940), 125, and see another copy of the agreement in *Birkat-ha-Areẓ* by Baruch David ha-Kohen (1904), 61). This study group ceased to function when Vital moved to Jerusalem, where he served as rabbi and head of a yeshivah from late 1577 to late 1585. In Jerusalem he wrote the last version of his presentation of the Lurianic system. He returned to Safed early in 1586, staying there until 1592. According to tradition, he fell seriously ill in Safed around 1587; during his long period of unconsciousness the scholars of Safed are said to have bribed his younger brother Moses, who allowed them to copy 600 pages of Ḥayyim Vital's writings which were then circulated among a select group (according to a letter written by Shlomel Dreznitz in 1606, in *Shivḥei ha-Ari*).

In 1590 Vital was "ordained" as rabbi by his teacher Moses Alshekh. (The text of the ordination is published in *Sefer Yovel le-Y. Baer* (1961), 266.) He was in Jerusalem once more in 1593 and perhaps stayed there several years, returning to Safed from time to time. According to the tradition of the rabbis of Jerusalem, he moved from Jerusalem to Damascus; in any case, he was in Damascus in 1598 (*Sefer ha-Ḥezyonot* (1954), 87) and remained there until his death. For a time he served as rabbi of the Sicilian community there (*ibid.*, 92, 116). After a severe illness in 1604, his sight was impaired and at times he was even blind. During his final years a kabbalistic group gathered around him. Vital was married at least three times and his youngest son, Samuel, inherited his writings. While he was in Damascus, mainly between 1609 and 1612, Ḥayyim Vital assembled autobiographical notes which he called *Sefer ha-Ḥezyonot*, mainly stories and testimonies to his greatness, but also including his dreams and those of others; these form an important source for the study of the course of his life and the complexities of his soul. The work is preserved in his handwriting and was published by A.Z. Aešcoly (1954), from the autograph in the possession of Rabbi A. Toaff of Leghorn. From this work it is apparent that strained relations existed between Vital and Jacob Abulafia, one of the rabbis in Damascus, who doubted Vital's claims to be the sole interpreter of Lurianic Kabbalah. The early editions of *Sefer ha-Ḥezyonot* were published from fragmentary and corrupt copies, in Ostrog (1826) as *Shivḥei R. Ḥayyim Vital*, and in Jerusalem (1866) as *Sefer ha-Ḥezyonot*. Vital's epitaph was published in David Zion Laniado's *La-Kedoshim Asher be-Areẓ* (1935), 43. Besides his son, his other disciples in Damascus included Japheth ha-Miẓri, *Ḥayyim b. Abraham ha-Kohen of Aleppo, and Ephraim Penzieri. Many legends about Vital circulated even during his lifetime, and are preserved in *Toledot ha-Ari* and in the letters of Shlomel Dreznitz, first published in 1629 in *Ta'alumot Ḥokhmah* by Joseph Solomon *Delmedigo. In subsequent generations many other legends were added.

Vital was a prolific writer. His proficiency in exoteric subjects is attested by his ordination and by his rabbinical function in Jerusalem. However, few of his talmudic teachings have been preserved: one responsum from Damascus was published in the responsa of Joseph di *Trani (Constantinople, 1641 ed., 88c.) and ten halakhic responsa are included in Samuel Vital's *Be'er Mayim Ḥayyim* (Ms. Oxford Neubauer Cat Bod no. 832). His commentaries on the Talmud are extant, together with those of his son (in Ms. Guenzburg 283) and have been published at the end of every tractate of the El ha-Mekorot Talmud, appearing in Jerusalem since 1959. A complete volume of his sermons on esoteric subjects and popular Kabbalah is preserved in *Torat Ḥayyim* (unpublished Ms. in the written list of the collection of R. Alter of Gur, no. 286) and several of his sermons can also be found in Badhab Mss. collection 205, now in the Hebrew University, and in Columbia University (Ms. H533, foll. 150ff., New York). His *Sefer ha-Tekhunah* on astronomy was published in Jerusalem in 1866. His own manuscript of his major work on practical Kabbalah and alchemy was extant in the Musayoff collection in Jerusalem in 1940.

According to his son, Vital assembled his major writings into two vast works *Eẓ ha-Ḥayyim* and *Eẓ ha-Da'at*. The former is the inclusive name for all those writings in which he elaborated on the teaching of Isaac Luria. These works went through several versions and adaptations, for Vital began to arrange what he had heard from Luria immediately after his death, and, according to Meir *Poppers, remained absorbed in this task for more than 20 years. This first edition of *Eẓ ha-Hayyim* was organized into eight sections, called "gates" (*she'arim* in Hebrew). "Gate" one contains everything in Luria's own handwriting that Vital could find; no published version of this "gate" exists but it was preserved in several manuscripts (see G. Scholem, in: KS, vol. 19 (1942–43), 184–96); "Gate" two, *Sha'ar ha-Hakdamot*, includes the doctrine of emanation and the creation of the world; in "Gate" three, *Sha'ar Ma'amerei Rashbi ve-Razal*, Vital's commentaries on the *Zohar and on talmudic tractates according to Lurianic principles are arranged; "Gate" four, *Sha'ar ha-Pesukim*, contains commentaries on all parts of the Bible; "Gate" five, *Sha'ar ha-Kavvanot*, covers mystical customs and meditations on prayers; the reasons for the *mitzvot* according to the order of the sections of the Torah are set out in "Gate" six, *Sha'ar ha-Mitzvot*. "Gate" seven, *Sha'ar Ru'aḥ ha-Kodesh*, deals with meditation, customs, acts of magical contemplation (called "unification," *yiḥudim*), the *tikkun* of sins, and the principles of physiognomy; "Gate" eight, *Sha'ar ha-Gilgulim*, covers the doctrine concerning the soul and its transmigrations. The first version (*mahadurah kamma*) remained in Damascus with Vital's son, who did not permit it to be copied for many years. He himself reedited and rearranged the *Shemonah She'arim* and this version was widely circulated from around 1660. The Middle Eastern kabbalists, especially those in Palestine, considered this the most authoritative version of Lurianic Kabbalah, and some confined their studies to this version only. In Samuel Vital's version of the *Shemonah She'arim* the first "gate" was cut out and its contents dispersed throughout the rest of the work, mainly in the third "gate" which was then divided into two, *Sha'ar Ma'amerei Rashbi* (on the Zohar) and *Sha'ar Ma'amerei Razal*. For 200 years this edition circulated in manuscript form only, being copied by many scribes and kabbalists. Finally the work was printed in seven volumes in Jerusalem (1863–98) with the support of the kabbalists of the Bet-El yeshivah. A new and revised edition was published in Tel Aviv (1961–64). A magnificent manuscript written in large letters, which served as the paradigm for other copies, is preserved in the National Library in Jerusalem (4ø674, three folio vols.). So that it might have greater authority, this manuscript, which was actually written in the late 17th century, had false dates added to it to make it appear that it was copied in Aleppo and Damascus in 1605.

The copies of Ḥayyim Vital's works which circulated during his lifetime among the kabbalists in Palestine were not arranged in good order. Around 1620 Benjamin ha-Levi and Elisha Vestali (or Gastali) assembled them into a three-volume edition. This, too, was not printed but was very popular in subsequent generations. It included *Sefer ha-Derushim*, mainly composed of material belonging to *Sha'ar ha-Hakdamot* and *Sha'ar ha-Gilgulim; Sefer ha-Kavvanot*; and *Sefer ha-Likkutim*. Vital's writings first reached other countries in this edition, which is extant in several libraries. The torn and tattered pages of the "last version" (*mahadurah batra*) which Vital arranged in Jerusalem were discovered by Abraham *Azulai and his colleagues, apparently shortly after 1620, in a *genizah* in Jerusalem. From these writings Jacob *Ẓemah arranged several books, such as *Oẓerot Ḥayyim* (Korets, 1783), *Adam Yashar* (1885), and *Olat Tamid* on meditations in prayers (1850). Another version of Vital's system which corresponds to the *Sha'ar ha-Hakdamot* was discovered and published as *Mevo She'arim* or *Toledot Adam*. His grandson, Moses b. Samuel Vital, reports that he found the author's own manuscript in Hebron (Ms. British Museum, Margoliouth CMBM no. 821). Copies reached Italy in the middle of the 17th century, but it was first published in Korets in 1783. Parts of the beginning of the work are missing in both the printed and manuscript editions, but a complete version was still extant in Jerusalem in 1890, and was also preserved in the collection of Isaac Alter of Gur.

From all the previous editions that reached the Jerusalem kabbalists, Meir Poppers, the disciple of Ẓemaḥ, arranged the final edition of Vital's writings, which was completed (according to testimony in some of the copies) in 1653. All matters pertaining to the *Sha'ar ha-Hakdamot* were arranged in *Sefer Derekh Eẓ Ḥayyim*, in five major sections and 50 sub-sections including the "first version" and the "last version" and even at times other versions (third and fourth), side by side. This book alone was given the name of *Sefer Eẓ Ḥayyim* when it was published in Korets in 1782 by Isaac Satanov (of Moses *Mendelssohn's circle). The best editions are those published in Warsaw (1890) by Menahem Heilperin, and Tel Aviv (1960), by Y.Z. *Brandwein. Everything pertaining to matters of prayer and mystical meditations (*kavvanot*) was arranged in *Sefer Peri Eẓ Ḥayyim* in four sections: *Kavvanot*; the reasons for the *mitzvot* (*Ta'amei ha-Mitzvot*); *Tikkunei Avonot*; and *Yiḥudim*. The section on mystical meditations alone was published under the name *Peri Eẓ Ḥayyim* (Dubrovno, 1803). The book which was published earlier under this name in Korets in 1782, is not based on Poppers' edition but was a separate adaptation by his colleague Nathan Shapira called *Me'orot Natan*. The third and fourth sections were published together under the name *Sha'ar ha-Yiḥudim* and *Tikkun Avonot* in Korets in 1783. All material pertaining to other matters was arranged in *Sefer Nof Eẓ Ḥayyim* in four sections: *Perushei ha-Zohar; Perushei Tanakh; Perushei Aggadot*; and *Gilgulim*. A complete manuscript of this work is found in Oxford (Neubauer, Cat Bod no. 1700). The first section was never published in this form; the second section (which also included the *ta'amei ha-mitzvot*) was published as *Likkutei Torah Nevi'im u-Khetuvim* (Zolkiew, 1773); an incomplete version of the third section was published as *Likkutei Shas* (Korets, 1785); and the fourth section was published earlier than all Vital's other works as *Sefer ha-Gilgulim* (Frankfurt on the Main, 1684). A version in 70 chapters revised according to Nathan Shapira's version was published in Przemyśl in 1875. Hence it is clear that Vital's writings exercised their main influence on kabbalists through manuscript copies, despite the fact that all his works were later published several times. In a few places in Palestine, Turkey, Poland, and Germany, Vital's writings were copied wholesale. *Sefer ha-Kavvanot* (Venice, 1620) was merely an abridgment and adaptation of one of the copies which circulated in Palestine during Vital's lifetime. The major part of the first section on *Perushei ha-Zohar* was published as *Zohar ha-Raki'a* (Korets, 1785).

In all these works Vital's presentation is dry and matter of fact, quite unlike the flowery language common in his day. In one place in *Sefer Eẓ Ḥayyim* (39:16) he inserted an adaptation from Moses *Cordovero's *Pardes Rimmonim* without mentioning that it was not Luria's teaching. In most parts of the *Shemonah She'arim* Vital added statements from Luria's other disciples, mainly on matters which he himself did not hear directly, but he rarely mentions them by their full names. Vital was most exact in transmitting Luria's teachings, pointing out on many occasions that he could not remember exactly, or that he had heard different statements on different occasions, or that he had forgotten. It would seem that on first hearing them he recorded many statements in copybooks and notebooks which were occasionally cited. He also presents some statements of which he admits that he cannot recall their meaning. Indeed, his works include more than a few contradictions, some of which have their source in his teacher and others in the development of Vital's views while he was editing. These contradictions gave rise to a kind of "*pilpul*" literature on Vital's statements comprising many volumes.

Before his association with Luria, Vital wrote a commentary on the Zohar according to the system of Cordovero, to which he later added occasional remarks alluding to Luria's views. Discovering this commentary in Jerusalem, Abraham *Azulai inserted it in his compilation, *Or ha-Ḥammah* (1896–98). Vital's affinity to Cordovero's teaching can also be recognized in his second major work, *Sefer Eẓ ha-Da'at*, only parts of which are extant. It apparently included commentaries on most of the books of the Bible, but what he calls *peshat* ("the literal meaning") and *remez* ("the allegorical meaning") are in many cases Kabbalah, although closer to the literal meaning of the Zohar. According to one testimony, he began this work as early as 1563 at the age of 20, but according to another he wrote it in 1575. Chapters 2 and 6 of this work were preserved in his own handwriting in the collection of R. Alter of Gur (no. 185; dated 1575). His commentary on Psalms was published from this manuscript, *Sefer Tehillim* (1926). The part on the Torah was published as *Eẓ ha-Da'at Tov* (1864). The second part, including various eulogies, sermons for weddings, circumcisions, on repentance, and commentaries on Proverbs and Job, was published in Jerusalem in 1906 from a manuscript preserved in the kabbalistic yeshivah Bet-El. Vital himself arranged various editions of this work. In addition to these works, he also wrote moralizing tracts; the most important, *Sha'arei Kedushah*, was first published in Constantinople in 1734 and many times afterward. His work *Lev David* was published from his own manuscript by H.J.D. *Azulai (Leghorn, 1789) and several other times. It is assumed that in addition to these works Vital wrote many pamphlets on Kabbalah not included in the printed editions, such as *Hakdamah Kodem Derush Mayim Nukvin* quoted by his son and partly published in the introduction to Meir *Bikayam's *Me'ir la-Areẓ* (Salonika, 1747). Of doubtful attribution is *Goral Kodesh*, on geomancy according to the Zodiac (Czernowitz, 1899). *Arba Me'ot Shekel Kesef* (Korets, 1804) is apparently an extract from Vital's known works with additional autobiographical remarks and allusions to other works but it is highly doubtful that Vital could have written them. The book purports to be written in 1615 but it cites names of later versions arranged by Benjamin ha-Levi and Ḥayyim Ẓemaḥ. It would seem that in fact it was written in the second half of the 17th century, and was known in Morocco in the early 18th century. A scroll containing descriptions of the celestial worlds of the Kabbalah written by Vital and brought from Damascus was found in Yemen, and in 1858 was sold to the traveler Jacob Saphir (*Sefunot*, 2 (1958), 270). Writings of Israel *Sarug, such as *Limmudei Aẓilut* and a commentary on *Sifra di-Ẓeni'uta* (1897), were erroneously attributed to Vital. Vital was also interested in early kabbalistic literature, although he hardly used it in his works. His anthology of early works was found in his own handwriting as late as 1930 in Tunis (Ms. Tanuji). His son Samuel's copy is preserved in manuscript in the Jewish Theological Seminary in New York.

Although he possessed no truly creative powers, Vital was one of the most important influences on the development of later Kabbalah, attaining this position as the chief formulator of the Kabbalah of Luria. No thorough study of his personality and activities has yet been attempted.

BIBLIOGRAPHY: N. Shapira, *Tuv ha-Areẓ*, ed. by J. Hirschensohn (1891), appendix 23–25 (based on a complete manuscript of *Mevo She'arim*); G. Scholem, in: *Zion*, 5 (1940), 113–60; M. Benayahu, in; *Sinai*, 30 (1952), 65–75; idem, *Sefer Toledot ha-Ari* (1967), index; D. Tamer, in: *Tarbiz*, 25 (1956), 99f.

[Gershom Scholem]

VITAL, SAMUEL BEN ḤAYYIM (1598–c. 1678), kabbalist, youngest son of Ḥayyim *Vital. Vital grew up in Damascus where he studied under his father and other rabbis. He married a daughter of Josiah *Pinto. Vital was considered among the important talmudic authorities of Damascus. For many years he reedited his father's writings and added many of his own annotations (which begin *Amar Shemu'el*: "Samuel said"). Many kabbalists went to Damascus to study these writings at his home, but they were not given permission to copy them. From 1650 on Samuel prepared copies, some of which have been preserved. Around 1664 he went to Cairo where he served as rabbi. He was in close contact with the wealthy Raphael Joseph Chelebi. During the heyday of the Shabbatean movement (in 1666), he was responsible for the *tikkun* of repentance of the faithful in Egypt, "going about fasting, praying, and practicing flagellation from the beginning of these events." A protocol on his exorcism of an evil spirit (**dibbuk*) in the summer of 1666 was published at the end of *Sha'ar ha-Gilgulim* (1903), fol. 77–78.

Samuel's writings include: *Ḥayyim Shenayim Yeshalem* (Ms. Guenzburg 283), his own and his father's novellae on the Talmud, the Shulḥan Arukh, *Sifrei ha-Levush*, and *Maimonides. The novellae appear in the Vilna edition of the Talmud, published in Jerusalem; *Be'er Mayim Ḥayyim*, responsa, is arranged according to the dates of the replies, in the handwriting of the author (MS. Oxford 832; *Ha-Maggid*, 15 (1871), 45). In his introduction to the responsa Samuel also mentions *Sha'ar ha-Shamayim*, a collection on astronomy and astrology, and *Ta'alumot Ḥokhmah*, amulets, practical Kabbalah, and incantations – which have been lost; *Toẓe'ot Ḥayyim*, sermons on the Torah, was written between 1630 and 1648. The author's own manuscript copy from 1674 is found in the Alliance Israélite Universelle Library, Paris, 128. The author's copies from previous years were in the library of the rabbi of Gur, 284 and 285; *Mekor Ḥayyim* (Leghorn, 1792), sermons for the new moon (Rosh Ḥodesh), was completed in 1649; *Ḥokhmat Nashim* (Badhab MS. 112, Jerusalem), on the laws of divorce, was completed in 1659; *Ḥemdat Yisrael* (Munkacs, 1901), on the *kavvanot* ("intentions of prayers") according to Isaac *Luria, was completed in 1663, apparently still in Damascus; another part of *Ḥemdat Yisrael*, still in manuscript (in the library of the rabbi of Gur), contains special prayers for epidemics and locust plague, and also *piyyutim*.

BIBLIOGRAPHY: Scholem, Shabbetai Ẓevi, 1 (1957), 224, 227; 2 (1957), 539 and index.

[Gershom Scholem]

VITAL STATISTICS.

Introduction

GENERAL EXPLANATION. Population changes reflect the natural facts of life: births and deaths. Births, in turn, have long been largely governed by the mechanisms of family formation. Vital statistics are compilations of data on marriage, divorce, birth, and death. Births and deaths directly determine changes in the size of a population; marriages and divorces create and dissolve, respectively, the conditions under which most births occur. The surplus of births over deaths is called natural increase; under unfavorable demographic conditions, deaths may exceed births, in which case a natural decrease occurs.

Vital events constitute one of the components of population dynamics; the others are migration and, for a group like the Jews, adhesion and withdrawal. In a "closed" population, unaffected by migrations and by adhesions or withdrawals, the numerical evolution depends entirely on the balance of births and deaths. The natural increase (or decrease) is indeed of fundamental importance for the future of any population, but the migratory changes may counteract the vital balance for some time. For example, despite strong natural increase, there was probably no growth in the total number of Jews in Eastern Europe at the beginning of the 20th century because of extensive emigration, mostly to America. On the other hand, among Jewish populations in Central and Western Europe throughout the 20th century prevailing natural decrease was outweighed or at least compensated by a positive migratory balance.

The figures of vital events in any population are strongly affected by its age composition. In a population containing a very large proportion of young adults, as may be the case where there has been large immigration, birth figures may be high in spite of a modest level of fertility (for definition of this term, see measurement, below); on the other hand, under conditions of advanced aging frequently found at present in Jewish populations, actual death figures may be high even though the specific mortality in each age group is comparatively low. All these factors need to be considered in evaluating the causes and consequences of population trends. The age composition of a population at any specific time is itself the result of the demographic dynamics of preceding decades: unless migratory influences or adhesions/withdrawals were particularly conspicuous, it largely depends on past fertility. A prolonged decrease in births leads to the aging of a population. In the early phases of aging the proportion of children decreases while that of all adults, including the adults of procreative age, increases. This in turn tends to sustain the crude birth rate while deaths of children will be relatively fewer per 1,000 of the population (which may reduce the crude death rate especially if child mortality is still conspicuous). In later phases of aging, the proportion of elderly and old persons in the population grows, and consequently, the crude birth rate is depressed and the crude death rate rises. Age composition thus intervenes as both the consequence and the cause of the frequency of vital events in a population.

MEASUREMENT. Absolute figures of births, deaths, etc., are important for calculating up-to-date estimates of population size and for planning such social services as schools, hospitals, etc. For demographic analysis, it is necessary to consider the frequency of vital events in relation to the population in which they occur. The resulting figures are called demographic rates. "Crude" rates usually indicate the frequency of vital events per 1,000 of mean population in a specified year. The commonly mentioned "birth rate" and "death rate" are of this nature. Crude rates make no allowance for age and sex composition of a population. Consequently, if this composition is markedly distorted, crude rates are liable to lead to misconceptions about the intrinsic demographic situation. Unfortunately, crude rates are often the best available information on vital events among Jewish populations, especially prior to the last few decades.

To overcome the shortcomings inherent in crude rates, age-sex specific rates are calculated to show correctly the frequency of vital events in any specified age-sex group of the population during a certain period. These rates can be synthesized by the use of appropriate techniques. Demographic indicators thus obtained – e.g., "fertility rates" for the measurement of reproduction and "mean life expectancy at birth" for the measurement of mortality – are unaffected by peculiarities in the age-sex composition of any population. They depend, however, on the availability of data broken down by small age groups and by sex, with regard to both the total population and the persons involved in the given vital events (such as the women giving birth, the deceased, etc.). Under present conditions of documentation on Jewish vital statistics, such data are only very partially available. In addition, if the absolute numbers for vital events are broken down by age and sex, very small figures, which are liable to irregularities, result in all but the larger Jewish populations. It is also possible to calculate "standardized rates," assuming, for the sake of comparison, the same age distribution for several demographic groups, e.g., the Jews and the general population of the respective country. The concept of "fertility" relates the births not to the entire population of both sexes and all ages but to the women of reproductive age. It means basically, the number of children born, on the average, to women throughout their reproductive period.

SOURCES. Vital statistics on Jews in Diaspora countries come from either official or Jewish sources. Official statistics of this kind now exist only for a minority of the Jews in Diaspora countries. Data on vital events either come from current statistics reflecting the administrative registration of births, deaths, etc., or are obtained from censuses and surveys. In the latter instances, some of the relevant information may be derived from retrospective questions on age at marriage of the persons ever married, on the number of children born to the enumerated women, etc. Under present conditions, current vital statistics from Jewish sources tend to reflect the frequency of religious functions, such as weddings, divorces, circumcisions, and burials, rather than give a full demographic picture, because some Jews recur to civil ceremonies alone.

DEMOGRAPHIC TRANSITIONS. The widely prevalent descriptive model of the demographic transition divides the modern evolution of the populations of the technologically advanced countries into four stages. In the first stage, which represents the conditions of the past, both fertility and mortality were very high, so that only limited natural increase could materialize. In stage two, which fell mainly into the 19th and early 20th centuries, mortality declined, while fertility continued to be high; considerable natural increase resulted, and the respective populations grew rapidly. In stage three fertility also declined due to the diffusion of birth control; population growth consequently diminished, with a low being reached in the 1930s. The fourth stage – in the context of a generally moderate or low mortality level – resulted in repeated upward and downward fertility fluctuations (such as a "baby boom" in some Western countries and an ensuing "baby bust") reflecting response to changing circumstances. Eventually fertility subsided again, yet maintained itself at somewhat different levels in different countries. In Europe, stages two and three did not begin at the same time in the various countries but spread, on the whole, from west to east. Even within the same country, the timing of the changes differed according to social group and geographical location: the educated, well-to-do, and urban elements were involved earlier than the other groups. By 1970 nearly all the populations in the developing countries of Asia, Africa, and Latin America had entered upon stage two which expresses itself by a "population explosion," and some had already entered upon stage three. By 2000 all countries were moving through one or another stage of demographic transition. Significantly, a fifth stage had emerged mostly among European societies, showing a negative balance between birth and death rates and reflecting a progressive aging of age composition.

It is noteworthy that the Jews of Europe preceded the general population of the respective countries in effecting the transition from stage one to two, lowering mortality, from stage two to three, adoption of family planning, from stage three to four, fertility response to changing environment, and from stage four to stage five, population erosion due to a negative balance of births and deaths. In this, as well as in the subsequent developments, the Jews intensively displayed the characteristics of the social and ecological strata in which they were largely concentrated – the educated and urbanized, with a tendency to white-collar occupations. Besides these compositional effects, additional and more specifically Jewish determinants in the cultural and socio-psychological realm played an important role in the demographic evolution of the Jews.

Mortality

The limited data available from some European cities in the 18th century give the impression that Jewish mortality was already declining. There is ample documentation to show the systematic decline of Jewish mortality all over Europe throughout the 19th century, though there was some time lag between this development among the Jews in the countries of Central and Western Europe, on the one hand, and of Eastern Europe, on the other. In any country of Europe and at any time during the 19th century, the crude death rate of the Jews was almost always lower than that of the entire population of the respective country (see Table 1). This was largely

Table 1: Births, Deaths, and Natural Increase (Rates)[1] (Selected Data)

		Births		Deaths		Natural Increase	
Country or City	Period	Jews	General Population	Jews	General Population	Jews	General Population
Amsterdam[2]	1899–1900	25	30	12	17	13	13
	1919–1922	19	22	11	11	8	11
Switzerland	1959–1961	11	18	16	10	–5	8
Prussia	1822–1840	36	40	22	30	14	10
	1876–1880	32	39	18	24	14	15
	1906–1910	17	32	14	17	3	15
	1921–1925	14	23	13	14	1	9
	1926–1927	12	20	14	12	–2	8
	1933	7	15	16	11	–9	4
Berlin	1925	12	12	14	11	–2	1
Germany (F.G.R.)	1960–1962	6	18	21	11	–15	7
Vienna	1880	28	40	14	28	14	12
	1901–1910	18	27	14	18	4	9
	1921–1923	14	16	13	15	1	1
	1934	4	6	14	12	–10	–6

Table 1: Births, Deaths, and Natural Increase (Rates)[1] (Selected Data) (cont.)

Country or City	Period	Births		Deaths		Natural Increase	
		Jews	General Population	Jews	General Population	Jews	General Population
	1960–1962	6	18	31	16	–25	2
Italy	1851–1875	29	37	24	31	5	6
	1876–1900	23	36	20	26	3	10
	1901–1910	18	33	17	22	1	11
	1921–1930	16	28	17	17	–1	11
	1931–1935	11	24	17	14	–6	10
	1951–1955	10	18	15	10	–5	8
	1961–1965	11	19	16	10	–5	9
Hungary	1891–1895	36	42	19	33	17	9
	1906–1910	29	36	15	25	14	11
	1926–1930	13	26	14	17	–1	9
	1931–1935	11	22	14	16	–3	6
Budapest	1931–1934	8	16	15	16	–7	0
Czechoslovakia	1931–1933	18	21	13	14	5	7
Bohemia	1930	7	18	15	13	–8	5
Galicia	1882	46	48	29	36	17	12
	1901–1902	38	44	19	27	19	17
	1910	32	39	16	24	16	15
Russian Poland[2]	1906	29	39	16	23	13	16
Poland	1926–1930[3]	21	32	11	17	10	15
	1931–1936	19	28	10	15	9	13
Warsaw[2]	1930–1936	13	14	10	12	3	2
Lithuania	1927	17	30	10	17	7	13
Latvia	1926–1927	17	22	11	15	6	7
European Russia	1900–1904[3]	34	49	16	31	18	18
St. Petersburg (Leningrad)	1910–1913	18	28	11	22	7	6
U.S.S.R.	1926	24	43	9	20	15	23
Romania	1881–1886	47	41	26	26	21	15
	1906–1910	30	40	17	26	13	14
	1926–1928	20	36	13	22	7	14
	1936–1938	14	31	13	19	1	12
Bulgaria	1891–1895	38	38	23	28	15	10
	1904–1907	34	43	14	22	20	21
	1925–1928[4]	22	35	11	18	11	17
	1933–1936	17	28	10	15	7	13
Canada	1930	15	24	6	11	9	13
	1940	14	22	7	10	7	12
	1950	20	26	8	9	12	17
	1957–1959	15	28	8	8	7	20
Tunisia[2]	1921	41	...	21	...	20	...
	1946[5]	37	39	15	19	22	20
Israel	1923–1925	35.8		14.1		21.7	
(Palestine)	1931–1935	30.3		9.3		21.0	
	1936–1940	25.7		8.0		17.7	
	1946–1947	29.4		6.2		23.2	
	1949–1950	31.2		6.6		24.6	
	1965	22.6		6.4		16.2	
Israel-Jews of European origin[6]	1965	15		8			7
Jews of Asian- African Origin[6]	1965	30		5			25

1 Rates per 1,000 of population. Some of the figures are only approximate or based on different definitions.

2 Jews and non-Jews, respectively.

3 Corrected version of official figures for Jews.

4 1926–1928 for general population.

5 1945 for non-Jews.

6 Estimates.

Main Sources: Compilations contained in the publications listed in the Bibliography; Statistical Abstract of Israel (various issues). The vital statistics are official ones, except for those on the Jews of Italy which are based on registration by the Jewish communities.

due to the reasons adduced above for the peculiar position of the Jews in the framework of modern demographic transitions: their concentration in towns and particularly in large cities, which by the 19th century in Europe had better hygienic conditions and health services than rural areas; their higher educational level; and their other socioeconomic characteristics. Additional cultural factors, that were specific to the reduction of mortality, may have included the hygienic influence of the observance of some traditional Jewish precepts in the selection and preparation of food, washing of hands, and ablutions, etc.; the rarity of venereal diseases and alcoholism among Jews; the comparative frequency of physicians among them; and perhaps also greater attention to health and especially to the health of children, the reduction of whose previously high mortality was a major feature in the overall improvement of the mortality situation. The differentials in the death rate of Jews and non-Jews were smaller for towns than for entire countries where the non-Jewish rural population is included in the comparisons.

The differentials between Jews and non-Jews were sometimes particularly conspicuous with regard to infant mortality (see Table 2).

Comparing cause-of-death distributions and morbidity patterns of Jews and non-Jews in the 19th and early 20th centuries, one finds lower proportions of infectious diseases and diseases of the digestive system among the Jews. An often observed difference was the lower frequency of tuberculosis among Jews.

During the Holocaust, Jewish mortality in Europe was on an altogether catastrophic scale: the majority of Jews there perished. The age groups most affected were the old and the very young. The deficiency of persons whose childhood coincided with the Holocaust period continues to make itself felt in the age distribution of European Jews. It was aggravated by a great reduction in Jewish births before, and even more so during the persecutions.

While the Jews in Europe and in technologically advanced countries of other continents preceded their neighbors in the reduction of mortality, the majority of populations closed the gap in the course of time and the respective differentials narrowed substantially. This had already happened in some cities and countries even before the Holocaust. Because of the increasing aging of many Jewish populations, these developments cannot be studied properly from crude rates, and more refined methods must be resorted to. In particular, it has been possible to calculate the mean life expectancy at birth which is based on age-specific rates and not affected by the actual age composition for several Jewish populations. In recent decades, the life expectancy of Jews in advanced countries has been growing by about one year of life every five calendar years, and around the year 2000 it reached 80 years for women and 75 years for men. Although only little different from that of the general population in the corresponding countries or cities, a tendency for infant mortality to be lower among Jews persisted. On the other hand, crude mortality rates of Jews considerably exceed those of the respective general populations, mainly due to the overaged composition of the respective Jewish groups.

The Israel population census of 1961 was instrumental in furnishing information on the mortality conditions of the Jews in Asian and African countries. The census contained a question addressed to women who were ever married: "How many of their children born abroad before immigration to Israel died below the age of 5?" The available data provide relevant information for the participants in the mass migration of 1948–54 (see Table 3). Child mortality among the Jews was still very high in Yemen but reached various stages of decrease in other countries of major Jewish residence in Asia and Africa. Younger women had been affected by lower child mortality than older women, whose experience stretched back into earlier decades.

Table 2: Infant Mortality (Rates)[1] (Selected Data)

Country or City	Period	Jews	General Population
Amsterdam	1907–1909	75	90
	1919–1923	41	50
Switzerland	1947–1954	26	32
	1959–1963	12	21
Berlin	1924–1926	43	90
Florence	1838–1847	149	218
Rome	1901–1907	72	138
Italy	1965	33[3]	38
Hungary[2]	1925–1926	96	170
Budapest	1880	159	271
	1904–1905[2]	103	166
	1930	63	114
Poland	1927	73	151
	1931–1936	49	138
Lithuania	1927	35	156
	1935–1937	46	124
Latvia	1926–1927	38	89
European Russia	1900–1904	119	254
U.S.S.R.	1926	57	174
St. Petersburg (Leningrad)	1900–1904	109	260
	1922–1924	78	178
Montreal	1931	43	113
	1941	24	70
	1951	10	43
	1961	(6)	23
Israel (Palestine)	1923–1925	121	
	1931–1935	78	
	1946–1947	30	
	1949–1950	49	
	1955	32	
	1965	23	

1 Deceased under 1 year per 1,000 live births. Some of the figures are only approximate or based on different definitions.
2 Jews and non-Jews, respectively.
3 The three principal Jewish communities in Italy.
Main Sources: Compilations contained in the publications listed in the Bibliography; Statistical Abstract of Israel (various issues). The vital statistics are official ones, except for those on the Jews of Italy which are based on registration by the Jewish communities.

Table 3: Mortality below Age Five per 100 Children Born in Asia and Africa (Born to Jewish Women who Subsequently Immigrated to Israel during 1948–54)

Women's Country of Birth		Women's Age at Immigration	
		20–24	45–49
Asia and Africa – Total		21	27
There of:	Yemen, Aden	47	46
	Iraq	14	20
	Iran	17	(26)
	Turkey	14	19
	Egypt	9	(34)
	Libya	22	29
	Tunisia, Algeria	27	37
	Morocco, Tangier	22	32

Source: Israel Population Census, 1961, vol. 32.

Table 4: Mean Age of Jews at Marriage[1] in Europe (Persons who Subsequently Immigrated to Israel)

Period of Marriage	Men	Women
Up to 1961 – total	28.0	24.0
Up to 1915	24.5	21.8
1916–1925	26.7	23.6
1926–1930	27.1	23.9
1931–1935	27.5	24.2
1936–1940	28.4	24.5
1941–1945	29.2	24.2
1946–1950	29.3	24.6
1951–1955	29.9	25.3
1956–1961	29.4	25.1

1 At first marriage.
Source: Israel Population Census, 1961, vol. 26.

In Palestine, Jews achieved a remarkable reduction of mortality during the Mandatory period (1918–48), largely due to the strong immigration of European elements and the establishment of active and highly qualified health services. In the latter part of the 1940s, the Jewish population in Palestine was already counted among the very advanced in the world insofar as lowering of mortality was concerned. Some temporary setback, especially in infant mortality, was caused by the mass immigration of Jews from less developed countries in Asia and Africa in the early years of the State of Israel, but it was overcome with astonishing speed. The whole Jewish population had a mean life expectancy in excess of 70 years for females since 1951, and for males since 1959.

Marriage and Divorce

Among the European Jews in the past, as far as is ascertainable from available information, marriage was widespread. Few people did not marry at all unless prevented by official restrictions. Persons of both sexes contracted their (first) marriage at a rather early age. Though high mortality led to frequent instances of widowhood, this was often followed by remarriage, especially of men. In this case, the average age difference between spouses was greater than in the first marriage. Women used to spend a very large proportion of their reproductive years in married life, and this favored high fertility. In addition, there was hardly any out-marriage. Among the Jews in Europe and later among Jews of European origin who settled in America and in other areas of immigration changes developed in this traditional marriage pattern in the course of time. These changes were connected, among other things, with the spread of secularization and the modern complexion of Jewish life. There emerged some tendency for a larger proportion of Jews to remain unmarried which was already particularly marked in Central and Western Europe between the world wars and has again become conspicuous since the 1970s. There was also a systematic rise in age at first marriage, very clearly shown by retrospective census data on the large body of European Jews, mainly from Eastern Europe, who settled in Israel (see Table 4). Between the world wars, Jews in Central and Eastern Europe already had a higher marriage age than the general population of the respective countries. In the United States, Jews participated in a general reduction of the marriage age, but according to an official sample survey of 1957, their median age at first marriage was somewhat higher than among the rest of the population. It is obvious that these trends among Jews of European origin, namely the increase in the proportion never married and in marriage age, were bound to have a depressing influence on fertility levels.

A major trend in the modern marriage pattern of Diaspora Jews is the increase in out-marriage. Because of the inconsistency in the use of words like *intermarriage* and *mixed marriage* the term *out-marriage* will be used here for all unions in which only one partner is, or was, a Jew. The statistical information available on this topic has been scanty and unsatisfactory because of both the paucity of sources and difficulties in measurement. In relation to measurement, it should be noted that most available data reflect the religious diversity of marriage partners at a specified time while ignoring previous diversity that was overcome by change of religion on the part of one of them. Therefore, the data tend to give an underestimate of the real extent of out-marriage among Jews. There are two main types of sources: statistics of current weddings and statistics of couples in the population as ascertained by censuses or surveys. Because of the rising trend of out-marriages, their proportion is higher in the data derived from the former source.

An increase in out-marriage among Jews was observable in European countries of strong Jewish assimilation and in immigration countries overseas as early as the 19th century. Out-marriage reached considerable proportions in some larger Jewish populations of Europe between the world wars. Since World War II, a rise in the proportion of out-marriages has been noticeable among the Jews in Europe, America, South Africa, and Australia. There are, however, great differences in the actual extent of out-marriage. While it spells the disintegration of some smaller Jewish groups in Europe where most marrying Jews contract out-marriages, it used to be much more limited in America until the early 1960s (see Table 5).

Table 5: Recorded Out-Marriages of Jews (Selected Data)

Country or City	Period	Per 100 Jewish	
		Grooms/Husbands	Brides/Wives
		Current Weddings	
Amsterdam	1926–1927	14	13
Netherlands	1951–1962	41	36
Switzerland	1951–1965	46	26
Prussia	1875–1884	5	5
Germany	1901–1904	8	7
	1926–1930	27	17
Berlin	1951–1964	75	32
	1876–1880	16	12
	1901–1904	18	12
	1925–1926	30	18
Vienna	1926–1927	12	11
Italy	1951–1964	61	29
	1936–1937	35	34
Milan	1934–1936	43	33
	1952–1955	52	39
Hungary	1895–1899	3	3
	1925–1926	13	11
Budapest	1896–1900	7	7
	1926–1927	18	16
Latvia	1925–1927	1	2
U.S.S.R.[1]	1924–1926	7	6
R.S.F.S.R.[1]	1924–1926	21	12
Ukraine	1924–1926	4	5
Belorussia	1924–1926	2	4
Canada	1926–1930	4	1
	1941–1945	7	3
	1951–1955	8	4
	1961–1965	12	6
		All Existing Couples	
Netherlands	1954	30	22
Switzerland	1880	3	2
	1910	5	4
	1930	9	8
	1950	19	10
	1960	25	12
Austria	1961	36	15
Italy	1965	22	10
U.S.A.	1957	5	3
Australia	1911	28	15
	1933	21	12
	1961	12	6

[1] European territories only.

Main Sources: Compilations contained in the publications listed in the Bibliography. The data are official ones, except for those on "all existing couples" in the Netherlands and Italy which were obtained through Jewish-sponsored population surveys.

Since then it has been on the increase there also, as shown particularly by current country-wide data from Canada, by intergenerational comparisons made from data of local Jewish community surveys in the United States, and especially by the National Jewish Population Surveys of 1970, 1990, and 2001. The proportion of recorded out-marriages was generally higher among Jewish men than Jewish women, but over time the gap has narrowed.

The basic causes of out-marriage are the growing interaction of Diaspora Jews with surrounding society, the weakening of religious links and of ethnic identity, and assimilation. There are also contributory demographic factors: the limited size of many Jewish populations, especially after the Holocaust; the increased geographical dispersion of the Jews; and distortions in the age-sex composition of Jewish populations which themselves are partly connected with their smallness as well as with the aftereffects of the Holocaust and other factors. It is noteworthy that even before the middle of the 19th century in America and in the early part of this century in Australia, a marked tendency toward out-marriage prevailed in the then small Jewish populations but its frequency greatly diminished after the arrival of large waves of new Jewish immigrants. Similarly, it is found that at present out-marriage among the Jews of a given country is more frequent in localities or regions with fewer Jews.

Out-marriage is of great importance to the demography of the Jews. It often spells demographic losses through the drop-out of out-marrying Jewish spouses or of the children of such marriages. The direct statistical information available on the balance of demographic losses and gains occasioned by out-marriage generally indicates a loss to the Jewish side in Western and Eastern Europe and in the United States. The affiliation balance may turn in favor of the Jewish community in the case of some Latin American countries such as Mexico or Venezuela where the incidence of out-marriage is quite low.

Conversions to Judaism prompted by marriage pose problems of identity in the present and following generations. Some data on ex-Jews and persons of mixed (Jewish and non-Jewish) origin are available from Germany. In relation to 100 infants born to all Jewish couples including the out-married, those with only one parent whose religion was recorded as Jewish were 13 percent in Prussia during 1925–28 and 51 percent in West Germany during 1951–64 (both figures do not include illegitimate births by Jewish women). According to the Nazi census of 1939, 307,600 persons of Jewish religion were enumerated in Germany, Austria, and the Sudeten region, but there were a total of 330,600 "Jews according to race" and another 112,600 "mixed" persons with one or two Jewish grandparents of whom only 7,200 were Jews by religion. From the accession of the Nazis to power in Germany until that census (1933–39), the number of Jews by religion had dropped to less than one-half in the enumerated areas, mainly through emigration. It may be assumed that the relative extent of emigration was smaller for the other categories of persons with one or two Jewish grandparents. It might be roughly conjectured that their number corresponded to about one-quarter of the Jews by religion at the beginning of the 1930s.

Glimpses of the traditional marriage patterns of the Jews in Asia and Africa are found in Israel statistics, particularly in the data of the 1961 population census (see Table 6). First marriages had been practically universal and occurred at an early age, especially among the girls, and remarriage was frequent, primarily because of the rather high mortality. Among the

Table 6: Marriage Patterns of Jews in Asia-Africa (Persons who Immigrated to Israel), 1961

Country Of Birth	Age at Marriage[1]		Percent Ever Married at age 45–49[3]	Percent Married More than Once by Age 65+[3]
	Mean Age	Percent Married Young[2]		
		Men		
Asia and Africa – total	24.2	22	97	24
Thereof: Yemen, Aden	20.8	44	99	43
Iraq	26.5	15	95	16
Iran	24.3	22	98	29
Turkey	25.8	10	99	21
Egypt	26.5	7	95	15
Libya	23.5	22	97	22
Tunisia, Algeria	24.0	19	99	24
Morocco, Tangier	22.5	27	99	22
		Women		
Asia and Africa – total	19.4	39	98	10
Thereof: Yemen, Aden	17.0	55	97	20
Iraq	19.8	36	97	6
Iran	18.4	48	99	12
Turkey	23.1	14	97	10
Egypt	21.8	19	95	13
Libya	19.3	37	(100)	7
Tunisia, Algeria	20.7	27	99	7
Morocco, Tangier	17.4	54	99	12

1 Age at first marriage of persons who married before migration to Israel.
2 Married up to age 19 for men, and up to age 17 for women.
3 Per 100 persons born in Asia-Africa and living in Israel in 1961.
Source: Israel Population Census, 1961, vols. 22, 32.

Asian-African Jews enumerated in Israel in 1961, the proportion of individuals who had married at an early age was particularly high among those married in Yemen. Yet, the Israel data also show some rise in the age of Asian and African Jews at first marriage in the period prior to the mass migration to Israel and a higher marriage age among the better educated. Out-marriages were apparently rare among the Jews in Asia and Africa. In Mandatory Palestine and Israel, virtually all Jews have been in the habit of marrying, including those of European origin. The marriage age of the Jews from Asia and Africa went up, especially among women; the marriage age of the Jews from Europe, on the other hand, somewhat dropped and a tendency clearly emerged toward standardization of the respective patterns of all Jews in Israel. Out-marriage was rare in Israel until the arrival of a substantial number of non-Jewish immigrants in the framework of the major exodus from the former Soviet Union after 1989.

Data on Jewish divorces can be obtained from statistics reflecting current registration of such events or from information supplied by censuses and surveys on the composition of a Jewish population according to marital status. Sources of the latter kind usually show a higher proportion of divorced persons among women than among men, because of the greater tendency of men to remarry. In comparing the frequency of divorce among Jews and the general population of a country in the Diaspora, the religious orientation of the latter and prevailing legal arrangements must be taken into account. The Roman Catholic Church does not permit divorce, whereas it is not infrequent in Muslim societies. In some countries a status of separation is recognized. For an assessment of the relative frequency of divorce among the Diaspora Jews of European origin, their urbanization and socioeconomic stratification must be taken into consideration. The data available point to an increase in divorce in the Jewish populations of Europe and America during the 20th century but there were considerable differences between various countries in the actual proportion of divorced Jews. There also were marked differences between countries in the relative frequency of divorce among the Jews and among the general population, respectively. In Canada, an increase in the proportion of divorced Jews occurred from 1931 to 1961, and the Jews there had somewhat higher proportions of divorces than the general population. In the United States, considerable differences emerged in the extent of divorce among Jews according to the data available from local studies. The overall prevalence of divorce was lower among Jews than among the total U.S. population, but over time Jews tended to close that gap. Divorce was not rare among the Jews in Asia and Africa.

Births

Data on birth and on fertility can be derived either from current statistics, based on registration of the births that take place, or from censuses and surveys. In the latter case, retrospective questions may be asked about the children born to each woman. Failing such a specific inquiry, the sex-age distribution obtained from a census or population survey permits calculation of the "fertility ratio" also called "child-woman ratio" which is the ratio of the number of young children alive to the number of women of reproductive age. For improved measurement, child mortality up to the date of enumeration is accounted for. The average number of children living in each family is a rough indication obtainable from censuses. The ratio between the number of 0–4-year-old children and that of 5–9-year-old children shows recent changes in the frequency of births.

In Europe, the birth rate of the Jews was, on the whole, high in the past. As early as the first half of the 19th century, however, birth rates found among the Jews were somewhat lower than those among the general population in some countries and cities of Central Europe. In large parts of Eastern Europe, the birth rate of the Jews continued to be very high and similar to that of the respective general populations until near the end of the 19th century.

The Jews preceded the general population of their countries of residence in the reduction of natality and in the adoption of family planning through birth control methods. The reasons for this differential may be the above-mentioned greater concentration of Jews in those social strata which, in general, reduced births more rapidly such as the urban, were better educated, engaged in white-collar occupations; the fact that mortality of the Jews went down more rapidly causing Jewish families to experience the economic pressure exercised by the survival of more children at an earlier date; possibly also the greater concern of Jews for the proper upbringing of their children, as well as the eagerness of Jews for upward social mobility, and other related factors.

The decrease in Jewish births was a gradual process. In some countries, however, it proceeded rather quickly. In Europe, this development spread, on the whole, from west to east. As early as the eve of World War I, there were cities in Europe where the Jewish birth rate had dropped so low that it was barely able to balance the current deaths. This situation intensified in the 1920s and became still more acute and widespread during the general slump in births in the 1930s when the economic and political crisis was aggravated for the Jews in Europe by ever more menacing manifestations of antisemitism. In North America as well, the high fertility of the Jewish immigrants from Eastern Europe quickly gave way to drastic birth limitation. Retrospective fertility data, subsequently obtained in the United States and Canada, show that Jewish women who had spent their most fertile years during the 1930s and early 1940s had borne, on the average, less than two children – not enough for demographic replacement. Then the Shoah overtook European Jewry; births became rare and most young children perished.

After World War II, Jews in Western Europe, America, and Australia participated in the "baby boom" characteristic of those years. The survivors in Europe had the special reason of wishing to reconstitute their families. However, this upsurge of natality among the Jews was rather short-lived. In the United States by the late 1950s and in Western Europe by the early 1960s it was followed by another decline in births. In Eastern Europe, barely any postwar birth-rate recovery emerged. The ensuing data from all over the world show that natality and fertility were lower among Jews than among the general population of their respective countries of residence. This can be seen from decreasing absolute figures and crude birth rates, as well as from the age breakdown of Jewish children (the ratio of 0–4-year-olds to 5–9-year-olds), according to censuses and surveys. It is true that the age structure of the Jewish adults was unfavorable to current births, because the prospective mothers belonged to the comparatively small cohorts born during the great slump in births of the 1930s. But when the age composition turned to be more favorable to Jewish natality for a while as the comparatively large cohorts born during the "baby boom" around 1950 were reaching procreative age, the expected rise in the Jewish birth rate did only partially materialize. Fertility indicators which are less affected by the actual age composition, also pointed to a decline in Jewish fertility. Indeed, birth rates and fertility levels also registered declines in the general population of many technologically advanced countries during the 1950s or 1960s, and even more significantly during the 1970s. Low fertility levels, anticipated by Jewish populations, lead nearer to, or aggravate, insufficient demographic replacement all across developed countries.

There are variations in the actual levels of fertility and natality of Jews throughout their global geographical dispersion. Yet these levels are universally rather low when assessed as a source for the growth, or even for the mere maintenance, of Jewish population size. The present low fertility of the Jews in most Diaspora countries is a major cause of concern for the demographic future of large sections of the Jewish people.

Among Jews of European origin in Mandatory Palestine and Israel, there was a rapid decline in fertility in the 1920s and 1930s to a low at about 1940. Yet the crude birth rate remained substantial because of the comparatively young age composition of this immigrant population. There, too, a "baby boom" was followed by a renewed drop in fertility; however, fertility remained above replacement level. It is noteworthy that the European Jews who immigrated after the establishment of the State of Israel increased their fertility from its level abroad, which was quite insufficient for demographic replacement, to a level which, though moderate, was sufficient for this end.

The Jews of Asia and Africa used to have high fertility in their countries of residence. Retrospective data from Israel on fertility of immigrants abroad prior to immigration show that women gave birth to six or seven children on the average. Though differentiation of fertility according to educational level of women had already set in, the great majority of women had not attended school or had reached only low educational attainment and were very prolific. Jews in Egypt and Turkey had markedly lower fertility, just as they differed in socioeconomic status from other Asian-African Jews. The overwhelming majority of the Jews from Asia and Africa moved to Israel or to France and other countries of Europe and America. Israel data show a rapid fertility decline throughout the 1950s, 1960s, and 1970s under the influence of the new surroundings, and similar developments took place in other countries where the socioeconomic status of Jewish migrants from Asia and Africa was generally higher than that of their peers who had moved to Israel.

Illegitimate births, insofar as statistical data are available, were on the whole less frequent among Jews than among the respective general populations. However, percentages of such births recorded from Central Europe in the period between the world wars and again in recent decades were not negligible. An altogether different matter was the lack of an officially recognized status for many religious Jewish marriages in some parts of Eastern Europe, which led to the offspring of such unions being registered by the authorities as "illegitimate."

Natural Increase

In the past, mortality, and especially child mortality, was so high as to almost offset high fertility; as a consequence, natural increase was small and population growth was slow. On the whole, this may also be presumed to have been the situation of the Jews before the modern demographic evolution. As mortality declined, while fertility continued to be high or at least moderately high, considerable natural increase was generated. This was the demographic situation of most of European Jewry during a great part of the 19th century. East European Jewry, which adopted widespread birth control comparatively late, displayed natural increase on such a substantial scale that its numbers rose from about five and a half million to seven million during 1880–1914, despite the emigration of more than 2,500,000 persons overseas or to Western Europe. As the Jews had preceded the general population of their countries of residence in the reduction of mortality, they enjoyed, for a considerable time, relatively higher natural increase.

When the subsequent fertility decline among Jews became more acute, their natural increase dwindled and became smaller than that of the corresponding general populations. Extreme instances were Jewish populations in Central Europe that already had a yearly surplus of deaths over births from some time in the 1920s before the accession of the Nazis to power. In the United States and Canada in the 1930s, Jewish fertility was insufficient for demographic replacement in the long run.

The Shoah liquidated not only about one-third of the Jewish people, but also had aftereffects that were highly detrimental to the further demographic development of the survivors. Distortions in the age-sex distribution and the reduced size of the Jewish communities extant in Europe or scattered through migration to other regions of the Diaspora enhanced the chances of out-marriages with their consequent demographic losses to the Jewish people.

After the short-lived Jewish "baby-boom" following World War II, the growth prospects of Jewish Diaspora populations became far from encouraging. In Central and Western Europe all the evidence shows an outright deficit in the balance of births and deaths. For Eastern Europe including the Soviet Union, direct evidence and statistics available on the age composition of immigrants to Israel show that fertility was long below replacement level. As regards the Jews in the United States and Canada, a decline in births since the late 1950s and early 1960s is clearly documented. It is evident that the rate of natural increase cannot be very considerable. This is also the conclusion from data available for South Africa and Australia.

The small natural increase, or even decrease, of Diaspora Jews is the more disquieting from the viewpoint of the demographic future of the Jewish people. Since World War II, and more especially since the 1970s when an unmistakable tendency to increasing out-marriages and some withdrawals emerged, a small natural increase in a Jewish population became insufficient to maintain Jewish population size irrespective of migratory influences. Aggravating circumstances were low fertility; advanced aging; out-marriages and withdrawals. Only by viewing all of these negative factors together, is a realistic picture obtained of the demographic situation and perspectives of most Jewish Diaspora communities in Europe, North America, and other overseas countries.

Until mass emigration following Israel's independence in 1948, the Jews in Asia and Africa were in a stage of rapid and accelerating demographic expansion. Exceptions to this generalization were presented by the Yemenites, whose mortality was still too high to leave much room for natural increase, and on the other hand, the Jews in Turkey and Egypt, whose fertility had already been reduced considerably. The first effect of migration to Israel and to France was a reduction in mortality, which boosted natural increase for a while; however, the fertility decline, which soon set in, operated in the opposite direction. While the transfer of many Jews from Asia and Africa to Israel, France, etc., raised the average fertility and natural increase among the Jewish population in the receiving countries, it tended to lower the fertility and natural increase of the Jewish people as a whole.

Into the 21st Century

Over the last quarter of the 20th century, distinct erosion in conventional marriage patterns among Jews reflected similar general trends among developed Western societies. Propensities to marry significantly diminished. An increase in unmarried couples living together overwhelmingly composed by one Jewish and one non-Jewish partner in the Diaspora, did not compensate for fewer and later marriages. Divorce rates increased and tended to approach the higher rates of non-Jews. In Israel such trends were more conservative, but they could be observed too, as demonstrated by the presence of over one million non-married individuals among the adult Jewish population around 2005.

Among Jews who married since the 1990s, in the United States 50 percent or more had a non-Jewish partner, between 35 and 45 percent did in France and the U.K., and higher percentages approaching 70 and 80 percent did in the FSU and other Eastern European countries. The differential frequency of out-marriages of Jewish men and women tended to disappear, equalling the higher levels previously recorded for men. The majority of children of out-marriages were not identified as Jews. During the 1990s, similar relatively low proportions of children of out-marriages (about 20 percent) were identified by the respective parents as Jewish in Russia (with rather underdeveloped Jewish community resources), as in the United States (with highly developed Jewish resources). In 2001, that percent had risen to about one-third in the U.S. As a compound consequence, the configuration of Jewish households was characterized by an increasing share different from the conventional nuclear family inclusive of two Jewish parents living with their Jewish children. In the Diaspora this comprised an ever smaller minority of all Jewish households.

In a general context of low and declining death rates, life expectancy at birth surpassed 80 years for women and 75 for men. Fertility was quite stable among Jews in Israel, while it turned to be about one half lower among the rest of

Jewish communities worldwide. The latter reflected or even often anticipated the general decline of fertility in the more developed countries. Jews in Israel were an exception, becoming with 2.6–2.7 children on average the population with the highest fertility among developed nations. Jews from similar countries of origin who migrated to Israel or to Europe ended up adopting the quite different social norms and behaviors on fertility of their countries of absorption. In Israeli society, community was an important intervening factor in fertility trends resulting in larger families than could be found among Jews with similar backgrounds that moved to other countries. Cultural, religious, and community related determinants of higher fertility in Israel led to a unique surplus of natural increase and helped to maintain a comparatively young age composition among the Jewish population. The number of Jewish births in Israel was higher than the number of Jewish deaths by over 45,000 in 1990, by over 58,000 in 2001, and by over 67,000 in 2004.

In the Diaspora low fertility was the main determinant of rapid Jewish population aging. This in turn significantly contributed to a negative balance between Jewish births and deaths. Among the better documented examples, in the Russian Republic the number of Jewish deaths exceeded the number of Jewish births by over 10,000 in 1988, and by 7,600 in 2000 among a greatly diminished Jewish population. In Germany, the excess of Jewish deaths over Jewish births was over 300 in 1990, and had grown nearly over threefold in 2004 while the Jewish population itself had grown by three thanks to the steady inflow of immigrants from the FSU. In the U.K., each year the number of Jewish deaths surpassed by over 1,000 the number of Jewish births. The spiral of low fertility, aging, and partial erosion of the younger generation through the non-affiliation with Judaism of a large portion of the children of out-marriage foreshadowed significant further changes in the demographic profile of world Jewry.

While the world's developing countries continue to experience fast population growth rates and also the populations of many of the technologically advanced countries recorded substantial growth – increasingly due to international migration rather than to natural increase – the Jewish Diaspora at the beginning of the 21st century was in a rather precarious demographic situation. Thanks to the persisting natural increase in Israel, world Jewish population kept close to zero population growth.

See also *Demography; *Migrations; *Population; *Statistics.

BIBLIOGRAPHY: J. Lestschinsky, *Probleme der Bevoelkerung-Bewegung bei den Juden* (1926); A. Ruppin, *Soziologie der Juden*, 1 (1930); A. Ruppin, *The Jewish Fate and Future* (1940); U.O. Schmelz and P. Glikson (ed.), *Jewish Population Studies 1961-1968* (1970), 11–94; L. Hersch, in: *The Jewish People, Past and Present*, 2 (1948), 1–34; R. Bachi, in: JJSO, 4 (1962), 172–91; U.O. Schmelz, *ibid.*, 8 (1966), 49–63; M. Davis, *ibid.*, 10 (1968), 177–203. **ADD. BIBLIOGRAPHY:** S. DellaPergola, *La trasformazione demografica della diaspora ebraica* (1983); idem, *World Jewry Beyond 2000: The Demographic Prospects* (1999); idem, "World Jewish Population 2005," in: AJYB, 105 (2005), 87–122; M. Tolts, "The Post-Soviet Jewish Population in Russia and the World," in: *Jews in Russia and Eastern Europe*, 1–52 (2004), 37–63.

[Usiel Oscar Schmelz / Sergio DellaPergola (2nd ed.)]

VITEBSK, capital of Vitebsk district, Belarus. The first Jewish settlement appears to have been established in Vitebsk at the end of the 16th century. The charter given to the residents of Vitebsk in 1597 by Sigismund III Vasa forbids Jews "in accordance with long-held practice" to dwell within the city. Still, it appears that some Jews did live there, under the protection of the local nobility, both before and after 1597. The Jewish community developed, though not without conflict with the Christian population of the city over Jewish rights and privileges. In 1627 the local ruler S. Sangushko granted permission for the construction of a synagogue in the city. A document from the 17th century takes note of "the Jew's gate."

During the war between Poland and the government of Moscow in 1654, Jews fought in the defense of the city. When it fell to the Russians, their property was confiscated and they were taken captive, not being released until peace was achieved with Poland (1667). Upon the Jews' return they had to enter into litigation with their neighbors who had appropriated their property. In 1679 King John III Sobieski granted a charter to the Jews, restoring their former privileges and promising them freedom of religion and commercial rights. This charter was renewed and confirmed by the kings of Poland in 1729 and 1759. In 1708, during the war with Sweden, the Jewish quarter of Vitebsk was destroyed by fire. The local residents then occupied the plot where the synagogue had been and built a church upon it. The Lithuanian supreme court ordered them to return the land to the Jews and pay damages of 13,500 gold pieces. The Jewish community of Vitebsk was part of the Council of the *Lands. It was under the jurisdiction of the *Brest-Litovsk community and through it was subject to the Lithuanian Council. The Vitebsk Jewish community kept a *pinkas (minute-book) from 1706.

With the first partition of Poland in 1772 Vitebsk was annexed to Russia. At that time the community numbered 1,227 persons, or about a quarter of the town's population. Most of Vitebsk's trade in flax and tobacco was conducted with Riga by way of the Dvina River. With the completion of the Orel-Vitebsk-Dvinsk railroad during the 1860s the commerce of Vitebsk with regional towns and villages increased and the Jewish community grew accordingly. After their expulsion from Moscow in 1891 some of the Jews transferred their businesses to Vitebsk. In 1897 the city had 34,420 Jews (52.4% of the total population).

Vitebsk was a stronghold of Orthodox Judaism, containing elements of Lithuanian Jewish scholarship, and even stronger ḥasidic influences. At the end of the 18th century the founders of Lithuanian Ḥasidism, Menahem *Mendel of Vitebsk and Shneur Zalman of Lyady, were active in the city. Strong *Ḥabad ḥasidic influences were present. The rabbi of the city from 1803 to 1860 was Yiẓḥak Isaac Behard, who was both kazyonny *ravvin (government-appointed rabbi) and the choice of the *admor.* Jekuthiel Zalman Landau succeeded him in the rabbinate serving also as head of the yeshivah of Vitebsk. After Landau moved to St. Petersburg the community did not select a new chief rabbi, as a result of a dispute between the Ḥasidim and **Mitnaggedim.* During the last years of the 19th century 72% of the school-age children studied in the *ḥeder* and *talmud torah* schools of Vitebsk.

The settlement of Jews in Vitebsk who had been expelled from Moscow strengthened the *Haskalah elements in the city. The Ḥibbat *Zion movement began to develop, as did the Socialist movement at a later date. Vitebsk was one of the first centers of the *Bund. In 1901 the Zionist leader Grigori (Ẓevi Hirsch) *Bruck was selected as *kazyonny ravvin* of Vitebsk. He had great influence upon the life of the community, even after he was deposed by the authorities. This occurred as a result of his position as a delegate to the *Duma, in which he signed the Wyborg Proclamation. The Zionist and *Po'alei Zion movements flourished, causing the *talmud torah* to be converted into a Hebrew school. After 1905 several private gymnasia opened in the city, most of the students being Jewish. The artist Y. Pen opened an art school which trained hundreds of young people, including Marc *Chagall and S. Yudovin. S. *An-Ski and C. *Zhitlovsky were both from Vitebsk. During World War I Vitebsk served as a way station for tens of thousands of Jews who had been expelled from Lithuania. Several thousands of them settled there permanently.

With the advent of Soviet rule the Vitebsk Jewish community began to decline. Thousands of residents who had come from Lithuania and Latvia used their rights of relocation and emigrated from the Soviet Union. The *Yevsektsiya established one of its centers in Belorussia in Vitebsk, publishing the paper *Der Royter Shtern* ("The Red Star") until 1923. In 1921 a public trial "over the *ḥeder*" was conducted in Vitebsk and several synagogues in the city were confiscated. The Vitebsk *He-Ḥalutz movement was harassed and came to an end during the middle of the 1920s. Vitebsk had a semi-legal Ḥabad yeshivah until 1930. In 1923 there were 39,714 Jews (43.7% of the total population). In 1926 there were 37,013 (37.5%).

With the Nazi conquest of the city in July 1941 part of the Jewish population fled into the interior of Russia. The city was destroyed in a fire started by the retreating Red Army. The 16,000 Jews who remained behind were imprisoned in a ghetto. On October 8, 1941, their systematic liquidation began. After the liberation of the city from the Germans Jews began to return. In the later 1960s the Jewish population was estimated at about 20,000 but there was no synagogue. Most left during the large-scale emigration of the 1990s.

BIBLIOGRAPHY: *Vitebsk Amol* (Yid. 1956); *Sefer Vitebsk* (Heb. 1957).

[Yehuda Slutsky]

VITERBO, town in central Italy. Documents show Jews living in the town in 1272; in 1294 the loan-banker Elia resided there, and a few years later the number of Jews had increased to such an extent that in 1313 a Christian proposed setting up an institution that would collect all the Jews together to convert them. In the 14th century some of the moneylenders left Viterbo to found the settlement at Urbino and others moved to Orvieto. In 1427 the Franciscan friar Bernardino da *Siena delivered inflammatory sermons in Viterbo. The town came under the rule of the Church in 1435 and 15 years later the Jews were compelled to wear the *badge. In 1538 the banking permits were withdrawn. At that time, the Jews owned two synagogues and a medicinal spring called the "bath of the Jews." As in the other Church possessions, a ghetto was established in Viterbo in 1555, and the community leaders were thrown into prison. After Pius V was elected to the papacy, the Jews were expelled from all the minor cities of the papal states (1569). Ten families were readmitted to Viterbo in 1586, but in 1593 they were definitely banished. Later, Jewish merchants were allowed to visit the town only during the fair; at one of these, in 1705, a group of Jews were accused of a blood *libel but they were acquitted the following year. A number of notable copyists and physicians came from Viterbo, including the talmudist Theodorus de Sacerdotibus (Eliezer ha-Cohen), physician to Pope Julius III.

BIBLIOGRAPHY: Milano, Italia, index; Roth, Italy, index: Milano, in: *Scritti... Guido Bedarida* (1966), 137–49; Roth, in: RMI, 20 (1954), 367–71.

[Attilio Milano]

VITERBO, CARLO ALBERTO (1889–1974), leader of Italian Jewry. Born in Florence, Viterbo studied law at the University of Pisa, coming under the influence of S.H. *Margulies and A. *Pacifici. An early Zionist, he participated in numerous congresses and was president of the Italian Zionist Federation and of Keren Hayesod. In 1936–37, he went on a study tour of North African Jewish communities on behalf of the Italian Jewish community. He also made contact with the *Falashas in Ethiopia, then under Italian rule, and published new documents he had found on their history (*Annuario di Studi Ebraici*, 2 (1937), 125ff.). From 1944 Viterbo edited the weekly *Israel.* He also published some Hebrew language textbooks (1933, 1955, 1968).

BIBLIOGRAPHY: *Israel*, 54 (1969), no. 14, 5–6 (It.). **ADD. BIBLIOGRAPHY:** F. del Canuto (ed.), *Israel un decennio: 1974–1984* (1984).

[Alfredo Mordechai Rabello]

VITERBO, JEHIEL ḤAYYIM (c. 1766–c. 1842), a rabbi of Ancona, scholar, and poet. Among his poems is a eulogy of 26 stanzas on the death of Ḥayyim Joseph David *Azulai in which he alludes to the 31 works of the latter.

He published two volumes of sermons in Leghorn, *Yiḥyu Dagan*, for Sabbaths and festivals (1830), and *Va-Yeḥi Od*, which includes a commentary on *Pirkei Avot* and responsa (1839). After his death, *Va-Yeḥi va-Yitten* (1843) appeared. Viterbo was in close contact with the *yishuv* in Ereẓ Israel. Many of his letters and poems remained in manuscript and are in the archives of the Budapest rabbinical seminary.

BIBLIOGRAPHY: A.N.Z. Roth, in: M. Benayahu, *Sefer ha-Ḥida* (1959), 64–67; C. Roth, in: *Sinai*, 21 (1947), 326.

VITKIN, JOSEPH (1876–1912), precursor of the Second Aliyah, teacher, and communal worker. Born in Mogilev, Belorussia, he went to Ereẓ Israel in 1897, where he worked as a laborer. Later he became a teacher and headmaster at a Gederah school, where his reforms led to his being invited to become headmaster of the school in Rishon le-Zion. In 1904 he became headmaster of the school at Kefar Tavor (Mesḥah), and two years later he returned to teaching in Rishon le-Zion, where he remained for the rest of his life. Vitkin was the precursor of the Second Aliyah both chronologically and in his ideological contribution to the pioneering movement in Ereẓ Israel. His influential pamphlet entitled *Kol Kore el Ẓe'irei Yisrael Asher Libbam le-Ammam u-le-Ẓiyyon* ("A Call to the Youth of Israel whose Hearts are with their People and with Zion," 1905), signed Ḥavurat Ẓe'irim me-Ereẓ Israel ("A Group of Young People from Ereẓ Israel") contains all the principles of the labor movement of the Second Aliyah. He forcefully rejected "diplomatic" Zionism and condemned a Zionism that merely entailed shekel- and share-buying by Jews in the Diaspora. He demanded that Diaspora youth unite for *aliyah* and sacrifice for their homeland, as other nations do for their countries. He even outlined plans for a new type of settlement based on self-employed labor on nationally owned land. He ended the pamphlet with the appeal: "Hasten, Heroes of Israel, renew the days of the Biluim with even greater strength and vigor, for otherwise we shall be lost." When the *Ha-Po'el ha-Ẓa'ir Party was formed, he became a member and was the first to demand that, in addition to "conquest of labor" by Jewish workers as wage earners on Jewish-owned farms, the party should advocate "conquest of the soil," i.e., agricultural settlement by Jewish worker-pioneers. He developed a theoretical and practical educational system uniting Jewish values with love of nature.

A selection of his writings appeared in 1912. A new comprehensive edition, containing letters, an appraisal, and a detailed bibliography, edited by E. Shoḥat, appeared in 1961. Kefar Vitkin in the Ḥefer Plain is named after him.

BIBLIOGRAPHY: M. Braslavsky, *Tenu'at ha-Po'alim ha-Ereẓ-Yisre'elit*, 1 (1955), 130–1, 314–5; B. Ḥabas (ed.), *Ha-Aliyah ha-Sheniyyah* (1947), index.

[Getzel Kressel]

VITORIA, town in N. Spain, S.E. of Bilbao. Vitoria was founded in 1181 by King Sancho I of Portugal, the "City Builder" (1185–1211), and destroyed by fire in 1202. The town recovered in the days of Alfonso *X (1252–84) of Castile, and it appears that the Jews helped to develop it anew. The Jewish quarter was situated in the eastern part of the city, along the battlements. Isaac ibn *Ẓadok (Çag de la Maleha) was a tax farmer there in 1276. Toward the end of the 13th century the community was one of the moderately important Castile communities. Little is known about the community in the 14th century. In 1439 Don Shem Tov ibn Naḥmias collected dues from the fairs held in the Basque country and taxes from the whole of Castile. From 1482 the anti-Jewish decrees issued by the Cortes of *Toledo (1480) were put into effect in Vitoria also. Nevertheless, the crown often intervened on behalf of the Jews there, granting them a charter of protection as late as 1488. Following the edict of expulsion (May 1492), the community leaders of Vitoria negotiated with the municipal authorities regarding the fate of Jewish communal property. The Jewish cemetery was given to the town council, which undertook to take care of it and never to build on it. The place was subsequently known as the *Judimendi* ("Jews' Mount"). The synagogue was also given to the town council and turned into a school. In July 1492 the majority of the Jews of Vitoria left the town for nearby Navarre. In order to speed up their assimilation, in 1493 the Conversos who had remained were scattered throughout the town and not allowed to live in a separate quarter. In 1952, the Jews of *Bayonne, descendants of the Jews of Vitoria, reached an agreement with the town releasing it from its duties toward former Jewish property. The remains in the old cemetery were collected and reburied in a common grave, with a monument to commemorate the old community of Vitoria.

BIBLIOGRAPHY: Baer, Toledot, index; Baer, Urkunden, 2 (1936), index; M. Kayserling, *Geschichte der Juden in Navarra…* (1861), 116–32, 213; J. Amador de los Rios, *Historia… de los judíos de España y Portugal*, 2 (1876, repr. 1960), 130; *Sefarad*, 12 (1952), 442–3; Suárez Fernández, Documentos, index.

[Haim Beinart]

VITORIA, FRANCISCO DE (d. 1592), Marrano prelate. He was the son of the New Christian Duarte Nuñes, and two of his brothers lived as Jews in Safed and Tripoli respectively, under the names of Abraham and Jacob Curiel. Many other members of his immediate family also reverted to Judaism, while Isaac de Mattathias *Aboab was his great nephew. Entering holy orders, Francisco became bishop of Tucumán (now in Argentina) in 1583 and was later nominated archbishop of Mexico. He aroused great enmity, however, and was recalled for investigation to Madrid, charges both of corruption and of Judaizing being involved. He died before the inquiry was concluded.

BIBLIOGRAPHY: Révah, in: *Boletim Internacional Lusco-Brasileiro*, 2 (1961), 297–9; J. Caro Baroja, *Los Judios en la España Moderna…*, 2 (1962), 243–4; I. da Costa, *Noble Families Among the Sephardic Jews* (1936), index, s.v. *Curiel*.

[Cecil Roth]

°**VITRUVIUS, POLLO** (or **Mamurra**; first century B.C.E.), Roman architect and engineer, author of a work on architecture. In it (8. 3. 8) he says that at Joppa in Syria and in Nomad Arabia there are lakes of immense size producing much bitumen which is gathered by the neighboring tribes. The reference, which seems to be to the Dead Sea, is similar to that in *Zenophilus (Xenophilus), who likewise speaks of a lake near Joppa with bitumen.

[Louis Harry Feldman]

VITRY (**le-Brûlé**, today **Vitry-en-Perthois**, not to be confused with Vitry-le-François) town in the department of Marne, N. France. When Louis VII, king of France, sacked the town in 1142, he is said to have spared the Jews, who therefore constituted the majority of the population for a while. In 1230, when Thibaut IV, count of Champagne, granted a communal charter to Vitry, he retained for himself the "guard and jurisdiction" over a number of categories of its inhabitants, particularly the Jews. In 1321, after having been accused of poisoning the wells together with the lepers, 77 Jews were immediately massacred, a large number succeeded in escaping, and another 40 were imprisoned. Once the prisoners realized the hopelessness of their situation, they chose death at the hands of one of their companions, who was then killed by the Christians. There is today a small Jewish community in Vitry-le-François, founded in the 16th century as a refuge for the inhabitants of Vitry-le-Brûlé which had been destroyed by fire. Vitry-le-François was built a few miles away from the burnt town. Simḥah b. Samuel, who is said to be the author of the talmudical and liturgic compendium known as *Maḥzor Vitry, was a native of the town.

BIBLIOGRAPHY: Gross, Gal Jud, 195–7; C.-M. Detorcy, *Fragments Tirés d'un Manuscrit Contenant des Recherches Chronologiques et Historiques sur l'Ancienne Ville de Vitry-en-Partois* (1839), 15ff.; A.C. Boitel, *Histoire de l'Ancien et du Nouveau Vitry* (1841), 92ff.; E. Jovy, *La Charte Communale de Vitry* (n.d.) 19.

[Bernhard Blumenkranz]

VITTA, CINO (1873–1956), Italian jurist. Vitta was professor of administrative law first at the Florence Institute of Social Science and then professor at the universities of Cagliari, Modena, and Turin. An authority on all branches of public law his treatise *Trattato di diritto amministrativo* (2 vols., 1954–55⁴), on administrative law, ran into several editions. He also taught international law and lectured at the Hague Academy in 1930, 1934, and 1936. During World War II, Vitta was president of the Jewish community of Florence, a position that had been held by his father and grandfather before him. During the Nazi occupation he and his wife were hidden in the Siena mental hospital. After the war he returned to teaching.

Among his publications: "Il Diritto pubblico degli Ebrei," in: *Accademia Mazionale dei Lincei*, 6 (1951), 109ff.

BIBLIOGRAPHY: *Recueil des Cours de l'Académie de Droit International de la Haye*, 56 (1936), 303f. **ADD. BIBLIOGRAPHY:** *Novissimo Digesto Italiano*, 20 (1975), 1033 f.

[Giorgio Romano / Alfredo Mordechai Rabello (2nd ed.)]

VITTORIO VENETO, town in N. Italy, formed in 1866 by the union of the two adjacent towns of Serravalle and Ceneda. The presence of Jews in Serravalle is attested in 1398, but nothing is known of their subsequent history. In 1597 Israel di Conegliano was authorized to open a loan-bank in Ceneda; in spite of two expulsion attempts, in 1631 and 1638, the *Conegliano family remained in the town throughout the 17th century. In the 18th century a number of Jews were enclosed in a small ghetto. There were 45 Jews (11 families) in Ceneda in 1765, out of a total population of 7,946. Their status was then superior to that of the other Jews in Veneto, as shown by the fact that in 1770 they obtained the revocation of a 1767 prohibition to trade in grain. About the second half of the 18th century a "council of Jews" (*corpo degli ebrei*) was formed, which was comparatively influential at the beginning of the following century, when it included the important Luzzatto, Romanin, Gentili, Fontanella, Valenzin, Conegliano, and Pincherle families. Lorenzo da *Ponte (Conegliano) was born in Ceneda. However, in 1870 only 50 Jews remained in Vittorio Veneto and their number progressively decreased, although there was a Gemilut Ḥasadim society. The cemetery at Vittorio Veneto was not established until the second half of the 19th century; before then the Jewish cemetery of *Conegliano was used. A private synagogue existed from 1646; it was completely renovated in 1701, in a style similar to the synagogue of Conegliano. It has been transferred to the Israel Museum in Jerusalem.

BIBLIOGRAPHY: Milano, Bibliotheca, nos. 1171f., 1418f.; Milano, Italia, index; Roth, Italy, index; idem, *Venice* (1930), index; J. Pinkerfeld, *Battei Keneset be-Italyah* (1954), 40; F. Luzzatto, in: RMI, 22 (1956), 42–43, 122–3, 274–5; idem, *Cronache storiche della Università degli Ebrei di San Daniele del Friuli* (1964), 74, 132; U. Nahon, *Aronot Kodesh ve-Tashmishei Kedushah me-Italyah be-Yisrael* (1970), 20–26.

[Alfredo Mordechai Rabello]

VIVANTE, CESARE (1855–1944), Italian jurist. Born in Venice, Vivante graduated in law from the University of Padua and in 1882 at the age of 27 became professor of commercial law at the University of Parma, and in 1889 at the University of Bologna. From 1898 he was professor of commercial law at the University of Rome, a post he held for over 30 years until his retirement. He presided over numerous legislative commissions and was chairman of the Italian Commission for the Reform of the Commercial Law Code.

Vivante is considered the founder of the modern Italian school for the study of commercial law. He developed a new inductive approach to its study, establishing the principles from the agreed rules of law while at the same time coordinating commercial law principles with those of civil law. His works include *Trattato di diritto commerciale* (4 vols., 1893), *Il Contratto di assicurazione* (3 vols., 1894), which ran into several printings and was translated into many languages, and his classic *Instituzioni di diritto commerciale* (1891), a standard textbook which attained 60 printings. Vivante was a cofounder of the *Rivista del diritto commerciale* in 1903, the leading Italian journal on commercial law. Among his pupils was Tullio *Ascarelli who succeeded him as professor of commercial law at Rome.

In Bari, at the beginning of 1980s, the "Istituto Commerciale C.V." was founded and in Catania a way was dedicated to his name. The *Rivista della Scuola Superiore dell'economia e delle finanze* published on the Internet his speech (1888) for "un codice unico delle obbligazioni."

BIBLIOGRAPHY: *Studi in Onore di Cesare Vivante*, 2 vols. (1931). **ADD. BIBLIOGRAPHY:** *Novissimo Digesto Italiano*, 20 (1975), 1034.

[Giorgio Romano / Alfredo Mordechai Rabello (2nd ed.)]

VIVANTI, DAVID ABRAHAM (1806–1876), Italian rabbi. Born in *Ancona, Vivanti came from a well-known Italian-Jewish family, originally from Mantua, which had settled in Ancona in the first half of the 18th century. When still a youth, he was ordained as a rabbi and appointed to the *bet din* at Ancona, and in 1840 became rabbi of the community.

Vivanti wrote commentaries on the Pentateuch and Psalms, both of which are unpublished. His annotations to the *Shulḥan Arukh*, arranged in alphabetic order and containing halakhic decisions both of his own and earlier authorities, and annotations to the *Sefer ha-Ḥinnukh* (according to the Venice edition of 1600), together with a *kinah* composed by him for the 24 martyrs of Ancona and some homilies, were published by H. Rosemberg, *Keẓat mi-Kitvei ... David Avraham Ḥai* (1932); and in Italian *Saggio degli Scritti degli Rabbini David Abraham Vivante* (1929).

[Alfredo Mordechai Rabello]

VIVANTI CHARTRES, ANNIE (1868–1942), Italian novelist. Annie Vivanti was born in London, the daughter of an Italian political exile, her mother being a German writer. In 1890 she became famous with the publication of *Lirica*, a volume of verse, prefaced by the eminent Italian poet Giosuè Carducci. Abandoning verse for fiction, she wrote several novels including *Circe* (1912); *Vae victis!* (1917), a dramatic though naïve account of the relationship between the victors and the vanquished of World War I; *Naja tripudians* (1920) and *Fosca, sorella di Messalina* (1922). In a novel in English, *Marie Tarnowska* (1915), she analyzed the problem of crime, which she considered a hereditary physical disease devoid of any moral implication. Her years in England, Switzerland, and the U.S. inspired a collection of short stories, *Zingaresca* (1918). She also wrote two plays: *L'Invasore* (1916) and *Le bocche inutili* (1918).

A representative of Italian romanticism at its most decadent, Annie Vivanti was true to the fashion of her times even in her private life. She married an Irish lawyer and journalist, John Chartres, whom she supported in his campaigns for Irish independence. Her daughter, Vivien Chartres, a talented violinist, inspired her best novel, *The Devourers* (1910). The "devourers" are the infant prodigies who sacrifice their parents to their own talents. Vivien Chartres died during an air raid in London in 1941. Annie Vivanti herself suffered from Mussolini's antisemitic laws: her books were banned in Italy, and she spent some time in internment. She died a lonely woman in Turin.

BIBLIOGRAPHY: B. Croce, *La letteratura della nuova Italia*, 6 (1940), 305–15; P. Pancrazi, *Scrittori d'oggi*, 6 (1953), 287–374; Allason, in: *Nuova Antologia*, 454 (1952), 369–81.

[Giorgio Romano]

VIVES, JUAN LUIS (1492–1540), Spanish humanist. A recent study by Pinta y Llorente and Palacio, *Procesos Inquisitoriales contra la familia judía de Luis Vives* (1964), established that his mother became a Christian only in 1491, that she was said to have continued Jewish practices after her baptism, that she was condemned by the Inquisition 24 years after her death, and that her remains were burned and her property confiscated. Vives' father was delivered in 1524 "to the secular arm" by the Inquisition, which usually meant death. This evidence indicates that Vives was of Jewish origin and that he must have been fully aware of this through the fate of his parents.

Vives studied Latin and Greek at Valencia and then, in 1509, went to the University of Paris. He found the scholasticism taught there sterile, and later bitterly attacked his studies and teachers. He said the university was like "an eighty-year-old lady, sick, senile, and in imminent danger of death." Vives' first major work, *Adversus pseudodialecticos* (1520), was a strong attack upon the school. In 1512 he moved to Bruges where he studied and taught children of influential families. In 1517 he began teaching at the new University of Louvain and became a close friend of Erasmus, whom he had long admired. The religious struggles in the Low Countries, Erasmus' departure for Basle, and the condition of the university led Vives to go to England, where he was immediately received by the humanists and by the court. Vives was offered a post at Alcalá, but refused to return to Spain. Instead he became a professor at Oxford. Political problems involving Henry VIII and Catherine of Aragon finally led to Vives' dismissal. He returned a bitter and poor man to Bruges, where he wrote his major works in isolation and discontent.

Vives' writings include criticisms of scholasticism, reform of education, the classics, social problems, philosophy, and religion. His most famous works, extremely popular in the 16th century, were his commentaries on Saint Augustine (1522); *De Anima et Vita* (1538); *Dialogi: Exercitatio Lingae Latinae* (1538; trans. W.H.D. Rouse, *Scenes of School and College Life*, 1931); *De Institutione feminae Christianae* (1524; trans. R. Hyrde, *The Instruction of a Christen Woman*, 1541); *Introductio ad Sapientiam* (1524; trans. R. Morison, *An Introduction to Wysedome*, 1540); and *De Veritate Fidei* (posthumous, 1543). Vives was the first advocate of secular education and state, rather than Church, social welfare. His philosophical concern was not to find ultimate truth (since he believed that metaphysics could only yield conjectures), but rather a basis for human conduct. He was the first modern to investigate human psychology empirically, and developed an early form of naturalism. Though many of his writings deal with Christian religious subjects (including a criticism, mild for the time, of Judaism in *De Veritate Fidei*), he was not concerned with doctrinal or institutional elements of Christianity, but mainly with morality. Like Erasmus, he advocated a nontheological religion as a way of life. Vives' philosophical-ethical religion may represent a Marrano compromise with Christianity, interpreting it as an ethic rather than as a set of dogmas.

BIBLIOGRAPHY: C.G. Norena, *Juan Luis Vives: A Humanistic Conception of Philosophical Knowledge* (Thesis, San Diego, 1967), incl. bibl.

[Richard H. Popkin]

VIZHNITSA (Rom. **Vijnita**; Yid. **Vizhnits**), town in Chernovtsy district, Ukraine. Before World War I Vizhnitsa belonged to Austria, and between the world wars to Romania. The town derives its fame from the local ḥasidic rabbis (see hasidic dynasty *Vizhnitz). Jews began to settle in the town under Moldavian rule in the mid-18th century. In 1774, under Austrian administration, there were 60 Jewish families (191 persons); by 1782 there were 61 families, and in 1807 there were 64. Later many Jewish settlers were attracted by the Vizhnitsa rabbis and by 1900 there were 4,738 Jews and in 1930, 2,666. A *ḥevra kaddisha* existed from 1768. After the Austrian annexation the Jews were subject to restrictions and persecutions; 19 families were expelled in 1774 on the claim that they did not contribute to the town's agricultural development. In 1789 the authorities ordered the expulsion of all the Jews for the same reason, but this order was not carried out entirely.

During World War I the town was nearly destroyed. The Jews fled to Vienna and some did not return. The rabbi at that time, Israel Hager of the *Kosov dynasty, moved to *Oradea, where he established his court. Vizhnitsa now ceased to be a ḥasidic center.

Under early Austrian rule the community was affiliated with the *Chernovtsy congregation and became independent only in the mid-19th century. By 1888 there were already eight prayer houses, classed according to the congregants' professions. There was a large yeshivah, and in 1921 a Hebrew elementary school was founded. Between the world wars Zionist youth and adult groups were active. Several descendants of the ḥasidic dynasty settled in Israel, where they established yeshivot and ḥasidic centers in Haifa and Bene Berak. From 1941 the Jewish community suffered drastically, and in August of that year 2,800 Jews were deported to death camps. About 800 remained alive and most of them immigrated to Israel.

In 2005, the city had a Jewish community center.

BIBLIOGRAPHY: N.M. Gelber, in: H. Gold (ed.), *Geschichte der Juden in der Bukowina*, 1 (1958), 89–90; *ibid.*, 2 (1962), 120–2.

[Yehouda Marton]

VIZHNITZ, ḥasidic dynasty, founded by MENAHEM MENDEL BEN ḤAYYIM HAGER (1830–1884). After the death of his father, the *ẓaddik* of Kosov (1854), Menahem Mendel began to lead the community of Vizhnitz (Vizhnitsa) where he also served as *av bet din*. He became famous as a miracle worker and a distributor of amulets. He headed *Kolel Vizhnitz and Maramuresh, a fund for the poor in Ereẓ Israel. He also attempted to settle the dispute between R. Ḥayyim *Halberstam of Zanz (Sandz) and the sons of R. Israel of *Ruzhin. His book *Ẓemaḥ Ẓaddik* (1885) was written in the spirit of ḥasidic Kabbalah.

His oldest son BARUCH (1845–1893) served as a ḥasidic rabbi in Vizhnitz for eight years, and gathered around him many Ḥasidim. A collection of his writings was published as *Imrei Barukh* (1912). Seven of his nine sons and three of his sons-in-law were ḥasidic rabbis, a fact which contributed to divisions among the Ḥasidim and gave rise to controversy. He was succeeded by his son ISRAEL (1860–1938). R. Israel was very popular and had thousands of ḥasidic followers. He founded a big yeshivah called Bet Israel and moved to Grosswardein (Hung. Nagyvarad) which became a center of Ḥasidism in Hungary. His publications include *Ahavat Yisrael* (1943) and *Or Yisrael* (1938). Other sons of R. Baruch with many followers included ḤAYYIM OF ITINIA (1864–1935) and PHINEHAS OF BORSA (d. 1941). The successors of the Vizhnitz dynasty in Bene-Berak, Israel, the sons of R. Israel, include: ḤAYYIM (1881–1979); whose teachings are in *Kunteres ha-Likkutim* (1949); ELIEZER (1889–1946), author of *Dammesek Eliezer* (1949); and BARUCH, of Siret-Vizhnitz (1895–1972). The *Ẓaddikim* of Vizhnitz were active in spreading Torah learning; in Israel they established yeshivot and housing for their Ḥasidim.

BIBLIOGRAPHY: H. Cahana, *Even Shetiyyah* (1930); Y.H. Schwartz, *Evel Yisrael* (1936); M.A.H. Horowitz, *Zikhron Yisrael* (1937); I. Alfasi, *Tiferet she-be-Malkhut* (1961).

[Avraham Rubinstein]

VLADECK, BARUCH CHARNEY (1886–1938), U.S. journalist, civic leader, and public official; brother of Daniel *Charney and Shmuel *Niger. Born in Dukor, near Minsk, Belorussia, Vladeck abandoned religious study in his teens in favor of political action. A lifelong socialist, he had been a revolutionary in Russia, but became a moderate in the United States. Between 1904 and 1908, he agitated extensively for the Jewish Labor *Bund, and was imprisoned three times. He wrote Yiddish poetry and prose. In 1908, he immigrated to the United States, becoming city editor of the *Jewish Daily Forward* in 1916, and business manager of that newspaper from 1918. From 1918 to 1921, he sat on the board of aldermen in New York City as a Socialist member. Long active in the public housing movement, Vladeck was appointed to the New York City Housing Authority in 1934. In 1938, he served on the City Council, leading a coalition of its pro-La Guardia members. President of ORT from 1932 to 1938 and chairman of the Jewish Labor Committee from 1934 to 1938, Vladeck was an opponent of Communist influence in the labor movement and was influential in helping to align Jewish labor with other segments of the Jewish community.

BIBLIOGRAPHY: M. Epstein, *Profiles of Eleven* (1965), 323–56; J. Herling, in: AJYB, 41 (1939), 79–93, includes portrait; AJYB, *Index to Volumes 1–50* (1967), 348; Rejzen, Leksikon, 1 (1926), 999–1001; A. Liesen, *Zikhroynes un Bilder* (1954), 295–311; LNYL, 3 (1960), 469–75, incl. bibl.

[Franklin Jonas]

VLADIMIR VOLYNSKI (formerly **Lodomira**, Pol. **Wlodzimierz**; in Jewish sources: **Lodmer**, **Ladmir**, or **Ludmir**), city in Volhynia district, Ukraine. Jews from *Kiev, *Khazaria, and other eastern communities settled in the city in the 12th century. They established an important station there on the trade route between eastern and western Europe, which was subsequently visited by Jewish merchants from *Ashkenaz. The Jewish community was destroyed by Tatars in the 1240s but it was renewed on a small scale in the early 15th century under Grand Duke Witold of Lithuania. An organized community was founded in the early 16th century and it developed rapidly after the Polish annexation of *Volhynia (1569).

In the charter of privileges given to the city in 1570 by King Sigismund II Augustus, the Jews were granted equal rights with gentile citizens. During the 16th century the Jews of Vladimir Volynski traded at the fairs in Lublin, Poznan, and Cracow, where they sold furs, woolen cloth, and wax. The richer Jews engaged in estate-leasing and tax-farming. From the middle of the 16th century several famous rabbis lived in Vladimir Volynski, e.g., *Isaac b. Bezalel, who served from 1547 to 1570, Menahem Isaiah b. Isaac (known as Menahem-Mendel R. Avigdors; 1591), who later became rabbi of Cracow (d. 1599), and the talmudist *Isaac ben Samuel ha-Levi (1580–1646), who was born in Vladimir Volynski. The outstanding talmudist and author, Yom-Tov Lipmann *Heller, was rabbi of the community from 1634 to 1643.

The community suffered greatly during the *Chmielnicki massacres (1648–49) in which many Jews were murdered. After repeated attacks in 1653 and 1658, the heads of the community were forced to borrow large sums to save the Jews from impoverishment. Their economic situation improved in the late 17th century. In 1700 Augustus II awarded Fishel Lewkowicz of Vladimir Volynski the title of "royal agent and purveyor and official secretary for the Council of the Four Lands." In 1765 1,327 Jews paid the poll tax.

The economic crisis which befell the Polish kingdom in its last years affected the Jewish population in Vladimir Volynski. By 1784 there were only 340 Jews in the city. In 1795 it was annexed by Russia. In the 19th century the Jewish population increased, numbering 3,930 in 1847 and 5,854 (66% of the total) in 1897. They traded in grain and lumber, and engaged in shopkeeping, tailoring, hatmaking, and shoemaking. The hasidic movement became influential in the community, especially under the direction of Moses Solomon Karliner and the Maid of *Ludomir.

There were 5,917 Jews there in 1921 comprising 51% of the population, and by 1931, 10,665 (44%). In 1926, 84% of the businesses were in Jewish hands. There were *Tarbut, *Beth Jacob, and Yavneh schools. The Jews of Vladimir Volynski organized *self-defense against the attacks of May 1923, and in the 1930s they protested vigorously against the antisemitic boycott. In the city council elections of 1929, 12 of the 24 seats were won by Jews.

[Arthur Cygielman]

Holocaust Period

When the war broke out between Germany and Poland on Sept. 1, 1939, thousands of Jews from western Poland sought refuge in the city, bringing the number of Jews in the city to 25,000. When the city passed to Soviet rule (1939–41), a unique effort was made by the Jews of the city to guarantee a Hebrew education for the children. The Tarbut leaders successfully acquired the local authorities agreement to run a Hebrew language school, on condition that all religious studies be removed from the program. However, the school only functioned for two months for in November 1939 the regional Soviet authorities in Rovno intervened and the language of instruction became Yiddish. In the summer of 1940 many Zionist leaders and refugees were exiled to the Soviet interior. The Germans entered on June 25, 1941. On July 5, 150 Jews were rounded up by the Germans and Ukrainians and murdered in the prison courtyard. A *Judenrat was established in 1941, headed by Rabbi Morgenstern. When he died two months later, his post was filled by a lawyer, Weiler. Weiler refused to hand over the victims to the Germans and committed suicide together with his family. In August–December 1941 the Germans continued to murder the Jews, disposing of their victims in mass graves in the prison courtyard. On Feb. 27, 1942, 250 Jews were taken for forced labor to the Kiev area. On April 13, 1942 a ghetto was set up in two sections: one for skilled craftsmen, nicknamed by the Jews "the ghetto of life", and a second ghetto for the non-productive, called the "ghetto of the dead." They contained altogether about 22,000 Jews. In the summer of 1942 some young people made attempts to contact the partisans operating in the vicinity. On Sept. 1, 1942, an *Aktion* ("action") began, lasting two weeks, in which 18,000 Jews were murdered. Four thousand Jews were killed in the prison courtyard and 14,000 in pits prepared in the Piatydni area. Following this *Aktion*, the area of the ghetto, now reduced in size, contained only 4,000 persons. Leib Kudish, who collaborated fully with the Germans, was placed at the head of the Judenrat. On Nov. 13, 1942, another *Aktion* began, lasting several weeks, following which only 1,500 Jews were left alive and registered while a group of "illegals" continued to exist. During the last *Aktion* an armed group of young Jews took up a fortified position in a bunker near Cygielnia, but they were discovered by the Germans, and 13 fell in the fight. In 1943 the Germans continued in their hunt-down of "illegals" i.e., those who did not possess work permits. The victims were shot in prison. On Dec. 13, 1943, the last of the Jewish community was liquidated, and many of those who tried to escape were killed by Ukrainian peasants or members of the Polish underground Armia Krajowa. The city was freed from the Germans on July 22, 1944, at which time only a few dozen Jews were found alive. A society of former residents of the city functions in Israel.

BIBLIOGRAPHY: Halpern, Pinkas, index; N.N. Hannover, *Yeven Meẓulah* (1966), 65, 66; R. Mahler, *Yidn in Amolikn Poyln in Likht fun Tsifern* (1958), index; E. Ringelblum, in: *Miesięcznik żydowski*, no. 11/12 (1933), 233; idem, *Projekty i proby przewarstwowienia żydow w epoce stanislawowskiej* (1934), 35–36; B. Mark, *Di Geshikhte fun Yidn in Poyln* (1957), index; M. Tikhomirov, *Drevniye russkiye goroda* (1946), index; B. Wasiutyński, *Ludność żydowska w Polsce w wiekach XIX i XX* (1930), 81, 82, 84, 88; I. Schiper, *Dzieje handlu żydowskiego na ziemiach polskich* (1937), index; H.H. Ben Sasson, *Hagut ve-Hanhagah* (1959), 56, 136, 138, 163, 178–9.

[Aharon Weiss]

VLADIVOSTOK, city in Maritime Territory, formerly Russian S.F.S.R., now Russian Federation. Jews began to arrive in Vladivostok at the close of the 19th century, forming part of those exiled to the Russian Far East regions. In 1897 there were 290 Jews in Vladivostok (1 percent of the total population), representing an organized community administered by the Zionists until the Soviet occupation in 1922. In 1926 the community numbered 1,124 (1 percent of the total population). Although it is known that with the development of the city and the growth of the Jewish settlement of the nearby region of *Birobidzhan, the number of Jews increased, in 1970 no information was available concerning any organized Jewish life in Vladivostok. In 2005 the original synagogue was again in use and a Sunday school was being run by the community.

[Yehuda Slutsky]

VOET, ANDRIES (1907–1982) U.S. physical chemist. Born in Amsterdam, Voet was chief chemist at an inks works in Hilversum until he went to the U.S. He joined the General Printing Ink Corporation and then (from 1943) the J.M. Huber Corporation in Borger, Texas, heading their physical research from 1950. He was a consultant to the U.S. Industrial Intelligence Agency in Germany (1945). Voet was an authority on the theory and practical applications of printing inks, carbon black, pigments, resins and their reactions with the surfaces on which these are imprinted. He took out over one hundred patents. His book *Ink and Paper in the Printing Process* (1952) is a classic in this field.

[Michael Denman (2nd ed.)]

VOGEL, ARTHUR ISRAEL (1905–1966), British organic chemist. Born and educated in London, he spent his career at Woolwich Polytechnic (London) from 1932. In 1934 he became head of the department of chemistry. He was the author of textbooks known and used throughout the world: *Elementary Practical Chemistry* (1936), *Textbook of Qualitative Chemical Analysis* (1937), *Textbook of Quantitative Chemical Analysis* (1939), *A Textbook of Practical Organic Chemistry* (1948), and *Elementary Practical Organic Chemistry* (1957), each of which ran to several editions.

VOGEL, DAVID (1891–1944), Hebrew poet and writer. Born in Satanov, Russia, he spent his youth in Vilna and Lvov and in 1912 settled in Vienna. Upon the outbreak of World War I, Vogel was imprisoned in Austrian detention camps as an enemy (Russian) national. He was released in 1916 but thereafter lived a solitary life, finding refuge in the seclusion to which he had already given expression in his youthful Hebrew diary, and which is the cornerstone of all his poetry.

His poems were published from 1918 onward in Hebrew journals in various countries, and the only volume of poems he ever published, *Lifnei ha-Sha'ar ha-Afel* ("Before the Dark Gate"), appeared in Vienna in 1923. Vogel settled in Paris in 1925, immigrated to Palestine in 1929, but left a year later. After traveling to Warsaw, Vienna, and Berlin he returned in 1932 to his beloved Paris. During these years he published his stories *Be-Veit ha-Marpe* (1927; "In the Sanatorium"); a novel *Ḥayyei Nissu'im* (1929–30; "Married Life"); *Le-Nokhaḥ ha-Yam* (1932 34; "Facing the Sea"), and prepared a second volume of poems for publication which he did not live to publish. When World War II broke out Vogel was incarcerated in French detention camps as an enemy national (now an Austrian). These experiences are described in the manuscript of his diary (in Yiddish). After the capitulation of France, Vogel was released (1941) and lived in Hauteville near Lyons. There he was arrested by the Nazis in February 1944, and most likely perished in a concentration camp.

Vogel's poetry is completely introspective and describes a dream world, disjointed and purposeless. The main subjects are love, lost childhood, and fear of oblivion, which fuse together to create a sense of alienation and isolation. The constant presence of death becomes the basic sense of existence. The poems are extremely restrained in tone but their lack of pathos serves only to intensify the dread. Vogel's imagery is startling and elliptic and most of his poems are written in free rhythm, without ordered rhyming. Their framework appears loose: unequal sections, and only vague hints as to the affinity between them. Both the external and the inner-psychological plots of his prose works are developed within a framework of time and a given society. *Be-Veit ha-Marpe* creates an atmosphere of despair and aimlessness against a background of life in a tuberculosis sanatorium (Vogel and his wife were both stricken with this disease). *Ḥayyei Nissu'im*, a psychological novel set in Vienna after World War I, depicts a pathological love affair between a Jew and a gentile baroness. Vogel's stories generally were favorably received but had little influence.

His poetry, on the other hand, aroused varied and conflicting reactions, reflecting the changing trends in Hebrew literary criticism. His first poems already won him admirers (among them J.Ḥ. *Brenner), but also dismayed more traditionalist critics (including Ḥ.N. Bialik), who found them entirely illogical. In the 1930s and 1940s he was almost totally ignored as a literary figure but was "rediscovered" in the 1950s. Unlike his early admirers who spoke of his "gentle delicacy," the new critics pointed out the power of his allusive expression and regarded him as an important forerunner of Hebrew modernism.

His complete poems have been published, with an introduction and bibliography by Dan Pagis: *Kol Shirei David Vogel* (1966). Since the 1980s there has been a growing interest in the works of Vogel, who is considered by literary critics to be one of the seminal innovators of modern Hebrew prose. Menaḥem Peri rediscovered and published (1986) the novel *Ḥayyei Nissu'im* (English translation: *Married Life*, 1988 and 1998) and *Taḥanot Kavot* (novellas and diaries, 1990; *Extinguished Stations*) in his series Ha-Sifriah ha-Ḥadashah. The collected poems were published in 1971, 1975 and 1998. An English translation of the novella *Facing the Sea* is included in A. Lelchuk and G. Shaked (ed.), *Eight Great Hebrew Short Stories* (1983). Vogel's diaries and autobiographical notes

1912–1922 and 1941/42 were published in German as *Das Ende der Tage*, with a forward by Amir Eshel. A list of other works translated into English appeared in Goell, Bibliography, 56, and further information concerning translations is available at the website ITHL at iwww.thl.org.il.

ADD. BIBLIOGRAPHY: G. Shaked, "A Viennese Author Who Wrote in Hebrew: D. Vogel," in: *Modern Hebrew Literature*, 12:1 (1986), 20–27; G. Shaked, *Ha-Sipporet ha-Ivrit*, 3 (1988), 93–103; M. Peri, *"Ibbed Fogel et Fogel,"* in: *Taḥanot Kavot* (1990), 327–50; A. Feinberg, "I Have Without Doubt Lost This War: David Vogel," in: *Modern Hebrew Literature*, 6 (1991), 38–40; G. Shaked, "D. Vogel: A Hebrew Novelist in Vienna," in: *Austrians and Jews* (1992), 97–111; G. Abramson, "Poet of the Dark Gate: The Poetry of D. Vogel," in: *Jewish Book Annual*, 50 (1992), 128–42; A. Komem, *Ha-Ofel ve-ha-Pele: Iyyunim bi-Yẓirato shel David Fogel* (2001).

[Dan Pagis]

VOGEL, SIR JULIUS (1835–1899), prime minister of New Zealand. Born in London, Vogel was attracted to Australia by the gold-rush and settled in Melbourne in 1852. Unable to make a fortune in the mines, he immigrated to New Zealand in 1861, became a journalist, and edited the colony's first daily newspaper, the *Otago Daily Times*. In the following year he was elected to the Otago provincial council. In 1863 Vogel became a member of the house of representatives where his mastery of financial issues brought him to the fore. He was made colonial treasurer in 1869 and acquired great prestige by successfully negotiating a loan with the British government for the construction of roads and railways. In 1873 Vogel became prime minister and set about reducing the autonomy of the New Zealand provinces with the intention of abolishing the regional system and strengthening the hand of the central government. This policy lost him considerable popularity and in 1875, while on a visit to London to negotiate fresh loans, he resigned. He was briefly prime minister again in the following year, and from 1876 to 1881 was agent-general of New Zealand in London. There he succeeded in persuading the British government to pass the Colonial Stock Act, thereby allowing for the inscription of colonial loans. Vogel returned to New Zealand in 1884 and became colonial treasurer for a second time. However, bitter criticism of his policy of public borrowing forced him to resign in 1887 and he left for London shortly afterward. He took no further part in New Zealand politics. Vogel was knighted in 1875, and died in East Molesley, Surrey. In 1889 Vogel published a novel, *Anno Domini 2000; or, Women's Destiny,* in which he predicted that women would rule and poverty would be abolished.

BIBLIOGRAPHY: JC (March 18, 1899); P.H. Emden, *Jews of Britain* (1943), 440–3; L.M. Goldman, *The History of the Jews in New Zealand* (1960). **ADD. BIBLIOGRAPHY:** ODNB online; R. Dalziel, "Julius Vogel," in: *Dictionary of New Zealand Biography*; R.M. Burdon, *The Life and Times of Sir Julius Vogel* (1948); R. Dalziel, *Julius Vogel, Business Politician* (1986).

VOGEL, KAREL (1897–1961), Czech-English sculptor. Born in Bohemia, educated in Prague, Vogel fled to England in 1939. He gained success as a portraitist and executed a number of public commissions. He also did a series of small nudes in bronze which showed the influence of Rodin. Vogel worked at London's Camberwell School of Arts and Crafts, where he was head of sculpture. His work is in important museums in London and in Prague.

VOGEL, SIMON (1850–1917), Hungarian soldier. Born in Karczag, Vogel joined the Austro-Hungarian army as a private but was selected for the officers' school and fought in the Bosnian campaign. Teaching at the Kassa cadet academy, Vogel was introduced to Emperor Francis Joseph I and was promoted to colonel with command of a regiment. He was made governor of Sarajevo in 1903 and represented the Austrian army at the marriage of King Alphonso XIII of Spain in 1906. In 1909 he became a major general and retired soon afterward.

VOGEL, WLADIMIR (1896–1984), composer. Born in Moscow, Vogel studied piano and theory privately, and was influenced by Scriabin, whom he saw performing at a concert. During World War I he was interned in the Urals and later went to Berlin, where in the 1920s he studied with Thiessen and Busoni. In 1935 he settled in Switzerland and taught composition privately. After World War II he became an honorary member of the Academia Sta. Cecilia in Rome and an ordinary member of the Akademie der Kuenste in Berlin. He won several prizes, including the composer's prize of the Schweizerischer Tonkűnstlerverein. Vogel experimented a great deal with the use of "speaking choirs," being influenced by Communist agit-prop, melodrama, and Expressionist music. He wrote a number of dramatically impressive oratorios and cantatas using this technique, such as *Wagadus Untergang durch die Eitelkeit* (1930) and *Thyl Claes, fils de Kolldraeger* (1938–45). Starting with his Violin Concerto (1937) Vogel used 12-note technique. In some of his later works he was inspired by architectural, pictorial, and graphic images (*Inspiré par Jean Arp*, 1965; *Graphique*, 1976; *Verstrebungen*, 1977).

BIBLIOGRAPHY: NG²; M.Geering and P. Ronner (eds.), *Wladimir Vogel (1896–1984): Verzeichnis der musikalischen Werke* (1992).

[Claude Abravanel / Yulia Kreinin (2nd ed.)]

°**VOGELSANG, KARL VON** (1818–1890), Austrian conservative clerical publicist, and antisemite. Vogelsang was born in Liegnitz (Legnica), Silesia, and studied jurisprudence. A Protestant by upbringing, Vogelsang embraced Catholicism like many other citizens in Mecklenburg after the crisis of the 1848 revolution. In 1850 he therefore lost his position. In the 1860s he and his family moved to Austria. He finally settled in Vienna in 1875 and became the editor of *Vaterland*, an ultra-conservative and clerical daily, the ideological organ of the antisemitic Christian Social movement. His first year was devoted, inter alia, to attacking the minister of justice, Julius *Glaser (a converted Jew), and defending the striking Brno textile workers (many of whose employers were Jewish). A fierce opponent of liberalism and capitalism, which he blamed for all the ills of society, he identified modern Jewry with capitalism, the disrupter of the ideal Christian, feudal, corporative, social fabric. Though not a racial antisemite, he prepared the grounds for modern conservative antisemitism by furnishing it with a wide social appeal: castigating the insolent "*Judenpresse*," despising godless and greedy "*Reformjuden*," and thundering against the "*Judenboerse*." The demagogic talent and later mayor of Vienna, Karl Lueger, took over Vogelsang's political objectives and popularized them. Notwithstanding his antisemitic ideology, Vogelsang was highly respected by the Austrian Conservatives even after the Shoah; in 1990 a special Austrian stamp recalled the 100th anniversary of his death.

BIBLIOGRAPHY: P.G.J. Pulzer, Rise of Political Anti-Semitism in Germany and Austria (1964), index; D. van Arkel, *Anti-Semitism in Austria*, (Ph.D. thesis, Leiden University, 1967), 56–66. **ADD. BIBLIOGRAPHY:** E. Bader (ed.), *Karl v. Vogelsang…* (1990); W. Pollak, *Tausend Jahre Oesterreich* (1973), 250–55; *Christliche Demokratie*, 2 (1991–92).

[Albert Lichtblau (2nd ed.)]

VOGELSTEIN, family in Germany, active in the Reform-Liberal movement.

HEINEMANN VOGELSTEIN (1841–1911) was rabbi at Pilsen and Stettin (Szczecin) and founder and president of the Association of Liberal Rabbis and a vice president of the Association for Liberal Judaism (Vereinigung fuer das Liberale *Judentum). He published a prayer book (1894–96) eliminating references to the restoration of Jewish nationhood. A strong anti-Zionist, he was among the *Protestrabbiner in 1897 and published in 1906 a pamphlet *Der Zionismus, eine Gefahr fuer die gedeihliche Entwickelung des Judentums*. He also wrote *Kampf zwischen Priestern und Leviten seit den Tagen Ezechiels* (1889).

His son HERMANN VOGELSTEIN (1870–1942) occupied rabbinical posts at Oppeln (Opole), Koenigsberg, and Breslau. In 1938 he emigrated to the United States. His writings include *Die Landwirtschaft in Palaestina zur Zeit der Misnah – Der Getreidebau* (1894); *Militaerisches aus der israelitischen Koenigszeit* (1906); *Zur Vorgeschichte des Gesetzes ueber die Verhaeltnisse der Juden vom 23. Juli 1847* (1909). With Paul *Rieger he wrote the standard history of the Jews in Rome (*Geschichte der Juden in Rom*, 2 vols., 1895–96) of which a revised edition in English (by M. Hadas) appeared in the Jewish Communities Series of the Jewish Publication Society of America (JPSA; 1940).

Another son of Heinemann, Ludwig *Vogelstein, became a metal magnate and philanthropist.

THEODOR VOGELSTEIN (1880–1957) also a son of Heinemann, was a banker, industrialist, and cofounder of the Democratic Party of the German Weimar Republic. During the Nazi regime he emigrated to Paris where he later died.

JULIE VOGELSTEIN-BRAUN (1883–1971) a daughter of Heinemann, was a writer. She edited Otto Braun's writings after his death (*Schriften eines Frueh-Vollendeten*, 1920), and wrote *Geist und Gestalt der abendlaendischen Kunst* (1957) and *Was niemals stirbt* (1966).

MAX VOGELSTEIN (1901–) son of Hermann, served as rabbi in Frankfurt on the Main and Koblenz (1935–38), and taught at the Jewish Teachers' Academy in Berlin (1934–35). In 1938 he emigrated to the United States. He made a special study of biblical chronology, on which he published, among other works, *Fertile Soil: A Political History of Israel…* (1957).

VOGELSTEIN, LUDWIG (1871–1934), U.S. business executive, philanthropist, and communal leader. Vogelstein, who was born in Pilsen, Czechoslovakia, went to the U.S. in 1896 as the representative of the metal firm of Aaron Hirsch & Sohn of Halberstadt. He later founded his own metal-dealing firm, which subsequently merged with the American Metal Co., Ltd. (1920). In 1924 Vogelstein became that firm's first vice president and later chairman of its executive board. He also founded and developed several large mining and metal companies in the U.S. and Canada. A vigorous supporter of Reform Judaism, Vogelstein predicted the eventual merging of all movements of Judaism. He was a staunch anti-Zionist. Extremely active in Jewish communal life, Vogelstein served as chairman of the Union of American Hebrew Congregations; trustee-at-large for the support of Jewish Philanthropic societies; vice president of the World Union for Progressive Judaism; governor of Hebrew Union College; director of the Jewish Publication Society; and president of Temple Beth-El (New York City), and a trustee after its merger with Emanu-El.

°VOGÜÉ, CHARLES EUGENE MELCHIOR, COMTE DE (1829–1916), French architect and archaeologist. De Vogüé was born in Paris into one of the oldest families of the French aristocracy. In 1853/54 he went on research trips in Ereẓ Israel and Syria, discovering many ruined cities in Hauran and Northern Syria with well-preserved remains. His books *Mélanges d'architecture orientale* (1866) and *L'architecture civile et religieuse du Ier au Vieme siècle dans la Syrie centrale* (2 vols., 1866–77) opened a new chapter in the architectural history of the Roman-Byzantine period in Ereẓ Israel and Syria. De Vogüé also published sketches of the Temple enclosure, *Le Temple de Jérusalem* (1865–67), including a restoration of the Second Temple which is still of value today. The inscriptions found on his travels are translated and clarified in *Inscriptions sémitiques* (1869–77). After the establishment of the Third Republic he became the French ambassador in Constantinople (1871) and Vienna (1875–79).

BIBLIOGRAPHY: *Florilegium: ou, Recueil de travaux d'érudition, dédiés à … de Vogüé…* (1909).

[Michael Avi-Yonah]

VOHRYZEK, JOSEF (1926–1998), Czech literary critic, translator, and prose writer. Born in Prague, Vohryzek was sent by his parents (who perished in the Holocaust) to Sweden in 1940, where he lived until 1950. In 1956 he graduated from Charles University in Prague, where he studied Czech and literary sciences. In his articles in the literary monthly *Květen* ("May"), where he worked from 1956 to 1985, he refused to adopt the Marxist-Communist dogma. In 1959 he had lost his job at the Institute for Czech literature of the Czechoslovak Academy of Sciences because of his criticism of the Communist Party's policies. Vohryzek worked as a translator (especially from Swedish – Lindgren, Bergman, Strinberg, Ibsen) and an editor. After 1970 he was forced to do only manual jobs. He signed Charter 77 and became its spokesperson in 1987. A collection of his articles from the 1960s was published as *Kniha Josefova* (1986 in *samizdat* "The Book of Josef"; in 1995 as *Literární kritiky* ("Literary Criticism")). His experimental prose work *Chodec* ("The Walker," 1964) was inspired by his stay in Sweden. After 1989 he was fully occupied with literary criticism and with the issue of antisemitism. He wrote excellent critical works on the books of J. Kovtun; I.B. *Singer; S. *Wiesenthal; and V. Černý.

BIBLIOGRAPHY: J. Lehár, *Česká literatura od počátků k dnešku* (1998); *Slovník českých spisovatelů* (1982); *Slovník českých spisovatelů* (2000).

[Milos Pojar (2nd ed.)]

VOLCHKO (Pol. **Wolf**, **Wólczko**, also known as **Tsolner**; d. 1441?), Polish merchant, revenue officer, banker, purveyor to the king, and founder of settlements. Although the date of his birth is unknown, he originated in the town of Drogobych. A wealthy Jew, he became the banker and official agent (*Officialis Noster*) of Ladislaus II Jagello (1386–1434), king of Poland. Volchko was very successful in financial affairs, tax-collection, commerce, and the founding of settlements (*locator*). The earliest evidence of his activities is a document (1404) which names him as executor of a large sum of money in the king's name for the town of *Lvov (Lemberg). For the next 30 years his affairs also involved the lease of the king's and the town's revenues in Lvov, and those of the customs stations of *Chelm and the salt mines of Drogobych. In addition to granting credit to the king and his court, Volchko also lent money to members of the feudal aristocracy with the king's consent. In 1419 he built himself a magnificent house in the Jewish quarter of Lvov which, at the close of the 16th century, finally became the property of the *Nachmanovich family who later built a synagogue in it. Volchko also engaged in the import of spices, silk, furs, and English cloth as well as in the export of wax. In 1423 the king granted him administrative rights and jurisdiction over the village of Werbiz (near *Sambor), which he developed most successfully on the strength of privileges similar to those of the *Magdeburg Law. To show his satisfaction, the king extended Volchko's rights to other estates in the vicinity. In letters-patent of the king in 1425, however, it was hinted that Volchko converted to Christianity. Volchko gave cause for disappointment in this hope and thus gave Church officials pretext to demand his removal from the estates on the basis that it was forbidden for a Jew to have jurisdiction over Christian settlers. Until 1432 Volchko succeeded in establishing more villages but in time he was compelled to retire from these activities and his rights were taken over by Christians.

BIBLIOGRAPHY: Lemberg, Archivum, *Akta grodzkie i Ziemskie*, 2 (1870), nos. 42, 45, 46, 49, 53, 55, 58;12 (1887), nos. 219, 821, 1096; 19 (1906), no. 2820; I. Schiper, *Studya nad stosunkami gospodarczymi żydów w Polsce podczas średniowiecza* (1911), index, s.v. *Wołczko Czolner*; M. Balaban, *Miscellanaea. Dwa przycznyki do stosuknow Jagielly żydami Iwowskimi* (n.d.).

[Arthur Cygielman]

VOLCKER, PAUL A. (1927–), U.S. economist. Volcker, who was born in Cape May, N.J., was educated at Princeton, Harvard, and the London School of Economics. He began at the New York Federal Reserve Bank as a summer research assistant in 1949, returned as an economist in the research department in 1952, and became a special assistant in the securities department in 1955. Two years later he became a financial economist at Chase Manhattan Bank and returned there in 1965 as a vice president. He served as undersecretary of the treasury for international monetary affairs from 1969 to 1974. He played an important role in the decision surrounding the American decision to suspend gold convertibility in 1971, which resulted in the collapse of the Bretton Woods system. In general Volcker acted as a moderating influence on policy, advocating the pursuit of an international solution to monetary problems. From 1979 to 1987, Volcker served as chairman of the Federal Reserve System, under presidents Jimmy Carter and Ronald Reagan, and president of the Federal Reserve Bank of New York from 1975 to 1990. Volcker's tenure at the Fed was credited with ending the United States inflation crisis of the early 1980s by constricting the money supply through a sharp increase in interest rates. Inflation, at 9 percent in 1980, was lowered to 3.2 percent by 1983. This was predictably accompanied by a decrease in growth, a recession, and by an increase in unemployment, which rose to the highest levels since World War II. When the inflation was resolved and interest rates were lowered, unemployment and domestic economic growth returned to their normal levels. In the late 1990s Volcker headed a panel that looked to mediate a dispute between Swiss banks and Holocaust survivors. The panel was created by the World Jewish Restitution Organization and the Swiss Bankers Association in 1996 to investigate the dormant accounts. The Jewish groups had accused the Swiss banks of hoarding the wealth of Holocaust victims. Hundreds of auditors pored over bank records for three years, identifying nearly 54,000 accounts that may have belonged to victims of the Nazis. The commission's report lent credence to long-standing charges that the Swiss banks had turned a deaf ear to the needs of Jewish depositors while responding to the orders issued by officials in Nazi Germany. The commission also concluded that it saw no reason to revise the $1.25 billion settlement that Swiss banks agreed to in 1998 to pay Holocaust-era claims. In April 2004 Volcker was assigned by the United Nations to research possible corruption in the Iraqi Oil for Food program. In a report summarizing the research,

Volcker accused Kojo Annan, son of United Nations secretary general Kofi Annan, and the Swiss company Cotecna Inspection, Annan's employer, of trying to conceal their relationship. The report accused more than 2,200 companies and prominent politicians of colluding with Saddam Hussein's regime to bilk the humanitarian mission of $1.8 billion. It blamed shoddy management for allowing the corruption to go on for years. The investigators found that companies and individuals from 66 countries paid illegal kickbacks using a variety of methods, and those paying illegal oil surcharges came from, or were registered in, 40 countries. Volcker maintained his interests in the business world. He served on the board of the Nestlé Corporation from 1988 on and was chairman of the Washington-based Group of Thirty.

[Stewart Kampel (2nd ed.)]

VOLHYNIA (Rus. **Volyn**; Pol. **Wolyá**), historic region in N.W. Ukraine. Under czarist rule most of it was incorporated into the province of Volhynia. Today, the greatest part of it is divided up into the oblasts of *Zhitomir, *Rovno, and Volyn in the northwest part of Ukraine. The earliest information on Jews in Volhynia is in a report on the mourning of the Jews of the town of *Vladimir Volynski over the death of the prince of Volhynia, Vladimir Vasilkovich (d. 1288). However, there is reason to believe that there was already a Jewish settlement there in the 12th century. The Jews continued to live in Volhynia after it was annexed by *Lithuania. Among the Jewish communities whose members were granted rights of residence by the Lithuanian Grand Duke Witold were those of Vladimir-Volynski and *Lutsk.

During the first half of the 15th century, a wealthy Jew leased properties in the town of Vladimir-Volynski and even received an estate from the duke. Jewish landowners in the district of Lutsk are also mentioned during the second half of that century. In 1495, the grand duke of Lithuania, Alexander Jagellon, expelled all the Jews from his country, including those of Volhynia. In 1503, Alexander authorized the Jews to return to Lithuania and restituted their property, with the exception of their estates. In 1507 the ancient rights of residence of the Jews were again ratified by the authorities, and from then until the incorporation of Volhynia into the territories of the Polish Crown (1569), there was a considerable increase in the Jewish population of the region. During this period there were 13 Jewish settlements in Volhynia, including four principal communities (*Ostrog, Vladimir-Volynski, Lutsk, *Kremenets) which together numbered 3,000 members.

The Jews of Volhynia engaged mainly in commerce, but there were also some craftsmen, such as tailors and furriers, among them. Tension arose between them and the townsmen over Jewish economic activities. At the time the authorities, and particularly Queen Bona (1493–1557) – within the limits of her estates – defended the rights of the Jews. The general policy of the authorities toward the townsmen was marked by a tendency to increase their obligations, which also affected the Jews. During the second half of the 16th century, the Jews began to lease inns and engaged in various branches of the economy connected with the estates.

The expansion and consolidation of the Jewish settlement during this period made Volhynia a center of Jewish culture. By the middle of the 16th century, the area already boasted such distinguished scholars as Solomon *Luria, who held rabbinical office in Ostrog, and *Isaac b. Bezalel, the rabbi of Vladimir-Volynski. The golden era of Volhynian Jewry was the period between the annexation of the area to the Polish Crown in 1569 and the massacres of 1648. The establishment of towns on the steppes in the wake of the rapid settlement of the Ukraine and improved conditions of security led to the expansion of the Jewish population of Volhynia into new areas; especially due to migration from the towns to the townlets. In 1648 there were 46 Jewish settlements in Volhynia with a population of 15,000.

After the annexation, the Jews of Volhynia received legal status, equal to the Jews of Poland, whose rights surpassed those of the Jews of Lithuania. The Jews of Vladimir-Volynski (1570) and Lutsk (1579) were exempted from the payment of custom duties throughout the Polish kingdom. The Jews of Volhynia enjoyed the protection of the royal officials, who even defended their rights before the aristocracy and all the more so before other classes. With the weakening of royal authority at the close of the 16th and early 17th centuries, the Jews had the protection of the major landowners, mainly because they had become an important factor in the economy of Volhynia. At the close of the 16th century, the noblemen began to lease out their estates to Jews in exchange for a fixed sum which was generally paid in advance. All the incomes of the estate from the labor of the serfs, the payments of the townsmen and the Jews (who lived in the towns which belonged to the estate), innkeeping, the flour mills, and the other branches of the economy were handed over to the lessee. During the term of his lease, the Jew governed the estate and its inhabitants and was authorized to penalize the serfs at his discretion. During that period, a Jew named Abraham who lived in the town of Turisk became renowned for his vast leases in Volhynia. However, with the exception of these large leases, which were naturally limited in number and on which there is no further information from the beginning of the 17th century, many Jews leased inns, one of the branches of the agricultural economy of the estates, or the incomes of one of the towns or townlets. A lessee of this kind was actually the agent and confidant of the owner of the estate and the financial and administrative director of the economy of the aristocratic class. As a result of his functions, such a lessee exerted administrative authority and great economic influence, a situation which embittered the peasants, the townsmen, and the lower aristocracy. The lease of estates, together with the trade of agricultural produce derived from them, constituted the principal source of livelihood of the Jews of Volhynia.

Cultural and social life also prospered between 1569 and 1648. Each one of the four principal communities became an important Jewish center, and leading personalities, such as Mordecai b. Abraham *Jaffe (author of the *Levushim*), R. Isaiah b. Abraham ha-Levi *Horowitz' (SHe-La-H), R. Samuel Eliezer b. Judah ha-Levi *Edels (Ma-Ha-RSHA), R. Yom Tov Lipmann *Heller (author of *Tosefot Yom Tov*), *David b. Samuel ha-Levi (Ta-Z), and many others, held rabbinical office in them. The rabbis of the principal communities and the leaders of the province (Volhynia was one of the "provinces" of the *Council of the Lands) convened from time to time to discuss affairs of common interest, but every principal community retained its independence, a fact which caused controversies between the communities. The above-mentioned rabbis and leaders also participated in the conventions of the provinces from the inception of the "Council of the Lands" in Poland in the 1580s. It also appears that earlier, before 1569, they participated in the Lithuanian conventions. In Volhynia, as in the other "provinces", there was a supreme bet *din whose seat was in Ostrog and before which any person who refused to be judged by the *bet din* of his town could present his case; disputes between communities were also brought before this *bet din*.

The rebellion of the peasants and the Cossacks in 1648, led by *Chmielnicki, undermined the very foundations of the Jewish settlement in Volhynia. The Jews of Volhynia, unlike those of the Dnieper region and the plain, knew of the defeats suffered by the Polish army and the massacres of Jews, and the overwhelming majority of them sought refuge in the fortified cities. However, after the fall of the fortress of Polonnoye into the hands of the rebels, as a result of the treason of the Ukrainian townsmen, and the massacre of the Jews of the town, a mass exodus toward the west began. The few who remained in Volhynia were put to death or converted, and Jewish homes and property were thoroughly ransacked. Although those who had fled returned to their residences after a few months (the first of them even before the end of 1648), the Jewish settlement in Volhynia, like the region as a whole, did not recover completely. Volhynia was transformed from a region which served as an economic, social, and administrative hinterland for the extensive colonization of the Ukrainian plain, into a border area of the kingdom, and its importance declined even further after the wars of the middle of the 17th century.

During the 1660s, when a period of relative calm dawned on Poland, the Jewish settlement of Volhynia appears to have regained its former dimensions. In the late 1670s there were about 20,000 Jews living in Volhynia. Thereafter, the number of Jews grew steadily, due to natural increase and to settlement in townlets and small villages. A total of 51,736 Jews were counted in 116 localities in Volhynia in 1765. However, there is reason to believe that their numbers were actually greater because a section of the population evaded the census, which was carried out for purposes of tax collection. About 30% of the Jews lived in over 2,000 villages; in three communities there were between 2,000 and 2,500 people, and in six communities there were between 1,000 and 2,000.

Large leases of whole estates are not in evidence during this period, but a considerable number of Jews leased inns or individual branches of the agricultural economy. Some of the Jews acted as the agents of various landowners, whereas others traded with the farmers. A number of them also traded with other parts of Poland or even traveled abroad to attend fairs. The percentage of craftsmen was also on the rise. In the main towns (the so-called royal towns), the townsmen succeeded in completely undermining the position of the Jews, but the Jews established themselves from the economic point of view in smaller towns (the so-called private towns) owned by noblemen. The owners of these towns compelled the townsmen to do agricultural labor for them; and many of the town dwellers therefore gradually moved over to the suburbs, which became semi-agricultural settlements, while in the town centers the Jewish population that kept its distinct urban character continued to increase. This evolution further strained the relations between townsmen and Jews, and there were ample opportunities for anti-Jewish incitement by the clergy.

From the beginning of the 18th century, a series of misfortunes and persecutions befell the Jewish population of Volhynia: a rebellion of the Cossacks broke out in 1702 and several bands penetrated into Volhynia; the Polish armies and the Cossacks of Mazeppa, who came to suppress the rebellion, also robbed the Jews and molested them. During the Great Northern War between Sweden, Poland, and Russia, Swedish regiments invaded the area (1706) and imposed heavy levies on the population. They were followed by the Russian and Polish armies, which continued to exact extortion from the Jews. From the 1730s onward, the Jews of Volhynia were the victims of repeated attacks by the *Haidamacks. From the 1740s to 1760s, there were most frequent blood libels in eastern Poland, possibly against the background of the rivalry between the Catholic and Russian Orthodox clergies. In 1747, there was a *blood libel in Zaslavl; in 1755 an attempted blood libel in Kremenets; and in 1756 a blood libel in Yampol.

The great revolt of the Haidamacks in 1768 affected the Jews of Volhynia to a relatively slight degree. Two years later, however, "the plague – may we be saved from it – broke out, while a conflagration raged in many districts through innumerable towns and villages, so that the Jews deserted their lands, abandoned their houses, and animals and fled to the forests and the fields; this confusion also struck the province of Volhynia" (Jacob Israel ha-Levi, *Aguddat Ezov*, 2 (1782), 24). After the massacres of 1648, the importance of Volhynia declined but its cultural organization was strengthened. During this period, the autonomous province of Volhynia remained one of the provinces of the Council of the Lands, and its representatives attended meetings. The activities of the provincial council, which met every three years with the participation of the delegates from the principal communities, also continued. During this period, the communities of Dubno and *Kovel were added to the provincial council. Toward the middle of the 18th century there were frequent disputes within Volhynia; for example, the trustees of the province complained against the communities of Ostrog ("the first and leading one among the communities of Volhynia") and Lutsk for their refusal to contribute toward the province's expenses. Controversies also broke out between the principal communities and the petty communities ("the environs"), which sought to liberate themselves from the authority of the former. It is worth noting that even after the dissolution of the Council of the Lands in 1764, the principal communities of the province continued to convene and deliberate.

Volhynia (together with neighboring *Podolia) was also the first arena of *Ḥasidism. Several members of Israel Baal Shem Tov's company were of Volhynian origin, and during the following generation, Ḥasidism made rapid progress in Volhynia. *Jacob Joseph, one of the most prominent disciples and followers of the tradition of the Baal Shem Tov, lived in Polonnoye; the leader and successor of the Baal Shem Tov, *Dov Baer, in Mezhirech and Rovno; and R. Phinehas in *Korets (where an important press of the Ḥasidim was established); *Levi Isaac in Berdichev; R. *Wolf in Zhitomir; *Moses Ḥayyim Ephraim in Sudilkov; R. Feivish in *Zbarazh; R. Samson in *Shepetovka; R. Zeev Wolf in Zbarazh; R. Mordecai in Kremenets; R. Moses in Zvahi; R. Isaac in Radziwill; R. Joseph in Yapol (the last five were the sons of R. Mekhel of *Zolochev); R. Abraham in Trisk. In the 1760s, the Ḥasidim already exerted much influence in Volhynia and Dov Baer was a decisive authority in the public affairs of Volhynia. The administration of the communities of Volhynia was subsequently controlled by the Ḥasidim, and all appointments required the consent of the *ẓaddikim*. The first partition of Poland in 1772 and the separation of Volhynia from Galicia, to which it was attached mainly by social and economic ties, left a considerable imprint on the Jewish population of the region. The great fair of *Lvov was transferred to Dubno and helped the development of that community. Fairs also flourished in several other towns of Volhynia. At the close of the century, Berdichev became an important commercial center for the whole vicinity.

In the second (1793) and third (1795) partitions of Poland, sections of Volhynia were annexed by the Russian Empire, and the province of Volhynia was created from them in 1799. At first the political changes did not affect the sources of livelihood of the Jews or even the organizational systems of the communities; the proximity to the Austrian border, particularly to the important commercial town of *Brody, encouraged the Jews to establish commercial relations with Austria, even to the point of smuggling. This situation was brought to the attention of the Russian authorities during the first years after the annexation, and in 1812 the governor of the province of Volhynia suggested that the Jews be removed from a border strip 50 versts wide to prevent them from smuggling. This proposal received royal assent in 1816. In 1825, it was extended to all the western provinces of Russia, though in practice it was never fully applied. In 1843, an order was published to remove the Jews from the border region "without any excuses." At that time, Jews from the provinces of Lithuania and Belorussia began to immigrate to Volhynia. In 1847, there were 174,457 Jews in Volhynia. Industry began to develop among the Jews, and toward the middle of the 19th century a number of wealthy Jews leased the alcoholic beverage excise from the government. As a result, the number of Jewish innkeepers also increased. Many Jews traded in agricultural produce and tobacco. In 1885 there were no Christian merchants of the first and second guilds in Volhynia, whereas the number of Jews who belonged to these guilds amounted to 113; in the third guild, there were 3,749 Jewish and 56 Christian inhabitants of Volhynia.

In 1821, R. Isaac Dov (Baer) *Levinsohn returned from Galicia to his native town of Kremenets, and a center of the *Haskalah was thus created in Volhynia. In the early 1830s, through the initiative of the physician Rutenberg of Berdichev, a circle of *maskilim* named "Ḥevrat Shoḥarei Or ve-Haskalah" ("Society of the Seekers of Light and Enlightenment") was organized in Volhynia. At that time, the author Abraham Baer *Gottlober, who influenced many youths in the spirit of the Haskalah, was living in Volhynia. The Haskalah also made progress among the wealthy, including the lessees of the tax on alcoholic beverages. From the 1840s, the Russian government endeavored to propagate education among the Jews of Russia. Zhitomir, where one of the two Hebrew presses permitted by the government to function (in 1845) and the government rabbinical seminary (opened in 1848) were located, became an important center of the Haskalah movement in southwestern Russia.

The emancipation of the peasants in 1861 and the Polish rebellion of 1863 caused far-reaching changes in the economic and social development of Volhynia that affected the Jews. The decline of the estates of the Polish nobility, the construction of railways, and the creation of direct lines of communication with the large commercial centers deprived the Jewish masses of their traditional sources of livelihood and impoverished them. This prompted the Jews to develop industry. Of the 123 large factories situated in Volhynia in the late 1870s, 118 were owned by Jews. The number of craftsmen also increased. In 1862, a vocational school, the first of its kind in Russia, opened in Zhitomir. In 1897, there were 395,782 Jews living in Volhynia constituting 13.21% of the total population; 30% of them lived in the towns, 49% in the townlets, and 21% in the villages. The Jews constituted one half of the population of the towns. Forty per cent of Volhynia's Jews earned their livelihood from commerce, 25% from crafts, 12.5% from public and private services, 3.7% from haulage, and 2.3% from agriculture. The industries in which they engaged were light and nonmechanized and consisted essentially of the processing of agricultural produce, wood, hides, soap, etc. During the last quarter of the 19th century, the Jews of Volhynia, together with those of other parts of Russia, organized their public life and entered upon a political struggle for their rights. By the 1880s cells of the Ḥovevei Zion had already been established in the towns and townlets of Volhynia, and at the beginning of the 20th century branches of the *Bund and the Zionist parties were organized. Ḥasidism, however, continued to exert the most decisive influence.

The Jews of Volhynia were not harmed directly by the pogroms in Russia during the 1880s and in 1905–06. Many disasters befell them during World War I and the Russian civil war, however. In 1915 the Russian soldiers perpetrated pogroms in Volhynia, as in the other regions within proximity of the front, when they enforced the expulsion of the Jews because of their supposed disloyalty to Russia. In the summer of 1917, soldiers fleeing from the front murdered and robbed Jews in various parts of Volhynia. The situation deteriorated in the wake of the hostilities between the Ukrainians and the Bolsheviks in 1918, and the disorders reached their climax in a series of pogroms against the Jews by armed bands and in the frequent changes of regime in 1919–20. Many thousands died in these pogroms. During the Polish-Soviet war of 1920, the Jews of Volhynia suffered at the hands of both sides. In the peace treaty signed between Russia and Poland, the greater part of Volhynia went to the Poles, while the towns of Zhitomir, *Ovruch, and their surroundings remained under Soviet rule. In the 1926 census 65,589 Jews were counted in Russian Volhynia, while some 300,000 Jews lived in Polish Volhynia in the early 1930s. The economic discrimination against Jews by the Polish government was evident in Volhynia as in other parts of Poland, but Jewish cultural and social life prospered there. Jewish educational institutions, parties, the courts of ḥasidic *ẓaddikim*, etc., developed freely. The Jews of Volhynia, as in other parts of Poland, played an important role in *aliyah* to Palestine and the support to the *yishuv*.

The situation in the Soviet part of Volhynia was rather different. A brief period of cultural awakening in the 1920s was followed by the decline and the apathy of the 1930s, when many active Jews abandoned the townlets for the larger towns of the Ukraine and inner Russia. After the division of Poland in September 1939 according to the Hitler-Stalin agreement, the whole of Volhynia was annexed by the Soviet Union, and a policy of liquidation of the Jewish parties, organizations, and institutions was pursued until the German attack on the Soviet Union in June 1941.

Holocaust Period

The extermination of the Jews of Volhynia began in the first days after the outbreak of the war between Germany and the Soviet Union. In many places, the Ukrainians perpetrated acts of murder before the arrival of the Germans or immediately after it. In Zhitomir, 2,500 Jews were exterminated during the last week of July 1941, while several thousands were confined to a ghetto which was liquidated on September 19 of the same year (mainly by Ukrainians). Ghettos were set up in various towns in formerly Polish Volhynia. They continued to exist until the autumn of 1942, and during the months of September–November the Jews were exterminated and the ghettos of Rovno, Kremenets, and Dubno were liquidated. It is difficult to estimate the number of Jews who perished in Volhynia, but there is no doubt that it reached tens of thousands. After World War II, some of the few survivors returned to the towns of Volhynia, but the Holocaust and the Soviet policies of the 1950s and 1960s had completely obliterated the communal and public Jewish life that had existed in Volhynia for about eight centuries.

In 2005, two Holocaust monuments were erected in the city.

BIBLIOGRAPHY: S. Ettinger, in: *Zion*, 20 (1955), 21 (1956); S. Bershadski, in: *Yevreyskaya Biblioteka*, 7 (1879); 8 (1880); *Arkhiv Yugo-Zapadnoy Rossii*, pt. 5 vol. 2 (1890); S. Dubnow, in: *Voskhod*, 14, nos. 4 and 12 (1894) Vseukrainska Akademiya Nauk, *Zbirnyk prats zhydivskoy istorychno-arkheografichnoy komisii*, 1 (1928); V.P. Rybynsky, *ibid.*, 2 (1929); V.P. Ikhtyussky, *ibid.; Sifrei Zikkaron* for most of the communities mentioned.

[Shmuel Ettinger]

VOLKOVYSK (Pol. **Wolkowysk**), city in Grodno oblast, Belorus. Jews were first mentioned as living in the environs of Volkovysk in 1577. In 1766 the Jews paying poll tax in the city and its environs numbered 1,282. Volkovysk was annexed by Russia in 1795, and by 1797 there were 1,477 Jews and Karaites, comprising 64% of the population. There were 1,429 Jews in 1847; 5,445 (64% of the total) in 1897; and 5,130 (46%) in 1921. In the 19th century the Jews engaged in shopkeeping, crafts, and marketing agricultural products; they founded textile plants, sawmills, a brewery, a tannery, and manufactured tobacco products. Many Jews earned their livelihood by providing services and purveying to the nearby Russian army camp. The Jewish proletariat began to organize in 1897 under the influence of the *Bund, which began its activities when a strike broke out in the tanneries. A large yeshivah was founded in Volkovysk in 1887 and existed up to World War I. Between the world wars all the Jewish parties were active in the city, as well as a branch of *He-Ḥalutz. The educational institutions of the community comprised a school and kindergarten of the *Tarbut network, a Hebrew high school named Herzliyya (founded 1927), Taḥkemoni and Yavneh schools, a *talmud torah*, and a CISHO (see *Education) school. There was also a cooperative farmers' union (with 35 farms) for the purchase of equipment and marketing of their produce. Between 1924 and 1929 a Yiddish weekly, *Volkovisker Lebn*, was published. The rabbis of the community included Jonathan b. Mordecai *Eliasberg in the 1890s; Isaac Elhanan *Spektor lived there in the 1830s. Eliyahu *Golomb, Raphael Klatzkin (the Habimah actor; d. 1987), and Naḥman Rachmilewitz (Lithuanian minister for Jewish affairs), were originally from Volkovysk.

[Dov Rubin]

Holocaust Period

With the outbreak of the German-Soviet war (June 22, 1941), Volkovysk was heavily bombed by the Germans. Several hundred Jews were among those killed. A few escaped with the retreating Soviet army. From the start of the Nazi occupation many Jews were massacred, some of them denounced by Poles. A ghetto was set up on Dec. 13, 1941. In May 1942 about 2,000 Jews were exterminated near the town. The head of the *Judenrat, Ajzik Weinberg, attempted to alleviate the suffering of the community and established contact with the partisans. A Jewish underground movement organized groups to join the partisans in the forests. Discovering that Jewish doctors had helped the partisans, the Germans arrested all 11 doctors in the ghetto, severely tortured them, and, when they refused to denounce their colleagues, hanged them in the town square. On Nov. 2, 1942 all of the Jews were rounded up in a former prisoner-of war camp, joined within a few days by all the Jews of the surrounding areas – a total of 20,000 persons. They lived in overcrowded huts below ground level. By the end of 1942, about 18,000 people were deported for extermination to the death camp of *Treblinka. The Volkovysk camp was liquidated on Jan. 12, 1943, and the remnants of the town's community were transferred to *Auschwitz.

[Aharon Weiss]

BIBLIOGRAPHY: *Ḥurban Wolkowysk* (1946); B. Wasiutyński, *Ludność żydowska w Polsce w wiekach XIX i XX* (1930), 83, 87, 89; I. Schiper, *Dzieje handlu żydowskiego na ziemiach polskich* (1937), index; O. Margolis, *Geshikhte fun Yidn in Rusland* (1930), 281; M. Einhorn (ed.), *Volkovisker Yisker-Bukh*, 2 vols. (1949); J.S. Hertz et al. (eds.), *Geshikhte fun Bund*, 1 (1956), 38.

VOLKSPARTEI, JUEDISCHE (Jewish National Party; **Juedisch-nationale** or **Juedische Partei**), political arm of the Zionist movement for domestic policy (Landespolitik) in Austria from 1906 to 1934. The party had branches throughout Austria, excepting Galicia, which had an independent organization after 1908. It stressed Jewish pride and rejected the participation of Jews in other national movements. Accepting the idea of an Austrian multinational state, it demanded recognition of the Jews as one of the peoples therein and the transformation of their religious communities into national communities. The Jewish National Party found many adherents in eastern Austria. In the west, it was largely popular among university students. It published weekly papers in several places and from 1919 to 1927 the daily *Wiener Morgenzeitung*. In 1908 Benno Straucher was elected Reichsrat deputy from Bukovina and formed the Jewish Club with three deputies from Galicia (Heinrich Gabel, Arthur Mahler, and Adolf Stand). In 1911 only Straucher's seat was retained. With the break up of the Austrian Empire in 1918, the party lost most of its followers and was virtually limited to Vienna. There it succeeded in 1919 in electing its leader, Robert *Stricker, to the Austrian parliament, where he cast the only vote against proclaiming Austria to be a part of Germany. He vigorously defended equality of rights for Austrian Jews, but he failed to be reelected in the Reichsrat election of 1921 owing to changes in the parliamentary election law. In 1919 the party gained three seats in the city council, to which Leopold Plaschkes, Jakob Ehrlich, and Bruno Pollack-Parnau were elected. In 1923 it lost two of the three seats, with Plaschkes remaining city councilor. In 1927 it lost the last seat. The party participated in subsequent elections with ever diminishing returns. It was successful in the Vienna religious community, however, where it obtained a change in the electoral rules, first gaining strong representation in the 1920s, and finally reaching a majority when Desider *Friedmann was elected community president in 1933.

BIBLIOGRAPHY: J. Kreppel, *Juden und Judentum von heute* (1925); R. Stricker, *Wege der juedischen Politik* (1929); A. Boehm, *Zionistische Bewegung*, 2 vols. (1935–372); J. Fraenkel, *Robert Stricker* (1950). **ADD. BIBLIOGRAPHY:** A. Gaisbauer, *Davidstern und Doppeladler* (1988); H.P. Freidenreich, *Jewish Politics in Vienna 1918–1938* (1991).

[Hugo Knoepfmacher / Evelyn Adunka (2nd ed.)]

VOLLI, GEMMA (1900–1971), Italian historian and teacher. Born in Trieste, Gemma Volli devoted herself to Jewish studies, and especially to the history of Italian Jewry in its relations with the Church.

Of particular interest are her papers on the *Mortara case in the *Rassegna Mensile d'Israel* (26, 1960 and 28, 1962) and in the *Bollettino del Museo de Risorgimento* (5 (1960), 1087ff.). Her articles and lectures on the cult of Simon of Trent (in *Il Ponte*, 19 (1963), 1396ff.; and RMI, 31 (1965), 570ff.) led to its abolition by the Church (Oct. 26, 1965); as a consequence, the Jewish *ḥerem* on the city of Trent lost its validity. Volli did the same service in exposing the cult of Lorenzino da Marostica (RMI, 34 (1968), 513ff., 564ff.). Her other works include *Breve storia degli Ebrei d'Italia* (1961); "*La vera storia del protocolli dei Savi anziani di Sion*" (Il Ponte, 13 (1957), 1649ff.); and *Gli Ebrei a Lugo* (1970).

Her name was commemorated in the preface to the theatrical story about Simonino from Trento, "Shalom Alechem" by A. Zanotti – R. Fracalossi (Rovereto, 2005) for her contribution to the abolition of the cult of Simonino. Her *Gli Ebrei a Lugo* has been republished.

BIBLIOGRAPHY: *Israel* (May 13, 1971); JC (May 21, 1971); A. Perugia, RMI, 37 (1971), 335–42.

[Alfredo Mordechai Rabello]

VOLOS (Volo), principal port city of Thessaly, Greece. The community of Volos was founded in the 19th century by a considerable number of Jews who came from the Peloponnesus after the Greek Revolution and the destruction of all of its Jewish communities. The community numbered 35 families in 1850. A new Romaniot synagogue was built in 1865 with the assistance of the Barons Rothschild and Hirsch of Paris. The rabbi was Samuel Molcho. One of the first schools to be opened by the *Alliance Israélite Universelle was in Volos (1864), which was also attended by many Greek children. Due to financial problems, communal apathy, defective instruction, dwindling enrollment, and abhorrent sanitary conditions, the school closed permanently in 1878. In 1889 and 1893 the community suffered from blood libels. At the end of the Turko-Greek war in 1897, anti-Jewish riots broke out, and many Jews fled to *Salonika. In 1909 there were 150 Jewish families and in 1913 about 1,000 persons. In 1910, the Zionist organization Po'alei Zion was founded, and in 1933 the Maccabi scout movement was founded. In 1940 the Jewish population of the city was 882. In 1943 the Jews dispersed themselves in the surroundings, but 130 of them fell into the hands of the Nazis and were included in a transport to the death camps. Rabbi Moshon Pessah, in consultation with the local Greek-

Orthodox Metropolit Ioachim, decided that he would not turn over communal lists to the German commander, and had the insight and courage to advise his community members to flee to the Pelion Mountains and elsewhere outside of Volos in the Thessaly region. Mainly the very poor, old, or those who returned to the city because of the rigors of mountain village life or to get supplies were caught and deported to Birkenau. Some of the Jews of Volos were in a special ELAS Jewish unit in the Pelion Mountains, and throughout Thessaly the Jews cooperated with the British in sabotage against German targets. In 1948 there were 565 Jews in the town; in 1958, 230; and in 1967, 210. In the earthquakes of 1955 and 1957, damage was done to the synagogue. It was decided to rebuild it on the same site, and money was raised from the Greek Board of Jewish Communities, the Salonikan Jewish community, the American Jewish Joint Distribution Committee, and private donors. In 1987, antisemitic graffiti were sprayed on the synagogue and Jewish stores in Volos.

BIBLIOGRAPHY: *Bulletin de L'Alliance Israélite Universelle*, 12 (1887), 34–37; E.N. Adler, *Von Ghetto zu Ghetto* (1909), 102; N. Leven, *Cinquante ans d'histoire. L'Alliance Israélite Universelle 1860–1910*, 2 (1920), 61–65; M. Molho and J. Nehama, *In Memoriam; Hommage aux victimes juives des Nazis en Grèce*, 2 (1949), 58–60, 164. **ADD. BIBLIOGRAPHY:** B. Rivlin, "Volos," in: *Pinkas ha-Kehillot Yavan* (1999), 101–9.

[Simon Marcus / Yitzchak Kerem (2nd ed.)]

VOLOZHIN (Pol. **Wołożyn**), city in S. Molodechno oblast, Belarus; in Poland before 1793 and between 1921 and 1945. Jews were living in Volozhin in the 16th century. They numbered 383 in 1766, 2,452 in 1897 (including the Jews in the vicinity), and 1,434 (54.5 percent of the total population) in 1921; out of 5,600 inhabitants in 1931, the large majority were Jews. They were mainly occupied in small-scale commerce, forest industries, flour milling, tanning, brickmaking, and crafts for the requirements of the agricultural locality. In World War II, on the eve of the Holocaust, according to estimates by survivors, there were approximately 3,000 Jews in Volozhin. They were "liquidated" in three Aktionen, the first following the German occupation of the town, the second on May 10, 1942, and the third in September 1942.

Volozhin Yeshivah

Volozhin acquired importance in Jewish life in Lithuania and Russia in the 19th century from its yeshivah, founded by Ḥayyim *Volozhiner and named Ez̦ Ḥayyim in his honor. It was mainly established to serve as a barrier to the spread of *Ḥasidism, especially among the youth when it became clear that the strong opposition to Ḥasidism had been unable to halt its advance. R. Ḥayyim considered that it was the *pilpul* (casuistic) method of yeshivah teaching, divorcing study of the Talmud from its halakhic foundations, that was the reason for the dissatisfaction among the youth and that pushed many of them into the arms of Ḥasidism because of the religious stimulus and inspiration it offered. Hence the yeshivah he envisaged was to educate its pupils in the methods taught by *Elijah b. Solomon Zalman, the Gaon of Vilna: analysis of the text and understanding of its plain meaning. According to one tradition, the yeshivah was founded on the instructions of the Gaon, although it was established in 1803, several years after he died.

Two yeshivot already existed in Vilna when R. Ḥayyim decided to establish the yeshivah in Volozhin for reasons unknown – possibly to remove it from the influence of the *Vilna community administration, then rent by severe internal discord, and so that he could guide it in accordance with his own views. His opposition to the students' boarding out and the responsibility he took upon himself for their gaining a means of livelihood (about the time the yeshivah was founded he called on the Jewish communities to support it), despite the heavy burden which this devolved on him, evinced his concern to prevent the students from coming under external influence. R. Ḥayyim's endeavors prevented the yeshivah from becoming a merely local institution, and made it into a foundation supported by the whole of Jewry; it thus became a prototype for the Lithuanian yeshivot founded subsequently.

Teaching in the yeshivah began with only ten students, but it rapidly acquired a name among the Jewish public. It became so highly esteemed that the military governor of Lithuania in 1813, during the Napoleonic wars, issued a document of protection to R. Ḥayyim instructing all military units "to safeguard the chief rabbi of Volozhin, Ḥayyim ben Isaac, his schools and educational institutions… and to extend to the above-mentioned chief rabbi every assistance and protection…" The number of students had already risen to 100. In the meantime a special building for the yeshivah had been erected (of wood). The main lectures were given by R. Ḥayyim himself, his son-in-law R. Hillel, rabbi of Horodono (Grodno), and his son R. Isaac.

After R. Ḥayyim's death in 1821 his son R. Isaac served as principal of the yeshivah. Around this time (1824) the Russian authorities decided to close the yeshivah for reasons that are not clear. However, despite the official order prohibiting its existence, the yeshivah continued to function and expand. The number of students rose to 200 and its buildings were enlarged. The head of Volozhin yeshivah was considered at the time to be among the leaders of Russian Jewry, even by the authorities, and when in 1843 the government decided, in line with the recommendations of its "Jewish Committee," to convene a conference of rabbis to discuss problems of Jewish education, R. Isaac was invited to attend. He took this opportunity to obtain official recognition of the yeshivah through the record at the ministry of education of the letter of protection which had been issued at the time to his father. Since R. Isaac was then occupied with public matters and the administrative and financial affairs of the yeshivah, the task of teaching was principally delegated to his two sons-in-law, R. Eliezer Isaac Fried and Naphtali Z̦evi Judah *Berlin (Ha-Nez̦iv). By then a controversy had already begun in the yeshivah, because, in contradiction to the tradition laid down by its founder,

R. Eliezer Isaac inclined to favor *pilpul*, and had a following among the students.

After the death of R. Isaac in 1849, R. Eliezer Isaac Fried was appointed principal of the yeshivah and R. Naphtali Ẓevi Judah Berlin the vice principal. R. Eliezer Isaac did not live much longer, and after his death in 1854, when both R. Berlin and R. Ḥayyim's grandson, R. Joseph Baer *Soloveichik, were both appointed principals, a severe disagreement broke out over the method of instruction, in which R. Joseph Baer favored the *pilpul* method, and had many supporters among the yeshivah students. When the controversy threatened to endanger the existence of the yeshivah, a delegation of prominent Lithuanian rabbis, including David Tevele of Minsk, Joseph of Slutsk, Isaac Elhanan *Spektor of Kovno, and Ze'ev the *Maggid* of Vilna, went to Volozhin in order to settle the controversy. The committee ruled that R. Berlin should be the principal of the yeshivah while R. Joseph Baer should serve as his deputy. From then on the yeshivah was headed by two persons – the principal of the yeshivah and his vice principal. In 1865 R. Joseph Baer left the yeshivah to serve as rabbi of Brest-Litovsk (Brisk). R. Raphael Shapira, son-in-law of R. Berlin, was appointed in his place, serving in this position until 1881. His successor was R. Ḥayyim *Soloveichik, son of Joseph Baer and grandson of R. Berlin.

At the end of the 1850s the government renewed the campaign against the *ḥadarim* and yeshivot. It was helped by a number of the *maskilim* who sent memoranda to the state-appointed Jewish Committee requesting that the yeshivot should be closed down as "nurseries of fanatical rabbis." The government evidently considered that so long as the yeshivot continued, the graduates of the state rabbinical seminaries would not be accepted to rabbinical offices, and that the Volozhin yeshivah was the chief rival of these seminaries. Thus in April 1858 the yeshivah was closed down by order of the authorities on the ground that its syllabus had not been submitted for approval to the ministry of education. Prominent Jews in Vilna and Minsk sent a request to the authorities to permit the yeshivah to reopen since "the Volozhin yeshivah, because of the esteem in which its founder was held, had acquired a high reputation from its foundation. By faithfulness to its mission it had made a noteworthy contribution to the spiritual education of our people. We owe a debt of gratitude to the large number of rabbis in various towns, many of whom have become prominent as authors of important works in rabbinical literature." Despite all the efforts on the part of the Jews, the authorities did not rescind their decision. However, like the order of closure of 1824, it did not have noticeable practical effects.

R. Berlin proved a most able administrator, and he was assisted in this by his wife Batya Miriam. The number of pupils continued to grow, reaching 300 at the end of the 1870s and 400 at the end of the 1880s, by then also attracting students from outside Russia – from England, Germany, Austria, and even America. Berlin also considerably expanded the budget of the yeshivah, which in 1885 reached 16,675 silver rubles, of which some 6,000 were expended on support of the students (the juniors received two to four rubles monthly, and the seniors four to ten), and 3,618 rubles on teachers' salaries. At the end of the 1860s R. Berlin went to collect funds for a new building and library, and sent emissaries to all parts of the Diaspora. The appeal succeeded, and a stone building of three stories was built with the funds.

A daily program was established for the students. Prayers were held at 8 A.M., and they then took breakfast. Afterward the weekly portion was read and explained by the principal of the yeshivah. Study proceeded from 10 a.m. to 1 p.m., during which the supervisor ensured that none of the students missed study. A lecture followed (delivered in the 1880s by R. Ḥayyim Soloveichik, son of R. Joseph Baer, in the first part of the week, and by R. Berlin in the second) and then came the midday meal. The students returned to the yeshivah at 4 P.M., held *Minḥah*, and studied until 10 P.M. *Ma'ariv* was then held, preceding supper. Many would return to the yeshivah and study until midnight. They would sleep until 3 A.M. and return to study until morning. The atmosphere of the yeshivah was created by the study circle of young students devoted in their enthusiasm for Torah study. At certain periods the principal of the yeshivah would examine the students once in each term (*zeman*).

In the 1860s opposition began to be voiced in the Jewish press to the yeshivot. Only the extreme *maskilim* demanded that they should be closed down; others criticized their system of study and its contents and wished to introduce general subjects, as had been instituted in the rabbinical seminaries in Germany and in Western countries. R. Berlin adamantly opposed any changes of this nature. However, when the Pahlen Commission was sitting in St. Petersburg and discussing the Jewish question, a number of Jewish communal leaders regarded it necessary to demonstrate to the authorities that the Jews were ready to make changes. On pressure from them in 1887 a number of prominent rabbis, including Isaac Elḥanan Spektor, Joseph Baer Soloveichik, and R. Berlin, convened in St. Petersburg, and at this meeting it was decided on the appointment of a special teacher to instruct the yeshivah students in Russian and arithmetic, provided that these studies would not be conducted within the yeshivah, but outside it. Volozhin yeshivah refrained from translating this decision into practice.

Despite the vigilance of the supervisors and the severe discipline in the yeshivah, external influences began to infiltrate there. At first the influence of the *Musar movement had begun to be felt. Study of ethical works like *Ḥovot ha-Levavot* and *Mesillat Yesharim* won acceptance by many. This opened the doorway to a religious awakening in the *musar* spirit despite the reservations of the heads of the yeshivah. On the other hand the ideas of *Haskalah were increasingly disseminated in the yeshivah and in the 1880s the Ḥovevei Zion also attracted many students. R. Berlin's sympathy with the latter helped to propagate its ideas in the yeshivah.

However, the spiritual excitement raised by these influences did not end there. A growing number of students read

Haskalah literature in Hebrew and other languages despite the energetic opposition of the principal. The *maskilim* began to demand changes in the yeshivah's regime, which finally brought intervention by the Russian educational authorities. On Dec. 22, 1891, the Russian minister of education published the "Regulations concerning Volozhin Yeshivah," which defined the yeshivah as a private open educational institution, and its pupils were required to study general subjects to elementary school standard. The regulations stated that any digression from them would lead to the closing down of the institution. R. Berlin did not agree to the regulations, and on Jan. 22, 1892, the authorities announced the closure of the yeshivah. R. Berlin and the students were expelled from Volozhin.

However, a few years later the yeshivah was reopened. In 1895 the government permitted use of the yeshivah building as a place of prayer. The students reassembled and laid the foundation for reviving the yeshivah. It continued to expand and develop until World War I (from 1899 under R. Raphael Shapira as principal). When the battle zone reached the vicinity of Vilna, the heads of the yeshivah left Volozhin with the rest of the Jewish refugees for the Russian interior (Minsk). The yeshivah did not resume activity until 1921. It existed, though with reduced numbers and influence, until the liquidation of the last 64 students in the Holocaust. The last to head the yeshivah were R. Jacob Shapira (d. 1936) and his son-in-law Ḥayyim Wulkin, who perished in the Holocaust. Many of the students of Volozhin yeshivah distinguished themselves in Hebrew literature and public leadership, including Ḥ.N. *Bialik, who left an enduring monument to the yeshivah in his poem "*Ha-Matmid*" and M.J. *Berdyczewski.

BIBLIOGRAPHY: A.A. Sh-n (Sirotkin), in: *Ha-Shaḥar*, 8 (1877), 112–9, 161–9; *Ha-Meliẓ*, 15 (1879) nos. 28, 32, 35; 16 (1880), no. 36; 25 (1885) no. 9; 32 (1892) nos. 46, 47, 50; M. Berdyczewski, in: *Ha-Asif*, 3 (1887), 231–42; idem, in: *Ha-Kerem* (1887), 63–77; M.M. Horowitz, *Derekh Eẓ Ḥayyim* (1895); Z. Epstein, *Kitvei…*, 1 (1904), 117–26; M. Shmukler, *Toledot Rabbenu Ḥayyim mi-Volozhin* (1909); S.L. Citron, in: *Reshummot*, 1 (1925), 123–5; B. Epstein, *Mekor Barukh*, 4 (1928), 1766–74, 1813–22, 2019–28; I. Nissenbaum, *Alei Ḥeldi* (1929), 40–46; I.I. Rivkind, in: *Sefer Turov* (1935), 232–9; M. Berlin, *Mi-Volozhin ad Yerushalayim*, 1 (1939), 1–119; M. Rabinowitz, in: *Koveẓ al Yad*, 15 (1951), 221–33; I. Schapiro, *Ge'on Ya'akov* (1953); S.K. Mirsky (ed.), *Mosedot Torah be-Eiropah be-Vinyanam u-ve-Ḥurbanam* (1956); *Sefer ha-Partizanim ha-Yehudiyyim*, 1 (1958), 478–98; *Yahadut Lita*, 1 (1960), 206–13; J. Katzenelson, in: *Voskhod*, 13 (1893) no. 6; M. Ryvkin, *ibid.*, 15 (1895) nos. 1, 3, 5; Yu. Hessen, in: *Perezhitoye*, 1 (1908), 19–22; *ibid.*, 2 (1910), 281–5; I. Tenenbaum, in: *Yevreyskaya Letopis*, 12 (1924); A. Leoni (ed.) *Sefer Volozhin* (1970).

[Shmuel Ettinger]

VOLOZHINER, ḤAYYIM BEN ISAAC (1749–1821), rabbi and educator, leading disciple of R. Elijah b. Solomon Zalman the Gaon of Vilna and of R. Aryeh *Gunzberg (author of *Sha'agat Aryeh*). R. Ḥayyim was the acknowledged spiritual leader of non-ḥasidic Russian Jewry of his day. Ḥayyim distinguished himself both in the theoretical and practical spheres. In 1802 he founded the renowned yeshivah of *Volozhin (later to be named Eẓ Ḥayyim in his honor), which became the prototype and inspiration for the great talmudic academies of Eastern Europe of the 19th and 20th centuries, and similar schools in Israel, the United States, and elsewhere. His yeshivah, which the poet Ḥ.N. *Bialik was later to call "the place where the soul of the nation was molded" transformed the whole religio-intellectual character of Lithuanian Jewry. Imbued with his educational philosophy, it raised religious scholarship in Lithuania to the unique status it was to enjoy there until the Holocaust. It attracted students from afar enhancing the dignity of their calling. Ḥayyim set high standards for admission, insisting on extreme diligence and constancy of study, and instituted in the yeshivah the system of collegial study (*ḥavruta*), preferring it to self-study. The talmudic methodology, which was introduced by Ḥayyim into the yeshivah, was that of internal criticism of texts which he had learned from the Vilna Gaon. Though humble and of pleasant disposition, Ḥayyim was fearlessly independent in his scholarly endeavors. His insistence upon "straight thinking" (*iyyun yashar*), as opposed to the complicated dialectics common to much of the talmudic discourse of his time, led him occasionally to disagree even with decisions of the Shulḥan Arukh, albeit with appropriate reverence. The theological framework for Ḥayyim's educational philosophy is contained in his posthumously published *Nefesh ha-Ḥayyim* (Vilna, 1824), which is addressed primarily to "the men of the yeshivah." Quoting widely from Kabbalistic as well as rabbinic sources. R. Ḥayyim elevated the study of the Torah to the highest value it had ever been accorded in Judaism. He held the hypostatized Torah to be identified with the mystical *Ein Sof*, and he therefore considered study of Torah as the most direct form of unmediated communion with God. In reaction to the ḥasidic thinkers, he defined *Torah li-Shemah* as study for the sake of understanding, rather than as ecstasy or mystical theurgy, regarding this as the ideal form of motivation for study. This cognitive teleology of Torah study was allied with an emphasis on the objective performance of the commandments and a corresponding devaluation of the subjective, experiential component of religious observance. In the great polemics of his day between the Ḥasidim and the *Mitnaggedim*, R. Ḥayyim was the acknowledged leader of the latter. He was the leading ideological spokesman for classical rabbinism, his critique of Ḥasidism being thorough and deliberate. Yet in the communal aspects of the controversy, he was a decided moderate. Thus, despite his enormous reverence for the Vilna Gaon (rivaling the loyalty of Ḥasidim to their *ẓaddikim*), he did not sign the ban against the Ḥasidim. Both these attitudes, that of theological firmness and personal mellowness, were revealed in the *Nefesh ha-Ḥayyim*, which thus became a mitnaggedic response to the dialogue begun by the ḥasidic teacher, R. *Shneur Zalman of Lyady, and the beginning of the reconciliation of the two groups. The ḥasidic reaction to R. Ḥayyim's critique was reflected in the pseudonymous *Meẓaref Avodah*, published in Koenigsberg, 1858. R. Ḥayyim was also the author of a number of important responsa, published in *Ḥut ha-Meshullash* and

Kedushat Yom Tov; Ru'aḥ Ḥayyim, a commentary on Mishnah *Avot* (and, like the *Nefesh ha-Ḥayyim*, posthumously published by his son and successor, R. Isaac); and of a number of introductions to works of the Vilna Gaon.

[Norman Lamm]

VOLOZHINER, ISAAC BEN ḤAYYIM (d. 1849), talmudist and yeshivah head. Son of the founder of Volozhin yeshivah, popularly known as "Itzele of Volozhin," he acquired some secular knowledge, including foreign languages. Isaac taught at the yeshivah during his father's lifetime, and, upon his father's death, succeeded him as principal and became rabbi of the Volozhin community. After the Russian government closed the yeshivah in 1824, Isaac continued to maintain it, the local authorities closing their eyes to his activities. He exercised a profound influence on all the Lithuanian communities, particularly among the *Mitnaggedim*. Eliezer Isaac and Naphtali Ẓevi Judah *Berlin, both of whom taught in the yeshivah, became his sons-in-law, and on his death assumed the leadership of the yeshivah. Volozhiner took an active part in communal affairs. In 1824 M. *Lilienthal sought his support in the establishment of Jewish schools under government auspices. In the summer of 1843, together with M.M. *Shneersohn, Jacob Halpern, and B. Stern, he participated in the conference called by the government on the education of Jews, and defended the stand of the Orthodox circles, who objected that government-run schools might prove a danger to Jewish education and would be fruitless without political rights for Jews. In the end, however, he was compelled to submit to the demands of the government. He was one of those who gave approvals to the textbooks published by the government for Jewish children. He also gave his approval for the publication in Vilna of Mendelssohn's *Biur.* When asked for his reaction to the Russian government's degree ordering the style of clothing to be changed, he ruled that "the law of the government is binding" provided that it applied to all the inhabitants of the state. While taking part in the conference, Isaac obtained the government's permission to maintain the Volozhin yeshivah. He published *Nefesh ha-Ḥayyim* (Vilna, 1824), his father's ethical work, with his own glosses and a biographical introduction. He died in Ivenitz, in the district of Minsk. *Millei de-Avot* (1888), his homiletical commentary on *Avot*, was published posthumously.

BIBLIOGRAPHY: Berdichevski (Bin Gorion), in: *Ha-Asif*, 3 (1887), 233–4; Y. Lipschuetz, Zikhron Ya'akov, 1 (1924), 82–83, 100–2; S.K. Mirsky, *Mosedot Torah be-Eiropah be-Vinyanam u-ve-Ḥurbanam* (1956), 31–34; Bialoblocki, in: *Yahadut Lita*, 1 (1959), 190–1.

[Yehuda Slutsky]

VOLPA (Pol. **Wolpa**; Yid. **Volp**, **Volpe**), town in Grodno district, Belarus. A Jewish community existed there from the early 17th century. In 1766 there were 641 Jews in Volpa who paid the poll tax; they numbered 700 in 1847; 1,151 (58% of the total) in 1897; and 941 (54.3%) in 1921. In the 17th century the community built a wooden synagogue which became famous for its original beauty. Besides their traditional occupation with commerce and crafts the Jews in Volpa engaged in domestic farming. In 1886 there were two tanneries, a dye works, and a brewery. Lack of rail connections prevented further industrial development and the Jews of Volpa took to gardening and tobacco growing, becoming expert in these fields. Before World War I there were 29 Jewish farms on an area of 242 hectares (597 acres); 73 hectares (180 acres) were Jewish owned and the rest were rented from gentile farmers. In 1921, 429 of the 941 local Jews made their living by farming. With the beginning of Polish rule in 1919 the armies stationed near Volpa incited much anti-Jewish activity. In 1929, the Jews were forbidden to grow tobacco, their main source of livelihood. Some of them turned to vegetable farming, cucumbers for pickling being their special crop.

Zionist organizations such as Ereẓ Yisrael ha-Ovedet were active in Volpa between the two world wars. There were a Hebrew *Tarbut school and a Hebrew and Yiddish library each containing 3,000 volumes. The community was annihilated in the Holocaust.

BIBLIOGRAPHY: S. Dubnow (ed.), *Pinkas ha-Medinah* (1925), index; Ẓ. Kaplan, in: *Volkovisker Yisker-Bukh*, 2 (1949); D. Davidovich, *Battei Keneset be-Polin ve-Ḥurbanam* (1960), 9.

[Dov Rubin]

VOLPE, ARNOLD (1869–1940), conductor. Born at Kovno, Lithuania, Volpe emigrated to the U.S. in 1898. There he conducted the Young Men's Symphony Orchestra (1902–19), the Volpe Symphony Orchestra (1904–1914) founded by him, the Washington D.C. Opera Company (1919–22), and the University of Miami Symphony Orchestra (1926–40). He was also director of the orchestral school of the Kansas City Conservatory (1922–25). In 1918 he founded the celebrated summer concerts at the Lewisohn Stadium, New York.

°VOLTAIRE (**François-Marie Arouet**; 1694–1778), French philosopher. No writer contributed so much as Voltaire to the destruction of the traditional beliefs fundamental to European society before the French Revolution: belief in the divine right of monarchy, in the legitimacy of the privileges of the nobility, and in the infallibility of the Church. Voltaire's philosophical convictions were those of a deist, not an atheist. It is also noteworthy that he attacked the biblical belief in the unity of mankind; to blacks, for instance, he attributed an inferior and separate origin. The better to ridicule the established Church, or, in his own words "Écraser l'Infâme," Voltaire preferred to concentrate his attacks on the Old Testament and its followers, the Jews; this he did in such a manner that in antisemitic campaigns in the following centuries he was used as an authority and frequently quoted. From the psychological point of view it seems that the antisemitism of Voltaire, far from being a tactical stratagem, expressed in the facility of his attacks against the Jews, was primarily a result of his hatred for the Church. For instance, it is characteristic of Voltaire that in his polemics with Isaac de *Pinto, he forgot the habitual formula which followed his usual way of signing, "Écrasez l'Infâme," and signed instead: "Voltaire, chrétien gentilhomme de la chambre du Roi très-chrétien." Historically speaking, Voltaire's outlook was a powerful contribution to the creation of the mental climate which made possible the emancipation of the Jews, but at the same time it prepared the ground for the future racial antisemitism. Just after Voltaire's death, Zalkind *Hourwitz, librarian to the king of France, wrote: "The Jews forgive him all the evil he did to them because of all the good he brought them, perhaps unwittingly; for they have enjoyed a little respite for a few years now and this they owe to the progress of the Enlightenment, to which Voltaire surely contributed more than any other writer through his numerous works against fanaticism." Two centuries later this judiciously balanced judgment seems to have been only partially warranted. Recent scholars such as A. Hertzberg (see bibliography) have seen Voltaire as one of the founders of modern secular antisemitism (see *Antisemitism).

BIBLIOGRAPHY: A. Guénée, *Lettre de quelques Juifs ... à M. de Voltaire* (1769); many editions; also translated: *Letters of Certain Jews...* (1777); W. Klemperer, *Voltaire und die Juden* (1894); P. Stauff, *Voltaire ueber die Juden* (1913); H. Oppenheimer (Emmrich), *Das Judentum bei Voltaire* (1930); L. Poliakov, *Histoire de l'antisémitisme*, 3 (1968); A. Hertzberg, *The French Enlightenment and the Jews* (1968), index.

[Leon Poliakov]

VOLTERRA, Italian family especially prominent during the Renaissance. In 1408, BONAVENTURA, son of Genatano of Bologna, was invited to open a loan-bank in Volterra and the name of the city became his own and his descendants'. He may have been the copyist of a Hebrew work on logic. His son MANUEL opened a loan-bank in Florence in 1459. He was very affluent but his family apparently lost its wealth. One of his sons was the traveler MESHULLAM DA *VOLTERRA. Another son, ABRAHAM, opened a loan-bank in Gaeta, southern Italy. Another, LAZZARO (ELIEZER), continued in banking in southern Italy, in Siena and in Florence. His wife Hannah was the daughter of Jehiel b. Isaac da *Pisa. He was in touch with Johanan *Allemanno on philosophical questions. He also wrote poetry, including love poetry. ḤAYYIM (VITA) BEN MOSES of Venice and later Finale, Senigallia, and Ancona, engaged enthusiastically in rabbinic disputes. About 1714 he got into trouble with the Inquisition and took refuge for a time in London (Ms. Roth 262). VITO *VOLTERRA was an Italian jurist.

BIBLIOGRAPHY: Roth, Italy, 483: Milano, Italia, index; C. Roth, *Jews in the Renaissance* (1959), index; U. Cassuto, *Ebrei a Firenze nell' età del Rinascimento* (1918), 264–70; Ghirondi Neppi, index; Mortara, Indice, s.v.; *Enciclopedia Italiana*, s.v.

[Menachem E. Artom]

VOLTERRA, EDOARDO (1904–1984), Italian jurist. Born in Rome, he was the son of Vito *Volterra, the Italian mathematician. He became professor of Roman law successively at the universities of Cagliari, Parma, Pisa, and Bologna. Volterra was removed from his teaching posts in 1938 under the Fascist antisemitic laws. He was decorated for his bravery in fighting the Germans during the last year of the war. He returned in 1945 to Bologna where he was rector until 1947. He became professor of law at the University of Rome in 1951.

Volterra's numerous publications include *Collatio Legum Mosaicorum et Romanarum* (1930), *La Conception du mariage d'après les juristes romains* (1940), and *Instituzioni di Diritto Romano* (1961). He also wrote many articles on family law which were notable for their clarity and wide range of knowledge.

[Giorgio Romano]

He was appointed constitutional justice of Italy (1971–1980); in 1971 the University of Rome published six volumes in his honor, *Studi in onore di Edoardo Volterra;* his books were very popular among scholars. Republished in 1980 was his *Istituzioni di Dirito Romano* as was in 1983 his *Diritto Romano e Diritti Orientali* (originally published a few months before the racial legislation). In 1991 six volumes of his *Scritti giuridici* were published. The British Academy's Research Projects hosted an important internet site called *Project Volterra Database* in honor of his memory. In 2005 the University of Rome commemorated the 100th anniversary of his birth.

[Alfredo Mordechai Rabello (2nd ed.)]

BIBLIOGRAPHY: *Novissimo Digesto Italiano*, 20 (1975), 1048.

VOLTERRA, MESHULLAM BEN MENAHEM, DA (Bonaventura di Manuele; 15th century), Italian traveler. Volterra was partner and later owner of his father's affluent loan-bank in Florence; he also traded in precious stones. He was interested in Jewish literature and philosophy, and was friendly with Lorenzo de Medici to whom he once sent a gift of game. In the spring of 1481 he set out for Ereẓ Israel in order to fulfill a vow made when he got into trouble in Florence. He sailed from Naples to Egypt by way of Rhodes, and then went by land over the Sinai peninsula, arriving in Jerusalem on July 29, 1481. After remaining about a month, he returned via Venice, where he arrived in October. Volterra wrote in Hebrew an account of his journey (Massa Meshullam mi-Volterra be-Ereẓ Yisrael, ed. A. Yaari, 1949; abridged English translation in E.N. Adler (ed.), *Jewish Travellers* (1930), 156–208) which contains a wealth of information about the cities he visited – Alexandria, Cairo, Gaza, Hebron, Jerusalem, Jaffa, Beirut, Damascus – their Jewish communities and traditions; he also gives much information of economic interest. While occasionally noting local legends, he is often skeptical about them. He shows also some familiarity with classical literature. His style is readable and attractive although containing some grammatical errors and numerous Italian expressions. In 1487 Meshullam again left for a trip to the east for commercial reasons, traveling part of the way with R. Obadiah di *Bertinoro. Another Meshullam da Volterra, according to Abraham Portaleone, drew up in 1571 a price list of gems in the world market.

BIBLIOGRAPHY: V. Cassuto, *Ebrei a Firenze nell' età del Rinascimento* (1918), 266–8; idem, in: *Miscellanea storica della Valdesa*, 27

(1919), 66–70; Sestieri, in: RMI, 10 (1935/36); 478–92; Milano, Italia 667.

[Menachem E. Artom / Avraham Yaari]

VOLTERRA, VITO (1860–1940), Italian academic. Born in Ancona, he studied in Florence and graduated in mathematical, physical, and natural sciences from the University of Pisa. When 23 years old he taught rational mechanics at the University of Pisa, where he became dean of the Faculty of Sciences. He moved to the University of Turin in 1893. Volterra became a member of the Academy of the Lincei, of which later he was also president. He was dean of the faculty of sciences at the University of Rome in 1907. Volterra was always anti-Fascist. A subscriber to the "Croce Manifesto" drawn up by the anti-Fascist intellectuals, he was among the very few Italian professors to refuse to swear allegiance to the Fascist regime, thus losing his chair. He died in Rome. The department of mathematics at the University of Rome was dedicated in his name.

BIBLIOGRAPHY: G. Fabre, *L'Elenco: Censura Fascista, Editoria e Autori Ebrei* (1998).

[Massimo Longo Adorno (2nd ed.)]

VOLYNSKI, AKIM LEVOVICH (pseudonym of **A.L. Flexer**; 1863–1926), Russian literary critic and art historian. Volynski studied law, but abandoned an academic career which would have required his conversion to Christianity. His early writings dealt with Jewish themes and appeared in Russo-Jewish periodicals. In 1884 he co-edited an anthology entitled Palestina. His works include books about *Spinoza, S.S. *Frug, the Bible in Russian poetry, Dostoevski, and religious philosophy. He wrote a definitive essay on L.O. *Levanda, the historian of Russian Jewry. Volynski's opposition to the "progressive" critics and their philosophy of materialistic positivism aroused tremendous controversy, and he was branded "decadent." After the 1917 Revolution, he abandoned literary criticism and became head of the Choreographic Institute in Leningrad.

Critical essays which he wrote as an editor of the monthly *Severny vestnik* ("Northern Courier") appeared in two collections: *Russkiye kritiki* ("Russian Critics," 1896) and *Borba za idealizm* ("The Fight for Idealism," 1900). Volynski's last books dealt with ballet. Among his works is a book on the aesthetics of dance, *Kniga Likovanii* ("The Book of Exultations," 1923). He also wrote a volume on Leonardo da Vinci.

BIBLIOGRAPHY: M.J. Olgin, *Guide to Russian Literature 1820–1917* (1920), 192–4.

[Yitzhak Maor]

°**VOLZ, PAUL** (1871–1941), German Bible scholar. Born in Lichtenstern (Wuerttemberg), Volz was professor in Tuebingen from 1909.

He wrote a comprehensive exposition of Jewish eschatology, which in opposition to the religio-historical school, he considered as genuinely "biblical-Israelite" (*Juedische Eschatologie von Daniel bis Akiba*, 1903; second edition: *Die Eschatologie der juedischen Gemeinde im neutestamentlichen Zeitalter*, 1934). In his work *Mose, Ein Beitrag zur Untersuchung ueber die Urspruenge der israelitischen Religion* (1907), Volz concludes from the post-mosaic pre-prophetic religion that Moses was the founder of a YHWH League; in the second edition (*Mose und sein Werk*, 1932) he regards Moses as the founder of the people and the Decalogue as his authentic program. He anticipated S. Mowinckel's explanation of the Festival of Tabernacles as a New Year Festival of YHWH, in analogy with the Babylonian New Year Festival (*Das Neujahrfest Jahwes*, 1912). With his disciple W. Rudolph, Volz opposed the prevailing theory of the Pentateuch in that he contested the existence of the Elohist source (*Der Elohist als Erzaehler*, 1933). Another well-known work by Volz is *Der Prophet Jeremia* (1922, 1928^2).

BIBLIOGRAPHY: A. Weiser, in: *Deutsche Theologie* (1941), 79–89.

[Rudolf Smend]

VON FURSTENBERG, DIANE (1946–), U.S. fashion designer. Von Furstenberg, the daughter of a Holocaust survivor, became an internationally celebrated designer whose achievements were predicated largely on one simple dress. She was born Diane Halfin in Brussels, 18 months after her mother, Liliane, was liberated from Auschwitz. Her father, Leon, a Russian émigré, raised the family in Belgium and Diane was educated in Spain, England, and Switzerland. While studying economics at the University of Geneva, she met Egon von Furstenberg, a Swiss-born German prince. They married in 1969 and moved to New York. In 1970, shortly after the birth of her first child, Alexandre, she launched Diane Von Furstenberg Studio. A year later, her daughter, Tatiana, was born. By 1972, she had created the dress that was to catapult her to fame. Made of Italian printed jersey, it was a simple wrap-around style designed to cling to the body without looking vulgar. It seemed to symbolize the vast changes in sexual and social attitudes then taking place in the U.S. and was a nationwide success, landing Von Furstenberg on the covers of *Newsweek* and the *Wall Street Journal*. By 1976, the modestly priced dress – known simply as The Wrap – had sold in the millions. A version was hung in the Smithsonian Institution in Washington, D.C. But by the late 1970s, von Furstenberg's marriage had dissolved and the market had become oversaturated with the dress. Demand dwindled. She sold her apparel business to Carl *Rosen of Puritan Fashions and licensed her name for products ranging from luggage to cosmetics. In 1979, she created Tatiana, a fragrance that became a best seller. But she was forced to sell her cosmetics and fragrance business in 1983 because it was undercapitalized. Von Furstenberg left the U.S., traveled widely, lived in Bali, then Paris and returned to New York in 1990. In 1992, she created a company called Silk Assets and offered its products on QVC, a television shopping channel. QVC was eventually acquired by Barry *Diller, the founder of Fox Broadcasting and a long-time intimate who would become Von Furstenberg's second husband. In her first appearance on the channel, Von Furstenberg sold $1.3 million worth of silk separates in one hour. In the late 1990s, she revived her wrap dresses and found a receptive new audience in the daughters of her earliest customers. Her company expanded into jewelry and cosmetics and by 2005, Diane von Furstenberg boutiques were in New York, Miami, London, and Paris. Von Furstenberg has also produced books and been involved in movies. In 1998, she published a memoir, *Diane: A Signature Life*. Earlier, she had produced a series of home furnishing books. She was an executive producer of *Forty Shades of Blue*, a drama that won a prize at the 2005 Sundance Film Festival. She was elected to the boards of the Council of Fashion Designers of America and U.S.A. Network Inc. in 1999 and was awarded a CFDA Lifetime Achievement Award in 2005. Von Furstenberg, an early supporter of the U.S. Holocaust Memorial Museum in Washington, was honored by the Anti-Defamation League and by Israel's Shenkar College.

[Mort Sheinman (2nd ed.)]

VON WEISL, ZE'EV (Wolfgang) (1896–1974), physician, Zionist leader, journalist and writer. Born in Vienna and an active Zionist from youth, during World War I he was a lieutenant in the Austro-Hungarian army, and after the collapse of the monarchy led a Jewish defense unit to forestall attacks on the Jewish Quarter of Vienna.

He graduated as a physician in 1921 and emigrated in 1922 to Palestine where he was a laborer as well as a practicing physician. In 1923 he returned to Vienna, resuming his Zionist activities and contributing to the *Neue Freie Presse* and the *Wiener Morgenzeitung*. He was correspondent for the *Vossische Zeitung* and *Chicago Tribune* for the Middle East, traveling extensively there, interviewing numerous Moslem leaders including Kings Ibn Saud, Feisal and Fuad. He was imprisoned in Persia as a suspected British spy. Lecturing extensively in Europe on behalf of the Revisionist Movement, he was among its founders and leaders in Palestine, a member of the editorial board of *Do'ar ha-Yom*, and editor of *Ha'am*. In 1936 he was elected president of the New Zionist Organization (NZO). In 1940 he escaped from Paris and resumed his political and journalistic activities in Palestine. In 1942 he was chairman of the Palestine NZO. In June 1946 he was interned in the detention camp at Latrun and was released after a prolonged hunger strike, but in 1947 he was again interned together with other Jewish leaders. He was wounded in the War of Independence.

Among his numerous works are *Der Kampf um das Heilige Land* (1925), *Allah ist gross* (1937), and *Tish'im u-Shenaim Yemei Ma'aẓar ve-Ẓom* (1947).

BIBLIOGRAPHY: Tidhar, D. 2 (1947), 969–71; 15 (1966), 4802.

[Joseph Nedava (2nd ed.)]

VOORSANGER, JACOB (1852–1908), U.S. Reform rabbi. Voorsanger, born in Amsterdam, Holland, received his rabbinical education there and in 1872 settled in the United States. After holding several pulpits, he became associated with Emanu-El Congregation in San Francisco in 1886, first as assistant to Rabbi Elkan *Cohn, and, upon the latter's death in 1889, as rabbi. Well versed in Jewish literature, an energetic worker, and an able preacher and writer, Voorsanger became the foremost rabbi on the West Coast. He knew 13 languages and taught at the University of California Berkeley. He was classically Reform in his religious orientation and actively opposed Zionism. Among the rabbis he influenced were boys in his own congregation, Judah L. Magnes, Martin A. Meyer, who was his successor, and his son Elkan Voorsanger. In 1895 he founded the weekly *Emanu-El*, which achieved prominence on the West Coast. He published *Chronicles of Emanu-El* (1900) and also compiled a Sabbath evening service. Voorsanger's *Sermons and Addresses*, ed. by O.I. Wise, was issued in 1913. He was not open to the immigration of Eastern European Jews and proposed a quota on the number of immigrants, especially to San Francisco.

[Sefton D. Temkin / Michael Berenbaum (2nd ed.)]

VORARLBERG, autonomous province in W. Austria. Jews lived in the village of Feldkirch in the early 14th century. Seven Jewish families who moved without permission, in 1343, to Bludenz, continued to remain the property of their former lord, Duke Ulrich I of Montfort, according to a decision of the court. Virtually no Jews lived in the isolated and mountainous region in the following century. In 1559 the city of Bregenz received the privilege of not tolerating Jews within its walls; nonetheless, a **Schutzjude*, Wolf, was given permission to settle there in 1584. In 1617 Jewish refugees from Burgau were invited to settle in *Hohenems, where they soon constituted a flourishing community; by 1624 a Hebrew printing press was in operation in the city. In 1676, however, they were expelled. Jews first came to Sulz in 1637 but the community assumed permanent form only in 1676, when refugees from Hohenems settled there. Between 1676 and 1688 the community numbered about 65. Only the three richest Jewish families were allowed to remain in Sulz in 1688 when an expulsion order of the Vorarlberg estates was modified by the emperor; by 1743 their number had grown to ten. In 1744 the local militia, after a victory against French invaders, plundered the synagogue and Jewish homes and expelled the ten Jewish families, who thereafter found asylum in Hohenems. The refugees appealed to *Maria Theresa when the Vorarlberg estates attempted to forbid their return. The empress's decision on restitution was never carried out.

Severe economic restrictions which forbade the Jews to engage in trade within the semi-autonomous province forced them to become large-scale exporters and importers of goods (mainly textiles) from neighboring Switzerland, Italy and Bavaria. The Jewish community of *Saint Gall, Switzerland, was founded by merchants from Hohenems. The Jews established and developed the textile industry in Hohenems and later, in Bregenz. After all economic and civil disabilities were abolished in 1867 in Austria, a sharp numerical decline subsequently set in as the Jews moved to the major cities. The Jewish population declined from 246 in 1869 to 126 in 1910 and 42 in 1934 and ended in the Nazi period. After World War II

(1946) 400 *displaced persons (DPS) were temporarily interned in Bregenz.

BIBLIOGRAPHY: A. Taenzer, *Die Geschichte der Juden in Tirol und Vorarlberg* (1905); J. Scherer, *Die Rechtsverhaeltnisse der Juden in den deutsch-oesterreichischen Laendern* (1901), 668–71.

[Harry Wasserman]

VORENBERG, JAMES (1928–2000), U.S. lawyer. Vorenberg, the son and grandson of presidents of the Gilchrist Company department store in Boston, graduated from Harvard College and its law school, where he was president of the *Law Review.* He served in the United States Air Force and then became clerk for Justice Felix *Frankfurter of the Supreme Court in 1953 and 1954. He joined the Boston law firm of Ropes & Gray in 1954 and returned to Harvard as a professor of criminal law in 1962. He was active in legal and public affairs. From 1965 to 1967 he served as executive director of a commission appointed by President Lyndon B. Johnson to study the growing problem of crime in America. The report the commission produced reflected Vorenberg's observation that fighting crime required solutions such as rehabilitation services and larger court staffs that were far more complex than those that had been relied upon traditionally, such as larger budgets for the police. He published an article suggesting that the American tradition of giving prosecutors unfettered power had gone too far and proposed limits on their authority. At Harvard, he worked to broaden police understanding of legal principles. In 1973 Vorenberg was selected as one of the senior assistants to Archibald Cox, helping to organize the office that had been established to investigate the burglary at Democratic Party headquarters at the Watergate complex and assertions of campaign sabotage by the Committee to Re-Elect President Richard M. Nixon. Vorenberg set up the staff that continued the investigation that led to Nixon's resignation. In 1981 Vorenberg became dean of the Harvard Law School. His eight-year tenure was somewhat stormy because of bitter disputes over tenure decisions involving professors who advocated a school of legal thought known as critical legal studies, which asserted that law was not neutral. Critical legal scholars argued that law was an oppressive tool of the rich and powerful. While the battles raged, some black Harvard law students protested, saying that there were not enough minority members on the law school faculty. Vorenberg was largely credited with keeping the law school intact during that period. He also was an advocate of affirmative action, to increase the number of minority faculty and students.

[Stewart Kampel (2nd ed.)]

VORONCA, ILARIE (originally **Eduard Marcus**; 1903–1946), Romanian and French poet. Born in Brăila, Romania, Voronca published his first verse in Lovinescu's review Sburătorul Literar in 1921. He himself edited Integral and contributed to many of the avant-garde publications of his time. His books of poetry, beginning with *Restristi* ("Hard Times", 1923) provoked varied reactions among critics.

An outstanding pioneer of modernism, Voronca wove futurism, Dadaism, and surrealism into his Romanian verse collections which include *Ulise* (1928), *Brățara nopților* ("Bracelet of the Night," 1929), *Zodiac* (1930), *Incantații* ("Incantations," 1931), *Petre Schlemihl* (1932), and *Patmos* (1934). In two volumes of essays, *A doua lumină* (1930) and *Act de prezență* (1932), Voronca termed the poet a "*Wandering Jew without a shadow" and a "Peter Schlemihl without a homeland," who could be certain only of universal uncertainty and whose sole religion should be poetry.

During the early 1930s Voronca immigrated to France, where he began writing in French, eventually publishing some two dozen volumes of verse. He made important contributions to periodicals such as the *Nouvelles littéraires, Cahiers du Sud*, and *Cahiers juifs*. Collections of this period include *Permis de séjour* (1933), *Ulysse dans la cité* (1933), *La joie est pour l'homme* (1936), and *Beauté de ce monde* (1940). During World War II Voronca was active in the French Maquis and allegedly converted to Catholicism. This abandonment of Judaism – if it indeed took place – did little to relieve the poet's inner anxiety which, in the form of a profound restlessness, appears in such later titles as *Les témoins* (1942), *Souvenirs de la planète terre* (1945), and *Contre solitude* (1946). Voronca finally committed suicide.

BIBLIOGRAPHY: J. Rousselot, in: *Europe*, 34 (Fr., Sept.–Oct. 1956); G. Călinescu, *Istoria Literaturii Române* (1941), 782–4; idem, *Ulysse* (1967), 136–40, E. Lovinescu, *Evoluția poeziei lirice* (1927), 438–48; I.M. Rașcu, *Convingeri literare* (1937), 72–8.

[Dora Litani-Littman]

VORONEZH, city and region in Southern Central Russia. The province of Voronezh lay outside the Jewish Pale of *Settlement, and until 1917 Jews were forbidden to settle there. The Russian authorities also took special steps at the beginning of the 19th century to remove Jews from the province, in order to prevent them from influencing those Russian sectarians who inclined toward Judaism (the Subbotniki, who were numerous there). Small groups of Jews, entitled to settle outside the boundaries of the Pale, nevertheless found their way into the province during the 19th century. In 1874, 319 Jews lived in the town and obtained permission to maintain a synagogue in a private house. The constitution of their community received official authorization in 1890. In 1897 there were 2,888 Jews in the Voronezh province, of whom 1,708 resided in the town of Voronezh. The Jewish population of the town was assaulted during the wave of riots which broke out in Russia in October 1905, and the community was attacked again during the Russian Civil War (1918–20). After World War I, the number of Jews in Voronezh increased and by 1926 had reached 5,208 (4.3% of the general population). The community suffered severely during the Nazi occupation (July 1942 to January 1943). According to the 1959 census, there were 6,179 Jews in the Voronezh district, most of whom lived in the city of Voronezh, though their real number was estimated at close to 10,000. There was no synagogue, as the old synagogue was turned into a storehouse for building material (reported in the *New York Times*, June 19, 1959). When the Jews attempted to repossess the synagogue, the authorities said that they must first purchase a new storehouse and then renovate the building, but the community lacked the necessary funds. In 1959 the Star of David was removed from the synagogue wall. There was no separate Jewish cemetery. In 2002 there were 1,522 Jews in the Voronezh district.

[Abraham N. Poliak]

VORONOFF, SERGE (1866–1951), surgeon and physiologist. Born in Russia, he was educated in Paris, where he served as chief surgeon of the Russian Hospital. He was later appointed director of the biological laboratory of Ecole des Hautes Études and director of experimental surgery at the Collège de France at Nice. When the Nazis occupied France. he fled to Portugal and later to the United States.

Among Voronoff's early successes was an increase in the yield of wool from sheep by gland transplants. Encouraged by the results, he tried to find a means to rejuvenation, attempting to stimulate the flow of sex hormones by the transplantation of glands from higher primates to human subjects. He claimed that the human life-span could thus be prolonged to 140 years. Voronoff attempted to cure thyroid deficiencies by similar means. His publications include *Traité des greffes humaines*... (1916); *Conquest of Life*... (1928); *Sources of Life* (1943); *Love and Thought in Animals and Men* (1937); and *From Cretin to Genius* (1941).

VORSPAN, AL (1924–), a leading Jewish spokesperson and author on social justice concerns during the second half of the 20th century. *Vorspan served as the long-time senior vice president for social justice of the Union of American Hebrew Congregations (now the Union for Reform Judaism). His social justice textbooks (*Justice and Judaism*, *The Prophets*, *Tough Choices*, *Jewish Dimensions of Social Justice*) have been widely used for 50 years in Reform religious schools, adult education programs, and social action committees. For a quarter century, he taught popular social justice seminars for rabbinical students at HUC-JIR in N.Y.

Raised in St. Paul, Minnesota (along with his brother Rabbi Max *Vorspan, a Conservative Rabbi who served as the vice president of the California-based University of Judaism), he was greatly influenced by the liberal politics of Hubert Humphrey (senator and vice president). After serving in the U.S. Navy during World War II, he began working in New York City at the National Jewish Community Relations Advisory Council. Quickly developing a national population for his eloquence, writing and programmatic skills, in 1953 he was hired as the deputy to Rabbi Eugene J. Lipman in heading the Reform Movement's new social justice program, of which he assumed leadership from 1961 to 1993.

He is credited with playing a key role in stimulating the creation of congregational social action committees, helping to make them a norm in American Jewish life and being a defining expositor of the social justice emphasis of Reform Judaism. The impact was significant. According to J.J. Goldberg in his book *Jewish Power*, "The Reform [C]ommission [on Social Action], ... [r]un on a shoestring from the New York offices of the Reform synagogue union, could mobilize an army of congregants through the social-action committees of hundreds of Reform temples nationwide." He played a leading role in the efforts that led to the creation of the Religious Action Center of Reform Judaism, the Reform Movement's social justice center in Washington, D.C.

In the national social justice battles of the mid-century, Vorspan was constantly at the forefront of Jewish efforts. One of the Jewish community's leading proponents of civil rights, Vorspan was part of a 16-person delegation of prominent Reform leaders (all the others, rabbis) who traveled at Dr. Martin Luther King's invitation to St. Augustine, Florida, in 1964 to protest racial discrimination. They were arrested and issued a widely discussed public letter calling the Jewish community to arms in the civil rights struggle.

An outspoken critic of the Vietnam War, he helped, with Rabbi Maurice Eisendrath, to lead the Reform Movement to condemn the war in 1965, several years before other national Jewish organizations did so. Similarly, on Soviet Jewry, domestic poverty, anti-apartheid efforts, women's rights, Middle East peace and the United Nations (at which he served as the NGO representative of the UAHC/URJ), his prolific writings and eloquent speeches shaped and mobilized the social justice activities of large segments of the political liberal Jewish community.

[David Saperstein (2nd ed.)]

VORSPAN, MAX (1916–2002), U.S. rabbi and administrator. Born in St. Paul, Minnesota, Vorspan was ordained by the Jewish Theological Seminary in 1943. During his senior year, he served first as assistant director of the Seminary School of Jewish Studies (1943) and then as the program director of the 92nd Street Young Men's Hebrew Association. Upon graduation, he enlisted in the army as a chaplain, serving in Saipan until the end of World War II. Discharged when the war was over, he accepted a pulpit in Pasadena, California, where he established the first Reconstructionist Congregation in the West. He then joined the Brandeis Camp Institute as an associate director, where he established a reputation as a creative administrator and popular lecturer.

In 1954, Vorspan was invited to become the first full-time registrar and instructor at the University of Judaism, which was then the West Coast branch of the Jewish Theological Seminary. He remained there for some 40 years, retiring in the early 1990s as associate professor of American Jewish history and senior vice president. Universally liked, he was instrumental in establishing the Pacific Southwest Coast Region of the United Synagogue, Camp Ramah in California, and the University's School of Fine Arts.

In addition to his classes at the university, Vorspan lectured widely throughout the West. He published a number of popular articles and cowrote *The History of the Jews of Los Angeles*.

[David L. Lieber (2nd ed.)]

VORST, LOUIS J. (1903–1987), chief rabbi of Rotterdam, Holland. The son of a diamond worker, Vorst entered the Amsterdam Rabbinical and Teachers' Seminar in 1914 and obtained the degree of "*Maggid*" in 1924. He taught at Jewish elementary schools in Amsterdam and in 1927 became head of Jewish studies at the new Jewish post-elementary school there. In 1931 he was invited by Chief Rabbi A.B.N. Davids of Rotterdam to head Jewish education in that city. When Chief Rabbi Davids died in Bergen-Belsen in 1945, Vorst, who had survived although seriously weakened, returned after the liberation to Rotterdam where he took over most of the duties of Chief Rabbi Davids as well as resuming his own duties. He was given the personal title of rabbi, although he had not obtained the rabbinical diploma entitling him to become a chief rabbi. In 1959 he passed the rabbinical examination at the Amsterdam Ashkenazi Seminar and was then appointed chief rabbi of the Rotterdam District. He retired in 1971 and went to live in Israel. On his retirement he was made a Commander in the Order of the Netherlands Lion.

On his promotion to the position of chief rabbi, the Jewish Congregation of Rotterdam in September 1959 published a volume of essays (*Opstellen*) in his honor.

[Henriette Boas]

VOS, ISIDOR H.J. (1887–1942), Dutch physician and liberal politician. Vos was head of the hygiene department of the Netherlands army headquarters (1914–18), and later an Amsterdam councilor and alderman. From 1928 to 1940 he was a member of the second chamber of the Dutch parliament. Given the opportunity to leave Holland after the German invasion in World War II, he sent his family away but he stayed, and died in a concentration camp.

VOSKHOD (Rus. "Dawn"), a periodical in the Russian language published in St. Petersburg from 1881 to 1906. The magazine was established by Adolph *Landau, who transformed his annual literary-scientific publication *Yevreyskaya Biblioteka* ("Jewish Library") into a monthly. Early in 1882 Landau added a weekly supplement to *Voskhod* called *Nedelnaya khronika Voskhoda* ("Voskhod Weekly Chronicle"). From 1885 to 1899, this was the only Jewish periodical published in Russian and it served as the vehicle for the Russian-Jewish intelligentsia which had not severed its ties with Judaism. Although the subscribers (who numbered more than 4,000 in the 1890s) were scattered throughout Russia, they were especially numerous in the southern districts of the Jewish Pale of Settlement.

Among the most important associates of the magazine were S. Grusenberg, who edited the weekly *Chronicle*, and S. *Dubnow. In the late 1890s, when Landau had to interrupt his work with *Voskhod* for prolonged periods because of ill health, Grusenberg served as its editor. Dubnow commenced his work with *Voskhod* by writing sharp polemical articles on religious and educational reform for Jews and later edited its department of literary criticism. He also published certain historical studies, as well as "Letters on Old and New Judaism," first stating his theory of *autonomism, which ran counter to the views of the editors of *Voskhod* and their sympathizers.

Two principles guided the editorial policy of *Voskhod*: confidence in progress and faith in the ultimate triumph of Russian Jews in their struggle for complete emancipation, and the conviction that because Russia was the homeland of its Jewish citizens, solutions to both internal and external Jewish problems had to be found within Russia itself. Although *Voskhod* was not against the idea of a limited settlement of Jews in Ereẓ Israel, it opposed the *Ḥibbat Zion movement and was particularly antagonistic to Zionism. At the same time, the journal opposed total assimilation, advocating the preservation of national-religious Jewish values while encouraging Jews to become more familiar with the Russian language and culture. It also fostered the idea of developing a Jewish literature in the Russian language. *Voskhod* called upon the Russian Jewish intelligentsia to remain close to the masses of the Jewish people and to devote themselves to the public struggle for Jewish rights, participating as individuals in organized Jewish community life, education, and social welfare. The magazine also hoped to raise the standards of the rabbinate in Russia by establishing a theological seminary similar to those of Western Europe. It also suggested a plan for increasing the productivity of Russian-Jewish economic life by having Jews engage in physical labor, especially in agriculture.

Between 1881 and 1884 *Voskhod* courageously called for a Jewish self-defense organization. Its polemic outcries against the Russian authorities, anti-Jewish laws and acts, and the hostile Russian press were regarded as one of the chief tasks of the editorial board, which devoted a special section to the problem, "Echoes of the Press." In 1891, after two warnings, the magazine was suspended by the government for six months. When it was resumed, it had to submit the material of its weekly edition to the censors prior to each publication, a procedure which sharply curtailed its freedom of expression.

Voskhod published studies by A.A. *Harkavy, the basic historical research of S. *Bershadski on Lithuanian Jews and of V. *Nikitin on Jewish agricultural settlements in Russia, and the essays of S. Dubnow on the history of Ḥasidism. It also introduced the works of the historians S. *Ginsburg, Y. *Hessen, P. *Marek, S. Posner, I. *Zinberg, and others. Translations from the literature of the Wissenschaft des Judentums which appeared in Western Europe were also included. As supplements, it offered basic works on the history of the Jewish people, including the writings of Josephus, the *Geschichte der juedischen Literatur* by Gustav *Karpeles, the *History of the Jews* by S. Dubnow, an *Anthology of Jewish Folk Songs* by S. Ginsburg and P. Marek, and a "Systematic Bibliographical Guide to the Literature Pertaining to Jews in the Russian Language." In its "Literary Chronicle" (whose editors included I.L. Gordon, S. Dubnow, and S. Ginsburg), *Voskhod* reviewed new books on Jews and Judaism in Hebrew and other languages. The attitude of the editors toward the Yiddish language changed in the course of time, moving from a complete negation of its value to an appreciation of Yiddish as a positive factor in shaping both the Jewish image and the way of life of the Jewish masses. *Voskhod* also gave its attention to textbooks and children's literature. In its "Literary Chronicle," it published translations from the works of K.E. *Franzos, L. *Kompert, I. *Zangwill, E. *Orzeshkowa, and others, as well as numerous historical novels. Among the Russian-language short-story writers who contributed to *Voskhod* were I.L. *Levanda, G. *Bogrov, M. *Ben-Ami, N. Pruzhanski, and S. Yaroshevski (a prolific, though superficial, writer whose works generally preached assimilation). Articles and reports of events in both the Diaspora and Ereẓ Israel (including correspondences from H. Hissin, M. Meirovitz, and Ḥemdah *Ben-Yehuda) also found their way into the journal.

In the summer of 1899 Landau sold the magazine to a group of young writers (including J. *Brutzkus, L. *Bramson, S. Ginsburg, and M. *Vinawer), some of whom were nationalists and even Zionists. M.N. *Syrkin became the official editor. The declared aim of the new owners was to serve Jews through "… developing [their] national consciousness, [and] raising the cultural level of the masses." In order to compete with the Russian daily press for the attention of Jewish intellectuals in the provinces, the editors attempted in 1900–01 to publish the weekly supplement (whose name was itself changed to *Voskhod*) as a semiweekly. The new *Voskhod* carried Zionist articles and many translations from Yiddish and Hebrew. The number of subscribers reached 5,000. In 1903, after the pogroms in *Kishinev, issues 16 and 17 of the weekly were confiscated because of an article advocating Jewish *self-defense. In 1904 the weekly was suspended for six months and some of the material that had been prepared for it was published in the monthly. From 1900, the new *Voskhod* had to compete with *Budushchnost* ("The Future"), published by S. Grusenberg. Gradually, an anti-Zionist group led by M. Vinawer took over the direction of the *Voskhod*; the Zionists left it and in 1904 began publishing a Russian-language periodical of their own, *Yevreyskaya Zhizn* ("Jewish Life"). In 1906 *Voskhod* ceased publication.

BIBLIOGRAPHY: Y. Slutsky, *Ha-Ittonut ha-Yehudit-Rusit ba-Me'ah ha-19* (1970); S. Ginzburg, *Amolike Peterburg* (1944), 170–83.

[Yehuda Slutsky]

VOSKOVEC, GEORGE (1905–1981), Czech actor. Voskovec, born in Sazava, worked with Jan Werich at the "Liberated Theater for Prague," 1927–38. He spent the war years in the U.S., and returning to Prague in 1946 he adapted several American plays before finally leaving Czechoslovakia in 1953. In 1956 he acted in *Uncle Vanya* in New York and *The Diary of Anne Frank* in London. He also appeared in *The Tenth Man* in New York (1959), in Shakespeare at Stratford, Connecticut, and in *The Physicists* (1964). His films included *Twelve Angry Men*, *The Bravados*, and *The Spy who came in from the Cold.*

VOTICE (Ger. **Wotitz**), town in S. Bohemia, Czech Republic. The first evidence of a Jewish community dates from a document of 1538 concerning a Jewish cemetery. In 1570 there were 13 Jewish families in Votice. A synagogue was built in 1661 and renovated in 1724. The synagogue was torn down in 1949–50. Fifty families lived there in 1799. Votice was an agricultural center, and many Jews earned their livelihood as grain merchants and as **arendas* ("land-leasers") on the surrounding estates. There were 340 Jews in Votice proper in 1869 and 1,015 in the district; in 1902 there were 560 Jews living in 12 localities; in 1910 there were 163 Jews in the town and 348 in the district; in 1930 the community numbered 76. The community had an active cultural life. Outstanding among its rabbis were Jedidiah Tia Weil and Moses Bloch (1847–53). The family names Wotizky and Utitz probably indicate origin in this community. Under the Nazi occupation in 1942 all the Jews were deported to extermination camps. The community's synagogue equipment was sent to the Jewish Central Museum in Prague. A Jewish community was not reestablished after World War II. The synagogue and the cemetery, with gravestones dating from the 18th century, were still in existence in 1970. The names of the victims of the Holocaust were included in the memorial at *Tabor.

BIBLIOGRAPHY: Klein, in: H. Gold (ed.), *Die Juden und Judengemeinden Boehmens in Vergangenheit und Gegenwart* (1934), 705–28. **ADD. BIBLIOGRAPHY:** J. Fiedler, *Jewish Sights of Bohemia and Moravia* (1991).

[Jan Herman / Yeshayahu Jelinek (2nd ed.)]

VOWS AND VOWING. The Hebrew נֶדֶר (*neder*), a vow, is used in the Bible for a promise made to God to perform some deed (e.g., Gen. 28: 20) as well as for a prohibition which a person imposes upon himself to abstain from something which is otherwise permitted. The former is contrasted in the Mishnah with the *nedavah*, the free will offering (Kin. 1:1) while the latter is differentiated from the *shevu'ah*, the oath. The distinction between these two appears to be largely technical, but it has far-reaching consequences in the practical sphere. In the vow the person prohibits the thing to himself by declaring, "I take upon myself"; in the oath he prohibits himself to the thing by saying, "I swear to do this, or not to do this." It is with the second category, of vow, that the Talmud largely concerns itself, and to which this entry is confined.

The enormous importance of the vow and its serious consequences are reflected in the fact that a whole tractate of the Talmud, consisting of 11 chapters in the Mishnah and 91 folios in the *Gemara*, is devoted to it (see **Nedarim*), excluding the *Nazirite vow, to which a separate tractate is devoted. The biblical laws of vowing are to be found in Numbers 30: 1–16. No explicit provision is made there for absolution from vows (*hattarat nedarim*), the Bible permitting only the voiding of a vow (*hafarat nedarim*) in the case of an unmarried woman by her father, and a married woman by her husband, providing he did so "in the day that he heareth." Nevertheless, the rabbis evolved an elaborate machinery for the absolution of vows, although they frankly admitted that "the rules about the absolution of vows hover in the air and have nothing to support them" (Ḥag. 1:8). The first vow mentioned in the Bible is that of Jacob (Gen. 28:20) and it receives the indirect assent of God (Gen. 31:13). So with regard to the tragic vow of Jephthah (Judg. 11:30–40) there is no suggestion that it was wrong of him to make it, although the Midrash declares that he could have been absolved from it by Phinehas the high priest, and only the personal foolish pride of both prevented it being done (Gen. R. 60:3).

In Ecclesiastes, however, the first doubt, though a qualified one, is expressed about the advisability of making vows. "When thou vowest a vow unto God, defer not to pay it… better is it that thou shouldst not vow, than thou shouldst vow and not pay" (5:3–4). There is a difference of opinion in the Talmud (Ḥul. 2a) as to the implication of this verse. R. Judah states, "Better than both is he who vows and pays," and in the Mishnah (Dem. 2:3) confines this injunction not to be profuse in vows to the *ḥaver*, while R. Meir is of the opinion, "Better than both is he who does not vow at all." Both views find their expression in rabbinic literature. The Midrash (Lev. R. 37:1, which reverses the authors) states: "He who vows and pays receives the reward both for his vow and its fulfillment," and "he who vows and pays his vow will be vouchsafed to pay his vow in Jerusalem" (*ibid.* 37:4). The weight of opinion, however, especially in the Talmud, is in favor of completely refraining from vows. Samuel goes so far as to say, "Even when one fulfills his vow he is called wicked" (Ned. 22a), while R. Dimi calls him a sinner (Ned. 77b). It is even said that as a punishment for taking vows one's children die young (Shab. 32b).

It was as a result of this view that the elaborate procedure for the absolution of vows, which annulled them *ab initio*, was developed. The annulment depended on finding a "door of regret," the establishment of circumstances which the person taking the vow had not taken into consideration or known about at the time when he took the vow – had he done so he would not have take the vow. The annulment had to take place before a properly constituted *bet din* of three, and the formula of absolution is: "It is absolved to thee, it is absolved to thee" (Sanh. 68a). On the question of the application of the vow, it is emphasized that one follows the popularly accepted connotation of the word used, and not its literary or biblical meaning. The whole of the sixth chapter of Mishnah *Nedarim* and half of the seventh confine themselves to examples. For instance, a vow to abstain from milk does not include whey, "meat" excludes soup, "wine" only grape wine, and "clothes" excludes sackcloth or sheets.

Vowing has practically disappeared from Jewish practice. A curious exception is the accepted formula for making offerings when called up to the reading of the *law (see *Torah, reading of). The donation is introduced by the words *ba'avur she-nadar* ("inasmuch as he has vowed") – which is the origin of the Yiddish word "*shnodder*" for an offering.

Despite the accepted formula which established a promise or an undertaking as a vow, the sanctity of the word was so highly regarded that the verse "that which is gone out of thy mouth thou shalt observe and do" (Deut. 23:24) was taken as a separate injunction, independent of the words which follow "according as thou hast vowed." Even more, it was interpreted as meaning that "the mere utterance of thy lips is equivalent to a vow," giving a simple statement of intention the force of a vow (Ned. 7a), as a result of which the custom developed of adding to any such statement the disclaimer *beli neder* ("without it being a vow"). The Shulḥan Arukh (YD 203:7) permits the taking of vows when its purpose is to rid oneself of bad habits.

BIBLIOGRAPHY: A. Wendel, *Das israelitisch-juedische Geluebde* (1931); J.H. Hertz, *The Pentateuch and Haftorahs* (1950), 730–1; Z. Taubes, in: MGWJ, 73 (1929), 33–46; Eisenstein, Dinim, 258–60.

[Louis Isaac Rabinowitz]

VOZNESENSK, city in Nikolayev district, Ukraine. The Jewish settlement in Voznesensk was founded during the first half of the 19th century by several of the numerous Jews who migrated from northwestern Russia to "New Russia" (Ukraine). There were 1,249 Jews in Voznesensk in 1864; 5,932 in 1897; and by 1926 the 5,116 Jews formed 23.7% of the total population. The Jews of Voznesensk suffered severely during the Russian Civil War (1918–20) and were exterminated when the Germans occupied the town during World War II. In 1959 there were again Jews in Voznesensk (900, forming about 3% of the population). Most left in the 1990s.

[Abraham N. Poliak]

VOZNITSYN, ALEXANDER ARTEMYEVICH (d. 1738), a proselyte officer in the Russian navy. The Russian authorities accused Voznitsyn of having converted to Judaism under the influence of the Jew Baruch b. Lev of Dubrovno, who had already been suspected of proselytizing. Both Voznitsyn and Baruch were brought before the "Bureau of Secret Investigations" of St. Petersburg, which made extensive use of torture in interrogating persons suspected of plotting against the state. The matter was made known to Czarina Anna, who ordered that the bill of indictment be transferred to the senate. Under the pressure of the czarina and despite the opinion of the ministry of justice that evidence to condemn the two men was insufficient, both were burnt at the stake. The entire episode only served to intensify the already hostile Russian policy toward Jews. The legal dossier, taken from the archives of the Holy Synod of Russia, was published by I. Markon as a supplement to the collection *Perezhitoye* (with vols. 2–4, 1910–13).

BIBLIOGRAPHY: Dubnow, Divrei, 7 (1958), 147–8.

[Abraham N. Poliak]

VOZROZHDENIYE (Rus. "Renaissance"), Jewish nationalist and socialist group in Russia between 1903 and 1905. It was also connected with groups of Russian Jewish students in Western Europe. Some of the former members of the "Ḥerut" group of Berlin (whose leader had been Nachman *Syrkin) were among the members and supporters of Vozrozhdeniye, e.g., M. *Silberfarb and Z. *Kalmanovitch; members of *Po'alei Zion and of similar orientation also took part, e.g., S. *Dobin, M. Levkovski, J. Novakovski, *Ben-Adir (A. Rosin), N. *Shtif,

B. Friedland, P. *Dashewski, J. Bregman, and W. Fabrikant, and such personalities as M.B. *Ratner, Ch. *Zhitlowsky, and A. Mandelberg. At a meeting of Zionist-socialist students in Rovno (Passover, 1903), the initiative was taken for the convocation of the Vozrozhdeniye foundation conference in Kiev (Sukkot, 1903), which became its center. The detachment from political indifferentism, which had prevailed in Po'alei Zion (particularly within its Minsk trend) was shattered by the *Kishinev pogrom, the Jewish *self-defense movement, and the wave of political strikes and demonstrations which began to engulf Russia. Political activism against the czarist regime became predominant. Simultaneously, during and after the *Uganda controversy, the crisis in the Zionist concept of settling Ereẓ Israel encouraged territorialist trends.

In Vozrozhdeniye the divergence between the territorialist and the autonomist ideologies became apparent, and the autonomist trend gradually gained the upper hand. Its general theory was that the national factor in history would not disappear because it was immanent in human experience in every generation, and was of a progressive nature. Capitalism not only fails to bring about the erosion of national existence by cosmopolitan amalgamation but even enhances national separateness in human society. This process is nurtured, among others, by the democratization of life and by the social and cultural activization of the popular classes, who thus also develop their own natural national forms of existence and creativeness. This is also the background of the national liberation movements of oppressed peoples. National differences will not disappear in the future socialist system, but they will coexist in greater harmony. Within this conceptual framework, Vozrozhdeniye integrated its doctrine of Jewish national life and future. It rejected the pessimism of the Zionist "negation of the Exile." There were opportunities for revival under Diaspora conditions by positive initiatives in various spheres of life and culture: education, productivization, organization of social classes, and political-ideological trends of which the nation was composed. Above all, it claimed that it was possible to attain a recognized official status of the Jews in their countries of residence as part of the state in the form of a national-political autonomy, which would be headed by national Jewish assemblies or diets ("Sejms"). The ultimate territorial concentration of the Jews was an ideal and the final objective, which would be achieved in an undetermined time and place. However, there existed an immanent, organic relationship between the achievement of this final aim and the day-to-day "activity of the present" in its various forms. The Zionist objective – in fact, the territorialist one – would be achieved not as a result of negative factors or of catastrophic misfortune. It would be a gradual evolution of events reflecting the growth of vital and positive forces within the nation in the lands of its dispersion, after it had organized and consolidated itself in the framework of national-political autonomy. The Jewish labor movement should be based on three principles: socialism (as the final objective); revolutionary struggle against absolutism and the bureaucratic regime; and national autonomy (both as an end in itself and as a way for gaining territory for the Jewish people in the future). This ideological system was developed in the Russian organ of the group which bore its name. Numbers 1–2 were published abroad (also in Yiddish under the title *Di Yidishe Frayhayt*) at the beginning of 1904, and issue numbers 3–4 were published at the end of 1904; a third issue (St. Petersburg, 1905) contained a comprehensive essay by Ben-Adir on the "National Ideal and the National Movement." In December 1904 (January 1905), the *Zionist Socialist Workers' Party was founded with the participation of delegates of Vozrozhdeniye. However, because of their rejection of "Sejmism," Dobin, Novakovski and Levkovski resigned from the new party and remained active within Vozrozhdeniye. The second conference of Vozrozhdeniye was held in September 1905. It was attended also by the young Berl *Katznelson. The attempt to establish a joint party with the Ereẓ Israel-oriented Po'alei Zion was unsuccessful because of the issue of affiliation to the Zionist Organization. After the establishment of the Jewish Social Democratic Party *Po'alei Zion under the leadership of B. *Borochov the members of Vozrozhdeniye held the foundation conference of the Jewish Socialist Workers' Party (Sejmists) in Kiev (April, 1906), after which the group disbanded. The autonomism promoted by Vozrozhdeniye influenced not only Borochov's Po'alei Zion but also the Zionist Organization of Russia, as reflected in the *Helsingfors Program.

BIBLIOGRAPHY: Ben-Adir, in: *Sotsialistisher Teritoryalizm* (1934), 17–51, 134–9; N. Shtif, *ibid.*, 130–3; M.S. Silberfarb, *ibid.*, 57–78; idem, *Gezamlte Shriftn*, 1 (1935), 5–50, 199–258; O. Janowsky, *The Jews and Minority Rights*, 1898–1919 (1933), index; B. Borochov, *Ketavim*, ed. by L. Levite and D. Ben-Naḥum, 1 (1955), 377–82, 560–7, index to notes; 2–3 (1958–66), indexes to notes; B. Katznelson, *Ketavim*, 5 (1947), 385.

[Moshe Mishkinsky]

°**VRCHLICKÝ, JAROSLAV**, pseudonym of **Emil Frída** (1853–1912), Czech poet, playwright, and translator. Vrchlický was born in Louny, Bohemia. The most prolific and perhaps the greatest Czech writer of the 19th century, he wrote more than 160 books, and was professor of literature at the Czech University of Prague. Vrchlický was interested in Judaism and Jewish literature (Torah, Talmud) from his earliest years; at least a hundred of his poems and three of his plays are based on Jewish themes.

One of Vrchlický's greatest works is his dramatic 400-page poem *Bar Kochba* (1897). This was translated into German, as was his comedy *Rabínská moudrost* ("Rabbinic Wisdom," 1886), based on the life of R. *Judah Loew of Prague. Samson is the hero of a dramatic *Trilogie o Simsonovi* (1901), one part of which was set to music by J.B. Foerster. He translated many important poetic works from French, Italian, German, English, Spanish, and Portuguese into Czech. Vrchlický also translated into Czech many poems on Jewish themes by great foreign authors. In addition to *Byron's *Hebrew Melodies*, Vrchlický published translations of poems by *Judah Halevi and Ibn *Gabirol, and Morris *Rosenfeld's *Songs of the Ghetto*.

To Rosenfeld he also dedicated two poems and an essay, *Básník žargonu* ("The Poet of Jargon," 1906). Vrchlický's Czech translations of the Hebrew poets were based on Selig Heller's German renderings, those from Rosenfeld's Yiddish on the English version by Leo Wiener. Vrchlický's *Bar Kochba* was translated into Hebrew by Abraham *Levinson. For a time, Vrchlický was a member of the Austrian parliament's Upper House. While practically all histories of Czech literature written before World War II state that Vrchlický was of Jewish origin on his father's side, later studies reject this claim and the formerly accepted theory of Vrchlický's Jewishness seems now to be at least disputable.

BIBLIOGRAPHY: F.X. Šalda, *Duše a dílo* (1913); F.V. Krejčí, *Jaroslav Vrchlický* (1913); Weingart, in: *Sborník společnosti Jaroslava Vrchlického* (1917); O. Donath, *Židé a židovství v české literatuře 19. století* (1923); P. Váša and A. Gregor, *Katechismus dějin české literatury* (1925). **ADD. BIBLIOGRAPHY:** A. Mikulášek et al., *Literatura s hvězdou Davidovou*, vol. 1 (1998); J. Hrabák, *Dějiny české literatury III* (1961); *Slovník českých spisovatelů* (2000).

[Avigdor Dagan]

°VRIEZEN, THEODORUS CHRISTIAAN (1899– 1981), Dutch biblical scholar and Semitist. Born in Dinxperlo, Vriezen was a teacher of religion at The Hague from 1929 to 1941, and graduated as doctor of theology in 1937, the title of his thesis being *Onderzoek naar de paradijsvoorstelling bij de oude semietische volken*. In 1940 he taught Babylonian-Assyrian language at the University of Utrecht; in 1941 he became ordinary professor of Old Testament studies at the State University of Groningen, and in 1965 at the State University of Utrecht.

Of his many articles and books written on the Old Testament and the *Umwelt* of Israel, the best known are his *De Literatuur van Oud-Israel* (1961), *De godsdienst van Israel* (The Religion of Israel, 1963) and his *Hoofdlijnen van der theologie van het Oude Testament* (1954), which was translated into many languages.

[Adam Simon Van Der Woude]

VROMAN, AKIVA (1912–), geologist. Born in Holland, Vroman graduated from the University of Utrecht in 1935. Upon immigration to Ereẓ Israel, he made a geological survey of the southwest region of the Carmel in 1936. He received his doctorate from the Hebrew University in 1938. From 1948 to 1955 he made extensive geological surveys of Israel, including a geological mapping of the Negev with Dr. J. Bentor. He received the Israel Prize for science in 1955.

VROMAN, LEO (1915–), Dutch poet and biologist. Born in Gouda, Vroman fled to England when the Germans invaded Holland and then spent the war years in the Dutch East Indies. In 1945 he went to the U.S., where he worked as an animal physiologist until he retired. After a stay in New Jersey he settled in New York. In 1938 he became engaged to Tineke Sanders. Separated during WWII, they married in 1947, one day after their reunion. She played a colorful role in his poetry and prose ever since. Vroman has a unique place in Dutch experimental poetry, his language – a mixture of colloquial and extremely sophisticated speech – being notable for a biological terminology that creates surrealistic effects. His best-known works are *Gedichten* (1946), written between 1942 and 1945, and *Gedichten, vroegere en latere* (1949), poetry of the years 1935–40 in Holland, of 1940–41 in the Dutch East Indies, and of 1946–48 in the U.S. Memories of his youth were expressed in the epic poem *Inleiding tot een leegte* (1955); war experiences in *De adem van Mars* (1956); and the secret of life and death in *De Ontvachting* (1960). Much of Vroman's verse is included chronologically in the prize-winning collection *126 Gedichten* (1964). Vroman also composed English verse, collected in *Poems in English* (1953). His prose works include the short story *Tineke* (1948), and the collection *Snippers van Leo Vroman* (1958). He further published diary notes under the title *Vroeger donker dan gisteren. Herfstdagboek* (Amsterdam 2004). Of particular note are his letters from the U.S.: *Brieven uit Brooklyn* (1975). His collected poetry appeared in 1985, *Gedichten 1948–1984* (Amsterdam), a feat that by no means signified the end of his activity as a poet. He published new volumes almost every year, such as *Psalmen en andere gedichten* (Amsterdam 1995). Leo Vroman's gifts were not confined to literature – he was a fine artist, and throughout his work his poems were regularly accompanied by subtle drawings.

BIBLIOGRAPHY: J. Kuijper, *Het Vroman-effect: over leven en werk van Leo Vroman* (1990); B.J. Peperkamp, *Over de dichtkunst: een lezing met demonstraties* (1995); H.U. Jessurun d'Oliveira, *Het gedicht als wereld. Essays over Lucebert, Leo Vroman en Rutger Kopland* (2003).

[Gerda Alster-Thau / Maritha Mathijsen (2nd ed.)]

VUGHT (also called **Kl Herzogenbusch**), the site of a minor Nazi camp for Dutch Jewry in the province of Brabant, Holland. It was established in 1942 under the supervision of WVHA. Karl Chmielewski, who was a veteran of Mauthausen, was its commandant. He was joined by a staff of 80 Kapos, but unlike the situation in Mauthausen, these Jews were not to be mistreated. Two categories of Jews were interned in Vught: textile and diamond workers who had lost their original status as "privileged" Jews; and those who in April and May 1943 had to leave certain provinces which were being "cleansed" of Jews. Originally, the camp was said to be a labor camp; most were employed outside the camp in fur and clothing manufacturing; others worked in construction of fortifications. There was a unique arrangement with the Philips Company, which employed some 1,200 prisoners. The company insisted that the inmates who worked for them be given a hot meal each day and not be deported. Dr. Arthur Lehmann served as the head of the Jewish administration of the camp and he functioned as best he could given his limited and derivative powers to treat his fellow Jews well. He kept a detailed record of life in Vught. Conditions deteriorated when Adam Grunewald replaced Chmielewski; he in turn was removed for excessive punishments, which bespeaks the unusual situation of the camp. Grunewald was replaced by Hans Huttifg.

From Jan. 13, 1943, until Sept. 6, 1944, Vught served as a transit point for Jews who were sent on to death camps. Approximately 12,000 Jews passed through Vught. Transports reduced the camp population and then others arrived. Most notorious of all the transports from Vught was one that took place via *Westerbork to *Sobibor on June 5, 1943, consisting of 1,266 children under the age of 16. They were murdered upon arrival. In the end even the Philips Company could not protect its Jews from deportation, but not for want of trying. Those who were sent to Auschwitz were selected for work for Telefunken by an agreement between the two corporations. But conditions in Auschwitz were so harsh that of the 517 Philips workers who were deported to Auschwitz, only 160 – less than one in three – survived. Among them were nine children and more than 100 women.

BIBLIOGRAPHY: J. Presser, *Ashes in the Wind: Destruction of Dutch Jewry* (1968), 464–78, index; *Vught, Poort van de hel* (1945). **ADD. BIBLIOGRAPHY:** J. Michman, "Vught," in: Y. Gutman (ed.), *Macmillan Encyclopedia of the Holocaust*, vol. 4 (1990), 1584–86.

[Abel Jacob Herzberg / Michael Berenbaum (2nd ed.)]

VULGATE (Latin *Vulgata* (*versio*); "common version"), *Jerome's translation into Latin of the Bible, Apocrypha, and New Testament. Jerome's translation enjoyed general appreciation and acceptance in Western Christendom during the Middle Ages, thus becoming known as the Vulgate. Until recently the Vulgate was the only text used in the Roman Catholic liturgy. For a full discussion, see *Bible, Translations.

VULTURES, a number of carrion-eating birds. They are recognizable by their blunt claws, in which they differ from other birds of prey, and their bald heads (except for the bearded vulture). These are useful birds since they act as scavengers, and formerly were very common in Israel. In recent times, however, they have diminished in number, and some species are in danger of extinction due to the use of chemical pesticides to kill various animals (like jackals and mice), causing the vultures to die from eating the poisoned carcasses. Four species of vulture are mentioned in the Bible: *nesher* (AV, "eagle"; JPS, "great vulture"), *ozniyyah* (AV and JPS, "osprey"), *peres* (AV, "ossifrage"; JPS, "bearded vulture"), and *raḥam* (AV, "gier-eagle"; JPS, "common vulture"). The first three are mentioned together as forbidden for food (Lev. 11: 13, Deut. 14: 12).

There is no doubt that the *nesher* (נֶשֶׁר) of the Bible is the griffon vulture – *Gyps fulvus*. It is the largest of Israel's carnivorous birds, its outstretched wings sometimes attaining a span of ten feet. It does not prey on living things but feeds on carcasses; as mentioned in Job (39: 27–30): "She dwelleth… on the rock…. From thence she spieth out the prey; her eyes behold it afar off… and where the slain are, there is she." It has no feathers on its neck to prevent the blood of the carcass from congealing when the vulture puts its head inside it, and hence its designation of "baldhead" (Micah 1: 16). It is one of the longest-lived birds (cf. Ps. 103: 5). The pair of vultures builds its nest on the peaks of lofty rocks (Jer. 49: 16; etc.). The fledgling develops slowly, and the parents tend it with devotion and train it to fly (cf. Deut. 32: 11). (On the identification of the *nesher* with the eagle, see *Eagle.) The name *ozniyyah* (עָזְנִיָּה) appears to be connected with the bird's strength; it is called *oz* ("strength") in the Mishnah, which states that articles used to be made from its wings (Kel. 17: 14). Whereas the griffon vulture was common near settlements, it was pointed out that the *ozniyyah* was found only in places far away from settlements (Ḥul. 62a). The reference is to the black vulture, which is similar in build to the griffon vulture, but has only a bald head and not a bare neck. Two species are found in Israel, the *Aegypius monachus*, which is dark brown and very rare, and the *Aegypius tracheliotus*, found in the Negev and distinguished from the former by its brightly colored belly.

The Talmud (*ibid.*) notes that like the *ozniyyah* the *peres* (פֶּרֶס) is not found in inhabited localities. It is identified with the bearded vulture, the *Gypaetus barbatus*. It is presumed that the name *peres* derives from the fact that it breaks (*pores*, פּוֹרֵס) the bones of carcasses by dropping them from a height in order to eat the marrow. It is recognizable by the hairy beard fringe at the end of its beak, and is widely dispersed geographically, being found in southern Europe, Africa, and Asia, although in all these places it is rare. In Israel too, in the mountains of the Negev, only solitary pairs are found. The *raḥam* (Deut. 14: 17, רָחָמָה) is also mentioned as a bird forbidden as food (Lev. 11: 18), and its similar name in Arabic is the basis of its identification with the *Neophron percnopterus*, the Egyptian vulture. It is the smallest of Israel vultures and is found in flocks near garbage heaps where it feeds on carcasses and insects. When young it is brown in color and later becomes white. In the Talmud the *raḥam* is identified with a bird called the *sherakrak*, which, according to the *aggadah*, if it will sit upon the ground and chirp, thus gives a sign of the advent of the Messiah (Ḥul. 63a). Apparently the reference is to a bird of the genus *Merops* which is never seen resting on the ground.

BIBLIOGRAPHY: R. Meinertzhagen, *Birds of Arabia* (1954), 382f.; J. Feliks, *The Animal World of the Bible* (1962), 63–71. **ADD. BIBLIOGRAPHY:** Feliks, Ha-Ẓome'aḥ, 256, 259.

[Jehuda Feliks]

VYGOTSKI, LEV SEMYONOVICH, (1896–1934), Soviet psychologist and author. Vygotski joined the Institute of Psychology in Moscow in 1924. In 1932 he founded the laboratory of psychology at the All-Union Institute of Experimental Medicine in Moscow, where studies by psychologists and psychiatrists were carried out on disintegration of personality in various neuropsychiatric disorders. He advanced the psychological diagnostics of mental disturbances (Vygotski's blocks for the study of concept formation) and methods for teaching mentally retarded children. His main concern was a theory of historicocultural development of man's highest mental functions, such as conceptual thinking and voluntary control of behavior. After his premature death the creative impetus he imparted to Soviet psychology was carried on by a group of his close associates including A.R. *Luria and B.V. Zeigarnik.

His publications in English included "The Problem of the Cultural Development of the Child," in *Journal of Genetic Psychology*, 36 (1929), 415–34; "Thought in Schizophrenia," in: *Archives of Neurology and Psychiatry*, 31 (1934), 1063–77; and *Thought and Language* (trans. from Russian with introd. by J.S. Bruner, 1962). His publications in Russian include: *Pedagogicheskaya psikhologiya* ("Educational psychology," 1926); *Pedologiya v shkol'nom vozraste* ("Paedology of the School Age") 1928; *Voobrazheniye i tvorchestvo v detskom vozraste* ("Imagination and Creativity in Children," 1930); *Umstvennoye razvitiye detey v protsesse obucheniya* ("Effects of Schooling on the Child's Mental Development," 1935); and *Psikhologiya iskusstva* ("Psychology of Art," 1965).

BIBLIOGRAPHY: A.R. Luria, in: *Journal of Genetic Psychology*, 46 (1935), 224–6; E. Kaufmann and J. Kasanin, in: *Journal of Psychology*, 3 (1937), 521–40; A.N. Leontyev and A.R. Luria, in: B.B. Wolman (ed.), *Historical Roots of Contemporary Psychology* (1968), 338–67.

[Josef Brozek]

VYSOKOYE (Pol. **Wysokie Litewskie**), city in W. Brest oblast, Belorus; in Poland-Lithuania before 1795 and between the two world wars. Jews were living in Vysokoye from the late 16th century. A community was organized in the early 17th century, which by decision of the Lithuanian Council (see Councils of *Lands), came under the jurisdiction of the Brest community. The synagogue, built of stone in 1607 was enlarged in 1828. In 1650 a meeting of the Lithuanian Council took place in Vysokoye. Jewish economic activity in the second half of the 18th century was encouraged by the owner of the town, Duchess A. Jablonowsky (1728–1800), in accordance with her policy toward Jews in Semiatycze and *Kock. A bet midrash was established in 1757. A new building was completed to house the bet midrash in 1837 and a new cemetery was opened in 1898. A *talmud torah* was founded in 1853. The Jewish population numbered 1,475 in 1847 and 2,876 (85% of the total) in 1897. In the 19th century Jews engaged in the trade of agricultural products, tailoring, tanning, carpentry, and transportation. Between the two world wars, when it was part of independent Poland, there was a Hebrew *Tarbut school. The community, which numbered 1,902 (91%) in 1921, was annihilated in World War II.

BIBLIOGRAPHY: S. Dubnow (ed.), *Pinkas ha-Medinah* (1925), index; B. Wasiutyński, *Ludność żydowska w Polsce w wiekach XIX i XX* (1930), 83; R. Mahler, *Yidn in Amolikn Poyln in Likht fun Tsifern* (1958), index.

[Arthur Cygielman]

Illuminated "W" used to represent the sound of the initial letter of the Latin word Vere. *The figures represent Ecclesia and Synagoga. Detail from the* Missal of Paris, *France 12th century, Paris, Bibliothèque Nationale, Ms. Lat. 8884, fol. 130.*

WA-WEI

WACHNER, LINDA JOY (1946–), U.S. apparel industry executive. Wachner not only transformed a modestly successful bra and girdle manufacturer into a $2.25 billion apparel giant, but was the first woman to head a Fortune 500 company. She was born in Manhattan, the daughter of Herman Wachner, a furrier, and his wife, Shirley, a saleswoman at Saks Fifth Avenue, and raised in Queens. When she was 11, severe scoliosis put her in a full-body cast for a year, an experience, she says, that developed her tenacious nature and taught her to be self-reliant. She graduated from high school at 16, then earned a B.S. in economics and business at the University of Buffalo in 1966. After joining Associated Merchandising Corp., a New York City buying office for department stores, at $90 a week, she became an assistant buyer at Foley's, a store in Houston, Texas, in 1968. A year later, she was a bra buyer at R.H. Macy's in New York City. In 1973, she met and married Seymour Appelbaum, a man 31 years her senior. In 1974, she joined Warnaco, becoming a vice president in 1975. In 1978, she was recruited to run the U.S. division of Max Factor, a money-losing cosmetics company. Wachner cut costs, laid people off, and produced a $5 million operating profit in her second year. In 1983, Wachner's husband, who had a serious heart condition, died. Wachner tried to buy the Max Factor business, but her offer was rejected and she was forced out. Eager to run her own show, Wachner engineered a $550 million hostile takeover of Warnaco in 1986 and quickly began to remake the 113-year-old company, which had a stable of prestigious brand names but did not market them effectively. Annual volume was $425 million when Wachner took over. Becoming chief executive in 1987 and chairman in 1991 – the year she took the company public – she was called "America's most successful businesswoman" by *Fortune* magazine. The same publication also anointed her one of America's "toughest bosses." In 1997, Wachner acquired Designer Holdings, a company licensed to make Calvin *Klein jeans. A year later, Warnaco business began to suffer, a victim of dwindling demand for its products, lower market share, a weakening economy, and several problematic licensing deals. In addition, Wachner's difficult personality was blamed for many top managers leaving the company. Perhaps most important was a nasty, headline-making fight with Calvin Klein over the way his jeans, which accounted for 25 percent of Warnaco's overall sales, were made and marketed. Klein said Warnaco was not only selling the high-prestige jeans to low-end discount houses, but altering designs and skimping on quality. Wachner counter-sued and a settlement was reached in January 2001. Warnaco stock, which had traded at $44 a share in 1998, was down to 39 cents a share in 2001, and Wachner's personal stake in the firm had fallen from some $200 million to $1.8 million. The company filed for bankruptcy in 2001 (emerging in 2003) and Wachner was fired. She sued for $25 million in severance pay, but settled for $452,000.

[Mort Sheinman (2nd ed.)]

WACHSTEIN, BERNHARD (**Dov Ber Wachstein**; 1868–1935), historian, bibliographer, and genealogist. Born in Tłuste, Galicia, he was educated in the Vienna rabbinical seminary and University of Vienna. In 1903 he became librarian of the Vienna community. He broadened the Judaica collection and was made assistant director in 1906; later he became director of the library, which he built up to 50,000 volumes, making it one of the richest and best ordered in Europe. In 1912 and

1917 he published his two-volume master work, *Die Inschriften des alten Judenfriedhofes in Wien*, a scholarly study of the tombstones of the Viennese Jewish community dating from 1540 to 1783. Wachstein subsequently rendered a similar service to the community of *Eisenstadt (*Die Inschriften des alten Judenfriedhofes in Eisenstadt*, 1922) and also published a number of monographs on Moravian communities. He compiled a bibliography of Hebrew eulogies in the holdings of the community library in Vienna (*Mafteach Ha-hespedim. Zur Bibliographie der Gedaechtnis- und Trauervorträge in der hebraeischen Literatur*, 4 vols., 1922–32) as well as bibliographies of the writings of G. *Wolf and M. *Guedemann. Together with Alexander Kristianpoller and Israel Taglicht, he published an anthology on Hebrew journals in Vienna (*Die Hebraeische Publizistik in Wien*, 3 vols., 1930). In 1939, a few years after his death, YIVO published the *Vakhsteyn-bukh*, a compilation in his memory.

BIBLIOGRAPHY: S. Chajes, *Bibliographie der Schriften Bernhard Wachsteins* (1933); N.M. Gelber, in: S. Federbusch (ed.), *Ḥokhmat Yisrael be-Ma'arav Eiropah*, 1 (1958), 232–40; A.M. Habermann, in: *Yad la-Koré*, 5 (1957–59), 163–5; S. Wachstein, *Hagenberggasse*, 49 (1996; Eng. *Too Deep Were Our Roots*, 2001).

[Mirjam Triendl-Zadoff]

WACHTLER, SOL (1930–), U.S. jurist, chief judge of the New York State Court of Appeals. He was born in Brooklyn, New York, and received his B.A. cum laude and his law degree from Washington and Lee universities. He was in private law practice in Jamaica, Long Island, until his appointment as a justice of the New York Supreme Court in 1968; later that year he was elected to a full term in the court. In 1972 he was elected to the New York State Court of Appeals, the state's highest court, and in January 1985 Governor Cuomo appointed him chief judge of the State of New York and the Court of Appeals. In this position he supervised a system that included some three thousand judges and about twelve thousand non-judicial personnel.

As chief judge of the Court of Appeals, Wachtler said that he set for himself two chief missions: to achieve collegiality for the court, so that it may speak with "one voice" and win for itself again the reputation it enjoyed under the leadership of Benjamin N. *Cardozo; and to streamline and modernize the administration of the state's judicial system.

In 1992 Wachtler's career came to a grinding halt when he was arrested by the FBI for stalking and harassing the woman with whom he had been having an affair for several years. In 1993 he was indicted on five counts of extortion, mailing threats, and lying to a government agency. He pleaded guilty to harassment and was sentenced to 11 months in a medium-security federal prison, which followed a year of home confinement. This harrowing experience is chronicled in his book *After the Madness: A Judge's Own Prison Memoir* (1997).

His own personal demons notwithstanding, in his capacity as a jurist Wachtler initiated reforms in a number of controversial areas. For example, he declared it unconstitutional that a man could rape his wife and go unpunished; he extended the human rights law to prohibit discrimination against obese people; he provided women with more power to fight gender bias; and he endorsed gay rights.

Wachtler went on to teach law at the Law School at Touro College in Huntington, New York. In 2000 he received the President's Award of the New York State Mental Health Association for the work he did on behalf of the mentally ill. Wachtler co-authored the novel *Blood Brothers* (2003) with David Gould, a former assistant district attorney.

BIBLIOGRAPHY: J. Caher, *King of the Mountain: The Rise, Fall, and Redemption of Chief Judge Sol Wachtler* (1998).

[Milton Ridvas Konvitz / Ruth Beloff (2nd ed.)]

WADDINGTON, MIRIAM (**Dvorkin**; 1917–2004), Canadian poet. Waddington was born and raised in Winnipeg, Manitoba. She attended high school in Ottawa and earned a B.A. from the University of Toronto in 1939. Subsequently, she earned an M.S.W. from the University of Pennsylvania in 1945, and an M.A. from the University of Toronto in 1968. She married the journalist Patrick Waddington in 1939 (from whom she was later divorced) and had two sons.

In 1945, Waddington moved to Montreal, where she was employed as a social worker and participated in the city's literary life. She contributed poems to *First Statement* and *Preview* and published her first book of poems with First Statement Press. In 1960, she returned to Toronto, where she worked for North York Family Services. From 1964 until her retirement in 1983, Waddington was a professor of English at Toronto's York University.

Waddington published 12 books of poetry. Her earliest collections (*Green World*, 1945; *The Second Silence*, 1955; *The Season's Lovers*, 1958) established her reputation as a lyricist. Waddington's poetry mines the historical past and individual memory. Her work is characterized by intensely visual images that evoke landscape and daily life. At the same time, her oeuvre reflects a lifelong engagement with social issues, which she attributed to her Jewish upbringing, particularly as they affect women. Throughout several decades, she experimented with form and language in poems that reveal – with increasing concision and gentle irony – the contradictory meanings of ordinary life (*The Glass Trumpet*, 1966; *Say Yes*, 1969; *Dream Telescope*, 1972; *Driving Home*, 1972). By celebrating small pleasures, her poems on aging (in *The Price of Gold*, 1976; *Mister Never*, 1978; *The Visitants*, 1981; *The Last Landscape*, 1992) subdue the pain of loneliness. Her *Collected Poems* was published in 1986, and an excerpt from one of her poems appears on the Bank of Canada $100 note. Waddington won the Montreal Jewish Public Library's J.I. Segal Foundation Award in 1972 and 1986.

Waddington also published *Summer at Lonely Beach and Other Stories* (1982), a collection that draws on her childhood and youth in southern Manitoba, and *Apartment Seven* (1989), a volume of essays. She wrote *A.M. Klein* (1970), a pioneering critical study of the Canadian poet, and edited *The Collected*

Poems of A.M. Klein (1974), as well as *John Sutherland: Essays, Controversies and Poems* (1972).

[Ruth Panofsky (2nd ed.)]

WADI AL-NAṬṬŪF, site of the first discovery of the prehistoric Natufian culture in Ereẓ Israel. Starting in the Judean hills c. 12½ mi. (20 km.) north of Jerusalem, Wadi al-Naṭṭūf joins Naḥal Ayalon in the coastal plain near Or Yehudah, and near the village of Shuqbā the wadi turns sharply to the southwest; on the northern side of this turn is the Shuqbā Cave, 72 ft. (22 m.) above the wadi-bed and 656 ft. (200 m.) above sea level. The cave, composed of three chambers, measures 131×131 ft. (40×40 m.); the vault, 82 ft. (25 m.) above the floor of the cave, contains two open chimneys.

The Shuqbā Cave was excavated in 1928 by D. Garrod in one of the earliest cave excavations in Ereẓ Israel. The cave was the first to reveal a Mesolithic cultural stage, dating to about 10,000 years ago, which Garrod called Natufian after the name of the wadi. Four stages were distinguished in the cave, including, from bottom to top: layer D, with an upper Mousterian industry; layer C derived from D and redeposited with abraded implements; layer B containing the Natufian industry; and the uppermost layer A with pottery dating from the Early Bronze Age to recent times. The Natufian of layer B is characterized by an important group of microliths – tiny stone implements – of which the majority are lunates (crescentshaped blades) and also including triangles, trapezes, and various small-backed blades. Among the non-microlithic artifacts were scrapers, gravers, borers, etc., as well as sickle blades which make their first appearance in the Natufian culture. Bone tools, mainly awls, are also typical of this stage. The Natufian tool kit is regarded as representing a more or less intensive collection of wild cereals in conjunction with the traditional food supply acquired through hunting and food gathering. The report that a domesticated dog was found in the Natufian culture at Shuqbā is dubious.

BIBLIOGRAPHY: Garrod, in: *Proceedings of the Prehistoric Society*, 8 (1942), 1–20.

[Avraham Ronen]

WADI DĀLIYA, valley 12 mi. (c. 19 km.) N.W. of Jericho. In 1962 Bedouin discovered a number of papyri in the Maghārat Abu Shinjah in Wadi Dāliya. The cave was cleared in 1963 by P. Lapp. The finds included over 200 skeletons, jewelry, 128 seals of documents, and a number of legal documents from Samaria, dated 375 (or 365) B.C.E. The Aramaic documents mention Yoshua son of Sanballat (II) the (hereditary) governor of Samaria, and the prefect Hananiah. They mention conveyances of land, manumissions, and the sale of slaves (including one Nehemiah to the Samaritan noble Yehonur). The people in the cave seem to have fled there during the Samaritan revolt against Alexander the Great and appear to have perished in a Macedonian attack.

BIBLIOGRAPHY: F.M. Cross, in: D.N. Freedman and J.C. Greenfield (ed.), *New Directions in Biblical Archaeology* (1969), 41–63.

[Michael Avi-Yonah]

WAGENAAR, LION (1855–1930), Dutch rabbi. Wagenaar served as chief rabbi of Friesland (1886) and Gelderland (1895), and as rector of the Nederlands Israelietisch Seminarium, the Jewish theological seminary of Amsterdam, from 1918 until his death. A disciple of J.Z. *Duenner, he published many historical-critical articles on talmudic-halakhic subjects and translated the prayer book into Dutch, with a commentary and historical expositions.

A jubilee volume (*Feestbundel*) in his honor was issued in 1925 by the Genootschap voor de Joodsche Wetenschap in Nederland, with a bibliography of his writings. After his death a collection of 31 articles was published (*Ellu le-Ahavah*, 1932).

BIBLIOGRAPHY: Wininger, Biog, s.v.; S. Dasberg, in: *Bijdragen en Mededeelingen van het Genootschap voor de Joodsche Wetenschap in Nederland*, 5 (1933), 19–26.

[Frederik Jacob Hirsch]

°**WAGENSEIL, JOHANN CHRISTOPH** (1633–1705), Christian Hebraist. While professor at the University of Altdorf, he published a series of writings on Judaism and the Jews whose missionary intention is manifest. His most important work was *Tela ignea Satanae, Hoc est: arcani, et horribles Judaeorum adversus Christum Deum et Christianam religionem libri* ("Flaming Arrows of Satan; that is, the secret and horrible books of the Jews against Christ, God, and the Christian religion"; Altdorf, 1681), a collection of works written by Jews for use in Jewish-Christian disputations and controversies. Wagenseil published these for the first time, with a Latin translation and his own introduction, with the intention of making Christians aware of the Jewish objections to Christianity and thus to refute them. Since this compilation of Jewish polemical writings made Jewish criticism of Christianity widely known, it was used in anti-Jewish propaganda, but these same criticisms were also employed by some opponents of religious fanaticism, such as *Voltaire and the Encyclopedists. Later, in *Denunciatio christiana de blasphemiis Judaeorum in Jesum Christum* (Altdorf, 1703), Wagenseil appealed to the Protestant rulers to prevent the Jews from blaspheming Christianity and to try to convert them (though without persecutions and forcible means, to which he was opposed). A varied collection of essays on Jewish matters, *Benachrichtigungen wegen einiger die gemeine Juedischkeit betreffenden Sachen* (Leipzig, 1705), included a missionary essay and a work against *blood libel.

Earlier in his life Wagenseil published Latin translations of the mishnaic tractate *Sotah* (Altdorf, 1675) and extracts from the Talmud and *Ein Ya'akov* with the sources. Corrections to *Sefer ha-Nizzahon* by Yom Tov Lippmann Muelhausen are incorporated at the end of this book. In his determination to understand Judaism in all its ramifications, Wagenseil learned Yiddish and studied its literature. His collection, *Belehrung der juedisch-teutschen Red- und Schreibart* (Koenigsberg, 1699), includes Passover songs in Yiddish, the *Megillat Vinz* of Elhanan b. Abraham Hellen (describing the *Fettmilch uprising in Frankfurt), a Yiddish version of the Arthurian legend, and a Yiddish version of *Hilkhot Derekh Ereẓ Rabbah ve-Zuta*. Wagenseil was on friendly terms with some Jews, and an interesting correspondence with his teachers has survived. Considered the father of Scandinavian Hebrew studies, he trained a group of Hebrew scholars who were interested in acquiring information on Judaism, such as J.J. *Schudt.

BIBLIOGRAPHY: J. Weissberg, in: *Zeitschrift fuer Deutsche Sprache*, 25 (1969), 154–68; Graetz, Hist, 5 (1895), 185–8; H. Thompson, *Wagner and Wagenseil* (1927); B. Weinryb, in: *Gedank un Leben*, 2 (1944), 109–18; H.J. Schoeps, *Philosemitismus im Barock* (1952), index; Fuerst, Bibliotheca, 489; ADB.

[Judah M. Rosenthal]

WAGENSTEIN, ANGEL RAYMOND (1922–), Bulgarian novelist and screenwriter. Born in Plovdiv, Bulgaria to a Jewish workers' family, Wagenstein was active in the partisan resistance movement in World War II. Captured and tortured, he was sentenced to death and only saved by the rapid advance of the Red Army in August 1944.

After the war he studied cinema in Moscow and went on to write more than 50 screenplays for feature films, documentaries, and animated cartoons produced in Bulgaria, Germany, Russia, the Czech Republic, Greece, China, and Vietnam. *Stars* (*Zvezdi*), dealing with the fate of the Jews during the Holocaust, won a special prize at Cannes in 1959. As a novelist he wrote the prizewinning trilogy *Petoknizie Isaakovo* ("Isaac's Pentateuch") on Jewish life in the 20th century, *Avram Karkacha*, and *Sbogom Shanhai* ("Good-bye Shanghai"), which won the Jean Monet Prize in 2004.

Wagenstein was one of the 12 dissidents invited to the historic meeting with President Mitterand at the French Embassy in Sofia before the collapse of totalitarianism in Bulgaria. After the changes in 1989 he was elected as a deputy in the National Assembly, which produced the new democratic constitution of Bulgaria. He was named a chevalier in the French Order of Merit.

[Emil Kalo (2nd ed.)]

WAGG, British family of stockbrokers and merchant bankers. This prominent English financial dynasty was founded by JOHN WAGG (1793–1878), a German Jewish immigrant who began the family City of London stockbroking firm of Helbert, Wagg & Co. in 1823. Wagg was a relative of the *Rothschilds and acted as their stockbrokers. His sons ARTHUR WAGG (1842–1919) and EDWARD WAGG (1843–1933) developed the firm into a merchant bank dealing with the distribution and arbitrage of international securities. The firm was notable for treating its staff well, introducing a pioneering pension scheme. Arthur's son ALFRED RALPH WAGG (1877–1969) served as chairman of the firm from 1922 until 1954. In 1962 Helbert, Wagg merged with the famous non-Jewish City merchant bank J. Henry Schroder & Co. to form J. Henry Schroder, Wagg & Co. In 2000 Citigroup, the American bank, acquired the firm, renaming it Citigroup Global Market Ltd.

BIBLIOGRAPHY: ODNB online; R. Roberts, *Schroders: Merchants and Bankers* (1992).

[William D. Rubinstein (2nd ed.)]

WAGG, ABRAHAM (1719–1803), loyalist merchant. Wagg was probably born in London. He settled in New York in about 1770 and became a wholesale grocer and chocolate manufacturer. In that year he married Rachel Gomez (1739–1809), daughter of Mordecai Gomez (1688–1750). He remained in New York City during the English occupation of the city in 1776. As a member of the militia and fire watch, he suffered severe injuries which caused him to become lame. He took an oath of allegiance to Great Britain in 1777 and two years later sailed for England. He settled in Bristol and from there unsuccessfully sought restitution for his properties seized in New York.

BIBLIOGRAPHY: C. Roth, in: AJHSP, 31 (1928), 33–75.

[Leo Hershkowitz]

WAGHALTER, IGNATZ (1882–1940), conductor and composer. Born in Warsaw, Waghalter studied in Berlin, where he became conductor of the Comic Opera. From 1912 to 1923 he was conductor and general musical director of the German Opera House in Berlin-Charlottenburg. In 1925 he visited the United States and conducted the New York State Symphony Orchestra for one season. In 1933 he moved to Prague, in 1934 to Vienna, and after 1938 he settled in New York. As a composer he was best known for his operas, particularly *Mandragola* (1914), based on Machiavelli's comedy. He also wrote operettas, works for strings, piano works, a vaudeville (*Bibi*), songs to Yiddish texts, and piano arrangements of Yiddish songs. Waghalter wrote an autobiography, *Aus dem Ghetto in die Freiheit* (1936).

°**WAGNER, RICHARD** (1813–1883), German composer. Disillusioned by the failure of the 1848 revolution, in which he had played an active part, Wagner (like *Proudhon and other early socialists) made a bitter attack on the Jews, whom he portrayed as the incarnation of money power, symbolized by the Rothschilds and commercialism (he published "Das Judentum in der Musik" anonymously in *Neue Zeitschrift fuer Musik*, 1850). This common stereotype and the composer's emotional aversion to Jews were given a kind of rationalization in his racial deterministic theories. He transferred his dislike to the cultural field, denying Jewish cultural creativity in general and, in particular, that the composers Giacomo *Meyerbeer and Felix *Mendelssohn or Heinrich *Heine could be considered truly creative. In ambiguous terms, under the guise of speaking of their redemption, he conceived the idea of the extinction (*Untergang*) of the Jews. Under his own name Wagner republished the article as a separate pamphlet with a supplement, "Enlightenment on Jewry in Music," in 1869, blaming his current problems on the alleged control of the press, theater, and cultural life by Jews, and including in his strictures those non-Jewish writers and editors who were opposed to his chauvinism. Identifying modern materialism with alleged Jewish influence, he envisaged the forced removal of Jews from cultural life or, alternatively (since he was inconsistent), their complete assimilation by means of art and music. Like the original article, the pamphlet, the ideas of which were eagerly seized on by Eugen

*Duehring, provoked a storm of controversy. In a series of articles entitled "German Art and Politics" (1867) in the semiofficial Bavarian *Sueddeutsche Presse*, Wagner expounded his ideas of the pure-blooded German mission, opposed to "alien" French and Jewish materialism. Founding his own paper, the *Bayreuther Blaetter* (1878), he (and his disciples) used it as a platform for his notion that the pastoral Germans of romantic idyll were economically dominated by Jewish speculators and bankers, and reiterated his view on the control of cultural life by Jews, borrowing phrases from the antisemite Wilhelm *Marr. In "Know Thyself," a supplement to *Religion und Kunst* (1881), Wagner deplored the granting of civil rights in 1871, applauded political antisemitism, and branded the Jews as the "demon causing mankind's downfall" (*Untergang*).

Wagner's antisemitism was shared by his devotees, and above all by his wife, Cosima, trustee of his estate for 47 years. She and Houston Stewart *Chamberlain, who married Wagner's youngest daughter in 1908, established the "Wagner cult" as a faith adumbrating the Nazi Fuehrer principle. Wagner Clubs were founded on an international scale from the 1860s on. Wagner began publishing his *Collected Works* in 1871; by 1912 they comprised 12 volumes. The articles and pamphlets on Jews and antisemitism are reprinted in volumes 5, 8, and 10. Wagner's works, which circulated widely among the educated classes, made antisemitism culturally respectable, and generally spread racialist doctrines, popularizing those of *Gobineau, with whom he was personally acquainted. Wagner's political writings were among the great ideological influences on Adolf Hitler, and his favorite reading. He was an admirer of his operas from his early youth and had them regularly performed at Bayreuth in connection with the Nazi Party conventions. The question of Wagner's parentage – whether he was the son of his legal father, Carl Friedrich Wagner, or the actor Ludwig Geyer (whom his mother married eight months after the former's death) – led to the widely circulated rumor that he was of Jewish origin. According to recent research, Wagner was Geyer's illegitimate son. But Geyer was the descendant of German Protestants whose ancestry could be traced back to the late 17th century. The genealogical investigation was undertaken by the Nazis to remove all doubts concerning their cultural and ideological hero.

In the State of Israel, Wagner's music remained excluded from the repertoire of its Philharmonic Orchestra and broadcasting program, in spite of divergent opinions and even protests.

BIBLIOGRAPHY: R.W. Gutman, *Richard Wagner* (1968); E. Newman, *Life of Richard Wagner*, 4 vols. (1933–46), index, esp. v. 4 index: *Wagner, Richard, Anti-semitism*; F. Kobler (ed.), *Juden und Judentum in deutschen Briefen* (1935), 323–4; M. Boucher, *Political Concepts of Richard Wagner* (1950), 50–55, 72; L. Stein, *Racial Thinking of Richard Wagner* (1950); T.W. Adorno, *Versuch ueber Wagner* (1952), 17–19; O. Kulka, in: BLBI, 4 (1961), 281–300; R.E. Herzstein, in: *Zeitschrift fuer die Geschichte der Juden*, 4 (1967), 119–40 (Eng.); E. Friedmann, *Das Judenthum und Richard Wagner* (1869); A. Holde, *Jews in Music* (1959), index.

[Toni Oelsner]

WAGNER, SIEGFRIED (1878–1952), Danish sculptor. Born in Lyngby, Wagner had a special position among Danish sculptors because his work showed the influence of the old Oriental style rather than the modern Danish tradition, and because of his immense productivity. His work adorns squares in Copenhagen and many other towns. His memorial in the Jewish cemetery, Copenhagen, to the Jews who died in *Theresienstadt concentration camp consists of the Lion of Judah. Wagner often used Jewish motives in his work.

WAGNER, STANLEY M. (1932–), U.S. rabbi, academician, and community leader. Born in Brooklyn, New York, Wagner was educated at Yeshiva University, where he was ordained (1956) and wrote his doctoral dissertation on "Religious Non-Conformity in Ancient Jewish Life" (1964), a study of talmudic terms and categories for deviant religious behavior. After holding pulpits, as well as university teaching positions, in Lexington, Kentucky (1957–61) and Baldwin, New York (1961–70), Wagner served as executive vice president of the Religious Zionists of America (Mizrachi – Ha-Poel ha-Mizrachi (1970–72). In 1972, he was appointed rabbi of the Beth HaMedrosh HaGodol (BMH) congregation, the oldest traditional congregation in Denver (founded in 1897), serving there until his retirement in 1997. At the beginning of his tenure, Wagner led the BMH into affiliation with the Union of Orthodox Jewish Congregations. At the end of his tenure, another traditional congregation, Beth Joseph, merged with the BMH and was housed in its facility.

In his 25 years in the Denver rabbinate, Wagner played a major role in reinvigorating communal Jewish life in Denver, due to his rabbinic, academic, and inter-religious activism, reflecting his interest in ideological diversity, first evident in his doctoral research. While serving as a congregational rabbi, Wagner also served as professor of Jewish history at the University of Denver (1972–99), where in 1975 he founded and directed the Center for Judaic Studies, which sponsored, in addition to its academic program at the university, courses in Judaica at local Christian seminaries, the Rocky Mountain Jewish Historical Society, and Beck Archives of Rocky Mountain Jewish History, a Holocaust Awareness Institute, and community cultural outreach programs. In 1982 he founded the Mizel Museum of Judaica, and served as its director until 2000. Wagner was also the only rabbi to serve as chaplain of the Colorado State Senate (1980–98). He was an outstanding example in the United States during last third of the 20th century of a rabbi as communal leader, institutional builder, and chief executive officer.

Wagner's publications include *A Piece of My Mind* (1979), and several volumes which he edited, including *Great Confrontations in Jewish History* (1977), *Traditions of the American Jew* (1977), and (with Raphael Jospe) *Great Schisms in Jewish History* (1981). He also served as general editor of a six-volume series on *Christian and Jewish Traditions in the 20th Century*. After his retirement, Wagner collaborated with Israel Drazin on a multi-volume English translation of and commentary on Targum Onkelos, *Understanding the Bible Text: Onkelos on the Pentateuch.*

Wagner's commitment to community-wide service, transcending denominational divisions, led him to write a halakhic study validating the "Denver Conversion Program," in which Orthodox, Conservative, Reform, and Reconstructionist rabbis cooperated in a joint educational program preparing candidates for conversion, and delegating authority for conversion to an Orthodox Bet Din which accepted candidates for conversion from all movements, and who were to be recognized, in turn, by the entire community. The program, which led to widespread controversy and was ultimately rejected by many Orthodox authorities (see the discussion in Samuel Freedman, *Jew vs. Jew: The Struggle for the Soul of American Jewry* (2000) and the symposium "The Denver Conversion Experience," in: CCAR *Yearbook* XCVI (1986), 47–58), provided a precedent and paradigm for the official Neeman Commission, charged by the government of Israel with developing an effective mechanism for resolving the difficulties of conversion in the Jewish state.

[Raphael Jospe (2nd ed.)]

WAHB IBN MUNABBIH (d. ca. 110/728), Yemenite scholar and ascetic, probably of Jewish origin. Wahb was one of the most important conduits of Isrāʾīliyyāt or biblical materials (both Jewish and Christian), including "Tales of the Prophets" (Arabic: *qiṣaṣ al-anbiyāʾ*) into Islamic tradition; in his days the gates were still wide open. He claimed to have read the "books" *(kutub)* of the famous Jewish converts to Islam, ʿAbdallāh ibn Salām and *Kʿab al-Aḥbār. According to one of Wahb's contemporaries, who was critical of his immodesty, he boasted that he commanded the combined knowledge of these two scholars. Wahb was born in *Sanʿa or in Dhimār south of Sanʿa. His mother was of the aristocratic tribe of Ḥimyar. As to his father, the least prestigious, and hence the most trustworthy, version has it that he was a mawlā or client of the Abnāʾ, i.e. the descendants of the Sassanian warriors who conquered the *Yemen in the sixth century C.E. Other versions have it that his father was of the Abnāʾ themselves, or even a descendant of one of the Sassanian emperors. After converting to Islam, his father became a disciple of *Muhammad's Companion Muʿādh ibn Jabal who was one of Muhammad's envoys to the Yemen. There were many scholars among Wahb's relatives and direct descendants. His brother Hammām (d. 101/719 or 102/720), for example, left a collection of *ḥadīths, i.e., sayings and accounts ascribed or related to Muhammad and his Companions.

Under the caliph ʿAbd al-Malik, Wahb officiated as a salaried preacher (*qāṣṣ*, until 75/694). He was an expert reader of the *Koran, besides being one of the earliest compilers in Islam; his biography of Muhammad, which is replete with miracles, reveals a Shīʿite bias. Wahb's traditions are often quoted in Koran exegesis, and many of them deal with the merits of Jerusalem and Palestine (or Syria; Arabic: Shām). Under the caliph Omar II, the former salaried preacher was appointed qadī or judge of Sanʿa, an office he also held at the beginning of Yazīd ibn ʿAbd al-Malik's caliphate (more precisely until 103/721). His appointment was frowned upon by those who deplored any form of cooperation with the government. Also under Omar II, probably in conjunction with his judgeship, Wahb was in charge of the treasury (probably in Sanʿa). Taking the government's side, Wahb engaged in polemics against rebellious Khārijites who argued that it was illegitimate to pay taxes to oppressive rulers. Still, under the caliph Hishām ibn ʿAbd al-Malik, Wahb was jailed and died as a result of flogging ordered by the governor of the Yemen. Wahb's adherence to the doctrine of *qadar* or free will was probably behind his chastisement, since there is in this context a reference to an ordeal he underwent (*umtuḥina*). In addition to human informants, Wahb relied on written materials: his brother Hammām is said to have bought for him "books." A prominent Yemenite scholar figuratively warned a pupil of his against the "saddle-bag" of Wahb and another scholar, since they were "owners of books, i.e. they transmitted from leaves." Wahb is rarely quoted in the canonical collections of ḥadīth, although most experts on the quality of ḥadīth transmitters considered him trustworthy.

BIBLIOGRAPHY: Entry on Wahb, in Ibn ʿAsākir, *Taʾrīkh madīnat Dimashq*, ed. al-ʿAmrawī, 53:366–403; al-Rāzī, *Kitāb taʾrīkh madīnat Ṣanʿāʾ*[2], ed. Ḥusayn ibn ʿAbdallāh al-ʿAmrī (1981); J. Horovitz, "Wahb b. Munabbih", in: EIS s.v., 1084a–1085b; R.G. Khoury, "Wahb b. Munabbih," in: EIS[2] and the bibliography cited there; J. van Ess, *Theologie und Gesellschaft im 2. und 3. Jahrhundert Hidschra: Eine Geschichte des religiösen Denkens im fruehen Islam* (1991), 702–6.

[Michael Lecker (2nd ed.)]

WAHL, ISAAK (1915–2004), Israeli agronomist. Wahl was born in Kherson, Ukraine, and after immigrating to Palestine in 1933 studied botany at the Hebrew University. In 1939 he began to teach natural science at the Ben Shemen Youth Village, while writing his doctoral thesis on the biology of a local mushroom in the Herzl Forest under the supervision of Prof. Israel Deisers, the father of phytopathology (plant diseases) in Israel. In 1946 he left Ben Shemen and began to teach at the Mikveh Israel Agricultural School, where he gained his practical knowledge of agriculture. Inspired by Aaron *Aaronson's discovery of the wild ancestor of wheat, Wahl began to take an interest in native species of wild cereal grains and the ability to withstand disease that they had developed over thousands of years.

While doing research at the University of Minnesota in 1949, Wahl was invited by Senator Hubert Humphrey to join a research group investigating the state's declining grain production. Wahl came up with a hybrid of American and sturdier Mediterranean strains that resolved the problem. In 1951 Wahl returned to Israel and became an associate professor at the Aaronson School of Agriculture (later the Faculty of Agriculture) in Rehovot. In 1966 Wahl moved to Tel Aviv University, where he established the Cereal Crops Research Institute.

Wahl was the recipient of many prizes, including the Technion's Harvey Prize for Science and Technology (1978) and the Bruno Kreisky Human Rights Prize (1985) for research that led to increased food production in the third world. In 1992 he was awarded the Israel Prize in agriculture. The Awards Committee cited Prof. Wahl as "one of the fathers of phytopathology in Israel and one of the greatest researchers in the field the world over." His work made possible the establishment of the Wild Cereals Gene Bank, the source for improved grain harvests all over the world.

[Ruth Rossing (2nd ed.)]

WAHL, JACQUES HENRI (1932–), French civil servant. Wahl was born in Lille, N. France, where his father had a small business. After graduation from the prestigious School for National Administration, he entered the French civil service and held a senior position in the Ministry of Finance. From 1970 to 1972 he was economic minister at the French embassy in Washington and was a member of the board of the International Monetary Fund. In 1978 he was appointed secretary-general of the Elysée Palace, a post regarded as equivalent to that of chief of staff at the White House.

WAHL, JEAN (1888–1974), French philosopher. Wahl was born in Marseilles, studied at the Sorbonne, and taught at Besançon, Nancy, and Lyons. In 1941 he was imprisoned in a concentration camp, but was rescued and went to the U.S., where he taught at the New School for Social Research in New York City, Mount Holyoke, and Smith College. After World War II, he became a professor at the University of Paris and also developed the Collège Philosophique for the presentation and discussion of philosophical themes.

Wahl wrote many important works, both on traditional philosophy and on existentialism, of which he became a leading exponent. He wrote *Les Philosophies pluralistes d'Angleterre et d'Amérique* (1920; *The Pluralistic Philosophies of England and America*, 1925), on Descartes and Hegel, and the important *Etudes Kierkegaardiennes* (1938), which brought Kierkegaard's thought to the attention of the French intellectual world. He followed this with a series of works developing the existentialist position, both in terms of its history and of his own ideas. Wahl stressed the role of traditional philosophy in his major work, *Etude sur le Parménide de Platon* (1926). He also wrote a volume of poems.

BIBLIOGRAPHY: Blin, in: *Fontaine* (1946), 632–48, 808–26.

[Richard H. Popkin]

WAHL, SAUL BEN JUDAH (in state documents of Poland-Lithuania, **Saul Judycz**; 1541–c. 1617), merchant and *parnas* of *Brest-Litovsk Jewry; son of Samuel Judah b. Meir Katzenellenbogen, rabbi of *Padua, where he was born. In his youth Saul Wahl went to Brest-Litovsk to study, and remained there, becoming a wealthy merchant. In 1578 King Stephen Bathory leased him the salt pans in the grand duchy of Lithuania with the sole right to sell their products and in 1580 also the salt mine at *Wieliczka near Cracow. Later Wahl farmed the king's revenues in the Brest-Litovsk region, and in 1589 King Sigismund III granted him the status of servus regis. From the 1580s Saul Wahl was among the *parnasim* of the Brest community and a leader of Lithuanian Jewry, taking an important part in the *Council of the Lands from the beginning of its existence. In 1593, through the mediation of Wahl, the Brest-Litovsk community was granted the right to adjudicate lawsuits between Jews, despite strong opposition from the city council. He built the women's gallery in the Brest-Litovsk synagogue in memory of his wife. Little is known of the last years of his life; S.A. *Bershadski has argued (in Voskhod, 5 (1889), 1–4) that Wahl died after 1622.

A number of legends grew up around the figure of Saul Wahl. Some scholars regard them as an expression of the economic and political achievements of the Jews in Poland before the catastrophe of the *Chmielnicki persecutions of 1648. One legend relates that, during the interregnum of 1587, before the election of King Sigismund III to the throne of Poland, Saul Wahl was chosen to perform a high royal function; another legend even attributes to him the title of king for a day before the final ratification of the election of Sigismund. The legends explain Wahl's rise to greatness in the patronage accorded to him by Prince Radziwill (apparently Mikolaj Krayszto f "the orphan," 1549–1616) who at a critical time during a pilgrimage to Padua received immediate aid from R. Judah, Saul Wahl's father. Of Saul Wahl's sons, Meir Katzenellenbogen-Wahl was rabbi of Brest and one of the founders of the Council of Lithuania in 1623, and Abraham (Abrashka) was rabbi of Lvov for many years. According to legend, Saul Wahl married his beautiful daughter to a rabbi of Brest-Litovsk of the same name as his.

BIBLIOGRAPHY: Halpern, Pinkas, index; S. Dubnow (ed.), *Pinkas ha-Medinah* (1925), index; *Akty vilenskoy arkheologicheskoy kommisyi*, vol. 3, no. 204; H. Edelmann, *Gedullat Sha'ul* (1925²); M. Balaban, *Skizzen und Studien zur Geschichte der Juden in Polen* (1911), 24–44; idem, *Historja Żydów w Krakowie i na Kazimierzu*, (1931–36), index; I.S. Eisenstadt and S. Wiener, *Da'at Kedoshim* (1897–98), 82–90; P. Bloch, in: *Zeitschrift der historischen Gesellschaft fuer die Provinz Posen*, 4 (1889).

[Alexander Carlebach]

WAHLE, RICHARD (1857–1935), Austrian philosopher and psychologist. He was professor at Czernowitz and then at Vienna. He was a critic of traditional metaphysics, insisting that all that is knowable are "occurrences," but not their causes. Philosophically he was a skeptical agnostic about the possibility of knowing reality. In psychology he rejected any theory concerning psychic entities or powers. He also wrote on the philosophy of culture and history and on Spinoza.

His major writings include *Gehirn und Bewusstsein* (1884); *Das Ganze der Philosophie und ihr Ende* (1894, 1896²); *Ueber den Mechanismus des geistigen Lebens* (1906); and *Die Tragikomoedie der Weisheit* (1915, 1925²).

BIBLIOGRAPHY: F. Flinker, *Die Zerstoerung des Ich; eine kritische Darlegung der Lehre Richard Wahles* (1927); S. Hochfeld, *Die*

Philosophie Richard Wahles und Johannes Rehmkes Grundwissenschaft (1926); F. Austeda, in: *Encyclopedia of Philosophy*, 8 (1967), 275–6, incl. bibl.

[Richard H. Popkin]

WAHRMANN, ABRAHAM DAVID BEN ASHER ANSCHEL (c. 1771–1840), ḥasidic rabbi. Born in Nadvornaya, Ukraine, Wahrmann was a disciple of *Levi Isaac of Berdichev and *Moses Leib of Sasov. He served as rabbi in Jazlowce (Jazlowice) from 1791, and when his father-in-law Ẓevi Hirsch Kro, author of *Neta Sha'ashu'im* (1829) and *av bet din* in Buchach, died in 1814, Abraham was appointed to his position. While living in Buchach, he began to behave like a *ẓaddik*, prayed according to *nusaḥ Sefarad*, and prolonged the morning prayer to noon. Scholars in the town opposed him, but many gathered round him to enjoy his teachings and blessings. He trained many disciples and wrote the following important halakhic and ḥasidic works: *Da'at Kedoshim*, in three parts (part one 1871); *Maḥazeh Avraham* (1876); *Tefillah le-David* (1876); *Divrei Avot* (1879); *Eshel Avraham* (1931); and *Divrei David* (1892).

BIBLIOGRAPHY: A.S. Schmerler, *Toledot ha-Rabad* (1890), incl. bibl.

[*Encyclopaedia Hebraica*]

WAHRMANN, ISRAEL (1755–1826), Hungarian rabbi and grandfather of Moritz *Wahrmann. Wahrmann, who was born in Obuda, Hungary, studied at the yeshivot of *Eisenstadt, Pressburg (*Bratislava), and *Prague. He subsequently served as rabbi in Posen, Bodrogkeresztur, and Pest (from 1799), where he had been living since 1796. As a result of his efforts, the first Jewish elementary school was opened in Pest in 1814. In 1825 Wahrmann obtained an edict ordering that Jewish secondary school students should receive instruction in their own religion even when attending schools maintained by Christian denominations. He introduced regular synagogue services for young people on the Sabbath, preaching the sermons himself. The first constitution of the Jewish congregation of Pest was a result of his efforts, as was the foundation of the Shi'ur Society for the promotion of learning, and other communal institutions (such as Bikkur Ḥolim). Land for the Jewish cemetery of Pest was acquired during Wahrmann's ministry. Two of his sermons were published.

BIBLIOGRAPHY: I. Reich, *Beth-El, Ehrentempel verdienter ungarischer Israeliten*, 1 (1868), 123–7; S. Büchler, *A zsidók története Budapesten* (1901), 381–98.

[Jeno Zsoldos]

WAHRMANN, MORITZ (1831–1892), Hungarian economist and businessman. Wahrmann, who was born in Pest, Hungary, entered his father's textile business and in 1859 became the sole owner. His articles in *Pester Lloyd* attracted the attention of F. *Deák, who subsequently supported him in the election campaign which made him the first Jewish member of the Hungarian parliament (1869). There, he served as chairman of the finance committee. At the same time, he was president of both the Pester Lloyd Co. and the Budapest Chamber of Commerce and Industry. Wahrmann advocated the acquisition of landed property by Jews, regarding it both as a profitable investment and as a means of gaining a foothold in the landed gentry class. He believed that it would promote the assimilation and social equality of Jews, but failed to realize the dangers of the inevitable hostile reaction. As vice chairman of the first General Congress of Hungarian Jews (1868–69), he supported an autonomous religious and educational establishment for Hungarian Jewry; he also spoke in favor of this in parliament. From 1883 until his death he was president of the Jewish community of Pest, where he instituted various organizational reforms. His term of office was also marked by the founding of the Jewish hospital and the Jewish community center of Budapest (1889 and 1891).

BIBLIOGRAPHY: S. Büchler, in: *Magyar Zsidó Szemle*, 10 (1893), 7–15; L. Venetianer, *A magyar zsidóság története* (1922); Gy. Mérei, in: IMIT (1943), 313–43; N. Katzburg, *Ha-Antishemiyyut be-Hungaryah* (1969).

[Jeno Zsoldos]

WAISMANN, FRIEDRICH (1896–1959), Austrian philosopher. One of the original members of the Vienna Circle, he was born in Vienna. He was assistant of the German neopositivist philosopher Moritz Schlick at Vienna University (1929–36), and then lectured at Cambridge (1937–39). He then went to Oxford as reader in the philosophy of mathematics, and later as reader in the philosophy of science. Waismann's philosophy began as a rather orthodox version of logical positivism, but under the influence of Wittgenstein's later views changed radically, moving away from an emphasis upon formalism to a type of extreme informalism. His later work, such as the series of articles entitled "Analytic-Synthetic" (*Analysis*, 1949–53) and "Language Strata" (*Logic and Language*, 1953), attempts to relieve philosophical perplexity by contrasting the rigid caricatures of language use developed by traditional philosophers with the flexible, subtle, and fluid use of language in its everyday employment. The high point in this development is to be found in his paper "How I See Philosophy" in *Contemporary British Philosophy* (1956) where he contends that philosophy is "very unlike science in that in philosophy there are no proofs, no theorems and no questions that can be decided."

Apart from these influential papers, Waismann's main contributions are to be found in *Einfuehrung in das mathematische Denken* (1936; *Introduction to Mathematical Thinking*, 1951), and *The Principles of Linguistic Philosophy*. The latter work was unfinished at Waismann's death, and was edited by R. Harre and published in 1965.

BIBLIOGRAPHY: S. Hampshire, *Friedrich Waismann 1896–1959* (Eng., 1960); B.F. Mc-Guiness (ed.), *Wittgenstein und der Wiener Kreis von Friedrich Waismann* (1967).

[Avrum Stroll]

°**WAKEFIELD, ROBERT** (**Wakfeldus**; d. 1537), English Hebraist and Orientalist. Born in Pontefract, Yorkshire, Wakefield was educated at Cambridge and then served as professor of Hebrew at Louvain (1519) and at Tuebingen (1520–23) before being recalled to England to serve as a chaplain to Henry VIII. He taught at Cambridge from 1524 and in 1530 was appointed first professor of Hebrew at the University of Oxford, where his students included the future Cardinal Pole. His pioneering work, *Oratio de laudibus et utilitate trium linguarum, Arabicae, Chaldaicae, et Hebraicae, atque idiomatibus hebraicis quae in utroque testamento inveniuntur* (London, 1524), "On the value of Arabic, Aramaic, and Hebrew," was the first English publication to contain Hebrew and Arabic type. Dedicated to Henry VIII, it displays Wakefield's considerable rabbinic scholarship and his familiarity with medieval Hebrew literature. A supplementary work, *Syntagma de Hebraeorum Codicum incorruptione…* (London, c. 1530), was published with an address on the study of Hebrew which the author delivered at Oxford in the same year. Both works were printed by Caxton's successor, Wynkyn de Worde. Wakefield also wrote a Paraphrasis in Librum Koheleth (n.d.). Wakefield held the leading Jewish writers of the Middle Ages in high regard and believed that Hebrew was God's own language.

His younger brother, THOMAS WAKEFIELD (d. 1575), was appointed first regius professor of Hebrew at the University of Cambridge in 1540. His temporary replacement in this post by Paulus *Fagius (1549–53) is thought to have been brought about by his loyalty to Catholicism. In 1569 Thomas Wakefield was finally replaced by the convert Immanuel *Tremellius.

BIBLIOGRAPHY: R. Loewe, in: V.D. Lipman (ed.), *Three Centuries of Anglo-Jewish History* (1961), 138; Steinschneider, Cat Bod, 2713 no. 7357. **ADD. BIBLIOGRAPHY:** ODNB online.

[Godfrey Edmond Silverman]

WAKSMAN, SELMAN ABRAHAM (1888–1973), U.S. microbiologist and Nobel Prize winner. Born in Priluki, Russia, he was taken to the United States as a child. From 1925, he taught at Rutgers University, heading its Institute of Microbiology from 1949. Although Waksman's research interests involved various aspects of soil microbiology, he is best known for his investigations of antibiotics, particularly streptomycin. The term antibiotic, a substance produced by one microorganism that kills other microorganisms, was coined by Waksman. When he began his search for antibiotic substances in the 1930s, he had already many years of experience with a group of fungi known as the actinomycetes, and he was very familiar with their abundance, distribution, taxonomy, and activities. In the course of their work Waksman and his colleagues developed many specialized techniques which were valuable in the cultivation of microbes, as well as the isolation and purification of active antibiotics.

Streptothricin, the first antibiotic substance he isolated from an actinomycete, was too toxic for therapeutic use. Returning to a species of fungus that he had first described in 1916, he found a strain that produced a substance possessing antibacterial activity but was less toxic. The fungus, *Streptomyces griseus*, was grown in submerged culture. The isolation of the new antibiotic, which he named streptomycin, was done by adsorption on charcoal, removing it from the charcoal by treatment with dilute acid, followed by drying and crystallization. Using standardized strains of bacteria, a series of laboratory tests were performed to investigate the bacteriocidal properties of streptomycin. It proved to be effective against a great variety of bacteria, including the tubercle bacillus, and was categorized as a broad-spectrum antibiotic. Waksman and his coworkers began the work of elucidating the chemical structure of streptomycin, but the task was completed by other investigators. Streptomycin, one of the most useful antibiotics to be discovered, was considered a major breakthrough in the area of chemotherapy. Following this work, Waksman and his coworkers continued the search for antibiotics and succeeded in finding several more. He was elected to the National Academy of Sciences and in 1952 was awarded the Nobel Prize for Medicine and Physiology. His autobiography, *My Life with the Microbes*, appeared in 1954.

BIBLIOGRAPHY: T. Levitan, *The Laureates: Jewish Winners of the Nobel Prize* (1960), 164–8; H.B. Woodruff (ed.), *Scientific Contributions of Selman A. Waksman; selected articles published in honor of his 80th birthday* (1968).

[Norman Levin]

WALBROOK, ANTON (1896–1967), Austrian actor. Born Adolf Wilhelm Anton Wohlbruck in Vienna, Walbrook was the son of a Jewish mother and a non-Jewish circus clown whose family had been actors since the 18th century. He was educated at Catholic schools and was an officer in the German army during World War I, held as a prisoner of war by the French for several years. He began his career under Max *Reinhardt and later starred in German films. He settled in England in 1937 and won acclaim for his stage performances in *Design for Living* (1939) and *Watch on the Rhine* (1942). His film career, spanning three decades, included roles as Prince Albert in *Victoria The Great* (1937); *Sixty Glorious Years* (1938); *Dangerous Moonlight* (1941), where he gave the first performance (through an offstage pianist) of the famous *Warsaw Concerto*; *The 49th Parallel* (1941); *Colonel Blimp* (1943); *The Queen of Spades* (1948);*The Red Shoes* (1948); and *I Accuse!* (1958), based on the *Dreyfus Case. Walbrook gave part of his earnings from each film to help Jewish refugees. He became a British subject in 1947 but then went frequently to Germany for film and television roles, dying in Bavaria.

ADD. BIBLIOGRAPHY: ODNB online.

WALD, ARNOLD (1932–), Brazilian lawyer. Born in Guanabara, Wald lectured at the universities of Rio de Janeiro and Niteroi and in 1966 became professor of civil law at the University of Guanabara, where he lectured for more than 30 years. From 1966 to 1967 he was attorney general of the state of Guanabara, secretary general and vice president of the Institute of Brazilian Lawyers and the Brazilian Committee of Comparative Law. Wald was Brazilian delegate to several international congresses on comparative law and published a number of books and papers on his specialty including *Influência do di-*

reito francês sôbre o direito brasileiro no domînio da responsabilidade civil (1953), *O Mandado de Segurança* (1968), *Direito de familia* (1998,) and *O novo direito de familia* (2000).

[Israel Drapkin-Senderey]

WALD, GEORGE (1906–1997), U.S. biologist and biochemist; Nobel Prize winner. Born in New York City, he received his B.Sc. in 1927 from New York University and his Ph.D. from Columbia University in 1934, where he developed his continuing interest in the biochemistry of vision. In 1934 he joined the Biological Sciences Department at Harvard University, where he rose to the rank of full professor in 1948. After discovering vitamin A in the retina, he showed that a derivative of this substance (retinene) is the primary lightsensitive pigment. Retinene is joined to specialized retinal proteins (opsins) in the visual pigments which abound in tiny structures of the retina called rods. Upon exposure to light, this attachment is broken as a result of chemical rearrangement of the retinene molecule, and ultimately vitamin A is produced. The significance of this fundamental biochemical cleavage pattern was enhanced by Wald's demonstration that it underlies the visual process in all organisms which possess a highly structured eye. Specific modifications of retinene and vitamin A characterize the lower vertebrates and provide biochemical insights into evolutionary relationships. He was the recipient of many honors and in 1967 was awarded the Nobel Prize for physiology and medicine. He wrote a widely acclaimed laboratory manual for general biology and co-authored *General Education in a Free Society* (1945). He was also active in the political arena and played a leading role in mobilizing opposition to U.S. involvement in the Vietnam war.

BIBLIOGRAPHY: *Current Biography Yearbook, 1968* (1969), 412–4.

[George H. Fried]

WALD, HENRI (1920–2002), Romanian philosopher; regarded as an authority on trends in contemporary philosophy and dialectical logics. Born into a Jewish family of humble means, Wald lectured at Bucharest University on logic and the theory of knowledge from 1948 to 1962, and in 1953 was appointed director of the department of dialectical materialism at the Institute of Philosophy of the Rumanian Academy.

Wald's works included *Rolul limbajului în formarea și desvoltarea ideilor* ("The Role of Speaking in the Formation and Development of Ideas," 1956); *Filozofia Deznădejdii* ("The Philosophy of Desperation," 1957); *Structura logică a gindirii* ("The Logical Structure of Thought," 1962); and *Realitate și limbaj* ("Reality and Speaking," 1968). Later he also became interested in linguistics and semantics, fields to which his contribution was a most important one.

Wald was also interested in the development and criticism of Marxian theory that did not follow the Leninist line. He also published several valuable contributions to the history of Jewish culture in the publications of the Jewish community.

[Dora Litani-Littman / Paul Schveiger (2nd ed.)]

WALD, HERMAN (1906–1970), South African sculptor born in Hungary, the son of a rabbi. Wald settled in South Africa in 1937. Among his principal works are a monument to martyred European Jewry, "Kria," which stands at the entrance to the Witwatersrand Jewish Aged Home, Johannesburg, and a memorial to the Six Million, in the grounds of the West Park Jewish Cemetery, Johannesburg. His later works include municipal fountains and decorations for synagogues in Johannesburg and Cape Town.

WALD, JERRY (1912–1962), U.S. screenwriter and producer. Wald was born in Brooklyn, N.Y. During 1934–41 Wald wrote or coauthored a number of scenarios, including *They Drive by Night*. Then, as an associate producer (1941) and producer (1942–50) for Warner Brothers, he turned out a number of successful films, including *Destination Tokyo, Objective, Burma!*, and *Johnny Belinda*. In 1950 he formed the independent Wald-Krasna Productions with the writer Norman Krasna, an arrangement which ended in 1952. Wald then became production vice president at Columbia. From 1956 he headed Jerry Wald Productions at Twentieth Century-Fox.

WALD, LILLIAN (1867–1940), U.S. social worker. Lillian Wald was born in Cincinnati, Ohio, to a German-Jewish immigrant family and was raised in Rochester, N.Y. As a child, Lillian Wald had all the comforts of upper middleclass life. Her decision to become a nurse led ultimately to contact with the immigrants of New York's Lower East Side, and she soon resolved to bring nursing care and hygienic instruction to the needy. These activities led to a concern for the total needs of the individual and to the establishment of the Nurses (Henry Street) Settlement in 1895. Combined with nursing services were campaigns for improved sanitation, pure milk and the control of tuberculosis, plus the full range of educational, recreational, and personal services offered by the settlement.

Lillian Wald was the very prototype of the liberal reformer of the early 20th century. She disliked millennialism because it too often traded present gains for future hopes; she was deeply interested in people but demanded that reform proceed from fact and sound argument, not sympathy; and she realized that charity could make no dent in social problems since it left both the individual and the environment unchanged. Instead, the state must take the responsibility for creating the proper conditions for a decent and humane society. Thus she campaigned for the end of child labor, supported trade unions, and was an important member of most of the leading social reform organizations of the day.

Vigorously opposed to U.S. entry into World War I, Lillian Wald was president of the American Union against Militarism. In destroying the brotherhood of man and stirring national and ethnic hatreds, war attacked her basic beliefs and the work of a lifetime. Once the United States entered the conflict, she did her best to preserve civil liberties and maintain the social welfare gains of the previous two decades. Although in close contact with the Jewish community of the Lower East

Side, Lillian Wald never identified with her coreligionists as such. She urged a fundamental brotherhood among men, for she had found "that the things which make men alike are finer and stronger than the things which make them different." She wrote *House on Henry Street* (1915) and *Windows on Henry Street* (1934).

BIBLIOGRAPHY: R. Duffus, *Lillian Wald* (1938); A.F. Davis, *Spearheads for Reform…* (1967).

[Irwin Yellowitz]

WALDEN, AARON BEN ISAIAH NATHAN (1838–1912), ḥasidic author and bibliographer in Poland. Born in Warsaw, Walden was a Ḥasid of R. Menahem Mendel of Kotsk and R. Isaac Meir Alter of Gur. For many years he worked as proofreader at Ephraim Baumritter's publishing house in Warsaw. He became particularly well known for his bio-bibliographical work, *Shem ha-Gedolim he-Ḥadash*, following the same structure and augmenting the *Shem ha-Gedolim* of Ḥ.J.D. *Azulai. It was published in several editions and widely circulated. The first part of the work is an alphabetical list of over 1,500 rabbis and authors, the second part lists over 1,600 works, also in alphabetical order (1864; 1870^2; 1879^3; with additions and corrections by Walden's son JOSEPH ARYEH LEIB, and subsequent editions).

Walden also published Simeon b. Isaac ha-Levi Oshenburk's *Devek Tov* on *Rashi's commentary on the Pentateuch with many emendations (1895); a new edition of *David b. Solomon ibn Abi Zimra's (Radbaz) responsa, Parts 1–7 (1882); Moses *Alshekh's commentary on the Five Scrolls (1862); and *Mikdash Me'at* (1890–93), an anthology of the *aggadah* on the Psalms in five parts. He died in Kielce.

Walden's son MOSES MENAHEM published several works on the history of Ḥasidism in Poland: *Ohel ha-Rabbi* (1913), including tales about Jacob Isaac ha-Ḥozeh ("the Seer") of Lublin; *Beit ha-Ḥayyim* (1930–31) on rabbis who died in Kielce; *Ve-Khabbed Av*, supplements to *Shem ha-Gedolim he-Ḥadash* (1923); *Nifle'ot Yiẓhak* (1914), on the brothers Mordecai Menahem and Jacob David Kalish; and *Nifle'ot ha-Rabbi* (1911), also on Ha-Ḥozeh of Lublin.

BIBLIOGRAPHY: M. Steinschneider in: *Ha-Mazkir*, 8 (1865), 108–9; J.H. Kalman, in; *Ha-Karmel*, 6 (1866), 181–2, 190–1; B.Z. Eisenstadt, *Dor Rabbanav ve-Soferav*, 3 (1901), 13–14; M.M. Walden, *Beit ha-Ḥayyim* (1931), 110–1; H.D. Friedberg, *Toledot ha-Defus ha-Ivri be-Polanyah* (1950^2), 113; J. Rubinstein, in: *Hadorom*, 16 (1963), 140–50.

[Naphtali Ben-Menahem]

WALDEN, HERWARTH (originally **Georg Lewin**; 1878–1941), German author and editor. Born in Berlin, Walden studied music in Italy and Berlin. In 1907 he founded a society for the cultivation of the arts (Verein fuer Kunst) – a forum for progressive poets, artists, architects, and scientists – and edited the literary and theatrical sections of several German periodicals. But it was as the founder and editor of *Der Sturm* (1910–32) that he was most influential in propagating his theories of expressionism in art, music, and literature. Walden's first novel, *Das Buch der Menschenliebe* (1916), and his first drama, *Weib* (1917), were followed by two more novels and eight plays. These, however, were less significant for his generation than was his theory of abstract art or his aid to early expressionists, futurists, and cubists, who had been rejected by the official artists' associations and important galleries alike. *Der Sturm* reproduced drawings and woodcuts by members of the Bruecke, and in particular works by the fiery young Austrian, Oskar Kokoschka, Walden's special protegé. In 1912 he opened a gallery dedicated to everything new and provocative from a number of countries. The names of the artists sponsored by the Sturm Gallery in its first decade included Albert Bloch, Ludwig *Meidner, Jakob *Steinhardt, and, above all, Marc *Chagall. His last work was a collection of lyrics, *Im Geschweig der Liebe* (1925). Walden was associated with the German left-wing intelligentsia and was himself pro-Communist. In 1932 he emigrated to the U.S.S.R., where he worked as a teacher of German. He published articles in the German exíle press in publications such as *The Word* (*Das Wort*) and *International Literature* (*Internationale Literatur*) until 1938. He became a victim of Stalinist police persecution, dying after seven months in jail. His wife (from 1901 until 1911) was the poet Else *Lasker-Schueler. In 2002 the correspondence between Herwarth Walden and Karl Kraus was published, entitled *Feinde in Scharen: ein wahres Vergnügen dazusein; Karl Kraus – Herwarth Walden; Briefwechsel 1909–1912*, by G.C. Avery.

BIBLIOGRAPHY: N. Walden and L. Schreyer (eds.), *Der Sturm: Ein Erinnerungsbuch* (1954); Nationalgalerie, Berlin, *Der Sturm: Herwarth Walden und die europaeische Avantgarde, Berlin 1912–1932* (1961); N. Walden, *Herwarth Walden* (1965). **ADD. BIBLIOGRAPHY:** G. Bruehl, *Herwarth Walden und "Der Sturm"* (1983); M. Jones, *"Der Sturm": A Focus of Expressionism* (1984); H. Boorman, "Herwarth Walden and William Wauer: Expressionism and "Sturm" Politics in the Post-War Context," in: R. Sheppard (ed.), *Expressionism in Focus* (1987); M. Godé, *Der Sturm de Herwarth Walden; l'utopie d'un art autonome* (1990); idem, *Herwarth Waldens Werdegang von der "autonomen Kunst" zum Kommunismus*, in: *Etudes germaniques*, 46:3 (1991), 335–47; F. Muelhaupt, *Herwarth Walden. 1878–1941. Wegbereiter der Moderne* (1991); P. Sprengel, "Institutionalisierung der Moderne: Herwarth Walden und 'Der Sturm'," in: *Zeitschrift fuer deutsche Philologie*, 110 (1991), 247–81; idem, "Nachtraegliches zu Herwarth Waldens Cabaret fuer Hoehenkunst 'Teloplasma'. Eine Miszelle in eigener Sache," in: *Zeitschrift fuer deutsche Philologie*, 111 (1992), 256–61; G. Heinersdorff, *Bruno Taut und Herwarth Walden* (1996); M. Godé, "De la Spree à la Volga. L'itinéraire d'Herwarth Walden (1878–1941)," in: *Crises allemandes de l'identité*, ed. under the direction of M. Vanoosthuyse (1998); S. Bauschinger, "'Ich bin Krieger mit dem Herzen, er mit dem Kopf.' Else Lasker-Schueler und Herwarth Walden," in: G. Seybert (ed.), *Das literarische Paar* (2003), 245–56.

[Sol Liptzin / Konrad Feilchenfeldt (2nd ed.)]

WALDENBERG, ELIEZER JUDAH (1912–), rabbi. Born in Jerusalem, Rabbi Waldenberg is the author of the multivolume series of responsa entitled *Ẓiẓ Eliezer* dealing with actual problems of life in Israel and abroad and published several other books on questions of *halakhah*. From 1957 he was president of the District Rabbinical Court of Jerusalem. In 1976 he was awarded the Israel Prize for rabbinical scholarship.

WALDHEIM AFFAIR. The "Waldheim Affair" is the term conventionally applied to the controversy surrounding the disclosure of the previously unknown past of Kurt Waldheim, former secretary general of the United Nations, which arose during his campaign for the Austrian presidency in 1986. The affair not only focused international attention on Waldheim personally, but also raised broader questions relating to the history of antisemitism in Austria and the role Austrians played in the Nazi dictatorship and the "Final Solution." A concomitant of the Waldheim affair was the reemergence in Austrian political culture of the appeal to antisemitic prejudice for political ends. Employing a coded idiom more appropriate to "post-Auschwitz" political debate, the Waldheim camp (principally the Christian Democratic Austrian People's Party [ÖVP], which had nominated him) helped construct a hostile image of Jews ("Feindbild") which served both to deflect criticism of Waldheim's credibility and to explain the international "campaign" against him. The central assumption of this "Feindbild" was that Waldheim and Austria were under attack from an international Jewish conspiracy.

Kurt Waldheim had enjoyed an exceptionally successful career in the Austrian foreign service after World War II. Taken on as secretary to Foreign Minister Karl Gruber in 1946, Waldheim served in various posts abroad and in Vienna, including two stints as Austrian representative to the UN, and was appointed foreign minister in January 1968 by Chancellor Josef Klaus (ÖVP). His term as minister ended in March 1970, when the Socialists (SPÖ) under Bruno Kreisky won the parliamentary elections. Shortly thereafter, Waldheim returned to New York as Austria's ambassador to the UN. In January 1971, he was again in Vienna temporarily to run as the ÖVP candidate for president, which in Austria is a largely ceremonial post for which elections are held every six years. Though he made a very respectable showing, Waldheim lost to the incumbent Socialist Franz Jonas and afterward returned to his post in New York. On December 22, 1971, Waldheim was elected secretary general of the UN, and reelected to a second term in 1976. His bid for a third term, however, failed, and in March 1982, Waldheim, described by one journalist as "the most successful Austrian diplomat since Metternich," finally came home to Austria.

Waldheim's international prominence and personal ambition left few in doubt that he would run for the Austrian presidency in 1986, but it was unclear whether as the candidate of the ÖVP, or as a consensus candidate of the two major parties. The ÖVP hoped to draw maximum political advantage from Waldheim's candidacy for itself, without identifying him so closely with it that it would endanger either Waldheim's election as president or the hoped-for attendant political "turn." Then chairman Alois Mock pushed through Waldheim's nomination by the ÖVP as a "non-partisan" candidate in March 1985, more than a year prior to the elections, very early by traditional Austrian standards. The SPÖ, also conscious of Waldheim's electoral appeal, had not ruled out a joint candidacy until confronted with the ÖVP's fait accompli. One month later, the SPÖ presented Kurt Steyrer, then minister for health and environment, as its standard bearer. Two minor candidates, Freda Meissner-Blau from the Greens, and Otto Scrinzi, former FPÖ member of parliament and representative of the (German) nationalist far right in Austria, also entered the race.

The relatively uneventful early phase of the campaign, in which Kurt Waldheim was the clear front runner, ended abruptly in March 1986. Indeed, the Waldheim affair may be properly said to date from March 3, 1986, when the Austrian weekly *Profil* published documents first revealing details of Waldheim's unknown past. *Profil*'s disclosures were followed on March 4 by nearly identical revelations by the *World Jewish Congress (WJC), and the *New York Times* (NYT). The key to unlocking the evidence was said to be a picture published by an army unit, which placed Waldheim in Yugoslavia at a specific time and thus could unlock his wartime record. This gave historian Robert Herstein, who was commissioned by the World Jewish Congress, a place to begin.

Waldheim had always denied any affiliation with the Nazis of any kind, and, in both his public statements and in the relevant passages in his memoirs, had claimed that his military service ended in the winter of 1941–42, with his wounding on the eastern front. The evidence made public by *Profil*, the WJC, and the NYT suggested on the contrary that the former secretary general had been a member of the Nazi Student Union and that he had also belonged to a mounted riding unit of the Sturmabteilung, or SA, while attending the Consular Academy in Vienna between 1937 and 1939. Other documents revealed that Waldheim had been declared fit for duty in 1942, after his wound had healed. By the end of March 1942, Waldheim had been assigned to Army High Command 12 (which became Army Group E in January 1943), then based on Thessalonika (Salonica), and remained attached to it until the war's end. Army Group E, commanded by Alexander Löhr, was known for its involvement in the deportations of Jews from Greece and for the savagery of its military operations against Yugoslav partisans and their suspected civilian supporters.

For his part, Waldheim denied membership in any Nazi organization and offered evidence suggesting his ideological hostility to Nazism. He conceded having served in Army Group E, but denied participation of any kind in atrocities committed by units under Löhr's command, and claimed to have known nothing of the deportation of the Jews of Thessalonika.

The more general strategy pursued by Waldheim and his supporters was to brand the disclosures as part of a "defamation campaign" designed to inhibit his chances in the presidential election. Waldheim's argument ran along the following lines: the accusations of the WJC and the NYT represent a continuation of a slander campaign which the SPÖ had been waging against him for some time. The Socialists or their accomplices had fed documents to the WJC and the NYT in order to damage Waldheim's international reputation, his main advantage over Steyrer. Such allegations were all the less credible, since Waldheim had been cleared by the Austrian secret service at the time he entered the diplomatic service 40 years previously. Moreover, during his candidacy for UN secretary general, the CIA, the KGB, and the Israelis all investigated him and would not have allowed his election had there been anything in the least incriminating against him. He had not mentioned his tour of duty in the Balkans in his memoirs, Waldheim claimed, because he had had such a minor function and also because his injury on the eastern front had represented a major caesura in his life. He also said that he knew nothing of Jewish deportations and had had nothing to do with other atrocities. But if Waldheim were to be blamed for such things, then truly every Wehrmacht soldier would also come under suspicion.

Although the Waldheim affair became an international media extravaganza, the principal source of documents relating to Waldheim's past, as well as his most vocal critic, was the WJC, an organization based in New York whose primary activities involve campaigning to defend threatened Jewish communities throughout the world and lobbying for what it perceives as the common interests of Jews. The series of press releases and disclosures of documents (24 between March 4 and July 8, date of the second round of the Austrian presidential election) by the WJC set the pace and largely the terms for the debate on Waldheim in the United States. In the early phase of the controversy, the WJC published evidence relating to Waldheim's membership in the SA and Nazi Student Union, which it believed amounted to proof of his "Nazi past." The material on Waldheim's wartime past the WJC first presented was patchy and inconclusive, but over the next several months it made public dozens of additional documents which helped complete the picture of Waldheim's various duties in the Balkans.

On March 22, the WJC published a copy of the Central Registry of War Criminals and Security Suspects (CROWCASS), a list compiled by the U.S. Army of persons suspected of war crimes, showing that Waldheim had been sought by Yugoslavia after the war for, among other things, murder. The basis for the CROWCASS listing was a file of the United Nations War Crimes Commission (UNWCC), and this latter file was in turn based on a dossier prepared by the Yugoslav authorities and submitted to the UNWCC shortly before it concluded its deliberations in 1948.

With the publication of the Yugoslav file, known as the Odluka, or "Decision," the debate on Waldheim's past acquired a far more serious dimension: allegations of war crimes had been leveled against Waldheim by the Yugoslav War Crimes Commission, and these had been reviewed and endorsed by the UNWCC. The WJC's subsequent disclosures as well as the discussion on Waldheim's past in general were heavily influenced by this new discovery.

On March 25, 1986, the WJC presented the findings of Robert E. Herzstein, the historian it had commissioned to look into Waldheim's past. Herzstein had discovered that Waldheim had served as a staff officer in the military intelligence department of Army Group E and had been assigned to the Battle Group West Bosnia, whose troops were responsible for the slaughter of thousands of Yugoslavs in the Kozara Mountains in 1942. Waldheim had also received an award for valor (the King Zvonimir medal) from the puppet Croatian government at the end of this campaign.

The WJC continued to offer documents it felt corroborated the findings in the Odluka, and pressed U.S. Attorney General Edwin Meese to place Waldheim's name on the so-called "watch list" of undesirable aliens, effectively barring him from entering the U.S. In the international media, calls for the publication of Waldheim's UN file were coupled with more intensive efforts to find a "smoking gun."

The issues involving Waldheim's possible criminality were in any event never self-evident. The possibilities for inferring something opprobrious about Waldheim's service in the Wehrmacht from his previously concealed "Nazi past" were legion, while the publication of the CROWCASS and the Yugoslav Odluka transformed vague intimations about his military duties into concrete juridical suspicion.

Embarrassing, if not necessarily incriminating, documents were surfacing daily, but there were few around who could reliably interpret what they meant. Moreover, merely keeping track of Waldheim's whereabouts in the Balkans was difficult: he had served in seven different posts in at least ten locations in Serbia-Montenegro, Albania, and Greece. The issue of Waldheim's possible war criminality was also complicated by ignorance about the practice of the Nuremberg Tribunal. On the one hand, much of what the Wehrmacht did to Yugoslav partisans was gruesome but "legal." On the other hand, the conditions under which an officer of Waldheim's rank and position could even incur criminal liability were narrowly circumscribed. Categories of guilt, complicity, responsibility, etc., easily elided, while the suspicious background to the compilation of the Odluka, which undermined if not vitiated the charges made in it, only became known later.

In Austria itself, Waldheim and his supporters continued to portray all new claims about his wartime role as slander, and Waldheim as the victim of a coordinated international "defamation campaign," initiated by socialists, led by the World Jewish Congress, and promoted by the international press, particularly the *New York Times*. In the course of the election campaign, the WJC became the main object of abuse, and the abundant political invective arrayed by politicians of the ÖVP against it as scapegoat helped promote and legitimate antisemitic prejudice in public discourse to an extent unseen since 1945. Waldheim also attempted to identify his own fate with that of his generation and country by claiming that he, like thousands of other Austrians, had merely done his "duty" under Nazi Germany, an appeal which struck a responsive note among many Austrian voters. In the election on May 4, 1986, Waldheim polled 49.7% of the votes, just short of the majority needed to win. During the six weeks leading up to the second round, the Socialists emphasized their candidate's ability to reconcile a divided nation, but to no avail. Waldheim won the second round handily: his 53.9% of the votes was the largest of its kind (i.e., when not running against an incumbent) in the Second Republic.

Whatever actually determined Austrian voting behavior is open to a great deal of speculation, but the result was almost certainly not affected in any significant way by a negative backlash against the Waldheim camp's antisemitic wager. At the same time, the election does not appear reducible to a moral referendum on Waldheim or his past, for it is doubtful either that Austrian voters conceived the election in such ethico-political terms or that their votes reflected their respective moral choices. Dissatisfaction with government policies or the desire to deliver a protest vote for any one of several reasons seem to have motivated voters at least as much as a reflexive national spite or even antisemitic prejudice. What cannot be doubted is that Waldheim's diminished credibility and his perceived trivialization of Nazi atrocities (in the eyes of his critics, if not his supporters) did not cost him the election.

Contrary to Waldheim's expectations, interest in the unanswered questions about his past did not disappear after his election. Waldheim received no official invitations from any country in Western Europe, and some official government visitors to Austria even avoided traveling to Vienna, as protocol would otherwise have required them to pay a courtesy call on the Austrian president. Some prominent private individuals, such as political scientist Ralf Dahrendorf, also boycotted events where Waldheim would have been present. In April 1987, the U.S. Department of Justice announced that it was placing Waldheim on the watch list, further reinforcing his pariah status.

Since Waldheim's election, three independent research efforts, a commission of seven historians established at the request of the Austrian government, a panel of five international jurists engaged by British and U.S. television production companies, and a commission of the British Ministry of Defense, have illuminated Waldheim's wartime career in great detail, and none found anything in Waldheim's behavior which could implicate him personally in any criminal activity. Waldheim himself considered these judgments a complete vindication, and he and his supporters found the stigma which still attached to him incomprehensible.

Waldheim's diplomatic isolation was broken initially by Pope John Paul II, who received Waldheim officially in June 1987, and Waldheim subsequently visited a few Arab countries, some of whose papers had defended Waldheim against ostensible Zionist attacks. Though in April 1990 the U.S. Justice Department confirmed its decision to bar Waldheim, an indication of a possible thaw in attitudes toward Waldheim came the following July, when presidents Richard von Weizsäcker of Germany and Vaclav Havel of Czechoslovakia publicly met Waldheim at the Salzburg Festival, where Havel gave the ceremonial address in which he, albeit, indirectly attacked Waldheim by speaking of those who distort their memoirs.

In Austria itself, President Waldheim did not become the kind of integrative figure he had wished. Waldheim was initially an irritation and embarrassment to many, and was even forced by opponents in the government into remaining silent at the official commemoration of jubilee of the Austrian *Anschluss* in March 1988. During the second half of his term, which ended in 1992, on the other hand, Waldheim's treatment in the press suggested that increasing numbers of Austrians had accepted Waldheim as president, even though he would never be accorded the respect and affection his predecessors had enjoyed.

More broadly conceived, the Waldheim affair symbolizes the postwar unwillingness or inability adequately to confront the complications of the Nazi abomination. It remains to be seen whether current infelicitous images of Austria's Nazi past will be supplanted by the more prosaic Trapp family pendant, or whether the Waldheim affair becomes the occasion for a more general effort on all sides to come to terms with the past. If so, then Waldheim may indeed be said to have performed an important function.

[Richard Mitten]

There were two collateral impacts of the Waldheim Affair. Simon *Wiesenthal, a citizen of Austria, refused to join the World Jewish Congress in its assessment that Waldheim was a war criminal. Always cautious before making such an accusation, he remained unconvinced. His hesitation was not shared by the *Simon Wiesenthal Center, which joined the WJC in pressing the case. It was rumored that this cost him the Nobel Peace Prize that was awarded to Elie *Wiesel that year. Secondly, the U.S. ambassador to Austria was a then young American Jew, descendent of a family that traced its roots to the Austro-Hungarian Empire and heir to a great cosmetics fortune. Ronald *Lauder experienced antisemitism directly for the first time. This experience aroused in him the desire to act affirmatively on behalf of the Jewish people and gave rise to his important efforts to rebuild Jewish life in Central and Eastern Europe through the foundation he established.

[Michael Berenbaum (2nd ed.)]

BIBLIOGRAPHY: R. Mitten, *The Waldheim Phenomenon in Austria. The Politics of Anti-semitic Prejudice* (1991); R. Wodak, P. Nowak, J. Pelikan, R. de Cillia, H. Gruber, and R. Mitten, *'Wir sind alle unschuldige Täter!' Studien zum Nachkriegs Anti-semitismus* (1990); R. Seheide, K. Gruber, and F. Trauttmansdorff (eds.), *Kurt Waldheim's Wartime Years. A Documentation* (1987); H. Born, *Für die Richtigkeit. Kurt Waldheim* (1987); H. Czernin, "Waldheims Balkanjahre," seven-part series on Waldheim's Balkan year, *Profil*, nos. 49–52 (1987), 1–4 (1988); J.L. Collins, Jr., H. Fleischer, G. Fleming, H.R. Kurz, M. Messersehmidt, J. Vanwelkenhuyzen, and J.L. Wallach, *Der Bericht der internationalen Historikerkommission Vienna: Supplement to Profil* 7 (February 15, 1988); R.E. Herzstein, *Waldheim. The Missing Years* (1988); M. Palumbo, *The Waldheim Files: Myth and Reality* (1988).

WALDINGER, ERNST (1896–1970), Austrian poet. Born in Vienna, Waldinger had both a secular and an Orthodox education. He volunteered for military service in 1915 and two years later was severely wounded on the Romanian front. After hospitalization he studied at the University of Vienna, where he received his Ph.D. in 1921. He then turned to poetry, choosing classical forms rather than the free verse of the dominant expressionists. Although he published individual poems from 1924, Waldinger's first verse collection, *Die Kuppel*, did not appear until 1934. It was followed by others, notably *Der Gemmenschneider* (1937), and in later years by *Musik fuer diese Zeit* (1946); *Glueck und Geduld* (1952); *Zwischen Hudson und Donau* (1958), a volume of selected poems; and *Gesang vor dem Abgrund* (1961). Forced to immigrate to the U.S. in 1938, Waldinger first lived in New York and worked in a library, in a department store, and for the U.S. government during World War II. In 1947 he was appointed professor of German literature at Skidmore College, Saratoga Springs, New York, where he taught until 1965. A master of the sonnet and the ode, he drew his inspiration chiefly from classical myths, musical compositions, war experiences, and the Austrian and American landscapes. His Jewish background inspired poems such as "Jehuda Halevis Tod," "Die Opferung Isaaks," and "Der Sabbat." *Ich kann mit meinem Menschenbruder sprechen* (1965) was his outstanding book of verse.

BIBLIOGRAPHY: Schoenwiese, in: E. Waldinger, *Gesang vor dem Abgrund* (1961), 5–24; H. Zohn, *Wiener Juden in der deutschen Literatur* (1964), 95–100. **ADD. BIBLIOGRAPHY:** J. Holzner, "Das Verschwinden der Aurora. Die Lyrik Ernst Waldingers und ihre Rezeption in Oesterreich," in: H.F. Pfanner (ed.), *Kulturelle Wechselbeziehungen im Exil* (1986), 202–13; E.R. Robert, "Ernst Waldinger," in: J.M. Spalek (ed.), *Deutschsprachige Exilliteratur seit 1933*, vol. 2 (1989), 985–96; K.M. Gauß (ed.), *E. Waldinger, Noch vor dem juengsten Tag. Ausgewählte Gedichte und Essays* (1990); J. Holzner, "Friedensbilder in der oesterreichischen Exilliteratur. Ueber Stefan Zweig, Vicki Baum, Ernst Waldinger und Theodor Kramer," in: *Zagreber germanistische Beiträge*, 4 (1995), 35–60; H. Zohn, "The Austro-American Jewish Poet Ernst Waldinger," in: H. Zohn, *Austriaca and Judaica* (1995), 153–67; H.F. Pfanner, "Weinheber oder Waldinger. Oesterreichische Lyrik im Licht und Schatten des Nationalsozialismus," in: J. Thunecke (ed.), *Deutschsprachige Exillyrik von 1933 bis zur Nachkriegszeit* (1998), 67–82; S. Schlenstedt, "Heimat im Gedicht des Verbannten. Über Theodor Kramer mit einem Seitenblick auf Ernst Waldinger," in: H. Staud and J. Thunecke (eds.), *Chronist seiner Zeit – Theodor Kramer* (2000), 187–98.

[Sol Liptzin]

WALDMAN, LEIBELE (c. 1907–1969), *ḥazzan*. Born in New York City, Waldman was recognized as a child prodigy and officiated as a *ḥazzan* and appeared in concerts while still a youth. He held positions in Boston, Passaic, and New York and sang regularly on the radio, rapidly becoming most popular. He possessed a warm, well-rounded, lyric baritone voice which, together with his clear diction and easy-flowing style, was particularly suited to the liturgical pieces and Yiddish religious folksongs which he performed in concerts and on his numerous records.

WALDMAN, MORRIS DAVID (1879–1963), U.S. social worker. Born in Bartfa, Hungary, Waldman was taken to the United States when he was four years old. He lectured at Columbia University (1916–18). He was rabbi of Temple Anshe Emeth in New Brunswick, New Jersey, in 1900–03, and in 1906–08 he directed the *Galveston Movement which was created to direct eastern European immigrants from the East Coast of the United States to less populous areas. Waldman was managing director of the United Hebrew Charities of New York from 1908 to 1917, vice president of the New York State Conference of Charities and Correction (1912), president of the New York City Conference of Charities (1915), and in 1927 was president of the National Conference of Jewish Charities. He traveled widely in the United States, setting up federations of Jewish charities to coordinate local Jewish philanthropy. Waldman spent 1921–22 in organizing relief for Central European Jewish communities, and was European director of the war orphans department and of the medico-sanitary department of the Joint Distribution Committee. In 1928 he became executive secretary of the American Jewish Committee, serving until 1945. From 1942 to 1945 he served as executive vice president of the Committee.

Waldman was responsible for many innovations in social work, including the District Service Plan in Boston, geared to serve family units rather than individual members of families; a planned parenthood clinic in Detroit; and bureaus of Jewish education based on the principle of community control. He helped to create the Bureau of Philanthropic Research and the National Desertion Bureau (of which he was the first chairman). He was also instrumental in having a human rights provision put into the United Nations charter. Additionally, he was active in the non-Zionist section of the Jewish Agency for Palestine; in the British-Zionist negotiations on Palestine, he represented the non-Zionist views. He opposed Jewish nationalism which he defined as the "organization of the scattered Jewry of the world into an international political unit or entity," although at the American Jewish Committee he tried unsuccessfully to bring agreement between Zionists and the non-Zionists in the organization. He later favored the establishment of Israel. Waldman's activities are recorded in *Not By Power* (1953), an autobiography. He also wrote *Sieg Heil* (1962), about Hitler's treatment of the Jews.

WALDMAN, MOSHE (1911–1996), Yiddish poet, journalist, and editor. Born in Ozorkow near Lodz, Waldman attended a Polish school and a modern Hebrew institution. After spending several years in Lodz (1927–31), where he edited the children's literary magazine *Lomir Kinder Lernen* and co-edited the journal *Di Fraye Yugnt*, he moved to Warsaw and then to Paris and Brussels. After publishing an article about Zishe *Bagish in the Brussels Yiddish press and a poem in a Philadelphia journal (1932), Waldman contributed poetry, criticism, and articles about education issues to various journals in Lodz, Warsaw, Cracow, Paris, New York, Buenos Aires, Mexico, and Tel Aviv. On his return to Warsaw (1933), he led various cultural activities of Po'alei Zion until World War II. In 1938 his first collection of poems, *Fartunklte Frimorgns* ("Darkened Mornings"), appeared. The original tone of the then still unknown poet attracted the attention of Dov *Sadan, who printed Hebrew translations of two poems in the Tel Aviv daily *Davar*. In September 1939 Waldman fled to Bialystok and from there was deported by the Soviets to Komi; he lived in Bukhara (1941–46). Among the survivors of the Holocaust who returned to Lodz, he tried to rebuild a Jewish life there, but in 1949 he immigrated to Paris, which became a flourishing postwar center of Yiddish culture. Waldman's interests then focused on promoting the survival of Yiddish culture. In Paris, he initiated educational and cultural projects, and helped Yiddish writers and artists arriving from eastern Europe. For decades he had a vitalizing effect on young people whom he inspired to take responsibility for the Yiddish cultural heritage. His indefatigable efforts played an important role in the growing interest in Yiddish literature and culture in Paris among young researchers and translators. His poem *Gang aroyf tsu Yerusholayim* ("Ascending to Jerusalem," 1976) was accompanied by French and Hebrew translations. A splendid volume of his collected poetry, *Fun Ale Vaytn* ("From All Remote Regions," 1980), appeared with an introduction by D. Sadan and illustrations by various artists. In 1983 he was awarded the Manger Prize. Two collections of his poetry in Hebrew translation appeared (1985, 1986). Later in life, he often went for longer sojourns to Israel with his wife, the Yiddish novelist Menuha Ram.

BIBLIOGRAPHY: LNYL, 3 (1960), 269; B. Kagan, Leksikon, 228; H.L. Fuks, *Fun Noentn Over*, 3 (1957), 250–5; D. Sadan, *Moznaim*, 43:2 (July 1976), 133–9; M. Yungman, *Di Goldene Keyt*, 103 (1980), 191–3.

WALDMANN, ISRAEL (1881–1940), Zionist, active in the Ukrainian government-in-exile. Waldmann was born in Chortkov, east Galicia. In 1897 he was forced to leave school before completing his studies because of his connections with Zionism. He worked as a legal assistant to the Ukrainian leader Dr. V. Holubovych in Ternopol, and through the latter's influence became acquainted with the Ukrainian intelligentsia and its fledgling nationalist movement. (The Zionist movement stayed neutral in the struggle for Ukrainian self-determination.) Waldmann engaged in Zionist politics during the elections to the Austrian parliament in 1907 and 1911. During World War I he left for Vienna, where he continued his close contacts with the Ukrainian nationalists who had set up their national council in Vienna under Dr. Petrushevych. At that time he published a daily, *Lemberger Zeitung*, supporting Jewish national claims. He was chosen to serve as Jewish representative for eastern Galicia in the Ukrainian national government which was organized in 1918 in Stanislav, but, before his appointment was officially recognized, the expansionist Polish regime annexed Galicia, and the Ukrainian administration was transferred to Vienna in May 1919. Waldmann continued as a propagandist for the Ukrainian leadership and accompanied their representative to the peace talks between Russia and Poland held in Riga in 1921.

In the *Steiger case (1924–25), when a Jew was accused of attempting to kill the Polish president, Waldmann tried to induce the Ukrainian nationalists to admit publicly their responsibility for the act. When his pleadings were ignored, he decided to reveal the Ukrainians' guilt to the public, thereby dissolving his connections with their movement. He testified before the court in Lvov, and several days later Steiger was acquitted. Waldmann was denied residence in Poland and thereafter lived in Vienna until 1935, when he went to Palestine. He died in Jerusalem.

BIBLIOGRAPHY: EG, 3 (1955), 145; R. Fahn, *Geshikhte fun der Yidisher Natsional-Autonomie inem Period fun der Mayrev Ukrainishen Republik* (1933); N.M. Gelber, *Toledot ha-Tenu'ah ha-Ẓiyyonit be-Galizyah*, 2 vols. (1958), index.

[Moshe Landau]

WALDTEUFEL, EMIL (1837–1915), composer. He was born in Strasbourg, where his father, Lazare Waldteufel (Wallteufel), was a piano teacher at the conservatory, and his brothers were also active as musicians. Emil Waldteufel studied at the Paris Conservatory, but left before graduating and began to write dance music. His waltzes became perennial favorites, including *Très Jolie* (op. 154), *Dolores* (op. 170), *Estudiantina* (op. 191), and especially *España* (op. 286) and the "Skaters' Waltzes" (*Les Patineurs*, op. 183). In 1865 Waldteufel was appointed chamber musician to Empress Eugénie and director of the court balls.

WALES, country of the United Kingdom. No Jewish communities are recorded there during the Middle Ages. However, individual Jews are mentioned in places where English influence was prevalent, such as Caerleon and Chepstow. The charters of newly created boroughs in northern Wales in 1284 included the "liberty" to exclude Jews. In the 18th century Jews began to resettle in Wales. They are found in *Swansea from 1731, a community being organized in 1768. The *Cardiff community followed in 1840. In the second half of the 19th century other communities were established, especially after the beginning of the Russian-Jewish influx to Britain in the 1880s. The newly arrived immigrants set up small businesses and pawnbroking establishments in the mining towns of Tonypandy, Tredegar, Aberdare, Llanelly, Merthyr Tydfil, Pontypridd, Porthcawl, and elsewhere. An attempt to introduce Polish Jews into the coal mines failed owing to local opposition, which had some antisemitic undertones. The disorders in South Wales during the miners' strike in 1911 took on an anti-Jewish tinge. On August 18–19 several Jewish-owned shops and houses were looted and wrecked in Tredegar, and the disorders swiftly spread to other mining towns in the area, driving hundreds of Jews to seek refuge elsewhere. Winston *Churchill, then home secretary, was responsible for sending troops to put down the disorders. These anti-Jewish riots, virtually the only example of violent antisemitism in modern British history, have been the subject of much dispute among historians. They also contrast starkly with the long-established Welsh Protestant tradition of philo-semitism and pro-Zionism, which produced such figures as David *Lloyd George, who promulgated the Balfour Declaration. With the change in economic circumstances in

South Wales after World War I, many of the small communities in the mining centers ceased to exist. While the parent community of Welsh Jewry, Swansea, decayed, Cardiff became a considerable Jewish center. Llanelly, Bangor, and the resort town of Llandudno (in northern Wales) had small communities. The total number of Jews in Wales in 1967 was estimated at 4,300 (3,500 in Cardiff).

In later years the Jewish population of Wales declined considerably. The 2001 British census found 941 declared Jews in Cardiff, 170 in Swansea, 39 in Newport, and smaller numbers in other towns, about 1,300 in all. Cardiff (the capital of Wales) has an Orthodox and a Reform synagogue and a number of representative institutions. There are also Orthodox synagogues in Llandudno, Newport, and Swansea.

BIBLIOGRAPHY: Roth, England, 82, 92; idem, *Rise of Provincial Jewry* (1950), 102–4; Lehmann, Nova Bibl, index; O.K. Rabinowicz, *Winston Churchill on Jewish Problems* (1956), 167–72. **ADD. BIBLIOGRAPHY:** U. Henriques (ed.), *The Jews of South Wales: Historical Studies* (1993); W.D. Rubinstein, "The Anti-Jewish Riots in South Wales: A Re-examination," in: *Welsh History Review*, 18 (1996–97); G. Alderman, "The Anti- Jewish Riots of August 1911 in South Wales: A Response," ibid., 20 (2000); G. Davies (ed.), *The Chosen People: Wales and the Jews* (2002).

[Zvi Zinger (Yaron)]

WALETZKY, JOSH, U.S. filmmaker and musician. Waletzky was born in New York City. Early on his father, Sholom Waletzky, introduced him to Yiddish melodies. Waletzky studied piano and composition at the Juilliard School from 1959 to 1965 and spent a semester studying under Peter Schickele. He graduated from Harvard College in 1969 with a bachelor's degree in linguistics and mathematics. Waletzky sang with the Yugntruf Ensemble, and in 1970 he wrote and directed the Yiddish operetta *Chelm, Undzer Shtetl* with Zalman Mlotek, which was staged at New York's 92nd Street Y. He performed with the Yiddish Youth Ensemble on *Yiddish Songs of Work and Struggle* (1972), a recorded collection of hymns and ballads from the Jewish workers' movements. At NYU Film School, he composed the music for and directed the Yiddish-language film *Dos Mazl* (1974). Waletzky worked as a sound editor on the documentary *Ibeorgun* (1975), followed by work on the Oscar-winning *Harlan County, U.S.A.* (1976), directed by Barbara *Kopple. He composed music for the film *Circle in the Square* (1976), as well as for two shorts, *Car Wash* (1977) and *Body Shop* (1977), for the PBS children's show *Sesame Street*. He served as musical director for a production of *The Jewish Woman* (1977) at the American Jewish Theatre, and scored *The Good Omen* (1978). Waletzky returned to sound editing for two Oscar-nominated documentaries, *With Babies and Banners: The Women's Emergency Brigade* (1978), which recounted the 1937 sit-down strike against General Motors, and *The War at Home* (1979), which followed the antiwar movement in Madison, Wisconsin. After working on the album *Past and Present* (1980) with Kapelye, a klezmer band he helped found, Waletzky starred with the band in the film and on the soundtrack for *The Chosen* (1981). In 1981, he was producer-director of *Image Before My Eyes*, a documentary about Jewish life in prewar Poland, and he served as script and musical consultant for the Barbra *Streisand film *Yentl* (1983). In 1986, Waletzky directed, scored, and cowrote the Jewish resistance documentary *Partisans of Vilna* (1986) with Aviva Kempner. Later Waletzky focused his attention on directing musical documentaries, including *Pavarotti and the Italian Tenor* (1991), *Music for the Movies: Bernard Herrmann* (1992), *Music for the Movies: The Hollywood Sound* (1995), and *Sacred Stage: The Mariinsky Theater* (2005). Other documentaries have included *Dashiell Hammett: Detective, Writer* (1999) and *The Endurance: Shackleton's Legendary Antarctic Expedition* (2000). In 2001, he released a CD of Yiddish songs, *Crossing the Shadows*.

[Adam Wills (2nd ed.)]

WALEY, family of English Jews, active in various branches of public and intellectual life. The Waley family traces its descent from Benjamin Levi (d. 1784), an engraver from Wiesbaden who settled in Portsmouth in 1740. His son Jacob (d. 1817) married ELIZABETH WALEY, and their son SOLOMON JACOB (d. 1864), a successful stockbroker, adopted his mother's original family name in 1834. JACOB WALEY (1818–1873), eldest son of Solomon Jacob, was educated at London University and was among the first Jews called to the English bar. He achieved an eminent position as a lawyer and, in addition, was professor of political economy at University College, London, 1853–66. He was an active member of the Jewish community, being a founder of the United Synagogue, first president of the Anglo-Jewish Association, and president of the Jews' Hospital and Orphan Asylum. His brother, SIMON WALEY (1827–1875), was prominent as a stockbroker, but was also a talented musician. He composed for both piano and orchestra and wrote some pieces for the synagogue. His son ALFRED JOSEPH WALEY (1861–1953), a leading member of the London Stock Exchange, was treasurer of the Royal Academy of Music (1924–46) and chairman of its committee of management from 1946. Jacob's daughter JULIA MATILDA (1854–1917) married Nathaniel Louis Cohen (1846–1913) and was mother of Sir Robert Waley *Cohen. She was president of the Union of Jewish Women and active in many other public bodies, and she wrote devotional literature for Jewish children. A sister, RACHAEL SOPHIA WALEY, married David Frederick Schloss (1850–1912), a prominent Fabian who wrote studies of the London poor; after the outbreak of World War I their sons assumed their mother's family name. SIR (SIGISMUND) DAVID WALEY (1887–1962), who was educated at Rugby and Oxford, spent his working life in the British Treasury, where he became one of its highest officials. Seriously wounded in World War I, he became an expert in external finance; after World War II he was attached to the European Recovery Department of the Foreign Office and during 1951–52 represented the United Kingdom on the Commission on German Debts. He was knighted in 1943. His brother Arthur *Waley was a poet and translator of Chinese and Japanese literature.

BIBLIOGRAPHY: JC (June 27 and July 4, 1873; Jan. 7 and 21, 1876); DNB, s.v. *Waley Jacob, Waley Simon*; *The Times* (Jan. 5, 1962); R. Henriques, Sir Robert Waley Cohen (1966); Ḥ. Bermant, *Troubled Eden* (1969), index. **ADD. BIBLIOGRAPHY:** ODNB online.

[Sefton D. Temkin]

WALEY, ARTHUR (1889–1966), English poet and translator of Oriental literature. Originally named Arthur David Schloss, Waley was born in Tunbridge Wells and was educated at Rugby and at Cambridge University. The family changed its name to Waley in 1918. From 1912 to 1930 he was assistant keeper of the Department of Prints and Drawings at the British Museum but devoted much of his time to the translation of Chinese and Japanese literature. In 1918 he published his translation of *One Hundred and Seventy Chinese Poems* and between 1925 and 1933 the classic Japanese romance, *The Tale of Genji*. The Chinese poems were a genuine popularization of material previously accessible only to specialists, and many poets derived inspiration from the technical adroitness of Waley's free verse. The modern British interest in syllabics – poetry measured by syllable rather than stress – derived from Waley's Chinese translations, just as the extraordinary popularity of the haiku in English arose from his translations from the Japanese. Through his translations, Waley brought something new into English poetry; a quiet, meditative tone, far removed from the crude Orientalizing of the 19th century. However, Waley never visited China. He apparently felt that his detachment from the immediate scene would enable him to concentrate upon more permanent issues and values. Waley's later work is mainly of interest to specialists, much of it lying in fields remote from creative literature.

He wrote several books on Chinese philosophy, notably *Three Ways of Thought in Ancient China* (1939). His last publications were mostly biographical and historical – *The Opium War Through Chinese Eyes* (1958), studies of the Chinese poets Li Po and Po Chu-I, and *The Secret History of the Mongols* (1963). He was made a Companion of Honor (CH) in 1956. His *Madly Singing in the Mountains*, edited by Ivan Morris (1970), is an anthology of writings with an appreciation of his work.

ADD. BIBLIOGRAPHY: ODNB online.

[Philip D. Hobsbaum]

WALINSKY, family of U.S. Jews in public service. OSSIP JOSEPH (1886–1973) was a U.S. labor leader and a journalist. Born in Grodno, Russia, Walinsky in his youth was involved in the Jewish socialist underground (1903) and was arrested. He immigrated to London, England, where he was active in the trade union movement (1904–07), edited Jewish trade union publications (1907–09), and became one of the founders of the Jewish fraternal order, the *Workmen's Circle (1912). From 1912 to 1915 Walinsky lived in Toronto, Canada, as a union manager. In 1915 he arrived in New York, again starting as union manager, and became a regular contributor to the Jewish press. In 1918 Walinsky became president of the International Leathergoods, Plastics and Novelty Workers Union. During the same year he presided over the first American Labor Conference for Palestine and remained an active leader in the National Committee for Labor Israel. In 1956 he published a book of Yiddish poems, *Lament and Song*. Walinsky retired from his union presidency in 1957, concentrating on leading about 2,600 *landsmanschaften*, fraternal orders, and folk organizations in their campaigns for Israel Bonds, UJA, and Histadrut.

His son LOUIS JOSEPH (1908–2001) was a U.S. economist. Born in London, England, and educated in the United States, Walinsky from 1931 was a teacher and lecturer. From 1943 to 1947 he was economic consultant and director of the Materials Division, U.S. War Production Board, and director of the Office of Economic Review and Analysis of the Civilian Production Administration. After that (1947–49) Walinsky became financial director of the latter organization, director of Germany-Austria Operations, and secretary general of the World ORT Union. Subsequently he was economic adviser to the governments of many Asian, African, and Latin American countries, as well as Australia. From 1953 to 1958 he served as an adviser to the government of Burma. In the 1960s he was a consultant to the World Bank. Among his publications are *Economic Development in Burma* (1962); *The Planning and Execution of Economic Development* (1963); and *Issues Facing World Jewry* (1981).

Ossip's daughter ANNA WALINSKA (1906–1997) was an artist. She ran the Guild Art Gallery in New York in the 1930s, traveled around the world in the 1950s, and created more than 1,000 works on canvas and paper over nine decades. A well-known portrait artist, she painted such subjects as Eleanor Roosevelt, Arshile Gorky, Mark Rothko, and U Thant. Her work is exhibited in galleries and museums around the world, including the Smithsonian Art Museum, the National Portrait Gallery, the Holocaust Museum, and Yad Vashem.

Louis' son ADAM (1937–) was a U.S. attorney. Born in New York, he joined the U.S. Department of Justice under Attorney General Robert F. Kennedy. He was Kennedy's legislative assistant and main speechwriter, accompanying him on his trips to South Africa and Latin America. After Kennedy's death he ran unsuccessfully for the office of attorney general of the State of New York (1970). From 1971 to 1995, Walinsky practiced law with the New York firm of Kronish, Lieb, Weiner & Hellman. He was a member and chairman of the New York Commission of Investigation from 1978 to 1981. In 1995, he began to serve full time as president of the Center for Research on Institutions and Social Policy, which concentrates on issues affecting law enforcement and social change. He is considered the father of the Police Corps, a program that strengthens American law enforcement by adding citizens to the police force; they serve four-year terms and receive four-year college scholarships in exchange for their commitment to serve as police officers. The Police Corps became law in 1994 as part of the Omnibus Crime Bill. Walinsky is a trustee of the Robert F. Kennedy Memorial.

[Frederick R. Lachman / Ruth Beloff (2nd ed.)]

WALKIN, AARON (1865–1942), Lithuanian rabbi, communal leader, and author. Born in Shumyachi, Belorussia, Walkin received his education at the Volozhin yeshivah where he studied under R. Naphtali Ẓevi Judah *Berlin. After the yeshivah was closed in 1892, he continued his studies in Kovno under R. Isaac Elhanan *Spektor. Walkin served successively as the rabbi of the communities of Gruzdziai and Seduva in Lithuania, and Mstislavl in Belorussia. After World War I he became the rabbi of the important Jewish community of Pinsk. He was active in *Agudat Israel and, with Meir *Hildesheimer, visited the United States on its behalf in 1914. Walkin and most of his family were murdered by the Nazis during the summer of 1942.

Walkin was considered a leading writer of responsa of this period, and his published responsa appeared in two volumes under the title *Zekan Aharon* (1932, 1938; reprinted in the U.S., 1951, 1958). His talmudic novellae *Beit Aharon* were published in four volumes (to *Bava Mezia*, 1905, reprinted 1965; to *Ketubbot*, 1911; to *Bava Kamma*, 1923, reprinted 1963; to *Gittin*, 1939, reprinted 1955). Walkin also published *Ḥoshen Aharon*, a commentary to the Shulḥan Arukh *Hoshen Mishpat* in three volumes (1927, 1928, 1930). His sermons entitled *Mezaḥ Aharon* were published in two volumes, the first of which was reprinted by war refugees in Shanghai (vol. 1, 1902, 1908, 1928, 1945; vol. 2, 1926). He also issued a new edition of the *Sefer Yere'im* of Eliezer b. Samuel of Metz, which included his own commentary entitled *Saviv li-Yre'av* (1935, reprinted 1960).

BIBLIOGRAPHY: H. Seidmann, in: *Elleh Ezkerah*, 1 (1956), 64–71; *Yahadut Lita*, 3 (1967), 47.

[Aaron Rothkoff]

WALKOMITZ, SIMḤAH ḤAYYIM (sometimes pronounced **Wilkomitz**), (1871–1918), Hebrew teacher and educator. Born in Nesvizh, Belorussia, Walkomitz became interested in the *Haskalah movement and went to Vilna, where he broadened the scope of his studies. He joined the *Benei Moshe Association and in 1896 went to Ereẓ Israel. As a teacher, he helped to lay the foundations of Hebrew education, stressing the labor ideal. He taught in Reḥovot, Metullah, Rosh Pinnah, and Jaffa, devoting his major efforts to the establishment and development of the school at Rosh Pinnah, where, from 1902, he was headmaster for 16 years. The first rural educational institution in Ereẓ Israel, this school served as a model for the entire country. Walkomitz was among the founders of the *Teachers' Association in Ereẓ Israel, delivering a comprehensive lecture at its first meeting in 1903 on the image of the Hebrew rural school. The anthology *Ha-Moreh* ("The Teacher," 1959), dedicated to his memory, contains appreciations of Walkomitz, as well as his own articles and model lessons, which had previously appeared in various periodicals. His son, AMI ASSAF (1903–1963), a member of the moshav *Bet Yehoshua, was a *Mapai member of Knesset and served as deputy minister of education and culture from 1958 to 1963.

[Gedalyah Elkoshi]

WALKOWITZ, ABRAHAM (1878–1965), U.S. painter. Walkowitz, who was born in Tumen, Russia, was taken as a boy to New York, where he lived on the Lower East Side. Jacob *Epstein was a neighbor and close friend. He eked out a living by lettering diplomas and shingles for doctors' offices. By 1906 he had saved enough to study for two years in Paris. When he returned to New York and showed his paintings in a basement storeroom, they were dismissed by most of the critics as "monstrosities." In 1913 Walkowitz was invited to exhibit ten works in the historic Armory Show in New York. One of his earliest backers was Alfred *Stieglitz, the art dealer. As the public grew used to the anti-academic manner of the new painters, he began to be a success, and his paintings were acquired by leading American museums. Walkowitz drew and painted assiduously until the 1930s, when failing eyesight made it difficult for him to work, and by the mid-1940s he stopped painting completely. As his own creative powers declined, he devoted his time to posing for colleagues, and in 1944 the Brooklyn Museum mounted an exhibition, "One Hundred Artists and Walkowitz" consisting of paintings and sculptures with himself as subject. Walkowitz' style ranges from Romanticism to abstract art. He began by painting dark, misty landscapes but changed in time to warmer and fresher colors. His subjects were confined mainly to outdoor scenes with figures, and for many years his favorite model was the dancer Isadora Duncan.

BIBLIOGRAPHY: Savin, in: *Arts Magazine*, 39 (1964), 42–45.

[Alfred Werner]

WALLACE, IRVING (1916–1990), U.S. writer. Born in Chicago, Ill., Wallace grew up in Kenosha, Wis., where his father, an immigrant from Russia, was a clerk in a general store. He always wanted to be a writer, Wallace said. He sold his first article, *The Horse Laugh*, to *Horse and Jockey Magazine* for $5 while in high school. He attended the Williams Institute in Berkeley, Calif., where he took creative writing courses, and then moved to Los Angeles and began to write full-time in 1937. After service in World War II, where he wrote scripts for training films, Wallace wrote fiction and nonfiction articles for a number of periodicals. Unable to make ends meet as a magazine writer, he moved into screenwriting. Among the films he worked on were *Split Second, The West Point Story, Meet Me at the Fair*, and *The Big Circus*. Turning to fiction, he wrote two books that were ignored by the critics. But in 1960, he published *The Chapman Report*, a novel about the impact of a sex survey on some Los Angeles suburban women. It became a bestseller, and, as a film in 1962 starring Jane Fonda, Shelley Winters, and Efrem Zimbalist, Jr., it was a big moneymaker. In addition to his own books, Wallace collaborated with his wife, Sylvia, his daughter, Amy, and his son, David Wallechinsky, who used the name the family had in Russia. Wallace wrote 15 novels all told, including *The Prize* (1962), *The Nympho and Other Maniacs* (1971), and *The Guest of Honor* (1989).

[Stewart Kampel (2nd ed.)]

WALLACE, MIKE (**Myron Leon**; 1918–), U.S. television journalist. Born in Brookline, Massachusetts, Wallace received a B.A. from the University of Michigan in 1939. He gained prominence in 1956 for his penetrating interviews on New York television. He wrote a column for the *New York Post*, "Mike Wallace Asks" (1957–58; published as a book under the same title in 1958), ran the radio series *New Beat* (1959–61), and worked as staff correspondent for CBS News (1963–64). He hosted several TV series, such as *Night Beat* (1956); *The Mike Wallace Interview* (1957–58); and *Biography* (1961–64). He was the anchor on the CBS *Morning News* from 1963 to 1966. From 1968 he was one of the main correspondents on the popular news magazine series *60 Minutes*. In 1990 CBS News presented the one-hour special *Mike Wallace Then and Now*, which highlighted his 40 years of reporting and interviewing.

Wallace also hosted the TV series *20th Century with Mike Wallace* (1995) and appeared in such TV documentaries as *The Uncounted Enemy: A Vietnam Deception* (1982); *Watergate: The Secret Story* (1992); *The Real Malcolm X* (1992); *Hugh Hefner: Once upon a Time* (1992); *Rod Serling: Submitted for Your Approval* (1995); *Ayn Rand: A Sense of Life* (1997); *Dead Blue: Surviving Depression* (1998); *Breaking the News* (2001); and *The 100 Most Memorable TV Moments* (2004).

Wallace interviewed kings, presidents, and prime ministers, dictators and divas, musicians and millionaires. Among his many honors and awards are 19 Emmy Awards, three Peabody Awards, and the Robert F. Kennedy Journalism Award. In 1989 he was honored by Chicago's Museum of Broadcast Communications for his lifetime contribution to radio and television. In 1991 he was inducted into the Television Academy Hall of Fame and was honored by the Radio/Television News Directors Association with the Paul White Award. In 1993 he was named Broadcaster of the Year by the International Radio and Television Society. In 2002 he received a Lifetime Achievement Emmy.

Wallace's published works include *Close Encounters: Mike Wallace's Own Story* (with G.P. Gates, 1985) and *Between You and Me: A Memoir* (with G.P. Gates, 2005).

[Ruth Beloff (2nd ed.)]

WALLACH, ELI (1915–), U.S. actor. Born in Brooklyn, New York, Wallach received a B.A. from the University of Texas. He got his dramatic training with the Actors Studio and the Neighborhood Playhouse. He was in the Broadway cast of *Mister Roberts* in 1949, and in 1951 won a Tony Award for his portrayal of the Sicilian lover in the Tennessee Williams play *The Rose Tattoo*. In 1954 he appeared in London in *Teahouse of the August Moon*. With his wife, Anne Jackson, to whom he has been married since 1948, he shared several successes, notably on Broadway in *Rhinoceros* (1961) and *Luv* (1964). He also appeared in *Staircase* (1968); *Promenade, All* (1972); *The Waltz of the Toreadors* (1973); *Saturday Sunday Monday* (1974); *Twice around the Park* (1982); *Café Crown* (1989); *The Price* (1992); and *The Flowering Peach* (1994).

Wallach made his film debut in 1956 in *Baby Doll* and had roles in more than 100 movies. Among them are *The Lineup* (1958); *Seven Thieves* (1960); *The Magnificent Seven* (1960); *The Misfits* (1961); *How the West Was Won* (1962); *Lord Jim* (1964); *How to Steal a Million* (1966); *The Good, the Bad and the Ugly* (1966); *The Tiger Makes Out* (1967); *How to Save a Marriage* (1968); *Mackenna's Gold* (1969); *The Angel Levine* (1970); *Cinderella Liberty* (1973); *Crazy Joe* (1974); *The Deep* (1977); *Movie Movie* (1978); *The Salamander* (1980); *The Hunter* (1980); *Tough Guys* (1986); *Nuts* (1987); *Terezin Diary* (1989); *The Godfather, Part 3* (1990); *Mistress* (1992); *Night and the City* (1992); *Two Much* (1995); *The Associate* (1996); *Keeping the Faith* (2000); *Advice and Dissent* (2002); *The Root* (2003); and *King of the Corner* (2004).

He also appeared in a host of TV series and TV movies. In 1967 he won a Best Supporting Actor Emmy for his role in the TV movie *Poppies Are Also Flowers*. His autobiography *The Good, the Bad, and Me: In My Anecdotage* was published in 2005.

[Jonathan Licht / Ruth Beloff (2nd ed.)]

WALLACH, MOSHE (**Moritz**; 1866–1957), pioneer of medicine in Ereẓ Israel. Wallach, born in Cologne, Germany, received an Orthodox education and studied medicine at Berlin and Wuerzburg. In 1891 he settled in Jerusalem and opened a clinic in the Old City. With financial support from Amsterdam and Frankfurt, he purchased land at a deserted spot outside the city walls for the establishment of a modern hospital. Named Sha'arei Ẓedek ("Gates of Righteousness"), the hospital was opened in 1902. Attached to it was a small farm. He served as director of the hospital until his retirement in 1947, giving it its Orthodox stamp.

BIBLIOGRAPHY: Rabbi Binyamin (B. Radler-Feldmann), in: *Hadoar* (Jan. 20, 1947); E. Porush, *Sha'arei Zedek* (Heb., 1952).

[Getzel Kressel]

WALLACH, OTTO (1847–1931), German organic chemist and Nobel Prize winner. Wallach was born in Koenigsberg and worked in Bonn from 1870. He was appointed professor in Berlin (1876) and head of the department of pharmacy (1879–89). From 1889 until he retired in 1915 he was professor at Goettingen and director of the university's chemical institute, continuing his research until he was 80.

In 1884 knowledge in the field of "ethereal oils" was in a state of utter confusion. Wallach, after many years of work, characterized 12 terpenes which were different from one another, in place of the far greater number of products previously thought, and charted their interrelationships and determined their structures, based on rings with six carbon atoms as the basic skeletons. He received the 1910 Nobel Prize for Chemistry for "his pioneer work in the field of alicyclic compounds." His work was scientifically important in clarifying a field of natural products, and also (through his students) led to the industrial synthesis of camphor and artificial perfumes. He wrote *Terpene und Kampfer* (1909, 1914). Wallach received many honors and was president of the German Chemical Society.

BIBLIOGRAPHY: T.N. Levitan, *Laureates, Jewish Winners of the Nobel Prize* (1960), 34–35; Partridge and Schierz, in: *Journal of Chemical Education*, 24 (1947), 106–8; Blumann, in: *Proceedings of the Chemical Society* (1964), 387–9.

[Samuel Aaron Miller]

WALLACH, YONA (1944–1985), Israeli poet. Wallach was born in Tel Aviv and was an active member of the literary group known as the "Tel Aviv poets," a circle which emerged around the literary journals *Akhshav* and *Siman Keriah* in the 1960s, with the aim of imbuing Hebrew poetry with an avant-garde, daring spirit. Her first collection, *Devarim* ("Things"), appeared in 1966, followed during her lifetime by *Shenei Ganim* ("Two Gardens," 1969), *Shirim* (1976), and *Or Pere* ("Wild Light," 1983). She also wrote for and appeared with an Israeli rock group, and in 1982 some of her poems were set to music and recorded. Wallach, one of the most original, venturesome voices in contemporary Hebrew poetry, explores inner processes of emotion and perception, reflects on the energies of the feminine body, on the ambiguities of sexual fulfillment, and is indeed one of the first feminine revolutionaries in Israeli writing. Written in fluid lines, her lyrical verse defies conventional poetic structures, offering her readers deliberately provocative, subversive lines of utmost intensity. Little wonder then that her poetry was considered obscene and tasteless, as when she mentioned the *tefillin* in a poem describing the sexual act. Yigal Sarnah wrote her biography (1993), portraying a woman who in her habits and life-style, as well as in her artistic work (be it poetry or performance of rock music) always sought the extreme. After her early death, "Selected Poems 1963–1985" was published. An English volume with poems appeared in 1997 and individual poems have been translated into a number of languages. For information concerning translation, see the ITHL website at www.ithl.org.il.

BIBLIOGRAPHY: D. Zilberman, *Ha-Ivrit Hi Ishah Mitḥappeset: Sheloshah Perakim al Shiratah shel Y. Wallach* (1990); Y. Mazor, "The Sexual Sound and the Flowery Fury: The Role of Y. Wallach in Contemporary Hebrew Poetry," in: *Modern Judaism*, 16:3 (1996), 263–90; L. Rattok, *Al Shirat Y. Wallach* (1997); R. Kartun-Blum, *Profane Scriptures* (1999); E. Feliu, "*Yona Wallach o la Ilum salvatge*," in: *Tamid*, 3 (2000–2001), 119–54; E. Negev, *Close Encounters with Twenty Israeli Writers* (2003); Z. Cohen Lidovsky, "*Loosen the Fetters of Thy Tongue, Woman": The Poetry and the Poetics of Y. Wallach* (2003).

[Anat Feinberg (2nd ed.)]

WALLANT, EDWARD LEWIS (1926–1962), novelist. Although Wallant's writing career was brief, he earned a reputation for craftsmanship and concern for moral values in his works, which included *The Human Season* (1960), *The Pawnbroker* (1961; made into a film after its publication), *The Tenants of Moonbloom* (1963), and *Children at the Gate* (1964), which dealt compassionately with the lives of ordinary people. Wallant's presentation of Judaism often focuses on a love for the marginalized, the stranger, and the "other," as well as Judaism's demands for dignity and justice. His works are often the ground in which Judaism and Christianity meet, suggesting that there is a common situation for faith as well as a common ground in which they encounter one another.

BIBLIOGRAPHY: D. Galloway, *Edward Lewis Wallant* (1979).

[Lewis Fried (2nd ed.)]

°**WALLENBERG, RAOUL** (1912–?), Swedish diplomat who became a legend through his work to save Hungarian Jewry at the end of World War II. Descended from a long line of bankers and diplomats, he was an architect by profession, a graduate of the University of Michigan. In 1936, he spent six months in Haifa, where he studied management at the Holland Bank, and first met with Jewish refugees from Germany. Upon his return to Stockholm, he became the foreign representative of a central European trading company, whose president was a Hungarian Jew, K. Lauer.

In July 1944, the Swedish Foreign Ministry, at the request of the American *War Refugee Board, sent him on a rescue mission to Budapest as an attaché to the Swedish Embassy. By this time, 437,000 Hungarian Jews had already been deported to death camps, and deportation had been ordered for Budapest Jewry. He had a great deal of cash, provided by Jewish organizations, since the WRB was to be financed by private contributions, and permission to employ unorthodox methods to save Jews. He had one other advantage. He was operating in a climate where everyone knew that Germany would lose the war and the only remaining question was when. Hence neutral countries, including Sweden, and even some German allies, were positioning themselves for the postwar world.

Wallenberg's chief operation was the distribution of Swedish certificates of protection ("Wallenberg Passports" or *Schutz-Paesse*), which were initially granted to Jews who had some link with Sweden. Wallenberg applied pressure on the Hungarian government and gained friends and assistants for his work. His department, "Section 3 – for Humanitarian Aims," employed 300 Jews. When the *Arrow Cross seized power in October 1944, Wallenberg initiated the establishment of the "international ghetto." About 33,000 Jews, 7,000 of whom had Swedish protection, thus found refuge in houses flying the flags of neutral countries. Wallenberg did not work alone. His efforts were joined by Carl Lutz, a Swiss diplomat, and by Giorgio Perlasca, an Italian businessman who posed as a Spanish diplomat and worked with the Zionist underground. Without any authorization or authority, Perlasca offered Spanish safe passes to Jews and established children's houses. He explained his motivation: "I simply cannot understand why a man can be persecuted because he is of a different religion from mine."

When threats did not work Wallenberg offered bribes, or even stood between Jews and their captors, saying they would have to take him first. When Jews had no authentic identification papers, Wallenberg came up with forged papers or driver's licenses. Anything that looked like an official paper, document, or list of names was flourished by an imperious Wallenberg with an air of authority that intimidated even Nazi officials. Wallenberg did not back down even in the face of personal danger. *Eichmann made threatening noises, saying, "Accidents do happen, even to a neutral diplomat." Wallenberg's car was rammed.

In November 1944, thousands of Budapest Jews, including women and children, were forced on a "death march" via the town of Hegyeshalom, to the Austrian border. Wallenberg and Per Anger, the Embassy's secretary, followed after them with a convoy of trucks carrying food and clothing, and he himself distributed medicine to the dying and food and clothing to the marchers. By superhuman efforts he managed to free some 500 persons and return them to Budapest. He saved several hundred members of labor detachments who had been put on the deportation train. In Budapest, he organized "International Labor Detachments" and even a "Jewish Guard" consisting of Aryan-looking Jews dressed in ss and Arrow Cross uniforms, and established two hospitals and soup kitchens. Eichmann threatened to kill him, referring to him as "*Judenhund Wallenberg*." Wallenberg formulated a comprehensive plan to restore the Hungarian economy when peace came. When the Soviet army entered Budapest on January 16, 1945, 100,000 Jews were still alive. Many, if not most of them, owed their lives to Wallenberg and his colleagues. At that moment, Wallenberg's struggle seemed to be over. He should have been able to look forward to returning home in honor. He approached Soviet officials with a plan for the postwar rehabilitation of Hungarian Jews. On January 17, 1945, Wallenberg was seen by Dr. Erno Peto, one of his closest collaborators, in the company of Soviet soldiers. He said: "I do not know whether I am a guest of the Soviets or their prisoner." He was never seen as a free man again. During the liberation, he had presented himself to Soviet army guards, who were reconnoitering the streets of Budapest.

For ten years, the Soviet Union denied that Wallenberg was in their custody. But after the death of Stalin and the thaw of the Khrushchev years, the Soviet Union formally announced that Wallenberg had been arrested. They produced a death certificate to substantiate their claim that he had died of a heart attack in 1947.

Yet up until the 1980s, there were occasional reports from former political prisoners who said they had seen an aging Swede in various Soviet prisons. In 1991, on the eve of the collapse of the Soviet Union, Mikhail Gorbachev presented the Wallenberg family with Wallenberg's diplomatic passport.

In 1981 the United States Congress gave Raoul Wallenberg honorary citizenship, an honor previously accorded only to Winston Churchill. The United States Holocaust Memorial Museum is located on Raoul Wallenberg Place and Yad Vashem has named him Righteous Among the Nations.

BIBLIOGRAPHY: R. Philipp, *Raoul Wallenberg, Fighter for Humanity* (1947); J. Lévai, *Raoul Wallenberg* (Hung., 1948); J. Wulf, *Raoul Wallenberg* (Ger., 1958); R.L. Braham (ed.), *The Hungarian Jewish Catastrophe: ...annotated bibliography* (1962), index. **ADD. BIBLIOGRAPHY:** K. Marton, *Wallenberg* (1982); idem, *Wallenberg: Missing Hero* (1995); P. Anger, *With Raoul Wallenberg in Budapest: Memories of the War Years in Hungary* (1995); A. Gersten, *Conspiracy of Indifference: The Raoul Wallenberg Story* (2001).

[Livia Rothkirchen / Michael Berenbaum (2nd ed.)]

WALLENROD, REUBEN (1899–1966), Hebrew writer on American Jewish life. Born in Vizno, Belorussia, he emigrated to Ereẓ Israel in 1920, but shortly afterward left to study in France and the United States. Wallenrod served as instructor and later professor of Hebrew literature at Brooklyn College in New York. From 1929, he frequently contributed stories and essays to Hebrew periodicals.

His novels *Ki Fanah Yom* (1946; *Dusk in the Catskills*, 1957) and *Be-Ein Dor* (*At Ein Dor*, 1953), as well as his collections of short stories *Ba-Deyotah ha-Shelishit* (1938) and *Bein Ḥomot New York* (1952), describe the life of immigrant Jews in the United States and their difficulty in adjusting to their new surroundings. Among his works are essays and literary criticism *Mesapperei Amerikah* (1958), a travelogue *Derakhim va-Derekh* (1951), and others. He was coauthor, with Abraham Aharoni, of *Fundamentals of Hebrew Grammar* (1949) and *Modern Hebrew Reader and Grammar* (1945). In English he wrote *The Literature of Modern Israel* (1956) and in French, *Dewey, l'éducateur* (1932).

BIBLIOGRAPHY: M. Ribalow, *Im ha-Kad el ha-Mabbu'a* (1950), 250–5; A. Epstein, *Soferim Ivrim ba-Amerikah*, 2 (1952), 370–90; Kressel, Leksikon, 1 (1965), 692; A. Zeitlin, *Ha-Ẓofeh* (Feb. 2, 1968), 4; Waxman, Literature, 5 (1960), 204–6.

[Jerucham Tolkes]

WALLENSTEIN, ALFRED (1898–1982), U.S. cellist and conductor. Born in Chicago, Wallenstein was taken when still a child to California, where he played the cello in theater orchestras and later in the San Francisco Orchestra. After studying the cello and medicine in Europe, he became first cellist of the New York Philharmonic under Toscanini (1929) and, from 1931, began appearing on the radio as conductor. Two years later he formed the Wallenstein Sinfonietta, a radio orchestra which became famous for its high standard of performance and its extensive repertoire of classical and contemporary music. From 1943 to 1956 Wallenstein conducted the Los Angeles Philharmonic and, after 1952, was also music director of the Hollywood Bowl.

WALLENSTEIN, MEIR (1903–1996), Orientalist. Born in Jerusalem, Wallenstein taught in Palestine (1925–29) and in Manchester, England (1932–38). From 1946 he was reader in medieval and modern Hebrew at Manchester University, and in 1970 he settled in Jerusalem.

Wallenstein's works include studies on Moses Judah Abbas and his contemporaries in *Melilah*, 1–4 (1944–50); *Hymns from the Judean Scrolls* (1950); *Some Unpublished Piyyutim from the Cairo Genizah* (1956); *The Neẓer and the Submission in Suffering Hymn from the Dead Sea Scrolls* (ed., with translation, 1957); and he edited J. Jaffe's *Ahavat Ẓiyyon vi-Yrushalayim* (1946).

WALLICH, German family that produced many scholars, rabbis, and physicians. The family origin can be traced to the 13th century. The name of Walch is first mentioned in 1349. It applies to a physician who appears in the register of Jews exiled from Worms and Speyer. ABRAHAM WALCH was the authority responsible for the observance of customs within the Worms community and signed, as chairman, the "Worms Judenordnung" in 1584. JOSEPH BEN MEIR WALLICH, also known as Pheibusch, obtained his doctorate at Padua around 1600 and was appointed by the emperor "Jew Doctor" of Worms. His medical activity is also mentioned in *Mainz about 1605. Soon thereafter, he had to defend himself before the Senate against a charge of poisoning, brought by his non-Jewish colleagues. ISAAC (d. 1632) left a catalog of folksongs of his day, written in Hebrew letters. MOSES WALLICH (d. 1739) is the author of the so-called *"Ku-Bukh"* published in Frankfurt in 1687, which is a collection of fables in the Yiddish dialect.

From Worms the family spread to Metz, Frankfurt, Bonn, Coblenz, Mainz, Copenhagen, and many other places. In 1747, SOLOMON EMMANUEL WALLICH, who studied in Heidelberg, was appointed "Jew Doctor" in Mainz by the elector Frederick Charles. He, too, had to overcome opposition of non-Jewish as well as Jewish non-qualified colleagues. ABRAHAM WALLICH, who resided in Frankfurt, compiled a popular medical booklet named "Harmonica Wallichia Medicia," which was published only posthumously (1700) by his son, JUDAH LOEB, also a physician, under the title: *Sefer Dimyon ha-Refu'ot, Terufot le-Khol Minnei Ḥola'im, u-Mashveh Refu'ot ha-Guf bi-Refu'ot ha-Nefesh.* Because of the Wallichs' reputation, one of them was even called to the sickbed of Louis XV of France. The name is also mentioned in the records of other German cities, e.g., in an antisemitic leaflet with woodcuts representing the desecration of the *Host in *Passau (1470). NATHANIEL WALLICH (1787–1854), born in Copenhagen and well known as a physician and botanist, as well as director of the Calcutta Botanical Gardens, specialized in the flora of India, Hindustan, and Burma. Other descendants were the Jerusalem pioneer and director of the Sha'arei Ẓedek hospital, Moshe (Moritz) *Wallach, and the chemist and Nobel Prize winner, Otto *Wallach.

BIBLIOGRAPHY: G. Wolf, *Zur Geschichte der Juden in Worms* (1862); F. Rosenberg, in: ZGJD, 2 (1888), 232–96.

[B. Mordechai Ansbacher]

WALSTON, SIR CHARLES (1856–1927), British archaeologist and writer. Born Charles Waldstein in New York and educated at Columbia University and in Germany, Walston (as he was known from 1918) came to England in 1880 and taught classical archaeology at Cambridge University from 1883 to 1907. He was director of the Fitzwilliam Museum, Cambridge (1883–89), and as director of American School of Archaeology in Athens (1889–93) led the excavations at Plataea, Eretria, and the Hera sanctuary at Argos. His interests included contemporary art history, art education, psychology, and ethics, and among his varied writings was *The Jewish Question and the Mission of the Jews* (1899). He was knighted in 1912. His son, BARON HENRY WALSTON (1912–1991), a farmer and agricultural researcher, was given a life peerage in 1961 and, in 1964–67, served as a junior minister in Harold Wilson's Labour government. From 1968 until 1981 he served as chairman of the Institute of Race Relations.

ADD. BIBLIOGRAPHY: ODNB online.

[Penuel P. Kahane / William D. Rubinstein (2nd ed.)]

WALTER, BRUNO (**Bruno Walter Schlesinger**; 1876–1962), conductor. He was born in Berlin, where he studied at the Stern Conservatory. At 17 he became voice coach at the Cologne Opera and the following year assistant conductor, under Gustav *Mahler, at the Municipal Theater in Hamburg. He conducted in various German towns until 1900, when he became conductor at the Berlin Opera, but he left after a year to become Mahler's assistant at the Vienna Opera, where he remained until 1912. In 1917 he was engaged as general director of the Munich Opera, which gained a brilliant reputation for its fine repertory and high standard of performance. From 1922 he worked as a guest conductor, making his American debut and conducting at the Salzburg Mozart Festival. In 1925 he became conductor of the Municipal Opera in Berlin-Charlottenburg, and in 1929 of the Leipzig Gewandhaus Orchestra. In 1932 he was a guest conductor of the New York Philharmonic and was reengaged for the next three seasons under Toscanini. Meanwhile, the Nazis came to power and he lost his German engagements. In 1936 he accepted the post of musical director of the Vienna Opera, but when the Nazis overran Austria in 1938 he moved to France. On the outbreak of World War II he emigrated to the United States, settling in California, and from 1947 to 1949 was conductor and musical adviser of the New York Philharmonic.

Walter was equally eminent as a conductor of orchestral and operatic music. A classicist among conductors, his interpretations were characterized by a contemplative, lyrical quality and by sensitive color and phrasing. He excelled as an interpreter of Mozart and above all of Mahler, with whom he had worked in close friendship for so many years. He conducted the first performances of *Das Lied von der Erde* and of Mahler's ninth symphony, and remained a lifelong champion of his music. Walter was also a composer, but discouraged the performance of his own works. A man of wide culture, he wrote several books: *Von den moralischen Kraeften der Musik* (1935); *Theme and Variations* (1947; autobiography); *Gustav Mahler; ein Portraet* (1957); and *Von der Musik und vom Musizieren* (1957; *Of Music and Music-Making*, 1961).

BIBLIOGRAPHY: P. Stefan, *Bruno Walter* (Ger. 1936); T. Mann, in: *Musical Quarterly* (1946), 503–8; A.L. Holde, *Bruno Walter* (Ger., 1960); MGG, s.v.; Riemann-Gurlitt, s.v.; Grove, Dict, s.v.; Baker, Biog Dict, sv.; H.W. Freyhan, in: *AJR Information* 25 (Aug. 1970), 5–6.

WALTERS, BARBARA (1931–), U.S. broadcast journalist. Born in Boston, Massachusetts, Walters received a B.A. in English from Sarah Lawrence College in New York in 1953. She began her career as a writer for local television stations on the

East Coast. In 1961 she joined NBC's *Today* show, and in 1964 she became its lead female correspondent. She was already earning a reputation as a skilled reporter and interviewer at a time when women's function on news programs was usually subordinated to the male anchors. She hosted the TV series *Not for Women Only* (1971–76). In 1974 NBC accorded her the status of co-host on *Today*, a position she retained until 1976. Walters had a string of exclusive interviews with personalities of international status – including Fidel Castro, Anwar Sadat, and every U.S. president since Richard Nixon. In 1976 she joined ABC as co-anchor of its evening news with Harry Reasoner, at a salary of $1 million per year for five years. She thus became the first female to anchor a news broadcast on a major network and the first anchorperson to earn a million dollars a year. While Walters' arrival did not signal the ratings boost for which ABC had hoped, she remained on contract to the network and flourished with a series of interview specials and as a correspondent on the newsmagazine *20/20*, of which she was the co-host from 1984 until 2004. Among her many television stints and appearances, she hosted the running interview series *The Barbara Walters Specials* (which began in 1976); served as substitute anchor on *ABC News Nightline* (1991–2004); hosted the TV series *Turning Point*, along with such journalists as Peter Jennings and Diane Sawyer (1993–97); and hosted the music show in a *New Light '94* (1994); the TV special *A Celebration: 100 Years of Great Women* (1999); and the TV talk show *The View* from 1997, serving as its executive producer in 1999–2000.

Among her many honors and awards, Walters was nominated for 18 Emmy Awards and won one in 2003 for *The View*. She was inducted into the Television Academy Arts and Sciences' Hall of Fame in 1990; she received a Lifetime Achievement Award from the International Women's Media Foundation (1991); was honored by the American Museum of the Moving Image (1992); received a Lifetime Achievement Award from Women's Project and Productions (1993); and in 1996 was honored by the Museum of Television and Radio for her contributions to broadcast journalism. Walters wrote *How to Talk with Practically Anybody about Practically Anything* (1970).

BIBLIOGRAPHY: M. Fox, *Barbara Walters: The News Her Way* (1980); M. Malone, *Barbara Walters: TV Superstar* (1990); J. Oppenheimer, *Barbara Walters: An Unauthorized Biography* (1992); H. Remstein, *Barbara Walters* (1998).

[Rohan Saxena and Ruth Beloff (2nd ed.)]

°**WALTON, BRYAN** (1600–1661), English churchman and Orientalist. Born in Yorkshire, Walton studied at Cambridge University and became active in ecclesiastical affairs. As a result of his High Church views and undisguised royalist sympathies, he retired to Oxford in 1639 and there devoted himself to Oriental studies during the 1640s. When a new Polyglot Bible was published in Paris in 1645, Walton began preparing a project of the same kind, but of greater scope and quality, and as the *Biblia Sacra Polyglotta*, this eventually appeared in six volumes (London, 1654–57). The outstanding work of its type, Walton's London Polyglot contained texts in nine languages, including the Hebrew Old Testament, the Greek Septuagint, the Latin Vulgate, the Samaritan Pentateuch, the Targums, Ethiopic versions of Psalms and Song of Songs, and a Persian translation of the Pentateuch. It also contained the Apocrypha, with Hebrew versions of Tobit by Paulus *Fagius and Sebastian *Muenster. Among the scholars who contributed to the London Polyglot were Edmund *Castell and John *Lightfoot. Walton's own *Prolegomena*, one of the outstanding early introductions to the Old Testament, later appeared separately and, in this form, went through several editions. The Polyglot as a whole still retains much scholarly value and interest. As a reward for his loyalty to the crown, Walton was made bishop of Chester after the restoration of Charles II in 1660.

WALZER, MICHAEL (1935–), U.S. philosopher and professor. Born in New York to parents Joseph and Sally, Walzer graduated summa cum laude from Brandeis University and holds a B.A. in history. He continued his studies as a Fulbright Fellow at Cambridge University, and then earned a Ph.D. in political science and history from the Kennedy School of Government at Harvard University. From 1962 to 1966, he was an assistant professor of politics at Princeton University, before he moved to Harvard and taught as a professor of government. He became a UPS Foundation Professor of Social Science at the Institute for Advanced Study in 1980 at Princeton. In addition to teaching, Walzer acted as both co-editor of *Dissent* and a contributing editor of *The New Republic*, as well as a member of the editorial board for *Philosophy and Public Affairs*, an academic journal. He was also a member of the board of governors at The Hebrew University.

An accomplished writer on topics of multiculturalism, political theory, and moral and social philosophy, Walzer was often hailed as one of the country's foremost political thinkers. His writing and speeches often tackled some most vexing topics of the current era, namely war and the reasoning, or justification, behind the wars and clashes of recent years. Walzer's theories look to historical thought and events to create understanding of today's issues; his current work includes a collaborative project on the history of Jewish political thought, and a study of "difference" in its many forms.

Walzer's body of published work includes more than 20 works written or edited by Walzer, among them *Just and Unjust Wars: A Moral Argument with Historical Illustrations* published in 1977 and reprinted in 1992; *Spheres of Justice: A Defense of Pluralism and Equality* (1983); *The Jewish Political Tradition*, edited by Walzer and two others (2000, Volume 1 and 2003, Volume 2); and *Arguing About War* (2004). His dozens of articles on topics such as political action, equality, war, Israel, and multiculturalism were published in a variety of scholarly and political journals.

Walzer was a member of the American Philosophical Society, International Affairs Committee of the American Jewish Congress, and the Institute for Jewish Policy Planning and Research at the Synagogue Council of America. He was also a member of the Conference for the Study of Political Thought and the Society of Ethical and Legal Philosophy. He had a special relationship with the Shalom Hartman Institute, where he has worked with Judaic scholars to shape a new understanding of the Jewish political tradition.

[Lisa DeShantz-Cook (2nd ed.)]

WALZER, RICHARD RUDOLF (1900–1975), scholar of Greek and Arabic philosophy. Born in Berlin, Walzer left Germany when Hitler came to power and, from 1933 to 1938, was lecturer in Greek philosophy at the University of Rome. He went to Oxford where he lectured in Greek, Arabic, and Hebrew philosophy. Walzer discovered much lost Greek material in Arabic philosophical writings, and contributed both to the understanding of Greek thought and of its use and development by medieval Islamic thinkers.

Walzer's publications include *Magna Moralia und Aristotelische Ethik* (1929); *Aristotelis Dialogorum Fragmenta* (1934, 1963^2); *Studi su Al-Kindi* (with H. Ritter and M. Guidi, 2 vols., 1938–40); *Eraclito: Raccolta dei frammenti* (1939); *Al-Farabius: De Platonis Philosophia* (with F. Rosenthal, 1943): translations of Galen, *On Medical Experience* (1944), and *Galen on Jews and Christians* (1949); and he edited *Galeni Compendium Timaei Platonis* (with P. Kraus, 1951), and *Greek into Arabic: Essays on Islamic Philosophy* (1962).

[Richard H. Popkin]

WANAMAKER, SAM (1919–1993), U.S. actor, director, producer. Born in Chicago, Wanamaker attended Drake University and studied acting at the Goodman Theater in Chicago. Despite a rich career in acting and directing, Wanamaker gained his greatest notice for his efforts to build an exact reconstruction of William Shakespeare's Globe Theatre, originally erected and used in the 17th century on the banks of the Thames River. Before his death in 1993, Wanamaker had raised over $10 million for the building, completed in 1997. For this effort, Wanamaker was posthumously awarded the 1994 Society of London Theatre Award for Outstanding Achievement. Wanamaker got his start as a stage actor in summer stock productions during the 1930s. From 1943 to 1946, he served in the U.S. armed forces. By the 1950s, he had expanded his talents to directing, including *Purple Dust, The World of Sholem Aleichem*, and *The Three Penny Opera*. In Liverpool, he directed and acted at the New Shakespeare Theatre in the plays *A View From the Bridge, Tea & Sympathy, Finian's Rainbow, Cat on a Hot Tin Roof, King of Hearts, Bus Stop,* and *The Rose Tattoo*. He is well known for his depiction of Iago in *Othello*. Concurrent with his stage directing and acting, he established a film career in *Taras Bulba* (1962), *Those Magnificent Men in Their Flying Machines* (1965), *Death on the Nile* (1978), *Private Benjamin* (1980), *The Competition* (1980), and *Irreconcilable Differences* (1984). He began acting in TV in the 1970s, including roles in the TV series *Berringer's* (1984) and in the award-winning TV drama *Holocaust*.

[Amy Handelsman (2nd ed.)]

WANDERING JEW, figure in Christian legend condemned to wander by Jesus until his second coming for having rebuffed or struck him on his way to the crucifixion. The story has given rise to a variety of folktales and literature still flourishing into the 20th century. Like the image of the Jew in popular conception, the personality of and tales about the Wandering Jew reflect the beliefs and tastes of the age in which he is described. While in the era of Church dominion he inspires religious horror and exhortations to piety, the character is later used as a vehicle for social satire, and even appears as a tragic figure expressing a spirit of revolt against the Church and the established order. He also appears in his old role as a target for modern *antisemitism. The name Wandering Jew has been given to a card game, a game of dice, plants, and birds. The legend has obvious affinities with other tales of eternal wanderers, primarily Cain (with whom the Jewish people as a whole is identified by Christian homilists, beginning with *Tertullian (150–230)).

Origin

At first the legend had only indirect connections with the Jews. Its beginnings have been traced (by L. Neubauer, see bibliography) to the New Testament story of the high priest's officer who struck Jesus (John 18: 20–22); it subsequently became linked and equated with other figures and elements, and in particular was associated with sayings attributed to Jesus foretelling his second coming (Mat. 16: 28; John 21: 20). The legend changed, and details were added. This story of the sinner doomed to eternal life apparently circulated in oral tradition in the Near East and eastern Mediterranean as late as the 15th century.

When the legend appeared in Europe, it readily gave expression to the prevailing medieval anti-Jewish hostility. The first written account specifically mentioning a Jew condemned for his sin to live until Jesus' second coming is recorded in a 13th-century chronicle of Bolognese origin. This states that, in 1223, some pilgrims at the monastery of Ferrara related "that they had seen a certain Jew in Armenia who had been present at the Passion of the Lord, and, as He was going to His martyrdom, drove Him along wickedly with these words 'Go, go, thou tempter and seducer, to receive what you have earned.' Jesus is said to have answered him: 'I go, and you will await me until I come again.'" The Jew subsequently repented of the deed, converted to Christianity, and led an ascetic life while enduring his punishment (*Ignoti Monachi Cisterciencis S. Mariae de Ferraria Chronica…* ed. A. Gandenzi, 1888). The English chronicler Roger of Wendover relates in his *Flores Historiarum* for 1228 that an Armenian bishop visiting the monastery of St. Albans told substantially the same story, adding that the man had struck Jesus. The tale was incorporated by Matthew Paris (d. 1259) in his widely circulated *Chronica Majora*, and in many other writings – in entirety or mentioned – in chronicles, poems, tractates, pilgrim itineraries, and miracle plays, from the 13th to 16th centuries in Italy, Spain, France, and England. The scene with Jesus is said to have been painted by Andrea Vanni of Siena (d. 1414).

At the beginning of the 17th century a chapbook was printed in German which accentuated the anti-Jewish implications of the legend, and was to popularize it further and inaugurate its transposition to further literary genres. Evidently based on Matthew Paris' chronicle, it first appeared under different imprints in Germany dated 1602, entitled *Kurtze Beschreibung und Erzehlung von einem Juden mit Namen Ahasverus*. In the copy published under the imprint of "Christoff Creutzer of Leyden" it is related that Paulus von Eitzen, bishop of Schleswig, in the winter of 1542, when attending church in Hamburg, saw a tall man, dressed in threadbare garments, with long hair, standing barefoot in the chancel; whenever the name of Jesus was pronounced he bowed his head, beat his breast, and sighed profoundly. It was reported that he was a shoemaker named Ahasuerus who had cursed Jesus on his way to the crucifixion. On further questioning he related the historical events that had occurred since. He conversed in the language of the country he happened to be visiting. This version shows "Ahasuerus" as a fully fledged personification of the Jewish people, incorporating the themes of participation in the crucifixion, condemnation to eternal suffering until Jesus' second coming, and the bearing of witness to the truth of the Christian tradition. The description of his person suggests the well-known figure of the Jewish *peddler.

In former versions of the legend, the man who assailed Jesus is referred to by various names: Cartaphilus, Buttadeus, Buttadeo, Boutedieu, Votadio, Juan Espera en Dios. Subsequently the name Ahasuerus (then a cant name for Jew through the familiarity it achieved in *Purim plays) became the most common appellation of the Wandering Jew in later literature, though in French he is frequently called Isaac Laquedem (corrupted Hebrew for "Isaac the Old" or "from the East"). In the German connotation he appears in a distinctly anti-Jewish light, referred to as the "Eternal Jew" (Ger. *Der ewige Jude*), which in English and French versions became the "Wandering Jew" (*le Juif errant*).

Numerous reissues of the chapbook appeared in German in varying versions in the 17th century, nine of which are attributed to the authorship of a (pseudonymous) Chrystostum Dudulaeus Westphalus. It was translated or paraphrased into French (notably the *Histoire admirable du juif errant*, c. 1650, reprinted well into the 19th century), Danish (*Sandru Beskriffuelse*, 1621), Swedish (*Jerusalems Skomager*, 1643), Estonian (printed at Reval, 1613), and Italian (*Narrazione d'un Giudeo errante*, and others).

In Folktale

Well over 100 folktales have invested the legend of the Wandering Jew with many local variations in places far apart, e.g., when the moon is old, he is very very old, but when the moon is young he turns young again (Ukraine); he may only rest for as long as it takes to eat a morsel of white bread (Westphalia), and can only rest on two harrows or a plowshare (Denmark, Sweden). Throughout the Alps his appearance presaged some calamity. In France his passing was connected with storm, epidemics, or famine; 19th-century museums in Ulm and Berne even exhibited large shoes allegedly worn by the Wandering Jew. Mark Twain, in his *Innocents Abroad* (1869), summarizes a local version of the legend told in Jerusalem by his guide in the Via Dolorosa.

After 1600 the Jew was reported to have made his appearance in localities in numerous countries at various dates (among many: Luebeck, 1603; Paris, 1604; Brussels, 1640; Leipzig, 1642; Munich, 1721; London, 1818).

In Literature

In the 17th and 18th centuries the Wandering Jew was the subject of *complaintes* or lyric laments by French popular singers. In England a 17th-century ballad entitled "The Wandering Jew" was printed in Percy's *Reliques* (1765). *The Wandering Jew or Love's Masquerade*, a comedy by Andrew Franklin, was produced at Drury Lane, London, in 1797.

From the end of the 17th century the Wandering Jew was used to describe "at first hand" events in world history or remote corners of the earth. *Goethe planned an epic poem based on the legend to survey events in history and religion and the Church (begun c. 1773; pub. by J. Minor, *Goethes Fragmente vom ewigen Juden*... 1904). The Wandering Jew became a popular theme in Romantic literature, ushered in by the Swabian poet Christian Friedrich Daniel Schubart's *Der ewige Jude* (1783), a poem in which Ahasuerus, standing on Mt. Carmel and overcome by despair, recounts how he has vainly sought death in battle, fire, flood, and tempest. Shelley invests him in *Queen Mab* (1813) with Promethean dimensions as the rebel against the dictates of a tyrannical deity.

Other literary treatments of the legend include, in French, Edgar Quinet's modern morality play *Ahasverus* (1833); Eugène Sue's highly colored novel *Le Juif errant* (1844–45), an anti-Jesuit satire (filmed in France in 1926); and a novel by Dumas Père, *Isaac Laquedem* (Paris, 1853). Gustav Doré published 12 engravings illustrating the legend in 1856. There is a short satirical story by Guillaume Apollinaire (1910; translated into English by R.I. Hall, *The Wandering Jew*, 1965). In Danish, Hans Christian Andersen's drama, *Ahasverus*, was first staged in 1847. Among German writers, Karl Gutzkow (*Plan eines Ahasvers*, 1842) identifies him with the evil attributes of Judaism. Kierkegaard in his notes (1835–37) depicts Ahasuerus as a man whom God cursed and outlawed. To Maxim *Gorki Ahasuerus is a symbol of all Jews in "The Jewish Massacre." August Strindberg in a short poem dealt with Ahasuerus' difficulties in coping with the complexities of modern life (in *Ordalek och Smakonst*, Stockholm, 1905).

English and American literary treatments include George Croly's historical novel *Salathiel* (1827), Nathaniel Hawthorne's story in *Mosses from an Old Manse* (1846), Rudyard Kipling's "The Wandering Jew" (in *Life's Handicap*, 1891), a yarn by A.T. Quiller Couch (in *Old Fires and Profitable Ghosts*, 1900), and short stories by William Sydney Porter (O. Henry; in *Sixes and Sevens*. 1911), and John Galsworthy (*A Simple Tale*, 1914), and E. Temple Thurston's popular play *The Wandering Jew* (1920).

Another popular work was the erotic interpretation in the U.S. novel *My First Two Thousand Years* by G.S. Viereck and P. Eldbridge (1928).

Among Jewish authors who have used the legend as a symbol are Jaroslav Vrcblický, the Czech poet (in three poems between 1872 and 1902), Abraham Goldfaden (poem in Yiddish, *Evige Yude*, Frankfurt, 1880s), and David Pinski (a one-act Yiddish play *The Eternal Jew*, 1906). The Wandering Jew appears as the narrator in the biography of Jesus by Edmond Fleg (1933).

Movies include the Yiddish film *The Wandering Jew* (1933), starring Jacob Ben-Ami, and an English film of the same name with Conrad Veidt (1935).

The hatred of the old superstition is turned into understanding and blessing in the Danish Hans Hartvig Seedorf's poem "Ahasuerus and the Plough" (1961), in which Ahasuerus is bidden to rest on his plow and thus bless the earth: for by the Jew "stones become grapes/ and figs grow from sand./ Pass between lilies, thou son of Israel,/ into the Promised Land of desire."

BIBLIOGRAPHY: J. Gaer, *Legend of the Wandering Jew* (1961); G.K. Anderson, *Legend of the Wandering Jew* (1965); Baron, Social^2, 11 (1967), 177–82; J. Karlowicz, in: *Biblioteka Warszawska*, 3 (1900), 1–13; 214–32; F. Rosenberg, *From Shylock to Svengali* (1960); L. Neubauer, *Die Sage vom ewigen Juden* (1893); A. Yarmolinsky, in: *Studies in Jewish Bibliography and Related Subjects* (1929; Slavic treatments of legend); A. Scheiber, in: *Midwest Folklore*, 4 (1954), 221–35; 6 (1956), 155–8 (Hungarian treatments); F. Kynass, *Der Jude im deutschen Volkslied* (1934); H.C. Holdschmidt, *Der Jude auf dem Theater des deutschen Mittelalters* (1935).

[Yvonne Glikson]

WANDSBECK, a district of Hamburg, N.W. Germany. Jews were permitted to settle in Wandsbeck in about 1600 by Count Breido Rantzau, when he saw the usefulness of the Jews in nearby Hamburg. The Wandsbeck community was Ashkenazi; they consecrated a cemetery in 1634. When in 1649 the Ukrainian refugees from the *Chmielnicki massacres were expelled from Hamburg, some of them settled in Wandsbeck. Jews from Wandsbeck visited the Leipzig fairs between 1678 and 1748. From 1671 until 1811 the *Altona, *Hamburg, and Wandsbeck communities were united (AHW). From 1688 some Ashkenazi Jews from Hamburg belonged to the Wandsbeck community, but from 1710, when Ashkenazi Jews were allowed to live in Hamburg, the importance of the Wandsbeck community declined. In 1734 there were 123 Jewish families; they had a synagogue in Peterstrasse.

A number of Hebrew books were printed in Wandsbeck between 1688 and 1722. With the arrival in Wandsbeck in 1726 of Israel b. Abraham Halle, the proselyte printer, a serious printing venture began, which owed its inspiration to Moses *Ḥagiz, who was the official censor. Between 1726 and 1733 not fewer than 23 (Bamberger), but perhaps as many as 40, items were issued here, many of them works of Ḥagiz himself.

After the disbandment of the united communities (AHW), the Wandsbeck Jews came under the jurisdiction of the Altona rabbi until 1864, when they elected their own rabbi. In 1905 there were 60 Jewish families in Wandsbeck.

BIBLIOGRAPHY: E. Taeubler, in: MGADJ, 1 (1908), 42–44; H. Kellenbenz, *Sephardim an der unteren Elbe* (1958), index; M. Grunwald, *Hamburgs deutsche Juden…* (1904), 165ff.; idem, in: MGJV, 14 (1904), 33–35; MGJV, 3 (1899), 29–33; S. Bamberger, in: *Festschrift… A. Freimann* (1935), 101–8; Ḥ.D. Friedberg, *Toledot ha-Defus ha-Ivri… u-ve-Arim she-be-Eiropah ha-Tikhonah* (1937), 104f.

[Zvi Avneri]

WANNEH, ISAAC BEN ABRAHAM (**Mahariv**; mid-17th century), Yemenite kabbalist. His works and the kabbalistic books which Wanneh copied assisted the propagation of *Kabbalah in *Yemen. His most important enterprise was the arranging of the Yemenite *maḥzor* on the basis of the Kabbalah and its interpretations. With the penetration of the printed *maḥzorim* of the Sephardi rite into Yemen, Wanneh ranked among the faction which was inclined toward the newer version that was inspired by the sanctity of Ereẓ Israel and the mystic conceptions of the kabbalists of *Safed. He enlarged the text of the prayers of Yemenite Jewry with numerous additions of prayers and *piyyutim* which were written by kabbalists, especially those for the Sabbath and festivals. The *maḥzor* which he introduced is a synthesis of the old and the new. His commentary, which is based on the plain and homiletic meanings and the Kabbalah, is the first commentary to have been written to the Yemenite prayer book. He entitled this book Pa'amon Zahav ve-Rimmon (Ms. Sassoon, 337), but it is called *Ḥiddushin* ("Novellae") by the copyists.

His other works include a commentary on *Maimonides' laws of ritual slaughter and the forbidden foods (Bodleian Library, Ms. Heb. f. 8, fol. 187); *Rekhev Elohim*, an explanation on the subjects of the *sefirot* and the Divine chariot; *Tikkun Seder Hashkamat ha-Keri'ah ba-Laylah; Bat Melekh; Mevasser Tov*, which appears to deal with the Messiah and the Redemption, but only its name is known. He is also renowned in popular legend as a miracle worker.

BIBLIOGRAPHY: Y. Ratzaby, in: KS, 28 (1952/53), 277 no. 146, 395 no. 169, 396 no. 175.

[Yehuda Ratzaby]

WANNSEE CONFERENCE. The "Wannsee Conference," as it became known after the war, was a high-level meeting that took place on January 20, 1942, to discuss the "Final Solution" of the Jewish Question. The meeting had been called by Reinhard *Heydrich, the head of the Reich Security Main Office (Reichsicherheitshauptamt, or RSHA), which controlled both the Nazi Security Police (Gestapo and Kriminalpolizei) and the SS intelligence service (Sicherheitsdienst, or SD). Heydrich had invited some 14 senior SS officers, Nazi Party officials, and civil servants to meet originally on December 9, 1941, but fallout from the Japanese invasion of Pearl Harbor and a temporary worsening of the situation on the Eastern Front led to postponement. The gathering finally convened on January 20 in a splendid villa on the shores of Berlin's Lake

Wannsee. One of Heydrich's subordinates, Adolf *Eichmann, took minutes, 30 copies of which were evidently distributed among the participants and other interested parties in the following weeks. The only surviving copy, marked No. 16 out of 30, was found in March 1947 among German Foreign Office files by American War Crimes investigators. After that discovery, the minutes, or "Wannsee Protocol," rapidly attained postwar notoriety.

The document's resonance derived above all from the coldly bureaucratic clarity with which it articulated a pan-European plan of genocide. The minutes are summary rather than verbatim, so we cannot be sure of all that was said, but the principal element of the conference was evidently Heydrich's lengthy exposition of past, present, and future policies. Some parts of the minutes were shrouded in euphemism, as when Heydrich discussed what the Protocol refers to as "new possibilities in the East." A table slated 11 million European Jews, listed by country, for inclusion in these "possibilities." Because of such euphemisms, Holocaust deniers among others have claimed that murder was not on the agenda, but elsewhere the Protocol is unequivocal:

> In large, single-sex labor columns, Jews fit to work will work their way eastwards constructing roads. Doubtless the large majority will be eliminated by natural causes. Any final remnant that survives will doubtless consist of the most resistant elements. They will have to be dealt with appropriately, because otherwise, by natural selection, they would form the germ cell of a new Jewish revival.

As far as we can tell from the minutes, other contemporary sources, and postwar testimony, none of the participants, many coming from dignified, well-established ministries that had long predated the Nazi state – the Ministry of the Interior, the Ministry of Justice, the Foreign Ministry, and the Reich Chancellery – protested. For the U.S. investigators after the war, a leading member of whom was Robert Kempner, formerly a high-flying (Jewish) civil servant in the pre-1933 Prussian Justice Ministry, it was almost incredible that such educated and apparently civilized men, eight of them holding doctorates, had concurred with such a plan. As a symbol of the calm and orderly governance of genocide, the Protocol remains without parallel.

For all the minutes' shocking clarity, historians have found it hard to reach agreement over the Wannsee Conference's function and significance. Some copies of the invitations to the meeting survive, and both their wording and Heydrich's opening remarks suggest that the Wannsee gathering was needed to clarify fundamental issues before the full "solution" was inaugurated. For early postwar observers, credence was lent to the idea of Wannsee's centrality in planning the "Final Solution" by wartime statements of the governor general of German-occupied Poland, Hans *Frank, which had already come to light before the Wannsee Protocol itself was found. Around the time the Wannsee meeting had originally been scheduled to take place, Hans Frank had alluded to fundamental discussions on the Jewish question concurrently taking place in Berlin. When coupled with the Protocol's systematic listing of all European Jews slated for "solution," many postwar observers believed it was at the Wannsee Conference that genocide had been decided upon. Yet what made this unlikely was the fact that mass killings of Jews had begun on the territory of the Soviet Union six months *before* the meeting, and that by the time Heydrich and his guests convened in Wannsee preparations for the Belzec camp were well underway, and the Chelmno death camp was murdering at full tilt. Moreover, there was the question of who had the power to make such decisions in Nazi Germany. Neither Heydrich nor his guests were in a position to unleash the Final Solution. Historians tend to believe those decisions lay with Hitler and Himmler.

Historians have therefore long debated how to interpret a meeting that claimed fundamental significance yet came so late in the day. The absence of any record of a clear Fuehrer order to kill Europe's Jews, and the rather ragged process by which killings expanded from shootings in the Soviet Union to a pan-European shooting and gassing program, have led historians to a variety of interpretations of the Holocaust's origins. Thus their conclusions about Wannsee's function have differed in line with their broader understanding of the Final Solution. Those who believe a fundamental command to kill Europe's Jews was given in July 1941 or indeed earlier, for example, see the Wannsee meeting as at best of secondary interest and sometimes as an almost entirely symbolic affair. For those scholars, by contrast, who believe that a decision to murder all European Jews – as opposed to the Soviet killings – crystallized piecemeal over the second half of 1941, the meeting's timing makes more sense as a response to an emerging consensus among Nazi leadership about the way to go forward. Something that may also have affected the timing of the meeting was the negative reaction among some Berlin officials to the rapidly disseminated news that Berlin Jews had been included in mass shootings in the Soviet Union toward the end of November 1941. These shootings in Kovno and Riga in November signaled the first mass executions of German Jews, something that had a different psychological significance than the already familiar content of reports about the murder of Russian and East European Jews. Wannsee may thus have been convened partly to ensure that the Reich's ministries were on board with the program.

What we can say with certainty is that Heydrich had invited many of the agencies with whom he and his RSHA staff had regularly clashed over lines of authority. Indeed, representatives of Hans Frank's civilian authority in the Polish General Government were, along with their SS counterparts, added only as an afterthought after an SS representative from Poland visiting Himmler in Berlin complained about Frank's resistance to the SS mandate. Heydrich's aim was clearly to impose the SS' and specifically his leadership on the Jewish question. To suppress any latent opposition to the deportation of more German Jews, he wanted to obtain agreement on any special categories to be exempted – highly decorated Jewish veterans from World War I and so forth. A substantial element of the

Protocol consists of detailed discussion of how to deal with special and borderline categories. Echoing proposals long articulated by Party radicals, Heydrich sought to overturn most of the special exemptions for the so-called *Mischlinge* (half-Jews and quarter-Jews) and also for Jews in mixed marriages that the Ministry of the Interior and the Reich Chancellery had thus far managed to maintain. This was the one significant area in which the Protocol records any counter-proposals to Heydrich's own suggestions, although in advocating the "compromise" of sterilizing all half-Jews, the Interior Ministry's Wilhelm Stuckart went much further in Heydrich's direction than had previously been the case.

Historians disagree too about the Conference's impact. Some contemporary documents as well as postwar testimony suggest that Reinhard Heydrich was very pleased with the meeting's outcome. It is certainly the case that both the deportation of German Jews, and the killing rate of Polish Jews rapidly accelerated in the spring, though how far this had been facilitated by the meeting itself is unclear. On the matter of the *Mischlinge,* follow-up meetings showed that considerable resistance to their being equated with "full Jews" remained, and in this regard Heydrich did not achieve the breakthrough he had hoped for.

BIBLIOGRAPHY: C. Gerlach, "The Wannsee Conference, the Fate of German Jews and Hitler's Decision in Principle to Exterminate All European Jews," in: O. Bartov (ed.), *The Holocaust. Origins, Implementation, Aftermath* (2000), 106–61; H.R. Huttenbach, "The Wannsee Conference Reconsidered 50 Years After: SS Strategy and Racial Politics in the Third Reich," in: H. Locke and M. Littell (eds.), *Remembrance and Recollection. Essays on the Centennial Year of Martin Niemoeller and Reinhold Niebuehr and the 50th Year of the Wannsee Conference* (1996), 58–79; J. Eberhard, "On the Purpose of the Wannsee Conference," in: J. Pacy and A.P. Wertheimer (eds.), *Perspectives on the Holocaust. Essays in Honor of Raul Hilberg* (1995), 39–50; M. Roseman, *The Villa, the Lake, the Meeting: Wannsee and the Final Solution* (2000).

[Mark Roseman (2nd ed.)]

WAQQĀṢA (or **Ruqqasa**), Moroccan family known in *Ceuta and *Fez from the 13th century. The Waqqāṣa family maintained contacts with the first *Merinid princes, particularly with the future sultan Abū-Yaʿqūb Yūsuf, whose private affairs they managed. According to the historian Ibn Khaldūn (14th century), the family encouraged the ruler's desire for wine. The Waqqāṣas' influence grew within the retinue of the prince, and when Abu-Yaʿqūb ascended the throne in 1286, he chose KHALIFA BEN ḤAYUN BEN WAQQĀṢA, known as Khalīfa al-Kabīr (Khalifa the Elder), first as *qahramān al-dār* (palace intendant) and then officially as chamberlain with very extensive powers. From then onward the Waqqāṣas dominated the viziers and other Muslim officials of the government and provided a growing number of intendants and stewards. Khalīfa al-Kabīr, who was very favorably looked upon by the sovereign and had amassed an immense fortune, acted as a dictator with unlimited powers. He was assisted by his brother ABRAHAM, his brother-in-law Moses Sebti, and his cousin KHALĪFA AL-ṢAGHĪR (Khalifa the Younger), who shared their relative's powers in every sphere. The vizier Abdallah ben Abu-Medyen, who was jealous of their position, plotted against them, succeeded in slandering them before the sovereign, and suggested a method of striking out at them. They were suddenly disgraced and arrested near *Tlemcen, which was besieged at the time by the Merinid army. Khalīfa al-Kabīr and all his relatives were executed in 1302, the only exception being Khalīfa al-Ṣaghīr. The latter subsequently entered the service of another sultan, Abu Rabīʿa, and became an all-powerful chamberlain. The kings of Aragon flattered this great personality and sent emissaries to him to assist them in inducing the sultan to join in an alliance against the kingdom of Grenada. Prior to this, Khalīfa al-Ṣaghīr found the opportunity to take vengeance against the vizier Abu-Medyen, who was put to death on the basis of the former's accusations. New intrigues subsequently resulted in the execution of Khalīfa al-Ṣaghīr and his entire retinue in 1309.

BIBLIOGRAPHY: D. Corcos, in: JQR, 56 (1964), 137–50; Hirschberg, Afrikah, 281–2, 389; C.E. Dufourcq, *L' Espagne Catalane et le Maghreb aux XIII et XIV siècles* (1966), 392–5.

[David Corcos]

WAR AND WARFARE.

TO THE DESTRUCTION OF THE FIRST TEMPLE

The methods of offensive and defensive warfare developed side by side in the Ancient Near East. The development of weapons was dependent upon the supply of raw materials, such as stone, metal, and wood; the technical developments of the period, e.g., the development of a metallurgical industry, the manner in which wood was treated, and that in which different materials, such as wood and metal, were joined; and the need, i.e., whether methods of warfare developed by one country necessitated corresponding developments to counteract them by a rival country.

Weapons

THE EARLY BRONZE AGE (C. 3150–2200 B.C.E.). The beginning of urbanization and the consequent development of more sophisticated armies in the Early Bronze Age also brought about the development of more sophisticated weapons, and the first metal weapons appear at this time. Several types of bows (Heb. קֶשֶׁת, *keshet* (*qeshet*)) are known in this period: the simple double-convex Egyptian bow; the early Mesopotamian bow, shaped like a simple curve; and the composite bow, developed by the Akkadians in the second half of the third millennium. Arrows (Heb. חֵץ, *ḥeẓ*) were hollow reed shafts, their bases usually feathered. Arrowheads were at first made of flint and later of metal. Tubular leather quivers (Heb. אַשְׁפָּה, *ʾashpah*) with circular bases have been found in Egypt. The spear (Heb. רֹמַח, *romaḥ*) was used for hand-to-hand combat (Num. 25:7–8) while the javelin (Heb. חֲנִית, *ḥanit*), a smaller and lighter weapon, was thrown from a distance (I Sam. 18:11). Spearheads found in Palestine (Kefar Monash and Tell el-Hesi) are triangular with a protuberant midrib and a tang terminating in a hood, which was fitted into the staff. The sword (Heb. חֶרֶב, *ḥerev*, also used for dagger), battle-ax, and mace were the principal weapons used on the battlefield. The technical limitations of the period for the production of long and tough metal blades were the main obstacle in the development of the sword as a basic weapon. At this time, swords were straight, double-edged, and pointed, an average of 10 in. (25 cm.) in length. They were designed mainly for stabbing, as if they were daggers. A second type of sword, the sickle-sword, developed in Mesopotamia in the second half of the third millennium B.C.E., was used for striking. There were two types of axes (Heb. גַּרְזֶן, *garzen*): the cutting ax and the piercing ax, developed as an answer to the metal helmet. Technically, they are divided into two groups according to the manner in which they were attached to the wooden staff: the shaft-holed axes and the tangled axes, both of which were developed in this period. The Sumerian infantry, for which there is the most information on military dress in this period, wore sleeveless leather vests with metal studs, presumably the earliest known coats of mail. Their metal helmets (Heb. קוֹבַע, *kova* (*qovaʿ*)) were slightly pointed, and they carried large rectangular shields (Heb. מָגֵן צִנָּה, *magen ẓinnah*) of wood and leather (?) to which a metal disk was attached.

Chariots (Heb. מֶרְכָּבָה, *merkavah*; רֶכֶב, *rekhev* is mostly collective, "chariotry") were not weapons in themselves but were used as mobile firing bases. They had to fulfill two basic requirements: stability and speed. These contradictory functions followed the development of the chariot, which was first evolved by the Sumerians at the beginning of the third millennium B.C.E. Two-wheeled and four-wheeled chariots are evident at this time, both drawn by two pairs of horses.

THE MIDDLE BRONZE AGE (THE AGE OF THE PATRIARCHS; C. 2200–1550 B.C.E.). The most advanced type of bow, the composite bow, was developed in Akkad in the second half of the third millennium (see above). While the highly technical skill that the bow required is not evident among the nomads who penetrated and conquered Syria and Mesopotamia, the appearance of the composite bow fully developed at the beginning of the Late Bronze Age shows that composite bows were in use in the Middle Bronze Age. Most of the data on bows comes from Egypt. The conservative Egyptians continued to use the simple double-convex bow, as seen in the wall paintings at Beni-Hasan, and the Asiatics in the same painting also carry this bow. Also portrayed is a workshop for the manufacture of bows, and the use of the bow in battle. Quivers did not change much, and the Egyptian ones have the same form as earlier ones. The same type of quiver is carried by one of the Asiatics in the Beni-Hasan wall painting.

Spears and javelins are divided into two types according to the method of attachment to the wooden staff: the tanged head and the socketed head. Tanged javelin heads have been found mainly in the tombs of the nomadic peoples of Middle Bronze Age I. The blade is typically leaf-shaped, with a long tang ending in a hook. With the javelin-heads have been found pointed metal skewers, also with long hooked tangs, which were presumably the butt ends of the javelin (Heb. אַחֲרֵי הַחֲנִית, *ʾaḥarei ha-ḥanit*), used either as weapons (II Sam. 2:23) or to stick the weapon into the ground when not in use (I Sam. 26:7). The socketed javelin head appears at the time of the Hyksos. Both the javelin head and the socket were cast in the same mold, the socket being wrought into shape afterward. The sicklesword, used for striking, was modified in the Middle Bronze Age, when it was made in a mold and the handle was attached to the hilt by a metal rivet. The length of the handle was twice as long as the blade. Several well-preserved examples have been found at Byblos, Shechem, and in Egypt. The dagger-sword was also developed in this period. Those of Middle Bronze Age I, found mostly in tombs, are straight and narrow, with a prominent central spine. The hilt was made together with the blade and had up to ten rivets. From their length of approximately 12 to 15 in. (30 to 40 cm.) it can be assumed that they were used for striking and thrusting. While the sickle-sword was used for striking, broader and shorter daggers for stabbing also appear at this time (Middle Bronze Age II B-C). In accordance with their function, they were strengthened by ribs and a central spine. The hilt was made together with the blade and a crescent-shaped stone or metal piece served as a pommel. While the development of the sword as the main weapon of the infantry lagged because of technical difficulties, the battle-ax that replaced it in hand-to-hand combat made rapid technical advances. The blade of the lugged, tanged ax is narrower and longer than previously, and the cutting edge is shaped like a crescent, and is wider than the rest of the blade. Such axes were used by the Egyptian army as piercing axes until the beginning of the New Kingdom. The triple-tanged ax was used at the beginning of the Middle Kingdom in Egypt mainly as a cutting ax. Demand for a special ax for piercing metal helmets gave rise to several changes in this ax. One of the axes developed to serve this need was the "eye ax," used in the 20th–19th centuries B.C.E. The three tangs of this ax ended in a semicircular shaft, thus forming two "eyes." Such axes were used in the 12th dynasty period and in Palestine, Syria, and Anatolia, and a group of ceremonial gold "eye-axes" have been found at Byblos. In Syria and Palestine in the 19th century, the "eye-ax" was developed into the "duck-bill" ax, which had a longer blade, a narrower cutting edge, and narrower oblong "eyes," which gave the ax its name. The haft was curved to prevent its slipping from the hand. Such axes were found mainly in Syria, and one of the Asiatics in the Beni-Hasan wall painting carries one. Shaft-holed axes, the typical piercing battle-ax, appear in Syria and Palestine in the 18th century B.C.E. and were used throughout Middle Bronze Age II. The forerunner of this ax was used in the Akkadian army. It has a long and very narrow blade, with a shaft no wider than the blade. Technical changes usually consisted of a strengthening of the shaft and a better means of connection between the haft and the blade.

Data from the Middle Bronze Age provide no information on the development of the means for personal protection and the chariot. However, the highly technical advances made at the beginning of the Late Bronze Age could not have been developed in a vacuum and presumably the personal equipment of this period was similar to that of the succeeding period (see below).

THE LATE BRONZE AGE (1550–1200 B.C.E.). The composite bow, made of wood from birch trees (?), tendons of wild bulls, horns of wild goats, and sinews from the hocks of bulls (Aqhat A, tablet 6, lines 20–23; Pritchard, Texts, 151), was the only type of bow used by archers in this period. The highly technical skill required for its manufacture made it the weapon of the armies of the empires and of the wealthy ruling class of the city-states. The two basic types, triangular and bi-concave, were both used during the same period. The triangular bow is shaped like a shallow isosceles triangle with a wide-angled peak. The arms of the bi-concave bow curve near the ends at the points to which the string is attached. A special bow case was attached to the Egyptian chariot, the bow being the main weapon of Egyptian charioteers. The charioteer had a quiver attached to the right side of the chariot and sometimes additional ones on his shoulders. Quivers, made of leather with a shoulder strap, remained long and cylindrical, and each contained 25 to 30 arrows. Arrowheads were leaf-shaped with a central ridge. To train soldiers in the operation of the bow, on foot or while driving a chariot, special training programs were devised, in which ranges and target shooting were employed (I Sam. 20:20–22). Spears and javelins did not change much from those of the Middle Bronze Age. They were used by the infantry of all armies, especially by the assault phalanx. They were the main weapon of Hittite charioteers, while Egyptian charioteers used the bow, as is clearly seen in the reliefs portraying the battle of Kadesh. Improvements in the melting and casting of metal are evident in the swords and daggers of this period. For the first time, the complete weapon – blade, hilt, and handle – was cast in a single mold for additional strengthening of the weapon. The sickle-sword remained the main type of sword, but the relative sizes of the hilt and handle became 1:1. Daggers were straight and narrow, the handle becoming part of the blade. The handle of both the sickle-sword and the dagger was molded with side flanges, the resulting recess in the center of the handle perhaps being filled by plates. At the end of the period, due to the influence of the Sea Peoples, a straight, long sword took the place of the sickle-sword. The two main types of battle-axes continued in this period. The Egyptians still used the tanged ax-head with extended lugs for better attachment to the wood haft. This ax-head, with a crescent-shaped cutting edge, was used throughout the period with only small changes. The blade was shortened and the cutting edge narrowed. The socketed battle-ax, mainly used by armies of the northern countries, underwent slight changes. The blade was widened and prongs were attached to the socket opposite the blade. This type of ax disappeared at the beginning of the Iron Age.

The development of the piercing battle-ax and the composite bow necessitated a development in personal defense. Body armor was composed of leather or rough cloth, to which oblong scales made of thin leaves of bronze were attached. The size of the scales varied according to their position on the coat. According to the Nuzi tablets, each coat of chain mail contained 400 to 600 scales. Such armor had several disadvantages: weight, cost, and the joints at the sleeves, between the scales, and at the collar, which were the weakest points (I Kings 22:34). Chain mail was used by charioteers and archers, as well as for protection of the chariots and horses. Several outfits have been found in Egypt, Syria, Palestine, and Mesopotamia, and they are represented in the wall reliefs of the Egyptian kings, especially in the chariot reliefs of Thutmose IV and those of Ramses II portraying the battle of Kadesh. Several types of helmets were used by the Late Bronze Age soldiers. The Canaanites wore a round metal helmet that covered the back of the neck but exposed the ears, as represented on the carved ivory plaque from Megiddo. The Asiatics that fought Thutmose IV wore slightly pointed helmets covered by feathers or decorated leather, with a tassel attached to the crown and knotted at the back like a plait. The Hittite helmet as represented on the King's Gate at Boghazköy is pointed with well-defined ear and neck shields and a long tassel. Another type of Hittite helmet is shown in the reliefs of the battle of Kadesh, in which Hittite charioteers wear round helmets covering the neck and exposing the ears. The pharaoh had a special battle crown known as the Blue Crown. The development of armor resulted in a reduction in the size of the shield, which was composed of a wooden frame covered with leather. The Egyptians used a small oblong shield with a round top. A metal disk was later added at the top. The Hittites carried a shield shaped like the number eight. The Canaanite shield was small and rectangular and was later replaced by a small round shield.

The chariot reached a high point of development in this period. It was brought to Egypt by the Hyksos, and the Egyptian chariots of the 16th–15th centuries are imitations of the Canaanite ones. The Egyptian chariots were light, with two wheels, a pole, and a yoke to which two horses were harnessed. The earlier chariots were lighter, with four-spoked wheels and an axle-rod placed near the rear of the body. The frame was constructed of wood and partly covered with leather or light wood. The pole ran underneath the body for additional support, and a double-convex yoke was nailed at the forward end. Chariots of the 14th–13th centuries B.C.E., such as that of Ramses II, were heavier with six-spoked wheels and an axle-tree at the rear of the body. The Egyptian chariot was built to carry a driver and an archer. A bow case and quiver were attached to it. While Canaanite chariots were copied by the Egyptians at the beginning of the period, under Egyptian rule in Canaan, Egyptian chariots were copied by the Canaanites, as seen in the ivory plaque from Megiddo. Hittite chariots, as represented on the reliefs of Ramses II portraying the battle of Kadesh, were heavier, with six-spoked wheels and an axle-tree placed under the middle of the chariot or near the rear. Two horses were harnessed to it, and a driver, a javelin hurler, and a shield bearer rode in it. While the Egyptians employed their chariots as mobile bases for the archers, the Hittites used them as mobile bases for the infantry, which was armed with javelins and capable of fighting as infantry without the chariots.

The principles of warfare as known today were also employed in the Ancient Near East. The techniques included surprise attack, ambush, concentration of power, methods to ensure maximum mobility, and the interconnected use of different forces of the army. Battles usually were fought on the main roads, such as the battle of Megiddo between Thutmose III and the Syro-Palestine coalition headed by the king of Kadesh. Prior to this battle in the summer of 1468 B.C.E., Thutmose III and his army, which included chariots and infantry, camped at Yehem (Kh. Yama (?)), where the pharaoh received the latest intelligence information concerning the king of Kadesh and his allies, who were reportedly waiting for him near Megiddo. A staff meeting with the Egyptian commanders was held and the three possible approaches to Megiddo were discussed. The commanders preferred to march along the easier routes, the southern one, via Taanach, or the northern one, via Djefti. They argued against the use of the main route via the wadi ʿAruna, because the way becomes narrow and they would be forced to march "one man behind the other, and one horse behind the other." Thutmose III, however, decided to take the more dangerous route on principles of honor and for the sake of achieving a tactical surprise. The entire Egyptian force marched through the pass, in a long procession without encountering any resistance or harassment, regrouped, chose the ground on which the battle would be fought, and won the battle. The Egyptian army, instead of pursuing the fleeing Canaanites, began to loot the camp. Thus the Canaanites managed to take refuge in Megiddo, and it took the pharaoh seven more months of siege to conquer the city and break the rebellion.

Further data concerning the conduct of war are given in the Egyptian description of the battle of Kadesh on the Orontes. In the summer of 1286 Ramses II marched to Syria to check the advance of the Hittites, taking with him four brigades. Before he crossed the Orontes, two *Shosu* (Bedouin) came to his camp and gave him false information – that the Hittites were camping at Aleppo to the north of Kadesh. Acting on this information, Ramses II divided his forces and headed for Kadesh with only two brigades, those of Amon and Re. He arrived at Kadesh with the leading Amon brigade, and while he encamped, his scouts discovered the Hittite army hidden beyond the city of Kadesh. The Hittite chariots then attacked, destroyed the Re brigade while it was marching unawares toward the city, and then struck north, breaking into the fortified camp of the pharaoh. Only the leadership and valor of Ramses and the employment of his reserve brigade saved the Egyptians from total defeat. A mere glimpse of the military tactics of the armies is given in the descriptions of these two battles. However, they reveal that these armies were aware of the advantages of surprise attack, the importance of military intelligence, the deployment of armies marching into battle (with or without a defended flank according to the terrain and the time of day), the division of the army into separate chariot and infantry units, and military discipline.

THE IRON AGE (THE PERIOD OF THE JUDGES AND THE UNITED KINGDOM; 1200–900 B.C.E.). After a period of decline at the beginning of the period, the bow continued in the tradition of the Late Bronze Age. The composite bow was used by all armies. Changes in the shape of quivers and arrows were marginal. Arrowheads lost their protruding spine and some of those found in Palestine and Syria carried inscriptions, such as "the arrow of ʿAbdlabiʾat" (חץ עבדלבאת). The sling, essentially a shepherd's weapon, also appears on the battlefield, as in the confrontation of David and Goliath (I Sam. 17).

The spear and the javelin, along with the sword and the bow, were the basic weapons of the infantry. Deborah lamented that her army was not prepared because it lacked spears: "Was there a shield or spear among forty thousand in Israel?" (Judg. 5:8). The main type was a shaft-holed spearhead with a long blade and a very broad midrib. The finest description of these weapons occurs in that of Goliath's armament (I Sam. 17:5–7): he had a special hurling javelin, with a finger-loop like a "weaver's beam" on the shaft. Under the influence of the Philistines, the sickle-sword changed into a long, straight iron sword used for cutting and thrusting. Since the smiths at that time were all Philistine, the Israelites were not able to produce similar swords (I Sam. 13:19). The new type of sword, described in Judges 3:16, replaced the sickle-sword as the basic weapon.

The Philistines brought with them weapons that had been developed in the Aegean. In the wall reliefs of Ramses III at Medinet Habu, each group of Sea Peoples wore slightly different helmets and armor, perhaps as a tribal distinction. The Philistines wore feather-crested helmets, while the other groups wore horned helmets or helmets with disks and horns. The body was protected by a coat of armor made of numerous metal strips laid at angles to each other, thus forming inverted V's or V's, depending upon the tribe. The lower part of the body was protected by a kilt with two strips of leather (?) forming a cross in the front. The Philistine army fought in groups of four, each soldier armed with either a long sword or a pair of spears, and protected by a round wood and leather shield. In hand-to-hand combat, the duelist, like Goliath, was protected by a man-sized shield carried by a special shield bearer (I Sam. 17:7). The bow and the battle-ax were not included in the Philistine arsenal. While the bow remained a decisive weapon on the battlefield, the long, straight-bladed sword took the place of the ax. It is interesting to compare the dress and weapons of Goliath with those of David. The former had, besides a sword (I Sam. 17:51), "a helmet of brass upon his head, and he was clad with a coat of mail, and the weight of the coat was 5,000 shekels of brass. And he had greaves of brass upon his legs, and a javelin of brass between his shoulders. And the shaft of his spear was like a weaver's bow; and his spear's head weighed six hundred shekels of iron; and his shield bearer went before him" (I Sam. 17:5–7). David was clad in Saul's "apparel, and he [Saul] put a helmet of brass upon his head, and he clad him with a coat of mail. And David girded his sword upon his apparel" (I Sam. 17:38–39).

While the Egyptian army continued to use the same type of chariot as was used in the Late Bronze Age, the Philistines employed a heavy chariot with six-spoked wheels and a crew of three, armed with hurling javelins like the Hittite charioteers. The Israelite tribes, when settling in the hill country, "drove out the inhabitants of the hill country, for he [Judah] was unable to drive out the inhabitants of the valley, because they had chariots of iron" (Judg. 1:19). The tribal army of Deborah and Barak was victorious over the chariots of Sisera in a battle in the Jezreel Valley (Judg. 4:13–15). David and Solomon were the first to form chariot squadrons in the Israelite army, and Solomon built special cities for chariots (I Kings 10:26; II Chron. 1:14). At the same time, Solomon was the main trader in horses and chariots between Egypt and the Hittites (I Kings 10:28–29).

The technique of night attack can be seen in the description of the battle between Gideon and the Midianites (Judg. 6–8), the latter being mounted on camels. The army of Gideon encamped "beside En-Harod; and the camp of Midian was on the north side of them, by Gibeath-Moreh, in the valley." After the Israelites had assembled, Gideon chose only 300 of them, for a surprise night attack requires only a small number of men. Before the attack, Gideon reconnoitered outside the Midian camp. His plan of attack was simple, with the 300 men divided into three companies under the leadership of Gideon, an agreed signal, and the battle cry of "For the Lord and for Gideon." After a timetable for the attack was set, the Israelites attacked the enemy camp during the changing of the guard. The attack was executed according to plan and the enemy was put to flight. Gideon asked the Ephraimites to block the retreat of the Midianites across the Jordan, while he and his army pursued the fleeing enemy until it was destroyed and the Midianite kings captured.

THE IRON AGE: THE KINGDOMS OF ISRAEL AND JUDAH (900–586 B.C.E.). The main sources of this period for information on the military organization are the wall reliefs found in the palaces of the Assyrian kings. The prophet Isaiah describes the character and great strength of the Assyrian army (5:26–28), which was imitated by the other armies of the ancient Near East. The army was divided into three forces – infantry, cavalry, and chariots – as described in the Bible: "And muster an army like the army that you have lost, horse for horse, and chariot for chariot" (I Kings 20:25); "For there was not left to Jehoahaz of the people save fifty horsemen and ten chariots and 10,000 footmen" (II Kings 13:7). Besides his special weapons, each soldier had a basic armament of a sword, a coat of mail, and a helmet. The design of this basic armament was slightly changed from the reign of one king to the other. The iron sword was long and straight with a double edge, and the handle was constructed to fit to the fingers. It was carried in a sheath shaped like the sword, and a floral decoration was occasionally added near the opening and the base. The sheath was hooked to the belt on the left side and held in place by a leather strap that circled the left shoulder. The coat of armor, shaped like a sack with an opening for the head and short sleeves, was full-length in the ninth century B.C.E. A special scarf of scales used by archers connected the helmet to the armor. In the eighth and seventh centuries the chain mail dress was shortened into a shirt. The shape of metal helmets varied from conical and pointed to feather-crested, according to the troops wearing them and the reigning king.

The infantry (Heb. *ragli, ish ragli*; I Kings 20:29) was divided into four groups: archers (Heb. *dorekhei qeshet*; Jer. 50:14; *nosheqei qeshet*; I Chron. 12:2), slingers (Heb. *kalla'im*; II Kings 3:25), spearmen (Heb. *'orekhei ẓinnah wa-romaḥ;* I Chron. 12:9), and auxiliaries. While the spearmen, the assault troops of the army, defended themselves with shields which were rectangular, round, or curved with a round top, depending upon the period, the archers and the slingers were without shields, and special shield bearers were attached to their companies. The infantry took part in battles in the open field and in assaults on fortified cities with no change in their equipment. The cavalry (Heb. *parashim*) only participated in open field engagements and were equipped with either bows or spears. While mounted spearmen defended themselves with round shields, mounted archers, who needed the use of both hands in combat, were protected by mounted shield bearers. The cavalry operated either as independent units or as a mobile defense for the chariots. Chariots (Heb. *rekhev, ḥeil rekhev*) as the main assault force underwent many changes in Assyrian military history. The earliest known ones, those of Ashurnaṣirpal II (883–859 B.C.E.), were heavier than those known from the preceding period. Each had six-spoked wheels of medium size, an axle-rod at the rear of the body, and a heavy pole. Two horses were harnessed to it and a third, riding as an outrigger, was held in reserve. The crew consisted of a driver, who also served as a spearman, and an archer. A shield bearer was added to the king's chariot. The chariots of Tiglath-Pileser III (745–727 B.C.E.) are heavier still, and the wheels are larger with eight spokes. A driver, archer, and shield bearer rode in the chariot, the latter protecting the others with two round shields. The number of horses and, correspondingly, of yokes was increased to four. The tendency of the kings following Tiglath-Pileser III was to build heavier chariots. In the time of Ashurbanipal (668–630 B.C.E.), the crew numbered four – a driver, an archer, and two shield bearers.

A complicated description of the battle between Ahab and Ben-Hadad of Aram is given in I Kings 20:1–23. This battle took place in the Samarian Hills, and the Arameans blamed their defeat on the fact that the Israelite God "is a God of the hills; therefore they were stronger than we; but let us fight against them in the plain, and surely we shall be stronger than they." Subsequently, a second battle was fought in the plain of Aphek in the Golan (I Kings 20:23–30). The two armies faced each other for seven days before finally joining battle, which the Arameans again lost.

Fortifications

THE EARLY BRONZE AGE (C. 3150–2200 B.C.E.). The widespread urbanization which had its beginnings in this period created a need for a developed civic organization, a central administration, and the means for defense of the city. Armies were created, and military engineers designed city walls and inner citadels, fortified city gates and bastions. Posterns were built into the city wall for use in counterattack. The achievements of these engineers have been preserved in the monuments and remains uncovered by archaeologists. The earliest plans of fortified cities are preserved on the ceremonial slate palettes of the late pre-Dynastic period in Egypt (late 4th millennium). These show square or rectangular fortified cities with wide walls, square towers, and a parapet around the top for protection of the defenders. Three fortified enclosures dating to the Second Dynasty in Egypt were found at Hierakonpolis and Abydos. Incomplete fortifications that have been uncovered in Palestine usually have very thick walls, 13–26 ft. (4–8 m.) thick, built of the materials available in the region, i.e., of either stone or brick or a combination of the two, the stone forming the foundation and the brick the superstructure. Such walls were found at Megiddo, Ai, Bet-Yeraḥ, and Jericho. They were fortified with semicircular towers, as at Ai, Arad, and Jericho (and as represented in a wall relief from Deshashah in Egypt, detailing the Egyptian assault of a Syrian city), and/or with rectangular towers as at Tell el-Far'ah (biblical Tirzah), Jericho, and Ai. City gates are of two types. At Tell el-Far'ah and Jericho passageways flanked by two protruding towers were found. The second type, as found at Khirbet et-Tabaik (Rosh ha-Nikrah), features an indirect approach between the inner and outer entrances, thus forcing the attacker to turn in the middle of the attack. The forerunners of certain methods of fortification which occur in a more advanced form in the Middle Bronze Age were found in this period. Thus a primitive glacis was uncovered at Gezer, Tel ʿAierani, and Taanach, and a small fosse (moat) at Jericho.

Three methods were employed to conquer a fortified city: direct approach, i.e., penetrating the wall by breaching, climbing it, or digging a passage underneath it; siege; indirect approach, i.e., penetration by ruse. Only when the first method was employed does material evidence remain; for evidence of the other two, written documents must be used. Direct approach was employed to either penetrate the wall in an undefended spot or to attack the gate, the most vulnerable point in the wall. In such an attack, ladders were used for scaling the wall, or axes, spears, and later the battering ram were used for breaching it, all under the covering fire of archers. The weapons of this period were primitive, but even the large walls of the cities crumbled in front of them, as attested by the many layers of destruction found in excavated sites. Hoes and battering poles for breaching the city wall, and mobile and non-mobile ladders for scaling them were widely used by the Egyptian army.

THE MIDDLE BRONZE AGE (2200–1550 B.C.E.). This period is divided into the pre-Hyksos period (Middle Bronze IIA in Palestine, the 12th Dynasty in Egypt; c. 2000–1750 B.C.E.) and the Hyksos period (Middle Bronze IIB–C in Palestine, the 13th–17th Dynasties in Egypt; cf. 1750–1550 B.C.E.). An excellent example of Egyptian fortifications of the first period was excavated at Buhen in northern Nubia. The citadel measures approximately 170 × 180 m. and has four lines of defense: an inner wall, outer wall, moat, and fortified gate. The brick inner wall is approximately 16½ ft. (5 m.) thick and approximately 33 ft. (c. 10 m.) high. At intervals of 16½ ft. (5 m.) square bastions protrude from the face of the wall. Battlements and balconies crown the top of the wall. The outer wall, lower than the inner one in the typical Egyptian style of this and the preceding period, has a series of semicircular bastions at intervals of 33½ ft. (10 m.). On top of the wall and the bastions are two rows of embrasures, one above the other. A dry moat was excavated at the foot of the outer wall, with a counterscarp on the opposite side. The gate complex consisted of two rectangular towers, which protruded beyond the counterscarp and flanked a narrow passageway leading to a two-doored gate. Remains of a wooden drawbridge were found over the moat. While the ground outside the wall was covered by the archers from at least three directions, the weakest point of the defenses was the gate, and burnt layers at this spot show that the citadel was breached here. A citadel represented on a wall painting at Beni-Hasan in Egypt has a wall sloping outwards at the bottom and topped by balconies and two gates with battlements. A fortified gate excavated at Megiddo was reached by a stairway protected by a wall. The outer and inner entrances are on an indirect axis, which, together with the nearby gate tower, provided an ample means of defense against attack. The appearance of the chariot and a developed battering ram changed the nature of fortifications. The gates could no longer be built with an indirect approach or with a stepped passageway, as chariots could not maneuver under such conditions. Means to protect the wall and its base against the battering ram had to be devised. The walls were built upon large ramparts of terre-pisée, as found at sites as far afield as Syria and Egypt, and at *Sharuhen (Tell al-Fāriʿa), Tell el-ʾAggul (Beth-Egliam), Lachish, Hazor, Tel Dan, and Jericho in Palestine. The outer face of the rampart was made into a glacis, which was constructed of several layers of terre-pisée, in a sandwich pattern, and was faced with bricks, stones, or hardened clay. A fosse was excavated at the foot of the glacis and a counterscarp built on the outer edge. The gates were built against the inner face of the city wall. Three pairs of pilasters flanked the passageway, creating two guardrooms, while also serving as piers for the upper stories of the gate tower. The gate was protected by two multistoried rectangular towers, usually not protruding from the outer face of the wall. This type of gate has been found in almost every excavated site of this period, such as Hazor, Gezer, Beth-Shemesh, and Shechem in Palestine, and Alalakh and Qatna in Syria.

The main development in offensive weapons was the battering ram (Heb. כַּר). Primitive ones are represented in the relief from Deshasheh, but the first representation of one whose users are covered against arrows from the wall by a hut-shaped enclosure appears in the Beni-Hasan wall painting. The battering ram is also mentioned in the Mari letters and the Boghazkőy archives, which deal with problems of use, special methods of construction, and mobility.

THE LATE BRONZE AGE (1550–1200 B.C.E.). The cities of this period occupied the same sites as those of the Middle Bronze Age and where the defenses were still standing, they were reused, with generally only small changes being made. The main feature which emerges in this period is a citadel built inside the city on the highest point. A palace and temple were built inside the citadel. Elevations of Canaanite cities are shown in the wall reliefs of the 19th Dynasty, whose kings, Seti I and Ramses II, conquered many of them. The cities are stereotyped, being built on a mound with two main features of defense – an outer city wall and an inner citadel, both with semicircular battlements and rectangular balconies. The cities had one or two rectangular gates of the same type as the Middle Bronze II gates, at Megiddo, Hazor, and Gezer. Archaeological remains that exhibit the new developments in military engineering are scarce. One of them is the eastern city gate at Shechem, which is constructed of two pairs of pilasters, with a guardroom between them. The pilasters served as piers for the upper stories of the gate tower. Remains of citadels and fortified temples, called *migdal* in the Bible (Judg. 9:46–49, 50–52), were found at Shechem, Megiddo, and Beth-Shean. The rectangular temples at Megiddo and Shechem were protected by thick walls, with a pair of square towers flanking the entrance. According to biblical descriptions and archaeological evidence, they were multistoried. The fortifications of Boghazkőy, the Hittite capital, exhibit several new features in military architecture. The walls were constructed as casemates, with a low outer wall in front of them. Several underground posterns were found underneath the walls. The gates, known as the King's Gate and the Lion's Gate, were formed by two pairs of pilasters with a guardroom between them and a passageway flanked by two multistoried towers.

Most information on war of offense in this period comes from Egyptian wall reliefs and documents and from the Bible. The Egyptians employed all the three possible methods of offense: direct and indirect approach and siege. While assaulting a city, the shock troops, protected by shields, used scaling ladders to climb the wall or attempted to breach the city gates with battle-axes. No battering ram appears in Egyptian reliefs. When direct approach was impossible or too dangerous, the Egyptians laid siege to the city, which sometimes lasted up to three years, as that of ʿAhmose (Amasis), the founder of the 18th Dynasty, against Sharuhen in Southern Palestine. Ruse was also employed in the conquest of cities. One of the most well-known is the Trojan horse, which ended the siege of Troy. Joshua employed ruses at least twice. That used against Jericho (Josh. 6) is still obscure. A clearer stratagem is that used against Ai (Josh. 8:3–8), in which Joshua and the Israelites drew the inhabitants out of the city by feigning retreat. Burnt levels, found at Beth-El, Lachish, Tell Beit Mibsim, and Hazor, indicate the destruction caused by the Israelites in their conquest of the land.

THE IRON AGE (1200–900 B.C.E.). Excavation has revealed remains of the fortifications of the kings of the United Monarchy, Saul, David, and Solomon. Geba, or Gibeath-Shaul (present-day Tell el-Ful) was the capital of Saul's kingdom. The citadel, dating from the second half of the 11th century, was built with a casemate wall and a corner tower with three chambers. Architectural remains from the time of David are scant. Although remains of fortifications have been found in Jerusalem, it is difficult to attribute any of them to David with certainty. From the Bible it is known that he fortified the city after the expulsion of the Jebusites (II Sam. 5:9). Solomon continued to build in Jerusalem. Besides the erection of the Temple and the palace, he completed the Millo (the fill between the city of David and the Temple Mount) and fortified the city (I Kings 11:27). Remains of two towers, a huge stone glacis, and a gate found in Jerusalem are attributed to the time of David and Solomon. Solomon built extensively throughout the country as well (I Kings 9:15). Excavations at the three cities, Hazor, Megiddo, and Gezer, have shown that all were built according to the same general plan, with almost identical gates. The cities were fortified by casemate walls, a type of construction introduced into Palestine possibly by the Hittites via Syria. The casemates in such walls were used as garrisons and for storage. The gates of these cities were designed with an entrance flanked by two square towers, which led to a roofed passageway with three guardrooms on either side. The walls of the guardroom served as piers for support of the upper story.

The destruction of many cities in the devastating campaign of Pharaoh Shishak in approximately 920 B.C.E. and the appearance of the mighty war machines of the Assyrian army changed the methods of fortification under the divided monarchy. Each kingdom built a peripheral defense (II Chron. 11:6–12). Besides these cities, a chain of citadels was built along the main roads and trade routes and on the frontiers (II Chron. 26:9–10). Casemate walls remained only in nonstrategic places, such as Tell Beit Mirsim in southwest Judah. This was the main feature of citadels in the wilderness, i.e., the Negeb. A fine example of such citadels is that at Kadesh-Barnea, which is rectangular, 100 × 166½ ft. (30 × 50 m.), and fortified by a casemate wall, with square towers at the corners and in the middle of each side. Similar citadels have been found in the Negeb, such as at Arad and Khirbet Uzzah. Inner citadels and fortified palaces, as the palace of Ahab in Samaria and a palace excavated at Ramat Raḥel (Beth-Cherem) near Jerusalem, were also fortified by casemate walls. Defense of the main cities changed with the reappearance of the battering ram, for which there is no extant evidence in the Late Bronze Age and the time of the United Monarchy. The hollow casemate wall was unable to withstand the breaching power of this weapon. The space between the wall was hastily filled with stones, and later a new solid stone wall was built. The outer face of the wall was constructed with salients and recesses. Secondary defenses took the form of a low outer wall, towers and bastions in the weak spots, and a stone glacis. Battlements and balconies were built on top of the walls. A wooden frame to hold the shields of the defenders was added to the battlement to protect the upper body of the warrior, and a screen of shields was thus formed. This structure is clearly seen in the reliefs portraying Sennacherib's assault against Lachish and is described in the Bible (II Chron. 26:15). Gates also changed, usually following the design of gates in Syria and Assyria. The depth of the entrance was lessened, and a gate with two chambers on either side and two protruding towers was constructed. This style was typical of the ninth century, while a gate with a single chamber on either side and two towers was typical of the eighth century. Gates with a broken approach to the main entrance are also known from this period, especially at Samaria, Lachish, Tell el-Far'ah, and Tell-Muqana' (Ekron). The preparations taken by King Hezekiah of Judah in the face of the coming siege of Jerusalem by Sennacherib are described in II Chronicles 32:3–5 and included the construction of new waterworks, known as the Siloam tunnel, to bring water directly into the city (II Kings 20:20; II Chron. 32:30).

The development of the battering ram in the time of the Judges and the United Monarchy is not known, and the casemate walls constructed at this time were not built to withstand the attack of battering rams. It must be assumed that attacks were carried out along traditional lines, i.e., by means of siege, scaling the walls, and indirect approach, especially surprise attacks. When Shechem rebelled against Abimelech the son of Gideon, who had usurped the kingship there, he divided his troops into three groups and by means of ambush and surprise, stormed the outer city walls (Judg. 9:43–45). After the conquest of the outer city walls, only the citadel remained, which Abimelech destroyed by fire (Judg. 9:48–49). David's campaigns against fortified cities consist of the conquest of Jerusalem by an obscure method (II Sam. 5; I Chron. 11) and the classic battle of Rabbath-Ammon, which can be divided into five stages. The first phase was a battle in the open field, with the purpose of destroying the armies of the Ammonites and their allies, thus preventing a counterattack on the exposed flanks and rear of the Israelites when it later laid siege to the city (II Sam. 10). The second phase was the besieging of the city (*ibid.* 11:1). In the third stage the Israelites tried to breach the walls while the Ammonites counterattacked (*ibid.* 11:23–25). The conquest of the "royal city" and the "city of waters" (*ibid.* 12:26–28) constituted the fourth stage, and the conquest of the inner citadel, the last (*ibid.* 12:29).

The Assyrians were the dominant military power in the Near East at the time of the divided kingdom. Their military might was organized into units, each with a defined purpose, and it was under them that the art of siege was developed. From the reign of Ashurnaṣirpal II (883–859 B.C.E.) onward, the battering ram reappeared as a decisive siege machine. Both mobile and stationary battering rams were used by the Assyrian army at this time. The mobile type had six wheels and a body built on a wooden frame, with the sides covered by rectangular shields. The front was protected by sheets, probably of metal, behind which a turret rose. Inside the turret hung a rope to which the battering ram was attached like a pendulum. The top of the turret was protected by a metal (?) dome with embrasures. The metal cutting head of the ram was shaped like an ax-head, which could be inserted with force between the bricks or stones of the wall and, by levering on all sides, could remove them from the wall, causing collapse. The battering rams were protected by archers mounted on mobile towers. Ashurnasirpal's methods of siege are portrayed in the wall reliefs in his palace at Nimrud. There, the covering fire of archers protects the assault troops, which use four methods of penetration: battering rams breach the main wall of the city; sappers dig underground tunnels; armored sappers demolish the outer wall with pikes and spears; and spearmen scale the wall with scaling ladders. In the reign of Shalmaneser III (858–824 B.C.E.), two new mobile battering rams appear, as seen in the reliefs of the bronze gates at Balawat. These rams have four or six wheels, a turret, and a fixed battering head, shaped like a boar's snout. This type of battering ram was presumably used mainly against city gates. Those of Tiglath-Pileser III (745–727 B.C.E.) and Sargon (721–705 B.C.E.) were light and very maneuverable. They have four wheels and the wooden frame was covered with metal-studded hides. The turret was lower and the cutting edge of the battering ram was shaped like a spearhead. These machines were often operated in pairs and were placed on special man-made ramparts, on which they were driven toward the wall. Several improvements were made in the battering rams of Sennacherib (704–681 B.C.E.), which have a longer pole and higher turret. One member of the crew was a fireman, who poured water onto the front of the battering ram with a long spoon to extinguish the torches thrown by the defenders. The siege of Jerusalem by the Babylonians is summarized by the prophet Ezekiel (21:27): "In his [the king of Babylon] right hand is the lot of Jerusalem, to set battering rams, to open the mouth for the slaughter, to lift up the voice with shouting, to set battering rams against the gates, to cast up mounds [i.e., for the battering rams], to build forts."

[Yitzhak Margowsky]

SECOND TEMPLE TO 614

In the period of the Second Temple, Judea was incorporated in the Persian Empire and had no independent army. Jews served as mercenaries of the Persian king at *Elephantine (Yeb) in Upper Egypt; they were organized in companies (called a *degel* – "flag") and had their own temple. In Judea proper, the Persian governor (who was normally a Jew) had a bodyguard; Nehemiah came with Persian troops, but Ezra refused such protection. In case of need, the governor (as in the case of Nehemiah) could mobilize the entire able-bodied population. During the building of the wall of Jerusalem, the people were armed with swords, spears, and bows and had coats of mail (Neh. 4:10). A trumpeter was kept ready for signaling.

In the Hellenistic period Jews served in the Ptolemaic armies; they were holders of military cleruchies; they were classified as "Persians of the Epigone," one rank below the Macedonians and Greeks and above the native Egyptians. Two of them, *Ananias and Helkias, were generals of Cleopatra III and their standing influenced the policy of the Egyptian government in relation to Alexander Yannai. In Perea, east of the Jordan, the Jewish family of the *Tobiads had its own cleruchs, as known from the Zeno papyri. The militant nature of Jason, the former high priest, who was allied with the Tobiads, shows their readiness to fight. During the conquest of Jerusalem by Antiochus III, the Jews actively supported the Seleucid attack on the Egyptian garrison in the Temple citadel. The Seleucid king settled Jewish cleruchs in Asia Minor as reliable and good soldiers. However, until the Hasmonean revolt the Jews as a nation fought no wars.

Driven by necessity the rebels under Judah Maccabee gradually acquired the necessary military skills. It is not clear whether the strategic and tactical genius shown by the Jewish leader was the result of his service with some Hellenistic army or of a natural ability. In the beginning the Jewish rebels were badly armed; Judah himself had to pick up and use the sword of his first defeated enemy, Apollonius the governor of Samaria, after the battle. The Jewish forces were properly organized only at Mizpeh; on the eve of the battle of Emmaus Judah used the biblical grouping into "thousands and hundreds and fifties and tens" (I Macc. 3:55) and appointed the "scribes of the people" (*grammateis tou laou*) as a kind of military police. The wars of Judah Maccabee were distinguished by his aptitude for strategic thinking, as witnessed in the blockade of Jerusalem and his swift movements on the inner line of communications which headed off successive Seleucid attempts (four in all) to break through to the besieged city. In his tactics Judah knew how to use the ground; he selected for his attacks the passes leading up to Judea (Lebonah?, Beth-Horon, and Emmaus) and was a master of surprise in the field. His campaign against Nicanor was marked by an attack from an unexpected direction and a massive pursuit which led to the disintegration of the enemy forces. Judah's last battle at Elasa was fought against overwhelming forces and even then he achieved a partial success.

Jonathan, the second leader of the revolt, was for some time forced to carry on an "underground" guerrilla warfare from his stronghold in the Judean Desert. His strength lay in mobility and surprise attacks; the operation against the people of Medeba and his subsequent escape from the army of Bacchides, which had cornered him between the Jordan and the Dead Sea, show a high degree of tactical skill. When besieged in Beth-Bassi Jonathan wisely refused to play the enemy's game and concentrated on harassing him from outside the siege lines. Like his brother Judah, Jonathan had the advantage of a superior intelligence, the fighting being in his own country and among his people. Once installed in Jerusalem as governor and high priest, Jonathan was de facto independent and was able to train a regular force. He fortified Jerusalem (one of his towers can be still seen on the Ophel hill). During his time the Jews attained military superiority in the south of the disintegrating Seleucid empire and moved at will all over Coele-Syria. Jonathan's crowning achievement was the battle near Jamnia (Jabneh) against the forces of the Syrian general, Apollonius. Hitherto, the Jews had been successful mainly on hilly ground, where the Seleucid phalanx could not properly operate. Apollonius invited Jonathan to fight in the plain and prepared an ambush; his cavalry attacked the Jewish forces from the rear, while the infantry held them in front. Under these unfavorable conditions the Hasmonean army showed its mettle; while the enemy "cast their darts at the people from morning till evening," the Jewish ranks remained unbroken till the enemy's cavalry wearied. It was now evident that the Hasmonean army could fight the Greeks under any conditions. In the time of Simeon, the last of the Hasmonean brothers, the Jews developed their skill in siege warfare of the Hellenistic type. They constructed a siege tower (*helepolis*) which was instrumental in the taking of Gezer. Such knowledge must have been most useful in the wars of Simeon's successors, John Hyrcanus (135–104 B.C.E.), Judah Aristobulus I (103 B.C.E.), and Alexander Yannai (103–76 B.C.E), as their conquests were mainly of fortified places. Hyrcanus' sons besieged Samaria for a whole year; the evidence of the destruction wrought by them is still visible. Alexander Yannai, who gradually obtained control of almost all of Ereẓ Israel, was singularly unlucky in the open field; he lost his battles against Ptolemy Lathurus, king of Cyprus, at Zaphon, east of the Jordan; against the Seleucids, Antiochus XII and Demetrius III (at the Yarkon and at Shechem); and against the Nabatean Obodas at Gedor. Nevertheless, by dint of perseverance and skill in siege warfare, he took Gaza, the northern coast including the Carmel, and most of the lands east of the Jordan, turning the Dead Sea into an inland Jewish lake. One ominous development in his time was the employment of foreign mercenaries, Pisidians, Cilicians, and others, in the Hasmonean service. They stood by the king in his war with the Pharisees when the latter allied with a Seleucid invader, but this use of mercenaries was in itself a sign of the increasing Hellenization of Jewish military life and the loss of the moral qualities which had hitherto distinguished it. Under Salome Alexandra, the armed forces were neglected by the ruling Pharisees, and this nearly led to a revolt under her second son *Aristobulus. The civil war which followed the death of the queen and the Roman intervention diminished the fighting capacity of the Judean army, although it still gave a good account of itself with Antipater, Herod's father, when coming to the aid of Julius Caesar in Egypt.

Herod's superior military capacity defeated his Hasmonean rival Mattathias Antigonus. Once king, Herod was able to raise some Jewish and Idumean troops, with which he defeated the Nabatean Arabs. He settled Idumeans and Babylonian Jews to police Batanea and Trachonitis and thus secured these lands for peaceful colonization. He also raised cohorts from his cities Caesarea and Sebaste. His bodyguard was composed of non-Jews, with an addition of Thracian mercenaries and of German and Gaulish soldiers, the gift of Augustus. Herod also had a navy with which he came to help the Romans in the Black Sea.

Augustus had released the Jews from the obligation to serve as auxiliaries in the Roman armies, and with the decline of the Herodian house their troops also diminished, although even Agrippa II still maintained some cavalry. What fighting was done until the first Roman War was by Zealot guerrillas, who were as a rule suppressed without much difficulty by the local levies of the procurators. Only in specially difficult situations, such as at the annexation of Judea and the first census, did the legate of Syria intervene with his legions.

The first war against Rome (66–73 C.E.) was begun by the Zealots, but the command soon passed to the aristocratic circles who planned the creation of an army able to meet the Romans in the field. At the beginning of the struggle Judea and Galilee were divided into military districts, with Josephus being given the command of Galilee. Their unexpected victory over Cestius Gallus, the legate of Syria, on his retreat from Jerusalem by the pass of Beth-Horon, provided the insurgents with much needed arms and siege engines. Their efforts to attack Ascalon failed, however. In Galilee, the most exposed part of the territory in revolt, Josephus made an effort to train a field army, only to see it dispersed at the first encounter with Vespasian. In his despair he fled to the fortress of Jotapata, which fell after a siege of 47 days, although he displayed most of the ruses of siege warfare. The failures in Galilee exposed the weakness of the tactical conception of the Jewish leadership; unable to hold the field they preferred to lock themselves up in strongholds, which were bound to fall when attacked systematically by the Romans. The Jewish war effort dissolved into a series of siege operations against Gamala, then Jerusalem, and finally Masada. The Zealot leaders John of Giscala and Simeon bar Giora were unable to make headway until it was much too late. The Jews fought with great bravery, which is attested also by Josephus, who saw the siege of Jerusalem from the Roman side. They turned the Roman siege machines against their makers, succeeded in burning down the Roman apparatus and in undermining and destroying the siege dams. In the end, however, the methodical warfare of the Romans, coupled with starvation, prevailed in Jerusalem; Masada, which was provided with food and water, succumbed to a high siege dam and tower. The scanty evidence of the weapons used in defending these places show that the Jews used the standard equipment of the Roman army and its auxiliaries. There were even some naval combats in this war, near Jaffa and on the Sea of Galilee, probably in the style of the naval battle from Yannai's days depicted on a wall of Jason's Tomb, Jerusalem.

The second war with Rome (or the war of *Bar Kokhba, 132–135) was preceded by a Jewish rising in Cyrenaica and Egypt against Trajan. Its leader, Lucuas or Andreas, penetrated into Egypt from Cyrenaica; although Alexandria was saved at the beginning of the revolt (115), it lasted until 117 when it was crushed by a special Roman army commanded by Marcus Turbo. The fight was waged with great ferocity. At the same time the Jews of Mesopotamia defended their cities against Trajan, and although they could not stop him, they upset his timetable.

The war of Bar Kokhba was the last great armed struggle of the Jews as a nation until modern times. Its history shows that the Jews had learned well the lessons of the earlier war. The war was carefully prepared; the Jews tendered offers to supply the Roman army with weapons and deliberately delivered them sub-standard; the arms were rejected and went to arm the insurgents. Bar Kokhba avoided sieges; positions in the field were prepared, probably connected with each other, in order to hold up the Roman advance. The command of the Jewish army remained from beginning to end in the hands of Simeon bar Kosiba (Bar Kokhba). When the war broke out, the Jews soon seized Jerusalem and the whole of Judea, possibly even parts of Samaria; they were joined by gentiles who rebelled against Roman society. In the course of the war one Roman legion, the XXII Deioteriana, was probably destroyed completely; it disappears from the Roman army lists. In the end the Romans had to concentrate an army of several legions (including parts of legions from Moesia). Bar Kokhba's army was finally besieged in Bethar, but some of the insurgents fled to the caves above the Dead Sea. Their archives, discovered in 1960–61, throw much light on the military, civil, and religious organization of Bar Kokhba's army and administration. While he took care of sequestrating food and arresting malcontents, Bar Kokhba also ordered the collection of the "four species" for making *lulavim*. The Bar Kokhba war marks the last great military effort of the Jewish nation in Ereẓ Israel. It was followed by two minor occasions on which the Jews took up arms against their oppressors. One was the revolt which broke out at Sepphoris in 351 against Gallus Caesar, the tyrannical emperor Constantinus II. The rebels, led by a certain Patricius, seized the armory and were able for some months to maintain a semblance of government in Galilee (Sepphoris and Tiberias) and Lydda. The revolt was suppressed by the Roman general Ursicinus, who defeated the Jews near Acre and advanced into Galilee.

In 614, at the approach of the Persian armies, the Jews rose again. Their force numbered some 20,000 men from the mountains of Galilee and around Jerusalem. They succeeded this time in taking Acre, but failed before Tyre. Nevertheless they were useful allies in the siege of Jerusalem by the Persians, which ended with the capture of the city and the establishment of a short-lived government there. The Jewish leader in this war is known to us only under the pseudonym "Nehemiah son of Ḥushi'el." The Persians soon dissolved their alliance with the Jews, and this last military effort came to nought.

[Michael Avi-Yonah]

For modern period see: *Israel, State of: Israel Defense Forces; *War of Independence; *Sinai Campaign; *Six-Day War; *Yom Kippur War; *Lebanon War.

BIBLIOGRAPHY: Y. Yadin, *The Art of Warfare in Biblical Lands* (1963); idem, in: EM, 2 (1954), 179–262 (incl. bibl.); 5 (1968), 462–71, 931–70 (incl. bibl.); idem, in: *World History of Jewish People* ed. by B. Mazar, 2 (1970), 127–59; J. Liver (ed.), *Historyah Ẓeva'it…* (1964). SECOND TEMPLE TO 614: Besides general histories (Schuerer, Noth, Abel) see F.M. Abel, *Les livres des Macchabées* (1949); A. Avissar, *Milḥamot Yehudah ha-Makkabbi* (1968); M. Avi-Yonah, in: *Massot u-Meḥkarim bi-Ydi'at ha-Areẓ* (1965), 57–72; idem, *Atlas Carta li-Tekufat ha-Bayit ha-Sheni…* (1966); idem, *Bi-Ymei Roma u-Bizantiyyon* (1970), 153–8, 223–33; A. Galili, *Kavvim le-Ma'arekhot Yisrael bi-Ymei ha-Bayit ha-Sheni* (1951); A. Schalit, *Hordos ha-Melekh* (1962), 94–101; V. Tcherikover and A. Fuks, *Corpus papyrorum judaicarum*, 1 (1957), 13–15, 86–92; S. Yeivin, *Milḥemet Bar-Kokhva* (1957); M. Gichon, *Atlas Carta le-Toledot Ereẓ Yisrael mi-Beitar ve-ad Tel-Ḥai, Historyah Ẓeva'it* (1969).

WARBURG, family of German and U.S. Jews.

PAUL MORITZ WARBURG (1868–1932) was a banker and philanthropist. Born in Hamburg, Germany, he became a partner in 1895 in his family's banking house, M.M. Warburg and Co. In the same year he married Nina Loeb, daughter of Solomon Loeb of Kuhn, Loeb and Co. of New York. In 1902 Warburg moved to the United States and became a member of the Kuhn, Loeb firm. Warburg's contribution to the U.S. banking system was considerable. One of the chief architects of the legislation establishing the Federal Reserve System in 1913, he served as a member of the Federal Reserve Board (1914–16) and as its vice governor (1917–18). Although he declined reappointment and returned to private banking, Warburg maintained an active interest in the board by serving as a member (1921–23) and president (1924–26) of its advisory council. He also wrote several books expounding his belief in the necessity for a strong, politically independent central banking system in the United States. Active in philanthropic and civic affairs, Warburg was a leading figure in the work of the *American Jewish Joint Distribution Committee, the Federation for the Support of Jewish Philanthropic Societies in New York City, the American Society for Jewish Farm Settlement in Russia, the Juilliard School of Music, the National Child Labor Committee, Tuskegee Institute, and many others. He wrote *Federal Reserve System – Its Origin and Growth* (1930).

Paul Warburg's son, JAMES PAUL (1896–1969), was also a banker. He was born in Hamburg, Germany, and was taken to the United States in 1902. After service with the Navy Flying Corps in World War I, Warburg pursued a career in finance, serving as president of the International Acceptance Bank and director of the Bank of the Manhattan Company. He was also one of the major backers of the highly successful Polaroid Corporation. A liberal Democrat, Warburg was a member of President Franklin D. Roosevelt's "brain trust" during the early years of the New Deal. At the same time, he entered a new phase of his career as a prolific writer, first of poetry and technical works on textiles, later of popular volumes on economics, public affairs, and foreign policy. In the late 1930s, Warburg urged U.S. intervention against Nazi Germany and during World War II served as deputy director of the Office of War Information. Disenchanted with the Cold War atmosphere of the 1950s, Warburg consistently championed the cause of peaceful coexistence of the major powers, awareness of the dangers of German rearmament, and the necessity for an independent, progressive U.S. foreign policy. He wrote the autobiographical *The Long Road Home* (1964).

FELIX MORITZ (1871–1937), a brother of Paul M. Warburg, was also born in Hamburg, Germany. He moved to the United States in 1894, married Jacob H. Schiff's daughter Frieda (see below) in 1895, and became a partner in his father-in-law's banking firm, Kuhn, Loeb and Co. Although Warburg participated, as partner and later as senior partner in Kuhn, Loeb and Co., in the financial aspects of the economic and industrial transformation of the U.S., his chief interests were philanthropy, education, and culture, and his contributions in these fields were considerable. He was one of the earliest supporters in New York City of the Educational Alliance and the Henry Street Settlement, organizations facilitating the absorption of immigrants. He served on the New York City Board of Education (1902–05) as a New York State probation commissioner, and he was active in movements to combat juvenile delinquency and family desertion. Deeply interested in music and art, he was a leader in the development of the Juilliard School of Music, the New York Philharmonic Symphony Orchestra, and the erection of the Fogg Museum of Art at Harvard University. His educational activities included service as a trustee of Teachers College of Columbia University, financial support of the Horace Mann and Lincoln Schools, presidency of the American Association for Adult Education, and trusteeship of the American Museum of Natural History.

A key figure in the German-Jewish elite which dominated the U.S. Jewish community in the early decades of the 20th century, Warburg's manifold activities displayed a wide range of sympathetic interests. He was chairman of the American Jewish Joint Distribution Committee from its establishment in 1914 until 1932, a major contributor to the American Society for Jewish Farm Settlement in Russia, and founder of the Refugee Economic Corporation. At home, he led in the formation in 1917 and subsequent administration of the Federation for the Support of Jewish Philanthropic Societies of New York City and was president of the Young Men's Hebrew Association of New York. He generously supported Jewish education, including the Hebrew Union College and, especially, the Jewish Theological Seminary and the Graduate School for Jewish Social Work. Not a Zionist, Warburg nevertheless was active in promoting Jewish settlement in Palestine through major support of the Palestine Economic Corporation and The Hebrew University. He cooperated with Louis *Marshall, president of the American Jewish Committee (of which Warburg was a member), and Chaim *Weizmann in the broadening of the *Jewish Agency for Palestine to include non-Zionists. Chairman of the Agency's administrative committee, he resigned in 1930 in protest against British policies restricting Jewish immigration, and, in 1937, he protested the British plan for the partition of *Palestine.

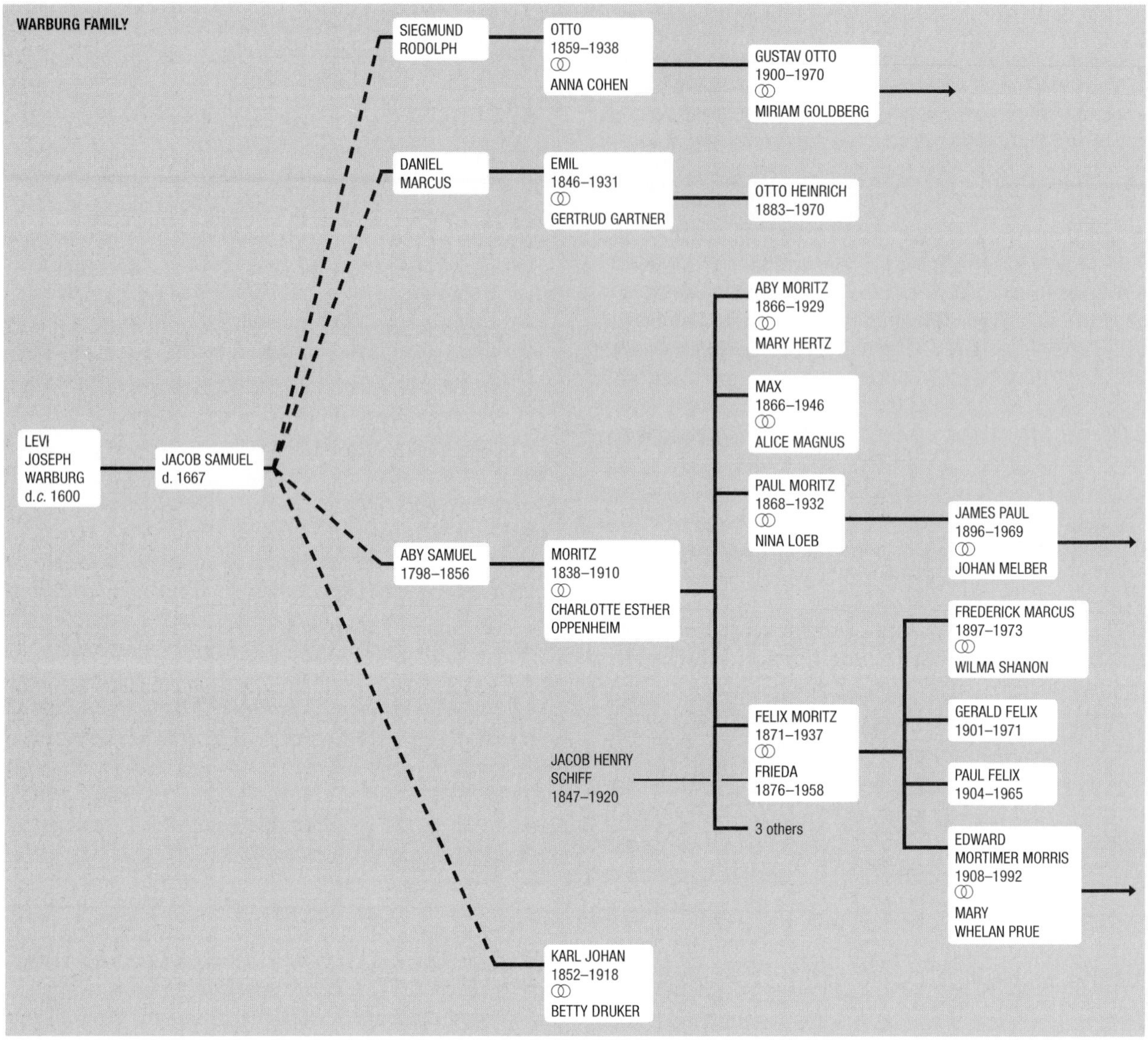

Felix Warburg's wife, FRIEDA (née SCHIFF; 1876–1958), was a philanthropist and communal leader. She was associated with her husband in numerous philanthropies and was also a leading figure in her own right. Among her major interests were the Young Women's Hebrew Association and the Visiting Nurse Service of New York. Although a non-Zionist, she was active in the work of Hadassah, especially its Youth Aliyah and the hospital in Jerusalem, and the American Friends of The Hebrew University. Her largest single gift was $650,000 in 1951 to the United Jewish Appeal to aid in the absorption of immigrants to Israel.

Felix and Frieda Warburg's son FREDERICK MARCUS (1897–1973) was a banker. After service in the U.S. Army during World War I, he was an investment banker, serving with the American International Corporation (1919–21), M.M. Warburg and Co. (1922–27), and Lehman Brothers (1927–30). In 1931 he became a partner of Kuhn, Loeb and Co. Among the civic and communal groups in which he served as officer or trustee were the American Museum of Natural History, Boy Scout Council, National Recreation Association, and the Federation of Jewish Philanthropies of New York. During World War II Warburg rose to the rank of colonel in the U.S. Army Special Service Division.

His brother GERALD FELIX (1907–1971) made his debut as a cellist with the New York Philharmonic in 1925, was a member of the Stradivarius Quartet from 1930 to 1936, and organized the Stradivarius Society. He was also a founder and conductor of the Brooklyn Symphony Orchestra and served as an officer of the New York City Center and Carnegie Hall.

Another brother PAUL FELIX (1904–1965) was active in banking and related fields, including service with the International Acceptance Trust Company, Bank of the Manhattan Company, J.S. Bache and Company, and, from 1951 to 1961, Carl M. Loeb, Rhoades and Co. He was a founder and president of the Federation Employment Service. During the 1930s he was active in bringing child refugees from Nazi Germany to the United States, and during World War II he served in the army as an intelligence officer and military attaché at the U.S. embassy in Paris. From 1946 to 1950 he was a special assistant at the U.S. embassy in London. A prominent member of the Republican Party, he was a director of the United Republican Finance Committee.

Another brother EDWARD MORTIMER MORRIS (1908–1992) graduated from Harvard University in 1930. He did not engage actively in the family's banking business, but was immersed in a variety of cultural, communal, and philanthropic activities. His interest in the fine arts was expressed through teaching at Bryn Mawr College (1931–33), extensive foreign travel, a notable private art collection, service as a founder and trustee of the Museum of Modern Art in New York, and chairmanship of the American Patrons of the Israel Museum. He was a member of the Board of Regents of New York State, a trustee of the Institute of International Education, and special assistant to the governor of New York on cultural affairs. Most significant in Warburg's career was his outstanding Jewish philanthropic leadership. He was chairman of the *American Jewish Joint Distribution Committee (1941–66) as well as chairman (1950–55) and honorary chairman from 1956 of the United Jewish Appeal. In 1967 he became president of the United Jewish Appeal of Greater New York. Warburg's interest in Israeli institutions included trusteeship in the American-Israel Cultural Foundation and membership in the Board of Governors of The Hebrew University. During World War II he served in the U.S. Army, rising to the rank of major.

BIBLIOGRAPHY: DAB, 19 (1936), 412–3 (on Paul Moritz Warburg); 22 (1958), 694–5; Adler, in: AJYB, 40 (1938/39), 23–40 (on Felix Moritz Warburg); M. Warburg, *Aus meinen Aufzeichnungen* (1952); E. Rosenbaum, YLBI, 7 (1962), 121–49; D. Farrer, *The Warburgs* (1975).

[Morton Rosenstock]

WARBURG, ABY MORITZ (1866–1929), German historian of art and civilization. Warburg was born in Hamburg. His main field of study was the intellectual and social context of Renaissance art. His works such as *Bildniskunst und Florentinisches Buergertum* (1902); *Die Grablegung Roger van der Weydens in den Uffizien* (1903); and *Francesco Sassettis letztwillige Verfuegung* (1907) were concerned with the relationship between classical antiquity and the Christian religion in the Renaissance. *Italienische Kunst und internationale Astrologie im Palazzo Schifanoja zu Ferrara* (1912) revealed the importance of classical astrology in Renaissance art. *Heidnisch-antike Weissagung in Wort und Bild zu Luthers Zeiten* (1920) and *Orientalisierende Astrologie* (1926) also discussed the beliefs and superstitions of the period. In these works and in numerous essays, Warburg developed an interdisciplinary approach to art history, which aimed to investigate the psychological and cultural role of symbolism in general. Warburg founded the Kulturwissenschaftliche Bibliothek Warburg, which opened officially in Hamburg in 1926, and was transferred to London in 1933 when Hitler came to power. In London it became known as the Warburg Institute and was incorporated in 1944 into the University of London. It consisted of 60,000 volumes and 20,000 photographs, and its purpose was to extend Warburg's own researches by tracing the influence of classical antiquity on all subsequent civilizations. The work was carried out by a group of mainly Jewish scholars which included Erwin *Panofsky and Ernst *Cassirer. The lectures given at the Institute were published as *Vortraege der Bibliothek Warburg*. The Institute publishes the journals *Studies of the Warburg Institute* and the *Journal of the Warburg and Courtauld Institutes*, and the Warburg Haus publishes Warburg's own papers under the title *Gesammelte Schriften*.

BIBLIOGRAPHY: G. Bing, *Aby M. Warburg* (1958); F. Saxl, in: *Vortraege der Bibliothek Warburg, 1921–1922* (1923); K.G. Heise, *Persoenliche Erinnerungen an Aby Warburg* (1947). **ADD. BIBLIOGRAPHY:** E.H. Gombrich and F. Saxl, *Aby Warburg: An Intellectual Biography* (1986); A.M. Meyers, "Aby Warburg in His Early Correspondence," in: *American Scholar*, 57 (1988); H. Liebeschuetz, "Aby Warburg as Interpreter of Civilization" in *Leo Baeck Institute Year Book* (1971); C. Naber, "Pompeji in Neu-Mexico: Aby Warburg's amerikanische Reise," in *Freibeutere, 38* (1988); B. Roeck, *Der junge Aby Warburg* (1997); C. Schoell-Glass, *Aby Warburg und der Antisemitismus: Kulturwissenschaft als Geistespolitik* (1998); U. Raulff, *Wilde Energien: vier Versuche zu Aby Warburg* (2003); E.R. Woodfield, *Art History as Cultural History: Warburg's Projects* (2001).

WARBURG, FREDERICK (1898–1981), British publisher. Warburg was born in London. He was not directly related to the famous German banking family and attended a leading public school, Westminster, on a scholarship. After serving as an officer in World War I, he attended Oxford University and then entered the publishing firm of George Routledge & Sons, but was dismissed in 1935 after the death of its head. With a friend, Roger Senhouse, he purchased the failing publishing firm of Martin Secker, renaming it Secker & Warburg, and developed it into one of the most influential and prestigious firms in Britain. It is most famous for publishing George Orwell's great works *Animal Farm* and *1984*; its other authors included such luminaries as H.G. Wells and Thomas Mann. In 1952 Warburg helped found the influential magazine *Encounter*, and, in 1954, defended an important obscenity lawsuit over the publication of Stanley Kaufman's *The Philanderer*. In later years his firm published a new string of notable works, among them *The Bridge on the River Kwai* and William L. Shirer's *Rise and Fall of the Third Reich*. Warburg published two volumes of autobiography, *An Occupation for a Gentleman* (1959) and *All Authors Are Equal* (1973).

BIBLIOGRAPHY: ODNB online.

[William D. Rubinstein (2nd ed.)]

WARBURG, GAVRIEL REUBEN (1927–), Israeli Orientalist. Warburg, a grandson of Otto *Warburg, was born in Berlin, Germany, but immigrated with his parents to Palestine in 1934. From 1946 to 1964 he was a member of kibbutz Yeḥi'am. In 1968 he was appointed lecturer in the Department of Middle Eastern History of the University of Haifa, was chairman of the department from 1969 to 1972, senior research Fellow at the Research Institute on Communist Affairs and at the Middle East Institute at Columbia University in New York from 1972 to 1973, and in the latter year was appointed associate professor at Haifa. In 1974 he was appointed rector of the University. Warburg published *The Sudan under Wingate* (1971); *The Rise and Decline of the Sudanese Communist Party* (1974), *Egypt and Sudan* (1985), and *Islam, Sectarianism and Politics in the Sudan Since the Mahdiyya* (2003).

WARBURG, KARL JOHAN (1852–1918), Swedish literary historian. Warburg was born in Göteborg, where his father was the Danish consul. Warburg became professor of literature and art history at the Göteborg Academy in 1890. He moved to Stockholm ten years later and from 1901 organized and administered the Swedish Academy's Nobel Library. In 1906 he was elected to the chair of literature at the University of Stockholm, succeeding Oskar Ivar *Levertin. As a literary critic and contributor to the liberal press, Warburg had a considerable influence on Swedish cultural life. His outstanding achievement was the monumental *Illustrerad svensk litteraturhistoria* (1896–97; 6 vols., 1926–30^{3}), an authoritative history of Swedish literature written in collaboration with Johan Henrik *Schück. This was the first serious attempt to investigate the subject from its 17th-century beginnings, and was characterized by keen psychological insight. Warburg also played an active part in Jewish communal affairs and, from 1905 until 1908, was a member of the Swedish parliament.

BIBLIOGRAPHY: *Svenska män och kvinnor*, 8 (1955); M. Lamm, *Karl Warburg, ord och bild* (1919).

[Hugo Mauritz Valentin]

WARBURG, MAX M. (1867–1946), German banker. His family, the *Warburgs, had been successful in private banking for more than a generation. After studying business in Germany, Great Britain, and the Netherlands, Warburg worked in his family's M.M. Warburg Bank in Hamburg. He became one of the leading personalities in late Imperial Germany concerning international industrial banking. Interested in the welfare of the Reich, he concentrated on colonial affairs. From 1903 he was a member of the Hamburg parliament. In the same year he became one of the rare Jews who could directly contact German Emperor Wilhelm II. Though he followed the path of acculturation, Warburg was a member of the Jewish community in Hamburg. Compared to his elder brother, the famous art historian Aby *Warburg, who agreed with his younger brother to forgo leading the family bank – though always receiving enough money to buy books for his library – Max M. Warburg developed a more uncomplicated and direct relation towards his own Jewishness. During World War I Warburg was – together with Albert *Ballin – one of the main promoters and founders of the "Reichseinkauf" (later "Zentraleinkaufsgesellschaft"), a state-owned central organization to buy food for Germany in foreign countries during the war years. Later, Warburg was attacked by antisemites for this activity. Together with his brother Felix M. Warburg, who was a successful banker in the U.S., Max M. Warburg organized financial aid for Jews in Eastern Europe. As the war led to increasing antisemitism, Warburg started to ask officials to protect Jews against discrimination. During the war Warburg came to be one of the leading figures to advise German politicians, diplomats, and the military in financial matters. In October 1918 he was appointed a financial advisor to the chancellor (*Reichskanzler*) Prinz Max von Baden. In 1919, Warburg served the German delegates during the negotiations on the Versailles peace treaty as an economic specialist. Warburg preferred to keep a low profile. When Walther *Rathenau asked him in early 1922 to join the cabinet (*Reichsregierung*) as minister of finance he refused, saying that two Jewish ministers would be too much for Germany. After the assassination of Rathenau the murderers planned also to kill Warburg. In 1924 he was appointed a member of the board (*Generalrat*) of the Reichsbank. The Warburg Bank was still one of the most important banking companies in Germany. From the late 1920s on Warburg intensified his interest in Zionism.

From World War I on, his brothers Felix M. and Paul M. Warburg opened the doors to the leading financial circles in North America for their brother. This was – again – especially helpful, when Germany urgently needed fresh capital during the world economic crisis between 1930 and 1932. After the Nazis came to power in Germany, the Warburg Bank came under increasing pressure. Max M. Warburg focused on helping Jewish emigrants to get their money out of Germany via the Palaestina-Treuhand GmbH. After the Warburg Bank was closed by the National Socialists, Warburg himself immigrated in 1938 to New York, where he died.

BIBLIOGRAPHY: M.M. Warburg, *Aus meinen Erinnerungen* (1952, edited by Eric M. Warburg); E. Rosenbaum et al., *Das Bankhaus M.M. Warburg & Co. 1798 bis 1938* (1976); R. Chernow, *The Warburgs* (1993).

[Christian Schoelzel (2nd ed.)]

WARBURG, OTTO (1859–1938), botanist and the third president of the World Zionist Organization. Born in Hamburg to a wealthy, assimilated family, *Warburg received an exclusively secular education. He completed his studies in the natural sciences in 1883 and decided to become a botanist, beginning his scientific career with studies in plant physiology and anatomy and specializing in tropical plants and plant geography and development. From 1885 to 1889 he conducted research expeditions in southern and eastern Asia and on the southeast Asian islands as far as East Australia. His observations on these expeditions provided the basis for his research work, as he discovered many hundreds of new types and species of plants. In 1892 he was appointed to a professorship at the University of Berlin. The most important of his scientific works are his books *Kulturpflanzen der Weltwirtschaft* (1908) and *Die Pflanzenwelt* (3 vols., 1916–23), a storehouse of botanical information on plant families and species, with special emphasis on their uses. A number of plant species are named after Warburg (*warburgia, warburgiella, warburgina*).

Warburg became a Zionist through the influence of his father-in-law, Gustav Cohen. In 1894 he was a member of the committee of *Ezra, the Berlin society of Ḥovevei Zion (see *Ḥibbat Zion). Together with his father-in-law, he joined *Herzl's supporters. He regarded the large-scale settlement of Ereẓ Israel as the basis for a Jewish state and, though a political Zionist, he was opposed to delaying settlement until the granting of a charter. Warburg also favored large-scale Jewish settlement in the countries close to Ereẓ Israel, since he believed that Ereẓ Israel would thus have a reservoir of political, economic, and demographic assistance. He participated in the attempts to settle Jews in Anatolia beginning in 1900, planning to settle there 100,000 Jews in 500 villages, and undertook the financial support of two Jewish settlements from his personal funds. From 1900 to 1906 Warburg dealt with Jewish agricultural and urban settlement in *Cyprus and encouraged the *Jewish Colonization Association (ICA) in its initial steps in this venture. In 1905–06 he planned the settlement of a million Jews in Mesopotamia (now Iraq), but opposed Herzl's proposals regarding *El-Arish and refused to join the Zionist El-Arish expedition. After his first visit to Ereẓ Israel, he drew closer than ever to Herzl and became his adviser on matters pertaining to settlement, providing him with the relevant material for his utopian novel *Altneuland*. From the Sixth Congress (1903), at which he supported the *Uganda Scheme, Warburg became active in the Zionist Organization. At the same Congress he was elected chairman of the Palestine Commission which later became the primary factor in the settlement program of the Zionist Organization, and initiated its publication *Altneuland*.

Warburg's main contribution to Zionism was his role in advancing practical settlement work in the Zionist Organization. He urged the Jewish Colonization Association and the *Jewish National Fund to purchase land, and encouraged the investment of private Jewish capital in agriculture, industry, and commerce. On Warburg's initiative, the Zionist Organization established the *Palestine Office under the direction of Arthur *Ruppin in 1905, as well as the Palestine Land Development Company. He played a large part in the establishment of the experimental agricultural station at Athlit under the direction of Aaron *Aaronsohn.

After Herzl's death (1904), Warburg was elected to the Zionist Executive. He disagreed with the views of David *Wolffsohn, who remained faithful to the doctrine of political Zionism. With the emergence of the leadership of the practical Zionists, Warburg was elected president of the World Zionist Organization in 1911 and technically remained in office through World War I, until 1920, while during the war years the center of world Zionist activity moved first to Copenhagen and then to London. He was elected primarily for fostering practical settlement work in Ereẓ Israel. However, he had to cease activity of this kind completely when war broke out, and he concentrated instead on purely political efforts, e.g., by using his influence with the German Foreign Ministry to restrain Turkish persecution of the Jews in Palestine. After the war, Warburg dedicated himself to scientific work in Palestine. From 1921 he directed the agricultural research station at Rehovot, and from 1925 he also headed the botany department of The Hebrew University. During the 1930s Warburg divided his time between Palestine and Germany, due to his wife's illness. Severely ill himself, he spent his last years bedridden in Berlin, where he died a lonely death under Nazi rule. Sedeh Warburg, a moshav on the coastal plain, is named after him.

BIBLIOGRAPHY: J. Thon, *Otto Warburg* (Heb., 1948); I. Reichert, in: *Palestine Journal of Botany*, Reḥovot series 2 (1938), 2–16; N. Sokolow, in: *Davar* (Aug. 9, 1928), 2; idem, *History of Zionism*, 2 (1919), index; A. Boehm, *Die zionistische Bewegung*, 1 (1935), index; M. Bodenheimer, *Prelude to Israel* (1963), 171–5, 179–83 and index.

[*Encyclopaedia Hebraica*]

WARBURG, OTTO HEINRICH (1883–1970), German biochemist and Nobel Prize winner; Warburg was born in Freiburg, Baden, the son of the physicist Emil Warburg (1846–1931), and, like his father, was baptized. He worked on radiation physics in the Physikalische Reichanstalt Berlin-Charlottenburg, of which his father was president from 1906 to 1922. In 1918 he went to the Kaiser Wilhelm Institut fuer Biologie in Berlin-Dahlem, and for over 30 years from 1930 was director of the Kaiser Wilhelm Institut fuer Zellphysiologie. He was one of the very few scientists of Jewish descent who remained undisturbed in his position during the Nazi period. He never taught, except for directing his research associates. Warburg was awarded the Nobel Prize for Physiology and Medicine in 1931 "for his discovery of the nature and mode of action of the respiratory enzyme." Warburg also designed a manometric apparatus for measuring the respiration of cells, tissues, or extracts of tissues, and an inhibition technique employing carbon monoxide, which are both widely used by biochemists all over the world.

Warburg contributed to scientific journals, and wrote several books, including *Stoffwechsel der Tumoren* (1926; *The Metabolism of Tumours*, 1930); *Katalytische Wirkungen der lebendigen Substanz* (1928); and *Heavy Metal Prosthetic Groups and Enzyme Action* (1949).

BIBLIOGRAPHY: T.N. Levitan, *Laureates: Jewish Winners of the Nobel Prize* (1960), 141–3.

[Samuel Aaron Miller]

WARBURG, SIR SIEGMUND (1902–1982), British merchant banker. Warburg was born at Tubingen, Germany, a member of the famous German banking family, although from one of its less affluent branches. Nevertheless, in 1919 he entered the family bank, M.M. Warburg & Co. of Hamburg, spending long periods in London and New York as he learned his trade during the 1920s. He was made a partner in 1930. The way ahead seemed clear when Hitler came to power in 1933. Warburg immediately left for London, where he founded a small merchant bank, the New Trading Company; he became a British subject in 1939. In 1946 his bank was renamed S.G. Warburg & Co. By a process of meticulous research, information-sharing on a daily basis among all executives, and a painstaking personal approach to its clients, it gradually became an important force in the City of London. In 1957 it became a member of the Accepting House Committee, thus joining the City's financial elite. Warburg pioneered new (and perhaps surprising) takeover techniques, especially in the 1958 purchase of British Aluminium, and spent much of the rest of his life trying to create a genuinely global merchant bank. He was knighted in 1966 and spent most of his last years in Switzerland.

BIBLIOGRAPHY: ODNB online; R. Chernow, *The Warburgs* (1993).

[William D. Rubinstein (2nd ed.)]

WAR CRIMES TRIALS.

Crystallization of the Principles of International Criminal Law

Immediately after the outbreak of World War II, when the first Nazi violations of the laws and customs of war as defined by the Hague and Geneva Conventions were revealed (and in particular as they affected the noncombatant population and prisoners of war), the Allies began to publish official notes, warnings, and declarations. On September 3, 1939, Czechoslovakia's president-in-exile, Eduard Beneš, sent a letter to the British prime minister Neville Chamberlain, reporting the persecution of his country's civilian population at the hands of the Nazis. In 1940 several statements were published by the governments of the United Kingdom, Poland, Czechoslovakia, and France on the violations of the laws of war in Poland. Crimes against Jews were likewise mentioned. These governments warned Germany and stressed the responsibility of the Nazi regime for the criminal acts. On October 25, 1941, President Franklin D. *Roosevelt of the United States – then a neutral nation – stated that "the Nazi treatment of civilian population revolts the world," while British prime minister Winston *Churchill declared that "retribution for these crimes must henceforward take its place among the major purposes of the war." But this was more an expression of outrage in a propaganda war than a concrete plan of action for a postwar world. After the German invasion of the Soviet Union in June 1941 and the ensuing crimes against the civilian population and prisoners of war, the Soviets also began to publish statements on the subject. The Soviet foreign minister, Vyacheslav Molotov, declared in his notes of November 7, 1941, and January 6, 1942, inter alia, that the Soviet government held the leaders of Nazi Germany responsible for the crimes committed by the German army. One of the important steps toward punishment can be seen in the St. James Declaration made in London on January 13, 1942, in which the representatives of the governments-in-exile – of Belgium, Netherlands, Yugoslavia, Norway, Greece, Luxembourg, Poland, Czechoslovakia, and the Free French – declared that the punishment, through the channels of organized justice, of criminal acts perpetrated by the Germans against civilian populations was among the principal war aims of the signatories. Also present at the St. James Conference were representatives of belligerent but nonoccupied countries, among them the United Kingdom and the United States. The St. James Declaration did not specifically mention the crimes against the Jews. This policy of *Totschweigen* ("hushing up" the Jewish tragedy) aroused Jewish opinion in the U.S. and Britain, and a protest against this policy was lodged on February 18, 1942. Only on December 17, 1942, did the British foreign secretary, Anthony Eden, make a statement in the House of Commons (published simultaneously in London, Moscow, and Washington) on the physical destruction of Jews, of which the Allies had a growing awareness, as it developed, in 1941 and 1942 (see *Holocaust).

Another important step toward this objective was the publication of the Moscow Declaration of November 1, 1943, in which the three principal powers, Britain, the United States, and the Soviet Union, solemnly committed themselves to the punishment of those responsible for war crimes. The Moscow Declaration distinguished between criminals whose acts were committed within the boundaries of specific countries and the "major criminals" whose "offenses have no particular geographical location and who will be punished by a joint decision of the governments of the Allies."

The first international body to make preparations for punishment of the criminals was the United Nations War Crimes Commission (UNWCC). A proposal for its formation was announced in October 1942 and it was constituted on October 20, 1943. Its objects were to investigate the atrocities and record the names of the individuals responsible. Participants in the commission were representatives of Australia, the United States, Belgium, Britain, Denmark, the Netherlands, Yugoslavia, Greece, Luxembourg, Norway, New Zealand, China, Poland, Czechoslovakia, France, and Canada. The Soviet Union, embroiled in controversy over the composition of its representation, did not join the commission.

At the Yalta Conference in February 1945, the last attended by Roosevelt, the president advanced the idea that an international tribunal should be convened to try Nazi leaders for planning and waging a war of aggression and for war crimes. Soviet leader Joseph *Stalin favored the legalist approach but wanted to confine the process to crimes committed in war; Churchill and Eden preferred summary trial and execution.

The various Allied activities culminated in the London Agreement of August 8, 1945, which established the International Military Tribunal, and in the Tribunal's charter, which dealt with substantive and procedural rules. One of the decisive contributions toward the formulation of the revolutionary principles of Nuremberg was made by Hersch *Lauterpacht, a British Jewish law professor originally from Galicia. Lauterpacht defined the three crimes in the charter: crimes against peace, war crimes, and crimes against humanity. In his studies and books, Lauterpacht, who later became a judge of the International Court of Justice, formulated the "Nuremberg principles," which were accepted not only in the London

Charter but also in the development of international criminal law in general.

The first comprehensive description of violations of international military law was offered by Raphael *Lemkin – a Polish Jewish legal scholar who had lost his family in the Holocaust – in his book *Axis Rule in Occupied Europe* (1944). It was Lemkin who coined the term "genocide," which was not adopted by the courts but served as the subject of a special international convention. The main theoretical and practical work in the field by world Jewish institutions was done by the *Institute of Jewish Affairs of the *World Jewish Congress. The political department of the *Jewish Agency also collected incriminating material, prepared lists of war criminals, and presented them to the institutions of the Allies dealing with the location and trial of Nazi criminals.

There were differences of opinion among the Allies as to what to do with the Nazi leadership. As the war was ending, President Roosevelt was at first convinced by Henry *Morgenthau, his Jewish secretary of the Treasury, that the top Nazi leaders should be summarily shot once caught. At the Quebec Conference in September 1944, Churchill also supported this approach. A list of 2,500 "archcriminals" set for execution by military firing squad was being created by Morgenthau's assistants. Secretary of War Henry Stimson strongly argued, however, for holding trials. After a great deal of intracabinet dueling, Roosevelt eventually abandoned the so-called Morgenthau Plan (which also called for destroying Germany's industrial capacity and turning it into "a country primarily agricultural and pastoral in its character") in favor of Stimson's legalist approach. Murray Bernays, a young Jewish lawyer in Stimson's office, drafted the first outline of how the Nazi archcriminals should be tried. Bernays also came up with the idea of putting on trial not just individuals but also Nazi organizations, using the Anglo-American legal doctrine of conspiracy liability. Stalin also favored trials, but the kind of show trials mounted by the regime in the Soviet Union, in which guilt was predetermined. The Soviet Union and France were uninterested in conspiracies and Britain shied away from conspiracies against the peace. The Soviet Union wanted to restrict the trials to the war years alone. Ambiguity papered over diplomatic differences. The importance of the trials was enhanced when President Harry S. Truman named Supreme Court Justice Robert Jackson, who took leave from the Court, as the chief American prosecutor. The move was virtually unprecedented and it enhanced the stature of all that was to follow.

Number of Nazi Criminals and Their Collaborators

As it is not possible to establish exactly the number of German criminals who participated in the annihilation of the Jews; only an estimate is possible. One ordinarily thinks of two main groups of criminals: the instigators, planners, and commanders who directed the killing operations or with whose knowledge, agreement, or passive participation these acts were committed; and the actual implementers of the plans and commands at various levels of authority and initiative. But there was also a wider circle of persons involved, including those who designed and engineered the gas chambers and the crematoria and those who built the economic infrastructure that allowed the camps to flourish. Also involved were the corporations that invested in these camps, and that used slave laborers there and worked them to death. The first group, to which the leadership of the German government belonged – the heads of ministries, the Nazi Party, the armed forces, the Gestapo, the SS, and the RSHA (*Reichssicherheithauptamt*, Reich Central Security Office) – numbered many hundreds. The second group included hundreds of thousands – members of the Gestapo, the SS, the Waffen SS, the SD, the police with its many branches, the armed forces; officials from special departments of the Foreign Ministry and Ministry of the Interior who dealt with Jewish matters, the staffs of the concentration camps, doctors who practiced in the concentration camps, lawyers, judges, and many others. The estimate of hundreds of thousands who participated actively in the annihilation of the Jews and other crimes is no exaggeration. This number, furthermore, does not include collaborators from the conquered territories – Croats, Ukrainians, Latvians, Lithuanians, Estonians, Byelorussians, Russians, and others. Many tens of thousands of collaborators who participated in the planning and execution of the murder of Jews, Soviet prisoners of war, and local civilian populations were able to retreat together with the Germans as they fled from Eastern Europe, and later escaped – posing as innocent refugees – to the United States, Canada, Great Britain, Australia, and Latin America. During the war, many of these killers were organized in special units – often referred to as *Schutzmannschaft* units – mostly within the framework of the Security Police (SD), among them such notorious murder squads as the "Special Detachment" (*Ypatingas burys*) and the 12th Lithuanian Auxiliary Police Battalion in Lithuania and the Arajs Kommando in Latvia. They not only carried out the orders of the Nazis, but also killed tens of thousands of Jews on their own initiative. The murder of the Jews of Kaunas and other areas in Lithuania, for example, began immediately upon the evacuation of the Soviet army from these places, even before the first German soldiers entered. The same was true in the parts of Poland that had been occupied by the Soviet Union in 1939, in western Ukraine, and elsewhere.

Trials in Allied Military Tribunals

Nazi war crime trials began during World War II itself. The first trial of perpetrators of crimes against civilian populations was conducted in the liberated territories of the Soviet Union. The trial dealt with the abominable actions committed by the German invaders in the city of Krasnodar in the northern Caucasus. It opened on July 14, 1943, after the liberation of the area, with eleven accused, of whom eight were sentenced to death. The second trial dealing with annihilation of civilian populations and prisoners of war took place in the city of Kharkov, Ukraine, in December 1943. Three Germans,

*SS men and police, and a Russian collaborator were tried, and all were sentenced to death by hanging. At this trial, for the first time, documentation of the annihilation of civilian populations by gas was shown.

THE INTERNATIONAL MILITARY TRIBUNAL (THE FIRST NUREMBERG TRIAL). The specific question of war crimes and crimes against Jews, defined then as "crimes against humanity" under the general policy of the infamous Final Solution, was considered only after World War II, first by the International Military Tribunal (IMT) at Nuremberg that tried the heads of the Nazi regime who had been captured by the Allies.

The IMT trial, the first of the Nuremberg trials, was conducted from November 1945 to October 1946. The defendants included Hermann *Goering, the most prominent Nazi the Allies had captured, who officially held the title of Commander of the Luftwaffe and several departments of the SS; Hans *Frank, governor general of occupied Poland; Ernst *Kaltenbrunner, head of the RSHA; Joachim von *Ribbentrop, Reich minister for foreign affairs; Julius *Streicher, gauleiter of Franconia and editor of *Der *Stuermer*, the infamous antisemitic publication; Martin *Bormann, chief of the chancellery of the Nazi Party and Hitler's private secretary, who was tried *in absentia*. (Some of the most prominent Nazi criminals and German government leaders managed to evade justice and were not brought to trial at Nuremberg, including *Hitler, *Himmler, *Goebbels, and Robert Ley, who committed suicide [the latter hanged himself in his cell while awaiting trial at Nuremberg]; Reinhard *Heydrich, charged by Goering with the implementation of the Final *Solution, was assassinated in 1942; Heinrich *Mueller, one of the heads of the *Gestapo, disappeared without a trace. Martin Bormann, tried in absentia, was never found. Having fled from the chancellery bunker on May 1, 1945 as the Red Army was closing in, he was said to have been killed by the Russians; his death in Berlin was supposedly confirmed by evidence found in 1972, but he was also rumored to have escaped to South America.)

In accordance with the principles of the London Charter of August 8, 1945, an indictment was brought by the principal prosecutors of the four main Allied powers, detailing the accusations against each of the defendants as well as against six organizations defined as criminal: the Reich cabinet, the Leadership Corps of the Nazi Party, the SS, the SA, the Gestapo and SD, and the General Staff and High Command of the German armed forces. In preparing the material, as well as during the trial, the four prosecutors had the cooperation of the delegations of the other members of the anti-Nazi alliance and some representatives of Jewish organizations, in particular the World Jewish Congress' Institute of Jewish Affairs, founded as a documentation center in 1941, headed by Jacob *Robinson. The latter assisted in the preparation of the material and in the formulation of the statement concerning the persecution and murder, which the Germans called "extermination," of the Jews. Nuremberg was chosen as the site of the trial not because of the Nuremberg Laws or its role as the location of grand Nazi Party rallies but because the city had not been completely ruined during Allied bombing raids and was in good enough condition to host the trials, with a standing courthouse (still in use today). Courtroom 600 of the Palace of Justice, where both the IMT trial and subsequent American zonal trials were held, is still in use as a working courtroom.

The proceedings began on November 20, 1945 and were concluded on October 1, 1946 – the date of Yom Kippur (the Jewish Day of Atonement) that year – with a judgment in which twelve defendants were sentenced to death, three to life imprisonment, four to prison terms, and three acquitted. The death sentences were carried out by hanging on October 16–17, 1946, except for that of Goering, who took poison before he could be executed.

Justice Jackson set the scene in his opening statement:

> In the prisoners' dock sit twenty-odd broken men. Reproached by the humiliation of those they have attacked, their personal capacity for evil is forever. It is hard to perceive in these miserable men as captives the power by which as Nazi leaders they once dominated much of the world and terrified most of it. Merely as individuals, their fate is of little consequence…
>
> What makes this inquest significant is that these prisoners… are the living symbols of racial hatreds, of terrorism and violence, and of the arrogance and cruelty of power… Civilization can afford no compromise with the social forces which would gain renewed strength if we deal ambiguously or indecisively with the men in whom those forces now precariously survive.

The charter of the International Military Tribunal at Nuremberg served as a basis for domestic laws later enacted in countries in which trials of war criminals were conducted (except for the Federal Republic of [West] Germany, which did not officially adopt the Nuremberg principles). The Tribunal, and four-power cooperation in general, did not continue after the judgment, due to the deteriorating relations between the Western Allies and the Soviet Union, leading to the onset of the Cold War.

British historian David Cesarani has assessed the importance of these trials: "The Nuremberg tribunal established a model for the future. It generated a detailed record and accumulated a mass of material, which ensured that the history of the Nazi era would not be forgotten easily and would make political distortions more difficult. The tribunal… satisfied the popular desire for retribution… and made, for the first time[,] the political echelon accountable in a court of international law for the planning and conduct of war." In 2005–06, on the sixtieth anniversary of the trials, conferences were held around the world commemorating their significance to the growth of international criminal law. A conference in Washington, D.C. cited the Nuremberg proceedings as "the birth of [modern] international law." The *ad hoc* international tribunals created by the UN Security Council in the late 1990s to try perpetrators of the atrocities in Yugoslavia and the genocide in Rwanda were directly modeled on the Nuremberg proceedings, and became the first international trials for war crimes and crimes against humanity since Nuremberg. The permanent International Criminal Court, established at the beginning of the twenty-first century, is also in a direct lineage from Nuremberg. The trials also led to subsequent action by the United Nations, such as the 1948 Genocide Convention and the Universal Declaration of Human Rights.

Certain dimensions of the IMT trial remained unclear. There was confusion between war crimes and crimes against humanity. The specific nature of what happened to the Jews became a background to the trial rather than its central theme; contrary to current popular belief, the crimes of the Holocaust played only a secondary role. The major emphasis, especially for the Americans, was to try the Nazi leadership for the crime of waging aggressive war.

Of significance also was that the Tribunal did not accept the defense of "merely following orders," though in many subsequent trials such a defense was invoked.

The proceedings also provided copious documentary evidence of the crimes committed by Nazi Germany. The material (trial transcripts, affidavits, and documents) was published in an official edition of 42 volumes in English, French, and German (English title: *Trial of the Major War Criminals*) between 1947 and 1949 (the "Blue Series") and constituted an invaluable contribution to the administration of justice to Nazi criminals in various countries, as well as to the study of the Nazi Party and the German administrative apparatus that implemented the "Final Solution to the Jewish Question" that is now known as the Shoah or Holocaust.

The Nuremberg judgment constitutes an important historical turning point, one of the great landmarks in the development of international law and international relations, whose importance has grown in recent years. Despite Nuremberg not being a trial specifically of the Holocaust, the IMT proceedings did expose the criminal measures against the Jewish people and did not submerge the victimization of the Jews in the general category of "racial persecution," "stateless persons," or other euphemisms. In this respect, it served as a binding precedent that was followed in subsequent trials almost everywhere. On the other hand, the IMT followed the provisions of the charter and considered as crimes against humanity only such crimes that were somehow connected with "crimes against peace" or war crimes – in other words with crimes committed after the outbreak of the war. Consequently, no attention was paid to such crimes as the April 1, 1933 boycott, the Nuremberg laws, *Kristallnacht*, etc.

There were many who found the trial problematic. Some Germans considered it victors' justice. Others regarded it as *ex post facto* law. The role of the Soviet Union in the invasion of Poland was deliberately ignored. Still others felt that Nuremberg was a distraction because they wanted to focus on the future and the swiftly developing Cold War – the next war – and not the last war. Others felt that the punishment given the convicted defendants, however great, was inadequate given the magnitude of the crimes. In subsequent years, as the punishments meted out to subsequent defendants became less severe, some questioned whether any real justice was achieved or merely the appearance of justice.

On December 20, 1945, the four Allied governments in occupied Germany enacted Control Council Law No. 10, which had special significance for the continuation of the Nazi trials and the definition of crimes against humanity. This law, with minor modifications, eliminated the connection between crimes against humanity and the two remaining crimes (crimes against peace and war crimes), and raised crimes against humanity to a level equal to that of the other two. This also extended the period covered by the law from the war years alone to the entire Nazi period. Control Council Law No. 10, whose articles dealt mainly with crimes against humanity, enabled each of the Allies, as well as military and civilian tribunals, to hold trials in conquered territories in Germany.

INDIVIDUAL ALLIED MILITARY TRIBUNALS. The 1945–46 trial at Nuremberg of the surviving Nazi leadership was the only one conducted by the IMT. Later trials, called Subsequent Nuremberg Proceedings or zonal trials (and also widely known as "Nuremberg Trials") were conducted by military tribunals of the four occupying Allied powers within their own occupation zones, under the terms of Control Council Law No. 10.

Twelve trials of special significance were conducted at Nuremberg by U.S. military tribunals ("Nuremberg Military Tribunals," composed of American judges) in 1946–49. (Other U.S. military tribunal trials were held at Dachau, also in the U.S. Occupation Zone, during the same period.) Justice Jackson's deputy, Telford Taylor, a lawyer serving in the U.S. Army and given the rank of brigadier general, took over the job as chief counsel for the prosecution after Jackson's return to the U.S. Supreme Court at the conclusion of the IMT proceedings.

The twelve cases were brought against groups of important Nazis who bore the chief responsibility for some of the most serious and significant of Nazi crimes. They were:

1. The Medical Case, November 21, 1946–August 20, 1947
2. The Milch Case, December 20, 1946–April 17, 1947
3. The Justice Case, February 17–December 4, 1947
4. The Pohl Case, March 10–November 3, 1947
5. The Flick Case, April 19–December 22, 1947
6. The I.G. Farben Case, August 14, 1947–July 30, 1948
7. The Hostage Case, July 8, 1947–February 19, 1948
8. The RUSHA Case, October 10, 1947–March 10, 1948
9. The *Einsatzgruppen* Case, July 3, 1947–April 10, 1948
10. The Krupp Case, September 17, 1947–April 10, 1948
11. The Ministry Case, November 15, 1947–April 14, 1949
12. The High Command Case, December 30, 1947–October 28, 1948

As noted above, the crimes committed against the Jews were not the main focus of the IMT trial. During the subsequent trials, however, much more attention was paid to acts of cruelty and the annihilation of Jews under the Nazi regime. The Jewish question had special significance in the following trials: the Pohl Case, in which Oswald Pohl and 17 others were tried for committing crimes against the inmates of the concentration and death camps, and especially against Jews; the *Einsatzgruppen* Case, the trial of 24 SS and Gestapo men from the *Einsatzgruppen* (special "mission units" or task forces) who headed firing squads that murdered approximately a million Jews in the conquered German territories in Eastern Europe, and particularly in the Soviet Union; likewise, the Ministries Case, with 21 defendants including three government ministers, molders of Reich policy, who were tried for abetting the preparation of the war and creating the conditions for the implementation of the crimes of the Nazi regime. In the last trial Robert *Kempner, one of the chief U.S. prosecutors, presented to the Tribunal and the entire world one of the most important Nazi documents from the files of the German Foreign Ministry relating to the annihilation of the Jews. It was the record of the *Wannsee Conference of January 20, 1942, during which cooperation was requested and received from all party and government institutions involved in the implementation of the Final Solution. The *Einsatzgruppen* trial was primarily a trial of documents. The chief prosecutor in the case, Benjamin Ferencz, a young American Jewish lawyer working under Taylor, was able to obtain conviction of the generals responsible for the murders by these mobile killing squads by introducing into evidence the operational field reports sent to Berlin from the killing fields of the Soviet Union. The Medical Case trial led to the enunciation of new principles of medical ethics, known in medical circles as the "Nuremberg Code" and taught now in every medical school in the United States. The ten-point Nuremberg Code prohibits experimentation on human subjects without their "informed consent" and gives the subject or patient the right to stop the experiment or treatment at any time.

One hundred seventy-seven Nazis were tried and convicted in these twelve trials. Of these, twelve were sentenced to death, 25 to life imprisonment, and the remainder to long prison terms. Proximity to the crime was taken as a measure of guilt. Those who were directly involved in the killing – doctors, concentration camp heads, *Einsatzgruppen* officers – received the most severe sentences. Thus, those who profited by the crime and developed the infrastructure that enabled the killings to proceed were treated more leniently.

The U.S. tribunals met in 1,200 sessions, and the trial transcripts cover 330,000 pages, aside from documents entered in evidence. This vast corpus of material supplements extensively that from the International Military Tribunal. A large part of the documentation of the military tribunal trials was published by the U.S. authorities in 15 volumes (*Trials of War Criminals* – "Green Series") in 1949–53.

In the U.S. military tribunal trials conducted in Dachau, 1,517 of the 1,941 defendants who were tried by 1949 were found guilty. Of these, 324 were sentenced to death, and 278 of these sentences were actually carried out.

In the British Occupation Zone, in Lueneburg, Hamburg, and Wuppertal, 1,085 defendants were tried before British military tribunals and 240 were sentenced to death. Among the more important trials in the British Zone, that of the SS guards at the *Bergen-Belsen concentration camp (the Bergen Trial, September 17–November 17, 1945) should be mentioned. Josef Kramer, the camp commandant, and his accomplices were convicted. Kramer was put to death.

In the French Zone, 2,107 defendants were tried and 104 sentenced to death.

The total number of Nazi criminals convicted in the three Western occupation zones between 1945 and 1949 was 5,025, of whom 806 were sentenced to death. Four hundred eighty-six death sentences were carried out; the remainder were commuted to prison terms of varying lengths.

Official or semiofficial figures are not available for the trials of Nazis in the Soviet Occupation Zone. It is assumed, however, that tens of thousands of Germans were tried there and that most of them were convicted and in large measure deported to Soviet territories to serve their sentences. (In 1955, in the wake of a Soviet-West German agreement, 8,877 criminals were freed. Another 749 were handed over to West Germany for further investigation.)

In the course of its work, the United Nations War Crimes Commission prepared 80 lists of war criminals, which together comprised 36,529 names (including Japanese). The Commission published a number of partial statistics on the period until March 1, 1948. The authorities of the United States, Great Britain, France, Greece, Netherlands, Norway, Poland, and Yugoslavia conducted 969 trials, in which 3,470 German defendants were tried. Death sentences were passed for 952; 1,905 were sentenced to varying prison terms, and 613 were acquitted.

Before the trials concluded, the political climate changed. The Cold War had begun and both the Americans and the Soviet Union were vying for the esteem of the German people. For some Americans, the Korean War made putting the Nazi period in the past ever more urgent. John J. McCloy, a former assistant secretary of war who became U.S. high commissioner for Germany in 1949, promulgated the Clemency Act in January 1951, commuting many of the convicted war criminals' sentences. By 1958 nearly all prisoners had been freed.

Trials in Liberated Countries and Israel

WEST GERMANY AND AUSTRIA. *West Germany.* Courts in postwar Germany began to function at the end of 1945, when some of the Allies reinvested the Germans with the right to hold trials. According to a summary prepared by the Federal Department of Justice in Bonn, indictments were issued by the West German authorities against 9,401 Nazi criminals between 1945 and Jan. 1, 1969. Of these, twelve were condemned to death (through 1949), 98 to life imprisonment, 6,002 to various prison terms, and the remainder acquitted or never brought to trial. All in all, during the above period, investigations were carried out against 79,401 accused Nazi criminals. 13,000 were tried and 6,487 were convicted; 6,197 were sentenced to prison (thirteen to life terms) and 23 to death. Among the most important trials were those of the Treblinka guards (1959–65); the Auschwitz SS personnel (1963–79 and 1963–64); Franz Stangl, commandant of Sobibor and Treblinka (1974–75); the Majdanek case (1975–81); and Josef Schwammberger, commandant of the Mieliec, Rozvadow, and Przemysl forced labor camps in Poland, who also destroyed the Przemysl ghetto (1991–92).

Three periods are discernible in the trial and punishment of Nazi criminals in West Germany: 1) from the close of the war until 1952, the "denazification period"; 2) 1952–57, a period of relative cessation of legal activities in this area; and 3) from 1958 on, with the establishment of the Central Office of the State Judicial Authorities (*Zentralstelle der Landesjustizverwaltungen*) in Ludwigsburg.

Immediately after the end of World War II, the Allies realized that in the interests of international security, Germany must be thoroughly purged of its Nazi elements. "Denazification," the process of purging the German state and civil society of their Nazi elements, began in 1945 and had several aspects: military, political, and legal. In the military sphere, the magnitude of the German defeat ensured that the German military posed no threat to the occupying armies; the Allied military governments in occupied Germany further secured themselves by means of preventive arrest of members of all Nazi government, military, police, and party bodies. In the political sphere, denazification proceedings were intended to prevent Nazis not included in the list of war criminals from assuming influential positions in the political, economic, and social life of Germany, and to assure the process of German democratization. In the legal sphere, investigations of Nazi functionaries were carried out and those accused of crimes prosecuted, when the evidence warranted (trials and denazification were not the same thing). More than 3,000,000 Germans were obliged to undergo this process, and trials were conducted against accused Nazi criminals in both Allied and German courts. From 1946 to 1952, trials were held by the West German states of, inter alia, participants in the **Kristallnacht* riots (November 9–10, 1938), and the number of accused reached several hundred.

When a state and civil society are dominated so totally by a ruling party that all officials either willingly or by necessity adhere to its expressed ideology, it is difficult to purge these people from its institutions, including the judiciary and legal community and the government bureaucracy, and still have a functioning system. Denazification, therefore, was not at all successful, and most former Nazis, especially in the judiciary, returned to their old posts.

After 1953, denazification ceased in West and East Germany. Searching for criminals not yet brought to trial abated, and many were able to flee Germany and go elsewhere. Latin America was a frequent destination, as were Arab countries. As a result murderers lived freely and with only vague fears throughout the world – Adolf Eichmann lived in Argentina; the physician Josef *Mengele lived in Argentina until 1960 and later in Paraguay and Brazil; Horst Schumann, who performed medical experiments on Jewish prisoners in the concentration camps, lived in Ghana until his extradition; Franz Stangl, commandant of the *Treblinka and *Sobibor death camps, lived in Syria and Brazil until his extradition; and there were plenty of others. And many lived freely in East and West Germany as well. West German authorities rationalized this by claiming that the Nuremberg trials, even though they had been held in Germany, did not evoke the appropriate reaction in the country. After its overwhelming defeat, the German nation was busy repairing the ravages created by the war. Appropriate documentation was lacking, as the victors had taken all the German archives that remained after the war. The reservoir of potential witnesses that existed in Germany between 1945 and 1950 and constituted an important element in gathering complaints and evidence, disappeared with the elimination of Displaced *Persons camps and the migration of the refugees to Israel and other countries. Most importantly, the Cold War became a central concern of the Allies and the politics of fighting it predominated. There was less incentive for the Western allies to pursue war crimes trials. In addition, Germans in general, and their official institutions, maintained that they were not completely aware of the extent of the crimes committed by the Nazis. It was only in the wake of the 1958 Ulm trial against the members of the *Einsatzkommando Tilsit*, which operated in Lithuania, that most Germans learned of the extent of the crimes – or so it was argued.

Whatever the validity of this claim, it is a fact that 1958 marked a turning point in the attempt to bring Nazi criminals to justice within the territory of the Federal Republic of Germany, and, to a far lesser extent, in Austria. In a number of places suitable conditions and tools were created for renewed activity in this field, especially in West Germany, Israel (where Yad *Vashem, the memorial institution whose work includes documentation of the Holocaust, was established, as was a special police unit for Nazi criminals), and the United States (where the Institute of Jewish Affairs concentrated exclusively on assistance to German and Austrian judicial authorities). In the Ulm trial, it became clear to the prosecution that until that time the crime of the Final Solution was barely considered by the German courts and that those mainly responsible for its planning and execution were not tried at all. This had to do with the restrictions placed by the Allies on the authority of the West German courts, which were loosened only later.

As a result of this trial, there was an awakening among liberal jurists in Germany. Thirteen years after the end of the war, a special meeting of the ministers of justice of the 13 *Laender* (states) then constituting the Federal Republic was held in city of Ludwigsburg, near Stuttgart. Following the suggestion of the minister of justice of Baden-Wuerttemberg, the ministers of the federal Laender decided in October 1958 to create the aforementioned *Zentralestelle der Landes-*

justizverwaltungen zur Aufklaerung der NS-Verbrechen (Central Office of the State Judicial Authorities for the Investigation of National Socialist Crimes – Central Office, for short). This authority started its work in Ludwigsburg on December 1, 1958.

According to the administrative agreement of the Laender, the task of the Central Office consisted of collecting and sifting all obtainable records about relevant criminal acts under investigation, examining crimes, classifying them and determining the whereabouts of the perpetrators. The office was obliged to coordinate preliminary inquiries and transmit relevant information to the appropriate public prosecutors and to be of further assistance to them.

As the Central Office itself was not a public prosecution office, it could not prefer charges, apply for arrest warrants, or examine property, but was obliged to pass its findings to the public prosecutors. The Central Office had no competence to investigate genuine war crimes. It also did not initially possess any jurisdiction to investigate killings in those concentration camps which were located in the area of the Federal Republic. Later on – at the end of 1964 – its jurisdiction was extended and it then investigated such crimes committed in German territory, with the exception of those committed by the Reich Central Security Office, which remained within the jurisdiction of the Chief State Prosecutor at the Supreme Court of Justice.

Under the terms of the Administrative Agreement, public prosecutors were obliged to forward to the Central Office all the findings they obtained during proceedings and present the minutes of the examination sessions of accused and witnesses, as well as other relevant documents together with their concluding notes. The Central Office registered these documents in card indexes. In January 1985, the central card catalogue in the Central Office contained more than 1.3 million cards arranged alphabetically as well as by the sites at which the acts were committed and by which division (*Dienststelle*). The data was obtained from witnesses, the accused, and other persons. The document collection included more than half a million individual documents about the Nazi era (mainly photocopies) and more than 500 microfilms. These were also available for use through separate document catalogues.

Initially, the Central Office was entrusted with the investigation, in addition to murders, of crimes classified as manslaughter. The statute of limitations ran out on these as of May 8, 1960. As a result only those murders which are defined as willful murders can be prosecuted. A law of December 1979 lifted limitations for all murders, not only Nazi killings.

The employees of the Central Office were generally prosecutors and investigating judges; the majority were devoted young people, who were not adults when the Nazi crimes were committed. They began their work by becoming acquainted with the problem, gathering documentary material and establishing ties with Israel and Jewish institutions in the United States. This office did not deal with crimes committed within German territory itself; those crimes were prosecuted by the regular judicial authorities in the states in which the alleged perpetrators resided, as were crimes committed outside Germany – the Central Office gathered information, and individual states undertook investigations and trials.

The Central Office came up against many problems. On the one hand, its activities were an annoyance and a threat to German circles that included many influential figures who wanted to forget the past, e.g., ex-Nazi politicians, judges and police officials, and adherents of *neo-Nazism. On the other hand, prosecutors encountered many difficulties and obstacles in gathering documentary material scattered in many countries. Certain countries, for political reasons, were not always willing to assist by placing the material in their possession at the disposal of the German authorities.

In addition, in dealing with Nazi crimes, investigation authorities had to take into consideration further difficulties. Many witnesses who were victims of National Socialism were no longer alive or were unwilling to give testimony about their terrible experiences, especially in the oppressive atmosphere of a courtroom. Proof becomes more difficult to establish over time. Some survivors refused to return to Germany even for a trial. Others were angry at what they considered the disrespectful tone of cross-examination. Ordinary victims had usually been in contact only with low-level perpetrators and not with those in charge, the leaders. In cases of culprits who were not known to their victims either by name or by appearance verification could be arrived at only through documentary evidence. Documents often arrived in the form of photocopies from the archives of Eastern European states and were therefore distrusted, or flatly rejected, by certain circles in the Federal Republic. In some trials in which such documentary evidence was introduced, counsel for the defense asked the courts not to accept it. (When, however, incontestable originals were placed at the courts' disposal, no further attempts were made to dispute the authenticity of these documents.) Unfortunately, in several cases, such documentary proof was entirely missing, as the documents had been destroyed shortly before the end of the war or never existed. These proceedings were almost always dependent on the testimony of witnesses. But it is only natural that, decades after the events, the value of such testimony becomes more and more questionable. In addition, the exterminations of the National Socialist era were not carried out openly, but in specially chosen localities, behind walls and fences and under the strictest secrecy.

The problem of locating witnesses was even greater with respect to German nationals, who were unwilling to give incriminating testimonies against their accomplices. The reservoir of witnesses was therefore usually limited to the circles of the perpetrators or the victims. Many of those who witnessed such acts or were in contact with those who committed them were afraid to expose themselves to investigation; they remained silent, because of misguided solidarity with the perpetrators, or because they had suppressed the terrible events from their memory. The victims were often able to recall the essentials, but had forgotten details which seemed to them at the time unimportant and which might have been crucial for the proceedings. They often instinctively substituted for their imperfect knowledge hearsay evidence and conclusions reached later, often after discussion with other survivors. Perpetrators, times, and places became confused, especially as many of the victims had passed through a dozen or more camps. Still, even in these cases remarkably precise testimonies were often given which could be – sometimes through documentation – unequivocally verified. It has also been repeatedly established that witnesses for the accused contacted each other, sometimes in an organized fashion, to coordinate their exonerating statements.

Many of the investigations handed over for legal action were completed with the trial and conviction of the accused, e.g., the trials of the SS men from the staff of the *Chelmno death camp; the members of the *Einsatzgruppen* who operated in Belorussia; the Heuser trial involving the destruction of the Jews of Minsk; the trials of the murderers of the Treblinka, Auschwitz, and Sobibor death camps and the Tarnopol, Czestochowa, Lvov, and Stanislav ghettos. Special units of the criminal police were established to assist the Central Office; their task was to interrogate witnesses in Germany, locate criminals, and make arrests on the basis of the office's data. Among the important cases dealt with by the Central Office are those of the *Einsatzgruppen*, with all their units, that operated mainly in the German-occupied Soviet territories, and the infamous *Aktion Reinhard* case, the operation aimed at murdering Polish Jews. The Central Office also investigated the crimes committed in the ghettos in Poland and in all German-occupied countries of Europe. Again, it is important to note that an enormous amount of investigatory work was also undertaken by each state prosecuting attorney's office – for example, in the Auschwitz trial, most of the investigation was done by the prosecution and the court in Frankfurt.

An important limitation of the prosecution of Nazi killings was the amendment of Article 50, Paragraph 2 of the Penal Code passed in October 1968, whereby persons who had participated in such murders could be punished only if their own special criminal characteristics, such as delight in murder, avarice, or other base motives such as racial hatred or lust for revenge, were proved. Failure to prove these meant that the act was covered by the statute of limitations and was not actionable as of May 8, 1960. Other related manifestations, such as extreme cruelty and malice, were, however, excluded from the above amendment.

In performing its functions the Central Office cooperated from the outset with private and state institutions in Germany and elsewhere – especially with institutions in Israel, the U.S., and France – to obtain documentary proofs or testimonies of witnesses. From 1965 the Central Office was also given the opportunity, after appropriate agreements were reached, to cooperate with states of the Eastern Bloc and to make use of the extensive documentary material in their archives. Difficulties arose with regard to cooperation with the states of the Middle East, South American countries, and also the German Democratic Republic (East Germany). Interpol had declined to help in clarifying Nazi crimes, as it classified these in the category of political offenses, with which, according to its constitution, it is not supposed to deal. As a not insignificant number of persons sought for had succeeded, equipped with false personal documents and in some cases helped by the Vatican, in disappearing into Arab or South American countries, which as a rule declined extradition of these persons, proceedings against these accused often remained unsettled. For example, Walter Rauff, former *SS-Standartenfuehrer* and director of the technical department of the RSHA dealing with the use of gas, lived until his death in 1984 in Chile, and could not be extradited. It is also possible that some accused lived unidentified in the Federal Republic.

In comparatively numerous cases the accused committed suicide in detention or died during the proceedings. Often, the inability of a defendant to stand trial – supported by official medical examinations – resulted in the suspension of the proceedings. The fact that these suspensions have occurred more frequently in Nazi trials than in other legal proceedings is related not to the indulgence of the courts, but to the age of the defendants. 2005 was sixty years after liberation and thus a thirty-year-old officer in 1945 was by then 90 and likely to plead ill health and feebleness. With defendants at death's door, some have suggested that no trials be held and that the courts simply wait for time to take its toll.

All these circumstances now necessitate an especially careful and precise examination of testimonies by the courts. Proceedings have often terminated – in spite of very lengthy searches throughout the world for witnesses – with verdicts of acquittal because of possible errors in testimony, following the principle "*in dubio pro reo*" (when in doubt, favor the accused). As over the years the number of living witnesses has decreased and their memories have deteriorated, the proportion of acquittals in forthcoming cases will undoubtedly increase.

The fall of the Berlin Wall and the incorporation of the German Democratic Republic into the Federal Republic did not lead to identification or prosecution of East Germans now under the jurisdiction of the Central Office. The unified German government was more interested in trying former East German Communist Party leaders and former Berlin Wall guards responsible for the killing of East Germans attempting to escape than in prosecuting aged pensioners with a Nazi past.

As of 2004, the Central Office had 35 suspected Nazi war criminals under review. In 2003, two new indictments were filed for murder, and these were the only murder charges outstanding against former Nazis or collaborators anywhere in the world.

Chances of obtaining additional convictions, moreover, remain small, for reasons apart from failing memories. As the Canadian historian Rebecca Wittmann has pointed out, the conservative German judiciary has always been loath to convict aging German pensioners for wartime acts. A prominent example is the case of Friedrich Engel, a former Nazi SS officer known as the Butcher of Genoa, for his part in the wartime massacre of 59 Italian POWs. In 2002, a Hamburg court found Engel guilty of murder and sentenced him to seven years' imprisonment. In 2004, however, Germany's Federal Court of Justice threw out the conviction. Although the appellate court agreed that Engel ordered the execution, it held that the charge of murder had not been sufficiently proven and would have required a retrial which would not take place because of Engel's advanced age. In 2006, Engel died of natural causes at age 97 in Hamburg.

Austria. Despite the proclamations and claims of government circles in Austria about the desire to eradicate traces of Nazism and antisemitism from the country, the acts of the Austrian courts attest to the opposite. Only isolated trials against Nazi criminals were held in Austria in the 1960s, and all the verdicts constituted a mockery of justice and law, to the point of arousing wrath the world over. Among those brought to trial were Franz Novak, an SS member and aide to Adolf Eichmann, who organized the transport of tens of thousands of Jews to the gas chambers (he was tried in 1964 and sentenced to eight years. A new trial was held in 1966 and he was acquitted. He was tried again in 1969 and sentenced to nine years and a fourth trial was held in 1972 when he was found guilty and sentenced to seven years); Franz Murer, the murderer of Vilna Jewry, who was acquitted by the court in Graz of a charge of murder and is free; Erich Raja Rajakowitsch, another of Eichmann's aides, responsible for sending tens of thousands of Dutch Jews to the death camps, who was sentenced to two and a half years' imprisonment; and the Mauer brothers, criminals who committed atrocities and murdered the Jews of the city of Stanislav, Poland (now in the Ukraine).

While Austria as of 2004 had 27 ongoing investigations, the only convictions obtained there have been those discussed in the preceding paragraph. In February 2006, Ephraim Zuroff of the *Simon Wiesenthal Center called Austria "a paradise for Nazi criminals" after failing to convince the Austrian government of Prime Minister Wolfgang Schuessel to take more active measures to investigate and prosecute suspected former Nazis still living in Austria.

Former United Nations Secretary-General Kurt Waldheim, who later became President of Austria, was known to have lied about his whereabouts during World War II (he served in Yugoslavia in the vicinity of the places where atrocities were committed). He was placed on the "Watch List" for Nazi War Criminals by the Department of Justice of the United States, but his personal responsibility for crimes has not been established by a Court of Law.

Punishment of Criminals Tried in West Germany and Austria. In contrast to the period immediately after the war, when membership in a Nazi organization was sufficient for a prima facie case, current German criminal law stipulates that proof must be given that an individual defendant committed acts of murder or was an accomplice to such acts. The Federal Republic's Justice Ministry did not adopt any of the international criminal provisions and chose instead to try Nazi criminals under the existing pre-Nazi German penal code that had been established in 1871. Although it was still possible to find Jewish eyewitnesses to testify against low-ranking Nazis, it was almost impossible to do so in the case of high-ranking officials, those who gave the commands. Jews were seldom in direct, eyewitness contact with the leaders, merely with the lower-level officials who operated in the vicinity of Jews. Thus, it was only on the basis of testimony given by accomplices or documents from the period that they could be brought to trial, and these were often unavailable or nonexistent. The verdicts of trials against accused Nazi criminals in West Germany, and even more so in Austria in the 1950s, often reflected the tendency to acquit them or spare them severe punishment on the ground that they had committed their criminal acts out of "an error of conscience." Defendants were tried as either perpetrators of or accomplices to murder; they could not be tried for manslaughter after 1960, as noted above, because of the 15-year statute of limitations on manslaughter. There was a 20-year limitation on charges of murder, which was hotly debated throughout the 1960s and the 1970s but was ultimately never invoked vis-à-vis Nazi crimes. Defendants who were convicted were largely convicted as accomplices, because in order to convict them as perpetrators (earning an automatic life sentence) the prosecution had to show their inner motivations. Elements of inner motivation included lust for killing, sexual drive for killing, cruelty, treachery, base motives (defined in Nazi trials as racial hatred, and very hard to prove). Above all, the prosecution had to prove the individual initiative of the defendant in order to get a conviction of murder. This led to a strong focus on defendants who committed brutal acts in excess of their orders. The "just following orders" defense had already been thrown out at Nuremberg, as it had been proven there that no Nazi or SS officer or enlisted man had ever been punished or even investigated for refusing to carry out these kinds of orders.

Despite the substantial amounts of documentary material and testimony presented against them, many of the criminals convicted nonetheless received sentences that did not stand in any reasonable proportion to the extent of their crimes. Tens of thousands of other defendants enjoyed the immunity afforded by the German statute of limitations, twice extended. Prior to the 1979 amendment it was only 30 years in the case of murder. The reasons for this leniency included the fact that many German and Austrian judges or jurors themselves served the Nazi regime and some of them had been members of the Party. Even those who were not Nazis were not inclined to mete out severe punishments to their neighbors. The indifference of the bulk of the German and Austrian public to the question of Nazi criminals also played a role in this matter.

Various circles in Germany and a large part of the German press protested more than once against the absurdity of the light punishments or acquittals of the criminals in comparison to punishments meted out to ordinary thieves, murderers, and others. In contrast, the voices of Nazi sympathizers encouraged the acquittals and the lenient sentences. The response to the German broadcast of the American television docudrama *Holocaust* in 1978, and to growing international pressure, led West Germany to decide not to invoke the statute of limitations on crimes of murder committed during the Holocaust.

Nevertheless, as discussed above, the overly strict legalistic approach adopted by German judges and the lack of political will or popular support to continue investigations and prosecutions of aged Nazis, has resulted in the failure to bring many Nazis to justice. As Rebecca Wittmann observes, "[C]hanges to the law made it easier and easier for those who had the most power in the Nazi regime – the desktop murderers – to go free or escape trial, and in the end only the most sadistic – and exceptional – of Nazi criminals, usually camp guards, were tried and convicted of murder. On the one hand, there were thousands of trials. On the other hand, the continuities in the judicial personnel made the sentences and interpretation of the laws extremely favourable to the defendants.... The law was not the setting in which Germans would come to recognize the wholesale complicity of an entire generation."

OTHER LIBERATED COUNTRIES. In the years after the end of the war, many countries that had been occupied by the Germans conducted a large number of trials of Nazi occupiers and their collaborators, most in accordance with special legislation, but the number of defendants of German origin was relatively low. The reason is that the Nazi criminals, except those who had been captured before the end of the war, were not always found within the borders of the countries in which the crimes were committed. Through 1949, hundreds of Nazi criminals were extradited to the legal authorities of these countries, but others remained free because no extradition agreements were in place. Extradition activities continued only until 1950 when the cold war set in. Summarized below are several trials, held in countries that are of special interest from a Jewish perspective.

In Poland, trials of Nazi criminals were held from 1944 in accordance with special legislation. Special tribunals were established that functioned until 1946, after which the accused were tried by ordinary courts. During the two years 2,471 defendants were convicted (out of about 10,000); 631 were sentenced to death and the remainder to varying prison terms. Especially significant in their bearing on the Holocaust were the cases of Amon Goeth, commandant of the *Plaszow concentration camp, in 1946, who was sentenced to death; of Ludwig Fischer, governor of the Warsaw district, who was found guilty and executed in Poland in 1947; and Rudolf *Hoess, commandant of the *Auschwitz death camp (Hoess was hanged on a gallows outside the gas chamber at Auschwitz; the gallows is still there as a kind of memorial to his crimes); of SS General Jakob Sporrenberg, responsible for the *Majdanek death camp, in 1950, who was found guilty and executed; and of SS General Juergen *Stroop, suppressor of the Warsaw ghetto uprising, in 1951, who was also found guilty and executed. According to unofficial statistics Polish tribunals dealt with about 40,000 persons, both Germans and collaborators, accused of Nazi crimes.

In Czechoslovakia, the following, inter alia, were tried for war crimes: Dieter *Wisliceny, an aide to Eichmann; Karl *Frank, commander of the police and the SS in Czechoslovakia; Monsignor Josef Tiso, president of the Nazis' Slovak puppet state, and Alexander Mach and Anton Vasek, leading collaborators responsible for the annihilation of Jews in Slovakia, who were found guilty and hanged. According to available statistics, 19,000 persons were brought to trial for Nazi crimes and collaboration in Czechoslovakia, the vast majority of them local collaborators.

In Hungary, according to official statistics of the Ministry of Justice, up to March 1, 1948, the Hungarian government instituted proceedings against 39,514 persons, of which 31,472 had been completed and 8,042 were still pending in 1948 when the regime changed. The courts dismissed 5,954 cases, 9,245 cases resulted in not guilty verdicts, and 19,273 defendants were sentenced to prison terms. Three hundred twenty-two persons were sentenced to death and 149 actually executed. No official data is available for post-1948 trials. The swift execution of the Holocaust in Hungary – the Germans occupied the country in March 1944, Jews were ghettoized in April and 437,402 deported between May 15 and early July – was an important ingredient in the war crimes trials in that country. Among the minor war criminals were those of the "labor battalions" and people involved in the deportation of the Jews. As to major war criminals, a former prime minister, László Bárdossy, was held responsible for the deportation of Jews to *Kamenets-Podolski and for the *Novi Sad massacre; he was executed. Another former prime minister, Béla Imrédy, was charged with responsibility for, among other things, the anti-Jewish laws and for the destruction of Hungarian Jewry; he, too, was executed. Three leading men of the Ministry of Interior – the minister, Andor Jaross, and the state secretaries, László Baky and László Endre, who played a leading part in the destruction of Hungarian Jewry – were sentenced to death and executed. Practically all members of the Szálasi and Sztójay governments (including the prime ministers) were tried and sentenced to death.

In the Netherlands, most of the trials took place between 1948 and 1952. More than 200 accused collaborators were tried, as well as several Germans. Among the latter, the trials of the following should be mentioned: Hans Rauter, commander of the police and SS in the Netherlands, in 1948; Wilhelm Harster, commander of the SD in the Netherlands, who bore the chief responsibility for the deportation of Dutch Jews to the death camps, and Ferdinand aus der Fuenten, Harster's aide, also responsible for the deportation of the Jews, both in 1949. Rauter was sentenced to death, and after being denied a pardon, was executed on March 25, 1949. Harster was sentenced to twelve years imprisonment (he was later sentenced to an additional 15 years in another trial in Munich). Aus der Fuenten's original death sentence was later commuted to life imprisonment.

Many trials were also held in Denmark, Belgium (610), Norway (81), and France (2,345), among them those of Karl Oberg and Helmut Knochen, police and SS commanders responsible for the deportation of French Jews to the death camps. All in all, according to West German sources, about 80,000 Germans were convicted in all countries (including the then Soviet Union and East Germany) for committing crimes against humanity. The number of local collaborators reached the tens of thousands. For example, 13,600 collaborators were tried in Denmark alone. More than 90 percent of all collaborators were sentenced to fewer than four years' imprisonment.

THE SOVIET UNION. The Soviet Union played a major role in the prosecution of Nazi war criminals and collaborators in Eastern Europe. During the initial decade after the war, thousands of accused perpetrators were put on trial in the Soviet republics that had been under German occupation – although not always for their role in the murder of the Jews. Unfortunately, no exact figures exist on the number of such trials and their results, but from the information available in the post-Communist era, it is clear that the number of those punished is relatively high when compared to Western countries. Since numerous local Nazi collaborators in these areas actively participated in the mass murder of Jews, these trials and the transcripts, documents and secondary sources published in their wake are of great importance for Holocaust history. Unfortunately, the trials were not, and the publications are not, entirely free of Soviet propaganda, which diminishes their value. The Soviets' policy of denying or minimizing (depending on the era) the singularity of the fate of the Jews and their suffering during World War II must also be considered in evaluating these sources.

Many of those convicted by Soviet courts were executed for their crimes, while others were sentenced to lengthy terms in prison camps or in exile. Many were freed in the 1955 amnesty granted by Nikita Khrushchev. Trials were held in the Soviet Union of Soviet citizens who collaborated in occupied territories during the war. Inasmuch as official publications and documents on these trials are not available, information about them was gleaned primarily from publications of the Soviet information agency, Tass. Also implicated in these trials were collaborators who had previously been Soviet citizens, i.e., those who had fled from the Soviet army – both deserters and Soviet POWs who were recruited by the Germans and later found asylum in Western countries. Trials since 1961 have not dealt explicitly with the annihilation of Jews *qua* Jews, while in trials held previously, Jews were submerged in the broad category of Soviet citizens, in keeping with the Communist interpretation of the war. There were notable exceptions such as the October 1965 trial in Riga, Latvia that considered the annihilation of the Jews and the role of Latvian collaborators in it.

The breakup of the Soviet Union led to the opening of wartime archival materials in Moscow and other Russian cities, and newly discovered Soviet documents became quite useful in the prosecution of aging collaborators living in the United States. Russia itself did not hold any trials, and there was no call for such trials to be held in Russian territory. But there were unprosecuted Holocaust perpetrators still living in Latvia, Lithuania, Estonia, and Ukraine at the end of the twentieth century. Unfortunately, these countries showed little or no interest in investigating their local populace. Latvia and Lithuania did mount some investigations and Lithuania was able to obtain one conviction of a local collaborator in the 1990s.

Trials Outside Continental Europe

Trials also occurred outside continental Europe, at a distance from the site of the crime.

ISRAEL. In spite of all their problematic features and limitations, the trials recorded above can lay claim to notable achievements. A vast store of documentary material on the criminal policies of the Nazi regime toward the Jewish population and on the responsibility of the leaders for the crimes was collected by the Allies. Likewise, trial records and collections of documents from the main trials, in various languages, were also published. In all these trials, the specific persecution of Jews was considered as only one of the many facets of Nazi criminality, all of which were required to establish the responsibility of the accused for various violations of international law: crimes against peace, war crimes, and crimes against humanity. In contrast, the only trial that dealt specifically and comprehensively with the Final Solution was the *Eichmann trial held in Jerusalem in 1961–62. The Eichmann trial had important implications for the trials of Nazi criminals and their aides in those countries where such trials were still being conducted (West and East Germany, Austria, and the U.S.S.R.). In the wake of renewed interest in the prosecution of Holocaust perpetrators generated by the Eichmann trial, Simon *Wiesenthal opened an office in Vienna and relaunched his efforts to bring Nazi war criminals to justice. He had closed his first office in Linz in 1954 after the Cold War dampened Allied enthusiasm for the prosecution of Nazi war criminals in West Germany.

A second trial in Israel, that of death camp guard John Demjanjuk, was held more than a quarter of a century later, in 1988. Demjanjuk was tried as "Ivan the Terrible," who operated the gas chambers at Treblinka, but his original conviction and death sentence were overturned when doubt was cast on his identification as Ivan, doubt which also raised questions regarding the accuracy of survivor testimony. The Demjanjuk trial obviously had significantly less impact than the Eichmann trial, but by then the memory of the Holocaust was less dependent on trials and more institutionalized and broadly based on scholarship, writing and film. Demjanjuk, a naturalized American citizen, later returned to the United States after serving seven years in Israel for his role as a concentration camp guard (he was kept in prison while his case was being appealed, the death sentence triggering an automatic Supreme Court appeal in Israel). Late in 2005, he was ordered deported from the United States for concealing his wartime past when applying for immigration and naturalization.

THE UNITED STATES. Since the passing of the most intense phase of the Cold War in the 1950s and early 1960s, and the Eichmann trial in 1961–62, the country that has been most active in pursuing Nazi war criminals has been the United States, where the presence of many Nazi war criminals and collaborators was first exposed in the mid-1970s. Because of doubts about whether they had jurisdiction to prosecute crimes committed overseas in which neither the suspects nor the victims were American citizens, American legal authorities decided to press only civil charges against suspected war criminals, for immigration and naturalization violations. Thus, in effect, Nazi war criminals have been tried for concealing their wartime activities when they applied to enter the United States and/or when they applied for U.S. citizenship. In 1978 Congress passed the Holtzman Amendment, sponsored by Representative Elizabeth *Holtzman of New York, that enabled the United States to deport aliens if they had been Nazi criminals or accessories to Nazi crimes; in 1979 the U.S. Justice Department established its Office of Special Investigations (OSI) for this purpose. As of 2006, OSI has won verdicts against more than one hundred Nazi war criminals, with more than eighty having been denaturalized and more than sixty having been removed or deported.

The Demjanjuk case was a matter of overreach by OSI, which did not pursue him merely as a camp guard, which was easily provable, but as Ivan the Terrible. After Demjanjuk's conviction in Israel, the Supreme Court of Israel overturned the verdict because of questions relating to an essential document supplied by the Soviet Union supposedly identifying him as the notorious Ivan, and Demjanuk was freed and returned to the United States. OSI moved against him again and won both denaturalization and deportation rulings. In December 2005, after exhausting all his appeals, the 85-year-old Demjanuk was ordered by an immigration judge to be deported from the United States, presumably to Ukraine, his place of birth.

A statistical summary of OSI's activities since 1979 shows the following results as of early 2006:

Persons whose denaturalization and/or removal have been sought: 132

Persons denaturalized or removed to date: 101 (81 denaturalized and 60 removed, of whom 19 had never become citizens)

Persons placed on the "watch list" for possible exclusion from the U.S.: nearly 70,000

Persons excluded at U.S. ports of entry: 170 (during 458 border stops or inquiries)

Cases in litigation: 20

Peak number of cases in litigation: 28 (in 1984)

Persons under investigation: 94

Preliminary inquiries underway: 167

Investigations opened to date: 1,517

Investigations closed to date: 1,423

[Emmanuel Brand / Rebecca Wittmann and Michael J. Bazyler (2nd ed.)]

THE UNITED KINGDOM. The presence of suspected Nazi war criminals in the United Kingdom was first exposed by Zuroff, who compiled an initial list of 17 suspects which was submitted to the British consul in Los Angeles by Rabbis Marvin Hier and Abraham Cooper on October 22, 1986 with a request that the U.K. government conduct a comprehensive investigation of the scope of the problem. Although the government initially refused to even consider any legal action in these cases, it ultimately agreed to the establishment of an official commission of inquiry following a series of exposés by Scottish Television on Nazi war criminals living in the U.K., pressure brought to bear by the All-Party War Crimes Group headed by Members of Parliament Merlyn Rees and Greville Janner, and groups such as the Wiesenthal Center.

On February 8, 1988, Home Secretary Douglas Hurd announced the appointment of an official War Crimes Inquiry, to be headed by Sir Thomas Hetherington and William Chalmers. The War Crimes Inquiry completed its report on June 16, 1989, and it was presented to Parliament in July 1989. The report confirmed that a number of persons implicated in Nazi crimes had managed to enter the U.K. after the war and were still alive, and recommended that legislation be introduced to give domestic courts jurisdiction over "acts of murder and manslaughter, or culpable homicide" committed as war crimes in Germany or in German-occupied territory during World War II by persons found in the United Kingdom. "Consideration should be given," it stated, to prosecution "in three cases in which there appears to us to be a realistic prospect of conviction on the evidence already available." Other cases, the report stated, merited investigation.

The proposed legislation twice passed in the House of Commons only to be rejected by the House of Lords. It became law on May 10, 1991, after it passed the Commons a third time, enabling U.K. courts to try British citizens and residents for murder and other culpable homicides committed between 1933 and 1945 in Germany and German-occupied territory. Later in 1991, war crimes units were set up in the Crown Prosecution Service and the Metropolitan Police (New Scotland Yard).

On July 13, 1995, the British government instituted its first prosecution, a criminal case brought against Semyon Serafimovich, the alleged former chief of police in the city of Mir, Byelorussia (Belarus), for complicity in the mass murder of Jews in 1941 and 1942. The case had originally been expected to go to trial in 1996. At the committal hearing, the prosecution's key witness was Oswald Rufeisen, a Jew who, while masquerading as a Pole, had actually worked for a time as an interpreter for Serafimovich. (Rufeisen, who saved the lives of several hundred Jews in Mir by tipping them off to the planned liquidation of the community, converted to Catholicism after the war and settled in Israel, where he was known as Brother Daniel. He died there on July 30, 1998). On January 17, 1997, however, Serafimovich was adjudged by the court mentally incompetent to stand trial, reportedly on the basis of Alzheimer's disease. He died in hospital seven months later, on August 7, 1997.

On September 26, 1997, the government made its second arrest, taking into custody Anthony (Andrzej) Sawoniuk, 76, of East London. Sawoniuk was charged with murdering three unnamed Jewish women and two named Jewish men in 1942 in the vicinity of the town of Domachevo, Byelorussia (now in Poland), while serving as deputy commander of the *Schutzmannschaft* in Domachevo. Committal hearings began in London on April 20, 1998. On May 29, 1998, magistrate Graham Parkinson committed Sawoniuk for trial on four of the five charges brought by the government, and granted him bail. The fifth charge failed because the necessary witness was unable to travel from Poland to testify. The defense conceded that there was sufficient evidence for indictment with respect to three of the charges. In April 1999, at the conclusion of an Old Bailey trial, Sawoniuk was convicted of multiple murders and was sentenced to two life terms. On February 10, 2000, a three-judge panel of the Court of Appeal unanimously affirmed the conviction, rejecting Sawoniuk's contention that it was impossible to obtain a fair trial on charges involving events of so long ago. Sawoniuk died in a Norwich prison more than five years later, in November 2005.

At the conclusion of the Sawoniuk trial, Scotland Yard announced that the War Crimes Unit, which had once employed eleven police officers, two historians and a support staff, was being scaled down to a small staff to conclude its work, and that any new allegations received would be investigated by Scotland Yard's Organised Crime Group. On October 13, 1999, Scotland Yard announced that it had been advised by the Crown Prosecution Service that there was insufficient evidence to mount a prosecution in the one remaining case that it had referred to the CPS under the War Crimes Act of 1991. The same day, a Scotland Yard spokesperson announced that in light of the CPS's decision in the case, all of the War Crimes Unit's inquiries had now been exhausted and the unit would be shut down, and by year's end it was closed.

Ironically, the case which had been instrumental in convincing the British government to take legal action against the Nazi war criminals in the U.K. – that of Lithuanian police battalion officer Anton Gecas (Antanas Gecevicius) of Edinburgh, whose unit murdered thousands of Jews in Lithuania and Belarus – was never brought to trial. Gecas had worked for British intelligence following his arrival in the U.K., a factor that apparently influenced the authorities. The Lithuanian government sought Gecas' extradition, but he died in 2001 before he could be sent to Vilnius for trial.

CANADA. In April 1987, special units were set up within the Canadian Justice Department and the Royal Canadian Mounted Police to handle war crimes cases.

In September 1987, Canada's criminal code was amended to allow prosecution of persons implicated in war crimes and crimes against humanity committed anywhere outside Canada at any time before or after the law's enactment. The legislation received Royal Assent on September 16, 1987. This amendment was possible despite the fact that the Canadian Constitution's Charter of Rights and Freedoms, adopted in 1982, contains a provision, Section 11(g), barring the enactment of ex post facto criminal legislation, because the same section allows conviction for acts or omissions that were criminal "according to the general principles of law recognized by the community of nations."

During the period 1987 through 1994, six proceedings were initiated, four of them criminal cases. Only the two civil cases were successful. It was the 1994 decision in the case of the Hungarian gendarmerie commander Imre Finta, in which his defense of "superior orders" was accepted by the Supreme Court of Ontario, that ultimately forced the Canadian government to switch to the model employed by the United States. Thus on January 31, 1995, the Canadian government announced that it would henceforth emphasize the bringing of civil cases – citizenship revocation and deportation actions – rather than criminal prosecutions, since all previous criminal cases had been unsuccessful. This change meant that Canadian prosecutors would now be proceeding much as the U.S. Justice Department's Office of Special Investigations had since its inception in 1979. As of early 2005, a total of 21 civil cases have been brought with the following results: eight denaturalizations; two cases in which defendants voluntarily left Canada; three cases lost by the government. None of those denaturalized has yet been removed from the country.

AUSTRALIA. The presence in Australia of Nazi war criminals was first exposed in April 1986 by journalist Mark Aarons. In response the government established an official commission of inquiry, headed by retired civil servant Andrew C. Menzies, which confirmed the suspicions raised by Aarons and others. These others included the Wiesenthal Center, which submitted to the Australian government on September 1, 1986 a list of forty suspects known to have emigrated to Australia. In April 1987, the authorities established a Special Investigations Unit (SIU) in the federal Attorney-General's Department to handle these cases. More importantly, in January 1989, the Australian War Crimes Act of 1945 was amended to permit the prosecution in ordinary Australian courts, rather than military tribunals, of persons who committed war crimes outside the country during World War II.

The government closed down the SIU on June 30, 1992, despite its being clear that the problem of Nazi criminals in Australia had hardly been solved. In fact, at that point, 841 persons had been investigated (of whom 542 had been located) but only three had been brought to trial, none of whom was convicted.

Subsequently, additional allegations against suspected Nazi war criminals living in Australia were raised, primarily by Zuroff, and extradition requests for two Australian residents accused of Nazi crimes were submitted, one by Latvia (for Arajs Kommando officer Konrad Kalejs) and one by Hungary (for the soldier Karoly Zentai). As of early 2006, however, Australia had failed to take successful legal action against a single Holocaust perpetrator living in the country.

Cancellation of Pardons Granted to Holocaust Perpetrators. One of the byproducts of the efforts to bring Nazi war criminals to justice has been the attempt to prevent the granting of pardons and "rehabilitations" to convicted Nazi war criminals. Following the demise and dismemberment of the Soviet Union, each of the former Soviet Baltic republics launched an extensive rehabilitation program that included legal pardons and generous financial compensation for those considered illegally convicted by Soviet courts. Even though Nazi war criminals were not supposed to be eligible for such pardons, in practice at least dozens of such criminals were rehabilitated in Lithuania and Latvia. The Simon Wiesenthal Center exposed this process in Lithuania and Latvia and played a leading role in the efforts to cancel the pardons. So far, over 160 pardons for Nazi-era crimes have been cancelled in Lithuania and two in Latvia thanks to these efforts.

[Michael Berenbaum (2nd ed.)]

The Impact of the Trials

After 1958, and especially after the capture and trial of Adolf Eichmann, a change became noticeable in the pursuit of Nazi criminals. In Germany and in other countries, investigations were renewed against a number of Nazis who had long ceased to be of official interest; the search for Nazi criminals who had thus far succeeded in avoiding imprisonment was intensified; the possibilities for Nazis to exploit the rights of asylum in other countries were diminished; there was an increased awareness that the crimes of the Nazis must not be forgotten and that the criminals must be punished in order to prevent a recurrence of the crimes. Although the sentences meted out to Nazi criminals in most of the trials in West Germany, and especially in Austria, were in no way proportionate to the crimes (if proportion were at all possible), the careful preparation of the trials by the prosecution and the openness and thoroughness of the substantiated verdicts, based, inter alia, on testimony given by Jewish victims, resulted in their contributing significantly to the research of Holocaust history for the education of the German people, and especially German youth.

[Emmanuel Brand]

The investigation of Nazi crimes has remained a controversial chapter of postwar German history, both in private discussion and public debate. All nuances of opinion are represented, starting with the reproach of "fouling one's own nest" from right-wing, neo-Fascist, neo-Nazi circles, through the widespread criticism heard in Germany and elsewhere (and not only in Eastern Europe) that the investigation of Nazi crimes was, from the outset, carried out only half-heartedly, and ending with the repeatedly voiced opinion that people should try to forget what happened in those wretched times. Martin Hirsch, a former German federal judge, has said about the reproach of "mud-slinging" that he finds it shocking that the same people who "fouled the nest" in those days in such a terrible way should now level this accusation against those who try to cleanse it.

Oftentimes, trials in the latter years of the twentieth century had an unintended disquieting impact on the societies in which they were held. In France, Klaus Barbie, the former head of the Gestapo in Lyon – known as the "Butcher of Lyon" – was brought to trial after a decade of work by Nazi hunters Serge and Beate *Klarsfeld. French politicians had preferred to ignore the issue, as it once again raised questions about Vichy France and the participation in its government by postwar French politicians. Barbie stood trial in Lyon between May 11 and July 4, 1987. The evidence brought exposed the cooperation between fleeing SS men and Allied intelligence services (Barbie had worked for the Americans after the war, and they had helped him escape prosecution). The defense contested the moral standing of those who tried Barbie and the discrepancies in memory some four decades after the fact between resistance leaders and Jews. Barbie was found guilty but the trial was less than a clear success in the battle for memory.

Another French trial, that of Paul Touvier, was also disruptive to French self-perception. Touvier had been a high-ranking officer in the Vichy government. Convicted of collaboration in 1946 and sentenced to death, he went into hiding with the assistance of the Roman Catholic Church. In 1967 there was an attempt to clear his record, but it backfired as resistance veterans and Jews demanded that he be tried. He then disappeared, certainly not unassisted. He was tried and found not guilty because he had been an agent of Vichy France, but the outrage that greeted the verdict led to an appeal which overturned the verdict and Touvier was found guilty, the first Frenchmen to be found guilty of crimes against humanity.

The trial of Maurice Papon, another high-ranking functionary of the Vichy regime, was held in 1997 for his role in the deportation of the Jewish men, women and children from Bordeaux. A high-ranking civil servant in postwar France – he was chief of the Paris police and eventually became a minister in the cabinet of President Valery Giscard d'Estaing – Papon was found guilty of complicity in crimes against humanity and sentenced to ten years' imprisonment. (While Papon was chief of police, he was responsible for the murder of Algerian demonstrators – the number is disputed – in 1961.) He was released in 2002 on grounds of ill health and was still living as of early 2006.

No trial was held for Vichy police chief René Bosquet, who was finally indicted after being protected from prosecution for years. He was assassinated in 1993 by a deranged assailant shortly before his trial was scheduled to begin.

Ongoing Investigations

Zuroff is the last of the Nazi hunters. He has brought considerable pressure to bear on various governments, especially following the demise of the Soviet Union and the fall of Communism. Among his important initiatives has been "Operation Last Chance," a joint project of the Simon Wiesenthal Center and the Targum Shlishi Foundation of Miami, founded by philanthropist Aryeh Rubin, which offers financial rewards for information that will facilitate the prosecution and punishment of Holocaust perpetrators. Besides leading to the issuing of three arrest warrants, two extradition requests, and dozens of new investigations, the project, which by 2005 had been launched in nine countries (Germany, Austria, Lithuania, Latvia, Estonia, Poland, Romania, Croatia, and Hungary), raised public consciousness in these countries regarding the complicity of the local population in the mass murder of Jews during World War II by employing media ads that focused on this issue.

Each year the Wiesenthal Center issues an Annual Status Report on the investigation and prosecution of Nazi war criminals worldwide. In 2005 it reported that the investigation and prosecution of Nazi war criminals continued in sixteen countries, among them countries such as Germany, Austria, Lithuania, Latvia and Poland – where the crimes of the Holocaust were committed – and others, like the United States, Britain, Canada and Australia, which afforded postwar havens to Holocaust perpetrators. From April 1, 2004 until March 31, 2005, five convictions of Nazi war criminals were obtained, all in the United States. Most of those convicted served as armed guards in death camps and/or concentration camps in Poland and Germany. The number of convictions is lower by two than the number achieved during the previous year. From January 1, 2001 through March 31, 2005, a total of thirty-two convictions of Nazi war criminals were obtained all over the world. Of these convictions, 23 were in the United States, where the violations are civil, relating to providing false information on visa applications rather than to the actual crime, with the others in Germany (3), Canada (3), Poland (1), France (1) and Lithuania (1).

During the period from (April) 2004 through March 2005, legal proceedings were initiated against at least six Nazi war criminals in four countries – three in the United States, one in Hungary, one in Denmark and one in Lithuania. The number of indictments obtained in this period is lower by four than the figure achieved during the previous year. From January 1, 2001, through March 1, 2005, 33 new indictments have been submitted against Nazi war criminals, the majority in the United States. New investigations were initiated in eleven countries against at least 663 suspected Holocaust perpetrators. In 2005, there were ongoing investigations against more than 1,252 suspected Nazi war criminals in 16 countries, with the largest number of cases being investigated in Poland (450), the United States (246), Austria (199), Canada (190), Latvia (58) and Germany (46).

The Ukraine will not address the issue of Holocaust perpetrators, and Austria is unwilling to prosecute Milivoj Ašner, who served as police chief of Pozega, Croatia during World War II and played an important role in the persecution and deportation to concentration camps, where they were murdered, of hundreds of Jews, Serbs and Gypsies. Sweden and Norway no longer investigate Nazi war criminals due to existing statutes of limitation.

[Michael Berenbaum (2nd ed.)]

Implications for the Twenty-First Century

There is much about international criminal law in the twenty-first century that tends to be taken for granted: ousted tyrants such as Slobodan Milosevic, of Serbia and Yugoslavia, and Saddam Hussein, of Iraq, being brought to trial at the bar of justice; tribunals of various sorts springing up as the result of human rights violations in places such as Rwanda, Sierra Leone, and Cambodia; perpetrators of Nazi-era atrocities being hauled before courts in the United States, stripped of their citizenship and deported; and the existence of a permanent International Criminal Court, with wide-ranging jurisdiction to try the most serious offences in the international legal lexicon, though its authority is not accepted by all. Additionally, terms such as "crimes against humanity," "genocide," and "war crimes" have become part and parcel of the daily vocabulary, and are encountered with great frequency. In various ways, the world has become blasé about such matters – to the extent that it is often forgotten what a recent phenomenon all of this is. New generations growing up in the modern era could easily be forgiven for thinking that it has always been this way.

Yet, as recently as 1945, it would have been unthinkable. On November 20 of that year, Sir Geoffrey Lawrence of the British Court of Appeals, presiding over the opening of the International Military Tribunal trial of major war criminals at Nuremberg, solemnly intoned, "The trial which is now about to begin is unique in the history of the jurisprudence of the world…"

The uniqueness began with the very fact that there were trials at all. Thanks in large measure to President Truman and Justice Robert Jackson, who took leave from the Supreme Court of the United States to be the chief prosecutor, the British view favoring a "political solution" (translation: just take them out, put guns to their heads and shoot them) did not prevail.

The U.S. rationale was threefold: precedents had to be established in international law to place the relevant legal principles as well as the process of justice on a firm, well-established footing, and to send an unequivocal message to future would-be Hitlers of the fate that potentially awaited them; a high moral plane had to be established, in marked contrast to the wanton brutality practiced by the defendants, signifying that civilized society would not respond in kind; and a comprehensive historical record had to be collated systematically for the benefit of future generations, thereby enabling them to learn the lessons of the Nazi era.

Besides being the first international tribunal in history to try criminal offences, the IMT at Nuremberg also established two other precedents of a procedural nature: "Crimes… are committed by men, not by abstract entities...," thereby resoundingly affirming the charges against the leaders of the Nazi regime, who argued that since, under international law, only states had legal personality, it was the state of Germany that should have been tried. In the process, too, it was made abundantly clear that heads of state, heads of government and other national leaders could not hide behind claims of immunity in an international tribunal.

At the substantive level, Nuremberg added two major criminal offenses to the canons of international law: planning and conducting aggressive warfare, the culmination of the work of some three decades of whittling away at the unfettered right of states to declare and conduct wars; and crimes against humanity, contemplating acts such as extermination, enslavement, and other inhumane acts directed against civilian populations. The body of international law dealing with such crimes which was thereby established on a sound foundation was further enlarged in 1948, with the adoption of the Genocide Convention, directed against acts intended to wipe out whole populations, defined by race, religion, nationality, or ethnicity.

The precedents thus created have reverberated into the twenty-first century. The tribunals for Rwanda and Yugoslavia were based directly on the Nuremberg tribunals, while seeking to improve on the original model, for instance by conferring jurisdiction to investigate and prosecute alleged crimes by all sides to the conflict, not just the losers. In addition, other models have developed. National courts exercise jurisdiction to try the very same crimes referred to above, most famously in the trial of Adolf Eichmann in Jerusalem over his central role in the Final Solution. In Sierra Leone, what was established was a hybrid tribunal, combining national as well as international elements. In the "Pinochet model" a Spanish magistrate almost succeeded in having the former Chilean dictator extradited from Britain to face trial over atrocities committed by his regime. In 1998, the Rome Statute creating the new, permanent International Criminal Court was adopted by 120 nations, thus addressing yet another shortcoming of Nuremberg, namely the ephemeral nature of the tribunals. (It should be noted that the United States has refused to ratify the Rome Statute and thus exempts itself from the International Criminal Court's jurisdiction, while Israel, which has signed on to the Court, is currently refusing to obey a ruling against it declaring illegal the separation wall it is building on occupied Palestinian territory.)

The evolution of the procedural dimension has been matched at a substantive level. Thus, although crimes against humanity and genocide lie at the heart of prosecutions of large-scale human rights violations, both have evolved over the decades. For instance, the modern definition of crimes against humanity expressly includes rape. And, in patrilineal societies, rape may also constitute genocide, where it takes place across ethnic lines, with the aim of producing offspring which take on the father's ethnicity and prevent the mother's group from reproducing itself.

The Nuremberg model lay largely dormant for some 45 years. Beginning in the 1990s, however, prosecution of international crimes gained considerable momentum, to the extent that the world began to become a small and distinctly uncomfortable place for tyrants, or at least some of them. In this fashion, profound meaning began to be breathed into the remarks of Lord Justice Lawrence that followed his above-quoted opening: "... and it is of supreme importance to millions of people all over the globe." The revolution wrought by Nuremberg, and its abiding legacy, is indeed that.

[Harry Reicher (2nd ed.)]

BIBLIOGRAPHY: United Nations War Crimes Commission, *History of the United Nations War Crimes Commission* (1948); World Jewish Congress, *Unity in Dispersion* (1948); J. Robinson, *And the Crooked Shall be Made Straight* (1965); idem and P. Friedman, *Guide to Jewish History under the Nazi Impact* (1960), 176–221; idem, in: *Kovez̧ Meḥkarim ba-Mishpat ha-Beinle'ummi ha-Pumbi le-Zekher Sir Hersch Lauterpacht* (1961), 84–91; N. Robinson, *Report on the Activities of the Institute of Jewish Affairs, World Jewish Congress, in the Field of the Prosecution of War Criminals in Germany* (1961); idem, in: *Gesher*, 7 no. 2 (1961), 38–50; idem, in: *Le Monde Juif*, 26, no. 60/61 (1971), 16–23; E. Brand, in: *Yad Vashem Bulletin*, 14 (1964), 58–62; 19 (1966); 36–44; 20 (1967), 14–29; 21 (1967), 18–21; L'vai, in: R.L. Braham, ed., *Hungarian Jewish Studies*, (1969), 253–96; German Federal Republic, Bundesministerium fuer Justiz, *Die Verfolgung nationalsozialistischer Straftaten im Gebiet der Bundesrepublik Deutschland seit 1945* (1964); R. Vogel, ed., *Ein Weg aus der Vergangenheit: Eine Dokumentation zur Verjaehrungsfrage und zu den nationalsozialistischen Prozessen* (1969), *Probleme der Verfolgung und Ahndung von nationalsozialistischen Gewaltverbrechen* (1967); R. Henkys, *Die nationalsozialistischen Gewaltverbrechhen* (1964); Deutscher Bundestag, *175. Sitzung, Bonn, 25. 3. 1965; J. Gorzkowska and E. Zakowska, Zbrodniarze hitlerowscy przed sądami* NRF (1964); N.S. Alekseyev, *Otvetstvennost natsistskikh prestupnikov* (1968). **ADD. BIBLIOGRAPHY:** G.J. Bass, *Stay the Hand of Vengeance* (2000); D. Bloxam, *Genocide on Trial: War Crimes Trials and the Formation of History and Memory* (2003); R. Wittmann, *Beyond Justice* (2005).

WARENDORF, town in the former Prussian province of Westphalia, N.W. Germany, after 1945 in North Rhine-Westphalia. In the Middle Ages Jews from Warendorf are mentioned only once, in 1387 in Cologne. From the early 16th century many Jews settled in the bishopric of Muenster; they are first mentioned in Warendorf in 1553. After 1628, jurisdiction over the Jews in the bishopric of Muenster passed to the bishop, and under his protection a Jewish community gradually developed in Warendorf. It was one of the largest in the bishopric and remained its main community until the abolition of episcopal rule in 1802, as no Jews were allowed to reside in the city of Muenster until the Emancipation. Warendorf was the seat of the *Obervorgaenger* (elder) of the Muenster **Landjudenschaft*, founded in 1651, as well as of the Muenster **Landrabbiner* after the Muenster rabbinate had become separated from that of Cologne. The first *Landrabbiner* was Samuel Michel Essingen (1742), known as a disciple of Jonathan *Eybeschuetz. His successor was Michael Meyer Breslau of Hildesheim (1771–89), *Court Jew and mint supplier to the Muenster bishop; Michael Meyer was followed by his son David Breslau (1790–1815). A synagogue is first mentioned in 1709; it was renovated in 1808 and 1897. The community of Warendorf owned a cemetery from 1773; after 1823 a new cemetery was acquired. From one or two Jewish families living in Warendorf, their number grew to 18 (88 persons) in 1803 when the bishopric came under Prussian rule. Since neighboring Muenster was now open to Jewish settlement, a number of Jews left Warendorf. The community later increased slightly. It numbered 99 in 1833; 55 in 1849; 85 in 1880; 43 in 1933; and 15 in 1939.

The synagogue was destroyed in 1938. The last six Jews from Warendorf who had not emigrated were deported, with other Jews of the Muenster region, to Riga on Dec. 13, 1941, and murdered there. A memorial to the martyrs was consecrated in the cemetery in 1970.

The community was not reconstituted after the war. In 1971 two Jews were living in the town. The synagogue building was used as a dwelling. A plaque commemorates the former synagogue.

BIBLIOGRAPHY: B. Brilling, in: H.C. Meyer (ed.), *Aus Geschichte und Leben der Juden in Westfalen; eine Sammelschrift* (1962), 241ff., esp. 257; B. Brilling (ed.), *Westfalia Judaica*, 1 (1967), 212; F. Lazarus, in: MGWJ, 80 (1936), 106–17; C. Rixen, *Geschichte und Organisation der Juden im ehemaligen Stift Muenster* (1906); H. Schnee, *Die Hoffinanz und der moderne Staat*, 3 (1955), 54ff.; W. Zuhorn, in: *Warendorfer Blaetter fuer Orts-und Heimatskunde*, 13 (1914), nos. 1–3; nos. 5–7. **ADD BIBLIOGRAPHY:** M. Broemmelhaus, "Nach unbekannt verzogen," in: *Die Geschichte der Warendorfer Juden in der Zeit des 3. Reiches* (Quellen und Forschungen zur Geschichte des Kreises Warendorf, vol. 19) (1988).

[Bernhard Brilling]

WARFIELD, DAVID (1866–1951), U.S. actor. His roles ranged from a youthful burlesque, "Solomon Yankel," to a controversial portrayal of Shylock. His Jewish specialty was developed by David *Belasco into the role of Solomon Levi in *The Auctioneer* (1901) which Warfield played for three years, establishing the type of sentimental Jewish hero. Another of his long-playing roles was that of the German musician in *The Music Master*, a play which ran from 1903 to 1907, and again in 1917–18. In 1922 at the height of Warfield's popularity, Belasco produced *The Merchant of Venice*, and Warfield portrayed Shylock as a man crazed by persecution. The adverse criticism which greeted this interpretation was said to have influenced his retirement in 1924. Warfield was a collaborator in a volume of sentimental sketches, *Ghetto Silhouettes* (1902).

[Samuel L. Sumberg]

WARHAFTIG, ZERAH (1906–2002), lawyer and leader of the National Religious Party in Israel. Born in Volkovysk, Belorussia, Warhaftig became active in the Mizrachi movement and at the outbreak of World War II fled to Lithuania and, through Japan, to the United States, where he became deputy director of the Institute for Jewish Affairs of the *World Jewish Congress. In 1947 he settled in Palestine, became a member of the Va'ad Le'ummi, and in 1948 a member of the Provisional State Council, serving as one of the framers of its constitution. He was also a signatory of Israel's Declaration of Independence. In 1948 he set up and directed the Institution of Hebrew Law at the Ministry of Justice. From 1948 to 1963 he was a lecturer of law at the Hebrew University. Warhaftig was repeatedly elected to the Knesset on the Ha-Po'el ha-Mizrachi (later *National Religious Party) list and served in the Israel government as minister of religious affairs from 1960. In 1970, Warhaftig was elected chairman of the *curatorium* of Bar Ilan University. In 1983 he was awarded the Israel Prize for special contribution to law and society.

Warhaftig published articles on religious and political affairs and, while in the United States during World War II, published in English *Starvation over Europe* (1943), *Relief and Rehabilitation* (1944), and, after the war, *Uprooted* (1946). His works in Hebrew are *Ha-Ḥazakah ba-Mishpat ha-Ivri* ("Presumption in Hebrew Law," 1954) and *Al ha-Shipput ha-Rabbani be-Yisrael* ("Rabbinical Judgment in Israel," 1955).

BIBLIOGRAPHY: Tidhar, 4 (1950), 2030.

[Joshua Gutmann]

WARKA, hasidic dynasty in Poland. Its founder, ISAAC (KALISH) OF WARKA (1779–1848), became one of the most noted *ẓaddikim* in central Poland in the first half of the 19th century. Born at Zolochev, after his marriage at the age of 14 he moved to Zarek (Bremberg). He officiated as rabbi in Gowanczow and then in the village of Ruda. His teacher, David of *Lelov (Lelow), would travel with him to the "courts" of *ẓaddikim*, and in this way he became a student in the *bet midrash* of *Jacob Isaac ha-Ḥozeh (the "Seer") of Lublin, and a disciple of *Simḥah Bunem of Przysucha and his son, Abraham Moses. After the early death of the latter in 1829, Isaac settled in *Przysucha, becoming the acknowledged leader of the Ḥasidim there. Some time later he moved to the small town of Warka (Warsaw district), where he gathered many disciples round him, including *ẓaddikim* and *admorim* such as Jacob Aryeh of *Radzymin, Dov Baer (Berish) of Biala, Shraga Feivel of Goerits (Gorzyca), Jehiel of *Aleksandrow, and others. He was also a friend of Menahem Mendel of *Kotsk and Mordecai Joseph of *Izbica Lubelska, and often visited Israel *Ruzhin and Meir of Peremyshlyany.

Isaac of Warka negotiated with influential people on behalf of the Jews to obtain the abrogation of hostile decrees, including the conscription of young Jews for military service (*Cantonists; 1827), and the prohibition forbidding the Jews to wear their traditional dress (1845). To achieve these he attempted to invoke the assistance of Sir Moses *Montefiore and the British government in influencing Czar *Nicholas I. In 1846 Isaac met Sir Moses when the latter passed through Poland.

Because of his activities Isaac was given the appellation "Lover of Israel." A characteristic story relates that Menahem Mendel of Kotsk sought Isaac of Warka in the upper world after the latter's death, and passed through the *heikhalot* (upper halls) until he found him in a field by a river, where he was standing, bent, leaning on his stick and looking at the river – made by the tears of the Jewish people – unable to move from there. Tales concerning him and his novellae on the Torah were collected in *Ohel Yizḥak* (Piotrkow, 1814) by Meir Walden, and in *Huẓẓak Ḥen* (1947), by Noah Weintraub.

Isaac of Warka's son, JACOB DAVID OF AMSHINOV (1814–1878), founded the Amshinov dynasty. Born at Zarek, he was a pupil of Menahem Mendel of Kotsk. After his marriage he lived at Gur (*Gora Kalwaria), and later at Przysucha, becoming in 1849 the leader of a large group of Ḥasidim at Amshinov. Like his father he was active in Jewish affairs. Following enactment of the law prohibiting Jews from growing a beard and sidelocks, he was put in prison with R. Isaac Meir of Gur on the charge of inciting the masses to revolt against the government. However, he succeeded in obtaining revocation of the decree and received a personal certificate of protection from a minister in Warsaw, forbidding anybody to harm him. He died in Italy where he had gone for medical treatment. His son MENAHEM (1860–1918), continued to head the Amshinov dynasty for 40 years.

The second son of Isaac, MENAHEM MENDEL OF WARKA (1819–1868), continued the Warka ḥasidic dynasty. He was known as the "silent *ẓaddik*." In contrast to his brother Jacob David, in his youth he was not very studious. After his father's death he refused to take over the leadership. However, Shraga Feivel of Goerits, who substituted for him, died six months later, and Menahem Mendel then became the leader against his will. He usually secluded himself and conversed and taught little on Torah, mainly speaking briefly and by implication. Most of the time he spent in silence in accordance with the scriptural saying, "To thee silence is praise" (Ps. 65:2). In Menahem Mendel's opinion, one should not speak of the Torah unless one is overflowing with it. The real cry of prayer is worship within the heart, without uttering a sound, and on this point he would preach with quotations from many biblical verses. In his words, man possesses three fine things: an erect bow, a silent shout, and a motionless dance. From what his pupils related it would appear that silence was his mode of speech. Tales describe meetings between him and contemporary *ẓaddikim* where not a word was uttered, all sitting in complete silence. His pupil, Dov Baer of Biala, testified that he sat with the rabbi and all his Ḥasidim around the table in dead silence: "I felt that all my blood vessels were about to burst, so closely did he examine me, but I passed the test and gave replies to all his questions." Menahem Mendel was even gay in his silence, preaching forgetfulness of the cares of the morrow, and was given to strong drink, which in his opinion led to the love of God, and joy.

Menahem Mendel's son, SIMHAH BUNEM (1851–1907), emigrated to Ereẓ Israel in 1887. He was imprisoned by the Turks and expelled after spending some months in Tiberias. He went back to Poland, staying in Otwock, and returned to Ereẓ Israel in 1906. At first he lived in Jerusalem but settled in Tiberias shortly before his death.

BIBLIOGRAPHY: A.Y. Brombeg, *Mi-Gedolei ha-Ḥasidut*, 3 (1952); N. Benari, *Ha-Ẓaddik ha-Shotek* (1965); R. Mahler, *Ha-Ḥasidut ve-ha-Haskalah* (1961), index; J. Shatzky, *Geshikhte fun Yidn in Varshe*, 2 (1948); M. Buber, *Tales of the Ḥasidim*, 2 (1966^3), 290–302; L.I. Newman, *Hasidic Anthology* (1963), index.

[Esther (Zweig) Liebes]

WARNER, family of pioneers of the motion picture industry and founders of Warner Bros. Pictures, Inc. The Warners date their entrance into the industry from 1903, when they rented a vacant store in New Castle, Pennsylvania. There were nine children in this Polish immigrant family, but only four were active in the business: Harry, the eldest (1881–1958), born in Poland; Albert (1883–1967), born in Baltimore; Sam (1884–1927), and Jack, born in London, Ontario (1892–1978). As their enterprise prospered, the brothers opened more theaters. In 1912, they decided to produce films themselves. Sam became technical chief of the studio, Albert handled distribution, Harry was business head, and Jack, the showman, was in charge of production.

In 1917 they scored a coup by filming *My Four Years in Germany*, from the book by U.S. Ambassador James W. Gerard, who had been ordered home from Berlin. It was at that time one of the most significant pictures yet made.

In 1923 they became incorporated as Warner Brothers Pictures, Inc. By 1925 the company was a leader in the silent film business. That year they bought the Vitagraph Company, which owned an invention that synchronized sound with action, called Vitaphone. In 1927 Warner Brothers issued *The Jazz Singer*, thus marking the official debut of talking pictures and revolutionizing the industry.

During the 1930s the Warners acquired the Stanley Company of America, which controlled 250 cinema buildings. This guaranteed them an outlet for all their films. They set the scale for film musicals with the lavish *Gold Diggers* series and films built around "headline" news, such as *G-Men* (1935) and *China Clipper* (1936), and spectacles such as *A Midsummer Night's Dream* (1935) and *The Adventures of Robin Hood* (1938). They also used the screen for presenting social issues such as *The Life of Emile Zola* (1937) and *The Black Legion* (1937), which involved racial and religious bigotry.

In 1951 the company was forced to divest itself of its theaters after the film industry lost a 13-year suit brought by the U.S. Government on anti-trust charges. The Warner studios continued to be one of the leaders in Hollywood through the 1960s. Branching out into television, Warner has produced a wide variety of sitcoms and action series, such as *Maverick*; *Murphy Brown*; and *Lois and Clark*. By 1993 Warner Bros. was ranked as Hollywood's largest supplier of television programs. In 1995 Warner and the Tribune Company launched the WB television network, targeting the teenage viewing audience with such weekly series as *Buffy the Vampire Slayer* and *Dawson's Creek*. In the late 1990s Warner obtained the rights to the immensely popular *Harry Potter* novels and released four film adaptations between 2001 and 2005.

Acquisitions held by Warner include the television cartoons of Hanna-Barbera Productions; the TV and film holdings of Lorimar; and rights to the majority of the film library of Castle Rock Productions.

BIBLIOGRAPHY: A.W. Pearce, *The Future Out of the Past: An Illustrated History of the Warner Brothers Company* (1964); J.L. Warner, *My First Hundred Years in Hollywood* (1965). **ADD. BIBLIOGRAPHY:** C. Higham, *Warner Brothers: A History of the Studio* (1975); J. Silke, *Here's Looking at You, Kid: 50 Years of Fighting, Working, and Dreaming at Warner Brothers* (1976); C. Hirschorn, *The Warner Bros. Story* (1982); R. Behlmer, *Inside Warner Bros.* (1987).

[Stewart Kampel / Ruth Beloff (2nd ed.)]

WAR OF INDEPENDENCE (Heb. מִלְחֶמֶת הָעַצְמָאוּת *Milḥemet ha-Aẓma'ut*, or מִלְחֶמֶת הַקּוֹמְמִיּוּת *Milḥemet ha-Komemiyyut*, or מִלְחֶמֶת הַשִּׁחְרוּר *Milḥemet ha-Shiḥrur* (the War of Liberation)), war waged by the Jews of Palestine for survival, freedom, and political independence against the Arabs, mainly from the neighboring countries, between the end of November 1947 and July 1949.

The war was divided into two distinct phases: the first began on Nov. 30, 1947, the day after the UN General Assembly adopted its resolution on the partition of Palestine, and ended on May 15, 1948, when the British forces and administration were withdrawn from the country; the second started on the day after the British evacuation and came to an end on July 20, 1949, when the last of the armistice agreements was signed (with Syria). In the first phase, the *yishuv* and its defense forces, organized in the *Haganah, were under attack by Palestinian Arabs, aided by irregular volunteers from Arab countries. In the second phase, the army of newly independent Israel – officially established on May 28 as the Israel Defense Forces (see *Israel, State of: Defense Forces) – fought primarily against regular troops from Egypt, Iraq, Transjordan, Syria, and Lebanon, who were supported by volunteer detachments from Saudi Arabia, Libya, and the Yemen. In both phases, the avowed purpose of the Arabs was to frustrate the UN partition resolution and prevent the establishment and consolidation of the Jewish state.

THE FIRST PHASE: NOVEMBER 30, 1947–MAY 14, 1948

The Jewish Forces

At the beginning of the first phase, Arab attacks were carried out by loosely organized bands led by representatives of the Palestine Arab political organizations. As early as October 1947, however, the *Arab League had instructed its member states to train volunteers and collect money and arms for the Palestine Arabs. The first Arab onslaughts were resisted by the mobilized units and active reserves of the Haganah, which consisted, in addition to headquarters, service units, and a small ordnance industry, of four battalions of *Palmaḥ, consisting of 2,100 men and women and 1,000 reserves (in October); Ḥish (Ḥeil Sadeh – field force or infantry), with 1,800 on active service and 10,000 reserves; and Ḥim (Ḥeil Mishmar – guard or garrison force), with 32,000 registered members, responsible for static defense. The Ḥish was organized mainly in area commands named after the region (e.g., Givati, Golani, Carmeli), which later developed into brigades. There were also the *Gadna, trained in auxiliary functions, who would later fill the ranks of the Palmaḥ and the Ḥish. On the eve of the war, the Haganah had in its secret arsenals over 15,000 rifles of various makes, a small quantity of light machine guns, and a few dozen medium machine guns and 3-inch mortars, as well as hand grenades, explosives, and Sten submachine guns manufactured in its clandestine workshops. There were also two other armed underground organizations that operated independently during the first phase: the IẒL (*Irgun Ẓeva'i Le'ummi), with 5,000 members at the beginning of the war, and Leḥi (*Loḥamei Ḥerut Israel), with 1,000 members.

Repelling the Arab Offensive: November 29, 1947–March 1948

From the start, the nature of the Arab offensives was determined by a number of factors: the existence of a considerable number of Jewish settlements in predominantly Arab areas, the mixed Arab-Jewish population of several cities, and Arab control of most of the hill region and of the major road arteries. The first attack took place on Nov. 30, 1947, when a Jewish bus was ambushed near Lydda. The next day, the Arab Higher Committee declared a general strike, and on December 2 an Arab mob attacked and destroyed the commercial center in Jerusalem. There was also Arab firing in Haifa and on the border between Tel Aviv and Jaffa. After Arab attacks, on December 10, on Jewish vehicles in the Negev and on the Jerusalem–Kefar Eẓyon road, Haganah and IẒL forces started to hit back at concentrations of Arab bands. During December, Arab- and Jewish-controlled areas were gradually demarcated; in the mixed cities, areas between Jewish and Arab residential quarters were evacuated and contested. In the battle for the roads, which was gaining in intensity, the Arabs had the upper hand, largely as a result of the attitude of the British forces, which were neutral in theory and pro-Arab in fact. For political reasons, 33 Jewish settlements, which according to the partition resolution were to be included in the Arab state, were not evacuated.

On January 10, a 900-man force of the Arab Liberation Army, commanded by Fawzī al-Qāwuqjī and trained on the other side of the border, attacked Kefar Szold and was repulsed. The following days were marked by attacks on isolated Jewish settlements in the Jerusalem and Hebron hills, Upper Galilee, and the Negev. A platoon of 35 men, on its way to reinforce the isolated Eẓyon bloc of settlements (Kefar Eẓyon, Massu'ot Yiẓḥak, Ein Ẓurim, and Revadim) was wiped out in a fierce engagement near Beit Nattīf. There were continual attacks against Jewish population centers and Jewish workers in enterprises employing both Arab and Jewish labor. Explosive charges were set off in Jewish areas of Haifa and Jerusalem; in the capital, the targets were the offices of *The Palestine Post* (February 1), Ben-Yehuda Street, one of the principal shopping thoroughfares (February 22), and *Jewish

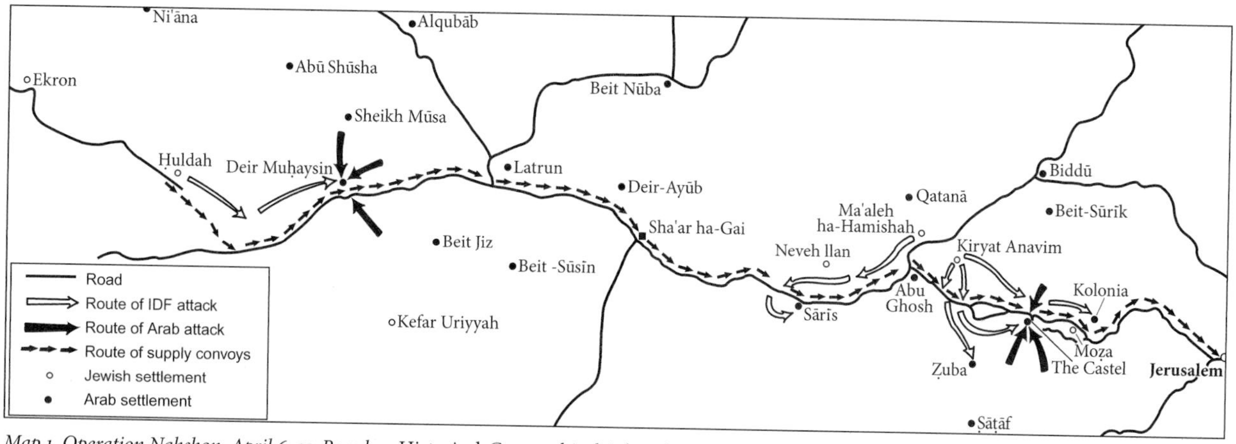

Map 1. Operation Naḥshon, April 6–15. Based on Historical-Geographical Atlas of Ereẓ Israel.

Agency headquarters (March 11). The outlying Jewish quarters in the southeastern part of Jerusalem were cut off from the center. On most of the roads, Jewish communications were maintained by means of armored vehicles and convoys, which left at odd hours, usually at night, and used circuitous routes. In March, Jewish traffic to several quarters of Jerusalem and on some of the country's principal roads came to an almost complete standstill.

On February 16, the Arab Liberation Army attacked Tirat Ẓevi and was forced to withdraw with heavy losses. In March, having failed to capture Jewish settlements, the Arab forces concentrated on the battle for the roads, while continuing their attacks on outlying districts in the mixed towns and on settlements in the north, the Jerusalem mountains, and the Negev. Nevertheless, a convoy of armored trucks succeeded in making the trip from Negbah to Gat, which had been cut off for a long period, and an Arab arms convoy was ambushed and destroyed near Kiryat Motzkin. In general, the Arabs scored considerable success in the battle for the roads: on March 26 Jewish traffic on the coastal road leading to the Negev came to a complete stop; a convoy on its way back to Jerusalem from the Eẓyon bloc was trapped near al-Nabī Dāniyāl and another, which tried to reach Yeḥi'am, was ambushed and wiped out.

Throughout this period, however, the Jewish defense forces made substantial progress in organization and training. By the end of March, 21,000 men aged 17–25 were under arms. The manufacture of antitank projectors, submachine guns, and explosives was greatly stepped up, and large quantities of light arms, purchased in Czechoslovakia, were expected to arrive. The *yishuv*'s air force consisted of 30 light planes for reconnaissance, transportation, and supply to isolated areas. The Arab forces – both the locally organized National Guard and the volunteers from the Arab states – were also growing.

Jewish Forces Take the Initiative: April 1948–May 15, 1948
The hour of military decision was fast approaching. The impending British evacuation made action imperative in order to gain control of the area allotted to the Jewish state and to improve the Jewish position in the face of the expected Arab invasion, while the growth of its strength made it possible for the Haganah to take the initiative. A comprehensive operational plan ("Plan D") had been adopted for execution in stages, depending upon the rate of British withdrawal and developments on the various fronts. The first objective was to open the road to Jerusalem. For this purpose Operation Naḥshon was planned; a force of 1,500 men was mobilized and equipped, in part with Czech arms which had been secretly landed on April 1. Two preparatory actions were carried out: the blowing up of the headquarters of Hasan Salāma, the Arab area commander, near Sarafand, and the capture of Qasṭal (Castel), an Arab village dominating the approaches to Jerusalem. Operation Naḥshon began on April 6, Haganah forces taking the Arab village of Ḥuldah, the Wadi al-Ṣarrār Camp, and Deir Muḥaysin (Beko'a). They encountered fierce opposition, especially on the Qasṭal hill, which changed hands several times until April 10, when the Arabs finally withdrew; on the previous day, the commander of the Arab forces in the Jerusalem area, ʿAbd al-Qādir al-Husseini, was killed in battle. By April 15, when Naḥshon came to an end, three large convoys carrying food and arms had reached Jerusalem.

Meanwhile the Arab Liberation Army, still under Qāwuqjī's command, had made another attempt to capture a Jewish settlement. On April 4 it had shelled Mishmar ha-Emek, following up with an infantry attack, which was beaten back. A second attack, next day, was halted by the intervention of British troops, and a cease-fire was proclaimed, during which the women and children were evacuated. At the end of the cease-fire, Haganah forces counterattacked, capturing several strongholds southeast of the village on April 12 and routing an Arab force which was trying to renew the attack. Qāwuqjī appealed for help to the commander of a battalion of Druze mercenaries encamped at Shfāʾ ʿAmr (Shefaram). This force attacked two strongholds east of Ramat Yoḥanan between April 12 and 14, but was repulsed with heavy losses and took no further part in the war. Qāwuqjī was now in danger of being cut off from his base, and he decided to withdraw to Jenin. The artillery at his disposal was transferred to Jeru-

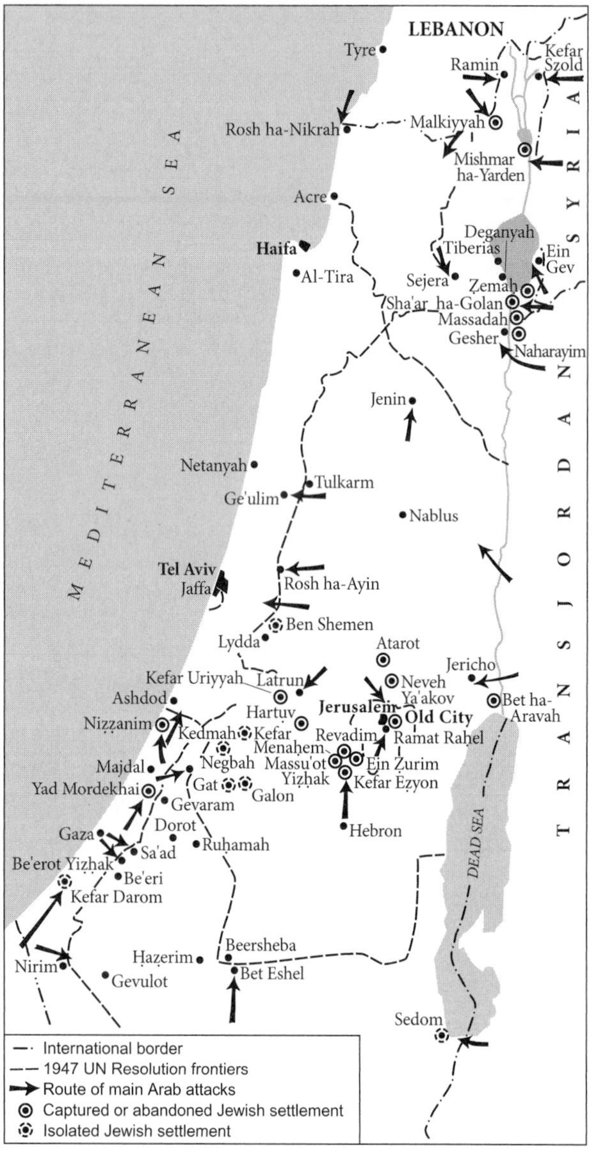

Map 2. From the invasion to the first truce, May 15–June 11, 1948. Ibid.

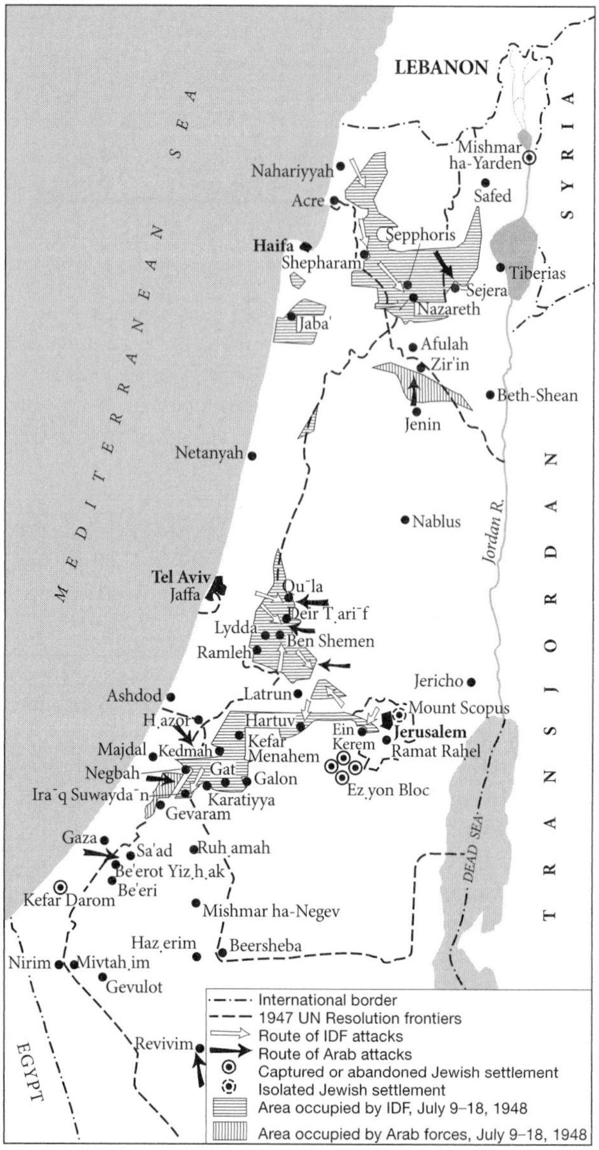

Map 3. The "Ten Days," July 9–18, 1948. Ibid.

salem and at the beginning of May began shelling the Jewish quarters of the city.

The success of Naḥshon and the defeats inflicted on the Arabs at Mishmar ha-Emek and Ramat Yoḥanan encouraged the Haganah to continue the implementation of Plan D. On April 18, troops of the Golani area command (later the Golani Brigade) and the Palmaḥ cut in two the Arab part of Tiberias, where the Jewish quarter was under heavy attack. The Arabs decided to leave the town and were evacuated with British aid. On April 21, when the British started to concentrate their remaining forces in the Haifa port area, the battle for Haifa began. The Jewish forces captured it within 24 hours and most of the Arab inhabitants left, despite Jewish assurances that no harm would befall them if they stayed.

The capture of Tiberias and the opening of roads leading to eastern Galilee made it possible to reinforce the Haganah troops in "the finger of Galilee" at the northern tip of the country. On April 14, a Palmaḥ unit infiltrated into Safed, bolstering the defenses of the besieged Jewish quarter. As part of Operation Yiftaḥ – designed to win Upper Galilee and gain control of its major arteries – Haganah forces occupied the Rosh Pinnah police fortress and a neighboring army camp as soon as these were evacuated by the British (April 28). Two attempts were made to capture al-Nabī Yūshaʿ, the fort on a ridge dominating the Ḥuleh Valley, which had been handed over to the Arabs by the British, but failed, with the loss of 28 Haganah men. On May 1 the Arabs launched an attack on the beleaguered village of Ramat Naftali, with the support of Lebanese army artillery and armored cars. With the help of a few Piper Cub airplanes, the settlers managed to hold out, and Operation Yiftaḥ could proceed according to plan. On May 3, a second Palmaḥ battalion entered Safed, but the first Jewish

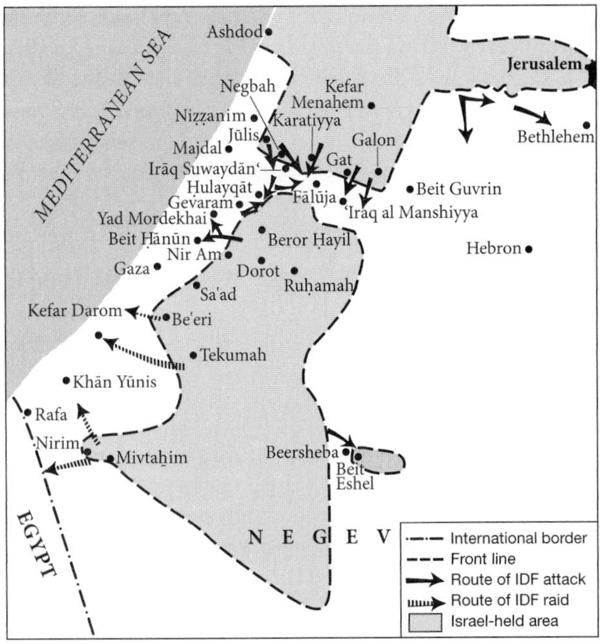

Map 4. Operation Yo'av, Oct. 15–22, 1948. Ibid.

attack, on May 6, ended in failure; the Arabs brought in reinforcements and began using artillery. A new attack, on May 10, resulted in the capture of the key positions in the town. The Safed Arabs, numbering some 10,000, fled en masse, followed by the Arab villagers of the Ḥuleh Valley, and on the eve of the Arab states' invasion the Jewish forces were in control of a continuous area in eastern and upper Galilee.

Further south, Golani troops occupied the Arab town of Samakh (Ẓemaḥ) and the police fortresses at Samakh and Gesher as soon as the British had withdrawn from them

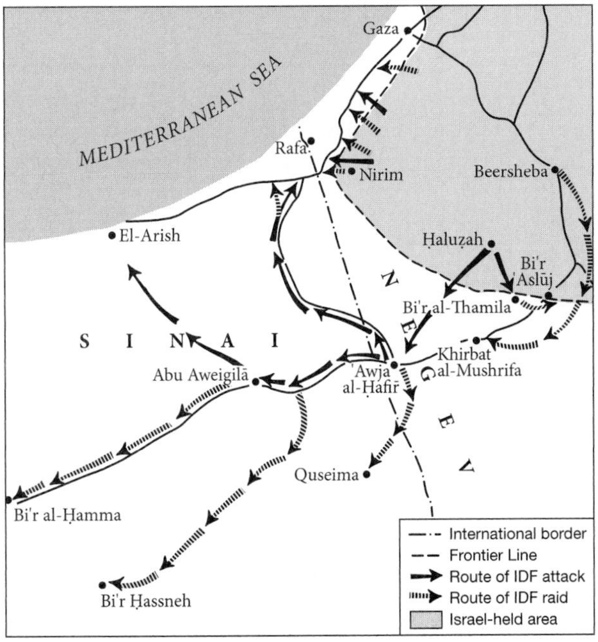

Map 5. Operation Ḥorev, Dec. 22, 1948–Jan 7, 1949. Ibid.

(April 29). Arab Legion troops, supported by artillery and armored cars, attacked Gesher but were beaten back. Beisan (Beth-Shean) fell to the Haganah on May 12; so did a number of villages in the Mount Tabor area, Arab Shajara, Bethlehem (in Galilee), the erstwhile German colony of Waldheim, and Umm al-Zīnat in the southern Carmel. In Operation Ben-Ami, troops of the Carmeli area command captured the strongholds dominating Acre, A-Ziv (Akhziv), and Basah (Beẓet), and reestablished overland connection with Yeḥi'am and the Ḥanitah group of settlements. (Acre itself was taken on May 17.)

In the Tel Aviv area, the Alexandroni, Kiryati, and Givati brigades launched Operation Ḥamez on the eve of Passover and occupied several Arab villages, including Hiriya, Sakiya,

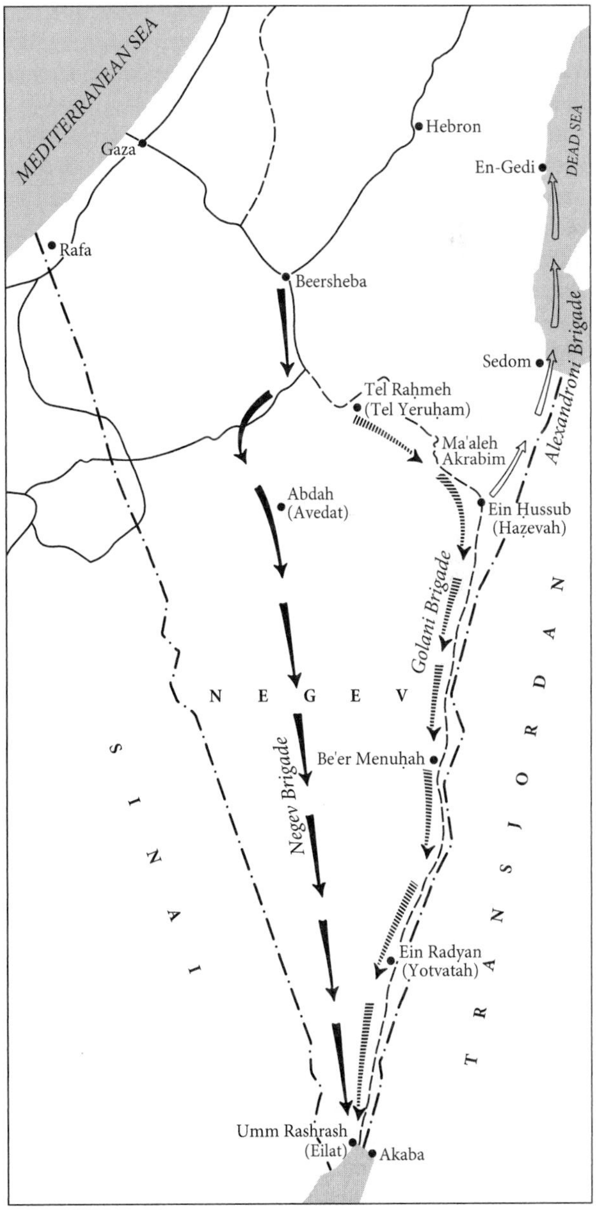

Map 6. Operation Uvdah, March 3–10, 1949. Ibid.

Salame, and Yazur, and encircled Jaffa, which had been included in the area of the Arab state envisioned in the partition resolution. Meanwhile, I.Ẓ.L. forces attacked Manshiye and other northern quarters of Jaffa, but met with heavy resistance, and British forces intervened. The attack was renewed on April 26 and Manshiye was cut off. The encirclement of Jaffa was completed on April 29, and most of its 70,000 Arab inhabitants fled. Its final surrender came on May 13, when the British troops had left.

On April 9, a combined IẒL and Leḥi force attacked Deir Yassin, an Arab village on the outskirts of Jerusalem. Two hundred Arabs, including women and children caught up in the fighting, were killed. The heavy casualties were given wide publicity in the Arab world as a deliberate massacre and intensified the panic among the Arab population, which was one of the causes of their flight. On April 13, a convoy to the Hadassah Hospital on Mt. Scopus was attacked by Arabs and 77 people – mainly doctors and other medical personnel – were massacred. British troops stationed nearby made no attempt to interfere with the slaughter. In view of rumors that the British intended to advance the date of their evacuation of Jerusalem, the Harel Brigade of the Palmaḥ was transferred to the capital. As soon as the brigade convoy had passed through, the Arab Liberation Army seized the strongpoints dominating the road to Jerusalem, and once again the city was cut off. Although the rumors of an earlier British withdrawal proved false, it was decided to launch Operation Yevusi to reestablish the links with the isolated quarters and nearby settlements: Neveh Ya'akov, Atarot, and Mount Scopus in the north, and Mekor Ḥayyim, Ramat Raḥel and Talpiyyot in the south. An attack on Nebi Samwil, on April 22, ended in failure, and while Harel troops succeeded in taking the Sheikh Jarraḥ quarter of Jerusalem on April 26, British troops forced their withdrawal. Two days later, an attempt was made to capture the Augusta Victoria buildings on the Mount of Olives and thereby gain control of the road to Jericho, but this, too, was unsuccessful. An attack on the St. Simon Convent in the Katamon quarter, launched on April 29, was successful, however. Both sides had reached the point of exhaustion when Haganah reinforcements were sent in and decided the issue. The resulting capture of Katamon made it possible to reinforce the isolated Mekor Ḥayyim quarter. Another attempt to open the road to Jerusalem, Operation Makkabbi, also failed: although the Harel Brigade took the village of Beit Maḥsir and Givati captured the *Latrun detention camp, only a few dozen trucks got through to Jerusalem before the road was once more blocked.

On May 4 the Arabs attacked the Eẓyon bloc with the support of an Arab Legion armored unit and four British tanks. The attack was beaten off, but the defenders suffered heavy losses, which were irreplaceable owing to the complete isolation of the four villages. On the eve of May 12 the Arab forces succeeded in cutting the block in two; the following day they captured a strongpoint dominating the area between Kefar Eẓyon and Massu'ot Yiẓḥak, and Arab Legion armored cars penetrated into Kefar Eẓyon. After the defenders had surrendered, many were massacred by Arab villagers from the Hebron area, and on May 14 the survivors were taken captive by the Arab Legion. On May 14, when the last British troops left Jerusalem, forces of Eẓyoni, the capital's infantry brigade, launched Operation Kilshon ("Pitchfork") to seize the areas evacuated by the British and prevent their being taken over by the Arabs.

In the six weeks preceding the establishment of the State of Israel and the invasion by regular Arab armies, the Jewish forces had taken over Haifa, Jaffa, Safed, and Tiberias, encircled Acre, and captured about 100 Arab villages. Apart from the Latrun sector of the Jerusalem road, the Jewish armed forces could move freely on most of the major arteries of communication. The Palestine Arab forces had been routed, and the Arab Liberation Army had suffered heavy defeats in the north and in the Jerusalem Corridor. The Jews had lost several hundred men, but they now had 30,000 young men under arms, ready to meet the invaders. The arrival of the first boatload of Czech arms and the acquisition of antitank and antiaircraft guns had considerably improved the quantity and quality of the arms at their disposal, but they still lacked field artillery and fighter planes.

[Netanel Lorch]

THE SECOND PHASE: MAY 15, 1948–JULY 20, 1949

The Arab Armies Invade

On May 15, 1948, the day the British Mandate over Palestine ended, the regular armies of five neighboring Arab states invaded the new State of Israel, which had proclaimed its independence the previous afternoon. The invasion, heralded by an Egyptian air attack on Tel Aviv, was vigorously resisted. From the north, east, and south came the armies of Lebanon, Syria, Iraq, Transjordan, and Egypt. (Saudi Arabia sent a formation that fought under Egyptian command; Yemen considered itself at war with Israel but sent no contingent.)

The Jews found themselves in a precarious situation. The invading forces were fully equipped with the standard weapons of a regular army of the time – artillery, tanks, armored cars and personnel carriers, in addition to machine guns, mortars and the usual small arms in great quantities, and full supplies of ammunition, oil, and gasoline. Egypt, Iraq, and Syria had air forces. As sovereign states, they had no difficulty (contrary to the pre-state Jewish defense force) in securing whatever armaments they needed through normal channels from Britain and other friendly powers.

The Jews had no matching artillery, no tanks, and no warplanes in the first days of the war. Some supplies of these weapons arrived in the days that followed, however, and turned the tide. Little more than small arms – and not enough of those to go round – a few homemade, primitive armored cars, and some light training planes were all that had been available to the *Haganah, the underground defense force controlled by the responsible Jewish authorities during the British Mandate. However, it could now emerge aboveground as the army of the sovereign State of Israel, though the constitutional formalities establishing the army were completed only on May 28 with the publication by the Provisional Government of the Israel Defense Forces (IDF) Establishment Order. Haganah's general staff and commanders continued their functions in the IDF, with the difference that their identities were now no longer secret. The two dissident organizations, Irgun Ẓeva'i Le'ummi (IẒL) and Loḥamei Ḥerut Israel (Leḥi), agreed to discontinue their independent activities, except in Jerusalem, and to the absorption of their members into the IDF. Their units in Jerusalem were disbanded in September, following an ultimatum by the IDF.

Invaded from all directions, Israel had suddenly to cope, as it were, with the outbreak of a thousand fires, and to do so with limited means. Numerous settlement outposts in Galilee and the Negev were isolated, open on all sides to Arab attack, and had to rely on their own tenacity and meager armories to stave off defeat. The hastily mobilized army had to engage in offensive action to dislodge the enemy from key positions, block the advance of their columns, and rush to seal gaps in Israel's defenses.

Until the First Truce: May 15–June 11, 1948

THE EGYPTIAN ADVANCE. In the south, Egyptian forces jumped off from their advance bases in Sinai and crossed the frontier. Passing through Arab-populated territory, one formation moved up the coastal road to Gaza; another was landed by ship at Majdal further north; a third drove up from Abu Aweigila northeast to Beersheba, some of its units pressing on later to the Arab towns of Hebron and Bethlehem, where they linked up with Transjordan's Arab Legion and took up positions just south of Jerusalem. The major enemy forces were those at Gaza and Majdal, and their main thrust was aimed at Tel Aviv, though they could also penetrate from Majdal to other vital sectors in the interior of the country. To stop them, Israel deployed the Negev Brigade, operating south of the Majdal–Bet Guvrin line, and part of the Givati Brigade deployed north of it. There were also some 27 settlements scattered in the area, 22 of which had less than 30 defenders. Five of these kibbutzim lay alongside what was later known as the Gaza Strip. The Egyptians decided to wipe them out before proceeding to Tel Aviv, to protect their rear and flanks. Their first target was Kefar Darom (see *Benei Darom), a religious kibbutz 7 mi. (11 km.) south of Gaza, which had already withstood attacks by units of the extremist Egyptian movement, the Muslim Brothers, in the pre-state fighting. In an assault only a few days earlier, the Orthodox Jewish defenders had filled the small bags that held their *tefillin* with TNT and flung them at their assailants, after they had exhausted their stock of hand grenades. On the morning of May 15, eight Egyptian tanks approached the kibbutz, their guns blazing, followed by infantry. Having no artillery, the 30 defenders had no other course but to wait until the enemy came within range of their small arms, and then they opened fire. One Piat antitank weapon that had been rushed to the kibbutz during the night was quickly put in to action, and direct hits were scored on the enemy lead tanks. The remaining tanks thereupon turned around in retreat, exposing the infantry to fire from the kibbutz. Enemy armored vehicles returned later, but only to cover the retreat of the infantry. As a parting gesture, they mortared and shelled the kibbutz but made no further attempt to take it, contenting themselves with occupying positions covering its perimeter.

While Kefar Darom was under attack, another formidable Egyptian column attacked kibbutz Nirim, with its 40 defenders, further to the south. Nirim lost more than half its men in killed and wounded, but repulsed the enemy. Next day the Egyptians returned to their attack, accompanied by air bombardment. They were again driven back. Thereafter they did not attempt a ground assault, but kept the settlement isolated and subjected it to periodic shelling and air bombardment. The pattern at Kefar Darom and Nirim was to be typical of all but a few of the encounters between the enemy and kibbutzim on all fronts throughout the country.

There was, however, one kibbutz which the Egyptians considered it vital to liquidate if they were to proceed with their drive on Tel Aviv. This was Yad Mordekhai, close to the coastal highway between Gaza and Majdal and blocking the linkup of these two Egyptian bases. After their bitter experience, the Egyptians prepared the attack more carefully and assigned larger forces – two infantry battalions, one armored battalion, and one artillery regiment. Nevertheless, it took them five days of hard fighting to overcome the defenders, who numbered, together with reinforcements from the Negev Brigade, no more than one infantry company. Shortly before dawn on May 24, their plight desperate, with many killed and wounded, ammunition spent, and their last machine gun out of action, the defenders abandoned the settlement, creeping through the enemy lines under cover of darkness and carrying their wounded with them. Although Yad Mordekhai fell, the five days of resistance proved crucial. It held up the main Egyptian advance, and in that time the IDF was able to strengthen the defenses nearer to Tel Aviv, dispatch reinforcements to the south, and acquire heavier weapons and some fighter planes, which were to play a key role in the major confrontation.

The major phase of this confrontation began on May 29, when the Egyptian forces had regrouped after the Yad Mordekhai battle and a column of brigade strength, numbering some 500 vehicles, moved north from Majdal, passed Ashdod, and halted at the Ashdod bridge 2 mi. (3 km.) to the north. The IDF units in this area were from the Givati Brigade, and their sappers had blown up the bridge the night before. With the column held up, the IDF GHQ sent the first four Messerschmidt fighter planes, which had just arrived and been hastily made ready for action, to attack it. It was the first time the enemy had seen Israeli fighter planes, and this new factor made the column vulnerable. The Egyptians accordingly proceeded to dig in. Now they were subjected to another weapon that they had not encountered from Israel before – some 65 mm. artillery which had just been landed and rushed into action. These guns shelled the column, while other Givati units harassed it continuously. The destroyed Ashdod bridge, only some 20 mi. (32 km.) from Tel Aviv, was to prove the northernmost limit of the Egyptian advance throughout the war. Though halted and harassed, the Egyptian brigade had not lost its fighting capacity, and during the next few days it sought out targets in the vicinity. Attacks on the kibbutz of *Negbah failed. The attack on kibbutz *Niẓẓanim, launched on June 7, succeeded, however. Givati also had its gains and failures in attacks and counterattacks.

By now, after feverish efforts at the United Nations, it was evident that a truce would soon be called. Each side tried desperately to improve its positions before the cease-fire. The most important Israeli failure was the unsuccessful attempt to take the ʿIrāq Suwaydān police fort and breach the east-west line from Majdal through Suwaydān to Fālūja. This meant that the Negev was cut off from land communication with the north. On June 11, the first truce went into effect. It lasted a month.

THE FIGHT FOR JERUSALEM. Jerusalem and the corridor to the west were the scenes of continuous bitter fighting throughout the four weeks that ended with the June truce. The Israelis suffered heavy losses and several serious setbacks, the most important of which were the loss of the Jewish Quarter of the Old City and the failure to take Latrun at the western end of the corridor. But they emerged with West Jerusalem intact and in possession of a tenuous link with the coast. The Arabs had several military successes, but they failed in their major objective – the conquest of West Jerusalem (the New City), with its 100,000 Jews, whose citizens were holding out on starvation food rations and the troops on "starvation rations" of ammunition. They now had to cope not only with hunger, but with a military onslaught from all directions and with the constant shelling of their homes by Arab Legion 25-pounders and Egyptian heavy artillery and mortars from positions near Bethlehem. As the British departed and the Arab Legion came in, the Eẓyoni Brigade succeeded, in "Operation Pitchfork," in consolidating all the Jewish areas in the New City and beating off all penetration attempts by the enemy. But the perimeter of these areas was now the front line. The main Jewish outpost in the south, the Eẓyon Bloc, had fallen on May 14. On that night and the next, the two northern settlements in the heart of the Arab hills, *Atarot and Neveh Ya'akov, were evacuated. On May 21, there was a powerful attack by units of the Arab Legion and the Egyptian Muslim Brothers on *Ramat Raḥel at the southern edge of Jerusalem, which changed hands three times in the next four days, being captured during the day and recaptured at night. On the 25th, the defenders, assisted by a unit from the Harel Brigade, fought a daylong battle and routed their assailants. Successive Arab Legion attempts to break into the New City were all repelled, often in hand-to-hand fighting, while armored cars were knocked out at close range with Molotov cocktails.

In the most desperate position was the Jewish Quarter of the Old City, close to the *Western Wall, whose strategic situation was far outweighed by its deep meaning for Jewry. The Jews living there, mostly elderly folk engaged in religious study, with their families, were completely surrounded by Old City Arabs and Arab Legion forces. The Jews had been strengthened during the previous months by some 80 members of the Haganah, some of whom had been there for months, and others who had fought their way through the walled city to help organize the defenses. There were also some IẒL personnel. On May 16 the Arab Legion attacked from all directions, and although the Jews resisted with homemade incendiary bombs, hand grenades, submachine guns, and a meager quantity of explosives, they were steadily pressed back from house to house, as each was destroyed by the powerfully armed Legion. On May 19 a Harel unit managed to blast the Zion Gate and reach the Jewish Quarter; but it withdrew the following day. Legion pressure mounted, but renewed attempts to reinforce the beleaguered defenders failed. On May 28 the Jewish Quarter surrendered.

To break the siege of Jerusalem, it was essential to capture Latrun, astride the highway from the coast. The Israel GHQ set up a special brigade, the 7th, for this task. It was composed of one hastily assembled armored battalion, with half-tracks that had just reached Israel's shores; one infantry battalion with men drawn from existing formations; and one battalion made up of new immigrants who had also just arrived in the country and who had received some training with dummy weapons in the displaced persons' camps in Europe and the immigrant camps in Cyprus.

The 7th Brigade was thrown into action immediately, without time to organize and train together. At the last minute, a veteran battalion of the Alexandroni Brigade was included. A two-battalion attack was launched on May 25, Alexandroni making a frontal assault on the Latrun police fort and village, with the battalion of new immigrants assigned to secure its right flank. The assault should have started in darkness, but there was a delay and it was past dawn when they approached the fortified Arab Legion positions. The element of surprise was lost, and the assault came under such fierce fire that they were forced to retire with heavy casualties. The brigade tried again on May 30, the Alexandroni battalion being replaced by a battalion from Givati. The armored battalion made the main assault this time, fighting its way right up to the police fort, and even succeeding in breaking into the courtyard. But the battalion sappers, who were to breach the wall of the fort, were hit by Legion shells, and the untrained infantry units failed to reach them. The battalion retired. The third attempt to capture Latrun was made on the nights of June 9 and 10, the Yiftaḥ Brigade of the Palmaḥ, which had been operating in Galilee, replacing the 7th Brigade, and a Harel battalion also taking part. This attack also failed, and it was about to be resumed when the cease-fire took effect at 10:00 on June 11.

In the meantime, however, an alternative link between Jerusalem and the coast had been discovered and rendered serviceable. This was a rough dirt track, broken by a steep wadi, on which hundreds of elderly men worked night after night to make it fit for vehicles. They dubbed it the "Burma Road." With the truce, Jerusalem was joined to the coastal plain, its siege days over.

IN THE COASTAL STRIP. In the central sector, the narrow coastal strip in the Sharon was gravely threatened by the tough-fighting Palestinian Arabs in the Samarian bulge, stiffened by the surviving irregulars of the Arab Liberation Army under Fawzī al-Qāwuqjī. Their chief centers were the towns of Nablus, Jenin, and Tulkarm, the point of a dagger thrusting at nearby Netanyah on the coast. On May 24 one Iraqi armored brigade and two infantry brigades occupied this "triangle" and prepared for offensive operations. The Iraqi forces had started crossing the Jordan on May 15 and were active in the southern part of the Jordan Valley, south of the Syrian invaders. But they had suffered two severe setbacks, being repulsed at kibbutz *Gesher and by a Haganah unit at *Belvoir. When the Arab Legion moved its main forces in the "triangle" to the Latrun and Jerusalem sectors, the Iraqis moved in. Defense of the Sharon was in the hands of the Alexandroni Brigade.

On May 25, the Iraqis tried to cut through to Netanyah, capturing one kibbutz and attacking three others near Tulkarm. The captured kibbutz was retaken by Alexandroni and the Iraqi drive was temporarily stopped. But it was evident that the only way for the Israel forces to prevent an all-out assault toward the coast by so powerful an enemy force was to keep it on the defensive. On May 29, the Golani Brigade penetrated the "triangle" from the north, taking several villages plus the strongholds of *Megiddo and al-Lajjūn, which offered a good base for an attack on Jenin. This was undertaken on the nights of May 31 and June 1 by one battalion from Golani and two battalions of the Carmeli Brigade, which had been operating in western Galilee. Golani captured all enemy positions in the valley leading to Jenin, and on the following night the Carmeli formations seized the two key hills southeast and southwest of the town, holding them against fierce counterattacks throughout the next day. Then the men of Golani entered and took the town. The Iraqis rushed up more reinforcements, and the fighting was heavy. But the Israel troops held firm. Since the IDF could spare no forces for an operation to take the whole of the Arab bulge, it decided on an orderly withdrawal from Jenin. This was carried out on June 4, with the Israeli units taking up defensive positions on the southern slopes of Mt. Gilboa. Shortly thereafter, an Alexandroni unit captured the key village of Qāqūn just north of Tulkarm. The only Iraqi gain before a truce was the seizure of the headwaters of the Yarkon river and the pumping station at *Rosh ha-Ayin (Raʾs al-ʿAyn).

THE SYRIAN ATTACK REPULSED. In the north, the Syrians crossed into Israel just south of Lake Kinneret and spearheaded their invasion on the night of May 15 with a crack infantry brigade, a battalion of armored cars, one of artillery, and a company of tanks. Facing them in the Jordan Valley were a cluster of kibbutzim, whose members were a kind of Haganah garrison force and a Haganah battalion for offensive action drawn from the Golani Brigade. The Syrian aim was to rout the kibbutzim, cross the Jordan, and then make a lightning dash westward through mostly Arab-held territory of Lower Galilee to Haifa. The first Syrian targets were Ẓemaḥ, at the southern tip of Lake Kinneret, and *Shaʾar ha-Golan, and *Massadah (not to be confused with Masada on the Dead Sea), the two easternmost kibbutzim in the area. Though they suffered heavy losses, the Jewish defenders held all three positions. On the 18th the enemy again assaulted Ẓemaḥ in full force. It fell after stubborn fighting; Shaʾar ha-Golan and Massadah had been evacuated shortly before. The front line now shifted to *Deganyah, the very first kibbutz to have been established (in 1909). The attack on Deganyah was launched early on May 20 by a Syrian infantry company, five tanks, and numerous armored cars, after the kibbutz had been heavily shelled. They managed to reach the outer perimeter and came steadily on. Then one tank was knocked out. A second, which had got right through to the kibbutz, was halted by a Molotov cocktail (the remains of the tank are still there), and a third was disabled by a three-inch mortar. Armored cars that reached the trenches were put out of action by Piats and Molotov cocktails. The infantry was dealt with by small-arms fire. At noon two old pieces of artillery, which had just arrived in the country, were rushed to Deganyah and put into action against Syrian concentrations of armor and support units. This probably tipped the balance, for the Syrians then retired, also evacuating Ẓemaḥ and taking up positions in the hills to the east.

Apart from minor clashes, the Syrians made no further attacks in this sector, and their aim of a lightning drive to Haifa was abandoned.

Instead, they sought to make local territorial gains and use their powerful force to nip off the northeastern tip of Upper Galilee. While they were regrouping, a huge supply base was blown up by a Haganah sabotage squad, and the Syrian assault was postponed. It came, however, on June 6, directed against *Mishmar ha-Yarden, north of Lake Kinneret, and was accompanied by heavy shelling and air bombardment of the kibbutzim in the area. The attack was repelled with heavy losses on both sides; but a renewed attack on June 10 was successful, so that the truce found the Syrians with a foothold on the Israel side of the Jordan. On the same day, *Ein Gev, the only Jewish kibbutz on the eastern shore of Lake Kinneret at the time, fought off a heavy enemy attack, and did so again when it was attacked the next day despite the truce. The cease-fire became effective in this sector only on June 12.

THE LEBANESE ASSAULT. The invasion route chosen by the Lebanese army was through Malkiyyah, just west of the powerful, Arab-held police fort of Nabī Yūshaʿ, on the ridge dominating the Ḥuleh Valley. Jewish defense in this sector was the responsibility of the Yiftaḥ Brigade of the Palmaḥ, which had effected the remarkable capture of *Safed a few days earlier. On the night of May 14/15, a Yiftaḥ battalion cut across the mountains on foot toward the Lebanese border, skirted the Nabī Yūshaʿ fort, and, without resting, went straight in to storm Malkiyyah and nearby Kadesh. Both fell after heavy fighting. But the next day the Lebanese put in a determined counterattack, and the Palmaḥ men were forced to retire, taking up positions between the border and Nabī Yūshaʿ. That night, a unit of the battalion infiltrated deep into Lebanon and cut an important supply route. This action, together with their casualties in retaking Malkiyyah and Kadesh, stopped the Lebanese from pursuing the Yiftaḥ battalion, which accordingly attacked Nabī Yūshaʿ the next night and was successful. (In an earlier, heroic but unsuccessful, attempt just before independence, 28 Yiftaḥ men had lost their lives.) On the 18th the Palmaḥ launched the attack on Malkiyyah, taking the enemy by surprise by approaching from the rear – from inside Lebanese territory. Malkiyyah fell. With the Lebanese advance halted, the Yiftaḥ Brigade was rushed south to take part in the urgent actions in Jerusalem and the Corridor. Replacing Yiftaḥ was the newly formed Oded Brigade, consisting of men from local settlements, a Haifa Haganah battalion, and new recruits.

In western Galilee, the Carmeli Brigade, ready to meet a possible Lebanese invasion through *Rosh ha-Nikrah on the coast, cleared the stretch from Haifa to the border, taking Acre on May 17. Carmeli later operated in the Jordan Valley and in the Jezreel Valley just north of Jenin.

On June 6, simultaneously with the Syrian attack on Mishmar ha-Yarden, a combined two-brigade force of Syrians, Lebanese, and Qāwuqjī's reorganized Arab Liberation Army attacked Malkiyyah and overran the small Israel garrison that had been left there. Through this gap poured units of the Liberation Army that proceeded to consolidate themselves in heavily Arab-populated Central Galilee and remained there when the truce went into effect.

The First Truce: June 11–July 9

The truce was supervised by Count Folke *Bernadotte, the mediator for Palestine who had been appointed by the UN General Assembly on May 21, together with teams of UN observers made up of army officers from Belgium, France, Sweden and the United States. It was to last 28 days (the UN hoped it would be extended), and the observers were to ensure that neither side gained any "military advantage" during the truce by the acquisition of additional arms or "fighting personnel."

On the tenth day of the truce, a grave intra-Jewish incident occurred when an IẒL arms vessel, the *Altalena*, attempted to land its weapons on the shores of Israel. It had left a French port early in June, and IẒL refused to hand it over to the Israel government. When IẒL persisted in its refusal to agree to the government's conditions, the landing was resisted by force. The ship was set on fire just off the Tel Aviv beach by IDF troops, who then waded into the water to rescue IẒL personnel. There were casualties on both sides.

In the meanwhile, both the Arab and Israel armies used the truce to improve their positions. The IDF engaged in more rigorous training of its men – established settlers, new immigrants (*Gaḥal), and volunteers from overseas (*Maḥal) with World War II battle experience; regrouping its forces; and readying for action more of the newly arrived heavy weapons and planes (flown by local pilots and overseas volunteers). Toward the end of the truce period it became clear that the truce would not be prolonged. The one agreement Bernadotte was able to arrange between the two sides was the demilitarization of the Mount Scopus area in Jerusalem. The truce ended at 6 A.M. on July 9 and hostilities were resumed. They lasted ten days and were followed by the second truce.

The "Ten Days": July 9–18

ON THE EGYPTIAN FRONT. In the south, the Egyptians had taken advantage of the truce to bolster their Majdal-Bet Guvrin line, cutting northern Israel off from the Negev. Their strength was now four brigades. Twenty-four hours before the truce ended, on the morning of July 8, they launched a series of attacks on both sides of the line, ejecting an IDF unit from Kawkaba to the south, but being badly mauled when they tried to take Beit Darās to the north. That night, Givati units attacked the line from the north, capturing the villages of ʿIrāq Suwaydān, Beit (Bayt) ʿAffa, and ʿIbdis – the last in a tough battle in which they routed two Egyptian companies and captured large quantities of weapons and ammunition. A Negev Brigade unit, attacking the line from the south, was less successful; it seized several positions but failed in its assault on the ʿIrāq Suwaydān police fort. (Suwaydān village and, later, Belt ʿAffa had, accordingly, to be abandoned.) For the next eight days, the two IDF brigades fought continuously to contain the more powerful Egyptians, break their line, and join in the defense of local kibbutzim, notably Negbah and *Be'erot Yiẓḥak, which held out miraculously against overwhelming enemy forces. On the night of July 17, with another truce about to be called, the IDF launched a determined attack on two positions astride the Egyptian line, Ḥatta and Karatiyya, located between ʿIrāq Suwaydān and Fālūja. Taking a key role in the combined Givati-Negev brigades action was a commando battalion from a newly created armored brigade that had made a spectacular dash through the town of *Lydda a few days earlier and had been rushed down to reinforce Givati. Ḥatta and Karatiyya fell, thereby breaching the Majdal-Fālūja line. When the truce came on the evening of July 18, Egyptian east-west communications were thus severed, and the Israelis had a direct land connection with the Negev.

ON THE CENTRAL FRONT. The IDF's greatest offensive effort during the ten days of fighting was directed against the Arab Legion on the central front, the area between Tel Aviv and Jerusalem. With the major objective of taking the two towns of Lydda and *Ramleh, clearing the central area, and then, if there was still time, attempting the capture of Ramallah and Latrun, the IDF organized a strong force, headed by the commander of the Palmaḥ, consisting of the Yiftaḥ Brigade, the new 8th Armored Brigade – comprising a tank battalion, a commando battalion of jeeps and half-tracks – and two battalions from the Kiryati and Alexandroni Brigades, as well as additional artillery and engineering units. The action was called "Operation Dani." Two forces struck in a pincer movement, one moving on Lydda and Ramleh from the northwest, the other from the southwest. Yiftaḥ, the southern force, captured ʿInāba and Jimzū and by the afternoon of the 10th fought its way through to *Ben Shemen, to the rear of Lydda. One unit turned westward to take Kefar Daniel, which cut off Ramleh from the east. The armored brigade moved off along the northern arc on the morning of the 10th and captured Wilhelma, Ṭīra, and other villages en route and then swung south to Deir Ṭarīf, ready to meet the southern pincer forces at Ben Shemen. During this advance, a small force darted off to capture al-Sāfiriyya and then pushed on to capture the Lydda airport. Thus, within a day and a half of the resumption of hostilities, the largest airport in the Middle East and a dozen key villages had fallen to the IDF in the first engagements in which Israel units had used armor. At Deir (Dayr) Ṭarīf the tank battalion was held up by strong Arab Legion forces based on Beit Nabālā across the road, on the western slopes of the hills. Fighting there was heavy, and Deir Ṭarīf fell only on the following day. The commando battalion did get through to Ben Shemen, however, on the afternoon of the 10th, having bypassed Deir Ṭarīf. Then, without pausing to rest or wait for the required artillery support, it made a surprise dash to Lydda, breaking into the city past Arab positions, driving right through it and shooting it up, and repeating the same maneuver on its way back. This was one of the most daring actions of the war and caused utter confusion in the enemy ranks. They were still dazed when Yiftaḥ troops moved in to effect the city's capture. The Arab Legion counterattacked the next day without success. On July 12, Kiryati units took Ramleh, which surrendered after a brief engagement, and, north of this sector, Rosh ha-Ayin, which had been seized by the Iraqis in June, was recaptured.

The Arab Legion now regrouped its forces to strengthen the defenses of Ramallah and Latrun. With reinforcements brought from Jerusalem, the Legion held the Latrun enclave with a full brigade and considerable armor. For the next few days it fought stubbornly – and effectively – being saved by the truce from the attacks of the Yiftaḥ and Harel units. But north of Latrun, Israel units pressing southward from Lydda and Ramleh captured Shiltā, Barfīlyya, Burj, Bīr (Bi'r) Maʿin, and Salbit. This brought them to positions from which they dominated the Ramallah-Beit Nūba-Latrun road. Southeast of Latrun, Harel, again responsible for the Jerusalem Corridor, widened it by capturing important positions on its southern edge, including Hartuv. In and around Jerusalem, *Ein Kerem and Malḥa were captured by local Jerusalem units, who had been engaged in heavy fighting throughout the ten days in different quarters of the city. But the truce found the Old City still held by the Arab Legion. The one Legion gain was the capture of a building belonging to a certain Mr. Mandelbaum. This later became the celebrated Mandelbaum Gate, the crossing point between Jordan and Israel during the period from the armistice to the *Six-Day War.

OPERATIONS IN THE NORTH. The most spectacular operation in the north during the ten days of fighting was "Operation Dekel," which culminated in the capture of Nazareth. It was carried out by a group consisting of the 7th Brigade and a battalion from Carmeli, with some support from Golani. After capturing several Arab positions between the coast and the foothills southeast of Acre, the force successfully attacked the Shefaram (Shefāʿ Amr) on July 14 and pressed on southeast to take Ẓippori the following day after stubborn fighting. The opposing Arab force in this region was Qāwuqjī's Arab Liberation Army, which at that moment was placing very heavy pressure on *Sejera, to the east. With the fall of Ẓippori, and Qāwuqjī's main force still being resisted by the Jewish settlement of Sejera, the people of Nazareth began to panic as the main brigade column advanced on the city. At the same time, a small unit from Golani moved toward Nazareth from the Jezreel Valley, suggesting to Qāwuqjī that he was also threatened by a strong force from the south. When the brigade was less than a mile from the town, however, the commander of Nazareth sent out an armored car unit to block its advance. The brigade column went straight on without pausing, firing as it moved. After desultory fighting, the city surrendered on the evening of July 16. Qāwuqjī himself, together with the bulk of his forces, succeeded in escaping into the mountains to the north through trails that IDF troops had not yet had a chance to seal. The result of "Operation Dekel" was to free the entire belt of Lower Galilee from Haifa Bay to Lake Kinneret.

Further north, the Carmeli Brigade undertook operations whose major aim was the elimination of the Syrian salient at Mishmar ha-Yarden, and whose lesser purpose was the containment of the enemy within the area of the bridgehead. Fighting was intense throughout the entire ten days, with positions like Dardara and Hill 223 changing hands as many as three times. The battles ended in a stalemate, with the Syrians still in Mishmar ha-Yarden; but the Syrians were stopped from advancing even the short distance westward to cut the Rosh Pinnah-Metullah road.

AIR AND NAVAL OPERATIONS. The Israel air force, with its newly acquired warplanes, though inferior in number and type to those of the enemy, was very active during these ten days, carrying out support, pursuit, and bombing missions. Three World War II Flying Fortresses carried out air attacks on Egypt en route to Israel on July 14, one bombing Cairo and the others attacking Rafa and El Arish. Damascus was also bombed. The Israel navy, having feverishly reconditioned the hulks of "illegal" immigrant boats, bombarded Arab centers along the Carmel coast, sabotaged ships near Gaza, and shelled the Lebanese port of Tyre. Most of the navy's casualties, however, were suffered on land when an amphibious company was rushed to the southern front during the critical operation to break the Egyptian Majdal-Fālūja line to reinforce Givati.

The Second Truce

Breaches of the second truce, which went into effect at 7 P.M. on July 18, began almost from the first day. In the Jerusalem area the Arab Legion intensified its bombardment of the New City, and during the remainder of July, August, September, and October, Jerusalem was shelled, mortared, and machine-gunned almost every night. (The attacks stopped only on November 30, when both sides agreed to a "sincere cease-fire.") On August 12, the Legion destroyed the Latrun pumping station, even though it was under UN control, but Israel quickly laid a pipeline along the "Burma Road" and kept Jerusalem supplied with water. In the north, Qāwuqjī's Arab Liberation Army kept up sporadic harassment of Jewish positions.

Clearing the Road to the Negev: October 15–22

In the south, the Egyptians soon ignored the truce provisions and denied Jewish convoys passage through the Ḥatta-Karatiyya gap in their line. They seized positions outside the truce boundaries and then extended their attacks to several IDF posts that covered the gap. On October 15, the Israel army and air force turned to the offensive after the Egyptians had attacked a convoy proceeding south and raided inter-kibbutz communications. In a brisk seven days' campaign, the road to the Negev was opened and the Negev was cleared of Egyptian troops.

During this period, Operation Yo'av (also known by its preliminary name, Operation Ten Plagues) was carried out. In the reorganization that the army had carried out during the preceding truce months (when, incidentally, officers had been given ranks for the first time), the country had been divided into four military commands. The southern front command, headed by the Palmaḥ commander, was responsible for Operation Yo'av. The force consisted of three infantry brigades, Negev, Givati and Yiftaḥ, plus an armored battalion from the 8th Armored Brigade and the largest artillery formation that had ever been available to the IDF. (The Oded Brigade joined the command on October 18.) During the truce months, Yiftaḥ was flown south in an extraordinary airlift – since the Egyptians had blocked the road – to relieve the Negev Brigade, which was lifted north to rest, reorganize, and prepare for resumed action.

On the night of October 15 the Israel Air Force bombed bases from which Egyptian assaults had been launched and also attacked Egypt's advanced airfield at Rafa. This action kept most of the Egyptian front-line fighters out of the skies and gave the IDF air superiority for the first time. The Israel navy also took part in these southern engagements, shelling enemy coastal installations, preventing supplies from reaching Gaza and Majdal by sea, and scoring a spectacular triumph on the very eve of the truce, when its special unit sank the *Amir Fārūq* ("Emir Farouk"), flagship of the Egyptian navy, off the shores of Gaza.

On the ground, Yiftaḥ troops led off by carrying out a series of raids and sabotage actions against Egyptian concentrations and communications in the coastal strip north and south of Gaza, to the links between Rafa and Gaza, and between Gaza and Majdal. The Givati and the armored battalion went into action to break the Majdal-Bet Guvrin line. In heavy fighting, the tank unit failed to take ʿIrāq al Manshiyya, just east of Fālūja. Next night, Givati units made a breakthrough west of Fālūja, fighting their key battles at Hill 113 and nearby Egyptian strongholds dominating the crossroads between Majdal and Fālūja. After stiff hand-to-hand engagements, the positions were captured and held against heavy Egyptian counterattacks. On the night of the 16th, Givati advanced southward and took the Heights of Kawkaba, commanding the road running north–south. But Yiftaḥ failed to take the Heights of al-Ḥulayqāt further south, which also commanded that road. Ḥulayqāt fell only on October 20, after other Yiftaḥ units had succeeded in capturing several nearby positions. The road to the Negev was now clear, in spite of the fact that the ʿIrāq Suwaydān police fort had successfully resisted a further Israel attack to capture it.

Meanwhile, the Security Council was anxiously trying to effect a cease-fire, and the IDF recognized that it had little time to exploit the successful opening of the Negev road. At 4:00 on the morning of October 21, the IDF moved to capture Beersheba. Taking part were the bulk of the 8th Brigade; a Negev Brigade battalion, which had dashed south along the road within hours of the capture of Ḥulayqāt; and the Negev Brigade's commando battalion, which had already been operating in the south, harassing the enemy in the Gaza-Rafa region. While some units took up blocking positions north and south of the town to hold up Egyptian reinforcements, and another carried out a diversion action in the direction of Hebron, the main IDF force advanced on the city from the west. There was stiff fighting inside the city, but at 8:00 a.m. a white flag went up on the police fort, and by 9:15 the capture of Beersheba was complete.

During Operation Yo'av, the Harel Brigade was active in the mountainous area between the Jerusalem Corridor and Bet Guvrin, greatly widening the approaches to Jerusalem and cutting the Egyptian artery from Bet Guvrin to Bethlehem. Detachments from the Eẓyoni and Givati Brigades took part in some of these actions. A truce was ordered for 3:00 p.m. on October 22, but there was some action in the days immediately following. The police fort of Bet Guvrin fell on October 27, and after the Egyptians had retreated southward from Ashdod (October 28) and Majdal (November 6) to Gaza, IDF troops occupied the coastal strip down to Yad Mordekhai. Trapped in a pocket, which was centered around Fālūja and included ʿIrāq Suwaydān on the west and ʿIrāq al Manshiyya on the east, was an entire Egyptian brigade, consisting of some 4,000 troops headed by a brave Sudanese commanding officer who refused to surrender. On November 9, the area of the "Fālūja Pocket," as it came to be called, was reduced by IDF's capture of the village and police fort of ʿIrāq Suwaydān, in one of the numerous actions in which both sides engaged to improve their positions despite the truce.

The Arab Liberation Army Driven Off: October 29–31

In the north, Qāwuqjī's Arab Liberation Army which did not consider itself bound by the United Nations truce, carried out local attacks during the cease-fire months. On October 22, thinking that the IDF would be too preoccupied with actions in the Negev, Qāwuqjī launched a strong attack on the outpost of kibbutz *Manarah, a kibbutz on the ridge near the Lebanese border above the Ḥuleh Valley. They captured the strongpoint of Sheikh ʿAbbād, repelled a counterattack by the local IDF unit, and ambushed the reinforcements who were rushed in to relieve Manarah, inflicting heavy casualties on them as they tried to negotiate the steep heights. Israel's protests to the UN were unavailing. The Arabs continued to hold Sheikh ʿAbbād and captured further hill positions, cutting the Manarah-Nabi Yūshaʿ track and dominating the *Rosh Pinnah-*Metullah road. On the night of October 28, the IDF initiated Operation Ḥiram, striking not at the point of attack selected by Qāwuqjī, but at his main bases, in an effort to rout his army. The forces available to the northern front commander were four brigades: the 7th (together with the armored battalion that had fought with it in Operation Dekel), Oded, Golani, and Carmeli. The air force was active in bombing and ground-support missions. The main action fell to the 7th Brigade, which pushed off from Safed in a western and northwestern drive on Sasa, the heart of Upper Galilee. In less than 24 hours of hard fighting, they made a lightning advance through the rugged hills and captured Meron (succeeding in the second attack); took Safsāf; sped on to the powerful stronghold of Jish, which had been reinforced by a Syrian battalion and which they overcame in stiff combat; and by nightfall on the 29th were in Sasa. In a coordinated action, Oded started eastward at zero hour from bases near Nahariyyah also aiming for Sasa, so that the Arab Liberation Army would be encircled and squeezed by Oded thrusting from one direction and the 7th Brigade from the other. Oded's first objective was Tarshīḥa. Several outposts near the approaches to the town were captured, but Tarshīḥa itself held firm. It surrendered only on the morning of the 30th, after Golani had undertaken a series of diversionary actions in the south that sent the Liberation Army northward.

In a quick change of plan, Golani was ordered to exploit its success and push on to ʿAylabūn, which it captured, while the 7th Brigade, further north, also exploited its success by advancing northeastward on Malkiyyah. Oded detachments, who by now were driving eastward beyond Tarshīḥa, engaged Arab forces retreating from the south, and then, after reaching the frontier road with Lebanon, changed direction and pushed due west, clearing the entire road up to the Mediterranean coast. The 7th Brigade took Malkiyyah by surprise, coming at it from the south, and captured it. This relieved the pressure on Manarah, and the Carmeli Brigade, covering the eastern sector to prevent a Syrian breakthrough from Mishmar ha-Yarden, now moved to the offensive. It crossed into Lebanon and captured a number of villages lying near the Manarah road. Some of its detachments reached the Litani River. (The Lebanese villages were given up by Israel in the *armistice agreement which was signed in March 1949.) When the survivors among Qāwuqjī's forces realized that they were being squeezed from the east, south, and west, and particularly after the fall of their key centers at Jish, Sasa, and Tarshīḥa, they started evacuating the pocket, using little-known tracks to make their way northward into Lebanon. When the cease-fire was ordered on October 31, 60 hours after the start of the action, the entire Galilee was clear of the Arab Liberation Army.

Expelling the Egyptians: December 22–January 7

In the south, there were infractions of the truce by both sides throughout November and December; but those of the Egyptians were more serious, as they had more to gain, having lost so much. They attacked Jewish settlement communications, sabotaged the inter-settlement water pipeline, and tried to seize Negev outposts in order to improve their military positions. They also refused to implement a Security Council order (which Israel accepted) to start armistice talks, unless Israel first allowed the release of the trapped Fālūja brigade. Israel said it would release the force as soon as talks got under way. Egypt remained adamant, and its forces continued their harassing activities in the Negev. Israel then decided to launch Operation Ḥorev, aimed at expelling the Egyptians from the borders of the country. The forces taking part, under the commander of the southern front, were the 8th Armored and the Negev brigades, which had participated in Operation Yo'av; the Alexandroni and Golani brigades, which replaced Givati and Yiftaḥ; and two battalions and an additional unit from the Harel Brigade. The Egyptians were entrenched along two main wings, the western and stronger of the two, forking north from ʿAwjā al-Ḥafīr along the Sinai border into the coastal strip through Rafa to Gaza, and the eastern one curving in an arc northeast from ʿAwjā through al-Mushrifa and Bīr (Bī'r) ʿAslūj to 15 mi. (24 km.) south of Beersheba. The main effort called for in the first phase of IDF's operation was the destruction of the eastern arm, with its heavily defended strongpoints ranged all along the main, hard-topped Beersheba-ʿAwjā highway. To effect surprise, the IDF decided to use a little known old Roman road cutting directly across the desert through Wadi al-Abyaḍ from Beersheba to ʿAwjā, which would bring its forces in the rear of ʿAwjā and of the Mushrifa and Bīr ʿAslūj bases. This ancient track had to be prepared by the engineers to take vehicles, however, and such work could not be started without losing the element of surprise until the campaign was under way. It was accordingly decided to start operations with feinting and diversionary attacks on the western Egyptian wing, which would also promote the impression that this was the main objective, and then deliver the principal punch to the east wing.

On the afternoon of December 22, the coastal strip was heavily shelled, and that night Golani units went into action cutting enemy communications between Rafa and Gaza and trying to seize key hills. For the next 48 hours IDF fought bitter battles and suffered many casualties in strong Egyptian counterattacks, displaying particular heroism in the battle for Hill 86 (from which they eventually had to retreat). But they fulfilled their task of diverting the enemy's attention from the eastern wing and misleading them as to IDF's true intentions.

On the morning of December 25 (a storm and flooding forced a postponement of zero hour by a day) the 8th Armored and Negev brigades set forth from al-Khalaṣa, south of Beersheba, on their appointed tasks. The Negev Brigade cut southward, aiming for Mushrifa, and had to fight a series of stiff battles for the well-defended group of hills round al-Thamila, close to the ʿAwjā-Bīr (Biʾr) ʿAslūj road. The Egyptians counterattacked heavily, and one Negev unit lost half its men trying to hold one key height. But it was soon regained, and by the morning of December 26 the key middle bastions of the Egyptians between ʿAwjā and Bīr ʿAslūj were in Israeli hands, with Bir ʿAslūj, the northeastern terminal of the Egyptian line, cut off and the rear of ʿAwjā exposed.

Meanwhile, the Armored Brigade had had a very difficult drive southwest across the Roman road to the south, and despite the brilliant work of the engineers in making the track passable, there were delays. The main force, which was to have reached the ʿAwjā area by dawn on the 26th, did not get there until the late afternoon, when it engaged ʿAwjā's outposts but was not in a position to launch its main attack. The offensive was carried out on the morning of the 27th, after roadblocks had been established north and west of ʿAwjā. The attack, in which the commando battalion of the Armored Brigade played a key part, was heavily resisted; Egyptian ground forces were aided by their air force, which bombed and strafed the Israeli units. But by 8:00 A.M., ʿAwjā fell, and thereafter Egyptian troops began evacuating their strongholds in the rear of ʿAwjā, with Israeli units in hot pursuit. The Negev Brigade completed its task of clearing the entire line up to and including Bīr ʿAslūj, which it occupied just after midday, and then raced westward along the paved road, joining up with the Armored Brigade at ʿAwjā in the afternoon. The Beersheba-ʿAwjā highway was now open, and no Egyptian troops were left on Israeli soil.

IDF then continued westward and northwestward from ʿAwjā into Sinai in pursuit of the Egyptian forces. On the night of the 28th, the Negev Brigade plus the Armored Brigade's tank battalion carried out an attack on Abu Aweigilā, some 30 mi. (48 km.) west of the international border, commanding the important junction of the road west to Ismailia and the road northwest to El-Arish. Golani units assisted by carrying out operations to halt enemy reinforcements. Captured enemy transport was used for the fast move (which led to a mishap soon after they crossed the border when, with enemy markings still on them, they were attacked by Israeli planes). The column advanced, battling defensive strongpoints en route, until they reached the outposts of Abu Aweigilā itself. There was stubborn fighting through the night, but the outposts were finally captured, and by dawn Negev units entered Abu Aweigilā. Almost without pause, part of the force pressed forward to raiding operations, though subjected to Egyptian air bombing. The tanks and commando units advancing northwest reached the El-Arish airfield, destroying installations and capturing one Spitfire intact, and went on to fight a brisk battle with the battalion-held outpost of Bīr Laḥfan, which they captured. But with no supporting troops, and the tanks badly in need of maintenance, the units returned to Abu Aweigilā on December 30. On the previous day as well, a light mobile unit sped westward to raid the air base at Bīr Ḥamma more than 50 mi. (80 km.) west of Abu Aweigilā, and returned. The 30th was spent in capturing Egyptian defense positions between Abu Aweigilā and El-Arish, between ʿAwjā and Rafa, and al-Quṣayma, some 20 mi. (32 km.) south of ʿAwjā.

By this time, however, with IDF forces inside Sinai in pursuit of the enemy, strong diplomatic pressure was being exercised on the government of Israel. Britain even threatened to activate the Anglo-Egyptian Treaty of 1936 unless the IDF withdrew to the international boundary. The front command was accordingly given orders to evacuate Sinai by January 2, 1949, but to continue operations within the boundaries of mandatory Palestine. The last Israeli actions inside Sinai were a Harel raid on Bīr Ḥassneh and the destruction of a large bridge spanning the Ismailia-Abu Aweigilā road. The next few days were spent in bitter fighting in the Rafa area, mostly by the Golani and Harel brigades, supported by the Armored and Negev brigades, in which several outposts of Rafa, stubbornly contested by both sides, kept changing hands. With the enemy squeezed back toward the coast, the IDF prepared to attack Rafa itself, but was prevented from doing so by the cease-fire, which became effective on the afternoon of January 7. On that day, five British fighters zoomed low over Israel battle positions and were shot down by Israeli planes. It transpired later that they were on armed reconnaissance flights, but they had been taken for Egyptian warplanes, which had been strafing Israeli units daily. This action caused a furor in the British parliament, where the government was strongly criticized – particularly by Winston Churchill, who was then leader of the opposition – for sending planes over the battle area in what seemed an open act of British intervention.

The Alexandroni Brigade had been assigned to contain and then subdue the Egyptian brigade trapped in the Fālūja Pocket. It attacked ʿIrāq al-Manshiyya on the night of December 27 and fought a hard battle. But the defenders under their Sudanese commander put up very stout resistance, battling with bravery and skill and effecting determined counterattacks when any position fell. The Israelis withdrew. The Fālūja Brigade was released only with the signature of the Israel-Egypt armistice agreement at Rhodes on February 24, and was saluted for its bravery by its Israeli adversaries as it left.

Under that agreement, Israel was permitted to maintain only defensive troops in the western Negev, from Fālūja to Eilat. They were free, however, to maintain whatever forces they considered necessary in the eastern half of the Negev. Up to then, Israel had controlled the Negev by regular patrols, without having a permanent force at the southern tip on the Gulf of Akaba. Early in March, the Negev Brigade set off from the northern Negev to trek south along interior tracks through sand and rock, hill barriers, and canyons, while the Golani Brigade moved along the Arabah. On the afternoon of March 10, 1949, the Israeli flag was hoisted on a few mud buildings, abandoned by a Transjordanian detachment, at what was known then as Umm Rashrash and now as Eilat. The spearheads of both brigades arrived almost simultaneously. The armistice agreement with Transjordan was signed, also at Rhodes, on April 3, 1949. On March 23 an agreement was signed with Lebanon at Rosh ha-Nikrah; and the last armistice agreement, with Syria, was signed on July 20. These acts officially ended Israel's War of Independence.

[Moshe Pearlman]

BIBLIOGRAPHY: N. Lorch, *The Edge of the Sword* (1968^2), includes bibliography; M. Pearlman, *Army of Israel* (1950); E. O'Ballance, *Arab Israeli War 1948* (1956); J. Kimche, *Seven Fallen Pillars* (1950); J. and D. Kimche, *Both Sides of the Hill* (1960); W. Eytan, *First Ten Years* (1958); J.R. Carlson, *Cairo to Damascus* (1951). **ADD. BIBLIOGRAPHY:** U. Millstein, *History of Israel's War of Independence*, 4 vols. (1996–99).

WAR REFUGEE BOARD, a United States government agency established to assist refugees during World War II. In the autumn of 1943, at the initiative of the Emergency Committee to Save the Jewish People of Europe (the Bergson group), members of Congress introduced a resolution urging the creation of a government agency to rescue refugees from Hitler. At the same time, aides to Treasury Secretary Henry *Morgenthau, Jr., discovered that the State Department had been obstructing opportunities to rescue Jewish refugees and blocking the transmission to the U.S. of information about German atrocities. With pressure building in Congress and the press, Morgenthau, armed with a report from his staff about the State Department's actions, brought the issue to President Roosevelt in January 1944. FDR pre-empted Congressional action by establishing the War Refugee Board.

The WRB was handicapped from the outset. By the time it was established, more than four million Jews had already been slaughtered. As its agent in Istanbul, Ira Hirschmann, put it, the agency was created "at five minutes to twelve [midnight]." Moreover, Roosevelt had established the WRB primarily as a political gesture, and gave the new agency little financial or other support. Private Jewish organizations contributed more than 90 percent of its budget. Fortunately, the board, led by executive director John Pehle, was staffed largely by the same Treasury Department officials who helped lobby for the agency's creation in the first place. Their creativity, determination, and zeal helped overcome some of the administrative and other obstacles they encountered. The WRB's representatives in Turkey, Switzerland, North Africa, Portugal, and Italy energetically employed unorthodox means of rescue, including bribery of border officials and the production of forged identification papers and other documents needed to protect refugees from the Nazis.

The WRB's agents arranged for some 48,000 Jews to be moved from Transnistria, where they would have been in the path of the retreating German army, to safe areas in Romania. About 15,000 Jewish refugees, and about 20,000 non-Jewish refugees, were evacuated from Axis-occupied territory, and at least 10,000 more were protected through various WRB-sponsored activities.

As the German deportation of Hungarian Jews to Auschwitz got underway in the spring of 1944, the WRB launched a campaign of psychological warfare aimed at the Hungarian authorities, whose cooperation was crucial to the success of the deportations. The WRB engineered a series of threats of postwar Allied retribution against collaborators, including public statements to that effect by President Roosevelt, Congressional leaders, and other prominent Americans. Their warnings were conveyed to Hungary through diplomatic channels, radio broadcasts, the European press, and the dropping of leaflets by Allied planes. The WRB's efforts also helped elicit pleas to the Hungarian leadership from the Vatican, the International Red Cross, and the king of Sweden. When the Hungarians finally succumbed to these pressures, about 120,000 Jews remained alive in Budapest. Many had been sheltered by the Swedish diplomat Raoul *Wallenberg, who, with financial and logistical backing from the WRB, organized a network of safe houses in the city.

The WRB took action in other areas, as well. It arranged for the shipment of tens of thousands of food parcels to concentration camp inmates during the final months of the war. The board also helped Herbert Pell, the U.S. representative to the Allied War Crimes Commission, put pressure on the State Department to take a stronger stand on the postwar prosecution of Nazi war criminals.

Some of the board's efforts met with less success. For months, it sought to persuade President Roosevelt to establish temporary shelters for refugees in the United States, but in the end he agreed to just one token shelter for a group of 982 refugees in Oswego, New York. The board repeatedly asked the War Department to bomb the railroad lines leading to Auschwitz or the gas chambers and crematoria, but the requests were rejected. The State Department, too, often refused, or delayed, cooperating with the board's requests for assistance, despite the fact that the president's executive order creating the WRB specifically required such cooperation. The British government likewise responded coldly to the board's efforts and sometimes even impeded them.

Given the magnitude of the Nazi genocide, WRB director John Pehle was correct in his later assessment of the board's accomplishments as "late and little." Still, the WRB deserves credit for playing a major role in the rescue of more than 200,000 refugees during the final 15 months of the war despite numerous and daunting obstacles.

BIBLIOGRAPHY: D.S. Wyman, *The Abandonment of the Jews* (1984); I.A. Hirschmann, *Lifeline to a Promised Land* (1946); D. Halasz, "The War Refugee Board and the Destruction of Hungarian Jewry" (Ph.D. dissertation, Texas Christian University, 2000).

[Rafael Medoff (2nd ed.)]

°**WARREN, SIR CHARLES** (1840–1927), British army officer, police commissioner, and archaeologist. Warren entered service in the Royal Engineers in 1857. He carried out a survey of Gibraltar from 1861 to 1865 and conducted excavations at Jerusalem from 1867 to 1870. Together with C.R. *Conder, he published the results of the survey of western Palestine which Conder had completed in 1881. Warren also conducted a survey of southern Transjordan. In his archeological work in Jerusalem Warren concentrated on excavating the outer wall of the Temple enclosure. Digging a series of underground tunnels, he labored under vast difficulties. Among his discoveries was the wall of the Ophel. Warren recorded the results of his excavations with great care, and they provided the main source of information on the Herodian wall down to its foundation until excavations were again undertaken there in 1968. He also preserved and registered every object he uncovered – a new departure at that time – which gave his work lasting value. His topographical and historical theories, on the other hand, have for the most part become obsolete.

Among his publications are *The Recovery of Jerusalem* (1871), *Underground Jerusalem* (1876), *The Survey of Western Palestine* (with C.R. Conder, 1884), and several works on problems of ancient weights and measures (especially *The Early Weights and Measures of Mankind*, 1913). Warren was one of the founders of the Palestine Exploration Fund and a member of its Executive Committee from 1871 until his death.

Warren was among those who advocated the Jewish settlement of Palestine (in *The Land of Promise*, 1875). In his opinion the country with its natural borders could absorb 15 million people if all its resources were exploited properly. Warren is most famous today for his time as commissioner of the Metropolitan Police from 1886 until 1889, when, among other things, he had to deal with the "Jack the Ripper" murders in Whitechapel. Warren acted with great sensitivity towards the large Jewish community in London's East End, ordering that antisemitic graffiti found near the scene of one murder be immediately erased, for fear that it would stir up anti-Jewish hostility. His role is discussed in all of the many accounts of the "Ripper" crimes, generally regarded as the most famous unsolved murders in history.

BIBLIOGRAPHY: W.W. Williams, *The Life of General Sir Charles Warren* (1941). **ADD. BIBLIOGRAPHY:** ODNB online; P. Begg, *Jack the Ripper: The Definitive History* (2003), index.

[Michael Avi-Yonah]

WARRENS, ROSA (1821–1878), Swedish poet and translator. Born in Karlskrona, she spent much of her life in Hamburg and died in Copenhagen. Apart from important contributions to the study of Scandinavian folklore and Norse legend, she published Nordic verse in German translation: *Schwedische Volkslieder der Vorzeit* (1856), *Daenische Volkslieder* (1858), and *Schottische Volkslieder* (1861). Her other works include three volumes of Norwegian, Icelandic, and Finnish folk songs and a collection of original verse (1873).

WARSAW (Pol. **Warszawa**), originally capital of the Masovia region; from the 16th century, capital of Poland. Jews were apparently living in Warsaw by the end of the 14th century, but the first explicit information on Jewish settlement dates from 1414. In 1423 the records show ten Jewish families paying tax in Warsaw, and about the same number exempted. The hostility of the townsmen of Warsaw to Jewish settlement in the capital was particularly strong. In 1483 the Jewish inhabitants were expelled, although some were living there three years later. There is no information about Jews in the city between 1498 and 1524; evidently they had either been driven from the city entirely or remained in the outskirts on property owned by the Polish magnates from where they could enter the city for business purposes. Eventually, in 1527, the townsmen of Warsaw obtained the privilege *de non tolerandis Judaeis*, authorizing the exclusion of Jews from the city. Because of its importance as a political and commercial center, however, their connection was not entirely severed. A number of Jews were able to continue to reside in the outskirts, and some managed to gain access to Warsaw itself. When the national Sejm (diet) transferred its sessions to Warsaw in 1572 Jews were permitted to enter the city during its conventions. The time permitted for their sojourn was subsequently extended to a period of two weeks before and after the sessions. In addition, Jewish representatives (*shtadlanim*) of the *Councils of the Lands, empowered to negotiate with royalty and the nobility, also visited Warsaw. A number of other Jews obtained authorization by various means to enter the city temporarily even while the Sejm was not sitting. One of the customary "arrangements" was the "daily ticket" system, which gave the holder of a ticket the right to stay in Warsaw for 14 days. A census of 1765 records that there were 2,519 Jews in Warsaw.

During the *Haidamack attacks of 1768 fugitives from the eastern districts of Poland flocked to the outskirts. The census for 1792 records 6,750 Jews in Warsaw, forming 9.7% of the total population: 30.4% of those economically active were engaged in commerce or as taverners, 26.7% in craft or industry, 41.4% in undefined occupations, and 1.5% in domestic employment or as simple laborers. Several scores of Jewish entrepreneurs engaged in flourishing business as moneylenders, court factors of royalty or the nobility, army suppliers, or agents for foreign embassies. These were the nucleus of the great Jewish bourgeoisie which subsequently formed in Warsaw; they were mainly immigrants from abroad or from other towns in Poland.

Throughout the period of unofficial settlement the townspeople spared no efforts to drive the Jews from the capital. A partial expulsion of the Jewish residents was enforced, in conjunction with organized street attacks, in 1775 and 1790. After the first partition of Poland (1772), Warsaw Jewry, in particular the poorer sector, took an energetic part in the Polish uprising against the Russians. Many Jews volunteered for guard duties, and a number joined in the fighting in the Jewish legion formed under Berek *Joselewicz. In their onslaught the Russian troops massacred the Jewish civilian population, in particular in the Praga suburb where resistance was fierce. Legend associates the name of Joseph Samuel *Zbitkower with large-scale rescue operations during the massacre.

After Warsaw passed to Prussia in 1796, Warsaw Jewry was subjected to the *Juden Reglements* of 1797. Only Jewish residents of the city prior to 1796 were allowed to stay; the others were only permitted the right of temporary domicile, in a reversion to the old "daily ticket" system. In 1805 fresh attacks on Jews in Warsaw were made by the Polish populace. Nevertheless, there was now continuous immigration of German-speaking Jews from Prussia, Silesia, and other places to Warsaw, and the Jewish population increased from 7,688 (12% of the total) in 1797 to 11,630 (17.4%) in 1804.

Within the Duchy of Warsaw (1807–13)

After the formation of the Napoleon-sponsored duchy of Warsaw the Jews were not deprived of the rights of citizenship, but in 1808, under the "infamous decree" of *Napoleon, restrictions were imposed on Jewish rights for ten years. During this period Warsaw Jewry was burdened with heavy taxes. In 1809 a "Jewish quarter" was established outside in which the only persons permitted to reside were Jewish owners of real estate, wholesale merchants, manufacturers, bankers, army suppliers, and doctors, on condition that they wore European dress, were able to read and write Polish, German or French, and sent their children to general schools. The "daily ticket" was abolished in 1811. The vicissitudes of war between 1812 and 1815, and the inimical attitude of the government of the duchy, led to a reduction of the number of Jewish residents in Warsaw, who in 1813 numbered 8,000.

From 1527 until the Prussian conquest no authorized community (*kehillah*) had existed in Warsaw. However, the Jews living in the city and environs met for prayers, established prayer houses and charitable associations, and appointed a *syndic-parnas*, to direct the tax administration, exercise judicial power, and organize the census, among other duties. He was assisted by *dayyanim* and a sworn-in *meturgeman* (interpreter). Rabbis had also officiated without authorization. The Prussian administration had appointed a representation for Warsaw Jewry with the right to exercise the **ḥerem* (excommunication) to facilitate tax collection. Thus the Warsaw community was revived and had the opportunity of appointing authorized rabbis. During the existence of the duchy of Warsaw the community extended its authority until it was transformed in practice from a local body to an institution representative of the Jewry of the whole duchy.

*Ḥasidism spread to Warsaw toward the latter part of the 18th century. A celebrated public disputation between spokesmen of the Ḥasidim and *Mitnaggedim* was held in the Praga suburb in 1781. On the other hand, a small circle of *maskilim* also formed in this period, which included a number of wealthy arrivals from abroad, physicians, and others. In 1802 Isaac Flatau founded the "German Synagogue," in which traditional services were held but sermons were delivered in German. A government-sponsored rabbinical seminary was established in 1826, which the Orthodox members of the community strongly opposed. It continued for 37 years, until the Polish uprising of 1863, and became a center for assimilationist and reformist tendencies.

Within Congress Poland (1815–1915)

During the existence of Congress Poland, the size of the Warsaw community increased to become the largest in Europe. The Jewish population numbered 15,600 (19.2% of the total) in 1816, 72,800 (32.7%) in 1864, 130,000 (33.4%) in 1882, 306,000 (39.2%) in 1910, and 337,000 (38.1%) in 1914. Natural increase was responsible for only part of this growth, which was mainly the outcome of the migration to Warsaw beginning in the 1860s and particularly after the *pogroms in Russia of 1881, when 150,000 Jews moved to Warsaw, a substantial number coming from Lithuania and Belorussia, and from the Ukraine.

From 1815 there was a sharp deterioration in the status of Warsaw Jewry. The area of the "Jewish quarter" was further restricted, the system of "daily tickets" was reintroduced, and the animosity of the general populace increased. The second half of the 19th century inaugurated a change for the better, and was marked by some rapprochement between certain Jewish and Polish circles. In 1862 the restrictions relating to all the Jews of Congress Poland were lifted. The Jews of Warsaw took an active part in the two Polish uprisings against Russia, especially in the second in 1863.

At the end of the 1870s there was a recrudescence of anti-Jewish feeling in Warsaw and throughout Poland. In December 1881 a pogrom broke out in Warsaw in the wake of the Russian pogroms, motivated in particular by the notion that the "Litvaks" (Lithuanian Jews) were the promoters of russification in Poland. The elections to the fourth Imperial *Duma of 1912, in which Warsaw Jewry returned a left-wing candidate, further aggravated anti-Jewish hostility.

Throughout this period, the Warsaw Jews considerably extended their activities in the economic sphere, and the social and economic differences within the community grew more marked. Jews played an important role in finance and all sectors of commerce and also in industry. Of the 20 bankers in Warsaw in 1847, 17 were Jews. Jewish bankers initiated and developed various industries in the state, participated in the construction of railroads, held the monopoly for the sale of *salt and alcoholic beverages, leased the Jewish taxes, and engaged in other activities. In 1849 Jews formed 52% of the total persons engaged in commerce. Nevertheless this *haute bourgeoisie*, despite its economic importance, formed a negligible percentage in the total Jewish population of Warsaw, in 1843 forming 2.2% of the number of Jews actively employed there. In this year about 30% of the Jews earned a livelihood from commerce, mainly as shopkeepers or peddlers, about one-third as artisans and laborers, 13.5% as carters, porters or day laborers, and 12.5% as domestic workers. The proportion of Jews engaged in commerce increased until the 1870s but afterward dropped in face of growing Polish competition.

In 1862 the main source of livelihood for the Jewish proletariat was commerce and crafts: 31.7% were employed in commercial establishments, 27.9% in crafts, and 4.5% in industry; the number in industry later increased, although mainly in small or medium industry, large industries, even under Jewish ownership, taking a smaller number of Jewish workers; 2.8% of the Jews were employed in finance, 1.9% in transportation, and 1.9% in the liberal professions. The large percentage of domestic workers (29.3%) reflects the migration of unemployed women to the metropolis. Later, part of this number was absorbed into the garment and tobacco industries.

Social and Cultural Developments

Ḥasidism spread rapidly in Warsaw. In 1880 two-thirds of the 300 approved synagogues, and many prayer rooms, were ḥasidic, and this also reflected the proportion of Ḥasidim to the total Jewish population in the city. The *Mitnaggedim* were augmented by the end of the 19th century with the advent of the "Litvaks."

The tendency to *assimilation in Warsaw began with the penetration of German cultural influences, in which an important role was played by the wealthy arrivals from the West at the end of the 18th century and the beginning of the 19th, whose ranks were reinforced by wealthy Jews of Polish birth. Later the attachment of the assimilationists became closely orientated to Polish culture and society, and in the second half of the 19th century the tendency spread to the youth of wider circles. The assimilationists took an active role in the leadership and cultural life of the community. The incidence of conversion in Warsaw became the highest in Eastern Europe: in the first half of the 19th century 70 bankers, industrialists and large-scale merchants, 15 printers, and 20 officials adopted Christianity.

In 1883 the society of She'erit Israel of the Ḥovevei Zion was established in Warsaw, led by Israel Jasinowski and Saul Phinehas *Rabinowitz, and in 1890 the society Menuḥah ve-Naḥalah was founded, led by Eliyahu Ze'ev *Lewin-Epstein, which established the moshavah of *Reḥovot in Ereẓ Israel. The Geulah Company, formed in 1904, participated in acquiring land for the society of Aḥuzzat Bayit which pioneered the building of Tel Aviv. The circles of Ḥovevei Zion in Warsaw concentrated in particular in the synagogue of Ohel Moshe, founded in 1885, and subsequently in the Moriah synagogue founded in 1908, at which Isaac *Nissenbaum served as preacher.

A number of Zionist youth and student circles, whose leadership included Jan Kirshrot, Yiẓḥak *Gruenbaum, and Yosef *Sprinzak, combined in the society Ha-Teḥiyyah in 1903. Its ranks included supporters of differing national and socialist ideologies who soon separated. Some of its members joined the Zionist Democratic Fraction, under the leadership of Gruenbaum. Another group became a formative influence in the Po'alei Zion, under the leadership of Yiẓḥak *Tabenkin and Ben-Zion Raskin, and in Ẓe'irei Zion, led by Sprinzak. After the split in the Sixth Zionist Congress over the *Uganda scheme (1903), the supporters of Theodor *Herzl and the political Zionists joined in the Meginnei ha-Histadrut which established its headquarters in Warsaw.

At the end of the 19th century Jewish socialist societies and workers' circles were consolidated into the *Bund, under the leadership of Leo Goldman, John Mill, and Ẓiviah Hurvitz, originally from Vilna. The Bund conducted its activities among the Jewish workers, organized strikes and May 1st demonstrations, and promoted Yiddish culture: it was opposed to Zionism and the movement to revive Hebrew.

Until the end of the 1860s the Warsaw community leadership was mainly Orthodox, excepting for the periods 1841–44 and 1856–58, when the president of the community was Matthias Rosen, an assimilationist who was acceptable to all groups of the community. After a financial criterion was established in the elections, the assimilationists assumed the leadership of the community by agreement with the Ḥasidim, and controlled its affairs for over 50 years, between 1871 and 1926. Zionist opposition to the assimilationists was organized for the first time in 1899.

Four rabbis served for the whole of Warsaw and its vicinity, all *Mitnaggedim*: Solomon Zalman *Lipshitz, 1819–39; Ḥayyim *Dawidsohn, 1839–54; Dov Berush *Meisels, 1854–70; and Jacob *Gesundheit, 1870–73, who was not accepted by the Ḥasidim and was removed from office with the help of the assimilationists. The rabbis served in conjunction with *dayyanim*. Attempts to establish a *Reform synagogue in Warsaw were unsuccessful. The only innovation introduced by the "modernized" congregations was that sermons in their synagogues were preached in German or Polish. Rabbis in these synagogues were Abraham Meir Goldschmidt, Isaac Kramsztyk, Mordecai *Jastrow, Isaac Cylkow, Samuel Abraham *Poznanski, and Moses *Schorr.

The main trend of Jewish education in Warsaw was Orthodox. In the middle of the 19th century, 90% of all Jewish children of school age attended *ḥeder*. Subsequently the percentage decreased, and by the end of the century only 75% attended *ḥadarim*. In 1896 there were 433 authorized *ḥadarim*, in Warsaw and a large number of unauthorized ones. In 1885 circles of Ḥovevei Zion established the first *ḥeder metukkan*, or modern *ḥeder*, in Warsaw. In 1820 three state schools for Jewish children had been opened under the supervision of Jacob *Tugendhold, but the Orthodox opposition curbed the development of general schools. On the threshold of World War I there were 20 elementary schools in Warsaw in which the language of instruction was Russian. Attempts to open private schools for boys met only with limited success. On the other hand, the girls' secondary schools, which disseminated Polish culture, were more popular; even Ḥasidim, who normally insisted on an extreme Orthodox education for their sons, sent their daughters to them. In 1895, 19 schools of this type existed in Warsaw. Vocational training courses, a secondary school with a scientific trend (1878–88), and a trade school were also opened. The first Hebrew kindergarten was founded by Jehiel Heilperin in 1909, in conjunction with a course for kindergarten teachers, opened in 1910.

Jewish Press

The Haskalah literature in Warsaw was of an inferior standard and made little impact. However, in the 1880s, Warsaw became the center for Hebrew publishing in Poland and throughout Russia. The daily and weekly press, the many literary organs, and other periodicals which now began to burgeon, marked the transition from the world of Haskalah to the new Hebrew literature. They provided a platform for the elite of the writers, poets, scholars, and journalists. In 1862 the Hebrew periodical **Ha-Ẓefirah* was established as a weekly by Ḥayyim Selig *Slonimski, which after a series of intervals and setbacks became a daily in 1886 and the central organ for Russian Jewry. Other daily or weekly Hebrew newspapers also published in this period did not continue for long, generally for lack of readership; the heavy hand of the censor also proved a stumbling block. The pioneer of Hebrew publishing in Warsaw was A.L. Ben Avigdor (see *Shalkovich) while the most active personality in journalism and literature was Nahum *Sokolow.

The first Yiddish (and Polish) weekly was *Der Beobakhter an der Weykhsel*, published in 1823–24 by assimilationist circles. The transition in *Yiddish literature to new forms and contents originated with Y.L. *Peretz and his circle and the literary publications which they founded, *Yidishe Bibliotek* (1891–95) and *Yontev Bletlakh* (1894–96). After a number of unsuccessful attempts, two Yiddish periodicals became established which soon began to overtake the Hebrew press: Samuel Jacob Jackan began to publish the daily *Yidishes Tageblat* in 1906, changed in 1908 into **Haynt*. Zevi *Prylucki established the daily **Moment* in 1911. Polish periodicals also appeared, first sponsored by the assimilationists, among them the weekly *Jutrzenka*. At the beginning of the 20th century national newspapers were also published in Polish.

World War I and the Polish Republic

During World War I thousands of refugees arrived in Warsaw. In 1917 there were 343,400 Jews (41% of the total population). The German occupation brought improvement from the political standpoint, but the concentration of refugees and the havoc wrought by war increased the economic distress.

During the period of renewed Polish independence (1918–39) the Jewish population of Warsaw showed marked growth, but a decrease compared with the general population. In 1918 the total was 320,000 (42.2%), and in 1938, 368,400 (29.1%). The tendency of the Polish state to centralize economic activity in its own institutions, the antisemitic direction of its policy and the antisemitic feelings rife among the Polish public, as well as the economic action taken against the Jews (see *Poland), severely affected Jewish life in Warsaw. The number of Jewish unemployed reached 34.4% in 1931, while that of those without means of livelihood was even greater. In 1933 half of the members of the Warsaw community were exempted from the communal tax as they were unable to furnish the minimal payment of five zlotys a year. Consequently the pressure of emigration increased, in particular to Palestine.

Warsaw was the headquarters of Jewish parties and movements in Poland, the arena of the struggle for Jewish representation in the state Sejm and Senate, and the center of Jewish cultural and educational activities, of the arts, scholarship and literature, and of the Jewish national press. A fierce political struggle was waged over the character that Jewish life in Warsaw should assume. Ḥasidism continued to be an important factor in Jewish affairs. Many of the ḥasidic *admorim* of various dynasties settled in Warsaw. Assimilation became a less important issue, and the chief political struggle was between the Zionist factions and the Orthodox-ḥasidic groups, which combined in the *Agudat Israel. Between 1926 and 1936 the direction of Warsaw communal affairs was in the hands of Agudat Israel and the Zionists, either in coalition or alternately. However, in 1936 the Bund gained the lead in both the elections to the communal leadership and the Jewish representation on the Warsaw municipality. The Polish government annulled the results of the democratically held communal elections and appointed another community board (*kahal*) which continued in office until the German occupation in World War II.

JEWISH EDUCATIONAL INSTITUTIONS. During the inter-war period a number of Jewish school systems existed: six Hebrew-national elementary schools, established by the Zionist Tarbut organization; four Yiddish secular schools established by the CYSHO supported by the Bund and the left Po'alei Zion; a Yiddish-Hebrew school of the Shulkult organization, separated from the CYSHO; an Orthodox school of Agudat Israel (Ḥorev for boys and *Beth Jacob for girls) – the exact number of their schools is not known but the number of the pupils exceeded that for other schools; two bilingual (Polish-Hebrew) elementary schools and one secondary school of the Yavneh founded by *Mizrachi; and numerous private secondary schools. Most Jewish children attended the state schools. In neighborhoods where there were Jewish concentrations, some of these schools were solely intended for Jewish pupils: lessons were held on Sundays instead of the Sabbath, and the schools were known as *szabatówki*. In 1928 the Institute for Jewish Studies, Makhon le-Ḥokhmat Yisrael, was opened, and the name was subsequently changed, as its sphere of activity expanded, to Makhon le-Madda'ei ha-Yahadut. Moses Schorr, Meir *Balaban, Abraham *Weiss, and Menahem (Edmund) Stein served as principals.

During this period Hebrew literature and press declined. Many of the Hebrew writers emigrated to Ereẓ Israel. Attempts to continue publication of Hebrew dailies were unsuccessful; not one lasted for an appreciable time. The most important publishing house of Hebrew books in Warsaw was that of A.J. *Stybel. On the other hand, the Yiddish and Polish Jewish press increased its output. Other Yiddish dailies were published alongside the *Haynt* and *Moment*, including party organs and unaffiliated papers, with a wide public and considerable influence on their readers. In 1917 *Nasz Kurjer* was published under the editorship of Jacob Apenszlak, which changed to *Nasz Przegląd* in 1920, a national independent daily. Other weeklies and periodicals were also published.

[Avraham Rubinstein]

Hebrew Printing

The beginning of Hebrew printing in or near Warsaw was due to the desire of the government to stem the outflow of capital abroad for the import of Hebrew books. In Warsaw the first Hebrew book (Ẓevi Hirsch b. Ḥayyim's notes on the Yalkut Shimoni *Ẓemah le-Avraham*) was printed by Peter Zawadzki in 1796. After his death his widow continued printing – mainly anti-hasidic literature – until 1801. Another non-Jewish Hebrew printer was V. Dombrowsky (to 1808). The first Jewish-owned press was that of Ẓevi Hirsch Nossonowitz of Lutomirsk, who printed, with Krueger's Novydwor type, from 1811, in partnership with Avigdor Lebensohn 1818–21, and afterward the two of them separately, Nossonowitz now changing his name to Schriftgiesser ("type-caster"). He died in 1831, succeeded by his son Nathan; the firm continued for another century, printing a Talmud edition (1872). Lebensohn and his descendants were active to 1900. More than 30 additional presses were established in Warsaw during the 19th century, including that of S. Orgelbrand and sons, who printed Talmud editions as well as *Turim*, Maimonides' *Yad*, the Shulḥan Arukh, and a Mishnah edition.

Among the moving spirits of Hebrew printing in Warsaw was Isaac Goldmann (1812–1887), who ran his own press from 1867 producing more than 100 books, among them Talmud tractates. In 1890 the brothers Lewin-Epstein established a Hebrew printing house, which is still active in Israel. A dozen or so more presses were set up in the first quarter of the 20th century. At the outbreak of World War II in 1939 more than 1,000 workers were engaged in the Hebrew printing works in Warsaw.

Holocaust Period

When German forces entered the city on Sept. 29, 1939, there were 393,950 Jews, comprising approximately one-third of the city's population, living in Warsaw. Between October 1939 and January 1940 the German occupation authorities issued a series of anti-Jewish measures against the Jewish population. These measures included the introduction of forced labor; the order that every Jew should wear a white armband with a blue star of David, and the special marking of Jewish-owned businesses; confiscation of Jewish real estate and other property; and a prohibition against Jews using the railway and other public transportation.

THE GHETTO. In April 1940 the Germans began constructing a wall to enclose the future Warsaw ghetto. On October 2, the Germans established a ghetto for all Warsaw Jews and Jewish refugees from the provinces. Within six weeks all Jews or persons of Jewish origin had to move into the ghetto, while all "Aryans" residing in the assigned area had to leave. The ghetto originally covered 340 hectares (approximately 840 acres), including the Jewish cemetery. As this area was gradually reduced by the Germans, the walls were moved, and the number of gates changed. In the autumn of 1941 the ghetto was divided into two parts, joined by a bridge over Chlodna Street. The gates were guarded by German and Polish police from the outside and by the Jewish militia (*Ordnungsdienst*) from the inside and only those with a special permit could enter or leave the ghetto. In the beginning, the Warsaw city hall, German political authorities, and a special office, the "*Transferstelle*," responsible for financial affairs, dealt with the ghetto's administration. However, from April 1941 a German commissioner, Heinz Auerswald, was appointed over the ghetto. The head of the Jewish community council was Adam *Czerniakow, an engineer who had been appointed by the mayor of Warsaw during the siege (Sept. 23, 1939). By order of Hans Frank (Sept. 28, 1939), a *Judenrat was created, consisting of 24 members, and presided over by Czerniakow. Czerniakow carried out his functions for the general good under trying conditions, often interceding with the German authorities to ameliorate the repressive regulations. He tirelessly supported social and cultural institutions in the ghetto and provided relief wherever possible.

Originally some 400,000 Jews were crowded into the area of the ghetto. The reductions in its size necessitated internal shifting and further overcrowding, so that thousands of families were often left without shelter. The situation was further aggravated when some 72,000 Jews from the Warsaw district (see *Poland) were transferred to the ghetto, bringing the total number of refugees to 150,000 (April 1941). The average number of persons per room was 13, while thousands remained homeless. The ghetto population during various periods prior to July 1942 is estimated to have been between 400,000 and 500,000. The confiscation and plunder of Jewish property was conducted by the "*Transferstelle*." In January 1942, Jewish goods valued at 3,736,000 zlotys ($747,200) were confiscated; in February – 4,738,000 zlotys ($947,600); in March – 6,045,000 zlotys ($1,209,000); and in April-6,893,000 zlotys ($1,378,000). The ghetto population received a food allocation amounting to 184 calories per capita a day, while the Poles received 634, and the Germans 2,310. The price per large calorie was 5.9 zlotys (about $1) for Jews, 2.6 zlotys (50 cents) for Poles, and 0.3 zlotys ($.06) for Germans. The average allocation per person in the ghetto was four pounds of bread and a half pound of sugar a month. The dough was mixed with sawdust and potato peels.

The ghetto suffered from mass unemployment. In June 1941, 27,000 Jews were active in their professions, while 60% of the Jewish population had no income at all. A small number of Jews who had their own tools and machines found employment in factories taken over by Germans. Wages were minimal. For 10–12 hours of strenuous labor, a skilled worker earned 2½–5 zlotys ($0.50–1.00) daily. There was an acute shortage of fuel to heat the houses. In the winter of 1941–42, 718 out of the 780 apartments investigated had no heat. These conditions led to epidemics, especially typhoid. The streets were strewn with corpses due to starvation and disease. Bands

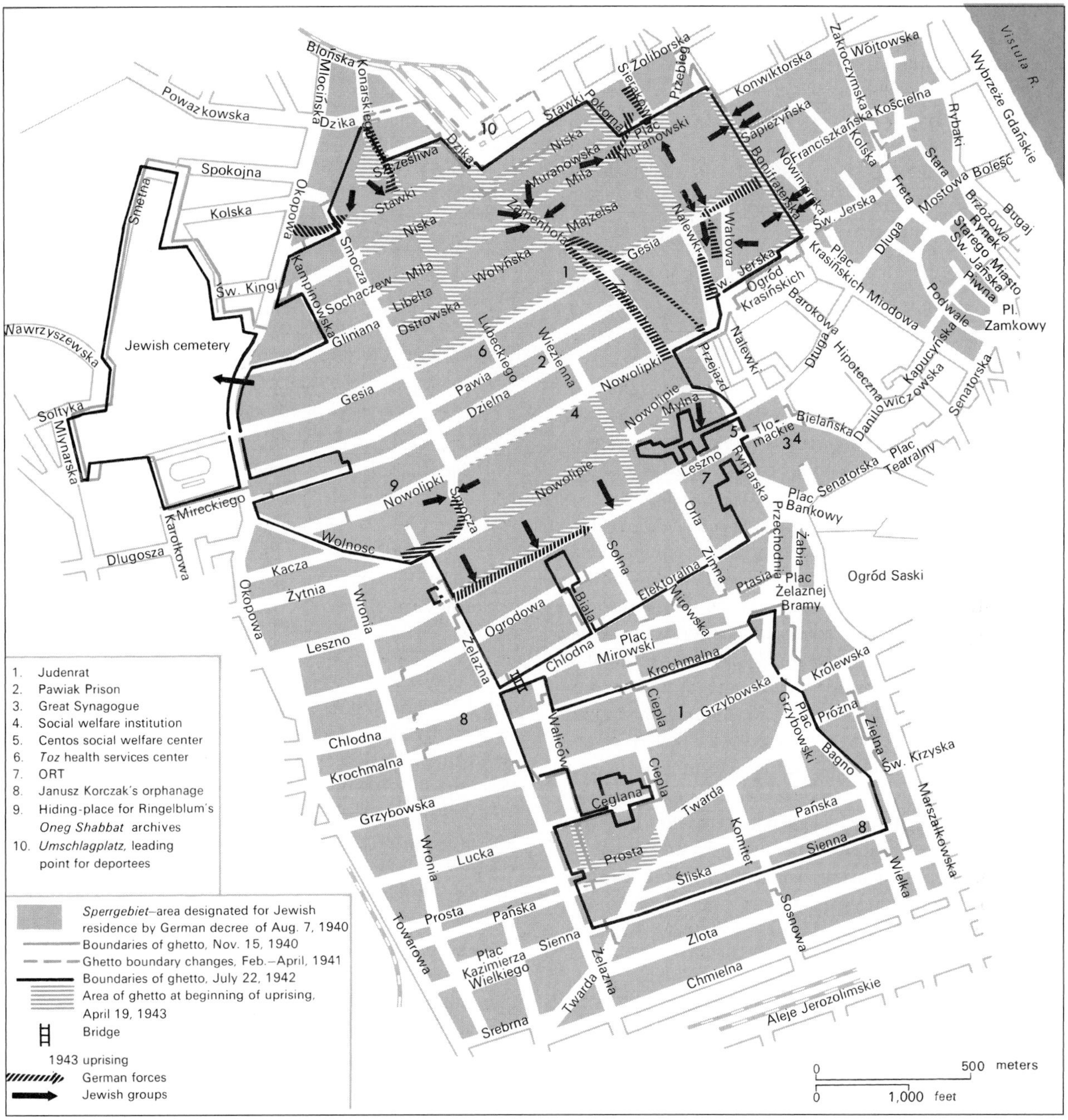

Plan of Warsaw ghetto, 1940–43, after J. Ziemian, The Borders of Warsaw Ghetto, *Jerusalem, 1971.*

of children roamed the streets in search of food. A few women and children occasionally slipped across to the "Aryan" side, in an attempt to find food or shelter. The Polish police usually seized them and turned them over to the Germans. In October 1941 the authorities declared that leaving the ghetto without permission was punishable by death.

From time to time the authorities rounded up able-bodied people in the streets and sent them to slave labor camps. In April 1941 some 25,000 Jews from the Warsaw ghetto lived in these camps under conditions that rapidly decimated their numbers. After the outbreak of the German-Soviet War (June 1941), many of the inmates in the camps were executed.

It is estimated that by the summer of 1942, over 100,000 Jews died in the ghetto proper. Nevertheless, the morale of the ghetto inhabitants was not broken, and continual efforts were made to overcome the German decrees and organize relief. Illegal workshops were gradually established for manufacturing goods to be smuggled out and sold on the "Aryan" side. These included leather products, metals, furniture, textiles, clothing, and millinery. At the same time raw materials were smuggled in. In this way thousands of families were sustained. The smuggling of foodstuffs into the ghetto, carried out by Jewish children, was especially intensive. In December 1941 the official import of foodstuffs and materials into the ghetto was valued at 2,000,000 zlotys ($400,000) while illegal imports totaled 80,000,000 zlotys ($16,000,000). Social welfare institutions were active to combat hunger and disease. The *Centos for social welfare, the *Toz for health services, and other organizations re-formed and established hospitals, public kitchens (daily providing over 100,000 soup rations), orphanages, refugee centers, and recreation facilities. In each block of houses a committee for charitable work functioned and also engaged in cultural and educational activities, such as reading groups, lectures, and musical evenings. A network of schools, both religious and secular, as well as trade schools functioned in the ghetto. Some of these schools were illegal and could operate only under the guise of soup kitchens. Similarly, medical, technical, and scientific training was given under the guise of trade courses. By the end of 1940 the Jewish historian, Emmanuel *Ringelblum, established a secret historical and literary society under the code name of *Oneg Shabbat*. This group set up secret archives on the life and martyrdom of the Polish Jews under the Nazis. These archives, which were hidden in several places, were discovered after the war. Despite the closing down of all synagogues and the prohibition against public worship, clandestine services were held, especially on holidays. Yeshivot secretly functioned. The *ẓaddikim* of *Aleksandrow and *Ciechanow were hidden and cared for by their followers. Many religious Jews held the view that their sufferings were preliminary to the coming of the Messiah. There were many instances of heroism by ultra-Orthodox Jews in the face of death. Hillel *Zeitlin, the famous religious writer, arrived at the "*Umschlagplatz*" (assembly point) during the 1942 deportation, proudly dressed in his religious garb. Janusz *Korczak, the director of the Jewish orphanage, continued to give hope and courage to his wards until he boarded the death train together with the children.

FORMATION OF RESISTANCE. The main form of resistance in the ghetto revolved around the underground political life which existed throughout the German occupation. The most active were the Zionist groups – *Po'alei Zion, *Ha-Shomer ha-Ẓa'ir, Deror, *Betar, *Gordonia, as well as the Bund and the Communist-inspired Spartakus organization. As early as Passover 1940 the Germans, with the cooperation of Polish hooligans, provoked a pogrom in the Jewish district. Underground Jewish groups organized effective self-defense. After the ghetto was established, underground activity increased, as the purely Jewish environment offered better security against denunciations and infiltration of German police agents into the ranks of the underground. The political underground movements in the ghetto engaged in such activities as disseminating information, collecting documents on German crimes, sabotaging German factories, and preparing for armed resistance. A series of illegal periodicals appeared in Hebrew, Yiddish, and Polish. Among the best known were the following Hebrew publications: *Deror*, circulated by the *He-Halutz organization; *El Al, Itton ha-Tenu'ah*, and *Neged ha-Zerem* by Ha-Shomer ha-Ẓa'ir: *Magen David* by Betar; *Sheviv* by the General Zionists; Yiddish publications: *Bafrayung* by He-Halutz; *Morgenfray* and *Biuletin* by the Bund: and Polish publications: *Awangarda* by Po'alei Zion; *Jutrznia* and *Plomienie* by Ha-Shomer ha-Ẓa'ir.

The first Jewish military underground organization, Swit, was formed in December 1939 by Jewish veterans of the Polish army. Most of its members were Revisionists. The organization was headed by David Apelbaum and Henryk Lipszyc, aided by a Polish major, Henryk Iwanski.

Early in 1942 a second underground fighting organization emerged, created by four Zionist groups: Po'alei Zion, Ha-Shomer ha-Ẓa'ir, Zionist Socialists, and Deror, as well as the Communist organization. It soon became known as the anti-Fascist bloc. Its leaders were Szachna Sagan, Aron Lewartowski, Josef Kaplan, and Josef Sak. Four commanders were appointed: Mordecai *Anielewicz, Pinkus Kartin, Mordecai Tenenbaum, and Abram Fiszelson. The Bund did not join the bloc but created its own fighting organization "Samo obrona" (self-defense) under the command of Abraham Blum. None of the three military organizations of the ghetto succeeded in acquiring arms prior to July 22, 1942, when mass deportations to *Treblinka death camp were initiated by the Nazis.

FIRST MASS DEPORTATIONS. The deportations were preceded by a series of terrorizing "actions," when scores of people were dragged out of their homes and murdered in the streets. Just one day before the mass deportations to Treblinka began (July 21, 1942), 60 hostages were taken to the Pawiak Prison. Three days later, the president of the Judenrat, Adam Czerniakow, committed suicide following a demand by the Nazis that he cooperate with them in the deportations. His successor, Maksymilian (Marek) Lichtenbaum, also an engineer, obeyed the Nazi orders. The number of deportees averaged 5,000–7,000 daily, sometimes reaching 13,000. Some of the victims, resigned to their fate as a result of starvation, reported voluntarily to the "*Umschlagplatz*," lured by the sight of food which the Germans offered to the volunteers, and by the promise that their transfer to "the East" meant they would be able to live and work in freedom. In the beginning, the Germans exempted from deportation employees of the ghetto factories, members of the Judenrat and Jewish police, and hospital personnel, as well as their families. Thousands of Jews made feverish attempts to obtain such employment certificates. In the course of time even these "safe" categories were subject to deportation. The number of victims, including those murdered in the ghetto and those deported to Treblinka, totaled approximately 300,000 out of the 370,000 inhabitants in the ghetto prior to July 1942. This major *Aktion* lasted from July 22 until Sept. 13, 1942. Following the deportations, the ghetto area was drastically constricted so that some factories and several blocks of buildings were left outside the new walls and cordoned off with barbed wire to prevent anyone finding shelter there. The Germans also fixed the number of inhabitants allowed to remain in the ghetto at a maximum of 35,000 persons.

ACTIVE RESISTANCE. The leaders of the underground movements appraised the new situation. At their first meeting, they decided to create the Jewish Fighting Organization (Żydowska Organizacja Bojowa-ZOB), and take active steps to oppose further deportation. A few members of the underground managed to escape from Treblinka, and brought to the ghetto information about the real fate that awaited the deportees, namely physical annihilation. Because of the blockade it was not even possible to pass this information on to the non-Jewish population.

Some 30,000–35,000 Jews, most of them factory workers and their families, legally remained in the ghetto and were employed within or outside the ghetto. In addition, there were between 20,000 and 30,000 Jews living on in the ghetto "illegally." By the end of 1942 there was an influx of several thousand Jews from the labor camps which had been closed. At this time some Jews hiding on the "Aryan" side were seized and returned to the ghetto. In this period intensive preparations were made for armed resistance. The Bund also joined the ZOB, while the Revisionists continued to adhere to their separate organization, Swit. Appeals were made to several Polish underground organizations for the acquisition of weapons. An emissary of the ZOB, Arie (Jurek) Wilner, succeeded in persuading the commanders of one of the Polish underground armies (Armia Krajowa) of the necessity of supplying weapons to the ghetto underground and, after long negotiations, about 100 firearms and some hand grenades were sent into the ghetto. Another small quantity of arms was supplied by the Communist "People's Guard." The Revisionists also obtained several loads of arms from two Polish underground organizations led by Major H. Iwanski and Captain Szemley (Cesary) Ketling. Several secret workshops were established in the ghetto to manufacture homemade hand grenades and bombs, and some additional arms were bought on the black market. At the same time, a network of bunkers and subterranean communication channels was constructed to enable combat against the superior German forces and to protect the non-fighting population.

The second wave of deportations began on Jan. 18, 1943, when the Nazis broke into the ghetto, surrounded many buildings, and deported the inhabitants to Treblinka. They liquidated the hospital, shot the patients, and deported the personnel. Many factory workers who had been employed outside the ghetto were included among the deportees. The underground organizations, insufficiently equipped and ill-prepared, nevertheless offered armed resistance, which turned into four days of street fighting. This was the first case of street fighting in occupied Poland. The Germans, fearing the impact of this outburst on other parts of Poland, stopped the deportations, and attempted to carry out their aim by "peaceful" means, namely by voluntary registration for the alleged labor camps. The underground, in turn, conducted an intensive information campaign about the real intentions of the Nazis. As a result the second wave of deportations was suspended after four days, during which the Germans managed to send only 6,000 persons to Treblinka. About 1,000 others were murdered in the ghetto itself.

THE GHETTO UPRISING. After this *Aktion*, daily life in the ghetto was paralyzed. Walking in the street was punishable by death. Only groups of workers marching under armed guard were to be seen. Social institutions ceased to function and the Judenrat, most of whose members were killed in the January *Aktion*, were reduced to a small office. The underground organizations, however, were preparing for armed resistance in case a further attempt would be made by the Germans to liquidate the ghetto. Mordecai Anielewicz now headed the ZOB. The members of his command were: Itzḥak (Antek) *Cukierman, Herz Berlinski, Marek Edelman, Zivia Lubetkin, and Michal Rojzenfeld. The entire force was divided into 22 fighting units, each unit affiliated with one of the political groups. Israel Kanal was commander of the units operating in the central area of the ghetto; and Eleazar Geller and Marek Edelman commanded the factory units. The ZOB underground headquarters were at 18 Mila Street. The Revisionist commanders were Leon Rodal, Pawel Frenkiel, and Samuel Luft.

On April 19, 1943, a German force, equipped with tanks and artillery, under the command of Col. Sammern-Frankennegg, penetrated into the ghetto in order to resume the deportations. The Nazis met with stiff resistance from the Jewish fighters. Despite overwhelmingly superior forces, the Germans were repulsed from the ghetto, after suffering heavy losses. Sammern-Frankennegg was relieved of his command, and Gen. Juergen *Stroop, appointed in his stead, immediately resumed the attack. Street fighting lasted for several days, but when the Germans failed in open street combat, they changed their tactics. Carefully avoiding any further street clashes, the Germans began systematically burning down the houses. The inhabitants died in the flames, while those hiding in the canals and bunkers were killed by gas and hand grenades. Despite these conditions, the Jewish fighting groups continued to attack German soldiers until May 8, 1943, when the ZOB headquarters fell to the Germans. Over a hundred fighters, including Anielewicz, died in this battle. Several units continued to fight even after the fall of the ZOB and Revisionist headquarters. Armed resistance lasted until June 1943. With the help of the Polish "People's Guard" some 50 ghetto fighters escaped from the ghetto and continued to fight the Germans in the nearby forests as a partisan unit named in memory of Anielewicz.

The Warsaw ghetto uprising had an enormous moral effect upon Jews and non-Jews throughout the world, especially since it was prepared and carried out under conditions which practically excluded *a priori* any attempt at armed resistance. Despite the vastly unequal forces, the uprising continued for a long time and constituted the largest battle in occupied Europe before April 1943 (excepting in Yugoslavia). This battle also had its impact upon the Polish population, resulting in the intensification of resistance by the Poles as well as by Jews throughout the country. On May 16, 1943, Stroop reported to his superiors on the complete liquidation of the Warsaw ghetto. As a token of his victory he blew up the Great Synagogue on Tlomacka Street. According to his report, the Germans in the course of one month's fighting had killed or deported over 56,000 Jews. The Germans themselves officially suffered 16 dead and 85 wounded between April 29 and May 15, but it is conjectured that the German casualties were in fact much higher. In the course of the following months, the Germans penetrated the empty ghetto and hunted down the remnants hiding in the ruins, often using fire to overcome sporadic resistance, which continued until August 1943.

The Warsaw ghetto uprising became an event of world history when details of what happened became known after the war. Among the writers who depicted life in the ghetto and the underground fighters were Yiẓḥak L. Katznelson, John Hersey, and Leon *Uris.

After the liquidation of the ghetto, the surviving members of the ghetto leadership continued underground work on the "Aryan" side of Warsaw. The underground's main activity was to assist Jews living on the "Aryan" side, either in hiding or by means of forged documents. According to their figures, the number of Jews on the "Aryan" side reached 15,000 (May 1944). They also established contact with Jewish organizations abroad and received financial assistance. Among their leaders were Adolf *Berman of Po'alei Zion and Leon Fajner of the Bund. Emmanuel *Ringelblum continued his scientific work of collecting evidence on Nazi crimes until March 1944, when he was seized and executed. Hundreds of Jews were active in the Polish underground of Greater Warsaw, particularly Hanna Szapiro-Sawicka, Niuta Tajtelbaum, Ignacy Robb-Narbutt, Menasze Matywiecki, and Ludwik Landau. When the Polish uprising in Warsaw broke out on Aug. 1, 1944, over 1,000 Jews in hiding immediately volunteered to fight the Germans. Hundreds of them fell in the battle, among them a member of the high command of the People's Army, Matywiecki, and Pola Elster, a member of the Polish National Council. In addition, the remnants of the ZOB, under the command of Cukierman, and a group of liberated prisoners from the city concentration camp, participated in the uprising.

[Danuta Dombrowska]

Post-War Developments

About 6,000 Jewish soldiers participated in the battle for the liberation of Warsaw. Warsaw's eastern suburb, Praga, was liberated in September 1944, and the main part of the city on the left bank of the Vistula on Jan. 17, 1945. On that day only 200 Jewish survivors were found in underground hideouts in the ruins of destroyed Warsaw. By the end of 1945 about 5,000 Jews had settled in Warsaw. That number was more than doubled, when Polish Jews, who had survived the war in the Soviet Union, returned. Warsaw became the seat of the Central Committee of Polish Jews. On April 19, 1948 (the fifth anniversary of the Warsaw ghetto uprising) a monument executed by N. Rapaport in memory of the ghetto fighters was unveiled in the square called "The Ghetto Heroes' Square." In 1949 a number of Jewish cultural institutions (The Jewish Historical Institute, the Jewish Theater, editorial staffs of the Yiddish papers *Folksshtime* and *Yidishe Shriften*) were transferred from Lodz to Warsaw. A club for Jewish youth, "Babel," was opened there and one synagogue was rebuilt. After the war Warsaw Jews left Poland in three main waves: in 1946–47 after the great pogrom in *Kielce; in 1957–58; in 1967–68 when the Polish government launched its official antisemitic campaign. After 1968 Jewish institutions, although officially not closed, had actually ceased to function. The number of remaining Jews, mostly aged people, was estimated at 5,000 in 1969.

[Danuta Dombrowska / Stefan Krakowski]

In the following two decades Jewish life in Warsaw was dormant, as in all of Poland, with one synagogue open and no rabbi. With the fall of Communism Jewish life revived. Poland now had a chief rabbi whose seat was in Warsaw. A primary school and kindergarten were opened and Jewish courses were offered at the university. Warsaw's Jewish Historical Institute housed Emanuel *Ringelblum's famous ghetto archive as well as a 60,000-volume library while the Warsaw Yiddish Theater was the only regularly functioning Yiddish theater in the world, though most of the actors were non-Jews. In the early 21st century the majority of Poland's 8,000 registered Jews lived in Warsaw, though it was believed that there were many more people of Jewish ancestry.

BIBLIOGRAPHY: S. Dubnow, *History of the Jews in Russia and Poland*, 3 vols. (1916–20), index; R. Mahler. *Divrei Yemei Yisrael, Dorot Aḥaronim*, 1, pt. 3 (1955); pt. 4 (1956); 2, pt. 1 (1970), indexes: idem, *Toledot ha-Yehudim be-Polin* (1946), index; A. Levison, *Toledot Yehudei Varshah* (1953); EG (1953, 1959); *Pinkas Varshe* (Yid., 1955); E. Ringelblum, in: *Historishe Shriftn*, 2 (1937), 248–68; idem, in: *Zion*, 3 (1938), 246–66, 337–55; idem, in: *YIVO Bleter*, 13 (1938), 124–32; idem, *Kapitlen Geshikhte…* (1953); idem, *Geshikhte fun Yidn in Varshe*, 1–3 (1947–53); A. Kraushar, *Kupiectwo warszawskie* (1929); H.D. Friedberg, *Toledot ha-Defus ha-lvri be-Polanyah* (1950^2), 109 15; B. Weinryb, in: MGWJ, 77 (1933), 273ff.: H. Lieberman, in: *Sefer ha Yovel… A. Marx* (1943), 20–21. See also bibl. Poland. E.Ringelblum, *Zydzi w Warszawie podczas sredniowiecza* (1932); G.Zalewska, *Ludnosc zydowska w Warszawie w okresie miedzywojennym* (1996);Y. Gutman, A.Wein, S. Netzer,*Toledot Yehudei Varsha,me-Reshitam ad Yameinu* (1991), M.Fuks, *Prasa zydowska w Warszawie 1823–1939*, (1979). HOLOCAUST: For a full bibliography see Holocaust, General Survey-Sources and Literature, Sections 3, 4; G. Reitlinger, *Final Solution* (1968^2), 260–326, and passim, incl. bibl.; R. Hilberg, *Destruction of European Jews* (1961), index: Central Commission for War Crimes, *German Crimes in Poland*, 2 vols. (1946–47); American Federation for Polish Jews, *Black Book of Polish Jewry* (1943); American Jewish Black Book Committee, *Black Book* (1945); A. Czerniakow, *Yoman Geto Varshah* (1968); C.A. Kaplan, *Scroll of Agony: Warsaw Ghetto Diary* (1965); J. Tenenbaum, *In Search of a Lost People* (1949); idem, *Underground, the Story of a People* (1952); B. Mark, *Der Aufstand im Warschauer Ghetto* (19593); idem, (ed.). *The Report of Juergen Stroop* (1958), includes introduction and notes; J. Kermish (ed.), *Mered Getto Varshah be-Einei ha-Oyev* (1968^2), Eng. introd. and notes; P. Friedman, *Martyrs and Fighters*

(1954); Y. Gruenbaum (ed.), *Varshah* (1953), 601–815; J. Sloan (ed.), *Notes from the Warsaw Ghetto. The Journal of Emmanuel Ringelblum* (1958); B. Goldstein, *Five Years in the Warsaw Ghetto* (1961); idem, *The Stars Bear Witness* (1950); D. Wdowinsky, *And We Are Not Saved* (1963); A. Donat, *The Holocaust Kingdom* (1965); N. Blumental and J. Kermish (eds.), *Ha-Meri ve-ha-Mered be-Getto Varshah* (1965), Eng. introd.: M. Berland, *300 Sha'ot ba-Getto ha-Do'ekh* (1959). **ADD. BIBLIOGRAPHY:** Y. Gutman, *Mered ha-Neẓorim* (1963), idem, *Yehudei Varsha 1939–1943, Getto, Makhteret, Mered* (1977); Kh.A. Kaplan, *Megilath Yesurin, Yoman Getto Varsha* (1966), Y. Cukierman (Antek), *Sheva ha-Shanim ha-Hen, 1939–1946* (1990); T. *Prekerowa, Konspiracyjna Rada Pomocy Zydom w warszawie 1942–1945* (1967).

WARSCHAWSKI, MAX (1925–), rabbi and scholar, chief rabbi of Bas-Rhin (Alsace, France), Warschawski was born in Bischeim, a suburb of Strasbourg, to an Alsatian family whose roots go back to Eastern Europe. He was a student of Chief Rabbi Abraham Deutsch, and during World War II studied in the Jewish Seminary of Limoges, to where the Alsatian Jewish community was evacuated in 1939. After the liberation, he completed his studies in Paris and London and became rabbi of his hometown Bischeim. He was in charge of religious teaching in Strasbourg. He was appointed rabbi of Strasbourg in 1954; then he became deputy chief rabbi in 1961 and chief rabbi in 1970. He was active and successful in developing Jewish education both in Jewish schools and in state schools. He was also active in welcoming in Alsace Jews from North Africa, mostly from Algeria, who massively emigrated in 1962. His aim was to avoid what had happened in the inter-war period, when Alsatian Jews had refused to welcome Jewish immigrants from Eastern Europe and from Germany. The old Jewish community of Strasbourg became more diverse in the 1960s, and Warschawski struggled to maintain its unity. Under his guidance, Jewish life flourished in Strasbourg: many students engaged in Jewish learning and were of a strong Zionist bent; new synagogues were built in the city and its suburbs. Warschawski, together with his wife, Mireille (born Metzger), tried to be a rabbi for both secular and Orthodox Jews. He maintained strong ties with the Jewish scouts (Éclaireurs Israélites de France). Warschawski also worked as a historian of the Jews of Alsace, studying the traditions of this ancient, deeply rooted community, saving the artifacts he could find (delivering them to Strasbourg museums), and writing numerous articles in the Jewish press on these old rural communities. With his wife, he wrote a textbook for young Jewish students about the Bible, *Ma Bible illustrée* (1957). With his wife, he immigrated to Jerusalem in 1988.

[Jean-Marc Dreyfus (2nd ed.)]

WAR SCROLL, manuscript comprising 18 columns found among the manuscripts in Qumran Cave 1 in 1947 and acquired by E.L. *Sukenik for the Hebrew University; it is now in the Shrine of the Book, Jerusalem. Two fragments of the scroll were discovered when the cave was officially inspected early in 1949; further fragments of a different recension of the same work were found in Cave 4.

Summary

The work contains prescriptions for the eschatological warfare, lasting 40 years, which will end with the extermination of wickedness (embodied in the "sons of darkness") and the triumph of righteousness (embodied in the "*sons of light"). It is in some degree a Midrash on Daniel 11:40ff., describing in detail how the last great enemy of the people of God, together with his supporters, "shall come to his end, and none shall help him" (Dan. 11:45), and how Michael will stand up to champion the cause of God (Dan. 12:1). The exiles will return from "the wilderness of the peoples" to encamp in "the wilderness of Jerusalem" and in the first instance they will give battle to the *Kittim and their allies, extirpating them first from Syria and then from Egypt. This phase of the war lasts six years. A pure sacrificial worship is established in Jerusalem, organized by a worthy priesthood. There remain 29 years for fighting (for every seventh year is free from war); during these remaining years the other enemies of Israel are attacked and wiped out in turn: those of the family of Shem in the first nine years, the family of Ham in the next decade, and the family of Japheth in the final decade.

The Holy War

The whole campaign is envisaged in terms of the ancient institution of the holy war; slogans emphasizing this are inscribed on the trumpets and on the standards of the sons of light. Some of these slogans have the character of "orders of the day," as when Judah Maccabee, before joining battle with Nicanor, gave the watchword "God's help" (II Macc. 8:23). The "great standard at the head of all the people" was to bear the inscription "Peoples of God" (1QM 3:13), which may be compared with Simeon's official title *sar am El* (I Macc. 14:28). As Judah, before leading his troops into battle, reminded them how divine help had come to their ancestors in similar crises, in the destruction of Sennacherib's army (II Macc. 8:19), so encouraging episodes from Israel's history are invoked in the *War Scroll*: "Goliath of Gath, a mighty man of valor, Thou didst deliver into the hand of David Thy servant, because he trusted in Thy great name" (1QM 11:1ff.). As Judah and his men, returning from victory, "sang hymns and praises to heaven" (I Macc. 14:24), so the *War Scroll* prescribes a hymn of thanksgiving to be sung after battle (1QM 14:4ff.) as well as blessings to be pronounced before and during the action itself by the high priest and the priests and levites (1QM 10:1ff.). As befits a holy war, the priesthood plays a leading part; special vestments are prescribed for its members to wear during battle, in which they accompany the fighting men to strengthen their hands and blow the trumpets for advance, engagement, and return. But when the rout of the sons of darkness begins, "the priests shall sound from afar when the slain fall, and they shall not come to the midst of the slaughter lest they be defiled by unclean blood, for they are holy and must not profane the oil of their priestly anointing with the blood of a nation of vanity" (1QM 9:7–9). Ceremonial purity is insisted upon throughout; not only are the men engaged in a holy war but the holy angels go with their armies. The soldiers must therefore abstain from sexual intercourse while on active service; latrines must be separated from the camp by 2,000 cubits; physical blemishes incapacitate a man from military service as rigorously as they do from ministry in the sanctuary (1QM 7:3–8).

Contemporary Models

While the fundamental principles of the action are those of the holy war, the detailed directions about battle formation, tactics, and weapons are fairly closely related to contemporary practice. It does not appear that the author of the work had ever seen a battle; as in Chronicles, the sons of darkness remain passive and allow the sons of light to carry out their plan of war against them without offering much resistance. Yet the author and his associates had made it their business to study contemporary military manuals, and the results of their study are incorporated in the *War Scroll*. It is debated whether their models were Hellenistic or Roman, but the battle formation has more in common with the Roman *triplex acies* than with the Hellenistic phalanx, and the arms for defense and attack resemble those which are attested for the Roman armies in the age of Caesar. That Jewish generals did adopt Roman models is evident from Josephus' account of his training and equipping the forces which he commanded in Galilee at the beginning of the war against Rome (Jos., Wars, 2:577ff.); a comparison between this account and the *War Scroll* shows some impressive points of resemblance, except that Josephus was more of a realist than the author of the *War Scroll* and tried to anticipate the probable action and reaction of the enemy. The detailed way in which the prescriptions are particularized makes it quite improbable that the conflict with which the *War Scroll* is concerned is an allegorical conflict against spiritual forces of wickedness (like John Bunyan's *Holy War*); fighting with material weapons against foes of flesh and blood is envisaged, even if the course of the action turned out differently from that anticipated in this blueprint when at last the sons of light declared war on the Kittim.

BIBLIOGRAPHY: Y. Yadin, *Scroll of the War of the Sons of Light Against the Sons of Darkness* (1962); J. Carmignac, *La règle de la guerre* (1958); J. van der Ploeg, *Le rouleau de la guerre* (1959); H.A. Brongers, *De rol van de strijd* (1960); Atkinson, in: BJRL, 40 (1957–58), 272ff.; G.R. Driver, *Judaean Scrolls* (1965), 168–225.

[Frederick Fyvie Bruce]

WARSHAVSKY, YAKIR (1885–1942), Yiddish and Hebrew novelist and journalist. Born in Mlawa, Poland, to a ḥasidic merchant family, Warshavsky received a traditional education and studied secular subjects on his own. He worked as a Hebrew teacher, an official in Jewish institutions, and a Zionist organizer, as well as writing articles, stories and sketches for various Yiddish and Hebrew periodicals, influenced by his townsman and classmate, Joseph *Opatoshu. Articles about his 1914 trip to Palestine became the basis for his first book, *Min ha-Moledet* ("From the Homeland," 1919). His collection of tales, *Di Letste* ("The Last Ones," 1929), described Polish ḥasidic life vividly and sympathetically. He lived in Warsaw, continuing to work and write during World War II in the Warsaw Ghetto until his murder by the Nazis in the summer of 1942.

BIBLIOGRAPHY: Rejzen, Leksikon, 1 (1926), 921–3; LNYL, 3 (1960), 314–5; *Pinkes Mlave* (1950), 216, 280–6; Kressel, Leksikon, 1 (1965), 709–10. **ADD. BIBLIOGRAPHY:** S. Liptzin, *A History of Yiddish Literature* (1985), 431.

[Melech Ravitch/ Lily O. Kahn (2nd ed.)]

WARSHAWSKI, MARK (1848–1907), Yiddish poet and song-writer. Born in Odessa, he practiced law in Kiev. He wrote both the words and the music of his songs, improvised couplets and sang them at various gatherings, but remained unaware of the literary and folk quality of his songs until *Sholem Aleichem encouraged him to publish them and wrote the introduction to Warshawski's *Yudishe Folkslider mit Notn* ("Jewish Folksongs with Music," 1900). A second edition, with additional poems and biographical information, was published in Odessa (1914) and a third edition in New York (1918). A fourth edition, edited by S. Rozhansky (Rollansky), appeared in Buenos Aires in 1958. Warshawski's songs and poems, written in a simple, unsophisticated style, describe the joys and sorrows of everyday life. In contrast to many writers of his period, who were generally critical of Jewish ways, he wrote with enthusiasm about customs and modes of life. "Oyfn Pripetshik," glorifying the old-fashioned *ḥeder*, became one of the most popular Jewish songs, attaining the status of a folk song. His wedding songs and his hymns to Zion brought cheer, comfort, and hope to Russian Jews under czarist oppression.

BIBLIOGRAPHY: Rejzen, Leksikon, 1 (1928), 918–21; LNYL, 3 (1960), 316–8; Liptzin, *Flowering of Yiddish Literature* (1963), 72–5; I. Manger, *Noente Geshtaltn* (1938), 163–9; E.H. Jeshurin, *Mark Varshavski-Bibliografye* (1958); J. Leftwich (ed.), *The Golden Peacock* (1961), Eng. trans. **ADD. BIBLIOGRAPHY:** S. Leichter (ed.), *Anthology of Yiddish Folksongs*, 6 (2002).

[Elias Schulman / Tamar Lewinsky (2nd ed.)]

WARSHAWSKY, ISAAC (pseudonym **Ben Asher**; 1832–1903), Hebrew writer and linguist. Born in Odessa, Warshawsky taught Hebrew at a *talmud torah*, Judaism at a government school there, and supervised several charitable institutions. He published articles in the Hebrew and Russo-Jewish press.

A proponent of the purity of the Hebrew language, he wrote the polemic, *Li-Teḥiyyat Sefat Ever* (2 vols., 1893, 1902), attacking those who were developing the language without due regard to its grammar. Among his other works are *Ha-Ḥoker* (vol. 1, 1863 in Hebrew, vol. 2, 1866 in German) and a history of Israel until the building of the Second Temple, *Toledot Yisrael* (1867, and many other editions).

BIBLIOGRAPHY: N. Sokolow (ed.), *Sefer Zikkaron le-Soferei Yisrael* (1889), 37f.

[Gedalyah Elkoshi]

WARSKI-WARSZAWSKI, ADOLF (1868–1937), Polish Communist leader. Born in Cracow into an assimilated family which favored Polish independence, he was connected from early youth with the Polish workers' movement. Warski-Warszawski was one of the founders of the Polish Labor Union, and organized the Social Democratic Party of Poland and Lithuania. He took an active part in the Russian revolution of 1905 and was arrested by the czarist authorities on several occasions. During World War I Warski-Warszawski represented the Polish Democrats at the anti-war conferences of Zimmer-Wald and Kiental (Switzerland). After the war he was one of the founders of the Polish Communist Party and was a member of its central committee and political bureau. He was elected as a Communist member of the Sejm, and won a reputation for his courageous speeches and sharp criticism of the authorities. When the Communist Party was made illegal in 1930 he emigrated to the Soviet Union, where he became a prominent figure in the Polish section of the Communist International. In 1937, during the great purges in the U.S.S.R., he was accused of treason and of being a counterrevolutionary, and he was imprisoned and executed.

[Abraham Wein]

WARSZAWSKI, OSER (**Varshavsky**; 1898–1944), Yiddish novelist. Born in Sochaczew, Poland, he astounded the Yiddish literary world with his youthful novel *Shmuglares* ("Smugglers," 1920), dealing with Polish-Jewish life under German occupation during World War I. The language is laced with dialect and vulgarity; the focus skips from one underworld character to another; the descriptions are bloodily expressionistic. The influence of his patron, the naturalistic novelist I.M. *Weissenberg, is obvious. Five Yiddish, three Russian, and one Hebrew edition of *Shmuglares* appeared within a decade. In 1924 Warszawski settled in Paris, where he edited with Peretz *Markish the second issue of the Yiddish avant-garde journal **Khalyastre*, and associated with the foreign, often Jewish, artists of Montparnasse. From the Nazi occupation of France until his arrest by the Gestapo in Rome in May 1944, Warszawski penned fictionalized chronicles of Jewish life in occupied Paris and Vichy France. After his murder at Auschwitz and the liberation of France, his widow Marie published his wartime writings in both Yiddish and (French) translation, which posthumously transformed Warszawski from the author of a paradoxical Yiddish bestseller into one of the rare writers who, like Isaiah *Spiegel, produced Holocaust fiction simultaneously with the incomprehensible events they recount and rework.

BIBLIOGRAPHY: Rejzen, Leksikon, 1 (1926), 921–3; LNYL, 3 (1960), 318–21; M. Ravitch, *Mayn Leksikon*, 1 (1945), 80–82; I. Papiernikov, *Heymishe un Noente* (1958), 230–77.

[Melech Ravitch / Alan Astro (2nd ed.)]

WARWICK, town in central England. Jews are not mentioned there until the 13th century. They were excluded in 1234, but subsequently the community seems to have attained relative importance and was the seat of an *archa. The local synagogue was in the house of an active financier named Elijah, but the Elijah of וורויק referred to in a medieval Hebrew source is probably Elijah of York. No Jewish community has existed in Warwick since the expulsion of the Jews from England in 1290.

BIBLIOGRAPHY: Roth, England, 3, 121–2, 238, 277; idem, *Intellectual Activities of Medieval English Jewry* (1949), 57; M.D. Davis, *Shetaroth: Hebrew Deeds of English Jews*, 1 (1888), 53, 95, 211; Rigg, Exchequer, passim.

[Cecil Roth]

WASHINGTON, a Pacific Northwest state of the United States, with a Jewish population – including Seattle – of approximately 45,000 Jews (2003). A Latvian adventurer, Adolph Friedman, who came to Washington in the late 1840s, is considered the first Jew to have settled in the new territory. Others soon followed – German-speaking Jews in the 1850s; Yiddish-speaking Jews in the 1880s; and Judeo-Spanish (Ladino) speaking Jews in 1902. By 1889, when Washington became the 42nd state, Jews had been contributing to the state's economy and growth for four decades. One of them, Edward S. Salomon, became territorial governor in 1870, others joined state legislators and/or became city mayors. Successful entrepreneurs, such as the Schwabacher family, had businesses throughout the state.

By 1920 just over 10,000 Jews called Washington State home. They would be joined by immigrants fleeing Hitler's Germany before World War II, survivors from Hitler's death camps, and people who moved west to take advantage of Washington's mild climate, beautiful lakes and mountains, welcoming businesses, excellent medical facilities, and, in Seattle, opportunities and amenities of the University of Washington. Unlike the first three groups who were mainly businessmen and women, the latter group were or became physicians, professors, teachers, rabbis, cantors, musicians, artists, and business and health workers of all kinds. They would invigorate Jewish life and add to the state's culture and economy.

The first Jewish organizations in Washington were benevolent societies rather than temples or synagogues. The desire for a Jewish cemetery led Jews in Olympia and small towns around Puget Sound to establish the Hebrew Benevolent Society of Puget Sound in 1873. They also made clear that the society would "aid and assist poor and distressed co-religionists." The Hebrew Benevolent Association of Tacoma

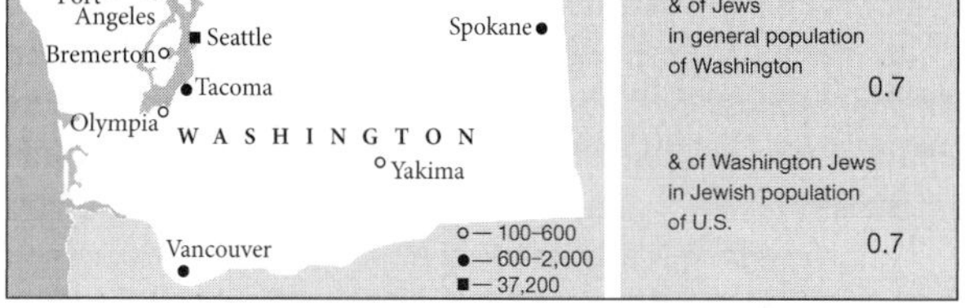

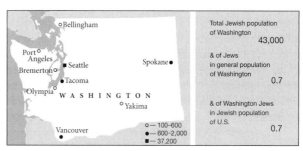

Jewish communities in Washington. Population figures for 2001.

also followed that example. Soon other Jewish communities throughout the state set up a myriad of voluntary organizations to help the unfortunate as well as to enhance the lives of Jews in the state.

Tacoma, Spokane, and Seattle all had religious congregations before 1900. All were Reform, sometimes modified to contain elements of an Orthodox service. Others, like Bellingham and Everett, chose Orthodox. The small community of Aberdeen followed Reform, but services included Orthodox rituals. All the cities except Spokane were in the western part of the state, the largest population area.

After World War II, Jewish religious life in Washington expanded. Newcomers and the maturing new generations of Americanized Jewish children either established new congregations in cities such as Richland, Wenatchee, and Vancouver, or changed the status of existing ones. For example, in Tacoma and Spokane the Reform and Orthodox combined to form one place of worship.

Another great expansion of Jewish religious life started in the 1970s and accelerated into the 1990s. In many congregations, half the couples had only one partner who was Jewish, a reflection of the growing trend of interfaith marriages throughout the United States. The founding of a temple or synagogue for a special group of people, say gays or lesbians, or becoming Reconstructionist became unremarkable and Reform and Conservative congregations welcomed women rabbis and cantors. In 2003 there were 41 religious congregations offering services.

BIBLIOGRAPHY: M. Cone, H. Droker, J. Williams, *Family of Strangers: Building a Jewish Community in Washington State* (2003).

[Jacqueline Williams (2nd ed.)]

WASHINGTON, D.C., capital of the United States. Jewish population (est. 2005), 27,735; general population, 572,059; Jewish population of the Washington metropolitan area, 215,000; general population: 5,162,029; sixth largest Jewish community in the nation.

Early Arrivals and First Congregations

In contrast to U.S. cities where the first Jews, often Sephardi in origin, arrived in the 17th and 18th centuries, Washington's Jewish community got a later start. The diamond-shaped area along the shores of the Potomac River was not designated as the future home of the federal district until 1790; the federal government arrived 10 years later. Washington's economy, based largely on the presence of the federal government, lacked the manufacturing of other cities. Jewish residents in the first decades of the 19th century, and many of those who followed later, were attracted by the growing capital's economic opportunities or arrived to pursue federal service. As Washington was not a port of entry, 19th- and early 20th-century immigrants did not arrive in the city directly. Most had previously spent time in port cities such as New York and Baltimore.

Among the earliest Jewish residents was land speculator and builder Isaac Polock, grandson of a founder of the Newport, Rhode Island, synagogue, who arrived from Savannah, Georgia, in 1795. Anticipating the ensuing needs of the federal government, Polock completed a row of buildings near the President's House. Known as the Six Buildings, they initially housed the U.S. State Department and the Secretary of the Navy. In 1828, Captain Alfred Mordecai, of North Carolinian colonial lineage, was assigned to the Washington Arsenal and made his home in Washington. His daughter, Rosa (b. 1839), was the first known Jewish child born in Washington. Mordecai became superintendent of the Arsenal during the Mexican-American War (1846–1848). Rather than fight against his native South, he resigned from the army at the start of the Civil War.

For decades, the numbers of Jews in Washington remained small, estimated at only 25 in 1847. The population grew significantly in the late 1840s and the 1850s with the arrival of German-speaking immigrants fleeing dwindling economic prospects, harsh restrictions, and failed revolutionary movements in Central Europe. Many of the new arrivals were merchants who catered to the growing federal city. In 1852, 21 German-speaking men met in a Pennsylvania Avenue home to form Washington's first Jewish congregation, which would become known as the Washington Hebrew Congregation. The congregation petitioned Congress (constitutionally responsible for local law) for legislation ensuring its right to own property in Washington. President Franklin Pierce signed "An Act for the Benefit of the Hebrew Congregation in the city of Washington" on June 2, 1856. U.S. Navy Captain Jonas P. Levy, a president of the congregation and a popular hero of the Mexican-American War, assisted the congregation in that endeavor. Today one of the nation's largest Reform synagogues, Washington Hebrew, is the only congregation in the country with a Congressional charter.

During the Civil War (1861–1865), the city's Jewish population grew from 200 to almost 2,000, with some soldiers staying in Washington after completing their service. Most Jewish newcomers were merchants arriving to serve the wartime boom. One newspaper reported six kosher restaurants operating in the capital during the 1860s. Washingtonians organized the first Washington lodge of B'nai B'rith (the Elijah Lodge) in 1864. During the war, the women of the Washington Hebrew Congregation raised money for the U.S. Sanitary Commission, and the congregation's visiting nursing corps ministered to injured soldiers. Among the Jewish Civil War soldiers cared for by the Washington Hebrew nurses was Leopold Karpeles who was awarded the Medal of Honor for his service during the Battle of the Wilderness (1864). After the war, Karpeles married his nurse, Sarah Mundheim, and became a clerk in the U.S. Post Office Department.

Changes to the liturgy and the introduction of a melodeon (an organlike keyboard instrument) at the Washington Hebrew Congregation upset a small group of like-minded traditionalists who resigned to found Adas Israel Congregation in 1869. President Ulysses S. Grant attended the 1876 dedication of its synagogue, the first building constructed as a synagogue in Washington. Grant's presence at the dedication was particularly meaningful. During the Civil War, General Grant had issued Order No. 11 (1862) expelling Jews "as a class" from Mississippi, Tennessee, and Kentucky on charges of war profiteering.

In 1861 the Washington Hebrew Congregation established the city's first Jewish school, an all-day program that compensated for the lack of public schooling in the District of Columbia. By 1870, with a new public school system in place, the Jewish elementary school closed. For more than half a century Jewish education in the nation's capital would consist of supplementary classes meeting on weekday afternoons and on weekends.

New Immigrants, New Congregations

By 1880, many of Washington's 1,500 Jews were second-generation Americans, including shopkeepers, clerks, established merchants, and a smattering of professionals. They were soon joined by a new wave of Jewish immigrants, Orthodox Jews fleeing Eastern Europe's pogroms, poverty, and forced military service.

The influx of newer immigrants in the 1880s and 1890s made necessary new philanthropic institutions, including the Hebrew Relief Society (1882; later the United Hebrew Relief Society), United Hebrew Charities (1890), the Jewish Foster Home (1908), the Hebrew Free Loan Society (1909), and the Hebrew Home for the Aged (1914). One of the outstanding leaders in these endeavors was Minnie Lansburgh Goldsmith (1871–1971), daughter of department store owner Gustav Lansburgh. She served as president of the United Hebrew Charities, led fundraising efforts for the Jewish Foster Home and the Hebrew Home for the Aged, and helped create Washington's Community Chest, predecessor to the United Way. The arrival of new immigrants increased Washington's Jewish community to 10,000 by 1920.

Zionist activity in Washington dates to the early 20th century, with the founding of the Washington Zionist Organization, the local chapter of the Zionist Organization of America (c. 1901), Washington Poale Zion Society, and Washington's first Hadassah chapter (1919), formed shortly after a visit to the city by Hadassah founder Henrietta Szold.

Jews principally settled where existing commercial development suggested the viability of small businesses, running grocery stores, meat markets, dry goods establishments, hardware stores, and the like across the city. Families often lived above their shops and formed congregations in the neighborhoods. One of the largest concentrations of Jewish residents clustered around Seventh Street NW, one of the city's main business districts. Amid small furniture, fancy goods, jewelry, and millinery shops, several Jewish merchants expanded their businesses into fashionable department stores such as Lansburgh's, Hecht's, and S. Kann & Co. In the early 20th century, enough families lived in the Seventh Street neighborhood to support three synagogues within as many city blocks: Washington Hebrew Congregation, Adas Israel Congregation, and Ohev Sholom Congregation (1886), the first congregation in Washington founded by Russian Jews.

New immigrants also joined the handful of German-speaking Jewish merchants in Georgetown and Southwest Washington. In Georgetown, German-speaking Jews had established the Mount Sinai Society (1860s), later absorbed into Washington Hebrew. In 1910, Orthodox Russian immigrants founded Kesher Israel Congregation, which remains on the same site today.

In the early 20th century, close to 200 Jewish families in Southwest D.C. supported two synagogues, Talmud Torah Congregation (1887) and Voliner Anshe Sfard (1908). Al Jolson (born Asa Yoelson) attended synagogue at Talmud Torah, where his father, Moshe Yoelson, served as a cantor, *mohel* and *shoḥet*. Many Russian Jewish immigrants also settled along H Street NE in the early 1900s and founded Ezras Israel Congregation (1907). A small community of Orthodox Jews living nearby on Capitol Hill established the Southeast Hebrew Congregation (1909).

Wartime Washington and the Great Depression

World War I introduced a new wave of soldiers and government war workers to the capital. A group of young men who had formed the Young Men's Hebrew Association (YMHA; 1911) organized activities for arriving government workers and the first servicemen's club in the United States. The YMHA and the Young Women's Hebrew Association (1913) hosted dances, Sabbath services, and recreational opportunities for the thousands of Jewish servicemen and servicewomen posted in Washington during the war. After the war, national and local leaders raised money to build an impressive Jewish Community Center (JCC) on Sixteenth Street (1926), one mile from the White House. A local Jewish newspaper, the *National Jewish Ledger* (now *Washington Jewish Week*), began publication in 1930. The Jewish Community Council organized in 1938 as a unified voice for communal organizations on issues of importance to the Washington Jewish community.

As Jews became more established, they moved uptown into neighborhoods made possible by the development of streetcar suburbs in the northernmost areas of Washington and in nearby Maryland. New congregations were also founded in these uptown neighborhoods. The move northward was restricted in part by developers who placed covenants in real estate deeds prohibiting sale or lease to Jews, African Americans, and other racial and ethnic groups in areas like Spring Valley, an upscale neighborhood, and parts of Chevy Chase, Maryland. Although the Supreme Court ruled restrictive covenants unconstitutional in 1948, their effects lingered in many neighborhoods.

Although the presence of the federal government spared Washington the worst of the Great Depression, organizations like the Hebrew Sheltering Society provided kosher meals, a change of clothes, and lodging for those newly arrived in Washington and looking for work. The 1930s and 1940s saw a more than doubling of Washington's Jewish population, as young professionals arrived to work on President Franklin Delano Roosevelt's New Deal, for the war effort, and in an expanding civil service. Many of them first-generation Americans, they helped shape and implement New Deal policies and programs of social relief and reform.

As Hitler's grip tightened on Europe in the 1930s, Washington became a fulcrum of Zionist and rescue activity. Washingtonians worked to rescue European Jewish children and to support a Jewish homeland in Palestine as a haven for refugees. In 1938, 4,000 protesters packed the Daughters of the American Revolution's (DAR) Constitution Hall to pressure the British government to open Palestine to Jewish immigration. Local clergy of many faiths, civic leaders, and congressmen addressed the crowd and attendees petitioned President Roosevelt to intercede on behalf of Jews seeking to immigrate. The Women's Auxiliary of B'nai B'rith's Argo Lodge, whose anniversary luncheon in 1938 was attended by First Lady Eleanor Roosevelt, raised money on behalf of European Jewish refugees. Denise Tourover, Hadassah's first Washington representative, led lobbying and fundraising efforts to rescue the "Teheran children" – 700 Polish orphans stranded in Persia after making their way out of Europe. In 1943 she pleaded with State Department officials and ambassadors until British ships finally transported the children to Palestine.

As the nation mobilized for war, Jews were among the tens of thousands of soldiers and war workers who arrived to serve at the epicenter of the Allied war effort. In 1941 alone, the JCC room registry helped find housing for 4,000 Jews in local boarding houses, some of which catered to Jewish residents with kosher-style meals. Local organizations and synagogues sponsored religious services for military personnel.

Like American Jews in general, Washington Jews held differing views about Zionism. In 1940 and 1941, leaders of the Washington chapter of the Zionist Organization of America (ZOA) worked to build local membership. The Washington apartment of Supreme Court Justice Louis D. Brandeis served as a salon for national and local Zionist leaders. Rabbi Norman Gerstenfeld of the Washington Hebrew Congregation spoke ardently against the idea of a Jewish state. Local Zionists – such as Edmund I. Kaufmann, Zionist Organization of America president (1940–1941), and Rabbi Isadore Breslau, director of the American Zionist Bureau's lobbying efforts – rose to prominence on Washington's national stage.

In the aftermath of World War II, many of the most influential members of Washington's Jewish community participated in a secret fundraising campaign to support the Haganah in its war for independence. Men and women raised money to provide ships and crews to support Aliyah Bet (illegal immigration to Palestine), to purchase machinery for a munitions factory, and supply World War II surplus weapons and explosives for the Haganah. The local United Jewish Appeal met its first million-dollar campaign in 1946 to help meet the overwhelming economic and social needs of Jewish immigrants in Palestine. In 1947, Washington Jews tapped personal connections in the embassies and the White House to influence the UN vote on the partition of Palestine.

As David Ben-Gurion proclaimed the independence of Israel in Jerusalem on May 14, 1948, an exuberant crowd of Washington Jews gathered at the Jewish Agency building on Massachusetts Avenue NW. They danced and sang as the new flag was raised. Local Jews selected and purchased Israel's first embassy near Embassy Row shortly after statehood. Formerly non-Zionist and anti-Zionist organizations and individuals, including Rabbi Gerstenfeld, came to support the new nation. The presence of the Embassy of Israel in Washington reinforced the community's ties to Zionism, with the ambassador and his family playing an active role in local religious and community life.

Suburbanization

With the expansion of the federal bureaucracy in the postwar period, returning veterans and newly arrived government workers contributed to the transformation of Washington from capital city into metropolitan region. Seeking new homes, many Jewish residents joined an exodus to the Maryland and Virginia suburbs. By 1956, half of the area's 81,000 Jews lived outside the city limits. Many Jewish-owned businesses followed. Synagogues also moved to follow their congregants, and suburban residents formed new congregations, including the Arlington Fairfax Jewish Center (now Etz Hayim), which began meeting in Arlington, Virginia, in the early 1940s, and the Montgomery County (Maryland) Jewish Center (now Ohr Kodesh), founded in 1947. Jewish builders and real estate developers played a major role during Washington's postwar building boom. When it opened in 1944, Hebrew Academy (Orthodox) became the first day school in the Washington area in nearly a century. A number of smaller schools, including Beth Jacob School and a Yeshiva High School, operated in Washington for a number of years in the 1950s and 1960s.

In the late 1950s community leaders made plans to move communal agencies to the Maryland suburbs to serve the burgeoning suburban population. In 1969, the Jewish Community Center, the Hebrew Home for the Aged, and the Jewish Social Services Agency (later joined by the United Jewish Appeal (UJA) and the Jewish Community Council) relocated to a centralized campus of Jewish institutional life in Rockville, Maryland. The process was accelerated by the urban riots in the late 1960s. As Jews left Washington, D.C. neighborhoods and fled to the suburbs, so, too, did Jewish institutions. B'nai Israel relocated to Rockville – as part of a cluster of Jewish institutions that included the JCC of Greater Washington, the Hebrew Home for the Aged and the Charles E. Smith Jewish Day School. Adas Israel almost moved from its Quebec Avenue NW site, save for the objection of some donors, who had only recently contributed to its construction. Within several years, it was again thriving, as the Metro opened almost at its front door.

The Jewish Community Council placed civil rights issues at the forefront of its activities in the 1950s and 1960s.

The Council lent its name to the Thompson's Restaurant court case, decided by the Supreme Court in 1953, which ended segregation in public accommodations in Washington. Following *Brown v. Board of Education* (1954), which declared segregated public schools unconstitutional, the Council worked with city and religious leaders to encourage peaceful integration.

Washingtonians joined thousands in the national Jewish community who protested the treatment of Soviet Jews with massive demonstrations on the Mall in the 1970s and 1980s and maintained a daily vigil outside the Soviet embassy from 1970 to 1991. Church groups took over the vigil on Shabbat and on the High Holidays.

The 21st Century Community

In 2005, 83 percent of greater Washington's 215,000 Jews lived in the Maryland and Northern Virginia suburbs. Although the Jewish community is clustered most densely in lower Montgomery Country, Maryland (36 percent), the community now extends to the far reaches of the Greater Washington, D.C. metropolitan region. Northern Virginia experienced a 111 percent growth in its Jewish population between 1983 and 2003. In 2004, Congregation Sha'are Shalom built the first Jewish house of worship in Loudoun County, Virginia (25 miles from Washington, D.C.). Over 70 congregations and three JCCs serve the metropolitan area. The Washington-Baltimore corridor is virtually one continuous city, yet the Jewish communities of Washington and Baltimore are quite separate and the Jewish community of Columbia, Maryland, is also independent, though more linked to Baltimore than to Washington.

In addition to synagogue religious schools, serving the community in the area of Jewish education are the Hebrew Academy (1944), which had moved from 16th Street in Washington to nearby Silver Spring, and then again out closer to the Orthodox community in Kemp Mill; Charles E. Smith Jewish Day School (1972; a community day school, which evolved out of a Solomon Schechter Day School established in the 1960s), one of the largest day schools in the Diaspora, located in Rockville; the Jewish Primary Day School, first housed at Adas Israel congregation and later at the 16th Street home of the Hebrew Academy (1987; an independent, community K-6 school); and Gesher (Northern Virginia's community day school).

The Jewish Community Relations Council of Greater Washington, comprised of over 210 constituent organizations in the early 21st century, encourages collaborative partnerships within the area's Jewish community and between the Jewish community and the broader society. One local project has provided tours of the U.S. Holocaust Memorial Museum for Washington, D.C. police officers. The United States Holocaust Memorial Museum is a major presence of Jewish memory adjacent to the National Mall and has drawn almost four out of five American Jews as pilgrims.

Although the majority of the Jewish community lives in the suburbs, a resurgence of interest in maintaining a Jewish presence downtown has occurred over the last decades. District residents formed a new downtown Jewish Community Center in the late 1970s, and in the 1990s purchased, restored, and reopened the original JCC building. The first building constructed as a synagogue in Washington is listed on the National Register of Historic Places and is maintained by the Jewish Historical Society of Greater Washington as the Lillian and Albert Small Jewish Museum. The second home of Adas Israel, a church for half a century, has been restored and reopened as the Sixth and I Historic Synagogue, providing a downtown meeting place for the community.

Jews and the Federal City

Jewish Washingtonians have served in elected and appointed positions in the local and federal governments since the 19th century. Adolphus Solomons (1826–1910), publisher and proprietor of a Washington bookstore, served in the Washington, D.C. House of Delegates (1871). He turned down the offer of the governorship of the District, as the position would have required working on the Sabbath. Simon Wolf, who moved to Washington in 1862 after receiving his law degree, served as recorder of deeds for the District of Columbia. In the 20th century, local Jews have served in the district government and as ambassadors, policy advisors, heads of federal agencies and Supreme Court justices. Many have joined local synagogues and taken part in the life of the Washington Jewish community. Senator Joseph Lieberman, the first Jewish candidate for vice president (2000), is a member of Kesher Israel Congregation in Georgetown. Many Jews who come to Washington for what they think to be a brief stay in elective office or government service make Washington their permanent home. Senators and congressmen, Supreme Court justices, cabinet officials, ambassadors to the United States from foreign countries and high-ranking staff of the executive branch, the judiciary and the Congress, and their spouses and children, are found in synagogues and schools, ordinary participants in Jewish life.

Washington's confluence of religious, civic, and political life and its status as national and international capital have made it a fitting backdrop for national Jewish dialogues. In the 19th century, Adolphus Solomons counseled local and national Jewish leaders and played a pivotal role in convincing President Lincoln to allow Jews to become military chaplains during the Civil War. Simon Wolf, one of the most influential Jewish leaders of his time, advocated on behalf of Jewish issues worldwide through his work with the Board of Delegates of American Israelites. When the Board merged with the Union of American Hebrew Congregations in 1878, Wolf served as chairman of the UAHC's Board of Delegates of Civil and Religious Rights for over 30 years. In 1913, Carrie Simon, wife of Rabbi Abram Simon of the Washington Hebrew Congregation, created the National Federation of Temple Sisterhoods.

Lobbyists, activists, dignitaries, and philanthropists convene in Washington to discuss support for Israel and legislative issues of concern to the American Jewish community. Many national Jewish organizations and lobbying groups, including the American-Israel Public Affairs Committee (AIPAC), the national office of the Jewish War Veterans, the Union of Reform Judaism's Religious Action Center, B'nai B'rith International (which established its national office in Washington in 1943), and Hillel: The Foundation for Jewish Campus Life, are headquartered in the capital.

[Laura Burd Schiavo (2nd ed.)].

°**WASHINGTON, GEORGE** (1732–1799), commander in chief of the American forces in the Revolutionary War and first president of the United States. So far as can be ascertained, Washington's Jewish associations were exclusively official, and despite claims in earlier Jewish sources, no Jew ever served him as aide-de-camp.

Three members of the Franks family had dealings with him. In 1758, when Washington took command of Braddock's defeated forces in western Pennsylvania, he applied to David *Franks (1720–1794) of Philadelphia for supplies. Franks served as agent for a British syndicate quartermastering British colonial forces and was banished behind the British lines for his loyalist sympathies in 1778. The Jew whom Washington came to know best was David Solebury *Franks (c. 1742–1793), who joined the patriot forces in Montreal in 1776. By June 1778 he was aide-de-camp to General Benedict Arnold, commandant at Philadelphia. Two years later Franks was on Arnold's staff when the latter turned traitor, but he was later exonerated from all charges. Franks continued functioning as a military and diplomatic courier, rising to the rank of lieutenant-colonel. In November 1789, as secretary of a commission to the Creek Indians, he dined with the commissioners at Washington's table. The yellow fever epidemic that killed Franks brought Washington in touch with Isaac W. Franks (1759–1822). In the fall of 1793 Washington sought a suburban presidential mansion outside disease-ridden Philadelphia; he rented Franks' Germantown house.

Solomon *Bush (1753–1795) served under Washington as a captain of a Pennsylvania battalion in the Battle of Long Island. He rose to lieutenant-colonel, the highest rank achieved by a Jew on active duty. Philip Moses Russell (1747–1830) served as surgeon's mate with Virginia regiments from 1775 to 1778, becoming ill as the result of his ministrations at Valley Forge. In applying for a pension his widow stated that he had received a letter of commendation from General Washington. The Prager family, merchants from Holland, settled in Philadelphia, ignoring their Jewish origins. In July 1784 Washington furnished one of them with letters of introduction and, three years later, while attending the Constitutional Convention, Washington dined at the Prager home.

Washington was inaugurated as president of the United States on April 30, 1789. Within one week, Levi Sheftall, as president of the newly reorganized *Savannah Hebrew congregation, penned a congratulatory letter which Washington acknowledged. Savannah's hasty action embarrassed Shearith Israel Congregation, located in the then capital city of the U.S., New York. Its leadership delayed until June 1790 before inviting the congregations in Newport, Philadelphia, Charleston, and Richmond to join in preparing a message to the president. Newport declined because Rhode Island had not yet ratified the Constitution. However, when Washington made a visit to Newport on August 17, 1790, Moses *Seixas, as president of that congregation, and also as grand master of the masonic lodge, presented two letters to Washington. For the congregation he wrote extolling a government, "which to bigotry gives no sanction, to persecution no assistance…." In his response, Washington repeated these phrases. When Shearith Israel continued to procrastinate, Manuel *Josephson, president of the Philadelphia congregation, took the occasion of the government's move to Philadelphia to present the congratulations of the four remaining Hebrew congregations on December 13, 1790.

BIBLIOGRAPHY: J.C. Fitzpatrick (ed.), *Writings of George Washington*, 39 vols. (1931–44^2), index; idem, *Diaries of George Washington*, 4 vols. (1925), index: F.B. Heitman, *Historical Register of Officers of the Continental Army* (1914, repr. 1967), index; J.R. Marcus, *Early American Jewry*, 2 vols. (1952–55), index; idem, *American Jewry: Documents Eighteenth Century* (1959), index; E. Wolf II and M. Whiteman, *History of the Jews of Philadelphia* (1957), index; M.U. Schappes, *Documentary History of the Jews in the U.S. 1654–1875* (1952^2), index.

[Malcolm H. Stern]

WASHOFSKY, MARK E. (1952–), U.S. Reform rabbi, academician. Washofsky was born in New Orleans, Louisiana, and received his B.A. from the University of Alabama in 1974. In 1980, he was ordained at *Hebrew Union College, where he earned a Ph.D. in 1987. He served as rabbi of Beth Israel Synagogue in Hamilton, Ohio (1981–85), while also teaching homiletics at the Cincinnati campus of HUC-JIR. In 1985, he was appointed associate professor of rabbinics and elevated to professor in 2001. A scholar in the field of the literature of the Talmud and *halakhah*, his subspecialty is the divergent traditions of Ashkenaz and Sepharad. In the Reform movement, Washofsky has been the chairman of the Committee on Responsa of the *Central Conference of American Rabbis since 1996. He was a major contributor to *The Oxford Dictionary of the Jewish Religion* and is the author of *Jewish Living: A Guide to Contemporary Reform Practice* (2001). He also co-edited (with Gunther *Plaut) *Teshuvot for the Nineties: Recent American Reform Responsa* (1997).

[Bezalel Gordon (2nd ed.)]

WASIT, city in S. Iraq, founded about 703 by al-Ḥajjāj, governor of Babylonia on behalf of ʿAbd al-Malik, the *Umayyad caliph. Situated in a fertile region on the banks of the Tigris, Wasit was a populous center under the Umayyads and *Abbasids; it retained its importance during the Late Middle Ages up until the 16th century when the city fell into ruins as a result of the Tigris changing its course to a more eastward one. Under the Abbasid caliphs, Wasit had one of the leading Jewish communities in Babylonia, and, as reported by *Nathan ha-Bavli, paid an annual tax of 150 dinars to the *Sura academy. It was still a flourishing community in the 13th century; in 1201 R. Daniel b. Eleazar b. Ḥibat Allah, the head of the Baghdad academy, addressed himself to the communities of Basra and Wasit (in connection with *Beit Keneset shel Ezra*), from which it appears that these were the two outstanding communities in southern Babylonia. Some of the members of the *Ibn al-Barqūlī family, a prominent Jewish family of Wasit in this period, served in government posts. Judah *Al-Harizi visited Wasit and in his report praised the dignitary Samuel, who may be identical with Samuel ibn al-Barqūlī. The poet *Eleazar b. Jacob composed many poems in honor of Joseph ibn al-Barqūlī, a resident of Wasit. *Matteh Oz*, a work dating from this period, is a collection of sermons given by Isaac Sar-Shalom in Wasit and other southern Babylonian towns from 1210 to 1232 (Neubauer, Cat, no. 1001).

BIBLIOGRAPHY: G. Le Strange, *The Lands of the Eastern Caliphate* (1930), 39ff.; S. Assaf, in: *Tarbiz*, 1 no. 1 (1930), 122; no. 3, 54, 64; J. Leveen, in: JQR, 16 (1925/26), 395–7.

[Eliyahu Ashtor]

WASKOW, ARTHUR (1933–), founder of the American movement for Jewish Renewal. As the leading proponent and founder of the American religious movement for Jewish Renewal, Waskow's midrashic interpretations of Jewish texts have sparked a renaissance of interest in the connection between Jewish spirituality and social justice in contemporary America.

Born in Baltimore, Md., Waskow received his bachelor's degree from Johns Hopkins University in 1954 and a master's degree (1956) and doctorate (1963) in U.S. history from the University of Wisconsin. From 1959 to 1982, he worked in Washington, D.C., on public policy concerning military strategy and disarmament, race relations, nonviolent action, the Vietnam War, and renewable energy sources. He also served as a founder and fellow of the Institute for Policy Studies from 1963 to 1977.

Throughout the 1960s, he was active in writing, speaking, electoral politics, and nonviolent protests against racism and the Vietnam War. In 1981 and 1986, along with eight other plaintiffs from the Washington area, he won a lawsuit against the FBI for illegal and unconstitutional harassment of his antiwar work, under its COINTELPRO program.

In 1969, Waskow's life took a new turn, toward leadership in the renewal of Jewish life in America. This work first began when Waskow wrote *The Freedom Seder*, a Passover *Haggadah* that wove together the traditional text with passages from leaders of social justice movements, such as Martin Luther King. Waskow continued to work as a writer, teacher, and organizer in the movement to renew Judaism. His other notable titles include *These Holy Sparks: The Rebirth of the Jewish People* (1983), *Tales of Tikkun: New Jewish Stories to Heal the Wounded World* (1997), and *A Time for Every Purpose Under Heaven: The Jewish Life-Spiral as a Spiritual Path* (2002), the latter two coauthored with Phyllis Berman.

In 1982, Waskow moved to Philadelphia to become a member of the faculty of the Reconstructionist Rabbinical College, where he founded The Shalom Center, a think tank concerned with Jewish thought and action in response to the dangers of the nuclear arms race and other global environmental threats. During this era, he founded the journal *Menorah: Sparks of Jewish Renewal*, of which he was editor since its inception. In 1993 The Shalom Center left the Reconstructionist Rabbinical College and merged with P'nai Or, founded by Rabbi Zalman *Schachter-Shalomi, to form ALEPH: Alliance for Jewish Renewal. In 1995, after five years of directed study and writing, Waskow was ordained privately as a rabbi by four individuals (three rabbis – one ḥasidic, one Conservative, and one Reform – and a feminist theologian) in the custom of Jewish renewal. In 2005, The Shalom Center became an independent organization, with Waskow as rabbinic director.

Waskow devoted his life's work to raising questions of social justice in the Jewish community. In addition to his pioneering work on eco-Judaism and public opposition to the wars in Vietnam and Iraq, Waskow may be best known for his writing and teaching on behalf of a two-state solution for peace between Israel and the Palestinian people. He was among the leaders of Breira in the 1970s and of New Jewish Agenda in the 1980s, and was one of the peace activists invited to the White House to witness the signing of the Israeli-Palestinian Declaration of Principles in September 1993.

[Michael Berenbaum (2nd ed.)]

WASSER, DENNIS M. (1942–), U.S. lawyer. Born in Brooklyn, N.Y., Wasser and his family moved to California, where he earned a bachelor's degree from the University of California, Los Angeles, and a law degree from the University of Southern California. A member of the firm Wasser, Cooperman & Carter in Los Angeles, Wasser first gained fame when he represented the tennis star Billie Jean King, who was sued by her former lover, a woman, who sought property and support for the rest of her life. King and her husband won the suit, and Wasser's reputation in family law was established. Over the years, he represented a galaxy of Hollywood celebrities in divorce actions, including Steven *Spielberg, Clint Eastwood, Tom Cruise, James Woods, Jane Fonda, Richard *Dreyfus, Lionel Richie, Jennifer Lopez and the wife of Michael *Douglas. Wasser also successfully represented the baseball star David Justice in a "palimony" suit and negotiated on behalf of Kirk Kerkorian, who was sued for child support by a woman he lived with but whose baby he had not fathered. Wasser wrote and lectured widely on family and divorce law.

[Stewart Kampel (2nd ed.)]

WASSERMAN, DALE (1917–), U.S. playwright. Born in Rhinelander, Wisconsin, Wasserman came to the fore when he adapted Ken Kesey's novel *One Flew Over the Cuckoo's Nest* (1963) for the stage. This was followed by *Man of La Mancha* (1965), for which Wasserman received many awards, including a Tony Award and a Critics Circle Award. His other plays include *Western Star*; *An Enchanted Land*; *Players in* *the Game*; *Beggar's Holiday*; *Boy on Blacktop Road*; and *The Stallion Howl*.

Wasserman also wrote screenplays for such feature films as *The Vikings* (1958); *Cleopatra* (1963); *Quick, before It Melts* (1964); *Mister Buddwing* (1966); *A Walk with Love and Death* (1969); and his own *Man of La Mancha*, which he also co-produced (1972).

For television, Wasserman wrote the adaptations for the productions of *The Citadel* (1960) and *The Power and the Glory* (1961), as well as *Long after Summer* (1967). He also wrote for a number of television series, such as *Studio One* (1948); *Armstrong Circle Theatre* (1950); *Kraft Television Theater* (1953); *The DuPont Show of the Month* (1957); and *G.E. True* (1962). Wasserman's book *The Impossible Musical: The Man of La Mancha Story* was published in 2003.

[Ruth Beloff (2nd ed.)]

WASSERMAN, DORA (1919–2003) and **BRYNA** (1947–), Yiddish theater directors. Dora Wasserman was born Dora Goldfarb in Chernikhov in the U.S.S.R. to a poor family. After graduating from high school, she studied voice and went on to train with the Moscow Yiddish Academy under Solomon *Mikhoels. She worked with the Tyuz children's theater in Kiev, the Kiev State Theater, and the Zhitomir Theater until the Soviet Union entered World War II. On the road in 1944, she met and married her husband, Shura Wasserman, in Kazakhstan. They had two daughters, Bryna and Ella. After the war, Dora formed a theater troupe and performed in DP camps in Austria. Wasserman immigrated to Montreal in 1950 and organized children's Yiddish theater groups. In 1957 she formed the Yiddish Drama Group, an adult ensemble created under the auspices of the Montreal Jewish People's Schools. She received support for the theater from the Jewish community, as well as from the wider theater community. The well-known Québecois actor Gratien Gélinas provided technical and material support. In 1967 the company was invited to join the new Saidye Bronfman Centre.

Wasserman went on to produce or direct more than 70 plays for the Yiddish theater. She worked closely with many of the writers who presented works at the company or whose works she adapted for the Yiddish theater. She acquired exclusive stage rights to the works of Isaac Bashevis *Singer. She had Ted Allan's play, *Lies My Father Told Me*, translated into Yiddish (1984), and then staged Michel Tremblay's Quebec classic, *Les Belles Soeurs* (1992). She produced *Fiddler on the Roof* for the first time in Yiddish (1993). The company toured in Israel, the United States, Austria, and Russia. Wasserman was invested as a member of the Order of Canada and the Order of Quebec. In 1996, after Dora Wasserman suffered a stroke, her daughter Bryna took over the artistic directorship of the Yiddish Theatre.

Bryna Wasserman grew up around productions at the Yiddish Theatre. She received a BFA and an MFA in directing from the Tisch School of Fine Arts (NYU), and worked at English and Yiddish theaters, including the Vivian Beaumont at Lincoln Center, Mercer Street, Vancouver Opera House, American Place, and the Folksbiene Playhouse. In 1998 she was appointed artistic director of the English-language theater program for the Theatre of the Saidye Bronfman Centre for the Arts. Under her direction, both the SBC Theatre and Dora Wasserman Yiddish Theatre have received MECCA (Montreal English Critics' Circle) Awards. The Dora Wasserman Yiddish Theatre remains North America's only Yiddish theater company in permanent residence.

BIBLIOGRAPHY: J. Larrue, *Le théâtre yiddish à Montréal/ Yiddish Theatre in Montreal* (1996).

[Rebecca E. Margolis (2nd ed.)]

WASSERMAN, ELHANAN BUNIM (1875–1941), Lithuanian talmudic scholar, yeshivah head, and communal leader. Wasserman received his education at the yeshivot of Volozhin and Telz, which were headed at the time by Eliezer *Gordon and Simeon *Shkop, respectively. In 1899 he married the daughter of Meir Atlas, rabbi of Salant, and spent some years studying in his father-in-law's home. In 1903 he was appointed head of the yeshivah of Amtshilov, where he proved an outstanding teacher, greatly influencing his students. He joined the *kolel* of the Ḥafeẓ Ḥayyim in Radun in 1907 and remained there until 1910, when he was appointed rabbi of Brest-Litovsk. During World War I he returned to Radun, and when the war reached that town the yeshivah moved to Smilovichi, where Wasserman was appointed its head. After the war he moved to Poland and established a yeshivah at Baranowicze, which became one of the most famous in eastern Europe. He was one of the main pillars of the *Agudat Israel movement, together with Ḥayyim Ozer *Grodzinski and the Ḥafeẓ Ḥayyim, and was regarded as the latter's spiritual successor. Wasserman emerged as one of the outstanding leaders of Orthodox Jewry. In addition to his academic activities, he played a major role in communal affairs, contributing extensively to the Jewish press, and figuring prominently at Agudat Israel conferences.

He wrote *Ikvata di-Meshiḥa* (1942), and published the responsa of Solomon b. Abraham *Adret (the Rashba) with annotations (1936^2). His talmudic novellae appeared in the rabbinic journal *Sha'arei Ẓiyyon* (1929–34) and in other publications. At the outbreak of World War II he fled to Vilna and, in June 1941, while on a visit to Kovno, was arrested by the Nazis together with 12 other rabbis and sent to his death. On their last journey he encouraged his fellow victims to walk proudly and with head erect. "The fire which will consume our bodies will be the fire through which the people of Israel will arise to a new life," he assured them.

BIBLIOGRAPHY: Ha-Makhon le-Ḥeker Be'ayot ha-Yahadut ha-Ḥaredit (ed.), *Elleh Ezkerah*, 1 (1956), 82–91; Y.D. Kamson (ed.), *Yahadut Lita*, 1 (1960), 223, 233.

[Mordechai Hacohen]

WASSERMAN, LEW (1913–2002), U.S. entertainment executive. Born Lewis Robert Wasserman in Cleveland, Ohio, to Russian immigrant parents, Wasserman worked as an usher at a vaudeville theater during high school. After graduating in 1930, he worked as a promoter for the Mayfair Casino nightclub. The Music Corporation of American (MCA) talent agency hired him in 1936 as national director of advertising and publicity, and two years later Wasserman moved to Los Angeles. As vice president of MCA's motion picture division, Wasserman brought in such A-list celebrities as Billy *Wilder, Bette Davis, Jimmy Stewart, Gene Kelly, and Ronald Reagan, and won greater control for his clients by doing away with the standard seven-year studio contract and earning them a percentage of the box office. By 1946 he had risen to president of MCA, and in the early 1950s Wasserman branched out with an MCA motion picture division. In 1958, Wasserman purchased a portion of Paramount Pictures' film library for $10 million, and then sold the broadcast rights to television stations for more than $30 million. MCA purchased Universal Studios and Decca Records in 1962, and soon found itself under the scrutiny of the Justice Department, which forced MCA to divest itself of its talent business. Subsequently, Wasserman became involved in politics, holding fundraisers for political campaigns, and courting presidential candidates; Wasserman was also active in donating to Jewish and Catholic charities. In 1973, Wasserman was named chairman of MCA, following Jules Stein's retirement. Soon after he launched the phenomenon of the "summer blockbuster" with such films as *Jaws* (1975) and *Star Wars* (1977). In the late 1970s and 1980s, MCA expanded its television stake by producing such programs as *The Rockford Files*, *Columbo*, *Kojak*, and *Miami Vice*. In 1990, MCA was sold to the Japanese electronics company Matsushita, which allowed Wasserman to maintain his chairmanship. Matsushita sold its stake in MCA to Seagram in 1995, which all but ended Wasserman's control of the company. That same year, Wasserman, in his trademark thick black frame eyeglasses, was presented with the Presidential Medal of Freedom by President Clinton. Wasserman has been the subject of many books, including *When Hollywood Had a King* by Connie Bruck (2003), as well as a documentary, *The Last Mogul* (2005).

BIBLIOGRAPHY: "Wasserman, Lew," in *Newsmakers*, Issue 3 (Gale Group, 2003); "Wasserman, Lew," in: *International Dictionary of Films and Filmmakers*, vol. 4: *Writers and Production Artists* (2000^4). **WEBSITE:** Lew Wasserman, Internet Movie Database, www.imdb.com.

[Adam Wills (2nd ed.)]

WASSERMANN, AUGUST VON (1866–1925), bacteriologist and immunologist. Born in Bamberg, he studied medicine and worked initially at the Institute for Infectious Diseases in Berlin, under Robert Koch. In 1906 he was appointed head of the Serum Department in the institute, and in 1913, head of the Institute of Experimental Medicine at Dahlem near Berlin. Wassermann was one of the founders of immunology, his great discovery being the reaction for the sero-diagnosis of syphilis, which bears his name. This test, which he published in 1906 together with Albert Neisser and Carl Bruck, became one of the most important methods of the sero-diagnosis, and Wassermann used it to prove the syphilitic nature of the tabes dorsalis and progressive paralysis. He developed specific antisera for determining the origin of proteins and blood cells originating from different animals; he also investigated, with Paul *Ehrlich, methods for the determination of the potency of therapeutic sera. He co-edited the first encyclopedia of medical bacteriology and immunology, *Handbuch der pathogenen Mikroorganismen* (1903–13). In 1913 he was ennobled. Throughout his life he remained linked to Judaism.

BIBLIOGRAPHY: S.R. Kagan, *Jewish Medicine* (1952), 252–3; W. Bullock, *History of Bacteriology* (1938; repr. 1960).

[Aryeh Leo Olitzki]

WASSERMANN, JAKOB (1873–1933), German novelist and essayist. In his autobiography, *Mein Weg als Deutscher und Jude* (1921; *My Life as German and as Jew*, 1933), Wassermann reviews his life from his birth in Fuerth, an industrial center of Franconia and the seat of an ancient Jewish community. He had an unhappy childhood and youth and, during his years of penury, found escape from despair in literary visions. In Munich, Wassermann joined the staff of *Simplizissimus*; from 1898 he lived in Vienna. In time he became friendly with Hugo von *Hofmannsthal, Arthur *Schnitzler, and Thomas *Mann. For his first novel, *Die Juden von Zirndorf* (1897; *The Dark Pilgrimage*, 1933), Wassermann utilized personal experiences interwoven with old myths and legends of Franconian Jewry to present a vivid portrait of changing Jewish life in his native province. He won wider recognition with *Caspar Hauser oder die Traegheit des Herzens* (1908; *Caspar Hauser*, 1928), the tragic story of a foundling. The unusual individual at odds with society was also the main theme of *Das Gaensemaennchen* (1915; *The Goose Man*, 1922), a novel about a musician and composer burdened with guilt and tragedy through his concentration on his art and withdrawal from life.

Wassermann's international vogue dates from *Christian Wahnschaffe* (2 vols., 1919), a grandiose epic of Europe on the eve of World War I, which became an American best seller under the title *The World's Illusion* (1920). The novels that followed include *Ulrike Woytich* (1923; Eng. *Gold*, 1924), a critical analysis of materialistic greed; *Der Fall Mauritius* (1928; *The Mauritius Case*, 1929), which castigated the worship of legalism; *Etzel Andergast* (1930; Eng. 1932) and its sequel, *Joseph Kerkhovens dritte Existenz* (1934; *Joseph Kerkhoven's Third Existence*, 1934), clinical studies set against the political and moral chaos after the German defeat of 1918; and many other less profound, but popular, works. He also wrote biographical sketches of Christopher Columbus (1929) and Hofmannsthal in *Hofmannsthal der Freund* (1930).

Wassermann was preeminently a gifted storyteller. In his long prose epics he drew characters from various social strata who seek God despite their horrible experiences, and eventually find salvation after perilous adventures.

Wassermann was an articulate exponent of German-Jewish assimilation and an implacable foe of Jewish nationalism. He believed in a Jewish priestly and prophetic mission among the nations, yet held the "Chosen People" idea to be "plainly absurd and immoral." In his view, the Jews were unfitted for common action and had no talent for politics. Reconstituted as a nation in line with Zionist aspirations, they would be an international laughingstock. Wassermann insisted that his own work exemplified the synthesis of Germanism and Judaism which others should follow, but he abhorred apostasy. The triumph of Nazism and the burning of his books in German towns brought Wassermann back to the spiritual ghetto from which he had always fled and to a common destiny with the eastern European Jews with whom he had always denied kinship. Wassermann published a second autobiographical work, *Selbstbetrachtungen* (1933), but *Ahasver*, a novel intended to describe the epic history of the Jews, was never completed.

BIBLIOGRAPHY: E. Poeschel, in: G. Krojanker (ed.), *Juden in der deutschen Literatur* (1926), 76–100; A.L. Sell, *Das metaphysischrealistische Weltbild Jakob Wassermanns* (Thesis, Marburg, 1932); S. Bing, *Jakob Wassermann* (Ger., 1933^2); M. Karlweis, *Jakob Wassermann* (Ger., 1935); J.C. Blankenagel, *The Writings of Jakob Wassermann* (1942; includes bibliography); W. Voegeli, *Jakob Wassermann und die Traegheit des Herzens* (1956), includes bibliography; S. Liptzin, *Germany's Stepchildren* (1944, repr. 1961), 173–83.

[Sol Liptzin]

WASSERMANN, OSCAR (1869–1934), German banker active in Jewish organizations. The scion of an old established family of Jewish merchants in Bavaria, which in 1880 founded the bank A.E. Wasserman in Bamberg, he opened its Berlin branch in 1900 and served as its director, together with his cousin Max, until 1912, when he became a member of the board of directors of the Deutsche Bank. Chosen in 1923 to stand at the head of the board as its "speaker," a post he held until his dismissal in 1933, Wassermann became one of the central German bankers, serving on many governmental and official committees, such as the Council of the Reichsbank. Unlike most descendants of the *Court Jews who severed their ties with the Jewish community, Wassermann was a learned and conscious Jew, albeit not orthodoxly observant, who knew Hebrew and the Bible and was a patron of many Jewish institutions of learning and philanthropy. Although an alleged "non-Zionist," Wassermann was among the founders (1922) of the German *Keren Hayesod and served as its president and a member of its world board of directors. In 1927/28 he took part, together with Lord *Melchett, Felix *Warburg, and Lee *Frankel, in the Joint Palestine Survey Commission, that prepared the ground for enlarging the *Jewish Agency in 1929 by adding non-Zionist representatives. As one of the signatories of the new Agency's charter, Wassermann occupied leading positions in its administrative and financial committees.

BIBLIOGRAPHY: D.E. Fitz, *Vom Salzfaktor zum Bankier* (1992); A. Barkai, *Oscar Wassermann und die Deutsche Bank* (2005)

[Avraham Barkai (2nd ed.)]

WASSERMAN SCHULTZ, DEBBIE (1966–), first Jewish congresswoman ever elected from Florida. Born and raised on Long Island, N.Y., she ran for student council each year and lost. She attended the University of Florida and graduated with a bachelor's degree in political science in 1988 and with a master's degree in 1990. At 26 she became the youngest woman ever elected to the State House. She served eight years in the House, two as minority leader, and then moved to the State Senate from 2000 to 2004. During her last year in the Florida Senate, Wasserman Schultz was among Democratic lawmakers who presented a plan for overhauling the state's education system, but it was ignored in the Republican-controlled Legislature.

She also was an outspoken opponent of a proposed state constitutional amendment that the legislature has put on the ballot to require parental notification before minor girls can obtain abortions. "History has shown that we have had terrible, terrible results when abortion wasn't safe and legal, and that's what we're going to be forcing here," she said.

She ran on a liberal platform that included promises to spend more on health care and education. "We live in the greatest country in the world," Wasserman Schultz said. "Yet we have sick children whose families cannot afford to take them to a doctor." She wants to extend health care for every child and young adult up to age 25, not just those from low-income families. She has been critical of Congress for failing to fully fund federal education programs.

She stepped up to a Congressional seat when Peter Deutsch, the incumbent Congressman, ran for an open Senate seat. She won the election without a primary opponent, a rarity for an open seat, and swamped her opponent in the general election from her heavily Democratic, heavily Jewish District.

Wasserman Schultz was appointed to the Financial Services Committee, the committee in the House of Representatives that oversees the entire financial services industry, including the securities, insurance, banking, and housing industries. The committee also oversees the work of the Federal Reserve, the Treasury, the Security and Exchange Commission (SEC) and other financial services regulators. Most recently, Wasserman Schultz was appointed to the Committee on the Judiciary, with responsibility for the administration of justice in Federal courts, administrative bodies, and law enforcement agencies. It also handles issues relating to bankruptcy, espionage, terrorism, the protection of civil liberties, constitutional amendments, immigration and naturalization, claims against the United States, presidential succession, antitrust law, revision and codification of the statutes of the United States, state and territorial boundary lines, and patents, copyrights and trademarks. Particularly important in our time is the committee's oversight responsibility for the Departments of Justice and Homeland Security.

Wasserman Schultz has been a critic of the war in Iraq, saying it has diverted the United States from fighting terrorism and been too costly in lives and treasure. She also is committed to supporting Israel as "the lone democracy in the Middle East."

WASSERSTEIN, BERNARD (1948–), British historian. Born in London and educated at Oxford University, Wasserstein taught at Brandeis and Glasgow Universities and was president of the Oxford Centre for Hebrew and Jewish Studies from 1996 to 2000. In 2003 he became professor of history at the University of Chicago. Wasserstein has written prolifically on modern Jewish history in such works as *The British in Palestine* (1978), *Britain and the Jews of Europe, 1939–1945* (1979), *The Secret Life of Trebitsch Lincoln* (1989), *Vanishing Diaspora* (1996), and *Divided Jerusalem: The Quest for the Holy City* (2001). In 2000–2 he was president of the Jewish Historical Society of England.

[William D. Rubinstein (2nd ed.)]

WASSERSTEIN, BRUCE (1948–), U.S. entrepreneur. Wasserstein, who was born in Brooklyn, N.Y., graduated from the University of Michigan and then earned two degrees from Harvard, one from the business school and one from the law school. In addition he was a Knox traveling fellow at Cambridge University, earning a graduate diploma in comparative legal studies in economic regulation. Wasserstein's first job was at the white-shoe law firm Cravath, Swaine & Moore, but he was recruited by Joseph R. Perella to join the First Boston Corporation in 1977. Two years later Perella stunned his boss by asking him to make Wasserstein co-head of mergers and acquisitions, his equal. In 1988 the pair formed Wasserstein, Perella & Company, which became one of the most prominent mergers-and-acquisitions advisers. They helped broker more than 1,000 transactions worth $250 billion, including Texaco's acquisition of Getty Oil. When Perella left the firm in 1993, he sold all his stock, although, for contractual reasons, his name stayed on the door. In 1992 the firm took Maybelline, a cosmetics company, private and then spun it off in a public offering in 1992. In 1994 the firm owned Collins & Aikman, an automotive supplies maker that filed for bankruptcy protection. In 2000, at the top of a bull market, Wasserstein sold his boutique investment bank Wasserstein, Perella to Germany's Dresdner Bank for $1.5 billion. Wasserstein pocketed more than $600 million on the deal. Over the years, Wasserstein wrote four books: *With Justice for Some: An Indictment of the Law by Young Advocates* (1972), *Corporate Finance Law* (1978), *Big Deal: The Battle for the Control of America's Leading Corporations* (1988), and *Big Deal: Mergers and Acquisitions in the Digital Age* (2001). He also had a hand in publishing, owning American Lawyer Media's collection of 29 legal newspapers and magazines around the country, and *The Deal*, a publication covering the mergers marketplace. In 2004 he added *New York* magazine to his media empire. After Wasserstein left the Dresdner Bank, he took the top position at Lazard Frères, the famously secretive investment bank. Michel David-Weill, the patriarch of Lazard, and Wasserstein had a public feud over the direction of the firm. In 2005 Wasserstein succeeded in taking Lazard public after David-Weill was bought out. Wasserstein and Lazard made a substantial profit on the initial deal.

[Stewart Kampel (2nd ed.)]

WASSERSTEIN, WENDY (1950–2006), prize-winning U.S. playwright and the first woman to receive the Tony Award for Best Play. Wasserstein, the youngest of four children of Lola (Schleifer) and Morris Wasserstein, a prosperous textile manufacturer, was born in Brooklyn and grew up in Manhattan. She received a B.A. from Mount Holyoke College in 1971 and an M.F.A. from the Yale School of Drama in 1975. Her plays, which have strong feminist themes tempered with humor and compassion, include *Uncommon Women and Others* (1975); *Tender Offer* (1983); *Isn't It Romantic* (1983); and *The Heidi Chronicles* (1989), which won both a Tony Award and the Pulitzer Prize. While many of her plays had distinctively Jewish elements, *The Sisters Rosenzweig* (1992) explicitly portrays the different ways three sisters come to terms with their Jewish heritage. Other plays include *An American Daughter* (1997), *Old Money* (2000), and *Third* (2005).

Wasserstein was also a prolific writer in other genres, including television and film. Collections of her essays include *Bachelor Girls* (1991) and *Shiksa Goddess* (2001). She was the author of *Sloth* (2005), part of a series on the seven deadly sins published by Oxford University Press. Wasserstein died of cancer in New York City, leaving behind a daughter born in 1999. Her papers are collected at the Mount Holyoke Archives, South Hadley, Massachusetts.

BIBLIOGRAPHY: J. Balakian, *The Dramatic World of Wendy Wasserstein* (1998); idem, "Wasserstein, Wendy," in: P.E. Hyman and D.D. Moore (eds.), *Jewish Women in America*, vol. 2 (1997), 1456–59.

[Judith R. Baskin (2nd ed.)]

WASSERZUG (Lomzer), ḤAYYIM (1822–1882), cantor and composer. Born in Sieradz, Poland, Wasserzug became cantor in Konin at the age of seventeen. In his years at Nowy Dwor, near Warsaw (1841–54), he introduced four-part choral music to the Polish synagogue, despite the bitter opposition of the Ḥasidim. He pursued his innovation as cantor in Lomza (1854–59) and Vilna (1859–67). In 1868 he emigrated to England, and, until his death, officiated at the North London Synagogue. In 1878 he published *Shirei Mikdash*, with his own compositions and some older melodies all simply harmonized for cantor and choir. Wasserzug had a voice remarkable for its quality and compass, and he drew great crowds wherever he sang. He was offered a contract to sing in opera, but refused it on religious grounds.

BIBLIOGRAPHY: JC (Sept. 1, 1882), 7; E. Zaludkowski, *Kultur-Treger fun der Yidisher Liturgie* (1930), 84–87; Wininger, Biog, 6 (1935), 217–8.

[David M.L. Olivestone]

WAT, ALEXANDER (**Szymon Chwat**; 1900–1967), Polish author, editor, and translator. Born in Warsaw, Wat was an active pamphleteer for the Polish "New Art," futurist movement, coediting *Nowa Sztuka* (1921–22) and the *Almanach Nowej Sztuki* (1924–25). From 1929 onward he edited the leftist literary monthly *Miesięcznik Literacki* and worked as a literary editor in the Gebethner and Wolff publishing house (1932–39). During World War II he lived in Soviet Kazakhstan, returning to Warsaw in 1946. He subsequently took a lead in postwar Polish literary life, but emigrated to France in 1963.

His works include *Bezrobotny Lucyfer* ("The Unemployed Lucifer," 1927), collected stories; *Ucieczka Lotha* ("Lot's Escape," 1948–49), a novel; and *Wiersze* ("Poems," 1957). Wat's painful experiences in the U.S.S.R. and during the Stalinist period in postwar Poland shattered his Communist ideals. His last works, such as the verse collection *Ciemne świecidło* ("The Dark Spangle," 1968), which appeared posthumously in Paris, display a swing to religious feeling and mysticism, with the writer seeking a new road to an understanding of the world and its many complexities. Wat also published many translations from Russian and Western literature.

[Stanislaw Wygodzki]

WATCHERS. In Daniel 4:7ff., Nebuchadnezzar, king of Babylon, relates a strange dream of his and its interpretation by the Jewish savant, Daniel. A baleful message is delivered by a heavenly being, referred to as an *ʿir we-qaddish*, the so-called "Holy Watcher" (4:10). The exact interpretation of the name of this being is somewhat problematic. Rashi explains it to mean an angel, deriving the word from the Hebrew *ʿr* "to be awake," and explains that an angel is always awake. The Greek versions of Aquila and Symmachus translate the term, "Wakeful One," a translation which is the source of our English, "Watcher" (Fitzmyer, in bibl., p. 72), an archaic word for one who is awake. However, the Septuagint has simply angel. That the term means angel can be shown from the *Genesis Apocryphon* of the Dead Sea Scrolls, where the word *ʿir* is in clear parallelism with "sons of heaven" (2:1). Also in the *Zadokite Documents*, the "Watchers" are associated with the legend of angelic intercourse with women (A 2:17–18). In Daniel itself, they seem to be some sort of heavenly council (4:14). The "Watchers" figured prominently in pseudepigraphic and later mystical literature.

BIBLIOGRAPHY: J. Montgomery, *Daniel* (ICC, 1927), 234ff.; Ch. Rabin, *The Zadokite Documents* (1958), col. II 1:17–18; J. Fitzmyer, *The Genesis Apocryphon of Qumran Cave One* (1966), 72.

[Daniel Boyarin]

WATEN, JUDAH (1911–1985), Australian novelist and critic. Born in Odessa, Waten was taken to Ereẓ Israel shortly after his birth, but in 1914 the family immigrated to Australia. An active anti-Fascist, he did much during and after World War II to assist refugees seeking a haven in Australia. He was a fervent Communist, and some of his journalistic work was devoted to cultural aspects of left-wing politics. Unlike many intellectuals who supported Communism, Waten became closer to the Soviet Union after 1956. His political writings were often viewed as propaganda, especially his repeated denials of Soviet antisemitism.

Several of his novels deal with Jewish characters and settings. His best-known work, *Alien Son* (1952), was one of the first Australian novels to deal with Jewish themes and is seen as a landmark in Australian literature. He also wrote *The Unbending* (1954), *Distant Land* (1962), and *From Odessa to Odessa* (1969). Three other novels were *Shares in Murder* (1957), *A Time of Conflict* (1961), and *Season of Youth* (1966). Waten was an important literary critic and also translated works by Hertz *Bergner and Pinchas *Goldhar from Yiddish into English. His own novels have been translated into Russian, German, Dutch, and Chinese. Although an anti-Zionist, Waten retained his links with the Jewish community. He published an autobiography, *Scenes of a Revolutionary Life*, in 1982.

BIBLIOGRAPHY: J. Hetherington, *Forty-two Faces* (1962), 153–8. **ADD. BIBLIOGRAPHY:** W.D. Rubinstein, Australia II, index; D. Carter, *A Career in Writing: Judah Waten and the Cultural Politics of a Literary Career* (1997); idem, *Judah Waten: Fiction, Memoirs, Criticism* (1998).

[Greer Fay Cashman / William D. Rubinstein (2nd ed.)]

WATTASIDS (Banu Wattas), Moroccan dynasty related to the *Merinids. The Wattasids ruled much of eastern *Morocco in the 13th century and replaced the Merinids in the years 1472 to 1554. Their capital, court, and administrative center were situated in *Fez. During the Wattasids' reign the Jewish community expanded demographically and prospered, as the waves of immigration of the *megorashim* (the ones expelled) from Spain resettled in parts of Morocco beginning in 1492. Several Jews were diplomats, financial advisers, and ministers in the Wattasid court. The most noted among them were Jacob Rosales, Abraham Cordovi, and R. Jacob Roti, the **nagid* of the Fez Jewish community during the 1530s and 1540s. Roti was an affluent merchant with international connections who carried on extensive and delicate negotiations with *Portugal – then a vital commercial and military power – which occupied key Moroccan towns. In the 1530s he even served as foreign minister. Another Jewish diplomat was Moses Abutam. In 1554, the Sharifian Saʿdi dynasty overthrew the Wattasids. The Saʿdis claimed to be descendants of the Prophet *Muhammad and dominated Morocco until 1660.

BIBLIOGRAPHY: H.Z. Hirschberg, *A History of the Jews in North Africa*, 1 (1974); M.M. Laskier, *The Alliance Israélite Universelle and the Jewish Communities of Morocco: 1862–1962* (1983); N.A. Stillman, *The Jews of Arab Lands* (1979).

[Michael M. Laskier (2nd ed.)]

WATTERS, LEON LAIZER (1877–1967), U.S. scientist, teacher, writer, and communal leader. Watters was born in Salt Lake City, Utah. After teaching chemistry at Columbia University (1898–1900) and the University of Cincinnati (1901–2), he became a food and drugs investigator for the City of New York and presented papers on that subject before the American Association for Advancement of Science. Watters developed a method for sterilizing catgut used as sutures in surgery. He founded the Watters Laboratories and Hospital Supply Company, which he later sold to the Air Reduction Company (1948). During World War I he built the first portable disinfectors for the U.S. Army and Navy. In World War II he designed a mobile hospital unit that was used in North Africa by the British. A civic-minded scientist, Watters was a founder and president of the Utah Club of New York, head of the advisory committee of Cooper Union, and a member of the Chemists Club of New York. At the suggestion of his friend Albert Einstein, he endowed the Watters Memorial Research Laboratory for experimental research in pure physics at the California Institute of Technology and established scholarships and students' loan funds at the University of Utah. Active in Jewish life, Watters was chairman of the New York section of the Jewish Welfare Board during World War I. He served at one time as vice president of the Hebrew Technical Institute and as treasurer of the New York YMHA. Watters' nontechnical writings included *Pioneer Jews of Utah* (1952); his papers are at the American Jewish Archives at Hebrew Union College in Cincinnati, Ohio.

BIBLIOGRAPHY: L. Watters, in: *Western Humanities Review*, 2 (1948), 10–25; J. Dumond and J.P. Youtz, in: *Review of Scientific Instruments*, 8 (1937), 291–307; *New York Times* (April 19, 1967), 45; AJYB, 69 (1968), 613.

[Isidore S. Meyer]

°WATZINGER, CARL (1877–1948), German archaeologist. Watzinger taught as lecturer in Berlin (1905), assistant professor in Tostock (1905–09), and professor in Giessen (1909–16) and Tuebingen (from 1916 until his death). Together with E. *Sellin, he directed excavations at Jericho and published the excavation report (1913). He also collaborated with H. Kohl in clearing ancient synagogues in the Galilee; the publication of their results *Antike Synagogen in Galilaea* (1916) remains to this day the basic study of the earlier type of synagogues in Israel.

During World War I Watzinger participated in German surveys. He was the author of two works on Damascus – *Damaskus, die antike Stadt* (1921), and *Damaskus, die islamische Stadt* (1924). After the war he published a study of the finds of Megiddo (1921) and a work on the antiquities of Ereẓ Israel, *Denkmaeler Palaestinas*, 2 vols. (1931–35).

[Michael Avi-Yonah]

WAWELBERG, HIPOLIT (1843–1901), banker and philanthropist. Born in Warsaw, he was a son of the merchant banker and *maskil*, Ẓevi Hirsch Wawelberg. From his youth he advocated the assimilation of Polish Jewry into the gentile population, but his longtime residence in St. Petersburg (from 1869), where he managed a branch of his father's bank, brought him into close contact with Jewish public workers and Jewish affairs. He was appointed a member of the Committee for the Struggle Against Civil Discrimination against Russian Jews, headed by Baron Horace *Guenzburg. He was also active in the *Society for the Promotion of Culture among the Jews of Russia and contributed liberally to various Jewish cultural and charitable institutions. Wawelberg displayed particular concern for the settlement program of Baron de *Hirsch in Latin America, and in 1899 he donated a large sum to the *Jewish Colonization Association (ICA) for this purpose. ICA responded by renaming the settlement Santa Elena (in Argentina) "Wawelberg." He also generously supported the school for crafts of the Warsaw Jewish community and founded a Jewish agricultural school in *Czestochowa. Wawelberg sided with those Polish circles that advocated a compromise with the Russian regime, and, to encourage this tendency, he founded a liberal Polish weekly *Kraj*, in St. Petersburg. It was outstanding for its literary standard. He financed the publication of the Warsaw Polish daily *Kuryer Polski*, whose trend was also liberal, advocating sympathy for Russia and fighting antisemitism. Wawelberg donated large sums for the publication of inexpensive editions of the works of classical Polish writers and is still considered one of the greatest Maecenases of Polish literature. He believed that a cultural and social rapprochement between Polish Jewry and their gentile neighbors could be effected through the establishment of institutions in which Jews and Poles would work together. In 1895 he contributed to the establishment of an industrial school in Warsaw. When the school reverted to the Polish government (1918), Wawelberg's heirs inserted a clause into the agreement stating that Jewish students were not to be discriminated against, although this was not abided by. Before his death, Wawelberg established a fund at the University of Lvov to encourage research in Jewish history in Poland. This fund was helpful to several Jewish historians, such as M. *Schorr, M. *Balaban, and I. *Schiper.

BIBLIOGRAPHY: *Lu'aḥ Aḥi'asaf* (1902/03), 32 ("*Keronikah Ivrit*"); I.L. Peretz, *Avnei Pinnah* (1952), 91–98; J. Shatzky, *Geshikhte fun di Yidn in Varshe*, 3 (1953), 88–94; M. Turkow, *Di Letste fun a Groysn Dor* (1954), 151–99.

[Gedalyah Elkoshi]

WAXMAN, AL (1936–2001), Canadian actor, director, teacher. Waxman was born in Toronto. His parents, immigrants from Poland, owned and operated a small restaurant in downtown Toronto. His mother continued in the food service industry after her husband died when Al was only nine years old. From his early teens Waxman wanted to be an actor and, by the time he was 17, he was performing in live CBC radio dramas. He gathered together enough money to study theater at New York's Playhouse Theater before moving to London in 1961 for further study. He struggled to find acting jobs in London and Hollywood and appeared in several films. His acting breakthrough came after his return to Toronto, where he was hired for a starring role in the sitcom *The King of Kensington*, a successful Canadian series that ran for five seasons. He added to his own celebrity as a regular character in the American television detective series *Cagney & Lacey*, which ran for 125 episodes beginning in 1981. Waxman never again lacked for work as an actor on televison, in films, or on stage. After a career that spanned more than 50 years, Waxman is regarded as a pioneer in Canadian theater, television, and film. He acted in, directed, produced, or wrote more than 1,000 radio, television, theater, and film productions. He also taught theater for 10 years at York University in Toronto. In the years before his death, Waxman was drawn to the stage. In 1997 he played the role of Willy Loman in the Stratford Festival production of *Death of a Salesman*. The year before his death, he directed a well-received production of *The Diary of Anne Frank*, and at the time of his death, Waxman was about to play Shylock in the Stratford production of *The Merchant of Venice*.

Waxman was honored with many awards and was active in many Jewish and larger community organizations. In 1997 he was named to the Order of Canada, the highest award Canada can bestow on a citizen.

[Joel Greenberg (2nd ed.)]

WAXMAN, MEYER (1887–1969), scholar of the history of Jewish literature and rabbi. Born in Slutzk, Russia, Waxman received a traditional yeshivah education. He emigrated to the United States in 1905 and studied at the Jewish Theological Seminary, where he was ordained as a rabbi in 1913. After serving for some years in rabbinical posts, he became principal of the Mizrachi Teachers Seminary (1917–21) and director of the Mizrachi Zionist organization (1921–24). In 1924 he joined the faculty of the Hebrew Theological College in Chicago, where he served as professor of Hebrew literature and philosophy until his retirement in 1955, also teaching at the College of Jewish Studies in Chicago. He moved to New York where he continued his literary and scholarly activities until his death. Waxman was an extremely prolific writer on the history of Jewish thought and literature, publishing hundreds of articles in Hebrew, Yiddish, and English. Many of his articles were collected in volumes of essays, *Ketavim Nivḥarim* (2 vols., 1943–44), *Galut u-Ge'ullah* (1952), and *Moreh ha-Dorot* (1963). He wrote studies in the history of Jewish philosophy, including the *Philosophy of Don Hasdai Crescas* (1920) and a translation, with introduction, of Moses Hess's *Rome and Jerusalem* (1945). Waxman's works, *A Handbook of Judaism* (1947) and *Judaism-Religion and Ethics* (1958), were widely used. His major work was *History of Jewish Literature* (4 vols., 1941; 5 vols., 1960^2), a comprehensive detailed account of the main trends in Jewish literature from the end of the biblical period until the present day. In this work Waxman summarizes and evaluates the works of Jewish literature in all fields. On the occasion of his 75th birthday a jubilee volume was published containing articles in English and Hebrew, *Meyer Waxman – Jubilee on the Occasion of his 75th Birthday* (ed., Judah Rosenthal, 1967), which includes an evaluation of Waxman's achievements by Chaim Rothblatt and a bibliography compiled by L. Mishkin.

[Seymour Siegel]

WAXMAN, MORDECAI (1917–2000), U.S. Conservative rabbi, interfaith activist. Waxman was born in Albany, N.Y., and received his B.A. from 1937. In 1941, he was ordained at the *Jewish Theological Seminary, which awarded him an honorary D.D. in 1968. After serving as rabbi of Temple Beth Israel in Niagara Falls, N.Y. (1941–42), he became founding rabbi of North Park Congregation Shaare Tikvah in Chicago, Illinois (1942–46), leaving the synagogue for two years during World War II to serve as a chaplain in the U.S. Army. In 1947, he was appointed rabbi of Temple Israel in Great Neck, Long Island, where he remained for 55 years, until his death. Under his leadership, Temple Israel grew from 100 member families to 1,300 families.

Waxman emerged as a leader in the Conservative movement after he edited and wrote the introduction to *Tradition and Change* (1958), the definitive anthology of writings on the views and philosophy of *Conservative Judaism. He became chairman of the Membership Committee of the *Rabbinical Assembly (1966–68) and subsequently editor of the journal *Conservative Judaism* (1969–74). He also chaired the RA's Committee on the Study and Reevaluation of the Community Service Program (1969–70) – a requirement that JTS graduates enter the military chaplaincy or a designated alternative equivalent that had become so unpopular during the Vietnam War that it was terminated. In 1974, Waxman was elected president of the Rabbinical Assembly, where he worked to strengthen RA representation in the World Council of Synagogues, the official representative of Conservative Judaism in the *World Zionist Organization. Seeking to establish Conservative Judaism in Israel, he pressed for greater coordination among the various Israel programs sponsored by the RA, the JTS, and United Synagogue. Also during his term of office, the RA approved the plan to publish a new commentary on the Torah for use in Conservative synagogues.

Following his term in office, Waxman became president of the Conservative movement's World Council of Synagogues (1980–85) as well as president of the Synagogue Council of America (1983–85). As president, and later as chairman of the National Council of Synagogues (1996–97), he participated in the annual assemblies on world Jewish affairs convened by the presidents of the state of Israel, as well as in the deliberations of The Hebrew University's Diaspora Institute headed by Moshe *Davis. He was also instrumental in obtaining the funding for the first headquarters of the United Synagogue of America in Jerusalem.

Waxman, who served as chairman of the International Jewish Committee for Interreligious Consultation (1985–87), was particularly active in Catholic-Jewish relations. In 1987, he led a delegation of Jewish leaders that met with Pope John Paul II at Castel Gondolfo to resolve the *Waldheim affair. Soon after, he spoke for American Jewry in welcoming the pope to the United States. For many years thereafter, Waxman and Cardinal William Keeler of Baltimore co-chaired an annual series of Catholic-Jewish dialogues. He helped draft the welcoming Jewish response to the Vatican document *We Remember: A Reflection on the Shoah* and worked to implement its mandate that Jews and Catholics sponsor joint educational programs on the Holocaust. His efforts were instrumental in bringing about the establishment of diplomatic relations between the Vatican and the State of Israel (1993). In 1997 he was awarded the Nostra Aetate Award, and in 1998 he became the first rabbi to be named by the pope a Knight Commander of the Order St. Gregory the Great.

Concerned about widening differences within the American Jewish community, Waxman joined with Reform, Orthodox, and Reconstructionist rabbis in the 1986 "Symposium for Unity" – a traveling panel that discussed Jewish issues from the perspectives of the four denominations. He was also a contributor to numerous publications, including the *Encyclopedia Judaica*. In recognition of his many contributions, he was named Rabbi of the Year in 1991 by the New York Board of Rabbis – the first rabbi to receive the $10,000 Finkle Prize that accompanies this designation. Other honors bestowed on him were the Lifetime Achievement Award from the Ziegler Rabbinic School of the University of Judaism (2001), and the Louis Finkelstein Award from the Jewish Theological Seminary of America (2002).

[Bezalel Gordon (2nd ed.)]

°**WAY, LEWIS** (1773–1840), British missionary. Way was educated at Eton and Oxford and became a barrister. At the age of 40, out of religious inclination, he became interested in Jews and Judaism and joined a British missionary society. He visited Jewish settlements in eastern Europe and came to the conclusion that the Jews should be granted civil rights and their economic situation improved, so that they would become attracted to Christianity. During his stay in Russia, Way heard about the interest of Czar *Alexander I in the conversion of Jews. In 1818, during the assembly of the heads of the European states (Congress of Aix-la-Chapelle (Aachen)), he submitted several memoranda to Alexander I and other participants in which he suggested granting Jews equal rights and access to public office, compulsory military service, apportionment of land for Jewish agricultural settlement, and encouragement of the settlers through exemption from taxes and granting of loans. He suggested compelling poor Jews to teach their sons a craft, the opening of educational institutions to Jews, and the establishment of elementary schools for Jewish children. On the other hand, Way proposed taking strong measures against those Jews engaged in nonproductive professions. Under the influence of Alexander I the participants at the conference adopted a favorable attitude to Way's memoranda, though without any practical results. The memoranda were published in 1819 under the title *Mémoire sur l'état des israélites dédiés a leurs Majestés Impériales et Royales réunies au congrès d'Aix-la-Chapelle*. It probably had a certain influence on Czar *Nicholas I and his government in determining their Jewish policy.

BIBLIOGRAPHY: J.F.A. de Le Roi. *Geschichte der evangelischen Judenmission seit Entstehung des neueren Judentums* (1899; = *Die evangelische Christenheit und die Juden* ..., vols. 2–3, 1891), indexes; Dubnow, Divrei, 9 (1958[2]), 90–91. **ADD. BIBLIOGRAPHY:** ODNB online.

[Yehuda Slutsky]

WAYNE AND SHUSTER, Canadian comedy team often regarded as the founding fathers of English Canadian TV comedy. FRANK SHUSTER (1916–2002) and JOHNNY WAYNE (John Louis Weingarten; 1918–1990) were both born in Toronto. Johnny Wayne, son of a successful clothing manufacturer, was raised in downtown Toronto, the eldest of seven children. Frank Shuster grew up in Niagara Falls, Ontario, where his father operated a local theater before returning to Toronto. The two first met in Toronto's legendary Harbord Collegiate, high school to many in Toronto's inner-city Jewish community. Wayne and Shuster each went on to complete a degree in English at the University of Toronto, where they also wrote, produced, and starred in a number of student variety shows. They worked briefly at CBC radio in the early 1940s before joining the Canadian infantry in 1942. In the military they wrote and performed for the Big Army Show, which entertained Canadian troops across Canada and, after the invasion of Europe, in the Netherlands, Belgium, and France. After the war, they returned to CBC, where they remained Canada's premier comedy team until Wayne's death in 1990. During their early years they wrote all their own material, but they later hired other writers to work with them. In general, their comedy was literate, middle-brow, and upbeat. They never resorted to cruel humor, preferring the send-up to the put-down.

Relentlessly loyal to Canada and the Canadian "voice," the comedy team resisted the temptation to relocate to the United States. But Wayne and Shuster's comedy became well known in the United States. They made a record-setting 67 appearances on *The Ed Sullivan Show*. After first appearing on the *The Ed Sullivan Show* in 1958, Sullivan was so enamored of the pair that he agreed to a one-year contract granting them complete freedom to decide on the length, frequency, content, sets, and supporting cast of all their sketches. They proved to be Sullivan's most popular act in 10 years of broadcasting. Edited versions of their many CBC television specials were also highly popular in American syndication, and Wayne and Shuster made frequent appearances on the BBC. The pair won numerous awards, including the illustrious Silver Rose of Montreux. In 1998 the Margaret Collier Award paid tribute to the duo's routines at the Gemini Awards, and twice TV critics and editors in the United States chose Wayne and Shuster as the best comedy team in North America. In 1999, their names became part of the Canadian Walk of Fame in Toronto. A year later, the duo was also among the first six inductees into the Canadian Comedy Hall of Fame.

BIBLIOGRAPHY: P. Rutherford, *When Television Was Young: Primetime Canada 1952–1957* (1990).

[Joel Greenberg (2nd ed.)]

WAŻYK (Wagman), ADAM (1905–1982), Polish poet and novelist. A member of the *Awangarda* group, he published poems and prose and coedited the "New Art" *Almanach Nowej Sztuki* (1924–25). After World War II, Ważyk coedited *Kuźnica* and *Twórczość* and wrote many verse collections, plays, novels, and essays. His *Poemat dla dorosłych* ("Poem for Adults," 1956) heralded Poland's anti-Stalinist campaign.

WDOWINSKI, DAVID (1895–1970), participant in the Warsaw Ghetto Uprising and founder of the Zydowski Zwiazek Wojskowy (ZZW; Jewish Military Union). Born in Bedzin, Wdowinski studied psychiatry at the universities of Vienna, Brno, and Warsaw. He became very involved in the Zionist Revisionist movement. Whereas many Jewish leaders fled in the wake of the German invasion of Poland, Wdowinski remained in Warsaw and was very active in underground activities in the ghetto. In particular he was the Revisionist representative in the Zydowski Towarzystwo Opieki Spolecznej (Jewish Mutual Aid Society), which engaged in welfare work. Around the time the great deportation was drawing to a close, and nearly 265,000 Jews had been deported to Treblinka, the ZZW was formed by Wdowinski, Dr. Michael Strykowski, and Leon (Arie) Rodal. Pawl Frankiel, of Betar, was made the military commander of the organization and Wdowinski apparently set its political tone. The ZZW never integrated into the main underground fighting organization in Warsaw, the Zydowska Organizacja Bojowa (The Jewish Fighting Organization), but the two groups did coordinate their activities to a certain extent during the spring of 1943. The ZZW did not participate in the first armed clash in the ghetto, in January 1943. During the April uprising its fighters fought fiercely near Muranowska Square, in one of the major battles of the rebellion. Other ZZW men fought in the Brushmakers' area of the ghetto, and still others in the area where supplies were kept. Wdowinski was captured by the Germans during the uprising and was sent to various concentration camps but survived. He settled in the United States after the war and in 1961 was a witness at the Eichmann Trial. He published his memoirs, *And We Are Not Saved* (1963).

BIBLIOGRAPHY: I. Gutman, *The Jews of Warsaw, 1939–1943: Ghetto, Underground, Revolt* (1982).

[Robert Rozette]

WEBB, JACK (1920–1982), U.S. actor, director, producer. Born Jack Randolph Webb in Santa Monica, California, Webb graduated from Belmont High School, and served in the Air Force from 1942 to 1945. Webb began his entertainment career as a radio announcer in San Francisco, followed by roles in the radio dramas *Pat Novak for Hire* (1946) and *Johnny Modero* (1947). He married actress Julie London (née Julie Peck) in July 1947, but they divorced in 1953. Webb made his feature film debut in *He Walked by Night* (1948), followed by roles in such films as *Sword in the Desert* (1949), *The Men* (1950), and *Sunset Boulevard* (1950). In 1949, he created the radio drama *Dragnet*, which was the first series based on actual police files. While the show moved to television in 1951, he continued to produce the radio version until 1955. Webb played the cool, emotionless Sgt. Joe Friday throughout the series' incarnations, including the highly rated television runs from 1951 to 1959 and 1967 to 1970, as well as the 1954 feature film. Webb began directing and starring in his own films, *Pete Kelly's Blues* (1955), *The D.I.* (1957), and *-30-* (1959). In 1958, he published a book about the Los Angeles Police Department, *The Badge: True and Terrifying Crime Stories That Could Not Be Presented on TV*. Webb followed up his success on *Dragnet* by producing such television dramas as *Adam 12* (1968–70), *The D.A.* (1971), *Emergency!* (1971–75), and *Project Blue Book* (1978). In respect for the man who became so closely associated with the department, the LAPD lowered its flags for Webb when he died, an honor traditionally reserved for fallen police officers and government officials.

[Adam Wills (2nd ed.)]

WEBER, KOLOMAN (d. 1931), Czechoslovakian Orthodox rabbi. Weber attended yeshivot in Pressburg (*Bratislava), where he received *semikhah*. He served first as rabbi of Rete but made his name as rabbi of *Piestany, Slovakia, where he remained for 29 years, waging a bitter battle against *Neologists and *Zionists. After World War I, Weber was instrumental in organizing the autonomous Orthodox *Zentralkanzlei* of Jewish communities in Slovakia, which he headed autocratically for 12 years. In March 1926, Emil *Margulies accused Weber in the *Selbstwehr* of expropriating for his own use large sums from the American Jews' Central Relief Committee, and Weber took legal action against him. In the course of the trial it came out that Weber and Rabbi Simon Hirschler had received 100,000 crowns in order to split the Jewish vote in Subcarpathian Ruthenia by creating a "Jewish Economic Party," thus keeping the Zidovska strana (the "Jewish Party") out of parliament and benefitting the ruling Agrarian party. Although he lost his suit, neither his power nor combativeness suffered. He died a few years later in an accident.

[Henry Wasserman]

WEBER, MAX (1881–1961), U.S. painter. Weber was born in Bialystok, Poland, and taken to New York at the age of ten. From 1905 to 1909 he worked and exhibited in Paris. He was a pupil of Henri Matisse and a close friend of Henri Rousseau. Back in New York, he arranged the first American Rousseau exhibition. Weber's work, highly controversial and often attacked by critics, was shown at avant-garde galleries but was unappreciated for many years. The artist had to support himself and his family by teaching, mainly at the Art Students League. His breakthrough finally came in 1948 with a comprehensive retrospective exhibition at the Whitney Museum of American Art, New York. In the years to follow, he received many prizes and awards and in 1955 was elected member of the National Institute of Arts and Letters.

His compositions grew bolder, more abstract, but without severing completely the link to nature. In sensuous, rich colors, geometrical patterns, they seemed to catch the dynamism of the metropolis. His subject matter included somber and melancholy landscapes with trees; well-arranged still lifes; plump and unseductive, yet disturbing, nudes; musicians; sweating workmen; and Orthodox Jews. Weber frequently stressed the dynamism of Jewish groups in action, using their eloquent hands to underline an argument, or dancing ecstatically in the *shul*. He was also a distinguished sculptor, whose three-dimensional work veers toward the abstract. He published *Cubist Poems* (1914), and *Essays on Art* (1916).

BIBLIOGRAPHY: H. Cahill, *Max Weber* (1930); L. Goodrich, *Max Weber* (1949); New York Museum of Modern Art, *Max Weber Retrospective Exhibition* (1930); *Max Weber* (1945), introd. by the artist.

[Alfred Werner]

WECHSLER, DAVID (1896–1981), U.S. psychologist. Born in Lespedi, Romania, he was taken to the United States in 1902. He was chief psychologist, Bellevue Psychiatric Hospital (1932–66). He was also clinical professor of the NYU College of Medicine (1942). He was the originator of several widely used intelligence tests. Wechsler's greatest contribution was in the field of mental measurement. He demonstrated that there is a change and a differential decline with age in human abilities. His intelligence tests are based upon the concept of intelligence as being much more than the sheer ability to reason, deal with symbols, abstract, and conceptualize. He stressed that there were also volitional and non-intellective factors in intelligence. Thus his tests combining verbal and performance items were based on a non-hierarchical concept of intelligence, and the IQ was derived from the average of tested abilities in which equal credit was apportioned to subtests measuring abstract as well as concrete tasks. WAIS or Wechsler Adult Intelligence Scale was prepared in such a way as to underemphasize speed of response and present items of interest to most adults. The use of his scales made it possible to make quantitative as well as qualitative observations of behavior and thought processes, and permitted, through pattern analysis, a diagnostic approach to intellectual deficiencies, organic brain disorders, schizophrenia, etc. These tests were adapted for use in many countries, and hundreds of publications describing and discussing them have appeared in almost all languages.

He was the author of articles and of books on adult intelligence: *The Measurement of Emotional Reactions* (1925, includes bibl.); *Wechsler-Bellevue Intelligence Scale* (1939); *Wechsler Intelligence Scale for Children* (1949); *The Range of Human Capacities* (1955^2); *Wechsler Adult Intelligence Scale* (1955); *The Measurement and Appraisal of Adult Intelligence* (1958^4); and *Wechsler Pre-school and Primary Scale of Intelligence* (1968).

BIBLIOGRAPHY: A. Anastasi, *Psychological Testing* (1968^3).

[Boris M. Levinson]

WECHSLER, ELINA (1952–), Argentinean poet. Born in Buenos Aires, she was a psychoanalyst by profession. She left Argentina in 1977 as a consequence of the military dictatorship that unleashed extreme political repression and violence and took up residence in Madrid. Wechsler was the author of four collections of poetry: *El fantasma* (1983), *La larga marcha* (1988), *Mitomanías amorosas* (1991), and *Progresiones en un cierto mes de julio* (1995). Her poetry is characterized by her questioning approach, most likely influenced by her training in psychology. Her early volumes are linked rather directly to her exile and the political repercussions she suffered in her personal life as a result. Likewise, her writing focuses on issues of identity that specifically deal with being a woman and Jewish. She often seeks to examine these aspects of her identity through the lyrical treatment of such female figures as Lilith, Eve, and Lot's wife. She is also the co-author of *La metáfora milenaria: una lectura psicoanalítica de la Biblia* (1993), an insightful reading of the Bible that has much in common with many of the questions she raises in her poetry.

[Darrell B. Lockhart (2nd ed.)]

WECHSLER, HERBERT (1909–2000), U.S. legal scholar. Wechsler was born in New York City and graduated from Columbia University Law School in 1931. A member of the Columbia Law School faculty from 1933 until 1978, he was at the time of his death the Harlan Fiske Stone Professor of Constitutional Law Emeritus. Wechsler specialized in criminal and constitutional law, and in the practice of law. During his career he served as law secretary to Supreme Court Justice Harlan F. Stone and as counsel to Senator Robert F. Wagner, when the latter was minority leader in the N.Y. State constitutional convention of 1938. During World War II he was assistant attorney general in charge of the war division of the U.S. Department of Justice. Wechsler participated in the establishment of the International Military Tribunal at Nuremberg in 1945, and then served as principal technical adviser to the U.S. judges in the Nuremberg war-crime trials. During 1941–45 he also served by appointment of the U.S. Supreme Court on the committee that drafted the federal rules of criminal procedure and on that court's advisory committee to revise its rules of practice. He was a member of the President's Commission on Law Enforcement and Administration of Justice, which reported in 1967.

In 1952 Wechsler was appointed chief reporter in the preparation of the model penal code, which was approved by the American Law Institute (ALI) in 1962. He became director of the institute and also chairman of the permanent editorial board for the Uniform Commercial Code. From 1961 he was a member of the temporary commission of the New York State Legislature to draft a revision of the state's penal law and code of criminal procedure. Wechsler appeared as counsel in many important cases before the U.S. Supreme Court. He served as director of the ALI from 1963 to 1984, after which he became director emeritus. In 1993 he was awarded the Institute's Henry J. Friendly Medal for his "outstanding achievement in promoting reform and clarification of the law" and for the extent to which his "outstanding intelligence, integrity, and devotion to the law enriched the areas of constitutional law, criminal law, and federal jurisdiction."

He wrote *Principles, Politics, and Fundamental Law* (1961), *Criminal Law and its Administration* (with Jerome Michael, 1940), *Federal Courts and the Federal System* (with Henry M. Hart, Jr., 1953), *The Nationalization of Civil Liberties and Civil Rights* (1968), and many articles in professional periodicals. Wechsler believed that "the main constituent of the judicial process is precisely that it must be genuinely principled, resting with respect to every step that is involved in reaching judgment on analysis and reasons quite transcending the immediate result that is achieved." Thus judicial review, if it is to be faithful to its function or its authorization, must operate in accordance with what Wechsler styles "neutral principles."

[Julius J. Marcke / Ruth Beloff (2nd ed.)]

WECHSLER, ISRAEL (**Spanier**; 1886–1962), U.S. neurologist, born in Lespedi, Romania. He was taken to the U.S. at an early age and educated in New York. He taught at Columbia University (professor of clinical neurology, 1931) and served as consulting neurologist at various New York hospitals. He was president of the American Neurological Association (1958). He was a member of the Board of Governors of The Hebrew University of Jerusalem from 1930 and president of the American Friends of The Hebrew University.

Wechsler made special studies on various aspects of epilepsy. He recommended the use of ephedrine in the treatment of autonomic epilepsy and paraldehyde intravenously for status epilepticus. He also did research on Vitamin E in amyotrophic lateral sclerosis. He is the author of *Textbook of Clinical Neurology* (1927, 1958⁸) and *The Neurologist's Point of View: Essays on Psychiatric and Other Subjects* (1945).

BIBLIOGRAPHY: S.R. Kagan, *Jewish Medicine* (1952), 405–6; Baron, in: JSOS, 25 (1963), 100–1.

[Suessmann Muntner]

WECHSLER, JAMES ARTHUR (1915–1983), U.S. editor and author. Born in New York, Wechsler graduated from Columbia University in 1935. In his early years Wechsler wrote for the *Student Advocate, The Nation*, and the New York liberal daily, *P.M.*, where he served as assistant editor and Washington bureau chief. In 1946 he joined the staff of the *New York Post* as Washington correspondent. He was particularly concerned with civil liberties and labor relations. In 1948 he was appointed editor of the *Post*. Under his editorship the paper assumed the role of crusader, taking on such issues and public figures as J. Edgar Hoover, Senator Joseph McCarthy, Richard Nixon's slush fund, and the mass evictions incurred by Robert Moses' slum clearance program. He served as editor until 1961, when the reins were turned over to executive editor Paul Sann, and Wechsler became a columnist and chief of the editorial page.

Wechsler's books include *Revolt on the Campus* (1935); *Labor Baron* (1944); *The Age of Suspicion* (1953); *Reflections of an Angry Middle-Aged Editor* (1960); and *In a Darkness* (1972).

[Ruth Beloff (2nd ed.)]

WECHSLER, JUDAH (1832–1907) U.S. Reform rabbi, journalist, interfaith and civil rights activist. Wechsler was born in Bavaria and studied at the yeshivah of Würzburg, where he was ordained an Orthodox rabbi. Arriving in the United States in 1857, he served the Jewish community of Portsmouth, Ohio, as **ḥazzan* and **shoḥet,* before becoming rabbi of the Reform Indianapolis Hebrew Congregation in Indianapolis, Indiana (1861–64). A pioneer in conducting interfaith services, he was the first rabbi to preach in the city's Methodist church. When the congregation was having financial difficulties, Wechsler took the pulpit of a congregation in Richmond, Virginia (1864–67), returning to Indianapolis in 1867. In 1869, he served a congregation in Columbus, Ohio, moving to New Haven, Connecticut, in 1872, and then to Temple Mt. Zion in St. Paul, Minnesota (1882–92). His final pulpit was in Meridian, Mississippi (1892–97); in retirement, he moved back to Indianapolis, where he remained until his death.

In St. Paul, Wechsler – who was a member of the *Central Conference of American Rabbis from its founding in 1889 – strove to bring his temple into the *Union of American Hebrew Congregations and the mainstream of Reform Judaism. He also became the patron of a utopian-style colony in Painted Woods, South Dakota, populated by immigrants fleeing czarist Russia. The colony grew to nearly 250 people; but when it ultimately failed, Wechsler moved on to another tremendous challenge in Meridian, Mississippi, where he took a courageous stand on behalf of improving the education and status of African-Americans. He was so instrumental in the building of a high school for blacks that the school bears his name.

In 1884, Wechsler traveled to the West Coast and chronicled his visits to Jewish communities in Portland and San Francisco. He was a regular contributor to the **American Israelite* and the *Jewish Messenger,* and his articles were frequently translated into Hebrew for publication in the European Jewish press.

BIBLIOGRAPHY: K.M. Olitzky, L.J. Sussman, M.H. Stern, *Reform Judaism in America: A Biographical Dictionary and Sourcebook* (1993).

[Bezalel Gordon (2nd ed.)]

WECHSLER, MAX (pseudonyms: **Germanicus**; **I.H. Văleanu**; **Ieşau**; 1870–1917), Marxist theoretician and leading member of the general and Jewish socialist movement in Romania. In the 1890s he was among the founders of the first independent Jewish socialist society, which was formed in *Jassy under the name of *Lumina. Wechsler fought against the refusal of the Romanian Social-Democratic Party to conduct a special campaign for the emancipation of the Jews. He was among the signatories to the memorandum of the society to the Fourth Congress of the Second International in London (1896). Wechsler was one of the editors of the society's organs in Romanian (*Lumina*) and Yiddish (*Der Veker*). He rejected the demand for assimilation and conversion as a condition for the civic emancipation of the Jews. After the establishment of the new Social-Democratic Party, a few years before World War I, Wechsler joined its ranks. In May 1917 he was accused by revolutionary soldiers of complicity in the liberation of the party's leader, his friend Christian Rakovski (the future president of Soviet Ukraine). He was imprisoned by the Romanian military authorities and put to death.

BIBLIOGRAPHY: J. Kisman, *Shtudyes tsu der Geshikhte fun Rumenishe Yidn in 19-tn un Onheyb 20-tn Yorhundert* (1944), index; I. Popescu-Puțuri et al. (eds.), *Presa muncitorească si socialistă din Rominia*, 2 vols. (1964–66); indexes; S. Bernstein, *Die Judenpolitik der rumaenischen Regierung* (1918), 185–7.

[Moshe Mishkinsky]

°WEDGWOOD, JOSIAH CLEMENT, FIRST BARON (1872–1943), British statesman and supporter of Zionism. Wedgwood was a member of the famous pottery family and was educated at Clifton College. He first worked as a naval architect and a military officer. He was a member of Parliament from 1906 to 1942, when he received the title baron; until 1919 he was a member of the Liberal Party, and from then on a member of the Labour Party. While serving on the Gallipoli front as an artillery officer in 1915, Wedgwood met the men of the Zion Mule Corps, commanded by Joseph *Trumpeldor, and from then on took an active interest in Zionism. He participated in the political efforts which led to the *Balfour Declaration in 1917 and was among those who influenced President Wilson's delegate at the Versailles Peace Conference, Colonel House, to take a sympathetic stand toward Zionism. Between the two world wars, he visited several countries on Zionist missions and made two visits to Palestine in 1926 and in 1934. Wedgwood envisaged a Jewish state on both sides of the Jordan that would be a member of the British Commonwealth. He was among the founders of the "League for the Seventh Dominion" and in 1928 published *The Seventh Dominion*, a work on this subject. He realized at an early stage that the British government would abandon its pro-Zionist policy and concluded that the Jews must fight the British administration with all the means at their disposal – including illegal ones. He was close to V. *Jabotinsky and the *Revisionist movement and often voiced criticism of the Zionist and *yishuv* leadership for their loyalty to the British authorities. He even drew up a plan for war against the Mandatory government that provided, inter alia, for "illegal" *immigration and for armed resistance to repressive acts perpetrated against the Jews by the British authorities. On the outbreak of World War II, Wedgwood called for the establishment of a Jewish fighting force within the framework of the British army.

Wedgwood published a number of books, including *Testament to Democracy* (1943), *Forever Freedom* (with A. Nevins, 1940), and *Palestine: The Fight for Jewish Freedom and Honor* (1926), a collection of speeches made in America. One of the leading gentile pro-Zionists of his time, he wrote an autobiography, *Memoirs of a Fighting Life* (1940). Dame C.V. Wedgwood (1910–1997), the famous historian, was his niece.

BIBLIOGRAPHY: C.V. Wedgwood, *The Last of the Radicals* (1951). **ADD. BIBLIOGRAPHY:** ODNB online.

WEEDS. Israel abounds in species of weeds, the climatic and soil conditions causing the speedy proliferation of both cultivated plants and weeds. Many of them are *thorns. The prophets frequently warned that because of sin, misfortunes would befall Israel's agriculture and the land would produce weeds in place of cultivated plants. Isaiah in particular warns against the transformation of the sown and planted area into *shamir* and *shayit* ("briars and thorns"), a general term for all the species of weeds that flourish among cultivated crops. These weeds start as annual plants, then lowly shrubs grow, and finally the field turns into a forest (cf. Isa. 7). Normally weeds grow in fields of grain in Israel, the most conspicuous being *tares, species of *mustard, Scolymus thistle (*ḥo'aḥ*), and *Ridolfia segetum* (*boshah*, "noisome weeds"). Job (31:40) swears that if he has indeed sinned, then let him be cursed, "Let *ḥo'aḥ* grow instead of wheat, and *boshah* instead of barley." The *amora* Oshaiah observes that it can be deduced from this verse "that a field that produces *ḥoḥim* is good for wheat, while a field that produces *boshah* is good for barley" (Tanḥ. B. Deut. 25), showing that these weeds are indications to cultivate plants.

BIBLIOGRAPHY: J. Feliks, *Olam ha-Ẓome'aḥ ha-Mikra'i* (1957), 204–17.

[Jehuda Feliks]

WEEGEE (1899–1968), U.S. photographer. Born Usher Fellig in what is now the Ukraine, Weegee went to the United States, where he was renamed Arthur, as a boy. He was the second of seven children of Jewish parents who fled antisemitic pogroms spreading throughout the Russian *Pale of Settlement. Weegee became the ultimate crime-news photographer in a newspaper career that ran from 1935 to 1946.

Weegee attended local public school on the Lower East Side up to seventh grade. At 15 he left home and earned his living selling candy to factory workers and working in restaurants. He became an assistant to a photographer, loading glass-plate holders and magnesium flash power. For a time he accompanied silent films on the violin, and he later wrote that he loved playing on the audience's emotions. One critic said he simply switched instruments. After years on the fringes of photography as a street portraitist, darkroom assistant, printer, and technician, he set out as a freelancer, hanging out at Manhattan police headquarters, waiting to fill the needs of picture-hungry tabloids and magazines. He specialized in the night shift, from 10 P.M. to 5 A.M. He lived in a rundown room near a police station and woke up as night fell. He was the first photographer given a permit to install a short-wave radio for police and fire calls in his car, and he had a small darkroom in his trunk. He was usually the first to arrive at a murder scene, a fire, an arrest, or a rescue. Gangland killings became a trademark, but he had remarkable range, from the homeless, to strivers, to freaks, politicians, and celebrities to tender shots of people afflicted or uplifted by everyday life. He exposed the faces of accident victims, survivors, and helpless sufferers. In one famous image, two women watching relatives burn to death in a fire are convulsed with grief and horror. In his book *Naked City*, Weegee said he cried when he took the picture. A critic said he combined "instincts of a bloodhound, a Peeping Tom, a showman and a human-interest editor." Weegee himself said, "Crime was my oyster, and I like it, my postgraduate course in life and photography."

Weegee used infrared film to register in the dark or low light to catch lovers in the movies and on the beach at night. His artless, mostly unposed, shots not only made him famous but also inspired a generation of younger photographers, from Diane *Arbus to Andy Warhol. One of Weegee's more famous photographs, "The Critic," of 1943, shows two elegantly clad women, furred and jeweled, sweeping grandly past a shabby, angry-looking bystander as they arrive at the opera. The truth, as Weegee revealed in his 1947 book, *Weegee's World*, is that he asked an assistant to ply the "bystander," a regular at bars on the Bowery, with cheap wine and then pose her near the curb as the socialites emerged from their limousines. Disheveled and barely able to stand up, she stared drunkenly at the women as Weegee's flashbulbs popped.

His only steady affiliation, with the newspaper *PM*, lasted 4½ years, beginning in 1940. Some of his most important work appeared in *PM*. After the publication of *Naked City*, Weegee went to Hollywood, where he served as a consultant on the film made from his book and played some minor film roles. He was the set photographer and technical consultant for Stanley *Kubrick's antiwar classic *Dr. Strangelove* (1963). Kubrick originally ended the film with a pie fight in the war room. He didn't like that ending, so he destroyed the negative and replaced it with the final wild cowboy ride on a nuclear bomb. The only record of the pie-fight sequence is Weegee's photographs.

No one is sure where he got the name Weegee, which he adopted in 1938. Some said it came from his job as a "squeegee boy," removing excess water from prints before they were put in darkroom dryers. Others suggested that it reflected a craze in the 1930s for the supposedly clairvoyant Ouija board, whose fanciful border was illustrated by fictional characters, one of whom resembled the photographer. Weegee himself said the name reflected his own clairvoyance at sensing photo opportunities, but his statements were not always trustworthy. Later he elaborated the name to Weegee the Famous.

[Stewart Kampel (2nd ed.)]

WEGROW (Pol. **Węgrów**; in Jewish documents: **Vengrove**), town in Warszawa province, E. Poland. Jews settled there at the beginning of the 16th century, when it was under Lithuanian rule. They engaged in trading both locally and abroad, and in tax farming. An organized community was established soon after the middle of the 16th century. After the town was incorporated within the kingdom of Poland in 1569, the community developed rapidly to achieve a leading position among the communities of the region. The owner of the town, Jan Kazimierz Kraniński, in an attempt to attract new Jewish settlers, granted the community in 1655 a privilege confirming its right of judicial autonomy, freedom to engage in trade and crafts, and exemption from municipal taxes. It imposed on the Jews an annual tax of two zlotys per household, and a one-time payment of six zlotys by new families as a domiciliary fee. At the beginning of the 17th century the Wegrow community had jurisdiction over the communities of Ciechanowiec, *Sokolow, and later Miedzyrzec *Podlaski and others. After a prolonged struggle against the *kahal* of *Tykocin, the Wegrow *kahal* obtained official representation at the *Council of Four Lands, and from the 1660s headed the independent *galil* (province) of Wegrow, which survived until 1764. In 1715 the Ciechanowiec community broke free of the authority of Wegrow, to be followed by Miedzyrzec in 1753. In 1765 there were 3,623 poll-tax payers under the community's jurisdiction, of whom 581 lived in the town. In 1764 the Wegrow community was the sixth largest in the Polish kingdom. Up to 1788 the Jewish community of the Praga suburb of Warsaw was affiliated to that of Wegrow as regards the payment of the poll tax.

In the second half of the 18th century Jews of the town traded in cattle, participated in the fairs of Breslau, Berlin, and Koenigsberg, and were occupied as tailors, weavers, furriers, bakers, and carters. The Jewish artisans were mostly organized in independent guilds. The *pinkas* of the *dayyanim* of Wegrow for 1781 to 1814 (now in the National and University Library in Jerusalem) provides an important source for the social and economic life of the community. In the 1790s Jewish entrepreneurs established workshops for wool weaving and tanning, and wealthy merchants were purveyors to the Polish and Russian armies. In 1794 a branch of the Hebrew printing press of *Nowy Dwor, founded by J.A. Krieger, printed books in Wegrow, including *Josippon.

In 1815 Wegrow was incorporated within Congress Poland. The community numbered 1,463 (48% of the town's population) in 1827; 2,343 (61%) in 1857; and 5,150 (62%) in 1897. From the 1870s many Jews took up occupations as jewelers, manufacturers of luxury goods and ritual articles, and engaged in transportation. At the beginning of the 20th century many Jews in Wegrow were occupied in the knitting and tanning industries. The *Bund gained considerable influence among the local workers in 1905.

In 1918 the *Po'alei Zion established Bet Borochov; later Tarbut, Central Yiddish School Organization (CYSHO), Yavneh, and Beth Jacob schools were established. In Orthodox circles the Gur (*Gora Kalwaria) Ḥasidim became influential. The Jewish population numbered 5,227 (55%) in 1931.

[Arthur Cygielman]

Holocaust Period

At the outbreak of World War II there were about 6,000 Jews in Wegrow. Immediately after the German army entered the town, attacks were made on the Jewish population, and on Sept. 23, 1939 (the Day of Atonement), the rabbi of Wegrow, Mendel Morgenstern, was tortured to death. During 1940 about 1,500 Jews from other parts of Poland were forced to settle in Wegrow, and the number of Jews there had grown to about 7,500 by the beginning of 1942. On Sept. 22, 1942, several thousand Jews from Wegrow and the vicinity were transferred to the *Treblinka death camp, where they perished. However, the majority of the Jewish population had managed to escape to the surrounding forests the previous day. Almost all of them were eventually caught and shot by German armed units who searched them out. The last 100 Jews, who had remained in a local forced-labor camp, were executed on May 1, 1943.

The community was not reconstituted after the war.

[Stefan Krakowski]

BIBLIOGRAPHY: Halpern, Pinkas, index; L. Loewenstein, *Index approbationum* (1923), 15, 18, 85, 102, 132, 140, 143–4; E. Ringelblum, *Projekty i próby przewarstwowienia Żydów w epoce stanisławowskiej* (1934), 94; idem, *Di Poylishe Yidn in Oyfshtand fun Kościuszko* (1937), 123; R. Mahler, in: *YIVO Historishe Shriftn*, 1 (1937), 644; Z. Rubashow (Shazar), *ibid.*, 187, 189; M. Baliński and T. Lipiński, *Starożytna Polska*, 3 (1845), 412; R. Rybarski, *Handel i polityka handlowa Polska, w XVI stuleciu*, 2 (1928), 89, 93, 149, 155–8; M. Kremer, in: *Zion*, no. 3–4 (1936), 311; *Yevreyskaya Starina*, 4 (1911), 286; B. Wasiutyński, *Ludność żydowska w Polsce w wiekach XIX i XX* (1930), 35, 66, 72, 77.

WEICHERT, MICHAEL (1890–1967), Yiddish theatrical producer, who worked in the Warsaw ghetto during World War II. Born in Galicia, Weichert studied drama in Vienna, and in Berlin under Max *Reinhardt. After World War I he returned to Poland and joined the *Vilna Troupe, which by then had moved to Warsaw. Among his productions for them was his dramatization of Sholem *Asch's *Kiddush ha-Shem* (1928). He also helped to run a Yiddish drama school, and when the Vilna Troupe broke up continued to work as teacher and producer, introducing Jewish audiences to modern social drama. When the Germans invaded Poland in World War II, Weichert accompanied the Jewish masses into the Warsaw ghetto and played an important part in organizing Jewish life while this was still possible. He left an account of his work there in *Yidishe Aleynhilf 1939–1945* ("Jewish Self-Help"), a two-volume work published in 1962. He survived the Holocaust, and in 1957 went to Israel, where he wrote his memoirs in three volumes (*Zikhroynes*, 1960–63).

BIBLIOGRAPHY: Z. Zylbercweig (ed.), *Leksikon fun Yidishn Teater*, 1 (1931), 676–8.

[Joseph Leftwich]

WEICHMANN, HERBERT (1896–1983), German politician. The son of a doctor in Silesia, Weichmann became an official in the Weimar government. He was a provincial judge from 1926 to 1927 and from 1927 to 1933 held a number of important governmental posts. With the advent of the Hitler regime, Weichmann left Germany for France, Spain, and finally the United States, where he became a university lecturer. In 1948 Weichmann returned to Germany. At the invitation of the burgomaster of Hamburg he joined the city's administration. He held high positions and was himself eventually elected burgomaster (1965–71). In 1965 Weichmann entered the Bundesrat (the Federal Upper House) as a Social Democrat and became its president. In this capacity, he was acting president of federal Germany in the absence of the president from the country. Weichmann, whose family was killed by the Nazis, regularly attended synagogue services and emphasized his Jewishness at every opportunity. He always rejected the frequent suggestion that he be considered for the presidency of the Federal Republic because he felt that, as Jew, he would be a burden on relations with the Arab world.

BIBLIOGRAPHY: W. Schaber, in: *Aufbau*, 33, no. 26 (1967), 7; W. Winfried, in: *Hamburger Bibliographien*, 17 (1974); H. Fahning (ed.), *Herbert Weichmann zum Gedächtnis...* (1983); E. Presser, in: *Neues Lexikon des Judentums* (2000), 849.

[Monika Halbinger (2nd ed.)]

WEIDENFELD, (Arthur) GEORGE, Baron (1919–), British publisher. Weidenfeld was born in Vienna. Following the Anschluss in 1938, he immigrated to Great Britain and joined the BBC where he worked in overseas intelligence and as a commentator on European affairs. Weidenfeld was a lecturer at Chatham House and in 1945 founded *Contact*, a journal of contemporary affairs and the arts. In 1948, together with Nigel Nicolson, he set up Weidenfeld and Nicolson, a large British publishing house, whose program is divided equally between general literature, academic books, and art and illustrated productions, and publishes the works of many Israeli scholars. In 1969 a subsidiary company was established in Jerusalem.

Weidenfeld was political adviser to President Chaim *Weizmann from 1949 to 1950, and his close association with Israel dates from that period. He was later chairman of the Board of Governors of Ben-Gurion University of the Negev and a member of the Board of Governors of the Weizmann Institute of Science. In 1969 Weidenfeld was knighted and in 1976 given a life peerage. Weidenfeld was one of the best known and most successful of postwar British publishers and produced many works of Jewish interest by a range of Jewish notables, among them Moshe *Dayan, Dr. Henry *Kissinger, Golda *Meir, and Sir Martin *Gilbert. He was the author of an autobiography, *Remembering My Good Friends*, in 1994.

[Asher Weill]

WEIDENREICH, FRANZ (1873–1948), German anatomist, physical anthropologist, and paleontologist. Born in the Palatinate, Weidenreich taught anatomy at Strasbourg from 1899 to 1918 and at Heidelberg from 1921 to 1924. In 1928 he was appointed professor of anthropology at Frankfurt University. In 1935, during the Nazi regime, he left Germany and took a position at Union Medical College in Peking (Beijing), China. He settled in the United States in 1940, and from 1941 until his death was affiliated with the Museum of Natural History in New York City. A leading scholar of human evolution and morphology, Weidenreich became internationally known for his studies of *Homo Sinanthropus*, the human fossil remains discovered in China in 1927 of which he gave the first description in 1943. He also investigated the later *Homo Sapiens* group found at Chou Kou Tien in north China, Neanderthal skeletons from Europe and Central Asia and, together with the Dutch paleontologist Gustav Koenigswald, the remains of *Pithecanthropus, Maganthropus* and *Paleojavinicus* from Java.

Among the problems dealt with by Weidenreich in his articles were the relation of erect posture to the evolution of the foot, hand, pelvis, and skull, and the influence of the expansion of the brain on human development. His shorter anthropological papers written from 1939 to his death were published in 1949 (Eng.; ed. by S.L. Washburn and D. Wolffson).

[Ephraim Fischoff]

WEIDER, BEN (1924–), Canadian businessman, physical fitness enthusiast, and Napoleon scholar. Weider was born into a working-class Montreal family. After serving in the Canadian military during World War II, and with only an elementary school education, he joined his brother Joe, who was publishing a bodybuilding magazine. Together the brothers expanded into the manufacture and sale of bodybuilding equipment. Their business now includes the manufacture of nutritional food and health supplements. Though Joe eventually moved to the United States, while Ben stayed in Canada, their holdings have become a sport, physical fitness, and bodybuilding empire. Two Weider companies, Weider Sports Equipment and Weider Health and Fitness, are estimated by some industry analysts to control as much as 25 percent of the worldwide health and fitness market.

To generate interest in bodybuilding and bring recognized standards to international weightlifting, in 1946 Ben Weider established the International Federation of Bodybuilders (IFBB). It has since become the world's oldest organization for bodybuilders and fitness competitors, active in over 170 countries. As the president of the IFBB, Weider worked to have bodybuilding and the IFBB recognized on the world sports stage. In 1998 the International Olympic Committee granted the IFBB official recognition as the international governing body of weightlifting.

From his home in Montreal, Weider was active in the Montreal and Canadian Jewish communities and an advocate of building political, ethnic, and religious understanding through sports and physical fitness. His efforts have been widely recognized in Canada and abroad. The Montreal YMHA is named in his honor. He was also granted several honorary degrees and the Order of Canada, the nation's highest citizen award.

Weider is also an acknowledged Napoleon scholar and served as president of the International Napoleonic Society. He is credited with groundbreaking research on the French emperor. He published several books on Napoleon, including *The Murder of Napoleon*, which was translated into 39 languages and sold over a million copies.

[Avi Hyman and Brenda Cappe (2nd ed.)]

WEIDMAN, HIRAM (**(Chaim) Leib**; 1862–1933) and **MORDECAI S.** (1864–1952), businessmen and Winnipeg communal leaders. Born in Orla near Bialystok in Russian Poland, the brothers moved to Winnipeg in 1882, where they lived for two years, and then worked on farms in the Jewish agricultural colony of New Jerusalem in present-day Saskatchewan. They returned to Winnipeg in 1887, when Hiram opened a grocery and jewelry business and Mordecai ran a fruit store. Both brothers branched out into other areas of retail, but their most enduring business began in 1909 when together they opened a wholesale grocery business, with Hiram as president and Mordecai as vice president.

Hiram and Mordecai shared strong anti-socialist sentiments, and were both opponents of the Winnipeg General Strike of 1919. But there were also some political differences between the brothers. An advocate of free trade, Hiram supported the Liberal Party and was a founder of the Hebrew Liberal Club in 1908. Mordecai, in contrast, supported the Conservative Party. He helped organized Jewish support in Winnipeg for the Conservatives, and in 1908 was chosen as one of three vice presidents of the Hebrew Conservative Club of Winnipeg. In 1910 he was elected to the executive committee of the Hebrew Conservative Association. Although an ardent Conservative, that same year Mordecai voted for Solomon Hart Green, a Liberal who became the first Jew elected to the Legislative Assembly of Manitoba.

Both men were active in communal affairs, together founding the Shaarey Zedek Synagogue in 1889, with Hiram serving as synagogue president from 1920 to 1921. They were both strong supporters of Jewish education, and together were founders of a Hebrew literary society. Hiram also was a moving force behind the establishment of a *talmud torah*. Both were committed Zionists: Hiram was a founder of Winnipeg's Zionist society in 1898, and helped found the Federation of Canadian Zionist Societies a year later. In response to the 1903 Kishinev pogrom, Hiram spearheaded the formation of a committee to raise relief funds. In 1923, Hiram and Mordecai traveled to Poland, where they made donations to Jewish institutions and charities, and from there to Palestine, where their parents had immigrated in 1904. The brothers deeded the Jerusalem home of their parents to a Jewish maternal aid society, and donated money towards the home's upkeep.

In the 1920s, even as a new generation of Weidmans moved into the family business, Hiram and Mordecai retained their positions in the family firm, and continued to do so until they died. At the time of his death, Mordecai was one of the last of the Russian Jewish immigrants to Winnipeg.

[Henry Trachtenberg (2nd ed.)]

WEIDMAN, JEROME (1913–1998), U.S. novelist. Born in New York City, Weidman obtained first-hand knowledge of the Jewish garment industry while working his way through college. In his first novel, *I Can Get It for You Wholesale* (1937), later made into a musical, he described the rise of an unscrupulous go-getter in the dress trade. His second novel, *What's in It for Me?* (1938), which had a similar setting, aroused a storm of protest because of its unpleasant portrayals of Jewish characters. During World War II, Weidman worked for the Office of War Information and there found material for his satire on war propaganda, *Too Early to Tell* (1946). In his novel, *The Enemy Camp* (1958), Weidman analyzes relations between Jews and non-Jews on the basis of his own experiences as a young man. The short stories of *My Father Sits in the Dark* (1961) contain nostalgic glimpses of East Side Jews. Weidman's style is restless, naturalistic, and colored with slang and satiric overtones. In his portrayal of Jewish types, he takes his place beside other Jewish writers of his age group such as Budd *Schulberg, Norman Katkov, and Albert *Halper, but was less unkind than some of his contemporaries. Hedonistic in his attitude, Weidman remained generally aloof from the strivings of the Jews of his generation. Weidman also wrote the book for a musical, *Fiorello* (1959), which was awarded a Pulitzer Prize. Later works included *Back Talk*, essays (1963), a short story collection entitled *The Death of Dickie Draper and Nine Other Stories* (1965), *Fourth Street East: A Novel of How It Was* (1970), and the autobiography *Praying for Rain*.

BIBLIOGRAPHY: R. Newquist, *Counterpoint* (1964), 626–34; J. Barkham, in *Saturday Review* (July 28, 1962), 38–39: S.J. Kunitz (ed.), *Twentieth Century Authors*, first suppl. (1955), s.v.; L. Nichols, in: *New York Times Book Review* (June 15, 1958), 8.

[Sol Liptzin]

WEIDNER, PAULUS (c. 1525–1585), physician and rector of Vienna University. Born in Udine, Italy, as Asher Judah b. Nathan Ashkenazi (the physician and diplomat Solomon *Ashkenazi was his brother), he studied medicine at Padua and was invited by the estates of Carinthia to practice there, in a province where Jews were not allowed to reside. After a period of spiritual struggle he embraced Christianity in Vienna in 1558. His first book, *Loca praecipua fidei christianae* (1559), was an attempt to persuade the Jews of the truth of Christianity; the work showed his mastery of Hebrew and Christian sources. Weidner enjoyed the substantial patronage of the Austrian emperors, whom he served as physician. On March 13, 1560, *Ferdinand I, after repeatedly postponing the expulsion of Bohemian Jewry, ordered all its Hebrew books to be brought to Vienna; they were checked by Weidner, who found no fault in them and had them returned. A year later the Jews of Prague were forced to listen to a series of conversionary sermons preached by him. Weidner's last published work was *Sententiae Hebraicae* (1563), a collection of proverbs, mainly from Pirkei *Avot, in Hebrew, German, and Latin. After his conversion he was accepted by the University of Vienna, where he became dean of the faculty of medicine six times and thrice rector of the university. The title "von Billerburg" was granted him in 1582.

BIBLIOGRAPHY: P.J. Diamant, *Paulus Weidner von Billerburg 1525–1585* (1933; repr. from: *Mitteilungen des Vereines fuer Geschichte der Stadt Wien*, 13/14, 1933).

°**WEIGAND, THEODOR** (1864–1963), German archaeologist. Weigand went on expeditions for the Prussian Oriental Museum from 1895 and for a time was the scientific attaché in the German embassy in Constantinople. During World War I Weigand served as a staff member of the German Denkmalschutz-Kommando for the preservation of antiquities in Syria and Palestine and conducted a survey of the Negev – the first in which air photography was used in archaeological work – and of Petra. From 1911 to 1931 he was director of the antiquities department of the Berlin Museum, and from 1932 until his death the head of the German Archaeological Institute.

[Michael Avi-Yonah]

WEIGEL (Zaluszowska), CATHERINE (c. 1460–1539), martyr in Poland. Catherine was the wealthy widow of Melchior Weigel, a merchant-patrician and member of the Cracow municipal council. In 1530, at an advanced age, she was accused of Judaizing. She recanted, but in 1539, on further accusation, refused to do so again, and was burned at the stake. According to the chronicler Lukasz Gornicki, as well as eyewitnesses, the 80-year-old woman went to her death courageously. Asked "Do you believe in His [God's] only son, our Lord Jesus Christ?" she said: "God had neither wife nor son, nor does He need this; for only mortals need sons. We are His children … and all who walk in His ways are His children" (*Dzieje w Koronie Polskiej* (1637), 5). Whether Catherine was a Jewess to the full or a radical anti-Trinitarian, her death made a great impression. On the king's order the heads of the Cracow community were arrested, and a number of Jews fled. The rabbi of the town, the physician Moses Fishel, suffered so much in prison that he died a short time after his release. This event started off a Judaizing scare, and a hunt for proselytes to Judaism which was relentlessly pursued in *Poland-*Lithuania in 1539–40.

BIBLIOGRAPHY: M. Balaban, *Historja Żydów w Krakowie i na Kazimierzu*, 1 (1931), 125–30.

[Arthur Cygielman]

WEIGEL, HELENE (1900–1971), actress and intendant of the Berliner Ensemble. Born in Vienna, she went to Frankfurt after her training and later to Berlin, where she was taught by Max Reinhardt and appeared at the Volksbühne and at the Deutsches Theater.

In the early 1920s she met Bertolt Brecht. The couple married in 1929 and had two children. Weigel inspired the female figures in her husband's work and played them on stage. In 1933 the family emigrated to the United States (via Prague, Vienna, Paris, Switzerland and Scandinavia), where Weigel dedicated herself to her family.

A year after the family's return from the U.S. in 1947, Weigel played the main character in the world première of Brecht's *Die Antigone des Sophokles* in Switzerland. In the same year the couple went to East Berlin. In 1949 Weigel became intendant of the newly established Berliner Ensemble, which she and Brecht led to an international reputation.

In 1950 Weigel was a founding member of the Deutsche Akademie der Künste (German Academy of Arts) in East Berlin. In 1954 she ran as a candidate of the SED for the Berlin parliament. Three times (1949, 1953, 1960) she was awarded with the National Prize of the GDR. She also received the "Vaterländischer Verdienstorden in Silber" (Patriotic Order of Merit in Silver) and the "Clara-Zetkin-Medal."

BIBLIOGRAPHY: W. Hecht, *Helene Weigel...* (2000); C. Herold, *Mutter des Ensembles. Helene Weigel...* (2001); S. Kebir, *Abstieg in den Ruhm. Helene Weigel...* (2000); Munzinger, *Internationales Biographisches Archiv* 31 (1971).

[Monika Halbinger (2nd ed.)]

WEIGERT, CARL (1845–1904), German pathologist. Born in Muensterberg, he worked as an assistant to famous anatomists and pathologists, including Julius *Cohnheim. In 1897 he was appointed professor of pathological anatomy at the Senckenberg Institute of Frankfurt (director from 1884).

He discovered and developed methods for the staining of tissues and bacteria, and these methods helped greatly in the development of histology and bacteriology. Weigert's staining methods are still used in histology. He made important studies on tissue degeneration, on embolism and on miliary tuberculosis.

BIBLIOGRAPHY: R. Rieder, *Carl Weigert und seine Bedeutung fuer die medizinische Wissenschaft* (1906).

[Joshua O. Leibowitz]

WEIGERT, FRITZ (1876–1947), German physical chemist and biochemist. Born and educated in Berlin, he was the nephew of Paul *Ehrlich and of C. *Weigert. He was on the staff of Berlin University from 1908. From 1914 until the Nazis forced him to leave in 1935, he was professor of photochemistry in Leipzig University. He immigrated to Britain and from 1936 was director of the Physiochemical Department of the Cancer Research Institute at Mount Vernon Hospital, Northwood.

He elucidated the metabolism of the carcinogenic hydrocarbon 3, 4-benzpyrene by fluorescence spectroscopy. His books included *Die chemischen Wirkungen des Lichts* (1911) and *Optische Methoden der Chemie* (1927).

BIBLIOGRAPHY: Berenblum and Halban, in: *Nature*, no. 159 (1947), 733.

[Samuel Aaron Miller]

WEIGHTS AND MEASURES. From the earliest period of their history the Jews were alive to the necessity of an accurate system of weights and measures, and an honest handling of them. The first legislation in the interest of economic righteousness in general is found in Leviticus 19:35 and Deuteronomy 25:13–16, and the prophets constantly denounced the use of false measures (Amos 8:5; Hos. 12:8; Micah 6:10; see also Prov. 11:1; 16:11; 20:10). Rabbinic legislation went so far as to demand the periodic cleaning of weights, scales, and measures lest their true standard be impaired by dirt (BB 5:10; see also BB 89a-b).

Metrological Systems in the Bible and the Ancient Near East

An authoritative and accepted system of weights for buying and selling, building, measuring areas, and the like is a necessity of civilized life. Therefore even in very ancient periods fixed measurements were established, initially for barter, estimation of distances, etc., and later for more complex needs such as building, the division of land, the digging of canals, and others. For that reason, most of the first measures were natural or common physical phenomena, such as the palm of the hand, a day's journey, seeds of grain, and simple utensils. As time progressed, the measures were improved and made more precise, but they were still called by their ancient names. Various systems of measurement developed in the large cultural centers of Egypt and Mesopotamia from a very early period. There, even complex reckoning was carried out to determine the equivalence between the different categories, that is, to reckon volume in terms of weight or area, and the like.

This type of reckoning is not found in the Bible though it was certainly known in Israel. An allusion to a similar reckoning is found in the Bible in a verse which expresses acreage in terms of volume of seed requirement: "And he made a trench about the altar, as great as would contain two measures of seed" (I Kings 18:32; see also Jer. 27:16; Isa. 5:10b (see *Targum), and later sources down to modern Palestine Arab usage).

The weights and measures in the Bible are in large part based upon the weights and measures which were accepted by the ancient peoples, the names of the measures also being the same. In Israel, measures of several peoples were used simultaneously: from Mesopotamian measures, the kor, *se'ah*, shekel, and others; from Egyptian measures, the ephah, hin, and others; and measures whose names were borrowed from the Canaanites such as *letekh* and *kikkar*. Apparently the Israelites adopted the measures from the Canaanites, who lived in the land before them, along with the names which were originally Egyptian and Mesopotamian. For this reason Egyptian measures have been found that have Mesopotamian names. Some measures, since they are not found among the neighboring countries, were apparently established in Israel.

In biblical measures, it is customary to distinguish between natural measures (measures established in reference to parts of the human body, utensils, average sizes of burdens loaded on animals, etc.) and between measures established by reckoning which were fixed and precise. In some cases the Bible explains the relationship between measures, but it is difficult today to establish their absolute values because as early as the days of the Second Temple the biblical measures were abolished, and later translators and commentators were inclined to identify them with their contemporary measures without being precise as to their values.

In the metrology practiced in the Ancient Near East, there were measures which differed in their absolute value but were identical in name, for example: in Egypt and Mesopotamia, the short cubit was in use along with the long cubit, and there were also different weights, light and heavy, called by the same name, such as the mina. Double weights of this sort were in use also in Palestine, as has been proven from the Bible and from archaeological finds, and were in use there almost until modern times.

Aside from these, there were measures confined to specific localities. Ancient documents provide evidence of weights named for cities: "Alalakh weight," "Carchemish weight," and the like. This custom, too, was practiced in Palestine. In addition to the already-mentioned difficulties, there is the problem of the durability of these weights, since it is likely that with the passage of time many changes took place in them. The ascertaining of biblical measures and the determination of their values in terms of present-day measures is done mainly on the basis of archaeological finds. In the excavations carried out in Palestine, many weights have been uncovered and also fragments of vessels upon which measurements of volume have been written. Linear measure can be reckoned according to ancient structures whose measurements are marked. In the neighboring countries – mainly Egypt, Syria, and Mesopotamia – actual measuring rods of wood and stone were uncovered, along with weights and economic documents, all of which are valuable aids in determining the biblical measures. However, it still cannot be known whether these measures are identical with biblical measures and which of the various standards the Bible used. The Bible demands the use of correct measures and promises long life to one who is careful in this matter (Deut. 25:13–16; Amos 8:5, et al.).

Linear Measure

The units of length mentioned in the Bible, as well as those used by other ancient peoples, are derived from average measures of the length of human limbs. Names of measures based on the limbs of the body are in use in some languages even to this day.

It appears that in the early period it was customary to measure with the limbs themselves: the part of the arm from the elbow to the tip of the middle finger is the "standard cubit [lit. by a man's forearm]" (Deut. 3:11); the span (*zeret*) was the distance between the tip of the little finger and the tip of the thumb with the fingers straddled. The measurement of the handbreadth was the width of the four fingers, and the fingerbreadth was measured according to the width of the finger. As time progressed, absolute and more precise values and relationships were established for these natural measures, though these were still named according to the parts of the body.

The large measures mentioned in the Bible are based upon crude estimates such as the range of the bowshot (Gen. 21:16), i.e., the distance which the bow is able to shoot the arrow. In several places in the Bible, the expression *kivrat ʾerez*, "a short distance," is mentioned (Gen. 35:16; 48:7; II Kings 5:19) which seems to mean a journey of two hours. Greater distances were measured by days' journey (Gen. 30:36; 31:23; et al.).

Among the instruments used for measuring small units of length, the Bible mentions: *ḥut*, "thread" (Jer. 52:21); *ḥevel*, "rope" (Amos 7:17); *ḥevel middah*, "measuring line" (Zech. 2:5 [1]; *kav* (*qav*) *ha-middah*, "measuring line" (Jer. 31:38 [39]; *petil pishtim... u-qeneh ha-middah*, "line of flax... and measuring reed" (Ezek. 40:3). It is likely that all or some of these instruments were used regularly for linear measure and it should be noted that the rope served as a standard measurement of length among several ancient peoples.

Five small units of length are mentioned in the Bible. Their exact length is not explicit but their interrelations are generally established: *kaneh* (*qaneh*), "reed"; *ʾammah*, "cubit"; *zeret*, "span"; *ṭefaḥ/ṭofaḥ*, "handbreadth"; and *ʾeẓbaʿ*, "fingerbreadth." The most important and basic measure was the cubit. It appears that there were two values for the cubit which were in use in different periods: the short cubit is implicit in II Chronicles 3:3 in the description of the Temple, "in cubits of the old standard," and the meaning of the verse is that the measurements of the Temple are given in terms of the ancient cubit and not the longer royal cubit which was in use in this time. In the description of the future sanctuary in Ezekiel 40:5 (see also 48:13), the second or long cubit is mentioned: "and the length of the measuring reed in the man's hand was six long cubits, each being a cubit and a handbreadth in length." The cubit in this description exceeds the normal cubit by one handbreadth and thus contains seven handbreadths and not six like the short cubit. Ezekiel uses the long Persian cubit, which was in use also in Mesopotamia, and which may have come into use in Palestine during the time of the Return. (See Table: Units of Length-Bible.)

Table 1. Ratio between the Units of Length in the Bible

	reed	cubit	handbreadth	fingerbreadth
According to the short cubit				
reed	1			
cubit	6	1		
handbreadth	36	6	1	
fingerbreadth	144	24	4	1
According to the long cubit				
reed	1			
cubit	6	1		
handbreadth	42	7	1	
fingerbreadth	168	28	4	1

Attempts have been made to learn the value of the cubit in terms of present-day measures by comparisons with ancient structures whose measurements are noted, such as the tunnel of Siloam dating to the reign of Hezekiah; or on the basis of the measurements of buildings which, in the opinion of their excavators, were built in whole cubits, such as the walls of Hazor, Megiddo, and Gezer from Solomon's time (I Kings 9:15); or by estimating the volume of "the molten sea" which stood in the Temple (I Kings 7:23 – 26; II Chron. 4:2). However, all of these calculations are unreliable. Various scholars (e.g., R.B.Y. Scott) – some on the basis of comparisons with Egyptian and Mesopotamian standards, and some according to parallels from Hellenistic sources – established the values shown in Table: Value of the Cubit.

Table 2. Conjectured Value of the Cubit

long cubit (28 fingerbreadths)	–	521.0 mm.
short cubit (24 fingerbreadths)	–	446.0 mm.
handbreadth (4 fingerbreadths)	–	74.0 mm.
fingerbreadth	–	18.6 mm.

These figures probably approximate the actual values of the measures, but they cannot be considered precise.

Volume

As was the case with linear measures, human limbs were initially used to measure volume. The small units were: *komeẓ* (*qomeẓ*, "handful"; Lev. 2:2; 5:12), which is the measure of the grasp of three fingers and perhaps is the *shalish* mentioned in Isaiah 40:12; *ḥofen* (Ex. 9:8, et al.), which is the entire palm of the hand; and *ḥofnayim*, which is two handfuls. They were also accustomed to measuring with receptacles which the farmer used at home and in the field; the omer (*ʿOmer*) is a bundle of ears of corn; a quantity of wine in the measure of a skin (jar) is also mentioned (I Sam. 1:24). The values of these measures cannot be established, for it is certain that they were not precise; later on some of them did become fixed, their previous names being preserved. It is likely that various foods used to be prepared in fixed portions, and therefore the Bible notes quantities of food, liquid and dry, in numbers of portions without designating the volume (I Sam. 25:18; II Sam. 16:1, et al.).

The units of volume mentioned in the Bible are the following:

homer (Lev. 27:16; Isa. 5:10; Ezek. 45:11; 13:14; Hos. 3:2);
kor (Ezek. 45:14);
letekh (Hos. 3:2);
ephah (Ex. 16:36; Ezek. 45:11, 13; 46:14, et al.),
bath (Ezek. 45:11, 14; II Chron. 2:9);
se'ah (Gen. 18:6; I Sam. 25:18; I Kings 18:32; II Kings 7:1, 18, et al.);
hin (Ex. 29:40; Ezek. 45:24; 46:11, 14, et al.);
omer (Ex. 16:16, 36; Lev. 23:10 – 14, et al.);
ʿissaron (Ex. 29:40; Lev. 14:21; Num. 15:4, et al.);
qav (II Kings 6:25);
log, which is the small liquid measure (Lev. 14:10, 12, 15, 21, 24).

(See Table 3: Measures of Volume and Their Ratios).

It is worth noting the mixture of the decimal system which was used in Egypt and the sexagesimal system of Mesopotamia which is most characteristic of the scale of weights and measures in Palestine. Also the names – as was noted – are in part from Egyptian measures and in part from Mesopotamian measures.

If a distinction is made between liquid and dry measures, the following tables can be set up as seen in Table: Dry and Liquid Measures.

Table 4. Distinction between Dry and Liquid Measures

Dry		Liquid	
homer	1	kor	1
letekh	2	bath	10
ephah	10	hin	60
se'ah	30	*log*	720
omer – *ʿissaron*	100		
qav	180		

Scholars no longer attempt – as in previous generations – to equate these measures with Greek and Roman measures and thereby determine their absolute values, because this was based on conjecture only. The only method by which modern scholars can determine the values of these weights is to measure the volume of vessels discovered in excavations in Palestine whose capacity is marked on them, such as fragments of vessels with the words *bt*, "bath," or *bt lmlk*, "royal bath," written upon them. According to W.F. Albright's calculations, which are accepted by most scholars today, the "royal bath" has a capacity of 22 liters. (See Table: Scale of Measures of Volume.)

Table 5. Scale of Measures of Volume (Dry and Liquid)

homer – kor	220.0 liters
letekh	110.0 liters
ephah – bath	22.0 liters
se'ah	7.3 liters
hin	3.6 liters
omer – ʿissaron	2.2 liters
qav	1.2 liters
log	0.3 liters

Aside from the inscriptions "bath" and "royal bath," some potsherds were discovered during excavations with inscrip-

Table 3. Measures of Volume and Their Ratios

	Homer – kor	*letekh*	ephah – bath	*se'ah*	hin	omer – *ʿissaron*	*qav*	*log*
homer – kor	1							
letekh	2	1						
ephah – bath	10	5	1					
seʿah	30	15	3	1				
hin	60	30	6	2	1			
omer – *ʿissaron*	100	50	10	3 1/2	1 2/3	1		
qav	180	90	18	6	3	1 4/5	1	
log	720	360	72	24	12	7 1/5	4	1

tions which in general designate the type of goods and the quantity; however, for the most part, the names of the units of volume are missing from these inscriptions (a common practice in the Bible also; see I Sam. 25:18; II Sam. 16:1). A shard was found at Tell Qasileh bearing the inscription (according to the reading of B. Mazar), "To the king, 1,100 [measures of] oil, from Aḥiyahu." The liquid measure is not explicit: in the opinion of Mazar, the *log* is intended. Another inscription, discovered in Kadesh-Barnea, reads 51, and according to M. Dothan, it designates five measures of oil and the hin is intended. Also discovered in Samaria were tens of ostraca upon which measures of oil and wine are mentioned by the *nbl*, "skin" (biblical, *nevel*, cf. I Sam. 1:24; 25:18; II Sam. 16:1, et al.). The units of volume mentioned in the Elephantine papyri from the fifth century B.C.E. are *se'ah* and *qav*, the measure being designated by the first letter only. This way of designating measures continued in Palestine until the end of the Second Temple, as a vessel uncovered in the ruins of Qumran reveals. Upon it is inscribed: "two *se'ah* and seven *log*." This vessel has the capacity of 35.65 liters.

Area Measure

The main measure of area in the Bible is the *ẓemed* (I Sam. 14:14; Isa. 5:10), which refers to the area which a pair of oxen can plow in one day. This method of measuring area persists into the Mishnah and the Talmud Ancient Near East and later passed on to the Romans. In Rome the unit of area used was called *jugerum* from *jugum*, "yoke" (Pliny, *Naturalis Historia*, 18:9), while the modern measures feddan and acre have similar meanings. These measures, which in the beginning were not precise, in time became more clearly defined.

There was also another system of measuring area mentioned in the Bible, based upon the quantity of seeds sown in it (Lev. 27:16; I Kings 18:32; Isa. 5:10b (see *Targum)); and, needless to say, this measurement was not precise. This system was especially prevalent in Mesopotamia, and a formulation of this measure there reads: *bīt 1 imēru*, "property measuring one homer." This method of measuring area persists into the Mishnah and the Talmud (BB 7:1; 2:5, et al.) and is also attested in a deed from the time of the Bar Kokhba revolt. The Bible uses more precise measurement in its description of a rectangular area, noting the measure of the length and width in cubits or parts of cubits, and also adds the adjective *ravu'a*, "square" (Ex. 27:1; 28:16, et al.). Ezekiel also notes the areas of the entire complex of buildings in the Temple in cubits (Ezek. 40).

Weights

WEIGHT IN THE BIBLE. The verb shql ("to weigh") is shared by all Semitic languages; and generally the system of weights used by Semitic peoples is the same. Weights, for the most part, were made of stone, hence the Bible refers to weights generally as "stones" ('even). In Akkadian, weights are called also aban kīsi, "stones from the bag," which consist of stones placed in a cloth bag (Micah 6:11; Prov. 16:11, et al.). In Ugaritic too the word *'abn*, "stone," signified weights; but there have also been found many cast metal weights from the biblical period. During the Persian period, the metal weight became a coin and indication of this process can be seen in the Septuagint where the word for shekel, σίκλος, is changed to the word for the coin didrachm, δίδραχμον. Similarly they translated beka (beqaʿ), δραχμή, and gerah, ὀβολός.

In some ancient countries, especially in Mesopotamia, the old unit of weight was a seed of grain. Although the Bible used the names of early Mesopotamian weights, it does not mention this particular weight since the reciprocal relationship between Israel and Mesopotamia in weights, as in measures of volume, appears only in a relatively late period (apparently the Neo-Babylonian; see below).

Seven weights are mentioned in the Bible: talent, mina, shekel, beka, gerah, *pim*, and *kesiṭah*. A scale of the relationships between the first five weights mentioned can be established on the basis of the Bible and other sources; the absolute and relative value of the *pim* can be determined from archaeological finds (see below). The seventh weight, the *kesiṭah* (Gen. 33:19; Josh. 24:32; Job 42:11), seems to be an archaic weight and the origin of its name and its metrological value are not known. (Some believe it means rather "a sheep or goat.")

The basis of the biblical system of weights becomes clear by investigating the interrelationships of the three most important weights, the talent, shekel, and gerah.

The talent (*kikkar*), was the largest unit of weight in the Bible, and was already known by the same name in Ugaritic. In Ugaritic it was pronounced *kakaru*, as has been shown from Akkadian documents from Ugarit and Alalakh where the Canaanite name appears in the forms *qaq(q)aru(m)*, *kakaru(m)*. The very name *kikkar* testifies to the round shape of the weights. The relation between the talent and the shekel becomes clear in Exodus 38:25–26. The half shekel brought by 603,550 men amounted to 100 talents and 1,775 shekels. Thus the following calculations can be made as seen in Table: Shekel and the Talent.

Table 6. Relation between the Shekel and the Talent

603,550 half-shekels	=	300,000 + 1775 shekels
300,000 shekels	=	100 talents
3,000 shekels	=	1 talent

This system of dividing the talent into 3,000 shekels differs from the Mesopotamian system which divides the talent into 3,600 parts, and is the same as the Ugaritic system where the talent is also divided into 3,000 shekels. From this it follows that the biblical division is based upon an ancient Canaanite tradition.

The shekel (Akk. *šiqlu*; Ugaritic, *ṯ~ql*; early Aram. *shql*; late Aram. *tql*) is the most basic weight, as its name, which means simply weight, testifies. Since the shekel is the definite weight, an expression such as "1,000 silver" (Gen. 20:16) can be explained as 1,000 shekels of silver, and the name of the weight is omitted since it is self-explanatory. Abbreviations like these are also found in other Semitic languages. The fundamental nature of the shekel can also be seen in the fact that all weights which the Bible explains are explained only in terms of the shekel.

The gerah is known in Akkadian as *girû*. The basic meaning of the Akkadian word is a grain of carob seed. The value of the gerah is the 20th part of a shekel (Ex. 30:13), unlike the Akkadian *girû* which is the 24th part of a *šiqlu*. S.E. Loewenstamm noted that the ratio 24:20 is identical with the ratio 3,600:3,000, and therefore he holds that the division of the shekel into 20 gerah is based upon the same ancient Canaanite tradition according to which the talent was divided into 3,000 shekels.

The mina (Heb. *maneh*; Sum. *mana*; Akk. *man* –; Ugaritic, *mn*), which designates a weight of approximately 50 or 60 shekels (see below), is found in the Bible primarily in the late books (Ezek. 45:12; Ezra 2:69; Neh. 7:70, 71). In the period preceding the destruction of the First Temple, the mina is mentioned only once, in the verse about Solomon's shields (I Kings 10:17). From this it is reasonable to assume that in ancient times in Israel reckoning was done in shekels and talents only, and the mina was not used except in unusual situations. It appears that this practice too had its roots in an ancient Canaanite tradition, for in Ugaritic writings many calculations are found involving shekels and talents and very few involving the mina. The value of the mina is defined in Ezekiel 45:12. From this verse it follows that the mina is equivalent to 60 shekels like the Akkadian *man* –. However, there is reason to assume that Ezekiel's definition was influenced by his Mesopotamian environment, and that the Canaanite-Israelite mina was equivalent to only 50 shekels. First, it appears that there are two systems intertwined in Ezekiel's words. Portions of 15 and 20 shekels are appropriate for a mina of 60 shekels, as they equal a fourth and a third of it. Not so a portion of 25 shekels which is appropriate only for a mina of 50 shekels, of which it would comprise half. F. Thureau-Dangin found support for the existence of a Canaanite mina of 50 shekels in Ugaritic weights which contain 50 Ugaritic shekels. He regarded these as weights of a mina. According to this, the ratio of the Mesopotamian weight to the Canaanite weight would be 60:50, like the ratios 3600:3000 and 24:20 which were dealt with above. Support for this system can also be found in the passages which speak of payment of 50 or 100 shekels (Deut. 22:19, 29, et al.), which probably refer to payments of one or two minas. Moreover, there are signs that the Mesopotamian system of Ezekiel did not succeed in supplanting the Canaanite system. The Septuagint (LXXA) reads for Ezekiel 45:12: "five shekels shall be five shekels, and ten shekels shall be ten shekels, and your mina shall be fifty shekels"; and although Borrois advanced proofs to show that this version should not be preferred over the Masoretic Text, this version is significant. It provides evidence that at the time of the translation, the mina consisted of 50 shekels.

The beka is mentioned twice in the Bible (Gen. 24:22; Ex. 38:26) and its value is explicitly determined as one-half a shekel. Its name is derived from the root *bqʿ*, "to break, to divide," and its basic meaning is "a part." According to the reckoning of a mina as 50 shekels, the Table: Weight and their Ratios 1 may be set up:

Table 7. Measures of Weight and Their Ratios (mina = 50 shekels)

	talent	mina	shekel	beka	gerah
talent	1				
mina	60	1			
shekel	3,000	50	1		
beka	6,000	100	2	1	
gerah	60,000	1,000	20	10	1

However, on the basis of Ezekiel 45:12 according to which the mina contains 60 shekels and on the assumption that Ezekiel divided the talent (*kikkar*) into 60 minas, the Table: Weight and their Ratios 2 may be set up.

Table 8. Measures of Weight and Their Ratios (mina=60 shekels)

	talent	mina	shekel	beka	gerah
talent	1				
mina	60	1			
shekel	3,600	60	1		
beka	7,200	120	2	1	
gerah	72,000	1,200	20	10	1

This table is arranged according to the Mesopotamian system and contains nothing from the Canaanite-Israelite system except the division of the shekel into 20 gerah instead of 24.

In addition to being divided into the beka and gerah, the shekel is also divided into a fourth and a third (I Sam. 9:8; Neh. 10:33). There is support for this division both inside and outside Palestine. From Assyrian documents found at Calah it is evident that the shekel was very often divided there into many more subunits, but there is no proof that this was so in Israel as well.

Also mentioned in the Bible is the *peres* (Dan. 5:25, 28), and C. Clermont-Ganneau has suggested that it is half a mina. This weight is mentioned also among bilingual weights (Akkadian-Aramaic) from the Persian period and its written form is פרש. The *peres* is also mentioned in the Mishnah (Pe'ah 8:5; Ḥul. 11:2) and its value there is half a *zuz*.

In establishing the value of the shekel there is an additional complication in that the Bible mentions at least three kinds of shekels: in Genesis 23:16, a shekel of silver "at the going merchant's rate [*ʿover la-soḥer*]," which is similar to the Akkadian expression *ina manê ša tamkari*, "in the merchant's mina"; in Exodus 30:13, "shekel by the sanctuary weight [*ha-qodesh*]"; and in II Samuel 14:26, "shekels by the king's weight [*be-ʾeven ha-melekh*]," that is, shekels stamped by the royal treasury as proof that they are perfect. Also in the Elephantine papyri from the Persian period it is said "royal weight" (באבני המלכא or במתקלת מלכא). It cannot be determined whether these shekels were equivalent in value, but on the basis of evidence from external sources, it appears that there were differences between them.

ARCHAEOLOGICAL FINDS. In excavations carried out in Palestine many weights have been uncovered – some with the weight marked on them, but most without any notation. The shape of the weights, for the most part, is semicircular (dome-shaped). There are also some cast metal weights that are rectangular and cube-shaped, and some that are oval or in the shape of animals. Most of the weights found in Palestine are from the end of the period of the monarchy (the seventh to sixth centuries B.C.E.).

Very few weights and inscriptions with the word shekel written explicitly have been found in strata from the Israelite period. A bronze weight in the shape of a turtle was found in the coastal plain; on its reverse side it bears the inscription (according to the reading of A. Reifenberg) פלג שקל, and on the front, פלג רבעית, and its weight is 2.63 gm. And in fact, a weight of this sort (one-quarter shekel) is mentioned in I Samuel 9:8. Another bronze weight from Samaria, also in the shape of a turtle, bears the inscription חמש ("five"), and this has been interpreted to mean five gerahs, that is one-quarter of a shekel, and its weight is 2.49 gm. Another weight from Samaria is marked on one side רבע ש[ק]ל and on the other רבע נצף, and its weight is 2.54 gm. (see below). At Tell Qasileh an ostracon was found with the following inscription engraved upon it: [ז]הב אפל לבית חרן and here too, B. Mazar interprets the letter *sin* to mean shekels. Two ostraca containing calculations in shekels were also found in Yavneh-Yam. Many weights found in excavations bear a special mark in the form of ≡ ש, with another sign next to it which in general designates the number of units. These weights have for some time been considered shekels. They were discovered for the most part at localities in the Kingdom of Judah, in the following places: Gibeon, Jerusalem, Ramat-Raḥel, Gezer, Tel Zechariah, Tell Jedideh, Lachish, En-Gedi, Tel Malḥatah, and Arad; and others in the coastal plain; Tel Jemmeh, Nebi Rubin, Yavneh-Yam, and Ashdod. Only one weight of this type is known from the area of Samaria, and it was discovered at Shechem. Many others of unknown provenance are in private collections.

Scholars have been greatly divided as to the interpretation of the sign x̲ which appears on the weights. Thompson thought that this sign was taken from the Egyptian *nb* ("gold") weight which weighs approximately 12 gm. On the basis of a bronze weight of 12.28 gm. which was discovered at Gezer and upon which is written the number two and next to it *lmlk*, Diringer and Borrois maintain that the purpose of this sign is to designate the royal shekel which was fixed at 11.3 gm.; and this was the accepted opinion among scholars in the past. Recently the debate was revived when R.B.Y. Scott suggested that the sign be interpreted as a schematic drawing symbolizing the word *ẓeror*, that is, a cloth bag, tied at the top, in which precious metals were wrapped. Y. Yadin, basing his opinion on these weights from Gezer and upon the image of a scarab found in the Elephantine Papyri upon which the word למלך, *lmlk*, also appears, maintains that this sign is merely a schematic drawing of the well-known royal scarab which is found on common *lmlk* seals. In his opinion, in every case where this sign is written, it serves as a recognized sign designating the word *lmlk*, that is, the official royal standard.

Alongside this sign is usually written an additional sign which all scholars interpret as a number which notes the quantity of royal shekels contained in each weight. By examining the average weight of all the weights of this kind which have been discovered up till now, it becomes evident that they were clearly divided into weights of one unit (11:3 gm.); two units (22.6 gm.); four units (45.5 gm.); eight units (91.2 gm.); 16 units (188.5 gm.), and 24 units (268.24 gm.). In line with this, Yadin assumes that the numerical signs are Hebrew and signify parallel units (that is, they designate the numbers 1, 2, 4, 8, etc.). Against this, Aharoni, following Scott, conjectures that these numbers are actually Egyptian-hieratic which were copied on weights of the Judahite kingdom and stand for the values 5, 10, 20, and 30. The contradiction between the division of the weights into units of 4, 8, 16, and 24 and the values of the Egyptian numbers he explains by saying that the basic weight, that of eight shekels, is identified with the Egyptian *dbn* which was chosen by Josiah for international trade. Since the *dbn* weight is divided into 10 *qdt*, it means that Judahite weights of 4, 8, 16, and 24 units are equivalent to 5, 10, 20, and 30 *qdt*. The hypothesis of Scott and Aharoni that the signs on the large units are Egyptian is reasonable, all the more so since much important evidence has been gathered concerning the use of hieratic numbers in Israel during this period (from an ostracon from Arad, among other sources). However, in spite of this, it is difficult to assume that the Egyptian system itself was adopted in Israel, since the basic unit in the shekel system – as Aharoni also notes – is a weight of eight shekels. This division, different from that practiced in Egypt (division by tenths) or Mesopotamia (division by sixths), and which is evidence of Phoenician-Israelite local distinctiveness, is the same phenomenon which was found in the biblical system of weights. Likewise, it is difficult to imagine that they used one system for weighing and actually meant a different system (an uncommon situation in the metrological systems of the Ancient Near East). Another suggestion which Aharoni himself raised, and then rejected, is more reasonable; it is that the Egyptian numbers were carved on the weights because of their simple form (it is difficult to carve complex numbers on small stone weights) without paying attention to their original values, and that the Egyptian number five was understood to be four in Israel. Support for this interpretation is found on an ostracon from Yavneh-Yamon which, according to the reading of J. Naveh, is inscribed "the weight of four [shekels of] silver" and next to it is the common sign for the unit of four shekels, which is to say that they did not read this number five and intend four, but rather also read the number as four.

Weights with Designations Discovered in Israel. Three other types of weights, also from the end of the Kingdom of Judah, have been discovered in Israel and their names are inscribed on them in full: *nẓp*, *pym*, and *bqʿ*.

The word *nẓp* does not appear in the Bible and is known only from the inscriptions on these Hebrew weights, and also from Ugaritic. The word *nẓp* is explained on the basis of the Arabic *nisf*, "half." If this interpretation is accepted, the weight of the *nẓp* unit is half of 19.75 gm. since the average weight of the *nẓp* is 9.8 gm. This unit of weight is not known in Israel. In R. de Vaux's opinion, the *nẓp* is half the weight of the Ugaritic shekel, which is known as the "heavy shekel" and weighs from 18.7 to 23.4 gm. It is also possible that the *nẓp* does not belong at all to the metrological system based on the shekel but rather to a different and unknown system. At least one weight which is a subunit of the *nẓp* was found in Samaria. On it is written רבע נצף, "one quarter," and it weighs 2.54 gm. According to this, the whole *nẓp* weighs 10.16 gm. However, on the second side of the weight is written ל[ק]רבע ש, "one-quarter shekel," and some see this as additional proof that two standards existed side by side in Israel, and one weight could be at the same time one-half shekel according to one standard and a whole shekel according to the other. Seventeen *nẓp* weights have been discovered.

The *pim* is mentioned once in the Bible (I Sam. 13:21). *Pim* (*pym*) weights which were uncovered in excavations helped to clarify the obscure verse I Samuel 13:21, but not to explain the name. Several scholars tried, unsuccessfully, to explain it. Clermont-Ganneau suggested: *pi* (*shenayi*)*m* (according to Zech. 13:8), that is two portions, i.e., two-thirds. E.A. Speiser held that its source is from the Akkadian *šinipu*, that it means two-thirds (of a shekel), and that in Canaan they borrowed the last part of the word from Mesopotamia, interpreted it as a third, and made it dual. Diringer and Borrois also think that the *pim* is two-thirds of a standard shekel but that Speiser is correct that the source of the word is foreign and that it has no meaning in Hebrew. Twelve such weights have been discovered, and their average weight is 7.8 gm.

The beka is the one unit of weight mentioned in the Bible whose value has been determined. It is half a shekel (see above). However, this value does not correspond to the beka (*bqʿ*) weights found in excavations. In Israel, seven weights have been found with the name beka written on them. On some the name is written in full, and on some only the letter ב (*beth*) appears. Their average weight is 6.03 gm. more than the value of the half-shekel of 11.3 gm. The heaviest one is 6.65 gm. and the lightest 5.55 gm. Petrie believes that the beka is an extremely ancient unit of weight which was used in Egypt and has been discovered in pre-dynastic graves of the Amration period (the fourth millennium B.C.E.). In his opinion, the beka was the common weight used in Egypt for gold and its weight was 12.28–13.90 gm. If Petrie's opinion is accepted the Israel beka would be half the weight of the Egyptian weight which Petrie established as the Egyptian beka. Reifenberg publicized a coin from the Persian period bearing the inscription beka; its weight is 3.88 gm.

Weights Marked with Numbers. In addition to the aforementioned weights, some 20 weights marked with numbers (either letters or numerals) have been uncovered in excavations, and their weights range from 1.52 to 7.05 gm. Recently, Scott has gathered all the above-mentioned finds, sorted them into groups, and tried to determine their precise relationships to the perfect weights mentioned above. However, all attempts – those of Scott as well as his predecessors – to determine the exact value of these small weights, are very unreliable since there are no written sources about the detailed division of the Israelite shekel into small subunits.

A large number of weights have been discovered which contain no inscription, no number, and no sign whatsoever. Examination of these weights has not led, in general, to sufficient clarification. Among them, it is worth noting in particular two weights. One was found at Tell Beit Mirsim, weighing 4,565 gm., and in W.F. Albright's opinion has the value of eight minas of 50 shekels each (that is, the weight of 400 shekels). The second is a basalt stone weight from the area around Taanach which weighs 4,780 gm. This weight is decorated with the relief of a winged lion and in addition bears the personal name *Šmʿ*. In N. Avigad's opinion, the value of this weight is eight minas of 50 shekels, that is, 400 shekels, which, he believes, is a standard weight (compare "four hundred shekels of silver at the going merchant's rate," Gen. 23:16). Scott's explanation as noted above is that the shekel weights were established according to the Egyptian standard and interprets the unit of 400 shekels as 50 *dbn*. In his opinion, that is the reason for the special Israelite system of weights which contains only 50 shekels in a mina. However, we have already found this division at Canaanite Ugaritic and it is more plausible that the special Israelite system was based upon the ancient Canaanite system and not the Egyptian system.

[Eliezer Bashan (Sternberg)]

In the Talmud

After a long and complex development (cf. Jos., Ant., 14:105; 3:144), the talmudic system emerges. In it the Italian mina was equated with 100 *denarii* (TJ, Shek. 2:4, 46d; mina = *litra* = Roman *libra* originally; TJ, Ter. 10:7b), thus equaling 1½₄ Roman pounds (Tanḥ. B., Ex. 109). However, the Talmud mentions yet another maneh of 40 shekels (160 *denarii*; Ḥul. 137b–138a), and there were also regional variations (Ḥul. 12b). The biblical gerah was identified with the current *me'ah* ("obol" = ⅙ drachma; Bek. 50a). The syncretist system was linked to the Tyrian standard and conveniently dovetailed with the monetary system. (See Table: Syncretist System in the Talmud.)

Besides the rough and ready measures, e.g., *komeẓ* ("three-fingers full"; Lev. 2:2), or *ḥofen* ("handful"; Ex. 9:8, etc.), a carefully graduated system, primarily of Mesopotamian origin, was used from earliest times both for dry and liquid measures. The relationships between the various denominations are amply attested, revealing the system. (See Table: Measures of Volume in the Talmud.)

Table 9. Syncretist System of Weights and Measures in the Talmud

	Kikkar ("talent")	mina	Italian mina	*tartimar* (=⅓)	*Unkiyyah* "uncia")	sela ("hetra- drachm")	Shekel ("½ biblical shekel")	*zuz* ("denar- ius")
Kikkar ("talent")	1	37	60	120	750	1,500	3,000	6,000
mina		1½	1⅗	3⅕	20	40	80	160
Italian mina			1	2	12½	25	50	100
tartimar (=⅓)				1	6¼	12½	25	50
Unkiyyah ("uncia")					1	2	4	8
sela ("hetra-drachm")						1	2	4
Shekel ("½ biblical shekel")							1	2
zuz ("denar-ius")								1

Table 10. Measures of Volume (Dry and Liquid) in the Talmud

A. Dry	B. Liquid	1 homer kor	2 *letekh* –	3 ephah bath	4 *se'ah* –	5 – hin	6 omer *'issaron*	7 *qav* –	8 – *log*
1 homer	kor	1	2	10	30	60	100	180	720
2 *letekh*	–		1	5	15	30	50	90	360
3 ephah	bath			1	3	6	10	18	72
4 *se'ah*	–				1	2	3⅓	6	24
5 –	hin					1	1⅔	3	12
6 omer	*'issaron*						1	1⅘	7⅕
7 *qav*	–							1	4
8 –	log								1

The table shows the influence of the sexagesimal system with a parallel decimal subdivision, while philological analysis shows the terms to be derived from Mesopotamian (e.g., 1AB, 4), Egyptian (3A, 5B), and Canaanite (2) sources. In rabbinic times the *log* was further subdivided as follows: 1 *log* = 2 *toman* = 4 *revi'it* = 6 *beiẓah ukl a* = 36 *mesurah* = 64 *kurtov*. According to *Eruvin* 83a there were at least three standards current (with a 30% variation; cf. Jos., Ant., 3:197, 321; 8:57; 9:86), but the basic standard was probably linked to the Roman one (Kelim 17:11), so that the *log* equaled the *sextarius* (Gr. *xestes*), giving a *se'ah* of 1½ *modii-16 sext.* = 1 *mod.*-(but cf. TJ, Ter. 5:1, 43c). For cubic equivalents see TJ, *Pesaḥim* 10:1, 37c, where 1 *revi'it* = 7⅓ cu. *eẓba* ("digit"), while *Eruvin* 14b states that a *mikveh* containing 40 *se'ah* is 3 cu. *ammah*. However, in view of the differing standards of length (see below), it is difficult to reach any absolute value for these measures.

Alongside this developed system of exact measures, the rabbis introduced a series of "rule of thumb" measures, readily recognizable by all. Thus one was punishable for eating (most) forbidden foods only after having had an amount equal to a medium-sized olive (*ke-zayit*). The standard for (transgressing the stricture on) leavened bread on the Passover and for eating on the Day of Atonement was a (large) *kotevet* (a certain species of date), while that for carrying on the Sabbath was a *gerogeret* ("dried fig"). These measures bore no easy relationship to the established metrological system. They themselves were at most ready and approximate, and their relationship to the exact measures likewise. Thus the *ke-zayit* was probably about half a *beiẓah*, the *gerogeret* larger than the *ke-zayit* but smaller than the *kotevet*, and the *kotevet* larger than the *gerogeret* but still smaller than a *beiẓah*. In recent years the size of these measures has been the subject of considerable controversy.

Length. The most common metrical denominations are measures of length derived from parts of the human body: the finger-breadth (digit), handbreadth or palm, cubit (from *cubitum*, elbow) or length of the forearm. It is this latter, in Hebrew *ammah*, which appears to be the basic unit of the Palestinian system (Kelim 17:9–10). Normally the *ammah* consisted of handbreadths (*tefaḥ*, pl. *tefaḥim*); however, Ezekiel 40:5 and 43:13 suggest that there was also an *ammah* of seven *tefaḥim*. This seems to be paralleled by the Egyptian system, which had a "short" cubit of six handbreadths, and a "royal" one of seven. The Mishnah too tells of different *ammot* (Kelim, *ibid.*). There is considerable discussion as to the precise length of the *ammah* (or *ammot*), as different sources yield varying results, and much has been written on the subject. All that can be stated with real certainty are the relationships between the different units:

1 *ammah* = 3 *zeret* = 6 *tefaḥ* = 24 *eẓba*. The only multiple of the *ammah* mentioned in the Bible is the *kaneh* ("reed") of Ezekiel 40:5, which according to *Menaḥot* 97a equals six *ammot*. Longer measures were approximate, e.g., a bowshot (Gen. 27:16), day's journey (Gen. 30:36, etc.; see also Gen. 35:16). In the Greco-Roman period there was a syncretistic system for the longer measures, in which the *mil* (Roman mile, *milion* in Matt. 5:41) of 2000 *ammah* was reckoned at 7½ *stadia* (Heb.

ris, Yoma 6:4), giving a convenient division of the *parasang* (Heb. *parsah*) into 30 *stadia*.

Surface. In biblical times the concept of area was expressed by squaring the length, i.e., "x *ammot* squared" (*ravu'a*, passive participle from *arba*, "four"). In the Mishnah it is expressed in the form "x *ammot* by [*al*] × *ammot*." In antiquity two methods were used to measure land:

(a) a standard was based on the area plowed by a yoke of oxen in a given time (cf. Roman *jugum, jugerum*);

(ii) an area was judged by the amount of seed required to sow it (a method of Mesopotamian origin).

Both methods were known and practiced in biblical times, the former being alluded to in Isaiah 5:10, the latter in I Kings 18:32 (cf. Lev. 27:16). In the Mishnah the size of a field is uniformly calculated by the second method. The whole series of dry measures (see above) was employed in this system. The size of these surface measures may be in terms of *ammot* from certain talmudic equations. Thus from *Eruvin* 96a it emerges that a "*beit se'atayim*" (2 *se'ah* plot) equaled the area of the Tabernacle's court, 5,000 sq. *ammot*. Hence, a "*beit se'ah*" = 2,500 sq. *ammot* (BB 26b). The obscure *ma'anah* of I Samuel 14:14 is identified with a four *se'ah* plot (= *beit ha-peras*; Oho. 17:1), and said to be 10,000 sq. *ammot*. (See Table: Measures of Surface.)

The *ammah* varied between the approximate limits of 45.75 and 53.34 cm. (18 and 21 in.), but the upper limit may be even higher (21½ in., for example). The *beit se'ah*, which was 2,500 sq. *ammot* would therefore be equal to 1,143 – 1,333.5 sq. m. However, the variation in *se'ah* measures would affect this calculation.

The basic measure of capacity is the *log*:

1 *log midbarit* = 503.5 cc. = grm (= 30.7 cu. in.)

1 *log yerushal mit* = 699.4 cc. = grm (= 39.6 cu. in.)

1 *log sepphorit* = 777.4 cc. = grm (=47.4 cu. in.)

The basic weights were the *sela* = 224 grains and the mina (40 selas) = 8,960 grains. All other measures may be calculated from these, according to the ratios given. However, the resultant calculations will only have a "probability truth-value," as the range of variation grows in the higher multiples.

As measures (*shi'urim*) are of great halakhic importance, there were throughout the ages constant attempts to reevaluate them in current terms. There has thus grown up over the years a considerable body of halakhic material dealing with metrology, which affords much valuable information.

[Daniel Sperber]

Criminal Law. The biblical injunction, "You shall not have in your pouch alternate weights, larger and smaller; you shall not have in your house alternate measures, a larger and a smaller; you must have completely honest weights and completely honest measures" (Deut. 25:13–15) was interpreted not as prohibiting any fraud by means of false weights and measures (which is dealt with in Lev. 19:35–36), but as applying to the manufacture or possession of any weights or measures, including utensils (such as pots or pitchers), which might be used for weighing or measuring and cause false weighing or measuring (BB 89b; Maim. Yad, Genevah 7:3; Sh. Ar., ḤM 231:3). While the manufacture of false weights and measures may be punishable with *flogging, the mere possession thereof is not, the violation of a negative injunction being so punishable only where an act is committed, as distinguished from the omission to get rid of the prohibited utensils. In order effectively to enforce the prohibition, courts in talmudical times appointed market inspectors charged with the control of all weights and measures even in private houses (BB 89a). There are detailed provisions for the manner in and the materials with which weights and measures are to be manufactured or repaired so as to be and remain accurate (Maim. Yad, Genevah, 8:4–11; Sh. Ar., ḤM 231:4–11). It is said that the crime of false measures is graver than even those crimes (like incest) which are punishable with *karet* (*Divine Punishment); the latter can be expiated by repentance and flogging, whereas in the case of the former repentance is of no avail, since neither the damage caused or the persons to whom restitution has to be made can be ascertained (BB 88b and Rashi ad loc., Maim. Yad. Genevah 7:11).

[Haim Hermann Cohn]

The Approach in Jewish Law

The dominant approach in Jewish law to the subject of weights and measures is the insistence that any doubt be resolved by the merchant in favor of the customer. Where the price is established by weight according to a scale, the merchant compares the two sides of the scale – the weight as opposed to the merchandise. However, if it is difficult to be certain of the comparison, the merchant must make his estimation in favor of the customer. Where the custom was not to make such a

Table 11. Measures of Surface and Their Ratios

	beit-kor	*beit- letekh*	*beit- peras*	*beit- zemed*	*beit-se'ah*	*beit-kav*	*beit-rova*	square *ammot*
beit-kor	1	2	7½	10	30	180	720	75,000
beit-letekh		1	3¾	5	15	90	360	37,500
beit-peras			1	1⅓	4	24	96	10,000
beit-zemed				1	3	18	72	7,500
beit-se'ah					1	6	24	2,500
beit-kav						1	4	416⅔
beit-rova							1	104⅙
square *ammot*								1

determination, the merchant must add an additional amount of merchandise for which he does not charge, and there is also a minimum amount that is required to be added. This law is derived from the verse in Deuteronomy 25:15: "A perfect and just weight…" and, as explicated in the Talmud, "'just' – [take] of yours and give him" (BB 88b; Sh. Ar., ḤM, 231:14). Due to the stringency of the requirements, the question arises as to whether imprecision in weights and measures may be pardoned. Tosefta BB 5:4 states: "…one sells to another one *log* [liquid measure or dry measure] and a half [*log*], a quarter [*log*], an eighth [*log*]: when he calculates the bill he may not say fill up this measure and say, sell me this (*kortov*) (1/64 portion) for the science of measures is not dependent on people, and it is God who has set his name upon them, because the verse ends with 'I am the Lord your God' [Lev 19:36]." Some commentators are of the opinion that agreeing to pardoning inexactitude is not effective, insofar as it may mislead people into thinking that this is the local custom, from which they will learn to cheat. Others are of the opinion that pardoning is effective, based on the Mishna in BB 7:2 (BB 103b), regarding one who sells a *bet kor* (area of land in which one can sew a particular amount of produce) and says to the buyer that the measure is "more or less." Even if he sold less or more, up to a certain percentage of the quantity a deviation of certain amount is permitted, and the transaction is valid (see Sh. Ar., ḤM 231:1 and *Kesef Kedoshim*; *ibid*; 209.1, Sh. Ar., ḤM 209:1; *Teḥumin* 3, p. 338).

The question arises today in the context of factories requesting a certain acceptance of imprecision on their part. The term for this is "scale tolerance." For example, a factory packages a line of products on a production line; each box or bag is stopped at a particular point on the line for a predetermined number of seconds, is filled with a predetermined amount from a container that is poured into it, is automatically closed, and continues on the line. The manufacturers claim that on occasion, unpredictably, the measurements in this process will be imprecise, as in the case where some of the product is spilled or the bag's progress is off schedule on the production line by a second more or less. They therefore demand that they not be checked on the basis of a single bag, but rather according to the average of a number of bags. The European Market has approved this arrangement – one which seems to require an act of pardoning imprecision in advance. If, on the other hand, we were to require the manufacturers to take into consideration the "determination" in favor of the consumer, they would raise the price of the product accordingly. It may be that an arrangement could be used whereby the labeling states that the package contains 98 to 102 tea bags, as in the case of the declaration of "more or less" cited above, or perhaps 98 to 103 tea bags, in order to fulfill the obligation of the determination in favor of the customer (see *Teḥumin* 3, *supra*).

[Itamar Warhaftig (2nd ed.)]

BIBLIOGRAPHY: GENERAL BIBLIOGRAPHY: G. Cardascia, *Les Archives des Murash* – (1951), 199; S. Moscati, *Epigrafia ebraica antica* (1935–50), 83–98; A.E. Berriman, *Historical Metrology* (1953); D.J. Wiseman, *Alalakh Tablets* (1953), 14–15; A. Goetze, *The Laws of Eshnunna* (1956), 186; C.F. Nims, in: *Journal of Egyptian Archaeology*, 44 (1958), 56–65; J.B. Pritchard, *Hebrew Inscriptions and Stamps from Gibeon* (1959), 29–30; R.B.Y. Scott, in: BA, 22 (1959), 22–40. MEASURES OF LENGTH: Clarke-Engelbach, *Ancient Egyptian Masonry* (1930), s.v. *measurements*; C.L. Wodley, *Ur of the Chaldees* (1954), pl. 10b; R.B.Y. Scott, in: JBL, 77 (1958), 205–14. VOLUME MEASUREMENTS: K. Sethe, in: *Zeitschrift fuer aegyptische Sprache und Altertumskunde*, 62 (1926), 61; F. Thureau-Dangin, in: *Revue d'assyrologie et d'archéologie*, 25 (1928), 115–8;27 (1930), 65–71;28 (1931), 109–19; 29 (1932), 189–92; 32 (1935); 1ff.; 34 (1937), 80–86; C.H. Gordon, in: BASOR, 78 (1940), 10–11; E.L. Sukenik, in: *Kedem*, 1 (1942), 32–36; H. Lewy, in: JAOS, 64 (1944), 65–73; D. Diringer, in: BA, 12 (1949), 76 86; N. Avigad, in; IEJ, 3 (1953), 121–2; V.R. Grace, in: S. Weinberg (ed.), *The Aegean and the Near East* (1956), 86–109; R.T. Hallock, in: JNES, 16 (1957), 204–6; B. Parker, in: *Iraq*, 19 (1957), 125–38; J.T. Milik, in: *Biblica*, 40 (1959), 985ff.; P.W. Lapp, in: BASOR, 158 (1960), 11–12. AREA MEASUREMENTS: K. Baer, in: JNES, 15 (1956), 113ff.; S.E. Loewenstamm, in: IEJ, 6 (1956), 221–2. WEIGHTS: Cowley, Aramaic; F. Thureau-Dangin, in: *Revue d'assyrologie…*, 24 (1927), 68–75; A. Reifenberg, in: JPOS, 16 (1936), 39; idem, in: *Matbe'ot ha-Yehudim* (1948); 7–10; idem, in *Yedi'ot*, 15 (1950), 70; M. Narkiss, *Matbe'ot ha-Yehudim* (1936); A.S. Hemmy, in: JEA, 23 (1937), 39ff; D. Diringer, in: PEQ, 74 (1942), 82–103; J. Friedrich, in: *Wiener Zeitschrift fuer die Kunde des Morgenlandes*, 49 (1942), 17–9; A.J. Sachs, in: BASOR, 96 (1944), 29–39; idem, in: JCS, 1 (1947), 67–71; H. Lewy, in: BASOR, 98 (1945), 25; W.F. Albright, *ibid.*, 110 (1948), 74, n. 21; S.R.F. Glanville, *The Legacy of Egypt* (1953), s.v. *weights*; E.G. Kraeling, *The Brooklyn Museum Aramaic Papyri* (1953); J.J. Finkelstein, in: *Anatolian Studies*, 7 (1957), 137; N. Glueck, in: BASOR, 153 (1959), 35–38; R.B.Y. Scott, *ibid.*, 32–35; Y. Yadin, in: *Scripta Hierosolymitana*, 8 (1960), 1–17; J. Naveh, in: IEJ, 12 (1962), 27–32. IN THE TALMUD: ET, 1 (1951), 343, s.v. *Eifah ve-Eifah*; EM, (1950), 272f., s.v. *Eifah ve-Eifah*; 4 (1962), 846–78, s.v. *Middot u-Mishkalot*; M. Bloch, *Das mosaisch-talmudische Polizeirecht* (1879), 35ff.; Y. Gilat, *Mishnato shel R. Eliezer b. Hyrcanus* (1968), 11–20; idem, in: *Tarbiz*, 28 (1958/59), 230ff.; A. Segré, *Metrologia* (It., 1928), 55–93; S. Ganzfried, *Kiẓẓur Shulḥan Arukh*, ed. by D. Feldman (1927), 169–208 (second pagin.); A. Naeh, *Shi'urei Torah* (1947); B, Naeh, in: *Shanah be-Shanah* (1962), 89–99; Sperber, in: *Journal of the Economic and Social History of the Orient*, 8 (1965), 266–71. **ADD. BIBLIOGRAPHY:** M. Elon, *Ha-Mishpat ha-Ivri* (1988), 1:558, 560, 567, 584, 592, 610ff., 701, 821; 2:846, 879, 881, 1000, 1223; idem, *Jewish Law* (1994), 2:679, 681, 689, 719, 732, 754ff., 865, 1006; 3:1034, 1074, 1210, 1465; I. Wahrhaftig, *Haganat ha-Ẓarkhan le-Or ha-Halakhah, Teḥumin*, 3 (1982), 334–82.

WEIL, A. LEO (1858–1938), U.S. lawyer and civic reformer. Weil was born in Keysville, Charlotte County, Virginia. He practiced law in Bradford, Pennsylvania, from 1879 until he moved to Pittsburgh in 1888. There he organized the Voters' League of Pittsburgh and was its president for almost 30 years. The league's purpose was to fight corruption in public office and ensure honest elections. Weil believed that if leaders were honest, the ills of society could be cured without radical changes, maintaining that religious teachings and the laws of the land were sufficient to supply the maximum good. One Voters' League campaign resulted in 149 indictments, and led to the abolition of the city's councils (150 members) and the establishment of a new nine-member body in its place. An investigation of the city's school system led to its reorganization and substantial improvement. Weil became known for his successes in these activities and was invited to help organize reforms in other states.

An active participant in Jewish life, Weil served on the board of Temple Rodef Shalom, Pittsburgh, and was its vice president. He was one of the incorporators of the American Jewish Committee and a member of the executive committee, as well as a trustee of the Jewish Publication Society of America. Weil was vice president of the National Municipal League, of the World Union for Progressive Judaism and of the Union of American Hebrew Congregations. He was on the executive committees of the Pennsylvania Civil Service Association and of the Federated Jewish Philanthropies of Pittsburgh.

WEIL, ANDRÉ (1906–1998), U.S. mathematician. Born in Paris, Weil was appointed professor at the Aligarh Muslim University in India at the age of 24. He returned to Europe to join the faculty of science at the University of Strasbourg in 1933. He was a lecturer at Haverford College and Swarthmore College in the U.S. from 1940 to 1942, and in 1945 joined the faculty of philosophy at the University of São Paolo in Brazil as professor of mathematics. He returned to the U.S. in 1947 to join the department of mathematics at the University of Chicago, and from 1958 was at the Institute of Advanced Studies in Princeton until he retired.

Weil contributed widely to many branches of mathematics, including the theory of numbers, algebraic geometry, and group theory. Among his books are *Foundations of Algebraic Geometry* (1946, 1962), *Introduction l'étude des variétés kaehlériennes* (1958), *Adeles and Algebraic Groups* (1961), and *Basic Number Theory* (1967). In 1979 Weil was awarded the Wolf Prize, and the following year the American Mathematical Society awarded him its Steele Prize. In 1994 he received the Kyoto Prize from the Inamori Foundation of Japan.

[Maurice Goldsmith]

WEIL, ERIC (1904–1977), German philosopher. Born in Hamburg, he worked for his doctorate under Ernst *Cassirer. In 1933 Weil immigrated to France and in 1945 was appointed Maître de Recherche at the Centre National de la Recherche Scientifique and professor at the École Pratique des Hautes Études of the Sorbonne. In 1956 he took up the post of professor of philosophy in Lille and in 1968 was appointed professor of philosophy at Nice. Weil represents a classical tradition in philosophy according to which man is a rational but finite being. Although considering that past philosophical systems form the main stages of the development of the human spirit, Weil, unlike Hegel, does not think that Reason realizes itself entirely in the historical process. Philosophy is confronted by an eternal task: to grasp violence and to come to terms with it. In application, philosophy is not an Olympian and harmonious activity, but a moment of peace and reflection between violent events. In politics there is no reasonable attitude other than the desire for success, and success can result only from a certain capacity for thinking. Philosophers can locate reason in political actions and show that pure violence can never be a permanent scheme of action. Politics is always involved with morality, which for Weil is the refusal of the individual to accept foreign values and external influences. Man lives in inner (intellectual) freedom, and he wants his legitimate wishes to be satisfied. Dissatisfaction – even if no more than a vague sentiment – introduces a dialectical element into society, causing a dangerous antagonism between man and man. So, like politics, morality too is exposed to violent eruptions, and humanity needs philosophy in order to understand the nature of real human satisfaction. The latter consists in leading a meaningful life and attaining true knowledge of an ever-present reality.

He wrote *Logique de la Philosophie* (1950), *Hegel et l'État* (1950), *Philosophie Politique* (1956), *Philosophie Morale* (1961), and *Problèmes Kantiens* (1963).

[Eugene Jacob Fleischmann]

WEIL, FRANK LEOPOLD (1894–1957), U.S. lawyer and communal leader. Weil founded the law firm of Weil, Gotshal and Manges in 1926. Weil led many Jewish and general community efforts in a voluntary capacity. Long active in scouting, he was a member of the national executive board of the Boy Scouts of America and chairman of the Jewish Committee on Scouting. He was president of the 92nd Street YM-YWHA, New York, 1932–40 and of the N.Y. Metropolitan Section of the National Jewish Welfare Board (JWB). From 1940 to 1950 he served as president of the National Jewish Welfare Board and in this capacity convened the first meeting which created the United Service Organizations (USO), becoming a vice president and later chairman of the President's Committee on Religion and Welfare in the Armed Forces. As president of the JWB during World War II, he succeeded in mobilizing U.S. Jewry for moral and religious support of the military on an unprecedented scale and received the Medal of Merit, the highest U.S. government civilian award.

Weil was also instrumental in initiating the historical study of JWB and the Jewish community center movement with a view to determining their postwar objectives. The significant recommendations of the JWB survey were adopted in 1948. During Weil's presidency, JWB undertook the sponsorship of the Jewish Book Council of America; the National Jewish Music Council; and, for several years, the American Jewish Historical Society. He was a founder and president of the World Federation of YMHAs, Jewish Community Centers, and of the National Social Welfare Assembly. In 1952 he was chairman of the National Citizens Committee for UN Day. A vice president of Temple Emanu-El, New York, he was elected chairman of the board of governors of Hebrew Union College-Jewish Institute of Religion, which established the Frank L. Weil Institute of Advanced Studies in Religion and the Humanities in his memory.

[Philip Goodman]

WEIL, GOTTHOLD (1882–1960), Orientalist. Born in Berlin, Weil began his academic career at the Berlin State Library in 1906, and in 1918 became director of its Oriental department, which he had founded. Teaching post-biblical Jewish history and literature at Berlin University from 1912, he was appointed professor in 1920. In 1931 he was appointed professor of Semitic languages at the University of Frankfurt, in succession to Josef *Horovitz. Weil was dismissed by the Nazis with the rest of his Jewish colleagues in 1934. From 1935 to 1946 he was head of the National and University Library in Jerusalem and also held the chair of Turkish studies at The Hebrew University (to 1952).

Weil's main field was Arabic studies, but he had wider Jewish interests as well and was on the board of various Jewish cultural institutions in Germany, and a governor of The Hebrew University. World War I directed his interest to Turkish studies. Tatar prisoners of war gave him the opportunity to conduct linguistic research, and he also published a *Grammatik der osmanischtuerkischen Sprache* (1917). His work in the field of Arab philology was concerned in the main with the history of Arab grammar (*Abul Barakat ibn al-Anbari, Die grammatischen Streitfragen der Basrer und Kufer*, 1913), and he also wrote about Arabic prosology (*Grundriss und System der altarabischen Metren*, 1958). In 1953 he published *Maimonides Responsum ueber die Lebensdauer* (text with German translation). On the occasion of his 70th birthday a *Festschrift* was issued by the Institute for Oriental Studies of The Hebrew University.

BIBLIOGRAPHY: *Gotthold E. Weil Jubilee Volume on the Occasion of his Seventieth Birthday* (Articles in Hebrew with summaries in Eng., 1952); D. Goldschmidt, in: *Yad la-Koré*, 6 (1961), 172–3. **ADD. BIBLIOGRAPHY:** J.M. Landau, "Gotthold Eljakim Weil," in: *Die Welt des Islams*, 38/3 (1998), 278–85.

[Lothar Kopf]

WEIL, GUSTAV (1808–1889), Orientalist. Born in Sulzburg, Baden, to a rabbinical family, he was schooled at home and at Metz, and later studied at Heidelberg, where he began his work in Arabic which he continued in Paris. As a correspondent he went with the French forces to *Algeria (1830) and proceeded to *Cairo, where he spent over four years as French instructor at a medical school, devoting most of his time to enriching his Arabic and mastering Persian and Turkish. He spent some time at Constantinople. Upon his return to Heidelberg, he was employed as librarian, later as teacher, and, after two decades, was awarded a professorship. His extensive literary output attempted to present a general survey of Arab letters and history, often on the basis of manuscript material. It can be divided into (1) work on the *Koran and tradition, e.g., the first introduction to the Koran (*Historischkritische Einleitung*, etc., 1844) and a study tracing the rabbinic background of much of the biblical lore of the Muslims (*Biblische Legenden der Muselmaenner*, 1845; English tr. 1846); (2) translations (of the Arabian Nights; the biography of the Prophet by Ibn-Isḥāk); (3) history, especially *Geschichte der Chalifen* (5 vols. 1846–62); a shorter work was translated by S. Khuda Bukhsh as *History of the Islamic Peoples* (Calcutta, 1914).

BIBLIOGRAPHY: JE; J. Fueck, *Die arabischen Studien in Europa* (1955), 175f.

[Moshe Perlmann]

WEIL, JACOB BEN JUDAH (d. before 1456), German rabbi and halakhic authority in the first half of 15th century. The name Weil was derived from the town of that name in the Neckar district. Weil's main teacher was Jacob *Moellin (the Maharil), who ordained him and appointed him rabbi of Nuremberg. Moellin granted him permission to establish a yeshivah there, but he refrained out of respect for Zalman Katz, who had previously been appointed to this office (Responsa Weil, no. 151). It appears, however, that from 1422 he served in both offices. Weil also refers to Zalman Ronkel of Mainz as "my teacher" and states that he studied in his yeshivah (*ibid.*). After Nuremberg he was in *Augsburg, then in *Bamberg for a short period, and from 1444 he was rabbi of *Erfurt. Scholars from various communities, including Israel *Isserlein, addressed their halakhic problems to him. Weil became renowned through his volume of responsa (Venice, 1523, frequently republished) which contains 193 responsa. They were copied during his lifetime and some are found among the responsa collections of other rabbis. Particularly well known is his *Hilkhot Sheḥitah u-Vedikah* ("laws of slaughtering and examination"), which was accepted as halakhic practice by the Ashkenazim and has been republished more than 70 times. These laws were first published in his responsa (Venice, 1549), and various scholars, among them Solomon *Luria (the Maharshal), added glosses, explanations, and novellae. The section *Bedikot* (Venice, 1552) was first published separately, but from the Mantua, 1556, edition, it was published together with the laws of slaughtering and given the title *Shehitot u-Vedikot*.

Apart from their halakhic importance, Weil's responsa are a valuable source for the social and religious history of German Jewry. They reflect the various problems that occupied the Jews of Germany during his era and, in particular, throw light on the internal organization of the communities. Particularly noteworthy is his responsum in connection with the rabbinic office. In his view the claim of presumptive right (*ḥazakah) does not apply to the rabbinical office, and any scholar has the right to take up residence in a town where there is a rabbi whose authority has been accepted by the community and may act as rabbi in the same manner as the incumbent; "and we have also seen in our own generation several places where there are two rabbis, and we have never heard that one had a greater right than the other" (Responsum 151). In one responsum he complains about the decline in the honor of the rabbinate and attacks those rabbis "who declare their own importance [and] administer their office in a high-handed manner, treading upon the heads of ordinary Jews and imposing monetary fines upon them in order to promote their own honor." In answer to the query of a contemporary scholar who complained that certain litigants refused to accept him as *dayyan* over them, he points out that nowadays "the generations have degenerated, understanding has declined, the *dayyanim* have deteriorated, and there is not a single scholar in the world who is an acknowledged expert." He attests of himself that "during my whole life I have never acted as judge over any one against his will, and always refrain with all my might from acting as a judge" (no. 146).

His *Hilkhot Shehitah u-Vedikah* was intended primarily for *shoḥatim*, to enable them to revise the laws. For this reason the sources are not given, nor does the work contain halakhic novellae, but merely gives the ruling in the briefest terms. He stresses the final halakhic ruling but also gives the local customs. Also appended to his Responsa is *Dinim ve-Halakhot*, in 71 sections, on the laws of divorce, **ḥaliẓah*, redemption of the firstborn, repentance, and the festivals, giving the halakhic ruling and relegating the sources to the end of his responsa. Two additional pamphlets appended to the responsa are: a collection of the novellae of the author of the *Aguddah* and the *Nimukkim* of *Menahem of Merseburg. Weil permitted the use of *pilpul merely as an aid to study, but in his practical halakhic rulings he relied only upon "clear proofs, clarified and complete, and elucidated from the plain meaning" (no. 164). Solomon Luria states that Weil was the chief of the **aḥaronim* and that all his successors relied upon his rulings. The *aḥaronim*, especially Moses *Isserles, attached great importance to his rulings, accepting them as binding. Of the many commentaries on his *Hilkhot Sheḥitah u-Vedikah*, the *Ohel Yisrael* (Wandsbek, 1733) of Israel of Copenhagen should be noted. It contains additions by later authorities and also includes questions "that should be asked of those coming to receive ordination," so that they can show their familiarity with the subject.

BIBLIOGRAPHY: Michael, Or, no. 1061; Graetz, Gesch, 8 (n.d. 4), 209f., 213, 264f.; M. Wiener, in: MGWJ, 17 (1868), 390f.; A. Berliner, *ibid.*, 18 (1869), 318; D. Kaufmann, *ibid.*, 42 (1898), 424; S. Neufeld, *ibid.*, 69 (1925), 285, 289f.; Guedemann, Gesch Erz, 3 (1888), index; Weiss, Dor, 5 (1904[4]), 242–6; J. Freimann (ed.) Joseph b. Moses, *Leket Yosher*, 2 (1904), introd. 33f.; S.M. Chones, *Toledot ha-Posekim* (1910), 200, 569; Waxman, Literature, 2 (1960[2]), 173; C. Tchernowitz, *Toledot ha-Posekim*, 2 (1947), 257, 261–4; Zinberg, Sifrut, 2 (1956), 128f.

[Yehoshua Horowitz]

WEIL, JIŘI (1900–1959), Czech writer, journalist, and translator. Born in Praskolesy, Bohemia, Weil completed his studies of Slavonic philology and comparative literary history at Charles University in Prague in 1928. As a student, he became a member of the Communist Party of Czechoslovakia and began to work at the Soviet embassy. In 1933 he left for Moscow, where he translated Russian, Soviet, and Marxist literature (Gorky, *Pasternak, Lenin, Majakovsky). His critical letters about the conditions of life in the Soviet Union may have contributed to his sudden expulsion from the Soviet Communist Party and later from the Czechoslovak party. He was sent to the Soviet East (Alma-Ata and a labor camp in Central Asia) as a reporter and returned to Czechoslovakia in 1935. After the German occupation of Czechoslovakia, he lost his job and started to work in the Jewish Museum in Prague. When in 1942 he was summoned, as a Jew, for deportation to Theresienstadt, he feigned suicide in the Vltava River and lived in hiding until 1945. After the war he worked as an editor, as he was out of favor with the dogmatic Communists who took power in 1948. Some of his books could be published only in the 1960s and after 1989.

Weil belonged to the modernist literary group Devětsil, whose avant-garde members took inspiration from France and the Soviet Union. From 1933 he was a co-editor of the progressive magazine *Tvorba* ("Creation"). In 1924, Weil published his literary survey "Russian Revolutionary Literature," followed by "Czechs Are Building in the Land of the Five-Year Plans," 1937. His novel *Moskva – hranice* ("Moscow – the Border," 1937, 1991) was the first to tell the truth about the purges and trials under Stalin's rule. Both style and content were met with anger from the Communists, and Weil was criticized severely. He therefore did not dare to publish his next novel, "Wooden Spoon" (1977, in *samizdat*, 1992), which was set in the *Gulag*. His historical novel *Makanna, otec divů* ("Makanna, Father of Wonders," 1945, 1948) appeared after the war; he also published collected stories from the Protectorate, *Barvy* ("Colors," 1946); another series of stories, containing two with Jewish themes, *Vězeň chillonsk* ("Prisoner of Chillon," 1957), and "Elegy for 77,297 Victims," 1958, 1999. The fate of Czech Jews under the Nazis is described in Weil's two novels *Life with a Star* (1989, 1991, 1998, with a preface by Philip *Roth) and, posthumously, *Mendelssohn on the Roof* (1998). The first one is a Kafkaesque and existentialist account of human suffering in the form of a Jew in Nazi-occupied Prague attempting to hold on to his humanity. The second book is also dedicated to the Jewish tragedy of that time.

BIBLIOGRAPHY: R. Grebeníčkov, *Jiří Weil a normy česk· przy po patncti letech*, in: Plamen (1963); R. Grebeníčkov, "Jiří Weil a modern roman," in: Preface to *Jiří Weil ivot s hvězdou* (1967); A. Mikulek et al., *Literatura s hvězdou Davidovou*, vol. 1 (1998); *Slovnok českch spisovatelů* (1982); S. Vondráčkov, *Mrazilo-tlo. O Jiřím Weilovi* (samizdat 1979).

[Milos Pojar (2nd ed.)]

WEIL, JOSEPH (1897–1977), U.S. electrical engineer. Born in Baltimore, Weil received his B.A. from Johns Hopkins in 1918 and his M.S. from Pittsburgh in 1926. Weil joined the faculty at the University of Florida in 1921, and was professor and head of the department of electrical engineering from 1931, and dean of the college of engineering, 1937–63. He was a consulting engineer to municipalities, industrial organizations, radio stations, and U.S. government agencies; he was closely involved in defense training courses, civilian pilot training, and manpower commissions. Weil was the first, and for many years the only, Jewish faculty member at the University of Florida.

[Sharon Zrachya (2nd ed.)]

WEIL, NETHANEL BEN NAPHTALI ẒEVI (1687–1769), German rabbi. In his youth Weil studied at the yeshivah of

Abraham *Broda in Prague, and in Metz. Later, he served as head of a yeshivah in Prague. On the expulsion of the Jews from Bohemia in 1744, he was appointed rabbi of the Schwarzwald (Black Forest) district. In 1750 he became rabbi of Karlsruhe.

He is known mainly for his *Korban Netanel*, a comprehensive commentary on *Asher b. Jehiel's commentary to *Mo'ed* and *Nashim*. This was the first Hebrew book printed and issued in Karlsruhe (1755) and has been printed in all editions of the Talmud containing the *Rosh*. He also wrote *Netiv Ḥayyim* (Fuerth, 1779), annotations to the Shulḥan Arukh, *Orah Ḥayyim*, and *Torat Netanel*, responsa and sermons (2 vols., Fuerth 1795).

BIBLIOGRAPHY: Azulai, 1 (1852), 148 no. 39; 2 (1852), 131 no. 103; S.M. Chones, *Toledot ha-Posekim* (1910), 455.

[Zvi Meir Rabinowitz]

WEIL, R. ADRIENNE (1903–?), French naval engineer, Adrienne Weil was born in Paris, where her father was professor of philosophy at the Sorbonne, and her mother a senior official in the Ministry of Education. From 1940 to 1944 she was at the Cavendish Laboratory, Cambridge University. From 1951 she was contractual engineer for arms and construction in the French Navy.

WEIL, SIMONE (1909–1943), French philosopher. Simone Weil was one of those rare thinkers whose life and thought were inseparable. Born into an upper-class Paris family (her brother was André *Weil), she lived most of her adult life in circumstances of physical deprivation. In 1934, wishing to share the experiences of the poor, she gave up teaching philosophy to become a factory worker. The fruit of this experience was *La Condition Ouvrière*, published posthumously in 1951. In 1936 she joined the Republicans in the Civil War in Spain, and in 1940, after the Nazi invasion, she worked as a farm laborer in southern France. In 1942, she left the U.S., where she had immigrated with her family, intending to return to France and join the Resistance. She never got further than England where, weakened by the hardships of her earlier life, she permitted herself to die of starvation. Most of Simone Weil's writings, published posthumously, consist of fragments from her notebooks, letters, articles, and memoranda, and can perhaps best be regarded as the testimony of a life of relentless dedication to the search for absolute truth and social justice. She was a mystic in the tradition of the 14th-century German theologians Meister Eckhart and St. John of the Cross, both of whom influenced her thought. Although she never actually converted to Catholicism, she experienced a mystical encounter with Jesus in 1938. Her main reason for not converting was that she found it impossible to accept the unchristian historical role of the Church. On the other hand, her attitude towards Judaism was one of total and blinding rejection. She considered it a racial, nationalistic, and cruel religion, and attributed all the evil in Christianity, such as the Inquisition and the killing of heretics, to its Jewish sources.

Published selections of her writings include: *Cahiers* (3 vols., 1951–56; *Notebooks*, 2 vols., 1956); *La pesanteur et la grâce* (1946; *Gravity and Grace*, 1952); *L'Enracinement* (1949; *The Need for Roots*, 1952); *Attente de Dieu* (1950; *Waiting on God*, 1951); and *Lettre à un religieux* (1951; *Letter to a Priest*, 1953).

BIBLIOGRAPHY: J. Cabaud, *Simone Weil* (Eng., 1964); R. Rees, *Simone Weil; a Sketch for a Portrait* (1966); G. Kempfer, *La Philosophie mystique de Simone Weil* (1960); I.R. Malan, *L' Enracinement de Simone Weil* (1961).

[Myriam M. Malinovich]

WEILER, JACK D. (1904–1995), U.S. realtor and communal worker. Weiler, who grew up in New York City, held leadership positions in several Jewish organizations, particularly in the UJA since its inception in 1939. From 1953 he was a national chairman of the organization. He represented the UJA in this capacity on the Joint Distribution Committee and became the committee's vice chairman and director. Also on the UJA's Executive Committee, the organization's top policy-making body, he became chairman of trustees for the Greater New York UJA, a select group of New York community leaders. A real estate man, Weiler joined with his brother-in-law, Benjamin *Swig, in 1937 to form one of the most successful real estate firms in the country, with one office in San Francisco and another in New York. The partners bought and sold real estate in cities throughout the United States. He also served as chairman of the finance committee for Senator Herbert H. Lehman in 1950 and for New York City Mayor Robert Wagner in 1956. Weiler's holdings included 5 million square feet in New York City; 1.5 million in California; and a community of more than 2,000 homes on the southern ridge of Jerusalem.

Other organizations in which Weiler held leadership positions include the State of Israel Bond Organization, the Federation of Jewish Philanthropies, the New York Board of Rabbis, and the Jewish Theological Seminary of America. Some of the institutions that Weiler contributed to are the Jack D. Weiler Hospital of Yeshiva University's Albert Einstein College of Medicine in New York City; the chaplaincy of the New York Board of Rabbis; and, in Israel, the architecture department of Bezalel Academy of Art, and the Jack D. Weiler Fund for Research into Halakhic Philosophy at Bar-Ilan University.

WEILL, ALEXANDRE ABRAHAM (1811–1899), French author. Born in Alsace, Weill trained for the rabbinate in Frankfurt, where he also studied languages and literature. Abandoning rabbinics in 1836, he went to Paris where, armed with an introduction from Heinrich *Heine, he gained admittance to the principal literary salons. His friends included Balzac (whom he later criticized), Gérard de Nerval, Victor Hugo, and *Meyerbeer. Weill was a prolific author, publishing over 40 books and hundreds of articles in a variety of French and German journals. His subjects ranged from religious polemic and historical studies to linguistic speculation, mediocre poetry, and autobiography. His *Sittengemaelde aus dem elsaessischen Volksleben* (1847), tales of village life in Alsace, provides invaluable source material for the Jewish social historian.

His biographical studies include *Ludovic Boerne* (1878) and *Souvenirs intimes de Henri Heine* (1883). *La France Catholique* (1886) was his energetic reply to Edouard *Drumont's notorious antisemitic libel. Weill's kabbalism, later formulated in *Mystères de la Création* (1855), probably influenced the last book of Hugo's *Contemplations*. One of his many biblical publications maintained that the altar of the Tabernacle was in effect an electrical device. In 1890 he published an autobiography, *Introduction à mes mémoires*.

BIBLIOGRAPHY: M. Bloch, *Alexandre Weill, sa vie, ses oeuvres* (1905); R. Dreyfus, *Cahiers de la Quinzaine*, Série 9 (1908); D. Saurat, *Victor Hugo et les dieux du peuple* (1948), 18–32.

WEILL, KURT (1900–1950), composer. The son of a *ḥazzan*, Weill was born in Dessau and studied under the composer Busoni in Berlin. He at first wrote operas and symphonic and chamber music, but later turned to social satire in the theater. Weill formed an association with the German dramatist Bertolt Brecht, with whom he produced a "singspiel," *Aufstieg und Fall der Stadt Mahagonny* (1927–29), a savage satire on American life. In 1928 he composed, again with Brecht, *Die Dreigroschenoper*, a modern version of the English 18th-century ballad-opera *The Beggar's Opera*. This was an extraordinary success in Europe and the United States. After the Nazis seized power in Germany, Weill, accompanied by his wife, the actress Lotte Lenya, moved to Paris and then to London, finally settling in the U.S. in 1935. Unusually adaptable, Weill became acclimatized to American theatrical ways and produced a number of successful musical works, including the Jewish opera *The Eternal Road* (1937) based on the historical pageant *Der Weg der Verheissung* written by Franz Werfel; *Knickerbocker Holiday* (1938), *One Touch of Venus* (1943), and *Love Life* (1948). He also wrote a one-act American folk opera, *Down in the Valley* (1948), and the music for Ben *Hecht's pageant in honor of the State of Israel, *A Flag is Born* (1948). With Hindemith, Kurt Weill was instrumental in shaping the genre of *Gebrauchsmusik* (utilitarian music), which aimed at producing music accessible to the masses and capable of performance by non-professional groups. This did not, however, exclude the application of dissonant counterpoint and harmony. Weill made liberal use of modern dance rhythms, particularly jazz, often combining these modern resources with nostalgic and even sentimental ballad forms. Weill's music paved the way for many experiments of his younger German contemporaries, including B. Blacher, C. Orff, and H.W. Henze; it also impressed and inspired his American colleagues, such as Aaron *Copland. Today Weill is rightfully considered one of the most influential German composers of his generation.

ADD. BIBLIOGRAPHY: MGG²; NG²; Baker, Biog Dict; J. Schebera, *Kurt Weill: eine Biographie in Texten, Bildern und Dokumenten* (Ger. 1990, Eng. 1995); S. Hinton (ed.), *Kurt Weill: The Threepenny Opera* (1990); H. Edler and K.H. Kowalke (eds.), *A Stranger Here Myself: Kurt Weill Studien* (1992); J. Schebera, *Kurt Weill* (2000); F. Hirsch, *How Can You Tell an American? Kurt Weill on Stage from Berlin to Broadway* (2000).

[Nicolas Slonimsky / Yulia Kreinin (2nd ed.)]

WEILL, MICHEL AARON (1814–1889), French rabbi. Weill, who was born at Strasbourg, studied at the Ecole Rabbinique at Metz and at the Sorbonne in Paris. In 1845 he was appointed teacher and subsequently chief rabbi at Algiers, the first Frenchman to hold this office (1846–64). In 1876, after a period of temporary retirement, Weill became rabbi of Toul. He resigned in 1885 and settled in Paris to devote himself to writing.

His chief works are *Le Judaisme, ses dogmes et sa mission* (4 vols., 1866–69) and *La morale du Judaïsme* (2 vols., 1875–77). His son GEORGES WEILL (1865–1942) was a historian, author of *L'éveil des nationalités et le mouvement libéral 1815–1848* (1930, 1962).

WEILL, RAYMOND (1874–1950), French Egyptologist and historian. He directed excavations in Egypt, in the Sinai Peninsula, and, under the auspices of Baron Edmond de Rothschild, in Jerusalem on the hill of Ophel (1913–14; 1923–24). The latter expedition revealed a large area of the southern part of the city of David, including a great part of its eastern fortifications and a complex of tombs, which Weill thought to be those of the kings of Judah. These excavations are described in *La Cité de David* (2 vols., 1920–47). In 1920 he was appointed professor of Egyptology at the Ecole des Hautes Etudes in Paris, and in 1931 he became professor of Oriental history at the Sorbonne.

Among his numerous publications are: *Recueil des inscriptions égyptiennes du Sinai* (1904); *Les origines de l'Egypte pharaonique* (1908); *Les décrets royaux de l'ancien empire égyptien* (1912); *La fin du moyen empire égyptien* (1918); *L'installation des Israélites en Palestine* (1924); *Bases, méthodes et résultats de la chronologie égyptienne* (1926); *La Phénicie et l'Asie occidentale* (1939; 1949^2).

WEILL, SANFORD I. (1933–), U.S. banker, financier, and philanthropist. The son of Polish immigrants, Weill was born in Brooklyn, N.Y. When his parents could not find housing, they enrolled him at the Peekskill Military Academy. He attended Cornell University, where he was a member of the Air Force ROTC. Although he wanted to be a pilot, that was not to be. In 1955 he got his first job on Wall Street as a runner for Bear Stearns. While there he became friends with Arthur Carter, who was working at Lehman Brothers, and he became a licensed broker. In 1960, Carter, Roger Berlind, Peter Potoma, and Weill formed Carter, Berlind, Potoma & Weill. After the New York Stock Exchange brought disciplinary proceedings against Potoma, he left the firm. In 1968 the firm became Cogan, Berlind, Weill & Levitt (Marshall Cogan, Roger Berlind, who later became a Broadway producer, Arthur Levitt). Weill was chairman from 1965 to 1984, a period in which the firm completed over 15 acquisitions to become the country's second largest securities brokerage firm. The company became CBWL-Hayden, Stone in 1970, Hayden Stone in 1972, Shearson Hayden Stone in 1974, when it merged with Shearson Hammill & Co., and Shearson Loeb Rhoades in 1979, when it merged with Loeb Rhoades Hornblower. With capital totaling $250 million, Shearson Loeb Rhoades trailed only Merrill Lynch as the securities brokerage industry's largest firm. In 1981 Weill sold the company to American Express for about $930 million in stock. He began serving as president of American Express in 1983 and as chairman and chief executive of its insurance subsidiary, Fireman's Fund Insurance, in 1984. Frustrated with the direction of the company, Weill quit American Express in 1985. The following year he went to Minneapolis to persuade Control Data to spin off its subsidiary, Commercial Credit, in a public offering worth $850 million. Weill took over as chief executive, investing $7 million of his own money. He also acquired its subsidiary, a property and casualty insurance concern called Gulf Insurance. By 1988 Weill and his team had turned Commercial Credit around and acquired the Primerica Corporation for $1.5 billion along with its holdings, the brokerage Smith Barney and the A.L. Williams insurance company, renamed Primerica Financial Services. Over the next two years Primerica absorbed the consumer lending operations of Barclays American/Financial. In 1992 alone, Primerica raised $625 million by selling nonstrategic assets. Weill then bought 27 percent of Travelers Insurance for $722 billion. He personally earned $67.6 million that year, most of it from stock options, making him the second highest-paid executive in the United States. The following year Weill realized an old dream. He regained control of Shearson (now Shearson Lehman), buying it back from American Express for $1.2 billion. By doing so, he acquired Shearson's 8,400 brokers and state-of-the-art back office, while leaving behind Shearson's litigation liability. In 1996 Weill added to his holdings, at a cost of $4 billion, the property and casualty operations of Aetna Life & Casualty, and the following year he acquired Salomon, the parent company of Salomon Brothers, for over $9 billion in stock. In April 1998 Travelers announced an agreement to undertake the $76 billion merger between Travelers and Citicorp, the parent company of Citibank, to create Citigroup. Citicorp was the world's largest supplier of credit cards, and Citibank was the second largest bank in the United States. At the beginning of the day the merger was announced, the two companies were valued at $70.6 billion. By the end of the day the value had jumped to $83.6 billion. In 2002 the company was rocked by a wave of scandals that followed the stock market downturn. Weill was replaced as chief executive of Citigroup in 2003. He served as chairman until 2006. Weill's career was also marked by extensive philanthropy. He endowed Cornell's medical school in 1998 with a $100 million pledge, and it was named the Joan and Sanford I. Weill Medical College and Graduate School of Medical Sciences. As chairman of Carnegie Hall he raised $60 million for renovation of its facilities, and one of the concert halls is named for him. He was the principal sponsor of the High School of Economics and Finance in New York and worked with the Disney Company to create, at the children's museum in Baltimore, Md., a game to teach youngsters about capitalism.

[Stewart Kampel (2nd ed.)]

WEILL, SHRAGA (1918–), Israeli artist. Weill was born in Nitra, Czechoslovakia. He first studied sculpture with a local sculptor, but continued at the Prague School of Art. His first graphic works were produced during World War II, part of which he spent in prison, having been convicted of membership in the underground movement. Weill immigrated to Israel in 1947 and settled in kibbutz Ha-Ogen. During 1949–1955 he worked as an illustrator, illustrating several books of poems and biblical stories, such as Lea *Goldberg's "The Love of Samson," "The Song of Songs," and the "Dead Sea Scrolls," with drawing depicting desert landscapes or local people. In 1954, he studied in Paris at the Ecole des Beaux-Arts. Weill worked in many artistic media – painting, drawing, illustration, mural painting, and reliefs. In 1965, he illustrated *Kohelet* (the Book of Ecclesiastes) with more abstract stylization, but a continuity of his earlier style is still noticeable. He was commissioned to prepare several large works for public buildings, including metal reliefs for the doors of the main entrance to the Knesset building in Jerusalem (1966), in which he used popular symbols and motifs, diffusing them in an abstract composition with biblical and Jewish subjects; a relief for the Hilton Hotel, Tel Aviv; one for the Wolfson House at the Weizmann Institute, Reḥovot; and another for the Israel Pavilion at "Expo 67," Montreal, Canada. His works are represented in the Israel Museum, Jerusalem, the Nelson-Atkins Gallery of Art, Kansas City, Mo.; the William Hayes Fogg Art Museum, Harvard University; and Los Angeles County Museum.

[Judith Spitzer]

WEIN, GEORGE (1925–), U.S. pianist, jazz festival organizer, record label founder and owner, entrepreneur. George Wein is nothing if not a realist. When he realized that despite his family pedigree (his father was a prosperous doctor in Newton, Mass., who also played piano) he was more drawn to music than to grad school, he dropped out of Harvard to play jazz wherever he could in the Boston area. When he realized that, as he himself has said, he was not a great musician, merely a highly professional one despite training with Margaret Chaloff and Teddy Wilson, he started a Boston jazz club, Storyville, which quickly became a mecca for music both old and new. Wein was adept at finding and filling gaps in the music community; his most famous invention, the Newport Jazz Festival, first staged in 1954, was the first regular outdoor jazz festival in the world. When Newport became a less convivial venue in the 1970s, he moved it to New York without hesitation (although a small version has continued in Newport throughout). His programming has always been an inventive balance between the commercial and artistic, mixing every possible genre of jazz and related musical crossovers. As Wein has said, a jazz festival should offer "a broad spectrum of what jazz is in any given year." Wein also pioneered the concept of corporate sponsor association with music events, putting sponsors' names on his festivals long before the practice became the norm. Among his many honors it should be noted that he was both a member of the Legion d'Honneur in recognition of his creation of the contemporary jazz festival, and a recipient of a Jazz Masters award from the National Endowment for the Arts. This is only appropriate for someone who single-handedly remade the business end of jazz. "Not many people can say they changed the world and make it stick," remarked Gene Santoro in *Nation*. "Without Wein everything from Woodstock to Jazz at Lincoln Center might have happened differently – if it happened at all."

BIBLIOGRAPHY: R.J. DeLuke, "George Wein: Dinosaur Walks the Earth," in: *All About Jazz*, at: www.allaboutjazz.com; N. Hentoff, "George Wein, a Life in and for Jazz," in: *Jazz Times*, at: www.jazztimes.com; F. Jung, "A Fireside Chat With George Wein," in: *All About Jazz*, at: www.allaboutjazz.com.

[George Robinson (2nd ed.)]

WEINBAUM, MARK EFIMOVICH (Veinbaum, 1890–1973), U.S. journalist. Born in Proskurov, Ukraine, Weinbaum went to the U.S. in 1913. He was associated with several Russian-language publications, joining the staff of *Russkoye Slovo* in 1914, and later founding his own journal *Russkiy Golos* (1917–20). In 1925 he became editor and co-owner of the influential *Novoye Russkoye Slovo*. From 1948 he was director and president of the Fund for the Relief of Russian Writers and Scientists in Exile.

WEINBERG, GLADYS DAVIDSON (1909–2002), U.S. archaeologist and daughter of Hebrew literary scholar Israel *Davidson and Carrie Dreyfuss Davidson, editor of *Outlook* magazine of the United Synagogue of America's Women's League. Weinberg was raised in New York City and received her B.A. from New York University in 1930 and her Ph.D. from Johns Hopkins in 1935 for a dissertation on the excavations at Corinth. In 1931, she joined the Johns Hopkins University expedition to Olynthus and continued her research in Greece from 1932 to 1939 as a Fellow of the American School of Classical Studies at Athens, and then as a member of the American School Excavations at Corinth. From 1940 to 1943, she worked as assistant curator of ancient art at the Princeton Art Museum. After marrying fellow archaeologist Saul Weinberg, she worked as translator and librarian in the Foreign Service Auxiliary of the U.S. State Department in Istanbul and Athens (1943–45), and then as librarian of the American School of Classical Studies in Athens (1946–48). Serving as editor of the magazine *Archaeology* (1952–67), Gladys Weinberg conducted excavations searching for ancient glass factories in the eastern Mediterranean, becoming a leading authority on glassmaking technology in ancient Greece, Crete, and Israel. Cofounder of the Museum of Art and Archaeology at the University of Missouri-Columbia, after 1962 she served as its curator of ancient art, then as assistant director and research fellow; she also founded and edited the museum's annual, *Muse*, from 1966–77.

In addition to publishing numerous articles, Weinberg coauthored and/or edited several important archaeological publications, including *Small Finds from the Pnyx*, I (1943); *Corinth: The Minor Objects* (1952); *The Antikythera Wreck Reconsidered* (1965); *Excavations at Jalame, Site of a Glass Factory in Late Roman Palestine* (1988); and *Selected Glass Vessels in Ancient Greece* (1992). She was made an honorary life member of the American Association of University Women and the Archaeological Institute of America. In 1985, Gladys Davidson Weinberg, together with her husband Saul Weinberg, received the Gold Medal for Distinguished Archaeological Achievement from the Archaeological Institute of America. The following year, she became the recipient of the Percia Schimmel Award for Archaeological Exploration in Biblical Lands from the Israel Museum. The Saul and Gladys Weinberg Papers can be found in the archives of the American School of Classical Studies at Athens.

BIBLIOGRAPHY: A. Fishman. "Weinberg, Gladys Davidson," in: *Jewish Women in America* 2:1462–63; "Archaeological Institute of America: Award for Distinguished Archaeological Achievement," in: *American Journal of Archaeology*, 90 (April 1986), 173; "Columbia Archaeologists Discover Glass Slab on Israeli Expedition," in: *Columbia Missourian* (May 15, 1966), 39.

[Harriet Pass Freidenreich (2nd ed.)]

WEINBERG, HARRY (1908–1990), U.S. philanthropist. Born in Sambur, Galicia, Weinberg immigrated to America at the age of four. He grew up in Baltimore in absolute poverty but, by the age of 40, he was a millionaire and, by the time he was 50, he was a billionaire. He lived in Hawaii for the last 20 years of his life where, for a time, he was the largest individual landowner in the state.

With all his money, Weinberg never indulged himself. In the 1950s, after purchasing the Scranton, Pennsylvania, bus lines, he lived in a rented, second-floor apartment, even though he could have bought the entire block the house stood on.

Weinberg was known for working seven days a week, and his main interest appeared to be in acquiring as much as he could. His chief hobby was charity. In the late 1930s, he pledged support from his then meager assets to enable many German Jews to reach safe haven in America. When his wealth had increased, he gave annual grants to yeshivot and Orthodox synagogues in Baltimore, even though he was not Orthodox. He donated $3 million to the Honolulu congregation for its building and an endowment fund. He aided the Associated Jewish Community Federation of Baltimore in many ways. He also gave funds to many non-Jewish institutions.

He established two foundations. The first, the Harry and Jeanette Weinberg Foundation established in 1959, had assets at his death of almost $1 billion and was the 11th largest private foundation in the U.S. By 2005 it was still one of the largest such institutions in the U.S., with assets of approximately $2 billion. The other foundation, the Harry Weinberg Foundation, was worth $90 million and was devoted solely to the benefit of the Associated Jewish Community Federation in Baltimore.

The larger foundation disburses $100 million annually. Its charter stipulates that 25% of its disbursements go to organizations that primarily benefit Jews and 25% to organizations that primarily benefit non-Jews. The remaining 50% goes to any groups – Jewish or non-Jewish – deemed worthy by the foundation's trustees. There are no geographical limitations on disbursements, and it was intended that both Israel's and Baltimore's homeless would benefit. It has expanded to include Hawaii, northeastern Pennsylvania, New York, and the former Soviet Union, providing grants for such needs as food, shelter, health, and socialization, and to enhance the individual's ability to meet those needs for himself.

[David Geffen / Ruth Beloff (2nd ed.)]

WEINBERG, JACOB (1879–1956), composer and pianist. Weinberg taught in his native Odessa from 1915 to 1921 and emigrated to Ereẓ Israel in 1922. He left for the United States in 1926.

His works include the opera *The Pioneers* (Philadelphia, 1926; *He-Ḥalutz* 1932), one of the first operas based on life in Ereẓ Israel; music for the Sabbath morning service, *Shabbat ba-Areẓ* (1939), an experiment in the use of Palestinian folk melodies in modern style in the synagogue; and *Tefillot le-Shabbat* ("Prayers for the Sabbath"). He also wrote oratorios, *Isaiah* (1953), and *The Life of Moses* (1955); music for texts from the Dead Sea Scrolls, and *The Gettysburg Address* (1954).

BIBLIOGRAPHY: L. Appleton (ed.), *Four American Jewish Composers – Their Life and Work: Gershon Ephros, Solomon Rosowsky, Heinrich Schalit, Jacob Weinberg* (1962–63), 25–33, includes bibliography; Sendrey, Music, index; Baker, Biog Dict s.v.

[Edith Gerson-Kiwi]

WEINBERG, JEHIEL JACOB (1885–1966), talmudic authority, thinker, and teacher. Weinberg studied in the yeshivot of Mir and Slobodka. In 1907 he was appointed rabbi in his native Pilwishki (in Lithuania). While there, he lectured to a group of advanced Talmud students and contributed articles to the periodical *Yagdil Torah*. With the outbreak of World War I, Weinberg went to Germany and studied at the University of Giessen, where he was granted his doctorate for his thesis on the masorah. He was appointed rabbi of the Charlottenburg district of Berlin and in 1924 began to lecture in Talmud and *halakhah* at the *Rabbiner-Seminar Fuer Das Orthodoxe Judentum, of which he later became rector. In his lectures and essays, Weinberg introduced German Orthodoxy to the viewpoints of the eastern European yeshivot. Following the closing of the Rabbiner-Seminar by the Nazis, he returned to eastern Europe and was later interned in various concentration camps. After the war, broken in health, he settled in Montreux, Switzerland, from where he exercised considerable influence, primarily through his writing. A profound talmudic scholar, at home in the critical-historical approach of modern scholarship, well read in general literature, and familiar with current problems, he educated a generation of intellectuals who became rabbis and communal leaders. He maintained close relations with the leading talmudists of his time and was held in respect by European scholars, becoming a link between eastern and western Jewry.

Weinberg's most important work is his responsa *Seridei Esh* (1961–69) in four volumes, the third and fourth volume appearing posthumously. Among the practical problems discussed are whether animals may be electrically stunned before *sheḥitah*, whether it is permitted to have a bat mitzvah ceremony for girls corresponding with the boys' bar mitzvah, and whether Jews may lecture on Jewish law to gentiles. In the course of his responsa, which reflect his independent and incisive reasoning, Weinberg elucidates many talmudic themes. He was considered an authoritative halakhist, and problems were addressed to him from all parts of the world. His essays (published in *Li-Ferakim*, 1936, and *Das Volk der Religion*, 1949) reveal not only his own originality, but the profound influence upon him of the ideas of Israel *Lipkin (Salanter) and Samson Raphael *Hirsch. His talmudic genius is apparent in *Meḥkarim ba-Talmud* (1937–38). Weinberg was also a frequent contributor to rabbinic periodicals. He died in Montreux and was buried in Jerusalem.

BIBLIOGRAPHY: Soreski, in: J.J. Weinberg, *Et Aḥai Anokhi Mevakkesh* (1966), 17–42; Berkovits, in: *Tradition*, 8, no. 2 (1966), 5–14; idem et al., in: *Hadorom*, 24 (1966/67), 6–20; Cohen et al., in: *De'ot*, 31 (1966/67), 7–23; Atlas, in: *Sinai*, 58 (1966), 281–96; H.H. Greenberg, *Mi-Gedolei ha-Dor* (1967); *Yahadut Lita*, 3 (1967), 46; I. Grunfeld, *Three Generations* (1958), 78–79, 103.

[Mordechai Hacohen]

WEINBERG, SAUL S. (1911–1992), U.S. educator and archaeologist. Born in Chicago, Weinberg received an M.S. in architectural history from the University of Illinois in 1933 and a Ph.D. from Johns Hopkins in 1935. He spent much time in Greece between 1936 and 1948. In 1948 he began his academic career at the University of Missouri and was appointed professor of classical archaeology in 1956. In 1957 he and his wife Gladys founded the Museum of Art and Archaeology at the University of Missouri, and in 1961 he became its director. Weinberg distinguished himself as a teacher, excavator, scholar, and museologist. He participated in or directed excavations in Greece (at Corinth and Elateia), Cyprus (at Kourion and Episkopi), Crete (at Tarrha), and Israel (at Tel Anafa and Shamir). In 1969 he became chief curator of the Biblical and Archaeological Department of the Israel Museum and also taught prehistory at The Hebrew University. In 1975 he was made a fellow of the American Academy of Arts and Sciences. In 1985 he and Gladys received the Gold Medal of the American Institute of Archaeology, and in 1986 they received the Percie Schimmel Award of the Israel Museum, Jerusalem, for archaeological exploration in Bible lands.

In addition to numerous articles, Weinberg published two volumes of the American School of Classical Studies at Athens publications, *Geometric and Orientalizing Pottery* (1943) and *The Southeast Building, The Twin Basilica, The Mosaic House* (1960), and also published *The Stone Age in the Aegean* (Cambridge Ancient History, 1 (1965^2), ch. 10). He edited *The Aegean and the Near East: Studies Presented to Hetty Goldman…* (1956).

Gladys Davidson Weinberg (1909–2002), also an archaeologist, was one of the foremost authorities on ancient and medieval glass. She specialized in ancient miniature art. She was the editor of *Archaeology* magazine from 1952 to 1967 and curator of Ancient Art of the Museum of Art and Archaeology at the University of Missouri from 1962 to 1973. She served as assistant director of the museum from 1973 to 1977, after which she was a research fellow. She was made an honorary life member of the Archaeological Institute of America. Her books include *Small Objects from Pnyx* (with Dorothy Burr Thompson, 1942); *Corinth: The Minor Objects* (1952); *Excavations at Jalame, Site of a Glass Factory in Late Roman Palestine* (1988); and *Selected Glass Vessels in the National Museum, Athens, Greece* (1992).

[Penuel P. Kahane / Ruth Beloff (2nd ed.)]

WEINBERG, SIDNEY J. (1891–1969), U.S. investment banker. Weinberg was born in New York City and at the age of 16 entered the Wall Street investment banking house of Goldman, Sachs & Co. After serving in the navy during World War I, Weinberg rejoined Goldman, Sachs. He subsequently bought a seat on the New York Stock Exchange (1925) and became a firm partner (1927). Weinberg's reputation as a corporate finance expert was such that he once sat simultaneously on the boards of directors of 31 companies. In 1956 Weinberg supervised the $650 million sale of Ford Motor Company stock, then the greatest such undertaking in business history. A Roosevelt supporter from 1932, he was offered, but declined, the post of ambassador to the U.S.S.R. in 1936. In 1933 he founded the Business Council, a forum for presenting the business view on the state of the nation and economy to Washington. He served as assistant director of the War Production Board during World War II, special assistant in the Office of Defense Mobilization during the Korean War, and as unofficial financial and economic advisor to U.S. presidents from Roosevelt through Kennedy.

WEINBERG, STEVEN (1933–), U.S. physicist and Nobel Laureate in physics. Born in New York, Weinberg graduated A.B. from Cornell University (1954) and studied at Copenhagen Institute for Theoretical Physics before receiving his Ph.D. in physics from Princeton University (1957) under the direction of Sam Treiman. After appointments at Columbia University (1957–59) and the Lawrence Radiation Laboratory, Livermore, California (1959–60), he was successively professor of physics at the University of California at Berkeley (1959–69) and at the Massachusetts Institute of Technology (1969–73). He was Higgins Professor of Physics at Harvard University and Senior Scientist at the Smithsonian Astrophysical Observatory (1973–83) before moving to the University of Texas at Austin as Jack S. Josey – Welch Foundation Professor, Regental Professor of Science, and founding director of the Theory Group in the College of Natural Sciences. His research concerns the interactions between strong electromagnetic force and the weak forces which allow beta decays of the nucleus, and hence radioactivity. Neutrinos and, to a lesser extent, electrons account for these interactions. Weinberg's theoretical concept of these processes has been largely validated experimentally. This field has fundamental implications for understanding the formation of complex inorganic and biological molecules from elements formed in the evolution of the universe, with the ultimate objective of explaining the physical basis of matter throughout the universe. He was awarded the Nobel Prize (1979) jointly with Abdus Salam and Sheldon Glashow. His many honors include membership in the U.S. Academy of Sciences (1972), the JR Oppenheimer Prize (1973), foreign membership in the Royal Society of London (1982), the U.S. National Medal of Science (1991), and the Benjamin Franklin Medal of the American Philosophical Society (2004). He was visiting professor at the Weizmann Institute (1985). Among his many national and international commitments to scientific education and planning, he was director of the Jerusalem Winter School of Theoretical Physics from 1983. Weinberg was also active in teaching and writing on the social and philosophical implications of modern science. He served as consultant for the U.S. Arms Control and Disarmament Agency. His books for general readers include *The First Three Minutes: a Modern View of the Origin of the Universe* (1977), *Elementary Particles and the Laws of Physics* (with R.P. Feynman) (1987), *Dreams of a Final Theory* (1993), *Facing Up – Science and Its Cultural Adversaries* (2001), and *Glory and Terror – the Growing Nuclear Danger* (2004). His contributions to the field of scientific writing have been recognized by his receipt of the American Institute of Physics and U.S. Steel Foundation Science Writing Award (1977) and the Lewis Thomas Prize honoring the scientist as poet (1999).

[Michael Denman (2nd ed.)]

WEINBERG, ẒEVI ZEBULUN (1883–1971), Hebrew author. Born in Praga, near Warsaw, he became an instructor in Jewish subjects in Augustov, Suvalki, and Warsaw. In Warsaw, he established a Hebrew high school and was among the founders of the Polish Association of Hebrew Authors and Journalists, which he headed for a short time. In 1934 he emigrated to Ereẓ Israel, where he taught at the Tel Mond School.

His first story, *Nissayon* ("Test"), was published in *Ha-Zeman* (1905); subsequent stories appeared in various Hebrew periodicals. He served as an editor of the monthlies *Kolot* (1924) and *Reshit* (1933). While his early stories realistically describe Jewish life in Poland, those of his post-migration period relate the Israel experience. His books are *Bayit u-Reḥov* (1931);

Bi-Derakhim Afelot (1942); *Meḥizot* (1943); *Asher Avar* (3 vols., 1950–56); *Poh ve-Sham* (1954); *Adam be-Oholo* (1955).

BIBLIOGRAPHY: A. Ben-Or, *Toledot Ha-Sifrut ha-Ivrit ha-Ḥadashah*, 3 (1946), 244–51; Keshet, in: *Moznayim*, 33 (1960), 35–40.

[Jerucham Tolkes]

WEINBERGER, JAROMIR (1896–1967), composer. Born in Prague, Weinberger studied at the Prague Conservatory and with Max Reger in Leipzig. In 1922 he visited the U.S., and on his return to Europe he taught in various cities, but his center was in Prague. In 1937 he emigrated to the U.S., settling in St. Petersburg, Fla. Although best known for his operas, Weinberger also wrote orchestral, choral, and instrumental works. His early compositions were in the style of the French impressionists, but later works were inspired by Czech folk music and the school of Dvorak and Smetana. His picturesque folk-opera *Švanda dudák* ("Schwanda the Bagpiper," 1927), written in the tradition of Smetana, won Weinberger immediate popularity, and was translated into 17 languages and performed throughout Europe and the U.S. The opera's "Polka and Fugue" is a concert staple.

Other operas are *Lidé z Pokerflatu* ("The Outcasts of Poker Flat," after Bret Harte, 1932) and *Wallenstein* (1937), a lyric tragedy after Schiller. After leaving Europe, Weinberger became deeply influenced by American culture and completely changed his style. Among his later works are *Variations and Fugue on Under the Spreading Chestnut Tree* (1939), *Lincoln Symphony* (1941), *Ecclesiastes*, for soprano, baritone, mixed chorus, and organ (1945), *Prelude and Fugue on Dixie*, and *Legend of Sleepy Hollow*. Some of his music on Jewish subjects is still unpublished.

BIBLIOGRAPHY: MGG, incl. bibl.; Baker, Biog Dict; Riemann-Gurlitt, incl. bibl.; Grove, Dict; *New York Times* (Aug. 11, 1967), 21.

WEINBERGER, MOSHE (1854–1940), rabbi. Born in Hungary, he studied with Samuel Ehrenfeld, Elazar Loew, Moses Sofer, and Meir Perles and immigrated to the United States in 1880 for reasons unknown. Fervently Orthodox, deeply learned, and highly unsuccessful, he was in the wrong place at the wrong time, or he was the wrong man for his place and his time. A sense of his experience in the United States can be found in his book written in Hebrew, not Yiddish, on Jews and Judaism in New York (1887), in which he bemoans Jewish life in New York City and criticizes its materialism, its impiety, the low level of Jewish learning and Jewish life, and the terrible standards of *kashrut*. "Great cantors, but empty synagogues" is the way he characterized Jewish life. His message to those who had not yet come to the United States was simple: Don't! It was not a happy report, but it did not stem the tide of immigration. Jonathan Sarna describes his book as the best "single source for Orthodox Jewish life among early East European immigrants." It is a non-romantic portrait. The heroes resist and do not embrace Americanization.

He then became rabbi in Scranton, Pennsylvania, in 1890 and moved on to Philadelphia three years later, and his career was on the upswing. He then returned to New York to be rabbi of the Beth Hamidrash Hagadol, Anshei Ungarn (Hungary). He attempted to organize a Yeshivat Or-Hayyim but, in the end, could not open the school. His experience with his congregation was no better. His congregation was appreciative neither of his learning nor of his educational interests. He hung on but was not supported adequately, so he had to earn additional money elsewhere. In 1906 there was violence directed at him toward the end of Passover and the police were called in to settle the matter. He resigned, entered the *matzah* business and wrote an open letter to his congregation.

He wrote *Kuntres Halakhah le-Moshe* (1884), *Rosh Divrei Moshe* (1895), *Ho'il Moshe* (1895), *Halakhah le-Moshe* (1902); *Divrei Shalom ve-Emet* (1908), and *Dorosh Darash Moshe* (1914).

BIBLIOGRAPHY: J. Sarna, *People Walk on Their Heads, Moses Weinberg's Jews and Judaism in New York* (1982); M.D. Sherman, *Orthodox Judaism in America: A Biographical Dictionary and Sourcebook* (1996); S.Z. Leiman "Yeshivat Or-Hayyim: The First Talmudical Academy in America?" in: *Tradition*, 25:2 (Winter 1990).

[Michael Berenbaum (2nd ed.)]

WEINER, ANTHONY (1964–), U.S. congressman. Born in Brooklyn, New York, Weiner attended Brooklyn Tech High School, then earned his bachelor's degree from the State University of New York at Plattsburgh in 1985. Following graduation, he relocated to Washington, D.C., to work for U.S. congressman Charles *Schumer, serving in various positions, including budget director, press assistant, and foreign affairs assistant. Weiner returned to Brooklyn as Schumer's district office liaison and later became his chief advisor.

In 1991, following a New York City charter revision that created new City Council districts, Weiner ran in the newly created Forty-Eighth District. He was elected, becoming at 27 the youngest person ever elected to the New York City Council. Weiner served on the City Council until 1998, winning reelection by large margins and earning a reputation as a gifted speaker and a leading consumer advocate. He chaired the Subcommittee on Crime in Public Housing.

In 1998 Charles Schumer vacated his seat in Congress to run for the U.S. Senate, and he endorsed Weiner's campaign to fill the Congressional seat. After winning the hotly contested Democratic primary, Weiner easily won election over his Republican opponent, Louis Telano. Weiner has since served as the representative of the Ninth District of New York, winning three successive reelections.

Weiner serves on Congress's Judiciary Committee, where his legislative efforts have included an increase in funding for DNA testing to solve crimes, as well as measures to protect women from sexual predators. He was a sponsor of the "COPS" program to increase police presence on city streets nationwide.

Following the September 11, 2001, terrorist attacks on New York and Washington, D.C., Weiner was appointed to the Homeland Security Task Force, the only Task Force member from New York. He worked to pass legislation that would increase the flow of information between state and federal authorities, and to overhaul building collapse investigations. In 2004, following conflicting statements from the Department of Justice, the Federal Bureau of Investigation, and the Department of Homeland Security regarding the likelihood of an impending al-Qaeda attack, Weiner called on President Bush to clarify the chain of command, stating that the conflicting statements suggested "an intelligence community in disarray."

In 2005 Weiner ran for the Democratic nomination for mayor of New York City, coming in second to Fernando Ferrer. When it initially appeared that the results might force a runoff election, Weiner withdrew and endorsed Ferrer, purportedly at the urging of high-ranking Democrats, including Schumer. Though absentee ballots in fact placed Ferrer's results over the required 40 percent, Weiner's withdrawal was seen as a politically savvy move that could serve him well in the next mayoral race.

[Dorothy Bauhoff (2nd ed.)]

WEINER, LAZAR (1897–1982), composer and conductor. Born at Cherkassy, near Kiev, Weiner immigrated to the United States at the age of 17. He settled in New York, where he conducted choral societies and the Mendelssohn Symphony Orchestra of Brooklyn. Weiner was also conductor at the Central Synagogue, New York City, on the Message of Israel radio programs, and of a YMHA chorus. From 1952 he taught at the Hebrew Union School of Education and Sacred Music. His compositions include the cantatas *Legend of Toil* (1933), *Fight for Freedom* (1943), and *To Thee, America* (1944), several Friday evening services, a Saturday morning service, ballets on Jewish subjects, and choral arrangements of Jewish folk songs. His son, YEHUDI (1921–), was also known as a composer. Weiner's musical score to a Yiddish play, *Generations of Green Fields*, played by the Folksbiene, was produced in 1974 and was widely acclaimed.

WEINER, LEO (1885–1960), composer and teacher. Born in Budapest, Weiner was professor at the Budapest Academy from 1908 to 1949, and gained a reputation as a teacher. As a composer, Weiner was a moderate modernist of a stature recognized beyond the borders of his country. His music, written in a Hungarian idiom, has a light and vivacious touch and shows the influence of both the French and German schools. Weiner wrote orchestral works, chamber music, piano pieces, incidental music, and music for children. He also published several books on music theory.

WEINER, RICHARD (1884–1937), Czech poet, author, and journalist. Weiner was born in Písek, Bohemia. Although for many years Paris correspondent of the leading Czechoslovak newspaper *Lidové Noviny*, Weiner was essentially a poet. His books of verse, *Pták* ("The Bird", 1913), *Usměvavé odříkání* ("Smiling Abandon," 1914), *Mnoho nocí* ("Many Nights," 1928), *Zátiší s kulichem, herbářem a kostkami* ("Still Life with Owl, Herbarium and Dice," 1929), and *Mezopotámie* (1930, 1965), made an original, substantially Jewish contribution to modern Czech poetry. In his short stories he displays typically Jewish qualities of irony and self-criticism and a desire to reconcile opposites. Weiner's prose, often reminiscent of *Kafka's in his use of a psychoanalytic technique, often, like a cubist painter, showing things simultaneously from different angles, provides a surprising contrast between the simplicity of his plots and the complexity of his characters. His short story collections include *Netečný divák* ("The Apathetic Spectator," 1917), *Lítice* ("Furies," 1916), *Škleb* ("The Grimace," 1919, 1993), *Lazebník* ("The Barber", 1929, 1967, 1974), and *Hra doopravdy* ("A Play in Earnest," 1933, 1967, 1974). His deep interest in the Jewish problem is revealed in a number of his essays. Weiner repudiated Jewish assimilation and admired Zionist ideals, without, however, joining the Zionist movement, and he remained a solitary, split character, like many of the characters he described in his stories. An anthology of Weiner's poems, *Sluncem svržený sok* ("The Rival Toppled by the Sun"), was published in 1989. After the fall of the Communist regime Weiner's collected works began to be published.

BIBLIOGRAPHY: P. Váša and A. Gregor, *Katechismus dějin české literatury* (1925); O. Donath, *Židé a židovství v české literatuře 19. a 20. století* (1930); J. Chalupecký, *Richard Weiner* (Czech, 1947); Hostovský, in: *Jews of Czechoslovakia* (1967), 441f. **ADD. BIBLIOGRAPHY:** V. Linhartová, "Doslov," in: R. Weiner, *Hra doopravdy* (1967); A. Mikulášek, *Literatura s hvězdou Davidovou* vol. 1(1998); B. Novák, *O Richardu Weinerovi* (1932); *Slovník českých spisovatelů* (2000).

[Avigdor Dagan / Milos Pojar (2nd ed.)]

WEINFELD, EDWARD (1901–1988), U.S. federal judge. Born in New York City and raised on Manhattan's Lower East Side, Weinfeld attended law school at night while working at various jobs. He received his LL.B. degree in 1921 and his LL.M. in 1922, both from New York University. Entering private practice in New York, he was active in the Democratic Party. In 1935, he served as chief counsel for the New York State Legislative Committee Investigating Bondholders Commission. In 1939, Governor Herbert *Lehman named Weinfeld as New York State's first housing commissioner, a post he held until 1942. He served as vice president and director of Citizens Housing and Planning Council for New York State from 1943 until 1950, when President Harry Truman appointed him as a judge in the U.S. District Court in the Southern District of New York.

Weinfeld gained a reputation as a dedicated jurist whose decisions were rarely reversed. His long career saw many notable cases, including the bribery trial of James Marcus, a former New York City Water Commissioner, and the Quentin Reynolds-Westbrook Pegler libel trial. In another prominent case, he ruled that Senator Joseph R. McCarthy's Committee on Government Operations lacked the authority to investigate author Corliss Lamont. Yet Weinfeld maintained that "every case is important"; he was known for his extensive research and precisely written decisions.

A member of the American Bar Association and the New York State Bar Association, Weinfeld received numerous awards and honors, including the American Law Institute's Henry Friendly Medal in 1987 for outstanding contributions to the law, and New York's LaGuardia Medal in 1988. Justice William J. Brennan, Jr., of the U.S. Supreme Court, stated that "there is no better judge on any court." Weinfeld's biographer William Nelson, who holds the position of Edward Weinfeld Chair at New York University Law School, has described him as the "preeminent trial judge in twentieth-century America." Though many had hoped that Weinfeld would be named to the Supreme Court, he expressed pride in serving on the district court. At the time of his death in 1988 at age 86, he was the oldest active federal district judge in the United States.

[Dorothy Bauhoff (2nd ed.)]

WEINGARTEN, JOAB JOSHUA (1847–1922), Polish rabbi. Regarded by Abraham Bornstein of Suchaczew as his most brilliant pupil, he and his teacher exchanged numerous responsa. Weingarten had strong leanings toward Ḥasidism; from 1880 he was rabbi in several Polish cities and finally in Konskie, being thereafter known as "the Rabbi of Konskie." He was considered one of the greatest halakhic authorities in Poland, and many Polish rabbis addressed halakhic questions to him, but in his replies, contrary to the usual practice, he does not mention the name of his correspondents. His replies were always brief and to the point; he justified this brevity by stating that his decisions might not be regarded as the final *halakhah*. He was the author of *Ḥelkat Yo'av* on the four parts of the Shulḥan Arukh (2 pts., 1903–05). A second, revised, edition, with a supplement containing his glosses to the Babylonian and Jerusalem Talmuds, was published in Jerusalem in 1950. In this work he disagreed, at times in disparaging terms, with the views of several accepted halakhic authorities, charging them in the introduction with being ignorant of the stylistic features of Hebrew. His work became a classic among Polish scholars, among whom his novellae circulated. In the appendix to the work, entitled *Kabba de-Kashyata*, he lists 103 insoluble problems (the numerical value of *kabba* (קבא) being 103). His son Meir, who succeeded him as rabbi of Konskie, was killed by the Nazis.

BIBLIOGRAPHY: J.J. Weingarten, *Ḥelkat Yo'av* (1950^2), introd.

[Itzhak Alfassi]

WEINGREEN, JACOB (1908–1995), Hebrew and Bible scholar. Born in Manchester, he graduated from Trinity College, Dublin, where he became professor of Hebrew in 1939 and served until his retirement in 1978. During the period immediately following World War II, he served as director of education in the Displaced Persons' Camp in Bergen-Belsen.

Weingreen's best-known publication, *A Practical Grammar for Classical Hebrew*, was published in 1939 and remained in general use 50 years later. A French edition, *Hébreu Biblique*, appeared in 1984. His other works included *Classical Hebrew Composition* (1957), *From Bible to Mishna – The Continuity of Tradition* (1976), and *Introduction to the Critical Study of the Text of the Hebrew Bible* (1982). His writings, as well as his teaching, were distinguished by their lucidity.

He received many honors and was president of the Society for Old Testament Studies, Great Britain and Ireland (1961), of the British Association of Jewish Studies (1976), and governor of the *Irish Times* Trust from 1974.

An abiding interest in archeology led to his foundation of what, on his retirement, was named the Weingreen Museum of Biblical Antiquities in Trinity College, Dublin. His contention that the Book of Deuteronomy is not, as widely believed, one of the main sources of the Pentateuch, because it bears the characteristic of a mishnah, caused a stir among biblical scholars.

[Asher Benson]

WEINHEIM, town in Baden-Wuerttemberg, Germany. In the latter half of the 13th century it had a relatively large Jewish community, but in 1298 the synagogue, in which 70 Jews had sought refuge from the *Rindfleisch persecutions, was burnt down. Among the martyrs were several of the *Kalonymus family. A smaller community was established soon afterward. During the *Black Death persecutions (1349), Duke Rupert I granted asylum to Jewish refugees. In his reign a synagogue and cemetery were in existence. After his death (1390) the community declined and left few traces until the late 17th century, when a synagogue was built for the 15-family community by its leader, Oppenheim. At that time a guild was organized which was against Jewish bakers and millers; market regulations assigned them a special quarter. In 1906 a new synagogue, financed by the Hirsch family, who owned the tanning factory, was dedicated. The community comprised 188 persons in 1910 (1.3 percent of the total population) and 168 in 1933; subsequently a decline set in. On Nov. 10, 1938, the furnishings of the synagogue were demolished by axe-wielding Nazis; later it was blown up. On Oct. 22, 1940, 40 Jews were deported to *Gurs. In 1967 two Jews were living in Weinheim. A plaque (mounted in 1967) commemorates the destroyed synagogue. Another memorial (mounted in 1999) is dedicated to the victims of the Nazi era. The 17th-century synagogue (which was sold in 1906) is now a residential building.

BIBLIOGRAPHY: D. Horsch (ed.), *Die juedische Gemeinde in Weinheim* (1964); *Germania Judaica*, 2 (1968), 870–1; 3 (1987), 1563–65; **ADD BIBLIOGRAPHY:** C. Fischer, "Geduldet, vertrieben, ermordet. Die Juden in Weinheim bis 1933," in: *Die Stadt Weinheim zwischen 1933 und 1945* (*Weinheimer Geschichtsblatt*, vol. 38) (2000), 351–444; C. Modig, "Die juedischen Buerger Weinheims 1933–1945," in: *Die Stadt Weinheim zwischen 1933 und 1945* (*Weinheimer Geschichtsblatt*, vol. 38) (2000), 445–567. **WEBSITE:** www.alemannia-judaica.de.

[Larissa Daemmig (2nd ed.)]

WEINHOUSE, SIDNEY (1909–2001), U.S. biochemist. Weinhouse was born in Chicago and obtained his B.S. (1933) and Ph.D. (1936) in biochemistry from the University of Chicago. After postdoctoral studies in Chicago, he joined Temple University Medical School, Philadelphia (1947), becoming professor at (1950) and director of the Fels Institute for Cancer Research (1963–75). His research interests concerned carbohydrate metabolism, leading him to discover the enzyme glucokinase and enzyme expression in cancers. Weinhouse was a lifelong gifted teacher, and his honors included election to the U.S. National Academy of Sciences (1979).

[Michael Denman (2nd ed.)]

WEININGER, OTTO (1880–1903), Austrian psychologist and philosopher. Weininger was born in Vienna. From 1898 he studied philosophy, biology, psychology, physics, and mathematics at the University of Vienna. He rejected his original positivistic view, and, influenced by, among others, Plato, Kant, St. Augustine, Neoplatonism, and Wagner, he converted to Protestantism the day he received his Ph.D. in 1902. He then wrote his major work, *Geschlecht und Charakter* (1903; *Sex and Character*, 1906), a philosophical justification of male superiority expressing misogynistic and antisemitic views. After its publication, he sank into a deep depression, culminating in his suicide, at the age of 23, in the same house in which Beethoven had died. Shortly after his death, his unpublished essays and aphorisms appeared under the title *Ueber die letzten Dinge* (1904^1) and in a second edition with a biographical introduction by Moriz Rappaport (1907^2). Much later, two other works were published: *Otto Weininger, Die Liebe und das Weib* (1917), and *Taschenbuch und Briefe an einen Freund*, ed. by A. Gerber (1919). In 1990 Weininger's collected works and letters appeared under the title *Eros und Psyche* (1990), ed. by H. Rodlauer. Weininger's *Geschlecht und Charakter* became well-known after his death; following Max Nordau's discussion of it in the *Vossische Zeitung*, it had almost 30 editions in German (Hebrew ed. 1953). Weininger's theory is based on a fundamental relationship between sex and character. Every human being is a combination of male and female elements. He saw Man as the positive, productive, logical, conceptual, ethical, spiritual force capable of genius, while Woman is the negative one, incapable of any of these virtues. Woman is either interested purely in sexual pleasure (the Prostitute) or in procreation (the Mother). As a result, the ideal Woman depends on Man, on the Phallus, and her emancipation, as well as the spiritual progress of Man, depends upon ending coitus.

In his discussion of Judaism, Weininger saw the characteristics of the Jew as even worse than those of Woman. The Jew is a force which exists within people, not just in individual Jews (it is found also in non-Jews). The disadvantage of the Jew compared to Woman is that the latter at least believes in the Male while the Jew believes in nothing. Hence the Jew gravitates towards Communism, anarchism, materialism, empiricism, and atheism. Zionism, Weininger claimed, could only come about after the rejection of Judaism, since Jews could not grasp the idea of a state. The Jewish religion he saw as belief in nothing, in contrast to the positive faith he found in Christianity. Weininger's views combined elements of romanticism, Wagnerianism, Nietzscheanism, modern psychology, and biology, with many original insights. His opinions and arguments were taken over by Nazi thinkers as justification for their views. After the war the attitude towards Weininger's work and figure shifted from an ideological use of his ideas towards a search for an understanding of his thoughts and behavior within the framework of the humanities and social sciences. In 1982 the Israeli playwright Y. Sobol wrote for the stage *Nefesh Yehudi: ha-Layla ha-Aḥaron shel Otto Weininger* (*Weiningers Nacht*, 1986, 1988^2).

BIBLIOGRAPHY: J. Sachs, *The Jewish Genius* (1939), 237–43; S. Liptzin, *Germany's Stepchildren* (1944), 184–90; S. Freud, *Origins of Psychoanalysis: Letters to Wilhelm Fliess* (1954), index (incl. bibl.); D. Abrahamsen, *The Mind and Death of a Genius* (1946), incl. bibl.; H. Kohn, in: YLBI, 6 (1961), 152–69. **ADD. BIBLIOGRAPHY:** J. Le Rider and N. Leser (eds.), *Otto Weininger* (1984); J. Le Rider, *Der Fall Otto Weininger* (1985); A. Janik, in: I. Oxaal et al. (eds.), *Jews, Antisemitism and Culture in Vienna*, 75–88; S. Beinssen-Hesse, in: J. Milfull (ed.), *Why Germany?* (1993), 9–28; H. Schroeder, in: C. Kohn-Ley, I. Korotin (eds.), *Der Feministische "Suendenfall"?* (1994), 60–83; N.A. Harrowitz and B. Hyams (eds.), *Jews & Gender* (1995); R. Robertson, in: B. Cheyette and L. Marcus (eds.), *Modernity, Culture and 'the Jew'* (1998), 23–39; R.S. Wistrich, in: *Der Juedische Echo*, 48 (1999), 93–113; C. Sengoopta, *Otto Weininger* (2000).

[Richard H. Popkin / Noam Zadoff (2nd ed.)]

WEINMANN, JACOB (1852–1928), Bohemian industrialist. Born in Dobra, near Klatovy (Bohemia), in 1874 Weinmann was placed in charge of the Aussig (Usti nad Labem) coal business which was then owned by the Prague Bankverein. After the collapse of that bank, he took over the coal business under the name of Eduard J. Weinmann and subsequently developed it into one of the largest enterprises in Europe. He was instrumental in the great expansion of the coal industry in northwestern Bohemia. He was also very active in charitable and humanitarian pursuits, both Jewish and non-Jewish, providing them with considerable financial support.

Jacob's son, FRITZ, conducted unsuccessful negotiations with the Nazis, who confiscated the Weinmann concern for the Hermann Goering Werke. His brother, HANS, was held as surety in Prague but escaped. Both arrived in America in 1941; Fritz changed his name to Frederick Wyman, and Hans' son, Charles, joined the Unitarian Church. A foundation bearing the Weinmann name was established in 1947.

BIBLIOGRAPHY: J. Stoessler, in: H. Gold (ed.), *Juden und Judengemeinden Boehmens in Vergangenheit und Gegenwart*, 1 (1934), 21–22; R. Hilberg, *Destruction of the European Jews* (1967^2), 72ff.

[Oskar K. Rabinowicz]

WEINPER, ZISHE (pseudonym of **Zise Weinperlech**; 1893–1957), Yiddish poet, short story writer, editor, and essayist. Weinper was born into a ḥasidic family in Turisk (Ukraine). His father was a cantor and a member of the Trisker rebbe's inner circle. As a youth, Weinper wandered throughout the Ukraine and Poland and in 1910 moved to Warsaw, where he began his literary career. In 1913 he emigrated to the U.S., where he became associated with the Yiddish literary group Di *Yunge. He continued his literary activities while also working as a house painter and elementary school teacher. In 1917, he edited the literary journal *Der Onheyb*, which included his own works as well as those of his contemporaries such as B.J. *Bialostotsky, Aaron *Nissenson, and Naphtali *Gross. In 1918, Weinper joined the British *Jewish Legion and served in the Middle East. After returning to New York, he resumed publishing his poems, short stories, and essays in Yiddish publications such as *Morgn-Zhurnal, Fraye Arbeter Shtime,* and *Tsukunft*. The Depression of the early 1930s and the rise of Hitler in 1933 led him to join the radical left, and he became the poet and moving spirit of the Yidisher Kultur Farband, the leftist Yiddish cultural federation. His lyric volumes *Poemen Vegn di Neviim* ("Poems about the Prophets," 1951) and *Leyd un Freyd* ("Sorrow and Happiness," 1954) gave expression to his later, less optimistic moods.

BIBLIOGRAPHY: Rejzen, Leksikon, 1 (1926), 949f.; LNYL (1960), 369–71; *Dos Z. Weinper-Bukh* (1962), 3, incl. bibl.; Z. Zylbercweig, *Leksikon fun Yidishn Teater*, 4 (1963), 3586–89.

[Sol Liptzin / Marc Miller (2nd ed.)]

WEINREB, FRIEDRICH (Fryderyk, Freek, Fischel; 1910–1988), economist. An unprecedented controversy developed in the Netherlands in the 1960s over the World War II activities of Friedrich Weinreb, a native of Lemberg whose family had settled in Scheveningen during World War I. When the Nazis occupied the Netherlands in 1940 Weinreb was a senior staff member of the Netherlands Economic Institute in Rotterdam. In 1941, shortly after losing his job due to anti-Jewish measures, he started a swindle, telling fellow Jews that the Nazis had permitted him to set up emigration destined for unoccupied France and Portugal. Three to four thousand Jews paid him to be on his – unfortunately, only imaginary – emigration list. He also managed to deceive the Nazis, collaborating with them in a second imaginary emigration plan that helped the Nazis track down Jews and Jewish valuables. He went into hiding with his family in 1944.

After the liberation Weinreb was sentenced to six years of imprisonment for swindling and betraying fellow Jews. Some sympathizers regarded him as a second Dreyfus and campaigned for his release. Owing to Queen Wilhelmina's jubilee he was released in December 1948.

The debate about his war past began in 1965, when the Dutch-Jewish historian J. Presser, basing his opinions mostly on Weinreb's voluminous memoirs, declared him an alternative hero who had resisted the Nazis with cunning and deceit. After the publication of Weinreb's memoirs in 1969 many journalists, politicians, historians, and critical intellectuals became involved in a public debate. Two publicists, Renate Rubinstein and Aad Nuis, and a Weinreb Committee dedicated themselves to the cause of Weinreb's rehabilitation. The dispute split society into Weinreb believers and non-believers, the latter being a minority. In particular, the novelist W.F. Hermans and journalist and high school teacher Henriëtte *Boas became fierce opponents of Weinreb. The 1976 report issued by the Rijksinstituut voor Oorlogsdocumentatie (Netherlands Institute for War Documentation) determined that he was a fantasizer and swindler, whose memoirs were largely false, and that his collaboration had resulted in 70 deaths. His activities did contribute to some Jews' survival, but most Jews who fell for Weinreb's swindle were deported and killed.

The enigma of Weinreb's beguiling talents is the more interesting because he proved to be a charlatan in other spheres of life as well, conning high-ranking officials of the Dutch Ministry of Foreign Affairs, leading a group of religious followers from 1948, and being convicted in 1957 and 1968 for posing as a medical doctor and for sexual offenses. Eventually, to avoid imprisonment, Weinreb left the country in 1968. He settled in Switzerland, where he continued to be a religious guru until his death in 1988.

Weinreb inspired extreme characterizations ranging from "messianic" to "the embodiment of evil." He won goodwill and stirred up trouble wherever he went. For a small group of followers Weinreb remains a hero and a guru. In fact, he was both a villain and a victim, and his historical accounts proved a miscellany of fact and fabrication, hardly suitable as a reliable historical source.

His memoirs cover the following: on World War II, *Collaboratie en Verzet* (1969); on the aftermath, *De gevangenis, Herinneringen 1945–1948* (1989); on religion, *De Bijbel als schepping* (1963) and *Ontmoetingen met mensen en engelen* (religious memoirs; 1982).

BIBLIOGRAPHY: J. Presser, *Ondergang* (1965) (the paragraph on Weinreb was omitted in the English edition); D. Giltay Veth, A.J. van der Leeuw, *Rapport… inzake de activiteiten van drs. F. Weinreb…* (1976); R. Grüter, *Een fantast schrijft geschiedenis* (1997) (with extensive bibliography).

[Regina Grüter (2nd ed.)]

WEINREICH, MAX (1894–1969), Yiddish linguist, historian, editor. Born in Kuldiga (Latvia), Weinreich made his debut as a Yiddish writer at the age of 13, and became a contributor to various Yiddish, Russian, German, and later English publications. After studying at the universities of St. Petersburg and Berlin, he completed a doctoral thesis on the history of Yiddish philology at the University of Marburg (1923; *Geschichte der jiddischen Sprachforschung*, 1993).

Early in his career Weinreich became a prominent educator in various capacities, ranging from the teaching of Yiddish literature at the Vilna Yiddish Teachers' Seminary to serving as leader of a Yiddish scouting movement, Di Bin ("The Bee"). He was instrumental in giving Yiddish linguistics a solid, scholarly footing. Co-founder with Nokhem *Shtif, Elias *Tcherikover, and Zalmen *Rejzen of the *YIVO Institute (1925), and YIVO's guiding spirit, he was largely responsible for its achieving a worldwide reputation. As director of YIVO's Research Training Division and organizer of its graduate school, Weinreich successfully educated young Yiddish scholars, among them, his son, Uriel *Weinreich. At the World Congress of Linguistics in Copenhagen (1936), he lectured on "Yiddish as an Object of General Linguistics," and in 1940, he immigrated with his son Uriel to the U.S., where he became the country's first university professor of Yiddish, teaching Yiddish language, literature, and folklore at the College of the City of New York and Columbia University, while serving as the scholarly director of YIVO.

Weinreich's wide array of books and studies include his *magnum opus*, *Geshikhte fun der Yidisher Shprakh* ("History of the Yiddish Language," 4 vols., 1973; Engl. transl. of vols. 1–2, 1980), the culmination of a half century of research on Yiddish sociolinguistics, tracing the thousand-year development of Ashkenazi culture and the Yiddish language as integral to the Jewish way of life. He studied the development of Yiddish from its origins in Germany, through Eastern Europe and into the second diaspora, creating the basic concepts and theoretical tools of the linguistic study of Jewish languages. Prominent among his other works are *Hitlers Profesorn* (1947; English transl. 1946) – probably the best documented indictment of German scholarship during the Nazi regime; *Shturemvint* ("Tempest," 1927), sketches on 17th-century Jewish history; *Bilder fun der Yidisher Literatur-Geshikhte* ("Sketches from the History of Yiddish Literature," 1928); *Der Veg tsu Undzer Yugnt* ("Path to Our Youth," 1935), a socio-psychological study of Jewish youth in Eastern Europe; and *Di Shvartse Pintelekh* ("Black Dots," 1939), a history of alphabets. Weinreich translated Homer, Freud, and Ernst Toller into Yiddish and edited the periodicals *Yidishe Filologye* (1924–26), *Filologishe Shriftn* (1926–29), *Yivo-Bleter* (1931–50), and the critical edition of S. *Ettinger's works, N. Stutchkoff's *Oytser fun der Yidisher Shprakh* ("Thesaurus of the Yiddish Language"), Y.L. Cahan's *Shtudyes vegn Yidisher Folkshafung* ("Studies in Yiddish Folklore"), and *Yidishe Folkslider mit Melodyes* ("Yiddish Folksongs with Melodies").

BIBLIOGRAPHY: *For Max Weinreich on his Seventieth Birthday: Studies in Jewish Languages, Literature and Society* (1964), incl. bibl.; LNYL, 3 (1960); M. Schaechter, in: *Goldene Keyt*, 50 (1964), 157–71; L.S. Dawidowicz, in: AJYB, 70 (1969), 59–68. **ADD. BIBLIOGRAPHY:** J.C. Frakes, in: M. Weinreich, *Geschichte der jiddischen Sprachforschung* (1993), vii-xxiv.

[Mordkhe Schaechter / Jean Baumgarten (2nd ed.)]

WEINREICH, URIEL (1925–1967), Yiddish and general linguist, editor, and educator. Despite his early death, he left behind him the equivalent of several lifetimes of research and creativity – an unbelievably wide range of investigations.

Born in Vilna, the son of Max *Weinreich and a well-known editor-educator, Regina Weinreich (Szabad), the young Weinreich was exposed from earliest childhood to the best Vilna had to offer intellectually. Uriel Weinreich went to the United States in 1940 and as a linguist he was an immediate success ("The twenty minutes that it took him to read, before a well-attended annual meeting of the Linguistic Society of America, his paper '*Sabesdiker Losn*: A Problem of Linguistic Affinity' transformed a practically unknown young man into an enthusiastically applauded leader of the new generation" [Y. Malkier]). The monograph *Languages in Contact: Findings and Problems* (1952), based on his doctoral dissertation, became a standard reference work in its field; the textbook *College Yiddish: An Introduction to the Yiddish Language and to Jewish Life and Culture* (1949) went through five editions and ten printings within a 10-year span. Appointed professor of Yiddish language, literature, and culture at Columbia University in 1959, Uriel Weinreich was also chairman of the university's Department of Linguistics (1957–65). His extraordinary teaching capabilities are attested to by the fact that some of his students became leading linguists at various universities. Equally impressive were Weinreich's achievements as editor of, for example, the U.S. State Department's *Problems of Communism* (1950–51), of the linguistic journal *Word* (1953–60), of the first three volumes of *The Field of Yiddish: Studies in Yiddish Language, Folklore, and Literature* (1954, 1963², 1969³), and of the *YIVO's *Yidisher Folklor* (1954–62). He was the editor of the Yiddish section in the Encyclopaedia Britannica's *World Language Dictionary* (1954). Special mention should be made of his *Yiddish Language and Folklore (A selective bibliography for research)* (1959), compiled jointly with his wife, Beatrice Weinreich.

Uriel Weinreich's research papers, written and published in Yiddish, English, Hebrew, French and Russian, ranged topically from a cultural history of Yiddish rhyme through such fields as phonology, grammatical theory, bilingualism, language standardization, dialectology, semantics, and lexicology. Almost every research paper and lecture of his was a trail-blazing venture, greeted by acclaim on all sides.

The two crowning achievements in Uriel Weinreich's work are the pioneering *Language and Culture Atlas of Ashkenazic Jewry* (at Columbia University, 1950–) – one of the world's largest collections of spoken language – and the *Modern English-Yiddish, Yiddish-English Dictionary* (1968). The atlas, initiated, organized and directed by U. Weinreich under a grant from the National Science Foundation, is an ongoing, large-scale project designed to record and study Yiddish dialects by harnessing the methods of advanced linguistic research and computer data processing. The dictionary is a climax in the history of Yiddish lexicography, both in its unsurpassed scholarly quality and its immediate wide popularity.

BIBLIOGRAPHY: LNYL, 3 (1960), 366–7; Marvin I. Herzog, in: *Language*, 43 (1967), 607–10 (a bibliography); L. Kahn, in: *Yugntruf*, no. 17/18 (1969), a bibliography; Y. Malkiel, in: *Language*, 43 (1967), idem, in: *Romance Philology*, 22 (1968), 128–32; M. Schaechter, in: *Goldene Keyt*, 66 (1969).

[Mordkhe Schaechter]

WEINRUB, MATVEY, Soviet lieutenant general, Hero of the Soviet Union. In World War II, at the battle of Stalingrad, he commanded the armor of the 62nd army, and his small tank force twice succeeded in preventing the Germans from reaching the Volga. Weinrub was promoted to major general with command of the armored division of the 8th guards army which recaptured the Donets coalfield and Odessa and advanced to Berlin.

WEINRYB, BERNARD DOV SUCHER (1900–1982), economic and social historian. Born in Turobin, Poland, Weinryb studied in Breslau at the Jewish Theological Seminary and at the university, was librarian at the seminary in 1931–33, and worked on the editorial staff of the *Encyclopaedia Judaica* in Berlin and Zurich (1933–34). In 1934 he emigrated to Palestine, where he lectured at the School of Social Work and School of Economics to 1939. Moving to the United States, he taught at the Herzliah Teachers' Seminary and at the Jewish Teachers' Seminary, New York (1941–48). Weinryb was lecturer at Brooklyn College (1948–51), worked as an economist for the State Department (1951–55), and lectured at Columbia University (1950–56), Yeshiva University (1948), and as professor of Jewish history and economics at Dropsie College (from 1949).

To the economic history of Russian and Polish Jewry Weinryb contributed *Studien zur Wirtschaftsgeschichte ...* (1933); *Neueste Wirtschaftsgeschichte ...* (1934; Hebrew and English summary, 1939); *Te'udot le-Toledot ha-Kehillot ha-Yehudiyyot be-Polin* ("Texts and Studies in the Communal History of Polish Jewry," 1951, introduction and notes in English); *Be-Reshit ha-Sozyalizm ha-Yehudi* ("In the Beginnings of Jewish Socialism," 1940). On the sociology of the yishuv in Palestine he wrote *The Yishuv in Palestine: Structure and Organization* (1947); *Jewish Vocational Education* (1948); *Ha-Dor ha-Sheni be-Ereẓ Yisrael ve-Darko ha-Mikẓo'it* ("The Second Generation in Ereẓ Israel and its Occupational Status," 1954). Together with S.D. Loewinger, Weinryb prepared a *Catalogue of Hebrew Manuscripts in the Jewish Theological Seminary, Breslau* (1965) and *Yiddische Handschriften in Breslau* (1936). He also wrote *The Jews of Poland* (1972) and *Studies and Documents in Modern Jewish History* (1975). Weinryb edited (and contributed to) *Studies and Essays in Honor of A.A. Neumann* (1962). He published over 300 articles in periodicals.

WEINSHALL, Ereẓ Israel family. BEN ZION ZE'EV (Vladimir; 1863–1943) was born in Grodno, studied at the Russian Military Academy of Medicine, and served as a government doctor in the Caucasus. He was employed among the "*Mountain Jews" to fight cholera, while his permanent residence was in Baku, where he worked for 20 years (1902–22). He was a member of the Zionist movement from its inception, having joined Ḥovevei Zion in Minsk during the Bilu period (1882–83). During 1917–20 he edited the Russian-language Zionist newspaper in the Caucasus, *Yevreyski Kavkazski Vestnik*. He settled in Palestine in 1922, and, after serving as village doctor in Reḥovot (1923–24) and municipal doctor of Tel Aviv (until 1926), he settled in Haifa, where he opened a private practice. In 1928, he was elected president of the Haifa branch of the Medical Society.

His son JACOB (1891–?) was born in Tiflis in the Caucasus. Serving in the Russian army as medical officer in 1916, he joined Joseph *Trumpeldor in his attempt, after the Russian Revolution, to organize Jewish soldiers of the Russian army to effect a breakthrough on the Caucasus front and conquer Palestine. In 1922 he settled in Palestine, serving as a doctor in the *kuppat Ḥolim of the Histadrut until 1932. He was a member of the municipal council of Tel Aviv (1925–28), a delegate to the first and second Asefat ha-Nivḥarim, and a member of the Va'ad Le'ummi. He took part in the establishment of the Union of Zionist Revisionists at its founding conference in Paris (1925) and was chairman of its central committee in Palestine until 1928. After the assassination of Chaim *Arlosoroff, he published a novel based on the murder and trial, entitled *Ha-Mishpat Yatḥil Maḥar* ("The Trial Will Begin Tomorrow"), which appeared in the Revisionist newspaper *Ha-Am*. In 1939 he founded the biweekly *Ha-Ḥevrah*. A prolific writer, he favored the biographic and historic-novel form, including *Hans Herzl* (1945), *Marco Baruch* (1949), *Aggadat Onkelos* ("The Onkelos Legend," 1951), and others. He wrote a book about *Jabotinsky (*Jabo*, 1954).

His second son ABRAHAM (1893–1968) was born in the Caucasus. In 1920 he settled in Haifa, where he was appointed municipal legal adviser. An expert on questions concerning real estate, he was instrumental in the acquisition of valuable land for Jewish settlement, including the land for Nahariyyah, Shavei Zion, and a new commercial center in Haifa. Weinshall's legal essays were published in the professional organ *Ha-Peraklit*. He became chairman of the Revisionist central committee in Palestine. During 1925–31 he was a member of the Jewish community council of Haifa, also serving in 1927–33 as a member of the Asefat ha-Nivḥarim and the Va'ad Leummi. He published and edited the first newspaper of Haifa, *Ha-Ẓafon*, during 1926–27. In 1937 Abraham dissociated himself from the Revisionists and submitted a memorandum to the British government on the solution of the Palestine problem in the name of a group headed by him called Benei Ḥorin. In 1947 he was detained in the Latrun camp by the British authorities, together with other political leaders.

BIBLIOGRAPHY: Tidhar, 2 (1947), 602, 879–90, 901.

WEINSTEIN, AARON (known as **Yerahmiel** or **Rahmiel**; 1877–1938), *Bund leader in Russia. He was born in Vilna, and, while a student at the teachers' training college, he joined a secret socialist circle. In the late 1890s he headed the Bund organization in Warsaw. He was a delegate at the third (1899) and fourth (1901) conventions of the Bund and was a member of its executive committee from 1901 to 1920. Weinstein was among the Bund delegates at the Russian Social-Democratic congress held in London in 1907. He directed the authorized publishing house of the Bund "Di Velt," contributed to the Bundist press, and, during the period of reaction after the abortive revolution in 1905–06, supported the "legalist" trend in the Bund. He was among the four Bundists who took part in the meeting of Jewish communal leaders held in Kovno in 1909, and a delegate at the All-Russian Convention of Craftsmen in 1911. Weinstein was jailed for political activities on several occasions, and during World War I was exiled to Siberia, from where he was released after the February Revolution in 1917. At the tenth conference of the Bund (April 1917), he was elected chairman of its central committee, and moved to Minsk. There he was also elected to head the town council. Up to 1918 Weinstein had identified himself with the right wing of the Bund, but at its 11th conference (March 1919) he veered to the left. With his sister-in-law, Esther (Malkah) Frumkin, he headed the pro-Communist majority at the 12th conference of the Bund (April 1920), but opposed hostile government action against the socialists. He played a decisive role in the incorporation of the Kombund (Communist Bund) within the Communist Party (1921). After this, he held important state functions: chairman of the Popular Economic Council in Belorussia; vice chairman of the Council of Popular Commissars in Kirghizia (1922–23); member of the Collegiate of the Commissariat of Finances, and other positions in the government and economic administration. His Jewish activities were essentially connected with the agricultural settlement schemes; he was vice chairman of Komerd and chairman of Gezerd in Moscow. At the time of Stalin's purges in the 1930s, he was accused of "Bundist nationalism" and arrested. He committed suicide in prison.

BIBLIOGRAPHY: LNYL, 3 (1960), 385–8; J.S. Hertz et al. (eds.), *Geshikhte fun Bund*, 3 vols. (1960–66), index; Ch. Shmeruk (ed.), *Pirsumim Yehudiyyim bi-Verit ha-Mo'aẓot* (1961), index; R. Abramovich, *In Tsvey Revolutsyes*, 1 (1944), 196–7, 328–33; 2 (1944), 310–19.

[Moshe Mishkinsky]

WEINSTEIN, BERISH (1905–1967), Yiddish poet. Born to a ḥasidic family in Rzeszow (western Galicia), he moved to Vienna in 1923 and to New York two years later. His first book, *Brukhvarg* ("Fragments," 1936), is a masterpiece of rough expressionism. In long, Whitmanesque lines, elliptical syntax, and Galician dialect, Weinstein describes the depths of eastern Europe and New York, a world of sailors, thieves, and bloodthirsty gentiles. In his second book, *Reyshe* ("Rzeszow," 1947), in which he recreates his vanished birthplace, a noted center of religious learning, Weinstein began an autobiographical trilogy, continuing with *Amerike* (1955) and *Dovid Hameylekhs Giter* ("King David's Estates," 1960), where he glorifies the formation of the State of Israel. In 1949 Weinstein collected his early poems into *Lider un Poemes* ("Poems and Long Poems"), where few pieces from *Brukhvarg* reappear, and even they are severely shorn of their roughness and descriptive detail: Weinstein had elided his original and daring modernism in order to write in the vein of nostalgia and nationalist Jewish unity demanded by conservative critical taste after the Holocaust. His last book of verse, *Basherte Lider* ("Destined Poems"), appeared in 1965.

BIBLIOGRAPHY: B. Weinstein, *Reisha* (Heb. 1951), 5–29 (introd. by D. Sadan); I. Howe and E. Greenberg (eds.), *A Treasury of Yiddish Poetry* (1969), 291–3. **ADD. BIBLIOGRAPHY.** J. Glatstein, in: *Oyf Greyte Temes* (1967) 123–7; B. and B. Harshav (eds.), *American Yiddish Poetry* (1986), 628–73; B. Kagan, *Leksikon fun Yidish-Shraybers* (1986), 239–41.

[Leonard Prager / Itay Zutra (2nd ed.)]

WEINSTEIN, HARVEY (1952–) and **BOB** (1954–), U.S. entertainment executives. The brothers were raised in Flushing, New York. Harvey enrolled at the University of Buffalo, while Bob went to the State University of New York at Fredonia; however, neither Weinstein graduated. Harvey became involved in concert promotion on campus, and eventually purchased a theater where he booked music acts and featured films between performances. The Weinsteins went to the Cannes Film Festival in 1979 and purchased the soft-core film *Goodbye, Emmanuelle*, which enabled them to start Miramax. The studio, named for the Weinstein's parents and set up at first in Harvey's one-room apartment in New York, distributed independent and foreign films other studios refused to handle. The Weinsteins' first Academy Award win was for the Danish film *Pelle the Conqueror* (1987), which took the 1988 Oscar for best foreign film. When Miramax received a $5 million investment from Midland Montague in 1988, the brothers began producing their own films, such as *Scandal* (1989), about the British Profumo scandal. However, Miramax first major successes were *sex, lies and videotape* by Steven Soderbergh, which cost $1.1 million to make and pulled in $24 million in the North American box office, and the Oscar wins for *My Left Foot* (1989). *The Crying Game* (1992) led to another hit for Miramax, garnering six Oscar nominations and one win for the studio. In 1993, Bob Weinstein founded Dimension Films, a studio for genre films, such as *Scream* (1996) and *Spy Kids* (2001). *The Piano* (1993) was the next hit for Miramax, with three Academy Award wins and Cannes' Palme d'Or. In 1993, Disney purchased Miramax for $65 million, but left the Weinsteins in control of projects under $12 million. When the Motion Picture Association of America's Ratings Board handed down an X rating to the film *Tie Me Up! Tie Me Down!* (1990), the Weinsteins sued, which led the board to create the NC-17 rating for films featuring adult content that was not pornographic in nature. Miramax continued to rack up hits with *Pulp Fiction* (1994), *Il Postino* (1994), *Trainspotting* (1996), *The English Patient* (1996), *Good Will Hunting* (1997), and *Shakespeare in Love* (1998), among many other titles. In all, Miramax projects received 243 Academy Awards nominations and the studio enjoyed 57 wins before Disney took full control of the company and its film library in 2005. The Weinsteins still retained control of Dimension Films, and launched a new venture called the Weinstein Co.

[Adam Wills (2nd ed.)]

WEINSTEIN, JACK B. (1921–), U.S. federal judge. Born in Wichita, Kansas, Weinstein graduated from Brooklyn College of the City University of New York in 1943 and served as an officer in the U.S. Navy during World War II. He received his law degree from Columbia University in 1948. In 1949 and 1950 he served as law clerk to Judge Stanley H. Fuld of the New York Court of Appeals. In 1953 Weinstein entered private practice and began teaching at Columbia Law School, where he continued to teach until 1998. From 1956 to 1967 he was County Attorney of Nassau County, New York.

Weinstein served as special counsel to the New York Joint Legislative Committee on Motor Vehicle Problems, and as counsel to New York State Senator Seymour Halpern. He was secretary of the Nassau County Board of Ethics, and he served as consultant and reporter for the New York Temporary Commission on Courts in 1966. In 1967 he served as adviser to the New York State Constitutional Convention.

That same year he was appointed by President Lyndon Johnson as a federal judge in the Eastern District of New York. Weinstein served as chief judge of the Eastern District from 1980 to 1988, becoming senior judge in 1993. He ruled on many high-profile mass tort cases, including those involving asbestos, Agent Orange, tobacco, and handguns, and the 1999 case of *Hamilton v. Accu-Tek*, in which damages were awarded based on negligent marketing. He is considered to have had a significant influence on the law of mass tort litigation. The *New York Times* called Weinstein the "quintessential activist judge."

Judge Weinstein was considered an authority on a wide range of issues, including procedure, legal ethics, judicial administration, and the role of science in the courts. He was the author of numerous articles for law reviews, and his works include widely cited treatises and casebooks on New York civil procedure and federal evidence rules, including *Reform of Federal Court Rule Making Procedures* (1976), *Basic Problems of State and Federal Evidence* (1976), *Mass Torts: Cases and Materials* (1994), and *Individual Justice in Mass Tort Litigations* (1995).

A member of the New York State Bar Association, Judge Weinstein was the recipient of numerous awards and honors, including the Judicial Recognition Award of the National Association of Defense Lawyers, the Edward J. Devitt Distinguished Service to Justice Award, the Columbia Law School Excellence Award, the Honorable William J. Brennan Award of the New York State Association of Criminal Defense Lawyers, and the *National Law Journal*'s Lawyer of the Year Award.

[Dorothy Bauhoff (2nd ed.)]

WEINSTEIN, JACOB (1902–1974), Reform rabbi. Born in Stephin, Russia, he immigrated to the United States at the age of seven with his family to Portland, Oregon, where he became a protégé of Charles E. Wood, the city's most prominent civil liberties and labor lawyer, whose clients included Jewish anarchist Emma *Goldman.

He went to Reed College in Oregon and then the Hebrew Union College, where he was ordained in 1929.

He was rabbi of Congregation Beth Israel in Austin, Texas, from 1929 to 1930. A year later he moved to San Francisco, where he was rabbi of Congregation Shearith Israel. He became involved in the Mooney Billings case, defending striking longshoremen, as well as urging higher wages for department store employees to a congregation that included the owners of these stores. His career in San Francisco did not last for long. He went to New York for three years and then returned to San Francisco, not as a congregational rabbi but as director of the School for Jewish Studies in San Francisco from 1935 to 1939.

Jacob Weinstein became rabbi of KAM in Chicago, Illinois, in 1939 and served there until 1967. He was a leading spokesman for Judaism's mission of social action in American society. A fervent opponent of racism, he helped integrate the Hyde Park neighborhood as a paradigm of solidarity and cooperation. He nudged the labor movement in the United States and in Israel toward egalitarian and humanitarian goals. He influenced such politically well-known Chicago figures as Arthur J. Goldberg and Abner Mikva, as well as Democratic presidential candidate (in 1952 and 1956) Adlai Stevenson and a host of younger rabbis and lay leaders in the Chicago and national communities.

During the years of World War II, Rabbi Weinstein served as public member of the Chicago area War Labor Board, which arbitrated a crushing load of contract disputes between workers and their employers. This experience led to subsequent arbitration assignments in the labor relations field. He served on the Public Review Board of the United Auto Workers, established by legendary Labor leader Walter Reuther in 1957 to mediate and adjudicate disputes within the union. Among his colleagues on that board were Msgr. George Higgins, chair of the Catholic Conference on Social Research; Prof. Frank McCulloch, formerly head of the Labor Education Division at Roosevelt University, and Dr. Robin Flemming, labor arbitrator and president of the University of Michigan.

He was president of the Chicago Board of Rabbis from 1947 to 1949, during the time in which the post-war transformation of the Jewish community was taking root and when the State of Israel was established. He was president of the Hyde Park Council of Churches and Synagogues from 1948 to 1950. Admired by his colleagues, nationally as well as locally, he was president of the Central Conference of American Rabbis, from 1965 to 1969. An ardent laborite and Zionist, he was President of the National Committee for Labor Israel in 1974. President John F. Kennedy, under the influence of Secretary of Labor Arthur J. Goldberg, appointed him to the President's Commission on Equal Employment Opportunity. He also served on the Business Ethics Advisory Committee to the secretary of commerce.

He is the author of *A Rabbi's Rabbi: The Life of Solomon Goldman*, his Conservative Colleague in Chicago, a tribute to their friendship and to his scholarship. An avid letter writer, he was both a serious pastor, writing to congregants in the army or after losses and at milestone occasions, and a significant and courageous, liberal political and religious leader.

BIBLIOGRAPHY: J. Feldstein, *Rabbi Jacob J. Weinstein: Advocate of the People* (1980).

[Michael Berenbaum (2nd ed.)]

WEINSTEIN, LEWIS H. (1905–1996), U.S. attorney and communal leader. Weinstein, born in Arany, Lithuania, was taken to the United States as an infant and grew up in Portland, Maine. He received his law degree from Harvard Law School in 1930. He was admitted to the Massachusetts bar and practiced law. During World War II he served in the army, in 1944 on General Eisenhower's staff as liaison to General Charles de Gaulle, and in 1945 as a lieutenant colonel and chief of the liaison section in the European Theater of Operation. He was among the Allied troops that took part in the liberation of the concentration camp prisoners at the end of the Holocaust. Weinstein returned to a Boston law practice and was active in local, state, and national bar associations.

Among his many interests was housing; he served as counsel for urban renewal agencies and on city, state, and federal housing agencies, and taught city planning at Massachusetts Institute of Technology and law at Harvard and other professional institutions. His wide-ranging interest in Jewish life led to his service as chairman of four national Jewish agencies: the Council of Jewish Federations and Welfare Funds (1965–66); the National Community Relations Advisory Council (1960–64); the American Jewish Conference on Soviet Jewry, which he helped found and which he served as cochairman from its inception and from 1968 as chairman; and the Conference of Presidents of Major American Jewish Organizations (1963–65). He also served a number of local, state, and national organizations, including the Temple Mishkan Tefila board, Boston's Hebrew College (president, 1946–53), and the Combined Jewish Philanthropies of Greater Boston as president and general campaign chairman.

At Harvard's Center for Jewish Studies, Weinstein established the annual Selma and Lewis Weinstein Prize in Jewish Studies, awarded to the best undergraduate essay in Jewish studies. Weinstein's autobiography *Masa: Odyssey of an American Jew,* which chronicles his journey from the shtetl to Harvard Law School, was published in 1989. His book *My Life at the Bar: Lawyer, Soldier, Teacher, and Pro Bono Activist* appeared in 1993.

WEINSTOCK, SIR ARNOLD, BARON (1924–2002), British industrialist. Born in London, the son of a tailor, Weinstock studied statistics before becoming a junior administrative officer in the Admiralty in 1944. He left government service in 1947 to engage in finance and real estate development, and in 1952 became the managing director of Radio and Allied Industries. In 1949 he married the daughter of Martin (later Sir Martin) Sobell, the head of the General Electric Company (GEC). He became a director of GEC in 1961 and served as its managing director from 1963 to 1996. Under his direction, after many economies in production and management, GEC quadrupled its earnings. In 1967 Weinstock won a prolonged, bitter battle for control over Associated Electrical Industries. GEC and AEI were merged into General Electric Ltd., which thus became the biggest telecommunications and electronics combine in Britain. In 1970 he received a knighthood for his contribution to the expansion of his country's exports. He was then invited by the British Government to head a new company responsible for the development of Britain's domestic nuclear power, in which GEC holds a 50% interest. He was described as "the ablest young industrialist in England" and became one of the most successful British industrialist of his time. He was given a life peerage in 1980.

BIBLIOGRAPHY: *Fortune* (1967), 61–62; *Business Week* (Aug. 24, 1968), 70–72. **ADD. BIBLIOGRAPHY:** S. Aris, *Arnold Weinstock and the Making of GEC* (1998).

[Morton Mayer Berman]

WEINSTOCK, HARRIS (1854–1922), U.S. businessman and communal leader. Weinstock, who was born in London, emigrated to the U.S. and settled in California in 1869. Entering business with his half brother David Lubin in Sacramento and San Francisco, he established the Weinstock, Lubin Company in 1888, which became known for its one-price policy and enlightened employee relations. In 1908 Weinstock established an automobile supply business in San Francisco, and was also vice president of the Weinstock-Lubin Real Estate Company. Weinstock's interest in labor relations and in civic government brought him invitations to participate in numerous civic activities. He was a member of the Board of Trustees of the State Library, the Board of Freeholders of the State Board of Horticulture, the Executive Board of the National Civic Federation, and others. In 1908 he was appointed by Governor Gillet to investigate labor conditions throughout the world, publishing his conclusions in *Strikes and Lock-Outs* (1911). President Wilson appointed him to the Industrial Relations Commission in 1913, and he also served on the Industrial Accident Commission at the invitation of Governor Hiram Johnson, a close friend. In 1915 he was appointed State Market Director. Weinstock, who was active in the California Progressive movement, was often called upon to mediate strikes. With David Lubin he was an influential supporter of cooperative marketing and agriculture reform.

Deeply interested in Jewish life, Weinstock served for a number of years as president of his congregation in Sacramento, where on occasion he conducted the service and delivered the sermon. He was author of a number of articles on Judaica, including religious and economic essays entitled *Jesus the Jew and Other Addresses* (1902). During World War I Weinstock led fund raising for the American Jewish Relief Committee.

[Max Vorspan]

WEINSTOCK, HERBERT (1905–1971), U.S. writer and musicologist. Weinstock was born in Milwaukee and attended the University of Chicago. He became a music editor at the New York publishing firm of Alfred A. Knopf (1943–59 and

1963–71). Weinstock was also a prolific writer and published books on *Tchaikovsky* (1943), *Handel* (1946), *Chopin* (1949), and *Music as an Art* (1953). However, most of his writings were more especially on operatic subjects, including *The Opera: a History of its Creation and Performance, 1600–1941* (New York, 1941; 1962² as *The World of Opera*); *Donizetti and the World of Opera in Italy, Paris and Vienna in the First Half of the Nineteenth Century* (1963), as well as his later works dedicated to the biographies of *Rossini* (1968) and *Bellini* (1971). From 1966 he was also New York correspondent for the British journal *Opera*.

[Max Loppert / Amnon Shiloah (2nd ed.)]

WEINTRAUB, SOLOMON (1781–1829), Polish cantor; also known as Solomon Kashtan, after his native town in Volhynia. He was cantor in Dubno, but often traveled from town to town giving performances, and was noted for his fervor and singular coloratura. He was the first cantor to leave written compositions, and he created an Eastern European style. Most of his works remained in manuscript (Hebrew Union College, Cincinnati), but a selection was edited and published in modern form by his son, ZEVI HIRSCH ALTER WEINTRAUB (1811–1882). The latter succeeded him as cantor in Dubno (1830–35), and was cantor in Koenigsberg (1838–80). He made his father's work part three of his *Schire Beth Adonai oder Tempelgesaenge* ... (3 pts., Leipzig, 1860; 1955³).

BIBLIOGRAPHY: Idelsohn, Music, 266–9; H. Harris, *Toledot ha-Neginah ve-ha-Ḥazzanut be-Yisrael* (1950), 395–6, 408–10; Sendrey, Music, index; Z.H.A. Weintraub, in: *Ha-Maggid* (April 7, 1875).

[Ernst Daniel Goldschmidt]

WEINZWEIG, HELEN (**Tenenbaum**; 1915–), Canadian author. Weinzweig was born in Poland and immigrated to Canada at the age of nine with her divorced mother. She did not know her father until she was an adult. Weinzweig grew up in the Jewish immigrant district of Toronto and deliberately abandoned her native Polish and Yiddish languages. In Toronto, she attended school for the first time. Her mother remained a single parent and was sole provider at a time when women rarely found themselves in such circumstances. Weinzweig's story "My Mother's Luck," included in her short story collection and adapted as a one-act play, records the difficult life and dynamic character of her mother.

During adolescence, Weinzweig spent two years at a sanatorium while recuperating from tuberculosis. It was during this period that she developed the love of reading that continued throughout her life. After completing high school, Weinzweig was forced by the Depression to work successively as a stenographer, receptionist, and salesperson. She married the composer John *Weinzweig in 1940 and they had two sons.

Weinzweig's first novel, *Passing Ceremony* (1973), published when she was 58, is highly experimental in form and presents a somber, ironic picture of the ritual of marriage, the "passing ceremony" of its title. As an expressionistic work, *Passing Ceremony* employs strategies from other genres – film, painting, and music – to bring meaning and unity to an otherwise senseless marriage between a homosexual and a promiscuous woman. Weinzweig's narrative style blends the surreal and the gothic and communicates her belief in the paradox that tragedy always lurks beneath the comfortable and conventional surface of everyday life.

Basic Black with Pearls (1980), Weinzweig's second novel and winner of the City of Toronto Book Award, is an ingenious work of puzzles that also exposes the vacuousness of traditional marriage. Written as a highly subjective interior monologue, its protagonist is the respectable Shirley Kaszenbowski, née Silverberg, alias Lola Montez, a middle-class, middle-aged, married woman in a basic black dress and pearls who travels the world to meet her elusive lover, Coenraad, an alleged spy for an unidentified "Agency." Shirley's chameleon-like transformations imply that all behavior is mere acting, and Weinzweig's innovative use of the mask motif heightens the interplay of reality and illusion that is at the heart of this novel.

A View from the Roof (1989) is a collection of thirteen short stories whose range of themes and styles evoke Weinzweig's novels. The short story "The Sea at Bar" appeared in the journal *Parchment* (vol. 2, 1993–94).

[Ruth Panofsky (2nd ed.)]

WEINZWEIG, JOHN (**Jacob**; 1913–2006), Canadian composer and teacher. Born in Toronto to Polish immigrant parents, Weinzweig first studied music at the Workman's Circle Peretz School, at Toronto high schools, and privately. In 1934–37 he studied with Healey Willan at the University of Toronto, where he founded and conducted the University of Toronto Symphony Orchestra. At the invitation of Howard Hanson, he completed a M.Mus. (1938) in composition at the Eastman School of Music. Weinzweig's *Suite for Piano* (1939) contains Canada's first 12-tone writing.

Except for a 1943–45 stint in the RCAF, Weinzweig taught at the Toronto Conservatory from 1938 to 1960. Having composed music for four National Film Board movies (1941–45) and for about 100 CBC Radio dramas (1941–51), he taught composition and orchestration at the University of Toronto in 1952–78. Among his many renowned students were Murray Adaskin, Harry Freedman, Srul Irving Glick, and Brian Cherney.

Among his concert works are Divertimento No. 1 (1946) for flute and orchestra, which won the Silver Medal at the 1948 Arts Olympiad; the Cello Sonata "Israel" (1949); *Dance of the Massadah* (1951) for baritone and piano, based on Yiẓḥak *Lamdan poems and commissioned by the Canadian Jewish Congress; *Am Yisrael Chai!* (1952) for chorus, based on Weinzweig's translation of Malke *Lee's text; *Wine of Peace* (1957) for soprano and orchestra, dedicated to "the United Nations, where the dreams of mankind for peace on earth become a reality"; *Dummiyah/Silence* (1969) for orchestra, which he described as a reaction to the horrors of the Holocaust; and the choral "Prisoner of Conscience" (1986) dedicated to Amnesty International.

Weinzweig played a central role in founding both the Canadian League of Composers (1951) and the Canadian Music Centre (1959). In 1967, he was awarded the B'nai Israel Beth David Synagogue Scroll of Honour for outstanding contributions to Canadian culture. Other accolades include honorary doctorates from the Universities of Ottawa (1969) and Toronto (1982), an appointment as Officer of the Order of Canada (1974) and Member of the Order of Ontario (1988). A recipient of the Canadian Music Council Medal in 1978, Weinzweig was designated "President Emeritus" by the Canadian League of Composers in 1981. He is also the first composer to receive the Canada Council's Molson Prize (1981) and the Roy Thomson Hall Award (1991). Subsequently Weinzweig received the Toronto Arts Award for Music (1998) and the SOCAN (Society of Composers, Authors and Music Publishers) Lifetime Achievement Award (2004). He married the fiction writer Helen *Weinzweig.

BIBLIOGRAPHY: E. Keillor, E. *John Weinzweig and His Music: The Radical Romantic of Canada* (1994).

[Jay Rahn (2nd ed.)]

WEISBERGER, BERNARD ALLEN (1922–), U.S. historian. Born in New York, Weisberger taught at several universities before being appointed adjunct professor of history at New York University. Weisberger won many awards and wrote books in a popular style supported by careful research and profound thought. He was a member of the National Hillel Commission and a dedicated participant in the civil rights movement. After teaching at such universities as Wayne State, the University of Chicago, and the University of Rochester, he gave up the classroom and dedicated his time to writing. He was a contributing editor for *American Heritage*, where he wrote a column entitled "In the News" for more than 10 years.

Among his many books are *They Gathered at the River* (1958), a provocative study of Protestant revivalism; *The New Industrial Society* (1969); *The American Heritage History of the American People* (1971); *Pathways to the Present* (1976); *The Impact of Our Past* (1976); *Reaching for Empire* (1980); *From Sea to Shining Sea* (1981); *The Statue of Liberty* (1985); *Many People, One Nation* (1987); *The La Follettes of Wisconsin* (1994); and *America Afire* (2000).

[Ruth Beloff (2nd ed.)]

WEISENBURG, THEODORE H. (1876–1934), U.S. physician. Weisenburg was born in New York City and, having suffered from a nervous disorder as a child, he determined to devote himself to the field of neurosurgery. In 1908 be was chairman of the American Medical Association's section on nervous and mental disorders.

Weisenburg taught at the University of Pennsylvania (1904–07) and at the Medico-Chirurgical College in Philadelphia. After the college became a part of the university, he became a professor of neurology (1918) and in 1920 a vice dean of the college. He became particularly noted as a pioneer in the use of moving pictures for the study of patients with nervous and mental disorders.

From 1905, Weisenburg was an active member of the American Neurological Association and became its president in 1918. In 1919 he became editor of *Transactions*, the association's journal. Weisenburg also edited the *Archives of Neurology and Psychiatry* from 1920 until his death.

With the aid of a grant from the Commonwealth Fund of New York City, Weisenburg embarked on a planned program of research, which included adult intelligence tests. In 1933–34 he was made president of the Association for Research in Nervous and Mental Diseases. He was also a member of the Examining Board for Certification of Specialists in Neurology and Psychiatry. His books *Aphasia* (1935) and *Adult Intelligence* (1936) were published posthumously.

WEISER-VARON, BENNO (1913–), journalist, author, diplomat, and university lecturer. Born in Czernovitz (Austro-Hungarian Empire), after the outbreak of World War I he moved with his family to Vienna. In 1938 he had almost completed medical studies. As a student he was active together with Teddy *Kollek and Ehud *Avriel in diverse Zionist student organizations.

After the annexation of Austria to the Third Reich, he left in autumn 1938 for Ecuador via Amsterdam and settled in Quito, where he succeeded in obtaining visas for his family and his fiancée. As one of the only European refugees to be proficient in Spanish, he was hired in April 1940 by the leading newspaper of Quito, *El Comercio*, to cover the events in Europe, on which he had a daily column, "El Mirador del Mundo" ("Observer of the World").

In 1945 he attended the first Latin American Zionist Congress in Montevideo and established close ties with leading Zionist activists in Latin America – among others Moshe Toff (later Tov). As a newspaperman he met for an interview in Buenos Aires Juan D. Peron, at that time Argentina's vice president. In spring 1946 he established, at the request of Nachum Goldmann, a regional agency for the Jewish Agency in Bogota. In June 1947 he was called to New York as acting director (for Tov), and later director, of the Latin American Department of the Jewish Agency. His main mission was to create and maintain Latin America's support at the UN for the Zionist cause and later for the State of Israel. Weiser succeeded in securing Ecuador's crucial vote, on November 29, 1947, at the special session of the UN General Assembly, in favor of the UNSCOP partition plan for Palestine, the decision for the establishment of a Jewish state.

In 1957, as ambassador of the State of Israel, he represented the country at the inauguration of Luis Somoza Debayle as president of Nicaragua. In 1960 he was asked to take over the Israel-Iberoamerican Institute of Cultural Relations in Jerusalem and moved with his family to Israel. He reported on the Eichmann trial for several newspapers. In 1964 Weiser was appointed the first ambassador of Israel to the Dominican Republic and adopted, on the advice of Prof. Efraim E. Urbach, the name Varon, and in 1966 he was also named nonresident ambassador to Jamaica. As a result of the Six-Day War of 1967, Weiser was asked to proceed to New York to join the Israeli delegation to the UN, headed by Abba Eban. When Paraguay was elected to the UN Security Council for 1968–69, Weiser was appointed as the first Israeli ambassador to Paraguay. On May 4, 1970, the embassy offices in Asunción were invaded by two Palestinians intent on killing the Israeli ambassador. After shooting Edna Peer dead and wounding Diana Zawluk with five bullets (she survived), the invaders had no bullets left for the ambassador. Weiser-Varon terminated his diplomatic activities for the State of Israel in 1972.

In 1973 he moved to Boston and wrote articles for publications such as *Commentary, Midstream*, the *New York Times*, and the *Boston Globe*. In 1986 he joined the department for Jewish Studies at Boston University, retiring in 2001.

Among his writings are *El Mirador del Mundo* (1941), *Yo era Europeo* (1942), *Visitenkarte* (1957), and *Professions of a Lucky Jew* (1992).

[Gabriel E. Alexander (2nd ed.)]

WEISGAL, ABBA JOSEPH (1885–1981), *ḥazzan*. Weisgal was born in Poland where his father, the local *ḥazzan*, was his first teacher. After serving as *ḥazzan* in Ivancice, Czechoslovakia, he emigrated to the United States in 1920 and became *ḥazzan* of the Chizuk Amuno congregation of Baltimore, Maryland, officiating for more than 50 years. Joseph Levin, a *ḥazzan* and musician, wrote a work entitled *Emunah Abba* about Weisgal's compositions and published it together with those compositions in a volume called *Shirei Ḥayyim ve-Emunah* (1982). Weisgal was the brother of Meyer *Weisgal and the father of Hugo *Weisgal.

[Akiva Zimmerman (2nd ed.)]

WEISGAL, MEYER WOLF (1894–1977), Zionist. Born in Kikol (near Lipno), Poland. Weisgal emigrated to the U.S. in 1905. From 1921 to 1938 he served as national secretary of the Zionist Organization of America, and became Chaim *Weizmann's personal political representative in the U.S. In 1940 he participated in the establishment of the U.S. section of the Jewish Agency for Palestine, serving as its secretary general until 1946. He was appointed organizing secretary of the *American Jewish Conference in 1943. In 1944 Weisgal began his dynamic public relations activities on behalf of the *Weizmann Institute of Science. He established his residence in Israel in 1949 on the campus of the Institute at Reḥovot and took over the management of its affairs as chairman of the Executive Council. He served as president from 1966 to 1969 and then as chancellor. Weisgal was closely connected with the arts in the U.S. and Israel. He edited several newspapers and books of Jewish interest (*The Maccabean*, 1918–21, and *New Palestine*, 1921–30), and produced a number of plays, including Franz Werfel's *The Eternal Road*, directed by Max Reinhardt in 1937 in the U.S. He edited the book *Theodor Herzl, a Memorial* (1929), and two books on Weizmann: *Chaim Weizmann: Statesman, Scientist, Builder of the Jewish Commonwealth* (1944), and *Chaim Weizmann: A Biography by Several Hands* (1963^2). Weisgal's autobiography, ... *So Far*, was published in 1971 and the Hebrew translation, *Ad Kan*, in 1972. He was buried on the grounds of the Weizmann Institute.

BIBLIOGRAPHY: E. Victor (ed.), *Meyer Weisgal at Seventy: an Anthology* (1966).

[Rinna Samuel]

WEISGALL, HUGO (1912–1997), composer, conductor, and teacher. Born in Ivancice, Czechoslovakia, Weisgall emigrated to the United States in 1920. He conducted orchestras in Baltimore and was active in Jewish musical life, directing the Har Sinai Temple Choir (1931–42) and the Youth Alliance Orchestra (1935–42). From 1946 to 1947 he was a cultural attaché at the U.S. embassy in Prague. Weisgall also taught in New York City at the Juilliard School of Music (1956–60) and at Queen's College (1960–1983), and from 1952 was faculty chairman of the cantors' institute of the Jewish Theological Seminary of America. He was a nephew of Meyer *Weisgal.

His compositions include operas, such as *Six Characters in Search of an Author* (1956), *Athaliah* (1964), and *Nine Rivers from Jordan* (1968), as well as ballets, and choral and orchestral works.

BIBLIOGRAPHY: Baker, Biog Dict, incl. bibl.; MGG, incl. bibl.

WEISS, ABRAHAM (1895–1970), East European talmudic scholar and Zionist. Weiss was born in Podhajce, eastern Galicia. He completed his studies in history and classical philology at the University of Vienna in 1921 and received ordination at the Vienna Rabbinical Seminary in 1922. He taught Talmud and rabbinics at the Institute for Jewish Science in Warsaw (1928–1940) and at Yeshiva University in New York 1940–1967. In 1967 he settled in Israel, lecturing at Bar-Ilan University. From 1935 to 1940 Weiss was vice president of the Mizrachi Organization in Poland; he was also active in the World Zionist Organization for many years. Weiss was noted for his pioneering talmudic research, embodied in several articles dealing with the complete range of tannaitic, amoraic, and early gaonic literature. Most noteworthy for his examination of the Talmud's history and development are *Hithavvut ha-Talmud bi-Shelemuto* (1943), *Le-Ḥeker ha-Talmud* (1954), and *Al ha-Yeẓirah ha-Sifrutit shel ha-Amora'im* (1962). The application of scientific methodology to the clarification of talmudic law and literature and his resultant conclusions are best exemplified in *Seder ha-Diyyun; Meḥkarim be-Mishpat ha-Talmud* (1957), and *Diyyunim u-Verurim be-Bava Kamma* (1966). His views on the Mishnah's composition and structure are given in *Le-Ḥeker ha-Sifruti shel ha-Mishnah* (HUCA, 16 (1941), 1–33, Heb. sect.). His findings on the Babylonian Talmud's evolvement and the saboraic and early gaonic activities opened many new avenues in talmudic jurisprudence and historiography.

BIBLIOGRAPHY: *Abraham Weiss Jubilee Volume* (1964), 1–80 (Eng. sec.), 1–72 (Heb. sec.). incl. bibl.

[Meyer S. Feldblum]

WEISS, ALBERT PAUL (1879–1931), psychologist and social philosopher, Weiss, who was born in Steingrund, Germany, went to the U.S. as a child. He spent most of his teaching and research career at Ohio State University. He was one of an important group in the U.S. who demanded an objective and natural science approach to all behavior, including human. Weiss held a reductionist view that psychology is a sector of biology, and biology ultimately a sector of physics, but he also especially emphasized the key role of social factors in determining human behavior. Terms such as "biosocial behavior" and "social status" were used by Weiss to describe the human being as a social reactor in a social context without compromising his belief in the physical nature of man, as well as of man's environment. Thus, even in his treatment of human learning and processes of behavior modification, Weiss dwelt more on social variables than on neurophysiological ones. Weiss sought to realize a mission for scientific psychology in practical human affairs, the goal being to achieve greater human welfare in a stable, rational, and peaceful society under the guidance of "behavioristic ethics." Weiss' major works include: *A Theoretical Basis of Human Behavior* (1925); and "Feeling and Emotion as Forms of Behavior," in: *1st International Symposium on Feelings and Emotions, 1927* (Wittenberg, 1928).

[William N. Schoenfeld]

WEISS, AURELIU (1893–1962), Romanian literary critic. A leading Bucharest lawyer, Weiss wrote original and scholarly studies of Romanian and foreign authors collected in *Studii literare* (1922) and *Autori si păreri* ("Authors and Opinions," 1929). Weiss made his reputation, however, when he settled in Paris after World War II. His later works, many of which appeared posthumously, include *Le destin des grandes oeuvres dramatiques* (1960; Eng., 1965); *Le théatre de Luigi Pirandello dans le mouvement dramatique contemporain* (1964); and *Le monde théatral de Michel de Ghelderode* (1966).

WEISS, AVI (1944–), Orthodox Jewish activist. Avraham "Avi" Weiss was born in New York City and received his rabbinical ordination at the Rabbi Isaac Elchanan Theological Seminary (Yeshiva University) in 1968. He quickly established a reputation as an activist on behalf of Jewish communities everywhere and served for 10 years as Chairman of the Student Struggle for Soviet Jewry (SSSJ).

Through the 1980s, Weiss extended his passionate but non-violent activism to a wide range of Jewish causes. In 1985, he traveled to Bergen-Belsen to protest President Reagan's visit to the Bitburg military cemetery. In 1989, Weiss led demonstrations at the site of a Carmelite convent that had been established at Auschwitz, which, he asserted, threatened to "Christianize the memory of the Holocaust," and which had already desecrated the burial site of over a million murdered Jews. In 1991, he rose to the defense of the Lubavitch community of Crown Heights after anti-Jewish riots broke out there, accusing the mayor of New York and the city's police department of turning a blind eye and allowing the rioters to vent. He went on to found the grassroots organization AMCHA/Coalition for Jewish Concerns, of which he continues to serve as national president.

On issues pertaining to the State of Israel, Weiss was a vocal opponent of any recognition of the Palestinian Liberation Organization or of its leader, Yasir Arafat. He led numerous public demonstrations against the PLO and Arafat in front of the PLO's offices in Manhattan, and was an outspoken critic of the 1993 Oslo Accords. In 1994, he was arrested in Oslo while protesting the awarding of the Nobel Peace Prize to Arafat.

In addition, Weiss emerged as a Modern Orthodox visionary due to his position as congregational rabbi at the Hebrew Institute of Riverdale. Under Weiss' leadership, HIR quickly grew into a formidable synagogue. Weiss taught and practiced a unique inclusive philosophy, throwing open the doors of his Orthodox synagogue to the Orthodox and the non-Orthodox alike, as well as to the physically and mentally challenged. He launched innovative programs to include women in Orthodox practice, establishing a Women's Prayer and Torah Reading Service in 1974, and, in 1999, naming a *madrikhah ruḥanit* (religious mentor) at HIR, the first woman to serve an Orthodox congregation in a quasi-rabbinic role. At the same time, Weiss mentored numerous assistant rabbis and rabbinic interns at HIR, many of whom went on to assume major pulpits of their own.

In 2000 Weiss founded Yeshivat Chovevei Torah (YCT), the Modern and Open Orthodox Rabbinical Seminary. The mission of YCT is to produce rabbis who are classically trained and dedicated to strict halakhic observance, and who are open and inclusive in their construction of Orthodox communities, sensitive to the religious aspirations of women, and welcoming of Jews of all backgrounds.

Weiss is the author of two books, *Principles of Spiritual Activism* (2002), and *Women at Prayer: A Halakhic Analysis of Women's Prayer Groups* (1990).

[Yosef Kanefsky (2nd ed.)]

WEISS, ERNST (1884–1940), Austrian novelist. Born in Bruen, Weiss studied medicine and traveled to the Orient as a ship's doctor. During World War I he served as a medical officer in the Austrian army on the eastern front. After achieving some success as a playwright, he devoted himself to literature, working in Berlin and Munich. A pupil of *Freud and a friend of *Kafka, *Werfel, and *Brod, Weiss was a master of the psychological novel. His basic theme is strife between individuals – son against father, husband against wife, lover against beloved. The heroes are often physicians.

His novels include *Der Kampf* (1916), *Tiere in Ketten* (1918), *Nahar* (1922), *Georg Letham, Arzt und Moerder* (1931), and *Boëtius von Orlamuende* (1928). He also wrote a successful drama, *Tanja* (1920); *Das Versoehnungsfest* (1920), a verse collection; and several volumes of short stories. During the Third Reich, Weiss fled from Vienna to Prague, and from Prague to Paris. Two of his last novels were *Der Gefaengnisarzt oder Die Vaterlosen* (1934) and *Der Verfuehrer* (1938). When the Nazis entered Paris, the embittered and lonely writer committed suicide. *Der Augenzeuge* (1963), a posthumous novel, describes the ordeal of a Jewish physician whose ex-patient, an unbeloved World War I soldier, becomes the *Fuehrer* of the Third Reich. In 1982 an edition of selected works appeared in 16 volumes, edited by P. Engel and Volker Michels.

BIBLIOGRAPHY: W. Bedel, Sieben Dichter (1950), 102–7; F. Lennartz, Die Dichter Unserer Zeit (1952[5]), 544–6. **ADD. BIBLIOGRAPHY:** M. Wollheim, *Begegnung mit Ernst Weiß. Paris 1939–1940* (1970); U. Längle, *Ernst Weiß. Vatermythos und Zeitkritik. Die Exilromane am Beispiel des "Armen Verschwenders"* (1981); M. Versari, *Ernst Weiß. Individualität zwischen Vernunft und Irrationalismus. Ein Werk zwischen "Mythologie" und "Aufklärung"* (1984); F. Haas, *Der Dichter von der traurigen Gestalt: zu Leben und Werk von Ernst Weiß* (1986); R. Mielke, *Das Böse als Krankheit. Entwurf einer neuen Ethik im Werk von Ernst Weiß* (1986); F. Trapp, "*'Der Augenzeuge' – ein Psychogramm der deutschen Intellektuellen zwischen 1914 und 1936*" (1986); S. Adler, *Vom "Roman expérimental" zur Problematik des wissenschaftlichen Experiments. Untersuchungen zum literarischen Werk von Ernst Weiß* (1990); M. Streuter, *Das Medizinische im Werk von Ernst Weiss* (1990); P. Engel and H.-H. Müller (eds.), *Ernst Weiß. Seelenanalytiker und Erzähler von europäischem Rang*, Beiträge zum Ersten Internationalen Ernst-Weiß-Symposium aus Anlaß d. 50. Todestages, Hamburg 1990 (1992): M. Pazi, *Ernst Weiß. Schicksal und Werk eines jüdischen mitteleuropäischen Autors in der ersten Hälfte des 20. Jahrhunderts* (1993); A. Steinke, *Ontologie der Lieblosigkeit. Untersuchungen zum Verhältnis von Mann und Frau in der frühen Prosa von Ernst Weiß* (1994); K.-P. Hinze, "Ernst Weiss," in: D.G. Daviau (ed. and introd.), *Major Figures of Austrian Literature* (1995), 487–519; E. Krückeberg, "Jeder ist ein Stück Hamlet: Ernst Weiß' Roman 'Georg Letham' und der Hamlet der Dreißiger Jahre," in: H. Arntzen (ed.), *Ursprung der Gegenwart* (1995), 364–418; J. Golec, "Prag – Berlin – Paris. Ernst Weiß' Lebensstationen auf der Suche nach der Identität," in: M. Katarzyna Lasatowicz and J. Joachimsthaler (ed.), *Nationale Identität aus germanistischer Perspektive* (1998), 133–41; H.-H. Müller, "'Das Klarste ist das Gesetz. Es sagt sich nicht in Worten.' Ernst Weiß' Roman 'Die Feuerprobe'. Eine Interpretation im Kontext von Weiß' Kritik an Kafkas 'Proceß'," in: *Euphorion*, 92 (1998), 1–23; H. Berke, "Wer sagt hier 'Ich'? Zur Rollenambivalenz in 'Der Verführer' von Ernst Weiß," in: M. Godé and M. Vuillaume (eds.), *Qui parle dans le texte? Études réunies* (2000), 169–76; T. Taterka, "'Wir dürfen nicht nachlassen, solange wir atmen.' Literarische Augenzeugenschaft und Widerstandswille bei Ernst Weiß," in: F.L. Kroll (ed.), *Deutsche Autoren des Ostens als Gegner und Opfer des Nationalsozialismus*, (2000), 203–218; Y.P. Alefeld, "Macht und Ohnmacht. Zu den 'Arztromanen' von Ernst Weiß," in: M. Zybura (ed.), *Geist und Macht* (2002), 203–16.

[Sol Liptzin]

WEISS, ISAAC HIRSCH (1815–1905), scholar and writer on the history of the Oral Law. Weiss, who was born in Gross-Meseritsch (Velke Mezirici), Moravia, studied in the yeshivot of Trebitsch and Eisenstadt. He subsequently engaged in business, corresponded on halakhic topics with leading rabbis, and for a short time headed a yeshivah in his native town. In 1846 he began publishing Hebrew poems and studies on the Talmud. After losing his wealth, he migrated to Vienna and became a proofreader in a printing press. In 1864 he was appointed lecturer in talmudic literature in the Vienna Bet ha-Midrash founded by A. *Jellinek. Weiss was opposed both to the conservative spirit prevailing in the Hungarian yeshivot and to extreme Reform. His aim was to blend fundamental talmudic condition with secular culture and the critical scientific method. His moderate position aroused against him not only the anger of the rabbis of the older generation and the Orthodox, but also the criticism of the Reformers. He was opposed to the Ḥibbat Zion movement and to the idea of settling Ereẓ Israel, regarding them as dangerous since they accorded with the view of the antisemites that there was no place for Jews in Europe. In his opinion the nationhood of Jews consisted of their Torah and religion, and they must await in exile the redemption of Heaven. On the other hand he understood the importance of the Hebrew language and wrote his compositions in it.

Weiss' scholarly work was wholly devoted to the study of the Oral Law. He published two **midreshei-halakhah* with introductions and notes: the **Sifra* (1862) and the *Mekhilta* (1865), and wrote a grammar book, *Mishpat Leshon ha-Mishnah* (1867). He published many articles, some of which appeared in periodicals which he founded and edited (both *Beit ha-Midrash* (1865–66) and *Beit Talmud* (1881–86; founded jointly with M. *Friedmann)).

Weiss' largest and most important work is the five-volume *Dor Dor ve-Dorshav* (1871–91). This work, in which he described the history of the Oral Law from its beginning (before the Written Law) until after the expulsion from Spain, deals not only with the sequence of the *halakhah*, but also with the development of the *aggadah*, with the history of talmudic and rabbinic literature and with the character traits of important sages. From his critical approach to the sources, Weiss understood the development of the *halakhah* and its historical background. Into this vast amount of material Weiss brought system and order without multiplying small details. The work is distinguished by its picturesque and fluent language and by its vivid descriptions. At times, however, there are errors in his conclusions and it is also tendentious. Weiss, who belonged to the *Haskalah generation, frequently imposed his own view upon the sources and described the characters of scholars and works in accordance with his own views. Sometimes he drew general conclusions from particular points or concepts without properly examining the material. N. *Krochmal's *Moreh Nevukhei ha-Zeman* gave Weiss the impetus to write this work. He also transferred from the domain of history to that of rabbinic literature, though without justification, the view of Krochmal that a period of decline in Jewish history began from the 13th century. In its time *Dor Dor ve-Dorshav*, which was published a number of times and had a large circulation, particularly in eastern Europe, exercised great influence. However, there were also among the scholars of the older generation radical opponents who wrote works critical of it, some of them attacking Weiss personally. (The most important of his critics was Isaac *Halevy in his *Dorot ha-Rishonim*.) Despite all its faults – or perhaps just because of them – its contribution to the study of the Talmud was great. Its very composition was audacious, and nothing similar has subsequently been written. "There are things which Weiss completely demolished; and there are also things which he built permanently" (L. Ginzberg). Weiss also composed an autobiography with the title *Zikhronotai* (1895); it appeared in serial form in *Genazim* (1, 15–53 (1961)) with an introduction and notes by G. Kressel.

BIBLIOGRAPHY: S. Schechter, *Studies in Judaism*, 1 (1896), 182–212; J. Klausner, *Yoẓerim u-Vonim*, 1 (1925), 1–17; L. Ginzberg, *Students, Scholars, and Saints* (1928), 217–40; F. Lachower, *Rishonim ve-Aḥaronim*, 1 (1934), 56–60.

[Moshe David Herr]

WEISS, ISAAC JACOB (1902–1989), rabbinical scholar. Born in Dolina, Poland, Weiss studied in various yeshivot and became head of the Yeshivah of Munkacs (Mukachevo; then Czechoslovakia, now Soviet Ukraine), at the age of 20. In 1929 he was appointed *dayyan* of the important Jewish community of *Oradea.

During World War II, he and his family escaped deportation and found refuge in Romania. Returning after the war, he became the spiritual leader of what was left of the community and took a prominent part in its reconstruction. In 1949 he immigrated to Britain where he was appointed senior *dayyan* of the Manchester and Salford Jewish Community, and was soon recognized as an outstanding halakhic authority. His first halakhic work, *Divrei Yiẓḥak*, appeared in 1941. From 1955 successive volumes of his responsa (*Minhat Yiẓḥak*) began to appear, and a six-volume edition was published in Jerusalem (1973–75), including homiletic material, which also appeared in a separate volume under the same title. An appendix to the first volume of the second edition, titled *Pirsumei Nisa* (pp. 265 ff.), gives a moving description of life under the Nazi-dominated Hungarian regime and of his miraculous escape into Romania. In 1968 Weiss was appointed head of the *bet din* of the ultra-Orthodox Ashkenazi community (*Edah Ḥaredit*) of Jerusalem.

[Alexander Carlebach]

WEISS, JIŘÍ (1913–2004), Czechoslovak film director. Weiss made documentaries and won an international prize in 1934 at the Venice Biennale and the Czechoslovak Stage prize in 1937. During World War II, he made films for the exiled Czechoslovak government in London. He returned to Prague in 1945 and won the State film prize for the historical picture *Vstanou noví bojovníci* ("New Fighters Will Rise," 1951) a film on coal miners without professional actors. He also won the Critics Prize, Berlin, for *31 ve stínu* ("31 Degrees in the Shade," 1965). His best film, *Romeo, Julie a tma* (1961) was based on an anti-Nazi novel by Jan Očenášek. In 1966 he made *Razda po nazdem* ("Murder Czech Style"). After the Soviet invasion in 1968 he fled the country, returning in 1989 to make *Martha und Ich*, his first film in 23 years. In the interval he lived in the United States, teaching at Hunter College, New York, and Santa Barbara, Calif., and writing two plays and a volume of memoirs.

BIBLIOGRAPHY: R. Bergen, Obituary, in: *The Guardian* (May 27, 2004).

WEISS, JOSEPH G. (1918–1969), researcher of Ḥasidism and Jewish mysticism. Weiss was born in Budapest, Hungary, to a *Neologist family. In 1939 he immigrated to Palestine and studied medieval Jewish-Spanish literature at The Hebrew University of Jerusalem. Under the influence of Gershom *Scholem he changed his field of interest to Jewish mysticism and specialized in the doctrines of Rabbi *Naḥman of Bratslav. In 1951 he immigrated to England. He studied and taught in Oxford, Leeds, Manchester, and London, where he stayed for the rest of his life. From 1959 Weiss was the head of the Institute of Jewish Studies and, later on, also a professor at the University College London, as well as editor of the *Journal of Jewish Studies*. Throughout his life Weiss maintained a close and complex relationship with his teacher Gershom Scholem, and was considered by Scholem as one of his closest and most talented pupils. The results of Weiss' works in the field of research of Bratslav Ḥasidism and the Ḥasidic Movement in general, published in many articles, were innovative and influenced by his unique personality. He had an existential view of the figure and doctrines of Rabbi Naḥman ("*Ha-Kushya be-Torat Rabbi Naḥman*," in: *Alei Ayin* (1952)), which changed over time to psychological and mythological analysis ("*Iyyunim bi-Tefisato ha-Aẓmit shel R. Nahman*," in: *Tarbiz* (1958)). In this article he emphasized the notion that all the writings of Rabbi Naḥman, especially his stories, are actually a mythological autobiography of Rabbi Naḥman himself, and the figures mentioned in the texts are reflections of his tormented personality. Weiss' work was collected after his death in a Hebrew volume *Meḥkarim be-Ḥasidut Braslev* (1974), ed. by M. Piekarz, and in *Studies in Eastern European Jewish Mysticism* (1985, 1997), ed. by D. Goldstein.

BIBLIOGRAPHY: G. Scholem, in: JJS, 20 (1969), 25–26; H.H. Ben Sasson, in: *Zion*, 34 (1969), 261–64; J. Katz, in: A. Rapoport-Albert (ed.), *Hasidism Reappraised* (1996), 3–9; S.O. Heller Wilensky, in: *ibid.*, 10–41; J. Dan, in: *Studies in East European Jewish Mysticism and Hasidism* (1997), ix–xx

[Noam Zadoff (2nd ed.)]

WEISS, JOSEPH JOSHUA (1907–1972), British radiation chemist. Weiss was head of the chemistry department in the Textile Institute, Sorau, Germany (1928–30) and worked at the Kaiser Wilhelm Institute for Physical Chemistry, Berlin-Dahlem (1930–33) and then at University College, London (1934–39). He was professor of radiation chemistry at the University of Newcastle (1956). Weiss was an authority on chemical reactions induced by atomic radiations, particularly gamma rays.

WEISS, JOSEPH MEIR (1838–1909), Hungarian rabbi and author. Weiss was born in Munkacz (Mukachevo), where his father Samuel Ẓevi was the head of the *bet din*. He studied under his uncle Yiẓḥak Izak Weiss in the small town of Svalyava (now in the Ukraine), later at the yeshivah of Meir Eisenstadt and his son in Ungvar, and subsequently in the yeshivah of Shmelkel Klein in Nagyszőllös (Vinogradov). After his marriage he conducted a yeshivah in Brusa, Turkey. On the death of his wife he returned to his parents' home in Munkacz. After his remarriage, he stayed with his father-in-law. Weiss was an adherent of the ḥasidic rabbi Isaac Izak Eichenstein of Zydaczow (Galicia), whom he considered to be his teacher in *Kabbalah, and with whom he stayed for a time. After Eichenstein's death many of his Ḥasidim regarded Weiss as his successor and began to attend upon him frequently in great numbers. He also visited Ḥayyim Halberstam, the ḥasidic rabbi of Zanz, whose authority he accepted. He became the founder of the ḥasidic dynasty of *Spinka, which combines the characteristics of those of Zydaczow and Zanz. Many legends and remarkable stories circulated about him, some of which are given in the *Pe'er Yosef*, and he was the author of *Imrei Yosef*, a work on the Pentateuch. He also published *Likkutei Torah ve-ha-Shas* of his teacher and uncle, Yiẓḥak Izak of Zydaczow.

BIBLIOGRAPHY: J. Weiss, *Turei Yosef*, 1 (1910), introd.; A. Feuer, *Zikhron Avraham* (1924); A.S. Weiss, *Pe'er Yosef* (1934); *Ḥasidut Spinka ve-Admoreha* (1958); J.L. Levin, *Beit Spinka* (1958); A. Stern, *Meliẓei Esh*, 1 (1962), 206, no. 120.

[Samuel Weingarten-Hakohen]

WEISS, MANFRÉD (1857–1922), industrialist and a pioneer of industry in Hungary. Born in Pest, Weiss founded, together with his brother Berthold, the first canning factory in Hungary, which was later enlarged and converted into the armaments factory at Csepel, a suburb of Budapest. The latter enterprise was capable of supplying all the armaments of the Hapsburg Empire in the event of war, and during World War I, 30,000 workers were employed in it. After Hungary's defeat in World War I, Weiss began to manufacture household appliances, agricultural machines, and motorcars. He was the founder of the national union of Hungarian industrialists (GYOSZ) and was also involved in Jewish public life, founding several charitable institutions, among them a Jewish maternity home (named after his wife), and a hospital for chronic diseases. He also fostered such Jewish public activities as the national council for the preparation of a united Jewish autonomy (1912), which included both *Neologist and Orthodox members.

BIBLIOGRAPHY: *Egyenlöség*, no. 52 (1922), 21–3; J. Dálnoki Kováts, *Ipari öntudatunk ébresztöi és munkálói* (1943), 250–2.

[Jeno Zsoldos]

WEISS, MEIR (1902–1998), Bible scholar. Born in Budapest, he became a rabbi and received a doctorate from the Royal Science University of Hungary in Semitic linguistics, history of the Ancient Near East, and Roman history. He immigrated to Israel in 1945 and worked as a teacher and principal in various schools. From 1957 he lectured in Bible at Bar-Ilan University and from 1960 at The Hebrew University, where he became a professor in 1972. He was a pioneer among modern biblicists in his holistic appreciation of each book for its own sake; he published collections of articles and a commentary on Job. In 1990 he received the Israel Prize for Jewish studies. Among his writings are *Ha-Mikra ki-Demuto* (1967, 1987); *The Story of Job's Beginning* (1983); *Mikra'ot ke-Havanatam* (collected essays; 1987); *Sefer Amos* (1992); *Emunot ve-De'ot be-Mizmorei Tehillim* (2001).

[Fern Lee Seckbach]

WEISS, MELVYN I. (1935–), U.S. lawyer. Born in the Bronx, N.Y., and educated at City College's Baruch School and New York University Law School, Melvyn Irwin Weiss practiced law in New York while building his firm, Milberg Weiss Bershad Hynes & Lerach, into the country's premier securities class-action law firm. Its lawyers became corporate America's most aggressive and nettlesome private legal adversaries. Weiss embodied one of Wall Street's worst nightmares: the shareholder lawsuit. He was one of the first to test a 1966 law that permitted them, and he became dean of the practice. Along the way, he forced Wall Street to be more accountable to investors. He won nearly $30 billion from more than 1,000 companies, including Prudential and Drexel Burnham Lambert as well as Charles Keating's failed savings and loan empire. His later targets included several public investment banks and Enron, the energy company that bilked states and others with false companies. Weiss also earned the enmity of the accounting profession for his long-standing accusations of laxity in corporate oversight, and accompanying lawsuits. After working together for nearly three decades Weiss and one of his partners, William S. Lerach, parted bitterly as both came under investigation by Federal prosecutors. Weiss was honored many times, and his awards included the Anti-Defamation League humanitarian award, the United Jewish Appeal's Proskauer award, and the B'nai B'rith of Argentina Dignity and Justice Award. He served as a director and member of the executive committee of the Israel Policy Forum and the American Jewish Congress.

[Stewart Kampel (2nd ed.)]

WEISS, PAUL (1901–2002), U.S. philosopher. Weiss was born in New York and studied under Morris Raphael *Cohen. He received his Ph.D. from Harvard University in 1929, where he studied with philosopher Alfred North Whitehead. He lectured for a year at Harvard and Radcliffe and then taught at Bryn Mawr. Weiss began as a logician and later went into metaphysics, art, and aesthetics. In 1946 he was the first Jew to be appointed to the faculty of the undergraduate college at Yale, and from 1963 he was professor until he retired in 1969 as professor emeritus. In 1947 he founded the Metaphysical Society of America and its academic journal *The Review of Metaphysics*, which he edited until 1964. Through his teaching and writing Weiss was influential in the revival of interest in metaphysics in the United States and played an important role in the Peirce Society and the Metaphysical Society of America. Together with Charles Hartshorne he edited *The Collected Papers of C.S. Peirce*. He was active in Jewish affairs.

After his retirement from Yale, Weiss began to challenge the issue of age discrimination. He was offered a chair at Fordham University, but it was later revoked because he was too old (69). Weiss sued the university in 1971 for age discrimination but lost the controversial $1 million suit. Again, after having taught for many years as the Heffer Visiting Professor of Philosophy of Catholic University in Washington, he discovered that the university's refusal to renew his contract was due to his advanced age. After an official inquiry into the matter by the Equal Opportunity Commission, the university reinstated him for two more years, after which he retired. Weiss was elected to the Library of Living Philosophers, which published *The Philosophy of Paul Weiss* in 1995 as part of a series of volumes devoted to influential philosophers.

The man who staunchly fought against age discrimination lived to be 101.

Weiss's major works include *Reality* (1938); *Nature and Man* (1947); *Man's Freedom* (1950); *Modes of Being* (1958); *Nine Basic Arts*; and *The World of Art* (both 1961); *Religion and Art* (1964); *The God We Seek* (1964); *Making of Men* (1967); *First Considerations* (1977); *You, I, and the Others* (1980); *Privacy* (1983); *Toward a Perfected State* (1986); *Being and Other Realities* (1995); *Emphatics* (2000); and *Surrogates* (2002).

BIBLIOGRAPHY: I. Lieb (ed.), *Experience, Existence, and the Good: Essays in Honor of Paul Weiss* (1961); T. Krettek (ed.), *Creativity and Common Sense: Essays in Honor of Paul Weiss* (1987).

[Richard H. Popkin / Ruth Beloff (2nd ed.)]

WEISS, PETER (1916–1982), German playwright and author. A half-Jew, Weiss, who was born near Berlin, left Germany in 1934, spending two years in England and two more in Prague, before settling in Sweden in 1939. There he made his career as a painter, film producer, and writer. At first he wrote stories such as *Der Schatten des Koerpers des Kutschers* (1960) and *Abschied von den Eltern* (1961; *Leavetaking*, 1966), but broadened his scope in the novel, *Fluchtpunkt* (1962; *Vanishing Point*, 1966; together with *Leavetaking* as *Exile*, 1968). This last is an autobiographical work of passionate intensity covering the career and successive exiles of the hero from the age of 18 until his 30th year. The book reveals the young art student's rebellion against middle-class conformity, and the anguish of a Jewish manufacturer's son who, on his mother's side, belongs to the nation of the persecutor. As a dramatist, Weiss gained international fame with his play, *Die Verfolgung und Ermordung Jean Paul Marats …* (1964; *The Persecution and Assassination of Jean-Paul Marat as Performed by the Inmates of the Asylum of Charenton under the Direction of the Marquis de Sade*, 1965). In his *Die Ermittlung* (1965; *The Investigation*, 1966), Weiss made use of the documentation produced at the Frankfurt trial of the Nazi war criminals responsible for the brutalities at Auschwitz.

His other works include *Der Gesang vom lusitanischen Popanz* ("Song of the Lusitanian Bogey," 1966), *Diskurs ueber die Vorgeschichte und Verlauf des lang andauernden Befreiungskrieges in Viet Nam* (1968), and, in Swedish, *Sangen om Utysket* ("The Song of the Scarecrow," 1968), and *Trotskij i exil* ("Trotsky in Exile," 1970).

BIBLIOGRAPHY: L. Kahn, *Mirrors of the Jewish Mind* (1968), 232–6.

WEISS, SAMSON (1910–1990), U.S. rabbi and Orthodox leader. Born in Emden, Germany, Weiss received his rabbinical diploma at the yeshivah of Mir. He received his Ph.D. summa cum laude at Dorpat University, Estonia, after studying at the universities of Breslau, Berlin, and Zurich. He headed the Hebrew department of the Jewish teachers' college in Wuerzburg, Germany, before immigrating to the United States in 1938. After teaching at the Ner Israel Yeshivah in Baltimore (1938–40), Weiss moved to Detroit to direct Yeshivath Beth Yehudah in that city (1941–44). He moved to New York in 1944 where he became rabbi of Congregation Orach Chaim and organized *Torah Umesorah, a national association for the promotion of Hebrew day-school education. In 1945 he founded and became director of Young Israel's Institute for Jewish Studies and two years later was made director of the National Council of *Young Israel, serving in this position until 1956, when he became executive vice president of the *Union of Orthodox Jewish Congregations of America. Weiss resigned from the latter position in 1972 to settle in Israel. He maintained his position as professor of Jewish philosophy at Touro College and was first chairman of the Department for Judaica Studies at Touro.

WEISS, SAMUEL ARTHUR (1902–1977), U.S. congressman and judge. Weiss, born in Krotowica, Poland, went to the United States as an infant and was educated at Duquesne University (1927). He played football while in college, retaining a devotion to athletics throughout his subsequent career. Admitted to the Pennsylvania bar in 1927, he organized a private practice in Pittsburgh. He was elected to the state legislature as a Democrat in 1934 and served there from 1935 to 1939. Weiss represented the 31st Congressional District in the U.S. House of Representatives from 1941 to 1946, the first Jew elected by the district. His congressional activities reflected a continuing interest in Jewish matters, as well as in promoting physical fitness. He resigned from Congress when he was elected judge of the Allegheny County Court of Common Pleas, sitting on that bench from 1946 to 1967.

He was a referee for the National Football League from 1942 to 1954 and officiated in collegiate football as well. Long associated with B'nai B'rith in his home state, Weiss served as national vice president from 1949 to 1967. He was tri-state regional chairman of the United Jewish Appeal from the 1950s.

WEISS, YAACOV (1924–1947), Jew executed by the British in Palestine. Weiss was born in Nove Zamky, Czechoslovakia, and joined the local Betar as a boy of ten. In 1945 he was apprehended in attempting to enter Ereẓ Israel "illegally" and was imprisoned in Athlit. On his release he joined the IẒL and took part in many of its operations, the last being the break into Acre prison when, with Avshalom Ḥaviv and Meir Nakar, he was captured, sentenced to death, and hanged.

BIBLIOGRAPHY: Y. Nedava, *Olei-ha-Gardom* (1966); Y. Gurion, *Ha-Nizzaḥon Olei Gardom* (1971).

WEISSBERG, ISAAC JACOB (1840–1904), Hebrew writer and linguist. He was born in Polonka in Minsk district and contributed to various publications, including **Ha-Meliz*, **Ha-Maggid*, and *Ha-Asif. He opposed both modern Hebrew style, because of the linguistic innovations it contained, and the infiltration of European literary movements into Hebrew literature. His own style is biblical and florid.

He collected and published the letters of J.L. *Gordon (2 vols., 1894), the letters of I.B. *Levinsohn to Dr. R. Kalischer (1896), and the letters of Isaiah Tugendhold (*Divrei Yeshayah ben Ya'akov Tugendhold*, 1896). His works include *Ga'on ve-Shivro* (1883); *She'elat ha-Nashim al pi ha-Talmud* ("The Question of Women According to the Talmud," 1890); *Dalet Tekufot le-Divrei ha-Yamim li-Venei Yisrael* ("Four Periods in the History of the Children of Israel," 1898); and *Mishlei Kadmonim*, ("Ancient Proverbs," 1900).

BIBLIOGRAPHY: Kressel, Leksikon, 1 (1965), 672–3; *Lu'aḥ Aḥi'asaf*, 9 (1902), 361–2; Ha-Mashkif (pseud. J. Klausner), in: *Ha-Shilo'ah*, 14 (1904), 193–4.

[Gedalyah Elkoshi]

WEISSBERG (Veysberg), JULIA LAZAREVNA (1878/80–1942), composer and critic. Born in Orenburg, Russia, she studied at the historico-philological faculty of the Women's University and graduated from St. Petersburg Conservatory in 1912, where she studied composition under Rimsky-Korsakov, whose son, Andrei, she later married. From 1912 to 1914 she studied in Berlin with Humperdinck and Reger. From 1915 to 1917 she was coeditor of the periodical *Muzykalny Sovremennik*. Not evacuated from German Nazi-blockaded Leningrad, she perished during the siege. Her compositions were often lyrical and sometimes in an exotic vein. She also wrote music for children. Among her works were operas, including *Rusalochka* ("The Little Mermaid"; 1923), *Gusi-lebedi* ("Geese-Swans"; 1937) and others; a cantata for chorus and orchestra *The Twelve* (1925); a symphonic poem, *At Night* (1935), and songs.

BIBLIOGRAPHY: NG^2; M.F. Gnesin, *Moi vospominania o N.A. Rimskom-Korsakove* ("Thoughts and Reminiscences on Rimsky-Korsakov"; 1956), incl. Weissberg's writings and correspondence with A.K. Glazunov.

[Marina Rizarev (2nd ed.)]

WEISSBERG, MEIR (Max; 1856–1930), scholar and historian of modern Hebrew literature. Born at Bukaczowce in Galicia, he was appointed teacher in the public school system in Galicia in 1884, became headmaster of the Stanislav public school and, from 1888 until 1925, served as instructor in Jewish religion and the German language at the government high school of the city. He devoted himself to the study of Hebrew Haskalah literature, especially that of Galicia with which, being one of its products, he was thoroughly familiar.

He published a large number of essays on the subject in German, Polish, and Hebrew. His principal works are: *Die neuhebraeische Aufklaerungsliteratur in Galizien* (1898); *Wo-elwel Zbarazer, der fahrende Saenger des galizisch-juedischen Humanismus* (1909).

BIBLIOGRAPHY: Rejzen, Leksikon, 1 (1929), 963–5; G. Bader, *Medinah va-Ḥakhameha* (1934), 90; R. Fahn, in: *Arim ve-Immahot be-Yisrael*, 5 (1952), index.

[Gedalyah Elkoshi]

WEISSENBERG, ALEXIS (Sigismond; 1929–), pianist. Weissenberg was born in Sofia. He studied piano with his mother and then with Pancho Vladiguerov. During the German occupation he and his mother were briefly confined in a concentration camp. He was taken to Ereẓ Israel in 1945, where he gave his first performance with an orchestra. In 1946, he entered the Juilliard School of Music as a pupil of Olga Samaroff, and also studied with Arthur *Schnabel and Wanda *Landowska. Having won the Leventritt Award (1947), he made his New York debut with G. *Szell and the New York Philharmonic, and thereafter commenced his American, and later (1951) his European career. He settled in France and in the early 1950s retired from the concert hall in order to study and teach (at the Accademia Chigiana, Siena, where his pupils included Rafael Orozco); he returned only in 1966, with performances in Berlin. From that time he refashioned an important international career as a virtuoso pianist of great (if sometimes eccentric) prowess, noted for his interpretations of Romantic music.

ADD. BIBLIOGRAPHY: Grove online; *Baker's Biographical Dictionary* (1997); J. Holcman, "The Tangled Talents of Sigi [Alexis] Weissenberg," in: *Pianists, On and Off the Record: The Collected Essays of Jan Holcman* (2000), 155–61.

[Max Loppert / Naama Ramot (2nd ed.)]

WEISSENBERG, ISAAC MEIR (Itshe; 1881–1938), Yiddish novelist and dramatist. Weissenberg was born in Zelechow, Poland, and began his literary career in 1904 as a disciple of Y.L. *Peretz, with realistic tales of small town life in Poland. In his earliest story, *"Dor Hoylekh ve-Dor Bo"* ("One Generation Passeth Away and Another Generation Cometh," 1904), he depicted an undernourished father who collapsed in a shoe factory, his son being expected to replace him as an object of exploitation. In *"Di Meshugene in Dorf"* ("The Village Madwomen," 1905), he showed a young girl desperately resisting her mother's efforts to compel her submission to the unloved husband imposed on her. His best work of fiction was his novella *A Shtetl* ("A Town," 1906), which dealt with the conflict between the older Jewish generation, steeped in tradition and following the guidance of religious leaders, and the rising generation which was receptive to new ideas, especially Bundism and Socialism, and which relied more upon pistols than upon the Psalms. In Weissenberg's stories, Jewish workers were beginning to become class-conscious, engaging in strikes, organizing demonstrations, rebelling against Czarist officials and local bosses.

Weissenberg edited *Yudishe Zamlbikher* (1918–20) the literary organ of the Yiddish intellectuals of Warsaw after the death of Peretz. As editor and critic he was an embattled figure, engaging in constant polemics with the outstanding Yiddish writers, but also encouraging young novelists, such as Oser *Warszawski and Simon Horenczyk, to follow in his footsteps and to write in a purely naturalistic style. Weissenberg visited the U.S. in 1923, but returned to Warsaw to continue the struggle for his ultra-realistic literary approach. His dramas, praised by the discerning critic *Baal-Makhshoves, did not meet with general acclaim. His translation of the *Thousand and One Nights* in six volumes (*Tauzent un Eyn Nakht*, 1922) achieved considerable popularity. A full list of his works appears in his *Geklibene Verk* (1930).

BIBLIOGRAPHY: Rejzen, Leksikon, 1 (1926), 967–72; LYNL, 3 (1960), 415–8; A.A. Roback, *Story of Yiddish Literature* (1940), 223–7; M. Ravitch, *Mayn Leksikon* (1947), 80–5; I. Howe and E. Greenberg, *A Treasury of Yiddish Literature* (1954), 295–307. **ADD. BIBLIOGRAPHY:** I. Oren (ed.), *Kratkaia evreĭskaia entsiklopediia*, 1 (1976), 599; G.G. Branover (ed.), *Rossiĭskaia evreĭskaia entsiklopediia*, 1 (1994), 200–1; G. Estraikh, *In Harness: Yiddish Writers' Romance with Communism* (2005), 79, 171.

[Sol Liptzin]

WEISSENBERG, SAMUEL ABRAMOVICH (1867–1928), Russian physician and anthropologist. He was born in Elizavetgrad in the Ukraine. After Cesare *Lombroso, Weissenberg was perhaps the most distinguished of that first generation of Jewish anthropologists who became interested in Jewish ethnic and physical characteristics. For his anthropometric research on the Jews of southern Russia, which was published in *Archiv fuer Anthropologie* in 1895, he was awarded a gold medal by the Moscow Society for Natural Sciences. His research culminated in his book *Wachstum des Menschen nach Alter, Geschlecht und Rasse* ("Growth of Man as Related to Age, Sex, and Race," 1911). Weissenberg traveled extensively, amassing material for anthropological studies of the Jews of Palestine, Syria, Iraq, North Africa, and Yemen, as well as of various Karaite communities. Many of his essays on Jewish folklore, proverbs, and folk music were published in the influential journal *Globus*.

BIBLIOGRAPHY: Wininger, Biog, 6 (1925), 249–50, includes bibliography; Rejzen, Leksikon, 1 (1926), 973–5.

[Ephraim Fischoff]

WEISSER, ALBERT (1918–1982), U.S. musicologist, composer, editor, and choral conductor. Born in New York City of Russian-Jewish parentage, he attended high school in Queens and sang in the choir of his uncle, the renowned cantor Joshua S. *Weisser. He studied piano with Isaiah Seligman and played with various dance and jazz bands prior to entering New York University in 1940. In 1942 he was drafted into the U.S. Army, and later earned a Purple Heart for wounds received during the Normandy invasion. While convalescing in England, he studied privately with composer Ralph Vaughn Williams. He resumed his studies in composition (at NYU) under Miriam Bauer and Philip James. Upon graduating in 1948, he entered the master's program in musicology. Under the guidance of Curt Sachs, he wrote his thesis on "The Jewish National Music in Russia," which was later published as *The Modern Renaissance of Jewish Music: Events and Figures, Eastern Europe and America* (1954). He also studied privately with Lazare *Saminsky, who encouraged his work on the St. Petersburg School. He was music director of Temple Israel (Great Neck) until 1960. He taught at Brooklyn College from 1959 to 1969 and at the Jewish Theological Seminary (New York), where he taught the history of Jewish music and music theory from 1970 until his death. While serving as first president of the newly founded *American Society for Jewish Music (1974–82), he conceived the scholarly journal *Musica Judaica*. He published *Bibliography of Publications and Other Resources on Jewish Music* (1969), and "The Music Division of the Jewish-Ethnographic Expedition in the Name of Baron Horace Guinsbourg (1911–1914)," in *Musica Judaica*, 4 (1981–1982), 1–7.

BIBLIOGRAPHY: I.J. Katz: "In Memoriam: Albert Weisser (1918–1982)," in: *Musica Judaica*, 4 (1981–1982), 87–98 (includes his complete writings and compositions).

[Israel J. Katz (2nd ed.)]

WEISSER (Pilderwasser), JOSHUA (1888–1952), *ḥazzan* and composer. Born in Novaya Ushitsa, Ukraine, Weisser studied with several notable *ḥazzanim*, including Eliezer *Gerovich, before taking his first position as *ḥazzan* in Vinnitsa at the age of 20. He emigrated to the United States in 1914 and officiated in various New York synagogues. Weisser composed music for each synagogue service, including the usually neglected weekday service.

He published several collections of liturgical music, including *Ba'al Tefillah* (2 vols., 1936–40) and *Shirei Beit ha-Keneset* (2 vols., 1951–52). His work *Avodat ha-Ḥazzan* (2 vols., 1943–48) is a valuable reconstruction of the east European cantorial style. Weisser was also active in publishing ḥasidic songs, including those of *Modzhitz and *Ḥabad, and notated the music in S. Zalmanoff (ed.), *Sefer ha-Niggunim*, 1 (1948).

BIBLIOGRAPHY: E. Zaludkowski, *Kult-Treger fun der Yidisher Liturgye* (1930), 279–81; M. Wohlberg, in: *Cantors Voice* (Sept. 1952), 2, 7; A. Weisser, *Modern Renaissance of Jewish Music* (1954), 144–5; P. Kavon, in: *Journal of Synagogue Music* (Jan., 1968), 16–42.

WEISSKOPF, VICTOR F. (1908–2002), physicist. He was born and educated in Vienna before gaining his Ph.D. in physics at the University of Goettingen under the supervision of Eugene *Wigner (1931). He worked with Erwin Schroedinger and Werner Heisenberg at the University of Berlin (1931–32) and in Niels *Bohr's laboratory in Copenhagen (1932–33), supported by a Rockefeller scholarship and supplemented by a stipend from the Carlsberg brewery. He next worked with Wolfgang *Pauli at the Federal Institute of Technology in Zurich (1934–36). Aware that the rise of Nazism precluded a career in Germany, Weisskopf went first to Kharkov, Ukraine (then in the Soviet Union), where he worked with Lev *Landau. After eight months he was offered both a position at the University of Rochester, New York, and a better-paid post in the University of Kiev, Ukraine. His impressions of the Soviet Union persuaded him to move to Rochester (1937). In 1944 he joined the Manhattan Project in Los Alamos as a group leader in the Theoretical Division. After World War II Weisskopf joined the Massachusetts Institute of Technology (MIT) (1946–60) before moving to the Centre Européenne pour la Recherche Nucleaire (CERN) in Geneva, initially as one of five directors but as director-general after one year (1961–65). He returned to MIT as head of the department of physics (1967–73), but he taught in Geneva every summer. He continued his research after 1973. Weisskopf was a theoretician who entered the then very small and illustrious coterie of nuclear physicists. He was admired for his ability to reformulate abstruse mathematical concepts in comprehensible physical language. In the 1930s he was concerned with the application of quantum mechanics to electromagnetic fields and devised mathematical solutions that accelerated progress in this contentious subject. His main contribution to the Manhattan Project was to calculate the effects of nuclear fission explosions, but he also worked on the peaceful applications of nuclear energy. In Geneva, despite the physical problems of a hip injury sustained in a traffic accident, he presided over the introduction of the challenging and ultimately highly successful program in accelerator physics designed to study the interaction of subatomic particles colliding at high velocity. Weisskopf was renowned for his helpfulness to his colleagues, regardless of their status. His books for students and laymen were highly influential, and *Knowledge and Wonder: The Natural World as Man Knows It* (1962) was selected as the science book of the year for young people. Weisskopf's concerns over nuclear weapons began in 1944, and he was a founder member of the Federation of Atomic Scientists. These concerns were heightened when he witnessed the Trinity test, and by the Hiroshima and Nagasaki bombs. He was present at the first Pugwash meeting (1957) and prominent in the subsequent organization. His honors included membership in the U.S. National Academy of Sciences and the (70-member) Pontifical Academy of Sciences (1975). His awards included the Max Planck Medal (1956), the U.S. National Medal of Science (1980), the Wolf Prize in physics (1981), the Oppenheimer Medal (1983), and the Public Welfare Medal of the U.S. National Academy of Sciences (1991). He was also a Mozart scholar.

[Michael Denman (2nd ed.)]

WEISSLER, BARRY and **FRAN**, U.S. theatrical producers. Fran Weissler majored in drama at New York University, while her husband, she said, dropped out of Rutgers Law School after a year. Both started out in retailing but formed the National Artists Management Company in 1970 to bring classic plays to children. Beginning in 1982 with *Othello*, the Weisslers produced 19 plays on Broadway through to a revival of *Sweet Charity* in 2005. Their presentations on Broadway, including *Medea* (1982), *Your Arms Too Short to Box With God* (1982), *Zorba* (1983), *Cabaret* (1987), *Macbeth* (1988), *Gypsy* (1989), *Cat on a Hot Tin Roof* (1990), *Fiddler on the Roof* (1990), *Grease* (1994), and *Chicago* (1996), which ran for 10 years as a revival. They received five Tony awards, for *Chicago, Othello, Fiddler on the Roof, Gypsy,* and *Annie Get Your Gun* (1999).

[Stewart Kampel (2nd ed.)]

WEISSMAN, BARUCH MORDECAI (1887–1966), Russian Yiddish and Hebrew writer. Weissman was born in Slovechno, Ukraine, where his father was a poor farmer. Before and during World War I he taught Hebrew in Jewish religious schools in Bessarabia, but in 1917 he lived in Odessa where he became friendly with Ḥayyim Naḥman *Bialik and Ahad *Ha-Am. He abandoned an attempt to leave secretly for Ereẓ Israel via Romania in 1919, fearing that the authorities might not let his family join him, and in the mid-1920s he moved to Kiev where he taught in Jewish schools. Having become an ardent advocate of the Soviet regime, he published articles in Soviet periodicals in Yiddish, mainly condemning the Jewish religion. In 1933 he went with his family to Birobidzhan, where he taught at a secondary pedagogical school and also contributed to the local *Birobidzhaner Shtern*, but returned to Kiev in the late 1930s. Under the influence of the state-inspired antisemitism of the Stalin regime in 1937–38, the Holocaust, and especially after the establishment of the State of Israel, however, Weissman came to terms with the Jewish religion again. In 1952 he began writing a diary in Hebrew, which he continued until September 1956. Some of the entries are in the form of letters to the future reader. Toward the end of 1955 they started reaching Israel by devious ways and were published in the newspaper *Davar* under the title *El Aḥi bi-Medinat Yisrael* ("To my Brother in the State of Israel") and were also broadcast. In 1957 a limited edition of a book with the same title was published containing extracts from the diary "by an anonymous Soviet Jew," without the author's name, and his authorship was revealed only after his death. He was nevertheless arrested in 1957 and sentenced to five years imprisonment in labor camps on charges of Zionist activity. In 1960 he was released on account of old age and poor health, and settled in Boyarka, near Kiev. A posthumous edition of Weissman's diary, which included only part of the 1,300 manuscript pages, was published in 1973 under the title *Yoman Maḥteret Ivri* ("Hebrew Underground Diary"). The diary is further evidence of the continuing tradition of the literary activities in Hebrew in the U.S.S.R., decades after it was forced underground by Soviet authorities. Simple and unsophisticated in form, written in the Hebrew style of the beginning of the 20th century, the diary is a moving human document full of sorrow for the cultural traditions of the Jewish people, ruthlessly persecuted in the U.S.S.R., imbued with indignation and sarcasm directed against those responsible for the state antisemitism in the U.S.S.R., and filled with a profound love for Israel which he saw as the sole assurance of Jewish survival.

[Michael Zand (2nd ed.)]

WEISSMANDEL, MICHAEL DOV (1903–1956), rabbi and Jewish resistance leader. An Orthodox rabbi, son-in-law and close associate of Rabbi Unger of Nitra, Weissmandel began his public and social activities during the Nazi period when Jews were deported from Slovakia, engaging non-Jewish emissaries to send food, clothing, and money to the deportees temporarily "settled" in the territories of the General Government in Poland. Weissmandel belonged to the core of the underground "Working Group" and was the initiator of the *Europa Plan to rescue the remnants of European Jewry, seeking to bribe Nazi officials to forestall the deportation of Jews. When an initial $20,000 ransom to Dieter Wisliceny, Eichmann's deputy in Slovakia, which he reported to his superiors, halted a limited deportation, the Working Group and Weissmandel in particular thought they had hit upon a formula that might save Jews. When the vast sums promised were not forthcoming from the West, most particularly from the *American Jewish Joint Distribution Committee, which was prohibited by law from transmitting funds behind enemy lines during wartime, Weissmandel turned bitter and interpreted the slow responses that he was receiving from Switzerland as indifference born of assimilation. In a remarkable and extraordinary situation, he worked closely with a woman Zionist leader, Gisi *Fleischman, in a rare display of cooperation. Fleischmann and Unger were cousins and this certainly helped mediate the vast political divide. His letters, addressed to the Jewish leadership of the free world "in the style of the Marranos," castigated indifference and begged for action to save the Jewish remnants from extermination. He was frantic and he communicated this both in his letters and his postwar memoirs. He sought $200,000 as a down payment on a $2 million ransom. In April 1944, he warned Hungarian Jewry of the impending deportations. He was part of the group that received the report from Rudolf Vrba and Alfred Wetzler, who had escaped from Auschwitz on April 7 and reported both on the activities of Auschwitz and of the plans for the impending arrival of Hungarian Jews. On May 27 two more Jews, Czeslaw Mordowicz and Arnost Rosin, escaped; their report was direct evidence of what was happening to Hungarian Jews (437,000 Jews were deported on 147 trains from May 15 to July 8, 1944, mostly to Auschwitz, where most were gassed upon arrival). The Working Group passed on this information to world leaders, the government of Slovakia, and the Catholic Church. Weissmandel implored world Jewish leaders to demand that the Allies bomb the murder installations at Auschwitz. In the autumn of 1944, the deportations from Slovakia resumed. He was deported with his family but jumped from the transport on its way to Auschwitz. His wife and children were killed at Auschwitz. Later he was on the Kasztner train that went to Switzerland. After the war he lived in the United States and reestablished the Nitra Yeshiva in Mount Kisco, New York, where he died. His book of memoirs, *Min ha-Meẓẓar* ("From the Depths"), was published posthumously in 1960. It is a bitter, condemnatory work, powerful and furious. It is also a problematic work for historians as it is difficult to tell what he wrote and what was written by his brother and students after he died.

BIBLIOGRAPHY: L. Rothkirchen, *Ḥurban Yahadut Slovakya* (1961), index (comprehensive English summary); O.J. Neumann, *Be-Ẓel ha-Mavet* (1958), passim; N. Levin, *The Holocaust* (1968), 535–47. **ADD. BIBLIOGRAPHY:** Y. Bauer, *Jews for Sale: Nazi-Jewish Negotiations, 1933–1945* (1994).

[Livia Rothkirchen / Michael Berenbaum (2nd ed.)]

WEISSMANN, ADOLF (1873–1929), music critic and writer. Born in Rosenberg, Silesia, Weissmann settled in Berlin, and became music critic of the *Berliner Tageblatt* and the *Berliner Zeitung am Mittag*. He died in Haifa while on a lecture tour. His lively and original books include studies of Bizet, Chopin, Verdi, Puccini, *Die Musik in der Weltkrise* (1922; *The Problems of Modern Music*, 1925), *Die Musik der Sinne* (1925), and *Die Entgoetterung der Musik* (1928; *Music Come to Earth*, 1930).

WEISS-ROSMARIN, TRUDE (1908–1989), U.S. editor, scholar, author, lecturer. Born in Frankfurt am Main, she was the daughter of Jacob Weiss, a prosperous wine merchant, and Celestine Mulling. Although her parents attended Jewish religious services, they were highly acculturated to German bourgeois life. In Frankfurt, Weiss-Rosmarin studied at the Freie Jüdische Lehrhaus established by Franz *Rosenzweig. She was a university student in Berlin, Leipzig, and Würzburg, where she received her doctorate in 1931 in Semitics, archaeology, and philosophy. Her dissertation, "Mention of Arabia and the Arabs in Assyrian-Babylonian Texts" was later published. In 1930 she married Aaron Rosmarin, a Russian Jewish scholar; they immigrated to the United States in 1931 and had one son. Unsuccessful in obtaining a university position in Assyriology, Weiss-Rosmarin established in Philadelphia, under the auspices of Hadassah, the School of the Jewish Woman, modeled on Rosenzweig's Frankfurt Lehrhaus; she served as director from 1933 to 1939. Weiss-Rosmarin designed a rigorous curriculum for Jewish women, based on Hebrew, Yiddish, biblical studies, rabbinic sources, Jewish history, and philosophy. As an intellectual feminist, she hoped that serious education would overcome women's traditional exclusion from Jewish learning. Hadassah withdrew its support in 1936, following disputes with Weiss-Rosmarin, and the school closed in 1939. However, Weiss-Rosmarin and her husband continued publication of the school newsletter, *The Jewish Spectator*. Weiss-Rosmarin became sole editor in 1943, and over the next 40 years the journal became an influential voice for rabbis and Jewish professionals on a wide range of topics. Weiss-Rosmarin was a popular and provocative lecturer; she contributed widely to other publications and she also taught Jewish history at New York University. Her books include *Religion* *of Reason: The Philosophy of Hermann Cohen* (1936); *Hebrew Moses: An Answer to Sigmund Freud* (1939); *The Oneg Shabbat Book* (1940); *Jewish Women Through the Ages* (1940); *Jewish Survival* (1949); *Saadia* (1959); and *Jewish Expressions on Jesus: An Anthology* (1977). Weiss-Rosmarin was a national co-chair of education for the Zionist Organization of America and served on the advisory boards of the National Jewish Curriculum Institute and the Jewish Book Council. Her first marriage ended in divorce in 1951; she later married Nissim Sevan. Weiss-Rosmarin moved to Santa Monica, California, in 1978; she died there of cancer. Her papers are in the American Jewish Archives in Cincinnati, Ohio.

BIBLIOGRAPHY: J. Breger, "Weiss-Rosmarin, Trude," in: P.E. Hyman and D. Dash Moore (eds.), *Jewish Women in America: An Historical Encyclopedia*, vol. 2 (1997), 1463–65; D. Dash Moore, "Trude Weiss-Rosmarin and the *Jewish Spectator*," In: C.S. Kessner, *The "Other" New York Jewish Intellectuals* (1994), 101–21.

[Carole S. Kessner (2nd ed.)]

WEISZ, MAX (1872–1931), Hungarian rabbi and scholar. Weisz was born in Budapest, where he received rabbinic ordination at the Landesrabbinerschule. He became a rabbi in Pest and professor at the Landesrabbinerschule. A pupil of David *Kaufmann, Weisz did research in Jewish history, history of civilization, and literature. When the Kaufmann library became the property of the Hungarian Academy of Sciences, Weisz was named its archivist.

He prepared the *Katalog der hebraeischen Handschriften und Buecher in der Bibliothek des Prof. Dr. David Kaufmann* (1906), and edited, from this collection, the ritual book *Seder Troyes* by Menahem ben Joseph (in: *Sefer Yovel … Moses Aryeh Bloch* (1905), 97–137, Heb. pt., and in the same year also separately), and an Italian-Jewish *minhag* book from the 13th century (in *Ha-Ẓofeh, le-Ḥokhmat Yisrael*, 13 (1929), 217–45). As a result of his studies of the Kaufmann *genizah*, he published letters he had discovered, the liturgic compositions of a *paytan* he called Samuel (*Seridim me-ha-Genizah*, 1924), geonic texts (in: *Ve-Zot li-Yhudah … li-Khevod … Yehuda Aryeh Blau* (1926), 159–63), and *Festschrift … der … Landesrabbinerschule* (Heb. pt., (1927), 77–97).

BIBLIOGRAPHY: E. Zsoldos, *Harminc év Isten szolgálataban* (1925); S. Groszman, in: *Magyar Zsidó Szemle*, 48 (1931), 299–314; L. Salgó *ibid.*, 315–7 (bibl.).

[Alexander Scheiber]

WEISZ, VICTOR ("**Vicky**"; 1913–1966), British caricaturist whose incisive drawings and gift for portraying political personalities in mock-heroic attitudes won him a wide following. Born in Berlin of Hungarian parents, he was trained at the Berlin Art School and worked for German newspapers. He immigrated to England in 1935, became attached to the *New Chronicle* in 1941, and later joined the *Daily Mirror*. He was naturalized in 1946. He did much of his best work for the *New Statesman* from 1954, and for the *Evening Standard* from 1958.

He illustrated several books and also published several collections of his work: *Stabs in the Back* (1952); *New Statesman Profiles* (1957); *Vicky's World* (1959); *Vicky Must Go* (1960); *A Selection of "Evening Standard" Cartoons* (1962); and *Home and Abroad* (1964). "Vicky" was one of the most famous political cartoonists in modern Britain. He was termed "the fifth estate of the realm" by Michael Foot, and was responsible for such popular political images as that of Harold Macmillan (British prime minister, 1957–63) as "Super-Mac." In private life, however, Weisz was extremely insecure. He was married four times, suffered from depression, and committed suicide at the age of 52.

BIBLIOGRAPHY: Le Foe, in: *Contemporary Review*, 208 (1966), 134f. **ADD. BIBLIOGRAPHY:** ODNB online.

WEITER, A. (pseudonym of **Eisik Meir Devenishski**; 1878–1919), editor, political agitator, and Yiddish writer. Born in a village near Vilna, Weiter early joined the revolutionary movement, becoming active in the Jewish Labor *Bund. Imprisoned in 1899 and in 1902–04, he participated in the 1905 Revolution. In 1910 he became the first editor of the Vilna-based Boris Kletzkin Yiddish publishing house. He proposed its strictly non-profit character and aspiration to maximize the author's royalties. In 1912, he was exiled to Siberia, where he remained until the outbreak of the 1917 Revolution. He then lived in Petrograd and Nizhni Novgorod and at the end of 1918 settled in Vilna, where he was shot by the Polish Legionnaires who occupied the city in 1919.

Weiter wrote plays, short stories, and essays. In his early period (1898–1906), most of his writings were of a political nature, but in his second period (1906–19) his plays were free of any political motifs. In his blank-verse play, *Fartog* ("Dawn," 1907), he displayed in symbolic form the moods of the Jewish intellectuals on the eve of the 1905 Russian Revolution. In his second play, *In Fayer* ("In Fire," 1910), Weiter expressed the alienation and loneliness of the younger generation and their longing for a full and creative Jewish life. In his third drama, *Der Shtumer* ("The Mute," 1912), he portrayed the suffering of his generation, whose expectations of a new freedom were not fulfilled. Weiter was one of the first writers to give expression to the estranged Jewish intellectual's longing to return to Jewishness and to his renewed search for Jewish roots and Jewish values.

In 1908, A. Weiter, together with S. Gorelik and Samuel *Niger, edited and published the *Literarishe Monatshriftn*, a journal which became a rallying point for the young writers who believed in a renaissance of Jewish life and letters and a revitalized Jewish culture. Among the works that Weiter translated were Gorki's *My Childhood* and Max Halbe's *In Stream* (together with Z. *Rejzen). Weiter's works were published in a one-volume edition in Vilna (1923), edited, with a full biography, by A.J. Goldshmidt.

BIBLIOGRAPHY: Rejzen, Leksikon, 1 (1926), 929–38; LNYL, 3 (1960), 338–43; S. Liptzin, *Flowering of Yiddish Literature* (1963), 162–4; *Weiter-Bukh* (1920); *Bikher-Velt*, 1 no. 4–5 (Kiev 1919), 118–20.

ADD. BIBLIOGRAPHY: E. Gordon-Mlotek, in: YIVO *Bleter*, New Series, vol. 2 (1994), 43–66.

[Elias Schulman / Gennady Estraikh (2nd ed.)]

WEITZ, JOSEPH (1890–1972), Hebrew author and a director of the *Jewish National Fund (JNF). Born in Burmel, Volhynia, Weitz went to Ereẓ Israel in 1908. He worked as an agricultural laborer and watchman and in 1911 was one of the founders of the Union of Agricultural Laborers in Ereẓ Israel (Histadrut ha-Po'alim ha-Ḥakla'im be-Ereẓ Yisrael). In 1915 he was appointed manager of the *Sejera farm, and between 1919 and 1932 he was inspector of plant and afforestation in the JNF settlements. From 1932 Weitz was director of the JNF's Land Development Division and, from 1950, a member of its board of directors. In these capacities he played an important role in the acquisition and development of land for the JNF and in the planning of agricultural settlement.

Weitz's literary work is varied and encompasses both Israeli agriculture and children's stories. He is outstanding in his descriptions of the landscape of Israel, which are noteworthy for their lyricism as well as their profound knowledge of the country. He wrote books and pamphlets of belles lettres and on various agricultural and land settlement themes. His principal work is *Yomani ve-Iggerot la-Banim* ("My Diary and My Letters to My Sons," 5 vols., 1965). *Bi-Netiv ha-Hagshamah*, a collection of essays published in 1950 in honor of his 60th birthday, included a biography, a bibliography, and an appraisal of his work. *Adam im Aẓmo* ("Man by Himself") appeared in 1966 in honor of his 75th birthday and includes a bibliography of his writings.

His son RA'ANAN (1913–1998), who was born in Reḥovot, held the posts of the head of the Land Settlement Department of the *Jewish Agency, chairman of the National and University Institute of Agriculture, and head of the Settlement Study Center. Among his works are *Derakheinu ba-Ḥakla'ut u-va-Hityashevut* (1958), *Agriculture and Rural Development in Israel: Projection and Planning* (1963), *Ideology and Farming – Characteristic Variables in the Moshavim* (with D. Solomanica and U. Shaked, 1975), and *The Southern Project, A Proposal for the Development of a Rural Region in the South of Israel* (1975), and numerous publications on agriculture and rural development. In 1973 Weitz was appointed a member of the Council for Higher Education, as well as professor of regional development theory in the School of Social Work, Haifa University, relinquishing the position in 1978 when he was appointed to a similar position at Bar-Ilan University. He lectured on the subject at many international conferences held in Germany, Italy, Brazil, Costa Rica, Venezuela, Mexico, and South Africa. Upon his 70th birthday, friends presented him with the book *Ḥaverim Mesiḥim im Ra'anan* (1983). In 1990 he was awarded the Israel Prize for exemplary lifelong service to society and the State.

Another son, YEḤIAM (1918–1946), who was born at Yavne'el, was killed during the struggle against the British regime while dynamiting the bridge at Achzib in Western Galilee. A book of his letters appeared in 1948 and in 1966, and kibbutz Yeḥi'am in Western Galilee is named for him.

BIBLIOGRAPHY: Tidhar, 11 (1961), 3876. **ADD. BIBLIOGRAPHY:** R. Weitz, *Hashkafato shel Josef Weitz* (1995).

[Gedalyah Elkoshi]

WEITZ, NAPHTALI (1866–1935), physician and *yishuv* leader. Born in Odessa, Weitz was active in the *Ḥovevei Zion movement from 1884. He studied medicine at Kharkov University, where he became a member of a Jewish national student association in 1885. From 1888 Weitz studied at the Sorbonne in Paris. He attended an international conference of Ḥovevei Zion in Paris in 1894 and was elected to the movement's central committee. In 1898, at the request of Baron Edmond de *Rothschild, he and his wife, Hannah, who was also a physician, went to Ereẓ Israel, where Weitz was employed as a physician in the settlements of Upper Galilee and in *Zikhron Ya'akov, and they worked hard to eradicate malaria. In 1907 he moved to Jerusalem, where he practiced medicine in various medical institutions. He was a founder of the Jerusalem Hebrew Gymnasium (high school) and the Bet ha-Am cultural center. As a Russian national, he was deported to Egypt during World War I; there he served on the Refugee Aid Committee and helped found the Zion Mule Corps. When the British conquered Palestine, he was the first to receive a permit to return.

BIBLIOGRAPHY: I. Klausner, *Mi-Katoviẓ ad Basel*, 2 (1965), index.

[Israel Klausner]

WEIZMAN, EZER (1924–2005), Israeli air force commander, politician, and seventh president of Israel, member of the Ninth, Eleventh, and Twelfth Knessets. A nephew of Chaim *Weizmann, he was born in Tel Aviv. He learned flying at the Haifa Aviation Club, joined the British Air Force in 1942, obtained his pilot's wings in 1944, and served in Egypt and India. In 1946 he joined the IẒL. In 1947 he joined the Haganah's air service, which preceded the establishment of the Israel Air Force of which he was one of the founders. At the beginning of the War of Independence he was sent to Czechoslovakia to learn to fly Messerschmidt planes and fly one of them back to Israel. In the course of the war he participated as a fighter pilot on all fronts, and flew ammunition and supplies to the Negev and to *Gush Etzyon. He was appointed squadron leader in 1949, and in 1950 was named head of operations of the Air Force staff. The following year he attended the RAF Staff College in England and became wing commander in 1953. Weizman was appointed commander of the Israel Air Force in 1958, serving in that position until 1966. During his tour of duty he formulated the air-force strategy that was successfully implemented in the first hours of the Six-Day War of 1967. From 1966 to 1969 Weizman served as head of the Operations Branch in General Headquarters, and was appointed deputy chief of staff with the rank of major general under Chief of Staff Yitzhak *Rabin. When Rabin suffered a 24-hour breakdown at the outbreak of the Six-Day War, he asked Weizman to take command but soon returned to active service. In 1969 Weizman retired from the army, and joined the *Ḥerut Movement. Though not elected to the Seventh Knesset in 1969 he was appointed minister of transportation on behalf of Gaḥal in the second government established by Golda *Meir, resigning from the government, along with other members of Gaḥal, against the background of Meir's willingness to consider the Rogers Plan. From 1971 to 1972 he served as chairman of the Ḥerut movement but resigned over a controversy with Menaḥem *Begin on the distribution of seats in the party's Central Committee. He rejoined the Ḥerut Movement in May 1973. After his son Shaul was wounded in the course of the Yom Kippur War, Weizman started to become more moderate in his approach to the conflict with the Arabs. In the 1977 elections he served as the Likud's campaign manager, and was elected to the Knesset and appointed minister of defense.

He played a major role in the peace process with Egypt, establishing warm relations with Egyptian President Anwar *Sadat and Prime Minister Mustafa Halil. He was a member of the delegation, headed by Begin, which negotiated the Camp David Agreement with Egypt in September 1978, and participated in the negotiations leading up to the Peace Agreement with Egypt in March 1979. He was responsible for the Litani Operation in Lebanon in March 1978 but soon thereafter proposed the establishment of a National Peace Government – an idea rejected by Begin. Weizman became increasingly critical of the government's attitude toward a settlement with the Palestinians and clashed with Ariel *Sharon over his settlement activities. In May 1980 he resigned from the government, allegedly over cuts in the defense budget, but in fact because he disagreed with Begin over the way in which the negotiations on autonomy for the Palestinians were being conducted. In November 1980 he voted against the government in a vote on a motion of no-confidence. As a result he was expelled from the Ḥerut Movement, but refused to relinquish his Knesset seat. From 1980 to 1984 Weizman engaged in business, but before the elections to the Eleventh Knesset in 1984 he decided to form a new party by the name of Yaḥad, which won three seats. Soon after the elections, however, he joined the Alignment, and thus helped tip the balance in favor of the establishment of a National Unity Government based on parity between the two main political blocs and a rotation in the premiership. From 1984 to 1988 Weizman served as minister without portfolio, in charge of Arab affairs. In the government formed by Yitzhak *Shamir in 1988 Weizman was appointed minister of science and technology. However, at the end of 1989 Shamir threatened to fire him from the government because he had had unauthorized contacts with PLO members. After the breakup of the National Unity Government in March 1990 he decided to distance himself from politics, and in February 1992 resigned his Knesset seat, calling upon Shimon *Peres and Yitzhak *Rabin to do the same.

The following year he was elected as Israel's seventh president. He was Israel's most political president, frequently speaking his mind and being criticized for it. When Rabin was prime minister, Weizman was disappointed with the way the peace process with the Syrians was progressing and hoped to meet with President Hafiz al-*Asad in Jerusalem or Damascus, feeling that he had much in common with the Syrian president, since both were presidents, both had been pilots, and both had lost sons in accidents. But Asad did not respond, and Weizman adopted a more rigid position toward Syria. After the Palestinian terrorist attacks in the beginning of 1996, he called for the suspension of talks with the Palestinians. After Binyamin *Netanyahu was elected prime minister he criticized him for the way he was conducting the peace process, and enraged Netanyahu by visiting President Hosni *Mubarak of Egypt to discuss ways of getting the peace process out of the stalemate it had entered. He was also criticized by Yosef Tomi *Lapid for going to see the mentor of Shas, Rabbi Ovadiah *Yosef, to try to convince him to support the peace process. Weizman managed to enrage many women by expressing chauvinist positions regarding the place of women in society, the homosexual community by making homophobic remarks, and many citizens for his frequent refusal to reduce the sentences of prisoners imprisoned for criminal offenses. Nevertheless, due to his charm and sincerity, and his practice of visiting the families of fallen soldiers, and visiting many of the wounded in the hospital, he was extremely popular in the general public, and was viewed by many as "the ultimate Israeli" – for better or for worse. Weizman was elected to a second term as president in 1998, and could have remained president until 2003. However, following a police investigation over alleged improper financial contacts with the French millionaire Eduard Sarousi (the investigation was closed for lack of evidence), and failing health, he decided to resign in July 2000, and retired to his home in Caesarea.

He wrote *On Eagles' Wings: The Personal Story of the Leading Commander of the Israeli Air Force* (1979); *The Battle for Peace* (1981); with Dov Goldstein, *Lekha Shamayim, Lekha Ereẓ* (1993); and *Rut Sof: Biografiyah* (2002).

BIBLIOGRAPHY: S. Eilati (ed.), *Yaḥad Shivtei Yisrael: Rav Si'aḥ im Nesi Medinat Yisrael* (1996); Y. Kotler, *Hapolet: Ezer Weiẓman Kemot Shehu* (2000).

WEIZMANN, Russian family, one of whose members, Chaim *Weizmann, became the first president of the State of Israel. There were 15 children in the family. OZER (1850–1911), the head of the family, was a timber transporter and the only Jew appointed *starosta* (head of the village) in Motol. In about 1894 he moved to Pinsk and succeeded in business there. He was a *maskil*, versed in Judaism, and an early Zionist, as well as representative to the Sixth Zionist Congress (1903). RACHEL-LEAH (1852?–1939), his wife, settled in Palestine in 1920 and established the first home for the aged in Haifa. Their daughter ḤAYA (later LICHTENSTEIN; 1878–1959), a teacher, settled in Palestine in 1921 and taught at the Herzlia High School in Tel Aviv, and later in the Levinsky Teachers' Seminary in Tel

Aviv. She was the president of the Benot Berit Society from 1946 to 1950 and published her memoirs in two volumes (1947–48 and 1952–53). Another daughter GITA (later DOUNIE; 1884?–?), a music teacher, studied at the Warsaw Institute of Music (1901–05) and settled in Haifa in 1911. She was one of the founders of the Haifa School of Music (1924), now known as the Dounie-Weizmann Conservatory. A son MOSES (MOSHE; 1879–1957), a chemist, settled in Palestine in 1924, lived in Jerusalem, and in 1947 was appointed the head of the organic chemistry laboratory of The Hebrew University, where he became professor. Another brother, MIKHAIL (YEḤIEL MIKHL; 1892–1957), an agronomist and the father of Ezer *Weizman, settled in Ereẓ Israel in 1914, becoming director of the Palestine Government Department of Agriculture and Fisheries (1920–28) and manager of the Imperial Chemical Industries, Middle Eastern Zone (1928–35). Later he worked independently in industry in the development of Tel Mond. Another brother SAMUEL (SAMUIL; 1882–?), an engineer, joined the Zionist Socialist Workers' Party (Territorialist) c. 1906. He was engaged as an engineer in Kiev and during World War I in the Moscow Machine Tool Factory. After the Russian Revolution he directed industrial plants in Soviet Russia. He died after World War II in a penal camp. ANNA (ḤANNAH; 1886?–1963), a chemist, worked on the staff of the Moscow Institute of Biochemistry. She settled in Palestine in 1933 and was appointed to the staff of the Sieff Research Institute in Reḥovot (later the Weizmann Institute of Science).

WEIZMANN, CHAIM (1874–1952), first president of the State of Israel, president of the (World) Zionist Organization (1920–31 and 1935–46), and distinguished scientist. He was born on Nov. 27, 1874 (8 Kislev 5635), in the village of Motol near Pinsk, in the Russian Pale of Settlement. He was the third child of Ozer Weizmann, a timber merchant, who made his living by floating logs to and along the Vistula for processing and export in Danzig, and of Rachel-Leah, daughter of Michael Tchemerinksy (see *Weizmann family). They were married when the husband was 16 years of age and his bride less than 14. Chaim was one of 15 children, of whom 12 survived infancy and lived to old age. Chaim's childhood years were typical of the Jewish *shtetl*, an autonomous island within the vast and hostile Russian world. In his autobiography *Trial and Error* he wrote: "We were strangers to their ways of thought, to each other's dreams, religions, festivals, even languages. There were times when the non-Jewish world was practically excluded from our consciousness, as on the Sabbath, and still more on the spring and autumn festivals.... We were separated from the peasants by a whole inner world of memories and experiences. My father was not yet a Zionist, but the house was steeped in rich Jewish tradition; and Palestine was at the center of the ritual.... The return was in the air, a vague deep-rooted Messianism, a hope which would not die" (1949 edition, pp. 10–11). Weizmann's early education was imparted by a *melammed* who taught him the Bible and Hebrew grammar, and immersed him in memories of departed Jewish glory. The Weizmann Archives in Reḥovot display a Hebrew letter which young Chaim wrote at the age of 11, containing this stirring call: "For why should we look to the Kings of Europe for compassion that they should take pity upon us and give us a resting-place? In vain, all have denied: The Jews must die, but England will nevertheless have mercy upon us. In conclusion to Zion Jews to Zion let us go."

At the Realschule in Pinsk, he showed an early talent for scientific studies. His family had fallen on hard times, and the boy had to give private lessons in Hebrew and other subjects to children of wealthier Jewish families. On completing his secondary school course at the age of 18, he already displayed a versatile intellectual energy. He was known for hard and tenacious labor and was prominent among his contemporaries for a bent for ironic humor and a tendency to dominate any company in which he found himself. As it was difficult for Jews to obtain entry to Russian universities, where a *numerus clausus* was strictly applied, Weizmann set out in 1892 to study in Germany, where he enrolled at Darmstadt Polytechnic, supplementing his frugal means by teaching Russian at a Jewish school in a neighboring town. After two terms at Darmstadt, he moved to Berlin to study biochemistry at the Institute of Technology in Charlottenburg.

First Zionist Steps

In Berlin, he joined a glittering circle of Zionist intellectuals, Der Juedisch-Russische wissenschaftliche Verein, including Nachman *Syrkin, Leo *Motzkin, and Shemaryahu *Levin. It was a period of strong ideological conflict within the Zionist Movement, and Weizmann and his friends soon came under the spell of *Aḥad Ha-Am, who defined the object of Jewish nationalism in cultural and spiritual terms. In 1896, the Jewish world was electrified by the appearance of Theodor *Herzl with his revolutionary vision of separate Jewish nationhood and the establishment of the Jewish State. Weizmann and his followers were already steeped in this concept, which was not new to his generation of Russian Jews, but they were attracted by the political sweep and emotional depth of Herzl's call, despite his lack of roots in the authentic Hebrew traditions. Above all, the Russian Zionists were elated by the unexpected adherence to their cause of a sophisticated Western Jew, whose dignity of bearing contrasted with the somewhat bohemian and untidy atmosphere in which Russian Zionism flourished. Owing to a visit to Moscow during the summer vacation of 1897, Weizmann was unable to get back in time for the First Zionist Congress at Basle, but he was a delegate to the second in 1898. In the same year, he went to Fribourg University, Switzerland, to complete his doctorate. He sold his first chemical patent and, in 1901, laid the foundations of his academic career, when, at the age of 27, he became an assistant lecturer at Geneva University. From this point onward, his life was to be divided between his Zionist passion and his scientific vocation. He soon became a prominent figure in the Zionist Movement. He did not doubt Herzl's primacy, and admired the patience with which the leader pursued his political aims; but he developed a critical attitude to Herzl's emphasis on the external forms of diplomacy and his relative indifference to the need for creating tangible social facts. On the eve of the Fifth Zionist Congress in Basle in 1901, Weizmann and his friends created the *Democratic Fraction whose aim was to break out of Zionism's diplomatic emphasis, in order to develop cultural, educational, and social institutions in Ereẓ Israel which would both symbolize and stimulate the concrete work of state-building. At this formative stage in his political evolution, Weizmann was already displaying the skeptical, hard-headed empiricism which held his visionary emotions in check. While Herzl pursued a charter from the sultan of Turkey and worked himself toward an early grave amid ceaseless interviews with European dignitaries, Weizmann and his group devoted themselves to the dissemination of Hebrew culture and published a pamphlet, *Eine juedische Hochschule*, calling for the establishment of a Hebrew university which would be Zionism's spiritual center and scientific bulwark. Hundreds of Weizmann's early letters are devoted to this project.

In 1903, the Movement was torn apart by the *Uganda controversy. The British foreign secretary, Lord Lansdowne, had tentatively suggested Jewish settlement in an area of 5,000 square miles in the East African Protectorate. The most powerful state in the Western world had taken Jewish nationalism seriously enough to offer it a territorial abode, at a time when the fearful persecution of Russian Jews seemed to make their physical rescue more urgent than anything else, and Herzl was inclined to accept the offer as a *Nachtasyl* – a temporary shelter – on the road to Zion. The Russian Jews, however, led by *Ussishkin, would not agree to a Zionism without Zion. Weizmann, deeply rooted in Jewish tradition and East European Jewry, ultimately came down on the side of Herzl's opponents. The great leader died in 1904, a broken and frustrated man, and yet a splendid figure, bequeathing his legend to the Jewish people as the symbol and portrait of its future sovereignty.

Zionism was in the doldrums, and Weizmann's post in Geneva was petering out. He felt the need for a new start and decided to leave for England in 1904 to open the second chapter in his Zionist and scientific life. In 1906 he married Vera Chatzmann (see below), a medical student from Rostov-on-the-Don, whom he had known for five years and wooed in an ardent correspondence. He had started research at Manchester University in 1905 and began to lecture and hold tutorial classes in his subject. In 1907, he was appointed senior lecturer. He maintained his ties with the Zionist Movement, and at the Seventh Zionist Congress, in 1905, was elected to the Larger Actions Committee (later called the General Zionist Council), the supreme body in inter-Congress periods. For the greater part of his remaining years, English life and culture were to excite his admiration. He was deeply impressed by the order, courtesy, reticence, symmetry, and tranquil superiority of the English temperament in its best expressions, and he had a premonition that the decisive turning point in Jewish history would come through intersection with British interests. In 1906, he had a sudden opportunity of explaining the Zionist idea in Manchester to the prime minister, Arthur James *Balfour. Balfour had been puzzled by the Zionist rejection of the Uganda opportunity and wanted to meet an anti-Ugandist who would explain this quixotic step. When Balfour asked Weizmann why he was against Uganda, the younger man, with some effrontery, asked Balfour whether, if he were offered Paris, he would abandon London. Balfour answered, "No, but London is the capital of my country." Weizmann replied, "Jerusalem was the capital of our country when London was a marsh." It was from that date that Balfour became a captive of the Zionist dream.

In Manchester, Weizmann's scientific work became more fertile than ever before. He strove to break down the social barriers which cut him off as a young foreigner from the life of British Jewry, and to make contact with a group of young Manchester Jews, Simon *Marks, Israel *Sieff, and Harry *Sacher, who, in their subsequent affluence, were to help carry him forward to the full expression of his powers. These three, together with some London colleagues, Leonard *Stein, Leon *Simon, and Samuel Landman, formed a nucleus around which British Zionism was to grow. Weizmann soon resumed touch with European Zionism. In 1907, the year in which his eldest son, Benjamin, was born, he delivered an important speech at the Eighth Zionist Congress at the Hague, making a fervent plea for practical work in Ereẓ Israel, in addition to diplomatic activity. "If we achieve a synthesis of the two schools of Zionism," he said, "we may get past the dead points … If you tell me that we have been prevented by local difficulties, by the Turkish authorities, I will not accept it. It is not wholly the fault of the Turks. Something can always be done." He pleaded that, even if a charter, such as Herzl had dreamed of, were possible "… it would be without value unless it rested, so to say, on the very soil of Palestine, on a Jewish population rooted in that soil, on institutions established by and for that population" (*Trial and Error*, p. 122).

This "synthetic Zionism," as it came to be known, was thenceforward the principle of his Zionist work and exercised a significant influence on the Movement as a whole. At the end of the Congress, he paid his first visit to Ereẓ Israel. He was acutely depressed by the experience. Zionism had hardly made any visible impression on the country's landscape. The Turkish government and the major Western powers – Britain, France, and Germany – regarded the Movement as a wild obsession. It was also held in visible contempt by the powerful Jewish communities in London, Paris, and Berlin. But it was this contact with the realities of Ereẓ Israel that stimulated him to press with redoubled energy for immediate practical work there; it was then that he laid out the program of his Zionist work for the next eight years. As chairman of the Standing Committee, he was now able to exercise more influence on the proceedings of the Congresses. At the same time, he was strengthening his roots in English life. In Manchester, he became reader in biochemistry and began to make his mark as a teacher and research worker. The course of his life and, therefore, of Zionist history was nearly changed when he was frustrated in the hope of obtaining a professorship in Manchester, but he sought to balance academic disappointment by intensified Zionist activity. In 1914, he joined in the struggle to ensure that the language of the new Technical School (*Technion) in Haifa, established by the German-Jewish community, should be Hebrew and not German. As a scientist, he knew the limitations of the Hebrew language, but he felt that the Movement would lose its spirit once it cut itself off from its roots in the Jewish past.

World War I

The outbreak of World War I brought Weizmann from the margin to the center of Jewish history. He was now 40 years of age, holding no executive position in the Zionist Movement. Indeed, the Zionist Executive in Berlin found it necessary to reinforce its position in London by sending Nahum *Sokolow and Jehiel *Tschlenow to London. Supported by the English Zionists, by Aḥad Ha-Am, by Haham Moses *Gaster, spiritual head of the Sephardi community, and by Vladimir *Jabotinsky, who shared a flat with him in South London for a time, Weizmann embarked upon an independent effort to win political support for Zionist aims. He paid no attention to his own hierarchical deficiencies. There seemed to be a promise in the air of new opportunities to be snatched from the changing interests and fortunes of the powers. He gathered his friends around him, watched and nursed his chances, and then intervened in the central political arenas with such massive authority and sureness of timing as to change the direction of his people's history.

The link between him and the British government was created by C.P. *Scott, editor of the *Manchester Guardian*, who maintained close relations with cabinet ministers, and especially with *Lloyd George. Weizmann charmed Scott into the understanding and support of Zionist aims. The first contacts which Scott made for him were with Herbert *Samuel and Lloyd George. Samuel was then head of the Local Government Board in Asquith's Cabinet; later he was to hold the posts of postmaster-general and home secretary. To Weizmann's surprise, this cool, rational, unsentimental Jew had already been fired by the emotion of Zionism, and was even preparing a memorandum proposing the establishment of a Jewish state in Palestine after the defeat of the Turkish Empire. The prime minister, Mr. Asquith, and most of his colleagues were unimpressed by the memorandum, but Lloyd George enthusiastically accepted Samuel's approach. More surprisingly, the foreign secretary, Sir Edward Grey, revealed a sympathetic attitude. Thus, Weizmann found his field already plowed to good effect.

It was not until 1916 that he took the initiative of Zionist advocacy in British governmental circles. In that year, when the prospect of Allied victory was dim, his access to British ministers was facilitated by his successful establishment of a process that would yield acetone, a solvent needed for the production of munitions, which brought him into contact with all kinds of people in the British government, including such men as Winston *Churchill, the first lord of the admiralty, and Lloyd George, minister of munitions. In connection with his work, he moved to London, where he had more leisure for his political work. When the Asquith government resigned, Lloyd George became prime minister and Balfour, foreign secretary. Fortune had smiled broadly on Weizmann's efforts; the two British statesmen, a Welshman and a Scot, most sensitively attuned to his ideas, now held the central place in Britain's international relations.

The practical calculations which drove British statesmanship to support of the Zionist program have never been precisely explained. It is certain that one of the aims was to strengthen the British sympathies of American Jews, and especially of Zionist leaders such as Justice *Brandeis of the Supreme Court, who was a friend of President Wilson. But British policy was also inspired by the hope of keeping Palestine out of the hands of France, which, through its traditions of ecclesiastical protection, had a stronger status in the Levant. This was certainly the chief impulse which moved Sir Mark Sykes, one of the secretaries of the British War Cabinet, who met Weizmann in the early part of 1917 at the house of Moses *Gaster. Some military commentators and strategists were sponsoring an idea of a Jewish homeland in Palestine as an assurance of British interests at a strategic point along the route to India. Others were impressed by the ardor of Zionist conviction in Russia. Thus, they came together in a somewhat quixotic alliance to create a strong movement on Zionism's behalf in Whitehall. Opposition, however, came from some British Jews, led by Edward *Montagu, later to be secretary for India, and Claude *Montefiore, president of the Anglo-Jewish Association, who feared that recognition of Jewish nationhood would cast a shadow on the allegiance of Jews to countries of which they were citizens. At one stage, in 1917, Weizmann felt so frustrated by this opposition, as well as by bureaucratic obstruction to his scientific work in the admiralty, that he decided to resign his chairmanship of the English Zionist Federation, to which he had been elected that year. It was at this stage that his friend and mentor, Aḥad Ha-Am, commanded him in paternal tones to follow his destiny to the end, arguing that, since he had never been appointed by anybody to lead the Zionist Movement, there was nobody to whom he could properly submit his resignation; nothing but the commanding attributes of his own personality and the new opportunities of Jewish history had laid the charge upon him.

Weizmann went on building his structure of support and brought his efforts to a triumphant consummation in the early fall of 1917. Despite the opposition of some British Jews and skepticism in some parts of the British Cabinet, Lloyd George and Balfour eventually approved his request for a statement of sympathy for Zionist aims, and the famous *Balfour Declaration was issued on Nov. 2, 1917. The Declaration, which was Weizmann's primary achievement, was a turning point in modern Jewish history. The idea of restoring Jewish political nationhood had passed from fantasy into the world of politics. A leading diplomatic historian has described Weizmann's role as "the greatest act of diplomatic statesmanship of the First World War," declaring that "not even … Masaryk and Venizelos can compare in stature with Weizmann" (Sir Charles Webster, *The Art and Practice of Diplomacy* (1961), 114). The spectacular nature of his achievement had made him the central figure in the public life of the Jewish people; he was recognized as such by Jews and non-Jews alike. His position in international life even conveyed a premonition of Jewish sovereignty. Heads of state, ministers, and high officials, behaved toward him as though he were already president of a sovereign nation equal in status to their own. He and they knew that this was not strictly true; but something in his presence and in their own historic imagination forbade them to break the spell.

Weizmann's Jewish and international eminence was immediately reflected in the tasks now laid upon him. In 1918, he was appointed head of the Zionist Commission then sent to Palestine by the British government to advise on the future settlement and development of the country. He was ceremonially received in audience by King George v beforehand. After a reunion with Jabotinsky in Cairo, he arrived in Palestine, where he was greeted rhapsodically by the Jewish community and with greater reserve by the British military authorities. The conqueror of the Holy Land, General *Allenby, showed a respectful deference, but both he and other British authorities were skeptical of Weizmann's prospects of success, unless he could achieve an understanding with Arab nationalism. Weizmann crossed to Akaba to meet Emir Feisal, son of the sharif Hussein of Mecca, and undisputed leader of Arab nationalism, to whom the British government had made promises of Arab independence throughout Syria and Iraq, but not in Palestine. Feisal made written pledges to Weizmann promising to recognize Zionist aims in Palestine, provided that the aims of Arab nationalism were achieved in Iraq and Syria. The hour of grace was short. Feisal did not obtain what he had hoped from the Allies in Syria and Iraq. He therefore felt released from his promises to Weizmann. The Arab-Jewish alliance was frustrated because its basis and conditions had been undermined by the Western Powers. In 1918, Weizmann laid the foundations of The Hebrew University of Jerusalem. In 1919, he led the Zionist delegation to the Peace Conference at Versailles, where the committee of ten victorious Allies heard him, together with Sokolow and Ussishkin, plead for international ratification of the Balfour Declaration. By this time, the influential supporters of Zionism were not confined to Britain. President Wilson, General *Smuts, and others helped Weizmann to bring about the adoption of the Mandate for Palestine. In this document, whose preamble referred to the historical connection of the Jewish people with Palestine, the realization of the Zionist dream became an integral part of international law.

The Balfour Declaration had been greeted by world Jewry as a kind of Magna Carta; the caution and ambivalence of its formulation could not dim its inner glow. When the Mandate embodying the Declaration was ratified by the international community, Jewish hopes had no bounds. In some parts of the Diaspora, the messianic fervor was so intense that Weizmann found it necessary to sound a cautious note: "A state cannot be created by decree, but only by the forces of the people and in the course of generations. Even if all the governments of the world gave us a country, it would be a gift of little worth, but, if the Jewish people will go and build Palestine, the Jewish state will become a reality."

The 1920s and 1930s

During the 1920s and 1930s, he worked within the gap between the dream and the reality. He was confronted by formidable difficulties, not all of them from without. In 1920, at the Zionist Conference in London, he was elected president of the Zionist Organization, thus achieving formally a position already unchallenged in practice. But now, for the first time, his leadership was disputed. The American Zionists, led by Justice Brandeis, openly questioned his empirical, pioneering approach and the centralized character of the organization. He was forced to defend the principles which had inspired his Zionism from the days of his youth. He could not compromise with the concept of organizational centrality; unless the Jewish people were a single historic unit, there would be no reason to justify its specifically national claims. He was convinced that a nation cannot be arranged from above; it must build itself from below. In the economic sphere, he believed that there should be an attempt to enhance the status of national institutions in the hope that they would evolve into sovereign authorities. He was suspicious of excessive emphasis on financial orthodoxy. He attached vital importance to the social originality of the cooperative villages (moshavim) and collective settlements (kibbutzim), just as he continued to foster and promote the seed of an independent Jewish culture. From his own humble origins and from the atmosphere of the Pale of Settlement he had absorbed a populist emphasis which remained with him at every stage of his career.

In any case, he was now politically indispensable. He was universally recognized as the most authoritative figure in Jewish life, and after much argument and contention he usually got his way. The position was different in his contact with the Mandatory power. The appointment of the Jew, Sir Herbert Samuel, as the first high commissioner of Palestine had messianic implications for Jews in Palestine and elsewhere. But the British administration in Palestine soon fell away from the generous visions which had inspired Balfour and Lloyd George. Its main objective now was not so much to promote the Jewish national home as to mitigate Arab resentment at its progress. Immigration was cut down. Little protection was offered to Jews attacked by Arab gunmen, and embarrassed efforts were often made to persuade the Arabs that the Balfour Declaration meant even less than it said. In these conditions, every Jewish immigrant brought to Palestine and every acre of land purchased there were the fruit of a bitter struggle which Weizmann and his colleagues had to wage with the Mandatory administration in Jerusalem and with the Colonial and Foreign Offices in Whitehall.

Weizmann bore the fatigue of this effort with stoic dignity and patience. He did not believe that spectacular turns of fortune, such as that which he had instigated in 1917, were part of normal historic development. He faced his querulous people with the harder doctrine of gradual evolution to be maintained by sheer hard work. A Jewish national society could be built only "house by house, dunam by dunam." The political struggle would only be resolved if diplomatic efforts were reinforced by facts more substantive than diplomacy. If the reality of a Jewish nation were created, then the recognition of it would only be a matter of time and fortune. Not all Zionists shared this view. No sooner had Weizmann emerged victorious from his struggle with Brandeis than a more serious conflict broke out between him and his friend Jabotinsky, who, in Weizmann's eyes, attached an excessive importance to the declaratory aspects of diplomacy and gave less attention to the prosaic construction of social facts. Jabotinsky's *Revisionist Party, as well as some other Zionist groups, also opposed Weizmann's proposals for the establishment of an "enlarged" *Jewish Agency, incorporating the Zionist Organization and providing a framework for enlisting the support of all Jews, Zionists, and non-Zionists, for the development of the national home. However, Weizmann, who attached historical importance to the scheme, persisted, and in 1929, after bitter and prolonged debates in the Zionist Movement and negotiations with non-Zionist bodies and personalities, the first conference of the enlarged Jewish Agency for Palestine met in Zurich, with some of the most glittering figures in Jewish life standing behind him on a common platform.

Weizmann attached great importance to the Arab problem. He thought that a major effort should be made to secure regional harmony. The key to the situation, he said, lay in "genuine friendship and cooperation with the Arabs to open the Near East for Jewish initiative. Palestine must be built without violating the legitimate interests of the Arabs. Not a hair on their heads shall be touched. The Zionist Congress … has to learn the truth that Palestine is not Rhodesia, and that 600,000 Arabs live there, who, before the sense of justice of the world, have exactly the same right to their homes in Palestine as we have to our National Home." This utterance was later to have a prophetic ring. It did great credit to Weizmann's statesmanship; on the other hand it elicited no response from Arab leaders. In 1920, 1921, 1929, and 1936, murderous attacks were launched upon Jewish communities, often with heavy loss of life. On each occasion the British government responded by penalizing the victims and rewarding the authors of the assaults.

In 1930, the British abandonment of obligations toward the Zionists was so blatant that Weizmann angrily resigned his office. A vast wave of public protest rose up against the colonial secretary in the British Labour government, Lord Passfield, whose White Paper threatened to strangle the Jewish national home. Ramsay MacDonald, the prime minister, had to acknowledge the force of public dissent by sending a letter to Weizmann in which he renewed the main assurances which Zionists considered essential in the policy of the Mandatory power.

A year later there was a stormy Zionist Congress meeting in Basle at which Weizmann was not reelected to office. He had undermined his position by refusing to placate his critics; he had even been quoted in a newspaper as holding no special brief for the idea of a Jewish majority in Palestine. This was undoubtedly a misrepresentation of his philosophy; his empirical mood always forbade him to adopt slogans which were not effective for the task at hand. He believed that a Jewish majority would ultimately be brought about, not by premature incantation but by the assiduous addition of immigrant to immigrant, house to house, village to village, city to city. The paradox of Weizmann's dismissal was underlined by the election of his closest colleague, Sokolow, as president of the Jewish Agency. This was a confession that no policy other than that of Weizmann could command support.

Hitler had now come to power in Germany; the shadow of future Jewish disaster was growing longer. Weizmann devoted the years of his removal from office to projects closest to his heart. He undertook fund-raising tours for Zionist agencies, threw himself into the work of rescuing refugees, and made special efforts to salvage for Ereẓ Israel some of the Jewish scientific talent being destroyed in Nazi Germany. In 1935, after four years of non-presidency in which his preeminence was, if anything, emphasized by lack of office, he was restored to the helm. The story of Weizmann's life between the two world wars is one of patient accumulation against obstacles created by Arab hostility, British coldness, and Jewish dissension. He saw, in spite of everything, the contours of Jewish nationhood becoming firmly set, the national home growing in cohesion and individuality: by 1939 it had a population of 450,000; its economic and technological levels were spectacular by Middle Eastern standards, although well below the best European average; but it was a source of pride for the Jewish people and, for the world, a fascinating and original spectacle. Here, and only here, the Jews faced history in their own authentic image; they were not a marginal gloss on other societies.

To preserve his personal and intellectual independence, Weizmann had clung tenaciously to his scientific interests; in the early 1930s he laid the foundations of the Daniel Sieff Institute at *Reḥovot, which later burgeoned into the *Weizmann Institute of Science, and in 1937 he made his home in Reḥovot.

A significant Zionist breakthrough was achieved in 1937, when a British Royal Commission headed by Lord Peel agreed, under Weizmann's prodding, to recommend the establishment of a Jewish state in a part of Palestine. In that plan the territorial provisions for Jewish statehood were very disappointing; the area allotted for Jewish sovereignty was little more than 2,500 square miles. But, once Jewish statehood had been proposed as a serious and practicable solution, it was never to leave the international agenda. It may even be said that from 1937 onward the establishment of a sovereign Jewish state was only a matter of time. This brilliant achievement owed much to a remarkable oratorical success by Weizmann. Appearing before the Royal Commission, for over two hours he delivered an address of towering majesty and deep pathos. One passage in particular was never to be forgotten: "There are in this part of the world 6,000,000 people doomed to be pent up in places where they are not wanted and for whom the world is divided into places where they cannot live and places which they cannot enter." At the Zionist Congress in 1937, Weizmann proposed that the principle of partition be accepted while an effort be made to improve its territorial provisions. The Arabs rejected the entire proposal. In Britain, a majority of the House of Commons supported the plan; but the government gradually retreated from it, under the impact of Arab resistance and in obedience to a growing national timidity.

Weizmann, together with *Ben-Gurion and most – but not all – of the Palestine labor leaders, was fully aware of the limitations of the truncated state that was offered to them, but they were obsessed by the idea that the whole future of the Jewish people was in the balance. With civil war in Spain, Italian aggression in Abyssinia, and the German *Anschluss* with Austria, the international horizon was growing darker. The spirit of appeasement and cowardice to be later reflected in the Munich Agreement had its reflection in the British attitude toward the Jewish national home. In 1939, after conferences at St. James' Palace, in which the Jewish delegation was again led by Weizmann, a White Paper was published which effectively proposed to bring an end to Zionist aims. Severe restrictions were imposed upon the purchase of land by Jews; and after five years, during which a maximum of 75,000 immigrants were to be admitted, no further immigration could be admitted except in the improbable contingency of Arab consent.

In the summer of 1939, Zionist leaders assembled at Geneva for their biennial Congress in a mood of tragic expectation. A great doom was in the making, and it seemed to be coming on relentlessly. While the Congress was debating the British betrayal of its obligations to a small people which in Weizmann's words was "battered and bleeding from a million wounds," the news came of the Soviet-German agreement which heralded the assault on Poland and the outbreak of World War II. In the closing moments of the Congress Weizmann loomed with tragic tenderness above the delegates, many of whom knew that their own fate, as well as that of the communities of which they were members, was horribly sealed.

World War II

When World War II broke out, Weizmann immediately promised the British government all possible aid by the Jewish population in Palestine and the Jewish people outside. He also tried to renew the scientific cooperation which had enhanced his political status in Britain in World War I. His efforts now were less fruitful. Although hard pressed for manpower, the British government found ways of delaying the proposed formation of a Jewish military unit. Weizmann's scientific offers were rebuffed. In 1942 his son Michael was killed in action with the Royal Air Force over the English Channel. In the early years of the war, his influence and pressure did not enable him to prevent such tragedies as that of the vessel *Struma*, which sank with Jewish refugees aboard in the Black Sea, owing to the refusal of the Mandatory government to give them entry to Palestine.

The national home was not static during the war years. Its population grew by immigration, authorized and unauthorized; its manpower increased its defensive capacity by massive enrollment in the British forces; and its incipient industrial potential found an outlet through supplies and manufacture in support of the Allied war effort in the Middle East. But the main thrust and accent of Weizmann's work were aimed at obtaining a satisfactory political settlement at the end of the war. In London, he invested much effort and persuasion on Winston Churchill, who gave him frequent and sometimes dramatic assurance that he would not let Zionism down. But there was nothing in the daily practice of Whitehall, or of the administration in Jerusalem, which gave any support or reinforcement to Zionist hopes. In any case it was evident that the balance of world power was changing. To Weizmann, as well as to Ben-Gurion, it was evident that the United States was destined to have a strong and perhaps decisive voice in the Middle Eastern future. In 1941 and 1942, Weizmann spent much time in New York and Washington in a sustained effort to enlist American leadership on behalf of Zionist aims. In a notable article, written in the New York quarterly, *Foreign Affairs*, he outlined the project for the establishment of a Jewish commonwealth in Palestine. In April 1942, under Ben-Gurion's initiative, this concept became official Zionist policy. The resolution, adopted at a conference in the Biltmore Hotel (the *Biltmore Program), spoke of a Jewish commonwealth in the entire area of Western Palestine. When the physical danger to Palestine was removed through British victories against Rommel's armies in the western desert, Zionist prospects appeared temporarily to improve. In August 1944, Churchill instructed his secretary of state for war to reply affirmatively to Weizmann's request for the formation of a Jewish fighting force. At the same time, it became known that British ministers were actively discussing and analyzing various partition plans, which would involve the establishment of an independent Jewish state as soon as the war came to an end.

But these hopes were fragile and transient. As the fearful dimensions of the Jewish Holocaust in Europe became known, Weizmann began to wonder whether any victory for Zionism would come in time to save his people from a fatal and horrible depletion of its resources and strength. The assassination of the British minister of state in Cairo, Lord Moyne, by Jewish underground fighters acting against the will and authority of the Jewish Agency, brought about a temporary alienation of Churchill from his Zionist sympathies. The work on partition proposals was suspended, and the British government turned instead to the task of suppressing the growing movements of Jewish resistance in Palestine.

To add to his burdens, Weizmann found that his leadership was no longer unquestioned throughout Palestine Jewry. He arrived in Jerusalem on Nov. 15, 1944, and later celebrated his 70th birthday amid a deep chorus of public affection. But among the leadership there was a different story. New forces were jockeying for position, and Ben-Gurion no longer found himself working in fraternal association with his older chief. In particular, there was a demand, even in responsible Zionist circles, for a more militantly anti-British attitude than Weizmann, with all his frustrations, seemed willing to accept. When the war with Germany ended in May 1945, Weizmann's troubles were compounded by the first serious breakdown of his health. He became affected by glaucoma and was condemned to temporary blindness and tense, agonizing operations. Less than two months after the end of the German phase of World War II, he was shatteringly disappointed by a letter that he received on June 9, 1945, from Churchill, stating: "There can, I fear, be no possibility of the question being effectively considered until the victorious allies are definitely seated at the peace table." Weizmann's hope that a substantive move would be made as soon as the German war was over, had thus been shattered. Churchill was winding up his historic ministry with the 1939 White Paper unabrogated, with no commitment on the record, and with Weizmann left high and dry, standing before the Jewish people baffled, enraged, and empty-handed. A week later Churchill was out of office and, a few months after that, his voice from the opposition benches was castigating the new Labour government for not giving Zionism its due. By this time President Roosevelt was dead. He had shown an ominous coolness toward Zionism at the end of his final presidency; but his administration contained many stalwart supporters of Weizmann's cause. Now, with Churchill and Roosevelt both gone, Weizmann had to begin again.

The Bevin Period

In London, he was to know nothing but discouragement and defeat. The Labour government, under Prime Minister *Attlee and Foreign Minister *Bevin, turned its back drastically on previous British commitments and on its own far-reaching promises of support for Zionism. In the United States the Zionist cause prospered more; but when President Harry S. *Truman urged the Attlee-Bevin government to admit 100,000 Jewish *displaced persons from refugee camps in Europe to Palestine, he met with a flat refusal. A joint Anglo-American commission of enquiry recommended the immediate entry of 100,000 immigrants, but Attlee and Bevin found reasons for evading the recommendations of a body which they themselves had appointed. The deadlock was sharp. It was constantly deepened by an almost inevitable growth in Jewish resistance activities in Palestine. The relations between Britain and organized world Jewry became so embittered that the years of grace, beginning with the Balfour Declaration and the Mandate, were almost entirely lost from memory. It was against this unpromising background that Weizmann's position as leader of the Zionist Movement came to an end. When the first postwar Zionist Congress assembled in Basle, in 1946, the British connection and the Zionist attitude toward the Mandatory power were the fundamental issues before it. Weizmann returned to London, defeated as a champion of the "Anglocentric" point of view, although he had in fact no illusions left about the attitude of the British government toward Zionism.

With leadership passing into other hands, it seemed as if Weizmann's public life was finished. There was, however, to be a dramatic and moving series of epilogues. In February 1947, the last Zionist efforts at reaching a solution within the British Mandatory framework ended in failure. The British government submitted the future of Palestine to discussion and recommendation by the General Assembly of the United Nations. Weizmann now held no official position in the Zionist Movement, but it was taken for granted that he must be a principal spokesman of the Jewish national cause in what was evidently going to be a crucial and decisive phase. When a United Nations special committee went to Palestine in the summer of 1947, its members conferred in detail and at length with Weizmann, who now openly advocated a partition compromise. Later in the year, despite the burdens of age and illness, he went to New York, where he made a moving and unforgettable appeal to the General Assembly. He knew that this would be his last appearance at the bar of the nations. He showed all his old qualities of eloquence and sardonic humor. He made light of the Arab spokesmen's assertion that the Jews were the descendants not of the Hebrew kingdoms, but of the Khazars of southern Russia. "It is very strange, all my life I have been a Jew, felt like a Jew, and I now learn that I am a Khazar." On the idea that the Jewish national home should accept minority status within an Arab state, he said, "Those of us who made our homes in Palestine did not do so with the object of becoming Arab citizens of the Jewish persuasion." In a final grand and weary gesture he reminded the General Assembly's committee that it was meeting under the providence of history. "The Lord shall set His hands the second time to recover the remnants of His people, and He shall set up an ensign for the nations and shall assemble the outcasts of Israel and gather together the dispersed of Judah from the four corners of the earth."

In the next few months he was destined to be the primary architect of two achievements: the retention of the Negev area in the United Nations plan for a Jewish state; and the spectacular recognition of Israel by the United States. He secured these results by capturing the trust and imagination of President Truman. In each case the president, under Weizmann's urging, overruled powerful interests within his own administration which favored a more reserved attitude toward Zionism and a purposeful attempt to win Arab support for American policies. Thus, on Nov. 29, 1947, when the United Nations voted the partition proposal with the Negev included in the Jewish state, and on May 14, 1948, when Palestine Jewry proclaimed its statehood, Weizmann stood in the center of his people's gratitude. He had been specially insistent that the Palestine Jewish leadership proclaim Jewish statehood on the withdrawal of the British, no matter what was said or proposed by the United Nations or the major powers. It was a strange role for the so-called "moderate" to be summoning the Jewish people to the utmost intransigence and tenacity. His feeling was that war with the Arab world had become inevitable. For that very reason it was essential that the ordeal be faced from the starting point of an existing Jewish statehood.

May 14, 1948, was a red-letter day for Weizmann in New York. His colleagues and rivals in Tel Aviv had proclaimed the Jewish state to whose establishment he had dedicated his life and dreams; and President Truman, in direct response to Weizmann's letter, had authorized the recognition of Israel by the United States. Moreover, before the day was out, a telegram had come from Israel on behalf of the Palestine labor leaders, expressing their intention to propose him for the presidency of the new state. "Mine eyes have seen the coming of the glory of the Lord," wrote Justice Felix Frankfurter; "happily you can now say that and can say what Moses could not." Albert Einstein wrote to him, "I read with real pleasure that Palestine Jewry has made you the head of their state and so made good, at least in part, their ungrateful attitude toward you." A few days later Weizmann went to Washington, where he was received by President Truman with the full trappings belonging to his presidential status. He secured from Truman a promise to finance Israel's early economic development by a loan of $100,000,000; and to establish full diplomatic relations with Israel once its first government was democratically elected.

First President of Israel

In February 1949, the first elected parliament of Israel, meeting specially in Jerusalem, elevated Weizmann from the presidency of the Provisional State Council to the title of president of the State of Israel. But age and sickness had now overtaken him at a point at which he could give little consecutive service to the state. He was sufficiently alert and competent to express fierce resentment and surprise at the rigid limitations of his office. He found himself virtually confined to those ceremonial activities in which he had at no time in his life shown the slightest interest. The Israel government of the time showed a lack of imagination and a failure of historic deference. Weizmann's name was not included among those who had signed the *Declaration of Independence; and even his request to receive the Cabinet minutes regularly was not fully answered.

His final months were spent in sharp ambivalence of feelings. On the one hand, he had, unlike Moses, passed beyond Pisgah into the Promised Land. His historic imagination could not fail to be stirred by the thought that he had come the full circle, from Motol, near Pinsk in the Russian Pale of Settlement, to the presidency of an independent Jewish state, which to less sensitive minds had seemed such a wild and chimerical dream. The Weizmann Institute of Science, which was inaugurated on Nov. 2, 1949, as a growing complex of laboratories and libraries, already showed promise, later amply fulfilled, of placing Israel high in the universal enterprise of scientific research. On the other hand, he chafed at his inability to impress the new society with his own message of social progress, intellectual integrity, aesthetic refinement, and manifest dedication to peace. Israel had been born in violence and conflict; it continued to live an embattled existence.

There were times when Weizmann was seized by a poignant concern for Israel's inner quality; but, whenever he fell into doubts and regrets, he looked through his window at Reḥovot upon the verdant rolling plains and rich orange groves surrounding the scientific laboratories established under his inspiration. On a clear day his gaze would go as far as the Judean Hills. The landscape in between was dotted with villages and townships indicative of the new impetus given to Jewish national vitality. And then a deep contentment would come upon him, and his mind would become serene, as befitted a man who to a degree unshared by any figure in contemporary history had seen an improbable vision translated, largely through his own effort, into vibrant and solid reality. After a long and painful illness, which for some months left him entirely incapacitated, he died on Nov. 9, 1952. He was survived by his wife, whose implacable loyalty and devotion had sustained and consoled him throughout the years; and by his elder son, Benjamin. His grave was situated at his own wish in the garden of his home in Reḥovot. At the initiative of his closest friend, Meyer *Weisgal, who had helped him found the Weizmann Institute, a graceful plaza was constructed in his memory by *Yad Chaim Weizmann* (Weizmann National Memorial), with the assistance of the government and the Jewish Agency. His archives and library were established in the Weizmann memorial area.

Weizmann's autobiography, entitled *Trial and Error*, appeared in 1949. A selection of his speeches from 1901 to 1936, entitled *Devarim*, appeared in four volumes in 1937. Some of his speeches and essays include: *Eine juedische Hochschule* (1909) written together with M.M. *Buber and B. *Feiwel; *Die Hebraeische Universitaet in Jerusalem* (1913), a speech at the laying of the cornerstone for The Hebrew University (1919); *The Jewish People and Palestine*, a statement made before the Palestine Royal Commission on Nov. 25, 1936, on Palestine's role in the solution of the Jewish problem in *Foreign Affairs*, 20 (1942), 324–38; *We Do Not Want to Return to the Past* (1946); *We Warned You, Gentlemen* (1947). His letters and papers are being prepared for publication. The first volume of the *Letters and Papers of Chaim Weizmann* appeared in 1969 and publication was completed in 1980 with the 23rd volume.

[Abba Eban]

As Chemist

In 1910 Weizmann became associated with a British team seeking (unsuccessfully) to make synthetic rubber. A possible starting point was butanol. Weizmann, who had been studying chemical reactions effected by bacteria, isolated a starch-decomposing anaerobic organism *Clostridium acetobutylicum* which produced butanol, acetone, and ethyl alcohol by fermenting a mash of cooked corn. In World War I the ministry of munitions needed great quantities of acetone, and Weizmann went to work in the Lister Institute and at the Admiralty Cordite Factory, Poole. His efforts were directed toward developing his laboratory work into a technical process – the first use of a biological process for industrial production (other than the age-old procedures for making alcoholic beverages). Because there was insufficient grain in wartime Britain, plants were set up also in India, Canada, and the U.S. After the war the U.S. plants became the Commercial Solvents Corporation, which went on making acetone by the Weizmann process for many years, until overtaken by purely chemical processes. Later he worked on naphthacene derivatives from phenols and phthalic anhydride, on the photochemistry of aqueous solutions of amino acids, and on the reaction of acetylene with ketones, but mainly on the production of aromatic hydrocarbons by high-temperature cracking of petroleum. This process was developed after the war at Partington, Lancashire, by the Manchester Oil Refinery and Petrochemicals Ltd., the plant being later acquired by Shell. Weizmann wrote many papers and took out some 100 patents (in which he called himself Charles Weizmann).

[Samuel Aaron Miller]

His wife, VERA (née Chatzman; 1882–1966), was the daughter of an assimilated well-to-do Jewish family beyond the *Pale of Settlement in Rostov-on-Don. She studied medicine at the University of Geneva, where she met Weizmann, and she married him in 1906. Soon after their marriage they went to Manchester, where she worked for a number of years as a medical officer at Manchester clinics for schoolchildren. At all times she was of great help to her husband in his Zionist work. She was a co-founder of *WIZO, for many years the chairman of its executive, and later its honorary president. During World War II she was chairman of *Youth Aliyah, and after 1948 she devoted much of her time and effort to Magen David Adom and the organization for disabled veterans. Her memoirs, *The Impossible Takes Longer*, were published in 1967.

BIBLIOGRAPHY: M. Weisgal and J. Carmichael (eds.), *Chaim Weizmann: A Biography by Several Hands* (1962); M. Weisgal (ed.), *Chaim Weizmann: Statesman, Scientist, Builder of the Jewish Commonwealth* (1944); P. Goodman (ed.), *Chaim Weizmann: A Tribute on His Seventieth Birthday* (1945); I. Berlin, *Chaim Weizmann* (1958); L. Stein, *The Balfour Declaration* (1961); idem, *Weizmann and England* (1964); idem, *Weizmann and the Balfour Declaration* (1964); H. Sacher, *Chaim Weizmann* (1955); R. Baker, *Chaim Weizman, Builder of a Nation* (1950); I. Berlin and I. Kolatt, *Chaim Weizmann as Leader* (1970). **ADD. BIBLIOGRAPHY:** J. Reinharz, *Chaim Weizmann: The Making of a Zionist Leader* (1985); idem, *Chaim Weizmann: The Making of a Statesman* (1992).

WEIZMANN INSTITUTE OF SCIENCE, a center of scientific research and graduate study, is located on 300 acres (1.2 sq km) of lawns and gardens in the town of Reḥovot, Israel – 14 miles (22 km) south of Tel Aviv and 35 miles (50 km) west of Jerusalem. In 1996, the Institute community numbered 2,400 scientists and support staff, including more than 850 scientists-in-training pursuing advanced degrees at Weizmann's Feinberg Graduate School. In 2005 it numbered 2,500 scientists.

The Institute's campus of some 40 buildings grew out of the Daniel Sieff Research Institute, founded in 1934 by Dr. Chaim *Weizmann, the distinguished scientist and Zionist leader President of Israel. The Sieff Institute was established in memory of Daniel Sieff by his parents, Israel and Rebecca *Sieff of the United Kingdom. On November 2, 1949, with the agreement of the Sieff family, the Institute was renamed and formally dedicated as the Weizmann Institute of Science.

The Institute is administered by a board of governors and an executive council. It is headed by a president assisted by four vice presidents and the deans of the five faculties and the Feinberg Graduate School.

The Institute consists of 18 research departments grouped into five faculties: Biology (Biological Regulation, Immunology, Molecular Cell Biology, Molecular Genetics and Neurobiology), Biophysics-Biochemistry (Biochemistry, Membrane Research and Biophysics and Plant Genetics), Chemistry (Chemical Physics, Environmental Sciences and Energy Research, Materials and Interfaces, Organic Chemistry and Structural Biology), Mathematical Sciences (Applied Mathematics and Computer Science, and Theoretical Mathematics), and Physics (Condensed Matter Physics, Particle Physics and Physics of Complex Systems).

To promote the interdisciplinary contacts which increasingly characterize today's front-line science, the Institute has created 19 research centers, generally organized as intellectual rather than physical entities.

The presidents of the Institute have been: Chaim Weizmann (1949–52); Abba *Eban (1959–66); Meyer W. *Weisgal (1966–69); Albert B. *Sabin (1969–72), Israel Dostrovsky (1973–75), Michael Sela (1975–85), Aryeh Dvoretzky (1985–88) and Haim Harari (1988–2001), and Ilan *Chet (2001–). From 1952 to 1959, Meyer *Weisgal headed the Institute as chairman of the Executive Council.

The Institute's budget (approximately $181 million in 2004/5) is covered mainly by funds from the Israel government (36%), private donations and research grants (24%), as well as financial and other revenues.

Institute scientists acted as pioneers in various areas of science locally. They were the first to introduce cancer research in Israel, to design and build the first computer in Israel and one of the first anywhere, to establish the first nuclear physics department, the first research accelerators for the study of atomic nuclei, the first and, so far, only, submicron research facility for advancing the electronics industry, and the first advanced solar energy research facility in Israel and one of only a handful worldwide.

More than half of all Institute research is aimed – in one way or another – at battling cancer. Among past achievements is the identification of the genetic origins of some types of leukemia as well as of genes that induce or suppress malignancies. Major efforts are directed at the study of autoimmune diseases, and two medications for multiple sclerosis based on Institute research are already reaching patients. Basic research is elucidating brain structure and function and neurological disease.

At the solar facilities, researchers pursue the development of new ways to harness the sun's energy. Scientists engaged in environment-related studies analyze local aquifers, develop water protection and purification systems. Institute chemists work in areas ranging from basic investigation of the elements to the development of new materials. Photochromic materials that reversibly darken when exposed to sunlight are the result of a Weizmann Institute discovery.

Accomplishments of Institute mathematicians include the development of "smart cards" and decoders that prevent unauthorized access to confidential computer data and commercial satellite TV, and software architecture allowing people to meet "virtually" through the Internet.

Institute physicists first proposed the existence of an elementary particle called the top quark, and contributed to the identification of another particle called a gluon. They now conduct advanced experiments at the European Laboratory for Particle Physics (CERN) in Geneva and at the DESY Laboratory in Hamburg. In the new field of submicron research, scientists are growing crystals in layers no more than a few atoms thick which will result in smaller and faster computer chips for the electronics industry.

The Institute's Feinberg Graduate School, operating under charter from the State of Israel and the Board of Regents of the State of New York, confers M.Sc. and Ph.D. degrees in the life sciences, chemistry, physics, mathematics, computer science and science teaching. More than 10 percent of the student body hails from abroad and English is the official language of instruction. Over the years the Feinberg Graduate School has produced more than 30% of Israel's Ph.D.'s in science and its alumni hold key positions both in Israel and overseas.

The Science Teaching Department has played a pioneering role in raising the level of science teaching in primary and secondary schools, and the Youth Activities Section's extracurricular programs introduce thousands of Israeli youngsters each year to the thrill of scientific discovery. The Section also runs the Institute's Garden of Science, a unique hands-on outdoor science park.

The Institute's Yeda Research and Development Company was founded in 1959 to promote the commercial applications of Institute research. By the mid-1990s some 10% of the Institute's operating budget was derived from Yeda's activities. Yeda has been involved in the licensing of scores of patents and technologies to industry, and in the establishment of numerous spin-off companies in Israel and abroad.

The Weizmann Institute played a key role in the founding of Israel's first high-tech industrial park, Kiryat Weizmann, and a new science-based industrial park now under construction near the campus.

The Institute maintains strong ties with preeminent research institutions throughout the world, attracts many foreign scientists (about 600 a year work in its laboratories for varying periods of time), and is a venue for international scientific conferences.

Yad Chaim Weizmann is a memorial area covering Dr. and Mrs. Weizmann's private estate, their graves near their former home and a memorial plaza. It was established after Weizmann's death in 1952 by the government of Israel and the Jewish Agency Executive and incorporated as a separate institution in 1955. The primary objective of Yad Weizmann was to promote the "Weizmann heritage" in humanitarian, cultural and aesthetic terms. To this end, the memorial foundation has, among other programs, sponsored lectures in the sciences and humanities by leading world scholars and savants, and organized a variety of events. The foundation is responsible for maintaining the Weizmann Archives and for publishing more than 25,000 of Weizmann's papers and letters in 25 volumes. Its permanent exhibition reflects Weizmann's lifelong activities as scientist and statesman. Yad Weizmann conducts tours of the historic home of Dr. Weizmann designed in the 1930s by architect Erich Mendelsohn.

BIBLIOGRAPHY: R. Calder, *The Hand of Life: The Story of Weizmann Institute* (1959); J. Wechsberg, *A Walk through the Garden of Science: A Profile of the Weizmann Institute* (1967); L. Shultz (ed.), *Gateway to Science: The Weizmann Institute at Twenty-Five* (1970); The Annual Report; Scientific Activities (annual). **WEBSITE:** www.weizmann.ac.

[Meyer Wolf Weisgal]

ABBREVIATIONS

GENERAL ABBREVIATIONS

This list contains abbreviations used in the Encyclopaedia (apart from the standard ones, such as geographical abbreviations, points of compass, etc.). For names of organizations, institutions, etc., in abbreviation, see Index. For bibliographical abbreviations of books and authors in Rabbinical literature, see following lists.

*	Cross reference; i.e., an article is to be found under the word(s) immediately following the asterisk (*).
°	Before the title of an entry, indicates a non-Jew (post-biblical times).
‡	Indicates reconstructed forms.
>	The word following this sign is derived from the preceding one.
<	The word preceding this sign is derived from the following one.

ad loc.	*ad locum*, "at the place"; used in quotations of commentaries.
A.H.	*Anno Hegirae*, "in the year of Hegira," i.e., according to the Muslim calendar.
Akk.	Addadian.
A.M.	*anno mundi*, "in the year (from the creation) of the world."
anon.	anonymous.
Ar.	Arabic.
Aram.	Aramaic.
Ass.	Assyrian.
b.	born; *ben, bar.*
Bab.	Babylonian.
B.C.E.	Before Common Era (= B.C.).
bibl.	bibliography.
Bul.	Bulgarian.
c., ca.	Circa.
C.E.	Common Era (= A.D.).
cf.	*confer*, "compare."
ch., chs.	chapter, chapters.
comp.	compiler, compiled by.
Cz.	Czech.
D	according to the documentary theory, the Deuteronomy document.
d.	died.
Dan.	Danish.
diss., dissert,	dissertation, thesis.
Du.	Dutch.
E.	according to the documentary theory, the Elohist document (i.e., using Elohim as the name of God) of the first five (or six) books of the Bible.
ed.	editor, edited, edition.
eds.	editors.
e.g.	*exempli gratia*, "for example."
Eng.	English.
et al.	*et alibi*, "and elsewhere"; or *et alii*, "and others"; "others."
f., ff.	and following page(s).
fig.	figure.
fl.	flourished.
fol., fols	folio(s).
Fr.	French.
Ger.	German.
Gr.	Greek.
Heb.	Hebrew.
Hg., Hung	Hungarian.
ibid	*Ibidem*, "in the same place."
incl. bibl.	includes bibliography.
introd.	introduction.
It.	Italian.
J	according to the documentary theory, the Jahwist document (i.e., using YHWH as the name of God) of the first five (or six) books of the Bible.
Lat.	Latin.
lit.	literally.
Lith.	Lithuanian.
loc. cit.	*loco citato*, "in the [already] cited place."
Ms., Mss.	Manuscript(s).
n.	note.
n.d.	no date (of publication).
no., nos	number(s).
Nov.	Novellae (Heb. *Ḥiddushim*).
n.p.	place of publication unknown.
op. cit.	*opere citato*, "in the previously mentioned work."
P.	according to the documentary theory, the Priestly document of the first five (or six) books of the Bible.
p., pp.	page(s).
Pers.	Persian.
pl., pls.	plate(s).
Pol.	Polish.
Port.	Potuguese.
pt., pts.	part(s).
publ.	published.
R.	Rabbi or Rav (before names); in Midrash (after an abbreviation) – *Rabbah.*
r.	recto, the first side of a manuscript page.
Resp.	Responsa (Latin "answers," Hebrew *She'elot u-Teshuvot* or *Teshuvot),* collections of rabbinic decisions.
rev.	revised.

Rom.	Romanian.
Rus(s).	Russian.
Slov.	Slovak.
Sp.	Spanish.
s.v.	*sub verbo, sub voce*, "under the (key) word."
Sum	Sumerian.
summ.	Summary.
suppl.	supplement.
Swed.	Swedish.
tr., trans(l).	translator, translated, translation.
Turk.	Turkish.
Ukr.	Ukrainian.
v., vv.	*verso*. The second side of a manuscript page; also verse(s).
Yid.	Yiddish.

ABBREVIATIONS USED IN RABBINICAL LITERATURE

Adderet Eliyahu, Karaite treatise by Elijah b. Moses *Bashyazi.
Admat Kodesh, Resp. by Nissim Ḥayyim Moses b. Joseph |Mizraḥi.
Aguddah, Sefer ha-, Nov. by *Alexander Suslin ha-Kohen.
Ahavat Ḥesed, compilation by *Israel Meir ha-Kohen.
Aliyyot de-Rabbenu Yonah, Nov. by *Jonah b. Avraham Gerondi.
Arukh ha-Shulḥan, codification by Jehiel Michel *Epstein.
Asayin (= positive precepts), subdivision of: (1) *Maimonides, *Sefer ha-Mitzvot;* (2) *Moses b. Jacob of Coucy, *Semag.*
Asefat Dinim, subdivision of *Sedei Ḥemed* by Ḥayyim Hezekiah *Medini, an encyclopaedia of precepts and responsa.
Asheri = *Asher b. Jehiel.
Aeret Ḥakhamim, by Baruch *Frankel-Teomim; pt, 1: Resp. to Sh. Ar.; pt2: Nov. to Talmud.
Ateret Zahav, subdivision of the *Levush*, a codification by Mordecai b. Abraham (Levush) *Jaffe; *Ateret Zahav* parallels Tur. YD.
Ateret Ẓevi, Comm. To Sh. Ar. by Ẓevi Hirsch b. Azriel.
Avir Ya'akov, Resp. by Jacob Avigdor.
Avkat Rokhel, Resp. by Joseph b. Ephraim *Caro.
Avnei Millu'im, Comm. to Sh. Ar., EH, by *Aryeh Loeb b. Joseph ha-Kohen.
Avnei Nezer, Resp. on Sh. Ar. by Abraham b. Ze'ev Nahum Bornstein of *Sochaczew.
Avodat Massa, Compilation of Tax Law by Yoasha Abraham Judah.
Azei ha-Levanon, Resp. by Judah Leib *Zirelson.

Ba'al ha-Tanya – *Shneur Zalman of Lyady.
Ba'ei Ḥayyei, Resp. by Ḥayyim b. Israel *Benveniste.
Ba'er Heitev, Comm. To Sh. Ar. The parts on OḤ and EH are by Judah b. Simeon *Ashkenazi, the parts on YD AND ḤM by *Zechariah Mendel b. Aryeh Leib. Printed in most editions of Sh. Ar.
Baḥ = Joel *Sirkes.
Baḥ, usual abbreviation for *Bayit Ḥadash*, a commentary on Tur by Joel *Sirkes; printed in most editions of Tur.
Bayit Ḥadash, see *Baḥ*.
Berab = Jacob Berab, also called Ri Berav.
Bedek ha-Bayit, by Joseph b. Ephraim *Caro, additions to his *Beit Yosef* (a comm. to Tur). Printed sometimes inside *Beit Yosef*, in smaller type. Appears in most editions of Tur.
Be'er ha-Golah, Commentary to Sh. Ar. By Moses b. Naphtali Hirsch *Rivkes; printed in most editions of Sh. Ar.
Be'er Mayim, Resp. by Raphael b. Abraham Manasseh Jacob.
Be'er Mayim Ḥayyim, Resp. by Samuel b. Ḥayyim *Vital.
Be'er Yiẓḥak, Resp. by Isaac Elhanan *Spector.
Beit ha-Beḥirah, Comm. to Talmud by Menahem b. Solomon *Meiri.
Beit Me'ir, Nov. on Sh. Ar. by Meir b. Judah Leib Posner.
Beit Shelomo, Resp. by Solomon b. Aaron Ḥason (the younger).
Beit Shemu'el, Comm. to Sh. Ar., EH, by *Samuel b. Uri Shraga Phoebus.
Beit Ya'akov, by Jacob b. Jacob Moses *Lorberbaum; pt.1: Nov. to Ket.; pt.2: Comm. to EH.
Beit Yisrael, collective name for the commentaries *Derishah, Perishah,* and *Be'urim* by Joshua b. Alexander ha-Kohen *Falk. See under the names of the commentaries.
Beit Yiẓḥak, Resp. by Isaac *Schmelkes.
Beit Yosef: (1) Comm. on Tur by Joseph b. Ephraim *Caro; printed in most editions of Tur; (2) Resp. by the same.
Ben Yehudah, Resp. by Abraham b. Judah Litsch (ליטש) Rosenbaum.
Bertinoro, Standard commentary to Mishnah by Obadiah *Bertinoro. Printed in most editions of the Mishnah.
[Be'urei] Ha-Gra, Comm. to Bible, Talmud, and Sh. Ar. By *Elijah b. Solomon Zalmon (Gaon of Vilna); printed in major editions of the mentioned works.
Be'urim, Glosses to Isserles *Darkhei Moshe* (a comm. on Tur) by Joshua b. Alexander ha-Kohen *Falk; printed in many editions of Tur.
Binyamin Ze'ev, Resp. by *Benjamin Ze'ev b. Mattathias of Arta.
Birkei Yosef, Nov. by Ḥayyim Joseph David *Azulai.
Ha-Buẓ ve-ha-Argaman, subdivision of the *Levush* (a codification by Mordecai b. Abraham (Levush) *Jaffe); *Ha-Buẓ ve-ha-Argaman* parallels Tur, EH.

Comm. = Commentary

Da'at Kohen, Resp. by Abraham Isaac ha-Kohen. *Kook.
Darkhei Moshe, Comm. on Tur Moses b. Israel *Isserles; printed in most editions of Tur.
Darkhei No'am, Resp. by *Mordecai b. Judah ha-Levi.
Darkhei Teshuvah, Nov. by Ẓevi *Shapiro; printed in the major editions of Sh. Ar.
De'ah ve-Haskel, Resp. by Obadiah Hadaya (see *Yaskil Avdi).*

Derashot Ran, Sermons by *Nissim b. Reuben Gerondi.
Derekh Ḥayyim, Comm. to *Avot* by *Judah Loew (Lob., Liwa) b. Bezalel (Maharal) of Prague.
Derishah, by Joshua b. Alexander ha-Kohen *Falk; additions to his *Perishah* (comm. on Tur); printed in many editions of Tur.
Derushei ha-Ẓelaḥ, Sermons, by Ezekiel b. Judah Halevi *Landau.
Devar Avraham, Resp. by Abraham *Shapira.
Devar Shemu'el, Resp. by Samuel *Aboab.
Devar Yehoshu'a, Resp. by Joshua Menahem b. Isaac Aryeh Ehrenberg.
Dikdukei Soferim, variae lections of the talmudic text by Raphael Nathan*Rabbinowicz.
Divrei Emet, Resp. by Isaac Bekhor David.
Divrei Ge'onim, Digest of responsa by Ḥayyim Aryeh b. Jeḥiel Ẓevi *Kahana.
Divrei Ḥamudot, Comm. on *Piskei ha-Rosh* by Yom Tov Lipmann b. Nathan ha-Levi *Heller; printed in major editions of the Talmud.
Divrei Ḥayyim several works by Ḥayyim *Halberstamm; if quoted alone refers to his Responsa.
Divrei Malkhi'el, Resp. by Malchiel Tenebaum.
Divrei Rivot, Resp. by Isaac b. Samuel *Adarbi.
Divrei Shemu'el, Resp. by Samuel Raphael Arditi.

Edut be-Ya'akov, Resp. by Jacob b. Abraham *Boton.
Edut bi-Yhosef, Resp. by Joseph b. Isaac *Almosnino.
Ein Ya'akov, Digest of talmudic *aggadot* by Jacob (Ibn) *Habib.
Ein Yiẓḥak, Resp. by Isaac Elhanan *Spector.
Ephraim of Lentshitz = Solomon *Luntschitz.
Erekh Leḥem, Nov. and glosses to Sh. Ar. by Jacob b. Abraham *Castro.
Eshkol, Sefer ha-, Digest of *halakhot* by *Abraham b. Isaac of Narbonne.
Et Sofer, Treatise on Law Court documents by Abraham b. Mordecai *Ankawa, in the 2nd vol. of his Resp. *Kerem Ḥamar.*
Etan ha-Ezraḥi, Resp. by Abraham b. Israel Jehiel (Shrenzl) *Rapaport.
Even ha-Ezel, Nov. to Maimonides' *Yad Ḥazakah* by Isser Zalman *Meltzer.
Even ha-Ezer, also called *Raban* of *Ẓafenat Pa'ne'aḥ,* rabbinical work with varied contents by *Eliezer b. Nathan of Mainz; not identical with the subdivision of Tur, Shulḥan Arukh, etc.
Ezrat Yehudah, Resp. by *Isaar Judah b. Nechemiah of Brisk.

Gan Eden, Karaite treatise by *Aaron b. Elijah of Nicomedia.
Gersonides = *Levi b. Gershom, also called Leo Hebraecus, or Ralbag.
Ginnat Veradim, Resp. by *Abraham b. Mordecai ha-Levi.

Haggahot, another name for *Rema.*
Haggahot Asheri, glosses to *Piskei ha-Rosh* by *Israel of Krems; printed in most Talmud editions.
Haggahot Maimuniyyot, Comm,. to Maimonides' Yad Ḥazakah by *Meir ha-Kohen; printed in most eds. of Yad.
Haggahot Mordekhai, glosses to *Mordekhai* by Samuel *Schlettstadt; printed in most editions of the Talmud after *Mordekhai.*
Haggahot ha-Rashash on Tosafot, annotations of Samuel *Strashun on the Tosafot (printed in major editions of the Talmud).
Ha-Gra = *Elijah b. Solomon Zalman (Gaon of Vilna).
Ha-Gra, Commentaries on Bible, Talmud, and Sh. Ar. respectively, by *Elijah b. Solomon Zalman (Gaon of Vilna); printed in major editions of the mentioned works.
Hai Gaon, Comm. = his comm. on Mishnah.
Ḥakham Ẓevi, Resp. by Ẓevi Hirsch b. Jacob *Ashkenazi.
Halakhot = Rif, *Halakhot.* Compilation and abstract of the Talmud by Isaac b. Jacob ha-Kohen *Alfasi; printed in most editions of the Talmud.
Halakhot Gedolot, compilation of *halakhot* from the Geonic period, arranged acc. to the Talmud. Here cited acc. to ed. Warsaw (1874). Author probably *Simeon Kayyara of Basra.
Halakhot Pesukot le-Rav Yehudai Ga'on compilation of *halakhot.*
Halakhot Pesukot min ha-Ge'onim, compilation of *halakhot* from the geonic period by different authors.
Ḥananel, Comm. to Talmud by *Hananel b. Ḥushi'el; printed in some editions of the Talmud.
Harei Besamim, Resp. by Aryeh Leib b. Isaac *Horowitz.
Ḥassidim, Sefer, Ethical maxims by *Judah b. Samuel he-Ḥasid.
Hassagot Rabad on Rif, Glosses on Rif, *Halakhot,* by *Abraham b. David of Posquières.
Hassagot Rabad [on Yad], Glosses on Maimonides, *Yad Ḥazakah,* by *Abraham b. David of Posquières.
Hassagot Ramban, Glosses by Naḥmanides on Maimonides' *Sefer ha-Mitzvot;* usually printed together with *Sefer ha-Mitzvot.*
Ḥatam Sofer = Moses *Sofer.
Ḥavvot Ya'ir, Resp. and varia by Jair Ḥayyim *Bacharach
Ḥayyim Or Zaru'a = *Ḥayyim (Eliezer) b. Isaac.
Ḥazon Ish = Abraham Isaiah *Karelitz.
Ḥazon Ish, Nov. by Abraham Isaiah *Karelitz
Ḥedvat Ya'akov, Resp. by Aryeh Judah Jacob b. David Dov Meisels (article under his father's name).
Heikhal Yiẓḥak, Resp. by Isaac ha-Levi *Herzog.
Ḥelkat Meḥokek, Comm. to Sh. Ar., by Moses b. Isaac Judah *Lima.
Ḥelkat Ya'akov, Resp. by Mordecai Jacob Breisch.
Ḥemdah Genuzah, , Resp. from the geonic period by different authors.
Ḥemdat Shelomo, Resp. by Solomon Zalman *Lipschitz.
Ḥida = Ḥayyim Joseph David *Azulai.
Ḥiddushei Halakhot ve-Aggadot, Nov. by Samuel Eliezer b. Judah ha-Levi *Edels.
Ḥikekei Lev, Resp. by Ḥayyim *Palaggi.
Ḥikrei Lev, Nov. to Sh. Ar. by Joseph Raphael b. Ḥayyim Joseph Ḥazzan (see article *Ḥazzan Family).
Hil. = Hilkhot ... (e.g. *Hilkhot Shabbat).*
Ḥinnukh, Sefer ha-, List and explanation of precepts attributed (probably erroneously) to Aaron ha-Levi of Barcelona (see article *Ha-Ḥinnukh*).
Ḥok Ya'akov, Comm. to Hil. Pesaḥ in Sh. Ar., OḤ, by Jacob b. Joseph *Reicher.
Ḥokhmat Sehlomo (1), Glosses to Talmud, *Rashi* and Tosafot by Solomon b. Jehiel "Maharshal") *Luria; printed in many editions of the Talmud.
Ḥokhmat Sehlomo (2), Glosses and Nov. to Sh. Ar. by Solomon b. Judah Aaron *Kluger printed in many editions of Sh. Ar.
Ḥur, subdivision of the *Levush,* a codification by Mordecai b. Abraham (Levush) *Jaffe; *Hur* (or *Levush ha-Hur)* parallels Tur, OḤ, 242–697.
Ḥut ha-Meshullash, fourth part of the *Tashbeẓ* (Resp.), by Simeon b. Zemaḥ *Duran.

Ibn Ezra, Comm. to the Bible by Abraham *Ibn Ezra; printed in the major editions of the Bible *("Mikra'ot Gedolot").*
Imrei Yosher, Resp. by Meir b. Aaron Judah *Arik.
Ir Shushan, Subdivision of the *Levush,* a codification by Mordecai b. Abraham (Levush) *Jaffe; *Ir Shushan* parallels Tur, ḤM.
Israel of Bruna = Israel b. Ḥayyim *Bruna.
Ittur. Treatise on precepts by *Isaac b. Abba Mari of Marseilles.

Jacob Be Rab = *Be Rab.
Jacob b. Jacob Moses of Lissa = Jacob b. Jacob Moses *Lorberbaum.
Judah B. Simeon = Judah b. Simeon *Ashkenazi.
Judah Minz = Judah b. Eliezer ha-Levi *Minz.

Kappei Aharon, Resp. by Aaron Azriel.
Kehillat Ya'akov, Talmudic methodology, definitions etc. by Israel Jacob b. Yom Tov *Algazi.
Kelei Ḥemdah, Nov. and *pilpulim* by Meir Dan *Plotzki of Ostrova, arranged acc. to the Torah.
Keli Yakar, Annotations to the Torah by Solomon *Luntschitz.
Keneh Ḥokhmah, Sermons by Judah Loeb *Pochwitzer.
Keneset ha-Gedolah, Digest of *halakhot* by Ḥayyim b. Israel *Benveniste; subdivided into annotations to *Beit Yosef* and annotations to Tur.
Keneset Yisrael, Resp. by Ezekiel b. Abraham Katzenellenbogen (see article *Katzenellenbogen Family).
Kerem Ḥamar, Resp. and varia by Abraham b. Mordecai *Ankawa.
Kerem Shelmo. Resp. by Solomon b. Joseph *Amarillo.
Keritut, [Sefer], Methodology of the Talmud by *Samson b. Isaac of Chinon.
Kesef ha-Kedoshim, Comm. to Sh. Ar., ḤM, by Abraham *Wahrmann; printed in major editions of Sh. Ar.
Kesef Mishneh, Comm. to Maimonides, *Yad Ḥazakah,* by Joseph b. Ephraim *Caro; printed in most editions of *Yad Ḥazakah.*
Kezot ha-Ḥoshen, Comm. to Sh. Ar., ḤM, by *Aryeh Loeb b. Joseph ha-Kohen; printed in major editions of Sh. Ar.
Kol Bo [*Sefer*], Anonymous collection of ritual rules; also called *Sefer ha-Likkutim.*
Kol Mevasser, Resp. by Meshullam *Rath.
Korban Aharon, Comm. to *Sifra* by Aaron b. Abraham *Ibn Ḥayyim; pt. 1 is called: *Middot Aharon.*
Korban Edah, Comm. to Jer. Talmud by David *Fraenkel; with additions: *Shiyyurei Korban;* printed in most editions of Jer. Talmud.
Kunteres ha-Kelalim, subdivision of *Sedei Ḥemed,* an encyclopaedia of precepts and responsa by Ḥayyim Hezekiah *Medini.
Kunteres ha-Semikhah, a treatise by *Levi b. Ḥabib; printed at the end of his responsa.
Kunteres Tikkun Olam, part of *Mispat Shalom* (Nov. by Shalom Mordecai b. Moses *Schwadron).

Lavin (negative precepts), subdivision of: (1) *Maimonides, *Sefer ha-Mitzvot;* (2) *Moses b. Jacob of Coucy, *Semag.*
Leḥem Mishneh, Comm. to Maimonides, *Yad Ḥazakah,* by Abraham [Ḥiyya] b. Moses *Boton; printed in most editions of *Yad Ḥazakah.*
Leḥem Rav, Resp. by Abraham [Ḥiyya] b. Moses *Boton.
Leket Yosher, Resp and varia by Israel b. Pethahiah *Isserlein, collected by *Joseph (Joselein) b. Moses.
Leo Hebraeus = *Levi b. Gershom, also called Ralbag or Gersonides.
Levush = Mordecai b. Abraham *Jaffe.
Levush [Malkhut], Codification by Mordecai b. Abraham (Levush) *Jaffe, with subdivisions: [*Levush ha-] Tekhelet* (parallels Tur OḤ 1–241); [*Levush ha-] Ḥur* (parallels Tur OḤ 242–697); [*Levush] Ateret Zahav* (parallels Tur YD); [*Levush ha-Buẓ ve-ha-Argaman* (parallels Tur EH); [*Levush] Ir Shushan* (parallels Tur ḤM); under the name *Levush* the author wrote also other works.
Li-Leshonot ha-Rambam, fifth part (nos. 1374–1700) of Resp. by *David b. Solomon ibn Abi Zimra (Radbaz).
Likkutim, Sefer ha-, another name for [*Sefer] Kol Bo.*

Ma'adanei Yom Tov, Comm. on *Piskei ha-Rosh* by Yom Tov Lipmann b. Nathan ha-Levi *Heller; printed in many editions of the Talmud.
Mabit = Moses b. Joseph *Trani.
Magen Avot, Comm. to *Avot* by Simeon b. Ẓemaḥ *Duran.
Magen Avraham, Comm. to Sh. Ar., OḤ, by Abraham Abele b. Ḥayyim ha-Levi *Gombiner; printed in many editions of Sh. Ar., OḤ.
Maggid Mishneh, Comm. to Maimonides, *Yad Ḥazakah,* by *Vidal Yom Tov of Tolosa; printed in most editions of the *Yad Ḥazakah.*
Maḥaneh Efrayim, Resp. and Nov., arranged acc. to Maimonides' *Yad Ḥazakah* , by Ephraim b. Aaron *Navon.
Maharai = Israel b. Pethahiah *Isserlein.
Maharal of Prague = *Judah Loew (Lob, Liwa), b. Bezalel.
Maharalbaḥ = *Levi b. Ḥabib.
Maharam Alashkar = Moses b. Isaac *Alashkar.
Maharam Alshekh = Moses b. Ḥayyim *Alashekh.
Maharam Mintz = Moses *Mintz.
Maharam of Lublin = *Meir b. Gedaliah of Lublin.
Maharam of Padua = Meir *Katzenellenbogen.
Maharam of Rothenburg = *Meir b. Baruch of Rothenburg.
Maharam Shik = Moses b. Joseph Schick.
Maharash Engel = Samuel b. Ze'ev Wolf Engel.
Maharashdam = Samuel b. Moses *Medina.
Maharḥash = Ḥayyim (ben) Shabbetai.
Mahari Basan = Jehiel b. Ḥayyim Basan.
Mahari b. Lev = Joseph ibn Lev.
Mahari'az = Jekuthiel Asher Zalman Ensil Zusmir.
Maharibal = *Joseph ibn Lev.
Mahariḥ = Jacob (Israel) *Ḥagiz.
Maharik = Joseph b. Solomon *Colon.
Maharikash = Jacob b. Abraham *Castro.
Maharil = Jacob b. Moses *Moellin.
Maharimat = Joseph b. Moses di Trani (not identical with the Maharit).
Maharit = Joseph b. Moses *Trani.
Maharitaẓ = Yom Tov b. Akiva Ẓahalon. (See article *Ẓahalon Family).
Maharsha = Samuel Eliezer b. Judah ha-Levi *Edels.
Maharshag = Simeon b. Judah Gruenfeld.
Maharshak = Samson b. Isaac of Chinon.
Maharshakh = *Solomon b. Abraham.
Maharshal = Solomon b. Jeḥiel *Luria.
Mahasham = Shalom Mordecai b. Moses *Sschwadron.
Maharyu = Jacob b. Judah *Weil.
Maḥazeh Avraham, Resp. by Abraham Nebagen v. Meir ha-Levi Steinberg.
Maḥazik Berakhah, Nov. by Ḥayyim Joseph David *Azulai.

*Maimonides = Moses b. Maimon, or Rambam.
*Malbim = Meir Loeb b. Jehiel Michael.
Malbim = Malbim's comm. to the Bible; printed in the major editions.
Malbushei Yom Tov, Nov. on *Levush*, OḤ, by Yom Tov Lipmann b. Nathan ha-Levi *Heller.
Mappah, another name for *Rema.*
Mareh ha-Panim, Comm. to Jer. Talmud by Moses b. Simeon *Margolies; printed in most editions of Jer. Talmud.
Margaliyyot ha-Yam, Nov. by Reuben *Margoliot.
Masat Binyamin, Resp. by Benjamin Aaron b. Abraham *Slonik
Mashbir, Ha- = *Joseph Samuel b. Isaac Rodi.
Massa Ḥayyim, Tax *halakhot* by Ḥayyim *Palaggi, with the subdivisions *Missim ve-Arnomiyyot* and *Torat ha-Minhagot.*
Massa Melekh, Compilation of Tax Law by Joseph b. Isaac *Ibn Ezra with concluding part *Ne'ilat She'arim.*
Matteh Asher, Resp. by Asher b. Emanuel Shalem.
Matteh Shimon, Digest of Resp. and Nov. to Tur and *Beit Yosef*, ḤM, by Mordecai Simeon b. Solomon.
Matteh Yosef, Resp. by Joseph b. Moses ha-Levi Nazir (see article under his father's name).
Mayim Amukkim, Resp. by Elijah b. Abraham *Mizraḥi.
Mayim Ḥayyim, Resp. by Ḥayyim b. Dov Beresh Rapaport.
Mayim Rabbim, , Resp. by Raphael *Meldola.
Me-Emek ha-Bakha, , Resp. by Simeon b. Jekuthiel Ephrati.
Me'irat Einayim, usual abbreviation: *Sma* (from: *Sefer Me'irat Einayim*); comm. to Sh. Ar. By Joshua b. Alexander ha-Kohen *Falk; printed in most editions of the Sh. Ar.
Melammed le-Ho'il, Resp. by David Ẓevi *Hoffmann.
Meisharim, [*Sefer*], Rabbinical treatise by *Jeroham b. Meshullam.
Meshiv Davar, Resp. by Naphtali Ẓevi Judah *Berlin.
Mi-Gei ha-Haregah, Resp. by Simeon b. Jekuthiel Ephrati.
Mi-Ma'amakim, Resp. by Ephraim Oshry.
Middot Aharon, first part of *Korban Aharon*, a comm. to *Sifra* by Aaron b. Abraham *Ibn Ḥayyim.
Migdal Oz, Comm. to Maimonides, *Yad Ḥazakah*, by *Ibn Gaon Shem Tov b. Abraham; printed in most editions of the *Yad Ḥazakah.*
Mikhtam le-David, Resp. by David Samuel b. Jacob *Pardo.
Mikkaḥ ve-ha-Mimkar, Sefer ha-, Rabbinical treatise by *Hai Gaon.
Milḥamot ha-Shem, Glosses to Rif, *Halakhot*, by *Naḥmanides.
Minḥat Ḥinnukh, Comm. to *Sefer ha-Ḥinnukh*, by Joseph b. Moses *Babad.
Minḥat Yiẓḥak, Resp. by Isaac Jacob b. Joseph Judah Weiss.
Misgeret ha-Shulḥan, Comm. to Sh. Ar., ḤM, by Benjamin Ze'ev Wolf b. Shabbetai; printed in most editions of Sh. Ar.
Mishkenot ha-Ro'im, *Halakhot* in alphabetical order by Uzziel Alshekh.
Mishnah Berurah, Comm. to Sh. Ar., OḤ, by *Israel Meir ha-Kohen.
Mishneh le-Melekh, Comm. to Maimonides, *Yad Ḥazakah*, by Judah *Rosanes; printed in most editions of *Yad Ḥazakah.*
Mishpat ha-Kohanim, Nov. to Sh. Ar., ḤM, by Jacob Moses *Lorberbaum, part of his *Netivot ha-Mishpat;* printed in major editions of Sh. Ar.
Mishpat Kohen, Resp. by Abraham Isaac ha-Kohen *Kook.
Mishpat Shalom, Nov. by Shalom Mordecai b. Moses *Schwadron; contains: *Kunteres Tikkun Olam.*
Mishpat u-Ẓedakah be-Ya'akov, Resp. by Jacob b. Reuben *Ibn Ẓur.
Mishpat ha-Urim, Comm. to Sh. Ar., ḤM by Jacob b. Jacob Moses *Lorberbaum, part of his *Netivot ha-Mishpat*; printed in major editons of Sh. Ar.
Mishpat Ẓedek, Resp. by *Melammed Meir b. Shem Tov.
Mishpatim Yesharim, Resp. by Raphael b. Mordecai *Berdugo.
Mishpetei Shemu'el, Resp. by Samuel b. Moses *Kalai (Kal'i).
Mishpetei ha-Tanna'im, Kunteres, Nov on *Levush*, OḤ by Yom Tov Lipmann b. Nathan ha-Levi *Heller.
Mishpetei Uzzi'el (Uziel), Resp. by Ben-Zion Meir Hai *Ouziel.
Missim ve-Arnoniyyot, Tax *halakhot* by Ḥayyim *Palaggi, a subdivision of his work *Massa Ḥayyim* on the same subject.
Mitzvot, Sefer ha-, Elucidation of precepts by *Maimonides; subdivided into *Lavin* (negative precepts) and *Asayin* (positive precepts).
Mitzvot Gadol, Sefer, Elucidation of precepts by *Moses b. Jacob of Coucy, subdivided into *Lavin* (negative precepts) and *Asayin* (positive precepts); the usual abbreviation is *Semag.*
Mitzvot Katan, Sefer, Elucidation of precepts by *Isaac b. Joseph of Corbeil; the usual, abbreviation is *Semak.*
Mo'adim u-Zemannim, Rabbinical treatises by Moses Sternbuch.
Modigliano, Joseph Samuel = *Joseph Samuel b. Isaac, Rodi (Ha-Mashbir).
Mordekhai (Mordecai), halakhic compilation by *Mordecai b. Hillel; printed in most editions of the Talmud after the texts.
Moses b. Maimon = *Maimonides, also called Rambam.
Moses b. Naḥman = Naḥmanides, also called Ramban.
Muram = Isaiah Menahem b. Isaac (from: Morenu R. Mendel).

Naḥal Yiẓḥak, Comm. on Sh. Ar., ḤM, by Isaac Elhanan *Spector.
Naḥalah li-Yhoshu'a, Resp. by Joshua Ẓunẓin.
Naḥalat Shivah, collection of legal forms by *Samuel b. David Moses ha-Levi.
*Naḥmanides = Moses b. Naḥman, also called Ramban.
Naẓiv = Naphtali Ẓevi Judah *Berlin.
Ne'eman Shemu'el, Resp. by Samuel Isaac *Modigilano.
Ne'ilat She'arim, concluding part of *Massa Melekh* (a work on Tax Law) by Joseph b. Isaac *Ibn Ezra, containing an exposition of customary law and subdivided into *Minhagei Issur* and *Minhagei Mamon.*
Ner Ma'aravi, Resp. by Jacob b. Malka.
Netivot ha-Mishpat, by Jacob b. Jacob Moses *Lorberbaum; subdivided into *Mishpat ha-Kohanim*, Nov. to Sh. Ar., ḤM, and *Mishpat ha-Urim*, a comm. on the same; printed in major editions of Sh. Ar.
Netivot Olam, Saying of the Sages by *Judah Loew (Lob, Liwa) b. Bezalel.
Nimmukei Menaḥem of Merseburg, Tax *halakhot* by the same, printed at the end of Resp. Maharyu.
Nimmukei Yosef, Comm. to Rif. *Halakhot*, by Joseph *Ḥabib (Ḥabiba); printed in many editions of the Talmud.
Noda bi-Yhudah, Resp. by Ezekiel b. Judah ha-Levi *Landau; there is a first collection *(Mahadura Kamma)* and a second collection *(Mahadura Tinyana).*
Nov. = Novellae, Ḥiddushim.

Ohel Moshe (1), Notes to Talmud, *Midrash Rabbah*, Yad, *Sifrei* and to several Resp., by Eleazar *Horowitz.

Ohel Moshe (2), Resp. by Moses Jonah Zweig.
Oholei Tam. Resp. by *Tam ibn Yaḥya Jacob b. David; printed in the rabbinical collection *Tummat Yesharim.*
Oholei Ya'akov, Resp. by Jacob de *Castro.
Or ha-Me'ir Resp by Judah Meir b. Jacob Samson Shapiro.
Or Same'aḥ, Comm. to Maimonides, *Yad Ḥazakah,* by *Meir Simḥah ha-Kohen of Dvinsk; printed in many editions of the *Yad Ḥazakah.*
Or Zaru'a [the father] = *Isaac b. Moses of Vienna.
Or Zaru'a [the son] = *Ḥayyim (Eliezer) b. Isaac.
Or Zaru'a, Nov. by *Isaac b. Moses of Vienna.
Orah, Sefer ha-, Compilation of ritual precepts by *Rashi.
Oraḥ la-Ẓaddik, Resp. by Abraham Ḥayyim Rodrigues.
Oẓar ha-Posekim, Digest of Responsa.

Paḥad Yiẓḥak, Rabbinical encyclopaedia by Isaac *Lampronti.
Panim Me'irot, Resp. by Meir b. Isaac *Eisenstadt.
Parashat Mordekhai, Resp. by Mordecai b. Abraham Naphtali *Banet.
Pe'at ha-Sadeh la-Dinim and Pe'at ha-Sadeh la-Kelalim, subdivisions of the *Sedei Ḥemed,* an encyclopaedia of precepts and responsa, by Ḥayyim Hezekaih *Medini.
Penei Moshe (1), Resp. by Moses *Benveniste.
Penei Moshe (2), Comm. to Jer. Talmud by Moses b. Simeon *Margolies; printed in most editions of the Jer. Talmud.
Penei Moshe (3), Comm. on the aggadic passages of 18 treatises of the Bab. and Jer. Talmud, by Moses b. Isaiah Katz.
Penei Yehoshu'a, Nov. by Jacob Joshua b. Ẓevi Hirsch *Falk.
Peri Ḥadash, Comm. on Sh. Ar. By Hezekiah da *Silva.
Perishah, Comm. on Tur by Joshua b. Alexander ha-Kohen *Falk; printed in major edition of Tur; forms together with *Derishah* and *Be'urim* (by the same author) the *Beit Yisrael.*
Pesakim u-Khetavim, 2nd part of the *Terumat ha-Deshen* by Israel b. Pethahiah *Isserlein' also called *Piskei Maharai.*
Pilpula Ḥarifta, Comm. to *Piskei ha-Rosh, Seder Nezikin,* by Yom Tov Lipmann b. Nathan ha-Levi *Heller; printed in major editions of the Talmud.
Piskei Maharai, see *Terumat ha-Deshen,* 2nd part; also called *Pesakim u-Khetavim.*
Piskei ha-Rosh, a compilation of *halakhot,* arranged on the Talmud, by *Asher b. Jehiel (Rosh); printed in major Talmud editions.
Pitḥei Teshuvah, Comm. to Sh. Ar. by Abraham Hirsch b. Jacob *Eisenstadt; printed in major editions of the Sh. Ar.

Rabad = *Abraham b. David of Posquières (Rabad III.).
Raban = *Eliezer b. Nathan of Mainz.
Raban, also called *Ẓafenat Pa'ne'aḥ* or *Even ha-Ezer,* see under the last name.
Rabi Abad = *Abraham b. Isaac of Narbonne.
Radad = David Dov. b. Aryeh Judah Jacob *Meisels.
Radam = Dov Berush b. Isaac Meisels.
Radbaz = *David b Solomon ibn Abi Ziumra.
Radbaz, Comm. to Maimonides, *Yad Ḥazakah,* by *David b. Solomon ibn Abi Zimra.
Ralbag = *Levi b. Gershom, also called Gersonides, or Leo Hebraeus.
Ralbag, Bible comm. by *Levi b. Gershon.
Rama [da Fano] = Menaḥem Azariah *Fano.
Ramah = Meir b. Todros [ha-Levi] *Abulafia.
Ramam = *Menaham of Merseburg.
Rambam = *Maimonides; real name: Moses b. Maimon.
Ramban = *Naḥmanides; real name Moses b. Naḥman.
Ramban, Comm. to Torah by *Naḥmanides; printed in major editions. ("Mikra'ot Gedolot").
Ran = *Nissim b. Reuben Gerondi.
Ran of Rif, Comm. on Rif, *Halakhot,* by Nissim b. Reuben Gerondi.
Ranaḥ = *Elijah b. Ḥayyim.
Rash = *Samson b. Abraham of Sens.
Rash, Comm. to Mishnah, by *Samson b. Abraham of Sens; printed in major Talmud editions.
Rashash = Samuel *Strashun.
Rashba = Solomon b. Abraham *Adret.
Rashba, Resp., see also; *Sefer Teshuvot ha-Rashba ha-Meyuḥasot le-ha-Ramban,* by Solomon b. Abraham *Adret.
Rashbad = Samuel b. David.
Rashbam = *Samuel b. Meir.
Rashbam = Comm. on Bible and Talmud by *Samuel b. Meir; printed in major editions of Bible and most editions of Talmud.
Rashbash = Solomon b. Simeon *Duran.
*Rashi = Solomon b. Isaac of Troyes.
Rashi, Comm. on Bible and Talmud by *Rashi; printed in almost all Bible and Talmud editions.
Raviah = Eliezer b. Joel ha-Levi.
Redak = David *Kimḥi.
Redak, Comm. to Bible by David *Kimḥi.
Redakh = *David b. Ḥayyim ha-Kohen of Corfu.
Re'em = Elijah b. Abraham *Mizraḥi.
Rema = Moses b. Israel *Isserles.
Rema, Glosses to Sh. Ar. by Moses b. Israel *Isserles; printed in almost all editions of the Sh. Ar. inside the text in Rashi type; also called *Mappah* or *Haggahot.*
Remek = Moses Kimḥi.
Remakh = Moses ha-Kohen mi-Lunel.
Reshakh = *Solomon b. Abraham; also called Maharshakh.
Resp. = Responsa, *She'elot u-Teshuvot.*
Ri Berav = *Berab.
Ri Escapa = Joseph b. Saul *Escapa.
Ri Migash = Joseph b. Meir ha-Levi *Ibn Migash.
Riba = Isaac b. Asher ha-Levi; Riba II (Riba ha-Baḥur) = his grandson with the same name.
Ribam = Isaac b. Mordecai (or: Isaac b. Meir).
Ribash = *Isaac b. Sheshet Perfet (or: Barfat).
Rid= *Isaiah b. Mali di Trani the Elder.
Ridbaz = Jacob David b. Ze'ev *Willowski.
Rif = Isaac b. Jacob ha-Kohen *Alfasi.
Rif, *Halakhot,* Compilation and abstract of the Talmud by Isaac b. Jacob ha-Kohen *Alfasi.
Ritba = Yom Tov b. Abraham *Ishbili.
Riẓbam = Isaac b. Mordecai.
Rosh = *Asher b. Jehiel, also called Asheri.
Rosh Mashbir, Resp. by *Joseph Samuel b. Isaac, Rodi.

Sedei Ḥemed, Encyclopaedia of precepts and responsa by Ḥayyim Ḥezekiah *Medini; subdivisions: *Asefat Dinim, Kunteres ha-Kelalim, Pe'at ha-Sadeh la-Dinim, Pe'at ha-Sadeh la-Kelalim.*
Semag, Usual abbreviation of *Sefer Mitzvot Gadol,* elucidation of precepts by *Moses b. Jacob of Coucy; subdivided into *Lavin* (negative precepts) *Asayin* (positive precepts).
Semak, Usual abbreviation of *Sefer Mitzvot Katan,* elucidation of precepts by *Isaac b. Joseph of Corbeil.

Sh. Ar. = *Shulḥan Arukh,* code by Joseph b. Ephraim *Caro.
Sha'ar Mishpat, Comm. to Sh. Ar., ḤM. By Israel Isser b. Ze'ev Wolf.
Sha'arei Shevu'ot, Treatise on the law of oaths by *David b. Saadiah; usually printed together with Rif, *Halakhot;* also called: *She'arim of R. Alfasi.*
Sha'arei Teshuvah, Collection of resp. from Geonic period, by different authors.
Sha'arei Uzzi'el, Rabbinical treatise by Ben-Zion Meir Ha *Ouziel.
Sha'arei Ẓedek, Collection of resp. from Geonic period, by different authors.
Shadal [or Shedal] = Samuel David *Luzzatto.
Shai la-Moreh, Resp. by Shabbetai Jonah.
Shakh, Usual abbreviation of *Siftei Kohen,* a comm. to Sh. Ar., YD and ḤM by *Shabbetai b. Meir ha-Kohen; printed in most editions of Sh. Ar.
Sha'ot-de-Rabbanan, Resp. by *Solomon b. Judah ha-Kohen.
She'arim of R. Alfasi see *Sha'arei Shevu'ot.*
Shedal, see Shadal.
She'elot u-Teshuvot ha-Ge'onim, Collection of resp. by different authors.
She'erit Yisrael, Resp. by Israel Ze'ev Mintzberg.
She'erit Yosef, Resp. by *Joseph b. Mordecai Gershon ha-Kohen.
She'ilat Yavez, Resp. by Jacob *Emden (Yaveẓ).
She'iltot, Compilation arranged acc. to the Torah by *Aḥa (Aḥai) of Shabḥa.
Shem Aryeh, Resp. by Aryeh Leib *Lipschutz.
Shemesh Ẓedakah, Resp. by Samson *Morpurgo.
Shenei ha-Me'orot ha-Gedolim, Resp. by Elijah *Covo.
Shetarot, Sefer ha-, Collection of legal forms by *Judah b. Barzillai al-Bargeloni.
Shevut Ya'akov, Resp. by Jacob b. Joseph Reicher.
Shibbolei ha-Leket Compilation on ritual by Zedekiah b. Avraham *Anav.
Shiltei Gibborim, Comm. to Rif, *Halakhot,* by *Joshua Boaz b. Simeon; printed in major editions of the Talmud.
Shittah Mekubbeẓet, Compilation of talmudical commentaries by Bezalel *Ashkenazi.
Shivat Ẓiyyon, Resp. by Samuel b. Ezekiel *Landau.
Shiyyurei Korban, by David *Fraenkel; additions to his comm. to Jer. Talmud *Korban Edah;* both printed in most editions of Jer. Talmud.
Sho'el u-Meshiv, Resp. by Joseph Saul ha-Levi *Nathanson.
Sh[ulḥan] Ar[ukh] [of Ba'al ha-Tanyal], Code by *Shneur Zalman of Lyady; not identical with the code by Joseph Caro.
Siftei Kohen, Comm. to Sh. Ar., YD and ḤM by *Shabbetai b. Meir ha-Kohen; printed in most editions of Sh. Ar.; usual abbreviation: *Shakh.*
Simḥat Yom Tov, Resp. by Tom Tov b. Jacob *Algazi.
Simlah Ḥadashah, Treatise on *Sheḥitah* by Alexander Sender b. Ephraim Zalman *Schor; see also *Tevu'ot Shor.*
Simeon b. Ẓemaḥ = Simeon b. Ẓemaḥ *Duran.
Sma, Comm. to Sh. Ar. by Joshua b. Alexander ha-Kohen *Falk; the full title is: *Sefer Me'irat Einayim;* printed in most editions of Sh. Ar.
Solomon b. Isaac ha-Levi = Solomon b. Isaac *Levy.
Solomon b. Isaac of Troyes = *Rashi.

Tal Orot, Rabbinical work with various contents, by Joseph ibn Gioia.
Tam, Rabbenu = *Tam Jacob b. Meir.
Tashbaẓ = Samson b. Zadok.
Tashbeẓ = Simeon b. Zemaḥ *Duran, sometimes also abbreviation for Samson b. Zadok, usually known as Tashbaẓ.
Tashbeẓ [*Sefer ha-*], Resp. by Simeon b. Ẓemaḥ *Duran; the fourth part of this work is called: *Ḥut ha-Meshullash.*
Taz, Usual abbreviation of *Turei Zahav,* comm., to Sh. Ar. by *David b. Samnuel ha-Levi; printed in most editions of Sh. Ar.
(Ha)-Tekhelet, subdivision of the *Levush* (a codification by Mordecai b. Abraham (Levush) *Jaffe); *Ha-Tekhelet* parallels Tur, OḤ 1-241.
Terumat ha-Deshen, by Israel b. Pethahiah *Isserlein; subdivided into a part containing responsa, and a second part called *Pesakim u-Khetavim* or *Piskei Maharai.*
Terumot, Sefer ha-, Compilation of *halakhot* by Samuel b. Isaac *Sardi.
Teshuvot Ba'alei ha-Tosafot, Collection of responsa by the Tosafists.
Teshjvot Ge'onei Mizraḥ u-Ma'aav, Collection of responsa.
Teshuvot ha-Geonim, Collection of responsa from Geonic period.
Teshuvot Ḥakhmei Provinẓyah, Collection of responsa by different Provencal authors.
Teshuvot Ḥakhmei Ẓarefat ve-Loter, Collection of responsa by different French authors.
Teshuvot Maimuniyyot, Resp. pertaining to Maimonides' *Yad Ḥazakah;* printed in major editions of this work after the text; authorship uncertain.
Tevu'ot Shor, by Alexander Sender b. Ephraim Zalman *Schor, a comm. to his *Simlah Ḥadashah,* a work on *Sheḥitah.*
Tiferet Ẓevi, Resp. by Ẓevi Hirsch of the "AHW" Communities (Altona, Hamburg, Wandsbeck).
Tiktin, Judah b. Simeon = Judah b. Simeon *Ashkenazi.
Toledot Adam ve-Ḥavvah, Codification by *Jeroham b. Meshullam.
Torat Emet, Resp. by Aaron b. Joseph *Sasson.
Torat Ḥayyim, , Resp. by Ḥayyim (ben) Shabbetai.
Torat ha-Minhagot, subdivision of the *Massa Ḥayyim* (a work on tax law) by Ḥayyim *Palaggi, containing an exposition of customary law.
Tosafot Rid, Explanations to the Talmud and decisions by *Isaiah b. Mali di Trani the Elder.
Tosefot Yom Tov, comm. to Mishnah by Yom Tov Lipmann b. Nathan ha-Levi *Heller; printed in most editions of the Mishnah.
Tummim, subdivision of the comm. to Sh. Ar., ḤM, *Urim ve-Tummim* by Jonathan *Eybeschuetz; printed in the major editions of Sh. Ar.
Tur, usual abbreviation for the *Arba'ah Turim* of *Jacob b. Asher.
Turei Zahav, Comm. to Sh. Ar. by *David b. Samuel ha-Levi; printed in most editions of Sh. Ar.; usual abbreviation: *Taz.*

Urim, subdivision of the following.
Urim ve-Tummim, Comm. to Sh. Ar., ḤM, by Jonathan *Eybeschuetz; printed in the major editions of Sh. Ar.; subdivided in places into *Urim* and *Tummim.*

Vikku'aḥ Mayim Ḥayyim, Polemics against Isserles and Caro by Ḥayyim b. Bezalel.

Yad Malakhi, Methodological treatise by *Malachi b. Jacob ha-Kohen.

Yad Ramah, Nov. by Meir b. Todros [ha-Levi] *Abulafia.
Yakhin u-Vo'az, Resp. by Ẓemaḥ b. Solomon *Duran.
Yam ha-Gadol, Resp. by Jacob Moses *Toledano.
Yam shel Shelomo, Compilation arranged acc. to Talmud by Solomon b. Jehiel (Maharshal) *Luria.
Yashar, Sefer ha-, by *Tam, Jacob b. Meir (Rabbenu Tam); 1st pt.: Resp.; 2nd pt.: Nov.
Yaskil Avdi, Resp. by Obadiah Hadaya (printed together with his Resp. *De'ah ve-Haskel).*
Yaveẓ = Jacob *Emden.
Yehudah Ya'aleh, Resp. by Judah b. Israel *Aszod.
Yekar Tiferet, Comm. to Maimonides' *Yad Ḥazakah,*by David b. Solomon ibn Zimra, printed in most editions of *Yad Ḥazakah.*
Yere'im [*ha-Shalem*], [*Sefer*], Treatise on precepts by *Eliezer b. Samuel of Metz.
Yeshu'ot Ya'akov, Resp. by Jacob Meshullam b. Mordecai Ze'ev *Ornstein.
Yiẓhak Rei'aḥ, Resp. by Isaac b. Samuel Abendanan (see article *Abendanam Family).
Ẓafenat Pa'ne'aḥ (1), also called *Raban* or *Even ha-Ezer*, see under the last name.
Ẓafenat Pa'ne'aḥ (2), Resp. by Joseph *Rozin.
Zayit Ra'anan, Resp. by Moses Judah Leib b. Benjamin Auerbach.
Ẓeidah la-Derekh, Codification by *Menahem b. Aaron ibn Zerah.
Ẓedakah u-Mishpat, Resp. by Ẓedakah b. Saadiah Huẓin.
Zekan Aharon, Resp. by Elijah b. Benjamin ha-Levi.
Zekher Ẓaddik, Sermons by Eliezer *Katzenellenbogen.
Ẓemaḥ Ẓedek (1) Resp. by Menaham Mendel Shneersohn (see under *Shneersohn Family).
Zera Avraham, Resp. by Abraham b. David *Yiẓḥaki.
Zera Emet Resp. by *Ishmael b. Abaham Isaac ha-Kohen.
Ẓevi la-Ẓaddik, Resp. by Ẓevi Elimelech b. David Shapira.
Zikhron Yehudah, Resp. by *Judah b. Asher
Zikhron Yosef, Resp. by Joseph b. Menahem *Steinhardt.
Zikhronot, Sefer ha-, Sermons on several precepts by Samuel *Aboab.
Zikkaron la-Rishonim . . ., by Albert (Abraham Elijah) *Harkavy; contains in vol. 1 pt. 4 (1887) a collection of Geonic responsa.
Ẓiẓ Eliezer, Resp. by Eliezer Judah b. Jacob Gedaliah Waldenberg.

BIBLIOGRAPHICAL ABBREVIATIONS

Bibliographies in English and other languages have been extensively updated, with English translations cited where available. In order to help the reader, the language of books or articles is given where not obvious from titles of books or names of periodicals. Titles of books and periodicals in languages with alphabets other than Latin, are given in transliteration, even where there is a title page in English. Titles of articles in periodicals are not given. Names of Hebrew and Yiddish periodicals well known in English-speaking countries or in Israel under their masthead in Latin characters are given in this form, even when contrary to transliteration rules. Names of authors writing in languages with non-Latin alphabets are given in their Latin alphabet form wherever known; otherwise the names are transliterated. Initials are generally not given for authors of articles in periodicals, except to avoid confusion. Non-abbreviated book titles and names of periodicals are printed in *italics*. Abbreviations are given in the list below.

AASOR	*Annual of the American School of Oriental Research* (1919ff.).
AB	*Analecta Biblica* (1952ff.).
Abel, Géog	F.-M. Abel, *Géographie de la Palestine,* 2 vols. (1933-38).
ABR	*Australian Biblical Review* (1951ff.).
Abr.	Philo, *De Abrahamo.*
Abrahams, Companion	I. Abrahams, *Companion to the Authorised Daily Prayer Book* (rev. ed. 1922).
Abramson, Merkazim	S. Abramson, *Ba-Merkazim u-va-Tefuẓot bi-Tekufat ha-Ge'onim* (1965).
Acts	Acts of the Apostles (New Testament).
ACUM	*Who is who in ACUM [Aguddat Kompozitorim u-Meḥabbrim].*
ADAJ	*Annual of the Department of Antiquities, Jordan* (1951ff.).
Adam	Adam and Eve (Pseudepigrapha).
ADB	*Allgemeine Deutsche Biographie,* 56 vols. (1875–1912).
Add. Esth.	The Addition to Esther (Apocrypha).
Adler, Prat Mus	1. Adler, *La pratique musicale savante dans quelques communautés juives en Europe au XVIIe et XVIIIe siècles,* 2 vols. (1966).
Adler-Davis	H.M. Adler and A. Davis (ed. and tr.), *Service of the Synagogue, a New Edition of the Festival Prayers with an English Translation in Prose and Verse,* 6 vols. (1905–06).
Aet.	Philo, *De Aeternitate Mundi.*
AFO	*Archiv fuer Orientforschung* (first two volumes under the name *Archiv fuer Keilschriftforschung)* (1923ff.).
Ag. Ber	*Aggadat Bereshit* (ed. Buber, 1902).
Agr.	Philo, *De Agricultura.*
Ag. Sam.	*Aggadat Samuel.*
Ag. Song	*Aggadat Shir ha-Shirim* (Schechter ed., 1896).
Aharoni, Ereẓ	Y. Aharoni, *Ereẓ Yisrael bi-Tekufat ha-Mikra: Geografyah Historit* (1962).
Aharoni, Land	Y. Aharoni, *Land of the Bible* (1966).

Ahikar — Ahikar (Pseudepigrapha).
AI — *Archives Israélites de France* (1840–1936).
AJA — *American Jewish Archives* (1948ff.).
AJHSP — *American Jewish Historical Society – Publications* (after vol. 50 = AJHSQ).
AJHSQ — *American Jewish Historical (*Society) *Quarterly* (before vol. 50 =AJHSP).
AJSLL — *American Journal of Semitic Languages and Literature* (1884–95 under the title *Hebraica,* since 1942 JNES).
AJYB — *American Jewish Year Book* (1899ff.).
AKM — Abhandlungen fuer die Kunde des Morgenlandes (series).
Albright, Arch — W.F. Albright, *Archaeology of Palestine* (rev. ed. 1960).
Albright, Arch Bib — W.F. Albright, *Archaeology of Palestine and the Bible* (1935^3).
Albright, Arch Rel — W.F. Albright, *Archaeology and the Religion of Israel* (1953^3).
Albright, Stone — W.F. Albright, *From the Stone Age to Christianity* (1957^2).
Alon, Meḥkarim — G. Alon, *Meḥkarim be-Toledot Yisrael bi-Ymei Bayit Sheni u-vi-Tekufat ha-Mishnah ve-ha Talmud,* 2 vols. (1957–58).
Alon, Toledot — G. Alon, *Toledot ha-Yehudim be-Ereẓ Yisrael bi-Tekufat ha-Mishnah ve-ha-Talmud,* I (1958^3), (1961^2).
ALOR — Alter Orient (series).
Alt, Kl Schr — A. Alt, *Kleine Schriften zur Geschichte des Volkes Israel,* 3 vols. (1953–59).
Alt, Landnahme — A. Alt, *Landnahme der Israeliten in Palaestina* (1925); also in Alt, Kl Schr, 1 (1953), 89–125.
Ant. — Josephus, *Jewish Antiquities* (Loeb Classics ed.).
AO — *Acta Orientalia* (1922ff.).
AOR — *Analecta Orientalia* (1931ff.).
AOS — American Oriental Series.
Apion — Josephus, *Against Apion* (Loeb Classics ed.).
Aq. — Aquila's Greek translation of the Bible.
Ar. — *Arakhin* (talmudic tractate).
Artist. — Letter of Aristeas (Pseudepigrapha).
ARN^1 — *Avot de-Rabbi Nathan,* version (1) ed. Schechter, 1887.
ARN^2 — *Avot de-Rabbi Nathan,* version (2) ed. Schechter, 1945^2.
Aronius, Regesten — I. Aronius, *Regesten zur Geschichte der Juden im fraenkischen und deutschen Reiche bis zum Jahre 1273* (1902).
ARW — *Archiv fuer Religionswissenschaft* (1898–1941/42).
AS — *Assyrological Studies* (1931ff.).
Ashtor, Korot — E. Ashtor (Strauss), *Korot ha-Yehudim bi-Sefarad ha-Muslemit,* 1(1966^2), 2(1966).
Ashtor, Toledot — E. Ashtor (Strauss), *Toledot ha-Yehudim be-Miẓrayim ve-Suryah Taḥat Shilton ha-Mamlukim,* 3 vols. (1944–70).
Assaf, Ge'onim — S. Assaf, *Tekufat ha-Ge'onim ve-Sifrutah* (1955).
Assaf, Mekorot — S. Assaf, *Mekorot le-Toledot ha-Ḥinnukh be-Yisrael,* 4 vols. (1925–43).
Ass. Mos. — Assumption of Moses (Pseudepigrapha).
ATA — Alttestamentliche Abhandlungen (series).
ATANT — Abhandlungen zur Theologie des Alten und Neuen Testaments (series).
AUJW — *Allgemeine unabhaengige juedische Wochenzeitung* (till 1966 = AWJD).
AV — Authorized Version of the Bible.
Avad. — *Avadim* (post-talmudic tractate).
Avi-Yonah, Geog — M. Avi-Yonah, *Geografyah Historit shel Ereẓ Yisrael* (1962^3).
Avi-Yonah, Land — M. Avi-Yonah, *The Holy Land from the Persian to the Arab conquest (536 B.C. to A.D. 640)* (1960).
Avot — *Avot* (talmudic tractate).
Av. Zar. — *Avodah Zarah* (talmudic tractate).
AWJD — *Allgemeine Wochenzeitung der Juden in Deutschland* (since 1967 = AUJW).
AZDJ — *Allgemeine Zeitung des Judentums.*
Azulai — Ḥ.Y.D. Azulai, *Shem ha-Gedolim,* ed. by I.E. Benjacob, 2 pts. (1852) (and other editions).

BA — *Biblical Archaeologist* (1938ff.).
Bacher, Bab Amor — W. Bacher, *Agada der babylonischen Amoraeer* (1913^2).
Bacher, Pal Amor — W. Bacher, *Agada der palaestinensischen Amoraeer* (Heb. ed. *Aggadat Amora'ei Ereẓ Yisrael),* 2 vols. (1892–99).
Bacher, Tann — W. Bacher, *Agada der Tannaiten* (Heb. ed. *Aggadot ha-Tanna'im,* vol. 1, pt. 1 and 2 (1903); vol. 2 (1890).
Bacher, Trad — W. Bacher, *Tradition und Tradenten in den Schulen Palaestinas und Babyloniens* (1914).
Baer, Spain — Yitzhak (Fritz) Baer, *History of the Jews in Christian Spain,* 2 vols. (1961–66).
Baer, Studien — Yitzhak (Fritz) Baer, *Studien zur Geschichte der Juden im Koenigreich Aragonien waehrend des 13. und 14. Jahrhunderts* (1913).
Baer, Toledot — Yitzhak (Fritz) Baer, *Toledot ha-Yehudim bi-Sefarad ha-Noẓerit mi-Teḥillatan shel ha-Kehillot ad ha-Gerush,* 2 vols. (1959^2).
Baer, Urkunden — Yitzhak (Fritz) Baer, *Die Juden im christlichen Spanien,* 2 vols. (1929–36).
Baer S., Seder — S.I. Baer, *Seder Avodat Yisrael* (1868 and reprints).
BAIU — *Bulletin de l'Alliance Israélite Universelle* (1861–1913).
Baker, Biog Dict — *Baker's Biographical Dictionary of Musicians,* revised by N. Slonimsky (1958^5; with Supplement 1965).
I Bar. — I Baruch (Apocrypha).
II Bar. — II Baruch (Pseudepigrapha).
III Bar. — III Baruch (Pseudepigrapha).
BAR — *Biblical Archaeology Review.*
Baron, Community — S.W. Baron, *The Jewish Community, its History and Structure to the American Revolution,* 3 vols. (1942).

Baron, Social	S.W. Baron, *Social and Religious History of the Jews*, 3 vols. (1937); enlarged, 1-2(1952²), 3-14 (1957–69).
Barthélemy-Milik	D. Barthélemy and J.T. Milik, *Dead Sea Scrolls: Discoveries in the Judean Desert*, vol. 1 *Qumram Cave* I (1955).
BASOR	*Bulletin of the American School of Oriental Research.*
Bauer-Leander	H. Bauer and P. Leander, *Grammatik des Biblisch-Aramaeischen* (1927; repr. 1962).
BB	(1) *Bava Batra* (talmudic tractate). (2) *Biblische Beitraege* (1943ff.).
BBB	Bonner biblische Beitraege (series).
BBLA	*Beitraege zur biblischen Landes- und Altertumskunde* (until 1949–ZDPV).
BBSAJ	*Bulletin,* British School of Archaeology, Jerusalem (1922–25; after 1927 included in PEFQS).
BDASI	*Alon* (since 1948) or *Hadashot Arkhe'ologiyyot* (since 1961), bulletin of the Department of Antiquities of the State of Israel.
Begrich, Chronologie	J. Begrich, *Chronologie der Koenige von Israel und Juda* (1929).
Bek.	*Bekhorot* (talmudic tractate).
Bel	Bel and the Dragon (Apocrypha).
Benjacob, Oẓar	I.E. Benjacob, *Oẓar ha-Sefarim* (1880; repr. 1956).
Ben Sira	see Ecclus.
Ben-Yehuda, Millon	E. Ben-Yedhuda, *Millon ha-Lashon ha-Ivrit,* 16 vols (1908–59; repr. in 8 vols., 1959).
Benzinger, Archaeologie	I. Benzinger, *Hebraeische Archaeologie* (1927³).
Ben Zvi, Eretz Israel	I. Ben-Zvi, *Eretz Israel under Ottoman Rule* (1960; offprint from L. Finkelstein (ed.), *The Jews, their History, Culture and Religion* (vol. 1).
Ben Zvi, Ereẓ Israel	I. Ben-Zvi, *Ereẓ Israel bi-Ymei ha-Shilton ha-Ottomani (1955).*
Ber.	*Berakhot* (talmudic tractate).
Beẓah	*Beẓah* (talmudic tractate).
BIES	Bulletin of the Israel Exploration Society, see below BJPES.
Bik.	*Bikkurim* (talmudic tractate).
BJCE	Bibliography of Jewish Communities in Europe, catalog at General Archives for the History of the Jewish People, Jerusalem.
BJPES	Bulletin of the Jewish Palestine Exploration Society – English name of the Hebrew periodical known as: 1. *Yedi'ot ha-Ḥevrah ha-Ivrit la-Ḥakirat Ereẓ Yisrael va-Attikoteha* (1933–1954); 2. *Yedi'ot ha-Ḥevrah la-Ḥakirat Ereẓ Yisrael va-Attikoteha* (1954–1962); 3. *Yedi'ot ba-Ḥakirat Ereẓ Yisrael va-Attikoteha* (1962ff.).
BJRL	*Bulletin of the John Rylands Library* (1914ff.).
BK	*Bava Kamma* (talmudic tractate).
BLBI	*Bulletin of the Leo Baeck Institute* (1957ff.).
BM	(1) *Bava Meẓia* (talmudic tractate). (2) *Beit Mikra* (1955/56ff.). (3) British Museum.
BO	*Bibbia e Oriente* (1959ff.).
Bondy-Dworský	G. Bondy and F. Dworský, *Regesten zur Geschichte der Juden in Boehmen, Maehren und Schlesien von 906 bis 1620,* 2 vols. (1906).
BOR	*Bibliotheca Orientalis* (1943ff.).
Borée, Ortsnamen	W. Borée *Die alten Ortsnamen Palaestinas* (1930).
Bousset, Religion	W. Bousset, *Die Religion des Judentums im neutestamentlichen Zeitalter* (1906²).
Bousset-Gressmann	W. Bousset, *Die Religion des Judentums im spaethellenistischen Zeitalter* (1966³).
BR	*Biblical Review* (1916–25).
BRCI	*Bulletin of the Research Council of Israel* (1951/52–1954/55; then divided).
BRE	*Biblical Research* (1956ff.).
BRF	*Bulletin of the Rabinowitz Fund for the Exploration of Ancient Synagogues* (1949ff.).
Briggs, Psalms	Ch. A. and E.G. Briggs, *Critical and Exegetical Commentary on the Book of Psalms,* 2 vols. (ICC, 1906–07).
Bright, Hist	J. Bright, *A History of Israel* (1959).
Brockelmann, Arab Lit	K. Brockelmann, *Geschichte der arabischen Literatur*, 2 vols. 1898–1902), supplement, 3 vols. (1937–42).
Bruell, Jahrbuecher	*Jahrbuecher fuer juedische Geschichte und Litteratur,* ed. by N. Bruell, Frankfurt (1874–90).
Brugmans-Frank	H. Brugmans and A. Frank (eds.), *Geschiedenis der Joden in Nederland* (1940).
BTS	*Bible et Terre Sainte* (1958ff.).
Bull, Index	S. Bull, *Index to Biographies of Contemporary Composers* (1964).
BW	*Biblical World* (1882–1920).
BWANT	*Beitraege zur Wissenschaft vom Alten und Neuen Testament* (1926ff.).
BZ	*Biblische Zeitschrift* (1903ff.).
BZAW	*Beihefte zur Zeitschrift fuer die alttestamentliche Wissenschaft,* supplement to ZAW (1896ff.).
BŻIH	*Biuletyn Zydowskiego Instytutu Historycznego* (1950ff.).
CAB	*Cahiers d'archéologie biblique* (1953ff.).
CAD	*The* [*Chicago*] *Assyrian Dictionary* (1956ff.).
CAH	*Cambridge Ancient History*, 12 vols. (1923–39)
CAH²	*Cambridge Ancient History,* second edition, 14 vols. (1962–2005).
Calwer, Lexikon	*Calwer, Bibellexikon.*
Cant.	Canticles, usually given as Song (= Song of Songs).

Cantera-Millás, Inscripciones	F. Cantera and J.M. Millás, *Las Inscripciones Hebraicas de España* (1956).
CBQ	*Catholic Biblical Quarterly* (1939ff.).
CCARY	Central Conference of American Rabbis, *Yearbook* (1890/91ff.).
CD	*Damascus Document* from the Cairo *Genizah* (published by S. Schechter, *Fragments of a Zadokite Work*, 1910).
Charles, Apocrypha	R.H. Charles, *Apocrypha and Pseudepigrapha . . .*, 2 vols. (1913; repr. 1963–66).
Cher.	Philo, *De Cherubim.*
I (or II) Chron.	Chronicles, book I and II (Bible).
CIG	*Corpus Inscriptionum Graecarum.*
CIJ	*Corpus Inscriptionum Judaicarum,* 2 vols. (1936–52).
CIL	*Corpus Inscriptionum Latinarum.*
CIS	*Corpus Inscriptionum Semiticarum* (1881ff.).
C.J.	Codex Justinianus.
Clermont-Ganneau, Arch	Ch. Clermont-Ganneau, *Archaeological Researches in Palestine*, 2 vols. (1896–99).
CNFI	*Christian News from Israel* (1949ff.).
Cod. Just.	Codex Justinianus.
Cod. Theod.	Codex Theodosinanus.
Col.	Epistle to the Colosssians (New Testament).
Conder, Survey	Palestine Exploration Fund, *Survey of Eastern Palestine*, vol. 1, pt. I (1889) = C.R. Conder, *Memoirs of the . . . Survey.*
Conder-Kitchener	Palestine Exploration Fund, *Survey of Western Palestine*, vol. 1, pts. 1-3 (1881–83) = C.R. Conder and H.H. Kitchener, *Memoirs.*
Conf.	Philo, *De Confusione Linguarum.*
Conforte, Kore	D. Conforte, *Kore ha-Dorot* (1842^2).
Cong.	Philo, *De Congressu Quaerendae Eruditionis Gratia.*
Cont.	Philo, *De Vita Contemplativa.*
I (or II) Cor.	Epistles to the Corinthians (New Testament).
Cowley, Aramic	A. Cowley, *Aramaic Papyri of the Fifth Century B.C.* (1923).
Colwey, Cat	A.E. Cowley, *A Concise Catalogue of the Hebrew Printed Books in the Bodleian Library* (1929).
CRB	*Cahiers de la Revue Biblique* (1964ff.).
Crowfoot-Kenyon	J.W. Crowfoot, K.M. Kenyon and E.L. Sukenik, *Buildings of Samaria* (1942).
C.T.	Codex Theodosianus.
DAB	*Dictionary of American Biography* (1928–58).
Daiches, Jews	S. Daiches, *Jews in Babylonia* (1910).
Dalman, Arbeit	G. Dalman, *Arbeit und Sitte in Palaestina*, 7 vols.in 8 (1928–42 repr. 1964).
Dan	Daniel (Bible).
Davidson, Oẓar	I. Davidson, *Oẓar ha-Shirah ve-ha-Piyyut*, 4 vols. (1924–33); Supplement in: HUCA, 12–13 (1937/38), 715–823.
DB	J. Hastings, *Dictionary of the Bible*, 4 vols. (1963^2).
DBI	F.G. Vigoureaux et al. (eds.), *Dictionnaire de la Bible*, 5 vols. in 10 (1912); Supplement, 8 vols. (1928–66)
Decal.	Philo, *De Decalogo.*
Dem.	*Demai* (talmudic tractate).
DER	*Derekh Ereẓ Rabbah* (post-talmudic tractate).
Derenbourg, Hist	J. Derenbourg *Essai sur l'histoire et la géographie de la Palestine* (1867).
Det.	Philo, *Quod deterius potiori insidiari solet.*
Deus	Philo, *Quod Deus immutabilis sit.*
Deut.	Deuteronomy (Bible).
Deut. R.	*Deuteronomy Rabbah.*
DEZ	*Derekh Ereẓ Zuta* (post-talmudic tractate).
DHGE	*Dictionnaire d'histoire et de géographie ecclésiastiques*, ed. by A. Baudrillart et al., 17 vols (1912–68).
Dik. Sof	*Dikdukei Soferim,* variae lections of the talmudic text by Raphael Nathan Rabbinovitz (16 vols., 1867–97).
Dinur, Golah	B. Dinur (Dinaburg), *Yisrael ba-Golah*, 2 vols. in 7 (1959–68) = vols. 5 and 6 of his *Toledot Yisrael,* second series.
Dinur, Haganah	B. Dinur (ed.), *Sefer Toledot ha-Haganah* (1954ff.).
Diringer, Iscr	D. Diringer, *Iscrizioni antico-ebraiche palestinesi* (1934).
Discoveries	*Discoveries in the Judean Desert* (1955ff.).
DNB	*Dictionary of National Biography,* 66 vols. (1921–222) with Supplements.
Dubnow, Divrei	S. Dubnow, *Divrei Yemei Am Olam*, 11 vols (1923–38 and further editions).
Dubnow, Ḥasidut	S. Dubnow, *Toledot ha-Ḥasidut* (1960^2).
Dubnow, Hist	S. Dubnow, *History of the Jews* (1967).
Dubnow, Hist Russ	S. Dubnow, *History of the Jews in Russia and Poland,* 3 vols. (1916 20).
Dubnow, Outline	S. Dubnow, *An Outline of Jewish History,* 3 vols. (1925–29).
Dubnow, Weltgesch	S. Dubnow, *Weltgeschichte des juedischen Volkes* 10 vols. (1925–29).
Dukes, Poesie	L. Dukes, *Zur Kenntnis der neuhebraeischen religioesen Poesie* (1842).
Dunlop, Khazars	D. H. Dunlop, *History of the Jewish Khazars* (1954).
EA	El Amarna Letters (edited by J.A. Knudtzon), *Die El-Amarna Tafel,* 2 vols. (1907 14).
EB	*Encyclopaedia Britannica.*
EBI	*Estudios biblicos* (1941ff.).
EBIB	T.K. Cheyne and J.S. Black, *Encyclopaedia Biblica,* 4 vols. (1899–1903).
Ebr.	Philo, *De Ebrietate.*
Eccles.	Ecclesiastes (Bible).
Eccles. R.	*Ecclesiastes Rabbah.*
Ecclus.	Ecclesiasticus or Wisdom of Ben Sira (or Sirach; Apocrypha).
Eduy.	*Eduyyot* (mishanic tractate).

EG — *Enziklopedyah shel Galuyyot* (1953ff.).
EH — *Even ha-Ezer.*
EHA — *Enziklopedyah la-Ḥafirot Arkheologiyyot be-Ereẓ Yisrael,* 2 vols. (1970).
EI — *Enzyklopaedie des Islams,* 4 vols. (1905–14). Supplement vol. (1938).
EIS — *Encyclopaedia of Islam,* 4 vols. (1913–36; repr. 1954–68).
EIS² — *Encyclopaedia of Islam, second edition (1960–2000).*
Eisenstein, Dinim — J.D. Eisenstein, *Oẓar Dinim u-Minhagim* (1917; several reprints).
Eisenstein, Yisrael — J.D. Eisenstein, *Oẓar Yisrael* (10 vols, 1907–13; repr. with several additions 1951).
EIV — *Enẓiklopedyah Ivrit* (1949ff.).
EJ — *Encyclopaedia Judaica* (German, A-L only), 10 vols. (1928–34).
EJC — *Enciclopedia Judaica Castellana,* 10 vols. (1948–51).
Elbogen, Century — I Elbogen, *A Century of Jewish Life* (1960²).
Elbogen, Gottesdienst — I Elbogen, *Der juedische Gottesdienst ...* (1931³, repr. 1962).
Elon, Mafte'aḥ — M. Elon (ed.), *Mafte'aḥ ha-She'elot ve-ha-Teshuvot ha-Rosh* (1965).
EM — *Enẓiklopedyah Mikra'it* (1950ff.).
I (or II) En. — I and II Enoch (Pseudepigrapha).
EncRel — *Encyclopedia of Religion,* 15 vols. (1987, 2005²).
Eph. — Epistle to the Ephesians (New Testament).
Ephros, Cant — G. Ephros, *Cantorial Anthology,* 5 vols. (1929–57).
Ep. Jer. — Epistle of Jeremy (Apocrypha).
Epstein, Amora'im — J N. Epstein, *Mevo'ot le-Sifrut ha-Amora'im* (1962).
Epstein, Marriage — L M. Epstein, *Marriage Laws in the Bible and the Talmud* (1942).
Epstein, Mishnah — J. N. Epstein, *Mavo le-Nusaḥ ha-Mishnah,* 2 vols. (1964²).
Epstein, Tanna'im — J. N. Epstein, *Mavo le-Sifruth ha-Tanna'im.* (1947).
ER — *Ecumenical Review.*
Er. — *Eruvin* (talmudic tractate).
ERE — *Encyclopaedia of Religion and Ethics,* 13 vols. (1908–26); reprinted.
ErIsr — *Eretz-Israel,* Israel Exploration Society.
I Esd. — I Esdras (Apocrypha) (= III Ezra).
II Esd. — II Esdras (Apocrypha) (= IV Ezra).
ESE — *Ephemeris fuer semitische Epigraphik,* ed. by M. Lidzbarski.
ESN — *Encyclopaedia Sefaradica Neerlandica,* 2 pts. (1949).
ESS — *Encyclopaedia of the Social Sciences,* 15 vols. (1930–35); reprinted in 8 vols. (1948–49).
Esth. — Esther (Bible).
Est. R. — *Esther Rabbah.*
ET — *Enẓiklopedyah Talmudit* (1947ff.).
Eusebius, Onom. — E. Klostermann (ed.), *Das Onomastikon* (1904), Greek with Hieronymus' Latin translation.
Ex. — Exodus (Bible).
Ex. R. — *Exodus Rabbah.*
Exs — Philo, *De Exsecrationibus.*
EẒD — *Enẓiklopeday shel ha-Ẓiyyonut ha-Datit* (1951ff.).
Ezek. — Ezekiel (Bible).
Ezra — Ezra (Bible).
III Ezra — III Ezra (Pseudepigrapha).
IV Ezra — IV Ezra (Pseudepigrapha).

Feliks, Ha-Ẓome'aḥ — *J. Feliks, Ha-Ẓome'aḥ ve-ha-Ḥai ba-Mishnah* (1983).
Finkelstein, Middle Ages — L. Finkelstein, *Jewish Self-Government in the Middle Ages* (1924).
Fischel, Islam — W.J. Fischel, *Jews in the Economic and Political Life of Mediaeval Islam* (1937; reprint with introduction "The Court Jew in the Islamic World," 1969).
FJW — *Fuehrer durch die juedische Gemeindeverwaltung und Wohlfahrtspflege in Deutschland* (1927/28).
Frankel, Mevo — Z. Frankel, *Mevo ha-Yerushalmi* (1870; reprint 1967).
Frankel, Mishnah — Z. Frankel, *Darkhei ha-Mishnah* (1959²; reprint 1959²).
Frazer, Folk-Lore — J.G. Frazer, *Folk-Lore in the Old Testament,* 3 vols. (1918–19).
Frey, Corpus — J.-B. Frey, *Corpus Inscriptionum Iudaicarum,* 2 vols. (1936–52).
Friedmann, Lebensbilder — A. Friedmann, *Lebensbilder beruehmter Kantoren,* 3 vols. (1918–27).
FRLT — *Forschungen zur Religion und Literatur des Alten und Neuen Testaments* (series) (1950ff.).
Frumkin-Rivlin — A.L. Frumkin and E. Rivlin, *Toledot Ḥakhmei Yerushalayim,* 3 vols. (1928–30), Supplement vol. (1930).
Fuenn, Keneset — S.J. Fuenn, *Keneset Yisrael,* 4 vols. (1887–90).
Fuerst, Bibliotheca — J. Fuerst, *Bibliotheca Judaica,* 2 vols. (1863; repr. 1960).
Fuerst, Karaeertum — J. Fuerst, *Geschichte des Karaeertums,* 3 vols. (1862–69).
Fug. — Philo, *De Fuga et Inventione.*

Gal. — Epistle to the Galatians (New Testament).
Galling, Reallexikon — K. Galling, *Biblisches Reallexikon* (1937).
Gardiner, Onomastica — A.H. Gardiner, *Ancient Egyptian Onomastica,* 3 vols. (1947).
Geiger, Mikra — A. Geiger, *Ha-Mikra ve-Targumav,* tr. by J.L. Baruch (1949).
Geiger, Urschrift — A. Geiger, *Urschrift und Uebersetzungen der Bibel* 1928²).
Gen. — Genesis (Bible).
Gen. R. — *Genesis Rabbah.*
Ger. — *Gerim* (post-talmudic tractate).
Germ Jud — M. Brann, I. Elbogen, A. Freimann, and H. Tykocinski (eds.), *Germania Judaica,* vol. 1 (1917; repr. 1934 and 1963); vol. 2, in 2 pts. (1917–68), ed. by Z. Avneri.

GHAT	*Goettinger Handkommentar zum Alten Testament* (1917–22).
Ghirondi-Neppi	M.S. Ghirondi and G.H. Neppi, *Toledot Gedolei Yisrael u-Ge'onei Italyah ... u-Ve'urim al Sefer Zekher Ẓaddikim li-Verakhah . . .*(1853), index in ZHB, 17 (1914), 171–83.
Gig.	Philo, *De Gigantibus.*
Ginzberg, Legends	L. Ginzberg, *Legends of the Jews,* 7 vols. (1909–38; and many reprints).
Git.	*Gittin* (talmudic tractate).
Glueck, Explorations	N. Glueck, *Explorations in Eastern Palestine,* 2 vols. (1951).
Goell, Bibliography	Y. Goell, *Bibliography of Modern Hebrew Literature in English Translation* (1968).
Goodenough, Symbols	E.R. Goodenough, *Jewish Symbols in the Greco-Roman Period,* 13 vols. (1953–68).
Gordon, Textbook	C.H. Gordon, *Ugaritic Textbook* (1965; repr. 1967).
Graetz, Gesch	H. Graetz, *Geschichte der Juden* (last edition 1874–1908).
Graetz, Hist	H. Graetz, *History of the Jews,* 6 vols. (1891–1902).
Graetz, Psalmen	H. Graetz, *Kritischer Commentar zu den Psalmen,* 2 vols. in 1 (1882–83).
Graetz, Rabbinowitz	H. Graetz, *Divrei Yemei Yisrael,* tr. by S.P. Rabbinowitz. (1928 1929^{2}).
Gray, Names	G.B. Gray, *Studies in Hebrew Proper Names* (1896).
Gressmann, Bilder	H. Gressmann, *Altorientalische Bilder zum Alten Testament* (1927^{2}).
Gressmann, Texte	H. Gressmann, *Altorientalische Texte zum Alten Testament* (1926^{2}).
Gross, Gal Jud	H. Gross, *Gallia Judaica* (1897; repr. with add. 1969).
Grove, Dict	*Grove's Dictionary of Music and Musicians,* ed. by E. Blum 9 vols. (1954^{5}) and suppl. (1961^{5}).
Guedemann, Gesch Erz	M. Guedemann, *Geschichte des Erziehungswesens und der Cultur der abendlaendischen Juden,* 3 vols. (1880–88).
Guedemann, Quellenschr	M. Guedemann, *Quellenschriften zur Geschichte des Unterrichts und der Erziehung bei den deutschen Juden* (1873, 1891).
Guide	Maimonides, *Guide of the Perplexed.*
Gulak, Oẓar	A. Gulak, *Oẓar ha-Shetarot ha-Nehugim be-Yisrael* (1926).
Gulak, Yesodei	A. Gulak, *Yesodei ha-Mishpat ha-Ivri, Seder Dinei Mamonot be-Yisrael, al pi Mekorot ha-Talmud ve-ha-Posekim,* 4 vols. (1922; repr. 1967).
Guttmann, Mafte'aḥ	M. Guttmann, *Mafte'aḥ ha-Talmud,* 3 vols. (1906–30).
Guttmann, Philosophies	J. Guttmann, *Philosophies of Judaism* (1964).
Hab.	*Habakkuk* (Bible).
Ḥag.	*Ḥagigah* (talmudic tractate).
Haggai	*Haggai* (Bible).
Ḥal.	*Ḥallah* (talmudic tractate).
Halevy, Dorot	I. Halevy, *Dorot ha-Rishonim,* 6 vols. (1897–1939).
Halpern, Pinkas	I. Halpern (Halperin), *Pinkas Va'ad Arba Araẓot* (1945).
Hananel-Eškenazi	A. Hananel and Eškenazi (eds.), *Fontes Hebraici ad res oeconomicas socialesque terrarum balcanicarum saeculo XVI pertinentes,* 2 vols, (1958–60; in Bulgarian).
HB	*Hebraeische Bibliographie* (1858–82).
Heb.	Epistle to the Hebrews (New Testament).
Heilprin, Dorot	J. Heilprin (Heilperin), *Seder ha-Dorot,* 3 vols. (1882; repr. 1956).
Her.	Philo, *Quis Rerum Divinarum Heres.*
Hertz, Prayer	J.H. Hertz (ed.), *Authorised Daily Prayer Book* (rev. ed. 1948; repr. 1963).
Herzog, Instit	I. Herzog, *The Main Institutions of Jewish Law,* 2 vols. (1936–39; repr. 1967).
Herzog-Hauck	J.J. Herzog and A. Hauch (eds.), *Real-encyklopaedie fuer protestantische Theologie* (1896–1913^{3}).
HḤY	*Ha-Ẓofeh le-Ḥokhmat Yisrael* (first four volumes under the title *Ha-Ẓofeh me-Ereẓ Hagar)* (1910/11–13).
Hirschberg, Afrikah	H.Z. Hirschberg, *Toledot ha-Yehudim be-Afrikah ha-Zofonit,* 2 vols. (1965).
HJ	*Historia Judaica* (1938–61).
HL	*Das Heilige Land* (1857ff.)
ḤM	*Ḥoshen Mishpat.*
Hommel, Ueberliefer.	F. Hommel, *Die altisraelitische Ueberlieferung in inschriftlicher Beleuchtung* (1897).
Hor.	*Horayot* (talmudic tractate).
Horodezky, Ḥasidut	S.A. Horodezky, *Ha-Ḥasidut ve-ha-Ḥasidim,* 4 vols. (1923).
Horowitz, Ereẓ Yis	I.W. Horowitz, *Ereẓ Yisrael u-Shekhenoteha* (1923).
Hos.	Hosea (Bible).
HTR	*Harvard Theological Review* (1908ff.).
HUCA	*Hebrew Union College Annual* (1904; 1924ff.)
Ḥul.	*Ḥullin* (talmudic tractate).
Husik, Philosophy	I. Husik, *History of Medieval Jewish Philosophy* (1932^{2}).
Hyman, Toledot	A. Hyman, *Toledot Tanna'im ve-Amora'im* (1910; repr. 1964).
Ibn Daud, Tradition	Abraham Ibn Daud, *Sefer ha-Qabbalah – The Book of Tradition,* ed. and tr. By G.D. Cohen (1967).
ICC	International Critical Commentary on the Holy Scriptures of the Old and New Testaments (series, 1908ff.).
IDB	*Interpreter's Dictionary of the Bible,* 4 vols. (1962).
Idelsohn, Litugy	A. Z. Idelsohn, *Jewish Liturgy and its Development* (1932; paperback repr. 1967)
Idelsohn, Melodien	A. Z. Idelsohn, *Hebraeisch-orientalischer Melodienschatz,* 10 vols. (1914 32).
Idelsohn, Music	A. Z. Idelsohn, *Jewish Music in its Historical Development* (1929; paperback repr. 1967).

IEJ	*Israel Exploration Journal* (1950ff.).
IESS	*International Encyclopedia of the Social Sciences* (various eds.).
IG	*Inscriptiones Graecae,* ed. by the Prussian Academy.
IGYB	*Israel Government Year Book* (1949/50ff.).
ILR	*Israel Law Review* (1966ff.).
IMIT	*Izraelita Magyar Irodalmi Társulat Évkönyv* (1895 1948).
IMT	International Military Tribunal.
INB	*Israel Numismatic Bulletin* (1962–63).
INJ	*Israel Numismatic Journal* (1963ff.).
Ios	Philo, *De Iosepho.*
Isa.	Isaiah (Bible).
ITHL	Institute for the Translation of Hebrew Literature.
IZBG	*Internationale Zeitschriftenschau fuer Bibelwissenschaft und Grenzgebiete* (1951ff.).
JA	*Journal asiatique* (1822ff.).
James	Epistle of James (New Testament).
JAOS	*Journal of the American Oriental Society* (c. 1850ff.)
Jastrow, Dict	M. Jastrow, *Dictionary of the Targumim, the Talmud Babli and Yerushalmi, and the Midrashic literature,* 2 vols. (1886 1902 and reprints).
JBA	*Jewish Book Annual* (19242ff.).
JBL	*Journal of Biblical Literature* (1881ff.).
JBR	*Journal of Bible and Religion* (1933ff.).
JC	*Jewish Chronicle* (1841ff.).
JCS	*Journal of Cuneiform Studies* (1947ff.).
JE	*Jewish Encyclopedia,* 12 vols. (1901–05 several reprints).
Jer.	Jeremiah (Bible).
Jeremias, Alte Test	A. Jeremias, *Das Alte Testament im Lichte des alten Orients* 1930^{4}).
JGGJČ	*Jahrbuch der Gesellschaft fuer Geschichte der Juden in der Čechoslovakischen Republik* (1929–38).
JHSEM	Jewish Historical Society of England, *Miscellanies* (1925ff.).
JHSET	Jewish Historical Society of England, *Transactions* (1893ff.).
JJGL	*Jahrbuch fuer juedische Geschichte und Literatur* (Berlin) (1898–1938).
JJLG	*Jahrbuch der juedische-literarischen Gesellschaft* (Frankfurt) (1903–32).
JJS	*Journal of Jewish Studies* (1948ff.).
JJSO	*Jewish Journal of Sociology* (1959ff.).
JJV	*Jahrbuch fuer juedische Volkskunde* (1898–1924).
JL	*Juedisches Lexikon,* 5 vols. (1927–30).
JMES	*Journal of the Middle East Society* (1947ff.).
JNES	*Journal of Near Eastern Studies* (continuation of AJSLL) (1942ff.).
J.N.U.L.	Jewish National and University Library.
Job	Job (Bible).
Joel	Joel (Bible).

John	Gospel according to John (New Testament).
I, II and III John	Epistles of John (New Testament).
Jos., Ant	Josephus, *Jewish Antiquities* (Loeb Classics ed.).
Jos. Apion	Josephus, *Against Apion* (Loeb Classics ed.).
Jos., index	*Josephus Works,* Loeb Classics ed., index of names.
Jos., Life	Josephus, *Life* (ed. Loeb Classics).
Jos, Wars	Josephus, *The Jewish Wars* (Loeb Classics ed.).
Josh.	Joshua (Bible).
JPESB	Jewish Palestine Exploration Society Bulletin, see BJPES.
JPESJ	Jewish Palestine Exploration Society Journal – Eng. Title of the Hebrew periodical *Kovez ha-Ḥevrah ha-Ivrit la-Ḥakirat Erez Yisrael va-Attikoteha.*
JPOS	*Journal of the Palestine Oriental Society* (1920–48).
JPS	Jewish Publication Society of America, *The Torah* (1962, 1967^{2}); *The Holy Scriptures* (1917).
JQR	*Jewish Quarterly Review* (1889ff.).
JR	*Journal of Religion* (1921ff.).
JRAS	*Journal of the Royal Asiatic Society* (1838ff.).
JHR	*Journal of Religious History* (1960/61ff.).
JSOS	*Jewish Social Studies* (1939ff.).
JSS	*Journal of Semitic Studies* (1956ff.).
JTS	*Journal of Theological Studies* (1900ff.).
JTSA	Jewish Theological Seminary of America (also abbreviated as JTS).
Jub.	Jubilees (Pseudepigrapha).
Judg.	Judges (Bible).
Judith	Book of Judith (Apocrypha).
Juster, Juifs	J. Juster, *Les Juifs dans l'Empire Romain,* 2 vols. (1914).
JYB	*Jewish Year Book* (1896ff.).
JZWL	*Juedische Zeitschift fuer Wissenschaft und Leben* (1862–75).
Kal.	*Kallah* (post-talmudic tractate).
Kal. R.	*Kallah Rabbati* (post-talmudic tractate).
Katz, England	*The Jews in the History of England, 1485-1850 (1994).*
Kaufmann, Schriften	D. Kaufmann, *Gesammelte Schriften,* 3 vols. (1908 15).
Kaufmann Y., Religion	Y. Kaufmann, *The Religion of Israel* (1960), abridged tr. of his *Toledot.*
Kaufmann Y., Toledot	Y. Kaufmann, *Toledot ha-Emunah ha-Yisre'elit,* 4 vols. (1937 57).
KAWJ	*Korrespondenzblatt des Vereins zur Gruendung und Erhaltung der Akademie fuer die Wissenschaft des Judentums* (1920 30).
Kayserling, Bibl	M. Kayserling, *Biblioteca Española-Portugueza-Judaica* (1880; repr. 1961).
Kelim	*Kelim* (mishnaic tractate).
Ker.	*Keritot* (talmudic tractate).
Ket.	*Ketubbot* (talmudic tractate).

Kid.	*Kiddushim* (talmudic tractate).
Kil.	*Kilayim* (talmudic tractate).
Kin.	*Kinnim* (mishnaic tractate).
Kisch, Germany	G. Kisch, *Jews in Medieval Germany* (1949).
Kittel, Gesch	R. Kittel, *Geschichte des Volkes Israel,* 3 vols. (1922–28).
Klausner, Bayit Sheni	J. Klausner, *Historyah shel ha-Bayit ha-Sheni,* 5 vols. (1950/512).
Klausner, Sifrut	J. Klausner, *Historyah shel haSifrut ha-Ivrit ha-Ḥadashah,* 6 vols. (1952–582).
Klein, corpus	S. Klein (ed.), *Juedisch-palaestinisches Corpus Inscriptionum* (1920).
Koehler-Baumgartner	L. Koehler and W. Baumgartner, *Lexicon in Veteris Testamenti libros* (1953).
Kohut, Arukh	H.J.A. Kohut (ed.), *Sefer he-Arukh ha-Shalem,* by Nathan b. Jehiel of Rome, 8 vols. (1876–92; Supplement by S. Krauss et al., 1936; repr. 1955).
Krauss, Tal Arch	S. Krauss, *Talmudische Archaeologie,* 3 vols. (1910–12; repr. 1966).
Kressel, Leksikon	G. Kressel, *Leksikon ha-Sifrut ha-Ivrit ba-Dorot ha-Aḥaronim,* 2 vols. (1965–67).
KS	*Kirjath Sepher* (1923/4ff.).
Kut.	*Kuttim* (post-talmudic tractate).
LA	Studium Biblicum Franciscanum, *Liber Annuus* (1951ff.).
L.A.	Philo, *Legum allegoriae.*
Lachower, Sifrut	F. Lachower, *Toledot ha-Sifrut ha-Ivrit ha-Ḥadashah,* 4 vols. (1947–48; several reprints).
Lam.	Lamentations (Bible).
Lam. R.	*Lamentations Rabbah.*
Landshuth, Ammudei	L. Landshuth, *Ammudei ha-Avodah* (1857–62; repr. with index, 1965).
Legat.	Philo, *De Legatione ad Caium.*
Lehmann, Nova Bibl	R.P. Lehmann, *Nova Bibliotheca Anglo-Judaica* (1961).
Lev.	Leviticus (Bible).
Lev. R.	*Leviticus Rabbah.*
Levy, Antologia	I. Levy, *Antologia de liturgia judeo-española* (1965ff.).
Levy J., Chald Targ	J. Levy, *Chaldaeisches Woerterbuch ueber die Targumim,* 2 vols. (1967–68; repr. 1959).
Levy J., Nuehebr Tal	J. Levy, *Neuhebraeisches und chaldaeisches Woerterbuch ueber die Talmudim . . .,* 4 vols. (1875–89; repr. 1963).
Lewin, Oẓar	Lewin, *Oẓar ha-Ge'onim,* 12 vols. (1928–43).
Lewysohn, Zool	L. Lewysohn, *Zoologie des Talmuds* (1858).
Lidzbarski, Handbuch	M. Lidzbarski, *Handbuch der nordsemitischen Epigraphik,* 2 vols (1898).
Life	Josephus, *Life* (Loeb Classis ed.).
LNYL	*Leksikon fun der Nayer Yidisher Literatur* (1956ff.).
Loew, Flora	I. Loew, *Die Flora der Juden,* 4 vols. (1924 34; repr. 1967).
LSI	*Laws of the State of Israel* (1948ff.).
Luckenbill, Records	D.D. Luckenbill, *Ancient Records of Assyria and Babylonia,* 2 vols. (1926).
Luke	Gospel according to Luke (New Testament)
LXX	Septuagint (Greek translation of the Bible).
Ma'as.	*Ma'aserot* (talmudic tractate).
Ma'as. Sh.	*Ma'ase Sheni* (talmudic tractate).
I, II, III, and IVMacc.	Maccabees, I, II, III (Apocrypha), IV (Pseudepigrapha).
Maimonides, Guide	Maimonides, *Guide of the Perplexed.*
Maim., Yad	Maimonides, *Mishneh Torah (Yad Ḥazakah).*
Maisler, Untersuchungen	B. Maisler (Mazar), *Untersuchungen zur alten Geschichte und Ethnographie Syriens und Palaestinas,* 1 (1930).
Mak.	*Makkot* (talmudic tractate).
Makhsh.	*Makhshrin* (mishnaic tractate).
Mal.	Malachi (Bible).
Mann, Egypt	J. Mann, *Jews in Egypt in Palestine under the Fatimid Caliphs,* 2 vols. (1920–22).
Mann, Texts	J. Mann, *Texts and Studies,* 2 vols (1931–35).
Mansi	G.D. Mansi, *Sacrorum Conciliorum nova et amplissima collectio,* 53 vols. in 60 (1901–27; repr. 1960).
Margalioth, Gedolei	M. Margalioth, *Enẓiklopedyah le-Toledot Gedolei Yisrael,* 4 vols. (1946–50).
Margalioth, Ḥakhmei	M. Margalioth, *Enẓiklopedyah le-Ḥakhmei ha-Talmud ve-ha-Ge'onim,* 2 vols. (1945).
Margalioth, Cat	G. Margalioth, *Catalogue of the Hebrew and Samaritan Manuscripts in the British Museum,* 4 vols. (1899–1935).
Mark	Gospel according to Mark (New Testament).
Mart. Isa.	Martyrdom of Isaiah (Pseudepigrapha).
Mas.	Masorah.
Matt.	Gospel according to Matthew (New Testament).
Mayer, Art	L.A. Mayer, *Bibliography of Jewish Art* (1967).
MB	*Wochenzeitung* (formerly *Mitteilungsblatt*) *des Irgun Olej Merkas Europa* (1933ff.).
MEAH	*Miscelánea de estudios drabes y hebraicos* (1952ff.).
Meg.	Megillah (talmudic tractate).
Meg. Ta'an.	*Megillat Ta'anit* (in HUCA, 8 9 (1931–32), 318–51).
Me'il	*Me'ilah* (mishnaic tractate).
MEJ	*Middle East Journal* (1947ff.).
Mehk.	*Mekhilta de-R. Ishmael.*
Mekh. SbY	*Mekhilta de-R. Simeon bar Yoḥai.*
Men.	*Menaḥot* (talmudic tractate).
MER	*Middle East Record* (1960ff.).
Meyer, Gesch	E. Meyer, *Geschichte des Alterums,* 5 vols. in 9 (1925–58).
Meyer, Ursp	E. Meyer, *Urspring und Anfaenge des Christentums* (1921).
Mez.	*Mezuzah* (post-talmudic tractate).
MGADJ	*Mitteilungen des Gesamtarchivs der deutschen Juden* (1909–12).
MGG	*Die Musik in Geschichte und Gegenwart,* 14 vols. (1949–68).

MGG² — *Die Musik in Geschichte und Gegenwart, 2nd edition (1994)*
MGH — *Monumenta Germaniae Historica* (1826ff.).
MGJV — *Mitteilungen der Gesellschaft fuer juedische Volkskunde* (1898–1929); title varies, see also JJV.
MGWJ — *Monatsschrift fuer Geschichte und Wissenschaft des Judentums* (1851–1939).
MHJ — *Monumenta Hungariae Judaica,* 11 vols. (1903–67).
Michael, Or — H.Ḥ. Michael, *Or ha-Ḥayyim: Ḥakhmei Yisrael ve-Sifreihem,* ed. by S.Z. Ḥ. Halberstam and N. Ben-Menahem (1965²).
Mid. — *Middot* (mishnaic tractate).
Mid. Ag. — *Midrash Aggadah.*
Mid. Hag. — *Midrash ha-Gadol.*
Mid. Job. — *Midrash Job.*
Mid. Jonah — *Midrash Jonah.*
Mid. Lek. Tov — *Midrash Lekaḥ Tov.*
Mid. Prov. — *Midrash Proverbs.*
Mid. Ps. — *Midrash Tehillim* (Eng tr. *The Midrash on Psalms* (JPS, 1959).
Mid. Sam. — *Midrash Samuel.*
Mid. Song — *Midrash Shir ha-Shirim.*
Mid. Tan. — *Midrash Tanna'im* on Deuteronomy.
Miége, Maroc — J.L. Miège, *Le Maroc et l'Europe,* 3 vols. (1961 62).
Mig. — Philo, *De Migratione Abrahami.*
Mik. — *Mikva'ot* (mishnaic tractate).
Milano, Bibliotheca — A. Milano, *Bibliotheca Historica Italo-Judaica* (1954); supplement for 1954–63 (1964); supplement for 1964–66 in RMI, 32 (1966).
Milano, Italia — A. Milano, *Storia degli Ebrei in Italia* (1963).
MIO — *Mitteilungen des Instituts fuer Orientforschung* 1953ff.).
Mish. — Mishnah.
MJ — *Le Monde Juif* (1946ff.).
MJC — see Neubauer, Chronicles.
MK — *Mo'ed Katan* (talmudic tractate).
MNDPV — *Mitteilungen und Nachrichten des deutschen Palaestinavereins* (1895–1912).
Mortara, Indice — M. Mortara, *Indice Alfabetico dei Rabbini e Scrittori Israeliti ... in Italia ...* (1886).
Mos — Philo, *De Vita Mosis.*
Moscati, Epig — S, Moscati, *Epigrafia ebraica antica* 1935–1950 (1951).
MT — Masoretic Text of the Bible.
Mueller, Musiker — [E.H. Mueller], *Deutisches Musiker-Lexikon* (1929)
Munk, Mélanges — S. Munk, *Mélanges de philosophie juive et arabe* (1859; repr. 1955).
Mut. — Philo, *De Mutatione Nominum.*
MWJ — *Magazin fuer die Wissenshaft des Judentums* (18745 93).

Nah. — Nahum (Bible).
Naz. — *Nazir* (talmudic tractate).
NDB — *Neue Deutsche Biographie* (1953ff.).
Ned. — *Nedarim* (talmudic tractate).
Neg. — *Nega'im* (mishnaic tractate).
Neh. — Nehemiah (Bible).
NG² — *New Grove Dictionary of Music and Musicians* (2001).
Nuebauer, Cat — A. Neubauer, *Catalogue of the Hebrew Manuscripts in the Bodleian Library ...,* 2 vols. (1886–1906).
Neubauer, Chronicles — A. Neubauer, *Mediaeval Jewish Chronicles,* 2 vols. (Heb., 1887–95; repr. 1965), Eng. title of *Seder ha-Ḥakhamim ve-Korot ha-Yamim.*
Neubauer, Géogr — A. Neubauer, *La géographie du Talmud* (1868).
Neuman, Spain — A.A. Neuman, *The Jews in Spain, their Social, Political, and Cultural Life During the Middle Ages,* 2 vols. (1942).
Neusner, Babylonia — J. Neusner, *History of the Jews in Babylonia,* 5 vols. 1965–70), 2nd revised printing 1969ff.).
Nid. — *Niddah* (talmudic tractate).
Noah — Fragment of Book of Noah (Pseudepigrapha).
Noth, Hist Isr — M. Noth, *History of Israel* (1958).
Noth, Personennamen — M. Noth, *Die israelitischen Personennamen.* ... (1928).
Noth, Ueberlief — M. Noth, *Ueberlieferungsgeschichte des Pentateuchs* (1949).
Noth, Welt — M. Noth, *Die Welt des Alten Testaments* (1957³).
Nowack, Lehrbuch — W. Nowack, *Lehrbuch der hebraeischen Archaeologie,* 2 vols (1894).
NT — New Testament.
Num. — Numbers (Bible).
Num R. — *Numbers Rabbah.*

Obad. — Obadiah (Bible).
ODNB online — *Oxford Dictionary of National Biography.*
OḤ — *Oraḥ Ḥayyim.*
Oho. — *Oholot* (mishnaic tractate).
Olmstead — H.T. Olmstead, *History of Palestine and Syria* (1931; repr. 1965).
OLZ — *Orientalistische Literaturzeitung* (1898ff.)
Onom. — Eusebius, *Onomasticon.*
Op. — Philo, *De Opificio Mundi.*
OPD — *Osef Piskei Din shel ha-Rabbanut ha-Rashit le-Ereẓ Yisrael, Bet ha-Din ha-Gadol le-Irurim* (1950).
Or. — *Orlah* (talmudic tractate).
Or. Sibyll. — Sibylline Oracles (Pseudepigrapha).
OS — *L'Orient Syrien* (1956ff.)
OTS — *Oudtestamentische Studien* (1942ff.).

PAAJR — *Proceedings of the American Academy for Jewish Research* (1930ff.)
Pap 4QSᵉ — A papyrus exemplar of IQS.
Par. — *Parah* (mishnaic tractate).
Pauly-Wissowa — A.F. Pauly, *Realencyklopaedie der klassichen Alertumswissenschaft,* ed. by G. Wissowa et al. (1864ff.)

PD	*Piskei Din shel Bet ha-Mishpat ha-Elyon le-Yisrael* (1948ff.)
PDR	*Piskei Din shel Battei ha-Din ha-Rabbaniyyim be-Yisrael.*
PdRE	*Pirkei de-R. Eliezer* (Eng. tr. 1916. (1965^{2}).
PdRK	*Pesikta de-Rav Kahana.*
Pe'ah	*Pe'ah* (talmudic tractate).
Peake, Commentary	A.J. Peake (ed.), *Commentary on the Bible* (1919; rev. 1962).
Pedersen, Israel	J. Pedersen, *Israel, Its Life and Culture,* 4 vols. in 2 (1926–40).
PEFQS	*Palestine Exploration Fund Quarterly Statement* (1869–1937; since 1938–PEQ).
PEQ	*Palestine Exploration Quarterly* (until 1937 PEFQS; after 1927 includes BBSAJ).
Perles, Beitaege	J. Perles, *Beitraege zur rabbinischen Sprach- und Alterthumskunde* (1893).
Pes.	*Pesaḥim* (talmudic tractate).
Pesh.	Peshitta (Syriac translation of the Bible).
Pesher Hab.	Commentary to Habakkuk from Qumran; see 1Qp Hab.
I and II Pet.	Epistles of Peter (New Testament).
Pfeiffer, Introd	R.H. Pfeiffer, *Introduction to the Old Testament* (1948).
PG	J.P. Migne (ed.), *Patrologia Graeca,* 161 vols. (1866–86).
Phil.	Epistle to the Philippians (New Testament).
Philem.	Epistle to the Philemon (New Testament).
PIASH	*Proceedings of the Israel Academy of Sciences and Humanities* (1963/7ff.).
PJB	*Palaestinajahrbuch des deutschen evangelischen Institutes fuer Altertumswissenschaft,* Jerusalem (1905–1933).
PK	*Pinkas ha-Kehillot,* encyclopedia of Jewish communities, published in over 30 volumes by Yad Vashem from 1970 and arranged by countries, regions and localities. For 3-vol. English edition see Spector, *Jewish Life.*
PL	J.P. Migne (ed.), *Patrologia Latina* 221 vols. (1844–64).
Plant	Philo, *De Plantatione.*
PO	R. Graffin and F. Nau (eds.), *Patrologia Orientalis* (1903ff.)
Pool, Prayer	D. de Sola Pool, *Traditional Prayer Book for Sabbath and Festivals* (1960).
Post	Philo, *De Posteritate Caini.*
PR	*Pesikta Rabbati.*
Praem.	Philo, *De Praemiis et Poenis.*
Prawer, Ẓalbanim	J. Prawer, *Toledot Mamlekhet ha-Ẓalbanim be-Ereẓ Yisrael,* 2 vols. (1963).
Press, Ereẓ	I. Press, *Ereẓ-Yisrael, Enẓiklopedyah Topografit-Historit,* 4 vols. (1951–55).
Pritchard, Pictures	J.B. Pritchard (ed.), *Ancient Near East in Pictures* (1954, 1970).
Pritchard, Texts	J.B. Pritchard (ed.), *Ancient Near East Texts* ... (1970^{3}).
Pr. Man.	Prayer of Manasses (Apocrypha).
Prob.	Philo, *Quod Omnis Probus Liber Sit.*
Prov.	Proverbs (Bible).
PS	*Palestinsky Sbornik* (Russ. (1881 1916, 1954ff).
Ps.	Psalms (Bible).
PSBA	*Proceedings of the Society of Biblical Archaeology* (1878–1918).
Ps. of Sol	Psalms of Solomon (Pseudepigrapha).
IQ Apoc	The *Genesis Apocryphon* from Qumran, cave one, ed. by N. Avigad and Y. Yadin (1956).
6QD	*Damascus Document* or *Sefer Berit Dammesk* from Qumran, cave six, ed. by M. Baillet, in RB, 63 (1956), 513–23 (see also CD).
QDAP	*Quarterly of the Department of Antiquities in Palestine* (1932ff.).
4QDeut. 32	Manuscript of Deuteronomy 32 from Qumran, cave four (ed. by P.W. Skehan, in BASOR, 136 (1954), 12–15).
$4QEx^{a}$	Exodus manuscript in Jewish script from Qumran, cave four.
$4QEx^{\alpha}$	Exodus manuscript in Paleo-Hebrew script from Qumran, cave four (partially ed. by P.W. Skehan, in JBL, 74 (1955), 182–7).
4QFlor	*Florilegium,* a miscellany from Qumran, cave four (ed. by J.M. Allegro, in JBL, 75 (1956), 176–77 and 77 (1958), 350–54).).
QGJD	*Quellen zur Geschichte der Juden in Deutschland* 1888–98).
IQH	*Thanksgiving Psalms* of *Hodayot* from Qumran, cave one (ed. by E.L. Sukenik and N. Avigad, *Oẓar ha-Megillot ha-Genuzot* (1954).
$IQIs^{a}$	Scroll of Isaiah from Qumran, cave one (ed. by N. Burrows et al., *Dead Sea Scrolls* ..., 1 (1950).
$IQIs^{b}$	Scroll of Isaiah from Qumran, cave one (ed. E.L. Sukenik and N. Avigad, *Oẓar ha-Megillot ha-Genuzot* (1954).
IQM	The *War Scroll* or *Serekh ha-Milḥamah* (ed. by E.L. Sukenik and N. Avigad, *Oẓar ha-Megillot ha-Genuzot* (1954).
4QpNah	Commentary on Nahum from Qumran, cave four (partially ed. by J.M. Allegro, in JBL, 75 (1956), 89–95).
IQphyl	Phylacteries *(tefillin)* from Qumran, cave one (ed. by Y. Yadin, in *Eretz Israel,* 9 (1969), 60–85).
4Q Prayer of Nabonidus	A document from Qumran, cave four, belonging to a lost Daniel literature (ed. by J.T. Milik, in RB, 63 (1956), 407–15).
IQS	*Manual of Discipline* or *Serekh ha-Yaḥad* from Qumran, cave one (ed. by M. Burrows et al., *Dead Sea Scrolls* ..., 2, pt. 2 (1951).

IQS^{a}	The *Rule of the Congregation or Serekh ha-Edah* from Qumran, cave one (ed. by Burrows et al., *Dead Sea Scrolls* ..., 1 (1950), under the abbreviation IQ28a).
IQS^{b}	*Blessings* or *Divrei Berakhot* from Qumran, cave one (ed. by Burrows et al., *Dead Sea Scrolls* ..., 1 (1950), under the abbreviation IQ28b).
4QSam^{a}	Manuscript of I and II Samuel from Qumran, cave four (partially ed. by F.M. Cross, in BASOR, 132 (1953), 15–26).
4QSam^{b}	Manuscript of I and II Samuel from Qumran, cave four (partially ed. by F.M. Cross, in JBL, 74 (1955), 147–72).
4QTestimonia	Sheet of Testimony from Qumran, cave four (ed. by J.M. Allegro, in JBL, 75 (1956), 174–87).).
4QT.Levi	*Testament of Levi* from Qumran, cave four (partially ed. by J.T. Milik, in RB, 62 (1955), 398–406).
Rabinovitz, Dik Sof	See Dik Sof.
RB	*Revue biblique* (1892ff.)
RBI	*Recherches bibliques* (1954ff.)
RCB	*Revista de cultura biblica* (São Paulo) (1957ff.)
Régné, Cat	J. Régné, *Catalogue des actes . . . des rois d'Aragon, concernant les Juifs* (1213–1327), in: REJ, vols. 60 70, 73, 75–78 (1910–24).
Reinach, Textes	T. Reinach, *Textes d'auteurs Grecs et Romains relatifs au Judaïsme* (1895; repr. 1963).
REJ	*Revue des études juives* (1880ff.).
Rejzen, Leksikon	Z. Rejzen, *Leksikon fun der Yidisher Literature,* 4 vols. (1927–29).
Renan, Ecrivains	A. Neubauer and E. Renan, *Les écrivains juifs français* ... (1893).
Renan, Rabbins	A. Neubauer and E. Renan, *Les rabbins français* (1877).
RES	*Revue des étude sémitiques et Babyloniaca* (1934–45).
Rev.	Revelation (New Testament).
RGG^{3}	*Die Religion in Geschichte und Gegenwart,* 7 vols. (1957–65^{3}).
RH	*Rosh Ha-Shanah* (talmudic tractate).
RHJE	*Revue de l'histoire juive en Egypte* (1947ff.).
RHMH	*Revue d'histoire de la médecine hébraïque* (1948ff.).
RHPR	*Revue d'histoire et de philosophie religieuses* (1921ff.).
RHR	*Revue d'histoire des religions* (1880ff.).
RI	*Rivista Israelitica* (1904–12).
Riemann-Einstein	*Hugo Riemanns Musiklexikon,* ed. by A. Einstein (1929^{11}).
Riemann-Gurlitt	*Hugo Riemanns Musiklexikon,* ed. by W. Gurlitt (1959–67^{12}), Personenteil.
Rigg-Jenkinson, Exchequer	J.M. Rigg, H. Jenkinson and H.G. Richardson (eds.), *Calendar of the Pleas Rolls of the Exchequer of the Jews,* 4 vols. (1905–1970); cf. in each instance also J.M. Rigg (ed.), *Select Pleas* ... (1902).

RMI	*Rassegna Mensile di Israel* (1925ff.).
Rom.	Epistle to the Romans (New Testament).
Rosanes, Togarmah	S.A. Rosanes, *Divrei Yemei Yisrael be-Togarmah,* 6 vols. (1907–45), and in 3 vols. (1930–38^{2}).
Rosenbloom, Biogr Dict	J.R. Rosenbloom, *Biographical Dictionary of Early American Jews* (1960).
Roth, Art	C. Roth, *Jewish Art* (1961).
Roth, Dark Ages	C. Roth (ed.), *World History of the Jewish People,* second series, vol. 2, *Dark Ages* (1966).
Roth, England	C. Roth, *History of the Jews in England* (1964^{3}).
Roth, Italy	C. Roth, *History of the Jews in Italy* (1946).
Roth, Mag Bibl	C. Roth, *Magna Bibliotheca Anglo-Judaica* (1937).
Roth, Marranos	C. Roth, *History of the Marranos* (2nd rev. ed 1959; reprint 1966).
Rowley, Old Test	H.H. Rowley, *Old Testament and Modern Study* (1951; repr. 1961).
RS	*Revue sémitiques d'épigraphie et d'histoire ancienne* (1893/94ff.).
RSO	*Rivista degli studi orientali* (1907ff.).
RSV	Revised Standard Version of the Bible.
Rubinstein, Australia I	*H.L. Rubinstein, The Jews in Australia, A Thematic History, Vol. I (1991).*
Rubinstein, Australia II	*W.D. Rubinstein, The Jews in Australia, A Thematic History, Vol. II (1991).*
Ruth	Ruth (Bible).
Ruth R.	*Ruth Rabbah.*
RV	Revised Version of the Bible.
Sac.	Philo, *De Sacrificiis Abelis et Caini.*
Salfeld, Martyrol	S. Salfeld, *Martyrologium des Nuernberger Memorbuches* (1898).
I and II Sam.	Samuel, book I and II (Bible).
Sanh.	*Sanhedrin* (talmudic tractate).
SBA	Society of Biblical Archaeology.
SBB	*Studies in Bibliography and Booklore* (1953ff.).
SBE	*Semana Biblica Española.*
SBT	*Studies in Biblical Theology* (1951ff.).
SBU	*Svenkst Bibliskt Uppslogsvesk,* 2 vols. (1962–63^{2}).
Schirmann, Italyah	J.Ḥ. Schirmann, *Ha-Shirah ha-Ivrit be-Italyah* (1934).
Schirmann, Sefarad	J.Ḥ. Schirmann, *Ha-Shirah ha-Ivrit bi-Sefarad u-vi-Provence,* 2 vols. (1954–56).
Scholem, Mysticism	G. Scholem, *Major Trends in Jewish Mysticism* (rev. ed. 1946; paperback ed. with additional bibliography 1961).
Scholem, Shabbetai Ẓevi	G. Scholem, *Shabbetai Ẓevi ve-ha-Tenu'ah ha-Shabbeta'it bi-Ymei Ḥayyav,* 2 vols. (1967).
Schrader, Keilinschr	E. Schrader, *Keilinschriften und das Alte Testament* (1903^{3}).
Schuerer, Gesch	E. Schuerer, *Geschichte des juedischen Volkes im Zeitalter Jesu Christi,* 3 vols. and index-vol. (1901–11^{4}).

Schuerer, Hist	E. Schuerer, *History of the Jewish People in the Time of Jesus,* ed. by N.N. Glatzer, abridged paperback edition (1961).
Set. T.	*Sefer Torah* (post-talmudic tractate).
Sem.	*Semaḥot* (post-talmudic tractate).
Sendrey, Music	A. Sendrey, *Bibliography of Jewish Music* (1951).
SER	*Seder Eliyahu Rabbah.*
SEZ	*Seder Eliyahu Zuta.*
Shab	*Shabbat* (talmudic tractate).
Sh. Ar.	J. Caro Shulḥan Arukh. OḤ – *Oraḥ Ḥayyim* YD – *Yoreh De'ah* EH – *Even ha-Ezer* ḤM – *Ḥoshen Mishpat.*
Shek.	*Shekalim* (talmudic tractate).
Shev.	*Shevi'it* (talmudic tractate).
Shevu.	*Shevu'ot* (talmudic tractate).
Shunami, Bibl	S. Shunami, *Bibliography of Jewish Bibliographies* (1965[2]).
Sif.	*Sifrei Deuteronomy.*
Sif. Num.	*Sifrei Numbers.*
Sifra	*Sifra* on Leviticus.
Sif. Zut.	*Sifrei Zuta.*
SIHM	Sources inédites de l'histoire du Maroc (series).
Silverman, Prayer	M. Silverman (ed.), *Sabbath and Festival Prayer Book* (1946).
Singer, Prayer	S. Singer *Authorised Daily Prayer Book* (1943[17]).
Sob.	Philo, *De Sobrietate.*
Sof.	*Soferim* (post-talmudic tractate).
Som.	Philo, *De Somniis.*
Song	Song of Songs (Bible).
Song. Ch.	Song of the Three Children (Apocrypha).
Song R.	*Song of Songs Rabbah.*
SOR	*Seder Olam Rabbah.*
Sot.	*Sotah* (talmudic tractate).
SOZ	*Seder Olam Zuta.*
Spec.	Philo, *De Specialibus Legibus.*
Spector, Jewish Life	*S. Spector (ed.), Encyclopedia of Jewish Life Before and After the Holocaust (2001).*
Steinschneider, Arab lit	M. Steinschneider, *Die arabische Literatur der Juden* (1902).
Steinschneider, Cat Bod	M. Steinschneider, *Catalogus Librorum Hebraeorum in Bibliotheca Bodleiana,* 3 vols. (1852–60; reprints 1931 and 1964).
Steinschneider, Hanbuch	M. Steinschneider, *Bibliographisches Handbuch ueber die . . . Literatur fuer hebraeische Sprachkunde* (1859; repr. with additions 1937).
Steinschneider, Uebersetzungen	M. Steinschneider, *Die hebraeischen Uebersetzungen des Mittelalters* (1893).
Stern, Americans	M.H. Stern, *Americans of Jewish Descent* (1960).
van Straalen, Cat	S. van Straalen, *Catalogue of Hebrew Books in the British Museum Acquired During the Years 1868–1892* (1894).
Suárez Fernández, Docmentos	L. Suárez Fernández, *Documentos acerca de la expulsion de los Judios de España* (1964).
Suk.	*Sukkah* (talmudic tractate).
Sus.	Susanna (Apocrypha).
SY	*Sefer Yeẓirah.*
Sym.	Symmachus' Greek translation of the Bible.
SZNG	*Studien zur neueren Geschichte.*
Ta'an.	*Ta'anit* (talmudic tractate).
Tam.	*Tamid* (mishnaic tractate).
Tanḥ.	*Tanḥuma.*
Tanḥ. B.	*Tanḥuma.* Buber ed (1885).
Targ. Jon	Targum Jonathan (Aramaic version of the Prophets).
Targ. Onk.	Targum Onkelos (Aramaic version of the Pentateuch).
Targ. Yer.	Targum Yerushalmi.
TB	Babylonian Talmud or Talmud Bavli.
Tcherikover, Corpus	V. Tcherikover, A. Fuks, and M. Stern, *Corpus Papyrorum Judaicorum,* 3 vols. (1957–60).
Tef.	*Tefillin* (post-talmudic tractate).
Tem.	*Temurah* (mishnaic tractate).
Ter.	*Terumah* (talmudic tractate).
Test. Patr.	Testament of the Twelve Patriarchs (Pseudepigrapha). Ash. – Asher Ben. – Benjamin Dan – Dan Gad – Gad Iss. – Issachar Joseph – Joseph Judah – Judah Levi – Levi Naph. – Naphtali Reu. – Reuben Sim. – Simeon Zeb. – Zebulun.
I and II	Epistle to the Thessalonians (New Testament).
Thieme-Becker	U. Thieme and F. Becker (eds.), *Allgemeines Lexikon der bildenden Kuenstler von der Antike bis zur Gegenwart,* 37 vols. (1907–50).
Tidhar	D. Tidhar (ed.), *Enẓiklopedyah la-Ḥalutẓei ha-Yishuv u-Vonav* (1947ff.).
I and II Timothy	Epistles to Timothy (New Testament).
Tit.	Epistle to Titus (New Testament).
TJ	Jerusalem Talmud or Talmud Yerushalmi.
Tob.	Tobit (Apocrypha).
Toh.	*Tohorot* (mishnaic tractate).
Torczyner, Bundeslade	H. Torczyner, *Die Bundeslade und die Anfaenge der Religion Israels* (1930[3]).
Tos.	*Tosafot.*
Tosef.	Tosefta.
Tristram, Nat Hist	H.B. Tristram, *Natural History of the Bible* (1877[5]).
Tristram, Survey	Palestine Exploration Fund, *Survey of Western Palestine,* vol. 4 (1884) = *Fauna and Flora* by H.B. Tristram.
TS	*Terra Santa* (1943ff.).

TSBA	*Transactions of the Society of Biblical Archaeology* (1872–93).
TY	*Tevul Yom* (mishnaic tractate).
UBSB	United Bible Society, *Bulletin*.
UJE	*Universal Jewish Encyclopedia*, 10 vols. (1939–43).
Uk.	*Ukẓin* (mishnaic tractate).
Urbach, Tosafot	E.E. Urbach, *Ba'alei ha-Tosafot* (1957^{2}).
de Vaux, Anc Isr	R. de Vaux, *Ancient Israel: its Life and Institutions* (1961; paperback 1965).
de Vaux, Instit	R. de Vaux, *Institutions de l'Ancien Testament*, 2 vols. (1958 60).
Virt.	Philo, *De Virtutibus*.
Vogelstein, Chronology	M. Volgelstein, *Biblical Chronology (1944)*.
Vogelstein-Rieger	H. Vogelstein and P. Rieger, *Geschichte der Juden in Rom*, 2 vols. (1895–96).
VT	*Vetus Testamentum* (1951ff.).
VTS	*Vetus Testamentum* Supplements (1953ff.).
Vulg.	Vulgate (Latin translation of the Bible).
Wars	Josephus, *The Jewish Wars*.
Watzinger, Denkmaeler	K. Watzinger, *Denkmaeler Palaestinas*, 2 vols. (1933–35).
Waxman, Literature	M. Waxman, *History of Jewish Literature*, 5 vols. (1960^{2}).
Weiss, Dor	I.H. Weiss, *Dor, Dor ve-Doreshav*, 5 vols. (1904^{4}).
Wellhausen, Proleg	J. Wellhausen, *Prolegomena zur Geschichte Israels* (1927^{6}).
WI	*Die Welt des Islams* (1913ff.).
Winniger, Biog	S. Wininger, *Grosse juedische National-Biographie …*, 7 vols. (1925–36).
Wisd.	Wisdom of Solomon (Apocrypha)
WLB	*Wiener Library Bulletin* (1958ff.).
Wolf, Bibliotheca	J.C. Wolf, *Bibliotheca Hebraea*, 4 vols. (1715–33).
Wright, Bible	G.E. Wright, *Westminster Historical Atlas to the Bible* (1945).
Wright, Atlas	G.E. Wright, *The Bible and the Ancient Near East* (1961).
WWWJ	*Who's Who in the World Jewry* (New York, 1955, 1965^{2}).
WZJT	*Wissenschaftliche Zeitschrift fuer juedische Theologie* (1835–37).
WZKM	*Wiener Zeitschrift fuer die Kunde des Morgenlandes* (1887ff.).
Yaari, Sheluḥei	A. Yaari, *Sheluḥei Ereẓ Yisrael* (1951).
Yad	Maimonides, *Mishneh Torah (Yad Ḥazakah)*.
Yad	*Yadayim* (mishnaic tractate).
Yal.	*Yalkut Shimoni*.
Yal. Mak.	*Yalkut Makhiri*.
Yal. Reub.	*Yalkut Reubeni*.
YD	*Yoreh De'ah*.
YE	*Yevreyskaya Entsiklopediya*, 14 vols. (c. 1910).
Yev.	*Yevamot* (talmudic tractate).
YIVOA	*YIVO Annual of Jewish Social Studies* (1946ff.).
YLBI	*Year Book of the Leo Baeck Institute* (1956ff.).
YMḤEY	See BJPES.
YMḤSI	*Yedi'ot ha-Makhon le-Ḥeker ha-Shirah ha-Ivrit* (1935/36ff.).
YMMY	*Yedi'ot ha-Makhon le-Madda'ei ha-Yahadut* (1924/25ff.).
Yoma	*Yoma* (talmudic tractate).
ZA	*Zeitschrift fuer Assyriologie* (1886/87ff.).
Zav.	*Zavim* (mishnaic tractate).
ZAW	*Zeitschrift fuer die alttestamentliche Wissenschaft und die Kunde des nachbiblishchen Judentums* (1881ff.).
ZAWB	*Beihefte* (supplements) to ZAW.
ZDMG	*Zeitschrift der Deutschen Morgenlaendischen Gesellschaft* (1846ff.).
ZDPV	*Zeitschrift des Deutschen Palaestina-Vereins* (1878–1949; from 1949 = BBLA).
Zech.	Zechariah (Bible).
Zedner, Cat	J. Zedner, *Catalogue of Hebrew Books in the Library of the British Museum* (1867; repr. 1964).
Zeitlin, Bibliotheca	W. Zeitlin, *Bibliotheca Hebraica Post-Mendelssohniana* (1891–95).
Zeph.	Zephaniah (Bible).
Zev.	*Zevaḥim* (talmudic tractate).
ZGGJT	*Zeitschrift der Gesellschaft fuer die Geschichte der Juden in der Tschechoslowakei* (1930–38).
ZGJD	*Zeitschrift fuer die Geschichte der Juden in Deutschland* (1887–92).
ZHB	*Zeitschrift fuer hebraeische Bibliographie* (1896–1920).
Zinberg, Sifrut	I. Zinberg, *Toledot Sifrut Yisrael*, 6 vols. (1955–60).
Ẓiẓ.	*Ẓiẓit* (post-talmudic tractate).
ZNW	*Zeitschrift fuer die neutestamentliche Wissenschaft* (1901ff.).
ZS	*Zeitschrift fuer Semitistik und verwandte Gebiete* (1922ff.).
Zunz, Gesch	L. Zunz, *Zur Geschichte und Literatur* (1845).
Zunz, Gesch	L. Zunz, *Literaturgeschichte der synagogalen Poesie* (1865; Supplement, 1867; repr. 1966).
Zunz, Poesie	L. Zunz, *Synogogale Posie des Mittelalters*, ed. by Freimann (1920^{2}; repr. 1967).
Zunz, Ritus	L. Zunz, *Ritus des synagogalen Gottesdienstes* (1859; repr. 1967).
Zunz, Schr	L. Zunz, *Gesammelte Schriften*, 3 vols. (1875–76).
Zunz, Vortraege	L. Zunz, *Gottesdienstliche vortraege der Juden …* 1892^{2}; repr. 1966).
Zunz-Albeck, Derashot	L. Zunz, *Ha-Derashot be-Yisrael*, Heb. Tr. of Zunz Vortraege by H. Albeck (1954^{2}).

TRANSLITERATION RULES

HEBREW AND SEMITIC LANGUAGES:

	General	*Scientific*
א	not transliterated[1]	ʾ
בּ	b	b
ב	v	v, b̲
גּ	g	g
ג		ḡ
דּ	d	d
ד		d̲
ה	h	h
ו	v – when not a vowel	w
ז	z	z
ח	ḥ	ḥ
ט	t	ṭ, t
י	y – when vowel and at end of words – i	y
כּ	k	k
כ, ך	kh	kh, k̲
ל	l	l̲
מ, ם	m	m
נ, ן	n	n
ס	s	s
ע	not transliterated[1]	ʿ
פּ	p	p
פ, ף	f	p, f, ph
צ, ץ	ẓ	ṣ, ẓ
ק	k	q, k
ר	r	r
שׁ	sh[2]	š
שׂ	s	ś, s
תּ	t	t
ת		t̲
ג׳	dzh, J	ğ
ז׳	zh, J	ž
צ׳	ch	č
ָ		å, o, ȯ (short) â, ā (long)
ַ	a	a
ֲ		a, [a]
ֵ		e, ẹ, ē
ֶ	e	æ, ä, ę
ֱ		œ, ě, [e]
ְ	only *sheva na* is transliterated	ə, ě, e; only *sheva na* transliterated
ִ ִי	i	i
ֹ וֹ	o	o, o, o
ֻ וּ	u	u, ŭ û, ū
ֵי	ei; biblical e	
‡		reconstructed forms of words

1. The letters א and ע are not transliterated.
An apostrophe (') between vowels indicates that they do not form a diphthong and are to be pronounced separately.
2. *Dagesh ḥazak* (forte) is indicated by doubling of the letter, except for the letter שׁ.
3. Names. Biblical names and biblical place names are rendered according to the Bible translation of the Jewish Publication Society of America. Post-biblical Hebrew names are transliterated; contemporary names are transliterated or rendered as used by the person. Place names are transliterated or rendered by the accepted spelling. Names and some words with an accepted English form are usually not transliterated.

YIDDISH

א	not transliterated
אַ	a
אָ	o
ב	b
בֿ	v
ג	g
ד	d
ה	h
ו, וּ	u
וו	v
וי	oy
ז	z
זש	zh
ח	kh
ט	t
טש	tsh, ch
י	(consonant) y (vowel) i
יִ	i
יי	ey
ײַ	ay
כּ	k
כ, ך	kh
ל	l
מ, ם	m
נ, ן	n
ס	s
ע	e
פּ	p
פֿ, ף	f
צ, ץ	ts
ק	k
ר	r
ש	sh
שׂ	s
תּ	t
ת	s

1. Yiddish transliteration rendered according to U. Weinreich's Modern *English-Yiddish Yiddish-English* Dictionary.
2. Hebrew words in Yiddish are usually transliterated according to standard Yiddish pronunciation, e.g., חזנות = *khazones.*

LADINO

Ladino and Judeo-Spanish words written in Hebrew characters are transliterated phonetically, following the General Rules of Hebrew transliteration (see above) whenever the accepted spelling in Latin characters could not be ascertained.

ARABIC

ء ا	a[1]	ض	ḍ
ب	b	ط	ṭ
ت	t	ظ	ẓ
ث	th	ع	c
ج	j	غ	gh
ح	ḥ	ف	f
خ	kh	ق	q
د	d	ك	k
ذ	dh	ل	l
ر	r	م	m
ز	z	ن	n
س	s	ه	h
ش	sh	و	w
ص	ṣ	ي	y
ـَ	a	ـَا ى	ā
ـِ	i	ـِي	ī
ـُ	u	ـُو	ū
ـَو	aw	ـِيّ	iyy[2]
ـَي	ay	ـُوّ	uww[2]

1. not indicated when initial
2. see note (f)

a) The EJ follows the *Columbia Lippincott Gazetteer* and the *Times Atlas* in transliteration of Arabic place names. Sites that appear in neither are transliterated according to the table above, and subject to the following notes.

b) The EJ follows the *Columbia Encyclopedia* in transliteration of Arabic names. Personal names that do not therein appear are transliterated according to the table above and subject to the following notes (e.g., Ali rather than ʿAlī, Suleiman rather than Sulayman).

c) The EJ follows the *Webster's Third International Dictionary, Unabridged* in transliteration of Arabic terms that have been integrated into the English language.

d) The term "Abu" will thus appear, usually in disregard of inflection.

e) Nunnation (end vowels, *tanwīn*) are dropped in transliteration.

f) Gemination (*tashdīd*) is indicated by the doubling of the geminated letter, unless an end letter, in which case the gemination is dropped.

g) The definitive article *al-* will always be thus transliterated, unless subject to one of the modifying notes (e.g., El-Arish rather than al-ʿArīsh; modification according to note (a)).

h) The Arabic transliteration disregards the Sun Letters (the antero-palatals (*al-Ḥurūf al-Shamsiyya*).

i) The *tā-marbūṭa* (o) is omitted in transliteration, unless in construct-stage (e.g., *Khirba* but *Khirbat Mishmish*).

These modifying notes may lead to various inconsistencies in the Arabic transliteration, but this policy has deliberately been adopted to gain smoother reading of Arabic terms and names.

GREEK

Ancient Greek	*Modern Greek*	*Greek Letters*
a	a	*Α; α; ᾳ*
b	v	*Β; β*
g	gh; g	*Γ; γ*
d	dh	*Δ; δ*
e	e	*Ε; ε*
z	z	*Ζ; ζ*
e; e	i	*Η; η; ῃ*
th	th	*Θ; θ*
i	i	*Ι; ι*
k	k; ky	*Κ; κ*
l	l	*Λ; λ*
m	m	*Μ; μ*
n	n	*Ν; ν*
x	x	*Ξ; ξ*
o	o	*Ο; ο*
p	p	*Π; π*
r; rh	r	*Ρ; ρ; ῥ*
s	s	*Σ; σ; ς*
t	t	*Τ; τ*
u; y	i	*Υ; υ*
ph	f	*Φ; φ*
ch	kh	*Χ; χ*
ps	ps	*Ψ; ψ*
o; ō	o	*Ω; ω; ῳ*
ai	e	*αι*
ei	i	*ει*
oi	i	*οι*
ui	i	*υι*
ou	ou	*ου*
eu	ev	*ευ*
eu; ēu	iv	*ηυ*
–	j	*τζ*
nt	d; nd	*ντ*
mp	b; mb	*μπ*
ngk	g	*γκ*
ng	ng	*γγ*
h	–	‘
–	–	’
w	–	*Ϝ*

RUSSIAN

А	A
Б	B
В	V
Г	G
Д	D
Е	E, Ye[1]
Ё	Yo, O[2]
Ж	Zh
З	Z
И	I
Й	Y[3]
К	K
Л	L
М	M
Н	N
О	O
П	P
Р	R
С	S
Т	T
У	U
Ф	F
Х	Kh
Ц	Ts
Ч	Ch
Ш	Sh
Щ	Shch
Ъ	omitted; see note [1]
Ы	Y
Ь	omitted; see note [1]
Э	E
Ю	Yu
Я	Ya

1. Ye at the beginning of a word; after all vowels except ***Ы***; and after **Ъ** and ***Ь***.
2. O after ***Ч***, ***Ш*** and ***Щ***.
3. Omitted after ***Ы***, and in names of people after ***И***.

A. Many first names have an accepted English or quasi-English form which has been preferred to transliteration.
B. Place names have been given according to the *Columbia Lippincott Gazeteer*.
C. Pre-revolutionary spelling has been ignored.
D. Other languages using the Cyrillic alphabet (e.g., Bulgarian, Ukrainian), inasmuch as they appear, have been phonetically transliterated in conformity with the principles of this table.

GLOSSARY

Asterisked terms have separate entries in the Encyclopaedia.

Actions Committee, early name of the Zionist General Council, the supreme institution of the World Zionist Organization in the interim between Congresses. The Zionist Executive's name was then the "Small Actions Committee."

*__Adar__, twelfth month of the Jewish religious year, sixth of the civil, approximating to February–March.

*__Aggadah__, name given to those sections of Talmud and Midrash containing homiletic expositions of the Bible, stories, legends, folklore, anecdotes, or maxims. In contradistinction to **halakhah*.

*__Agunah__, woman unable to remarry according to Jewish law, because of desertion by her husband or inability to accept presumption of death.

*__Aharonim__, later rabbinic authorities. In contradistinction to **rishonim* ("early ones").

Ahavah, liturgical poem inserted in the second benediction of the morning prayer *(*Ahavah Rabbah)* of the festivals and/or special Sabbaths.

Aktion (Ger.), operation involving the mass assembly, deportation, and murder of Jews by the Nazis during the *Holocaust.

*__Aliyah__, (1) being called to Reading of the Law in synagogue; (2) immigration to Ereẓ Israel; (3) one of the waves of immigration to Ereẓ Israel from the early 1880s.

*__Amidah__, main prayer recited at all services; also known as *Shemoneh Esreh* and *Tefillah*.

*__Amora__ (pl. **amoraim**), title given to the Jewish scholars in Ereẓ Israel and Babylonia in the third to sixth centuries who were responsible for the **Gemara*.

Aravah, the *willow; one of the *Four Species used on *Sukkot ("festival of Tabernacles") together with the **etrog, hadas*, and **lulav*.

*__Arvit__, evening prayer.

Asarah be-Tevet, fast on the 10th of Tevet commemorating the commencement of the siege of Jerusalem by Nebuchadnezzar.

Asefat ha-Nivḥarim, representative assembly elected by Jews in Palestine during the period of the British Mandate (1920–48).

*__Ashkenaz__, name applied generally in medieval rabbinical literature to Germany.

*__Ashkenazi__ (pl. **Ashkenazim**), German or West-, Central-, or East-European Jew(s), as contrasted with *Sephardi(m).

*__Av__, fifth month of the Jewish religious year, eleventh of the civil, approximating to July–August.

*__Av bet din__, vice president of the supreme court (*bet din ha-gadol*) in Jerusalem during the Second Temple period; later, title given to communal rabbis as heads of the religious courts (see **bet din*).

*__Badḥan__, jester, particularly at traditional Jewish weddings in Eastern Europe.

*__Bakkashah__ (Heb. "supplication"), type of petitionary prayer, mainly recited in the Sephardi rite on Rosh Ha-Shanah and the Day of Atonement.

Bar, "son of . . . "; frequently appearing in personal names.

*__Baraita__ (pl. **beraitot**), statement of **tanna* not found in *Mishnah.

*__Bar mitzvah__, ceremony marking the initiation of a boy at the age of 13 into the Jewish religious community.

Ben, "son of . . . ", frequently appearing in personal names.

Berakhah (pl. **berakhot**), *benediction, blessing; formula of praise and thanksgiving.

*__Bet din__ (pl. **battei din**), rabbinic court of law.

*__Bet ha-midrash__, school for higher rabbinic learning; often attached to or serving as a synagogue.

*__Bilu__, first modern movement for pioneering and agricultural settlement in Ereẓ Israel, founded in 1882 at Kharkov, Russia.

*__Bund__, Jewish socialist party founded in Vilna in 1897, supporting Jewish national rights; Yiddishist, and anti-Zionist.

Cohen (pl. **Cohanim**), see Kohen.

*__Conservative Judaism__, trend in Judaism developed in the United States in the 20th century which, while opposing extreme changes in traditional observances, permits certain modifications of *halakhah* in response to the changing needs of the Jewish people.

*__Consistory__ (Fr. *consistoire*), governing body of a Jewish communal district in France and certain other countries.

*__Converso(s)__, term applied in Spain and Portugal to converted Jew(s), and sometimes more loosely to their descendants.

*__Crypto-Jew__, term applied to a person who although observing outwardly Christianity (or some other religion) was at heart a Jew and maintained Jewish observances as far as possible (see Converso; Marrano; Neofiti; New Christian; Jadīd al-Islām).

*__Dayyan__, member of rabbinic court.

Decisor, equivalent to the Hebrew *posek* (pl. **posekim*), the rabbi who gives the decision (*halakhah*) in Jewish law or practice.

*__Devekut__, "devotion"; attachment or adhesion to God; communion with God.

*__Diaspora__, Jews living in the "dispersion" outside Ereẓ Israel; area of Jewish settlement outside Ereẓ Israel.

Din, a law (both secular and religious), legal decision, or lawsuit.

Divan, diwan, collection of poems, especially in Hebrew, Arabic, or Persian.

Dunam, unit of land area (1,000 sq. m., c. ¼ acre), used in Israel.

Einsatzgruppen, mobile units of Nazi S.S. and S.D.; in U.S.S.R. and Serbia, mobile killing units.

*__Ein-Sof__, "without end"; "the infinite"; hidden, impersonal aspect of God; also used as a Divine Name.

*__Elul__, sixth month of the Jewish religious calendar, 12th of the civil, precedes the High Holiday season in the fall.

Endloesung, see *Final Solution.

*__Ereẓ Israel__, Land of Israel; Palestine.

*__Eruv__, technical term for rabbinical provision permitting the alleviation of certain restrictions.

*__Etrog__, citron; one of the *Four Species used on *Sukkot together with the **lulav, hadas*, and *aravah*.

Even ha-Ezer, see Shulḥan Arukh.

*__Exilarch__, lay head of Jewish community in Babylonia (see also *resh galuta*), and elsewhere.

*__Final Solution__ (Ger. *Endloesung*), in Nazi terminology, the Nazi-planned mass murder and total annihilation of the Jews.

*__Gabbai__, official of a Jewish congregation; originally a charity collector.

*__Galut__, "exile"; the condition of the Jewish people in dispersion.

*__Gaon__ (pl. **geonim**), head of academy in post-talmudic period, especially in Babylonia.

Gaonate, office of *gaon.

*__Gemara__, traditions, discussions, and rulings of the *amoraim*, commenting on and supplementing the *Mishnah, and forming part of the Babylonian and Palestinian Talmuds (see Talmud).

*__Gematria__, interpretation of Hebrew word according to the numerical value of its letters.

General Government, territory in Poland administered by a German civilian governor-general with headquarters in Cracow after the German occupation in World War II.

*__Genizah__, depository for sacred books. The best known was discovered in the synagogue of Fostat (old Cairo).

Get, bill of *divorce.

*__Ge'ullah__, hymn inserted after the *Shema* into the benediction of the morning prayer of the festivals and special Sabbaths.

*__Gilgul__, metempsychosis; transmigration of souls.

*__Golem__, automaton, especially in human form, created by magical means and endowed with life.

*__Ḥabad__, initials of *ḥokhmah, binah, da'at*: "wisdom, understanding, knowledge"; ḥasidic movement founded in Belorussia by *Shneur Zalman of Lyady.

Hadas, *myrtle; one of the *Four Species used on Sukkot together with the *etrog*, *lulav*, and *aravah*.

*__Haftarah__ (pl. **haftarot**), designation of the portion from the prophetical books of the Bible recited after the synagogue reading from the Pentateuch on Sabbaths and holidays.

*__Haganah__, clandestine Jewish organization for armed self-defense in Ereẓ Israel under the British Mandate, which eventually evolved into a people's militia and became the basis for the Israel army.

*__Haggadah__, ritual recited in the home on *Passover eve at seder table.

Haham, title of chief rabbi of the Spanish and Portuguese congregations in London, England.

*__Hakham__, title of rabbi of *Sephardi congregation.

*__Hakham bashi__, title in the 15th century and modern times of the chief rabbi in the Ottoman Empire, residing in Constantinople (Istanbul), also applied to principal rabbis in provincial towns.

Hakhsharah ("preparation"), organized training in the Diaspora of pioneers for agricultural settlement in Ereẓ Israel.

*__Halakhah__ (pl. **halakhot**), an accepted decision in rabbinic law. Also refers to those parts of the *Talmud concerned with legal matters. In contradistinction to *aggadah*.

Ḥaliẓah, biblically prescribed ceremony (Deut. 25:9–10) performed when a man refuses to marry his brother's childless widow, enabling her to remarry.

*__Hallel__, term referring to Psalms 113-18 in liturgical use.

*__Ḥalukkah__, system of financing the maintenance of Jewish communities in the holy cities of Ereẓ Israel by collections made abroad, mainly in the pre-Zionist era (see *kolel*).

Ḥalutz (pl. **ḥalutzim**), pioneer, especially in agriculture, in Ereẓ Israel.

Ḥalutziyyut, pioneering.

*__Ḥanukkah__, eight-day celebration commemorating the victory of *Judah Maccabee over the Syrian king *Antiochus Epiphanes and the subsequent rededication of the Temple.

Ḥasid, adherent of *Ḥasidism.

*__Ḥasidei Ashkenaz__, medieval pietist movement among the Jews of Germany.

*__Ḥasidism__, (1) religious revivalist movement of popular mysticism among Jews of Germany in the Middle Ages; (2) religious movement founded by *Israel ben Eliezer Ba'al Shem Tov in the first half of the 18th century.

*__Haskalah__, "enlightenment"; movement for spreading modern European culture among Jews c. 1750–1880. See *maskil*.

*__Havdalah__, ceremony marking the end of Sabbath or festival.

*__Ḥazzan__, precentor who intones the liturgy and leads the prayers in synagogue; in earlier times a synagogue official.

*__Ḥeder__ (lit. "room"), school for teaching children Jewish religious observance.

Heikhalot, "palaces"; tradition in Jewish mysticism centering on mystical journeys through the heavenly spheres and palaces to the Divine Chariot (see Merkabah).

*__Ḥerem__, excommunication, imposed by rabbinical authorities for purposes of religious and/or communal discipline; originally, in biblical times, that which is separated from common use either because it was an abomination or because it was consecrated to God.

Ḥeshvan, see Marḥeshvan.

*__Ḥevra kaddisha__, title applied to charitable confraternity (*ḥevrah*), now generally limited to associations for burial of the dead.

*__Ḥibbat Zion__, see Ḥovevei Zion.

*__Histadrut__ (abbr. For Heb. **Ha-Histadrut ha-Kelalit shel ha-Ovedim ha-Ivriyyim be-Ereẓ Israel**). Ereẓ Israel Jewish Labor Federation, founded in 1920; subsequently renamed Histadrut ha-Ovedim be-Ereẓ Israel.

*__Holocaust__, the organized mass persecution and annihilation of European Jewry by the Nazis (1933–1945).

*__Hoshana Rabba__, the seventh day of *Sukkot on which special observances are held.

Ḥoshen Mishpat, see Shulḥan Arukh.

Ḥovevei Zion, federation of *Ḥibbat Zion, early (pre-*Herzl) Zionist movement in Russia.

Illui, outstanding scholar or genius, especially a young prodigy in talmudic learning.

*__Iyyar__, second month of the Jewish religious year, eighth of the civil, approximating to April-May.

I.Ẓ.L. (initials of Heb. *__Irgun Ẓeva'i Le'ummi__; "National Military Organization"), underground Jewish organization in Ereẓ Israel founded in 1931, which engaged from 1937 in retaliatory acts against Arab attacks and later against the British mandatory authorities.

*__Jadīd al-Islām__ (Ar.), a person practicing the Jewish religion in secret although outwardly observing Islām.

*__Jewish Legion__, Jewish units in British army during World War I.

*__Jihād__ (Ar.), in Muslim religious law, holy war waged against infidels.

*__Judenrat__ (Ger. "Jewish council"), council set up in Jewish communities and ghettos under the Nazis to execute their instructions.

*__Judenrein__ (Ger. "clean of Jews"), in Nazi terminology the condition of a locality from which all Jews had been eliminated.

*__Kabbalah__, the Jewish mystical tradition:
 Kabbala iyyunit, speculative Kabbalah;
 Kabbala ma'asit, practical Kabbalah;
 Kabbala nevu'it, prophetic Kabbalah.

Kabbalist, student of Kabbalah.

*__Kaddish__, liturgical doxology.

Kahal, Jewish congregation; among Ashkenazim, *kehillah*.

*Kalām (Ar.), science of Muslim theology; adherents of the Kalām are called *mutakallimūn*.

***Karaite**, member of a Jewish sect originating in the eighth century which rejected rabbinic (*Rabbanite) Judaism and claimed to accept only Scripture as authoritative.

***Kasher**, ritually permissible food.

Kashrut, Jewish *dietary laws.

***Kavvanah**, "intention"; term denoting the spiritual concentration accompanying prayer and the performance of ritual or of a commandment.

***Kedushah**, main addition to the third blessing in the reader's repetition of the *Amidah* in which the public responds to the precentor's introduction.

Kefar, village; first part of name of many settlements in Israel.

Kehillah, congregation; see *kahal*.

Kelippah (pl. **kelippot**), "husk(s)"; mystical term denoting force(s) of evil.

***Keneset Yisrael**, comprehensive communal organization of the Jews in Palestine during the British Mandate.

Keri, variants in the masoretic (*masorah) text of the Bible between the spelling (*ketiv*) and its pronunciation (*keri*).

***Kerovah** (collective plural (corrupted) from **kerovez̩**), poem(s) incorporated into the **Amidah*.

Ketiv, see *keri*.

***Ketubbah**, marriage contract, stipulating husband's obligations to wife.

Kevuz̩ah, small commune of pioneers constituting an agricultural settlement in Erez̩ Israel (evolved later into *kibbutz).

***Kibbutz** (pl. **kibbutzim**), larger-size commune constituting a settlement in Erez̩ Israel based mainly on agriculture but engaging also in industry.

***Kiddush**, prayer of sanctification, recited over wine or bread on eve of Sabbaths and festivals.

***Kiddush ha-Shem**, term connoting martyrdom or act of strict integrity in support of Judaic principles.

***Kinah** (pl. **kinot**), lamentation dirge(s) for the Ninth of Av and other fast days.

***Kislev**, ninth month of the Jewish religious year, third of the civil, approximating to November-December.

Klaus, name given in Central and Eastern Europe to an institution, usually with synagogue attached, where *Talmud was studied perpetually by adults; applied by Ḥasidim to their synagogue ("*kloyz*").

***Knesset**, parliament of the State of Israel.

K(c)ohen (pl. **K(c)ohanim**), Jew(s) of priestly (Aaronide) descent.

***Kolel**, (1) community in Erez̩ Israel of persons from a particular country or locality, often supported by their fellow countrymen in the Diaspora; (2) institution for higher Torah study.

Kosher, see *kasher*.

***Kristallnacht** (Ger. "crystal night," meaning "night of broken glass"), organized destruction of synagogues, Jewish houses, and shops, accompanied by mass arrests of Jews, which took place in Germany and Austria under the Nazis on the night of Nov. 9–10, 1938.

***Lag ba-Omer**, 33rd (Heb. **lag**) day of the **Omer* period falling on the 18th of *Iyyar; a semi-holiday.

Leḥi (abbr. For Heb. ***Loḥamei Ḥerut Israel**, "Fighters for the Freedom of Israel"), radically anti-British armed underground organization in Palestine, founded in 1940 by dissidents from *I.Z.L.

Levir, husband's brother.

***Levirate marriage** (Heb. *yibbum*), marriage of childless widow (*yevamah*) by brother (*yavam*) of the deceased husband (in accordance with Deut. 25:5); release from such an obligation is effected through *ḥaliz̩ah*.

LHY, see Leḥi.

***Lulav**, palm branch; one of the *Four Species used on *Sukkot together with the **etrog*, *hadas*, and *aravah*.

***Ma'aravot**, hymns inserted into the evening prayer of the three festivals, Passover, Shavuot, and Sukkot.

Ma'ariv, evening prayer; also called **arvit*.

***Ma'barah**, transition camp; temporary settlement for newcomers in Israel during the period of mass immigration following 1948.

***Maftir**, reader of the concluding portion of the Pentateuchal section on Sabbaths and holidays in synagogue; reader of the portion of the prophetical books of the Bible (**haftarah*).

***Maggid**, popular preacher.

***Maḥzor** (pl. **maḥzorim**), festival prayer book.

***Mamzer**, bastard; according to Jewish law, the offspring of an incestuous relationship.

***Mandate, Palestine**, responsibility for the administration of Palestine conferred on Britain by the League of Nations in 1922; mandatory government: the British administration of Palestine.

***Maqāma** (Ar. pl. **maqamāt**), poetic form (rhymed prose) which, in its classical arrangement, has rigid rules of form and content.

***Marḥeshvan**, popularly called Ḥeshvan; eighth month of the Jewish religious year, second of the civil, approximating to October–November.

***Marrano(s)**, descendant(s) of Jew(s) in Spain and Portugal whose ancestors had been converted to Christianity under pressure but who secretly observed Jewish rituals.

Maskil (pl. **maskilim**), adherent of *Haskalah ("Enlightenment") movement.

***Masorah**, body of traditions regarding the correct spelling, writing, and reading of the Hebrew Bible.

Masorete, scholar of the masoretic tradition.

Masoretic, in accordance with the masorah.

Meliz̩ah, in Middle Ages, elegant style; modern usage, florid style using biblical or talmudic phraseology.

Mellah, *Jewish quarter in North African towns.

***Menorah**, candelabrum; seven-branched oil lamp used in the Tabernacle and Temple; also eight-branched candelabrum used on *Ḥanukkah.

Me'orah, hymn inserted into the first benediction of the morning prayer (*Yoz̩er ha-Me'orot*).

***Merkabah**, *merkavah*, "chariot"; mystical discipline associated with Ezekiel's vision of the Divine Throne-Chariot (Ezek. 1).

Meshullaḥ, emissary sent to conduct propaganda or raise funds for rabbinical academies or charitable institutions.

***Mezuzah** (pl. **mezuzot**), parchment scroll with selected Torah verses placed in container and affixed to gates and doorposts of houses occupied by Jews.

***Midrash**, method of interpreting Scripture to elucidate legal points (*Midrash Halakhah*) or to bring out lessons by stories or homiletics (*Midrash Aggadah*). Also the name for a collection of such rabbinic interpretations.

***Mikveh**, ritual bath.

***Minhag** (pl. **minhagim**), ritual custom(s); synagogal rite(s); especially of a specific sector of Jewry.

***Minḥah**, afternoon prayer; originally meal offering in Temple.

*__Minyan__, group of ten male adult Jews, the minimum required for communal prayer.

*__Mishnah__, earliest codification of Jewish Oral Law.

Mishnah (pl. **mishnayot**), subdivision of tractates of the Mishnah.

Mitnagged (pl. ***Mitnaggedim**), originally, opponents of *Ḥasidism in Eastern Europe.

*__Mitzvah__, biblical or rabbinic injunction; applied also to good or charitable deeds.

Mohel, official performing circumcisions.

*__Moshav__, smallholders' cooperative agricultural settlement in Israel, see moshav ovedim.

Moshavah, earliest type of Jewish village in modern Ereẓ Israel in which farming is conducted on individual farms mostly on privately owned land.

Moshav ovedim ("workers' moshav"), agricultural village in Israel whose inhabitants possess individual homes and holdings but cooperate in the purchase of equipment, sale of produce, mutual aid, etc.

*__Moshav shittufi__ ("collective moshav"), agricultural village in Israel whose members possess individual homesteads but where the agriculture and economy are conducted as a collective unit.

Mostegab (Ar.), poem with biblical verse at beginning of each stanza.

*__Muqaddam__ (Ar., pl. **muqaddamūn**), "leader," "head of the community."

*__Musaf__, additional service on Sabbath and festivals; originally the additional sacrifice offered in the Temple.

Musar, traditional ethical literature.

*__Musar movement__, ethical movement developing in the latter part of the 19th century among Orthodox Jewish groups in Lithuania; founded by R. Israel *Lipkin (Salanter).

*__Nagid__ (pl. **negidim**), title applied in Muslim (and some Christian) countries in the Middle Ages to a leader recognized by the state as head of the Jewish community.

Nakdan (pl. **nakdanim**), "punctuator"; scholar of the 9th to 14th centuries who provided biblical manuscripts with masoretic apparatus, vowels, and accents.

*__Nasi__ (pl. **nesi'im**), talmudic term for president of the Sanhedrin, who was also the spiritual head and later, political representative of the Jewish people; from second century a descendant of Hillel recognized by the Roman authorities as patriarch of the Jews. Now applied to the president of the State of Israel.

*__Negev__, the southern, mostly arid, area of Israel.

*__Ne'ilah__, concluding service on the *Day of Atonement.

Neofiti, term applied in southern Italy to converts to Christianity from Judaism and their descendants who were suspected of maintaining secret allegiance to Judaism.

*__Neology; Neolog; Neologism__, trend of *Reform Judaism in Hungary forming separate congregations after 1868.

*__Nevelah__ (lit. "carcass"), meat forbidden by the *dietary laws on account of the absence of, or defect in, the act of **sheḥitah* (ritual slaughter).

*__New Christians__, term applied especially in Spain and Portugal to converts from Judaism (and from Islam) and their descendants; "Half New Christian" designated a person one of whose parents was of full Jewish blood.

*__Niddah__ ("menstruous woman"), woman during the period of menstruation.

*__Nisan__, first month of the Jewish religious year, seventh of the civil, approximating to March-April.

Niẓoẓot, "sparks"; mystical term for sparks of the holy light imprisoned in all matter.

Nosaḥ (nusaḥ) "version"; (1) textual variant; (2) term applied to distinguish the various prayer rites, e.g., *nosaḥ Ashkenaz*; (3) the accepted tradition of synagogue melody.

*__Notarikon__, method of abbreviating Hebrew works or phrases by acronym.

Novella(e) (Heb. **ḥiddush (im)*), commentary on talmudic and later rabbinic subjects that derives new facts or principles from the implications of the text.

*__Nuremberg Laws__, Nazi laws excluding Jews from German citizenship, and imposing other restrictions.

Ofan, hymns inserted into a passage of the morning prayer.

*__Omer__, first sheaf cut during the barley harvest, offered in the Temple on the second day of Passover.

Omer, Counting of (Heb. *Sefirat ha-Omer*), 49 days counted from the day on which the *omer* was first offered in the Temple (according to the rabbis the 16th of Nisan, i.e., the second day of Passover) until the festival of Shavuot; now a period of semi-mourning.

Oraḥ Ḥayyim, see Shulḥan Arukh.

*__Orthodoxy__ (Orthodox Judaism), modern term for the strictly traditional sector of Jewry.

*__Pale of Settlement__, 25 provinces of czarist Russia where Jews were permitted permanent residence.

*__Palmaḥ__ (abbr. for Heb. *peluggot maḥaẓ*; "shock companies"), striking arm of the *Haganah.

*__Pardes__, medieval biblical exegesis giving the literal, allegorical, homiletical, and esoteric interpretations.

*__Parnas__, chief synagogue functionary, originally vested with both religious and administrative functions; subsequently an elected lay leader.

Partition plan(s), proposals for dividing Ereẓ Israel into autonomous areas.

Paytan, composer of **piyyut* (liturgical poetry).

*__Peel Commission__, British Royal Commission appointed by the British government in 1936 to inquire into the Palestine problem and make recommendations for its solution.

Pesaḥ, *Passover.

*__Pilpul__, in talmudic and rabbinic literature, a sharp dialectic used particularly by talmudists in Poland from the 16th century.

*__Pinkas__, community register or minute-book.

*__Piyyut__, (pl. **piyyutim**), Hebrew liturgical poetry.

*__Pizmon__, poem with refrain.

Posek (pl. ***posekim**), decisor; codifier or rabbinic scholar who pronounces decisions in disputes and on questions of Jewish law.

*__Prosbul__, legal method of overcoming the cancelation of debts with the advent of the *sabbatical year.

*__Purim__, festival held on Adar 14 or 15 in commemoration of the delivery of the Jews of Persia in the time of *Esther.

Rabban, honorific title higher than that of rabbi, applied to heads of the *Sanhedrin in mishnaic times.

*__Rabbanite__, adherent of rabbinic Judaism. In contradistinction to *Karaite.

Reb, rebbe, Yiddish form for rabbi, applied generally to a teacher or ḥasidic rabbi.

*__Reconstructionism__, trend in Jewish thought originating in the United States.

*__Reform Judaism__, trend in Judaism advocating modification of *Orthodoxy in conformity with the exigencies of contemporary life and thought.

Resh galuta, lay head of Babylonian Jewry (see exilarch).

Responsum (pl. ***responsa**), written opinion (*teshuvah*) given to question (*she'elah*) on aspects of Jewish law by qualified authorities; pl. collection of such queries and opinions in book form (*she'elot u-teshuvot*).

***Rishonim**, older rabbinical authorities. Distinguished from later authorities (**aḥaronim*).

***Rishon le-Zion**, title given to Sephardi chief rabbi of Ereẓ Israel.

***Rosh Ha-Shanah**, two-day holiday (one day in biblical and early mishnaic times) at the beginning of the month of *Tishri (September–October), traditionally the New Year.

Rosh Hodesh, *New Moon, marking the beginning of the Hebrew month.

Rosh Yeshivah, see *Yeshivah.

***R.S.H.A.** (initials of Ger. *Reichssicherheitshauptamt*: "Reich Security Main Office"), the central security department of the German Reich, formed in 1939, and combining the security police (Gestapo and Kripo) and the S.D.

***Sanhedrin**, the assembly of ordained scholars which functioned both as a supreme court and as a legislature before 70 C.E. In modern times the name was given to the body of representative Jews convoked by Napoleon in 1807.

***Savora** (pl. **savoraim**), name given to the Babylonian scholars of the period between the **amoraim* and the **geonim*, approximately 500–700 C.E.

S.D. (initials of Ger. *Sicherheitsdienst*: "security service"), security service of the *S.S. formed in 1932 as the sole intelligence organization of the Nazi party.

Seder, ceremony observed in the Jewish home on the first night of Passover (outside Ereẓ Israel first two nights), when the *Haggadah is recited.

***Sefer Torah**, manuscript scroll of the Pentateuch for public reading in synagogue.

***Sefirot, the ten**, the ten "Numbers"; mystical term denoting the ten spheres or emanations through which the Divine manifests itself; elements of the world; dimensions, primordial numbers.

Selektion (Ger.), (1) in ghettos and other Jewish settlements, the drawing up by Nazis of lists of deportees; (2) separation of incoming victims to concentration camps into two categories – those destined for immediate killing and those to be sent for forced labor.

Seliḥah (pl. ***seliḥot**), penitential prayer.

***Semikhah**, ordination conferring the title "rabbi" and permission to give decisions in matters of ritual and law.

Sephardi (pl. ***Sephardim**), Jew(s) of Spain and Portugal and their descendants, wherever resident, as contrasted with *Ashkenazi(m).

Shabbatean, adherent of the pseudo-messiah *Shabbetai Ẓevi (17th century).

Shaddai, name of God found frequently in the Bible and commonly translated "Almighty."

***Shaḥarit**, morning service.

Shali'aḥ (pl. **sheliḥim**), in Jewish law, messenger, agent; in modern times, an emissary from Ereẓ Israel to Jewish communities or organizations abroad for the purpose of fund-raising, organizing pioneer immigrants, education, etc.

Shalmonit, poetic meter introduced by the liturgical poet *Solomon ha-Bavli.

***Shammash**, synagogue beadle.

***Shavuot**, Pentecost; Festival of Weeks; second of the three annual pilgrim festivals, commemorating the receiving of the Torah at Mt. Sinai.

***Sheḥitah**, ritual slaughtering of animals.

***Shekhinah**, Divine Presence.

Shelishit, poem with three-line stanzas.

***Sheluḥei Ereẓ Israel** (or **shadarim**), emissaries from Ereẓ Israel.

***Shema** ([Yisrael]; "hear… [O Israel]," Deut. 6:4), Judaism's confession of faith, proclaiming the absolute unity of God.

Shemini Aẓeret, final festal day (in the Diaspora, final two days) at the conclusion of *Sukkot.

Shemittah, *Sabbatical year.

Sheniyyah, poem with two-line stanzas.

***Shephelah**, southern part of the coastal plain of Ereẓ Israel.

***Shevat**, eleventh month of the Jewish religious year, fifth of the civil, approximating to January–February.

***Shi'ur Komah**, Hebrew mystical work (c. eighth century) containing a physical description of God's dimensions; term denoting enormous spacial measurement used in speculations concerning the body of the **Shekhinah*.

Shivah, the "seven days" of *mourning following burial of a relative.

***Shofar**, horn of the ram (or any other ritually clean animal excepting the cow) sounded for the memorial blowing on *Rosh Ha-Shanah, and other occasions.

Shoḥet, person qualified to perform **sheḥitah*.

Shomer, *Ha-Shomer, organization of Jewish workers in Ereẓ Israel founded in 1909 to defend Jewish settlements.

***Shtadlan**, Jewish representative or negotiator with access to dignitaries of state, active at royal courts, etc.

***Shtetl**, Jewish small-town community in Eastern Europe.

***Shulḥan Arukh**, Joseph *Caro's code of Jewish law in four parts:
Oraḥ Ḥayyim, laws relating to prayers, Sabbath, festivals, and fasts;
Yoreh De'ah, dietary laws, etc;
Even ha-Ezer, laws dealing with women, marriage, etc;
Ḥoshen Mishpat, civil, criminal law, court procedure, etc.

Siddur, among Ashkenazim, the volume containing the daily prayers (in distinction to the **maḥzor* containing those for the festivals).

***Simḥat Torah**, holiday marking the completion in the synagogue of the annual cycle of reading the Pentateuch; in Ereẓ Israel observed on Shemini Aẓeret (outside Ereẓ Israel on the following day).

***Sinai Campaign**, brief campaign in October–November 1956 when Israel army reacted to Egyptian terrorist attacks and blockade by occupying the Sinai peninsula.

Sitra aḥra, "the other side" (of God); left side; the demoniac and satanic powers.

***Sivan**, third month of the Jewish religious year, ninth of the civil, approximating to May–June.

***Six-Day War**, rapid war in June 1967 when Israel reacted to Arab threats and blockade by defeating the Egyptian, Jordanian, and Syrian armies.

***S.S.** (initials of Ger. *Schutzstaffel*: "protection detachment"), Nazi formation established in 1925 which later became the "elite" organization of the Nazi Party and carried out central tasks in the "Final Solution."

***Status quo ante** community, community in Hungary retaining the status it had held before the convention of the General Jewish Congress there in 1868 and the resultant split in Hungarian Jewry.

*__Sukkah__, booth or tabernacle erected for *Sukkot when, for seven days, religious Jews "dwell" or at least eat in the *sukkah* (Lev. 23:42).

*__Sukkot__, festival of Tabernacles; last of the three pilgrim festivals, beginning on the 15th of Tishri.

Sūra (Ar.), chapter of the Koran.

Ta'anit Esther (Fast of *Esther), fast on the 13th of Adar, the day preceding Purim.

Takkanah (pl. ***takkanot**), regulation supplementing the law of the Torah; regulations governing the internal life of communities and congregations.

*__Tallit (gadol)__, four-cornered prayer shawl with fringes (*ẓiẓit*) at each corner.

*__Tallit katan__, garment with fringes (*ẓiẓit*) appended, worn by observant male Jews under their outer garments.

*__Talmud__, "teaching"; compendium of discussion on the Mishnah by generations of scholars and jurists in many academies over a period of several centuries. The Jerusalem (or Palestinian) Talmud mainly contains the discussions of the Palestinian sages. The Babylonian Talmud incorporates the parallel discussion in the Babylonian academies.

Talmud torah, term generally applied to Jewish religious (and ultimately to talmudic) study; also to traditional Jewish religious public schools.

*__Tammuz__, fourth month of the Jewish religious year, tenth of the civil, approximating to June-July.

Tanna (pl. ***tannaim**), rabbinic teacher of mishnaic period.

*__Targum__, Aramaic translation of the Bible.

*__Tefillin__, phylacteries, small leather cases containing passages from Scripture and affixed on the forehead and arm by male Jews during the recital of morning prayers.

Tell (Ar. "mound," "hillock"), ancient mound in the Middle East composed of remains of successive settlements.

*__Terefah__, food that is not **kasher*, owing to a defect on the animal.

*__Territorialism__, 20th century movement supporting the creation of an autonomous territory for Jewish mass-settlement outside Ereẓ Israel.

*__Tevet__, tenth month of the Jewish religious year, fourth of the civil, approximating to December–January.

Tikkun ("restitution," "reintegration"), (1) order of service for certain occasions, mostly recited at night; (2) mystical term denoting restoration of the right order and true unity after the spiritual "catastrophe" which occurred in the cosmos.

Tishah be-Av, Ninth of *Av, fast day commemorating the destruction of the First and Second Temples.

*__Tishri__, seventh month of the Jewish religious year, first of the civil, approximating to September–October.

Tokheḥah, reproof sections of the Pentateuch (Lev. 26 and Deut. 28); poem of reproof.

*__Torah__, Pentateuch or the Pentateuchal scroll for reading in synagogue; entire body of traditional Jewish teaching and literature.

Tosafist, talmudic glossator, mainly French (12–14th centuries), bringing additions to the commentary by *Rashi.

*__Tosafot__, glosses supplied by tosafist.

*__Tosefta__, a collection of teachings and traditions of the *tannaim*, closely related to the Mishnah.

Tradent, person who hands down a talmudic statement on the name of his teacher or other earlier authority.

*__Tu bi-Shevat__, the 15th day of Shevat, the New Year for Trees; date marking a dividing line for fruit tithing; in modern Israel celebrated as arbor day.

*__Uganda Scheme__, plan suggested by the British government in 1903 to establish an autonomous Jewish settlement area in East Africa.

*__Va'ad Le'ummi__, national council of the Jewish community in Ereẓ Israel during the period of the British *Mandate.

*__Wannsee Conference__, Nazi conference held on Jan. 20, 1942, at which the planned annihilation of European Jewry was endorsed.

Waqf (Ar.), (1) a Muslim charitable pious foundation; (2) state lands and other property passed to the Muslim community for public welfare.

*__War of Independence__, war of 1947–49 when the Jews of Israel fought off Arab invading armies and ensured the establishment of the new State.

*__White Paper(s)__, report(s) issued by British government, frequently statements of policy, as issued in connection with Palestine during the *Mandate period.

*__Wissenschaft des Judentums__ (Ger. "Science of Judaism"), movement in Europe beginning in the 19th century for scientific study of Jewish history, religion, and literature.

*__Yad Vashem__, Israel official authority for commemorating the *Holocaust in the Nazi era and Jewish resistance and heroism at that time.

Yeshivah (pl. ***yeshivot**), Jewish traditional academy devoted primarily to study of rabbinic literature; *rosh yeshivah*, head of the yeshivah.

YHWH, the letters of the holy name of God, the Tetragrammaton.

Yibbum, see levirate marriage.

Yiḥud, "union"; mystical term for intention which causes the union of God with the **Shekhinah*.

Yishuv, settlement; more specifically, the Jewish community of Ereẓ Israel in the pre-State period. The pre-Zionist community is generally designated the "old yishuv" and the community evolving from 1880, the "new yishuv."

Yom Kippur, Yom ha-Kippurim, *Day of Atonement, solemn fast day observed on the 10th of Tishri.

Yoreh De'ah, see Shulḥan Arukh.

Yoẓer, hymns inserted in the first benediction (*Yoẓer Or*) of the morning **Shema*.

*__Ẓaddik__, person outstanding for his faith and piety; especially a ḥasidic rabbi or leader.

Ẓimẓum, "contraction"; mystical term denoting the process whereby God withdraws or contracts within Himself so leaving a primordial vacuum in which creation can take place; primordial exile or self-limitation of God.

*__Zionist Commission (1918)__, commission appointed in 1918 by the British government to advise the British military authorities in Palestine on the implementation of the *Balfour Declaration.

Ẓyyonei Zion, the organized opposition to Herzl in connection with the *Uganda Scheme.

*__Ẓiẓit__, fringes attached to the **tallit* and **tallit katan*.

*__Zohar__, mystical commentary on the Pentateuch; main textbook of *Kabbalah.

Zulat, hymn inserted after the **Shema* in the morning service.

ISBN-13: 978-0-02-865948-0
ISBN-10: 0-02-865948-1